A

GENERAL INDEX

TO THE PUBLICATIONS OF

𝕿𝖍𝖊 𝕻𝖆𝖗𝖐𝖊𝖗 𝕾𝖔𝖈𝖎𝖊𝖙𝖞.

The Parker Society.

Instituted A.D. M.DCCC.XL.

For the Publication of the Works of the Fathers and Early Writers of the Reformed English Church.

A

GENERAL INDEX

TO THE

PUBLICATIONS OF THE PARKER SOCIETY.

COMPILED FOR

The Parker Society,

BY

HENRY GOUGH,
OF THE MIDDLE TEMPLE, ESQ., BARRISTER AT LAW.

WIPF & STOCK · Eugene, Oregon

Wipf and Stock Publishers
199 W 8th Ave, Suite 3
Eugene, OR 97401

General Index to the Publications of The Parker Society
By Gough, Henry
ISBN 13: 978-1-60608-436-6
Publication date 4/22/2010
Previously published by Cambridge University Press, 1855

THE
THIRTEENTH & FINAL REPORT

OF THE

Council of the Parker Society,

FOR THE PUBLICATION OF THE WORKS OF THE FATHERS AND EARLY WRITERS OF THE REFORMED ENGLISH CHURCH.

IN closing the proceedings of the Parker Society, the Council desire to express their thankfulness to God that a very important object has been attained, that the works of the leading English Reformers have been made for all future time easily accessible to the theological student, and a fuller light thereby thrown upon the principles of the Church of England. Heretofore the writings of the divines of the Reformation age were so rare, that it was difficult for any but those who had ready access to the large libraries of the country to obtain an extended acquaintance with them. It is true that some few pieces, such as the Apology of Bishop Jewel and the Sermons of Bishop Latimer, were popularly known: the selections also published by the late Rev. Legh Richmond were in many hands. But these and other volumes of the kind were little more than specimens, and served mainly to indicate that the mine was rich, if it only could be worked out. The design, therefore, of the Parker Society (originated by a friend and colleague, whose memory the Council affectionately cherish, the late GEORGE STOKES, Esq.) was new. It was not merely to cull out two or three celebrated productions: it was not to give the writings of a single author, or to select portions from a number: it had a wider range: it proposed to re-publish the entire mass of the printed works of the leading divines of our reformed church, who flourished in the age when the Roman yoke, which pressed so grievously upon our forefathers, was broken, and to add the pieces from their pens, if any such could be found, that were still lying in manuscript unpublished.

If the Society has not accomplished all that it designed, if it has left untouched the works of some valuable authors, if it has in one or two cases been unable to comprehend in its volumes the whole of the writings of divines it undertook to re-print, the Council, though it may feel some regret, cannot express surprise. Such publications could not be of a popular character. Those who were acquainted with the authors of that date knew that their language was frequently uncouth, their learning ponderous and of a scholastic cast, their matter for the most part controversial, and that, in short, they lacked much, from the very fact of their belonging to another age, of that which gives currency to modern literature, even modern theological literature. It was no matter of surprise, therefore, that some of the subscribers expressed a degree of disappointment when the Parker Society volumes began to appear, that men accustomed to the current style of the present day could not bring themselves to grapple with the solid, perhaps heavy, productions of the elder divines. The very cheapness, too, of the Society's publications, multiplying them so rapidly upon subscribers' shelves, was not without its influence.

It is needless to advert further to reasons why some part—it is comparatively a small part—of the original plan has not been completed; the Council would rather turn with thankfulness to what has been accomplished. They reverently acknowledge God's blessing on their proceedings, evidenced in the harmony in which they have worked together, the public support which has been afforded, the satisfactory results of their labours. Fifty-three volumes, the list of which has repeatedly been printed in the Reports, several of them of large size, have been issued, and are within every one's reach. They have been distributed through the United Kingdom, the colonies, and many foreign countries. They are a library in themselves. They comprise the complete works of the most eminent prelates, and others, who suffered imprisonment, exile, or death, in the sixteenth century, for the gospel's sake; and those of their immediate successors when religion was re-established under Queen Elizabeth. They contain proved weapons for the whole encounter with popery, and maintain the doctrine and order of the Church of England against those who afterwards rose up from her own bosom to assault her. They have shed light upon contemporary history. They are documents, which have already been frequently appealed to in the Ecclesiastical Courts, and which will ever remain as evidences of Reformation truth. It is a curious fact, that the Parker Society publications alarmed the Roman Catholics of this country, and induced them—so it was stated in a prospectus—to establish a counter-society for re-printing the works of Romish writers against whom the Reformers had contended. A few volumes were issued; but the plan met with little support, and it is believed was soon given up.

The fifty-three Parker books are now augmented by a General Index, the value and importance of which every reader will be prepared to appreciate.

The Council have only to add that the final statement of accounts will be completed as speedily as possible, and will then be made public.

33, *Southampton Street, Strand, December,* 1855.

THE COUNCIL AND OFFICERS.

President.

THE RIGHT HONOURABLE THE EARL OF SHAFTESBURY.

Treasurer.

SIR WALTER R. FARQUHAR, BART.

Council.

THE LORD BISHOP OF LINCOLN.—REV. G. E. CORRIE, D.D., Master of Jesus College, Cambridge.—REV. R. G. BAKER.—REV. C. BENSON, Canon of Worcester.—JOHN BRIDGES, ESQ.—JOHN BRUCE, ESQ.—REV. GUY BRYAN.—REV. RICHARD BURGESS, Canon of St. Paul's.—REV. T. TOWNSON CHURTON, late fellow of Brasenose College. Oxford.—HON. WILLIAM COWPER.—REV. W. HAYWARD COX, Oxford.—REV. J. W. CUNNINGHAM.—REV. THOMAS DALE, Canon Residentiary of St. Paul's.—REV. W. GOODE.—JOSEPH HOARE, ESQ.—REV. T. HORNE, Canon of St. Paul's.—HON. ARTHUR KINNAIRD.—HENRY POWNALL, ESQ.—REV. JOSIAH PRATT.—REV. M. M. PRESTON.—REV. DR. ROBINSON.—REV. DANIEL WILSON.

General Secretary and Librarian.

REV. JOHN AYRE.

Secretary for General Business.

WILLIAM THOMAS, ESQ., at the Office of the Parker Society, 33, Southampton Street, Strand, London, to whom all cheques and Post Office Orders are to be made payable.

Auditors.

HON. A. KINNAIRD, H. POWNALL, ESQ., and F. LOWE, ESQ.

Bankers.

MESSRS. HERRIES, FARQUHAR, AND CO., No. 16, St. James's Street.

PREFACE.

The publications of the Parker Society are brought to a conclusion with the present volume, which, it is trusted, will afford means of easy access to the contents of the entire series, and so increase its value.

Little need be said in explanation of the plan on which this Index is framed. At all events it has been endeavoured—it is hoped not unsuccessfully—to make it explain itself.

In the event of any medieval writer not being found mentioned under his supposed surname, recourse may be had to his Christian name; and there may be cases in which the converse of this rule should be applied. It is likewise possible that information as to given subjects may sometimes be found under the names of their contraries, or other correlatives. It is believed, however, that such cases are generally provided for by the cross-references. Some omissions, of these and other kinds, may have arisen from the necessity there was of printing portions of the MS. before the revision of the whole; but it is apprehended that such omissions are few.

Spurious and doubtful writings attributed to the Fathers are generally indicated as such, but possibly not always. It has not been considered necessary to describe the Decretal Epistles in the names of the early Popes, as pseudonymous, since the fact of their being so, with but few exceptions, is sufficiently notorious[1].

[1] Oudin. Comment. de Scriptoribus Ecclesiæ Antiquis, Tom. ii. p. 46, &c.

Extracts from the Fathers and from other writers, will, it is hoped, be found, though in many cases compressed, always accurate in substance. Nevertheless, in so large a work, executed in a time comparatively short, and with the subordinate assistance of several other persons, the compiler hardly ventures to pledge himself to the verbal exactness of every particular citation.

The material of this Index, as of the books to which it refers, is of course mainly theological. There are, however, but few subjects to which it has not some relation. The publications of the Society include a considerable amount of historical and biographical information; they may also prove serviceable to the topographer and the antiquary; certainly they are not likely to be overlooked by any who may hereafter direct their attention to English lexicography.

The compiler has, in conclusion, to acknowledge his obligations, and to return his best thanks, to several gentlemen who have favoured him with valuable suggestions.

H. G.

[The bracketted reference to R. de Diceto, p. 183, col. 1, proves on examination to be unfounded.]

GENERAL INDEX.

A

A: *v.* A-life, A per se, &c. *infra.*
A: used for Ah! 2 *Tyn.* 156
A. (A.): *v.* Aless (A.)
A. B. C. &c.: written on the ground at the consecration of a church, according to the Romish ritual, *Calf.* 209
A. B. C. for Children, otherwise called The A.B.C. against the Clergy: ascribed by More to Barnes, 1 *Tyn.* 3,
A. (R.): *v.* Allison (R.)
A. (W.), a chantry priest: 2 *Cran.* 249
A. (W.), author of the Special Remedy, 1579: notice of him, *Poet.* li; a prayer of a repentant sinner (in verse), *ib.* 508
Aachen: *v.* Aix-la-Chapelle.
Aaron: referred to, 2 *Bul.* 142, 195, 198, 4 *Bul.* 30, 225, 232; he fell, 1 *Hoop.* 23; his idolatry, 3 *Bul.* 222, 4 *Bul.* 37; he was consecrated before the people, 4 *Bul.* 132; a good priest, *Sand.* 148; his office, *Whita.* 417; how he blessed the people, 2 *Bul.* 140; his priestly garments, 2 *Brad.* 380; his priesthood ended with the law, 2 *Hoop.* 30; his rod, 2 *Bul.* 132, 154, 4 *Bul.* 262, 276, *Calf.* 335; it was a type of discipline, *Sand.* 372; he was a figure of Christ, 2 *Bul.* 132, 138, 1 *Tyn.* 208, 209, 412, 427, but Fisher says he was a type of Peter and of the pope, 1 *Tyn.* 208, 209; death of his sons, 4 *Bul.* 239; Moses and Aaron associated as rulers, *Pil.* 35
Aaronism: brought into the church, 4 *Bul.* 139
Abaddon: the term applied to Rome, *Rid.* 69
Abanne: to curse, 2 *Jew.* 697
Abba, Father: *v.* Adoption.
Abbas Cluniacensis: *v.* Peter of Cluny.
Abbas Panormitanus: *v.* Tudeschi (N. de).
Abbas Urspergensis: *v.* Liechtenaw (C. à).
Abberforde (Tho.): servant to Cranmer, 2 *Cran.* 257 n., 260, 284, 285
Abbes (James): martyred at Bury, *Poet.* 163
Abbeys, Priories, and other Religious Houses: of monasteries and monks, 4 *Bul.* 513, &c.; why first founded, 1 *Bul.* 286, 2 *Ful.* 19, 25; ordained for the poor, 1 *Lat.* 93; founded through fear of purgatory, 2 *Lat.* 362; built as compensation for sin, 1 *Tyn.* 249, 260; monasteries of solitary women, why first set up, 2 *Bec.* 376; the original institution of hospitals, &c., 1 *Tyn.* 231; the building of abbeys, cloisters, colleges, chantries, &c. alleged to have led to the decay of the realm, 3 *Tyn.* 78; abbeys had a shew of holiness, but were naught within, 1 *Lat.* 392; their midnight prayers, *Pil.* 528; their hospitality and alms, *ib.* 610; their gluttony and outrage, *ib.*; abominable enormities therein, 1 *Lat.* 123, 2 *Lat.* 240; children's skulls found in them, *Pil.* 687; abbey lubbers, *ib.* 447; abbeys were enriched by massmongers, 1 *Lat.* 522; the popes endowed bishopricks and cathedrals from abbey-lands, 2 *Tyn.* 277; their wealth, *ib.* 288; Henry VIII.'s injunctions to all monasteries, 2 *Lat.* 240 n., doubt respecting one of them, 2 *Cran.* 317; the lesser monasteries suppressed, *ib.* 321 n., 2 *Lat.* 245 n.; the suppression begun by Wolsey and Fisher, 4 *Jew.* 800, 801; some of the bishops desired that the king should have only such as were founded by his ancestors, and that the rest should be applied towards education, the relief of the sick and poor, &c., 2 *Cran.* 16; Henry VIII. desires certain bishops to select twelve monasteries as places of education, 3 *Zur.* 614; abbeys were destroyed for covetousness, *Pil.* 43; made stables for the king's horses, 1 *Lat.* 93; their lands looked for by carnal gospellers, *ib.* 256, taken away, *ib.* 291; suppression of cathedral colleges lamented, *Hutch.* 203; demand of the Devonshire rebels respecting abbey lands, 2 *Cran.* 186; Nowell says one house in each shire should have been reserved for soldiers, and one for scholars, *Now.* 227; application of their revenues, *Park.* 215; monasteries abolished in Scotland, 2 *Zur.* 116
Abbot (Rob.), bp of Salisbury: his Antilogia, *Calf.* 6 n
Abbots: none in the church at first, 4 *Jew.* 909; some sat in parliament, *Pil.* 628; six

1

mitred abbots in Gloucestershire, 2 *Tyn.* 288 n.; abbots kept the monks in ignorance, *ib.* 290; some were made bishops, 1 *Lat.* 123; several executed, 3 *Zur.* 317, 614, 627

Abdias: *v.* Obadiah.

Abdias of Babylon: a new found old doctor, 2 *Ful.* 149; called scholar to the apostles, *Rid.* 221; the Historia Apostolica, or Historia Certaminis Apostolici, *Calf.* 69 n., otherwise called the Acts of Abdias, *Rog.* 82; it is a forgery, 1 *Jew.* 85, 112, 113; its contents discussed, and the work proved to be an imposture, *Calf.* 126—135; when first published, *ib.* 126 n.; interdicted, but afterwards allowed, *ib.*; the writer says that Matthew celebrated mass, 1 *Jew.* 108; speaks of the whole church receiving it, *ib.* 115, and of Thomas dividing the sacrament to the people, *ib.*; his account of Matthias, *ib.* 245; says Bartholomew entered through shut doors, *ib.* 483; gives the words of Andrew to his cross, *ib.* 535; mentions a saying of Peter respecting Simon Magus, 4 *Jew.* 1076; speaks of Paul arming himself with the sign of the cross, 2 *Ful.* 172

Abecedarius: perhaps a learner of A, B, C, D, 2 *Hoop.* 487

Abel: referred to, 2 *Bul.* 130, 3 *Bul.* 399; a chosen vessel, *Pil.* 168; the image of the church, *Sand.* 378; his offering, 2 *Hoop.* 325 n.; in what sense he offered a greater (or more excellent) sacrifice than Cain, 1 *Cov.* 27, 28; by signification he bare Christ in his hands (says Gregory), 3 *Jew.* 467; he was the first martyr, 1 *Cov.* 29; killed by Cain for the love that God bore him, 2 *Hoop.* 268; the meaning of his name is vanity, *ib.* 281

Abel (Jo.), an English merchant: mentioned, 1 *Zur.* 8, 9, 25, 2 *Zur.* 20, 22, 74, 108, 117, 3 *Zur.* 541 n., *et sæpe;* notice of him, 2 *Cov.* 504 n.; his character, 1 *Zur.* 172; he aids the exiles, *Jew.* xiii; the boy Cranmer left with him at Strasburgh, 4 *Jew.* 1198, &c.; his death, *ib.* 1278, 1 *Zur.* 211, 224, 226, 232; letters by him, 2 *Zur.* 108, 117

Abel (Tho.?): a priest, executed for denying the king's supremacy, 2 *Cran.* 310 n., 3 *Zur.* 209

Abelard (Pet.): a heretic, 3 *Jew.* 212—214; compelled to recant in the council of Sens, 1 *Bec.* 337; his errors refuted by Bernard, *ib.* n

Abelke (Mr.): saluted, 3 *Zur.* 617

Aben Ezra (R. Abr.): *v.* Abraham.

Abergavenny (Geo. and Hen. lords of): *v.* Neville.

Abgarus, king of Edessa: *Bale* 612, 2 *Ful.* 53, 204; fable of the picture sent to him by our Saviour, *Calf.* 41; the second Nicene council relies upon the fiction, *ib.* 171; mistake in the Caroline books with regard to it, *ib.*; More alludes to the legend, 3 *Tyn.* 79 n

Abiathar, high priest: displaced by king Solomon, 1 *Bul.* 330, 2 *Ful.* 265, 4 *Jew.* 987, 988; not lawfully the high priest, 2 *Ful.* 265 n

Abihu: *v.* Nadab.

Abijah, or Abijam, king of Judah: 1 *Bul.* 325, 384, 2 *Bul.* 7

Abila, a town in Israel: proverb respecting it, 1 *Jew.* 421

Abimelech, king of Gerar: punished for taking Sarah, 1 *Bul.* 410; relieved by Abraham's prayer, 4 *Bul.* 224

Abimelech, son of Jerubbaal: *Pil.* 451

Abinadab, a Levite: 2 *Bul.* 148

Abington (......): *v.* Abyngton.

Abiram: *v.* Korah.

Abishag: was David's wife, 1 *Lat.* 113, 116.

Abishai: 1 *Bul.* 276

Abomination of desolation: *Coop.* 180, 2 *Jew.* 988, 991, 994, 4 *Jew.* 727, &c; whether the Roman ensigns, *Bale* 208; the mystical exposition of Chrysostom, *Whita.* 633, (and elsewhere *v.* Chrysostom); declared to be the popish mass, *Bale* 165; set up in England, *Rid.* 63

Abowan (Howell), [ap Owen?]: 2 *Cran.* 263

Abra, daughter of St Hilary: 2 *Jew.* 728

Abracadabra: an amulet used by the Basilidian heretics, *Calf.* 285

Abraham: his call, *Poet.* 287, 4 *Jew.* 1122; his faith, 1 *Bul.* 59, 87, 89, *Pil.* 352; the father of faith, 2 *Bul.* 18; justified by faith, 1 *Bul.* 115, 3 *Bul.* 44, 49, 4 *Bul.* 318—320; 2 *Cran.* 209, 1 *Ful.* 406, &c., 2 *Ful.* 385; 2 *Hoop.* 89, 1 *Tyn.* 497; justified by works, 1 *Tyn.* 119; justified before he was circumcised, 4 *Bul.* 311; his life, as well as his faith, to be followed, 1 *Hoop.* 57; with all his obedience he was infirm and imperfect without Christ, 2 *Hoop.* 89; a prophet, 1 *Bul.* 40; a preacher, 4 *Bul.* 102; God's promises to him, 4 *Bul.* 434, 2 *Hoop.* 6; who are his children, 2 *Hoop.* 325; the consolation promised to them, *ib.*; he delivers Lot, 1 *Bul.* 308; God's covenant with him, 4 *Bul.* 245; he receives the sign of circumcision, 2 *Bul.* 169—172, 175; before his circumcision he was called Abram, *ib.* 176; his hospitality, *ib.* 59; his

afflictions, 2 *Bul.* 103; preserved by God in the matter of his wife Sarah, 2 *Hoop.* 296; Abraham and his two wives, the history allegorized by Paul, *Whita.* 406; he swore reverently, 1 *Bul.* 210, 246, 247; with constancy of faith he would have killed his son, 2 *Hoop.* 219; his sacrifice of Isaac mystically expounded, *Phil.* 257; burial of Sarah, &c., 3 *Bul.* 399; his age, 1 *Bul.* 41; his burial, 4 *Bul.* 523; invoked by the rich man, 3 *Bul.* 400; Christ took his flesh, 2 *Hoop.* 12; the God of Abraham, 3 *Bul.* 136.
— Abraham's Bosom: *v.* Hell (ᾅδης).

Abraham Aben Ezra (R.), otherwise R. Abraham Hispanus: mentioned, 1 *Ful.* 313, 315, 535; his opinion respecting the images stolen by Rachel, *ib.* 106; records the custom of Egypt in the punishment of swearing, and censures that vice in Israel, 1 *Bec.* 363, 364; declares the truth to be in the expositions of the rabbins, 3 *Jew.* 248

Abraide: to upbraid, 1 *Hoop.* 289

Abramus (Barth.): set forth the acts of the council of Ferrara in Latin, 2 *Jew.* 689

Abre (Dr): *v.* Aubrey.

Abrech (אַבְרֵךְ, Gen. xli. 43): its meaning, 1 *Tyn.* 405

Abridges (Sir Tho.): *v.* Bridges.

Absalom: slew Amnon, 1 *Bul.* 413; deceived the people, 2 *Hoop.* 269, 270, *Pil.* 289, 309; his rebellion and end, 1 *Bul.* 280, 290, 376, 413, 2 *Bul.* 104, 431, 2 *Hoop.* 105, *Now.* 223, 224, *Sand.* 407

Absolution: *v.* Confession, Pardons.

Not to be rejected, *Hutch.* 243; on the power of the keys, or binding and loosing, 1 *Bec.* 101, 102, 2 *Bec.* 556, 557—568, 4 *Bul.* 39, 44, 127, 146—148, 1 *Cov.* 373, 374, 2 *Hoop.* 51, *Hutch.* 44, 96—98, 100, 108, 109, 199, 243, 3 *Jew.* 351, &c., 361, &c., 1 *Lat.* 30, 31, 423, 424, *Now.* (57), 100, 176, *Pil.* 131, 271, 494, *Rog.* 255, 256, 1 *Tyn.* 205, 243, 264, 267—271, 320—322, 342, 427, 2 *Tyn.* 159, 160, 282—284, 287, 3 *Tyn.* 103, 141; it is the preaching of God's word, or the law and the gospel, 3 *Bul.* 51, 88, 94, 4 *Bul.* 127, 146, 1 *Ful.* 459, 3 *Jew.* 363, &c., 1 *Lat.* 424, 1 *Tyn.* 91, 119, 205, 243, 269, 342, 2 *Tyn.* 159, 160, 282—284, 287, *Whita.* 425; absolution consists in the declaration of forgiveness, sometimes also in the open reconciliation of penitent sinners, 3 *Jew.* 354, &c.; examples of it in scripture, 2 *Bec.* 567, 568; how the apostles did bind and loose, 4 *Bul.* 148; how the minister executes the authority of binding or shutting, 3 *Jew.* 361, &c., 1 *Lat.* 423; it is analogous to the Mosaic law of leprosy, 1 *Ful.* 274, 1 *Tyn.* 217 n., 264, 269, 427; there is no absolution but in Christ, 2 *Lat.* 13; God only forgives sin, *Bale* 117, 2 *Bec.* 172, 173, 557, &c., 2 *Hoop.* 60; though he sometimes forgives by his ministers, *Hutch.* 108; Christ's ministers have power to bind and loose, 1 *Ful.* 273, 486, 3 *Jew.* 351, &c.; the priest or minister must absolve in such way as he is commanded, 1 *Lat.* 423, 2 *Lat.* 363; the office is common to all pastors, 1 *Jew.* 360; Cyprian ascribes it to the apostles, to the churches which they founded, and to bishops, *Whita.* 418 n.; on the absolution of the priest, *Hutch.* 44; ministers forgive and retain sins only by declaring the word of God, *ib.* 96; absolution depends not on the worthiness of the minister, *ib.* 97; how man ministers forgiveness, *ib.* 199; how absolution may be given by a layman, 3 *Jew.* 356; this is allowed by the pope's canon law in case of necessity, *ib.* 357; general and particular absolution, *Pil.* 131; private absolution may be sought if a man cannot be satisfied in the public sermon, 1 *Lat.* 423, 2 *Lat.* 13; the mode of absolving penitents in the ancient Latin church, 1 *Ful.* 431; absolution by imposition of hands, 2 *Bec.* 556, 2 *Ful.* 83, 3 *Jew.* 360, 374, *Pil.* 271, 3 *Whitg.* 255; no outward sign avails without repentance, *Hutch.* 109; absolution ought not to be given without consent of the church, and prayer, 2 *Hoop.* 51; absolution of the sick, *Lit. Edw.* 188, 314, 1 *Ful.* 458, 459, 2 *Zur.* 356; of madmen, 3 *Jew.* 359; whether a man may be absolved against his will, *ib.*; post mortem absolution, *ib.*; the Novatians' doctrine on absolution, 1 *Ful.* 272; the popish doctrine, *Hutch.* 98, *Rog.* 255, 256; the pope hath not Peter's key, but a picklock, *Hutch.* 100; Antichrist's use of the keys, 2 *Jew.* 911; some sins absolved by priests, others by bishops, archbishops, or the pope, *Pil.* 494; absolution à pœna et culpa, granted for thousands of years, *Rid.* 55, 418; the pope professes to forgive the guilt of sin either with or without the pain, 1 *Tyn.* 271, 3 *Tyn.* 103, 141; papists say that God absolves only à culpa, 1 *Tyn.* 271, but he absolves à pœna et culpa, 2 *Bec.* 174, 3 *Bec.* 144, 233, 3 *Tyn.* 154; the power of absolution unduly claimed by popish priests, 2 *Bec.* 556, 557; Romish absolution avails not, whether in Latin or English, for the priest rehearses no promise, but speaks his own words, 1 *Tyn.* 268; absolution ought not to be mumbled in the Latin tongue, 2 *Bec.* 568; there was a

1—2

general one at Pentecost, 1 *Lat.* 135; absolution pronounced at Paul's cross, 1 *Lat.* 140; form at daily prayer, *Lit. Edw.* 219; forms at the communion, *ib.* 7, 91; form at the visitation of the sick, *ib.* 138, 314; on the form in the Latin Prayer Book of 1560, *Lit. Eliz.* xxviii; on the words of the bishop in the ordination service, 1 *Whitg.* 489; Bradford's declaration of the forgiveness of sins to Careless, 2 *Brad.* 237; that of Careless to Bradford, *ib.* 240; absolution of certain excommunicated foreigners, *Park.* 247

Abster: to deter, 1 *Bec.* 63
Abstinence: *v.* Fasting.
Abstract of Chronicles: *v.* Chronicles.
Abulensis (......): on the Apocrypha, *Whita.* 65
Abulinis (Jo.): probably a clerical error for Jo. ab Ulmis (*q. v.*), 3 *Zur.* 389 n
Abundance: *v.* Riches.
Abuses: of Christian liberty, 2 *Bul.* 314; of church-goods, 4 *Bul.* 503; of holy things, 1 *Jew.* 5, &c.; abuses in the church, 3 *Whitg.* 277; in attire, diet, &c. to be repressed, *Sand.* 49
Abyngton (......), a free-willer: letters to him, 2 *Brad.* 180, 181; mentioned, *ib.* 244
Abyssinia: *v.* Prester John.
Acacius, bp of Amida: 2 *Ful.* 115
Acacius, bp of Cæsarea: *Pil.* 601 n
Acacius, patriarch of Constantinople: erased the name of pope Felix, 4 *Jew.* 650
Accaron: *v.* Ekron.
Accend: to set fire to, 1 *Bec.* 141
Accession: *v.* Elizabeth.
   Notes on accession services, *Lit. Eliz.* 463
Accidents and Substances: 1 *Cran.* 45, 254, 256, 260, 261, 267, 273, 274, 284, 301, 323, 324, 326, 328, *Grin.* 44, 2 *Jew.* 562, &c.; Gardiner's joke upon them, 1 *Cran.* 256
Accite: to summon, 3 *Bec.* 237
Accius Navius: a wizard, *Calf.* 316
Accusations: false and wrongful, 2 *Bul.* 114; just ones, *ib.* 117
Acephali, or Acephalians: *Calf.* 141; denied the properties of the two natures in Christ, *Rog.* 54; said women might be deacons, *ib.* 240; would not yield obedience to bishops, *ib.* 330
Acesius, a Novatian bishop: 2 *Ful.* 387
Achates: provisions, *Park.* xii
Achatius: *v.* Acacius.
Acheri (Luc d'), Spicilegium, 1 *Hoop.* 160
Acknown: known, acknowledged, *Bale* 366, 1 *Whitg.* 242; be not acknown, i. e. let it not be known, 2 *Brad.* 6
Ackworth (Geo.), public orator at Cambridge: notice of him, *Park.* 440 n.; answers N. Sanders, 1 *Zur.* 281 n.; makes an oration in honour of Bucer and Fagius, 2 *Zur.* 51 n

Acolythes: their office, 4 *Bul.* 114, 115; 3 *Jew.* 273, *Whita.* 509; they waited on the bishop as witnesses of his conversation, 3 *Jew.* 274; mentioned by Eusebius, 2 *Whitg.* 174; one of the popish orders, *Rog.* 258
Acon: *v.* Aix-la-Chapelle.
Acontius (......), an Italian: 1 *Zur.* 9, 58, 78
Acrased: crazed, damaged, sick, 1 *Jew.* 367
Acrostics: an acrostic on "God save the Queen," signed I. C., *Lit. Eliz.* 561; of "John Norden," *Nord.* 150
Act: an academical term, 1 *Tyn.* 232 n., 3 *Tyn.* 264
Acta Eruditorum: 2 *Ful.* 33 n., 287 n
Acta Sanctorum: 2 *Ful.* 81 n., 355 n.; *Jew.* xxxiv
Actius Sincerus: his saying on envy, *Pil.* 336
Acton family: Sutton, in Tenbury, co. Worc., their seat, 2 *Lat.* 416
Acton (Rich.): recommended to Cromwell, 2 *Lat.* 387, 389, 405; Cromwell favours him, *ib.* 410
Acton (Sir Rob.), son of Richard: 2 *Lat.* 388, 401
Acton (Sir Roger): imprisoned, *Bale* 50; hanged and burned, *ib.* 10, 51, 351, 394
Acts of the Apostles: *v.* Luke.
ACTS OF CHRIST AND OF ANTICHRIST, by T. Becon, 3 *Bec.* 498, &c.
Acts of Parliament: *v.* Statutes.
Acts of Pilate: *v.* Pilate.
Adam: *v.* Eve, Man.
   Referred to, 2 *Bul.* 120, 169; meaning of his name, *Pil.* 94, 95, 219; his creation, 1 *Cov.* 16; *Now.* (32) 148; Gardiner's argument from his creation out of clay, 1 *Cran.* 266: Adam and Eve made after God's image, *Lit. Edw.* 501, 502, (551); their marriage, 1 *Bul.* 394, 400, 409; to what end God gave the law to him, 2 *Bul.* 375; he had no infirmity before he sinned, *ib.* 377; his fall, 1 *Bec.* 46, 1 *Brad.* 59, 2 *Bul.* 361, &c., 1 *Cov.* 17, 2 *Hoop.* 24, 71, 1 *Lat.* 5, *Lit. Edw.* 502, (551), *Now.* (33, 34), 148, 149, *Pil.* 447; curious and unprofitable questions respecting it, *Rog.* 98; his fall foreknown, 2 *Bul.* 377, and provided for, 3 *Zur.* 327, yet it was wilful, 1 *Brad.* 214; he lost the image of God thereby, *ib.* 215; death came thereby, *Sand.* 168; his spiritual death, 1 *Bec.* 46; his misery, *ib.* 72; Adam and Eve, how their eyes were opened, *Whita.* 477; in

Adam we fell, *Sand.* 168, and became bondmen, *ib.* 178; we are all condemned in him, 1 *Bec.* 46, 47, 68, 1 *Brad.* 330; proof of our being dead in him, 1 *Bec.* 68, &c.; from the miserable state into which we were cast by him, we cannot deliver ourselves, *ib.* 389; through his wickedness we were born the children of wrath, *ib.*, 1 *Tyn.* 14, 17, 22; through his fall we sin naturally, 3 *Tyn.* 209; what man is by natural descent from Adam, 1 *Tyn.* 113; the old Adam remains in us as long as we live, *ib.*; it is to be cast away, *Nord.* 163; of the fall of man in Adam; verses by Cha. Best, *Poet.* 471; our fall in Adam and restoration in Christ, *Phil.* 285; God's love shewn to Adam and Eve, 1 *Brad.* 69; God's revelation of mercy to him, 1 *Cov.* 18—24; life promised to him, 4 *Bul.* 434; God's promise of a Saviour, 2 *Hoop.* 5, *Now.* (34), 150; Adam saved though Christ, 2 *Lat.* 5; the first minister of God, 4 *Bul.* 28, 102; he and Eve faithful Christians, 1 *Cov.* 24—27; "When Adam dalve," &c., *Pil.* 125; he called his best son Abel, i. e. vanity, 2 *Hoop.* 281; caused his sons to hear of his own fall, and of redemption, *ib.* 325; the length of his life, 1 *Bul.* 40; supposed to be buried in Jerusalem, *Pil.* 373; compared with Christ, 1 *Bul.* 113, *Pil.* 374, 1 *Tyn.* 70, 500

Adam (Melch.): Vitæ, 3 *Zur.* 611 n., 681 n., 712 n.

Adam (Mich.), a Jew: 3 *Zur.* 641

Adamites: the ancient sect so called, 2 *Brad.* 385, *Phil.* 420; the old Adamites and the new, *Whita.* 229 n., 1 *Whitg.* 62; the new Adamites (or Picards, *q. v.*), a Bohemian sect of the sixteenth century, 2 *Bec.* 379, 2 *Jew.* 689; both old and new said they were without original sin, *Rog.* 101; and pure as Adam before his fall, *ib.* 135

Adams (Mr), a bedel at Cambridge: *Sand.* iii

Adams (Jo.): martyred, 3 *Zur.* 41 n

Adase: to dazzle, 1 *Tyn.* 221

Adauctus: overthrew idols in Phrygia, 2 *Bec.* 305

Addlington (......): martyred, *Poet.* 168

Adela, queen of Henry I.: gave Aston, Herts, to Reading abbey, 2 *Cran.* 275 n

Adelman, bp of Bresse: 1 *Hoop.* 118

Adelme (St), bp of Sherborne: *Pil.* 590

Adelstane: *v.* Athelstan.

Ademarus: gives a list of popes, 4 *Jew.* 648

Adheral (Will.): martyred, *Poet.* 168

Adiaphora, and pseudodiaphora: 2 *Brad.* 388

Adiaphorists: a sect, 2 *Jew.* 686, 3 *Jew.* 621; the adiaphoristic controversy, 2 *Zur.* 125 n

Adlam (Jo.): burned, *Bale* 142, 243

Adminicles: helps, supports, 1 *Cran.* 37

Admonition: *v.* Gospel.

It should go before punishment, 1 *Bul.* 361; an admonition respecting infection, to be read by ministers, *Grin.* 270; a friendly admonition, by Rich. Hill, *Poet.* 305

ADMONITION TO THE PARLIAMENT: a book issued by the Puritans, *Grin.* 348, *Now.* ix, *Rog.* 8, 1 *Zur.* 284 n., 291 n., 297 n., 2 *Zur.* 140 n.; contained in *Whitg.* passim; twice reprinted, *Park.* 395; cited, *Rog.* 326, 327, 331, 332, 334, 343; a proclamation against it, 2 *Zur.* 253 n.; some account of it, 3 *Whitg.* x; it was written by Field and Wilcocks, *ib.*; the additions, detractions, and alterations, made by the admonitors, 3 *Whitg.* 468, &c.; Certain Articles collected...by the Bishops out of...An Admonition, etc., *ib.* 498; a Second Admonition, ascribed to Cartwright, *ib.* x; a view of the Second Admonition, *ib.* 506; Whitgift's Answer, 1 *Whitg.* 48, 3 *Whitg.* x, 2 *Zur.* 227 n.; Cartwright's Reply to an Answer, *Park.* 453 n., 3 *Whitg.* xi; Whitgift's DEFENCE, *Whitg.* passim; noticed, 3 *Whitg.* xi; Cartwright's Second Reply, *ib*; Cartwright answered by Dering, *Park.* 434; by Hooker, 3 *Whitg.* xvi; books on the controversy, *ib.* xxiv

Adnihilation of the sacramental bread: 1 *Cran.* 305, 306

Ado, abp of Vienne: referred to, *Calf.* 114 n., 2 *Ful.* 360, 1 *Jew.* 159, 160, 4 *Jew.* 1050, 1055

Adolph, duke of Holstein: a suitor to queen Elizabeth, 1 *Zur.* 34 n.; visits England, and is made K. G., *ib.* 89

Adoni-bezek: *Pil.* 226, 257

Adonijah: his ambition, 1 *Lat.* 113

Adoption: *v.* Faith.

The word explained, 2 *Bec.* 25; the Spirit of adoption, 1 *Ful.* 412, *Pra. B.* xiii, 160, *Sand.* 185; we are the children of God by adoption, 2 *Lat.* 99; it is the work of the Spirit, *Lit. Edw.* 514, (562); Abba, Father, a joyful song, 2 *Hoop.* 344

Adoration: *v.* Worship.

Adoration of the Sacrament: *v.* Mass.

Adrade: adread, afraid, *Phil.* 373

Adrastus: 1 *Hoop.* 184

Adrian, emperor: changed the name of Jerusalem, 2 *Lat.* 48, or built Ælia instead thereof, *Pil.* 372, 375; would have had temples erected to Christ, 2 *Jew.* 646 n.; granted the Christians one church within the city of Rome, 4 *Jew.* 892

Adrian I. pope: his history, 2 *Tyn.* 262;

upheld image-worship, 1 *Zur.* 156 n.; his reasons for it, 2 *Jew.* 657, 658; miraculous preference of the Roman liturgy in his time, *Pil.* 508, 509; his additions to the mass, 2 *Brad.* 308 n., 311; said to have devised the surplice, 3 *Whitg.* 109; his feet kissed by Charlemagne, 4 *Jew.* 688; his acts abrogated by Leo, *ib.* 1110; he (or another Adrian) says no man may judge the pope, *ib.* 752

Adrian II., pope: his history, 2 *Tyn.* 267; father of Talarus, afterwards pope, 2 *Ful.* 98 n., or, according to Jewel, son of a bishop named Taralus, 3 *Jew.* 394

Adrian III. pope: his history, 2 *Tyn.* 267

Adrian IV. pope [Nicholas Brekespere, an Englishman]: was wont to say, we succeed not Peter in teaching, but Romulus in murdering, 2 *Jew.* 993, 1020, 4 *Jew.* 1009; claimed the right to dispose of the empire, 2 *Jew.* 917; his vaunts over the emperor Frederick, 4 *Jew.* 677, 682, 837, *Pil.* 22

Adrian VI. pope: meant well, 2 *Cran.* 78; confessed (amongst other things) that all the ill of the church came first à culmine pontificio, 3 *Jew.* 182; 4 *Jew.* 737, 1107; his offers to Zuinglius, *Pil.* 142, 684; Legatio in Conventu Norembergensi, *Jew.* xxxii, 4 *Jew.* 1079

Adrian: alias John Byrte, *q.v.*

Adrian (Friar): *Bale* 429

Adultery: *v.* Commandments.

What is forbidden under the name, 2 *Bec.* 97, &c., 3 *Bec.* 611, 1 *Brad.* 166, 1 *Bul.* 410, &c., 2 *Bul.* 227, 1 *Hoop.* 374, *Now.* (19), 133; against adultery and fornication, with sentences and examples out of scripture condemning them, 1 *Bec.* 450, &c.; adultery and uncleanness prevalent, 1 *Bec.* 41; their prevalence lamented, 2 *Bec.* 643, &c., 1 *Lat.* 244, 257, 3 *Zur.* 647 n.; adulterers warned, 1 *Bec.* 126; they must forsake their wicked living, *ib.* 256; adultery condemned, 2 *Bec.* 98; a damnable thing, 2 *Tyn.* 50; plagued with punishment, 2 *Bec.* 100, 101, 647, 648; the incommodities that flow from it, *ib.* 646, &c.; it should be punished by law, *Sand.* 50, with death, 1 *Lat.* 244, according to the law of Moses, *ib.* 258; laws of various nations against it, 2 *Bec.* 649, 1 *Bul.* 203; the names of adulterers to be presented to the ordinary, *Grin.* 143; punished by penance, 2 *Zur.* 360; fornication allowed in the church of Rome, 3 *Jew.* 157, 158, or but lightly esteemed, 4 *Jew.* 627, &c.; reckoned among small faults by Gregory IX, *ib.* 638; some doctors have doubted whether it be sin, 2 *Tyn.* 50; fornication called better than marriage, 4 *Jew.* 627, 640, &c.; fornication to be abstained from, 2 *Jew.* 850: remedies whereby to avoid adultery, 2 *Bec.* 101, &c., 650, 1 *Cov.* 523; a prayer against whoredom, 3 *Bec.* 58; on divorce for adultery, 2 *Tyn.* 51, 52; an adulteress absolved by Christ, 1 *Bul.* 413; adultery as committed in the heart, 2 *Tyn.* 49; spiritual adultery, 4 *Bul.* 91

Advent: *v.* Christ.

Sermons on putting off the works of darkness, &c., 2 *Jew.* 1035, *Sand.* 197; on signs in the sun, &c. (Luke xxi.), 2 *Lat.* 44, *Sand.* 346; on the end of all things, *ib.* 386; sermon on John sending his disciples to Christ, 2 *Lat.* 65

Adversaries: *v.* Enemies.

Adversary (The): *v.* Satan.

Adversity: *v.* Affliction.

It is profitable, 1 *Tyn.* 197; against unbelievingly supposing that God sends it in anger, with sentences and examples out of scripture against this, 1 *Bec.* 475, &c.; the temptation of it, 2 *Bec.* 188, &c., more profitable than that of prosperity, *ib.* 188, 189; what we ought to do in it, *ib.* 189, 191; God assails not only sinners, but also his servants with it, *ib.* 190; it is peculiarly the lot of those who are beloved of God, *Now.* (18), 132; why God lets his children be tempted with it, 2 *Tyn.* 110; it is sent to teach self-knowledge, 1 *Hoop.* 89; sometimes adversity is an impediment that leadeth from God, *ib.* 303; why God punisheth therewith, *ib.* 304, 305; two good things in it, *ib.* 305; we should not despond in it, *ib.* 493; consolation from God shines in the deepest adversity, *ib.* 498; it is better than prosperity, *Hutch.* 308; we may pray to be delivered from it, 2 *Whitg.* 473; a prayer in adversity, *Lit. Edw.* 480; a prayer for grace in prosperity and adversity, *Lit. Eliz.* 253

Advertisements: notice of a book of Advertisements (or Articles, or Ordinances) devised by certain bishops, 1564, *Park.* 236, 271; references to it, 2 *Zur.* 149, 163

Advouries: *v.* Avowries.

Advoutry: adultery, 1 *Tyn.* 17; advouters, 1 *Bec.* 12; advouterer, *Lit. Edw.* 6, 79; advoterer, *Pil.* 642; advoterous, *Calf.* 330

Advowsons: *v.* Benefices, Patrons, Simony.

Ægeria: *Calf.* 14

Ægidius: *v.* Egidius.

Aelfer, or Elfere, prince of Mercia: expelled monks and restored married priests, *Pil.* 575

Ælfric, abbot of St Alban's: 2 *Ful.* 20

Ælfric, abp of Canterbury: did not hold transubstantiation, 2 *Ful.* 20; Ussher's mistake concerning his Liber Canonum, *ib.* 22 n.; Alfricus, probably this Ælfric, 4 *Jew.* 1274

Ælia: *v.* Jerusalem.

Ælian (Cl.): on the law of Zaleucus against adultery, 2 *Bec.* 649 n

Ælius Lampridius, *q. v.*

Ælmer (Jo.): *v.* Aylmer.

Æmilius: placed by Tiberius over Egypt, *Sand.* 135

Æmylia: turned into a man, 4 *Jew.* 656

Æmylius (Geo.): the Lord's prayer in Latin verse by him, *Pra. Eliz.* 403; notice of him, *ib.* n.; he wrote on the Apocalypse, *Bale* 258

Æmylius (Paulus): referred to, 1 *Jew.* 112, 4 *Jew.* 683, 684, 685, 686, 690, 1051, 1101; speaks of a duke of Athens, 4 *Jew.* 653; says that Michael Paleologus was refused Christian burial because he submitted to the pope, *ib.* 740; relates that the ambassadors of Sicily invoked the pope as taking away the sins of the world, *ib.* 752

Æneas Sylvius Piccolomini: *v.* Pius II.

Ænon: 4 *Bul.* 357

Æpinus (Jo.), or Hippinus: notices of him, 1 *Cran.* 365 n., 3 *Zur.* 616 n.; quoted by Gardiner as supporting the real presence, although an enemy of the church of Rome, 1 *Cran.* 20, 159; says that the eucharist is called a sacrifice, because it is a remembrance of the true sacrifice offered on the cross, and that in it is dispensed the very body and blood, yea the very death of Christ, *ib.* 20, 160; Gardiner alleges that he considered the Lord's supper a sacrifice propitiatory, *ib.* 365; Cranmer denies this, *ib.*; named, 2 *Cran.* 421 n.; letter to him, 3 *Zur.* 616

Aerians: followers of Aerius, 1 *Whitg.* 61; said there was no difference between bishops and priests, *Rog.* 330; their doctrines, 2 *Brad.* 382 n.; their factious disposition,*ib.* 387

Aerius: his doctrines, 2 *Ful.* 67, 388, *Phil.* 405, 425; the statement of Augustine, 2 *Whitg.* 292; he rejected prayers for the dead, 3 *Bul.* 399, 3 *Jew.* 166; denied any difference between a bishop and a priest, 2 *Whitg.* 290; but he was an Arian, and otherwise heretical, 3 *Bul.* 399; erroneously cited for Aetius, 2 *Ful.* 43

Æschylus: the remarkable manner of his death, *Grin.* 8, *Wool.* 112

Æthelbert: *v.* Ethelbert.

Æthiopia: *v.* Liturgies.

Aetians: cast off all grace and virtue, *Rog.* 118

Ætiological sense: *v.* Scripture.

Aetius: his heresy, 2 *Ful.* 43; denied fornication to be sin, 4 *Jew.* 630

Ætna: *Rog.* 215

Affectionately: warmly, or partially, 2 *Whitg.* 185, 436

Affections: *v.* Man, &c.

Divers good affections in religion, *Pil.* 127; the affections of the mind shewn in the face, *ib.* 292, 312; must be kept under, *ib.* 313

Affects: affections, *Bale* 437

Affiance in darkness: 4 *Jew.* 1038

Affinity: *v.* Marriage.

Afflict: a conflict, 2 *Bec.* 542

Affliction: *v.* Adversity, Calamity, Cross, Mourning, Oppression, Patience, Persecution, Prayers, Sickness, Sorrow, Temptation, Tribulation.

Two sermons of oppression, affliction, and patience, *Hutch.* 295, &c.; meditations on affliction, 1 *Brad.* 253, *Lit. Eliz.* 488; on affliction, verses, 2 *Brad.* 368; the kinds of calamities, 2 *Bul.* 65; in exile, *ib.* 101; in famine, *ib.*; in wars, *ib.* 102; examples out of the word of God of patience in adversity, 1 *Cov.* 169; examples taken out of natural things, and of heathen men, *ib.* 174; affliction cometh from God, *ib.* 95, 2 *Cran.* 107, or by his sufferance, 2 *Bul.* 92, not of chance, but by the counsel of God, 2 *Bec.* 572; all estates of men are subject to it, *Hutch.* 298; it comes on good and evil, 2 *Bul.* 66; there are two kinds of affliction, of sinners, and of saints, *Hutch.* 299, 307; some afflictions are common to all, *Sand.* 376, some peculiar to the elect, *ib.* 377; examples of the patriarchs, 2 *Bul.* 103; of the church of old, *ib.* 104, &c.; the afflictions of Christians foretold, *ib.* 107; they are called thereto, *Hutch.* 314, 2 *Jew.* 844; chastening is the portion of all God's children, 1 *Tyn.* 140; afflictions laid on the general body of the church, *Sand.* 378; on particular members, and especially on principal members, *ib.* 379; causes of the storms which trouble the church, *ib.* 380, and of those which trouble men in particular, *ib.* 381; the affliction of the godly, an argument of God's judgment against the wicked, 2 *Bul.* 79; to be without affliction is a bad sign, 1 *Lat.* 435, 483; causes of affliction in the wicked, 2 *Bul.* 79; its effect on the unfaithful, 1 *Cov.* 149; the end, or causes, of affliction, 2 *Brad.* 23, 2 *Bul.* 68,

69, 73, 93, *Hutch.* 58, 73, 74; 2 *Lat.* 184; 1 *Tyn.* 135, &c.; its benefits, 1 *Hoop.* 509, *Nord.* 28, 1 *Tyn.* 197; it is better than prosperity, 1 *Lat.* 467, *Phil.* 226; a bitter medicine, 1 *Brad.* 431, 2 *Cov.* 247; yet the cup of health, 1 *Bec.* 283; not to be thought strange, 1 *Brad.* 416, &c., 2 *Cov.* 233, &c.; a necessary preparation for heaven, 1 *Lat.* 464; a token of God's love, 2 *Brad.* 221, 2 *Bul.* 572, 1 *Cov.* 103, sometimes of God's anger and mercy, 2 *Brad.* 35, not necessarily of his anger, 2 *Lat.* 106; permitted in mercy to us, 1 *Tyn.* 280; sent to subdue the old Adam in us, 2 *Bul.* 572; sent for the punishment of our sins, 1 *Cov.* 97; less than our sins, *ib.* 100; God for Christ's sake, of mercy, love, and favour, doth correct and punish us, *ib.* 105; similitudes declaring how God doth chasten us of very love, *ib.* 108; Christ, through his passion, hath blessed and sanctified affliction, *ib.* 106; afflictions serve to prove us, *ib.* 116; help us to the knowledge of ourselves, and of God, *ib.* 119, and to the knowledge of our sins and to repentance for them, *ib.* 121, to the exercising and increasing of our faith, *ib.* 123; give occasion to pray to God, and to praise him, *ib.* 127; further us in virtue and godliness, *ib.* 129; help and further us toward the fear and love of God, *ib.* 134; trouble and affliction make men hard and strong, *ib.* 139; teach men to despise the world, *ib.* 140; help to much quietness and commodity in this world, *ib.* 142; a furtherance to eternal life, *ib.* 145; testimonies of the doctrine of faith, 2 *Bul.* 70; we are tried thereby, *ib.*; what afflictions teach us, *ib.* 633, patience, *ib.* 572, 573, also meekness and lowliness 1 *Cov.* 136, pity, compassion, and patience toward others, *ib.* 138; affliction manifests God's children, 2 *Brad.* 41, *Hutch.* 302; none can separate the godly from their Lord, 2 *Bul.* 98, nor hurt God's children, 1 *Brad.* 419, 2 *Cov.* 235; God's people have the victory by suffering, *Pil.* 197; we do not, however, obtain salvation for our sufferings, 2 *Lat.* 432; the time of affliction is a special time for receiving grace, *Sand.* 307, &c.; consolation under it, 2 *Brad.* 106, 108, &c., *Park.* 453; companions in trouble and adversity, 1 *Cov.* 150; how trouble and adversity may be overcome, *ib.* 153; promises made to the afflicted, 2 *Bul.* 95; we must conceive a good hope in affliction, *ib.* 573; support in adversity, 1 *Cov.* 156; examples of the help of God, *ib.* 161; God's faithfulness in times of extreme distress, 2 *Cran.* 457; God's providence most comfortable to all his afflicted, 2 *Hoop.* 216; their comfort when God seemeth to have forsaken them, *ib.* 220; the afflicted by the commandment of God take courage to approach his mercy, *ib.* 257; no comfort to the afflicted but God alone, *ib.* 323; in adversity we must direct our faith, hope, and confidence towards God, 1 *Cov.* 164; of prayer in adversity, *ib.* 166; repentance and amendment of life in adversity, *ib.* 168; by what means patience may be gotten, kept, and increased, *ib.* 174; the fruit of patience, *ib.* 188; the time of affliction short, the reward ample, 2 *Bul.* 97; we are delivered out of afflictions by the goodness of the Lord, *ib.* 69

Affliginensis (Gul.): *v.* Gulielmus.

Africa: *v.* Councils.

On the languages used there, 1 *Jew.* 292, &c.; the ancient churches of Africa, 4 *Bul.* 32, *Whita.* 223; separate from Rome for a hundred years, 1 *Jew.* 416; the reconciliation, *ib.* 416—418; dissensions therein about rebaptizing, 1 *Ful.* 35; the church not extinct there, 4 *Bul.* 20, 73

Agabus: 4 *Bul.* 105

Agag: spared by Saul, 2 *Jew.* 855

Agapæ, or Feasts of Charity: church-feasts so called in old time, 2 *Bec.* 251, 4 *Jew.* 1089, 2 *Lat.* 263, 2 *Whitg.* 70, 548; mentioned in the Apostolical Constitutions, *Whita.* 568; Ignatius gives the name (as it seems) to the Lord's supper, 1 *Bec.* 231 n

Agapetus I. pope: son of a priest, 2 *Ful.* 98 n.; inaccurately stated to have introduced processions, *Calf.* 295, 2 *Ful.* 184; consecrated Menna, bishop of Constantinople, 1 *Jew.* 408, 3 *Jew.* 331

Agapetus II. pope: 2 *Tyn.* 269 n

Agatha: *v.* Councils.

Agatha (St), or Agasse: account of her, 1 *Bec.* 139 n., 3 *Tyn.* 61 n.; invoked for the fire, 1 *Bec.* 139, i. e. to save persons from burning, 2 *Bec.* 536, also by those who had sore breasts, *Rog.* 226; her letters, 2 *Cran.* 148, *Pil.* 177, 536, 563; they were believed to be a charm against fire, 3 *Tyn.* 61; we are taught by God's word not to trust in Agasse, 3 *Bec.* 43

Agatho, pope: did not claim universal jurisdiction, 2 *Cran.* 487; his alleged decree declaring that all the constitutions of the apostolic see must be received as if they were confirmed by the voice of Peter, 3 *Bec.* 511, 513, 1 *Jew.* 304, 4 *Jew.* 855, *Rog.* 202 n.; confessed himself a sinner, but not a heretic, *Pil.* 642

Agathos, abbot: 1 *Hoop.* 144 n
Agde, Agathense : *v.* Councils.
Age, Aged: what kind of age is honourable, 2 *Bec.* 373, 3 *Bec.* 607; covetousness reigns chiefly in age, 2 *Bec.* 373; it is bent to much babbling, *ib.* 375; the aged are included in the term parents, 1 *Bul.* 269; the honour due to old men, 1 *Bul.* 285; their duty, with probations of scripture, 2 *Bec.* 521; they must shine as lights among younger folks, *ib.* 372; they must declare their affection to God's word in their talk, *ib.* 373; they must avoid the whole lump of sin, *ib.*; what St Paul requires of them, *ib.* 373, 374; petitions for elder men and women, 3 *Bec.* 38; the duty of old women, with probations of scripture, 2 *Bec.* 521; they must wear becoming raiment, *ib.* 375; and not abuse their tongue, *ib.*; nor give themselves to wine, *ib.* 375, 376; they must teach honest things, but not in the congregation, *ib.* 376
Ager (Ant.): servant to Cromwell, perhaps Sir Ant. Aucher, 2 *Cran.* 313
Agesilaus, king: stories respecting him, 1 *Jew.* 84, 101, 2 *Jew.* 996, *Pil.* 428
Aggeus : *v.* Haggai.
Agilbert, an Anglo-Saxon bishop : 2 *Ful.* 16, 119, *Pil.* 512 n
Agletts: Fr. aiguilettes; figuratively, finishing touches, *Park.* 12
Aglionby (Edw.): lent Parker a MS., *Park.* 388 n
Agnadello: the battle there, 3 *Bec.* 510 n
Agnes (St), or Annes: account of her, 1 *Bec.* 139 n.; invoked for a husband, *ib.* 139, 2 *Bec.* 536; we are taught by God's word not to trust in Annesse, 3 *Bec.* 43
Agnise: to recognise, acknowledge, or confess, 1 *Bec.* 245, 1 *Jew.* 227, *Wool.* 12
Agnoites: their heresy, *Rog.* 48
Agnus Dei: appointed, in the mass, by Sergius I., 2 *Brad.* 310, 2 *Jew.* 586, *Pil.* 503; not to be said before the communion, 2 *Hoop.* 128, *Rid.* 319
Agnus Dei: a charm, 1 *Cov.* 511, 1 *Jew.* 6, 2 *Jew.* 1045; said to break sin, &c. *Rog.* 111; made of wax, *ib.* 223; one produced in the pulpit by Jewel, 2 *Jew.* 1045
A-good: of good, in reality, 1 *Tyn.* 456, 462
Agreement : *v.* Unity.
Agricola (Jo.), of Eisleben: assisted in drawing up the Interim, 2 *Zur.* 125 n., 3 *Zur.* 383 n (where he is called Julius.)
Agrime: algorithm, arithmetic, 2 *Brad.* 177
Agrippa I.: commonly called Herod, *q. v.*
Agrippa II.: Paul pleads before him, 4 *Bul.* 95, 97; he is troubled at Paul's preaching, *Pil.* 1, 41; he despised justification by faith, *Rog.* 113

Agrippa (Hen. Corn.) de Nettesheym: his works, *Jew.* xxxii; his book De occulta Philosophia ungodly, 1 *Hoop.* 327; De Vanitate Scientiarum, 4 *Jew.* 846; says the Council of Nice commanded that no Christian should be without the Bible in his house, 2 *Jew.* 670; *Whita.* 221; accused of slandering the pope as receiving pensions from courtezans, 4 *Jew.* 643, 644; says the priests of the Greek church marry, *ib.* 807; says that a dispensation was granted to consecrate the sacrament in Norway without wine, 1 *Jew.* 137, 222; agrees with Cranmer about the king's divorce, 1 *Cran.* xi; praises ignorance, 2 *Jew.* 803; quotes Carnotensis (John of Salisbury), 1 *Jew.* 385, 3 *Jew.* 130, 250, 4 *Jew.* 679, 846, 939, 1147
Ague: prevalent in Yorkshire, *Grin.* 325 n
Aguilar (Don Juan d'): defeated in Ireland, 2 *Zur.* 335 n
Aguirre (Jos. Saenz card. de): Not. Conc. Hisp. *Calf.* 154 n
Agylæus (Hen.): 2 *Ful.* 42 n
Ahab, king of Israel: 1 *Bul.* 242, 307, 4 *Bul.* 71; takes Naboth's vineyard, 2 *Brad.* 371, 2 *Hoop.* 303
Ahasuerus, king: identified with Astyages, 1 *Bul.* 51; taken to be husband to Esther and father of Darius, *Pil.* 14
Ahaz, king of Judah: 1 *Bul.* 236, 2 *Bul.* 9, 4 *Bul.* 30, 70; the dial of Ahaz, 4 *Bul.* 231
Ahijah: a prophet, 1 *Bul.* 335; none of his writings lost, *Whita.* 525
Ahimelech, high priest: 2 *Bul.* 149
Ahithophel: his treason, 2 *Hoop.* 105, *Now.* 223, *Pil.* 242; deceived the people by lies, 2 *Hoop.* 270; hanged himself, *Now.* 224
Aidan (St): 2 *Ful.* 12, 16, 18, 26, 27
Aide (The): one of Frobisher's ships, 2 *Zur.* 291 n
Ailewarde (Will.), called by Foxe Jo. Aleworth: died in prison at Reading, *Poet.* 163
Ailbert, a bishop: *Pil.* 625 n
Ailly (P. d'): *v.* Alliaco.
Ainsworth (Ralph), master of Peter-house: *Pil.* 38 n
Air: its corruption the cause of pestilence, 1 *Hoop.* 318, 2 *Hoop.* 160, 383
Aix-la-chapelle, Aachen, or Acon: *v.* Councils.
   The emperor's seat, 4 *Jew.* 677; legend respecting Charlemagne's residence there, 2 *Tyn.* 265
Ajax: his blasphemy (Sophocles), 1 *Lat.* 491
Aknowen of (To be): to acknowledge, 1 *Tyn.* 465, 3 *Tyn.* 38

Akon: *v.* Alkhen.
Alabaster (Will.): on the marks of the true church, *Rog.* 176
Alan (Will. card.): *v.* Allen.
Alaric I., king of the Wisigoths: 2 *Bul.* 109
Alasco (Jo.): *v.* Lasco (Jo. à).
Alba: *v.* Alva.
Alban (St): a victory ascribed to his intercession, 2 *Ful.* 10; his patrimony, 2 *Tyn.* 124
Alban's (St): *v.* Saint Alban's.
Albany (Hen. duke of): *v.* Henry.
Albe: a vestment, 1 *Whit.* 488, 2 *Whitg.* 49, 3 *Whitg.* 472, 1 *Zur.* 345; of old the habit of a deacon, 2 *Ful.* 113; its first appointment, 2 *Brad.* 308; the alleged signification thereof and of the flaps thereon, 3 *Tyn.* 73; appointed for the ministration of the communion, *Lit. Edw.* 76, 97, 157, 174, 217; albes to be destroyed, *Grin.* 135, 159; the word used by Tyndale in translating Exodus, 1 *Tyn.* 419
Albert, abp of Mentz, 3 *Jew.* 193
Albert, marq. of Brandenburg, 3 *Zur.* 58 n., 113, 682
Albertinus (......): de Eucharistia, *Grin.* 60 n
Albertus Magnus: mentioned, 4 *Bul.* 485; held the virgin to be without original sin, *Rog.* 99; on the manner of Christ's benediction of the bread, *Calf.* 231, 2 *Ful.* 167; says the body of Christ is not in many places by reason of union, but by reason of consecration, 1 *Jew.* 496; says that in times past all that came together to the church communicated together, 2 *Bec.* 239, 240, 3 *Bec.* 417; maintains that in the eucharist Christ is offered in human nature as a sacrifice for all, *Rog.* 300 n; his remark respecting the inscription upon the cross, 1 *Jew.* 277; wrote on the Apocalypse, *Bale* 257; calls those that govern the church for the most part thieves and murderers, &c., 4 *Jew.* 746; his book De Secretis Mulierum, 1 *Tyn.* 394
Albigenses: *Bale* 322, 563; one burned in London, *ib.* 3; said to have rejected the Old Testament and denied the resurrection, *Whita.* 31
Albini (Will. de), earl of Arundel: ambassador to Rome about Becket, *Pil.* 589
Albohazen Haly: an Arabian astrologer, 2 *Jew.* 872
Albright (Ann), alias Champness: her martyrdom, *Poet.* 165; 3 *Zur.* 175 n
Albuin (St): *v.* White.
Albumazar: an Arabian astrologer, 2 *Jew.* 872
Alcherus: the probable author of a work ascribed by some to Augustine, 2 *Jew.* 618 n

Alciatus (Andr.): asks what needeth his presence that understandeth not what is done? 1 *Jew.* 178; tells what a minion was made bishop of Comum, Paulus Jovius being put aside, 4 *Jew.* 659; on Justinian, *Calf.* 305
Alciatus (Jo. Paul): his blasphemous heresy, *Rog.* 44
Alcoran: *v.* Mahomet.
Alcoranus Franciscanorum: *v.* Franciscans.
Alcuin (Flaccus): declares that no man can have peace with God but by Christ, 3 *Bec.* 420; on the continual reading of scripture, 2 *Jew.* 681 n.; wrote on the Apocalypse, *Bale* 256; said to have composed the Caroline books, 2 *Ful.* 23, 154; Charlemagne writes to him, 2 *Jew.* 704
Alcumine: a mixed metal, *Bale* 527
Alcyona tempora: *Calf.* 307
Aldborough, co. Suffolk: contest between Levers and Willoughby about the benefice, *Park.* 404; the chancel quite down, &c., *ib.*
Aldegonde (P. lord of Mont St): *v.* Marnix (P. de).
Alder first: first of all, *Phil.* 379, 417
Aldermen: become colliers, 1 *Lat.* 279
Alderney: the race of Britain, i. e. of Alderney, 1 *Hoop.* 497
Aldhelm (St): *v.* Adelme.
Aldington, co. Kent: the parson an abettor of the maid of Kent, 2 *Cran.* 272; it was a manor of Cranmer's, *ib.* 325
Aldrich (Rob.), bp of Carlisle: Dr Aldryche sent to France, 2 *Cran.* 246; when provost of Eton he signed a declaration respecting a general council, *ib.* 486
Aldrich (Tho.), master of Benet college, Cambridge, *Park.* 358; a great maintainer of Mr Cartwright, *ib.* 427, 429; sent for by the ecclesiastical commissioners, *ib.* 433; he and the fellows appeal to lord Burghley as chancellor of the university, *ib.* 436, 438; his insolence too great, *ib.* 436; most of the heads against him, *ib.* 439; resigns his prebend at Westminster, *ib.*; doubts as to the mode of determining the controversy, *ib.* 440; desires to resign rather than be deprived, *ib.* 443
Aleberry: a beverage, 1 *Bec.* 373
Alehouses: *v.* Taverns.
Alen (Fra.): 1 *Zur.* 93 n
Alen (......): dead, 3 *Zur.* 150
Alençon (Fra. duke of): *v.* Francis.
Ale-pole: the pole supporting a sign-board? 1 *Tyn.* 416
Ales (Alex. de): *v.* Alexander.
Aless (Alex.): notice of him, 2 *Lat.* 277 n.; took away adoration in the sacrament, *ib.* 278; his learning and piety, 2 *Cran.* 79 n.;

translated the Order of the Communion, and also king Edward's first Prayer Book, into Latin, 2 *Cov.* 525 n., 2 *Lat.* 277 n., 3 *Zur.* 31 n.; notice of his version of the Prayer Book, 1551, *Lit. Eliz.* xxiv, &c.

Aleworth (Jo.): *v.* Ailewarde (Will.)

Alexander the Great: his impartiality, 2 *Bec.* 308; his tyranny, *ib.* 441; thought himself able by natural strength to conquer his enemies, 2 *Hoop.* 85; would not sort his people by Greeks and barbarians, 1 *Jew.* 268; an ambitious saying of his, *ib.* 377; how he knew that he was a mortal man, 4 *Jew.* 689; how a woman appealed from him, *Pil.* 98; his answer to Darius, *ib.* 187; his punishment of Bessus, *ib.* 188; spares the house of Pindar, 2 *Brad.* 372 n.; answer made to him by a pirate, *Sand.* 226; his visit to Jerusalem, and interview with Jaddus the high priest, *Calf.* 117, *Pil.* 69, 148, 196; his golden coins used as amulets in the days of Chrysostom, *Calf.* 285

Alexander Severus, emperor: *v.* Severus.

Alexander [de Medici,] duke of Florence: 2 *Cran.* 331

Alexander [Farnese], 3rd duke of Parma: governor of the Netherlands, 2 *Zur.* 308 n.; compels Henry IV. of France, to raise the blockade of Paris, *Lit. Eliz.* 471

Alexander I. pope: made part of the mass, 2 *Brad.* 308, 1 *Jew.* 9; used the epistle and gospel, 3 *Whitg.* 74; directed the use of unleavened bread in the communion, *ib.* 82, 83, and prescribed the mixing of water with the wine, 3 *Bec.* 359; speaks of the passion of Christ being mingled with the oblations, 1 *Jew.* 473, 474; his first spurious epistle, 2 *Ful.* 81, 84, alleged for the use of holy water, *Calf.* 16 n., 2 *Ful.* 117, which he is said to have instituted, 1 *Lat.* 75, *Pil.* 601, *Rid.* 500 n

Alexander II. pope: his character, 2 *Hoop.* 240; sent a banner to William duke of Normandy to conquer England, 2 *Tyn.* 294; says it is sufficient for a priest to say mass once in a day, 2 *Jew.* 633; willed no man to hear the mass of any priest keeping a concubine, 4 *Jew.* 801; on excommunication, 3 *Jew.* 203

Alexander III. pope: 4 *Jew.* 1045; sets his foot on the neck of the emperor Frederick Barbarossa, *Grin.* 21; 1 *Jew.* 414, 3 *Jew.* 298, *Lit. Eliz.* 450; this event called in question by some modern authors, *Grin.* 21 n.; betrayed the emperor Frederick to the Turk, 3 *Whitg.* 592; moved men to sedition till Henry II. was content to be under him, 2 *Hoop.* 240; affirms that adultery is but a trifling offence, *Calf.* 18; his decrees called Alexandrines, 1 *Lat.* 212

Alexander V. pope: says that the adoration of the sacrament should be conditional on its consecration, 1 *Jew.* 13; poisoned, *Bale* 593

Alexander VI. pope: 1 *Lat.* 49 n.; bought the popedom, 1 *Lat.* 185; his incontinency, *Rog.* 304; verses against him, *Rid.* 54

Alexander, bp of Alexandria: 4 *Jew.* 993; disputes with Arius, *Phil.* 295 n.; allowed the validity of baptism ministered by Athanasius when a child, *Hutch.* 115, 116, 2 *Whitg.* 527

Alexander, bp of Antioch: reconciled, 1 *Jew.* 417—419.

Alexander ab Alexandro: speaks of the kissing of the emperor's feet, 4 *Jew.* 689; on lictors, *ib.* 805

Alexander Alensis, or de Hales, the irrefragable doctor: notice of him, 4 *Bul.* 485 n.; 1 *Tyn.* 150 n.; his works, *Jew.* xxxii; his works disallowed, 2 *Cran.* 383; says that communion is greater than consecration, 1 *Jew.* 124, 166; declares that whole Christ is not sacramentally contained under each kind, 1 *Jew.* 207; says that although receiving the sacrament under one kind be sufficient, yet to receive under both kinds is of greater merit, *ib.*; notes that the laity for the most part receive in one kind, *ib.* 261; says some erroneously hold Christ's body to be under the sacrament, not according to quantity, *ib.* 485; cited as to many strange miracles in the mass, *ib.* 509; declares that in the sacrament there appears flesh, sometimes by the conveyance of men, sometimes by the working of the devil, 3 *Jew.* 197, 554; his irreverent speech about a dog, swine, or mouse eating Christ's body, 2 *Jew.* 783, 3 *Jew.* 454, 517, *Rog.* 293; on the Sursum corda, *ib.* 535; declares that the sacrament of confirmation (as a sacrament) was ordained neither by Christ nor the apostles, but by the council of Melda, 2 *Jew.* 1125, 3 *Jew.* 459; says knowledge (in one sense) is not a key, 3 *Jew.* 382; maintains that, if a man suffer the frailty of the flesh, without doubt he shall be punished, but not perish, 4 *Jew.* 635; wrote on the Apocalypse, *Bale* 258

Alexander (And.), keeper of Newgate: his cruelty to Philpot, *Phil.* 159

Alexander (Mr): *i. e.* A. Citolini, *q. v.*

Alexander (Natalis): *Calf.* 42 n., 63 n., 96 n.; rejects the fabulous acts of the synod of Sinuessa, 2 *Ful.* 364 n.; the unacknowledged source of Gother's Nubes Testium, *Calf.* 63 n

Alexander (Peter), of Arles: notices of him, 2 *Cran.* 428, 1 *Zur.* 79 n., 119, 2 *Zur.* 50 n., 3 *Zur.* 67; reinstated in his prebend at Canterbury, 4 *Jew.* 1234, 1 *Zur.* 79; letter from him to Fagius, 3 *Zur.* 329

Alexandria: *v.* Councils, Patriarchs.

Formerly called No, 4 *Jew.* 694; destruction of pagan temples there, 2 *Jew.* 648; Jerome's account of the election of the earlier bishops, 2 *Whitg.* 222, 428; the newly-elected bishop laid the hand of his deceased predecessor on his head, and put on St Mark's cloak, 1 *Jew.* 409; the bishop made a patriarch, 4 *Bul.* 112, *Phil.* 43, *Rid.* 263, 2 *Whitg.* 220, 221 n.; a nominal patriarch still appointed by the pope, 4 *Jew.* 842; jurisdiction of the see, 2 *Whitg.* 144, 148, 161, 164, 429; election of ministers there, 1 *Whitg.* 409; factions in the church, *ib.* 465; what the people said to Timotheus (a bishop of the Arians), 1 *Jew.* 99, 144; an ecclesiastical school there, 4 *Bul.* 199, 483

Alexandrines: *v.* Alexander III.

Alexius I? emperor of the East: prayed for in the mass ascribed to Chrysostom, 1 *Jew.* 114

Alexius III, called Angelus, emperor of the East: notice of him, 2 *Jew.* 1028 n

Alfonsus de Castro: *v.* Castro.

Alforde (Jo.), or Halforde: witness against H. Totehill, 2 *Cran.* 387, 388

Alfred, king of England: *v.* Asser (Jo.)

He translated the scriptures, 1 *Tyn.* 149 n.; caused the Psalter to be turned into English, 2 *Jew.* 694, *Whita.* 222; translated Bede, 4 *Jew.* 779

Alfred (St), king of Northumberland: at a synod at Whitby, 2 *Ful.* 16, *Pil.* 625 n

Alfric: *v.* Ælfric.

Algar (St): his bones, 1 *Lat.* 55

Algates: at any rate, notwithstanding (perhaps all gaits), 2 *Ful.* 183, 1 *Jew.* 153, *Phil.* 328

Algerus, monk of Clugny: wrote on the sacrament against Berenger, 1 *Hoop.* 118; his treatise commended by Erasmus, 1 *Cran.* 20; on the spiritual food of Christ's body, *Bale* 154, 155 n

Aliaca, Sicily: taken by the French, 3 *Zur.* 741

Aliaço (Pet. de): *v.* Alliaco.

A-life: as my life, exceedingly, 2 *Bul.* 117

Aliote (Mr): probably Sir Tho. Elyot, 2 *Cran.* 307

Alkerton (Dr): reproved by Will. Thorpe, *Bale* 119

Alkhen, in the Netherlands: 1 *Tyn.* lxx.

Allatius (Leo): his Confutatio Fabulæ de Joanna Papissa, *Calf.* 6 n

Allchurch, co. Worcester? Latimer's park there, 2 *Lat.* 394

Allegories: *v.* Types.

Many in scripture, 4 *Bul.* 243; how to be handled, 1 *Cov.* 511; their use exemplified, 1 *Tyn.* 428; Paul's allegory of Hagar, *ib.* 307; bp Fisher deduces the pope's supremacy from the types of Moses and Aaron, *ib.* 208; the manna, the rock, the brasen serpent, &c., 2 *Jew.* 969; the history of Christ healing Malchus allegorized, 1 *Tyn.* 306; allegories prove nothing, and need to be proved, *ib.*; cautions against their misapplication, *ib.* 425, 428; reasons grounded on them uncertain, 2 *Whitg.* 92; employed by heretics to set aside the meaning of scripture, *Phil.* 426; the faith was lost through allegories, 1 *Tyn.* 307

Allegorical sense: *v.* Scripture.

Alleine (Edm.): *v.* Allen.

Alleluia: *v.* Hallelujah.

Allen (......), clerk of the council: 1 *Brad.* 487

Allen (......), tutor of Christ's college: 2 *Zur.* 192

Allen (......), of C. C. C. Oxon: *Jew.* ix

Allen (Edm.): he and his wife Catharine martyred at Maidstone, *Poet.* 169

Allen (Edm.), or Alleine: an exile for religion, 1 *Cran.* (9); designed for bishop of Rochester, 1 *Zur.* 40; his death, *ib.* 46; letter to him, 3 *Zur.* 541; notice of him, *ib.* n

Allen (Fra.): *v.* Alen.

Allen (Rose): her hand burnt, 1 *Jew.* 59 n

Allen (Tho.), skinner: *Park.* 211. (*v.* Attyn)

Allen (Will.): martyred at Walsingham, *Poet.* 164

Allen (Will.) or Alan, a cardinal: notice of him, *Lit. Eliz.* 657 n.; professor at Rheims, *Whita.* 15; writes various tracts in furtherance of the Spanish invasion, *Grin.* 169; maintains that there is no salvation out of the Roman church, *Rog.* 152; his opinions respecting the English reformation, *ib.*, 169; calls the reformed bishops incircumcised Philistines, &c., *ib.* 230; speaks of the protestant ministry as pretended, and sacrilegious, *ib.* 333; affirms that in matters of religion kings are not superior to bishops, *ib.* 343; calls the pope the father of all Christians, &c., *ib.* 348; his Apology, 1 *Ful.* 277; writes on purgatory, 1 *Ful.* ix, 2 *Ful.* 104; books by him answered by Fulke, 1 *Ful.* xi, 2 *Ful.* 3, 4

Allenson (Jo.), of St John's Coll. Camb.: *Whita.* xi, xii
Allerton (Raufe): prisoner in Lolers' tower, 2 *Brad.* 363; burned at Islington, *Poet.* 171; (there called Rafe Glaiton)
Alley (Will.), bp of Exeter: his share in the Bishops' Bible, *Park.* 335 n.; his death, *Jew.* xx
All Hallows: *v.* All Saints.
Alliaco (Pet. de), card. abp of Cambray: notice of him, *Sand.* 249 n.; maintains that the bread was Christ's body before he pronounced the words, "This is my body," 2 *Jew.* 788, 3 *Jew.* 451; allows it to be more agreeable to the truth of God's word to suppose that in the eucharist very bread and very wine remain, 2 *Bec.* 269, 3 *Bec.* 426; he complained in the council of Constance of the covetousness and pride of the court of Rome, 4 *Jew.* 1105
Allison (R.): his Plain Confutation cited, *Rog.* 230, 231, 281
Allix (Peter): asserts that the four last chapters of Zechariah were written by Jeremiah, 2 *Ful.* 386 n
All Saints: succeeded all the gods, *Calf.* 67
All Saints' day: sermon on the gospel, 1 *Lat.* 474; the practice of ringing bells on Alhallows' night forbidden, 2 *Cran.* 414, 415, *Grin.* 136, 160, nevertheless observed in Elizabeth's time, 2 *Zur.* 361
All Souls' day: injunctions against observing it, *Grin.* 136, 2 *Hoop.* 147
All-to: entirely, 1 *Brad.* 137, 2 *Bul.* 9, *Calf.* 91, *Pra. Eliz.* 504, 2 *Tyn.* 114, *et sæpe.*
Allyn (Tho.): *v.* Attyn.
Almanack: *v.* Kalendar.
Almany: Germany, 1 *Tyn.* 186, 2 *Tyn.* 244
Almaric: deemed a heretic, 3 *Jew.* 212—214
Almary, or Almerie: 1 *Bec.* 468, *Calf.* 136
Almesse: alms, 1 *Brad.* 66
Almous: the same, 1 *Bec.* 20
Alms: *v.* Chest, Collections, Oblations, Poor.
What is to be understood by alms, 1 *Bec.* 163, 1 *Tyn.* 72, 77, 96, *Wool.* 136; almsdeeds commended, 1 *Bec.* 161, *Wool.* 136; a part of true religion, *Rid.* 60; a Christian duty, *Rog.* 354; alms, prayer, and fasting, go together, 2 *Tyn.* 93, 94, and are our spiritual sacrifices, 1 *Bec.* 138; almsgiving garnishes prayer, *ib.* 162; alms and fasting are the wings of prayer, *ib.* 163; the objection taken from some being unable to give alms answered, *ib.*; no man is poorer for giving, 1 *Lat.* 303, 408, 410, 414; giving is gaining, 1 *Lat.* 409, 546; the blessedness of almsgiving, 1 *Lat.* 411; directions for it, 2 *Tyn.* 72, &c.; to whom alms should be given, 1 *Tyn.* 99; it is not true alms to maintain the idle, *Pil.* 608; bountifulness to the poor a fruit of mercy, *Sand.* 229, 230, and the effect of compassion to our neighbour, 1 *Tyn.* 118; the liberality of Cornelius, *Sand.* 265; almsgiving refused by certain heretics, *Rog.* 355; said by some to purge sin, 3 *Zur.* 233, 234; alms stolen from the poor by the clergy, 2 *Tyn.* 276; exhortation to aid the exiles at Zurich, 3 *Zur.* 748—750
Almsmen: almsgivers, 1 *Bec.* 108
Alnwick, co. Northumberland: *Rid.* 489, 492
Alogians: heretics so called, *Phil.* 420; they rejected the writings of St John, 1 *Ful.* 7, 8, *Whita.* 34
Aloisius Lippomanus, *q. v.*
Aloisius (Petrus), duke of Parma: *v.* Peter.
Alpha and Omega: *Bale* 589, 631, 632
Alphege (St): *v.* Elphege.
Alphonsus de Castro: *v.* Castro.
Alphonsus V. king of Arragon: a saying of his, 1 *Bec.* 398, 2 *Bec.* 5 n.; his speech about the flourishing state of his kingdom, 2 *Bec.* 5; erroneously said to have kept the sacrament about him till it putrefied, 2 *Jew.* 556
Alphonsus X. king of Castile: an error, 1 *Bec.* 398, 2 *Bec.* 5 n
Alsa (Will.), or Asa: a rebellious priest, 2 *Cran.* 187 n
Alsop (Mr), of Alsop in the Dale, co. Derby: 1 *Bec.* ix. 2 *Bec.* 420
Altar, Altars: *v.* Tables.

i. *The term:* diversely taken, *Phil.* 193; use of the word in scripture, *Pil.* 547; translations concerning it examined, 1 *Ful.* 110—112, 515—519; priest, sacrifice, and altar, inseparable consequents, *ib.* 240, 253; altar, or θυσιαστήριον, the name how derived, *Rid.* 323; faith called an altar, 2 *Jew.* 735

ii. *Before Christ:* one made by Jacob, and called The mighty God of Israel, *Grin.* 41; Jewish altars not to be of hewn stone, 4 *Bul.* 419; the one altar and place of sacrifice, what signified thereby, 1 *Cov.* 45; the altar of incense, 2 *Bul.* 145, 157; that of burnt-offering, *ib.* 158; altars abolished by Christ's death, *Calf.* 124

iii. *The cross:* the altar of the cross, 3 *Bec.* 138, 139, 253, 1 *Ful.* 241, *Phil.* 193

iv. *The heavenly altar:* Irenæus says our altar and temple are in heaven, *Coop.* 92, 1 *Jew.* 128; Christ alone is our altar, 3 *Bec.* 258, 1 *Ful.* 114; the souls of the martyrs beneath the altar, *Bale,* 323; Christ the

ALTAR — ALTHAMERUS

golden altar, *Bale*, 358, the gospel its four corners, *ib.* 359

v. *Altars amongst Christians:* intolerable, 3 *Bec.* 229, 4 *Bul.* 418, 1 *Hoop.* 488, 2 *Jew.* 735; objections against their use for ministration of the Lord's supper, 2 *Bec.* 297, not needed for that purpose, 3 *Bec.* 364, 365; P. Martyr against them, 2 *Zur.* 33; "we have an altar,"—what it signifies, *Phil.* 119; how the table may be called an altar, *Rid.* 322, 2 *Lat.* 276

vi. *In the early church:* altars not used by Christ, the apostles, or the primitive church, *Rid.* 88, 323; that church used no proper altars, but tables at the Lord's supper, 3 *Bec.* 258, 2 *Ful.* 112; Origen admits that Christians have no altars, *Calf.* 79; none amongst Christians in the time of Arnobius, 1 *Ful.* 104; but the communion table was often called an altar metaphorically, 1 *Ful.* 262, 516—518, 1 *Jew.* 311, 2 *Jew.* 709, *Rid.* 280; it was called reverend, &c. but this does not prove the real presence of Christ there, 1 *Cran.* 228; what kind used in the primitive church and by us, 1 *Jew.* 98; only one in an ancient church, and that in the midst, 1 *Jew.* 311, 2 *Jew.* 636; only one in a Greek church now, 2 *Jew.* 636; called by Eusebius the holy of holies, and said to be placed in the midst, 1 *Jew.* 311; in Augustine's time made of wood, *ib.*; he approves of the burial of martyrs beneath them, 2 *Jew.* 756; those broken down by ancient heretics were of wood, 3 *Jew.* 601, 602; erected in Britain, as Cyril mentions, *Rid.* 280; none in Northumberland for 600 years after Christ, *Pil.* 583

vii. *Altars in the Romish sense:* when first brought into the church, 3 *Bec.* 262, 365, 1 *Jew.* 310; said to have been introduced by pope Sixtus II., 2 *Bec.* 297, 1 *Jew.* 310; stone altars commanded by Sylvester, *ib.*; when hallowing of them was introduced, 3 *Bec.* 262; when censing of them was brought in, *ib.* 264; the altar made of stone because Christ is a rock, 1 *Jew.* 15; said to denote the cross, or the grave, 3 *Tyn.* 74; relics deposited beneath it, 1 *Ful.* 268 n.; many in one church, *Pil.* 529; prayers said at the high altar foolishly imagined better than those said in the quire, &c. 1 *Hoop.* 491; hallowing of the altar, 2 *Hoop.* 129; superstitions connected with the altar-stone, and the chalice, 1 *Tyn.* 209, 225; altar-stones washed with wine on Maundy Thursday, *Bale*, 528; what the washing signified, 1 *Bec.* 116; super-altars, 2 *Cran.* 525, 2 *Bec.* 297, *Rid.* 55, 319; mass might not be celebrated without an altar, or at least a super-altar, *Rid.* 322; Bullinger could not approve of the altar and mass vestments if they were commanded, 1 *Zur.* 345

viii. *In the reformed church:* the term used in The Order of the Communion, temp. Edw. VI. *Lit. Edw.* 4; "altar" and "table" used interchangeably in king Edward's first Prayer Book, *Rid.* 322; "altar," *Lit. Edw.* 77, &c.; "the Lord's table," *ib.* 77; "God's board," *ib.* 91; two candles on the high altar in king Edward's time, 2 *Cran.* 155, 499; in king Edward's second Prayer Book "altar" is changed to "Lord's table," *Lit. Edw.* 265, &c.; whether an altar or a table should be used, 4 *Bul.* 418; altars should be turned into tables, 1 *Hoop.* 488; they should be abolished, 2 *Hoop.* 128; reasons why the Lord's board should rather be after the form of a table than of an altar, 2 *Cran.* 524, *Rid.* 321; that form tends to superstition, *Rid.* 322; letter from the council to bishop Ridley, to take down altars and place communion tables instead of them, 2 *Cran.* 524; king Edward writes to Ridley requiring the taking down of some that remained, *Rid.* 507; altars pulled down, and tables substituted, 2 *Cran.* x. 524, 1 *Jew.* 90, *Rid.* 280, 281, 529, 2 *Zur.* 159 n., 3 *Zur.* 72, 79, 384, 466; Ridley's determination concerning altars, *Rid.* 324; the Lord's board not to be made in the form of an altar, *ib.* 320; by-altars or tables forbidden, *ib.*; super-altars forbidden, *ib.* 319; altars set up again in Mary's time, *ib.* 409; removed again temp. Eliz., 1 *Zur.* 63; dispute between Sandys and Sir Jo. Bourne, concerning a stone altar, *Sand.* xviii; altars to be taken down, and the stones to be broken, defaced, and bestowed to some common use, *Grin.* 134; inquiry respecting altars, *ib.* 158

Altar (Sacrament of the): v. Supper of the Lord.

Altar-cloths: linen coverings introduced by pope Boniface (III. or IV.), 3 *Bec.* 262, 2 *Brad.* 311; popish linen cloths not to be used, *Grin.* 155; what sort convenient, 2 *Ful.* 113

Altel [Fr. autel]: altar, 2 *Brad.* 314

Alteserra (Ant. Dadin.): 2 *Ful.* 103 n

Altham (James): patron of Buckland, Herts, 1 *Bec.* xii

Althamerus (And.): refused the epistle to the Hebrews and that of James, *Rog.* 84; on the Swermerians, *ib.* 237 n., 337 n

ALTHOUGH — AMBROSE

Although: as though, 3 *Bec.* 259
Altissiodorense concilium: *v.* Councils, Auxerre.
Alt-Sax (John Phil. baron of): comes to England, 2 *Zur.* 214; character of the baron his father, *ib.*; copy of his diploma from Oxford, *ib.* 216; leaves England, *ib.* 260
Alum: the pope's merchandise, 1 *Lat.* 180; the art of boiling it, *ib.* 181 n
Alured: *v.* Alfred.
Aluric: *v.* Ælfric.
Alva (Fernando duke of): called the duke Dalby, 2 *Cran.* 236; comes into the Netherlands with the forces of the king of Spain, 2 *Zur.* 165; his standard baptized by Pius V., and named Margaret, *Rog.* 266; he puts to death the counts of Egmont and Horn, and other nobles, 1 *Zur.* 204, being irritated at the defeat at Groningen, *ib.* 205; his cruelty and tyranny in the Netherlands, *ib.* 208, 209, 273 n., 274, 2 *Zur.* 207; arrests the English at Antwerp, 1 *Zur.* 209 n., 2 *Zur.* 182; recalled to Spain, 1 *Zur.* 275
Alvarus de Caturco: wrote on the Apocalypse, *Bale* 258
Alvey (Jo.): an exile, 1 *Cran.* (9)
Alvey (Rich.): an exile, 3 *Zur.* 755, 763; master of the Temple, 2 *Zur.* 255 n.; applies to Parker about Corranus, *Park.* 476
Alyaco (Pet. de): *v.* Alliaco.
Alypius, bp of Tagasta: opposed the encroachments of the see of Rome, 1 *Jew.* 358; addressed by Paulinus as placed in an apostolic see, and as a prince of God's people, *ib.* 365, 4 *Jew.* 824; passages from him and Augustine on justification, 2 *Cran.* 203
Amadeus VIII., duke of Savoy: elected pope [Felix V. antipope, 1439], 4 *Jew.* 1105; thought himself happy that of a pope he was made a cardinal, *ib.* 1111
Amadys (......), a goldsmith of London: *Calf.* 36, 2 *Ful.* 128
Amalarius: referred to, *Pra. Eliz.* 27 n
Amalekites: conquered, 2 *Bul.* 165, 429, 4 *Bul.* 224, *Grin.* 41, 4 *Jew.* 1180
Amand (St): *v.* Saint-Amand.
Amaral (And. d'): grand-master of Rhodes, 2 *Lat.* 33
Amasis, king of Egypt: his law against idleness, *Sand.* 117
Amasius: so the civil law calls one who keeps a concubine, 4 *Jew.* 632
Amathas: scholar to St Anthony, 4 *Bul.* 514
Amaziah, king of Judah: 1 *Bul.* 384, 2 *Bul.* 8
Amaziah, priest of Bethel: 4 *Bul.* 71
Ambages: dark sayings, *Bale* 260

Ambarvalia: processions in honour of Ceres, 2 *Zur.* 40 n
Ambition: said by Cyprian to sleep in the bosom of priests, 1 *Jew.* 354; the evil of it, 2 *Lat.* 27, 32, 33; remedy against it, 1 *Cov.* 525
Ambleteuse: the camp near it taken, 3 *Zur.* 658 n
Ambletons (The): meaning Hamiltons, 1 *Zur.* 203 n
Ambrose (St): *v.* Athanasius, Liturgy, Maximus Taurinensis, Sylvester II.
   i. *His life.*
   ii. *His works.*
   iii. *On God, and Christ.*
   iv. *Scripture, Word of God, Truth.*
   v. *Sin, Repentance, Absolution, &c.*
   vi. *Grace, Justification, Faith, &c.*
   vii. *The Church.*
   viii. *Apostles, Bishops, Ministers.*
   ix. *Peter, Rome.*
   x. *Saints.*
   xi. *Sacraments.*
   xii. *Baptism.*
   xiii. *The Eucharist.*
   xiv. *Prayer, Praise, &c.*
   xv. *Fasting.*
   xvi. *Virginity, Marriage.*
   xvii. *The Cross, Images.*
   xviii. *Heresies, Antichrist.*
   xix. *The Civil Power, the Emperor.*
   xx. *Miscellanea.*
   i. *His life*: reference to him, 4 *Bul.* 199; he was a nobleman, 3 *Jew.* 410; bishop of Milan, *Rog.* 330; his election, 1 *Whitg.* 461; chosen before his baptism, *ib.* 323; asserts that all the bishops, of the East and West, consented to his election, 1 *Jew.* 407; whether a metropolitan or a simple bishop, 2 *Whitg.* 155; being made bishop, he began to rebuke the nobles, 1 *Jew.* 407; took order for the service of the church of Milan, *ib.* 265; ordained that hymns and psalms should be sung after the manner of the East, 4 *Bul.* 195; opposed the empress Justina, who favoured the Arians, *Calf.* 301; sought to turn the emperor Gratian from error, 3 *Jew.* 236, &c.; present at the council of Aquileia, 2 *Whitg.* 362; the means of Augustine's conversion, 1 *Brad.* 540 n., 1 *Lat.* 201; he expelled Theodosius from the church, and why, 3 *Bec.* 478, &c., 1 *Jew.* 311, *Pil.* 381, 491, 555, 3 *Whitg.* 242, &c.; his language to him when excommunicate, with his reply, 3 *Jew.* 374; exhorted him to repentance, 3 *Whitg.* 244; brought him to it by ecclesiastical discipline, *Sand.* 72; his boldness in this matter commended, *Rid.*

95; he declared that Theodosius enjoyed perpetual light, *Grin.* 25; that emperor's opinion of him, 1 *Jew.* 362; he settled disputes, *ib.* 382; used funeral sermons, *Pil.* 543; applied the sacred vessels of the church to the redemption of captives, 2 *Bul.* 45; he often differs in opinion from other fathers, *Whita.* 455; erred in some points, 1 *Hoop.* 28; his house of salutations (ἀσπαστικὸν οἶκον), 2 *Whitg.* 386, 388, 390; legendary story of his leaving a rich man's house who had never tasted adversity, 3 *Bec.* 103, 1 *Lat.* 435, 483; how he received the communion on his death-bed, 1 *Jew.* 162, 242, 250; his dying words, 1 *Jew.* 243, *Jew.* xxii; year of his death, 2 *Ful.* 81; Jerome scoffs at him and his writings, 1 *Jew.* 314, 3 *Jew.* 176

ii. *His works*: 4 *Bul.* 587, *Calf.* 401, 2 *Ful.* 395; Hexaëmeron, 3 *Bul.* 150; De septem Tubis, *Bale* 256; De Sacramentis, libri sex; their genuineness questioned or denied, 4 *Bul.* 248, *Calf.* 202 n., 1 *Cran.* 180, 210 n., 2 *Ful.* 239, 1 *Hoop.* 234; he speaks of only two books of his on the sacraments, 2 *Jew.* 1103; the books De Mysteriis Initiandis not his, 1 *Cran.* 180, 210 n., 318; nor the books De Vocatione Gentium, 1 *Bec.* 81 n., *Calf.* 295, 2 *Cran.* 142 n., 2 *Ful.* 353 n.; the spurious commentary on St Paul's epistles, *ib.* 183, 367, 1 *Bul.* 213 n.; the commentary on Titus not his, *Calf.* 235 n.; a sermon De Cruce, by Maximus Taurinensis, attributed to him, *ib.* 177 n., 2 *Ful.* 154, 155; a sermon attributed both to him and Augustine, 2 *Ful.* 284; one ascribed to him, to Augustine, and to Maximus, *ib.* 340 n.; hymns ascribed to him;—Jam lucis orto sidere, *Pra. Eliz.* 134 n.; Rerum Creator omnium, *ib.* 148; Consors paterni luminis, *ib.*; Te Deum laudamus; hymnus Ambrosii et Augustini, *ib.* 250, and in the Prayer Books.

iii. *On God, and Christ* (see also x.): he records a saying of Symmachus on the unity of God, 3 *Jew.* 622; shews how man is the image of God, *Calf.* 156; defends the term ὁμοούσιον, 3 *Bul.* 246, *Whita.* 535; on the omnipresence of Christ, 1 *Jew.* 493; says, to be in the form of God, is to be in the nature of God; to take the form of a servant is to take the perfection of human nature, 3 *Jew.* 261; says Christ appeared in human figure, 2 *Jew.* 569; supposes the word footstool, Psa. xcix. 5, to denote our Lord's humanity, *Calf.* 165, 1 *Cran.* 236, 237, 1 *Jew.* 540; calls the body of Christ the body of the divine Spirit, 3 *Bec.* 445, 446; calls Christ alone our mouth, our eye, and our hand to the Father, 2 *Bec.* 135; says of the wise men, they knew the star that signified him unto them who was both man and God, but they adored the little One, 1 *Jew.* 515; says, we have seen Him with our eyes, and have thrust our fingers into the holes of the nails, &c., 2 *Jew.* 570; on "that which is behind of the afflictions of Christ," (Col. i. 24—pseud.), 2 *Bul.* 333; on Christ's entry when the doors were shut, 1 *Jew.* 483; shews that we must not seek Christ in the earth, nor after the flesh, like Mary, but in heaven as Stephen did, 2 *Bec.* 274, 277, 3 *Bec.* 451, 1 *Cran.* 96, (49), *Grin.* 54, 1 *Hoop.* 234, 2 *Hoop.* 483, 1 *Jew.* 12, 490, 2 *Jew.* 1118; says that we cannot see Christ now truly, 3 *Jew.* 531, but that Christ is touched and seen by faith, 1 *Jew.* 499, 542, 2 *Jew.* 1043, 3 *Jew.* 525, 529, 531, 548, *Sand.* 153; speaks of carrying Christ, 3 *Jew.* 545; he (or Leo) speaks of the faithful as eagles flying to the body with spiritual wings, 1 *Jew.* 451; says that Christ, here in image, is there in truth, when as an advocate he intercedes for us, 2 *Bec.* 277, 3 *Bec.* 451; says, first the shadow went before, the image followed, the truth will be; the shadow in the law, the image in the gospel, the truth in heaven, 2 *Jew.* 598, 730; observes that, when the Son of man shall come, shall faith be rare, 4 *Jew.* 723; compares the glory of the gospel of Christ with the power of Rome, 1 *Jew.* 368, 369

iv. *Scripture, Word of God, Truth*: he says the Jews see the ink, but not the Spirit of God, 3 *Jew.* 498; speaks of the word of God as a lamp, *Whita.* 384; says it is the living meat of our souls, 2 *Cran.* 28; on the crumbs which fall from the Master's table, viz. the doctrines of scripture, *Whita.* 701; asserts that the foundation of the apostles and prophets means the two testaments, *ib.* 349; on faith, and the authority of scripture, addressed to Gratian, *ib.* 357, 702; says that all truth, by whomsoever spoken, is of the Holy Ghost, 2 *Whitg.* 465, 589, 590; remarks that it pleased not God by logic to save his people; for the kingdom of God is in simplicity of faith, not in contention of speech, 4 *Jew.* 911; shews that the simple truth of fishermen confounds the words of philosophers, *ib.*; another passage much to the same effect, *ib.*; his high estimation of the LXX. version, 1 *Ful.* 51, 53; in the New Testament, he asserts the greater authority of the original Greek, *Whita.* 157; tells the people that Moses accuses them, they have heard him read, 4 *Jew.* 857; appeals to the people, knowing them to be skilled in scripture, against Auxentius the Arian, *Whita.* 465; speaking of the Arians, he says, Let them come to the church; let them hearken with the people; not that any man may sit as judge, but that every man may have the examination of his own mind, 4 *Jew.* 913; desires not that the people should believe him, but the scriptures, 3 *Jew.* 231, 238; says that we must ask Peter and Paul if we would find the truth, 1 *Jew.* 25; teaches that to discover truth, we must ask the scriptures, the prophets, the apostles, and Christ, *Coop.* 191, 3 *Jew.* 236, 237, *Whita.* 702; says, Let our judgment stand apart, let us inquire of Paul, 3 *Jew.* 238; shews that even the apostles' preaching beside the Gospel, is not to be heard, 2 *Cran.* 29; declares that we justly condemn all new things which Christ has not taught, and that such teaching is detestable, 2 *Bec.* 261, 3 *Bec.* 391, 398, 404, 2 *Cran.* 28; speaking of some doctrine he says, so our fathers have said according to the scriptures, 3 *Jew.* 238; proves the ὁμοούσιον from scripture, *Whita.* 535; likewise the perpetual virginity of Mary, *ib.* 539; on the profundity of scripture, *ib.* 372; on the perspicuity of scripture, *ib.* 398; remarks that Paul interprets himself, *ib.* 492; says heretics impugn the law by the words of the law, 3 *Jew.* 151; on the Arians' misuse of scripture, *ib.* 241; on the term "tradition" as used by St Paul, *Whita.* 555; on human tradition, 1 *Ful.* 171; calls those who make themselves subject to men's superstitions the slaves of men, 3 *Jew.* 615; against false prophets, and writers of false gospels, *ib.* 441; shews that nothing is to be added to the word of God, even for a good purpose, 2 *Cran.* 28, *Phil.* 373; on the caution against adding to the Apocalypse, *Whita.* 622; on Cain and Abel, 1 *Ful.* 395; on Noah's flood, 3 *Jew.* 595; on Melchisedech, 2 *Jew.* 731; on the division of the Red sea and Jordan, &c., 1 *Cran.* 318, *Hutch.* 276, 3 *Jew.* 502; contrasts the manna with the bread which God now gives, that is, the word which he has ordained, 3 *Bec.* 340; division of the ten commandments (pseud.), 1 *Bul.* 213, 1 *Hoop.* 349; on Elisha causing iron to swim, 1 *Cran.* 318, *Hutch.* 39, 276; says that Herod burnt the records, in order to conceal the baseness of his house, 4 *Jew.* 762, *Sand.* 16; on the reception of the word of God by the Thessalonians, *Whita.* 337; on the deliverance of the creature, or creation, (Rom. viii.—pseud.), 1 *Brad.* 352; in what sense he calls the book of Tobit divine, *Whita.* 80

v. *Sin, Repentance, Absolution, Excommunication:* he maintains the doctrine of original sin, 2 *Bul.* 390; calls pride the greatest sin, *Sand.* 137; condemns usury, 2 *Jew.* 853, 856; calls it killing a man, to deny him the things which should preserve his life, 1 *Bec.* 25; says Paul calls those impudent that are contentious, &c., 2 *Jew.* 607; reprobates unthankfulness towards God, *Sand.* 156; says that he that preaches Christ must be estranged from all kinds of vices, 1 *Bec.* 386; says it is a shameful lie to call oneself a Christian, and not to do the works of Christ, *ib.* 387; remarks that when a man begins to live wantonly, he begins to decline from the true faith, 3 *Jew.* 584; asks, how can the word of God be sweet in thy mouth in which is the bitterness of sin? *Grin.* 381; says God verily foreknew to what end the fury of the mad man (Cain) would come, nevertheless he was not urged by necessity of sinning (pseud.), 2 *Bul.* 378; says the soul overcome with the pleasure of the flesh is made flesh, 2 *Jew.* 566; on the frailty of the flesh, 4 *Jew.* 635; Ambrose (or Prosper) on the law of the mind, and the conflict between the flesh and the spirit, 3 *Jew.* 464; passages describing true repentance (pseud.), 1 *Bec.* 93, *Sand.* 140; says that none can rightly repent, unless he trust in God's mercy, *Wool.* 145; remarks on the penitence of Peter, 1 *Ful.* 438; he exhorts sinners to humble themselves, and to let the church weep for them, 3 *Jew.* 361; referred to on penance, 3 *Jew.* 456; remarks on absolution, with reference to the doctrine of the Novatians, 1 *Ful.* 272, 273; he declares that he alone forgives sins, who alone died for our sins, 2 *Bec.* 173, 174 n.; says that to forgive sin and to give the Holy Ghost is only in the power of God, *ib.* 173, 219, 227, 3 *Bec.* 468; declares that no man can be partner with Christ in forgiving sins, 3 *Jew.* 380; cited as saying that the word of God forgives sin, the priest is the judge, 2 *Bec.* 174; his words are that sins are forgiven by the word of God, the expounder whereof is the Levite, *ib.* n., 3 *Jew.* 358, 364, 378—81; on Paul's absolution of the incestuous person, 1 *Ful.* 485; he asserts that he who receives not remission of his sins here, shall not have it in another life, 2 *Bec.* 395, 3 *Bec.* 461, 3 *Jew.* 563; on excommunication, 3 *Whitg.* 239; his conduct towards Theodosius; see i, above.

vi. *Grace, Justification, Faith, Works, Merit :* he says that without the worship of the true God that which seems to be virtue is sin (pseud.), 2 *Cran.* 142; he asserts that the grace of the Holy Spirit knows nothing of slow struggles, *Whita.* 38, 102; says it is ours to remove the stone, it is God's to raise the dead, 3 *Jew.* 379; maintains justification by faith only, 2 *Bec.* 639, *Wool.* 34; passages on justification, 2 *Cran.* 204—206, 210, 211; asks whence he should have merit, mercy being his crown, 1 *Ful.* 369, 2 *Ful.* 92; says that the redemption of Christ's blood would wax vile, if justification were due to merits, 3 *Bec.* 170; says that he who believes in Christ shall be saved without works, 2 *Cran.* 130; says it was decreed of God that, the law ceasing, the grace of God should require only faith for salvation, 3 *Jew.* 244; and again, that faith alone is appointed for salvation, *ib.*; says, I will not glory because I am just, but because I am redeemed; not because I am void of sins, but because my sins are forgiven me, &c. 3 *Jew.* 246 (see also n. 4); says (believers) are freely justified, because working nothing, and rendering nothing again, they are justified by faith only, by the gift of God (pseud.), 2 *Bul.* 341, 3 *Jew.* 244; says the grace of God through Christ hath justified men, not from one sin alone, but from many, 1 *Bec.* 337; sees the doctrine of justification by faith in the history of Jacob obtaining the blessing, *Wool.* 36; says he fulfils the law that believes in Christ, 2 *Bec.* 638; exclaims that faith is richer than all treasures, 1 *Bec.* 207; 3 *Bec.* 165; says faith is the mother of good will and righteous working, 1 *Bec.* 80; calls faith the root of all virtues, 1 *Bec.* 207, 3 *Bec.* 165; asserts that they who are the workmanship of God are no more sluggish (pseud.), 1 *Bec.* 80, 81, 2 *Cov.* 243; says the gifts of virtues cannot be idle, *ib.*; says that he who repudiates the faith, and limits the rights of the law is an unjust man, for, "The just shall live by faith," *Phil.* 34; speaks of Gentiles believing in Christ by the leading of nature, 3 *Jew.* 198

vii. *The Church :* he says God's house is where he is feared according to his will, 1 *Jew.* 434; that the church shines not by her own light, but by the light of Christ, 4 *Jew.* 750; that all the children of the church are priests, *ib.* 984; asks what can be more honourable, than that the emperor (Valentinian) should be called a child of the church? 1 *Jew.* 369, 3 *Jew.* 376; says that the law (i. e. the civil law) did not gather the church, but the faith of Christ did, 2 *Jew.* 1023, *Phil.* 27, 34; held that things used in the primitive church are not of necessity to be observed always, 1 *Jew.* 39, 74—76; speaks of differences between the apostolical church and the church of his day, 1 *Whitg.* 218; says they who should have been the vicars of the apostles are become the fellows of Judas, 4 *Jew.* 1009; would rather have the stony temples want their precious furniture, than the living temples of God their necessary food, 1 *Bec.* 31, 32; declares that the church has gold, not to hoard, but to bestow upon the poor, 1 *Bec.* 23, 3 *Bec.* 362; says that the disputation of faith ought to be in the congregation before the people, *Phil.* 16; approves provincial synods, 4 *Jew.* 1049, 1054

viii. *Apostles, Bishops, Ministers :* he ascribes the creed to the apostles, *Whita.* 604; says that the apostles mentioned in Eph. iv. are bishops, 2 *Whitg.* 230, 355; on apostles, prophets, evangelists, and pastors and teachers, 1 *Whitg.* 494, 503, 504; on the apostleship of Epaphroditus, 1 *Whitg.* 497; said to mention archbishops (pseud.), 2 *Whitg.* 153, 430; intimates that Timothy was bishop of Ephesus, 2 *Whitg.* 295; extols the episcopal power, 3 *Bec.* 508 n.; calls the bishop the highest priest, 4 *Jew.* 823; tells Felix, bp of Comum, that he has taken the government of the highest priesthood, *ib.*; says that all orders are in a bishop, and that he is prince of priests, 2 *Whitg.* 171 n., 432; "a bishop must be ...of good behaviour" (κόσμιον),—this he refers to the ornaments of the mind, 1 *Zur.* 157; says to one, Unless thou embrace the good work, a bishop thou canst not be, 3 *Jew.* 309; charges bishops of his time with simony (pseud.), *Sand.* 44, 136, 2 *Whitg.* 153 n.; speaks of a bishop being chosen by the whole church, 1 *Whitg.* 443, 446; said to confound bishops and priests, 2 *Whitg.* 250; says the ordination of a bishop and of a presbyter is one, both are priests, but a bishop is first, 3 *Jew.* 439; calls presbyters or elders vicars of Christ, and God's prelates, 3 *Whitg.* 152; on elders in the synagogue and the church, *ib.* 154; speaks of government by seniors as discontinued in his time, *ib.* 199, 203; on the promotion of deacons to a higher grade, *ib.* 70; on the injunction to lay hands suddenly on no man, 1 *Whitg.* 426, 433; thinks that ministers should abstain from worldly merchandise, *ib.* 485; maintains that he who preaches Christ must be estranged from all kinds of vices, 1 *Bec.* 386; says, in the beginning it was permitted to every one to preach, baptize, &c., 1 *Whitg.* 412, 2 *Whitg.* 526

ix. *Peter, Rome:* he says Peter exercised his primacy; the primacy of confession, not of honour; of faith, not of order, 1 *Ful.* 41, 2 *Ful.* 256, 257, 310; says Andrew received not the primacy, but Peter, 1 *Jew.* 366; speaks of Esau's primacy, *ib.*; affirms that what was said to Peter was said to the apostles (pseud.), 2 *Ful.* 284; explains how Christ looked on Peter after his denial of him, and caused his tears to flow, 1 *Bec.* 93, 94; mistaken in supposing that Peter was the first who saw our Lord after his resurrection, 2 *Ful.* 304; intimates that the command to feed Christ's sheep was given to all the apostles, 3 *Jew.* 384; says Christ left Peter as the vicar of his love, 2 *Ful.* 320, 321, 3 *Jew.* 282; speaks of Peter ruling others, 2 *Ful.* 256; credits and repeats an old tradition concerning Peter, *Rid.* 221; says they have not Peter's inheritance who have not his faith, (but the later editions for "fidem" read "sedem",) 4 *Jew.* 929; denies that Paul was inferior to Peter, though the latter was the foundation of the church, 2 *Ful.* 256; says Paul had the primacy in preaching among the Gentiles, 3 *Jew.* 328; says it is uncertain whether Peter or Paul should be placed first (pseud.), 1 *Jew.* 367, 375, 1 *Tyn.* 216 n.; calls pope Damasus ruler of God's house, 1 *Jew.* 429; and simply, bishop of Rome, *ib.* 433; addresses pope Syricius as a brother, 1 *Jew.* 433, 1 *Tyn.* 216 n.; says that reference was made to himself, after determination of the bishop of Rome, 1 *Jew.* 382, 421, 4 *Jew.* 1044; desired in all things to follow the church of Rome, but claimed the faculty of judging whether anything were better observed elsewhere, 4 *Jew.* 1046; calls Rome the head of superstition, 1 *Jew.* 421

x. *Saints, &c.* (see also ix. and xvii.): he says that, except Christ be our intercessor, neither we nor all the saints can have anything to do with God, 1 *Bec.* 150, 3 *Bec.* 356; thinks that as the angels are over (nations), so shall they be who have deserved the life of angels, 3 *Jew* 572; says the virgin obtained the grace to be replenished with the Author of grace, 1 *Ful.* 528; (as to her perpetual virginity see iv. supra); his reading of Gen. iii. 15, "ipsa conteret," 1 *Ful.* 533; a spurious passage on the honour due to martyrs, 3 *Jew.* 575; on the apparition of Gervasius, Protasius, and Paul (pseud.), 2 *Jew.* 654; praises Helena, the mother of Constantine, 1 *Jew.* 306; calls her "stabularia," *Calf.* 322; how he speaks of Constantine, 4 *Jew.* 1004; how of the soul of Valentinian, 2 *Jew.* 742, (and see xii.); how of Theodosius, *Grin.* 25

xi. *Sacraments:* he treats of two sacraments only, 3 *Jew.* 459; yet he calls the washing of the disciples' feet a sacrament, 2 *Cran.* 79, and applies the same term to penance, 3 *Jew.* 456; he says that the sacraments do not require gold, and that their ornament is the redemption of captives, 3 *Bec.* 362, 4 *Bul.* 419, *Pil.* 156, 157; calls him who is not present at the sacraments a forsaker of the Lord's tents, (pseud.), 3 *Bec.* 473

xii. *Baptism:* he addresses baptism as the water that has washed the world stained with man's blood, 1 *Jew.* 535; calls it the pledge and image of resurrection, 3 *Jew.* 470; calls the words of baptism heavenly words, 2 *Jew.* 620; says that in baptism we crucify in ourselves the Son of God, *ib.* 727, 3 *Jew.* 448; asserts that the water is made sweet unto grace by the preaching of the Lord's cross, *ib.* 565; says, the water of the holy font has washed us, the blood of the Lord has redeemed us, *ib.* 595; says, thou hast seen the font, thou hast seen the priest, &c., but those things which work, thou hast not seen, *ib.* 1106; remarks that we should not look at the things which are seen, but at those which are not seen, *ib.* 569, 3 *Jew.* 503; exhorts to believe that the presence of the Godhead is in baptism, and that Christ is there, 3 *Jew.* 468, 503; calls baptism a mystery which eye hath not seen, nor ear heard, &c., 2 *Jew.* 565, 570; observes that in baptism one thing is done visibly, another wrought invisibly, 1 *Jew.* 466; says that is better seen which (with our bodily eyes) is not seen, *ib.* 467, 490, 540, 2 *Jew.* 576; shews that in the water there is the image of death, but in the Spirit the pledge of life, and that therefore, if there be any grace in the water, it is of the presence of the Holy Ghost, 3 *Bec.* 468; says (inter alia) that water cleanses not without the Spirit, 2 *Jew.* 565; says the water healeth not, unless the Holy Ghost descend and consecrate it, *Calf.* 202, 2 *Jew.* 1102, 3 *Jew.*

445, that all water heals not, but only that which has the grace of Christ and the presence of the Trinity, 1 *Jew.* 466, 2 *Jew.* 781, 3 *Jew.* 443, 500, that the priest makes his prayer that the font may be sanctified, and that the presence of the Eternal Trinity may be in it, 2 *Jew.* 763; shews that in baptism the minister cleanses not, 3 *Bec.* 469; says the grace of baptism forgave Constantine all his sins at the end of his life, 4 *Jew.* 1004; allows that forgiveness of sins has been granted without baptism, 2 *Bec.* 219, 3 *Bec.* 468; expresses his belief that Valentinian, though he died unbaptized, yet died in the Lord, 2 *Bec.* 224, 2 *Jew.* 1107, 3 *Jew.* 359; expounds the texts of which the heresy denying remission of sins after baptism has been gathered, 1 *Bec.* 95, 96; on the text, "Christ sent me not to baptize," &c., 2 *Whitg.* 456; affirms that baptism ought necessarily to be given to young children, 2 *Bec.* 210; explains the rites used in baptism, *Whita.* 603; speaks of trine immersion, 2 *Bec.* 227

xiii. *The Eucharist* (see also iii.): he asserts that the eucharist is not the Lord's supper, 2 *Lat.* 263; the first who used the term "missa" for the eucharist, 2 *Ful.* 81, 239, *Pil.* 507; an extract (spurious) on saying mass, 1 *Brad.* 512; on St Paul's command to tarry one for another, 1 *Jew.* 17; calls the element one thing, consecration another, 3 *Jew.* 500, 501; his opinion as to the words of consecration, 1 *Ful.* 505, *Rid.* 18; says that when the priest consecrates the sacrament, he uses the words of Christ, 1 *Ful.* 270, 3 *Jew.* 497; speaks of St Laurence the deacon as consecrating the Lord's blood, 1 *Jew.* 240; on Christ's presence in the sacrament, *Rid.* 202; refers the words "Taste and see that the Lord is gracious," to Christ in the eucharist, 2 *Jew.* 765; calls that sacrament the grace and virtue of Christ's very nature, 1 *Brad.* 98; 3 *Jew.* 487; says that by receiving Christ's flesh, we become partakers of his divinity, *Hutch.* 240 n., 3 *Jew.* 466; cited in the canon law as saying that although the forms of bread and wine be seen, we must believe that nothing else remains after consecration, but the flesh and blood of Christ, 2 *Jew.* 568, and as saying that the bread is that body which was formed in the virgin's womb, *ib.* 791; his words upon the eating of Christ's body, &c. are to be understood figuratively, 1 *Cran.* 55, 179; he calls the sacrament a creature, 1 *Jew.* 547, 2 *Jew.* 569, 772; teaches that the substance of the sacramental elements remains, *Hutch.* 273; asks whether the word of Christ, which of nought could make what was not, cannot change things which are into what they were not, 3 *Bec.* 424, 1 *Cran.* 276 n., 318; says that there is such power in the word of the Lord Jesus...that (the elements) are what they were, yet changed into another thing, 1 *Cran.* 276, (31), *Grin.* 69, 1 *Jew.* 458, 2 *Jew.* 566, 569, 1115, 3 *Jew.* 482, 497, 513; says that the power of benediction is greater than the power of nature, because by benediction even nature itself is changed, 1 *Cran.* 318, *Hutch.* 275—277, 2 *Jew.* 566, that the word of God changes the kinds of the elements, 2 *Jew.* 595, that the bread before the words of the sacraments is bread, when consecration cometh, of bread is made the body of Christ (pseud. ?), 1 *Cran.* 177, 320, (72), 1 *Hoop.* 233, 2 *Jew.* 568; says that which is offered before the words of Christ is called bread, but afterwards it is called Christ's body (pseud. ?) 1 *Cran.* 178; affirms that the forms of bread and wine are changed, 1 *Cran.* 323; says, before the blessing of the heavenly words, another kind is named, but after consecration the body of Christ is signified (pseud. ?), 2 *Bec.* 285, 3 *Bec.* 436, *Coop.* 207, 1 *Cran.* 122, 178, 179, (50), 2 *Hoop.* 405 n., 1 *Jew.* 448, 2 *Jew.* 569, 570, 595, 597, 599, 699, 766, 775, 794, 1113, 3 *Jew.* 452, 500, 503; shews how the eucharist is the new testament in Christ's blood, 1 *Cran.* 122, 1 *Hoop.* 234 n.; says, when Moses called the blood the soul, doubtless he meant the blood to be one thing, and the soul another, 2 *Jew.* 612; says it is not the bread that goeth into the body...that strengthens the substance of the soul, 2 *Jew.* 572, 760, 3 *Jew.* 471, 474, 517, 524, 593; affirms that the body of Christ is spiritual meat, and spiritually eaten, 1 *Cran.* 178; says the sacrament is not corporal, but spiritual food, 3 *Bec.* 445; distinguishes between the flesh which was crucified, and the sacrament of that flesh, *ib.* 444, 445; calls the sacrament a type of the body of Christ, *Grin.* 69; designates the oblation the figure of Christ's body and blood, 2 *Bec.* 285, 3 *Bec.* 436, *Coop.* 207, 1 *Cran.* 122, (59), 2 *Jew.* 570, 3 *Jew.* 500; calls it an image, figure, type, similitude, &c., 2 *Jew.* 609; his use of the word simulacrum, 1 *Ful.* 102; speaks of receiving the sacrament for a similitude, 3 *Bec.* 436, *Coop.* 208, 1 *Cran.* 122, (59), 2 *Jew.* 570, 3 *Jew.* 487, 500; shews how in

AMBROSE

signification and figure of the divine benefit we take the mystical cup, 3 *Bec.* 436, 1*Cran.* 122, 2 *Jew.* 570; speaks of drinking the similitude of Christ's precious blood, 3 *Bec.* 436, 1 *Cran.* 122 (59), *Hutch.* 259, 2 *Jew.* 570; mentions that the priest ministered the sacrament saying, "The body of Christ," to which the recipient answered, "Amen," 1 *Jew.* 286 n., 2 *Jew.* 698; affirms that the cup after consecration was called blood, and that the people answered, "Amen," 2 *Jew.* 699; says, because we are delivered by the Lord's death, in eating and drinking we signify the flesh and blood which were offered for us (pseud.), 3 *Bec.* 436, 4 *Bul.* 440, 1 *Cran.* 122, (59), *Grin.* 65, 2 *Jew.* 570, 591, 597, 3 *Jew.* 493, 500; teaches that the wicked do not eat Christ's flesh nor drink his blood, *Hutch.* 265; says, the bread of life which came down from heaven doth minister everlasting life, and is the body of Christ, 1 *Cran.* 210, (81); remarks that he who ate the manna died, but that he who eats this body shall have remission of sins, and shall not die for ever, 2 *Bec.* 293, 3 *Bec.* 463, 1 *Cran.* 210, (81); says, Jesus is the bread that is the meat of saints, and he that takes it dies not a sinner's death, for it is the remission of sins, 2 *Bec.* 293, 3 *Bec.* 463, 1 *Cran.* 210, (81), 2 *Jew.* 1120, 3 *Jew.* 493, 4 *Jew.* 895; shews who are guilty of the Lord's body, (pseud.), *Grin.* 55, *Hutch.* 281; says, he is unworthy of the Lord who celebrates the mystery otherwise than it was delivered of the Lord (pseud.), *Coop.* 76, *Grin.* 57, 1 *Jew.* 205, 3 *Jew.* 444; asks Theodosius, after the slaughter at Thessalonica, how he will receive the body and blood of the Lord? which implies that the cup was given to the laity, *Coop.* 140, *Hutch.* 282, *Sand.* 455; says that as often as we drink, we have remission of our sins, 1 *Cran.* 210, (81); blames certain Greeks who came to the communion but once a year, *Coop.* 102, 1 *Jew.* 168; urges to receive the Lord's bread daily, and declares him who is not worthy to receive it every day, not worthy once a year, 2 *Bec.* 259, 3 *Bec.* 473, 1 *Jew.* 17, 120; speaks of offering up the eucharist once or twice in the week, 1 *Jew.* 129, 169, 2 *Jew.* 635, 636; interprets "our daily bread" of the sacrament daily consecrated, also of Christ the bread of life, 2 *Jew.* 772; says Christ gives bread always, 1 *Jew.* 450; calls the sacrament a spiritual medicine, and memorial of our redemption, 3 *Bec.* 389, 436; urges to receive it as the medicine of the wound of sin, *ib.* 473; says that because we sin always, we ought always to have the medicine, 2 *Bec.* 259, 3 *Bec.* 470; declares that we offer unto the remembrance of Christ's death, 2 *Bec.* 249, 3 *Bec.* 457; speaks of the oblation of many offered together, 1 *Jew.* 105, 202, 2 *Jew.* 737, 3 *Jew.* 477; says Christ, as a priest, now offers himself, that he may forgive our sins; here in a figure, there (viz. in heaven), in truth, 2 *Ful.* 83, 84; exhorts priests to follow the Chief Priest in offering sacrifice for the people, 1 *Jew.* 490, 2 *Jew.* 729, 742, 2 *Lat.* 274; speaks of Christ's body as offered on earth, 1 *Jew.* 490; says Christ is daily sacrificed, 2 *Jew.* 726, our minds being altars, *ib.* 730; says that the flesh of Christ is offered for the salvation of the body, and the blood for the soul, 2 *Bec.* 244, 3 *Bec.* 413; he offered for the emperor Valentinian, though assured of his salvation, *Coop.* 96, 2 *Jew.* 742; commends his brother Satyrus, who, in shipwreck, hanged the sacrament about his neck, *Coop.* 27, 134, 141, 2 *Ful.* 105, 2 *Jew.* 554, 3 *Jew.* 552, 554; disallows a private reception of the sacrament, *Hutch.* 229 n

xiv. *Prayer, Praise, &c.*: he prescribes times for praying, 1 *Bec.* 172; speaks of supplications, prayers, intercessions, and giving of thanks, as observed in all the world (pseud.), *Calf.* 295; compares the voice of prayer in the church to the sound of the waves of the sea, 4 *Jew.* 812, *Whita.* 271 n.; warns against babbling in prayer, since unto God not words but thoughts do speak, 1 *Bec.* 133, 135; says we are brought into the presence of the king by officers, but to obtain God's favour we only need a devout mind, 1 *Jew.* 97, 3 *Jew.* 578; on unknown tongues (pseud.), *Whita.* 273; asserts that those things ought to be spoken which the hearers may understand, 2 *Bec.* 254; 3 *Bec.* 407, 408, for an ignorant person hearing what he understands not, knows not the end of the prayer, and does not answer, Amen, 3 *Bec.* 407, 1 *Jew.* 282, 312; says that the unlearned, when he understands, perceives the truth of the Christian religion, 3 *Bec.* 408; on praying and giving thanks "with the spirit," 1 *Jew.* 313—315, 2 *Hoop.* 564; he prays for the repose of Theodosius, 2 *Ful.* 87

xv. *Fasting*: he supposes that Lent was instituted by Christ, *Whita.* 604; on abstinence from wine, &c., *Wool.* 136; asks, what is fasting but a substance and a heavenly image? 3 *Jew.* 507; speaks of the merit of fasting, 1 *Whitg.* 224; yet he cautions against boasting of a fast, else it will profit nothing, 2 *Bec.* 541; asks whether he can be thought to fast aright, who, instead of going to the church, goes to the chase, *ib.* 548; no fasting in his time between Easter and Whitsuntide, *Pil.* 556; his advice respecting different local customs of fasting, 3 *Jew.* 285, *Pil.* 557

xvi. *Virginity, Marriage:* he speaks of many heretics who feign chastity, 4 *Jew.* 767; says, we may desire virginity, but cannot command it, 3 *Jew.* 428, and that it may be counselled, but not enjoined, *ib.* 398; calls the minds of virgins altars on which Christ is daily offered for the redemption of the body, 1 *Jew.* 491, 730, 3 *Jew.* 470; affirms that a veiled virgin may not marry, 3 *Jew.* 418, and calls a lapsed virgin twice an adulteress, *ib.* 402; says a virgin is dependent on the judgment of her parents in respect to marriage, *Sand.* 455; says that the bands of matrimony are good, yet they are bands, 3 *Jew.* 415; observes that we see both virgins careful for the world, and married persons careful for the works of the Lord, *ib.* 417; on St Paul's words respecting virgins, *ib.* 422; remarks that the apostle had no commandment to give on this subject, but he had an example, *ib.* 423; says all the apostles were married, John and Paul excepted, 2 *Jew.* 727, 989, 3 *Jew.* 392, 4 *Jew.* 803; cites a canon of Nice on the second marriage of clerks, 2 *Whitg.* 152; allows that the second marriage of a priest is valid, *Pil.* 566; commends the married life of Gratian, *Pil.* 18; says that marriage with a niece is forbidden, 2 *Cran.* 329; allows diversity of religion to be a sufficient cause of divorce, 1 *Hoop.* 385; asserts that polygamy was without sin under the old law, 2 *Cran.* 405

xvii. *The Cross, Images:* he intimates that the standard of Abraham prefigured the cross, *Calf.* 103; describes the invention of the cross by Helena, *ib.* 325, 2 *Ful.* 190, 193, and declares that when she found it, she worshipped the King, not the wood, and intimates that the worship of the latter would have been a Gentile error and vanity of the wicked, 2 *Bec.* 72, *Calf.* 192, 377, 1 *Ful.* 212, 2 *Ful.* 202, 2 *Jew.* 650, *Park.* 8; tells what she did with the nails, *Calf.* 327; he numbers the second commandment among the ten, and holds it for a moral law, 2 *Bec.* 60; says the heathen worship wood as the image of God, 2 *Jew.* 646; false testimony for image-worship adduced as if from him at the second council of Nice, 2 *Ful.* 207

xviii. *Heresies, Antichrist:* on the serpentine discourse of heretics, *Whita.* 18; he says they put all the force of their poisons in dialectical disputations, 3 *Jew.* 237; alleges the Nicene council against the Arians, 3 *Jew.* 237, 238; opposed the empress Justina, who favoured them, *Calf.* 301; abhorred the council of Ariminum, *ib.* 345; wrote against the Novatians, 1 *Bec.* 95; his words against Apollinarius, 2 *Jew.* 578; against Eutyches, 1 *Jew.* 482 n.; he considered that the Roman kingdom was that which hindered the revelation of Antichrist, 2 *Jew.* 913; says "the abomination of desolation" is the cursed coming of Antichrist, 4 *Jew.* 728

xix. *The Civil Power, the Emperor* (and see i.): he calls it a great point of teaching whereby Christian men are taught to be subject to the higher powers, 1 *Bec.* 221; says, if the temporal governor demand tribute, the church denies it not, *ib.*; that those who have worldly riches are (peculiarly) subject to Cæsar, 4 *Jew.* 835; teaches that the things of God are not subject to the power and authority of princes, *Phil.* 11; appeals to the emperor against laymen judging priests, 1 *Ful.* 268; says even an heretical emperor may consider what sort of a bishop he is, who lays the priestly right under laymen's feet, 2 *Fulk.* 380; on the behaviour of Constantine in the Nicene synod, *Whita.* 436; says Constantius, the Arian emperor, took upon himself to judge of faith within the palace, *Grin.* 388; speaks of the council of Aquilæa as assembled by command of the emperor, 4 *Jew.* 1005; commends Gratian, *Grin.* 18; also Valentinian, and Theodosius, *ib.* 11; words to Valentinian, *Grin.* 376, 4 *Jew.* 1027, whom he blames for assuming the cognizance of ecclesiastical matters, 1 *Ful.* 268, *Whita.* 441; he exhorts him to be subject to God, 4 *Jew.* 670; tells him that in a cause of faith bishops were wont to judge of Christian emperors, not emperors of bishops, 2 *Ful.* 267, *Grin.* 388; and that conference about faith ought to be left to the priests, *Grin.* 388; refused to be tried by Valentinian, and warned him that he had no power over things pertaining to God, 4 *Jew.* 898, 1028, 3 *Whitg.* 308; offered himself and his goods to the pleasure of that emperor, 2 *Ful.* 266; speaks of his people addressing Valentinian, "We beseech thee, Augustus, we do not fight; we fear thee not, but we beseech," 3 *Jew.* 173; tells Theodosius that it neither becomes an emperor to deny liberty of speech, nor a priest not to say what he thinks, &c., *Park.* 94; and that in matters of religion, he (the emperor) should consult the priests of the Lord, *Grin.* 388; the law which Theodosius made at his suggestion, *Pil.* 409; he speaks of the labarum, or imperial banner, 2 *Jew.* 648

xx. *Miscellanea:* speaking of heavenly things, he says, the mind fails, the voice is silent, not mine only, but also the angels', &c., 3 *Jew.* 238; says, not the anciency of years, but of manners, is commendable, *Calf.* 192; said his arms were tears, 3 *Jew.* 170; declares it often against godly honesty to perform the oath that is made, 1 *Bec.* 372, 1 *Bul.* 250; remarks that it is no shame to go to the better, 4 *Jew.* 876; against giving heed to flattery, 3 *Whitg.* 578; on the evil consequences of forbearing things lawful (pseud.), *Sand.* 316; says it is a miserable necessity which is paid by parricide, 2 *Cran.* 216; shews how the outward man perishes, 3 *Jew.* 561; declares that there is no difference between the carcases of the dead, unless it be that the rich stink most, 2 *Bec.* 436; speaks of Julian's attempt to rebuild the temple, 4 *Jew.* 1075; speaks of converted Jews using sometimes the Syrian tongue, sometimes the Hebrew, 1 *Jew.* 290; on the bear, 1 *Ful.* 60 n

Ambrose of Alexandria: a deacon and a martyr, and the friend of Origen, *Whita.* 124

Ambrose of Camaldula: 2 *Ful.* 110 n

Ambrose of Duisburg: saluted, 2 *Zur.* 42

Ambrose (......): martyred, *Poet.* 166

Ambrose (......): died in Maidstone gaol, *Poet.* 170

Ambrosians: the orthodox so termed by Arians, 4 *Jew.* 713, 807

Ambrosiaster: this name is applied to the author of a commentary on St Paul's epistles, sometimes ascribed to St Ambrose, but perhaps written by Hilary the deacon, 2 *Ful.* 183 n

Amel: enamel, *Bale* 527; ameled, 3 *Bec.* 518

Amen: meaning of the word, 4 *Bul.* 218, 2 *Jew.* 698, 699; what it signifies at the end of the creed, 2 *Bec.* 51; what at the end of the Lord's prayer, *ib.* 197, 198, 4 *Bul.* 218, *Now.* (81), 202; mentioned as a response by Paul, Justin, and others, *Whita.* 259, 260; remarks of several fathers on it, 1 *Jew.* 286; not used of old after the Benedicite, *Pra. Eliz.* 27 n.; Stapleton says Protestant preachers made their hearers cry, Amen, 2 *Ful.* 117

Amendment of life: 1 *Bec.* 102, 103; for general amendment, each should amend one, *ib.* 257; a disposition to it is necessary in preparation for the Lord's supper, 2 *Bec.* 236; and must continue for ever, *ib.* 237

Amenusing: aminishing, diminishing, *Phil.* 352 n., 424

Amerbach (Boniface): letter to him, 3 *Zur.* 767; notice of him, *ib.* n

Amerbach (Bruno): on the blunders of the vulgar Latin Psalter, *Whita.* 191, 192; condemns as fictitious the commentary on the Psalms attributed to Jerome, 2 *Ful.* 208

America: not regarded as a fourth quarter of the world for many years after its discovery, *Rid.* 279 n

Amerius (Ant.), i.e. Rob. Barnes, *q. v.*

Amerus, one of the magi: *Whita.* 560 n

Ames (Jos.): Typogr. Antiq. ed. Herbert, 2 *Bec.* 423 n., 4 *Bul.* xv. &c., *Coop.* vi, *Grin.* 201 n.; corrected, *Pra. Eliz.* xix. n

Ames (Will.), a Puritan divine: 1 *Brad.* 564

Amice (amictus): a vestment, 1 *Tyn.* 419; the alleged signification thereof, and of the flap thereon, 3 *Tyn.* 73; amices of calaber and cats' tails, *Bale* 527; the grey amice forbidden, 2 *Whitg.* 50—52

Amit: to leave out, 1 *Hoop.* 534 n

Ammian (......): saluted, 1 *Zur.* 30, 3 *Zur.* 379, 421, 615

Ammianus Marcellinus: tells of the vain attempt of the Jews to rebuild their temple, *Sand.* 347 n.; mentions the bath of Constantine, 2 *Ful.* 360 n.; describes the contest between Damasus and Ursinus, 1 *Jew.* 355

Ammonites: children of Lot, *Pil.* 409

Ammonius Saccas: his system, 1 *Lat.* 202

Amnon: 1 *Bul.* 413

Amnon, king of Judah: 2 *Bul.* 10

Amorites: overthrown, 4 *Jew.* 1180

Amos: prophesies, 4 *Bul.* 70, 494; slain with a bar, 2 *Jew.* 839

Amount: to surmount, 3 *Bec.* 606

Amphilochius, bp of Iconium: his zeal against the Arians, *Sand.* 41, 73, 232; he confutes the Messalians, 1 *Jew.* 192, 193, 2 *Whitg.* 165; his jurisdiction, 2 *Whitg.* 430; says, as alleged by Cyril, that unless Christ had been born carnally, we had not been born spiritually, 1 *Jew.* 475; declares representations of saints to be needless, 2 *Jew.* 659, *Calf.* 145, 149; the fragments ascribed to him, *Whita.* 256 n.; the Life of Basil falsely ascribed to him, 1 *Jew.* 85, 187, &c., 242, 244, 245, 2 *Jew.* 559, 560, 585, 586, 3 *Jew.* 315, 4 *Jew.* 652, 1090; it calls Basil chief priest, &c.,

1 *Jew.* 373, 4 *Jew.* 824; it is cited for the elevation of the host, 1 *Jew.* 508; the writer says it is the natural provision of those who are deceived to take out of the way testimonies of the truth, 2 *Jew.* 672; to the writer of this Life of Basil, Jewel ascribes a Life of Becket, 1 *Jew.* 189; this book speaks of a maid who lived 36 years as a monk, 4 *Jew.* 650

Amplect: to embrace, 1 *Bec.* 66, 2 *Brad.* 9

Ampthill, co. Bedford: prince Edward lived there, 2 *Cran.* 413 n

Ampton (Sir Edw.), K.B.: married Anne, daughter of the protector Somerset, 3 *Zur.* 340 n

Amram: 1 *Bul.* 42

Amri: *v.* Omri.

Amsdorff (Nich.): complains of sects among professors of the gospel, 2 *Jew.* 686, 3 *Jew.* 621, 623

Amulets: *Calf.* 284, &c.

Amurath, the Great Turk: terms our Saviour, the crucified God, *Rog.* 49

An' (and): used for if, *Calf.* 245

Anabaptists: *v.* Baptism, Catabaptists, Enthusiasts, Family of Love, Swermerians, Beza (T.), Bullinger (H.), Calvin (J.), Gualther (R.), Hemmingius (N.), Zuinglius (H.).

The history of Anabaptism, 4 *Bul.* 393; imperial laws against rebaptizing, 4 *Bul.* 394; the rise of the Anabaptists not to be attributed to the reformers, *Phil.* 401; many in popish countries, 3 *Jew.* 189; six sorts of them in Germany, 2 *Jew.* 686; their turbulent proceedings, 1 *Hoop.* 246; a great trouble to many commonwealths, 2 *Hoop.* 76; alleged their success as a proof that they verily had the truth, 2 *Lat.* 209; seized the city of Munster, and committed great atrocities, *Grin.* 256 n.; their heresy preached by popish emissaries, 1 *Lat.* 151 n.; some burned in Smithfield, 1 *Tyn.* lxx; met their death boldly, 1 *Lat.* 160; a commission against them and other sectaries, in king Edward's time, 2 *Cov.* xiii; the errors of the English Anabaptists described by Hooper, 3 *Zur.* 65; by Micronius, *ib.* 574; their frenzy prevalent in Kent and Essex, *ib.* 87; inquiry concerning them, *Rid.* 531; many sprung up in England in queen Mary's time, 4 *Jew.* 1241; 1 *Zur.* 92; their prevalence, 3 *Bec.* 6, 293, 401, 1 *Zur.* 277, 285; they apply to Grindal for the free exercise of their religion, *Grin.* 243; a great number taken in 1575, on Easter-day, *Park.* 479; reference to them, *Nord.* 114; notes and properties of Anabaptists, collected out of Zuinglius and others, 1 *Whitg.* 125; their errors described and condemned, 2 *Bec.* 207, 215, 226, 2 *Brad.* 382, 383, 1 *Cov.* 51, *Rid.* 120, 3 *Whitg.* 552—554, 3 *Zur.* 65; their opinions pernicious, 1 *Lat.* 106; very pernicious and damnable, 2 *Hoop.* 121; their hypocritical humility, 1 *Whitg.* 8; they were liars, 1 *Bec.* 280; disturbers of the church and of the gospel, 1 *Whitg.* 16, 78, &c.; being contentious, *ib.* 40, 46; a crafty heresy, 3 *Whitg.* 134; their irreverence, *Rid.* 265; the devil builds his chapel in them and other heretics, 3 *Bec.* 401; they should be excommunicated, and given over to the magistrates, *Hutch.* 201; they denied the incarnation, 2 *Cov.* 347, &c., *Hutch.* 144; revived the heresy of Valentinus, 1 *Bec.* 412, 418, asserting that Christ took not flesh of the virgin, 2 *Bec.* 446, *Grin.* 69 n., 444, *Rog.* 52; Hooper's LESSON OF THE INCARNATION OF CHRIST, written against them, 2 *Hoop.* 2; they were Arians, *Phil.* 314; renewed the Pelagian heresy respecting original sin, *Lit. Edw.* 527, (573); thought they were able to save themselves, 2 *Hoop.* 76; affirmed that there is naturally in man free-will unto the best things, *Rog.* 106; also that man is justified by works, *ib.* 114; and may perfectly keep the law of God, *ib.* 123; contemned the sacraments as of no account, *ib.* 246; their errors on baptism, 3 *Whitg.* 23; in these opinions they followed certain ancient heretics, *Phil.* 274; they numbered baptism amongst things indifferent, *Rog.* 275; asserted that baptism does no more than civilly discern one man from another, *ib.* 278; they denied baptism to infants, and rebaptized, 4 *Bul.* 382, *Rid.* 367, *Rog.* 202, 265; by what arguments they denied baptism to infants, 4 *Bul.* 385, 395; they said that the apostles did not baptize infants, 2 *Bec.* 209; their use of Matt. xxviii, 2 *Whitg.* 516; their exposition of Acts xix, *Hutch.* 116; they feigned the baptism of children to be the pope's commandment, *Phil.* 280; said it was of the devil, or the invention of pope Nicholas, *Rog.* 280, and that infants believe not, therefore are not to be baptized, *ib.* 281; these and other arguments confuted, 4 *Bul.* 385, &c., 395, *Whita.* 506; they denied the validity of baptism by papists, 2 *Whitg.* 520; asserted that sin after baptism is unpardonable, 2 *Bec.* 170, &c., 3 *Bul.* 66, *Hutch.* 112, 113, *Rog.* 141; they considered the Lord's supper a bare sign, 2 *Lat.* 252, and made no difference between the Lord's table and their own, *Rid.* 9; their king and queen administered the Lord's supper, *Rog.* 234; they denied the scriptures, *Whita.* 298; rejected the book of Job, *Rog.* 81; and ridiculed it, *Whita.* 33; rejected the Psalms, *ib.* 31; and the Song of Solomon, *ib.* 32; deemed not the Bible to be the word of God, *Rog.* 78; yet burned the books of learned men, reserving only the scriptures, *ib.* 326; some asserted the scriptures to be too hard for any to interpret, *ib.* 194; they relied on the Spirit without the scriptures, 1 *Brad.* 329, rather on their own dreams, &c., *Rog.* 158, 196; they looked to new revelations for instruction, *Sand.* 115; a sect of them called Enthusiasts, 4 *Bul.*94 n.; their raving, 2 *Cov.* 521; their wicked fancies, 3 *Whitg.* 576; their books, *Rog.* 82; they asserted the visible church (i. e. themselves) to be free from sin, *ib.* 167, 179; pretended absolute pureness, 4 *Bul.* 168, *Sand.* 90; and declared all but themselves to be wicked, *Rog.* 169; rejected the testimony of the church, *Rid.*129 ; took on themselves the reformation and ordering of the church, *Rog.* 343; forsook it on account of wicked ministers, 4 *Bul.* 53; segregated themselves from society, 2 *Lat.* 197; their conventicles, 1 *Bul.* 293, *Sand.* 191; their error respecting wicked ministers, 2 *Brad.* 345, 4 *Bul.* 53, 161; said that evil ministers cannot loose, *Hutch.* 97; they hated the order of ministers for the faults of some of them, *ib.* 310; presumed to teach without authority, *Rog.* 231; said there should be no public preaching, *ib.* 232, 325; that there is no calling to the ministry but the immediate calling from God, *ib.* 239, 240, 1 *Whitg.* 412, 413; that no man who is himself faulty can preach the truth to others, *Rog.* 271; termed preachers, letter-doctors, *ib.*325; affirmed that all Christians should be equal, *ib.* 330, 2 *Whitg.* 326, 397, 398; and that goods should be common, 2 *Bul.* 18, 21, 4 *Bul.* 18, 2 *Hoop.* 42, 1 *Whitg.* 352; this error condemned by one of the Articles, *Lit. Edw.* 536, *Rog.* 353; in consequence of this opinion they give no alms, *ib.* 355; their doctrine on going to law, magistracy, and excommunication, *Hutch.* 323, 330; their mischievous tenets respecting magistracy, 1 *Bec.* 211—214, 1 *Bul.* 308 n., 385, &c., 1 *Cov.* 51, 2 *Hoop.* 76, 78, *Rog.* 337, 3 *Whitg.* 591, 593; their doctrine on this point is barbarous and wicked, *Sand.* 85; they allowed no judges on earth, 1 *Lat.* 151, 157, 273; some however allowed that magistrates are needful, 1 *Whitg.* 20; but said that Christians may not be magistrates, *ib.* 155, 156, that Christians have no need of magistrates, 3 *Whitg.* 274, 408; they thought it absurd that temporal rulers should reign over the spirituality, 1 *Bec.* 217; and affirmed that God's people are free from all laws, *Rog.* 317; thought that before the resurrection there shall be no magistrates, because the wicked shall be rooted out, *ib.* 346; they refused to take lawful oaths, 1 *Bul.* 245, 2 *Hoop.* 54, *Phil.* 83, 85, *Rog.* 358; denied the lawfulness of capital punishment, 1 *Lat.* 496, *Rog.* 349; affirmed war to be unlawful, 1 *Bul.* 370, 1 *Lat.* 495, *Rog.* 351; condemned allowable pleasures, 2 *Bul.* 57

Anablatha: the village where Epiphanius (*q. v.*) destroyed the picture, 2 *Cran.* 178, et al.

Anacharsis, a philosopher: on barbarians, 1 *Jew.* 267

Anacletus, bp of Rome: *v.* Soter.

His order in succession, *Whita.* 573; the epistles ascribed to him are plainly counterfeit, 1 *Jew.* 342, 354, *Rid.* 180, 182, 2 *Whitg.* 345; in them he (rather the writer in his name) commands all to communicate that will not be excommunicated, 3 *Bec.* 416, 474, 2 *Bul.* 238, 258, *Coop.* 128, 1 *Jew.* 19 n., 183, 186, *Rid.* 105, 317; this decree is also ascribed to Calixtus, 1 *Jew.* 19 n., 3 *Jew.* 472, 473, 476; claims superiority not from the apostles, but from Christ, *ib.* 355, 3 *Jew.* 306; speaks of the supremacy of Peter, 1 *Jew.* 341, 343, 351, 3 *Jew.* 195, 196, 306; derives Cephas from κεφαλή, 2 *Ful.* 301 n.; mentions archbishops, &c., 4 *Jew.* 1299, 2 *Whitg.* 136, 339; does not claim universal jurisdiction, 3 *Jew.* 333; speaks of some bishops as subject to the apostolic see, 4 *Jew.* 707; commands all bishops (of the province) to visit a certain church in Rome once a year, 1 *Jew.* 173, 409; gives directions respecting ordination of bishops, *ib.* 407; says the apostles left but two orders of priests, viz. bishops and elders, 3 *Jew.* 272; says, bishops are in the place of the apostles, and priests are in the place of the disciples, 2 *Jew.* 677; orders that the bishop at the ministration shall be attended by deacons, subdeacons, &c., 1 *Jew.* 176; says, that priests should be ordained by their own bishops, that the people may consent, *ib.* 408; cited for the minor orders, *Rog.* 260 n.; he speaks of the invisible power of the Spirit being mingled with oil, 1 *Jew.* 473

Anacletus II. antipope [Peter Leoni]: 1 *Jew.* 382
Anagogical sense: *v.* Scripture.
Anakims: called Enacke, 1 *Tyn.* 446
Analogical sense: *v.* Scripture.
Analogy of Faith: what it is, *Rog.* 195, *Whita.* 472; all our expositions must accord with it, *Whita.* 472; Stapleton says it means unwritten tradition, *ib.* 485
Ananias: Paul sent to him, 4 *Bul.* 95
Ananias, or Ananus, high-priest: 2 *Ful.* 246 n
Ananias, and Sapphira: 1 *Bul.* 242, 359, 3 *Bul.* 302, 4 *Bul.* 8, *Grin.* 8, 1 *Jew.* 384, 1 *Lat.* 407, 502, 3 *Whitg.* 447
Anastasius, emperor of the East: it is said that he commanded a quarternity of persons to be worshipped, *Rog.* 44; excommunicated by pope Anastasius II, *Pil.* 601 n
Anastasius I. bp of Rome: commanded that, while the gospels were read, the people should stand and diligently hear the Lord's word, 3 *Bec.* 409, 2 *Brad.* 308, 3 *Whitg.* 384; exhorts to worship the Lord's words, 1 *Jew.* 514; his judgment of Ruffinus, 4 *Jew.* 1006; cited for relics, *Calf.* 311; he (?) speaks of the states of the world as members of his body, 4 *Jew.* 920 n
Anastasius II. bp of Rome: excommunicated the emperor Anastasius, *Pil.* 601 n.; became a great heretic himself, *ib.*; favoured the Nestorians and Photinus, 1 *Jew.* 381, 3 *Jew.* 343, 4 *Jew.* 926; forsaken of his clergy for communicating with the latter, 1 *Jew.* 400, *Pil.* 601 n.; he was a sorcerer, *Bale* 593; an Arian, 3 *Jew.* 345
Anastasius III. bp of Rome: Bradford says he ordered standing at the gospel, but this is a mistake for Anastasius I, 2 *Brad.* 308
Anastasius Bibliothecarius: whether the author of the Pontifical, 2 *Ful.* 98 n
Anathema: *v.* Curse.
That of Paul against false preachers, 3 *Bul.* 52; how he wished himself accursed, *Pil.* 424
Anatolius, bp of Constantinople: 3 *Jew.* 220
Anaxagoras: his idea of the heavens, 3 *Jew.* 131; feigned snow to be black, *Phil.* 357; his death (or that of Anaxarchus?), *Hutch.* 80, 320
Anaxarchus: his death, *Hutch.* 80, 320
Anaximenes: on love to fathers, 1 *Bul.* 273
Ancestors: *v.* Forefathers.
Ancher (Ant.): *v.* Aucher.
Anchor: sacra anchora, shot anchor, sheet anchor, *Pra. Eliz.* 93 n.; shot anchor, 1 *Cran.* 158, 3 *Tyn.* 46
Ancona: a bishop thereof, not of Antioch, as stated by Becon, deprived for niggardliness, 1 *Bec.* 23 n., 2 *Bec.* 325, 326
Ancre: an anchorite, 2 *Tyn.* 42; "anchor," 2 *Bec.* 390
Ancyra: *v.* Councils.
And: used for if, 1 *Bec.* 204, *Calf.* 5, 245; for than, *Phil.* 339
Andabates: fencers who fought on horseback hood-winked, 1 *Bec.* 331
Andelot (Fra. d'): *v.* Coligni.
Andernach (Quinter): 2 *Cran.* 435, 2 *Zur.* 52, 3 *Zur.* 27 n., 28, 54, 334
Anderson (Chr.): his Annals of the English Bible, 2 *Cov.* viii. &c.; 2 *Cran.* 346 n., 395 n., 396 n.; *Park.* 262 n., 1 *Tyn.* xiii. n., &c.
Anderson (Tho.), minister of Montrose: 2 *Zur.* 365
Andradius (Jac.): *v.* Payva.
Andre (M. le mareschal St): *v.* Saint Andre.
Andreas (Jac.): was professor at Tubingen, 2 *Zur.* 98 n., 100 n., 101, 274 n.; and head of the Ubiquitarians in Germany, 1 *Zur.* 302; his form of concord rejected, *ib.* 321 n.; on dissensions amongst the reformed, 3 *Jew.* 623; on the judgment of à Soto and Hosius concerning the holy scripture, 3 *Jew.* 757, 758; cites a saying that Christ presides in heaven, the pope sits on earth, 4 *Jew.* 855; on the headship of the church, 1 *Whitg.* 392; his work against Hosius, 4 *Jew.* xxxii. 855, 899, 3 *Whitg.* xxiv.
Andreas (Jo.): on Christ's presence in the sacrament, 2 *Jew.* 798; he avouches that the pope receives money from courtezans, 4 *Jew.* 644; records a verse alluding to the name of Rome, *ib.* 867, 1082; maintains very extravagant pretensions of the pope, 3 *Jew.* 600, 4 *Jew.* 921; termed Jack of Andrew, 4 *Jew.* 838
Andree (Theod.): *v.* Theodoricus.
Andrew (St): falsely said to have celebrated mass, 1 *Jew.* 108; the succession of bishops of Constantinople traced to him, *Whita.* 510; his martyrdom, *Calf.* 127, 128, 2 *Whitg.* 303; his cross, *Calf.* 105; his address to it, 1 *Jew.* 535; why the tutelary saint of Scotland, 1 *Hoop.* 314; collect for his intercession, *Rog.* 227; a sermon on the gospel for his day, 2 *Lat.* 23; the apocryphal Gospel called his, *Bale* 314, *Rog.* 82, *Whita.* 108, 312; his Acts, *Rog.* 82
Andrew (Will.), or Androwes: died in prison, *Poet.* 164
Andrewes (Lanc.), bp of Winchester: referred to, *Calf.* 25 n., 65 n.; on the meaning of the Hebrew Thau, *ib.* 108 n.; mentions nine manifestations of the Spirit, *ib.* 226 n

Andrews (St): v Saint Andrews.
Andrews (......): brought in Sanders's book, *Park.* 409.
Androcides: calls wine the blood of the earth, 3 *Jew.* 522
Andronicus, and Junia: 1 *Whitg.* 498
Andronicus, emperor: says the common people are delighted with the dispraise of others, &c., 3 *Whitg.* 572
Androwes (Will.): *v.* Andrew.
Anempst: anent, concerning, 2 *Brad.* 4
Angel: a gold coin, 2 *Brad.* 172, 1 *Lat.* 181, *Pil.* 428; those of Edward IV., 1 *Hoop.* 333 n.; a silver (?) coin, *Phil.* 234
Angelica Summa: *v.* Angelus de Clavasio.
Angelici: heretics who worshipped angels, 3 *Bul.* 348, 2 *Ful.* 41 n., 375, *Phil.* 420; their doctrine condemned by the council of Laodicea, 2 *Ful.* 42 n.; the canon against them shamefully corrupted, *ib.*
Angelomus: compares Christ's body to hay, 1 *Jew.* 463; says, God the Father had his only-begotten Son Jesus Christ hidden in the letter of the law, the Jews not knowing it, 2 *Jew.* 594; wrongly cited for Julianus, *ib.* 724, *Jew.* xxxix. n
Angels: *v.* Saints, Prayer.

i. *More particularly the holy angels:* meaning of the word, 3 *Bul.* 327, *Now.* 99; translations of the word ἄγγελος examined, 1 *Ful.* 483—485; that there are angels, 3 *Bul.* 328; angels and spirits denied by Sadducees and Libertines, *Hutch.* 134; what they are, 3 *Bec.* 605, 3 *Bul.* 328; they are created, 3 *Bul.* 329; Augustine thought that light and darkness in Gen. i. referred to angels, *Whita.* 462; some heretics ascribed the work of creation to them, *Rog.* 40; they are not redeemed by Christ, 2 *Lat.* 109; the elect angels, 1 *Brad.* 322; angels are substances, not mere inspirations, 3 *Bul.* 329, *Hutch.* 139; what manner of substances, 3 *Bul.* 330; what bodies they take, *ib.* 331, *Hutch.* 82; they are incorruptible, 3 *Bul.* 332; most swift and free, *ib.* 334; but they cannot be at one time in two places, 1 *Cran.* 97; their strength, 3 *Bul.* 335; their happiness, *Pil.* 61; their knowledge, 3 *Bul.* 336; their multitude, and order, *ib.*; seven orders enumerated, 1 *Brad.* 274, 338, 341, *Pra. B.* 108; Dionysius and others treat of the ranks of the heavenly hierarchy, *Whita.* 576; Irenæus condemns the folly of those who pretend to describe them, *ib.* 577; Augustine confessed his ignorance of the difference between the orders, 3 *Bul.* 336, *Whita.* 577, 3 *Jew.* 278; these ranks are no pattern for the government of the church, 3 *Jew.* 279; the names given to them; archangels, thrones, &c., 3 *Bul.* 337; God useth the ministry of angels, *ib.* 338; they are his messengers, *Pil.* 134; ready to execute his commands, 1 *Lat.* 386; their obedience and diligence, 2 *Lat.* 85; what their ministries are, 3 *Bul.* 340, *Calf.* 199, *Lit. Edw.* 473, *Now.* (65,) 85, *Sand.* 267; the opinions of Origen on this, 1 *Jew.* 326; the ministry of angels, verses by Edmund Spenser, *Poet.* 30; they were the first preachers, 2 *Lat.* 118; they minister unto the elect, 2 *Tyn.* 167, 169; rejoice for our salvation, 2 *Lat.* 123; are appointed to defend us, *ib.* 86; guardian angels, *Wool.* 97; a prayer to God for the help of angels, 3 *Bec.* 84; the same, *Lit. Edw.* 474; angels are present at our worship, 2 *Jew.* 741; too much must not be attributed to them, 3 *Bul.* 344; they will not have themselves worshipped, *ib.* 210, 344; they are not to be worshipped, or prayed to, *Bale* 544, 626, 2 *Bec.* 58, 59, 3 *Bul.* 347, *Calf.* 375, 2 *Lat.* 86, 2 *Tyn.* 169; they do not offer prayer as intercessors, 3 *Bul.* 219; their intercession taught by Chrysostom, 2 *Jew.* 741; the angels mentioned in various parts of the Apocalypse, *Bale* 641; apocryphal fables respecting angels, 1 *Ful.* 21; Clement Alex. taught that the souls of men are transformed into angels, *Coop.* 146; angels are said to have ministered the sacrament, consecrated a bishop, and answered Arnulph at his matins, 1 *Jew.* 191; nothing touching religion can be proved by oracles, or visions of angels, 2 *Cran.* 40, 64; popish images of angels, *Rog.* 223; the mount of angels, (Mons Garganus,) 3 *Bul.* 348; angels declared to be subject to the pope, 4 *Jew.* 846

ii. *Evil angels* (*v.* Demons, Satan): what they are, 3 *Bec.* 605, 3 *Bul.* 348; Sadducees and Libertines deny their existence, *Hutch.* 134; or assert that they are mere bad affections, 3 *Bul.* 353, *Hutch.* 140; on the fall of some of the angels, 2 *Brad.* 102, 3 *Bul.* 349, 1 *Lat.* 27, *Now.* (31), 147; Clement Alex., Justin, and others, taught that they fell through the love of women, *Coop.* 146; strange opinions of Lactantius on this point, 3 *Zur.* 233; Augustine supposed the darkness mentioned in Gen. i. to mean evil angels, *Whita.* 462; evil angels are sent to try the godly, and to punish the wicked, *Sand.* 267

Angelus (St): a martyr in Sicily, *Bale* 586

Angelus de Clavasio: his Summa Angelica, *Jew.* xxxii; extract on public and private mass, 1 *Jew.* 174; on cases of doubtful consecration, *ib.* 550, 3 *Jew.* 454; he says the mass, in respect of the work wrought, is nothing else than the application of Christ's merit, and that it avails for those to whom the priest by intention applies it, 2 *Jew.* 747; on the power of the pope, *ib.* 907; asserts that the pope may, in certain cases, dispense with all the precepts of the Old and New Testament, 3 *Jew.* 219, 599; says, Martin V. dispensed with a man who had married his sister, *ib.* 599, 4 *Jew.* 1245; on the question whether the pope can commit simony, *ib.* 147, 4 *Jew.* 865, 866, 867

Angelus (Jo.), or Parisiensis: says purgatory is the peculiar possession of the pope, 3 *Jew.* 560, 4 *Jew.* 845

Anger: anger, strife, &c. forbidden, 2 *Bec.* 95, 96; against anger, with sentences and examples of scripture condemning it, 1 *Bec.* 458, &c.; anger (in an evil sense) is murder in God's sight, *Now.* (19), 133; a kind of madness, *Pil.* 408; what kind of anger is allowed, 1 *Bul.* 300; when good, *Pil.* 391, 477; when sinful, *ib.* 478; anger may proceed from love, 2 *Tyn.* 45; when it is to be restrained, *ib.* 46; that of Jonah, 1 *Hoop.* 551

Angle: see 2 *Bec.* 428 n

Anglicus (Jo.): *v.* John.

Anglo-Saxon tongue: *Park.* 253, 266, 271; type cast for Day, *ib.* 468 n.; MS. of Gregory's Pastoral, 4 *Jew.* 1273 n

Anglo-Saxons: *v.* England.

Anglus (Michael): i. e. Miles Coverdale, *q. v.*

Angus (Archib. earl of): *v.* Douglas.

Anhalt (Wolfg. prince of): *v.* Wolfgang.

Anicetus, bp of Rome: differed from Polycarp, but without a breach of communion, 4 *Bul.* 57, 58, *Calf.* 269, 270; he permitted Polycarp to administer (or receive?) the communion in his church, 1 *Jew.* 146, *Whita.* 217; stated to mention archbishops, 2 *Whitg.* 136

Anjou (Fra. duke of), sometime of Alençon: *v.* Francis.

Anjou (Hen. duke of): *v.* Henry III.

Anna, the prophetess: 3 *Bul.* 278, 4 *Bul.* 182

Anna Comnena: says, the Latins think and speak of the pope as lord of the whole world, 4 *Jew.* 828

Anna of Oldenburg, countess of East Friesland: patroness of John à Lasco, 3 *Zur.* 513

Anna, wife of Julius Sancterentianus, *q. v.*

Annals, or Annuals: masses so called, 1 *Lat.* 56 n.; injunction against anniversaries for the dead, 2 *Hoop.* 146

Annandale: ravaged by the English, 1 *Zur.* 225 n

Annas, high-priest: had the spirit of prophecy, 4 *Jew.* 941

Annates: *v.* Tot-quots in *Hutch.* index. How much the English bishops paid to the pope for annates or first-fruits, 4 *Jew.* 1078

Anne (St): *v.* Joachim.

St Anne of Buckstone, 1 *Hoop.* 40

Anne Boleyn, second queen of Henry VIII: slanders respecting her prior to her marriage, 3 *Zur.* 552, 553; not married by Cranmer, 2 *Cran.* 246; her marriage confirmed by Cranmer, *ib.* 244 n., and by act of parliament, *ib.* 285 n., and by a pope's bull, *Park.* 414, 420; ceremonies at her coronation, 2 *Cran.* 245; Tyndale sends her a copy of his New Testament, printed on vellum, 1 *Tyn.* lxiv; her letter to Cromwell on behalf of a merchant who was persecuted for abetting the publication of the New Testament in English, *ib.*; she lends Tyndale's Obedience, and reclaims it from Wolsey, *ib.* 130; sends for Parker, *Park.* 1, 2, 482; her liberality towards students, *ib.* 2; Latin letter from her to Rich. Nix, bp of Norwich, *ib.* 4; her charge to Parker about her daughter Elizabeth, *ib.* 59, 391, 400; her favour to Parker, *ib.* 70, 178; she is endowed by the king, 3 *Zur.* 202; Cranmer's letter to the king on the reports against her conduct, 2 *Cran.* 323; the succession of her children opposed by sir Tho. More, and bp Fisher, *ib.* viii; her divorce, *ib.*; hopes of the Romish party on her death, *ib.* 328 n

Anne of Cleves, fourth queen of Henry VIII: her reception at Calais, Canterbury, and elsewhere, 2 *Cran.* 400; her marriage, 3 *Zur.* 201, 529 n., 627; her repudiation, *ib.* 201; attempt to reconcile the king to her, 2 *Cran.* 409, 410; her marriage declared null, *ib.* 410 n.; the act to dissolve it, 3 *Zur.* 205; dedication to her, 3 *Bec.* 74; notice of her, *ib.* n

Anne of Hungary, wife of the emperor Ferdinand I: *Grin.* 3 n., 14 n

Anne, queen of Great Britain, &c.: notice of a prayer in her writing, now at Lambeth, *Pra. Eliz.* xx.

Annebault (Claude), baron de Rets: French ambassador and lord admiral, 2 *Cran.* 416 n (misprinted Annehault).

Annesse (St): *v.* Agnes.

Annius (Jo.): wrote on the Apocalypse, *Bale* 258
Anniversaries: *v.* Annals.
Annonius of Paris: 4 *Jew.* 648; or Antonius, *ib.* n
Anodynes: 2 *Cov.* 245
Anoiling, Anointing: *v.* Unction.
Anointed: *v.* Christ, Christs.
Another: used in a peculiar sense, *Hutch.* 316, 341
Ansbertus (Ambr.): wrote on the Apocalypse, *Bale* 256, *Jew.* xxxiii; tells how the chosen people of God go out of Babylon, 4 *Jew.* 876; calls Rome a second Babylon, *ib.* 1064
Ansegisus, abbot of Lobies: compiled the decrees of Charlemagne and Louis, 1 *Hoop.* 228, 4 *Jew.* xxxiii. 816, 1031, *Pil.* 536
Anselm (St), abp of Canterbury: named, *Pil.* 484; obliged William II. to surrender the investiture of bishops to the pope's vicar, 2 *Tyn.* 294; accused for acknowledging pope Urban, *Pil.* 589; attends a council at Rome, 1 *Tyn.* 380 n.; styled traitorous, 1 *Whitg.* 482; his works, 4 *Jew.* xxxiii. 808; only some of them printed at Cologne, *ib.* 809; MS. of his Offendiculum Sacerdotum, at C.C.C.C., 3 *Jew.* 130 n., 4 *Jew.* 808 n.; certain commentaries commonly ascribed to him were written by Anselm of Laon (*q. v.*), 1 *Jew.* 315 n.; some are supposed to have been written by Herv. Natalis, 2 *Cran.* 207 n.; Anselm defines original sin as the want of original righteousness, 2 *Bul.* 385; passages on justification (probably by Herv. Natalis), 2 *Cran.* 207, 209; says Peter was chosen to the salvation of the Jews, Paul to that of the Gentiles (pseud.), 3 *Jew.* 328; says, Linus was the first bp of Rome (pseud.), *Pil.* 588; says that God's law forbids to follow the steps of the catholic or universal faith, any further than the judgment of the canonical truth commands, 2 *Cran.* 35; says that in Latin a bishop is called superintendens (pseud.), 4 *Jew.* 906; forbade priests' marriages, *Pil.* 571, 573, 588; his remarkable dialogue on that subject, 4 *Jew.* 808; in it he refers to the question of clerical celibacy as discussed through the whole world in his time, 3 *Jew.* 130, 387, 4 *Jew.* 808; his epistle to Ernulph, prior of Canterbury, forbidding the marriage of priests, *Pil.* 571; his letter to Gundulph, bp of Rochester, the said Ernulph, and William archdeacon of Canterbury, on certain priests separated from their wives, *ib.* 573; pope Paschal's letter to him on the promotion of priests' children to holy offices, *ib.* 572; his letter to Waleram, on diversity of rites, *ib.* 538; reference to it, *ib.* 620; on St Elphege, *Bale* 191

Anselm of Laon: author of certain commentaries commonly ascribed to St Anselm (*q. v.*), 1 *Jew.* 315 n.; he says, we break and divide the bread into many parts, to declare the unity of the love of them that receive it, 1 *Jew.* 142, 2 *Jew.* 589; his reading of a text on the cup and the bread, 1 *Jew.* 236; exposition of 1 Cor. xiv. 16, "my spirit prayeth," &c. *ib.* 315; on the mystery of iniquity, 4 *Jew.* 729; says, Antichrist shall feign himself to be holy, and call himself God, *ib.* 843; foretells the departure of many churches from the church of Rome on account of her wickedness, *ib.* 875, 876

Anselm Ryd: *v.* Ryd,
Anselm (......): 2 *Zur.* 298
Answer: An Answer for the Tyme, &c., 3 *Whitg.* xxiv
Answers: to be given to those who ask for a reason of the hope that is in us, 3 *Tyn.* 55
Anterus, or Antherus, bp of Rome: cited, 1 *Jew.* 68; the epistles called his mention some who lived a long time after him, *ib.* 173, 342
Anthemius, emperor: 1 *Bul.* 264, 4 *Bul.* 130
Anthems: *v.* Antiphons.
Anthems sung in the steeple at St Paul's, *Pil.* 483, 522; why in the steeple, *ib.* 529: an anthem or prayer (in verse) for the preservation of the church, the queen's majesty, and the realm, *Lit. Eliz.* 560
Anthonius (......): was one of the ministers in the Dutch church at Norwich, 1 *Zur.* 256 n., 266 n
Anthony: *v.* Antonius
Anthony (St): account of him, 1 *Bec.* 139 n.; his life, among the works of Athanasius, *Calf.* 74 n.; he understood the scriptures without any knowledge of letters, 2 *Jew.* 684; was notably learned in them, 3 *Jew.* 430, 435; God's creatures were his books, *Pil.* 146; he says that in prayer our minds should be absorbed in divine meditations, *Whita.* 266; he used the sign of the cross, 2 *Ful.* 144, 172; story of him and the cobbler, 1 *Lat.* 392, 2 *Lat.* 94; his vision of swine standing at altars, 3 *Bec.* 280, 390; Jerome's opinion respecting the monster which appeared to him, *Calf.* 252; in a trance he saw the whole earth covered with snares, and on asking who could walk safely there, was answered, Only humility, 2 *Jew.* 1094; his burial, 4 *Bul.* 514; invoked, *Pra. Eliz.* 392 n., 535; for pigs,

1 *Bec.* 138, 2 *Bec.* 536, *Pil.* 92; his pig, *Calf.* 287; invoked for the burning, 2 *Jew.* 922; represented as vindictive, 2 *Tyn.* 561; his fast, *ib.* 98

Anthony, king of Navarre: mentioned, 2 *Zur.* 53; called the second Julian, *Grin.* 253; died of a wound received at the siege of Rouen, *ib.* n., 1 *Zur.* 118 n

Anthony (Jo.): one of the visitors of monasteries, 2 *Cran.* 271

Anthony (Mr), i. e. A. R. Cavallerius, *q. v.*

Anthropomorphites, or Humaniformarians (called by Epiphanius, Audiani, and by Augustine, Vadiani): heretics who supposed God to be in the form of man, 1 *Bul.* 225, 230, 3 *Bul.* 138, 315, 1 *Cran.* 172, 173, 191, 2 *Ful.* 391, 1 *Hoop.* 160, *Hutch.* 12, 24, 25, 4 *Jew.* 793, *Rog.* 38, *Whita.* 569; the origin of their heresy, *Whita.* 229; refuted by Theophilus of Alexandria, *ib.* 596; by Rutherius, 1 *Hoop.* 160 n

Anthropophagi: cannibals, *Rid.* 199

Antichrist, Man of Sin: *v.* Augustine, Bernard, Gregory, Hilary, Hippolytus, Irenæus, Jerome, Joachim.

THE ACTS OF CHRIST AND OF ANTICHRIST, by Tho. Becon, 3 *Bec.* 498; on the prophecies respecting him, 4 *Jew.* 727, &c.; foretold by Daniel, 2 *Cran.* 62, 63, 2 *Jew.* 911, 918, by Zechariah, *ib.* 918; described in the Sybilline oracles, *ib.* 914, 915, 4 *Jew.* 743; figured by Antiochus, 2 *Cran.* 63; foretold by St Paul, 2 *Jew.* 887, 902, 988, *Rog.* 178, 1 *Tyn.* 517, 3 *Tyn.* 104; described by St John, 2 *Tyn.* 181; the account of Joachim Abbas, 2 *Jew.* 915, 4 *Jew.* 714, 744; what he is, 3 *Bec.* 607; divers opinions concerning him, 2 *Jew.* 903, 914; that of Hippolytus, 1 *Jew.* 116; Hilary, Augustine, and Bernard, on Antichrist, *Coop.* 184, 185; whether one man, 2 *Ful.* 367; Tyndale denies a personal Antichrist, and says that he was in the times of the Old Testament, and shall continue to the world's end, 1 *Tyn.* 42, 147, 148; Antichrist declared to be the pope, or the pope and his followers, *Bale* 38, 1 *Brad.* 435, 441, 2 *Brad.* 142, 2 *Ful.* 269, 366, &c., 2 *Hoop.* 44, *Hutch.* 304, 1 *Jew.* 109, 2 *Jew.* 903, &c., *Lit. Eliz.* 619 n., *Nord.* 123, *Phil.* 152, 244, 338, *Poet.* 270, 282, *Rid.* 53, 263, 414, &c., *Sand.* 11, 389, 1 *Tyn.* 147, 148, 185, 191, 208, 232—252, 266, 340, 2 *Tyn.* 178, 179, 181, 182, 196, 197, 3 *Tyn.* 96, 102—107, 171; the pope so proclaimed by a council at Rheims, *Rog.* 182, 347; many popish writers have plainly confessed that the pope is Antichrist, 4 *Jew.* 1115; the returned exiles preached this doctrine, 1 *Zur.* 27; the pope declared by the legislature of Scotland to be very Antichrist, *ib.* 199; a sure token that he is so, 3 *Tyn.* 102; popery is Antichristianism, but covertly, *Whita.* 20, 21; Bale's opinion of one universal Antichrist, comprehending as well Mahomet as the pope, *Bale* 426, whom he calls the two monarchs of his kingdom, *ib.* 562; the Turk and the pope his two horns, 2 *Cran.* 62; Sanders says Protestants are members of Antichrist, 2 *Ful.* 373; the apostacy preceding him, 2 *Lat.* 320; on that which delayed his coming, 2 *Jew.* 908, &c.; *Whita.* 553, 554; the Roman empire removed before the pope was thoroughly installed, 2 *Ful.* 368; on the time of his coming, *ib.* 370, viz. before the second advent, 1 *Tyn.* 215; asserted to have begun in the apostles' time, 2 *Lat.* 321, 2 *Tyn.* 179, 2 *Whitg.* 181; that he is revealed, 1 *Bec.* 29, 1 *Lat.* 172; marks or signs by which he may be known, *Bale* 203, 2 *Hoop.* 44, 56, 512, 2 *Jew.* 913, 921, 991, 992; called ὁ ἄνομος, 2 *Jew.* 919; his name Λατεῖνος, 1 *Jew.* 915, 4 *Jew.* 714, 743; seated in the temple of God, i. e. the church, *Bale* 208, 1 *Brad.* 505, 523, 529, *Coop.* 180, 2 *Jew.* 991, 4 *Jew.* 727—729, *Poet.* 466, at Rome, 2 *Jew.* 915, 4 *Jew.* 743, 744; long the pilot of the ship (i. e. the church), 2 *Jew.* 994; his subtlety and secret working, *ib.* 909, &c., 1 *Tyn.* 224; his false and seducing miracles, *Bale* 233, *Calf.* 318, 2 *Cran.* 46, 2 *Hoop.* 45, 1 *Tyn.* 287, 3 *Tyn.* 262, 263; a fable concerning wonders to be wrought by him, 2 *Jew.* 991; whether to be received by the Jews, 2 *Ful.* 369; on his subjugation of three kings, *ib.* 370; his reign of three years and a half, *ib.* 233, 370; whether Elijah shall come in his time, *ib.*; his acts, life, and doctrine, as contrasted with those of Christ, 3 *Bec.* 504, &c., *Sand.* 12; his swarm of hypocrites, 3 *Bec.* 506; his church, *Sand.* 371; signs by which the church of Christ may be known from his synagogue, 2 *Bec.* 42; his tail, 3 *Whitg.* 495; he denies Jesus Christ, 2 *Ful.* 368; how he denies that he is come in the flesh, 2 *Tyn.* 196; he turns the root upward, 1 *Tyn.* 295; his kingdom a persecuting kingdom, *Rid.* 62; the great persecution to take place under him, *Pra. Eliz.* 26 n.; a prayer on behalf of those persecuted by him, *Pra. B.* 161; he feigns chastity, 2 *Jew.* 990; Antichrist's kingdom is large, 2 *Bec.* 151; we desire in the Lord's prayer that it may be brought to confusion, *ib.* 152; he shall shortly be confounded, *ib.* 409, 410; but shall bear rule till Christ come to judgment, 2 *Brad.* 361; how to be destroyed, 4 *Bul.* 34, 162, 2 *Ful.* 393, 2 *Jew.* 927, 928, 1 *Tyn.* 312; types of his destruction, 2 *Jew.* 928, 929; St John's account of it, *ib,* 930—932; his destruction began already, *Sand.* 389; Bradford wrote a treatise on Antichrist, 2 *Brad.* 146

Antichrists: denounced by St John, 1 *Tyn.* 530, 2 *Tyn.* 179; Hilary says he who repudiates the authority of scripture is antichrist, *Sand.* 15; false Christians so called by Augustine, 2 *Lat.* 316, 345; he that takes on him to save others by his merits is an antichrist, 1 *Tyn.* 95; so are the false-anointed, *ib.* 232; antichrists warned, 1 *Bec.* 127; many antichrists are risen up, 2 *Bec.* 555; their doctrines must be fought against, *ib.* 556; the pope one, the Turk another, 1 *Zur.* 269; Hacket, a counterfeit Christ, *Nord.* v. 110

Antidico-Marianites: an ancient sect, *Whita.* 539

Antididagma: a book set forth in 1545 by the canons of Cologne, in opposition to abp Herman's reformation, 2 *Cran.* xv.; 3 *Jew.* 186; ascribed to Jo. Gropper, 2 *Zur.* 18 n.; quoted on justification, 2 *Cran.* 210; it asserts that Christ's words without the canon of the mass are not sufficient to work consecration, 3 *Jew.* 451

Antigonus: his speech when he put on a diadem, *Sand.* 36

Antilochus: 1 *Hoop.* 184

Antilogia Papæ: 3 *Jew.* 427, 4 *Jew.* xxxiii. 910, *Pil.* 686

Antimonians: heretics, followers of Artemon, 1 *Bec.* 418

Antinomians: called Antinomi, 2 *Jew.* 686; would not have God's laws to be preached, *Rog.* 92; think outward calling a sufficient proof of election, *ib.* 152

Antioch: v. Councils, Patriarchs.

Alleged to have been the first see of St Peter, 2 *Brad.* 144, 145, 2 *Tyn.* 285; its primacy, 1 *Jew.* 366; its name of honour taken away by Theodosius, 3 *Jew.* 315; called by Chrysostom the head of all the world, 1 *Jew.* 422, 439; more esteemed by him than Rome, 4 *Jew.* 876; a patriarchate, 4 *Bul.* 112, *Rid.* 263, 2 *Whitg.* 221 n.; a nominal patriarch still appointed by the pope, 4 *Jew.* 842; riots at the election of bishops, 1 *Whitg.* 464; (alleged deposition of a bishop, for niggardliness, *v.* Ancona); bishops subject to the patriarch, 2 *Whitg.* 201; the church of Antioch, 4 *Bul.* 43, 105, 131, 199; the school there, *ib.* 483; the altar there set towards the West, 4 *Bul.* 500; the people rescued from imminent danger by a monk, *Calf.* 22; the crusaders' victory there, *Lit. Eliz.* 449

Antiochus IV., called Epiphanes: his history, 2 *Jew.* 977; his tyranny and persecution, 1 *Brad.* 283, 1 *Bul.* 377, 2 *Bul.* 162, 211, 413, *Pil.* 4; he burned the scriptures, 2 *Bul.* 13, 2 *Jew.* 690, 4 *Jew.* 1165; desecrated the temple, 2 *Jew.* 994, *Pil.* 88; called himself God, 4 *Jew.* 842; his death, 1 *Bul.* 318, 2 *Bul.* 79, 110, 4 *Jew.* 1126, *Whita.* 99; foretold by Daniel, *Bale* 261; a figure of Antichrist, 2 *Cran.* 63

Antipas, the martyr: *Bale* 279

Antipater: on the advantages of marriage, 1 *Bul.* 398, 408

Antiphon, a pagan opponent of Christianity: 3 *Jew.* 159

Antiphoners: to be abolished and destroyed, 2 *Cran.* 523, *Grin.* 135, 159

Antiphons: v. Anthems.

Antiphons or anthems, what, *Lit. Eliz.* 304 n.; ordained by pope Gregory, 2 *Brad.* 306

Antiquity: true and false, *Coop.* 61, &c; in what sense antiquity is a test of truth in matters of religion, 2 *Ful.* 64, 175; how not a test of truth, 2 *Cran.* 62; truth most ancient, *Rid.* 158; that of Christ and his apostles to be followed, *Pil.* 579; fallacy of Romish pretensions to antiquity, 4 *Jew.* 782, &c., *Sand.* 66

Antisthenes: on true nobility, 2 *Bec.* 436

Antithesis: 4 *Bul.* 184

Antitype: used by Basil and Theodoret for the sacrament of the body and blood of Christ, 2 *Hoop.* 406

Antonian: objections of an Antonian against Ridley, *Rid.* 117, &c; the name alludes to one Antony, an Arian bishop, *ib.* 147

Antonianus: Cyprian writes to him, 4 *Bul.* 131

Antoninus: v. Marcus Aurelius.

Antoninus, abp of Florence: his works, *Jew.* xxxiii.; Instructio Simplicium Confessorum, *Calf.* 64 n.; his opinion on the Apocrypha, *Whita.* 65; on the sufficiency of scripture, *ib.* 704; calls Timothy bishop of Ephesus, 2 *Whitg.* 294; says the office of a bishop is not of its very nature opposed to matrimony, 3 *Jew.* 404; testifies that the army of William the conqueror received the sacrament in both kinds, 1 *Jew.* 261; on the body of Christ remaining under the accidents, &c., 2 *Jew.* 777; on a mouse eating the sacrament, *ib.* 783, 784; speaks of all things being put under the feet of the pope, 3 *Jew.* 247; says no less honour is due to the pope than to the angels of

ANTONINUS — APOCRYPHA

God, 4 *Jew.* 689; says the pope's power is greater than any other power that God ever made, &c., *ib.* 846; says the Greeks believe not (the pretensions of the pope), *ib.* 842; acknowledges that pope Liberius communicated with heretics, *ib.* 929; cited respecting pope Gregory and John bishop of Constantinople, 2 *Hoop.* 233, 234; denies the authenticity of Constantine's donation, 4 *Jew.* 678; his account of pope Joan, *ib.* 651—656; speaks of the heresy and misdeeds of pope John XXII., *ib.* 932, 936; reproves the error of those who say simple fornication is no sin, *ib.* 635; shews how Dominic was preferred to Paul, 3 *Jew.* 576

Antoninus Marinarius, *q. v.*

Antonius (Nic.): Bibliotheca Hispana, 2 *Lat.* 349 n

Antonius Julianus, *q. v.*

Antonius (Marcus Constantius): *v.* Gardiner (S.)

Antonius Panormitanus: 2 *Bec.* 5 n

Antonius Parisiensis: *v.* Annonius.

Antonius de Rosellis, *q. v.*

Antonius, sometime bp of Tamallume: an Arian, *Rid.* 147

Antony (Mark): 3 *Bul.* 18

Antony (Mr), i.e. A. R. Cavallerius, *q. v.*

Antony (Rob.), sub-cellarer of Ch. ch. Canterbury: 2 *Cran.* 334; his journey to Rome, *ib.* 373, 375

Antwerp: Tyndale's Testament printed there, 1 *Tyn.* xxxiii.; Tonstal and More there, *ib.* xxxvii.; Tyndale there, *ib.* xxxvii. lx. lxv.; English merchants there, *ib.* lxiv. lxix.; they make efforts in Tyndale's behalf, *ib.* lxx.; the mart should have been at Calais, 2 *Tyn.* 319; martyrs at Antwerp, 1 *Tyn.* lix. 3 *Zur.* 578; opposition to the establishment of the Inquisition there, 3 *Zur.* 417 n.; Lutheran and Calvinist churches, 1 *Zur.* 174; a tumult, 2 *Zur.* 136 n., 146; popish recusants, *Grin.* 169 n

Anxiety: *v.* Care.

Apamea (A bishop of): 4 *Jew,* 685

Apaused: struck, *Phil.* 86

Apayd: content, *Bale* 116

Apelles: how he painted Antigonus, 2 *Jew.* 556

Apelles, the heretic: referred to, 3 *Bec.* 401; he denied that Christ took flesh of the virgin, 1 *Bec.* 412, 418, 2 *Bec.* 446, 3 *Bul.* 256; said that angels had a bodily substance derived from the stars, 2 *Cran.* 23; denied the resurrection, 2 *Cov.* 186

Apellitæ: their opinions, 2 *Cov.* 150 n., 184; they esteemed neither the law nor the prophets, *Rog.* 81

Apellius, one of the magi: *Whita.* 560 n

A per se A: explained, 2 *Brad.* 139

Apex: the word strangely misunderstood by Thomas Valois, 1 *Jew.* 150

Aphthartodocetæ: heretics who held that Christ's body was always glorious, 1 *Jew.* 497

Aphthonius: defines an active χρεία, 4 *Bul.* 232

Apiarius, an African priest: his appeal to Rome, 2 *Ful.* 70, 1 *Jew.* 356, 417

Apion: his Disputation with Peter, 1 *Jew.* 111, *Whita.* 315

Apish: trifling, 1 *Cov.* 4

Apocalypse: *v.* John (St), and Apocrypha, ii.

Apocrypha:

i. *Old Testament* (see the names of the several books, or their alleged authors, and the Index of texts; also Scripture, Canon): the books called Apocrypha not canonical, 4 *Bul.* 538, &c., 2 *Ful.* 220, 384, *Whita.* 39, &c., though sometimes, and in a certain sense, called canonical, *Whita.* 44, 49, and scripture, *ib.* 69, 76; called by some deutero-canonical, *ib.* 49; Cyprian (or rather Ruffinus) calls some of the books ecclesiastical, others apocryphal, 2 *Cran.* 23; some divide them into two classes, the first called deutero-canonical, *Whita.* 305, the second, apocryphal, *ib.* 312; on the church's rejection of apocryphal writings, 3 *Whitg.* 621; why they are rejected, 1 *Ful.* 18, 20; they were not written by prophets, *Whita.* 49, nor in Hebrew, *ib.* 51; they are not cited by Christ or his apostles, *ib.*, nor are they received by the Jews, *ib.* 52; rejected by Josephus, *ib.* 60, 61; also by fathers and doctors, *ib.* 56—66; forbidden to be read in churches by the council of Laodicea, 2 *Cran.* 39, *Whita.* 54; Jerome's opinion on the Apocrypha, 1 *Ful.* 24 (and *v.* Jerome); Augustine's opinion, 4 *Bul.* 539 (and *v.* Augustine), when apocryphal books were first received, 1 *Ful.* 18, &c.; some of the books declared canonical by the third council of Carthage, 2 *Cran.* 39, 3 *Whitg.* 349, 350, others received as such by the council of Trent, *Whita.* 29; on the books allowed by papists to be apocryphal, *ib.* 103, &c.; Alph. de Castro calls it heresy to reckon men's writings among the divine scriptures, 3 *Jew.* 211; consent of the reformed churches respecting these books, *Rog.* 81; some of them are read in the English church, 1 *Ful.* 21, but not as canonical, *ib.* 24; on reading them in the church, 3 *Whitg.* 338, &c., 491; false doctrines in the Apocrypha, 1 *Ful.* 21,

22; writings have been set forth under the names of Adam, Cain, and Seth, 2 *Jew.* 894; the Ascension of Isaiah, *Rog.* 82

ii. *New Testament:* counterfeit gospels made by various heretics, *Bale* 314, 2 *Jew.* 894, 3 *Jew.* 441, *Rog.* 82, *Whita.* 108; why the pseudo-gospels and other apocryphal books were rejected by Eusebius, *Whita.* 314; Gospel of the Twelve Apostles, *Rog.* 82, of Andrew, *Bale* 314, *Rog.* 82, *Whita.* 108, 312, of Barnabas, *Bale* 314, 2 *Jew.* 894, *Rog.* 82, of Bartholomew, *Bale* 314, 2 *Jew.* 894, 3 *Jew.* 441, *Rog.* 82, *Whita.* 531, of James the Less, *Rog.* 82, of Matthias, *Bale* 314, *Whita.* 312, of the Nazarenes, *Whita.* 108, of Nicodemus (otherwise called the Acts of Pilate), 3 *Jew.* 441, *Rog.* 82, *Whita.* 108, 560 n., it speaks of the finding of the cross by Seth, *Calf.* 321 n.; Gospel of Peter, *Bale* 314, 3 *Jew.* 442, *Rog.* 82, *Whita.* 304, published by philosophers, *ib.* 312, formerly read in some churches, but rejected by Serapion, *ib.* 326; Gospel of Thaddeus, *Bale* 314, *Rog.* 82, of Thomas, *Bale* 314, 2 *Jew.* 894, 3 *Jew.* 441, *Whita.* 108, 312, 531, of the Hebrews, mentioned by Origen and Eusebius, and translated by Jerome, 1 *Jew.* 238, accounted as deutero-canonical by Stapleton, *Whita.* 305; Gospel after the Egyptians, *Rog.* 82; Gospel of Judas Iscariot, *Whita.* 312; Acts of Abdias, Andrew, Philip, Thomas, &c., *Rog.* 82; Acts of Paul, *ib.*; Acts or Travels of Paul and Thecla, 2 *Ful.* 339, *Whita.* 304; Stapleton deems them deutero-canonical, *ib.* 305; the story of Thecla condemned (says Jerome) by St John, *ib.* 311; Acts of Peter, *Rog.* 82, *Whita.* 304; Preaching of Peter, and Judgment of Peter, *ib.*; Peter's Dispute with Apion, a book falsely ascribed to Clement, 1 *Jew.* 111, rejected by Eusebius because not apostolic in its doctrine, *Whita.* 315; Itinerary of Peter, otherwise the Recognitions, falsely ascribed to Clement (*q.v.*), *Calf.* 380, 387, 1 *Jew.* 111, 112; Epistle to the Laodiceans, testimonies against it, *Whita.* 108, 302—304, 531; no such genuine epistle ever existed, *ib.* 469, 526; the piece now so called is a modern forgery; the epistle so designated by Marcion is that to the Ephesians, *ib.* 303 n.; Epistles of Barnabas, accounted deutero-canonical by Stapleton, *ib.* 305; Revelation of Paul, *Rog.* 82, *Whita.* 312, condemned by Augustine, *ib.* 315; Revelation of Peter, *Rog.* 82, *Whita.* 304; Revelations of Stephen, and Thomas, *Rog.* 82; Hermas (*q.v.*), his Shepherd, publickly read in the church of old, *Whita.* 325, reckoned deutero-canonical by Stapleton, *Whita.* 305, who says it might be made canonical, *ib.* 109, 330

Apollinarians: wrongly said to have held a quarternity of persons in the Godhead, *Rog.* 44; they maintained that the carnal body of Christ was consubstantial with the Father, *ib.* 52, that Christ had a body without a soul, *ib.*, that he suffered in both natures, *ib.* 57, and that original sin is from nature, *ib.* 99

Apollinaris, (perhaps Claudius Apollinaris bp of Hieropolis, but possibly the heretic): says there is no martyrdom, where the truth of Christ is not, 1 *Hoop.* vii.; his testimony to the perfection of scripture, *Whita.* 688; Apollinarius, a millenarian, believed to be the same, 4 *Bul.* 537

Apollinaris, the elder, father of the next: a married priest, 4 *Jew.* 805; excommunicated, 3 *Whitg.* 240, 241

Apollinaris, or Apollinarius, bp of Laodicea: his Apology condemned by Julian, 3 *Jew.* 203; he turned the Psalms into Greek verse for children, 1 *Jew.* 332; included Psalm cli. in his Metaphrase, *Whita.* 104; taught by questions, *Lit. Edw.* 495, (545); became a heretic, 1 *Cran.* 262, 277, *Phil.* 424; excommunicated, 3 *Whitg.* 240, 241; his heretical doctrine, 3 *Bul.* 260, 374; he maintained the Godhead and manhood in Christ to be so mixed and confounded together as to make but one nature, 1 *Cran.* 286, 338, and held Christ's body to be of one substance with the Deity, 1 *Jew.* 497, 2 *Jew.* 578; his heresy was deduced from Jo. i. 14 ("the Word was made flesh"), 2 *Jew.* 11; Valla thinks he was the author of books ascribed to Dionysius the Areopagite, *Whita.* 576; many of his works anciently ascribed to Athanasius, *Calf.* 268

Apolline (St): *v.* Apollonia.

Apollo: oracle of the Pythian Apollo, 4 *Jew.* 1068, 1113; description of God, *Hutch.* 178

Apollonia (St), or Apolline: invoked for the tooth-ache, *Bale* 348, 498, 1 *Bec.* 139, 2 *Bec.* 536, 2 *Jew.* 923, *Pil.* 92, 3 *Tyn.* 181, *Rog.* 228; account of her, 1 *Bec.* 139 n.; she leaped into the fire alive, 2 *Bul.* 106; we are taught by God's word not to trust in Apolline, 3 *Bec.* 43

Apollonius: admonished his brethren to communicate every day, 3 *Bec.* 474; attributes the introduction of stated fasts to Montanus, 1 *Bul.* 434, *Whita.* 665; says an idle monk may be compared to a thief, 4 *Jew.* 798, 800; falsely accused, *Sand.* 129

Apollonius Tyanæus: his advice to Domitian on the reformation of the empire, 2 *Jew.* 1001

Apollos: said to have been bishop of Corinth and Achaia, *Rog.* 329

Apologies: written by ancient fathers, 3 *Jew.* 115, 185, *Pil.* 361

APOLOGY FOR SPITTING UPON AN ARIAN, by Jo. Philpot, *Phil.* 293

APOLOGY MADE BY ... JOHN HOOPER, &c., 2 *Hoop.* 550

APOLOGY OF PRIVATE MASS: *Coop.*; referred to, 2 *Ful.* vii. ix, 3 *Jew.* 186; bp Cooper's ANSWER, *Coop.*; reference thereto, 2 *Ful.* vii, ix

APOLOGY OF THE CHURCH OF ENGLAND, by bp Jewel, Latin and English, 3 *Jew.*; the DEFENCE thereof, 3 and 4 *Jew.*

Aposcopi: a play upon episcopi, 4 *Jew.* 1199 n

Apostasy, Apostates: apostasy a dreadful sin, 2 *Bul.* 425, 2 *Jew.* 809, 1074, 2 *Lat.* 440, 441, 2 *Tyn.* 212; kinds of it, 4 *Bul.* 77; before Christ's advent, 2 *Jew.* 896; predicted by Christ, 1 *Tyn.* 227, by St Paul, *Phil.* 28, 2 *Jew.* 896, 897, 1 *Tyn.* 228; the apostasy of Mahomet and that of the pope began about the same time, *Sand.* 388; the reformed have fallen from him who fell from Christ, *ib.* 389; the meaning of the word apostata, *Rid.* 341; some apostates named, 2 *Jew.* 803, 808; the great peril of apostates, *Hutch.* 112; fearful examples, *Sand.* 362; letter to one fallen from the known truth of the gospel to Antichrist and his damnable religion, 2 *Hoop.* 605

Apostles: *v.* Bishops, Canons, Creeds, Disciples, Peter, &c., Tradition; their Acts, *v.* Luke:

Meaning of the name, 4 *Bul.* 105, 1 *Ful.* 464, 2 *Ful.* 309, *Now.* 99; who and what they were, 1 *Bul.* 52; why fishers were chosen, 2 *Lat.* 24; they were called more than once, *ib.* 26; they received their commission directly from Christ, 1 *Tyn.* 211; he held nothing back from them, 1 *Cov.* 77; their ignorance while Christ was bodily present, 2 *Cran.* 54, 1 *Tyn.* 453; they were afterwards baptized with fire, 4 *Bul.* 355; anointed not with oil, but with the Spirit, 1 *Tyn.* 229; they were endued with the same fellowship as Peter, 1 *Jew.* 360, and were equal in power and authority, 3 *Jew.* 286, &c., 384, 2 *Tyn.* 283; on their office, 1 *Whitg.* 471, 492—500, 504; it was spiritual, 1 *Bec.* 213; the office of apostles and preachers, 3 *Bec.* 616; the apostolic office not a lordly one, 2 *Brad.* 255; they were not Christ's vicars, 1 *Hoop.* 21, 22; what he sent them to do, 2 *Bec.* 320, 321; he commanded them to feed the flock, *ib.* 320; their authority very great, 1 *Bul.* 53; they represented the whole church, 2 *Lat.* 264; "apostles and prophets," Eph. ii. 10, how the foundation of the church, *Whita.* 347—349, 640; the apostles were the masterbuilders of the church, 4 *Bul.* 105; they had authority over all others in it, *Rog.* 328; they first taught repentance, then faith, 2 *Bec.* 13; preached faith in Christ, 1 *Cov.* 77; ministered the sacraments, *ib.* 79; did not overcharge the people with ceremonies, *ib.* 80; baptized in water not consecrated, 4 *Bul.* 310; baptized infants, *ib.* 388, 391; how they did bind and loose, *ib.* 148; determined nothing concerning festivals, *Whita.* 540; would not offend the weak, 1 *Cov.* 81; their care of the churches, *Sand.* 235; they chose men anointed with the Spirit for teachers, 1 *Tyn.* 229; their office different from that of bishops, 2 *Jew.* 908; they were not particular bishops, 1 *Brad.* 506, 2 *Ful.* 308, &c., though some affirm that they at length became so, 2 *Whitg.* 302; their office has expired, 2 *Ful.* 310; the name was not used in the primitive church for a bishop, *ib.* 309; Cranmer, however, wished the English bishops to style themselves apostles of Jesus Christ, 2 *Cran.* 305; the apostles' successors, whether bishops only, or priests also, *Calf.* 219, 221; bishops only are their successors according to Anacletus, 2 *Jew.* 677; Jerome says bishops hold their place, *Whita.* 417; how succeeded by bishops, *ib.* 417, 418; ordinary ministers, in what respect their successors, 1 *Whitg.* 497; Bellarmine says that Peter was an ordinary pastor, the other apostles extraordinary, *Whita.* 417; the apostles were mostly married men, 3 *Bec.* 235, 1 *Bul.* 396, 402, 2 *Jew.* 727, 2 *Jew.* 989, 3 *Jew.* 392, 421, 4 *Jew.* 803; their doctrine respecting marriage, 3 *Jew.* 421, &c.; they held two councils (Acts ii. and xv.), 3 *Bul.* 52; reference to the latter, 2 *Cran.* 76, 4 *Jew.* 917, 2 *Whitg.* 232, 276, 277; their ordinances nowhere kept, 2 *Cran.* 55; their prayers, 4 *Bul.* 225; their faith, *Pil.* 352; their trials and temptations, 3 *Tyn.* 37—39; their doctrine mocked by the heathen, *ib.* 28; why they had things in common, 1 *Lat.* 406; their doings not always an example to us, 1 *Whitg.* 368; where they preached, 1 *Jew.* 267; their wages, 4 *Bul.* 491: More alleges that they spoke with reserve, 3 *Tyn.* 28 n.; they set down in writing the whole doctrine of godliness, 1 *Bul.* 63; left nothing necessary to salvation unwritten, 3 *Tyn.* 26—30; did not write without a divine command, nor on slight occasions, *Whita.* 527; things alleged to be spoken by them, without writing, are not to be believed, 2 *Cran.* 52; their special office with regard to the canon of scripture, *Whita.* 311; writings falsely ascribed to them, 2 *Jew.* 894, *Rog.* 82 (and *v.* Apocrypha, ii.); their names borrowed to avouch heresies, &c., 1 *Jew.* 111

Apostles (False): their doctrine, 2 *Bul.* 273; they denied the resurrection, *Rog.* 64; required the observance of Jewish ceremonies, *ib.* 314

Apostolic: *v.* Church.
  Import of the term, *Rid.* 414; what churches should be so called, 4 *Bul.* 76

Apostolical Constitutions: *v.* Clement of Rome.

Apostolics, or Apotactitæ: ancient heretics, 2 *Ful.* 375, 376, 391, *Phil.* 420, *Whita.* 597, 1 *Whitg.* 61, 2 *Whitg.* 87; described by Augustine, 2 *Brad.* 381 n., 2 *Bul.* 24, *Phil.* 420 n.; they condemned marriage, *Rog.* 261, 306; excommunicated all married people, *ib.* 311; enjoined community of goods, *ib.* 353

Apostolics, or Henricians, *q. v.*

Ap Owen (Howell): *v.* Abowan.

Appairing: impairing, 2 *Bec.* 116

Apparel: *v.* Jews.
  Against costly apparel, 1 *Bec.* 204, 2 *Bec.* 437, *Pil.* 55, 56; why clothing was given to us, 2 *Bec.* 437, 438; gorgeous apparel forbidden in scripture, 2 *Lat.* 82, by the seventh commandment, 1 *Hoop.* 377, continency therein, 1 *Bul.* 421; a rule for apparel, 2 *Bec.* 440; the apparel of a Christian, 2 *Lat* 19; madness of Englishmen in their apparel, 1 *Bec.* 204, 2 *Bec.* 438, *Nord.* 172, *Pil.* 56; laws relating to it, 1 *Lat.* 372; not enforced, 2 *Lat.* 19; abuses in attire should be repressed, *Sand.* 49; sobriety in attire, *ib.* 394; the apparel of kings, dukes, marquises, &c., *Pil.* 56; of magistrates, &c., 2 *Whitg.* 20; of aldermen, judges, &c., *Grin.* 210; that of ministers to be sober, 2 *Hoop.* 147 (and see Vestments); inquiry about that of deans, prebendaries, &c., *Grin.* 179; gallant apparel of the Roman prelates and clergy, 4 *Jew.* 971, 972; that of labouring men must be decent and seemly, 2 *Bec.* 400; that of women, what it should be, *ib.* 438, 439; their love of costly apparel reproved, *Pil.* 385—387; many women apparel themselves far above their degrees, 1 *Lat.* 252; their heads should be covered in token of subjection, *ib.* 253; their tussocks, tufts, &c. condemned, *ib.* 254; also their bracelets, vardingals, &c., 2 *Lat.* 108, 118; writhen hair a mark of pride, *Sand.* 142; the apparel of maids must be seemly, 2 *Bec.* 370, 371, 439; that of the princesses Mary and Elizabeth, and the lady Jane Grey, 3 *Zur.* 278; on mourning apparel, 3 *Whitg.* 368, &c.; on supposed holiness of apparel, 3 *Jew.* 614, &c.

Apparitions: *v.* Spirits.

Appeals: *v.* Pope.
  Appeals from equal to equal, 1 *Jew.* 395; to princes, *ib.* 396

Appelbie (Jo.): in exile, 1 *Cran.* (9)

Appellatio: *v.* Paris, *University.*

Appelles: *v.* Apelles.

Appian: says Julius Cæsar refused the name of king, 3 *Jew.* 318; on the image of murdered Cæsar, 2 *Jew.* 661

Appius Claudius: *Calf.* 316

Appleby (......): he and his wife martyred at Maidstone, *Poet.* 169

Apples: a dainty dish of apples, 1 *Lat.* 186

Application: viz. of the virtue of Christ's death and passion by means of the mass, 2 *Jew.* 746, &c.

Appose: to pose or question, *Pil.* 160; (oppose in *Now.* 109)

Apprentices: inquiries respecting their instruction, *Grin.* 161

Appropriations: need reformation, 1 *Lat.* 100; sacrilegious, *Grin.* 382

Aprice (......): martyred, *Poet.* 167

Aprigius, bp of Pacem: wrote on the Apocalypse, *Bale* 255

Apuleius: defends himself against the accusation of necromancy, 1 *Hoop.* 327; speaks of the gods going on men's feet, 3 *Jew.* 555

Aquablanca (Pet. de), bp of Hereford: the pope's agent, 4 *Jew.* 1080

Aquapendente: a city, *Pra. Eliz.* 392 n

Aquarii: heretics who used only water in the communion, *Coop.* 74, 110 n., 132, 136, 1 *Ful.* 522, 1 *Jew.* 154, 215, *Rog.* 296; opposed by Cyprian, *Whita.* 498, 602

Aquila: some account of him, and of his Greek version of the Old Testament, *Whita.* 123; referred to, *Calf.* 107 n., 2 *Ful.* 390, 2 *Jew.* 692

Aquila (Pet. de), a school doctor: 2 *Jew.* 667

Aquila (The bp of): ambassador from Spain, 4 *Jew.* 1248, 1 *Zur.* 102; instigates the conspiracy of Arthur Pole, &c., *ib.* 102 n.; desires a conference with abp Parker, *Park.* 201

3—2

Aquileia: v. Councils.
How the church of Aquileia worded the article of the creed respecting the resurrection of the body, 2 *Bec.* 49
Aquinas (St Tho.): v. Thomas.
Aquisgranum: v. Aix-la-chapelle.
Aquitaine: belongs of right to England, 2 *Zur.* 293
Arabia: its geography, 2 *Zur.* 89, 95; after hearing the godly voice of Paul it received Mahomet, *Phil.* 337; the church not extinct there, 4 *Bul.* 20; law of the Arabians against adultery, 2 *Bec.* 649¦
Arabici: denied the consciousness of the soul between death and the resurrection, 4 *Jew.* 930—932, 935
Arad: 1 *Bul.* 378
Aratus: supposed the soul to die with the body, 3 *Bul.* 385; cited by St Paul, 4 *Jew.* 737, *Whita.* 70, 2 *Whitg.* 36
Arau, Switzerland: 1 *Zur.* 22 n.; the English congregation there in queen Mary's time, 1 *Zur.* 88 n., 3 *Zur.* 165; the church of St Ursula appropriated to the English, 3 *Zur.* 167 n.; they beg leave to depart, 2 *Zur.* 2
Arausica: v. Councils, *Orange.*
Arbrothe (The lord of): 1 *Zur.* 219 n
Arcadius, emperor of the East: 1 *Bul.* 331; not saluted by Amphilochius, *Sand.* 232
Archangels: 3 *Bul.* 337
Archbishops, Metropolitans: v. Bishops, Canterbury, Pall.

Archbishops, their office, 4 *Bul.* 112, 117, 118; of archbishops, metropolitans, &c. 2 *Whitg.* 77; equivalent terms among the Jews, 4 *Jew.* 1299; the title archbishop pertains to Christ, ib. 81, 82, 85; as applied to a chief bishop it is a name of jurisdiction, not of a new ministry, ib. 89, 236, a difference of dignity, not of order, ib. 122; archbishops are not heads generally of the church, 2 *Hoop.* 237; the names of metropolitan, archbishop, &c. not antichristian, 2 *Whitg.* 118; the archbishop's authority distinguished from the pope's, ib. 99, 415, 245, &c.; ancient meaning of the name metropolitan, according to Cartwright, ib. 147, 167; whether the same as archbishop, ib. 150; Cartwright thinks the archbishop's office was of old temporary, ib. 157; the office is local, ib. 271; antiquity of the name, ib. 118, 190, &c.; the so called canons of the apostles require the bishops of every country to have a chief, ib. 145; so the council of Antioch, ib.; archbishops asserted to have been in England, A.D. 180, ib. 146; councils which mention archbishops, primates, and metropolitans, ib. 158, 160; fathers and historians who do so, 160, &c.; archbishops and metropolitans instituted in the time of Constantine, 2 *Hoop.* 237; the name of archbishop allowed by the council of Nice, 2 *Whitg.* 142; the office mentioned or referred to by Cyprian, 1 *Whitg.* 70; on the right reserved to each metropolitan of confirming the election of bishops within his own province, 3 *Jew.* 333; the consecration of archbishops, 2 *Whitg.* 91 n.; their authority in England, ib. 234; their prerogatives, ib. 360; some wished the name abolished, 4 *Jew.* 1299, *Park.* 373; list of the chief metropolitans in Europe, *Bale* 505

Archbold (Will.): witnesses Grindal's will, *Grin.* 463
Archdeacons: their office, 1 *Bec.* 20, 4 *Bul.* 112, 114, 115, 3 *Jew.* 109, 1 *Whitg.* 304; not of divine appointment, 2 *Whitg.* 100; ancient instances of the name, ib. 173; what the office was of old, ib. 175, &c.; archdeacons were anciently chosen by the deacons, ib. 177; the name allowed by the council of Nice, ib. 142; the office named by Chrysostom, 1 *Jew.* 198, and by Jerome, 2 *Whitg.* 431; the archdeacon is the eye of the bishop, *Phil.* 130; some wished the name abolished, 4 *Jew.* 1299; archdeacons directed to appoint portions of the New Testament to the clergy to be conned without book, *Grin.* 184; an archdeacon not in orders, *Park.* 142 n
Archduke: on the title, *Grin.* 12
Arches Court: v. Court.
Archery: shooting commendable for exercise, 1 *Lat.* 196; a gift of God, ib. 197; great importance of the bow in war, *Pil.* 428; the archery of ancient nations, ib.; the glory this realm hath gotten thereby, ib. 427, 428; an act passed for maintaining artillery, and debarring unlawful games (33 Henry VIII.), 1 *Lat.* 197 n.; archery at the battle of Pinkey, 3 *Zur.* 43; its decay lamented, *Pil.* 427; the outfit of archers, *Park.* 15; bow-staves imported from Switzerland, 3 *Zur.* 628, 629, 632; what they should be, ib. 629, 630; a serving-man may shoot sometimes, 2 *Lat.* 37
Archflamines: v. Flamines.
Archidamus, the Lacedæmonian: reproved by Nicostratus, 3 *Jew.* 103, 4 *Jew.* 1067
Archidiaconus: v. Guido de Bayso.
Archidiaconus Florentinus: denies that the pope can commit simony, calls him the lord of all worldly goods, and ascribes to Peter certain words of Satan, 4 *Jew.* 869

Archilochus: his books banished by the Lacedemonians, 2 *Bec.* 382
Archimedes: *Hutch.* 73
Archippus: 4 *Bul.* 153
Architecture: *v.* Building.
Archontici: their opinions on the resurrection, 2 *Cov.* 184; their monkery, 2 *Ful.* 390; their Symbonia, *Rog.* 202
Archpriests: 4 *Bul.* 117, 546; mentioned by Jerome, 2 *Whitg.* 431
Archytas Tarentinus: his mathematical dove, 2 *Jew.* 561
Ardeley (Jo.), or Ardite: martyred at Rayleigh, *Poet.* 162
Arden (......): executed in Smithfield for treason, *Lit. Eliz.* 658 n
Arden (Jo.): deprived by bp Sandys, *Park.* 125
Ardington (Hen.): *v.* Arthington.
Ardite (Jo.): *v.* Ardeley.
Ardres, near Calais: the meeting of Henry VIII. and Francis I. at the field of the cloth of gold, 2 *Tyn.* 313
Aread: to judge, pronounce, or reckon, 1 *Cov.* 277; arete, *Phil.* 350; areted to, *ib.* 386
Aretinus (Guido): notice of him, 1 *Hoop.* 118
Aretinus (Leon.): translates Basil, *Calf.* 59 n
Argentine: *v.* Strasburgh.
Arguments: ab auctoritate negativè, 1 *Whitg.* 61, &c., 176, &c., 2 *Whitg.* 147, 233, 574; à consequenti, *Calf.* 73; that a thing is not commanded, therefore forbidden, not good, 2 *Whitg.* 14, 15; from effect to cause, 1 *Tyn.* 58; à facto ad jus, 1 *Whitg.* 351, &c., 2 *Whitg.* 233; ex solis particularibus, 1 *Whitg.* 181, 182; commune argumentum, 3 *Jew.* 160; examples of vicious or foolish arguments, 2 *Brad.* 384, 388, 1 *Jew.* 14—16, 77, 78; various, 2 *Whitg.* 18, 115, 228, 229
Argus: 2 *Bul.* 218
Argyle (Earls of): *v.* Campbell.
Arians: *v.* Anabaptists, Arius.

Their heresy described and confuted, 1 *Cran.* 63, 67, 273, 339, 2 *Hoop.* 73, 74, *Hutch.* 162, 179, 182, 188, 206, 207, &c.; the subtlest of heretics, *Phil.* 141; Philpot's APOLOGY FOR SPITTING UPON AN ARIAN, *ib.* 293; their detestable impiety, *ib.* 296, &c.; their heresy and that of the Socinians distinguished, *ib.* 298 n.; blinder than the Jews, *Whita.* 482; they alleged scripture, 4 *Bul.* 21; but they corrupted it, 1 *Ful.* 11; false translations by them, *ib.* 12; some rejected the epistle to the Hebrews, *ib.* 8, *Whita.* 323; they wrested scripture, but were refuted by the fathers out of scripture, *Whita.* 481, 534, &c., 562, &c.; their interpretation of 1 John v. 7, *Hutch.* 168; they denied the consubstantiality of the three persons of the Godhead, *Rog.* 201, and the deity of the Son, 4 *Bul.* 21, *Pil.* 638, *Rog.* 45, 47; some were called Douleians, because they called our Lord the servant of God, *Rog.* 47; they said that our Lord had not a human soul, *ib.* 52; denied the Godhead of the Holy Ghost, *Phil.* 302, *Rog.* 45, 47; hence they were by-named Pneumatomachons, *ib.* 45; some affirmed the Holy Ghost to be inferior to the Son, *ib.* 72; others said he was one and the same person with Christ, *ib.* 74; they rebaptized, 4 *Bul.* 393, denied that they had sin, *Phil.* 310—312, and declared sin after baptism to be unpardonable, *ib.* 313; they condemned marriage, *Rog.* 306; history of the heresy, *Phil.* 295 n.; whence it sprung, *Grin.* 41; conventicles of the Arians, *Calf.* 298, *Sand.* 191; the council of Nice convened against the Arians, 2 *Bec.* 305; after this council they waxed great, 4 *Jew.* 908; they were very numerous, 4 *Bul.* 155; took upon themselves the name of Catholics and persecuted the church, *Coop.* 183, and gave sectarian names to the orthodox, 2 *Ful.* 375, 2 *Jew.* 807, *Phil.* 424; they cited Origen, 1 *Jew.* 83, 3 *Jew.* 226; mighty nations were converted by them, 2 *Ful.* 60; their heresy confirmed by the council of Ariminum, *Rog.* 209; how they were confuted, *Rid.* 283; Hilary against them, 1 *Jew.* 127; how they were refuted by Ambrose and Augustine, 3 *Bul.* 246; the persecution of Constantius, *Pil* 637; their heresy occasioned the doxology Gloria Patri, 2 *Whitg.* 481; the creed of Athanasius, as well as that of Nice, devised against them, *Rog.* 93; it is evident that Christ's bodily presence in the sacrament was unknown in the church in the time of the old Arians, 1 *Hoop.* 520; they appear and spread in England, 2 *Brad.* 213, *Rid.* 367, 2 *Lat.* 98, 1 *Zur.* 285, 2 *Zur.* 182; many sprung up in queen Mary's time, 4 *Jew.* 1241, 1 *Zur.* 92; dispute with them in the foreign churches in London, 1 *Zur.* 93, 3 *Zur.* 574
Arians (Semi-): affirmed the Holy Ghost to be a mere creature, *Rog.* 70
Arias Montanus (Bened.): defends the Hebrew points, 1 *Ful.* 55; confesses that there are many various readings in the Vulgate, *ib.* 74; his opinion on the Apocrypha, *Whita.* 66
Ariminum: *v.* Councils.
Aristæus: the account of the LXX. ascribed to him is spurious, *Whita.* 117 n.; it says

their version was exactly conformable to the Hebrew, *ib.* 121; it only mentions the Pentateuch, 1 *Ful.* 80

Aristides: 1 *Hoop.* v. vi; accused of justice, 1 *Ful.* 457

Aristobulus, bishop of Britain: *Rog.* 329

Aristobulus: seems to say that there was a Greek version of the scriptures before that of the LXX, *Whita.* 118 n

Aristocracy: what it is, 1 *Bul.* 310, 1 *Whitg.* 390

Aristophanes: calls Jupiter king (τύραννον) of the gods, 1 *Ful.* 201; what he says of Cleon, 2 *Hoop.* 86; what of Philippides, 3 *Jew.* 183; cited, 4 *Jew.* 716

Aristotle: referred to, 1 *Cran.* 331; Philip's letter to him, 2 *Bec.* 5, 386; his authority with his scholars, 1 *Hoop.* 44; his speech to his physician, 2 *Jew.* 1023; his dying prayer to One God, *Hutch.* 176; his great authority with Papists, 2 *Lat.* 317, 1 *Tyn.* 157, 276; more honoured than Christ, 1 *Tyn.* 76; thought necessary to interpret the scriptures, *Bale* 350, 1 *Tyn.* 154, though he teaches many things directly opposed to them, 1 *Tyn.* 154, 155; called by Luther sceleratus nebulo, 2 *Ful.* 57 n.; he teaches that God does all things of necessity, 1 *Tyn.* 154; disapproves all corporal likenesses of God, *Wool.* 26; calls religious worship the principal thing, 1 *Hoop.* 352; his doctrine on works and free-will like that of the Papists, 1 *Tyn.* 108, 155, 276; by δικαίωμα he means a just work, 1 *Ful.* 336; references to his political writings, 1 *Hoop.* 78, 80, 351; he speaks of three forms of government, 1 *Bul.* 309, 310, 2 *Whitg.* 134; on monarchy, 2 *Whitg.* 244; on the qualifications of a rule, 1 *Hoop.* 361; calls a king ruler of the things that pertain to the gods, 4 *Jew.* 991; shews that princes should excel in virtue, 2 *Zur.* 169; calls the magistrate a keeper of the law, 1 *Bul.* 309, 2 *Hoop.* 86; calls the law a canon, *Whita.* 27; says it is not servitude to live after the form of the commonwealth, but safety, 1 *Hoop.* 372; remarks that what is common to all is neglected of all, 1 *Whitg.* 521; on money, 3 *Zur.* 284; on usury, 4 *Jew.* 1295; says a city cannot consist of bastards, 4 *Jew.* 907, 908; his opinion of felicity, 1 *Cov.* 175, 176, 2 *Hoop.* 299, 1 *Tyn.* 155; on friendship, 2 *Zur.* 293; on friendships dissolved through want of intercourse, *ib.* 279, 3 *Zur.* 309 n.; his saying, Socrates is my friend, and so is Plato, but the friendship of truth is best of all, 2 *Jew.* 808; says that some falsehoods seem more probable than some things which are true, &c., 1 *Jew.*

83; tells what is gained by lying, 3 *Jew.* 141, 4 *Jew.* 640; condemns the external act when the mind consents not, 1 *Hoop.* 283; declares that justice (?) is more beautiful than the day-star, *Wool.* 13; says that the commoner a good thing is the better, *Calf.* 357; advises to look to small things, 2 *Whitg.* 96; his opinion of the human understanding, *Whita.* 277; references to his logical writings, 1 *Whitg.* 63, 84; speaks of an ill argument à consequenti, *Calf.* 73; shews that arguments ab auctoritate hold only affirmatively, 1 *Whitg.* 178; speaks of ten predicaments, 1 *Hoop.* 274; his rule of καθόλου πρῶτον, 2 *Whitg.* 45, 46; calls the authorities of men uncunning proofs, 1 *Whitg.* 427, 435; his vain sophisms, 1 *Hoop.* 325; calls names imitations of things, 2 *Whitg.* 81; says it is a mark of contempt to forget the name of another, *ib.* 146; ridicules uncunning painters who have to write the names of what they paint, *ib.* 194; on physical knowledge, 1 *Brad.* 359; obscurity of his physical writings, *Whita.* 706; he allows one primum mobile, 1 *Brad.* 361, 1 *Cran.* 251, *Hutch.* 170, 1 *Tyn.* 154; maintains that the world is eternal, *Rog.* 40, 1 *Tyn.* 154; on generation and corruption, 1 *Hoop.* 124; his opinion of substances, 2 *Hoop.* 473; his school admits no accident without subject, 1 *Hoop.* 123; his definition of invisible, *ib.* 70; on health, *ib.* 349; speaks of a certain philosopher who did not know his own voice, 1 *Whitg.* 144; says seven hours' sleep suffice, *Sand.* 395; mentions one who died with sudden joy, 1 *Hoop.* 297; on the terror of death, 4 *Jew.* 1073; on the piety of the stork, 1 *Hoop.* 359 n.; on the nature of the palm-tree, 1 *Bec.* 112; on sound, 3 *Jew.* 260; on νέμεσις, 1 *Whitg.* 166, 167; his ὀβελισκολύχνιον, 3 *Whitg.* 428; a mistake of his, 4 *Jew.* 635

Arithmetic: not a forbidden art, 1 *Hoop.* 330

Arius, the heretic: 1 *Bec.* 278, 3 *Bec.* 401, 1 *Cov.* 194 n.; notice of him, *Phil.* 295 n.; he separated from Alexander, his bishop, 1 *Ful.* 261; said he had abundance of grace above all others, *Phil.* 108; his heresy, 1 *Bul.* 12, 3 *Bul.* 243, 260, 4 *Bul.* 77, 2 *Jew.* 1110, *Phil.* 382 n.; he denied the consubstantiality of the Son with the Father, *Phil.* 299 n.; affirmed the Holy Ghost to be a mere creature, *Rog.* 70; took away a clause from John x, *Bale* 638; defended heresies by mistaking of scripture, 1 *Hoop.* 162, 282, 402; alleged tradition as his authority, 3 *Jew.* 440; complained of persecution, 1 *Jew.* 523, 4 *Jew.* 1073; was banished by Theodosius, *Sand.* 41; vanquished by a council, 4 *Jew.* 1095; spoken of as confuted by an unlearned man, but the story refers to another, *Pil.* 267; compared by Jerome to an idolater, 1 *Ful.* 213; his horrible death, *Phil.* 318, *Pil.* 29, *Sand.* 362; wonderful prevalence of his heresy, 2 *Jew.* 909; it was followed by the bishops of Rome and Constantinople, and by the emperor, *Phil.* 384

Ark of Noah: meaning of the word ark in Genesis, 1 *Tyn.* 405; the ark a type of Christ, 1 *Cov.* 32; a type of the church, *Sand.* 361, 2 *Whitg.* 92, 499; why so long in building, 2 *Cran.* 200

Ark of the Covenant: meaning of the word ark in Exodus, 1 *Tyn.* 419; it was kept in the most holy place, 2 *Bul.* 145; its history, *ib.* 148; its mystic signification, *ib.* 153; its use and abuse, *ib.* 155; too highly exalted by the Israelites, 4 *Bul.* 294; it was touched by the priests only, 2 *Jew.* 704; though carried away by enemies, it lost not its holiness, *ib.* 781

Arles: *v.* Councils.

Arles (The bp of): came to England, *Grin.* 300 n

Armachanus: *v.* Richard of Armagh.

Armada: *v.* Spanish Armada.

Armageddon: *Bale* 488

Armagh: persons proposed for the archbishoprick, 2 *Cran.* 438 (see also Dorrell, Dowdall, Lancaster, Wauchop.)

Armagnac, an earldom in Guienne: 2 *Tyn.* 303

Armarium: an almonry, or ambry, *Calf.* 136; what Cicero means by the word, 2 *Ful.* 150

Armasius: 1 *Bul.* 264, 4 *Bul.* 130

Armenia, Armenians: *v.* Liturgies.

Oppressed by Maximin, 1 *Bul.* 378; revolted against the Romans, and afterwards against the Persians, 3 *Zur.* 746; the Armenian church disallows the mixed cup, 1 *Ful.* 523, has prayer in the vulgar tongue, *Whita.* 269, denies purgatory, *Rog.* 213 n.; error of the Armenians respecting the intermediate state, 4 *Jew.* 931, 932, 935; they hold that the law ceremonial is yet in force, *Rog.* 89; the Instructio Armeniorum of Eugenius IV., *Calf.* 248 n.; account of a cross brought from Armenia, 2 *Zur.* 45

Arminians: opposed by Whitaker, *Whita.* x

Armour of God: sermons on it, 1 *Lat.* 26, 490

Armour of light: 2 *Hoop.* 115, 2 *Jew.* 1035, *Sand.* 214

Arms, Armour, Weapons: *v.* War.

The different parts of armour for the body, 1 *Lat.* 499; weapons of war, ancient and modern, *Pil.* 427; their use lawful, *Pil.* 436, *Rog.* 350; armours of war not to be neglected, 1 *Bec.* 244, 245; how to be provided by the clergy, *Park.* 345—348

Arms, or Coat-armour: not forbidden by the second commandment, 2 *Ful.* 202; a mark of gentility, 2 *Bec.* 436; carried at funerals, *Pil.* 317; metaphorically referred to, 4 *Bul.* 314, *Phil.* 260; given to kings by the pope, 1 *Tyn.* 187; the royal arms set up in churches, "down with the arms of Christ [the rood], and up with a lion and a dog," 2 *Cran.* 217

Armuyden, a village of Zeeland: laid waste by the Walloons, 1 *Zur.* 273

Arnobius Afer: says the authority of religion must be weighed by God, and not by time, for what is true is never too late, 4 *Jew.* 477; speaks of the name of Christ as diffused throughout all countries, 3 *Jew* 596; calls the sacrament of the Lord's supper divine, 3 *Bec.* 388, 389; mentions the heathen objection that Christians had neither temples, images, nor altars, and admits the fact, 1 *Ful.* 104, 1 *Jew.* 310, 2 *Jew.* 658, *Park.* 86, *Rid.* 88; against the images of the Gentiles, *Calf.* 39, 40, 373, 374; says the heathen worshipped Jupiter conditionally, 1 *Jew.* 551; calls Etruria the mother of superstition, *ib.* 421; calls the Latin tongue sermo Italum, *ib.* 56, 281; he is confounded by Erasmus, Fulke, and others, with Arnobius Junior, 2 *Ful.* 319 n.; mistaken for Minucius Felix (*q. v.*), *Calf.* 178, 2 *Ful.* 206

Arnobius Gallus, or Junior: on Christ's charge to Peter after his repentance, 2 *Ful.* 319, 320; he calls Peter a bishop of bishops, *ib.* 319, 320, 322; says he who goes forth from the church of Peter shall perish for thirst, *ib.* 347, 348; confounded with Arnobius Afer, *ib.* 319 n

Arnold (James): recommended for the office of sword-bearer of London, 2 *Cran.* 307, 332

Arnoldus Carnotensis, or of Chartres: the real author of twelve treatises attributed to Cyprian, 1 *Brad.* 548 n., *Calf.* 200 n., 1 *Cran.* 308, 2 *Ful.* 163, 238; referred to, 4 *Jew.* 777 n.; on the command to love God, *Whita.* 27 n.; he calls it a horrible abomination to wish to serve Christ and Baal together, *Pil.* 631; says, let us, standing around the cradle of the Saviour, taste the first dish of his childhood, 3 *Jew.* 474; on the baptism of Christ, and on remission of sins, *Calf.* 201—203; he says that whether it be Judas or Paul who baptizes, it is Christ who puts away the sin, 2 *Bec.* 226, 3 *Bec.* 468; on the signs which make the visible sacrament of baptism, 2 *Ful.* 163; shews that baptism by effusion is sufficient, 1 *Jew.* 223, 226; on the sign of the cross in baptism, *Calf.* 200; says the sacrifice of Christ on the cross is no less acceptable to-day than on the day when blood and water ran from his wounded side, 2 *Jew.* 720; says the law forbids the drinking of blood, the gospel commands it, 2 *Lat.* 269; speaks of cleaving to the cross, and sucking up the blood of the Redeemer, 2 *Jew.* 570, 1042, 3 *Jew.* 619; exclaims, thy blood, O Christ, seeks not for vengeance, 2 *Jew.* 1135; says the Lord's blood washes our sins and pardons our trespasses, 3 *Jew.* 562; asserts that the wicked have no gain by the death of Christ, 4 *Jew.* 894; censures the unbelief of those who understood in a carnal sense the expressions of our Lord about eating his flesh, 3 *Bec.* 431, 432; shews that the flesh of Christ is to be eaten spiritually, 1 *Hoop.* 232 n.; says, in the presence of this body tears crave not forgiveness in vain, 2 *Jew.*739,740,746; affirms that we are made the body of Christ both by the sacrament, and by the thing thereby signified, 1 *Jew.* 132; says the conjunction between Christ and us does not mingle persons...but knits affections and wills, 1 *Jew.* 477, 3 *Jew.* 496; says the bread which the Lord gave to his disciples, being changed in nature, not in form, is, by the omnipotency of the Word, made flesh, 1 *Brad.* 543, 1 *Cran.* 106, 308, (37), 2 *Ful.* 238, *Hutch.* 38, 276, 1 *Jew.* 519, 537, 2 *Jew.* 564, &c., *Rid.* 162, 163, and adds, that as in the person of Christ the manhood was seen and the divinity hidden, so the divine essence hath infused itself into the visible sacrament, *Hutch.* 38, 273, 2 *Jew.* 762; says our Lord at the table gave bread and wine, but on the cross he gave his own body, that the apostles might declare to the nations how bread and wine may be his flesh and blood, 2 *Bec.* 285, 3 *Bec.* 437 n., 1 *Cran.* 121, (58), 2 *Jew.* 718, 1115; says that in the sacrament we whet not our teeth to bite, but with pure faith we break the holy bread, 2 *Bec.* 295, 3 *Bec.* 432, *Grin.* 46; calls Christ's body food for the mind, not the belly, 1 *Jew.* 141, 449, 2 *Jew.* 141, 572, 1120, 3 *Jew.* 525; says it is called bread because it is the nutriment of life, 2 *Jew.* 596 n.; calls it the nourishment of immortality, the portion of everlasting life, &c., 3 *Bec.* 388 n.; and says, being changed into flesh and blood, it procures life and increase to our bodies, 1 *Brad.* 97 n., 1 *Cran.* 311; says, that bread is the life of the soul and the health of the mind, 2 *Jew.* 760; remarks that no multitude consumes this bread, *Rid.* 243; speaks of the wonderful nourishment in the bread and wine as the ineffable work of God, 1 *Cran.* 341; shews that the eating is our dwelling in him, and the drinking as it were a certain incorporation, 3 *Bec.* 432, 462 n., 1 *Cran.* 27, 209 n., (80); that the eating of this flesh is a certain greediness, and desire of remaining in him, 3 *Bec.* 432, 1 *Cran.* 209 n., (80), 3 *Jew.* 486, 530; that there is one house of the church, in which the Lamb is eaten; and that none partake thereof but true Israelites, 2 *Bec.* 292, 3 *Bec.* 462 n., 475 n., 1 *Cran.* 209 n., (80), 1 *Jew.* 130, 132, 133; says the weakness of our faith is taught by the understanding of the sacrament, 3 *Jew.* 370; shews that the faithful receive the Lord's Supper with longing after God, abhorrence of sin, thanksgiving for pardon, and holy delight, 1 *Cran.* 208, (79); says the poor in spirit, being content with this only dish, despise the dainties of the world, 3 *Jew.* 474; declares that the hallowed bread entered into the wicked mouth (of Judas), 2 *Bec.* 267, 3 *Bec.* 424 n., but shews that the wicked do not partake of the body of Christ, 2 *Hoop.* 497; says the holy banquet requires pure minds, 3 *Bec.* 475 n.; declares that a natural man is not admitted among the guests of the Lord's table, *ib.* n.; speaks of the bread as received, and not shut up, 2 *Jew.* 553, 3 *Jew.* 555; says, in sacraments the divine power works mightily; the truth is present with the sign, 2 *Jew.* 763; speaks of God's anointing pouring the fulness of grace into the ministerial sanctification, 3 *Jew.* 443; says that those things which signify, and those which are signified, may be called by one name, 2 *Bec.* 285, 3 *Bec.* 271 n., 437, 1 *Brad.* 87 n., 2 *Jew.* 608, 3 *Jew.* 508; declares that it is the power of God that gives effect to the element of oil, *Hutch.* 237 n., 266, 2 *Jew.* 567, 3 *Jew.* 503; declares that remission of sins, by whatever sacrament given, is the work of the Holy Ghost, 3 *Bec.* 468 n., *Calf.* 201, 2 *Jew.* 1106, 3 *Jew.* 463; on the washing of feet, 1 *Jew.* 223; observes that as meat is to the flesh, so is faith to the soul, 3 *Jew.* 533; says, all Christians offer up unto God daily sacrifice, being ordained of God priests of holiness, 2 *Jew.* 737, 3 *Jew.* 336; says vices are dried up by fasting, 1 *Bec.* 104; says prayer is mighty in operation, if fasting go before, 1 *Bec.* 162, 2 *Bec.* 548; denies that godly men ever took any great thing in hand except they first fasted, 2 *Bec.* 548; a confession of sins by him, *Pra. Eliz.* 498; he declares that God refuses not repentance even at the latest moment of life, 3 *Jew.* 562

Arnoldus de Nova Villa: notice of him, 1 *Tyn.* 153 n

Arnstadt: convention there, 3 *Zur.* 529

Arnulph, king of Bavaria: his death, 4 *Jew.* 684.

Arnulph, or Ernulph, prior of Canterbury afterwards bp of Rochester: Anselm's letter to him against the marriage of priests, *Pil.* 571; another, to him and others, *ib.* 572; story of angels responding at his (?) matins, 1 *Jew.* 191

Arnulphus, another: his speech in the council of Rheims, concerning the pope, 4 *Jew.* 744; he bewails the state of Rome, *ib.* 874; censures the pope and cardinals for ignorance of the scriptures, *ib.* 1046

Arow: in a row, successively, 3 *Bec.* 11

Arran (Jas. earl of): *v.* Hamilton.

Arras (Ant. cardinal of): *v.* Perrenot.

Arrian: speaks of nations that have no bread, 1 *Jew.* 222; surveyed the Red Sea, &c., 2 *Zur.* 89, 95

Arsacius, bp of Constantinople: 1 *Zur.* 350 n.; Chrysostom's unworthy successor, 4 *Jew.* 1070; his name erased by Innocent bishop of Rome, *ib.* 650

Arschot (The house of): *v.* Croy.

Arsennius, bp of Hipsell: submits to Athanasius, 1 *Jew.* 420, 2 *Whitg.* 162; calls him governor of the catholic church, 1 *Jew.* 434

Art, Arts: graving and painting not forbidden by the second commandment, 1 *Hoop.* 44, *Now.* (10), 123; to art; verses by Tho. Scott, *Poet.* 315

Artaxerxes: a name common to all the Persian kings, *Pil.* 14, 307; one of them received gifts of his subjects, 1 *Bec.* 236

Artaxerxes Longimanus, king of Persia: befriends the Jews, *Pil.* 307, 1 *Bul.* 318; sometimes called Darius, 1 *Bul.* 326, 2 *Bul.* 13, *Pil.* 14

Artemius: translates the bones of Andrew, Luke, and Timothy, 2 *Whitg.* 303

Artemon: his heresy, 1 *Bec.* 278, 418 n., 4 *Bul.* 77, 1 *Cran.* 278

Arthington (Hen.), or Ardington: beguiled by Hacket, *Nord.* 113; published that the said Hacket was come to judge the world, *Rog.* 68; his pretended visions, *ib.* 196 n.; his rebellion, *ib.* 344

Arthur, king of Britain: his knights, *Calf.* 271

Arthur (......): 2 *Tyn.* 320, 3 *Tyn.* 166

Article: *v.* Greek.

Articles (The Six): referred to, *Bale* 510, 1 *Bec.* viii, 399 n., 2 *Cran.* 16, 1 *Lat.* xi, 487, *Pil.* 531, *Rid.* 129, 131; a bill drawn, but not adopted, 2 *Cran.* 315 n; opposed by Cranmer, 2 *Cran.* ix, and by Latimer, 1 *Lat.* xi, 319; the act passed, 3 *Zur.* 527 n., copy of the Articles, 2 *Cran.* 168 n.; one of them prescribed auricular confession, 1 *Bec.* 102 n.; provisions against the marriage of priests, 2 *Cran.* 393 n.; bill to moderate them, 3 *Zur.* 204 n.; Cranmer succeeds in procuring their mitigation, 2 *Cran.* ix; they were totally repealed on the accession of king Edward, *ib.* x; the rebels in Devon demand their re-enactment, 2 *Cran.* 168; Cranmer shews that they are not agreeable to the old councils, *ib.*; not to be maintained or taught, 2 *Hoop.* 129, *Rid.* 320

Articles (The XXXIX.*): the successive changes made in them, *Lit. Edw.* xi; Cranmer's part in them, 2 *Cran.* xi; the articles of 1552 sent to Cheke and Cecil for consideration, 2 *Cran.* 439, and to the lords of the council, *ib.* 440; submitted to the king's chaplains, 2 *Cran.* xi; ARTICLES, &c., 42 in number, as set forth in 1552, *Lit. Edw.* 526; ARTICULI, &c., (the same in Latin,) *ib.* 573; subscription commanded, 2 *Cran.* 441 n., 3 *Zur.* 594; copies of the mandates, 2 *Cran.* 532, 533; the doctrine of the Articles agreeable to holy scripture, *Rid.* 400; subscribed by the exiles at Frankfort, 3 *Zur.* 754; revised in 1562, *Now.* iii, and allowed by convocation, and authority of the prince and state, *Rog.* 6; a bill introduced, 1566, respecting subscription to the Articles, *Park.* 291—294; they are again revised, 1571, *Jew.* xx; enjoined to be read in churches, *Grin.* 128; the bill for subscription passed, *Park.* 293 n.; subscription required, *Grin.* 164, *Rog.* 7; refused by divers inferior ministers, *ib.* 8; the Puritans agree to subscribe, *ib.* 10; the Articles allowed by Cartwright, 3 *Whitg.* 461, 462; subscription called for a second time in 1584, which some called the woeful

---

* Originally XLII.

year of subscription, *Rog.* 11, 14; subscription again urged, 1604, *ib.* 22; refused in part by the Puritans, *ib.* 25, &c.; THE CATHOLIC DOCTRINE OF THE CHURCH OF ENGLAND, AN EXPOSITION OF THE XXXIX. ARTICLES, by T. Rogers, *Rog.* passim; notes on the sixth, 2 *Ful.* 221 n., 222 n.; on the citation of Augustine in the 29th, *Park.* 381

Articles (The Lambeth): copy of them, with remarks by abp Hutton, 3 *Whitg.* 612; their history, *ib.* xvii

Articles of Inquiry, Injunctions, &c.: *v.* Advertisements.

Henry VIII's injunctions to religious houses, 2 *Lat.* 240 n.; doubt respecting one of them, 2 *Cran.* 317; bp Latimer's injunctions to the prior and convent of St Mary's, Worcester, 1537, 2 *Lat.* 240; his injunctions to the diocese of Worcester, *ib.* 242; reference to lord Cromwell's injunctions, 1538, 3 *Zur.* 231 n.; abp Cranmer's injunctions to the diocese of Hereford, 1538, sede vacante, 2 *Cran.* 81 (and see 2 *Lat.* 242 n.); references to injunctions set forth by Bonner, bp of London, 2 *Jew.* 993 n., 2 *Lat.* 242 n.; injunctions given by king Edward VI. to all his subjects, 2 *Cran.* 498; his injunctions to the bishops, *ib.* 504; articles to be inquired of within the diocese of Canterbury, in the visitation of abp Cranmer, 1548, *ib.* 154; articles of inquiry at his visitation of the cathedral church of Canterbury, 1550, *ib.* 159; his injunctions to the dean and chapter there, *ib.* 161; articles to be inquired of in the visitation of the diocese of London, by bp Ridley, 1550, *Rid.* 529; his injunctions to the diocese of London, 1550, *ib.* 319; articles concerning Christian religion given by bp Hooper to the clergy of the diocese of Gloucester, 1551, 2 *Hoop.* 120; Hooper's injunctions to the same, *ib.* 130; orders for the bishops and clergy, drawn up by Sandys when bp of Worcester, and subscribed in convocation, 1562, *Sand.* 434; queen Elizabeth's injunctions referred to, *Grin.*128, &c.; directed to be read quarterly, *ib.* 129; articles of inquiry for strangers in and about the city of London, 1567, *ib.* 296; injunctions given by Grindal, abp of York, in his visitation of that province, 1571; — for the clergy, *ib.* 123; — for the laity, *ib.*132;—for the dean and chapter, *ib.* 145; articles enjoined by abp Grindal to be put in execution within the archdeaconry of York, *ib.* 154; articles agreed on in the convocation of the province of Canterbury, 1575-6, touching the clergy, *ib.*185; Grindal's mandate for their publication, *ib.* 190, 191; articles to be inquired of within the province of Canterbury, in the visitation of abp Grindal, 1576, *ib.* 156; articles to be inquired of in the same visitation in all cathedral and collegiate churches, *ib.* 178; injunctions by Grindal to the dean and chapter of Bangor, 1576, *ib.* 183; articles of inquiry for recusants, 1580, *ib.* 418; the like, 1581, *ib.* 424; reference to articles of inquiry at bishops' visitations, 1 *Brad.* 277

Articles of Accusation, &c.: articles to which Latimer was required to subscribe, 1531, 2 *Lat.* 218; another copy, *ib.* 219; the Latin copy, *ib.* 466; articles imputed to Latimer by Dr Powell, 1533, *ib.* 225; reply to them, *ib.* 225, 358; articles of accusation against Parker, sent to lord chancellor Audley, 1539, with Parker's replies, *Park.* 7; articles subscribed by Will. Phelps, curate of Cirencester, 1551, ministered to him by bp Hooper, 2 *Hoop.* 152; officium et sententia contra Jo. Bradford, 1 *Brad.* 585; interrogatories objected to Cranmer, with his answers, 2 *Cran.* 219; the process in Latin, *ib.* 541; articles objected against Ridley and Latimer, 1555, *Rid.* 270, 271; the Latin copy, *ib.* 486; articles objected against Philpot, *Phil.* 83, 146, 150

Articles (Various): articles in Latin, probably drawn up for the agreement of the English and German divines, 1538, 2 *Cran.* 472, 480; fifteen articles containing the demands of the rebels in Devon, 1549, with Cranmer's answer, *ib.* 163, &c.; antichristian articles were procured from queen Mary, 3 *Bec.* 234; a book of articles was presented to Elizabeth by the returned Marian exiles, *Park.* 290; articles were sent from some learned men in Germany soon afterwards, *ib.* 118; articles treated of by Jewel in reply to Harding, 1 *Jew.* 103; CERTAIN ARTICLES OF CHRISTIAN RELIGION PROVED AND CONFIRMED, by T. Becon, 3 *Bec.* 396

Artificers: the king's artificers and labourers oppressed by delay in payment, 1 *Lat.* 261

Artillery: *v.* Archery.

Artopæus (Pet.): Bradford's preface to his Places of the Law and of the Gospel, 1 *Brad.* 5.

Artotyrites: a sect who ministered bread and cheese in the sacrament, 4 *Bul.* 410, 1 *Jew.* 252 n., 2 *Jew.* 588, *Phil.* 420, *Rog.* 295

Arts: *v.* Art.

Arundel, co. Sussex: the forest of Arundel, 2 *Cran.* 255

Arundel (Earls of): *v.* Albini, Fitzalan, Howard.

Arundel (Humf.), governor of St Michael's Mount: executed, 2 *Cran.* 163 n., 186 n., 187 n

Arundel (Tho.), abp of Canterbury: his rebellion against Richard II., 3 *Jew.* 171, and consequent temporary exile, *Bale* 125, 2 *Tyn.* 295; his examination of Will. Thorpe, *Bale* 44 n., 60, &c.; edited by Tyndale, 1 *Tyn.* xxvi., *Rid.* 494 n.; he calls Wicliffe a great clerk, *Bale* 81; sends Thorpe to prison, *ib.* 126; his constitution against translating the scriptures into English, or reading any unallowed translation, 1 *Tyn.* 132 n.; summons a synod in 1413, *Bale* 15; his process against lord Cobham, *ib.* 6, 15, &c.; he complains of him to the king, *ib.* 17; cites him, *ib.* 18; lord Cobham is brought before him, *ib.* 23; again, *ib.* 28; extract from the examination, 3 *Tyn.* 243 n.; he reads lord Cobham's sentence, *Bale* 41; the archbishop's death, *ib.* 9 n., 51

Arundel (Sir Tho.): receives Hooper as his steward, and sends him to Gardiner, *Hoop.* viii.; 3 *Zur.* 35 n.; executed, 3 *Zur.* 33 n., 577 n., 579 n

Arundell (Mr): *Park.* 448

Arvernense concilium: *v.* Councils.

Asa, king of Judah: 1 *Bul.* 221, 384, 2 *Bul.* 7

Asa (Will.): *v.* Alsa.

Asaph, the psalmist: *v.* Psalms.

Appointed by David to be a musician, till the building of the temple, 2 *Hoop.* 324; mentioned, 3 *Bul.* 207

Asaph (St): *v.* Saint Asaph.

Ascanius (...... card.): had a popinjay that could say the creed, 3 *Jew.* 255

Ascension: *v.* Christ.

Ascension-day: *v.* Thursday (Holy).

Ascham, (Roger): at St John's coll., Cambridge, *Hutch.* i. ii. ix; his account of the state of the university, 1 *Lat.* 178 n., 179 n. a friend of Dr Redman, 2 *Lat.* 297 n.; reference to his Toxophilus, *Pil.* 429; letters by him, 2 *Zur.* 64, 90; his account of queen Elizabeth, *ib.* 66, &c.; letter to him, 3 *Zur.* 150.

Ascham (Sturmius): 2 *Zur.* 90

Asclepiades, a Roman judge: 3 *Bul.* 225

Asconius Pedianus: on Θ and T, *Calf.* 107

Ashby (Mr): 2 *Zur.* 285

Ashdon (......): Ashdon's wife, martyr at Lewes, *Poet.* 170

Ashen, co. Essex: Parker's rectory, *Park.* vii, viii, 482

Ashes: *v.* Holy Ashes, Wednesday (Ash).

Ashford, co. Kent: martyrs there, *Poet.* 169

Ashley, co. Worcester: the hermitage at Redstone Ferry able to lodge 500 men, 2 *Lat.* 401

Ashley (Sir Jo.): 2 *Lat.* 415

Ashridge (......), a rebel: 2 *Cran.* 187 n

Ashtaroth, an idol: 3 *Tyn.* 92 n

Ashton (Jo.): died in prison, 1382, *Bale* 133; his body burned, as it seems, *ib.* 394

Ashton (Obad.): *v.* Assheton.

Ashton-under-Line, co. Lanc.: 1 *Brad.* 454

Ashwell, co. Herts: tithes there given by abp Grindal to Pembroke hall, *Grin.* 458

Ash-Wednesday: *v.* Wednesday.

Asia: comment on the epistles to the seven churches, *Bale* 265, &c.; Asia Minor had the service in Greek, 1 *Jew.* 272; on the dialects there, *Whita.* 256, 257; persecutions in Asia, 2 *Bul.* 105; the church not extinct there, 4 *Bul.* 73

Asiatici: sacrificed swine, and changed the beginning of the year, 2 *Brad.* 387

Asile: asylum, 1 *Bec.* 128

Ask (Mr), a gentleman of Yorkshire: *Grin.* 325

Aske (Rob.): his rebellion in Yorkshire (called the Pilgrimage of Grace, *q.v.*) 2 *Cran.* 332 n., 1 *Lat.* 25 n., 29

Askewe (Anne): born in Lincolnshire, of a noble stock, *Bale* 141; reads the Bible in Lincoln minster, *ib.* 173; account of her marriage with Mr Kyme, *ib.* 198, 199; her FIRST EXAMINATION, described by herself, with observations by Bale, *ib.* 136, &c.; questioned by Chr. Dare at Saddlers' hall, *ib.* 148; taken before the lord mayor, *ib.* 153; sent to the Counter, *ib.* 156; while there prentices and others send her money, *ib.* 222; brought before bp Bonner, *ib.* 163, 229; she is bailed, *ib.* 178, and set free, *ib.* 179; her voice, out of the 54th Psalm, *ib.* 184; her LATTER EXAMINATION, described by herself, with observations by Bale, *ib.* 186, &c.; prefixed is her letter to a friend, written from prison, on the Lord's supper, *ib.* 196; she is examined before the king's council at Greenwich, *ib.* 198; sent to Newgate, *ib.* 206; her confession of faith in Newgate, *ib.* 207; her prayer, *ib.* 210; she is condemned at Guildhall, *ib.* 212; her letter to lord chancellor Wriothesley, *ib.* 216; her confession of faith, written to the king, *ib.* 217; she is counselled to recant, *ib.* 218; sent to the Tower, *ib.* 220; racked by Wriothesley and Rich, *ib.* 224; she argues with the former, *ib.* 225; her patience under sufferings, *ib.* 227; her answer to John

Lassels's letter, *ib.* 228; her confession of faith made in Newgate before she suffered, *ib.* 231; her prayer, *ib.* 237, 238; her ballad made in Newgate, *ib.* 239; burned in Smithfield, *Bale* 243, 2 *Hoop.* 376, *Phil.* 249 n., 3 *Zur.* 41 n.; thunder at her death, *Bale,* 243, &c.; compared with Blandina, *ib.* 141; contrasted with Becket and other popish martyrs, *ib.* 190

Askewe (Edw.): was son to Sir Will. Askewe, and servant to Cranmer, 2 *Cran.* 399

Askewe (Sir Will.): was father of Anne Askewe, *Bale* 141, 198; his son Edward servant to Cranmer, 2 *Cran.* 399

Askue (......): martyred at Newbury, *Poet.* 168

Aslacton, co. Notts: the birthplace of Cranmer, 1 *Cran.* vii, 2 *Cran.* vii

Asotus (Pet.): *v.* Soto (P. à).

Asplyn (......): purposed to kill Day, *Park.* 449

Assayed: satisfied, *Phil.* 376

Assemannus (Jo. Sim.): 1 *Hoop.* 457 n

Assembled: resembled, compared, *Bale* 379

Assemblies: *v.* Church.

Asser (Jo.), bp of Sherborne: his Ælfredi Res Gestæ, published by abp Parker, *Park.* 468

Asses (The Feast of): Jan. 14, 1 *Tyn.* 91 n

Assheton (Obad.): wrote the life of Whitaker, *Whita.* xi

Assistance (Ready): a flower of the Nosegay, 1 *Bec.* 222

Assizes: a sermon at an assize, *Sand.* 216

Assoil: to solve, *Bale* 148, *Now.* 125; to absolve, *Bale* 29; so assoyle, *Calf.* 242; assoiled, for solved, 2 *Ful.* 48

Assoil: a releasing, 1 *Brad.* 283

Assurance: *v.* Faith, Grace, Peace, Prayers, Predestination.

Assurance of pardon, salvation, and eternal life declared or treated of, 3 *Bec.* 172, &c, 531, 1 *Brad.* 252, 344, 436, 2 *Brad.* 118, 132, 154, 1 *Ful.* 415, &c., 420, 421, 2 *Hoop.* 40, *Pra. B.* 14, *Sand.* 447, 1 *Tyn.* 89, 113, 2 *Tyn.* 186, 207, 3 *Whitg.* 622; it is the doctrine of scripture, 3 *Jew.* 245, and of the old fathers, *ib.*, and the earnest-penny of our salvation, *Pra. B.* 89; the full assurance of faith, 1 *Ful.* 416, 417; it belongs to believers, *Sand.* 184, 185; they may be assured of glory everlasting who are not ashamed to take up the cross of Christ, *Phil.* 265; it is the mark of a perfect Christian, *ib.* 266; the work of the Spirit, 1 *Tyn.* 101; how assurance of pardon is to be obtained, 2 *Tyn.* 84; prayer a means thereof, 3 *Bec.* 157; it produces holiness, 1 *Brad.* 77; the devil labours to subvert it, *ib.* 316; the pope wrests texts against certainty of salvation, 3 *Bec.* 531; Papists deny it, 3 *Bec.* 174, 2 *Ful.* 229, *Rog.* 113, and say we should always doubt the pardon of our sins, *Rog.* 285; the certainty of grace and salvation termed presumption, by Harding, 3 *Jew.* 241, &c., but it is not so, 3 *Bec.* 174, 3 *Jew.* 245, &c.; examples of some who have had it, 3 *Bec.* 177, 178; Philpot's assurance of God's favour, *Phil.* 140; a prayer for sure hope of the life everlasting, *Lit. Eliz.* 253

Assyrians: their monarchy, 3 *Bec.* 9, 10, 1 *Cov.* 34, *Pil.* 186, 187; an angel slays 185,000 of them, 4 *Jew.* 1180; mentioned by Judith, 4 *Bul.* 181

Astall (Rich.), parson of Chevening: 2 *Cran.* 255 n., 257 n.; letter to him, *ib.* 260; another, requiring him to reform a bad husband, *ib.* 278

Astaroth: *v.* Ashtaroth.

Asterius, a bishop: 2 *Jew.* 661

Astesanus Astensis: wrote on the Apocalypse, *Bale* 258

Aston, co. Herts: the manor and church belonged to the monks of Reading, 2 *Cran.* 275 n

Aston (Jo.), a follower of Wicliffe: *Bale* 81

Astrology: *v.* Nostradamus (M.)

Astrology condemned, 2 *Cran.* 100, 1 *Hoop.* 328, 329, 331; a sin against the first commandment, 1 *Hoop.* 308; calculation by astronomy a great evil, 2 *Hoop.* 294; astrology refuted, *Hutch.* 77—88; astronomers censured for calling some days unfortunate, *Pil.* 17, 18; Pilkington allows that the stars may have some power on the body and for physic, *ib.* 17; astrologers named, and their predictions condemned, 2 *Jew.* 872; Wolsey and other prelates used astrology, 2 *Tyn.* 308, 312; it was practised by Bomelius, *Park.* 364; treatises against it, by W. Fulke, 1 *Ful.* ii, v, vi

Astronomy: various astronomical notes are annexed to some of the Calendars (*q. v.*); see particularly, *Pra. Eliz.* 225, &c.

Asturia, a part of Spain: 1 *Bul.* 416

Astyages, king of Persia: *v.* Ahasuerus.

Astyages, and Harpagus: their history, 1 *Lat.* 457

Astyrius: his conduct at an idolatrous sacrifice, 2 *Brad.* 339, 341

Athaliah: slain, 1 *Bul.* 388, 2 *Bul.* 8

Athanasians: the orthodox so called by Arians, 2 *Ful.* 375, 4 *Jew.* 713

Athanasius (St): *v.* Creeds.

i. *His life:* when a child he ministered baptism, and it was held valid, *Hutch.* 116,

ATHANASIUS

2 *Whitg*. 528; present at the council of Nice, being then a deacon, 4 *Jew*. 1009; erroneously stated to have presided there, *Phil*. 77, *Grin*. 223; bishop of Alexandria, *Rog*. 329, or archbishop, 2 *Whitg*. 161; persecuted, *Rid*. 63, 74; falsely accused, 1 *Bec*. 18, *Sand*. 129; condemned in a council at Tyre, 1 *Jew*. 392; appealed to Constantine, 2 *Ful*. 358, 379, 1 *Jew*. 392, 3 *Whitg*. 309; banished by that emperor, at the instigation of priests, 2 *Cran*. 12; some account of his banishment and restoration, 1 *Jew*. 414—416: complained of his deposition to Julius bp of Rome, 2 *Ful*. 346, 347; also to Felix, 1 *Jew*. 386, 391, &c.; banished again by Julian, *Pil*. 440; he refused to attend councils, 4 *Jew*. 951, &c., 1100; as archbishop of Alexandria, he corrected Ischaras, a pretended clerk, 2 *Whitg*. 161, (see 3 *Jew*. 321), and received the submission of Arsennius, a bishop, *ib*. 162, and visited churches, *ib*.; his jurisdiction, *ib*. 165, 430; high titles ascribed to him, 3 *Jew*. 315; called "lord" (δεσπότης), and "most reverend," 2 *Whitg*. 387; called by Ruffinus the greatest, or highest bishop, 4 *Jew*. 823; he (not Ambrose as Jewel states), was called by Gregory Nazianzen the eye of the world, the archpriest of priests, the foundation of the faith, 3 *Jew*. 219; called orbis oculus, 4 *Jew*. 1045; denominated by Socrates the great star of Egypt, 3 *Jew*. 125; written to by Basil, *ib*. 301—304; his funeral sermon made by Gregory Nazianzen, *Grin*. 10

ii. *His works*: see *Calf*. 402, 2 *Ful*. 396; he writes an epistle to Eupsychius of Cæsarea, 3 *Jew*. 410; references to the Life of St Anthony found amongst his works, 3 *Bec*. 280 n., *Calf*. 74 n.; the spurious Questiones ad Antiochum, *Calf*. 73, 74, 268, 272, 2 *Ful*. 143, 177, 193, 206; Martiall falsifies this book, *Calf*. 376; the fictitious Liber de Passione Imaginis Christi, 2 *Ful*. 200; forged epistles in his name, 1 *Jew*. 367, 4 *Jew*. 937, 994, 1001; many works of Apollinarius anciently ascribed to him, *Calf*. 268; Latin graces after meat, taken from his works, *Pra. Eliz*. 400, 401; Simler makes collections from his writings, 1 *Zur*. 62; misalleged by Dr Cole, *Phil*. 24

iii. *God*: he mentions two ways of coming to the knowledge of God, *Calf*. 46; his doctrine respecting Christ (Creed), 3 *Bul*. 260: he maintains the deity of the Holy Ghost, *ib*. 304; says, notwithstanding the words (persona, homousios, &c.,) are not found expressed in scripture, yet they have the meaning that the scripture wills, 3 *Jew*. 440; says, nature, essence, kind, and form, are all one (pseud.), *ib*. 261, 513

iv. *Scripture*: he says that the holy scriptures are sufficient to all instruction of the truth, 2 *Cran*. 24; the same and other testimonies to the like effect, *Whita*. 680; says, we must learn of the holy scriptures, wherein are proofs sufficient, 3 *Jew*. 228; speaking of certain truths, he says, these things we have drawn from the divinely inspired masters who unrolled the sacred books, *ib*. 238; his saying, if I be deceived, thou hast deceived me, 2 *Jew*. 1059; he numbers the second commandment among the ten, and holds it a moral law, 2 *Bec*. 60; says Christ composed the Old Testament and the New, *Whita*. 528, that the gospel is the presence of our Lord Jesus Christ, 2 *Jew*. 616, that the Lord is in the words of the scriptures, 3 *Jew*. 467, 541, and that the child is kept among us whom Herod laboured to destroy, *ib*. 545; asserts that the Hebrew gospel of Matthew was translated into Greek by the apostle James, *Whita*. 126; on the authority of what Paul delivered by word of mouth, 2 *Cran*. 57; his testimony for tradition considered, *Whita*. 588; on the canon of scripture, and the books which are not canonical, *ib*. 57, 62; mentions the fourth book of Maccabees, *ib*. 103

v. *Eucharist*: he explains the distinction between the flesh and the spirit, and speaks of Christ's flesh as called celestial meat, and spiritual food, 2 *Bec*. 289, 3 *Bec*. 431, 1 *Jew*. 141, and see 1 *Brad*. 97 n., *Rid*. 201; asks, for how many men Christ's body could have sufficed, that he should be the food of all the world? and says that he spoke of his ascension that he might withdraw men from corporal understanding, 1 *Cran*. 209, (80), *Grin*. 67, 68, 1 *Jew*. 464, 2 *Jew*. 1120, 3 *Jew*. 539; calls the Lord's supper the conservatory to the resurrection of everlasting life, 3 *Bec*. 388, 1 *Cran*. 209; says that the image of a king is called the king, though it is not so, 3 *Jew*. 545, 546

vi. *Councils* (see also i.): false statements in his name respecting the council of Nice, 1 *Jew*. 354, &c., 2 *Whitg*. 151; says the Arians falsified that council, 1 *Jew*. 357; says bishops (amongst others), of Britain came to the council at Sardica, 3 *Jew*. 165; cited respecting a council in the time of pope Julius, 4 *Jew*. 695; tells of the pride and ambition that reigned in the councils of the clergy in his days, 2 *Cran*. 53; tells of bishops who sent priests to councils as their deputies, 4 *Jew.* 999; says letters for summoning a council were sent out from the emperor and his lieutenants, *ib.* 1005; describes an assembly gathered by compulsion of the civil power and falsely termed a synod, *ib.* 1028; calls for a synod far from the palace, *ib.*; tells how Constantius made a show of referring matters to the judgment of bishops, *ib.* 1029.

vii. *Bishops, Rome:* he speaks of metropolitans, 2 *Whitg.* 163; on the jurisdiction of the bishop of Alexandria, *ib.* 165; he calls Eupsychius bishop of Cappadocia, 4 *Jew.* 805; asks what need there is of men who are bishops in title only, 3 *Jew.* 310; his use of the word παροικία, 1 *Jew.* 160; he calls Rome the metropolis of the Roman jurisdiction, 1 *Jew.* 403, 3 *Jew.* 307, 4 *Jew.* 707, 828; says that Julius, bishop of Rome, by the counsel of all the bishops of Italy, sent unto the bishops of the East, 1 *Jew.* 394; he calls the bishop of Rome brother, 4 *Jew.* 841; how Liberius wrote to him, *ib.* 841, 1044; he beseeches the help of the apostolic see (pseud.), 1 *Jew.* 351, 353; complains that Constantius had no reverence for the bishop of Rome, 2 *Ful.* 362, 379; regards it a foolish thing to suppose that religion stands in the greatness of cities, 4 *Jew.* 1069; speaks of many bishops as not married, 3 *Jew.* 409

viii. *Saints, Cross, Images:* against the worship of creatures, *Calf.* 144, 149; the Index Expurgatorius of card. Zapata condemns a reference to his declaration that God alone is to be adored, *ib.* 375 n.; why the virgin was called "full of grace," 1 *Ful.* 529, 530; cited, in the second Nicene council, as saying that Christ dwells in relics and dead men's bones, 2 *Jew.* 664; ascribes the conversion of wicked men to the faith of Christ and the sign of the cross, 2 *Ful.* 198, 199; asks why believers make figures of the cross, but not of the spear, or the reed, which are as holy as the cross itself (pseud.), *Calf.* 272, 273, 2 *Ful.* 177, 193, and see 206; speaks of devils flying when they see the cross (pseud.), *Calf.* 73, 74, 2 *Ful.* 143; says the invention of images came not of good, but of evil, 2 *Jew.* 646, 656, *Park.* 83, *Rid.* 85; falsely alleged for image-worship, 2 *Jew.* 662, and as recording a story of an image of Christ made by Nicodemus, *ib.* 651; a spurious passage on Christ's image, *ib.* 655; he refutes the heathen argument for images, *Calf.* 21 n., 1 *Hoop.* 42

ix. *Heretics:* on heresy, *Bale* 218; he says heretics use the words of scripture for a bait, 4 *Jew.* 752; states the heretical opinion of the Arians, 3 *Jew.* 258; records words of Arius relating how he learned his doctrine, *ib.* 440; says the Arians erred through taking spiritual things in a corporal sense, *ib.* 499; observes that they being themselves guilty, took upon them to be judges, 4 *Jew.* 918; says they carried forth and burnt the seats, the wooden table, &c., 3 *Jew.* 602; on the Apollinarian heresy, *Rog.* 52 n., 99 n.; on the Tropicks, *ib.* 70 n

x. *Miscellanea:* shews that harlots, murderers, &c., are changed by the faith of Christ, *Calf.* 353; affirms that those who worship the Lord and live not worthy of him, are guilty of the Lord's death (pseud.?), 4 *Jew.* 894; says, it is the part of Christians to be persecuted, but to persecute Christians is the office of Pilate and Caiaphas, 2 *Jew.* 890, 4 *Jew.* 1075; how he made the reader utter the psalm, 4 *Bul.* 194; he (not as Jewel says, Theodoret), declares the knowledge of heavenly things to be useful to a prince, 2 *Jew.* 681 n.; he recommends the study of godly things to Jovinian, 3 *Jew.* 194; denies that the judgment of the church receives its authority from the emperor, *Whita.* 439; how he was willing to submit his cause to the emperor, 4 *Jew.* 1028; on hell-fire, 2 *Lat.* 235; he extols Hosius of Corduba, 4 *Jew.* 999, 1003

Atheists: numerous, 3 *Bul.* 112; they deny the general judgment, *Rog.* 67; reject the scriptures, *ib.* 78; understand not salvation through Christ, *ib.* 109; cast off all grace and virtue, *ib.* 118; assert that there is no hell but opinion, *ib.* 148; their licentiousness, *Wool.* 44

Athelstan, king of England: caused the scriptures to be translated into English, 2 *Jew.* 690, 694, 1 *Tyn.* 149, *Whita.* 222; his laws, *Bale* 447; he gave a palace to Wulstan, abp of York, 1 *Zur.* 259 n

Athenæus: on the licence of poets, 2 *Jew.* 660

Athenagoras: calls second marriage a fair kind of adultery, 3 *Jew.* 390; on the fury of the heathen against the Christian name, *Wool.* 19

Athens, Athenians: Athens called by Thucydides Græcia of all Græcia, 1 *Jew.* 420; its walls rebuilt, 4 *Jew.* 1104; its schools of learning, 4 *Bul.* 480, 2 *Jew.* 981; the proverb, γλαῦκας εἰς Ἀθήνας, 3 *Zur.* 435; custom at the feast of Prometheus, 1 *Zur.* 123 n.; law of the Athenians against adul-

ATHENS — AUGUSTINE 47

tery, 2 *Bec.* 649; they swore to fight for religion, 2 *Brad.* 105; their spies, 4 *Bul.* 106; pope Joan brought up at Athens, 4 *Jew.* 648, 652; how long learning remained there, *ib.* 652; sundry dukes and bishops thereof in modern times, *ib.* 653; the city taken by the sultan Mahomet, *ib.* 653
Atherton (Mr): *Grin.* 462
Athol (Jo. earl of): *v.* Stuart.
Athos (Mount): defied by Xerxes, 4 *Jew.* 845
Atkins (Anth.), fellow of Merton college: committed to the Tower, *Park.* 75
Atkinson (......), vice-provost of King's college, Cambridge: *Park.* 18
Atkynson (......): sentenced to do penance at St Paul's for errors about the sacrament, 2 *Cran.* 372
Atonement: at-one-ment, concord, *Phil.* 330, 1 *Tyn.* 9
Ator, one of the magi: *Whita.* 560 n
Attalus (St): the history of Attalus and Blandina, 2 *Lat.* 80
Attfelld (Mr): 2 *Cran.* 301
Atticus, bp of Constantinople: 1 *Jew.* 356, 3 *Jew.* 340, 4 *Jew.* 937
Attila: called Atthilas, 2 *Bul.* 109
Attire: *v.* Apparel.
Attrition: a feigned word, 1 *Tyn.* 265, 342; the definition of the council of Trent, *ib.* 265 n.; attrition and contrition, 1 *Brad.* 46, 51
Attyn (Tho.), perhaps Allyn: letter signed by him, 3 *Zur.* 170
Aubertin (Edm.): L'Eucharistie, 1 *Hoop.* 161 n
Aubrey (Will.): an insatiable cormorant, *Park.* 267; called Dr Abre, *ib.* 285; Grindal's officer, *Grin.* 402, 408, 415 n
Aucher (Sir Ant.): mentioned as Ant. Ager, 2 *Cran.* 313; mayor of Dover, 3 *Zur.* 614, 630 (misprinted Ancher).
Auckland (Bishop), co. Durham: Pilkington died there, *Pil.* xi, and was buried there, but afterwards removed, *ib.* xii; a prebend, *ib.* 574
Audians: *v.* Anthropomorphites.
Audientes: *v.* Hearers.
Audius, a heretic: 1 *Hoop.* 160
Audley (Edm.), bp of Salisbury: of noble birth, 3 *Jew.* 410
Audley (Jo.): *v.* Awdelie.
Audley (Tho.), lord Audley of Walden, and lord chancellor: notice of him, 3 *Zur.* 36 n., 317 n.; he examines Frith, 2 *Cran.* 246; articles sent to him against Parker, *Park.* 7; he was learned and eloquent, *ib.* 315; letters to him, 2 *Cran.* 264, 291 (?); his heiress, 1 *Zur.* 137 n (misprinted Dudley)

Auerstadt (The bp of): 2 *Zur.* 70
Augmentation court: *v.* Court.
Augsburgh: *v.* Confession.
    Conferences or diets there, 2 *Bul.* 399, 3 *Jew.* 208, 235, 557, 4 *Jew.* 783, 3 *Zur.* 667, 669; the Interim forced upon it, 3 *Zur.* 335; the city taken, *ib.* 456 n
Augures: their art, 1 *Hoop.* 327, 328.
Augustine (St): *v.* Cæsarius, Eligius, Evodius, Fulgentius, Gennadius, Guigo, Ivo, Paulinus, Vigilius Tapsensis.
    i. *His Life.*
   ii. *His Works.*
  iii. *On God; the Father, the Son, and the Holy Ghost.*
  iv. *Angels.*
   v. *Scripture, Word of God, Truth.*
  vi. *Tradition.*
 vii. *Sin.*
viii. *Grace, Justification, Works, &c.*
  ix. *The Church.*
   x. *Bishops and other Ministers.*
  xi. *Peter, Rome.*
 xii. *Saints.*
xiii. *Sacraments.*
xiv. *Baptism.*
 xv. *The Eucharist.*
xvi. *Ceremonies.*
xvii. *Prayer, Praise, Worship.*
xviii. *Tongues.*
xix. *Miracles.*
 xx. *Festivals, Fasts.*
xxi. *Marriage, &c.*
xxii. *Confession, Penance, Absolution, Excommunication.*
xxiii. *Affliction, Persecution.*
xxiv. *The Soul.*
xxv. *Death, Judgment, Heaven, Hell; also Burial, Purgatory, Resurrection, &c.*
xxvi. *Images, the Cross.*
xxvii. *Heresies.*
xxviii. *Antichrist.*
xxix. *Kings, Civil Power.*
xxx. *Miscellanea.*
    i. *His life*: born at Tagasta, *Hutch.* 349; his mother Monica (*q. v.*), 2 *Bec.* 344 n., 1 *Brad.* 540; how he learned Latin, 1 *Jew.* 295; reclaimed by reading Cicero's Hortensius, 3 *Jew.* 558; he speaks of himself as nearly nine years a Manichee, *ib.* 156; writes of his going to Rome, and teaching there, 4 *Jew.* 654; his conversion from the Manichean heresy, 3 *Tyn.* 50, *Whita.* 320, 698; it was through hearing Ambrose, 1 *Lat.* 201, and by reading the scriptures, 2 *Jew.* 676, 3 *Whitg.* 38; his account of his conversion, 2 *Jew.* 1018, 1019, 4 *Jew.* 1169;

he narrates how he sought a way to get strength, that he might be able to enjoy God, but found it not until he embraced Jesus Christ, 3 *Jew.* 537; legendary account of his baptism by Ambrose, *Pra. Eliz.* 250 n.; how he became a perfect Christian, 2 *Jew.* 1062; coadjutor to Valerius at Hippo, 1 *Hoop.* 508; bishop of Hippo, *Rog.* 330; called pope, 1 *Jew.* 362; Jerome addresses him as the most notable bishop in the world, 4 *Jew.* 1044; he styles himself a servant of Christ and of the servants of Christ, 1 *Jew.* 424; he determined secular causes, 4 *Jew.* 1300, 2 *Whitg.* 358, 3 *Whitg.* 441, 442, 450—452, 456; the verses he wrote over his table, *Sand.* 399; his dispute with Jerome, 1 *Jew.* 532, *Phil.* 401; his advice to him, 1 *Jew.* 80; he subscribed at several councils, 3 *Jew.* 296; took part in the third council of Carthage, *Whita.* 39; his church became separate from the see of Rome, 1 *Jew.* 416; he often differs in opinion from other fathers, *Whita.* 455; in some things he erred, 1 *Hoop.* 28, 29; he was not ashamed to acknowledge this, 1 *Bec.* 279, 2 *Hoop.* 154; cited by Papists in defence of open abominations, 2 *Jew.* 806; he was ignorant of Hebrew, 1 *Ful.* 391, 1 *Jew.* 329; he appointed Eradius as his successor, 4 *Bul.* 133, 1 *Whitg.* 443, 445; on his death-bed he desired to hear the seven penitential Psalms, *Pra. Eliz.* 45 n.; he died out of communion with the church of Rome, 2 *Ful.* 71 n., just before the taking of Hippo, *Pil.* 612; the date of his death, 4 *Bul.* 515; he was yielding in matters not affecting the frame of Christian faith, 4 *Jew.* 1306; a great discloser of the forgery and pride of the bishop of Rome, 1 *Jew.* 418; he maintained the innocence of pope Marcellinus, 2 *Ful.* 365 n.; condemned by Boniface II., as accursed and set on by the devil, 1 *Jew.* 418, 3 *Jew.* 295, 296; likewise by some heretical councils, *Rid.* 134

ii. *His works*: see 4 *Bul.* 587, *Calf.* 402, 2 *Ful.* 396, *Jew.* xxxiii; commendation of them, *Pil.* 682, 1 *Tyn.* 154; our faith is not grounded on them, 1 *Hoop.* 127; his writings on free-will, grace, and predestination, occasioned by the heresy of Pelagius, *Coop.* 148; some of his works translated by Rogers, *Rog.* viii; his book De Civitate Dei, *Phil.* 386; his reason for writing it, 1 *Tyn.* 164 n.; commentators on it, 1 *Hoop.* 314; object of his Speculum, 2 *Jew.* 690, 691; the Homilia de Pastoribus wrongly rejected by Fulke, 2 *Ful.* 291; his treatise De Cura agenda pro Mortuis, 3 *Tyn.* 272 n.; his Retractationes, 4 *Jew.* 1173, *Phil.* 403; he acknowledged that there were many things in his works which might justly be reproved, 3 *Bec.* 391, 2 *Cran.* 33, and revoked many things which he had written, 1 *Tyn.* 154; spurious addresses to Catechumens, *Calf.* 84 n.; the Sermones de Sanctis, falsely ascribed to him, 1 *Ful.* 353; a questionable homily of Chrysostom, De Cruce et Latrone, mistakenly assigned to him, *Calf.* 63 n., 277, 2 *Ful.* 180 n.; a sermon attributed both to him and Ambrose, 2 *Ful.* 284; a sermon ascribed to him, to Ambrose, and to Maximus Taurinensis, *ib.* 340 n.; the sermon De Visitatione Infirmorum not his, *Calf.* 361; a spurious sermon among those De Diversis, 2 *Ful.* 82; words falsely assigned to him in the Canon Law, *Calf.* 54; notice of meditations doubtfully ascribed to him, *Pra. Eliz.* xxi. xxii. 373 n.; Liber Soliliquiorum Animæ, *ib.* 374 n.; the Scala Paradisi not his, 3 *Jew.* 379 n.; nor the Manuale, 2 *Cov.* 404 n.; the treatise De Mirabilibus S. Scripturæ, considered spurious, 1 *Jew.* 481 n.; Basil's prologue to the Psalms wrongly ascribed to him, *ib.* 325 n.; he is stated to have written on the Apocalypse, *Bale* 255, but the work seems a collection from various writers, 2 *Jew.* 760 n.; De vera et falsa Penitentia, not his, 2 *Cov.* 343 n.; Contra Felicianum Arianum, not genuine, 3 *Bul.* 265; counterfeit Tractatus contra quinque Hæreses, 2 *Ful.* 147 n.; the treatise De Fide ad Petrum Diaconum, sometimes ascribed to him, is by Fulgentius, 3 *Bec.* 455 n., *Coop.* 94, 2 *Cov.* 200 n, 2 *Ful.* 86 n.; his words wrongly alleged by Gardiner, 1 *Jew.* 53; altered by Pighius, *ib.* 53, 54; misreported by Harding, 1 *Jew.* 371, 436, 437; wrongly cited for Jerome, 1 *Bec.* 383

iii. *God; the Father, the Son, and the Holy Ghost*: on the co-eternity of the Father and the Son, and the everlasting procession, from them both, of the Holy Spirit, 3 *Bul.* 306, 307; another passage, *ib.* 308; speaking of the Holy Trinity he says, this is my faith, because this is the catholic faith, 2 *Jew.* 799 n.; he says, in that high Trinity there are no distances of times [meaning that the persons are co-eternal together], 3 *Bul.* 300; referred to about false views of God, *ib.* 124; he warns against believing that the nature of God may be changed, since sometimes the thing which signifies takes the name of the thing which it signifies, 3 *Bec.* 442, 443; says God is in himself as A and Ω, in the world as governor and author, in the angels as sweetness and comeliness, in the church as the good-man in his house, &c., *Wool.* 96; says, my God is everywhere present, everywhere whole, nowhere shut up, 3 *Jew.* 555, 4 *Jew.* 662; shews that the will of God is the first cause of all things, *Pil.* 674; and that what is done by God's will cannot be against nature, 1 *Jew.* 501; mentions things which God cannot do because he is almighty, *Hutch.* 111; maintains that God is not the author of evil, 1 *Ful.* 563; shews that there is nothing which is not subject to the providence of God, 2 *Cov.* 112; says, God fulfils his own good purposes by the evil purposes of wicked men, 3 *Zur.* 327; inquires who dare reply to God, 4 *Jew.* 831; remarks that he who gives the kingdom of heaven only to the godly, gives this earthly kingdom both to the godly and the godless, as he pleases, *Calf.* 113; confesses that all God's works are very good, *ib.* 131; says it is no injury to the holy hills to say that our help is not in them but in the Lord, *ib.* 67; calls God the Father, the Son, and the Holy Ghost, bread, 2 *Jew.* 766, 767, 3 *Jew.* 492; speaks of God as the inward bread of his soul, 2 *Jew.* 768, 1110, 3 *Jew.* 492; says, God shall be the end of our longing and desire, 2 *Cov.* 216; against the error of the Anthropomorphites, viz. that God has bodily parts, 1 *Bul.* 225, 3 *Bul.* 138; asks, what is the image of God, but the countenance of God? *Calf.* 172; shews how man is the image of God, *ib.* 156, 157; on the right hand of God, 3 *Bec.* 452, 1 *Bul.* 147, 150, 151, 2 *Cov.* 154, 155; referred to respecting the "back parts" of God, 3 *Bul.* 145 n.; says, every substance which is not God is a creature...and what is less than God is not God, 1 *Jew.* 482; observes that he loves God the less who loves anything besides God, 2 *Jew.* 583; shews why the Romans, who received the gods of almost all the Gentiles, never received the God of the Hebrews, 3 *Bul.* 203

He says, let no man believe of Christ but that which Christ has commanded him to believe of him, 3 *Jew.* 122, 4 *Jew.* 845; on the two natures in Christ, 1 *Jew.* 482; he declares that Christ, when he came to the virgin, was everywhere whole, everywhere perfect; wholly in the womb, wholly on the cross, &c., 1 *Hoop.* 224; observes that when Christ said, "I and My Father are one," the Jews rushed to take up stones, and that they understood what the Arians do not, *Whita.* 481, 482; affirms that as concerning the form of God, Christ says, "I and My Father are one," 3 *Jew.* 261, and that the form is one, because the Godhead is one, *ib.*; expounds "form" by "substance," *ib.* 262; shews that the doctrine of homousion is contained in scripture, though the word is not, 3 *Bul.* 246; says the word was confirmed in the council of Nice, 1 *Jew.* 533; asks, how do you touch God? because "the Word became flesh, and dwelt among us," 3 *Jew.* 492; calls the Word the everlasting meat, says the angels feed upon it, and shews that the Word was made flesh that man might eat, 1 *Jew.* 530; remarks that if Christ came as God he would not be known, 3 *Jew.* 493; on the text "Adorate scabellum pedum ejus," (Psal. xcix. 5), which he interprets of our Lord's humanity, 1 *Cran.* 236, *Hutch.* 254, 2 *Lat.* 273, 1 *Jew.* 541, *Rid.* 233, 234; he observes that we must beware not so to maintain the divinity of the man, that we take away the truth of his body, 2 *Bec.* 277, 3 *Bec.* 451, 3 *Bul.* 264, 265, 1 *Cran.* 94, 186, *Grin.* 52, 1 *Jew.* 482, 495 n., 497, 505, 3 *Jew.* 259, 623; writes, when thou thinkest of the form of a servant in Christ, think of the fashion of a man, if thou hast faith, 1 *Jew.* 496, 3 *Jew.* 261; says, Christ as concerning his manhood is a creature, 1 *Jew.* 482; mentions that Nestorius taught that Christ was man only, and that Eutyches denied his manhood, 1 *Cran.* 293; (see more as to our Lord's humanity lower down, after the passages respecting his ascension); on Christ alone without sin, 3 *Jew.* 581; why our Lord was named Christ, and of his offices as King and Priest, 3 *Bul.* 296, 297; asserts that there is no other way to the Father than by him, 1 *Bec.* 150; he speaks of him as the corner-stone, joining two walls, viz. the Jews and the Gentiles, 3 *Jew.* 280; writes largely of Melchisedec as a type of Christ, 2 *Jew.* 731; how Abraham saw Christ's day, 1 *Hoop.* 212; remarks that it is not said that the rock signified Christ, but that it "was Christ," 2 *Jew.* 563 (and see v. and xiii. below); says the rock was Christ for its firmness, and the manna was Christ, because it came down from heaven, *ib.* 765; affirms that the godly in manna understood Christ, *ib.*; on Christ's sleep in the ship, *Sand.* 382 n.; shews that when Judas departed, the Son of man was glorified, that departure being a figure of the time when the tares shall be separated from the wheat, 4 *Bul.* 284, 285; explains in what sense Christ confessed himself to be a king when before Pilate, 1 *Hoop.* 79; maintains that Christ's death was not of necessity, but of his own will, *ib.* 168; speaks of the victim tied by the horns, as a type of Christ crucified, 1 *Jew.* 503; says Christ was both the priest and the sacrifice, and his cross the altar, 2 *Jew.* 733; writes, there were three on the cross, one the Saviour, another to be saved, another to be damned; the punishment of all was alike, but the cause diverse, 3 *Jew.* 188; shews that Christ could not be bodily present in the sun and moon, and upon the cross at one time, 1 *Jew.* 495, 3 *Jew.* 257, 535; teaches that only Christ could offer for the remission of sins, and no other thing than his own body, 2 *Hoop.* 505; asserts that no man takes away the sins of the world but Christ alone, 2 *Bec.* 173, 3 *Bec.* 419; calls the blood of Christ the ransom of the whole world (Prosper), *ib.* 419, 422; says that Christ by his death, that one true sacrifice, has put away whatsoever sins there were, *ib.* 419; declares that the Lord sent his Son, who giving to all remission of sins might offer them being justified to God, *ib.*; affirms that Christ's body died without sin, that the obligations of all faults might be put out, *ib.* 418; invites to behold Christ that we may be healed from sin, 3 *Bec.* 172, 422; reposes all his hope in the precious blood of Christ, *ib.* 171; observes that Christ is slain to every man, when he believes that Christ was slain, 2 *Jew.* 726, 733; shews that of the very remnant of our thoughts, that is, of our very memories, Christ is daily sacrificed unto us, 3 *Jew.* 469; speaks of every man offering up the sacrifice of our Lord's passion for his sins, *ib.* 336; says that Christ crucified is milk for babes, and meat for the strong, 1 *Jew.* 463; on Christ crucified as milk for babes, 3 *Jew.* 493; he calls the cross of Christ our feast and spiritual fair, &c. (dub.), *Calf.* 277; on the title upon the cross, 1 *Jew.* 275; the descent into hell not in the creed which he expounds, 1 *Bul.* 137; his opinion on that subject, *ib.* 138; he confesses his ignorance of the reason of it, *Whita.* 537, but calls him an infidel who denies it, 1 *Ful.* 280; his doctrine respecting the true resurrection of our Lord, 2 *Cov.* 145; he shews how the body of our Lord in respect of the substance of it, is even after the resurrection called flesh, 1 *Jew.* 461; says that our Saviour, after the resurrection, though now in the spiritual flesh, yet in the true flesh did eat and drink with the disciples, 2 *Cov.* 193; speaks of Christ as slain and rising daily, 1 *Jew.* 128; on Christ's words to Mary, "Touch me not," *ib.* 477; his doctrine relative to the ascension of our Lord, 2 *Cov.* 153; on the Son of man ascending where he was before, &c., 1 *Jew.* 524, 525; he says, now thou findest not Christ to speak on earth, 3 *Jew.* 254; shews that Christ, by his ascension, would secure us against those whom he foretold as saying, "Lo, here is Christ," 1 *Jew.* 495; cautions against listening to those who say that the body of Christ which rose and ascended was not that which was buried, 3 *Bul.* 265; on his session at God's right hand, 1 *Bul.* 150, 151; he warns against listening to those who deny that Christ sits at the right hand of God, 3 *Bec.* 452, 453; on what is meant by that expression, 2 *Cov.* 154, 155; he proves that after the form of Christ's human nature, we may not think that he is everywhere, 2 *Bec,* 277, 278, 3 *Bec.* 451, 1 *Cran.* 94, 95, 96, (48), *Grin.* 52, 1 *Jew.* 505, 2 *Jew.* 797, 3 *Jew.* 259; speaks of Christ being absent in his manhood, 3 *Bec.* 452, 1 *Cran.* 73; affirms that as to the flesh which the Word assumed, as to that which was born of the virgin, taken by the Jews, fixed on the cross, &c. (Christ said) "Me ye have not always," 2 *Bec.* 273, 274, 3 *Bec.* 272, 273, 274, 427, 428, 452, 4 *Bul.* 454, 455, 1 *Jew.* 505, 506, 2 *Jew.* 1118, 3 *Jew.* 263, *Phil.* 187, 188, *Rid.* 42, 43, 176; says our Lord absented himself in body from all the church, and ascended into heaven, 3 *Jew.* 263; teaches that we must believe and confess that Christ as to his humanity is visible, corporeal, local, &c., 2 *Hoop.* 491, 3 *Jew.* 261; says he is gone, and yet is here…for he has carried his body into heaven, but has not taken from the world his majesty, 1 *Jew.* 505; says Christ went as man, but remained as God: he went as to that which was in one place; he remained as to that which was everywhere, 3 *Jew.* 263; speaks of Christ as absent in body, but present in the power of his majesty, and as hearing what the consciences of the people have said, 4 *Jew.* 976; declares that Christ has left the world by his bodily departure, but not with the governance of his divine presence, 3 *Bec.* 428, 452; says, after Christ is risen and ascended, he is in us by the Spirit, 1 *Jew.* 477, 479; asserts that a body must needs be in some certain place, 2 *Bec.* 278, 281, 3 *Bec.* 454, 3 *Bul.* 264, 265, 4 *Bul.*

444, 1 *Cran.* 97, 101, (50), 1 *Hoop.* 194, 1 *Jew.* 484, 3 *Jew.* 259; says, Christ's body in which he rose must be in one place, but his truth is dispersed in all places, 2 *Bec.* 278, 3 *Bec.* 452, 1 *Brad.* 91, and see 591, 1 *Cran.*140, *Grin.* 53, 2 *Hoop.* 488, 1 *Jew.* 486, 494, 2 *Jew.* 776, 1118, 3 *Jew.* 146, 252, 254, 257, 259, 262, 535, *Rid.* 176, 215, 216; corruption of this testimony in some copies, 1 *Hoop.* 192, 3 *Jew.* 254; says, according to his body he is in heaven and passes from place to place, 3 *Jew.* 485; says that we ought not to inquire, where and how the body of our Lord is in heaven, but we must believe that it is only in heaven, 2 *Bec.* 278, 3 *Bec.* 273, 452, 2 *Cov.* 156; declares that Christ is everywhere as God, but in a certain place of heaven because of the measure of a true body, 2 *Bec.* 278, 3 *Bec.* 430, 1 *Bul.* 148, 1 *Cran.* 94, 3 *Jew.* 257; other words to the same purport, *Grin.* 53, 3 *Jew.* 535; he asserts that Christ is in every place in that he is God, but in heaven in that he is man, 3 *Bec.* 273, 451, 1 *Cran.* 186, 1 *Jew.* 505, 3 *Jew.* 259; says, Christ by his Godhead is ever with us; but, unless he had bodily departed from us, we should always carnally see his body, 1 *Jew.* 505; says, we have Christ always, as regards the presence of his majesty, but not as to that of his flesh, 1 *Brad.* 90 n., 3 *Bul.* 265, 3 *Jew.* 485, *Rid.* 42, 43; asserts that the Son of God as concerning his divinity is incircumscriptible, but as concerning his humanity he is contained in a certain place (pseud. ?) 3 *Bec.* 428, 453; says that until the world be ended Christ is above, yet that his truth is even here, 1 *Jew.* 494, 2 *Jew.* 1118; says that it becomes us to have the glorious body of our Lord in high and worthy estimation, 2 *Cov.* 157; declares that they sin no less who blaspheme Christ reigning in heaven, than they who crucified him walking on the earth, 1 *Bec.* 359, 363; says, the priesthood of Aaron is now found in no temple, but that of Christ continues always in heaven, 2 *Jew.* 736; "where the body is, there shall the eagles be gathered together," this, says he, was spoken of spiritual men, who by imitating his passion and humility are filled as it were with his body, 3 *Jew.* 546; asked by Consentius whether the body of Christ in heaven have blood in it, 1 *Jew.* 206; he says Christ reigns not carnally in heaven, 1 *Cran.* 139; declares that the body of our Lord...hath received an heavenly change; and we ourselves are commanded at the last day to hope for the same, 1 *Jew.* 461; says Christ gave immortality to his body, he did not take away its nature, 2 *Cov.* 160, 1 *Jew.* 461, 502, 505, 3 *Jew.* 252, 254, 259; says, this is my whole hope and all my trust, for in Christ Jesus our Lord is flesh and blood, which is a portion of each of us, therefore where a portion of mine reigns, there I believe I reign too, 3 *Jew.* 592; Augustine (or Honorius of Autun) on Stephen's vision of Christ, 1 *Jew.* 542; says, the Wisdom of God, the Word of God, our Lord Jesus Christ, is everywhere present, &c., 1 *Jew.* 493; asks a persecutor to find, if he can, a place of exile whence he may command Christ to depart, *ib.* 499; says that Christ is present by grace to the godly, *Rid.* 226; you have Christ, says he, at present by faith, at present by the sacrament of baptism, at present by the meat and drink of the altar, (see xv. b. below); shews that Christ's presence is not seen by the eyes, but realized by faith, *Bale* 31; says, our life is Christ, who dwells in our hearts, now by faith, afterwards by sight, 2 *Jew.* 598; often speaks of touching Christ, i.e. believing in him, 1 *Jew.* 500, 506, 3 *Jew.* 548; says, that we touch not Christ with our hands, 1 *Cran.* 153, but may touch him with our faith, 1 *Jew.* 506; in reply to the inquiry, How shall I hold Christ, being absent? he says, send up thy faith, and thou holdest him, 2 *Bec.* 274, 3 *Bec.* 428, 452, 2 *Hoop.* 489, 1 *Jew.* 448, 2 *Jew.* 776, 1121, 3 *Jew.* 469, 547, 548, 549, *Sand.* 88; writes, the absence of our Lord is not absent, have faith, &c., 3 *Jew.* 549; speaks of some who could not lay hold on him, because they had not the hands of faith, 3 *Jew.* 548; says, there are certain spiritual hands in the heart, *ib.*; exhorts to come to Christ, i.e. to believe in him, 2 *Jew.* 764, 3 *Jew.* 548; says, he that believeth in Christ...is united to him and made a member of his body, 1 *Jew.* 476, 3 *Jew.* 495; repeatedly declares that by faith we are incorporated in Christ, 1 *Jew.* 477, 3 *Jew.* 494; declares that we are (not only made Christians) but also made Christ, i.e. his members, 1 *Jew.* 474, 2 *Jew.* 566, 3 *Jew.* 495; exclaims, behold him ascending, believe in him absent, hope in him coming; yet by his secret mercy feel him to be present, 3 *Jew.* 258, 535; exhorts to maintain the Christian profession that he arose from the dead, ascended into heaven, &c., 2 *Bec.* 277, 278, 3 *Bec.* 451, 1 *Cran.* 94 1 *Jew.* 505, 3 *Jew.*

485; maintains that Christ shall so come again as he was seen to go into heaven, i. e. in the same form and substance, 1 *Jew*. 495, 3 *Jew.* 259; and that Christ will come from heaven, and not from any other place, to judge the quick and the dead, 1 *Brad.* 392 n., 3 *Bul.* 264, 265, *Grin.* 52, 3 *Jew.* 485, *Rid.* 177; by the word "nations" (Luke xxi. 25), he understands those who shall be on Christ's left hand, *Sand.* 364; gives reasons why the time of the world's end is hidden from us, *Sand.* 352; on the burning and renewal of the world, 1 *Brad.* 357

He proves the godhead of the Holy Ghost by Peter's words to Ananias, 3 *Jew.* 264; and by words of Paul, *ib.*; says if the Holy Ghost were not God, he would not be placed before the church in the rule of faith (i.e. the creed), *Whita.* 485; proves the procession of the Holy Ghost from the Son, *ib.* 536; his explanation of Gen. i. 2, "the Spirit of God moved," &c., *Hutch.* 65, 196; sin against the Holy Ghost, see below; how the Holy Ghost descended in the form of a dove, and as cloven tongues of fire, 4 *Bul.* 285, 286

iv. *Angels, good and evil:* he says, angel is a name of office, not of nature (dub.), 3 *Bul.* 327; presumes not to say when angels were created, *ib.* 329; supposes "light" and "darkness" in Gen. i. to have reference to good and evil angels, *Whita.* 462; confesses his ignorance of the difference between the orders of the heavenly hierarchy, 3 *Bul.* 336, 337, 3 *Jew.* 278, *Whita.* 577; says, when the angels of God hear, he heareth in them, as in his temple, 3 *Bul.* 345; shews that they are not unchangeable by nature, but by grace, *ib.* 332, 333; maintains that angels, and indeed all creatures, are corporeal, *ib.* 330, 331; on the bodies in which they have appeared, *ib.* 331, 332; against trusting in their intercession, *ib.* 347; he says good angels require sacrifice not to themselves, but to God, *ib.*; and that if angels require sacrifice to be done to them, they are by no means to be obeyed, though they work miracles, *Calf.* 319; and shews that they are not holy angels who accept worship, but malignant spirits, 3 *Bul.* 210; he affirms that if we should build a temple to the most excellent angel, we should be accursed, 3 *Bul.* 348, 4 *Bul.* 501, *Calf.* 129; ascribes the fall of the devil to pride and disobedience, 3 *Bul.* 352; shews that he had no power against Job, but by God's permission, *ib.* 364; in what sense Satan is "the prince of this world," *ib.* 358; how he is "cast out," *ib.* 358, 359; his transformation into an angel of light, 1 *Jew.* 549; he speaks of Origen's error that the devil and his angels after great torments should be delivered and be placed with the holy angels, 3 *Jew.* 560

v. *Scripture, Word of God,* (see ix. below): (*a*) On the canon of Scripture, *Whita.* 51; he says, we should prefer those books which are received by all churches to those which some do not receive, &c., 1 *Ful.* 19, *Whita.* 45, 308; denounces an anathema on all who should receive any scriptures but those which the church had received, *Whita.* 331; he does not however, make the difference between canonical and apocryphal writings dependent on the judgment of the church, *ib.* 309, 315, but teaches that the canonical authority of the Old and New Testament was established in the days of the apostles, *ib.* 310; he uses the word canonical in a large sense, *ib.* 46, 48; on the preservation of the scriptures by Christ's enemies the Jews, 4 *Jew.* 980; they say, we have no law of our own, but only theirs, *ib.* 763; he says, the Jews help us with their books, but they are our enemies in their hearts, *ib.* 763; another passage to the like effect, *ib.*; he held those books to be of less authority which are not in the Jewish canon, *Whita.* 46; says, but few prophets left any writings, *ib.* 302; asserts that Enoch wrote some things before Moses, *ib.* 114, 516; calls Tobit and Judith, &c. canonical, 4 *Bul.* 539, 1 *Ful.* 20; praises the book of Wisdom, *Whita.* 56 n.; once thought it was Solomon's, *ib.* 46; cites it, *ib.* 89; what he says of Ecclesiasticus, *ib.* 93; he once thought this was Solomon's, *ib.* 46; he reckons the books of the Maccabees canonical, admitting, however, that they were not accounted so of old, 4 *Bul.* 539; confesses that they were not esteemed by the Jews as the Law and Prophets, 1 *Ful.* 23, 2 *Ful.* 221, *Whita.* 51; says, the church allows them as canonical on account of the terrible and wonderful passions of certain martyrs, 3 *Jew.* 433, *Whita.* 94; though he calls them canonical, yet he does not allow them to be divine, *Whita.* 93—95; says, although something may be found in the books of the Maccabees worthy to be joined with the number of miracles, yet hereof he will have no care, intending only to speak of the miracles contained in the books of the holy canon, 3 *Jew.* 432; speaks of a reckoning not found in the holy scriptures that are called canonical, but in certain other books, among which are the books of the Maccabees, 3 *Jew.* 432, *Whita.* 94; declares the case of suicide commended in the Maccabees to be an example of folly not to be imitated by Christ's martyrs, *Grin.* 24; on certain writings rejected from the canon, *Whita.* 304; he gives reasons why, although many had written of the deeds of Christ and the apostles, only four Gospels and the Acts are received, *ib.* 315, 532; says, in opposition to the Manichees, that believing the Gospel he must needs believe the Acts, both being alike commended to him by catholic authority, *ib.* 318; says, if you ask us how we know that these are the apostle's writings? we know them by the same means as you know the writings of Manichæus, 3 *Jew.* 441; speaks of the Manichees reading certain books written in the names of the apostles, by some stitchers together of fables, *Whita.* 315; speaks of the contents of some of these books, 1 *Jew.* 113; disallows the Apocalypse of Paul, *Whita.* 315; does not reckon the Decretal Epistles as holy scripture (as falsely stated in Gratian), *ib.* 109; distinguishes between canonical scripture and the writings of the doctors, 2 *Lat.* 248; various arguments, shewing holy scripture to be divine, *Whita.* 319

(*b*) The authority of holy scripture asserted, 2 *Bec.* 261, 1 *Hoop.* 566, 1 *Whitg.* 224 n.; he declares that scripture is placed on an elevated throne, demanding the obedience of every faithful and pious understanding, *Whita.* 353, 663, he calls it a letter from God, 2 *Bec.* 549; another passage, *Pil.* 286; shews that God speaks to us in scripture, which must therefore be reverently received, 2 *Bec.* 549; says that God speaks therein as a familiar friend, without dissimulation, to the heart of learned and unlearned, 2 *Jew.* 671, 4 *Jew.* 897, 1187, *Whita.* 374; says that he who sent the prophets before his incarnation sent the apostles after his ascension, 2 *Cran.* 29; tells us that whatever the apostles wrote, Christ wrote, he being the Head, *Whita.* 527, 528; makes Christ the judge of controversies, *ib.* 461, or his apostles (he speaking in them), *ib.* 461, 462; says, holy scripture hath laid a rule unto our doctrine, that we may not dare to understand more than is meet, 4 *Jew.* 772; expresses his belief in the infallible authority of the writers of the scriptures, and maintains that they were free from error, but that all other writings are to be judged by scripture and reason, 3 *Bec.* 403, *Coop.* 145, 146, 2 *Cran.* 32, *Phil.* 352, 1 *Whitg.* 173; asserts that the evangelists were free from all error, *Whita.* 37, and says that to admit the smallest lie would invalidate the authority of scripture, *ib.*; exhorts to yield and consent to holy scripture, which can neither deceive nor be deceived, 2 *Cov.* 335, 3 *Jew.* 231; he owned scripture as the rule of faith, 2 *Jew.* 1000; what he means by that expression, *Whita.* 486, 487; speaks of scripture as a foundation against insidious errors, *ib.* 697; says, let us not bring deceitful balances...but let us bring the divine balance from the holy scriptures, 2 *Cran.* 30, *Whita.* 28, 659; speaks of some who use not the equal balance of the divine scriptures, but the deceitful balance of their own customs, 1 *Jew.* 260, 3 *Jew.* 480; says, our mind ought not to swerve from the authority of the divine scriptures, *Calf.* 27, 28; affirms that the canonical books may not be doubted, but that the writings of bishops may be reproved by better authority, 3 *Bec.* 403, 404, 2 *Cran.* 31; declares that we hold not the disputations of men, though never so catholic and worthy, as the canonical scriptures, 3 *Bec.* 391, 2 *Cran.* 33, 3 *Jew.* 176, 216, 4 *Jew.* 1173; passages shewing how other writers are to be read, *Calf.* 58, 2 *Cran.* 32, 33, 3 *Jew.* 227, *Rid.* 114, *Whita.* 463; he says, this kind of writings is to be read not with a necessity of believing, but a liberty of judging, 2 *Cran.* 32, 3 *Jew.* 227, 4 *Jew.* 1174; says the words of the creed are scattered through the scriptures, *Whita.* 529, 553; in a disputation on the term homousion, he appeals not to councils, but to scripture, *ib.* 535, (and al. see ix.); against heretics, he cites the scriptures, 2 *Ful.* 230; says, the scribes and Pharisees, sitting in Moses' seat, teach the law of God; but if they teach any thing of their own, they are not to be heard, 2 *Cran.* 30, 54, 3 *Jew.* 323, 4 *Jew.* 710, 775, 1117; says, they spake good things unto the people, &c., 4 *Jew.* 710; speaks of bishops sitting in the chair, i.e. teaching the law of God, 1 *Jew.* 402; says that to follow reason is very dangerous, and that the safer way is to walk by the scriptures, 1 *Jew.* 377, 2 *Jew.* 793; shews that we must not allege natural reason against the authority of the holy scriptures, 1 *Jew.* 378; teaches that if we live after men's reason, we do not live after the will of God, *Rid.* 133; says it is lawful for pure minds to know the eternal law of God, but not to judge it, *Whita.* 353, 354; shews that although a man be spiritual, yet he ought to be a doer, not a judge of the law, &c., 3 *Jew.* 442; says that in any case in which clear and certain instruction is not afforded by the scriptures, human presumption should restrain itself, *Cran.* 17, *Whita.* 695; asks, when the Lord hath been silent, who of us shall say such or such things are? 2 *Cran.* 528, 3 *Jew.* 239, 440; made great difference between the holy scriptures and other writings, 2 *Cran.* 77; said he owed his consent without gainsaying only to the canonical scriptures, 2 *Cran.* 29, 3 *Jew.* 228, 239, *Whita.* 702; affirms that we may lawfully dissent from all doctrines but those of scripture, 2 *Cran.* 30; according to these books, says he, we freely judge of all other writings, whether of the faithful or unfaithful, *Whita.* 659, 660, 3 *Jew.* 238, 1 *Whitg.* 224; says that a doctrine confirmed by the clear authority of canonical scripture should be believed without doubt; not so other witnesses, 2 *Bec.* 261, *Whita.* 702; writes, I seek the voice of the Shepherd: read me this out of a prophet, or the law, or a psalm, &c., 3 *Jew.* 239, *Sand.* 14; says to the Donatists, after the voice of our Shepherd, uttered most plainly by the mouths of the prophets, his own mouth, and the mouths of the evangelists, we cannot admit your voices, 1 *Jew.* 262, 4 *Jew.* 865; says, away with man's writings, let the divine words sound, 3 *Jew.* 223, *Whita.* 697; exclaims, let our writings be taken from among us, let the book of God come among us; hear what Christ says, hear the Truth speaking, 3 *Jew.* 231, 4 *Jew.* 1173, *Whita.* 699; that we should not hear, I say, but, Thus saith the Lord, 2 *Cran.* 31, 1 *Jew.* 79, 2 *Jew.* 1000, 3 *Jew.* 229, 4 *Jew.* 750, *Sand.* 95; he did not account Cyprian's writings as canonical, but weighed them by the scriptures, 2 *Cran.* 33, *Whita.* 601; says, we do no wrong to Cyprian when we distinguish his writings from the canonical authority of the divine scriptures, 3 *Jew.* 233, 4 *Jew.* 1174; says to Jerome, I reckon not, my brother, that thou wouldst have thy books read as those of the apostles and prophets, 3 *Bec.* 403, 2 *Cran.* 32, 3 *Jew.* 176, *Phil.* 353; exhorts him to take unto him Christian severity to correct and amend a book of his, 3 *Jew.* 607; men not to trust to his own writings as if they were canonical scripture, *Calf.* 58, 2 *Cran.* 33, 2 *Ful.* 134, 3 *Tyn.* 136; allows appeal to scripture against himself, 1 *Hoop.* 132; asks, how do they know when they hear me speak of myself, whether I speak the truth? 3 *Jew.* 373; suggests to his opponents the laying aside of all authorities except the divine canonical scriptures, since he would wish the church to be shewn not by the doctrines of men, but by the divine oracles, 3 *Jew.* 230; again, hear this, Thus saith the Lord, not Thus saith Donatus, Rogatus, Vincent, &c., 3 *Jew.* 231, 4 *Jew.* 1173; he asserts that what Faustus says upon the birth of Mary is not to be held binding, because it is not canonical, 2 *Cran.* 30; asks Faustus why he does not submit himself to the authority of the gospel, 4 *Jew.* 865; on the way in which some treated the scriptures, 1 *Jew.* 447; charges heretics with taking away the authority of the scriptures, and leaving every man to his own fancy, 4 *Jew.* 775; speaks against striving for man's fancy, and negligently considering God's word, *ib.* 850; grieves that the holy scriptures are not regarded, and so many presumptions of men are enforced, 3 *Jew.* 569, and so many servile burdens, *ib.* 570, (see xvi. below); his speech to Petilian, who burned the holy gospel (the words are in fact those of Petilian himself), 4 *Jew.* 764, see 1 *Jew.* 463, *Sand.* 16 n.; says, let him be thought to have cast the holy scriptures into the fire, who, when they are read, is proved not to consent to them, 4 *Jew.* 762; intimates that to quarrel with the will of him who made the testament is as bad as to commit the testament to the flames, 4 *Jew.* 765

(c) On the sufficiency of scripture:—references to several passages, 1 *Whitg.* 224; his testimonies to this, 2 *Cran.* 29, *Whita.* 694, &c.; he says that whatsoever things Christ wished us to read, he enjoined the apostles to write, *Whita.* 630, and that amongst the things plainly set down in scripture, are all things which relate to faith and manners, hope and charity, 2 *Cran.* 17, 31, 32, *Whita.* 28, 374, 394, 694, 3 *Whitg.* 55; another passage to the like effect, *Whita.* 695; he declares that what is to be retained and what is to be shunned are to be found in scripture, 2 *Cran.* 29; asserts that the scriptures are plain upon every point that a man could not be ignorant of without danger to his salvation, *ib.* 31; says that not all things which Christ did are written, but certain chosen things sufficient for the salvation of believers, 2 *Cran.* 30, *Phil.* 360, *Whita.* 547, 629, 630; speaking of Paul's anathema against preachers of another Gospel, he pronounces a like anathema against all who teach anything concerning Christ or his church, or whatever pertains to our faith and life, except that which we have received in the legal and evangelical scriptures, 3 *Jew.* 230, 4 *Jew.* 772, 1174, 2 *Lat.* 261, *Rid.* 113, 631, 696, *Whita.* 624; other words on Paul's anathema, 2 *Cran.* 29, *Whita.* 627; on the caution against adding to the Apocalypse, *Whita.* 622; he says that we should seek no farther than is written, 2 *Cran.* 33; on the littleness of all knowledge gathered out of the books of Gentiles, compared to the knowledge of the scriptures, *ib.* 30

(*d*) The original text, and versions thereof:—he commends Hebrew and Greek learning for finding out the meaning of the Latin, 1 *Ful.* 47, 48, *Whita.* 468, 493; on the superior authority of the original Greek and Hebrew, *Whita.* 157; he maintains that Hebrew was the original tongue, *ib.* 113; he asserts the inspiration of the Septuagint, 1 *Ful.* 51, 53; his high opinion of that translation, *Whita.* 119; he affirms the miraculous unanimity of the translators, *ib.* 120; on certain alleged errors of their version, *ib.* 122; he was not entirely addicted to the Latin Bible, 1 *Ful.* 70; says many Latin versions were made from the LXX, *ib.* 73; his opinion of the old Latin versions, *Whita.* 128; he tried to persuade Jerome from translating the scriptures from the Hebrew, 1 *Ful.* 25, 48; his account of Jerome's version, *Whita.* 131; he speaks (in several places) of the scriptures being published in various tongues, 4 *Jew.* 896; does not say that the scripture was read in three languages only, *Whita.* 220; his testimony to the use and value of vernacular versions, *ib.* 245; lays down critical rules respecting MSS. and versions, 4 *Bul.* 542, 543

(*e*) On the study and interpretation of scripture:—he says they require not rash and proud accusers, but diligent and pious readers, 2 *Hoop.* 493; advises to seek the meaning of scripture by reading, meditation, prayer, contemplation, *Whita.* 467; he (or more probably Alcuin) says, continual reading purges all things; whoso will ever be with God, must evermore pray and read, 2 *Jew.* 681; reading without meditation is barren, meditation without reading erroneous, prayer without meditation is cold (pseud.), 3 *Jew.* 435; speaks of some men who, when they hear they should be humble, will learn nothing, 2 *Jew.* 680, 4 *Jew.* 897; rules for interpreting scripture from his four books of Christian Doctrine and other writings, *Whita.* 462, 492—494; on the four senses of scripture, viz. the historical (or literal), the ætiological, the analogical, and the allegorical, *ib.* 403; Augustine (or Alcherus) on the literal sense, 2 *Jew.* 618; he says we should not be content with the letter, *ib.* 595; how he uses the phrase "secundum literam," 1 *Jew.* 504; he shews that the spiritual understanding of Paradise, Hagar and Sarah, &c. is not inconsistent with a literal sense, *Calf.* 101; on the tree of life, and the tree spoken of in the first Psalm, *ib.* 102; (as to figurative speeches see also xiii. and xv. below); cautions against taking a figurative speech according to the letter, *Grin.* 63, 1 *Jew.* 448, 2 *Jew.* 594, 1113; it is to this (he says) Paul refers when he says "the letter killeth," for when the thing that is spoken figuratively is taken as if it were plainly spoken it savours of the flesh, 3 *Jew.* 447; he calls it a wretched bondage of the soul to take words for things, 4 *Bul.* 287, *Whita.* 470, (and see xiii. below); notes a rule to be observed in every allegory, 2 *Jew.* 1112; warns not to think a speech figurative unless it be repugnant to charity, as the command to heap coals of fire on the head of an enemy, 4 *Bul.* 288, 289; gives examples of figurative speeches, 4 *Bul.* 440, 441, *Whita.* 379; observes that our Lord said of John, "He is Elias;" but John himself said, "I am not Elias;" John answering plainly, our Lord speaking figuratively, 3 *Jew.* 500; remarks that all things signifying appear in a certain manner to bear the persons of the things signified; e.g. "The rock was Christ," 3 *Jew.* 545; explains how to distinguish literal from figurative expressions, 2 *Bec.* 290, 291, 3 *Bec.* 431, 1 *Cran.* 115, 137, *Grin.* 63, 1 *Hoop.* 162; distinguishes figurative speaking from lying, 1 *Brad.* 547 n.; says the grace of God lay hidden in the Old Testament, 2 *Jew.* 618, 797, and that the New Testament is hidden in the Old Testament, or in the Law, *ib.* 595, 604, 619, 797; says the Old Testament is unveiled in the New, and the New veiled in the Old, *Whita.* 620, that Christ came, not to add what was wanting, but to accomplish what was written, *ib.*, the times are altered, not the faith, 2 *Cran.* 138, there was a veil placed over the face (of the Jews) that they might not see Christ in the scriptures, 3 *Jew*. 531; he shews that if anything apparently contrary to truth is found in the canonical writings, it is to be attributed to an error in the copy, or to its being misunderstood, 2 *Cran*. 32; on things mentioned in scripture by way of anticipation, *Whita*. 378; he says, it is written in Genesis, " These be the children of Israel, that were born to him in Mesopotamia;" and yet Benjamin was born long afterward, 4 *Jew*. 694; again, we say that Paul the apostle was born at Tarsus in Cilicia, and yet Paul at the time, when he was born, was no apostle, 3 *Jew*. 206, 4 *Jew*. 694; so, when we hear that Christ's disciples were bidden to the marriage at Cana, we must understand that they were not then his disciples, but became so afterwards, 4 *Jew*. 694; remarks that sometimes a thing is told after that was done before, 1 *Cran*. 248; and that the circumstance of the scriptures is wont to open the meaning, 3 *Jew*. 227, *Whita*. 494; says we ought not always to approve whatever we read men that are praised to have done, *Calf*. 281; passages on the plainness of scripture, *Whita*. 393, 394; he says God has made the scriptures stoop to the capacity of babes and sucklings, *ib*. 393; shews that God feeds us with the plain places of scripture, and exercises us with the hidden; and adds that there is scarcely anything in the obscure parts which is not found elsewhere very plainly, 1 *Ful*. 558, *Whita*. 393; passages on the depths of scripture, *ib*. 374, 375, 393; he says things easily investigated are generally held cheap, *ib*. 374; reproves Julian the Pelagian, for exaggerating the difficulties of scripture, 4 *Jew*. 897, 1182, *Whita*. 395; says the scriptures expound themselves, 3 *Tyn*. 249; advises to let scripture be compared with scripture, &c., 3 *Whitg*. 466, 467, see also *Rid*. 113; shews that conference of scriptures will make a perfect preacher, 2 *Ful*. 132; says that one place of scripture ought to be understood by means of many, *Phil*. 138; on the exposition of the obscurer parts of scripture, 4 *Bul*. 292; he repeatedly affirms that dark places in scripture are to be expounded by those that are more plain, *Calf*. 57, 2 *Cran*. 17, 31, 32, 1 *Ful*. 10, *Grin*. 197, 2 *Hoop*. 494, *Phil*. 138; says man's words do not cause the word of God to be understood, 2 *Jew*. 982; in teaching, he disclaims doing more than expounding the words of the great Teacher, *Whita*. 659, 698; acknowledged that there were more things in scripture which he knew not, than that he knew, *ib*. 375; says that he who loves the law of God honours in it even what he understands not, 1 *Jew*. 327; so he read Paul, and Isaiah, *ib*.; he says that he who supposes himself to understand the scriptures, and is without love to God and his neighbour, as yet understands nothing, 1 *Bul*. 77, 4 *Bul*. 55; on the eloquence of the inspired writers, *Whita*. 150; his definition of a testament, *Hutch*. 246 n.; he calls scripture a glass which flatters no man, 1 *Brad*. 55

(*f*) Expositions of some particular passages:—in Gen. iii. 15, he corruptly reads " ipsa conteret," &c., and refers the text to Eve, and to the church, 1 *Ful*. 533, *Whita*. 164; he follows the LXX. in Gen. iv. 7, reading "conversion" for "desire," 1 *Ful*. 390; on the division of languages (Gen. xi.), *Whita*. 112, 378; he says "lex" is sometimes used for morals, 2 *Lat*. 348; sometimes he reckons but three precepts in the first table, sometimes he reckons four, 1 *Bul*. 214, 1 *Hoop*. 349, 350; shews that Gideon's fleece (Jud. vi.) was a type of the Jewish nation, 2 *Bul*. 287; strangely expounds 1 Sam. xxi. 13, being misled by an erroneous translation, *Whita*. 469, (and al. see xv. b. below); calls Isaiah rather an evangelist than a prophet, 1 *Bul*. 51; (Apocrypha; see above); he harmonized the gospels, *Whita*. 377; speaks of "the mountains" of holy scripture (Matt. xxiv. 16), *Whita*. 684, compare *Rid*. 63; refutes an heretical punctuation of John i. 1, by the rule of faith, *Whita*. 487; on John vii. 52, "search and look," &c., 3 *Jew*. 242; on John xx. 30, where it is said that Jesus did many signs which are not written, *Whita*. 547, 629, 630; he says the apostolic epistles were written not only to them who heard them, but to us, 4 *Jew*. 858; places Paul above all doctors and writers, 3 *Jew*. 233; differs from Jerome on Gal. ii. 14, (Paul's contest with Peter), 1 *Ful*. 35; his interpretation of Jacob's staff (Heb. xi.), *ib*. 539, 540, 542; he supposed that John's first epistle was written to the Parthians, *Whita*. 218; origin of the mistake, *ib*. n.; on Gog and Magog (Rev. xx.), *Bale* 571

(*g*) He directed the scriptures to be read to the people, 1 *Jew*. 270; frequently refers to the public reading of scripture, 3 *Whitg*. 47, 48, (and see xvii. below); admonishes the people to read the scriptures at home, 2 *Jew.* 670; exhorts to feed on the hills of scripture, 2 *Cran.* 31; says that by the scriptures that faith is conceived whereby the just liveth, and by which we walk so long as we sojourn absent from the Lord, *Whita.* 664, 696; exhorts to read the holy scriptures, because God willed them to be written that we might be comforted by them, 2 *Jew.* 696; says, if we do not read or hearken to the divine scriptures, our very medicines are turned into wounds, 4 *Jew.* 796; declares that the instruction of scripture is so modified that none shall be unable to draw enough for himself, if he approach with piety and devotion, *Whita.* 394; on God's word as a lamp, *ib.* 384; says the truth, by which holy souls are lightened, is one, &c., 1 *Jew.* 493; says that before our Lord came righteous men believed in him that was to come, as we believe in him that is come; the times are changed, not the faith, 4 *Bul.* 299; says, truth is sweet and bitter, &c., *Pil.* 475; allows some room for diversity of opinion in matters not essential to Christian faith, 2 *Bul.* 400, &c., 4 *Jew.* 1306

vi. *Tradition* (see ix. below): he denies that antiquity and old custom can prevail against the truth, 4 *Jew.* 777; declares we ought to follow the truth rather than the custom, 1 *Bec.* 376, 3 *Bec.* 390, *Calf.* 191; says custom must give place when the truth is once opened, 3 *Bec.* 390, 2 *Cran.* 51, 1 *Jew.* 49; on the authority of traditions, 2 *Cran.* 58, and the ordinances of our elders, *ib.* 59; he says heretics built their falsehoods on that saying of Christ, "I have many things to say unto you, but ye cannot bear them now," 1 *Jew.* 125, 3 *Jew.* 439; thinks that what is universally observed, but not written in the scriptures, nor coming from general councils, is tradition from the apostles, 2 *Cran.* 56 n., 59, and says that what the universal church holds, not being instituted by councils but always retained, is justly ascribed to apostolic authority, 2 *Jew.* 587, 3 *Jew.* 338, *Whita.* 507, 2 *Whitg.* 187; ascribes the great anniversary solemnities and other universal customs to apostolic tradition or to general councils, *Whita.* 605, 606, 1 *Whitg.* 230, 2 *Whitg.* 186; declares that all things neither contained in scripture, nor found in the statutes of councils, nor confirmed by the universal custom of the church...should be cut away, *Calf.* 194; his alleged testimony in favour of tradition considered, *Whita.* 219, 605, &c.

vii. *Sin*: he gives several definitions of sin, 2 *Bul.* 360; distinguishes between "peccatum," "delictum," and "crimen," *ib.* 359; cautions that when we hear that all things are of God, we must not think that sin is of him, *ib.* 383; shews how God is said to do evil (Amos iii.), not sin, but punishment, *ib.* 382, 383, and see 1 *Ful.* 563; why God forbade Adam to eat of the tree of knowledge, 2 *Bul.* 376; he shews that there is no sin without will, *ib.* 388; another passage, 1 *Lat.* 195, and that the beginning of vices is in the will of man, though the hearts of men are moved by various accidental causes, 2 *Bul.* 404; says there are two things which work all sin in man; desire and fear, *ib.*; and three things by which sin is accomplished; suggestion, delectation, consent, *ib.* 405, 406; shews that voluntary sin is hereditary, *ib.* 388; treats largely of original sin, *ib.* 386, 387; Pighius says he had a wrong opinion on the subject, 4 *Jew.* 786, 787; shews that all the old fathers confessed it, 2 *Bul.* 390; calls it "alienum peccatum," yet shews that it is proper to all, *ib.* 397; proves that infants have original sin, 4 *Bul.* 376; quotes Jerome on the universality of sin, even in babes, 2 *Bul.* 391; describes the errors of Cœlestius and Pelagius on original sin, *ib.* 386; shews that sin and death from the first man went through all men, 1 *Bec.* 69, and how men are evil by nature, 2 *Bul.* 362; remarks that it is not said the wrath of God shall *come* upon the sinner, but that it "abideth upon him," and again, "we ourselves were sometime the children of wrath," referring to the corruption of our nature, 2 *Jew.* 1104; his view of Rom. vii. "I am carnal," &c., *Whita.* 455; on concupiscence remaining after baptism, 2 *Bul.* 418; he affirms that in men who are baptized, and justified, there remains a conflict with the world, the flesh, and the devil, 2 *Cov.* 385; teaches that although our sins are forgiven in baptism, concupiscence remains in us as long as we live, 4 *Bul.* 399, and that on account of it we cannot do what we would, 2 *Cov.* 385; observes that the concupiscence of the flesh, against which the good Spirit lusts, is both sin, and the pain of sin, and the cause of sin, 3 *Jew.* 389, 464; says, as long as thou livest there must be sin in thy members, *ib.* 464; reproves the contrary opinion in the Pelagians, &c., 2 *Cov.* 387; shews that sin is left in man in this life for the conflict of faith, 2 *Bul.* 430, 431; says that holy men truly pronounce themselves to be sinners, and shews why, 2 *Cov.* 385, 386; explains how the Christian, though all his sins are put away, yet says, "Forgive us our debts," 3 *Bec.* 419; says, let the apostles of Christ themselves say, O Lord, forgive us our offences, 3 *Jew.* 562; declares that except Christ there was never a man without sin in this life, nor ever will be, *ib.* 581; against weighing sins with deceitful balances, 2 *Bul.* 407; shews that things done amiss through ignorance, are sins, and how, *ib.* 410; on the saying of our Lord about having a "cloak for sin," *ib.* 411; shews that in them who will not understand, ignorance is sin, and in those who cannot understand, the penalty of sin, so that both are justly condemned, 4 *Jew.* 897; argues that the reprobate sense of the heathen is a just punishment, 2 *Bul.* 380; remarks that not to suffer unjustly, but to do unjustly, is sin, 2 *Bul.* 414; other passages to the same effect, *ib.*; speaks of vices nigh to virtues, 2 *Whitg.* 393 n.; against talebearers, 1 *Hoop.* 407; explains the word "mammon," 1 *Tyn.* 68 n.; he condemns usury, 2 *Jew.* 852, 860; on those who seek Jesus that they may gain something by him, 3 *Whitg.* 581, 582; he (or Maximus) says, there is no difference before God, whether a man hold another's goods by open violence, or by guile, 4 *Jew.* 1077, 1078; on sacrilege, 4 *Jew.* 802; on flattery, 3 *Whitg.* 572; he condemns the flatterer's tongue, *Sand.* 132; warns that no man must flatter himself, 1 *Bec.* 83; says a proud man is a son of the devil, 2 *Lat.* 170; tells Julian, the Pelagian, that his pride is fain to cover itself with sorry clouts, 4 *Jew.* 850; says pride itself has a certain desire of unity and omnipotence, 3 *Jew.* 277; and that in the pomp of this world man desires to have many things subject to him, a perverse imitation of almighty God, *ib.* 279; says that he takes the name of God in vain, who for the love of a temporal thing takes God for a witness, 1 *Bec.* 379; praises Regulus for keeping his oath, 1 *Hoop.* 336; commends David for breaking his rash oath, 1 *Bec.* 374, 1 *Bul*, 251; writes terribly of lying, 1 *Lat.* 503; observes that lies have a covert to lurk in, 1 *Jew.* 84; says, when thou speakest untruth under the colour of humility, if thou wert not a sinner before, by lying thou art made a sinner, 4 *Jew.* 847; mentions eight kinds of lies, 2 *Bul.* 114; on the officious lie, 2 *Whitg.* 59 n.; shews that no lie can possibly be righteous, 2 *Bul.* 116; teaches that we should choose death rather than deny the truth, *ib.* 413; against hypocrisy, or the false shew of holiness, 4 *Jew.* 798; on counterfeit innocence, *Wool.* 47 n.; he has many godly sayings of cursing, 2 *Hoop.* 561; censures drunkenness, 2 *Jew.* 1040; condemns necromancy, 1 *Hoop.* 327; tells the servants of God that there is nothing worse than idleness, and that they must work in the name of the Lord, 4 *Jew.* 800; says, he is guilty not of a small price, but of the blood of Christ, who defiles his soul which was made clean by the blood and passion of Christ (pseud.), *ib.* 894; asserts that (the adulterer) is guilty of eternal death, because he despised in himself the blood of the Redeemer (pseud.), *ib.* 895; says, the cry of Sodom and Gomorrha is multiplied, *ib.* 634; disallows self-murder in order to escape sin, 2 *Bul.* 415, 416; says we do not find in the canonical scriptures any permission to take away our own lives, *Whita.* 95; states various opinions on the sin against the Holy Ghost, 1 *Lat.* 463 n.; cited by Gratian as saying that the sin against the Holy Ghost is final impenitence (pseud.), 2 *Bul.* 425; on the punishment of the wicked, *Bale* 576 (see also xxv. below); says he is an enemy of righteousness who sins not, only for fear of punishment, 1 *Bec.* 93; writes that there is as great a diversity of punishments as of sins, 2 *Bul.* 427; declares that no sinner is to be loved as such, 1 *Bul.* 185; says it is in the power of the wicked to sin, but to produce this or that effect by sinning is not in their power, but in God's, who ordains even darkness, 3 *Zur.* 326, 327

viii. *Grace, Justification, Works,* &c.: he says grace is so called because given gratis, *Sand.* 297, and affirms that that cannot be grace, which is not every way free, *ib.* 11; declares that the faithful Jews before Christ were under grace, *Hutch.* 326; refutes the errors of Pelagius on grace, 3 *Bul.* 11 (and see xxvii. below); asks what is meant by the words "For nothing thou shalt save them"? and replies, thou findest nothing in them why thou shouldest save them, and yet thou dost save them, &c., 3 *Jew.* 588; shews that salvation is the free gift of God, 3 *Bec.* 170; recommends thanks to be given to God for free redemption, 1 *Bec.* 75; shews that God gives not the pain that is due, but the grace which is not due, *ib.* 73; declares that deserved punishment would throw all men into death unless the undeserved grace of God delivered them, 3 *Jew.* 588; denies that our merits have caused salvation to be sent to us, and says that if our merits did anything, it should come to our damnation, 2 *Ful.* 92; says, let no man say that the grace of God is given to him for the merits of his works, or the merits of his prayers, or the merits of his faith, &c., *Wool.* 79; writes, let us be glad to be healed...let us not boast of health, 2 *Cov.* 390; observes that he has profited much in this life, who by his profiting has learned how far he is from the perfection of righteousness, 3 *Jew.* 581; says, we may receive the gift according to our portion, but cannot pour it out upon others; yet on their behalf we call upon God, 4 *Jew.* 829; teaches that all who receive eternal life receive it only by Christ, 1 *Bec.* 75; says, all my hope is in the death of my Lord; his [death is my merit, my refuge, health, life, and resurrection (pseud.), 2 *Cov.* 404; exclaims, let only the price of the blood of my Lord avail me to the perfection of my deliverance, 3 *Jew.* 566; "They washed their robes in the blood of the Lamb,"—that is (says he), in the grace of God through Christ, *ib.* 487; remarks that God's mercy is greater than our iniquity, 1 *Lat.* 267; expounding Rom. v. 18, says that the grace of Christ hath loosened not only the faults of infants, but many afterwards added, 1 *Bec.* 337, 3 *Bec.* 418, 419; asserts that in Christ we receive the remission of all sins, 3 *Bec.* 418; let none be doubtful (says he) lest anything be not forgiven, 3 *Jew.* 566; declares salvation to be both by grace, and by justice, 1 *Ful.* 339; affirms that Christ shall not, because of the wicked, remain without his inheritance; "The Lord knoweth them that are his," 4 *Jew.* 724, 725; says, the number of the predestinate is certain, and can neither be increased nor diminished, 3 *Whitg.* 612; writes that the gospel is preached to some unto reward, to some unto judgment, 3 *Jew.* 362; shews how some hear the gospel inwardly, some outwardly, and that to the former it is given to believe, but not to the latter, 2 *Jew.* 822; says that according to God's secret predestination, there are many sheep without the church, and many wolves within the church, 4 *Jew.* 667, 890; declares that the reprobate, though called, justified, and renewed by the laver of regeneration, perish because not called according to God's purpose, *Whitg.* 613; refutes the notion of destiny, 2 *Bul.* 864; refuses not to employ the word (prædestinatio?), *Phil.* 403; affirms that as we do not by memory compel things past, so God does not by his foreknowledge compel things future, 2 *Bul.* 378; says we may not ask why (true religion came) so late, for the counsel of him who sent it is impenetrable, 4 *Jew.* 777; declares that, as the nature of man could not keep the health it had, it certainly cannot get again that which it lost, 1 *Bec.* 70; expounding Rom. iii. 23, says, no man of himself is able to recover the life lost, *ib.* 315, 316; his memorable saying, give what thou commandest, and command what thou wilt, 1 *Lat.* 387, 433, *Pil.* 208, *Sand.* 133; he maintains, against the Pelagians, that God commands what we cannot do, 2 *Cov.* 388; shews that although we are commanded to depart from evil and do good, we can of ourselves do neither, *ib.* 389; why God commands this, viz. that we may know what we ought to ask him, *ib.*; he declares that free-will avails to evil, but not without God's help to good, 1 *Bec.* 70, *Sand.* 133; shews that there is free-will both to evil and to good, but that none can have the latter unless the Son make him free, 3 *Bul.* 103; exclaims, O evil free-will without God! 3 *Jew.* 168, and says that man misusing his free-will lost both himself and his will, *ib.*, that the possibility of nature (i. e. free-will), is wounded, mangled, lost, *ib.*, that free-will being enslaved avails only to sin, *ib.*, that what we do well, or understand aright, we owe to God; we have nothing of our own but sin, *ib.*; he remarks that we will, but it is God that worketh in us to will; we do, but it is God that worketh in us to do, &c., that our confession may be humble and lowly, and that the whole may be ascribed to God, &c., *ib.*; on the office of man's will in justification— the passage in which occurs the question, he that made thee without thee, shall he not justify thee without thee? 1 *Brad.* 217, 1 *Ful.* 386; this passage perverted by Romanists, 1 *Brad.* 217 n., 1 *Ful.* 386, &c.; he says that faith (as to which see also iii. above,) is the beginning of man's salvation, 1 *Bec.* 207, 3 *Bec.* 165; affirms that it is the foundation of repentance, 2 *Cov.* 343; maintains that it is the gift of God, *Wool.* 37 n.; ascribes it not to man's will, nor to any merits going before, but confesses it to be God's free gift, 2 *Ful.* 43; acknowledges that he once erroneously supposed that faith was not the gift of God, but of ourselves, 1 *Bul.* 100; says of some that they have their hearts shut because they have not the key of faith, 3 *Jew.* 358; declares that that ought to be called the key whereby the hardness of hearts is opened unto faith, *ib.* 364, 373; says that God speaks to the heart of every one of us, *Whita.* 290; writes that when we become strong in faith, we believe by God himself internally confirming and illuminating our minds, *ib.* 321; on the inward assurance of faith—I would hear and understand how thou madest heaven and earth, &c., *ib.* 356; he shews that in order to obtain an understanding of what we believe, it is requisite that our minds should be inwardly confirmed and illuminated by God himself, *ib.* 357; on the "unction from the Holy One," *ib.* 452, and the necessity of the inward teaching of the Holy Ghost, *ib.* 453; he speaks of Christ as an inward Teacher, *ib.*; on being "taught of God," 4 *Bul.* 99; another passage, *Whita.* 454 (see also x. below); he says the word of God works in our hearts, not because it is spoken, but because it is believed, 1 *Jew.* 328; remarks that faith hath eyes of her own, 1 *Jew.* 451, 3 *Jew.* 531; on reason and faith (pseud.), 1 *Jew.* 504; he says the multitude is saved, not by quickness of understanding, but by simplicity of believing, 1 *Jew.* 323, *Whita.* 240; another passage to the same effect, *Whita.* 241; writes that if Christ died only for those who have sure intelligence, our labour is almost in vain, 1 *Jew.* 323; speaks of the unlearned as rising up, and catching heaven away from us, 2 *Jew.* 693; distinction between believing "illi," "illum," and "in illum" (pseud.), *Calf.* 86 n.; he says we believe Paul, we do not believe in Paul; we believe Peter, &c., 3 *Jew.* 256; remarks, he that hath faith without hope and charity believes that there is Christ, but he believes not in Christ, *ib.* 584; in reply to the inquiry what it is to believe in God, he says, by believing to love, by believing to go into him, and to be incorporated with his members, *ib.* 253; declares that when we believe in Christ, of the very remnants of our thought, Christ is sacrificed unto us every day, 2 *Jew.* 724; says, have faith, and he whom thou seest not is present with thee, *ib.* 741; exhorts to approach Jesus, not in the flesh, but with the heart, not with presence of body, but with power of faith, *ib.* 740; asks, what is it to approach unto him, unless to believe in him? 3 *Jew.* 548; says, let us now shew the Jews where Christ is, would God they would hear and lay hold on him, *ib.* 547; addresses one, thou wilt say, How shall I hold Christ being absent? how shall I reach my hand unto heaven, that I may hold him sitting there? Send up thy faith and thou holdest him; thy fathers held him in the flesh, hold thou him in thy heart, *ib.* 469, 548, (and see p. 51, col. 2, above); on Christ's dwelling in our hearts by faith, 1 *Jew.* 476; he tells the widow Italica not to think herself desolate while Christ dwells in her heart by faith, *ib.* 499; says the faith of absent things is present, and the faith of things that are without is within, 2 *Jew.* 740, 3 *Jew.* 469; writes, the things that we understand are more certain than the things that we see, 3 *Jew.* 470; shews that things to come were foreseen by the prophets with the same spirit of faith as that by which we believe those things now they are come, 2 *Bul.* 287; says, it is possible that a man may hold all the words of the creed, and yet not believe rightly, 3 *Jew.* 255; on the faith of devils, spoken of by James, 3 *Tyn.* 201 n.; he says a foolish faith not only doeth no good, but hurteth, 2 *Jew.* 926, 3 *Jew.* 122, 553, 4 *Jew.* 845; explains what repentance is, 1 *Bec.* 92; declares that God wills not the sacrifice of a slain beast, but of a slain heart, *ib.* 97; says that penitence ought to be desired which is evidently grounded on faith, *ib.* 98; observes that the dead man cannot be raised unless the Lord cry within him, 3 *Jew.* 358; said to compare fear to the bristle on the shoe-maker's thread, *Pil.* 104, 3 *Jew.* 199; mentions the signs of true repentance, 1 *Bec.* 77, 78, 92; justification by faith defended by him in many places, 2 *Cov.* 340; references to several passages, *ib.*; sentences on justification collected from his works, 2 *Cran.* 203—208, 210 *bis*, 211 *bis*, his third treatise on St John's epistles referred to on the subject, 2 *Lat.* 313; he uses the vulgar term "satisfaction," but plainly rejects the false doctrine, *Calf.* 75; speaks of faith alone justifying, 2 *Bec.* 639; calls justification and glorification the gift of God, not of merits, 1 *Bec.* 72, 73; says that the medicine of the soul's wounds is to believe in Christ, *ib.* 79; tells that all who are justified by Christ are righteous not in themselves but in him, 2 *Bec.* 638; says all the commandments are accounted to be done when the thing

AUGUSTINE

that is not done is forgiven, 3 *Jew*. 581; writes, " if righteousness be by the law, then is Christ dead in vain," but if Christ died not in vain, the ungodly is justified by him alone, *Wool*. 35; shews that Paul by "the deeds of the law" meant not only ceremonies but morals, 2 *Bul*. 248; alleged to say that of all that Paul taught nothing is more difficult than what he wrote concerning the righteousness of faith, *Whita*. 360; shews that the teaching of James is not opposed to that of Paul, 3 *Jew*. 244, *Wool*. 30; says the objection of difference between Paul and James is made by those who understand neither, 4 *Jew*. 765; on the prayer, "Enter not into judgment with thy servant, O Lord," 3 *Jew*. 586, 587; he commends not the works of his hands, *ib*. 587; he (or rather Ambrose) says, presume not of thy working, but of the grace of Christ,...this is not arrogance, but faith; to declare that thou hast received, is not pride but devotion, 3 *Jew*. 246; warns those who will be partakers of the grace of God not to boast their merits, 2 *Bec*. 637, *Wool*. 78; asks, what are the merits of men? 3 *Jew*. 587; alleged to speak of the reward of merits, but the passage is spurious, 1 *Ful*. 353; remarks that merits are of God, not of man, 1 *Ful*. 353; says, let men's merits be still, and let the grace of God reign, 3 *Bec*. 170, 2 *Cov*. 432; writes, when a man sees that whatever good he has is not of himself but of his God, he sees that all that is praised in him is of the mercy of God, not of his own merits, *Wool*. 78; says if God were to deal with us after our merits, he would find nothing but that he might condemn, 3 *Jew*. 587; confesses that his merit is the mercy of the Lord, 1 *Bec*. 54, 75, 3 *Bec*. 171; shews that the Lord at the judgment will crown the righteous with favour and mercy, 3 *Jew*. 587, 588; shews (at length) that God crowns not our merits, but his own gifts, 2 *Bul*. 347—350; expresses the same sentiment in other places, *Bale* 590, 631, 2 *Cov*. 432, 1 *Ful*. 340, 353; shews that although life eternal will be rendered to good works, those works must be referred to the grace and gift of God, 2 *Bul*. 328; says, if God has covered sins, he has determined not to observe... to consider, or to punish, 2 *Lat*. 246; asks, what shall I render to the Lord, for that I call my sins to remembrance, and yet my soul is not afraid thereof? 3 *Jew*. 246; says, it is not of my presumption, but of his promise, that I shall not come into judgment, *ib*.; shews that self-righteousness is the cause of heresies and schisms, 4 *Jew*. 852; teaches that good works are inseparable from true faith, 2 *Cran*. 137, but that we must set no good works before faith, *ib*. 141, and that there is no light in works done without a godly intent and true faith, *ib*. 142; says there is no good without the chief good, *Wool*. 51, 52; he (?) says that a good work maketh not a good man, but a good man maketh a good work (cited by W. Tracy), 3 *Tyn*. 273; declares that good works follow, and shew a justified man, 2 *Ful*. 386; and that they spring from charity, *Pra. Eliz*. 568; he says, when grace is given, then our works (merita) begin to be good, and that through grace, 2 *Bul*. 325; teaches that every work which comes not of faith is sin, 2 *Cran*. 142, that all the life of them that believe not is sin, *ib*., that pagans and heretics cannot do good works, *ib*., and that the virtues of unbelievers deserve punishment, *Wool*. 49; he says that good things (in themselves) may be done, and yet not be done well by those who do them, 2 *Bec*. 541, and that there is no virtue but obedience, *Sand*. 145; but he asserts that there is one work in which are all good works, viz., faith which worketh by love, 2 *Cran*. 142, and that good life can never be divided from such faith, 3 *Jew*. 584; he says, if we are the children of God we are led by God's Spirit to do good, 2 *Cov*. 389; declares that he takes upon him the name of a Christian man in vain, that follows not Christ (pseud.), 1 *Bec*. 387, *Wool*. 9; shews in what sense the virtue which is now in a just man is called perfect, 3 *Jew*. 581; tells that the just are so called, not because they are void of all sin, but because they are furnished with the greater part of virtues, *ib*.; says our very righteousness itself is such in this life, that it stands rather in forgiveness of our sins, than in perfection of virtues, *ib*. 582; declares that the true sacrifice is every good work, *Coop*. 91; on brotherly love as an evidence of the love of God, *Sand*. 286; he shews that we should, from the consideration of our own failings, ever be ready to excuse our brethren, *ib*. 106; says we must verily take heed, lest in the storm of contention the fairness of charity be not obscured, 1 *Whitg*. 230; calls alms-deeds works of justice, 1 *Ful*. 446; on the sin of giving stolen things as alms, *Wool*. 138; passages on the necessity of restitution, 2 *Bul*. 50, 1 *Hoop*. 404, 1 *Lat*.

11, 405, 2 *Lat.* 211, 427, *Pil.* 471; amongst alms-deeds he reckons the forgiveness of injuries, *Wool.* 137; praises humility, 1 *Bec.* 201

ix. *The Church* (see v. and viii. above): he says, we believe (not we believe in) the holy church, and explains the difference, 1 *Bul.* 159, 3 *Jew.* 434; affirms that Cain and Abel represent the false church and the true, *Phil.* 106; writes, sometime the church was only in Abel, and sometime only in Enoch, 4 *Jew.* 724; says the synagogue was a congregation, the church a convocation, yet calls the former "ecclesia," 1 *Ful.* 227; affirms that the Israelites were Christians, and that Christians are Israelites, 2 *Jew.* 614; says the Lord has set the church (his tabernacle) in manifestation (Ps. xix.), 2 *Ful.* 54; 'on the apparel of "the queen," in Ps. xlv., 4 *Jew.* 814; on the two cities, Babylon, which is confusion, and Jerusalem, the vision of peace, and their respective citizens, 1 *Cov.* 199; he says we are all citizens of one or the other, *Bale* 253; on the stones of New Jerusalem, *ib.* 609; he says all that belong to the body of Christ, the chief and true Prince of priests, are consecrated with the royal priesthood, 4 *Jew.* 984; and again, all are priests, because they are members of the one Priest, 1 *Ful.* 242 n., 4 *Jew.* 984; says the church is often compared to the moon, 4 *Jew.* 724; writes, until the end of this world, the church goes forward as a pilgrim, between the persecutions of the world and the comforts of God, 3 *Jew.* 160; and again, the whole city of God is a pilgrim in the earth, *ib.*; he speaks of persecution increasing the church, *Rid.* 100 (and see xxiii. below); observes that the church has learned of her Redeemer to put no trust in man, 4 *Jew.* 1057; says the church is called catholic because she is universally perfect, and halteth in nothing, and is spread throughout the world, 2 *Ful.* 36, 3 *Jew.* 268, *Phil.* 136; his definition of the catholic faith, *ib.* 38; speaks of asking the way to the catholic church in a city, 1 *Ful.* 222; confesses that the name of catholic (amongst other things) stayed him in the right faith, 2 *Ful.* 241; on the unity of the church, 3 *Whitg.* 595; he speaks of the sacramental bread as a figure thereof, 2 *Hoop.* 426; says the unity of the church stands by the power which Christ hath reserved to himself only, of which (unity) it is said, "My dove is one," 4 *Jew.* 751; on union with the church, 1 *Whitg.* 95; he says, let no man think he knows Christ unless he be a partaker of his body, i. e. of the church, 1 *Jew.* 234; affirms that there can be no good men separate from the church, *Pil.* 617 n.; states that whoever is separate from the church, however well he may live, shall not have (eternal) life, *Rid.* 122; says he shall not have God for his Father, who will not have the church for his mother, *ib.*; cautions against seeking the conventicles of the just separated from the unity of all the world, which, he says, can never be found, 2 *Ful.* 62; reprehends the setting up altar against altar, 1 *Jew.* 90 (and see corrig.); shews whence schisms come, 4 *Jew.* 852, (see xxvii. below); says there is no security of unity except the church be declared out of the promises of God, &c., 2 *Ful.* 62; writes that when heresy has prevailed there is no other proof of true Christianity but the scriptures, and that the true church can be known by them only, *Whita.* 684 (comp. the Opus Imperfectum, cited *Coop.* 187); advises him who fears he may be deceived, to consult that church which the scripture points out, *Rid.* 127, *Whita.* 442; having alleged succession of bishops, &c. as marks of the church, he says, we do not so much presume of those documents as of the holy scriptures, 2 *Ful.* 242, 351; says the church must not be sought in our own righteousness, but in the scripture, 2 *Cran.* 29; and that the true church is shewn not by signs and wonders, miracles and visions, not by catholic consent even, but by the scriptures and the voice of the Shepherd, *ib.* 47, 48; desires the holy church to be pointed out, not by human documents, but by the divine oracles, 3 *Jew.* 153, 4 *Jew.* 750, 864; in the holy scriptures (says he) the church is manifestly known, 4 *Jew.* 864; we must know the church as we know the Head, in the holy canonical scriptures, *ib.*; holy scripture points out the church without any doubtfulness, 3 *Jew.* 326, 4 *Jew.* 750, 864; the church is best sought in the words of him who is the Truth, and who best knows his own body, *Coop.* 186, 187, 4 *Jew.* 750, 864; by the mouth of Truth (says he) I know the church that is partaker of the truth, 4 *Jew.* 864; says to the Donatists, let the Head, on whom we agree, shew unto us his body, on which we disagree, *ib.* 749; and again, in the scriptures we learn Christ, in the scriptures we learn the church; these scriptures we have indifferently between us; why do we not after one sort hold Christ and the church by them? 2 *Jew.* 1000; again, let Christ be asked that he may shew his own church, 3 *Jew.* 223; whether they (the Donatists) have the church or not, let them shew by the scriptures, *Coop.* 188, 4 *Jew.* 749, 2 *Ful.* 54; and again, let them, if they can, shew us their church, not in the speeches and rumours of the Africans, nor in councils of their bishops... but in the injunction of the Law, &c., *Whita.* 51; there are (says he) certain books of the Lord, to the authority of which both parties agree; let us there seek the church, 3 *Jew.* 153, 4 *Jew.* 748; his declaration that he had not believed the gospel unless the authority of the catholic church had moved him, 4 *Bul.* 67, 2 *Cov.* 419—421, 2 *Cran.* 59, 4 *Jew.* 864, 865, *Phil.* 135, 347, &c., *Rid.* 125, 3 *Tyn.* 49, 50, *Whita.* 319, &c.; the context of this passage, 2 *Cov*, 421, *Phil.* 348; the saying well-explained by Melancthon, *Rid.* 128; Driedo and Bellarmine thereon, *Whita.* 322; his reasons for adherence to the church, viz. consent of nations, succession from Peter, the name of catholic, &c., 1 *Brad.* 526, 2 *Ful.* 350, *Phil.* 137, 141, 142, *Pil.* 617 n.; he states these reasons in opposition to the Manichees, *Phil.* 141, and urges the same points against the Donatists, *ib.* 144; says the church ought not to set herself above Christ, 2 *Jew.* 638; ascribes more to truth of doctrine than to the authority of the church, *Whita.* 321; says that ecclesiastical judges, being men, are oftentimes deceived, 1 *Jew.* 228, 3 *Jew.* 176, 4 *Jew.* 1174; observes that the earthly seat is one thing, the judgment seat of heaven another, 3 *Jew.* 180; declares the authority of general councils to be most healthful, 3 *Jew.* 223, but does not own them as the rule of faith, 2 *Jew.* 996 (see 1 *Zur.* 162); will not have the council of Nice or Ariminum urged, but rather the authority of scripture, *Calf.* 10, 2 *Cran.* 36, 2 *Ful.* 130, 2 *Jew.* 638, 996, 3 *Jew.* 217, 228, *Rog.* 210, *Whita.* 535, 563, 698; says the general councils themselves are often corrected by later ones, 2 *Cran.* 36, 3 *Jew.* 176, 177, *Rid.* 134; speaks of certain synods as councils of quarrelling bishops, &c., 4 *Jew.* 1052; considers that customs universally observed, as the great yearly festivals, were either delivered by the apostles, or decreed by general councils, *Whita.* 605, 606, 1 *Whitg.* 230, 2 *Whitg.* 186; says that what the whole church holds, not being appointed by councils, must be believed to be of apostolic authority, 2 *Jew.* 587, 3 *Jew.* 338, *Whita.* 507, 2 *Whitg.* 187; teaches that in things not determined by scripture the custom of the people of God is to be taken for a law, 1 *Whitg.* 222, &c.; exhorts Christians to keep the customs of the church of the place where they live, *ib.*; another passage, *ib.* 286; calls it madness not to observe anything observed by the whole church, *Whita.* 506, 1 *Whitg.* 202; maintains that changes disturb through novelty, *ib.* 227; on order, 2 *Whitg.* 311, 334; he speaks of the mingled church, *Rid.* 126; shews that not all who are in the visible church are in the body of Christ, 4 *Bul.* 341; says there are many sheep without, many wolves within, 4 *Jew.* 667, 890; distinguishes true Christians from mere professors, 2 *Lat.* 346; calls false Christians antichrists, *ib.* 316, 345; declares that neither heretics, nor hypocritical professors have either a true faith, or are to be counted among the members of Christ, 1 *Cran.* 211, (81); counsels to tolerate evil men for the good's sake, *Rid.* 136, 137; says, oftentimes God's word rebukes the wicked sort of the church as though all were such, and none at all remained good, 4 *Jew.* 722; advises men quietly to correct what they may, and what they cannot to suffer till God amend it, 4 *Bul.* 61; divides the church into penitents, reformers, and the perfect, 1 *Cov.* 202, 203; supposes the judgment spoken of in Rev. xx. to denote the government of the church at present, 3 *Jew.* 367; says the church, after a certain manner, eateth those whom she hath gotten, 1 *Jew.* 503; he replies to the vaunt of the heathens that Christianity should perish, 3 *Jew.* 180

x. *Bishops and other Ministers, Ministry, Monks, &c.*: he says bishops were made instead of apostles, 2 *Ful.* 309; speaks of the apostles as fathers, and of bishops as their children, *Rog.* 329 n.; claims for the governors of the church the power given to the apostles, 1 *Jew.* 385; his use of the word pope, 2 *Hoop.* 236; declares the name bishop to be the same as superintendent, 4 *Jew.* 906; inquires what a bishop is, but the first presbyter, i.e. the highest priest, 3 *Jew.* 315, 439, 4 *Jew.* 823, 2 *Whitg.* 432; exhorts one to follow his bishop, 1 *Whitg.* 226; says, a bishop's office is a name of labour, not a name of honour, that he who wishes to be foremost, not to do good, may know he is not a bishop, 2 *Jew.* 1020, 3 *Jew.* 308,

4 *Jew.* 972, 1103; on the election of bishops in his time, 2 *Zur.* 229; he writes that our heavenly Master forewarned the people of evil rulers, lest on their account the seat of wholesome doctrine should be forsaken, &c., 1 *Jew.* 398; says he that neither rules himself, nor has washed off his sins, nor corrected his children, may rather be called a filthy dog than a bishop, 1 *Jew.* 399, 3 *Jew.* 309, 4 *Jew.* 972; affirms that the character (of a bishop) many wolves give to wolves, 3 *Jew.* 281, 349, 4 *Jew.* 972; warns that we may not consent even to catholic bishops if they be deceived, and determine contrary to the canonical scriptures, 3 *Jew.* 227, 285, 4 *Jew.* 875; remarks that bishops' letters, if they swerve from the truth, may be reprehended by the discretion of any one more skilful, *ib.* 1054; acknowledges himself, though a bishop, to be inferior in many respects to Jerome, a presbyter, 1 *Ful.* 264; says the bishop's office is higher than the presbyter's after the names of honour which the use of the church has obtained, 3 *Jew.* 294; mentions that Aerius denied any difference between a bishop and a presbyter, *Rog.* 330 n., 2 *Whitg.* 292; says every man should be a bishop in his own house, 1 *Lat.* 14; (as to the priesthood of all Christians, see ix. above); on evangelists, 2 *Whitg.* 302; on Philip the deacon, 3 *Whitg.* 60; he intimates that the deacons of Rome advanced themselves above their estate, 1 *Jew.* 355; mentions one Falcidius, who foolishly sought to make deacons equal to priests, 3 *Jew.* 293; says evil men resist Christ, when they blaspheme his ministers who blame them, 2 *Lat.* 347; cautions against spiritual pride, and the despising of human ministry, 1 *Bul.* 86; says, let us hear the gospel as if the Lord were present, 4 *Bul.* 103; asserts that preachers deliver Christ unto their learners, 3 *Jew.* 545; says that to minister the word and sacraments the minister is somewhat, but to make clean and justify he is nothing, 2 *Bec.* 227, 3 *Bec.* 469; shews that conversion is not the work of the minister but of God, 4 *Bul.* 98, 99; address the people, saying, we speak in your ears, but how do we know what may be wrought in your hearts? whatsoever is wrought within you is wrought not by us but by him, 3 *Jew.* 373; tells the people that so far from seeing the thoughts of their hearts, he cannot see what they do in their houses, 4 *Jew.* 976; shews how men preach outwardly, and how God reveals inwardly, 1 *Bul.* 86; says that God who by his ministers warns us outwardly with the signs of things, by himself teaches us inwardly with the very things themselves, *ib.*; shews that outward teaching is nothing without the inward teaching of the Spirit, 4 *Bul.* 99; paraphrases the charge " Feed my sheep "— think not to feed thyself, but my sheep, feed them as mine, not as thine; seek my glory in them, not thine, &c., 3 *Jew.* 281; remarks that Christ said not unto Peter, Feed thy sheep, but, Feed mine, 4 *Jew.* 918; says, whosoever they be that feed the sheep to make them theirs, not Christ's, they love themselves and not Christ, 3 *Jew.* 175, 4 *Jew.* 919; declares that pastors must recall wandering sheep, even with stripes, (the passage not found,) *Sand.* 72; on the pastoral watch-tower, 1 *Jew.* 370—372; on compelling men to come in, *Sand.* 46; he warns the people not to ridicule their pastors if they should express themselves ungrammatically in their prayers and sermons, 1 *Jew.* 295, *Whita.* 224; wills the priests to correct their Latin speech, that the people may understand, and say, Amen, 1 *Jew.* 268, 295; on a priest learning from a layman, *Bale* 118; he speaks of the continency of clerks, as an example to others, 2 *Ful.* 94, 95; mentions Paul's anathema against false teachers, (see v. *c.* above); describes the miserable state before God of unfaithful ministers, 1 *Hoop.* 551; says that he who for fear of any power hides the truth, provokes the wrath of God, 2 *Lat.* 298; declares that the hearers despise the words of doctrine when they see the works of the preacher differ from the words of his preaching, 1 *Bec.* 16; if (pastors) will teach their own things, be cautious not to hear or do them, 3 *Jew.* 202; on the sin of negligent pastors, 2 *Whitg.* 459; on priests who sell their prayers, and receive the gifts of widows (pseud.), 2 *Jew.* 628; he says there is no reason why the sheep should hate their clothing, because they sometimes see wolves disguised in it, 3 *Jew.* 152; speaks of deans (decani), 2 *Whitg.* 178 —180; referred to respecting abbots and monks, 4 *Jew.* 909; as to the latter, 4 *Bul.* 515; he says, let no brother placed in a monastery say, I will depart out of the monastery, 2 *Ful.* 102; remarks that the devil has scattered abroad a multitude of hypocrites under the habit of monks, 4 *Jew.* 800; speaks of monks who desire idle

hands and full altars, *ib.*; complains of their hypocrisy, idleness, and wickedness, *Hutch.* 203; several passages against the idleness and hypocrisy of monks, 4 *Jew.* 797, 798, 799; he did not institute an order of friars, 2 *Ful.* 102, 103; his advice to certain virgins or nuns, respecting their apparel, discipline, prayers, &c., 2 *Ful.* 100

xi. *Peter, Rome:* he allows Peter's primacy, and considers that he was a figure of unity or of the whole church, 2 *Ful.* 294, 295, 317; but he also speaks of Esau's primacy, 1 *Jew.* 366; he calls Peter the first of the apostles, *ib.* 428, and prince of the apostles, *ib.* 430, and (as Harding says) head of the church, *ib.* 436; he says, Peter was an eye in the head, *ib.* 370; asks, who is honoured in Peter, but he that died for us? for we are Christians, not Petrians, *ib.* 369; remarks that the devil confessing Christ was bidden to hold his peace, but that Peter's confession was allowed, *Rog.* 272 n.; asserts that Peter takes his name from the rock, not the rock from Peter, 4 *Jew.* 1119, 1 *Tyn.* 217 n.; he declares that Christ was the rock, upon which foundation Peter himself was also built, 2 *Ful.* 298, 1 *Jew.* 340; imagines our Lord as saying, "I will build thee upon me," 2 *Ful.* 298, 1 *Jew.* 340, 2 *Jew.* 895, 1000, 4 *Jew.* 1119; "upon this rock," i.e. (says he) upon the rock which thou hast confessed, 2 *Jew.* 895, 1 *Tyn.* 217 n.; or (as he writes in his Retractations) upon him whom Peter confessed,...the rock was Christ, 1 *Ful.* 226, 4 *Jew.* 1118; in the work last mentioned he leaves it to the reader to choose between two interpretations, viz. that the rock is Peter as a figure of the church, or Christ whom Peter confessed, 2 *Ful.* 287; see further, *ib.* 273, 294; he says, when Christ said unto Peter, "unto thee will I give the keys of the kingdom of heaven," he signified the whole church, 3 *Jew.* 356; other passages to the same effect, 3 *Jew.* 384, *Phil.* 44, 75, 1 *Tyn.* 218 n.; he writes that wretched men, while in Peter they understand not the rock, and are unwilling to believe that the keys of the kingdom of heaven are given unto the church, have lost them out of their hands, 3 *Jew.* 385; says Peter spake for all, and received with all, 1 *Jew.* 368; he says Peter paid tribute as the head of them (the apostles), 1 *Jew.* 436, 437; shews that Christ prayed not for Peter only, 4 *Jew.* 711, 717, 929; asks whether he did not also pray for John and James, 3 *Jew.* 219, 4 *Jew.* 710, 717, 917;

quoting Ambrose, he explains how Christ looked on Peter after his denial of him, 1 *Bec.* 93, 94; affirms that when he said unto Peter, "Lovest thou me? Feed my sheep," he said it to all, 2 *Ful.* 295, 3 *Jew.* 385; his exposition of the threefold precept, *Hutch.* 102, 1 *Tyn.* 218 n.; another exposition, 2 *Ful.* 291; he says Peter and his fellow-disciples lived together in concord, 3 *Jew.* 288; writes, we have learned in the holy scriptures that Peter, in whom the primacy of the apostles has the pre-eminence, &c. was corrected by Paul, 2 *Ful.* 313; observes that God taught Peter by Paul, who was called after him, 3 *Jew.* 284; speaks of the agreement between Peter and Paul as to preaching, *ib.* 327; says, Christ without respect of persons gave to Paul to minister among the heathens, what he gave to Peter to minister among the Jews, *ib.* 288; shews that Paul could not be the root or the head of those whom he planted, and that he was a member, not the head, 1 *Jew.* 379, 432, 440, 3 *Jew.* 270; calls Rome Babylon, *Rog.* 181, the second Babylon, 4 *Jew.* 1063; shews who are the citizens of Babylon, *ib.*; why Rome was called the metropolis, 1 *Jew.* 433; he says the imperial city imposed not only her yoke but her language on the vanquished nations, *Whita.* 225; expounds Rom. i. 7, "to all that be in Rome," 1 *Bec.* 73; proves the church of Rome to be apostolical, *Phil.* 78, 79; speaks of princes coming to Rome, and going to the memory (shrine) of a fisher, 2 *Ful.* 111; he yielded great reverence to the see of Rome, and why, 1 *Jew.* 370; he declares that in the church of Rome the principality of the apostolic chair has always flourished, 2 *Ful.* 351, 1 *Jew.* 369, 4 *Jew.* 822, 824; on the succession of bishops there, 1 *Jew.* 398; he speaks of succession from Peter as a mark of the church (see ix. above); says that in the succession of bishops of Rome, there was no Donatist, 1 *Jew.* 94, 3 *Jew.* 321, 325, 4 *Jew.* 886, *Whita.* 427; mentions that Constantine referred the Donatists to Melchiades, bishop of Rome, *Whita.* 436, 437; speaks of the matter of Cæcilian as committed to the same and other bishops by the emperor, 1 *Jew.* 397; but he disallowed appeals to Rome, *Park.* 111, rejected the pretended Nicene canon on that subject, 2 *Ful.* 70, 353, and decreed, among other bishops, that it should not be lawful to appeal to Rome, 1 *Jew.* 370; quoted as saying that all Christian countries beyond sea are subject to the church of Rome, *Rid.* 260; but the passage is spurious or interpolated, *Rid.* 260 n.; disputes on it, *ib.* 263, 265, 279; his language respecting Innocent I. is incompatible with papal supremacy and infallibility, 1 *Tyn.* 216 n.; when he speaks of the chair of heavenly doctrine, he does not mean the see of Rome, 2 *Ful.* 350; he says the faith sprang from the Greeks, or from the Eastern churches, 1 *Jew.* 280, 353; 4 *Jew.* 883

xii. *Saints* (see iv. above): he says, the blood of martyrs has been sown, the crop of the church has sprung up, *Pil.* 144 n.; another like passage, 2 *Cov.* 313 n.; the sentiment often occurs in his writings, 1 *Lat.* 361 n.; of the faithful he says, they were bound, imprisoned, beaten, tortured, burnt, yet they multiplied, 3 *Jew.* 189, 4 *Jew.* 1181, *Pil.* 144, 269; affirms that not the death but the cause makes a martyr, 1 *Hoop.* vii. 2 *Hoop.* 504; denies that the blood of any martyr was shed for the remission of sins, 3 *Bec.* 419; controverts the notion that men may obtain pardon by the merits of holy friends, 3 *Jew.* 566; writes that Paul does not make himself a mediator between God and the people, but intreats them to pray one for another, being all members of Christ's body, 3 *Jew.* 575; asks what Christian could bear John if he had made himself the mediator, 2 *Jew.* 634, 3 *Jew.* 575; says, we honour the saints with love, not with service, neither do we build temples to them, &c., 2 *Ful.* 149, 150; writes, we do not erect temples to our martyrs as unto gods, but memorials as unto dead men, &c., 3 *Bul.* 221; says, we make not temples, &c. to martyrs, because not they, but their God is our God, 4 *Bul.* 501, *Calf.* 129; shews that the priest does not offer sacrifice to the martyrs, but to God, 3 *Bul.* 221, 1 *Ful.* 269; asks, who ever heard of a priest sacrificing to Peter, Paul, or Cyprian? 1 *Ful.* 268, 269; passages on the honour due to martyrs and on the reasons for their commemoration, 2 *Cran.* 483, 2 *Ful.* 88, 2 *Whitg.* 580; he censures the excesses that were committed in honouring dead saints, 1 *Jew.* 158; on their monuments, 2 *Tyn.* 161 n.; he condemns superstition at the tombs of martyrs, 2 *Ful.* 44; on burial near a martyr's tomb, *ib.* 105; he speaks of the martyrs who lie underneath the altar of God in heaven, 2 *Jew.* 754, 755, 756, and approves of their burial under the altar on earth, *ib.* 756; somewhat sanctions the commendation of departed souls to the saints, 3 *Tyn.* 126 n.; mentions a saying of the heretic Faustus, that idols were changed into martyrs, 4 *Jew.* 949; speaks of some honoured on earth as saints, whose souls are tormented in hell, *Bale* 58; cited to the same effect, 1 *Hoop.* 345; mentions some who sold the bones of doubtful martyrs, 1 *Hoop.* 345, 1 *Jew.* 158; he says Moses was a priest, 4 *Jew.* 981, 982; affirms that no man knew the grave of Moses, lest the people should adore it (pseud.?), *ib.* 1047; (as to the ghost of Samuel, see xxv. below); he commends David for breaking his rash oath, 1 *Bec.* 374, 1 *Bul.* 251; on his seeming madness, 3 *Jew.* 250; he commends the Maccabees, *Rid.* 139; referred to in connexion with the dispute respecting the immaculate conception of the virgin Mary, 4 *Jew.* 1046, 1053; he pronounces all men sinners except the virgin, of whom, for the honour of the Lord, he will have no question, 1 *Bec.* 317; says, she was more blessed in that she received the faith of Christ, than in that she conceived the flesh of Christ, &c., 3 *Jew.* 578; observes that her maternal nearness would have profited her nothing, had she not borne Christ in her heart, 2 *Jew.* 757; thinks she was a little vainglorious, 1 *Lat.* 383, 515, 2 *Lat.* 163, 164; (Peter, see xi. above, where Paul is also named); he declares that Christ sacrificed Paul with his voice, and, after a certain manner, did eat him, 3 *Jew.* 495; on the charge of madness against the same apostle, *ib.* 250; he did not blindly receive the writings of Cyprian, 1 *Ful.* 39 (and see xiii. *b*); his story of Firmius, bishop of Tagasta, *Hutch.* 54; his account of St Anthony of Egypt, 2 *Jew.* 684; he commends his knowledge of the scriptures, 3 *Jew.* 430, 435; on the works of Epiphanius, 2 *Whitg.* 288, 289, his commendation of Jerome, 2 *Bul.* 390, 1 *Jew.* 278 (see xiii. *b*); describes Paulinus as rich for the poor, 1 *Hoop.* 397

xiii. *Sacraments*: he declares that men cannot be gathered into any name of religion, either true or false, unless they are knit together in some fellowship of visible signs or sacraments, 4 *Bul.* 332, 1 *Jew.* 131, 2 *Jew.* 1100; defines a sacrament as a holy sign, *Bale* 212, 1 *Jew.* 458, or a sign of a holy thing, *Phil.* 92, as the visible form of an invisible grace, *Bale* 213, 4 *Bul.* 234, *Grin.* 43, and n., 1 *Jew.* 515, 2 *Jew.* 1099, as a visible word, 1 *Bec.* 12, 3 *Bec.* 255, 2 *Jew.* 620, *Wool.* 22; in another place he asks, what are corporal sacraments, but, as it were, visible words? 4 *Bul.* 317, 1 *Jew.* 547; again, the sacraments are words visible, for in them as in lively images the death of Christ is sensibly set before our eyes, 3 *Jew.* 365: he calls them signs of things, being one thing and signifying another, *Bale* 148, 2 *Bec.* 284,¦3 *Bec.* 441, 1 *Cran.* 221, 3 *Jew.* 500, 501, *Rid.* 42, *Sand.* 454; says they are visible signs of divine things, *Bale* 213, 4 *Bul.* 291, 292, 2 *Hoop.* 405, 1 *Jew.* 458, 546; observes that signs, when applied to divine things, are called sacraments, 4 *Bul.* 234, 1 *Jew.* 219, 2 *Jew.* 591, 1099, 1100; defines a sign, 4 *Bul.* 227, 1 *Jew.* 219, 458, 515, 2 *Jew.* 605, 1099; says we universally call those things signs, which signify anything, 4 *Bul.* 227; speaks of everything that is either done or spoken in a figure shewing forth that which it signifies, 4 *Jew.* 764; terms sacraments holy seals, *Hutch.* 252; declares that unless sacraments had a certain likeness of those things of which they are sacraments, they would indeed be no sacraments; and shews that forasmuch as sacraments bear the names of those things of which they are sacraments, after a certain manner, the sacrament of Christ's body is Christ's body,...and the sacrament of faith is faith, 2 *Bec.* 283, 3 *Bec.* 440, 441, 1 *Brad.* 88, 533, 4 *Bul.* 284, *Coop.* 203, 1 *Cran.* 124, 225, 1 *Ful.* 270, *Grin.* 61, 1 *Hoop.* 515, 2 *Hoop.* 462, *Hutch.* 36 n., 237, 266, 1 *Jew.* 167, 458, 489, 503, 518, 2 *Jew.* 570, 600, 609, 718, 793, 1100, 1113, 3 *Jew.* 446, 456, 462, 471, 512, 602, *Rid.* 41, *Sand.* 453, 454, 3 *Whitg.* 111, &c.; a very similar passage, from the Canon Law, 1 *Cran.* 126, 282; says that a thing which signifies is wont to be called by the name of that which it signifies, and gives examples, 2 *Bec.* 282, 3 *Bec.* 441, 4 *Bul.* 284, 1 *Cran.* 125; 1 *Lat.* 167; also that images are wont to be called by the names of those things whereof they are images, 2 *Bec.* 249; writes that in sacraments we must not consider what they are, but what they signify, 1 *Cran.* 126, 221, 2 *Hoop.* 405, 1 *Jew.* 150, 467, 515, 545, 547, 2 *Jew.* 569, 1113, 3 *Jew.* 455, 497, 509, 526, *Rid.* 42; again, he says of signs, let no man consider in them what they are, but rather what signs they are, i. e. what they signify, 2 *Jew.* 594, 3 *Jew.* 500; teaches that the sacraments of the Jews and ours are all one in signification, 4 *Bul.* 299, 300, 1 *Cran.* 75, 76, 2 *Hoop.* 520, that is, the same faith in different signs, 4 *Bul.* 300, 1 *Jew.* 219; the faith remains, the signs are changed, 2 *Jew.* 709; again, the times are changed, not the faith, 4 *Bul.* 299,

2 *Cran.* 138; he thinks those mad who see diversity of things because of diversity of signs, 1 *Cran.* 76; declares that the Jews had one thing, we another,...but both signify the same, 2 *Jew.* 595; says, these things (the manna, &c.), were sacraments; different in signs, but in the thing which is signified, equal, 4 *Bul.* 299, 1 *Cran.* 75, 2 *Jew.* 610, 1119, 3 *Jew.* 447; the law and the prophets ...had sacraments foreshewing a thing to come; but the sacraments of our time witness that to have come, which those foretold as coming, 4 *Bul.* 297, 2 *Jew.* 610; he calls the old sacraments promises of things to be performed, ours, tokens of things which are performed, 4 *Bul.* 297, 2 *Jew.* 610, 3 *Jew.* 448; then, it was "Christ is about to come," now, "Christ hath come," 1 *Cran.* 76, 2 *Jew.* 709; he says, the sacraments of the new testament give salvation, those of the old testament promised a Saviour, 4 *Bul.* 297, 1 *Cran.* 77, *Hutch.* 250, 2 *Jew.* 616; on the meaning of circumcision, 2 *Bul.* 173; speaks of the Red Sea as consecrate in the blood of Christ, 2 *Jew.* 732; says, unto the Jews the rock was Christ, *ib.* 726, 731; observes that (Paul) says not the rock signified Christ, but, "the rock was Christ," 1 *Hoop.* 127, though it was not Christ in substance, but by signification, 1 *Jew.* 447, 2 *Jew.* 600, 4 *Jew.* 765; he says that while the faith remains, the signs vary; the rock was Christ to the Jews, to us Christ is what is laid on the altar of God, 2 *Jew.* 617; declares that manna, and the altar of God, signified the bread which descended from heaven, 4 *Bul.* 299; says of Moses, Aaron, and others, that they understood the visible manna spiritually, 2 *Jew.* 619; on "the same spiritual meat," 3 *Bec.* 443, 2 *Jew.* 602; remarks that "our fathers" (did eat it), not *their* fathers, *Hutch.* 249; says that as many as in the manna understood Christ ate the same spiritual meat as we do, 1 *Cran.* 76, 1 *Jew.* 545, 2 *Jew.* 617; speaks of the sacraments of the church as two (gemina), 2 *Jew.* 1103, 3 *Jew.* 459, and says of God, he has knit together the fellowship of a new people with sacraments very few in number, very easy in observation, very excellent in signification, as baptism... and the communion,...and whatsoever else is commended to us in the canonical scriptures, 4 *Bul.* 247, 2 *Hoop.* 124, *Pil.* 130; says the Lord has not burdened us with signs, but...delivered a few things instead

of many..., as the sacrament of baptism, and the celebration of the Lord's body and blood, 2 *Bec.* 291, 3 *Bec.* 441, 4 *Bul.* 246, 286, *Calf.* 223, 1 *Cran.* 134, 2 *Jew.* 1103, 3 *Jew.* 459, 1 *Whitg.* 267; mentions that the Punic Christians called baptism "salvation," and the sacrament of the body of Christ "life," 1 *Jew.* 294, 3 *Jew.* 482 n.; declares that holy men receive Christ in their hands and in their forehead, 2 *Jew.* 760, 3 *Jew.* 545, 467; uses the term sacrament in a wide sense, 4 *Bul.* 247, 248; speaks of the sacraments of the scriptures, i. e. their dark sayings, *Calf.* 235; speaks of holy bread given to catechumens before their baptism, and calls it a sacrament, 1 *Cran.* 180, 3 *Jew.* 458, *Rid.* 30; calls chrism a sacrament, *Calf.* 215; says the washing of feet is the sacrament of daily sins, 3 *Jew.* 458; declares that in the figure of the cross is contained a sacrament, *ib.* 457; speaks of the sacrament of marriage, *ib.*; mentions the sacrament of ordination, 4 *Bul.* 247; speaks of baptism and orders, as sacraments not to be repeated, 1 *Brad.* 534; says the word comes to the element and it becomes a sacrament, 1 *Bec.* 12, 2 *Bec.* 270, 3 *Bec.* 255, 1 *Brad.* 87, 4 *Bul.* 240, *Calf.* 205, 1 *Hoop.* 516, *Hutch.* 40, 1 *Jew.* 123, 2 *Jew.* 795, 1100, 1125, 3 *Jew.* 452, 458, *Phil.* 65, 3 *Whitg.* 129, 130; *Wool.* 22, 2 *Zur.* 232; distinguishes the sign from the thing signified, 2 *Jew.* 592, 759; he says the sacrament is one thing, the thing of the sacrament another, *Grin.* 43, 1 *Jew.* 516, 520, 2 *Jew.* 1122, 3 *Jew.* 501, 526; warns that all mysteries must be viewed with inner eyes, 2 *Jew.* 594; notes that in sacraments one thing is seen, another understood, 3 *Bec.* 440, 2 *Jew.* 594, 3 *Jew.* 514; observes that the thing which is seen has a corporal shew; that which is understood, spiritual fruit, *ib.* 595; says, if we apply our mind to the visible things wherein the sacraments are administered, who is ignorant that they are corruptible? but if to that which is wrought by them, who does not see that they are incorruptible? 3 *Jew.* 484, 514, 517; says it is a miserable servitude of the soul to take the signs for the things signified, 3 *Bec.* 435, 1 *Jew.* 448, 456, 516, 2 *Jew.* 591, 1113, 3 *Jew.* 472, 526, 540 (compare p. 55, col. 2, above); declares that as to follow the letter and to take the signs for the things signified is (a point) of servile infirmity; so to expound the signs unprofitably is (a point) of evil-wandering error, 4 *Bul.* 272, 286, 287, *Coop.* 210, 1 *Cran.* 134, 2 *Hoop.* 428; writes that he serves under a sign, who works or worships any sign, not knowing what it signifies, 1 *Cran.* 134; says that he who worships a profitable sign divinely appointed, and understands its power and meaning, does not worship that which is seen and passes away, but that unto which all such things have relation, 1 *Jew.* 548; he says this of baptism and the celebration of the body and blood of the Lord, *ib.*; teaches that sacraments must be venerated not with a carnal bondage, but with a spiritual freedom, 2 *Bec.* 291, 3 *Bec.* 441, and that they are to be honoured, not wondered at, *Grin.* 49; his doctrine on the efficacy of sacraments, 2 *Brad.* 405, 1 *Cov.* 459, 460; he says, those of the new testament give salvation, 3 *Jew.* 447 (and see p. 67, col. 2); in what sense, *ib.*; he taught not that they give grace (ex opere operato), 4 *Bul.* 297; he declares that God is present with his words and sacraments, 2 *Jew.* 763; argues that, if any grace be given in the sacraments, it is God's alway, 3 *Bec.* 469; says although the sacraments were common to all, yet their grace was not common to all, which is the power of the sacraments, 3 *Jew.* 487; avers that men are not to be thought to be in the body of Christ because they are corporally partakers of his sacraments, 4 *Bul.* 341; shews, by examples of scripture, that the visible sacraments profit not without the sanctification of invisible grace, 2 *Bec.* 218, 3 *Bec.* 466, 467, 1 *Brad.* 98, 4 *Bul.* 273, 347—349; teaches that sacraments received without faith in Christ are unprofitable to the receiver, 4 *Bul.* 341, 342; mentions some in his time who taught that if a man had been baptized and had received the communion, though he lived wickedly, &c., yet he could not be condemned, 2 *Jew.* 750; concludes that all are condemned who are not partakers of baptism and the eucharist, 2 *Whitg.* 521 (but see xiv. below); says that the sacraments worthily used bring reward, unworthily, judgment, 1 *Cran.* 68, 69; shews that they are spirit and life, even when carnally received, but not to the carnal receiver, 4 *Bul.* 343; writes that the wickedness of men cannot make them less holy, though to the ungodly they are a testimony of damnation, *ib.*; remarks that the faith of the receiver has nothing to do with the integrity of the sacrament, though very much with his salvation, *ib.*; says that the ways of evil men do not obstruct the sacraments of God, but that the sacraments hinder the ways of evil men, 1 *Cran.* 58; shews that the Donatists and Petilians did not esteem sacraments holy unless given by holy men, *Rog.* 270 n.; teaches that it is not communion with bad men in the participation of sacraments that defiles a man, but consent to their deeds, *Rid.* 121; declares that Christ left it to the apostles to order how the sacraments, &c. (see xv. *h*) should be used; speaks of brethren celebrating the same sacraments, and answering "Amen," 2 *Jew.* 699; intimates that pagans see the good works of Christians, though their sacraments are hidden from them, *ib.* 706; tells how the people desired the rites of the church in times of trouble, 1 *Jew.* 244; says, visible sacraments are instituted on account of carnal men, &c., 3 *Jew.* 370, and shews that when Christ shall have delivered up the kingdom, we shall have no need of bodily mysteries, 2 *Jew.* 615

xiv. *Baptism:* he exhorts catechumens to dispose their minds against the time of their baptism, 1 *Jew.* 119; mentions a mystical meat given to catechumens before baptism, 3 *Jew.* 458, *Rid.* 30; in the fictitious addresses to catechumens there is mention of crossing before baptism, 2 *Ful.* 145, they being mentioned as after a certain manner sanctified by the sign of Christ, 3 *Jew.* 359, and conceived by the sign of the cross, *ib.*; he says, baptism is no God, but it is a great thing because it is a sacrament of God, 2 *Jew.* 771, 3 *Jew.* 481, 482; writes that when the element has received the Holy Ghost it becomes a sacrament, and is not water of drinking but of sanctification, not common water but the water of refreshment, 3 *Jew.* 500; calls baptism the sacrament of Christian fellowship, 4 *Bul.* 400; says, ye have Christ at present by the sign, by faith, by the sacrament of baptism, (see xv. *b*); calls baptism the sacrament of faith, and declares that after a certain manner it is faith, *Coop.* 203 (and see p 67, col. 1); another passage, *ib.* 205; speaks of Christ's baptism as red, 2 *Jew.* 732; says, we honour the baptism of Christ wheresoever it be, 1 *Jew.* 514, 547; remarks that the apostle says, "we are buried with Christ," &c. not, we signify burial, 2 *Bec.* 283, 3 *Bec.* 444, *Coop.* 203, 1 *Cran.* 124, *Hutch.* 37 n., 2 *Jew.* 600, *Sand.* 454; shews that heretics lose not their baptism, and maintains that they are not to be baptized again, 4 *Bul.* 393, *Whita.* 607—609, 3 *Whitg.* 141, 576; opposed Cyprian's views on rebaptizing heretics, *Whita.* 507; says, the baptism of the church may be without the church, but the gift of blessed life is not found but within the church, 3 *Jew.* 444; affirms that a catechumen, how much soever he profiteth, bears the burden of his iniquity so long as he is unbaptized, *ib.* 355; condemns the Pelagians for promising to infants dying unbaptized a blessed life without the kingdom of God, *ib.* 564; on the condition of such infants after death, *ib.*; he repeatedly maintains that infants cannot be saved without baptism, 1 *Hoop.* 132, 4 *Bul.* 375, 376, 377; yet in other places he speaks dubiously, 4 *Bul.* 380, 381; and he says baptism is fulfilled invisibly when not contempt of religion, but necessity excludes it, 2 *Bec.* 224, 4 *Bul.* 381, 3 *Jew.* 355; says Paul baptized as a minister,...the Lord as the power itself, and shews the difference, 4 *Bul.* 42, 368, 369, 1 *Jew.* 455; and again, the Lord continues baptizing still; not by the ministry of his body, but by the invisible work of his majesty, 1 *Jew.* 455; says, my Master hath assured me of whom his Spirit saith, "This is he who baptizeth," 3 *Jew.* 461; again he says, the Lord retained to himself the power of baptizing, the ministry he gave to his servants, *ib.* 380; again, it is Christ that baptizeth, *ib.* 480; declares that God has retained to himself alone the power in baptism to forgive sins, 2 *Bec.* 219, 3 *Bec.* 469, 3 *Jew.* 379; says the water outwardly shews the sacrament of grace, and the Spirit inwardly works the benefit of grace, 2 *Jew.* 604; asserts that good and bad baptize visibly, but that God baptizes invisibly by them, 2 *Bec.* 227, 3 *Bec.* 469; affirms that baptism is holy though ministered by unholy men, 4 *Bul.* 350; shews, against the Donatists, that baptism is no less effectual when ministered by wicked men than by good men, since grace belongs to God, *ib.* 369, 370; his doubts respecting baptism by laymen, 4 *Bul.* 380; 2 *Whitg.* 536; he admits that baptism is given by them, though not rightly given, 2 *Whitg.* 532, and allows lay-baptism in cases of necessity, *ib.* 526; mentions the baptizing of young children, 4 *Bul.* 392; extract from his sermon De Bapt. Infantum, *Calf.* 243, 244; he says the baptism of young children was derived not from the authority of councils, but from the apostles, 2 *Bec.* 210, 4 *Bul.* 392, *Phil.* 280; maintains it from scripture, 2 *Cran.* 59, *Whita.* 506; mentions Cyprian's decree on the subject, 4 *Bul.* 392, *Phil.* 279; recites also the opinion of John, bp of Constantinople, *Phil.* 279; intimates that the Pelagians rejected it, *Rog.* 280 n.; he reckons young children, not yet baptized, in the number of those who believe, 2 *Jew.* 1105; says children are rightly called faithful, because they confess the faith, in a certain manner, by the words of those who bring them, 4 *Bul.* 344; observes that they are carried unto Christ the Physician to receive the sacrament of everlasting salvation, 2 *Jew.* 764; asserts that it is holy and right to believe that the faith of those by whom the child is offered is profitable to him in baptism; our mother the church, he adds, lends them the feet of other men that they may come, and the heart of other men that they may believe, 3 *Jew.* 462, *Phil.* 106 n., 1 *Zur.* 180 n.; and he says that as they are born again by the ministry of baptizers, so also they believe by the hearts and mouths of the confessors; they have faith on account of the sacrament of faith, 3 *Jew.* 462; speaks of children being baptized in the faith of their godfathers, *Phil.* 106; remarks on sponsorship, 2 *Bec.* 283, 3 *Whitg.* 111—113; his reply to Boniface, who asked him how parents and friends could answer for an infant in baptism, 1 *Cran.* 124 (59); in his time the sponsors answered for the infant, who was at once admitted to the Lord's supper, *Calf.* 213; Grindal and Horn say that the questions put to infants seem to be borrowed from him, 1 *Zur.* 179; on the exorcism of infants, *ib.* 178 n.; he speaks of baptism by trine immersion, 2 *Bec.* 227; several passages describing the prayers and rites then used, including exorcism, exsufflation, sponsors, and oil, 4 *Bul.* 360, 361; shews that we ought to long and mourn for that unspeakable thing to come which the sacrament points to, 2 *Jew.* 615; says the water is enriched almost with a greater gift than Mary (pseud.?) 3 *Jew.* 443; declares, against the Pelagians, that baptism washes away all sins...but takes not away the infirmity which the regenerate resists, *ib.* 461; says, the holiness of baptism cannot be defiled; the heavenly power is assistant unto the sacrament, 1 *Jew.* 537, 2 *Jew.* 763; teaches the use of this ordinance, viz. that the baptized may be incorporate into Christ, 1 *Jew.* 473; says that by baptism we are joined as members unto the body of Christ, 4 *Bul.* 377, 400; affirms that the baptized are incorporate into Christ, and made his members, 1 *Jew.* 141, 3 *Jew.* 467; he (or Fulgentius) unhesitatingly declares that every faithful man is partaker of the body and blood of the Lord, when in baptism he is made a member of Christ, 3 *Bec.* 443, *Coop.* 121, *Grin.* 68, 69, 1 *Jew.* 132, 450, 529, 2 *Jew.* 767, 3 *Jew.* 530 (*v.* Bede); he says, the sacrifice of the Lord's passion every one offers for his sins when he is dedicated in the faith of his passion, 2 *Jew.* 727, 737, 748; and again, that the Lord's sacrifice is in a manner offered for each, when in baptism he is marked with the name of Christ, *ib.* 727; and again, "there remaineth no more sacrifice for sin," i. e. he can be no more baptized, *ib.*; he declares that true baptism consists not so much in the washing of the body, as in the faith of the heart, *ib.* 1105, 3 *Jew.* 462; asks why Christ does not say, "Ye are clean because of the baptism wherewith ye are washed," but, "for the word which I have spoken unto you," saving for that it is the *word* that cleanseth in the water? take away the word, and what is the water but water? 1 *Cov.* 459, 2 *Jew.* 757, 1105, 3 *Jew.* 353, 357, 365; inquires whence is the virtue of the water, that it touches the body and washes the heart, unless by the working of the word, not because it is spoken, but because it is believed? 4 *Bul.* 258, *Calf.* 205, 2 *Hoop.* 407, 1 *Jew.* 123, 3 *Jew.* 462, 558; speaks of the water of baptism giving us outwardly the sacrament of grace, 3 *Jew.* 463; from the words "Baptism doth now save us," he shews that the visible sacrament alone is not sufficient, 4 *Bul.* 341, 3 *Jew.* 462; says the laver of regeneration is common to all who are baptized, but the grace thereof, by which the members of Christ are regenerated with their head, is not common to all, 4 *Bul.* 300, 301 n.; writes that many have baptism, not to life eternal, but to eternal punishment, not well using so good a thing, 4 *Jew.* 893; teaches that it is available to some unto the kingdom, to some unto judgment, *ib.* 893, 894; says, he who receives baptism unworthily receives judgment, not health (pseud.), 1 *Jew.* 517; declares that visible baptism did nothing profit Simon Magus, 4 *Bul.* 347, 348; says holy things (baptism and priesthood) fly from evil men, 2 *Jew.* 761; mentions the opinion of the Manichees that baptism is of no avail, 4 *Bul.* 397, *Rog.* 275 n.; holds, in opposition to the Pelagians, that baptism is necessary for the remission of original sin, *Rog.* 277 n.; he wrote on this sacrament against the Donatists, 1 *Cran.* 221; says Donatus did not believe baptism to be, except in his communion, 1 *Jew.* 132; on the baptism of those bereft of reason, 3 *Jew.* 355 n.; he mentions one who was baptized as he lay in a trance, in deadly pain, and unconscious, *ib.* 358; speaks against baptizing unborn infants, 1 *Jew.* 6, 3 *Jew.* 358

xv. *The Eucharist* (see also xiii.):

(*a*) Name, institution, &c.:—he calls the sacrament "signaculum" and "signum," 2 *Hoop.* 405; terms it a figure, *Grin.* 195, the sacrament of bread and wine, 2 *Jew.* 795, 3 *Jew.* 483, a sacrament of memory, 1 *Hoop.* 529, *Rid.* 39, the Lord's morsel, 2 *Jew.* 772; speaks of it as a sermon, 1 *Jew.* 121; his use of the word "communion," *ib.* 132; (as to the word "missa," see (*h*) below;) on Luke's account of the institution, 1 *Cran.* 248, *Grin.* 197; why it is not spoken of in John xiii., 4 *Bul.* 463; his exposition of Christ's saying, that he would drink of the wine in the kingdom of his Father, *Hutch.* 269; intimates that the breaking of bread in going to Emmaus was hospitality, 1 *Brad.* 548, 1 *Jew.* 232; elsewhere he interprets it of the sacrament, 2 *Ful.* 234; says (the eucharist) is blessed and sanctified, 1 *Ful.* 504; speaks of the sacrament causing us to be moved as if we saw the Lord present on the cross, 1 *Jew.* 467, 539, 2 *Jew.* 600, 726; another passage, somewhat similar, 1 *Jew.* 491

(*b*) Of the sign and the thing signified, and how the elements are Christ's body and blood:—he distinguishes between Christ's body and the sacrament thereof, 2 *Bec.* 293, 1 *Cov.* 427, 2 *Jew.* 767; speaks of the visible and invisible sacrament, 1 *Cran.* 201, 204; says (eternal life) pertains to the virtue of the sacrament, not to the visible sacrament, 3 *Bec.* 432, 2 *Jew.* 619, 1120; declares that although the sacrament be visibly ministered, yet it must be invisibly understood, 1 *Cran.* 230, 231, (87); he (or rather Fulgentius) speaks of the figurative character of the eucharist, *Rid.* 40; speaks of Christ ordaining a similitude or representation of his sacrifice, 3 *Bec.* 458, 459; says the sacrament is a figure, commanding us to communicate with the passion of Christ, &c., (see (*c*) below); referred to on Christ's presence therein, *Rid.* 251; he says we have Christ at present, by faith, by a sign, by the sacrament of baptism, by the meat and drink of the altar, 3 *Bec.* 452, 1 *Jew.* 491, 537, 2 *Jew.* 740, 3 *Jew.* 484, 529; cited in the Canon Law as saying that the elements are before consecration bread and wine, afterwards the flesh and blood of Christ, 1 *Jew.* 545, 2 *Jew.* 571; he says we receive Christ's flesh covered with the form of bread, &c., 2 *Jew.* 617, 796, 3 *Jew.* 525; affirms that Christ gave his flesh to be eaten which he took of the earth, &c., *Rid.* 234; declares plainly, in many places, that Christ's body is not corporally present, nor corporally eaten in the sacrament, 1 *Cran.* 232; his exposition of the word "corporaliter," (not with reference to this subject), 1 *Jew.* 476; he denies that there is any miracle in the sacrament, 1 *Hoop.* 225, 2 *Hoop.* 410; declares that we call that the body and blood of Christ which is taken of the fruit of the earth, and consecrated by mystical prayer, 3 *Bec.* 442, 1 *Cran.* 105, (54); says the bread by a certain consecration becomes mystical unto us, 2 *Hoop.* 426; shews that inasmuch as sacraments have the name of the things whereof they are sacraments, the sacrament of Christ's body is Christ's body, and the sacrament of Christ's blood, the blood of Christ (see p. 67, col. 1); declares that the heavenly bread is called Christ's body, when indeed it is the sacrament of his body, 2 *Bec.* 250, 284, 3 *Bec.* 437, 458, *Coop.* 204, 2 *Jew.* 619, 620, 794, 3 *Jew.* 508, *Rid.* 42; gloss on this passage, 2 *Jew.* 621; he explains how the bread is Christ's body and the cup his blood, one thing being seen and another understood, 3 *Bec.* 440, 3 *Jew.* 514; says, the fathers (i. e. before Pelagius) expressed the sacraments of so great a thing none otherwise than by the name of the same thing, *Hutch.* 37, 3 *Jew.* 499; imagines Christ as saying, understand what I say spiritually; ye shall not eat this body that ye see...I have delivered you a certain sacrament, 2 *Bec.* 296, 3 *Bec.* 443, *Coop.* 211, 1 *Cran.* 231, *Grin.* 44, 45, 70, 1 *Hoop.* 235, 2 *Hoop.* 463, 495, 1 *Jew.* 451, 479, 525, 542, 2 *Jew.* 621, 622, 775, 895, 1111, 3 *Jew.* 529, *Rid.* 39; says that Christ, by speaking (in John vi.) of his ascension, shewed what he meant in saying he would give his body, 1 *Jew.* 454; shews that "the flesh profiteth nothing," 1 *Jew.* 526; on 1 Sam. xxi. 13, "Ferebatur in manibus suis," he says that Christ after a certain manner bare himself in his own hands, 3 *Bec.* 442, 4 *Bul.* 438, 439, 1 *Cran.* 59, 61, 1 *Ful.* 544 n., *Grin.* 61, 198, 1 *Jew.* 502, 503, 2 *Lat.* 274, *Rid.* 243, 244, *Whita.* 469; he says the Lord held bread, 1 *Jew.* 503; declares that the Lord did not hesitate to say, "This is my body," when he gave the sign of his body, 2 *Bec.* 282, 285, 3 *Bec.* 271, 369, 435, 442, 1 *Brad.* 590, 4 *Bul.* 441, *Coop.* 201, 211, *Grin.* 65, 1 *Hoop.* 127, 231, 2 *Hoop.* 405, 463, 1 *Jew.* 219, 2 *Jew.* 563, 592, 612, 1112, 3 *Jew.* 169, 243, 512, 4 *Jew.* 765, *Rid.* 41, 3 *Tyn.* 259, 260; speaks of the sacrament as the partaking of the body and blood of the Lord, 3 *Bec.* 389; says, our Lord by the sacrament of wine commends unto us his blood, 3 *Jew.* 521; exhorts to drink Christ's blood, 2 *Lat.* 269; asserts that Paul says to those who receive the body and blood of the Lord, "Seek those things which are above," 1 *Jew.* 542, 3 *Jew.* 534; says "the blood is the soul," as "the rock was Christ," 2 *Bec.* 282, 3 *Bec.* 442, 2 *Jew.* 612; calls the elements bread and wine after consecration, 2 *Jew.* 571; exclaims, come boldly, it is bread, and not poison, 3 *Bec.* 424; says, that which you see is the bread and the cup, which also your eyes do shew you; but faith sheweth further, that the bread is the body of Christ, and the cup his blood, 2 *Bec.* 267, 268, 3 *Bec.* 424, 1 *Cran.* 277, (31), 1 *Jew.* 11, 150, 564, 2 *Jew.* 579, 776, 791, 1066, 1115, 3 *Jew.* 482, 483, 512, see also *Bale* 93; says the bread is spent in receiving the sacrament, 2 *Bec.* 252, 3 *Bec.* 456, 2 *Hoop.* 425; speaks of the visible species of the elements, 2 *Jew.* 793, 794; deems the words "daily bread" to include, that which is needful for the body, the visible consecrated bread, and the invisible bread of God's word, 1 *Brad.* 100; takes it to mean either the sacrament of the body of Christ, which (says he) we receive daily, or the spiritual food, the meat which perisheth not, 1 *Jew.* 169, 2 *Jew.* 767, not the bread that passes into the body, but that bread of everlasting life, which sustains the substance of the soul (pseud.), 1 *Jew.* 169, 2 *Jew.* 571; (see also (*h*) below); he says, no man eats the flesh of Christ, unless he first adore, (i. e. worship him in heaven), 1 *Cran.* 230, 1 *Jew.* 11, 12, 541; on "the poor" and "the rich of the earth" eating at Christ's table, and adoring, 1 *Jew.* 543, 544; he says (in the Canon Law) we honour in form of bread and wine, things invisible, 1 *Jew.* 545; declares that (the elements) may have honour as things pertaining to religion, but not wonder as things marvellous, 1 *Jew.* 481, 2 *Jew.* 1122; says he is no less guilty who hears God's word negligently, than he who suffers the body of Christ to fall upon the ground (pseud.), 1 *Brad.* 100, 1 *Cran.* 146, 1 *Jew.* 151, 2 *Jew.* 771

(*c*) Of eating Christ's body, &c. (see the preceding paragraph; also p. 67, col. 2): he speaks of Christ's flesh as the true food, and of his blood as truly drink, 1 *Cran.* 24; shews how the eating and drinking thereof must be spiritually understood, 2 *Bec.* 293, 296, 1 *Cran.* 27; his words about eating the body of Christ with our mouths are to be understood figuratively, 1 *Cran.* 55; he means not that Christ's flesh is to be eaten carnally, but spiritually, at the Lord's supper as well as at all other times, *ib.* 118, 208; he teaches (in many places) that sacraments are food for the mind, not for the mouth, 1 *Hoop.* 233; declares that Christ's words about eating his flesh (John vi.) must be understood figuratively, since otherwise they would seem to command a horrible wickedness, 1 *Brad.* 91, 4 *Bul.* 289, 461, 1 *Cran.* 22, 27, 115, (57), *Grin.* 70, 1 *Jew.* 525, 2 *Jew.* 622, 624, 1113, 3 *Jew.* 487, *Rid.* 21, 32, *Whita.* 472, and see 2 *Lat.* 266; calls the sacrament a figure commanding us to partake of his passion, 1 *Cran.* 115, 212, 2 *Hoop.* 429, 463, 1 *Jew.* 452, 463, 2 *Jew.* 624, 3 *Jew.* 619; he shews that to keep in our minds that Christ was crucified and wounded for us, is to eat his flesh and drink his blood, 1 *Cran.* 115, 212, 232, (57); remarks that the people took the saying (in Jo. vi.) foolishly; but they were hard, not the saying, 2 *Bec.* 296, 3 *Bec.* 443, 2 *Jew.* 895; declares the words of Christ to be spirit and life, though not to him who carnally understands them, 1 *Cran.* 206; imagines Christ as saying, understand what I speak spiritually; ye shall not eat this body which ye see, &c. (see (*b*) above), and, when ye shall see the Son of man ascending where he was before, even then truly shall you see that he bestows his body not in that manner which you think, 3 *Jew.* 487, 539; quotes Christ's saying, "he that eateth me shall live through me," 2 *Jew.* 766; speaks of him as shewing us what it is to eat his body...not only in the sacrament, but in very deed, i. e. to dwell in him, 2 *Bec.* 293, 3 *Bec.* 434, 463, 464, 1 *Jew.* 450, 3 *Jew.* 542; calls Christ the food of great ones, 2 *Jew.* 786; calls him the bread of our heart, 1 *Jew.* 475, 2 *Jew.* 1117, 3 *Jew.* 530; says, Christ hath called us unto his gospel, and he himself is our meat to be tasted in the heart, 2 *Jew.* 768; again, Christ is our meat, than which there is nothing more savoury if a man have a sound taste in his heart, 3 *Jew.* 549; exclaims, hunger within, thirst within, *ib.* 530; says, this bread requires the hunger of the inner man, 2 *Bec.* 295, 1 *Jew.* 451, 2 *Jew.* 572, 3 *Jew.* 467, 488, 589; speaks of him who eats inwardly, not outwardly, who eats in the heart, not who presses with the teeth, 3 *Bec.* 432, 1 *Hoop.* 233, 2 *Jew.* 619, 1120, 3 *Jew.* 487, 542; writes, he that eateth not eateth, and he that eateth eateth not, 3 *Jew.* 531; speaks of drinking inwardly, 1 *Jew.* 451, 2 *Jew.* 572; declares that Christ cannot be devoured with teeth, 3 *Bec.* 434; asks, why preparest thou thy teeth and belly? believe, and thou hast eaten, 2 *Bec.* 295, 296, 3 *Bec.* 432, 1 *Brad.* 105 n., 4 *Bul.* 460, 1 *Cran.* 118, 208, *Grin.* 44, 1 *Hoop.* 233, 530, *Hutch.* 242, 1 *Jew.* 141, 449, 468, 475, 528, 2 *Jew.* 776, 1110, 1119, 3 *Jew.* 466, 486, 492, 530, 589, *Sand.* 88, 3 *Tyn.* 228; again, prepare not thy jaws, but thy heart, 1 *Cran.* 118, 208, 1 *Hoop.* 233, 2 *Hoop.* 497, 2 *Jew.* 1110, 3 *Jew.* 486, 539; he asserts that the grace of Christ is not consumed by morsels, 3 *Jew.* 487, 530, 539; declares that he who believes eats, 2 *Bec.* 295, 296, 3 *Bec.* 434, *Hutch.* 263, 3 *Jew.* 488; speaks of making Christ come into the bowels of the hungry by preaching him, 4 *Jew.* 790; asserts that the centurion received Christ into his heart, *ib.*; calls Christ the bread of which he that eats lives for ever, 3 *Bec.* 463; exclaims, brethren, behold the heavenly bread, eat it with a spiritual mouth, 3 *Jew.* 530; says, to believe in him, that is to eat the living bread, &c., 2 *Bec.* 295, 296, 3 *Bec.* 465, 1 *Hoop.* 233, *Hutch.* 263, 1 *Jew.* 452, 468, 2 *Jew.* 776, 3 *Jew.* 533, 549, 589, 3 *Tyn.* 228; says, when Christ is eaten, life is eaten, 1 *Jew.* 458; exclaims, eat life, drink life, 1 *Brad.* 97, *Rid.* 161, 201

(d) That Christ's body is eaten by the righteous, but not by the wicked:—he admonishes that he that comes to the holy banquet must come full of holiness, 3 *Bec.* 476; shews that those only who are cleansed may receive the meat of the body of Christ, *ib.* 475; says, the sacrament is received from the Lord's table, of some unto life, of some unto destruction; but the thing itself whereof it is a sacrament (that is, the body of Christ) is received of every man unto life and of no man unto destruction, whosoever be partaker of it, 3 *Bec.* 463, 465, 1 *Cran.* 212, 1 *Cov.* 428, 1 *Jew.* 193, 453, 524, 2 *Jew.* 759, 1122, 3 *Jew.* 449, 494, 4 *Jew.* 895; admonishes not to eat the flesh and drink the blood of Christ only in the sacrament, which many evil men do, 3 *Bec.* 433; affirms that he who is in the unity of the body of Christ truly eats his body and drinks his blood, *ib.* 463, 464; approves the judgment of those who say that he eats not the body of Christ, who is not in the body of Christ, 2 *Bec.* 293, 3 *Bec.* 464, 1 *Brad.* 91, 542, 4 *Bul.* 465, 1 *Cran.* 216; says this is the eating of that meat and the drinking of that drink,—for a man to dwell in Christ, and to have Christ abiding in him, 2 *Bec.* 293, 3 *Bec.* 463, 1 *Cran.* 26, 212, 1 *Jew.* 212, 2 *Jew.* 786, 3 *Jew.* 454, 619, 4 *Jew.* 893; declares that he that dwells not in Christ and in whom Christ dwells not, without doubt, neither spiritually eats his flesh nor drinks his blood, although he carnally and visibly presses the sacrament thereof with his teeth, 2 *Bec.* 293, 3 *Bec.* 463, 4 *Bul.* 460, 465, 470, 1 *Cov.* 428, *Grin.* 58, 2 *Hoop.* 498, 2 *Jew.* 759, 4 *Jew.* 895, and see *Hutch.* 264; on the citation of this passage in the 29th article of the church of England, *Park.* 381; again, he who abides not in me and in whom I do not abide, let him not say or think that he either eats my body or drinks my blood, 2 *Jew.* 1120, 3 *Jew.* 532, and see 1 *Cran.* 26; again, he that agrees not with Christ neither eats his flesh, nor drinks his blood, though he daily receive the sacrament of so great a thing to the condemnation of his presumption, 2 *Bec.* 292, 3 *Bec.* 433, 434, 463, 464, 1 *Cran.* 205, 210, (81), *Grin.* 59, *Hutch.* 265 n., 1 *Jew.* 519, 2 *Jew.* 1120; he says they (the wicked) have the sacrament outwardly, but do not hold the thing itself inwardly...so they eat and drink judgment, 2 *Jew.* 604, 4 *Jew.* 894; yet he speaks of evil men receiving the body of Christ *quodam modo*, *Phil.* 133, and says it was the body of the Lord even to them who ate unworthily, 1 *Cran.* 222; says that those without the church may have the sacrament, but the matter of it they cannot have, 2 *Bec.* 293, and that heretics and schismatics receive the same sacrament (as the church does), but it is not profitable to them, but very hurtful, 3 *Bec.* 464, 1 *Cran.* 216, *Pil.* 632; shews that it is hurtful to those who use it ill, 1 *Cran.* 221, (85); remarks that bread feeds man, but kills the hawk, 2 *Hoop.* 424; says it is death, not life, to him who thinks that (Christ) the Life was a liar, 2 *Jew.* 699; what it is not to discern the Lord's body, 4 *Bul.* 471; he says, he that is blind within sees not Christ the

AUGUSTINE

bread, 2 *Jew.* 1121, 3 *Jew.* 474; avouches that Judas was present at the last supper, 4 *Bul.* 464; says, the Lord himself tolerates Judas, and suffers a devil, a thief, and his betrayer, to receive among his innocent disciples our price, 4 *Jew.* 892, 893; declares that he admitted Judas to the feast, in which he commended and delivered to his disciples the figure of his body and blood, 2 *Bec.* 285, 3 *Bec.* 369, 435, *Coop.* 202, *Grin.* 65, 2 *Hoop.* 405, *Hutch.* 259, 1 *Jew.* 447, 2 *Jew.* 592, 609, 775, 1113, 3 *Jew.* 169, 527, 532, 4 *Jew.* 893, *Rid.* 40; he says that they (the disciples) did eat the bread that was the Lord, he, (Judas), the bread of the Lord against the Lord, 2 *Bec.* 294, 297, 3 *Bec.* 463, 466, 1 *Brad.* 512, 537, 542, 4 *Bul.* 405, 1 *Cran.* 213, 224, 2 *Hoop.* 497, 2 *Jew.* 767, 3 *Jew.* 455, 481, 532; declares that good men eat both, *Rid.* 247; nevertheless he speaks of Judas (in one sense) receiving the body and blood of the Lord, 2 *Bec.* 296, 1 *Cran.* 222, *Hutch.* 265, 266; tells how Judas received the morsel (non malum sed male), 2 *Bec.* 296, 3 *Bec.* 432, 1 *Cran.* 221, *Rid.* 246; shews that the Lord's supper was the same to Peter and to Judas, but that the effect differed in them; the table (says he) was one to both, but it availed not to both for one thing, 1 *Brad.* 542, 1 *Cran.* 57

(*e*) Benefits, &c.:—referred to on the grace of the Lord's supper, *Rid.* 202; he says, whosoever with faith and fear hears the word of God, is comforted by the breaking of bread, 3 *Jew.* 549; teaches that they who eat and drink Christ eat and drink life, 3 *Bec.* 414, 433, 465; says to eat him is to be refreshed, to drink him is to live, 3 *Bec.* 414, 433, 465; a like passage, to eat *that*, &c., 1 *Cran.* 203, 212, 1 *Jew.* 528; he says he who eats not the flesh of Christ...has not life, and he who eats it has life eternal, 1 *Cran.* 212, see also 2 *Jew.* 1121, 1122, 3 *Jew.* 449, 493, 592; writes of certain heretics who affirmed that whoever once received the sacrament could not be damned, 1 *Hoop.* 161; he erroneously maintains that is is necessary for salvation to infants, 3 *Bul.* 398, 4 *Bul.* 379, *Calf.* 259, 2 *Ful.* 41, 158, 392; mentions an instance of the practice of giving it to them, 1 *Jew.* 6; a spurious passage alleged for infant communion, *ib.* 250; shews, however, that those who depart hence without receiving the sacrament of Christ's body and blood, are not deprived of the benefit of that sacrament if they have that which is thereby signified (Fulgentius), 3 *Bec.* 443, 1 *Jew.* 132, 2 *Jew.* 1107

(*f*) The sacrament as a type of unity:—he speaks of the sacrament of bread as denoting unity, 1 *Jew.* 232, 234; shews that it declares the unity of Christians, &c., *Grin.* 55, 56; calls it the mystery of unity, 1 *Jew.* 141; blames him who takes the mystery of unity, and does not hold the bond of peace, *Grin.* 56, 1 *Jew.* 204; says, we receive together, we drink together, because we live together, 1 *Jew.* 261, 3 *Jew.* 479; passages on the "one bread and one body," *Coop.* 120, 2 *Hoop.* 426; he says the Lord calls bread, made by the kneading of many grains, his body, *Grin.* 56 n., 2 *Hoop.* 426, and see 1 *Cov.* 445, 1 *Cran.* 249; declares that the Lord would have his meat and drink understood to be the fellowship of his body and members, 1 *Jew.* 134; shews that he must be in the body of Christ, who would receive the body of Christ, 1 *Brad.* 91, 542 (& *al.* see (*d*) above); another passage, 1 *Jew.* 141; he says, we are made Christ's body, and by his mercy we are that which we receive, 1 *Hoop.* 230, *Hutch.* 240; hence he tells the faithful communicants, ye are there upon the table, ye are there in the cup, 1 *Hoop.* 230, *Hutch.* 240, 1 *Jew.* 468, 522, 539, 3 *Jew.* 542, 602

(*g*) The eucharist as a sacrifice:—he affirms that Christ was once offered in himself, and yet is daily offered sacramentally, 2 *Bec.* 250, 3 *Bec.* 458, 2 *Jew.* 718; declares that Christ is the priest, himself offering, and himself the oblation; the sacrament of which thing the church will have to be the daily sacrifice, 2 *Ful.* 80 n.; says, Christ is sacrificed, i. e. the sacrifice of Christ is represented, and remembrance is made of his passion, 2 *Jew.* 726; shews how Christ is sacrificed by the people every day, 1 *Hoop.* 529 n., 1 *Jew.* 167; says that by our remembrance of Christ, he is sacrificed to us daily, 1 *Jew.* 23 (similar passages will be found in iii. p. 50); affirms that every man offers the sacrifice of the Lord's passion for his own sins, (see p. 70, col. 2); shews in what way the sacrament is called a sacrifice, 4 *Bul.* 432, 1 *Cran.* 87, 124, 2 *Hoop.* 528, 529; says, the church offers up the sacrifice of bread and wine, 2 *Hoop.* 429, 2 *Jew.* 1114, 3 *Jew.* 349; asserts that the sacrifice of the church consists of two things, the visible shape of the elements, and the invisible flesh and blood of our Lord, 2 *Bec.* 268, 1 *Cran.* 277, 282, 2 *Jew.*

AUGUSTINE

592, 594; says, the visible sacrifice is a sacrament, i. e. a holy sign, of the invisible sacrifice, 1 *Cov.* 451 n., 1 *Cran.* 351, 2 *Hoop.* 405, 528, 2 *Jew.* 736, 737, and that what is called of all men the sacrifice, is a sign of the true sacrifice, 1 *Cran.* 351, (95), 2 *Ful.* 80 n., 2 *Hoop.* 528, 529, 2 *Jew.* 710, 737; he says, the sacrifice of the flesh of Christ made by the hands of the priest is called Christ's passion, death, crucifixion; not really, but in a significant mystery, 2 *Bec.* 250, *Coop.* 204, 2 *Jew.* 711, 794, 4 *Jew.* 893; contrasts the carnal sacrifices of the Law, wherein there was a figure of the flesh of Christ which he should offer, with our sacrifice, in which there is a thanksgiving for and memorial of the flesh of Christ which he has offered for us (Fulgentius), 3 *Bec.* 441, 442, 456, 457, 1 *Cran.* 77, *Grin.* 68, 2 *Hoop.* 429, 430, 1 *Jew.* 491, 2 *Jew.* 602, 610, 708, 709, 716, 3 *Jew.* 350; says, the flesh and blood of (Christ's) sacrifice was, before the advent of Christ, promised by sacrifices of resemblance; in the passion it was given in truth; since his ascension it is celebrated by a sacrament of remembrance, 2 *Bec.* 249, 3 *Bec.* 441, 457, 2 *Jew.* 710, 736; observes that all the sacrifices of the old testament in many and various ways signified the one sacrifice whose memory we now celebrate, 2 *Jew.* 708; says that now Christians celebrate the memory of his finished sacrifice by the holy oblation and participation of his body and blood, 3 *Bec.* 456, *Rid.* 179; now we offer not his flesh with our hands, but with our heart and mouth we offer praise, 4 *Jew.* 1047; he declares that the church offers sacrifice, not to martyrs, but to God alone, 3 *Bec.* 356; again, he speaks of this sacrifice as the (mystical) body of Christ, which is not offered to martyrs, since they themselves are that body, *Coop.* 93; another passage, wherein he speaks of the people as the oblation, *ib.*; on Melchisedec's offering, 1 *Ful.* 148; he says he gave Abraham the eucharist of the Lord's body and blood, 2 *Jew.* 732; writes, Christ has given an image of his sacrifice to be celebrated in his church in memory of his passion, that he might be a priest, not after the order of Aaron, but of Melchisedec, 2 *Jew.* 656, 736, 3 *Jew.* 336, 4 *Jew.* 715; says that the same sacrifice which Melchisedec offered is now offered throughout the world, 2 *Jew.* 736; declares that the priest offers up the sacrifice of praise, not after the order of Aaron, but after the order of Melchisedec, *ib.* 737; on the offering foretold by Malachi, *ib.* 723; he calls upon the Jews to behold the accomplishment of that prediction, *ib.* 736; terms the Lord's supper the sacrament of the altar, *Phil.* 119; speaks of the altars of our hearts (dub.), 2 *Jew.* 735

(*h*) Rites :—he says the Saviour left the circumstances of the sacrament to his apostles, &c., 1 *Jew.* 39, 74, 122, 125, 1 *Whitg.* 237; relates that the heathen supposed Christians to worship Bacchus and Ceres in the sacrament, 1 *Jew.* 544; 3 *Jew.* 552, 4 *Jew.* 709, *Rid.* 236; his writings contain some vestiges of the primitive forms, 4 *Bul.* 409; he speaks of daily communion, 1 *Jew.* 125, 174, 202; speaks of some communicating every day, some on certain days, some only on the Lord's day, 2 *Bec.* 258, 3 *Bec.* 381, *Coop.* 101, 1 *Jew.* 17; affirms that the sacrament is prepared in some places every day, in some places on certain days, 2 *Bec.* 258, 3 *Bec.* 381, 1 *Jew.* 169, 2 *Jew.* 759; says, the "daily bread" may be taken for the sacrament of Christ's body, which we receive every day, 1 *Jew.* 169, 202 (see (*b*) above); states that many in the Eastern parts did not communicate daily, *ib.* 169; neither praises nor blames daily communion (pseud.), 2 *Bec.* 258, 3 *Bec.* 470, 1 *Jew.* 199, but counsels men to receive every Sunday, if the mind be without desire to sin (pseud.), 2 *Bec.* 258, 3 *Bec.* 470, *Pil.* 542; his advice to parties differing about the frequency of celebration, 4 *Bul.* 424, 425; he speaks of the communion as celebrated twice in some places, on the Thursday before Easter, 2 *Jew.* 631; replies to questions as to its celebration on that day, 1 *Whitg.* 236; shews that in the primitive church the priest and people sometimes communicated after supper, 1 *Jew.* 136; mentions the table of the Lord set in the midst, 1 *Jew.* 311, 2 *Jew.* 636; speaks of the Donatists breaking the altar-boards, 1 *Jew.* 311, 3 *Jew.* 602; on the mode of celebration at Carthage, 1 *Jew.* 208; he uses the term "missa" for the dismissal of the catechumens, 2 *Ful.* 82 n., see *Phil.* 93; speaks of the exhortation "Sursum corda," as used throughout the world, 1 *Cov.* 456 n., and as used in the holy mysteries, 1 *Jew.* 119, 3 *Jew.* 534; he says the hearts of the faithful are in heaven, because daily lifted up to heaven, and mentions the response, "Habemus ad Dominum," 3 *Bec.* 266, 360; declares that in the sacraments of the faithful it is said that we should lift up our hearts unto the Lord, and that the people responded, 3 *Bec.* 407, 3 *Jew.* 534; says that the faithful know when it is said, "Let us give thanks unto our Lord God," 3 *Bec.* 407; affirms that prayer should be made for the dead, 3 *Bul.* 397; says the souls of the dead are relieved by the devotion of the living, when the sacrifice of the Mediator is offered, 2 *Lat.* 275; mentions the kiss of peace, 1 *Jew.* 154; says the bread is broken that it may be distributed, &c., 1 *Jew.* 203, 2 *Jew.* 588, 4 *Jew.* 819; referred to to shew that the bread and the cup were given into the hands of the communicants, 2 *Bec.* 301 n., 3 *Bec.* 411, 1 *Jew.* 154; speaks of the host being broken, and the blood from the chalice poured into the mouths of the faithful, 3 *Bec.* 413, 1 *Jew.* 167, 209, 2 *Jew.* 599, 600, 729; mentions that the minister said, "The body of Christ," and that the recipient replied "Amen," 1 *Jew.* 141; addresses the communicants as receiving the cup of Christ together, 3 *Bec.* 413; seems to imply that the sacrament was not received, 2 *Jew.* 554; he (or Cæsarius) speaks of the care used in receiving the sacrament to be carried home, 1 *Jew.* 148, 151, 248; referred to (the passage also attributed to Gregory) as naming private mass, 1 *Jew.* 106; tells of the expulsion of evil spirits from the house of Hesperius by the offering of the sacrifice of the body of Christ, 2 *Ful.* 86

xvi. *Ceremonies* (see also ix. and xiii.): on the burden of Jewish ceremonies, *Rid.* 138; he declares that in his time ceremonies so oppressed religion ... with servile burdens, that the condition of the Jews was more tolerable, 2 *Bul.* 126, 1 *Jew.* 138, 2 *Jew.* 992, 3 *Jew.* 570, 4 *Jew.* 797, *Lit. Edw.* 198, 3 *Tyn.* 74, *Whita.* 607, 2 *Whitg.* 577; this passage not noticed in the very copious index of the Benedictine editors, 3 *Tyn.* 74 n.; he is grieved that many things wholesomely commanded in the holy scriptures are not regarded, and that all things are full of presumptions, *Calf.* 268, 3 *Jew.* 569, 571; advises Januarius to conform to the customs of the church where he comes, they being not contrary to faith and good manners, 4 *Bul.* 58, 504, 3 *Jew.* 285, 1 *Whitg.* 236; says that in matters not determined by scripture, custom must be taken for law, 1 *Jew.* 254; commends whatever tends to the increase of faith or charity, *Grin.* 29; allows that changes may be made in respect of times, &c., 2 *Brad.* 389, *Calf.* 196; would have ceremonies whose causes are doubtful, cut away, 1 *Jew.* 509, 2 *Jew.* 589, 3 *Jew.* 570, 1 *Whitg.* 238, 241; speaks of holy bread given to catechumens, and calls it a sacrament, 1 *Cran.* 180, 3 *Jew.* 458, *Rid.* 30; asks what else is imposition of hands but prayer over a man? *Calf.* 215; on the ceremony of washing the feet, 1 *Jew.* 223, 225; calls it a sacrament, 3 *Jew.* 458; says his mother left bringing wine and cakes to the church not because it was ungodly or unlawful, but because it resembled the superstition of the heathen, 3 *Jew.* 616; speaks of some vowing oil and wax for the lights at night, *ib.* 178

xvii. *Prayer, Praise, Worship*: he mentions the opinion of Socrates that every god should be worshipped according to his own commandment, *Calf.* 34, 3 *Jew.* 553, *Sand.* 87; calls prayer a help to him that prayeth, a sacrifice to God, a scourge to the devils, *Sand.* 263; observes that if Stephen had not prayed, Paul had not been converted, 3 *Jew.* 556, 1 *Lat.* 338 n.; says that God is to be sought and prayed unto in the secret places of a reasonable soul, 1 *Bec.* 133, 134, 3 *Bec.* 407; declares that one about to pray should prepare a secret place in the peace of his heart, 1 *Bec.* 159; admonishes to ask in prayer of none but the Lord God, *ib.* 167; says we must think it no great thing to be heard at our will, but for our profit, *ib.*; declares that the prayer which is not made by Christ is very sin, 1 *Bec.* 149, 2 *Bec.* 135, 3 *Bec.* 356; asserts that the prayer of an envious man is put away from the ears of God, 1 *Bec.* 138; says that prayer without devotion is as the bellowing of oxen, *ib.* 163, 164; states that there is nothing which the Lord's prayer does not comprehend, 4 *Bul.* 203, 2 *Whitg.* 469, 486; on the petition "deliver us from evil," 2 *Whitg.* 484; he does not mention the doxology to the Lord's prayer, 4 *Bul.* 220; says that in some prayers of his time there were many things contrary to the catholic faith, 1 *Jew.* 316; allows that prayers which have something heretical in them may yet be profitable to those who recite them in simplicity, *Whita.* 265; says, I have a sacrifice within, with which I may persuade my God, 4 *Jew.* 1047; shews how we must ask for bodily health, 2 *Whitg.* 474; he prayed for tribulation in this world, that he might be spared hereafter, 3 *Bec.* 104; he says the souls of the dead are relieved by the devotion of the living, (see xv. (h), and xxv.); calls fasting and alms the two wings of prayer, 1 *Bec.* 163, 4 *Bul.* 179; shews that we may pray standing, kneeling, sitting, or lying, 4 *Bul.* 185, 186; distinguishes between praying much and babbling much, *ib.* 205; shews that words are needful to us, but not to God, *ib.* 204, and that there is no need of voice in prayer, except in public, 1 *Jew.* 57, 284, 285, *Whita.* 271; says we should pray with intelligence, not as birds utter sounds which they have been taught, but do not understand, 1 *Jew.* 8, 282, 283, 330, *Whita.* 272; (as to the use of unknown tongues, see the next division); on the use of "Amen," 1 *Jew.* 312, 317; exhorts men to understand the joyful sound, *Whita.* 272; shews that we should sing with understanding and with the heart, 4 *Jew.* 812; he (or rather Basil) asks, how can he sing duly unto God, who knows not what he sings? 1 *Jew.* 333; (the same) on singing the psalms, *ib.* 332; (the same) says the psalms were made for young men and children to sing, *ib.* 332; says, we sing one psalm, and answer one Amen, *ib.* 286; inculcates the offering of the sacrifice of praise to God, 1 *Bec.* 186; calls it the sacrifice of the new testament, 2 *Jew.* 735; on blessing the Lord at all times, *Calf.* 250; he desired that over melodious tunes might be removed from his ears and from the church, and approved the mode of singing prescribed by Athanasius, 4 *Bul.* 194; mentions that Ambrose ordained singing after the manner of the East, *ib.* 195; describes the singing in the church of Milan, 1 *Jew.* 265; on giving thanks "with the spirit," *ib.* 313; repeatedly speaks of the reading of the gospel, and the lesson, 4 *Jew.* 857; says, behold God's emmet; she riseth daily, goeth to the church of God, prayeth, heareth the lesson, singeth the hymn, &c., *ib.* 858; (as to temples, see iv. and xii. above)

Prayers taken or adapted from his writings, or ascribed to him: (præcatio) pœnitentis et divinam misericordiam implorantis, *Pra. Eliz.* 373; the same in English, with the title, a prayer in commendation of God's mercy received, *ib.* 501; pro tollenda morum pravitate, et vita melius instituenda, *ib.* 380; the same in English, *ib.* 438; viri fidelis oratio de se humiliter sentientis, *ib.* 381; oratio afflicti in tribulatione, *ib.* 382; oratio, qua nos Deo commendamus, et gratiam ab eo poscimus, *ib.* 383; de vitæ hujus miseriis querela, *ib.* 395; a prayer to God the Father, in Jesus Christ, our Redeemer, *ib.* 453; a prayer for forgiveness of sins, ascribed to him, *ib.* 494; a complaint of a sinner, in that he sinneth again after repentance, *ib.* 503; a prayer for continuance in seeking after Christ, *ib.* 528; the fear of the Judge and the judgment day (a prayer), *ib.* 557; one of his prayers turned into Latin verse by Walter Haddon, *ib.* 382 n.

xviii. *Tongues:* on the division of languages (Gen. xi), *Whita.* 112, 378; he asks, what profits the integrity of speech, if the hearer's understanding follows not? 4 *Jew.* 810, 811; other like passages, *ib.* 811; observes that we hear these words, "vita beata," and the thing itself we all confess ourselves to long for; but we have no pleasure in the sound, &c., *ib.* 813; says no man is edified by hearing what he understands not, *ib.* 858, *Whita.* 265; remarks that a man would rather dwell with his dog than with a man of an unknown tongue, 4 *Jew.* 768; says the diversity of tongues is no schism, *ib.* 814; "Astitit regina a dextris tuis in vestitu deaurato, circundata varietate" (Psalm xlv. 9); this he expounds of the variety of tongues in all nations, *ib.*; a spurious treatise quoted by Eckius with reference to the three holy tongues, 3 *Bec.* 410 n.; he maintains that the original tongue was Hebrew, *Whita.* 113; on the employment of an unusual Greek word by Cresconius, 1 *Ful.* 589; he remarks that the imperial city imposed not only her yoke but her language on the vanquished nations, *Whita.* 225; passages from his works shewing that Latin was commonly spoken in his time in Africa, *ib.* 224, 225; he says, now I will speak Latin, that all may understand, 1 *Jew.* 56, 296; he often spoke words that were not good Latin, that he might be the better understood, *ib.* 295, *Whita.* 224; he would (e. g.) call a bone "ossum" to avoid the ambiguity of "os," 1 *Brad.* 562; on the Punic tongue, 1 *Jew.* 294; he states that the eucharist was in that tongue called "life," and baptism, "health," 1 *Jew.* 294, 3 *Jew.* 482 n.; other remarks on the Latin and Punic tongues, *ib.* 268, 296, 297; on speaking with tongues, *ib.* 313

xix. *Miracles:* he says that when it pleased God, even Balaam's dumb ass spake reasonably; yet men are not commanded in their doubts to seek counsel of an ass, 4 *Jew.* 943; addresses Faustus, ye work no miracles, and if ye did, at your hands we would take heed of them, *Calf.* 319, 2 *Cran.* 46, 3 *Brad.* 197; he would not receive a thing as true on account of miracles, seeing that they might be the feigned devices of lying men, or the wonders of deceitful spirits, *Calf.* 333, 2 *Cran.* 47, 4 *Jew.* 1040; cautions against miracle mongers, seeing that in the last days there shall rise up false prophets, 4 *Jew.* 662, 1041; on the lying wonders which shall be wrought by Antichrist, 2 *Cran.* 46; whoever (says he) now requires prodigies that he may believe is himself a great prodigy, 4 *Jew.* 1041; he observes that although the blind flesh does not open its eyes by a miracle of the Lord, yet the blind heart opens its eyes by the word of the Lord, *ib.*; a similar passage as to the ears, *ib.*; still he asserts that there were miracles in the church in his time, referring particularly to the case of a blind man restored to sight at Milan, 2 *Cran.* 48; mentions a woman named Innocentia who was healed by the sign of the cross, 2 *Ful.* 157

xx. *Festivals and Fasts*: on St Paul's reproof for observing days (Gal. iv.), 2 *Whitg.* 594; he says that the day of the Lord's nativity is not to be celebrated in a sacrament (or figure), but it is only to be called to memory that he was born, *ib.* 577; on the institution of the great yearly solemnities, viz. those of the passion, resurrection, ascension, and descent of the Spirit, 1 *Whitg.* 230, 2 *Whitg.* 592; he shews in what sense Easter is the time of the Lord's passion, &c., 2 *Bec.* 283, 3 *Bec.* 440; judges that Easter is authorized by scripture, 2 *Whitg.* 568; nevertheless he says, Christ rises to thee every day, 2 *Jew.* 733; quotes Seneca respecting the sabbath of the Jews, 1 *Hoop.* 346; speaks of it as a type of eternal rest, *ib.* 339; says that of all the ten commandments only that concerning the sabbath is to be taken figuratively, 2 *Bul.* 255, 2 *Cran.* 61, and affirms that we are not commanded to keep the day according to the letter, but spiritually, 2 *Cran.* 102; condemns those who when they hear of the sabbath, understand nothing thereby but one day in the seven, 1 *Bul.* 287; distinguishes the sabbath and the Lord's day, and thinks that fasting is not positively unlawful on either, though very inexpedient on the latter, *Whita.* 573, 1 *Whitg.* 228, 229; ascribes the institution of the Lord's day to apostles and apostolic men, and says that the doctors of the church transferred to it all the glory of the Jewish sabbath, 2 *Brad.* 391 n.; mentions but few saints' days, 1 *Hoop.* 347; he recommends the taming and mortifying of the flesh, 2 *Bec.* 544; shews the necessity of fasting for that purpose, *ib.*; allows that days of fasting are not limited by our Lord or his apostles, 3 *Jew.* 438; says the apostles determined nothing concerning fasting, *Whita.* 665; observes, it is written that we ought to fast, but not on what days we should fast, *Pil.* 558; mentions fasting between Easter and Whitsuntide as unlawful, 3 *Jew.* 436; speaks of the contention about a certain fast as interminable, &c., *Calf.* 262; applies to Ambrose respecting different local customs of fasting, *Pil.* 557; mentions that in the Lent season most men abstained not only from flesh, but also from certain fruits, 3 *Jew.* 438; says, I ask not what thou eatest, but what thou likest, *ib.* 170; says, in our fasting nothing is better than this, that he who eateth not despise not him who eateth, 4 *Jew.* 1142; maintains that the fasts of Christian men are to be observed spiritually rather than carnally, 1 *Bec.* 105, 106, 2 *Bec.* 540; shews that the great and general fast is to abstain from iniquities and unlawful pleasures of the world, 1 *Bec.* 106, 2 *Bec.* 540; declares it of no profit to pass a whole day in fasting, if afterward the soul be oppressed with superfluity of meats, 2 *Bec.* 535; recommends that what is not eaten on fasting-days be bestowed on the poor, *ib.* 546; remarks that mercy commended the prayer and fasting of Cornelius, who fed those that wanted, *ib.*

xxi. *Marriage, &c.*: he wrote a work in defence of marriage, 1 *Jew.* 157; affirms that it is holy, 4 *Jew.* 804; calls it a sacrament, 1 *Ful.* 492; speaks of the band of marriage, and the sacrament of marriage, 3 *Jew.* 457; speaks of marriage as chastity, &c., 1 *Bul.* 402; compares Abraham with John Baptist in respect of marriage, *Pil.* 575, 576, *Sand.* 322; observes that holy Samuel begat children, and Zachariah, 3 *Jew.* 416; on the chastity of John, and that of Peter, *Park.* 159; he affirms that sometimes chastity is good, sometimes marriage, 3 *Jew.* 415; says it is the special gift of God that men will and are able to live continently, 1 *Ful.* 389; on the text "a sister, a wife," (1 Cor. ix. 5) arguing that the latter word should be rendered "woman," *ib.* 471 n.; on a bishop being "the husband of one wife," *Whita.* 455; shews that a Christian wife is holy, 3 *Jew.* 405, 416; recounts the behaviour as a wife of his mother Monica, 2 *Bec.* 344 n.; says Paul would dissuade from marriage, not as from a thing bad and unlawful in itself, but as from a thing burdensome and troublesome, 3 *Jew.* 389; declares that men had better marry than burn, *ib.* 400, 421; charges the Manichees with forbidding marriage, as Paul foretold, 2 *Jew.* 1129, 3 *Jew.* 158, 420, 4 *Jew.* 642, *Rog.* 261 n.; writes, he forbids marriage who says it is an evil thing, not he who prefers what is better, 3 *Jew.* 418, 420; relates that the Hieracites admitted to their communion none but single persons, *Rog.* 306 n.; mentions that the Cathari did not allow second marriages, *Rog.* 262 n., 307 n.; declares lapse from a vow of chastity to be worse than adultery, 3 *Jew.* 386, 401, yet he rejects the opinion that the marriage of such persons is no marriage, but rather adultery, 4 *Bul.* 513, 3 *Jew.* 401, 4 *Jew.* 640, 788, and maintains that they sin grievously who put such persons asunder, 3 *Jew.* 399, 4 *Jew.* 642, 786, 797; denies that such persons are to be condemned for marrying, but for that they have violated their first faith, (or promise of continency), 4 *Bul.* 513, 3 *Jew.* 402; remarks on some who have made vows of celibacy, 3 *Jew.* 400; he requires the mother's consent to be asked for a damsel's marriage, *Sand.* 326: shews that the judicial law of Moses is not in force with reference to adultery, 1 *Whitg.* 273; says that concubinage was without sin under the old law, 2 *Cran.* 405; writes, although men have no wives, yet it is not lawful for them to have concubines, whom they may afterward put away, 4 *Jew.* 633; denies any distinction between concubine and harlot, *ib.*; his book De Ordine, (written before his conversion) cited by Harding in favour of the allowance of harlots, 3 *Jew.* 157, 4 *Jew.* 643, 645; he says, the worldly city has made the filthiness of harlots lawful, 4 *Jew.* 645, (see also vii. above.)

xxii. *Confession, Penance, Absolution, Excommunication*: he shews why God requires confession, 3 *Jew.* 369; asks, what have I to do with men, that they should hear my confessions, as if they could heal my griefs? and speaks of a sort of men curious in searching out the life of others, and slothful in correcting their own, 2 *Jew.* 1134, 3 *Jew.* 359, 4 *Jew.* 976; shews that Peter's penitence was not ecclesiastical penance, 1 *Ful.* 438; on penance (or repentance) before and after baptism, and the daily penance of all believers, *ib.* 436—488; he exhorts sinners to do penance, as it is done in the church, that the church may pray for them, &c., 3 *Jew.* 356, 361; advises one to make satisfaction by public penance, that he may be received into communion, having been reconciled by the judgment of the priest, *ib.* 360, 374; says that forasmuch as for the most part the grief of one man's heart is unknown to another,... it is very well that by those that have the oversight of the church, certain times of penance are appointed, that the congregation may be satisfied, *ib.* 374; applauds the provision that open penance in the church should be done but once, *ib.* 354; speaks of the more grievous penance, whereby penitents were suspended from the eucharist, 1 *Ful.* 431; refers to false penitents, 2 *Jew.* 1068; says the fruit worthy of penance is to lament past sins, and not to do them again, 1 *Bec.* 93; (see passages on repentance and restitution in viii. above); approves moderation in discipline, 4 *Bul.* 508, but accounts it sometimes mercy to punish, and cruelty to spare, *Sand.* 148, 1 *Zur.* 261 n.; says, the will of the priest can neither further nor hinder, but the merit of him that desires absolution, 3 *Jew.* 381; declares that the priests do not forgive sin, but the Holy Ghost through them, 2 *Bec.* 174; seems to ascribe binding and loosing to all Christian people, 3 *Whitg.* 258; says that the church received the keys from Christ, i.e. the power of binding and loosing, *Whita.* 425; shews what binding and loosing is, 3 *Jew.* 356; calls excommunication the condemnation of episcopal judgment, than which there is in the church no greater punishment, *ib.*; speaks of excommunication by the bishop and the whole church, 3 *Whitg.* 256, 257; shews that none should be excommunicated unless convicted, *ib.* 263; thinks excommunication altogether in vain, where the infection is general, *ib.* 259; asks, what is a man harmed if human ignorance strike him out of the table (of the church), unless an evil conscience blot him out of the book of the living, 4 *Jew.* 650, 890

xxiii. *Affliction, Persecution* (see ix. and xii.): he tells why God hath filled the world with calamities, 1 *Cov.* 141; admonishes that we (like Job) should think adversity to be from God, 2 *Cran.* 107, not from the devil, *ib.*; says that sufferings are no proof of righteousness, *Sand.* 378; shews that the godly are afflicted that they may seek help, and ultimately that they may praise God, 1 *Cov.* 128; describes the different effects of affliction on the righteous and on the wicked, 2 *Bul.* 75—79; speaks of the wicked conspiring against the just, not because they love one another, 4 *Jew.* 956; says the false prophets were not persecuted by Elijah, as he was by the wicked king, 3 *Jew.* 183; enumerates ten persecutions of the church, 2 *Bul.* 105; mentions a common proverb that rain fails because of Christians, 3 *Jew.* 214; compares the blood of Christians to the seed of gospel fruits, 1 *Lat.* 361; shews that the oppressed suffer for a time, but that the oppressor heaps up for himself wrath against the day of wrath, *Pil.* 474.

xxiv. *The Soul* (see xxv.): he doubts whether souls are created, or whence they come, 3 *Bul.* 374; confesses that he cannot name the substance of the soul, *ib.* 372; argues that the soul is incorporeal, *ib.* 369—371; says that only man has a substantial soul, living after the body, *ib.* 385; denies that there are two souls in man, as Jacobus and certain Syrians affirmed, *ib.* 367; on the operations and powers of the soul, *ib.* 377, 378; tells of a man who lay in a trance seven days, 1 *Lat.* 539; on the knowledge of souls departed with regard to what they do who are alive, 2 *Cov.* 218; he judges that the spirit raised by the witch of Endor, was not the soul of Samuel, but the devil in his likeness, 2 *Cran.* 45; shews that the soul is mortal, and that its death was its revolt from God in paradise, 3 *Bul.* 381, 2 *Cov.* 201; says the soul has its death when it lacks a blessed life, and shews that (in another sense) it is immortal, 3 *Bul.* 381

xxv. *Death, Judgment, Heaven, Hell; also Burial, Purgatory, Resurrection, &c.*: he prefers a good life to a long life, 2 *Cov.* 129; thinks death rather to be chosen than a repetition of life, 1 *Brad.* 337; on looking for death, *Sand.* 173 n. (and 171); he affirms that he cannot die ill who has lived well, *Grin.* 30, *Sand.* 173; speaks of corruption and worms as the dishonour of man's state, 1 *Tyn.* 159 n.; says that in what state every man shall be found the last day of his life, so shall he be taken the last day of the world, 3 *Bec.* 460, *Grin.* 5, 3 *Jew.* 568, *Sand.* 162, and that the day of the Lord shall find him unprovided, whom the last day of this life finds unprovided, 3 *Jew.* 568; as our Lord finds a man when he calls him hence, even so he judges him, 3 *Jew.* 568; says the bodies of the dead, specially of the faithful, are not to be despised or cast away, 3 *Bec.* 125; on the causes of solemnizing funerals, *Sand.* 161, 162; declares that funeral rites are rather the comforts of the living than the helps of the dead, 3 *Bec.* 125, 462, *Lit. Eliz.* 431, *Pil.* 320, *Sand.* 162, 3 *Tyn.* 272; passages on hell (inferi), particularly as the abode of Abraham, &c. before Christ's death, 1 *Ful.* 289—295; what the term inferi means, *ib.* 298, 309; he says whatever separates brethren is to be called infernus, *ib.* 299; on the lower hell, *ib.*; his doctrine concerning memorials for the dead, 2 *Cov.* 270; he erred respecting prayer for the dead, 3 *Bul.* 398, affirming that prayers for their souls are not to be neglected, *ib.*; he declares, that it is not to be denied that the souls of the departed (faithful) are benefited by the sacrifice and alms of survivors, 2 *Jew.* 750, 752; he condemns Aerius and the Arians for denying its efficacy, 3 *Jew.* 564; (see also xv. (h) above); Augustine (or Chrysostom?) on mourning apparel, 3 *Whitg.* 369, 370; he (or Eligius?) declares that when the soul is separated from the body it is immediately placed in paradise for its good deserts, or cast into hell for sin, 2 *Bec.* 277, 2 *Lat.* 247; teaches that since the ascension of our Lord the souls of saints go straightways to heaven, and of sinners to hell (pseud.), 2 *Bec.* 394, 3 *Bec.* 460; states his belief in heaven and hell, but declares himself utterly ignorant of a third place, not finding it in the holy scriptures (pseud.), 2 *Bec.* 394, 3 *Bec.* 461, 1 *Ful.* 278, 2 *Ful.* 241, 293, 3 *Jew.* 564, 567, *Phil.* 415; he (or Cæsarius?) affirms that there are two places, and a third is not seen; he who has not deserved to reign with Christ shall doubtless perish with the devil, 3 *Bec.* 277, 2 *Lat.* 246; asserts that there are two dwelling-places, one in fire, the other in the eternal kingdom, 2 *Bec.* 394, 3 *Bec.* 461; declares that there is no other place to correct our manners but only in this life, 3 *Bec.* 461, 462; tells that the souls of the godly are in rest, while those of the ungodly suffer punishment, *ib.* 462; says, some will have no punishments after death but the pains of purgatory, 3 *Jew.* 560; again he says, some suffer pains temporal in this life only, some after death, some both now and also then, yet before that most severe and last judgment, 3 *Jew.* 564; a supposititious sentence ascribed by Gratian to Augustine respecting purgatory, 2 *Ful.* 240; he doubted of it, 2 *Ful.* 240, 241, 3 *Jew.* 563—568, 1 *Tyn.* 269 n.; he says, for example, that some such thing after this life is not incredible, but it is questionable whether it be or not, 3 *Jew.* 565; again, that the spirits of the dead find a fire of transitory tribulation I do not disprove, for perhaps it is true, *ib.*; another passage expressive of doubt, *ib.*; he speaks of the Arabici, who affirmed that souls are dissolved with bodies, and raised again at the end, 4 *Jew.* 930, 932, 935, 937; says, every one sleeps with his own cause, and with his own cause shall rise again, 2 *Bec.* 395, 3 *Bec.* 460, 1 *Hoop.* 571, 3 *Jew.* 568; declares that as all who die, die no otherwise than in Adam, so all who are made alive (in the resurrection) are made alive in Christ, 4 *Bul.* 374; his mind concerning the resurrection of the flesh, 2 *Cov.* 192—194; he maintains the resurrection of the same body, 1 *Bul.* 169, 2 *Cov.* 169; yet declares that our resurrection shall not be carnally, 2 *Cov.* 192, 193, 1 *Cran.* 139; in what sense our bodies will be spiritual after the resurrection, 2 *Cov.* 182, 193, 194; on errors concerning the resurrection of the body, *ib.* 183; on the glory of the bodies of the righteous after the resurrection, *ib.* 179; he cannot tell what their action, rest, and ease will be, *ib.* 213; declares that the saints in the spiritual body shall see God, 1 *Bul.* 179, 2 *Cov.* 215; Augustine (rather Fulgentius) on the resurrection of the ungodly, 2 *Cov.* 200; he says that whosoever in this life shall not please God, shall in the world to come have repentance for his sins, but pardon in the sight of God he shall not find, because, although there will be the sting of repentance, yet there shall be no amendment of the will, 3 *Jew.* 568; supposes "the uttermost farthing" to mean that punishment which is called eternal, *ib.* 563; shews that living bodies may continue in hell-fire, 2 *Cov.* 204; refutes those who deny punishment to be everlasting, *ib.* 208; says, none can tell the nature of the fire there, unless God shew him, 2 *Lat.* 236, 361; on Psalm lxxiii. 20, he affirms that God will bring their image to nought in his (celestial) city, who have brought his image to nought in his earthly city, *Calf.* 164

xxvi. *Images, the Cross:* he cautions against the love of visible things in religion, *Calf.* 41; shews that whatever the soul serves as God, must needs be better than herself, and thence argues that we may not worship the earth, the sun, the stars, &c., 3 *Bul.* 229, 230; speaks against images, 1 *Hoop.* 47; cautions against the worship of man's handy-work, observing that better are the workmen themselves, 3 *Bul.* 202, 203, *Calf.* 378; shews that worship (latria) is not to be given to angels nor men, much less to stones, 1 *Hoop.* 320; says, Jacob did not erect the anointed stone to adore it, 1 *Jew.* 551; commends king Hezekiah for destroying the brazen serpent, 1 *Ful.* 183; mentions various evil consequences of images, *Calf.* 43; cites Varro as saying that the Romans worshipped for more than 170 years without any, 1 *Bul.* 201, 202, 1 *Hoop.* 319, and approves his opinion that religion might be more purely observed without them, *Calf.* 43, 2 *Ful.* 127, 1 *Hoop.* 319, *Park.* 86, *Rid.* 89, likewise his saying that they who first erected the images of gods took away fear, and increased error, 1 *Hoop.* 319, 2 *Jew.* 659; cites his statement that the knowledge of the gods were useful, if a man knew what power and authority each god had in every thing, for thus, he said, we should be able to know what god to call upon and whom to pray to, 3 *Jew.* 576; shews why scripture so frequently reminds us that images have mouths and speak not, &c., 2 *Jew.* 665, *Park.* 87, *Rid.* 89; disallows images amongst Christians, 2 *Ful.* 128; calls it a detestable thing to place a likeness of God in a Christian temple, much more in the heart, 1 *Bul.* 150, 151, *Calf.* 42, 2 *Cran.* 101, *Hutch.* 24, 2 *Jew.* 644, 4 *Jew.* 794; says, they deserved to err who sought Christ and his apostles not in holy books, but in painted walls, *Calf.* 188, 4 *Jew.* 792; speaks of certain heretics who favoured images, 2 *Jew.* 646; mentions Marcellina, a follower of the Carpocratian sect, as worshipping images of Jesus, Paul, Homer, and Pythagoras, 1 *Bul.* 229, 2 *Jew.* 667, 4 *Jew.* 950; says, that images are of more force to crook an unhappy soul than to straighten and amend it, *Calf.* 187, 188, *Park.* 87, *Rid.* 89; states how the heathen defend image-worship, and shews it to be idolatry, *Calf.* 185—187, 1 *Hoop.* 319; says, let no man tell me, it is not a god, 2 *Jew.* 667, 4 *Jew.* 950; shews that temples, idols, groves, &c. should not be converted to private use, 2 *Whitg.* 31, 54; his use of the word "simulacrum,'" 1 *Ful.* 103; distinguishes δουλεία from λατρεία, *ib.* 258 n., but he is no authority in Greek, *ib.* 260; thinks that the two sticks gathered by the widow of Sarepta prefigured the cross, 2 *Ful.* 146; says, Christ has left us the cross in remembrance of his passion, &c., *Calf.* 185; refers the height, length, and depth of the love of Christ (Eph. iii.) to hope, patience, and humility, and to the figure of the cross, *ib.* 205; says, let me not have a naked forehead; let the cross of Christ my Lord cover it, *ib.* 75, 76; again, thou must be marked in thy forehead with the sign of the passion and cross, &c. *ib.* 224; shews that the cross was honoured by the Romans when they became Christians, 2 *Ful.* 202; speaks of catechumens as signing themselves with the cross, 2 *Jew.* 706; cited as saying that no sacrament is solemnly done without the cross, *Calf.* 206, 234; a spurious book in his name says, that by the mystery of the cross churches are dedicated, the ignorant instructed, the font hallowed, &c. *ib.* 184, 204, 207; on resisting the enemy with the sacrament of the symbol (or creed) and the banner of the cross (pseud.), *ib.* 84

xxvii. *Heresies:* he speaks of the kingdom of ignorance, i. e. the kingdom of error, 2 *Jew.* 800; he fled from what was proved to be error, 4 *Jew.* 876; his alleged saying, I may err, but will not be a heretic, 3 *Jew.* 210, *Pil.* 620, 1 *Whitg.* 8, 2 *Whitg.* 539; 3 *Whitg.* 460; he remarks that heresy is very hard to be defined, 3 *Jew.* 211; says, they are heretics who, in the church of Christ, savour anything corrupt, and stubbornly resist when admonished, *ib.* 210; declares him to be a heretic who for the sake of any temporal good, especially of vain-glory and pre-eminence, breeds or follows false and new opinions, *Bale* 218, 1 *Brad.* 539, *Rid.* 155, 2 *Hoop.* 540; refers to the fact that Jesus Christ the righteous is our advocate and propitiation, and adds, he that held this never made heresy, or schism; whence then come schisms? when men say, We are righteous, we sanctify the unclean, we justify the wicked, &c. 3 *Jew.* 380, 4 *Jew.* 852; says, all heretics abused those words of our Lord, "I have yet many things to say unto you," 1 *Jew.* 125, 3 *Jew.* 439, *Whita.* 544; reckons up at least eighty-eight heresies, 1 *Jew.* 334 n., 2. *Jew.* 687 n., 3 *Jew.* 603; on the difference between heretics and schismatics, 4 *Bul.*

63; declares it to be the property of error to suppose that what displeases one's-self, is displeasing to God, 1 *Jew.* 100 n.; says of some, whatever they love they will have to be the truth, 4 *Jew.* 740; imagines certain heretics as saying, What we will is holy, &c. 3 *Whitg.* 593; describes the practices of schismatics, 4 *Bul.* 60, 61; writes, none would make schisms if they were not blinded with hatred of their brethren, 1 *Whitg.* 7; on leaders of sects, *ib.* 136; rejoices on heretics being delivered from their old errors, 2 *Bec.* 316; says, far be it from us to compel any man to our religion, 1 *Bul.* 364, but elsewhere he allows the persecution of heretics, *Hutch.* 329 (see xxix. below); affirms that those who are not willing, should be forced to the truth, *Phil.* 105; would have heretics both taught and terrified, 3 *Whitg.* 528; but he says it pleases no good men in the catholic church for any one thought a heretic to be killed, 2. *Bec.* 317, 4 *Jew.* 770; prescribes in respect of heretics to love the men but kill the errors, 2 *Bec.* 316; would have them killed with the two-edged sword (the holy word); killed unto themselves, that they might live unto God, 4 *Jew.* 770, 771; says he once thought that heretics should not be compelled to the unity of Christ, but that the case of his own city (Hippo) changed his mind, 1 *Bul.* 365; his opinions on compulsion in matters of religion, at length, *ib.* 366—369; holds that whatever good we meet with in any heresy is not to be rejected, 1 *Zur.* 158; writes of certain heretics who affirmed that whosoever had received the Lord's supper could not be damned, 1 *Hoop.* 161; says heretics turn upside down, by allegories, whatever is contained in the Bible against their errors, *Phil.* 426; derides certain carnal heretics, 1 *Jew.* 463; his words to a heretic named Emeritus, 4 *Jew.* 703; speaks of the Adamites, 2 *Brad.* 385 n.; his account of Aërius, 2 *Brad.* 381 n., 3 *Bul.* 399, 2 *Whitg.* 292; he condemns the Angelici, 3 *Bul.* 348, 2 *Ful.* 42 n., *Phil.* 420 n.; speaks of the Anthropomorphites, whom he calls Vadiani, 1 *Hoop.* 160 n.; refutes their heresy, 1 *Bul.* 225, 3 *Bul.* 138; describes the heresy of Apollinarius, 3 *Bul.* 260; speaks of the Apostolics, 2 *Brad.* 381 n., 2 *Bul.* 24, *Phil.* 420 n.; mentions the Arabici, who affirmed that souls are dissolved with bodies, and raised again at the end, 4 *Jew.* 930, 932, 935, 937; on the Arians, *Rog.* 72; tells how they called themselves catholics, 4 *Jew.* 713, and termed the orthodox Homoüsians, 1 *Jew.* 465; on Carpocrates, *Rog.* 154 n. (as to the idolatry of his sect, see xxvi. above); as to the Cathari, see p. 79, col. 1; on the heresy of the Cerdonians, *Whita.* 31; he describes the errors of the Cerinthians, 2 *Jew.* 566 n.; on the Circumcellions, *Rog.* 77, 118, 3 *Whitg.* 57; writing of the Donatists, he shews that some of them were Arians, and some Circumcellions, 1 *Whitg.* 113; speaks of their error on free-will, *Rog.* 106; declares that they not only said they were just, but even the justifiers of men, *ib.* 135; mentions their opinion that the church remained only in Africa, 3 *Jew.* 151, *Rog.* 171, and their notion of its purity, *Rog.* 167; censures them as worse than the Jews who persecuted the flesh of Christ walking on earth, seeing that they persecuted the gospel of Christ sitting in heaven, 3 *Jew.* 183; records that they brake the altar-boards, *ib.* 602; says, that in an assembly they laboured that nothing should be done, *ib.* 209; that they said to him, Dispute we will not, but baptize we will, 4 *Jew.* 898, and that they subscribed their articles with the names of the dead, 1 *Jew.* 184; speaks of their complaining of persecution, 2 *Brad.* 379; he maintains, by the example of Nebuchadnezzar, that Christian princes rightly punished them, 1 *Bul.* 358; he reproves Cresconius the Donatist, 3 *Jew.* 315; his saying to Tyconius the Donatist, 1 *Ful.* 147 (as to this sect, see also p. 69, col. 1, 2, p. 71, col. 1, and xxix. below); he speaks of the Ebionites, 2 *Jew.* 566 n.; on the opinions of Eutyches, 2 *Cov.* 348 n., 1 *Cran.* 293; he says the Helvidians supposed that Mary had other children besides our Lord, 4 *Bul.* 437 n.; writes of the Heracleonites, *Phil.* 424 n.; as to the Hieracites, see p. 79, col. 1; on the heresy of Jovinian, 2 *Bul.* 407; he copiously refutes the Manichees, *Whita.* 31; his account of their founder Manes, *Phil.* 421 n.; says he had twelve disciples, *ib.* 422 n.; mentions that he was said to be the Paraclete, 4 *Jew.* 843 n.; speaks of the Manichean opinion that there were two gods, one good, one evil, *Rog.* 37, and that the world was made by the latter, *ib.* 41; refers to their notion that the princes of darkness held fast the light lest it should flee from them, 4 *Jew.* 870; mentions their error that Christ suffered and died only in appearance, *Rog.* 51, and that in fact demons suffered, *ib.* 57; records their false doctrine with respect to original sin, *ib.* 99; their error as to men being driven to sin, *ib.* 105; and their denial of the resurrection of the body, *ib.* 64, 145; says they denied many things in the holy scriptures, *Rog.* 80, 3 *Jew.* 158 n., ascribed the Law of Moses to the prince of darkness, *Rog.* 92, and rejected the Acts, *ib.* 84; says they read apocryphal scriptures, written by cobblers of fables under the name of the apostles, 1 *Jew.* 113, 2 *Jew.* 894, 3 *Jew.* 442; says they commended the sacrament of bread and the cup, 1 *Jew.* 258; on their profanation of that sacrament, *Rog.* 295 n.; he says, they bore a countenance of continent life and notable chastity, 4 *Jew.* 767; on their pretended fasting, 3 *Jew.* 159; he says they that among them are called auditores eat flesh, till the ground, and, if they will, marry, none of which they do who are called electi, 3 *Jew.* 419, *Rog.* 303 n.; maintains, against this heresy, that Christians may possess property, *Rog.* 353 n.; intimates that they gave no alms to men not of their sect, *ib.* 355 n.; records their saying that it should not be inquired what men professed their sect, but what was the profession, 4 *Jew.* 940; mentions their notion that herbs and trees live, understand, and feel pain when they are hurt; and that (for a similar reason) they ate no eggs, 3 *Jew.* 511; says, thus the Manichees rave, but let them repent and be not Manichees, *ib.* 624; his prayer for them, *Pil.* 510; he says to them, let them persecute you who know not with what labour the truth is found, and how hardly errors are avoided, 4 *Jew.* 1075; against Faustus the Manichee, 1 *Jew.* 461; his saying to this man, 1 *Ful.* 146, 147 (as to this sect, see also v. (*a*), xxi. and xxix.); on the idleness of the Messalians, 1 *Jew.* 193; on the (Montanist or) Cataphrygian heresy, *Phil.* 421 n.; he mentions their assertion that Paul knew in part, &c. for the perfection (which was in Montanus) was not yet come, 4 *Jew.* 760; says Nestorius taught that Christ was man only (pseud.), 1 *Cran.* 293; on the Passalorynchites, *Phil.* 421 n.; on the Patripassians, *Rog.* 57; his controversy with Pelagius and his sect, 3 *Bul.* 11, 2 *Cov.* 387, 388, &c., 2 *Hoop.* 73 n., and with Celestius his partner, 2 *Bul.* 386, 2 *Cov.* 387; he describes the errors of the Pelagians respecting original sin, 2 *Bul.* 386, and reproves them for affirming that the righteous are utterly without sin, 2 *Cov.* 387; their errors on original sin, *Rog.* 99, on baptism, see pp. 69, 70, on free-will, *Rog.* 105; he cites fathers against Julian the Pelagian, 3 *Jew.* 230; tells him that his pride is fain to cover itself with sorry clouts, 4 *Jew.* 850; as to the Petilianites, see p. 69, col. 1; Petilian their leader is named p. 54, col. 2; on the Priscillianists, *Rog.* 119 n.; he tells that they supposed the members of man's body to be governed by the twelve signs, 2 *Bul.* 363; on the Rhetorians, *Rog.* 161; on the heresy of the Timotheans, 2 *Jew.* 566; his opinion of the ancient Traditors, 1 *Tyn.* 144 n.; he tells how pagans are to be won, 2 *Whitg.* 32, 34

xxviii. *Antichrist*: on St Paul's allusion to that which delayed the coming of Antichrist, *Whita.* 553, 554; he considers that it was the Roman empire, 2 *Jew.* 913; calls Antichrist, the prince, and the last Antichrist, 2 *Ful.* 367; says false miracles shall attend his presence, 2 *Cran.* 46; maintains that he shall subdue all kings, and obtain the kingdom himself alone, 2 *Jew.* 917, 4 *Jew.* 681; expresses his belief that he shall come to such a height of vain-glory, that many weak men shall think God has forsaken the care of the world, 4 *Jew.* 681; says he shall place his seat in the holy temple (pseud.), 3 *Jew.* 348; mentions an opinion that by the phrase "sitteth in the temple of God" is meant sitteth as if he were the temple of God, i.e. the church, *Coop.* 184, 2 *Jew.* 918, 4 *Jew.* 729; says the temple in which he shall sit is not the temple of any idol, 2 *Jew.* 916, 4 *Jew.* 729

xxix. *Kings, Civil Power*: he condemns those who will not obey the laws of temporal governors, 1 *Bec.* 216; shews how men are called gods, 1 *Jew.* 462; writes about Constantine and Theodosius, 1 *Bul.* 385; told Boniface that princes have many temporal friends, but few who care for their souls, 1 *Zur.* 64; on good and evil magistrates (pseud.), 3 *Whitg.* 588; on the duty and conduct of the Jewish kings and Nebuchadnezzar in matters of religion, 2 *Brad.* 379; he shews, from the second psalm, how kings should "serve the Lord with fear," 1 *Bul.* 367—369, 4 *Jew.* 976, 1145, *Pil.* 641 n., *Sand.* 41; another passage, *Pil.* 641; he says, kings serve God...if within their kingdom they command what is good, and forbid what is evil, not only in civil matters but in religion, 2 *Cran.* 479, 4 *Jew.* 986; again, he says that kings serve Christ by making laws for Christ, 4 *Jew.* 1033, 3 *Whitg.* 414, 592; words on appealing to the emperor, 1 *Jew.* 396, 3 *Whitg.* 592; he asks, is it not lawful for the emperor to speak in a case of religion? 1 *Jew.* 396, 4 *Jew.* 964, 966, 1029, 3 *Whitg.* 309; yet he reproves the Donatists for desiring to have an earthly king to be judge of their cause, 2 *Ful.* 357; mentions that they chose the emperor to be their judge, and then despised him, 4 *Jew.* 965; he says, if it is no fault to appeal to the emperor, it is no fault to be heard by the emperor, *ib.* 966; speaks of one Felix, a bishop, being purged before the emperor, *ib.*; passages on the duty of the magistrate with reference to heretics, 1 *Bul.* 365—369; says when emperors hold the truth, and by the truth give commandment against error, whoso despises it procures judgment against himself, 4 *Jew.* 992; shews that worldly possessions are holden by the right of kings, *ib.* 835; mentions a law made in Rome, called Lex Voconia, that no man should convey his inheritance to a woman, not even to his only daughter, *ib.* 665; on going to law, &c., *Hutch.* 327; on the legal penalty of a false suggestion by a plaintiff, 1 *Jew.* 101, 102; he intimates that the Manichees spoke against the payment of tribute, *Rog.* 337 n.; says if any thinks, because he is a Christian, he ought to pay no tribute, he falls into a great error, 1 *Bec.* 220, 221; shews that magistrates may restrain men from crimes, *Rog.* 345 n.; does not disallow the punishment of death, *ib.* 349 n.; shews that war is lawful, 1 *Bul.* 371—373; maintains this point in opposition to the Manichees, *Rog.* 351 n.; shews that God has blessed faithful kings with great victories, &c. 2 *Bul.* 13; but he is not always consistent with himself on the question whether Christians should engage in war, *Whita.* 456; referred to on oaths, 1 *Bul.* 252 n., 1 *Hoop.* 336; he asserts that they ought to be had only in necessary things, 1 *Bec.* 379 (and see the case of David in xii. above).

xxx. *Miscellanea*: he says the ark of God, though taken captive, lost not its holiness, 2 *Jew.* 781; derives the word religion à religando, 1 *Bul.* 233, 3 *Bul.* 231; describes the conduct of a peaceful man in religious contentions, *Pil.* 661; defines charity, or love to God and man, 1 *Bul.* 180; tells who our neighbour is, *ib.* 184; says all men are to be loved alike, but as we cannot do good to all, we must especially do good to them to whom we are more nearly joined, *ib.* 186; sayings about conscience, 2 *Hoop.* 574; he calls it a point of great wisdom for a man to recall that which he has evil spoken, 1 *Bec.* 372; prescribes a rule of discipline in reproving inferiors, 3 *Bec.* 508 n.; remarks that words are not ordained that men should deceive each other with them, 4 *Bul.* 264; more on the use of words, *ib.* 265; says, I fear lest we should appear to do injury to our senses, when we would by speaking prove that wherein the evidence of truth surpasses speech, 3 *Jew.* 514; writes, it is easy for any one to conquer Augustine, but you should see whether by truth or by clamour, *ib.* 543; declares that it is much less evil to be unlearned than to be unapt to learn, 4 *Jew.* 910; mentions with disapprobation a saying of Varro, that it is useful to states that their valiant men believe themselves, though falsely, to be the children of gods, *ib.* 783; exclaims, O vanity, selling vanity to them that will hear vanity, *ib.* 851; says it pertains nothing to the city (of God) in what apparel, &c. any follow the faith; therefore when philosophers become Christians they are not compelled to change their apparel, &c. 3 *Jew.* 615, 2 *Whitg.* 37; he admonishes clerks or monks against remarkable apparel, 3 *Jew.* 617; his own apparel, *ib.* 618; he says, we may conjecture from a man's other works whether he wear mean clothing in contempt of superfluous apparel or for ambition, *ib.*; says that even hypocrites counterfeit homely and necessary apparel to deceive the unwary, *ib.*; tells one that his pride is fain to cover itself with sorry clouts, 4 *Jew.* 850; speaks against women painting their faces, 3 *Jew.* 402; against the desire of worldly things, 3 *Whitg.* 584; says good men use the world that they may enjoy God; evil men do the contrary, *ib.* 580; observes that justice is the inheritance of children, &c., *Wool.* 14; says that when any thing which decays not by giving, is had and not given, it is not had as it ought to be, *Coop.* 7; writes against superstitious charms for the cure of diseases, 4 *Bul.* 260; remarks that the ground is rent by the share alone, but that this may be done, the other parts of the plough are also necessary, 2 *Jew.* 983; mentions that in the East sheep bear twice a year, 2 *Lat.* 119 n.; says sound may be extended and divided by delay, 3 *Jew.* 261; remarks that frozen snow cannot be hot, for as long as it is snow, it is not possible for it to be hot, *ib.* 623; asks, if one know not which way to go, what profits it to know where to go? 4 *Jew.* 796; the dates he assigns to Mercurius Trismegistus and Rhadamanthus, 2 *Bul.* 218 n.; explains why Gentiles are called Greeks, 1 *Jew.* 278; says that the intention of a question is to be considered, 1 *Lat.* 272; asks what availeth a key of gold if it will not open what we desire, and what hurteth a key of wood if it will do this? 1 *Jew.* 316, 2 *Jew.* 983; a garbled extract, 1 *Ful.* 38

Augustine (St), abp of Canterbury: 2 *Ful.* 186, *Park.* 425; called the apostle of the English, 1 *Ful.* 464, *Poet.* 280, but he was not so, *Poet.* 289; sent to Britain by Gregory, 1 *Jew.* 280, 299, 3 *Jew.* 163—166, 4 *Jew.* 778—782, *Pil.* 482, 483, 515; he submits certain questions to Gregory, 1 *Jew.* 301, 4 *Jew.* 1045, *Pil.* 517; Gregory gave him advice, *Calf.* 197, and "codices plurimos," 2 *Ful.* 113; copy of the Hebrew Psalter said to have been his, 1 *Ful.* 46; the time of his coming, 1 *Jew.* 307; in what state he found the Britons, *Calf.* 305, 306; his reception, *Pil.* 516; his doctrine, 2 *Ful.* 7, &c.; he brought in popery, *Pil.* 618, *Rid.* 100; his litany and cross, *Calf.* 308, 2 *Ful.* 120; though he and his companions carried a cross, there is not (as Collier remarks, and Manning admits) the least intimation given that they worshipped it, 2 *Ful.* 17 n.; he used St Martin's church at Canterbury, 1 *Jew.* 299; he christened in the river Swale, *Pil.* 518; his arrogant and cruel deeds, 3 *Jew.* 164, 4 *Jew.* 778; his proud reception of the British bishops, 1 *Jew.* 300; his demands, *Calf.* 307; his authority denied by the bishops of this country, *Park.* 111; his doctrine not received by them, *ib.* 265, 266; he is stated to have incited the slaughter of the monks of Bangor, at Westchester, *Bale* 189, 3 *Jew.* 165, 4 *Jew.* 778, &c.; whether chargeable with this crime, *Calf.* 306 n.; defended by Bede with reference to this event, 2 *Ful.* 6, 186, but Jewel says Bede is corrupted, 4 *Jew.* 779; miracles ascribed to him, *ib.* 5, but denied by the British historians, *ib.* 76; the date of his death, 4 *Jew.* 780; table of his acts, *ib.*; how he and the ancient ascetics differed from popish monks, 2 *Ful.* 17, 18; England declined from his steps, *Pil.* 522

Augustine of Ancona: wrote on the Apocalypse, *Bale* 257

Augustine, an Irish monk: the supposed author of a treatise ascribed to St Augustine, *Whita.* 92 n

Augustine of Rome: wrote on the Apocalypse, *Bale* 257

Augustinians: v. Friars.
Augustinus (Ant.): De emend. Gratiani, *Calf.* 137 n
Augustinus Steuchus, *q. v.*
Augustus Cæsar, emperor: his proclamation and taxation, 2 *Lat.* 96; he built a temple and library in honour of Apollo, 2 *Jew.* 981; found Rome of brick, left it of marble, 1 *Bec.* 245, *Grin.* 17, 2 *Jew.* 1015; forbade necromancy, 1 *Hoop.* 329; his warning to Tiberius, 1 *Jew.* 292
Augustus, elector of Saxony: he summons the convocation at Thorgau, 1 *Zur.* 315 n.; hostile to the Calvinists, 2 *Zur.* 274; marriage of his daughter, *ib.* 173
Aulus Gellius: speaks of Theodectes, 1 *Bul.* 48 n.; relates how Diagoras died of joy, 1 *Hoop.* 297; on swearing among the Romans, 1 *Bul.* 202; he speaks of the punishment of false witnesses, *ib.* 204; gives as example of a deceitful oath, *ib.* 249; records a saying of Cato on private thieves and public ones, 2 *Bul.* 47; speaks of the word ceremony as derived à carendo, 2 *Bul.* 125 n., 3 *Bul.* 230 n., and of religion as from relinquendo, 3 *Bul.* 230 n.; describes physiognomists, 1 *Hoop.* 329, and writes against Chaldeans or astrologers, *ib.* n
Aumâle: the dukedom, 1 *Zur.* 124 n
Aureitas: a term used by the schoolmen, 1 *Tyn.* 158 n
Aurelia: v. Councils, *Orleans.*
Aurelian, emperor: cured himself by thin diet, *Sand.* 393; his tyranny and death, 2 *Bul.* 106
Aurelian of Rheims: the disciple and biographer of Martial, *Calf.* 69 n
Aurelius, bp of Carthage: had the care of many churches, 2 *Whitg.* 165, 430; withdrew from the Roman jurisdiction, 1 *Jew.* 416, 418; condemned by Boniface II, 3 *Jew.* 128, 295, 296; blessed Augustine and his company, 2 *Ful.* 108
Aurelius (Marcus): v. Marcus.
Aurelius Victor (Sextus): records Sapor's treatment of Valerian, 4 *Jew.* 701
Aureolus (Pet.): wrote on the Apocalypse, *Bale* 258
Aureum Speculum Papæ: v. Speculum.
Aureus de Universo: an old chronicle mentioned by Caxton, *Pil.* 598 n
Auricular Confession, *q. v.*
Auscoo (James), or Austoo: he and Margery his wife, martyrs at Islington, *Poet.* 171
Ausonius: against usury, 1 *Bul.* 204; he uses the word metancœa, 1 *Ful.* 434, 435
Austin, Latimer's servant: v. Bernher (A.).

Austoo (James): v. Auscoo.
Austria: the communion received there in both kinds by the pope's dispensation, 2 *Ful.* 243
Austria (Archdukes of): v. Charles, Leopold.
Authentica: v. Law (Civil).
Authority: v. Apostles, Kings, Parents, &c. How it began, *Pil.* 125; it shews what a man is, 1 *Lat.* 177
Auxentius, bp of Milan: 2 *Ful.* 266; deprived for heresy, 1 *Whitg.* 461; favoured by Constantius, 4 *Jew.* 1049, 1101; he professed to believe as he had been taught from childhood, 2 *Jew.* 694; alleged the consent of multitudes against Hilary and the catholics, 4 *Jew.* 1053; called Hilary a heretic, *ib.* 952; would not allow him to be a bishop, *ib.* 1052; denied the baptism of infants, 4 *Bul.* 382; one of the first who did so, *Phil.* 274; Helvidius was his disciple, 1 *Hoop.* 161 n
Auxerre: v. Councils.
Availing their bonnets: lowering them, *Bale* 41
Avant: to vaunt, 1 *Jew.* 7
Avarice: v. Covetousness.
Avarice, a poem by Hen. Lok, *Poet.* 138
Ave Maria: v. Mary.
Avenar (Jo.): *Rog.* viii. ix.
Aventinus (Jo.): Annales, *Jew.* xxxiii; he says Lucius, St Paul's companion, went into Germany, 1 *Jew.* 280; tells that the heathen called Christ the most beggarly of all the gods, 4 *Jew.* 971; referred to on the council of Frankfort, *ib.* 1055, *Rog.* 204 n.; records a saying in the council of Worms respecting the usurpations of the pope, 4 *Jew.* 825; speaks of the fruits of Hildebrand's popedom, 3 *Jew.* 426, 4 *Jew.* 699, 700, 744; on the virtues of the emperor Henry IV, 4 *Jew.* 698; reports two verses written of the emperor Lotharius II, *ib.* 692; records Adrian IV.'s arrogance towards the emperor Frederick, *ib.* 677, 682, 837, 847, 1152; referred to on the poisoning of the emperor Henry VII, *ib.* 687; speaks of the priests of Liburnia using the Slavonic tongue, 3 *Bec.* 410
Averroes, an Arabian philosopher: 1 *Hoop.* 70, 332; he rejected Christianity on account of transubstantiation, 3 *Bec.* 278 n., *Wool.* 27
Avicenna, an Arabian philosopher: 1 *Hoop.* 70, 332
Avignon: pope Clement V. removes thither, 4 *Jew.* 933; the schism, *Pil.* 545
Avims (עוים, Deut. ii. 23): what, 1 *Tyn.* 445

Avowries, or Advouries: saints chosen as protectors, 1 *Brad.* 284, 1 *Lat.* 225, 2 *Tyn.* 166
Avowry: justification, 2 *Cov.* 478
Awake: what it is to be so, 3 *Bec.* 610
Away with: bear, 1 *Brad.* 316, 1 *Tyn.* 505
Awdelie (Jo.): notice of him, *Poet.* liv; portion of his epitaph on master John Viron, preacher, *ib.* 540
A worth: at worth, having a value, 1 *Tyn.* 463, 3 *Tyn.* 195
Axe: to ask, 1 *Bec.* 22 n. & al.
Axholme, co. Linc.: the Carthusian priory, or Charterhouse, 2 *Cran.* 299; its lands, *ib.* 337; the prior condemned for treason, *ib.* 303; Cranmer purposes to get a prior to resign, *ib.* 363
Axiothea: went in man's apparel to hear Plato, 4 *Jew.* 651
Ayenst: against, 2 *Brad.* 31
Aylmer (Jo.), or Elmer, bp of London: account of him, *Phil.* 171, 3 *Zur.* 275 n.; tutor to the family of the marquis of Dorset, including the lady Jane Grey, 1 *Bec.* ix, 2 *Bec.* 424, 3 *Zur.* 429, 431; archdeacon of Stow, 3 *Zur.* 373 n.; an exile, 1 *Cran.* (9); his Harborowe, in reply to Knox on the government of women, 2 *Ful.* 37 n., 2 *Zur.* 34 n.; appointed to attend a disputation in 1559, 4 *Jew.* 1200, 1 *Zur.* 11; mentioned, 1 *Zur.* 69, 2 *Zur.* 179; a fit person to answer the book De Disciplina (ascribed to Travers), *Grin.* 353; he declines to do so, *Park.* 477; recommended for the see of London, *Park.* 350; succeeds Sandys therein, *Sand.* xxii; occasional forms of prayer set forth by him, *Lit. Eliz.* 466, &c.; letter concerning a form of prayer on the earthquake, 1580, *ib.* 562 n.; president in the convocation of that year, 1 *Grin.* xiii; his contribution to Geneva, *ib.* 432 n.; two letters to Bullinger, 3 *Zur.* 275, 277; letters to him, *Grin.* 404, 406, 421; a sermon dedicated to him, 2 *Jew.* 948
Aylmer (Tho.), son of the bishop, and archdeacon of London: 1 *Bul.* viii., 4 *Bul.* xxx.
Aylond (......): *Park.* 38
Ayre (Jo.): editor of Becon's Works, Jewel's Works, and Sandys' Sermons, 1, 2, 3 *Bec.*, 1, 2, 3, 4 *Jew., Sand.*; on the authority and office of bishops being depressed by Romanists, 1 *Brad.* 506 n.; reference to his life of Jewel, 2 *Brad.* 45 n.; on Æneas Sylvius, or Pius II, *ib.* 160 n
Ayscough (Anne): v. Askewe.
Azariah, or Ahaziah, king of Judah: 2 *Bul.* 7
Azariah, or Uzziah, *q. v.*

B

B.: v. Bernher (A.).
B. (D.): i. e. Dr N. Bownde, *q. v.*
B. (G.), author of The Ship of Safeguard: possibly Barnaby Googe, or Bernard Garter, *Poet.* xxxv; stanzas from his poem, *ib.* 388
B. (I.), a sectary: *Rog.* 203
B. (T.): notice of him, *Poet.* li; two exhortations to the praise of God, to be sung before morning and evening prayer, from the O.V. of the Psalms, *ib.* 501, 502
Baal: the 7000 who bowed not to him, 4 *Bul.* 71, 3 *Zur.* 39; his priests, 4 *Bul.* 73, 75, 481; none but Baalites promoted in queen Mary's time, 3 *Bec.* 244
Baal-peor: Belphegor, *Bale* 629, 2 *Hoop.* 451
Baal-shalisha: firstfruits brought thence to Elisha, 4 *Bul.* 489
Baasha, king of Israel: 2 *Bul.* 12; his stock, 1 *Bul.* 235
Babbling: what babbling in prayer is, 1 *Bec.* 169; censured, *ib.* 134, 135, 4 *Bul.* 204
Babel: the tower of Babel, 4 *Bul.* 499, *Pil.* 30, 231; Sibylline testimony respecting it, *Whita.* 112
Babington (......), warden of the Fleet: his cruel treatment of bp Hooper, and his servant Will. Downton, 2 *Hoop.* 619, 3 *Zur.* 101 n., 292 n
Babington (sir Ant.): also Elizabeth his daughter, 1 *Bec.* 37 n
Babington (Ant.): his plot, in conjunction with Ballard, *Lit. Eliz.* 468, 658; form of thanksgiving on the discovery of it, *ib.* 595; sermon on the conspiracy, *Sand.* 403
Babington (Fra.), rector of Linc. coll. Oxon: Dr Babington, at Oxford, probably the above, *Park.* 138 n
Babington (Zacharias): controversy between him and Dr Beacon for the chancellorship of Coventry and Lichfield, *Grin.* 370, 371
Bable: a bauble, the fool's ensign, 3 *Jew.* 133
Babthorp (Sir Will.): *Grin.* 325
Babylon: v. Babel.
The origin or monarchy, 1 *Cov.* 34, 1 *Lat.* 356; the country, *Pil.* 281, &c.; captivity of the Jews there, 4 *Bul.* 11, 73, 75, 481, *Pil.* 12, its length, *ib.* 127; cruelty of the Babylonians to the Edomites, *ib.* 235, &c.; they had famous schools, 4 *Bul.* 480; the city was 16 miles square, *Pil.* 231
Babylon (Mystical): v. Beast, Rome.
Prophecies concerning Babylon to be spiritually understood, *Rid.* 70; why St John uses the name, *Phil.* 428; it means confu-

sion, 1 *Cov.* 199; the church of the wicked may be so called, 4 *Bul.* 11; Babylon declared to be Rome, 1 *Brad.* 443, 2 *Brad.* 329, 1 *Ful.* vii, 4 *Jew.* 1061, &c., *Phil.* 428, *Rid.* 415; so Jerome and others explain it, 2 *Ful.* 371, 4 *Jew.* 1063, 1 *Lat.* 173; Babylon named in 1 Peter, whether Rome, 2 *Ful.* 336—338; Babylon prayed against, 3 *Bec.* 22; the captivity a figure of Romish slavery, *Pil.* 4, 277, or of the captivity of sin, 1 *Cov.* 400; what signified by the deliverance therefrom, *ib.*; departure from it, 4 *Jew.* 881; the whore of Babylon, *Bale* 498, 1 *Brad.* 390, *Phil.* 428, *Rid.* 418, 1 *Tyn.* 188; Let go the whore of Babylon, verses, 2 *Cov.* 586; the wares of Babylon, *Bale* 524 &c.; the fall thereof, *ib.* 458, 517, 2 *Jew.* 930—932, 4 *Jew.* 1181; Primasius on this fall, 2 *Jew.* 896; how bewailed, *Bale* 524, 533

Bacchus: his sieve, 4 *Bul.* 238; Augustine mentions that in celebrating the holy mysteries, Christians were thought by some to worship Bacchus and Ceres, 4 *Jew.* 709, et al.

Bachelors: a prayer of single-men, *Lit. Edw.* 464; a prayer for the unmarried, 3 *Bec.* 27

Backbiting: pernicious, 2 *Bul.* 118

Backere (Romanus de): excommunicated from the strangers' church at Sandwich, *Park.* 247

Backsliders: sliders back from the truth of God's word censured, 1 *Bec.* 256; how they should behave themselves, *ib.* 257; their danger, 2 *Bec.* 206, 207; hardly to be converted, *Pil.* 448; intercession for them, 3 *Bec.* 248

Bacon (Fra. lord), visc. St Albans: his opinion on prophesyings, *Grin.* xi. n

Bacon (Jo.): v. Baconthorpe.

Bacon (sir Nich.): referred to, *Poet.* lii; a commissioner for the suppression of colleges, &c., *Park.* 33 n.; recommended by Cranmer for town-clerk of Calais, 2 *Cran.* 384; grantee of abbey lands, *ib.* n.; his house in Noble street, London, *Park.* 49 n.; lord keeper, *ib.* 155, 156, 179, 328 n., 357, 381, *Grin.* 405, 1 *Zur.* 5 n., 2 *Zur.* 132; co-president with abp Heath of the Westminster conference, *Grin.* v, 1 *Zur.* 16 n.; at variance with Parker, *Park.* 309—316; libelled, *ib.* 444; letters from him to Parker, *ib.* 49, 53, 68, 69, 71, 76, 120; letters from Parker to him, *ib.* 50, 52, 57, 171; his death, *Poet.* 511

— Anne his wife (dau. of sir A. Cook): translates Jewel's Apology, *Jew.* xviii, *Park.* 219; Parker's dedicatory letter to her, with her translation of that book, 3 *Jew.* 51; sneered at by Harding, *ib.* 254, 313 n., 4 *Jew.* 941 n.; defended by Jewel, 3 *Jew.* 262; letters from Parker to her, *Park.* 219, 309

Bacon (Roger): mentioned, *Pil.* 80 n.; his remarks on the woeful state of the church in his time, 4 *Jew.* 735; called by Harding a conjuror and necromancer, *ib.* 736; his learning, *ib.*; false miracles by means of his books, *Bale* 190

Baconthorpe (Jo.), or Bacon: reference to him (?), *Pil.* 80; account of him, *Bale* 304 n.; he wrote on the Apocalypse, *ib.* 257

Baden: Parkhurst there, 4 *Jew.* 1196

Baden (Margr. of): v. Cecilia, Christopher.

Bader (......): forces a minister on the church at Lindau, 2 *Cov.* 519

Badge: v. Livery.

Badius (Claudius): acted as a notary at Cranmer's examination, 2 *Cran.* 542, 555

Badlesmere (The barons): *Bale* 19 n

Bagard (Tho.): chancellor of Worcester, &c. 2 *Lat.* 376 n

Bagnal (Sir R.): desires a commission against the clergy, *Park.* 413, 424

Bagshaw (D.): the pope's Judas or pursebearer, *Lit. Eliz.* 681

Bail (Louis): rejects the spurious inventory of canonical books which Carranza ascribes to the council of Florence, 2 *Ful.* 222 n

Bailie (J.): v. Baylie.

Baillet (Adr.): Jugemens des Savans, *Calf.* 200 n

Baily (Tho.), or Hall? his Life of bp Fisher, 2 *Lat.* 356 n

Bain (......): v. Banosius.

Baine (Ralph), or Baines, bp of Coventry and Lichfield: notice of him, *Phil.* xxvi; he opposes Latimer, 1 *Lat.* iv, 2 *Lat.* xii; at Philpot's examination, *Phil.* 148, 152; a great hinderance, 1 *Zur.* 10 n.; he disputes, on the Romish side, at Westminster, *ib.* 11 n.; his death, *ib.* 69

Baines (Edw.): Hist. of Lancashire, 2 *Brad.* xii

Baines (......): probably Paul Bayne, 1 *Brad.* 564

Bainham (Geo.): martyred, *Bale* 394, 586

Bainham (James): compelled to confess that he had Tyndale's writings, and condemned to the fire, 1 *Tyn.* 35, 36; visited in Newgate by Latimer and others, 2 *Lat.* 221; burnt, *ib.* 224

Baker (......): married Parker's mother, *Park.* 18 n

Baker (Jo.), recorder of London: letter to him, 2 *Cran.* 293

Baker (Jo.), Parker's treasurer and half-brother: *Park.* 18 n
Baker (Sir Jo.), a Kentish justice: 2 *Cran.* 349 n.; witness to a writ, *ib.* 489; Baker of Kent, a persecutor, believed to be the same, *Bale* 395
Baker (Phil.), provost of King's coll. Cambridge: misdemeanors objected against him, *Grin.* 308; being deprived by the queen's commissioners, he fled to Louvaine, *ib.*
Baker (Tho.), of Smarden, Kent: 2 *Cran.* 367 n
Baker (Tho.), ejected fellow of St Jo. coll. Cambridge: 2 *Cov.* 39, *Pra. B.* v; his manuscripts, 2 *Lat.* 295 n
Balaam: could not curse Israel, but blessed them, 1 *Jew.* 399, *Sand.* 149; his followers, *Bale* 259, 280; the bishop of Rome, 2 *Cov.* 4
Balbis (Jo. de): *v.* Joannes.
Balduinus (Fra.), or Baudouin: notices of him, 4 *Jew.* 1254, 1 *Zur.* 118 n., 2 *Zur.* 156; his apostasy, 2 *Jew.* 803, 808, *Sand.* 362; on his fitness to attend the conference at Poissy, *Grin.* 245; he slanders Beza, Calvin, &c., 2 *Ful.* 73; acknowledges an interpolation in Optatus, *ib.* 302 n.; he added the seventh book against Parmenian in small type, *ib.* 323 n
Baldus (Pet.) de Perusio: works, *Jew.* xxxiii; he says, the pope is doctor of both laws, by authority not by knowledge, 1 *Jew.* 381, 4 *Jew.* 768; calls the fulness of the pope's power plenitudo tempestatis, *ib.* 832; affirms that the pope is not guilty of simony though he take money, 4 *Jew.* 868; observes that a man may say he believes what the church believes, but not what the pope believes, *ib.* 928; cited on the question whether a courtezan can make a testament, *ib.* 647
Baldwin I. emperor of the East: compels the Greek church to agree to the supremacy of Rome, 2 *Hoop.* 238
Baldwin I. king of Jerusalem: his victory at Antioch, *Lit. Eliz.* 449
Baldwin, abp of Canterbury: puts out the monks there, *Pil.* 610
Bale (Jo.), bp of Ossory: his birth and education, *Bale* vii; his conversion, *ib.*; protected by lord Cromwell, *ib.* ix; he retires to Germany, *ib.*, with his wife and children, *ib.* 494; returns, *ib.* ix; rector of Bishopstoke, vicar of Swaffham, *ib.*; meets Edward VI, *ib.*; made bishop of Ossory, *ib.* x; leaves his diocese, *ib.* xi; taken by pirates, and sold for a slave, *ib.*; his persecutions and deliverance, 2 *Zur.* 79 n.; in exile, 1 *Cran.* (9), *Grin.* 221, 224, 228, 3 *Zur.* 755; his preferment at Canterbury, *Park.* 197 n., 199, 202; he dies there, *Bale* xi; possessed many ancient MSS., *Park.* 140, 198, 287; they were bought by abp Parker, 2 *Zur.* 78 n.; his works, *Bale* vii, xi, *Pil.* 682 (misprinted Bate); his SELECT WORKS, edited by the Rev. H. Christmas, *Bale*; he wrote under the name of Hen. Stalbrydge, 1 *Bec.* viii; his Scriptorum Britanniæ Catalogus, *Bale* xii, 2 *Brad.* xi. n.; the Image of both Churches was written in exile, *Bale* 254, 494; his Mystery of Iniquity cited, on free-will, *Rog.* 114, on the communism of the Anabaptists, *ib.* 355 n.; his plays, *Bale* ix; his Interlude of king Johan, *ib.*, 2 *Cran.* 388 n.; his tragedy of Pammachius, *Bale* vii; he tended to write against Peryn, *ib.* 236; referred to about pope Zosimus, 3 *Jew.* 340, 341; cited respecting the election of Leo VIII., 1 *Whitg.* 402; he says that Roma spelt backwards is a preposterous Amor, *Rog.* 179; his statement as to the giving of names to bells, *Calf.* 15 n.; on the origin of bishops' prisons, 3 *Whitg.* 405, 449
— Dorothy his wife, *Bale* viii.
Balfour (James), minister of Guthrie: 2 *Zur.* 365
Balion (Malatest): lost his head, *Phil.* 426
Balkius (Isbrandus): minister in the Dutch church at Norwich, afterwards at Stamford, 1 *Zur.* 256 n., 266 n
Ball (Jo.): martyred, *Bale* 394
Ball (Jo.), a puritan divine: 1 *Brad.* 564
Ballads: the Song of Solomon called a Ballad by the older translators, 1 *Ful.* 571, 572, 2 *Ful.* 43, 2 *Hoop.* 257, or Ballets, *Phil.* 317; a ballad made by Anne Askewe, *Bale* 239; notice of A proper new Ballad wherein are contayned Catholike Questions to the Protestant, *Poet.* xxiv; complaint of lewd ballads, 2 *Cov.* 538, 3 *Whitg.* 527
Ballard (Cha.): concerned in Babington's conspiracy, *Lit. Eliz.* 468, 595, 658; sermon on that plot, *Sand.* 403
Ballard (Phil.), or Hawford, *q. v.*
Ballerinus (Hieron. and Pet.), 2 *Ful.* 70 n
Balliol Family: *v.* Scott.
Balsamon (Theod.): Canones, *Jew.* xxxiii; his character, 3 *Jew.* 305, 306; referred to for the right reading of a sentence in the African council, *ib.* 295; passages on the emperor's power over bishops, &c., 4 *Jew.* 967, 1030, 1036
Baltasar, or Balthazar: one of the three kings, or magi, *Whita.* 560; prayer to him *Rog.* 228

Baltazar, an Anabaptist: answered by Zuinglius, 1 *Whitg.* 130; Balthasar Pacimontane, apparently the same, 3 *Jew.* 265

Balthasar: *v.* Belshazzar.

Balthasor (Dr), surgeon to Henry VIII.: letter to him, 2 *Cran.* 248

Baltinglas (The lord): *v.* Eustace.

Baluzius (Steph.): *Calf.* 16 n., 154 n

Baly: its inhabitants worship false gods, *Rog.* 37

Bamberg: the bishoprick invaded, 3 *Zur.* 682 n

Bamford (Will.): martyred, *Poet.* 163

Banbury, co. Oxon: hospital of St John, near it, 2 *Lat.* 250 n.; Banbury glosses, i.e. corruptions of the truth, *ib.* 299

Bancor: *v.* Bangor.

Bancroft (Rich.), abp of Canterbury: his Survey of the pretended Holy Discipline, 1 *Zur.* 285; dedications to him, 4 *Jew.* 1314, *Rog.* 3; he says that at Geneva the elder ministers the cup, *ib.* 235 n.; speaks of a multitude being excommunicated at Edinburgh for some disorders about a Robin Hood, *ib.* 311, 312 n.; on the Presbyterian classis, *ib.* 334 n.; A brief Discovery of the Untruths ... contained in D. Bancroft's Sermon, *ib.* 331 n

Bandog: 1 *Brad.* 38

Bands: enjoined to be worn with the cap and gown, 2 *Zur.* 121

Banger (Ann): martyred at Colchester, *Poet.* 172

Bangor, co. Caernarvon: *v.* Missale.

The diocese much out of order, *Park.* 257; Grindal's injunctions to the dean and chapter, and the clergy of the diocese, *Grin.* 183; as to sermons in the cathedral, *ib.*; the grammar-school, *ib.* 184

Bangor, or Bancor, co. Flint: number of monks there, according to Bede, 1 *Jew.* 306; they were subject to abbot Dinoth, *Pil.* 516; many of them slaughtered at Chester, *Calf.* 306, 2 *Ful.* 6, 186, 3 *Jew.* 165, 4 *Jew.* 778, 780

Banishment: *v.* Exile.

Banks (Jo.): mentioned, 3 *Zur.* 293, 296, 297; three letters from him to Bullinger, 3 *Zur.* 303—308

Banks (Will.): a friend of Sandys, *Sand.* xii.

Banners: *v.* Labarum, Processions.

Henry V. set up a banner with a cross against the disciples of Wickliffe, *Bale* 51; banners used in processions, *Grin.* 141, 3 *Whitg.* 276, 495; that borne in the war in Saxony, 1551, 3 *Zur.* 677; those of the Scots confederate lords, 1 *Zur.* 195; of the rebels in the North of England, *ib.* 214 n., 218, 2 *Jew.* 883

Bannester (Tho.), skinner: *Park.* 211

Bannister (......) said that Christ endured in hell the very pains of the damned, *Rog.* 61; his error respecting the law, *ib.* 92

Bannisterians: think there will be a time in this world when we shall need no sacraments, *Rog.* 251; say the water at baptism is not holy, *ib.* 278; consider common and rash swearing but a trifle, *ib.* 357

Banns: *v.* Marriage.

Banosius (......): called Bain, 2 *Zur.* 293, 298

Banquets: *v.* Feasting.

A CHRISTMAS BANQUET, by T. Becon, 1 *Bec.* 59

Bantoun: *v.* Hepburn of Bantoun.

Baptism: *v.* Ambrose, Arnold, Athanasius, Augustine, and other fathers; also Anabaptists, Prayers.

   i. *Baptism generally.*
   ii. *Its Signification; Types and Analogies.*
   iii. *It is One, &c.*
   iv. *Its general Necessity.*
   v. *The Minister.*
   vi. *Baptism by Heretics.*
   vii. *Its Proper Subjects.*
   viii. *Its supposed Prerequisites.*
   ix. *The Baptismal Formula.*
   x. *Rites, Circumstances.*
   xi. *The Profession made in it.*
   xii. *The Grace of Baptism.*
   xiii. *Sin after Baptism.*
   xiv. *Baptism for the Dead, &c.*

i. *Baptism generally:* Tyndale writes thereof in his Brief Declaration of the Sacraments, 1 *Tyn.* 345, Becon, in his Catechism, 2 *Bec.* 202, and in his Principles of Christian Religion, *ib.* 507, Jewel, in his Treatise of the Sacraments, 2 *Jew.* 1104, Nowel, in his Catechism, *Now.* (86), 207, Rogers, on the 16th and 27th Articles, *Rog.* 136, 274; Bullinger writes largely on the subject, especially in his 5th Decade, 4 *Bul.* 351; an article on baptism, 2 *Cran.* 474 (and see Articles); de sacro baptismo; verses by Jo. Sauromanus, *Pra. Eliz.* 404; meaning of the word, 4 *Bul.* 352; its primary signification, 1 *Ful.* 110, 218; its ecclesiastical use, *ib.* 110; it is rightly retained in English, *ib.* 256; translations concerning baptism examined, *ib.* 450—457; whether intended by "water" in John iii, 2 *Whitg.* 521, 522; denoted by "the water," 1 *Jo. v.* 6, 2 *Tyn.* 209; on the baptism mentioned in Acts xix. (see iii. below); instituted by

God the Father, 2 *Bec.* 203, 4 *Bul.* 352, by Christ, 1 *Cov.* 78; when instituted, 4 *Bul.* 353; exposition of the words "he that believeth and is baptized shall be saved," *Phil.* 281, 3 *Tyn.* 276 ; what baptism is, 2 *Bec.* 202, 507, 508, 3 *Bec.* 612, 616, 617, 1 *Brad.* 121, 4 *Bul.* 352, *Lit. Edw.* 516, (563), *Now.* 85, (207); its essence and accidents (see x. below); lofty terms applied to baptism by the fathers, 2 *Jew.* 763, 764, 3 *Jew.* 463, 468, &c. 503; Gregory Nyssen calls it the divine bath, 2 *Jew.* 620; in the Punic tongue called health, 1 *Jew.* 294; it is God's livery, 1 *Hoop.* 75 ; a peculiar covenant and sign, 2 *Bec.* 573, 574; the sign of the new league between God and us made by Jesus Christ, and the mark of Christians, 2 *Hoop.* 46; a sacrament to be reverently received of all, 2 *Bec.* 215; why it is called a sacrament, 1 *Hoop.* 128; it is coupled in scripture with the Lord's supper, 1 *Brad.* 88, 534; it is the sacrament or sign of repentance, *Calf.* 242, 2 *Tyn.* 161, 3 *Tyn.* 171; the sacrament or seal of faith, *Coop.* 203, 204, 3 *Whitg.* 113; a seal of righteousness, 2 *Bec.* 217; the sacrament of adoption, *Pra. B.* 14; its parts, the word and the water, 2 *Bec.* 202, 1 *Hoop.* 533, or, the sign and the thing signified, 2 *Bec.* 199, 573, 4 *Bul.* 250, 328, 353, 1 *Hoop.* 74; why we are baptized, 2 *Bec.* 203, 508, 2 *Tyn.* 173; three kinds of baptism mentioned by the fathers; of the Spirit, of blood, of water; yet there is but one baptism, 2 *Bec.* 225, 226, 2 *Jew.* 1107; baptism with fire, what, 4 *Bul.* 355, 396; baptism is less than the gospel, *Phil.* 276 ; on the text, "Christ sent me not to baptize," &c., 2 *Whitg.* 456; popish doctrines no small derogation and injury to baptism, 1 *Cran.* 25, 34, 45; on Philpot's views of baptism, *Phil.* xix ; Hooper's judgment, 2 *Hoop.* 88, 89; Cartwright's errors, 3 *Whitg.* 553, 554; it was derided by the Family of Love, *Rog.* 177

ii. *Its Signification; Types and Analogies:* what it signifies or declares to us, 2 *Cran.* 176, 2 *Lat.* 133, *Lit. Edw.* 517, (564), 1 *Tyn.* 26, 359, 409, 426, 2 *Tyn.* 90, 3 *Tyn.* 171, 245, 247; it denotes tribulation, 1 *Tyn.* 138, and death, 2 *Tyn.* 228, death unto sin and new life unto righteousness, 1 *Tyn.* 253, 261, 500, 2 *Tyn.* 189; it preaches the mortification of the flesh and the vivification of the spirit, 2 *Bec.* 205, 206; it represents our washing in the blood of Christ, 2 *Jew.* 1101 (see xii. below), being a figure of his death and passion, *Hutch.* 115, 1 *Jew.* 521, 4 *Jew.* 893; the deluge, and the Red Sea, types of it, 4 *Bul.* 364, 2 *Jew.* 1106; also Noah's ark, 1 *Tyn.* 426; it takes the place of circumcision, 1 *Brad.* 82, 2 *Bul.* 269, 2 *Jew.* 1104, 1105, *Phil.* 277, 1 *Tyn.* 350, 356, 425, 3 *Tyn.* 246, and is the seal of God's covenant, as circumcision was, 1 *Brad.* 149; it is "the circumcision made without hands," 4 *Bul.* 299 ; compared with the Lord's supper, *Rid.* 275, 3 *Tyn.* 245, &c.

iii. *It is One, and given once for all* (see vi. below): the baptism of John, of Christ, and of the apostles declared to be one and the same, 4 *Bul.* 354, 1 *Ful.* 453, &c., 3 *Whitg.* 17; opinion that Paul did not rebaptize with water those baptized by John (Acts xix.), 4 *Bul.* 356, 1 *Ful.* 453, *Hutch.* 116, 3 *Whitg.* 17; baptism is but one, though three kinds are often mentioned by the fathers, (see i. above), 2 *Bec.* 225, 226, 2 *Jew.* 1107; it is one and the same everywhere, *Coop.* 117; it is into the one catholic faith, 4 *Bul.* 22, *Phil.* 16, 73, not into the faith of sponsors, *Phil.* 105; it is given once for all, 2 *Hoop.* 46, and remains perpetual, 4 *Bul.* 398, 3 *Whitg.* 141, for though the washing be past, the power (i. e. the word of God) lasteth ever, 1 *Tyn.* 267; the Holy Ghost comes to us, not in baptism only, but so long as we dwell in Christ, 1 *Cran.* 71 ; it may not be repeated, 2 *Bec.* 226, *Hutch.* 114, 115, *Phil.* 380; Harding admits the validity of baptism in the church of England, 3 *Jew.* 443, 444; but papists (sometimes) rebaptize children baptized by Protestant ministers, *Rog.* 236, 266

iv. *Its General Necessity:* baptism is generally, but not absolutely, necessary, 1 *Brad.* 90, 503, 4 *Bul.* 366, 1 *Hoop.* 131, 2 *Hoop.* 47, 2 *Whitg.* 521, 523, 537, &c.; its necessity shewn by the baptism of Christ, *Hutch.* 152; it is not neglected by the faithful, 1 *Cov.* 411; wilful rejection or neglect of it is damnable, 2 *Bec.* 215, 224, 226, 2 *Jew.* 1107; to die without it a probable token of reprobation, 2 *Whitg.* 538; still God's grace is not tied to it, 1 *Ful.* 456, 2 *Jew.* 1107; Papists say that none are saved who depart unbaptized, *Rog.* 137, 249, 250, but this doctrine is injurious, 2 *Bec.* 215, &c., and dissents from the verity of God's word, *ib.* 220, &c.; baptism is of the same necessity that circumcision was, *ib.* 216; unbaptized infants buried in a certain middle place between the profane and holy ground (in cæmiterio innocentum),

4 *Bul.* 380; infants dying unbaptized are not necessarily condemned, 2 *Bec.* 214, 215, 3 *Bec.* 617, 1 *Brad.* 503, 2 *Ful.* 392, 1 *Hoop.* 129, 132, 2 *Hoop.* 47, 2 *Jew.* 1107, 1 *Tyn.* 350, 2 *Whitg.* 521, 522; nor is a believing Turk who cannot be baptized, 1 *Tyn.* 351; some may be spiritually baptized among the Turks and heathen, 2 *Bec.* 221, 222; blessed martyrs have died without it, being excluded by necessity, *Coop.* 73, 2 *Jew.* 1107; martyrdom said to supply its place, 2 *Zur.* 195

v. *The Minister:* who should baptize, 4 *Bul.* 369; what the minister works, *ib.* 367; it ought to be administered by lawful ministers, 1 *Hoop.* 131, *Rog.* 235; article of convocation to this effect, *Grin.* 188; it is neither the better nor the worse on account of the goodness or badness of the minister, 2 *Bec.* 226, 227, 2 *Jew.* 1106, *Pil.* 171, 2 *Whitg.* 520, 525, 528, 553, 576; deacons may baptize, 2 *Whitg.* 519, 525, 3 *Whitg.* 58, &c. 72; on baptism by laymen, *Rog.* 235, 236, 1 *Tyn.* 256; it is valid, 2 *Whitg.* 525; opinions of the fathers on this, *ib.* 526, 536; examples from ecclesiastical history, *ib.* 527, &c.; on the ministration of baptism by women, 4 *Bul.* 370, *Grin.* 340, *Rog.* 235, 236, 2 *Whitg.* 495, &c., 521, &c., 3 *Whitg.* 492, 546, 1 *Zur.* 164, 2 *Zur.* 356; said to have been appointed by pope Victor I, 2 *Whitg.* 495, 507, 523; testimonies of fathers against the practice, 4 *Bul.* 370, 2 *Whitg.* 535, 536; baptism by women admitted in case of necessity, 3 *Tyn.* 18, 29, 30, 98; its validity maintained, 2 *Cran.* 58, 2 *Whitg.* 532; whether allowed by the Prayer Book, 2 *Whitg.* 496; permitted by some reformers in time of necessity, *ib.* 503; objections to it, 2 *Zur.* 149, 357, 361; it was disapproved by Grindal and Horn, 1 *Zur.* 178 (see 358), by Sandys, *Sand.* 433, 448, by Beza, 2 *Zur.* 130; its validity denied by Cartwright, 2 *Whitg.* 525

vi. *Baptism by Heretics:* baptism by heretics is valid, 2 *Whitg.* 532, 2 *Zur.* 194; heretics have true baptism, 1 *Brad.* 504; they do not lose their baptism, 3 *Whitg.* 141; converted heretics, therefore, are not to be rebaptized, *Whita.* 497; Cyprian in error on this point, 4 *Bul.* 349, 363, *Whita.* 506 (and see Cyprian); his opinion opposed by Augustine, *Whita.* 507, 607—609; dissensions in Africa on the question, 1 *Ful.* 35; the church of Rome has true baptism, 1 *Brad.* 505, 4 *Bul.* 69; it has been preserved in the midst of the gulf of papistry, 3 *Whitg.* 144

vii. *The proper Subjects of Baptism:* who are to be baptized, 4 *Bul.* 381, 3 *Whitg.* 132; the commandment to baptize all nations refers to all sorts of men, *Phil.* 96; baptism is not, however, to be administered to untaught Gentiles, *ib.* 281; it was denied by the Marcionites to married folks, *Rog.* 265; infants are to be baptized, 2 *Bec.* 207, &c., 3 *Bec.* 617, 1 *Brad.* 82, 2 *Brad.* 213, (parallel with *Rid.* 367), 253, 4 *Bul.* 343, 1 *Hoop.* 132, 2 *Hoop.* 46, 1 *Jew.* 224, 227, 2 *Jew.* 764, 1104, 1105, 3 *Jew.* 460, 461, 462, *Rog.* 278—281, 1 *Whitg.* 363, 368; this was denied by Auxentius, Pelagius, and other heretics, *Phil.* 274, by the Servetians, and Anabaptists (*q. v.*), *Rog.* 265, not by the Puritans, 1 *Whitg.* 99; answer to the Anabaptists' argument from Matt. xxviii., 3 *Whitg.* 24; the baptism of infants is of God, 4 *Bul.* 388, and may be proved from scripture, 2 *Cran.* 59, 60, *Now.* (87,) 209, *Phil.* 274, 380, *Whita.* 506, 515, 540, and from antiquity, *Phil.* 278, from circumcision, 2 *Bec.* 207, 208 (and see ii. above), from the fact that children have been from their cradle endued with the Holy Spirit, *ib.* 208; from the fact that the apostles baptized households, *ib.* 209, 4 *Bul.* 391; the baptism of children has lasted from the time of the apostles, 4 *Bul.* 392; Origen refers it to apostolic tradition, *Whita.* 587; yet baptism was delayed by some of old till the approach of death, *Sand.* 152; a letter by Philpot concerning the baptism of infants, *Phil.* 271; whether the children of wicked men may be baptized, 3 *Whitg.* 135, &c.; whether the infants of papists, 2 *Zur.* 243; Whitgift says the children of papists and excommunicated persons are to be baptized, 3 *Whitg.* 576; baptism is much profaned through want of discipline, *Poet.* 466; on the baptism of insensible persons, 3 *Jew.* 358, 359

viii. *Its supposed Prerequisites:* baptism consequent on election, 2 *Brad.* 123; what it requireth, 1 *Brad.* 121, viz. assurance, 2 *Brad.* 167, or faith, 3 *Jew.* 462, *Pra. B.* 14; God's election in infants, faith in those of age, 2 *Brad.* 290; it requires that we should be regenerate, 1 *Brad.* 297, and confirms or seals our regeneration, 2 *Brad.* 289, 2 *Cov.* 267; penance and faith said to precede it, 1 *Hoop.* 74; this is explained by the ceremony of coronation, *ib.* 75; it is a sign and seal of remission of sin already received by faith, *ib.* 128, the confirmation of Christ's promise received before admission thereto, *ib.* 130, 133; it presupposes repentance, *Hutch.* 109; it declares we are in the favour of

God, 2 *Bec.* 205, 3 *Bec.* 173; of itself it brings not grace, but testifies that he who is baptized has received grace, 2 *Bec.* 220; the grace is received only by the faithful, *Now.* (87), 208; being incorporate into Christ by faith, that incorporation is assured unto us and increased in our baptism, 1 *Jew.* 140, 141; it is (says Cartwright) the seal of grace before received, 2 *Whitg.* 525 n., the public reception of him (says Hooper) who has been previously received by grace, 3 *Zur.* 47; infants, though they have no faith when they are baptized, yet have their faith confirmed by their baptism, even to their lives' end, 2 *Ful.* 169

. ix. *The Baptismal Formula :* baptism should be ministered with the words commanded, 4 *Bul.* 357, 358, 2 *Hoop.* 47; what it is to be baptized in the name of the Father, the Son, and the Holy Ghost, 2 *Bec.* 203; "in" and "into," 4 *Bul.* 357; Glin affirms that baptism doth not consist in the word "I" or in the word "baptize," &c. but in all the words spoken in order, *Grin.* 197; instances of the perversion of the proper form of words, 1 *Jew.* 316, 3 *Jew.* 444, 445; baptism "in the name of Jesus Christ," and the like, 4 *Bul.* 357; the apostles did not baptize in the name of Jesus only, 1 *Jew.* 224, 225; what it is to be baptized in the name of Christ, 2 *Bec.* 13

x. *Rites, Ceremonies, and Circumstances* (v. Chrisom, Cross, Exorcism, Fonts, Sponsors, Unction) : of the rite or ceremony, 4 *Bul.* 356, 2 *Hoop.* 47; there can be no sacrament of baptism without water, as well as the Holy Ghost, spiritually regenerating, 1 *Cran.* 304; Harding asserts that the apostles departed from the letter of Christ's institution, 1 *Jew.* 223; rites used in Tertullian's time, *Calf.* 270, 2 *Cran.* 56, 1 *Whitg.* 216; Victor I. on the celebration of baptism, 2 *Whitg.* 507; papists have added many ceremonies, 1 *Bec.* 11, 2 *Bec.* 207, 3 *Bec.* 231, 524, 4 *Bul.* 310, 359, &c., *Calf.* 212—214, &c., 3 *Tyn.* 20, 3 *Whitg.* 87 ; yet it is not so much corrupted by them as the other sacrament is, *Pil.* 171 ; even when performed in Latin, it has all the requisite parts, *Rid.* 140 ; the people's erroneous belief respecting it, 1 *Tyn.* 276; their superstitious attention to the ceremonial, *ib.* 277; rites, as crossing, sponsors, and the like, no parts of it, 2 *Cran.* 58, 2 *Jew.* 1106, 2 *Whitg.* 528 ; rites used in the church of England, 2 *Brad.* 383; baptismal services, in the Prayer Books, *Lit. Edw.* and *Lit.*

Eliz.; the English service described by bp Horn, 2 *Zur.* 356; inquiry as to the use of popish rites, *Grin.* 160; objections of the Puritans to the service for public baptism, 3 *Whitg.* 381; order for its public ministration in Denmark, 1 *Cov.* 478, 479 ; catechumens were of old exhorted to prepare themselves for baptism, 1 *Jew.* 119; on the time of it, 4 *Bul.* 366; celebrated in Victor's time at Easter only, 1 *Whitg.* 513, afterwards at Easter and Pentecost, 2 *Cran.* 56 n., 175, *Whita.* 592, 1 *Whitg.* 513; of old the unbaptized were not suffered to be present at its ministration, 2 *Jew.* 706; of the place of it, 4 *Bul.* 365; to be administered openly, 2 *Bec.* 200; celebrated near the church-door, 2 *Whitg.* 461, 463 ; on baptism in private places, *Grin.* 340, *Rid.* 534, 1 *Whitg.* 207, &c., 2 *Whitg.* 496, 508, &c., 516, 533 ; article of the convocation of 1576 about private baptism, *Grin.* 188 ; it may be ministered to one person, *Phil.* 96; fathers should be present at the baptism of their children, 2 *Bec.* 228; not necessarily associated with preaching, 3 *Whitg.* 15, &c., 2 *Zur.* 232; a certain mystical meat was anciently given to catechumens before baptism, *Rid.* 30 ; of sponsors (*q. v.*), 1 *Whitg.* 130, 3 *Whitg.* 118; their origin, *Calf.* xi. 211, 212, 3 *Whitg.* 109, 120, 473, 514 ; the practice of having godfathers and godmothers declared to be a commendable old custom, 2 *Bec.* 228, defended, 2 *Zur.* 233; the Puritans objected to it, 1 *Zur.* 281; of parents presenting and answering for their children, 3 *Whitg.* 134, 138; how parents and friends can answer for an infant, 1 *Cran.* 124; children are not baptized into the faith of sponsors, *Phil.* 105; Basil says those who are baptized should renounce Satan, *Whita.* 593; of interrogatories to infants, *Grin.* 340, 3 *Whitg.* 109, &c., 1 *Zur.* 164; from the response, Volo, the people called baptism volowing, and a priest a volower, 1 *Tyn.* 253, 276, 3 *Tyn.* 72; the interrogations to infants, &c., tolerated, say bishops Grindal and Horn, until better times, 1 *Zur.* 179 (see 358); on giving names, 4 *Bul.* 329; remarks on the choice of them, 2 *Jew.* 1108; the fountain of water, 4 *Bul.* 257; baptism to be performed at the font, not in basins, 2 *Zur.* 149 n.; Cyprian declares that the water must first be sanctified by the priest, *Calf.* 225, but the apostles did not do this, 4 *Bul.* 310, and it not needful, *Whita.* 592; on trine immersion, 2 *Bec.* 227, 4 *Bul.* 364, *Calf.*

213, 2 *Zur.* 122, mentioned by Tertullian, 1 *Whitg.* 216, also by Basil, Gregory, Gratian, &c., but not apostolical, *Whita.* 592, forbidden by the 4th council of Toledo, 2 *Cran.* 58, *Whita.* 593, and not observed in Spain, 2 *Cran.* 58, directed by king Edward's first Prayer Book, *Lit. Edw.* 111; papists use trine sprinkling, *Whita.* 593; Cyprian approves aspersion, *ib.* 592; affusion or sprinkling sufficient, 2 *Bec.* 227, 288, 4 *Bul.* 364, 1 *Jew.* 223, 226; superstition about total immersion, 1 *Tyn.* 277; an Arian being about to baptize a man, the water dried up, 2 *Jew.* 761; baptism in rivers (the Swale, &c.), *Pil.* 518; on the use of the sign of the cross (*q. v.*), *Calf.* 200, &c., 2 *Cran.* 56, 1 *Zur.* 164, 179, 358; it is only a rite, not of the essence of the sacrament, *Calf.* 206, tolerated, say bishops Grindal and Horn, until better times, 1 *Zur.* 179, disliked by abp Sandys, *Sand.* 433; some of old erroneously supposed (from Matt. iii.) that children should be marked with a hot iron at their baptism, 2 *Jew.* 1110; anointing anciently joined with it, *Calf.* 224, 225 (*v.* Unction); milk and honey anciently given after it, 2 *Cran.* 56; abstaining from washing infants for a week after, and other traditions relating thereto, *ib.*; Romanists take away half the effect of baptism by their confirmation, *Calf.* 216, 217, teaching that the latter is a greater sacrament, *ib.* 221, 222

xi. *The Profession made in Baptism and its Obligations:* baptism represents our profession, and is a mark of difference, 2 *Lat.* 315, 342, *Rog.* 274—276; it is the common badge of Christians, 1 *Tyn.* 426; it serves for our confession, and reminds us of the duties of godliness, 4 *Bul.* 400; the profession which we made therein, 1 *Brad.* 384, 396, 410, 418 (parallel with 2 *Cov.* 234), 2 *Brad.* 105, 203, 217, 235, *Rid.* 57, 1 *Tyn.* 469, 2 *Tyn.* 136; we entered into the profession of Christianity, *Sand.* 212, and bound ourselves to fight under the standard of Christ, and never to forsake him, 1 *Cov.* 495; he that hath the profession of his baptism written in his heart, can be no heretic, 2 *Tyn.* 140; the knowledge of our baptism is the key and light of scripture, *ib.* 138, &c.; its obligations, 1 *Tyn.* 350; to be baptized and not to keep God's commandments, is worse than a Turk, 1 *Lat.* 346; all engagement contrary to our baptismal obligations are void, *Pil.* 621; confessions of the breach of baptismal engagements, *Lit. Eliz.* 505, *Poet.* 509

xii. *The Grace of Baptism:* it was not instituted in vain, 1 *Cov.* 411; how we are made new therein, 1 *Cran.* 176; how it saveth, namely, as preaching does, 1 *Tyn.* 253, 424, and by faith, *ib.* 426; the fruit, effect, or grace of it, 2 *Bec.* 203, &c., 3 *Bec.* 173, 4 *Bul.* 397, 2 *Cov.* 267, 2 *Cran.* 95 (Inst. of a Chr. Man), 2 *Ful.* 388, 391, *Hutch.* 137, 2 *Jew.* 1106, *Now.* (86), 207, 208; on God's invisible working, 1 *Jew.* 455, 465, 466; that the Holy Ghost works regeneration therein, *Hutch.* 156, 199, 200; the washing outwardly teacheth the washing God worketh inwardly, 1 *Cran.* 17; the baptizer gives visibly the sacrament of regeneration, the grace is given invisibly by God alone, 4 *Bul.* 367; passages from the fathers on the grace of baptism, 2 *Jew.* 1102 (and see their names); its efficacy ascribed to the power and presence of God, 2 *Jew.* 565, 771, 781, 1106, 3 *Jew.* 443, 463; on the effects of baptism in young children, 2 *Brad.* 404; they, being baptized, and dying in their infancy, are washed from sin by Christ's sacrifice, 2 *Cran.* 128; baptism is not the cause of salvation to them, *Rog.* 250; it is called salvation, life, regeneration, &c., and why, 2 *Jew.* 1105, 3 *Jew.* 470 (and see i.); it is a token of the grace of God, 2 *Cov.* 86, the entry of the church, a washing into a new birth, and a renewing of the Holy Ghost, 2 *Hoop.* 46; by it we are joined to the church, 3 *Tyn.* 246, 247, brought into the church, *Pra. B.* 140, planted in the church, 1 *Cov.* 370, *Phil.* 221, incorporated into the church, *Sand.* 87, made members of the church, through faith, 1 *Brad.* 347; by it we put on Christ 2 *Lat.* 19, whom, continues Philpot, if we endeavour to represent, we are indeed the sons of God and inheritors with Christ, *Phil.* 286; through it we receive Christ, 1 *Cov.* 410, are joined to Christ, 1 *Jew.* 131, 132, 450, 529, 2 *Jew.* 767, are incorporate into Christ, 1 *Jew.* 473, 3 *Jew.* 467, are grafted into Christ's mystical body, 1 *Brad.* 89, that is, outwardly engraft into Christ, *ib.* 503; by it men become Christians, 1 *Lat.* 7; it gathers us together to be the people of God, 4 *Bul.* 399; by it we are removed, says Becon, from the fierce judging-place to the court of mercy, 2 *Bec.* 635, 636; of the remission of sins in baptism, 1 *Bec.* 333, 339, 2 *Bec.* 204, 1 *Brad.* 89, 94, 4 *Bul.* 282, 398, *Calf.* 15, 16, 1 *Cov.* 410, especially of original sin, 2 *Cran.* 132, the after pains thereof continue, *ib.* 182; baptism is a sacrament of the remission of sins, 3 *Jew.* 460, an assurance of the remission of sins, 2 *Lat.* 127; Arians spoken of as having been once by baptism delivered from the bondage of sin, *Phil.* 309; baptism and regeneration, 1 *Bec.* 178, 1 *Brad.* 218, 260, *Hutch.* 11, 115, 219, 229, *Rid.* 57, 238, 240, 3 *Whitg.* 23; Leo on this point, 1 *Jew.* 474; in it, says Cranmer, we be regenerated and pardoned of our sin by the blood of Christ, 2 *Cran.* 116; Gardiner's statement respecting the effect of Christ's sacrifice on the cross dispensed in baptism, 1 *Cran.* 360; in the bath of holy baptism, says Hutchinson, we are regenerate, *Hutch.* 11; on the meaning of "water and the Spirit," 1 *Ful.* 455, 456, and "the washing of regeneration," *ib.*; baptism the sacrament, sign, or seal of regeneration, 2 *Brad.* 92, 1 *Jew.* 140, 487, 2 *Jew.* 567, 1104, 1117, *Rog.* 276—278, 2 *Whitg.* 538, not a sign or seal only, 3 *Jew.* 460; it is the water of regeneration, 4 *Bul.* 441, 2 *Cran.* 176; it is therefore called regeneration, 2 *Brad.* 271, 2 *Cov.* 250, 253, 1 *Cran.* 150, 153, *Whitg.* 382; it is regeneration, as the eucharistic bread is Christ's body, 1 *Brad.* 533, the water being sacramentally changed into the fountain of regeneration, *Rid.* 12; the water is not mere water, 1 *Jew.* 149, 515, 519, 545, 2 *Jew.* 565, 566, 570, 575, but, in a certain sense, Christ's blood, *Grin.* 62, 1 *Jew.* 518, yet there is no change in the water, *Now.* (91), 214, save that the water is changed in the use, 1 *Cran.* 180, 308, or changed sacramentally, *ib.* 254, 322; all the ancient authors speak of this change, *ib.* 311; Christ and the Holy Ghost not in the water, *ib.* 148; Christ present as well in baptism as in the Lord's supper, *ib.* 76, 92, 228, 342, 356, 366; Christ is not only in them that duly receive the sacrament of the Lord's supper, but in them that duly receive the sacrament of baptism, and in true Christian people at other times, *ib.* 140; we are regenerated as well in the one sacrament as in the other, *ib.* 176; in every part of the water in baptism is whole Christ and the Holy Spirit sacramentally, *ib.* 64; Christ is manifested and exhibited in it spiritually *ib.* 156; baptism ministered to children in token of their spiritual birth, *Sand.* 253; the grace of adoption and regeneration said to be received through it, *Calf,* 217; if any have not the seal of regeneration, we cannot say that he is born the child of God, 2 *Jew.* 1108; regeneration is by Christ's resurrection, whereof baptism requireth faith, *Pra. B.* 64; baptism considered in connexion with justification, 2 *Tyn.* 90; "baptized or justified," 2 *Cran.* 133 (Homily of Salvation); the relation of the baptism of infants to faith, *Whita.* 540; how baptism sealeth, 4 *Bul.* 321; John gave not remission of sins to all whom he baptized, 3 *Zur.* 48; the outward washing declares the inward purging of the Spirit, *Sand.* 302; Dionysius says, the natural purgation by water teaches the purgation of the soul, 1 *Jew.* 476; outward baptism does not give grace by any power that it has, 2 *Bec.* 217; without the baptism of the Holy Ghost it profits nothing, *ib.* 203, 218; all who are contained in the visible church are not baptized alike, *ib.* 225; those that come feignedly, and those that come unfeignedly, both be washed with the holy water, but both be not washed with the Holy Ghost, 1 *Cran.* 221; the outward sign does not contain grace, 3 *Whitg.* 382, nor does it justify, 2 *Tyn.* 90, or cleanse us from sin, 1 *Cov.* 411, 1 *Hoop.* 74; it does not bring grace ex opere operato, 2 *Jew.* 751, 757, *Rog.* 278; the water does not cleanse the soul; we must seek salvation in Christ alone, not in any outward thing, 2 *Jew.* 1106; answer to such as allege John iii. 5, in proof that the Holy Spirit is present in the water, and that therefore the work of baptism putteth away sin, 1 *Tyn.* 423, 424; what it is to be baptized with the Holy Ghost, 2 *Bec.* 202; the inward baptism of the heart, 2 *Tyn.* 12; none other availeth, *ib.* 13; those who are baptized in the flesh only, are baptized unto greater damnation, 1 *Tyn.* 358, for he that receives baptism unworthily, receives judgment, 1 *Jew.* 517, 4 *Jew.* 893, 894; they who are baptized in the flesh and not in heart have no part in Christ's blood, 1 *Tyn.* 351; wicked men may receive the external sign, and yet remain members of Satan, 3 *Whitg.* 383

xiii. *Sin after Baptism:* concupiscence remaining after it is sin, 3 *Jew.* 463, 464, but not unpardonable: *v.* Sin.

xiv. *Baptism for the Dead, of the Dead, &c.:* Christian men said to have been baptized over dead men's graves, in token that the dead should rise again, *Hutch.* 138; vicarious baptism for the dead practised by some ancient heretics, 1 *Jew.* 5, 23 n., 2 *Jew.* 744, *Rog.* 266; Paul's argument from baptism for the dead, 1 *Jew.* 67; baptism of the dead, *ib.* 6, *Rog.* 266; of children unborn, 1 *Jew.* 6, 3 *Jew.* 358, 359; the baptism of

bells, standards, ships, *Rog.* 266, *Sand.* 19 (and see Bells).
— Baptism of blood: *v.* i. supra.
— Baptism of fire: *v.* i. supra.
— Baptism of John: *v.* iii. supra.
Baptista Mantuanus (Spagnolus): works, *Jew.* xxxiii; speaks of scandalous crimes of the Romish priesthood, 3 *Jew.* 427, 4 *Jew.* 1106; affirms that at Rome, everything is lawful, except to be good, 4 *Jew.* 628; complains of papal pride, *ib.* 740; says the faith of the Roman church is sick and almost dead, *ib.* 724, 907; declares that at Rome all things are sold, *ib.* 1082; says Hilary was married, 3 *Jew.* 391, *Pil.* 570; speaks of a novelty which is not a novelty, but true antiquity, *Pil.* 586
Barath (Jo.): wrote on the Apocalypse, *Bale* 257
Barbara (St): invoked for aid against gunshot, *Bale* 348, or in war, 1 *Hoop.* 457; also to keep from thunder and lightning, 1 *Bec.* 139, 2 *Bec.* 536; account of her, 1 *Bec.* 139 n.; 1 *Hoop.* 457 n
Barbara, Celarent, &c., *Grin.* 43 n
Barbarians: *v.* Tongues.
Use of the term by Paul, and other ancient writers, 1 *Jew.* 267, *Whita.* 267, 356
Barbary: barbarity, barbarism, 3 *Bec.* 42
Barbatius (And.): proves the antiquity of cardinals from the first book of Kings, 4 *Jew.* 783; says as the door is ruled by the hinge, so is the church of Rome by the council of cardinals, *ib.* 855
Barbelitæ: a name given to the Gnostics, 2 *Ful.* 375
Barbelrode: Matthew, the prefect there, 2 *Cov.* 510, 521, &c.
Barber (Jo.), Cranmer's official: treacherous to him, 2 *Cran.* 360 n.; to be sent to Canterbury to inquire about Becket's blood, *ib.* 378; letter in his behalf to Cromwell, *ib.* 386
Barber (Rich.), warden of All Souls' college: letters to him, *Park.* 296, 297, 300, 320, 324; enjoined to deface superstitious plate, &c., *ib.* 301 n
Barcara: *v.* Bracara.
Barclay (Will.): replies to Buchanan's book, De Jure Regni, 2 *Zur.* 311 n
Barcobas, and Barcolf: false prophets, *Rog.* 82
Bardesanes: notice of him, 2 *Bul.* 363
Barenger: *v.* Berengarius.
Baret (R. and W.): *v.* Barret.
Bargaining: *v.* Buying.
Barkeley, (Alice): married Geo. Whetenhall, 1 *Bec.* 191 n

Barker (Ambrose): 2 *Cran.* 364
Barker (Anne), daughter of William: married to two husbands, 2 *Cran.* 364
Barker (Anth.), warden of the collegiate church of Stratford-on-Avon: 2 *Lat.* 383 n.; Latimer complains of him, *ib.* 413
Barker (Chr.), printer: 2 *Hoop.* 20, 63
Barker (Will.), of Cheswicke: Anne his daughter, 2 *Cran.* 364
Barker (Will.), servant to the duke of Norfolk: *Park.* 391
Barking, co. Essex: first appointment of a place of burial there, 2 *Ful.* 13; when the nuns sung their lauds, *ib.* 123; More relates how certain relics were discovered there, including some kerchiefs worked by our lady, 3 *Tyn.* 124 n.; Barnes preaches there, 2 *Cov.* 350, 351; Latimer to preach at Barking [Essex?] for Mr Manworth, 2 *Lat.* 409
Barkley (......): prosecuted for saying mass, as chaplain to the princess Mary, 2 *Cran.* 529
Barley (Rob.), of Barley: Elizabeth (Hardwick) his wife, *Park.* 301 n
Barlings, co. Lincoln: the prior heads an insurrection, *Park.* 8 n
Barlow (Jerome), sometime a friar at Greenwich: his escape, 1 *Tyn.* xxxv
Barlow (Tho.), bp of Lincoln: his Brutum Fulmen, 2 *Ful.* 286 n., 290 n
Barlow (Will.), successively bishop of St Asaph, St David's, Bath and Wells, and Chichester: account of him, 3 *Bec.* 501 n., 1 *Brad.* 290 n.; mentioned as bishop of St David's, 3 *Zur.* 626; his Dialogue betwixt the Gentleman and the Ploughman, 3 *Tyn.* 258 n; his views on the eucharist, 3 *Zur.* 72, 76; he submits for a while to popery, 1 *Brad.* 290 n., 473, 481, 3 *Zur.* 171; his escape, 3 *Zur.* 171 n.; mentioned as an exile, 1 *Cran.* (9); he goes into Poland, 3 *Zur.* 687, 692; made bishop of Chichester, 1 *Zur.* 23, 40, (63 cancelled), *Grin.* vi. n.; he signs letters to the queen, *Park.* 101, 294; his share in the Bishops' Bible, *ib.* 335 n.; dedication to him, 3 *Bec.* 501; his death, *Park.* 331
— his daughter Frances marries Matthew, son of abp Parker, x., *Park.* 484, 2 *Zur.* 263 n.; all his five daughters eventually married bishops, 3 *Bec.* 501 n., 2 *Zur.* 263 n
Barlow (Will.), son of the bishop: sometime at Heidelberg, 2 *Zur.* 217; mentioned, 1 *Zur.* 302; his letters to Simler, 2 *Zur.* 224, 259, 268, 272; notice of him, 2 *Zur.* 263 n
Barlow (Will.), another?: Summe of the

Conference at Hampton Court, *Calf.* 199 n.; *Rog.* 317 n

Barnabas (St): *v.* Apocrypha (ii).
Sent forth by the church of Antioch, 4 *Bul.* 43, 132; with Paul at Lystra, 3 *Bul.* 209; cited by Jerome, *Whita.* 572 n.; his opinion on the seven ages of the world, 1 *Lat.* 365 n.; his epistles accounted by Stapleton as deutero-canonical, *Whita.* 305; the epistle to the Hebrews ascribed to him by Tertullian and others, 1 *Ful.* 29, 31, 33, *Whita.* 106

Barnack, co. Northampton: the advowson, 2 *Cran.* 239, 269 n

Barnard Castle, co, Durham: besieged by the rebels, 1569, 1 *Zur.* 247 n

Barnarde (Jamys): Cranmer's secretary, 2 *Cran.* 294

Barnes (Barnaby): notice of him, *Poet.* xv; twenty sonnets by him, *ib.* 41, &c.; hymn to the glorious honour of the most blessed Trinity, *ib.* 51

Barnes (Sir Geo.), lord mayor of London: commended, *Rid.* 410, 411

Barnes (Rich.), bishop of Carlisle, afterwards of Durham: father of Barnaby, *Poet.* xv; letter to him, *Park.* 392

Barnes (Rob.): notices of him, 2 *Cran.* 380 n., 1 *Tyn.* liii, 3, 33; prior of the Augustines at Cambridge, 1 *Cov.* vii, 2 *Cov.* vii; the friend of Coverdale, *ib.* viii; ambassador to Smalcald, 2 *Cran.* 332 n.; known abroad as Antonius Anglicus, and Antonius Amerius, and hence called by Luther, Antony Barnes, 3 *Zur.* 616 n.; his preaching, 2 *Cran.* 339, 2 *Lat.* 378, 389, 3 *Zur.* 215, 317, 627; he was a Lutheran, though More incorrectly charges him with the doctrine of Zuinglius, 1 *Tyn.* 3; his works on popery, 2 *Cov.* 341, &c., *Pil.* 682; his Vitæ Rom. Pont. cited, 1 *Whitg.* 404; the reputed author of the A. B. C. for Children, otherwise called the A. B. C. against the Clergy, 1 *Tyn.* 3; letter from him to Æpinus, 3 *Zur.* 616; prisoner in the Tower, *ib.* 632; exempted from the general pardon, *ib.* 207; burned, *Bale* 394, 586, 3 *Bec.* 11, 1 *Brad.* 283, 288, 2 *Cov.* 322, 2 *Hoop.* 376, 3 *Zur.* 209; persons burned with him, 2 *Cran.* 310 n.; his protestation at that time, 2 *Cov.* 322; extracts from it, *ib.* 331, &c.; it was printed in German, 3 *Zur.* 211; attacked by Standish, 2 *Cov.* 320, 323; Coverdale's CONFUTATION of Standish's treatise, including copious extracts therefrom, *ib.*; Barnes had the spirit of Elias, *Bale* 138

Barnet, co. Herts: the battle, 2 *Tyn.* 304 n.; a martyr there, *Poet.* 163

Barney (Eliz.), afterwards Grymeston, *q. v.*

Baro (Pet.), Margaret professor at Cambridge: his part in the controversy respecting Barret of Caius, 3 *Whitg.* xvii, xviii; the queen offended with him, *ib.* 617 (*v.* Dr Barrow)

Baron (Jo.), a Scottish minister: Anne Goodacre his wife, *Park.* 205, 209

Baronius (Cæsar card.): his Annales referred to, 1 *Bec.* 17 n., 2 *Ful.* 71 n., 328 n., *Sand.* 193 n.; he sanctions the irrational derivation of Cephas from κεφαλή, 2 *Ful.* 302 n.; vainly relies on the corrupted Chronicon of Eusebius to prove that Peter was 25 years at Rome, *ib.* 337 n.; endeavours to uphold the credibility of the acts of Paul and Thecla, *ib.* 339 n.; refuses to admit the alleged antiquity of the pseudo-Hegesippus, *ib.*; adduces the valueless Acts of the martyr Pontius, *ib.* 355 n.; on Paul of Samosata, *Hutch.* 132 n.; his confession as to the imaginary acts of the synod of Sinuessa, 2 *Ful.* 365 n.; his falsehood respecting the continuance of Eusebius's tendency to Arianism, *ib.* 359 n.; his extraordinary proof from the same writer of the antiquity of shaven crowns, *ib.* 115 n.; he alleges a falsified translation of that historian, *Calf.* 321 n.; denies that Paphnutius opposed compulsory celibacy in the council of Nice, 1 *Hoop.* 376 n.; speaks of the preservation of the font of Constantine, 2 *Ful.* 360 n.; disregards the counterfeit Liber de Passione Imaginis Christi, which bears the name of Athanasius, *ib.* 200 n.; maintains the genuineness of the spurious epistle to Oceanus, ascribed to Jerome, *ib.* 97 n., 339 n.; considered that father shamefully astray respecting the primacy of Peter, *ib.* 292 n.; rejects an epistle of Epiphanius, *Calf.* 42 n.; also a sermon, In Adorationem ven. Catenarum, ascribed to Chrysostom, 2 *Ful.* 110 n.; on the Opus Imperfectum ascribed to the same saint, *Calf.* 95 n.; referred to respecting the Scripta de Inventione S. Crucis, condemned by the Gelasian decree, *ib.* 324 n.; on the grant of Phocas to the pope, *Pil.* 76 n.; he is the authority for the common opinion as to that grant 2 *Ful.* 365 n.; his account of Jo. Moschus and the Limonarium, *Calf.* 174 n.; he derived from William of Malmesbury an interpolated letter ascribed to Sergius I., 2 *Ful.* 119 n.; calls Compostella a great storehouse of miracles, 1 *Hoop.* 455 n.; the fictitious St Synoris in his first edition of the Roman Martyrology, 2 *Ful.* 44 n.; he exhibits the figure of an amulet, *Calf.* 285 n.;

considers the name Papist to be a sublime title of glory, *Calf.* 290
Barons (Dr): *v.* Barnes (Rob.)
Barow (Jo.): *v.* Barrow.
Barr (Jo.): a letter to him, 1 *Brad.* 591, 2 *Brad.* 194
Barrel breeches: 2 *Ful.* 209
Barret (Dr): rejected by Cranmer at Cambridge, 1 *Cran.* viii
Barret (Rog.), or Baret: a rebellious priest, 2 *Cran.* 187 n
Barret (Will.), of Caius college: his prosecution, *Whita.* x; letter to the vice-chancellor concerning him, 3 *Whitg.* 611; his sermon gives rise to the Lambeth Articles, 1 *Whitg.* xvii; copy of those articles, 3 *Whitg.* 612; a brief touching him, *ib.* 614
Barrow: *v.* Bergen-op-Zoom.
Barrow (Dr): concerned in a controversy at Cambridge about the regularity of certain graces, *Grin.* 365—369 (qu. if Pet. Baro?)
Barrow (Hen.): preached without authority, and taught that any layman might do so, *Rog.* 231; his opinion on ministry and sacraments, *ib.* 176; he said there was no ministry of the gospel in all Europe, *ib.* 238; asserted parsonages and vicarages to be popish and antichristian, *ib.* 332; denied the visible church to be mixed, *ib.* 167; said that every member of a church has power to examine the manner of administering the sacraments, and to forsake a church which will not reform upon private admonition, *ib.* 273; thought the people might reform the church, *ib.* 344; on discipline and excommunication, *ib.* 310 n.; he asserts that a prince contemning the censures of the church should be excommunicated, *ib.* 311; intimates that baptism should not be given to the children of whores and witches, *ib.* 280; declares sin after baptism to be unpardonable, *ib.* 141; calls the apostles' creed a forged patchery, *ib.* 93; he maintained the perpetuity of the law, *ib.* 90 n., yet declared the observing of times to be an error fundamental, *ib.* 187; against liturgies and forms of prayer, *ib.*
Barrow (Isaac): his very learned treatise on the Pope's supremacy, 2 *Brad.* 145 n.; he calls Chrysostom the prince of interpreters, and ascribes to him a counterfeit Sermo in Pentecosten, 2 *Ful.* 285, 286 n
Barrow (Jo.), or Barow: a rebellious priest, 2 *Cran.* 187 n
Barrowists: *v.* Barrow (Hen.).
    Said to have had neither preaching nor sacraments, *Rog.* 176

Barrugh: *v.* Bergen-op-Zoom.
Barsham, co. Norfolk: Henry VIII. walked barefoot thence to Walsingham, 3 *Zur.* 610 n
Barston (......): legacy to him, *Grin.* 462
Bartelett (Tho.): *v.* Berthelet.
Barthelot (Jo.): letter by him and Geo. Withers, 2 *Zur.* 146
Barthius (Caspar): his conjecture about the epistles and life of Martial of Limoges, *Calf.* 69 n
Bartholinus (Tho.): works, *Calf.* 181, 258, 287
Bartholomæus Lucensis: *v.* Ptolomy.
Bartholomew (St): *v.* Apocrypha (ii).
    he preached in Armenia, 1 *Jew.* 267; how he confounded the demon which inhabited the idol Astaroth, 3 *Tyn.* 92; tales concerning him told by the false Abdias, *Calf.* 132, 133, 1 *Jew.* 483; the place and manner of his death, *Calf.* 133; proverb on his day, *Rog.* 8 n
— Massacre of St Bartholomew: *v.* Paris.
— Bartholomew Fair: *v.* London.
Bartholomew Iscan, bp of Exeter: *Pil.* 589
Bartholomew of Pisa: wrote concerning St Francis, *Bale* 205
Bartholus (......): *v.* Bartolus.
Bartie (......): a fellow-prisoner of Sandys, *Sand.* xii
Bartlet (......): answers the Hatchet of Heresies, 2 *Ful.* 4
Bartlett (......): took on him to read his divinity lecture at St Giles's Cripplegate, though suspended by the bishop, *Grin.* 288
Bartlow (Frere): does much hurt in Cornwall and Devon, 2 *Lat.* 406
Bartolus (......): In Jus Civile, *Jew.* xxxiii; on the civil rights of a harlot, 4 *Jew.* 647; he affirms that the pope is not said to commit simony, *ib.* 868; referred to, *ib.* 802
Barton (......): Cranmer's cousin, 2 *Cran.* 323
Barton (Eliz.), called the holy maid of Kent: *Bale* 139, 440, 1 *Tyn.* 483; account of her impostures, 2 *Cran.* 65, 271—274, 1 *Tyn.* 327, 3 *Tyn.* 91, 92; letter of Cranmer to bring her before him, 2 *Cran.* 252; her ghostly father, *ib.* 273; she is consulted about the king's marriage, and impedes its progress, *ib.*; Latimer engaged in her detection, 1 *Lat.* xi; she confesses her impostures, 2 *Cran.* 274; her execution, 1 *Tyn.* 327 n., 3 *Tyn.* 91 n
Barton (Geo.), parson of Abchurch, London: deprived by Grindal, *Grin.* 266, 274
Baruch (Book of): its claims to be canonical considered, *Whita.* 67, &c.; mentioned by

the council of Laodicea in conjunction with Jeremiah, *ib.* 54; taken by Cyril of Jerusalem for part of that book, *ib.* 58

Barwycke (Humf.): condemned for treason, 1 *Zur.* 129 n

Baschurche (Tho.): notice of him, 2 *Cran.* 255; his insane proceedings, *ib.* 319

Bash: to be abashed, *Phil.* 303

Basil: *v.* Basle.

Basil, emperor: *Whita.* 438

Basil (St), the Great: *v.* Amphilochius, Liturgies.
  i. *His life.*
  ii. *His works.*
  iii. *On God.*
  iv. *Scripture, Tradition.*
  v. *Justification, &c.*
  vi. *Bishops, &c.*
  vii. *Angels, Saints, Images.*
  viii. *Baptism.*
  ix. *Eucharist.*
  x. *Prayer, Praise, Worship.*
  xi. *Alms, Fasting, Penance, Celibacy.*
  xii. *Miscellanea.*

i. *His life*: his father, 3 *Jew.* 412; Basil studied at Athens, 4 *Jew.* 652; he was bishop of Cæsarea, *Rog.* 329; styled a metropolitan, 2 *Whitg.* 166, 431, yet possessed only a few books and an old gown, *ib.* 167; called prince of priests, 4 *Jew.* 824, the canon of faith, *ib.* 1045, and the doctor of the world, *Whita.* 233; he rebuked Demosthenes the cook for prating about theology, *ib.* 232; erred on some points, 1 *Hoop.* 28; his funeral sermon made by Gregory Nazianzen, *Grin.* 10; writers of his life, 1 *Jew.* 189; errors in the life falsely ascribed to Amphilochius, *ib.* 190, &c.

ii. *His works*: *Calf.* 59 n., 403, 2 *Ful.* 397, *Jew.* xxxiii; some works of his discovered, 3 *Zur.* 447; De Spiritu Sancto; the version of Erasmus, and his judgment concerning the work, *Calf.* 266 n., *Whita.* 589; object of his book of Morals, 2 *Jew.* 690, 691; he wrote on the work of the six days, 3 *Bul.* 150; the Ascetica not his, 1 *Jew.* 194; the Regulæ contractiores, Bellarmine's uncertainty as to the author, 2 *Ful.* 161

iii. *On God*: he wrote an epistle on the difference between essence and subsistence, 3 *Bul.* 159; extract from it, *ib.* 165; asks, what ear is worthy of the greatness of the things that are spoken of God? 2 *Jew.* 721, 722; says we may, by knowledge, become like God, *ib.* 670; says Christ is the life, the way, the bread, the vine, the light, a sword, &c., *ib.* 762; calls Christ indeed the sure and firm rock, 1 *Jew.* 447; says, we are partakers of the Word and Wisdom by his incarnation, 2 *Cran.* 209, 1 *Jew.* 472; shews that Christ is in us by his Spirit, *ib.* 477; his exposition of Gen. i, "The Spirit of God moved," &c., *Hutch.* 64, 137, 196; he proves that the Holy Ghost is God, by his being at one time in different persons, which angels cannot be, 2 *Bec.* 280, 3 *Bec.* 454, 1 *Cran.* 97, (50), *Phil.* 209; on an error respecting the Holy Ghost, *Rog.* 74 n

iv. *Scripture, Tradition*: his diligent study of scripture, *Whita.* 371; he speaks of a rule or canon, *ib.* 662; said to call scripture the canon of rectitude, &c., but see xii. below; says the chief thing for the finding of the truth is meditation on the scriptures, *Calf.* 144, 149; teaches that a man may not do what he thinks good, without their testimony, 2 *Cran.* 24, 2 *Ful.* 161; says, that whoso forbids us to do what the Lord commands, &c., should be execrable to all who love the Lord, 1 *Jew.* 207, 2 *Jew.* 653; denies that custom is the rule of doctrine, ascribes that office to the judgment of the scriptures, and exhorts to stand by their arbitration, *Whita.* 2, 463, 682; some other passages on their authority, 2 *Hoop.* 435—438; he says it is the property of a believer to assent to the word of God, to reject nothing, to add nothing, *Whita.* 621, and he adds, that whatsoever is beside the scriptures is sin, 2 *Ful.* 239, 2 *Lat.* 261, *Whita.* 621, 648; says it is a manifest piece of infidelity, either to reject what is written, or to add to it, *Whita.* 681; writes that every word and deed must be confirmed by the scriptures, for the full persuasion of the good and the confusion of the ungodly, 2 *Cran.* 24, 1 *Ful.* 418, 2 *Jew.* 688; teaches that the obscure parts of scripture are to be interpreted by those which are plainer, *Whita.* 491; compares the scripture to an apothecary's shop, 2 *Jew.* 671, 691, 4 *Jew.* 1174, *Whita.* 399; on the sin of wilful ignorance of scripture, *Whita.* 398; he says the gospel, without an interpretation, is a mere name, *ib.* 534; remarks, that hearers who are skilled in scripture should examine what is delivered by their teachers, *ib.* 624; says, our Lord hath so taught, the apostles have preached, the fathers have observed, the martyrs have confirmed, 2 *Ful.* 177; on the creation of light, 2 *Jew.* 581, 582; he calls it a tradition to believe in the Father, the Son, and the Holy Ghost, *ib.* 674; speaks of the tradition of baptism, meaning the written command, 3 *Jew.* 437, *Whita.* 498; distinguishes between scripture and tradition, *ib.* 499; speaks of worldly wisdom opposed to God's wisdom, 2 *Jew.* 1023; enumerates various traditions asserted to be apostolical, but which are not so regarded by papists, 3 *Jew.* 436, *Whita.* 666; on things indifferent, or not settled in Scripture, *ib.* 594; on ecclesiastical usages, 1 *Whitg.* 218; a passage on traditions wherein it is said that if we reject customs, not written, we may condemn things necessary to salvation (dub.), *Calf.* 266, 2 *Cran.* 58, 3 *Jew.* 430; testimonies alleged from his works in favour of tradition considered, *Whita.* 588—594

v. *Justification, &c.*: he confesses original sin, 2 *Bul.* 390, 3 *Jew.* 588; his words on justification by faith alone, wherein he speaks of Paul boasting of the contempt of his own righteousness, 2 *Cran.* 130, 205, 3 *Jew.* 246; he remarks that one who trusts not to good deeds, nor hopes to be justified by works, has no other hope of salvation but the mercies of God, 2 *Jew.* 1041, 3 *Jew.* 246, 583; says (the believer) knows himself to be void of true righteousness, but, only by faith in Christ, to be justified, 3 *Jew.* 244; a similar passage, *ib.* 588; he shews that the just even now drinks of the living water, 2 *Jew.* 598, 615; maintains that faith is produced by the energy of the Holy Ghost, *Whita.* 357

vi. *Bishops, &c.*: he says, Christ appointed Peter pastor of his church after him, and gave the same power unto all pastors, 1 *Jew.* 360, 3 *Jew.* 384; declares that Peter is a rock through Christ the rock, 2 *Ful.* 284, and says he received the building of the church upon him for the excellency of his faith, *ib.* 289, see also 4 *Jew.* 1118; speaks of the many bishopricks as knit together by a garland, 3 *Jew.* 301; speaks of the safety of the church of Antioch depending on Athanasius of Alexandria, 1 *Jew.* 403, 3 *Jew.* 304; writes to Athanasius on the expediency of the bishop of Rome giving his counsel in certain matters, and desiring his own help, 1 *Jew.* 393, 3 *Jew.* 135, 301—304, *Whita.* 439; he also desires counsel of all the bishops of the West, 1 *Jew.* 393, 3 *Jew.* 303; nevertheless he asks, what help shall the pride of the Western (bishops) give us? 3 *Jew.* 294, 303, 304; speaks of certain young men who preached against bishops, 3 *Whitg.* 594; mentions that the Arians denied the catholic bishops to be bishops, 4 *Jew.* 1052, 1053

vii. *Angels, Saints, Images*: he affirms that an angel cannot be at one time in divers places, 2 *Bec.* 280, 3 *Bec.* 454, 1 *Cran.* 97, (50), *Phil.* 209; says the angels are present in the church, and mark those who keep their fast, 2 *Jew.* 741; did not deem the perpetual virginity of Mary an article of faith, *Whita.* 502, 539; on the imitation of saints and martyrs, 2 *Cran.* 483; his statement respecting Zacharias who was slain, *Whita.* 589; his account of Julitta the martyr, 1 *Brad.* 554; on the sign of the cross, *Whita.* 590; a creed erroneously ascribed to him approves image-worship, 2 *Jew.* 657; cited as saying that the honour given to an image passes to the prototype, *ib.* 662; on the pictorial art, *ib.* 660; he exhorts painters (meaning orators?) to set forth the deeds of martyrs, 2 *Ful.* 199

viii. *Baptism*: he says the people were baptized in Moses, and believed in him, 3 *Jew.* 256; speaks of baptism as a power to resurrection, 1 *Jew.* 529, 3 *Jew.* 470, 532, 593; says that in it the kingdom of heaven is set open, 1 *Jew.* 466; says the grace is not of the nature of water, but of the presence of the Spirit, 2 *Jew.* 565, 3 *Jew.* 510, mentions many traditional observances in the celebration of baptism, 2 *Cran.* 56 n., as the blessing of the water, *Whita.* 592, and trine immersion, 2 *Bec.* 227, *Whita.* 592; he says those who are baptized should renounce Satan, *Whita.* 593

ix. *Eucharist* (v. Liturgies): on "Taste and see that the Lord is gracious," 1 *Jew.* 451, 3 *Jew.* 530; he says Christ called his mystical doctrine his flesh and blood, 1 *Cran.* 209, 2 *Jew.* 656; writes, there is a spiritual mouth of the inner man, whereby he is nourished by receiving the Word of life, the bread that came from heaven, 1 *Jew.* 529, 2 *Jew.* 1117, 3 *Jew.* 530; his reading of Luke xxii. 20, "This cup," &c., 1 *Ful.* 133, 512; on the sacrament as a remembrance, 2 *Jew.* 591; he calls it the mystical advent of Christ, 1 *Brad.* 98, *Rid.* 202, and the antitype of the body of Christ, *Grin.* 69; says it is divine, undefiled, heavenly, 3 *Bec.* 388, and that he that comes to it must be pure from filthiness, *ib.* 476; he shews that reverence is needful, 2 *Hoop.* 433; on "the fruit of the vine," 3 *Jew.* 521; referred to about substance and accidents, 1 *Cran.* 324, 326; on the benefits of receiving the Lord's body and blood, *Coop.* 141; he speaks of receiving the sacrament with the hand,

1 *Jew.* 155; thinks that the number of communicants is a part of Christ's institution, and that it should be at least twelve, 1 *Jew.* 122, 135, 183, 2 *Whitg.* 549; speaks of hermits receiving the sacrament by themselves, and of the reservation thereof in private houses, 1 *Jew.* 152, 154, 155, 248; mentions that in Egypt almost every man had the sacrament in his house, *ib.* 152, 2 *Jew.* 554; he was not author of private mass, 1 *Hoop.* 226, 1 *Jew.* 155; cited in support of the elevation of the host, but erroneously, 1 *Brad.* 514 n.; 1 *Jew.* 508; mentions the practice of communicating four times a week, 1 *Jew.* 155

x. *Prayer, Praise, Worship:* he describes the customs used in worship in all Christian congregations, 3 *Bec.* 408; disallows prayer in an unknown tongue, *Whita.* 264, 265; mentions the singing of psalms in various languages, 2 *Jew.* 692; speaks of the common prayer and worship of the Egyptians, Lybians, Thebans, &c., 1 *Jew.* 290; mentions the custom of standing in prayer on Sundays, and from Easter to Whitsuntide, *Whita.* 587, his reasons for this practice, *ib.* 593, and for turning to the East in prayer, *ib.* 591; he likens the sound of the people praying in the church to the roaring of the waves, 1 *Jew.* 56, 281, 282, 2 *Jew.* 1059, *Whita.* 271, 2 *Whitg.* 493; shews how the people joined in the psalm of confession, 1 *Jew.* 290, 333, *Whita.* 270; exhorts to let the tongue sing, but to let the mind search out the meaning, 1 *Jew.* 284, 333; says, he sings not unto the Lord who merely utters the words of the psalm, *ib.* 328, and that piety is not in the sound of the air, *Whita.* 402; says that a psalm puts demons to flight, and invites angels to help us, 1 *Jew.* 325 n., 327; exhorts artificers to sing psalms, *ib.* 331, 332; mentions the alternate singing of psalms, 1 *Jew.* 266, 3 *Whitg.* 385; teaches that Christian mysteries should not be exposed to the profane, 2 *Jew.* 702, 703; *Whita.* 253; says, let superfluous things be put to silence in the church of God (pseud.), 3 *Jew.* 617

xi. *Alms, Fasting, Penance, Celibacy:* he calls him a thief who makes that his own which he has received to distribute, 1 *Bec.* 25, 108, 2 *Bec.* 538; rebukes covetous men who while alive will give nothing, but at their death bequeath largely to the poor, 2 *Bec.* 396, 3 *Bec.* 460; part of this quoted by Jo. Damascene, 3 *Bec.* 366 n.; compares alms to seed sown, *Wool.* 137; a remark on carity through want of charity, borrowed from him, 1 *Zur.* 301; he praises fasting, 1 *Bec.* 104; says that it is necessary when we desire to obtain anything of the Lord, 2 *Bec.* 548; defines the true and Christian fast, 1 *Bec.* 104, 106, 2 *Bec.* 539, 1 *Bul.* 431 (see also vii.); rebukes drunkards, 1 *Bec.* 106; tells how the people confessed their sins to John the Baptist and the apostles, 3 *Jew.* 352; says the order of conversion (or penance) must be suited to the sinner, *ib.* 374; on repentance in sackcloth and ashes, 1 *Ful.* 429, 430, 444; on marriage and celibacy, that both are allowed by God, *Phil.* 404 n.; a spurious passage on the marriage of veiled virgins, 3 *Jew.* 386; he allowed monasticism, 1 *Hoop.* 28; (order of St Basil: v. Monks).

xii. *Miscellanea:* he calls the creed (not, as Whitaker alleges, the scripture) the canon of right and the standard of truth, *Whita.* 28, 659 n.; compares doctrines to a chain of united links, 1 *Jew.* 89; speaks of the gospel as first springing up in his parts, 4 *Jew.* 883; against the heresy of Valentinus, 2 *Jew.* 791; he defends Gregory of Neocæsarea against the Sabellians, *ib.* 607; his use of the word πληροφορία, 1 *Ful.* 418; calls the world the school of our souls, 1 *Jew.* 501; shews how profane authors should be read, 2 *Ful.* 134; says we must be partakers of men's sayings after the manner of the bees, *Calf.* 59; on the evils of wicked company, *Wool.* 127; he says we should answer cavils, 3 *Whitg.* 577; remarks that he who would please the people had need be like a certain Egyptian sophist, *ib.* 570; speaks of Antichrist, 2 *Ful.* 374

Basil (Theodore): Becon's feigned name, 1 *Bec.* viii, xi, xiv, xv, 28, 195

Basilides, bp of Astorga: 1 *Ful.* 40, 2 *Ful.* 342, 343, 3 *Jew.* 332

Basilides, the heresiarch: 3 *Bec.* 401, 1 *Cran.* 277; he espoused the heresy of the Gnostics, *Grin.* 59, said that Christ suffered in appearance only, *Rog.* 57, and that Simon of Cyrene was crucified in his stead, *Phil.* 417, *Rog.* 57; he rejected the Old Testament, *Rog.* 80, 87; said that men are elected and saved by nature, *ib.* 149; his new prophets, *ib.* 82, 202

Basilidians: feigned divers gods, *Rog.* 37; cast off all virtue, *ib.* 118; allowed perjury to escape persecution, *ib.* 119, 357; their traditions, *Whita.* 667; they used amulets, *Calf.* 285; wrongly referred to on justification by works, *Rog.* 126, 160

Baskerville (Dr), or Baxterville: *Park.* 171
Basle, or Basil: *v.* Councils.
    Destroyed by an earthquake, *Pil.* 607; the English exiles there, 3 *Zur.* 164, 166 n.; a church granted to them, *ib.* 766 n.; instructive pictures in the town-house, 1 *Hoop.* 507
Basnage (Jac.): Hist. des Juifs, 2 *Ful.* 101 n
Bassefontaine (......): 3 *Zur.* 741
Basset (Fra.): named, 2 *Cran.* 254; letter to him, *ib.*; Cranmer's servant, *ib.* 321; dispossessed of lands by the earl of Shrewsbury, *ib.* 366; the archbishop begs an abbey lease for him, *ib.* 380, 387
Basset (Fulke), bp of London: opposed the pope's legate, 4 *Jew.* 1080
Bassus: ministered the sacrament to Simeones, 1 *Jew.* 244
Bastard (T.): notice of him, *Poet.* xxvii; English verses by him, de Microcosmo, and, ad Johan. Whitegift, *ib.* 306
Bastards: their condition under the law of Moses, 2 *Bul.* 230; on dispensations enabling them to take orders, &c., *Grin.* 450
Bate-makers: makers of discord, *Grin.* 181
Bateman (Tho.): excommunicated from the strangers' church at Sandwich: *Park.* 247
Bath: queen Elizabeth there, 2 *Zur.* 258
Bath (Jo. earl of): *v.* Bourchier.
Bath (The): *v.* Knights.
Bathsheba: *v.* David.
Batman (Steph.): notice of him, *Poet.* xxxvi; stanzas from The Travayled Pilgrime, *ib.* 389
Batt (......): saluted, 3 *Zur.* 621
Battersea, co. Surrey: a house there occupied by the archbishops of York, *Sand.* xxii
Battle: *v.* War.
Battle (adj.): rich, fertile, *Sand.* 301
Batus, prince of Tartary: sends ambassadors to Rome, *Wool.* 28
Battus: a babbling poet, whence βαττολογεῖν, 3 *Whitg.* 514, 516
Baudouin (Fra.): *v.* Balduinus.
Bauger: barbarous, *Bale* 42
Bavande (Will.): translates a book by Jo. Ferrarius Montanus, *Wool.* 28
Bavaria: the house of Bavaria, 2 *Zur.* 274 (v. Louis, William); articles of the Bavarian inquisition, 1 *Zur.* 110 n., 278
Baxter (Rich.): Key for Catholics, *Calf.* 42 n
Baxterville (Dr): *v.* Baskerville.
Baxterly, or Bexterly, co. Warwick: the seat of Jo. Glover, 2 *Lat.* 84, 419 n
Bayard: a horse, *Calf.* 51, 1 *Ful.* 137, 457; "as bold as blind Bayerd," *Pil.* 610
Bayfield (Rich.), monk of Bury: condemned to the fire, the possession and distribution of the writings of Tyndale, &c., being counted among his crimes, 1 *Tyn.* l. 33, 42 n., 3 *Tyn.* 258 n
Bayle (Pierre): Dictionnaire, 2 *Ful.* 37 n
Bayley (Rich.): *v.* Baylis.
Baylie (Julian): charged with lewdness, 2 *Cran.* 394
Baylis (Rich.), or Bayley: priest at Malling, 2 *Cran.* 249
Bayne (Paul): *v.* Baines (......).
Bayne (Ralph): *v.* Baine.
Baynton family: 2 *Lat.* 322 n
Baynton (... lady): desires Cobham college, 2 *Cran.* 411 (wife of the next?)
Baynton (Sir Edw.): attends on queen Catharine Howard, 2 *Cran.* 409; letters from Latimer to him, 2 *Lat.* 322, 334; notice of him and his family, *ib.* 322 n.; his death, 3 *Zur.* 36
Baynton (Jo.), Carmelite: wrote on the Apocalypse, *Bale* 257
Bayso (Guido de): *v.* Guido.
Bazzanis (Menelaus de): 2 *Cran.* 555
Beach (Joan): *v.* Beche.
Beach (Jo.), abbot of Colchester: executed, 3 *Zur.* 317 n., 614 n
Beach (Steph.): *v.* Beiche.
Beacon: *v.* Cresset.
Beacon (Jo.): his controversy with Babington for the chancellorship of Coventry and Litchfield, *Grin.* 370, 371
Beadroll: a list of persons to be prayed for, 1 *Tyn.* 148 n., 2 *Tyn.* 287; beadrolls prohibited, 2 *Hoop.* 129, 135, 142, *Rid.* 320; beadrow, a catalogue, 1 *Bul.* 356
Beads: prayer on them, *Poet.* 281, 2 *Tyn.* 113; order for preaching and bidding of the beads in all sermons, 1534, 2 *Cran.* 460; the king's ordinance about bead-telling to be obeyed, 2 *Lat.* 243; order of bidding appointed by king Edward, 2 *Cran.* 157; injunction against wearing or praying upon beads or knots, *Grin.* 140
Beadsman: one who says prayers for his patron, *Calf.* 6; bead-men, prayer-men, 1 *Tyn.* 331
Beaksbourne: *v.* Bekesbourne.
Beale (Rob.): notices of him, 2 *Zur.* 292 n., 296
Bear-baiting: practised on Sundays, &c.; 1 *Brad.* 31, 2 *Brad.* xxxviii, *Lit. Eliz.* 574; bear-gardens tolerated, *Nord.* 177
Beard (......), vicar of Greenwich: *Park.* 197
Beard (Tho.): on the transient sign, and permanent erection of the cross, *Calf.* 197 n
Beards: "maugre their beards," 1 *Brad.* 421, 2 *Brad.* 2

Beaseley (Rich.): v. Beesley.
Beastly: obstinate, or carnal, 2 *Brad.* 130
Beasts: varieties of them, 2 *Bul.* 213; their disobedience reminds us of our sin, *Pil.* 91; the plague of beasts threatened to despisers of God's word, 1 *Bec.* 469, 470
Beasts (τέσσαρα ζῶα): spoken of in the Apocalypse, *Bale* 300—302, 475, 540
Beasts (θηρία): the beasts of Daniel, *Bale* 423; the beast of the Apocalypse, 2 *Jew.* 915, or of Babylon, *Rid.* 50, 53; he is so called for his cruel and beastly manners, *ib.* 70; he rises out of the bottomless pit, *Bale* 392; out of the sea, *ib.* 420, &c.; speaks blasphemies, *ib.* 430; another beast, *ib.* 436; the mark of the beast, *ib.* 447, *Phil.* 222, *Rid.* 69; this is declared to be the shaven crown or tonsure, 2 *Brad.* 43, 1 *Tyn.* 173, 236; the number of the beast, *Bale* 448; solutions, ἀντεμος, ἀρνοῦμαι, τειτάν, dic lux, *ib.*; others, *ib.* 449; the woman seated on the beast, *ib.* 496; the beast and the false prophet taken, *ib.* 554
Beatitudes, the eight beatitudes expounded, 1 *Lat.* 476, &c., 2 *Tyn.* 16, &c.
Beaton (Dav. card.), abp of St Andrews: 3 *Tyn.* 187 n
Beaton (James card.), abp of Glasgow: 1 *Zur.* 193 n., 3 *Zur.* 37, 240
Beatus: v. Rhenanus (B.)
Beauchamp (Rich.), bp of Salisbury: of noble birth, 3 *Jew.* 410
Beauchamp, lord Saint-Amand: the family, 2 *Lat.* 322 n
Beaufort (Hen. card.), bp of Winchester: quarrels with Humphry duke of Gloucester, 1 *Lat.* 118; made cardinal at Calais, *ib.*; his acts in France, 2 *Tyn.* 303; sent to Germany to seek aid against the Hussites, 2 *Jew.* 979
Beaufort (Mons. de): a name assumed by the earl of Arran, 1 *Zur.* 57 n
Beaumont (Rob.), master of Trin. coll. Cambridge: 1 *Zur.* 137 n.; extract from a letter by him as vice-chancellor, *Park.* 226 n.; to preach at Paul's cross, *ib.* 264, 275; joins in a remonstrance against the habits, 3 *Whitg.* vii; his death, 1 *Zur.* 194
Beauty: a vain thing, and not to be rejoiced in, 2 *Bec.* 437; an enticement to uncleanness, *ib.*; an hymn of heavenly beauty, by Edm. Spenser, *Poet.* 15
Beaven (James): Account of St Irenæus, 2 *Ful.* 69 n., 340 n
Bebbington, co. Chester: the advowson, *Grin.* 346 n
Becanus (Mart.): quotes as genuine a fictitious catalogue of canonical books, ascribed by Carranza to the council of Florence, 2 *Ful.* 222
Beccles, co. Suffolk: the rotten rood of Beccles, *Bale* 528, and see 2 *Ful.* 210; a man and two women, martyrs there, *Poet.* 167
Beche (Jone): martyred, *Poet.* 166
Becket (Gilb.): his fire, *Pil.* 606
Becket (Tho. à), abp of Canterbury: his history, according to Will. of Newbridge, 3 *Jew.* 574, 4 *Jew.* 960; his kindred, *Pil.* 606; born in Cheapside, London, 1 *Lat.* 201 n, *Pil.* 527; some account of his career and military prowess, 2 *Tyn.* 274, 292; incorrectly said to have been made a bishop in the field of battle, *ib.* 273, 274, 292; he writes that Rome is become a harlot, 4 *Jew.* 1083; his quarrel with Henry II. and disgrace, 2 *Cran.* 388, *Pil.* 640; accused before the pope, *Pil.* 589; a traitor to his prince, 2 *Lat.* 223, *Pil.* 488, 589; no saint, but a rebel, 2 *Cran.* 378 n.; the pope's martyr, 2 *Hoop.* 240; he shed his blood in an earthly quarrel, *Sand.* 359; the true cause of his death, 3 *Jew.* 575; his death compared with lord Cobham's, *Bale* 55, &c.; Becket contrasted with Anne Askewe, *ib.* 190; alleged miracles at his tomb, 3 *Tyn.* 131; his shrine, v. Canterbury; his blood at Canterbury, 2 *Cran.* 378; his bones burned, *ib.* n.; his service, *Pil.* 535, 536; he had two days in the calendar, *ib.* 19; his name, &c. ordered to be obliterated from church-books, 2 *Cov.* 499, 2 *Cran.* 157; complaint respecting his picture in a window at Henley, 2 *Cov.* 501; declared to be set over the works of God's hands, *Rog.* 38; blasphemous invocations of him, 1 *Bec.* 328, 329, *Rog.* 226; collect for his intercession, *Rog.* 227; prayer for salvation by his blood, 2 *Jew.* 1082, 3 *Jew.* 135, 573, *Rog.* 111; his image set up at Mercer's chapel, 3 *Zur.* 177 n., which stands on the site of his birthplace, 1 *Lat.* 201 n.; a life of him in MS., 1 *Jew.* 189; Epistolæ et Vita, *Jew.* xxxiii
Becket (Tho.), a monk of Canterbury in Cranmer's time: 2 *Cran.* 333
Beckman (J.): Hist. of Inventions, 1 *Lat.* 181 n
Beckwith (Mr): *Grin.* 325
Beckynsall (Mr): studies in Paris, 2 *Cov.* 496
Becon (Theodore), and the other children of Tho. Becon: 1 *Bec.* xiv, 2 *Bec.* 4, &c.
BECON (Tho.): WORKS, edited by the Rev. Jo. Ayre, 1, 2, 3 *Bec.*; biographical notice, 1 *Bec.* vii—xix; his birthplace uncertain, *ib.* vii; his country, *ib.* 235; he is sent to Cambridge, *ib.* vii; a hearer of Latimer,

ib.; ordained, and made vicar of Brenzett, *ib.* viii; published under the name of Theodore Basil, *ib.* viii, xi, xiv, xv, 28, 195; troubled under the Six Articles, and compelled to recant, *ib.* viii, 102 n.; retired into the Peak of Derbyshire, *ib.* ix, 2 *Bec.* 419, 420; joined Wisdome in Staffordshire, 1 *Bec.* ix, 2 *Bec.* 422; in Warwickshire, where he met Latimer, and Leicestershire, 1 *Bec.* ix, 2 *Bec.* 424; repaired home on hearing of the death of his step-father, 1 *Bec.* x, 2 *Bec.* 426; the books he wrote and translated while in the country, 1 *Bec.* x, 2 *Bec.* 427; his books condemned, 1 *Bec.* x, 28; malice of the papists against him and his writings, 2 *Bec.* 419; made rector of St Stephen's Walbrook, on the accession of king Edward 1 *Bec.* x; other promotions; *ib.*; professed divinity at Oxford, *ib.* xi; committed to the Tower in the reign of Mary, but shortly delivered, *ib.*; Ridley asks about him, 2 *Brad.* 83; his exile, 3 *Bec.* 204, 1 *Cran.* (9), 3 *Zur.* 755, 763; from Strasburgh he addressed an Epistle to the afflicted People of God, 1 *Bec.* xi; a proclamation against his books, *ib.* xii; his return to England after Mary's death, *ib.*; restored to his London living, made prebendary of Canterbury, rector of Buckland, &c., *ib.*; he dedicates his Catechism to his children, 2 *Bec.* 4; his part in the convocation of 1562, 1 *Bec.* xii; after some hesitation he subscribed, xiii; his letter to abp Parker, *ib.*; a preacher at Paul's cross, *ib., Park.* 275; published his Postils, 1 *Bec.* xiii; his death, *ib.*; his maxims, xiv; his wife and family, *ib.*; his poverty, *ib.* xiv, 61, 235, 2 *Bec.* 7; the sum of his doctrine, 1 *Bec.* 27, 28; his works, *ib.* xv, 29, 2 *Bec.* 421; their popularity, 1 *Bec.* xv; attacked by Dr Rich. Smith, *ib.*; Tanner's account of them, *ib.*; changes made in his revision of them, *ib.* xvii, xviii; he quoted faithfully from the fathers, *ib.* xix; references to his works, *Calf.* 10, 19, 52, 175, 190 nn., *Lit. Eliz.* 565 n., *Poet.* 272 n., 286 n., *Pra. Eliz.* xxii n.; quoted about St Erasmus, 1 *Hoop.* 310 n., about a pardon bowl, 1 *Lat.* 75 n.; his account of Latimer's sermons, *ib.* iii; he predicts the removal of the gospel from England, 3 *Bec.* 12

Bed: *v.* Meditations, Prayers.

The figure of the grave, *Poet.* 403; how we ought to behave ourselves when we go to bed, 1 *Bec.* 175; on going to bed, and prayers for it, *ib.* 403; before we go to bed; verses by Jo. Norden, *Nord.* 159, *Poet.* 463

Beddell (Hen.), *v.* Bedell.
Beddingfield (Sir Hen.): *v.* Bedingfield.
Bede (The Venerable):
  i. *His Works.*
  ii. *Scripture, Doctrine.*
  iii. *Prayer, Sacraments, &c.*
  iv. *Church History.*
  v. *Miscellanea.*

i. *His Works*: *Calf.* 403, 1 *Hoop.* 118 n., *Jew.* xxxiii: his History translated by king Alfred, 4 *Jew.* 779, by Stapleton, 2 *Ful.* 5; variations in the numbering of its chapters, *ib.* 9 n.; he translated John's gospel, 2 *Jew.* 694, *Whita.* 222; wrote on the Apocalypse, *Bale* 255; his Collectanea, 2 *Lat.* 313; lessons from his works in Romish service books, 4 *Bul.* 201

ii. *Scripture, Doctrine*: he says the lifting up of the brasen serpent is the passion of our Redeemer on the cross, 2 *Jew.* 726; on the building of the old gate (Neh. iii. 6), *Pil.* 383; on the troubles attending the building of the second temple, *ib.* 447; on the Cainan mentioned Luke iii. 36, and on some discrepancies between the different copies of the scriptures, 1 *Ful.* 53, 56, 57; explains why Christ sent lepers to the priest, 1 *Tyn.* 264; on our Saviour's words to Peter, and the power of the keys, 1 *Jew.* 401, 1 *Tyn.* 218 n., which he affirms was given to all the apostles, 3 *Jew.* 385; he teaches that the church is built, not on Peter, but on his faith, 4 *Jew.* 1119; on the opposition of the scribes and Pharisees to Christ, 3 *Jew.* 324; he says the hairs of Christ's head were persecuted, *Bale* 195; asserts that Christ was taken up in his humanity, but concerning his divinity he abides still on the earth, 2 *Bec.* 275, 3 *Bec.* 429; declares that Christ forsook those corporally, whom concerning his divine majesty he never left, 2 *Bec.* 275, 278, 3 *Bec.* 429, 455; on the words of Christ, "A little while ye shall see me," *Grin.* 54; he says the Son of God prays for us as our Priest, in us as our Head, and is prayed to by us as God, 2 *Jew.* 733; on the people of God coming out of Babylon, 4 *Jew.* 881; on the forerunners of Christ's second advent, *Bale* 137; [some of the wood-cuts and legends in the margin of the Book of Christian Prayers seem to have been suggested by his account of the fifteen days of judgment; see Neale's Hierologus, 107, *Pra. Eliz.* 490, &c.]; his interpretation of the sun and moon being obscured, *Sand.* 357; his opinion on the dissolution of the heavens and the earth, *ib.* 366; he says that if any man speak, he is to speak the will of God, lest he say anything besides that which is commanded, 2 *Cran.* 35; on James's doctrine of justification, *ib.* 208, 209

iii. *Prayer, Sacraments, &c.*: he says, he prays always that does good always, 1 *Bec.* 170; calls the tongue barbarous, that cannot praise God, 1 *Jew.* 268; on the speech of Galilee, *ib.* 273; says that in his time this island searched out the knowledge of one truth with five tongues, 2 *Jew.* 692, 693, *Whita.* 222; cites Augustine on the participation of Christ's body and blood in baptism, *Coop.* 121 n., 1 *Jew.* 132, 2 *Jew.* 767, 3 *Jew.* 530; he knew not of transubstantiation or private mass, 1 *Hoop.* 227; was not a massing priest, 1 *Ful.* 277; he speaks of Christ instituting the sacrament of his flesh and blood in the figure of bread and wine, 2 *Bec.* 286, 3 *Bec.* 436, shewing that the bread has mystical relation to the body of Christ, the wine to his blood, 2 *Brad.* 590, *Grin.* 47, *Hutch.* 239, 1 *Jew.* 206; says the creature of bread and wine, by the ineffable sanctification of the Spirit, is turned into the sacrament of Christ's flesh and blood, 2 *Jew.* 568, 3 *Jew.* 497, 503; declares that we ourselves are made the body of Christ, 2 *Jew.* 566; he did not hold the outward sacrament of the Lord's supper to be absolutely necessary in all cases, 1 *Jew.* 132 n.; says that the wicked do not eat Christ's body, *Hutch.* 265; cited by P. Lombard on confession, 3 *Jew.* 357, 372; reports an opinion of Augustine on excommunication, 3 *Whitg.* 263, referred to on extreme unction, 3 *Jew.* 457

iv. *Church History:* he says Paul compared the gospel which he preached in a council of the apostles, 4 *Jew.* 914; asserts that a bishop is called superintendens in Latin, *ib.* 906; mentions the Swiss martyrs Felix and Regula, 2 *Bul.* 106; names six general councils, 1 *Bul.* 14; on the time of the Nicene synod, 4 *Jew.* 1000; records the death of Augustine of Hippo, 4 *Bul.* 515; his statement as to the relationship between Gregory the Great and Felix III, 2 *Ful.* 99; he preserves a testimony of Gregory about the fourfold distribution of church goods, 4 *Bul.* 488; gives the story of Augustine the monk, 1 *Jew.* 299–301, 306, 4 *Jew.* 778; his testimony exonerates him from the guilt of murder, *Calf.* 306 n., 2 *Ful.* 6, 186; Jewel erroneously denies this, and says that the history is corrupted, 4 *Jew.* 779; on Augustine's demands, *Calf.* 307; he mentions the Christian queen Bertha, 1 *Jew.* 306, 3 *Jew.* 165; speaks of churches in Britain not subject to the pope, 2 *Ful.* 374; shews that the Britons kept Easter with the Greeks, 1 *Jew.* 145, *Pil.* 512; speaks of the tonsure of the Greeks, 2 *Ful.* 115; examples of the consecration of bishops from his writings, *ib.* 118, 119; relates a miracle wrought by Germanus, *ib.* 116; his account of the abbot Benedict, 1 *Jew.* 303; on certain teachers of psalmody in Britain, and the introduction of singing in our churches, 1 *Jew.* 303, 305; his account of Cædmon, 1 *Jew.* 304, 2 *Jew.* 694

v. *Miscellanea:* he advises rather to forswear ourselves than, for the eschewing of perjury, to fall into any more grievous sin, 1 *Bec.* 374, 1 *Bul.* 251; cited by Rabanus Maurus as to the appearing of spirits, 3 *Bul.* 400; his exposition of S. P. Q. R., 1 *Jew.* 421, of PPP. SSS. RRR. FFF., *ib.* n.; his journey to Rome a fiction, 2 *Ful.* 119 n

Bedell (A.?): A. B. chapl. challenged of false doctrine, *Grin.* 204

Bedell (Hen.), of St Pancras: *Park.* 278

Bedell (Mr), clerk to the ecclesiastical commissioners, *Grin.* 318 n (perhaps identical with the next).

Bedell (Tho.): v. Bedyll.

Bedford (Earls of): v. Russell.

Bedingfield (Sir Hen.): one of queen Mary's privy council, 1 *Zur.* 5 n

Bedlam: v. London.

Bedrot (Mr): saluted, 3 *Zur.* 607; named by Calvin, *ib.* n

Bedyll (Tho.), clerk of the council: 2 *Cran.* 242 n., 244 n., 261, 271, 272, 560

Beehive of the Romish Church: on St Patrick's purgatory, *Rog.* 215 n.; on the worship of the spear and nails, *ib.* 225 n

Beelzebub: v. Satan.

Beersheba: 4 *Bul.* 372

Bees (St): v. Saint Bees.

Beesley (Rich.), or Beaseley: one of the six preachers at Canterbury, 1 *Bec.* x. n

Bega, an Anglo-Saxon nun: 2 *Ful.* 26

Beggars: v. Fish (Simon).

Poor honest beggars and begging friars, 3 *Tyn.* 76; the craft of begging slothfully, 2 *Cran.* 108; sturdy beggars serve the devil, 1 *Lat.* 376; those who can work and will not are thieves, 2 *Bec.* 108; the duty of beggars, *ib.* 115; we all are beggars, 1 *Lat.* 413

Beguardi, or Begadores: said they were impeccable, *Rog.* 101; condemned by the council of Vienne, *ib.* n.; the Beguardi would have no reverence given on the elevation of the sacrament, 1 *Jew.* 513; the United Brethren persecuted as Beghards, 2 *Brad.* 161 n.; Bogardi, 2 *Jew.* 689. [All these names appear to belong to the same sect, which is sometimes confounded with that of the Picards, *q. v.*]

Beguinæ: would have no reverence given on the elevation of the sacrament, 1 *Jew.* 513; condemned by the council of Vienne, *Rog.* 101 n

Behem (Theobald), merchant at Strasburgh: 2 *Zur.* 305

Behesteth: promiseth, *Phil.* 379

Behold! use of the word in scripture, *Pil.* 72, 225, 459, in the prophecy of Isaiah concerning the virgin Mary, 2 *Hoop.* 8

Beiche (Steph.): confers with Bradford, 1 *Brad.* 499; named, *ib.* 541, 552

Bekesbourne, co. Kent: letters dated thence, 2 *Cran.* 411, &c.; it formerly belonged to Ch. ch. Canterbury, *ib.* 458; Parker desires to take down a part of his house at Ford to enlarge his house at Bekesbourne, *Park.* 419; repairs intended, *ib.* 446, 448

Bel and the Dragon: an apocryphal addition to the book of Daniel, *q. v.*

Bele, or Bield: a den or covert, *Sand.* 64

Belenian (Nic.): martyred, 3 *Zur.* 41 n

Beleth (Jo.): *Jew.* xxxiii; his opinion on the consecration of the sacrament in silence, 2 *Jew.* 703; cited on tongues, 1 *Jew.* 291

Belfry: poor Magdalene in the belfry, 1 *Lat.* 16, a poor woman, *ib.* 167

Belial (בְּלִיַּעַל): the word explained, 3 *Bul.* 357, 1 *Tyn.* 445

Belief: *v.* Creeds, Faith.

Believers: *v.* Christians, Faithful, Righteous, Saints.

Belisarius: conquered the Vandals, 1 *Jew.* 416; took Rome, 2 *Bul.* 109; caused Vigilius to be chosen bishop, 1 *Zur.* 18 n.; his wretched estate at last, 2 *Bec.* 441; named, 4 *Jew.* 1030

Bell (To bear the) away: 1 *Brad.* 480 n., 2 *Brad.* 84, 3 *Jew.* 415, *Rid.* 360

Bell, book, and candle: *v.* Excommunication.

Bell (......): *v.* Bill (W.)

Bell (Jo.), bp of Worcester: employed as a civilian in the matter of the king's divorce, 2 *Cran.* 244; two letters to him, *ib.* 254; he resigns the collegiate church of Stratford-on-Avon, 2 *Lat.* 383 n.; referred to as bishop, 3 *Zur.* 626

Bellamy (Jo.): brother of Jewel's mother, *Jew.* v

Bellarmine (Rob. card.): some account of him and his works, *Whita.* 5, 6; Whitaker writes against him, *ib.* xii. & passim; his opinion of Whitaker, 1 *Ful.* 14 n.; he kept the portrait of him in his study, *Whita.* x; his opinion on the inspiration of the sacred writers, *ib.* 102; he admits that the scriptures are to be believed, not on account of the church, but on account of the revelation of God, *ib.* 358; says that scripture is a commonitory, not a rule, *ib.* 657; pronounces the histories of the Old Testament unnecessary, *ib.* 660; admits the scripture is a partial rule, *ib.* 662; his rules for the interpretation of scripture, *ib.* 414; his Jesuitical glosses on several passages of scripture, *ib.* 6, &c.; he maintains the general purity of the Hebrew text, *ib.* 160, 161; his opinion as to how far the Vulgate is the work of Jerome, *ib.* 130; his defence of the Apocrypha, *ib.* 53; he ascribes Bel and the Dragon to a second Daniel, *ib.* 79; on the chronology of Judith, *ib.* 84; he denies that the faithful can obtain assurance of their forgiveness, 1 *Bul.* 91 n.; holds the supremacy of the pope to be an article of faith, *Rog.* 203; referred to on images, 1 *Hoop.* 47, on purgatory, 3 *Bul.* 393, 395, *Rog.* 215 n., on prayer for the dead, 3 *Bul.* 396, 399; he defends these doctrines by referring to the appearance of spirits, *ib.* 400; denies that bells are baptized, *Calf.* 15 n.; borrows arguments from the old heretics, *Whita.* 614; garbles quotations from the fathers, *ib.* 374; quotes an interpolated passage in the chronicle of Eusebius as proof that Peter continued for 25 years at Rome, 2 *Ful.* 337; cites the fictitious epistles of Martial of Limoges, *Calf.* 70 n.; his unsatisfactory account of the writings of the pseudo-Areopagite, *ib.* 211 n.; he relies on the testimony of the pseudo-Hegesippus, 2 *Ful.* 339; his timidity in speaking of the counterfeit epistles of the early popes, *Calf.* 222 n.; stamps as ambiguous a feigned epistle bearing the name of pope Eusebius, *ib.* 323 n.; his dishonesty with regard to a poem assigned to Lactantius, *ib.* 181 n.; his opinion of the emperor Constantine, 2 *Ful.* 380; he adopts a glaring corruption of a passage in Eusebius's life of that emperor, *Calf.* 278 n.; alleges a falsified version of Eusebius respecting the invention of the cross, *ib.* 321 n.; adduces the fictitious Liber de Passione Imaginis Christi, bearing the name of Athanasius, 2 *Ful.* 200; condemns, and yet relies on, a work falsely ascribed to the same, *Calf.* 74 n.; his doubt as to the author of the Regulæ Contractiores ascribed to Basil,

2 *Ful.* 161; endeavours to discredit an epistle of Gregory Nyssen De iis qui adeunt Hierosolymæ, *ib.* 109 n.; rejects an epistle of Epiphanius, *Calf.* 42 n.; adduces from Chrysostom a homily which he elsewhere confesses not to be authentic, *ib.* 63 n.; acknowledges that Chrysostom sometimes speaks hyperbolically, *ib.* 64 n.; his opinion on the Opus Imperfectum, *ib.* 96 n.; he maintains the genuineness of the spurious treatise Contra quinque Hæreses attributed to Augustine, 2 *Ful.* 147 n.; on the sermon De Visitatione Infirmorum, untruly assigned to the same father, *Calf.* 361 n.; alleges, on two occasions, the fabulous acts of the council of Sinuessa, 2 *Ful.* 364; rejects Gratian's corruption of a Milevitan decree, *ib.* 71 n.; on a canon of the Quinisext council, *Calf.* 137 n.; admits that the council of Basil allowed the cup in the eucharist to the Bohemians, 2 *Bec.* 245 n.; cites as authentic a counterfeit catalogue of canonical books assigned by Carranza to the council of Florence, 2 *Ful.* 222; misrepresentation as to the memorable Instructio Armeniorum, *Calf.* 248 n.

Bellasis (Ant.), or Bellows, master in Chancery: 3 *Zur.* 289 n

Bellasis (Sir Will.): v. Bellewes.

Bellerivus (Ant.), Corranus: v. Corranus.

Bellewes (Sir Will.): 1 *Zur.* 213 n (probably Bellasis).

Bellievre (...... Pompon de): v. Pompon.

Bello-Loco (Gaufridus de): 1 *Lat.* 95

Bellon (P.): speaks of priests using the Armenian tongue in divine service, 3 *Bec.* 411

Bells: very numerous in England, 1 *Lat.* 498; Latin verses on their duties, *Calf.* 15 n.; bells baptized by papists, 1 *Bec.* 11, 4 *Bul.* 502, *Calf.* 15, 16, 17, 1 *Hoop.* 533, *Rid.* 55, *Rog.* 266, *Sand.* 19, 1 *Tyn.* 274; that at Christ church, Oxon, baptized Mary, *Jew.* x; superstitions respecting hallowed bells, 4 *Bul.* 502, 1 *Hoop.* 197, 1 *Tyn.* 225, 283, 3 *Tyn.* 258; bell-ringing, 1 *Brad.* 160, 4 *Bul.* 502, 1 *Hoop.* 197; it is not damnable while the world is out of order, 2 *Tyn.* 73; not now a mark of antichristianity, 2 *Whitg.* 38, 55; the bells were better preachers than the massers, 3 *Bec.* 256; bishops rung into towns; a bishop much offended at a broken bell, 1 *Lat.* 207; bells not to be knolled or rung in service-time, 2 *Cran.* 158, *Grin.* 160, 2 *Hoop.* 136, 146, except one bell before sermon, 2 *Cran.* 502; ringing after matins, 3 *Whitg.* 384 (see 2 *Hoop.* 136, 146); bell-ringing on All-hallows day at night forbidden, 2 *Cran.* 414, 415, *Grin.* 136, 160; yet in Elizabeth's time bells were tolled on vigils, on that of All Saints through the night, 2 *Zur.* 361; the passing-bell permitted, 2 *Hoop.* 137, enjoined, *Grin.* 136, 160; forth-fares, or knells, not to be rung for the death of any man, but one bell might be tolled, 2 *Hoop.* 137; bells tolled at funerals, 2 *Zur.* 361; one short peal rung before burial, another after, *Grin.* 136, 160; threefold peal at funerals, 3 *Whitg.* 362; bells rung to stay storms, 4 *Bul.* 502, *Pil.* 177, 536, 2 *Whitg.* 67, to drive away the devil, and evil spirits, 1 *Lat.* 498, 1 *Tyn.* 225; the curfaye (curfew) bell forbidden by Hooper, 2 *Hoop.* 136; the saunce (or sanctus) bell, 1 *Jew.* 292; the sacring bell, *Bale* 91, 1 *Brad.* 160 n., forbidden by Hooper, 2 *Hoop.* 128, by Ridley, *Rid.* 319, ordered to be destroyed, *Grin.* 135, 159; hand-bells to be destroyed, *ib.*; they were carried on gang days, *ib.* 141, and at funerals, *ib.* 136

Belly: made a god, 1 *Tyn.* 299, 300; the great evils of belly-care, 2 *Bec.* 602

Belphegor: Baal-peor, *Bale* 629, 2 *Hoop.* 451

Belshazzar: his sacrilege, 2 *Ful.* 114; the handwriting on the wall, 2 *Hoop.* 266; his destruction, 2 *Bul.* 13

Bembo (Pet. card.): works, *Jew.* xxxiii; his history of Venice, 4 *Jew.* 693; he calls Mary our lady and goddess, 3 *Jew.* 577, 4 *Jew.* 949; what Leo X. said to him, *Rog.* 181 n

Bemeland: Bohemia, 3 *Jew.* 604, 4 *Jew.* 995

Benbowe (Jane): her suit with Pery, 2 *Cran.* 249, 252, 253

Benbrike (Tho.): martyred at Winchester, *Poet.* 173

Bendel (Jo.): in exile, 1 *Cran.* (9)

Benden (Alice): martyred at Canterbury, *Poet.* 169

Benedicite: v. Daniel.

Benedict V. pope: his election, 1 *Whitg.* 401, 402; he (not Benedict I. as stated) was deposed by Otho, *Pil.* 640

Benedict VIII. pope: an enchanter, *Rog.* 180 (Benedict IX. is probably intended).

Benedict IX. pope: his history written by card. Benno, 2 *Hoop.* 240; his shameful life, 4 *Jew.* 702; his sorcery, *Bale* 593 (see Benedict VIII.); appearance of his ghost, 4 *Jew.* 702, *Pil.* 603 n

Benedict XI. or XII. pope (1334—42): reckoned by Onuphrius as X, 4 *Jew.* 934; cited about the state of faithful souls departed, *ib.* 925, 930, 931

Benedict XIII. antipope: two other popes at the same time, 1 *Tyn.* 325 n., *Whita.* 510

Benedict (St), abbot of Cassina: founded the Benedictine order, 3 *Bul.* 295, 4 *Bul.* 515, 516; ministered the communion to a person who was dead, 1 *Jew.* 6, 192, 2 *Jew.* 751; a fable concerning him, *Pil.* 80; a prayer to him, *Rog.* 224; invoked against poison, *ib.* 226; St Benet's bowl, *Bale* 527

Benedict, abbot of Aniane: restored the rule of St Benedict, 1 *Hoop.* 227 n

Benedict, a British abbot: 1 *Jew.* 303

Benedict, the Levite: *Calf.* 297 n

Benedictines: their founder, 3 *Bul.* 295, 4 *Bul.* 515; monks under Benedict's rule, 4 *Bul.* 516; popes and prelates of the order *ib.*; writers on the Apocalypse, *Bale* 255; the order once observed in all cathedrals, 1 *Jew.* 39, 74; their silence, *Phil.* 421; the rule restored by Benedict of Aniane, 1 *Hoop.* 227 n.; the Carthusians a branch of this order (*v.* Carthusians); the order of Fontevraud, a new sect of Benedictines, founded by one Robert or Rodbert, 3 *Bul.* 295

Benedictio mensæ: *v.* Graces.

Benediction: *v.* Blessing.

Benedictus (Luke i.): its use defended, 2 *Whitg.* 477, 482

Benedictus (Jo.), and
Benedictus (Renatus): deemed 3 and 4 Esdras canonical, *Whita.* 104

Benefactors: fôrm, in commendationibus benefactorum, *Lit. Eliz.* 432

Benefices: *v.* Appropriations, Dispensations, Impropriations, Ministers, Non-residence, Patronage, Pluralities, Simony.
How bestowed by popes, 4 *Bul.* 144; bought and sold, 1 *Lat.* 186, 203; Latimer freely spoke against this, 2 *Bec.* 425; farmed, 2 *Cran.* 254, 258, 260, 268, 278, 279, 284, 2 *Jew.* 1012, 1 *Lat.* 203; made a provision for families, 1 *Lat.* 317; archbishop Grindal's dislike to the granting out of advowsons (expectationes) especially by ecclesiastical persons, *Grin.* 329; spiritual livings swallowed up by laymen, 1 *Lat.* 317; given to secular men, *ib.* 269, and even to boys, *Grin.* 167, 2 *Zur.* 360; pensions granted out of rectories, 1 *Lat.* 203 n.; benefices covetously sought for, 2 *Tyn.* 108, obtained by court favour, 2 *Tyn.* 336; St Paul not a benefice hunter, 1 *Lat.* 507; many were so poor, that seven or eight scarcely furnished a pastor with convenient expenses, 1 *Bec.* 21; mandate for a return of them, 2 *Cran.* 489; Godfrey's book, *Park.* 348; informations for non-residence, *ib.* 312; on dispensations for pluralities, non-residence, &c., *Grin.*
449, 450; inquiry respecting advowsons in the province of Canterbury, *ib.* 179; Jewel laments pluralities, and the abuse of patronage, 2 *Jew.* 999, 1000

Benefit of Clergy: *v.* Clergy.

Benefits: thanksgiving for all God's benefits, 3 *Bec.* 68, 85; they are to be acknowledged, 4 *Bul.* 221

Benet (St): *v.* Benedict.

Benet (Rich.), a rebellious priest: 2 *Cran.* 187 n

Benett (Dr), patron of Barnack: 2 *Cran.* 239, 269 n

Benett (Mr), chaplain to Latimer: 2 *Lat.* 416

Benett (Rob.), rector of Barnack: 2 *Cran.* 269 n.

Benger (Dr): depositions against him for speaking for the pope, 2 *Cran.* 300, 301

Ben-Gorion (Jos.): *v.* Hegesippus.

Benis (Tho.), rector of St Clement's, Norwich: *Park.* vi, 481

Benjamin (Tribe of): war against it, 1 *Bul.* 375, 417

Benjamin, a tailor: helps Sandys to escape, *Sand.* xiii, xiv

Bennet (Rich.), alderman of Calais: 2 *Cran.* 373

Bennett (Dr): in convocation 1555, living 1563, *Park.* 196

Bennett (Will.): was prebendary of Southwell, and ambassador at Rome, 2 *Cran.* 233 n., 261, 262, 269, 275, 290

Benno (Card.): wrote the life of Hildebrand (Gregory VII.), *Jew.* xxxiii; says that pope wanted some sign for the certainty of transubstantiation, 1 *Jew.* 534; relates that he wickedly burned the sacrament, 1 *Hoop.* 123, 2 *Jew.* 773; speaks of his misdeeds, 3 *Jew.* 250, 346, 4 *Jew.* 700; wrote concerning other popes, 2 *Hoop.* 240; mentions several who were enchanters, *Rog.* 181 n

Benson (Will.), alias Boston, *q. v.*

Bentham (Tho.), bp of Coventry and Litchfield: sometime in exile, *Grin.* 224, 3 *Zur.* 752; minister of a congregation in London in queen Mary's time, 4 *Jew.* 1198, 1 *Zur.* 7, 2 *Zur.* 160 n.; appointed bishop, 1 *Zur.* 63; signs a letter to the queen, *Park.* 294; his share in the Bishops' Bible, *Park.* 335 n.; a book dedicated to him, 4 *Bul.* xxi

Benvenutus Imolensis: *Jew.* xxxiii; his account of Charlemagne and some of his successors, 4 *Jew.* 683, 684

Beor, king of Ethiopia: said to have been christened by St Matthew, 1 *Jew.* 112

Berdiseley (Will.), of Calais: 2 *Cran.* 320

Bereans: praised for searching the scriptures, *Whita.* 457

Berengarius II. king of Lombardy: 2 *Tyn.* 269

Berengarius, abp of Compostello: 1 *Jew.* 550 n

Berengarius, of Tours: an excellent and learned man, *Bale* 398, 1 *Hoop.* 124, 230; wrote on the Apocalypse, *Bale* 256; his opinion on the sacrament, 1 *Jew.* 193, 457, &c., 3 *Jew.* 215; a witness against transubstantiation, *Bale* 563, 1 *Hoop.* 118, 3 *Jew.* 166, *Phil.* 398, *Rid.* 156, 158; his doctrine condemned, 3 *Bec.* 361, 2 *Cran.* 537, *Grin.* 73 n., 1 *Hoop.* 524, 2 *Hoop.* 48 n.; his compulsory recantation, 2 *Bec.* 264 n., 1 *Hoop.* 525, 526, 1 *Jew.* 95 n., 446, 459, 3 *Jew.* 613, *Wool.* 27; remarkable gloss upon it, 1 *Jew.* 459; writers against him, 1 *Hoop.* 118

Bergen: *v.* Mons.

Bergen-op-Zoom: called Barrugh, 1 *Tyn.* xlii, or Barrow, *ib.* lx, lxvi, lxix, lxx

Bergomensis (J. P. F.): *v.* Forestus.

Bergzabern, in the duchy of Deux-ponts: Coverdale pastor there, 1 *Cov.* viii, 2 *Cov.* xii, xiv, 503, &c. 3 *Zur.* 247, 483 n

Berinber: *v.* Berryn-Arbor.

Berington (Jos.): Faith of Catholics, by him and Kirk, 2 *Ful.* 282 n

Berkeley (......): *v.* Barkley.

Berkeley (Gilb.), bp of Bath and Wells: mentioned, *Park.* 408; he complains of Dr Turner, 1 *Zur.* 206 n.; Jewel's legacy to him, *Jew.* xxv

Berkshire: lord Cromwell employs Coverdale to investigate superstitions there, 2 *Cov.* 498—501

Bernard (St), abbot of Clairvaux: *v.* Guillermus.
 i. *His Life and Works.*
 ii. *On Christ.*
 iii. *Sin.*
 iv. *Grace.*
 v. *The Church.*
 vi. *Peter, Rome.*
 vii. *Saints.*
 viii. *Sacraments.*
 ix. *Miscellanea.*

i. *His Life and Works:* works, *Jew.* xxxiv; story of him and his hostess, 1 *Lat.* 519; he compelled Peter Abelard to recant, 1 *Bec.* 337; compounded a great dispute in the church of Rome, 1 *Jew.* 382; erred in some points, 1 *Hoop.* 28; said to have excommunicated flies, *Rog.* 311; though he had done many good works, yet when he came to die he acknowledged he had lived unthriftily, and called upon the favourable grace of God, 2 *Bec.* 637

ii. *On Christ:* touching Christ's nativity, he says, the body of Christ is of my body, and is mine, 1 *Jew.* 472; he declares that Christ is touched with devotion, not with the hand; with faith, not with sense, 1 *Jew.* 500, 2 *Jew.* 769; he (or Guillermus) desires to see whole Christ, and to touch Him; and also to come to the holy wound of His side, &c., 2 *Jew.* 608; on Christ's presence in divers places, *Rid.* 217, 226 (see also vii, below).

iii. *Sin:* he declares that in the fall of the first man we all fell, 1 *Bec.* 69; explains why we feel in ourselves unlawful motions of concupiscence, *ib.*; says man is but a stinking seed, and the meat of worms, 1 *Bec.* 204, 2 *Bec.* 442; declares that no man is saved without the knowledge of himself, whereof springs humility, 1 *Bec.* 205; he calls pride the beginning of sin, *ib.* 201; defines humility, *ib.* 198; denominates it the stedfast foundation of virtues, *ib.* 201; calls idleness the mother of toys, *Sand.* 117; says, they must needs be (occupied) in the work of devils, who are not (engaged) in the work of man, 4 *Jew.* 800; declares that it is not safe to be secure in heaven, or in paradise, much less in the world, *Sand.* 210; tells of some who falsely profess to love chastity, 2 *Jew.* 1129, 4 *Jew.* 642; declares that nothing displeases God so much as ingratitude, 1 *Bec.* 185, which he calls the enemy of the soul, *ib.* 186; confesses that the zeal of those who serve avarice, love pleasures, and follow the vain praises of men, convict us of negligence and lukewarmness, 1 *Cov.* 181; speaks of certain things as pastures for demons rather than for sheep, 4 *Jew.* 972; a confession of sins by him, *Pra. Eliz.* 494; another, *ib.* 495; remarks on the torments of conscience, *Wool.* 99

iv. *Grace:* he says man is created, healed, and saved, not by himself, *Pil.* 445; maintains justification of faith only, *Wool.* 35; says grace justifies freely, 1 *Bec.* 73, 2 *Cran.* 206; exclaims, how greatly we were indebted to Christ, who yet pays our debt, 1 *Bec.* 177; declares that the labour of a natural man for attaining the things of the Spirit is to no purpose, 2 *Jew.* 679; says mercy reposes not save in the vessel of faith, 2 *Cran.* 210; affirms that we must give thanks to God for the good things we do, 1 *Bec.* 179, 180; describes good works (which, he says, we call our merits) as...the tokens of hidden predestination, the presages of future happiness, the way to the kingdom, not the cause of reigning; and says that God does not find men just, but justifies them, *Sand.* 214 n.; speaks of his merit being the mercies of the Lord, &c. 3 *Jew.* 588; declares that what he lacks he is bold to take out of the bowels which abound with mercy, 3 *Bec.* 423; asks, what safe and firm security and rest is there for the weak, but in the wounds of our Saviour? 3 *Jew.* 246; says that when troubled he hides himself in the wounds of Christ, 3 *Bec.* 172; asks, what is of so mighty force to heal the wounds of the conscience as the remembrance of Christ's wounds, *ib.* 172, 423; calls the passion of Christ the last refuge and singular remedy, *ib.* 423

v. *The Church; its corruptions:* he asks, what greater pride can be, than for one man to esteem his judgment more than that of the whole congregation? 4 *Jew.* 921; remarks that the apostles stood to be judged, but did not sit to judge, 1 *Brad.* 481; declares that temporal lordship was forbidden to them, 4 *Jew.* 819, 985; says, outward peace brought in lordly pride, *Pil.* 158; speaks of his days as the unhappy times foreseen by the apostle, in which men would not abide sound doctrine, 3 *Jew.* 596; says, the whole company of Christian people seems to have conspired against God, from the least to the greatest, 4 *Jew.* 724, 735; declares of the church, from the foot to the head there is no soundness in it, 1 *Jew.* 382, 2 *Jew.* 555, 769, 807, 992, 4 *Jew.* 724, 735, 742, 856, 907, 1106; laments its wound as within the bowels, and past recovery, 3 *Jew.* 596, 4 *Jew.* 906; says, ill men go forward, good men backward, 1 *Jew.* 382, 2 *Jew.* 807, 3 *Jew.* 195, 4 *Jew.* 1106; writes, they are not all the Bridegroom's friends that are now the spouses of the church; of many he says that they are not the friends, but the rivals of the Bridegroom, 3 *Jew.* 271; says all are friends (in profession), all enemies (in reality), 2 *Jew.* 1021, 1082, 4 *Jew.* 735; declares that those called Christians have become persecutors of Christ, &c., *ib.* 638, and that they are the chiefest in persecuting God, who love the highest rooms, and to bear rule, *ib.* 992, 1021, 1082, 4 *Jew.* 735; says the servants of Christ serve Antichrist, 1 *Jew.* 382, 2 *Jew.* 707, 769, 1082, 3 *Jew.* 196, 4 *Jew.* 799, 1112; complains largely of the pride and corruption of the clergy, 3 *Bul.* 117; 4 *Jew.* 735; speaks of the priests as worse than the people, 1 *Jew.* 121, 2 *Jew.* 685, 4 *Jew.* 735; finds fault with their dainty apparel, 4 *Jew.* 971; speaks of some as soldiers in their apparel, clerks in their gain, neither in their acts, *ib.* 972; says, holy degrees are given over to lucre, &c., *ib.* 867; affirms that spiritual ministers, who maintain their own pomp on that which should be bestowed on the poor, sin grievously two ways, 1 *Bec.* 24; asks, what avails it that they be chosen in order, if they live out of order? 3 *Jew.* 349; speaks of the bishops and priests of his time as unchaste, and given over to a reprobate mind, *ib.* 426, and as abstaining from the remedy of marriage, *ib.*; says, it is a shame to speak of the things done by them in secret, 4 *Jew.* 628; calls them the darkness of the world, *ib.* 747, 750; says they not only save not, but destroy, 4 *Jew.* 873, that they do not feed the Lord's flock, but kill and devour it, 3 *Jew.* 286, 4 *Jew.* 873; calls them not pastors but traitors, 3 *Jew.* 286, 4 *Jew.* 746; says doctors are become seducers, pastors impostors, prelates Pilates, 1 *Jew.* 162, 2 *Jew.* 992, 993, 1081, 4 *Jew.* 745, 746, 1112, *Sand.* 168; calls the clergy not hirelings, nor wolves, but devils, 1 *Jew.* 121, 2 *Jew.* 642, 1081; the corruption of the clergy in his time led him to expect the revelation of Antichrist, *Coop.* 185, 2 *Jew.* 638, 769, 897, 1082, 4 *Jew.* 735; he writes against the heretics called Apostolics or Henricians, 3 *Jew.* 151, *Rog.* 119 n., 330, 331 n

vi. *Peter, Rome:* Philpot refers to him as saying that the Holy Ghost is Christ's vicar, *Phil.* 108; he calls Peter by that name, *ib.* n.; he was deceived, as to Peter's supremacy, with the common error of his time, 2 *Ful.* 321; on Peter's reception of the keys, 3 *Jew.* 368; he supposed that Christ's prayer for Peter secured the infallibility of the Roman see, *Whita.* 430; a strange argument of his for the pope's supremacy, 4 *Jew.* 747; he addresses the pope as in primacy Abel, in government Noah, &c., 1 *Jew.* 438 n., 4 *Jew.* 745, 882, allows him two swords, 4 *Jew.* 825, and ascribes to him the plenitude of power, 2 *Brad.* 144 n., 3 *Jew.* 284, 4 *Jew.* 745, 746, 829, yet intimates that there may be the fulness of power without the fulness of justice, 4 *Jew.* 832; denies that the pope derives the right (of crowning the emperor) from Peter, *ib.* 836; speaks of the credit arising to himself on account of the advancement of

Eugenius, *ib.* 1045; tells that pontiff that in some things he succeeded not Peter, but Constantine, *ib.* 1009; addresses him as the shepherd shining in gold and gorgeous attire, but caring not for the sheep, 2 *Jew.* 1020; tells him that ambition through him strives to reign in the church, 3 *Jew.* 294, 4 *Jew.* 867, and that his ecclesiastical zeal burned only for the maintenance of his dignity, 4 *Jew.* 707; writes strongly to him on the confusion of appeals, 1 *Jew.* 391; admonishes him that his power is in offences, not in possessions, 3 *Whitg.* 410; speaks of a certain pope as a follower of Judas, 1 *Hoop.* 312; writes of the pope's court, that it more easily receives good men than makes them, &c., 4 *Jew.* 657; says the beast of the Apocalypse occupies the chair of Peter, as a lion prepared for his prey, 2 *Jew.* 915, 4 *Jew.* 743; calls the Romans hateful and wicked, *Rog.* 182

vii. *Saints:* expressions respecting the virgin, 2 *Jew.* 900 n., 3 *Jew.* 572; he interprets Gen. iii. 15 ("ipsa conteret") of her, 1 *Ful.* 534; Bernard (or Gillebert?) shews that the church is taught by the sufferings of martyrs, *Bale* 187

viii. *Sacraments:* he says a sacrament is called a holy sign, the invisible grace being given with a visible sign, 3 *Bec.* 449; calls the washing of feet a great sacrament, 1 *Jew.* 223, 225, a sacrament of the remission of daily sins, 2 *Jew.* 1103, and applies the term sacrament to a painted cross (Gaufrid?), 1 *Jew.* 225; speaking of baptism he says, let us be washed in Christ's blood, 1 *Jew.* 466, 475, 2 *Jew.* 768, 3 *Jew.* 496, 529; mentions some who in his time denied the baptism of infants, 4 *Bul.* 382, *Phil.* 274; says the will is taken for the deed (in baptism) when necessity excludes the deed, 2 *Bec.* 224; observes that a ring is given to invest one with an inheritance; so Christ, when he drew nigh to his passion, gave his disciples seisin of his grace, by a visible sign, 2 *Jew.* 1102; the sealing-ring, he says, is nothing worth; I sought for the inheritance, 1 *Jew.* 449; says, that in the communion, not only the priest sacrifices, but the whole company of the faithful, *ib.* 177; exhorts daily to receive the sacrament as the medicine of the wound of sin, 2 *Bec.* 259; passages on the presence of Christ in the sacrament, 1 *Jew.* 492, *Rid.* 217, 218; he says the flesh of Christ is given to us spiritually, not carnally, 2 *Bec.* 286, 3 *Bec.* 449; asks what it is to eat the flesh of Christ and drink his blood, but to be partaker of his passion and follow his conversation, 3 *Bec.* 433; a spurious work in his name says, angels eat the Word born of God, men eat the Word made flesh (fœnum), 2 *Jew.* 768, also that the priest holds his God, and gives him to others, *ib.*, and touches him with hand and mouth, *ib.*, and that the sacrament is God, and the wine the Creator of wine, *ib.*; remarks on these passages, *ib.* 769

ix. *Miscellanea:* on the way to understand the scriptures (pseud.), *Whita.* 451; on the straight paths of the Lord, *ib.* 400; he says, thou hast appealed unto the gospel, unto the gospel thou shalt go, 3 *Jew.* 565; declares that a rule which does not agree with the gospel is no rule at all, *ib.* 600; speaks of a so-called novelty which is not new, but the ancient inheritance of the church of God, 4 *Jew.* 777; his resolution, Never, O Lord, will I depart from thee without thee, 1 *Brad.* 559; he shews how we may know that God is with us in trouble, *Cov.* 120, and that it is better to be in trouble, with his presence, than to be even in heaven without him, *ib.* 165; he says faith must be by persuasion, not by force, 2 *Jew.* 1023, *Phil.* 105; declares that the seeing of the soul is understanding, 3 *Jew.* 531; calls it a vanity to garnish the stones of the church with gold, and leave her children naked, 1 *Bec.* 23; would not have honourable marriage taken from the church, 4 *Jew.* 645, 646; says that what has been unadvisedly vowed must not be kept; it is a wicked promise that is performed with wickedness (pseud.), 3 *Jew.* 428; writes to an archbishop about subjection to the higher powers, 4 *Jew.* 706; on the uncertainty of the time of death, *Sand.* 170; reference to a prayer on death by him, *Pra. Eliz.* 537 n.; St Barnard's verses, 2 *Cran.* 148; the saying, "Bernardus non vidit omnia," 3 *Jew.* 177

Bernard, abbas Augiensis: *v.* Berno.

Bernard of Morlaix, or Morlanensis, a Cluniac monk, *Jew.* xxxiv; verses on Rome, 4 *Jew.* 1083

Bernard, bp of St David's: submitted to the see of Canterbury, 3 *Tyn.* 158 n

Bernard, abp of Toledo: *Jew.* xxxiv; probably the author of the four sermons Super Salve Regina, 3 *Jew.* 596 n

Bernard of Trilia: wrote on the Apocalypse, *Bale* 257

Bernard (......): at Oxford, *Pil.* 682

Bernardine, i. e. B. Ochinus, *q. v.*

Bernardinus (St), Senensis: devota oratio

ad Jesum Christum, *Pra. Eliz.* 202; the same in English, *ib.* 108; an adaptation of a devout prayer by him, *Lit. Eliz.* 251; he wrote on the Apocalypse, *Bale* 258

Bernardinus de Busti: his Mariale, 2 *Jew.* 900, 3 *Jew.* corrig., *Jew.* xxxiv; his blasphemous expression respecting the virgin, 2 *Jew.* 900; referred to on purgatory, *Rog.* 215 n

Berne: the lords of Berna never subjects to the duke of Savoy, 4 *Jew.* 665; a public disputation at Berne, 4 *Bul.* x, 3 *Zur.* 718; the republic at war with Geneva, *Phil.* 389; letter from the council to king Edward, 3 *Zur.* 717; election of ministers there, 1 *Whitg.* 309, 418

Berners (......): *v.* Verney.

Bernher (Augustine): references to him, 1 *Brad.* 306, 2 *Brad.* 168, 398 n., 406, *Rid.* 362, 369, 371, 379, 384; some account of him and his writings, 2 *Brad.* 186 n., 1 *Lat.* 446, 3 *Zur.* 360 n.; he published the sermons of his master Latimer, 1 *Lat.* xiv, xvi, 446, 447 n., 455; his account of Latimer, *ib.* 319; he aids Jewel in his escape, *Jew.* xi; letter from him to Ridley, *Rid.* 381; to Bullinger, 3 *Zur.* 360; dedication to Katherine duchess of Suffolk, 1 *Lat.* 311; letters to him, 2 *Brad.* 34, 158, 172, 186, 251, *Rid.* 372, 380, 382

Bernius (Nich.): letter to bp Horn, 2 *Zur.* 264 (*v.* Bernus).

Berno, or Bernard, abb. Augiensis: 3 *Bec.* 415 n

Bernus (......): perhaps the same as Bernius, 2 *Zur.* 278, 284

Berny (......): *v.* Verney.

Bernye (Eliz.): *v.* Barney.

Berosus, the Chaldean: on Gog and Magog, *Bale* 571

Berryn-Arbor, or Berinber, co. Devon: Buden in this parish, Jewel's birth-place, *Jew.* v

Bertha, queen of Kent: attended by a Christian bishop, *Calf.* 306; worshipped at St Martin's, Canterbury, 1 *Jew.* 306; mentioned, 3 *Jew.* 165

Berthelet (Tho.), printer: 2 *Cran.* 395, 396

Berthlet (Tho.), or Barthelet: Cranmer's secretary (the same?), 2 *Cran.* 270, 300

Bertie (Pereg.), lord Willoughby de Eresby: sent to assist Henry IV. of France, *Lit. Eliz.* 470; his chaplain, 2 *Zur.* 327 n

Bertie (Rich.): an exile for religion, 2 *Zur.* 239 n.; husband of Katherine duchess of Suffolk (and father of the preceding), 1 *Lat.* 81 n.; (*v.* Bartie, perhaps the same).

Bertram, or Ratramn: his character by Trithemius, 3 *Bec.* 449; a learned and sound catholic, *Rid.* 206; his book De Corpore et Sanguine Domini, 1 *Hoop.* 524, *Jew.* xxxiv, *Rid.* 159; it was written against Paschasius, 1 *Hoop.* 118 n., 524 n.; written at the request of Charles the Bald, not of Charlemagne, *Grin.* 73 n., 1 *Hoop.* 524 n., *Rid.* 159 n.; insinuated by papists to be a recent forgery, *Rid.* 159 n.; but many passages from it are found translated into Anglo-Saxon in the Paschal homily, 2 *Ful.* 20 n.; this book brought Ridley from Romish error, *Rid.* ix, 206; that martyr, after his degradation, advised bp Brooks to read it, *ib.* 290; translated by Will. Hugh, *ib.* 159 n.; Bertram says that when we shall come to the sight of Christ, we shall have no need of instruments to put us in remembrance of his kindness, 3 *Bec.* 370, 371, 448; his doctrine on the sacrament, 1 *Jew.* 458; on the presence of Christ therein, *Rid.* 202; he allows that the sacrament is, after a certain manner, the body of Christ, 1 *Jew.* 503; says that as to the substance of the creatures, they remain after consecration what they were before, 2 *Bec.* 268, 3 *Bec.* 425, 2 *Jew.* 1116, *Sand.* 89; argues that if the mystery (of the sacrament) be not done under a figure, it is not rightly called a mystery, 3 *Bec.* 425, 2 *Hoop.* 405, and that if the wine when consecrated be turned into the blood of Christ, the water must be turned into the blood of the people, 3 *Bec.* 426, 447; calls the body and blood of Christ a spiritual meat and a spiritual drink, 2 *Bec.* 295, 296, 3 *Bec.* 434; says that he who now in the church spiritually turns bread and wine into his body and blood, once made his body of the manna, and his blood of the water from the rock, 1 *Jew.* 546, 2 *Jew.* 577, 3 *Jew.* 503; insists that the body of Christ in the sacrament is neither visible nor palpable, 3 *Bec.* 445, 446; expounds the distinction made by Ambrose between the flesh that was crucified, and the sacrament of that flesh, *ib.* 444, 445; argues from that father that the sacrament is not corporal but spiritual food, *ib.* 445; maintains, on the same authority, the difference between the body of Christ which suffered, and that which is received of the faithful in the sacrament, 3 *Bec.* 446, *Grin.* 73, 74; argues from Jerome that the flesh and blood of Christ are understood two ways, 3 *Bec.* 446; says that the body and blood of Christ used in the church differs from that known to be glorified in his body through his resurrection, *ib.* 447, 448; calls the bread and cup a figure, 3 *Bec.* 448, 449, 2 *Hoop.* 405; declares that without the spiritual working the mysteries of the body and blood of Christ profit nothing, 3 *Bec.* 469

Bertrand Parayte, *q. v.*

Bertrand (Pet.): in a gloss on the Decretals, he says, Christ would not have dealt discreetly, had he not left a vicar, 1 *Jew.* 380

Berub: to repair, 2 *Cran.* 186

Berwick on Tweed: *v.* Dialogue.

On the name Berwick, *Rid.* 489, 492; a congress there, 3 *Zur.* 429, 434, 454

Beryllus: a heretic, 3 *Bec.* 401; but he forsook his error, 2 *Jew.* 802

Bessarion (Card.): he flattered the pope, 1 *Jew.* 335; his conduct at the council of Florence, 3 *Jew.* 126, 341, *Rid.* 250 n.; made a cardinal, 2 *Jew.* 700; he declares that all churches but the Latin and Greek are full of heresies, 1 *Jew.* 334; confesses that there are only two sacraments plainly delivered in the gospel, 2 *Jew.* 1104, 1125; 3 *Jew.* 444, 459; shews that the proper order in the sacrament is first to consecrate, then to break, and after that to distribute, 1 *Jew.* 126, 4 *Jew.* 887; says, in the Latin church consecration is wrought by the words of Christ; in the Greek church, by prayers that follow, 1 *Jew.* 123, 139 n., 3 *Jew.* 451; speaks of the people saying "Amen" to the words of the priest, 1 *Jew.* 312, 2 *Jew.* 698; expresses his doubt of a work ascribed to Clement, 1 *Jew.* 112

Besides: apart from, 2 *Tyn.* 183

Bessus: punished by Alexander, *Pil.* 188

Best (Cha.): notice of him, *Poet.* xlv.; of the fall of man in Adam (verses), *ib.* 471

Best (Jo.), bp of Carlisle: ill-used in Cumberland, *Grin.* 268; recommended to Cecil, *ib.*; complains of want of preachers in his diocese, *ib.* 285

Beston (Eliz.): at Calais, 2 *Cran.* 320

Beswick (Rog.): Bradford's brother-in-law, 2 *Brad.* xli.

Bethel: 4 *Bul.* 165, 3 *Tyn.* 182; it came to be called Bethaven, 4 *Jew.* 1046

Bethesda: *v.* Jerusalem.

Bethlehem: *v.* Stars.

The house of bread, *Hutch.* 256; called by Prudentius the head of the world, 1 *Jew.* 439, 3 *Jew.* 270; Paula's visit to it, 2 *Jew.* 740

Bethlehem hospital: *v.* London.

Bethnal Green, co. Middlesex: *Sand.* xiv.

Bethsaida: denounced, 3 *Bul.* 112, 2 *Hoop.* 209

Bethshemesh: the ark there, 2 *Bul.* 148, 4 *Bul.* 295

Beti (Fr.): at Strasburgh, 1 *Zur.* 9

Betta (Thaddeus): saluted, 1 *Zur.* 305

Better: used (as in the Catechism) for superior in rank, 1 *Tyn.* 203

Bettes (Eliz.): *v.* Brown (E.).

Betts (Will.), of C. C. C., chaplain to Anne Boleyn: his death, *Park.* 1, 2

Betuleius (Xystus): *Calf.* 13 n

Beugnot (......): Hist. de la Destruction du Paganisme, 2 *Bec.* 305 n

Bever: drink? *Pil.* 446

Beveridge (Will.), bp of St Asaph: Pandecta, *Calf.* 137 n., 2 *Ful.* 50 n

Beverley, co. York: a place for pilgrimage, *Bale* 99

Beverley (Jo.): a persecuted priest, *Bale* 13, 50; hanged and burnt, *ib.* 51

Bevis of Hampton, or Southampton: *Calf.* 224, 1 *Hoop.* 77, 1 *Tyn.* 161

Bewray: to defile, 1 *Brad.* 137

Bexterley: *v.* Baxterley.

Beza (Theod.):

i. *His Life and Works:* his works *Jew.* xxxiv. 3 *Whitg.* xxv.; references to him, 1 *Zur.* 152, 2 *Zur.* 35; his ordination, 2 *Ful.* 73; Greek professor at Lausanne, 3 *Zur.* 153; his part in the conference at Poissy, *Grin.* 244 n., 1 *Jew.* 89; praises Cartwright, 1 *Zur.* 312 n.; mention of his letter to Grindal, 3 *Whitg.* 277, 278; testifies to the purity of doctrine in England, *Rog.* 7; letters by him to Bullinger, 2 *Zur.* 127, 153; letter of the church of Scotland to him, *ib.* 362; other letters to him, *ib.* 142, 152, 154, 170, 3 *Zur.* 741; letter to him and others, 2 *Zur.* 121

ii. *Biblical criticism:* his translation of the New Testament, 1 *Ful.* passim; a table of alleged corruptions therein, *ib.* 594 (and see the title Beza in the index to that volume); his translations not followed by the English, *ib.* 154; the Codex Bezae, *ib.* 57, 88; his criticisms on the Greek text of the New Testament, *ib.* 41, &c.; his opinion of the Vulgate version of the New Testament, *ib.* 175 n., *Whita.* 144; his rendering of Μετανοεῖτε, 1 *Ful.* 155; his interpretation of κατακυριεύουσιν and κατεξουσιάζουσιν in Matt. xx. 1 *Whitg.* 164; on Gal. ii. 2, "those of reputation," 2 *Whitg.* 411; on Eph. i. 23, "the fulness of him," &c. 1 *Ful.* 231 n., 232, &c.; exposition of Phil. i. 16, οὐχ ἁγνῶς, 1 *Whitg.* 294; his translation concerning temptation considered, 1 *Ful.* 561, &c.; he says the judicial law of Moses consists partly in external manner of worship, partly in the civil affairs of life, 1 *Whitg.* 268, and shews that its precepts are not binding on Christian states, *ib.* 277, 278; thinks we owe more to Paul's bonds than to his liberty, *Rog.* 324 n.; held John to be the writer of the Apocalypse, 1 *Ful.* 34; speaks of the dislike of Servetus and others to commentaries, *Rog.* 196 n

iii. *Doctrine:* on predestination, 3 *Whitg.* 142—145; on making our calling and election sure, 1 *Ful.* 85; he opposed the doctrine of free-will, *ib.* 377; on the impossibility of keeping God's commandments perfectly, *ib.* 399 n.; against the error of inherent justice, *ib.* 401 n., 404; on Christ's descent into hell, *ib.* 81; he amended his translation of a text respecting it, *ib.* 229, 230; his alleged omission of the article of the creed concerning it, *ib.* 278, 279; on the word שאול, *ib.* 310 n.; defence of his doctrine on Christ's descent into hell, 2 *Ful.* 377

iv. *Sacraments:* on circumcision as a seal of righteousness, 1 *Ful.* 451; he says that by circumcision the Jews became more guilty; so with respect to baptism, *ib.* 398 n.; rebukes Castalio for calling baptism "washing," *ib.* 255, 256; on John's baptism, *ib.* 453, &c.; on "water and the Spirit," *ib.* 455; against baptism in private, 3 *Whitg.* 548; on the baptism of the children of excommunicate persons, *ib.* 142—145; on the construction of Luke xxii. 20, "This cup," &c., 1 *Ful.* 132—139, 512, 2 *Ful.* 385—387; on the blessing or consecration of the sacrament, 1 *Ful.* 499—501; he declares that the sacraments are only two, 3 *Jew.* 455

v. *Church Polity:* on church government, 3 *Whitg.* 162, 217, 218; he says the apostles had authority, as twelve patriarchs, over the church, *Rog.* 328; on Peter's primacy, 1 *Ful.* 86; on the election of Matthias, 1 *Whitg.* 303, 357; on the corporal punishments inflicted by the apostles, 3 *Whitg.* 545; on Andronicus and Junia, 1 *Whitg.* 498; he allows difference of rank amongst ministers, 2 *Whitg.* 266, 332, 433; calls primates and archbishops the shadow and image of the Roman polity, *Rog.* 329 n.; on the office of Timothy, whom, in effect, he allows to have been bishop of Ephesus, 2 *Whitg.* 298, 300, 308; says πρεστώς was formerly the appellation of bishops, *ib.* 309; traces the growth of their civil jurisdiction, 3 *Whitg.* 544; on the calling and election of ministers, 1 *Whitg.* 365, 415—417; by χειροτονία he understands suffrage, *ib.* 345; expounds the peculiar duties of pastors, 2 *Whitg.* 457, 458; disallows the exercise of ministry against the will of the prince and bishops, *Grin.* 209; asserts that a discreet policy must be used in the church, that the apostles did not always use the same form of electing, and that therefore churches are not always bound to follow their form, 1 *Whitg.* 414, &c., 457, 458; on the choice of deacons (Acts vi.) *ib.* 303, 365, 417, 457, 458, 459; gives his opinion on their office, 2 *Whitg.* 457, 458, 3 *Whitg.* 65, 72; considers that Rom. xii. 8 has reference to them, 3 *Whitg.* 282 n.; on the συνέδριον (Matt. v. 22), *ib.* 228; on the presbytery or eldership, 1 *Whitg.* 488; says there should be a presbytery even under Christian rulers, 3 *Whitg.* 538; that princes and noblemen should be chosen into the presbytery, *ib.* 205; asks, who can exempt even kings and princes from the domination, not human but divine (of the presbytery)? *Rog.* 340; says one cause of councils was to make rules of discipline according to the diversity of time, 1 *Whitg.* 253, 287; approves provincial synods, 2 *Whitg.* 332; thought that private persons might summon assemblies about church causes, *Rog.* 206; warns against looking always at what the apostles did, 1 *Whitg.* 254, 287, 458, 3 *Whitg.* 195; says that not all apostolic rites are now to be received, 1 *Whitg.* 287; shews that canons about church-rites respect comeliness in external things, and hence are neither general nor perpetual, so that we find a contrariety in them, 1 *Whitg.* 253, 254, 287; allows that what is profitable to edify is not to be determined by the judgment of the common people, *ib.* 198, and that they who command or forbid the use of indifferent things without reason, or rashly judge men's consciences therein, offend God and their neighbours, *ib.* 198, 199; also that things otherwise indifferent may by some lawful commandment change as it were their nature, and become imperative, 1 *Whitg.* 209, 2 *Whitg.* 5; he disliked the sign of the cross, *Rog.* 321 n.; calls prayers in an unknown tongue a mockery of God, 1 *Jew.* 329; on excommunication, 3 *Whitg.* 142—145; on the keys (Matt. xvi.) *ib.* 542

vi. *Heresies:* on papism, 3 *Whitg.* 148; on Marcion's heresy, *Rog.* 51 n.; on the Enthusiasts, *ib.* 158; on the heretic Blandrata, *ib.* 49 n.; on the apostates Neuserus and Silvanus, *ib.* 162; on Osiander's error; *ib.* 115 n.; on Servetus, *ib.* 55 n., 70 n., 196 n.; he maintains that magistrates may punish heretics, 3 *Whitg.* 448

vii. *Marriage*: on 1 Cor. vii. 1, against Erasmus, 1 *Ful.* 115; he shews how celibacy is better than marriage, 2 *Ful.* 383; calls Ochinus a defender of polygamy, *Rog.* 307 n.; says the judgment of matrimonial causes pertains to the civil magistrate, 3 *Whitg.* 543

Bezaleel: 2 *Bul.* 150

Bianket (Jo.): a Bononois born, 2 *Cran.* 330

Bib: to drink, 3 *Bec.* 282

Bible: *v.* Law of God, Scripture, Word of God; also the names of the several books. The present title is bibliographical and historical.

POLYGLOT: the Complutensian Bible cited respecting the doxology to the Lord's prayer, 4 *Bul.* 219, 220 n

Anglo-Saxon: *v. English*, infra.

Armenian: it is alleged that Chrysostom rendered the scriptures into this tongue, *Whita.* 222; a version alluded to by Theodoret, *ib.* 245

British: *v. Welsh*, infra.

Coptic: Chrysostom says the Egyptians had scripture in their own tongue, *Whita.* 245; so Theodoret, *ib.*

Dalmatic: *v. Sclavonic*, infra.

Dutch: a version commenced by de Marnix, 2 *Zur.* 289 n

English: ancient vernacular versions, 2 *Cran.* 119; the Bible was translated for our Saxon forefathers, but it is questionable to what extent, 1 *Tyn.* 149 n.; Bede translated St John's Gospel, 2 *Jew.* 694; and he says the scriptures were read in his time in the languages of the English, the Britons, the Scots, the Picts, and the Latins, *Whita.* 222, & al.; his account of the poems of Cædmon, 2 *Jew.* 694, & al.; the Psalms translated by command of Alfred, 2 *Jew.* 694, *Whita.* 222; alleged translation by order of king Athelstan, 2 *Jew.* 690, 694, *Whita.* 222; reference to an old lawful translation before Wickliffe's, 3 *Tyn.* 168; Wickliffe's version, 2 *Cov.* ix. 1 *Tyn.* xx. xxviii.; this and other translations forbidden by abp Arundel, 1 *Tyn.* 132 n.; the reading of the scriptures by the people soon afterwards forbidden by law, *Bale* 50

Matthew and Mark, translated by Tyndale (c. 1524), 1 *Tyn.* xxvii.; Tyndale's New Testament with notes, in quarto, begun to be printed at Cologne, 1525, *ib.* xxviii. &c.; account of the only remaining fragment of this Testament, now in the British Museum, *ib.* 4, 5; the notes of that fragment, 2 *Tyn.* 227—236; Tyndale's New Testament, Worms, 1526, 12mo. without notes, (the first edition published), 1 *Tyn.* xxx.—xxxii.; specimen of it, 3 *Tyn.* 286; Tyndale's epistle subjoined to this edition, 1 *Tyn.* 389; third edition, Antwerp, Chr. Endhoven, 1526, *ib.* xxxiii.; bought up by abp Warham, *ib.*; fourth edition, Antwerp, Chr. Van Ruremund, 1527, *ib.*; Joye's surreptitious editions, 1534, *ib.* lxi.; revised edition, Antwerp, 1534, *ib.* lxii. 467; three editions printed at Antwerp in 1535; one of them for the use of ploughmen, *ib.* lxxiii.; specimen of the last-mentioned edition, 3 *Tyn.* 287; Tyndale's New Testament, 1536, the first volume of scripture printed in England, 1 *Tyn.* lxxv. 467; the edition of 1538, *ib.* 467; a copy of the New Testament, on vellum, sent by Tyndale to queen Anne Boleyn, *ib.* lxiv.; the books of Moses, by Tyndale, separately published, 1530, &c. *ib.* xl.; specimen, from the second edition of Genesis, 3 *Tyn.* 284; Tyndale's preface to the Pentateuch, 1 *Tyn.* 392; alleged translation of Jonah, by Tyndale, 1531 (no copy known to exist) *ib.* 447; Tyndale's Testament reviled by Tonstal and by Martin, *ib.* 228, 229, 1 *Ful.* 61; English Bibles and other books burned at St Paul's in the presence of Wolsey, bp Fisher preaching, 1 *Tyn.* xxxi.; translations inhibited by Tonstal, *ib.* 132 n.; their circulation forbidden by royal proclamation, 1 *Lat.* v., 1 *Tyn.* 131 n., the king being advised by More and the bishops, 1 *Tyn.* 34, 35; Latimer's letter to king Henry, for restoring the liberty of reading the holy scriptures, 2 *Lat.* 297; Papists condemn Tyndale's and all translations into common tongues, *ib.* 320

Coverdale's Bible (first printed 1535); translations used in this version, 2 *Cov.* 12; its publication, *ib.* ix.; it is stated that Henry VIII. ordered it to go abroad among the people, 1 *Ful.* 98, but probably it was never expressly sanctioned by him, 2 *Cov.* x.; different editions, *ib.* x. &c. 2, 1 *Ful.* 20 n., 67, 68; editions of his New Testament, 2 *Cov.* xi. 23, 497; dedication and prologue to the New Testament printed by Nycolson, 1538, *ib.* 24—31; dedication and prologue to the New Testament printed by Regnault in the same year, *ib.* 32—36; two copies of a Bible to be printed on parchment, one for the king, one for lord Cromwell, *ib.* 492; letters from Coverdale to lord Cromwell respecting his biblical labours, *ib.* & seq.

The Bible called Matthew's (Grafton, 1537), 2 *Cov.* x. 2 *Cran.* 344, 345, 1 *Ful.* 20 n., 21, 72, 91; edited, or commenced, by

Jo. Rogers the martyr, 2 *Cov.* x., 1 *Tyn.* lxxiv.; completed, *ib.* lxxv.; specimen of Tyndale's translation of the historic books of the Old Testament, from that edition, 3 *Tyn.* 285; the English Bible sanctioned by Henry VIII. 2 *Cran.* viii. 345; licence granted to read it, 2 *Lat.* 240; it is ordered to be set up in churches, 2 *Cran.* 346 n.; 2 *Lat.* 240 n.; Latimer orders it to be chained in the monastery of Worcester, and directs each monk to procure the New Testament, *ib.* 241; about this time Anne Askewe reads it in Lincoln minster, *Bale* 173; the clergy directed to procure Bibles for themselves, 2 *Lat.* 243; the Bible enjoined to be used in English as well as in Latin, and studied by the clergy and laity, 2 *Cran.* 81, 155, 161; the declaration to be read by curates upon the publishing of the Bible in English, *ib.* 391 n.; the injunctions for reading it abused at Calais, *ib.* 391; Cranmer's Bible disliked by Papists, 1 *Ful.* 190; price fixed for it, and proposed exclusive privilege for printing it, 2 *Cran.* 395, 396; Cranmer's prologue to the Bible, *ib.* 118; the Bible ordered to be provided in churches, 2 *Zur.* 158; vacillating conduct of the king, 2 *Cran.* ix.; the general reading of the English Bible prohibited, 1543, 3 *Zur.* 356 n.; Hooper orders a Bible to be provided in every church, 2 *Hoop.* 139, 142; desires a better version, *ib.* 393

The Geneva version (first printed 1560), 1 *Ful.* 118 n., 154; it was translated from the Hebrew and Greek, *ib.* 118; the translators, 3 *Zur.* 764 n.; Bodley has a special licence to print this version for seven years from Jan. 1560-1, *Park.* 261; edition of London, 1578, 1 *Whitg.* 203 n., 2 *Whitg.* 524; that of Edinb. 1579, 1 *Ful.* 67, 68; verses on the excellency of scripture, by Tho. Gressop, prefixed to the Geneva Bible, *Poet.* 469; various notes and translations, see 3 *Whitg.* 629

The Bishops' Bible (first printed 1568), 1 *Ful.* 113 n., *Grin.* viii.; Parker desires Cecil to revise an epistle, *Park.* 290; lists of the revisers, *ib.* 334—336 n.; instructions sent to them, *ib.* 336 n.; the revision completed, *ib.* 334; Parker's letter sent with this Bible to the queen, *ib.* 337; quarto edition, 1569, 1 *Ful.* 113 n.; this translation ordered to be read in churches, 1571, *ib.*; English edition of 1577, *ib.* 68

Bibles burned by the popish rebels in the North, 1569, 1 *Zur.* 214, 228; the Bible permitted to be read in English, but disregarded, 1 *Bec.* 38; it lieth always open (in churches) for men to read, *Lit. Eliz.* 571; leaves torn out of the Bibles in St Paul's church, 1 *Bec.* 322 n.; reference to a Bible printed by Rich. Jug, 1577, 1 *Ful.* 422

The Rhemish Testament (first printed 1582), 1 *Ful.* xiii. & passim, *Whita.* 141; strange words therein, e. g. "promerited," *Lit. Eliz.* 681; notes cited, *Rog.* 58 n., & passim (*v.* Rhemists).

Fulke's DEFENCE OF THE TRANSLATIONS OF THE HOLY SCRIPTURES INTO THE ENGLISH TONGUE (anterior to 1582), AGAINST THE CAVILS OF G. MARTIN, 1 *Ful.*; the English versions were translated from the common printed copies, *ib.* 74; what versions read in churches, *ib.* 190; alleged errors in English translations, 2 *Jew.* 831; alleged heretical additions to the text, 1 *Ful.* 547, &c.; alleged corruptions, *ib.* 557, &c.; other faults, *ib.* 571, &c.; on the general excellence of the English versions, *ib.* 591; mistake in Bagster's English Polyglot, and other English Bibles, (Jud. ix. 53), *Calf.* 91 n

Ethiopic: Chrysostom says the Ethiopians had scripture in their own tongue, *Whita.* 245

French: a translation published by Olivetan (Neuf. 1535), 3 *Zur.* 622 n.; the version of Seb. Chateillon, 1555, 4 *Jew.* xxxiv. 980

Gothic: the version of Ulphilas, 2 *Jew.* 690, *Whita.* 221

Greek (LXX. — *v.* Chronology): account of the Septuagint, *Whita.* 117; whether the LXX. translated the entire Old Testament or only the Pentateuch, *ib.* 118; Jerome doubts whether they translated more than the latter, 1 *Ful.* 80, 521; whether the version of the LXX. be still extant, *Whita.* 121; Fulke expresses a doubt as to its existence, 2 *Ful.* 166; it was caused to be made by king Ptolemy, 2 *Cran.* 183; Josephus and Epiphanius on the books sent by the Jews to that prince, *Whita.* 59; on the story of its translation, 1 *Ful.* 53, 80; the miraculous unanimity of the translators asserted by Irenæus and Augustine, but denied by Jerome, *Whita.* 120; when the Septuagint was published, *ib.* 118; the Psalter now extant said not to be of the LXX. translation, 1 *Ful.* 373; in what sense the Septuagint is authentic, *Whita.* 138; its authority, 2 *Ful.* 222; faults of the present copies, *Whita.* 121, 122; it differs widely from the Hebrew, 1 *Ful.* 521; the fathers endeavour to reconcile those copies, *ib.* 53; the Septuagint is not to be despised, though it has often corrupted the Hebrew, *Whita.* 180; venerated by Augustine and Ambrose, 1 *Ful.* 51; not so much esteemed by Jerome, *ib.* 49, 51; highly valued by the fathers generally, 1 *Ful.* 73, *Whita.* 119; the principal editions of the Septuagint, viz. Compl. 1517, Venet. 1518, Rom. 1585, and the Alexandrine, 1707, 2 *Ful.* 166 n

Greek (other versions of the O. T.): those of Aquila, Symmachus, Theodotion, &c., 2 *Jew.* 692, *Whita.* 123; some parts of Jerome's Latin version turned into Greek by Sophronius, *Whita.* 137

GREEK (N. T.): on the Greek edition of the New Testament, *Whita.* 125; conjectural emendations of the Greek text by Beza, 1 *Ful.* 41; he rejects Septuagintal phrases, *ib.* 43, &c.; the Codex Bezæ, *ib.* 88

HEBREW (*v.* Chronology): on the Hebrew text, *Whita.* 112; supported by Christ's citations, 1 *Ful.* 49; the points defended, *ib.* 55, 578; alleged errors in the present text, *ib.* 578, &c., *Whita.* 158, &c.

Indian (?): Chrysostom and Theodoret speak of the Indians as having scripture in their own tongue, *Whita.* 245

Italian: the version of Antonio Bruccioli, 1532, 4 *Jew.* xxxiv. 980

Latin (versions before Jerome): innumerable early Latin versions, 1 *Ful.* 73, 439, *Whita.* 128; the versio Itala preferred by Augustine to all other Latin copies, *Whita.* 128

Latin (Vulgate): on the Latin Vulgate edition, *Whita.* 128, &c.; Jerome's version read in the church in his own lifetime, *ib.* 129; the present Vulgate not entirely Jerome's, *ib.* 129; how far his according to Bellarmine, *ib.* 130; the Psalms, not of Jerome's version, but a translation from the Greek, *ib.* 180; the authors of the Vulgate were not sufficiently conversant with Latin, 1 *Ful.* 435; examples of its many solecisms and barbarisms, *Whita.* 150; the present Vulgate differs widely from the Hebrew, *ib.* 131; it does not always follow the LXX. 1 *Ful.* 73, 81; it often varies from the judgment of Jerome, *Whita.* 132, 146; Bellarmine's replies on this point considered, *ib.* 134; its various readings very numerous, 1 *Ful.* 74; it is very corrupt, *Whita.* 111; certain corrupt places therein set forth, *ib.* 163, &c.; errors in it, 1 *Ful.* 62, 70, 385, 591; on the manifold corruptions in the Psalms, *Whita.* 179; corruptions in the New Testament, *ib.* 193, &c.; opinions of Erasmus and Isidore Clarius on its corruptions, *ib.* 207; false doctrines based on its errors of translation, *ib.* 468; the Vulgate was not of the highest authority with Bede, 1 *Ful.* 57, but it is preferred by Romanists to the Greek and Hebrew, *Whita.* 111, and was declared authentic by the Council of Trent, *ib.*; arguments of the Romanists in favour of its authority refuted, *ib.* 135—140; arguments of Melchior Canus for its superiority, *ib.* 140; the ten arguments of the Rhemish translators answered, *ib.* 141; proofs that it is not authentic scripture, *ib.* 145; it is not altogether to be condemned, but to be tried by the originals, 4 *Bul.* 541, &c.; Coverdale's remarks on the Vulgate version, 2 *Cov.* 25, 26, 27, 28, 33, 35; Beza's opinion, 1 *Ful.* 175 n., *Whita.* 144; Fulke's opinion, 1 *Ful.* 176; reference to a text, 4 *Jew.* 989; some parts of Jerome's version turned into Greek by Sophronius, *Whita.* 137

Biblia cum Glossa Ordinaria et expositione Nic. de Lyra, 1502, *Jew.* xxxiv.

Biblia Sacra, adject. schol. auct. Isid. Clar. 1557, *Jew.* xxxiv.

Latin (other versions): the Bible by Pagninus and Vatablus, 1 *Brad.* 535, *Jew.* xxxiv.; reference to it, 4 *Jew.* 989; the version of Leo Judæ, completed by Bibliander, revised by Pellican, *Jew.* xxxiv., 3 *Zur.* 235 n., 623 n.; reference to it, 4 *Jew.* 980; the version of Seb. Castalio, 2 *Zur.* 261; Beza's Latin Testament, 1 *Ful.* 69, &c.

Persian: Chrysostom says the Persians had scripture in their own tongue, *Whita.* 245; so Theodoret, *ib.*

Polish: the (Socinian) Bible published at the cost of Nicholas Radzivil, palatine of Wilna, 3 *Zur.* 597

Sarmatian (?): Theodoret alludes to a version in the tongue of Sarmatia, *Whita.* 246

Sclavonic: the alleged Dalmatic or Sclavonic version by Jerome, 1 *Jew.* 270, 2 *Jew.* 690, 691, 692, *Whita.* 221

Scottish: Scottish and Pictish versions referred to by Bede, *Whita.* 223

Scythian (?): Theodoret alludes to a version in the tongue of the Scythians, *Whita.* 246

Spanish: the translation of scripture forbidden by Ferdinand and Isabella, 2 *Jew.* 689, 690; the version of Cassiodorus de Reyna (Bas. 1569, Amst. 1702), 2 *Zur.* 175, 176

Syriac: Chrysostom says the Syrians

had scripture in their own tongue, *Whita.* 245; Jerome speaks of the Psalms in Syriac, *ib.* 222

Welsh : a British version referred to by Bede, *Whita.* 223; the scriptures ordered to be translated into Welsh (5 Eliz. c. 28, 1563), 1 *Zur.* 124 n.; progress of the work, *Park.* 265; the New Testament, *Grin.* 188

Bibliander (Theod.), or Buchmann: notices of him, 1 *Zur.* 155 n., 3 *Zur.* 11 n.; saluted, 2 *Brad.* 406, 1 *Zur.* 30, 62, 136, 2 *Zur.* 107, 3 *Zur.* 38, 42, 49, 615, 621; invited to England, 3 *Zur.* 725; he completes the translation of the scriptures begun by Leo Judæ, *ib.* 235 n., 623 n.; his commentary on Genesis and Exodus, 1 *Zur.* 155, 355; he says the Jews used five sorts of bitter herbs with the paschal lamb, 3 *Bec.* 381; his wife, 3 *Zur.* 53

Bibliotheca:
Bibliotheca Patrum (Par. 1610), 2 *Ful.* 236 n.
Bibliotheca Magna Veterum Patrum (Col. Agr. 1618—22), 2 *Bec.* 252 n., 256 n., 258 n., 276 n., 3 *Bec.* 422 n., 425 n., 444 n., 456 n., 481 n., 2 *Ful.* 236 n., *Jew.* xxxiv.
Bibliotheca Patrum, per M. de la Bigne (Par. 1624), *Jew.* xxxiv.
Bibliotheca Patrum Gr. et Lat. (Par. 1624), *Jew.* xxxiv.
Magna Bibliotheca Patrum (Par. 1654), 2 *Ful.* 236 n
Maxima Bibliotheca Veterum Patrum (Lug. 1677), 2 *Bec.* 91 n., 256 n., 267 n., 289 n., 3 *Bec.* 415 n., 2 *Ful.* 236 n
Bibliotheca Vet. Patrum, studio Galland. (Venet. 1765—81), 2 *Bec.* 281 n., 3 *Bec.* 454 n., *Jew.* xxxiv.; several of the above follow a direction of the Vatican Expurgatory Index, 2 *Ful.* 236 n

Bickley (Tho.), bp of Chichester: sometime chaplain to Parker, *Park.* 261; sent to preach at Cripplegate, *ib.* 278; recommended for a prebend, *ib.* 290; warden of Merton college, proposed as bishop of Oxford, *ib.* 360

Biddenden, co. Kent: Frensham's bequest, 2 *Zur.* 21 n

Biddil (Jo.): in exile, 1 *Cran.* (9)

Bidding: *v.* Beads, Prayer.
The form of bidding the common prayers, 2 *Cran.* 504; form of bidding in a Latin sermon, 2 *Jew.* 951, in an English one, *ib.* 1025

Biel (Gab.): he flourished 1480, *Pil.* 80; his Sac. Canon. Miss. Expositio, 2 *Cov.* 254, 2 *Ful.* 22 n., *Jew.* xxxiv.; he maintains that the church has never erred, *Rog.* 179 n.; says that catholic verities are by their own nature immutably true, *Whita.* 357; that the pope has power to declare new articles of faith, 2 *Cov.* 254; he asserts free-will, *Rog.* 106 n., and justification by works, *ib.* 116; extols a priest above our lady and all saints, 1 *Jew.* 206; declares that since the council of Constance, it is heresy to say that the communion of both kinds is of necessity for salvation, 3 *Bec.* 415; says the church of Rome used leavened bread in opposition to an error of the Ebionites, 3 *Jew.* 616; on a petition in the canon of the mass, 2 *Jew.* 738; on consecration, 1 *Hoop.* 522, 529, 1 *Jew.* 126; acknowledges that scripture does not shew how Christ consecrated the elements, 3 *Jew.* 451; on transubstantiation, 2 *Brad.* 275, 2 *Cov.* 254; he says, how the body of Christ is under the kinds of bread and wine is not found expressed in the Bible, 2 *Bec.* 269, 3 *Bec.* 426, 2 *Jew.* 563, 3 *Jew.* 490; referred to on the body of Christ remaining under the accidents, &c., 2 *Jew.* 777; declares that the priest receives the sacrament as the mouth, and that the virtue passes into all the members of the church, 2 *Jew.* 744, 3 *Jew.* 557; passages on the application of Christ's passion by the mass, 2 *Jew.* 747; speaks of applying the mass through all the cases of declension, *ib.* 747, 748; acknowledges that Christ did not give the sacrament to be reserved, 2 *Jew.* 554, 3 *Jew.* 553; cites Paschasius on the sacrament, 2 *Bec.* 252 n.; 3 *Bec.* 456 n., says, the sacrifice requires not a spiritual life in act and deed, but only in possibility, 2 *Jew.* 751; on the sacrifice of the wicked, 3 *Jew.* 755; defines opus operatum, *ib.* 750, 751; maintains that sacraments confer grace ex opere operato, *Rog.* 248 n

Bield: *v.* Bele.

Bierus (Edm.): 2 *Cov.* 515, 516, 517, &c.

Bifurked: two-forked, *Bale* 440

Bigamus: in the canon law it means one who has been twice married, *Calf.* 19, 3 *Tyn.* 165; such were not admitted to orders, *Rog.* 241 n.; the canon against admitting them, 3 *Tyn.* 165 n

Bigamy: proclamation against it, 1548, 3 *Zur.* 263 n.; that of Philip, landgrave of Hesse, *ib.* 666 n

Biggar (Tho.), minister of Kinhorne: 2 *Zur.* 365

Bigotius (Americ): *Grin.* 72 n

Bilde (Beatus): *v.* Rhenanus (B.).

Bill: ancient meaning of the word, 1 *Tyn.* 45

Bill (Will.), successively master of St John's and Trin. coll. Cambridge, provost of Eton, and dean of Westminster: notice of him *Hutch.* 10 n.; unable to have his fellowship at St John's for want of money, *Park.* 3; master of St John's, *ib.* 38 n.; chaplain to king Edward, 2 *Brad.* xxvi., 2 *Cran.* xi.; made master of Trinity, 3 *Zur.* 150; his acts at Cambridge, *Sand.* ii. v.; he preaches at Paul's cross on the accession of Elizabeth, 1 *Zur.* 4 n.; preaches before the queen, 2 *Zur.* 16 n.; a commissioner for the revision of the Prayer Book, *Grin.* v. (printed Bell), and for other church affairs, *Grin.* vii., *Park.* 133; almoner to queen Elizabeth, *Lit. Eliz.* xxxiii.; verses on images by him, *Hutch.* 10

Bill of Fare: one agreed on by the church dignitaries, 2 *Cran.* 491

Billet (Jo.): *v.* Beleth.

Billicus (Eberh.): 1 *Ful.* 63 n

Billinger (Jo.): 3 *Zur.* 695, 697, 699

Billinus: founded Billingsgate, *Pil.* 345

Billmen: their outfit, *Park.* 15

Bilney (Tho.): mentioned, 1 *Tyn.* lix., 2 *Tyn.* 320; the means of Latimer's conversion, 1 *Lat.* 334, 2 *Lat.* x., *Rid.* 118; his friendship with Latimer, 1 *Lat.* i. ii. 222, 334, 2 *Lat.* xiii. 52; Latimer commends him, 2 *Lat.* 330; he visits the prisoners at Cambridge, 1 *Lat.* 335; his recantation, 1 *Tyn.* 129; he bears a faggot, and afterwards despairs, 2 *Lat.* 51; gives Tyndale's New Testament, &c. to an anchoress, 1 *Tyn.* 129; burned, *Bale* 394, 3 *Bec.* 11; once in great fear of death, but he died a martyr, 1 *Lat.* 222; Sir Thomas More wrote against him, or rather Tyndale, *ib.* 251, and defended his condemnation, 3 *Tyn.* 145, 146

Bilson (Tho.), bp of Winchester: his True Difference, an answer to Allen, 2 *Ful.* 283 n

Bilston, co. Suffolk: the manor, 2 *Cran.* 266

Binder (......): 3 *Zur.* 615, 621

Binding and loosing: *v.* Absolution.

Bindon (Tho. visc.): *v.* Howard.

Bing (And.): part of a letter to Dr S. Ward, 3 *Whitg.* xvii.

Bing (Tho.): recommended as visitor for St John's college, Cambridge, *Grin.* 359

Bingham, co. Notts: a free-school established there, 2 *Cran.* 262

Bingham (Hen.): a kinsman of Cranmer, 2 *Cran.* 265

Bingham (Jos.), 2 *Bec.* 9, 297, 298, 301, 319, 327, 3 *Bec.* 278, *Calf.* 29, 285, 297, 2 *Ful.* 82, 117, 183, 235, 238, 364, 1 *Lat.* 237, 1 *Zur.* 350 &c. nn.; relates how Romanists attempted to deny or suppress a passage of Chrysostom, *Grin.* 72 n.; distinguishes the ciborium from the pix, 2 *Jew.* 561 n.; referred to on memorials for the dead, 2 *Cov.* 249

Binius (Sev.): Concilia, *Calf.* 54, 66, 136, 137, 193, 255, 297, 323, 324, 2 *Ful.* 70, 71, 183, 288, 302, 364, 2 *Hoop.* 48, 234, 534, &c. nn.; his deceitfulness, or absurd mistake, concerning the baptistery of Constantine, 2 *Ful.* 360 n

Binnemann (Hen.): seeks a privilege for printing some school-books, *Park.* 352

Biographia Britannica: 2 *Brad.* xii. n

Biondi (Scipione): *v.* Scipio.

Biondo (Flav.): *v.* Blondus.

Birchet (Pet.): wounds one Hawkins, mistaking him for Sir Chr. Hatton, 2 *Whitg.* addenda, 1 *Zur.* 313 n

Birchington (Steph.): Hist. de Archiep. Cant., 2 *Tyn.* 294 n

Birckman (A. F. and J.): *v.* Byrchman.

Bird (Jo.), bp of Chester: his visitation book, 2 *Brad.* 1 n.; his preaching, 3 *Zur.* 80; he ordained Grindal, *Grin.* i. (there erroneously called bp of Winchester)

Bird (Will.): *v.* Byrd.

Birdbrook, co. Essex: 2 *Cov.* viii.

Birds: the guillemot, willocks, or sea-hen, *Rid.* 492 n

Birkman (A. F. and J.): *v.* Byrchman.

Birlingham: *v.* Burlingham.

Birmenstorf, near Bremgarten: 4 *Bul.* xi.

Biron (Sir Jo.): *v.* Byron.

Birrus: worn by Cyprian, 1 *Zur.* 350, but not peculiar to the clergy, *ib.* n

Birth (New): *v.* Regeneration.

Birthdays (Natalitia) of martyrs: the days of their martyrdom, *Calf.* 257

Biscay (Bay of): 2 *Zur.* 85

Bishop (Geo.): 2 *Ful.* 214

Bishop (Rich.): *v.* Busshop.

Bishop (Tho.): executed at York, 1 *Zur.* 225 n

Bishoping: the people's name for confirmation, *Bale* 528, *Pil.* 553, 1 *Tyn.* 277, 3 *Tyn.* 72

Bishopricks: *v.* Bishops, Cathedrals. Those of England enumerated, 3 *Jew.* 109; how much they paid the pope for first-fruits, &c., 4 *Jew.* 1078, 1079; the poverty of some of them, 2 *Cran.* 437, 2 *Whitg.* 167; they were much impoverished by Papists, *Pil.* 592, 594, 595; still much richer than those in Italy, 4 *Jew.* 971

Bishops: *v.* Archbishops, Chorepiscopi, Coadjutors, Prelates, Suffragans, Clergy, Ministers, Courts, Exhortation, Succession, Vestments.

BISHOPS

i. *The name, office, and order.*
ii. *Their election, consecration, &c.*
iii. *Their duty, &c.*
iv. *Their authority.*
v. *Their titles.*
vi. *Bishops in England.*
vii. *Miscellanea.*

i. *The name, office, and order :* what they are, 2 *Bec.* 317, &c.; Cicero uses "episcopus" in its original sense, 1 *Ful.* 217; the meaning of the word in scripture, &c., 1 *Ful.* 218, *Pil.* 494, 1 *Tyn.* 229; it is equivalent to superintendent, 4 *Jew.* 906; rendered "overseer" in Acts xx., 1 *Ful.* 110; in a sense we are all bishops one over another, 2 *Brad.* 342; the word used (in citing St Paul) for high-priest, *Hutch.* 173; it is a name of labour, not of honour, 3 *Jew.* 308; the apostles were not bishops, 1 *Brad.* 506; neither are bishops apostles, 2 *Ful.* 309; their office is different, 2 *Jew.* 908; Jerome says they hold the place of the apostles, *Whita.* 417; in what respect they may be said to do so, *ib.* 417, 418; on their succession to the apostles in government, 2 *Whitg.* 355; their office and character according to St Paul, 1 *Tyn.* 229, 479; how it is degenerated from the original in the scripture, 1 *Hoop.* 396, &c.; those described by Paul and popish bishops as like as black and white, *Pil.* 493; their office at first, 1 *Hoop.* 480; ancient and modern bishops compared, 2 *Whitg.* 372, 434; bishops in Jerome's days, 1 *Whitg.* 438; the character of a true one, *Pil.* 604; the office of a bishop, what, 1 *Lat.* 62; R. Gualter's remarks upon it, 2 *Zur.* 227; Fulke on the same, *Rog.* 332 n.; the names bishop and presbyter (or elder) used interchangeably in scripture, 2 *Cov.* 464, 1 *Ful.* 254, 267, *Pil.* 493, 3 *Tyn.* 17, 1 *Whitg.* 488, 2 *Whitg.* 251, 3 *Whitg.* 151; bishops and priests were one in the beginning of Christianity, 4 *Bul.* 109, 2 *Cran.* 117, 1 *Ful.* 264, 2 *Ful.* 388, 1 *Tyn.* 518, 2 *Tyn.* 253; the names used interchangeably by ancient fathers, 3 *Jew.* 272, 2 *Whitg.* 250, as by Irenæus, 1 *Jew.* 144, who speaks of presbyters who have received the succession of the episcopacy, 1 *Jew.* 402; the statement of Epiphanius, 2 *Whitg.* 290, 291; Jerome (*q. v.*) maintains that bishops and priests were all one at first, 1 *Ful.* 265, 3 *Jew.* 272, 3 *Tyn.* 152, 2 *Whitg.* 221, and he says that bishops are greater than priests rather by custom than by God's ordinance, 1 *Jew.* 340, 379; bishops and ministers the same, according to Bradford, Harpsfield, &c., 1 *Brad.* 506; bishops differ not, says Becon, from spiritual ministers, 2 *Bec.* 319; statement that the order has always been owned as superior to that of presbyters, *ib.* n.; Jewel says there is little difference between them, 3 *Jew.* 439; they are all one as to their ministry, 2 *Whitg.* 254, 261; bishops are not superior as to the word and sacraments, but only in government, 1 *Ful.* 461; they have no higher commission from Christ than other ministers, *Pil.* 493; Jerome and Chrysostom regard ordination as their only peculiar work, 1 *Whitg.* 439, 440; Hooper styled "compresbyter" by Ridley, *Rid.* 357; an article on the order and ministry of bishops and priests, 2 *Cran.* 484; all bishops equal as to their episcopacy, 3 *Jew.* 290, &c., 300; no one bishop should have preeminence, *Phil.* 394; the primitive church knew no high bishop under Christ; all were of like authority, 2 *Cov.* 464; their equality maintained by Cyprian and other fathers, 1 *Tyn.* 215, &c.; Romanists reckon three orders of them, patriarchs, archbishops, and bishops, 4 *Bul.* 117; on the government of the church by them in common, 1 *Jew.* 349, 350; there is but one bishoprick, whereof each bishop has a part, 2 *Jew.* 1001; in what sense they may be called the heads of their several churches, 3 *Jew.* 269

ii. *Their election, consecration, &c.:* they are not made by chance, *Sand.* 334; questions and answers concerning the appointment and power of bishops and priests, 2 *Cran.* 115, &c.; bishops made by the apostles, *Rog.* 328; on their election, 1 *Jew.* 407, 3 *Jew.* 320, &c.; how they were appointed at Alexandria, 2 *Whitg.* 222, 428; before there were any Christian princes they were elected by the people, 2 *Cran.* 117; ancient edicts for their election by the people, 1 *Whitg.* 396, 401; riots at popular elections, *ib.* 463, &c.; councils sometimes made bishops with the consent of the people, *ib.* 410, &c.; their election in the time of Cyprian, 1 *Jew.* 347, 349, 2 *Whitg.* 197; the oath of Romish bishops to the pope, 4 *Bul.* 141, 142, 530, *Pil.* 555; the election of bishops by the chapter, 3 *Jew.* 334; its confirmation by the primate, 3 *Jew.* 330, *Park.* 306; bishops chosen and consecrated by royal mandate, *Grin.* 340, 341; solemnities in their appointment not necessary, 2 *Cran.* 116; no promise of God that grace is given by their appointment, *ib.*; their lawful consecration, *Rog.* 332; they need none by the scripture, 2 *Cran.* 117; ancient canons require three bishops to perform it,

BISHOPS

1 *Jew.* 407, 3 *Jew.* 330; Jo. Major declares this to be an ordinance of man, 3 *Jew.* 334; one bishop sufficient, according to St Gregory, to maintain succession, 2 *Ful.* 118; Felinus declares that the pope can make a bishop by his word only, 3 *Jew.* 329; whether there may be more than one bishop in the same city, 2 *Whitg.* 214, 215, 378; this was disallowed by ancient canons, 1 *Jew.* 348, though scripture speaks of many in one city, 1 *Ful.* 264; the council of Syrmium willed Felix II. and Liberius to be bishops of Rome together, 1 *Jew.* 377; bishops forbidden to be appointed in little cities, 2 *Whitg.* 376; on the resignation of bishops; case of N. de Farnham, bp of Durham, *Grin.* 399; nullatenses, i. e. bishops without sees, at the council of Trent, 4 *Jew.* 997; the people are bound to judge heretical bishops, *Whita.* 440; whether princes may correct and depose them, 2 *Ful.* 378, &c.; they should have their office only so long as they behave well in it, 1 *Hoop.* 481; if negligent should be turned out, and laymen may be called to their office, 1 *Lat.* 122; bishops, popes and all others who enter not in by the door, are thieves and robbers, 2 *Lat.* 309—312

iii. *Their duty, &c.* (see also i.): the office or duty of bishops and spiritual ministers, 1 *Bec.* 224, 272, 286, 2 *Bec.* 114, 1 *Hoop.* 142, 146, *Hutch.* 105, 2 *Whitg.* 418; their duty, with probations of scripture, 2 *Bec.* 516, 517; if they do it not they are forsworn, 1 *Bec.* 371; those who neglect their duty are thieves, 2 *Bec.* 107; the office laborious, 1 *Hoop.* 505, *Pil.* 36, 494, 604; its weightiness, *Sand.* 331; its hardness, *ib.* 332; its poverty in ancient times, 2 *Whitg.* 381; at the first it was very perilous, 2 *Tyn.* 255; wherefore many good men endeavoured to avoid it, *Sand.* 333; they are taught by St Paul, in the 1st epistle to Timothy, 1 *Tyn.* 517; and in 2 Tim. and Titus, *ib.* 519; of their holy and unblameable life, 4 *Bul.* 158; examples of ancient ones, 1 *Bec.* 31, 32; a greater charge on them than on inferiors, to appoint godly ministers, *ib.* 4; their fault in ordaining unfit persons, 2 *Bec.* 423; their responsibility as to the appointment of curates, 1 *Lat.* 152; they must study the scriptures, preach them purely to the people, and pray fervently, 1 *Bec.* 382; must rebuke the sin of swearing in their sermons, *ib.* 380, 381; the chiefest part of their office is to teach, 1 *Hoop.* 19, 142, 511; their neglect of this, *ib.* 142, 143; preaching put down by lording, 1 *Lat.* 66; they left preaching, but reserved to themselves certain ceremonies, 1 *Tyn.* 274; appointed deputies to preach for them, 1 *Lat.* 77; it is their duty to govern the church, not the commonwealth, 1 *Hoop.* 142, 2 *Hoop.* 559; they must watch that the devil sow not his seed, 2 *Lat.* 189; they should reform the church, 2 *Jew.* 996; should lay aside tyranny, 1 *Bec.* 260; should not harass preachers, 2 *Lat.* 328; nor prescribe any thing prejudicial to their flocks, 2 *Cran.* 98; some deserve the name of bitesheep, 2 *Brad.* 146, *Pil.* 495; they must not be sluggish, 1 *Bec.* 381; must be liberal, *ib.* 23, 31; one deprived for niggardliness, *ib.* 23; they must shew hospitality, 1 *Bec.* 24, 2 *Bec.* 325, &c.; hospitality decayed among them, 2 *Bec.* 320; examples of the charity of ancient bishops to the poor, *ib.* 586; some sold the church utensils for the purpose of relieving the needy, *ib.*

iv. *Their authority:* what it is, 2 *Cran.* 98, *Pil.* 488, &c., more especially in England, 1 *Whitg.* 260, 2 *Whitg.* 209, 1 *Zur.* 179; their authority acknowledged in the times succeeding the apostles, *Rog.* 329; the church committed to their government, *Pil.* 482, 488; fathers who were not bishops deemed by papists of minor authority, *Whita.* 413, and the teaching of bishops is regarded by them as of no certain authority, unless delivered ex cathedra, *ib.*; bishops and clergy called ministers of God under the king, 2 *Cran.* 116, but their spiritual authority extends to princes, *Pil.* 491; according to Ignatius they are subject to no earthly power, *Whita.* 573; the Canon Law declares that they ought not to be set beneath kings and princes, 2 *Cran.* 73, and that they are to be judged of no laymen, *ib.*; on their authority to admit and ordain ministers, 1 *Bul.* 133, 1 *Whitg.* 425, 2 *Zur.* 129; ordination always principally committed to them, *Rog.* 332; what manner of examination the old bishops used, 4 *Bul.* 136; their blessing cannot make any place holy, *Pil.* 64, nor put away sin, 1 *Tyn.* 284; their agreement about doctrines proves nothing, 2 *Cran.* 48; how far they may exercise temporal jurisdiction, 1 *Whitg.* 153, 3 *Whitg.* 481, &c.; often greedy for, or burdened with, secular offices, 1 *Brad.* 428, 2 *Cov.* 244, 1 *Lat.* 67, 68, 176, 1 *Tyn.* 274; their temporal authority is derived from the prince, *Pil.* 492; when their prerogative began, 4 *Bul.* 110; their dignity and prerogative increased, *ib.* 112; their courts, *ib.*; bishops not permitted to make new laws, *ib.* 151; they should not govern worldly kingdoms, but devote themselves entirely to the word of God, 1 *Tyn.* 207

v. *Their titles:* extravagant names given to them in early times, 1 *Jew.* 427; they were often called ἀρχιερεῖς, 2 *Whitg.* 310; the name "summus pontifex" applied to them, 1 *Hoop.* 237; their titles as "primate of all England," "legate of the apostolic see," &c., 2 *Cran.* 304; "lord," and other names of temporal dignity, 1 *Whitg.* 152, 2 *Whitg.* 79, 188, &c. 385, &c., 3 *Whitg.* 405; Cranmer would have the bishops leave all their styles, and write themselves apostles of Jesus Christ, 2 *Cran.* 305

vi. *Bishops in England* (see the title passim): the investiture of bishops surrendered by William II. to the pope's vicar, 2 *Tyn.* 295; how much they paid to the pope for first-fruits, &c., 4 *Jew.* 1078, 1079; common proverbs respecting popish bishops, 1 *Tyn.* 304; they upbraided the people with ignorance, when they are the cause of it, 1 *Lat.* 137; bishops rung into towns; one much offended at a broken bell, *ib.* 207; old abbots made new bishops, *ib.* 123; they granted licenses to midwives, 2 *Lat.* 114 n.; their evil deeds late in Henry VIII.'s time, *Bale* 485; their laws often changed, 1 *Hoop.* 154; how godly bishops, &c. were under the reformation, 3 *Bec.* 236; enjoined to preach personally once a quarter, at the least, 2 *Cran.* 505; they complain to parliament of increased immorality, 1 *Lat.* 258; generally very poor, 2 *Cran.* 437; the Marian bishops deposed, and restrained or imprisoned, by Elizabeth, 4 *Jew.* 908, *Pil.* 621, 622, 623, 1 *Zur.* 101, 105, 113, 122, 2 *Zur.* 181, 182; letter to those deprived, *Park.* 109; Sampson's views as to the degeneracy of English bishops from the primitive institution, as regards their election, vestments, &c., 1 *Zur.* 1; scheme for the exchange of their lands for parsonages impropriate, *ib.* 20, 29; the new bishops to be consecrated without superstitious ceremonies, *ib.* 50; the first reformed bishops were opposed to the vestments and ceremonies retained, *ib.* 84 n., 149 n., 169; orders for the bishops and clergy subscribed in the synod, 1562, concerning alienation of lands, ordination, &c., *Sand.* 434; the council complains of their negligence, and of consequent disorder amongst the people, *Park.* 355; their conduct, 2 *Zur.* 161; regarded as persecutors of the Puritans, *Park.* 410; impoverished by their predecessors, *Pil.* 592, 594, 595; very poor, 2 *Whitg.* 167; bishops to whom Becon dedicated his works, 1 *Bec.* 1; on the authority of bishops in the church of England, 1 *Zur.* 179 (and see iv.); their power in ordination disapproved by Beza, 2 *Zur.* 129; bishops' prisons, 3 *Whitg.* 405, 449; their chancellors, commissaries, and officials, *ib.* 543; their consent not necessary to an act of parliament, *Pil.* 627; their alleged luxury, 2 *Whitg.* 382, 384

vii. *Miscellanea:* contest of bishops in the ancient church which should be greatest, 2 *Tyn.* 257; disputes between them were not always decided by the bishop of Rome, 1 *Jew.* 382; the names of bishops often struck out of the calendar, 4 *Jew.* 649; commonly spoken against, 3 *Whitg.* 594; poverty of bishops in Naples, 4 *Jew.* 971; Greek bishops, 4 *Bul.* 190; prayer for bishops and ministers, 3 *Bec.* 21, &c.; petitions for them, *ib.* 36, 37; they should be reasonably provided for, 1 *Hoop.* 398

— Bishops of Rome: v. Pope. The pope not a bishop, but a bite-sheep, 2 *Brad.* 146

— Universal Bishop: remarks on the title, 1 *Jew.* 422, &c., 3 *Jew.* 316, &c.; it was sharply denounced by St Gregory, 1 *Jew.* 32, et sæpe al. (v. Gregory I.); a proud name, 3 *Jew.* 310, &c.; a cursed name, *Pil.* 519; Harding denies that the pope claims the title, 3 *Jew* 316; "bishop of the universal church," 1 *Jew.* 422, not the same as "universal bishop," *ib.* 426

— Nicholas bishops, or boy bishops, 2 *Bec.* 320 n., 1 *Ful.* 218

Bishops' Book: v. Book.

Bishopsbridge (Rog. of): v. Roger.

Bishop's Cleeve, co. Glouc.: v. Cleeve.

Bishopstoke, co. Hants: Bale rector, *Bale* ix.

Bishopsthorp, near York: the palace of the archbishop, *Grin.* 325; an attempt made to alienate it, *Sand.* xxii.

Bisse (Βύσσος): fine white, whether silk or linen, 1 *Tyn.* 406

Bissweiler: the church there, 2 *Cov.* 517, 521

Bitonto (Corn. bp of): v. Cornelius.

Bizarro (Pietro), otherwise Peter of Perugia: notice of him, 2 *Brad.* xxi. n., 352, 353, 3 *Zur.* 338 n.; letter from him to Bullinger, 3 *Zur.* 338; on the faith of the Persians, *Rog.* 38

Blaarer (......): (probably an error for Blaurer), 1 *Zur.* 130

Black (......), a Dominican friar: slain with Rizzio, 1 *Zur.* 166

Black (Fra.): 3 *Zur.* 692

Black (Geo.): son of Francis, 3 *Zur.* 692

Blackburn, co. Lanc.: the vicar, *Pil.* vii.; an apparition there, *Park.* 222
Black friars: *v.* Dominicans.
Black guard (The): 1 *Jew.* 72, 4 *Jew.* 925
Blackheath, co. Kent: the Cornish rebels defeated at Blackheath field, 1497, 1 *Lat.* 101
Blackley, in Manchester, *q. v.*
Blackness: a port near Boulogne, 3 *Zur.* 728 n
Blackstone (Sir Will.): Commentaries, 1 *Lat.* 52, 74, 107
Blackwall, co. Middx.: 2 *Zur.* 290 n., 291 n
Blackwood (Adam): answers Buchanan's book De Jure Regni, 2 *Zur.* 311 n
Bladers: 2 *Bul.* 234
Blag (Jo.): was Cranmer's grocer, 2 *Cran.* 289
Blaise (St): account of him, 1 *Bec.* 139; invoked for the ague, *ib.*; for choking, 2 *Jew.* 922; also to save houses, *Pil.* 92; St Blesis's heart at Malverne, 1 *Lat.* 55
Blake, or Bleyke: bare, naked, *Bale* 321
Blake (......): 2 *Zur.* 335
Blanchers: spoken of, 1 *Lat.* 73, 75, 76, &c.; they patch truth with popery, *ib.* 290
Blanching: evading, 2 *Brad.* 131
Bland (......): he was Sandys's schoolmaster, *Sand.* i.; martyred, *Poet.* 162
Blandina (St): *v.* Attalus.
Her history, 2 *Lat.* 80; her constancy under persecutions, *Rid.* 74; compared with Anne Askewe, *Bale* 141
Blandrata (Geo.): was a partisan of Socinus, 4 *Bul.* xiii; he blasphemed the Trinity, *Rog.* 44, and denied the divinity of the Son, *ib.* 49
Blase (St): *v.* Blaise.
Blasphemy: condemned, 1 *Hoop.* 476; what it is properly, 2 *Bul.* 421; its prevalence lamented, 1 *Lat.* 231; blasphemy against the Son of man, 2 *Bul.* 422; against the Holy Ghost, *ib.*; the names of blasphemers to be presented to the ordinary, *Grin.* 143
Blastus: makes God the author of sin, *Rog.* 97
Blaurer (......): *v.* Blaarer.
Blaurer (Ambr.): noticed, 3 *Zur.* 392 n.; saluted, *ib.* 418
Blaurer (Dithelm): son of Thomas, 2 *Zur.* 28, 74, 107
Blaurer (Tho.): mentioned, 2 *Zur.* 27, 74, 3 *Zur.* 635 n.; letters to him, 2 *Zur.* 27, 3 *Zur.* 635
Bleacher (Rich.): 2 *Brad.* 121
Bleane (The): a wood in Kent, *Grin.* 364
Blederic, duke of Cornwall: *Pil.* 516
Blemish: an impediment to the Aaronic priesthood, 1 *Bec.* 8; spiritual meaning of this prohibition, *ib.* 8, 9, 12, 100, 101

Blennerhasset (Jo.): his daughter Anne, 1 *Bec.* 125 n
Blesdik (Nic.): Hist. Dav. Georgii, *Rog.* 307 n
Blesilla, daughter of Paula: 3 *Zur.* 5 n
Blessed: what it is to be blessed, 1 *Bec.* 74 (*v.* Beatitudes)
Blessing, Benediction: what it is to bless, 1 *Lat.* 301—303, *Now.* 99, 1 *Tyn.* 406; a new signification of the word, 2 *Ful.* 171—172; wrongly applied by papists, *Calf.* 231—233, 250; true blessing is prayer, 1 *Tyn.* 258, or thanksgiving, 4 *Bul.* 263; the benediction of the bishop, 2 *Ful.* 107; the moving of the bishop's hands over us cannot put away sin, 1 *Tyn.* 284; that of a pious layman is as good as the pope's, *ib.* 258; blessing with two fingers, 3 *Tyn.* 8 (see 1 *Lat.* 301—303), with the sign of the cross, 2 *Ful.* 171; Romish benediction in baptism, 4 *Bul.* 306; blessing of bread, 1 *Jew.* 238 (*v.* Supper)
Blessings: on those who obey God's word, 2 *Bec.* 617; why God sends temporal blessings, *Sand.* 61; if they are abused, plagues will follow, *ib.* 62
Blethin (Will.), bp of Llandaff: *Park.* 476
Bleyke: *v.* Blake.
Blindness: that of the world, whence it comes, 3 *Bec.* 488; of the papists, *ib.* 354
Blith (Dr), of King's hall, Cambridge: opposes Latimer, 2 *Lat.* xii
Blomefield (F.): Hist. of Norfolk, 2 *Lat.* 296 n
Blondel (Dav.): *Calf.* 69, 126, 222, 322 nn., 2 *Ful.* 71, 81, 160, 179, 236, 237, 301 nn
Blondus, (Flav.): mentions a woollen pallium, 1 *Zur.* 160
Blood: *v.* Murder.
Vengeance taken of it, 2 *Bul.* 108
Blood, and things strangled: forbidden to be eaten, 2 *Bul.* 214, 272, *Coop.* 10, 60, 1 *Jew.* 223, 228, *Hutch.* 231, 232, 2 *Lat.* 14, *Phil.* 379, *Rid.* 269, 2 *Whitg.* 43, 227, 3 *Whitg.* 187; blood forbidden by the council of Constantinople (691), *Whita.* 41
Bloomsbury: *v.* London.
Blore (T.): Hist. of Rutland, 2 *Lat.* 295 n., 296 n
Blount (James), 6th lord Montjoy: at the duke of Norfolk's trial, 1 *Zur.* 267 n
Blount (Cha.), 8th lord Montjoy: defeats the Spaniards in Ireland, 2 *Zur.* 335 n
Blount (Sir Jo.): his daughter Elizabeth, 2 *Bec.* 554 n
Bloxam (Jo.), a Carmelite: wrote on the Apocalypse, *Bale* 257
Blue (True): 2 *Cran.* 394

Blumen (Jo.), or Florus: 4 *Bul.* 546
Blush: resemblance, look, first sight, *Bale* 437, 496
Blyth (St): his bowl, *Bale* 527
Blyth (Dr), of King's hall: *v.* Blith.
Blyth (......), M.D.: *Park.* 18, 37
Blythe (Geoff.), bp of Coventry and Lichfield: his death, 2 *Cran.* 259 n
Boanerges: sons of thunder, *Pil.* 265
Boasting: *v.* Pride.

Vain-glory, a hindrance to unity, *Sand.* 101; there is nothing in us whereof we may boast, *ib.* 102; vain-glory is hardly bridled, *ib.* 102, 103
Boaying: bawling, 3 *Bec.* 233
Boaz: his marriage with Ruth, *Rid.* 84
Bobbing, co. Kent: the lazar-house, *Park.* 169
Bocardo: *v.* Oxford.

Use of the word in logic, *Grin.* 43 n
Bocardus (......) interprets scripture mystically, *Rog.* 197
Bocham (Rob.), or Bochim: a rebellious priest, 2 *Cran.* 187 n
Bochart (Matth.): Traitté des Reliques, *Calf.* 66 n
Bochart (Sam.): Hierozoicon, 2 *Lat.* 89 n
Bocher (......), of Oxford: 2 *Cran.* 384
Bocher (Joan), or Butcher, or Knel, commonly called Joan of Kent: her heresy, *Hutch.* ii., 3 *Jew.* 187, 2 *Lat.* 114, *Phil.* 55; Hutchinson's account of his interview with her, *Hutch.* 145; her burning, 2 *Cran.* x., *Hutch.* iii., *Rog.* 350, 3 *Zur.* 560; Foxe's erroneous statement respecting Cranmer's importunity for her death, *Hutch.* iv.; evidence that Foxe was in error, *ib.* v.
Bocking, co. Essex: Calfhill buried there, *Calf.* viii.
Bockyng (Edw.): an abettor of the maid of Kent, *Bale* 139, 2 *Cran.* 271, 272 n., 273 n
Bodenham (Cecil), last abbess of Wilton: 2 *Cran.* 258 n., 297
Bodenham (Jo.): notice of him, *Poet.* xlii.; of faith and zeal, verses, *ib.* 455; similes on the same subject, *ib.* 456; of life, *ib.* 457; similes on the same subject, *ib.* 458
Bodenstein (And.): *v.* Carolostadius.
Bodinus (Jo.): Method. ad facil. Hist. cogn. *Rog.* 337 n
Bodius (Herman.): notices of his book called Unio Dissidentium, 3 *Tyn.* 187, 213
Bodley (Jo.): specially licensed to print the Geneva Bible, *Park.* 261
Bodley (Laurence): 2 *Zur.* 270, 273
Body: *v.* Flesh, Health, Man, Meditations, Resurrection.

The care of the body, 2 *Bul.* 312; a vile body, 1 *Bul.* 175; a natural and a spiritual body, *ib.* 176; a clarified body, *ib.* 175; a glorious body, *ib.* 173
Body of Christ: *v.* Christ; also Church, Supper.
Boemus (Jo.): 1 *Bec.* 8 n., 391, 2 *Bec.* 649 n., 3 *Bec.* 123 n
Boethius (A. M. T. S.): quoted, *Phil.* 321
Boethius (Hector): 1 *Bec.* 390
Bogardi: *v.* Beguardi.
Bogging: botching up, *Phil.* 308
Bohemia: received the gospel from hearers of Wickliffe, *Pil.* 264, 654, upon whom More charges the utter subversion of the kingdom, 3 *Tyn.* 165; the Bohemians request to receive the communion under both kinds, 1 *Jew.* 212, *Rid.* 269; the council of Basil permitted them to continue the use of the cup, 1 *Jew.* 205, 3 *Jew.* 203 (and see Councils); they receive a letter from the church of Constantinople, 3 *Jew.* 196; the king was an elector of the empire, *Bale* 502, and umpire amongst the seven electors, 2 *Tyn.* 270
Boileau (Jac.): Hist. Flagell., 2 *Hoop.* 76 n
Boissise (......): sent as French ambassador to England, 2 *Zur.* 333 n
Bokkynge, (Edw.), *v.* Bockyng.
Bolen (Will.): archdeacon of Winton, *Phil.* ix.
Boleyn (......): *v.* Bullin.
Boleyn (Anne), queen: *v.* Anne.
Boleyn (Geo.), prebendary of Canterbury: *Park.* 319
Boleyn (Jane), lady Rochford (widow of Geo. visc. Rochford, son of the next): beheaded, 2 *Cran.* 408 n., 3 *Zur.* 226
Boleyn (Tho.), visc. Rochford, afterwards earl of Wiltshire and Ormond: sent ambassador to France, 2 *Cran.* 246; mentioned, *ib.* 270; a commissioner for a subsidy, *ib.* 301; he desires Rix as chaplain, *ib.* 302; letters to him, *ib.* 229, 259
Bolingbroke (Hen.), bp of Winchester: one of lord Cobham's judges, *Bale* 23, 28
Bollandus (Jo.): Acta Sanctorum, &c., 2 *Brad.* 291 n., 2 *Ful.* 81 n., 355 n., 360 n., *Jew.* xxxiv.
Bolmann (Theod.): *Calf.* 321 n
Bologna, in the Papal States: taken by Louis XII., 2 *Tyn.* 310
Bolseck (Hen.): denied predestination, *Rog.* 148, 150
Bolteby family: 1 *Tyn.* xiii.
Bolton, co. Lancaster: 1 *Brad.* 454; the queen of Scots imprisoned in the castle, 1 *Zur.* 210 n
Bolton (......): the first hatcher of Brown-

ism, *Rog.* 142; hanged himself in despair, *ib.* n
Bolton (R.): saluted, 2 *Brad.* 76
Bolton (Rob.), a Puritan divine: 1 *Brad.* 564
Bomelius (Eliseus): his astrology and imprisonment, *Park.* 363, 364; he desires to go to Russia, *ib.* 364 n.; ad lectorem epigramma, prefixed to Becon's works, 1 *Bec.* 33
Bona [Sforza], consort of Sigismund, king of Poland: 3 *Zur.* 602 n., 689 n
Bona (Jo. card.): referred to on the mass, 2 *Brad.* 306, &c., n., as to the books De Sacramentis, called Ambrose's, *Calf.* 202 n., with reference to the modern use of ancient words, *Phil.* 94 n.; his statement about the font of Constantine, 2 *Ful.* 360
Bonamy (Elias), of Guernsey: apparently son of the next, 1 *Zur.* 322, 2 *Zur.* 264
Bonamy (Pet.): a persecutor in the same island, 2 *Zur.* 264 n
Bonar (......), castellan of Bietz: 3 *Zur.* 602 n
Bonaventure (St), called the Seraphic Doctor: some account of him, 1 *Tyn.* 150 n.; his works, *Jew.* xxxiv.; he refers for the true form of consecration not to the gospel of Christ, but to the canon, 3 *Jew.* 451; his doubt as to the words thereof, *ib.* 452; on the fraction of the host, 1 *Hoop.* 228, 229; he affirms that grace is not contained in the sacraments essentially, as water in a vessel, 2 *Bec.* 219, 3 *Bec.* 469, 4 *Bul.* 307, 308, 1 *Jew.* 473, 2 *Jew.* 781, 3 *Jew.* 445, 448; says, the grace is in the soul, not in the visible signs, 3 *Jew.* 446; yet he maintains that sacraments confer grace ex opere operato, *Rog.* 248 n.; how the remission of sins is hid in baptism, 3 *Jew.* 446; he defines how long Christ's body remains in the sacrament, 2 *Jew.* 786; is of opinion that a brute beast eating the host does not receive the body of Christ, *ib.* 783; explains how the term eating, properly applied to corporeal things, is translated from them to spiritual things, 3 *Bec.* 434, 435; says, that by the alone faith of the passion of Christ all sin is forgiven, *ib.* 421; affirms that confession was insinuated by the Lord, instituted by the apostles, and openly proclaimed by James, 3 *Bul.* 84; intimates that to affirm the sufficiency of confession to God was not heretical till the time of Innocent III., *ib.* 89; asks whether a man can be absolved against his will, 3 *Jew.* 359; declares that the priests under the law of Moses were said to cleanse the leprosy, because they shewed who was cleansed, *ib.* 381, 448; says, almost all priests are as unlearned after the receiving of orders as they were before, *ib.* 363, 365; on the torments of purgatory, *Rog.* 216 n.; he ascribes the book of Wisdom to Philo, *Whita.* 88; his blasphemous Psalter, 1 *Brad.* 588, 1 *Ful.* 528, 1 *Tyn.* 150 n.; addresses to the virgin, 2 *Jew.* 899, 900, 1083, 3 *Jew.* 571
Bonchief: benefit, *Bale* 76
Bond: on a bond securing an annual sum to one till he should attain spiritual promotion, 2 *Cran.* 266
Bondage, Bonds: provisions of the judicial law of Moses respecting bondage, mancipation, &c., 2 *Bul.* 229; what bondage is, *ib.* 301; two sorts, *ib.* 302, bodily, *ib.*, spiritual, *ib.* 304; all are bondmen by nature, *Sand.* 178; we are redeemed from bondage by Christ, *ib.* 179; he hath delivered us from the bondage of Romish servitude, *ib.* 180; what bonds God hath broken, 1 *Bec.* 296, 297
Bondell (Jo.): 2 *Cran.* 382
Boner (Edm.): *v.* Bonner.
Bongeor (Will.): *v.* Banger.
Bonham (Will.): a leader of the separatists, *Grin.* 316; promise made by him, *ib.* 318; to be discharged, *Park.* 464
Boniface I., pope: son of a priest, 2 *Ful.* 98 n.; his claim to appellate jurisdiction, *ib.* 70, 71, 308, 2 *Hoop.* 236; he writes to Honorius the emperor, telling him that Rome was his city, 4 *Jew.* 678, 679, and desiring his aid to appease the tumults of the church, 2 *Ful.* 362; applies the term holy of holies to any consecrated thing, 1 *Jew.* 522; deposed by Honorius, 4 *Jew.* 1034
Boniface II., pope: brawls at his election, 1 *Whitg.* 463; he first divided the priest from the people in divine service, 1 *Jew.* 311; condemned Augustine and the council of Africa, 1 *Jew.* 402, 418, 3 *Jew.* 127, 128, 295, 607, 4 *Jew.* 938, and reconciled the African church to Rome, 1 *Jew.* 416 —418; his epistles to Eulalius, *ib.* 402, 417, 418
Boniface III., pope: said to have obtained the supremacy from Phocas, *Bale* 503, 2 *Ful.* 72, 365, 2 *Hoop.* 235, 555, 1 *Jew.* 184, 363, *Pil.* 76, 521, *Poet.* 284, 2 *Tyn.* 258; the nature of the evidence upon which it is believed that he obtained the title of œcumenical bishop, 2 *Ful.* 365, and see 371; took on him to be God's vicar, *Bale* 319; forbade the marriage of the clergy, 2 *Tyn.* 258; commanded altars to be covered with linen, 2 *Brad.* 311

Boniface VIII., pope: entered into the popedom as a fox, reigned as a wolf, died as a dog, 2 *Bul.* 267, 4 *Jew.* 684, 825, (the saying occurs with some variations); wore the crown imperial, and had two swords borne before him, 4 *Jew.* 820, 825; forbade princes to tax ecclesiastics without the pope's consent, 1 *Tyn.* 179 n.; instituted the jubilee at Rome, 2 *Bul.* 266—268, 1 *Lat.* 49 n.; burned the bones of St Herman, *Bale* 394, *Pil.* 18; his sorcery, *Bale* 593; his character, 4 *Jew.* 825; his bull, "Unam sanctam," *Rid.* 164 n.; Sextus Decretalium collected in his time, 1 *Hoop.* 568 n.; on Christ's charge to Peter, "Feed my sheep," 1 *Jew.* 433; cited as asserting that God took Peter into the fellowship of the undivided Trinity, *ib.* 439; he claims infallibility, 1 *Whitg.* 373; declares the pope to have all law in his own breast, 1 *Jew.* 68, 93, 442, 3 *Jew.* 598, 4 *Jew.* 768; his strange arguments for the pope's sovereignty, 1 *Jew.* 14, 143, 339, 377, 414, 4 *Jew.* 672; he claims for the pope the power of both swords, 1 *Jew.* 14, 442, 443, 3 *Jew.* 247, 4 *Jew.* 820; says, the material sword is to be drawn by princes at the beck of the priest, 3 *Jew.* 172, 4 *Jew.* 979, 992; affirms that though the pope carry innumerable souls with him to hell, yet he may not be judged (ascribed in the Canon Law to Boniface the martyr), 4 *Jew.* 833, *Rog.* 202, 1 *Tyn.* 328 n.; asserts that the pope is to be judged by no one (ascribed as the last), 3 *Bec.* 527, 528 n., 1 *Jew.* 77 n., 385, 1 *Tyn.* 328 n.; says, the pope is free from all human law, 2 *Jew.* 919; states that every human creature must be subject to the pope of the necessity of salvation, 1 *Jew.* 95, 368, 3 *Jew.* 196, 318, 325, 339, 4 *Jew.* 875, 1115, 1137, 1 *Whitg.* 181, 283; his decree against those who opposed any cardinal or clerk belonging to the pope's family, 2 *Cran.* 71; he says that what touches all must be allowed of all, 4 *Jew.* 1001; his rule of law as to a possessor malæ fidei, 1 *Jew.* 50

Boniface IX., pope: king Richard II.'s letter to him, *Pil.* 640

Boniface (St), abp of Mentz: appoints bishops in Germany, 2 *Whitg.* 377; his questions to pope Zachary, 4 *Jew.* 1045; receives the name Boniface (before called Winfred), 2 *Tyn.* 259 n.; put to death, *Bale* 190; words ascribed to him in the Canon Law against judging the pope, see Boniface VIII. above; his(?) expression concerning treen cups and golden priests, &c., 1 *Jew.* 120, 121, 2 *Jew.* 993, *Pil.* 157

Boniface, a Roman count: Augustine's remark to him about princes, 1 *Zur.* 64

Bonnam (Master): 2 *Lat.* 322

Bónner (Edm.), bp of London: notice of him, *Phil.* xxv.; Cranmer's letter to him, 1533, on appealing from the pope to a general council, 2 *Cran.* 268; suspected by Henry VIII. to be a favourer of the pope, 2 *Hoop.* 267, whereupon he purged himself by an epistle set before Gardiner's book De Vera Obedientia, 2 *Hoop.* 268, 557, 567, 1 *Jew.* 34, 60; this preface cited, 4 *Jew.* 1074; in it he declares that the pope's prey in England was almost as great as the revenues of the crown, *ib.* 1080, and says, notwithstanding the pope be a very ravening wolf, dressed in sheep's clothing, yet he calls himself the servant of servants, *ib.* 848; he succeeds Gardiner as ambassador at Paris, 2 *Cov.* 493 n., 495 n., 497; translated from Hereford to London, *ib.* 495 n.; references to injunctions set forth by him, 2 *Jew.* 993 n., 2 *Lat.* 242 n.; his tergiversation, 2 *Cran.* 17 n.; his conduct towards Anne Askewe, *Bale* 161, 163, 218, 229, &c.; Cranmer's letter to him about abolishing candle-bearing, ashes, and palms, 2 *Cran.* 417; Hooper's controversy with him, 3 *Zur.* 69, 70; his preaching at St Paul's, and conduct before the commissioners, *ib.* 557; he alleged that laws made during the king's minority were not binding, 1 *Lat.* 118 n., 3 *Zur.* 557; Latimer and Hooper complain of him to the council, 2 *Hoop.* xi.; he is imprisoned, 3 *Zur.* 69, 80, 558, 660; deposed, *ib.* 660; his acts in the convocation, 1553, *Phil.* xiii.; his injustice to Ridley's lessees, *Rid.* 291, 297, 427; homilies set forth by him, 2 *Cran.* 128 n.; his cruelty to Ridley, *Rid.* viii.; he examines Bradford, 1 *Brad.* 465; degrades Dr Taylor, *ib.* 496, likewise Hooper and Rogers, 2 *Hoop.* xxiv.; his examination of Philpot, *Phil.* 3, 14, 50, &c.; he entertains him, *ib.* 14; said to have been made the common inquisitor against his will, *ib.* 15; not the cause of Philpot's imprisonment, *ib.* 51; illegally declares himself to be Philpot's ordinary, and proceeds accordingly, *ib.* 83; ignorant in the law, *ib.* 149; his last exhortation to Philpot, *ib.* 151; his brutality to Tho. Whittle, *ib.* 13; his coal-hole used as a prison, *ib.* 12, 13, 70, 227, *Lit. Eliz.* 339 n., 352 n.; a commissioner against Cranmer, 2 *Cran.* 224; he sanctions the publication of Cranmer's recantations, *ib.* 563; extract from his register on the subject, *ib.* 567; called London Littlegrace, *Poet.* 167, a bloody butcher,

&c., *Pil.* 361, 400, 587; his cruelty, 2 *Zur.* 280, 3 *Zur.* 132; complaint of Ridley's executors against him, 1 *Zur.* 7; his cavil against the Ordinal of 1559, *Lit. Eliz.* xxi.; a great hindrance, 1 *Zur.* 10 n.; confined as prisoner to his house, 1 *Zur.* 7; deprived of his see, *ib.* 23; sent to prison, 4 *Jew.* 1234, 1 *Zur.* 79, 82; address of one of the prisoners in the Tower to him, 4 *Jew.* 1237; his easy life in the Marshalsea, *Pil.* 623 n.; his death, *Grin.* 307, 1 *Zur.* 79 n.; though he died excommunicate, he was buried in St George's churchyard, Southwark, privily by night, *Grin.* 307, 308; a paper written by him, 2 *Cran.* 152 n

Bonner (Mrs), mother of the bishop: kindly treated by Ridley, *Rid.* viii.

Bononia: *v.* Bologna, Furius.

Bonytoun (The young laird of): his execution, 2 *Zur.* 331, 332

Book (Bishops'): *v.* Institution.

BOOK OF CHRISTIAN PRAYERS, 1578: *Pra. Eliz.* 429; notes respecting it, *ib.* xvi.

Book of Common Order, (or John Knox's Liturgy): references to it, 1 *Brad.* 247 n., *Lit. Eliz.* 263—266, 483, 488, *Pra. Eliz.* 488, 517, 554 nn

Book of Common Prayer: *v.* Subscription.

King Edward's first book; THE BOOK OF COMMON PRAYER, &c. 1549, *Lit. Edw.* 9; notice of copies so dated, and their differences, *ib.* iii—vi.; it was drawn up at Windsor, 2 *Cran.* 450 n., 3 *Zur.* 322 n.; chiefly composed by Cranmer and Ridley, *Grin.* v.; finished in 1549, 2 *Cran.* x.; its preface, doubtfully ascribed to Cranmer, *ib.* 517; Bullinger desires to see the book, 3 *Zur.* 739; it was much disliked by Hooper, *ib.* 79; debates in parliament about it, *ib.* 322 n.; remarks in it, *ib.* 350; proposed amendments, *ib.* 281, 282

King Edward's second book; THE BOOK OF COMMON PRAYER, &c. 1552, *Lit. Edw.* 187; notices of copies so dated, and their differences, *ib.* vii.; the revision, 2 *Cran.* xi.; remarks on this book by P. Martyr, 2 *Brad.* 403; the English services (according to this book) described by bp Horn, 2 *Zur.* 354; Bullinger's remarks thereon, *ib.* 357; remarks and opinions on the two books of king Edward, 1 *Brad.* 471 n., 2 *Lat.* 262, 1 *Zur.* 234, 235, 2 *Zur.* 159; difference between them as to the rubric about the delivery of the elements, *Hutch.* 231 n

Queen Elizabeth's books: the Book of Common Prayer re-established by act of parliament, 1 *Zur.* 29, 84, having been revised, *Park.* 65; names of the divines who revised it, *Grin.* v., *Pil.* iii.; its use restored at the queen's chapel and St Paul's, *Grin.* v., 2 *Zur.* 17 n.; THE BOOK OF COMMON PRAYER, &c. 1559, *Lit. Eliz.* 23; notes respecting this and other Elizabethan Prayer Books, *ib.* xii. &c., as to editions published by the Puritans, *ib.* xv. &c.

Versions (see in the next sentence): both king Edward's Prayer Books were translated into French, 2 *Cran.* 439; the Prayer Book translated into Latin, for certain collegiate churches, 1560, *Park.* 133; the book itself, LIBER PRECUM PUBLICARUM, &c., *Lit. Eliz.* 299; notice respecting it, *ib.* xxi. &c.; farther notice, *Pra. Eliz.* xi. n.; the Prayer Book ordered to be translated into Welsh, 1563, 1 *Zur.* 124 n.; Liber Precum Publicarum, &c. Latine Græceque editus (by Will. Whitaker, 1569); notice of it, *Lit. Eliz.* xxii, *Whita.* xii.

Portions (see also Litany, Order of Communion, Ordination): the morning and evening prayer, litany, collects, and other parts of the public service adapted to private use, *Lit. Edw.* 383, &c.; the collects throughout the year (in king Edward's Primer), *ib.* 439; the general confession and prayer for the king from the public service, together with other prayers for use in schools, *ib.* 538; the general confession, absolution, and other portions in Latin (in the Orarium, 1560), *Pra. Eliz.* 132, &c.

The English service agrees with the ancient church, *Pil.* 533; follows the apostles and old fathers, *ib.* 541; alleged offer of Pius IV. to confirm it, *Lit. Eliz.* xxii.; approved by the cardinal of Lorraine, *Park.* 398; objections of the Puritans against it, 1 *Whitg.* 283, 1 *Whitg.* 119 n.; it is not absolutely perfect, 1 *Whitg.* 173; controversy respecting it, 2 *Whitg.* 438, &c.; an examination of the particular faults with which it is charged, *ib.* 465; of subscribing to the Communion Book, 3 *Whitg.* 326, &c.; whence it is taken, *ib.* 326, 490; declared by one to be patched out of the popish portass, *Grin.* 213; said to be sealed with the blood of martyrs, 3 *Whitg.* 327—330; directed to be provided by churchwardens, *Grin.* 133; inquiry respecting it, *ib.* 157; injunctions about its use, 2 *Hoop.* 130, &c.; in what parts of the church it is to be read, *Grin.* 132, 155; said by the priest in the chancel, his back to the people, 2 *Whitg.* 461; the communion service said at the further end of the chancel, *ib.*; custom as to other offices, *ib.* 461, &c.

Notice of several editions of the Newe

Forme of Common Praier, set forth by the Puritans, *Lit. Eliz.* xix. n
Book of Discipline: *Park.* 382
Book (King's): the name applied to the Necessary Doctrine and Erudition, likewise to the first Book of Common Prayer, *Hutch.* 231 n
Book of Life: *v.* Predestination.
Book of Oaths: 4 *Jew.* 1144 n., 2 *Lat.* 114 n
Book of the Wars of the Lord: *v.* Wars.
Bookbinder (Jo.), i.e. Jo. Byrte, *q.v.*
Books: *v.* Manuscripts.

The book with seven seals, *Bale* 304; an angel with a little book, *ib.* 370; John eats it, *ib.* 375; on the text "Of making of many books," *Sand.* 1; many English books printed at Paris by Regnault, 2 *Cov.* 495; many popish ones found in Berkshire, *ib.* 499; the high price of good books lamented, *Rid.* 488, 491; a catalogue of popish books written in the English tongue during the reign of Elizabeth, 2 *Ful.* 3; inquiry about popish books, *Grin.* 169; books ordered to be placed in churches, *Jew.* xxviii.; articles respecting church-books, *Grin.* 134, 157; books bequeathed by Grindal, *ib.* 459

Books of laymen: *v.* Images.
Books of service: *v.* Liturgies.
Booksellers: ordered not to sell books without permission, *Park.* 410
Bool: to bawl, 2 *Bec.* 390
Booth (Cha.), bp of Hereford: Cranmer's admonition to him about a dispute between a clergyman and the receiver of the see, 2 *Cran.* 263
Boots: an academic distinction, 1 *Tyn.* 232
Bopfingen: surrendered, 3 *Zur.* 638 n
Borbonius (Nich.); pia admonitio ad pueros, verses, *Pra. Eliz.* 413; he was a friend of Holbein, *ib.* n
Bordered: embroidered, *Sand.* 310
Borders of garments: *v.* Jews.
Bordesley, co. Worcester: the abbey demesne granted to lord Windsor, 2 *Lat.* 394 n
Boren (Kath. à), wife of M. Luther, *q. v.*
Borgest (......), the Spanish ambassador's secretary: hires two desperate men to murder lord Burghley and the queen, *Grin.* 332 n., 2 *Zur.* 198 n
Borough (......): *v.* Burgh.
Borrowing: *v.* Lending.
Borthwick castle, Scotland: 1 *Zur.* 193 n
Borthwike (Sir Jo.): charged with heresy, 3 *Tyn.* 187 n
Bosfell (Hen.): a proctor, 2 *Cran.* 492
Bosom: to conceal in privacy, 2 *Bul.* 28
Bossuet (Jac. Benigne), bp of Meaux: eulogizes the confession of Helvetia, 1 *Zur.* 169 n.; referred to, 3 *Zur.* 666 n
Bostius (Arn.): cited, *Bale* 168
Boston, co. Lincoln: famous for pardons, *Pil.* 551; indulgence granted to the church there, 1 *Tyn.* 244 n.; the rood, 2 *Ful.* 210
Boston (Will.), alias Benson, abbot, afterwards dean of Westminster: notice of him, 2 *Lat.* 370 n.; his pliability, 2*Cran.* 240; he attends Anne Boleyn's coronation, *ib.* 245; signs a declaration respecting a general council, 2 *Cran.* 468 [Benson according to the footnote, but qu. whether not Will. Reppes or Rugge, abbot of St Benet at Hulme?]; letters to him (Benson), *ib.* 240, 251, 270
Boter (Jo.): 2 *Brad.* xiii. n
Botergius (Jordanes): wrote on the Apocalypse, *Bale* 257
Botfield (Beriah): his Notes on the Cathedral Libraries cited, *Pra. Eliz.* xx.
Bothwell (Adam), bp of Orkney: *v.* Hepburn.
Bothwell (James earl of): *v.* Hepburn.
Bothwellhaugh: *v.* Hamilton (James).
Bottom-blessings: *Bale* 526
Bouchier (Hen.), earl of Essex, and others: *v.* Bourchier.
Bouchier (Tho.): De Martyrio Fratrum Ord. Min., 2 *Lat.* 392 n
Boughton under the Blayne, co. Kent: farmed of the convent of Feversham, 2 *Cran.* 374, 400
Boulogne: king Henry's camp there, 1 *Brad.* 32 n., 487 n., 2 *Brad.* xiii.; the siege, 1 *Brad.* 493 n., 2 *Tyn.* 305; the town taken by king Henry, *Park.* 15 n., 30 n., *Pil.* 70, 86; the keys delivered to him, *Hutch.* 99; homilies sent there, 2 *Cran.* 505; the women and children sent away in expectation of an attack by the French, 3 *Zur.* 264; some of the Swiss cantons engage to aid the French in its recovery, *ib.* 740; attacked by the French, *ib.* 652; surrendered to them on payment of a large sum of money, *ib.* 398 n., 410, 558 n., 559, 728; our lady of Bulloyne, 1 *Hoop.* 455
Boulting: sifting, *Phil.* 200
Boun: boon, 2 *Jew.* 1086
Bound (Nich.): *v.* Bownde.
Bounds: bonds, engagements, 3 *Bec.* 618
Bounty: *v.* Almsgiving.
Bourbon (Cha. duke of): *v.* Charles.
Bourbon (L. de), duke of Condé: *v.* Louis.
Bourbon (Nich.): *v.* Borbonius.
Bourcher (Arth.): notice of him, *Poet.* xxv.; his golden precepts, *ib.* 297
Bourchier (Fulke), lord Fitzwarine: Elizabeth his daughter, 1 *Bec.* 396 n

Bourchier (Hen.), earl of Essex: letter to Cranmer as to his dispossessing Richard Stansby of copyhold lands in Bilston, 2 *Cran.* 266; Cranmer's reply, recommending a reference to arbitration, *ib.*; Henry VIII.'s peremptory order to him to restore the lands, *ib.* 267 n.; his death, *ib.* 266 n., 3 *Zur.* 221

Bourchier (John), 2nd earl of Bath: one of queen Mary's privy council, 1 *Zur.* 5 n. (there erroneously called Henry).

Bourchier (Will.), earl of Eu: Anne (Plantagenet) his wife, 1 *Bec.* 396 n

Bourding: jesting, 1 *Brad.* 38

Bourgoyne (Fra.): notice of him, 3 *Zur.* 730 n.; two letters to Calvin, *ib.* 730, 731

Bourne (Gilb.), bp of Bath and Wells: notice of him, *Phil.* xxviii; his life saved by Bradford at Paul's cross, 1 *Brad.* 16 n., 465, 466, &c., 474, 485; 2 *Brad.* xxxi, *Rid.* 370 n., 3 *Zur.* 368 n.; said to have begged for Bradford's life, 1 *Brad.* 549, 2 *Brad.* 199, *Rid.* 370; prisoner in the Tower, *Park.* 122; afterwards in the custody of bp Bullingham, *ib.* 253

Bourne (Sir Jo.), brother of the bishop, and secretary of state: 1 *Brad.* 469, *Phil.* xxviii, *Rid.* 155; not of noble birth, 4 *Jew.* 1146; his dispute with Sandys, commencing about a stone altar, *Sand.* xviii.

Bourne (Phil.), father of the bishop and Sir John: *Phil.* xxviii.

Bovius (C.): on Easter, *Whita.* 569

Bow: *v.* Archery. Rainbow: *v.* Noah.

Bow down (To): *v.* Worship.

Bowed: bent, 2 *Bul.* 190

Boweland (Tho.), a Londoner: examined before the ecclesiastical commissioners, *Grin.* 201

Boweman (Nic.): notice of him, *Poet.* lvi; verses from his epitaph on bishop Juel, *ib.* 554; the Lenvoy (sic), *ib.* 555

Bowen (Mr): *Park.* 266, 267

Bowen (Walter), of Barnstaple: 4 *Jew.* v.

Bower (Jo.), or Bowyar: farms the parsonage of Petworth, 2 *Cran.* 278

Bowes (Sir Geo.): sent against the rebels in the North, 1 *Zur.* 213 n., 247 n.; executes many of them, *Lit. Eliz.* 538 n

Bowes (Joyce), or rather Lewes, *q. v.*

Bowes (Sir Martin): sheriff of London, *Phil.* 150

Bowes (Rich.): one of the royal visitors for the North, 1 *Zur.* 73 n

Bowes (Sir Rob.): surveys Norham castle, 2 *Tyn.* 278 n.; sent to France, 2 *Cran.* 411 n

Bowier (......), of the Temple: 2 *Brad.* 251, 253

Bowier (Tho.): *v.* Bowyer.

Bowing: *v.* Christ, Worship.

Bowler (Jo.): a gaoler in the Tower, converted through Bradford and Sandys, 2 *Brad.* xxxii, *Sand.* vii. viii.

Bowls: pardon-bowls, 3 *Bec.* 198 n., 1 *Lat.* 50 n., 75; pardon-masers [maizers], as St Benet's bowl, St Edmond's, St Giles's, St Blyth's, and Westminster bowl, *Bale* 527; bowl of St Leonard, *Calf.* 287

Bowls: injunctions respecting the game, *Grin.* 130, 138

Bowmer (......): Bowmer's wife, martyr at Chichester, *Poet.* 170

Bowers: archers, *Bale* 191

Bownde (Nich.): his opinions zealously opposed by Rogers, *Rog.* ix; the sum of Sabbatarian doctrine, as stated by him and others, *ib.* 19; he maintains that the law of the sabbath is moral and perpetual, *ib.* 90 n.; says the life of God (in Adam) could not continue without the seventh day, &c., *ib.* 97, 98; affirms that the church has no authority to sanctify any other day, *ib.* 187 n., 322 n.; says the sabbath must be sanctified by preaching, *ib.* 233 n., 271 n., 326; other statements, *ib.* 315, 327; he imposes his sabbatarian traditions on the church under pain of damnation, *ib.* 319 n

Bowne: ready, prepared, 1 *Brad.* 445; to bowne, *Pil.* 353

Bows: *v.* Archery.

Bowyar (Jo.): *v.* Bower.

Bowyer (Tho.): martyred, *Poet.* 168

Box: "in a wrong box," *Rid.* 163

Box (Will.): cousin to Hutchinson, *Hutch.* viii. x.

Boxall (Jo.), dean of Peterborough, Norwich, and Windsor: notice of him, 1 *Zur.* 255 n.; not of noble birth, 4 *Jew.* 1146; one of queen Mary's privy council, 1 *Zur.* 5 n.; he quarrels with the service-book, *Park.* 65; to be deprived if he refuse the oath, *ib.* 104; prisoner in the Tower, *ib.* 122; removed thence on account of the plague, *ib.* 192—195; lives with Parker, *ib.* 194 n., 203, 215, 217, 218; his death, 2 *Zur.* 183; his character, *Park.* 104 n

Boxhornius (Hen.): Harmonia Eucharistica, 2 *Ful.* 22 n

Boxley, co. Kent: the rood of grace destroyed at Paul's cross, 3 *Zur.* 604, 606, 609

Boy-bishop: *v.* Bishops.

Boyd (Rob. 4th lord), of Kilmarnock: 1 *Zur.* 262 n

Boyer (......): treacherously executed by Sir Ant. Kingston, 2 *Cran.* 187 n
Boyes (......): in exile, 3 *Zur.* 167 n
Boyes (Edw.): recommended as a justice, *Park.* 204
Boyle (Hon. Rob.): 1 *Zur.* viii. n
Boyneburgh (Geo. à): an envoy from Germany, 2 *Cran.* 377 n., 3 *Zur.* 612 n
Boys (Jo.): letter to him as steward of Parker's liberties, *Park.* 452
Boys (Jo.): Expos. of the Dominical Epistles and Gospels, *Calf.* 5 n., 25 n., 78 n
Boys (Tho.): witness in a cause, 2 *Cran.* 390
Boys (......): counsel to Cranmer (perhaps the last named), 2 *Cran.* 388
Bozius (Tho.): on the tokens of the Church, *Rog.* 176
Brabant: invaded by Charles V., 2 *Cov.* 512; martyrs there, 3 *Tyn.* 113; its affairs, 2 *Zur.* 165
Brabble: a brawl, 2 *Ful.* 142; to brabble, *Phil.* 305
Bracarense concilium: v. Councils, *Braga.*
Brachmanes, or Brahmins: 2 *Jew.* 981
Brackenbury (Edw.): recommended as a notary, *Park.* 393 n
Bradbridge (G.): martyred at Canterbury, *Poet.* 164
Bradbridge (Jone): martyred at Maidstone, *Poet.* 169
Bradford (......), mother of the martyr: letters to her, 2 *Brad.* 41, 72, 74, 249
Bradford (......), a sister of the martyr: 2 *Brad.* 197; the same, or another sister, *ib.* 252
Bradford (Ann), also a sister: 2 *Brad.* 76
Bradford (Eliz.), a married sister of the martyr: [perhaps the same as Eliz. Brown, *q. v.*], 2 *Brad.* 76
BRADFORD (Jo.): WORKS, edited by the Rev. Aubrey Townsend, B.D., 1 and 2 *Brad.*; biographical notice, 2 *Brad.* xi—xliv; (and see Sampson's account of him, 1 *Brad.* 29, &c.); his birth, 2 *Brad.* xi; early education, *ib.* xii; servant to sir Jo. Harrington at Boulogne, *ib.*; paymaster at the siege of Montreuil, *ib.* xiii; he enters the Inner Temple, *ib.*; his conversion, *ib.*; by Latimer's advice, he compels sir Jo. Harrington to make restitution for a fraud, *ib.* xiv—xvi, and loses his patronage, *ib.* xvi; said to have paid conscience-money, 1 *Lat.* 262 n.; he enters Catharine hall, Cambridge, 2 *Brad.* xvii; invited by Ridley to a fellowship at Pembroke hall, *ib.*; made M. A. by special grace, *ib.* xviii; his fellowship, *ib.* xviii; his holy life, *ib.* xix; tutor and patron of Whitgift, *ib.* xx, 3 *Whitg.* vi; his friendship with Bucer, 2 *Brad.* xx. xxi, 2 *Zur.* 72 n.; he visits Oxford with him, 2 *Brad.* xxii; ordained deacon by Ridley, *ib.*, who made him his chaplain, *ib.* xxiii; he attends the death-bed of Bucer, *ib.*; made prebendary of St Paul's, *ib.* xxv, *Rid.* 331, 336, and chaplain to the king, 2 *Brad.* xxv; his itinerant labours, *ib.* xxvi; appointed to attend Sir Miles Partridge before his execution, *ib.* xxvii; his last sermon in Manchester, *ib.*; preaches before the king, *ib.* xxviii. (and 1 *Brad.* 111); his warning of coming judgment, *ib.*; his faithful preaching, *ib.* xxix, *Rid.* 59; his private life, 2 *Brad.* xxix; he laments king Edward's death, *ib.* xxx; saves the life of bp Bourne (*q. v.*) at Paul's cross, *ib.* xxxi, and preaches at Bow church, *ib.* xxxii; is sent to the Tower, *ib.* xxxii, 2 *Lat.* 258, 3 *Zur.* 369; his fellow-prisoners, Cranmer, Ridley, and Latimer, 2 *Brad.* xxxiii, (and subsequently, Ferrar, Taylor, and Philpot, *ib.* 74 n., 96, 140; Becon, 1 *Bec.* xi, also Sandys, *Sand.* vii. viii. xii;) described by Latimer as "that holy man," 2 *Brad.* xxxiii; removed to the King's Bench, where he strengthens Ferrar, *ib.* xxxiv, *Rid.* 358; declaration concerning religion, signed by him and several other prisoners, 1 *Brad.* 374; he preaches in prison, 2 *Brad.* xxxiv, 116; favoured by his keepers, *ib.* xxxiv. xxxv; examined before Gardiner, *ib.* xxxvii; condemned, *ib.*; the proceedings and sentence, in Latin, 1 *Brad.* 585; awaits martyrdom, *Rid.* 380, 391, 3 *Zur.* 171; in the custody of lord Derby, *Rid.* 382; intention to send him to Manchester, 2 *Brad.* xxxvii; he confers with Romish divines, *ib.* xxxviii; his dreams in the Compter, *ib.*; he receives notice of his burning, *ib.* xxxix; taken to Newgate, *ib.* xl, and thence to Smithfield, *ib.*; his martyrdom, *ib.* xli. xlii, 1 *Brad.* 556, *Poet.* 162, 3 *Zur.* 772; references to him, 2 *Hoop.* 592, *Phil.* 235, *Pra. B.* v. vii, *Rid.* 337; his character and appearance, 2 *Brad.* xlii. xliii. and 1 *Brad.* x; Dr Wilkinson's account of him, 1 *Brad.* 558; his works, 2 *Brad.* xlii. xliii, 1 *Brad.* x; list of editions of his writings, 2 *Brad.* xlv; reference to his treatise on the communion, *Rid.* 363; his prayer for true mortification, *Pra. Eliz.* 526; he translates the prayers of Lud. Vives, *ib.* xxii; a letter by him or Latimer, 2 *Brad.* 45, 2 *Lat.* 435; his letter to certain godly men who helped him in his imprisonment, 1 *Brad.* 379; he wrote two

letters to the earl of Bedford in prison, 2 *Zur.* 215 n.; letters to him (see 2 *Brad.* contents), 2 *Hoop.* 592, *Lat.* 358, *Rid.* 358, 363, 366, 367, 369, 371, 377, 379, 537 (?)
Bradford (Margaret), a married sister of the martyr: [apparently the same as Margery Coke, *q.v.*], 2 *Brad.* 28, 76
Bradford (Roger), brother of the martyr: 2 *Brad.* 76, 250
Bradford (Rodolph): account of him, 2 *Lat.* 376 n
Bradgate, near Leicester: the seat of the Suffolk family, and birthplace of lady Jane Grey, 3 *Zur.* 275 n., 429 n
Bradock (Tho.): translates the Defence of the Apology into Latin, *Jew.* xxviii.
Bradshaw (James): 2 *Brad.* 41, 236
Bradshaw (Lau.): 2 *Brad.* 41
Brady (Hugh), bp of Meath: appointed, *Park.* 117 n.; he (or a titular bp of Meath his contemporary?) takes flight, 1 *Zur.* 309 n
Braga: *v.* Councils.
Brahmins: *v.* Brachmanes.
Bramford, co. Suffolk: martyrs there, *Poet.* 173
Bramhall (Jo.), abp of Armagh: mentions the fictitious council of Sinuessa, 2 *Ful.* 364; referred to on the council of Florence, *Calf.* 408
Brand (Jo.), minister of Holyrood: 2 *Zur.* 365
Brand (Jo.): Popular Antiquities, 2 *Bec.* 346, 438, 3 *Bec.* 126; 1 *Lat.* 71, 175, 207, 208, 498, 2 *Lat.* 100 nn
Brand (Will.), of the strangers' church at Sandwich: *Park.* 247
Brandenburg (Electors of): *v.* Albert, George, Joachim.
Brandon (St): his fast, 2 *Tyn.* 98; his legend, *ib.* n
Brandon (Cha.), duke of Suffolk: bore the crown at the coronation of Anne Boleyn, 2 *Cran.* 246; notice of him, 3 *Zur.* 36 n
— Katherine, duchess of Suffolk, his last wife (baroness Willoughby de Eresby in her own right): mentioned, 2 *Cov.* 528, 1 *Lat.* xiv, *Poet.* liii, *Pra. Eliz.* 239 n., notice of her, 1 *Lat.* 81 n., 2 *Zur.* 239; sermons preached before her by Latimer, dedicated to her by A. Bernher, 1 *Lat.* 309; helps Ridley in prison, "my good lady's grace," 2 *Brad.* 161, *Rid.* 374, 382; her life sought, *Bale* 220, 242; in exile with her husband, 2 *Cov.* 528; dedication to her by T. Some, 1 *Lat.* 81; the ecclesiastical commissioners send for one Brown, her chaplain, *Park.* 390

Brandon (Hen.), duke of Suffolk: death of him and lord Charles his brother, 3 *Bec.* 205, 2 *Cran.* 454, 496, 576, 727
Brandt (Ger.): Hist. of the Reformation, 3 *Zur.* 417 & al.
Brasen Serpent: *v.* Serpent.
Brassius (Egbert): 2 *Zur.* 106
Brast: to burst, 2 *Tyn.* 208; brast (participle), *Pil.* 264
Bray (Edm. lord): his daughter Anne, 1 *Bec.* 264 n
Bray (Sir Edw.), cousin to Sandys: his wife a zealous Protestant, *Sand.* xi.
Bray (Hen.), mayor of Bodmin: executed 2 *Cran.* 163 n., 186 n
Braybroke (Sir Gerard): his daughter Joan, 1 *Bec.* 264 n
Braybrooke (Rob. de), bp of London: his gentleness, *Bale* 125
Braye (Rich.), fellow of All Souls': *Park.* 300, 301 n
Brayley (Edw. W.): *Grin.* 273 n
Brayne (Edw.): 3 *Whitg.* 604 n., 608
Brazil: called Gallia Antarctica, 2 *Ful.* 61
Bread: the gift of God, 2 *Tyn.* 117; what it signifies in scripture, 2 *Bec.* 166; what it is to break it to the hungry, *ib.* 538, 539; among the Jews it signified all kinds of meats, &c., 4 *Bul.* 214; sent by one bishop to another, as by Paulinus to Augustine, in token of fellowship, 1 *Jew.* 145; Arrian and Strabo speak of whole nations who have no bread, *ib.* 222
— Breaking of bread: meaning of the phrase, 4 *Bul.* 276, 402, 429, *Grin.* 42, *Hutch.* 284, 1 *Jew.* 232, &c., 2 *Jew.* 584, &c., *Phil.* 117; and see Supper of the Lord, likewise Host.
— Daily Bread: variously understood, 2 *Bec.* 166, 1 *Brad.* 100, 131, 181, 4 *Bul.* 214, 1 *Lat.* 389, *Now.* (77), 197, 2 *Cran.* 109; and in every exposition of the Lord's Prayer, *q.v.*
— Holy Bread: 1 *Lat.* 497, 2 *Lat.* 286, 1 *Tyn.* 284; conjuration thereof, *Rid.* 106; Latimer's verses on giving it, 2 *Lat.* xviii. 294 (see also Holy).
— Shew Bread: its meaning, 2 *Bul.* 156; remarks of Origen thereon, 2 *Ful.* 85
Breast-plate: that of the high priest, 2 *Bul.* 135; the breast-lap of judgment, *ib.* 136; brest-flap, 1 *Tyn.* 419
Bredwell (S.): his Detection, quoted, *Rog.* 70, 92, 103, 147, 157, 274, &c.
Bremael, otherwise Brocinail, mayor of Chester: *Pil.* 516
Bremen: dissensions there, 3 *Zur.* 561; it holds out against the emperor, *ib.* 668 n

Bremgarten, near Zurich: Bullinger's birthplace, 4 *Bul.* vii.

Brenchley (Friar): his preaching against the king, 2 *Cran.* 302

Brenne: to burn, *Pil.* 595; brenning, 1 *Bec.* 18; brent, 1 *Bul.* 411, *Pil.* 481 n

Brentius (Jo.), or **Brentzen**: at the diet of Worms, 3 *Jew.* 621; the patron of Ubiquitarianism, and opponent of Bullinger (*q. v.*), 4 *Bul.* 447 n., *Coop.* 39, 3 *Jew.* 623, 4 *Jew.* 1258 n., 1263 n., 1 *Zur.* 98 n., 108 n., 121, 123, 131, 135, 139, 2 *Zur.* 97, 245, 314, 3 *Zur.* 132; he takes refuge with the duke of Wurtemberg, 3 *Zur.* 543; goes to the council of Trent, *Whita.* 10; states what dominion may be exercised by bishops, and what not, 1 *Whitg.* 153—155; on χειροτονία, *ib.* 345 n.; on the apostles' appointment of presbyters in every church, 3 *Whitg.* 156; on the power of remitting and retaining sin, *ib.* 236; on Romish contempt of scripture, 4 *Jew.* 757, 758; exemplification of this in Hosius, *ib.* 759, who replied to what he wrote against à Soto, *ib.* 941, 942; he wrote on the Apocalypse, *Bale* 258; letter to him, 3 *Zur.* 542

Brentius (Valentius): 2 *Cov.* 509

Brenzett, co. Kent: Becon's vicarage, 1 *Bec.* viii.

Brephotrophia: 1 *Bul.* 286, 4 *Bul.* 498

Brereley (Jo.): 2 *Ful.* 49, 57, 70, 71 nn

Brerewood (Edw.): Enquiries, 2 *Ful.* 328 n

Brest, in Bretagne: dispute concerning it between Richard II. and his lords, 2 *Tyn.* 296

Brether, or **Brethern**: brethren, *Pil.* 233

Brethren, Brother: who our brother is, 3 *Bec.* 610; import of the name, *Lit. Edw.* 524, (571); how the term is used in scripture, *Pil.* 187, 288; examples of desire for the saving health of brethren, 1 *Bec.* 196; we are bound to seek their salvation, 2 *Bec.* 176, 177; the Presbyterian party in the church of England called Brethren, *Rog.* 10

— Weak brethren (*v.* Faith): who are such, 3 *Bec.* 610; they are to be borne with, 1 *Tyn.* 452, 506, 507; they should be upheld, 2 *Tyn.* 8

— False Brethren: 2 *Jew.* 937, &c.

Brethren of Love: *v.* Family of Love.

Breton (Sir Nich.): notice of him, *Poet.* xix; stanzas, from A small Handful of Fragrant Flowers, *ib.* 179; a prayer for gentlewomen and other to use, *ib.* 180; a solemn and repentant prayer for former life misspent, *ib.* 181; a prayer, *ib.* 184; a prayer written for a gentlewoman, *ib.*; the praise of humility, *ib.*; gloria in excelsis Deo, *ib.* 187; stanzas from his poem upon the longing of a blessed heart, *ib.* 190; hymn, *ib.* 194; two sonnets, *ib.* 195; Mary Magdalen's lamentations, by some ascribed to him, *ib.* xl; extracts therefrom, *ib.* 447

Breton (Will.): *v.* Brito.

Breviary: sometimes called portess, porteux, portuis, &c., 1 *Tyn.* 230, & al. (see Portass); on the antiquity of the pope's portus, *Pil.* 534, 535; reference to a form entitled benedictio mensæ, *Pra. Eliz.* 399

— **Breviarium Romanum**: form of benediction of water for baptism, 4 *Bul.* 306, 307; the Roman Breviary records, as a fact, the fable of the baptism of Constantine by pope Silvester, 2 *Ful.* 359; contains matter taken from the imaginary acts of the synod of Sinuessa, *ib.* 364; collects from it for the days of St Laurence and St Stephen, 1 *Tyn.* 231 n.; legend of St Laurence, 2 *Tyn.* 254; legend of St Agatha, 3 *Tyn.* 61 n.; collect for the octave of SS. Peter and Paul, *ib.* 117 n

— **Breviarium ad usum Sarum**: rubric concerning the Lord's prayer, *Lit. Eliz.* 72 n.; references to it respecting hymns, *Pra. Eliz.* 134, 141, 145, 147, 148, 150, 153, 156, 269 nn.; Portiforium seu Breviarium ad usum Sarum (Par. 1510), invocations of Tho. à Becket, 1 *Bec.* 328 n., 2 *Jew.* 1082, 3 *Jew.* 573; editions omitting the word "pope," &c. (Lond. 1541, 44), 2 *Cran.* 366 n.; Portiforium ad usum Sarum, (Roth. 1556,) *Calf.* 17 n.; the Breviaries of Sarum, York, and Bangor, *Pil.* 535

— Breviary of the Franciscans, 2 *Lat.* 227 n

Brevint (Dan.): Saul and Samuel, *Calf.* 19 n

Brewers: at Cracow, 3 *Zur.* 689, 694, 697

Brewis, or **Brose**: a kind of pottage, 3 *Bec.* 208

Brian (Mr): 2 *Cran.* 241

Bribery: a kind of thieving, 1 *Lat.* 139; a secret fault, *ib.* 188; bribes are like pitch, *ib.*; a rich murderer escapes thereby, *ib.* 189; bribery of a jury in a case of murder, *ib.* 190, 380; another case, *ib.* 190; a warning to bribers, *ib.* 260; the prevalence of bribe-taking, 2 *Bec.* 307

Brice (Jo.), servant to Cranmer: 2 *Cran.* 297

Brice (Tho.) *v.* Bryce.

Brickman (Arn.): *v.* Byrchman.

Bride (St): *v.* Brigit.

Bridewell: *v.* Londen.

Bridges (Jo.), 1st lord Chandos: his creation, 2 *Cran.* 364 n.; lieutenant of the Tower (?), *Phil.* 50, *Rid.* 155; the order for Hooper's execution sent to him, 2 *Hoop.*

xxvi; one of the examiners of Philpot, *Phil.* 50, 56

Bridges (Edm.), 2nd lord Chandos: charged with Hooper's execution (then Sir Edm. Bridges,) 2 *Hoop.* xxvi; he writes to Parker, *Park.* 213 n.; at the duke of Norfolk's trial, 1 *Zur.* 267 n. (erroneously called Edward).

Bridges (Will.), 4th lord Chandos: his daughter Frances, 2 *Bec.* 480 n

Bridges (Agnes): pretending to be possessed, she is examined before abp Parker, and does penance at Paul's cross, *Park.* 465

Bridges (Jo.), bp of Oxford; answers Stapleton, 1 *Ful.* 75 n., 2 *Ful.* 3; Defence of the Godly Ministers against the Slanders of D. Bridges, *Rog.* 327 n

Bridges (Sir Tho.), or Abridges: converses with Ridley in the Tower, *Rid.* 155; (apparently the brother of lord Chandos, named, *Phil.* 56)

Bridges (Will.), brother to Sir John: his unlawful marriage, 2 *Cran.* 364

Bridoul (Toussain): *Calf.* 86 n

Briganden (Mr): *v.* Bryganden.

Briget: presumed to be W. Brito, *q. v.*

Brigit (St): *v.* Psalms.

Notice of her, 1 *Tyn.* 151 n.; a legend respecting her, 3 *Bec.* 390 n.; her revelations, 1 *Hoop.* 291; she threatens the clergy of Rome with the loss of Christ's blessing, 4 *Jew.* 874; notice of The XV. Oes of S. Bridget, *Pra. Eliz.* xxii; ten prayers ascribed to her, being a portion of the XV. Oes, *ib.* 507–512

Bright (Will.): *v.* Brito.

Brighthelmstone, co. Sussex: *Grin.* 359 n

Brill (The), in Holland: 2 *Bec.* 480 n.; taken by the lord of Lumey, 1 *Zur.* 273

Brill (Steph.), fellow of All Souls': *Park.* 300

Brimly: publicly, 3 *Bul.* 147

Brimstone: made from stuff gathered on the shore, *Park.* 341

Brinced: pledged, 3 *Jew.* 265

Brinnynge; burning, *Pil.* 481

Brion: *v.* Bruno.

Bristol: formerly called Bristow, 3 *Tyn.* 12; Tyndale preaches on St Austin's green, 1 *Tyn.* xviii; commotions there through the preaching of Latimer and others, 2 *Cran.* 308 n., 2 *Lat.* 225 n., 358; recommended to lord Cromwell's care, 2 *Lat.* 402; Holbeach made suffragan bishop, *ib.* 412 n.; the friars preachers, 2 *Cran.* 252; churches of St Thomas and St Nicholas, 2 *Lat.* 358 n.; the mint, 1 *Lat.* 263 n., 3 *Zur.* 649; queen Elizabeth at Bristol, *Lit. Eliz.* 666 n., 2 *Zur.* 258 n

Bristow (Rich.), a popish author: *Grin.* 169; on the marks of the true church, *Rog.* 176; he affirms that the pope may deprive heretical princes, *ib.* 348 n.; Fulke writes against him, 1 *Ful.* viii. ix. 15, 68, 76; some account of him and his works, *ib.* 95 u

Britain, Britons: *v.* England.

Britannia Sancta: a book published 1745, 2 *Tyn.* 216 n

Brito (Will.), or Breton: referred to, 2 *Lat.* 319

Brittayne (......): cousin to Anne Askewe, *Bale* 160, 162, 165, 177; surety for her, *ib.* 178

Britten (Dr): *v.* Brytten.

Broach: to pierce through, 1 *Brad.* 79

Broadgate hall: *v.* Oxford.

Broadway, co. Dorset: the rectory, *Park.* 136

Brocinail: *v.* Bremael.

Brocvale, king of Leicester: 4 *Jew.* 780

Brodbridge: *v.* Bradbridge.

Broided: embroidered, 1 *Hoop.* 377

Broke: a breach, 2 *Bec.* 94

Broke (James), or Brokes, bp: *v.* Brooks.

Broke (Jo.): suitor in Chancery against one Mares, 2 *Cran.* 257

Broke (Tho.): *v.* Brooke.

Bromham, co. Wilts.: 2 *Lat.* 322 n., 332

Bromley (G.): an ecclesiastical commissioner, *Park.* 383

Bromley (Sir Tho.): an ecclesiastical commissioner, *Park.* 370, 383; lord chancellor, 3 *Whitg.* xii; signature as such, *Grin.* 412, 414, 417, 423, 427, 429, 433, 435

Brooke (Tho.), 5th lord Cobham: Elizabeth his daughter married Sir Tho. Wyat the elder, 1 *Bec.* 232 n

Brooke (Geo.), 6th lord Cobham: commissioner for a subsidy, 2 *Cran.* 301; Cranmer's letter to him on a cause there, and to buy him wine, *ib.* 411; governor of Calais: *ib.* 330, 335, 3 *Zur.* 264; a privy councillor, 2 *Cran.* 531; dedication to him, 1 *Bec.* 264; notice of him, *ib.* n

Brooke (Will.), 7th lord Cobham: minister to the Netherlands, 2 *Zur.* 303 n.; lord warden of the Cinque Ports, *Park.* 202, 203, 379 n., 437; letter to him, *ib.* 379; Frances (Newton) his wife, *ib.* 341 n

Brooke (Sir Tho.): Joan (Braybroke) his wife, 1 *Bec.* 264 n

Brooke (Tho.), alias Cobham, brother to lord Cobham: servant to Cranmer, who begged for him the house of Grey Friars at Canterbury, 2 *Cran.* 330; married Susan Cranmer, *ib.* n

Brooke (Tho.), or Broke, customer of Calais: accused of heresy, 2 *Cran.* 390, 391 n., 292

Brooke (Fulke lord): *v.* Greville.
Brookesby (Humph.): *Park.* 297
Brooks (......): applies for the prebend of Rycall in the church of York, *Park.* 361
Brooks (James), bp of Gloucester: account of him, 2 *Cran.* 214 n., 383 n., *Phil.* xxviii, 1 *Zur.* 12 n.; a commissioner for the examination of Latimer, 2 *Lat.* 283, &c., also to examine Ridley, *Rid.* 255; exhorts him to turn, *ib.* 283; speaks of his singular wit, *ib.* xii, 283; refuses to deliver his letter to queen Mary, *ib.* 427; sits in judgment upon Cranmer, 2 *Cran.* 212, 225, 446 n., 447, 455, 456, 541, &c.; perjured, 2 *Cran.* 454; account of his death, 4 *Jew.* 1201
Brose: *v.* Brewis.
Brother: *v.* Brethren.
Brotherhoods: what, 1 *Tyn.* 212 n
Brotherly kindness: *v.* Love.
Brouage, near Rochelle: salt-works there, 2 *Zur.* 84
Brough (......): *v.* Browgh.
Broughton (Hugh): on hades, *Rog.* xiii.
Broughton (Sir Jo.): Anne his widow, 2 *Bec.* 622 n
Broughton (Rich.): *Calf.* 306 n
Broughty castle, Scotland: 3 *Zur.* 387
Broune (Tho.), poticary of Bristow: Marget his widow, 2 *Cran.* 275
Brouwershaven (Cunerus Petri de): *Calf.* 88, 3 *Jew.* 140
Browgh (......): citation to him, 2 *Cran.* 257
Browne* (Sir Ant.), K.G.: ambassador to France, 2 *Cran.* 246; named, *ib.* 490, 496; privy councillor to king Edward, *ib.* 505; his marriage, *Rid.* x. n (*v.* Clinton.)
Browne (Ant.), 1st visc. Montagu: privy councillor to queen Mary, 1 *Zur.* 5 n.; commissioner at Bruges, 2 *Zur.* 115 n.; saluted, *Park.* 285
Brown (Edw.): *v.* Fasciculus.
Brown (Eliz.), afterwards Bettes, and Rushbrough, [perhaps Bradford's own sister; *v.* Bradford (Eliz.)]: letters to her, 2 *Brad.* 70, 127
Browne (Geo.), abp of Dublin: he pulls down an image, *Park.* 96 n.; notice of him, 3 *Zur.* 428 n
Brown (Geo.): one of the royal visitors for the North, 1 *Zur.* 73 n
Brown (Sir Jo.): one of queen Mary's council, 1 *Zur.* 5 n
Browne (Jo.), esq.: persecuted, *Bale* 13, 50; hanged and burned, *ib.* 51
Browne (Jo.), fellow of Pembroke hall: legacy to him, *Grin.* 462

Brown (Rich.), a priest of Bristol: complains against Latimer, 1 *Lat.* viii, 2 *Lat.* 358 n
Brown (Rob.): affirms that a husband may leave his wife, or a wife her husband, on account of false religion, *Rog.* 273, 274 n.; "one Brown" (probably the celebrated Robert) chaplain to the duchess of Suffolk, *Park.* 390
Browne (Tho.): burned in Smithfield, *Poet.* 165, 3 *Zur.* 175 n
Brown (Tho.), of Bristow: *v.* Broune.
Browne (Tho.), a gentleman of Lincolnshire: 2 *Cran.* 369
Brown (Tho.), of Shrewsbury: archbishop Grindal's letter to the bishop of London, in pursuance of a letter from the council, respecting a collection to be made for him, *Grin.* 404; the council's letter, *ib.* 405
Brown (Tho.), of Swalecliff: 2 *Cran.* 388
Browne (Will.), a poet: 2 *Jew.* 627 n
Brownists: mentioned, *Nord.* 114, *Poet.* 268; some of them impugned the deity of the Holy Ghost, *Rog.* 70; they affirmed the laws judicial of Moses to belong to Christians, *ib.* 90; held the visible church to be devoid of sin, *ib.* 167; said to have had neither preaching nor sacraments, *ib.* 176; they declared that their discipline, and not the pure preaching of the word, &c., marked the true church, *ib.*; said that Christians should join only the people among whom the Lord's worship was free, *ib.* 185, that it would hardly be found in all the world that any minister was duly called, *ib.* 237, and that there is no calling but the immediate call from God, *ib.* 239, that no man is to communicate where there is a blind or dumb ministry, *ib.* 272, and that private persons have authority to depose unmeet ministers, *ib.* 273; their notions respecting the covenant of marriage, *ib.*; they denied baptism to the children of open sinners, *ib.* 280, and maintained that the baptism of children by the ministers of the church of England was not lawful, *ib.* 281; they excommunicated whole cities and churches, *ib.* 311; held that God's people are not to be bound with the bands of any jurisdiction of this world, *ib.* 317; said that no Apocrypha might be brought into Christian assemblies, *ib.* 326; some of their writers, *ib.* 203
Broxbourn, co. Herts.: *Grin.* 304, 331, 332
Broxup (Will.): notice of him, *Poet.* xxxvi; stanzas from St Peter's Path to the Joys of Heaven, *ib.* 390

---

* Brown and Browne are arranged together.

Broyle, co. Sussex: a park near Lewes, *Park.* 178

Braccioli (Ant.): his Italian Bible, *Jew.* xxxiv; his commentaries, *Whita.* 66

Bruce (Edw.), abbot of Kinloss: ambassador to queen Elizabeth, 2 *Zur.* 332

Bruce (Jo.): editor of Hutchinson's Works, *Hutch.*; one of the editors of the Correspondence of abp Parker, *Park.*

Brucker (Jo. Jac.): Hist. Crit. Philos., 2 *Ful.* 101 n

Bruerne (Rich.): was regius professor of Hebrew at Oxford, 2 *Cran.* 552; deprived of his professorship, 4 *Jew.* 1199 n., 1201, 1 *Zur.* 12, but had Peter Martyr's prebend, 1 *Zur.* 66; his irregular election as provost of Eton, *Park.* 150 n., 1 *Zur.* 12 n.; receiver of Christ church, *ib.* 240

Bruges, in Flanders: Wolsey goes thither, 2 *Tyn.* 314; the colloquy there, 1565, concerning commerce, 2 *Zur.* 115 n

Bruges family: *v.* Bridges.

Brunichilda, the French queen: a matter touching the purgation of a bishop committed to her by St Gregory, 1 *Jew.* 396, 4 *Jew.* 961, &c.

Bruno, founder of the Carthusians: 3 *Bul.* 295; he says that the scriptures are sufficient for instruction and salvation, 2 *Cran.* 34; on justification, 2 *Bec.* 639, 2 *Cran.* 206 bis; a witness against transubstantiation, *Bale* 563

Bruno (......): ambassador from Jo. Fred. duke of Saxony, 2 *Cran.* 416 n

Brunus (Conrad): De Cæremoniis, *Calf.* 97 n

Bruse (Peter): alleged to have been a heretic, 3 *Jew.* 161; Peterbrusians, *ib.* 212; their opinions and opponents, *ib.* 215

Brussels: its wretched state under the Spaniards, 3 *Zur.* 57; visit of Charles V., *ib.* 60; rejoicings in honour of the prince of Spain, *ib.*

Brust: *v.* Brast.

Brute: the founder of Britain, *Pil.* 125

Bruterer: a soothsayer, or maker of dismal days, 1 *Tyn.* 445

Bruton, co. Somerset: birthplace of Stephen Batman, *Poet.* xxxvi.

Brutus (Jun.): spared not his own sons, *Sand.* 227; his treason, 2 *Hoop.* 105

Bryan (......): *v.* Brian.

Bryan (Sir Fra.): ambassador to France, 2 *Cran.* 246

Bryan (Jos.): notice of him, *Poet.* xxix; three psalms in metre by him, *ib.* 334

Bryce (Tho.): notice of him, *Poet.* xix; his Compendious Register in metre; an account of the martyrs during the reign of queen Mary, *ib.* 161; the wishes of the wise, *ib.* 175

Brydges family: *v.* Bridges.

Bryganden (Mr): an opponent of Latimer, 1 *Lat.* iv.

Brygitta (St), or Brygot: *v.* Brigit.

Brytten (Dr): 2 *Cran.* 244

Bucardus (Fra.): *v.* Burckhardt.

Bucchingerus (Mich.): Hist. Eccles., *Calf.* 77 n

Bucer (Martin): *v.* Cambridge.

His views respecting the divorce of Henry VIII., 3 *Zur.* 551 n.; on divorce in general, *ib.* 665, 666; he confers with Gardiner about the royal supremacy, 1 *Ful.* 489; concerned in abp Herman's reformation, *Lit. Eliz.* xxix. n., 2 *Zur.* 18 n.; present at the marriage of the landgrave of Hesse, 2 *Cran.* 405 n.; at Strasburgh, 2 *Cov.* 510; father of the church there, 2 *Zur.* 72 n.; in trouble, 2 *Cov.* 513; he answers Gardiner's book on the celibacy of the clergy, *ib.* 512, 520; Gardiner writes against him, 3 *Zur.* 254; Hooper corresponds with him on the sacraments, 2 *Hoop.* ix; his dismissal from Strasburgh, 3 *Zur.* 538, 649, 651; mention of him, 1 *Hoop.* 246, 3 *Zur.* 640; invited to England, 2 *Cran.* 423, 3 *Zur.* 19, 37, 476; his arrival, 3 *Zur.* 330 n., 652; reception by Cranmer, 3 *Zur.* 535, 539; his intimacy with that prelate at Canterbury, 2 *Cran.* 421 n.; 3 *Zur.* 67; to go to Cambridge, 3 *Zur.* 536, 537, 539; made regius professor there, *ib.* 353; his acts in the university, 2 *Zur.* 18 n.; he declined to wear a square cap because his head was not square, *Pil.* 662; yet he opposed Hooper, 3 *Zur.* 675; his lectures and preaching at Cambridge (and perhaps elsewhere), 1 *Brad.* 31, 445, 3 *Zur.* 81, 266, 339, 401; he disputes with Jo. à Lasco on the eucharist, 3 *Zur.* 572; an intimate friend of Bradford, 1 *Brad.* 350, 558, 2 *Brad.* xx, and his father in the Lord, 1 *Brad.* 355; dangerously ill, 3 *Zur.* 401, 543, 558; his last illness, 2 *Brad.* xxiii; his death, 3 *Bec.* 205, 2 *Brad.* xxiii, *Park.* 42 n., 2 *Zur.* 71, 3 *Zur.* 5 n., 490, 495, 662 n., 724; account of his funeral, 3 *Zur.* 492; Parker preaches on that occasion, 2 *Brad.* xxiv; Parker and Haddon his executors, *Park.* 46, 47; some account of his goods, *ib.* 47, 3 *Zur.* 362 n.; his dead body excommunicated, *Rog.* 311, exhumed and burned, 1 *Jew.* 60, *Pil.* 65 n., 217, 652, 1 *Zur.* 4 n., 2 *Zur.* 20 n., 24, 51; all acts against him rescinded by the university on the accession of Elizabeth, 2 *Zur.*

51, 74; Pilkington's sermon at the restitution, *Pil.* 651; Bucer's excellent qualities, *Park.* 44; Burcher's opinion of him, 3 *Zur.* 662, 666, 678, 696; Sir John Cheke's opinion, 3 *Zur.* 666 n.; Cartwright's estimate, 2 *Whitg.* 533

His works, 3 *Whitg.* xxv. (some mentioned below); Psalmorum Explanatio, 1529, published under the name of Aret. Felinus, 2 *Whitg.* 475; notice of the Simplex ac pia Deliberatio, &c., 1535, drawn up by him and Melancthon, *Lit. Eliz.* xxix. n. 2 *Zur.* 18 n.; his Gratulatio, against Gardiner, 2 *Brad.* 19, 3 *Zur.* 178; his Censura of the English Prayer Book noticed, *Lit. Eliz.* xxv. n., 3 *Whitg.* 85, 124, 1 *Zur.* 234 n.; his Scripta Anglica, *Grin.* i. n., iii. n., 2 *Zur.* 17; Bradford's RESTORATION OF ALL THINGS, mostly translated from Bucer's commentary on the Romans, 1 *Brad.* 350; a passage from the Latin, *ib.* 355 n.; certain of his writings translated into English, 1 *Zur.* 162; letters by him, *Park.* 41, 42, 3 *Zur.* 520—549; letters to him, 2 *Brad.* 24 (?), 352, 353, 2 *Cran.* 426, 427, 428, 2 *Hoop.* xiv, 3 *Zur.* 219, 44, 468, 474, 552, 556; on the word Thora (תורה), the Law, 1 *Bul.* 49; on the word εὑρηκέναι, *ib.* 116; he shews that none of Christ's commands are to be neglected, 3 *Whitg.* 534; referred to on original sin, 2 *Bul.* 385; against deferring baptism, 2 *Whitg.* 533; he allows the use of the cross in that sacrament, 3 *Whitg.* 123; his way of speaking on the eucharist, 3 *Zur.* 544, 545; alleged to have defended Lutheran opinions, *ib.* 61; Harding asserts that he admitted a carnal presence in the sacrament, 1 *Jew.* 468, 469, 498; his words explained, *ib.* 499; on the abuse of the Lord's Supper at Corinth, 3 *Whitg.* 547; his opinion on communion under one kind, 1 *Jew.* 217, &c.; on the bread used in the communion, 3 *Whitg.* 84; on the communion at marriages, *ib.* 356; he approves communion of the sick, 2 *Whitg.* 545; on rulers in the church, 3 *Whitg.* 162; on bishops, 2 *Whitg.* 108, 231, 401, 402, 403; he says Timothy was a bishop, *ib.* 297; allows archbishops, patriarchs, &c., *ib.* 432; on subjection to ecclesiastical superiors, *ib.* 331; maintains that presbyters should be increased according to the number of the people, 3 *Whitg.* 540; on the secular business which ministers should not undertake, *ib.* 432; on the office of deacons, 2 *Whitg.* 64; on the same, with reference to Rom. xii. 8, 3 *Whitg.* 282 n.; on evangelists, 1 *Whitg.* 493; he speaks of seven kinds of preaching or teaching, 3 *Whitg.* 46; on the advantage of reading the scriptures in the church, *ib.* 30, 48, 51; approves the use of homilies, 1 *Bul.* 10, 3 *Whitg.* 346; on contention in the church, 1 *Whitg.* 138; on things indifferent, *ib.* 258; he advocates the reformation of ceremonies, 3 *Whitg.* 549; on holy-days, 2 *Whitg.* 584; on confirmation, 3 *Whitg.* 359, 360; on the marriage-ring, *ib.* 353; on the lawfulness of using things which were used by the Jews and Gentiles, 2 *Whitg.* 38; his views on vestments; he allows them, but is averse to their imposition, 2 *Hoop.* xiii, xiv, 2 *Whitg.* 57, 1 *Zur.* 161, 2 *Zur.* 120, 3 *Zur.* 488, 495, 585; thinks bells not necessarily a mark of Antichrist, 2 *Whitg.* 55; on binding and loosing, 3 *Whitg.* 236; on the excommunication of the incestuous person at Corinth, *ib.* 542; against the anabaptistical opinion that a Christian may not be a magistrate, 1 *Whitg.* 155, 156; he says no man is so wise and holy as to be able to exercise both the civil and ecclesiastical power, 3 *Whitg.* 545, 546; on new Romish writers, 2 *Jew.* 815; on the petition "deliver us from evil," 2 *Whitg.* 485; on the deceits of Satan, 1 *Whitg.* 97

— Wibrand Bucerin, his widow, 3 *Zur.* 28 n.; Cheke intercedes with the king for her, *Park.* 43, 44; she goes to Strasburgh, *ib.* 47; letter from her to Cranmer 3 *Zur.* 363; Cranmer's reply, 2 *Cran.* 434, 435, 3 *Zur.* 27; her children, 3 *Zur.* 364, 667; Bucer's grandson, W. Meier, 2 *Zur.* 322 n

Buchanan (Geo.): writes verses in praise of queen Elizabeth, 1 *Zur.* 115, and see 120; saying of Elizabeth respecting him,*ib.* 240 n.; he writes in praise of the queen of Scots, *ib.* 263; tutor of James VI., 2 *Zur.* 302 n.; his book De Jure Regni apud Scotos, 2 *Zur.* 311 n., 312; Rerum Scot. Hist. *Rog.* 360 n.; letters to Gualter, 2 *Zur.* 302, 310; letters addressed to him, *ib.* 294, 312

Buchmann (Theod.): *v.* Bibliander.

Buck (Dr), a prior at Cambridge: opposes Latimer, 2 *Lat.* xii.

Bucker (Geo.), alias Adam Damplippe, *q. v.*

Buckhurst, co. Sussex: 2 *Cran.* 259

Buckhurst (Tho. lord), afterwards earl of Dorset: *v.* Sackville.

Buckinghamshire: Knox preaches there, 3 *Zur.* 760 n.; superstitious processions there in gang week, *Grin.* 241 n

Buckland, co. Herts.: the rectory, 1 *Bec.* xii.

Buckland Newton, co. Dorset: the register, *Park.* 393 n

Buckstone: *v.* Buxton.

Buda: taken by the Turks, *Lit. Eliz.* 451
Budæus (Gul.): books by him, *Jew.* xxxiv; referred to as a critic, 1 *Ful.* 132, 4 *Jew.* 907; he defines faith, 1 *Bul.* 83 n., 436; 1 *Hoop.* 221; on the word παραλαμβάνω, 1 *Hoop.* 237; on δοκῶ, 2 *Whitg.* 411; he says that Sesostris forced kings to draw his chariot, 4 *Jew.* 702; on papal greediness, *ib.* 1082
Buden, co. Devon.: *v.* Berryn-Arbor.
Bugenhagius (Jo.): settled at Hamburgh, 1 *Tyn.* xl; his address to the faithful in England, *ib.*; he was opposed to the followers of à Lasco, 3 *Zur.* 513 n
Bugs: bugbears, objects of childish or superstitious terror, *Sand.* 192, 1 *Tyn.* 417, 2 *Tyn.* 87, 250, 3 *Tyn.* 110
Builders of God's house: must seek his glory, *Pil.* 363; must not fear mockers, *ib.* 365; their blessedness, *ib.* 366; they will have no fellowship with hypocrites, *ib.* 367
Building: the daughter of fancy, 2 *Bec.* 430; the practice of curious buildings declared to be a token that the day of judgment is at hand, *ib.*; continency therein, 1 *Bul.* 422
Bulkeley (Arth.), bp of Bangor: his death, *Phil.* xxix.
Bulkley (Edw.): 2 *Ful.* 74 n
Bull: a bubble, *Lit. Eliz.* 501 n
Bull (......), parson of Northfleet: "M. Bul," 2 *Cran.* 382
Bull (......), the younger: at Oxford, 3 *Zur.* 421
Bull (Geo.), bp of St David's: his Works referred to, *Calf.* 85 n., 1 *Lat.* xiv; mistaken in supporting the genuineness of a tract ascribed to Hippolytus, 2 *Ful.* 282; on the opinions of the Docetæ, 1 *Cov.* 21 n
BULL (Hen.): CHRISTIAN PRAYERS, *Pra. B.*; biographical notice of him, *ib.* viii; notice of his book, *Pra. Eliz.* xxii; he was editor of some works of bp Hooper, 2 *Hoop.* 182 n.; his preface to Hooper's Apology, *ib.* 551
Bulla aurea, &c.: *v.* Bulls.
Bullen family: *v.* Boleyn.
Bullin: *v.* Bullingham (N.)
Bullinger (Chr.), son of the reformer: notice of him, 3 *Zur.* 699
Bullinger (Hen.), father of the reformer: renounces popery, 4 *Bul.* x. n., and is formally married, *ib.* vii. n.; his death, *ib.* xi. n.; Anna Widerkehr, his wife, 4 *Bul.* vii; her death, *ib.* xii. n
Bullinger (Hen.), the reformer: biographical notice, 4 *Bul.* vii, &c.; birth, parentage, childhood, and early education, *ib.* vii; he studies at Cologne: *ib.* viii; lectures in the abbey of Cappel, *ib.* ix; writes numerous treatises, *ib.*; attends Zwingle's lectures at Zurich, *ib.* x; undertakes the pastoral office, *ib.*; marries Anne Adlishweiler, formerly a nun, *ib.* xi; on the defeat of Cappel he removes to Zurich, *ib.*; appointed preacher of the cathedral there, *ib.*; deputed to attend the conference at Basle, where he assisted in drawing up the first Helvetic Confession, *ib.* xii; he receives English visitors, *ib.*; turns Masters from popery, 2 *Zur.* 63; his friendship with Hooper, 4 *Bul.* xiii, 2 *Hoop.* ix; Hooper's prophetic words to him on leaving Zurich, *ib.* x; Cranmer writes to him about a synod of the reformed, 2 *Cran.* 430, 431; his kind reception of the English exiles at Zurich in queen Mary's time, 4 *Bul.* xiii, *Rid.* 387, 1 *Zur.* viii, and of Italian exiles from Locarno, 4 *Bul.* xiii; his reply to queries of a certain Scotsman (Knox or Goodman), about civil government in England and Scotland, 3 *Zur.* 745 (see 4 *Jew.* 665); engaged in combating various errors and heresies, 4 *Bul.* xiii, 1 *Zur.* 127 n.; his controversy with Brentius, 1 *Zur.* 98 n., (and see his works, below); he is attacked by the plague, 4 *Bul.* xiv, 1 *Zur.* 142, 143; death of his wife and daughters, 4 *Bul.* xiv, 1 *Zur.* 142 n., 144, 171 n.; his last illness, 4 *Bul.* xiv, 1 *Zur.* 317; his death, 4 *Bul.* xiv, 1 *Zur.* 318, 2 *Zur.* 268; eulogies on him, 4 *Bul.* xii. n., 1 *Zur.* 318, *Phil.* 391

His works, 3 *Whitg.* xxvi; list of the principal of them in chronological order, 4 *Bul.* xv; books of his cited or referred to in the editorial notes to the Decades, see *ib.* 588; his writings highly appreciated in England, 1 *Bul.* vii, 3 *Zur.* 618; some of them turned into English, 3 *Zur.* 396; Jo. Dudley, earl of Warwick, undertook that his works should be translated, *ib.* 422; his writings never published in a collected form, *ib.* xii. n.; De Origine Erroris in negocio Eucharistiæ ac Missæ, 1 *Zur.* 182, 208, 215, 4 *Bul.* xv. xviii; books against the Anabaptists, 1 *Zur.* 87, 95, 96, 110, 4 *Bul.* xv. xxiv; Commentaries on the Epistles, collected edition, 4 *Bul.* xvii; THE OLD FAITH, translated by Coverdale, 1 *Cov.* 1; notice of it, 4 *Bul,* xvii; on the authority of Holy Scripture, and on bishops, two treatises dedicated to Henry VIII., 3 *Zur.* 611, 4 *Bul.* xviii; their reception by the king, 3 *Zur.* 611; his treatise on the two natures in Christ, 1 *Zur.* 30 (see 4 *Bul.* xviii); the Christian state of matrimony, 1 *Bec.* 29, 4 *Bul.* xviii, 3 *Zur.* 406, 422, 427; THE HOPE OF THE FAITHFUL, translated by Coverdale from Bullinger (not as stated in 2 *Cov.* 137, from Wermuller), 2 *Cov.* 135, &c.; see 4 *Bul.* xix; Answer to Cochlæus on Scripture and Church Authority, 2 *Zur.* 194(?), 3 *Zur.* 244, 4 *Bul.* xix; his book on the Eucharist against Luther (Absoluta de Christi Domini...Sacramentis Tractatio), 3 *Zur.* 681 n., 3 *Bul.* xix; Commentaries on Luke, 3 *Zur.* 255, 4 *Bul.* xx; DECADES, translated by H. I., edited by the Rev. Tho. Harding, A.M., 1, 2, 3, 4, *Bul.*; dedication of a portion of them to the ministers of Zurich, 4 *Bul.* 546; a portion of them dedicated to king Edward VI., 3 *Zur.* 73, 78, 88, 269, 560, 662, 665, 4 *Bul.* xx. xxvii; this dedication, 2 *Bul.* 3; a portion dedicated to the marquis of Dorset (afterwards duke of Suffolk), 3 *Zur.* 3, 7, 77, 82, 90, 393, 399, 406, 409, 434; this dedication, 4 *Bul.* 528; references to the Decades, 2 *Zur.* 118, 242, 243, 3 *Zur.* 121, 123, 266; notice of the English translation, 4 *Bul.* xxvii; how far sanctioned by convocation, 1 *Bul.* viii, 4 *Bul.* xxviii; Whitgift's orders in regard to them, 3 *Whitg.* xvi, 4 *Bul.* xxviii; The Perfection of Christians, 3 *Zur.* 6 n., 4 *Bul.* xxi; his book on justification (De Gratia Dei justificante nos, &c.), 3 *Zur.* 744 (see 4 *Bul.* xxii); Sermons on the Apocalypse, 1 *Zur.* 99, 4 *Bul.* xxiii; Sermons on Jeremiah, 1 *Zur.* 122, 4 *Bul.* xxiii. xxiv; reply to the Bavarian articles (Institutio eorum qui propter D. N. J. C. de Fide examinantur), 4 *Jew.* 1242, 1 *Zur.* 110, 278, 4 *Bul.* xxiv; Catechism, its use recommended by statute in the university of Oxford, 1 *Bul.* vii, 4 *Bul.* xxiv; On Councils, 1 *Zur.* 97, 208, 215, 4 *Bul.* xxiv; works against Brentius and his followers, 1 *Zur.* 108, 110, 241, 243, 258, 266, 303, 305, 2 *Zur.* 245, 4 *Bul.* xxiv. xxv. xxvi; Homilies on Daniel, 1 *Zur.* 144, 145, 150, 151, 220, 2 *Zur.* 164, 4 *Bul.* xxv; it contains a retractation of a former work, 4 *Bul.* xv; Homilies on Isaiah, 1 *Zur.* 151, 172, 191, 194, 220, 2 *Zur.* 164, 4 *Bul.* xxv; German discourses on conversion (Von der bekerung, &c.), 1 *Zur.* 220, 224, 4 *Bul.* xxv; Refutation of the Bull against Elizabeth, *Grin.* 328, 4 *Jew.* 1129 n., 1 *Zur.* 221, 242—244, 258, 266, 268, 269, 2 *Zur.* 178 n., 179, 183 n., 192, 4 *Bul.* xxv; his exhortation to unity (Adhortatio ad omnes, &c.), 1 *Zur.* 270, 315, 4 *Bul.* xxvi; On the Persecutions of the Church, 1 *Zur.* 284, 300, 303, 308, *Bul.* xxvi; German homilies on Psa. cxxx. and cxxxiii, 1 *Zur.* 303, 308, 4 *Bul.* xxvi; his letter to Rob. Horn, bp of Winton, 3 *Whitg.* 496, 497; other letters by him, 1 *Zur.* 341, 345, 356, 357, 360, 2 *Zur.* 17 n., 136, 137, 152, 154, 166, 178, 240, 244, 3 *Zur.* 739—751; letters to him, 2 *Brad.* 400, 403, 2 *Cov.* 502, 2 *Cran.* 430, 431, 4 *Jew.* 1211, 1248, 1251, 1257, 1263, 1265, 1269, 1270, 1277, 1280; and see 1 *Zur.* contents, 2 *Zur.* contents, and 3 *Zur.* contents to each part; also *Grin.* 290 n.; saluted, 1 *Zur.* 12, 17, 22, 2 *Zur.* 90, 95, et sæpe.

He mentions that Hofman the Anabaptist thought salvation to be of man's own power, *Rog.* 298 n.; he differs in some respects from Calvin on the fall of Adam, 3 *Zur.* 327; on teaching and baptism, 3 *Whitg.* 19; he says the Anabaptists contemn the sacraments, *Rog.* 246 n.; on their indifference as to baptism, &c., *ib.* 275 n.; he says they declared the baptism of children to be of the pope and the devil, *ib.* 280 n.; on disorders at the Lord's supper in the church of Corinth, 2 *Whitg.* 72 n.; against hearing mass, 2 *Brad.* 297 n.; on apostles, prophets, evangelists, &c., 1 *Whitg.* 493, 494, 2 *Whitg.* 300; on Andronicus and Junia, 1 *Whitg.* 499; on the office of Timothy, 2 *Whitg.* 297; on the works of an evangelist, *ib.* 299; on the $\sigma\upsilon\nu\acute{\epsilon}\delta\rho\iota\upsilon\nu$, 3 *Whitg.* 227; on $\chi\epsilon\iota\rho\upsilon\tau\upsilon\nu\acute{\iota}\alpha$, 1 *Whitg.* 347, 349; on ordination by laying on of hands, *ib.* 431; he says the apostles chose ministers, *ib.* 343; mentions divers ways of appointing ministers in the apostles' time, *ib.* 429; on the election of ministers at Zurich, *ib.* 309; on the promotion of deacons, 3 *Whitg.* 70; against the anabaptistical errror that there ought to be no preaching, *Rog.* 232 n., 325 n.; on ministry, in opposition to the errors of that sect, 1 *Whitg.* 413; on the lawfulness of some things used by papists, 2 *Whitg.* 40; a passage on the wearing of ecclesiastical garments, *Grin.* 207; on their ancient use, 2 *Whitg.* 22, 1 *Zur.* 345, &c.; on the introduction of massing Levitical apparel, 3 *Whitg.* 550; on the observance of holy days, 2 *Whitg.* 583, 585; remarks on the service of the church of England, 2 *Zur.* 357; on excommunication, 1 *Whitg.* 186; passages against various errors of the Anabaptists, *Rog.* 67, 78, 87, 123, 141, 1 *Whitg.* 85, 91, 137, 383, 2 *Whitg.* 114, 3 *Whitg.* 276; he says that they held themselves to be free from all laws, *Rog.* 317 n.; relates that Muncer said that the sword of Gideon was given to him against

all tyrants, &c., *ib.* 343 n.; mentions that the Priscillianists allowed an open denial of the faith to avoid persecution, *ib.* 357 n.; says that many rich men are called, 1 *Whitg.* 34; on giving "with simplicity," 3 *Whitg.* 283; he follows the vulgar Jewish chronology, 1 *Bul.* 42 n
— His wife (see above), 1 *Zur.* 34, 165 n., 171 n.; his children and sons-in-law, (Zwingle, Lavater, Simler), 1 *Zur.* 30 n., 87, 142 n., 171 n., 258, 2 *Zur.* 165 n., 202, 3 *Zur.* 608, 698; his advice to his son, 3 *Zur.* 511 n
Bullinger (Hen.), the younger son of the reformer: saluted, 1 *Zur.* 105, 321; he (?) studies at Strasburgh, 3 *Zur.* 511 n.; letter to him, 2 *Zur.* 199
Bullinger (Jo.), brother to the reformer: 4 *Bul.* xi. xv.
Bullinger (Rodolph), son of the reformer: Parkhurst advises H. Bullinger not to send his son to Oxford till it should be reformed, 1 *Zur.* 29; Jewel does the like, *ib.* 33; Rod. Bullinger saluted, *ib.* 150
Bullingham (Jo.), afterwards bp of Gloucester and Bristol: to preach at Paul's cross, *Park.* 318; his preaching not suited to the court, *ib.* 378
Bullingham (Nich.), successively bp of Lincoln, and Worcester: archdeacon of Lincoln, in exile (" D. Bullin"), 1 *Cran.* (9), assists in the compilation of certain advertisements, *Park.* 233; has the custody of bp Bourne, *ib.* 253; signs a letter to the queen, *ib.* 294; his share in the Bishops' Bible, *ib.* 336 n.; an ecclesiastical commissioner, *ib.* 383; mentioned, *Grin.* 266
Bullock (......), of Qu. coll., Cambridge: opposes Latimer, 2 *Lat.* xii.
Bullock (Geo.), master of St Jo. coll., Cambridge: displaced, *Pil.* iv.
Bullock (Maur.), of New coll., Oxon, 2 *Cran.* 547
Bulls (Papal): 2 *Lat.* 378 n., 1 *Tyn.* 212, 1 *Zur.* 223; the Bulla aurea, 2 *Ful.* 269; there were eleven bulls for Cranmer's promotion, 2 *Cran.* 237 n.; one was issued confirming the marriage of Anne Boleyn, *Park.* 414, 420; copy of that of Pius V. against Elizabeth, 4 *Jew.* 1131; a bull in Spanish brought to Parker, *Park.* 397; the bull In Cœna Domini, usually published on Maunday Thursday, 2 *Cran.* 74, 167; the power of the keys often lapped up in a bull of lead, 3 *Jew.* 357 (see the names of the popes).
Bulstrode (James): his suit with Edwardes, 2 *Cran.* 253 bis, 261
Bulwiler (The count): 2 *Zur.* 207

Bumpstead (Steeple), or Bumpstead ad Turrim, co. Essex, 2 *Cov.* viii.
Bungay, co. Suffolk: *Bale* 443
Bungay (Friar): his supposed witcheries, *Bale* 190, 2 *Tyn.* 304
Bunge (Mr), of Norwich: *Park.* vii. 481
Bungey (Cornelius): martyred at Coventry, *Poet.* 164, 1 *Zur.* 86 n
Bungey (Jo.), prebendary of Canterbury: *Park.* 442
Bunnie (Mr), a Yorkshire gentleman: perhaps the next, *Grin.* 325
Bunny (Edm.), archdeacon of York: a form of prayer compiled by him, *Lit. Eliz.* 467, and see 548
Buonarrotti (Mich. Ang.): *Phil.* 381
Burcart (Fra.): *v.* Burckhardt.
Burchard, bp of Worms: Decretorum libri xx, *Jew.* xxxiv; recites a decree for burning the sacrament when it is mouldy, 3 *Bec.* 374 n.; referred to, *ib.* 373 n., 2 *Ful.* 301 n
Burcher (Jo.): mentioned, 4 *Jew.* 1250, 1252 n., 1 *Zur.* 49, 70, 73, 87, 90, 105, 2 *Zur.* 55, 3 *Zur.* 719; his flight from England, 3 *Zur.* 201; he lives at Basle, *ib.* 218, 223; seeks permission to export wood from Zurich for making bows, *ib.* 236 n., 632; desires the freedom of Zurich, *ib.* 246; lives there, *ib.* 40; partner with Hilles, *ib.* 259 n.; his scruples about portraits, *ib.* 191—194; at Strasburgh, *ib.* 511 n; his visit to Poland, *ib.* 687, &c.; divorced from his wife, 1 *Zur.* 98 (see 90); has a cure not far from London, 2 *Zur.* 109; his letters (with one exception) to Bullinger, 3 *Zur.* 637—701; letter to him, *ib.* 739; his character, *ib.* 247
Burcher (Rich.): sent to Rome to consult with Haller, 3 *Zur.* 165
Burckhardt (Fra.), vice-chancellor to the elector of Saxony: solicits Cranmer in favour of one sentenced to do penance for an error on the sacrament, 2 *Cran.* 371; envoy to Henry VIII. from the German princes, *ib.* 377 n., 3 *Zur.* 612 n.; sent to England to the marriage of Anne of Cleves, *ib.* 529 n
Burckhardt (M.), of Basle: 3 *Zur.* 767 n
Burdet (Rob.): notice of him, *Poet.* lii; the refuge of a sinner, *ib.* 514
Burdett (Sir Tho.), bart.: his ancestry, *Poet.* lii.
Buren (The count de): takes Darmstadt, 3 *Zur.* 639
Buren (Dan. à), a magistrate at Bremen: 2 *Zur.* 73
Burgart (Fra.): *v.* Burckhardt.
Burgavenny (Geo. lord of): *v.* Neville.

Burges (Jo.): answered by Dr Covel, *Rid.* 533; the same (?) Burges, in his letter to king James, 1604, states the number of nonconforming ministers in each of the counties of England, *Rog.* 317

Burges (......): martyred at Lewes, *Poet.* 170

Burgesses: they are become regraters, 1 *Lat.* 279

Burgh (Rich. de), 2nd earl of Clanricarde: 1 *Ful.* xi.

Burgh (Tho.), or Borough, 5th lord: at the trial of Tho. duke of Norfolk, 1 *Zur.* 267 (called by mistake Will.).

Burghley (Will. lord): *v.* Cecil.

Burgo (Jo. de): his Pupilla Oculi, *Jew.* xlii, 1 *Lat.* 414 n.; cases of non-consecration named therein, 1 *Jew.* 550; on the words "This is my body," 2 *Jew.* 788; he says that "enim" is not of the substance of consecration, 3 *Jew.* 507; on the intention to consecrate, *ib.* 454; he says a mouse may eat the body of Christ, 2 *Jew.* 783, *Rid.* 509

Burgo (Nich. de): Latimer suspects him, 2 *Lat*, 406

Burgo (Rich. de), or Bury, bp of Durham: 1 *Tyn.* 238 n

Burgon (Jo. Will.): Life of Sir T. Gresham, 1 *Zur.* 93, 139, 140, &c. nn

Burgoyne (Fra.): *v.* Bourgoyne.

Burgundy: called Burgaine, 2 *Tyn.* 303

Burhill (Rob.): Contra Eudæmon-Joannem, 2 *Ful.* 70 n

Burial, Burial places, Funeral rites: *v.* Dead. Of funerals and burials, 4 *Bul.* 523; scriptural examples, 3 *Bul.* 400, 4 *Bul.* 523; on the burial, and what is to be done towards the dead, 2 *Cov.* 108—110; of burial and matters thereto appertaining, 3 *Whitg.* 361, &c.; burials should be celebrated honourably, for the hope of our resurection, 3 *Tyn.* 280; the dead should be buried decently, 2 *Brad.* 279, 2 *Cov.* 258, *Pil.* 64, 317, reverently, 2 *Jew.* 999, with solemnity, 2 *Ful.* 13, but not with great cost and sumptuousness, *Pil.* 317, nor with superstition, *ib.* 318; the comely order required by Christian charity, *ib.*; burial should not take place too soon, 1 *Lat.* 538; examples shewing this, *ib.* 539; the solemnizing of funerals an ancient and commendable custom, *Sand.* 161; Augustine gives reasons for it, *ib.*; funeral rites help not the dead, but the living, *ib.* 162; offering for the dead in the ancient church was an offering of thanksgiving for their salvation, *Coop.* 96; Alleluia anciently sung at funerals, but forbidden by Papists, *Pil.* 320, 321, 543; Paula's funeral described by Jerome, *Whita.* 222; a funeral custom mentioned by the pseudo-Dionysius, *ib.* 580; popish funeral rites, *Rid.* 67; the Romish office for the dead called by different names, 1 *Brad.* 589; the funeral of a rich man described by Latimer, 1 *Lat.* 277; ringing, singing, and other funeral rites, *ib.* 305; disorderly funerals, *ib.* 547; that of the duchess of Norfolk, 1564, performed at Norwich without candles or torches, 1 *Zur.* 137; Crowley, of St Giles's, Cripplegate, turns out of his church divers clerks attending a funeral in surplices, *Park.* 275, 276; Grindal's directions for his funeral, *Grin.* 458; Sandys's directions, *Sand.* 447; on funeral trophies, *Pil.* 317; the English service, *Pil.* 543, 3 *Whitg.* 361, &c.; forms of burial, in the Prayer Books, *Lit. Edw.* and *Lit. Eliz.*; the Christian name of the deceased formerly introduced into the burial service, *Pra. Eliz.* 362 n.; the communion celebrated at burials, 1 *Lat.* 237 (and see Supper); funeral customs, 3 *Whitg.* 362, 368, 378; superstitions not to be allowed at burial, 3 *Bec.* 124, 125, 2 *Hoop.* 146, 147, *Pil.* 318; pardons buried with the dead, *Grin.* 29, *Pil.* 318; burial in friars' habits, *Bale* 329, *Calf.* 287, 2 *Cran.* 147, 2 *Ful.* 13, 1 *Lat.* 50, 2 *Lat.* 200, 332, 1 *Tyn.* 122 n., 2 *Tyn.* 92; dead men buried with the meteyard, *Pil.* 317; rites of the Russians, 3 *Zur.* 691; cemeteries and churchyards (*q. v.*), 2 *Ful.* 13, 1 *Whitg.* 534, 3 *Whitg.* 380; the names κοιμητήριον and Beth-haiaim, *Pil.* 319; in early times cemeteries were not consecrated, *ib.* 64; the dead were not anciently buried in the church or churchyard, *ib.*; burials should be without the city, as of old, 2 *Lat.* 66, 1 *Whitg.* 535; on the holiness of burial places, *Pil.* 316; the church superstitiously preferred to the churchyard, and the chancel to the church, 1 *Whitg.* 535; funeral sermons, made by Gregory Nazianzen, *Grin.* 10; disliked by some, *Pil.* 321, 1 *Whitg.* 251; controversy respecting the practice, 3 *Whitg.* 371, &c.; Gualter's remarks on them, 2 *Zur.* 234; a funeral sermon on Rev. xiv. 13, 1 *Hoop.* 559; one for the emperor Ferdinand, on Matt. xxiv. 44, *Grin.* 1; one for Charles IX. of France, on Job xiv. 14, *Sand.* 61; the burial of unbaptized infants, 4 *Bul.* 380; their burial place called cœmiterium innocentium, *ib.* 381 n.; burial refused to alleged heretics, *Bale* 394; exhumation and condemnation of dead bodies by Papists, *Pil.* 217, 652; the canon law commands that if an excommunicated

person have been buried in an ecclesiastical cemetery, the bones shall be dug up and cast out, 3 *Tyn.* 270; martyrs nothing the worse for wanting burial, *Pil.* 320
Burleigh : *v.* Burghley
Burlingham St Andrew's, co. Norfolk : *Park.* viii. 482
Burn (Jo.), minister of Musselburgh: 2 *Zur.* 365
Burnet (Gilbert), bp of Sarum : his account of the Zurich letters, *Zur.* viii ; other references, 2 *Bec.* 72, 319, 3 *Bec.* 205, 1 *Hoop.* xi, xii, 38, 41, 1 *Lat.* 321, 2 *Lat.* 240, 391, 1 *Zur.* 13, &c. nn
Burnham, co. Bucks.: 2 *Zur.* 172 n
Burning of heretics: inculcated by card. Hugo Charensis, 3 *Tyn.* 215; when first practised in England, *Bale* 3; the law of Henry V., *ib.* 50; the clergy deny that *they* burn heretics, *Phil.* 123, *Rid.* 267 (see 272); they deliver them over to the temporal power, 2 *Tyn.* 45; More affirms the burning of heretics to be lawful and well done, denies that the clergy procure it, 3 *Tyn.* 211, and says that a great many more should have been burned, *ib.* 97 n.; practice with regard to the writ de hæretico comburendo, *Hutch.* v; this writ was necessary for the exhumation and burning of a dead body, 3 *Tyn.* 270
Burntisland, Scotland: general assembly there, 2 *Zur.* 331 n
Burnt-offering : *v.* Sacrifices.
Burrey (Pet.): *Jew.* vi.
Burroughs (Will. lord): *v.* Burgh (T.)
Burton (Edw.): Hist. of the Chr. Ch., 2 *Bul.* 105 n.; Bampton Lectures, *Calf.* 343 n.; his remark about a supposed edition of Tertullian's works, 2 *Ful.* 64 n; referred to about the Therapeutæ, *ib.* 101 n
Burton (Rob.): Anatomy of Melancholy, 1 *Bul.* 8 n
Burton-on-Trent, co. Stafford : the relics of St Modwina there, 3 *Bec.* 240 n.; Annales Monasterii Burton., 2 *Hoop.* 522 n
Burwarde (Ant.): martyred at Canterbury *Poet.* 164
Burwell (Mrs. Frances) : *Pra. Eliz.* xx.
Bury (......), a rebel: 2 *Cran.* 187 n
Bury, co. Lancaster: 1 *Brad.* 454
Bury St Edmund's, co. Suffolk : a parliament held there, temp. Edw. I., 4 *Jew.* 904; the Benedictine monastery, 1 *Tyn.* 33 ; pardon bowl there, 3 *Bec.* 198 n., 1 *Lat.* 75 n.; some of the lands of the monastery granted to Nich. Bacon (afterwards lord keeper), 2 *Cran.* 384 n.; martyrs at Bury, *Poet.* 163, 172, 173
Bussæus (Jo.): publishes the Pontifical, 2 *Ful.* 98 n

Busby (......), a doctor of law: *Park.* 18
Busche (Herman von dem); 1 *Tyn.* xxx, xxxiv.
Busgradus (......) : says we must believe whatever the popes believe, *Rog.* 202
Bush: at a tavern-door, 2 *Tyn.* 184, 3 *Tyn.* 76, 253; ivy bush, 1 *Brad.* 94, 558, 1 *Ful.* 258, *Rid.* 10
Business: *v.* Occupation, Vocation.
Buskle: to bustle about, to prepare, *Bale* 554; said to be the same as busk, *Pil.* 353, buskel, 1 *Brad.* 445
Busshop (Rich.): 2 *Cran.* 547
Busti (B. de): *v.* Bernardinus.
Butcher (Joan): *v.* Bocher.
Butler (Alban): Lives of the Saints, *Calf.* 6 n., 305 n., 2 *Ful.* 70 n
Butler (Cha.): Book of the R. C. Church, *Calf.* 5 n
Butler (Hen.): some account of him, 2 *Cov.* 502; born at Zurich, but of English origin, 2 *Zur.* 192, 197; patronized by bp Parkhurst, 1 *Zur.* 241, 242, 271; a student in England, 1 *Zur.* 244, 258, 263, 2 *Zur.* 202, 204, 209; letter from him to Sandys, 2 *Zur.* 191
Butler (Jo.), doorkeeper of Hen. V.'s privy chamber : *Bale* 18; sent to cite lord Cobham, *ib.*
Butler (Jo.), Cranmer's commissary at Calais : 2 *Cran.* 275 n., 334, 348; letter to him, *ib.* 277; his letter to Cranmer on religious disputes there, *ib.* 373; sent to the Fleet, *ib.* 391 n
Butler (Jo.), father of Henry: notice of him, 3 *Zur.* 311, 621 n.; he sold his patrimony and went abroad, 2 *Zur.* 197, 3 *Zur.* 225; at Zurich, 4 *Bul.* xii; at Strasburgh, 3 *Zur.* 605, 609; courts a widow there, *ib.* 197, 218; saluted, &c., *ib.* 67, 70, &c.; his brother-in-law one of the stewards of the royal household, *ib.* 86, 225; Hooper desires his return to England, *ib.* 94, 97; mentioned, 2 *Zur.* 197, 3 *Zur.* 49, 56, 583; his letters, mostly to Bullinger, *ib.* 621, &c.
Butler (Mr), of Droitwich : 2 *Lat.* 390
Butrech (......): called doctor equestris, 2 *Zur.* 293 n.; mentioned, *ib.* 296, 300
Butter (......): martyred, *Poet.* 162
Butterworth (Edw.), of Rochdale : *Park.* 232
Buttes (Will.) : notice of him, *Poet.* xxvii; death certain, verses, *ib.* 309
Buttol (Greg.), a chaplain at Calais : 2 *Cran.* 376 n
Butts (Sir Will.), physician to Henry VIII.: 2 *Cran.* 293, 349 n.; he patronizes Latimer, 1 *Lat.* vi, 2 *Lat.* xv, xviii; his death, 3 *Zur.* 37, 150
Buxom : obedient, 1 *Brad.* 129, 239

Buxton, co. Derby (?): invocation there, 2 *Jew.* 923, viz. of St Anne of Buckstone, 1 *Hoop.* 40 n

Buying and selling: 2 *Bul.* 228; bargaining, whether lawful, *ib.* 29; the guile of buyers and sellers, 1 *Bec.* 254; what they should do, *ib.* 256

By and by: immediately, 1 *Tyn.* 241, 3 *Tyn.* 154

Byll (Will.): *v.* Bill.

Byng (And. and Tho.): *v.* Bing.

Byrchman* (Arn.): bookseller in London and Paris, 1 *Tyn.* xxviii. n.; he printed at Cologne, 1539, 3 *Jew.* 344; references to him, 4 *Jew.* 1231, 1234, 1 *Zur.* 70, 78, 3 *Zur.* 416

Byrchman (Fra.): 1 *Tyn.* xxviii. n (Byrckman)

Byrchman (Jo.): notice of him, 2 *Brad.* xxi. n., and see 352, 353, 405; references to him, 1 *Tyn.* xxviii. n.; 3 *Zur.* 452; letter from him to Bullinger, 3 *Zur.* 344

Byrchmans (The): the Byrkmans (probably A. and J.), not to be trusted, 3 *Zur.* 447; Birkman mentioned, probably Arnold, 1 *Zur.* 121

Byrd (Will.): notice of him, *Poet.* xxi; Psalm xiii. in metre, *ib.* 223; Psalm xv. in metre, *ib.* 222; care for thy soul, verses, *ib.* 223; the martyrs, *ib.* 224; notice of an anonymous contributor to his collection, 1587, *Poet.* li. 506

Byrkman (A. F. and J.): *v.* Byrchman.

Byron (Sir Jo.): mentioned, *Pil.* vii; possessor of Clayton, co. Lanc., and grantee of Newstead, *Park.* 232; lessee of the living of Rochdale, *ib.* 231 n

Byron (Sir Jo.), son of the last: he seems to be named as Mr Byron, *Park.* 231; letter to Mr Byron, *ib.* 232

Byrte (Jo.), otherwise called Adrian, otherwise John Bookbinder: 1 *Tyn.* lx.

By that: inasmuch as, 2 *Tyn.* 128

Byzantium: *v.* Constantinople.

Bzovius (Abra.): a remarkable addition made by him to a sentence cited from Cyprian, 2 *Ful.* 322 n.; he adduces the fabulous acts of the council of Sinuessa, *ib.* 364

C

C. *v.* Careless (Jo.)

C. (A.), a sectary: *Rog.* 203

C. (G.), author of A piteous Platforme: notice of him, *Poet.* xxiv; respice finem, verses, *ib.* 266

C. (H.), possibly Henoch Clapham: notice of him, *Poet.* xliv; lines by him, *ib.* 470

C. (H.), author of The Forrest of Fancy, 1579; possibly Hen. Constable: notice of him, *Poet.* xlvi; what misery and misfortunes mankind is continually subject unto, *ib.* 478; an exhortation to patience, *ib.* 479

C. (I.): *v.* Calfhill (J.)

C. (I.): acrostic on "God save the queen," *Lit. Eliz.* 561

C. (T.), i. e. Tho. Cartwright, *q. v.*

Cabala: what, 3 *Bul.* 131; cabalists, *ib.* 137

Cabasilas (Nic.): speaks of the priest standing at the altar, and lifting the gospel on high, 1 *Jew.* 512, and on his exclamation, "Holy things for the holy," *ib.* 511; says the bread of the sacrament is the body of our Lord itself, 2 *Jew.* 574; on the commemoration of Christ in the eucharist, *ib.* 717; he says the spirit is hid in the letter, *ib.* 618

Cabilon, the Lacedæmonian: would not treat with the courtiers of the king of Persia, because he found them playing at dice, 4 *Jew.* 1071

Cabrier: slaughter of the Waldenses there, *Pil.* 653

Caddow, or Kaddow: a jackdaw, *Bale* 153

Cade (Tho.): promoted at Calais, 2 *Cran.* 294

Cadiz: Sir Fra. Drake's victory there, *Lit. Eliz.* 469; Rob. earl of Essex and Cha. Howard lord admiral sent there, *ib.* 472; the town taken, *ib.*

Cadoc (St), of Cowbridge: *Bale* 191

Cadwallader, last king of the Britons: *Pil.* 482

Cadwan, or Caduane, duke of North Wales: *Pil.* 516

Cadwell (......): a friend of Jo. ab Ulmis, 3 *Zur.* 424

Cæcilian: *v.* Cecilian.

Cæcilius: *v.* Cecilius.

Caedmon: translated portions of scripture into English rhyme, 2 *Ful.* 14, 1 *Jew.* 304, 2 *Jew.* 694

Cælius (Lud.), Rhodiginus: Lectiones Antiquæ, *Jew.* xlii, thinks sacraments are called mysteries because they should be kept close, 4 *Bul.* 236, 237; says Rome was called the epitome of the world, 1 *Jew.* 420: speaks of a popinjay that could repeat the creed, 1 *Jew.* 283, 3 *Jew.* 255

Caer-Leon (Urbs legionum): a British archbishoprick, 3 *Jew.* 164 n., 2 *Whitg.* 128

Cæsar: *v.* Augustus, Julius, &c.

Sermons on Matt. xxii. 21, "Yield to Cæsar," &c., 1 *Lat.* 282, 296; the text explained, *Hutch.* 325, 1 *Lat.* 295, 511; "kaisar," emperor, 1 *Bec.* 31; "keser," *Sand.* 168

Cæsar (Phil.): *Rog.* viii.

Cæsarea: Cæsarea Stratonis, or Strato's tower,

---

* Thus the name is spelled by John, one of the three brothers, 3 *Zur.* 344

1 *Bul.* 85 n.; factions in the church, 1 *Whitg.* 464
Cæsaria: St Basil's epistle to her, 1 *Jew.* 152, 248
Cæsarius, brother of Gregory Nazianzen: his last words, 1 *Bec.* 32
Cæsarius of Arles: declares that tenths are not ours, but appointed for the church, 1 *Bec.* 24, 25; a homily ascribed to him, and to Chrysostom, *ib.* 77 n.; sermons ascribed to him, and Augustine, 2 *Bec.* 535 n., 540 n., 3 *Bec.* 277 n., 411 n., 1 *Whitg.* 224 n.; one also to Ambrose, 2 *Bec.* 540 n.; a homily, De Paschate, attributed both to him and to Eusebius Emissenus, *Calf.* 193 n
Cahathites: *v.* Kohathites
Caiani: referred to, 2 *Cov.* 184; they invoked angels, 2 *Ful.* 41, 86, 390, and avouched their follies and heresies, not by the scriptures, but by tradition, as they said, from St Paul, 3 *Jew.* 440
Caiaphas, high priest: mentioned, 1 *Bul.* 244, 3 *Bul.* 14, 23; not a Sadducee, 2 *Ful.* 246 n., 326 n.; he had the spirit of prophecy, 2 *Jew.* 3, 4 *Jew.* 941
Cain: of the name, 1 *Tyn.* 406; he contended for the birthright, 2 *Bul.* 131; his sacrifice, *ib.* 129; he slew his brother, 1 *Bul.* 210, 290, 306, for the love that God did bear him, 2 *Hoop.* 268; mercy offered to him, 1 *Brad.* 70; his punishment, 3 *Bul.* 152; the church of the devil began with Cain, 4 *Bul.* 11
Cainan (Lu. iii, 36): the clause rejected by Beza, 1 *Ful.* 43, 50, &c.
Caius, nephew of Augustus: his contemning of God the cause of a great dearth and famine, 2 *Hoop.* 166
Caius: his Fragmenta referred to, 2 *Cov.* 184 n., with regard to the death of Peter, 1 *Cov.* 362 n.; his enumeration of the Pauline epistles, *Whita.* 106
Caius (Jo.), master of Gonville hall (now Caius college): *Park.* 248; rash in expelling fellows, *ib.* 249, but worthy of respect as a founder, *ib.*; accused of atheism, *ib.* 251; mentioned, 2 *Brad.* 209 n.; apparently referred to as Mr Keyes, *Park.* 295; letter by him, *ib.* 298; his book De Antiq. Cantab. Academiæ, *ib.* n.; some account of him, 1 *Zur.* 31
Caius (Tho.): notices of him, 3 *Zur.* 394, 396, 415 n.; his Assertio Antiq. Oxon. Academiæ, *Park.* 298 n.; he translates writings by Bullinger, 4 *Bul.* xx.
Caius (Mr), a young clergyman: 2 *Zur.* 280
Cajetan (Tho. de Vio, card.): works, *Jew.* xxxiv; vehemently censured by Romish writers, *Whita.* 49; his judgment concerning the apocryphal books, *ib.* 48, 66; he deemed that only to be sacred scripture which the apostles wrote or approved, *ib.* 53; rejected a great part of the New Testament, *ib.* 105; refused (at least) some of the epistles, *Rog.* 84; admitted many faults in the Vulgate version, *Whita.* 169; he says that the exposition of scripture is not tied by God to the sense of the fathers, *ib.* 466; denies the genuineness of the works ascribed to Dionysius the Areopagite, *ib.* 576; declares that the councils of Constance and Basil were justly abrogate, 1 *Jew.* 69; on the "one faith," *Whita.* 671; on the deposit committed to Timothy, *ib.* 556; he denies faith to be necessary for receiving the sacrament, 2 *Jew.* 751, 752, yet speaks against the notion of opus operatum, *ib.* 752, 3 *Jew.* 557; admits that matrimony cannot be proved a sacrament from the word "sacramentum" in Eph. v. 32, *Whita.* 197; says, the apostle suffers a bishop to have one wife, others to have more, 3 *Jew.* 406; affirms that the pope may dispense with a priest of the Western church to marry, *ib.* 409; declares that it cannot be proved, either by reason or authority, that a priest offends God in marrying, *ib.* 396, 403, 4 *Jew.* 807, 808; says, our Lord appointed to his disciples no manner of vow, 3 *Jew.* 423; on the breaking of vows, 4 *Jew.* 788; he dislikes the use of Latin in the service of the church, *Whita.* 274; on the priesthood of Melchizedek, *ib.* 168; his remarks on Deut. xvii. 12, the judgment of the priest, *ib.* 420; he admits that James (v. 15) does not speak of extreme unction, *ib.* 199; referred to on the worship of the cross, *Calf.* 381 n.; his oration in the fifth council of Lateran, 1 *Jew.* 69 n., 94 n
Cakes: 3 *Zur.* 589, 594; what the casting down of cakes in the procession on Palm Sunday signified, 1 *Bec.* 114, 115
Calaber: a fur? *Bale* 527
Calabria: pillaged by the French, 3 *Zur.* 741
Calais: *v.* Spellache.
The siege, temp. Edw. III., 1 *Hoop.* 313 n.; the town long possessed by the English, 1 *Lat.* 5 n.; jurisdiction of the see of Canterbury there, 2 *Cran.* 275, 277, 345, 348, 349, 471; king Henry VIII's journey thither, 2 *Tyn.* 313 (v. Ardres); Wolsey endeavoured to remove the mart from Antwerp to this place, *ib.* 319; Cranmer desires to send chaplains to preach the word of God there, 2 *Cran.* 298 (see his letters to lord Lisle); the ignorance and blindness of the people, *ib.* 310; the church of St Peter by Calais, in the gift of the king, *ib.*;

unworthiness of the curate of St Mary within Calais, *ib.* 311; preachers sent to Calais, *ib.* 320, 376 n.; a seditious book brought therefrom, *ib.* 334; removal of images from the priory of Black Friars, *ib.* 372; the prior in Cranmer's custody, *ib.* 377; persecutions at this place, *ib.* 372, 373, 375, 376; an imposture there, *ib.* 375 n.; Nich. Bacon recommended as town-clerk, *ib.* 384; Cromwell sends for writings relating to the town, *ib.* 395; wine purchased there for Cranmer, *ib.* 316, 318, 411; Sir Hugh Paulet, the governor, has the Common Prayer translated into French, *ib.* 439; reception of Fagius on his way to England, 3 *Zur.* 331; the hangman of Calais, *Hutch.* 79, 3 *Zur.* 444, 449: message to the town from the French king, 3 *Zur.* 684; the town taken from the English by the duke of Guise, *Calf.* 114, *Pil.* 70, 86, 1 *Zur.* 91 n., 3 *Zur.* 139 n.; negociations for its restoration, 1 *Zur.* 8 n., 24, 91 n., 115 n.; "conveyed to Calais," a proverbial expression, 1 *Tyn.* 239

Calamities: *v.* Affliction.

Kinds of them, 2 *Bul.* 65; good and evil afflicted with them, *ib.* 66; their causes, *ib.* 68

Calder (......): murdered the regent Lennox, 1 *Zur.* 262 n

Caldwell (Rich.): *v.* Cawdewell.

Calendar: in king Edward's first Prayer Book, 1549, *Lit. Edw.* 23; in his second Prayer Book, 1552, *ib.* 207; in the Primer, 1553, *ib.* 360; in the Prayer Book, 1559, *Lit. Eliz.* 47; in the Primer, 1559, *Pra. Eliz.* 4; calendarium, in the Latin Prayer Book, 1560, *Lit. Eliz.* 317; in the Orarium, 1560, *Pra. Eliz.* 117; the new calendar, 1561, *Lit. Eliz.* 435; notices of the same, *ib.* xxxiii, *Park.* 133, 135; calendarium, with verses to each month, in the Preces Privatæ, 1564, *Pra. Eliz.* 213

Days and months now called by heathen names, *Pil.* 15, 16; on the calendar of the Roman church, *ib.* 15, 19; why the names of saints are inserted in our calendar, *Pra. Eliz.* 428; de anno et partibus ejus, *Lit. Eliz.* 323; verses on the immoveable feasts; Sex sunt ad Puri, &c., *ib.* 326; the Shepherd's Calendar, 2 *Jew.* 705, see *Grin.* xiii. n

Cales, i. e. Cadiz, *q. v.*: but sometimes it means Calais, as 2 *Cran.* 373

Caley (Rob.), a Romanist printer: *Park.* 295

Caleys (Jo. à): 2 *Cran.* 390

CALFHILL (James), or Calfield, bp elect of Worcester: biographical notice of him, *Calf.* vii; mention of him, *Grin.* 268; he preaches an injudicious sermon before the queen, *Park.* 218; his ANSWER TO JOHN MARTIALL'S TREATISE OF THE CROSS, edited by the Rev. Richard Gibbings, M.A. *Calf.*; references to it, *Coop.* iv, 1 *Ful.* 75 n., 2 *Ful.* 107; Fulke's REJOINDER TO JOHN MARTIALL'S REPLY, edited by the same, 2 *Ful.* 125—212; this book mentioned, 1 *Ful.* ix; source of Calfhill's error as to the date of the synod of Elvira, 2 *Ful.* 153; ad lectorem Jacobi Cathhilli (sic) carmen, 1 *Bec.* 33; in tria volumina operum Tho. Bæconi I. C[alfhilli?] carmen, *ib.*

—Margaret his wife, *Calf.* viii.

Calicut: 1 *Jew.* 22

Caligula, emperor: called himself God, and Jupiter, 4 *Jew.* 842; sometimes he took off the head of Jupiter and set on his own, 3 *Jew.* 280; his cruelty, 2 *Jew.* 1008; he locked up all the garners and storehouses of corn in Rome, and caused a general famine, 4 *Jew.* 879

Calil (כליל): what, 3 *Tyn.* 108

Calistus, a monk: accuses Aug. Mainard of heresy, *Phil.* 387

Calixtines: persecuted, 2 *Jew.* 979

Calixtus, bp of Rome: calls himself abp of the catholic church of the city of Rome, 1 *Jew.* 426; he (or Anacletus) enjoins all to communicate who would not be excommunicated, 3 *Bec.* 416, 474, 2 *Bul.* 238, 258, *Coop.* 128, 1 *Jew.* 19, 175, 183, 186, 3 *Jew.* 144, *Rid.* 105, 317; instituted certain fasts *Whita.* 501; condemned the marriage of priests, *Rog.* 181

Calk: to reckon, or calculate, *Bale* 443; calked, 2 *Tyn.* 308

Calling: *v.* Duty, Ministers, Vocation.

Calling on God: 1 *Bec.* 148

Calthrop (Mr): 2 *Brad.* 251

Caltrops: instruments used in war to wound horses' feet, 2 *Brad.* 214; (galtropes, *Rid.* 366)

Calvary: the mount, 2 *Bul.* 151; the highway to mount Calvarie, verses by S. Rowlands, *Poet.* 352

Calvin (Jo.):
   i. *Life and Works.*
   ii. *Scripture, the Jewish Dispensation, Christian Doctrine.*
   iii. *The Church and its Ministry.*
   iv. *Sacraments, Prayer, &c.*
   v. *Miscellanea.*

i. *Life and Works*: his ordination, 2 *Ful.* 73; his settlement at Geneva, banishment and return, 3 *Zur.* 622, see also *Phil.* 390; controversy with Anabaptists and P. Caroli, 3 *Zur.* 622 n.; he confutes the Interim, *Rid.* 120; complains of Melancthon's want of firmness, 2 *Zur.*

126 n.; Cranmer invites him to a conference for establishing uniformity of faith, 2 *Cran.* 431, 432; his answer, *ib.* 432 n.; reference thereto, *Rog.* 3; falsely slandered by Saverson, *Phil.* 46; his opinion on the troubles at Frankfort, 3 *Zur.* 756, &c. nn.; he opposed Knox, on the government of women, 4 *Jew.* 665; Parker desires his attendance at a conference in France, *Park.* 147; his illness, 2 *Zur.* 96; commendation of him, 2 *Bul.* 82; his character as a reformer, 1 *Whitg.* 247, as an interpreter of scripture, 436; his doctrine, 2 *Ful.* 377; character of his works, *Pil.* 682; their value, *Rog.* 324; references to them, 2 *Ful.* 398; his style, *Grin.* 235; his books studied in England, 2 *Zur.* 148; his commentaries, 2 *Bul.* 313 n., 1 *Lat.* 338 n.; his sermons on Job read in the reformed churches of Flanders and France, *Rog.* 325; his commentaries on 1 Cor. much disliked by Hooper, 3 *Zur.* 48; Bayle says he wrote on the Apocalypse, *Bale* 258; his Institutes, 1 *Bul.* 8, &c., 1 *Ful.* 21, 1 *Lat.* 478 n., 2 *Whitg.* 268, 502; his book on Relics, 2 *Ful.* 112; cited on Helena's search for the cross, *Calf.* 324 n.; it mentions at least fourteen nails, *ib.* 328; speaks of the contention about the body of St Denis, 4 *Jew.* 1046; his Catechism followed to some extent by Nowell, *Now.* vii.; publicly expounded in several reformed churches, *Rog.* 325; notices of his Strasburgh liturgy, *Pra. Eliz.* 458 n., 477 n., 488 n.; his book against Servetus, 3 *Zur.* 743 n.; he wrote a preface to a life of Spira, 2 *Brad.* 80 n.; letters by him to king Edward VI., 3 *Zur.* 707, 714; to lady Anne Seymour, *ib.* 702; to the protector Somerset, *ib.* 704; to Cranmer, *ib.* 711, 2 *Cran.* 432 n.; to lord Jo. Grey, 3 *Zur.* 715; to Cecil, on the government of women, 2 *Zur.* 34; letters to him, 2 *Cov.* 525, 2 *Cran.* 431, 432, 2 *Zur.* 49, 96, 3 *Zur.* 24, 31, 142, 147, 170, 328, 339, 545, 621, 730, 731, 737, 742, 743, 750, 751, 753, 755, 764, 766

ii. *Scripture, the Jewish Dispensation, Christian Doctrine:* on the evidences of the sacred scriptures, *Whita.* 293; his arguments concerning their authority defended against Stapleton, *ib.* 340, &c.; he shews that those who profess to speak or act by the Holy Spirit must be judged by scripture, *ib.* 354; his objections to the Vulgate Psalter vindicated, against Bellarmine, *ib.* 180, &c.; on the fall of Adam, 3 *Zur.* 327; he thinks Cain and Abel strove about the birthright, 2 *Bul.* 131 n.; mistakenly says that Abraham was nearly fifty years old, when Noah died, 1 *Bul.* 41 n.; referred to on the division of the decalogue, *ib.* 213 n., 214 n.; he says the promise of long life annexed to the fifth commandment pertains likewise to us, *ib.* 287; on the reason for the Jewish laws and ceremonies, 1 *Whitg.* 267, 268; he shews that the judicial law of Moses is not binding, *ib.* 275, 3 *Whitg.* 576; on the ceremonies of the law as a "handwriting," 2 *Bul.* 259 n.; on Moses being called a god, 2 *Whitg.* 82; on the tabernacle, *ib.* 94; on the expression "before the Lord" (Deut. xix.), 3 *Whitg.* 427; he shews that circumcision was performed in private houses, 2 *Whitg.* 516; proves that the Jewish polity is no authority for the popedom, *ib.* 347; on the dress of prophets, 2 *Whitg.* 12, 13; his view of Prov. xxv. 27, 1 *Bul.* 65 n.; referred to about Jonah, 1 *Bul.* 169, 170 n.; on Zech. xii. 2, 3, 2 *Bul.* 108 n.; referred to on the word עצב, which means both "trouble" and "an idol," 1 *Bul.* 223 n.; on the sanhedrim, or συνέδριον, &c., 2 *Whitg.* 91, 3 *Whitg.* 227; on the title Rabbono, 2 *Whitg.* 387; his opinion on the epistle of James, 1 *Ful.* 16 n.; thinks that "the epistle from Laodicea" was not written by Paul, but by the church of Laodicea, 1 *Bul.* 9; on "rightly dividing the word," 2 *Bul.* 16 n.; on the treatment of God's word by the Libertines, *Rog.* 197 n.; on Christ as a ransom, 1 *Bul.* 109 n.; on his fear or reverence (Heb. v. 7), 1 *Ful.* 324, 325; Calvin's opinion on the descent into hell, 1 *Bul.* 138 n., 1 *Ful.* 278, *Rog.* xii.; cited on the text "whom the heaven must receive," &c., 1 *Ful.* 131; on the word דעת, "knowledge" in Isa. liii. 11, 1 *Bul.* 110 n.; on the declaration that "no man can say that Jesus is the Lord, but by the Holy Ghost," and on regeneration, 2 *Whitg.* 590; he writes on predestination, 3 *Zur.* 325; his opinion on this point agreeable to that of all the doctors of the church, *Phil.* 46; he shews that even new-born babes are full of sin, 2 *Bul.* 397; yet declares that the children of the faithful are (in a sense) born holy, 3 *Jew.* 371; his definitions of faith, 1 *Bul.* 82, 83 n.; on justification, *Grin.* 255 n.; that it is by faith alone, 1 *Bul.* 114 n.; referred to on the blessedness of the justified, *ib.* 106 n.; on staggering in faith, *ib.* 88 n.; on repentance, 3 *Bul.* 71 n., and on confession, *ib.* 79 n., 85 n.; on rendering a reason of our faith, 3 *Whitg.* 133; on making our calling and election sure, 1 *Ful.* 85; on the duty of a good soldier of Jesus Christ, 3 *Whitg.* 413; on Paul's fulfilling that which was behind of Christ's sufferings for the sake of the church, 3 *Bul.* 94 n

iii. *The Church and its Ministry :* he discourses learnedly of the church, 2 *Ful.* 33; on the essential notes thereof, 1 *Whitg.* 185; on Noah's ark as a type of it, 2 *Whitg.* 92; alleged as saying that out of the church there is no light of the sound understanding of scripture, 3 *Jew.* 241; on the command, "Tell it unto the church," 3 *Whitg.* 171, 229; on submission to the church, *ib.* 89; on excommunication, against the Anabaptists, 1 *Whitg.* 186, 203; on the same subject, and on avoiding a heretic, 3 *Whitg.* 238; on keeping from the company of wicked members of the church, *ib.* 102; he shews that the power of excommunication pertains not to one man, *ib.* 541; against those who will tolerate no imperfection in the church, 1 *Whitg.* 387, 2 *Whitg.* 8; he declares that the ancient order of the church is for all ages, 3 *Whitg.* 532, yet allows that it may receive various alterations, *ib.* 217, 533; writes against setting up one church as a model for all, 2 *Whitg.* 452, 453, 3 *Whitg.* 398; on the universal practice of the church (from Augustine), 1 *Whitg.* 233; on the spiritual regimen of the church, 3 *Whitg.* 484; he affirms that Christ is the only Head of the church, 2 *Whitg.* 426; and dislikes the title of "supreme head," as applied to princes, 1 *Ful.* 488; on Christ's government of the church and the world, 3 *Whitg.* 483; on rulers in the church, *ib.* 162; he shews that the people left the decision of controversies to the apostles, 1 *Whitg.* 344; allows that one of the apostles was chief, 2 *Whitg.* 231, 247, 267, 278, 424, 425; on the conduct of Peter in the council at Jerusalem, *ib.* 276; on the election of Matthias, 1 *Whitg.* 296; on Paul's authority, 2 *Whitg.* 404; on apostles and evangelists, 1 *Whitg.* 494, 496, 497; on evangelists, 2 *Whitg.* 301; on the office of Timothy, 1 *Whitg.* 508, 2 *Whitg.* 297; his ordination, 1 *Whitg.* 432; on the prophecies respecting him, *ib.* 501: on Paul's "commandment" to him, 3 *Whitg.* 174; on the office of Titus, 2 *Whitg.* 282, &c.; he denies that Paul directed him to ordain bishops of his own authority, 1 *Whitg.* 427; says ancient synods command that bishops should be ordained by their metropolitans, *ib.* 439; on archbishops and patriarchs, 2 *Whitg.* 147, 419, 420, 422; he allows those titles, but dislikes the name of hierarchy, *ib.* 322—326; shews that primacy, though it may be profitable for one nation, is not proper for the whole world, *ib.* 245, 419, 424; disapproves the civil power of bishops, 3 *Whitg.* 544; on ancient dioceses, and chorepiscopi, 2 *Whitg.* 432, 3 *Whitg.* 272; he allows degrees of honour amongst ministers, 2 *Whitg.* 266, 404, 405; shews that they should not be occupied with secular affairs, 3 *Whitg.* 409, 433, though a temporal lord may be a preacher, 1 *Whitg.* 153; speaks against worldly rank in the church, *ib.* 159 n.; on Gal. ii. 6, οἱ δοκοῦντες, 2 *Whitg.* 410; on presbyters, 3 *Whitg.* 152; on colleges of elders, *ib.* 205, 400; on the office of deacons, *ib.* 65; on deacons with reference to Rom. xii. 8, *ib.* 282 n.; on Philip the deacon, *ib.* 59; he says the apostles did not altogether cast off care for the poor when deacons were appointed, *ib.* 422; asserts that we should have deacons such as the apostolic church had, *ib.* 538; on the election of ministers, 1 *Whitg.* 365, 3 *Whitg.* 537; on a canon of the council of Laodicea respecting it, 1 *Whitg.* 405, 407; on the term χειροτονία, *ib.* 347, 348; on imposition of hands in ordination, *ib.* 490; on Rom. x. 15, "except he be sent," 2 *Whitg.* 530; he thinks that women may preach if necessity require, *ib.* 502, &c.; on the women who prophesied at Corinth, *ib.* 505; on widows in the church, 1 *Whitg.* 321

iv. *Sacraments, Prayer, &c.:* his doctrine on the sacraments untruly reported by Harding, 3 *Jew.* 366, 370; defended by Jewel, *ib.* 370, 371; his definition of a sacrament, 4 *Bul.* 234; referred to on the benefit of sacraments, *ib.* 326 n.; he affirms that they are not to be esteemed by reference to the minister, 2 *Whitg.* 519, 520, 526; his views on baptism misrepresented, 1 *Ful.* 153; he does not debase it, 3 *Jew.* 241, &c.; calls it the sacrament of our redemption, *ib.* 243; on the baptism mentioned in Acts xix, 3 *Whitg.* 17; on the text, "Christ sent me not to baptize," &c., 2 *Whitg.* 457; on the baptism of infants, *ib.* 523; he records that Servetus rejected it, *Rog.* 265 n., 280 n.; on the minister of baptism, 2 *Whitg.* 498 n.; on baptism by women, *ib.* 503, 3 *Whitg.* 548; on "the washing of regeneration," 1 *Ful.* 455; passages against various errors of the Anabaptists, *Rog.* 141, 167, 1 *Whitg.* 81, 114, 138, 147, 221, 267, 387, 2 *Whitg.* 15, 3 *Whitg.* 76, 78; his doctrine on the eucharist, 2 *Zur.* 73 n.; his TREATISE ON THE

LORD'S SUPPER, translated by bp Coverdale, 1 *Cov.* 422; on "breaking bread," 3 *Whitg.* 83; on the rites used in the communion, *ib.*; on the disorderly celebration of the Lord's supper at Corinth, 2 *Whitg.* 507; he thought it an abuse to carry the sacrament, as Justin mentions, to those who were absent, 2 *Ful.* 237; on self-examination before communion, 3 *Whitg.* 80; on the intent and benefit of the Lord's supper, and on worthily receiving it, 4 *Bul.* 476, 477; his agreement with Bullinger and others respecting the eucharist, 3 *Zur.* 121 n., 267, 479 n; against hearing mass, 2 *Brad.* 297 n.; reference to an epistle of his about the mass, 4 *Bul.* xxvii; on giving thanks "with the spirit," 1 *Jew.* 313; on prayer in an unknown tongue, *ib.* 329; on kneeling at prayer, 1 *Whitg.* 240; on "much speaking" in prayer, 3 *Whitg.* 516; on the manner of prayer in the church of Corinth, *ib.* 387; on decent orders in divine service, *ib.* 106; says grave apparel is meet for doctors, 2 *Whitg.* 21; his opinion on confirmation, 3 *Whitg.* 477, &c.; on holy-days, 2 *Whitg.* 586, &c.; he allowed funeral-sermons, 3 *Whitg.* 371, 378; admits that some traditions of the apostles were not written, 1 *Whitg.* 221, 2 *Whitg.* 237; says that the use of many things is pure, the origin of which is evil, *ib.* 32, 465; on things indifferent, 1 *Whitg.* 221, 243, &c., *Wool.* 90, &c.; he defends the use of churches which were formerly polluted with idols, 2 *Whitg.* 33

v. *Miscellanea*: on the fall of Lucifer, 3 *Bul.* 350 n.; he tells why kings are called εὐεργέται (Luke xxii.), 1 *Whitg.* 151; shews that popular government tends to sedition, *ib.* 467; on Christian magistrates, 3 *Whitg.* 408—410; on the right use of God's gifts, *Wool.* 90, &c.; he alleges Anacletus, 2 *Whitg.* 137; speaks of a brief of Julius III. (or Paul III.?) respecting the council of Trent, 3 *Jew.* 207; on offences, 2 *Bul.* 320; on the doctrine of Brentius, 1 *Zur.* 108 n.; he attacks Fra. Baldwin, *ib.* 118 n., 119; opposes the doctrine of Stancarus, *ib.* 127 n.; on Osiander's error, *Rog.* 115; on false opinions of H. Bolseck, *ib.* 148, 149; on the Libertines, *ib.* 118 n.; on "the old leaven," 3 *Whitg.* 230; he tells of the obstinacy of the duke of Guise, *Rog.* 212 n.; mentions that the marriages and baptisms of the reformed were deemed invalid, *ib.* 362 n.; referred to on "forbidding to marry," &c., 1 *Bul.* 434 n.; against the indolence of the Stoics, 2 *Bul.* 82—85; referred to on נשך, usury, *ib.* 42 n

Calvinism: the reformed doctrine so called, 2 *Zur.* 128
Calvinists: the term used, *Calf.* 249, *Poet.* 268; disclaimed by Fulke as a nick-name, 1 *Ful.* 20; their struggles with the Lutherans, 2 *Zur.* 156 n.; Calvinists at Antwerp, 1 *Zur.* 174; Crypto-Calvinists, *ib.* 315 n
Camarine lake, in Sicily, 1 *Zur.* 161 n
Cambray: treaty made there between Henry VIII. and the princess regent, against the printing and selling of Lutheran books, 1 *Tyn.* xxxvii, xxxviii.
Cambridge: its fenny situation, 3 *Zur.* 190; old parliaments held there, *Park.* 300 n.; the merry monk of Cambridge, 1 *Lat.* 153, 170; letter by Cranmer to the mayor and his brethren, 2 *Cran.* 247; the disputation respecting the Lord's supper, 1549, *Grin.* 193—198; Ridley's determination thereon, *Rid.* 167; sweating sickness, 1551, 3 *Zur.* 727 [the duke of Suffolk and his brother did not die there, but at Buckden]; the gift of Faude, sometime mayor, and the case of Ward the painter, *Pil.* 656; the lady Jane proclaimed queen at Cambridge, *Sand.* ii; proposed disputation there, 2 *Brad.* 94, *Rid.* 363, 364; Bradford's farewell to Cambridge, 1 *Brad.* 441; a martyr there, *Poet.* 166; Puritan assemblies at Cambridge, in Sturbridge fair time, *Rog.* 206 n

University: v. Caius (Jo.), Universities. The proper style of the university, *Park.* 239; its power to license preachers, 2 *Lat.* 324, 329, *Park.* 238; list of the colleges and halls, 3 *Jew.* 110; the professorships, &c., *ib.* 111; the university considers the question of the king's divorce, 1530, 1 *Lat.* v; Latimer keeper of the university cross, 2 *Lat.* xxvii; account of Parker's election as vice-chancellor, 1544, *Park.* 17, 18; corrodies for decayed cooks, *ib.* 20; many things out of order, *ib.* 28; prayers and processions, 1545, for the king's success in war, *ib.* 30; copy of the commission from Henry VIII. to inquire into the possessions of the colleges, &c., 1546, *ib.* 34 n.; royal visitation, 1549, *Park.* 31, *Rid.* 327; the depressed state of the university described by Ascham, 1 *Lat.* 178 n., 179 n.; yet it favoured true religion more than Oxford, 3 *Zur.* 680; proceedings on the proclamation of queen Mary, *Sand.* ii—v; letter of that sovereign, on her accession, to Gardiner, respecting the condition of the university, *Park.* 54 n.; letter to the university from Gardiner, the chancellor, *ib.* 56 n.; popery restored there, *Rid.* 392 (as to the

10—2

intended disputation, see above); Bradford's farewell to the university and town, 1 *Brad.* 441; Ridley's farewell, *Rid.* 406; letter of Parker (archbishop elect) and others to the university, desiring the immediate election of a preacher, *Park.* 71; all acts against Bucer and Fagius solemnly rescinded, 2 *Zur.* 51; commemoration of them, 1560, *Pil.* iv. 651; comedies and tragedies performed, *Park.* 226 n.; dissensions about vestments, *ib.* 345; the study of Hebrew, *ib.* 348; Parker promises to do something for the increase of living for the Hebrew reader, *ib.* 467; devilish works there, *ib.* 353; not two men there able or willing to read the lady Margaret's lecture, *ib.* 374; Elizabeth prescribes a form of commendation of benefactors, *Lit. Eliz.* xxiii. n.; complaints of some young men against the masters of colleges, *Park.* 393; letter from the ecclesiastical commissioners to the vice-chancellor about Tho. Aldrich, master of Benet college, *ib.* 433; number of preachers bred at Cambridge in the time of Elizabeth, 1 *Whitg.* 313; where the scholars went for orders, *ib.* 310 n.; controversy respecting two graces, 1580, *Grin.* 365—369; pricking of officers, *ib.* 366; lord Stafford's advice to a foreign student, 2 *Zur.* 322

COLLEGES AND HALLS.

Benet or Corpus Christi college: letter from Henry VIII. to the fellows, recommending Parker as master, *Park.* 16; the mastership worth twenty nobles a year, *ib.* 51; revision of the statutes in king Edward's time, *ib.* 439; the Latin Prayer Book not favoured there, *Lit. Eliz.* xxxi; disorders there, *Park.* 343; proceedings about Tho. Aldrich, master—see his name; college leases, *ib.* 469; benefaction of archbishop Parker, *ib.* xiii; plate given by him, *ib.*

Buckingham college (now Magdalene): Cranmer reader there, 1 *Cran.* vii, viii, 2 *Cran.* vii.

Caius college: quarrels at Gonville hall, now Caius college, *Park.* 248, 252; Dr Jo. Caius the second founder—see his name; plate given by archbishop Parker, *ib.* xiii.

Christ's college: its foundation, 2 *Cran.* 279; a tragedy called Pammachius played there, and proceedings thereon, *Park.* 21—29; some there objected to the surplice, *ib.* 226 n

Clare hall: on the mastership, 2 *Lat.* 378, 382; intended union with Trinity hall, *Rid.* 327, 505; report of king Edward's visitors concerning this proposal, 2 *Brad.* 369; letter of Ridley deprecating the project, *ib.* 370; lord Exeter's benefaction, 2 *Bec.* 480 n

Clement hostel: named, 2 *Lat.* xii.

Corpus Christi college: otherwise Benet college, *q. v.*

Fistewick's hostel: seized by Henry VIII. and subsequently merged in Trinity college, 2 *Cran.* 318 n

Gonville hall: now Caius college, *q. v.*

Jesus college: it should have some lawyers, *Rid.* 506; letter to the master, with a buck, 2 *Cran.* 247; Cranmer writes to Cromwell respecting a farmer of this college, *ib.* 303

King's college: prayers were said there for the repose of Henry VI. the founder, 3 *Tyn.* 122; it should have six lawyers, *Rid.* 506

King's hall: named, 2 *Lat.* xii; seized by Henry VIII., and subsequently, with Michael house and Fistwick's hostel, merged in Trinity college, 2 *Cran.* 318 n.; *Rid.* 505

Magdalene college: Cranmer reader at Buckingham hall, now Magdalene college, 1 *Cran.* vii, viii, 2 *Cran.* vii.

Michael house: named, 2 *Lat.* xii; seized by Henry VIII., and subsequently merged in Trinity college, 2 *Cran.* 318 n., *Rid.* 505

Pembroke hall, or college: value of the mastership, 3 *Whitg.* 598; bp Wren's MS. account of the masters, 1 *Ful.* i. n., *Grin.* 37 n.; Bradford's fellowship, 2 *Brad.* 27; Ridley's farewell to Pembroke hall, *Rid.* 406; Ridley's walk, *ib.* 407 n.; contest between this society and the bishop of Norwich about the advowson of Soham, *ib.* 536; Grindal a benefactor to this house, *Grin.* 458, 459

Queens' college: should have one or two lawyers, *Rid.* 506; dispute about an election there, *Park.* 64, 65; Peacock resigns the headship to Dr May, *ib.* 67

St John's college: its foundation, &c., 2 *Cran.* 279; on the mastership, 2 *Lat.* 377, 382; eminent men educated there, *Hutch.* i; some there objected to the surplice, *Park.* 226 n.; proposal for the annexation to this house of the college of Manchester, *ib.* 365; disputes during the mastership of Nic. Shepherd, 2 *Zur.* 213; letter of bishop Grindal to lord Burghley on its visitation and reformation, *Grin.* 358

St Mary's hall: "hosp. D. Mariæ," *Park.* vii, 481

St Nicholas' hostel: named, 2 *Lat.* xii.
Trinity college: halls merged in it, 2 *Cran.* 318 n., *Rid.* 505; oath taken by the fellows, 1 *Whitg.* 15, 123, 507, 3 *Whitg.* 396; Whitgift's promotion to the mastership, *ib.* 597; his conduct in that office, *ib.* vii, viii, xi; expulsions, *ib.* 507
Trinity hall: intention to incorporate it with Clare hall, *Rid.* 327, 505; report of king Edward's visitors respecting the proposed union, 2 *Brad.* 369; letter of Ridley deprecating the project, *ib.* 370; plate given by archbishop Parker, *Park.* xiii.
The Schools: the highway to them, *Park.* 455

CHURCHES, &c.

Austin Friars' church: Latimer preaches there, 1 *Lat.* iii, 2 *Lat.* xi.
St Edward's church: Latimer preaches there, 2 *Lat.* xi.
St Mary the Great: Ridley in the university pulpit, *Rid.* 119; account of Bucer's funeral, 3 *Zur.* 492; his bones exhumed, *Pil.* 65 n., 2 *Zur.* 20 n.; his restitution, *Pil.* 651
St Michael's church: the disinterment of Fagius, *Pil.* 65 n., 2 *Zur.* 20 n

The Tower, or Castle: Latimer visits the prisoners there, 1 *Lat.* ii. 335, 2 *Lat.* xiii.
Inns: the Dolphin, 1 *Cran.* viii, 2 *Cran.* 557; the Falcon, 1 *Ful.* iii.

Cambuskenneth (The abbot of): tutor of James VI., 2 *Zur.* 302 n
Cambyses: flays a corrupt judge, 1 *Hoop.* 483, 1 *Lat.* 146
Camden (Will.), Clarencieux king of arms: his tutor at Oxford, 2 *Zur.* 329 n.; his Britannia, 1 *Lat.* 474 n.; Elizabetha, 1 *Zur.* 82, 89, 115, &c.; he describes the earthquake of 1580, *Grin.* 415 n.; wrote verses before a book by Rogers, *Rog.* v.
Camel (Matt. xix. 24): alleged to mean the cable of a ship, 2 *Lat.* 202
Cameracensis, i. e. P. de Alliaco, *q. v.*
Camerarius (Joach.): *Calf.* 22 n., 322 n., 2 *Ful.* 380 n
Camfield (......): 4 *Jew.* 1190
Camisado: a night-attack, in which the soldiers wore shirts over their armour, 1 *Jew.* 110
Camocensis, or Camotensis: a common error for Carnotensis, i. e. John of Salisbury; *v.* John.
Campbell (Archib.), 5th earl of Argyle: named, 1 *Zur.* 167 n., 197 n., 262 n.; he upholds the Protestant cause, *ib.* 149 n.; one of the confederate lords, *ib.* 193 n.; he arms in defence of the queen, *ib.* 205 n
— Jane (Stuart), countess of Argyle, his first wife: present at the seizure of David Rizzio, *ib.* 166 n., and at the christening of James VI., *ib.* 183 n
Campbell (Jo. lord): Lives of the Chancellors, 3 *Zur.* 506 n
Campeius (Lau. card.), or Campeggio: concerned in the matter of queen Catharine's divorce, 2 *Tyn.* 320 n.; deprived of the bishoprick of Salisbury by act of parliament, 2 *Cran.* 283 n., 330 n
Campeius (Tho.): De Cœlib. Sacerd. non abrogando, *Jew.* xxxiv; his evil doctrine respecting priests' marriage, 4 *Jew.* 628, 640, *Rog.* 304
Campeius (......): named, *Lit. Eliz.* 584 n
Campion (Edm.), named, 1 *Ful.* x, xi, 14, 66, 439, &c.; educated at Christ's hospital, *ib.* ii; his rank rhetoric, *ib.* 442; he could not construe Greek, *ib.* 508; Whitaker writes against him, *Whita.* xii; he comes into England, *Lit. Eliz.* 658 n.; the conference with him, *Now.* vii, viii; his treason and execution, 1 *Ful.* 440; he thought all councils were of equal authority with the word of God, *Rog.* 211; his History of Ireland, *Park.* 407
Camsele (Tho.), or Kampswell, prior of Coventry: 2 *Lat.* 386 n
Cana of Galilee: water changed into wine there, 4 *Bul.* 262
Canaan: promised to Abraham, 4 *Bul.* 245; a type of heaven, *Whita.* 407; the woman of Canaan, her faith and constancy, 2 *Hoop.* 259
Canaanites: punished for sin, 1 *Bul.* 374, 2 *Bul.* 429, 4 *Bul.* 496; Chananæi (Hos. xii. 7), merchants, Simoniacs, 2 *Bul.* 45; those mentioned in Obad. 20, said to be the Germans, *Pil.* 268
Canaglion (The bishop of): in 1593 he excommunicated the fishes, *Rog.* 311
Candace, queen of Ethiopia: 4 *Bul.* 94
Candia: *v.* Crete.
Candish (......): probably Tho. Cavendish, 1 *Poet.* xxvii.
Candlemas day: 1 *Tyn.* 91 n.; the blessing of candles on it, 2 *Cran.* 157, *Grin.* 140 n., *Rid.* 532; candles set up to the virgin, 1 *Zur.* 259 n.; candle-bearing forbidden, 2 *Cran.* 417, 509, *Grin.* 140; the ceremonies of this day borrowed from the heathen, *Calf.* 66, 3 *Jew.* 178
Candles, Tapers, Lights: the burning of tapers at noon-day, borrowed from the Gentiles,

Calf. 214, 3 *Jew.* 178; the imputation of doing so repudiated by Jerome. *Calf.* 214; tapers set upon the altar of Saturn, *ib.* 302; used (at night) by Chrysostom, *ib.* 298, &c., and the early Christians, *ib.* 301; forbidden in the day-time by the council of Elvira, *ib.* 302, 2 *Ful.* 185, and condemned by Lactantius, *Calf.* 302; the Romish use of lamps, cressets, torches, tapers, and candles, *Bale* 537; candles superstitiously used, 1 *Lat.* 70; their alleged signification, 3 *Tyn.* 74; set up before images, 1 *Hoop.* 317, 2 *Tyn.* 157, 165, 169, 3 *Tyn.* 81; use of candles in the Tenebræ service, on the Wednesday before Easter, *Calf.* 300; why that assigned to the virgin is not put out on that occasion, 3 *Tyn.* 39 n.; lights set before the Easter sepulchre, 3 *Zur.* 230—232; the Paschal taper, *Bale* 320, 2 *Cran.* 158; words sung at its consecration, 1 *Jew.* 468; holy candles brought to the death-bed, 1 *Lat.* 499, 1 *Tyn.* 48, 225, 3 *Tyn.* 140; some candles were called perchers, 1 *Bul.* 199, 238, *Calf.* 300; the use of candles defended by More, 3 *Tyn.* 80 n., and commended by Latimer, 1 *Lat.* 23, 24; forbidden, 1547, except two on the high altar, 2 *Cran.* 155, 499, and see 3 *Zur.* 72; Ridley forbids lights to be set on the Lord's board, *Rid.* 319; the use of tapers abolished in the church of England, 1 *Zur.* 178 (and see 358); articles against candles, 2 *Hoop.* 127, 129; tapers not to be used at baptism, *Grin.* 160; lighted candles retained in queen Elizabeth's chapel, *Park.* 97, 1 *Zur.* 63, 64; taken away, 1 *Zur.* 122; the candles brought back, but never lighted, *ib.* 129

Candlestick (The golden): 2 *Bul.* 156
Candlesticks: ordered to be destroyed, *Grin.* 135, 159
Canerner (Mr): *Park.* 18
Canfildus (......): *v.* Camfield.
Canisius (Pet.): on the authority of scripture, *Whita.* 358; on the authority of the church in respect to scripture, *ib.* 278; on apostolical traditions, *ib.* 512; his error respecting the descent into hell, *Rog.* 62; on faith, *ib.* 113 n.; on confirmation, *ib.* 253 n.; on penance, *ib.* 256 n.; on marriage as a sacrament, *ib.* 260 n.; his book called Mariana, 1 *Ful.* 527; his Catechism translated, 2 *Ful.* 4
Canndysh (Will.): *v.* Cavendish.
Canning: power, ability, 2 *Brad.* 28
Cannings (Tho.), and Agnes his wife: 1 *Tyn.* 212 n
Canon: *v.* Mass, Scripture.
  Meaning of the term when applied to scripture, *Whita.* 27, 662; the word sometimes used with reference to the creed, *ib.* 27 n
Canon Law: *v.* Law.
Canonical hours: *v.* Hours.
Canonization: *v.* Saints.
  It is judging before the time, 1 *Lat.* 149; the church of Rome divides departed saints into canonized and uncanonized, 3 *Tyn.* 121; canonizes such as are stout in the pope's cause, *Rid.* 55, 2 *Tyn.* 268
Canons: *v.* Councils.
  To be kept not precisely, but as edification shall require, *Park.* 389; ancient canons not observed, 2 *Cran.* 37; Canones Pœnitentiales, Lips. 1516, 2 *Ful.* 22 n
Canons of the Apostles.
  These canons having been variously divided by different editors, there are corresponding diversities of numeration. The canon, for example, which is here referred to as the 28th, is reckoned as the 29th by Beveridge, and by Dionysius Exiguus and Whiston as the 30th. The computation here adopted is that of the Corpus Juris Civilis, Antv. 1726; agreeing with that found at the end of the 1st volume of the Corpus Juris Canonici, Paris. 1687.

  [1] A bishop to be ordained by two or three bishops, 1 *Ful.* 261, 3 *Jew.* 330, 1 *Whitg.* 348, 459; [2] presbyters, deacons, and other clerks, to be ordained by one bishop, 1 *Ful.* 261, 1 *Whitg.* 348, 459; [3] bishops and presbyters offering upon the altar honey, milk, strong-drink, animals, pulse, &c. to be deposed, 3 *Bec.* 359 n.; [4] respecting other firstfruits; not cited; [5] bishops, presbyters, and deacons, not to put away their wives under the pretence of religion, 2 *Cran.* 37, 168, 2 *Jew.* 989, 3 *Jew.* 404, 422, *Whita.* 566; [6] nor to undertake secular business, 2 *Cran.* 38, (see also canons 80 and 82); [7] on Easter; not cited; [8] on the course to be pursued in case any of the clergy did not communicate, 3 *Bec.* 417, 2 *Cran.* 38, 171, 1 *Jew.* 176, 197, 3 *Jew.* 473, *Rid.* 317, *Whita.* 566; [9] those who came into the church and heard the scriptures, but remained not to prayers, and to the communion, to be excommunicated, 3 *Bec.* 416, *Coop.* 219, 2 *Cran.* 38, 171, 1 *Jew.* 19, 143, 202, 2 *Jew.* 989, 3 *Jew.* 475, 476, *Phil.* 61, *Rid.* 105, 317, *Whita.* 567, 2 *Whitg.* 552; [10—24]

not cited; [25] lectors and chanters who were single at their ordination permitted to marry, but no other clerks, 2 *Ful.* 95, 3 *Jew.* 386; [26, 27] not cited; [28] bishops, presbyters, and deacons, obtaining their office by money, as well as those ordaining them, to be cut off from communion as Simon Magus was by Peter, *Whita.* 42; [29] not cited; [30] against schismatical presbyters, 1 *Ful.* 261; [31] presbyters and deacons suspended by one bishop, not to be received by another, 3 *Whitg.* 260; [32] no bishop or clerk travelling to be received without letters commendatory, 2 *Cran.* 37; [33] that the bishops of each nation should have a primate, and of his authority, 2 *Whitg.* 145, 242, 367, 428; [34] on ordination, not cited; [35] bishops, presbyters, and deacons, not assuming the charge assigned to them, to be suspended from communion, 2 *Jew.* 1020, 1 *Whitg.* 359, 366, 459; [36] a synod of bishops to be held twice a year, *Whita.* 567 ; [37—45] not cited; [46] no bishop or presbyter to repeat true baptism, *Whita.* 567; [47, 48] not cited; [49] commands trine immersion in baptism, *Whita.* 592

Supernumerary canons: different statements respecting the number of the apostles' canons, *Whita.* 41, 42; [50] on abstinence from marriage, flesh, and wine, *Pil.* 566; [51] on communion of the sick, referred to by the council of Nice, 2 *Ful.* 105, 106; [52—62] not cited; [63] clerks or laymen entering a synagogue of Jews, or conventicle of heretics, to pray with them, to be deposed, *Pil.* 629 ; [64—67] not cited; [68] enumerates orders of ministers, 3 *Jew.* 273; [69—79] not cited; [80] forbids clergymen to meddle in worldly affairs, 4 *Jew.* 820, 3 *Whitg.* 430; [81] not cited; [82] forbids clergymen to be civil magistrates, 4 *Jew.* 803; [83] not cited; [84] recognizes the Gospel of St John, and speaks of the Acts of the Apostles, *Whita.* 42; differs from Rome as to the canon of scripture, *ib.* 43, 103

The canons of the apostles are not authentic, 1 *Ful.* 254, *Rog.* 82, *Whita.* 508, 2 *Whitg.* 121 ; spurious from internal evidence, *Whita.* 42; falsely alleged to have been written by the apostles at Antioch, *ib.* 566; a farrago, taken in part from the acts of the council of Antioch, *ib.* 567; ancient testimonies against their genuineness, *ib.* 41, 42; not kept or used, 2 *Cran.* 37; they often speak of bishops, presbyters, and deacons, 1 *Ful.* 253

Canons of 1571 (Liber quorundam canonum disciplinæ eccl. Angl.): not of legal authority, *Grin.* 327 ; abolished the grey amice, 2 *Whitg.* 50 n

Canons of 1603: approved by king James, *Rog.* 22 ; three of them, *ib.* 33

Canons of 1640 : cited respecting the observance of the day of the prince's inauguration, *Lit. Eliz.* 463

Canons (canonici): why so called, 4 *Bul.* 201; canons regular who have written on the Apocalypse, *Bale* 256

Canopy : of the hanging up the sacrament under it, 2 *Jew.* 553, &c.; only used in England, *ib.* 557, 559

Cantacuzene (Jo.): 2 *Jew.* 1028 n

Canterbury: burnt in the Conqueror's time, *Pil.* 607 ; the maid of Northgate, 2 *Cran.* 66; the rebels' camp near Canterbury, *ib.* 439 n.; martyrs in queen Mary's time, *Poet.* 163, 164, 165, 170, 173, *Sand.* i, 3 *Zur.* 175; a royal park there, *Park.* 178; scheme for making the river navigable, *ib.* 322; arrangements for queen Elizabeth's visit, *ib.* 441— 444; the visit described, *ib.* 475, 476; Grindal's legacy to the mayor and citizens for poor people, *Grin.* 459 ; Canterbury bells, *Bale* 101; Canterbury tales, *Calf.* 288, 2 *Cran.* 198, 1 *Lat.* 107

The cathedral and monastery of Christ church: the first archbishops buried in a porch [at St Augustine's], 2 *Ful.* 13; the monks put out by abp Baldwin, *Pil.* 610; the murder of Becket, *Bale* 55, &c.; his shrine, its riches, and the offerings there, 2 *Cran.* 378 n., 1 *Hoop.* 40, 41, 1 *Tym.* 436, 2 *Tyn.* 292, 3 *Zur.* 610 n.; the shrine destroyed, and Becket's bones burned, *Bale* 58, 2 *Cran.* 378 n.; pilgrimages to Canterbury, *Bale* 25; idolatry there, *Pil.* 63; relics set forth on St Blaise's day in the chapter-house, 2 *Cran.* 334;' Monachus Cantuariensis, a writer on the Apocalypse, *Bale* 256; the four great officers of the monastery, 2 *Cran.* 312 n.; the cellarer, weightiness of his office, *ib.* 312; letter from Cranmer to the prior, *ib.* 260; Cranmer enthroned, *ib.* 270 n.; trepidation of the prior and convent in consequence of the affair of the holy maid of Kent; they offer the king money, *ib.* 271; misdemeanor of certain monks, *ib.* 333, 334; dispute about the office of physician there, *ib.* 357 ; proceedings of the subcellarer, Antony, *ib.* 373, 375; letter from Cranmer to Cromwell respecting the new foundation, *ib.* 396; the proposed new establishment, *ib.* 398; exchange of prebends allowed, *ib.* 416;

Cranmer solicits the messuage of Bekisbourne belonging to Christ church, in exchange, *ib.* 458; articles of inquiry at the visitation, 1550, *ib.* 159; injunctions to the dean and chapter, *ib.* 161; the library, *ib.*; names of the fourteen preachers in king Edward's time, 1 *Bec.* x. n.; Ridley's farewell to the cathedral church, *Rid.* 407; church-plate, &c. sold by deans Wotton and Godwin, *Park.* 303, 304; Parker erects an organ, 2 *Zur.* 150; Elizabeth reserves prebends for her chaplains, *Park.* 319; the contribution of the chapter to the French church in London, 1 *Zur.* 288 n.; cardinal Coligny buried in the cathedral, having been poisoned, *ib.* 250 n.; custom on receiving princes, *Park.* 442; how queen Elizabeth was received, *ib.* 475; Grindal's legacy to the petty canons, &c., *Grin.* 459; the cross, a place for preaching, *Bale* 118

The archbishoprick (v. Court of Arches): mother to other bishopricks, *Rid.* 264; the archbishop a patriarch in England, *ib.* 263; his prerogative, 1 *Tyn.* 237; his courts and privileges, 2 *Zur.* 360; in crowning the king, he has no power to reject, or impose conditions on him, 2 *Cran.* 126; by prescriptive custom he visits throughout his province, *Park.* 115; his power to visit vacant dioceses, *ib.* 476; what the archbishop paid to the pope for his annates and firstfruits, and what for his pall, 4 *Jew.* 1078; his style changed by convocation from "legate of the apostolic see," to "metropolitan and primate," 2 *Cran.* 304 n.; the title of "primate of all England," no derogation to the king's authority, *ib.* 304; an exchange effected between the crown and the see, *Park.* 102 n.; contention for the stewardship of the liberties, *ib.* 285 n.; removed by the attainder of the duke of Norfolk, *ib.* 452; the steward to hold a court annually, citing all who hold of the palace of Canterbury by knight-service, *ib.*; reference to Steph. Birchington, Hist. de Archiep. Cant., 2 *Tyn.* 294 n

The archbishop's palace, &c.: the palace burned in Cranmer's time, repaired by Parker, *Park.* xiii; entertainments given by the latter in 1573, *Grin.* 347; the archbishop's mint, 2 *Cran.* 294, 357

The province and diocese (v. Convocation): articles to be inquired of in the visitation of the diocese, 2 Edw. VI., 2 *Cran.* 154; injunctions and articles of inquiry in Grindal's visitation of the province, *Grin.* 156, &c.

St Augustine's abbey: copy of the spurious charter of king Ethelbert, containing a donation of the site, [another copy in Somner's Cant. 47,] 4 *Jew.* 781; letter from Cranmer to the abbot, 2 *Cran.* 240; Anne of Cleves lodges there, *ib.* 400 n.; a royal palace, *Park.* 442; queen Elizabeth lodges there, *ib.* 475

St Gregory's, a priory of black canons: 2 *Cran.* 240

Black Friars: the prior replies to Cranmer's sermons against the pope, 2 *Cran.* 327

Grey Friars: their house suppressed 2 *Cran.* 330; grant of the site, *ib.* n

St Sepulchre's, a Benedictine nunnery: Eliz. Barton a nun there, 2 *Cran.* 252, 271

St Martin's church: used for service by Augustine the monk, 1 *Jew.* 299, and by queen Bertha, *ib.* 306

The Foreigners' church: its beginning, 2 *Cran.* 421 n

Hospitals, &c.: return of hospitals and schools within the diocese, *Park.* 163, 165 —170; lazar-house of St Lawrence by Canterbury, *ib.* 166; hospital of St John Baptist without the walls, *ib.* 167; hospital of poor priests, *ib.* 167; Maynerd's spittell, *ib.* 167; Eastbridge hospital, *ib.* 168, 3 *Zur.* 247 n.; the grammar-school, *Park.* 169 (see also 2 *Cran.* 160, 162, and Rush)

Cantilupe (Walter de), bp of Worcester: opposed the pope's legate, 4 *Jew.* 1080

Cantors: mentioned as an order in the apostolic canons, *Whita.* 509

Cantrells, i. e. Kentish-Town, *q. v.*

Canus (Melch.): mentioned, 2 *Lat.* 226 n.; his opinions opposed, *Whita.* passim; on inspiration, *ib.* 101; on the authority of scripture, *ib.* 277; on the advantages which attend a knowledge of the original scriptures, *ib.* 153; he says that traditions are of greater efficacy against heretics than scripture is, *ib.* 496; maintains the authority of the Vulgate, *ib.* 111, 140; on Abraham's purchase of a sepulchre, *ib.* 38; on the Apocrypha, *ib.* 53; on the book of Baruch, *ib.* 69; he maintains that without infused faith, we cannot certainly be persuaded of anything, *ib.* 358; rejects the canons of the council of Constantinople (691), 4 *Jew.* 41

Canute, king of England: commanded the water to retire, *Pil.* 51; his laws, 2 *Ful.* 22, *Jew.* xxxiv, 4 *Jew.* 905; complained to the pope that his bishops were vexed with exactions, 4 *Jew.* 1081

Cap: v. Caps.

Çape Farewell, Greenland: 2 *Zur.* 290 n

Capel (Rich.): his writings, 1 *Brad.* 564 n
Capellius (Car.): found a supposed book of Clement's, 1 *Jew.* 111
Capernaites; how they took Christ's words (Jo. vi.), 4 *Bul.* 447, *Grin.* 44, 2 *Hoop.* 191, 450, 1 *Jew.* 451, *Rid.* 175, *Rog.* 289
Capgrave (Jo.): his Legenda Nova Angliæ, 1 *Bec.* 139 n.; referred to about St Osyth, *Hutch.* 172 n.; on a synod held by Oswy at Whitby, *Pil.* 625; (see also Legenda); he wrote on the Apocalypse, *Bale* 257
Capistranus (Jo.): on the book of Wisdom, *Whita.* 89
Capito (Wolfg. Fabr.): notice of him, 3 *Zur.* 553 n.; mentioned, *ib.* 219, 520, 524; he sends a treatise to Henry VIII., 2 *Cran.* 340, 341; severely censures Jerome, 3 *Zur.* 235; letters to him, 2 *Cran.* 340, 341, 3 *Zur.* 15
Capnio (Jo.): *v.* Reuchlin.
Capon (Dr), or Caponer: 2 *Lat.* xxx.
Capon (Jo.), bp of Salisbury: otherwise called Salcot, *q. v.*
Capon (Will.), master of Jesus college, Cambridge; probably the Dr Capon above mentioned: Cranmer's letter to him with a buck, 2 *Cran.* 247
Cappel, Switzerland: the abbey reformed, 4 *Bul.* ix; Zwingle and Joner slain in the battle there, *ib.* x, n.; the defeat, *ib.* xi, xvi, xvii.
Cappellus (Marcus Ant.): 2 *Ful.* 70 n
Caps (Clerical): *Grin.* 207, 2 *Whitg.* 1, 2 *Zur.* 118; appointed by injunction, *Park.* 240; the cap and gown, tippet, hood, 1 *Whitg.* 72, 2 *Whitg.*1, &c., 1 *Zur.* 164, 2 *Zur.* 362; disputes about caps and surplices, 1 *Zur.* 142, 146; the round cap, whether lawful, 1 *Zur.* 134; the round or square cap, *ib.* 158, 345; square ones, *Grin.* 339; use of the square cap enjoined by Sandys, *Sand.* xx; a square cap worn by Hooper albeit (says Foxe) that his head was round, 3 *Zur.* 271 n.; Bucer declined to wear a square cap because his head was not square, *Pil.* 662; forked caps, 2 *Brad.* 225; different sorts of caps, 3 *Jew.* 612
Caps of maintenance: sent by popes to kings, 1 *Tyn.* 186, 204, 300
Captains: valiant ones, 1 *Bul.* 384; benefit of a stout captain, *Pil.* 377; duties of a good one, *ib.* 449
Captives: those of Satan warned, 1 *Bec.* 127; captive Christians, 4 *Bul.* 20
Captivity: *v.* Babylon.
Capuchins: the order established by Clement VII. in 1525, 4 *Jew.* 1106
Caput: caput, membra, corpus, *Now.* 99; diminutio capitis, 1 *Bul.* 356

Car (Nich.): writes to Sir Jo. Cheke on Bucer's last illness, 2 *Brad.* xxiii (see also ...... Carre)
Caraffa (Giampietro card.), afterwards Paul IV. *q. v.*
Caraffa (Jo.), bp of Theate: founded the order of Theatines, 4 *Jew.* 1106 n
Carbanell (Jo.), dean of Warwick college: 2 *Lat.* 396 n
Carbuncle: a jewel, erroneously supposed to be self-luminous, 2 *Brad.* 211
Card of ten: what, 1 *Bul.* 312
Cardillus (Gaspar): *Jew.* xxxiv; calls the pope terrenum Deum, 4 *Jew.* 843
Cardinals: the college of cardinals, *Whita.* 415; they have their name à cardine, 4 *Bul.* 117; called cardines mundi, 2 *Jew.* 1020; their antiquity, 2 *Tyn.* 257; curious proof of their antiquity, adduced by Barbatius, from the first book of Kings, 4 *Jew.* 783; when they began to flourish, *Bale* 561; their general character, *ib.* 520; followers of Judas, 1 *Lat.* 211; compared to the seventy disciples of Manes, *Phil.* 422; they have always been pernicious to England, 2 *Cran.* 184; Romish hats never brought good hither, 1 *Lat.* 119; princes' and kings' sons made cardinals, 4 *Jew.* 970; boys raised to the dignity, 2 *Cran.* 39, 2 *Ful.* 269; pillars and pole-axes carried before them, 2 *Jew.* 1020; cardinal of the pit (i. e. card. de Puteo), 2 *Cran.* 225
Cardmaker (Jo.), canon of Wells: his case, *Phil.* 6; his supposed submission, 1 *Brad.* 290, 473, 481, 554, 3 *Zur.* 171; burned in Smithfield, 1 *Brad.* 290 n., *Rid.* 391, 3 *Zur.* 171 n
Cards: *v.* Gaming.
Sermons on the card, 1 *Lat.* 1, &c.; Foxe's remarks on these sermons, 2 *Lat.* xi; the game of triumph, 1 *Lat.* 8 n.; hearts trump, *ib.* 13; the game of post, 1 *Jew.* 429; injunctions respecting playing at cards, *Grin.* 130, 138
Cardwell (Edw.): Conferences, *Grin.* v. n.; Documentary Annals, *Grin.* 142 n., 173 n., 241 n., 473 n., 1 *Lat.* 122 n.; Two Books of Common Prayer, *Lit. Edw.* viii. n
Care, Carefulness: against pensiveness and thought-taking for the life, with sentences and examples of scripture, 1 *Bec.* 439, &c.; against temptations from carefulness of living, with similar sentences and examples, *ib.* 441, 442; proper carefulness not forbidden, 2 *Bec.* 164; that which is forbidden is not labour, but careful pensiveness, *ib.* 617; anxious care forbidden, 2 *Tyn.*

109—111; what we ought to care for, *ib.* 110, 111; care and thought, what, 3 *Bec.* 607; a prayer against worldly carefulness, *Lit. Eliz.* 250; care of the body, 2 *Bul.* 312; carefulness, a part of repentance, 3 *Bul.* 106; care for others, a mean to maintain concord, *Sand.* 107; in some it is merely pretended, *ib.*; it must be hearty, *ib.* 108; specially the duty of princes, *ib.* 108, and of counsellors, *ib.* 110

Care (Hen.): Modest Enquiry whether St Peter were ever at Rome, 2 *Ful.* 336 n.; Weekly Pacquet, *Calf.* 52 n

Careless (Jo.): account of him, 2 *Brad.* 237 n.; he informed Latimer of coming danger, 1 *Lat.* 321, 2 *Lat.* xxi; died in prison, 1 *Lat.* 321 n., *Poet.* 168, 1 *Zur.* 86 n.; letters from him to Bradford, 2 *Brad.* 238, 354; letter to Latimer, *ib.* 406; letter to Philpot, *Phil.* 231; letters to him, 2 *Brad.* 34, 237, 242, *Phil.* 225, 227, 247; play upon his name, *ib.* 230

Carelessness: *v.* Negligence.

Carew (......): Mr archdeacon Karow, at Paris, 1538, 2 *Cov.* 496

Carew (Geo.), or Cary: being dean of Exeter, he has charge of bishop Bourne, *Phil.* xxviii; as dean of Windsor, he aids Geneva, *Grin.* 430 n., 432 n., 433

Carew (Sir Fra.): his interest in Croydon, *Grin.* 403

Carew (Sir Nich.), K.G.: notice of him, 3 *Zur.* 625 n

Carew (Sir Peter): apprehended, 3 *Zur.* 132 n., 133 n.; mentioned, *Grin.* 299

Carey (Hen.), lord Hunsdon: mourner at the funeral of the emperor Ferdinand, *Grin.* 32; he goes against the rebels in the North, *Park.* 388 n., 1 *Zur.* 214 n., 247 n.; invades Scotland, 1 *Zur.* 225; signature as privy councillor, *Grin.* 412, 414, 429, 433, 435; extract from a letter to lord Burghley, 1 *Zur.* 219 n

Carey (Rich.): mentioned, *Poet.* xxxix.

Carey (T.): notice of him, *Poet.* xxx; Psalm xci. in metre, *ib.* 338

Cargill (Tho.), schoolmaster of Aberdeen: 2 *Zur.* 334

Caria: 1 *Tyn.* 186 n

Carion (Jo.): references to his Chronicon, *Calf.* 78 n., 2 *Hoop.* 293, & al. *Jew.* xxxiv, 2 *Jew.* 981, 982, 4 *Jew.* 565, 699; speaks of defections from the empire in the days of Phocas, 1 *Jew.* 364; declares that the pope has neither possession nor jurisdiction, but he has received it from the French kings or the emperors, 4 *Jew.* 825; on the second council of Nice, *ib.* 1051; on pope Hildebrand, and his disputes with the emperor, *ib.* 699; he says the bishops enticed the son of Henry IV. to depose his father, *ib.* 698; records a speech of Adrian IV., 2 *Jew.* 993, 1020; tells of the treatment of the emperor Frederick by pope Alexander III., 3 *Jew.* 299, 4 *Jew.* 701; says pope Boniface VIII. entered as a fox, reigned as a wolf, and died as a dog, 4 *Jew.* 825; records the poisoning of emperor Henry VII. in the sacrament, *ib.* 687; relates that pope John XXIII. excommunicated the emperor Louis, *ib.* 825; on cardinals, *Bale* 561

Carle: one of low birth, *Pil.* 125

Carleton (Geo.), bp of Chichester: on the seven sacraments, *Calf.* 237 n

Carleton (Will.), a doctor of canon law: *Bale* 28

Carlile (Chr.): denies Christ's descent into hell, *Rog.* 61

Carlisle (Lodowick): *Pra. Eliz.* xx.

Carlisle (Nich.): Grammar-schools, *Now.* i.

Carlos (Don): *v.* Charles.

Carman (Tho.): martyred at Norwich, *Poet.* 172

Carmelites, or White Friars: a division of the Mendicants, 4 *Bul.* 516; their writers on the Apocalypse, *Bale* 257

Carmichael (......), warden of Liddisdale in Scotland: taken prisoner, sent into England, kept at York, and then sent home with honour and certain presents, *Grin.* 355 n

Carnal: *v.* Man.

Caro, carnalis, *Now.* 99; carnal bondage, 4 *Bul.* 287; carnal people, 2 *Bul.* 242; carnal security; against it, with sentences and examples of scripture, 1 *Bec.* 471, &c.

Carneades: his saying of Chrysippus, 4 *Jew.* 757, 1178; his speech against justice, *ib.* 1103

Carnisprivium: Shrovetide, 3 *Zur.* 627

Carnival: the first week in [before] Lent, so called by the Italians, 1 *Jew.* 107

Carnotensis: *v.* Arnoldus, Fulbertus, Ivo, John of Salisbury.

Caro (H. de S.): *v.* Hugo.

Carol: *v.* Christmas.

Caroli (Pet.): accuses Calvin, 3 *Zur.* 622 n

Caroline books: *v.* Charlemagne.

Carolostadius (And. Bodenstein): his opinion on "Hic est corpus meum," *Rid.* 158

Carosus: was an Eutychian heretic, 3 *Jew.* 226, 4 *Jew.* 783

Carpocrates: a heretic, *Bale* 265, 3 *Bec.* 401; he said the world was created by angels, *Rog.* 40, that Jesus was the son of Joseph, *ib.* 52, and rejected the Old Testament, *ib.* 80, 87

Carpocratians: heretics and idolaters, 1 *Ful.* 215; they denied original sin, *Rog.* 97; some boasted themselves to be as innocent as Christ, *ib.* 101, 135; their opinions on the resurrection, 2 *Cov.* 184; they said that none should be saved in soul and body together, *Rog.* 145; denied the resurrection of the body, *ib.* 154; held that Christ ascended, not in body, but in soul, *ib.* 65; they allowed whoredom, *ib.* 119; they had images, 2 *Ful.* 390, 2 *Jew.* 646; their traditions, *Whita.* 667, 668; comparison between them and the Papists, *Phil.* 417

Carr: see also Car, and Carre.

Carr (Sam.): editor of the Early Writings of Hooper, 1 *Hoop.*

Carranza (Barth.): confessor to king Philip, 2 *Brad.* xxxviii; references to his Summa Conciliorum, 2 *Ful.* 89, 151, 154, 184 nn., *Rog.* 204 n.; this book vitiated, *Calf.* 91 n.; possibly misunderstood by Calfhill respecting the synod of Elvira, *ib.* 154 n.; he shamefully corrupts an old canon, 2 *Ful.* 42 n.; on the Begadores, &c., *Rog.* 101; fictitious catalogue of canonical books ascribed by him to the council of Florence, 2 *Ful.* 222 n.; he says Monetarius, being a private man, took upon him the ordering and reformation of the church, *Rog.* 343 n

Carre (......), a master of Cambridge: [perhaps Nich. Car, *q. v.*], 2 *Brad.* xviii.

Carretus (Lud.): shews that the Jews deny the Trinity, *Rog.* 43 n., and Christ's divinity, *ib.* 49 n

Carriage: baggage, 4 *Jew.* 951

Carswell (Jo.), superintendent of Argyle and the Isles: 2 *Zur.* 364 n

Carte (Tho.): Hist. of England, 1 *Lat.* 25, 29, 99, 101, 102, 118, 119, 151, 163, 181, 183, 247, 263, 271 nn., *Now.* i, 1 *Zur.* 209, 219, 253, &c. nn

Carter (Dr): refuses the oath of supremacy, *Park.* 105

Carter (E.): Hist. Univ. Cambr., 2 *Brad.* xvii. n

Carter (Oliver): answers Riston's Challenge, 2 *Ful.* 3

Carter (Will.), chief printer for the Romanists: hanged at Tyburn, 1 *Ful.* xiii n., *Lit. Eliz.* 596 n

Carthage: *v.* Councils.
Seventy children offered up as a sacrifice to Saturn there, 2 *Jew.* 734; Scipio's lamentation over Carthage, 2 *Hoop.* 79; its tongue, 1 *Jew.* 293; the Carthaginian church, 2 *Bec.* 49

Carthusians: notice of them, 2 *Bul.* 57; a branch of the Benedictines: 1 *Tyn.* 302; beginning of the order, 1 *Whitg.* 482; their silence, *Phil.* 421; forbidden to speak, except at certain times, 1 *Tyn.* 302, 331; hence "sister of the Charterhouse," for a brawling woman, *ib.* 305, 331; they ate no flesh, *Phil.* 419, 3 *Tyn.* 8; thought that that the eating of fish pleased God, 1 *Tyn.* 278; some confined in Newgate, 2 *Lat.* 392; some executed for denying the king's supremacy, 1 *Hoop.* 202; an arm of one of them kept in a church as a relic, *ib.*; their writers on the Apocalypse, *Bale* 256

Cartwright (......), brother of Thomas: a lunatic, *Park.* 469, 470

Cartwright (Nich.): disputes with Latimer at Oxford, 2 *Lat.* 250, 272; notice of him, *ib.* 250 n

Cartwright (Tho.): *v.* Admonition, Whitgift (J.)

Notices of him, *Grin.* 323, 1 *Zur.* 312 n.; fellow of Trinity college, Cambridge, 1 *Whitg.* 15, 123 n.; his conduct in that position and as Margaret professor, 3 *Whitg.* viii; expelled from Trinity college by Whitgift, *ib.* 507; not to be permitted to read again in the university, *Grin.* 305; his positions, delivered to the vice-chancellor, *ib.* 323 n.; he lodges in Cheapside, *ib.* 347; Sandys complains of him, *Sand.* xx; his part in the Admonition controversy, *Park.* 434, 1 *Whitg.* 3 n., 13, &c., 3 *Whitg.* x, xi, 1 *Zur.* 297 n.; he escapes to Heidelberg, *ib.* 313 n.; favoured by Whitgift in his last days, 3 *Whitg.* xix; Whitaker's estimate of him, *Whita.* ix; his opinions, 1 *Whitg.* 6, &c., 3 *Whitg.* 598, 599; his dangerous points of doctrine collected, 3 *Whitg.* 552; his untruths and falsified authorities, *ib.* 555; he maintains that we are bound by the judicial law of Moses in part, *Rog.* 90; denies the calling of the English bishops, *ib.* 334 n.; affirms that the substance of the sacraments depends on their celebration by a minister, *ib.* 234 n., and says the laws of God require that none minister the sacraments who do not preach, *ib.* 235; mentions a decree of a council that in the minister's sickness, a deacon should read the homilies of the fathers, *ib.* 325 n.; intimates that the bare reading of the scriptures, without preaching, is not sufficient, *ib.* 326 n.; ascribes the power of excommunication to the church, *ib.* 310 n.; An Answere to M. Cartwright, ascribes it to ministers, *ib.* 310 n., 311 n.; he declares that the making of the orders and ceremonies of the church, pertains to the ministers of the church, and not to the civil magistrate, *ib.* 343 n., that magistrates are to ordain civil discipline only, *ib.* 344 n.; and that princes must be subject unto the church, *ib.* 340 n

Cartysdale (Rich.): *Bale* 16

Carucate: *v.* Plowland.

Carver (Dirick), martyr at Lewes: called by Bryce D. Harman, *Poet.* 162

Carvil (Nich.): his death, 1 *Zur.* 194

Casa (Jo.), abp of Beneventum: his disgraceful book, 4 *Jew.* 657—659

Casalius (Jo. Bapt.): *Calf.* 65 n

Casaubon (Isaac): Exercitationes ad Annales Baronii, *Calf.* 107 n., 225 n., 2 *Ful.* 292 n.; quoted with regard to the meaning of τὸ τέλειον as applied to the eucharist, 1 *Cov.* 203 n.; his MSS. in archbishop Marsh's library at Dublin, *Whita.* 276 n

Casaubon (Meric): 2 *Ful.* 311 n

Cashel (M. abp of): *v.* Gibbon.

Casimir (Duke): *v.* John Casimir.

Caspar (D.), more commonly known as Schvenfeldius, *q.v.*

Cassander (Geo): referred to on the cross, *Calf.* 362 n., 2 *Zur.* 43; he says the council of Trent bestowed a summer about the communion of the cup, 4 *Jew.* 948; works, *Jew.* xxxiv, 1 *Zur.* 118 n.; Armen. Lit. in his works, 2 *Bec.* 256 n., 3 *Bec.* 482 n., 4 *Jew.* 887; Aventinus, 3 *Bec.* 410 n.; B. Pal., *ib.*; P. Bell., *ib.* 411 n.; Gregory, 2 *Bec.* 256 n., 3 *Bec.* 482 n.; Vigilius, 2 *Bec.* 275 n., 279 n., 3 *Bec.* 273 n., 429 n., 430 n., 453 n.; letter to him, 2 *Zur.* 41; letter from him to bishop Cox, *ib.* 42

Cassanus, a Christian prince in the East: 4 *Jew.* 684

Cassian (St): Prudentius saw his history painted in a church, *Calf.* 30

Cassian (Jo.), a monk of the 5th century: *Jew.* xxxv; he often calls common prayer "missa," 1 *Jew.* 181; tells of one who at the commandment of his abbot threw out his child into a stream, 3 *Jew.* 615

Cassiander (......), a captain under Charles V.: 2 *Cran.* 235

Cassilis (Gilb. earl of): *v.* Kennedy.

Cassiodorus (Magn.* Aur.): notice of him, *Bale* 317 n.; works, *Jew.* xxxv; his Tripartite History compiled in Latin, from Socrates, Sozomen, and Theodoret, 2 *Brad.* 305 n., 3 *Zur.* 228 n.; in it he says the preachers of Christian doctrine came from the East, 4 *Jew.* 883; on Peter of Alexandria, 1 *Bul.* 34 n. he says Athanasius, when a deacon, was the greatest travailer in the council of Nice against the Arians, 4 *Jew.* 1009; his copy of the Nicene creed, 2 *Hoop.* 533; words of Constantius to Athanasius, *Pil.* 637; on the Arian council of Ariminum, 4 *Jew.* 1109; on Julian's robbery of the church, *Pil.* 596 n.; on the death of Julian, 2 *Hoop.* 292; the decree of Gratian, Valentinian, and Theodosius, on the catholic faith, *ib.* 540; he mentions that Chrysostom refused to be present at an Arian council, 4 *Jew.* 951; speaks of the sufferings of Olympia, *Pil.* 637; on a diversity in the church about fasting, 1 *Bul.* 433; respecting varieties in ceremonies, 2 *Brad.* 389; on penitents, and their readmission to communion, 1 *Jew.* 143, 3 *Jew.* 374; on idle monks, 4 *Jew.* 800; this history makes no mention of saints' days, 1 *Hoop.* 347; other references or citations, 3 *Bec.* 411, 420, 422, 2 *Brad.* 326, 1 *Bul.* 34, 35, 2 *Bul.* 45, *Calf.* 65, 87, 114, 198, 2 *Ful.* 64, 114, 116, 160, 346, 358, 2 *Hoop.* 292, 533, 539, 540, *Hutch.* 12, 1 *Jew.* 186, 187, 2 *Jew.* 977, 978, 3 *Jew.* 374, 409, 438, 4 *Jew.* 826, 994, 1001, 1009, 1015, 1019, 1020, 1054, 1109, *Rid.* 74, 500, *Sand.* 41, 1 *Whitg.* 410; Comment. in Psalmos, *Calf.* 81, 102, 2 *Ful.* 144; on the first Psalm, *Calf.* 102; in this work he speaks of the sign of the cross, *Calf.* 81, 2 *Ful.* 144, and exhorts to sing with intelligence, 2 *Bec.* 255, 3 *Bec.* 409, *Whita.* 273; he wrote on the Apocalypse, *Bale* 255; he says the soul of man is created of God, a spiritual and peculiar substance, &c., 3 *Bul.* 368, 372

Cassiodorus (......), a Spanish preacher in London: *Grin.* 310 n., 313 n

Cassius: his treason, 2 *Hoop.* 105

Cassock (camisia): worn by the Jewish priests, 2 *Bul.* 134

Cast: a calculated contrivance, 2 *Bec.* 575, 2 *Tyn.* 335

Cast: to calculate, 1 *Tyn.* 92; to add, *Phil.* 365

Castellane (Jo.): degraded, 1 *Tyn.* 233 n

Castellio (Seb.), or Castalio: his name, *Whita.* 32 n.; his version of the Bible, 2 *Zur.* 261 n.; a lax translator, 1 *Ful.* 163; he foolishly affects elegance of style, *ib.* 256; translates baptism, washing, *ib.* 255, 256; he despised the book of Canticles, *Rog.* 81; his opinion on this book, *Whita.* 32; he translated the Sibylline oracles, *Calf.* 95 n

---

* Or Marcus Aurelius.

Casterton (......), a Benedictine monk: wrote on the Apocalypse, *Bale* 256
Castle Camps, co. Cambridge: *Grin.* 266, 289
CASTLE OF COMFORT, by T. Becon: 2 *Bec.* 552
Castoldus (Jo. Bapt.): 2 *Cran.* 233
Castoll (Jo.): minister of the French church in London, 2 *Zur.* 326 n., &c.
Castriot (Geo.): v. Scanderbeg.
Castro (Alph. à): 1 *Brad.* 518; he confers with Bradford, *ib.* 530; preaches before king Philip against persecution, *ib.* 554; yet maintains (in his work De justa Hæret. Punit.) that heretics should be killed, *ib.* n.; his death, *ib.* 530 n.; he says, Paul has commanded us to submit our understanding only unto the obedience of Christ, 3 *Jew.* 615; against opinions of his, *Whita.* 343, &c.; on the interpretation of parables, *ib.* 409; he calls the translation of the scriptures the cause of all heresy, *ib.* 249; yet allows that Jerome translated the Bible into Dalmatic or Sclavonic, 1 *Jew.* 270, 2 *Jew.* 692; allusions to his work against heresies, 2 *Jew.* 689, 3 *Jew.* 161 n.; he says that they who rashly call everything heresy, fall into the same pit that themselves have digged for others, &c., 3 *Jew.* 211, 212; speaks of hearing a Dominican friar say in his sermon, that he was to be suspected as an heretic who in anything dissented from Aquinas, *ib.* 610, 619; allows that the pope may be a heretic, 3 *Jew.* 343, 4 *Jew.* 928, 1068, *Whita.* 431; says, every man, even the pope, may err in faith, and gives examples, 1 *Jew.* 399, 3 *Jew.* 343, 4 *Jew.* 926, 929; calls pope Liberius an Arian, 3 *Jew.* 127, 144, 342—344, 4 *Jew.* 929, 1117; says, pope Anastasius favoured the Nestorian heretics, 3 *Jew.* 342—344, 4 *Jew.* 926; condemns the opinion that a pope, when erring from the faith, is not a pope, 3 *Jew.* 119 n.; says many popes were ignorant of grammar, 1 *Jew.* 381, 4 *Jew.* 910, 1057, and asks how such grammar can expound the holy scriptures, 1 *Jew.* 381, 4 *Jew.* 925; says we are bound to believe that the true successor of Peter is the chief shepherd, but not to believe that Leo or Clement is such true successor, 3 *Jew.* 201, 4 *Jew.* 1013; places a general council above the pope, *Whita.* 415; declares that a simple priest absolves as much as the pope, 3 *Jew.* 385, 4 *Jew.* 977; his reasons against the use of the cup, 3 *Jew.* 597; he calls Epiphanius an iconoclast, *Calf.* 42 n.; admits that there is nothing about indulgences in the scripture or doctors, 4 *Jew.* 852; says that the Greeks do not receive purgatory, 3 *Jew.* 563, *Rog.* 213 n.; on the question whether fornication be deadly sin, 4 *Jew.* 629, 635, 636; he condemns a passage in Gratian, *Whita.* 109; what he states concerning Claudius of Turin, *Calf.* 379; on a sect termed Armenians, 4 *Jew.* 935; copied by Harding, 2 *Jew.* 682 n

Casulanus: 2 *Lat.* 298
Casure: cadence, *Calf.* 298
Casus Papales, Episcopales, Abbatiales: 2 *Ful.* 388
Cat of the mountain: leopard, *Bale* 423
Catabaptists: heretics, 1 *Bec.* 95, 1 *Whitg.* 87, 133; some denied the divinity of Christ, *Rog.* 49; they rejected the Old Testament, *ib.* 80; believed that themselves only should be saved, *ib.* 153; taught that the devils and ungodly shall finally be saved, *ib.* 67, 147
Catalogue: v. Books, Mendham (J.)
Catalogus Sanctorum: v. Petrus de Natalibus.
Catalogus Testium: 2 *Bec.* 261, 395, 3 *Bec.* 392, 398, 439, 459, 4 *Jew.* 1077 nn
Cataphrygians: v. Montanists.
Câteau Cambresis: peace concluded there, 2 *Zur.* 19
Catechisms, Catechizing: what the term catechism means, 2 *Bec.* 9, 4 *Bul.* 154, *Now.* 100; Socrates taught by questions, and Apollinarius, *Lit. Edw.* 495, (545); the teaching of catechisms ancient among Christians, 2 *Bec.* 9; the use and benefit of catechizing, 4 *Bul.* 154, *Now.* 109; catechising at Rivington school, *Pil.* 671; an uncertain catechism referred to by Coverdale, 1 *Cov.* 407

Becon's: A NEW CATECHISM SET FORTH DIALOGUEWISE, by T. Becon, 2 *Bec.* 1; the first part, *ib.* 10; the second, *ib.* 13; the third, *ib.* 53; the fourth, *ib.* 125; the fifth, *ib.* 199; the sixth, *ib.* 302; conclusion, *ib.* 408

Bullinger's Catechesis, recommended by statute to be used at Oxford, 4 *Bul.* xxiv.

Calvin's: taught at Rivington school, *Pil.* 671; partly followed by Nowell, *Now.* vii.

Canisii Catechismus: v. Canisius (P.)

Church of England Catechism: a catechism, that is to say, an instruction, &c. (in the several Prayer Books, and also) in the Primer, 1553, *Lit. Edw.* 369; catechismus, hoc est instructio, &c. (1560), *Pra. Eliz.* 127; another copy (1564), *ib.* 239; its contents and doctrine, *Pil.* 531, *Rid.* 141, *Whita.* 472; articles and injunctions respecting it, *Grin.* 124, 137, 162, 188, 2 *Hoop.* 126, 140, 144, 149, *Rid.* 320, *Sand.* 434; none that were single to be married that cannot say it, *Grin.* 163; Whitgift's circular letter to the bishops of his province, for the better observance of catechizing and confirming of youth, 3 *Whitg.* 610

Cranmer's: called the catechism of 1543, *Rid.* 160 n.; it was translated by Justus Jonas from German into Latin, and afterwards published in English with the sanction of Cranmer, 3 *Zur.* 381, 643; sent by Cranmer to Edward VI., 2 *Cran.* 420 n.; Cranmer added a short catechism to the Articles of 1552, 2 *Cran.* 220

Edward VI.'s: A SHORT CATECHISM; OR PLAIN INSTRUCTION, CONTAINING THE SUM OF CHRISTIAN LEARNING; set forth by king Edward VI., 1553, *Lit. Edw.* 485; notices of various editions, *ib.* x; mentioned, *Rid.* 160 n.; not put forth by Ridley, *ib.* 226; ascribed to Ponet or Nowell, *Phil.* 180 n.; made by bishop Ponet, 3 *Zur.* 142 n.; repudiated in 1553 by convocation, *Phil.* xiii; denounced by Philpot's examiners, *ib.* 88, 154, 179; condemned in every pulpit in queen Mary's time, *Rid.* 350; defended by Philpot, *Phil.* 180; this seems to be the godly and learned catechism referred to 3 *Bec.* 234; CATECHISMUS BREVIS (the same in Latin), 1553, *Lit. Edw.* 541; notice of various copies, *ib.* xii; mentioned, 1 *Brad.* 355 n., and see 3 *Bec.* 234

Heidelberg Catechism; compiled by Z. Ursinus, 2 *Zur.* 157 n

Householders: A Short Catechism for Householders, 1614, cited, *Rog.* 61 n. [By Jo. Stockwood? There is an edition of 1583.]

Nowell's: CATECHISMVS, SIVE PRIMA INSTUTIO DISCIPLINAQUE PIETATIS CHRISTIANÆ, 1570, *Now.* 1—104; A CATECHISM, &c.; the same translated by Tho. Norton, 1570, *ib.* 105—220; its history, and approval by convocation, *ib.* iv—vii, and see 1 *Brad.* 355 n.; injunctions respecting it, *Grin.* 142, 152; inquiry about it, *ib.* 174; of ministers learning of catechisms (viz. Nowell's), 1 *Whitg.* 336; named in the LXXIXth canon of 1603, as "the larger catechism heretofore by public authority set forth," 2 *Brad.* 355 n.; taught at Rivington school, *Pil.* 671

Trent: the Catechism of the council of Trent on the infallibility of the church, *Rog.* 179 n.; it allows that sacraments must be ordained by God, *ib.* 254 n.; on Christ's descent into hell, *Whita.* 537, 538; it says water must be mixed with the wine in the sacrament, *Rog.* 296 n.; calls the mass a propitiatory sacrifice, *ib.* 299 n.; on the pretended sacrament of confirmation, *ib.* 254 n.; on that of penance, *ib.* 256 n., 257, 258 n.; on that of extreme unction, *ib.* 263 n.; it teaches that we must always doubt of the forgiveness of our sins, *ib.* 285 n

Vaux's Catechism: 2 *Ful.* 4, *Rog.* 62, 110, &c. (v. L. Vaux).

Catechists: teachers so called of old, 2 *Bec.* 9, 4 *Bul.* 154, 2 *Jew.* 673, 3 *Jew.* 272, 2 *Whitg.* 340, 341

Catechumens: those newly come into the religion of Christ, and not yet baptized, 2 *Bec.* 9, 256, 1 *Ful.* 257, 1 *Jew.* 115, *Phil.* 283, 2 *Whitg.* 543; they signed themselves with the cross, 2 *Jew.* 706; warned to prepare their hearts for baptism, 1 *Jew.* 119; Chrysostom intimates that they may not join in the prayers of the church, 2 *Jew.* 706; not permitted to be present at baptism, *ib.*; not allowed to be present at the eucharist, 1 *Jew.* 182, 202, 2 *Jew.* 705, *Rid.* 160, 163; there are now none to be sent away, *ib.* 207

Categories: v. Predicaments.

Catena Aurea: *Jew.* xxxv.

Cates: provisions, 1 *Bul.* 424; "achates," *Park.* xii.

Cathari: v. Novatians.

Catharinus (Ambr.), abp of Canza: his works, *Jew.* xxxv; he admits that scripture is easy to the faithful, *Whita.* 401; on the term "barbarian" as used by Paul, *ib.* 268; on that apostle being "rude in speech," *ib.* 101; on "the epistle from Laodicea," *ib.* 303; on the Apocrypha, *ib.* 53; in the council of Trent he called Mary Christ's most faithful fellow, 3 *Jew.* 121, 135, 297, 451, 558, 577, 4 *Jew.* 1052; against the worship of images, 4 *Jew.* 950; condemned card. Cajetan for two hundred sundry errors, 3 *Jew.* 620; blamed him for asserting that Paul allows polygamy, *ib.* 406; and for saying that an infant, wanting instruction in faith, hath not perfect baptism, *ib.* 462; insulted him for disliking Latin prayers, *Whita.* 274; his contest with à Soto, 4 *Jew.* 956

Catharus: v. Novatian.

Cathedra (Ex): v. Bishops.

Cathedrals: v. Abbeys.

So called of cathedra, 4 *Bul.* 199; the order of St Benet observed in them, 1 *Jew.* 74; some endowed out of abbey lands, 2 *Tyn.* 277; their high steeples, 3 *Tyn.* 78; women sung songs of ribaldry in processions in cathedral churches, *ib.* 125; Cranmer's letter on the proposed new foundation at Canterbury, 2 *Cran.* 396; in the Marian times, they were dens of thieves, or worse, 4 *Jew.* 1217; their corrupt state on the accession of Elizabeth, 1 *Zur.* 45; on cathedral churches, 3 *Whitg.* 392, &c.; Cartwright would have had them turned into colleges, *ib.* 393; their order described, 3 *Jew.* 109; no women to live within their precincts, *Park.* 146, 151, 158; the statutes for the new cathedrals finished, *ib.* 395; articles to be inquired of respecting cathedrals and collegiate churches in the province of Canterbury, *Grin.* 178; their clergy and officers, *Grin.* 178, &c., 3 *Whitg.* 394

Catherine (St): account of her, 1 *Bec.* 139 n.; invoked for learning, *ib.* 139, *Rog.* 226; prayer to her, *ib.* 227; idolatrous altars builded to her, 3 *Bec.* 240; her knots, *Pil.* 80

Catherine of Arragon, first queen of Henry VIII. (*q. v.*): her parents, 2 *Tyn.* 304; her confessor, 1 *Lat.* 266 n.; her divorce, why sought by Wolsey, 2 *Tyn.* 319, 322; the wrong she suffered from the prelates, *ib.* 320, &c., 343; Tyndale's argument from seripture for the validity of her marriage, *ib.* 323, &c.; Cranmer declares her contumacious, 2 *Cran.* 241, 245; his fears lest she should appear at her sentence, *ib.* 242; his sentence of divorce against her, *ib.* 243 n.; his account of his proceedings against her, *ib.* 244; declared to be only princess dowager, *ib.* 277 n., 285 n

Catherine Howard, fifth queen of Henry VIII.: her stature diminutive, 3 *Zur.* 201; the king visits her at bishop Gardiner's, *ib.* 202; Cranmer states her confessions to the king, 2 *Cran.* 408; her execution, *ib.* 408 n., 3 *Zur.* 226

Catherine Parr, sixth queen of Henry VIII: married to the king, 3 *Zur.* 242; petition for her as queen, *Pra. Eliz.* 572; letter from her to Parker, *Park.* 16; letter to the dean and fellows of Stoke, desiring a lease for Edw. Waldegrave, *ib.* 19; letter to the university of Cambridge, *ib.* 36 n.; after the king's death she married the lord admiral Seymour, 1 *Lat.* 228; had daily prayer in her house, *ib.*; certain prayers from the service daily used there, *Lit. Eliz.* 252

Catherine, daughter of Edward IV., wife of Will. Courtenay (*q. v.*), earl of Devon.

Cathhill (James), believed to be Calfhill, *q. v.*

Catholic: *v.* Church, Faith.

The meaning of the word, *Bale* 178, *Now.* (54), 100, 173, *Phil.* 37, 38; Augustine explains it, *Phil.* 136; no party names are to be received, but only Christian and catholic, 1 *Ful.* 20; catholicity, a mark of the church, *Poet.* 269; why the church is so called, 2 *Bec.* 42; the catholic church of God stands not in multitude of persons, but in weight of truth, 3 *Jew.* 268; Elias believed contrary to the consent of very many, 3 *Tyn.* 89; the threefold universality of Vincent of Lirins, 3 *Jew.* 66; how the rule must be limited, *ib.* 267; the name assumed by Arians, *Coop.* 183; they (like the Papists) took to themselves the name of catholics, and gave sectarian names to the orthodox, *Phil.* 424; Augustine says that although all heretics desire to be called catholics, yet no heretic would dare to direct a traveller inquiring for the catholic church, to his own temple or house, *ib.* 141 n.; false catholicity, *Coop.* 171; the name wrongly applied to Papists, 2 *Ful.* 241; the catholic doctrine is the teaching of scripture, not the errors of the popish pseudo-catholics, *Whita.* 480; mass priests rob the church of her true name, *Rid.* 150; Romish doctrines and practices are not catholic, 1 *Jew.* 80; nor is the church of Rome the catholic church, 3 *Whitg.* 622; "your church cacolique," says Calfhill to Martiall, *Calf.* 214; the doctrine of the reformed is catholic, 2 *Jew.* 1030; Philpot avows himself a catholic, *Phil.* 131, 132; men are not to be counted as catholics who are not partakers of the Lord's supper thrice in the year, 3 *Bec.* 380; bishops of the catholic church, what, 1 *Jew.* 426; the catholic epistles, 1 *Ful.* 222, 223

Catholicon: *v.* Joannes de Balbis.

Catiline: his conspiracy, 2 *Cov.* 129, 2 *Hoop.* 105, *Wool.* 29

Catlyn (Sir Rob.), chief justice of the Queen's Bench: *Grin.* 272

Catmer (Geo.), alias Painter: martyred at Canterbury, *Poet.* 164

— Joan, his wife, also a martyr, *Poet.* 165, 3 *Zur.* 175 n

Cato: says there is great darkness in God's matters, 4 *Jew.* 683; charges to honour parents, 1 *Hoop.* 284; says, if any man praise thee, remember to be thine own judge, *ib.* 407; on consistency of conduct in a teacher, 1 *Bec.* 15, 2 *Bec.* 383; on money, 1 *Bec.* 222; he says, what is gotten in a long time, is spent in a little time, 2 *Bec.* 401; speaks of little thieves in fetters, and great thieves in purple and gold, 2 *Bec.* 600, 2 *Bul.* 47; on bearing the tongue of a wife, 2 *Bec.* 339; his remark on two augurs meeting, 1 *Jew.* 292; on Turrhenus, king of Etruria, *ib.* 294; he rebukes the brag of Pompey, 2 *Jew.* 1031; mentions an old saw among husbandmen, *ib.* 1023; his saying on idleness, *Wool.* 131; his anticipations of death, 3 *Bec.* 154

Catullus: 2 *Bec.* 419 n

Caturco (Alv. de): *v.* Alvarus.

Cautels: deceits, *Bale* 409

Cavallerius (Ant. Rod.), or Le Chevalier: notices of him, 2 *Cran.* 436 n., *Park.* 349 n., 3 *Zur.* 716 n.; recommended to king Edward, 2 *Cran.* 435; Hebrew professor at Cambridge, 2 *Zur.* 97 n., 190 n., 199, 218

Cavallerius (Pet.), or Chevalier: 2 *Zur.* 199

Cave (Dr): admitted in the Arches court, 2 *Cran.* 256; has a prebend at Oxford, *ib.* 386

Cave (Sir Ambrose): a tale ascribed to him about an island near Rhodes, [he was a knight of St John], 2 *Ful.* 155; one of queen Elizabeth's privy council, 1 *Zur.* 5 n.; signature as such, *Park.* 103, 106, 155, 298

Cave (Will.): 2 *Bec.* 173, 259, *Calf.* 41, 42, 48, 133, 306, 2 *Ful.* 147, 287 nn.; erred in rejecting the Testimonia adversus Judæos by Gregory Nyssen, 2 *Ful.* 295 n.; he attributes the books De Vocatione Gentium to Prosper of Orleans, *ib.* 353 n.; his unjust censure of Clichtoveus, *ib.* 277 n.; Discourse of ancient Church Government, *ib.* 70 n.; Lives of the Apostles, 1 *Hoop.* 455 n

Cavell (Jo.): martyred, *Poet.* 166

Cavendish (Geo.): his account of Wolsey's influence with the king, 2 *Tyn.* 307

Cavendish (Tho.), navigator: notice of one Candish, presumed to be the same, *Poet.* xxvii; verses by the said Candish; no joy comparable to a quiet mind, *ib.* 308

Cavendish (Sir Will.): grantee of Tutbury priory, 2 *Cran.* 379 n.; letter signed by him ("Willyam Candysh"), *Park.* 307

— Elizabeth (Hardwick), his wife, *ib.* 301 n.; his daughter Elizabeth married to the earl of Lennox, 2 *Zur.* 200 n

Cawdewell (Rich.), M.D.: 2 *Cran.* 543

Cawood, co. York: a palace of the archbishop, *Grin.* 325, 1 *Zur.* 259 n

Cawood (Jo.), printer: 2 *Jew.* 993

Caxton (Will.): continues the Polychronicon, *Pil.* 598 n

Cay (Jo.): *v.* Caius.

Ceadda (St): *v.* Chad.

Cechelles (......), or Secelles: 3 *Zur.* 112, 114

Cecil family: 2 *Bec.* 480 n

Cecil (Rich.), father of lord Burghley: 2 *Brad.* 397

Cecil (Rob.), 1st earl of Salisbury: 2 *Bec.* 480 n.; his harsh reception of Caspar Thoman, 2 *Zur.* 327; notice of him, *ib.* n.; his conduct with regard to the earl of Essex, *ib.* 332

Cecil (Tho.), afterwards 2nd lord Burghley, and 1st earl of Exeter: dedication to him, 2 *Bec.* 480; notice of him, *ib.* n

Cecil (Sir Will.), 1st lord Burghley: notice of him, 2 *Bec.* 480 n.; he was of St John's college, Cambridge, *Whita.* 13; master of the requests to the protector Somerset, *Hutch.* ii, 3 *Zur.* 77 n.; imprisoned in his house, 3 *Zur.* 77 n.; secretary to king Edward, *Rid.* 333; he favours the gospel, 3 *Zur.* 92; the Articles submitted to him, 2 *Cran.* xi; brought before queen Mary's council, *ib.* 442 n.; chancellor of Cambridge, *Park.* 54, *Whita.* 13; secretary of state and privy councillor to queen Elizabeth, 1 *Zur.* 5 n.; signature as privy councillor, *Grin.* 405, 408, 412, 414, 417, 427, 433, 435, *Park.* 46, 73, 74, 76, 77, 103, 106, 122, 155, 179, 328 n., 330, 357, 381; he favours the Reformation, 1 *Zur.* 55; desires P. Martyr's return, *ib.* 71; named, *ib.* 80, 2 *Zur.* 13; plenipotentiary for a peace with France, 1 *Zur.* 89 n.; restrains the queen from forbidding the marriage of the clergy, *Park.* 148; commended, 2 *Zur.* 66, 93; writes to Grindal concerning a fast for the plague, *Grin.* 79; interests himself with the queen in behalf of Coverdale, for the remission of the firstfruits of St Magnus, 2 *Cov.* xv; mourner at the funeral of the emperor Ferdinand, *Grin.* 33; instrumental in Sandys's promotion to the see of London, *Sand.* xix; created baron Burghley, *Park.* 381, and made lord high treasurer, *Grin.* 329; at the duke of Norfolk's trial, 1 *Zur.* 267 n.; two desperate men hired by the Spanish ambassador's secretary to murder him, *Grin.* 332, 2 *Zur.* 198; he sends Parker a book containing an attack on himself and the lord keeper, *Park.* 444; recommended as visitor for St John's college, Cambridge, *Grin.* 359; his message to archbishop Grindal, concerning his submission, *ib.* 469; letter from him to the heads of houses at Cambridge, *ib.* 368 n.; Grindal leaves him a cup, *ib.* 459; his opinion on Whitgift's proceedings against certain ministers, 3 *Whitg.* 604, 605; he corrects a form of prayer, *Lit. Eliz.* 472; dedication to him by Garbrand, 2 *Jew.* 966; one by Whitaker, *Whita.* 3; letter from him to Mr Herd, 2 *Cran.* 459; letters to Parker, *Park.* 53, 63, 67, 69, 77, 78, 104, 108, 138,

148, 161, 163, 172 bis, 183, 187, 223, 235, 301, 305, 354, 444; letters to Sturmius, 2 *Zur.* 210, 216; letters to him, 2 *Brad.* 395, 2 *Cov.* 529 n., 530, 531, 2 *Cran.* 429, 437—442, *Grin.* passim (see the contents), 2 *Hoop.* xviii, xix, 4 *Jew.* 1262, 1273, 1275 bis, 1276, *Now.* vi, *Park.* passim (see the contents), *Pil.* ix, *Rid.* 336, 532, 535, 3 *Whitg.* 597, 598, 601, 602, 607, 2 *Zur.* 34, 176, 320; extracts from his correspondence, *Sand.* xx, xxi, xxiii, xxvi, 1 *Zur.* 149 n., 2 *Zur.* 34 n, 91 n. 92 n

— Mary (Cheke) his first wife: 2 *Brad.* 396
— Mildred (Cook) his second wife: 2 *Zur.* 35 n

Cecilia (St): compared with Anne Askewe, *Bale* 141

Cecilia, margravine of Baden, sister of the king of Sweden: *Park.* xii, 1 *Zur.* 257 n

Cecilian, bp of Carthage: his contest with Donatus, 1 *Jew.* 396, 397, 3 *Jew.* 167; the Donatists called him a Traditor, 1 *Tyn.* 144

Cecilius à Bilta: in a council at Carthage, 2 *Jew.* 773

Cecilius (Lucius): perhaps the author of a work ascribed to Lactantius, *Calf.* 105 n., 2 *Ful.* 336 n

Cecrops: placed by Usher a little after the birth of Moses, 2 *Bul.* 218

Cedda: *v.* Chad.

Cednom: *v.* Caedmon.

Cedron (The brook): 2 *Brad.* 254, *Pil.* 345

Celestine I. pope: thought the clergy should be distinguished by their doctrine and conversation, not by garments, 2 *Brad.* 383, 3 *Jew.* 617, 2 *Zur.* 122; says the people must rather be taught than mocked, &c., 1 *Jew.* 319; his additions to the mass, 2 *Brad.* 305, 306, 308 n., *Pil.* 503, 3 *Whitg.* 73; he desired Cyril of Alexandria to represent him in the council of Ephesus, 4 *Jew.* 1002; his claim to appellate jurisdiction, 2 *Ful.* 70, 71, 308, 3 *Whitg.* 169; reproved of pride by the council of Africa, 3 *Jew.* 294, 295, 3 *Whitg.* 169; a heretic, 3 *Jew.* 127, 344, *Whita.* 431 n

Celestine III. pope: crowned the emperor Henry VI. with his feet, and then kicked the crown off again, 2 *Tyn.* 271; says the simple vow before God binds no less than the solemn, 4 *Jew.* 788

Celestines, old heretics: their opinion that the righteous have no sin in this life, 2 *Cov.* 387

Celestius, a heretic of the party of Pelagius: his errors, 2 *Bul.* 386, 1 *Ful.* 386, *Phil.* 427

Celibacy: *v.* Chastity, Marriage, Vows.

Far preferable to wedlock, *Hutch.* 148, 1 *Lat.* 393, 394, 1 *Tyn.* 21; in what respects, 2 *Ful.* 228, 383; especially good in time of persecution, 3 *Whitg.* 293; the true doctrine respecting it, 2 *Ful.* 99; false professions of it, 2 *Jew.* 830; abused by the mystery of iniquity, *ib.* 911; compulsory celibacy opposed to scripture, *ib.* 990; not annexed to holy orders, 3 *Jew.* 397; when first imposed on the English clergy, *ib.* 395; evil consequences of enforced celibacy, *Bale* 518, 531, 2 *Cov.* 484, 2 *Cran.* 37, 38, 2 *Ful.* 244, 3 *Jew.* 424, 427, *Poet.* 283, *Sand.* 316, 328, 1 *Tyn.* 278, 3 *Tyn.* 151, 157; spiritual virginity, *Bale* 454

Celius: *v.* Cælius, Cœlius.

Cellarer, or Sellerar: an office in a monastery, 2 *Cran.* 312 n., 2 *Tyn.* 287

Cellarii, a family: 1 *Zur.* 305

Cellarius (......), perhaps the individual next mentioned: 3 *Zur.* 194, 420, 424, 723

Cellarius (Jo.), Landavus: notice of him, *Pra. Eliz.* 412 n.; ad Deum Patrem: ad Deum Filium: ad Deum Spiritum S.: Latin verses, *ib.* 412; the same in English, by R. Wisdome, "Preserve us, Lord," &c., *ib.* n

Celsus: pretended to teach the truth, 3 *Jew.* 159; accused Christians of sedition and treason, 4 *Jew.* 666; objected that they had neither altars, images, nor temples, *Park.* 86, *Rid.* 88; spoke of their want of agreement amongst themselves, 1 *Lat.* 385; despised the religion of Christ because it came from the barbarous Jews, 3 *Jew.* 193, 194, 4 *Jew.* 667

Celsus (Aurel. Corn.): wrote on medicine, 1 *Hoop.* 297

Celsus (Juventius): defines law (jus), 1 *Hoop.* 273

Cemeteries: *v.* Burial.

Censers: to be destroyed, *Grin.* 135, 159

Centaur: his origin, 2 *Jew.* 784

Centum Gravamina: *v.* Germany.

Centuriators of Magdeburg: 2 *Ful.* 107 n., 109 n., 255, 1 *Jew.* 305 n., *Jew.* xxxv, *Whita* 380, 1 *Whitg.* 406, 413, 439; libraries searched for materials for them, 2 *Zur.* 77 n.; they call several apostles besides the twelve, 1 *Whitg.* 497, 498; allege a statement that Paul preached in Britain, 3 *Jew.* 128, 164; on Timothy's office, 2 *Whitg.* 295; they say that the early churches read openly certain epistles of Clement and Dionysius of Corinth, 1 *Bul.* 10, 3 *Whitg.* 345; on Origen, *Calf.* 78 n.; on the error of Apollinaris, *Rog.* 57; they say that Ambrose was a metropolitan, 2 *Whitg.*

11

155; on the works of Epiphanius, *ib.* 288; on the wide jurisdiction of Chrysostom, *ib.* 316; on Pelagian errors, *Rog.* 277 n., 354 n.; on the heresy of Theodore Mesethenus, *Rog.* 55 n.; on the Acephali, *ib.* 330 n.; on the banishment of idolatry by Leo III. and other princes, 2 *Bec.* 71 n.; on the antimagisterial principles of one Rabanus, *Rog.* 346 n.; on Louis IX.'s complaint of Romish exactions in France, 4 *Jew.* 1081; on bishops and metropolitans, 2 *Whitg.* 158; they say that bishops gave sentence in civil causes, 3 *Whitg.* 454; on chorepiscopi, *ib.* 271; they affirm that deacons preached, *ib.* 63; tell of a Jew baptized with sand by laymen, 2 *Whitg.* 528; in error concerning the origin of processions, *Calf.* 296 n.; their statement with respect to the first naming of bells, *ib.* 15 n.; on Romish service books, 4 *Bul.* 201

Cenwalch, king of Wessex: *v.* Coinualch.

Ceolfride, or Ceolfrith, abbot of Jarrow: his epistle to Naiton, king of the Picts, 2 *Ful.* 8; pope Sergius writes to him, *ib.* 119 n

Cephalæus (......): 2 *Cov.* 505, &c.

Cephas: *v.* Peter (St).

Cerdon: his heresy, 1 *Bec.* 412, 418, 2 *Bec.* 446, 3 *Bec.* 401, *Phil.* 418, 1 *Whitg.* 329; he espoused the heresy of the Gnostics, *Grin.* 59 n.; rejected a great part of the New Testament, *Whita.* 34; wrongly referred to, *Rog.* 57

Cerdonians: despised the Old Testament, and denied the resurrection, *Whita.* 31; their opinions on the latter subject, 2 *Cov.* 184; errors wrongly ascribed to them, *Rog.* 83, 145, 314

Ceremoniale Romanum: its proper title, Ceremoniarum sive Rituum ecclesiasticorum Romanæ Ecclesiæ libri tres (Col. Agrip. 1557), *Jew.* xxxv; it says the government of the Roman empire belongs to the pope, 4 *Jew.* 831; but allows that before Charlemagne no man ever received the crown of the Roman empire by the hands of the bishop of Rome, *ib.* 836; orders that the place where the emperor sits (in a general council) shall be no higher than the place where the pope sets his feet, *ib.* 957, 1017; gives the words used by the chief deacon at the consecration of the pope, *ib.* 828; mentions that the cardinal delivers him a book of the epistles and gospels, *ib.* 979; directs the epistle and gospel to be read in Greek when he says mass, *ib.* 842; shews the manner of his riding in pontificalibus, 3 *Jew.* 554; the pope addresses cardinals as senators of the city, hinges of the world, &c. 4 *Jew.* 855; the book declares that the patriarchs are now but as it were titular, *ib.* 1056; says abbots have right and authority to determine and subscribe in council as well as bishops, *ib.* 1009

Ceremonies: *v.* Augustine, and other fathers, Church, Superstitions, Tradition, Vestments, Worship.
  i. *Ceremonies generally.*
  ii. *Their institution, change and diversity.*
  iii. *Jewish rites.*
  iv. *In the early church.*
  v. *Romish ceremonies.*
  vi. *In England, &c.*

  i. *Ceremonies generally*: on ceremonies, 2 *Whitg.* 42, &c.; what they are, 2 *Bul.* 125; human ceremonies, *ib.* 126; divine ceremonies, *ib.* 127; to what end ordained, *ib.*; when God liketh, and when he misliketh them, *ib.* 128; the knowledge of them not unprofitable, *ib.* 129; the sum of them, *ib.* 130; ceremonies in the sacraments, 4 *Bul.* 252; the supper and baptism are not only ceremonies, but sacraments, 1 *Whitg.* 182; ceremonies are substantial or accidental, *ib.* 183; sacraments, signs, and ceremonies, are no service to God, but memorials unto men, 1 *Tyn.* 352, 362, 3 *Tyn.* 56; in themselves they are of small importance, *Sand.* 95; but they are to be rejected unless they teach good doctrine, 3 *Tyn.* 7; they are injurious to those who observe them without knowing their purport, 1 *Tyn.* 362; pernicious, unless required by scripture, *Whita.* 639; not understood by one among a thousand, 1 *Bec.* 111; unmeaning ceremonies condemned, 1 *Tyn.* 226, 3 *Tyn.* 7; dumb ceremonies edify not, but hurt altogether, 3 *Tyn.* 329; ceremonies cannot put away sin, 1 *Tyn.* 284, nor increase grace, *ib.* 286, nor give peace, 2 *Tyn.* 194; tested by their effects, 1 *Tyn.* 286; much observed by hypocrites, *Wool.* 45; ignorantly observed by the natural man, 3 *Tyn.* 8; the judgment of the vulgar concerning works ceremonial, *Wool.* 46; they are superstitiously watched by the common people, 1 *Tyn.* 277, 3 *Tyn.* 117; such as have lost their significations are salt which is to be trodden under foot, 2 *Tyn.* 33; no man to be judged for the non-observance of indifferent ceremonies, *ib.* 113—114; moderate ceremonies allowed by the fourth commandment, *Wool.* 69—71; ceremonies which serve to honesty and public order to be approved, 1 *Cov.* 461;

CEREMONIES

they are to be observed if allowed by lawful authority, and not repugnant to the word of God, *Rog.* 316, but not otherwise, *ib.* 318; such as tend to comeliness and edification are to be retained, *Rog.* 202, not to be contemned, 4 *Bul.* 249; how they serve to edifying, 2 *Whitg.* 56; their true use, 2 *Cran.* 157; the opinion of fathers and councils on things indifferent, 1 *Whitg.* 213; judgment of some foreign reformers on their use, 3 *Whitg.* 549—551; whether new ones may be introduced, and on the lawfulness of ceremonies generally, 1 *Zur.* 352

ii. *Their institution, change, and diversity:* the jurisdiction for ordaining them, 2 *Cran.* 98; on the church's power to decree them, *Rog.* 184—190; some are left to the ordering of the church, 1 *Whitg.* 190; examples, *ib.* 200; but one general rule given in scripture, *Whita.* 513; ceremonies may be ordained, changed, or abolished, by every particular church, so that all things be done to edifying, *Rog.* 321, 322; but the church may not ordain what rites she will, *ib.* 188; they may be altered as circumstances require, *Coop.* 61, 2 *Cran.* 55; 2 *Hoop.* 123, 520, *Hutch.* 232, 3 *Tyn.* 30, *Whita.* 513, 548; many old ones have been abrogated, 2 *Ful.* 174; some apostolical customs being abused were discontinued, as vigils and the kiss of charity, 1 *Tyn.* 219; all that were used by the apostles not now to be used, 1 *Whitg.* 287; Tyndale recommends the abolition of some, 3 *Tyn.* 126; their diversity, 4 *Bul.* 56; they are not necessarily alike in all places, *Rog.* 313, &c., 1 *Whitg.* 286, 288, 2 *Whitg.* 451; testimony of Anselm to this, *Pil.* 538, 620; their diversity hurts not, if the one faith be kept, 2 *Jew.* 1106, and it ought not to break the unity of faith, 2 *Brad.* 389

iii. *Jewish rites:* the outward ceremonies of the Jews, sacraments of heavenly things, 1 *Cov.* 445; why God ordained them, *ib.* 447; no ground for the abuses introduced by Romanists into the Lord's supper, *ib.* 461; why imposed upon the Jews, *Calf.* 122, 2 *Whitg.* 440; supposed by them to justify, 3 *Tyn.* 66—68; but they could not, 1 *Tyn.* 415, 416, 3 *Tyn.* 65; they were not given to justify men, but to prefigure Christ, 1 *Tyn.* 16, 414—416, 421, 422, 427; they were given to the Jews as toys to children, *ib.* 421; some of them were like a star-light of Christ, and some the daybreak, *ib.* 422; their meaning, 2 *Tyn.* 215; they were beggarly elements, 1 *Jew.* 137, 138; the middle wall of partition, 2 *Bul.* 358; the handwriting, *ib.* 259; how perpetual, *ib.* 262; some Levitical ordinances may still be used, 1 *Zur.* 347; Tyndale says the ceremonies of the law may still be observed if we will, provided we regard them as things indifferent, 2 *Tyn.* 327; fulfilled and taken away by Christ, *Pil.* 129

iv. *In the early church:* how they sprang up, 3 *Tyn.* 68, &c.; brought in by Jewish converts, *ib.* 70; some falsely ascribed to the apostles, 2 *Jew.* 991, 3 *Tyn.* 85; the apostles gave no blind ceremonies, *ib.*; unjustly thrust on the church, 2 *Bul.* 276; augmented in sacraments, 1 *Hoop.* 237; added to baptism, 4 *Bul.* 359; numerous in early times, 2 *Whitg.* 435; not very injurious at first, but they soon became a heavy yoke, 3 *Tyn.* 74—78; they had greatly multiplied in the days of Augustine, 2 *Jew.* 992 (*v.* Augustine, xvi); Augustine, Gerson, and Tho. Aquinas, sought to reduce their number, *Lit. Eliz.* xxvi; complaints of the later fathers and schoolmen, 1 *Jew.* 138; the multitude of ceremonies brought in ignorance of scripture, 3 *Tyn.* 75; ignorance made the people servants to ceremonies, *ib.* 76

v. *Romish ceremonies:* invented by man, *Pil.* 130; borrowed from the Gentiles, *Calf.* 66, 1 *Ful.* 564, *Phil.* 390; ceremonies in the pope's church and Mahomet's, *Bale* 262; vain and impious ones, *Rog.* 180; how it was believed that in practising them was salvation, 2 *Bec.* 414; the priests taught that Christ's death had purchased such grace for ceremonies that they could justify, 3 *Tyn.* 77, and encouraged ceremonies for fear of losing the offerings, 2 *Cran.* 465; they harden the hearts of Papists, 2 *Whitg.* 9; petitions against them, 3 *Bec.* 247; Sir Tho. More on "holy strange gestures," 3 *Tyn.* 85 n.; those used in the mass not primitive, 2 *Jew.* 991; ceremonies used in the church in Lent, 1 *Bec.* 110, &c.; absurd ones at Easter, 1 *Hoop.* 45, 46

vi. *In England, &c.:* disputes in Germany and England, *Rog.* 317; amendment of ceremonies recommended, 1 *Lat.* 52; an article de ritibus ecclesiasticis, 2 *Cran.* 477; those used in England, 1539, 3 *Zur.* 624; Book of Ceremonies, drawn up by Gardiner and others, 1539, 1 *Bec.* 110 n., 1 *Lat.* 132 n.; abolition of ceremonies by the gospellers, 3 *Jew.* 176; some retained under king Edward for a time, and why, 3 *Zur.*

535; inquiry concerning their abuse, 2 *Cran.* 158; proclamations commanding them not to be omitted unless forbidden, *ib.* 508; of ceremonies, why some be abolished and some retained: (first prefixed to king Edward's second Prayer Book), *Lit. Edw.* 197; the same, in the works of its supposed author, 2 *Cran.* 518; troubles about them at Frankfort, 3 *Zur.* 753, &c.; the "peaceable letter" of the church at Frankfort, *Pil.* iii; the order used in the church of England respecting them, 3 *Jew.* 569; the rites and ceremonies in it are not ungodly, though in some points they might be bettered, *Sand.* 448; they were strenuously opposed by the earlier reformed bishops,1 *Zur.* 84 n.; bishops Grindal and Horn on several ceremonies, *ib.* 178—180 (see 357); superstitious practices long retained in the North of England, *ib.* 259 n.; Sandys's advice concerning rites and ceremonies in the synod, 1562, *Sand.* 433; disorders in rites and ceremonies, under queen Elizabeth, *Park.* 224, 227; the prince has power by law to ordain ceremonies in certain cases, *Park.* 375; any rites might be imposed by the queen and the archbishop, 2 *Zur.* 130, 150, 161, 361; P. Martyr against superstitious rites, *ib.* 25, &c.; Beza feared the English ceremonies would bring the people back to superstition, *ib.* 134; common ceremonies or customs of Tyndale's day, 1 *Tyn.* 275
Ceres: *v.* Bacchus.
Cerinthians: ascribed the creation to angels, *Hutch.* 68; their supposed opinions on the earthly Jerusalem, 2 *Cov.* 184 n
Cerinthus: his heresy, *Bale* 265, 1 *Bec.* 278, 418, 3 *Bec.* 401, 1 *Bul.* 363, 4 *Bul.* 535, 1 *Hoop.* 17, 2 *Jew.* 566, *Whita.* 34 n.; he brought in his devices under the pretence of revelations, 3 *Jew.* 235; ascribed the world's creation unto angels, *Rog.* 40; taught that the law ceremonial continues in force, *ib.* 89, 160, 314; said that Christ was the son of Joseph and Mary, *ib.* 48; thought Christ's resurrection future, *ib.* 64; opposed by St John, 2 *Brad.* 263, who would not stay where he was, *ib.* 329
Certainty: *v.* Assurance, Faith.
Chabrias: his saying on the benefit of a valiant captain, *Pil.* 377
Chad (St), or Ceadda, abp of Lichfield, afterwards of York: 2 *Ful.* 26, 27; his consecration, *ib.* 118
Chaderton (Will.), bp of Chester, afterwards of Lincoln: a Latin letter to him by Sandys, *Sand.* 436; the same in English, *ib.* 439

Chafin (......): married two sisters, his case before the delegates, 4 *Jew.* 1262, *Park.* 176
Chagi: Turkish priests, *Rog.* 120, 359
Chairs: the chair of porphyry-stone, 4 *Jew.* 655, 689; a text appropriate to chairs and stools, 1 *Bec.* 65
Chalcedon: *v.* Councils.
Chalcedon (Jo. bp of): an English suffragan, 2 *Cov.* vii.
Chalcocondylas (Leonicus): Hist. Turcarum, 4 *Jew.* xxxv, 653, 656, 742
Chaldees: worshipped fire, 2 *Hoop.* 271
Chaldee tongue: 4 *Bul.* 189, *Whita.* 114; asserted by some to have become the vernacular language of the Jews after the captivity, *Whita.* 211, &c.; unknown to Jerome, *ib.* 81; the Chaldee paraphrasts, 2 *Ful.* 222, 2 *Hoop.* 474, *Whita.* 117, 214, 3 *Whitg.* 343, 344
Chaldean Christians: *v.* Nestorians.
Chalices: by whom introduced, 3 *Bec.* 262; on the vessels belonging to the Lord's supper, 4 *Bul.* 419; golden chalices, &c., often sold by godly bishops to redeem captives, and feed the hungry, *ib.* 502; Papists forbid the people to touch them, 3 *Bec.* 269; articles respecting the chalice, *Grin.* 133, 158, 159; one bequeathed by Grindal, *ib.* 460
Challenge: *v.* Jewel (Jo.), bp.
Challoner (Rich.), bp of Debra: *Calf.* 290 n
Challoner (Sir Tho.): 1 *Bec.* 232 n., *Grin.* 321, 322, 1 *Zur.* 185 n
Chalmers (A.): Biog. Dict., 2 *Brad.* xii n
Cham: *v.* Ham.
Cham: the ruler of Tartary, 2 *Ful.* 328
Cham: to chew, 3 *Tyn.* 163 (*v.* Champ)
Chamber: on praying in it, 4 *Bul.* 184
Chamber (Edw.): beneficed near Abington, *Park.* 96
Chamber (Rich.), or Chambers: notice of him, 3 *Zur.* 155 n.; his bounty, 4 *Jew.* 1302 n.; his assistance to Jewel, *ib.* vii, viii, xiii, 1196 n.; surety for Bradford at the Inner Temple, 2 *Brad.* xiii n.; he bears witness in favour of Latimer, 2 *Lat.* 421; a godly man of law, *ib.* 428; in Bread Street Counter, 2 *Hoop.* 613; in exile, *Rid.* 389, 394; at Frankfort, 4 *Jew.* xii, 3 *Zur.* 126; sent with a letter from the congregation of Frankfort to that of Strasburgh, 3 *Zur.* 296; at Zurich, *ib.* 752; letter from him and Horn to the senate of Zurich, *ib.* 126; named after his return to England, 1 *Zur.* 65, 141; his death, *ib.* 148, 155
Chambering and wantonness: 2 *Jew.* 1040, 2 *Lat.* 18, *Sand.* 138

Chamberlain (Mr), of Woodstock: 1 *Brad.* 486
Chamberlain (Sir Tho.): ambassador in the Low Countries, 3 *Zur.* 568 n
Chamberlain (Lord), or Grand Master of the king's house, 1 *Lat.* 93
Chamberlaine (......): martyred, *Poet.* 162
Chamberlayne (Robt.), a Dominican prior: *Bale* 28
Chamberleyn (Mr): process against him at Calais, 2 *Cran.* 348
Chambers (or champers?): large teeth, 2 *Jew.* 910
Chambers (Jo.), last abbot and first bp of Peterborough: 1 *Lat.* 123 n
Chambers (Jo.), chaplain to Grindal: *Grin.* 461
Chambers (Rich.): v. Chamber.
Chambers (Will.), servant and executor to Jewel, *Jew.* xxv.
Chamier (Dan.): Panstratia Catholica, *Calf.* 74 n., 287 n., 2 *Lat.* 359 n
Champ: to bite or devour, 1 *Brad.* 79 (v. Cham, Chambers)
Champion (......): one of Cranmer's chaplains, 2 *Cran.* 304, 317, 321, 339; sent to preach at Calais, *ib.* 376; letter to Cromwell in his behalf, for the living of Shepton Mallet, *ib.* 385
Champneis (Sir Jo.), lord mayor: notice of him, 2 *Cran.* 307 n.; named, *ib.* 332
Champness (Ann), alias Albright, q. v.
Chananæi: v. Canaanites.
Chance: v. Fortune.
Chancels: v. Burial.
 The chancel used for the celebration of divine service, 2 *Hoop.* 131, 1 *Jew.* 310, 311, 2 *Whitg.* 461, 2 *Zur.* 361; appropriated to clerici, 1 *Brad.* 527; the laity excluded therefrom by councils, 1 *Jew.* 198; the division disliked by Hooper, 1 *Hoop.* 492; to be maintained in order that the communicants may be separated from the rest of the people, *Rid.* 320; use of chancels upheld by Parker, *Park.* 132, 185, 186, 376, 450; to be repaired and maintained in good estate, *Grin.* 131; the choir anciently placed in the body of the church, 1 *Jew.* 311
Chancellors (Bishops'): 3 *Whitg.* 543
Chancery: v. Courts.
Chandos (The lords): v. Bridges.
Change: perilous, *Sand.* 35, 95; desired of all, *ib.* 167; what change desired by Job, *ib.* 168
Chanting: v. Music.
Chantries: 2 *Brad.* 279, 2 *Cov.* 258; many often united in one, 2 *Tyn.* 287, 288; embezzlement of their plate and other property, 2 *Cran.* 440
Chantry priests: enjoined to teach youth,

2 *Cran.* 504; made beneficed clergymen to save their pensions, 1 *Lat.* 123 n
Chapels: free chapels, 1 *Tyn.* 236; chapels royal, 3 *Whitg.* 392, &c. (and see Candles); private chapels or oratories sanctioned by the council of Agatha, &c. 1 *Jew.* 180, 184
Chaplains: what, 4 *Bul.* 116; permitted to hold pluralities, 2 *Tyn.* 336; their wicked career, 1 *Tyn.* 286 n., 2 *Tyn.* 336; given to flatter, 1 *Lat.* 381; too often idle, pluralists, &c., *Hutch.* 202; elbow-chaplains, 1 *Lat.* 264, 380
Chapman (Edm.), prebendary of Norwich: *Park.* 450
Chapmen: v. Merchants.
Chappell (Barth.): notice of him, *Poet.* xliii; a warning voice (on the signs of the times), *ib.* 465
Chapuys (......): ambassador from the emperor, 3 *Cran.* 375 n
Character: said to be conferred in ordination, *Calf.* 230; modern Romish definition of the word, 1 *Tyn.* 342 n.; conferred by the inward baptism, 2 *Tyn.* 12
Charelton (Sir W.): 2 *Brad.* 236
Charemon: was a married bishop, 3 *Jew.* 391
Charensis (Hugo): v. Hugo.
Charing, co. Kent: a lease of it obtained by Sir Rich. Sackville, *Park.* 372
Charis ($\chi\acute{\alpha}\rho\iota\varsigma$): what it signifies, 1 *Bee.* 311
Charities: inquiry concerning them, 2 *Cran.* 159
Charity: v. Love.
Chark (Will.): disputes against Campion in the Tower, *Whita.* 635 n
Charles I., emperor, commonly called Charlemagne: v. Councils (Frankfort), Creeds.
 His history, 2 *Tyn.* 262—265; made emperor, 2 *Hoop.* 238, 4 *Jew.* 672, 2 *Tyn.* 263, and styled most Christian king, 2 *Tyn.* 263; a strange legend respecting him, *ib.* 265; he erected five universities, 2 *Jew.* 981; summoned several councils, *Rog.* 204; especially one at Frankfort against images, 1 *Zur.* 156 n.; in this synod he condemned the second council of Nice, 4 *Jew.* 1049, *Rid.* 94; he called it a doltish and proud synod, *Calf.* 155; the Caroline Books, or Capitular, against images and the last mentioned council, *Calf.* 155, 4 *Jew.* 1054, 1055, *Park.* 92, 141; by whom and when composed, *Calf.* 42 n., 2 *Ful.* 23, 154, 188; their contents, *Calf.* 156—175; his account of the true ensign of Christ, *ib.* 311; quoted on the mystery of the cross, 2 *Zur.* 44 n.; he commanded that nothing should be read in the church but canonical scripture, 4 *Jew.* 1031, *Pil.* 536; church lessons chosen

at his request, 4 *Bul.* 201; he ordered that the people should offer their oblations, and receive the communion on Sunday, 1 *Jew.* 179, 4 *Jew.* 1031; no massing in his time, 1 *Hoop.* 227; he gives a reason for the consecration of the sacrament in silence, 2 *Jew.* 704; forbade that bells should be baptized, *Calf.* 16 n.; directed bishops to be chosen by the clergy and people, 1 *Whitg.* 396, 400, 403; permitted litigants to refer their disputes to the church, 3 *Whitg.* 455; his epitaph, 2 *Tyn.* 263 n.; statue of him at Zurich, 3 *Zur.* 192; mistaken for Charles the Bald, 1 *Hoop.* 524 n

Charles II., emperor: *v.* Charles II. king of France.

Charles V., emperor: heir to many kingdoms, 2 *Tyn.* 312; married by proxy to the princess Mary of England, sister to Henry VIII., *ib.*; the marriage broken off, *ib.* 313; his interviews with Wolsey, *ib.* 314 n.; he passes through England, *ib.* 315, 316 n.; pensions Wolsey, *ib.* 316; Wolsey's treachery to him, *ib.* 316, &c.; his book exposing Wolsey's conduct, *ib.* 322; he desired to hold the stirrup of pope Clement VII., 4 *Jew.* 690; the confession of Augsburgh presented to him, 2 *Zur.* 15; his proceedings, 1531—32, 2 *Cran.* 231—236; devastations committed by his army, *ib.* 233; at Genoa with many princes, *ib.* 331; spoiled the duke of Savoy, 4 *Jew.* 665, 672; his treaty with Henry VIII., 3 *Zur.* 36 n.; he invades the territory of William duke of Cleve, 2 *Cov.* 512; his wars with the German princes, 4 *Jew.* 669 n.; he takes several cities, 3 *Zur.* 638; an opposer of the gospel, *Pil.* 265, 653; the council of Trent assembled partly by his instigation, 4 *Jew.* 1102; his protest there, *ib.* 1052; the Interim drawn up at his command, 1 *Lat.* 305, 2 *Zur.* 125 n.; he deprives Constance of its privileges, 3 *Zur.* 385 n., 641 n., 642 n.; his persecuting acts, *Bale* 445, 446, 2 *Cov.* 526; he sends Scepper to carry away the lady Mary, 3 *Zur.* 568; besieges Metz, 2 *Zur.* 305; defeated by the French, 3 *Zur.* 687; recalled on his way to England, *ib.* 133; his abdication, *Grin.* 20 n.; buried in a friar's cowl, *Calf.* 287

Charles I., king of Great Britain, &c.: his birth, 2 *Zur.* 331; named as prince, *ib.* 334; he issues the fourth part of the homily against wilful rebellion, *Lit. Eliz.* 536 n

Charles Martel, ruler of France: his league with the pope, 2 *Tyn.* 260

Charles I., king of France: *v.* Charles I., emperor.

Charles II., king of France, surnamed the Bald (ultimately emperor): Bertram's book written for him, 3 *Bec.* 449, *Grin.* 73, 1 *Hoop.* 118 n., 524 n.; dedicated to him, *Rid.* 159 n.; what he wrote to pope Adrian, 4 *Jew.* 835; said to have been more fearful and cowardly than a hare, *ib.* 684

Charles III., king of France, surnamed the Simple: wanting both in strength of body and wisdom of mind, 4 *Jew.* 684

Charles IX., king of France: his accession, 2 *Zur.* 91 n.; makes peace with queen Elizabeth, 1 *Zur.* 273; cut off in his prime, *Sand.* 169; a sermon at the solemnization of his funeral at St Paul's, *ib.* 161

Charles, archduke of Austria, brother to the emperor Maximilian: suitor to queen Elizabeth, 1 *Zur.* 24, 34 n., 46, 144, 192

Charles, duke of Bourbon: chief captain to the emperor Charles V., 2 *Tyn.* 318

Charles, duke of Burgundy, called the Bold: *Grin.* 11

Charles, duke of Orleans, 2nd son of Francis I.: his proposed marriage with the princess Mary, 2 *Tyn.* 319 n

Charles (Emanuel) IV., duke of Savoy: besieges Geneva, *Grin.* 429 n., 1 *Zur.* 334 n., 2 *Zur.* 315 n

Charles, prince of Spain, son of Philip II.: 4 *Jew.* 1157, 3 *Zur.* 510 n

Charlier (Jo.), alias Gerson, *q. v.*

Charleton (Edw. lord): *v.* Cherleton.

Charms: *v.* Sorcery, Superstitions.

Charo (Hugo de S.): *v.* Hugo.

Charondas: what he says about dishonesty and lying, 1 *Bul.* 204; when he lived, 2 *Bul.* 219

Charta (Magna): *v.* Magna Charta.

Charterhouse: *v.* Carthusians, London

Chartres (Jo. of): *v.* John of Salisbury.

Chartres (Jo. vidame of): *v.* Ferriers.

Chasterlings: those who have kept themselves chaste, 3 *Bec.* 568

Chastening: *v.* Affliction.

That of God's children, 2 *Brad.* 184, 185, 222; God's chastisement is loving, 3 *Bec.* 94, &c.

Chastity: *v.* Celibacy, Marriage, Vows.

Of continency, 1 *Bul.* 419, &c.; wherein it consists, 1 *Hoop.* 375; enjoined on the priests of the old law, 3 *Tyn.* 164; commended, 2 *Lat.* 63; a singular gift of God, 3 *Jew.* 415, *Sand.* 316; it is not of man's free will, 1 *Tyn.* 430, but a gift, therefore not to be vowed, *ib.* 438, 439; the clergy of England not bound to a vow of chastity, 3 *Jew.* 395; counterfeit chastity, 4 *Jew.* 767; there is a false feigned chastity, 1 *Tyn.* 438; popish chastity, 2 *Tyn.* 123; that of the religious orders, 2 *Cran.* 147

Châtelherault, in Poictou: the French dukedom of the house of Hamilton, 1 *Zur.* 57 n
Châtillon (The lord): commissioner for peace with France, 3 *Zur.* 563, 565
Châtillon (Odet card. de): *v.* Coligni.
Châtillon (Seb.): *v.* Castellio.
Chattingdon, co. Kent: the manor granted to lord Cobham, 1 *Bec.* 264 n
Chaucer (Geof.): referred to, *Calf.* 288, *Rid.* 490, 494
Chaw: to grind with teeth, 1 *Brad.* 79
Chaws: jaws, 1 *Bul.* 4
Cheadsey (Will.): *v.* Chedsey.
Cheap: "good cheap," 1 *Tyn.* 122
Cheap, or Cheapside: *v.* London.
Check-mate: explained, *Bale* 233, 1 *Brad.* 7, 1 *Cov.* 50
Chedsey (Will.), president of C. C. C., Oxford: account of him, 2 *Cran.* 383 n., *Phil.* 168; threatens to burn the New Testament, 2 *Cran.* 383; disputes with P. Martyr, *Jew.* viii, *Rid.* 308 n.; in a disputation at Oxford, 2 *Cran.* 445 n.; present at Cranmer's condemnation, *ib.* 553; one of the examiners of Philpot, *Phil.* 50, 63, &c.; he disputes at Westminster, 4 *Jew.* 1199, 1200, 1 *Zur.* 11
Cheke (Sir Jo.): at St John's College, Cambridge, *Hutch.* i; a royal visitor of Cambridge, 2 *Brad.* 370, *Grin.* 194, *Rid.* 169; at a disputation, *Grin.* ii; a Greek scholar, *Pil.* iv; he translates a book De re militari, ascribed to the emperor Leo III., and dedicates it to Henry VIII., *Park.* 90, *Rid.* 93; named, 2 *Hoop.* xix, *Rid.* 389, 394, 2 *Zur.* 69, 3 *Zur.* 115, 449; tutor of king Edward VI., 3 *Zur.* 81, 465; secretary to the king, 2 *Cran.* 429, 438, 439, 440; made a knight, 3 *Zur.* 438 n.; the king prays for his recovery, and obtains it, *ib.* 456 n.; the Articles submitted to him, 2 *Cran.* xi; the supposed translator into Latin of Cranmer's Answer to Gardiner, 1 *Cran.* (2); indicted and sent to the Tower, 2 *Cran.* 441, 3 *Zur.* 142 n., 684; in exile at Strasburgh, *Jew.* xiii; again apprehended, 3 *Zur.* 132 n.; his recantation, repentance, and death, *ib.* 117 n., 132 n.; his remarks on the hurt of sedition, 2 *Cran.* 195 n.; letters to Bullinger, 3 *Zur.* 140, 145; letter to Calvin, *ib.* 142; letters to Parker, *Park.* 2, 39, 43, 48; letter to him, *Rid.* 331; letter to him and Cecil, 2 *Cran.* 429
Cheke (Peter): his wife, godmother to a child in prison, 1 *Lat.* 335; his daughter Mary, 2 *Bec.* 480 n
Chelius (Ulric): guardian of Bucer's children, 2 *Cran.* 435, *Park.* 46 n., 3 *Zur.* 27 n., 361, 364

Chelmsford, co. Essex: a martyr there, *Poet.* 170
Chelsea, co. Middlesex: the image of St Mary of Walsingham and other idols burned there, 2 *Brad.* 2 n., 2 *Lat.* 393 n.; Sir Thomas More's house, 1 *Tyn.* 33, 35; Anne of Cleves died at this place, 3 *Bec.* 74 n
Chemnitius (Mart.): Examen Concil. Trident., 1 *Hoop.* 47 n., *Jew.* xxxv, 2 *Lat.* 226 n.; gives the decree of the council about communion in both kinds, 3 *Jew.* 203, 204; against an argument of Eckius for the denial of the cup to the laity, 4 *Jew.* 766; he says the council held disputations, for seven months together about the justification of faith and works, *ib.* 948; mentions the opinion of Andradius that the heathen philosophers had faith, 3 *Jew.* 584
Chenies, co. Bucks.: 2 *Bec.* 622 n
Cheny (Sir Jo.): persecuted in the time of Rich. II., *Bale* 11
Cheny (Marg.): burned, *Bale* 509
Cheyne (Jo.): a commissioner, *Jew.* xv.
Cheyney (Rich.), bp of Gloucester: account of him, *Phil.* 170; sometime archdeacon of Hereford, *Phil.* 64, 3 *Zur.* 373 n; a disputant in the convocation, Oct. 1553, *Phil.* 170, 183; letter from him to Cecil, *Park.* 138 n.; letter to him, *ib.* 213; he avows Lutheran views respecting the eucharist, 4 *Jew.* 1271, 1 *Zur.* 185; Parker complains of him, *Park.* 332
Cheyney (Sir Tho.), or Cheney: grantee of Feversham abbey, 2 *Cran.* 374 n.; also of Davington nunnery, *ib.* 313 n.; lord warden of the Cinque Ports, *ib.* 441; privy councillor to [Henry VIII.], Edward VI., Mary, and Elizabeth, 2 *Cran.* 531, *Park.* 46, 1 *Zur.* 5 n
Cher (H. de St): *v.* Hugo.
Cheregatus (......): legate à latere, 4 *Jew.* 737, 738
Cherleton (Edw. de), lord Cherleton of Powys: recaptures lord Cobham, *Bale* 52
Cherubim: what they are, 3 *Bul.* 338; made by Moses in the tabernacle, 2 *Bul.* 154, *Calf.* 159, 2 *Jew.* 645; no precedent for images, 2 *Cran.* 178, 2 *Jew.* 646, 655
Cherubinus (Laert.): Bullarium, *Jew.* xxxv, 4 *Jew.* 1132
Cheshire: Bradford's farewell to Cheshire, 1 *Brad.* 448; his labours there, 2 *Brad.* xxvi; divers gentlemen of the county committed to ward for refusing to answer the bishop on oath, *Park.* 329
Chesible: a vestment, 3 *Jew.* 177
Chester: called West-chester, 1 *Brad.* 454, *Pil.* xv, 481 n., 487; slaughter of the British

monks, *Bale* 189, *Calf.* 306, *Pil.* 516 (*v.* Augustine of Canterbury); the bishops of Lichfield were sometimes called bishops of Chester, 2 *Cran.* 271 n., 274 n.; the rood of Chester, *Calf.* 35, 2 *Ful.* 210; martyrdom there, *Pra. Eliz.* 373 n.; a benefice annexed to the newly erected bishoprick, *Park.* 100; a seditious paper cast abroad there, *ib.* 163 n.; answered by bishop Pilkington, 2 *Ful.* 3, *Pil.* 481 n., 487

Chester (Sir Will.): sheriff of London, 2 *Brad.* 253

Chests: a common coffer for alms recommended in every parish, 2 *Tyn.* 73; articles and injunctions respecting alms-chests, *Grin.* 134, 158, 173, 2 *Hoop.* 149; the chest for the keeping of the register book, *Grin.* 134, 158

Chevalier (Ant. Rod. le): *v.* Cavallerius.

Chevenay (Will.), parson of Kingston by Canterbury: 2 *Cran.* 364

Chevening, co. Kent: *v.* Astall (R.)
 The benefice of Cheving, 2 *Cran.* 255; insane proceedings of Tho. Baschurche, 2 *Cran.* 319

Chevisance: enterprise, achievement, bargain, 1 *Jew.* 197, 2 *Tyn.* 297, 299

Chiavenna, Switzerland: meaning of the name, 2 *Zur.* 111; plague there, 1563, *ib.* 110 n., 113; heresy there, *ib.* 185

Chichele (Hen.), abp of Canterbury: succeeds archbishop Arundel, *Bale* 9 n., 52

Chichester: the diocese interdicted by bishop Ralph, 2 *Tyn.* 295; martyrs at Chichester, *Poet.* 162, 170

Chichester (Sir Jo.): *Grin.* 299

Chiete (The bp of): 2 *Cran.* 231

Childebert I., king of France: summoned councils at Paris and Orleans, *Rog.* 205

Childeric III., king of France: said to have been deposed by pope Zacharias, 2 *Cran.* 12, 4 *Jew.* 672, 681, and made a monk, 2 *Tyn.* 261

Children, Infants: *v.* Parents, Prayers, Youth.
 (*a*) What a child is, 3 *Bec.* 607; who are "little children," 2 *Tyn.* 247, 248; children said to have that which their fathers had; thus the later Jews are said to have been brought out of Egypt, *Pil.* 135; he who would have virtuous children must be cautious in choosing his wife, 2 *Bec.* 346, 347; the begetting of children, 1 *Bul.* 400, 408; why God gives them, 2 *Bec.* 4; the children of God's people, *ib.* 5; what is promised to the children of the godly, *Now.* (12,) 125; they are counted among the faithful, 4 *Bul.* 344; God will care for the children of those who suffer in his cause, 1 *Brad.* 398; those of unbelievers must be left to the judgment of God, 2 *Bec.* 214; children punished for the sin of their fathers, *Now.* (11,) 125; how this must be understood, 2 *Bec.* 74, 75

 (*b*) Infants are not free from sin, 1 *Brad.* 57 (and see Sin, Original); of their baptism (*q. v.*); why the Pelagians denied it, 4 *Bul.* 375—381; of their confessing or believing, *ib.* 385; remarks on the naming of them, 2 *Jew.* 1108; on sin remaining in them after baptism, 2 *Bul.* 417; on the salvation of infants departing without baptism, 2 *Bec.* 214, &c., 1 *Brad.* 90, 4 *Bul.* 372, 1 *Hoop.* 129, 1 *Whitg.* 521, &c.; on the salvation of those who died uncircumcised, *Whita.* 529, 530; on their salvation without faith, 1 *Brad.* 66, 67; elect infants, 2 *Brad.* 131; infants formerly received the Lord's supper, 1 *Jew.* 6, 250, but it was not intended for them, 4 *Bul.* 426 (see further under Supper of the Lord); their salvation depends not on sacraments, *Whita.* 530

 (*c*) How they should be brought up, 1 *Tyn.* 199, 391 (and see Education); how fathers should care for them, 2 *Jew.* 835—837; examples of bringing them up, 3 *Bec.* 234; the earnest study of the Gentiles for bringing up theirs, 2 *Bec.* 5; how and what they should be taught, 2 *Jew.* 1127; precepts for their instruction, 1 *Bul.* 293; injunctions respecting it, *Grin.* 124, 137; they must be brought up in the knowledge of God's word, 2 *Bec.* 348, 349, in Christian doctrine, *ib.* 378, in religion, 1 *Bul.* 291; good manners must be taught, 2 *Bec.* 349, 350, 1 *Bul.* 294; they must be sent to school, 2 *Bec.* 350; good books must be provided for them, *ib.* 351; chapters of the Bible to be read by them at dinner and supper, *ib.*; their plays and pastimes, *ib.* 349; they must be punished if they do amiss, *ib.* 353, 354; they should be corrected with stripes, 1 *Bul.* 296, 1 *Lat.* 501; many ruined by indulgence, 1 *Bul.* 296; their custom of swearing reprehended, 1 *Bec.* 362; company-keeping for them, 2 *Bec.* 349; they must learn an occupation, 1 *Bul.* 294; the lures of ambition should not be placed before them, 1 *Tyn.* 199

 (*d*) Their duty, 1 *Bec.* 287, 1 *Bul.* 297; children may have faith and please God, 2 *Bec.* 211, 212; they may have the Holy Ghost, *ib.* 213; their duty to their parents, with probations of scripture, *ib.* 519; they must honour and obey their parents, *ib.* 357, &c., 1 *Tyn.* 168; what it is for them to honour their parents, 2 *Bec.* 357, 358;

what it is to obey, *ib.* 358; reasons why they should so honour and obey, *ib.* 358, 359; their obedience, 1 *Tyn.* 168; the limit thereof, 2 *Lat.* 158, 164, 203; they must not follow their blind judgment in matrimony, nor marry without their parents' consent, 2 *Bec.* 355, 358, 371, 3 *Bec.* 199, 532, 1 *Lat.* 170, *Sand.* 50, 281, 325, 326, 455, 1 *Tyn.* 169, 170, 199, 3 *Zur.* 315; the sick man's exhortation to his children, 3 *Bec.* 131, 132

(*e*) Children under fourteen were, in old times, admitted to be readers in the church, 4 *Jew.* 911; their singing on Palm Sunday, what it signified, 1 *Bec.* 113, 114, 116; children made cardinals, archdeacons and deans, 2 *Cran.* 39

Children of God: *v.* Christians.
Chiliasts: *v.* Millennium.
Chillingworth (Will.): Relig. of Prot., 2 *Ful.* 331 n
Chilo: his counsel, 1 *Jew.* 91, 98
Chilton, co. Suffolk: two places so called, 2 *Zur.* 180
Chimere: an episcopal vestment, *Park.* 475; formerly scarlet, now black, 3 *Zur.* 271 n.; a scarlet one worn by Hooper, *ib.* 271 n., 585 n
Chimney: a text appropriate to one, 1 *Bec.* 63
China: a history of China translated from the Spanish by R. Parke, 1588, *Poet.* xxvii.
Chipley, co. Suffolk: a manor belonging to Stoke college, *Park.* 19
Chiromancy: condemned, 1 *Hoop.* 329
Chisleu, or Casleu: a Jewish month, *Pil.* 287
Chittenden (Nich.): *v.* Sheterden.
Chobham, co. Surrey: the retirement of archbishop Hethe, 2 *Zur.* 182 n
Choinecouch: chin-cough, 1 *Jew.* 344
Choir: *v.* Chancel.
Cholmley (Sir Roger): late chief justice, *Rid.* 163, 164; one of the commissioners for the examination of Philpot, *Phil.* 4
Chop (At the first): 1 *Tyn.* 241, 468
Chopological: 1 *Tyn.* 304, 308
Chopping and changing: *Sand.* 168
Chorazin: denounced by Christ, 3 *Bul.* 112, 2 *Hoop.* 299
Chorepiscopi: on their order, 4 *Bul.* 112, 4 *Jew.* 801, *Rog.* 329, 2 *Whitg.* 329, 374, 433, 3 *Whitg.* 270—272; mentioned by the council of Ancyra, 1 *Whitg.* 220, and in an epistle ascribed to Damasus, *ib.* 532
Choristers: *v.* Music.
Injunction respecting those at York, *Grin.* 152; inquiry about them in the province of Canterbury, *ib.* 180

Chremes: 4 *Jew.* 1260
Chria (χρεία): 4 *Bul.* 232
Chrism: *v.* Confirmation, Unction.
Chrismatories: vessels in which the chrism was kept, 3 *Bec.* 247; ordered to be destroyed, *Grin.* 135, 159
Chrisom: a white vesture put upon the newly baptized, 2 *Brad.* 383, *Calf.* 224, *Lit. Edw.* 112, 116, 149; used also in Romish confirmation, 1 *Tyn.* 225 n., and see 235
CHRIST (JESUS) our Lord: *v.* Prayer (The Lord's), Prayers.
  i. *What he is, &c.*
  ii. *His two natures, and his names JESUS, CHRIST, IMMANUEL.*
  iii. *His three great offices.*
  iv. *Other names and titles.*
  v. *Types of him.*
  vi. *His career, from the incarnation.*
  vii. *Christ and the church.*

i. *What he is, and his acts generally, &c.:* what he is, 2 *Bec.* 22, 3 *Bec.* 607, 1 *Hoop.* 16; A DECLARATION OF CHRIST AND HIS OFFICE, by bishop Hooper, 1 *Hoop.* 1; Christ as confessed in the creed (*q. v.*), 1 *Brad.* 142; a confession concerning him, 3 *Bul.* 242; of Christ; verses by W. Warner, *Poet.* 378; verses to Jesus Christ, by Tim. Kendall, *ib.* 384; "Christ is the only Son of God," verses, 2 *Cov.* 553; "I call on thee, Lord Jesus Christ," verses, *ib.* 560; two Latin verses on the knowledge of Christ, *Rid.* 124; modi quibus Christus se nobis exhibet; verses, *Pra. Eliz.* 416; he manifests the Father, 2 *Tyn.* 26, 176, 183; he is all in all, 1 *Tyn.* 19, 98, 110, 297—299; made all things to us, 2 *Jew.* 1042; all sufficiency for us in him, 1 *Bec.* 178; in him are found true nobility, pleasure, strength, praise, and wisdom, 1 *Cov.* 513: he is the fulness of all, 1 *Brad.* 280; commendation of him, 2 *Bec.* 444; none to be compared to him, 2 *Hoop.* 414; his various names, titles, and designations, *Bale* 548, 1 *Jew.* 526, *Sand.* 8, 2 *Tyn.* 180, 182 (see iv. below); he has compared himself to many of his creatures, *Calf.* 46, 47; he is the Holy One, *Pil.* 262, 2 *Tyn.* 180, 182, just, or righteous, 3 *Bul.* 218 (see also Righteousness in iv. below); the righteousness, truth and virtue of God, 1 *Bec.* 150; he came not to destroy the law, 2 *Tyn.* 38, but was the perfection, fulness, end, and accomplishment of the law, 4 *Bul.* 191, 2 *Hoop.* 26, which he fulfilled for us, 2 *Bul.* 249, 1 *Hoop.* 412, 2 *Lat.* 137, 147, 193;

he has taken off all burdens, 2 *Bul.* 293; blesses those with the gospel whom the law has condemned, 2 *Bec.* 630; no respecter of persons, 1 *Lat.* 545; his wonderful love, *Sand.* 298; his great love manifested, 1 *Brad.* 74; his gentleness towards us, 1 *Bec.* 329; his alluring kindness, 2 *Bec.* 446; his readiness to hear and help, 1 *Tyn.* 293; a psalm of rejoicing for the wonderful love of Christ, by W. Hunnis, *Poet.* 157; his work, 1 *Bec.* 51, &c., 2 *Tyn.* 152, 153, 156, 168—170; Christ and the pope compared, 2 *Tyn.* 273; THE ACTS OF CHRIST AND ANTICHRIST, by Tho. Becon, 3 *Bec.* 498; his life as contrasted with that of Antichrist, *ib.* 504, &c.; his doctrine as so contrasted, *ib.* 520; no image may be made of him, 1 *Bul.* 230, *Calf.* 45, 46; he is falsely asserted to have sent his picture to Abgarus, *Calf.* 41; it is said that Tiberius wished Christ to be numbered amongst the gods, *Pil.* 141, 683, 684; esteemed by the Turks almost as highly as by many Christians, 2 *Tyn.* 5; how he may be denied, 2 *Brad.* 331; he will deny those who deny him, 2 *Lat.* 440; on blasphemy against the Son of man, 2 *Bul.* 422; if we believe, his merits are ours, 1 *Lat.* 461, 2 *Lat.* 138, 140, 149, 193, 194, 1 *Tyn.* 79; they alone obtain remission and justification, 1 *Lat.* 521, 2 *Lat.* 138, 2 *Tyn.* 76, and salvation, *Sand.* 446, 447; his deeds have purchased a reward for us, 1 *Tyn.* 116; he has merited heaven for us, 1 *Lat.* 488, 2 *Lat.* 74; he has obtained all things for his people, 1 *Tyn.* 15, 19, 65, 433, 3 *Tyn.* 278; against plucking away our trust in his merits, with sentences and examples of scripture, 1 *Bec.* 420, &c.; how we may apply his benefits to ourselves, 2 *Lat.* 139; on faith in the Son of God, 1 *Bul.* 127; he is received by faith, 2 *Bec.* 295, &c., 3 *Bul.* 36, and not by works, 3 *Bul.* 37; probations out of the old fathers that he is received with the heart through faith, 3 *Bec.* 430, &c.; through faith we are engrafted in him, 2 *Bec.* 632; all true Israelites trusted in him, 1 *Cov.* 50; to see him (by faith) maketh blessed, 2 *Lat.* 4; not they who saw him with their bodily eyes were blessed, but they who saw him by faith 2 *Jew.* 1078; we may have firm faith and trust in him against death, 2 *Bec.* 576, 577; faith in Christ necessary to our support and comfort at that time, 2 *Cov.* 84, 85; to know him truly is the gift of God, 2 *Bec.* 428; a dialogue between Christ and a sinner, by W. Hunnis, *Poet.* 154

ii. *His two natures:*

(*a*) His divinity and humanity, 2 *Bec.* 26, 1 *Brad.* 142, *Calf.* 151, &c., 2 *Cran.* 473, 2 *Hoop.* 17, 27, 73, 130, 427, 454, 1 *Jew.* 482, &c., 497, &c., 1 *Lat.* 205, *Lit. Edw.* 507, 508, (556, 557), *Rog.* 53, 2 *Tyn.* 145; figures of scripture denoting his godhead and manhood, *Hutch.* 20; his two natures reflected in the literal and spiritual senses of scripture, *Whita.* 404; he was in the form, i. e. the nature, of God, and took the form of a servant, i. e. the nature of man, 3 *Jew.* 261; becoming man he retained his godhead, 1 *Hoop.* 17; the two natures united, 3 *Bul.* 261, 266, 267, 271, 4 *Bul.* 455, but not confounded, 3 *Bul.* 262, 264, 4 *Bul.* 456, 2 *Hoop.* 130; he is equal to the Father as touching his godhead, inferior to the Father as touching his manhood, *Phil.* 56; as man his knowledge is finite, though as God infinite, 2 *Lat.* 45; his humanity local, his godhead everywhere, 2 *Bec.* 272, 1 *Bul.* 151, 4 *Bul.* 453; the old fathers declare this, 2 *Bec.* 272, &c.

(*b*) His divinity (see also Homoüsion, and the title Lord, in iv. below):—he is a distinct person in the Godhead, *Hutch.* 132, 133, 143; very and eternal God, 1 *Brad.* 83, 2 *Brad.* 263, &c., 3 *Bul.* 18, 247, *Hutch.* 112, 2 *Lat.* 72, *Now.* (29), 145; not a creature, *Hutch.* 188; against the heresy of those who deny him to be God, with sentences and examples of scripture, 1 *Bec.* 406, &c.; his divinity proved, 2 *Bec.* 19, 20, *Rog.* 46; testified by the scriptures of the Old and New Testaments, 1 *Cov.* 222; he is declared by St John to be God, *ib.* 223; the true God and eternal life, *ib.*; all the attributes of Deity ascribed to him in scripture, *Hutch.* 187; he is eternal, *ib.* 190; his eternal pre-existence, 2 *Brad.* 264, 265; he was in the bosom of the Father, 1 *Cov.* 223; he was before Abraham, *ib.* 222; he came down from heaven, *ib.* 223; he is immutable, *Hutch.* 189; as to his deity he is omnipresent, *ib.* 33, 189 (and see in *a.* above); he is with the faithful always, 1 *Lat.* 494; not bodily, but by his Spirit and power, 1 *Hoop.* 21, 1 *Lat.* 530; knows all things as to his divinity, *Hutch.* 91, 191, 2 *Lat.* 45; he is almighty, 1 *Hoop.* 18, *Hutch.* 192; his might declared by creation, &c. 1 *Hoop.* 18; he created all things, 1 *Cov.* 222, *Hutch.* 62, 63, 190, *Lit. Edw.* 501, (550), and governs all things, *Hutch.* 191; he hath all power in heaven and earth, 1 *Cov.* 222; his divinity is also proved by his doctrine and miracles, *ib.*; by his own declaration, that we must believe in him, *ib.*; by his resurrection, *ib.* 346, 348, 406, for he is Lord over death, therefore very God, 1 *Lat.* 548, 550, 2 *Lat.* 67; his godhead is shewn by the declaration of Thomas, "My Lord and my God," 1 *Cov.* 222; by his ascension up to heaven, and sending the Holy Spirit, *ib.* 407, 408; he is the sole author of goodness, 1 *Bec.* 113 (as to his holiness, and his love, see i. above); he is the Son of God, 1 *Bul.* 127, 2 *Lat.* 75, 76; the eternal and co-equal Son of God, 2 *Lat.* 99; consubstantial and co-essential with the Father and the Holy Ghost, 1 *Bul.* 128, 3 *Bul.* 242, *Rog.* 201; his consubstantiality with the Father denied by Arians, *Phil.* 299 n., but proved from texts wrested by them, *Whita.* 481; why he is called the only Son of God, 2 *Bec.* 24, 25, *Now.* (37), 154; he alone is the Son of God by nature, we by adoption, 2 *Bec.* 145, 3 *Bec.* 615, 3 *Bul.* 247; called the first-begotten, 2 *Bul.* 131; his eternal generation, *Hutch.* 20, 123, 161, 162; none can declare it, *Phil.* 299; he is begotten unspeakably from everlasting, 3 *Bul.* 238; not the son of the Holy Ghost, *Hutch.* 149; he is the image of God, *ib.* 3, &c.; his glory, 3 *Bul.* 52; all things should give way to it, 1 *Cov.* 494; his glory in the church, *Pil.* 148; he is to be worshipped, *Hutch.* 191; how he is to be adored, 1 *Jew.* 530; to be prayed to, *Hutch.* 192; what his godhead profits, 2 *Bec.* 25; honoured by professors of the truth, but not by Papists, *Sand.* 289, 290, who in effect deny it, *Pil.* 142; a prayer to him, 3 *Bec.* 76; a confession of sins to him, *ib.* 16, &c. (as to prayer in his name, see iii. c. 2, below).

(*c*) His manhood (see also his incarnation and ascension in vi. below):—of his true humanity, 1 *Bec.* 74, 318, 406, 410, &c., 2 *Bec.* 26, 3 *Bec.* 137, 3 *Bul.* 254, 1 *Cov.* 257, 260, 1 *Hoop.* 113, 2 *Hoop.* 9, 13, *Hutch.* 143, &c., 1 *Jew.* 461, 472, 2 *Lat.* 101, 103, 110, 114, 115, 136, 182, 183, *Rog.* 50; it is denied by some, 2 *Lat.* 99; answer to those who deny it, 1 *Bec.* 318, &c.; against the heresy of those that deny him to have taken flesh, with sentences and examples of scripture, *ib.* 410, &c.; why he took our nature, *Hutch.* 154; he became man that man's mortal nature might be exalted to an immortal life, 2 *Cov.* 71; he is less than the Father as touching his manhood, *Phil.* 56, 3 *Tyn.* 232; his manhood is a creature, and therefore not omnipresent, 3 *Tyn.*

232, 254 (see *a.* above); it is like ours in all respects, sin alone excepted, *Phil.* 208, 209, 3 *Tyn.* 254; he was without sin, 2 *Bul.* 195, 201, 2 *Hoop.* 13, 124, 454, 2 *Lat.* 5, 110, *Rog.* 132; he took both body and soul, *Hutch.* 144; what his body is, 3 *Bec.* 612, 3 *Bul.* 248; no dead carcase, 1 *Brad.* 106; errors touching it, 4 *Bul.* 277, 1 *Jew.* 481, 497; on his body being said to be corporally, or naturally, in us, 1 *Jew.* 476, &c.; he has no body invisible, 1 *Hoop.* 112; that his body is to be worshipped, or honoured, and how, *Hutch.* 206, 255; how to make a difference of the Lord's body, 4 *Bul.* 470; he has a reasonable soul, 3 *Bul.* 259; he had, as a man, his own will, 3 *Tyn.* 224; as man he knew not the time of his coming, *Sand.* 352; he received our infirmities, 1 *Hoop.* 263, 1 *Lat.* 226; he was tormented in his manhood only, 1 *Hoop.* 17, 1 *Lat.* 223; made perfect by afflictions, *Phil.* 253; his voluntary humiliation, *Pil.* 341; his humility and lowliness, 2 *Bec.* 446, 447; considered by Tyndale to be the "least in the kingdom of heaven," 2 *Tyn.* 232, 3 *Tyn.* 116; what profit we have by his humanity, 2 *Bec.* 27, 28

(*d*) The power of his Name, *Calf.* 83; meaning of the name Jesus, 1 *Bec.* 51, 74, 312, 2 *Bec.* 21, 3 *Bec.* 136, 615, 1 *Bul.* 128, 2 *Lat.* 144, *Now.* (35), 151, *Sand.* 283, 1 *Tyn.* 182, 321, 2 *Tyn.* 152, 182, 227, *Whita.* 24; on bowing at that name, 2 *Ful.* 204, 3 *Whitg.* 384, 389, 390, 2 *Zur.* 161; what the name Christ or Messiah means, and why he is so called, 2 *Bec.* 22, 3 *Bec.* 136, 615, 1 *Bul.* 129, 326, 3 *Bul.* 21, 23, 283, 289, 296, 4 *Bul.* 228, *Lit. Edw.* 511, (559), *Now.* (35), 152, *Sand.* 283, 1 *Tyn.* 228, 2 *Tyn.* 153, 180, 182; it imports prophet, priest, and king, *Whita.* 21; proofs that Jesus is the Christ, 2 *Lat.* 75; the Greek monogram compounded of XP, 2 *Ful.* 140; the name Immanuel, 1 *Bul.* 130, 2 *Tyn.* 182

iii. *His three great offices.*

(*a*) He is our Prophet, Priest, and King, 3 *Bec.* 615, 2 *Hoop.* 29; these offices viewed in their antagonism to popery, *Whita.* 21; king and priest, 2 *Bul.* 158; priest, king, and Lord, 2 *Cran.* 87

(*b*) He is our Prophet and teacher (see also vi. *a.* below):—he is a Prophet, 2 *Bec.* 23, *Now.* (36), 153, *Sand.* 284, *Whita.* 22; the teacher of the church, 3 *Bul.* 283, 289, *Calf.* 289; our schoolmaster, 1 *Bec.* 321; the only schoolmaster, *Pil.* 81; that he is the alone teacher of truth, with probations out of scripture, 3 *Bec.* 312, &c.; chief contents of his doctrine, 1 *Bul.* 52; special points of it, 1 *Cov.* 74; it is perfect and sufficient for our salvation, 3 *Bec.* 260; he sends his hearers to the scriptures, and not to the church, 2 *Cran.* 18; his doctrine as contrasted with that of Antichrist, 3 *Bec.* 520, &c.; the benefit we have by Christ being our prophet, 2 *Bec.* 23, 24

(*c*) That he is a Priest, and of his priesthood, 1 *Brad.* 7, 2 *Brad.* 312, 3 *Bul.* 285, 1 *Ful.* 241, 1 *Hoop.* 19, 48, *Hutch.* 46, 49, *Now.* (36), 153, *Sand.* 27, 284, *Whita.* 23 (and see his passion in vi.); he is alone our priest, 2 *Bec.* 23; a priest after the order of Melchisedec, (*q.v.*) *Sand.* 411, 2 *Tyn.* 283; our great high-priest, 3 *Bul.* 282, 4 *Bul.* 96, 250, 1 *Cov.* 247, *Phil.* 395, 1 *Tyn.* 208; to be consulted as such, *Pil.* 679; typified by the high priest of Israel, *Whita.* 254, 2 *Whitg.* 346; his priesthood compared with Aaron's, 2 *Bul.* 154; comparison of him with the priests of the old law, 1 *Bec.* 334; not of the ordinary priesthood, 3 *Jew.* 324; he is the priest of the new testament, *Whita.* 423; his priesthood unchangeable or untransferable, 3 *Bul.* 216, 287, 2 *Ful.* 245; how he executes the office, 3 *Bul.* 283; blesseth, sacrificeth and sanctifieth, *ib.* 284; the profit of his priesthood, 2 *Bec.* 23

— (1) His sacrifice (*v.* Sacrifice):— how God's word teacheth of it, 2 *Brad.* 277, 2 *Cov.* 256; he is the sacrifice and the sacrificer, 1 *Brad.* 7, 2 *Brad.* 312, *Phil.* 408; he suffered willingly, 2 *Bec.* 30; he was made sin for us, i. e. a sacrifice for sin, or a sin-offering, *ib.* 575, 1 *Tyn.* 377; he took our sins upon himself, 1 *Lat.* 223, 330, 342, 2 *Lat.* 5, 113; he suffered for man's sin as though himself a sinner, 1 *Hoop.* 48, and was put to death by our sins, 1 *Bec.* 177; his humiliation, passion, and death, a proof of the greatness of sin, 1 *Brad.* 63; his sacrifice not Levitical nor carnal, but spiritual, 2 *Hoop.* 29; he is the only sacrifice for sin, 2 *Bec.* 250, 3 *Bec.* 138, 139, 265, 2 *Bul* 159, 166, *Rid.* 52; our satisfaction, 3 *Bul.* 91; the only satisfaction, 2 *Bec.* 574, 575, 1 *Brad.* 48, 2 *Cov.* 356, &c., 369, 370, 373, *Sand.* 221; opinions of Romanists destructive of this faith, 2 *Cov.* 358—360; he made satisfaction by his death, 1 *Hoop.* 48, a full satisfaction for all manner of sins, 2 *Hoop.* 123, 500, an everlasting satisfaction, 1 *Tyn.* 228, 267; his one sacrifice was offered once for all, 1 *Brad.* 393, 2 *Cran.* 150, 1 *Hoop.* 48, 2 *Hoop.* 123, 500, 501, 2 *Jew.* 718, &c., 738, 1131, 1 *Lat.* 73, 74, 253, 522, 2 *Lat.* 259, 292, *Pil.* 621, 622, *Rid.* 207, 211, 1 *Tyn.* 370, 3 *Tyn.* 149; it is all sufficient, 2 *Bec.* 247, 248; perfect and complete, 1 *Brad.* 393, 2 *Brad.* 313; finished upon the cross, *Rog.* 296—301; never to be repeated, *Coop.* 96, *Rid.* 178; its virtue never ceases, 1 *Bec.* 53; it endures for ever, 3 *Bec.* 258, 2 *Bul.* 195, 198, 1 *Jew.* 128, 129, 167, 1 *Lat.* 73; testimonies out of the old fathers, that his only sacrifice is sufficient without repetition, 3 *Bec.* 421, &c.; his sacrifice sufficient for the whole world, 2 *Bul.* 200, 1 *Lat.* 522, 2 *Lat.* 292, *Rog.* 297, (see also Redeemer in iv. below, and the head Redemption); his blood sufficient to cleanse all the sins that have ever been committed, 1 *Lat.* 417; Christ is the alone propitiatory sacrifice for all the sins of the world, with probations out of scripture, 3 *Bec.* 311, 312; he died for all, *Sand.* 79; he suffered for us, 1 *Lat.* 21; his sacrifice was made for all the elect, *Rid.* 52; he suffered for the fathers, 3 *Bul.* 42; for man only, not for the angels, 2 *Lat.* 123; not for the impenitent, 1 *Lat.* 331; yet Latimer says that he shed as much blood for Judas as for Peter, *ib.* 521; for whose sins his death is a satisfaction, 1 *Bec.* 102; he made satisfaction for all our sins, 2 *Cran.* 93; for the sins of all believers, 2 *Tyn.* 154, 218; to them alone his death is profitable, 2 *Lat.* 3; the benefit of his sacrifice, *Lit. Edw.* 500, (549); he is the only reconciliator, 3 *Bul.* 214; his death the means of our reconciliation, 1 *Hoop.* 257; he has thereby fulfilled that which the law requires, 2 *Bec.* 631, and put an end to legal ceremonies, 1 *Bul.* 59, *Calf.* 123; he alone is our propitiation, 1 *Brad.* 49, 2 *Bul.* 154, 196, 3 *Bul.* 391, 2 *Tyn.* 153; his atonement, *Bale* 569; he has taken and cleansed our sins, 1 *Bul*, 107; he alone purges our hands and our hearts, *Sand.* 139; he is the washing of the faithful, 2 *Bul.* 159; his blood, *ib.* 215; it purges, *ib.* 202, 1 *Tyn.* 285, 360; it is the only purgatory, 2 *Bec.* 381, 3 *Bec.* 66, 228; it alone purges from sin, 1 *Ful.* 429, 1 *Lat.* 343, 422, 2 *Lat.* 309; it purges from all sin, 3 *Bul.* 391, 2 *Cov.* 378; not from original sin only, but from all sins, and from both pain and fault; statement of this, with probations out of scripture, 3 *Bec.* 309, &c.; looking carnally on his blood would not avail us, 2 *Lat.* 364; he is the only remedy of all sins and sickness, 2 *Hoop.* 171; his sacrifice makes clean for ever, 2 *Bec.* 450, &c.; he died to

CHRIST. iii. iv.

procure peace, *Sand.* 288; his body given to be slain, not eaten, 1 *Hoop.* 156; he has by one oblation made perfect the faithful, 1 *Bec.* 96, 3 *Bec.* 368; the remembrance of his death makes us thankful to God the Father, 1 *Bec.* 65; the priesthood and sacrifice of Christ dishonoured and blasphemed by Rome, 2 *Brad.* 277, 2 *Cov.* 256, 1 *Hoop.* 500, 1 *Lat.* 231, *Sand.* 27; his death must not be depressed, 1 *Bec.* 337; how his passion is treated by Popish preachers, 2 *Tyn.* 12 (see also Mass, Priests, Sacrifice); his oblation said by Harding to be threefold,—in type, on the cross, in the sacrament, 2 *Jew.* 708, 709; comparison between Christ and the massmongers, 2 *Bec.* 451, 3 *Bec.* 267

— (2) He is our Mediator, Intercessor, Advocate:—Christ is our only mediator, 1 *Bec.* 55, 2 *Brad.* 294, 1 *Bul.* 130, 2 *Bul.* 192, 4 *Bul.* 68, 173, 2 *Cov.* 272, 1 *Hoop.* 34, 2 *Lat.* 234, 359, *Now.* (66), 186, 1 *Tyn.* 287; mediator or atonement-maker, 3 *Tyn.* 275; the alone mediator and intercessor, 2 *Bec.* 380, 381, 2 *Lat.* 85, 1 *Tyn.* 385; mediator and advocate, 3 *Bec.* 140; mediator, intercessor, and advocate, 2 *Bec.* 459, 460; mediator between God and man, 2 *Hoop.* 34, 1 *Jew.* 97; we must come unto the Father by him alone, 1 *Bec.* 150, 151; God accepts us and our works through Christ, 1 *Lat.* 167, 420, 453, 2 *Lat.* 85, 140; all good things are given to us of God for his sake, 1 *Bec.* 73, 83, 2 *Bec.* 45; all the promises were made in and for him, 1 *Hoop.* 257; all heavenly treasures are given in him, 1 *Bul.* 156; no mercy comes to us except through him, 1 *Tyn.* 11; our entrance into heaven comes only by him, 1 *Bec.* 115 (see Way, in iv. below); he is the mediator of the old and the new testament, 1 *Hoop.* 34; mediator of redemption and intercession, 3 *Bul.* 213; that he is the alone mediator and intercessor of the faithful, with probations out of scripture, 3 *Bec.* 308, 309; that he is the alone intercessor with God, and of his intercession, 3 *Bul.* 212—219, 284, 1 *Hoop.* 33, 34, 2 *Hoop.* 34, 1 *Tyn.* 385, 2 *Tyn.* 168, 169; the doctrine of Christ's intercession to be preached diligently, 1 *Hoop.* 34; his church is bound thereto, *ib.*; he prayed for his whole church, *ib.* 72; at God's right hand he ministers to saints, *ib.* 34; he alone is our advocate with the Father, 3 *Bul.* 218, 1 *Cov.* 384, 385, 2 *Cov.* 260, 425, 1 *Lat.* 330, 2 *Tyn.* 152; prayer must be made in his name, 2 *Bec.* 134; what it is to ask in his name, 1 *Bec.* 149, 2 *Bec.* 134

— (3) As a priest he blesses and sanctifies, 3 *Bul.* 284; his office is to consecrate and sanctify believers, 1 *Hoop.* 71, who, in him, are all priests (*v.* Priests).

(*d*) That he is a King, and of his regal office, 3 *Bul.* 274, 1 *Hoop.* 78, *Now.* (36), 152, *Sand.* 283, 2 *Tyn.* 168, *Whita.* 22; his seat as king, 3 *Bul.* 279; his kingdom, 1 *Brad.* 402; a meditation thereon, 2 *Brad.* 359; it is not of this world, 1 *Lat.* 360, 2 *Lat.* 91, *Lit. Edw.* 508, (556), (but the pope's is, 2 *Tyn.* 247, 273); the Jews looked for a temporal king, *Rid.* 70; Christ's kingdom shadowed forth by temporal conquests, *Pil.* 261; its difference from an earthly kingdom, *ib.* 269; it is spiritual, 2 *Bec.* 22, 2 *Brad.* 360, 1 *Hoop.* 79; Christ is king in the church, 4 *Bul.* 84, over which he has absolute power, *ib.* 42; he defends it by his power and his laws, 1 *Hoop.* 78, not by carnal weapons, *ib.* 79; he is king of all, 3 *Bul.* 237; how he reigns on earth, *ib.* 276, &c.; his kingdom not yet perfect, *Lit. Edw.* 520, (567); his kingdom desired, 1 *Lat.* 364; scripture calls the end of the world the fulfilling and performance of the kingdom and mystery of Christ, *Lit. Edw.* 510, (558); *v.* Millennium; when Christ will resign his mediatorial kingdom, 1 *Cov.* 385; how his kingdom is everlasting, 3 *Bul.* 280; the profit of his kingdom, 2 *Bec.* 22

iv. *Other names and titles :* Advocate, see iii. *c.* 2, above; All in all, see i. above; Altar, see v. below; called an Angel, *Pil.* 134, the angel from the altar, *Bale* 465; Anointed, see ii. above; Apparel, see Garment in this section; Book of life, see Life in this section; Bread, &c. (*v.* Supper of the Lord); he is the bread of life, 2 *Bul.* 192, 1 *Cov.* 212, 3 *Tyn.* 223, 226; our heavenly food, 2 *Bul.* 154, 156; the food of the soul, 2 *Bec.* 166, 232, *Hutch.* 242, not of the body, *Grin.* 44, 47, 2 *Jew.* 572; his flesh is meat, and his blood drink, 1 *Lat.* 457; the spiritual eating of him, 2 *Bec.* 294, 1 *Jew.* 528, 529, 543, *Whita.* 489; what it is to eat his flesh and drink his blood, 4 *Bul.* 457, *Hutch.* 244, 262, 1 *Tyn.* 369, 3 *Tyn.* 224, 226, 227, 236—238, 244; before his advent he was eaten by the fathers in their sacraments, 1 *Hoop.* 127, especially in the manna, 1 *Jew.* 545, 546, 2 *Jew.* 617, which was made Christ's body, 2 *Jew.* 577; his mystical body denoted by the bread in the communion, 3 *Tyn.* 257; he is not present corporally in sacraments, 4 *Bul.* 253; his body received by God's word, as well as by the Lord's supper, 1 *Brad.* 100; he is our table, bread, strong meat, herbs, milk, 1 *Jew.* 526; the Bridegroom of the church, *Hutch.* 101, 3 *Jew.* 265, *Sand.* 8; a husband, 1 *Brad.* 298—300; the church the Lamb's wife, *Bale* 542; Christ's marriage to the church, 1 *Lat.* 456, (see also Church, and Marriage, and vii. below); our elder Brother, *Lit. Edw.* 524, (571); Christ is our Brother, God our Father, 1 *Lat.* 328; the Comforter of the afflicted, 2 *Lat.* 67; Cornerstone, see Stone, below; Creator, see ii. above; Deliverer, see Saviour, in this section; promised as the Desire of all nations, *Pil.* 138, 147, 148; the promise connected with trouble, *ib.* 139; our Example, 1 *Cov.* 201, *Sand.* 288, 1 *Tyn.* 20, 72, 97, 2 *Tyn.* 28, 30; a perfect example, *Wool.* 5; we must imitate him, *Sand.* 375; his example teaches us all virtues, *Hutch.* 318; we must learn humbleness from it, 1 *Cov.* 213, and meekness, *ib.* 219, and patience, *ib.*; he is our example in afflictions, 2 *Bul.* 104; conformity to his sufferings necessary in order to our being partakers of his glory, 1 *Ful.* 441; on following him, 3 *Bec.* 609, 622, 1 *Brad.* 252; his shadow is to be followed rather than the body of councils or doctors, 1 *Hoop.* 25; but his example is to be followed in such things only as pertain to our vocation, 1 *Lat.* 516; First-begotten, see ii. above; Food, see Bread in this section; the Foundation, 2 *Bul.* 147, 3 *Bul.* 51, *Sand.* 386, (see also Peter, in the general alphabet, and Rock, and Stone, in this section); Fulness, see i. above; Garment,— to put on Christ, what, 2 *Bec.* 206, 2 *Hoop.* 116, 1 *Jew.* 526, 2 *Jew.* 1041; the Gift of God,—he was freely given to us of God, as a new-year's gift, 1 *Bec.* 307, 311, 348; as the gift of God he bringeth salvation, *ib.* 312; Head, see vii. below; Holy One, see i. above; our House, or dwellingplace, 1 *Jew.* 526; Husband, see Bridegroom, in this section; Intercessor, see iii. *c.* 2, above; Judge, see vi. below; Justice, see Righteousness, in this section; King, see iii. *a.* and *b.* above; the Lamb, *Bale,* 307, &c., *Hutch.* 217; the Lamb of God, *Sand.* 8; the Lamb slain from the beginning of the world, *Bale* 435, 1 *Brad.* 49, 1 *Ful.* 279, 2 *Jew.* 708, 718; our paschal lamb, or passover, 1 *Bec.* 117, 2 *Bul.* 164, 1 *Cov.* 211, 1 *Tyn.* 354, &c.; the Lamb opens the seals, *Bale* 312; the Lamb on mount Sion, *ib.* 451; the Lamb shall feed his servants, *ib.* 339; our Life, 3 *Bul.* 29, 2 *Tyn.* 146, being Lord over death, 1 *Lat.* 548, 550, 2 *Lat.* 67; Latimer says he is the book of life, 2 *Lat.* 175, 206; our Light, and the light of the world, 2 *Bul.* 137, 157, *Sand.* 212; light of light, 1 *Hoop.* 16; the knowledge of Christ is light, 1 *Tyn.* 490, 2 *Tyn.* 175; he is the Lion of the tribe of Judah, *Bale* 306; our Lord, 1 *Bul.* 129, *Now.* (37), 154; why he is called Lord, 3 *Bec.* 137; Lord of water as well as land, 1 *Lat.* 212; Lord of all, *Sand.* 284; what profit we have in that he is our Lord, 2 *Bec.* 26; Manna, see Bread, in this section; Master, see Lord, in this section, and Teacher, in iii. *b.* above; Mediator, see iii. *c.* 2, above; Messiah, see ii. *d.* above; Passover, see Lamb, in this section; our Peace, 1 *Tyn.* 330; sent from God to preach peace, *Sand.* 284; trust in aught but him cannot give peace, 1 *Tyn.* 330; how he sends not peace but a sword, 1 *Lat.* 377, (see also Prince, in this section); our Physician, 1 *Tyn.* 78; Priest, see iii. *c.* above; Prince of peace, 2 *Jew.* 1076; Prophet, see iii. *b.* above; Raiment, see Garment, in this section; Reconciler, see iii. *c.*'1, above; Redeemer,—the redemption effected by him, 1 *Ful.* 279; the ransom which he paid for our redemption, 2 *Cran.* 129; his death the only sufficient price and gage for sin, 1 *Hoop.* 50; by him we are redeemed from bondage, *Sand.* 179; he alone gave himself to redeem us from unrighteousness, 1 *Bec.* 328; redeemed us from *all* sin, *ib.* 330, &c., 3 *Bul.* 42; testimonies out of the old fathers, that by his death he not only delivered from original sin, but from all sins, 3 *Bec.* 418, &c.; whom he has redeemed, 3 *Bul.* 42, (see iii. *c.* 1, above; also Redemption); the Restorer of all things, 1 *Brad.* 352, 355, 362, 363; our Righteousness, 2 *Bul.* 154, 4 *Bul.* 68, 173, 1 *Tyn.* 95; our justice, wisdom, and sanctification, 1 *Ful.* 402, 403; his righteousness imputed makes believer perfect, *Sand.* 422; he is the mean wherein we are justified, 1 *Hoop.* 51, (see also Garment, in this section, and the references to the merits of our Lord in i. above); a Rock, 2 *Bul.* 174, 178, 2 *Cov.* 466; the rock whence water flows, 4 *Bul.* 285, 2 *Jew.* 563; the rock on which the church is built, 2 *Jew.* 1000, *Lit. Edw.* 513, (561), (see also Peter, in the general alphabet, and Stone, in this section); a Rose or flower, *Hutch.* 157; Ruler, see Lord, in this section, and Head in vii. below; Saviour,—his being promised as such is the beginning of

CHRIST. iv. v. vi.

our salvation, 1 *Bec.* 50; he came into the world not to rule, but to save, *ib.* 213; that Christ is the saviour of the world, is the sum of the Christian faith, 1 *Cov.* 408; he is our deliverer, 2 *Bul.* 301; the saviour of mankind, *Rog.* 55; the only saviour, 1 *Bec.* 51, 115, 312, 2 *Bec.* 21, 22, 380, 2 *Bul.* 195, 1 *Cov.* 72, 2 *Hoop.* 73, *Pil.* 81, *Rog.* 158; that he is the alone author of salvation, with probations out of scripture, 3 *Bec.* 305, &c.; there is none other name whereby we may be saved, 1 *Tyn.* 356, 2 *Tyn.* 214; Papists pervert this doctrine by introducing the merit of others, 2 *Bec.* 380; in what way he is a means of salvation to us, 2 *Hoop.* 477; God hath covenanted to give salvation through him, 3 *Tyn.* 275; all things requisite to salvation are given in him, 3 *Bul.* 27; his power saveth all, 1 *Cov.* 77; what manner of a saviour he is, 2 *Lat.* 124, 144, 168; a saviour from sin, 2 *Tyn.* 155; from all sin, original, actual, mortal, venial, 1 *Bec.* 336, 3 *Bec.* 418; a perfect saviour, *Sand.* 283; he works our salvation fully, 3 *Bul.* 30; he is the beginning and ending of our salvation, 1 *Bec.* 75; he delivers us from the fault (of sin), and from the pain due to it, *ib.* 102; a saviour, not only before, but after baptism, *ib.* 333, &c.; all salvation to be looked for in him, *ib.* 312; health, salvation, and comfort, to be sought only at his hand, *ib.* 313, 314, 315; to whom he is a saviour, *ib.* 44, 90, 317, 341, &c.; all God's elect are saved by him, 1 *Cov.* 70; the godly fathers of the old testament were saved by him, 1 *Bec.* 116; he is alone our eternal salvation, 3 *Bul.* 29; Schoolmaster, see iii. *b.* above; the Seed of the woman, 1 *Cov.* 21, 2 *Hoop.* 5, *Lit. Edw.* 503, (552), *Now.* (34), 151, *Sand.* 8, 1 *Tyn.* 10, (see also ii. *c.* above, and vi. below); our Shepherd, 2 *Cov.* 287, &c., *Poet.* 410; what comfort may be derived from the belief that he is such, 2 *Cov.* 294, &c.; the chief shepherd, 2 *Whitg.* 82; made Sin for us, see iii. *c.* 1, above; Son of God, see ii. *b.* above; Son of Man, see ii. *c.* above; the Stone on which we must build, *Bale* 128, (see also Foundation, and Rock, in this section); the corner-stone, 4 *Bul.* 82; compared to the Sun, *Lit. Edw.* 507, (556), *Sand.* 358; the sun of righteousness, *Bale* 327, 482, 552, whose beams are God's word and sacraments, *Rid.* 13; how obscured, *Sand.* 358, 359; as our Surety, he took our sins upon him, 1 *Lat.* 223; he voluntarily suffered as such, *Now.* (39), 156; he discharges our debts, 2 *Bec.* 636; Table, see Bread, in

this section; Teacher, see iii. *b.* above; he is the very Truth, 2 *Lat.* 298; the true Vine, *Hutch.* 35, 36, 43, 1 *Jew.* 526; the Way to God, 1 *Cov.* 248; the only way, *ib.* 221; the only way of acceptance, 1 *Lat.* 167; the only way to life eternal, 1 *Brad.* 502, (see also iii. *c.* 2); our Wisdom, 2 *Bul.* 154; the Wisdom of God, 2 *Brad.* 264, 265; the Word, 2 *Brad.* 264, 265, 4 *Bul.* 266, *Hutch.* 63, 132, 2 *Tyn.* 145; sentiments of Eusebius on this name, 3 *Zur.* 228

v. *Types*: Christ prefigured by Adam, 1 *Bul.* 113, *Pil.* 374, 1 *Tyn.* 70, 500; by Abel, *Sand.* 8; by Melchisedec, 1 *Brad.* 590, 1 *Cov.* 55, 56, 2 *Ful.* 260, *Sand.* 8, 454, *Whita.* 168, 169, & al.; by Isaac, *Sand.* 8; by Jacob's ladder, *Hutch.* 35; by Joseph, *Sand.* 8; by Moses, 1 *Tyn.* 209, *Whita.* 418; by Aaron, 2 *Bul.* 132, 138, 1 *Tyn.* 208, 209, 412, 427; by Joshua, 1 *Cov.* 50; by Gideon, *Sand.* 394; by Sampson, *Calf.* 336, *Sand.* 8, 370; by David, 2 *Brad.* 254, *Pil.* 371, 372, 389, especially in his conflict with Goliath, *Sand.* 371, *Whita.* 406; he is David's branch, 4 *Bul.* 85; Elijah compared to him, *Calf.* 336, *Phil.* 196, *Rid.* 196, 222—225; (see also the several names); typified by the paschal lamb, (see Lamb in iv.); by the manna (see Bread in iv.); by the rock, (see iv); by the brazen serpent, 1 *Cov.* 44, 1 *Tyn.* 426; by the door of the tabernacle (Lev. xvii), 1 *Brad.* 23; called by Irenæus, our altar, 1 *Jew.* 311; he is the golden altar, *Bale* 358; the holy of holies, 2 *Bul.* 137; signified by different gates of Jerusalem, *Pil.* 378, 579

vi. *His career, from the incarnation.*

(a) Generally:—CHRIST'S CHRONICLE, CONTAINING BRIEFLY...WHATSOEVER IS WRITTEN AT LARGE IN THE GOSPELS, by Tho. Becon, 2 *Bec.* 540, &c.; cursus vitæ D. N. J. C.; verses by Parkhurst, *Pra. Eliz.* 413; his first coming and his second, 2 *Lat.* 98, (and see Advent); psalmi, lectiones, et preces de nativitate, passione resurrectione, et ascensione Christi, &c., *Pra. Eliz.* 274; his incarnation, passion, resurrection, ascension, and coming again, 3 *Jew.* 252; his life, death, resurrection, ascension, and particularly his second coming to judgment, *Pra. B.* 10; his betrayal, condemnation, and death, *Now.* (39), 156; of his passion, descent into hell, resurrection, and ascension, *Lit. Edw.* 504, (553); FRUITFUL LESSONS UPON THE PASSION, BURIAL, RESURRECTION, AND SENDING OF THE HOLY GHOST, by bishop Coverdale, 1 *Cov.* 195; Christ's career of suffering, worse than ours can be, 2 *Lat.* 438; he was hated and troubled more than any man before or since his time, 2 *Hoop.* 214, slandered before he was born, and persecuted as soon as he was born, *ib.* 261; the Jews' enmity against him, 1 *Tyn.* 133, 2 *Tyn.* 72; his own kinsfolk raised against him, 2 *Hoop.* 261; he was often falsely accused, 2 *Tyn.* 30; persecuted, *Bale* 195; his words misreported, 2 *Lat.* 327; his extreme poverty, 2 *Lat.* 106, 300; he refused not to consort with sinners, 1 *Lat.* 15; was followed by the common people more than by scribes, *ib.* 199; why the multitude followed him, *Sand.* 338, &c.; he was diligent in his office, *ib.* 343; his prayers, 4 *Bul.* 225; he prayed, and taught others to pray, 1 *Bec.* 143; how he preached the gospel, 3 *Bul.* 37, (see also iii. *b.* above); an example to unpreaching prelates, 1 *Lat.* 199; his preaching was plain and simple, 2 *Lat.* 210; it was like a sword, 2 *Tyn.* 131; it was not all fruitful, 1 *Lat.* 155; he taught his disciples what to preach, 1 *Hoop.* 20; held nothing back from his apostles, 1 *Cov.* 77; revealed all things necessary to salvation, 1 *Hoop.* 20; spake and did many things which are not written, 1 *Bul.* 62, *Phil.* 359; why he worked miracles (*q. v.*), 2 *Lat.* 160; he confirmed his doctrine by them, 1 *Bec.* 52; his works bore witness to him, 2 *Lat.* 71, 73, 100; he raised the dead by his own power, 1 *Lat.* 550, 2 *Lat.* 67, 75; the purport, evidence, and manner of his miracles, all different from those alleged to be in the mass, 3 *Tyn.* 262; his three witnesses, 2 *Tyn.* 209

(*b*) More particularly :—he was revealed before he came, 2 *Lat.* 3; promised to the the fathers, *Now.* (35), 151; the promises touching him, 3 *Bul.* 13; he was the desire all nations, (see iv. above); Moses leads to him, 2 *Bul.* 240; he was foreshewn by the holy prophets, 1 *Cov.* 59, 1 *Tyn.* 422; his Spirit was in them, 1 *Bul.* 327; plainly foretold by Isaiah, *Sand.* 7; prophecies fulfilled in him, 3 *Bul.* 19; present with the fathers before his incarnation, *Pil.* 134; his coming or sending, what it is, *Hutch.* 150; being eternal God, he came in the flesh, 1 *Cov.* 222, and took on him the seed of Abraham, *ib.* 223; became poor to make us rich, 1 *Bec.* 51; his incarnation (as to which, see also ii. above), 3 *Bul.* 254, 260, 2 *Cran.* 88, 1 *Lat.* 456, *Now.* (34, 38,) 151, 154; A LESSON OF THE INCARNATION OF CHRIST, THAT HE TOOK HIS HUMANITY IN AND OF THE VIRGIN MARY, by Jo. Hooper, 2 *Hoop.* 1—18; the causes of his incarnation, 1 *Bec.* 51, 1 *Bul.* 130, 1 *Hoop.* 54; the effect and use of it, *ib.* 54; errors respecting it, 3 *Bul.* 260, 2 *Tyn.* 130; how denied by Antichrist and his members, 2 *Tyn.* 196; he was incarnate by the Holy Ghost, 2 *Bec.* 27; the manner of his conception, 1 *Bul.* 131, 2 *Hoop.* 9; he was conceived pure, 1 *Bul.* 133; his birth, *ib.*; on the birth of Christ; verses, 2 *Cov.* 562; he became true man of the virgin Mary, 1 *Bec.* 74, 318, 406, &c., 2 *Bec.* 28, *Hutch.* 145; why born of a woman, *Hutch.* 143; why of a virgin, *ib.* 147; why of a virgin betrothed, *ib.* 148; why born a babe, *ib.* 149; the day of his nativity uncertain, *Whita.* 667, (*v.* Christmas); his lineal descent, 1 *Bul.* 44, *Whita.* 560; his genealogy according to Matthew and Luke, 2 *Tyn.* 227; why he came in the end of the world, *Hutch.* 150, (*v.* Advent); peace throughout the world at his coming, *Sand.* 286; trouble at his birth, *Pil.* 140, 335, 359, 423; how he appeared, 1 *Bec.* 318; his birth announced to shepherds, 2 *Lat.* 84, 119; how the wise men saw and worshipped him, 1 *Jew.* 540; why he was circumcised, 2 *Lat.* 134, 135; his infancy, *ib.* 91; he laboured in his vocation as a carpenter, 1 *Lat.* 214, 2 *Lat.* 158; his baptism, *Hutch.* 121; why baptized, *ib.* 152; not because he had need thereof, but to give the church an example, *Phil.* 191; his temptation in the wilderness, 1 *Cov.* 73; why tempted, *Hutch.* 152; in order that he might succour those that are tempted, 2 *Hoop.* 12; he overcame the devil with the word, 1 *Lat.* 505; always answered objections by the word of God, 1 *Hoop.* 25; his citations from the Old Testament, 1 *Ful.* 44, 49; the miracle at Cana, 2 *Lat.* 160; he honoured wedlock, 1 *Bul.* 396; his discourse with Nicodemus, 1 *Hoop.* 52; all night in prayer, *Pil.* 340; was pitiful to those who had no shepherd, *Sand.* 344; his apostles (*q. v.*), 1 *Bul.* 52; his example in sending them forth, 1 *Lat.* 292; his choice of them, 2 *Bec.* 446; why he called fishers, 2 *Lat.* 24; his sermon on the mount, 1 *Lat.* 475; he reproves certain rich worldlings, 2 *Bec.* 587, 588; on his sleep in the ship, 2 *Jew.* 994, *Sand.* 370, &c.; he, and not his garment, cured the sick woman, 1 *Lat.* 542; he feeds five thousand (Jo. vi.), *Sand.* 340, &c.; pitiful to those who lacked food, *ib.* 344; his words in John vi. make much for the interpretation of the words of the supper, 4 *Bul.* 289, 462; he conveys himself away from being made a king, 1 *Bul.*

387; subject to the temporal power, 1 *Tyn.* 188, 2 *Tyn.* 245; he absolves adultery, 1 *Bul.* 413; why he refused to be a judge, *Hutch.* 324, 330; he came not as a judge or magistrate, 1 *Lat.* 273, 299; nor to deliver from civil burdens, *ib.* 282; he claimed no temporal power, 2 *Tyn.* 6; he foretells the destruction of Jerusalem, and the end of the world, 1 *Brad.* 39, 2 *Lat.* 45, *Sand.* 351; warns against surfeiting and drunkenness, 1 *Bul.* 423; his saying that we should not always have him with us, how spoken, *Phil.* 186, 187; his zeal for God's house, *Pil.* 5, 344; he purges the temple, 2 *Jew.* 1009, *Sand.* 236; signification of his casting out the sellers, 2 *Jew.* 708; he desires to eat the passover, *Rid.* 233; what he did when he ordained his holy supper, 3 *Bec.* 254; he alone ordained it, *ib.* 372, as an everlasting token of his passion and death, *ib.* 373, as a token of love among his people, *ib.*; he instituted not a sacrifice, but a memorial, *ib.* 372, 377; he sacrificed with thanksgiving to God, *ib.* 366; what he commanded to be done in the administration of his supper, *ib.* 358; his action therein is our instruction, *ib.* 383; he preached before he ordained his holy supper, *ib.* 254, 356; his foreknowledge exemplified in his prediction of the treachery of Judas, 1 *Cov.* 214; he called devoutly upon God his Father at his supper, *ib.* 356; he did not eat the supper alone, *ib.* 367; he did not admit all kinds of persons, but only apostles to receive, *ib.* 381, 382; ministered at a table, *ib.* 259, 356, without gorgeous furniture, *ib.* 362; he used neither cope nor vestment, but his daily apparel, *ib.* 259, 361; he ministered to his disciples sitting, *ib.* 364; he delivered the bread into the disciples' hands, *ib.* 363; he gave also the mystery of his blood, *ib.* 364; he used common bread and wine, *ib.* 359, 369; his words in ministering the supper, *ib.* 357; he pronounced them plainly, *ib.* 362; he took bread and made it his body, saying, "This is my body," that is to say, a figure of my body, *Grin.* 65; he declared that his body was broken and his blood shed for the remission of sins, 3 *Bec.* 367, 368; said, in a figure, to have borne himself in his own hands, 1 *Jew.* 502 & al.; probations out of the old fathers that his words, "This is my body," &c. must be figuratively understood, 3 *Bec.* 435, &c.; he did not eat his own body, *Phil.* 190; he said twice, "I will not drink of the fruit of the vine," *Grin.* 196; he gave the sacrament equally to all his disciples, 1 *Jew.* 130; after the supper he prepared for death, 3 *Bec.* 358; his last sermon, 1 *Lat.* 447; his commandment of love, *ib.* 453, 454; duration of his ministry, 1 *Bul.* 38; history of the three years of his preaching and miracles working, 3 *Bec.* 546, 548, 551; various assertions respecting his age, 4 *Bul.* 536, *Whita.* 665; his fear, or reverence, εὐλαβεία (Heb. v. 7), 1 *Ful.* 323, &c.; he had a natural fear of death, 2 *Cov.* 71, 2 *Hoop.* 225; his agony in the garden, 1 *Brad.* 63; the tears of our Saviour in the garden, a poem, *Poet.* 422; his agony and bloody sweat, a sermon for Good Friday, 1 *Lat.* 216; considerations from his agony, 1 *Cor.* 256, &c.; he is comforted by an angel, 1 *Lat.* 232; the betrayal of Christ; verses by Jo. Markham, *Poet.* 361; he bore the cross as an example to us, 2 *Lat.* 430; the highway to Mount Calvarie, verses by S. Rowlands, *Poet.* 352; Christ to the women of Hierusalem; verses by the same, *ib.* 357; as to the passion of our Lord, see also iii. *c.* above, the names Redeemer and Saviour in iv. above, and the heads Cross, Good-Friday, Prayers, Redemption, and Sacrifice; his passion, 1 *Bul.* 135, 2 *Cran.* 88; a meditation thereon, 1 *Brad.* 196, *Pra. B.* 116; another, 2 *Brad.* 254; he suffered, 1 *Bul.* 135, under Pontius Pilate, *ib.*; how great pains he suffered for us, 1 *Bec.* 53, 1 *Hoop.* 60, 2 *Hoop.* 261; his patient suffering, 1 *Cov.* 75; Psalms of the passion, *Pra. Eliz.* 75, (172); the passion, written by St John, *ib.* 81, (176); prayers of the passion, *ib.* 85, (180); why he suffered death, and why on the cross, *Hutch.* 153; his crucifixion, 1 *Bul* 135, *Now.* 100; the death of the cross reproachful, 1 *Bul.* 135, and accursed, 1 *Tyn.* 133; a prayer to Christ crucified, *Pra. B.* 149; stanzas from Christ's Crosse, by Jo. Davies, *Poet.* 250; the death of Christ, verses by the same, *ib.* 253; Saphickes upon the passion of Christ, by A. W., *ib.* 452; his coat without seam alleged as an authority for ecclesiastical vestments, 2 *Whitg.* 10, 11; his seven words on the cross, 2 *Cov.* 94; his exclamation, "Eli, Eli, lama Sabachthani," 2 *Ful.* 225, *Whita.* 216; he was touched with the horror of eternal death, *Now.* (42), 159; the darkness was not caused by an eclipse, *Whita.* 578; the earthquake, 1 *Cov.* 324; his death, 1 *Bec.* 52, 53, 2 *Bec.* 31, 32, 447, 3 *Bec.* 139; the water and the blood, 1 *Cov.* 75, 2 *Tyn.* 209, *Whita.* 499; considerations on the death of Christ, 1 *Cov.* 308—310; he died freely, 2 *Bul.* 201; his death was predetermined and concluded in the counsel of God, 1 *Cov.* 403; the day was specially foreordained, *Now.* (41), 158; he was to be slain in the latter days of the world, and at a certain time, as denoted by the day appointed for the Passover, 2 *Bul.* 180; yet the Jews were no less guilty, 1 *Cov.* 404; he was condemned and crucified by the visible church, 2 *Cran.* 15; the necessity of his death for us, 2 *Bec.* 229, 230, 1 *Cov.* 368; he died not in vain, 1 *Bul.* 114, 136; what profit we have by his passion, 2 *Bec.* 29—32, 1 *Cov.* 75, 220; *Now.* (42), 160; comfort from his passion, 2 *Cov.* 71; what he did and suffered was for our sake, 2 *Bec.* 29; he suffered for our redemption and example, *Hutch.* 316; by death he overcame death, 2 *Cran.* 92, 1 *Lat.* 550, 2 *Lat.* 145, *Now.* (39), 156, and destroyed the power of the devil, 1 *Lat.* 360, 2 *Lat.* 185; the death of death, sin's pardon, and soul's ransom; verses by S. Rowlands, *Poet.* 349; by his death we are delivered from our sins, 2 *Bec.* 230; the scriptures were opened thereby, and paradise was unclosed, *Whita.* 389; in his death is all our hope, 2 *Cov.* 404; his death is to be preached by the tongue of man from scripture, not from decrees of bishops, 1 *Hoop.* 31; his passion blasphemed, 1 *Lat.* 231; his burial, 2 *Bec.* 32, 1 *Bul.* 136, *Now.* (43), 160; what profit we have thereby, 2 *Bec.* 33; reflections thereon, 1 *Cov.* 316—321; the description of it by the evangelists, necessary for the assurance of our belief in his death and resurrection, *ib.* 317; his burial must needs be honourable, as foretold by Isaiah, *ib.* we must learn with Christ to die from the world, and to be buried in his death, *ib.* 318, 319; what we may learn from the conduct of the women, who brought spices for the burial of our Saviour, *ib.* 320, 321; his descent into hell, 2 *Bec.* 33, 3 *Bec.* 139, 1 *Bul.* 137, 2 *Cran.* 89, 1 *Ful.* 278, &c., 2 *Hoop.* 30, *Now.* (43), 160, *Rog.* 59, (see also Hell, ἄδης); various opinions respecting it, *Rog.* 60; difference between Papists, *Whita.* 536; the Romish view not provable by scripture, *ib.*; Latimer and others held that Christ descended to the place of torment, 1 *Lat.* 233, 234; a very gross opinion on the point maintained by a martyr [Latimer?], 1 *Whitg.* 29 n., see also 2 *Cran.* 89; the fact denied by some, 1 *Lat.* 233; supposed by some to mean no more than the burial, *Whita.* 537; the old metrical version of the creed thereon, 1 *Ful.* 283, 284; various opinions as to the reasons of Christ's descent into hell, *Whita.* 537, 538; our profit thereby, 2 *Bec.* 33; his resurrection from the dead, 1 *Bec.* 54, 2 *Bec.* 33, 34, 3 *Bec.* 139, 140, 1 *Bul.* 140, &c., 2 *Cov.* 142, &c., *Now.* (43), 161, *Rog.* 62, (and see Easter); of the resurrection, verses, 2 *Cov.* 563; another of the same, *ib.*; Christ rose on the third day, 1 *Bul.* 142; he rose again with his true body, 3 *Bul.* 257, 2 *Cov.* 142, 144, 145, which is called flesh, even after his resurrection, 1 *Jew.* 461; he raised his body by the power of his godhead, 1 *Hoop.* 18; the earthquake, 1 *Cov.* 324; the necessity of his resurrection, *Lit. Edw.* 505, (554); the doctrine thereof, 1 *Cov.* 76; whoso truly believes the resurrection of Christ is prepared to believe all that concerns Christ, *ib.* 323; comfort from it, 2 *Cov.* 71, 72; reflections, 1 *Cov.* 349, &c.; why it behoved Christ to rise again, *ib.* 369; it is a proof that he is the true Messiah, *ib.* 405; a strong argument to prove his godhead, *ib.*; it was discredited at first by the apostles, 3 *Tyn.* 37, 38; why Christ permitted this, 1 *Cov.* 327; why he led them gradually to the belief of it, *ib.* 328; the resurrection described by the evangelists, *ib.* 322, for the strengthening and stablishing of our faith in Christ, *ib.* 323; why they so distinctly describe the resurrection, *ib.* 327; why they do not all speak alike, *ib.* 323; evidence of the resurrection of our Lord, 2 *Cov.* 142—144; his appearings after it, *ib.* 144; why Christ would not suffer Mary to touch him, 1 *Cov.* 330; why he appeared so often after his resurrection, *ib.* 343; why he ate bread, *ib.*; what we learn from the doubting and confession of Thomas, *ib.* 345; our Saviour's appearance to the disciples at the sea of Galilee, *ib.* 348, &c.; what instruction we derive from the miracle wrought on that occasion, *ib.* 351, &c.; what instruction the ministers of the gospel derive from his discourse with Peter, *ib.* 355—361; the profit we have by our Lord's resurrection, 2 *Bec.* 34, 35, 2 *Cov.* 147, *Now.* (44), 161; we are thereby born again to a lively hope, 2 *Cov.* 148, and assured of our own resurrection, *ib.* 149; what Christ taught after his resurrection, *Whita.* 547; before his ascension he gave a charge to his servants, 1 *Bec.* 1, especially concerning ministers, *ib.* 2; his promises respecting his presence, 3 *Bec.* 273, *Pil.* 110; his presence in the sacraments is spiritual, 2 *Cran.* 176 n. (*v.* Supper); his ascension,

1 *Bec.* 54, 2 *Bec.* 35, 36, 3 *Bec.* 139, 140, 1 *Bul.* 143—146, 1 *Cov.* 380, &c., 2 *Cov.* 149, 162, 1 *Ful.* 322, *Now.* (45), 163, *Rog.* 65; Christ compared with Elijah, see v. above; why he ascended, 3 *Bec.* 139, &c., *Lit. Edw.* 505, 506, (554, 555); viz. to shew that his kingdom was not earthly, *Lit. Edw.* 508, (556), and for other causes, *ib.* 509, (557); the profit or fruit of Christ's ascension, 1 *Bec.* 54, 2 *Bec.* 36, 2 *Cov.* 164, *Now.* (46), 164; comfort from it, 2 *Cov.* 72, 229; he went into heaven, 1 *Bul.* 145, and opened it, 1 *Ful.* 287; he was, in the full sense, the first man who entered heaven, *ib.* 279; his ascension a pledge of ours, 3 *Bul.* 380, a cause of rejoicing, 2 *Bec.* 457, 458; heresies connected with Christ's ascension, 2 *Cov.* 150; he ascended not after his godhead, but after his manhood, 1 *Cov.* 382; he left the world in bodily presence, 3 *Bec.* 371, 372; why he did not tarry with us bodily on earth, *Now.* (46—48), 164, 165; his human nature is in one place, viz. in heaven, and not elsewhere, 2 *Bec.* 271, 280, 1 *Brad.* 90, 392, 3 *Bul.* 387, 4 *Bul.* 68, *Calf.* 152, 2 *Cov.* 157, 1 *Hoop.* 67, 70, 158, 159, 192, 2 *Hoop.* 36, 49, 90, 153, 444, 1 *Jew.* 505, 506, *Phil.* 209, *Rid.* 13, 3 *Tyn.* 251—254; not in divers places at one time, 2 *Bec.* 276, 277, 3 *Bec.* 272, &c., 2 *Hoop.* 36, 130, 445, 1 *Jew.* 480, &c.; probations of this out of scripture, 3 *Bec.* 314, &c.; testimonies of the old fathers, 2 *Bec.* 277, &c., 3 *Bec.* 451, &c.; his body must occupy space, 1 *Hoop.* 158; to teach that his body is in several places evacuates his humanity, which is a heresy, 2 *Bec.* 281; his ascent into heaven, a ground against transubstantiation (*q. v.*), *Rid.* 176, 213; the article of Christ's ascension much spoken of by the reformed, 3 *Jew.* 253, 257; Christ said to be whole here, and whole there, 1 *Jew.* 493, 3 *Jew.* 535; a prayer to Christ ascended, *Pra. B.* 149; another, *ib.* 150; his session at God's right hand, 1 *Bul.* 146, 147, 1 *Cov.* 384, 385, *Now.* (45), 163; the profit we have thereby, 2 *Bec.* 36, 37, *Now.* (46), 154; he is crowned for his suffering, 1 *Ful.* 374; he sends his Spirit to his church, 1 *Cov.* 385; he admits of no vicar on earth, 1 *Hoop.* 24; none other than the Holy Ghost, 2 *Hoop.* 39; Christ seen corporally after his ascension, *Rid.* 213, 218, &c.; how seen by Stephen, *Phil.* 189; his appearance to St John in Patmos, *Bale* 269; his vision of Christ on the white horse, *ib.* 312 (see also Lamb, in iv. above); Christ the judge, 1 *Brad.* 393, 1 *Bul.* 152, *Now.* (51), 169, *Sand.* 288, 353, 354, his second coming, and the day of judgment, *Bale* 267, 1 *Bec.* 55, 327, 2 *Bec.* 37, 38, 3 *Bec.* 141, 2 *Lat.* 44, *Now.* (50, 51), 168, 169, *Rog.* 66, (see also Advent, Judgment, World); a meditation of Christ coming to judgment, *Pra. B.* 98; a meditation of Christ coming to judgment, and of the reward of the faithful and unfaithful, 1 *Brad.* 185; his advent desired, 1 *Brad.* 275, 339, 439, 2 *Brad.* 228, 291, 2 *Cov.* 270, 1 *Lat.* 530, 2 *Lat.* 441, *Pra. B.* 23, 44, 86, 109, *Sand.* 174, 1 *Zur.* 277, 2 *Zur.* 269; it is the hope of the church, *Pra. Eliz.* 465; a cause of rejoicing to the faithful, 1 *Bec.* 55, 2 *Bec.* 460, 461, *Sand.* 390; the profit they will have by it, 2 *Bec.* 38; the time of it is unknown to us, 2 *Jew.* 871, *Sand.* 355, 356; to fix a time is vain and presumptuous, *Sand.* 356, but it is at hand, 3 *Bec.* 624, 1 *Brad.* 393, 2 *Brad.* 71, 249, 339, 2 *Jew.* 887, 1 *Lat.* 168, 169, 172, 364, *Lit. Eliz.* 501 n., 504, *Pra. Eliz.* 516, *Rid.* 116, *Sand.* 441—445, 3 *Zur.* 485; St Paul thought the day should have come in his time, 2 *Lat.* 59; we should continually look for it, *Sand.* 368, 2 *Tyn.* 185; an exhortation to watchfulness, *Nord.* 182; preparation for it, 2 *Lat.* 60; Jerome's prophetic view of the days before the second coming, 1 *Jew.* 327 (v. Antichrist); wars, pestilence, and other signs preceding it, *Bale* 137, 2 *Lat.* 51, *Lit. Eliz.* 504, 644, *Sand.* 171, 172, 356—358, 364, 365, 388, &c., 1 *Zur.* 325; state of the church and the world at Christ's coming, 2 *Brad.* 361; the manner of his coming, *Sand.* 365; he will come as a thief, *Grin.* 4, 2 *Lat.* 59; he will scarce find faith, 2 *Ful.* 207, 2 *Jew.* 869; his second coming foreshewn by the Flood, and the destruction of Sodom, 2 *Jew.* 868; the Son of Man sitting on the white cloud, *Bale* 463; how he shall descend, 2 *Jew.* 869; how the living shall be caught up, *ib.* 870; Christ's coming will put an end to heresies, 1 *Zur.* 307, to popery, *ib.* 320; righteousness shall then have the upper hand, *Rid.* 43; Christ's coming a cause of grief to the unfaithful, 2 *Bec.* 460, 461; he will take vengeance on the wicked, 1 *Brad.* 422, 2 *Cov.* 238; who will be confounded at his coming, 2 *Tyn.* 184; his kingdom; see above, also Millennium; when his mediatorial office shall terminate, God (the Holy Trinity) shall be all in all, 1 *Brad.* 272

vii. *Christ and the Church* (see also Church): he came to purge us a peculiar people to himself, 1 *Bec.* 340; men invited to him, *Sand.* 8, 9; how God draws unto him, 1 *Hoop.* 265; Christ sets his people free from bondage, 1 *Tyn.* 18, and makes them kings, priests, and disciples of God, 3 *Bec.* 615; what he is to them, 1 *Tyn.* 52, 296, 297, 300, 319, 3 *Tyn.* 274, (see iii. and iv. above); he is the perfectness of the faithful, 2 *Bul.* 249; Christ in Sion, or the church, *Pil.* 262, 264; what his church is, 3 *Bec.* 614, 615; his mystical body, 1 *Brad.* 353, *Phil.* 198, *Rid.* 17, 1 *Tyn.* 334; he is the head of the church, 1 *Brad.* 435, 1 *Jew.* 378, *Nord.* 99, *Now.* 99, 3 *Tyn.* 31, 2 *Whitg.* 84, 85, 426, 3 *Whitg.* 419, and ruler of the house of God, *Phil.* 394; the only head, 4 *Bul.* 67, 86, 3 *Jew.* 265; Christ the alone head of the catholic and apostolic church, with probations out of scripture, 3 *Bec.* 307, 308; the only ruler in the church, *Grin.* 205; he governs his church, being present therewith as God, though absent in body, *Lit. Edw.* 506, 507, (554, 555); how we are incorporated with the mystical body of Christ, 1 *Jew.* 140—142; he must be sought amongst the poor, 2 *Lat.* 127; he is still naked, hungry, and sick, in his members, *Sand.* 159; begs in our streets, and at our doors, *ib.* 187, 230, 266; lies in the streets of London, *Rid.* 535; his congregation always persecuted by the synagogue of Satan, 3 *Bec.* 194, 195; Christ is ours, 1 *Bec.* 52, 348; he must be received thankfully, *ib.* 57; what it is to follow him and leave all for his sake, 3 *Bec.* 609, 622; how he dwells in us, 1 *Jew.* 472, &c.; said to be mingled with us, *ib.* 474; he must be spiritually conceived in our hearts, and brought forth in our mouths and actions, 2 *Hoop.* 28; to be in him, what, *ib.* 432; his people are all one in him, 1 *Tyn.* 334, and all equal, 1 *Lat.* 249, 2 *Lat.* 199, 1 *Tyn.* 98, 200, 258, 296; they that will live in him must suffer persecution, 2 *Hoop.* 263; he allured his disciples to suffer for the glory of God, 3 *Bec.* 366; he is with the faithful in adversity, 1 *Cov.* 230; through him we have the victory over our enemies, 1 *Bec.* 114; Christians must rejoice in him, 2 *Bec.* 448; nothing can separate us from him, *Nord.* 97; what it is to die in him, 1 *Hoop.* 563; every believer is bound to die for his doctrine, 2 *Tyn.* 37; what it is to rest in him after this life, 3 *Bec.* 277

Christ-cross: 1 *Brad.* 264

Christen: Christians, 2 *Tyn.* 104, 254

Christen-catte (Bishop): 3 *Tyn.* 263

Christendom: the word used for christening, 1 *Tyn.* 277, 2 *Tyn.* 92

Christian II., king of Denmark: the Danish reformation begun under him, 1 *Cov.* 424; he was expelled from his kingdoms, 2 *Ful.* 121, 2 *Tyn.* 334 n

Christian III., king of Denmark: intercedes with queen Mary for Coverdale, 2 *Cov.* xiv; completes the reformation, 1 *Cov.* 424; sat openly in judgment, 1 *Lat.* 274

Christian doctrine: its excellence to a Christian commonwealth, 3 *Bec.* 597; in some places called heresy, *ib.*; honoured at Sandwich, *ib.*

CHRISTIAN KNIGHT, by Tho. Becon, 2 *Bec.* 620

Christian man: *v.* Christians, Doctrine, Institution.

Christian Religion: *v.* Religion.

Christians, Believers, Godly: *v.* Christ, Church; also Brethren, Christs, Godly, Heirs, Martyrs, Priests (ἱερεῖς), Righteous, Saints; likewise Adoption, Justification, Predestination, Redemption, Regeneration; and Affliction, Cross, Error, &c.

Of the name Christians, 3 *Bul.* 289; when given, *ib.* 291; antiquity of the name, *ib.*; some of the Jews of old were by faith Christians, *Hutch.* 218, 248, 325, 326; the great honour of the name, *Wool.* 15; Christians are named of Christ, 3 *Bul.* 50, *Now.* (1), 113; they are anointed, 2 *Tyn.* 180, 184, and bear the name by Christ's anointing, 2 *Hoop.* 29; Julian called them Galileans, 4 *Jew.* 667; Christian and catholic, the only names to be received, 1 *Ful.* 20; who are Christians in truth, 3 *Bec.* 602, 2 *Hoop.* 56, 2 *Lat.* 316; erroneous statements of Velsius, *Grin.* 474, &c.; what a Christian is, and how he is made such, Grindal's animadversions on those statements, *ib.* 436, &c.; there are but few, 3 *Bul.* 293, 1 *Tyn.* 204; a true Christian almost as rare as a black swan, *Wool.* 10; story of a Christian and a Jew, 3 *Bec.* 281, 282; opinions meet for a Christian man, 1 *Cov.* 514; Christians must leave man's word and cleave to God's, 1 *Hoop.* 139; their state and character, 2 *Brad.* 111, 114, 1 *Tyn.* 90, 97, 263, 2 *Tyn.* 170, 171, 189, 201, 210; in respect of God they are but passive, 1 *Tyn.* 197, 3 *Tyn.* 174; believers are not condemned, 2 *Cov.* 354, but justified, 1 *Bul.* 110, 2 *Lat.* 154; the godly are justified and received into favour, before they are made partakers of the sacraments, 4 *Bul.* 311; their righteousness imputative, 3 *Bul.* 46; all believers are perfect by imputation, *Sand.* 422; they are sinners and yet no sinners, 3 *Tyn.* 32, 33; they cannot err,

CHRISTIANS 181

and yet may err, *ib.* 32; the faithful though they slip, yet they fall not (utterly), *ib.* 35; why they sometimes fall, and how, 1 *Tyn.* 491; they are not servants but sons, *Sand.* 447; the sons of God, 2 *Bec.* 25, 2 *Tyn.* 27, 149, 190, 197, 200; why they are called saints, 2 *Bec.* 43; the faithful are saved, 3 *Bul.* 34, and have eternal life, 1 *Bul.* 110; they are not of this world, 1 *Brad.* 415, &c., 2 *Cov.* 231, &c., but crucified, dead, buried, risen, and ascended with Christ, *Now.* (48, 49), 166, 167; their bodies are God's temples, *Phil.* 257; they are kings, 2 *Bul.* 285, 3 *Bul.* 289; and priests, 2 *Bul.* 285, 3 *Bul.* 290; their sacrifice, viz. their goods, bodies, souls, *Sand.* 413, &c.; they are soldiers of Christ, 4 *Bul.* 236, 1 *Lat.* 490; pilgrims, 1 *Lat.* 474; addressed by John as children, young men, and fathers, 2 *Tyn.* 175, 176; they should not be always children, 2 *Lat.* 339, *Whita.* 243; they need leisure to grow, 1 *Tyn.* 454; young ones require milk, older ones strong meat, *ib.* 505; all are equal in Christ, 1 *Lat.* 249, 2 *Lat.* 199, 1 *Tyn.* 98, 200, 258, 296; they are called sheep, 2 *Cov.* 282, &c.; though sheep they are reasonable, 1 *Whitg.* 525; description of their life, 1 *Bec.* 324, *Wool.* passim; their office or duty, 1 *Cov.* 514, 1 *Hoop.* 15, 76, 2 *Hoop.* 99; they should consider their vocation, and seek to walk worthy of it, 2 *Bec.* 475, &c.; an wholesome warning for all men that bear the name of Christians to live Christianly, by Jo. Hall, M.D., *Poet.* 200; what Christ requires of them, 1 *Lat.* 8; two things requisite in a Christian, faith and works, 1 *Tyn.* 471; they live by faith, 3 *Tyn.* 206; they work because it is God's will, 1 *Tyn.* 77; faith and truth should reign among them, 1 *Bec.* 360; they must live holily, 1 *Hoop.* 77, 93, not in wilful sin, 2 *Tyn.* 189, 191, 212, 213, (although the godly have always acknowledged themselves sinners, 2 *Bec.* 637), but seeking in all things to honour Christ, 3 *Tyn.* 109; the children of God love righteousness, *ib.* 276; the good forgive injuries, *Pil.* 424; judge others to be like themselves, *ib.* 425; cannot but love, 1 *Tyn.* 298; to be a Christian is difficult, a science practive, not speculative, 1 *Hoop.* 137; none are worthy to be called Christians who are not ready to renounce all, *Phil.* 255; why the good dwell among the wicked, *Pil.* 424; their godly conversation has turned many to the faith, 1 *Bec.* 17; their study, *ib.* 82; they must labour for their living, 1 *Lat.* 211; they are bound to obey the law, 1 *Hoop.* 94, and must not resist tyrants, 3 *Tyn.* 188; Christ's sheep must not fight the wolves, 2 *Tyn.* 68; Christians may serve heathen masters, *Pil.* 311; THE OBEDIENCE OF A CHRISTIAN MAN, by Will. Tyndale, 1 *Tyn.* 127; Christians may be both rich and honourable, 2 *Lat.* 214; have been and may be magistrates, 1 *Bec.* 214, 1 *Bul.* 385; may use punishment of death and bear weapons, 2 *Hoop.* 127; how they prepare themselves to battle, 1 *Bec.* 252; in what sense they may seek to be avenged, 1 *Lat.* 145, 151; rules of Christian living, 1 *Cov.* 506; we must judge well of scripture, not doubting the promises of God, *ib.*; we must with a good courage enter in the way of salvation, *ib.* 507; we must despise whatsoever leadeth from the way of Christ, *ib.* 508; Christ must be the mark and ensample of our living, *ib.* 509; we must ascend from things visible to things invisible, *ib.* 510; we must follow Christ in his saints, *ib.* 512; we must vary from the common people, *ib.*; nothing should make us to go back from the truth, *ib.* 513; we must be climbing up unto godliness, *ib.* 515; we must ponder the incommodities of sin, *ib.* 516; we may not despair in God, *ib.*; we must ever keep watch, *ib.* 517; we must neither be fainthearted nor presumptuous, *ib.*; of temptation we must take occasion of virtue, *ib.* 518; after one temptation we must ever look for another, *ib.*; we must not favour ourselves in any vice, *ib.* 519; we must compare the bitterness of the fight with the pain that followeth sin, and the sweetness of sin with the pleasure of the victory, *ib.*; we must not despair though we be under, *ib.* 520; we must exercise ourselves in the cross of Christ, *ib.*; we must consider the filthiness of sin and the dignity of man, *ib.* 521; also the goodness of God and the malice of the devil, *ib.*; likewise the reward of sin, and the reward of virtue, *ib.* 522, as well as the misery of this life, *ib.*, and the extreme mischief of impenitence, *ib.* 323; the desire of Christians, 3 *Bec.* 226; their humility, prayer, fasting, &c., 1 *Tyn.* 75; how they give thanks to God, 4 *Bul.* 222; their praying, *ib.* 186; what they should pray for, 1 *Bec.* 167; their whole life should be a fervent desire of heavenly things, *ib.* 131; Christians cannot agree with the world, 2 *Lat.* 184; the faithful cannot want, *Pil.* 154; God will provide for them, 2 *Lat.* 154; their confidence in God, 2 *Tyn.* 159; nothing chances to the godly without the singular providence of God, 2 *Bec.* 158; it is in no tyrant's power to take away their lives till God appoints, 3 *Bec.* 218; they understand everything necessary to salvation, *Whita.* 392; their rich comfort, 2 *Cov.* 314; how Christ comforts believers under their trials, *ib.* 312, 313; he comforts them at his holy table, *ib.* 313; they find great consolation in the faithful service of God and earnest prayer, *ib.* 318; the joy of Christians, what it is, 1 *Bec.* 265; that they do not always experience the same degree of spiritual joy is shewn in the examples of David and St Paul, 2 *Cov.* 317; how believers win, *ib.* 312; what things are hoped for by them, 2 *Bec.* 13, 14, 2 *Bul.* 88; they shall judge the world, *Phil.* 264; their final joy, 2 *Bec.* 460, 461, 2 *Lat.* 195; the godly are punished for a time, *Pil.* 250; they are afflicted while the wicked live in pleasures, 2 *Bul.* 67; against the temptation arising from the misery of the godly in the world, and the wealth of the ungodly, with sentences and examples of scripture, 1 *Bec.* 463, &c.; how they behave in calamities, 2 *Bul.* 82; it is not expedient that Christians should be delivered from the troubles of the world, 2 *Hoop.* 230; Christians must bear the cross, 2 *Lat.* 429 &c., not give money to be exempt, *ib.*; their only way of deliverance is to cast their burden upon God, 2 *Cov.* 308; faithful ones will be hated and reviled, 1 *Bec.* 287, and must look to be rejected, as Christ was, 2 *Brad.* 109, 112; they must love their brethren, 2 *Tyn.* 137; all Christians are united by two bonds, *Pil.* 367; the cross tries who are true ones, 1 *Tyn.* 412; Christians are called to suffering, *ib.* 137; how it goeth with faithful believers, 2 *Cov.* 312; Christians are subject to two kinds of troubles, 2 *Hoop.* 230; every man is two men, flesh and spirit, which fight perpetually, 2 *Tyn.* 9; therefore every man must have his cross for the mortifying of his flesh, *ib.*; they have always had a care for the church, *Sand.* 235; dissensions among them, and the evil consequences thereof, 1 *Jew.* 532, 2 *Jew.* 687; they must remove false doctrine, and cut off springing evils, 2 *Hoop.* 3; they have many enemies in the world, 1 *Bec.* 125, 126; slanders and false charges brought against the early Christians, 3 *Jew.* 155, *Pil.* 359, *Sand.* 69, 1 *Tyn.* 164; some said they worshipped Bacchus and Ceres, 2 *Jew.* 1026; the first thing the ancient converts did was to proclaim defiance to paganism, *Sand.* 373

Christians (False): who are such, 3 *Bul.* 295, 2 *Jew.* 937, &c., 2 *Lat.* 316; there have ever been many, 1 *Tyn.* 165; but few of those designated Christians are under the everlasting testament of God in Christ, *ib.* 204; those who live not according to their profession are false Christians, and as far from eternal life as Jews and Turks, 2 *Lat.* 315, 342, 346; what a fire boils in their hearts, 2 *Bec.* 623

Christina (St): said to be the saviour of men and women by her passion, *Rog.* 298

Christina, landgravine of Hesse: 3 *Zur.* 666 n

Christison (Will.), minister of Dundee: 2 *Zur.* 364 n., 365

Christmas: on the observance of Christmas day, 1 *Bul.* 260, 2 *Whitg.* 576; the day of the nativity was observed in the time of Maximian, who burned a church where many were assembled to keep it, 2 *Jew.* 976; Augustine on the day, 2 *Whitg.* 576; Jerome (?) says it is uncertain whether this is the day on which Christ was born, or that of his baptism, *Whita.* 667; it was the only night on which mass might be said, 1 *Jew.* 117; sermons for Christmas day, 2 *Lat.* 84, *Sand.* 7; verses for Christmas day, by F. Kinwelmersh, *Poet.* 291; a Christmas carol, "My sweet little baby," &c., *ib.* 506; the season wickedly observed by many, 3 *Zur.* 285; the reformed service compared by the Devonshire rebels to a Christmas game, 2 *Cran.* 179; the Popish service more like one, *ib.* 180; Christmas pie, *Calf.* 158

CHRISTMAS BANQUET, by Tho. Becon, 1 *Bec.* 59

Christmas (Hen.): editor of bp Ridley's Works, *Rid.*; and of the Select Works of bp Bale, *Bale.*

Christopher (St): invoked for continual health, 1 *Bec.* 139, *Hutch.* 171; account of him, 1 *Bec.* 139 n., *Hutch.* 172 n.; his huge bulk, *Hutch.* 23

Christopher, pope: his brief pontificate, 1 *Hoop.* 217

Christopher, margrave of Baden: *Park.* xiii. n

Christopher, count Palatine: 2 *Zur.* 247

Christopher, prince of Wurtemberg: *Jew.* xiii.

Christopher (......): 1 *Zur.* 43, 3 *Zur.* 334 (qu. if Froschover?).

Christophers: supporters, *Bale* 317

Christopherson (Jo.), bp of Chichester: notice of him, *Phil.* xxx; at Cambridge, 1546, *Park.* 38; he tries to procure the arrest of Sandys, *Sand.* xii; one of the examiners of

Philpot, *Phil.*104,112; bishop of Chichester, 2 *Zur.* 20 n; he preaches a violent sermon at Paul's cross, and is committed to prison, 1 *Zur.* 4; his death, 4 *Jew.* 1196, 1197, 1 *Zur.* 4 n., 6; his version of a passage of Eusebius, *Whita.* 571; he translated Apollinaris, *ib.* 688

Christs: on "Touch not my Christs," Psa. cv. 15, *Wool.* 21; Augustine says we are made Christs, 2 *Jew.* 566

Christs (False): *v.* Antichrists.

Pseudo-christi, who they are, *Hutch.* 33; they shall arise in the end of the world, *Sand.* 365; several enumerated, *Bale* 384, *Rog.* 162; Tyndale calls them "false anointed," and applies the term to the Romish orders, 1 *Tyn.* 227, 232, &c.

Chromatius: the epistle of him and Heliodorus to Jerome not genuine, 1 *Jew.* 185 n.; Chrysostom cited for him, 1 *Bec.* 380 n

Chronicles (The two books of): 2 *Cov.* 18

Chronicles: the English chronicles censured, *Bale* 8; the Saxon Chronicle of Peterborough, 2 *Ful.* 23 n., 4 *Jew.* 780; Scala Cronica, *v.* T. Gray; Abstract of Chronicles,—perhaps the Booke of the Cronicles of England (Westm. 1480), *Jew.* xxxii, 3 *Jew.* 164, 4 *Jew.* 780 [qu. if the Abbreviationes Chronicorum ab initio mundi ad 1147, compiled by Ralph de Diceto?]; Chronicon Mundi, or Chronicon Chronicorum, commonly called the Nuremberg Chronicle, *v.* Schedel (H.); Supplementum Chronicorum, *v.* Forestus (I. P.)

Chronology: *v.* Calendar, and particularly *Pra. Eliz.* 225, &c.; also Year.

On the variance between the Hebrew chronology and that of the LXX, *Whita.* 121; that of the Samaritan text and the LXX, 1 *Cov.* 32 n; that of the books of Maccabees, *Whita.* 99 n

Chrysippus: named, 2 *Ful.* 204; his saying on government, *Sand.* 36

Chrysologus (Pet.): reprobates drunkenness, 2 *Jew.* 1040 n., *Sand.* 137

Chrysostom (St John): *v.* Liturgies.
  i. *His Life.*
  ii. *His Works.*
  iii. *On God, and Christ.*
  iv. *Angels.*
  v. *Scripture, Word of God.*
  vi. *Tradition.*
  vii. *Sin.*
  viii. *Grace, Justification, Works, &c.*
  ix. *The Church.*
  x. *Bishops and other Ministers.*
  xi. *Peter, Rome.*
  xii. *Saints.*
  xiii. *Sacraments.*
  xiv. *Baptism.*
  xv. *The Eucharist.*
  xvi. *Ceremonies.*
  xvii. *Prayer, Praise, Worship.*
  xviii. *Tongues.*
  xix. *Miracles.*
  xx. *Festivals, Fasts.*
  xxi. *Marriage, &c.*
  xxii. *Confession, Penance, Absolution, Excommunication.*
  xxiii. *Affliction, Persecution.*
  xxiv. *Death, &c.*
  xxv. *Images, the Cross.*
  xxvi. *Heresies.*
  xxvii. *Antichrist.*
  xxviii. *Kings, Civil Power.*
  xxix. *Miscellanea.*

i. *His life*: sent to Athens for instruction in his youth, 4 *Jew.* 652; his preaching at Constantinople, 1 *Jew.* 246; he preached but one day in the week, *ib.* 199; the extent of his jurisdiction, *Rog.* 329, 2 *Whitg.* 311, &c., 432; he deposed several bishops for simony, 2 *Whitg.* 315; blessed Theodosius, 2 *Ful.* 108; was exiled by the empress Eudoxia at the instigation of priests, 2 *Cran.* 12; his name struck out of the table of bishops of Constantinople, 4 *Jew.* 649; when he was banished, many of the people refused to communicate with his successor, *Coop.* 121; his appeal to pope Innocent, 1 *Jew.* 386, 387, 392, &c.; he would not attend an Arian council though called by the emperor Arcadius (not Constantius), 3 *Jew.* 38, 4 *Jew.* 1101; his death, *Lit. Eliz.* 452; commendation of him, 2 *Bul.* 395; Theodoret calls him the doctor of the world, 3 *Jew.* 282; he sometimes differs from other fathers, *Whita.* 455; not without his faults, *Calf.* 63, 64; condemned by heretical councils, *Rid.* 134; mentioned as Joannes Os Aureum.

ii. *His works*: *Calf.* 404, 2 *Ful.* 399, *Jew.* xxxv; MSS. of his homilies on Genesis, *Grin.* 291; his work on the gospels discovered, 3 *Zur.* 447; a phrase in one of his sermons upon Lazarus gave rise to the formation of an imaginary saint, 2 *Ful.* 44 n.; his first sermon De Cruce et Latrone wrongly assigned to Augustine, *Calf.* 63 n., 277, 2 *Ful.* 179, 180; some Latin homilies ascribed to him are mere compilations from his works, 2 *Brad.* 276 n.; on the genuineness of his epistle to Cæsarius the monk, first published by P. Martyr, *Rid.* 509; his hyperbolical language, *Calf.* 64, 77, 1 *Jew.* 473, 488; his many figurative speeches, 1 *Lat.*

274; his works praised, *Pil.* 682; quoted by Becon from the Latin editions, 1 *Bec.* 69 n.; falsified and untruly translated by Harding, 1 *Jew.* 393; an interpolation inserted by Possinus in the Catena Græcorum Patrum, 2 *Ful.* 286 n.; spurious treatises ascribed to him, *Calf.* 104 n.; five spurious homilies on Job, 2 *Ful.* 110, 139, 189; the Opus Imperfectum, 1 *Brad.* 529 n., 2 *Cran.* 18 n., 3 *Jew.* 311, 312, *Rid.* 33, *Sand.* 148 n.; opinions as to its authorship, *Calf.* 95 n.; it is ascribed by some to Maximus, an Arian, *Whita.* 684; Homiliæ ex variis in Matth. locis, not authentic, 2 *Ful.* 285 n.; spurious homilies on the gospel by Mark, *ib.* 147 n.; fictitious sermon De negatione Petri, *ib.* 285 n.; doubtful homily on Peter and Elias, *ib.*; spurious treatises respecting the cross, *Calf.* 63 n.; the first counterfeit Sermo in Pentecosten, alleged as genuine by Barrow, 2 *Ful.* 286 n.; counterfeit Oratio in principes Apost. Petrum et Paulum, *ib.* 110 n.; fictitious Sermo in adorat. venerabil. Catenarum, *ib.*; as to the Liturgy called his, *v.* Liturgies.

iii. *On God, and Christ:* he says it is a great matter to know which is the creature, and which the Creator, which the work, and which the Maker, 2 *Jew*, 1121, 3 *Jew.* 555; warns against confounding them, 3 *Jew.* 481; declares that to adore belongs to a creature, to be adored to the Lord, *Calf.* 378; shews that we are to honour Christ as he has willed us, 2 *Jew.* 559, 3 *Jew.* 553; says that if God had come in his manifest divinity, no creature could have borne his presence, 1 *Jew.* 530; declares that "the form of God" is the nature of God; "the form of a servant" verily is the nature of a servant, 3 *Jew.* 261; explains how Christ has profited us more largely than Adam hurt us, 3 *Bec.* 420; says, we see our Lord lying in a cradle, &c., 2 *Jew.* 608; his opinion respecting the hill on which Christ sat (Jo. vi. 3), *Sand.* 340; on the inconstancy of the people (Jo. vi), 3 *Whitg.* 568; on Christ's reply to them, *ib.* 577; on their greediness, *ib.* 582; on Christ's exhortation to them, not to labour for the meat that perishes, *ib.* 583, i. e. for worldly things, *ib.* 584; he remarks that Christ was heard in silence, 1 *Lat.* 204; says, both the winds and the sea bare witness to my Christ, 4 *Jew.* 662; shews why the Pharisees sought to keep men from Christ, 2 *Jew.* 1021; attributes the opposition of the Scribes and Pharisees to him to the fact that he was not of the priesthood, 3 *Jew.* 324; shews why the Jews sought to stone him, *Whita.* 481; says, Christ overthrew the exchangers' banks, meaning thereby that there may be no coin in the church, but spiritual, 4 *Jew.* 816; speaking of Christ before Caiaphas he says, there was a shew of judgment, but indeed the violence of thieves (O. l.), 4 *Jew.* 918; says Judas sold Christ's blood, 2 *Lat.* 271; Abraham saw Christ's day, i. e. (as Chrysostom understands it) the day of his death, 1 *Hoop.* 212; he thinks the narrative of Christ's passion sufficient to soften a stone, 2 *Jew.* 716, 717; explains the words, "Christ... crucified among you," 3 *Jew.* 542; says Christians were upbraided as worshippers of One who was crucified, 2 *Jew.* 649, and that that death was holden accursed among the Jews, and abominable among the heathen, *ib.*; shews that the devil and death have lost their sting by the body of Christ crucified, 3 *Bec.* 420; on Christ's blood shed for many, 2 *Jew.* 714; he says that the Father gave Christ an offering sufficient for the salvation of the whole world, 3 *Bec.* 421; on the weakness of the legal sacrifices and the perfection of that of Christ, 2 *Hoop.* 513; he contrasts the many sacrifices of the law with the one sacrifice of Christ in the gospel, 1 *Jew.* 171; speaks of the greatness of the one sacrifice of Christ, once offered, 3 *Bec.* 422; declares that there is none other sacrifice, one hath purged us, *ib.*; argues that if God have forgiven us our sins by one sacrifice, we have no need of a second, *ib.*; asserts that Christ has paid for us much more than we owe, *ib.*; says that the death of Christ has destroyed enmity, *ib.*; compares his sacrifice to a salve, 2 *Jew.* 720; on Christ's entering when the doors were shut, 1 *Jew.* 483; he says that the Lord drank wine and not water after his resurrection to root out a certain pernicious heresy, 2 *Hoop.* 438; speaks of Christ taking up his flesh and yet leaving it on earth, as Elijah did his mantle, *Phil.* 196; Philpot's explanation of this, *ib.* 197 (and see xv. *b.*); says Christ is here fully, and in heaven fully, one body, 3 *Jew.* 533; speaks of him as sitting above with the Father, and yet at the same time giving himself to those who will receive him, 1 *Jew.* 487; says, thou embracest the Lord himself, and being here beneath, art joined to that body that sits in heaven above, 3 *Jew.* 494, 496; declares that Christ is present in spirit unto faith, 1 *Hcop.* 224; affirms that he is evermore present with us; for, unless he were present, the church of God could not continue, 3 *Jew.* 486 ; understands the "one shepherd" to be Christ, *ib.* 280; says he is become our table, apparel, house, head, root, &c., 1 *Jew.* 526, 2 *Jew.* 1042; asks, what will not Christ be unto us? for by all manner of means he cleaves unto us, 3 *Jew.* 494; says, Christ moulds us, if I may so say, into one lump with himself, *ib.* 495 ; on the following of Christ, *ib.* 881, 882; on putting on Christ, 2 *Jew.* 1042; warns against believing reports that Christ has appeared, even in the true churches (O. I.), 3 *Jew.* 450, 451, 4 *Jew.* 865; his view of the signs going before the end of the world, *Sand.* 352; on the sign of the Son of Man (O. I.), *Calf.* 95, 96, 2 *Ful.* 137; on the deliverance of the creature from the bondage of corruption (Rom. viii), 1 *Brad.* 352 ; on the corruption and renewal of the world, 2 *Jew.* 577

iv. *Angels*: he says, the angels of God, be they never so great, are but servants and ministers, 3 *Jew.* 290, *Whita.* 627 ; declares that the angels and archangels are present at the sacrifice, 2 *Jew.* 739, and speaks of their intercession for us, *ib.* 741; affirms that the angels and martyrs are present in the church, *ib.*

v. *Scripture, Word of God* (see also ix)

(*a*) The origin and transmission of the scriptures:—he states that God the Creator of mankind spake many ways and in sundry sorts unto the fathers, 3 *Jew.* 434; shews why the scriptures are needful to us, though not to the patriarchs of old, *Whita.* 524; explains that it is for men's ungodliness that they have need of the scriptures, 3 *Jew.* 371; says, God minding to renew his favour towards man, sent his letters, thereby to reconcile man to himself, *ib.* 283; remarks that the prophets not only spoke, but wrote, and also prefigured events in real types, *Whita.* 648, 649; says to the Jews, you turn the leaves of the scriptures, made of the skins of dead cattle, but we have the Spirit that giveth life, 4 *Jew.* 763 ; declares that there remains now nothing among the Jews, but the writing contained in books, for all the observation of the law is passed from them, *ib.*; says, the letters of the law are with the Jews, but the sense and meaning with us, *ib.* 763, 980 ; writes, now-a-days there are some who cannot tell whether there be any scriptures, or no ; yet has the Spirit of God so provided that they are still preserved, *ib.* 763

(*b*) Scripture as a rule, &c.:—he exhorts to follow exactly the rule of holy scripture, *Whita.* 659 ; calls scripture an exact balance and standard, and the rule of all things, 2 *Jew.* 1058 n., *Whita.* 28, 662, 686 ; says that he is a true Christian whose confession agrees with the scriptures, 2 *Cran.* 26 ; declares that none can teach like the oracles of God, *Whita.* 701; on teaching with and without proof from scripture, *ib.* 685; he exhorts his hearers to read the scriptures, and try his doctrine by them, 3 *Bec.* 543; says that every preacher is a servant of the law, and must neither take away from nor add to it (O. I.), 2 *Cran.* 25; a genuine passage somewhat similar, *ib.* 27; he beseeches men not to hear preachers for amusement, but to follow the standard of holy scripture, *Whita.* 683 ; says, out of the true churches themselves go forth deceivers, and therefore warns against believing those who do not speak things agreeable to the scriptures (O. I.), 3 *Bec.* 391, 2 *Jew.* 688, 3 *Jew.* 228, 450, 451; cautions against believing men unless they speak things agreeable to scripture, 2 *Cran.* 27; on Paul's anathema against those who should preach another gospel, *Whita.* 627 ; another passage, 4 *Jew.* 1028; he says we may not believe Paul himself if he speak of his own, &c., see vi. below ; shews that the words of men who profess to speak by the Holy Spirit must be judged by scripture (pseud?) *Coop.* 191, 2 *Cran.* 25, 528, 3 *Jew.* 234, 4 *Jew.* 774, 775 ; says, on Matt. xxiii, the key is the word of the knowledge of the scriptures, by which the gate of truth is opened to men; the key-bearers are the priests (O. I.), 4 *Bul.* 149, 1 *Jew.* 331, 3 *Jew.* 357, 364, 4 *Jew.* 1134; asks, when thou seest the scriptures delivered into the hands of false priests, dost thou not understand that the word of truth is delivered unto the wicked princes and scribes? (O. I.), 4 *Jew.* 764; says heretic priests shut up the gates of truth, and shews why (O. I.), 2 *Jew.* 696, 4 *Jew.* 767, 892, 1039; shews 'the absurdity of refusing to trust others in the matter of money, and yet in more important matters to follow men's opinions, without reference to scripture, *Whita.* 686; he calls the scriptures continual schoolmasters, 1 *Whitg.* 524; says there is need of scripture because many corrupt doctrine, *Whita.* 683 ; declares that wheresoever the Bible lieth the devil can have no power, *Calf.* 258; speaks of fleeing, when heresy prevails in the church, to the scriptures (which he understands by "the mountains," Matt. xxiv), without which we cannot tell the true church, but shall fall into the abomination of desolation (O. I.), 2 *Cran.* 24, 25, 2 *Jew.* 688, 3 *Jew.* 153, 326, 4 *Jew.* 729, 1065, *Whita.* 683, 684; maintains that none can know which is the true church but by the scriptures (O. I.), 1 *Brad.* 528, 551, *Coop.* 187, 2 *Jew.* 985, 3 *Jew.* 153, 4 *Jew.* 750, 864, 1170, *Rid.* 123; speaks of scripture as the door of the sheepfold, and says that he who comes in another way is a thief, 3 *Jew.* 281, 4 *Jew.* 750, *Whita.* 700; speaks of the kingdom of God as inclosed in the scriptures (O. I.), 2 *Jew.* 604

(*c*) The sufficiency of scripture:—he asserts that all things are clear and plain in the divine scriptures; all needful things are manifest, 2 *Cran.* 18, 2 *Jew.* 683, 4 *Jew.* 1185, *Whita.* 396; he declares that all things may be determined by them, 2 *Cran.* 26; writes that all things needful to be known may be learned by them, *ib.* 27; says that whatever is required for our salvation is contained in them (O. I.), 2 *Cran.* 26, *Phil.* 361; on the expression "of all," in Acts i. 1, meaning, as he says, all things necessary for salvation, 1 *Hoop.* 106; he declares that the gospel contains all things both present and to come, 3 *Bec.* 404; says that the apostles did not write all things, because of their multitude, and because he that believes what they did write needs no more, 2 *Cran.* 27; compares the scriptures to an apothecary's shop, where every man may find a remedy, 1 *Whitg.* 516; on the sufficiency of scripture to those who will be ruled thereby, *Phil.* 362

(*d*) Versions:—he affirms that the original of the LXX. version of the prophets remained in his day, *Whita.* 119; he is said to have translated the scriptures into Armenian, *ib.* 222; he testifies to the existence of many vernacular versions of scripture in his time, 4 *Jew.* 896, *Whita.* 245

(*e*) The exposition and study of the scriptures, and that they are to be read by all:—he asks whether the power of the gospel is in the form of the letters, or in the understanding of the meaning (O. I.), 3 *Bul.* 261, *Calf.* 285, 2 *Hoop.* 407, 3 *Jew.* 445; says, God wills not that we should understand the words of holy scripture simply, but with great wisdom and discretion, 4 *Jew.* 764; observes that we have need of God's grace that we rest not on the bare words, for so heretics fall into error, 2 *Jew.* 577, 4 *Jew.* 764; declares that as God is covered in heaven, so is he hid in the scriptures, &c., (O. I.), 3 *Jew.* 541; warns that in a type or figure we are not to expect all things, 2 *Jew.* 1122, 3 *Jew.* 447; two reasons for the obscurity of scripture (O. I.), *Whita.* 372; he says the apostles had nothing dark in their life or doctrine, *ib.* 388; remarks that Paul, when he uses any obscure expression, explains himself, *ib.* 492; maintains that John's doctrine is clear and lucid, *ib.* 397; states that scripture expounds itself, 2 *Cran.* 27, *Whita.* 495 n., 659; asserts that not man's wisdom but the Holy Ghost is the true expositor, 2 *Cran.* 27; says that we must ask by prayer, &c., and inquire of the ancient writers, and divers priests, if we would know the truth of scripture (O. I.), 2 *Cran.* 17; calls the priests the key-bearers, (O. I. see *b.* above); says that we ought to confute false interpreters, and instruct inquirers (O. I.), 2 *Cran.* 26; affirms that our senses become practised by the use of the scriptures, and often hearing, 2 *Jew.* 682; says, that he who applies with fervent desire to the scriptures, cannot be neglected of God, 2 *Cran.* 17, 1 *Jew.* 321, 4 *Jew.* 1064; another like passage, 2 *Jew.* 681; on the command to search the scriptures, *Whita.* 236, 372; on Paul's command to Timothy to be diligent in reading, *ib.* 523; another passage on the apostle's commendation of scripture to him, *ib.* 637; exhorts all men and women to the study of scripture, *Calf.* 258, 1 *Jew.* 324, 2 *Jew.* 685, 696, *Whita.* 247; a long citation to this effect from his third sermon on Lazarus, 2 *Cran.* 119—121; says, I beseech you all...to search the scriptures, 3 *Jew.* 231; admonishes the people to get books, 2 *Jew.* 670; exhorts secular men, particularly heads of families, to procure the scriptures and study them with great diligence, 2 *Jew.* 670, 685, 696, 4 *Jew.* 1186, *Whita.* 239, 246, 1 *Whitg.* 525, 3 *Whitg.* 55; blames the people's negligence of scripture by the example of the woman of Samaria, *Pil.* 609; his rebuke of those who thought the scriptures were only for monks, 1 *Jew.* 324, *Pil.* 609; he says it is more necessary for the lay people to read God's word, than for monks or priests, 2 *Jew.* 672, 679, *Whita.* 395; remarks, the grace of the Holy Spirit has so disposed the scriptures that publicans, fishers, tentmakers, &c. might be saved by them, 4 *Jew.* 1183; says there is no need of logic, husbandmen and old women understand it, 2 *Jew.* 675, 676; affirms that the scriptures are easy to the slave, the husbandman, the widow and the child, 4 *Jew.* 897, 1183, *Whita.* 397; exhorts fathers to teach their children to sing psalms, 1 *Jew.* 332; in several places he exhorts the people to read the scriptures at home, *Calf.* 258, 1 *Jew.* 270, 2 *Jew.* 685, 4 *Jew.* 796, 1186, *Whita.* 247; says, let one of you take in hand the holy book, and call his neighbours, and water and refresh both their minds and his own, 4 *Jew.* 796; on the evils which arise from ignorance of the scriptures, *Whita.* 397; he says, this is the cause of all ills, that the scriptures are not known, 2 *Jew.* 680, 4 *Jew.* 1186, *Whita.* 701; observes, thou wilt say, "I have not read the scriptures;" this is no excuse but a sin, 1 *Jew.* 324, 4 *Jew.* 1178; says no man can attain to salvation, except he be always occupied in spiritual reading, 4 *Jew.* 1177; again, to know nothing of God's laws is the loss of salvation, *ib.* 1186; says, this is the working of the devil's inspiration; he would not suffer us to see the treasure, lest we should get the riches, 1 *Jew.* 324, 4 *Jew.* 1178; rebukes those who call ignorance of the scriptures simplicity, 1 *Jew.* 324; calls the reading of the scriptures a great fence against sin, 2 *Jew.* 695; declares that ignorance has brought in heresies and vicious living, and turned all things upside down, 2 *Jew.* 695, 4 *Jew.* 1186

(*f*) Remarks on some particular portions of the Bible:—on Cain and Abel, 1 *Ful.* 395; on Laban's complaint against Jacob, 2 *Jew.* 558, 559; he shews how the law had a shadow of good things to come, 2 *Jew.* 616; compares the state of the Jews to a candle, that of Christians to the sun, 2 *Jew.* 615; likens the Jewish state to the first draught of a picture set out only in bare lines, 2 *Jew.* 615, 616; numbers the second commandment among the ten, and holds it a moral law, 2 *Bec.* 60; says, David turneth the earth into heaven, and of men maketh angels, 3 *Jew.* 547, and that they who call in David with his harp, by means of him call in Christ, 4 *Jew.* 790; on Isa. viii. 7, and the metaphors used there, *Whita.* 379; on two texts in Matt. ii. (verses 15 and 23), *ib.* 525; he expounds the doxology in the Lord's Prayer, 4 *Bul.* 219, 220; mystical exposition of Matt. xxiv. from the O.I.—see *b.* above and ix. below; as to "the eagles," see xv. below; on John vii. 52, "search and look," 3 *Jew.* 242; his exposition of Eph. i. 23, "the fulness of him," &c., 1 *Ful.* 232, &c.; on the traditions of men (Colos. ii.), 1 *Ful.* 171; he vindicates the epistle to Philemon, *Whita.* 35

(*g*) Much of Cranmer's prologue to the Bible taken from him, 2 *Cran.* 118; he rebukes some who superstitiously hung the gospel about their necks as a charm (O. I.), 4 *Bul.* 261, *Calf.* 285, 1 *Jew.* 327, 328, 2 *Jew.* 750, 751; declares (in the Canon Law) that not only is he a betrayer of the truth who denies it, but also he who does not freely declare it, 1 *Jew.* 95, 2 *Lat.* 298

vi. *Tradition:* on Jewish traditions, added to the law, *Whita.* 618, 640; he states that the disciples observed the law, though not the traditions of the elders, 2 *Jew.* 1089, 3 *Jew.* 570; says, the mystery (or sacrament) were not divine nor perfect, if thou shouldest add anything to it, 2 *Jew.* 1100; affirms that the apostles delivered some things not in writing, *Whita.* 595, and (in other places) speaks in support of tradition, *ib.*; thinks a tradition of the church worthy of belief, 2 *Cran.* 57, 2 *Ful.* 231, *Whita.* 595; yet he says that to teach anything beside the doctrine of the apostles is to bring in dissensions and slanders, 2 *Cran.* 26; asserts that Paul delivered some things without writing, *ib.* 57, and that he calls his preaching, not written, by the name of the gospel, 3 *Jew.* 435, 437; but elsewhere he affirms that Paul wrote the same things which he had preached, 2 *Ful.* 231, and remarks that Paul says not, if they teach the contrary, or, if they overthrow the whole gospel, but, if they preach anything beside the gospel, let them be accursed, 4 *Jew.* 772; he declares that Paul himself is not to be believed if he speak anything of his own, 3 *Jew.* 290, 4 *Jew.* 711, 712, 773; asserts that good counsel is to be followed though it be not the custom, and that anything hurtful is to be rejected though it be the custom, *Calf.* 55, 2 *Cran.* 51

vii. *Sin:* he declares that every man is naturally not only a sinner, but sin, 1 *Bec.* 69; confesses original sin, 2 *Bul.* 390; his opinion on childbirth, 1 *Lat.* 252; he blames parents who lament their children's sickness, but make little account of their sin, *Sand.* 339; says the devil hides his snares under the colour of holiness, 3 *Jew.* 553; condemns flattery, 3 *Whitg.* 578; says, he who himself is a liar, thinks that nobody speaks the truth, not even God (O. I.), 3 *Jew.* 124 4 *Jew.* 1062; as to swearing, see xxviii. below; on concupiscence; contradictory statements ascribed to him, *Calf.* 64; on those shameless thieves who rob in the daytime, 3 *Jew.* 217; he compares an ill-gotten penny to a worm in an apple, *Pil.* 58, *Sand.* 231; condemns usury, 2 *Jew.* 853; calls it a great sin to desire evil against the brethren, 1 *Bec.* 154, 155

viii. *Grace, Faith, Works* (see also iii.): he says that mercy without justice is folly, &c. (O. I.), *Sand.* 147, 148; passages on justification, 2 *Cran.* 206 bis, 207; he speaks of faith alone justifying, 2 *Bec.* 639, 2 *Bul.* 342; declares that he who stayeth himself by only faith is blessed, 3 *Jew.* 244; says the thief was justified without works (dub.), *Wool.* 35, 36; observes that he needed not so much as one hour to repent, so great is the mercy of God, 3 *Jew.* 562, but he says that if he had lived, and not regarded faith and works, he would have lost his salvation (dub.), 2 *Cran.* 143; he declares that if we consider our own merits we are worthy of punishment, 3 *Bec.* 170; speaks of grace taking away all sins, *ib.* 420; maintains remission of sins without pilgrimage, 2 *Ful.* 111; speaks of being made worthy of the kingdom of heaven, 1 *Ful.* 360, 361, 364, 365; writes on Eph. i. 6, "hath made us accepted," *ib.* 410, 411; explains what repentance is, 1 *Bec.* 75, 76, 92, *Rog.* 256 n., (and see penance in xxii.); praises repentance, 1 *Bec.* 77, *Calf.* x. 64; declares that it alone cannot put away sins, *ib.* 78; but says that there is no sin which does not give place to the virtue of repentance, *ib.* 76; praises faith, *ib.* 79; says it gives things their substance, or rather is their substance, 3 *Jew.* 507; calls it a lamp, 1 *Bec.* 207, and the light of the soul, *ib.*; shews the necessity of having faith everywhere, *ib.* 79; his exposition of the words of St Paul, "I live in the faith of the Son of God," &c., 4 *Jew.* 662, 663; he says that without faith all things come to nought, 1 *Bec.* 79; declares that they who are sick should go to Christ with great faith, *ib.* 118, 119; says, we have offered this only gift to God...and by this only way we are saved, 2 *Ful.* 199; observes that Christ either is received or slain within us; for if we believe his word we receive him (O. I.), 4 *Jew.* 790; remarks on spiritual seeing, 3 *Jew.* 531; he says that where there is faith there is no need of questions, &c., 3 *Whitg.* 574; speaks against vain and impious questions, *ib.* 575; on the use of reason, 2 *Jew.* 793; he maintains that faith is full of good works, 2 *Cran.* 137; writes on the nature and reward of good works, 2 *Cov.* 432; shews that there can be no good works without faith, 2 *Cran.* 143; says, a work without faith is nothing (O. I.), 1 *Bec.* 79; terms faith the nurse of all good deeds, *Wool.* 37, 38; calls a pure mind the cause of all good things, 1 *Bec.* 138; on the necessity not only of faith, but of a virtuous life, 1 *Ful.* 418; he declares that the sons of God are not content to sit idle, 1 *Bec.* 208, 346; says that God wills not that a Christian man be contented with himself alone, but that he also edify others, *ib.* 356, 357; speaks of charity as enabling a man to be, in a sense, present in several places at once, 1 *Jew.* 494; on giving "with simplicity," 3 *Whitg.* 283; he says that such as one would have God to be to him, such he must shew himself to those that have offended against him, 1 *Bec.* 155; declares that nothing makes us more like unto God than to be easy entreated of them that hurt us, *ib.* 156; says the name only of Christ does not make a Christian (O. I.), 2 *Jew.* 819; exhorts the Christian soldier not to look for victory without conflict, *Wool.* 11

ix. *The Church* (see also v. &c.): he says Christians are sheep, but rational ones, 1 *Whitg.* 373, 525; describes sheep and wolves (O. I.), *Sand.* 397 n.; mentions that Christians were called Galileans by Julian, 4 *Jew.* 667; thinks the ship (Matt. viii. 23) denotes the church, *Sand.* 371; admonishes to understand by "Jerusalem" (in Matt. xxiv.) the church, which is called the city of peace, and founded on the mountains of the scriptures (O. I.), 4 *Jew.* 750, *Whita.* 683, 684; declares that the true church is only to be known by scripture (O. I.—see v. *b.* above); on the command "Tell it unto the church," i. e. as he explains it, to the presidents and prelates, 3 *Whitg.* 170, 226; shews the necessity of superiors in all societies, 2 *Whitg.* 259, 262, 3 *Whitg.* 588; on the things "set in order" by Paul, *Whita.* 550; he says, this day (viz. Pentecost) the earth is made heaven, &c. (pseud.), 3 *Jew.* 547; declares that the apostles dwelling in the earth had their conversation in heaven, *ib.*; says the church was at first a heaven, the Spirit of God ordering all things, but that only the vestiges of such things remained in his time, 2 *Jew.* 898, 899, 3 *Jew.* 192; compares the church to a woman fallen from her former modesty, and who keeps her boxes, but has lost the treasure that was in them, &c., 2 *Jew.* 899, 3 *Jew.* 192, 4 *Jew.* 723, 764; says, as every good thing proceeds from the temple, so every ill thing proceeds likewise from the temple (O. I.), 3 *Jew.* 596; declares that the church, by what way soever she do against the will of Christ, is worthy to be given over, 4 *Jew.* 727; says, of this head (i. e. Christ) the body hath both to be, and also well to be — what! cleavest thou to the members, and leavest the head? *ib.* 751; he affirms that we should not advance the church because of the increase of people, but endeavour to adorn her with virtue, *ib.* 723, 724; declares schism to be no less evil than heresy, 3 *Whitg.* 595; speaks of the infidel coming and saying, "I would be a Christian, but I know not whom I should follow, there is such dissension among you," 3 *Jew.* 609; says, for this cause we are scorned of Jews and Gentiles, while the church is rent into a thousand parts, *ib.*; commends the leaving the bodily church when the wicked by violence have invaded it (O. I.), 4 *Jew.* 876; says the church is not walls and roof, but faith and life, 2 *Lat.* 313 n.; as to the abomination of desolation standing in the holy places of the church, see xxvii. below; as to the dignity of Antioch, see xi. below; he says, in his time the British islands had felt the power of God's word, 1 *Jew.* 306, 3 *Jew.* 165

x. *Apostles, Bishops, and other Ministers:* he maintains that the prophets mentioned in Eph. ii. 20, are those of the Old Testament, *Whita.* 349; shews that different degrees were appointed in the church because equality engenders strife, 2 *Whitg.* 259, and that the rebellious nature of man made such degrees needful (O. I.), *ib.*; says the apostles were more mighty than kings, 1 *Jew.* 431, 4 *Jew.* 674; declares that Christ transferred all the judgment which he received of the Father unto the apostles and priests, 3 *Jew.* 355, 367, 368; says, heaven takes authority of judgment from the earth; in earth sits the judge, the Lord follows the servant, *ib.* 376; speaks of James as bishop of Jerusalem, 1 *Jew.* 428, 431, *Rog.* 328 n.; on the office of Timothy and Titus, 2 *Whitg.* 284, 285, 295, 296, 373, 427; on Paul's commandment to the former, (1 Tim. vi. 14), 3 *Whitg.* 174; observes, on 1 Tim. iv. 14, ("the laying on of the hands of the presbytery"), that Paul was speaking not of priests but bishops, 1 *Whitg.* 433, 487, 488; expounds 1 Tim. v. 22, as admonishing Timothy to be circumspect in appointing ministers, *ib.* 426, 430; writes on his hearing certain things from Paul "before many witnesses," *Phil.* 366; says Paul committed the ordination and government of bishops to Titus, 1 *Whitg.* 434, 2 *Whitg.* 353; shews why a bishop is so called, 4 *Jew.* 906; he declared that one city might not have two bishops, 1 *Jew.* 348, 2 *Whitg.* 215; speaks of the emperor ruling over the world, a bishop over one city, *ib.* 315, 317; says, the seat makes not the priest, but the priest the seat; the place sanctifies not the man, but the man the place (O. I., and in the Canon Law), 1 *Bec.* 6, 1 *Bul.* 333, 3 *Jew.* 327, 4 *Jew.* 1013, 1070, 1117; complains of the derision suffered by the bishops of his day, 3 *Whitg.* 594; distinguishes bishops from presbyters, 1 *Whitg.* 487; declares that between a bishop and a priest there is scarce any difference, and that the former is superior only by the power of ordaining, 3 *Jew.* 439, 1 *Whitg.* 440, 2 *Whitg.* 260, 261; what he understands by $\chi\epsilon\iota\rho o\tau o\nu i\alpha$, 1 *Whitg.* 346 n., 349; says, he that is appointed by men (only), before God is neither deacon nor priest (O. I.), 3 *Jew.* 309; he erred in styling ministers priests, 1 *Ful.* 251, but said his whole priesthood was to teach and preach the gospel, 2 *Jew.* 709; declares that every Christian is a priest, 3 *Jew.* 336; says, not every priest is holy, but every holy man is a priest (O. I.), 1 *Bec.* 6 n., and explains $\lambda\epsilon\iota\tau o\upsilon\rho\gamma o\acute{\upsilon}\nu\tau\omega\nu$, Acts xiii., to mean preaching, 4 *Jew.* 805; he says there are many priests, yet few priests; many in name, few in labour (O. I.), 1 *Bec.* 6, 2 *Jew.* 1020, 3 *Jew.* 309; calls priests the key-bearers (O. I., see v. *b.*); terms them the stomach of the people, *Bale* 109; speaks of the priest as bearing not fire, but the Holy Ghost, 2 *Jew.* 769, 3 *Jew.* 545; compares the office of the ministry to that of a herald, *Whita.* 284; shews that as in worldly affairs, so in spiritual matters, the message of the king is not to be despised on account of the baseness of the messenger, 4 *Jew.* 911; compares a pastor to one who wrestles naked, *Sand.* 332; on the words "our sufficiency is of God," 2 *Jew.* 982; shews why God puts "treasure in earthen vessels," *Hutch.* 305; calls it a shame for priests, when laymen are found more faithful than they (O. I.), 1 *Bec.* 386; his remarks on the virtue of preaching, 3 *Jew.* 595; he shews that preachers must teach first with works and then with words, 1 *Bec.* 15; cautions against hearing the word to destruction, 2 *Jew.* 1056; says that...if the ministry of man be wanting, the Lord himself will enlighten our mind, 2 *Jew.*1019; another similar passage, 2 *Cran.* 17, 1 *Jew.* 321, 4 *Jew.* 1064; referred to on evil ministers, 2 *Lat.* 347; tells how to know wolves in sheep's clothing, *Calf.* 292; shews the danger of ordaining unworthy men, 1 *Bec.* 6; says that if priests teach well but live ill, their doctrine, but not their manners, must be taken (O. I.), *ib.* 386, 387, 2 *Bec.* 324, 333; declares that he who lives other than he speaks, teaches God to punish him, *Sand.* 71; as to Paul's anathema against false teachers, see v. *b.* above; he laments superiorities and salutations in the church of God, 4 *Jew.* 688; says they who neither believe nor fear the judgment of God, abusing their ecclesiastical dignity in secular sort, turn the same into secular dignity (O. I.), *ib.* 971; defends the possession of lands by ministers, *Pil.* 596; on the election of deacons (Acts vi.), 1 *Whitg.* 340; he speaks of the public reading of scripture by the deacon, 3 *Whitg.* 47; describes the reader's office, 4 *Jew.*816; on the promotion of deacons to a higher grade, 3 *Whitg.* 70; he says that monks had their minds void of all affections, and their bodies like Adam's before the fall, *Calf.* 259; as to vowed women, see xxi. below.

xi. *Peter, Rome:* by the rock, he understood Peter, 4 *Bul.* 81; not his person, but his faith and confession, 2 *Ful.* 273, 285, 298, 1 *Jew.* 340, 2 *Jew.* 895; he thinks that Christ's gift of the keys to Peter was a gift of power to forgive sins, 3 *Whitg.* 235; does not consider that the keys were given to Peter only, for he speaks of them as committed to (John) the son of thunder, 2 *Ful.* 277; says Peter's crime was double, both for that he withstood Christ, and also for that he set himself before the rest, 3 *Jew.* 288; affirms that Christ shed his blood to purchase those sheep whose care he committed to Peter and his successors, 2 *Ful.* 326; his idea of Peter's primacy, *Whita.* 440; he designates him pastor and head, &c., 1 *Jew.* 435; often acknowledges Peter to be prince of the apostles, 2 *Ful.* 286, 304; calls him the head of the apostles, 1 *Jew.* 435, 3 *Jew.* 288; but he terms Elias head of the prophets, 1 *Jew.* 438, 3 *Jew.* 270, 288, 4 *Jew.* 1032, and styles the emperor the head of all men, 1 *Jew.* 438, 4 *Jew.* 975, 997, 1014; he calls Peter the ruler of the whole world, the teacher of the world, &c., 1 *Jew.* 428—430, 3 *Jew.* 269, 282; asks, how can he be a master that hath no scholar? (O. I.), 3 *Jew.* 309; declares that the apostles received the care of the whole world, 1 *Jew.* 430; states that the nation of the Jews was committed to Michael, but all the world to Paul, &c., *ib.* 430, 431, 3 *Jew.* 269; says Paul was moved with the care of all the churches, not of two or three, 3 *Jew.* 282, 319; asserts that he was as careful for the salvation of all, as if the whole world had been one house, *ib.* 319; calls him in a manner the common father of all the world, *ib.* 288; designates him the master of the world, and by other similar titles, *ib.* 282, 283, 319; calls John the pillar of all the churches in the world, *ib.* 319; says (to the people) let us take the care of the universal church, 1 *Jew.* 427; on Christ's inquiry of Peter, "Lovest thou me?" and his charge to him, 1 *Cov.* 356 n.; he says Christ asked Peter whether he loved him, to inform us how great care he takes of the government of the flock, 2 *Ful.* 317, 318; another like passage, *ib.* 326; thinks that Peter made James bishop of Jerusalem, 1 *Jew.* 428, 431; says Peter did all things (in the election of Matthias) with the consent of the disciples, 1 *Ful.* 466, 2 *Ful.* 286; says every Christian man who receives the word of Peter, is made Peter's chair, and Peter himself sits in him (O. I.), 4 *Jew.*929, 1013; sets it down as an undoubted truth that none has place before Paul, 3 *Jew.* 288; shews that Paul was equal with the highest, 2 *Ful.* 286, 3 *Jew.* 328; says Paul had no need of Peter...but was equal to him in honour, 1 *Jew.* 328, 375, 431, 3 *Jew.* 287, 288, 328, 4 *Jew.* 917; on the agreement between Peter, Paul, &c., as to their preaching, 3 *Jew.* 328; he speaks of certain women as the head of the church at Philippi, 4 *Jew.*975, 1 *Whitg.* 391; on the peculiar dignity of Antioch, where the disciples were first called Christians, 1 *Jew.* 369; another passage, 4 *Jew.* 883; he calls Antioch the head of all the world, 1 *Jew.* 421, 439, 4 *Jew.* 717, and the metropolis of the faith, 1 *Jew.* 433; considers it incongruous that they of Egypt should judge those of Thrace, 3 *Jew.* 303; says, whosoever desires primacy in earth, shall find in heaven confusion (O. I.), *ib.* 125, 126, 311, 312; observes that he who desires not vainglory, being made Christ's vicar, ought to preach the justice of Christ (O. I.), *ib.* 606

xii. *Saints:* he declares that God sooner

hears us, than others praying for us, 1 *Jew.* 97 (and see corrig.), and that he is easy to be entreated without a mediator, *ib.*; on the lifting up of Moses' hands (dub. and pseud.), *Calf.* 104; says Elijah changed the nature of water (by making iron swim), 2 *Jew.* 565; calls him head of the prophets, see xi; on the Zacharias who was slain in the temple, *Whita.* 590; referred to on the expression "full of grace," applied to the virgin Mary, 1 *Ful.* 529; thinks that she was a little vainglorious (two passages), 1 *Lat.* 383, 515, 2 *Lat.* 226, 3 *Tyn.* 207; oftentimes calls Paul sutorem pellium (σκηνοποιὸν), 3 *Jew.* 395; says it had been great folly for Paul, having received his doctrine from God himself, afterward to confer with men, 4 *Jew.* 901; observes, whithersoever a man come, he shall see Paul carried about in the mouth of every man, 3 *Jew.* 545; spurious passages on St Paul's chain, 2 *Ful.* 110, 139; as to this apostle see also xi; as to John see xi; he affirms that the tombs of Peter, Paul, John and Thomas, are well known, *Calf.* 130; says demons tremble not only at the Crucified, but at the ashes of those who are slain for him, *ib.* 77; rebukes Epiphanius for usurping authority in another church, 2 *Zur.* 242; tells how the monk Macedonius averted the rage of Theodosius from Antioch, *Calf.* 22 n

xiii. *Sacraments:* he observes that a figure must be not far from the truth, yet not the truth itself, 2 *Jew.* 594, and that if all things agreed, it would be no figure, *ib.* 1122; remarks on the rock being Christ, 3 *Jew.* 510; he says dyed wool is no longer called wool, but purple, or scarlet, &c. (pseud.), 2 *Jew.* 576; states that a sacrament is called a mystery because we see one thing, and believe another, *Calf.* 184, 2 *Jew.*, 619; speaks of the sacraments as things perceived by the mind, delivered in things sensible; and shews that our being in the body is the reason why the graces of the sacraments are not bestowed nakedly, but by means of outward signs, 2 *Bec.* 287, 3 *Bec.* 443, 1 *Brad.* 87 n., 491 n., 4 *Bul.* 242, 243, 249, 1 *Jew.* 464, 2 *Jew.* 595, 618, 759, 3 *Jew.* 371, *Sand.* 87; says all mysteries must be viewed with inward eyes, 2 *Bec.* 287, 297, 3 *Bec.* 430, 431, 438, *Grin.* 62, 64, 1 *Jew.* 463, 525, 2 *Jew.* 792, 1111, *Sand.* 454, or, as he elsewhere says, with the eyes of the understanding, 2 *Jew.* 572; he declares that the eyes of faith, when they behold the unspeakable good things, do not so much as mark the outward things, 3 *Jew.* 526; refers to the sacraments as stopping the mouths of heretics, see xv. below; speaks of the Lord's things as common to all, 1 *Jew.* 134; speaks of one baptism and one table, 2 *Jew.* 636; on our being baptized into one body, and drinking of one Spirit, 1 *Brad.* 88; warns that neither baptism, nor the holy table shall profit us, except we have a life pure from sin, 1 *Bec.* 341; denies that sacraments received by one, benefit others who receive them not, 2 *Jew.* 990; said to call penance a sacrament, 3 *Jew.* 456 n

xiv. *Baptism :* he intimates that catechumens may not join in the prayer of the church, 2 *Jew.* 706; refers to the words of baptism as not to be spoken in the presence of heathen men, *ib.*; calls them secret and dreadful words, *ib.* 716; terms baptism the seal of faith, 3 *Whitg.* 113; declares that the sick were healed at Bethesda, to shew the virtue of baptism, 3 *Jew.* 443; says the words of baptism pronounced by the priest regenerate him who is baptized, 2 *Jew.* 567, 706; declares that the element is sensible, but that what is wrought by it is spiritual, 4 *Bul.* 242, 243, 1 *Jew.* 465, 3 *Jew.* 513 n.; teaches that in baptism we receive, not the purple and the diadem, but the King himself for our clothing, 3 *Jew.* 544; considers that by baptism we are made flesh of Christ's flesh, and bone of his bone, 1 *Jew.* 131, 140, 477, 529, 3 *Jew.* 494, 529; says, as Christ was born by the Holy Ghost...even so in the font we are made the same, 1 *Jew.* 131, 3 *Jew.* 494; again, in thy baptism thou art made both a king and a priest and a prophet, 4 *Jew.* 984; speaks of the marvellous work therein effected as unspeakable, even by the angels, &c., 1 *Jew.* 487, 3 *Jew.* 498; shews that baptism is not to be judged by sight, 1 *Jew.* 466, 2 *Jew.* 594, 618, 619; says that an unbeliever, when he hears of the bath of baptism, thinks that it is nothing else but plain water, 1 *Jew.* 149, 466, 515, 2 *Jew.* 1101; what a Christian sees in baptism, 1 *Jew.* 515; he says simple water works not in us, but when it has received the grace of the Spirit, it washes away all sins, 2 *Jew.* 1102, 3 *Jew.* 443; declares that when the creature of water has received the Holy Ghost, it is made a sacrament, &c., 3 *Jew.* 500; calls it the water not of drinking, but of sanctification, 2 *Jew.* 576, 3 *Jew.* 500; says Christ by his baptism sanctified all water, *Whita.* 592; writes, when thou art baptized, it is not the priest that dippeth thee, but it is God that......holds thy head, 1 *Jew.* 454, 466, 2 *Jew.* 792, 3 *Jew.* 480; speaking of the change of the bread in the other sacrament, he adds, the like change is in the water of baptism, 3 *Jew.* 513; calls baptism Christ's passion, or his blood, (his words are, his baptism is a symbol of his passion), 1 *Jew.* 518, 521, 2 *Jew.* 727, 792, 1101, 3 *Jew.* 482, 502, 4 *Jew.* 893; teaches those who are to be baptized to hold the Saviour's feet, to wash them with tears, &c., 1 *Jew.* 487, 543; says baptism becomes to us, what the cross and grave were to Christ, *ib.* 521; on naming children; the example of the patriarchs, 2 *Jew.* 1108; on the text, " Christ sent me not to baptize," &c., 2 *Whitg.* 456; he speaks of some men deferring baptism to their death-beds, *Sand.* 152; condemns the Marcionites for baptizing living persons for the dead, 1 *Jew.* 23 n

xv. *The Eucharist* (see also iii. and vi.)

(*a*) Institution, &c.:—he speaks of the mysteries as stopping the mouths of heretics; for, he asks, if Jesus died not, whose sign or token is this sacrifice? 2 *Bec.* 288, 3 *Bec.* 438, 4 *Bul.* 317, 440, *Coop.* 206, *Grin.* 65, 1 *Jew.* 219, 258, 465, 2 *Jew.* 592, 609, 700, 775, 1101, 1112, 3 *Jew.* 468; writes of it as a memorial of the passion, &c., 2 *Jew.* 609; remarks that Christ, both in the bread and also in the cup, said, "Do this in remembrance of me," 3 *Jew.* 479; expounds those words as meaning, Do this in remembrance of my benefit, and of your salvation, 1 *Jew.* 166, 2 *Jew.* 591, 715; says that Christ participated in the mysteries of his body and blood, in which is a memory of himself, to induce his disciples to receive with a quiet mind, 3 *Bec.* 367, 438; expounds Christ's saying that he would drink of the fruit of the vine in his Father's kingdom, *Hutch.* 270; shews what " the fruit of the vine" is, see *b.* below; considers that the bread which Paul gave to eat in the shipwreck was merely sustenance, 1 *Jew.* 235; the Opus Imperfectum takes another view of it, *ib.*; Chrysostom denies that the eucharist is the Lord's supper, 2 *Lat.* 263

(*b*) Of the sign and the thing signified, and how the elements are Christ's body and blood (see xiii. above):—he cautions against understanding the words of Christ carnally, for that mysteries must be considered with inward eyes, i. e. spiritually, see xiii. above; explains what it is to understand carnally, 2 *Bec.* 287, 1 *Jew.* 452, 526; declares that there is no sensible thing delivered unto us by Christ (in these mysteries, but that) whatsoever things Christ has delivered are insensible, 3 *Jew.* 512, 3 *Tyn.* 260; speaks of Christ shewing bread and wine, after the order of Melchisedec, for a similitude of his body and blood, 2 *Bec.* 288, 3 *Bec.* 438, *Coop.* 206, 2 *Jew.* 580, 1115; states that Christ when he ascended left us his flesh in mysteries, *Phil.* 198; compares Christ's body to Elijah's mantle, 1 *Ful.* 510, 1 *Jew.* 488, 489, *Phil.* 196, *Rid.* 222—225; says, he that sits above with the Father is handled with the hands of all, 3 *Bec.* 411, 1 *Ful.* 510, 511, *Rid.* 223; declares that we receive in the mysteries the only begotten Son of God, 3 *Jew.* 543, 544; how he acknowledges Christ's very body to be present, 3 *Jew.* 544, 2 *Lat.* 274; he says, that royal body is worthy of the highest honour, 3 *Jew.* 523, 527; exhorts us, by the example of the magi, to worship the Lord's body, 1 *Jew.* 538, *Rid.* 250, 251; teaches how Christ's body is to be honoured, viz. by clothing the naked, &c., *Hutch.* 256, 257; prefers a poor man before the sacrament, and calls him the body of Christ rather than the other, *Grin.* 66; warns that the creature and the Creator must not be confounded, 3 *Jew.* 481; another passage to the same effect, 2 *Jew.* 1121, 3 *Jew.* 555, 556; says the bread is (in the Latin, signifies,) the body of Christ, and affirms the same of the receivers, 2 *Bec.* 287, 288, 3 *Bec.* 438, 2 *Hoop.* 405 n., 1 *Jew.* 135, 538, 765, *Rid.* 242; declares that not the true body of Christ, but a mystery of his body is contained in the hallowed vessels (O. I.), 2 *Bec.* 288, 3 *Bec.* 438, *Coop.* 205, *Grin.* 67, 198, 1 *Jew.* 151, 539, 2 *Jew.* 749, 771, 3 *Jew.* 467, 472, 523, 536, *Rid.* 32, *Sand.* 454; Gardiner's explanation of this passage, *Rid.* 33; its genuineness disputed, *ib.* 509; he reproves those who feared to touch holy vessels, yet dared to sin, 2 *Ful.* 115; says, the vessels are not partakers of him, nor feel him whom they contain, but we do truly, 3 *Jew.* 466; he says before the bread is hallowed we call it bread, but being hallowed, it is delivered from the name of bread, and deemed worthy to be called the Lord's body, although the nature of bread remains in it, 2 *Bec.* 265, 3 *Bec.* 423, 438, 1 *Brad.* 87 n., *Grin.* 72, *Hutch.* 275, 1 *Jew.* 545, 2 *Jew.* 564, 776, 792, 1066, 1106, 3 *Jew.* 501, 504, 509, *Rid.* 34, 174; Romish attempts to deny or suppress this passage,

Grin. 72 n.; he warns against supposing that the divine body is received at the hand of man, 2 *Bec.* 288, 3 *Bec.* 438, 2 *Jew.* 792; speaks of seeing the body of Christ with the eyes of the mind, 1 *Jew.* 150, and compare 515, see also the passage about the eagles, in *c.* below; he says Christ calls bread, either his doctrine or his body, for either of them makes the soul stronger, 2 *Jew.* 1111; declares that what is in the chalice is that which flowed out of Christ's side, 1 *Ful.* 511, 3 *Jew.* 519, 523, *Rid.* 237; but he says that when Christ gave the mystery of the sacrament he gave wine; the fruit of the vine, which produces wine, not water, 3 *Bec.* 359, 424, 1 *Brad.* 546, 2 *Jew.* 606, 3 *Jew.* 518, 521, 522, 523, *Rid.* 204; says David receiving of the water (that his men had gotten with great danger) would not drink of it; for it was not water, but blood (pseud.), 3 *Jew.* 499

(*c*) Of eating Christ's body, (see also *b.* and *d.*):—he writes, the greatest and worthiest thing that is, thou dost not only behold in the earth, but thou also touchest it, and eatest it, 3 *Jew.* 525, 531; speaks of our fastening our teeth in the flesh of Christ, 2 *Jew.* 608, 1042, 3 *Jew.* 613, 618, 619; calls Christ that great bread that feedeth the mind not the belly, 1 *Jew.* 452, 2 *Jew.* 572, 786, 3 *Jew.* 618; declares that he is our food, and the food of angels, 2 *Jew.* 786, spiritual food, &c., 2 *Hoop.* 500; says, we, being here beneath, taste him sitting in heaven above, 3 *Jew.* 546; considers that we are called eagles (Matt. xxiv.) to shew that he who cometh to the body of the Lord must climb up on high, 2 *Bec.* 295, 3 *Bec.* 360, 433, 1 *Jew.* 12, 448, 454, 467, 489, 539, 764, 2 *Jew.* 1121, 3 *Jew.* 528, 543, 546; speaking of the eagle's flight he says, wipe away all filth from thy soul, prepare thy mind to receive these mysteries, &c., 3 *Jew.* 543

(*d*) Exhortations to come to the communion; cautions to the wicked not to come, &c.:—his earnestness in exhorting to the eucharist, 2 *Brad.* 276, 2 *Cov.* 254 (see also *h.* below); he reproves his hearers for their slack coming to the holy table, 2 *Bec.* 259; complains, we stand at the altar for nought, &c., *Coop.* 14, 68, 1 *Jew.* 195, *Phil.* 97; his reproof of those who came but once or twice in the year, 3 *Bec.* 472, *Coop.* 101, 1 *Jew.* 170; his rebuke of those who stood by, not communicating, see *h.* below; he intimates that he who is not worthy of the communion is not worthy of the prayers, 3 *Bec.* 416, 473, 2 *Brad.* 276 n., 1 *Jew.* 19, 127; declares that he who has a pure conscience ought every day to come to the communion, 2 *Bec.* 258, 259; exhorts those that come with a pure conscience and clean mind, to come always to the holy table, 3 *Bec.* 472, 473; urges to come with great desire, *ib.* 473; declares that those ought to be pure who touch the King's cup, *ib.* 412; asks how any can touch Christ's body with impure hands, *ib.*; admonishes the wicked not to come at all to the holy table, 3 *Bec.* 472, 1 *Jew.* 170; cautions hypocrites against approaching the sacrament of Christ's body and blood, 1 *Bec.* 117; warns that no Judas or unclean person come to the holy table, 3 *Bec.* 476; charges ministers to repel impure persons, *ib.* 476, 477; shews that the admission of evil men to the mysteries is sinful in those that do not repel them, *ib.* 477, 478; speaks of the exclusion of those who are not meet to be partakers, *ib.* 478, 483; says, we forbid those to be present who are not perfect Christians, *ib.* 478, 483; affirms that the same punishment awaits those who receive the body of the Lord unworthily as those who crucified him, *Rid.* 247; says a wicked man eats and drinks damnation to himself, not to others, *Pil.* 636; affirms that Judas received Christ's true body no less than Peter, Andrew, &c., 3 *Jew.* 449; the Lord's supper greatly frequented in his time, 2 *Bec.* 258

(*e*) Benefits, &c.:—he calls the eucharistic mysteries a remembrance of many benefits, 3 *Bec.* 458; says, that in the sacrament we behold Christ's great benefit and our salvation, 1 *Jew.* 448; exhorts us to say, when we see the body of Christ set forth, Because of this body I am no longer dust and ashes, no longer captive, but free, 1 *Jew.* 537, 538, 2 *Jew.* 763; compares the eucharist to the coal from the altar (Isa. vi.), 2 *Bec.* 288 n., 1 *Brad.* 522; speaks of the people being made red with the blood of Christ, see *g.* below; speaks of the eucharist as the power and grace of God, 1 *Brad.* 97 n.; calls it the health of our souls, 1 *Bec.* 120; terms it the power of our soul, the sinews of the mind, &c., 3 *Bec.* 388; says, Christ calls us into heaven, unto the table of the great King, 3 *Jew.* 546, and see the passage about the eagles, in *c.* above; he says, this mystery makes earth heaven to us; ascend up therefore to the gates of heaven, &c., *ib.* 547;

on the grace received through the holy eucharist, 1 *Brad.* 97, 98, *Rid.* 202; he says we should depart from the table of the Lord God as lions that breathe fire, 1 *Bec.* 120, 121

(*f*) The sacrament as a type of unity:—he shews why we all partake of "one bread," *Coop.* 78, and why it is called not the participation, but "the communion of the body of Christ," *Rid.* 241; speaks not only of the bread, but of the receivers, as being the body of Christ, 2 *Bec.* 287, 288, 3 *Bec.* 438, 1 *Jew.* 135, 538, 765, *Rid.* 242; declares that we are made one body of Christ, 1 *Jew.* 132; says Christ reduces us, as it were, into one lump with himself, &c., *Hutch.* 240, 1 *Jew.* 470, (and corrig.) 473, 474

(*g*) The eucharist as a sacrifice:—he says Melchisedec brought forth bread and wine, but does not speak of it as a sacrifice, 2 *Jew.* 731; he shews that the oblation of the eucharist is a memorial of the sacrifice of Christ, 1 *Jew.* 171, 4 *Jew.* 804; says, our High Priest has offered up the sacrifice that cleanses us, and now we do the same in remembrance of him, &c., 2 *Jew.* 729; declares that we offer every day in remembrance of Christ's death; and that we offer not another, but the same sacrifice; rather we make a remembrance of that sacrifice, 2 *Bec.* 249, 3 *Bec.* 457, 458, *Coop.* 94, 1 *Cov.* 451 n., 2 *Hoop.* 530, 1 *Jew.* 171, 493, 2 *Jew.* 729, 3 *Jew.* 535, 4 *Jew.* 804, *Rid.* 215, &c., *Sand.* 454; says, the sacrifice is one, though offered in many places, because there is but one Christ everywhere, &c., 1 *Jew.* 492, *Rid.* 215; speaks of the death of Christ as wrought in the mysteries, 2 *Jew.* 726, 733, 3 *Jew.* 448, 527; speaks of Christ being crucified before our eyes, and the company being made red with his blood, &c., 1 *Jew.* 488, 2 *Jew.* 608, 792, 3 *Jew.* 546; says, in the mysteries blood is drawn from Christ's side, 2 *Jew.* 792; speaks of the priest standing at the altar, and commanding the people to offer thanks for all the world, &c., *Coop.* 97; mentions the sacrifice foretold by Malachi, as offered not by fire and smoke, but by the grace of the Spirit, 2 *Jew.* 724, 734, also as an unbloody sacrifice (pseud.), 2 *Jew.* 732; he says the sacrifice of the gospel ascendeth up without blood, without smoke, without an altar, *ib.* 735; yet he figuratively speaks of the mysteries as consumed by fire, *ib.* 791, 792; he considers "the offering up of the Gentiles" (Rom. xv. 16) to mean the preaching of the gospel to them, *Calf.* 230

(*h*) Rites, &c.:—he says, if thou shouldest add anything to the mystery it were not divine nor perfect, 2 *Jew.* 1100, 1125; declares that we are not, like the Jews, subject to the necessity of time, 3 *Bec.* 380; speaks of receiving the communion at the Epiphany, in Lent, at Easter, &c., *Coop.* 100, 101; at Easter, *ib.* 14; would call it presumption to be prepared for communion only one day in the year, 1 *Jew.* 120; speaks of offering daily, see in *g.* above; his meaning expounded, *Coop.* 104; he exhorts those who come to the communion after meat to be sober in behaviour, *Hutch.* 222; mentions the practice of the deacon calling the people to the communion, and shews how his voice separated the congregation, *Coop.* 107, 1 *Jew.* 172, 198, 2 *Jew.* 716; his exhortation to the communion,—we stand at the altar for nought, nobody will communicate, *Coop.* 14, 68, 1 *Jew.* 195, *Phil.* 97; he elsewhere uses the word "nobody" for "few," 1 *Jew.* 196; blames those who stand by at the communion, not partaking, 2 *Bec.* 257, 3 *Bec.* 416, 473, *Coop.* 107, 1 *Jew.* 119, 200, 2 *Jew.* 989, 3 *Jew.* 473, 474; shews that none who do not communicate must be present, 2 *Bec.* 257, 3 *Bec.* 483; says those who would not receive departed, &c., *Pil.* 542; mentions the unveiling of the altar at the sacrifice, 1 *Jew.* 508; cited as saying, in the time of the mysteries we embrace one another, that being many we may become one, *ib.* 132; says, we cry aloud in the sight of the oblation, "Lift up your hearts," 3 *Jew.* 534; on blessing the eucharist, i. e. giving thanks, *Calf.* 232, 2 *Ful.* 168; another passage, 1 *Ful.* 502, and see 504; he says that the sacrament is consecrated not by men, but by Christ himself, 1 *Ful.* 271; his opinion as to the words of consecration, *Rid.* 18; speaks of the host in the hands of the priest, 2 *Lat.* 274; refers to sacrifice for the dead, *ib.* 275; mentions the address, "Holy things for the holy," 1 *Jew.* 508, 511, *Pil.* 542; declares that the Lord's supper ought to be common, 2 *Bec.* 239, 3 *Bec.* 416; says the mysteries are set forth to rich and poor, 1 *Jew.* 202; affirms that in some cases the priest differs nothing from the layman, as in the use of the venerable mysteries, 1 *Jew.* 202, 205, 208, 230, 248, 261, 2 *Jew.* 737; refers to the priest and people speaking together in the mysteries, 1 *Jew.* 18, 57, 292, 312; does not sanction solitary masses, *Coop.* 99—107; says the things which belong to the eucharist, diverse from the old law, are all common between the priest and the people, 2 *Bec.* 245, 3 *Bec.* 413, *Coop.* 142, 143, *Hutch.* 282, *Sand.* 455; declares that priests and people receive equally of the holy table, 3 *Jew.* 477; says that in receiving the Lord's supper we ought to have golden minds, not golden vessels, 4 *Bul.* 419; the holy vessels are spoken of in *b.* above; he testifies that the sacrament was reserved in both kinds, 1 *Jew.* 241; speaks of the common supper after the communion, 2 *Bec.* 251

xvi. *Ceremonies*: he says these things (the traditions of men) are more regarded than the commandments of our Father, 3 *Jew.* 571; speaks of unction by the elders of the church, 1 *Ful.* 251, 3 *Jew.* 457; mentions the visible and spiritual oil, 2 *Jew.* 604; speaks of the priest lifting the gospel on high, 1 *Jew.* 512; mentions white (or clean?) garments, with reference, it is supposed to the clergy, 1 *Zur.* 350, but his meaning is disputed, *ib.* 160; speaks of priests going about in a white garment, 3 *Bec.* 476, 3 *Jew.* 616, 2 *Whitg.* 24, 26, 48; alleged to have introduced processions at Constantinople, and why, *Calf.* 298, &c.; did not consider pilgrimages needful, 2 *Ful.* 110, 111

xvii. *Prayer, Praise, Worship*: he says prayer is a great treasure, so that he that prays aright cannot sin, 1 *Bec.* 143; declares that prayer receives us full of sins, and cleanses us, *ib.* 144; asserts that by prayer all things are easy, *ib.* 143, 144; calls it the head of all goodness, terrible to the devils, and healthful to the godly, *ib.* 144; says that if we pray diligently God will enlighten us, without any interpreter, 1 *Jew.* 319, 321 (see v. *e.* and x.); declares that prayer is needful in order to prosperity, *Wool.* 135; asserts that the table which begins and ends with prayer shall never want, 1 *Bec.* 64, 175; says our prayers are acceptable to God only in Christ and for his sake, 2 *Jew.* 741; inculcates perseverance in prayer, 1 *Bec.* 153; prescribes times for daily prayer, *ib.* 172, 173; says, Paul the prince of the apostles calls upon us to be always praying, 4 *Jew.* 824; shews that a man may pray in any place, 1 *Bec.* 157—159; calls it the duty of a devout mind to pray, not so much with the voice as with the devotion of the heart, *ib.* 164; declares that, even though a man does not use external gestures, yet if he shew forth a fervent mind, he will make a perfect prayer, *ib.* 131, 158; says, he prays in the sight of God who gathers his mind quietly, and lifts up himself to heaven, *ib.* 136; maintains that in prayer there is not so much need of the voice as of the thought, *ib.*; explains battalogia, or babbling in prayer, *ib.* 169, 170; censures long prayers, while the mind is without fruit, *ib.* 135, 136; it is alleged that he says private prayer is more effectual than common prayer (sed qu.), 1 *Lat.* 338; two passages on the greater advantage of public prayer, 1 *Jew.* 333; he describes a Christian congregation, 2 *Lat.* 342; says communion of prayer and sacraments ought to be one, *Grin.* 263; often speaks of the priests and people joining in prayer, 1 *Brad.* 528, 1 *Jew.* 281, 282, 289, 292, 2 *Whitg.* 493, and mentions the response "And with thy spirit," 1 *Jew.* 282, 308, 312; cites Paul as thinking it no small inconvenience if the unlearned cannot say, "Amen," 3 *Bec.* 408, (see also xviii); speaks of the minister, before the reading of holy scripture, charging the people to keep silence and give ear, 4 *Jew.* 857; also mentions that before the reading of the lesson the deacon said, Πρόσχωμεν, "Let us mark," *ib.*; declares the reader's office, *ib.* 816; writes, he enters empty before God, who coming to prayer does no alms (O. I.), 1 *Bec.* 162, 163; his opinions on prayer for the dead, *Whita.* 596; he says, when the Lord is blessed, and thanks are given to him, then more plenteous blessing is wont to be given by him, *Calf.* 250; on giving thanks "with the spirit," 1 *Jew.* 313, 315; on the sacrifice of our bodies, *Sand.* 414; Latin graces after meat taken from his works, *Pra. Eliz.* 400, 401; Bradford's preface to his two orations on prayer, 1 *Brad.* 13

xviii. *Tongues* (see also xvii): on the multitude of languages, 1 *Jew.* 278; on the gift of tongues, and other extraordinary gifts of the Holy Ghost, *ib.* 307—309; some remarks on speaking with unknown tongues, 2 *Hoop.* 548, 564, 1 *Jew.* 329, 330, *Whita.* 238, 262, 264; on the term "barbarian," as used by St Paul, *Whita.* 268, 272; he shews that prayer in an unknown tongue profits not, 1 *Jew.* 178; asks what profit can there be of a voice not understood? 2 *Bec.* 254, 255, 3 *Bec.* 408, 1 *Jew.* 309, 329, *Whita.* 262; shews that the voice of a teacher profits nothing, if the hearers do not understand him, 3 *Bec.* 409; observes that he that understands not what he hears loses it (O. I.), 4 *Jew.* 858

xix. *Miracles*: speaking of miracles wrought by Peter, he says, before the knowledge of God was in men, there was reason that the power of God should be known by the holiness of men; but now it is madness, *Calf.* 112; shews that the faithful need no miracles, 2 *Cran.* 46; observes that a desperate mind stands still in the same frowardness though he see signs and miracles, *Calf.* 353, 2 *Ful.* 198; declares that Christ promised not to reward miracle-workers, but those that keep his commandments, 2 *Cran.* 49; calls the conversion of the world a miracle, 4 *Jew.* 1041; says, in old times it was known by miracles who were the true Christians, but now the working of miracles is taken quite away, and is rather found among false Christians (O. I.), 2 *Cran.* 46, 4 *Jew.* 1040, 1041, 1170; affirms that some miracles are wrought to try men, 2 *Cran.* 46; shews that the scriptures are of more force than the revelations of ghosts, *ib.* 43; affirms that sorcerers do not hold converse with dead men's souls, but with the devil, *ib.* 44; cites Clement as recording a declaration of Peter that Antichrist shall work miracles (O. I.), *ib.* 46; says, in the end power shall be given to the devil to work miracles (O. I.), 4 *Jew.* 1040

xx. *The Lord's day, Fasting*: he speaks of the first day of the week as the Lord's day, 1 *Hoop.* 342; shews that there are two kinds of fasting, a spiritual and a corporal fast, and that he who abstains from meat and not from evil works, though he appears to fast, fasts not in deed (O. I.), 1 *Bec.* 104, 105, 2 *Bec.* 539; says that fasting is abstinence from vices, and that abstinence from meat is received for this purpose, to make the flesh obedient to the spirit, 1 *Bec.* 105, 2 *Bec.* 545; asks what profit there is in fasting, if there be playing and trifling, &c. 4 *Jew.* 1141; calls fasting a help to prayer (O. I.), 1 *Bec.* 162; compares fasting and prayer to two wings, *Wool.* 136; explains what it is to anoint the head and wash the face in fasting, 1 *Bec.* 107, 108, 2 *Bec.* 537, 538; counsels that whenever we fast, we should be liberal to the poor, 2 *Bec.* 546; says that he who cannot fast, must give the larger alms, and be more diligent in prayer, *ib.* 546; says, thou dost fast, if thou despise money, if thou be fervent in love, if thou feed the hungry, and if thou forsake glory, 4 *Jew.* 1141; declares that those who so fast that they please men rather than God, through vain-glory have no reward of their labour, 2 *Bec.* 541; affirms that Christ commanded us not to follow his fasting, or to fast as he fasted, 3 *Jew.* 439; remarks on people voluntarily afflicting themselves with nails, &c., 4 *Jew.* 695, 696

xxi. *Marriage, &c.*: he says, the first degree of chastity is unspotted virginity; the second is faithful wedlock (O. I.), 1 *Bul.* 402, 1 *Hoop.* 375; passages from the same book in which marriage is spoken of as evil, 3 *Jew.* 388, 420; he declares that if a virgin, by a vow of chastity dedicated to God, marry, she sins much, 3 *Jew.* 418; shews that "marriage *is* honourable in all," 1 *Ful.* 478, 479; often commends it, 3 *Jew.* 416; says that it is void of fault, and no hindrance to virtue, 2 *Jew.* 1128, 4 *Jew.* 804; writes, marriage not only hindereth us nothing from the service of God if we will be sober, but also bringeth us great comfort, 3 *Jew.* 417, 4 *Jew.* 807; again, he denies that marriage hinders, and says, thy wife was given to thee to be thy helper, 3 *Jew.* 416; declares that though marriage have much trouble in it, yet may it be so taken that it shall be no hindrance to perfect life, 3 *Jew.* 416, 4 *Jew.* 806; speaks of the wonders wrought by Moses and Peter, who were married, as well as by Elias who was not (pseud.), *Pil.* 576, *Sand.* 322, and see 3 *Jew.* 416; remarks that Isaiah, the beholder of the celestial cherubim, was married, 3 *Jew.* 416; observes that Paul terms conjugal chastity and temperance holiness, 4 *Jew.* 804; says, use marriage with discretion, and thou shalt be chief in the kingdom of heaven, 1 *Jew.* 158, 2 *Jew.* 728; excuse not thyself on account of thy marriage; the Lord was at the marriage feast, &c. (pseud.), 3 *Jew.* 416; again, let no man make his excuse on account of his wife, or children; this excuse is the craft and deceit of the devil, 3 *Jew.* 417; says that parents should provide wives for their sons, *Sand.* 455; declares that a married man may be promoted to the holy throne (i. e. the bishop's chair), 2 *Jew.* 728, 1128, 3 *Jew.* 385, 387, 406, *Phil.* 405 n.; shews that Paul's direction that a bishop is to be "the husband of one wife" is permissive, not obligatory, 3 *Jew.* 406; considers that the case of a man married again after the divorce of his first wife is contemplated, *ib.* 387, 407; asks, why Paul said not that a bishop should be an angel, &c., *ib.* 422, *Park.* 159; says, Paul required this, not that the same should now be observed in the church (pseud.), 3 *Jew.* 412; does not think that Paul's "yoke-fellow" was his wife, 1 *Ful.* 475; remarks that if any man will open the souls of unchaste women, he shall see the devil tempered together with them, 3 *Jew.* 495; asserts that (the pretended) virginity of women amongst men is more reproved of all men than fornication itself, &c., *ib.* 402, 425

xxii. *Confession, Penance, &c.*: he declares that conscience is a judge, *Wool.* 99; says, let the examination of thy sins be in thine own thought, let this judgment be without witness, let God only see thee confessing, 1 *Jew.* 120, 2 *Jew.* 1133, 3 *Jew.* 360, 376, 605, 4 *Jew.* 977; again, before God confess thy sins; before the true Judge with prayer pronounce thy offences, 3 *Jew.* 360; again, take heed that thou tell not a man of thy sins,...but confess them to the Lord,... to him shew thy wounds, 3 *Bul.* 79; again, if thou art ashamed to tell thy sins to any man, then utter them daily in thine heart; I bid thee not confess them to thy fellow-servant, but to thy God, 3 *Bul.* 79, 1 *Jew.* 120, 2 *Jew.* 1133, 3 *Jew.* 376; imagines God as saying, Tell thy sin privately to me alone, that I may heal thy wound, 3 *Bul.* 79, 1 *Jew.* 120; and, This only I require, that (a sinner) confess his sins and forsake them, &c., 3 *Jew.* 566; another passage, *ib.* 567; he says, I bring thee not forth into the theatre of thy companions;...rehearse thy conscience before God, and declare it unto him, &c., 3 *Bul.* 79; again, here is the place of medicine, not of judgment, &c., 3 *Jew.* 360, 372; again, I say not that thou shouldst shew thyself openly, nor that thou shouldst accuse thyself before others, but... shew thy way unto the Lord, &c., 3 *Bul.* 78, 2 *Jew.* 1133, 3 *Jew.* 351, 360, 4 *Jew.* 977; as to repentance, see viii. above; he speaks of the penance of the Ninevites, 1 *Ful.* 432; he enforces reconciliation, *Sand.* 229; says that to deliver from the filthiness of sin is the mighty power of Christ, and that no man has power to forgive sin but God, 2 *Bec.* 173; cited as declaring that our priests have power utterly to cleanse the filth of the soul, 3 *Jew.* 352; declares that Christ has transferred the power of remitting sins to priests, *ib.* 355, 358, see also x. above; compares the power of priests in absolution to that of the Jewish priests in the matter of leprosy, 1 *Ful.* 272, 273; recites a text of James to prove that God forgives sins at the prayer of the elders, 2 *Ful.* 239, 240; declares that those who are notorious offenders must be cast out, 3 *Bec.* 478, 483; referred to on the excommunication of the incestuous person at Corinth, 4 *Jew.* 850; cautions against sparing a wolf (O. I.?) *Sand.* 413

xxiii. *Affliction, Persecution*: he describes the sorrows of all estates of men, *Hutch.* 298; maintains that adversity should not cause men to sin, *ib.* 319; cautions not to marvel if we bear many adversities, because we follow after and desire those things which are spiritual, 4 *Jew.* 1153; declares it unlawful for Christians with violence to overthrow errors, 3 *Bec.* 202; shews that, as the sheep does not persecute the wolf, Christians do not persecute heretics, but are persecuted by them (O. I.), 3 *Bec.* 302, 3 *Jew.* 182; says that he who rejoices in the blood of persecution is a wolf (O. I.), 3 *Jew.* 183, 189; describes the persecution of the church by the emperor, 1 *Jew.* 391

xxiv. *Death, &c.*: he says that God takes us away by death at the time most profitable for us, 2 *Cov.* 117; censures superfluous cost at funerals, 3 *Bec.* 125; explains that lamps and funeral hymns are used because God has delivered the dead from all labours, *ib.* 461; does not approve of mourning apparel, 3 *Whitg.* 371 n.; referred to on memorials for the dead, 2 *Cov.* 270; as to prayer for the dead, see xvii. above; he speaks of sacrificing for the dead, 2 *Lat.* 275; he does not mention purgatory, 1 *Lat.* 248; says there is nothing to do after the end of this life; this is the time of repentance, that of judgment, 3 *Bec.* 461; calls this the time of watching and striving, the other a time of requitings, *ib.* 459; advises men to prepare their works against their departure, as, when they are once departed, it lies not in their power to repent, or put away their offences, 2 *Bec.* 395, 3 *Bec.* 461; says that when we be once gone hence, though we would never so fain, yet shall we be able to do nothing, 3 *Bec.* 459; states that he who washes not away his sins in this life shall find no comfort afterward, *ib.* 129, 459; cautions against thinking that mercy will be granted in another world at the prayers of any, 2 *Bec.* 395, 3 *Bec.* 129, 459; says a soul separated from the body cannot wander in these regions, 3 *Bul.* 401, 402; declares that Abraham, Isaac, and Jacob were in hell ($ᾅδης$) until Christ's resurrection, 1 *Ful.* 294, 297; says that to be deprived of the fruition of God is greater pain than being in hell (the place of punishment), 2 *Lat.* 236; affirms that the greatest pain of the damned is to be separate and cut off from Christ for ever, *ib.* 362; says, he that feareth more hell than Christ is worthy of hell, 2 *Hoop.* 253

xxv. *Images, the Cross, Relics:* he speaks against images, saying that we through writings enjoy the presence of the saints, *Calf.* 144, 149; on Jacob and his staff (Heb. xi.), 1 *Ful.* 541; he affirms that Joseph commanded his bones to be carried out of Egypt, in order to prevent idolatry, 4 *Jew.* 1047; mentions a picture of an angel destroying the Assyrians (dub.), *Calf.* 173; referred to on the cross (pseud.), *ib.* 63, 68; on the sign of the cross, *ib.* 258; he commends the use of that sign, *ib.* 258; again, 3 *Whitg.* 126; says we must not merely print the cross on the body, but first, by faith, in the mind, *Calf.* 76; declares that the cross has made demons contemptible to men, *ib.*; speaks of pieces of the cross enclosed in gold and worn about the neck, *ib.* 284; mentions the cross as everywhere upon the walls of houses, &c., 2 *Jew.* 649 n.; his silver crosses, 2 *Ful.* 120, 184; on the Greek Tau (pseud.), *ib.* 147; against the veneration of portions of Christ's garments, &c. (O. I.), *Calf.* 286, 2 *Ful.* 181, *Park.* 8; as to relics, see also xii. above; his opinion on the silver shrines (ναοὶ) of Diana of Ephesus, 1 *Ful.* 204 n

xxvi. *Heretics:* he says, this tree (viz. of error) neither Paul planted, nor Apollos watered, nor God increased, 4 *Jew.* 886; cautions that even out of the true churches there oftentimes come deceivers, (O. I.), *ib.* 875; says heretics in their schism have churches, the scriptures, bishops, orders, baptism, the sacrament (viz. the communion) and in short Christ himself (O. I.), 2 *Jew.* 772; declares that error falls of itself, 1 *Jew.* 102; says Manes called himself the Holy Ghost (pseud.), 4 *Jew.* 842, 843, *Rog.* 71 n.; condemns the Marcionites for baptizing the living for the dead, 1 *Jew.* 23 n.; explains the opinions of Sabellius, Photinus, and others, *Hutch.* 121 n

xxvii. *Antichrist:* he considered that the Roman empire was that which hindered the revelation of Antichrist, 2 *Jew.* 913; says that he shall come into power on the dissolution of the empire, *ib.* 918, 4 *Jew.* 682; declares why he is called the abomination of desolation (O. I.), *ib.* 728, which (the same book says) shall stand in the holy places of the church, 3 *Jew.* 153, 160, 4 *Jew.* 729; he says Antichrist shall sit in the temple of God, not in that at Jerusalem only, but also in the churches everywhere, 3 *Jew.* 348

xxviii. *Kings, Civil Power:* he notes that even apostles, evangelists, and prophets are subject to the higher powers, and that this subjection is no hindrance to godliness, 2 *Jew.* 997, 4 *Jew.* 675, 703, 705, *Pil.* 23, 3 *Whitg.* 591; shews that priests are subject to the higher powers, 1 *Brad.* 478; declares that it is good even for the devils themselves to be obedient one of them unto another, (O. I.), 3 *Jew.* 622; says that God himself hath set the head of the prince under the hand of the priest, *ib.* 376; censures disobedience to princes, 3 *Whitg.* 590; says, he that defileth the emperor's image is injurious to the majesty of the emperor's person (cited in the 2nd council of Nice), 4 *Jew.* 894; speaking of the emperor he says, we have offended him that hath no peer on earth, and styles him the top and head of all men, 1 *Jew.* 438, 4 *Jew.* 975, 997, 1014; declares that tribute is not to be *given* to magistrates, but *paid, Sand.* 200; relates how Constantine overthrew the Jews who attempted to restore their temple, 4 *Jew.* 1074, 1075; mentions that Julian, in his proclamations, scornfully termed the Christians Galileans, *ib.* 667; his saying to Gaina, on the duty of a godly emperor, (in Euseb.), 1 *Bul.* 391; he besought the emperor to call a council, 4 *Jew.* 1005; refused to attend an Arian synod though summoned by the emperor, 3 *Jew.* 38, 4 *Jew.* 1101; marvels if any ruler can be saved, 1 *Lat.* 98, 158, 178; shews how evil it is for a realm to be without a ruler, 3 *Whitg.* 588; says, if the rulers be taken from the cities, we shall lead a life more unreasonable than the very brute beasts, 1 *Bec.* 215; calls a city without godly citizens more loathsome than any cave, 4 *Jew.* 876; compares the people to the waves of the sea, &c., 1 *Whitg.* 468, 3 *Whitg.* 274, 571; on swearing, *Bale* 111, 112; he explains how it first came up, 1 *Bec.* 377; declares that a dagger pricks not so sharply as the nature of an oath, and that a swearer is a condemned malefactor, *ib.* 365; says that an oath makes not a man worthy to be believed, but the testimony of his life, *ib.* 377, 378; he (rather Chromatius) declares that, as in an oath there must be no falsehood, so in words ought there to be no lie, *ib.* 379, 380

xxix. *Miscellanea:* he calls him the true nobleman that disdains to serve vices, 3 *Bec.* 436, 437; says that the nobility and goodness of our kinsfolk avail nothing, except we ourselves be good (O. I.), *ib.* 436; teaches that when more commodity comes by offending than hurt, we must not care for the offence, *Pil.* 45 ; remarks on apparel (O. I.), 3 *Jew.* 614; on mourning apparel, 3 *Whitg.* 371 n.; he says, he that falls into a pit that lies wide open, is not said to be negligent, but mad (O. I.), 3 *Jew.* 251; speaks of darkness, first in the vales, then on the hills (O. I.), 2 *Jew.* 1081; says that under brambles there rests nothing but serpents (O. I.), *Wool.* 126; speaks of the golden coins of Alexander used as amulets, *Calf.* 285; his frequent expression, ἴσασιν οἱ μεμυνημένοι, *Whita.* 615; mistakes of his, 4 *Jew.* 635

Chuff: a rough clown, 2 *Bul.* 15

Church: *v.* Augustine, and the fathers generally.

   I. THE CATHOLIC CHURCH.
 i. *What the Church is, generally.*
 ii. *The True Church.*
 iii. *The False Church, &c.*
 iv. *The two contrasted.*
 v. *The Outward Mixed Church.*
 vi. *Marks or Notes of the Church.*
 vii. *Names of the Church.*
 viii. *Its Authority.*
 ix. *Whether it may err.*
 x. *Its Government.*
 xi. *Its relation to the State.*
 xii. *Church property.*
   II. PARTICULAR CHURCHES.
 i. *The Greek Church.*
 ii. *Other Eastern Churches.*
 iii. *The Church of Rome.*
 iv. *The Church of England.*
 v. *Other Reformed Churches.*

  I. THE CATHOLIC CHURCH : *v.* Christ, Creeds.

i. *What the Church is, generally :* the church, congregation, or assembly, what it is, 1 *Bec.* 294, 2 *Bec.* 41, 3 *Bec.* 143, 608, 614, 615, 1 *Bul.* 158, 4 *Bul.* 3, 4, 5, *Coop.* 175, 1 *Cov.* 412, 2 *Cov.* 461, 1 *Cran.* 376, &c., 2 *Cran.* 11, 25, 2 *Hoop.* 40, 120, *Lit. Edw.* 511, 513, (559, 561), *Now.* (56, 101), 174, *Phil.* 136, 330, 332, *Pil.* 329, 330, 617, *Rid.* 122, &c., *Rog.* 164, &c., 2 *Tyn.* 12, 3 *Tyn.* 12, &c., *Whita.* 22, 299; translations concerning the church examined, 1 *Ful.* 225—239; Tyndale in his New Testament, preferred using the term "congregation," because the word "church" had been so greatly abused, 3 *Tyn.* 13—16 ; why sometimes rendered "congregation" in the English Bibles, 1 *Ful.* 90, 112, 226, &c.; the synagogue of the Jews called ἐκκλησία by Luke and Augustine, *ib.* 227 ; the word used in Acts for a congregation of heathen men, 3 *Tyn.* 15; sometimes rendered "congregatio" by Erasmus, and in one place "concio," *ib.* 16 n.; lord Cobham's belief concerning it, *Bale* 20, 21, 33 ; confession of Will. Thorpe, *ib.* 72, 90; Ridley's confession, *Rid.* 122, 123, 268 ; an article on it (1538), 2 *Cran.* 473, 474 ; another, viz. the 19th article of the Church of England, *Rog.* 164; confessions of the foreign churches on this point, *ib.* 165, &c.; Tyndale says the word has a double interpretation, viz. a carnal and a spiritual, 3 *Tyn.* 54, 113 ; Ridley states the word is used in three senses in scripture, *Rid.* 125, 126; to the same effect writes Philpot, *Phil.* 332; St Paul calls the poor the church of God, 3 *Tyn.* 257; the name church sometimes used for the governors of the church, *Coop.* 175, 3 *Whitg.* 501; though the Romish church be not the church, God hath one in the earth, 4 *Bul.* 72; he always hath a church, 4 *Bul.* 10, 2 *Lat.* 215 ; its original, 4 *Bul.* 26, 2 *Cran.* 514; Bradford says that it was from the creation, 1 *Brad.* 503 ; Sandys affirms that it began in paradise, *Sand.* 371; whether before Christ's incarnation, 1 *Brad.* 521; the old fathers before Christ asserted to have been one and the same church with us, 4 *Bul.* 50, *Phil.* 73, 3 *Tyn.* 245; according to Gregory it comprises the saints, before, under, and since the law, 1 *Jew.* 440; Hooper says the church of the prophets' time is one in effect with the church of the apostles' time, *ib.* 127 ; whether the church was before the scripture, *Phil.* 212, 3 *Whitg.* 621; whether before the gospel, *Phil.* 334, 340, 344, 3 *Tyn.* 24, 25 ; see also vi. below; we believe that the church is, we do not believe *in* it, 1 *Bul.* 158

ii. *The True Church* (see many of the definitions and confessions in section i; also sections iv, vi, &c.) : the true church described, 3 *Bec.* 393, 394, 1 *Bul.* 162, 2 *Cov.* 393, 461, 2 *Hoop.* 40, 120, 509, 3 *Jew.* 265, *Phil.* 220, 397, *Whita.* 613 ; the name is properly used for the elect church, which is the spouse of Christ, *Phil.* 332, the congregation of the truly faithful, who were forechosen, *Lit. Edw.* 511, (559), *Now.* (53, 54), 171, 172, 2 *Tyn.* 12, 3 *Tyn.* 12, 13, 30, 108—110, 113, *Whita.* 613; this church is the body of Christ, and the bride of Christ, see vii. below; it is Christ's inheritance, 2 *Hoop.* 229 ; it is said to be "in God the Father, and in the Lord Jesus Christ,"

2 *Jew.* 819; typified by Eve, *q.v.*; by Abel, *Phil.* 106; by Abel, Abraham, and others, *Sand.* 378; represented by Jerusalem, *q.v.*; a vision of the glorious church of Christ seen by Philpot, *Phil.* 272; Ridley's farewell to the universal church of the chosen, *Rid.* 427; what profit there is in believing that there is a holy universal church, 2 *Bec.* 43; its original is heavenly, 4 *Bul.* 26; it was not gathered by the law, but by the faith of Christ, 2 *Jew.* 1023; redeemed and defended by Christ, 1 *Hoop.* 21; crucified and risen with him, *Lit. Edw.* 509, (557); taught of God, *Whita.* 613; militant on earth, 4 *Bul.* 5, 2 *Cran.* 94, 2 *Hoop.* 43, *Nord.* 93, *Whita.* 22; commonly persecuted, 1 *Brad.* 526, *Nord.* 89, (*v.* Persecution); so the true church has ever been, 2 *Lat.* 290; its afflictions, 2 *Bul.* 104; the ten persecutions, *ib.* 105; it shall always be in affliction here, 1 *Hoop.* 80; by affliction it is tried, 1 *Cov.* 128; the church sent into the desert, *Bale* 254; the church under the seven seals, *ib.* 312, &c.; it shall be persecuted towards the end, 2 *Brad.* 360, 361; whence the storms arise which trouble it, *Sand.* 380; that which persecutes is of the devil, that which is persecuted, of God, 3 *Bec.* 201; the church's perpetuity and security, 1 *Hoop.* 201; God's faithful care of it, 2 *Cran.* 425, 3 *Zur.* 21; it shall continue to the world's end, 2 *Ful.* 30, &c.; it is preserved by the word of God, 4 *Bul.* 27; the Holy Ghost its guide, *Rid.* 123; he dwells in it, *Nord.* 89, and is its governor and protector for ever, 1 *Hoop.* 21; motion to prayer for the comfort and preservation of the church of Christ, *Nord.* 89; the prayer, *ib.* 98; a prayer for the whole church, *Pra. B.* 129; another, from the Book of Common Order, *Lit. Eliz.* 266, *Pra. B.* 126; petition for the preservation of God's congregation, 3 *Bec.* 247, 248; a praise of God's favour in protecting his church, verses by J. Norden, *Nord.* 104; we are members of the church by faith, 1 *Brad.* 346; out of it no pope nor prelate can cast us, *ib.* 347; Christ's elect church is holy and pure, and in the full favour of God, 3 *Tyn.* 142; how a true member of it sinneth not, though all men are sinners, *ib.* 113, 114; out of it there is no forgiveness of sins, 2 *Bec.* 44, and no salvation, 3 *Bec.* 144, 4 *Bul.* 51, 2 *Cov.* 393, 2 *Lat.* 182, 281, *Now.* (57), 176, *Phil.* 16, 40 (*v.* Salvation); the true church to be honoured, 3 *Bec.* 394; its glory, riches, and honour are not here, 1 *Brad.* 377; its beauty is inward, 1 *Brad.* 444, 2 *Brad.* 345, 346; the godly have always had a care for it, *Sand.* 235; the church triumphant, 4 *Bul.* 5, *Whita.* 24; its government, 3 *Jew.* 278

iii. *The False Church* (and false definitions of the church): *v.* Antichrist, Babylon, and sections iv. and ix. The name abused, 1 *Hoop.* 83; falsely assumed by many, *Coop.* 186, &c., *Phil.* 55; abused so as to comprehend none but the clergy, 3 *Tyn.* 12, 13; phrases and proverbs exemplifying this, *ib.* 12; hence Tyndale preferred using the word "congregation," in his New Testament, *ib.* 13—16; the clergy early set themselves up for the church, 2 *Cran.* 515; Romish prelates claim to be the church, 2 *Tyn.* 289; the name is always claimed by wicked priests in opposition to God's true prophets, 2 *Brad.* 199, *Rid.* 370; the laity are the church as well as the priests, 3 *Tyn.* 158; not all that call themselves the church are the church, *Rid.* 124; the carnal are not of the true church, whoever they be, 2 *Tyn.* 12, 3 *Tyn.* 31; the name sometimes used for the false church, the adversary of the true, *Phil.* 332; the church of the wicked, 2 *Jew.* 818; of Satan, *Rid.* 125, 126; of the devil and of Antichrist, 4 *Bul.* 10; where God builds his church the devil builds a chapel, 3 *Bec.* 400, &c.; errors about the church, 1 *Bec.* 294; a false definition of the name, *Phil.* 329; the church described by a Papist, *Rid.* 125; what Romanists intend by the term, *Whita.* 279; they mean first the consent of the fathers, secondly, the councils, thirdly, the pope, *ib.* 448, 449; practices of the false church, 2 *Cran.* 12

iv. *The two contrasted:* there have ever been two churches, the true and the false, *Phil.* 106, a church militant, and a church malignant, *Nord.* 93, the true church and the synagogue of Satan, 3 *Bec.* 608, 1 *Brad.* 376, *Sand.* 67; these were declared in Abel and Cain, *Phil.* 106, in Jerusalem and Babylon, *Bale* 250, 252, &c.; the true church distinguished from the false, 1 *Bec.* 296, 2 *Bec.* 42, 3 *Bec.* 392, 393, *Pil.* 129, *Sand.* 371; one is perfect and holy, the other false and ungodly, 2 *Cran.* 11; the catholic church and the Romish church two different things, 2 *Lat.* 290; Christ's church and the pope's church opposites, 2 *Brad.* 231; THE IMAGE OF BOTH CHURCHES, an exposition of the Revelation, *Bale* 249; comparison between the church of Christ and the synagogue of Antichrist, 1 *Bec.* 294, 295; another comparison between them

CHURCH

in respect of doctrine, ceremonies, &c., 3 *Bec.* 195, &c.; as they who depart from the true church are heretics, so they that depart from the church of heretics, are the true church, 3 *Tyn.* 45; an admonition for the true church and the false, 1 *Bec.* 294; the outward and inward church, *Whita.* 613; the visible and invisible, *Rid.* 129; the church and the world, 2 *Brad.* 124

v. *The Outward Mixed Church*: this is the whole number of those called Christians, *Phil.* 332, *Rid.* 125, 126, 3 *Tyn.* 13, 114, *Whita.* 613; what it has been in all ages, 2 *Cran.* 15; represented by the scribes, priests, and Pharisees, *ib.* 18; it will be mixed until the judgment, 2 *Brad.* 359, 361; good and evil in it, 4 *Bul.* 8, 2 *Hoop.* 41, *Pil.* 388; goats and sheep, *Rid.* 125, 1 *Whitg.* 183, 184, 373, 391; if we allow the outward and visible church to be the true, we make Christ the head of ungodly members, 2 *Cran.* 13; all that be in the church are not the church, 4 *Bul.* 16; all its members are not of the number of the elect, *Now.* (57), 175; Antichrist and false prophets therein, 1 *Brad.* 505; some (says a gloss of the Decrees) are in the church both nominally and really, some neither nominally nor really, some only nominally, and some really though not nominally, *Rid.* 127; the two classes in the church, viz. the spiritual and the carnal, described, 3 *Tyn.* 107—110, 113, 114, 144; the carnal always persecute the spiritual, *ib.* 54, 107, 110, 144; the church has never been idolatrous as a whole, *Rid.* 235; there always have been in it such as followed the truth, 1 *Hoop.* 170; there is no church absolutely perfect, 2 *Hoop.* 87; which is the purest, 1 *Hoop.* 343; Augustine divides the members of the church into penitents, reformers, and the perfect, 1 *Cov.* 202—206; the apostolic churches ravaged by the Turks, *Pra. Eliz.* 463

vi. *Marks or Notes of the Church*:

(*a*) What they are, in general, 1 *Cov.* 412—420, 2 *Ful.* 34—38, 215, 2 *Hoop.* 43, 87, *Phil.* 73, *Poet.* 269, &c.; outward marks, 4 *Bul.* 17, &c.; inward marks, *ib.* 23; marks mentioned by Augustine, viz. consent, succession, the name of catholic, &c., 1 *Brad.* 526, *Phil.* 141 n., 144; the three tokens of unity, antiquity, and consent, may be in the devil's church, 1 *Brad.* 551; the true church only to be known by the scriptures, 2 *Cran.* 25, 3 *Jew.* 153, *Rid.* 123, 3 *Tyn.* 44; the studies of the church, 4 *Bul.* 47

(*b*) The church is One, 2 *Bec.* 42; on its unity, 1 *Ful.* 237, *Phil.* 139, *Rog.* 167, 3 *Whitg.* 595; all churches are one, *Coop.* 117; Paul teaches the church's unity, but not under one earthly head, 2 *Brad.* 144; how the whole is knit together, *Nord.* 89; its faith is one, 1 *Brad.* 524, 2 *Hoop.* 519; no true church dissenteth from the general faith, 1 *Tyn.* 384; the church agrees in the substance of doctrine, but differs in ceremonies, *Pil.* 552; it never had one order of service, *ib.* 629; the unity of the Spirit, 2 *Hoop.* 52; the bond of peace, *Phil.* 248; the church compared to Christ's seamless coat, *Bale* 16, *Phil.* 283; its unity figured by "one loaf," *Hutch.* 37, by the bread and wine in the communion, *ib.* 239, 2 *Whitg.* 546 (*v.* Supper of the Lord); the church's unity must be maintained, 2 *Lat.* 340; for it we ought to suffer all things, 3 *Tyn.* 33; dissension and hostility about trifles deprecated, *Pra. Eliz.* 464; separation from the church a great crime, *Rid.* 119; Protestants have not departed from it, 2 *Ful.* 374; but Papists have, *Pil.* 618; communities which have not the whole ministry, or which are outwardly severed, may be parts of the true church, *Phil.* 385; a prayer for the concord of Christ's church, *Lit. Eliz.* 254, (see also Unity, and Schism).

(*c*) It is Holy, 2 *Bec.* 41, 1 *Bul.* 162, 4 *Bul.* 7, 17, 36, 49, *Now.* (54), 172; how it is without spot or wrinkle, 4 *Bul.* 36; it is called the fellowship of the saints, 2 *Bec.* 43, 2 *Cov.* 461 (*v.* Communion of saints); the chiefest points of true godliness in it, 4 *Bul.* 479; its belief concerning faith and good works, 2 *Bec.* 638, &c.

(*d*) It is Catholic, or universal: — why so called, 2 *Bec.* 42, 1 *Brad.* 146, 1 *Bul.* 161, 4 *Bul.* 5, 8, 2 *Cran.* 91, 2 *Ful.* 35, 2 *Hoop.* 41, *Lit. Edw.* 515, (562), *Now.* (54), 101, 173, *Phil.* 37, *Rid.* 266, *Rog.* 170, *Sand.* 254; Augustine names universality as a mark of it, *Phil.* 137, and states reasons why it is styled catholic, *ib.* 136; which is the catholic church, *Pil.* 617, 618; universality must be joined to verity, *Phil.* 137; no popish tradition observed by all churches, *Whita.* 504, 506; the catholic church was before Rome, and shall continue when Rome is gone, *Calf.* 261; it is not limited within certain bounds, 2 *Hoop.* 41, nor tied to any place, *Phil.* 138; the Lutheran catechisms say "Christian church" instead of "Catholic," 1 *Ful.* 222

(*e*) It is Apostolic, 1 *Jew.* 34, 61;

prophetical, apostolical, and orthodoxical, 4 *Bul.* 28; built upon the foundation of the apostles and prophets, *Whita.* 347—349, 649

(*f*) On Succession as a token of the church, (*v.* Succession), 1 *Brad.* 505, *Pil.* 597, *Poet.* 274; alleged by Augustine, *Phil.* 137; Lyra thereon, 1 *Brad.* 529; succession of bishops, 4 *Bul.* 28, 140, 2 *Ful.* 67, 74, 3 *Jew.* 320, &c., 339, *Pil.* 485, 597, 598, *Rog.* 330; consecration by one bishop sufficient, according to Gregory, to maintain it, 2 *Ful.* 118; not mentioned in scripture, though deemed essential by Papists, 1 *Brad.* 505, 2 *Brad.* 143; they affirm no church to be a true one, which does not stand by succession of bishops, 2 *Cran.* 11; this is affirmed by Bellarmine to exist in the Roman church alone, *Whita.* 510; that of the Roman church, not entire and uninterrupted, *Pil.* 600, *Whita.* 510; that of the early bishops of Rome doubtful, 3 *Jew.* 326; Papists have no lawful succession from the apostles, 2 *Ful.* 223; their bishops are successors of Judas, and in some respects of Peter (whom Christ once addressed as "Satan"), *Pil.* 604; succession in various countries, 1 *Brad.* 508; mere succession of bishops is no sign of the true church, which is not tied thereto, 1 *Brad.* 509, 2 *Cran.* 13, 2 *Ful.* 241, 242, 1 *Hoop.* 27, 82, 138, 2 *Hoop.* 90, 121, *Phil.* 139, 140, 144, 3 *Tyn.* 44; succession in place does not prove true bishops, *Pil.* 598; the good succeed the bad, and the bad the good, *ib.* 599; mere external succession not to be regarded, *Whita.* 510; the truth hangs not on it, *Pil.* 599; the right succession stands in true doctrine and sharp discipline, *ib.* 600, 604; no such succession in the Roman church, *ib.* 601—603; nor in any one see or country, *ib.* 597

(*g*) Visibility, &c.:—the church is both visible and invisible, *Phil.* 136, *Rog.* 164; how visible, 4 *Bul.* 8, 17, 2 *Ful.* 51, *Rid.* 125; visible, though sometimes eclipsed, *Poet.* 273, 274; not always equally visible, 1 *Brad.* 520; visible as Christ was, *ib.* 503, 551; how invisible, 2 *Hoop.* 41; the holy catholic church of the elect is not visible, *Now.* (56), 174; the true church not always a visible multitude, 1 *Brad.* 504, 520; multitude, no proof of it, 3 *Tyn.* 102, 103, 107, 109, 116, 122; it is not always represented by the greater number, *Rid.* 127, 131, *Whita.* 504; the true church is a small congregation, 1 *Hoop.* 84, or rather, it seems so, *Phil.* 392; the little flock contrasted with the great multitude who are not chosen, 3 *Tyn.* 109; where the church was before Luther, *Phil.* 391

(*h*) The Word and Sacraments as tokens of the church;—their true administration, together with discipline, are its essential outward mark, 1 *Brad.* 504, 2 *Brad.* 202, 4 *Bul.* 17, 2 *Cov.* 412—420, 2 *Ful.* 34, 2 *Hoop.* 43, 87, *Lit. Edw.* 513, (561), *Now.* (56), 175; *Phil.* 384, *Rog.* 174, 1 *Whitg.* 185; Christ's sheep hear his voice, *Coop.* 186; scripture allows no church which hearkens not thereto, 1 *Brad.* 394; probations out of scripture that the true holy catholic and apostolic church does not lean to the decrees of men, but to the doctrine of Christ, 3 *Bec.* 321, &c.; God is served therein by prayer, preaching, and the sacraments, *Sand.* 252; how it is taught, 4 *Bul.* 154; it needeth not legal instruction, *ib.* 524; it was never without its sacraments and sacrifices, 2 *Hoop.* 520; of holy assemblies, 4 *Bul.* 165, 499

vii. *Names, or figures, of the Church.*

(*a*) It is the Body of Christ, 4 *Bul.* 25, *Now.* (53, 100), 99, 172, *Phil.* 219, *Rid.* 125, 126, 3 *Tyn.* 31; shadowed out by man's body, 4 *Bul.* 84; the similitude should teach us love and unity, *ib.* 25, *Sand.* 98; Christ alone its Head, 1 *Brad.* 435, 4 *Bul.* 85, 2 *Cran.* 76, 2 *Ful.* 243, *Hutch.* 100, 3 *Jew.* 269, 270, *Lit. Edw.* 511, (559), *Nord.* 90, *Phil.* 332, 2 *Whitg.* 426, 3 *Whitg.* 198; he has no vicar, 4 *Bul.* 85; the notion of an earthly head condemned by Gregory the Great, 2 *Jew.* 992; queen Elizabeth refused to be called head of the church, 4 *Jew.* 1144, 1209; it is the image of Christ, *Nord.* 91

(*b*) It is spoken of as a Woman, the Bride of Christ, and our mother, (see Eve, Marriage): a virgin, 4 *Bul.* 91; a handmaid, 1 *Bec.* 295, being a handmaid to the laws of Christ, 1 *Jew.* 76; a woman clothed with the sun, *Bale* 404; the spouse of Christ, 1 *Bec.* 295, 296, 1 *Brad.* 370, 4 *Bul.* 90, *Hutch.* 101, 3 *Jew.* 151—153, 1 *Lat.* 456; the Lamb's wife, *Bale* 542; our mother, 1 *Brad.* 503, 4 *Bul.* 90; typified by Eve, 1 *Brad.* 503

(*c*) Other similitudes:—God's kingdom, 4 *Bul.* 84; the kingdom of heaven, 2 *Tyn.* 40; the spiritual tabernacle, *Sand.* 222, prefigured by that of Israel, 2 *Bul.* 147, 2 *Whitg.* 93; a holy temple, *Bale* 128, typified by the temple at Jerusalem, *Sand.* 240, 2 *Whitg.* 94; and also by the treasures therein, *Sand.* 371; the synagogue a figure of it, 2 *Whitg.* 345; it is God's house, 4 *Bul.* 79; Christ's household, 1 *Lat.* 35; the pillar and ground of the truth, 4 *Bul.* 37, 2 *Cov.* 422; 3 *Jew.* 151, *Phil.* 273, 306, *Rid.* 235, God's vine, 4 *Bul.* 83; often called a vineyard, *Sand.* 57; means used by foxes to destroy the vineyard, *ib.* 65; the field of the Lord, 2 *Hoop.* 41; a little flock, 3 *Tyn.* 108, 109; Christ's sheep-fold, 4 *Bul.* 88; the ark of Noah, 2 *Hoop.* 42, *Sand.* 361, 2 *Whitg.* 92, 499; often compared by the fathers to a ship, 2 *Jew.* 901, 994, *Sand.* 370, &c.; represented by the moon, *Sand.* 360; compared to the weakest things, 2 *Jew.* 994

viii. *Its authority* (v. Ceremonies, Councils, Discipline, Scripture, Tradition): the power of the church, wherein it consists, 4 *Bul.* 38—46; the authority of the church, *Rog.* 183; A DEFENCE OF THE TRUE AND OLD AUTHORITY OF CHRIST'S CHURCH, by C. S. Curio, translated by Jo. Philpot, *Phil.* 319; on the command, "Tell it unto the church," 3 *Whitg.* 169, 247; the church is to be heard, 1 *Brad.* 370; how we must hear the church, 3 *Tyn.* 100; the rule refers to fraternal admonition, *Whita.* 426; we must be sure that "the church" is the *true* church, *ib.*; the church not to be heard if it diverge from the revealed mind of Christ, *ib.*; to be heard, but tried, 2 *Brad.* 293, 2 *Cov.* 272; how far its judgment serves, *Phil.* 48; it is deemed by Papists the sole judge of controversies, *Rid.* 284; the authority of the church, as maintained by Romanists, means that of the pope, *Whita.* 414; they exalt the church above scripture, *ib.* 276; many of them say that it is older than the scripture, and therefore of greater authority, *ib.* 331; it is not above the word of God, *Phil.* 356, &c., *Rog.* 173, but subject to it, *Whita.* 352, not only as the term denotes the whole body of the faithful, but the pastors also, *ib.* 353; they only belong to the church who follow scripture, 1 *Hoop.* 139; the word does not derive its authority from the church, *Phil.* 134, 135; Augustine advises us, in doubtful questions, to consult the church which the scripture points out, *Whita.* 442; the church is tied to the word of God, 1 *Hoop.* 27, 31, 81, and to the doctrine of Christ, *ib.* 20; whatever authority it has depends entirely on the scriptures, *Whita.* 300, 335, 338; it must stay itself upon the word of God, 2 *Cran.* 52; its office in relation to the scriptures, 1 *Brad.* 519; this is but external and ministerial, *Whita.* 279, 286, 288, 299, 308; the church is as a notary, *Whita.* 283, a champion, *ib.*, a herald, *ib.* 284, an interpreter, *Phil.* 375, *Rog.* 193 —197, *Whita.* 284, 487; what power of interpreting scripture Papists claim for it, *Whita.* 410—415; it is not to judge scripture, *Rog.* 199, but only according to scripture, *Whita.* 353; it is not a judge, but a witness, *Rid.* 128, the witness and keeper of God's written word, *Rog.* 198; compared to a public office for records, 2 *Cran.* 59; likened to a clock, and scripture to the sun, 1 *Jew.* 80; Canus and Bellarmine allow that the church is not governed by new revelations, *Whita.* 504; yet Romanists maintain that it can even add a book to the canon of scripture, *ib.* 505; the authority and consent of the whole church a powerful argument against heretics, *ib.* 313, 316, 317; contentious spirits are repressed thereby, *ib.* 558; its authority may force men to acknowledge the scriptures, but cannot persuade them of their truth, *ib.* 317, 318; Augustine's use of the argument from the authority of the church considered, *ib.* 319, &c.; the faithful may be first moved by that argument, but rest finally upon firmer ground, *ib.* 322; how the church has authority in controversies of faith, *ib.* 190; we must receive no doctrine but that which agrees with the universal church of Christ, 2 *Cov.* 422; but the church has no authority to make a new article of faith, or to receive a doctrine contrary to God's word, *ib.* 418; it may not enforce anything to be believed contrary to, or besides, the word of God, *Phil.* 344, *Rog.* 201; More affirms that the church is to be believed in things for which no scripture can be shewn, 3 *Tyn.* 135, 139; on believing as the church believes, 2 *Lat.* 315; doctrines and practices alleged to rest upon church authority, 2 *Zur.* 194; the church is not a mistress over the sacraments, 4 *Bul.* 239; its power of consecration, *ib.* 39; power to administer, *ib.* 45; its authority is not to be objected in favour of the mass, 3 *Bec.* 392; its authority in rites and ceremonies, and things indifferent, *Rid.* 269, *Rog.* 184, *Whita.* 507, 1 *Whitg.* 175, 222, 2 *Whitg.* 64; it may not ordain what rites or ceremonies it will, *Rog.* 188; it cannot bind things left free by the gospel, 2 *Cov.* 338; may not forbid what the apostles permitted, *Phil.* 379; in indifferent traditions the order of the church should be followed, but with a limitation, *Calf.* 267, 1 *Whitg.* 222, &c.; every private man's consent said to be in the consent of the church, 2 *Whitg.* 573; the primitive church to be followed,

Phil. 273, 302; Cole maintains the example of the primitive church not to be binding, 1 *Jew.* 39, 74; its orders are not always so, *ib.* 75; the modern church not of greater authority than the ancient, *Whita.* 456; Romanists liken the apostolic church to an infant, and the later church to a full grown man, *Coop.* 10, 11, 1 *Jew.* 77; the fallacy of this comparison, *Coop.* 63; the absurdity of supposing that the later church knows the mind of God better than the apostles did, 1 *Jew.* 230; the testimony of the church too lightly esteemed by some in the days of Augustine, *Rid.* 128; disobedience to the church charged on Protestants, *Pil.* 484, 551; one church not to be set up as a model for all churches, 2 *Whitg.* 452, &c.; power of jurisdiction, 4 *Bul.* 39; in what points ecclesiatical jurisdiction consisteth, *ib.* 43; power of the keys, *ib.* 39, 44; they are given to the whole church, 2 *Hoop.* 51, (*v.* Absolution); power of judgment or judicial correction, 4 *Bul.* 40, 507; it is not the office of the ecclesiastical ruler to punish, 2 *Lat.* 196; the church's power to receive, 4 *Bul.* 40; to ordain ministers, *ib.* 43, 2 *Tyn.* 251; to preach, 4 *Bul.* 40; to teach, *ib.* 44; the church is the instrument whereby God teaches us, *Whita.* 286; whether Christ gave power to the church to teach anything besides that which he taught, *Phil.* 358; its power to judge of doctrines, 4 *Bul.* 45; to call a council, *ib.*; to dispose of its affairs, *ib.* 46

ix. *Whether it can err, &c.:* whether the church may err, and how, 4 *Bul.* 35, 2 *Hoop.* 90, 121, *Phil.* 332, 333, 382, &c.; Papists say dark passages in scripture are to be settled by the church, which cannot err, 2 *Cran.* 17; church-infallibility contended for by More, with Tyndale's replies, 3 *Tyn.* 93, &c., 170; infallibility affirmed to be necessary, to prove the authority of scripture, 2 *Tyn.* 289; the visible church, from time to time, hath erred, *Rog.* 177; its judgment is human, *Whita.* 338—340, not divine, save in a certain sense, *ib.* 341, 342; we should never be certain of our faith, if it rested upon the outward and glistering church, 2 *Cran.* 11; the outward and visible church has never continued the same for long, *ib.*; though the governors of it err, God reserveth to himself, 4 *Bul.* 69; the majority of the visible church may err, *Rid.* 129; the catholic church cannot err in doctrine, *Phil.* 38; it is preserved from all errors by the virtue and operation of the Holy Ghost, 2 *Hoop.* 74; the elect church cannot err damnably, 2 *Tyn.* 12, 3 *Tyn.* 30, 31; the catholic church has the promise of infallibility, particular churches have not, 2 *Jew.* 994; the primitive church was near to Christ in time, and like him in doctrine, 2 *Hoop.* 237; yet the visible church was corrupted even in the apostles' time, 2 *Whitg.* 183; the church of the apostles' times and of ours, 1 *Whitg.* 378; the latter church has dissented from that of the apostles, 2 *Jew.* 988, and may be compared to a woman who has lost her jewels, but keeps the boxes that contained them, *ib.* 899; its ruin was foretold, *ib.* 988; it has sometimes been heretical, 2 *Cran.* 15; verses on its decline and corruption, by Henoch Clapham, *Poet.* 466; it appeared near ruin in England, 1 *Lat.* 105; it is full of hypocrites, &c., 1 *Whitg.* 382, and Papists, Atheists, &c., *ib.* 385; the synagogue of Satan bears the greatest swing in Christendom, *Rid.* 126; corrupt state of the church in the last days, *Coop.* 180

On Reformation of the church (*v.* Reformation):—how the church should be reformed, 2 *Jew.* 1000; it should be purged as Christ purged the temple, *Sand.* 236, &c., 247, &c.; a sufficient platform of church reformation in scripture, 3 *Bul.* 122; whether they that will reform must stay for the determination of a council, *ib.* 116; things out of order may be reformed by every Christian church, *ib.* 119; the duty of reformation ascribed to civil rulers, *Sand.* 237, 238; it is perilous to introduce innovations, *Rid.* 137

x. *Its government* (see Archbishops, Bishops, Discipline, Ministers, Priests; also xi): it has two kinds of government, visible and invisible, 1 *Whitg.* 183, or internal and external, 3 *Whitg.* 485, 486, 554; how it is governed by Christ, *ib.* 483, &c.; he named no head to govern it, 2 *Cran.* 76; he has no vicar, 4 *Bul.* 85; the church militant is not governed like the church triumphant, 3 *Jew.* 278; its external government not particularly expressed in scripture, 1 *Whitg.* 6; there is no one certain kind of government which must be perpetually observed, 1 *Whitg.* 184, 3 *Whitg.* 214, &c.; how the church is a monarchy, an aristocracy, and a democracy, 1 *Whitg.* 390; its divers degrees of ministers, 4 *Bul.* 104, &c., 3 *Jew.* 271; Ephes. iv. not a perfect pattern of ecclesiastical government, 4 *Jew.* 1299; what officers the apostles ordained in the church, 2 *Tyn.* 253; in the apostles' days it was popular, 1 *Whitg.* 393; some of its institutions taken from the law, 2 *Whitg.* 126; on primacy or lordship in the church, 2 *Ful.* 251, &c.; it should not be ruled as earthly kingdoms are, *Phil.* 395; it is not burdened with infinite laws, 4 *Bul.* 478; its true liberty, 1 *Whitg.* 423

xi. *Its relation to the state* (see Kings, Magistrates, Statutes, Supremacy): whether, and how far, the care of religion belongs to the magistrate, 1 *Bul.* 323, &c., 1 *Hoop.* 31, 85, 4 *Jew.* 1027, &c., 2 *Zur.* 242, 251; whether ecclesiastical and civil government may reside in one person, 2 *Whitg.* 358; there are two swords or powers, the spiritual and the temporal, 2 *Hoop.* 53, 1 *Lat.* 85, 2 *Tyn.* 60; an example of the two regiments, 2 *Tyn.* 62; the duty of each, 1 *Hoop.* 142; the functions of king and priest not to be confounded, *Whita.* 424; spiritual things are not subject to the temporal power, *Phil.* 72; testimonies of emperors against the intervention of rulers in matters ecclesiastical, *Whita.* 436; temporal men ought not to be judges in spiritual cases, *Phil.* 32; the temporalty slack in the cause of God, 2 *Tyn.* 95; the spiritualty ought not to have temporal authority, *ib.* 247, &c., 273; ecclesiastics are subject to the temporal sword as well as the laity, 1 *Tyn.* 333, 2 *Tyn.* 67; in the apostles' time the church was not established, 1 *Whitg.* 389, &c.; how it may be established without a magistrate, *ib.* 392; its relations with the state or commonwealth, *ib.* 19, 386, 388; the government of every particular church asserted to be monarchical, 3 *Whitg.* 181, 198; when Christian assemblies may be held in secret, *Sand.* 191; the office of Christian magistrates in this particular, *ib.* 192; ecclesiastical privileges, 1 *Bul.* 333; ecclesiastical causes debated in parliament long before the Reformation, 4 *Jew.* 902, &c.

xii. *Church property* (see Benefices, Sacrilege, Tithes): church goods and revenues, 1 *Bul.* 286, 4 *Bul.* 486, &c.; they exist under the New Testament, 4 *Bul.* 487; to what uses church property may be applied, 2 *Zur.* 242, 259; its fourfold division in old time, 4 *Bul.* 488; ministers to be supported out of it, *ib.* 488, 503; students to be maintained, *ib.* 494; the poor to be relieved, *ib.* 494, 495, 503; for the goods of the church are the goods of the poor, 2 *Cran.* 500; they were given for the relief of the aged, the fatherless, &c., 1 *Bul.* 286; church goods are not to be abused or profaned, 1 *Bul.* 286, 4 *Bul.* 503, 2 *Ful.* 114 n.; the goods of the church not to be alienated nor its lands sold (Canon Law), 2 *Cran.* 73; inquiry whether church goods were alienated, 2 *Hoop.* 142; injunction respecting them, *Grin.* 171; church robbers censured, 2 *Bul.* 46; church lands, *Pil.* 592; an act passed empowering the crown to exchange them, *Park.* 98 n.; exchanges made by queen Elizabeth under it, 2 *Zur.* 39 n.

II. *Particular Churches.*

Particular churches, what, 4 *Bul.* 9, 51

i. *The Greek church:* v. Councils (especially *Florence*), Easter, Liturgies, Supper; also Antioch, Ephesus, &c.

The division of the church into Greek and Latin imperfect, 1 *Jew.* 271; the faith came to the West from Greece, 4 *Jew.* 883; succession of the Greek church, *Whita.* 510; difference between it and the Latin, *Pil.* 548; at any early period the Eastern churches differed from the Western as to the time of keeping Easter, *Whita.* 539; the ancient supremacy of the pope over the churches of the East asserted by Harding, 1 *Jew.* 402; the Greek church does not grant the pope to be the head, 4 *Jew.* 739, but abhors him, with the deformities of his church, *ib.* 740; rejects many Romish errors, *Coop.* 171, 3 *Jew.* 196, 4 *Jew.* 884, &c., *Pil.* 145, 205, 500, 3 *Tyn.* 133; the Greek rites followed by the early British church, 1 *Jew.* 306; separation of the Greeks from the Western church, 2 *Hoop.* 232, 397, 566, 4 *Jew.* 884, 2 *Tyn.* 259; they were compelled by Baldwin to acknowledge the supremacy of Rome, 2 *Hoop.* 238; the Greek church's opinion of the reformed churches (epist. ad Bohem.), 3 *Jew.* 196; the Greek church denies the procession of the Holy Ghost from the Son, *Rog.* 74; is contrary to the Romish church as to the sacraments, 2 *Jew.* 578; calls the Lord's supper σύναξις, 2 *Bec.* 240; Scotus and Innocent testify that it did not mix water with the wine, 1 *Jew.* 139; its doctrine on the consecration of the eucharist, *ib.* 123, 139; the priests consecrate with a loud voice, 2 *Jew.* 698; the Greek church said not to hold transubstantiation, 2 *Bec.* 266, 3 *Bec.* 232, 426, 618, 1 *Jew.* 139, *Rid.* 237, 249; has no private masses, 2 *Bec.* 239, 3 *Bec.* 418, *Coop.* 171, *Hutch.* 228, 1 *Jew.* 18, 2 *Jew.* 637, 4 *Jew.* 884, &c.; has mass but once daily, 2 *Jew.* 635; in Lent the sacrament was consecrated only on Saturdays and Sundays, 1 *Jew.* 128, 246; it never denied the cup to the laity, *Coop.* 171, *Hutch.* 283; never adopted the elevation, 1 *Jew.* 512; nor the adoration of the sacrament, *ib.* 516; the liturgy of St Chrysostom still used in this church, *Coop.* 97 n.; no man permitted to absent himself fourteen days from the sacrament, 2 *Bec.* 258, 3 *Bec.* 381, 474; the Greeks said by N. de Lyra to retain infant communion, 1 *Jew.* 249; the priests have ever been at liberty to marry, 3 *Bec.* 236, *Coop.* 171; auricular confession commenced in it, 1 *Tyn.* 263; but (now) the Greeks confess only to God, 1 *Jew.* 120, consenting not to ear-confession, pardons, &c., 3 *Tyn.* 170; they do not hold the doctrine of purgatory, 4 *Jew.* 885, &c., *Rog.* 213, 1 *Tyn.* 269; reject images, but allow pictures, 2 *Whitg.* 64; on the arrangement of a Greek church, 2 *Jew.* 636

ii. *Other churches of the East, &c.*

(*a*) *Africa* (see also *Egypt* and *Ethiopia*, below): the ancient churches of Africa, 4 *Bul.* 32, *Whita.* 223; dissensions therein on rebaptizing, 1 *Ful.* 35; they were separate from Rome for a hundred years, 1 *Jew.* 416; the reconciliation, *ib.* 416—418; the African church not extinct, 4 *Bul.* 20, 73

(*b*) *Armenia*: has prayer in the vulgar tongue, *Whita.* 269; like various other Eastern churches it receives not private mass, 1 *Jew.* 18; disallows the mixed cup in the communion, 1 *Ful.* 523; denies purgatory, *Rog.* 213 n.; error of the Armenians respecting the intermediate state, 4 *Jew.* 931, 932, 935; they hold that the law ceremonial is yet in force, *Rog.* 89; the Instructio Armeniorum of Eugenius IV., *Calf.* 248 n

(*c*) *Egypt* (*v.* Alexandria): the church there, 1 *Whitg.* 409; said to have prayer in the vulgar tongue, *Whita.* 269; the surplice worn by Christian priests there, 2 *Zur.* 166; Jerome's account of the three kinds of monks there, 2 *Tyn.* 42 n.; departed from Christ, *Phil.* 337

(*d*) *Ethiopia* (*v.* Prester John): the church there, 1 *Bul.* 292; said to have prayer in the vulgar tongue, *Pil.* 499, 500, *Whita.* 269; some old steps of Christianity perhaps remain there, *Pra. Eliz.* 463

(*e*) *Georgia*: the Georgian faith, 1 *Bul.* 98 n

(*f*) *India* (*v.* Thomas): Christianity there before the Jesuits, 3 *Jew.* 198; the Nestorian or Chaldean Christians on the coast of Malabar, *Phil.* 202 n.; the Indians said to have divine service in their own tongue, 1 *Jew.* 289; the Southern Indians in communion with Rome perform service in their own language, *Whita.* 269

(*g*) *Moravia*: converted to the faith by Cyril and Methodius, *Whita.* 269; allowed to have service in their own language, 1 *Jew.* 334, 335, *Whita.* 269; the Moravians, or United Brethren, persecuted as Waldenses, Beghards, and Picards, 2 *Brad.* 161 n (see 1 *Jew.* 227); their early apologies, 2 *Brad.* 161 n

(*h*) *Russia*: the church and religion of the Russians and Muscovites, 3 *Zur.* 690 &c.; they boast that they with the Grecians are the only church of God, *Rog.* 169; said to believe that themselves only shall be saved, *ib.* 153; they hold their church-traditions to be of equal authority with the scriptures, *ib.* 79; will not read the last four books of Moses, *ib.* 81; deny the procession of the Holy Ghost from the Son, *ib.* 74; hold that man is justified by faith and works, *ib.* 114; say all who die without baptism are damned, *ib.* 278; affirm that the Lord's supper can profit those who have no faith, as infants, *ib.* 285; priests there for lack of wine used to consecrate metheglin, 1 *Jew.* 222; they add warm water to the wine in the Lord's supper, *Rog.* 295, and mingle the bread and wine together, *ib.* 296; they have prayer in the vulgar tongue, 1 *Jew.* 334, 335, *Whita.* 269; have a liturgy compounded of the Greek and Sclavonian languages, *Rog.* 243; debar men who have been twice married from holy orders, *ib.* 240; think that none have now authority to call a general council, *ib.* 206; their churches and worship described, 3 *Zur.* 691; their funeral rites, *ib.*; persecution in Russia on account of the gospel, 3 *Zur.* 600; account of a Muscovite reformer, *ib.* 691

iii. *The church of Rome*: *v.* Catholic, Church I., Peter, Pope, Popery, Rome; also Councils, Easter, Mass, Priests, Sacraments, Scripture, Succession, Tradition, &c.

The division of the church into Greek and Latin imperfect, 1 *Jew.* 271; the see of Rome, how apostolical and yet not apostolical, *Phil.* 78; once apostolical, but now abominable, *Rid.* 414, 415; pure in the beginning, 2 *Cran.* 226, 1 *Jew.* 365; the primitive glory of the Roman church, *Rid.* 262; once it was most illustrious, *Poet.* 270; cautioned by Paul, 2 *Jew.* 201; its alleged lineal descent from Peter, *Rid.* 259, 261; its succession not without many interruptions, *Whita.* 510; the early bishops of Rome were simple men, *Bale* 502, learned and holy men, *Rid.* 180, 182, all slain from Peter to Sylvester, *Bale* 316; in the time of Irenæus Rome was the most illustrious of all churches, *Whita.* 439; not now as it was then, *Phil.* 25; its bishops were much honoured in early times, *Rid.* 262; the bishop recognized as a patriarch by the council of Nice, but the lowest of the four, *Phil.* 43; early assumptions of the church of Rome, 1 *Jew.* 304, 3 *Jew.* 152; its struggles for pre-eminence, 2 *Tyn.* 257; declared supreme by Phocas (*q. v.*), *ib.* 258; there have been men in the church of Rome who have pointed out the necessity of reformation, *Sand.* 249 (see especially Bernard); cardinals themselves have confessed abuses in it, 2 *Jew.* 683; its apostasy acknowledged in the council of Trent, by Cornelius, bishop of Bitonto, *ib.* 900; the chief points of difference between it and Protestants, 1 *Jew.* 26; the church of Rome propped up by the Jesuits, *Whita.* 4, 5, who have greatly changed its doctrine, *ib.* 18; Fulke's DISCOVERY OF THE DANGEROUS ROCK OF THE POPISH CHURCH, in answer to Sander, 2 *Ful.* 213, &c.; whether the pope and his sect be Christ's church or no, 3 *Tyn.* 9, 39—42; this party is not the church of Christ, 4 *Bul.* 22, 65, 2 *Ful.* 175; it has not the outward marks of God's church, 4 *Bul.* 66; nor the inward marks, *ib.*; the pope's church contrasted with Christ's little flock, 3 *Tyn.* 109; the Romish church is not the catholic church, 1 *Brad.* 395, 2 *Hoop.* 532, *Now.* (54), 173, *Phil.* 37, 3 *Whitg.* 622; it follows not the primitive catholic church, *Phil.* 40, but differs from the apostolic churches in almost all things, *ib.* 142; the pope's church was never universal, *ib.* 29, 41; Rome is the eldest church of the West, but not the mother of all Western churches, 1 *Jew.* 162; a mother church, but not therefore supreme, *Rid.* 264; not the holy mother church, 4 *Bul.* 92; not now the Latin church, *Whita.* 139; it is new and upstart, 4 *Bul.* 65; arguments used to prove it the true church, with Tyndale's answers to them, 3 *Tyn.* 42—52; viz. that all heretics came out of the true church, and the Lutherans came out of the papal church, *ib.* 42, and, that we receive the scriptures on her authority, *ib.* 45; false pretensions of the Roman church, *Rog.* 169, 172, &c.; a collection of tenets from the Canon Law shewing their extravagance, 2 *Cran.* 68; the church of Rome claims infallibility, 2 *Lat.* 279, *Phil.* 25, *Rog.* 182, 183, and to expound scripture, 4 *Bul.* 543; the doctors say that men must hold as she has determined, 2 *Bec.* 268, 269; Rome may err, 4 *Jew.* 726, and be cut off, 1 *Ful.* 39; hath erred especially, *Rog.* 179, in life, *ib.*, in ceremonies, *ib.* 180, in doctrine, *ib.*; she obeys not Christ's voice, 1 *Brad.* 527, but has shaken off his yoke, 1 *Jew.* 365, and breaks God's commandments to uphold her own traditions, *ib.* 366; consents not to God's law that it is good (especially with regard to matrimony), 3 *Tyn.* 40; sanctions unholy living, *ib.* 42; allows fornication, 4 *Jew.* 630, &c.; is disobedient to the higher powers, 3 *Tyn.* 41; repents not, but persecutes, *ib.*; her persecuting spirit, 1 *Tyn.* 132 n.; the church of Rome a tyranny, 4 *Bul.* 64; she curses as heretics those who do not worship images, *Rog.* 222, 223; has much more of the ceremonies of Aaron than of the ordinances of Christ, 1 *Jew.* 23; her beauty is outward, 2 *Brad.* 345, 346; she seeks her own glory, *Sand.* 23; desires outward pomp, *ib.* 26; maintains it by vile merchandise, *ib.*; robs God of his honour, *ib.* 27; attendance on her services sinful, 2 *Brad.* 201, 209, 297, &c. (and see Mass); Philpot's letter to the Christian congregations exhorting them to refrain from the idolatrous service of the Papists, &c., *Phil.* 217; as to the doctrines of the church of Rome, see especially *Cran. Jew.* and *Rog.* passim; truths which she denies, 2 *Ful.* 392; she is unsound in all things save the doctrine of the Trinity, *Phil.* 116; follows the errors of Pelagius, *ib.* 427; diminishes man's original corruption, *Sand.* 23; boasts of free-will, *ib.*; maintains justification by works, *ib.* 25; also merits and works of supererogation, *ib.*; labours to obscure the Son of God, *ib.* 358; the pope and his sect believe not to be saved through Christ, but trust in holy works, 3 *Tyn.* 39; the Romish church is neither a judge nor a witness of God's word, 2 *Hoop.* 467, 468; has corrupted the holy scriptures, 4 *Bul.* 69, 532, and mutilated them, 2 *Lat.* 283; forbids the reading of them, except by license, *Whita.* 209; blasphemies of Rome, *Bale* 431; Jewel's appeal against her errors to the fathers for 600 years after Christ, 1 *Jew.* 20, 21; there have been many dissensions, contentions and divisions in the church of Rome, 1 *Jew.* 532, 3 *Jew.* 610, &c., *Phil.* 401, 1 *Tyn.* 149, 158—160; many sects, 2 *Bec.* 415, 2 *Ful.* 375, *Sand.* 17, 1 *Tyn.* 124, 3 *Tyn.* 103, 128; many differences on most important points, *Pil.* 80, 81, 550; as on the eucharist, 1 *Jew.* 123, *Rid.* 307; the Roman church is no longer Bethel, but Bethaven, 2 *Jew.* 898, the mystic Babylon, *Phil.* 428, and the synagogue of Satan, 2 *Ful.* 175, the Babylonical church, not the catholic, *Phil.* 152; compared to the woman who in Solomon's time falsely challenged the true mother's child, *ib.* 139; of departing from the church of Rome, 4 *Bul.* 62; such departure confessed, *ib.* 65; commended, *ib.* 76; disagreement with Rome justified, *Phil.* 397

iv. *The Church of England:* v. England; also Articles, Book of Common Prayer, Canons, Homilies, and Bishops, Clergy, Ministers, Orders; likewise Benefices, Ceremonies, Convocation, Supremacy, Vestments, &c.

England did not receive the faith from Rome, 1 *Jew.* 279, 280; the British churches kept Easter with the Greeks, *ib.* 145; martyrs of the ancient British church, *Bale* 188; the Popish church planted by Augustine, *ib.*; doctrine of the Anglo-Saxon church, 2 *Ful.* 7, &c., 20, &c.; the evil life of the governors of the church of Rome was not the chief cause of our separation, *ib.* 175; the church of England half reformed in the time of Henry VIII., *Bale* 440, 485; its reformation under Henry and Edward, 2 *Zur.* 158; its condition in king Edward's days, *Rid.* 399; the first separatists from the reformed church of England, 2 *Brad.* 173 n.; Latimer desires the restoration of discipline and excommunication, 1 *Lat.* 258; abuses at this period, 3 *Zur.* 546, 547; sacrilege, pluralities, and other evils lamented, *Hutch.* 309; the clergy despised, *ib.* 310; the king acknowledged by the Articles of 1552 as supreme head in earth of the church of England and Ireland, *Lit. Edw.* 536, (580); bishop Horn's account of the services, &c. in king Edward's time, 2 *Zur.* 354; Bullinger's remarks in reply, *ib.* 357; A PITEOUS LAMENTATION OF THE MISERABLE ESTATE OF THE CHURCH OF CHRIST IN ENGLAND, IN THE TIME OF QUEEN MARY, by bp Ridley, *Rid.* 47; Sampson's question as to the lawfulness of the title "after Christ supreme head," &c., 1 *Zur.* 1; the title of supreme head declined by Elizabeth, *ib.* 24, 33; but she accepts the style of governor, *ib.* 29; reformation by Elizabeth, *Sand.* 58, 59, 250; the church spoken of as reformed, not transformed, 2 *Whitg.* 439; APOLOGIA ECCLESIÆ ANGLICANÆ, 3 *Jew.* 1; AN APOLOGY, Lady Bacon's translation, *ib.* 49; A DEFENCE OF THE APOLOGY, 3 and 4 *Jew.*; Jewel laments the prevalence of pluralities, the abuse of patronage, and the scarcity of ministers, 2 *Jew.* 999, 1000; account of the bishopricks, dignities, and order of the English church, 3 *Jew.* 109; its order explained to a French ambassador, *Park.* 215, 216; blemishes alleged by Humphrey and Sampson, 1 *Zur.* 163; Bullinger and Gualter thereon, *ib.* 357: reply by Grindal and Horn, *ib.* 178; the English church described by Beza, 2 *Zur.* 128, &c.; by Geo. Withers, *ib.* 157, &c.; by Withers and Barthelot, *ib.* 146, &c.; by Perceval Wiburn, *ib.* 358; undermined by Lutherans, *ib.* 157; seceders, 1568, *Grin.* 293; separation from the church condemned, *Sand.* 191, and magisterial constraint recommended *ib.* 192; confusion and schisms in the time of Elizabeth, *Nord.* 117, *Sand.* 95, 1 *Whitg.* 18, 3 *Whitg.* 496, 497; a view of Popish abuses (alleged as) yet remaining in the church of England, for the which godly ministers have refused to subscribe, 3 *Whitg.* 319; objections to its rites, &c. by the Puritans, 1 *Zur.* 280, 295; certain frivolous objections against its government answered, 4 *Jew.* 1299, 1300, 2 *Whitg.* 338; unhappy divisions described by Pilkington, 1 *Zur.* 287, who says that much Popish rubbish is left in the church, *Pil.* 417, 418; it is afflicted with Popery, and will be so, says bishop Horn, till Christ comes, 1 *Zur.* 320; still it is a favoured vineyard, *Sand.* 57, &c., possessing a learned ministry, *ib.* 245, but having many dissembling ministers, *ib.* 339; perverse opinions maintained by some of its teachers, *Nord.* 109; controversies instigated by the devil, *ib.* 117; its services allowed by a Romanist to be good, but not enough, *Sand.* 338; its doctrine, 1 *Whitg.* 3; Jewel's statement of its faith, 3 *Jew.* 252; the true faith maintained in it, *Sand.* 447; THE CATHOLIC DOCTRINE OF THE CHURCH OF ENGLAND, AN EXPOSITION OF THE XXXIX. ARTICLES, by T. Rogers, *Rog.* passim; purity of its doctrine admitted even by recusants, *ib.* 8; it agrees with all reformed churches, *Grin.* 208, *Rog.* passim.

v. *Other Reformed churches:* v. Confessions.

(*a*) The reformed churches too much estranged from each other, 3 *Zur.* 713; their unity much desired by Cranmer, 2 *Cran.* 420 n.; his design to unite them, 3 *Zur.* 17; foreign churches not condemned by the church of England, 1 *Whitg.* 5; as to the Lutheran churches, see Confession of Augsburgh, Consubstantiation, Lutherans.

(*b*) *Bohemia*: v. Confessions; also *Moravia*, above.

CHURCH — CHURCHES

(c) *Denmark*: v. Christian II. and III.: account of the reformation there, 4 *Bul.* xxii, 1 *Cov.* 424, 1 *Lat.* 274; order of the church there, as to government, 2 *Whitg.* 327; THE ORDER OF THE CHURCH OF CHRIST IN DENMARK, &c. FOR THE LORD'S SUPPER, BAPTISM, AND HOLY WEDLOCK, 1 *Cov.* 469, &c.

(d) *Flanders*, &c.: v. Confessions.

(e) *France*: v. Confessions, France: the reformation there, 3 *Whitg.* 314—316; Parker desires the re-edifying of the church there, *Park.* 147; the conference at Poissy (q. v.), *ib.* 147; the reformed religion, how tolerated, 1 *Zur.* 250; protected by royal authority, *ib.* n.; state of the reformed church, 1 *Whitg.* 311, 313, 379; six towns to one pastor, *ib.* 529

(f) *Ireland*: few willing to receive archbishopricks there, 2 *Cran.* 438; preaching there in English to walls and stalls, *ib.* 439; divine service ordered by an act of parliament to be said in Latin where the ministers did not know English (Edw. VI.), *Lit. Eliz.* xxiii. n.; state of the church, 1567, 2 *Zur.* 167

(g) *Saxony*: v. Confessions.

(h) *Scotland* (q. v.): the reformation there, 3 *Whitg.* 314—316, 1 *Zur.* 24, 39, 40, 46, 59, 67, 85, 149; its progress quicker than in England, *ib.* 91; summary of the laws establishing the reformation in Scotland, and concerning the patronage of churches, the punishment of fornicators, &c., *ib.* 198, &c.; the people firm in religion, the rulers ferocious, 3 *Zur.* 434; the confession of faith allowed, ratified, subscribed, 2 *Zur.* 363 n.; superintendents appointed, *ib.* 364 n.; the general assembly, *Rog.* 206; letter sent by order thereof to abps Parker and Young on the case of Jo. Baron's wife, *Park.* 205; Parker's view of the request contained in the same letter, *ib.* 209; state of religion and the church, *Grin.* 63, 1 *Zur.* 169, 2 *Zur.* 275; the gospel deeply rooted there, 1 *Zur.* 144; letter of many Scottish ministers to Beza, approving the Confession of Helvetia, 2 *Zur.* 362; some of the Puritans go to Scotland, but soon return dissatisfied, *Grin.* 295; subscription required of noblemen in king James's minority, *Rog.* 24, (see 2 *Zur.* 363 n.); renewal of the covenant at Burntisland, 1601, 2 *Zur.* 331; rites of the church of Scotland, *Grin.* 214; intercourse of this church with foreign churches, *ib.* 275; it is at unity with us, 2 *Ful.* 123

(i) *Sweden*: v. Confessions.

(j) *Switzerland*: v. Confessions, Berne, Geneva, Zurich: state of religion there, 2 *Brad.* 137

(k) *Wirtemberg*: v. Confessions.

Churches: v. Abbeys, Cathedrals, Temples; also Burial, Chancel, Consecration, Images, Pictures, Towers, Windows.

The word church derived from κυριακή, whence kyrke, 1 *Ful.* 231; of holy buildings (churches, schools, &c.), 4 *Bul.* 498; the temples of Christians, *ib.* 499; the building and decoration of churches, 1 *Lat.* 22, 23; they are not to be built for vain glory, *Pil.* 539; none built in apostolic times, 1 *Jew.* 310; God always provides a place for worship in time of persecution, *Pil.* 263; churches treated of by the pseudo-Dionysius, *Whita.* 577; heathen temples turned into churches, 2 *Whitg.* 53; Eusebius speaks not of temples, but of oratories, *Calf.* 182; the arrangements of a church described by him, 2 *Ful.* 149, 1 *Jew.* 311; Jerome complains that much cost was bestowed in adorning churches, and little regard paid to the choice of ministers, 1 *Whitg.* 482; Justinian commanded that none should be built till the bishop had set up a cross, *Calf.* 135, & al.; it is immaterial whether they are built towards the East or otherwise, 4 *Bul.* 500; the church at Antioch in Syria built towards the West, *ib.*; in some churches of Italy, &c., the priest turns Westward, 1 *Jew.* 312; churches gorgeously adorned, *Bale* 527, 528, 4 *Bul.* 499; Popish churches gorgeous, reformed ones simple, *Pil.* 129; comparison between them before the reformation and after, *ib.* 156; they should not be exorcised or conjured, *Bale* 611; they are hallowed by their use, 4 *Bul.* 499, *Calf.* 131; not to be built to saints, 4 *Bul.* 501; never so dedicated till the time of Constantine, *Calf.* 129; Calfhill condemns the custom, *ib.* 363; temples (according to Augustine) are not to be made even for any holy angel, nor for God, *ib.* 129, 130; they are not made for God, but for man, *ib.* 131; Gelasius mentions certain churches dedicated to dead men who were not altogether faithful, 1 *Jew.* 158; a case exposed by St Martin, *ib.*; the dedication feast, *Bale* 611; the proper use of churches, 2 *Jew.* 1005, *Pil.* 63, 64, 1 *Tyn.* 106, 2 *Tyn.* 170, 3 *Tyn.* 11, 84; they are places of prayer, 1 *Bec.* 156, *Sand.* 251, 3 *Tyn.* 86; they have no Jewish or Popish holiness, *Pil.* 63, and are not to be superstitiously venerated, 3 *Tyn.* 11, 88, as they are by hypocrites, *ib.* 67; blind unbelief can only pray in a church, 1 *Tyn.* 118, 3 *Tyn.* 11; but they are not to be despised, 1 *Bec.* 159; reverent behaviour in church enjoined, *Rid.* 321; churches profaned by lords of misrule, *Grin.* 175; the Romish ceremonies of Palm Sunday, 1 *Bec.* 116; the garnishing of the church on Easter-day, *ib.*; many churches desecrated by the protector Somerset and others, *Grin.* 29 n.; buying and selling in the church during divine service not to be permitted, 2 *Hoop.* 129, 142; enclosures, &c. to be removed, they being marks of Jewish imperfection and typical separation, *ib.* 135; texts against idolatry graven in churches, but erased on the accession of Mary, *Rid.* 52; churches much neglected, especially the chancels, *Park.* 132; injunctions respecting them, 2 *Cran.* 501, *Grin.* 133, &c., 157, 158; inquiry whether pulled down, or spoiled, *Grin.* 172; some offended with churches, 2 *Whitg.* 60; the steeple, the poor man's sign, 1 *Bec.* 21; churches were interdicted if blood was spilled there, 2 *Cran.* 281, until money was raised to pay for the hallowing, 1 *Tyn.* 340 (and see Interdict); difference between ecclesia parochialis, and ecclesia baptismalis, 1 *Jew.* 181; collegiate churches, 3 *Whitg.* 400; description of the churches of the Russians, 3 *Zur.* 691

On church furniture, ornaments, &c., 4 *Bul.* 499; an ancient church had but one altar, 2 *Jew.* 636; description of church ornaments, &c. by some ancient writers, *ib.* 654; injunction of abp Winchelsea respecting the provision of church books and furniture, *Grin.* 159 n.; church ornaments and utensils enumerated, 1 *Tyn.* 238; the table of affinity to be affixed in the parish church, *Grin.* 126; see also Altars, Chest, Font, Pulpit, &c.

Churching of women: on the ceremony, 2 *Whitg.* 557—564, 2 *Zur.* 356; derived from the Jewish law, 2 *Zur.* 358; superstitiously observed, 1 *Lat.* 336, 343, 2 *Lat.* xiv; objected to by Knox, *Rid.* 534; forms, in the Prayer Books, *Lit. Edw.* and *Lit. Eliz.*; on the use of veils, 3 *Whitg.* 490, 1 *Zur.* 164; unmarried women not to be churched till they have done penance, *Grin.* 127, 164

Churchwardens: great officers, 1 *Lat.* 533; how to be chosen, *Grin.* 133; their oath, *ib.* 177; their duties, *ib.* 133, 2 *Hoop.* 129, 134; to keep order in churches, *Rid.* 321; to make their accounts every year, 2 *Hoop.* 142

Churchyard (Tho.): notice of him, *Poet.* xxxviii; charity, verses by him, *ib.* 402; verses fit for every one to know and confess, *ib.* 403

Churchyards: *v.* Burial.

To be well fenced, *Grin.* 135, 158; none to dance in them, *ib.* 135; cœmiterium innocentium, the burial-place of unbaptized infants, 4 *Bul.* 381 n

Churton (Ralph): Life of Nowell, *Now.* viii

Ciampinus (Jo.): Examen Libri Pontificalis, 2 *Ful.* 99 n

Ciborium: not anciently the same as the pix, 2 *Jew.* 560 n.; the tabernacle so called by modern writers, 4 *Bul.* 449 n

Cicero (M. T.): gave counsel that Cæsar should be chief ruler of the people, 2 *Hoop.* 83; his advice to rule the commonwealth after reason and experience took not good effect for lack of the wisdom of God, *ib.* 85; Rome endangered by it, 1 *Hoop.* 490; he lamented that he had lived to see certain troubles in the state, 2 *Cov.* 129; speaks of his banishment, 1 *Jew.* 323; invented aids to memory, 2 *Hoop.* 461; scholars must exercise themselves in his works, 2 *Bec.* 386; his Latinity, *Now.* i*, ii*, 97, &c.; his book called Hortensius said to have led Augustine to Christ, 3 *Jew.* 558; he says it is bred and born together with men to think that there is a God, 3 *Bul.* 125; his definition of God, *Hutch.* 176; he asks, who is such a fool as to believe that what he eats is a god? 1 *Jew.* 544, *Wool.* 26; recites divers opinions on God and creation, *Hutch.* 176; alleges Pythagoras, 1 *Hoop.* 285; gives Cleanthes' reasons for God's providence, *Hutch.* 76; mentions that Democritus thought the sun infinite, *ib.* 161; on the image of Jupiter, 2 *Jew.* 664; on Saturn, why so called, 1 *Bul.* 215 n.; Lactantius states on his authority that there were five Mercuries, 2 *Bul.* 218; he declares what is the best worshipping of the gods, 1 *Bul.* 198; says the gods care for great things, and neglect small ones, *Rog.* 42 n.; was convinced of the folly of his own heathenism, 3 *Jew.* 198; describes certain infidels, *Rog.* 37 n.; mentions examples of Atheism, *Hutch.* 73, 75; describes the priests of the Romans, 2 *Whitg.* 128; remarks, that as by nature we think there are gods...so we hold opinion with the consent of all nations, that souls do still continue, 3 *Bul.* 385; on the nature of the soul, *Hutch.* 278; anticipations of death, 3 *Bec.* 148, 154, 2 *Cov.* 223; he observes that while the sick man has life he has hope, *Grin.* 4; on the death of Socrates, 2 *Cov.* 222; he speaks of the death of the aged as natural, *ib.* 128; records the wish of Diogenes respecting his burial, *Pil.* 317, and a saying of his, *Hutch.* 73; shews what is the lady and queen of all virtues, *Wool.* 13; on the performance of duty, *ib.* 107; maintains that nothing is disgraceful which is not dishonest, 1 *Cov.* 177; commends Regulus for keeping his oath, 1 *Hoop.* 336; translates an expression of Euripides on swearing with the tongue, not with the mind, 1 *Bul.* 249 n.; tells what is the divine and human punishment of perjury, 1 *Bec.* 375; thinks it wrong not to resist injustice, 2 *Hoop.* 66; on thieves, 2 *Jew.* 627; on temperance and continence, 1 *Bul.* 419; against punishing in anger, *Pil.* 408; on friendship, 1 *Bec.* 101; he cautions against flatterers, 1 *Hoop.* 407; on avarice, *ib.* 408, 2 *Jew.* 666; he recommends a mean in apparel, 1 *Hoop.* 378; on the origin of power and rule, *Pil.* 125; his use of the word "princeps," 1 *Jew.* 371, 430; on the bad example of a prince, *Wool.* 128; defines "lex," 1 *Bul.* 193, 1 *Hoop.* 273; says the opinion of the wisest was, that law was not invented by men's wits, but a certain eternal thing, ruling the whole world, 2 *Bul.* 219; calls laws the bonds of the city, the foundation of liberty, the wellspring of justice and perfect honesty, 1 *Bul.* 338; says the magistrate is the living law, and the law the dumb magistrate, *ib.* 339; explains why consuls were so called, 2 *Whitg.* 279; speaks of Asinius as a very willing senator, self-appointed and chosen by himself, 4 *Jew.* 675; declares that Verres, having bribed and spoiled all Sicily, thought it not good to suffer his name or his doings to come in hazard, but before a judge of his own, *ib.* 947; declares it to be sweet and seemly to die for one's country, 1 *Bec.* 233, 1 *Hoop.* 356; speaks of Thermopylæ, 1 *Hoop.* 356 n.; exclaims, cedant arma togæ, &c., *Pil.* 439; says an unjust peace is better than a just war, 1 *Whitg.* 39; calls the Jews and Syrians nations born to bondage, 4 *Jew.* 667; on civil discord, 1 *Hoop.* 390; said to call Catiline "pestis," *Hutch.* 141; ridicules soothsayers, 1 *Hoop.* 309; declares that the law of the twelve tables forbade magical arts (fragment quoted by Augustine?), *ib.* 327; mentions a case of necromancy, *ib.* 329; speaks of wonderful sights and prodigies, *Hutch.* 81; praises Epaminondas and Regulus, *ib.* 321, and Scipio, *Wool.* 94; mentions a saying of the latter, *Hutch.* 1; on Anaxagoras, *Phil.* 357 n.; his story of C. Fimbria and Q. Scævola, 3 *Whitg.* 323, of Ennius and Nasica, *Hutch.* 51; his account of Stilpho, *Wool.* 106; he speaks of the Greek tongue as read in almost all nations, 1 *Jew.* 278; declares that without words, there can be no meaning, *ib.* 283; says, in those tongues which we understand not, we are deaf, *ib.* 288; praises the great orators, 1 *Hoop.* 44; mentions a saying of Demosthenes, *Hutch.* 105; tells what Hannibal said of Phormio, 4 *Jew.* 885; declares that there is nothing so incredible that it may not be made probable by eloquence, 1 *Hoop.* 235; would have an advocate keep back what would prejudice his cause, 3 *Whitg.* 66; cautions that scurrilous chattering is to be avoided by an orator, 3 *Jew.* 159; blames Panetius, for not defining his terms, *Coop.* 57; defines "fides," 1 *Bul.* 81; explains ὁμολογία by "convenientia," 4 *Bul.* 244; his use of the word "armarium," 2 *Ful.* 150, of "episcopus," 1 *Ful.* 217, of "hæresis," 3 *Jew.* 214; of "quasi," 2 *Ful.* 173; of "simulacrum," 1 *Ful.* 101; on painters and poets, 2 *Jew.* 660; he mentions a common device of simple poets, *ib.* 581; declares that wise men say, whoso will take upon him to save others ought first to save himself, 4 *Jew.* 955; observes that in human things nothing is perfect so soon as it is invented, 1 *Hoop.* 27; mistakes of his, 4 *Jew.* 635; other citations and references, 1 *Hoop.* 352, *Hutch.* 13, 73, 1 *Jew.* 292, 465, 3 *Jew.* 219, *Now.* (69), 189, *Pil.* 679, *Sand.* 110, 2 *Whitg.* 483, 3 *Whitg.* 321, *Wool.* 32, 2 *Zur.* 293

Cimmerian darkness: 2 *Cran.* 118
Cinesias: 2 *Brad.* 387
Ciniphes (σκνίφες, Exod. viii): 1 *Jew.* 96
Cinque Ports: their names, *Pra. Eliz.* 428
Circe: 2 *Bul.* 213
Circumcelliones: ancient heretics, sprung from the Donatists, 1 *Whitg.* 113; their blind zeal, *ib.*; they rejected and burned the holy scriptures, *Rog.* 76; they cast off all grace and virtue, *ib.* 118; allowed suicide, 3 *Whitg.* 57; wandering preachers so called, *ib.* 53, 246, 250
Circumcision: its appointment and signification, 2 *Bul.* 168, &c., 2 *Lat.* 132, 1 *Tyn.* 349—351, 3 *Tyn.* 27, 65; its manner, 2 *Bul.* 173; given to infants, 4 *Bul.* 390; practised in private houses, 2 *Whitg.* 516; performed on one occasion by Zipporah, *ib.* 521, 524; neglected for forty years in the wilderness, 1 *Jew.* 224, 3 *Tyn.* 7; practised by the Ishmaelites, 3 *Whitg.* 147; it is called God's covenant, 4 *Bul.* 280, *Grin.* 41; it was the

sign, token, sacrament, or seal of the covenant, 1 *Brad.* 149, 2 *Bul.* 172, 1 *Ful.* 451, *Grin.* 41, 2 *Jew.* 1100, *Now.* (87, 88), 209, 210, *Rog.* 251; not a bare sign, 2 *Jew.* 1101; the seal of the justice that came by faith and not by works, 2 *Hoop.* 89; God's infallible truth and promises were confirmed to Abraham by it, not by his obedience, *ib.*; in itself it availed nothing, 1 *Tyn.* 349, 350, but increased the guilt of the Jew who hated the law, *ib.* 358; it was twofold, 2 *Jew.* 177; its spiritual character, 2 *Bec.* 216; its mystery, 2 *Bul.* 173; a sign of the blessed Seed to come, 4 *Bul.* 353; also of sanctification, *ib.* 383; the circumcised were gathered into one body by it, 2 *Bul.* 175; it put a man in mind of his duty, *ib.* 176; the grace of God was not tied to it, *ib.* 175; some that died without it were not condemned, 2 *Bec.* 215, 222, 223, *Whita.* 529, 530; it availed for women, *Whita.* 529; the sum of it, 2 *Bul.* 178; it figured baptism, 3 *Tyn.* 246, which is the "circumcision made without hands," 4 *Bul.* 299, 2 *Jew.* 1105; comparison between the ordinances, 1 *Tyn.* 350, 358; on re-circumcision, *Whita.* 123

Circumcision of Christ: the festival, 1 *Bul.* 260

Cirenius: *v.* Serenus.

Cistercians: beginning of the order, 1 *Whitg.* 482; called White Observant monks, *Pil.* 509; they used the liturgy of Ambrose, *ib.*; Hooper was a member of the order at Gloucester, 2 *Hoop.* vii.

Cisterciensis: on the first payment of tithes by Christians, *Bale* 104

Cities of Refuge: *v.* Sanctuaries.

Citolini (Ales.): an Italian Protestant exile, *Park.* 420 n., 421, 470

City of God: what, *Calf.* 164

Civil Law: *v.* Law.

Civil Offices: *v.* Offices.

Civility: citizenship, 2 *Cov.* 232

Clagett (Will.): *Calf.* 86 n., 246 n

Clamb: climbed, 2 *Tyn.* 256

Clamengiis (Nic. de), or Clavengiis: draws a fearful picture of the corruptions of the church, 2 *Jew.* 642, 1081 n.; mentions exactions for suffering concubines, 4 *Jew.* 644

Clanricarde (Rich. earl of): *v.* Burgh (R. de).

Clapham (Henoch): *v.* C. (H.)
Notice of him, *Poet.* xliii; verses on the decline and corruption of the visible church, *ib.* 466

Clapton (Will.): *v.* Clopton.

Clare (St): invoked by those who have sore eyes, *Rog.* 226; said by some to be the saviour of women, *ib.* 298; St Clare of Orchester, *Bale* 190

Clare, co. Suffolk: *Park.* 7, 8

Clarence (Geo. duke of): *v.* George.

Clarius (Isidorus), bp of Foligno: notice of him, 1 *Ful.* 62 n.; he reckoned 8000 errors in the Latin Vulgate, 1 *Ful.* 62, *Whita.* 207; his scholia on the Bible, *Jew.* xxxiv; he renders שאול, Gen. xxxvii. 36, "sepulchrum," 1 *Ful.* 287; on Hosea xii. 10, "assimulatus sum," *ib.* 579; on Hab. ii. 18, "imaginem falsam," *ib.* 211; on "the image that fell down from Jupiter," *ib.* 203; on giving thanks "with the spirit," 1 *Jew.* 313; on Eph. i. 23, "the fulness of him," &c., 1 *Ful.* 235; on "covetousness which is idolatry," *ib.* 100

Clark, and Clarke: *v.* Clerk.

Claudian: cited, 1 *Bec.* 369

Claudius Cæsar, emperor: mentioned in Acts, 4 *Bul.* 536; he abolished necromancy, 1 *Hoop.* 329

Claudius, bp of Turin: forbade the worship of the cross, *Calf.* 379, 2 *Ful.* 208

Clausures: inclosures, inclosed places, 3 *Bec.* 521

Clavasio (Ang. de): *v.* Angelus.

Clavengiis (Nic. de): *v.* Clamengiis.

Claw-backs: flatterers, 1 *Lat.* 133

Clay (Will. Keatinge): editor of *Lit. Eliz.*, also of *Pra. Eliz.*; his Book of Common Prayer Illustrated, *Lit. Edw.* ix. n

Claybroke (Dr): named, 2 *Cran.* 244; letter to him, *ib.* 254

Clayden (......): Bradford's keeper in the Compter, 1 *Brad.* 515, 516, 518, 538, 544, 552, 2 *Brad.* 251 n

Claydon (Jo.): hanged and burned, *Bale* 51

Clayson (Lucas): letter to R. Gualter the younger, 2 *Zur.* 213

Clayton (Tho.), regent of the Dominicans: *Bale* 16

Clean, &c.: *v.* Law of Moses, Purity.

Cleanthes: defends God's providence, *Hutch.* 76

Cleeve (Bishop's), co. Gloucester: Parkhurst's rectory, 4 *Jew.* 1190, 1191, 1 *Zur.* 48

Clemencet (Cha.): L'Art de vérifier les Dates, 2 *Ful.* 179 n.; an error noted, *ib.* 337 n

Clement I. bp of Rome: mentioned, 4 *Bul.* 31, 2 *Lat.* 280; account of him, 1 *Bec.* 139 n.; alleged as saying that he was next to Peter (pseud.), 3 *Jew.* 326; invoked for brewing beer, 1 *Bec.* 139, *Hutch.* 172, and for the bliss of heaven, *ib.* 172 n.; some suppose that he wrote or translated the epistle to the Hebrews, 1 *Ful.* 29, 31, 33, *Whita.* 125, 2 *Whitg.* 120; his genuine Epistle to the

Corinthians publicly read in the church of old, *Rog.* 324, 3 *Whitg.* 345; when first printed, 1 *Jew.* 111 n., 2 *Whitg.* 120 n.; many forged pieces published under his name, 1 *Jew.* 85, 111, 112, *Whita.* 565, 2 *Whitg.* 119; Epistle to James, 2 *Ful.* 322; Decretal Epistles, 2 *Ful.* 81 n., 1 *Jew.* 342, *Rid.* 180; the Itinerarium, quoted in Peter's name, *Calf.* 380, 387; the Recognitiones, *ib.* 20 n., 1 *Ful.* 475; a spurious work of his condemned by the sixth general council at Constantinople, *Whita.* 508; he is falsely said to have published the Canons of the Apostles, *ib.* 42; the so called Apostolical Constitutions, 1 *Jew.*111, 112, *Whita.* 43; they have not a grain of the apostolical spirit, *Whita.* 330, 331; they are spurious, and contain many falsehoods, *ib.* 567—569; Clement alleged for tradition (pseud.), 3 *Jew.* 240; says, he maketh no schism in the church that departeth from the wicked, but he that departeth from the godly (Const.), 4 *Jew.* 875; affirms that he who neglects ecclesiastical decrees shall suffer the torment of eternal fire (pseud.), *Pil.* 629; ordered that the clergy should have all things in common (pseud.), 1 *Jew.* 39, 74; says the mysteries are committed to three orders, the priest, the deacon, the minister (pseud.), 3 *Jew.* 272; referred to as saying that in some churches there were only bishops and deacons, and no presbyters, 2 *Tyn.* 256 n.; would have a bishop free from worldly cares (pseud.), 4 *Jew.* 819; addresses James as bishop of bishops, governor, &c. (pseud.), 1 *Jew.* 427, 3 *Jew.* 269; says Peter commanded primates or patriarchs to be placed where there had been chief flamines (pseud.), 3 *Jew.* 313, 2 *Whitg.* 118; on communion with foreign bishops (Const.), *Whita.* 217 n.; cited for minor orders, (pseud.), *Rog.* 260 n.; he speaks of chatechists (pseud.), 3 *Jew.* 272; on female priests (Const.), 2 *Whitg.* 522; catechumens required to prepare themselves for three months before their baptism (pseud.), 1 *Jew.* 119; said to have set forth (in the Const.) the mass as used by the apostles, *ib.* 108; the Constitutions intimate that Christ commanded his apostles to offer sacrifice, *ib.* 210, 521, 522, 2 *Jew.* 713, 716, and speak of offering up the sign of the body of Christ, *ib.* 715; quoted for the institution of the unbloody sacrifice, 1 *Jew.* 108; they say, We offer to thee, O King and God, according to Christ's institution, this bread and this cup, *ib.* 522; the words of offering cited for intercessory masses, 2 *Jew.* 743, 744; Clement commands that as many hosts be offered on the altar as will suffice the people (pseud.), 2 *Bec.* 239, 3 *Bec.* 416, 455, *Coop.* 151, 1 *Jew.* 16, 17, 202, 208, 2 *Jew.* 553, 585, 3 *Jew.* 477, and forbids the reserving of what remains (pseud.), 2 *Bec.* 251, *Coop.* 151, 2 *Jew.* 553; says, let not mice-dung be found among the fragments of the Lord's portion (pseud.), 3 *Jew.* 517; in a canon he forbids that the priest should offer any liquor but wine (pseud.), 3 *Bec.* 359; referred to on the water in the chalice (pseud.), 1 *Hoop.* 168; the Constitutions direct the subdeacons to give water for the priests' hands, and deacons are to stand at the altar with fans of parchment and peacocks' tails to drive away flies, 3 *Jew.* 273; their directions about the reception of the communion in order, 2 *Jew.* 744; notice of a prayer in the Constitutions, *Pra. Eliz.* 445 n.; on the use of the word Amen (Const.), 2 *Jew.* 698; Clement cited for confirmation (pseud.), *Rog.* 253 n.; for confession (pseud.), 3 *Jew.* 368; a book falsely ascribed to him maintains that wives should be common, *Pil.* 600; mentioned by Chrysostom as recording a declaration of Peter that Antichrist shall work miracles, 2 *Cran.* 46; cited as to images (pseud.), *Calf.* 21; on Egyptian idolatry (pseud.), *ib.* 369

Clement II. pope: set up by Henry the emperor, *Pil.* 640

Clement III. pope: his decrees, 1 *Hoop.* 228, 522

Clement V. pope: removed to Avignon, 4 *Jew.* 933, his profligacy, *ib.* 874; his treatment of Fra. Dandalus, ambassador of Venice, 4 *Jew.* 692, 931; his decretal epistles, or Clementines, 1 *Lat.* 212; he confirmed the adoration of the sacrament, 1 *Hoop.* 527 n., 1 *Jew.* 516, 549, and granted indulgences to keepers of the feast of Corpus Christi, 2 *Jew.* 774; remitted a part of the sins of those who were buried in the Minorite habit, 1 *Lat.* 50; he asserted all the right of kings to be from the pope, 1 *Jew.* 397, 4 *Jew.* 672, and declared himself to be heir of the empire, &c., 1 *Jew.* 443, 4 *Jew.* 682, 696; he(?) says all are subject to the pope's will, and are in him as members of a member, 3 *Jew.* 317

Clement VI. pope: shortened the jubilee to fifty years, 2 *Bul.* 268, 1 *Lat.* 49 n.; his jubilean bull cited with reference to indulgences, 1 *Tyn.* 74 n.; he commands the angels, 3 *Jew.* 560

Clement VII. pope: sometime bp of Worcester, 1 *Tyn.* xviii; he grants privileges to the church of Boston, 1 *Tyn.* 244 n.; Charles V. desires to hold his stirrup, 4 *Jew.* 690; he gives to the duke of Guelder the style of eldest son of the holy see, 2 *Tyn.* 264; meets Francis I. at Marseilles, 2 *Cran.* 246 n.; consequences of the interview, 4 *Jew.* 665; his conduct about king Henry VIII's first marriage, 2 *Cran.* 461, 462; mention of a bull (of this pope or Paul III. ?) confirming the marriage of queen Anne Boleyn, *Park.* 414; he caused Stuppino to be whipped for saying several masses in one day, 2 *Jew.* 633; ruined Florence, and spoiled Savoy, 4 *Jew.* 672; named, 4 *Bul.* 29

Clement VIII. pope: Missale, 2 *Ful.* 21 n.; Pontificale, *Calf.* 381 n.; Index Lib. Prohib., *ib.* 95 n., 126 n

Clement VIII. antipope [Giles de Mugnos, or Munion]: 1 *Tyn.* 325 n

Clement of Alexandria: his Pædogogus, lib. iii. cap. xii; an abridged translation, *Wool.* 147; he says, forasmuch as the Word itself is come to us from heaven, we may not seek unto the doctrine of men, 4 *Jew.* 901; thinks Christ preached but one year, *ib.* 695, *Whita.* 586, that he was thirty years old at his death, *Whita.* 665, and that he descended into hell to preach the gospel there, *ib.* 537, 586; teaches that angels fell through the love of women, *Coop.* 146, 3 *Jew.* 606; also that men's souls are transformed into angels, *Coop.* 146; declares that the word is hidden from no man, and that there is no darkness in it, 2 *Jew.* 683, 4 *Jew.* 1185, *Whita.* 398; says the scriptures deify us, 1 *Jew.* 462; supposes the Old Testament was lost in the captivity and restored by Ezra, *Whita.* 115; thinks it was read by Plato, *ib.* 118; tells how Minos imitated Moses, *Calf.* 13 n.; states how heretics misuse the scripture, 1 *Ful.* 9; describes the doctrine of Christ as most absolute, not wanting anything, *Sand.* 222; on the object of John's gospel, 2 *Brad.* 263 n.; he ascribes the epistle to the Hebrews to Paul, *Whita.* 106, and the Greek version of it to Luke, *ib.* 125; calls the second epistle of John, "ad virgines," *ib.* 218 n.; he says the tradition of the apostles, like their doctrine, was one, 2 *Jew.* 702; his testimony to tradition considered, *Whita.* 586; he says our faith is the key of the kingdom of heaven, 3 *Jew.* 358; declares that hope is as it were the blood of faith, *ib.* 245; cited with reference to τελείωσις, or Christian perfection, 1 *Cov.* 203 n.; referred to on the continuance of the church, 2 *Ful.* 67; he shews that the church was corrupted immediately after the apostles, 2 *Whitg.* 183; mentions how the heathen upbraided Christians for their dissensions, 3 *Jew.* 607; affirms that Christ says, Eat my flesh and drink my blood, meaning hereby under an allegory, the meat and drink that is of (our) faith and (his) promise, *ib.* 532, 533; says, when certain have divided the sacrament, they suffer each of the people to take part of it, 1 *Jew.* 153, 202, 2 *Jew.* 588; asserts that Christ shewed that which was blessed to be wine, by saying, "I will no more drink," &c., 2 *Jew.* 1116, 3 *Jew.* 521, 522; speaks of Christ's blood as double, fleshly and spiritual, 1 *Jew.* 463; says that to drink the blood of Jesus is to be partaker of his incorruption, 3 *Bec.* 434, 2 *Jew.* 1119, 3 *Jew.* 539; speaks of an oblation at the communion, *Coop.* 88; says that in the prayers all have one voice and one mind, 1 *Jew.* 289, 312; calls prayer an excellent and holy sacrifice, *Coop.* 91; shews that the voice is not essential to prayer, 1 *Jew.* 285; says marriage, as well as chastity, has its proper service pertaining to the Lord, 2 *Jew.* 1128, 3 *Jew.* 417; affirms that the apostles were married, 1 *Ful.* 472, 3 *Jew.* 392; particularly mentions Paul, whose "true yoke-fellow" he supposes to have been his wife, 1 *Ful.* 117, 476, 2 *Jew.* 727, 3 *Jew.* 414; affirms that perfect Christians do eat and drink and contract matrimony, 3 *Jew.* 393; declares that all the epistles, which teach sobriety and continent life, never forbid honest marriage, *ib.* 403, 423; speaking of certain old heretics, he says, these glorious braggers say they will follow the example of our Lord, that married no wife; unto them the scripture saith, "God withstandeth the proud, and giveth grace to the humble," *ib.* 423; considers painting and sculpture to be forbidden, 2 *Jew.* 658; speaks against image-worship, *Calf.* 370; his opinion as to the philosophical righteousness of the Greeks before Christ, &c., *Rog.* 126 n.; on the Gnostics, *ib.* 44 n.; on the Basilidians, *ib.* 37 n.; on an error of them and the Valentinians, *ib.* 149; on the Carpocratians, *ib.* 119 n.; he speaks of the Docetæ, 1 *Cov.* 21 n.; says the heretic Prodicas declared it lawful to commit open fornication, 4 *Jew.* 630; tells that Erectheus and Marius offered up their daughters, 2 *Jew.* 734; says Nicagoras made himself a pair of wings, and would be called Mercury, 4 *Jew.* 842; Clement's errors, *Coop.* 146, 3 *Jew.* 606, *Whita.* 586

Clement (Jo.), of Oxford, afterwards of Mechlin: tore leaves out of Theodoret, 1 *Jew.* 52, 4 *Jew.* 785

Clement (Jo.), or Clemente: died in prison for religion, *Poet.* 168

Clement (Ninian), or Clemett, minister of Aberbrothock: 2 *Zur.* 365

Clement (Sir Rich.), of the Mote, Igtham, Kent: 1 *Bec.* 125 n

Clement (Tho.), a prebendary: *Park.* 114

Clementines: *v.* Clement V.

Clements (......): saluted, *Phil.* 227

Clemett (N.): *v.* Clement.

Clenardus (......): on the Jews, *Rog.* 171

Cleobury (......): personates lord Devon, and is executed, 3 *Zur.* 133 n

Clepeth: calleth, 1 *Brad.* 105

Clergy, Clerks, Spiritualty: *v.* Ministers, Priests, &c., also Orders and Laity.

i. *Clergy, clerks, spiritualty, generally*: on ecclesiastical persons, 4 *Bul.* 93, &c.; κλῆρος originally signified all Christians, 1 *Ful.* 275; the name appropriated by ecclesiastics, 1 *Lat.* 314, who early set themselves up for the church, 2 *Cran.* 515; the laity are the church as well as they, 3 *Tyn.* 158; multitude of the clergy, 1 *Tyn.* 302; number at Rome, under Cornelius, 1 *Jew.* 197; Gregory Nazianzen complains of their number as too great, *ib.*; Justinian diminishes the number at Constantinople, *ib.*; anciently forbidden to perform secular business, 2 *Cran.* 38, 56 n.; nevertheless directed by the fourth council of Carthage to live by work, 2 *Whitg.* 381; against their holding temporal offices, *Hutch.* 338, or following secular pursuits, 2 *Lat.* 38; the spiritualty ought to be subject to the laws of the temporal government, 1 *Bec.* 216, 217, 2 *Tyn.* 67; dissension between the spiritualty and temporalty, 5 *Bec.* 255; they should not have temporal authority, 2 *Tyn.* 247, &c., 273; have no power to punish sin, 1 *Tyn.* 240; they are not all children of light, 1 *Lat.* 43; clerks were anciently students or candidates for the ministry, 4 *Bul.* 113; the name came at length to signify all who knew Latin, 1 *Brad.* 527, as the clerk who responds at mass in the name of the people, 2 *Brad.* 315, 334, being hired for a groat to stand beside the priest, *Whita.* 469; some maintain (from 1 Cor. xiv. 16) that it is sufficient if this one person, called the clerk, understand the prayers and say "Amen" thereto on behalf of all, *ib.* 259; the office unknown in the apostolic church, *ib.* 260

ii. *The Romish clergy in particular* (*v.* Regula, Stella Clericorum): they call themselves the spiritualty, 1 *Tyn.* 257, 2 *Tyn.* 177; who the true spiritualty are, *ib.* 128; on the clergy secular and regular, or priests and monks, *ib.* 277; the more wicked the people, the more they feared the clergy, 1 *Tyn.* 339; complaints of their degeneracy, by Romish writers, 1 *Jew.* 121; their alliance with wicked tyrants and usurpers, 2 *Tyn.* 268; they made rulers serve them, 1 *Tyn.* 282, 3 *Tyn.* 53; became a several kingdom, 1 *Tyn.* 147, 191; the shaven nation preached themselves, not Christ, and took away the authority of kings, *ib.* 213; their conspiracy against kings and the whole world, *ib.* 281; procure exemption from tribute, from the jurisdiction of lay courts, and from punishment, *ib.* 178, 180, 240, 2 *Tyn.* 124; they would not pay taxes, 1 *Tyn.* 189, 2 *Tyn.* 277, nor swear before a lay-judge, *ib.* 307; extracts from the Canon Law shewing their extravagant pretensions, 2 *Cran.* 72, &c.; according to this law, they ought to give no oath of fidelity to their temporal governors, except for temporalities, *ib.* 73, and all causes, spiritual or temporal ought to be determined and judged by them, *ib.*; forbidden by Urban II. to do homage to princes for their preferments, 1 *Tyn.* 380 n.; their jurisdiction according to the Romish Decretals, 2 *Cran.* 166; their spies everywhere, 1 *Tyn.* 191; their great wealth, and how obtained, *ib.* 236—239, 244, 249, 341, 424, 3 *Tyn.* 53; their ignorance, 1 *Tyn.* 146, 3 *Tyn.* 75; their evil doctrine, 2 *Tyn.* 123; their hostility to the circulation of the scriptures, 1 *Tyn.* 393; they set aside the scriptures, 2 *Tyn.* 103; corrupt the sense of it and the lives of the saints, 3 *Tyn.* 48; clerical falsifiers, &c., how to be punished by the Canon Law, *Calf.* 273; they frequent alehouses, 1 *Cran.* xiii, 1 *Tyn.* 394; their uncleanness, 2 *Tyn.* 123; their marriage forbidden, but their concubinage licensed, 3 *Tyn.* 40, (*v.* Celibacy, Marriage); their cruel and vindictive ways, 1 *Tyn.* 117, 340, 342; persecutors of God's word and its preachers, *ib.* 337, 3 *Tyn.* 48; they deny that they burn heretics, *Phil.* 122; their other evil ways, 1 *Tyn.* 336, 339—341; 3 *Tyn.* 40—42, 102—106; forms used in degrading them, *Pil.* 163, *Rid.* 289—291, 1 *Tyn.* 233

iii. *The clergy of England* (see Ministers, and the several Articles of Inquiry and Injunctions mentioned at p. 42): acts passed with reference to them, temp. Hen. VIII.,

2 *Lat.* 301 n.; they are enjoined to have Bibles of their own, 2 *Lat.* 243; enjoined not to resort to taverns, 2 *Lat.* 500; their marriage allowed by parliament, 3 *Zur.* 377, 468 n.; account of them in 1550, *ib.* 546, 547; their ignorance about the sacraments, 1 *Hoop.* 146; ignorance of those in the diocese of Gloucester, 1551, 2 *Hoop.* 151; illiterate clergymen styled Sir Johns, 1 *Lat.* 317; Hooper's letter to his clergy, 2 *Hoop.* 118; Latimer used to rebuke beneficed men in his sermons, 2 *Bec.* 425; the clergy enabled to hold the lands of their wives, and their children declared legitimate, 1 *Lat.* 529 n.; they were only half reformed in the days of Edward VI., *Rid.* 59; complaints of their impoverishment and its effects, 2 *Jew.* 999, 1012, 1 *Lat.* 100, *Park.* 374; some set up bills at Paul's or the Royal Exchange to see if they could hear of good masters, 3 *Whitg.* 246; armour to be provided by them, *Park.* 345—348; clerks' tolerations, what, *Sand.* xx. n.; complaints of their ignorance, temp. Eliz., 2 *Jew.* 1012; ministers enjoined to learn Nowell's Catechism, 1 *Whitg.* 336; commissions against them for discovery of concealed lands or goods, *Park.* 413; terrible things to be contrived against them in parliament, *Park.* 470

Clergy (Benefit of): the neck verse, 1 *Tyn.* 180, 181 n., 243; Sir Tho. More having been twice married, Tyndale said he was past the grace of his neck verse, 3 *Tyn.* 165

Clericus (Jo.), or Le Clerc: *Calf.* 10 n., 20 n., 2 *Ful.* 50 n., 353 n.

Clerk* (Barth.): engaged to refute Saunders, *Park.* 411, 412; some account of his answer, *ib.* 413, 414, 430, 1 *Zur.* 281 n.; he refuses to resign the deanery of the arches, *Park.* 427—432

Clerk (Jo.), bp of Bath and Wells: examines Jo. Tewkesbury, 1 *Tyn.* 42 n.; present at Anne Boleyn's coronation, 2 *Cran.* 245; he signs a declaration respecting a general council, 2 *Cran.* 468; recommended to Cromwell, 2 *Lat.* 386, 387

Clerk (Jo.), a proctor: 2 *Cran.* 492; the pope's notary at Cranmer's examination (probably the same), *ib.* 542

Clerke (Jo.): accuses Sir Tho. Rose, curate of Hadleigh, 2 *Cran.* 280 n

Clerke (Jo.): witness against Rich. Vulford, 1 *Tyn.* 13 n

Clarke (Sam.): Marrow of Eccl. Hist., 2 *Brad.* xii. n

Clark (Tho.), parson of St Mary Abchurch, London: 2 *Lat.* 324

Clerke (Walter): accuses Sir Tho. Rose, 2 *Cran.* 280 n

Clarke (W.): named as a Protestant writer, 1 *Ful.* x.

Clarke (Will.), of Cambridge: *Park.* 433

Clerk (Will.): letter to him and Dr Aubrey, who partly executed the office of vicar general during Grindal's sequestration, *Grin.* 408—412

Clerk (Will.), minister of Anstruther: 2 *Zur.* 365

Clarke (Mr): acts as notary at a disputation, 1 *Ful.* xi.

Clarke (......), fellow of Gonville hall: *Park.* 248

Clerk (......), niece of abp Parker: *Park.* xiii.

Clerks: v. Clergy.

Clerks (Parish): injunctions concerning their appointment and duties, *Grin.* 142, 168, 2 *Hoop.* 137; forbidden by Sandys to intrude into the priests' duty, *Sand.* xx; not to minister sacraments, &c., *Grin.* 132; they read the first lesson, the epistle, &c., *ib.* 142, 168

Cleve (Bishop's): v. Cleeve.

Cleves (Will. duke of): v. William.

Clichtoveus (Judocus): his argument from Virgil about "Hoc facite," 1 *Jew.* 15, 16; he declares that in the primitive church the faithful received the communion every day, 3 *Jew.* 477; in error about Philo, *Whita.* 89; his supplement to Cyril on John, 2 *Bec.* 173 n.; his conduct in this matter unjustly censured by Cave and others, 2 *Ful.* 277 n

Cliff (Will.), dean of Chester: 2 *Cran.* 264 n

Cliffe (Dr), of Clement hostel, Camb.: opposes Latimer, 2 *Lat.* xii. (v. Clyff).

Cliffe, co. Kent: the benefice annexed to the see of Rochester, *Park.* 100

Clifford (Lady Anne), afterwards countess of Pembroke: v. Herbert.

Clifford (Geo.): v. Clyfford.

Clifford (Rich.), bp of London, previously of Worcester: one of lord Cobham's judges, *Bale* 6, 7, 23, 28, 39; he sends to the bishop of Hereford a copy of lord Cobham's condemnation, *ib.* 44

Clifford (W.): grantee of part of Pontefract priory, 2 *Cran.* 363 n

Clifford moor, co. York: the rebellious earls assemble there, 1 *Zur.* 214 n., 247 n

Climacus (St Jo.): v. John.

---

* Clerk, Clerke, Clark, Clarke, are all arranged together.

Climates: seven climates of the world, *Bale* 501; four climates of the world, *ib.* 468
Clink: *v.* Southwark.
Clintanc (St): *v.* Clitank.
Clinton (Edw. lord), afterwards earl of Lincoln: privy councillor, 1 *Zur.* 5 n.; signature as such, 2 *Cran.* 524, 530, *Grin.* 414, 423, 427, 429, 433, 435, *Park.* 74, 77, 106, 122, 155, 330, 357, 381, *Rid.* 508; he commands troops against the rebels in the North, *Park.* 388 n., 1 *Zur.* 214 n., 247 n.; at the duke of Norfolk's trial, 1 *Zur.* 267 n.; created earl, *Park.* 447 n.; ambassador to France, 1 *Ful.* iii; 2 *Zur.* 201 n
Clinton (...... lady): previously married to Sir Ant. Browne, *Rid.* x. n. [not identified].
Clippings: embraces, *Bale* 544
Clitank (St): a saint of South Wales [probably Clintanc, king and martyr, Aug. 19], *Bale* 190
Cliva: a Cistercian monastery, 2 *Hoop.* vii. n
Clodovius: *v.* Clovis.
Cloning, or Cloyning: *v.* Cloyner.
Clopham (Dav.), a proctor: 2 *Cran.* 492
Clopton (Will.), or Clapton: injures a poor priest, 2 *Lat.* 383; Latimer complains of him to lord Cromwell, *ib.* 399
Closet: what it is to enter thereinto, 1 *Bec.* 130, 133
Closh: *v.* Cloyshe.
Cloth: particulars concerning English cloth, 1 *Zur.* 215, 241, 296, 2 *Zur.* 63, 225, 3 *Zur.* 62, 67, 69, 72, 216, 222, 613, &c. (see the letters of R. Hilles generally).
Clothes: *v.* Apparel.
Clothmakers: their fraudulent artifices, 1 *Lat.* 138
Clotworthy (Nich.): 2 *Brad.* 397 n
Clough (Sir Rich.): his account of Embden, 1 *Zur.* 140 n
Clout up: to join clumsily, *Phil.* 308
Clovis I., king of France: eldest son of the church, 1 *Tyn.* 187 n.; Clodovius (the same?) named the bishop of Rome a bishop as he did others, 2 *Hoop.* 237
Cloyner, Cloyning: what, *Bale* 391 n., see 170
Cloyshe, or Closh: a game, 1 *Hoop.* 393
Cluniacensis: *v.* Petrus
Clusius (......): saluted, 2 *Zur.* 293, 298
Clyff (Dr) : withholds the records of the see of Ely, 2 *Cran.* 264
Clyfford (Geo.): founded a lazar house at Bobbing, Kent, *Park.* 169
Coadjutors: bishops, &c. who cannot do their office should have helpers, 1 *Hoop.* 508, 1 *Lat.* 175; their duty, *Park.* 306
Coal: its price enhanced, 1 *Lat.* 279; coals of fire, meaning of the expression, *ib.* 439

Coat-armour: *v.* Arms.
Cob (Tho.): martyred at Thetford, *Poet.* 164
Cobham, co. Kent: the college bought by lord Cobham, 2 *Cran.* 411
Cobham, co. Surrey: named as the retirement and burial-place of abp Heath, 2 *Cran.* 276 n., *Phil.* xxvi, but it should be Chobham, as 2 *Zur.* 182 n
Cobham (The lord Reynolde of): called by Bale the father of Sir Jo. Oldcastle lord Cobham, [but this must be an error], *Bale* 7
Cobham (Jo. lord): *v.* Oldcastle.
Cobham (Geo. and Will. lords): *v.* Brooke.
Cobham (Tho.), alias Brooke, *q. v.*
Cocabas: an impostor, 2 *Ful.* 369
Coccius (Jod.): Thesaurus Catholicus, *Calf.* 70, 77, 81, 177, 231, 258, 2 *Ful.* 57, 85, 289 nn
Coccius (Ulric.): 2 *Zur.* 98 n
Cochlæus (Jo.): named, *Bale* 139; notice of him, 3 *Zur.* 244 n.; his views on the authority of scripture, *Whita.* 277; he mentions many things recorded in scripture which he says would not be credible but for the authority of the church, *ib.* 282; acknowledges that anciently all communicated together, 2 *Jew.* 625, 628, 3 *Jew.* 477; on the council of Constance and John Huss, *Rog.* 120 n.; writes against the confession of Augsburgh, 2 *Zur.* 103 n.; his account of Tyndale's labours at Cologne, 1 *Tyn.* xxviii; he is dismissed from Frankfort, *ib.*; answered by Bullinger, 4 *Bul.* xix.
Cockain (Sir Tho.): 2 *Lat.* 423
Cocket: the word explained, *Hutch.* 343
Cockraft (Hen.): in exile at Zurich, 3 *Zur.* 752
Cockrel (......): a shipowner, *Sand.* xv.
Cocks (Jo.), or Cokes: Cranmer's vicar-general, 2 *Cran.* 560; letter to him, *ib.* 288 (and perhaps 249, 252, 256, 259, 265)
Cock-sure: 1 *Brad.* 76, 2 *Brad.* 109, 1 *Whitg.* 149
Cocus (Rob.): *v.* Cooke.
Codenham (Jo.): proposed as suffragan of Dover, 2 *Cran.* 471
Codex: *v.* Law (Civil).
Codex Canonum vetus (Mogunt. 1525): 2 *Ful.* 107 n.; Codex Canonum eccl. Rom. (Par. 1609), *ib.* 179 n
Codrus, king of Athens: his death, 1 *Bec.* 233, 1 *Bul.* 278
Codrus Urceus, *q. v.*
Cods: husks, 1 *Bec.* 450
Cœlestine: *v.* Celestine.
Cœlestius: *v.* Celestius.
Cœlius: *v.* Curio (C. S.).

Cœnobia: what, 1 *Bul.* 286
Coffin (......), a rebel: 2 *Cran.* 187 n
Cognizance: *v.* Livery.
Coil: a noise, 3 *Bul.* 85
Coinage: *v.* Mint, Money.
    Angels, 2 *Brad.* 172, 1 *Lat.* 181, *Phil.* 234, *Pil.* 428; those of Edward IV., 1 *Hoop.* 333 n.; crowns of the sun, and of the rose, temp. Hen. VIII., 3 *Zur.* 615 n. (comp. "rosa solis," *Poet.* 193); depreciation of the coinage in the time of Henry VIII. and Edward VI., 2 *Lat.* 41, 112; testons reduced in value, 1 *Lat.* 137, 3 *Zur.* 727 n.; dandyprats, 2 *Tyn.* 306; anticipated renewal of the coinage, 3 *Zur.* 410; the new gold coinage of king Edward, *ib.* 53; description of a pretty little shilling, 1 *Lat.* 95; reference to the same, *ib.* 136, 137; a coin with the effigies of Ahab and Jezebel, i. e. Philip and Mary, 3 *Zur.* 115; the base coinage called in by queen Elizabeth, 1 *Zur.* 93, 104; restoration of the pure silver standard, 2 *Zur.* 67; a copper coinage first issued in England by James I., but used in Ireland long before, 2 *Tyn.* 231 n.; superstitious coins or medals, 1 *Ful.* 566
Coinualch, king of Wessex: ruled bishops, 2 *Ful.* 16, 24, 119
Coke (Sir Edw.): Institutes, 1 *Lat.* 69 n., 175
Coke (Margery): letter to her, 2 *Brad.* 100; named, *ib.* 197; [apparently Bradford's own sister: *v.* Bradford (Marg.)].
Coker (......): letter to him, 2 *Brad.* 58
Coker (W.): martyred at Canterbury, *Poet.* 163
Cokes (Jo.): *v.* Cocks.
Cokewold: cuckold, *Pil.* 629
Cokin (Sir Tho.), or Coking: *v.* Cockain.
Colbach (The margrave of): 3 *Zur.* 258
Colbyn (Tho.), of Beccles: letter signed by him, *Park.* 307; Mr Colby, Parker's steward, apparently the same, *ib.* 324
Colchester, co. Essex: martyrs there, *Bale* 586, *Poet.* 167, 170, 172; the abbot executed, *v.* Beach (J.); abp Harsnett's library in the castle, *Grin.* 478 n
Cole (Arth.), pres. of Magd. coll. Oxon: 2 *Cran.* 543
Cole (Hen.), warden of New coll. Oxon, afterwards dean of St Paul's: notice of him, *Phil.* xxix; he disputes with Ridley at Oxford, *Rid.* 191, 227; also with Latimer, 2 *Lat.* 276; directed to make a sermon for Cranmer's burning, 1 *Cran.* xxii; some account of it, *ib.* xxiv; at the disputation at Westminster, 1559, 4 *Jew.* 1199, 1200, 1 *Zur.* 11, 14, 27; Jewel's account of his harangue there, 4 *Jew.* 1203; he praised ignorance, 1 *Jew.* 57; an opponent of Jewel, *Coop.* 4, 50, *Pil.* 523; commencement of this controversy, 1 *Jew.* 2; his correspondence with Jewel on the challenge, *ib.* 26, &c.; he excuses his agreeing to the primacy of Henry VIII., *ib.* 60; holds with Gerson as to a general council being above the pope, *ib.* 67

Cole (James): mentioned as a notary, 1413, *Bale* 28

Cole (Rob.): letters to him, 1 *Brad.* 591, 2 *Brad.* 133, 194, 215; named, 2 *Brad.* 244; [perhaps identical with the next, who is mentioned by Strype as a freewiller].

Cole (Rob.), of St Mary le Bow: a Puritan, *Park.* 278

Cole (Tho.), archdeacon of Essex: one Cole (either Tho. or Will.) in exile, 1 *Cran.* (9); named as archdeacon, *Park.* 303 n.; letter to him, *Grin.* 240; his death, 1 *Zur.* 242, 256

Cole (Will.), LL.D.: present at the process against Cranmer, 2 *Cran.* 553

Cole (Will.), pres. of C. C. C., Oxon: notice of him, 1 *Zur.* 256 n.; an exile at Zurich, 3 *Zur.* 752, and see 1 *Cran.* (9); president of Corpus, 2 *Zur.* 218; letters from him to R. Gualter, *ib.* 222, 256, 307

Cole (Dr): at Cambridge, *Park.* 56

Cole (Dr): suspected of nonconformity (probably Tho.), *Park.* 264

Cole (Mr): at court in his hat and short cloak (probably Rob. or Tho.), *Park.* 237

Cole under candlestick: this implies deceitful secresy, 3 *Bec.* 260

Colen: *v.* Cologne.

Coler (......): 1 *Zur.* 30

Coles (R.): writes certain prayers, *Pra. B.* v.

Colet (Jo.), dean of St Paul's: founder of St Paul's school, 2 *Bec.* 383 n., *Pra. Eliz.* 171 n.; he calls for a reformation, 1 *Lat.* 58; is in danger of being burned, *Bale* 395, 1 *Lat.* 440, through translating the Pater-noster, 3 *Tyn.* 168; his opinion on Dionysius the Areopagite, 1 *Jew.* 113

Coligni (Fra. de), sieur d'Andelot: mentioned, 2 *Zur.* 132; his death, *ib.* n.; said to have been poisoned, *Sand.* 66

Coligni (Gaspard de), admiral of France: named, 2 *Zur.* 132, 247, 281 n.; apparently named as the lord Châtillon, 3 *Zur.* 563, 565, queen Elizabeth's contract with him and others, 1 *Zur.* 115 n.; he besieges Caen, *ib.* 124; murdered in the massacre of Paris, *Rog.* 8 n., 1 *Zur.* 291

Coligni (Odet de), cardinal de Châtillon: notice of him, *Grin.* 299 n., 1 *Zur.* 250 n.;

he arrives in England, *Grin.* 299 n.; his lodging at Canterbury, *Park.* 442; poisoned and buried there, 1 *Zur.* 250

Colin (......): *v.* Collin.

Coll: deceit, 3 *Bec.* 260 n

Collations: collections, the bringing together viz. of blasphemous and superstitious ceremonies, 2 *Bec.* 231

Collecta: "collectam facere;" to celebrate the holy communion, (mistranslated by Calfhill), *Calf.* xii, 253

Collections: collections for the poor to be made in every parish-church, 2 *Hoop.* 127

Collects : *v.* Book of Common Prayer, Prayers.

By whom ordained in the mass, 2 *Brad.* 307; collects of the saints, 1 *Tyn.* 290; examples from the Breviary, 1 *Tyn.* 231 n., 3 *Tyn.* 117 n

Colleges: *v.* Universities, Schools; also Cambridge, Oxford, &c.

No women to live within their precincts, *Park.* 146, 151, 158

Collenbeke (Hans): 1 *Tyn.* xxiv.

Colleth: embraceth about the neck, 2 *Brad.* 87

Collier : the collier's faith, viz. to believe as the church believes, 2 *Hoop.* 543 n

Collier (Geo.), warden of Manchester: 1 *Brad.* 538, 541

Collier (Jeremy): on the alleged embassy from Lucius to Rome, *Calf.* 53 n.; on Augustine the monk, 2 *Ful.* 399; he exposes the fraud of the blood of Hales, 1 *Hoop.* 41 n.; on prophesyings, *Grin.* xi, xii; on an address from convocation for Grindal's restoration, *ib.* 473 n.; other references, *Grin.* 239 n., 327 n., 1 *Lat.* 46 n., 258 n

Collier (R.): martyred at Canterbury, *Poet.* 163

Collin (......): 1 *Zur.* 30, 122, 3 *Zur.* 421

Collin (Nic.): adduces a false epistle of Alexander I. in defence of holy water, *Calf.* 16 n

Collins: a family so named, 2 *Zur.* 95, 107

Collins (......): burned for heresy, though insane, 3 *Tyn.* 39 n.; he had shot at a crucifix, 3 *Zur.* 200, 201

Collins (Dr): answered by Fitzherbert, 2 *Ful.* 294 n

Collins (Rob.): *v.* Colyns.

Collman (Jo.): was Cranmer's bailiff, 2 *Cran.* 259

Collo Torto (Rob. de): named, 2 *Jew.* 753

Collobium : a kind of tunic, 1 *Zur.* 350 n

Collyridians: heretics who worshipped the virgin Mary, 4 *Bul.* 371, *Calf.* 377, 2 *Ful.* 207, 215, 391, 3 *Jew.* 555, 576; the name, 2 *Ful.* 375

Colman (St), the bishop: 2 *Ful.* 16, *Pil.* 512 n

Cologne: the magi (*q. v.*) commonly called the three kings of Collen, 2 *Lat.* 143; Latimer marvels how the wise men came to Coleyne, *ib.* 132; what the archbishop paid for his pall, *Pil.* 583; the Simplex ac Pia Deliberatio, 1535, an interim service book drawn up for the diocese by Melancthon and Bucer, Hermann de Wied (*q. v.*) being then archbishop, *Lit. Eliz.* xxix; opposition to this prelate's attempts at reformation, *v.* Antididagma; printers at Cologne, 1 *Tyn.* xxviii; martyrs there, 3 *Tyn.* 113; the censors of Cologne write against Monhemius, *Whita.* 360; the college Bursæ Montis, 4 *Bul.* viii.

Colomesius (Paulus): 2 *Ful.* 338 n

Colossians (Epistle to the): *v.* Paul (St).

Colt (G.), of Clare: sends articles to lord chancellor Audley against Parker, *Park.* 7

Columna (Guido de): *Park.* 295

Colyns (Rob.): Cranmer's commissary, 2 *Cran.* 468

Combat: lord Cobham offers to purge himself from the charge of heresy by combat, *Bale* 23

Combefis (Fra.): *Calf.* 372 n

Comber : trouble, *Sand.* 308

Comber (Tho.): *Calf.* 89, 137, 287, 322, 2 *Ful.* 70, 289, 363 nn

Come yer, or come er: to come ere, or before, to anticipate, 2 *Bec.* 38

Comen: participle of come, 1 *Brad.* 317, *Sand.* 214

Comeracensis, or rather Cameracensis: *v.* Alliaco (Pet. de).

Comestible: that may be eaten, 1 *Bec.* 386

Comestor (Pet.): *v.* Petrus.

Comets: seen in 1531 and 1532, 2 *Cran.* 235; other appearances, *Lit. Eliz.* 570

Comfort, Consolation: *v.* Affliction, Castle.

What consolation rests in, 1 *Hoop.* 16; general consolations, 2 *Bul.* 91; an exhortation to rejoice and be of good comfort, *Sand.* 427; grounds of consolation in our spiritual trials, 1 *Cov.* 496, 497, under trouble and persecution, 2 *Hoop.* 578, &c.; consolation hidden by God for a time to try us, *ib.* 337; most needed by the greatest offenders, *Pil.* 131; lines by H. C. prefixed to R. Greenham's Comfort for an afflicted Conscience, *Poet.* 470; consolation under bereavements destroyed by the doctrine of purgatory, 1 *Hoop.* 562

Comity: courtesy, kindliness, 1 *Bec.* 232

Commandments (God's): *v.* Law.

Their purport, 1 *Tyn.* 434, 474; he is not a Christian that knows them not, 1 *Hoop.*

274; common excuses for ignorance of them taken away, *ib.*; keeping God's commandments is a sign of grace, 2 *Tyn.* 172; we are unable of ourselves to do that which we are commanded to do, *Sand.* 133, 139; they are not grievous to the righteous, though impossible, 2 *Cov.* 391; not heavy, 2 *Bul.* 252; those on bearing the cross, *ib.* 96; general and particular ones distinguished, 2 *Bec.* 69, 1 *Brad.* 490

Commandments (The X.): *v.* Law, Love.

The ten commandments with confirmations of scripture, 2 *Bec.* 497, &c; they occur in the catechism as originally drawn up, *Lit. Edw.* 122, and first appear in the communion service in 1552, *ib.* 266; exposition of them from the Institution of a Christian Man, with corrections by Henry VIII., and remarks by Cranmer, 2 *Cran.* 100—106; A DECLARATION OF THE TEN HOLY COMMANDMENTS OF ALMIGHTY GOD, by bp Hooper, 1 *Hoop.* 249—430; they are also expounded in king Edward's Catechism, *Lit. Edw.* 497, (546); in Becon's catechism, 2 *Bec.* 56, &c.; in Nowell's Catechism, *Now.* (8), 120; in Bullinger's Decades, 1 *Bul.* 209, &c.; a meditation on them, 1 *Brad.* 148; the commandments drawn into a prayer, 2 *Brad.* 256; they are an epitome of scripture, 1 *Hoop.* 144; all scripture a kind of commentary on the decalogue, *Whita.* 382, 388; they ought not to be altered from the words of scripture, 2 *Cran.* 100; excellence of their order, 1 *Bul.* 254; why they were given, 1 *Hoop.* 255, 2 *Hoop.* 26; for whom they were given, 1 *Hoop.* 256; expounded by Christ and the apostles, *ib.* 271; necessary rules as preparatives to them, *ib.* 286; how they are to be observed by us, 2 *Tyn.* 325; "If thou wilt enter into life, keep the commandments," this text explained, *Whita.* 471; they cannot be kept without the Spirit, 1 *Tyn.* 81, 82; to believe in Christ unfeignedly is to keep them, *ib.* 81; he that keeps them is entered into life, *ib.* 82; he who has the law of faith and love graven on his heart keeps them all spiritually, 2 *Tyn.* 325; he that submits not himself to keep them, has not the faith that justifies, 1 *Tyn.* 470; they are a rule or platform of good works, 2 *Bul.* 353, *Wool.* 69; the sum or substance of them, what they require and forbid, 2 *Bec.* 505, 506, 1 *Brad.* 55, 1 *Hoop.* 255, *Lit. Edw.* 497, (546, 547), *Now.* (7, 22), 120, 136, 1 *Tyn.* 24; they contain matter enough for every man to exercise himself in the exposition of, 1 *Hoop.* 272; all are broken by going to mass, 2 *Brad.*

317—327; the two tables, 1 *Bul.* 212, *Now.* (7), 120; holiness has relation to the first table, righteousness to the second, *Sand.* 190; the decalogue erroneously divided by Peter Lombard and others, following Augustine, 1 *Bul.* 213, 1 *Hoop.* 349, 350, who sometimes reckons but three precepts in the first table, sometimes four, 1 *Bul.* 214, 1 *Hoop.* 350; the erroneous division followed by the church of Rome, the Lutherans, and some English reformers, 2 *Brad.* 258 n.; the commandments read in churches, 1 *Brad.* 9; they should be explained to the people, 1 *Hoop.* 144, and diligently taught, 2 *Hoop.* 132, 133; written on the walls of churches, 1 *Brad.* 9; directed to be set up at the east end of the chancel, *Park.* 133, 135; a table of the commandments to be provided by churchwardens, *Grin.* 133; article respecting it, *ib.* 157; hung up in the house, 1 *Bec.* 66; the common people of the North have ever used the commandments in English metre, *Pil.* 501; the ten commandments of God, in verse, 2 *Cov.* 544; another of the same, *ib.* 545; in Latin verse, by Parkhurst, *Pra. Eliz.* 404; eadem breviss. compendio comprehensa, *ib.*

The first commandment (*v.* God), 2 *Bec.* 56, 497, 498, 1 *Bul.* 215, 1 *Hoop.* 293, *Lit. Edw.* 497, (546), *Now.* (8), 120; it is the foundation of all true religion, 1 *Hoop.* 294; it contains the mystery of our redemption by Christ, 1 *Bul.* 219; what God requires of us in it, and what he forbids, 2 *Bec.* 57, &c., 1 *Bul.* 217, 1 *Hoop.* 293; it is broken by going to mass, 2 *Brad.* 318, 324; a meditation on it, 1 *Brad.* 148, 150; prayer on it, 2 *Brad.* 257

The second (*v.* Idolatry, Images), 2 *Bec.* 59, 498, 499, 1 *Bul.* 222, 1 *Hoop.* 316, *Lit. Edw.* 497, (546), *Now.* (9), 122; what God requires and forbids in it, 2 *Bec.* 66, 1 *Hoop.* 317; no particular commandment (as that to make the brasen serpent) takes away the virtue of the general law, 2 *Bec.* 69; all the fathers teach that it is moral, not ceremonial, *Calf.* 42, 43; it is broken by going to mass, 2 *Brad.* 317; a meditation on it, 1 *Brad.* 152; it is omitted by some old writers, the tenth being divided into two, 2 *Bec.* 59, 60, 2 *Brad.* 258; gnawed out by Romish rats, 1 *Ful.* 42; suppressed in some Romish catechisms, 2 *Brad.* 258 n

The third (*v.* God, &c.), 2 *Bec.* 76, 499, 1 *Bul.* 237, 1 *Hoop.* 322, *Lit. Edw.* 497, (546), *Now.* (13), 126; what God requires and forbids in it, 2 *Bec.* 76, 1 *Hoop.* 322, &c.; it can be kept only by a reconciled sinner, 1 *Hoop.* 324; the vengeance of God against the transgressors of it, 2 *Bec.* 80; it is broken by going to mass, 2 *Brad.* 321; a meditation on it, 1 *Brad.* 154; prayer on it, 2 *Brad.* 258

The fourth (*v.* Sabbath), 2 *Bec.* 80, 500, 1 *Bul.* 253, 1 *Hoop.* 337, *Lit. Edw.* 497, (546), *Now.* (14), 128; persons rehearsed in it, 1 *Hoop.* 339; what God requires and forbids in it, 2 *Bec.* 80, 84, 1 *Hoop.* 337, &c.; all the commandments are moral and literally to be kept except the fourth, 2 *Cran.* 61, 102, or a part of it, *Rid.* 84; it is broken by going to mass, 2 *Brad.* 323; a meditation on it, 1 *Brad.* 157; prayer on it, 2 *Brad.* 259

The fifth (*v.* Parents, Kings, Magistrates, Ministers), 2 *Bec.* 85, 500, 501, 1 *Bul.* 267, 1 *Hoop.* 351, *Lit. Edw.* 497, (547), *Now.* (16), 130; what is commanded in it, 2 *Bec.* 85, &c.; who should be honoured, and how, 1 *Hoop.* 355, 356; the duty of superiors, *ib.* 360, &c.; this precept is broken by going to mass, 2 *Brad.* 326; a meditation on it, 1 *Brad.* 161; prayer on it, 2 *Brad.* 259

The sixth (*v.* Murder), 2 *Bec.* 94, 501, 502, 1 *Bul.* 298, 1 *Hoop.* 367, *Lit. Edw.* 497, (547), *Now.* (19), 133; what God forbids and requires in it, 2 *Bec.* 94, 95, 97, 1 *Hoop.* 368; it is broken by going to mass, 2 *Brad.* 326; a meditation on it, 1 *Brad.* 164; prayer on it, 2 *Brad.* 260

The seventh (*v.* Adultery, Marriage, &c.), 2 *Bec.* 97, 502, 503, 1 *Bul.* 393, 1 *Hoop.* 374, *Lit. Edw.* 498, (547), *Now.* (19), 133; what God forbids and requires in it, 2 *Bec.* 97, &c., 103, &c., 1 *Hoop.* 376 ; breach of matrimony too commonly accounted a thing unworthy of reprehension, *Grin.* 17; the precept is broken by going to mass, 2 *Brad.* 326; a meditation on it, 1 *Brad.* 166; prayer on it, 2 *Brad.* 260

The eighth (*v.* Theft), 2 *Bec.* 104, 533, 534, 2 *Bul.* 17, 1 *Hoop.* 387, *Lit. Edw.* 498, (547), *Now.* (19), 133; what God forbids and requires in it, 2 *Bec.* 104, &c., 111, &c., 1 *Hoop.* 388; it is broken by going to mass, 2 *Brad.* 326; a meditation on it, 1 *Brad.* 168; prayer on it, 2 *Brad.* 261

The ninth (*v.* Witness, Lying), 2 *Bec.* 116, 504, 505, 2 *Bul.* 111, 1 *Hoop.* 405, *Lit. Edw.* 498, (548), *Now.* (20), 134; what God forbids and requires in it, 2 *Bec.* 116, &c., 118, &c., 1 *Hoop.* 405; three kinds of lies forbidden, *ib.*; it is broken by going to mass, 2 *Brad.* 326; a meditation on it, 1 *Brad.* 170; prayer on it, 2 *Brad.* 260

The tenth (*v.* Covetousness), 2 *Bec.* 119, 505, 2 *Bul.* 120, 1 *Hoop.* 409, *Lit. Edw.* 498, (548), *Now.* (21), 136; what God forbids and requires in it, 2 *Bec.* 120, &c., 123, &c.; it specially declares our weakness, 1 *Hoop.* 410; no man can fulfil it, *ib.* 410; but it was fulfilled for us by Christ, *ib.* 412; broken by going to mass, 2 *Brad.* 326; a meditation on it, 1 *Brad.* 172; another, by Tho. Lever, *ib.* 569; prayer on it, 2 *Brad.* 261; those who omit the second, divide this commandment into two, 2 *Bec.* 59, 60, 1 *Bul.* 212

The ten commandments are comprised in two, 2 *Bec.* 123, 505, *Lit. Edw.* 499, (548), *Now.* (22), 136, 1 *Tyn.* 85, 470, *Wool.* 70; a man cannot sin without breaking the first great commandment, 1 *Tyn.* 490; of the love of God and of our neighbour, 1 *Bul.* 180

Commendams: *Grin.* 449, *Park.* 208

Commendations: an appendage to the Dirige, *Pra. Eliz.* 68

Commendone (Jo. Fra.), afterwards cardinal: sent to recall cardinal Pole to England, 3 *Zur.* 741 n

Comenty: community, 2 *Bec.* 307

Commerouse: cumbrous, *Park.* 249

Commination: in the Prayer Books, *Lit. Edw.* and *Lit. Eliz.*; when to be used, *Grin.* 127, 158, *Lit. Eliz.* 239 n

Commissions: *v.* Concealments, Courts, Reformatio Legum, Subsidy.

A commission for the establishment of religion, 1559, *Jew.* xv, 1 *Zur.* 24, 39, 73; many superstitious practices discovered by the commissioners, also many witches, 1 *Zur.* 44; other results of the inquiry, *ib.* 45; examination of certain Londoners, 1567, *Grin.* 199; letter from the ecclesiastical commissioners to Mr Earl, minister of St Mildred's, Bread Street, *ib.* 293; suggestions for a new commission, *Park.* 369, 370; letter from certain ecclesiastical commissioners to the vice-chancellor of Cambridge about Tho. Aldrich, *ib.* 433; letter from Parker and Sandys to a commissioner about the Puritans, *ib.* 434; the commissioners commit some to prison, *ib.* 447; the commission much abused, *ib.* 450; proceedings respecting Papists in the North, *Grin.* 350; proceedings against Puritans, *ib.* 353

Common: *v.* Goods.

Common Order: *v.* Book.

COMMON PLACES OF THE HOLY SCRIPTURE, by T. Becon, 3 *Bec.* 287

Common Prayer: *v.* Book.
Commons: *v.* People.
Commons, and their enclosure: commons enclosed by the rich, 2 *Bec.* 599, 2 *Cran.* 163 n., *Hutch.* 301; turned into parks, 1 *Tyn.* 202; complaints of taking them from the poor, 2 *Cran.* 195—197; their enclosure the pretext for rebellion, 3 *Zur.* 654; enclosures hurtful to the prince and people, 1 *Lat.* 99 n., 100; statutes touching commons and inclosures, *ib.* 101 n., 248
Commonwealths: preserved by force and law, 1 *Hoop.* 78; Satan an enemy to them, *ib.* 80; they should have only two governors, God and the prince, *ib.* 142; how to be appeased when troubled, *ib.* 459; the contempt of God's word is occasion of trouble to them, *ib.* 464; overmuch lenity in them is pestiferous, *ib.* 473; the commonwealth compared to a ship, *ib.* 497; that commonweal, where there is a good magistrate, a faithful preacher, a diligent schoolmaster, not likely to decay, 2 *Bec.* 377, 378
Commune sanctorum: *Pil.* 81
Communication of properties: 3 *Bul.* 270
Communion: meaning of the word, 1 *Hoop.* 148, 154, 1 *Jew.* 130, &c.; how used by Augustine and Jerome, 1 *Jew.* 132; offending clergymen anciently reduced to lay communion, *Coop.* 158, 159
Communion (Holy): *v.* Supper, and Order.
Communion of Saints: *v.* Church, Creeds, Saints.
 What it is, or wherein it consists, 1 *Bul.* 163, 4 *Bul.* 8, *Coop.* 116, 2 *Cov.* 430, 2 *Hoop.* 42, 1 *Jew.* 133, 140, *Lit. Edw.* 514, 515, (562), *Now.* (55), 173, *Pra. B.* 16, 65, *Wool.* 8; why the church is so called, 2 *Bec.* 43; it has communion with Christ, 4 *Bul.* 433, 1 *Hoop.* 154, and the fellowship of God's Spirit, 4 *Bul.* 23; communion in prayer, 1 *Lat.* 337, 338, 345; the advantage of Christian assemblies in troublous times, 2 *Hoop.* 589; a Romish writer on the communion of saints, *Coop.* 20; the phrase is an explication of "the holy catholic church," but applied by Bradford to the Lord's supper, 1 *Brad.* 107
Communion-tables: *v.* Tables.
Community: *v.* Goods.
Comnena (Anna): *v.* Anna.
Como (...... card.): *Lit. Eliz.* 584 n., 658
Compagni (Barth.), factor to Edward VI.: 1 *Zur.* 40, 58
Company: against keeping evil company, with sentences and examples of scripture, 1 *Bec.* 442, &c.; wicked company to be eschewed, 2 *Bec.* 102, *Pil.* 169, *Wool.* 126, &c.

COMPARISON BETWEEN THE LORD'S SUPPER AND THE POPE'S MASS, by T. Becon, 3 *Bec.* 351
Comparison between the old man and the new, also between the law and the gospel, 1 *Brad.* 297
Compendium Theologiæ: *v.* Epitome.
Complaint: the complaint of verity, verses, 2 *Brad.* 364; a complaint, by Edw. Hake, *Poet.* 369; the complaint of a sinner, from the O. V. of the Psalms, *ib.* 499; complaints in prayer, 4 *Bul.* 164
Compter: *v.* London.
Compline: its mystic import, *Pra. Eliz.* 154 n
Compostella, in Spain: pilgrimage to the shrine of St James, *Bale* 25, 633, 2 *Cov.* 479, 1 *Hoop.* 455, 1 *Tyn.* 281 n
Compton (Long), co. Warwick: Druidical stones there, 4 *Jew.* 655
Compton (Sir Will.): sheriff of Worcestershire for 19 years, 2 *Lat.* 398 n
Concalez (Fra. Ant.): Collectio Canonum Eccl. Hisp., *Calf.* 154 n., 302 n
Concealments: commissions against the clergy for discovery of concealed lands or goods, *Park.* 413; letter from Grindal to lord Burghley, complaining of injuries offered to the clergy by those who were sent down upon concealments, *Grin.* 343
Concomitantia: a term used by Romish writers on the sacrament, *Coop.* 130, 131, as by Harding, 1 *Jew.* 531, 533; remarks on the word, *ib.* 534
Concord: *v.* Unity.
 The concord of Wittemberg, 2 *Zur.* 102 n.; the Form of Concord, *ib.* 274 n
Concubines: *v.* Marriage.
 Difference between concubine and wife, 4 *Jew.* 631, &c.; how the word is to be taken, *ib.*; concubines allowed in the Romish church if kept secretly, 4 *Jew.* 802, 1 *Tyn.* 232, 3 *Tyn.* 40; a tax paid by priests to their bishops for permission to keep concubines, 2 *Tyn.* 295; Cranmer's letter to Osiander against concubinage, 2 *Cran.* 404, 406; pensionary concubinage continued in Wales after the Reformation, *Park.* 257
Concumbre (St): apparently a mock saint, 1 *Hoop.* 40 [Coucumbre?]
Concupiscence: described, 2 *Bul.* 121, *Now.* 100; condemned by the Gentiles, 1 *Bul.* 204; it is sin, 2 *Bec.* 120, 121, 3 *Jew.* 464, even in the regenerate, *Rog.* 101; why left and felt after baptism, 2 *Bec.* 204; errors respecting it, *Rog.* 102; it does not condemn unless we give place to it, 2 *Bec.* 204, 205

Concurrents: learned disputants in Italy, 2 *Ful.* 77
Condé (Princes of): *v.* Henry, Louis.
Conders (Fred.): 1 *Zur.* 273
Conducts (conducti): hired chaplains, *Grin.* 181
Confection: the making, i. e. of the body and blood of Christ, the act of consecration, 3 *Bec.* 389
Confectionary: *Pil.* 255, 2 *Tyn.* 97
Confession: meaning of the word generally, 3 *Bul.* 69, 1 *Tyn.* 261, 262
Confession of Faith: *v.* Baptism, Creeds, Faith.
  A confession of faith, by Dr Barnes, 2 *Cov.* 352; A GODLY CONFESSION AND PROTESTATION OF THE CHRISTIAN FAITH, by bishop Hooper, 2 *Hoop.* 64—92; a confession by Bradford, 1 *Brad.* 435; a declaration concerning religion, signed by Ferrar, Hooper, Bradford, Saunders, and others, *ib.* 367; a confession of Christian faith, by Becon, 2 *Bec.* 579, 580; notice of The Confession of a Christian Faith, borrowed from the Geneva Common Prayer Book, and often printed with that of the church of England, *Lit. Eliz.* xx; true and free confession of faith, in what it consists, 2 *Cov.* 461, 462; confession of God's word is followed by persecution, 1 *Bec.* 273
— Confessions of the Reformed Churches: several, 3 *Whitg.* xxvi; they approve of a return to the old constitution of the church, *ib.* 532; speak against primacy, lordship, and superiority in the church, *ib.* 535; on the election and ordination of ministers, *ib.* 537; against baptism by women, *ib.* 546; the Harmony, cited, *Rog.* 36 n., & passim, 1 *Zur.* 169 n., 2 *Zur.* 363 n
  Augsburgh: mentioned, 2 *Jew.* 686, 3 *Jew.* 455, 456, 2 *Zur.* 111, 3 *Zur.* 694, 697; the princes who signed it, 2 *Zur.* 15 n.; proposed for adoption in England, *ib.* 17, 48; disputes respecting it, *ib.* 81 n., 102, &c.; pressed at Strasburgh, *Grin.* 277 n.; cited, *Rog.* 36 n., & passim; a work in confutation of it drawn up by Faber, Eckius, and Cochlæus, to which Melancthon replied, 2 *Zur.* 103 n
  Basil: cited, *Rog.* 39 n., & passim.
  Belgium, *v.* Flanders.
  Bohemia: cited, *Rog.* 36 n., & passim.
  Flanders (Belg.): cited, *Rog.* 36 n., & passim; the confession of the Dutch church in London, on things indifferent, 2 *Whitg.* 5
  France: cited, *Rog.* 36 n., & passim.
  Helvetia: *v.* Switzerland.
  Holland: *v.* Flanders.
  Saxony: cited, *Rog.* 56 n., & passim.
  Scotland: when drawn up, and when ratified, 2 *Zur.* 363 n
  Strasburgh: translated into Latin by Jo. ab Ulmis, 3 *Zur.* 404
  Sweden: cited, *Rog.* 43 n., & passim.
  Switzerland (Helv.): first drawn up at Basle, 1536, 4 *Bul.* xii; enlarged and improved, 1566, 1 *Zur.* 169 n., 171, 172, 304, 2 *Zur.* 118; approved by the church of Scotland, 1 *Zur.* 304 n., 2 *Zur.* 362, &c.; heartily received by the church of England, 1 *Zur.* 169, 333 n.; approved by several other churches, *ib.* 304 n.; cited, *Rog.* 36 n., & passim; on apostles, prophets, evangelists, &c., 1 *Whitg.* 495; it says that the harmless simplicity of some pastors has profited more than the learning of others, 1 *Whitg.* 338, 542, 2 *Whitg.* 458; on diversities of rites, 1 *Whitg.* 288; on confirmation and extreme unction, 3 *Whitg.* 478, 481; on excommunication, *ib.* 221; it allows certain holy-days, 2 *Whitg.* 568
  Wirtemberg: cited, *Rog.* 36 n., & passim.
  Zurich: on St James's epistle, 2 *Ful.* 384; on holy days, 2 *Whitg.* 585
Confession of Sins: *v.* Absolution, Penance, Sin: for forms of confession, *v.* Prayers.
  i. *Generally:* of the confession of sins, what it is, 3 *Bec.* 618, 3 *Bul.* 69, 2 *Cov.* 481, 1 *Tyn.* 261—265; it is ordained of God, 3 *Bul.* 70; it is necessary, 1 *Bec.* 99, 2 *Hoop.* 349, 350, 2 *Lat.* 180; needful for those who come to the Lord's supper, 2 *Bec.* 234; without faith it is nothing worth, 2 *Hoop.* 350; the old fathers speak of it with modesty, 1 *Jew.* 120; divers kinds of confession, 1 *Bec.* 99, 3 *Bul.* 69, &c., 3 *Jew.* 351; what kind is ordained of God, 3 *Bul.* 70; what ordained by men, *ib.* 75; translations concerning it examined, 1 *Ful.* 457—459; Tyndale uses the word "knowledge" instead of "confession," 3 *Tyn.* 22
  ii. *Confession to God:* confessions should be made to him who is sinned against, 1 *Tyn.* 266, 3 *Tyn.* 23, namely, to God, 1 *Bec.* 99, 3 *Bul.* 71, 2 *Jew.* 1133, *Sand.* 157, 1 *Tyn.* 262; Chrysostom's doctrine on this point, 3 *Bul.* 78, & al.; lord Cobham's confession to God, *Bale* 29; in the mass confession is made to Mary, Peter, and all the saints, 3 *Bec.* 263
  iii. *Public confession:* before the congregation, 1 *Bec.* 100, 3 *Bul.* 73, 1 *Tyn.* 477; it was so made in the church of old, 2 *Ful.* 89, 2 *Jew.* 1135; Jerome mentions the

CONFESSION — CONFIRMATION

public confession of Fabiola, 3 *Tyn.* 313 n.; Erasmus's remarks on the passage, *ib.* 214 n.; public offences should be publicly confessed before the elders of the church, 2 *Ful.* 238; the general confession of the church of England, whether said openly, 2 *Hoop.* 146; the reformed manner of confession is the ancient way, *Phil.* 407

    iv. *Mutual confession:* James exhorts to it, 3 *Bul.* 84, 85, 2 *Cov.* 482, 1 *Ful.* 458, 2 *Jew.* 1133; on confession to our neighbour, 1 *Bec.* 100, 3 *Bul.* 74

    v. *Auricular confession:* what it is, 1 *Bec.* 100, 3 *Bul.* 80, 2 *Cov.* 481; not known under the law, nor by the apostles, 1 *Tyn.* 266; not commanded, 3 *Jew.* 377; not to be proved from scripture, 3 *Bul.* 83, 2 *Cov.* 481, 1 *Ful.* 458; not practised in the primitive church, *ib.* 274; nor mentioned in the ancient fathers, 3 *Jew.* 369; ordained of men, 3 *Bul.* 75; anciently used at Constantinople, but relinquished in consequence of the misconduct of a deacon, 2 *Ful.* 91, *Pil.* 553, 1 *Tyn.* 263, 3 *Tyn.* 172; no compulsory confession in the Anglo-Saxon church, 2 *Ful.* 9; it was first enjoined by the council of Lateran under Innocent III., 2 *Brad.* 310 n., 3 *Bul.* 82, 2 *Ful.* 90, 1 *Hoop.* 526, 2 *Jew.* 1133; whether necessary, 3 *Jew.* 366, &c.; whether to be received for discipline's sake, 3 *Bul.* 86; whether for private absolution's sake, *ib.* 88; advice respecting it, 2 *Brad.* 118; what it was at first, *ib.* 119; it is in itself a thing indifferent, *ib.*; not damnable, if rightly used, 2 *Tyn.* 150; its practice recommended, 2 *Cran.* 95; though no man is bound to confess deadly sins to a priest, *ib.* 117; confession to a minister able to instruct, sanctioned, *Rid.* 338; free confession approved, 1 *Brad.* 51; it may be used in certain cases, 2 *Lat.* 13; not to be reproved if rightly kept, 2 *Cov.* 481; confession to men not condemned, 2 *Jew.* 1133; a laudable custom if discreetly used, *Grin.* 57; the abuse to be taken away, not the thing itself, 1 *Bec.* 100; its commodities, *ib.* 101; the pope's earish confession condemned, 3 *Bec.* 4; it is unlawful and wicked, 2 *Brad.* 119; an abominable thing, 3 *Tyn.* 22, 172; a work of Satan, 1 *Tyn.* 263; an intolerable burden, *ib.* 245; an example of this, *ib.* 246; no man can confess all his sins, because no man can understand his sins, 1 *Brad.* 47; the numbering of our sins impossible, *ib.* 108; the Romish doctrine of confession, *Rog.* 255—257, 3 *Tyn.* 47; a modern definition of it, 1 *Tyn.* 342 n.; confession is a part of the Romish sacrament of penance, 1 *Brad.* 46, 588, 1 *Tyn.* 261, 267, 2 *Tyn.* 162; required before the reception of any other sacrament, 1 *Tyn.* 285, 337; alleged by Romanists to be needful in order to absolution, *ib.* 264; how it has been abused, 1 *Bec.* 100; 2 *Cov.* 482; the mischief of it, 3 *Bul.* 87; used as a rack of conscience, 1 *Jew.* 120; confessors lead away silly women, 3 *Tyn.* 105; by it priests discover the secrets of kings, &c., 2 *Lat.* 179; they know all men's secrets, 3 *Bul.* 87; 1 *Tyn.* 191, 281, 336, 337, 341; the secrets entrusted to a confessor have not been kept where the clergy had a purpose to serve, 1 *Tyn.* 337, 2 *Tyn.* 296, 3 *Tyn.* 171; confessions betrayed to Henry VII. by cardinal Morton and bishop Fox, 2 *Tyn.* 305; secrets of state, &c. betrayed by priests, *Pil.* 554; they have caused men to be cited before the ecclesiastical courts for offences revealed in confession, 1 *Tyn.* 238; the affiance that was placed in auricular confession, 2 *Bec.* 414; to die without it considered a sign of damnation, 1 *Tyn.* 246; seamen in peril of death confessed to the mast, *ib.* 245; archbishop Arundel's article concerning confession, *Bale* 27; lord Cobham questioned on confession, *ib.* 37; Will. Thorpe examined on it, *ib.* 116; Anne Askewe thereon, *ib.* 150; an injunction respecting it, 2 *Cran.* 81; resorting to a popish priest for shrift forbidden, *Grin.* 140, 168; confession enjoined not to be required of communicants, 2 *Hoop.* 146; it is not condemned in the church of England, abuses set apart, 3 *Jew.* 351, 363; permitted, but left free, *Pil.* 524; auricular confession allowed by the Communion book of Edw. VI., *Lit. Edw.* 4, and by the first Prayer Book, *ib.* 82; on the direction in the order of visitation of the sick, 1 *Ful.* 458; the danger of auricular confession creeping in again, 1 *Zur.* 342

Confessionists: a name given to the Lutherans, *Whita.* 379

Confidence: v. Assurance, Faith, Trust.

Confirmation: what it is, 3 *Bec.* 618; of the confirmation of children, 3 *Whitg.* 357, &c., 493; what kind to be allowed, *Calf.* 215, 2 *Cran.* 419, 2 *Jew.* 1126, 3 *Tyn.* 71, 2 *Zur.* 73; called by some a sacrament, 3 *Jew.* 456, but it is not so, *Calf.* 215, 2 *Jew.* 1125, 1126, *Rog.* 252—254; it hath no institution from God, *Rog.* 254; not ordained by Christ, 2 *Jew.* 1103, 1126; no scripture declares it to be instituted by Christ or his apostles, 2 *Cran.* 80; the example of the apostles no proof of it, *Calf.* 217, 218, 220,

2 *Jew.* 1126; Heb. vi. 2 considered as referring to it, *Hutch.* 114; how it came first into the church, 3 *Tyn.* 71; ordained of our ancient fathers, 2 *Jew.* 1126; its use in the ancient church, *ib.* 1125, *Rog.* 252; why appointed and used, *Now.* (89), 210, 3 *Whitg.* 494; Jerome thereon, 3 *Whitg.* 64; its ministration was not always limited to the bishop, 3 *Tyn.* 71; Gregory permits the chrism to be administered by priests where there are no bishops, *Calf.* 220; the case of Novatus, 2 *Ful.* 389; Tyndale's opinion on the rite, 1 *Tyn.* 273, 3 *Tyn.* 71; queries concerning it with Cranmer's answers, 2 *Cran.* 280; Calvin's views, 3 *Whitg.* 477, &c.; the opinion of Bullinger, 2 *Zur.* 357; that of Gualter, *ib.* 233; it is of such value as the prayer of the bishop is, 2 *Cran.* 80; on the Romish sacrament, *Calf.* 215—227, 2 *Jew.* 1125, 1126, *Rog.* 254, 255; it was ordained by the council of Melda, 2 *Jew.* 1125; declarations of the Canon Law thereon, *Calf.* 216, 219, 220, *Whita.* 609; of no value, by the Canon Law, unless performed by a bishop, *Calf.* 219, 2 *Cran.* 74; that Law says it is more to be had in reverence than baptism, 2 *Cran.* 74, and that no man is a Christian without it, *ib.*; other similar assertions of Romanists, 2 *Jew.* 1126; the Popish manner of confirming, 3 *Bec.* 234, *Now.* (89), 211, *Rog.* 253, 254, 1 *Tyn.* 225; Romish confirmation a dumb ceremony, 1 *Tyn.* 274; why reserved to bishops, *ib.*; the formula, 2 *Jew.* 1126, *Whita.* 610; chrism not in scripture, 2 *Cran.* 80, 116; the rite has been abused so as to become a confirming in ignorance and superstition, 3 *Tyn.* 72; commonly called bishoping, 1 *Tyn.* 277, 3 *Tyn.* 72; superstitious notions on it, 1 *Tyn.* 277, 3 *Tyn.* 72; confirmation in the English church, 3 *Bec.* 234, *Calf.* 215; the charge at the end of the baptismal office for the most part omitted, and confirmation much neglected by the bishops, 3 *Whitg.* 610; Whitgift's circular letter to the bishops on this, *ib.*; how children should be prepared for it, 2 *Jew.* 1127, *Now.* 109; forms of confirmation, in the Prayer Books, *Lit. Edw.* and *Lit. Eliz.*; the ceremony conceded as indifferent by the episcopal party at Frankfort, 3 *Zur.* 754; rejected by several Protestant churches, 3 *Whitg.* 478, 481; by the Puritans, 1 *Zur.* 281, comp. *Lit. Eliz.* xvi.
Confirmation of bishops: celebrated at St Mary le Bow, London, *Grin.* vi. n
Confiscation: a fit punishment in certain cases, *Sand.* 73

Confiteor: a part of the mass, ascribed to Damasus, 3 *Bec.* 263, 2 *Brad.* 306
Conflict: *v.* Enemies (Spiritual).
Confutation of four Romish doctrines: 2 *Brad.* 267, &c.
CONFUTATION OF UNWRITTEN VERITIES, by abp Cranmer, 2 *Cran.* 1
Congregation: *v.* Church.
That of the Jews at the feast of tabernacles, 2 *Bul.* 166
Congrue: fitting, proper, 1 *Jew.* 53
Congruity: a scholastic term, 1 *Tyn.* 466
Coningham (Alex.), earl of Glencairn: *v.* Conyngham.
Conject: thrown into, 1 *Bec.* 196
Conjunction: *v.* Union.
Conjurors: *v.* Sorcerers, Witchcraft.
Conradus: saluted, 2 *Cov.* 512
Conscience: *v.* Comfort, Peace.
What it is, 1 *Bul.* 194; Augustine's saying about it, 2 *Hoop.* 574; it is to be left free, 1 *Hoop.* 32; an evil conscience, what, 3 *Bec.* 604; when the conscience is admonished of sin it brings the body into a trembling and fear, 2 *Hoop.* 313; no trouble to be compared with this trouble, *ib.* 315; conscience is a judge and tormentor, *Wool.* 98; a creditor, *ib.* 100; that of godly men may be troubled, 2 *Bec.* 622; a comfort for afflicted consciences, 4 *Bul.* 475; a prayer for a quiet conscience, 3 *Bec.* 81, *Lit. Edw.* 469; a quiet one described, 3 *Bul.* 313, 2 *Hoop.* 327; how to be quieted, 2 *Bec.* 623, 624; peace only to be found in Christ, 1 *Hoop.* 50; a good conscience, what it is, 3 *Bec.* 604, 1 *Brad.* 255, *Phil.* 224
Conscience-money: *v.* Restitution.
Consecratio mensæ: *v.* Graces.
Consecration of churches: *v.* Churches.
How performed in Constantine's days, *Calf.* 207; how in Augustine's time, *ib.* 208; the Romish way of doing it, *ib.* 208—210, 1 *Jew.* 225 n.; the Canon Law says it is better not to consecrate the sacrament than to do so in a place not hallowed, 2 *Cran.* 74; Durandus on consecration, *Bale* 611, 2 *Ful.* 239, 1 *Jew.* 15, *Pil.* 63; the folly of Popish conjuration, *Rid.* 55, 1 *Tyn.* 274, 283, 340; places are made holy by holy use, not by magical enchantment, 4 *Bul.* 499, *Calf.* 131; consecration of altars, &c., 1 *Jew.* 15, *Rid.* 55, 1 *Tyn.* 274, 283; of churchyards *Pil.* 64; the consecration of churches, altars, &c. reserved to the bishop, by conc. Hisp. II., 2 *Whitg.* 374; hallowing of the fire or altar prohibited, *Rid.* 320
Consecration of bishops: *v.* Ordination.
Consecration of the elements: *v.* Supper.

Consensus Tigurinus: v. Zurich.
Consider: to give a price for, *Sand.* 22
Consideration: brings a man to the knowledge of his state, 1 *Bec.* 145
Consistory: v. Presbytery.
Consistory courts: v. Courts.
Consolation: v. Comfort.
Conspiracy: v. Rebellion.
Constable (Hen.): v. C. (H.).
Constable (Sir Rob.): in the Tower, 1 *Lat.* 163
Constance: v. Councils.
  Charles V. deprives it of its privileges, 3 *Zur.* 385 n., 641 n., 642 n.; its reported destruction, *ib.* 385, 435
Constance (The bishop of): possessed the tithes of Zurich, 2 *Zur.* 230, 231.
Constance, in France: v. Coutances.
Constancy: an address thereon, 1 *Brad.* 385; constancy in God's truth commendable, 3 *Bec.* 205
Constans I. emperor: wrote a menacing letter to his brother Constantius, requiring him to cease from persecuting the Christians, *Sand.* 109
Constans II. emperor: not the nephew of Heraclius, 2 *Ful.* 361
Constantia, empress: asks Eusebius for the image of Christ, *Calf.* 145, 150
Constantine I. emperor, called the Great: his birthplace, *Pil.* 413; he was a valiant soldier, 1 *Bul.* 380, 384; the sign of the cross seen by him in the sky, *Calf.* 110—112, 2 *Jew.* 647, &c.; the sign shewn to him exhibited the character of the name of Christ, 2 *Ful.* 139, 140, 148; his labarum or banner with the cross, *ib.* 140, 2 *Jew.* 650, 651; he respected the cross, but did not introduce it into churches, *Calf.* 278; abolished crucifixion, 2 *Jew.* 650; the true religion set forth and publicly preached in his time, 2 *Cran.* 15; he shewed favour to Christians, 1 *Hoop.* 276 n., *Sand.* 373; declared he would conceal the faults of the clergy, 2 *Bec.* 333; gave clerks the power of appealing from the civil magistrates to their bishops, 3 *Whitg.* 454; delegated a certain matter to Miltiades, bishop of Rome, 1 *Jew.* 397, 4 *Jew.* 965; he mentions the churches of Britain, 3 *Jew.* 165; the prayer which he taught his soldiers, *Pil.* 413; thanksgivings when he had obtained peace for the church, *Calf.* 294; his inauguration celebrated with a sermon by Eusebius, *Sand.* 56; his commendation of Eusebius, 1 *Jew.* 362; his acts in religious matters, 1 *Bul.* 327; his zeal for God, *Pil.* 8; his godly laws and exertions for the furtherance of religion, 2 *Bec.* 305; his pretended Donation to the pope, a Romish forgery, *Bale* 503, 2 *Brad.* 160, 4 *Bul.* 123, *Calf.* 174 n., 193, *Coop.* 170, 171, 2 *Ful.* 260, 261, 1 *Hoop.* 276, *Jew.* xxxv, 1 *Jew.* 357, 359, 403, 4 *Jew.* 678, 679, 838, &c., 2 *Lat.* 349, *Rid.* 374, 2 *Tyn.* 279; it commands the patriarch of Constantinople to be subject to the bishop of Rome, 4 *Jew.* 695; Lau. Valla's book upon it, 2 *Ful.* 361, *Rid.* 374; Constantine did not quit Rome, 2 *Ful.* 361; a voice of angels said to have been heard when he endowed the church, *Bale* 35, 2 *Jew.* 992; he is absurdly alleged to have done the office of a footman to pope Sylvester, 4 *Jew.* 690, 692, and stated to have called the pope God, *Calf.* 5 n., 1 *Jew.* 438, 2 *Jew.* 906, 3 *Tyn.* 231 n.; he wrote letters in behalf of Christians persecuted in Persia, *Sand.* 109, and waged war in behalf of the Christians against his sister's husband Licinius, *ib.*; made a law against the Donatists, *Pil.* 641; disburthened the church of heretics, *Sand.* 248; his words on this subject, *ib.*; punished blasphemers, 2 *Hoop.* 87; forbade idolatry, 2 *Bec.* 71, 312, 1 *Bul.* 359, 2 *Bul.* 281, 4 *Jew.* 1125; made an edict against witchcraft and other forbidden arts, 1 *Hoop.* 329; spoke against observing Easter with the Jews, 2 *Whitg.* 445; overthrew the Jews who attempted to restore their Temple, 4 *Jew.* 1074; built a church at Jerusalem, *Calf.* 182; how he hallowed it, *ib.* 207; there were no large and public churches before his time, 4 *Bul.* 418; his directions concerning the reparation of churches, 3 *Whitg.* 303—305; falsely said to have built a church in honour of St Paul, *Calf.* 193; sat as judge in an ecclesiastical case, 3 *Jew.* 167; ruled over bishops, 2 *Jew.* 997; called them the heads of the churches, 2 *Whitg.* 85; threatened unruly ones, 1 *Jew.* 405, 4 *Jew.* 675; summoned the council of Nice, 1 *Hoop.* 276 n., 4 *Jew.* 994, *Rog.* 204; his conduct with respect to this synod, *Whita.* 436, 3 *Whitg.* 306; his address to the priests there, 2 *Ful.* 356; by "sacerdotes" bishops are intended, 1 *Ful.* 268; he urged the bishops there assembled to decide everything by scripture, 2 *Cran.* 528, 2 *Ful.* 380, 3 *Jew.* 227, *Sand.* 15, 40, *Whita.* 435, 563, 678, 679; circulated the scriptures, 2 *Jew.* 690; presided over a disputation with the Arians, 2 *Hoop.* 385; thought to be an Arian, 4 *Jew.* 908; Athanasius falsely accused before him, *Sand.* 129; he was appealed to by that father, 2 *Ful.* 358, 379, whom he deprived,

1 *Jew.* 414; styled a pious and learned man, *Whita.* 678; not thoroughly reformed, *Calf.* 192; not baptized till near death, 2 *Jew.* 1107; he desired to be baptized in Jordan, *Whita.* 592; fable of his baptism by pope Sylvester, 2 *Ful.* 359; his so-called baptistry, in the Lateran, *ib.* 360; source of the fables respecting his leprosy, baptism, and donation, *Calf.* 174 n.; he did not receive the sign of the Lord's death till the close of his life, 3 *Bec.* 437

Constantine IV.* emperor, called Pogonatus: how he wrote to Donus, bishop of Rome, and how Agatho wrote to him, 4 *Jew.* 679; he governed the sixth general council at Constantinople, 3 *Whitg.* 307, and subscribed its acts, 4 *Jew.* 1024

Constantine V.† emperor, called Copronymus: summoned a council at Constantinople, *Calf.* xii, 46, 138, *Park.* 91; forbade image worship, 2 *Bec.* 71, 1 *Hoop.* 47, *Phil.* 407, *Rid.* 93, 3 *Tyn.* 183 n.; his bones burned by Irene, *Calf.* 175, 176, *Park.* 92, *Rid.* 94

Constantine VI.‡ emperor: was against images, *Phil.* 407; his eyes put out by his mother Irene, at the instigation of the pope, 2 *Cran.* 12, 2 *Jew.* 653, *Park.* 92, *Rid.* 94

Constantine I. pope: approved images, 2 *Bec.* 71 n

Constantine, bp of Constance in Cyprus: *v.* Constantius.

Constantine (Geo.): mentioned, *Bale* 64, *Rid.* 494 n., 1 *Tyn.* xxvi; examined by Sir Tho. More, 1 *Tyn.* xxxviii.

Constantinople: *v.* Councils, Creeds, Law (Civil), Patriarchs.

When the name was first heard of, 2 *Ful.* 339 n.; called New Rome, 1 *Jew.* 362, *Whita.* 510, 2 *Whitg.* 272 n.; how named by Justinian, 4 *Jew.* 883; a patriarchate, 4 *Bul.* 112, 2 *Hoop.* 234, 3 *Jew.* 334, *Phil.* 43, *Rid.* 263, 2 *Whitg.* 220; the decree of Chalcedon about this, 3 *Jew.* 220, 306; the bishop called universal patriarch, 1 *Jew.* 428; Socrates writes, "Without the consent of the bishop of Constantinople, let no man be chosen bishop," 3 *Jew.* 333; riots at the election of bishops, 1 *Whitg.* 463, 464; a nominal patriarch still appointed by the pope, 4 *Jew.* 842; privileges of the church, 1 *Jew.* 404; equal with the church of Rome, 2 *Hoop.* 237, 1 *Jew.* 363, the supremacy of which it never acknowledged, 1 *Hoop.* 226; it styled itself the mother and mistress of all that are catholic, 4 *Jew.* 883;

number of clergy in the church there, in the time of Chrysostom, 1 *Jew.* 197; a miracle there in his time, *ib.* 246; how auricular confession began there, and why it was abolished, 2 *Ful.* 91, *Pil.* 553, 1 *Tyn.* 263, 3 *Tyn.* 172; Const. ecclesiæ epist. ad eccl. Pragensem, *Jew.* xxxv; extract from this epistle, 3 *Jew.* 196; the basilica of St Sophia, 2 *Brad.* 311 n

Constantius, emperor (son of Constantine the Great): disliked his father's acts, 4 *Jew.* 678; became an Arian, with his wife and court, *Ful.* 361, 4 *Jew.* 908, *Whita.* 439; decreed that Christ was not God, 2 *Cran.* 15; would not suffer a dissembler in religion to be about him, *Sand.* 121; said that those who were faithless to God could not be faithful to their prince, *ib.* 97, 261, 441; bewailed that many waxed worse and worse after they had fallen to the religion of Christ, 3 *Jew.* 625; restored Athanasius, 1 *Jew.* 414, 415; his words to him, *Pil.* 631 n.; reinstated Liberius in the see of Rome, 3 *Jew.* 342; asked him what great portion of the world he was, *ib.* 187; his tyranny and persecutions, 2 *Ful.* 379, *Pil.* 637, *Sand.* 109

Constantius, bp of Constance: avowed, in the second Nicene council, that he worshipped images as he did the Holy Trinity, *Calf.* 167, 168, 2 *Jew.* 666 (Calfhill calls him Constantinus).

Constantius (Marcus Ant.): *v.* Gardiner (Steph.).

Conster: to construe, 2 *Cov.* 35

Constitutions: *v.* Canons, Law (Civil).

The term sometimes denotes despotic laws, 1 *Tyn.* 460

Constitutions (Apostolical) *v.* Clement of Rome.

Constitutions (Legatine): *v.* Lyndewode (W.)

Consubstantiality: *v.* Christ, ii.

Consubstantiation: *v.* Lutherans.

An erroneous doctrine, *Rog.* 289, 3 *Zur.* 37, 38; contrary to the analogy of faith, *Whita.* 473; disputes between the Swiss divines and those of Saxony, 3 *Zur.* 50 n

Consuls: what they were amongst the Romans, 2 *Whitg.* 279

Consultation: a part of repentance, 3 *Bul.* 75

Contarini (Gasp. card.): legate, *Bale* 449, 1 *Lat.* 58, *Phil.* 413

Contemplation: *v.* Heaven, Meditation.

Contention: *v.* Discord.

Contentment: we are required to be content

---

* Otherwise V. † Otherwise VI. Called IV. by Cranmer.

with what we have, 2 *Bec.* 114; contentment with regard to riches, *Pil.* 152; with God's will, *ib.* 153; verses (by Hum. Gifford,) in praise of the contented mind, *Poet.* 212; the praise of a contented mind, verses by Hen. Willobie, *ib.* 396

Contex: to weave together, 1 *Bec.* 143

Conti (Loth.) : *v.* Innocent III.

Continency: what, 1 *Bul.* 419; in tongue, *ib.* 420; in apparel, *ib.* 421; in buildings, *ib.* 422; in meat and drink, *ib.* 423

Contobabdites: allowed no bishops, *Rog.* 330

Contraries: to be holpen by contraries, 2 *Hoop.* 169

Contrition: what it is, 3 *Bec.* 618, *Now.* (100); its two parts, 1 *Bec.* 97; what it works in a truly penitent heart, *ib.*; without faith it leads to desperation, *ib.* 98; a part of penance, 1 *Brad.* 46, 1 *Tyn.* 265, 267, 2 *Tyn.* 162, 478; how distinguished from attrition, 1 *Brad.* 46, 51; a prayer for contrition, *Lit. Eliz.* 252

Controller: the word explained, *Hutch.* 343

Controversy: *v.* Faith (Rule), Scripture.

It hinders the preaching of the gospel, *Nord.* 117; scripture the only competent judge of it, *Whita.* 464

Convenable, or Covenable: agreeable, 1 *Jew.* 140

Convent: to come together, 2 *Brad.* 323; to summon, 3 *Bec.* 530

Conventicles: 1 *Whitg.* 95, 208; private meetings, when lawful and when not, *Sand.* 191, 192; keepers of secret conventicles, preachings, or lectures, to be presented to the ordinary, *Grin.* 144

Conventuals: a branch of the Franciscans, 2 *Cran.* 330 n., 1 *Lat.* 287 n.; viz. the unreformed Franciscans, so called in distinction from the Observants, 1 *Tyn.* 301 n

Conversation: that of gospellers ought to be honest and circumspect, 1 *Bec.* 83

Conversion: what it is, 3 *Bul.* 55; what they obtain that convert unto God, 1 *Cov.* 509; what degrees and orders the Lord uses in it, 2 *Hoop.* 204; ungodly doctrine and human tradition are a great hindrance to it, 1 *Hoop.* 448; that of the thief, 2 *Jew.* 1134; of Paul, *ib.*; against desperation for late conversion, with sentences and examples of scripture, 1 *Bec.* 478, 479

Conveyance: sleight of hand, fraudulent management, 2 *Tyn.* 297

Convocation: *v.* Articles, Canons.

The convocation described, 1 *Zur.* 179; called by the prince, 2 *Whitg.* 360; can do nothing without the consent of the sovereign and the archbishop, 2 *Zur.* 150; the convocation and the parliament, *Now.* i; the convocation is no part of the parliament, *Phil.* 52; not long separated therefrom, *Pil.* 628; its acts of no legal force till sanctioned by parliament, 2 *Ful.* 117; slow in its proceedings, *Park.* 9; what it has done, 1 *Lat.* 45; convocations variable in their decisions, *Rid.* 130; election of the prolocutor, 2 *Whitg.* 278, 280; Latimer called before the convocation at Westminster, 1531, 2 *Lat.* 218; the reading of the quarterly curse suspended, 1534, 2 *Cran.* 281; a sermon before the convocation, 28 Hen. VIII., 1 *Lat.* 33; judgment of the convocation concerning general councils, 2 *Cran.* 463; certain holy-days abolished, *ib.* 347 n., 348, 470; proceedings, 1550, 3 *Zur.* 314; meeting of convocation, Dec. 1551, 3 *Zur.* 444, 452; king Edward's Catechism set forth, *Rid.* 226; a new synod assembled Oct. 1553, *Phil.* xi; its proceedings, *ib.* xi—xiv, 3 *Zur.* 295, 508 n.; disputation in the Convocation house, Oct. 1553, *Phil.* 165—213; queen Mary's precept to Bonner for its dissolution, *ib.* 214; epistola ad episcopos, etc. in synodo Londinensi congregatos, 2 *Hoop.* 381; the convocation of 1562, *Grin.* vii, 257; Nowell was prolocutor, *Now.* iii; Sandys's advice concerning rites and ceremonies in this synod, *Sand.* 433; orders for the bishops and clergy drawn up by Sandys and subscribed in the same synod, *ib.* 434; the convocation of 1571, *ib.* xx; articles touching the admission of ministers, &c., 1576, *Grin.* 185; in the synod of 1580, bishop Aylmer presided, Grindal, the primate, being under sequestration, *ib.* xiii; proceedings on Grindal's sequestration, 1581, *ib.* 473 n.; the earlier registers of the convocation of the province of Canterbury destroyed in the fire of London, 4 *Bul.* xxviii.

Conygham (Will.), earl of Glencairn: taken prisoner at Solway, 3 *Zur.* 239 n

Conygham (Alex.), earl of Glencairn: one of the confederate lords, 1 *Zur.* 193 n., 197 n

Cooch (Robt.), or Cooke: letter to R. Gualter, 2 *Zur.* 236; account of him, *ib.* n

Cooe (Roger): martyred at Yoxford, *Poet.* 164

Cook * (Sir Ant.): named, *Grin.* 280, 4 *Jew.* 1222 n., 1225, 1226, 1 *Zur.* 59, 2 *Zur.* 64, 70, 93, 104, 114; called 'Αρχιμάγειρος, 4 *Jew.* 1207 n., 1223, 1 *Zur.* 21, 53; tutor to

---

* Cook and Cooke are arranged together.

king Edward, 3 *Zur.* 81; on his way to Italy, *ib.* 686; in exile at Strasburgh, *Jew.* xiii; he purchases Ponet's books of his widow there, 3 *Zur.* 118; his return to England, 1 *Zur.* 5; it was thought he would be lord chancellor, 4 *Jew.* 1198, 1 *Zur.* 8; an ecclesiastical commissioner, *Park.* 370 n., and visitor of colleges, *ib.* 439; letters by him, 2 *Zur.* 1, 13, 76, 3 *Zur.* 139
— His daughter Anne married Sir N. Bacon, *q. v.* His daughter Mildred married Sir Will. Cecil, *q. v.*
Cook (Jo.), registrar of Winton: the enemy of Philpot, *Phil.* ix..
Cooke (Jo.), alderman of Gloncester, 2 *Lat.* 418 n
— The lady Cooke, his widow, endows a school at Gloucester, *ib.*
Cooke (Rob.): *v.* Cooch.
Cooke (Rob.), or Cocus: Censura, *Calf.* 69, 89, 126, 137, 200, 248, 361, 2 *Ful.* 70, 90, 110, 165, 200 nn.; mistaken about the Pontifical, 2 *Ful.* 99 n
Cooke (Rog.), alias Taylor, *q. v.*
Cook (Will.?): one of the commissioners for the examination of Philpot, *Phil.* 9, 149
Cooke (......), chaplain to the earl of Sussex: *Park.* 458
Coole (Rob.): *v.* Cole.
Cooper (Eliz.): she was the woman who was burned at Norwich with S. Milner, *Poet.* 170
Cooper (Tho.), bp. of Lincoln, afterwards of Winchester: some account of him, *Park.* 316 n.; biographical notice of him, by Ant. à Wood, *Coop.* ix; when vice-chancellor of Oxford he instituted the first public celebration of the queen's accession, *Lit. Eliz.* 463; could not have the see of Oxford, *Park.* 360; preaches before the queen, being bishop of Lincoln, 1 *Zur.* 261 n.; consulted by Whitgift on his book against Cartwright, 3 *Whitg.* x, 600; meets the queen at Canterbury, *Park.* 475; list of his works, *Coop.* xi; his ANSWER IN DEFENCE OF THE TRUTH, AGAINST THE APOLOGY OF PRIVATE MASS, with the Apology prefixed, edited by the Rev. Will. Goode, M.A., F.S.A., *Coop.*; references to this Answer, 2 *Ful.* vii. ix. 4; his Brief Exposition of such Chapters of the Old Testament as usually are read in the church...on Sundays, *Park.* 462
Coot (Bald as a): 2 *Tyn.* 224
Coots (Mr): having preached at Hales, he is summoned before Cromwell, 2 *Lat.* 374
Cope [Lat. capa]: an ecclesiastical vestment, 1 *Brad.* 393 n., *Lit. Edw.* 217, 1 *Tyn.* 419, 2 *Whitg.* 50, 1 *Zur.* 158, 345; a golden one given, it is said, by Constantine to the church of Jerusalem, 2 *Ful.* 114; such a cope stated to have been sold by Cyril of Jerusalem, 2 *Whitg.* 23, 24; appointed by king Edward's first Prayer Book for the ministration of the communion, *Lit. Edw.* 76, 97, 217; forbidden by his second Book, *ib.* 217; worn at the Lord's supper in Elizabeth's time, 3 *Whitg.* 106, 1 *Zur.* 74, 164; but its use was optional after the queen's injunction, 1 *Zur.* 158 n.; used in the larger churches, 2 *Zur.* 361, as at St Paul's, *Grin.* 211; refused by some, 2 *Whitg.* 61; article against wearing it, *Grin.* 159; copes used as bed-coverings, 2 *Ful.* 114
Cope (Alan), i.e. N. Harpsfield, *q. v.*
Cope (Hen.): ambassador from Strasburgh to the emperor, 3 *Zur.* 664
Cope (Sir Walter): named, 2 *Zur.* 327 n
Cophti, or Copti: 2 *Ful.* 328, it should be Sophi, which is a title of the king of Persia.
Cophyne: coffin, *Calf.* 193
Copland (Will.), printer: 1 *Brad.* 247, 2 *Brad.* 351
Coppinger (Edm.): beguiled by Hacket, *Nord.* 113; published that the said Hacket was come to judge the world, *Rog.* 68; his visions, *ib.* 196 n.; his rebellion, *ib.* 344
Coptic language: *v.* Egyptian.
Copus (Alanus), i.e. N. Harpsfield, *q. v.*
Copy: copiousness, 2 *Hoop.* 345, *Phil.* 325, 390
Corage (coragium): the heart and its affections, 1 *Tyn.* 417, 2 *Tyn.* 74, 3 *Tyn.* 35, 278
Coram nobis: 2 *Tyn.* 32
Coranus (Ant.): *v.* Corranus.
Corbett (Hen.): *v.* Cortbeke.
Cordell (Sir Will.): one of queen Mary's privy council, 1 *Zur.* 5 n.; Woolton's epistle dedicatory to him, as master of the rolls, *Wool.* 3
Core: *v.* Korah.
Corell's Wood: belonged to the see of Canterbury, 2 *Cran.* 261
Coren (Hugh), or Curwen, abp of Dublin, afterwards bp of Oxford: being prebendary of Hereford, he is deputed to visit the diocese, 2 *Cran.* 81 n.; detects a false miracle at Dublin, *Park.* 95 n., 96 n.; bishop of Oxford, *ib.* 305; should have a coadjutor there, *ib.*
Coren (Oliver), Coryne, or Curwen: *Rid.* 536 n
Coren (Rich.), archdeacon of Oxford and Colchester: signs a declaration respecting a general council, 2 *Cran.* 468
Corier (Roger), martyr: *Poet.* 163
Corinth: the church there, 4 *Bul.* 105, 199;

it was much corrupted, *ib.* 59; dissensions in it, 2 *Jew.* 1047
Corinthians (Epistles to the): *v.* Paul (St).
Corle: *v.* Coy.
Corn: *v.* Hoarders, Husbandmen, Regraters.
Cornarius (Janus): *Calf.* 121, 251, 329, 377, 2 *Ful.* 100, 103, 286, 287 nn.; his works prohibited, *Calf.* 42 n.; his opinion on the writings of Epiphanius, 2 *Whitg.* 161, 289
Cornelia, daughter of Scipio: her reply about her children, 2 *Bec.* 5; how she bore the loss of her sons, 2 *Cov.* 125
Cornelius, the centurion: his character, *Sand.* 256, &c.; a good man though a centurion, 1 *Bul.* 387; his prayers and alms, 4 *Bul.* 179; he prayed on the housetop, 1 *Bul.* 292; his conversion, 4 *Bul.* 80, 95, 366; he had faith, *Sand.* 260; was justified by faith alone, 2 *Bul.* 342, 3 *Bul.* 44, 52; received the Holy Ghost before he was baptized, 4 *Bul.* 312, 348; nevertheless he was baptized, and that without delay, *ib.* 346, 366; baptized with fire, *ib.* 356
Cornelius (St), bp of Rome: his election, 1 *Jew.* 408, 2 *Whitg.* 199; addressed by Cyprian as his brother and fellow bishop, *Phil.* 42; his authority upheld by Cyprian, 2 *Whitg.* 193, 194; he differed from that father as to heretical baptism, 1 *Ful.* 35, 2 *Ful.* 77; enumerates the clergy, &c. of the church of Rome, 1 *Jew.* 197, 2 *Whitg.* 215; speaks of a schismatical bishop as reduced (on his return to the church) to lay communion, *Coop.* 159 n.; buried St Peter's body, 1 *Jew.* 173; his martyrdom, 2 *Bul.* 106; spurious epistles in his name, 2 *Ful.* 71 n., 81 n.; St Cornelis invoked for the foul evil, *Bale* 498; S. Cornely's horn, *Calf.* 287
Cornelius, bp of Bitonto: his speech in the council of Trent, *Jew.* xxxiv; he said that the pope was come a light into the world, 1 *Jew.* 385, 2 *Jew.* 831, 3 *Jew.* 145, 4 *Jew.* 752, 940, 1052; called bishops the stars of the churches, and the mighty army of God's angels, 4 *Jew.* 1057; yet spoke of the Romish church as having fallen from Christ to Antichrist, &c., 2 *Jew.* 900, 3 *Jew.* 196, 255, 325, 348, 4 *Jew.* 738, *Rog.* 210; lamented its filthiness, and the corruption both of the people and the priests, 4 *Jew.* 642; acknowledged that the Latin church owed everything to Greece, *ib.* 884
Cornelius Cornepolita: an author not identified, *Jew.* xxxv; referred to on the poisoning of Henry the emperor, 4 *Jew.* 686
Cornelius (......): named in conjunction with Cassander, 2 *Zur.* 41

Cornelius: i. e. C. Bungey, *q. v.*
Cornethwaite (Symone): 2 *Cran.* 364
Cornicius (James), a physician: 1 *Zur.* 28
Cornwall: *v.* Devonshire.
Its language, 3 *Zur.* 73; the Cornish rebels defeated at Blackheath, 1497, 1 *Lat.* 101; rebellion there, 1549, 2 *Cran.* 163, *Hutch.* 7 n., 3 *Zur.* 654; the Cornish men rejected the reformed service, &c., because they did not understand English, 2 *Cran.* 179, 183; their superstitious processions in gang week, *Grin.* 241 n.; the Spanish armada seen off the Lizard, *Lit. Eliz.* 469
Cornwalleys (Sir Tho.): one of queen Mary's privy council, 1 *Zur.* 5 n
Cornwell (Master): 2 *Lat.* 398
Coronation: the ceremony should be performed by the chief bishop, 2 *Cran.* 126; on the coronation oath, *ib.*; it did not permit the resignation of the crown to the pope or his legates, *ib.*; queen Mary took contradictory oaths at her coronation, *ib.* 454; anointing only a ceremony that might be omitted, *ib.* 126; the coronation of Anne Boleyn, queen consort, 2 *Cran.* 245
Corosy: a corrosive, 1 *Tyn.* 21, 3 *Tyn.* 195 (and see Corsie).
Corporal presence: *v.* Supper, Transubstantiation.
Corporal things: 4 *Bul.* 188; they may be prayed for, 1 *Bec.* 165
Corporass, Corporal, or Corporis-cloth: the linen cloth on which the host is laid, 2 *Brad.* 308, 2 *Jew.* 705, *Lit. Edw.* 85 n., *Pil.* 46; by whom devised, 3 *Bec.* 262; whence derived, 4 *Bul.* 419; its foolish signification, 3 *Tyn.* 73; foolish argument for it, 1 *Jew.* 15; articles respecting it, 2 *Hoop.* 145, 146
Corpus Christi day: *Rog.* 286, 291; the feast and service invented by Urban IV., *Bale* 168, 3 *Bec.* 274, 4 *Bul.* 423, *Grin.* 73, 1 *Hoop.* 527, *Pil.* 535, 1 *Jew.* 10, 516, 549, 2 *Jew.* 774
Corpus Juris Canonici: *v.* Law (Canon).
Corpus Juris Civilis: *v.* Law (Civil).
Corranus (Ant.), otherwise A. Bellerivus Corranus, or del Corro: notices of him, *Grin.* 309, &c., *Park.* 340 n., 2 *Zur.* 254 n., 261; his contest with one Hieronymus, *Grin.* 309, &c.; bishop Grindal's judgment on the case, *ib.* 313, 314; preferred to be reader of divinity at the Temple, &c., *ib.* 312 n.; thought to preach erroneous doctrine, *Park.* 476, *Grin.* 353 n., 2 *Zur.* 254, 255, 261; he disliked commentaries, *Rog.* 196; his death, *Grin.* 312 n.; his books, *Park.* 339 n.; letter from him to Bullinger, 2 *Zur.* 254; letter to him, *Park.* 339

Correction: why God corrects his children, 2 *Cov.* 367; the church's power of judicial correction, 4 *Bul.* 40; self-correction, 3 *Bec.* 619; the correction of children, 1 *Bul.* 295; things to be observed in it, 2 *Bec.* 354, 355; how a school-master must use it, *ib.* 384, 385

Corrichie, near Aberdeen: a battle there, 1 *Zur.* 129 n

Corrie (Geo. Elwes), master of Jesus coll. Cambridge: editor of Latimer's works, 1 and 2 *Lat.*; also of Nowell's Catechisms, *Now.*

Corringham, co. Lincoln: a prebend in the cathedral church, *Park.* viii, 482

Corrodies: for decayed cooks, *Park.* 20

Corruption: that of man's nature, 1 *Bec.* 46, 47, 3 *Bec.* 605; what, and how great, 2 *Bul.* 393; it includes the blotting out of God's image, *ib.* 394

Corser (Tho.): his library, *Poet.* viii.

Corsica: given to the pope, 2 *Tyn.* 261

Corsie: corrosive, 2 *Cov.* 335; corsive, the same, 3 *Bec.* 69, (and see Corosy)

Cortayne: curtain, *Calf.* 51

Cortbeke (Hen. ad), or Corbett, a Dutch priest: recommended to Cromwell, 2 *Cran.* 386; kept by Cranmer, *ib.* 395

Corunna: a new Spanish armada assembled there and at Ferrol, *Lit. Eliz.* 473

Corvinus (Ant.): 1 *Whitg.* 135; his Postil translated by Wisdom, 2 *Bec.* 423

Corwin (Hugh), abp: v. Coren.

Coryne (Oliver): v. Coren.

Coryphæus: the term applied to Peter, 2 *Ful.* 286 n

Cosin (Jo.), bp of Durham: Works, *Calf.* 19 n.; Private Devotions, or Hours of Prayer, *Pra. B.* iii, *Pra. Eliz.* x. n., xii, &c.; Prynne's Brief Survey and Censure of this book, *Calf.* 226 n.; Hist. of Transub., *ib.* 248 n., 2 *Ful.* 21 n.; Schol. Hist. of the Canon, 4 *Bul.* 539 n., *Calf.* 248 n., 2 *Ful.* 89 n., 221 n., 222 n., 3 *Whitg.* 350 n

Cosins (......): v. Cosyn.

Cosmus and Damian (SS): invoked for physic, 1 *Bec.* 139; account of them, *ib.* n

Cosmus (......), servant to the Dutch ambassador: fasts five or six days by Velsius's persuasion, that after his abstinence he might receive illuminationes à cœlo, and in the end falls mad, *Grin.* 255; Grindal's advice respecting him, *ib.*

Cosowarth (Mich.): notice of him, *Poet.* xxxix; Psalm xxx. in metre, *ib.* 406

Cosse: a kiss, 1 *Jew.* 154 n

Cossé (Arth. de), bp of Coutances: he appears to be the bp of Constance received by abp Parker, *Park.* 214

Costard: a species of apple, 3 *Bec.* 283; costardmongers, 2 *Whitg.* 115

Costasye (......): wrote on the Apocalypse, *Bale* 256

Costerus (Fra.): alleges that the scriptures are obscure, *Rog.* 199, *Whita.* 361, 366; affirms that Christ, by his descent, turned hell into paradise, *Rog.* 62; maintains the infallibility of the Roman church, *ib.* 179 n.; says that the pope cannot teach heresy, *ib.* 183; on the celibacy of the priesthood, *ib.* 241 n.; on the virtues of the cross, *ib.* 320 n.; he appeals to the pseudo-Hegesippus, 2 *Ful.* 339 n

Costerus (Jo.), editor of Ambrose's works: his authority alleged by Cartwright, 2 *Whitg.* 155 n

Costious: costly, 1 *Bec.* 204; costuous, *Bale* 527

Cosyn (......), or Cosins: was chaplain to Bonner, *Phil.* 18; he examines Philpot, *ib.* 92, &c.

Cosyn (Edw.): condemned for treason, 1 *Zur.* 129 n

Cotelerius (Jo. Bapt.): Patres Apostolici, 2 *Bec.* 546 n., *Jew.* xxxv, 1 *Whitg.* 223, 2 *Whitg.* 171, 304, 310, 428 nn

Cotes (Geo.), bp of Chester: notice of him, 2 *Cran.* 382 n

Coteswold, a tract of land in co. Gloucester: famous for sheep, 3 *Jew.* 415

Coton (......): preferred by Henry VIII., 2 *Lat.* 373

Cotray (Davy), of Pakring, monk of Byland: *Bale* 81

Cotta: confutes the Epicureans, *Hutch.* 13

Cottesford (Tho.): in exile, 1 *Cran.* (9), at Frankfort, 3 *Zur.* 763; his preparative unto prayer, *Lit. Edw.* 377; notice of it, *ib.* x, *Pra. Eliz.* ix.

Cotton (......): v. Coton.

Cotton (......): martyred at Bramford, *Poet.* 173

Cotton (Mr.), son of a knight: married Sir Rog. Woodhouse's daughter, *Park.* 401; very evil disposed, *ib.*; absconded, 402 n. 403, 415, 417

Cotton (Hen.): on Coverdale's Ghostly Psalms, 2 *Cov.* 535

Cotton (Roger): notice of him, *Poet.* xxxiv; stanzas from his Armour of Proof, *ib.* 372

Cottrell (Jo.): commissioned to visit Salisbury cathedral, *Jew.* xvii.

Cottrell (Eliz.): *Pra. Eliz.* xx.

Council (The Privy): v. Privy Council.

Councils: v. Creeds.

The names of those Councils which are for the most part

denominated General are printed in Italic capitals, as BASIL. Places are distinguished by their English names, as *Elvira*, but that no difficulty may occur in any case, other forms are inserted as cross-references*.

Councils in general:—of synods, 4 *Bul.* 505, &c.; how far to be allowed, *Phil.* 382, 383; councils are good, if of good men, 1 *Lat.* 288; of more weight than individual writers, 1 *Whitg.* 213; they have a twofold advantage, *Whita.* 434; on their office, *ib.* 436; two held by the apostles, 3 *Bul.* 52; see *Jerusalem*, p. 239; anciently held twice a year, 4 *Bul.* 506; various early councils speak of bishops, presbyters, and deacons, 1 *Ful.* 253; what sort of councils have been held in latter ages, 3 *Bul.* 116; councils cited in the Canon Law, see 4 *Jew.* 1332; Concilia, à Petro Crabbe, (*q. v.*) Col. Agr. 1551, *Calf.* 136 n., 2 *Ful.* 400, *Jew.* xxxv; he complains that the examples from whence he took them were wonderfully corrupted, &c., 1 *Jew.* 341; Sev. Binii Concilia, *Calf.* 403, 2 *Ful.* 398; Conciliorum Collectio, Par. 1644, 2 *Bec.* 210 n.; Concilia, studio Labb. et Cossart., Lut. Par. 1671, 1672, *Calf.* 138 n., 2 *Ful.* 23 n., *Jew.* xxxv; Foxe engaged in translating the Greek councils, 1 *Zur.* 43; many ancient ones possessed by Jo. Tilius, *Park.* 141; some not reputed lawful ones, 1 *Jew.* 410; on their authority, *Whita.* 194; Romish errors respecting them, *Rog.* 205, &c.; their liability to error denied, *ib.* 208, 210; wicked and heretical ones, *Rid.* 134; some of their errors, *Rog.* 208, 209; they are not the rule of faith, 2 *Jew.* 996; our religion is older than councils, *Pil.* 549; holy scripture their guide, 1 *Bul.* 13; all religious councils have ascribed the supreme decision to scripture, *Whita.* 434, 435; they must be tried by scripture, 3 *Tyn.* 99; they have no authority, except as they are confirmed by the word of God, 3 *Bec.* 391, 392; God grants as much to two or three gathered in his name as to thousands, 1 *Lat.* 288; the doctrine of Christ needs not the approbation of any council, yet councils are useful for the promotion of unity, *Phil.* 397; they meet not to define all controversies or to interpret scripture, but to condemn heresies, *Whita.* 449; the use of their decrees, *Now.* (3), 115; opinion of Gregory Nazianzen against councils, 2 *Cran.* 464, 4 *Jew.* 908, *Pil.* 532; the chief and oldest like cobwebs catch small flies only, 2 *Cran.* 39; on the power to call them, 4 *Bul.* 45; councils not to be gathered but by the commandment and will of princes, *Rog.* 204; instances of some which were so called, 1 *Jew.* 382, 411, 3 *Jew.* 225, 4 *Jew.* 902, &c., 996, &c., *Rog.* 204, 2 *Whitg.* 362; Parker owns councils called by religious princes, *Park.* 110; what councils were acknowledged by Bradford and others, 1 *Brad.* 371; we cannot certainly tell that councils were legitimately assembled, *Whita.* 449; they may be held without the pope's consent, 2 *Ful.* 160; ignorance of the members of some of them, *Whita.* 139; abuses reformed by provincial ones, 1 *Jew.* 322; according to Romanists only bishops (who are all sworn to the pope) have the right of suffrage, 3 *Jew.* 205; usually held in the pope's towns, 2 *Tyn.* 272; often confirmed by the pope, 1 *Jew.* 410; Rogers says that they have always (except in apostolic times) been confirmed by the sovereign, *Rog.* 205; proposed synod of the reformed churches, 2 *Cran.* 430, &c., 3 *Zur.* 23—26; opinions of the Disciplinarians, or Puritans, about councils, *Rog.* 206; Cartwright, on appeals to synods of shires, provinces, and nations, 3 *Whitg.* 263

General councils (see also above):—a general council is the church representative, *Whita.* 22, 415; they are not commanded, *Rid.* 132; on the number of general councils, *Phil.* 44; the first four, 1 *Bul.* 12, honoured by Gregory as the four gospels, 3 *Jew.* 225, 4 *Jew.* 1109; how many allowed by Protestants, 3 *Jew.* 176; four (says Harding) allowed in England by parliament, *ib.* 264; no council was ever truly general, 2 *Cran.* 76; on their authority, *ib.* 76, 77, *Rog.* 203; Augustine declares it to be most healthful, 3 *Jew.* 233; without the word of God, they are not sufficient to make articles of faith, 2 *Cran.* 36; their decrees are binding only so far as they are consonant with God's word, *Rog.* 210; Panormitan says we ought rather to believe a simple man bringing in scripture, than a whole general council, *Phil.* 357; not all gathered together in the Holy Ghost, 2 *Cran.* 515; laws made by them

---

* Various councils held at the same place are distinguished from each other as far as time and other circumstances have allowed. The years (which will sometimes be found to differ from those assigned by other writers) are taken from L'Art de verifier les Dates, as given in Sir N. H. Nicolas's Chronology of History.

COUNCILS

may be lawfully doubted, *ib.* 516; many good men may have been in them, and yet their decisions may have been erroneous, *ib.* 53; they may err, 2 *Ful.* 231, 1 *Jew.* 35, 65, 69, 254, 3 *Jew.* 176, 177, 4 *Jew.* 1109, *Rid.* 129, 130, 134, &c., *Rog.* 207; Cole maintains that no general council ever erred, 1 *Jew.* 38; they have erred in matters not trifling, 2 *Cran.* 11, 37, 39, even in things pertaining to God, *Rog.* 208; the relative authority ascribed to them and to the pope, 1 *Jew.* 67, &c., 4 *Jew.* 704, 922, 923, *Whita.* 414, 415; many Romanists have held that a general council may be called to depose an evil pope, 2 *Ful.* 160; who have summoned them, 3 *Jew.* 225, 4 *Jew.* 992, &c.; no one prince can now call one, 2 *Cran.* 467; the pope not always president, 1 *Jew.* 412, 4 *Jew.* 1003; the first place of signature not always given to him, 4 *Jew.* 1003; others besides bishops have given definitive sentence in them, 3 *Jew.* 206, 207; they have been confirmed by various bishops and lay princes, 4 *Jew.* 917, 998; their decrees may be altered by subsequent councils, *Pil.* 556, 557; some of them have rejected others, 2 *Cran.* 77; one has condemned another of heresy, *ib.* 11, 164; general councils have been overruled by provincial ones, 4 *Jew.* 1053; their decisions disregarded by Romanists, 1 *Jew.* 69, 70, or deceitfully adduced, *Pil.* 533; how they prove their general councils, 2 *Tyn.* 289; Popery cannot be proved by them, *Pil.* 531; councils of the pope and his flatterers called general, *Phil.* 396; general councils under the pope have never been free, 3 *Tyn.* 158; the churches of different Romish nations, assembled in a general council, would not believe each other, 3 *Tyn.* 99; judgment of the convocation respecting general councils, 2 *Cran.* 463; the opinions of Cranmer and several others of the bishops and clergy touching a proposed council, *ib.* 467; a general council looked for, 1560, 1 *Zur.* 90; Jewel desired a general council, Christ being president, 2 *Jew.* 995; we must not wait for general councils, 1 *Jew.* 322; what at this day Christians may look for by them, 3 *Bul.* 117

Achaia (250): held by Bacchylus, 4 *Jew.* 1125

Acon: v. *Aix-la-Chapelle.*

Africa: v. *Carthage, Hippo, Milevis.*

Agde (Agathense—506): mentioned, 2 *Bec.* 71; ordered that penitents, &c. should leave the church before the communion, 1 *Jew.* 181, 182; decreed that all catholics should communicate thrice a year, 2 *Bec.* 259, 3 *Bec.* 380, 2 *Cran.* 174, 1 *Jew.* 176, 177, *Pil.* 543; permitted mass in private oratories, provided that the owners came to the church on the great feasts, 1 *Jew.* 180, 181; decreed that upon certain days the country people should hold their communions only in great parishes or cities, 2 *Jew.* 631

Aix-la-Chapelle (...): declared it not lawful to minister the communion at home, but upon great necessity, 1 *Jew.* 184; affirmed that the voice and mind of them that sing unto the Lord in the church ought to agree together, 1 *Jew.* 309, *Whita.* 273; on reading in the church, *ib.* (see also *Melchidense.*)

Alexandria (321 or 324): refuted the Arians by scripture, *Whita.* 679

—— (340?): against the accusers of Athanasius, 1 *Jew.* 355

—— (363): condemns the followers of Macedonius, *Phil.* 382 n

—— (...): committed the visitation of all the churches in the West to Eusebius, bishop of Vercellæ, and those to the East to Asterius, 1 *Jew.* 386, 403; appealed to the bishops of the West, 3 *Jew.* 303, 304; defence of one Macarius, charged with breaking a holy cup, 1 *Jew.* 167; the epistle in defence of him shews that the sacrifice was not daily offered, *ib.* 200

Altissiodorense: v. *Auxerre.*

Ancyra (314): 4 *Jew.* 1049; canon respecting deacons who offered to idols, 1 *Jew.* 240; it allowed the clergy to marry if they stated their intention so to do at their ordination, 2 *Ful.* 96, 3 *Jew.* 396, 397, 408, 4 *Jew.* 806; on chorepiscopi, 1 *Whitg.* 220, 3 *Whitg.* 270; on simony, 1 *Whitg.* 220; canons referred to, 1 *Ful.* 434, 1 *Whitg.* 366, 459

Antioch (264): condemned Paul of Samosata, 4 *Jew.* 1007

—— (339 or 354): an Arian council against Athanasius, 1 *Jew.* 352, 410

—— (341): the so-called apostolical canons partly taken from its acts, *Whita.* 567; ordained that those who were present at the reading of scripture, but who did not communicate, should be put out of the church, 3 *Bec.* 416, 474, *Coop.* 219, 2 *Cran.* 171, 1 *Jew.* 70, 3 *Jew.* 477, *Phil.* 61; opposed to the reception of the sacrament by the priest alone, *Rid.* 317; ordered bishops and other ministers to be appointed by the metropolitan, 1 *Whitg.* 460; its canon on the office of metropolitan, 2 *Whitg.* 145, 146, 149, 159, 242, 360—362, 364, 365, 399, 430; forbade a priest or deacon to appeal from his bishop to the emperor, *ib.* 371; on the course to be pursued in judging a bishop in case the bishops of the province did not agree, *ib.* 370;· on the choice of ministers, 1 *Whitg.* 366, 459; against bishops, priests, and deacons, who, being condemned, should exercise any ministry, 2 *Whitg.* 371, or should set up separate altars, *ib.* 371; persons excommunicated by one bishop not to be received by another, 3 *Whitg.* 260; the acts of the council declared void by pope Julius I. because he was not called to it, 1 *Jew.* 412

Antissiodorense: v. *Auxerre.*

Aquileia (381): 4 *Jew.* 1020; summoned by the emperor, 2 *Whitg.* 362; did not own the bishop of Rome as supreme, *Phil.* 39; defended by Ambrose, 4 *Jew.* 1049, 1054

Aquisgranum: v. *Aix-la-Chapelle.*

Arausicanum: v. *Orange.*

Arelatense: v. *Arles.*

Ariminense: v. *Rimini.*

Arles I. (314): ordered that deacons should not minister the sacrament, 1 *Jew.* 240

—— *II.* (442?): on metropolitans, 2 *Whitg.* 159, 430; on the suspension of bishops, 3 *Whitg.* 262 n; divers canons mentioned, 1 *Whitg.* 220; the council cites a canon of Nice on libels, 2 *Whitg.* 152

—— *III.* (452?): enjoins penance to those through whose negligence the sacrament is eaten by a mouse or any beast, 2 *Jew.* 783

—— (813): summoned by Charlemagne, *Rog.* 204

Arvernense: v. *Clermont.*

Aurelianense: v. *Orleans.*

Auxerre (Altissiodorense—586): decree about the number of masses in one day, 2 *Jew.* 634, 635; it ordered that every woman, when she communicated, should have her dominical, 1 *Jew.* 179 n.; prohibited the Lord's supper to be given to the dead, 1 *Jew.* 7; direction about keeping chrism, *ib.* 249; against some horrible abuses, and wicked customs, 2 *Jew.* 635

Bᴀsɪʟ (1431): 2 *Cran.* 488, 4 *Jew.* 1105, 1110; its acts in Foxe, *Rid.* 374 n.; summoned expressly for the reformation of the clergy, 4 *Jew.* 1107; Augustinus de Roma bore the name of archbishop of Nazareth in it, *ib.* 1056; referred to on the eucharist, *Coop.* 39; it allowed the Bohemians to receive the sacrament under both kinds, 2 *Bec.* 245, 3 *Bec.* 415, 1 *Jew.* 205, 3 *Jew.* 128, 203; an argument used there to shew that the church cannot err, 1 *Jew.* 78; the synod declares that many popes have fallen into heresies, 1 *Jew.* 400, 3 *Jew.* 345, 4 *Jew.* 927; says, although the pope be the ministerial head of the church, yet is he not greater than all the church; if so, when he erred the whole church should err with him, 4 *Jew.* 734, 922; determined that a council of bishops is above the pope, 1 *Jew.* 38, 4 *Jew.* 704, 1110; deposed pope Eugenius IV. (for a time), 1 *Jew.* 35, 67, 406, 4 *Jew.* 927, 955, and put Amadeus in his place, 4 *Jew.* 1105, 1111; says, the Holy Ghost doth not give light to all men at one time, but breatheth where he will, and when he will, 3 *Jew.* 595; decrees that fornication is sin, 4 *Jew.* 634; Jo. de Torquemada defends the revelations of St Bridget, 1 *Hoop.* 291 n.; the council took part with the Scotists, 1 *Jew.* 70; opposed by Æneas Sylvius, 2 *Brad.* 160, *Rid.* 374; rejected by the Dominicans, 1 *Jew.* 233, and the Thomists, *ib.* 254; Pighius says it decreed against reason, &c., *ib.* 35, 38, 67, 4 *Jew.* 1109; a treatise annexed to its acts, 2 *Ful.* 294 n

Braga (Bracarense—563?): against antitrinitarian errors, *Rog.* 45 n.; against an opinion of the Manichees, *ib.* 41 n.; against an error of Paul of Samosata, *ib.* 48 n

—— *II.* (572): cited as commanding those who will not communicate to be put out of the church, 1 *Jew.* 118, 119, 2 *Whitg.* 553 (Capit. Mart. episc. Brac.), and as prohibiting the observance of Gentile holydays, and the decking of houses with green boughs, 2 *Whitg.* 446, 447 (id.)

—— *III.* (675): forbids the use of milk, &c. in the communion, *Coop.* 137 n.; condemns the practice of dipping the sacramental bread, 1 *Jew.* 252; censures bishops for carrying relics about their necks, 2 *Jew.* 555 n

Brixen (1080): charged pope Hildebrand (Gregory VII.) with many crimes, 1 *Jew.* 400, 3 *Jew.* 129, 345, 346; deposed him, 1 *Jew.* 406, 3 *Jew.* 129, 4 *Jew.* 700

Cabilonense: v. *Châlons.*

Cæsaraugustanum: v. *Saragossa.*

Carthage (or *Africa*): councils held here in Cyprian's time*, 1 *Bul.* 12 n., 4 *Jew.*

---

* These councils are not distinguished by numbers. This is also the case with many subsequent synods held at Carthage between the numbered ones, as well as with synods held at some other places.

909; his sentences therein, *Park.* 111; in one of them, A.D. 256, he said, "None of us makes himself a bishop of bishops," 2 *Ful.* 322 n., 3 *Jew.* 300; these synods denied the validity of baptism by heretics, and enjoined rebaptism, 1 *Ful.* 35, 4 *Jew.* 1109, 1 *Whitg.* 325, 2 *Whitg.* 208, 209, 365; saying of Cæcilius à Bilta in one of them, 2 *Jew.* 773

—— *II.* (390): referred to, *Phil.* 78 n.; Gennedius was president, 4 *Jew.* 1003; it did not first use the term "missa," 2 *Ful.* 81 n.; mentions a primate in every province, 2 *Whitg.* 159, 272, 431; on excommunicated priests, 3 *Whitg.* 260; it dissolved priests' marriages, 4 *Jew.* 1053; its words respecting matrimony perversely glossed by Harding, 3 *Jew.* 418, 423

—— *III.* (397): merely provincial, *Whita.* 40, 41; it abridged the council of Hippo, 3 *Jew.* 146; did not own the bishop of Rome as supreme, 2 *Hoop.* 540 n., *Phil.* 39; withstood his claims, *Rid.* 136; decreed that the bishop of the first see should not be called prince of priests, or high-priest, or the like; and declared that the Roman pontiff himself might not be called universal (bishop), 2 *Ful.* 322, 323, 2 *Hoop.* 235 n., 1 *Jew.* 355, 370, 425, 442, 3 *Jew.* 127, 143, 144, 312, 313, 314, &c., 355, 361, 370, 4 *Jew.* 824, 1110, *Whita.* 40, 2 *Whitg.* 168; the last clause suppressed by Crabbe, 1 *Jew.* 425; the synod disproves the alleged succession of the popes from Peter, *Poet.* 274 n.; it decreed that bishops should meet together in each of their provinces, at least once a year, 4 *Jew.* 1049; ordered nothing to be offered in the sacrament but bread and wine with water, 1 *Ful.* 261, 262; forbade sacraments to be administered to the dead, 1 *Jew.* 6, 7, 136, 192, 251, 2 *Jew.* 751, 3 *Jew.* 560, *Rog.* 266; on the use of forms of prayer, 2 *Whitg.* 468; it admitted children of fourteen to be readers in the church, 4 *Jew.* 911; ordained that nothing should either be read or sung in the church but the canonical scriptures, 4 *Bul.* 193, 1 *Jew.* 70, 265, 3 *Jew.* 87, 146, 4 *Jew.* 814, 815, 3 *Whitg.* 348, and the passions of martyrs on their days, 3 *Jew.* 146, 3 *Whitg.* 347; Carranza confesses that the mention of the passions of martyrs is an addition, 2 *Ful.* 89; on the canon of scripture; it received some apocryphal books as canonical or ecclesiastical, 4 *Bul.* 539, 1 *Ful.* 18, 19, 22, 23, *Whita.* 39, 46, 55, 3 *Whitg.* 350; forbade the observance of certain festivals, 2 *Whitg.* 447, 448; condemned night-wakes, 3 *Jew.* 167; forbade the children of bishops and clerks to exhibit or behold worldly spectacles, *Pil.* 566; in this (?) council Philippus and Asellus, the pope's legates, had the last place in subscription, 4 *Jew.* 999; confirmed by Leo IV., *Whita.* 39; Papists cling to it tooth and nail, to support purgatory and other errors, 2 *Cran.* 39; yet they receive not all its decrees, *Whita.* 40, 41

—— *IV.* (398): speaks of the Pelagians denying that infants are to be baptized, 4 *Bul.* 376; did not permit a woman to teach or to baptize, 4 *Bul.* 370, 2 *Whitg.* 536, 537; allowed the sacrament to be poured into the mouth of a man when sick or mad, 1 *Jew.* 251; its decree about receiving to penance one that fell mad, 3 *Jew.* 359; it gives directions about the appointment of a bishop, 1 *Whitg.* 411; how he should be first examined, 4 *Bul.* 136—138; the manner of his consecration, *ib.* 139; gives instructions concerning the houses and living of bishops, 2 *Whitg.* 381, 388; says a bishop ought to have mean furniture, *Grin.* 300; ordains that no bishop sitting, shall suffer a presbyter to stand, 2 *Whitg.* 383; on ordination, and the laying on of hands of the presbyters, 1 *Ful.* 249, 250, 261; clerks directed to live by trade or husbandry, 2 *Whitg.* 381; the deacon to wear an alb in the time of oblation and reading, *ib.* 49; what alb is spoken of, 2 *Ful.* 113; doorkeepers and readers mentioned, 4 *Bul.* 114 n

—— *V.* (401?): forbade leaving the principal chair and going to another church within the diocese, 1 *Jew.* 365

—— (416): addresses Innocent I. "domine frater," 2 *Ful.* 351, *Pil.* 78, and "most honourable brother," 1 *Jew.* 385; it styles the Roman see apostolical, *Phil.* 78

—— *VI.* (419): claims of the bishop of Rome, Boniface I., 2 *Cran.* 487; his craft with respect to certain alleged canons of the council of Nice, 2 *Hoop.* 236; the council charged pope Zosimus with corrupting the council of Nice, which was proved, 1 *Jew.* 356, 358, 3 *Jew.* 126, 300, 340, 341, 4 *Jew.* 789, 937; Augustine and many bishops here forbade appeals to Rome, and checked the presumption of the pope, 2 *Ful.* 70, 71, 353, 1 *Jew.* 353, 355, 361, 370, 386, 389, 418, &c., 3 *Jew.* 216, 300, 4 *Jew.* 1053, *Park.* 111, *Phil.* 27; on metropolitans, 2 *Whitg.* 148; it prescribed the order of the priests and deacons receiving the communion, 1 *Jew.* 197; on excommunicated priests, 3 *Whitg.* 261; decree respecting an excommunicate person who had been reconciled in sickness, 1 *Jew.* 136; this synod (and that of 425?) condemned by Boniface II. as led by the devil, 3 *Jew.* 127, 128, 295, 296

—— (425): reproved pope Celestine for pride and lordliness, 3 *Jew.* 294, 295; the epistle to him, against appeals beyond sea, in which he is desired not to send his clerks, lest the smoky puff of the world should be brought into the church of Christ, 2 *Ful.* 71 n., 353, 1 *Jew.* 356, 389, 417, 3 *Jew.* 135, 295, 307, 311, 4 *Jew.* 679, 1124, 2 *Whitg.* 169 (see also the council of 419, which is not always clearly distinguishable from the present); corrupted by Harding, 3 *Jew.* 135; it allowed the title of primate, 2 *Whitg.* 170

CHALCEDON (451): some account of it, 1 *Bul.* 14; summoned by Martian, 1 *Jew.* 411, 4 *Jew.* 995, *Rog.* 204; held at Chalcedon against the pope's petition, 4 *Jew.* 997; pope Leo was called to the council by the emperors, *ib.* 996; 630 bishops present, *ib.* 772; Philippus, one of the pope's legates, had 157 subscribe before him, *ib.* 999; its confession of faith, taken out of the book of Isidore, 1 *Bul.* 19, 2 *Hoop.* 535; shewn by the martyr Vigilius not to be contrary to the doctrine of Cyril, 1 *Bul.* 20; received by our divines, 1 *Brad.* 371, 2 *Hoop.* 74, *Phil.* 35; it confirmed the Constantinopolitan creed as to the two natures of Christ, 3 *Bec.* 455; Dorotheus consented and subscribed, 4 *Jew.* 1025; cry of the bishops, "We all believe thus," &c., 3 *Jew.* 220, 4 *Jew.* 1043; Rogers says it had erred if Jerome had been away, *Rog.* 207, but, in fact, he died before it, *ib.* n.; his opinion accords not with it, 1 *Jew.* 423; his opinion received against it, *ib.* 227, 3 *Jew.* 219; it condemned for heretics the bishops Dioscorus, Juvenalis, and Thalassius, 4 *Jew.* 1021, 1022; Dioscorus declared he had the fathers for him, 1 *Jew.* 83, 84, 3 *Jew.* 226, 4 *Jew.* 783; the heretic Carosus also referred to fathers in support of his doctrine, 3 *Jew.* 226, 4 *Jew.* 783; Eutyches did the same, 3 *Jew.* 226, 4 *Jew.* 783; the synod condemned Eutyches, 1 *Jew.* 366, 3 *Jew.* 224, *Phil.* 185 n., and Nestorius, 1 *Jew.* 374, *Phil.* 185 n.; outcry of the bishops of Egypt against Theodoret, 2 *Whitg.* 318, 319; the council restores him, *ib.* 320, acquitting him of Nestorianism, *Rid.* 36; Cyril observed that all heretics out of the divinely inspired scriptures gather occasions of their error, 4 *Jew.* 752; the bishops of the East said, "Accursed be he that parteth Christ; accursed be he that divideth him," 3 *Jew.* 598; the synod speaks of the council of Ephesus as a general one, 1 *Jew.* 66; referred to on primacy, 2 *Hoop.* 237; what sort of primacy it allowed to Leo, 2 *Ful.* 363; it did not own the bishop of Rome as supreme, *Phil.* 39; it says the fathers gave privileges to the see of old Rome on account of the empire, and gave like privileges to Constantinople, or New Rome, for the same reason, 3 *Jew.* 306, 4 *Jew.* 1023; claim of the bishop of Constantinople, 2 *Whitg.* 168; the synod decreed that he should be in dignity next to the bishop of Rome, with equal privileges, 2 *Ful.* 288, 289, 308, 327, 332, 363, 364, 1 *Jew.* 413, 3 *Jew.* 220; corruptions in the Latin text of this canon, 2 *Ful.* 289 n.; order respecting the jurisdiction of the bishops of Rome, Alexandria, and Antioch, 1 *Jew.* 361; on the primacy of Antioch, *ib.* 366; the council falsely stated to have called Leo universal bishop, 1 *Jew.* 422—426, 2 *Jew.* 629, 632, 3 *Jew.* 300, 316, *Pil.* 520; it appointed patriarchs, 2 *Whitg.* 221; mentions the patriarchs of every diocese, 2 *Zur.* 228 n.; speaks of archbishops, 2 *Whitg.* 160, 196, 316, 431; on the authority of the metropolitan, *ib.* 272; shews why it had been directed that bishops should assemble twice a year, 4 *Jew.* 1049; decrees that none be ordained without a title, 1 *Whitg.* 479, 480; forbids clergymen to undertake secular business without necessity, 3 *Whitg.* 430, 431, or to become soldiers, *ib.* 431; forbids one clerk to sue another in a temporal court, 2 *Cran.* 465; canon against pluralities, 1 *Whitg.* 531; consecrated monasteries forbidden to be made dwelling-houses for laymen, 2 *Cran.* 465; edict of the emperors in this synod, 1 *Jew.* 82, 229 n.; how it allowed the imperial authority, 4 *Jew.* 1023, 3 *Whitg.* 307, 308; titles applied to the emperors, 1 *Jew.* 432, 4 *Jew.* 1014, 1023; it speaks of cities being honoured by the royal letters with the metropolitan name, 3 *Jew.* 315; refers to Theodosius as confirming a general council, 1 *Jew.* 412; in it the civil magistrate condemned three bishops to be deposed, 3 *Jew.* 145, 4 *Jew.* 1021, &c.; Gratian's shameless depravation of its twenty-eighth canon and other corruptions noted, 2 *Ful.* 288, 289, 364; why the same canon was omitted by Dionysius Exiguus, *ib.* 288 n.; the council alleged to have sought the pope's confirmation, 1 *Jew.* 410; how it followed Leo, 3 *Jew.* 219, 220; he said he approved what it had decreed touching matters of faith, 4 *Jew.* 915, but censured it in some respects, 1 *Jew.* 413, 423, 3 *Jew.* 220—226, 4 *Jew.*1109; the emperor Martian says, "By the holy edict of our majesty we confirm this reverend council," 4 *Jew.* 917, 998; references to it, 4 *Jew.* 822, 1003; cited (probably by mistake instead of the council of Châlons) on fasting, 2 *Bec.* 533

Châlons-sur-Saône (Cabilonense—643, 4): on the election of bishops, 1 *Whitg.* 411; it used the word "missa" for any kind of prayer, 1 *Jew.* 185; cited as ordaining that none should be counted to fast who ate before evensong was done, 2 *Bec.* 533 n

Clermont (Arvernense—535 or 549): decreed that all country priests and wealthy citizens, should on certain feasts resort to the cities, and communicate with their bishops, 1 *Jew.* 180, 2 *Jew.* 631

Cologne (1536): says, that the priests may not only mumble their prayers, but also pronounce them from their hearts, let the book of the law never be laid from their hands, 4 *Jew.* 812; the same council (?) on the public reading of legends, 3 *Whitg.* 347, 348

CONSTANCE (1414—18): held in a time of schism, 2 *Cran.* 488; it deposed three popes, and elected a fourth, *Whita.* 510; condemned and deposed John XXII. (otherwise XXIII. or XXIV.), 2 *Ful.* 269, 1 *Jew.* 35, 67, 406, 4 *Jew.* 704, 934, 935, 955; said that from his youth he had been a man of ill disposition, unchaste, dishonest, &c., 4 *Jew.* 702; spoke of an error of his respecting the soul, 3 *Jew.* 144, 4 *Jew.* 935; declared that faith should not be kept with heretics, 4 *Jew.* 955; the case of John Huss, *Rog.* 119 n., 120 n.; it unjustly condemned him and Jerome of Prague, 2 *Cran.* 37, (see their names); murdered two witnesses of the Lord, *Phil.* 396; betrayed and murdered them, notwithstanding their safe conduct, 4 *Jew.* 955; denounced the doctrine of Huss, 3 *Jew.* 162; broke faith with Jerome of Prague and others, *Phil.* 426; condemned several witnesses for the truth, *Phil.* 393; censured opinions of Wickliffe, *Bale* 9, 3 *Jew.* 162, 308, 309; decreed against Christ, 1 *Jew.* 214; condemned the article that the divinity and humanity are one Christ, 2 *Cran.* 37; decreed that the cup should not be given to the laity, 2 *Bec.* 244, 3 *Bec.* 275, 414, 415, 4 *Bul.* 416, 2 *Ful.* 31, 387, 1 *Jew.* 28, 35, 38, 63, 64, 2 *Jew.* 989; its doctrine on the eucharist soon controlled, *Coop.* 38; it declared the example of the primitive church not to be binding, 1 *Jew.* 39, 74; affirmed it to be needful to salvation to believe that the pope is universal (bishop), 3 *Jew.* 320; anathematized those who denied the distinction between a bishop and a priest, *ib.* 430; the council is declared by cardinal Cajetan to be justly abrogate, 1 *Jew.* 69

CONSTANTINOPLE *I.* (381): account of it, 1 *Brad.* 371 n., 1 *Bul.* 13, 2 *Whitg.* 315; summoned by Theodosius I., 1 *Jew.* 411, 4 *Jew.* 994, *Rog.* 204, 2 *Whitg.* 362; one hundred and fifty bishops present, 4 *Jew.* 772; they wrote to the emperor, "We are come to Constantinople by your majesty's commission," *ib.* 1004; the council condemned Macedonius, 3 *Jew.* 224, *Whita.* 449; its creed, 1 *Bul.* 16, 2 *Hoop.* 534; it appointed bishops with the consent of the people, 1 *Whitg.* 410; commanded that all disputes should be decided by the bishops of the province or neighbourhood, 2 *Cran.* 486; did not own the bishop of Rome as supreme, *Phil.* 39; what authority Damasus had in it, 4 *Jew.* 994; the epistle to him and the Western bishops, *ib.* 1124; the synod says that Constantinople ought to have the honour of primacy after Rome, because it is New Rome, 1 *Jew.* 370, 2 *Whitg.* 272; reserves the primacy to the church of Antioch, 1 *Jew.* 366; on metropolitans, primates, and archbishops, 2 *Whitg.* 163, 431; the bishops present besought the emperor Theodosius to ratify their decrees, 1 *Jew.* 412, 4 *Jew.* 917, 1001; this council allowed by Damasus, 1 *Jew.* 410, 4 *Jew.* 1001; received by our divines, 1 *Brad.* 371, 2 *Hoop.* 74

—— (448): condemned Eutyches, *Phil.* 185 n

—— (536); the epistle of Justinian, 3 *Whitg.* 304, 307; this synod (referred to as Const. V.) speaks of the people coming around the altar to hear the lesson, 1 *Jew.* 311, 2 *Jew.* 636, 3 *Jew.* 856; mentions clerks...of the catholic holy church of God, 1 *Jew.* 426; salutes the bishop as universal patriarch, &c., *ib.* 427; pope Agapetus said that from the time of Peter the apostle, the East church had never received any bishop consecrated by the hands of a bishop of Rome, except Mennas, 3 *Jew.* 331; this Mennas, bishop of Constantinople, was president of the council, 4 *Jew.* 1003; Paulus, bishop of Apamea, said to Justinian on the death of Agapetus, "Our

COUNCILS

Lord hath taken the pope away, that he might reserve the whole fulness of order unto your majesty," *ib.* 1033

CONSTANTINOPLE II. (553): notice of it, 1 *Bul.* 14; it resisted the pope, 2 *Ful.* 308

—— (587): conduct of John, bishop of Constantinople, 2 *Whitg.* 171, 172, 637

CONSTANTINOPLE III. (680—81): notice of it, 1 *Bul.* 14; the bishop of Athens was present, 4 *Jew.* 652; pope Agatho excused his absence to the emperor, *ib.* 999; Constantine Pogonatus not only sat amongst the bishops, but also subscribed with them, *ib.* 1024; he sat as moderator, 3 *Whitg.* 307; the late pope Honorius was condemned for following Sergius the heretic, 1 *Ful.* 76, 2 *Ful.* 312, 1 *Jew.* 400, 406, 4 *Jew.* 926; the council calls the faith of the Trinity a tradition, and speaks of the faith of two natures in Christ as the lively tradition of the apostles, 2 *Jew.* 673; confirms a former decree rejecting the Apocrypha, 1 *Ful.* 18; enjoins the mixed cup in the eucharist, *ib.* 261, 523; proves that consecration was used by the Greeks in Lent, only on Saturdays and Sundays, 1 *Jew.* 129, 246; Latin mass at this council, 2 *Brad.* 311; it was decreed, that no man should presume to remove priests from the company of their lawful wives, 3 *Jew.* 404, 422; the council declared it not meet for the orthodox to mutilate the sayings of the holy fathers, 1 *Jew.* 344; condemned the worship of images, *Phil.* 407, *Rid.* 497; the sixth synod referred to about apparel, 1 *Zur.* 159, 348; frequently confounded with the Quini-Sext council, *Calf.* 137, *Whita.* 39, 41 n. (which is probably referred to just above); its acts alleged to be forged, *Calf.* 137 n

—— (691), the *Quini-Sext* council, held *in Trullo:* some account of its acts, *Calf.* x, xi, 137, *Whita.* 41; it confirmed the council of Laodicea, 1 *Whitg.* 406, and the third council of Carthage, 3 *Jew.* 313, *Whita.* 39, 41, 55, 63; forbade the title of prince of priests, or high priest, 3 *Jew.* 313; decreed that the bishop of Constantinople should have equal authority with the bishop of Rome, *ib.* 300, 307, 4 *Jew.* 841; forbade the reception of the sacramental bread by the communicants in golden vessels, 1 *Jew.* 154, 1 *Zur.* 179 n.; on the apostolical canons, *Whita.* 566; it mentions St James's Liturgy, 1 *Jew.* 108; permits the marriage of the clergy before ordination, 2 *Ful.* 95; speaks of clerical offenders being put into the place of laymen, *Coop.* 159 n.; cited on oratories, 1 *Jew.* 180;

it allowed pictures of the Saviour instead of typical representations of him by a lamb, *Calf.* 137 n.; made a canon against crosses in the pavement, *ib.* x, xl, 2 *Ful.* 151, 152; cited on apparel, 2 *Whitg.* 41; see also 1 *Zur.* 159, 348, where *this* council is probably referred to; its acts alleged to be forged, *Calf.* 137 n

—— (754): held under Constantine Copronymus, *Calf.* xii, 46; it anathematized Jo. Damascene, *ib.* 71 n.; condemned image worship, 2 *Jew.* 659, 4 *Jew.* 1110, *Park.* 91, 3 *Tyn.* 183 n.; it decrees against images of Christ and of the saints, and various heresies, *Calf.* 138—154

CONSTANTINOPLE IV. (869): referred to about image worship, *Whita.* 509; of no authority, *ib.* 564

Elvira (Eliberitanum; near Granada—c. 305): not general, 2 *Ful.* 126; mistake made by Calfhill, and in one of the homilies, as to its date, *Calf.* 154, 2 *Ful.* 153; annotations on its decrees, *Calf.* 302 n.; it requires communion thrice a year, 1 *Jew.* 176, but the canon is not regarded as genuine, *Coop.* 101, 102; forbade pictures in churches, 2 *Bec.* 71, 2 *Brad.* 308, *Calf.* 154, 2 *Cran.* 179, 2 *Ful.* 153, 154, 1 *Jew.* 69, 70, 2 *Jew.* 659, 990, 4 *Jew.* 791, 1110, *Park.* 93, *Phil.* 407, *Rid.* 94; prohibited the lighting of candles in the day-time in cemeteries, *Calf.* 302, 2 *Ful.* 185; forbade women to watch at burial places, 3 *Jew.* 167; this synod was condemned by the second council of Nice, *Calf.* 155

EPHESUS (431): account of it, 1 *Bul.* 13, 14; summoned by Theodosius II., 1 *Jew.* 411, *Rog.* 204; he writes to it, *Whita.* 437; denied by some to be general, 1 *Jew.* 38; two hundred bishops present, 4 *Jew.* 772; Cyril presided in it, *ib.* 995; it calls him head of the bishops there assembled, 1 *Jew.* 438; a confession made by him and sanctioned by the council, 1 *Bul.* 17, 2 *Hoop.* 534; the profession of John, bishop of Antioch, *Whita.* 678; the condemnation of Nestorius, 1 *Jew.* 527, 531, 3 *Jew.* 224; the Euchites censured, *Sand.* 263; the council alleged as authorizing communion under one kind, 1 *Jew.* 220, 296; it did not own the bishop of Rome as supreme, *Phil.* 39; mentions the metropolitan, 2 *Whitg.* 431; allowed by Celestine, 1 *Jew.* 410; received by our divines, 1 *Brad.* 371 n., 2 *Hoop.* 74

—— *II.* (449): not lawful, but heretical, 1 *Jew.* 410; called by the Greeks σύνοδος λῃστρική, *Calf.* 155 n.; Dioscorus bishop of Alexandria was president, 4 *Jew.* 1003; it did not own the bishop of Rome as supreme, *Phil.* 39; it absolved Eutyches the heretic, and condemned the godly Flavian, 1 *Jew.* 35, 65, 4 *Jew.* 1109, *Phil.* 185 n.; censured Theodoret in his absence, 2 *Whitg.* 320; the synod condemned, *ib.*; Pighius speaks of it as general, yet allows that it determined wickedly, 1 *Jew.* 35, 65

Ferrara (1438): its acts set forth by Abramus, 2 *Jew.* 689 n.; the bishops there declared that with whatsoever power the church of Rome is endued, yet is it inferior to the universal church, represented by a general council, 4 *Jew.* 922; its acts make mention of a mass said by fifteen Greek priests, *ib.* 888

FLORENCE (1439—42): a conventicle of Antichrist, *Whita.* 40; some account of it, 2 *Bec.* 266, 2 *Cran.* 488, *Rid.* 135; assembled instead of that at Basil, 4 *Jew.* 1105; some Oriental bishops there complained of the forgery of pope Zosimus, 3 *Jew.* 126, 341, 4 *Jew.* 937; it aimed to reunite the East and West, *Phil.* 29, and effected a temporary union, *Rid.* 250 n.; the Greek deputies were blamed by those who sent them for consenting to Romish doctrines, *Pil.* 145, 146; the Greeks would not allow transubstantiation, 3 *Bec.* 426, 1 *Jew.* 139, 533, 2 *Jew.* 564, 578; they would not deliberate on that point, *Rid.* 237, 249; they affirmed that the sacrament is made by the words "This is my body," 2 *Jew.* 699; the council referred to on the eucharist, *Coop.* 38, 1 *Lat.* 209; it admitted apocryphal books, *Whita.* 39; first asserted seven sacraments, *ib.* 512; spurious catalogue of canonical books, ascribed to it by Carranza, 2 *Ful.* 222 n.; a decree of Eugenius IV. wrongly attributed to it by Hooker, Stillingfleet, and others, [as Bramhall,—v. 211., Oxf. 1845], *Calf.* 247 n

Frankfort (794): some account of it, *Calf.* 155, 1 *Zur.* 156 n.; summoned by Charlemagne, 4 *Jew.* 1049, *Rog.* 204, 1 *Zur.* 156 n.; regarded in France as a general council, 1 *Zur.* 156 n.; called by Harding a false feigned matter, 4 *Jew.* 1050; denied by some to have been held, 4 *Jew.* 1270, 1 *Zur.* 156; proofs of its authenticity, 4 *Jew.* 1054, 1055; it forbade the worship of images, 4 *Jew.* 1049, &c., 1 *Zur.* 156; condemned the second synod of Nice, *Calf.* 155, 2 *Ful.* 154, 4 *Jew.* 1049, 1054, &c., *Rid.* 94; the Caroline Books, *Calf.* 155, 379, 2 *Ful.* 154, 4 *Jew.* 1054; their contents, *Calf.* 156—175; extracts from them, *ib.* 359, 363, 364

Gangra (3 . .): held between 325 and 341, 2 *Bul.* 24 n.; or, as some think, before Nice, 4 *Jew.* 1049; placed by some as late as 365 or 370, 1 *Zur.* 159 n.; it censured those who objected to the offering or communion of a married priest, 2 *Cran.* 39, 169, 2 *Jew.* 989, 3 *Jew.* 404, 4 *Jew.* 804, *Pil.* 570; made a canon on standing at prayer, 2 *Cran.* 39; cursed those that for justification wore a cloak instead of a byrrhus, 3 *Jew.* 614, 2 *Whitg.* 28, 1 *Zur.* 159, 350; condemned those who taught that faithful rich men could have no hope to be saved by the Lord, unless they renounced and forsook all their possessions, 2 *Bul.* 24; took those for heretics who regarded not the fast of Lent, 3 *Jew.* 430; condemned the pride and errors of Eustathius, *Coop.* 127, 2 *Ful.* 89, 1 *Jew.* 181, 186, 194, 1 *Zur.* 159, 350; divers canons mentioned, 1 *Whitg.* 220

Gironne (Gerundense—517): decreed that all little churches should conform themselves to the cathedral churches, &c., 1 *Jew.* 179

Granada: v. *Elvira.*

Hippo (393 or 395): abridged in the third council of Carthage, 3 *Jew.* 146; would have only the canonical scriptures read in the church, 4 *Jew.* 815; shews that children of fourteen were allowed to be readers in the church, *ib.* 911; said to disprove the alleged succession of the popes from St Peter, *Poet.* 274 n.; ordered that no priest should appeal to Rome, 3 *Jew.* 216; decreed that the bishop of the first see should not be called prince of priests, but only the bishop of the first see, 1 *Jew.* 355, 370; shews that the sacrament was sometimes put into dead men's mouths, *ib.* 251

Hispalense: v. *Seville.*

Illiberitanum: v. *Elvira.*

Jerusalem (52): the apostles' council here (Acts xv.), 3 *Bul.* 52, 2 *Ful.* 135, 249, 4 *Jew.* 917, 1007, *Whita.* 431, 432, 2 *Whitg.* 232; whether Peter or James was president, 2 *Ful.* 249, 4 *Jew.* 917, *Whita.* 432, 2 *Whitg.* 276, 277; no contest about headship, 2 *Cran.* 76; the decree, 2 *Bul.* 272, 275. Bullinger likewise reckons the Pentecostal assembly (A.D. 33, Acts ii.) as a council of the apostles, 3 *Bul.* 52

Laodicea (366): various dates assigned to it, 1 *Whitg.* 405 n.; on the election of bishops, &c., *ib.* 366, 405, 406, 408, 459; on metropolitans, 2 *Whitg.* 159; on baptism in Lent, 2 *Cran.* 39; it proves that the sacrifice was not daily offered, 1 *Jew.* 201; prescribed consecration in Lent only on Saturdays and Sundays, 2 *Cran.* 39, 1 *Jew.*

129; directed the priest to communicate in the holy place, 1 *Jew.* 198; forbade the sending abroad of the communion, *ib.* 161; prohibited the oblation to be made in private houses, *ib.* 184, 2 *Whitg.* 543; rejected apocryphal books, 1 *Ful.* 18, *Rog.* 81, *Whita.* 306; decreed that nothing should be read or sung in the church but the canonical scriptures, 4 *Bul.* 193, 2 *Cran.* 39, 2 *Ful.* 89, 1 *Jew.* 265, *Rog.* 81, *Whita.* 54, 3 *Whitg.* 347, 348; ordained that the gospel, with other scriptures, should be read on the sabbath-day (Saturday), 4 *Jew.* 815, 856; forbade Christians to take unleavened bread of the Jews, 2 *Whitg.* 446, 447; on the service of the Greek churches, 1 *Jew.* 264; on catechumens and penitents, 1 *Ful.* 257 n.; canons respecting penance, *ib.* 432; it censured superstition in dress, 1 *Zur.* 159, 348; condemned the Angelici, 2 *Ful.* 42 n.; shameful corruption of the canon against them ("angelos" changed into "angulos") *ib.*; this synod was approved by the third council of Constantinople, *Whita.* 55

LATERAN III. (1179): reference to its decrees, 4 *Jew.* 1045 n.; Tripartitum Opusculum, a work annexed to this council, *Jew.* xliii; it declares that the study of philosophy was translated from Athens to Rome, and afterwards from Rome to Paris, 4 *Jew.* 654; remarks that if the Greeks are by a certain schism divided from the Latins, so are the Latins from the Greeks, and allows that the latter do, in some respects, more duly keep the customs of the apostles, *ib.* 884; observes that in many briefs there are contained so many indulgences, that good men marvel, &c., *ib.* 852; says, so excessive is the riot, as well in the prelates and bishops, as in the clerks and priests, that it is horrible to be told, 3 *Jew.* 417, 426, 4 *Jew.* 657; complains of the great multitude of monks and friars, 2 *Jew.* 1019, 4 *Jew.* 801, 1106

LATERAN IV. (1215): account of it, 2 *Bec.* 260; its acts, *Bale* 506; Innocent III. published his creed there, 3 *Bul.* 82, 4 *Bul.* 557; the council referred to on the eucharist, *Coop.* 38; it settled the doctrine of transubstantiation, 2 *Bec.* 260, 262, 268, 3 *Bec.* 274, 361, 426, 1 *Brad.* 511 n., 545, 3 *Bul.* 82, 1 *Hoop.* 526, 2 *Hoop.* 48 n., 522, 2 *Jew.* 549, 564, 1067, 1116, *Rid.* 16 n., 246; the term first used there, 1 *Jew.* 11, 44, 3 *Jew.* 488; it ordained that the sacrament should be reserved, 2 *Bec.* 253 n., 3 *Bec.* 373 n., 2 *Brad.* 310 n., 2 *Jew.* 556; required communion once a year, 3 *Bul.* 82, 1 *Brad.* 490 n.; commanded the reservation of chrism, 2 *Bec.* 253 n., 2 *Brad.* 310 n., 2 *Jew.* 556; ordained auricular confession, 2 *Brad.* 310 n., 3 *Bul.* 82, 2 *Ful.* 90, 1 *Hoop.* 526, 1 *Jew.* 120, 2 *Jew.* 1133; advanced the pope and clergy above earthly princes, *Rog.* 209; directed that archbishops should have their palls from the pope, 2 *Brad.* 310 n.; decreed that lest too great a diversity of religions (i. e. religious orders) should bring great offence into the church of God, no man should thenceforth devise any new religion, 4 *Jew.* 801, 1106

LATERAN V. (1512—17): it was only summoned to overthrow the council of Pisa, 1 *Jew.* 70, 4 *Jew.* 1110; Egidius said that so often as councils were discontinued, so often was the church destitute of Christ, 4 *Jew.* 720; pope Julius affirmed that no council is of any credit, nor ever will be, unless confirmed by the authority of the church of Rome, *ib.* 1115; pope Leo declared the pope to have authority over all councils, *ib.* 919; Chr. Marcellus addressed the pope as another God on earth, 2 *Jew.* 906, 3 *Jew.* 284; Stephen, bishop of Patraca, ascribed all power to the pope, 1 *Jew.* 94, 3 *Jew.* 284, 4 *Jew.* 832, 846; Simon Begnius, bishop of Madrusia, called pope Leo the lion of the tribe of Juda, the root of David, and the saviour, 4 *Jew.* 752; card. Cajetan's declarations, 1 *Jew.* 69 n.; he said to the pope, "Gird thy sword upon thy thigh, O thou most mighty," *ib.* 94 n.; the pope decreed to be above the council, 4 *Jew.* 1110; he gave commandment to all preachers, that no man should dare to speak of the (time of the) coming of Antichrist, 4 *Jew.* 744; the council records the abhorrence of the Latin church by the Greeks, 3 *Jew.* 196

London (1255): on the great payments exacted of the clergy, 4 *Jew.* 1080

LYONS (Lugdunense—1274): named, 1 *Hoop.* 347; it condemned the errors of the Greeks, *Whita.* 536 [qu. for "Innocent the fourth," read "Innocent the fifth"?]

Macra in France (...): bishops said to be entangled in worldly affairs, 4 *Jew.* 971; it declares that only Christ can be truly priest and king, and that since his incarnation the offices are separate, *ib.* 985

Mantua: an intended general council, summoned for May 1535, but not held, 2 *Cran.* 331 n., 467 n

Martin (Council of pope): v. *Rome* (650).

Mascon II. (Matisconense, 585): summoned by Gunthranus, *Rog.* 204; referred to on baptism at Easter and Pentecost, 4 *Bul.* 367 n.; it decreed that every Sunday the oblation of the altar should be offered of all, 1 *Jew.* 179; its directions respecting what remained of the sacrament, 2 *Jew.* 554

Mayence (Moguntinum—813): summoned by Charlemagne, *Rog.* 204; it decreed that the greater litany should be used in procession for three days, *Calf.* 297, 2 *Ful.* 183

—— (...): referred to on baptism at Easter and Pentecost, 4 *Bul.* 367 n

—— (...): says, images are not set up to the intent we should honour or worship them, 2 *Jew.* 657; directed that if they were abused they should be notably altered or abolished, *ib.* 647, 668

Meaux (Meldense—845): ordained the sacrament of confirmation, 2 *Jew.* 1125

Melchidense & Aquisgranum (...): erred about matrimony, 2 *Cran.* 37

Milan (Mediolanense—3..): held by order of the emperor, 1 *Jew.* 382; Auxentius there, 4 *Jew.* 951; called by Hilary the synagogue of the malignant, *Rog.* 210

Milevis II. (416): mentions that the Pelagians affirmed that the petition "Forgive us our debts," was to be said humiliter non veraciter, *Rog.* 135 n.; erroneously cited respecting the grace of God (see *Orange II.*), 3 *Bul.* 10; it forbade appeals beyond sea, 2 *Cran.* 486, 2 *Ful.* 71, 1 *Jew.* 388, 3 *Jew.* 216, *Rid.* 136, 260 n.; how Gratian corrupted this canon, 2 *Ful.* 71 n.; on primates, 2 *Whitg.* 272; it sent its decrees to Rome, 2 *Ful.* 351, 352

Moguntinum : v. *Mayence.*

Nantes (660): says, it is a peevish thing to whisper those things to the walls that pertain to the people, 4 *Jew.* 812

Neocæsarea (314 or 315): more ancient than the first Nicene, 4 *Jew.* 1049, 2 *Whitg.* 376 n.; it prohibited the marriage of priests, and forbade adultery, 2 *Ful.* 96, 97; directed that priests should not be made under the age of 30 years, 2 *Cran.* 39, 1 *Whitg.* 220; on chorepiscopi, 3 *Whitg.* 272

Nice I. (325): notice of it, 1 *Bul.* 12; summoned and held by Constantine, 2 *Bec.* 305, 2 *Cran.* 15, 2 *Ful.* 358, 1 *Hoop.* 276, 1 *Jew.* 411, 4 *Jew.* 695, 993, *Rog.* 204, 2 *Whitg.* 362; its date, *Pil.* 549, 2 *Whitg.* 142; conduct of Constantine with relation to it, *Whita.* 436, 3 *Whitg.* 306; it was attended by 318 bishops, 2 *Brad.* 312 n., 1 *Bul.* 56, 4 *Jew.* 772; pope Sylvester sent legates there, 4 *Jew.* 993; some other bishops also sent deputies, *ib.* 999; the bishop of Rome did not preside, *Phil.* 77, but Eustachius, bishop of Antioch, 1 *Jew.* 412, 4 *Jew.* 1003; Constantine addressed the bishops as "sacerdotes," 1 *Ful.* 268, and exhorted them to decide everything by the authority of scripture, 2 *Ful.* 380, 3 *Jew.* 227, *Whita.* 435, 678, 679; the council did not follow the multitude, 2 *Ful.* 64; it anathematized Arius, *Phil.* 295 n.; condemned him by the scripture, *Whita.* 562; yet afterwards the Arians became more mighty than before, 4 *Jew.* 908; the synod approved the term ὁμοούσιον, *Whita.* 535; set forth the common creed, 2 *Cran.* 15 (v. Creeds); its doctrine allowed, 1 *Brad.* 371, 1 *Bul.* 12, 2 *Hoop.* 74; it censured Paul of Samosata, 1 *Hoop.* 64; anathematized the writings of Eusebius, 2 *Ful.* 359 n.; said to have commanded that no Christian should be without the Bible in his house, 2 *Jew.* 670, *Whita.* 221; did not receive the book of Judith as canonical, *Whita.* 82; catechumens mentioned, 2 *Jew.* 673 n.; it is written in this council that our baptism is not to be considered with bodily eyes, but with the eyes of the mind, and that we should consider the divine power which lies hid in the water, 4 *Bul.* 309, 310, 1 *Jew.* 545, 3 *Jew.* 445, 541, and that we should look on the water of baptism as full of heavenly fire, 1 *Jew.* 466, 2 *Jew.* 781, 3 *Jew.* 445; it refers to the Lamb of God lying on the holy table, 1 *Jew.* 464, 466, &c., 522, 3 *Jew.* 540, *Pil.* 546, *Rid.* 248—250; speaks of Christ as offered without sacrifice, 2 *Jew.* 710; admonishes not to look down to the bread and cup, &c., 2 *Bec.* 295, 3 *Bec.* 267, 433, 3 *Jew.* 540, 544; calls the holy mysteries the pledges or tokens of our resurrection, 3 *Jew.* 540, 593; falsely alleged as saying that none of the apostles called them a figure of the body of Christ, &c., *Rid.* 249; canon as to the order in which the clergy and people should receive the communion, 3 *Bec.* 417, *Coop.* 30, 103, 157, 2 *Cran.* 171, 1 *Ful.* 261, 2 *Hoop.* 395, 1 *Jew.* 197; it declares that deacons have not power to offer, 1 *Ful.* 261, 1 *Jew.* 240 n.; said to have allowed the deacons in the absence of the bishop and priests to take out the communion and receive it, 2 *Ful.* 107, 1 *Jew.* 239; allowed communion at the point of death, *Coop.* 29, 2 *Ful.* 105, 106, 2 *Whitg.* 544; but the canon refers only to excommunicated persons being penitent, *Coop.* 153, 2 *Ful.* 106, 2 *Whitg.* 544; it confirmed the distinctions of ecclesiastical grades, *Rog.* 329; canon on the jurisdiction of the bishops of Alexandria, Rome, and Antioch, 2 *Cran.* 38, 486, 1 *Jew.* 69, 359, 403, 3 *Jew.* 225, 304, &c.; erroneously said to have appointed *four* patriarchs, *Phil.* 43, 2 *Whitg.* 220, 221 n.; the *word* does not occur till above a century afterwards, 2 *Zur.* 228 n.; the council did not own the bishop of Rome as supreme, or as greater than the other patriarchs, 2 *Hoop.* 233—235, 4 *Jew.* 838, *Phil.* 39; it recognized the jurisdiction of the see of Rome within certain territorial limits only, 1 *Jew.* 386, 3 *Jew.* 216, 4 *Jew.* 828; pretended decree acknowledging the appellate jurisdiction of the bishop of Rome, 2 *Ful.* 70, 71, 308, 353, 2 *Hoop.* 236, 1 *Jew.* 351, &c.; the council ordered that bishops should assemble twice a year, 4 *Jew.* 1049; allowed the offices of metropolitan, archbishop, &c., 2 *Hoop.* 237, 2 *Whitg.* 142; on the office and jurisdiction of metropolitans, 2 *Whitg.* 144, 148, 158, 430; it appointed the election of bishops to bishops, 1 *Whitg.* 460; commanded that bishops should be ordained by their metropolitans, *ib.* 439 n.; decreed that if any man were made a bishop without the consent of his metropolitan, he might not be a bishop, 3 *Jew.* 333; wrote to the church in Egypt concerning the election of ministers, 1 *Whitg.* 408, 409; ordered priests found eating in taverns to be excommunicated, 2 *Cran.* 39; referred to on deacons, 2 *Whitg.* 177; the council forbade the clergy to have women residing with them, except relations, 1 *Ful.* 261; durst not dissolve priests' marriages, 2 *Ful.* 153, 4 *Jew.* 1053; a strong attempt to do so successfully resisted by Paphnutius, 1 *Bul.* 401, 2 *Cran.* 169, 1 *Ful.* 480, 2 *Ful.* 240, 1 *Hoop.* 376, 1 *Jew.* 227, 425, 1 *Lat.* 288, *Pil.* 532, 576, *Rog.* 207, 3 *Tyn.* 157 n., 165; the statement denied or doubted by some Romanists, 1 *Hoop.* 376 n.; the council ordained that on Sundays and at Pentecost Christians should pray standing, *Calf.* 257, 413, 2 *Cran.* 38, *Whita.* 593, 666, 2 *Whitg.* 451; public confession spoken of, 3 *Jew.* 369; canon respecting penance, 1 *Ful.* 432; persons excommunicated by one bishop not to be received by another, 1 *Jew.* 388, 3 *Whitg.* 260; the bishops shouted, "Let the ancient orders hold still," 1 *Jew.* 2, 320, 4 *Jew.* 1042; there were some unseemly contests there, 2 *Whitg.* 436; by whom the council was approved, 1 *Jew.* 412; many thousands consented to it, 1 *Jew.* 358; alleged to have sought the pope's confirmation, 1 *Jew.* 410, 4 *Jew.* 914; allusion in one of its decrees to the fifty-second apostolic canon, 2 *Ful.* 106; divers canons mentioned, 1 *Whitg.* 220; their number variously reckoned, 2 *Whitg.* 151; only twenty genuine ones remain, 1 *Jew.* 359; the fathers cite some canons not found amongst the twenty, 2 *Whitg.* 152; some, it is said, were burned by heretics, 1 *Jew.* 351, 354; some are corrupt and counterfeit, 4 *Jew.* 937, 2 *Whitg.* 150; an interpolation in the eighteenth canon, 2 *Ful.* 107; the council falsified by Zosimus, *q. v.*; condemned by heretical councils, *Rid.* 134; confounded by some with the second Nicene synod, *Calf.* 154 n

NICE II. (787): corrupt, idolatrous, and wicked, 1 *Ful.* 260, 2 *Jew.* 653, 1 *Whitg.* 531; an heretical conventicle, *Whita.* 564; many of the bishops of Greece were present, 4 *Jew.* 652; on the authorities alleged there, *Calf.* 345 n.; the fictitious Liber de Passione Imaginis Christi, 2 *Ful.* 200; false testimony adduced as if from Ambrose, *ib.* 207; the council anathematized imagebreakers, 1 *Ful.* 198—201, *Phil.* 406; an argument used there for images in churches, 1 *Jew.* 78; vanities and idolatrous fables in this council, 2 *Jew.* 658, 664; it affirmed that Christ dwelt in dead men's bones, *ib.* 594; denied that there were two kinds of worship, *ib.* 666; decreed the adoration of images, *Calf.* 48, 1 *Jew.* 548, 4 *Jew.* 791, 792, 1055, 1109, 1110, *Park.* 91, 92, *Rid.* 94, *Rog.* 209, 3 *Tyn.* 183, thereby contradicting scripture, general councils, and ancient doctors, *Whita.* 509; referred to respecting the picture sent to Abgarus, *Calf.* 41 n.; on the emperor's image, 2 *Jew.* 604; canon against pluralities, 1 *Whitg.* 530, 531; it allowed a clerk to labour with his hands rather than to have two benefices, 3 *Whitg.* 445; rejected the false epistle to the Laodiceans, *Whita.* 108, 303; Leontius said there, what an altar or a sacrifice is, Christians in a manner do not know, 2 *Jew.* 735; it condemned the council of Elvira, *Calf.* 155; recognized the Quini-Sext council, *ib.* 137 n.; decrees of the council of Constantinople, A.D. 754, preserved among its acts, *Calf.* 71 n., 138 n., *Park.* 91 n.; it declares that pope Honorius was condemned for a heretic in two general councils, 4 *Jew.* 926; calls Eupsychius a priest of the church of Cæsarea, 3 *Jew.* 125, 410, 4 *Jew.* 805; Petrus protopresbyter and Petrus presbyter, the pope's legates, subscribed before all the bishops, 4 *Jew.* 912; it was condemned by Charlemagne and the council of Frankfort, *Calf.* 155, &c., 2 *Ful.* 154, *Park.* 92, *Rid.* 94; contents of the Caroline Books in reply to it, *Calf.* 156—175; its decrees rejected in England and France, 2 *Ful.* 23

Orange I. (Arausicanum—441): forbade catechumens to enter the baptistery, 2 *Jew.* 706; prohibited the celebration of the eucharist on Good Friday and Easter eve, 1 *Jew.* 246

Orange II. (529): declares that to believe, to will, and to be able to do as we should do, is wrought by the Holy Ghost, 3 *Bul.* 10; subscribed by the prince's ambassadors and noblemen, 4 *Jew.* 1024, 1025

Orleans I. (Aurelianense—511): called litanies rogations, 2 *Ful.* 183; required communion thrice a year, 1 *Jew.* 176; this (?) synod ordered the sacrament to be burned when mouldy, 3 *Bec.* 374; it (?) decreed that every Christian man might have an oratory in his house, but not have mass said there, 1 *Jew.* 184; a canon relative to the erection of churches, attributed to the first council of Orleans, borrowed from a novel of Justinian, *Calf.* 135, 136, 2 *Ful.* 150

—— *II.* (538): summoned by Childebert, *Rog.* 205

Oxford (1222): a deacon degraded for apostasy, and afterwards burned, *Bale* 3

—— (....): forbade the sale of masses, 3 *Jew.* 552; the name of Christ omitted in its acts, and our lady's name put in its place, *ib.* 577

Paris (551?): in the time of Childebert, *Rog.* 205

—— *VI.* (...): referred to on baptism at Easter and Whitsuntide, 4 *Bul.* 367 n

—— (...): Probianus, bishop of Bourges, consented and subscribed at a synod here, 4 *Jew.* 1025; a council of Paris universally scoffed at, 1 *Jew.* 70

—— *Pisa* (1511): the Lateran council summoned to repeal its decrees, 1 *Jew.* 70, 4 *Jew.* 1110

Plaisance (Placentinum—1095): directed that none should be ordained without a title, 1 *Whitg.* 480—482; on archdeacons, 2 *Whitg.* 176

Quini-sext: v. *Constantinople* (691)

Ratisbon (....): a council at Reinspurg declared that pope Hildebrand, under a colour of holiness (by forbidding priests' marriage) had laid the foundation for Antichrist, 4 *Jew.* 744

Rheims (813): summoned by Charlemagne, *Rog.* 204

Rheims (9..): a council under Hugh Capet, in which Arnulphus proclaimed the pope Antichrist, 4 *Jew.* 744, *Rog.* 182, 347

—— (1119): Thurstan abp of York consecrated there, *Pil.* 584; in this council, or in one held about this time, Bernard is said to have severely censured the Romish clergy, 1 *Jew.* 121 (& al. v. Bernard).

Rimini (Ariminense—359): not allowed, and why, 1 *Jew.* 410, 3 *Jew.* 217; it most impiously decreed that Christ is not God, 4 *Jew.* 1109; confirmed the Arian heresy, *Rog.* 209; rejected the term ὁμοούσιον, *Whita.* 535; Ruffinus says none of the bishops there understood the word, *ib.* 139; condemned by a council at Rome in the time of Damasus, 1 *Jew.* 413; Basil's advice respecting its acts, *Whita.* 439; abhorred by Ambrose, *Calf.* 345; rejected by Augustine, *ib.* 10, 2 *Jew.* 638, 996; Gelasius cautions against it, 1 *Jew.* 111, 112

Rome (2..): councils here in Cyprian's time, 1 *Bul.* 12 n

—— (251): held against Novatian, 4 *Jew.* 1007

—— *II.* (325): a council alleged to have been held by pope Sylvester at the very time of the council of Nice, 4 *Jew.* 993; it is declared therein that the pope is to be judged of no man, 1 *Jew.* 68, 78, 3 *Jew.* 222, 339, 4 *Jew.* 1000; said to have decreed that no priest should make the chrism, for Christ of chrism hath his name, 4 *Jew.* 1000

—— (3..): a council under Damasus condemns the Arian synod of Ariminum, 1 *Jew.* 413

—— (496): seventy bishops sat there, *Calf.* 171 n.; the council received apocryphal books, *Whita.* 39, 44; denounced the Recognitions, *Calf.* 21; its opinion on the acts of Sylvester, *ib.* 174 n.; on the books of Lactantius, *ib.* 181; on the Scripta de Inventione S. Crucis, *ib.* 324 n

—— *III.* (502?): at a synod in the time of Symmachus, king Odoacer marvelled that anything was attempted without his knowledge, 4 *Jew.* 952, 1001

—— (650): the council of pope Martin [that of Rome, 650?] on metropolitans, 2 *Whitg.* 241

—— *V.* (731): confirmed image worship, *Calf.* 48

—— *VI.* (732): enjoined the worship of images, 2 *Brad.* 309, *Calf.* 48; this or the preceding council (or perhaps that of 769) said to have confuted the Iconomaches, *Phil.* 406

Rome (8..): a council under Nicolas I. prohibited any being present at the mass of an unchaste priest, 1 *Jew.* 70, 4 *Jew.* 801

—— (1050): condemned Berengarius, 2 *Hoop.* 48 n

—— (1059): referred to on the eucharist, *Coop.* 39; here Lanfranc opposed the opinions of Berengarius, 1 *Hoop.* 117 n., whom the council compelled to subscribe that Christ is in the sacrament sensibly, 1 *Jew.* 446, 459; remarkable gloss on the recantation, *ib.* 459; this synod seems to be that referred to *Grin.* 73 n. as the second of Lateran; reference to it with respect to unchaste priests, 4 *Jew.* 802

—— (1099): Urban II. here anathematized all clerks who should do homage to any prince for their preferments, 1 *Tyn.* 380 n

—— (1538): the assembly of eight cardinals, in the time of Paul III., 1 *Jew.* 469; report of the cardinals, &c. as to the state of the church, 4 *Jew.* 1107; on the corruption of manners at home, 2 *Jew.* 728, 807; they took order for the abating of the multitude of friars and monks, *ib.* 1019

Rouen (Rothomagense—1072?): first forbade that the eucharist should be delivered into the hands of the laity, 3 *Bec.* 412, *Hutch.* 230

Salegunstadiense: v. *Selingstad*.

Saragossa (Cæsaraugustanum— ...): censured those who received the sacrament, and did not eat it presently in the church, 1 *Jew.* 148 n., 242

Sardica (347): summoned by Constantius, 2 *Whitg.* 362; Cusanus says Augustine held not this for a catholic council, but rather for a council of Arian heretics, 4 *Jew.* 938; British bishops there, 3 *Jew.* 165; remarks on the famous decree attributed to it respecting appeals to Rome, 2 *Ful.* 70, 71, and see 308, 353; reference to the same, 4 *Jew.* 838; the synod ordered that clergy excommunicated by one bishop should not be received by another, 3 *Whitg.* 261; on excommunication by a bishop in anger, *ib.* 262; this council mistakenly alleged for Nice, 4 *Jew.* 937, 938

Seleucia (359): not lawful, 1 *Jew.* 410

Selingstad (Salegunstadiense—1022): forbade any priest to offer more than three masses in a day, 2 *Jew.* 626, 633

Sens (1140): Abelard compelled to recant, 1 *Bec.* 337

Sens (....): preferred images to books, 2 *Jew.* 660

Seville II. (Hispalense—619?): reserves the consecration of altars, churches, virgins, &c. to the bishop, and forbids priests to administer the sacraments or to preach in his presence, 2 *Whitg.* 374

Sinuessa (303): fabulous, 2 *Ful.* 364, 365 n., 3 *Jew.* 340 n.; said to have decreed that the pope should be judged by no man, 3 *Jew.* 339, 4 *Jew.* 833; yet Marcellinus is alleged to have been judged by it, 2 *Ful.* 364, 365, 3 *Jew.* 339, 340

Sirmich (Sirmiense, or Syrmiense—351, 357, 358): not lawful, 1 *Jew.* 410; condemned the orthodox as Homoousians, and subscribed to the impiety of the council of Ariminum, 4 *Jew.* 1109; willed Felix and Liberius to be bishops at Rome together, 1 *Jew.* 377; statement that Athanasius went away (qu. from Tyre?), 4 *Jew.* 961

Spain: v. *Braga*.

Strenaeshalch (now Whitby—6..): kings Oswine and Alfride there, 2 *Ful.* 16

Syrmiense: v. *Sirmich*.

Tela, in Spain (...): asserted to have forbidden appeals to Rome, 1 *Jew.* 388, 3 *Jew.* 216

Teuver: v. *Tribur*.

Toledo I. (400): anathematized those who should receive any other scriptures than those received by the church, *Whita.* 326; denounced heresies respecting the Godhead and manhood of Christ, 3 *Bul.* 268; condemned the Priscillianists, who thought man's body to be governed by the stars, 2 *Bul.* 363; its creed, 1 *Bul.* 22, 2 *Hoop.* 536; its doctrine approved, 1 *Brad.* 371 n.; this synod is stated to have permitted concubinage to the unmarried; Gratian says it enjoined it, but in editions of the Corp. Jur. Can. subsequent to the reformation, the passage has been altered, 4 *Jew.* 631, 3 *Tyn.* 40 n

—— *III.* (...): prescribed that the articles of faith should be recited, that the people might present hearts purified to receive the body and blood of Christ, 3 *Bec.* 414

—— *IV.* (633): called ignorance the mother of all errors, and declared it to be most of all to be eschewed in priests, 1 *Bec.* 384, 1 *Jew.* 57, 334, 2 *Jew.* 800; prohibited trine immersion in baptism, 2 *Bec.* 227 n., 4 *Bul.* 365, 2 *Cran.* 58, *Whita.* 593; directed the priests and deacons to communicate at the altar, the clerks in the choir, the people outside the choir, 1 *Jew.* 198; on the election of priests, 1 *Whitg.* 411; on certain priests who used the Lord's prayer only on Sunday, 1 *Jew.* 170; it decreed that women unlawfully joined with priests, should be removed by the bishop, and sold, 4 *Jew.* 639; its creed, 1 *Bul.* 24; its doctrine approved, 1 *Brad.* 371 n

Toledo VI. (638): in what sense the word primacy is used by it, 1 *Jew.* 366

—— *VIII.* (653): says it is better not to fulfil a vow than to commit wickedness, 1 *Bec.* 372, 3 *Jew.* 400

—— *XI.* (675): ordered that if any man received not the sacrament delivered by the priest, he should be excommunicated, 1 *Jew.* 251; on the communion of the sick, 2 *Bec.* 245, 1 *Jew.* 251

—— *XII.* (681): speaks of several masses as celebrated in a day, 2 *Jew.* 626, 638, &c.; sacrifice and receiving noted as sundry things, 1 *Jew.* 129; the use of images condemned, 2 *Bec.* 71 n., *Phil.* 407

—— *XVI.* (694?): referred to against images, 2 *Bec.* 71 n

Toulouse (1229): first forbade the laity to possess the scriptures in their own tongue, 1 *Tyn.* 132 n

Tours I. (461 *): forbids a clerk to become a layman, 2 *Whitg.* 382

—— *II.* (567): commanded the Lord's body to be laid up under the cross, *Calf.* 136, 2 *Ful.* 150; (this council?) referred to about providing a pix, 3 *Bec.* 373

—— *III.* (...): charged bishops not to give themselves to feasts, 2 *Whitg.* 382; its canon concerning the translation of homilies, 2 *Ful.* 15; this seems to be the council summoned by Charlemagne, *Rog.* 204

TRENT (1545 — 63): v. Catechisms, Chemnitius.

No general council, 4 *Jew.* 1051, *Whita.* 40, but a conciliabulum of a few popish heretics, 2 *Ful.* 231; an evil confederacy, *Lit. Eliz.* 619; assembled more by the instigation of the emperor Charles, than willingly, 4 *Jew.* 1102; the design of it, 3 *Bul.* 119, 4 *Bul.* 529; the indiction, or calling of the prelates, 4 *Bul.* 529, 530; the council opened by card. Hosius, 1 *Ful.* 8 n., 1 *Zur.* 113 n.; its decrees, sessions, and prorogations, 4 *Bul.* 531, 532, 2 *Zur.* 60, 83 n., 3 *Zur.* 23, 254; nothing done uprightly or by good order, 4 *Jew.* 1084; references to it, *Phil.* 397, *Pra. Eliz.* 420 n., 1 *Zur.* 136, 325, 2 *Zur.* 250; the pope wished it to be removed to Bologna, 3 *Zur.* 58; protest of the emperor Charles, the French king, and other Christian princes, 4 *Jew.* 905, 1052; slowness of its proceedings, 1 *Zur.* 118, 124, 341; only forty bishops present, 4 *Jew.* 905, 1056; only twenty-two at first, *ib.* 905 n.; Harding says there were nearly two hundred, *ib.* 1051; Pates, sometime bishop of Worcester, sat there, *ib.* 905, 1056, *Phil.* xxxvii, 1 *Zur.* 79 n., also Goldwell of St Asaph, *Phil.* xxxvii, also Wauchop, titular archbishop of Armagh, 4 *Jew.* 905, 1056; two of the bishops were slain in adultery, *ib.* 905, 913, 1056; Isidore Clarius was there, 1 *Ful.* 62 n.; the Protestants thought of attending, 2 *Cran.* 430 n.; Elizabeth refused to send representatives, 1 *Zur.* 101, see 4 *Jew.* 910 n.; why the English would not go there, 4 *Jew.* 898, 953; Melancthon and Brentius went to defend the confessions of their churches, *Whita.* 10; the reformed were not allowed a hearing, 1 *Jew.* 62, 3 *Jew.* 204, 207 n., 208, 4 *Jew.* 953, 1114; the pope's safe conducts, 4 *Jew.* 953, 954; the agreement of the Tridentine fathers, *ib.* 956; the freedom of the council, *ib.* 957; Jewel's Apology read there, 3 *Jew.* 186; two divines were ordered to reply to it, *ib.*; Orationes in Concil. Trident. habitæ (ed. Dudithius), *Jew.* xxxvi; for the speeches of Amb. Catharinus and Cornelius bishop of Bitonto, see Catharinus and Cornelius; Antonius Marinarius said, If the faith of the gospel were the rule of our life, we should be Christians indeed, as now by titles and ceremonies we are called Christians, 4 *Jew.* 874; what the French king's ambassador said about councils, *ib.* 908, 916, 947, 948, 949, *Rog.* 210; decree concerning the canon of scripture, 2 *Ful.* 222; rejecters of the Apocrypha accursed, *Rog.* 83 n.; what the council decreed concerning the authenticity of the Vulgate, 2 *Jew.* 831, 4 *Jew.* 907, *Whita.* 110, 111, 143, 145, &c.; it censured the translations of Isidore Clarius, 1 *Ful.* 287; its judgment as to vernacular versions, *Whita.* 209; it made no decree on the authority of scripture, *ib.* 275; its decree concerning the interpretation of scripture, *ib.* 402, 410; the reception of unwritten tradition commanded, *ib.* 502; it made tradition equal to the holy scriptures, *Rog.* 79, 200, 209; on freewill, *ib.* 106 n.; on works before justification, *ib.* 128; on original sin, 4 *Jew.* 786; from the decree on this point the virgin is excepted, *Rog.* 99 n., 134 n.; on concupiscence, 3 *Jew.* 464, *Rog.* 102 n., 103 n.; on sin

---

* The first council in Sir N. H. Nicolas's list, is that of 567.

after baptism, *Rog.* 139 n.; on justification, *ib.* 115, 116, 124, 127 nn.; on works before justification, *ib.* 127 n.; on works of supererogation, *ib.* 130; it says that we should ever doubt our election and justification, *ib.* 113 n., 151 n.; curses all who say that the sacraments of the new law were not all ordained of our Lord Jesus Christ, or that there are fewer or more than seven, 3 *Jew.* 460, and all who hold that grace is not given by the sacraments ex opere operato, 2 *Jew.* 751; a decree passed respecting the Lord's supper, 3 *Zur.* 24 n.; the council anathematizes all who should hold that it is necessary for infants to receive the communion, an opinion maintained by St Augustine and pope Innocent I., 2 *Ful.* 41 n.; allows either leavened or unleavened bread, according to custom, 1 *Jew.* 534 n.; on consecration in silence, 2 *Jew.* 697; on transubstantiation, 2 *Brad.* 227 n.; one whole summer spent about the communion of the cup, 4 *Jew.* 948; it granted the communion in both kinds to some countries on certain conditions, 1 *Jew.* 205, 3 *Jew.* 203; evaded the question by referring it entirely to the decision of the pope, *Grin.* 22 n.; accursed all who should maintain the need of communion in both kinds, 1 *Jew.* 231, 3 *Jew.* 597; provided that little sins need not be uttered in confession, 3 *Jew.* 372; on penance, 1 *Brad.* 46 n.; on attrition, 1 *Tyn.* 265 n.; it declared extreme unction to be a sacrament, *Calf.* 248; maintained the invocation of saints, *Rog.* 209; decreed that relics should be worshipped, *ib.* 224; ratified the doctrine of purgatory, 3 *Bul.* 389, *Rog.* 214; affirmed that Christ, descending into hell, liberated the fathers, *Rog.* 66 n.; its decree concerning Latin service, *Whita.* 250; arguments in defence of that decree refuted, *ib.* 251, &c.; it confessed the pope to be above the council, 1 *Jew.* 68; reserved, in all things, the authority of the apostolic see, 4 *Jew.* 773; discussions on the order of bishops, 2 *Bec.* 319 n., 1 *Brad.* 506 n.; it decreed that all bishops should preach the gospel, 4 *Jew.* 821, 1111; ordained that one man should not have two benefices at one time, *ib.*; cursed those who should say that they who minister neither the word of God nor the sacraments are no priests, 3 *Jew.* 309, 310; the legates complained that priests differed from laymen only in apparel, 4 *Jew.* 971; Jac. Nanchiantes bishop of Chioca obliged to crave pardon of the pope, *ib.* 955; the council condemned the cardinal de Châtillon, 1 *Zur.* 250 n.; its Index, *Calf.*

155 n.; the council ended, 4 *Jew.* 906; Jewel's letter to Scipio, a gentleman of Venice, about this council (Latin and English), *ib.* 1093—1126; proposed synod of the reformed churches in opposition to the Tridentine council, 2 *Cran.* 430—434, 3 *Zur.* 23, 502 n

Tribur (or Teuver—1036?): forbade the ministration of the sacrament in wooden vessels, 4 *Bul.* 420; referred to on private mass, 1 *Jew.* 106 n

Trullo (In): v. *Constantinople* (691)

Turonense or *Tyronense*: v. *Tours.*

Tyre (335): Athanasius said to have departed from it, 4 *Jew.* 951 n.; he was condemned by it, 2 *Ful.* 358, 1 *Jew.* 392; Constantine cited to his camp the bishops who had been present at it, 1 *Jew.* 396, 4 *Jew.* 963

Urbanum, i. e. of pope Urban II.: v. *Plaisance.*

Vaison II. (Vasense 529): referred to, 1 *Jew.* 106 n.; conc. Vas. III. al. II. (believed to be the same), allowed the reading of homilies, 3 *Whitg.* 345, 347, 348

Valence (374): ordered clerks defiled with mortal sin to be deposed, 3 *Jew.* 309

——— (1248): referred to on the eucharist, *Coop.* 39

Vangionum (In civitate): v. *Worms.*

Verceil (1050): condemned Jo. Scotus Erigena, 200 years after his death, *Grin.* 74; transubstantiation unknown until after it, 1 *Hoop.* 118, 524

VIENNE (1311, 12): decreed that there should be professors of Hebrew and Greek in all universities, *Whita.* 468

Whitby: v. *Strenaeshalch.*

Winchester (1076): enjoined celibacy on the clergy, 2 *Ful.* 23, 93

Worms (868?): referred to on baptism at Easter and Whitsuntide, 4 *Bul.* 367 n.; (the same synod?) says the dipping into the water in baptism is the going down into hell, and the coming out of the water is the resurrection, 3 *Jew.* 593

——— (1076): its charges against pope Hildebrand, 4 *Jew.* 641, 825

Counsel: good counsel, 2 *Bul.* 51

Counsellors: v. Lawyers.

The duty of counsellors of state, *Sand.* 110

Country: how greatly we are bound to it, 1 *Bec.* 232; it is included in the term "parents," in the fifth commandment, 1 *Bul.* 268; how to be honoured, *ib.* 275; on fighting in defence of it, *ib.* 276; we must pray for it, *ib.* 279; the fervent affection which some have had to their country, 1 *Bec.* 233, &c., 1 *Bul.* 278; the affection of Englishmen to theirs, 1 *Bec.* 235; that of Becon, *ib.*

Couper (Tho.), bishop: *v.* Cooper.

Couppage (......), a priest: 1 *Brad.* 517

Coursely: cursorily, 2 *Jew.* 601

Court: *v.* Courts.

Courtenay (Will.), abp of Canterbury: attends a parliament at Cambridge, *Park.* 300 n.; said to have enriched himself with money gathered to rebuild Paul's cross, *Pil.* 606; he persecuted Wickliffe, *Bale* 326

Courtenay (Will.), earl of Devon [so called, but he was attainted in his father's lifetime]: Catherine his wife, daughter of king Edward IV., 3 *Zur.* 625

Courtenay (Hen.), next earl of Devon, and marq. of Exeter: near to the crown, 3 *Zur.* 207, 625 n.; beheaded, 2 *Cran.* 386 n., 3 *Zur.* 207, 625 n

Courtenay (Edw.), next earl of Devon, and marq. of Exeter: excepted from an act of indemnity, 3 *Zur.* 207; in prison, *ib.* 220; released by queen Mary, *ib.* 367, 368; mentioned, after his restoration, *Now.* i, *Phil.* 182; personated by Cleobury, 3 *Zur.* 133 n.; his death at Padua, *ib.*

Courtiers: their character, *Pil.* 289, 309; examples of good ones, *ib.* 294; Nehemiah an example to them, *ib.* 288, 293

Courtop Street, in Kent: the residence of Elizabeth Barton, 2 *Cran.* 65, 252, 272; our lady of Court of Strett, *ib.* 272, 273 n

Courts (Civil): courts of law and conscience, *Pil.* 466; the court of Augmentations, 1 *Lat.* 261 n.; the court of Chancery, suits there, 2 *Cran.* 257, 306, 315; the Exchequer, a writ therefrom, *Park.* 163; the court of First-fruits and Tenths, 2 *Cran.* 489; the court of the Marches, 3 *Whitg.* 604; the Star-chamber, *Grin.* 344, 392, *Park.* 418, 427, 3 *Whitg.* 604; an order made there for the expulsion of sundry of the perverse sort in religion from the Inns of Court, *Park.* 384; the Court of Wards, 2 *Cran.* 368, 1 *Lat.* 69: (some local courts are mentioned under the names of the places where they are holden).

Courts (Ecclesiastical): *v.* Proctors.

The ecclesiastical courts briefly described, 2 *Zur.* 359, 360; of bishops' courts and their officers, 3 *Whitg.* 265; their process in the prince's name, *ib.* 267; their jurisdiction in matrimonial causes, 2 *Cran.* 249, 252, 253, (and see Marriage); dispensations sold therein, 2 *Zur.* 130; letter from Grindal to the officers of his courts, *Grin.* 361; the court of Arches, 1 *Lat.* 52 n., 2 *Lat.* 414, 1 *Tyn.* 235, 238, 2 *Zur.* 360; once sat in St Paul's, *Pil.* 540; a suit in this court, 2 *Cran.* 364; its licences, 3 *Whitg.* 276; letter to the dean, 2 *Cran.* 253; the Commissaries' court, *Rog.* 310, 3 *Whitg.* 279; the Consistory courts, 1 *Lat.* 52; the court of Faculties, 3 *Whitg.* 8, 11, 12, 265, 1 *Zur.* 164, 179, 180, 2 *Zur.* 149, 360; Grindal's account of it, *Grin.* 446; he and Parker desired its abolition, *Grin.* 448, *Park.* 363

Courts of the Lord's house: what is signified thereby, 1 *Bec.* 300

Cousins: included in the term parents in the fifth commandment, 1 *Bul.* 269

Cousin (Jo.), or Cousins: minister of the French church in London, *Grin.* 310 n., 313 n., 2 *Zur.* 96, 170

Coutances (Arth. bp of): *v.* Cossé (A. de).

Cove, near Dunwich, Suffolk: the birthplace of Bale, *Bale* vii.

Covel (Jo.): Acc. of the Gr. Ch., 2 *Bec.* 266 n

Covell (Will.): his answer to Jo. Burges, *Rid.* 533

Covenants, Testaments: *v.* Law, Gospel.

Tyndale's definition of the word testament, 1 *Tyn.* 9, 93 n., 409, see also 93, 105, 364, 365, 379, 476, 3 *Tyn.* 27; covenants were ratified by the slaying of beasts, 4 *Bul.* 245, 2 *Tyn.* 215; covenants amongst the Jews, 1 *Tyn.* 347, 348; covenant of God and man, 1 *Brad.* 322, 326, 2 *Bul.* 169, *Lit. Edw.* 503, (552), 1 *Tyn.* 403, 469, 470; some feign appointments between men and God to which he never subscribed, 2 *Tyn.* 103; the covenant made with Adam, 2 *Bul.* 169; with Noah, *ib.* 169, 1 *Tyn.* 348; with Abraham, 2 *Bul.* 169, 170, 1 *Tyn.* 349; how long this league should last, 2 *Bul.* 170; its conditions, *ib.* 170, 171; circumcision the sign or seal of it, *ib.* 172; the old and new covenants contrasted, 2 *Bul.* 293, &c., *Hutch.* 246, 1 *Tyn.* 363, 364, 476; both were of force from the beginning, *Hutch.* 326; both are yet operative, *ib.* 247; the old testament was confirmed with blood, 1 *Tyn.* 363; it was fearful and terrible, *ib.* 364; its rewards were temporal, *ib.* 415; its conditions, *ib.*; the new covenant, spoken of in Jer. xxxi, *Whita.* 561; made in Christ's blood, 1 *Tyn.* 363; it was from the beginning, *ib.* 417; ours and the fathers' are one, 2 *Bul.* 283, 293; it is gentle, and promising mercy, 1 *Tyn.* 364; its effects, when believed, *ib.* 417; the free promise is a covenant on God's behalf

COVENANTS — COVETOUSNESS

only, 1 *Brad.* 327; God's covenant in Christ's blood depends not on us, 2 *Brad.* 153; how God's covenant is with those that walk and are perfect before him, 1 *Bec.* 210; on the use of the word covenant with respect to sacraments, 4 *Bul.* 253; why the Lord's supper is called a testament, *ib.* 403; why God's word is called a testament, *Now.* (2), 114, *Whita.* 651; God's testament neither to be augmented nor diminished, 1 *Bul.* 114

— The Scottish covenant: renewed by James VI., 2 *Zur.* 331

Covent: convent, 2 *Tyn.* 24

Coventry, co. Warwick: monks put out in Richard I.'s days, *Pil.* 610; martyrs there, *Bale* 63, *Poet.* 164, *Rid.* 384 n., 1 *Zur.* 86; the queen of Scots removed thither from Tutbury, 1 *Zur.* 217, 247 n

Coverdale: a district in Richmondshire, 2 *Cov.* vii.

COVERDALE (Myles), bp of Exeter: *v.* Bible, English.

A short biographical notice, 1 *Cov.* vii, &c.; a more extended memoir, 2 *Cov.* vii, &c.; Tanner's account of him, *ib.* xix; Bale's, *ib.* xxii; his birth, *ib.* vii; sent to Cambridge, *ib.*; ordained priest, *ib.*; supports the reformation, *ib.* viii; said by Foxe (but it is believed erroneously) to have assisted Tyndale in his translations at Hamburgh, *ib.* ix, 1 *Tyn.* xxxix; he publishes his Bible, 2 *Cov.* ix; and new editions thereof, *ib.* x; goes to Paris to superintend lord Cromwell's Bible, *ib.*; interrupted by the Inquisition, *ib.*; returns to England, *ib.* xi; publishes the Bible of 1539, *ib.*; his declaration at Paul's cross concerning his translation, 1 *Ful.* 98; his Testament well read, 2 *Bec.* 420; he goes abroad, 2 *Cov.* xi, 3 *Zur.* 223; at Tubingen, 2 *Cov.* xii; appointed minister of the church at Bergzabern, *ib.*, 3 *Zur.* 483, having married Elizabeth Macheson, 2 *Cov.* xii; his character there, 3 *Zur.* 247; known abroad as Michael Anglus, *ib.* 245 n., so he sometimes wrote himself, 2 *Cov.* 505; returns to England, *ib.* xii, 3 *Zur.* 494; made chaplain to the king and almoner to the queen dowager, 2 *Cov.* xiii; on a commission against the Anabaptists and other sectaries, *ib.*; he publishes a new edition of his Bible, *ib.*; goes into Devonshire with lord Russell, *ib.*; appointed coadjutor to Veysey, bishop of Exeter, *ib.* xiii, 1 *Lat.* 272 n.; to be bishop of Exeter, 3 *Zur.* 483; consecrated, 2 *Cov.* xiii, 2 *Cran.* 429 n.; Cranmer's letter to Cecil in his behalf when elected, 2 *Cran.* 429; a bishop indeed, 1 *Lat.* 272; deprived on the death of king Edward, 2 *Cov.* xiii; summoned before the council, *ib.*; imprisoned, 3 *Zur.* 505; in peril, 1 *Brad.* 290; released on the intercession of the king of Denmark, 2 *Cov.* xiii; in exile, 1 *Cran.* (9); goes to Denmark, 2 *Cov.* xiii; preacher to the exiles at Wesel, *ib.*; returns to Bergzabern, *ib.*; his works proscribed, *ib.*; is at Geneva, *ib.*; returns to England, *ib.*; preaches at Paul's cross, *ib.* xv; assists at the consecration of abp Parker, *ib.*; named, 1 *Zur.* 131; recommended by Grindal for the see of Llandaff, 2 *Cov.* 529 n.; presented to St Magnus, London, *ib.* xv; his letter to Cecil on his appointment, *Grin.* 284 n.; absent from the Lambeth conference about the vestments, *Park.* 270 n.; he resigns St Magnus, 2 *Cov.* xv; permitted to officiate without the vestments, *Grin.* 203, 205, 1 *Zur.* 202 n.; his death and burial, 2 *Cov.* xvi.

WRITINGS AND TRANSLATIONS, edited by the Rev. Geo. Pearson, B.D., 1 *Cov.*; REMAINS, edited by the same, 2 *Cov.*; lists of his writings, 1 *Cov.* ix, 2 *Cov.* xix; the Spiritual and most Precious Pearl, referred to, 3 *Bec.* 34 n.; the Exhortation to the Carrying of Christ's Cross, ascribed to him, 1 *Brad.* 412 n., 2 *Cov.* 227, &c.; his Letters of the Martyrs, *Grin.* 211; he translated a book on matrimony by Bullinger, 1 *Bec.* 29; this may be the book referred to 3 *Zur.* 245; (The Old Faith, 1 *Cov.* 1, &c., and The Hope of the Faithful, 2 *Cov.* 135, are also translations from Bullinger, *q. v.*); remarks on his writings and translation of the scriptures, 2 *Cov.* xvii; letter from him to Calvin, 3 *Zur.* 31; to Fagius, *ib.* 32; Coverdale, Humphrey, and Sampson, to Farell, Viret, Beza, and others, 2 *Zur.* 121; letter from Bullinger to Coverdale, *ib.* 136

— Elizabeth (Macheson) his wife, 2 *Cov.* xii, xiv.

Coverham, co. York (N. R.): Coverdale's birthplace, 2 *Cov.* vii.

Coverte (Geo.): 2 *Cran.* 362

Covetousness, Avarice: *v.* Commandments.

Avarice, a poem, by Hen. Lok, *Poet.* 138; coveting forbidden by God, 1 *Brad.* 172, 2 *Bul.* 120, &c., 2 *Cran.* 105, *Now.* (21), 136; condemned in the Lord's prayer, 2 *Bec.* 164; against covetousness, with sentences and examples of scripture, 1 *Bec.* 453, &c.; that of the age reprehended, 2 *Bec.* 7; its prevalence, 1 *Bec.* 41, 3 *Bec.* 59, 60; that of the papal clergy, 3 *Tyn.* 53;

of the clergy and laity, *Hutch.* 338; this sin reigns chiefly in old men, 2 *Bec.* 373, 1 *Lat.* 431; on walking after it, *Sand.* 118; covetousness condemned, 2 *Jew.* 1043; it is a grievous sin, 1 *Lat.* 107, &c., 239, the sin of Nineveh, *ib.* 241, and of London, *ib.* 242; the evils which follow it, 2 *Tyn.* 99, 101, 102; it is the root of all evil, 1 *Lat.* 109, 184, 246, 280, *Nord.* 174; it is idolatry, *Sand.* 182; its evil effects on the nation, 1 *Lat.* 99, 317; often the cause of rebellion, *Cran.* 192, 1 *Lat.* 247; it is accursed, 2 *Tyn.* 17; it is insatiable, *Pil.* 51, 3 *Tyn.* 281; what the covetous delight in, 2 *Bec.* 428; they will hear nothing against covetousness, 2 *Lat.* 213; they become more covetous, 1 *Lat.* 278; they mock God when they pray, *ib.* 403; they believe not the promises, *ib.* 270, 2 *Lat.* 155; horrible death of a covetous man, 1 *Lat.* 277, 541; a lesson to the covetous, 2 *Lat.* 90; a warning, 1 *Bec.* 127; a prayer against covetousness, 3 *Bec.* 59, 60; a remedy against avarice, 1 *Cov.* 524

Coveyke (Will.), proctor: 2 *Cran.* 492

Cowbuck (Rob.), alias Parsons, *q.v.*

Cowling castle, co. Kent: the dwelling of lord Cobham, *Bale* 18

Cowper (Jo.): accused, 2 *Cov.* 499

Cowper (Rob.): Parker's tutor at C. C. C. C., *Park.* vii, 481

Cowper (Tho.), bp: *v.* Cooper.

Cox (D.): notice of him, *Poet.* li; the Lord's prayer paraphrased, *ib.* 503

Cox (Jo. Edm.); editor of Cranmer's works, 1 and 2 *Cran.*

Coxe (Rich.), bp of Ely: sometime dean of Ch. Ch. Oxon, *Park.* 118, *Phil.* 213 n.; chancellor of Oxford, 2 *Jew.* 952 n.; tutor to king Edward, *Phil.* 213 n., 3 *Zur.* 384; almoner to that prince, *ib.* 82; one of the compilers of the liturgy, *Rid.* 316, 1 *Zur.* 234 n.; his opinion thereof, *ib.* 235; patron of Jo. ab Ulmis, 3 *Zur.* 384, 389, 395; commissioner in the disputation on the eucharist at Oxford, *ib.* 391 n.; dean of Westminster, *ib.* 561; he attends the duke of Somerset at his execution, *ib.* 449; gives up the chancellorship of Oxford, *ib.* 457; intended to be made a bishop, *ib.* 458; arrested on the death of Edward VI., *ib.* 684; deprived of his preferments, *ib.* 373; he escapes in the same ship with Sandys, *Sand.* xv; an exile for religion, 1 *Cran.* (9).; at Frankfort, *Jew.* xii, *Rid.* 387, 3 *Zur.* 753, 755, 763; his firmness in the troubles there, *Grin.* 239, *Jew.* xiii; he preaches before the queen, 2 *Zur.* 16 n.; concerned in the disputation at Westminster, 1559, 1 *Zur.* 11; a commissioner for the revision of the Prayer Book, *Grin.* v; designed for the bishoprick of Norwich, 1 *Zur.* 23; appointed bishop of Ely, *ib.* 40; elected, *Park.* 101 n.; consecrated, *Sand.* xviii, 1 *Zur.* 63, 65 n.; he objects to the crucifix in the queen's chapel, and writes to her, *ib.* 66 n.; takes part in a disputation concerning images, *ib.* 67; advises the queen to marry, *Grin.* 19 n.; has the care of the deposed bishop Watson, *ib.* 281; assists in the compilation of certain Advertisements, *Park.* 233; to preach at Paul's cross, *ib.* 261; desires the enforcement of uniformity, *ib.* 270; his part in the Bishops' Bible, *ib.* 282, 336 n.; an ecclesiastical commissioner, *ib.* 383; defends the Prayer Book, the surplice, &c., 1 *Zur.* 235, &c.; his opinion of N. Sanders, *Park.* 410; libelled, *ib.* 474; required to surrender lands belonging to his see, 1 *Zur.* 319 n.; at Grindal's confirmation as abp of Canterbury, *Grin.* x; recommended as visitor of St John's college, Cambridge, *ib.* 359; mentioned, *Bale* 206, *Grin.* 267, 1 *Zur.* 59; letters by him, *Park.* 151, 281, 1 *Zur.* 26, 65, 112, 207, 220, 234, 243, 268, 279, 282, 284, 297, 306, 307, 314, 315, 316, 318, 328, 2 *Zur.* 41, 192, 3 *Zur.* 119—123; letter from him and others, exiles at Frankfort, to Calvin, 3 *Zur.* 753; he signs letters to the queen, *Park.* 101, 129, 294, and a letter to lord Burghley, *ib.* 394; letters to him, 1 *Zur.* 362, 2 *Zur.* 42, 225, 249, 258; letter to him, Grindal, and Jewel, from Bullinger, 2 *Zur.* 178

— He married the widow of Dr Turner, 2 *Zur.* 181, 204; his daughter Joanna married John, son of abp Parker, *Park.* x, 484

Coy, or Corle: to strike or pat with the hand, 2 *Bec.* 596

Cr...... (R...): *Poet.* xxx.

Crabbe (Pet.): Concilia, 2 *Ful.* 15, 107, 179, 200, 243, 288, 294, 363, 364, 400, *Jew.* xxxv, 3 *Jew.* 295, 4 *Jew.* 682, 739, 747, 752, 800, 834, 840, 878 bis, 926, 937, 938, 1033; he complains of the corruption of the councils, 1 *Jew.* 341; mutilates them, *ib.* 425; shamefully corrupts an old canon against the Angelici, 2 *Ful.* 42 n.; his reading in a remarkable canon of a council at Tours, *Calf.* 136 n

Crackenthorp (Rich.): Defence of Constantine, *Calf.* 174 n., 2 *Ful.* 359 n., 360 n.; Vigilius Dormitans, *Calf.* 290 n., 2 *Ful.* 307 n.; Defensio Ecclesiæ Anglicanæ, *Calf.*

96 n., 137 n., 2 *Ful.* 110 n.; Contra Archiep. Spalat., *Calf.* 64 n., 258 n
Cracow: 3 *Zur.* 689; the prince or lord, *ib.* 688, 701; the bishop's conduct towards a preacher of the gospel, *ib.* 700
Cradle crowns: 2 *Cran.* 37
Cradocke (Edw.): was Margaret professor of divinity at Oxford, *Coop.* iv.
Craiford (Jo.): *v.* Crayford.
Crafte (Geo.): *v.* Crofts.
Craig (Jo.), minister of Edinburgh: 2 *Zur.* 364; letter from him and others to abps Parker and Young, *Park.* 205
Crail, Scotland: the plague there, 2 *Zur.* 335
Craketh: boasteth, *Calf.* 351
Craling castle, Scotland: destroyed by the English, 1 *Zur.* 225 n
Crambe: cabbage, *Calf.* 320
Cramp-rings: *Rid.* 501
Cranbrook, co. Kent: Frensham's bequest, 2 *Zur.* 21 n
Crane (Jo.), fellow of Ch. coll. Cambridge, *Park.* 25, 26
Crane (Nich.): was a leader of the Separatists, *Grin.* 316 n., 318
Crank: sickly, 4 *Jew.* 945
Cranmer (Anne), dau. of the abp: 2 *Cran.* 219 n
Cranmer (Dorothy), sister of the abp, and wife of Harold Rosell, *q. v.*
Cranmer (Edm.), brother to the abp: made archdeacon of Canterbury, 2 *Cran.* 268 n.; sends informations against Dr Benger, *ib.* 301; he claims certain tithes at Davington, *ib.* 313; in exile, 1 *Cran.* (9)
Cranmer (Geo.): on Puritanism, 3 *Whitg.* xvi.
Cranmer (Jo.), of Aslacton, brother of the abp: Margaret (Fitz-Williams) his wife, 2 *Cran.* 330 n
Cranmer (Marg.), dau. of the abp: 2 *Cran.* 219 n
Cranmer (Susan), wife of Tho. Brooke, *q. v.*
CRANMER (Tho.), abp of Canterbury: *v.* Bible (*English*), Catechisms.

His life, state, and story, from Foxe's Acts and Monuments, 1 *Cran.* vii, &c.; biographical notice, by the Rev. J. E. Cox, 2 *Cran.* vii, &c.; his birth, 1 *Cran.* vii, 2 *Cran.* vii; education, *ib.*; first marriage, 1 *Cran.* vii, 2 *Cran.* vii, 219, 557; he retires to Waltham, 1 *Cran.* viii, 2 *Cran.* vii; sent for by the king, 1 *Cran.* ix, 2 *Cran.* vii; made archdeacon of Taunton, 2 *Cran.* vii; sent on an embassy to Rome, 1 *Cran.* x, 2 *Cran.* vii; ambassador to Charles V., 1 *Cran.* xi, 2 *Cran.* viii; his second marriage, 2 *Cran.* viii, 219, 550, 557, 3 *Zur.* 466; made archbishop, 1 *Cran.* xi, 2 *Cran.* viii; his consecration, 2 *Cran.* 237, 560, 561; the bulls for it, *ib.* 237; his oaths to the pope and his protestation, *ib.* 535, 537, 538, 559—562; he pronounces judgment for the king's divorce from Catherine of Arragon, *ib.* viii; his labours for reformation, *Pil.* 37, 3 *Zur.* 329, 480, 482; he unmasks the maid of Kent, 2 *Cran.* 66; describes idolatry at Walsingham, &c., 1 *Hoop.* 40; patronizes Latimer, 1 *Lat.* ix; divorces Anne Boleyn, 2 *Cran.* viii; receives a copy of Matthew's Bible, 1 *Tyn.* lxxv; commends it to Cromwell, and thanks him for procuring the king's sanction, *ib.* lxxv, lxxvi; gives injunctions to the diocese of Hereford, 2 *Cran.* 81, 2 *Lat.* 242 n.; takes cognizance of Dr Crewkehorne, 1 *Lat.* x; reproved by Grynæus, 3 *Zur.* 526; the Six Articles, 1 *Cran.* xii, xvi, 2 *Cran.* ix; charged with burning Rich. Mekins and others, 1 *Cran.* xxix, 3 *Zur.* 221; a conspiracy against him, and his deliverance, 1 *Cran.* xvii, 2 *Cran.* ix; the English litany of 1544, 2 *Cran.* ix, *Pra. Eliz.* xxiv; death of king Henry, 2 *Cran.* ix; the archbishop's change of views on the Lord's supper, 1 *Cran.* xix, 3 *Zur.* 13 n., 71, 89, 323, 383 n., 388; his proceedings in king Edward's time, 2 *Cran.* ix; his alleged dependence on Ridley, *Rid.* 283, 284; he patronizes Becon, 1 *Bec.* x; undertakes to educate the son of Fagius, 2 *Cov.* 526; Martyr, Tremellius, Bucer, Fagius, &c. with him at Lambeth, 3 *Zur.* 535; speaks of seditious priests in Devonshire, &c., 1 *Hoop.* 461; the controversy with Gardiner, 1 *Cran.* xx, 2 *Cran.* x, 3 *Zur.* 388 (and see below); signature as privy councillor, *Rid.* 508; he visits Joan Bocher, *Hutch.* iii; erroneously stated by Foxe to have urged Edward VI. to sign her death warrant, *ib.* iv, v; he was not present when the warrant was signed, *ib.*; blamed by the Familists for burning her, *Rog.* 350; he accuses Hooper before the council, 2 *Hoop.* xii; a dispensation granted to him by the king to depart from the usual forms of consecration in the case of that bishop, *ib.*; he writes to Bucer for his advice in the matter of garments, *ib.* xiii; he supports the foreign churches in London, 3 *Zur.* 568; his favour to the church of Zurich, *ib.* 93; he endeavours to secure unity of doctrine in all the reformed churches, *Rog.* 3; recommends a conference of protestant divines, 2 *Cran.* 430—434, 3 *Zur.* 23, 502 n.; in displeasure for shewing his conscience in the duke of

Somerset's case, and for opposing the spoil of church goods, 1 *Cran.* xii, *Rid.* 59; the Articles drawn up, 2 *Cran.* xi; he replies to Dr Smith, 3 *Zur.* 495; a commissioner for the reform of the ecclesiastical law, 3 *Zur.* 590; accession of queen Mary, 1 *Cran.* xx, 2 *Cran.* xi; his declaration against the mass, 1 *Cran.* xx, xxi, 3 *Zur.* 371, 505 n.; he is committed to the Tower on a charge of treason, 2 *Cran.* xi, 3 *Zur.* 371, 505, 506; Ridley, Latimer, and Bradford with him there, 2 *Brad.* xxxiii, 74 n., 2 *Lat.* 258; in peril of death, 1 *Brad.* 290; proceedings against him, 2 *Cran.* xi, 3 *Zur.* 343, 507, 743; he is attainted, 1 *Cran.* xxi, 2 *Cran.* xi, 442 n., 3 *Zur.* 374; sent to Oxford, with Latimer and Ridley, 1 *Cran.* xxi, 2 *Cran.* xi, 3 *Zur.* 515; the disputation there, 2 *Hoop.* 593, 1 *Jew.* 53, 2 *Jew.* 571, *Pil.* 400; his letter to the council on this disputation, 2 *Cran.* 445; record of it, *Park.* 160; his examination before Brooks, &c., 1 *Brad.* 494, 1 *Cran.* xxii, 2 *Cran.* 212—224; scandalous character of his judges, 1 *Zur.* 12; interrogatories against him, with his answers, 2 *Cran.* 219; the process against him, in Latin, *ib.* 541; he has Jewel and Mounson for his notaries or reporters, *Rid.* 194; cited to Rome, yet kept in prison at Oxford, 2 *Cran.* xii, 1 *Jew.* 59; burned at Rome in a mummery, 2 *Jew.* 629; his submissions and recantations, 1 *Cran.* xxii, 3 *Zur.* 173 n.; copies of them, 2 *Cran.* 563; extract from Bonner's register stating that he revoked them, *ib.* 567; his letter to a lawyer respecting his appeal, *ib.* 455, 456; in prison, ready to die, 1 *Brad.* 410, 445; his last sight of Latimer and Ridley, 3 *Zur.* 751 n.; Dr Cole's sermon at St Mary's, 1 *Cran.* xxiii, &c.; Cranmer's prayer, and exhortation to the people, *ib.* xxvi, 2 *Cran.* 565; his martyrdom, 1 *Cran.* xxviii, 2 *Cran.* xii, *Poet.* 166, 3 *Zur.* 143, 173; put to death unlawfully, 1 *Jew.* 59; his gentle nature, 1 *Cran.* xi, xiii; an example of it, *ib.* xiii; his singular patience, *ib.* xiii; his charity, *ib.* xvi; he was stout in God's cause, *ib.* xii, xvi; the order of his study, *ib.* xi.

WRITINGS AND DISPUTATIONS RELATIVE TO THE SACRAMENT OF THE LORD'S SUPPER, edited by the Rev. Jo. Edm. Cox, M.A., F.S.A., 1 *Cran.*; MISCELLANEOUS WRITINGS, edited by the same, 2 *Cran.*; lists of his writings, 1 *Cran.* xxx, 2 *Cran.* xii; homilies composed by him, 2 *Cran.* 128 n., 3 *Zur.* 626; they teach the necessity of good works, *Wool.* 31; the Catechism (*q. v.*) set forth by him, its doctrine, 3 *Zur.* 381, 643 n.; references to his Answer to Gardiner, 2 *Brad.* 274, 384 n., 2 *Cov.* 253, 262, 1 *Hoop.* 100, 4 *Jew.* 635, 2 *Lat.* 265, 272, &c., *Pil.* 523, 547, *Rid.* 160 n.; it was translated into Latin by Jo. Foxe, but only part of it printed, 1 *Zur.* 42 n.; his controversy with Gardiner never entirely printed, *Grin.* 232 n.; perhaps the writer of the Variations of Stephen Gardiner, published as Ridley's, *Rid.* 307, 543; another copy in 1 *Cran.* 380; Jenkyns's Remains, 1 *Cran.* iv, 444; some of his written books in private hands, *Park.* 186, 187; further particulars respecting his MSS., *ib.* 191; MS. note in his copy of Augustine, 4 *Bul.* 272 n.; his letters, 2 *Cran.* 229—458; their contents, *ib.* 581; some of these letters will be found in *Jew.* xii. n., *Park.* 39, 40, 43, 3 *Zur.* 11—29; letters to him, 2 *Brad.* 169, 190, 2 *Hoop.* xv, *Rid.* 361, 362, 3 *Zur.* 363, 520, 526, 531, 533, 711; dedications to him, 2 *Bec.* 525, *Hutch.* d; Cranmer railed at by Sanders, 2 *Ful.* 247

—Joan, his first wife, 2 *Cran.* vii, 219, 557; Anne, his second wife, the niece of Osiander, *ib.* 219, 550, 3 *Zur.* 466; his children, 2 *Cran.* 219 n

Cranmer (Tho.), son of the abp: 2 *Cran.* 219 n.; a youth left at Strasburgh, probably the same, 4 *Jew.* 1197, 1198, 1 *Zur.* 8

Cranmer hall, co. Lincoln: 1 *Cran.* vii.

Crantz (Alb.): *v.* Krantz.

Crashawe (Will.): his Sermon at the Crosse cited with reference to the baptism of bells, *Calf.* 15 n

Crassus: ridiculed by the Parthians, *Whita.* 218

Crates, the philosopher: anecdote of him, *Wool.* 85

Crauford (Jo. earl of): *v.* Lindsay.

Crawley (North), co. Bucks: Garbrand's rectory, 2 *Jew.* 816 n

Crayford (Jo.), master of Clare hall: 2 *Lat.* 378 n.; vice-chancellor of Cambridge, 2 *Cran.* 293

Crazed: ill, sickly, 2 *Brad.* 95, 116, *Rid.* 366

Creake: to cry creake, what, *Coop.* 22 n

Creake (Jo.), or Creke: servant to Cranmer, 2 *Cran.* 248, 255, 268, 270

— Mrs Creke, perhaps widow of the above, 2 *Cran.* 302

Cream: chrism, *Bale* 320

Creation: *v.* God.

The creation, 1 *Brad.* 140, 1 *Bul.* 43, 1 *Cov.* 14, *Now.* (30), 146, *Rog.* 39, &c.; its history contained in few words, 3 *Bul.*

174; God made all things of nothing, *Hutch.* 68; the making and preservation of the world, *Lit. Edw.* 501, (550), the fathers hold that nothing has been created since God rested, *Bale* 233; errors respecting the creation, *Rog.* 40—42; its end, *Now.* (31), 147; what it can teach, *Calf.* 355; David celebrates it, 3 *Bul.* 177; our thanks are due to God for it, 1 *Bec.* 176, 177; the creation of man, *ib.* 46, 1 *Brad.* 120, 141, 149, *Lit. Edw.* 501, (551), *Now.* (32, 100), 147; all things were made for man; and according to his state, so are they, 1 *Brad.* 352, &c.; creation shall be restored, *ib.* 355, &c.; there is a double creation,—in Adam, and in Christ, 1 *Bec.* 81; creation, preservation, grace, *Pra. B.* 12; creation is not permitted to man, 3 *Tyn.* 242

Creature (κτίσις, Rom. viii.): its subjection to vanity, and its deliverance, 1 *Brad.* 352, &c., *Pil.* 92

Creatures: all creatures praise God; verses by Tim. Pett., *Poet.* 386; the creatures obey God, *Pil.* 90; they refuse to serve man through sin, *ib.* 91; they are not to be considered in themselves, *ib.* 230

Credence: a pledge to be credited, 1 *Tyn.* 85

Credence table: 2 *Jew.* 636 n

Creeds: the three creeds, 2 *Hoop.* 120, 2 *Lat.* 332, *Rog.* 92; they may be proved by holy scripture, *ib.* 94; adversaries to them, *ib.* 93, 94; many creeds are mentioned in old writers, as those of Basil, Damasus, Jerome, Cyprian or Ruffinus, Gregory, &c., 3 *Jew.* 254, 255

APOSTLES': symbolum commune sive apostolorum, 2 *Hoop.* 533; the creed as translated by Cranmer, 2 *Cran.* 83; the creed in Latin verse, by A. Siberus, *Pra. Eliz.* 403; in verse, by Coverdale, 2 *Cov.* 546; another of the same, *ib.* 547; why it is called a symbol, *Lit. Edw.* 496, (546), *Now.* (26), 141, why the creed or symbol of the apostles, 2 *Bec.* 15, *Now.* (26), 142; sometimes called canon, *Whita.* 27 n.; Basil designates it the canon of right and the standard of truth, *ib.* 659 n.; Ambrose terms it the key of Peter, *ib.* 605; Augustine calls it the rule of faith, *ib.* 485; it is taken out of the word of God, 2 *Hoop.* 120, *Whita.* 529; its words are scattered through the scriptures, *Whita.* 529, 533; ascribed by some to the apostles themselves, 1 *Bul.* 123, *Whita.* 528; not collected by them, 2 *Cran.* 515; a brief summary of it early used in baptism, 1 *Tyn.* 253; its articles referred to by Irenæus, *Whita.* 520; it is given in substance by Tertullian, *ib.* 484, 1 *Whitg.* 217; it contains the one faith, 3 *Jew.* 253, &c.; it was sufficient at first, 1 *Bul.* 12; we maintain no other faith, 1 *Ful.* 415; it accords with the word of God, 1 *Brad.* 435, *Rog.* 92; the unity of the church consists in the twelve articles thereof, 1 *Brad.* 524; it refutes various heretics, *Whita.* 486; A BRIEF AND CLEAR CONFESSION OF THE CHRISTIAN FAITH, being an exposition of the creed, by bishop Hooper, 2 *Hoop.* 19, &c.; sermons on it, 1 *Bul.* 122—179; explanation from the Institution of a Christian Man, 2 *Cran.* 83, &c.; a meditation upon it, 1 *Brad.* 140; Jewel's paraphrase of it, 3 *Jew.* 252, &c.; Tho. Tusser, his belief, (a paraphrase of the apostles' creed), *Poet.* 258; other expositions, 2 *Bec.* 15, &c., *Lit. Edw.* 500, (550), *Now.* (27), 142; its sum, 2 *Brad.* 122; its parts, 2 *Bec.* 16, 1 *Bul.* 123, 2 *Hoop.* 21, &c.; the word "in" occurs but thrice, and why, *Bale* 33; its first clause expounded by the fathers in a threefold sense, " Credo Deo, credo Deum, credo in Deum," *Whita.* 300; it did not originally mention the descent into hell, *ib.* 536; in it we profess our belief, in [rather as to] the church; if, therefore, scripture be not the rule of faith because it is an article of faith, neither can the church be, *ib.* 352; it does not mention scripture, because it is itself an epitome of scripture, *ib.* 299; the four last articles often to be thought upon, 1 *Brad.* 346; its doctrine to be received and taught, *ib.* 370, 2 *Hoop.* 120; it should be daily explained, 1 *Hoop.* 144; it was the custom to recite it to the dying, 4 *Bul.* 74; reviled by Barrow, *Rog.* 93; the creed, Lord's prayer, and ten commandments, styled the sum of scripture, *Whita.* 388; the common people of the North have ever used them in English metre, *Pil.* 501

ATHANASIAN: symbolum beati Athanasii, 2 *Hoop.* 538; the same in English, 1 *Bul.* 29; ascribed by some to Eusebius Vercellensis, 3 *Jew.* 254; by others to Hilary of Arles, 1 *Brad.* 371 n.; probably written by Vigilius Tapsensis, an African bishop, 1 *Bul.* 29 n.; to be received, 1 *Brad.* 371, *Rog.* 92; its use defended, 2 *Whitg.* 481; cited, on God, 1 *Hoop.* 125; on Christ's two natures, 1 *Jew.* 485; it speaks of Christ's descent into hell, but omits the burial, *Whita.* 537; called Sathanasius' creed by some heretics, *Rog.* 93

Chalcedon: the creed of the council of Chalcedon, taken out of the book of Isidore, Greek and English, 1 *Bul.* 19; the same in Latin, 2 *Hoop.* 535; it is not contrary to the doctrine of Cyril, 1 *Bul.* 20; allowed, 1 *Brad.* 371, 2 *Hoop.* 74, *Phil.* 35

Charlemagne: says the gospel must be preached to all, that all may believe the Father, Son, and Holy Ghost, to be one Almighty God, 3 *Jew.* 256

Constantinople: the creed of the council held at Constantinople, A.D. 381, Engl., Gr., Lat., 1 *Bul.* 16; the same in Latin, 2 *Hoop.* 534; this creed cited, 3 *Bec.* 455, 1 *Bul.* 158, 436, 3 *Bul.* 310, 4 *Bul.* 356; allowed, 1 *Brad.* 371, 2 *Hoop.* 74

Cyril: the creed of Cyril, sanctioned by the council of Ephesus, see *Ephesus*, below.

Damasus: the creed of Damasus, taken from Jerome's works, Engl. and Latin, 1 *Bul.* 32; the same in Latin, 2 *Hoop.* 538; allowed, 1 *Brad.* 371; cited on Christ's ascension, 3 *Jew.* 257

Ephesus: the confession of faith set forth by the synod at Ephesus, Gr. and Engl., 1 *Bul.* 17; the same in Latin, 2 *Hoop.* 534; allowed, 1 *Brad.* 371, 2 *Hoop.* 74

Innocent III.: his creed is found in the Decretals, 4 *Bul.* 557

Irenæus: his creed or declaration of the faith, from his book against Valentinus, Gr. and Engl., 1 *Bul.* 26; the same in Latin, 2 *Hoop.* 537; allowed, 1 *Brad.* 371; reference to it, *Whita.* 520

NICE: the Nicene creed, as given by Socrates, Engl. and Gr., 1 *Bul.* 15; the same in Latin, 2 *Hoop.* 533; it was devised against the Arians, *Rog.* 93, 3 *Whitg.* 74; a creed substantially the same as that called the Nicene was drawn up by Hosius of Corduba, *Phil.* 310 n.; the Nicene creed was appointed by pope Marcus to be sung at the mass, 2 *Brad.* 308; used in our communion service, 3 *Whitg.* 74; allowed, 1 *Brad.* 371, 2 *Hoop.* 74; as to the expression "of one substance," see Homoüsion; why this creed omits the descent into hell, *Whita.* 537; as to the clause "Filioque," see Holy Ghost.

Tertullian: his creed, from his book De Præsc. Heret., Engl. and Lat., 1 *Bul.* 28; the same in Latin, 2 *Hoop.* 538; it is the apostles' creed in substance, 1 *Whitg.* 217; he calls it the rule of faith, *Whita.* 484; allowed, 1 *Brad.* 371

Toledo: the creed of the first council of Toledo, taken out of the book of Isidore, Eng. and Lat., 1 *Bul.* 22; the same in Latin, 2 *Hoop.* 536; creed of the fourth council of Toledo, also from Isidore, Eng. and Lat., 1 *Bul.* 24; both allowed, 1 *Brad.* 371

Creeping: v. Cross, ii.

Creke (Jo. and Mrs): v. Creake.

Crescens: said to have preached in France, 1 *Jew.* 267, & corr.; stated to have been bishop there, *Rog.* 329

Cresconians: thought that magistrates were not to punish malefactors, *Rog.* 345

Cresconius: v. Augustine, xxvii.

A Donatist heretic, 3 *Jew.* 226, 315

Cresset: a watch-fire, a light on a beacon, 2 *Bec.* 610, *Calf.* 298; creshet, *Bale* 346

Cressey: a family related to Cranmer, 1 *Cran.* viii, 2 *Cran.* vii.

Cressy (Hugh P.): Church History, 1 *Lat.* 55 n

Creswell (Percival): 1 *Brad.* 500, 514, 516

Crete: Jews there deceived by Satan, 2 *Cran.* 50; Candia subject to Venice, 4 *Jew.* 693

Crewkehorne (Dr): v. Cronkehorne.

Creyghton (......): 2 *Bec.* 266 n

Cribble: coarse flour, 1 *Bul.* 429

Cricamus: perhaps a mistake for Ochamus, 2 *Bec.* 639

Crinitus (Pet.): De honesta Disciplina, *Jew.* xxxv; this work expurgated, *Calf.* 190 n.; cited on the mistake about Longinus, 1 *Jew.* 150 n.; it records a decree of Valens and Theodosius against representations of the sign of Christ, 2 *Bec.* 71 n., *Calf.* 190, 2 *Ful.* 159, 2 *Jew.* 659, *Park.* 90, *Rid.* 92; on the learning of Jerome, 1 *Jew.* 278 n.; his name formerly printed Erinilus in one of the Homilies, 2 *Ful.* 159

Crisp (Sir Hen.), of the Isle of Thanet: *Park.* 204

Crispin (Edm.): notice of him, 2 *Cran.* 183 n

Crispin (Jo.), printer at Geneva: *Grin.* 327 n

Crispin (Rich.): notice of him, 2 *Cran.* 183 n

Crispin and Crispinian (SS.): invoked for shoes-making, 1 *Bec.* 139; account of them, *ib.* n

Crito: pseudonym of Jas. Hamilton, earl of Arran, 4 *Jew.* 1224, 1 *Zur.* 56, 57 n., 59, &c.

Croarius (Andr.), or Croarienses: 3 *Zur.* 311, 437, 496, 500

Crœsus: named, 1 *Hoop.* 184

Croft (Sir James), or Croftes: sent to Ireland, 3 *Zur.* 722 n.; one of the royal visitors for the North, 1 *Zur.* 73 n.; signature as privy councillor, *Grin.* 405, 408, 414, 417, 423, 427, 429, 433, 435, *Park.* 381; named, 2 *Zur.* 34 n

Crofts (Geo.), or Crafte, rector of Shepton Mallet, &c.: attainted, 2 *Cran.* 385 n

Croix (Pierre de): *Calf.* 85 n., 95 n
Croke (Rich.): called the Grecian, 2 *Brad.* 172, *Rid.* 373; notice of him, 2 *Brad.* 172 n.; witness against Cranmer, 2 *Cran.* 546; his deposition, *ib.* 547
Crome (Edw.): notice of him, 2 *Cran.* 339 n.; references to him, 2 *Brad.* 83, 2 *Lat.* 381; a gospeller, *Bale* 157, 161; his preaching and doctrine, 2 *Cran.* 339, 3 *Zur.* 211—213; charged with heresy, 2 *Lat.* 350; recommended by Cranmer for dean of Christ church, Canterbury, 2 *Cran.* 397; he intercedes with the king against persecution, 2 *Cran.* 208; in trouble, 1 *Lat.* xii, 3 *Zur.* 211, &c.; the king's judgment concerning him, 1540, 3 *Zur.* 214; compelled to recant, 2 *Cran.* 398 n.; opposes Hooper, 3 *Zur.* 80; a prisoner for the truth, 2 *Brad.* 95, *Rid.* 356, 363, 365; in peril of death, 1 *Brad.* 290; he signed a declaration concerning religion, *ib.* 374, but is said to have recanted, *Bale* 142, 441, 1 *Brad.* 529
Crome: preterite of cram, 1 *Tyn.* 264
Cromes: hooks, 3 *Bec.* 150
Crompe (Hen.): persecuted, *Bale* 43 n
Crompton (Will.): St Austin's Summes, 2 *Ful.* 80 n., 240 n
Cromwell (Gregory lord), son of the next: notice of him, 3 *Zur.* 203; his death, *ib.* 496 n
— Elizabeth (Seymour) his wife, sister of queen Jane, 3 *Zur.* 340 n
Cromwell (Tho. lord), earl of Essex: at court, 1 *Cran.* xiii, xiv; 3 *Zur.* 15, 611; he seems to have introduced Tyndale's works to the notice of the king, 1 *Tyn.* xli; his words to Cranmer, 1 *Cran.* xix; the early patron of Coverdale, 2 *Cov.* vii, 1 *Tyn.* xlii; he instructs S. Vaughan to persuade Tyndale to throw himself on the king's mercy, *ib.* xlii; his reply to Vaughan's letter respecting Tyndale, with interlined corrections, *ib.* xlv—xlviii; his acts with reference to Latimer, 1 *Lat.* vi, x, xi, 2 *Lat.* xv, xviii, 224; master of the rolls, 2 *Cran.* 306 n., *Park.* 5 n.; with Cranmer he unmasks the maid of Kent, 2 *Cran.* 66; chancellor of Cambridge, 2 *Lat.* 382; he writes letters for Tyndale's deliverance, 1 *Tyn.* lxix; a letter from him to Parker, *Park.* 5; he obtains licence for the scriptures to be read in English, 2 *Lat.* 240 n., 1 *Tyn.* lxxvi; undertakes the reprint of Matthew's Bible, at Paris, under the superintendence of Coverdale, 2 *Cov.* x; dedication to him of the New Testament, 1538, *ib.* xi, 32; vicar general, &c., 3 *Zur.* 618; he read the sentence against Lambert, 2 *Cran.* 218 n.; is made high steward of Cranmer's chases, &c., 2 *Cran.* 386; employs Coverdale in Berkshire, in the investigation of Popish superstitions in that country, 2 *Cov.* xi; obtains the earldom of Essex, 3 *Zur.* 221; he loved antiquities, 2 *Lat.* 375; his fall, 3 *Zur.* 202; Cranmer's letter to Henry VIII. lamenting to hear the charge of treason against him, 2 *Cran.* 401; his execution, 2 *Cov.* xi, 2 *Cran.* 401, 3 *Zur.* 202; his behaviour at his death, 3 *Zur.* 203; a prayer said by him, *Pra. Eliz.* 202 n. (the English of it, *ib.* 109); letters to him, 2 *Cov.* 490—501, 2 *Cran.* 237—600, 346 n., 360 n., 2 *Lat.* 367—418
Crones: old ewes, 2 *Bul.* 390
Cronkehorne (Dr), or Crewkehorne: his fanaticism, 2 *Cran.* 389, 1 *Lat.* x.
Crooch (Mr): saluted, *Phil.* 227
Crope: crept, 2 *Tyn.* 270, 3 *Tyn.* 78; cropen, *Grin.* 39
Crosier: the bishop's crose, a false sign, 1 *Tyn.* 252; used in king Edward's time, 3 *Zur.* 585; disused in the church of England, *Pil.* 584, 586 (cruch); what the crosier's staff signifies, 2 *Jew.* 1020
Cross: v. Crucifix, Images, Thau.
   i. *The Cross generally, Christ's cross in particular*: the cross of Christ, what it is, 3 *Bec.* 605; books on the cross, see *Calf.* index; Calfhill's ANSWER TO THE TREATISE OF THE CROSS (by Martiall), *Calf.* (see the Table, p. 393); Fulke's REJOINDER to Martiall's Reply, 2 *Ful.* 125, &c.; the cross prefigured in the law of nature, foreshewn by Moses and the prophets, and shewn from heaven in the time of grace, 2 *Ful.* 146, &c.; represented by the sail, the plough, the four winds, &c., *Calf.* 177, &c., 2 *Ful.* 164; passages of the Old Testament supposed to refer to it, *Calf.* 92—94, 103, 2 *Ful.* 136, &c.; prefigured by Jacob blessing his sons, 2 *Ful.* 171; by the lifting up of the hands of Moses, *Calf.* 104—106, 2 *Ful.* 147; by the two sticks gathered by the widow of Sarepta, &c., 2 *Ful.* 146; the figure found amongst the heathen, *Calf.* 178, as on the breast of the idol Serapis, *Calf.* 65, 91, 107, 276, 277, 2 *Ful.* 148; one of the Egyptian letters was cruciform, *Calf.* 276; so the Hebrew letter ת was anciently (v. Thau); the cross of Christ, on its true form, 2 *Zur.* 44; called an altar, 3 *Bec.* 138, 139, 253, 1 *Ful.* 241, *Phil.* 193; the material cross of Christ not valued by the apostles, 1 *Ful.* 212; the invention of the cross by Helena (*q.v.*), *Calf.* 287, 321, &c., 1 *Ful.* 212, 2 *Ful.* 190, 193, 194, *Pra. Eliz.* 529 n.,

3 *Tyn.* 124; witnesses agree not in their statements concerning it, *Calf.* 322—325; the Chronicle of Eusebius has been falsified respecting it, *ib.* 321 n.; five inventions are recounted in the Lombardic History, *ib.*; what Helena did with it, *ib.* 326, 327; on supposed fragments of it, *ib.* 325—327; their wonderful increase, *ib.* 326; pieces preserved as relics, *ib.* 280, &c., 2 *Ful.* 180, &c.; the reservation of such fragments compared to the use of Pharisaical phylacteries, *Calf.* 283; the nails, *ib.* 327; whether three or four, *ib.* 328; what Helena did with them, *ib.* 328, 329; their wonderful multiplication, 2 *Ful.* 194; the title, why written by Pilate in three languages, 1 *Jew.* 275, 277, *Whita.* 257; whether the cross is "the sign of the Son of Man," *Calf.* 95, 96; a cross gules, borne by the King of the heavenly Jerusalem, *Poet.* 429; what cross is the refuge of the faithful, *Calf.* 82; enemies of the cross of Christ, 1 *Lat.* 520, &c., *Sand.* 118

ii. *Visible and material crosses* (in some cases the crucifix is intended: *v.* Crucifix): instances of the miraculous appearance of the cross, *Calf.* 110, &c.; (*v.* Constantine, Julian); the cross set up everywhere on the overthrow of idols, 2 *Ful.* 171, &c., 2 *Jew.* 648; representations of the sign of Christ forbidden by Valens and Theodosius, 2 *Bec.* 71 n., *Calf.* 190, 2 *Ful.* 159, 2 *Jew.* 659, *Park.* 90, *Rid.* 92; a cross ordered by Justinian to be set up on the site of every intended church, *Calf.* 135, 136, 189, 2 *Ful.* 150, &c.; set upon churches, chapels, and oratories, *Calf.* 126, &c., 2 *Ful.* 149, &c.; its use in churches ancient and defensible, 2 *Zur.* 43, but its superstitious use to be guarded against, *ib.* 44; on its true form, and mystic signification, *ib.* 44, 46; how a wooden cross, or the sign of the cross, may be used with profit, 3 *Tyn.* 59, 60; such was the ancient use of these things, but their abuse is idolatry, *ib.* 60, 62; the sight of the cross should move us to mourning for our sins, *ib.* 85; it cannot teach effectually, *Calf.* 345, &c.; what kind of crosses Chrysostom introduced at Constantinople, *ib.* 298—301; Popish superstitions respecting the cross, *Rog.* 320, 321; the worship of it, *Bale* 39, 40; it is not to be honoured superstitiously, 3 *Tyn.* 185; we should not worship the wood and forget the mystery of the cross, *Park.* 7; its worship not allowed by the old fathers, *Calf.* 366, &c., 2 *Ful.* 201, &c.; the cross and instruments of the passion worshipped by Papists, *Rog.* 224, 225; proof that λατρεία is offered to it, *Calf.* 381 n.; the Belgic Index condemns the assertion, that it is manifest idolatry to adore it, *ib.* 376 n.; how it is prayed to, 2 *Ful.* 211, *Rog.* 228, 229; invoked for all things, *ib.* 226; greeting the holy cross, 2 *Lat.* 231; hymns to it of frequent occurrence in the Romish services, 2 *Bec.* 72, *Calf.* 381, 2 *Ful.* 211, 1 *Jew.* 534; the very cross of Ludlow, *Calf.* 35, 274; the rood of Chester, *ib.* 35; the rood of Winchester, *ib.* 274; the rood of grace in Kent, *ib.* 274, 3 *Zur.* 604, 606, 609; roods to be pulled down in every church, 2 *Cran.* 415 n.; what the cross signified when naked, 1 *Bec.* 113; veiling it, and kneeling to it abolished, 2 *Cran.* 414, 415; what it signified when carried in the ceremonies on Palm Sunday, 1 *Bec.* 112, 114; creeping to the cross, 1 *Brad.* 8, *Calf.* 9, 20; practised on Good Friday, *Calf.* 100, *Rid.* 497, 498; recognized by Henry VIII., 1 *Lat.* 132 n.; its omission sanctioned, 2 *Cran.* 509; the custom abolished, *ib.* 414; forbidden, 2 *Hoop.* 129, *Rid.* 320; practised at Dunbar in 1568, *Grin.* 295; its burial before Easter, *Rog.* 180; the cross borne in procession at the litany, 2 *Ful.* 182, &c.; borne before high prelates, 1 *Tyn.* 234; the university cross of Cambridge, Latimer keeper of it, 2 *Lat.* xxvii; crosses in market places, *Calf.* 25; in highways, 3 *Whitg.* 131; these, it is said, were formerly images of Mercury, *Calf.* 66; injunction against resting at crosses in carrying a corpse to burial, and against leaving little wooden crosses there, *Grin.* 140; crosses put on the corpse, 2 *Hoop.* 147, 3 *Whitg.* 362; the cross formerly worn by all soldiers, *Calf.* 113; assumed as a banner by the rebels in Yorkshire, 1 *Lat.* 29; set before the alphabet, 1 *Brad.* 264 n., 410, 459, 2 *Brad.* 204, 212, 351; drawn in the mass-book, *Calf.* 202; sworn by, 2 *Tyn.* 269; crosses to be destroyed, *Grin.* 135, 159

iii. *The sign of the cross*: the transient sign of the cross usual among Christians in ancient times, *Calf.* 195, &c.; had in great regard, 2 *Jew.* 649, 650; the apostles and primitive fathers alleged to have blessed themselves with it, 2 *Ful.* 171, &c.; it is not mentioned in scripture as part of the Christian's armour, *Calf.* 73; its use an ancient Christian custom, but much abused, *Whita.* 590; Tertullian on the sign of the cross, *ib.* 591, 3 *Whitg.* 125, 126; Basil thereon, *Whita.* 590; Cyril of Alexandria wrote upon it, *ib.* 597; Romish errors about it, *Rog.* 152; crossing without believing, mere enchanting, *Calf.* 76; Bullinger upon it, 2 *Zur.* 357; on its use in baptism, *Calf.* 200, &c., 2 *Cran.* 56, 3 *Whitg.* 123, 1 *Zur.* 164,179, 358; origin of the practice, 3 *Whitg.* 126; tolerated, according to bishops Grindal and Horn, until better times, but not to be defended, 1 *Zur.* 179, 180; disliked by Sandys, *Sand.* 433; not disallowed by Rogers, *Rog.* 321; judgment of the church of England, *Calf.* 199 n.; used in all Romish sacraments, *Calf.* 210, &c., 2 *Ful.* 160, &c.; formerly used in confirmation, *Lit. Edw.* 125, 3 *Tyn.* 72; the sign made over the dead, 1 *Lat.* 499; not to be used on entering any church, *Grin.* 140; the alleged commodity of this sign, 2 *Ful.* 196, &c.; miracles wrought by it, *ib.* 189, &c.; demons said to have been put to flight by it, 2 *Ful.* 143—145, 172, *Whita.* 591

iv. *The cross metaphorically:* v. Affliction, Persecution; also Exhortation.

What is meant by the cross, 3 *Bec.* 95, 605, 622; not voluntary sufferings, 1 *Lat.* 465; it may consist of sickness, poverty, or the like, 2 *Bec.* 468, or persecution, 3 *Bec.* 605; it is the sign of God's love to us, *Phil.* 245, the sure badge of his children, 2 *Hoop.* 214, the livery of Christ, *Pil.* 191, a token of election, 2 *Brad.* 229, the way to glory, 3 *Bec.* 95, &c.; Christ entered glory by it, *ib.* 96; the cross no strange thing to God's children, 1 *Brad.* 397; the saints have always suffered it, 2 *Bul.* 102; the New Testament is the word of the cross, 1 *Brad.* 264; it is promised to Christians in scripture, 3 *Bec.* 195; Christians prepare themselves unto it, *ib.* 203; each Christian must have his cross for the subduing of the flesh, 2 *Tyn.* 9; no true Christians can be without it, *ib.* 18; probations out of scripture that true Christians are seldom free from it, 3 *Bec.* 344, 345, that it is laid on them by God, *ib.* 345, that it ought to be borne of Christians patiently, *ib.* 346, &c., that pleasures and joys follow it, *ib.* 348; its commodities, 1 *Brad.* 423, &c., 2 *Brad.* 217, 2 *Cov.* 239, &c.; crosses call us to Christ, 1 *Lat.* 465; we may not try to avoid the cross, 2 *Brad.* 120, 2 *Lat.* 429, &c.; it must be embraced, *Rid.* 71; we must take it up, *Sand.* 377, 2 *Tyn.* 28, 76; (though the flesh is so weak that we can never do this of ourselves, 1 *Tyn.* 198); if we do not take it up, it will be placed upon us, 2 *Tyn.* 10; an exhortation to take up the cross, *Phil.* 251; if we take it up we may be assured of glory everlasting, *ib.* 265; on the bearing of it, 2 *Brad.* 60, 2 *Bul.* 96, *Poet.* 356; examples out of scripture of men bearing it, and the good end thereof, 3 *Bec.* 97, &c.; it must be borne patiently, 1 *Brad.* 375, 2 *Lat.* 185, 1 *Tyn.* 301, though it seem long, *Pil.* 127; the patient bearing of it declares who is a true member of Christ's church, 3 *Bec.* 203; a man cannot bear it of his own strength, 1 *Bec.* 283

Cross of St Andrew: *Calf.* 105
Cross-bitten: thwarted, *Calf.* 1
Cross-diggers: *Bale* 236
Cross-row: the alphabet, *Calf.* 52
Cross-week: rogation week, the week in which May 3 occurs, *Calf.* 66, *Grin.* 141, *Pil.* 556
Crotoaldus (Val.): *Rog.* 196 n
Crotone: Pliny says the pestilence was never there, 2 *Hoop.* 168
Crouch (......): *v.* Crooch.
Crouching: kneeling to a cross, 2 *Tyn.* 158
Crowick, co. Northumberland: *Rid.* 489, 492
Crowley (Rob.): a divine, a poet, and a printer, *Park.* 275 n.; some account of him, 2 *Zur.* 147 n.; in exile, 1 *Cran.* (9); called the vestments, the conjuring garments of popery, *Grin.* 211; expelled divers clerks from St Giles's, Cripplegate, who were attending a funeral in surplices, *Park.* 275, 276; his opinions declared to be anabaptistical, *ib.* 276; imprisoned in his own house, *ib.* 276, 278; he edited a treatise (ascribed to Tyndale) on the supper of the Lord, 3 *Tyn.* 220; answered two sermons by bp Watson, 2 *Brad.* 207 n; refuted an anonymous libel against God's providence and predestination, 2 *Ful.* 3

Crown: *v.* England, Scotland, Kings.
Crown: *v.* Coinage.
Crown (Shaven): *v.* Tonsure.
Croxden abbey, co. Stafford: its suppression, 2 *Cran.* 380, 387
Croy (... de), son of the duke of Arschot: wounds the prince of Spain in a tournament, 1549, 3 *Zur.* 61
Croy (Cha. Ph. de), marquis of Havre, brother of the duke of Arschot: commands troops in the Netherlands, 1577, 2 *Zur.* 290
Croydon, co. Surrey: examination of the vicar, Roland Philipps, before Cranmer, 2 *Cran.* 338; the vicar referred to, 2 *Tyn.* 302, 338; the priests neglect to obliterate the pope's name from the church-books, 2 *Cran.* 369; the priest of St Nicholas' chantry charged with lewdness, *ib.* 393, 394; archbishop Grindal desires to be buried in the choir, *Grin.* 458; his tomb, *ib.* xvi; his

gift to the poor, *ib.* 460; the archiepiscopal palace, 2 *Cran.* 348 n. &c.; Grindal desires to have it, and some lands adjacent, on his resigning, *Grin.* 399, 403; an earthquake thereabouts, *ib.* 354, 3 *Zur.* 433

Cruche: a bishop's crook, *Pil.* 584, 586

Crucifix: *v.* Cross, Images.
See *Calf.* passim; to be regarded very differently from a cross, *ib.* 185, 362 n.; not allowable, 2 *Zur.* 25, 26, 39, 41, 43, 47; disputation respecting the crucifix and images, 1 *Zur.* 67, 73; the holy rood, with St Mary and St John, 1 *Ful.* 190, 204; Elizabeth desires to retain them, 1 *Zur.* 73, 74; (as to the retention of the crucifix in her private chapel, *v.* Elizabeth); the crucifix disallowed by Bullinger, 1 *Zur.* 345; its use opposed by Jewel, *Jew.* xv.

Crucifixion: *Now.* (100); abolished by Constantine, 2 *Jew.* 650

Cruciger (......), superintendent of the reformed churches of Little Poland, 3 *Zur.* 602 n

Cruds: curds, *Bale*, 191

Crusades: the object of the clergy in promoting them, 1 *Tyn.* 338; this realm impoverished by them, *Pil.* 372

Crypto-Calvinists: 1 *Zur.* 315 n

Cubit: what, *Bale*, 602

Cuckoo: 1 *Brad.* 495

Cud: chewing thereof, 2 *Bul.* 13

Cullen (Pat. O'): *v.* O'Cullen.

Culpa: *v.* Absolution.
Difference between it and pœna, 3 *Bec.* 605, 3 *Bul.* 90

Culpepper (Jo.): recommended to the king, 2 *Cran.* 361

Culpepper (Tho.): executed, 2 *Cran.* 408 n, 3 *Zur.* 226 n

Culpepper (......): married the sister of Leonard Dacres, *Park.* 367; a suspected person, *ib.*

Culverwell (Nich.): *Jew.* xiv.

Cumberland: a lawless country, *Grin.* 257, 268

Cumnor, co. Berks: the seat of the earl of Leicester, *Coop.* xiv; death of Amy Robsart there, 2 *Bec.* 583 n

Cunner, i.e. Cunerus P. de Brouwershaven, *q. v.*

Cunning: learning, 2 *Tyn.* 336

Cunningham (Alex.), earl of Glencairn: *v.* Conyngham.

Cunningham (......): an astrologer, 1 *Ful.* v.

Cups: *v.* Chalices.
Text appropriate to a cup, 1 *Bec.* 64; the word is taken in Scripture for any thing that may happen to us, 2 *Hoop.* 229; many times for adversity, *ib.* 338; affliction called the cup of health, 1 *Bec.* 282, 283; we must take it at the Lord's hand, *ib.* 284; the cup running over (Psa. xxiii.), 2 *Cov.* 314

Cuperus (Gisb.), *Calf.* 105 n

Curates: *v.* Clergy, Manipulus, Ministers.
Ministers having cure of souls, 1 *Tyn.* 146, 300, 3 *Tyn.* 151; also ministers hired to perform the duties of others, 1 *Whitg.* 517, 527; great and little cures, 2 *Lat.* 350

Cure: office, 2 *Tyn.* 208; used for care, 2 *Bec.* 112

Curet: corslet, 2 *Bul.* 135

Curian (And.): 4 *Bul.* xv.

Curio (Cœlius Secundus): notices of him, *Phil.* 320, 3 *Zur.* 89 n., 595; his DEFENCE OF THE TRUE AND OLD AUTHORITY OF CHRIST'S CHURCH, translated by Jo. Philpot, *Phil.* 319; saluted or named, 3 *Zur.* 85, 89, 94, 327

Curiosity: dangerous in religion, *Phil.* 316; 3 *Whitg.* 573—577; an impediment to obedience, 1 *Hoop.* 419

Curius Dentatus (M. A.), 2 *Bec.* 308, 1 *Lat.* 44

Currency: *v.* Coinage.

Curse: scriptural meaning of the word, 1 *Tyn.* 406; the curse of God, 3 *Bec.* 604; it is fearful, 1 *Brad.* 57, &c.; cursings on those who disobey God's word, 2 *Bec.* 617, 618; that of Paul (*q. v.*) against false preachers, 3 *Bul.* 52; how he wished himself accursed, *Pil.* 424; whether cursing is allowed by God's law, *Bale* 103; the pope's blasphemous mode of cursing, with bell, book, and candle, 1 *Tyn.* 272; the general curse formerly read in the church four times a year, *ib.* 233, 337; copy of it from the Festival, 1532, 2 *Cran.* 281 n.; modus fulminandi sententiam, *ib.* 282 n.; its reading suspended, *ib.* 281—283; forbidden, *ib.* 461; a custom of cursing thieves in the marches of Wales, 1 *Tyn.* 273

Curry-Mallet, co. Somerset: the benefice 2 *Cran.* 255

Curteis, (i. e. courteous): Wolsey so called, 2 *Tyn.* 182

Curteys (Rich.), bp of Chichester: made dean of Chichester, *Park.* 290; recommended for the see, *ib.* 331; meet to serve the court, *ib.* 350; an ecclesiastical commissioner, *ib.* 383; he suspends Thickpenny, *Grin.* 359, 360

Curtius (Corn.), De Clavis Dominicis, *Calf.* 328 n

Curtopp (James), dean of Peterborough: notices of him, *Phil.* xxx, 3 *Zur.* 373; he assists Jewel, *Jew.* vii; disputes with Ridley at Oxford, *Rid.* 191; named, *ib.* 237; witness against Cranmer, 2 *Cran.* 546; his deposition, *ib.* 550; one of the commissioners to examine Philpot, *Phil.* 31

Curwen (Hugh and Oliver): *v.* Coren.

Cushion (To miss the): 1 *Whitg.* 516

Cuspinian (Jo.): De Turcarum origine, *Bale* 572; he says the Turks abhor images, *Calf.* 44, 45

Custody: things left in it, 2 *Bul.* 288

Custom: *v.* Dialogues.

It reconciles us to all things, 2 *Cran.* 118; how far to be followed, *Calf.* 54, 55; it must yield to truth, 1 *Jew.* 49, *Whita.* 613; custom without truth is the mother of error, 1 *Jew.* 154; it is, for the most part, on the side of Satan, 1 *Brad.* 376; its evil influence, 3 *Bec.* 379; it has not the same force in religion as in the state, *Whita.* 612; of no strength to prove a religion, 2 *Cran.* 50; not to be objected in favour of the mass, 3 *Bec.* 380; not a sufficient excuse for swearing, 1 *Bec.* 376; against wicked old customs, with sentences and examples of scripture, *ib.* 439; customs of Tyndale's time, 1 *Tyn.* 423

Cuthbert (St): his body translated, *Pil.* 591 n

Cuttle fish: 1 *Cran.* 24, *Rid.* 36

Cyaxares I. and II., kings of Persia: 1 *Bul.* 51 n

Cynus Pistoriensis: 4 *Jew.* xxxvi, 647

Cusa (Nich. de), cardinal: works, *Jew.* xxxv; he says, the mind cannot know God, and not love him, 3 *Jew.* 584; held that Christ descended into the place of torment, 1 *Lat.* 234 n.; terms the outward mixed assembly of professed Christians ecclesia conjecturalis, 4 *Jew.* 668; sets the church above scripture, *ib.* 1010; says, the commandments of Christ are no commandments, unless they are allowed by the church, *ib.* 759, 863, 901, 1013; states that a church may be without the scriptures, *Rog.* 199; declares that the scriptures follow the church, not the church the scriptures, 2 *Jew.* 987, 3 *Jew.* 223, 4 *Jew.* 863, 1010; maintains that the scriptures may have sundry understandings according to the times, 3 *Jew.* 248, 480, 600, 4 *Jew.* 719, 1012, *Rog.* 198; says, the priest did never celebrate without the deacon, 1 *Jew.* 198, 199; quotes Dionysius for the practice of the primitive church in not allowing non-communicants to be present, 3 *Bec.* 482; mentions certain ancient divines as saying that the bread in the sacrament is not changed in nature, but clothed with another substance more noble than itself, 3 *Jew.* 490; defends communion in one kind, 4 *Jew.* 1011; speaks of the compact made at the council of Basil, 3 *Jew.* 128, 203; affirms that Peter and Paul's primacy was given by Christ immediately, without the consecration and confirmation of any man, *ib.* 330; says the truth cleaves to Peter's chair, &c., 3 *Jew.* 221, 4 *Jew.* 720, 1009, 1011, &c., 1046, 1068, but denies that the inspiration of the Holy Ghost is wholly at the pope's commandment, 4 *Jew.* 916; declares that the judgment of faith is not always to be determined by the beck of the pope alone, for the pope may possibly be a heretic, 3 *Jew.* 344; says pope Liberius consented to the error of the Arians, *ib.* 342, 343, 4 *Jew.* 929; notes that Liberius, Honorius, and other popes being misled, fell into schismatical error, yet Peter's chair remained without fault, 3 *Jew.* 342, 4 *Jew.* 930; allows that the Donation of Constantine is forged, 1 *Jew.* 359, 4 *Jew.* 679, 839; speaks of the assumption of pope Eugenius, 3 *Jew.* 133; says, in general councils and in making of general laws, the bishop of Rome has no such power as certain flatterers would allow him, 4 *Jew.* 997; maintains that an universal council is above the pope and his apostolic see, *ib.* 922, 923; says, the bishop of Rome had always authority to be president in councils, otherwise they had not been general, *ib.* 1003; asserts that if the pope be negligent, or if he say nay, the emperor may command councils, *ib.* 998; affirms that the first eight general councils were summoned, not by the pope, but by the emperor, *ib.* 997; allows that in them the emperor presided, *ib.* 1018, 1019; says when the emperor was present in person, he was always president, *ib.* 1003; mentions that emperors sat in councils as judges, *ib.* 1015; says, that in the sixth council of Constantinople the emperor Basil, from humility, subscribed his name after the legates, the patriarchs, &c., *ib.* 1026, 1027; records that the council of Sardica was deceitfully alleged by the legates of pope Zosimus, instead of a canon of the council of Nice, *ib.* 938; says Augustine held not the council of Sardica for a catholic council, but rather for a council of Arian heretics, *ib.*; speaks of vices having grown in the church through overmuch obedience towards the prelates, *ib.* 875; calls obedience without reason the most perfect, *ib.* 719, 1011, 1012; affirms that the power of binding and loosing is no less in the church than in Christ, 3 *Jew.* 379; says, in the new testament, after a certain time, it was thought not reasonable for priests, &c , to contract matrimony, 4 *Jew.* 809; remarks on the life of monks, &c., *ib.* 799, 946; he declares that the virgin Mary was never under the dominion of the author of death, 3 *Jew.* 577; says that almost all our Christian religion is degenerated into a shew, 4 *Jew.* 874; asserts that the soul that will fly into the wilderness of contemplation must have two wings, the one of devotion, the other of knowledge, 3 *Jew.* 435; referred to on an interpolated passage in Gratian, *Calf.* 174 n.; he says, the last resolution of all things contained in the Alcoran is the sword, 4 *Jew.* 859

Cyprian (St): *v.* Arnoldus, Ruffinus.
 i. *His Life.*
 ii. *His Works.*
 iii. *On God, and Christ.*
 iv. *Scripture, Truth.*
 v. *Tradition.*
 vi. *Sin.*
 vii. *Grace, Faith, Works.*
 viii. *The Church.*
 ix. *Bishops, Priests, &c.*
 x. *Peter, Rome.*
 xi. *Sacraments.*
 xii. *Baptism.*
 xiii. *The Eucharist.*
 xiv. *Prayer, &c.*
 xv. *Marriage.*
 xvi. *Confession, Absolution, &c.*
 xvii. *Persecution.*
 xviii. *Death, &c.*
 xix. *Heresy and Schism.*
 xx. *Miscellanea.*

i. *His life*: he was bishop of Carthage, *Rog.* 329; addressed by the name of pope, 2 *Hoop.* 236, 1 *Jew.* 362, 2 *Whitg.* 86 n.; his wide jurisdiction, 2 *Whitg.* 164, 194, 205, 273, 428; he determined to do nothing as bishop, without the advice of the clergy and the consent of the people, 4 *Jew.* 909, 912, 3 *Whitg.* 255; disputes referred to him, 1 *Jew.* 382; his opinions, 3 *Zur.* 234; on some points he erred, *ib.*; he wrote to the church of Rome, 2 *Whitg.* 312; his examination by the proconsul, 2 *Lat.* 290; his thanksgiving when condemned to be beheaded, 2 *Bec.* 473; his martyrdom, 2 *Bul.* 106, 2 *Hoop.* 109; his apparel at that time, 2 *Whitg.* 22, 23, 25, 26, 1 *Zur.* 160, 350; his funeral oration made by Gregory Nazianzen, *Grin.* 10

ii. *His works*: *Calf.* 406, 2 *Ful.* 400, *Jew.* xxxvi; his treatise De Simplicitate Prælatorum, more correctly called De Unitate Ecclesiæ, *Phil.* 44 n., *Whita.* 418 n.; depravation of this tract, 2 *Ful.* 283 n., 290, 291; object of his treatise Ad Quirinum, 2 *Jew.* 690, 691; verses attributed to him, *Rog.* v. n.; some writings falsely ascribed to him, 3 *Tyn.* 48, 135; the fictitious Epistola ad Novatianum hæreticum, *Calf.* 227; twelve treatises, by Arnoldus Carnotensis, ascribed to him, 1 *Brad.* 548 n. & al.; the Exposition of the Creed attributed to him was made by Ruffinus, *Rog.* 42, *Whita.* 60; his writings to be judged by scripture, as Augustine teaches, 2 *Cran.* 33, *Whita.* 601

iii. *On God, and Christ*: he says it is dangerous to speak of God, 2 *Jew.* 675; asserts that God is not the God of all, but of believers, 4 *Jew.* 662; on his favour in permitting us to call him Father, 2 *Jew.* 722; on "the seed of the woman," *Whita.* 164 n.; he says, we should take care that when Christ comes he may find us holding what he admonished us of, observing what he taught, doing what he did, *Whita.* 692

iv. *Scripture, Truth* (see v.): he calls the word of God scripturas deificas, 1 *Jew.* 462; says all the rules of doctrine have emanated from scripture, *Whita.* 658; affirms that the gospel comprehends all things, and that nothing must be added, *Phil.* 373; on the rebaptizing of heretics, he appealed solely to the scriptures, *Whita.* 691, 692; he says, when we read the scripture, God speaks to us, when we pray, we speak to God, 3 *Whitg.* 39, 56; addresses the Novatians as reading the scriptures rather than understanding them (pseud.), 3 *Jew.* 222; on the public reading of scripture, 3 *Whitg.* 47; he declares that if we would walk in the light of Christ, we must not depart from his precepts, *Coop.* 115; advises to return to the head and source of divine tradition, &c., see xiii. and xix. below; how Deut. xvii. 12 is quoted by him, *Whita.* 421; on the excellency of the Lord's prayer, 4 *Bul.* 202, 203; he does not mention the doxology to it, *ib.* 220; cites the third book of Esdras, *Whita.* 68, 69; teaches that Christ only is to be heard, *Coop.* 62, *Whita.* 429, 643, but says that what the apostles delivered by the instruction of the Holy Ghost, is equal in authority to what Christ himself delivered, 2 *Cran.* 57; writes, forsaking error, let us follow the truth, 3 *Jew.* 351; asserts that no deliberation must be taken about adhering to the truth, 2 *Lat.* 290; says the truth is not to be dissembled, *Pil.* 631

v. *Tradition:* referred to on tradition, 2 *Ful.* 168; he uses the term for written teaching, *Whita.* 497, 498, (see iv. above); asks whether a certain tradition comes from the authority of the Lord or the gospel, &c., *Calf.* 233, 2 *Jew.* 674, 3 *Jew.* 437, *Whita.* 498; how he refers to Isa. xxix. 13,—"the precept of men," 1 *Cran.* 49, *Whita.* 639; he would not yield to custom without scripture, *Whita.* 611; says, we must not follow the custom of men, but the truth of God, *Calf.* 27, *Coop.* 161, 2 *Cran.* 50, 1 *Jew.* 49, 3 *Jew.* 351; counsels not to mark what any men before us thought best to be done, but what Christ did first, who is before all, 1 *Bec.* 376, 3 *Bec.* 394, *Coop.* 62, 161, 1 *Jew.* 49, *Phil.* 117, *Whita.* 429, 602; asserts that the Aquarii defended themselves by custom without truth, 1 *Jew.* 154; maintains that custom is not greater than truth, 2 *Cran.* 51; says that custom without truth is the antiquity of error, and that Christ called himself (not custom but) the truth, 1 *Bec.* 376, 3 *Bec.* 390, 2 *Cran.* 51, *Pil.* 537, see also 1 *Jew.* 64 n.; pronounces it sacrilege that by the appointment of man God's ordinance should be broken, 2 *Bec.* 261, 3 *Bec.* 398, 1 *Bul.* 208, 3 *Jew.* 235; speaks of the force of evil habits, *Wool.* 105

vi. *Sin:* he affirms that the Stoics and philosophers considered all sins equal, *Rog.* 137 n.; speaks of vices nigh to virtues, 2 *Whitg.* 393; says the blind love of their patrimony has deceived many, *Pil.* 630; declares that it is the work of the devil to defame God's servants, 3 *Whitg.* 606; cautions that lies cannot long deceive, 2 *Jew.* 810, 3 *Jew.* 251, 4 *Jew.* 721, 892; passages against adultery, 3 *Jew.* 402

vii. *Grace, Faith, Works:* he speaks of the substance of salvation, 3 *Jew.* 507; was wont to say we should boast of nothing, because we have nothing of our own, 2 *Bul.* 324; calls humility the groundwork of holiness, 1 *Brad.* 559; writes of God's readiness to forgive those who lament their faults, *Wool.* 142; cites scriptures concerning penitence, 1 *Ful.* 438, 439; describes its effects, 2 *Bul.* 87; says that faith only profits, 1 *Ful.* 353; affirms that to doubt, is not to know God, to offend Christ, &c., 3 *Jew.* 245; his opinion on merits, and the day of reward, 1 *Ful.* 351, 352; he observes that the testimony of a man's life is more effectual than that of his tongue, *Wool.* 8; says of Christians, they come that they may learn, they learn that they may live, 2 *Jew.* 1033, 1063; declares that no man is truly called a Christian, but he who labours to shew himself conformable to Christ, 1 *Bec.* 387; asks, how doth he say he believeth in Christ, that doth not the thing that Christ commanded? 3 *Jew.* 584; his doctrine on alms-deeds, 3 *Zur.* 234

viii. *The Church* (see iv. ix. &c.): he speaks of the mother and root of the catholic church, 2 *Ful.* 342; writing to Cornelius, bishop of Rome, he calls his church catholic, 4 *Jew.* 716; says that he who has not the church for his mother cannot have God for his father, 4 *Bul.* 51, 52, *Phil.* 317; asserts that he is not joined to the church, who is divided from the gospel; 1 *Jew.* 254, 2 *Jew.* 998, 3 *Jew.* 223, 430, 4 *Jew.* 876, *Sand.* 94, 456; declares that when we pray, we pray not for one, but for the whole people; for we, the whole people, are but one, 3 *Jew.* 301; says the church is one, as the light is one, though there are many rays, or as a tree, though it have many branches, 4 *Bul.* 49, 50, 3 *Jew.* 291, 300; speaks of one church divided into many members, and one bishoprick diffused abroad by the multitude of many bishops, 3 *Jew.* 301; thinks that the church is joined in one by consent of bishops, 1 *Jew.* 349, 372, 383, 3 *Jew.* 301, 2 *Whitg.* 211; what he means by universal brotherhood, 1 *Jew.* 349; he laments the decay of discipline and corrupt manners of his time, 3 *Jew.* 626; speaks against separation from the church, *Pil.* 617, 619; teaches that we must not depart from the church because we see cockle therein, but rather labour to be good corn, 4 *Bul.* 61, 62; says, whoever, separated from the church is joined to an adulterous church, is separated from the promises of the church, and from Christ's merits, &c., 4 *Bul* 51, 52; declares that out of the church there is no salvation, 4 *Jew.* 1072; alleged as saying that the blood of martyrs is the seed of the church, 2 *Ful.* 234, *Pil.* 144

ix. *Bishops, Priests* (see viii. x. xix.): he remarks that Christ never blamed the priests (of the Jews) except under the name of scribes and Pharisees, *Whita.* 427; holds that there ought only to be one bishop within one city, 1 *Jew.* 348, 2 *Whitg.* 214, 215; accounts every bishop within his own diocese the priest of God, 2 *Ful.* 253, 1 *Jew.* 348; says that they who are not with the bishop are not in the church, 1 *Jew.* 349; states that bishops who are made out of the church are not made by the will of God, *Pil.* 485, 597, 605; hence he denies Novatian's claim to be a bishop, 3 *Jew.* 322; calls himself and others presidents in God's church, 1 *Jew.* 434; says, deacons must remember that the Lord has chosen apostles, i. e. bishops, &c., 2 *Whitg.* 355; said to speak of the office of an archbishop, 1 *Whitg.* 70; he held bishops to be equal, 2 *Ful.* 315, 1 *Tyn.* 215 n.; condemns the tyranny of bishops over their fellows, 2 *Whitg.* 207, 208, 210, 212, 213, 265; says, we must firmly hold unity, especially (those of us who are) bishops, that we may declare our bishoprick to be but one, 3 *Jew.* 301; speaks of the bishoprick as one and undivided, 1 *Jew.* 349; says there is one bishoprick, a part of which is held in whole of every bishop, 2 *Ful.* 316, 1 *Jew.* 434, 2 *Jew.* 1001, 3 *Jew.* 284, 291, 300, 4 *Jew.* 1121, *Phil.* 73, 74; declares that a portion of the flock is committed to every pastor, 3 *Bul.* 120, 2 *Ful.* 344, 2 *Whitg.* 207, 208, 209, 265; writes, although we are many pastors, we feed one flock, and are bound to gather and to nourish all the sheep that Christ hath won by his blood, 3 *Jew.* 301; declares that priests are not made without the providence of God, *Sand.* 334; said to regard the consent of the people to the election of ministers as necessary, 1 *Whitg.* 358; he speaks of it as observed throughout almost all provinces, 1 *Jew.* 349, 1 *Whitg.* 360, 362, 469; allows that, generally speaking, a bishop should be chosen in the presence of the people, 1 *Whitg.* 362; while acknowledging that he was wont to take the advice of the clergy and people in the election of ministers, he says that the testimonies of men are not to be looked for when divine suffrages have gone before, *ib.* 444, 459; speaks of a bishop being chosen peaceably by the suffrage of all the people, 2 *Whitg.* 197, and in the presence of the people, *ib.* 198; speaks of Cornelius ascending through different degrees till made bishop (of Rome), by the testimony of his fellow bishops and the suffrages of the clerks and people, 1 *Jew.* 408, 2 *Whitg.* 198, 199, 205; on the election of Sabinus, a bishop of Spain, 1 *Jew.* 349, 409; he shews from Num. xx. and Acts i. that the ordering of ministers should be in the presence of the people, that they may object if needful, 1 *Bec.* 7, 4 *Bul.* 132, 1 *Whitg.* 361, 362, 2 *Whitg.* 198; says, the people ought to sever themselves from a wicked prelate, 1 *Jew.* 401; affirms that the people have power to choose worthy priests and to refuse unworthy, 1 *Bec.* 7, 4 *Bul.* 132, 1 *Jew.* 408, 3 *Jew.* 332; says the people ought to separate from a wicked priest, as they have power to choose, &c., 1 *Whitg.* 361; cautions the people against communicating with a sinful priest, and declares such communion to be sinful, *Pil.* 634; this opinion noted as an error, *Rog.* 270; he says that not only vicious priests shall perish, but all who favour them, *Bale* 131; says there are many priests in the church that if one promote heresy, the rest may help, 2 *Ful.* 345, 1 *Jew.* 383, 3 *Jew.* 284, 301, 2 *Whitg.* 211; held that those who had sacrificed to idols should not be permitted to minister in the church, 1 *Whitg.* 324; decreed in a council that clerks who in time of persecution had offered sacrifice should be no more admitted to the ministry, *ib.* 325, 2 *Whitg.* 310; directs them to be reduced to lay communion, *Coop.* 159 n.; confounds bishops and priests, 2 *Whitg.* 250; his use of the word "presbyterium," 1 *Ful.* 153; he translates πρεσβύτερος by "major," 4 *Jew.* 912; blames a priest who became executor of a will, 3 *Whitg.* 415; complains of the pride and ambition of priests, 1 *Jew.* 354, 442; says Paul was afraid, considering only the empty name and shadow of a priest, 3 *Jew.* 309

x. *Peter, Rome:* referred to respecting Peter as the rock, 4 *Bul.* 81 n., *Pil.* 44; he speaks of the church as founded on him, *Phil.* 75; says there is one God, and one Christ, and one church, and one chair founded on Peter (or on the rock) by the voice of the Lord, 2 *Ful.* 333, 334; affirms that the church, which is one, is founded by our Lord's voice on one that hath received the keys of it, *ib.* 290, 331; notes that the Lord gave first to Peter (or to Peter the first), on whom he built his church, the power of loosing, *ib.* 329; remarks that Peter, on whom the church had been builded by the Lord, as one speaking for all, said, "Lord, to whom shall we go?" *ib.* 330; alleged as saying that the keys were given to all in the person of Peter, *Phil.* 44, 75; he says Peter, on whom the Lord built his church, did not, when Paul disputed with him, challenge anything arrogantly, 1 *Jew.* 372, 4 *Jew.* 834, *Park.* 110; declares that the Lord after his resurrection gave equal power to all the apostles, and that the rest of them were the same that Peter was, endued with like fellowship, both of honour and of power, 2 *Ful.* 283, 291, 331, 1 *Jew.* 360, 367, 373, 384, 430, 3 *Jew.* 201, 286,

385, 605, 4 *Jew.* 1067, 1136, *Whita.* 418; observes that Christ prayed for the other disciples as well as Peter, 4 *Jew.* 929; he maintained (says Martin) that the church of Rome cannot err, 1 *Ful.* 38; the statement examined, *ib.* 39; he speaks of the apostle's praise of the Romans, and says unfaithfulness cannot have access to them (meaning that they would not listen to unfaithful reports), 1 *Ful.* 39 n., 2 *Ful.* 341, 342, 4 *Jew.* 720, 721, *Phil.* 113, 114; terms Rome the chair of Peter, and the principal church, whence priestly unity began, &c., 2 *Ful.* 341, 1 *Jew.* 428; calls Cornelius, bishop of Rome, his brother, companion and fellow-bishop, 1 *Jew.* 347, 385, 4 *Jew.* 841, *Phil.* 42; exhorts him not to shrink at the threats of the wicked, 1 *Jew.* 348, and see 3 *Whitg.* 322; (as to the election of Cornelius, see x.); calls pope Stephen his fellow-bishop, 2 *Ful.* 343; writes to him against Martian, bishop of Arles, 1 *Jew.* 405; reproves him, 2 *Ful.* 322 n., 4 *Jew.* 1046; speaks of him as in error, and a maintainer of the cause of heretics, 1 *Tyn.* 216 n.; mentions Basilides as deceiving him, 1 *Ful.* 40, 2 *Ful.* 342, 343; Cyprian differed from the bishop and church of Rome on rebaptization, 1 *Ful.* 35, 40, 2 *Ful.* 77, 345; was opposed to the pretensions of Rome, 2 *Hoop.* 236; declares it meet and right that every man's cause should be heard where the crime was committed, 3 *Bul.* 120, 2 *Ful.* 343, 344, 1 *Jew.* 389, 390, 3 *Jew.* 303, 4 *Jew.* 721; denies that the bishop of Rome has greater authority than other bishops, 4 *Jew.* 721; willed that Sabinus should continue a bishop in Spain, though disallowed by the pope, 3 *Jew.* 331; says that the authority of the bishops in Africa was no less than that of the bishop of Rome, 1 *Jew.* 390, 432, 3 *Jew.* 300; shews that bishops are not subject to the judgment of each other, but only to Christ, *Park.* 111; condemns Pupianus for making himself bishop of his bishop, 2 *Whitg.* 205, 206; says, none of us appoints himself bishop of bishops, &c., 4 *Bul.* 110, 2 *Ful.* 322, 3 *Jew.* 300; 4 *Jew.* 1119, 1 *Tyn.* 215 n., 2 *Whitg.* 208; language of the Roman clergy in an epistle to him, 2 *Ful.* 159, 160, 342

xi. *Sacraments :* he speaks of men being new born by both the sacraments, 3 *Jew.* 459; says, that sacraments declare Christians to be joined together with inseparable charity, 1 *Jew.* 134, 142; on sacramental communion with evil men, *Rid.* 121

xii. *Baptism :* he says "water" in the scriptures always means baptism, 3 *Zur.* 234; refers to three kinds of baptism, 2 *Bec.* 225 n.; calls baptism (or rather, as it seems, God) the fountain of life, 3 *Jew.* 482; used "tingentes" for "baptizantes," 1 *Ful.* 256; he, and sixty-six other bishops, assembled in council, concluded that baptism might be administered to infants before the eighth day, 2 *Bec.* 209, 4 *Bul.* 366, 392, *Phil.* 279; how the ordinance was celebrated in his time, *Calf.* 213, 225; he maintains that the water should be consecrated, *Calf.* 225, 4 *Bul.* 363; speaks of the interrogation, 1 *Whitg.* 217 n.; mentions the exorcism of infants, 1 *Zur.* 178 n.; approves aspersion, *Whita.* 592; says anointing is necessary, *Calf.* 225, *Whita.* 601, 602, 1 *Whitg.* 217 n.; on the baptism of the bed-ridden, *Calf.* 203; he thought baptism by heretics to be invalid, and maintained that those baptized by them should be baptized again, 1 *Bec.* 279, 1 *Brad.* 524, 4 *Bul.* 349, 363, 393, *Coop.* 147, 1 *Hoop.* 173, 4 *Jew.* 1109, *Whita.* 506, 507, 608, 611, 2 *Whitg.* 209, 210, 435; quoted as affirming that no minister could rightly baptize who was not himself endued with the Holy Spirit, *Rog.* 270; on the point of rebaptization he differed from the church of Rome, 1 *Ful.* 35, 40, 2 *Ful.* 77, 345; he was in error, but not a heretic, 2 *Ful.* 376; not obstinate in his error, 4 *Bul.* 393; he relates that the Novatians abused baptism by rebaptizing, *Rog.* 266 n., 277 n.; speaks dangerously of the lapsed, *Coop.* 147

xiii. *The Eucharist :* (some of the sentences in v. above refer to this subject); on Melchisedec and his offering, 1 *Cran.* 86, 158, 1 *Ful.* 148, 2 *Jew.* 730, 731; his exposition of "our daily bread," 3 *Bec.* 470, 1 *Hoop.* 232 n., 2 *Jew.* 762; he says that both the passover and the eucharist were Christ's, *Rid.* 233; teaches that none but Christ is to be followed in the sacrifice which Christ offered, *Coop.* 161, 162, 2 *Jew.* 725, *Phil.* 65; declares that we should celebrate the sacrament as our Lord did, *Coop.* 80; he calls it the holy thing of the Lord, &c., 3 *Bec.* 388, and the passion of Christ, 2 *Jew.* 792, 3 *Jew.* 527; said to maintain the real presence of Christ's body therein, *Rid.* 201; he says Christ's body is present by faith, 2 *Jew.* 741; confesses that the body of Christ is meat for the soul (pseud.), 3 *Jew.* 543, 544; says the Lord called the bread, made by the moulding together of many grains, his body, and the wine, pressed out of many grapes, his blood, 2 *Bec.* 267,

286, 3 *Bec.* 424, 437, 1 *Brad.* 590, 4 *Bul.* 336, 1 *Cran.* 33, 104, (54), *Hutch.* 239, 1 *Jew.* 516, 2 *Jew.* 795, 1115, 3 *Jew.* 483, see also *Coop.* 121 n.; compares the eucharistic bread, consisting of many grains, but one loaf, to the mystical body of Christ, the heavenly bread, *Rid.* 174, 175; says that not meal alone, nor water alone, can be the body of Christ, 1 *Cran.* 104; speaks of the sacrament as denoting unanimity, 1 *Jew.* 134, 142; his works contain traces of the ancient way of celebrating the eucharist, 4 *Bul.* 409; he shews the necessity of frequent communion, 3 *Jew.* 470; speaks of daily communion, 1 *Whitg.* 217; mentions the exhortation "Lift up your hearts," and the response thereto, 3 *Bec.* 266, 360, 407, 1 *Cov.* 456 n., 1 *Jew.* 285, 292, 3 *Jew.* 534, *Rid.* 318, *Whita.* 260; speaks of the chalice consecrated by solemn blessing, 1 *Ful.* 501; mentions the mixed cup as necessary, and as Christ's institution, *Coop.* 136 n., 1 *Jew.* 139, 3 *Jew.* 349, *Whita.* 498, 499, 602, 2 *Whitg.* 435, 3 *Zur.* 234; says it was foreshewn by Solomon, 1 *Ful.* 522; passages concerning it, 4 *Bul.* 411—414; he says, the wine expresses the blood, by the water the people is understood, &c., 1 *Cran.* 121, (58), 2 *Jew.* 726, 3 *Jew.* 350, 2 *Whitg.* 541 n.; opposes the Aquarii, who used only water in the eucharist, *Coop.* 62, 132; admonishes them to return to the root and beginning of the Lord's tradition or ordinance, *Coop.* 74, 75, 1 *Hoop.* 238, 1 *Jew.* 215; warns that the precepts of the gospel must not be departed from, *Coop.* 109, 110, and admonishes to return to the ordinance of the Lord and his apostles, *ib.* 131, 132; he did not so much advocate the mixing with water, as the use of wine, *Whita.* 498, 602; yet he estimates the practice too highly, *ib.* 603; passages on the wine in the eucharist, 2 *Hoop.* 421 —423, 500; writing against the aforesaid heretics he says, forasmuch as Christ said, "I am the true vine," therefore the blood of Christ is not water, but wine; nor can it be thought that his blood is in the cup, when wine is not in the cup, whereby the blood of Christ is shewed, 1 *Cran.* 267, (30), 1 *Hoop.* 232, 2 *Hoop.* 421, *Rid.* 204, *Whita.* 499 n.; affirms that it was wine that the Lord called his blood, and declares, that Christ's blood is not offered if wine be wanting, 2 *Bec.* 286, 3 *Bec.* 437, 1 *Brad.* 546, 1 *Cran.* 104, 267, (30), 2 *Hoop.* 421, *Hutch.* 272, 2 *Jew.* 606, 3 *Jew.* 521, 522; says further, how shall we drink with Christ new wine of the creature of the vine, if in the sacrifice we do not offer wine? 1 *Cran.* 267, (30), 2 *Hoop.* 421, 2 *Jew.* 795, 3 *Jew.* 522; referred to against separating the bread and the cup, 4 *Bul.* 416 n.; he testifies that the cup was given to the laity, *Coop.* 139, 140, 143, *Sand.* 455; warns against leaving Christians without the defence of the body and blood of Christ, 3 *Bec.* 414; asks how we make them meet for the cup of martyrdom, if we do not admit them to drink the cup of the Lord in the church? 2 *Bec.* 243, 3 *Bec.* 413, *Coop.* 139, 140, *Pil.* 542; in his time the Lord's supper was given to children, 1 *Hoop.* 172, *Whita.* 666; referred to to shew that the bread and the cup were given into the hands of the communicants, 2 *Bec.* 301 n.; he speaks of sacrificing for the martyrs, *Coop.* 96, 3 *Jew.* 561; says, drink sanctified into the blood of Christ burst out of the defiled bowels (of Judas), 2 *Bec.* 267, 3 *Bec.* 424; relates that an apostate coming to receive the sacrament, found instead thereof his hands full of ashes, 2 *Hoop.* 415, 1 *Jew.* 153, 2 *Jew.* 761, 785; tells of a woman who reserved the sacrament irreverently, and saw it burning in her coffer, *Coop.* 24, 1 *Jew.* 6, 148, 241, 242, 2 *Jew.* 554, *Phil.* 206; the story shews that God is displeased with the reserving of the sacrament, 1 *Jew.* 151; his account of a child, who having eaten meats sacrificed to idols, was brought to receive the sacramental cup, *Coop.* 33, 165, 1 *Hoop.* 172 n., 1 *Jew.* 6, 249, 250, *Sand.* 455, *Whita.* 666

xiv. *Prayer, &c.*: he calls God the hearer, not of the voice, but of the heart, 1 *Bec.* 133, 1 *Brad.* 34; describes the right affections of the mind in prayer, 4 *Bul.* 178; advises to pray with modesty, not with clamour, *ib.* 185; on the petition "deliver us from evil," 2 *Whitg.* 484; as to the Lord's prayer see also iv. and xiii; he speaks of the reader sounding out the lofty words, the gospel of Christ, 4 *Jew.* 856; as to the public reading of scripture see also v.

xv. *Marriage* (see vi.): he reprehends the marriage of vowed virgins, 3 *Jew.* 386; elsewhere he allows that virgins may marry, notwithstanding their resolution not to do so, 4 *Bul.* 512, 513, and recommends those who cannot or will not persevere in chastity, to marry, 3 *Jew.* 399, 401, 402, 4 *Jew.* 797; declares that to maintain (the pretence of) a continent life with reproach is worse than adultery, 3 *Jew.* 425

xvi. *Confession, Absolution, &c.:* he

speaks of exomologesis, i. e. confession, 1 *Ful.* 457 n.; writes of certain devout persons who confessed their sins to the priests of God sorrowfully and simply, 3 *Jew.* 368, 369; sets forth the order of confession, and describes the mode of absolving penitents, *ib.* 360; speaks of confession being made by the penitent, and his conscience being purged by sacrifice and the hand of the priest, 1 *Ful.* 457 n., 2 *Ful.* 83; declares that those who break canonical obedience must do penance, *Pil.* 629, and those who return from idol altars, *ib.* 630; says the Lord alone may shew mercy and forgive sins, 2 *Bec.* 172, 173; declares that the power of remitting sins was given to the apostles, to the churches which they founded, and to the bishops who succeeded them, *Whita.* 418 n.; speaks of things bound on earth being bound in heaven, &c., 3 *Jew.* 367 n.; uses the word "remissa" instead of "remissio," 2 *Jew.* 640; severely rebuked certain men who thought that other men's offences ought to be forgiven by the church for their merits, 3 *Tyn.* 199; on the undue absolution of Victor by Therapius, 3 *Whitg.* 254; he tells how a dying man being excommunicate should seek to be reconciled, 1 *Jew.* 244; reproves certain priests for too hastily receiving back some who had been excommunicated, 3 *Whitg.* 255, and declares his intention in such cases, *ib.* 256; says he is not a wise shepherd who gathers to his flock sheep that are diseased, *Pil.* 633; admonishes that ecclesiastical discipline is not to be left off because we are reviled, 3 *Whitg.* 322, and see 1 *Jew.* 348

xvii. *Persecution:* he says Christians were blamed for the calamities of his age, 1 *Tyn.* 164 n.; affirms that opprobrious speeches ought not to make us decline from the right way, 3 *Whitg.* 322; declares that (in time of persecution) God tries his family, &c., *Pil.* 632; says many have betrayed their faith at the first threats of the enemy, *ib.* 631; affirms that it is no shame to suffer of our brethren what Christ suffered, &c., 4 *Jew.* 859; writes on confessing the Lord when apprehended by the heathen, or in flight, *Grin.* 239, *Rid.* 387; says the priest of God, holding the gospel and keeping the commandments of Christ, may be killed, but cannot be conquered, 3 *Jew.* 189, 4 *Jew.* 770; exhibits the power of martyrdom, whereby persecutors are forced to believe (pseud.), 3 *Jew.* 558; said to call the blood of martyrs the seed of the church, 2 *Ful.* 234, *Pil.* 144

xviii. *Death, &c.:* he exhorts to repentance even at the very end of this temporal life, and warns that when we are departed hence, there is no place of repentance, 1 *Bec.* 326, 327, 3 *Bec.* 129, 277, 460; 3 *Bul.* 113, 114, 393; speaks of the profit of going out of the world, 3 *Bec.* 121; declares that departed brethren ought not to be mourned for, since they live with God, *ib.* 121, 461; shews that we should not mourn for those deceased as though they were lost, *ib.* 121, 122; on mourning apparel, 3 *Whitg.* 369, 370; he says, he fears death who will not go to Christ, 2 *Hoop.* 566; states that repentance after death shall be without fruit, 3 *Bec.* 129; says, such as God finds men when he calls them, such does he judge them, 2 *Bec.* 395, 3 *Bec.* 460; writes, we embrace the day of death, which assigns every one to his abode, &c., 2 *Lat.* 247; said not to mention purgatory, *ib.*; he speaks of purgation by fire, 3 *Zur.* 234; says he who acts against his conscience...builds for hell, *Grin.* 387

xix. *Heresy and Schism:* he says that the offences, through ignorance, of his predecessors, were no excuse for his continuance in error, and declares that he who errs of simplicity may be pardoned, but not he who perseveres in error after the revelation of the truth, *Coop.* 136, 1 *Jew.* 220, 3 *Jew.* 217, 349; exhorts men to flee from heresy as from the plague, *Whita.* 17; says the devil has devised a new fraud, under the very title of the name of Christ to deceive the unwary, 3 *Jew.* 152; speaks of some who teach night instead of day, destruction instead of safety, desperation under pretence of hope,...Antichrist under the name of Christ, 3 *Jew.* 247; shews how pride and self-will originate schisms and heresies, 3 *Whitg.* 605; says that heresies and schisms arise from not obeying God's priest, and because one priest and one judge at a time in the church (i. e. the bishop) is not considered as in the place of Christ, 2 *Ful.* 332, 1 *Jew.* 347, 349, 373, 3 *Jew.* 605, *Phil.* 73, 74, *Whita.* 441, 2 *Whitg.* 192, 193, 223, 240; again, he says that heresies and schisms arise from the bishop, who is one, and presides in the church, being despised by the arrogant presumption of certain persons, 1 *Jew.* 350, *Whita.* 441, 2 *Whitg.* 223; again, he says they arise because we go not to the origin of truth, nor seek the head, nor keep the doctrine of the heavenly Master, *Coop.* 62, 190, 2 *Cran.* 40, 1 *Jew.* 25, 79, 4 *Jew.* 1085; affirms that if we return to the head and origin of the divine tradition, all man's error will cease, 1 *Hoop.* 238, 1 *Jew.* 79, 80, 3 *Jew.* 236, 350, 4 *Jew.* 1047, 1169; calls them schismatics who usurp the office of a bishop, 4 *Bul.* 131; compares those who set up another altar, &c., to Korah and his company, *Pil.* 624, 628; on the heresy of the Cathari, *Rog.* 135; he wrote against the Novatians, 1 *Bec.* 94; says, Novatian, after the manner of apes, challenged to himself the authority of the catholic church, &c., 3 *Jew.* 150, *Whita.* 667; tells that his sect abused baptism by rebaptizing, *Rog.* 266 n., 277 n.; he refers to certain bishops drawn into his heresy, 2 *Whitg.* 211; speaks of Felicissimus a Novatian, being expelled from the church, *ib.* 202; relates that ninety bishops condemned Privatus, *ib.* 198, 200; as to the Aquarii, see v. and xiii. above, and as to Basilides, see x.

xx. *Miscellanea:* he takes the thau of Ezekiel for a mark, 2 *Ful.* 138; speaks of the origin and abuse of images, 2 *Jew.* 645, 646; relates how wicked spirits lurk in them, *Calf.* 317, 318; says that Satan changes himself into an angel of light to teach false doctrines, 2 *Cran.* 40; declares that evil spirits, being lost themselves, seek to destroy others, *ib.*; on man's upright posture, *Calf.* 371, 372; his high opinion of Tertullian, *Rid.* 37; referred to on legislators, *Pil.* 680; alleged by Gratian, as saying, Christ, by separate duties and distinct honours, hath set a difference between the offices of both powers, 4 *Jew.* 826, 985; on mourning apparel, 3 *Whitg.* 369, 370; on the holy oil (pseud.), 3 *Jew.* 510; Cyprian referred to, 1 *Brad.* 338; falsified by Harding, 1 *Jew.* 351

Cyprian of Antioch : 3 *Jew.* 333 n

Cyprian, bp of Rome: on holy water, 1 *Jew.* 15 n

Cyprianus (Ern. Sal.): *Calf.* 128 n

Cyprus: belonged to Venice, 4 *Jew.* 693; invaded by the Turks, 1 *Zur.* 239 n

Cyribiria : 4 *Bul.* 52

Cyril of Alexandria:
    i. *His Life and Works.*
    ii. *On God.*
    iii. *Scripture.*
    iv. *Grace, &c.*
    v. *The Church, Peter, &c.*
    vi. *Sacraments.*
    vii. *Miscellanea.*

i. *His life and works:* he was desired by pope Celestinus to represent him in the council of Ephesus, 4 *Jew.* 1002; called the head of the bishops assembled there, 3 *Jew.* 270; his confession sanctioned by this council, 1 *Bul.* 17, 2 *Hoop.* 534; the decree of Chalcedon not contrary to his doctrine, 1 *Bul* 20; he has been condemned by heretical councils, *Rid.* 134; referred to, *Whita.* 107, 678; his works, 2 *Ful.* 400, *Jew.* xxxvi; translation of his commentary on John by Geo. Trapezuntius, with the addition by Clichtoveus, 2 *Bec.* 173 n., 2 *Ful.* 277 n.; his rescript in the council of Africa, 1 *Jew.* 356, 358, 3 *Jew.* 340; he alleges Amphilochius, 1 *Jew.* 475; charges not to corrupt his writings, *Bale* 638; how alleged in the second council of Nice, *Calf.* 173; certain homilies ascribed to him seem to be Origen's, 2 *Jew.* 553 n

ii. *On God; the Father, the Son, and the Holy Ghost:* he cites Pythagoras respecting God, 1 *Bul.* 197, 198, 3 *Bul.* 124, 1 *Hoop.* 285; says Paul did rightly know the enumeration of the sacred Trinity, 3 *Bul.* 164; defines a true faith in the Trinity, *ib.* 168; his exposition of John i. 1, "In the beginning was the Word," *ib.* 240—242; he proves Christ's divinity by his adoration, *Calf.* 378; says, Christ would not be adored, unless we believed that the very Word was made flesh, 1 *Jew.* 530; asserts that the humanity and divinity of Christ joined in one must be honoured together, *ib.* 525; allows the title θεοτόκος, denied by Nestorius, 3 *Jew.* 224; imagines Christ as saying "I have taken mortal flesh upon myself; but forasmuch as I, naturally being life, dwell in the same, I have reformed that whole flesh unto my life," *ib.* 538; declares that Christ meant not to reign worldly, 1 *Hoop.* 79; shews why the Pharisees kept people from coming to Christ, 2 *Jew.* 1021, 3 *Jew.* 570, 595; attributes the opposition of the scribes and Pharisees to Christ, to the fact that he was not of the priesthood, *ib.* 324; says the Jews first bound Christ, then sought cause against him, 1 *Jew.* 58, 2 *Jew.* 629; declares that the flesh of Christ by nature hath power to give life, 3 *Jew.* 510; asserts that Christ was more than a common man, else his blood could not work salvation, *ib.* 538; speaks of his body after his resurrection, 3 *Bul.* 257—259; writes on his leaving the world and going to the Father, *Phil.* 195; says, Christ is present by the Spirit, 1 *Jew.* 486; speaks of him as saying, "Although I be absent in body, yet as God I will be present," 3 *Jew.* 486; affirms that he departed only according to the flesh, *ib.* 262;

declares that he took away the presence of his body, though in the majesty of his Godhead he is ever here, 2 *Bec.* 273, 3 *Bec.* 273, 274, 427; says he will evermore be with his disciples by the power of his Divinity, although not in body, 3 *Jew.* 535; states that he is absent from us as concerning his body, but by his power is present with all that love him, 3 *Bec.* 428, 429; says that, if the nature of the Godhead were a body, it must needs be in a place, 2 *Bec.* 281, 3 *Bec.* 454; affirms that Christ could not be conversant with the apostles in the flesh after he had ascended to the Father, 1 *Jew.* 495, 2 *Jew.* 776, 1118, 3 *Jew.* 257; speaks of us as corporally in Christ, and of Christ as corporally in us, 1 *Jew.* 476, 2 *Lat.* 273; says we are joined to Christ both spiritually and according to the flesh, 1 *Jew.* 471, and uses many other similar phrases, *ib.*; writes on the Divinity of the Holy Ghost, 3 *Bul.* 304; shews that he is the Spirit of the Son as well as of the Father, *ib.* 306

iii. *Scripture:* he affirms that it is needful to follow the holy scriptures, and in nothing to depart from what they prescribe, *Whita.* 687; says (in a mystical exposition ascribed also to Origen) that every word pertaining to God is to be sought out in the two Testaments, *ib.*; rejoiced that the faith of the church was agreeable to the divine scriptures and the traditions of the fathers, 3 *Jew*, 229; to prove the divinity of Christ he relied on scripture, *Coop,* 198; he says that certain councils concluded a controversy by the evangelistic and apostolic words (cited by Evagrius), 3 *Jew.* 228; affirms that the scriptures, that they may be easy to all men, are profitably set abroad in familiar speech, 4 *Jew.* 897, *Whita.* 399; declares that all things are plain and straight to them that have found knowledge; but to fools the most easy places seem hard, 4 *Jew.* 1184; speaks of young men being brought up in the scriptures, 2 *Jew.* 676, 681; says Julian complained that Christian women were skilled in the scriptures, *ib.* 676; declares that even children become devout by reading the scriptures, 1 *Jew.* 57, 3 *Jew.* 605; remarks that all things were not written which the Lord did, but those which the writers thought sufficient, as well for good manners as for doctrine, 2 *Cran.* 33, *Whita.* 547, 625, 630, 687; gives directions about the interpretation of scripture, *Whita.* 492; shews that the scriptures are difficult to heretics, 2 *Jew.* 683; says they gather occasion of error out of them, 4 *Jew.* 752

iv. *Grace, &c.:* on the severity of the law and the mercy of the gospel, 1 *Whitg.* 329, 330; he says that inwardly to quicken a sinner is the gift of God, 2 *Bec.* 173; declares Christ to be the beginning and foundation unto holiness and righteousness, by faith, and none otherwise; and shews that he dwells in us by faith, 3 *Jew.* 496, 539; says, if thou offer up thy faith as the price, thou shalt receive remission of thy sins from Christ, *ib.* 559; speaks of Christ as saying, "So I made you partakers of the divine nature, when I caused my Spirit to dwell in you;" for, he adds, Christ is in us by his Spirit, changing our corruption into incorruption, *ib.* 593; declares that Christ alone is to be followed as a master, 1 *Bec.* 88, 2 *Cran.* 33

v. *The Church, Peter, &c.:* he speaks of corporal union among Christians, 3 *Jew.* 495; says, it is not enough to be reckoned amongst the branches of the true Vine, &c., 2 *Cran.* 203, 204; declares that Christ gave full power to the apostles, and their successors, 1 *Jew.* 360; says Peter, as prince and head of the rest, first exclaimed, "Thou art the Christ," *ib.* 436; affirms that Christ by giving Simon the name of Peter, signified that he would build his church on him, 2 *Ful.* 277; thinks that Christ, by "this rock," meant Peter's faith, *ib.* 277, 278, 297, 1 *Jew.* 340, 4 *Jew.* 1119; on the charge to Peter, "Feed my sheep," *Hutch.* 103; he calls a bishop ἀρχιερέα, 2 *Whitg.* 310; says that a bishop is to teach those things that he has learned of God, and not of his own heart, 2 *Cran.* 33; a passage respecting the supremacy of Rome, ascribed to Cyril by Tho. Aquinas, *Whita.* 440, see *Coop.* 149; he addresses the bishop of Rome as his fellow-servant, 1 *Jew.* 373, and as his brother, 4 *Jew.* 841

vi. *Sacraments:* he speaks of only two sacraments (Cyr. Jer.?), 3 *Jew.* 459; he would not speak much of baptism in the presence of the unbaptized, 2 *Jew.* 706; says that heed must be taken not to deliver Christ in the sacrament of baptism unto catechumens before they be strong, 3 *Jew.* 544, 545; approves the baptizing of children, 4 *Bul.* 392, 393; illustrates, by the comparison of heated water, the communication of divine power to the water of baptism, 2 *Jew.* 565, 1102; condemns the iteration of baptism, 4 *Bul.* 392, 393, *Phil.* 280; says Christ was the very true manna, whom, under the figure of manna, God gave unto the fathers of the old testament, 3 *Jew.* 545; shews why manna is called the food of angels, 2 *Jew.* 620; his expressions on Christ's presence in his supper, *Rid.* 201, 202; he says Christ gave bread to his disciples, (τὸν ἄρτον, fragmenta panis), 2 *Bec.* 288, 3 *Bec.* 424, 439, 1 *Brad.* 590, 1 *Jew.* 149, 2 *Jew.* 580, 585, 606, 772, 795, 1116, 3 *Jew.* 483, 516; speaks of some who thought they were called to eat raw flesh, which is a horrible thing, 3 *Bec.* 443; denies (against Nestorius) that the sacrament is ἀνθρωποφαγία, the eating of a man, 1 *Jew.* 141, 150, 454, 475, 2 *Jew.* 623, 1120, 3 *Jew.* 537, 539; teaches that when we come to receive these mysteries, all gross imaginations must quite be banished, 3 *Jew.* 536, 538; speaks of the eucharist as a life-giving blessing, 1 *Brad.* 97 n.; says that he who eats the holy flesh of Christ has eternal life, &c., 2 *Bec.* 294, 1 *Brad.* 98 n., 1 *Jew.* 527—529, 2 *Jew.* 766; declares that when we eat the flesh of Christ we have life in us, 2 *Bec.* 294, 3 *Bec.* 464; asserts that the flesh of Christ makes them to live that are partakers of it, 3 *Bec.* 464; says that they who receive the bread of life shall obtain immortality, 2 *Bec.* 294, 3 *Bec.* 464; teaches that through the participation of Christ's body, men are nourished unto everlasting life, 3 *Bec.* 464; declares that, if men come seldom to church, and refuse to partake the mystical receiving of Christ, they debar themselves from everlasting life, *ib.* 470, 471; exhorts that, if we will obtain everlasting life, we gladly run to receive the blessing (in the sacrament), *ib.* 471, 472; describes the union of believers, through participation of the Lord's body, 1 *Jew.* 140; says that, as two molten waxes run into each other, so he that receives Christ's flesh and blood is joined with him, 3 *Bec.* 464; affirms that the Son of God, by the mystical blessing is united unto us as a man, 3 *Jew.* 484, 495; declares that we are of one body with Christ, *ib.* 491; calls the sacrament a table driving away all diseases, &c., 3 *Bec.* 388; affirms the handling and sanctification of Christ's body to be meet for those only who are sanctified in spirit, *ib.* 412; speaks of altars erected in Britain, and in far countries, *Rid.* 280; says they are mad who approve not of the reservation of the sacrament (dub.), *Coop.* 25, 149, 2 *Jew.* 780; calls the prayers of the angels and blessed spirits, unbloody sacrifices, 2 *Jew.* 734; speaks of our offering unto God, faith, hope, charity, as sweet savours, *ib.*

vii. *Miscellanea:* he declares that the working of miracles neither makes nor hinders holiness, 2 *Cran.* 50; says, unto such as cannot take the vow of chastity we ought to grant marriage, 3 *Jew.* 399; writes, when we come to our Lord and make a vow that we will serve him in chastity, we make an oath that we will chasten our flesh, *ib.* 398; advises him who has promised chastity and cannot keep it, to confess his sin, *ib.* 397, 398; declares that the judicial law of Moses as to adultery is not in force among Christians (Orig.), 1 *Whitg.* 274; shews why (id.), *ib.* 329, 330; says the relics of the dead were buried in the earth, 2 *Ful.* 89; states that although death be fallen into our nature because of sin, yet because the Son of God is made man, doubtless we shall all rise again, 3 *Jew.* 592; calls the Spirit of God in us the cause of resurrection, *ib.* 592, 593; teaches many things concerning the image of the cross, *Calf.* 361, *Whita.* 597; referred to on Christians making the sign at their doors, 2 *Ful.* 199; allows not images in churches, *Calf.* 362; thinks Antichrist will be an individual man, 2 *Ful.* 367; told the emperors that the welfare of the commonwealth depended on godliness, 2 *Jew.* 1014, 3 *Jew.* 194; speaks of the curiosity of the people (John vi.), 3 *Whitg.* 573; explains "natural union," 1 *Jew.* 476

Cyril, bp of Antioch: 3 *Whitg.* 455 n

Cyril of Jerusalem: he was bishop of that place, *Rog.* 329; said to have sold a golden cope, 2 *Whitg.* 23, 24; he called men back from the synod of the Patripassians, 4 *Jew.* 951; appealed from it, *ib.* 1101; his works, *Jew.* xxxvi; he teaches that scripture alone is the basis of our faith, *Whita.* 597; on the canon of the old Testament, *ib.* 58, 62; he tells what books were received by the Samaritans, *Rog.* 81; rejects the Apocrypha, *Whita.* 58, 62; speaks of only two sacraments, 3 *Jew.* 459 n.; refers to three kinds of baptism, 2 *Bec.* 225 n.; calls the water of baptism not simple water, 2 *Jew.* 575; speaks of baptism by trine immersion, 2 *Bec.* 227; referred to for an account of the mass used in Jerusalem, 1 *Jew.* 108, 109; cautions against considering the elements as bare bread and wine, 2 *Jew.* 573, 575, 579; speaks of Christ's body and blood as given in the figure of bread and wine, *ib.* 573; observes that, as the bread of the sacrament after the invocation of the Holy Ghost, is no longer common bread, but the body of Christ, so the holy oil is no longer bare oil, but the grace of Christ, *ib.* 575; writes on the error of the Jews (Jo. vi.), *ib.* 576; exhorts to drink the spiritual wine with the heart, *ib.*; on tasting (by faith) that the Lord is gracious, *ib.*; he compares Noah's ark to the cross, *Calf.* 103; on Valentinus the heretic, *Rog.* 37 n

Cyril the monk: he and his brother Methodius converted the Sclavonians, 1 *Jew.* 291, 334, 335, brought Moravia to the faith, *Whita.* 269

Cyril, a Carmelite: wrongly stated to be the author of Evangelium Æternum, *Rog.* 203

Cyrus, king of Persia: prophecy concerning him, 1 *Lat.* 457; he was raised up to deliver God's people, 1 *Bul.* 325, *Pil.* 4, 11, 12; he advanced true religion, 1 *Bul.* 318, 2 *Bul.* 13; restored the vessels of the temple, *Pil.* 8

Cyssel (Dav.): 2 *Bec.* 480 n

D.

D. (Master): letter to him from Ridley, 2 *Brad.* 398

D. (R.), author of An Exhortation to England: *Poet.* xxxviii; stanzas therefrom, *ib.* 399

Daare: to dazzle, *Phil.* 309; (v. Dare).

Dacre (Tho.), lord Dacre of Gillesland, or the North: his daughter Catharine, 1 *Bec.* 61 n

Dacre (Will.), lord Dacre of Gillesland: offered the queen £10,000 to spare Ridley's life, *Rid.* 395

Dacre (Leon.): son of Will. lord Dacre of Gillesland, *Park.* 367; his rebellion, 1569, *Grin.* 322; his sister married one Culpepper, *Park.* 367

Dacre (The lords) of the South: v. Fienes.

Dacres (Rich.), by Carlisle: *Grin.* 322

Dacres (Will.), son of Richard: married to Anne Grindal, niece of the archbishop, *Grin.* 321, 322

Dactylorynchitæ: v. Passalorynchitæ.

Dagon: his form, 1 *Bul.* 224

Daillée (Jean): references to his works, *Calf.* 96, 105, 202, 211, 246, 248, 278, 2 *Ful.* 44, 236 nn.; his mistake as to a Latin version of the acts of the second council of Nice, *Calf.* 138 n

Daily Bread: v. Bread.

Daintrel: a delicacy, 1 *Bul.* 424

Dale (......), chaplain to bishop Rugges: 2 *Cran.* 336

Dale (......): died in Bury gaol, *Poet.* 172

Dalgleesh (......): 1 *Zur.* 195 n

Dallison (Rich.): *Bale* 429

Dalmatian tongue: *Whita.* 221

Dalmatic: what, 1 *Zur.* 350 n.; said to have been worn by Cyprian, *ib.* 350, 351 n

Damage: the doing and receiving of it, 2 *Bul.* 230; by taking away, *ib.* 38

Damascene (St John): notice of him, *Rid.* 206 n.; reference to his life by Jo. patr. of Jerusalem, 3 *Jew.* 615; his works, *Jew.* xxxvi; Apolog. pro Venerat. SS. Imag., *Calf.* 22 n.; De orth. Fide, 2 *Ful.* 203; the Historia SS. Barlaami et Josaphati, supposititious, *ib.* 287 n.; on the canon of the Old Testament, *Whita.* 64; he ascribes the epistle to the Hebrews to Paul, *ib.* 107; reckons the canons of the apostles amongst canonical books, *ib.* 599; teaches that nothing is to be sought for and received but what was delivered by the law, the prophets, the apostles, and the evangelists, 2 *Cran.* 34, *Whita.* 703; compares the soul, irrigated by the scriptures, to a tree planted by the streams of water, *Whita.* 703; alleged in support of tradition, *ib.* 599; he cites Basil on that subject, *ib.* 589; speaks of baptism by trine immersion, 2 *Bec.* 227 n.; judges that the sacrament is called a figure before consecration, 2 *Jew.* 593, 3 *Jew.* 527; on the words, "This is my body," 2 *Jew.* 605; he defines substance, 3 *Jew.* 506; says, when the market (i. e. life) is once done, there is no more merchandise to sell, 3 *Bec.* 365; on the resurrection of the body, 2 *Cov.* 175; he affirms that the tree of life prefigured the cross, *Calf.* 101; mentions the blessing of Jacob as a type of it, *ib.* 103; compares the sign of the cross to circumcision, *ib.* 70; records portions of an edict of Leo Isauricus against images, *Park.* 90 n.; he contended for them, *Calf.* 71; regards them as the books of the unlearned, 1 *Hoop.* 39; would have the shape honoured, not the matter, 2 *Ful.* 203 n.; his remark on the conduct of Epiphanius in destroying a picture, *Calf.* 42 n.; on the Lampatians, *Rog.* 160; on light, 2 *Jew.* 581, 582; he was anathematized by council at Constantinople, *Calf.* 71 n

Damascus: one of the magi, *Whita.* 560 n

Damasus I. bp of Rome: contention between him and Ursinus, and riot at his election, 1 *Jew.* 355, 1 *Whitg.* 463; he entered his see with the slaughter of sixty persons, 2 *Ful.* 120; his creed, 1 *Bul.* 32, 2 *Hoop.* 538; approval of it, 1 *Brad.* 371, 4 *Bul.* 63; Jerome agreed in faith with him, 3 *Jew.* 608, &c.; the epistles ascribed to him are counterfeit, *Whita.* 435; said to have written to Jerome to know his counsel,

4 *Jew.* 1044; remark of Erasmus on the spurious correspondence, 2 *Ful.* 120 n.; the Liber Pontificalis, *Whita.* 43; he was not the author of it, 2 *Ful.* 98 n., 360; he speaks of Christ as having, through his passion, given to mankind full and perfect salvation, 3 *Bec.* 420, 422; censures the heresy that the Godhead suffered on the cross, 2 *Bul.* 268; said to refer to baptism by trine immersion (Damascene?), 2 *Bec.* 227; parts of the mass ascribed to him, 2 *Brad.* 306, 308; quotation from him respecting the body of Christ, *Grin.* 53; he is alleged to have been the inventor of prescript forms of prayer, 2 *Whitg.* 466; he says that at Rome on Sundays, there was nothing but some epistle, or chapter of the gospel, read openly to the people, 1 *Jew.* 174; ordained that the psalms should be sung interchangeably, and the Gloria Patri said at the end of each, *ib.* 264, 266, 2 *Whitg.* 469, 3 *Whitg.* 385; asked Jerome to send him the Greek psalmody, 1 *Jew.* 305; urged him to correct the Latin New Testament by the Greek, *Whita.* 157; said to have given directions about the reading of scripture in the church, 4 *Bul.* 201; mentions an order of St Peter, that no woman should come barefaced into the church, 1 *Jew.* 39, 74; commanded the bishops of the East to come to Rome, not in his own name but by the emperor's special letters, 4 *Jew.* 996; he (or Pelagius I.) ordered metropolitans to fetch their palls from Rome, 2 *Whitg.* 173; he states that many popes were the sons of priests, 3 *Jew.* 393; speaks of the teachers of the Roman jurisdiction, 1 *Jew.* 409, 3 *Jew.* 333; tells a story of king Lucius, *ib.* 267; compares bishops who neglect their people that they may follow worldly cares, to harlots, 3 *Jew.* 383; mentions chor episcopi, 4 *Jew.* 801, *Whitg.* 532; calls St Stephen an archdeacon, 2 *Whitg.* 173; said to speak of a decree of Milciades, 1 *Jew.* 159, 160; he does not mention the Epistles Decretal, *ib.* 173; calls it blasphemy against the Holy Ghost to violate the holy canons, *ib.* 184; speaking of certain ecclesiastical institutions he says, whatsoever wanteth reason must of necessity be rooted out, 3 *Jew.* 571, 4 *Jew.* 801

Damatria, or Dematria: slew her son, because he behaved as a coward in the wars, 1 *Bec.* 234

Damian (St), brother of Cosmus, *q. v.*

Damianus (St), or Dimianus: apostle of the Britons, 3 *Jew.* 163, 2 *Whitg.* 128; invoked by the sick, *Rog.* 226

Damn: anciently used for condemn, 1 *Tyn.* 15 n

Damnation: man's sin the cause of it, 1 *Hoop.* 264

Damp: astonishment, 1 *Bec.* 276

Damplippe (Adam), alias Geo. Bucker: notice of him, and the persecutions at Calais, 2 *Cran.* 372, 373, 375

Dan: on the opinion that Antichrist shall spring from this tribe, 2 *Ful.* 370

Dan: a title given to monks, 2 *Cran.* 333; Dane, *ib.* 310

Danæus (......): on the government of Elizabeth, *Rog.* 7

Dance of Death, or Dance Macaber: some account of it, *Pra. Eliz.* xvii—xix; rhymes referring to it, *ib.* 510, &c., marg.; references to it, *Poet.* 172, 300, *Pra. Eliz.* 403 n., 413 n.; how death is represented by painters, 1 *Lat.* 220

Dandalus (Fra.): chained under the pope's table, 3 *Jew.* 147, 4 *Jew.* 692, &c., 931

Dandelot (Fra.): *v.* Coligni.

Dandyprat: a small coin, 2 *Tyn.* 306

Dane: *v.* Dan.

Danes: vexed England, 2 *Tyn.* 268; claimed it even in Tyndale's time, 1 *Tyn.* 187, 2 *Tyn.* 334

Danet (Gerard): his unlawful marriage, *Park.* 353

Danger: peculiar use of the word for a state of dependence, 1 *Tyn.* 9, 502, 2 *Tyn.* 293, 3 *Tyn.* 186

Daniel: his three companions, 1 *Bul.* 270; his diet in Babylon, *Pil.* 52; he was the wisest man of all the East, 3 *Bul.* 180, though not a Levite, 4 *Bul.* 480; called polyhistor or philoïstoros, 1 *Bul.* 51, 4 *Bul.* 591; he exhorts Nebuchadnezzar to break off his sins, &c., 2 *Cov.* 367; his prayers, 1 *Bul.* 292, 4 *Bul.* 175, 225; he is cast into the lions' den, but delivered, 1 *Bul.* 171, 318; his visions of the four monarchies, *Bale* 423, *Hutch.* 147, *Pil.* 186; his confession, 2 *Bul.* 94, 4 *Bul.* 177, 179; thought to be mentioned by Nehemiah (iii. 7) as the "duke" or "governor," *Pil.* 384

— Book of Daniel: he was an evangelist rather than a prophet, 1 *Bul.* 51; the book attacked by Porphyry, *Whita.* 33; Coverdale's view of the seventy weeks, 1 *Cov.* 68, 69; reference to the opinion of Eusebius on them, 3 *Zur.* 229; his prophecy of Antichrist and his persecutions, *Poet.* 285, *Rid.* 76

— Apocryphal additions to this book; viz. the Song of the three Children, the story of Susanna, and Bel and the Dragon: their claims to be canonical considered,

1 *Ful.* 25, &c., *Whita.* 77, &c.; Jerome disallows them, 1 *Ful.* 26, *Whita.* 77—79; Bellarmine refers them to a second Daniel, *Whita.* 79; they are historically untrue, 1 *Ful.* 27

Daniel (......): Hymnologus Chr., 2 *Cov.* 316 n

Daniel (Sam.): notice of him, *Poet.* xxxvii; the vanity of riches; verses, *ib.* 397; the vanity of fame, *ib.* 398

Danists: a sect, 3 *Zur.* 560

Dante (Alighieri): calls Rome the whore of Babylon, 4 *Jew.* 744

Dantiscus (Jo.), bp of Vermein: 2 *Cran.* 401; letter to Cranmer condemning the conduct of Henry VIII., *ib.* 402, 403

Dantzic: Flemish exiles there, 2 *Zur.* 321

Danvers (Will.): an ecclesiastical commissioner, *Park.* 301 n

Darcy (Tho. lord) of Darcy: a leader in the rebellion called the pilgrimage of grace, 2 *Cran.* 363, 1 *Lat.* 163; Latimer confers with him in the Tower, 1 *Lat.* 163; his execution, 2 *Cran.* 363 n

Darcy (Tho. lord) of Chiche: signature as privy councillor, 5 Edw. VI., 2 *Cran.* 531

Darcy (Jo. lord) of ...... : goes on an expedition into Ireland, 1573, 2 *Zur.* 223 n

Darcy (Sir Arth.): writes to lord Cromwell, 1 *Lat.* 93 n.; Mr Arth. Darcy, presumed to be the same, *Jew.* xi.

Dare: to frighten, or to harm, &c., 2 *Brad.* 90; (*v.* Daare).

Dare (Chr.): questions Anne Askewe, *Bale* 148

Darell (Will.), of Canterbury: *v.* Dorel.

Darell (Will.), of Pageham: notice of him and his posterity, 1 *Bec.* 353 n

Dario (Silv.): ambassador from the pope, 2 *Cran.* 272 n.; deprived of the rectory of Ripple, 2 *Lat.* 375 n., 376 n

Darius, son of Hystaspes: favours the Jews, 1 *Bul.* 318, 325, 326, 2 *Bul.* 13, *Pil.* 14

Darius, the Mede: said to be the son of Esther, 2 *Jew.* 986, *Pil.* 14, of Astyages or Ahashuerus, 1 *Bul.* 51, 317, 325, 2 *Bul.* 13

Darius Codomannus: his embassy to Alexander, and his death, *Pil.* 187

Darkness: *v.* Works.

How used in scripture, 2 *Tyn.* 149, 175; darkness in doctrine, *ib.* 102—104; darkness of the former dispensation, 2 *Jew.* 1036; affiance in darkness, 4 *Jew.* 1038

Darlington, or Darnton, co. Durham: a prebend, *Pil.* 574

Darmstadt: taken by the count de Buren, 3 *Zur.* 639

Darnel: a weed, *Phil.* 229

Darnley (Hen. lord): *v.* Stuart.

Darrell (Will.): *v.* Darell, Dorel.

Dartford, co. Kent: a martyr there, *Poet.* 162

Dase, Dasing: *v.* Daze.

Dasipodius (......): 3 *Zur.* 509 n

Datary: an ecclesiastical officer, *Calf.* 331; the passage refers to N. Ormanet, *ib.* 413

Dathan: *v.* Korah.

Dathenus (Pet.): letter to him, *Park.* 471

Daughter: the sick man's exhortation to his daughter, 3 *Bec.* 133, 134

Daukin, or Dawkin: a slattern, *Calf.* 236

Dauncy (Sir Jo.): 1 *Tyn.* xxiii.

Daus (Jo.), of Ipswich: translated Bullinger on the Apocalypse, 4 *Bul.* xxiii, 1 *Zur.* 99

David, king of Israel: *v.* Psalms.

He kills Goliath, *Pil.* 30, 120, 246, 360, 415, *Sand.* 371, *Whita.* 406; his behaviour under Saul, 1 *Bul.* 316; a captain, *ib.* 384, 386; his hope, 2 *Bul.* 89; his feigned madness, 3 *Jew.* 250; when in exile he longed for the courts of the Lord, 4 *Bul.* 167, *Sand.* 294; he swore rashly against Nabal, 1 *Bul.* 251; had divers wives, 1 *Lat.* 113; performed the office of a true king, 1 *Bec.* 286; his reign was troublous, 2 *Hoop.* 81; yet he was the happiest of kings, 2 *Bul.* 6; his zeal for God, *Pil.* 7; his gratitude to God, 1 *Bec.* 280, 298; he paid his vows to the Lord by fulfilling his commandments, *ib.* 284, 285; would do nothing without the authority of God's word, *ib.* 299; an earnest promoter of God's glory, *ib.* 300; an example to his subjects in godliness, *ib.*; he ordered matters in religion, 4 *Jew.* 987; his zeal for the ark, *Pil.* 340; he brings it to its place, 1 *Bul.* 325; he offended in carrying it, 4 *Bul.* 22; brought music into the house of God, 1 *Bul.* 141, 191; divided the priests into twenty-four orders, *ib.* 141; collected for building the temple, *Pil.* 8; God promised him that Christ should be born of his seed, 2 *Hoop.* 6, 7; his sins, why recorded, *Whita.* 230; his adultery, murder, and repentance, 1 *Brad.* 70, 1 *Bul.* 413; he was reproved by Nathan, *Pil.* 12, 112, 161; his prayer on this occasion, 2 *Hoop.* 358; his sin ever before him, *ib.* 320; he was corrected for his sin after it was forgiven, 3 *Bul.* 91; the history a profitable one, 1 *Tyn.* 310; Absalom's rebellion against him, *Sand.* 408, &c.; his conduct during it, 2 *Bul.* 94, *Nov.* 223; by it he was humbled, 1 *Bul.* 431; cursed by Shimei, 2 *Cran.* 107; he prays to God as the only remedy against pestilence, 2 *Hoop.* 164; he numbers the people, his punishment and penitence, 1 *Lat.* 386; his afflictions, 2 *Bul.* 103; he patiently suffered the cross, 1 *Bec.* 283; was wonderfully exercised in worldly troubles, *Grin.* 105; but he confessed that God was ever his helper and deliverer, *ib.*; how constantly his soul waited upon the Lord, 2 *Hoop.* 247; he prayed seven times a day, 1 *Bec.* 171; he was heard, though a sinner, 4 *Bul.* 169; his desiring to be heard in prayer for his righteousness explained, 1 *Bec.* 150, 4 *Bul.* 175, *Sand.* 404; what he thought of justification, 3 *Bul.* 47, 49; his plain fidelity, 1 *Bec.* 276; his faith in Christ, 4 *Bul.* 551, 1 *Cov.* 53; "the sure mercies of David," what, *Sand.* 32; he was a prophet, 1 *Cov.* 53; what his trance or ecstasy (or "haste," Psa. cxvi. 11) signifies, 1 *Bec.* 276; DAVID'S HARP, by T. Becon; an exposition of Psa. cxvi., *ib.* 262; he excels all other musicians, *ib.* 264; the virtue of his harp, *ib.* 266; the excellency of his songs, *ib.*; his psalmody, the treasure-house of scripture, *ib.*; he celebrates the creation, 3 *Bul.* 177; declares how precious is the death of the saints, 1 *Bec.* 288; he was a type of Christ, 2 *Brad.* 254, *Pil.* 371, 372, 389, especially in his conflict with Goliath, *Sand.* 371, *Whita.* 406; his tomb, *Pil.* 389

David (St): his father, *Bale* 192

David Kimchi (R.): 1 *Ful.* 314, 315, 526, 527, 535, 576, 1 *Hoop.* 43, 4 *Jew.* 982

David's (St): *v.* Saint-David's.

Davidians, Davidists or Davi-Georgians: a sect of heretics, followers of David George, 2 *Bec.* 379, 415, *Rog.* 202, *Whita.* 229 n

Davidson (Jo.): writes a monitory letter to the assembly of the church of Scotland, 2 *Zur.* 332 n

Davies (Sir Jo.): notice of him, *Poet.* xvii; the immortality of the soul, verses, *ib.* 86; the dignity of man, *ib.* 95; worth of the soul, *ib.* 96; the soul, *ib.* 97; false and true knowledge, *ib.* 100

Davies (Jo.), of Hereford: notice of him, *Poet.* xxiii; seven sonnets, *ib.* 240; God eternal, *ib.* 243; those blessed who endure temptation, *ib.* 245; heavenly mansions, *ib.* 246; divine mercy as great as God's Divinity, *ib.* 247; God's glory and goodness inexplicable, *ib.*; grief for sin is a joyful sorrow, *ib.* 248; blessed be the merciful, &c., *ib.* 249; stanzas from Christ's Crosse, *ib.* 250; the death of Christ, *ib.* 253

Davies (Jo.), another: author of Sir Martin Mar-people, his Collar of Esses, *Poet.* xxxiii; stanzas therefrom, *ib.* 363

Davies (Rich.), bp of St Asaph, afterwards of St David's: his translation, *Park.* 137 n.; his part in the Bishops' Bible, &c., *ib.* 265, 267 n., 280, 335 n.; his letters to Parker, *ib.* 137, 265, 279; he signs a letter to the queen, *ib.* 294; letter to him, *ib.* 270; he was present at Grindal's confirmation as abp of Canterbury, *Grin.* x.

Davies (Tho.), bp of St Asaph: *Park.* 137 n.; he seeks a licence to hold a living in commendam, *ib.* 207; signs a letter to the queen, *ib.* 294; his death, *ib.* 446 n

Davington, or Daunton, co. Kent: lands of the priory claimed by the see of Canterbury, 3 *Cran.* 312, 313; deserted, and granted by the king to Sir Tho. Cheney, *ib.* 313 n

Davison (......): alleged dissolution of his marriage, 2 *Cran.* 277

Davison (Chr.), younger brother of the next: notice of him, *Poet.* xxix; Psalm xv. versified by him, *ib.* 332

Davison (Fra.): notice of him, *Poet.* xxix; eleven Psalms versified by him, *ib.* 318, &c.

Davy (Jo.): he and his brother martyred at Bury, *Poet.* 173

Dawes (Jo): *v.* Daus.

Dawkin: *v.* Daukin.

Day (Geo.), bp of Chichester: account of him, 2 *Lat.* 377 n., *Phil.* xxvii; named, *Park.* 18; once a Protestant, 1 *Brad.* 523; a commissioner for reforming the church-service, 2 *Cran.* 414, 415; committed to the Fleet for not removing altars, 2 *Zur.* 159 n.; visits judge Hales in prison, 2 *Hoop.* 378; confers with Bradford, 1 *Brad.* 518; his answers to certain questions, 2 *Cran.* 152

Day (Jo.), printer: account of him, 2 *Zur.* 183 n.; he has licence to print the works of Becon, 1 *Bec.* xv; other books printed by him, 1 *Cov.* 529, *Grin.* 2, 33, 1 *Hoop.* 558, 2 *Hoop.* 65, 92, *Now.* 105, *Lit. Edw.* 487, 540; *Pra. Eliz.* 430, & al.; his press stopped on the death of Edw. VI., *Hutch.* vii, 213, and he imprisoned in Newgate, *ib.* viii; perhaps the compiler of the Pomander of Prayer, 1558, *Pra. Eliz.* xxii; his address to the reader, prefixed to Hutchinson's Sermons on the Lord's supper, *Hutch.* 213; perhaps the compiler of the Christian Prayers, 1569, *Pra. Eliz.* xxii; letter from him to Bullinger, 2 *Zur.* 183; his new Italian letter, *Park.* 411; he obtains a lease of a shop in St Paul's churchyard, *ib.*; Asplyn attempts to kill him and his wife, *Park.* 449; Anglo-Saxon type cast for him, *ib.* 468; mention of him in certain verses, 3 *Whitg.* 498 n

Day (Rich.): martyred at Colchester, *Poet.* 172

Day (Rich.), son of Jo. Day the printer: *Pra. Eliz.* xxiii; his address on prayer, *ib.* 431—437
Day (Will.), bp of Winchester: sometime provost of Eton, *Park.* 162, 2 *Zur.* 263; his promotion to a bishoprick expected, 2 *Zur.* 270; meet for the see of London, *Park.* 360; proposed as a commissioner, *ib.* 370; his wife, 2 *Zur.* 263 n
Day of Judgment: *v.* Judgment, World.
Day (The Lord's): *v.* Sunday.
Day (New Year's): *v.* New Year's day.
Daying (Put in): submitted to arbitration, 3 *Jew.* 121
Days: called by heathen names, *Pil.* 16; against difference of days, 2 *Hoop.* 56; lucky and unlucky days, 2 *Cran.* 100; certain days improperly called unfortunate, *Pil.* 17, 18; "this day," what it means in the Lord's Prayer, 4 *Bul.* 215; "the evil day," what, 1 *Lat.* 28; man's last day, 3 *Bul.* 405; a time, times, and a half, *Bale* 374; the 1260 days, *ib.* 386, 410, 2 *Ful.* 233; the 42 months, *Bale* 432; three days and a half, *ib.* 394, 2 *Ful.* 233
Days (Holy): *v.* Holy days.
Days (Last): *v.* World.
Days' Minds: *v.* Minds.
Days of Offering: *v.* Offering.
Daze: to dazzle, *Calf.* 317; daseth, *Bale* 442; dased, *Calf.* 303; dasing, i. e. stupor, 1 *Bec.* 468; dazing, 1 *Cov.* 501, 1 *Tyn.* 167
Deaconesses: their office, 4 *Bul.* 107, 3 *Whitg.* 281
Deacons: *v.* Archdeacons, Subdeacons.
Meaning of their name, 1 *Tyn.* 230; the office said to have been taken from the Jews, 2 *Whitg.* 126; the word διάκονος, often means a minister generally, and therefore it is sometimes translated by that word, 1 *Ful.* 110, 254, &c., 460, &c.; the election of the seven, 1 *Whitg.* 298, 340; why they were appointed, 3 *Whitg.* 422, 423; viz. for the poor, *Pil.* 129; the office and duties of deacons, 2 *Bec.* 236, 4 *Bul.* 107, 112, 1 *Tyn.* 230, 231, 259, 2 *Tyn.* 253, 3 *Tyn.* 150, 1 *Whitg.* 299, 2 *Whitg.* 281, 341, &c., 3 *Whitg.* 422, 538, 539; what their office was of old, 2 *Ful.* 237, 2 *Whitg.* 525, 527, 3 *Whitg.* 61; it was highly honoured, 3 *Tyn.* 149; deacons mentioned by Justin, 1 *Jew.* 146; sometimes of old styled Levites, 1 *Ful.* 262; of their ministering and preaching, 3 *Whitg.* 58, &c.; they preached in the primitive church, but not in the time of Ambrose, 1 *Jew.* 75, who, however, says they may preach without a chair, 1 *Whitg.* 494; they may baptize, 2 *Whitg.* 519, 525, 3 *Whitg.* 58, &c., 71, 72; their office in the ministration of the sacrament, 3 *Whitg.* 64--67 (*v.* Supper); evidence that in the early church they sometimes consecrated the eucharist, 1 *Jew.* 240; they were prohibited from so doing by a council at Arles, *ib.*; they carried away the altar after the communion, 1 *Jew.* 311; in Chrysostom's time they used to call upon the people to pray, 1 *Jew.* 292; proof that they were sometimes promoted to a higher grade, 3 *Whitg.* 68—71; those of Rome advanced themselves above their estate, 1 *Jew.* 355; from them sprang the corruptions of the church, 2 *Tyn.* 256; what their office is in the pope's church, and such deacons contrasted with those of scripture, 2 *Bec.* 327, 1 *Ful.* 218, *Rog.* 259, 2 *Tyn.* 275; deacons mentioned as singing the gospel in cathedral churches, 3 *Whitg.* 288; their office now the first step to the ministry, *ib.* 68—71; they should continue in their office a year, *Grin.* 186; whether they ought to be in every congregation, 3 *Whitg.* 286, &c.; certain reformers would have had such restored as were in the primitive church, *ib.* 538, &c.; "to be made deacons," a phrase signifying to be executed, *Sand.* ii.
Dead: *v.* Baptism (xiv.), Burial, Death, Hell, Mourning, Prayer, Resurrection, Souls, Spirits.
Their state, 3 *Bul.* 386, &c.; dead men never return to tell their condition, 2 *Cran.* 43—45; souls departed know not what they do who are alive, 3 *Bul.* 212, 2 *Cov.* 238; Augustine's opinion, 2 *Cov.* 218—220; the blessedness of those who die in the Lord, *Bale* 462, 3 *Bec.* 181, &c., 3 *Bul.* 404, *Sand.* 162; they cease from sin, 2 *Cov.* 62, are delivered from this world, *ib.* 63, obtain salvation, *ib.* 64; Tyndale's protestation concerning his faith as to the state of departed souls, &c., 1 *Tyn.* lxii; they are not yet in glory, *ib.* lxiii; scripture says little on the state of the departed faithful before the resurrection, 2 *Tyn.* 185; the pope's doctrine concerning departed souls, (viz. that they are in heaven, hell, or purgatory,) is a mixture of Christian doctrine and heathen philosophy, and subversive of the scripture doctrine of the resurrection, 3 *Tyn.* 180, see 118, 127; they do not sleep, 3 *Bul.* 389; condemnation of the doctrine that the souls of the departed sleep until the resurrection (Article of 1552) *Lit. Edw.* 537, (581); against the opinion that the spirits of the saints are not in heaven but asleep, 2 *Hoop.* 63; probations out of the

old fathers that their state is not such that they can be delivered by Popish masses or the good works of others, 3 *Bec.* 459, &c.; we are not forbidden to mourn over them, 2 *Jew.* 864, 1 *Lat.* 547; how we are to mourn, 2 *Jew.* 866; unseemly sorrow is unprofitable and hurtful, 2 *Cov.* 125; grounds of consolation, *ib.* 111; the ancient practice of memorials of the dead, *ib.* 249, 270; it is opposed to the Romish doctrine of praying for the dead, *ib.*; memorial of the departed in the communion, 2 *Brad.* 291, 311, 2 *Cov.* 269; the Romish office for the dead, called by different names, 1 *Brad.* 582; dead men raised by Elijah and Elisha, 2 *Lat.* 68, 75

Dead men: monks so called, 2 *Tyn.* 182

Dead Sea: 1 *Bul.* 418

Deadly: mortal, *Bale* 97

Deadly sins: *v.* Sin.

Deal: to divide, 2 *Tyn.* 83, 3 *Tyn.* 250

Deal castle, co. Kent: *Park.* 203

Dean (Mr): *Park.* 258; Mr Dene, probably the same, *ib.* 285

Deans: their office not unlawful, 2 *Whitg.* 178; the name mentioned by Augustine, *ib.* 178—180; article to be inquired respecting them, *Grin.* 179

Deans rural: *Grin.* 176

Dearling: 1 *Brad.* 66; darling, *ib.* 108

Dearth: *v.* Famine.

Death: *v.* Dance, Dead.

What death is, 2 *Cov.* 47; four kinds of death—natural, spiritual, temporal, eternal, 1 *Brad.* 332, &c.; the death of the body, 2 *Bec.* 575; the death of souls, 3 *Bul.* 380, 4 *Bul.* 228; spiritual death, 1 *Brad.* 216, 332, 1 *Ful.* 397; the first death and the second, *Sand.* 31; the second death, *Bale* 580, *Sand.* 31; everlasting death, 3 *Bec.* 604, 1 *Brad.* 332; Wermuller's TREATISE ON DEATH, translated by Coverdale, 2 *Cov.* 37, &c.; death is a figure of sin, *Pil.* 111; it came by sin, 1 *Brad.* 333, 1 *Ful.* 397, and is the wages or penalty of sin, 2 *Cov.* 49, 1 *Lat.* 220, *Sand.* 168; death styled "nature's debt," 2 *Brad.* 51; death a due debt, verses, *Poet.* 311; it is God's pursuivant, 1 *Brad.* 346; it obeys none other, 1 *Lat.* 548; the death of Adam, and what it is, 1 *Bec.* 46; that of Christ, and what it is, *ib.* 52, 53, 65; in us death is the punishment of sin, in Christ it is obedience and love, 1 *Cov.* 230; on the death of young persons, 2 *Cov.* 128; on that of the aged, *ib.* 131; the death of the righteous (see below); the death and damnation of the ungodly, 2 *Cov.* 201; some men consent to the truth at their latter end, 3 *Tyn.* 36; God can turn a man's heart at the point of death, 1 *Lat.* 161; but death fixes our eternal state, 2 *Lat.* 56; for as every man departs hence, so he will be judged, *Sand.* 162; death often to be thought upon, 1 *Brad.* 345; the remembrance of our latter end is a bit to bridle carnal affections, 3 *Bec.* 90; the consideration of it profitable to virtue, 2 *Cov.* 60; in death we learn the knowledge of ourselves and of God, and the worthiness of the passion and death of Christ, *ib.* 61; we should not consider it in itself, or in our own nature, or in them that are slain through the wrath of God, but principally in Jesus Christ, and then in his saints who through him overcame death, *ib.* 80; a meditation of death, and the commodities it bringeth (from L. Vives), 1 *Brad.* 195, *Pra. B.* 114; three ditties, by Ant. Munday, on the coming of death, &c., *Poet.* 226—230; think to die; verses by D. Sand, *ib.* 299; verses by Lord Vaux, bethinking himself of his end, *ib.* 303; a short discourse of man's fatal end; by L. Ramsey, *ib.* 511; mors, tua mors, Christe, &c. themes for meditation, *ib.* 395; de vitæ hujus fragilitate, et spe resurrectionis vitæque æternæ; a meditation, from scripture and the burial service, *Pra. Eliz.* 358; death approaches, 2 *Lat.* 20; we ought not to fly from it, 2 *Cov.* 69; but no man may hasten it, 2 *Bul.* 413; its universal prevalence, 3 *Bec.* 147; it cannot be avoided, 2 *Cov.* 67, *Grin.* 6; neither the rich, the mighty, nor the wise, &c. exempt, *Grin.* 10; death certain; verses by W. Buttes, *Poet.* 309; all will not die, *Now.* (50), 168; it is necessary to prepare for death, 2 *Cov.* 77; it is profitable to do so while in health, *ib.* 80; how we should do so, *ib.* 96, (and see below); we should set our worldly affairs in order, 2 *Cov.* 99, 1 *Lat.* 540; the dangers of not expecting the change, *Sand.* 172, &c.; uncertainty of its time, 2 *Cov.* 48, *Grin.* 7; it may come any day, *Sand.* 170, 171; examples of sudden death, *ib.* 172, *Wool.* 111; strange sorts of death, *Bale* 579, 2 *Cov.* 131; why the time of death is hidden, 1 *Brad.* 346, 1 *Lat.* 416; performing our duty will not shorten our life, 2 *Lat.* 35, for the time of every man's death is appointed, 1 *Lat.* 416, and man dieth not before his time, *ib.* 265; in itself death is grievous both to body and soul, 2 *Cov.* 51; all men are commonly afraid of it, *ib.* 54; it is a terror to the wicked, and even to the godly, 1 *Lat.* 220; feared by two sorts, childish Christians, and customable sinners, *ib.* 549; some heathen feared it not, 3 *Bec.* 148; nor did the Jews and godly men of old, *ib.* 148, 149; Job desired his change, *Sand.* 168; it should not be feared by Christians, *Rid.* 425; their fear of death dishonours God, 2 *Cov.* 85; Satan's assaults when death approaches, 2 *Lat.* 148; the saints often meet it joyfully, 3 *Tyn.* 279; what it is to the believer, 1 *Brad.* 345; to the faithful it is but sleep, 1 *Lat.* 548; horrible death of a covetous man, *ib.* 227, 541; contempt of death no evidence of a good cause, *ib.* 160; the troubles of death not to be compared to the eternity that follows, 2 *Cov.* 75; what is to be done when the horror of it cometh, 1 *Lat.* 224, 227; against the fear of death, 2 *Brad.* 147—150, 183; a treatise against the fear of death, 1 *Brad.* 331; part of the same in Latin, *ib.* 581; against the terror of death, sin, and hell; with sentences and examples of scripture, 1 *Bec.* 479, 480; it is not to be feared, but desired, 2 *Bec.* 575; remedies against the fear of it, 3 *Bec.* 149, 150, against the pains of it, *ib.* 150, against thought-taking in departing from worldly goods, *ib.* 151, against thought-taking in departing from earthly friends, *ib.* 151, 152; death, hell, and desperation are overcome by Christ, 1 *Bec.* 297, 2 *Lat.* 145, *Now.* (39), 156; by means of the death and passion of Jesus Christ, God turns death into good, 2 *Cov.* 51; mortis et crucis collatio, Latin verses, *Calf.* 390; the same in English, *ib.* 391; the death of death, &c., verses by S. Rowlands, *Poet.* 349; how the sick and dying should be comforted, 2 *Bec.* 575, 576, 2 *Cov.* 104—108; consolation under death only to be found in scripture, 2 *Cov.* 41; the word of God ought to be practised and used, *ib.* 92; God can and will help us under death for Christ's sake, *ib.* 70; he has promised his help and comfort in death, *ib.* 73; the faithful cannot be separated by death from Jesus Christ, *ib.* 74; it is God who has laid the burden on us, *ib.* 49; he is more able to help, than the most horrible death to disturb or grieve, *ib.* 75; examples of God's help in death, *ib.* 76; witness that death is wholesome, *ib.* 67; it is turned into a blessing, 1 *Brad.* 410; to those who die, it is profitable to depart out of this life, 2 *Cov.* 114, death being a deliverance from this transitory life, *ib.* 56, from misery and trouble, 2 *Cov.* 57, 1 *Lat.* 347; it is the entrance into life, *Bale* 228; repentance and sorrow for sin are necessary to prepare for death, 2 *Cov.* 81; true faith is necessary, *ib.* 82, 100; the proper exercise of faith, *ib.* 84; it brings amendment of life, *ib.* 93; patience is necessary, 2 *Cov.* 94; the example of Christ and his saints in this, *ib.*; patience is promoted and sustained by faith, *ib.* 96; the exercise of hope in the hour of death, *ib.* 86; prayer is necessary for our support in death, *ib.* 88; faithful prayer is heard, *ib.* 92; (*v.* Prayers); the sacraments (received in time past) serve to the confirmation of faith and hope, *ib.* 86; opinions against the administration of the Lord's supper to the dying, 2 *Cov.* 86, 1 *Hoop.* 170—173; some in the hour of death rely on superstitious usages, 1 *Tyn.* 48; a dying Christian's exhortation to his son, 2 *Jew.* 1138, to his daughter, 3 *Bec.* 133, 134; how he is to be spoken to who is at the point of death, 2 *Bec.* 577, 578; pro beato vitæ exitu, verses by A. Flaminius, *Pra. Eliz.* 418; the death of the saints is precious in the Lord's sight, 1 *Bec.* 288, 290, 291; the felicity which they obtain thereby, 1 *Brad.* 340; joyful state of the faithful after death; places of scripture concerning it, 3 *Bec.* 182, &c.; the death of friends is profitable to the living, 2 *Cov.* 118, though painful, 1 *Hoop.* 561; how the pain may be alleviated, *ib.*; how persons ought to comfort themselves under the death of others, 2 *Cov.* 120; the departure of those who die in the Lord is not to be mourned, 3 *Bec.* 120, &c.; the heathen took the death of their friends patiently, *ib.* 123; sleep, the image of death, 1 *Lat.* 548, *Nord.* 153, *Poet.* 403, 404, *Pra. B.* 76; death, a figure of the end of the world, 2 *Lat.* 53; spoken of as Christ's coming, *ib.* 57; how represented by painters, 1 *Lat.* 220; death on the pale horse, *Bale* 321, 2 *Hoop.* 591

Death (Punishment of): *v.* Magistrates.

Commanded by God, 1 *Jew.* 228, *Sand.* 72; rulers may inflict it, 1 *Bul.* 352, 354, 1 *Lat.* 484, for grievous offences, *Rog.* 348—350; in what manner, 1 *Bul.* 356

Death-warnings: 2 *Zur.* 204

Debelleth: warreth against, 1 *Bec.* 201

Debile: infirm, weak, 1 *Bec.* 128

Deborah: 4 *Bul.* 371

Debts, Debtors: debts are to be paid, *Sand.* 200; debtors who will not pay when they can are thieves, 2 *Bec.* 108; their duty, *ib.* 115; on mercy towards debtors, 2 *Tyn.* 69; we must forgive them, 2 *Bec.* 179, 180; debts, or trespasses, i. e. sins, 1 *Brad.* 133, 182, 4 *Bul.* 216, v. Prayer (The Lord's); how we are to be delivered from them, 2 *Bec.* 178, 179

Decacordon of Quodlibetical Questions: *Rog.* 331 n
DECADES of Bullinger: 1, 2, 3, 4 *Bul.*; design and method of them, 2 *Bul.* 15, 4 *Bul.* 556
Decalogue: *v.* Commandments.
Decantate: to chant, or sing, 1 *Bec.* 182
Deceit, Fraud: *v.* Commandments.
 Robbery, deceit, and fraud forbidden, 2 *Bul.* 39, 230, 2 *Jew.* 850; that of officers, magistrates, and tradesmen, *Hutch.* 223; that of artificers, and statutes to correct it, 1 *Lat.* 138; various kinds of fraud condemned, *Pil.* 461, &c., 469, &c.; fraudulent practices exposed, 1 *Lat.* 400, 401; the reward of deceit and falsehood, 1 *Lat.* 402, 2 *Lat.* 190
Deceiver: a name of the devil, 3 *Bul.* 356
Decius, emperor: 2 *Bul.* 106, 4 *Bul.* 393, 514
Decius (Publius): 1 *Bec.* 234, 1 *Bul.* 278
Declaration: *v.* Christ, i., Commandments.
 A declaration concerning religion, signed by Bradford, Ferrar, Hooper, Sanders, and others, 1 *Brad.* 367; A Declaration in the name and defence of certain Ministers in London, *Park.* 285 n.; A brief Examination, &c., in reply to it, *ib.*
Decrees of God: *v.* Predestination.
Decretal epistles: *v.* Law (Canon), and the names of the popes.
Dedication: *v.* Churches, Consecration.
 The Jewish feast of the dedication, 2 *Bul.* 162; the dedication feast in England, a day of offering, 1 *Lat.* 23 n
Dee (Mr): chaplain to Bonner, *Phil.* 80; one of the examiners of Philpot, *ib.* 69
Deed: indeed, 1 *Cov.* 10
Deering (Edw.): *v.* Dering.
Defence: two doctrines noted by the word; one touching God, the other touching man, 2 *Hoop.* 262, 263
DEFENCE OF A CERTAIN POOR CHRISTIAN MAN, WHO ELSE SHOULD HAVE BEEN CONDEMNED BY THE POPE'S LAW, translated from the German by bp Coverdale, 2 *Cov.* 451
Defender of the Faith: Julius II. conferred the title on James IV. of Scotland, 2 *Tyn.* 187 n.; Leo X. afterwards gave it to king Henry VIII., 1 *Tyn.* 186, 2 *Tyn.* 264; extract from the bull, 1 *Tyn.* 187 n.; how the title was obtained, and its reception by the king, 2 *Tyn.* 338; the pope compared to Caiaphas in this affair, *Calf.* 5, 2 *Jew.* 3, 4; the title due to the king, 2 *Lat.* 380; a seeming allusion to it, *ib.* 308; Bale esteems it blasphemous, *Bale* 496; Martiall omits the title in addressing queen Elizabeth, *Calf.* 5
Defholdius (......): 2 *Zur.* 107
Defy: to disdain, 2 *Tyn.* 157; used, as in old French, for distrust, 3 *Tyn.* 38
Degradation: the mode of degrading priests, *Pil.* 163, 1 *Tyn.* 233; the degradation of Hooper and Rogers, 2 *Hoop.* xxiv; that of Ridley, *Rid.* 289—291
Degrees and states of men: appointed by God, 3 *Bec.* 36
Degrees (University): *v.* Doctors, Masters.
 Condemned by Wickliffe, 1 *Ful.* 568, and by the Puritans, 3 *Whitg.* 469, 470, 511
Deipara: *v.* Mary (B. V.).
Delamore (Humf.), parson of Kemisford: *Park.* 213
Delating: 3 *Bec.* 245
De la Warr (The lords): *v.* West.
Delay: its danger, *Sand.* 152
Deliberatio (Simplex ac Pia): *v.* Cologne.
Deliverance: examples of God's deliverance, 2 *Bul.* 96
Deloenus (Gualter), or Walter Delvin: a minister in the German church in London, 3 *Zur.* 575, 587 n
Deloenus (Pet.), or de Loene, minister of the same church: letter of bishop Grindal to him, *Grin.* 242
Deluge: *v.* Flood, Noah.
Delusion: sent by God to unbelievers, 2 *Jew.* 924
Delvin (Walter): *v.* Deloenus.
Demaratus: banished, *Pil.* 424
De Marca (Pet.): *v.* Marca.
Demas: put out of the church, 4 *Bul.* 8
Dematria: *v.* Damatria.
Demetriades: 4 *Bul.* 199
Demetrius, bp of Alexandria: 2 *Whitg.* 164, 373, 428, 531
DEMANDS OF HOLY SCRIPTURE, WITH ANSWERS, by T. Becon, 3 *Bec.* 595
Democracy: what it is, and how it began, 1 *Bul.* 310; popular government the worst that can be, 1 *Whitg.* 467; it leads to outrageous tumults, 1 *Bul.* 310; the sin of Korah, Dathan, and Abiram, *Sand.* 138, 139; Cartwright calls England a democracy in respect of the parliament, 1 *Whitg.* 390
Democritus: thought the sun infinite, *Hutch.* 161
Demons, or Devils: *v.* Angels, ii. Miracles, Spirits, Witchcraft.
 The word ($\delta\alpha\iota\mu\omega\nu$) used by the Gentiles in a good sense, *Now.* 100; its meaning according to Plato, &c., 1 *Brad.* 376 n., 3 *Bul.* 356; it is a name of Satan, 3 *Bul.* 356; there are devils, or evil spirits, *ib.*

348; they are very numerous, *ib.* 356, 1 *Lat.* 439; they were not created wicked, *Now.* (31), 147; they were angels, 1 *Lat.* 493; they are in the air, *ib.*; they are spirits and substances, 3 *Bul.* 353; what manner of bodies they take, *ib.* 354; they assume the names of dead men, 2 *Cran.* 41, 44; have wrought miracles to turn men from the truth, *Calf.* 317, 3 *Tyn.* 92; lead men astray, 2 *Cran.* 40, &c.; enforced celibacy is a doctrine of devils, 3 *Jew.* 417, &c.; bread and wine offered to them, 2 *Whitg.* 39; the mere words of scripture have no power against them, 1 *Jew.* 327; men who were possessed fled from Christ, and were brought to him by force, 3 *Tyn.* 92; they tremble when Christ is with us, 1 *Lat.* 494; why the devils who fear God do not enjoy profit thereby, 3 *Bec.* 619, or 91 n; on the faith of devils, 3 *Tyn.* 201; demoniacs, what, 3 *Bul.* 356; persons possessed were of old called energumeni (*q. v.*), 1 *Ful.* 258, & al.; cases; the maid of Ipswich, Sir Roger Wentworth's daughter, *Bale* 440, 2 *Cran.* 65, 1 *Tyn.* 327, 3 *Tyn.* 90; Elizabeth Barton, called the holy maid of Kent, 2 *Cran.* 272, 1 *Tyn.* 327, & al.; cases at Norwich described by bishop Parkhurst, 1 *Zur.* 303; the case of Agnes Bridges, examined by Parker, *Park.* 465; she and Rachel Pinder did penance at Paul's cross as impostors, *ib.* n.: books published on the subject of possession, *Park.* 465, 466; faith casts out devils, 1 *Tyn.* 82; foul spirits expelled by exorcists, 4 *Bul.* 114, 115, 3 *Jew.* 273: Bullinger thinks the gift ceased long ago, 4 *Bul.* 115; form of exorcism in the first Prayer Book of Edw. VI., 1 *Zur.* 178 n.; devils cast out in England, *Sand.* 60: exorcism by Mr Lane of Westchester, mentioned by Foxe, 2 *Ful.* 76; works on exorcism, *Calf.* 318 n.; devils said to be cast out by holy water, *Rid.* 500; they are stated to have fled from the cross, *Calf.* 87, *Whita.* 591; how they were driven from the house of Hesperius (Aug.), 2 *Ful.* 86; one is sometimes apparently ejected by another, but this is collusion, 2 *Jew.* 1027; the parable of the unclean spirit that returned, 1 *Tyn.* 473; the sin of consulting devils, or dead men's ghosts, *Sand.* 17; Christ refused the testimony of foul spirits, *Sand.* 17; the Manichees said devils suffered on the cross instead of Christ, *Rog.* 57; they have not their full torments till the last day, 1 *Lat.* 494; their redemption expected by some heretics, *Rog.* 58, 67

Demosthenes: endangered the commonwealth by his advice, 1 *Hoop.* 490; chose banishment rather than the place of government, *Sand.* 36; confessed laws to be the gift of God, 1 *Bul.* 338; sayings of his, *Calf.* 54, 1 *Ful.* 569, *Hutch.* 105

Demosthenes, the cook: rebuked by Basil, *Whita.* 233

Dene (Mr): *v.* Dean.

Denial: denial of God's truth in persecutions, no way to keep our goods, 2 *Bul.* 100; what it is for a man to deny himself, 3 *Bec.* 609, 622; the necessity of self-denial, 1 *Lat.* 464

Denis: *v.* Dionysius.

Denis (Father): ambassador from the pope to the king of Scots, 2 *Cran.* 331

Denison (Jo.): De Confess. Aur. vanitate, 2 *Ful.* 90 n., 91 n

Denly (Jo.): martyred at Uxbridge, *Poet.* 163

Denmark: *v.* Christian, Eric, Frederick.

The kings thereof style themselves kings of England, 1 *Tyn.* 187, 2 *Tyn.* 334; a king expelled in Tyndale's days, 2 *Tyn.* 334; the reformation there, 4 *Bul.* xxii, 1 *Cov.* 424, 1 *Lat.* 274; THE ORDER THAT THE CHURCH AND CONGREGATION OF CHRIST IN DENMARK...DOTH USE, at the Lord's supper, baptism, and wedlock, 1 *Cov.* 469; title to another edition, *ib.* 529; war with Sweden, 2 *Zur.* 106, 150

Denneshe (Jo.): *v.* Devenish.

Dennington, co. Suffolk: Fulke was rector there, 1 *Ful.* iii; his epitaph, *ib.* iv.

Denny (Sir Ant.): 1 *Cran.* xvii, 2 *Cran.* 349 n., 415 n., 416 n.; letter from him to the commissioners for the dissolution of colleges, *Park.* 33 n

— Joan his wife: her life sought, *Bale* 220, 242; she sends Anne Askewe money, *ib.* 222

Denny (Sir Hen.): 1 *Zur.* 230

Denny (Mr): *Bale* 177

Denny (......), vicar of North Elmham: *Park.* 247

Dens (Pet.): on the locality of purgatory, 2 *Tyn.* 287 n

Dent (Arth.): a great preacher, 1 *Brad.* 562

Dents (......): martyred at Lewes, *Poet.* 170

Denys (St): *v.* Dionysius.

Depart: to divide (v. a.), 3 *Tyn.* 34; to separate (v. n.), *ib.* 94; departed, i. e. separated, *Calf.* 303

Departed: *v.* Dead.

Deposing: *v.* Kings.

De Profundis: not to be said, *Grin.* 140

Depured: purified, *Bale* 195

Depravity: v. Man.
Derby (Earls of): v. Stanley.
Derbyshire: Becon goes into the Peak, 2 *Bec.* 420; a rude district, 1 *Bec.* ix; superstition and ignorance of the priests there, 2 *Bec.* 421, 422
Dereham (......): executed, 2 *Cran.* 408 n., see 409
Dereham, or Dirham, co. Gloucester: 2 *Lat.* 309 n
Dering (Edw.): a great learned man, *Park.* 410; he attempts to confute Saunders, *ib.*; answers Cartwright, *ib.* 434; the queen dislikes his reading, *ib.* 476; he is suspended from his lecture at St Paul's, *Sand.* xxi; his book against Harding, *Jew.* xx, 2 *Whitg.* 470
Dering (Jo.), monk of Canterbury: an abettor of the maid of Kent, 2 *Cran.* 271 n., 272; his treatise De Duplice Spiritu, *ib.* 277
Dering (Rich.), monk of Canterbury: executed, 2 *Cran.* 312 n
De Sainctes (Claud.): v. Sanctes.
Deserte: dizzard, 1 *Cov.* 4 n., 284
Deserts: v. Merit.
Desiderius, king of Lombardy, 2 *Tyn.* 262—264
Desiderius of Bordeaux: professed to be Christ, *Rog.* 162
Desirous: desirable, *Bale* 586
Desmond (Earls of): v. Fitzgerald.
Despair, Desperation: what it is, 3 *Bec.* 608; it comes of wilful sin, 2 *Tyn.* 76; examples of transgression driving men to it, 1 *Bec.* 146; trusting to works leads to it, 1 *Tyn.* 114; the godly are sometimes tossed with the waves of it, 2 *Bec.* 622, 623; how men yield to it, 1 *Hoop.* 422; it detracts from God's mercy, *ib.*; it is a hard matter to eschew it in great conflicts of the mind, 2 *Hoop.* 346; exhortations to the reformed against it, 3 *Bec.* 217, 218, 219; remedies against it, *ib.* 156; against desperation for late conversion, with sentences and examples of scripture, 1 *Bec.* 479, 480; how desperation is to be resisted, 2 *Bec.* 577, 578; notice of A godly and wholesome Preservative against Desperation, 2 *Brad.* 16
Despise: used for desire, 2 *Bec.* 626
Despisers of God's word: 1 *Bec.* 255; how they should behave themselves, *ib.* 257
Destiny: v. Fortune.
Detection of the Devil's Sophistry: v. Gardiner (S.)
Dethick (......), fellow of Gonville hall: *Park.* 248, 252, 298
Dethick (Sir Gilb.), Garter: grants arms to Whitgift, *Lit. Eliz.* 594 n

Dethick (Sir Will.), Garter: named, *Lit. Eliz.* 594 n
Dethlef (......): 3 *Zur.* 617
Deusdedit, pope: his father a subdeacon, 2 *Ful.* 98 n.; he appointed a second mass for the clergy, 2 *Jew.* 631, 635
Deuterius, an Arian bishop: on his being about to baptize a man the water dried up, 2 *Jew.* 761
Deuteronomy: some account of the book, 2 *Cov.* 17; Tyndale's prologue to it, 1 *Tyn.* 441; his explanation of certain words in it, *ib.* 445; as to the writer of the concluding paragraph, *Whita.* 519; meaning of the word "Deuteronomium" in Deut. xvii. 18, Vulg., 4 *Jew.* 978, 980
Deux-ponts: 2 *Cov.* 522
Devenish (Jo.), or Denneshe: burned in Smithfield, *Poet.* 171, 2 *Zur.* 160 n
Devenyshe (Will.?): a kinsman of Cranmer, 2 *Cran.* 279
Deventer: besieged by duke Casimir, 1 *Zur.* 325; betrayed to the Spaniards by Sir W. Stanley, *Lit. Eliz.* 656 n
Devereux (Walter) 1st visc. Hereford: one of the examiners of Philpot, *Phil.* 49
Devereux (Walter), 2nd visc. Hereford, afterwards earl of Essex: notice of him, *Poet.* xxviii; at the duke of Norfolk's trial, 1 *Zur.* 267 n.; his expedition into Ireland, *Grin.* 345, 2 *Zur.* 223 n., 224; his death and character, 1 *Zur.* 329; the complaint of a sinner, verses by him, *Poet.* 316
Devereux (Rob.), 2nd earl of Essex: lord lieut. of Hants, *Coop.* xv; sent to Cadiz with an armament, *Lit. Eliz.* 472; sent out with another fleet against the Spaniards, *ib.* 473; a book dedicated to him, *Poet.* liv; his correspondence with the king of Scots, 2 *Zur.* 332 n.; made earl-marshal, *Lit. Eliz.* 681 n.; Squire's attempt to kill him, *ib.*; made lord deputy of Ireland, *ib.* 473; his rebellion and execution, *ib.* 474, 2 *Zur.* 332 n
Devereux (Lady Penelope): admired by Sidney, 2 *Zur.* 297 n
Devil: v. Satan.
Devils: v. Demons.
Deven (Earls of): v. Courtenay.
Devonshire: v. Cornwall.
 The rebellion there, 1549, 2 *Bec.* 593 n., 596, 1 *Brad.* 395 n., 2 *Cov.* xiii, 2 *Cran.* x, 1 *Lat.* 118 n., 247 n., 275, 371, 3 *Zur.* 66, 409, 654; caused by mass-mongers, 2 *Bec.* 596; those who remained faithful suffered much, 1 *Lat.* 376; names of the principal leaders of the insurrection, 2 *Cran.* 187 n.; character of the rebels, *ib.* 194; answer to

their fifteen articles, *ib.* 163; the rebellion suppressed, *3 Zur.* 409; the stannaries, 2 *Jew.* 627

Devoterer: an adulterer, 1 *Bec.* 450

Devotion of the Sacred Heart: extract from a book of prayers so entitled, 3 *Tyn.* 117 n

Devotions: oblations devoted to charitable or pious purposes, *Grin.* 163

Deylingus (Salom.): *Calf.* 103 n

Diagoras, the Atheist: denied there was a God, *Rog.* 37; a story of him, *Hutch.* 75, 76

Diagoras (another): died of joy, 1 *Hoop.* 297

Dialects: *Whita.* 215, 256

Dialogues: a dialogue between Satan and our conscience, 1 *Brad.* 210; a fruitful dialogue between Custom and Verity, declaring these words of Christ, "This is my body," *Grin.* 35; a dialogue between Christ and a sinner, by W. Hunnis, *Poet.* 154; notice of A Dialogue between the father and the son; a translation by W. Roye, 1 *Tyn.* 39 n., of a dialogue in rhyme called, Rede me and be not wrothe, made by the same, *ib.*, of A new Dialogue wherein is contained the Examination of the Mass, &c., *Rid.* 510, of A newe Dialoge called the Endightment against Mother Messe, 1548, *ib.* 511; of A Dialogve wherein is plainly laide open the tyrannicall dealing of L. Bishopps, &c., [1589], 3 *Whitg.* xix, xxvii. (There are various treatises written dialogue-wise in the works of Becon).

Diana: shrines for Diana, what, 1 *Ful.* 566

Diazius (Alphonsus): murders his brother Jo. Diazius, 4 *Jew.* 657—659

Dice: *v.* Cards, Gaming.

Didymus of Alexandria: warns against gross conceptions of the Deity, 3 *Bul.* 315, 316; proves that the Holy Ghost is God, because he is in many places at one time, which no creature can be, 2 *Bec.* 281, 3 *Bec.* 454, 1 *Brad.* 90, 3 *Bul.* 302, *Phil.* 209; shews in what sense the Holy Ghost is sent by the Son, 3 *Bul.* 308; declares that although the Holy Ghost is called the multitude of good graces, yet he is not divided, *ib.* 310, 311; explains why he is called the Comforter, *ib.* 313; speaks of faith alone justifying, 2 *Bec.* 639; on a dead faith, 2 *Cran.* 135

Dieppe, in France: 1 *Zur.* 115 n., 2 *Zur.* 91 n., 131

Diet: *v.* Temperance.

That of maids, 2 *Bec.* 369

Dieu garde: may God defend, so help me God, 3 *Jew.* 396

Diffaming: defaming, *Grin.* 20

Differentia (De vera): books under this title, *Rid.* 512

Digby (Simon): executed at York, 1 *Zur.* 225 n

Digest: *v.* Law (Civil).

Dignities: *v.* Honours.

Church dignities, how obtained, 2 *Tyn.* 177

Dilapidation of churches, &c., *Grin.* 172, 178

Diligence: *v.* Idleness.

Dillenberg, Holland: the castle, 2 *Zur.* 207 n

Dimas, Dismas, or Ismas: the penitent thief so called, *Whita.* 560

Dimianus: *v.* Damianus

Diminutio capitis: what, 1 *Bul.* 356

Dinah: ravished, 1 *Bul.* 416; stated to have been the wife of Job, *Pil.* 244

Dingly: forcibly, *Phil.* 370

Dingy: meaning of the word, 1 *Brad.* 111 n

Dinner: *v.* Graces.

Prayer before it, 1 *Bec.* 401; another, 3 *Bec.* 18, 19; behaviour at table, 1 *Bec.* 402; thanksgiving after it, *ib.*; another, 3 *Bec.* 19; what is to be done after it, 1 *Bec.* 402

Dinoth, abbot of Bangor: *Pil.* 516

Dio Cassius: Rom. Hist., *Jew.* xxxvi; he mentions that the Jews would not fight on the sabbath, 1 *Jew.* 224; testifies that they had no images, 2 *Jew.* 646

Diocæsarea: 3 *Bul.* 257

Dioceses: at first the same as parishes, 1 *Whitg.* 534; said to have been divided by pope Dionysius, *ib.* 534, 535; diocesans, why so called, 1 *Hoop.* 143

Diocletian, emperor: persecution under him, 2 *Bul.* 73, 106, 1 *Jew.* 279, 2 *Jew.* 976, 1 *Tyn.* 144 n.; his law against bigamy, 1 *Hoop.* 386, 387; supposed inscriptions to him, 2 *Ful.* 217, 218; his jester, *Pil.* 401

Diodorus: died of shame, 1 *Hoop.* 298

Diodorus, a bishop: blessed Nectarius, 2 *Ful.* 108; he(?) and Flavian said to have originated antiphonal singing, 3 *Whitg.* 386

Diodorus, bp of Tarsus: supposed author of the Ζητήματα Ἀναγκαῖα ascribed to Justin, *Whita.* 583 n

Diogenes: sayings of his, 2 *Bec.* 600, *Hutch.* 73, *Pil.* 314; what he said about his burial, *ib.* 317

Diogenes Laertius: tells of the mistake of Anaxagoras, 3 *Jew.* 131

Dion (......): *Park.* 311

Dionysius I., tyrant of Syracuse: took away Jupiter's golden cloak, *Sand.* 155

Dionysius II., tyrant of Syracuse: lost his kingdom and became a schoolmaster at Corinth; hence the proverb "Dionysius Corinthi," 3 *Jew.* 199

Dionysius of Halicarnassus: *Calf.* 13 n., 362; he reports a speech of Julius Cæsar, 4 *Jew.* 670; Ascham's opinion concerning him, 2 *Zur.* 71, 72

Dionysius, bp of Alexandria: *Calf.* 211; his jurisdiction, 2 *Whitg.* 165, 429; he calls two bishops of Rome his brethren, 1 *Jew.* 385; speaks of one who heard the thanksgiving in the church, and answered "Amen," 2 *Jew.* 699; says, martyrdom suffered that the church may not be divided, is no less glorious than that which is suffered for not doing idolatry, 4 *Jew.* 872; speaks of receiving the sacrament with the hand, 1 *Jew.* 153; recites the story of Serapion, q. v.

Dionysius the Areopagite: his history, 2 *Whitg.* 130; said to have been made bishop or archbishop of Athens by St Paul, *Calf.* 211, *Rog.* 329, 2 *Whitg.* 130, 428

Dionysius, falsely called the Areopagite: his works, 2 *Brad.* 305, *Jew.* xxxvi; they are wrongly ascribed to the Areopagite, 4 *Bul.* 248, *Calf.* 211 n., 1 *Ful.* 431, 1 *Jew.* 113, 114, *Phil.* 45, *Rid.* 173 n., 3 *Tyn.* 48, 135, *Whita.* 252 n., 575—580, 3 *Whitg.* 110; they were not known for five hundred years after Christ, 2 *Ful.* 235; their credit cracked by Erasmus, *ib.* 165; Usher's judgment of their date, *Pil.* 585 n.; their character, 3 *Whitg.*110; their author is a writer of no authority, *Whita.* 509; he writes on the names of God, 3 *Bul.* 137; says, if we desire to have communion with God, we must behold the heavenly life that he led in the flesh, 3 *Jew.* 493; declares that lessons of the holy books were read in the churches, 4 *Jew.* 856; alleged in support of tradition, *Whita.* 499, 575; speaks of doctrine communicated from mind to mind, 2 *Jew.* 673; mentions numerous apostolical traditions, 2 *Cran.* 56 n.; titles applied by him to Peter, 1 *Jew.* 428; he reckons three orders in the church, bishops, priests, and deacons, 3 *Jew.* 272; calls Timothy bishop of Ephesus, 2 *Whitg.* 295; speaks of a bishop as turned into God ($\theta\epsilon\omega\theta\tilde{\eta}\nu\alpha\iota$), and explains his meaning, 1 *Jew.* 462; mentions the archpriest and the priest, 1 *Ful.* 268; calls presbyters sacrificers, 2 *Jew.* 709; describes the mode of ordination in his time, *Pil.* 585; refers the inferior orders to tradition, *Rog.* 260 n.; says, we are led by sensible outward tokens to the contemplation of heavenly things, &c., 1 *Jew.* 465, 466, 2 *Jew.* 591, 3 *Jew.* 370; states that the sacred mysteries are not to be imparted to the uninitiated, *Whita.* 253; cited as asserting that the Greeks call baptism the weed (garment) of immortality, 3 *Jew.* 470; his account of godfathers, 3 *Whitg.* 109; he says the sponsor, considering the greatness of the matter, is in horror, and hesitates, 2 *Jew.* 721; on the effect of baptism, 1 *Jew.* 473; he says, our regeneration by the natural purgation wrought by water in a certain bodily manner, teaches us the purgation of the mind, *ib.* 476; on the eucharist, 1 *Ful.* 503, 504; his account of its celebration, *Coop.* 82, 83, 1 *Jew.* 108, 115; he calls it σύναξις, 2 *Bec.* 240 n.; terms it a symbol, 2 *Jew.* 609, a figurative sacrifice, *ib.* 721, 724, a wholesome sacrifice and divine communion, 3 *Bec.* 387, 2 *Jew.* 720, 721; shews why it is called the communion, *Coop.* 20, 1 *Jew.* 130; addresses the sacrament as a divine and holy mystery, 1 *Jew.* 534; comment of Pachymeres on this, *ib.* 535; speaks of the bishop dividing the bread, 2 *Jew.* 584, 585, 588, 1115; shews that in his time the bread and cup were not received of the minister alone, but distributed to all, 2 *Bec.* 239, 1 *Jew.* 17; says, the priest both receives the holy communion and delivers it to others, and ends with thanksgiving, together with the whole multitude, 4 *Jew.* 812; speaks of the cup as well as the bread being delivered to all the people, 3 *Bec.* 412, 415, 416, 1 *Jew.* 261; declares that the distribution of one bread, and one cup, preaches a heavenly unity, 1 *Jew.* 131, 142; quoted for the elevation of the sacrament, *ib.* 507, 510, &c.; a witness against transubstantiation, *Rid.* 173; he calls the elements signs whereby Christ is signified and received, *Coop.* 207; says that those who did not communicate were not suffered to be present, 2 *Bec.* 256, 3 *Bec.* 475, 483; mentions catechumens, penitents, and the possessed, as excluded from the eucharist, 1 *Ful.* 431, 1 *Jew.* 115; speaks of those who were given to filthy lusts being put back from the holy mysteries, 3 *Bec.* 475; declares that the holy institution admits only those that are perfect, *ib.*; speaks of most divine oil, 2 *Jew.* 620; says mystical theology does not prove any thing, *Whita.* 410; quoted by N. de Cusa, 3 *Bec.* 482

Dionysius Carthusianus: In Nov. Test., *Jew.* xxxvi; he tells why Christ spoke to the people in parables, 2 *Jew.* 677; says it was real wine that Christ called his blood, 3 *Jew.* 522; on the "breaking of bread" at Emmaus, 1 *Jew.* 232; on the phrase "all scripture," *Whita.* 634; his explanation of Luke xv. 8, "evertit domum," *ib.* 202; on 1 Cor. xiv. 15, giving thanks "with the spirit," 1 *Jew.* 315; on Eph. ii. 20, "of the apostles and prophets," *Whita.* 349; he rejects the Apocrypha, *ib.* 65; testifies against unwritten traditions, 1 *Lat.* 209, 210; says the torments of some in purgatory will continue till the day of judgment, *Rog.* 217; speaks of the pains of lost souls, 2 *Lat.* 235 n.; mentions some as asserting that St Christina is the saviour of men and women by her passion, *Rog.* 298 n

Dionysius, bp of Corinth: reports that St Paul made Dionysius the Areopagite, bishop of Athens, *Calf.* 211 n., 2 *Whitg.* 130; speaks of epistles of Clement and Soter as read in the church, 3 *Whitg.* 345; complains of the apostles of the devil, 1 *Jew.* 418

Dionysius Exiguus: *Coop.* 223, 2 *Ful.* 97 n., 107 n.; his faithlessness with respect to a canon of the council of Chalcedon, 2 *Ful.* 288 n

Dionysius (St), or Denys, bp of Paris: patron of the French, 1 *Hoop.* 313; account of him, *ib.* n.; dispute about his relics, 4 *Jew.* 1046

Dionysius, bp of Rome: said to have divided parishes and dioceses, 1 *Whitg.* 534, 535

Dioscorus, bp of Alexandria: v. Theodosius. In some ecclesiastical affairs he was an earnest suitor to the emperor Theodosius, 4 *Jew.* 1001; he confounded the two natures in Christ, *Rog.* 54; alleged divers fathers, 1 *Jew.* 83, 3 *Jew.* 226; condemned for heresy, 3 *Jew.* 145, 4 *Jew.* 1022

Diotrephes: a forerunner of Antichrist, 2 *Jew.* 912; first claimed papal primacy, 4 *Jew.* 890; has more successors than all the apostles have, 2 *Cran.* 305

Diotrephes, i. e. bp Gardiner, *q. v.*

Diphyes: Cecrops so called, and why, 2 *Bul.* 218

Directorium sacerdotum: *Lit. Eliz.* 304 n

Dirige: the office for the dead, *Bale* 292, 1 *Lat.* 292 n., *Lit. Eliz.* 57, *Rid.* 55, 510, 1 *Tyn.* 148 n.; otherwise called the Placebo, &c., 1 *Brad.* 589; the dirige (in the Primer of 1559), *Pra. Eliz.* 57, &c.; when it was used, *ib.* n.; dirigies, i. e. dirges, 2 *Bec.* 394

Disard: *v.* Dizzard.

Disciples: no catalogue of the seventy is extant, *Calf.* 69 n.; they once were weak and worldly-minded, 1 *Tyn.* 165; priests said to be their successors, 4 *Bul.* 117; those at Ephesus baptized with fire, *ib.* 356, 396

Disciplinarians: *v.* Puritans.

Discipline: *v.* Book, Church, Excommunication, Keys, Penance, Priests (πρ.), Travers (W.)

Typified by the rod of Aaron, *Sand.* 372; the ordinance of Christ, and practised by the apostles, 2 *Hoop.* 43, 51; a mark of the church, *ib.*; the bond of the church, 2 *Jew.* 994; its use, expediency, and necessity, 1 *Hoop.* 91, 183, 2 *Hoop.* 43, 51, 2 *Jew.* 986, *Pil.* 129, 379, *Sand.* 71, 72, 1 *Whitg.* 21, &c.; the gospel can never produce its proper fruit without it, 3 *Zur.* 539; what discipline the church ought to have, 2 *Tyn.* 219, 251, 252; it must be regulated by scripture, *Rog.* 202, and administered in love, *Sand.* 419; it must be impartial, *Pil.* 67; order of judgment in the ancient church, *Phil.* 50, 59; its severe discipline, 2 *Whitg.* 542; the ancient discipline, which excluded penitents, &c., is abandoned, 2 *Jew.* 706; discipline much decayed, *Now.* (56), 175; Beza's views on discipline in England, 2 *Zur.* 129; none at all there, 1 *Zur.* 164; want of discipline deplored, *Pil.* 5, 6, 211, 382; insufficiency of the proposed consistories of seniors, *ib.* 380, 381; an exhortation to the exercise of ecclesiastical discipline, *Sand.* 440, &c.; Grindal's opinions and directions concerning it, *Grin.* 451; the ordinary names of church officers, &c., not to be rejected, *Rog.* 202; the discipline and correction of ministers, 4 *Bul.* 504; the discipline of schools, *ib.* 485

Discipulus, i. e. Jo. Heroldt, *q. v.*

Discommodities: those which the saints suffer, recompensed with commodities, 2 *Bul.* 99

Discord, Dissension, Division, Contention: *v.* Controversy, Schism, Unity.

Discord the ruin of kingdoms, 2 *Jew.* 1028, 1094; it brings all things to havoc, 3 *Bec.* 598; the evil of divisions, *ib.* 41; contention a hindrance to unity, *Sand.* 100; a bane of the heart, *ib.* 138; the harms of it, *Lit. Edw.* 522, (569); the names of contentious persons to be presented to the ordinary, *Grin.* 143

Discourse: a godly discourse; verses by Hum. Gifford, *Poet.* 215

Discovery of a Gaping Gulph, &c., 1579: a book written by Jo. Stubbs against the proposed marriage of queen Elizabeth with the duke of Anjou, *Grin.* 408—412

DISCOVERY OF THE DANGEROUS ROCK OF THE POPISH CHURCH, by W. Fulke: 2 *Ful.* 213

Diseases: *v.* Saints.

Dishes: text appropriate to them, 1 *Bec.* 65

Disinheriting: *v.* Inheritance.

Dismas: *v.* Dimas.

Disobedience: *v.* Kings, Magistrates, Obedience, Parents, Rebellion.
 Disobedience to God defiles all our doings, *Pil.* 172
Dispensations: *v.* Marriage.
 Those of the pope, 4 *Jew.* 1157, 1 *Tyn.* 147; the canon law and Romish writers say the pope may dispense with the divine law, the law of nature, yea with all the precepts of the Old and New Testament, 3 *Jew.* 218; on the dispensing power of the prince, and of the archbishop, *Park.* 351; dispensations granted by the primate, 2 *Zur.* 360; sold, *ib.* 130; account of those granted by the court of Faculties, *Grin.* 448, 449; which of them should be utterly abolished, *ib.* 450; some condemned as Romish rubbish, *Pil.* 418; dispensations for unlawful marriages sought of Cranmer, 2 *Cran.* 329 n.; Parker refuses one to allow a child to hold a benefice, *Park.* 136; a Roman dispensation to hold a prebend, whether still in force? *ib.* 176; a dispensation sought to make a child a prebendary, *ib.* 362
Dispiling: discipline, *Pil.* 381; displing, 2 *Whitg.* 556
DISPLAYING OF THE POPISH MASS, by T. Becon, 3 *Bec.* 251
Disputations: *v.* Cambridge, Convocation, Oxford, Westminster.
 Declaration, signed by Ferrar, Hooper, Bradford, Saunders, and others, containing reasons for declining to dispute, except as therein mentioned, 1 *Brad.* 367; public disputations recommended, *Hutch.* 201
Dissemblers, Dissimulation: *v.* Hypocrisy.
Dissension: *v.* Discord.
Distained: stained, polluted, 3 *Bec.* 137
Distinction: a scholastic term, borrowed from the canon law, 1 *Tyn.* 46 n
Disturbers: *v.* Worship.
Disworship: what, *Pil.* 103
Dite: a saying, *Phil.* 338
Ditty: a song, *Nord.* 150, *Poet.* xxii, 226, 420
Dive-doppel: the dive-dapper, or dab-chick, 3 *Bec.* 276
DIVERSITY BETWEEN GOD'S WORD AND MAN'S INVENTION, by T. Becon, 3 *Bec.* 484
Dives: *v.* Lazarus.
 Dives and Pauper: a book printed by Wynken de Worde; twice quoted, *Rog.* 298 n
Divinity: *v.* Schoolmen, Theology.
Divorce: *v.* Marriage.
 What it is, 1 *Hoop.* 382; when lawful, *ib.*; most divorces are on occasion of adultery, 2 *Bec.* 647; the Jewish law respecting divorce, 2 *Bul.* 228; the law of Christ, 1 *Hoop.* 378, 2 *Tyn.* 51, 52; on the cognizance thereof by church courts, 4 *Bul.* 511, 3 *Whitg.* 267; what man's law should do, 2 *Tyn.* 54, 55; divorce not so suffered by Papists as that the parties may marry again, 3 *Bec.* 532; proclamation respecting it, 1548, 3 *Zur.* 263 n.; Hooper's views on divorce, 1 *Hoop.* 378, &c., 2 *Hoop.* xxiii, 3 *Zur.* 64, 416, 422; Bucer's opinion, 3 *Zur.* 665, 666; lectures of P. Martyr, *ib.* 404
Dizzard: an idle fellow, a blockhead, 1 *Cov.* 4; disards, i. e. persons stupified, 4 *Jew.* 1091
Do on: *v. infra.*
Dobbs (Sir Rich.), lord mayor: his godly works, *Rid.* 60; concerned in the foundation of the royal hospitals, *ib.* 410, 411
Docetæ: *v.* Gnostics.
Dockery (Tho.), proctor: 2 *Cran.* 492
Doctors: *v.* Fathers, Schoolmen.
 Doctors or teachers, what, 4 *Bul.* 106; preaching their office, *ib.* 116; the four doctors of the church, viz. Gregory, Ambrose, Augustine, Jerome, 1 *Tyn.* 343 n.; Basil called the doctor or teacher of the world, *Whita.* 233; the old doctors and the school doctors, 2 *Lat.* 319; contrary doctors, 1 *Tyn.* 149—153; the diversity of doctors, *ib.* 158; list of many noted doctors who desired reformation, *Bale* 520
 The Union of Doctors: *v.* Unio Dissidentium; The Book of Doctors, a Latin pamphlet so called by Cartwright, 2 *Whitg.* 106, &c., 3 *Whitg.* 289; the angelic doctor, *v.* Thomas Aquinas: the divine doctor is Jo. Ruisbroeck: the doctor of grace, *v.* Augustine: the invincible doctor, *v.* Occam (Will.): the irrefragable doctor, *v.* Alexander Alensis: the mellifluous doctor, *v.* Ambrose: the profound doctor is Tho. Bradwardin, abp of Canterbury: the seraphic doctor, *v.* Bonaventure: the subtle doctor, *v.* Duns Scotus.
 Rings given to doctors on their creation, *Pil.* 192; doctors of divinity, specimen of exercises at their creation, 1 *Tyn.* 315; why they wore boots on that occasion, *ib.* 232; doctors of divinity in Romish universities abroad, 1 *Ful.* 568
Doctrine: *v.* Heresy, Scripture, Teaching.
 In what it consists, 4 *Bul.* 53, 54; whence to be fetched, *ib.* 149; that of Christ's faith is no new thing, 1 *Cov.* 4; that of the fathers before Christ and ours is one, 2 *Bul.* 283; it is foolishness to those that perish, but to those who are saved it is the power of God, 1 *Cov.* 5; we must put on the nature of Christ's doctrine, *ib.* 10; he that desires to do God's will, shall know

the true doctrine, 2 *Tyn.* 40; doctrine to be tried by scripture, *ib.* 103, 121, 195; power to judge thereof, 4 *Bul.* 45; comparison of the doctrines taught by the reformers with the Popish ones, 3 *Bec.* 227, &c.; those condemned by Romanists are no new or yesterday doctrines, *ib.* 404; that of Becon's Catechism is agreeable to the word of God, 2 *Bec.* 409, and dissents not from the teaching of the true catholic church, *ib.*; purity of doctrine was maintained through the reign of queen Elizabeth, *Rog.* 20; to sound doctrine must be joined an orderly life, *Sand.* 246; yet good doctrine is not to be rejected for the evil life of ministers, 4 *Bul.* 161; false doctrine causes evil works, true doctrine good works, 2 *Tyn.* 38; examples of darkness in doctrine, *ib.* 103; the teaching of false doctrine a work against the fourth commandment, 1 *Hoop.* 345; inquiry to be made respecting erroneous or seditious doctrine, *Grin.* 181

A necessary Doctrine and Erudition for any Christen Man, 1543, otherwise called the King's Book, 2 *Cran.* 16 n., 83 n., 337 n., *Hutch.* 231 n.; its authorship, *Rid.* 511; Anne Askewe questioned about the king's book, *Bale* 151

Dod (Hen.): notice of him, *Poet.* xli; Psalm cxxvii. in metre, *ib.* 449

Dod (Jo.), rector of Hanwell: 1 *Brad.* 562 n., 563 n., 564

Dodd (Cha.), [i. e. Hugh Tootle?]: Church History, *Calf.* 53 n., 290 n

Dodds (Greg.), dean of Exeter: appointed to preach, *Park.* 260, 275, 511

Doddy-poul: *v.* Dodypole.

Dodington (Rob.): an Augustine prior, *Bale* 28, 36

Dodkin: a little doit, a small coin, 2 *Bul.* 59, *Pil.* 607

Dodman (Jo.), master of a school at Bissweiler: 2 *Cov.* 505, 517, 521, 594 n

Dodwell (Hen.): *Calf.* 251 n

Dodypole: a blockhead, *Bale* 429; doddypoul, 1 *Lat.* 136; dodipole, *ib.* 245, 304; Dr Dodepole, the representative of folly in the old drama, *ib.* 245 n

Doe: *v.* Venison.

Doeg: was a peace-breaker, 1 *Lat.* 486

Dogbolt: a worthless fellow, 1 *Ful.* 469; used as an adjective, 2 *Ful.* 14, 212

Dogs: the self-righteous, 2 *Tyn.* 10; the obstinate, *ib.* 114; persecutors, *ib.* 230; those in Matt. xv. 27, and Mark vii. 28, said to be the faithful, *Whita.* 702; dumb dogs, who so called by the prophet, 2 *Hoop.* 357

Dominic (St): instituted the rosary or lady psalter, 1 *Brad.* 588

Dominica Judica: Passion Sunday so called, 1 *Jew.* 107

Dominical: a veil, or napkin, 1 *Jew.* 179 n

Dominicans, or Black Friars: 4 *Bul.* 517; they were Thomists, or followers of Aquinas, 3 *Jew.* 610, 1 *Tyn.* 159 n.; controversy between them and the Franciscans, 1 *Ful.* 35; they rejected the council of Basil, 1 *Jew.* 70, 233; controlled and cut off its determination touching the conceiving of our lady in original sin, 4 *Jew.* 1053; their writers on the Apocalypse, *Bale* 257

Dominicus à Soto: *v.* Soto.

Dominions: a name of angels, 3 *Bul.* 338

Dominis (Ant. de), abp of Spalato: 1 *Tyn.* 74 n.; Crackenthorp wrote against him, *Calf.* 64 n

Dominus, or Sir: a title assumed by priests, 1 *Tyn.* 277

Dominus vobiscum: 3 *Bec.* 257, 263, 2 *Brad.* 234, 4 *Bul.* 408, 1 *Jew.* 174, 175

Domitian, emperor: a gainsayer, 1 *Lat.* 129; a persecutor, 2 *Bul.* 105; a blasphemous title assumed by him, *Calf.* 6 n., 4 *Jew.* 842; a story respecting him and Apollonius Tyanæus, 2 *Jew.* 1001

Don (Jo.): *v.* Dunne.

Donald—, king of Scots: his law against swearing, 1 *Bec.* 390

Donat: a grammatical book, so called from the grammarian Donatus, 1 *Tyn.* 4

Donation: *v.* Constantine.

Donatists: their heresy, *Hutch.* 252, 1 *Lat.* 160, *Phil.* 79, 138, 426, 1 *Whitg.* 112, &c., 1 *Zur.* 285; they sought singularity, 2 *Brad.* 179 n.; separated from the church under the pretence of greater holiness, 4 *Bul.* 78; claimed to be the church exclusively, 3 *Jew.* 151, 190; said the church was only in Africa, 1 *Bul.* 161, 2 *Ful.* 32, 390, *Rog.* 171; affirmed the visible church to be free from sin, *Rog.* 167, and incapable of erring in manners, *ib.* 179; thought they were so perfect that they could justify others, *ib.* 135, 257; maintained free-will, *ib.* 106; their error respecting wicked ministers, 2 *Brad.* 345, 4 *Bul.* 56, 161; they declared the sacraments to be holy only when administered by holy men, *Rog.* 270, 2 *Whitg.* 520; said none could baptize who were not pure and holy, 4 *Bul.* 369; they denied baptism to infants, 2 *Cran.* 59, 60; re-baptized, *Bale* 316, 4 *Bul.* 393; what prayers they used at baptism, 4 *Bul.* 360; they taught that evil ministers could not loose, *Hutch.* 97; held conventicles, *Sand.* 191; alleged Cyprian, 1 *Jew.* 83; Augustine opposed them,

Phil. 137; they maintained the lawfulness of suicide, 1 *Ful.* 23; thought no man should be compelled in religion, 1 *Bul.* 357, and that no man should be put to death for any offence, *Rog.* 349; their cause judged by Constantine, 4 *Jew.* 964, &c.; he made a law against them, *Pil.* 641; they were punished by the civil power, 2 *Brad.* 379; went to death boldly, 1 *Lat.* 160

Donatus à Casis Nigris: 3 *Jew.* 167

Donatus, bp of Evoria: crossed himself, *Calf.* 252

Donatus, the grammarian, 3 *Whitg.* 500: Jerome's schoolmaster, 4 *Jew.* 653; referred to, *Whita.* 150; his book, 2 *Cov.* 509; a book called, after him, Donat, 1 *Tyn.* 4

Doncaster, co. York: a famous image there, 2 *Lat.* 395; the White Friars surrendered, the prior executed, *ib.* 392 n.; an army sent against the rebellious earls arrives there, 1 *Zur.* 247 n.; a plot against abp Sandys there, *Sand.* xxv.

Donel (Tho.): in exile, 1 *Cran.* (9)

Donkester (Tho.), sub-prior of Newesham: 2 *Cran.* 290, 291

Donne (Gabriel): a monk, who assisted Philips in the betrayal of Tyndale, connected with bp Gardiner, rewarded by bp Vesey, 1 *Tyn.* lxix. n

Donne (Jo.): *v.* Dunne.

Donne (Jo.): Sermons, *Calf.* 226 n.; Pseudo-Martyr, 2 *Ful.* 236 n

Donnes (Dr), of Jesus coll. Camb.: opposes Latimer, 2 *Lat.* xii.

Donse (Jo.), i. e. Jo. Duns Scotus: *Bale* 170

Doom, and Doomsday: *v.* Judgment.

Do on (To): to put on, 3 *Tyn.* 251; done on, *Bale* 404

Door-keepers: *v.* Porters.

Doors: text appropriate to one, 1 *Bec.* 63; the emblems of doors, locks, &c., explained, *Pil.* 382, 383

Dor: a drone, or beetle, 1 *Bul.* 332, 4 *Bul.* 266, *Calf.* 2; dories, drone-bees, *Phil.* 308

Dorbel (Nich.): *v.* Orbellis (N. de).

Dorcas, or Tabitha: 2 *Bul.* 21, 23, 321

Dorel (Will.?), prebendary of Canterbury: *Park.* 319; bishop Grindal advises that he should not be made abp of Armagh, *Grin.* 292

Dorell (Will.): *v.* Darell.

Doria (And.): his victories over the Turks, 2 *Cran.* 236

Dories: *v.* Dor.

Dorifall (Jo.): burned, *Poet.* 168

Doring (Matthias): his comments are with Lyra's, *Jew.* xxxvi; cited, 3 *Jew.* 590; Jewel accused of corrupting his words, *ib.* 589, &c.; he wrote on the Apocalypse, *Bale* 256

Dorix (Ecclus. xxiv. 30): said to be the name of a river in Armenia, but in fact a blunder (Gr. διώρυξ), *Whita.* 151

Dorman (Tho.): *Calf.* 2, 51, 4 *Jew.* 1263 n.; his books, 2 *Ful.* 3, *Grin.* 169, *Jew.* xxxvi; he writes against Jewel, *Grin.* 169, *Jew.* xx, xxxvi; calls Oza the poor Levite a king, 3 *Jew.* 409, 4 *Jew.* 695; asserts that the pope is the head, and kings the hands and arms, 3 *Jew.* 117, 120, 4 *Jew.* 898; his idea of the "kingly priesthood," 4 *Jew.* 985; he disapproves over-much antiquity, *ib.* 990; falsely alleges Theodoret, *ib.* 695; answered by Nowell, *Coop.* iv, 1 *Ful.* 75 n., *Now.* iii, iv, *Park.* 260, 1 *Whitg.* 22, &c., 2 *Whitg.* 195, 217, &c., 3 *Whitg.* 313

Dormi secure: a collection of sermons so called, 3 *Bec.* 200, 234

Dorotheus: a counterfeit writer, *Calf.* 126 n.; he calls Timothy bp of Ephesus, 2 *Whitg.* 294, and says he died there, *ib.* 303; states that Aristobulus was bishop of Britain, *Rog.* 329 n

Dorothy (St): invoked to save flowers, 2 *Bec.* 536; account of her, *ib.* n

Dorrell (Mr): *v.* Dorel.

Dorscheus (Jo. Geo.): *Calf.* 155 n., 181 n

Dorset (Tho.): 1 *Lat.* x.

Dorset (Hen. marq. of), afterwards duke of Suffolk: *v.* Grey.

Dorset (Frances marchioness of): *v.* Grey.

Dorset (Tho. earl of): *v.* Sackville.

Doted: rendered doting, 2 *Bec.* 646

Dotel: a dotard, *Pil.* 586

Dottrels: birds of a particular kind, also silly fellows, *Bale* 363

Douay: the seminary there, 1 *Ful.* viii, xii, *Lit. Eliz.* 656 n.; extracts from the Douay catechism, 1 *Tyn.* 342 n

Double-minded men: *Sand.* 130, &c.; they are commonly double-tongued, *ib.* 132

Doubt: *v.* Unbelief.

Douce (Fra.): his Dance of Death cited, *Pra. Eliz.* xvii. n., xviii. n., xix, xx, xxi, 403 n., 413 n

Douglas, in Scotland: besieged, 3 *Zur.* 387

Douglas (Archib.), earl of Angus: married Margaret, sister of king Henry VIII., 1 *Zur.* 102 n., 144 n

Douglas (James), 4th earl of Morton: present at the murder of Rizzio, 1 *Zur.* 166 n.; one of the confederate lords, *ib.* 193 n.; suspected of the murder of lord Darnley, *ib.* 197 n.; he sells the earl of Northumberland to the English, *ib.* 217 n

Douglas (Geo.): took part in the murder of Rizzio, 1 *Zur.* 166 n.; aided the queen of Scots in her escape from Lochleven, *ib.* 202 n

Douglas (Jo.), rector of the university of St Andrew's: 2 *Zur.* 364

Douglas (Lady Margaret), wife of Matth. Stuart (*q. v.*), earl of Lennox.

Douleians: some Arians so called, *Rog.* 47

Doulia: *v.* Worship.

Dounton (Will.): *v.* Downton.

Dove: its innocence and chastity, *Hutch.* 156; the mathematical dove of Archytas, 2 *Jew.* 561; the golden dove of Amphilochius, 1 *Jew.* 188, 2 *Jew.* 559, 560; gold and silver ones suspended over fonts and altars, *ib.* 559, 561

Dove (......), a prior at Calais, 2 *Cran.* 376 n

Dover, co. Kent: the emperor Charles V. lands there, 2 *Tyn.* 316 n.; state of the castle and town, *Park.* 203, 204; the pier and haven, *ib.* 258, 259; a strange person examined there, *ib.* 400; Parker sends a book about Dover to lord Burghley, *ib.* 436, 439. Suffragans of Dover: *v.* Ingworth, Rogers, Thornton.

Dover court, co. Essex: the rood there, *Bale* 442, 2 *Ful.* 210; the burning of it, 2 *Cran.* 280

Dowdall (Geo.), abp of Armagh: a Papist, 3 *Zur.* 428 n.; deprived, 1 *Bec.* viii. n

Dower: on right to it, 2 *Cran.* 360

Dowkings: duckings, 2 *Bec.* 455

Downes (Fra.), of East Tuddenham: *Park.* 402 n

Downes (Godfrey), chancellor of the church of York: letter to him, 2 *Cran.* 261

Downham (Geo.), bp of Derry: his Papa Antichristus, *Calf.* 6 n

Downham (Will.), bp of Chester: compounds for his visitation, *Park.* 222; signs a letter to the queen, *ib.* 294

Downton (Will.), servant to bp Hooper: 2 *Hoop.* 592, 597; how used by Babington, warden of the Fleet, 2 *Hoop.* 620, 3 *Zur.* 292 n

Dowriche (Ann): notice of her, *Poet.* xxxii; verses by her, *ib.* 359

Dowsepers: grandees, *Bale* 155, 317

Doxology: *v.* Gloria, Prayer (The Lord's).

Doyly (Tho.): married a neice of Parker, *Park.* xiii.

Draco: his laws, 2 *Bul.* 219

Draff: refuse, food for swine, *Bale* 285, 1 *Brad.* 289, *Calf.* 248, 2 *Hoop.* 206

Drafflesacked: filled with draff, 2 *Bec.* 591

Dragges: dregs or drugs, *Pil.* 121

Dragon: *v.* Satan.

A great red one, *Bale* 406; his seven heads, *ib.* 407; he stands before the woman, *ib.* 409; is overcome and cast out, *ib.* 412; pursues the woman, *ib.* 416; gives power to the beast, *ib.* 424; the dragon of St George perhaps symbolical, 1 *Hoop.* 313 n

Drake (Sir Fra.): his victories at Cadiz, &c., *Lit. Eliz.* 469

Drake (Rob.): martyred, *Poet.* 166

Drama: *v.* Interludes, Pammachius, Playhouses, Scaffold.

Suggestion of bishop Grindal, that histriones, or common players should be prohibited, at least for one whole year, *Grin.* 269

Drant (Tho.): notice of him, *Poet.* xl; Jeremie's prayer (Lam. v.) in metre, *ib.* 417

Draper (Sir Chr.): lord mayor, 1567, and an ecclesiastical commissioner, *Grin.* 201

Drayton (Mich.): notice of him, *Poet.* xvii; Solomon's song, chap. v, versified by him, *ib.* 117; the song of Annah, *ib.* 119; the prayer of Jeremiah, *ib.* 121; a song of Moses and the Israelites, *ib.* 124; a song of the faithful (Isa. xii.), *ib.* 126; a song of the faithful (Hab. iii.), *ib.* 127; the song of Jonah, *ib.* 129; the finding of Moses, *ib.* 130; the passage of the Red Sea, *ib.* 132; the law given on Sinai, *ib.* 134

Dreams: have deceived and destroyed many, 2 *Cran.* 43; not to be listened to, *ib.* 44; Bradford's dreams fulfilled, 2 *Brad.* xxxviii; a dream, by Hum. Gifford, *Poet.* 218

Dress: *v.* Apparel.

Dress: address, *Bale* 65

Driedo (Jo.) à Turnhout: De eccl.Script., &c., *Jew.* xxxvi; he tells why Scripture is called an instrument, *Whita.* 704; on the canon of Scripture, *ib.* 330; on the Latin Vulgate, *ib.* 129; on the book of Baruch, *ib.* 69; on the additions to Daniel, *ib.* 77; on the book of Wisdom, *ib.* 89; on the meaning of Augustine's declaration that he would not believe the gospel unless the authority of the catholic church moved him, *ib.* 322; he maintains that Gregory the Great did not disclaim supremacy, 1 *Jew.* 37, 47

Drinking: *v.* Drunkenness, Eating.

Drink-offerings: 2 *Bul.* 191

Drithe: *v.* Dryth.

Droitwich, co. Worcester: St Augustine's Friary, 2 *Lat.* 393 n., 395 n., 397

Druets (......): *Park.* 424

Druids: *Bale* 152, 2 *Jew.* 981

Drumslade: a musical instrument, 1 *Bec.* 449

Drunkenness: forbidden, condemned, 1 *Bec.* 324, 325, 1 *Bul.* 423, 1 *Lat.* 169, 254, 2 *Lat.* 15, 61, 81, *Sand.* 137, 393, 2 *Jew.* 1040; against it, with sentences and examples of scripture, 1 *Bec.* 449, 450; against drunkenness and banqueting, 1 *Lat.* 254; what drunkenness means in scripture, 2 *Bul.* 57; the names of drunkards to be presented to the ordinary, *Grin.* 143

Drury (Will.): commissary of the court of Faculties, *Grin.* 446; an ecclesiastical commissioner, *Park.* 277, 345; Parker's officer, *ib.* 363; letter to him, *ib.* 213

Drury (Sir Will.): 1 *Zur.* 202 n., 203 n.; takes the castle of Edinburgh, 2 *Zur.* 223 n.; Drury, marshal of Berwick (the same?), 1 *Zur.* 225 n

Druthmar (Christian), called Grammaticus, monk of Corbey: Expos. in Matth., *Jew.* xxxvi; speaks of Christ instituting the sacrament that the disciples might do that in a figure which he should do for them, 2 *Bec.* 286, 3 *Bec.* 437; says the blood of Christ is aptly figured by wine, 2 *Bec.* 286, 3 *Bec.* 437, *Grin.* 66, 3 *Jew.* 446

Dryander (Fra.), otherwise Duchesne, or Enzinas: 3 *Zur.* 77, 348 n., 463, 535; in England, 2 *Cran.* 421 n.; entertained by Cranmer at Lambeth, 3 *Zur.* 535; letters by him, *ib.* 348—354; his wife, *ib.* 562

Dryburgh (The abbot of): tutor of James VI., 2 *Zur.* 302 n

Dryth: dryness, 2 *Tyn.* 14; drithe, 1 *Jew.* 250

Duarenus (Fra.): on ancient colleges of presbyters, 3 *Whitg.* 202, 203; on certain laws of Theodosius and Charlemagne, *ib.* 455

Dubber (Dr): 1 *Lat.* 121

Dublin: a false miracle at Christ church, *Park.* 95 n.; abp Marsh's library at St Sepulchre's, *Whita.* 276 n

Ducæus (Fronto): 2 *Ful.* 110 n.; his edition of Chrysostom, 1 *Bec.* 69 n.; 2 *Bec.* 257 n

Du Cange (Car. du Fresne Dom); 3 *Bec.* 264 n., 2 *Ful.* 364 n

Duchesne(Fra.), alias Dryander, *q. v.*

Duddles: bundles of dirty rags, *Pil.* 212

Dudithius (Andr.): Orationes in conc. Trid., *Jew.* xxxvi, 4 *Jew.* 959 n

Dudley (Edm.): he and Empson, the rapacious ministers of Henry VII., 2 *Cran.* 298 n., 2 *Tyn.* 342

Dudley (Jo.), visc. Lisle, afterwards earl of Warwick, ultimately duke of Northumberland: mentioned as Sir Jo. Dudley, 2 *Cran.* 409; other references to him, 2 *Brad.* 89, 390, 3 *Zur.* 397, 399, 407, 409; as visc. Lisle he questions Anne Askewe, *Bale* 201; writes to Paget and the king about hostilities with the French, 2 *Cran.* 495 n.; being earl of Warwick he commands the archers at Pinkey, 3 *Zur.* 43; takes the part of Hooper, 2 *Hoop.* xii; favours the reformation, 3 *Zur.* 76, 82; termed a soldier of Christ, *ib.* 82; undertakes that Bullinger's works should be translated, *ib.* 422; Bullinger is advised to dedicate to him, *ib.* 445, 449, and receives information as to his style, *ib.* 440, 448; his opinion of the mass, 3 *Zur.* 439; his signature as privy councillor, 2 *Cran.* 524, 530, *Park.* 46, *Rid.* 508; his illness and recovery, 3 *Zur.* 89, 409; warden-general of the North, *ib.* 454 n.; Sion house granted to him, *ib.* 3 n.; Burcher accuses him of the murder of king Edward, *ib.* 684; his treason, *ib.* 366; he goes to Cambridge to proclaim the lady Jane, *Sand.* ii, iii; purposes to proclaim queen Mary there, but is arrested, *ib.* iv; his execution, 3 *Zur.* 367 n., 515, 742; he professed himself a Papist at his death, 1 *Brad.* 425, 426, 2 *Cov.* 241, 242; his dying speech printed in Latin, 3 *Zur.* 291 n.; his attainder confirmed by act of parliament, 2 *Cran.* 443 n.; his character, 3 *Zur.* 89; commended by Hooper, *ib.* 99; by Bullinger, 4 *Bul.* 545

Dudley (Ambrose), earl of Warwick: arraigned at Guildhall for adherence to the cause of the lady Jane, 3 *Zur.* 374 n., 507; sent with an army into Normandy to aid the Protestants, *Lit. Eliz.* 459; he holds Newhaven, *Park.* 179 n., 2 *Zur.* 92 n.; surrenders it, *Park.* 183; goes against the rebels in the North, *Park.* 388 n., 1 *Zur.* 214 n., 247 n.; at the duke of Norfolk's trial, *ib.* 267 n.; patron of Frobisher, 2 *Zur.* 290; a letter by him, *Park.* 319

— He married the lady Anne Seymour, dau. of the protector Somerset, 1 *Bec.* 396 n., 3 *Zur.* 340, 565 n.; she afterwards became the wife of Sir Edward Unton or Umpton*, K. B., 1 *Bec.* 396 n., 3 *Zur.* 340 n.; a book dedicated to her, *Poet.* xliii.

Dudley (Rob.), earl of Leicester: referred to, *Coop.* v, xiv, xv, 2 *Cov.* 530, 531, *Grin.* 391, *Park.* 236, 237, 2 *Zur.* 221, 283, 300; mentioned as suitor to queen Elizabeth, 1 *Zur.* 34 n., 216 n.; master of the horse, 2 *Zur.* 105; he procures Whittingham the deanery of Durham, 3 *Zur.* 764 n.; Parker intends to ask him for venison, *Park.* 177; he claims an advowson, *ib.* 266; signature as privy councillor, *Grin.* 405, 408, 417, 423, 427, 433, 435, *Park.* 328 n., 330, 357, 381; he seeks a dispensation to make a child a prebendary, *Park.* 362; patronizes Fulke, 1 *Ful.* iii; at the duke of Norfolk's trial, 1 *Zur.* 267 n.; slandered by a prisoner,

---

* Not Ampton as in 3 *Zur.* 340 n. and p. 24 of this Index.

Park. 400; offended with Parker, *ib.* 406, 408, 439; he supports the Puritans, *ib.* 428; Sandys writes to him concerning them, *Sand.* xx; expected to accompany the queen to Canterbury, *Park.* 442; visited by her *Coop.* xiv, *Park.* 468; he purposes to undo Parker, *Park.* 472; suspected of having poisoned the earl of Essex, 1 *Zur.* 329 n.; dedication to him by Garbrand, 2 *Jew.* 966; prayer offered for his success, when commanding in the Low Countries, *Lit. Eliz.* 467, 605; the prayer, *ib.* 605 n.; he quarrels with Whitgift, 3 *Whitg.* xiii; letters by him, *Park.* 190, 301; letters to him, *Grin.* 261, *Park.* 190, 405, *Pil.* 658, 3 *Whitg.* 624 (from Jewel); his cognizance, *Pra. Eliz.* xviii.

— Amy (Robsart), his wife, 2 *Bec.* 583 n

Dudley (Lord Guilford): arraigned and condemned, 2 *Cran.* 442 n., 3 *Zur.* 374 n., 507; beheaded, 2 *Brad.* 63, 3 *Zur.* 154, 515, 686

Dudley (Lord Hen.): Margaret (Audley) his wife, 1 *Zur.* 137 n

Dudley (Lady Mary), wife of Sir Hen. Sydney, *q. v.*

Duellius (Raim.): 1 *Bec.* 164 n

Dugdale (Sir Will.), Garter: Monast. Angl., 1 *Hoop.* 40 n., 4 *Jew.* 781 n.; Hist. of St Paul's, 1 *Lat.* 49 n.; Orig. Jurid., 2 *Lat.* 419 n., 428 n.; Hist. of Warwickshire, 1 *Lat.* 272, 2 *Lat.* 84, 383, 384, 388, 396, 419, 423 nn.; he suggested the re-interment of abp Parker, *Park.* xi.

Duglos (Geo.): *v.* Douglas.

Dulcetness: sweetness, 1 *Brad.* 338

Dulcius (Jo.): sent to England to the marriage of Ann of Cleves, 3 *Zur.* 529 n

Dulia: *v.* Worship.

Dumbarton, Scotland: the queen of Scots brought thence to France, 3 *Zur.* 643 n.; she desires to go to the castle, 1 *Zur.* 203 n., and see 204 n (Dunbritone); the castle taken by the regent Lennox, *ib.* 257 n., 262

Du Moulin (Pet.): *Calf.* 74, 137, 193, 257, 290, 322, 2 *Ful.* 71, 109, 347 nn

Dunbar, Scotland: taken by the English, 3 *Zur.* 645; creeping to the cross there, 1568, *Grin.* 295

Dunbritone: *v.* Dumbarton.

Duncan (Jo.), or Duncanson, minister of Stirling: 2 *Zur.* 365

Duncanson (Jo.), principal of St Leonard's coll., St Andrew's: 2 *Zur.* 364

Dundee, Scotland: besieged, 3 *Zur.* 387

Dungate (Tho.): martyred at Grinstead, *Poet.* 168

Dunne (Jo.), or Don: opposes the king's injunctions at Oxford, 2 *Cran.* 382—384

Duns-man: a follower of Duns Scotus, 1 *Tyn.* 108

Duns Scotus (Jo.): *v.* Scotists.

His works, *Jew.* xxxvi; he concludes that all things necessary for our salvation are contained in scripture, 2 *Cran.* 35, 36, *Whita.* 704; says, the certainty of faith is the greatest certainty, 2 *Lat.* 337; declares that the virgin was conceived without sin, 1 *Tyn.* 91, 3 *Tyn.* 131 n.; did no miracles, yet contradicted Aquinas, 3 *Tyn.* 131; says, touching the sacraments, we must hold as the holy church of Rome holds, &c., 2 *Jew.* 563, 578; treats of opus operatum, *ib.* 750, 751; confirms the opinion of transubstantiation, 1 *Jew.* 11, *Rid.* 16; admits that it was first explicitly set forth in the council of Lateran, 4 *Bul.* 277; citations and references shewing his view of it, 2 *Brad.* 275, 2 *Cov.* 254, 1 *Hoop.* 119, 167, *Rid.* 24; he allows the inconvenience of interpreting Christ's words in the eucharist literally, 1 *Jew.* 456, 2 *Jew.* 563; concedes that the words of scripture might be expounded more easily without transubstantiation, 2 *Bec.* 268, 269, 3 *Bec.* 426, 1 *Cran.* 302, (34), 2 *Jew.* 563; holds that the bread in the sacrament departs, and that in its place succeeds Christ's body, 1 *Jew.* 11, 534; says one body may be in divers places, &c., *ib.* 484; his opinion on the consecration of the eucharist, *Park.* 251; he says the bread is consecrated by the words, "This is my body," *Pil.* 635; states how these words are the words of consecration, 2 *Jew.* 789; says, the word "benedixit" works consecration, 1 *Hoop.* 518, 1 *Jew.* 123; mentions an opinion that any form of words written in the gospel is sufficient for that purpose, 3 *Jew.* 452; declares that neither Christ nor the church has defined which are the words of consecrating the cup, *Pil.* 635; testifies that the Greek church did not use the mixed cup, and that it is not necessary to do so, 1 *Jew.* 139; asserts that not only God applies the virtue of the sacrifice, but the priest also, 2 *Jew.* 747; his opinion on a mouse eating the sacrament, *Rid.* 509; he enumerates holy orders, 3 *Jew.* 273; treats of the origin of auricular confession, *Pil.* 554, 555; teaches that a man may make his confession in writing, and receive absolution by a substitute, 3 *Jew.* 357; writes on extreme unction, *Pil.* 527 n.; considers the vow of chastity, if not holding by the constitution of the church, not rigidly binding, 3 *Jew.* 428, 429; distinguishes between simple vows and solemn ones, 4 *Jew.* 788; his subtle quiddities, his disciples, &c., *Bale* 170, 1 *Hoop.* 325, 2 *Lat.* 317, *Pil.* 80, 550, *Rid.* 24; a Duns-man, what, 1 *Tyn.* 108; one described as "Dunsly learned," 2 *Lat.* 374; "Dunstical doctors," 1 *Ful.* 568

Dunstable, co. Beds: 2 *Cran.* 241, 242, 243, 244; "as plain as Dunstable way," a proverb, 1 *Lat.* 113; St Fremund of Dunstable, *Bale* 192; the sentence of divorce against queen Catherine of Arragon pronounced there, 2 *Cran.* 243 n

Dunstan (St), abp of Canterbury: a great helper of monks, *Pil.* 574; concerned in an imposture, *Calf.* 134

Dunstan (Ant.), alias Kitchen, *q. v.*

Du Pin (L. E.): *Calf.* 42, 202, 2 *Ful.* 71, 296, 302, 323 nn

Du Plessis (Phil.): *v.* Mornay.

Duræus (Jo.): *Calf.* 42 n.; he says no council ever had lawful authority which was not confirmed by the bishop of Rome, *Rog.* 205 n

Durandus (Gul.), bp of Mende: Rationale Divin. Officiorum, *Calf.* 98 n., 297 n., *Jew.* xxxvi, *Sand.* 224, 3 *Tyn.* 73 n.; he thinks that the office of settling the canon of scripture belonged only to the ancient church, *Whita.* 330; his opinion on worship, 2 *Jew.* 667; he says Hebrew was used in divine service by Christian Jews, 1 *Jew.* 289; allows that in times past all the faithful every day were partakers with the priest, 3 *Bec.* 414, 417, 3 *Jew.* 477; explains how in the primitive church all that were present were wont to communicate, 2 *Bec.* 239, 258, 3 *Bec.* 414, 417, 474; tells how the Roman missal was approved, and the Ambrosian missal rejected by a miracle, *Pil.* 509; gives very absurd reasons for the ceremonies of the mass, 1 *Jew.* 16, 78, 509, *Sand.* 224; explains the meaning of the vestments, 3 *Bec.* 259 n., 3 *Jew.* 614, 3 *Tyn.* 73 n.; tells why the altar must be of stone, 1 *Jew.* 15, 310; its position in his time, *ib.* 78, 311; on the position of the priest in churches having the door Eastward, *ib.* 212, 2 *Jew.* corrig.; gives a reason why the chalice must be of gold or silver, 1 *Jew.* 15; on the grail, 2 *Brad.* 306 n.; he affirms that the priest must say "Dominus vobiscum" under silence, 1 *Jew.* 175; explains why the host is made round, *ib.* 15, 78, 2 *Jew.* 587; says, in the primitive church they offered up one great loaf that might suffice all, as, it is said, the Greeks do still, 2 *Jew.* 587, 4 *Jew.* 888; on communion in one kind, 1 *Jew.* 256; he writes, in many places they communicate with bread and wine, i. e. with the whole sacrament, *ib.* 256 n., 261; says the bread signifies the body not the blood, and the wine the blood not the body, 3 *Bec.* 449; declares that Christ after consecration said, "This is my body," 3 *Jew.* 451; says some assert that the word "hoc" means nothing at all, 2 *Jew.* 788; reports a fable respecting certain shepherds using the words of consecration over their bread, *ib.* 705; speaks of the priest praying that God will favourably accept the transubstantiated host, 1 *Jew.* 97; gives reasons for the elevation of it, *ib.* 509, 512; on the adoration of the eucharist, *ib.* 11; he defines how long Christ's body remains in the sacrament, 2 *Jew.* 786; says the same body may be in divers places, 1 *Jew.* 485; explains why it is broken into three parts, and what they signify, 1 *Jew.* 18 n., 2 *Jew.* 585, 586, 588, 4 *Jew.* 818; speaks of a practice of dividing the host still observed in some churches, 3 *Bec.* 417; referred to on the missa sicca, *ib.* 372; says matrimony is only a sacrament of will, 2 *Jew.* 1125, 3 *Jew.* 459; his blasphemous doctrine on holy water, 2 *Cran.* 177, 1 *Jew.* 15; on a decree of the council of Agde respecting pictures, 2 *Bec.* 71 n.; he thinks the souls in purgatory have rest on Sundays and holy days, *Rog.* 217; referred to on ecclesiastical orders, 4 *Bul.* 114 n.; he ascribes plenitude of power to the pope, 2 *Brad.* 144 n.; compares him to Melchisedec, 1 *Jew.* 373; says he is borne on men's shoulders as the ark was, 2 *Jew.* 557; declares that bishops are derived from the pope as members from the head, and receive of his fulness, 4 *Bul.* 118, 1 *Jew.* 442 n., 3 *Jew.* 317, 4 *Jew.* 829, 939, 1137; describes a foolish ceremony used when the pope hallows agnos Dei, 4 *Jew.* 858; explains the title cardinal, 2 *Jew.* 1020; states why none but the bishop may dedicate churches, &c., 1 *Jew.* 15; referred to on singing, 4 *Bul.* 196; shews the mystic signification of bishops' boots, 1 *Jew.* 15, 2 *Jew.* 1020

Durandus (Gul.), junior: *Jew.* xxxvi; he would have priests' marriage left free by a council, 3 *Jew.* 428; says that simony reigns in the church of Rome as though it were no sin, 4 *Jew.* 867

Duren: taken by the imperialists, 3 *Zur.* 633 n

Durer (Albert): notice of wood-cuts ascribed to him and Agnes Frey his wife, *Pra. Eliz.* xvii, xviii

Durham: Continuatio Historiæ Dunelmensis, ab an. 1333 ad an. 1559, 1 *Tyn.* 238 n.;

intended division of the diocese in king Edward's time, *Grin.* iii; priests in that country wore swords, daggers, and coarse clothing, *Pil.* 659; the rebellion, 1569, *Pil.* ix, 1 *Zur.* 213 n., 214 n., 218, (*v.* Rebellion); the rebellious earls enter the city, *ib.* 247 n.; many of the rebels executed there, *Lit. Eliz.* 538 n., 1 *Zur.* 225 n.; the palatine rights of the bishop as to forfeited estates, disregarded by Elizabeth, *Pil.* x; the cathedral, secular priests ejected, and monks put in their place (1083), *ib.* 574; the church injured by fire, about 1520, *ib.* 607; its statutes signed by Philip and Mary, and sealed with the great seal, *Park.* 395; mass performed there by the rebels, *Pil.* ix; epitaphs on bp Pilkington, *ib.* xii, xiii.

During: enduring, 3 *Tyn.* 264

Durmeryght (Jo.), and Asleyne his wife: 2 *Cran.* 278

Dutch: *v.* Netherlands.

Dutch churches in England: *v.* London, Norwich, Sandwich, Stamford.

Dutchland: *v.* Germany

Du Tillet (Jean): published the Caroline Books, 2 *Ful.* 23 n

Duty: *v.* Vocation; also the names of all orders and degrees of men.

The word used for anything which is due, 1 *Tyn.* 82, 103; our duty must be followed, 2 *Lat.* 37; the danger of flying from it, 1 *Hoop.* 451; the offices and duties of all degrees, 2 *Bec.* 302, &c., 402, &c.; the duty of all estates, with probations of scripture, *ib.* 511, &c.; that of all degrees and estates to God and their neighbour, *ib.* 522; tabula œconomica, in qua quisque sui officii commonetur: (the duty of magistrates, subjects, pastors, hearers, parents, children, &c., in the words of scripture), *Pra. Eliz.* 235; a motion to a prayer that all estates may govern themselves according to their duties, *Nord.* 125; the prayer, *ib.* 129; another, *ib.* 180; verses on the same subject, *ib.* 133; the duty of all men to God to be fulfilled by exercising faith, 2 *Bec.* 402, 403, love, *ib.* 403, a new life, *ib.*, prayer with thanksgiving, *ib.* 403, 404; our duty to our neighbour to be fulfilled by shewing love, *ib.* 404; the office and duty of temporal magistrates, *ib.* 302, &c., *Pra. Eliz.* 235; to be learned in the laws of God, 2 *Bec.* 511; to maintain pure and Christian religion, *ib.* 511, 512; to punish, and, if they will not turn, kill, preachers of false doctrine, *ib.* 512; to judge equally, *ib.* 513; they must take no bribes, *ib.*; they must not oppress the common people, *ib.* 513, 514, but care for the commons as fathers for their children, *ib.* 514; they must defend the good and correct the evil, *ib.* 514, 515; the office and duty of subjects, *ib.* 327, &c., 515, 516, *Pra. Eliz.* 235; the office and duty of ministers of God's word, 2 *Bec.* 317; episcoporum et pastorum officium, *Pra. Eliz.* 235; the duty of bishops and ministers, 2 *Bec.* 516, 517, in respect to doctrine, *ib.* 516, in respect to life, *ib.* 516, 517, in respect to hospitality, *ib.* 517; the duty of a good pastor, 4 *Bul.* 153, that of deacons, 2 *Bec.* 326; quid debeant episcopis auditores suis, *Pra. Eliz.* 236; the duty of parishioners to ministers, 2 *Bec.* 517, 518; conjugum officium, *Pra. Eliz.* 236; the office and duty of husbands to wives, 2 *Bec.* 334, &c., 518; that of wives to husbands, *ib.* 340, &c., 518, 519; the office and duty of parents towards their children, *ib.* 346, &c., 519, 1 *Bul.* 291, *Pra. Eliz.* 236; that of children towards their parents, 2 *Bec.* 357, &c., 519, 1 *Bul.* 297, *Pra. Eliz.* 236; the office and duty of masters towards their servants, 2 *Bec.* 359, &c., 520, *Pra. Eliz.* 237; that of servants, &c., towards their masters, 2 *Bec.* 363, &c., 520, *Pra. Eliz.* 237; of schoolmasters, 2 *Bec.* 377, &c.; of scholars, *ib.* 385, &c.; the duty of young folk, *ib.* 521; of young men unmarried, *ib.* 366, 367; of maids and young unmarried women, *ib.* 367, &c.; of old men, *ib.* 372, &c., 521; of old women, *ib.* 375, &c., 521; the office and duty of widows, *ib.* 365, &c., 520, 521, *Pra. Eliz.* 237; of rich men, 2 *Bec.* 387, &c.; of poor labouring men, *ib.* 398, &c.; our duty to ourselves; we must keep the heart pure, *ib.* 405, sequester it from worldly things, *ib.*, call to remembrance our death, *ib.* 406, keep our words pure, *ib.*, and in order thereto pray for the taming of the tongue, *ib.*, we must soberly use our eyes, *ib.* 407, work no wickedness with our hands, *ib.*, direct our feet that they haste not to wickedness, *ib.*, use godly all our members, *ib.* 407, 408, take care that our life answer to our profession, *ib.* 408

Dyke (Dan.): was a great preacher, 1 *Brad.* 562

Dynewel (Anne), wife of Hen. Whitgift, *q. v.*

E

EADMER, monk of Canterbury, afterwards bp of St Andrews: 1 *Tyn.* 380 n

Eagles: the name, in Matt. xxiv, is applied

by several of the fathers to the faithful, 3 *Jew.* 546, & al. (Augustine, Chrysostom, Leo); an impious inscription beneath the German eagle, 3 *Zur.* 61; outcry in London against brasen eagles in churches, *Park.* 450

Eagles (Geo.), or Egles: unjustly hanged at Chelmsford, *Poet.* 170

Ear: to plough, 1 *Tyn.* 401, 2 *Tyn.* 101; earing, *Calf.* 177, 1 *Jew.* 520

Earconberct, king of Kent: commanded that all the idols in his kingdom should be destroyed, and that the fast of forty days should be observed, 2 *Ful.* 16, 24

Earl (Jo.): *v.* Erle.

Earl (Tho.), minister of St Mildred's, Bread Street: letter to him from the ecclesiastical commissioners, *Grin.* 293

Earls: the earldom of Exeter, 2 *Bec.* 480 n

Earnest: *v.* Holy Ghost.

Earnulph: *v.* Arnulph.

Ears: why two are given to us, 1 *Bec.* 370; they are made by God to be instruments to hear his will and pleasure, 2 *Hoop.* 329

Earshrift; auricular confession, *Calf.* 243, 2 *Whitg.* 556; earish confession, 3 *Bec.* 4

Earth: *v.* World.

Earthly things: what it is to despise them, 3 *Bec.* 620

Earthquakes: their natural causes, *Lit. Eliz.* 570; one felt at Croydon, 1551, *Grin.* 354, 3 *Zur.* 433; Ferrara partly destroyed by one, 1570, *Lit. Eliz.* 569; one in 1571 which turned a church to the clean contrary direction, &c., *ib.*; one in Yorkshire and the midland counties, 1574-5, *Grin.* 354, *Park.* 477; a terrible one in 1580, *Grin.* 415, *Lit. Eliz.* 464, 567; letter of the council to Grindal on it, *Grin.* 416; letter of Grindal to his officers concerning prayer on account of it, *ib.* 415; the form of prayer set forth on this occasion, *Lit. Eliz.* 562; bishop Aylmer's letter thereon, *ib.* n.; the earthquake, mentioned in Rev. xvi, *Bale* 490

Ease: *v.* Rest.

Easington, co. Durham: the manor (Esingtuna), *Grin.* 399 n

East: *v.* Empire.

East: on prayer towards the East, 4 *Bul.* 500, 2 *Cran.* 515, *Whita.* 591; a tradition, 2 *Cran.* 515; Basil mentions the practice, *Whita.* 591; pope Vigilius appointed that the priest should look Eastward at mass, 2 *Brad.* 311; in some churches of Italy, &c., the priest turns to the West, 1 *Jew.* 312, 2 *Jew.* corrig.; they turned towards the West at Antioch, *Whita.* 591

Easter: *v.* Irenæus, Victor; likewise Augustine, and other fathers.

The name applied to the Passover, *Sand.* 337; on keeping Easter, 1 *Bul.* 260; the feast observed by the apostles, 2 *Whitg.* 567; the observance of any day not of necessary obligation, *Whita.* 540; early disputes between the East and West concerning the time of its observance, 1 *Brad.* 525, 2 *Brad.* 389, 1 *Bul.* 432, 4 *Bul.* 57, 504, 537, *Calf.* 262, 269, 2 *Cran.* 77, 2 *Hoop.* 233, 1 *Jew.* 144, *Pil.* 512 n., *Whita.* 539, 540, 665, 2 *Whitg.* 445, 2 *Zur.* 339 n.; the Quartodecimans maintained that it need not be celebrated on Sunday, *Whita.* 539, 540; both parties alleged the example of apostles, *Sand.* 20, *Whita.* 539; Ignatius, Polycarp, &c., on the time of keeping it, *Whita.* 573; the so-called Apostolical Constitutions, and Epiphanius, on the same, *ib.* 569; reference to an edict of Constantine, 2 *Whitg.* 445; custom of the Britons and Scots, 1 *Jew.* 280, 306, *Pil.* 512; the synod at Whitby, called by Oswy, *Pil.* 625; Easter was of old a customary time for baptism, 4 *Bul.* 367; hence the Romish custom of hallowing the font on Easter even, 2 *Cran.* 158, 175, *Rid.* 532; a prayer used on that occasion, 2 *Jew.* 567; ceremonies used in churches at Easter, 2 *Cran.* 158, 1 *Hoop.* 45, 46; on garnishing the church, 1 *Bec.* 116, 117; the true meaning of Easter processions, *Park.* 7; the Easter sepulchre, 2 *Cran.* 158, 1 *Hoop.* 45, *Rid.* 67, 532; lights set before it, 3 *Zur.* 230—232; the paschal, or Paschal taper, *Bale* 320, 2 *Cran.* 158, 2 *Hoop.* 129, *Rid.* 320*; words sung at its consecration, 1 *Jew.* 468; inquiries about fire on Paschal, 1 *Cran.* 158, *Rid.* 532

Eating: *v.* Blood, Fasting, Food, Gluttony.

Its hedges or limits, 2 *Lat.* 14, &c.; what eating and drinking are allowed, 1 *Lat.* 169, 2 *Lat.* 14, 61, 80, 81; eating of flesh, why permitted after the flood, 2 *Lat.* 14

Eaton (......), servant to Cranmer, 2 *Cran.* 400

Eaton (Geo.), letters to him: 2 *Brad.* 51, 188

Eaton (Guy and others): *v.* Eton.

Eaton (Tho.), or Heton: he was a merchant of London who contributed to the afflicted professors of the gospel, and had been an exile at Strasburgh, *Jew.* xiii, 1 *Zur.* 47 n.; named or saluted, 2 *Cran.* 266 (?), *Grin.* 280, 4 *Jew.* 1197, 1198, 1214, 1215, 1 *Zur.* 2, 9, 40, 47, 65, 69, 80, 2 *Zur.* 104, 114; legacies to him and his wife, *Grin.* 462

---

* Here read, sepulchre, paschal.

Eberstein (Otto connt): 2 *Zur*. 207
Ebion: his heresy, 1 *Bec.* 278, 418, 3 *Bec.* 401, 2 *Brad.* 263, 1 *Hoop*. 17, 161, 2 *Jew.* 566; he rejected St Paul's epistles, 1 *Ful.* 7; praised Judas above all the apostles, 4 *Jew.* 700; yet would needs be called a Christian, *ib.* 713
Ebionites: their heresy respecting Christ, *Rog.* 48; they said he was the son of Joseph and Mary, *ib.* 52; deemed the ceremonial law to be still binding, and its observance necessary to salvation, *Phil.* 418, *Rog.* 89, 160; maintained that man is justified by faith and works, *Rog.* 114; received only the gospel of Matthew, *Whita.* 35, *Rog.* 83; they were opposed by St John, *Bale* 265, 1 *Bec.* 278
Eblie (Conrad): 3 *Zur.* 216, 219, 225
Ebuccinator: a trumpeter, 1 *Bec.* 43
Eccles: probably Etchells in Stockport, 1 *Brad.* 454
Ecclesia: *v.* Church.
Ecclesiastes: *v.* Solomon.
Ecclesiastica: the apocryphal books were so called, 1 *Ful*. 24
Ecclesiasticæ Historiæ Scriptores, *Jew*. xxxvi.
Ecclesiastical Law: *v.* Law.
Ecclesiasticus, otherwise called the Wisdom of Jesus the son of Sirach: not canonical, 1 *Ful.* 20, 77; its claims to canonical authority considered, *Whita.* 90, &c.; the Hebrew original lost; Jesus, son of Sirach, a mere translator, *ib.* 90; the book is mentioned in the Canons of the Apostles, *ib.* 43; spoken of by Epiphanius as doubtful, *ib.* 59; disallowed by Jerome, 4 *Bul.* 540, 1 *Ful.* 24; Augustine's opinion, *Whita.* 46; offence taken by a woman at a passage in it, *ib.* 229, 231
Ecebolus: an apostate in the time of Julian, 1 *Zur.* 169 n
Ecgfrid: *v.* Egfride.
Eckius (Jo.): notices of him, 1 *Ful.* 8 n., 3 *Zur.* 211 n.; his bastards, *Bale* 531; works of his, *Jew.* xxxvi; he writes against the confession of Augsburgh, 2 *Zur.* 103 n.; says, the scripture is not authentic, but by the authority of the church, 3 *Jew.* 247, *Whita.* 276; calls it the black gospel, and inken divinity, 1 *Ful.* 8, 4 *Jew.* 758; denies that John vi. refers to the sacrament, 3 *Jew.* 592; endeavours to prove transubstantiation from Aaron's rod, 1 *Hoop.* 166; his foolish arguments against communion in both kinds, 1 *Jew.* 15, 4 *Jew.* 766; he says the people drink spiritually by the mouth of the priest, 1 *Jew.* 213, 2 *Jew.* 744; his absurd arguments for the use of a strange tongue in common prayer, 1 *Jew.* 15; he speaks of divine service being chiefly performed in Hebrew, Greek, and Latin, 3 *Bec.* 410; allows that the Indians had service in their own tongue, 1 *Jew.* 289; holds that Romish ceremonies are necessarily to be observed, as well as the laws of God, *Rog.* 180 n.; his reason for organs, 1 *Jew.* 78; referred to on images, *Calf.* 21 n., 4 *Jew.* 1055; he places purgatory at the bottom of the sea, *Rog.* 215 n.; says that in it venial and mortal sins (for which in this life men have done no penance) are purged, *ib.* 217 n
Eclipses: what they portend, 2 *Jew.* 993, *Lit. Eliz.* 570; one before the death of Bucer, 2 *Brad.* xxiii.
Edda, surnamed Stephen, a chanter of Northumberland: 1 *Jew.* 303
Eden: the proper name of a place, *Whita.* 174; it signifies pleasure, 1 *Tyn.* 407
Eden (Rob.): editor of the Examinations and Writings of Jo. Philpot, *Phil.*
Edessa: Valens turned from his purpose of persecuting the church there, 2 *Brad.* 325, 326
Edgar, king of England: his laws, *Bale* 447, 4 *Jew.* 904
Edgar (Mr): 2 *Cov.* 440, 442
Edgecombe (Pearse), of Mount Edgecombe: *Poet.* xxxii.
Edgehill, co. Stafford: battle there, 1 *Brad.* 564
Edilred: *v.* Ethelred.
Edilwald: *v.* Ethelwald.
Edinburgh: pillaged by the earl of Hertford, 3 *Zur.* 37 n.; riots at Holyrood house, occasioned by the mass, 1 *Zur.* 104 n.; the city yields to the confederate lords, 1 *Zur.* 193 n.; the castle and town seized by the adherents of the queen of Scots, *ib.* 262; the castle taken by the English under Sir Will. Drury, 2 *Bec.* 480 n., 1 *Zur.* 290, 292, 2 *Zur.* 223 n.; disorders about a Robin Hood, *Rog.* 311 n.; the plague there, 2 *Zur.* 335
Eding (Adrian): 3 *Zur.* 583, 589
Edmund, a friend of Coverdale: 2 *Cov.* 515, 516, 520, 525
Edmund (St), king of East Anglia: martyred, *Bale* 192; St Edmund's bowl, *ib.* 527; his patrimony, 2 *Tyn.* 124
Edmund I., the Elder, king of England: his law against swearing, 1 *Bec.* 390
Edmund (St), abp of Canterbury: *Pil.* 484; legends respecting him, *ib.* 588; his constitution on priests' concubines, 4 *Jew.* 644; on vows by wives, 1 *Lat.* 54

Edmundes (Jo.?): in exile, 1 *Cran.* (9)
Edom, Edomites: the children of Esau, *Pil.* 218, 219; several prophesied against Edom, *ib.* 222; cruelty of the Edomites to Israel, *ib.* 223, 251, 252; they were deceived by their prosperity, *ib.* 232; beginning of their enmity, *ib.* 348; their utter destruction, *ib.* 235; Papists compared to them, *ib.* 211, 238, 255, 256
Edridge (Geo.), or Etheridge, Greek professor at Oxford: 2 *Cran.* 383, 547; he recommended that Ridley should be gagged, *Rid.* 289
Edward (St), the Martyr, king of England: *Bale* 190
Edward (St), the Confessor, king of England: his laws, *Jew.* xxxvi; St Edward's patrimony, 2 *Tyn.* 124
Edward I., king of England: a chaste prince, *Sand.* 81; he forbade bishops to go to Rome, *Pil.* 583; renounced the jurisdiction of the pope, *Rog.* 347
Edward II., king of England: subverted by wicked counsellors, *Wool.* 129
Edward III., king of England: loath to accept of foreign dominion, *Sand.* 81; he besieged Calais, 1 *Hoop.* 313 n.; founded the order of the Garter, *ib.*; endeavoured to restrain the use of copper coin in Ireland, 2 *Tyn.* 231 n.; renounced the jurisdiction of the pope, *Rog.* 347
Edward IV., king of England: a just prince, *Sand.* 81; affianced to a Spanish princess, but married to a knight's widow, and his marriage ascribed by Tyndale to the witcheries of a friar, 2 *Tyn.* 304; his natural son: *v.* Plantagenet (Arth.).
Edward V., king of England: murdered by king Richard, 3 *Zur.* 220
Edward VI., king of England: *v.* Articles, Catechisms, Privy Council, Statutes.
 Latimer's letter to lord Cromwell on his birth, 2 *Lat.* 385; his godly education, 1 *Lat.* 184; his learning, 3 *Zur.* 543; petition for prince Edward, 1544, *Pra. Eliz.* 572; never prince of Wales, *ib.* 19 n.; his letters to Cranmer before coming to the throne, with Cranmer's answers (Latin, with translations), 2 *Cran.* 412, 413 n.; he is proclaimed and crowned, 3 *Zur.* 257; no sermon at his coronation, but a speech by Cranmer, 2 *Cran.* 126 n.; he was the gift of God to England, 1 *Lat.* 91; his guardians or counsellors, *Hutch.* v, 3 *Zur.* 257; his injunctions to the clergy and laity, for the abolition of popery and superstition, 2 *Cran.* 498; injunctions to the bishops, *ib.* 504; proclamation against irreverent talking of the sacrament, *ib.* 505; proclamation respecting communion in both kinds, *Lit. Edw.* 1; reference to it, *ib.* iii. n.; anecdote of him, 3 *Zur.* 646; reference to him, *Hutch.* 128; proclamation for abstaining from flesh in Lent time, 2 *Cran.* 507; proclamation against omitting ceremonies not forbidden, *ib.* 508; letter from his council to all preachers against religious innovations and controversies, *ib.* 512; his proclamation forbidding all preaching for a time, *ib.* 513; reference to it, *Lit. Eliz.* xi. n.; Cranmer's letter to him on the necessity of religious education, 2 *Cran.* 418; his proposed marriage with the queen of Scots, *ib.* 154 n., 155 n.; lawless persons in his court, *Hutch.* 7; report of his attempted assassination by the lord admiral Seymour, 3 *Zur.* 648; he enjoins the clergy not to counterfeit the popish mass, 1 *Tyn.* 248 n.; three letters from the lords of his council at Windsor to those at London, 2 *Cran.* 520; his letter to the senate of Zurich, 3 *Zur.* 1; he sent a similar letter to Berne, *ib.* 717 n.; the answer of the provost and council, *ib.* 717; sermons before him, 1 *Hoop.* 432, &c., 1 *Lat.* 79, &c.; Latimer advises him on marriage, 1 *Lat.* 243, and admonishes him to look to his office himself, *ib.* 273; his youthful age no excuse to any man for errors in religion, 1 *Hoop.* 439, 539; Hooper earnestly exhorts him to virtue, and to beware of flattery, *ib.* 540, advises him to hear one sermon every Sunday, *ib.* 541; encourages him to purify the church, *ib.* 542; exhorts him to abolish all iniquity, to forbid the mass, &c., *ib.* 557; dedication of the Bible to him, 2 *Cov.* 3 n.; other dedicatory epistles, 2 *Bul.* 3, 3 *Bul.* 115, 1 *Cran.* (11), 1 *Hoop.* 435, 2 *Hoop.* 66; he erases a clause in the oath of supremacy, with his own hand, 2 *Hoop.* xii, 3 *Zur.* 416, 566; entry in his diary respecting the burning of Joan Bocher, *Hutch.* iv; evidence that he did not sign her death-warrant, *ib.* iv, v; entry in his diary on the marriage of lord Lisle, 3 *Zur.* 565 n.; note in it respecting a fleet sent out, *ib.* 564 n.; letter from his council to Ridley, *Rid.* 507; letter from the same to the princess Mary, on the use of the mass in her house, 2 *Cran.* 526; his account of Bucer's funeral, 3 *Zur.* 492; his interview with Bale, *Bale* x; letter to the bishops on occasion of the sweating sickness, 2 *Cran.* 531; his diary cited on the depreciation of certain coins, 3 *Zur.* 727 n.; his projected marriage with lady Jane Grey, 1 *Bec.* 396 n., 3 *Zur.* 430, 432; letters to him from Calvin, 3 *Zur.* 707, 714;

Cranmer's letter to him in behalf of Ralph Cavalier, 2 *Cran.* 435, 436; his progress after the execution of Somerset, *ib.* 438; he prays for Cheke's recovery, and obtains it, 3 *Zur.* 456 n.; his mandates for subscription to the Articles of 1552, 2 *Cran.* 532, 533; privilege for the Primer, 1553, *Lit. Edw.* 359; letters patent for the printing of the short Catechism and the little Catechism, *Lit. Edw.* 487; injunction to all schoolmasters to use the short Catechism, *ib.* 493, (544); his illness, 3 *Zur.* 593, 683; portents of his death, *ib.* 365; Cranmer endeavours to dissuade him from his last will, 2 *Cran.* 443; Sir James Hales refused to sign it, 2 *Brad.* 85 n., 89; tenor of it, 3 *Zur.* 273, 365; he devised the crown to the heirs of the duchess of Suffolk, 1 *Brad.* 62 n.; his dying prayer, *Phil.* 178; his death, 3 *Bec.* 207, *Hutch.* 293 n., 3 *Zur.* 100; announced to the lord mayor, &c., at Greenwich, *ib.* 272; report of his having been poisoned, *ib.* 365 n., 684; his death lamented, 1 *Brad.* 21, 38, 202, 279, 451; Cranmer officiates at his funeral at Westminster, using the Common Prayer, 3 *Zur.* 367; Gardiner sings a mass of requiem in the Tower, before the queen, *ib.* 368; his tomb, *Now.* 229; commendation of him, 3 *Bec.* 3, 4; his character, 3 *Zur.* 321, 324, 333, 543, 646; his wonderful qualities, 1 *Brad.* 61; he was a godly prince, *Rid.* 58, 3 *Zur.* 82; a noble and understanding king, 1 *Lat.* 118; his early zeal for the truth, 2 *Zur.* 6, 3 *Zur.* 561; compared to Josiah, *Calf.* 24, 2 *Cran.* 127, 3 *Bec.* 227; he renounced the jurisdiction of the pope, *Rog.* 347; his reformation, 2 *Zur.* 158, &c., 3 *Zur.* 141; state of religion in his time, 1 *Brad.* 59 n., 2 *Brad.* 42, *Rid.* 49, &c.; declaration of the prisoners for the gospel concerning his reformation, 1 *Brad.* 399; he founded three hospitals in London, *Rid.* xiii. n., 410, &c.; instituted sixteen grammar schools, and intended to establish twelve colleges, *ib.* xiii. n.; penal laws in his time, *Pil.* 614

Edward Fortunatus, son of Christopher, margrave of Baden: baptized by Parker, *Park.* xii.

Edwardes (......): suit with Bulstrode, 2 *Cran.* 253 bis, 261

Edwards (Jo.), M.A. Oxon: 2 *Cran.* 383

Edwards (Rich.): notice of him, *Poet.* xxv; of perfect wisdom, verses, *ib.* 295

Edwards (Rich.), last prior of the Black Friars, Worcester: 2 *Lat.* 406

Edwin (St), king of Deira: slain at Hatfield, *Bale* 190

Effingham (Will. baron of): *v.* Howard.

Eftsoons: soon afterwards, 1 *Brad.* 287; continually, *Phil.* 217

Egal: equal, 1 *Tyn.* 174; egally, 3 *Bec.* 243; egalness, 2 *Bec.* 510

Egbert, king of England: 2 *Ful.* 119

Egerton, co. Kent: 2 *Cran.* 289

Egesippus: *v.* Hegesippus.

Egfride, king of Northumberland: his wife Etheldreda, *Pil.* 590; he deposed bishop Wilfrid, 2 *Ful.* 17

Egidius (St): *v.* Giles.

Egidius of Rome: said that a certain council of Paris was too heavy to climb over the Alps, 1 *Jew.* 70

Egidius of Viterbo, a cardinal: said, in the council of Lateran, that as often as councils are discontinued, so often is the church destitute of Christ, 4 *Jew.* 720

Egidius (Jo.), a French Carmelite: wrote on the Apocalypse, *Bale* 257, [qu. whether Jo. Giles the first Englishman of the order of St Dominic is not intended].

Egidius (Jo.), canon of Seville: compelled to assent to the doctrine, that supreme adoration is to be offered to the cross, *Calf.* 381 n

Egles (Geo.): *v.* Eagles.

Eglinton (Hugh earl of): *v.* Montgomery.

Egmont (Count): *v.* Lamoral.

Egnatius (Jo. Bapt.): De Princ. Rom., *Jew.* xxxvi; on the poisoning of the emperor Henry of Luxembourg, 4 *Jew.* 687

Egueblank (Pet. de): *v.* Aquablanca.

Egylbertus: *v.* Agilbert.

Egyppus, king: *Bale* 612

Egypt: *v.* Alexandria, Church (II. iii.), Moses, Nile, Serapis.

The Egyptians said to have been called Ægophi, &c., 2 *Ful.* 328 n. [but Sophi is another word, see 410]; their wisdom, 4 *Bul.* 479, 480; their idolatry, *Calf.* 369; they worshipped a cat, 2 *Jew.* 830, a calf, an ox, &c., *Rog.* 37, serpents, 1 *Bul.* 224; witchcraft and sorcery held in great esteem among them, 2 *Hoop.* 271; their custom at feasts, *Sand.* 171; their law against swearing, 1 *Bec.* 363, 391; Egypt no refuge to the Jews, *Pil.* 240; the midwives, 2 *Bul.* 115; the plagues, *Pil.* 28, 29, 75; decem plagæ Ægypti; verses by Parkhurst, *Pra. Eliz.* 415; all the idol temples said to have been destroyed in the night of Israel's departure, 4 *Jew.* 880; Egyptian words occur in the book of Genesis, 1 *Tyn.* 409; the Egyptian name of God, Θωύθ, Θεύθ or Θωθ, 3 *Bul.* 131, 136; the Egyptian name of Joseph, *Whita.* 178;

Egypt is a figure of this sinful world, 1 *Brad.* 149, likewise of man's state by nature, *Now.* (8), 121; the deliverance out of it is a type of our redemption by Christ, 2 *Bec.* 57, 1 *Cov.* 39, *Sand.* 145; on the text, "Out of Egypt have I called My Son," *Whita.* 409, 525

Egyptians (The gospel according to the): *v.* Apocrypha, ii.

Eisel: vinegar, 1 *Bec.* 177; esel, 2 *Jew.* 652; eysil, 1 *Cov.* 520

Ekron, or Accaron: 3 *Bul.* 357

Elba: besieged by the Erench, 3 *Zur.* 741

Eldefride: *v.* Ethelfride.

Elders: *v.* Aged, Priests (πρ.)
What an elder is, 3 *Bec.* 607; the twenty four elders, *Bale* 299, 540; they worship God, *ib.* 303, 401; praise the Lamb, *ib.* 308; one speaks to John, *ib.* 338

Elderton (W.): notice of him, *Poet.* lii; his epitaph on bp Juell, *ib.* 512

Eldred (St), of Ramsey: he and his brother, martyrs, *Bale* 192

Eleazar, high priest: 2 *Bul.* 132, 141

Eleazar, an exorcist in the time of Solomon: 4 *Bul.* 114

Eleazar, martyr in the days of Antiochus Epiphanes, 2 *Bul.* 211

Election: *v.* Predestination and Election.

Election to office: *v.* Ministers, Ordination.
That of magistrates, 1 *Bul.* 318; of civil officers, 1 *Whitg.* 372

Elenchs: proofs, 2 *Jew.* 810

Elephant: Gregory's saying about the elephant and the lamb, 2 *Jew.* 684, *Whita.* 400

Eleutherius, bp of Rome: *v.* Lucius.
His alleged mission and fictitious epistle to Lucius, king of Britain, *Calf.* 52, 53, 305, 2 *Ful.* 128, 186, 366, *Jew.* xxxvi, 1 *Jew.* 163, 267, 306, 438, 4 *Jew.* 974, 1124, *Park.* 295, *Pil.* 482, 510—513, 2 *Whitg.* 128, 3 *Whitg.* 592; copy of this letter, *Pil.* 512, 513; it addresses Lucius as the vicar of Christ, 1 *Jew.* 438; letter from Eleutherius to the bishops of Gaul, *ib.* 427, 3 *Jew.* 283; his ordinance against refusing meats, *Pil.* 514

Eleutherius (St): martyred at Paris, 1 *Hoop.* 314 n

Elevate: to make light of, 2 *Hoop.* 141

Elevation: *v.* Mass.

Eleynye (......), gaoler of Lollards' tower: *Phil.* 292

Elfere: *v.* Aelfer.

Elfric: *v.* Ælfric.

Elfroy: *v.* Ethelfride.

Elgg, Zurich: 4 *Bul.* 546

Eli, high priest: wickedness of his sons, and his neglect to punish them, 1 *Bul.* 296, 4 *Bul.* 158, 486, 505, *Pil.* 35; troubles in his time, 1 *Bul.* 375, 2 *Bul.* 148, 149; Eli and Samuel compared, 1 *Lat.* 188

Eli Phili: 4 *Jew.* 1050, 1055

Eliad, a Familist: *Rog.* 202

Elias: *v.* Elijah.

Elias, bp of Crete: said, I do perfectly adore the holy images, and I accurse them that hold the contrary, 4 *Jew.* 792

Elias de Hanibalis, *q. v.*

Eliberis: *v.* Councils, *Elvira.*

Eliezer, servant of Abraham: 2 *Bul.* 18

Eliezer, son of Moses, 4 *Bul.* 378

Eligius: probably the writer of some treatises ascribed to Augustine, 1 *Bec.* 92 n., 3 *Bec.* 277 n

Eligius (St), otherwise Eloi, or Loy: account of him, 1 *Bec.* 139 n.; invoked for the cure of horses, *ib.* 139, 2 *Bec.* 536, 1 *Hoop.* 310

Elijah: he was ruler of a school, 4 *Bul.* 481; the power of his prayers, *ib.* 169, 186, 225; he stopped the rain, 1 *Lat.* 387; his contentment in his need, 2 *Hoop.* 302; he sacrificed out of the temple, 2 *Bul.* 152; slew the prophets of Baal, 1 *Ful.* 358; his zeal for God, 4 *Bul.* 71, *Pil.* 7, 98, 343; his complaint, 4 *Bul.* 71, *Pil.* 599; God's answer to him, 1 *Brad.* 552, 4 *Bul.* 71, 3 *Zur.* 39; his fasting, 1 *Bul.* 431, *Pil.* 54; he rebukes Ahab, *Pil.* 358; divides Jordan, *Calf.* 336; is translated, *Calf.* 312, 313; his mantle compared by Chrysostom to Christ's flesh, *Phil.* 196; a double portion of his spirit given to Elisha, 3 *Bul.* 311; his message (after his translation) to Joram, 2 *Bul.* 7; on his coming before Messiah, *Rid.* 70; how John the Baptist was Elias, 1 *Tyn.* 104; whether he shall come in the time of Antichrist, 2 *Ful.* 370

Eline (Jo.): *v.* Elyne.

Eliot (Margaret): died in prison, *Poet.* 167

Eliot (Nich.): with lord Cromwell, 3 *Zur.* 611, 612; he studies the law, *ib.* 225, 626; two letters from him to Bullinger, *ib.* 617, 619; his death, *ib.* 378

Eliot (Rog.): *v.* Elyott.

Eliot (Sir Tho.): *v.* Elyot.

Eliperius: a son of Peter Martyr, 4 *Jew.* 1232, 1 *Zur.* 78

Elisha: he received a double portion of Elijah's spirit, 3 *Bul.* 311; was ruler of a school, 4 *Bul.* 481; accepted a gift from a man of Baal-shalisha, *ib.* 489, but refused Naaman's present, *ib.* 124, 489; made an axe to swim, *ib.* 263; through his prayer the eyes of his servant were opened to see the angels, 3 *Bul.* 343; he anointed Jehu, to the end that he might slay the priests of Baal, 1 *Bul.* 358; a dead man raised on touching his bones, *Calf.* 313

Elizabeth, mother of John Baptist: her address to the virgin Mary, 2 *Hoop.* 13

Elizabeth, queen of England: *v.* Articles, Commissions, Privy Council, Statutes.

Her birth, 2 *Cran.* 274 n., *Lit. Eliz.* 452; proceedings on that occasion, 2 *Cran.* 255 n., 256 n.; Cranmer stood godfather at her baptism, *ib.* 274; her mother's charge to Parker, *Park.* 59, 391, 400; she resides at Hunsdon, and at Hatfield (1535—40), *ib.* ix, 483; mention of her as the lady Elizabeth, 1 *Lat.* 91; her simple apparel in king Edward's time, 3 *Zur.* 278; her reply to messengers sent by queen Mary shortly before she died, 1 *Zur.* 3; her accession, *ib.*; she was God's gift to England, *Nord.* 166, *Pra. Eliz.* 464, 477; letter to her on her accession, by R. Gualter, 2 *Zur.* 3; queen's day, or the anniversary of her accession, its origin, *Lit. Eliz.* 463; a thanksgiving (in verse) for that anniversary, *ib.* 558; sermons on it, *Sand.* 55, 75, 3 *Whitg.* 586; regna et regiones quæ sunt juris et imperii Elizabethæ, *Pra. Eliz.* 423; copy of her proclamation forbidding preaching till consultation should be had by parliament, 2 *Zur.* 16 n.; notices of it, *Lit. Eliz.* xi, 1 *Zur.* 7, 2 *Zur.* 29; she notifies her accession to the pope, *Lit. Eliz.* x. n.; her privy council, 1 *Zur.* 5 n.; her coronation, 2 *Zur.* 55; her prayer before proceeding to it, *Lit. Eliz.* 666 n.; her extreme caution in matters ecclesiastical, *ib.* x; she retains the mass, for a time, in her private chapel, 1 *Zur.* 18; contemplates the recall of Peter Martyr (*q. v.*), *ib.* 20, 53, 74; thinks of joining the league of Smalcald, *ib.* 21; she renounced and banished out of England the jurisdiction of the bishop of Rome, *Rog.* 347; her reformation of the church of England, *Sand.* 250; true religion restored by her, *Rog.* 6, 7; she appoints a commission for the establishment of religion, 1 *Zur.* 24; her injunctions (1559) allow the marriage of priests, *Pil.* 575; she declines being called head of the church, 4 *Jew.* 1144, 1209, 1 *Zur.* 24, 33, but accepts the title of governor, *ib.* 29; she declined the former title on Lever's suggestion, *Park.* 66; her numerous suitors, and rumours about her intention to marry, *Grin.* 408—412, 4 *Jew.* 1206, 1211, 1213, 1 *Zur.* 24, 34 n., 46, 68 n., 192, 239, 250, 331 n., 2 *Zur.* 66, 68; her suitors—*v.* Adolph, duke of Holstein; Charles, archduke of Austria; Dudley (Rob.), earl of Leicester; Eric XIV., king of Sweden; Fitzalan (H.), earl of Arundel; Francis, duke of Anjou; Hamilton (J.), earl of Arran; Philip II., king of Spain; Pickering (Sir W.), besides a Saxon prince mentioned, 1 *Zur.* 24; Parker's letter to her begging to be excused taking the archbishoprick, *Park.* 69; she makes a progress in Kent, 1 *Zur.* 40 n.; letter to her from Parker and others against images in churches, *Park.* 79—95; she consents to the casting out of images, *ib.* 96 n., but retains a crucifix, lighted tapers, &c. in her private chapel, *Calf.* ix, 7, 1 *Ful.* 204, 205, *Park.* 97, 105, 1 *Zur.* 55, 63, 64, 66; these were subsequently removed, but afterwards brought back again, *Park.* 379, 1 *Zur.* 122, 129; she desires the retention in churches of the rood with St Mary and St John, 1 *Zur.* 73, 74; her alienation of church lands, 2 *Zur.* 39 n.; letter to her from Parker and other bishops elect against the inequitable exchange of the lands of bishopricks, *Park.* 97; the queen's letter to the lord treasurer, &c., on this matter, *ib.* 101; letters patent authorizing the Latin Prayer Book, *Lit. Eliz.* 301; she dines with Parker at Lambeth, *Park.* 120; advised by Parker, Grindal, and Cox, to marry, *Grin.* 19 n.; their letter, *Park.* 129; similar advice by Nowell, *Now.* 228; her proclamation against strangers, *Grin.* 297; she reforms the currency, 1 *Zur.* 93, 104; letter to the ecclesiastical commissioners respecting a new calendar of lessons, tables of the commandments, &c., *Park.* 132; letter to Parker respecting the re-edifying of St Paul's, *ib.* 142; order prohibiting the residence of women in colleges and cathedral precincts, *ib.* 146; letter of bp Cox complaining of this order, *ib.* 151; letter of abp Parker severely condemning it, *ib.* 158; she disapproves the marriage of the clergy, but is restrained by Cecil from forbidding it, *ib.* 148; letter to Parker about the unauthorized election of a provost at Eton, *ib.* 149; Parker horrified by her words concerning holy matrimony, *ib.* 156; writ addressed to Parker commanding him to make a return of the hospitals and schools in his diocese, *ib.* 163; her progress through some Eastern counties, 2 *Zur.* 61 n.; she declines sending representatives to Trent, 1 *Zur.* 101, 4 *Jew.* 910 n.; reads with Ascham daily, 2 *Zur.* 93; purposes to go to York, 1 *Zur.* 109, 115; ill of the small pox, *ib.* 124; the question of succession to her debated in parliament, *ib.* 185 n.; she deter-

ELIZABETH

mines to assist the prince of Condé, *ib.* 115; aids the Protestants of France and Scotland, *Now.* 226, 227, *Pra. Eliz.* 484 n.; her letter to Mr Herd for a copy of Cranmer's common-place book, 2 *Cran.* 459; grant to abp Parker to retain forty persons with his livery badge, *Park.* 175; letter to the archbishop respecting prayer and fasting, 1563, *Grin.* 81, *Park.* 184; she sends Parker a deer killed with her own hand, *Park.* 190; letter to Parker on the reception of a French ambassador, *ib.* 212; she dines with Sackville, *ib.* 219; intends to go towards Stamford, *ib.*; letter to Parker on the correction of many disorders in opinions, and especially in rites and ceremonies, *ib.* 223; she disliked the church of Geneva, 2 *Zur.* 131; letter to her from the bishops praying that a bill for uniformity may be allowed to proceed, *Park.* 292; she chides Parker, *Park.* 311; rebukes dean Nowell, *Pra. Eliz.* xvii. n.; her letter to Parker charging him to make inquiry respecting the numerous strangers in England, *Park.* 321 (see 323); prayers on her sickness and recovery, *Lit. Eliz.* 516, 517; Parker's letter to her with the Bishops' Bible, *Park.* 337; her letter to Parker respecting a vacant prebend at Canterbury, *ib.* 340; bull of Pius V. (*q. v.*) against her, 4 *Jew.* 1132; she was excommunicated by three popes, *Rog.* 311, 348; Parker's letter to her respecting certain lands in Kent claimed by the crown and by the archbishop, *Park.* 371; her letter to Parker on the enforcement of uniformity in divine service, *ib.* 386; letter from Zanchius to her about the vestments, 2 *Zur.* 339; her life continually attempted, 1 *Zur.* 252; slandered by a prisoner, *Park.* 400; her progress in 1572, 2 *Zur.* 210 n.; she issues a proclamation against the Admonition to the Parliament, *ib.* 253 n.; two letters to her from Parker, about Dr Clerk, dean of the arches, *Park.* 428, 429; she visits Kent, &c., *ib.* 436, 437, 441, 2 *Zur.* 220 n.; received by the archbishop at Folkestone and Canterbury, *Park.* 475; ceremonies at the cathedral, *ib.*; she disallows prophesyings and discourages preaching, *Grin.* xi, xii, *Park.* 456, 457, 459 (and see below); her journey to Bristol, Sarum, &c., 3 *Zur.* 258 n.; her prayer at Bristow, *Lit. Eliz.* 667 n.; she returns from the West, *Park.* 466; comes to the earl of Leicester, *ib.* 468, *Coop.* xiv; proposes to go to the North, *ib.* 475; offended with archbishop Grindal in the matter of exercises or prophesyings, *Grin.* 372; letter from that prelate to her on the suppression of prophesyings and restraining the number of preachers, *ib.* 376; her letter to the bishops for suppressing prophesyings, &c., *ib.* 467; letter to her from Grindal against cutting timber in the woods of the see of Canterbury, *ib.* 364; letter to the confederate Swiss cantons on behalf of Geneva, 2 *Zur.* 315; letter to the four cities, Zurich, Berne, Basle, Schaffhausen, in the same cause, *ib.* 318; another letter to the Swiss cantons, for the same, 1 *Zur.* 333; her prayer of thanksgiving for the overthrow of the Spanish navy, *Lit. Eliz.* 622 n.; she assists Henry IV. of France with men and money, *ib.* 471; her letter to Sigismund, king of Poland, in favour of some Flemish exiles, 2 *Zur.* 321; she rebukes Whitgift respecting the Lambeth articles, 3 *Whitg.* xvii, xviii; a prayer made by the queen at the departure of the fleet, 1596, *Lit. Eliz.* 666, *Nord.* 188; letter from the state of Zurich to the queen on behalf of C. Thoman, 2 *Zur.* 323; a prayer on behalf of the queen, composed by Whitgift the day before her death, *Lit. Eliz.* 695; the queen called Theodosia, *Calf.* 11; called Glycerium, 4 *Jew.* 1228, 1 *Zur.* 82, 93, &c.; her character, *Rog.* 6, *Sand.* 57, 58, 80, 81, 2 *Zur.* 67; commended by Bullinger, 3 *Whitg.* 496, 497, by Parkhurst, *Rog.* 5; compared to Esther, *Pil.* 4; her learning, *Sand.* 57, 1 *Zur.* 64, 2 *Zur.* 67, 68, 3 *Zur.* 76; notice of her sacred poetry, *Poet.* xiii; Psalm xiv. versified by her, *ib.* 1; notice of prayers by her, *Pra. Eliz.* 475 n., 666 n.; letters by her to Sturmius, 2 *Zur.* 174, 257; his letters to the queen, *ib.* 175, 239; she was a gracious governor, *Sand.* 415; a peaceful queen, *ib.* 286; her wise and good government, 4 *Jew.* 1155, 2 *Zur.* 66, &c.; her government praised by Zanchius, Danæus, &c., *Rog.* 7; she delivered the oppressed, *Pil.* 473; but she was somewhat arbitrary in her conduct, 2 *Zur.* 144; prosperity in her reign, *Pil.* 613; her public acts, *ib.* 67; her clemency abused by Romanists, *Calf.* 6, 7; names of the principal traitors against her, *Lit. Eliz.* 657; another list of traitors, *ib.* 680; a list of forms of prayer on many special occasions during her reign, *ib.* 457; private prayers set forth during her reign, *Pra, Eliz.*; a motion to prayer for queen Elizabeth, *Nord.* 38; prayers for her, *ib.* 41, 45, *Pra. B.* 128, 130 (and see Prayers); Sandys prays for her protection, *Sand.* 416; a praise for her majesty's gracious government, *Nord.* 44; an anthem or prayer (in verse) for the preservation of the church, the queen's majesty, and the realm, *Lit. Eliz.* 560; verses of thanksgiving for her reign, by Edw. Hake, *Poet.* 368; a godly ditty to be sung for the preservation of her reign, by R. Thacker, *ib.* 420; a godly prayer given to her majesty, by Tho. Nelson, *ib.* 551; stanzas from Elisæ's Memorial, by Ant. Nixon, *ib.* 556; dedications to her, 2 *Bec.* 413, 1 *Ful.* 4, 3 *Jew.* 115, *Nord.* 3; sermons before her, 2 *Jew.* 965, *Now.* 223, *Sand.* 92, 112, 126, 144, 3 *Whitg.* 567; notice of a print of her at her devotions, *Pra. Eliz.* xvii, xix, 430

Elizabeth, queen of Bohemia: *Park.* 471 n., 2 *Zur.* 328 n., 334

Elizabeth, of Saxony: married to Jo. Casimir, count palatine, 2 *Zur.* 173

Elizabeth, queen of Spain: *v.* Isabella.

Elleker (Sir Ralph): 2 *Tyn.* 278 n

Ellingerus (And.): Latin verses de cœna Domini, *Pra. Eliz.* 405; notice of him, *ib.* n

Ellis (Dr): not a fit person for the see of Bangor, *Park.* 257, 261; sometime sheriff of the county, *ib.* 258

Ellis (G.): author of The Lamentation of the Lost Sheep, *Poet.* xxxix; stanzas therefrom, *ib.* 409

Ellis (Geo.): Early Engl. Met. Romances, 1 *Hoop.* 77 n

Ellis (Sir Hen.): Orig. Letters, *Lit. Eliz.* 657 n., 1 *Zur.* 103 n., 149 n., 166 n., &c.; Brand's Pop. Ant. by him, 3 *Bec.* 126 n

Elliston (Dr.): *v.* Elyston.

Ellys (Tho.): founder of Ellys's hospital, Sandwich, *Park.* 168

Elmer (Jo.), bp of London: *v.* Aylmer.

Elmham (North), co. Norfolk: the vicarage, *Park.* 247

Elohim: *v.* God.

Eloi (St): *v.* Eligius.

Eloquence: not to be despised, 4 *Bul.* 54

Elphege (St), abp of Canterbury: why slain, *Bale*, 191

Elsing (Mr): a harbourer of many preachers, 1 *Brad.* 36, 2 *Brad.* xxix; he provides Philpot some ease in prison, *Phil.* 242; letter to him, 2 *Brad.* 67

Eluiden (Edm.): notice of him, *Poet.* lv; a new-year's gift to the rebellious persons in the North parts of England, *ib.* 547

Elvan (St): sent from Rome to Lucius, *Park.* 295

Elvira: *v.* Councils.

Not quite the same as the modern Granada, *Calf.* 154 n

Elxeus: founder of the Ossenes, *Rog.* 242

Ely, co. Cambridge: the bishop's first fruits to the pope, 4 *Jew.* 1078; Dr May vicar general of the diocese, 2 *Cran.* 264; martyrs there, *Poet.* 164; but one prebendary resident, *Park.* 151

Ely house: *v.* London.

Ely (......): at Cranmer's burning, 1 *Cran.* xxviii.

Elymas: 1 *Bul.* 359, 363, 377

Elyne (Jo.): wrote on the Apocalypse, *Bale* 257

Elyot (Sir Tho.): ambassador to the pope, 2 *Cran.* 233 n.; apparently referred to as "Mr Aliote," *ib.* 307, as "Mr Eliot," *ib.* 332; employed to trepan Tyndale, 1 *Tyn.* li; Eliot's Latin dictionary, edited by bp Cooper, *Coop.* xi.

Elyott (Rog.), of All Souls' coll. Oxon: proctor, 2 *Jew.* 952 n

Elysian Fields: a Satanic counterfeit, *Calf.* 14

Elyston (Dr): 2 *Cran.* 248

Emanuel Philibert, duke of Savoy: wars against the Huguenots, 2 *Zur.* 171 n

Embden: two foreign churches established there, one English, the other French, 3 *Zur.* 513; a mart for English merchants, *Grin.* 266, 1 *Zur.* 139 n.; its religious character, *ib.* 140 n

Ember days: the four holy Fridays, 2 *Tyn.* 98; their appointment as ordination fasts, *ib.* n.; referred by some Papists to apostolic tradition, *Whita.* 501; letter of the archbishop and council respecting Ember days and Lent, *Grin.* 406, 407

Emblems: verses from Gef. Whitney's Choice of Emblemes and other Devises, Leyden, 1586, *Poet.* 203

Emilius: *v.* Æmilius.

Emims (Deut. ii. 10): 1 *Tyn.* 445

Emissenus, i. e. Eusebius (*q. v.*), bp of Emissa.

Emmanuel, a man skilful in Hebrew: *Sand.* xvi. [perhaps Tremellius].

Emmaus: the "breaking of bread" there, 1 *Jew.* 232, &c. (*v.* Bread); who the two disciples were, *ib.* 234

Emmerich, on the Rhine: 4 *Bul.* vii.

Emmerson (Marg. Van): Tyndale and Coverdale translate the scriptures in her house at Hamburgh, 1 *Tyn.* xxxix.

Emote: emmet, 4 *Jew.* 858

Emperors: *v.* Empire, Kings.

Emperowr (Marten), printer at Antwerp: 1 *Tyn.* lxii.

Empire: *v.* Rome, Germany.

Titles of the Roman emperors, 1 *Jew.* 424; liberal ones, 1 *Bec.* 26; some worthy of renown for learning, and encouragement of it, *ib.* 398; the division of the empire, 2 *Tyn.* 263; many countries severed from it, 2 *Jew.* 916; the imperial crown was not received from the pope till the time of Charlemagne, 4 *Jew.* 836; the empire erected in Germany, 2 *Ful.* 368, 2 *Tyn.* 269; the emperor an elected prince, 2 *Ful.* 268, 269; his election, *Bale* 502; the seven electors, 2 *Tyn.* 269; the election often influenced by the pope, 1 *Tyn.* 186; the emperor's dignity the highest in Christendom, *Grin.* 12; he was once the ruler of the world, 2 *Jew.* 916; he exercised ecclesiastical authority, 4 *Jew.* 977, &c., 1027, &c.; disputes between the emperor and the pope, 2 *Tyn.* 279, 280, 298, 301; the dominion of the former enfeebled and brought to nothing by the latter, *Bale* 502, 2 *Jew.* 916, 917; emperors compelled to perform menial offices to the pope, 4 *Jew.* 689, &c.

— The Eastern Empire: ruined by internal dissension, 2 *Jew.* 1028

Empires: the four great monarchies, *Bale* 423, *Hutch.* 147, *Pil.* 186

Empson (Sir Rich.): chancellor of Lancaster, 1 *Bec.* 37 n.; the rapacious minister of Henry VII., 2 *Cran.* 298 n., 2 *Tyn.* 342

Emser (......): wrote against Luther's Bible, 1 *Ful.* 60

Emulation: a bane of the heart, *Sand.* 138

Enallage: 3 *Bul.* 170

Enbasted: steeped in, *Phil.* 375

Enbourne, co. Berks: a libel left in the parish church, 1604 (called Euborn), *Rog.* 320

Enchantments: *v.* Witchcraft.

Enchiridion: *v.* Manuale.

Enchiridion (perhaps that of Erasmus, tranlated by Tyndale) not a prohibited book, 2 *Cran.* 288, see 1 *Tyn.* xvii.

Enclosure: *v.* Commons.

Encratites, or Tatians: the name Encratitæ, 2 *Ful.* 375; their heresy, 1 *Bul.* 432, 2 *Bul.* 24, 3 *Jew.* 236, *Phil.* 421 n.; they received only the Acts of the Apostles, *Rog.* 84; condemned marriage, *ib.* 261 n.; received no married person into their company, and ate no flesh, *Phil.* 419; used no wine in the Lord's supper, *Rog.* 295

End: *v.* Christ (vi.), World.

Endhoven (Chr.), printer at Antwerp: 1 *Tyn.* xxxiii.

Endor (The witch of): *v.* Samuel.

Endote: to endow, 1 *Tyn.* 249

Endurance: *v.* Perseverance.

Enemies: *v.* Prayers (especially the Lord's).

How it is an advantage to have one, 1 *Lat.* 427; kindness to them, *Pil.* 433; they must be overcome with good, 1 *Lat.* 440, 1 *Tyn.* 193; how to be forgiven, 1 *Lat.* 424; we are commanded to love our enemies, 3 *Bec.* 38, 2 *Tyn.* 70; a prayer for them, 3 *Bec.* 38

Adversaries of God's truth are many, 3 *Bec.* 39; enemies of God's word reproved and warned, 1 *Bec.* 182, 183, 184; they continually bark against lovers of the Lord's word, *ib.* 17; blaspheme through the wickedness of gross gospellers, *ib.* 347; are ready to accuse those that are wanting in hospitality, *ib.* 25; we must hate the enemies of God, 2 *Tyn.* 70; it is lawful to pray for God's justice on them, if we do it not maliciously, *Pil.* 404, 405; intercession against those who are enemies to the gospel of set malice, 3 *Bec.* 249, 250; intercession for those who are enemies for lack of knowledge, *ib.* 249; a prayer against the enemies of Christ's truth, *Lit. Eliz.* 255; enemies to religion have been converted by the godly communications of Christians, 1 *Bec.* 17, 18

Our spiritual enemies—the world, the flesh, and the devil (*v.* Temptations, &c.), 1 *Bec.* 125, 126, 2 *Bec.* 184; we must fight against them, 3 *Bec.* 49, *Sand.* 166, 167; how we are to do so, *ib.* 91; they can do no more than God suffers, 2 *Bec.* 193; the conflict of Christians with their adversaries most perilous in sickness, *ib.* 571; a prayer for victory over them, *Lit. Eliz.* 252; another, *Pra. B.* 124

Energumeni: persons possessed, 1 *Ful.* 258, 1 *Jew.* 115, 2 *Jew.* 705, 706, *Rid.* 160, 163; not allowed to be present at the eucharist, *ib.*

Enfarced: stuffed, filled, 1 *Bec.* 91

Enfield, co. Midd.: the chase, 2 *Cov.* 529 n., *Grin.* 285

Enfield (Will.): Hist. of Philosophy, 1 *Tyn.* 154 n., &c.

Enforming: forming, shaping, 2 *Brad.* 204

Engelhard (Hen.), pastor at Zurich: 4 *Bul.* x. n

Enghien (The duke d'), a French hostage: 3 *Zur.* 559 n

England: *v.* Church, II. iv., English, Kings, Parliament, Rebellion, Statutes, &c.

Lists of the counties (the names explained), cities, bishopricks, and chief rivers of England and Wales, with the names of the adjacent islands, *Pra. Eliz.* 423; the English chronicles censured, *Bale* 8 (*v.* Chronicles); Rerum Anglic. Scriptores post Bedam, *Jew.* xxxii; Britannia Sancta, a book published 1745, 2 *Tyn.* 216 n.; the first preaching of the gospel in this land, 1 *Jew.* 267, 279, 280, 305, 3 *Jew.* 163, &c., 4 *Jew.* 778, *Pil.* 482, 510 (*v.* Eleutherius); Cyril speaks of altars erected in Britain,

ENGLAND — ENGLISH

&c., *Rid.* 280; the testimony of Theodoret, 3 *Jew.* 128; of Nicephorus, *ib.* 129; this country received not the faith from Rome, *Pil.* 510; the Britons followed Greek rites, 1 *Jew.* 280, 306, *Pil.* 512; flamines (*q. v.*) changed for bishops, 2 *Whitg.* 127, 128, 428; it does not appear that there was any bishop of Britain at either of the first four councils, 4 *Jew.* 997; there were British bishops at Sardica, 3 *Jew.* 165; wickedness of the ancient Britons, and its fruits, 1 *Tyn.* 143; Gildas warned them to repentance and amendment of life, 3 *Bec.* 10, 11; they were displaced for their neglect of God's word; prodigious tokens beforehand, *Lit. Eliz.* 568; the land oppressed by Romans, Saxons, &c., *Pil.* 73; conquered by Danes and Normans, *ib.* 521; great warnings before the victories of the Danes, and the Norman conquest, *Lit. Eliz.* 568; England cursed by the Antichrist of Rome, 2 *Hoop.* 567; the injuries it has suffered from popes and popish prelates, 1 *Tyn.* 335—339, 2 *Tyn.* 53, 225, 294, &c., 3 *Tyn.* 138, 166; punished for the murder of Richard II., 2 *Tyn.* 53; the desolation caused by the wars of the roses, 1 *Tyn.* 458; the English were in great blindness when the bishop of Rome ruled, 1 *Bec.* 181, 2 *Bec.* 414, 415; Tyndale supposes that the clergy had, besides the tithes, one-third of the whole land, 1 *Tyn.* 236; England fortified through the wise provision of Henry VIII., 1 *Bec.* 245; state of religion in 1539, 3 *Zur.* 624; low state of morals, 1549, *ib.* 647; condition of religion in king Edward's time, 3 *Bec.* 3, 227, &c., 4 *Bul.* 528, *Rid.* 49, &c., 349, &c., 3 *Zur.* 635, 672; the country blessed with light, 2 *Bec.* 415; purged and made clean of its deformities, 1 *Bec.* 181; its felicity greater than that of the Israelites in the time of Solomon, *ib.* 193; a prospect of great felicity for the country if the reformation should go on, *ib.* 182; yet the land was miserable through the covetousness of the rich, 2 *Bec.* 434, 435; many towns had become desolate, *ib.* 434; signs declaring the destruction of true religion to be at hand, 3 *Bec.* 205; troubles under Mary, especially as to religion, 3 *Bec.* 225, &c., *Rid.* 49, &c., 349, &c.; the heavy plague of God fallen upon the land, *Rid.* 58; the English bewitched, like the Galatians, 1 *Brad.* 386; Philpot laments the state of the land, and says that great will be its plagues though the gospel be restored again, *Phil.* 259; its conduct in time of persecution reproved, *Pil.* 24; the Christian commonwealth de-formed in queen Mary's time, 3 *Bec.* 244, 245; misery of English Christians, *ib.* 245; signs and tokens in queen Mary's time, *Lit. Eliz.* 569; superstition lingered long in the North, 2 *Lat.* 16; rudeness of the people in those parts, *Park.* 123, 388; scarcity of preachers there, *Sand.* 154; the decay of godliness, and increasing corruption of the times, *Lit. Eliz.* 573, *Wool.* 141, 142; England's privileges, God's great mercies to it, 3 *Bec.* 11, 12, 206, 1 *Brad.* 13, *Nord.* 39, 166, *Pra. Eliz.* 464, 477, *Sand.* 217, 218, 349; its grievous sins, 1 *Bec.* 243, 244, 3 *Bec.* 225, &c., 1 *Brad.* 59, *Sand.* 158, 259, 350; disobedience, 2 *Hoop.* 86; ingratitude for the gift of God's word, 3 *Bec.* 4, &c., *Sand.* 219, 350; the land without excuse for despising communications with God, 1 *Bec.* 128; its long neglect of building God's house, *Pil.* 25, 37, 38; the land plagued for this neglect, *ib.* 58; called to repentance, 1 *Bec.* 243, 244, 3 *Bec.* 274, 1 *Brad.* 37, 38, &c., *Pil.* 82; warned, *Pil.* 89, 188, *Poet.* 375; An Exhortation to England, &c., by R. D., notice thereof, *Poet.* xxxviii; stanzas from it, *ib.* 399; intercession for England, 3 *Bec.* 245, &c.

— The crown, monarchy, &c. (*v.* Kings): the English constitution, 1 *Whitg.* 390, 393; the government a true monarchy, 3 *Whitg.* 197; the king of Denmark styled himself king of England, even in Tyndale's time, 1 *Tyn.* 187, 2 *Tyn.* 334; so the king of England styled himself king of France, 1 *Tyn.* 187; the crown entailed on the issue of Henry VIII. by Anne Boleyn, 2 *Lat.* 367 n.; preamble to the act of 25 Hen. VIII., 2 *Cran.* 285 n., it was objected to by bp Fisher and Sir Tho. More, *ib.*; on king Edward's will, *ib.* 443; the Protestant succession a matter of deep anxiety to the bishops under Elizabeth, *Grin.* 19 n.; the question of succession debated in parliament, 1 *Zur.* 185 n.; anticipated succession to the crown, 1572, 2 *Zur.* 200

Englefield (Sir Fra.): one of queen Mary's privy council, 1 *Zur.* 5 n.; he enters into the service of Spain, *Lit. Eliz.* 656 n

English: *v.* England.

They have nothing to boast of in their origin, *Pil.* 125; their character, 3 *Zur.* 420; their affection for their country, 1 *Bec.* 234, 235; they are bound above other nations to give God thanks, *ib.* 180; madness of their apparel, 1 *Bec.* 204, 2 *Bec.* 438, *Nov.* 172, *Pil.* 56

English language: the older English used in the North and in Scotland, *Bale* 63; the

old English tongue praised by Dr Turner, *Rid.* 490, 494; Jewel says the kingdom has five distinct tongues, 1 *Jew.* 275
English, a manor in Nuffield, *q. v.*
Engrossing: sinful, *Pil.* 457, 464
Enhalseth: embraceth, 1 *Bec.* 45
Enking: inking, *Pil.* 211
Ennius: says it is dangerous to be feared, *Hutch.* 8; Ennius and Nasica, *ib.* 51
Enno, count of East Friesland, 3 *Zur.* 512 n
Ennodius (M. F.): works, *Jew.* xxxix; he declares that Theodoricus deposed pope Symmachus, 4 *Jew.* 1034; mentions that the accusers of that pope said, that the successors of Peter, together with the privileges of their see, had also gotten free liberty to do ill, 3 *Jew.* 339, 4 *Jew.* 834, 918, 968
Enoch: cited by Jude in his epistle, 1 *Bul.* 39, *Whita.* 70; he did not write, but prophesied, *Whita.* 114; though Augustine thinks he wrote, *ib.* 516
Ens: a scholastic term, 1 *Tyn.* 158
Enthusiastæ: the Messalians or Euchites were so called, 4 *Bul.* 94 n., 345, 1 *Hoop.* 245; they preferred their own dreams, &c., to the word of God, *Rog.* 158, 196, and set baptism at nought, 4 *Bul.* 397; there was a sect of Anabaptists called by the same name, and professing very similar opinions, 4 *Bul.* 94 n., *Rog.* 158
Enunied: united, 1 *Bec.* 79
Envy: a grievous sin, 2 *Lat.* 18; described by heathen poets, 1 *Bul.* 301—303; its nature illustrated, *Pil.* 335, 336; that of the wicked against the good, *ib.* 398; against it, with sentences and examples of scripture, 1 *Bec.* 458, 459; an envious man, what, 3 *Bec.* 610
Enzinas (Fra.), alias Dryander, *q. v.*
Epaminondas: his death, *Hutch.* 321
Epaphroditus: called an apostle, 1 *Whitg.* 497; bishop of Philippi, *Rog.* 329
Ephesus: *v.* Councils.
Proclamation in the senate house, 3 *Jew.* 202; the twelve men of Ephesus, whether they were re-baptized, 4 *Bul.* 356, 396, 1 *Ful.* 453, *Hutch.* 116, 3 *Whitg.* 17; St Paul's epistle to the Ephesians, *v.* Paul; the apocalyptic epistle to the church there, *Bale* 273, *Phil.* 220; factions in that church 1 *Whitg.* 464; talk "ad Ephesios," 1 *Brad.* 541, 2 *Jew.* 579; Ἐφέσια γράμματα, 1 *Brad.* 592
Ephod: a Jewish priestly garment, 2 *Bul.* 135, 1 *Tyn.* 419
Ephphatha: the word used of old in connexion with baptism, 4 *Bul.* 361

Ephræm (St): when he lived, *Calf.* 258 n.; his works, *ib.* 407; the authenticity of many sermons attributed to him questioned, *ib.* 258 n.; his homilies read in churches, 1 *Jew.* 269; he knew no Greek, *ib.* 269; calls Christ a legislator, *Calf.* 258; terms the bread and wine a figure of Christ's body and blood, 2 *Jew.* 598, 599; speaks of the sign of the cross, *Calf.* 258; prays to the virgin Mary, *ib.* 258; his account of Basil, 1 *Jew.* 189
Epicharmus, a philosopher: 1 *Jew.* 178
Epictetus: 1 *Bec.* 392, 3 *Bul.* 386
Epicureans: admitted that there were gods, but denied that they regarded worldly affairs, *Phil.* 395; supposed God to be corporeal, *Hutch.* 12; held the fantasy that he sits in heaven idly and at ease, 1 *Jew.* 501, *Rog.* 42; denied his providence, *Hutch.* 69; enemies to the gospel, 3 *Bul.* 112; blasphemous, 1 *Hoop.* 324; their absurd notions respecting the sun, *ib.* 222; mentioned, 2 *Hoop.* 82, *Phil.* 404
Epicurus: wished his scholars to imagine him ever present, *Wool.* 94
Epimenides: his declaration that the Cretians are always liars, cited by St Paul, 2 *Jew.* 680, 4 *Jew.* 737, *Whita.* 70, 2 *Whitg.* 36
Epinus (Jo.): *v.* Æpinus.
Epiousion (Ἐπιούσιον): *Lit. Edw.* 521, (568)
Epiphanius (St):
    i. *His Works, &c.*
    ii. *On God.*
    iii. *Scripture, Tradition.*
    iv. *Bishops and other Ministers.*
    v. *The Eucharist.*
    vi. *Easter, Fasting, Marriage, &c.*
    vii. *Images, the Cross.*
    viii. *Angels, Saints.*
    ix. *Heresies.*
    i. *His works, &c.*: his works, *Calf.* 407, 2 *Ful.* 401, *Jew.* xxxvi; his Panarium, against heresies, *Calf.* 249 n.; the genuineness of this work impugned by Cartwright, but defended by Whitgift, 2 *Whitg.* 288; the second synod of Nice argued from it, *Calf.* 174; reply of the synod of Frankfort, *ib.* 175; his famous letter to John, bp of Jerusalem, 2 *Ful.* 173, 174; Jerome's approval of it, *Calf.* 254, 255; the spurious tract De vitis Prophetarum, 2 *Ful.* 207; Epiphanius was occupied in civil matters, 3 *Whitg.* 455; he erred in some points, 1 *Hoop.* 28; reproved by Chrysostom, 2 *Zur.* 242
    ii. *On God*: he proves that "substance," is in scripture as to the sense, 1 *Jew.* 533, 3 *Jew.* 227, 440, *Whita.* 535; supposes that

the magi came about two years after Christ's nativity, 2 *Lat.* 132 n.; condemns the opinion of Irenæus that Christ lived on earth forty years, *Whita.* 585; says Christ is the victim, priest, altar, God, man, king, highpriest, sheep, lamb, made all in all for us, 2 *Jew.* 733; declares that he sits at the right hand of the Father in glory, not putting away his body...even as our bodies ...shall be raised, &c., 1 *Jew.* 497

iii. *Scripture, Tradition* (as to the scriptures, see Alogians, Marcion, and Ptolomeans, in ix): his testimony to the sufficiency of scripture, *Whita.* 686; to its perspicuity, 2 *Jew.* 683, *Whita.* 399; he speaks of the treatment of scripture by heretics, *Calf.* 121, 122; his statement as to the canon of the Old Testament, *Whita.* 58, 59; he thought the LXX. to be in some sort prophets, *ib.* 119; his account of Aquila, and of Symmachus, *ib.* 123; he did not receive the books of Wisdom and Ecclesiasticus as canonical, *ib.* 59, 87; mentions an epistle to the Laodiceans, *ib.* 303; (as to tradition, see Caiani, in ix;) he says the scripture has need of speculation, and that it becomes us to use tradition, &c., 3 *Jew.* 240; on the apostles' traditions, 2 *Cran.* 57; he delighted too much in traditions and genealogies, *Whita.* 597; traditions mentioned by him, but rejected by Papists, *ib.* 598; on the Syriac tongue, 1 *Jew.* 276

iv. *Bishops and other Ministers:* he calls Peter the chief of the apostles, a sure rock on which the church of God is built, 2 *Ful.* 286; says that he visited and governed Pontus and Bithynia, 2 *Whitg.* 230; enumerates the first bishops of Rome, *Calf.* 251, 3 *Jew.* 326; sets forth the epistle of pope Marcellus to his most blessed fellowminister Julius, 2 *Ful.* 287; maintains that Timothy was bishop of Ephesus, 2 *Whitg.* 288, 295; on the jurisdiction of the bishop of Alexandria, *ib.* 429; calls him sometimes bishop, sometimes archbishop, *ib.* 160, 196; speaks of the churches of Egypt as under the jurisdiction of that see, *ib.* 161; says that in some churches there were only bishops and deacons, and no presbyters, 2 *Tyn.* 256 n.; states the difference between bishops and priests, with reference to the opinions of Aerius, 2 *Whitg.* 290, 291, see also 3 *Jew.* 430; declares that Jerome and Vicentius were hardly persuaded to accept the priesthood, 1 *Ful.* 263; speaks of Zacchæus, a pretended priest, 3 *Jew.* 321; says that Philip the deacon had not power to lay on hands so as to give the Holy Ghost, 3 *Whitg.* 59, 60; denies the right of women, not excepting Mary, to baptize or minister, 1 *Hoop.* 132, 2 *Whitg.* 535; see also Marcion, in ix. below.

v. *The Eucharist* (see Artotyrites, Encratites, Marcus, Severians, in ix): he does not say that Melchisedec offered bread and wine to God, but to Abraham, 2 *Jew.* 731; he says that Christ called a loaf, round and insensible, his body, 2 *Bec.* 288, 3 *Bec.* 439, 1 *Brad.* 590, 1 *Jew.* 535, 2 *Jew.* 772, 1122; on the reception of Christ's body, 1 *Brad.* 98, *Rid.* 202

vi. *Easter, Fasting, Marriage, &c.:* on the time of Easter, *Whita.* 569; he says that Christians in his time ate only bread and salt for some days before that feast, *ib.* 666; on the observance of the Lent fast in his time, 3 *Jew.* 170; he describes the austerity of the Pharisees, 2 *Jew.* 1017; reproves the simulated chastity of certain heretics who refused marriage, 2 *Ful.* 100, 2 *Jew.* 728, 830, 3 *Jew.* 425, 428; thinks it better for one who has vowed celibacy, openly to take a wife than to fall into other sins, 1 *Ful.* 481 n., 2 *Ful.* 103, 3 *Jew.* 399, 4 *Jew.* 797, *Whita.* 598 (see also Aetians, Apostolics, Gnostics, Saturnians, and Tatians, in ix).

vii. *Images, the Cross:* he calls images an abomination, 2 *Jew.* 990; says the superstition of images is unfit for the church of Christ, 4 *Jew.* 795; declares that it is a horrible wickedness for any man to set up any picture in the church, though it were the picture of Christ himself, *ib.* 792; says that to make an image of Christ is to make a creature of him who created all things, *Calf.* 249; he destroyed a picture of Christ, or of some saint hanging in a church at Anablatha, 2 *Bec.* 60, 61, 69, 71, 1 *Bul.* 229, *Calf.* 42, 253, &c., 376, 2 *Cran.* 178, 1 *Ful.* 194, 1 *Hoop.* 42, 2 *Jew.* 644, 655, 668, 4 *Jew.* 793, *Park.* 88, *Rid.* 91, 3 *Tyn.* 182; forbade the placing of images in churches, 2 *Cran.* 178, 2 *Jew.* 644, or their erection at the burial of the saints, or even in private houses, *Calf.* 144, 148, 4 *Jew.* 794; on the idolatry of certain heretics, 1 *Ful.* 194; see also Collyridians, and Valentinians, in ix); he says of certain Persians named Magusæi, they abhor the sight of idols, yet they fall down and worship idols, 4 *Jew.* 949; speaks of a woman who signed herself, *Calf.* 329

viii. *Angels, Saints:* he states there is nothing said in scripture as to the time when angels were created, 3 *Bul.* 329; see also Caiani, and Menander, in ix; he maintains the perpetual virginity of Mary from scripture, *Whita.* 539; blames some who too highly exalted her, 1 *Hoop.* 206, 208; says Christ called her "woman" lest any should think her of too great excellency, 3 *Jew.* 578; as to Mary, see also the last sentence in iv, and Collyridians, in ix; as to Peter, &c., see iv.; he relates that James wore a πέταλον, or plate of gold, 1 *Zur.* 160 n.; on the writings of Clement of Rome, *Whita.* 566

ix. *Heresies*: he reckons up eighty heresies, *Calf.* 249 n., 1 *Jew.* 334, 3 *Jew.* 603; describes the Adamites, 2 *Brad.* 385, *Rog.* 101 n., 135 n.; speaks of the Aerians, 2 *Brad.* 382 n., *Rog.* 330 n.; states the opinions of Aerius about bishops and priests, 2 *Whitg.* 290, 291; says he was an Arian, 3 *Bul.* 399; writes of the Aetians, *Rog.* 118 n.; tells that Aetius allowed fornication, 4 *Jew.* 630; states that the Alogians rejected the writings of St John, *Whita.* 35; speaks of the Angelici, 2 *Ful.* 41 n.; mentions their extinction, *Phil.* 420; calls the Anthropomorphites Audians, 1 *Hoop.* 160 n.; describes the Apostolics, 2 *Ful.* 376 n.; says they maintained community of goods, *Rog.* 354 n., that they condemned marriage, *ib.* 262 n., 306 n., and excommunicated all married persons, *ib.* 311 n.; refers to an error of the Arians, *ib.* 52 n.; notes the craft of Arius, 3 *Jew.* 450; tells that the Artotyrites added cheese to the sacramental bread, 4 *Bul.* 410, *Rog.* 295 n.; writes about the Barbelitæ, 2 *Ful.* 375 n.; says the Caiani avouched all their follies and heresies, not by the scriptures, but by tradition, as they said, from St Paul, 3 *Jew.* 440; amongst their errors he reckons invocation of angels, 2 *Ful.* 41, 86; speaks of the Carpocratians, *Rog.* 41 n., 119 n.; records that Carpocrates said he knew more than either Christ himself or his apostles, 4 *Jew.* 760; states the error of Cerinthus on creation, *Rog.* 41 n.; reproves the Collyridians for their worship of the virgin Mary, 3 *Jew.* 555, 576, and for making and using images, *Calf.* 377, 2 *Ful.* 207; says that Ebion, though he agreed with the Samaritans, would needs be called a Christian, 4 *Jew.* 713; referred to on his sect, 1 *Hoop.* 161 n.; he asserts that the Encratites used no wine in the Lord's supper, *Rog.* 295 n.; Enthusiasts, *v.* Messalians, infra; he says the Gnostics condemned marriage, *Rog.* 261 n.; describes the Helchesaites, *ib.* 71 n.; records errors of Hierax and his followers, *ib.* 71 n., 82 n., 137 n., 145 n.; writes of the Manichees, *Rog.* 137 n., *Whita.* 30, 31, and of Scythianus, the first originator of the Manichean heresy, *Rog.* 79 n.; tells of the doctrine of Marcion, *ib.* 44 n.; affirms that he permitted women to baptize, 4 *Bul.* 370, 371, *Rog.* 236 n.; mentions what books his sect rejected, *Whita.* 35; states that Marcus the heretic held the wine of the Lord's supper to be converted into blood, *Rog.* 287 n.; speaks of the heresy of Meletius, *Hutch.* 113; mentions the opposition of Peter, bp of Alexandria, to this error, 1 *Hoop.* 169; says Menander affirmed the world to be made by angels, *Rog.* 41 n., on the error of the Messalians, *ib.* 37 n., reference to them as Enthusiasts, 4 *Bul.* 397; on the Noetians' heresy, *Rog.* 45 n.; he notes the errors of Origen, *Rid.* 30; says the Ossenes prayed to God in a strange language, which they learned of Elxeus their founder, *Rog.* 242 n.; records the errors of Paul of Samosata, *ib.* 70; asserts that the Ptolomæans condemned the books of Moses, *Whita.* 31; tells how the heretic Ruffinus complained of persecution, 4 *Jew.* 1073; says the Saturnians condemned marriage, *Rog.* 306 n.; states the views of Saturninus, *ib.* 162 n.; affirms that the Severians used no wine in the Lord's supper, *ib.* 295 n.; on the blasphemies of Simon Magus, *ib.* 41 n., 64 n., 71 n.; he says the Tatians condemned marriage, *ib.* 261 n.; declares that the Valentinians feigned three sorts of men, *ib.* 122 n.; mentions their superstition with reference to the cross, 2 *Ful.* 139

Epiphanius, bp of Constantinople: Justinian the emperor esteemed him the more because his father and other ancestors had been priests and bishops, 3 *Jew.* 392

Epiphanius Scholasticus: translates Socrates, Sozomen, and Theodoret, 2 *Brad.* 305 n., *Jew.* xxxvi.

Epiphany: a sermon on that day, 2 *Lat.* 129

Episcopacy: *v.* Bishops, Ministers.

Episcopius (......), printer: *Grin.* 231

Epistle: A COMFORTABLE EPISTLE TO THE AFFLICTED PEOPLE OF GOD, by T. Becon, 3 *Bec.* 192

Epistles (Decretal): *v.* Law (Canon), and the names of the popes.

Epistles and Gospels: read at the communion, 3 *Whitg.* 74; by whom appointed, 2 *Brad.* 307; on standing at the gospel, 3 *Whitg.* 384; the practice ordained by Anastasius I. (not III.), 2 *Brad.* 308; an article against sitting at the epistle, and standing at the gospel, 2 *Hoop.* 146; both read from the pulpit, 2 *Cran.* 156, 501, *Grin.* 132; at the reading of the gospel in Poland, it was the custom for the king and others to stand up with naked swords, *Grin.* 56

Epitaphs: that of Similis, a late converted soldier, *Sand.* 173; an epitaph by Sir W. Raleigh on himself, *Poet.* 236

Epitheton: 1 *Hoop.* 124

Epitome alias Compendium Theologicæ Veritatis: *Jew.* xxxv; cited, 3 *Jew.* 458

Eposculations: kissings, 3 *Bec.* 283

Eppentianus (......): 2 *Zur.* 328

Equinoctial (The): what, 2 *Bul.* 180

Equitius, a deacon: *Rid.* 500, 504

Equity: epiky (ἐπιείκεια) softens the rigour of the law, 1 *Lat.* 182

Er : ere, before, 2 *Bec.* 38 n

Eradius, bp of Hippo: succeeded Augustine, 4 *Bul.* 133, 1 *Whitg.* 443, 445; called Evodius, 2 *Zur.* 230; perhaps Evodius wrote a treatise ascribed to Augustine, 1 *Jew.* 113 n

Erasmus (St): invoked by Papists, 1 *Hoop.* 339, *Rog.* 226; account of him, *ib.* 309, 310 n

Erasmus (Des.), Roterodamus:
  i. *His Life and Works.*
  ii. *Scripture.*
  iii. *Doctrine, Manners, &c.*
  iv. *Apostles, Bishops, Popes, &c.*
  v. *Ecclesiastical Writers, &c.*
  vi. *Sacraments, Worship, Prayer, Ceremonies.*
  vii. *Miscellanea.*

i. *His life and works*: he taught Greek at Cambridge, 1 *Tyn.* xv; a learned man, yet in error, *Coop.* 123; charged with causing dissension, 2 *Lat.* 341; Standish charges him with heresy, 1 *Lat.* 46 n.; disowned by Papists, though called by Leo X. his dear son, *Whita.* 66; Canus says Cajetan was deceived by his novelties, *ib.* 49: his Life, by Jortin, 2 *Ful.* 319 n.; his portrait bequeathed by Grindal to his successors, *Grin.* 459; his Adagia, 1 *Bul.* 272, &c., *Calf.* 2, 115, 251, 2 *Ful.* 299 nn., *Jew.* xxxii; Apophthegmata, *Calf.* 263 n.; Colloquia, 1 *Bul.* 129; sentenced to extinction, 2 *Ful.* 194 n.; Ecclesiastes, *Calf.* 360; his ENCHIRIDION MILITIS CHRISTIANI, an abridged translation by Coverdale, 1 *Cov.* 489; mistakenly attributed to Luther, *Calf.* 314 n.; translated by Tyndale, 1 *Tyn.* xvii, xxiv; Enchiridion (supposed to be the same) not a forbidden book, 2 *Cran.* 288; Modus Orandi Deum, *Calf.* 66 n., 389 n.; Paraclesis, 1 *Tyn.* 161; his Paraphrases, 2 *Brad.* 6, 1 *Lat.* 434, 1 *Tyn.* 162; to be provided in churches, 2 *Cran.* 155, 156, 499, 501, *Grin.* 134, 157, 2 *Hoop.* 139, 143; notice of his Precationes Aliquot, *Pra. Eliz.* 98 n. (see vi. below); Stultitiæ Laus, or Moriæ Encomium, *Calf.* 175 n., 255 n., 2 *Jew.* 803, 3 *Tyn.* 16 n.; Symboli Catechesis, 1 *Bul.* 230, 4 *Bul.* 236, *Calf.* 8, 34, 190 nn.; as to other labours of his, see iv. below; a note of his condemned by the Spanish inquisitors, 2 *Ful.* 290 n

ii. *Scripture*: he allows that in old time nothing was read in churches except the apostles' writings, and writings of apostolic authority, 4 *Jew.* 816; his account of the four senses assigned to holy scripture by schoolmen, 1 *Tyn.* 343; he allows that there are many gross errors in the Vulgate, 4 *Jew.* 907; would have laymen permitted to read the scriptures in their own tongue, 1 *Tyn.* 161, 162, *Whita.* 249; declares that the word Lord (Dominus) implies Redeemer and Vindicator, 1 *Bul.* 129; explains μετάνοια, (Matt. iii), 3 *Bul.* 55 n., 1 *Ful.* 155; expounds Matt. vi. 7, " vain repetitions," 3 *Whitg.* 515; thinks the concluding words of the Lord's prayer not inspired, 4 *Bul.* 219; expounds κατακυριεύουσιν and κατεξουσιάζουσιν, in Matt. xx, 1 *Whitg.* 163, 164; mentions an absurd exposition of the words, " Let these go their way," 2 *Jew.* 831; thinks that Matthew may have made a mistake as to the name of Jeremy (xxvii. 9), *Whita.* 37; on the darkness at the crucifixion, *ib.* 579; his exposition of 1 Cor. x. 13, " a way to escape," 1 *Bul.* 317; of 1 Cor. xi. 22, " have ye not houses," &c., 1 *Jew.* 158, 159; of Gal. ii. 2, 6—τοῖς δοκοῦσι, and οἱ δοκοῦντες, 2 *Whitg.* 411; he explains the word ἀνακεφαλαιώσασθαι, (Col. i. 19, Eph. i. 10), 1 *Bul.* 156; his opinion on the apocryphal books, *Whita.* 66; he declares that the dreams of monks, yea, every woman's doting fancies, were read amongst the holy scriptures, 4 *Jew.* 816, *Sand.* 18; censures Faber for supposing the epistle to the Laodiceans to be genuine, *Whita.* 303

iii. *Doctrine, Manners, &c.*: he says that in (ancient) times it was a great point of cunning to know how to be a Christian man, 3 *Jew.* 607; his words upon justification, 2 *Cran.* 207; he thought that some pagan philosophers, &c., were saved by their moral lives, *Rog.* 160; had a controversy with Luther on free-will, 3 *Tyn.* 233 n.; objects to the notion of the virgin having authority to command her Son, 1 *Tyn.* 316 n.; declares it a fault to blame another for what a man does himself, 1 *Bec.* 15; censures Jerome's language respecting chastity, 1 *Tyn.* 438 n.; observes that many counted godly men think little of fornication, 4 *Jew.* 634, 635; restricts the word "woman" in 1 Cor. vii. 1, to a wife, 1 *Ful.* 115; says Greek priests are married, 4 *Jew.* 807; calls idle people unprofitable lumps of unoccupied earth, 2 *Bul.* 33; says that ill-gotten goods are generally spent very lewdly, *ib.* 29; his story of a thief, 2 *Brad.* 393, 3 *Whitg.* 320; he calls thriftiness a very great revenue, 1 *Bul.* 297

iv. *Apostles, Bishops, Popes, &c.*: he says the doctors of Paris determined that Peter erred, 4 *Jew.* 927; speaks of the agreement between Peter and Paul as to preaching, 3 *Jew.* 328; on the office of Timothy, 2 *Whitg.* 296, and Titus, *ib.* 132, 352; on Jerome's opinions respecting bishops, 3 *Jew.* 292, 2 *Whitg.* 255, 258; he says episcopus, sacerdos, and presbyter were all one, 3 *Jew.* 293; declares that the title of high bishop of the world was not known to the old church, 2 *Hoop.* 237; calls popes the vicars of Julius Cæsar, of Alexander the Great, &c., not of Christ, nor of Peter, 4 *Jew.* 1009; says the Arian heresy entangled both pope and emperor, *ib.* 929, 930; asks, if the pope cannot err, what need we have for so many general councils, *ib.* 1068; deems the epistles of Innocent I. spurious, *Whita.* 435; how he characterizes the answer of pope Innocent to the council of Carthage, 4 *Jew.* 1046; says pope John XXII. and pope Nicolas in their decrees are contrary to each other in matters of faith, *ib.* 751; by χειροτονία he understands ordination by suffrages, 1 *Whitg.* 345, 346 n

v. *Ecclesiastical Writers, &c.*: he detected the spuriousness of many writings ascribed to the fathers, 3 *Tyn.* 135; shews that the Dionysius whose works are extant, was not the Areopagite, 2 *Ful.* 165, 1 *Jew.* 113, 114, 3 *Whitg.* 110; assigns the authorship of a commentary on the Psalms which he first published, to Arnobius Afer, instead of Arnobius Junior, 2 *Ful.* 319; his translation of the treatise De Spiritu Sancto, assigned to Basil, and his opinion on it, *Calf.* 266 n.; he thinks it interpolated, *Whita.* 589; supposes Eucherius to have been the writer of the books De Vocatione Gentium, sometimes ascribed to Ambrose, 2 *Ful.* 353 n.; says Theophilus calls Epiphanius an heresiarch, 3 *Jew.* 607; his Latin version and opinion of the treatise On Prayer ascribed to Chrysostom, *Calf.* 104 n.; he says Ruffinus was not clear from the Origenian heresy, 4 *Jew.* 1007; speaks of Jerome's education at Rome, *ib.* 654; on his railing against Vigilantius, 3 *Jew.* 167; he distinguishes the true from the false epistle to Demetrias attributed to that father, 2 *Ful.* 44 n.; his observation on the latter, 1 *Bec.* 205 n.; his remark on the spurious epistle to Oceanus attributed to Jerome, 2 *Ful.* 97 n.; his opinion as to the Commentary on the Psalms erroneously ascribed to him, *ib.* 208; what he thought of Jerome's Life of Paul the Hermit, *Calf.* 252; on the additions to Jerome's Catalogue of ecclesiastical writers, *Calf.* 128 n.; his Life of St Jerome expurgated, 2 *Ful.* 103 n.; he relates how Augustine exposed the Manichees, 4 *Jew.* 628; censures the spurious sermon De Visitatione Infirmorum bearing the name of that father, *Calf.* 361 n.; on Gratian, 3 *Jew.* 186; he blames the monstrous follies found in the commentaries of the late interpreters, 4 *Jew.* 878; declares it easier for a man to wind himself out of a maze than out of the shifts and corners of the Reals and Nominals, 3 *Jew.* 613; says, they that follow Thomas, and dissent from Duns and Gerson, almost account these as heretics, *ib.* 619; his flattering account of Tonstal, 1 *Tyn.* xxi, 395; he calls the reformers sharp physicians, *Bale* 183

vi. *Sacraments, Worship, Prayer, Ceremonies*: his explanation of the word sacrament, 4 *Bul.* 236; he says, to be baptized with the same baptism, is proverbially spoken of him that is partaker of the selfsame danger or misfortune, *ib.* 352; allows that the use of chrism in baptism was introduced by the fathers, *Whita.* 602; explains the phrase "breaking of bread," *Hutch.* 284; shews how in the ancient church the sacrament was partaken of in common, 3 *Bec.* 417, 418; reports that of old the sacrament was delivered into the hands of communicants to be taken home, *Coop.* 22; writing on a passage in Jerome, he declares that every one was wont to receive the body of Christ at home that would, 1 *Jew.* 156; says Christ in the sacrament ought not to be carried about the fields on horseback, 2 *Bec.* 253, 3 *Bec.* 359, 374, 375; censures those who deem themselves devout for looking at the body of Christ when the priest holds it up, 3 *Bec.* 360; says that anciently the people did not run to see what the priest held up, but lifted their minds to heaven, *ib.*; states that the worship of the sacrament was prior to Augustine and Cyprian, *Rid.* 236; says it was long and very late ere the church determined the article of transubstantiation, 4 *Jew.* 784; complains that the church does not follow Paul, so that the people hear only voices signifying nothing, 3 *Bec.* 410; would not have singing in an unknown tongue, 1 *Jew.* 315; on Christ and his disciples singing a hymn, 4 *Bul.* 191; he says that the singing used in the ancient churches was no other than a distinct and measured pronunciation, *ib.* 193; on giving thanks "with the spirit," 1 *Jew.* 313; he quotes Jerome for the custom of responding in the congregation, 3 *Bec.* 410; says the perpetual study of living godly is a continual prayer, 1 *Bec.* 170; two Latin prayers composed by him for St Paul's school, *Pra. Eliz.* 171, 372, 394; the same in English, *ib.* 483, 516; Latin prayers from his Precationes Aliquot, *ib.* 183, 190, 192, 202, 367, &c., 371, 372, 376, 377, 385, 389—393; English prayers from the same source, *ib.* 98, 441, 446, 450, 453, 456, 469, 483, 490, 518, 531, 533, 534, 536; Latin graces before and after meat, from the same, *ib.* 399, 402; notes respecting Latin prayers by him, *ib.* 154 n., 171 n., 197 n.; he speaks of the seventh day (the sabbath) being changed unto the eighth, 1 *Hoop.* 342; deplores that in fasting there is more superstition among Christians than ever there was among the Jews, 3 *Jew.* 528; speaks of certain heathen customs Christianized, *Calf.* 66; describes the shrines of St Thomas of Canterbury and our lady of Walsingham, 1 *Hoop.* 40 n., 1 *Tyn.* 436 n.; doubts whether it would not be better for the church if there were fewer monasteries, 4 *Jew.* 909; remarks that secret confession was unknown in the days of Jerome, 2 *Jew.* 1134, 3 *Jew.* 378, 3 *Tyn.* 214 n.; writes of the relics of saints, *Calf.* 314, 360; considers that people should not be taught by images, 1 *Hoop.* 46; says that there were men of good religion till Jerome's time, who would not allow pictures in churches, 1 *Bul.* 230, *Calf.* 8; declares they are not commanded even by man's law, 1 *Bul.* 229, *Calf.* 34; does not approve of images or relics being brought into the pulpit, *Calf.* 360

vii. *Miscellanea:* he speaks of some learned men who thought themselves half gods, and with high looks despised poor grammarians, 4 *Jew.* 1057; considered the discipline of the English universities preferable to the rules of monks, 3 *Jew.* 110; shews that bread means, among the Gentiles, all food, 2 *Hoop.* 240; on the word ἀντιπελαργέω, 1 *Bul.* 272; his story of the fiery dragon, 1 *Ful.* 368; adages explained; à remo ad tribunal, 3 *Jew.* 395; asini umbra, *Calf.* 115 n.; dares Entellum, *ib.* 2; Dionysius Corinthi, 1 *Bul.* 295; Euripus, a tempestuous gulf, 4 *Bul.* 212 n.; herbam præbens, 3 *Bul.* 69 n.; hinnulus leonem, *Calf.* 2; ne sutor ultra crepidam, *ib.* 263 n.; odium Vatinianum, 1 *Bul.* 340; omnem movere lapidem, 3 *Bul.* 182 n.; proterviam fecit, 1 *Hoop.* 484; similes habent labra lactucas, *Calf.* 251 n., *Whita.* 187 n.; summum jus summa injuria, 1 *Bul.* 341; picking out crows' eyes, *ib.* 343; avoiding the coal pit and falling into the lime-kiln, *ib.* 376; marry a wife of thine own degree, *ib.* 404; conscience a thousand witnesses, *ib.* 436; the fig-tree spoken of as infirm, 2 *Bul.* 428 n.; a proverb on deceit, 3 *Bul.* 97 n

Erasmus [Bierus]: a friend of Coverdale, 2 *Cov.* 514, 517; the same (?) Erasmus and his wife saluted, 3 *Zur.* 236; his death, *ib.* 255

Erasmus, bp of Strasburgh: 2 *Zur.* 92

Erastus, chamberlain of Corinth: 1 *Bul.* 387

Erbius (......): 3 *Zur.* 331

Erdfurt: conferences there, 2 *Zur.* 127

Erectheus: offered up his daughter, 2 *Jew.* 734

Eremites: *v.* Hermits.

Eric XIV., king of Sweden: a suitor of queen Elizabeth, 1 *Zur.* 24, 34 n., 46, 83, 89 n., 2 *Zur.* 66; expected in England, 1 *Zur.* 90 n., but he never came, 4 *Jew.* 1239 n.; his suit dismissed, 1 *Zur.* 102; he prepares for war with Denmark, 2 *Zur.* 106

Eric (Duke) of Brunswick, son of Eric duke of Hanover: 2 *Zur.* 106

Erigena (Jo. Scotus): *v.* Scotus.

Erinilus (Pet.): *v.* Crinitus.

Erith, co. Kent: an irruption of the Thames there, 3 *Tyn.* 77

Erithian sea: the Red sea, 4 *Bul.* 262

Erkenwald (St): account of him, 3 *Bec.* 43 n.; idolatrous altars built to him, *ib.* 240, 265; we are taught by God's word not to trust in him, *ib.* 43

Erlach (Benedict): mention of him and Erlach (Wolfgang) his son: 2 *Zur.* 333

Erle (Jo.), prebendary of Winchester: in prison for nonconformity, *Park.* 103

Erne (......): 2 *Zur.* 333, 335

Ernest, duke of Lunenburg: signed the confession of Augsburgh, 2 *Zur.* 15 n

Ernulph: *v.* Arnulph.

Errol (Andrew earl of): v. Hay.
Error: v. Heresy.
All errors are not damnable, 3 *Tyn.* 33; a good man may err in some things, and yet be saved, *ib.* 127; if men are in error, it does not follow that they are without the Holy Spirit, *Whita.* 296; the best men have fallen into error, 1 *Hoop.* 28; there was error in the apostolic church, 4 *Bul.* 303; there are some errors of doctrine and faith, some of life and manners, *ib.* 35; the error of those who will not have sacramental speeches expounded sacramentally, *ib.* 286
Erskine (... lord): at a conference at York, 1542, 3 *Zur.* 237 n
Erskine (Jo.), earl of Mar: one of the confederate lords, 1 *Zur.* 193 n., 197 n.; chosen regent of Scotland, *ib.* 262
Erskine (Jo.), next earl of Mar: ambassador to queen Elizabeth, 2 *Zur.* 332
Erskine (Jo.) of Dun, superintendent of Angus and Mearns: a layman, 2 *Zur.* 364
Erst: before, *Phil.* 14
Erythrea, the Sibyl: speaks of one God, the creator, &c., *Hutch.* 177
Esau: his birth, 2 *Bul.* 364; what he rejected, 1 *Tyn.* 523; his deception, 2 *Hoop.* 272; he banished Jacob, *Pil.* 256; Esau and his posterity, *ib.* 219
Esay: v. Isaiah.
Eschnavius (Matth.?), a prefect: 2 *Cov.* 517, 528; Lewis his son, *ib.* 524
Escot (Chr.): a commissioner for a royal visitation in the North, 1 *Zur.* 73 n
Esdras, i. e. Ezra, *q. v.*
Esel: v. Eisel.
Essence: meaning of the term, 3 *Bul.* 158, *Now.* (101); that of God one, 3 *Bul.* 154
Essenes: not identical with the Therapeutæ, 2 *Ful.* 101 n.; they enjoined community of goods, *Rog.* 353; deemed all swearing as bad as forswearing, *ib.* 358
Essex: a murder there discovered by a sheep, 1 *Zur.* 109
Essex (Earls of): v. Bourchier, Cromwell, Devereux, Parr.
Essex (Jo.), alias Sturvey, *q. v.*
Estate: a title of courtesy, *Hutch.* 344
Esther, queen: *Pil.* 310, 660; a fast ordained in her time, 2 *Bul.* 162; her prayers, 4 *Bul.* 225; Darius her son, *Pil.* 14
— The book of Esther, 2 *Cov.* 18; why omitted in some ancient catalogues of the Old Testament scriptures, *Whita.* 57, 58
— The Rest of Esther: its claims to be canonical considered, 1 *Ful.* 25, &c., *Whita.* 71, &c., disallowed by Jerome, 1 *Ful.* 26; contrary to the canonical book, *ib.* 27
Esthonia: its voluntary submission to Sweden, 2 *Zur.* 106 n
Estius (Gul.): Comm. in Sentent., 1 *Lat.* 384 n
Esto mihi: Quinquagesima Sunday so called, *Pra. Eliz.* 232
Estulphus, king of Lombardy: 2 *Tyn.* 261
Estwick (Rob.): Grindal's gentleman usher, *Grin.* 461
Etchells, in Stockport, co. Chester: v. Eccles.
Eternal: v. Ever.
Ethan, the Ezrahite: 3 *Bul.* 180
Ethelbert, king of Kent: his history, *Calf.* 306, 1 *Jew.* 299, 300, 4 *Jew.* 779, *Pil.* 516; called Adelbright, 3 *Jew.* 164 n.; he established Christianity by laws, 2 *Ful.* 123; copy of his charter (spurious) containing a donation of the site of St Augustine's abbey, 4 *Jew.* 781
Ethelbert (St), of Hertford: *Bale* 192
Etheldreda (St): was wife of king Egfride, but took the habit of a nun, 2 *Ful.* 12, *Pil.* 590
Ethelfride, king of Northumberland: 3 *Jew.* 164 n., 4 *Jew.* 780, *Pil.* 516
Ethelred, king of Mercia: Oftfor consecrated by his commandment, 2 *Ful.* 17, 24
Ethelwald, king of Northumberland: built a monastery, 2 *Ful.* 19
Ethelwold, bp of Winchester: thrust out married priests, *Pil.* 574
Etheridge (Geo.): v. Edridge.
Ethiopia: v. Church, Prester John.
The land of Prester John, 1 *Jew.* 334; form of the Ethiopic thau, *Calf.* 107 n
Ethnicks: Gentiles, 3 *Bec.* 602, 603, *Now.* (101), *Sand.* 256, &c.
Eton, co. Bucks: the French ambassador confined there 1 *Zur.* 132 n.; the college, 3 *Jew.* 111; prayers were said there for the repose of Henry VI., 3 *Tyn.* 122; letter by queen Elizabeth on the unauthorized election of a provost (R. Bruerne), *Park.* 149; letter from Parker to the provost and fellows, *ib.* 162
Eton (Guy): v. Eaton.
Eton (Jefere) and
Eton (Tho.), his brother, 2 *Cran.* 266
Eton (Tho.): v. Eaton.
Eu (Will. earl of): v. Bourchier.
Euangelion (Εὐαγγέλιον): v. Gospel.
Euborn: v. Enbourne.
Eubulus: 1 *Jew.* 194
Eucharist: v. Supper of the Lord.

EUCHARIST — EUSEBIUS

Meaning of the word as used by Irenæus, 1 *Jew.* 145

Eucherius of Lyons: affirms that the primitive language was Hebrew (pseud.), *Whita.* 113; says the kingdom of God is the church, wherein (Christ) every day drinks his blood by his saints, &c., 3 *Jew.* 520 n.; on posture in prayer, *Whita.* 591; on thunder, *Bale* 245; perhaps he was the author of the books De Vocatione Gentium, 2 *Ful.* 353 n.; the history of St Maurice under his name, 2 *Bec.* 91 n

Euchites: v. Messalians.

Eudæmon-Joannes (Andr.): *Calf.* 5 n

Eudo de Stella: professed to be Christ, *Rog.* 162

Eudoxia, empress: bore the charge of certain lights, *Calf.* 299; desired Chrysostom to bless Theodosius his godson, 2 *Ful.* 108; banished Chrysostom, 2 *Cran.* 12

Eudoxius, bp of Antioch, afterwards of Constantinople, his election to the former see, 1 *Jew.* 407; his heresy condemned, 1 *Bul.* 13

Eudoxius, a bishop: his saying in the council of Chalcedon, 3 *Jew.* 225, 229

Eugenius, a godly bishop: *Rid.* 147

Eugenius I. pope: brought in bishops' prisons, 3 *Whitg.* 405, 447, 449

Eugenius III. pope: v. Bernard, vi.

He allowed Gratian's decrees, 3 *Jew.* 312; calls him the foundation of canon law, *ib.* 132

Eugenius IV. pope: 2 *Ful.* 222 n.; condemned by the council of Basil, 1 *Jew.* 35, 67, 406, 4 *Jew.* 927, 955, 1105, 1111; he calls the council of Florence, *Rid.* 135 n.; determines the question of the Lord's supper there, 1 *Lat.* 209 n.; his Instructio Armeniorum wrongly ascribed to that council, *Calf.* 247 n.; he there in vain attempted to persuade the Greeks to allow transubstantiation, 3 *Bec.* 426; he says the sacraments of the old testament only shadowed forth salvation, but the sacraments of the new do confer and work salvation, *Rog.* 248 n

Eulalius, abp of Carthage: reconciled to the church of Rome, 2 *Ful.* 71 n., 1 *Jew.* 416, 417

Eulalius, bp of Thessalonica, or Alexandria: feigned letter of Boniface II. to him, 1 *Jew.* 417, 418

Eulogius, a heretic: 2 *Ful.* 381

Eulogius, a philosopher: 2 *Jew.* 981

Eunomians, heretics: 3 *Whitg.* 310; they divided the substance of the Trinity, *Rog.* 44; erred respecting the divinity of the Son, *ib.* 48; said that Christ had a body without a soul, *ib.* 52; opposed relics, *ib.* 224

Eunomius, bp of Cyzicus: his heresy, 1 *Ful.* 213, 2 *Ful.* 43, 387, *Phil.* 382 n., 424, 425; subdued by means of a council, 4 *Jew.* 1095

Eunuch (The Ethiopian): 1 *Bul.* 73, 387, 2 *Bul.* 23, 3 *Bul.* 24, 4 *Bul.* 94, 310, 311, *Pil.* 149; he believed before he was baptized, 4 *Bul.* 312; yet he was baptized, *ib.* 346

Eunuchs: on the text Matt. xix. 11, 1 *Ful.* 480

Euphemia (St): martyred, 2 *Jew.* 661

Euphrates: referred to in Nehemiah, *Pil.* 384; the four angels bound therein, *Bale* 359; the river dried up, *ib.* 484

Euphrosyna: dwelt thirty-six years in monk's apparel among monks, 4 *Jew.* 650

Eupsychius, bp of Cæsarea, and martyr: he was married, 3 *Jew.* 125, 409, &c., 4 *Jew.* 805

Eures (The lord): v. Evers.

Euripides: was torn of dogs, 2 *Cov.* 132; cited, 2 *Cov.* 110, 1 *Ful.* 201, 3 *Whitg.* 432; verses, in commendation of marriage, *ib.* 398; on those whose God is their belly, *Wool.* 44; his improper reflections on death, 2 *Cov.* 54; he says men are mad when they bestow vain cost on dead bodies, *ib.* 109

Euripus: a proverb on it, 4 *Bul.* 212

Eusebius, bp of Emissa: referred to, *Rid.* 200; his Homilies, *Jew.* xxxvi; he speaks of remission of sins in baptism, 1 *Jew.* 487, and of regeneration thereby, 2 *Hoop.* 430, *Hutch.* 241; says that the eucharist was consecrated that the thing once offered for our ransom might continually be had in remembrance through a mystery, 3 *Bec.* 444; speaks of Christ's everlasting sacrifice as evermore present by grace, 1 *Brad.* 97 n., 1 *Jew.* 467, 479, 486, 2 *Jew.* 741, *Rid.* 201; asserts that the invisible Priest turns the visible creatures into the substance of his body and blood, by his word, with secret power, 1 *Jew.* 519, 2 *Jew.* 573, 577; prescribes that we look upon the holy body and blood of our God with faith, 2 *Bec.* 295, 3 *Bec.* 432, 1 *Jew.* 12, 539, 3 *Jew.* 549; asserts a mutation of the recipient into Christ, 2 *Hoop.* 430, *Hutch.* 241; his homily on the abomination of desolation, 4 *Jew.* 728; a homily attributed to him and also to Cæsarius of Arles, *Calf.* 193 n

Eusebius, bp of Nicomedia: a chief pillar of the Arians, 1 *Jew.* 386, *Phil.* 310 n.; Arius writes to him, *ib.* 296 n.; he was convicted of blasphemy by the scriptures, *Whita.* 563; Jerome says he baptized Constantine, 4 *Jew.* 1004; he calls Paulinus, bishop of Tyre, "lord," 2 *Whitg.* 387

Eusebius Pamphilus, bp of Cæsarea: *v.* Hegesippus, Ruffinus.
   i. *His Life and Works.*
   ii. *Scripture, Doctrine.*
   iii. *Church history.*
   iv. *The Church and its Ministry.*
   v. *Sacraments, Worship, Ceremonies.*
   vi. *Heresies.*
   vii. *Miscellanea.*

   i. *His life and works:* he was a semi-Arian, *Phil.* 310 n.; but he forsook heresy, 2 *Jew.* 802; did not persist in favouring Arianism after the holding of the first Nicene council, 2 *Ful.* 359 n.; his opinions on various subjects, 3 *Zur.* 228, 229; he preached at Constantine's inauguration, *Sand.* 56; Constantius said he was worthy to be bishop of all the world, 1 *Jew.* 362; his works, *Jew.* xxxvi; why his writings were anathematized at the second council of Nice, 2 *Ful.* 359 n.; his Ecclesiastical History, *Pil.* 682; his Chronicle falsified, 2 *Ful.* 190, 236, 237, 337 nn.; Baronius and Bellarmine rely on a falsified translation of his Chronicle, *Calf.* 321 n.; Matthew Palmer, a Florentine, one of the continuators of it, 4 *Jew.* 733 n.; shameless corruption in a Latin version of his work De Vita Constantini, *Calf.* 278 n

   ii. *Scripture, Doctrine:* he calls the scriptures ἐνδιαθήκους, *Whita.* 28; on the canon of scripture, *ib.* 306, 307; on the date of St Matthew's gospel, *ib.* 520; he states that the church of Rome formerly denied the epistle to the Hebrews to be Paul's, *ib.* 106; says the Greek version of that epistle is ascribed to Luke or Clement, *ib.* 125, 2 *Whitg.* 120; seems to think James's epistle not written by him, 1 *Ful.* 16, 33, 222, 2 *Ful.* 384, 3 *Jew.* 433; his doubts concerning that of Jude, 1 *Ful.* 16 n., 222; on apocryphal books received by the old heretics, *Rog.* 82; his reasons for rejecting writings falsely ascribed to the apostles, *Whita.* 314; he rejects the gospel of Peter, *ib.* 327; says the gospels of Thomas, Bartholomew, and Nicodemus, were forged by heretics, 3 *Jew.* 441; names the gospel according to the Hebrews as a spurious book, 1 *Jew.* 238; rejects Peter's Dispute with Apion, *Whita.* 315; says that the Pastor of Hermas was publicly read in the church, *Rog.* 325 n.; records that the churches read openly certain epistles of Clement and Dionysius of Corinth, 1 *Bul.* 10, *Rog.* 324, 3 *Whitg.* 345; cited on apostolic tradition, *Whita.* 570, 571, 587; he declares it an evident token that men hate God, when they will have themselves to be called God, 2 *Jew.* 907, 4 *Jew.* 843; his sentiments on the Λόγος, 3 *Zur.* 228; on free-will, &c., *ib.* 229; he says the divine doctrines may be learned by women as by men, &c., *Whita.* 249; declares that Christians have no care of corporal circumcision, nor of keeping the sabbath, nor of abstaining from meats, 4 *Bul.* 292, 293

   iii. *Church history:* he commends Christianity for its antiquity, tracing it even to Adam, 3 *Bul.* 292, 2 *Jew.* 614, 4 *Jew.* 725, *Wool.* 15—18; mentions how carefully genealogies were kept by the Jews, 4 *Jew.* 761; calls Peter the greatest of the apostles, &c., 1 *Jew.* 428; mentions him as speaking before the rest, 1 *Whitg.* 160, 162; strange interpolation in Jerome's version of the Chronicon with regard to Peter's long-continued residence at Rome, 2 *Ful.* 337 n.; he says that Peter and the other apostles of Christ were married men, 3 *Jew.* 392; records Peter's exhortation to his wife at her martyrdom, 3 *Bec.* 235 n., 3 *Jew.* 421, 4 *Jew.* 1142; says that Peter was crucified at Rome under Nero, 1 *Bul.* 315 n., 1 *Cov.* 362 n., 2 *Cov.* 132 n.; states that Paul was married, 2 *Jew.* 727; thinks that by his "yoke-fellow" he meant his wife, 3 *Jew.* 414; says that he was slain with the sword, 1 *Bul.* 315 n., 2 *Cov.* 132 n.; asserts that the church of Rome was founded by Peter and Paul, *Phil.* 26; mentions that the knees of James grew hard, like those of a camel, with kneeling, 1 *Bec.* 143 n., 2 *Bec.* 140 n., *Sand.* 38; says that James ruled the church after the apostles, 2 *Whitg.* 252, and that he was bishop of Jerusalem, and after him Simeon son of Cleophas, *ib.* 136, 252; speaks of John's government of the churches after his return from Patmos, *Rog.* 328 n., 2 *Whitg.* 140, 230, 427, 428; relates how he sought out and recovered a young man departed from the right way, 1 *Hoop.* 170 n., *Hutch.* 114, 2 *Jew.* 945; tells how this apostle shunned Cerinthus the heretic, 2 *Bul.* 329, 1 *Bul.* 363, 4 *Bul.* 535, 4 *Jew.* 1100 n.; says he wore on his head a plate (πέταλον), 2 *Brad.* 380, 2 *Ful.* 113, 2 *Whitg.* 16, 22, 23, 25, 27, 1 *Zur.* 160 n., 350; his authority for this statement, 2 *Ful.* 113 n.; he says St Mark preached at Alexandria,

308 EUSEBIUS

1 *Jew.* 353; states that no list of the seventy disciples is found, *Calf.* 69; speaks of Dionysius the Areopagite being made the first bishop of Athens, 2 *Whitg.* 130, and of Crescens as sent to France, *Rog.* 329 n.; calls Timothy bishop of Ephesus, 2 *Whitg.* 294; cited with regard to a statue said to have been erected to Simon Magus, *Calf.* 343 n., 4 *Jew.* 843; he speaks of the flight of the Christians from Jerusalem to Pella, 1 *Whitg.* 380; relates that Tiberius desired Christ to be worshipped as a god, 1 *Jew.* 216, *Pil.* 683; says that the Christian religion from the beginning for very spite was called new and strange, 4 *Jew.* 776, and an impious heresy, *ib.* 1148, and the heresy of godless Christians, 3 *Jew.* 215; mentions Pliny's letter to Trajan about the Christians, 1 *Bec.* 17 n., *Pil.* 333; on writings falsely ascribed to Clement of Rome, 1 *Jew.* 111, *Whita.* 565; he says that when Polycarp by tradition had received certain things of them that had seen the life of the Word, he uttered the same, being all agreeable to the scriptures, 3 *Jew.* 437; describes the difference of judgment between Polycarp and Anicetus, *Calf.* 269; he says that when Polycarp stood to be judged, the people stirred up the president to slay all who professed the gospel, 3 *Jew.* 624; relates how he refused to deny his King, *Sand.* 218, and chose the flames rather than to swear by Cæsar's fortune, 1 *Bul.* 248, 1 *Hoop.* 478; narrates his martyrdom, *ib.* vi, *Pil.* 365 n.; mentions the gathering up of his bones, &c., 2 *Ful.* 188, 1 *Hoop.* 347; his account of the doctrines of Papias, 4 *Bul.* 537, 2 *Whitg.* 434 n., and those of Nepos, *Rog.* 154; he tells how Ignatius exhorted to adhere to the apostolic tradition, *Whita.* 570, 571; his account of the last exhortation of Ignatius, 1 *Ful.* 165; his Chronicle falsified for the purpose of maintaining that Lent was instituted by Telesphorus, and that Pius I. commanded that the feast of Easter should be kept on Sunday, 2 *Ful.* 236, 237; he records that Justin the martyr was first allured to the faith by the cruelty of tyrants, and the constancy and patience of God's saints, 3 *Jew.* 190, 558, 604; describes his apparel, *ib.* 615, 2 *Whitg.* 37; mentions the punishment inflicted on one who falsely accused Apollonius, *Sand.* 130; tells how rain, with thunder and lightning, was obtained by the prayers of the Christian soldiers of Marcus Aurelius, 1 *Bul.* 382, 383; his account of Hegesippus, *Whita.* 574; he says the contention about the keeping of Easter for a long time troubled the churches of the East and West, 4 *Bul.* 504; tells that Irenæus openly reproved pope Victor, 4 *Jew.* 1046; mentions a rash act of Origen when a boy, which Demetrius afterwards objected to him, 1 *Whitg.* 455; reports how Demetrius was displeased because Origen being a layman taught in the church, bishops being present, *ib.* 453, 454; shews how he was ordained in Cæsarea by bishops, *ib.* 454, 460; says he held a provincial council against Beryllus, in Arabia, 4 *Jew.* 1125; narrates the election of Fabianus to be bishop of Rome, a dove lighting on his head, so that the whole people proclaimed him bishop, 1 *Whitg.* 451; on the idolatrous priests appointed by Maximin, 2 *Whitg.* 392; he records a revolt of the Armenians, 1 *Bul.* 378, 3 *Zur.* 746; referred to about the emperor Philip, 2 *Ful.* 355; he says Valerian's court became a church of God, 2 *Jew.* 1033, 3 *Jew.* 194; records the destruction of oratories in Diocletian's time, *Calf.* 182; says the sins of the church were the cause of the bloody persecutions under Diocletian and Maximinian, 2 *Bul.* 73, 74; states that as many emperors, &c., as persecuted the preaching of the gospel, and advanced idolatry, died a foul and shameful death, 2 *Bul.* 13; notes the miserable end of Maximian, *ib.* 80; speaks of a copy of the emperor's writ whereby he commanded a council to be kept in Rome in the time of pope Miltiades, 4 *Jew.* 996, 1000; mentions the judgment of certain Donatists being committed to Miltiades and others, *ib.* 965; he preached at the inauguration of Constantine, *Sand.* 56; mentions the cross shewn to that emperor, *Calf.* 110, 111; describes his banner with the cross, 2 *Ful.* 140, 148, 2 *Jew.* 650, 651; records the prayer which he taught his soldiers, *Pil.* 413; mentions that he waged war against Licinius, his sister's husband, in the quarrel of the afflicted Christians, *Sand.* 109; tells how he disburthened the church of heretics, *ib.* 248; describes the thanksgivings offered when he had obtained peace for the church, *Calf.* 294; mentions that he used to say to the godly bishops, "Be you bishops within the church, and I will be bishop without," 4 *Jew.* 992; says that Constantine, as if he had been a common bishop appointed by God, assembled councils, 2 *Ful.* 358, 4 *Jew.* 1000, 1016; asserts that the council of Nice was called by him, *Rog.* 204 n.; describes his behaviour there, 4 *Jew.* 1015—1018, *Whita.* 436; says

that he confirmed that synod, 1 *Jew.* 412; mentions his instruction and commands against idolatry, 2 *Bec.* 71 n., 305 n.; states that he commanded all nations to rest from labour on Sundays, 2 *Jew.* 702; says that at the time of ecclesiastical sermons he stood upright, for the reverence that he bare to the word of God, 4 *Jew.* 1017; affirms that he was baptized, not in the flourishing state of his age, but only a little before he died, 4 *Jew.* 1003, 1004, and that he did not at once receive the sign of the Lord's death, 3 *Bec.* 437; the Latin translation of the Chronicle corrupted so as to make it bear witness to the invention of the cross, 2 *Ful.* 190; the continuation of his Chronicle mentions an order (an. 607) that the church of Rome should be head of all the churches, 4 *Jew.* 733

iv. *The Church and its Ministry* (see iii.): he says, the light and law of holy religion hath shined over the whole world, springing as it were from the bosom of the East, 4 *Jew.* 883; affirms that the diversity of ceremonies in the ancient church did not hinder their fellowship one with another, 4 *Bul.* 58; complains that the head rulers of the church thought they occupied the place of tyrants, rather than of priests, 2 *Cran.* 36; exposes the pride and contention that reigned in the councils of the clergy in his days, *ib.* 53; calls Demetrius bishop of the parishes of Alexandria and Egypt, 2 *Whitg.* 164, 205, 373, 428; speaks of other bishops governing several churches, *ib.* 165, 429; calls bishops of Rome elders and presidents, *ib.* 250; shews that recourse was not only had to Rome in doubtful cases, but to other churches, and to individuals, 4 *Jew.* 1044; declares how in the absence of Narcissus the governors of adjoining churches ordained another bishop, 1 *Whitg.* 450, and how Alexander was received as bishop of Jerusalem by consent of the bishops adjoining, *ib.*; shews that ministers had authority to choose bishops, *ib.* 451; referred to on a schismatical bishop being received back as a layman, *Coop.* 159 n.; describes evangelists as laying the foundations of churches, committing them to pastors whom they had ordained, and going to preach elsewhere, 1 *Whitg.* 502; speaking of Pantenus, he says there were still in his time many evangelists, *ib.* 503, 504; says Dorotheus, a priest, served the emperor in civil business, 3 *Whitg.* 455; describes an ecclesiastical school at Alexandria, 4 *Bul.* 199; speaks of noble schools at Alexandria in Egypt and in other renowned churches, *ib.* 483

v. *Sacraments, Worship, Ceremonies*: he records the baptism of Constantine, 2 *Ful.* 359, 4 *Jew.* 1003, 1004; mentions that Novatus, being baptized in sickness, did not receive the chrism, 2 *Ful.* 389; describes the sacrifice of the new testament, *Coop.* 92, 94, 1 *Jew.* 124; says that Christ made a marvellous oblation unto his Father, giving unto us to offer continually a remembrance instead of a sacrifice, 2 *Jew.* 716, 725, 735, 3 *Jew.* 337; calls the eucharist the sacrifice of praise, and the dreadful sacrifice, 2 *Jew.* 716; declares that we are taught to offer to the supreme God the sacrifices of Christ's table, *ib.* 715, 716; says, we burn the incense of prayer, and offer up the pure sacrifice, &c., *ib.* 713, 734; writes, we burn a sacrifice to God, a memorial of that great sacrifice, *ib.* 723, 724, 735; speaks of offering reasonable and unbloody oblations, *ib.* 725, 734, 735; calls prayer a pure sacrifice, *ib.* 725; he is a witness that the sacrament was anciently given to laymen in their hands, 3 *Bec.* 412, 1 *Zur.* 178 n.; cites an assertion of Irenæus that the bishops of Rome were wont to send the sacrament to other bishops in token of concord, 4 *Bul.* 430; mentions one who sent the sacrament, in one kind, to a sick person (viz. to Serapion, *q. v.*), *Phil.* 117 & al.; his account of the ministration of the communion by Novatus the heretic, 1 *Jew.* 153; the canon law says the mass was made by St James and him, *Pil.* 501, 502; he says that the Eastern churches immediately after the time of the apostles sang psalms and hymns to Christ our Lord, 4 *Bul.* 193; describes the churches of his day, and their furniture, 2 *Ful.* 149, 1 *Jew.* 311; speaks of one altar placed in the midst, 2 *Jew.* 636, and of the reverend, great, and only altar, *ib.*; mentions lights in the church, sufficient to afford light to the worshippers, 3 *Jew.* 178; cited with reference to the appointment of cemeteries, 1 *Whitg.* 535, 537; erroneously cited for the tonsure, 2 *Ful.* 115, 116

vi. *Heresies*: he mentions the sect of Artemon, 1 *Bec.* 418 n.; his account of Bardesanes and his heresy, 2 *Bul.* 363; he speaks of Basilides and his new prophets, *Rog.* 82 n.; mentions a council held against Beryllus, 4 *Jew.* 1125; says Cerinthus brought in his devices under the pretence of revelations, 3 *Jew.* 235; relates how St John shunned his company, 2 *Brad.* 329,

1 *Bul.* 363, 4 *Bul.* 535, 4 *Jew.* 1100 n.; describes the gross opinions of certain Chiliasts, 1 *Hoop.* 161 n. (as to Papias and Nepos, see p. 308, col. 1); he speaks of the judgment of certain Donatists being committed to Miltiades and others, 4 *Jew.* 965; on the Ebionite heresy, *Rog.* 48, 52, 114 nn.; on the Helchesaites, *ib.* 119 n.; on the pretensions of Manes, *ib.* 162 n.; he says the Montanists took bribes cunningly under the name of oblations, 3 *Jew.* 347; speaks of Montanus as the author of appointed days of fasting, 1 *Whitg.* 224; referred to about Novatus or Novatian, and the Novatian sect, 1 *Bec.* 94 n., 1 *Hoop.* 169 n., *Rog.* 138 n., 1 *Whitg.* 173 (see also v. above); on the heresy of Paul of Samosata, 1 *Hoop.* 83 n.; he describes his pride, 2 *Whitg.* 384; on the Severians, and their treatment of scripture, *Rog.* 84 n., 195 n., *Whita.* 35

vii. *Miscellanea:* he quotes a passage on fasting from Irenæus, 1 *Bul.* 433, 434; says, some think they ought to fast only one day, others two, others more (in Lent), 3 *Jew.* 439; disapproves of the marriage of the clergy, 3 *Zur.* 229; says, Dionysius, bishop of Corinth, wrote to Penytus, bishop of Gnosus, "Lay not that heavy burden of the necessity of chaste life upon the brethren," 3 *Jew.* 425; states that Cheremon, bishop of Nilus, was sent into banishment with his wife, *ib.* 391; records an instance of a woman who put away her husband for adultery, 1 *Hoop.* 383; referred to on image worship, *Rid.* 85; he speaks of the use of images as introduced from the heathen, 2 *Bec.* 61, *Calf.* 28, 2 *Jew.* 646, 652, 654, *Park.* 83; his reply to the empress Constantia, who asked him to send her the image of Christ, *Calf.* 145, 150; he relates stories of the impotency of the devil, 2 *Lat.* 149; describes a false miracle, 2 *Brad.* 341; says that martyrdom suffered that the church may not be divided, is no less glorious than that which is suffered for not doing idolatry, 4 *Jew.* 872; speaks of the repentance of Natalis, the martyr, after being seduced by heretics, 3 *Bul.* 76; narrates the martyrdom of Phileas, *Pil.* 565; his error with respect to the Therapeutæ, 2 *Ful.* 101

Eusebius, bp of Rome: the epistles in his name spurious, *Calf.* 322 n., 323 n.; a foolish argument from them, 1 *Jew.* 15 n.; they call Christ the head of the church, and priests his vicars, 1 *Jew.* 379; describe the invention of the cross, *Calf.* 322, 323; term confirmation a sacrament, 3 *Jew.* 456

Eusebius, bp of Samosata: called the standard of the truth, 4 *Jew.* 1045

Eusebius, bp of Verceil: supposed by some to have composed the Athanasian creed, 3 *Jew.* 254

Eusebius, presbyter of Cremona: a confession of sins ascribed to him, *Pra. Eliz.* 496; a prayer before the communion, *ib.* 519

Eusebius, the Philosopher: account of him, *Rid.* 200 n

Eusebius, a Christian man: 2 *Jew.* 1062

Eustace (James), visc. Baltinglas: his rebellion in Ireland, 1 *Zur.* 332 n

Eustathius, bp of Antioch: at Nice, 3 *Jew.* 225; condemned by heretical councils, *Rid.* 134

Eustathius, bp of Sebastia: allowed communion at home, *Coop.* 127: contemned the public churches and ministered in corners, 2 *Ful.* 89; depised married priests, *Pil.* 565; made religion to consist in a peculiar dress, 1 *Zur.* 159, 348; condemned by the council of Gangra, *Coop.* 127, 1 *Jew.* 194, 1 *Zur.* 360; deposed, 2 *Whitg.* 28, 29, 41; thought by some to have been the author of the Regulæ Contractiores ascribed to Basil, 2 *Ful.* 161 n

Eustathius, abp of Thessalonica: on Ἐφέσια γράμματα, 1 *Brad.* 592

Eustochium, daughter of Paula: 3 *Zur.* 5

Euthymius, patriarch of Constantinople (?): his alleged address to the girdle of the virgin, 1 *Jew.* 535 n., 536

Euthymius Zigabenus: Comm. in iv. Evangelia, *Jew.* xxxvi; he calls the sacrament the table on which lies the mystical supper of Christ, 3 *Bec.* 388; says the bread has a certain likeness to Christ's body, and the wine to his blood, 3 *Jew.* 510; writes, we may not look barely upon these things, but must imagine some other matter, and behold it with our inner eyes, *ib.* 470; admits that Mary was not faultless, 2 *Lat.* 226 n.; referred to on Simon being called Peter, 2 *Ful.* 278, 287; on the sign of the cross, *ib.* 167

Eutropius (Fl.): the continuations of Paul the Deacon and Landulphus Sagax mistaken for his history, 4 *Bul.* 515, *Calf.* 71 n., 138, 176, *Park.* 92

Eutropius, presb. Long.: Tract. de Jur. ac Priv. Imp., *Jew.* xxxvi, 1 *Jew.* 240, 3 *Jew.* 331, 4 *Jew.* 682, 1034

Eutyches: his heresy, 1 *Bec.* 278, 3 *Bul.* 261, 4 *Bul.* 455, 2 *Cov.* 348 n. & addenda,

1 *Hoop.* 64, 65, 2 *Hoop.* 74, *Lit. Edw.* 508, (557), *Now.* (48), 166, *Phil.* 185 n., 423, *Rid.* 176, 200 ; how he was deceived, 1 *Jew.* 497; he said that the body of the Lord which was born of Mary is not (now) of our substance, but made equal to his divinity, 1 *Jew.* 481, 482, 2 *Jew.* 699, 3 *Jew.* 258; his profession of faith, 3 *Jew.* 226; he alleged fathers, 1 *Jew.* 22, 498, 3 *Jew.* 226, 4 *Jew.* 783; expressed his desire to die in the faith of his ancestors, 2 *Jew.* 694; the second council of Ephesus took part with him, 1 *Jew.* 35; how he was rebuked by Eudoxius, 3 *Jew.* 229; how by Leo, *ib.* 468; refuted by Vigilius Tapsensis, 2 *Cov.* addenda; subdued by means of a council, 4 *Jew.* 1095; condemned by the council of Chalcedon, 1 *Bul.* 14, 1 *Jew.* 366, 461, 3 *Jew.* 224

Eutychian, bp of Rome: shews how certain heretics beguiled the simple, 1 *Jew.* 497; said to have ordained the offertory, 3 *Bec.* 264, 2 *Brad.* 308

Eutychius: disinterred the dead, *Pil.* 652

Eutychians: their heresy, 2 *Ful.* 391, *Phil.* 184 n.; they denied the true humanity of Christ, *Rog.* 51; confounded his two natures, *ib.* 54; denied the reality of his passion, *ib.* 57; how confuted, *Rid.* 283

Evagrius: his History, *Jew.* xxxvi; he is the first who speaks of the picture sent to Abgarus, *Calf.* 41 n.; he writes about the council of Ephesus, 1 *Jew.* 66, 374; says it was called by Theodosius the younger, *Rog.* 204 n.; records words of John bp of Antioch in that synod, *Whita.* 678; preserves words of Cyril, 3 *Jew.* 228, 229; speaks of the assembling of a council at Constantinople, 4 *Jew.* 1003; passages shewing that councils were subject to the emperor, *ib.* 1022, 1023, 1025; he records a revolt of the Armenians against the Persians, 3 *Zur.* 746; referred to about Justinian, *Calf.* 305 ; he says pope Vigilius accused pope Sylverius of treason because he would have betrayed the city of Rome to the Goths, 4 *Jew.* 1034; calls Euphemius, and Gregorias bishop of Antioch, the highest priests, *ib.* 823; speaks of divisions in the church at Alexandria, 1 *Whitg.* 465; referred to about the Acephali, *Rog.* 330 n.; declares that many works of Apollinarius were ascribed to Athanasius, *Calf.* 268; he speaks of Eutychius disinterring the dead, *Pil.* 652; testifies that young children were called to eat the remains of the sacrament, 2 *Bec.* 252, 3 *Bec.* 456

Evance (Tho. ?): 2 *Lat.* 385, 394, 399

Evangelics: Protestants were so called, *Lit. Eliz.* x.

Evangelion: *v.* Gospel.

Evangelists: what they are, 4 *Bul.* 105; their office and work, 1 *Whitg.* 299, 300, 493; they have an ordinary function, *ib.* 471; how they may be said to be in our time, *ib.* 500, &c.

Evangelium Æternum: wrongly ascribed to Cyril, a Carmelite, *Rog.* 203; written by Gerhardus, *ib.* n

Evans (......); proposed as bishop of Llandaff, 2 *Cov.* 529 n., *Grin.* 283

Evans (......): goes to Scotland, *Grin.* 295

Evans (Lewis): *Calf.* 276, 331; Mr [Lewis?] Evans answered by himself, 2 *Ful.* 4

Evaristus, bp of Rome: a spurious epistle ascribed to him declares marriage without the consent of parents to be no marriage, *Sand.* 50

Eve: *v.* Adam.
Her creation, 3 *Bul.* 375, *Now.* (32), 148, *Poet.* 253; she was deceived by Satan, *Now.* (33), 148; her unmeasurable talk was the cause of the fall, 2 *Lat.* 92; she repented and took hold of the promise, 1 *Lat.* 243; was a type of the church, 1 *Brad.* 508, 1 *Ful.* 533 n., *Poet.* 253

Eve, an anchoress of Leodium: *Bale* 168

Even: equal, 1 *Tyn.* 166

Evening: *v.* Prayers.

Evens: eves or vigils, 1 *Tyn.* 450

Ever: the word has two meanings in the Hebrew, 2 *Hoop.* 335

Everite (Mabel), a child: slain by an earthquake, *Lit. Eliz.* 567

Evers (Tho.* lord): in a commission for a royal visitation in the North, 1559, 1 *Zur.* 73 n.; sent against the rebels in the North, 1569, *ib.* 214 n

Everson (......): martyred, *Poet.* 162

Evesham, co. Worcester: Latimer's complaint of two monks there, 2 *Lat.* 389; the mitre, cross, &c., pawned, *ib.* 400; the abbey dissolved, *ib.* 389 n., 400 n

Evil: *v.* Prayer (The Lord's), Sin.
What the word means, *Now.* (80), 201; God not the author of it, 1 *Brad.* 213, 214, 321, 2 *Bul.* 365, 373, 2 *Cov.* 341, 1 *Ful.* 563, *Hutch.* 65, &c.; it to be imputed to man only, *Pil.* 613; the true cause of it, 2 *Bul.* 368, *Hutch.* 66; how God is said to cause

---

* Either the 1st or the 2nd baron Evre of Wilton; but both, according to Nicolas, bore the name of *William.* The date of the first lord's decease is not found recorded.

evil, 2 *Bul.* 382; the word sometimes means the sinful deed, sometimes the punishment thereof, *ib.* 383; all appearance of evil to be avoided, 2 *Jew.* 883; on the petition for deliverance from evil, 1 *Brad.* 136, 183, 4 *Bul.* 218 & al.; evils of the soul, 2 *Bec.* 195, 196, of the body, *ib.* 196; evils of the times displayed, *ib.* 593; what it is to be evil-minded, *ib.* 604; who are evil, *ib.* 603

Evington (......): martyred, *Poet.* 167

Evodius, bp of Hippo: *v.* Eradius.

Evre (The lord): *v.* Evers.

Ewelme, co. Oxon: this was the duke of Suffolk's estate, 3 *Zur.* 454

Examination: A briefe Examination for the Tyme of a certain Declaration, &c., 2 *Whitg.* 27, 36, 48, 57, 63, &c., 3 *Whitg.* xxvii; the nature and necessity of self-examination, *Nord.* 47

Example: God to be followed absolutely, men with caution, *Sand.* 375; the benefit of good example, *Pil.* 451; it is the most effectual way of teaching, 2 *Cran.* 124; pastors must give example of virtuous life, 1 *Bec.* 16, 17; those who teach soundly but live disorderly, kill by example, *Sand.* 246; barbarous nations impressed by the sober behaviour of captive Christian priests, *ib.*; whether examples of Jews appertain to Christians, 1 *Bul.* 326; examples of undoubted faith, *ib.* 91, (and see Faith, *h*), of repentance, 3 *Bul.* 111, 4 *Bul.* 549, 554, of afflictions in the patriarchs, 2 *Bul.* 103, of war, out of the scripture, 1 *Bul.* 384, of God's deliverance, 2 *Bul.* 96

Exceptio fori: what, *Phil.* 7, 35

Exchequer: *v.* Courts.

Excommunication: 2 *Cran.* 97 (Inst. of a Chr. man), 1 *Jew.* 143, 144, 3 *Jew.* 356, *Now.* (101), 1 *Whitg.* 84, 3 *Whitg.* 220, &c.; a sword, a key, and a rod, 2 *Hoop.* 51, 52; it was practised by the Jews, 1 *Ful.* 567; scriptural examples of it, 2 *Jew.* 943; it implies communion, *Coop.* 122; it is a principal part of the discipline of the church, 2 *Jew.* 942; whether an essential note of the church, 1 *Brad.* 185—187; not put away by the doctrine of election, 1 *Brad.* 327, 328; wrongful excommunication puts not out of the church, *ib.* 510, 522, 523; but right excommunication is the judgment of Almighty God, 2 *Jew.* 944; the right use of it, 1 *Tyn.* 273, 2 *Tyn.* 252, 3 *Whitg.* 101, &c.; this is now lost, *Hutch.* 323; lost by the church of Rome, through private masses, 1 *Jew.* 143; Papists excommunicate dead men, fishes, and flies, *Rog.* 311, locusts, snakes, caterpillars, &c., 1 *Jew.* 144; the ordinance much abused in England, *Grin.* 451, &c., 2 *Zur.* 163, 359; the English mode disapproved by Beza, 2 *Zur.* 129; civil excommunication, 3 *Whitg.* 266; excommunication for non-payment of costs, *ib.* 279; abuse of excommunication in some foreign churches, 2 *Zur.* 252; errors respecting it, *Rog.* 309, &c.; views of the Puritans, *ib.* 310, 311; opinion of the Anabaptists, *Hutch.* 323; its right use should be restored, 1 *Lat.* 258; argument propounded in the convocation concerning its ordinary use, *Grin.* 451; propositions for its reformation, *ib.* 454; against what persons and for what offences it should be exercised, 2 *Hoop.* 51, 52, 126, *Rog.* 308; proper against open offenders, 1 *Hoop.* 90; said to be always used against immoral persons, 1 *Whitg.* 382; such are in the church till they are cut off, *ib.* 386; on the excommunication of great men, *Pil.* 381; it is too often despised by such, *ib.* 382, 388; the ends of excommunication, *Grin.* 263, *Rog.* 312; the power of it, 4 *Bul.* 40; by whom it should be pronounced and executed, 2 *Cran.* 117, *Rog.* 308, 3 *Whitg.* 220, &c., 541, &c.; it should be by the lawful judgment of the church, *Now.* (95), 218; not to be given at the pleasure of some, but by consent of all the church, and to be done with prayer, 2 *Hoop.* 51, 52; whether the people's consent was required of old, 3 *Whitg.* 254, &c.; a form of excommunication, 2 *Jew.* 944; it was anciently for life in some cases, 1 *Jew.* 136; lugentes, audientes, and præcantes distinguished, *ib.* 143; killing an excommunicate no manslaughter by the canon law, 2 *Cran.* 74; how the excommunicate should humble themselves, 2 *Jew.* 943; how they are to be avoided, *Rog.* 307; they are to be received into the church again on repentance, *ib.* 312; whether the children of excommunicate persons may be baptized, 3 *Whitg.* 142; the excommunication of the martyr Bradford by Stephen Gardiner, 1 *Brad.* 492; that of certain members of the strangers' church at Sandwich, *Park.* 247; the δεσμὸς, or chain, a symbol of it, *Pil.* 381 n.; excommunication with bell, book, and candle, 1 *Brad.* 58, 2 *Cran.* 282 n

Excuses: vain excuses of negligence, *Pil.* 32, 41—43, 172

Execution of laws: the first and last part of good government, *Park.* 246

Execution of malefactors: *v.* Death (Punishment of).

A strange story of the execution of a traitor, 1 *Lat.* 149; another, *ib.* 163; other stories, *ib.* 164; execution of a gentleman falsely accused of murder, *ib.* 191; modes of execution, 1 *Bul.* 356; hanging, the English punishment for felony, 3 *Zur.* 205

Executors: often build churches and gild saints with another man's goods, 1 *Lat.* 22; Cyprian censures a priest for being executor of a will, 3 *Whitg.* 415

Exemption: that of monks, &c., *Calf.* 97, *Pil.* 380, 390

Exercises: *v.* Prophesyings.

Exeter: the bishop's first-fruits to the pope, 4 *Jew.* 1078; the city besieged by the rebels, 1549, 3 *Zur.* 655; letter to the chapter respecting divine service, *Park.* 107

Exeter (Marquises of): *v.* Courtenay

Exeter (Tho. earl of): *v.* Cecil.

Exhortation: we should exhort one another, 2 *Lat.* 87; An Exhortation unto Prayer, 1544, *v.* Litany; a general exhortation unto all men, *Lit. Edw.* 482; AN EXHORTATION TO THE CARRYING OF CHRIST'S CROSS, 2 *Cov.* 227, see also 1 *Brad.* 412 n., and 2 *Brad.* 267, 268, &c.; an exhortation to certain godly men, to be patient under the cross, &c., 1 *Brad.* 375; an exhortation to the brethren throughout the realm of England, *ib.* 414; two exhortations to the praise of God, by T. B.; to be sung before morning and evening prayer; from the old version of the Psalms, *Poet.* 501, 502; An Exhortation to the Byshops to deal brotherly with theyr Brethren, 3 *Whitg.* xxviii, 518 524, 1 *Zur.* 291 n.; an Exhortation to the Bishops and their Clergie to answer a little Booke, &c., 3 *Whitg.* xxviii, 518, 527, 1 *Zur.* 291 n

Exhumation: *v.* Dead.

Exile: *v.* Persecution.

A fit punishment in certain cases, *Sand.* 73; affliction in it, 2 *Bul.* 101

Exiles: *v.* Arau, Basle, Frankfort, Friesland, Geneva, Strasburgh, Zurich, &c.; also Strangers.

A list of exiles for religion, 1 *Cran.* (9); exiles at Zurich, Strasburgh, Frankfort, &c., *Grin.* 238, 239; names of some at Zurich, 3 *Zur.* 752, of some at Frankfort, *ib.* 755, 763, 764; exiles at Berne, *ib.* 162; some expelled from Wesel, *ib.* 163, 168; their removals, *ib.* 166 n.; some expelled from Basle, *ib.* 164 n.; some reside at Arau, 1 *Zur.* 88 n., 2 *Zur.* 2, 3 *Zur.* 165, 166, 167, 170, some at Vevay, 3 *Zur.* 167; dissensions amongst them, *ib.* 170; exhorted to walk without offence, *Sand.* 310,

&c.; they found many tokens of mercy, *ib.* 296; they prepare to return, *Grin.* 237; their honourable dismission from Geneva, 3 *Zur.* 765 n.; poor exiles of France and Flanders received by Elizabeth, 4 *Jew.* 1148; some in London, 1568, *ib.* 1274

Exodus: Tyndale's prologue to this book, 1 *Tyn.* 411; table expounding certain words therein, *ib.* 418; what we see in it, 2 *Cov.* 17

Exorcism: *v.* Baptism, Demons, Holy Water, Miracles.

Exorcists: ancient and modern ones, 4 *Bul.* 114, 115, 256; not mentioned in the apostolic canons, *Whita.* 509; the popish order, 3 *Jew.* 273, *Rog.* 258

Exordium commune: 3 *Jew.* 156, 159

Expectations, or Gratiæ expectativæ: papal instruments bestowing benefices prospectively, 1 *Lat.* 49 n

Expend: to weigh or consider, 3 *Tyn.* 247

Extended: confiscated, *Sand.* 82

Extortion: Zaccheus an example to extortioners, 1 *Lat.* 405, 414; extortioners warned, 1 *Bec.* 126

Extravagantes: *v.* Law (Canon).

Extreme Unction: *v.* Unction.

Extremities: God chiefly helps in great extremities; examples thereof out of the Old Testament, 3 *Bec.* 213, &c.; examples out of the New, *ib.* 215, &c.

Exuperius (St), bishop of Toulouse: carried the Lord's body in a wicker basket, 1 *Bec.* 32, 4 *Bul.* 419, 2 *Ful.* 115, 1 *Hoop.* 233, 1 *Jew.* 239, 245, 249, 2 *Jew.* 554; his liberality, 1 *Bec.* 32, 1 *Hoop.* 233; an epistle to him, 3 *Jew.* 386

Eycke (Corn. de): 1 *Zur.* 253 n

Eye (At): at a glance, *Park.* 130

Eyes: instruments to see God's will, 2 *Hoop.* 329; the eye of man, what it is, 3 *Bec.* 609; a single eye, what, *ib.*; a wicked eye, what, *ib.*

Eymericus (Nic.): Directorium Inquisitorum, 2 *Ful.* 21 n

Eysil: *v.* Eisel.

Ezechias: *v.* Hezekiah.

Ezra: when he repaired the ruins of the temple, he sent not to Ephesus; and when he purposed to restore the sacrifices, sent not to Rome, 4 *Jew.* 1047; he would not ask for a guard, *Pil.* 327; his reading of the law to the people, *Whita.* 212, 213; the sealing of the covenant, 4 *Bul.* 318; said by some to have restored the law, which, it is alleged, was lost in the captivity, *Whita.* 103, 114, 115; perhaps he arranged the scriptures, and added some things, *ib.* 116,

518, 519; said by Jerome to have changed the shape of the Hebrew letters, *ib.* 116

— Book of Ezra: its contents, 2 *Cov.* 18; Pilkington's exposition of it, not known to be extant, *Pil.* xvi, 308, 367; the name Esdras sometimes includes the books of Ezra and Nehemiah, 2 *Ful.* 222 n

— III. and IV. Esdras: not received by the church of Rome, *Whita.* 103, yet deemed canonical by some Romanists, *ib.* 103, 104; the former book cited by some fathers, *ib.* 68; fabulous stories in the latter, *ib.* 103

F

F. (A.): his preface to Hooper's Exposition, 2 *Hoop.* 181

F. (Sir Rob.): 2 *Cran.* 258

Faber (Basil): 2 *Zur.* 77 n

Faber (Geo. Stanley): *Calf.* 78 n

Faber (Guido): his speech in the council of Trent, whither he went as the French king's ambassador, *Jew.* xxxvi, 4 *Jew.* 908, 916, 947, 948, 949, *Rog.* 210

Faber (Jac.), Stapulensis: was in favour of translating the scriptures, 1 *Tyn.* 162 n.; he allows that there are many gross errors in the Vulgate, 4 *Jew.* 907; reproves the word "adjutores," 1 Cor. iii. 9, the rendering of συνεργοί, 1 *Ful.* 383; asserts the excellence of the Apocalypse, *Bale* 515; accounts the false epistle to the Laodiceans genuine, *Whita.* 303; declares that Christ gave his body to his disciples, but after a sacramental and spiritual manner, 3 *Bec.* 450; says that when he gives his flesh to eat and blood to drink, he gives them not after a carnal manner, *ib.* 435, 450; speaks against prayer in an unknown tongue, *Whita.* 273; finds fault with the forbidding of priests' marriage, 2 *Jew.* 993 n., 3 *Jew.* 417; his story of Valens the monk, 2 *Cran.* 42; he published a Latin version of a spurious epistle of Ignatius, *Calf.* 290 n., 2 *Ful.* 235 n., 237 n

Faber (Jo.), bp of Vienna: writes against the confession of Augsburgh, 2 *Jew.* 103 n.; cites Isidore on the mass, *Pil.* 503; notice of a pamphlet against him by Bullinger, 4 *Bul.* xvi.

Faber (Jo.), Dominican: a prayer pro vera fide, from his Precationes Christianæ, *Pra. Eliz.* 378

Faber (J.): his book on the religion of the Muscovites states that they added warm water to the wine in the Lord's supper, *Rog.* 295 n

Faber (Martin): 3 *Zur.* 539

Fabian (St), bp of Rome: his election, 1 *Whitg.* 451; fiction of his having baptized the Roman emperor Philip and his son, 2 *Ful.* 355 n.; said to have appointed seven deacons, and seven notaries, to record the acts of martyrs, *Bale* 187; cited as calling confirmation a sacrament, *Calf.* 222; said to have ordered that the oblation of all men and women should be made every Sunday, 1 *Jew.* 177; said to have decreed that all should communicate at least thrice a year, 2 *Bec.* 259, 3 *Bec.* 380, 1 *Jew.* 176; martyred at Rome under Decius, 2 *Hoop.* 109; his epistles forged, 1 *Jew.* 173; erroneously referred to, 3 *Bec.* 425

Fabian (Edw.): v. Fabyan.

Fabian (Rob.): his Chronicle, *Jew.* xxxvii; he says Lucius changed flamines for bishops, *Pil.* 597; describes the idols of the Saxons, *ib.* 16; narrates the acts of Augustine, *ib.* 516; speaks of his baptizing in the river Swale, *ib.* 518; says the bishop of St David's had no pall from Rome, *ib.* 583; records the rebellion of abp Arundel, 3 *Jew.* 171; affirms that for a thousand years, bishops and priests lived together with their wives, no law being to the contrary, *ib.* 395

Fabianis (Parius de): 2 *Cran.* 555

Fabius: his definition of a sign, 4 *Bul.* 227

Fabius Maximus: his fortitude, 2 *Cov.* 124

Fabius, bp of Antioch: *Coop.* 159 n

Fabricius (Erasmus), or Schmidt, canon of Zurich: perhaps referred to by his Christian name, 3 *Zur.* 236, 255, but see Erasmus [Bierus]; mention of his son, *ib.* 681

Fabricius (Geo.): poems by him, viz.—pro felici in literis successu, *Pra. Eliz.* 408; meditatio cubitum euntis, *ib.* 410; de vera Christianorum felicitate, *ib.* 416; the Tridentine Index censures a passage in his edition of the Christian Poets against image-worship, *Rog.* 222 n.; the Belgic Index condemns a statement in the same book, that to adore the wood of the cross is manifest idolatry, *Calf.* 376 n

Fabricius (Jo.): Hist. Bibl. Fabricianæ, 2 *Ful.* 18 n., 323 n

Fabricius (Jo.), Montanus: his oration against the council of Trent, *Jew.* xxxvii, 3 *Jew.* 208, 4 *Jew.* 956

Fabricius (Jo. Alb.): works of his, *Calf.* 407, 2 *Ful.* 401, 3 *Jew.* 560 n

Fabricius (Jo. Hen.), son of the standard-bearer of Zurich: account of him, 2 *Zur.* 53; sent to England, *ib.* 53, 54; his reception there, *ib.* 60—63; he was with the earl of Bedford, 1 *Zur.* 97, who placed him in the service of Sir Fra. Knowles, vice-chamberlain, 2 *Zur.* 54, 61; he visits bishop Parkhurst, 1 *Zur.* 108, 111; returns to his own country, 2 *Zur.* 74, 75, 76; saluted, 1 *Zur.* 258, 305, 2 *Zur.* 109

Fabricius (Wolfg.), Capito, *q. v.*

Fabrotus (Car. Ann.): 2 *Ful.* 99 n

Faburden: a high sounding tone, *Bale* 536

Fabyan (Edw.), sheriff of Oxon and Berks: letter to him, *Park.* 145

Fabyan (Rob.): *v.* Fabian.

Face: the command to wash the face (Matt. vi.) explained, 2 *Bec.* 539, 540

Faculties: *v.* Courts.

Fagan: *v.* Fugatius.

Faggots: borne by way of penance, by those charged with heresy, 2 *Lat.* 326, 333, 362, 2 *Tyn.* 45; the case of Tho. Bilney, 2 *Lat.* 51; that of Jo. Tewkesbury, 1 *Tyn.* 32

Fagius (Paul): saluted, 2 *Cov.* 520; dismissed from Strasburgh, 3 *Zur.* 538, 649, 651; invited to England, *ib.* 51, 329, 476; account of his journey thither, *ib.* 331, 332; his arrival, *ib.* 67, 330 n., 652; his reception by Cranmer, *ib.* 535, 539; to go to Cambridge, *ib.* 536, 537, 539; his illness, *ib.* 558, 659; his death, 3 *Bec.* 205, 2 *Cran.* 426, 3 *Zur.* 549, 675; Burcher's opinion of him, *ib.* 663; his dead body excommunicated, *Rog.* 311; his remains disinterred and burned, 1 *Jew.* 60, *Pil.* 65 n., 217, 652, 1 *Zur.* 4 n., 2 *Zur.* 20 n., 24 n., 51; all acts against him and Bucer solemnly rescinded by the university of Cambridge, 2 *Zur.* 51; commemoration of them, 1560, *Pil.* iv; Pilkington's sermon at the restitution, *ib.* 651; Fagius cited as to the Jewish monarch's copy of the law, 4 *Jew.* 979, 980; he translated the Chaldee Targum, 2 *Jew.* 679; says, the Jews at this day keep and use the law of God with all reverence, 4 *Jew.* 763; his opinion on marriage with two sisters, *ib.* 1243; three letters by him, 3 *Zur.* 331—333; letters to him, 2 *Cov.* 526, 3 *Zur.* 32, 329; letter to him and Bucer, 3 *Zur.* 2

— His sons Paul and Timothy, 3 *Zur.* 331; one of them educated by Cranmer, 2 *Cov.* 526, 3 *Zur.* 32; Paul mentioned, *ib.* 332, 355; his daughter Charity, *ib.* 330; his daughter Sarah married Jo. Ulstetter, *ib.* 331 n

Fain: to desire, 2 *Tyn.* 231

Fairfax (Edw.): his translation of Tasso, *Calf.* 47 n

Fairs: *v.* Markets.

Faith: *v.* Analogy of faith, Assurance, Christ, Creeds, Free-will, God, Justification, Prayers, Reason, Religion, Unbelief, Works.

(a) What faith is, its nature, &c., 1 *Bec.* 81, 208, 2 *Bec.* 13, 482, 3 *Bec.* 177, 602, 609, 615, 618, 1 *Bul.* 44, 81, 82, 84, 2 *Bul.* 336, 401, 4 *Bul.* 24, 1 *Cov.* 344, 345, 1 *Hoop.* 145, 265, 513, 1 *Lat.* 61, 2 *Lat.* 88, *Nord.* 17, *Now.* (100), *Phil.* 329, 1 *Tyn.* 407, 492, 2 *Tyn.* 14, 205, 3 *Tyn.* 198; its office, 2 *Tyn.* 14; homily of the true, lively, and Christian faith, 2 *Cran.* 135; of true faith, especially in the prospect of death, 2 *Cov.* 81—86; two chief points of it, 1 *Bul.* 94; it is the substance of things hoped for, the evidence of things which do not appear, 1 *Cov.* 5, an undoubted persuasion of the mind, 1 *Bul.* 87, assured hope and confidence in Christ's mercy, 2 *Cran.* 113, an assurance to the conscience of being predestinate to be saved, 3 *Bec.* 172, 173, 1 *Brad.* 313; it consists not in learning, but in simplicity of believing, *Phil.* 134; it stands not in disputing, 2 *Brad.* 121; faith is a principal part of Christian religion, *Now.* (6), 118; the very foundation of it, 1 *Bec.* 207, 269; it is the rock on which Christ built his church, 2 *Tyn.* 281, 3 *Tyn.* 31 (*v.* Peter); the eye of our soul, 1 *Jew.* 540; sight by faith surer than by the eye, *Pil.* 215; the certainty of faith the greatest certainty, 2 *Lat.* 337; the spiritual sight by it is the true sight, 1 *Bec.* 112; it beholds the truth of God, 2 *Jew.* 934; perceives the mysteries of God, *Lit. Edw.* 512, (560); it is the hand by which we receive the benefits of God, 2 *Lat.* 170, the mouth of the soul wherewith Christ is received and eaten, 2 *Bec.* 295, *Lit. Edw.* 517, (565), the marriage garment, 1 *Lat.* 286, a buckler, *ib.* 504, the altar of God, 2 *Jew.* 735; errors respecting faith, *Rog.* 113; vain braggers of it censured, 1 *Bec.* 81, 208; there is a blind imagination, falsely called by the name, 3 *Tyn.* 275, a faithless faith, 3 *Tyn.* 199; that of the multitude of professors is a different thing from true faith, *ib.* 69, 70, 107, 114; faith is resolved by some Papists into assent to the judgment of the church, *Whita.* 341, 342; the collier's faith, to believe as the church believes, 2 *Hoop.* 543 n.; the faith of hypocrites, 2 *Tyn.* 11, 130; that of swine, or the carnal, *ib.* 11; that of wicked men and devils, 2 *Cran.* 85, 86, 133, 135, 1 *Ful.* 419, *Phil.* 413, 1 *Tyn.* 278, 2 *Tyn.* 146, 201, 3 *Tyn.* 197; faith described by James, 1 *Tyn.* 120, 125; Paul and James (*q. v.*) speak of two different kinds of faith, *Phil.* 412; some Popish writers speak of ten different kinds, or more, *ib.*; true faith and false faith distinguished, 2 *Cran.* 133, 135, 1 *Lat.* 237, 421, *Now.* (27, 28), 142—144, 1 *Tyn.* 12, 53, 493, 2 *Tyn.* 11, 3 *Tyn.* 196; there are two kinds of faith, an historical faith, and a feeling, or real, faith, *ib.* 50, 51, *Whita.* 364; general, and particular, or special, faith, 1 *Bul.* 99, 4 *Bul.* 304; it must be special, as well as general, 1 *Ful.* 415, 2 *Lat.* 10, 124; faith inspired and gotten, 1 *Bul.* 100; true faith is infused by the Holy Ghost, and thence called by the schoolmen "fides infusa;" the faith we obtain from the church is not infused, but acquired, *Whita.* 355, 448; formal and informal faith, 1 *Bul.* 100, *Calf.* 85; faith is not, as many suppose, mere assent, 1 *Tyn.* 52, 121, 278, 2 *Tyn.* 146, 154, 201, 3 *Tyn.* 197; to believe that there is a God, is not to believe in God, 1 *Tyn.* 121, 2 *Tyn.* 146; faith is not a mere opinion, but a persuasion wrought by the Holy Ghost, 1 *Brad.* 371; it is not merely to believe the histories, but to believe that Christ died for ourselves, 1 *Lat.* 420, 421, 1 *Tyn.* 123; we must believe that Christ was born and gave himself for us, 2 *Bec.* 235; true faith is an appropriating faith, 1 *Tyn.* 224; it is hard to be found, 1 *Lat.* 168; how we may ascertain that we have it, 1 *Bec.* 346, 2 *Lat.* 194; dead faith is useless, *ib.* 312, 316; faith works miracles, 1 *Tyn.* 82; but the faith which does this is not necessarily saving faith, 3 *Tyn.* 197, 199; the decline of faith in the latter days, 1 *Brad.* 376; "first faith" (1 Tim. v.), not a vow of celibacy, *Whita.* 482, 483; infants may have faith, 2 *Bec.* 211, 212; it may dwell in children though not yet declared by works, *ib.* 213, 214; faith recommended, 3 *Bec.* 164, 165; an admonition for it, 1 *Bec.* 272; it is a duty which all men owe to God, 2 *Bec.* 402, 403; it is the will of God that it should be exercised, *ib.* 156; sentences and examples of scripture encouraging to it, 1 *Bec.* 405, &c.; "have faith in God," the text expounded, *ib.* 148; the necessity of faith, *ib.* 78, 79, 98, 99; we must have it to enjoy the benefits of God, *ib.* 118; without it God's goodness profits nothing, *ib.* 147; examples of this, *ib.* 147, 148; those who lack faith are called enemies of God, 1 *Hoop.* 262; want of faith is the cause of damnation, 2 *Lat.* 206

(*b*) Its unity:—faith is one alone, 1 *Bul.* 97; antiquity of the Christian faith, 1 *Cov.* 4, 14; it is older than the Jewish dispensation, *ib.* 35; that of the fathers before Christ one with ours, 2 *Bul.* 284 (*v.* Fathers before Christ); THE OLD FAITH, translated from Bullinger by bp Coverdale, 1 *Cov.* 1, &c.; faith in Christ as Mediator, is taught in the Old Testament, *Whita.* 612; the faith of the church is one and the same in all ages, 2 *Hoop.* 519; there is one faith for all sorts of men, *Whita.* 670, 671; we end by the same faith as we begin by, *Pil.* 132

(*c*) Of its origin, increase, &c.:—it is not attainable by free-will, but is the gift of God, and the work of the Holy Ghost, 2 *Bec.* 14, 212, 1 *Brad.* 65, 435, 536, 2 *Brad.* 133, 1 *Bul.* 84, 87, 363, 1 *Hoop.* 246, 2 *Hoop.* 59, 262, *Now.* (63), 183, *Pra. B.* 89, *Sand.* 268, 1 *Tyn.* 53, 56, 413, 488, 493, 3 *Tyn.* 51, 139, 140, 192, *Whita.* 342, 355—358, 454; it is in God only to appoint when and how it shall be given, 2 *Hoop.* 220; More's vain imagination that a man may captivate his understanding to believe, 3 *Tyn.* 140; though in the external way we perfectly hold the doctrines of religion, we have not learned any dogma aright without the teaching of the Holy Spirit, *Whita.* 364; faith not ours but by God's working in us, 2 *Cran.* 129; is God's seed, given to those that be ordained to everlasting life, *Pra. B.* 65; we can be stedfast only if God give and confirm our faith, 2 *Bec.* 632, 633; it must be laid as a sure foundation, *ib.* 638; it is the foundation of religion, 1 *Bec.* 207, 269; it ever is the companion of true repentance, *ib.* 78, 2 *Bec.* 12, 3 *Bec.* 209, 3 *Bul.* 35, 62, 1 *Hoop.* 33, 1 *Lat.* 370; a part of true repentance, 1 *Bec.* 97, 98, 1 *Tyn.* 478; the foundation of repentance, 2 *Cov.* 343; repentance without faith avails nothing, 1 *Bec.* 79, 2 *Cov.* 343; lady Faith and her gentleman usher, 1 *Brad.* 40, 41; lady Faith, her usher and train, 1 *Lat.* 168, 237; faith must be conjoined with reverent fear, 1 *Bec.* 207, 208; the ordinary way to it is the preaching of God's word, 2 *Bec.* 212, 1 *Bul.* 84; it cometh by hearing, 1 *Brad.* 65, 2 *Brad.* 78, 2 *Cov.* 308, 1 *Lat.* 200, 418, 2 *Lat.* 174, *Phil.* 104, *Pil.* 112, *Sand.* 153, 1 *Tyn.* 499, *Whita.* 648; it has not at all times like strength, 2 *Hoop.* 221, 222, 248; it is always imperfect in us, 1 *Hoop.* 22; faith and the feeling of it are different, 2 *Lat.* 207; weakness of faith no cause for despair, 2 *Hoop.* 221, 222, 248; right faith is accepted, though it be weak, 1 *Hoop.* 261, 2 *Tyn.* 9, 3 *Tyn.* 208; how the weak in faith are to be guided, 1 *Tyn.* 95, 506; they should be upheld by the stronger,

FAITH

2 *Tyn.* 8; they are chastised in pity, *ib.* 9; the disciples had not much faith, 2 *Lat.* 186; of its increase, 1 *Bul.* 98, 3 *Bul.* 191; it is increased by the same means as it is gotten by, viz. the word, *Pil.* 112; we must pray for it, 1 *Bul.* 86; it is confirmed by sacraments, 2 *Cov.* 308, 2 *Ful.* 169; perfection of faith is to be sought, *Sand.* 424; of the decrease of faith, 1 *Bul.* 98; David lost not his faith when he sinned, and therefore he repented, 3 *Tyn.* 203

(*d*) Its excellence, and the good that comes by it:—the excellence of faith, 2 *Brad.* 78; it is a treasure incomparable, 2 *Hoop.* 219; esteemed of God, 2 *Lat.* 201; its power and praise, 1 *Bec.* 79, 1 *Bul.* 101, 2 *Jew.* 740; it is mistress in the soul, 1 *Hoop.* 78; it is much, it is altogether, 2 *Bec.* 604; it is true knowledge, 1 *Bul.* 101; the certainty thereof is the greatest certainty, 2 *Lat.* 337; it may be perfect, though knowledge is not clear, *ib.*; the commodities it brings to us, 2 *Bec.* 14; the benefits we receive of God through it, with probations of scripture, *ib.* 482, 483; it quickens and joins us to God, 1 *Bul.* 103; it makes a Christian man, 1 *Bec.* 269; by it only comes salvation, 1 *Tyn.* 15, 471, 3 *Tyn.* 274—276; it applies the merits of Christ's death to us, 1 *Hoop.* 50; apprehends his righteousness, *ib.* 51; the forgiveness of sins comes by it, 1 *Hoop.* 50, 1 *Lat.* 370; by it we are justified, and receive other blessings, 2 *Bec.* 638 (*v.* Justification); it only justifies, 2 *Bec.* 176, 639, 3 *Bec.* 233, 1 *Bul.* 104, 118, 2 *Bul.* 339, 1 *Cov.* 5, 3 *Jew.* 583, &c.; *Poet.* 380, *Rid.* 259, 1 *Tyn.* 46, 278, 488, 499, 2 *Tyn.* 137, 3 *Tyn.* 195—206, 274; probations of this out the scripture, 3 *Bec.* 331, &c.; translations respecting special faith and only faith examined, 1 *Ful.* 415; whilst faith only justifies, faith that is alone justifies not, 3 *Tyn.* 196; we mean not faith without other virtues following, but without any other work or deed justifying, 1 *Cov.* 6; faith is not the efficient cause of justification, but the instrumental cause, 1 *Ful.* 405, 2 *Jew.* 748, 1 *Lat.* 235, 2 *Lat.* 147, *Now.* (61), 180, 2 *Tyn.* 89, *Wool.* 32; God accepts the believer as righteous, 2 *Bec.* 636, 1 *Tyn.* 478, 497; what faith comprehends and applies to us of Christ, 2 *Hoop.* 477; through it Christ's fulfilling of the law is ours, 2 *Bec.* 636; by faith we have remission of our sins, and are made partakers of peace with God, 1 *Hoop.* 50, 2 *Jew.* 748, 1 *Lat.* 370, *Sand.* 290, 1 *Tyn.* 294; it makes us at one with him, 1 *Tyn.* 118; makes us his children, 1 *Tyn.* 63, 2 *Tyn.* 145; filleth hungry souls, 3 *Tyn.* 223; brings tranquillity of conscience, 2 *Hoop.* 300; makes happy, 1 *Bul.* 102; causes the heart to feel joys and mirth unspeakable, 2 *Hoop.* 220; establishes the mind, 1 *Bec.* 147; where the heart believes in Christ, there he dwelleth, 1 *Tyn.* 369; faith certifies us of the Spirit's presence, *ib.* 489; fears no danger, 2 *Lat.* 152; is the demonstration of election, 3 *Bec.* 172, 173, 1 *Brad.* 313; by it we seek and obtain all good things of God, 2 *Bec.* 45, 46, 1 *Bul.* 95; he that hath it hath eternal life, 1 *Cov.* 249, 3 *Tyn.* 225; Gentiles, as well as Jews, justified by it, 1 *Bul.* 115

(*e*) Though justification is by faith alone (see *d*, above), true faith is not without works following, but is fruitful in all good deeds, 1 *Bec.* 80, &c., 270, 272, 2 *Bec.* 638, 3 *Bec.* 210, 1 *Brad.* 372, 1 *Bul.* 117, 118, 120, 2 *Bul.* 335, 336, 3 *Bul.* 32, 1 *Cov.* 6, 2 *Cov.* 342, 2 *Cran.* 136, 137, 140, &c., 1 *Ful.* 449, 1 *Hoop.* 33, 265, 2 *Hoop.* 59, 218, 571, 3 *Jew.* 583, &c., 1 *Lat.* 168, 237, *Lit. Edw.* 512, (560), *Now.* (61), 180; 1 *Tyn.* 13, 53, 55, 56, 59, &c., 118, 363, 489, 499, 2 *Tyn.* 187, 194, 3 *Tyn.* 142, 196, *Wool.* 32; according to More's doctrine, the best faith may be coupled with the worst life, 3 *Tyn.* 142, 150; the apostles wrote against the abusers of grace and faith, 2 *Bul.* 338; probations out of the scripture that faith is not idle, but fruitful in doing good works, 3 *Bec.* 334, 335; that faith which brings forth no good works is a dead faith, 2 *Cran.* 133, 135; faith purifies the heart, 1 *Lat.* 485, produces a new life, 2 *Tyn.* 77, 3 *Tyn.* 238, gives the desire and power to do good works, 1 *Tyn.* 115, 493, 494, 3 *Tyn.* 276, is the root of all goodness and obedience, 2 *Tyn.* 175, 194; true believers keep God's commandments, 1 *Cov.* 249; faith obeys, 2 *Bul.* 336; there can be no obedience without it, 1 *Tyn.* 26, 3 *Tyn.* 173, nor any true religion, *Sand.* 260; it makes deeds good, 1 *Tyn.* 120, 2 *Tyn.* 125, 126; it is such a precious jewel in God's sight that nothing is accepted without it, 3 *Bec.* 46; without it deeds are abominable, 2 *Tyn.* 126, all virtues are but sins, 2 *Bec.* 14; on the text "whatsoever is not of faith is sin," 2 *Brad.* 376, *Pil.* 168; faith is always accompanied by love, 1 *Bec.* 272, 2 *Cov.* 342, 1 *Lat.* 449, 454, 1 *Tyn.* 192, 223, 475, 2 *Tyn.* 88, 89, 130, 174, 204, 3 *Tyn.* 196—200; no man can have the right faith, unless he love

God in his heart, 2 *Cran.* 86; faith and love comprehend the whole law of God, 2 *Tyn.* 188; faith produces love, *ib.* 130; faith and hope, 2 *Bul.* 88; faith cannot, any more than hope and charity, stand with evil living, 2 *Cran.* 138, 139; many think they have faith, though their lives declare the contrary, *ib.*; they that continue in evil living cannot have true faith, *ib.* 133, 135; faith, hope, and charity, inseparable, *Lit. Edw.* 515, (562), *Nord.* 17, &c., 2 *Tyn.* 7, 13, 14, 3 *Tyn.* 95; of faith and zeal; verses by Jo. Bodenham, *Poet.* 455; exhortation to faith and good works, 1 *Bec.* 210

(*f*) The foundation of faith, and its objects:—true faith is founded on God's word and promises, *Coop.* 131, 1 *Cov.* 18, &c., 1 *Lat.* 544, 1 *Tyn.* 121, 278; it believes not every thing, 1 *Bul.* 90; believes neither too much nor too little, 3 *Tyn.* 95; leans to God and his word, 1 *Bul.* 92; beholds the truth of God, 2 *Jew.* 934; cleaves to the word of God only, 1 *Bec.* 270; believes the holy scriptures, 1 *Bul.* 96; pleads the promises, 2 *Tyn.* 89, lays hold of them, and relies upon them, 1 *Bec.* 98, 2 *Bec.* 604; some matters of faith are repugnant to reason, 3 *Tyn.* 234; the twelve articles of Christian faith, 2 *Bec.* 15—52, 483—489; in them stands the church's unity, 1 *Brad.* 524; to believe *in* God, what, 3 *Jew.* 253, 255, &c.; the fathers expound the first clause in the creed in a threefold sense,— " Credo Deo, credo Deum, credo in Deum," *Calf.* 86, *Whita.* 300; faith in God the Father, 2 *Bec.* 16, 483, 3 *Bec.* 135, 136, 1 *Bul.* 124, 2 *Hoop.* 23; in Jesus Christ our Lord, 2 *Bec.* 19, 484, 3 *Bec.* 136, &c., 1 *Bul.* 127, 2 *Hoop.* 27, 477; in the Holy Ghost, 2 *Bec.* 38, 487, 3 *Bec.* 141, 142, 1 *Bul.* 155, 2 *Hoop.* 39; as regards the church, 2 *Bec.* 41, 88, 3 *Bec.* 133, 134, 1 *Bul.* 158, 2 *Hoop.* 40, 519; as regards forgiveness of sins, 2 *Bec.* 43, 488, 3 *Bec.* 144, 1 *Bul.* 164, 2 *Hoop.* 58; as regards the resurrection of the body, 2 *Bec.* 46, 489, 3 *Bec.* 144, 145, 1 *Bul.* 168, 2 *Hoop.* 61; as regards everlasting life, 2 *Bec.* 49, 489, 3 *Bec.* 145, 1 *Bul.* 177, 2 *Hoop.* 62; the confession of Christian faith, 2 *Bec.* 579, 580; the sick man's confession of his faith, 3 *Bec.* 135, &c.; see also Confession of Faith, Creeds.

(*g*) The rule of faith : (*v.* Church, I. viii, Scripture, Tradition) :—multitude of adherents is no proof of a right faith, 3 *Tyn.* 102, 103, 107, 109, 116, 122; tradition not the rule of faith, *Whita.* 484, 485; Stapleton's definition, *ib.* 328, 485; how we may know the right faith without the aid of the outward church, 2 *Cran.* 13; God's word the rule of faith, 2 *Jew.* 998, *Whita.* 474, 484, 485; the catholic faith is based on scripture, 2 *Jew.* 988; faith cannot be reformed but by the word of God, 3 *Bul.* 121

(*h*) The life, conflict, and victory of faith :—the life of faith, 1 *Brad.* 253, 440; a godly Christian life is the trial of faith, 2 *Cran.* 139 ; we must have it in walking before God, 1 *Bec.* 207; true faith cannot be kept secret in the heart without confession, 2 *Hoop.* 218, 571, &c.; it is ever assailed, 3 *Tyn.* 34; the work of faith, 1 *Bec.* 78; the conflict of faith, 1 *Brad.* 254; its power and support in adversity, 1 *Cov.* 173; it is strengthened in affliction, *ib.* 125, 317 ; it overcomes the world, 2 *Tyn.* 197, 208, 209 ; it is a remedy to put away sin, 3 *Bec.* 209; a means to resist the devil, *ib.* 157 ; it gives us victory over death and the devil, 2 *Lat.* 148, 194; it is the victory of all Christians, 1 *Bul.* 120; victory is by it alone, *Sand.* 435

(*i*) Faith in respect to prayer and ordinances :—it is needful in prayer, 1 *Bec.* 148, 2 *Bec.* 132, 133, 4 *Bul.* 175, 1 *Lat.* 172, *Lit. Edw.* 523, (570), *Nov.* (67), 187, *Pil.* 295, *Pra. B.* xix; it gives the desire and power to pray, 1 *Tyn.* 118; stirs up to prayer, 4 *Bul.* 551; invocation springs from it, 3 *Bul.* 212; it pleads the promises, 2 *Tyn.* 89; we must pray for faith, 1 *Bul.* 86; prayer without faith is sin, *Nord.* 16; the life of him that prayeth must be answerable to his faith, 4 *Bul.* 177; faith is confirmed by sacraments, 2 *Cov.* 308, 2 *Ful.* 169; necessary in order to their reception, 1 *Cov.* 80, 1 *Hoop.* 134; it goes before baptism in those that have the use of reason, 2 *Bec.* 211; earnest faith must be given to the words of absolution, 1 *Bec.* 102; it is necessary for worthy preparation for the Lord's supper, 2 *Bec.* 234, 235

(*k*) Examples of faith :—Adam, 1 *Cov.* 25, 26, 2 *Hoop.* 325, 2 *Lat.* 5; Eve, 1 *Cov.* 25; Abel, *ib.* 27; Enoch, *ib.* 31; Noah, *ib.* 32; Abraham, 1 *Bul.* 59, 87, 89, 115, 2 *Bul.* 18, 3 *Bul.* 44, 49, 4 *Bul.* 318—320, 551, 1 *Cov.* 34, 35, 2 *Cran.* 209, 1 *Ful.* 406, &c., 2 *Ful.* 385, 2 *Hoop.* 89, 2 *Lat.* 171, *Pil.* 352, 1 *Tyn.* 497; Isaac and Jacob, 1 *Cov.* 36; Joseph, *ib.* 37; Moses, *ib.* 38, *Pil.* 341, 425; Joshua, 1 *Cov.* 50; Rahab, 1 *Tyn.* 119; David, 4 *Bul.* 551, 1 *Cov.* 53, 54, 3 *Tyn.* 203; the prophets, 1 *Cov.* 67; Zacharias,

Elizabeth, Simeon, *ib.* 69; the shepherds, 2 *Lat.* 88; the leper (Matt. viii.), *ib.* 169; the centurion (Matt. viii.), 1 *Bul.* 91, 1 *Lat.* 534; the woman with the issue of blood, 1 *Bul.* 92; Jairus, 1 *Lat.* 534; the woman of Canaan, 1 *Bul.* 92; Peter, 3 *Tyn.* 38, *Whita.* 430, 431

Faithful: *v.* Christians.

Falcidius: considered deacons equal to priests, 1 *Jew.* 355, 3 *Jew.* 293

Falckner (Hen.): 3 *Zur.* 199, 216, 241, &c., (*v.* Falconer).

Falcon (Mich.): 3 *Zur.* 638

Falconer (......): named, 1 *Zur.* 69; his death, *ib.* 79 (perhaps Hen. Falckner).

Falkner (......), a godly matron: 3 *Zur.* 42

Fall: *v.* Adam, Angels, ii, Man.

Fallenburg (Philip): 3 *Zur.* 719

Falling away: *v.* Apostasy.

Falsehood: *v.* Deceit, Lying.

False witness: *v.* Witness.

Fame: *v.* Vanity.

Families: *v.* Parents.

Familists, or Family of Love: a sect of Anabaptists, followers of H. Nicholas, *Grin.* 360 n., *Nord.* 114, *Poet.* 261, *Rog.* 13 n., *Sand.* 130; they said that God by them made heaven and earth, *Rog.* 41; affirmed all things to be ruled by nature, *ib.* 42; denied Christ's equality with the Father in his Godhead, *ib.* 49; made an allegory of his incarnation, *ib.* 52; understood his passion allegorically, *ib.* 58, 110; likewise his resurrection, *ib.* 64; denied or debased the estimation of the scriptures, *ib.* 78, *Whita.* 298; interpreted them allegorically, *Rog.* 197; taught that whatsoever is written of Christ must be fulfilled in us, *ib.* 59, 163; disliked written commentaries, *ib.* 196; preferred their own imaginations to the word of God, *ib.* 79, 158; held that the law ceremonial was still in force, *ib.* 89, 314; termed predestination a licentious doctrine, *ib.* 156; denied original sin, *ib.* 97; said that it comes by imitation, *ib.* 99; affirmed that the elect and regenerate sin not, *ib.* 101; said that men may perfectly keep the law of God, *ib.* 123; denied the possibility of sinning after having received the Spirit, 1 *Lat.* 229; asserted Christ and his righteousness to be inherent in the righteous, *Rog.* 115; held that the visible church is free from sin, *ib.* 167, 179, that themselves were free from sin, *ib.* 135, 141, that they only were the church of God, *ib.* 169; believed that themselves only should be saved, *ib.* 153; said that to be saved it was only necessary to have the heart and affections with them, *ib.* 160; taught that the sacraments might be received merely for obedience to magistrates, *ib.* 246, 284; derisively termed the water at baptism "elementish water," *ib.* 177, 278; maintained that none should be baptized until thirty years old, *ib.* 280; said there was no true baptism but among themselves, *ib.* 275; enjoined community of goods, *ib.* 353; gave alms only to their own sect, *ib.* 355; temporized in religion, *ib.* 320; allowed perjury to escape persecution, *ib.* 119, 357; condemned all war, *ib.* 351; prohibited the bearing of any weapons but staves, *ib.*; held that no man should be put to death or persecuted for his religion, *ib.* 350; charged Cranmer and Ridley with burning Joan of Kent, *ib.*; condemned magistracy, *ib.* 337; thought that before the resurrection there should be no magistrates, because the wicked should be rooted out, *ib.* 346; affirmed that none can minister the upright service or ceremonies of Christ but the regenerate, *ib.* 271; laboured to make contemptible the outward admission of ministers, *ib.* 333; denied all calling but the immediate call from God, *ib.* 239, 240; termed God's ministers "scripture-learned," "letter-doctors," "teaching-masters," &c., *ib.* 78, 177, 194, 233; their co-deified elders, *ib.* 202; they said there should be no preaching, *ib.* 325; called it presumption and unbecoming in any man to preach, *ib.* 233; held that the word is taught not by preaching but by revelation, *ib.* 231; said none understood the mysteries of the kingdom of God but their elders, *ib.* 194, and that none but them should busy themselves about the word, *ib.* 241; they called churches common houses, *ib.* 186, 320; held conventicles, *ib.* 191; contemned the Lord's day, *ib.* 187; made the promises of happiness to be accomplished in this life, *ib.* 88; acknowledged no triumphant state in heaven, *ib.* 166; taught that the righteous were already in godly glory, &c., *ib.* 68; denied the salvation of the body, *ib.* 145, and the resurrection of the wicked, *ib.* 67; declared hell to be only in the heart and conscience, *ib.* 148; said that they were a free people, *ib.* 185; declared to be half-Papists, *ib.* 187; books by and against them, *Rog.* notes, passim.

Famine: affliction therein, 2 *Bul.* 101; the prevalence of dearth, 2 *Bec.* 617; sent as a punishment for sins, *ib.* 617, 618; caused by covetousness, 1 *Lat.* 99; dearths in the time of popery, *Pil.* 611; a great one in

1550, 1 *Lat.* 527; one in England in queen Mary's time, *Lit. Eliz.* 569; Whitgift's letter to the bishops of his province, for fasting and prayer upon occasion of a dearth, 1596, 3 *Whitg.* 617

Famoust: famousest, 1 *Jew.* 13

Fanon, or Fannel: *v.* Maniple.

Farced: stuffed, filled, 2 *Bec.* 423

Fare: *v.* Bill.

Farel (Will.): notice of him, 3 *Zur.* 622 n.; mentioned, *ib.* 328, 548, 622; letter to him and others, 2 *Zur*, 121

Farewell: *v.* Sermons.

 Farewell to London, 1 *Brad.* 434; to Cambridge, *ib.* 441; to Lancashire and Cheshire, *ib.* 448; to Walden, *ib.* 455; the farewell; verses by Sir W. Raleigh, *Poet.* 233

Farewell (Cape): *v.* Cape.

Faringdon (Hugh), abbot of Reading: executed, 3 *Zur.* 317 n., 614 n., 627

Farley (My lord of): *v.* Hungerford (Sir W.).

Farming: *v.* Benefices.

Farnese (Alex.), duke of Parma: *v.* Alexander.

Farnham, co. Surrey: *Grin.* 260, 261

Farnham (Nich. de), bp of Durham: resigns his see, *Grin.* 399 n

Farr (Edw.): editor of Select Poetry, *Poet.*

Farrar (Rob.), bp: *v.* Ferrar.

Farringdon (Hugh): *v.* Faringdon.

Fasciculus Temporum: *Jew.* xxxvii; used by Caxton in his continuation of the Polychronicon, *Pil.* 598 n.; on the merits of St Benet, *ib.* 80; it rehearses twenty schisms between popes and their partakers, *ib.* 545; speaks of the kingdom of France being removed from the right heirs by pope Zachary, 4 *Jew.* 683; says there was no honour bestowed on pope Joan at her burial, *ib.* 650, 656

Fasciculus Rerum Sciendarum: a book printed at Cologne (the original edition of the work next mentioned), 4 *Jew.* 738

Fasciculus Rerum Expetendarum et Fugiendarum, ab Orthuino Gratio, stud. E. Brown: 2 *Brad.* 160, *Jew.* xxxvii, *Rid.* 374; referred to about Constantine's Donation, 2 *Ful.* 261 n., 4 *Jew.* 678 n.; Brown's error respecting this, 2 *Ful.* 360 n.; referred to about Gregory VII., 2 *Hoop.* 240 n.; this work contains the commentaries of Æneas Sylvius, 2 *Ful.* 302 n.; referred to about an assembly at Nuremberg, 4 *Jew.* 738 n.; on baptizing bells, *Calf.* 16 n.; on the confession of the Waldensian brethren, 2 *Brad.* 161, 1 *Jew.* 235, *Rid.* 374

Fast (adv.): stedfastly, 1 *Tyn.* 451

Fastidius: an early English bishop, 1 *Bec.* 367 n

Fasting: *v.* Meats.

(*a*) Its nature, intent, profit, &c.:—A FRUITFUL TREATISE OF FASTING, by T. Becon, 2 *Bec.* 523; he says none had written of it in English, *ib.* 527; of fasting, 1 *Bul.* 428, &c.; fasting defined, what it is to fast aright, 1 *Bec.* 105, 162, 163, 2 *Bec.* 528, &c., 537, 3 *Bec.* 609, 620, 621, 1 *Bul.* 428, &c., 1 *Hoop.* 348, 538, 1 *Tyn.* 75, 90, 2 *Tyn.* 91, &c.; the fast that God requireth, 2 *Tyn.* 48; that which is merely outward or constrained he abhors, 2 *Bec.* 529, 530; godly admonitions concerning fasting, 1 *Bec.* 109; several things to be observed in it, 1 *Bec.* 107, 2 *Bec.* 537, *Pil.* 559; the true fast rises of a heart contrite and sorrowful for sin, 1 *Bec.* 161, 2 *Bec.* 531, 532, of a mind given to godliness, 2 *Bec.* 532, 533; it is a fruit of repentance, *ib.* 542; it consists not only in abstinence of meats, but in forsaking of sin, *ib.* 539, 540; its dignity and excellence, 1 *Bec.* 103; the praise and profit of it, *ib.* 104; fasts are of two kinds, public and private, 1 *Bul.* 428; or, by commandment, and voluntary, *Pil.* 558; public fasts, 2 *Whitg.* 486; what it is to fast in secret, 1 *Bec.* 109, 2 *Bec.* 540, &c.; a third sort of fasting mentioned by Isaiah, *Pil.* 558; another division,—spiritual, and corporal fasting, 1 *Bec.* 104; the true use of fasting, 2 *Bec.* 542, &c.; *first*, to mortify and tame the flesh, 2 *Bec.* 543, &c., 3 *Bec.* 529, 1 *Bul.* 430, 1 *Tyn.* 90, 440, 2 *Tyn.* 91, 94, 137, 138, 3 *Tyn.* 80; a rule to be observed herein, 2 *Bec.* 545; to eschew evil, 1 *Bec.* 106; *secondly*, to have more liberally to give to the poor, 2 *Bec.* 545, 546, 3 *Bec.* 529; fasting is helpful to good works, *Wool.* 67, 88; the true fast is to exercise works of mercy, 1 *Bec.* 105; that pleases God best which is accompanied by such works, 2 *Bec.* 538, 539; *thirdly*, that, as godly men of old, we may be more apt to pray, 2 *Bec*, 546, &c., 1 *Bul.* 430; for this cause fasts were appointed of ancient fathers, 2 *Bec.* 548; spiritual exercises in fasting, *ib.* 528; Christ joined prayer with it, *ib.* 547; so did the apostles, &c., 4 *Bul.* 183; by prayer and fasting devils are cast out, 1 *Tyn.* 82; alms, prayer, and fasting, go together, 2 *Tyn.* 93, 94; they are our spiritual sacrifices, 1 *Bec.* 138, 161; fasting and alms are the two wings of prayer, *ib.* 163; *fourthly*, that we may the better hear and digest God's word, 2 *Bec.* 548, &c.; for this cause it was instituted on the evens of solemn feasts, *ib.* 549,

550; how fasting should be enjoined by priests, 2 *Tyn.* 95; against wicked and ungodly fasters, 1 *Bec.* 106

(*b*) The manner of fasting (see also *a* and *d*), 2 *Bec.* 528, 529, 537, &c., 1 *Bul.* 431; it stands not in abstinence from eating and drinking only, 1 *Bec.* 105, 163, 2 *Tyn.* 94; it is not a choice of certain kinds of meat, but a perpetual temperance, *Wool.* 135; godly men abstained in it not only from meat, but from all that might delight the flesh, 2 *Bec.* 529; the ancient custom was to fast from all meats till night, 1 *Bec.* 105; on abstinence from meats, *Phil.* 403; on eating fish, *Pil.* 558, 559; white meats (butter, eggs, cheese, &c.) allowed in Lent, 2 *Cran.* 508; some superstitious persons would not taste an egg in Lent, *Sand.* 104; difference between fasting and abstinence, 3 *Jew.* 169, 170

(*c*) The time of fasting (see also *d*; likewise Ember days, Friday, Holy-days, Lent), 1 *Bul.* 431; fasting on certain days is by a positive law only, 2 *Cran.* 156; fasting on Sundays anciently forbidden, 2 *Ful.* 237, accounted wicked by Tertullian, *Calf.* 257, deemed lawful by Augustine, *Whita.* 573; not expedient, 1 *Whitg.* 223, 228, 229; fasting on Wednesdays, *Park.* 235; on Wednesdays, Fridays, Saturdays, 2 *Tyn.* 93; on Fridays, *Park.* 216; this was required by a civil law, 2 *Lat.* 80, 81; an indifferent act in itself, 1 *Hoop.* 32; the golden Fridays, *Pil.* 80; abstinence on Fridays and Saturdays, 2 *Lat.* 16, 17; monkish fasting before Lent, 2 *Tyn.* 92; fasting used in Lent, 2 *Bec.* 526; fasting in honour of saints, 3 *Tyn.* 81; St Brandon's fast, lady-fasts, &c., 2 *Tyn.* 98; St Tronion's [Ronan's] fast, our lady's fast, &c., *Pil.* 80; Popish fast days, *ib.* 551; article respecting abrogated ones, *Grin.* 160; fasting days appointed by particular churches, *Pil.* 556

(*d*) Fasting in different ages and countries (see also *b* and *c*): — that of the fathers in the old law, 2 *Bec.* 528, 533, 2 *Tyn.* 97; it was not practised by them that they might be justified thereby, 2 *Bec.* 542; scriptural examples, 1 *Bec.* 103, 104, *Wool.* 136; Jewish fastings were solemn, 2 *Bul.* 162; the false fasting of the Jews, 3 *Tyn.* 68; why God cast away their fasts, 1 *Bec.* 109, 2 *Bec.* 539; fasting left free by scripture, 3 *Bec.* 529, 1 *Bul.* 434, 1 *Hoop.* 348; the apostles determined nothing about it, *Whita.* 665; but Montanus did, *Pil.* 558, *Whita.* 596, 665; the church of old taught that men should fast (except at the time of the taking away of the Bridegroom) of their own will, not by commandment: this was blamed by Tertullian when a Montanist, *Whita.* 666; differences in the early church, 1 *Bul.* 432; Epiphanius writes that in his day the custom was to eat nothing but bread and salt for some days before Easter, *Calf.* 270, *Whita.* 666; in Ambrose's time there was no fasting between Easter and Whitsuntide, *Pil.* 556; so in Augustine's time, *Calf.* 270; different customs at Rome and Milan in those days, *Pil.* 557; the Popish manner of fasting, 2 *Bec.* 533, &c., 2 *Tyn.* 124; this was wicked, 2 *Bec.* 542; it rose of custom or superstition, *ib.* 535, 536; Popish superstitious fasting, *Pil.* 559, 1 *Tyn.* 90; its vanity, *Poet.* 281; the fondness of the Papists in their fasting, 2 *Bec.* 536; different fasts among them, *Pil.* 80; their erroneous doctrine concerning fasting, 2 *Bec.* 542; how much it was trusted in, *ib.* 414; how it was abused by monks, 2 *Tyn.* 91; the eating of any kind of flesh forbidden to them by the canon law, *ib.* 276; the Carthusians thought the eating of fish pleasing to God, 1 *Tyn.* 278; story of a monk who was a great faster, 2 *Bec.* 534; a Popish feasting fast, 2 *Tyn.* 97; otter was counted as fish, *ib.* n.; Papists forbid flesh, but not wine, *Whita.* 596; diverse customs prevailed on the two sides of Cheapside, they being in different dioceses, *Pil.* 557; fasting not taken away by the reformers, but not bound to certain prescribed days, *Phil.* 405; not taken away, but reformed, 2 *Jew.* 1026, 4 *Jew.* 1140; abstinence from flesh at certain times required by law in England, 1 *Lat.* 372, 2 *Lat.* 17, 80, 81, 2 *Whitg.* 595; this was done for policy, 3 *Jew.* 169, &c., to encourage the fisheries, 2 *Cran.* 506, to maintain mariners and set men a fishing, *Grin.* 407, 408; Tyndale would have fasting to be so required by law for the commonweal's sake, 2 *Tyn.* 93; a proclamation of king Edward for abstinence from flesh on Fridays and Saturdays, and in Lent time, 2 *Cran.* 507; meat disallowed in Lent and on fast-days, except by dispensation, 1 *Zur.* 164, 358; on licences to eat flesh in Lent, &c., 3 *Whitg.* 276, 2 *Zur.* 360; Hooper desires licences to eat flesh on the fish days, for himself and Jo. Samford, 2 *Brad.* 396; increase of fish days in queen Elizabeth's time, 4 *Jew.* 1142; no flesh was to be had at inns on fast days, 2 *Zur.* 203; yet flesh was eaten on those days in spite of the queen's commandment, *Pil.* 484, 555; that fasting which is commanded of the high powers is to be kept, 2 *Bec.* 530, 531; why the law was enforced, 3 *Bec.* 621; orders respecting the mode of keeping a fast in 1563, *Lit. Eliz.* 489, 490; the form of prayer on that occasion, *ib.* 478; reference to this fast, 4 *Jew.* 1141; Grindal blames the neglect of fasting, *Grin.* 93 n., *Lit. Eliz.* 489 n.; the Wednesday fish day (in Lent) dispensed with at Oxford, Cambridge, and Winchester, *Park.* 235 ; Whitgift's letter to the bishops of his province, for fasting and prayer on occasion of a dearth, 1596, 3 *Whitg.* 617

Fate: *v.* Fortune.

Fathers: *v.* Forefathers, Parents.

Fathers before Christ: *v.* Church, Covenants, Faith, Jews.

The likeness and difference of the old and new testaments and people, 2 *Bul.* 282; the patriarchs, and the line of divine tradition, 1 *Bul.* 39—42, 4 *Bul.* 28; More alleges the faith of the patriarchs before the flood, to prove that scripture is not the necessary ground of a true faith, 3 *Tyn.* 133—135; the old fathers were under grace, *Hutch.* 247, 326; they were redeemed and justified even as we are, 1 *Ful.* 279, 1 *Lat.* 521; their faith one with ours, 2 *Bul.* 283, 284, 2 *Cran.* 138, 1 *Lat.* 378; how they saw God, 3 *Bul.* 142 ; they worshipped the Holy Trinity, *Hutch.* 122 ; looked for eternal happiness through Christ, *Rog.* 87 ; they looked beyond their sacrifices to him, 1 *Cov.* 46; Christ suffered for them, 3 *Bul.* 42; they were saved by him, 1 *Cov.* 72, 2 *Lat.* 5; salvation was not only promised to them, but performed, 2 *Bul.* 288; Christ was present with them, *Pil.* 134 ; they had one Spirit with us, 2 *Bul.* 285, and one manner of invocation, *ib.* 292; they had ceremonial and judicial laws, 1 *Bul.* 211; their sacraments (*q. v.*) were in effect the same as ours, 1 *Bul.* 58, 2 *Bul.* 292; they communicated with Christ, 4 *Bul.* 434; they did eat his flesh and drink his blood, *Hutch.* 248; their hope and inheritance the same as ours, 2 *Bul.* 288; the patriarchs exercised husbandry, 2 *Bul.* 31; their longevity, 1 *Bul.* 41; their hospitality, 2 *Bul.* 59 ; their afflictions, *ib.* 103

Fathers of the Church: *v.* Bibliotheca, Doctors, Vitæ Patrum.

How we should esteem them, 4 *Jew.* 1173; they are greatly to be honoured, *Coop.* 148; counsel of Vincentius Lirinensis concerning them, 2 *Ful.* 175; they were well esteemed by Ridley, *Rid.* 158; the reason of Becon's citing them, 1 *Bec.* 134; Jewel's celebrated appeal to the fathers for the space of 600 years after Christ, 1 *Jew.* 20, 21, 2 *Ful.* 28, 58; Calfhill reverenced them with all his heart, *Calf.* 260, and offered to abide by their decision, *ib.* 11; the cry " Fathers, fathers," 1 *Tyn.* 324; what authority is to be attributed to them, *Coop.* 145, 1 *Hoop.* 520; what authority is ascribed to them by the church of Rome, *Whita.* 412, 413; those who were not bishops deemed by Papists of less authority, *ib.* 413; with what judgment we should read their writings, *Calf.* 59; how they ought to be read and taken, *Phil.* 352; they are not to be followed in all things, 1 *Lat.* 218; they are to be treated differently from the canonical books, 2 *Cran.* 32, 33; they are not authors of doctrine, but witnesses and expounders, *Rid.* 28; without the written word of God they cannot prove any doctrine in religion, 2 *Cran.* 22, 51; their doctrine to be tested by scripture, 1 *Tyn.* 330, 3 *Tyn.* 133, 136; to be accepted if accordant with scripture, *Rid.* 114; not to be hearkened to, if they dissent from the doctrine of Christ, 1 *Bec.* 87, 3 *Bec.* 390; they would not have themselves further believed than this, *ib.* 390, 391, 402, 403; to interpret scripture by the doctors, is to measure the meteyard by the cloth, 1 *Tyn.* 153; their unanimous consent not the rule of interpretation, *Whita.* 448 (*v.* Scripture); this cannot be the rule, because there was a time when their writings were not extant, *ib.* 456; card. Cajetan denies that the exposition of scripture is tied by God to their unanimous consent, *ib.* 466; there is no such thing as their unanimous consent, *ib.* 455; they expounded scripture diversely, but were not therefore heretics, 1 *Tyn.* 384; their opinions and judgments, sometimes involve contrarieties, 3 *Jew.* 239; indeed they seldom agree, *Whita.* 414; examples of their variance, *ib.* 455; often as they differed in opinion, they always appealed to the scriptures, 2 *Cran.* 77 ; they allege the testimonies of the primitive church, not to establish faith, but to shew in what sense the word of God was used, 1 *Hoop.* 169; Christ built his church in them, the devil his chapel in heretics, 3 *Bec.* 401; being led by the Spirit of Christ they could teach nothing, in principal points, but that which is agreeable to the doctrine of Christ, 2 *Bec.* 277; while unwilling to adopt their fancies, we do not reject their exposition, *Calf.* 263; remarks on the opinions of several of them, 3 *Zur.* 228—235; in some points they erred, 1 *Bec.* 278, 3 *Bec.* 404, 3 *Bul.* 398, *Calf.* 258, 259, *Coop.* 146, 2 *Ful.* 41, *Rid.* 163, 2 *Whitg.* 435; they were often deceived, 3 *Jew.* 176; some were in error in holding that all who died without baptism were lost, 2 *Bec.* 214, 224; some spoke unadvisedly of repentance, &c., 1 *Ful.* 439, 441; in disputation against heretics they sometimes seem to approach the opposite errors, 2 *Jew.* 608; their faults in action, 2 *Whitg.* 436; it should not be our object to seek for proofs of their imperfection, *Calf.* 58, 226; they frequently used phrases which have been misunderstood, *ib.* 75; often employed hyperbole and metonymy, *ib.* 77; if the old doctors had foreseen controversies, they would have written more plainly, 2 *Lat.* 268; they are often misunderstood when they speak of the sacraments, *Rid.* 114; they moved no contentions about them, 4 *Bul.* 284; in treating of them they delighted in amplification of words, 2 *Jew.* 762; they called the sacraments by the names of the things signified, 1 *Hoop.* 523; termed the sacramental bread Christ's body, and the Lord's supper a sacrifice, *Grin.* 63, 1 *Tyn.* 370, 372; their words afterwards understood amiss, 1 *Tyn.* 372; they did not admit the carnal presence of Christ's body in the sacrament, 1 *Brad.* 99, 1 *Cran.* passim; their testimony against transubstantiation (*q.v.*), *Rid.* 28, &c., 173, &c.; the fathers were alleged by heretics, 1 *Jew.* 83, 3 *Jew.* 226, they are perversely used, and misquoted, by Papists, 1 *Jew.* 84, *Rid.* 115, *Whita.* 314, 315, 327; they have both herbs and weeds, but Romanists commonly gather the latter, *Rid.* 114; though alleged by Papists they are really adversaries to them, 3 *Bec.* 402, *Phil.* 115, 1 *Tyn.* 325, 3 *Tyn.* 132; the Romish profession of observing their injunctions to the utmost jot is a mere pretence, *Calf.* 260; an instance of the way in which Expurgatory Indexes, while apparently abstaining from censuring, effectually condemn their sentiments, *ib.* 375 n.; words of theirs against the pope's doctrine, *Grin.* 63 (and see above); fathers alleged in support of tradition, *Whita.* 564—610; against it, *ib.* 669—704; they taught that the second commandment is moral, *Calf.* 42, 43; held that faith only justifies, 2 *Cran.* 130, 133; their opinion on things indifferent, 1 *Whitg.* 213; saying of an ancient father about affliction, 3 *Bec.* 104; the elder fathers were diligent preachers, *Hutch.* 6; ignorantly condemned by some as new doctors, 2 *Lat.* 319; the writings of the fathers much corrupted, *Coop.* 170, 2 *Ful.* 59, 1 *Hoop.* 520, many spurious works ascribed to them, *Calf.* 268, *Coop.* 170, 1 *Jew.* 111, 173, 2 *Jew.* 894, 3 *Tyn.* 48, 1 *Zur.* 147; remarks on their respective styles of writing, *Whita.* 479; their works to be kept in church libraries, 2 *Cran.* 161.

Fathers (ghostly): learned ones to be sought, 1 *Bec.* 102

Fatherstone (......): *v.* Featherstone.

Faude (......), mayor of Cambridge: *Pil.* 656

Faustinus, a bishop: claimed supremacy for the bishop of Rome, 1 *Jew.* 355

Faustus, the Manichee: opposed by Augustine, 1 *Ful.* 146, 147; he affirmed that Mary was the daughter of Joachim, a Levite, 2 *Cran.* 30

Faustus, the Pelagian: his doctrine about faith and works, 2 *Tyn.* 104, 122; he says, we must not doubt that Christ gave himself for the whole world, 3 *Bec.* 422; a sermon amongst the works of Augustine ascribed to him by the Benedictine editors, *Sand.* 173 n

Favour: *v.* Grace.

Fawden (Tho.): *Hutch.* x.

Fear: *v.* God. The want of the fear of God is the root of all evil, 2 *Bec.* 416; the fear of God is of two sorts, 3 *Bul.* 60, *Pil.* 104; what fear we ought to have towards him, 1 *Bec.* 208; our fear must be childlike, not servile, *Sand.* 184—186; there is a servile fear, 2 *Whitg.* 475; this is the first cause of idolatry, 1 *Hoop.* 453; fearfulness condemned, *Pil.* 378, 432; fear goes before love, *ib.* 104; it is cast out by love, 2 *Tyn.* 203; there is a fear which must be joined with love, *Sand.* 186; the godly tremble at God's word, *ib.* 269; there are two sorts of fear in respect to rulers, 2 *Hoop.* 107; fear of the law is the last remedy, 1 *Tyn.* 185; fear of men is a great fault in a judge, 1 *Bul.* 348

Fear (v. a.): to terrify, 1 *Tyn.* 133

Feasting: banquets customably made at Christmas, 1 *Bec.* 61; worldly evil talk at them, *ib.* 62; banqueting and drunkenness condemned, 1 *Lat.* 254; banqueting a vain pleasure, not to be rejoiced in, 2 *Bec.* 440, 441; the evils it has brought, *ib.* 441

Feasts:

Jewish feasts (see their names): the holy times in general, 2 *Bul.* 159, &c.; the sabbath, *ib.* 161; the new-moon, *ib.* 162; the passover, *ib.* 163; pentecost, *ib.* 164;

the feast of the seventh month, or of tabernacles, *ib.* 165, 166; this (according to Bullinger's reckoning) included the feast of trumpets, *ib.* 165, the feast of cleansing, or day of atonement, *ib.* 165, the feast of tabernacles strictly so called, *ib.* 166, and the congregation or assembly, *ib.*; other yearly solemnities, of human institution, viz. the feast of purim, and the feast of dedication, *ib.* 162; the year of jubilee, *ib.* 166

— Christian festivals, *v.* Holy-days; also Christmas, Easter, Pentecost, &c.

—Feastful days appointed by magistrates are to be observed, 2 *Bec.* 83, such observance being in itself an indifferent act, 1 *Hoop.* 32; the feast of asses, Jan. 14, 1 *Tyn.* 91 n

Feat: employment, 2 *Bul.* 31

Feate: ingenious, *Calf.* 317

Featherston* (Alex.): slain by N. Ridley, *Rid.* ii. n

Fetherstone (Chr.): notice of him, *Poet.* xliv; a sonnet by way of exhortation to the Frenchmen, revolted from true religion, *ib.* 467

Featherston (Nich.): slays W. Ridle, *Rid.* ii. n

Fetherston (......): executed for denying the king's supremacy, 3 *Zur.* 209 n.; called Fatherstone, 2 *Cran.* 310 n

Featherstonehaugh family: their feuds with the Ridleys, *Rid.* i. n

Fechtius (Jo.): on the modern use of ancient words, *Phil.* 94 n

Feckenham, co. Worcester: a royal forest there, 2 *Lat.* 414

Feckenham (Jo.), or Fecknam, last abbot of Westminster: named, *Phil.* 154; at a disputation on the sacrament, 1551, *Grin.* ii; sent to the lady Jane and her husband in prison, 2 *Brad.* 63 n., 3 *Zur.* 294, 304; he belies Ridley at Paul's cross, *Rid.* 163; confers with him in the Tower, *ib.* 155; takes part in the disputation with Latimer at Oxford, 2 *Lat.* 263; disputes with Ridley there, *Rid.* 191; succeeds the martyr Bradford in his prebend at St Paul's, *Rid.* 331 n.; strives to hinder the reformation under Elizabeth, 1 *Zur.* 10 n.; one of the disputants at Westminster, 1558, 1 *Jew.* 60, 4 *Jew.* 1199, 1200, 1 *Zur.* 11 n.; he defends the monastic orders, in the house of lords, *ib.* 20; committed to the Tower, *ib.* 79 n.; prisoner there, *Park.* 122; placed under the care of Dr Goodman, dean of Westminster, *Grin.* 282; his enlargement, *ib.*

351; he is sent prisoner to Wisbeach, *Phil.* 168; his books, and replies to them by Horn, Fulke, Gough, and Tomson, 1 *Ful.* 75 n., 426, 2 *Ful.* 3, 378, 2 *Zur.* 147 n

Feeding: *v.* Pastors.

The word used in different senses in the scriptures, 2 *Hoop.* 197

Feet: *v.* Washing.

What they betoken in scripture, 3 *Bec.* 609, 610; "my feet were almost gone" (Psa. lxxiii.), what this signifies, 2 *Hoop.* 297

Feharde (......): 4 *Jew.* 1262, comp. *Park.* 177, ... charde.

Felding, or Fielding family: account of it, 3 *Bec.* 89 n

Felding (Basil): dedication to him, 3 *Bec.* 89; account of him, *ib.* n

Felicissimus, a Novatian: 2 *Whitg.* 201, &c.

Felicity: *v.* Happiness.

Felinus Sandeus: Comm. super Decretal., *Jew.* xxxvii; cites those words of Satan, "I will give thee all the kingdoms of the world," adduced to prove that the pope is lord of all things temporal, 4 *Jew.* 869, 1078; he asserts that the pope's authority is over all things, heavenly, earthly, and infernal, even the angels, good and evil, *ib.* 846; teaches that the pope may dispense against the law of God in particular cases, but not in general, 3 *Jew.* 599, that he may abolish the law of God in part, but not in whole, *ib.*, that he may dispense against the epistles of St Paul, *ib.*, that he may change the form of words in baptism, *ib.*; he states that the pope is said to have a heavenly judgment, and that therefore his will stands instead of reason, 4 *Jew.* 769; argues that he cannot commit simony, *ib.* 868, 869; says that if simony were stayed, the apostolic see of Rome would be despised, *ib.* 1082; declares that notwithstanding the fulness of power in the pope, he is not to be obeyed, when sin shall follow his bidding, 3 *Jew.* 202; says, if the pope commit an offence wherefore he should justly be deposed, he ought to be punished, as if he were a clown, 4 *Jew.* 834; affirms that he may not be deposed for lack of learning, *ib.* 910; testifies that Pius II. considered the Donation of Constantine a forgery, *ib.* 678 n., 840

Felix (St): martyred with his sister Regula, 2 *Bul.* 106, 4 *Bul.* xvii.

Felix (St), a martyr: pictures in the church at Nola where he was buried, *Calf.* 29

* Featherston, Fetherstone, &c. are arranged together.

Felix, a holy father: what he said about preaching, *Pil.* 184

Felix II.* pope: his name erased by Acacius, bishop of Constantinople, 4 *Jew.* 650; his epistle to the emperor Zeno, 1 *Jew.* 405

Felix III.† pope: son of a priest, 2 *Ful.* 98 n.; what relation to pope Gregory the Great, 2 *Ful.* 99, *Pil.* 527; he decreed that the communion should not be ministered at home, but upon great necessity, 1 *Jew.* 184

Felix II., anti-pope: an Arian, *Pil.* 601; his contention with Liberius about the popedom, 1 *Jew.* 377, *Rid.* 127

Felix V., anti-pope: *v.* Amadeus VIII.

Felix, bp of Aptungita: purged before the lord lieutenant, by the commandment of Constantine, 4 *Jew.* 966

Felix, bp of Aquitaine (?): leader at the synod of Elvira, *Calf.* 154

Fell (Jo.), bp of Oxford: 2 *Ful.* 290 n., 329 n

Fellowship: *v.* Communion.

Felly: fiercely, 2 *Brad.* 60

Felony: punished by hanging, 3 *Zur.* 205; accessories thereto, 1 *Brad.* 388

Felton (Dunstan): 2 *Zur.* 180

Felton (Jo.): executed in St Paul's churchyard, for affixing Pius V.'s bull of excommunication to the gate of the bishop of London there, 4 *Jew.* 1129, *Lit. Eliz.* 655 n., *Park.* 445 n., 3 *Whitg.* 503 n., 1 *Zur.* 221 n., 254

Felton (Tho.): a letter signed by him, *Park.* 307

Fenne (Sir Hugh): sub-treasurer of England, 1 *Bec.* 61 n

Fenner (Dudley): notice of him, *Poet.* xxxi; Solomon's Song, ch. iv, in verse by him, *ib.* 341; he thought that baptism should not be administered to the children of those who submitted not to church discipline, *Rog.* 280; teaches that tyrants may be deposed, *ib.* 361 n

Fenugreek: a medicinal herb, 3 *Zur.* 223

Ferdinand I., emperor: notice of him, *Grin.* 3 n.; his ancestry, *ib.* 11; he takes Milan from the French, 2 *Tyn.* 315; his wars against infidels, *Grin.* 13, 2 *Tyn.* 341; he valiantly defends Vienna against the Turk, *Grin.* 15; mentioned, before his succession to the empire, 2 *Cran.* 232, 234, 236, 3 *Zur.* 164, 258; crowned emperor without a mass, *Grin.* 20, 3 *Zur.* 182 n.; he cared little for the pope, *Grin.* 20—22; objected to the council being held at Trent, 4 *Jew.* 1097; requested the council, that liberty might be granted to have the communion administered in both kinds, *Grin.* 22; his tomb, *ib.* 17 n.; his funeral service at St Paul's, *ib.* viii; Grindal's sermon on that occasion, *ib.* 1, &c.; his gifts of mind, and godly virtues, *ib.* 12; commended for his chastity, *ib.* 17, 18; compared to David and Solomon, *ib.*

Ferdinand V., king of Spain: his conquest of Navarre, 2 *Tyn.* 310 n.; Ferdinand and Isabella forbade the translation of the Bible into Spanish, 2 *Jew.* 689, 690

Ferguson (Dav.), minister of Dunfermline: 2 *Zur.* 364 n., 365

Feria (The duke or count of): ambassador from Spain, 4 *Jew.* 1199, 1200, *Park.* 66, 1 *Zur.* 5 n., 10

Feries: *v.* Fery.

Feriol (St): invoked for geese, *Rog.* 226

Ferman (Rob.): *v.* Forman.

Fermer: one who farms the tithes, *Grin.* 161

Fernham (Nich. de): *v.* Farnham.

Fernihurst: *v.* Kerr (Tho.), of Fernihurst.

Fernihurst castle, Scotland: destroyed by the English, 1 *Zur.* 225 n

Feroe isles: 2 *Zur.* 290

Ferragutt (Aug.): 2 *Cran.* 555

Ferrar (Nich.), of Little Gidding: mention of his family, 1 *Brad.* 258 n., *Pra. B.* vi.

Ferrar (Rob.), bp of St David's: taken in hand by the council, *Park.* 281; consecrated bishop, 3 *Zur.* 645 n.; at a disputation in king Edward's time, *ib.* 645; in prison, 1 *Brad.* 403, 2 *Brad.* xxxiv, 74 n., 96; Sandys visits him, *Sand.* xii; he signs a declaration concerning religion, 1 *Brad.* 374; examined, *ib.* 465; ready to die, *ib.* 410; martyred, *Rid.* 391; his views on the eucharist, 3 *Zur.* 72, 76; a letter on election signed by him, 1 *Brad.* 305, 2 *Brad.* 169—171; letters to him and others, 2 *Brad.* 179, 2 *Hoop.* 592

Farrar (Sam.), son of the last: *Park.* 267

Ferrara: burning of the bones of Hermannus there, *Pil.* 18; the town partly destroyed by an earthquake, *Lit. Eliz.* 569

Ferrarius (Ambr.): sought for missing portions of Origen, 4 *Jew.* 789 n

Ferrarius (Jo.), Montanus: Woorke touchynge the good orderynge of a Common-weale, *Wool.* 28 n

Ferrers (Walter lord) of Chartley: *v.* Devereux (W.).

Ferriers (Jean de), vidame of Chartres: notice of him, *Grin.* 305; Parker's epistle to him,

---

* Otherwise III., martyred and canonized.   † Otherwise IV.

prefixed to Marlorat's Thesaurus, *Park.* 455

Ferrol: *v.* Corunna.

Ferte (M. le baron de la): *v.* La Ferte.

Ferus (Jo.): on Christ's descent into hell, *Rog.* 61 n

Fery [Lat. feria] : day of the week, *Calf.* 269, feries, *Pil.* 17

Festival (The) : some account of it, 1 *Hoop.* 182 n.; read in churches, 3 *Bec.* 199, 234, 519, 535, 1 *Hoop.* 182, 1 *Jew.* 265; cited on the adoration of the host, *Rog.* 291, about our lady's candle in the tenebræ service, *ib.* 172 n.; copy of the quarterly curse taken from it, 2 *Cran.* 281 n

Festivals: *v.* Holy-days.

Festus (Pomp.): mentions an opinion that ceremonies took their name of the town Cæres, or Cærete, 2 *Bul.* 125

Fet: to fetch, *Lit. Eliz.* 497 n., *Pil.* 78, 1 *Tyn.* 269; fet, i. e. fetched, 2 *Bec.* 304, 1 *Jew.* 146, 2 *Jew.* 1005; fett, 2 *Tyn.* 229; fette, *Calf.* 158

Fetherstone family: *v.* Featherstone.

Fetys, or Fetise: spruce, fine, *Phil.* 390

Feuguereius (Gul.): *Park.* 455

Feversham, co. Kent: the abbey surrendered, 2 *Cran.* 374

Feyld (Rich.), proctor: 2 *Cran.* 492

Fiacre (St): invoked for the ague, *Bale* 498

Ficino (Marc.): commends shooting as an exercise, 1 *Lat.* 197

Fidelitas, a Familist: *Rog.* 202

Fidus: his opinion that infants should not be baptized before the eighth day, disapproved by Cyprian and a council, 2 *Bec.* 209

Field (Jo.): a leader of the Puritans, *Sand.* xx; one of the compilers of the Admonition to the Parliament, 3 *Whitg.* x, 1 *Zur.* 284 n

Fielde (Jo.): reporter at a conference in the Tower, 1 *Ful.* xi. bis.

Field (Rich.): *v.* Feyld.

Field of the Cloth of Gold: *v.* Ardres.

Fielding family: *v.* Felding.

Fienes (Tho.), lord Dacre of the South: hanged for murder, 3 *Zur.* 220

Fienes (Greg.), next lord Dacre: ambassador to France, 2 *Zur.* 201 n

Fifteenth: a tax so called, 2 *Tyn.* 304

Figure-flingers: *Calf.* 14

Figures, Similitudes: similitudes a good kind of teaching, *Pil.* 161; their use, not to prove, but to illustrate, 1 *Tyn.* 312; they serve not throughout, 2 *Tyn.* 235; figurative speeches, 4 *Bul.* 283, 1 *Cran.* 181, 182; common in scripture, *Grin.* 42, 2 *Jew.* 1110, 1111; how to be received, 4 *Bul.* 288, 1 *Cran.* 115, 137, 138; heavenly things are shadowed forth by earthly things, *ib.* 243; one figure in the scripture represents different things, 1 *Tyn.* 208; how the word figure is used by old writers, 1 *Cran.* 116, 2 *Jew.* 569

Figurists: think nothing is received at the Lord's supper but bare signs, *Rog.* 289

File: to defile, 2 *Bec.* 62; filed, *Calf.* 132, 222

Fillol (Sir Will.): his daughter Catherine married the protector Somerset, 3 *Zur.* 340 n

Filmer (Hen.): martyred, 3 *Zur.* 242 n

Fimbria (C.): 3 *Whitg.* 323

Finan, bishop: 2 *Ful.* 16, 27

Finch (Jo.): letter from him to C. Humpard, 3 *Zur.* 605; ordained by Ridley, *ib.* n

Find : to provide for, 3 *Tyn.* 76

Finders: those who do not restore what they find, are thieves, 2 *Bec.* 108

Fine: end, or penalty, *Calf.* 125

Fineux (Sir Jo.): Elizabeth his wife (called "my lady Phines"), *Rid.* 407

Finland (Jo. duke of): *v.* John.

Fire: an image of God, *Hutch.* 163; it fulfils God's commandment, *Pil.* 607, 608; the might of the Holy Ghost so called, *ib.* 266, 342; fire threatened as a punishment against despisers of God's word, 1 *Bec.* 469, 470; a prayer on occasion of fire from heaven, *Pra. B.* 84; on the phrase "saved as by fire," 1 *Tyn.* 115, 116; strange fire, what, 1 *Bul.* 221; great fires in London and elsewhere, *Pil.* 606, 607

Firmament: meaning of the Hebrew word so translated, 1 *Tyn.* 407

Firmius, bp of Tagasta: refused to betray one whom he had hidden, *Hutch.* 54

First-born: *v.* Primogeniture.

First-fruits: why commanded by God, and offered by Israel, 2 *Tyn.* 215, 3 *Tyn.* 65; first-fruits and tenths, 2 *Cran.* 301, 305, 307; how much was paid for first-fruits by the English bishops to the pope, 4 *Jew.* 1078; restored to the crown, 2 *Zur.* 13 n.; burdensome, 1 *Zur.* 107

Fiscoke (Jo.), or Fishcock: martyred at Canterbury, *Poet.* 169

Fish: *v.* Fasting.

Fish (Simon): his Supplication of Beggars, 1 *Tyn.* 237 n., 2 *Tyn.* 335, 3 *Tyn.* 268 n.; he translated The Sum of the Scriptures [which appears to have been originally written in Italian] from the Dutch, 2 *Bec.* 421 n

Fisher (......): duo Fischeri, exiles, 1 *Cran.* (9)

Fisher (Jo.): *v.* Fysher.

Fisher (Jo.), bp of Rochester: preaches at the burning of Luther's works and Tyndale's New Testament, 1 *Tyn.* xxxi; editions of his sermon, *ib.* 189 n.; citations from it, *ib.* 190 n., 208, 209, 212, 213, 220—223; Tyndale's remarks upon it, *ib.* 208 — 223; character of it, *ib.* 341; he condemns Tho. Hitton, 2 *Tyn.* 340; once credited the holy maid of Kent, 1 *Tyn.* 327 n.; was one of the first suppressors of monasteries in this realm, 4 *Jew.* 800, 801; refused to swear to the preamble of the act of succession, 2 *Cran.* viii, 285; executed, *ib.* 349 n., *Pra. Eliz.* 318; a false martyr, *Bale* 139; his works, *Jew.* xxxvii, 4 *Jew.* 850; notices of his Psalmi seu Precationes, *Pra. Eliz.* x, 318; his book against Œcolampadius, 1 *Cran.* 46, 173, 190, 228, 344; he says the church is one because it has one head, viz. the pope, 1 *Jew.* 377, 1 *Tyn.* 212; regards Moses and Aaron as a shadow of Christ and his vicar, 1 *Tyn.* 208, 209, 412; argues that the pope is head of the church from Peter's payment of the tribute money, 1 *Jew.* 77, 1 *Tyn.* 190 n.; he says a council is sure to err if the pope of Rome be not present, *Rog.* 207, 208 n.; his reply to Velenus, 2 *Ful.* 336 n.; he allows that the real presence cannot be proved by any scripture, 1 *Jew.* 446; his view of purgatory, 3 *Jew.* 567, *Rog.* 216; reference to him on that subject, *ib.* 215 n.; he shews that the value of indulgences and pardons depends on purgatory, 1 *Jew.* 14, 101, 3 *Jew.* 568, 4 *Jew.* 851; charges the commons with heresy, 2 *Lat.* 301 n.; says that Luther and his followers would burn the pope and his favourers, 1 *Tyn.* 221; a letter to him, 2 *Cran.* 279; reference to him, 1 *Jew.* 92; his Life, by Bailey or Hall, 2 *Lat.* 356 n.

Fisking: dancing, 1 *Whitg.* 528
Fistewick's hostle: *v.* Cambridge.
Fit: canto or part, *Phil.* 18
Fittich (Vespasian): 1 *Zur.* 28
Fitton: fiction, 3 *Jew.* 217
Fitzalan (Will.), earl of Arundel: letter to him, 2 *Cran.* 255
Fitzalan (Hen.), earl of Arundel: privy councillor to [Edward], Mary, and Elizabeth, 1 *Zur.* 5 n.; signature as such, 2 *Cran.* 510, 511, *Park.* 73, 76, 2 *Zur.* 159 n.; ambassador from Mary to France and Germany, *Rid.* 394; suitor to queen Elizabeth, 1 *Zur.* 34 n.; mentioned, *Park.* 266; confined to his own house, 2 *Zur.* 172; he lent Parker a MS., *Park.* 388 n
Fitzgerald (Gerald), earl of Kildare: induces O'Neale to submit to queen Elizabeth, 1 *Zur.* 186 n

Fitzgerald (Tho.), earl of Desmond: his rebellion, 1 *Zur.* 332 n
Fitzgerald (Edw.), brother to the earl of Kildare: sent to arrest the duke of Norfolk, 2 *Zur.* 172
Fitzgerald (Will.): translator and editor of Whitaker's Disputation, *Whita.*
Fitzhamon (Rob.): 2 *Bec.* 480 n
Fitzherbert (Sir Tho.): his case alluded to, *Grin.* 274
Fitzherbert (Tho.): Obmutesce, 2 *Ful.* 294 n., 295 n
Fitzhugh (Geo.? lord): Catherine (Dacre) his wife, 1 *Bec.* 61 n
Fitzjames (Rich.), bp of London: shields the murderer of Richard Hunne, 3 *Tyn.* 166; would have made Colet a heretic for translating the Pater-noster, *ib.* 168
Fitzmaurice (James), brother of the earl of Desmond: leader of a rebellion in Ireland, *Lit. Eliz.* 657 n
Fitzpatrick (Barnaby), baron of Upper Ossory: previously styled (by Jo. ab Ulmis) comes Hiberniæ, 3 *Zur.* 423 n., 429
Fitzroy (Hen.), duke of Richmond: mentioned, 2 *Cran.* 259; notice of him, 3 *Bec.* 554 n.; his marriage, 2 *Cran.* 274, 359, 360; his death, *ib.* 359 n
— The lady Mary (Howard), his wife, 2 *Bec.* 554 n., 2 *Cran.* 274; on the validity of her marriage, and her right to dower, *ib.* 359, 360; letter from her to her father, *ib.* 360 n.; dedication to her, 2 *Bec.* 554
Fitzwarine (Fulke lord): *v.* Bourchier.
Fitzwilliam (Sir Will.): notice of him, 2 *Brad.* 135 n.; he favours Bradford in the King's Bench, *ib.* xxxiv; a privy councillor, *Park.* 364; letter to him, 2 *Brad.* 135
— Anne (Sidney), his wife, *Bale* 220, 242, 2 *Brad.* 135 n
Fitzwilliams (Jo.), of Sprotborough: his dau. Margaret, 2 *Cran.* 330 n
Flaccus, a Roman count: desired Petronilla to wife, 1 *Ful.* 475
Flacius (Matthias), Illyricus: notices of him, 1 *Ful.* 17 n., 2 *Zur.* 77 n.; his works, 2 *Ful.* 402, *Jew.* xxxvii, 3 *Whitg.* xxviii (and see Catalogus Testium); he was one of the writers of the Magdeburgh Centuries (*v.* Centuriators), 3 *Jew.* 128, 1 *Whitg.* 439; his criticisms, 1 *Ful.* passim; he defends Luther's translation of Rom. iii. 17,—"faith only," *ib.* 154; referred to on heaven, 1 *Lat.* 385 n.; said to be the father of those who would have no service or sacraments that they may be free from ceremonies, *Rog.* 186, 318; he speaks of Latomus asserting

that Socrates, Plato, and other heathen philosophers had as good understanding and faith in Christ as Abraham, 3 *Jew.* 583; calls Timothy and Titus bishops, 2 *Whitg.* 298, 427; writes on the work of an evangelist, *ib.* 299; speaks of the election of ministers as long continuing, 1*Whitg.* 448; says their ordination was proper to the bishop, *ib.* 439; cited on the appointment of metropolitans by the council of Nice, 2 *Whitg.* 148; the date he assigns to that synod, *ib.* 143; referred to on the degeneracy of Rome, *Rog.* 179 n., about the Nominals and Reals, 3 *Jew.* 613, about pope Joan, 4 *Jew.* 654; he mentions churches not subject to the pope, 2 *Bec.* 245 n., 4 *Jew.* 888; records that the bishop of Sidon, in the diet at Augsburgh, avouched openly, that the whole canon of the mass came from the apostles of Christ, word by word, 3 *Jew.* 235, 4 *Jew.* 783; referred to about Hosius, 4 *Jew.* 757, 758; he declares that the council of Trent was no lawful general council, *ib.* 1052; says there were forty bishops at it, *ib.* 1056; testifies that the Protestants were refused a hearing, 3 *Jew.* 208; on the conduct of the bishop of Chioca there, 4 *Jew.* 955; mentions that two bishops were taken and killed in adultery there, *ib.* 905, 913, 1056; he distributes the observing of days into four classes, 2 *Whitg.* 584; other references, 2 *Ful.* 232, 3 *Jew.* 340, 341, 1 *Whitg.* 398, 400; Cartwright acknowledges his obligations to a work of his, 1 *Whitg.* 448; letter from him to Parker, *Park.* 139; letters to him, *Park.* 286, 2 *Zur.* 77

Flagellants: notice of them, 2 *Hoop.* 76, 1 *Lat.* 465 n.; they said the baptism of voluntary blood was substituted for that of water, *Rog.* 277; condemned magistracy, *ib.* 337

Flamines: 3 *Jew.* 313, &c., *Pil.* 597, 2 *Whitg.* 124, 127, &c.; their jurisdiction a mere fantasy, 3 *Jew.* 315; archflamines, 2 *Whitg.* 123, &c.; the names archflamines and protoflamines not to be found in any allowed ancient writer, 3 *Jew.* 315

Flaminius (M. Ant.): poems by him, viz., hymnus matutinus, *Pra. Eliz.* 406; hymnus pœnitentialis, *ib.*; Dei beneficia prædicantis, *ib.* 407; hymnus meridianus, *ib.* 408; precatio cubitum ineuntis, *ib.* 409; hymnus ad Jesum Servatorem, *ib.* 410; pro pia vita, *ib.*; in morbo, *ib.* 417; pro beato vitæ exitu, *ib.* 418

Flanders: *v.* Netherlands.

Flattery: against it, 2 *Bul.* 119, 1 *Hoop.* 540, *Nord.* 175, 3 *Whitg.* 571—573; very evil in the clergy, 3 *Whitg.* 579; it is flattery to speak well of an evil man, *Hutch.* 224; flatterers are all double-tongued, *Sand.* 132; a lesson for them, 1 *Lat.* 231; Christ flattered not, 2 *Lat.* 187, but rebuked flattery, 3 *Whitg.* 578; Philip Flatterer, a proverbial name, 2 *Cov.* 436

Flavian, bp of Antioch: 1 *Whitg.* 410; he vanquished the Messalians, 1 *Jew.* 188, 193; the origin of antiphonal singing ascribed to him and Diodorus, 3 *Whitg.* 386

Flavian, bp of Constantinople: excommunicated by Dioscorus, assoiled by Leo, 1 *Jew.* 414—416; he describes the heresy of Eutyches, *ib.* 482, 3 *Jew.* 258; entreats pope Leo to make known the wickedness of that heretic to all the bishops under him, 4 *Jew.* 828; received the palm of a glorious death, 2 *Ful.* 363 n

Fleet prison: *v.* London.

Flegge (......), an English merchant at Antwerp, 1 *Tyn.* lxix.

Fleming (Malcolm 3rd lord): taken prisoner by the English at Solway, 3 *Zur.* 239 n

Fleming (Jo. 5th lord): named, 1 *Zur.* 203 n

Fleming (Abra.): notice of him, *Poet.* lv; a spiritual song by him, *ib.* 546

Flemming (Rich.): an inquisitor of heresies [probably afterwards bp of Lincoln], *Bale* 16

Flemyng (Jo.), curate of St Nicholas, Bristol: citation to him, 2 *Cran.* 257

Flesh: *v.* Enemies (Spiritual).

Flesh opposed to spirit (sometimes to the Spirit), *Now.* 99, 1 *Tyn.* 494, 504; the flesh and the spirit; verses by W. Warner, *Poet.* 378; what the flesh is, 3 *Bec.* 606, 1 *Tyn.* 139; it is the old man, 3 *Bul.* 98; all that is in man, before the Spirit of God come, 1 *Tyn.* 139; the nature of it, 1 *Bec.* 277; it remains in the regenerate, 3 *Bul.* 107; it profits nothing, 4 *Bul.* 461; it has a large kingdom, 2 *Bec.* 150, 151; we desire in the Lord's prayer that this kingdom may be plucked up, *ib.* 152; it is an enemy to the Christian, 1 *Bec.*126, 2 *Bec.* 184; its rebellion against the spirit, 2 *Bec.* 543; a declaration how the words flesh and spirit are to be understood in scripture, 1 *Brad.* 300; each termed a law by Paul, 1 *Tyn.* 504; their conflict, 1 *Brad.* 298, 301, 302, 1 *Lat.* 228, *Sand.* 167, 1 *Tyn.* 492, 500, 503, 2 *Tyn.* 160, 3 *Tyn.* 32, 113; the flesh oppresses the spirit, 2 *Tyn.* 9; the works of the flesh, brought forth by original sin, 2 *Bul.* 399; what it is to walk after the flesh, 2 *Bec.* 632, *Sand.* 118; the flesh is

tamed by fasting (*q.v.*), 2 *Bec.* 543, &c.; subdued by the cross, 2 *Tyn.* 9, 10
Flesh and blood, what, 3 *Bec.* 611; we should not put our trust in them, 2 *Hoop.* 278; they cannot be in heaven, 1 *Bul.* 176; all flesh is grass, *Sand.* 169
Holy flesh, Hag. ii. 12, what is meant thereby, *Pil.* 162
Fletcher: a maker of arrows, 1 *Bec.* 5
Fletcher (Anth.): notice of him, *Poet.* xlv; a simile, by him, *ib.* 475
Fletcher (Rob.), a gentleman of Cheshire: *Grin.* 345 n., 346 n
Fletcher (Will.), skinner: *Park.* 211
Fletcher (Will.), and the sweet rode: *Pil.* 628
Fleury (Claude): 2 *Ful.* 81 n., 183 n
Flinsbach (Cuman): 2 *Zur.* 98 n
Fliring: fleering, 2 *Bec.* 7
Flock (The little): Christ's flock a little one, 1 *Tyn.* 165, 363; this flock contrasted with the multitude who are not chosen, 3 *Tyn.* 109; they do not serve God after their own imagination, *ib.* 108, but seek the honour of Christ in all things, *ib.* 109; they are persecuted by the multitude, *ib.* 110
Flodden Field: before the battle the Scots played at dice for all the dukedoms and great cities in England, *Pil.* 251
Flood: *v.* Noah.
N. de Lyra and More were of opinion that many of those drowned in the flood were saved, 3 *Tyn.* 134 n.; the flood a type of baptism, 4 *Bul.* 364; a figure of Christ's second coming, 2 *Jew.* 868
Flood (......): martyred in Smithfield, *Poet.* 172
Florebell (Ant.): opposed by C. S. Curio, *Phil.* 319; his character, *ib.* 325
Florence: *v.* Councils.
Injured by Clement VII., 4 *Jew.* 672
Florence (Oct.): a pseudonym of Bullinger, 4 *Bul.* xv
Florentinus (Archidiaconus): *v.* Archidiaconus.
Florentius: Theodosius would have him present at the council of Chalcedon, 4 *Jew.* 1029
Floretus Liber: *Jew.* xxxvii; states that Christ's body in the sacrament of the altar may be in many places at one time, 1 *Jew.* 480 n.; mentions cases of non-consecration, *ib.* 550; gives a reason why the sacrament should not be consecrated on Good Friday or Easter eve, *ib.* 246; on opus operatum, 2 *Jew.* 750
Florian, vicar of Asia: 4 *Bul.* 394

Florian (......): 3 *Zur.* 187
Florin: its value, 4 *Jew.* 1079
Florinus, a heretic: *Whita.* 581; he made God the author of sin, *Rog.* 97
Florus (L. A.): says the Saguntines, &c. chose rather to die with fire and famine than violate an oath, 1 *Bul.* 252
Flottereth: fluttereth, or faltereth, 3 *Bec.* 94
Flotess: scum, 2 *Tyn.* 215
FLOWER OF GODLY PRAYERS, by T. Becon, 3 *Bec.* 1, &c.; referred to, *ib.* 186, 190
Flowers: what they signify in the ceremonies of Palm-Sunday, 1 *Bec.* 115
Flowers of speech: used by Harding, 3 *Jew.* 138, &c.
Flushing: troops sent thither, 1 *Zur.* 273; Spaniards executed there, 2 *Zur.* 207; pirates of Flushing, 1 *Zur.* 312; privateers, 2 *Zur.* 273
Foad off (To): what, 2 *Bul.* 38, 3 *Bul.* 106
Fogg (Mr): *Park.* 375
Foiled: trampled on, perplexed, puzzled, 2 *Bec.* 426
Foillanus (St), and his three brethren: *Bale* 192
Fokes (Mr): thanked for his law books, *Phil.* 230
Foliot (Gilb.), bp of London: *Pil.* 589
Foljamb (Jeffry): grantee of Croxden abbey, 2 *Cran.* 380 n
Folkerzheimer (Herman): saluted by the name of Herman, 4 *Jew.* 1241, 1242, 1 *Zur.* 9, 13, 17, 40, 47, & sæpe; he visits bp Jewel, 4 *Jew.* 1254, &c., 1 *Zur.* 119, 120, 2 *Zur.* 84, &c.; letters by him, 2 *Zur.* 84, 93, 105
Folkerzheimer (Ulric): 2 *Zur.* 105
Folkes (Tho.): Table of Coins, 1 *Lat.* 95 n., 137 n
Folkestone, co. Kent: Parker meets the queen there, *Park.* 475
Fond: (v. n.) to dote, *Bale* 114
Fons (Friar), i. e. Alph. à Castro, *q. v.*
Fontaine (Nic. de la): *v.* La Fontaine.
Fontevraud: the order so called, a sect of Benedictines, 3 *Bul.* 295 n
Fonts: of fonts, 3 *Whitg.* 122; said to have been invented by pope Pius, *ib.* 109; necessary in churches, 4 *Bul.* 501; superstitiously venerated, 1 *Tyn.* 225; hallowed on Easter eve, 2 *Cran.* 158, 175, *Rid.* 532; likewise on Whitsun eve, 2 *Cran.* 175; prayer at the hallowing, from the Salisbury Manuale, 2 *Jew.* 567; the water to be changed monthly, *Rid.* 532; fonts not to be removed, 2 *Zur.* 149 n.; diversely placed, 2 *Whitg.* 463; outcry against them in London, *Park.* 450

Food: *v.* Eating.
Moderation therein, *Pil.* 52; the miracle by which it nourishes, *ib.* 53; it is not enough to have temporal food, except it be blessed of God, 1 *Bec.* 174; the diet of maids, 2 *Bec.* 369

Fools: who is a fool, 3 *Bec.* 607; fools and jesters, 4 *Jew.* 860; the vicar of St Fools, *Calf.* 237

Forbes (Patr.): Full View, &c., 1 *Zur.* 56, 57, 69 nn

Force: to lay stress on, 2 *Cov.* 66

Forcelets: what, 1 *Jew.* 260 n

Ford, co. Kent: Parker desires to take down a part of his house at Ford, to enlarge his house at Bekesbourne, *Park.* 419, 424

Fore: previous, 2 *Tyn.* 5

Forefathers: we may not judge them; God knoweth his elect, 1 *Lat.* 305; many of our ancestors saved by God's grace notwithstanding the errors of their times, *ib.* 525; against following ungodly forefathers, with sentences and examples of scripture, 1 *Bec.* 437, &c.

Foreigners: *v.* Strangers.

Foreknowledge: *v.* God.

Forelette: to let or hinder, *Phil.* 346; forletteth, abandoneth, *ib.* 345

Foreman (Jo.): martyred at Grinstead, *Poet.* 168

Foreslowing: putting off, 1 *Jew.* 199, *Sand.* 172

Forespeaking: fortune-telling, *Now.* 127

Forest (Friar Jo.): account of him, 2 *Lat.* 391 n.; reference to him, 2 *Tyn.* 302; proceedings against him for denying the king's supremacy, 2 *Cran.* 365; burned, *Bale* 509, 2 *Cran.* 366 n., 1 *Lat.* xi, 266 n.; a false martyr, *Bale* 139; Latimer preaches at his execution, 2 *Lat.* 392 n

Forestus (Jac. Phil.), Bergomensis: Supplementum Chronicorum, *Jew.* xxxiii, 3 *Whitg.* xxv; calls Timothy bishop of Ephesus, 2 *Whitg.* 295; he relates the martyrdom of St Bartholomew, *Calf.* 133; tells how Helena disposed of the cross and nails, *ib.* 327, 328; mentions the transformation of the Pantheon at Rome into the church of All-hallows, *ib.* 67 n.; says Zosimus ordered that the deacon should not minister the eucharist in the presence of the bishop or priest, 1 *Jew.* 240; names pope Joan, 4 *Jew.* 656; speaks of the poisoning of Henry the emperor, *ib.* 687; referred to on the origin of friars, 2 *Ful.* 103 n.; probably mistaken for Sigebertus, *Calf.* 67 n., 323 n

Forgeries: *v.* Constantine, Zosimus, &c.

Forgiveness of others: *v.* Enemies, Prayer (The Lord's).
The duty of forgiving others, 2 *Bec.* 180, 574, 2 *Cran.* 110—112, *Hutch.* 333, 1 *Lat.* 424, 1 *Tyn.* 357; examples of it, 2 *Bec.* 179; we must forgive if we would be forgiven, 1 *Bec.* 153, 154, *Sand.* 229, 1 *Tyn.* 470; why we ought to forgive, 2 *Bec.* 182; our forgiveness of others is not the cause of God forgiving us, *ib.* 181, 182; for we must be forgiven by God before we can forgive, 2 *Cov.* 344; our forgiveness of those who trespass against us is, therefore, an evidence that we are forgiven, 1 *Tyn.* 76; how man forgives his neighbour, *Hutch.* 94, 95

Forgiveness of sins: *v.* Absolution, Sin.

Form, Forms: *v.* Meditations, Prayers.
Use of the word "form" in arguments for transubstantiation, 1 *Cran.* 251, 253, 254; remarks on the words "form" and "substance," 3 *Jew.* 261; "form" and "nature," often used for one thing, *ib.* 513

Form and manner, &c.: *v.* Ordination.

Form of concord: *v.* Concord.

Forman (Rob.), or Ferman, rector of All-hallows, Honey lane: harassed as a reformer, 3 *Tyn.* 193; his doctrine misrepresented by More, *ib.* 208

Formosus, pope: his body disinterred by a successor (the outrage is sometimes ascribed to Stephen VI., sometimes to Sergius III.), and cast into the Tiber, and his acts abrogated, *Bale* 394, 1 *Hoop.* 217, 218, 2 *Jew.* 586, 3 *Jew.* 249, 276 n., 277 n., 4 *Jew.* 1110, *Pil.* 652, 1 *Tyn.* 324 n

Forne: former, past, 4 *Jew.* 637

Fornication: *v.* Adultery.

Forrester (Andr.), or Forstar, minister of Dysart: 2 *Zur.* 365

Forslowing: *v.* Foreslowing.

Forstar (Andr.): *v.* Forrester.

Forster* (Mr), a gentleman of Hampshire: prisoner in the Fleet, 2 *Hoop.* 378

Foster (......), baily of Newark: 2 *Cran.* 316

Foster (Isabel): martyred in Smithfield, 3 *Zur.* 175 n.; called Annis Foster, *Poet.* 165

Forster (Jo.): his Dict. Hebr. cited on the name Pharisee, 3 *Whitg.* 522

Forster (Sir Jo.), warden of the Middle Marches: taken prisoner and carried into Scotland, *Grin.* 355 n

Foster (R.), of All Souls' college: *Park.* 297, 301 n.; his widow, *ib.* 320, 324

Fortalitium Fidei: *Jew.* xxxvii; the author

---

* Forster and Foster are arranged together.

was Alphonsus de Spina, 2 *Ful.* 5 n.; speaking of an opinion that latria is due only to God, he says that although this seems reasonable, common opinion holds the contrary, 2 *Jew.* 667; he affirms that Christ was sold in Joseph, hanged in the bunch of grapes, crucified in the serpent, *ib.* 765; his monstrous conclusion from transubstantiation, *ib.* 784; he says that although there remained but two faithful men in the world, in them the church, which is the unity of the faithful, should be saved, 3 *Jew.* 268, 4 *Jew.* 724, 877

Fortescu (Capt.): a name assumed by Ant. Babington, *q.v.*

Fortescue (Ant.), controller to cardinal Pole: condemned for treason, 1 *Zur.* 129 n

Forth: free course, *Sand.* 152

Forth-fares: 2 *Hoop.* 137

Forth on: thenceforward, 3 *Tyn.* 77

Forthink: to repent, 1 *Tyn.* 260, 3 *Tyn.* 23; forthinking, 1 *Brad.* 45

Fortress: the Fortalitium Fidei of Alph. de Spina, 2 *Ful.* 5 n. (*v.* Fortalitium); Stapleton's Fortress of the Faith, *ib.*; THE FORTRESS OF THE FAITHFUL, by T. Becon, 2 *Bec.* 581, &c.

Fortune, Fate, Destiny, Chance, Necessity: what fortune is, 3 *Bec.* 610; remarks on the doctrine of necessity, *Phil.* 402; God is not tied to it, 1 *Brad.* 212; things do not turn out by chance, but by providence, *Pil.* 309; false opinions respecting destiny or fate refuted, *Hutch.* 79, &c., 83, &c.; destiny not the cause of sin, 2 *Bul.* 363; nothing happens by fortune with respect to God, though it appears so to man, 1 *Brad.* 491; fortune is a word unseemly for Christians, *ib.* 213, a wicked fancy, *ib.* 423, 2 *Cov.* 240

For why: because, *Bale* 312

Fosbroke (T. D.): *Grin.* 273 n., 1 *Tyn.* 92 n

Fossarii: grave diggers, 3 *Jew.* 272

Foss-way: the Roman road from Bath to Lincoln, 2 *Lat.* 364

Foster (Isabel and others): *v.* Forster.

Foulis (Hen.): Romish Treasons, *Calf.* 6 n

Founceth: pounceth (probably a misprint), 4 *Jew.* 1061

Fountain (......), gaoler to bp Bonner: *Phil.* 292

Four: mystic import of the number, *Bale* 468

Fowler (Abr.): *Rog.* vi. n

Fowler (Jo.), groom of the privy chamber: sent to the Tower, 3 *Zur.* 648 n

Fowler (Jo.), or Fouler, printer at Louvaine:

2 *Ful.* 215 n.; translator of Frarine's attack on the Protestants of France, 1 *Ful.* x; his Psalter, answered by Sampson, 2 *Ful.* 3

Foxcroft (......): *Grin.* 266

Foxe * (Edw.), bp of Hereford: notices of him, 2 *Lat.* 379, 382, 3 *Zur.* 15 n.; almoner to Henry VIII., and concerned in the business of his divorce, 1 *Cran.* ix; ambassador to the pope, 2 *Cran.* 332 n.; provost of King's college, Cambridge, 1 *Lat.* iv; his book De Vera Differentia Regiæ Potestatis et Ecclesiasticæ, 2 *Brad.* 16, *Rid.* 512; he goes as ambassador to Smalcald, 3 *Zur.* 520 n., 527; his part in the Institution of a Christian Man, 2 *Cran.* 337 n., *Rid.* 511; his death, 2 *Cran.* 81 n

Foxe (Hugh): martyred in Smithfield, *Poet.* 171, 2 *Zur.* 160 n

Foxe (Jo.): mentioned, 1 *Zur.* 137 n.; tutor to Tho. duke of Norfolk, *Lit. Eliz.* 655 n., 2 *Zur.* 57 n.; in exile, 2 *Zur.* 21; much employed as a corrector of the press, *Grin.* 231, 2 *Zur.* 112 n.; he translated into Latin Cranmer's controversy with Gardiner about the eucharist, but only a part of it was printed, 1 *Zur.* 42 n.; being employed in collecting the history of the martyrs, he craves the assistance of B. Ochinus, *ib.* 26; engaged in translating the Greek councils, and on the history of the martyrs, *ib.* 43; assisted by Grindal in his work, *Grin.* iii; letters relating to it, *ib.* 219, &c.; his Rerum in Ecclesia gestarum Commentarii, 1559, the original of the Acts and Monuments, 2 *Brad.* xi. n., 2 *Hoop.* 381; publication of the Acts and Monuments, 1 *Zur.* 128; references to this work, 3 *Bec.* 11 n., *Calf.* 53 n., 246 n., 2 *Ful.* 23, 37, 61, 93, 209, 232, 247, 2 *Lat.* 505, *Wool.* 113 n.; cited on patriarchs, archbishops, &c., 2 *Whitg.* 125, 148, 150, 171, 333, &c.; he shews that the bishop of Rome was very anciently a metropolitan or patriarch, *ib.* 137, 220; on the mission of Eleutherius, *ib.* 128; on a place of Cyprian, *ib.* 217, 219; on the ancient use of funeral sermons, 3 *Whitg.* 375; he gives the history of the mass, *Pil.* 505; mentions the excommunication of the dead bodies of Wickliffe and others, *Rog.* 311 n.; his preface to Thorpe's examination,' *Bale* 64; he says Sixtus IV. built stews in Rome, *Rog.* 181 n.; account of Tyndale, 1 *Tyn.* xiv, &c.; mistake respecting Cranmer's urging Edward VI. to sign the death-warrant of Joan Bocher, *Hutch.* iv, v; life and acts of Latimer, 2 *Lat.* ix; prefaces to

---

* Fox or Foxe; these forms are arranged together.

the examination of Ridley, *Rid.* 189, 255; Dr Turner's letter to him concerning the Book of Martyrs, and especially on Ridley, *ib.* 487, 491; reference about Ridley, *Grin.* 211; preface to an account of the variations of Stephen Gardiner, *Rid.* 307; remarks on Grindal's Dialogue between Custom and Verity, *Grin.* 36; he mentions miracles in his time, 2 *Ful.* 76, 77; the Acts and Monuments slandered by Harding, 3 *Jew.* 187, 189; errors noted, 2 *Ful.* 98 n.; Bulkley's addition to Foxe, *ib.* 74 n.; he has been regarded (but as it seems incorrectly) as the compiler of the Christian Prayers, *Pra. Eliz.* xxi—xxiii; he publishes the Reformatio Legum Ecclesiasticarum, *Hutch.* 6 n.; part of his letter to the duke of Norfolk, dissuading him from marriage with the Scottish queen, 1 *Zur.* 216 n.; he attends the duke at his execution, 2 *Zur.* 198 n.; his friendship with Pilkington, who in 1572 gave him a prebend at Durham, *Pil.* xiii; the supposed editor of Day's edition of the works of Tyndale, &c., 1 *Tyn.* 370 n.; his remark on the Articles of alleged heresy extracted from Tyndale's Obedience, *ib.* 170, &c., nn.; his opinion on the perseverance of the saints, *ib.* 79 n.; his prayer for the church, and all the states thereof, made at Paul's cross, *Pra. Eliz.* 462; he finishes Haddon's second reply to Osorius, 4 *Jew.* 686 n., *Park.* 217 n.; his book De Christo gratis Justificante, appended to which is a sermon by Fulke, translated into Latin, 1 *Ful.* viii; his preface to Pilkington on Nehemiah, *Pil.* 277; letters by him, *Grin.* 230, 231, *Park.* 160, 230, 1 *Zur.* 22, 25, 35, 37 (see 2 *Zur.* xi), 41, 42, 216 n., 3 *Zur.* 767; letters to him, *Grin.* 219—237, *Rid.* 487, 491

Fox (Rich.), bp of Winchester: said to have betrayed the confessions of the nobility to Henry VII., 2 *Tyn.* 305; a Latin speech at Corpus Christi college, Oxford, in commemoration of him as founder thereof, 4 *Jew.* 1304

Foxe (Rich.), parson of Steeple-Bumpstead: 2 *Cov.* viii.

Foxes: enemies of the church so called, *Sand.* 62, &c.; the means they use to destroy the vineyard, *ib.* 65, &c.; they must be taken, and how, *ib.* 69, &c., 437, 441

Frame-house: 2 *Brad.* 54, 78, 86

Framlingham, co. Suffolk: St Michael's church, 2 *Bec.* 554 n.; Ridley had from Fremingham to the Tower, *Rid.* 155

Frampton (Rich.): Grindal's secretary, *Grin.* 421, 462

Framton (......), a vicar of the college of St Martin le Grand: 2 *Cran.* 240

France: *v.* Brabant, &c., Church, II. v, French.

Said to be Zarephath (Obad. 20), *Pil.* 268; evangelized, 1 *Jew.* 267, 280, 298; whether evangelized by Rome, *ib.* 162; various towns mentioned as the scenes of the labours of apostolic men, *ib.*; "Crescens to Galatia," 2 Tim. iv. 10, Epiphanius reads "Gallia," *ib.*; early persecutions there, 2 *Bul.* 105; epistle of the bishops of Gaul to Leo I., 1 *Jew.* 161; the title of king of France assumed by the kings of England, 1 *Tyn.* 187; our wars with France a heavy burden, *ib.*; acts of the English there in the time of Henry VI., 2 *Tyn.* 303; France ever the chief support of the papacy, *ib.* 260, 298; the kings styled Most Christian, 1 *Tyn.* 186, 2 *Tyn.* 263, and Eldest Son of the Holy See, 187 n.; Julius II. offered to transfer the title of Most Christian to Henry VIII., 2 *Tyn.* 187 n.; the king received the sacrament in both kinds, 1 *Jew.* 206; reflections of a certain king of France on his death bed, 2 *Cov.* 81; war with France, 2 *Tyn.* 316; peace, 1525, *ib.* 318; war against France, 1544, *Park.* 15, *Pra. Eliz.* 567 n.; treaty of peace, 1550, 3 *Zur.* 480, 559; France at war with the emperor, 3 *Zur.* 590; peace with England, 1559, 1 *Zur.* 24, and with Scotland, *ib.* 75 n.; troubles about the Huguenots, persecutions, and affairs of the country generally, 1 *Brad.* 571 n., 2 *Jew.* 840, 3 *Jew.* 193, *Nord.* 94, *Now.* 223, 228, *Pil.* 420, *Pra. Eliz.* 484 n., 1 *Zur.* 114, 2 *Zur.* 83, 84, 89, 128; massacres, *Rog.* 6; the Protestants aided by queen Elizabeth, *Now.* 226, 227; war declared against France, 1563, 1 *Zur.* 132; peace proclaimed, 1564, *ib.* 133, 139; wars of the Huguenots, *Lit. Eliz.* 578 n.; they did not burn the body of Irenæus, 4 *Jew.* 1047; they were defeated at Jarnac and Montcontour, 2 *Zur.* 250 n.; afterwards protected by royal authority, 1 *Zur.* 250 n.; peace with England, 1572, *ib.* 273; P. Frarine writes against the Protestants, 1 *Ful.* x; a sonnet by way of exhortation to the Frenchmen, which are revolted from true religion, by Chr. Fetherstone, *Poet.* 467; prayers used daily in the English army in France, 1589, *Lit. Eliz.* 626; capital punishments used in France, *Now.* 226; Bustum Anglorum Gallia, Gallorum Italia (proverb), *Calf.* 113

France (Abr.): *v.* Fraunce.

Francis (St): founder of the Minorites, 3 *Bul.*

295; termed the glory of God, *Rog.* 38; compared to Christ, *Bale* 205; said to be figured by Isaiah in his 6th chapter, *Rog.* 38 n., to be the Holy Ghost, *ib.* 71, to be free from all sin, *ib.* 134, 139, to have redeemed those saved since his days, *ib.* 298; eternal life promised to observers of his rules, 1 *Tyn.* 227; he commands that there be but one mass daily, 2 *Jew.* 635; his cord, 1 *Tyn.* 122 n.; his cowl, *Calf.* 287; burial in the coat or habit of his order, 1 *Tyn.* 122, 2 *Tyn.* 32

Francis I., king of France: his interview with Henry VIII. at Ardres near Calais, 2 *Tyn.* 313; war between him and England, *ib.* 316; taken prisoner at Pavia, *ib.* 318, but soon liberated, *ib.* 319; embassy to him, 2 *Cran.* 246; he met the pope at Marseilles, *ib.* n.; intended to have adopted the reformed religion, *ib.* 416 n.; his funeral sermon at St Paul's, London, *Rid.* v. n

Francis II., king of France, and consort of queen Mary of Scotland: styles himself king of Scotland and heir of England, 4 *Jew.* 1214, 1 *Zur.* 40; expected in Scotland with his army, 4 *Jew.* 1224, 1 *Zur.* 56; he renounces the title and arms of England, 4 *Jew.* 1238, 1 *Zur.* 89

Francis, duke of Anjou, Alençon, &c.: mentioned, 2 *Zur.* 278, 282, 305; his proposed marriage with queen Elizabeth, *Grin.* 408–412, 1 *Zur.* 239, 250, 331 n., 2 *Zur.* 308 n

Francis de Mayro: v. Maronis.

Francis, monk of Colen: counted concupiscence no sin, *Rog.* 102

Francis (Ant.): 2 *Zur.* 171

Francis (Tho.), regius professor of physic at Oxford, afterwards provost of Queen's college: 3 *Zur.* 420

Franciscans, Grey Friars, or Minorites: their order, 4 *Bul.* 517: their founder, 3 *Bul.* 295; the profession of their rule supposed to secure salvation, *Rog.* 152, 1 *Tyn.* 227; their great increase, 1 *Tyn.* 302; the order divided into Conventuals and Observants, 2 *Cran.* 330 n., 1 *Lat.* 287 n., 1 *Tyn.* 301 n.; they were Scotists, 1 *Tyn.* 159; controversy between them and the Dominicans, 1 *Ful.* 35; they set Christ but little above Francis (q. v.), 2 *Tyn.* 5; their writers on the Apocalypse, *Bale* 258; they received no bribes themselves, but had others to receive for them, 1 *Lat.* 189; story of a friar limitour, *ib.* 524; their excuse for ignorance, 1 *Whitg.* 33; turned out of their houses, 2 *Cran.* 330 n.; their Breviary, 2 *Lat.* 227 n.; Alcoranus Franciscanorum, *Rog.* 38, &c. nn.; Bouchier De Martyrio Fratrum Ord. Min.,
2 *Lat.* 392 n.; Pulton's Antiq. of Engl. Franciscans, 1 *Lat.* 287, 2 *Lat.* 319, 391

Franciscopolis, commonly called Havre-de-Grace, q. v.

Franciscus: saluted, 1 *Zur.* 119

Franciscus Zephyrus, q. v.

Francken (Chr.): *Rog.* 182 n

François (Rich.): v. Vauville (R.).

Francowitz (Matthias): v. Flacius.

Francus (Dan.): Disq. de Papistarum Indicibus, *Calf.* 96 n

Frank: a place to fatten boars in, a sty, *Bale* 467, 3 *Bec.* 375

Frank (Peter): martyred at Colchester, *Bale* 586

Frank-almoigne: 2 *Tyn.* 148

Franke (Sir), a martyr, *Poet.* 162

Frankfort: v. Councils.

The emperors were crowned there, *Grin.* 20; Tyndale's books printed and seized there, 1 *Tyn.* xxxv; the foreign church, 3 *Zur.* 110, 111; names of English exiles there, *ib.* 755, 763, 764; an English church, under Coxe and others, *Rid.* 387; subscription required of women in it, *Rog.* 24; the troubles there, *Grin.* iii, iv, 239, 4 *Jew.* xii, xiii, 1192, *Now.* ii, *Rid.* 533, 2 *Whitg.* 489 n., 1 *Zur.* 8 n., 3 *Zur.* 128, 753, &c.; McCrie ascribes them to Whittingham, 3 *Zur.* 764 n.; points conceded by the episcopal party, *ib.* 754, 757; the "peaceable letter" on ceremonies, *Pil.* iii; the French church, 3 *Zur.* 174; letter of bishop Grindal to the magistrates, in behalf of the congregation of Dutch Protestants, *Grin.* 247, 249; Frankfort fair, 1 *Zur.* 171, 184, 191, 2 *Zur.* 105, &c.

Frankincense: v. Magi.

Franklin (Rob.), fellow of All Souls': *Park.* 300

Franklings: freeholders, 1 *Lat.* 408

Frankweiler (......): 2 *Cov.* 519 n., 524

Frarine (Peter): rails against the Protestants of France, and is answered by Fulke, 1 *Ful.* x, 2 *Ful.* 4

Fraternities: 2 *Brad.* 279, 2 *Cov.* 258, 2 *Jew.* 912, 1 *Tyn.* 212 n

Fratricellians: a sect, *Pil.* 18; they condemned magistracy, *Rog.* 337; enjoined community of goods, *ib.* 353

Fratry: a refectory, 2 *Tyn.* 98; described, *Grin.* 272 n

Fratries: fraternities, 2 *Jew.* 912

Fraud: v. Deceit.

Fraunce (Abr.): notice of him, *Poet.* xxii; Psalm lxxii, (lxxiii), in hexameter verse, *ib.* 237

Freak (Edm.): v. Freke.

Freculphus Lexoviensis: *Calf.* 67 n., 87 n

Frederick I., emperor, called Barbarossa: his letter to pope Adrian, and the pope's arrogant reply, *Pil.* 22; that pope refused him a blessing for holding his left stirrup, 4 *Jew.* 692; he corrected four popes, *Pil.* 640; kissed the foot of pope Alexander III., *Grin.* 21; that pope trod upon him, 3 *Jew.* 299, 4 *Jew.* 696, 700, 701, *Lit. Eliz.* 450, and betrayed him to the Turk, 3 *Whitg.* 592; communion in both kinds not forbidden till his time, 1 *Hoop.* 229, *Hutch.* 283

Frederick II., emperor: miraculously hindered from destroying Catana, *Pil.* 536 n

Frederick I., king of Denmark: his reformation, 1 *Cov.* 424; story of king Frederick's physicians (supposed to be this king), *Pil.* 336

Frederick II., king of Denmark: prepares for war with Sweden, 2 *Zur.* 106

Frederick III., elector Palatine: *Park.* 471 n.; he favours Calvinism, 2 *Zur.* 156 n., 274 n.; patronizes Zanchius, 2 *Zur.* 185 n.; letter to him from Parker, *Park.* 317; another, from G. Withers, 2 *Zur.* 156

Frederick IV., elector Palatine: *Park.* 471 n

Frederick V., elector Palatine, and afterwards king of Bohemia: married Elizabeth, daughter of James I., *Park.* 471 n., 2 *Zur.* 328 n

Frederick (Duke): v. John Frederick.

Frederick of Venice, a Dominican: wrote on the Apocalypse, *Bale* 258

Freedom: v. Liberty.

Fremingham: v. Framlingham.

Freese (......): punished for selling the scriptures, 2 *Lat.* 306 n

Free-Will: v. Faith, Grace, Predestination. What it is, and how far man has it, 3 *Bec.* 608, 1 *Brad.* 216, *Rog.* 103, *Sand.* 24; errors on it, *Park.* 140, *Rog.* 104, *Sand.* 24; the thraldom of the will described, *Sand.* 21; the will of fallen man is not free, but bound unto the will of the devil, 1 *Tyn.* 17, 18, 23, 182; it is naturally bent to evil, 1 *Bec.* 151, 152, 2 *Bec.* 154, 3 *Bec.* 100, 1 *Hoop.* 152; it is not free to good naturally, but only when made so by grace, 3 *Bul.* 103, 3 *Jew.* 168, 3 *Tyn.* 174, 192; the will of Jonah was not free till made so, 1 *Tyn.* 454, 459; the will is free to run from God, but to draw near unto him is his grace and gift, *Sand.* 133; in respect of first birth, the will is only free to evil; in respect of second birth, only to good, 1 *Brad.* 251; the will is made free by grace, 1 *Tyn.* 183, 429, 489, 3 *Tyn.* 174; a good will the gift of God, 1 *Brad.* 23; the Spirit makes God's people willing, 2 *Tyn.* 250; after conversion men have two wills, *ib.* 76; probations out of scripture, that without the grace of God, free-will can do nothing in matters of faith and salvation, 3 *Bec.* 328, 329; examination of scriptures alleged for free-will, 1 *Brad.* 321; God's commands do not prove it, 1 *Ful.* 400; it is not proved by Luke ii. 14 (Vulg. "hominibus bonæ voluntatis"), *Whita.* 153, 468; translations concerning it examined, 1 *Ful.* 123—126, 375—400; a text in Ecclesiasticus alleged for it, *ib.* 21; the doctrine is set up by hypocrites, 1 *Tyn.* 430; it is Pharisaical, *ib.* 435; a false doctrine, *Bale* 427, 1 *Brad.* 372; a dark doctrine, 2 *Tyn.* 103; contrary to scripture, 1 *Tyn.* 111, 155, 2 *Tyn.* 190, 199; heretics, by their proud free-will knowledge, pervert the scriptures, *Phil.* 308; he, says Whitgift, that dieth in the opinion holdeth not the foundation, 1 *Whitg.* 188, 189, for it is clean contrary to free justification, 3 *Whitg.* 552; our own free-will cannot work righteousness, 1 *Tyn.* 494; what it doth when it taketh in hand to keep the law, *ib.* 429; repentance is not of man's free-will, 1 *Brad.* 53; faith is not attainable thereby, *ib.* 65; the will of man has no part in the working of faith, 3 *Tyn.* 140; it profits nothing, 1 *Bec.* 70, 72; it must be slain, 1 *Tyn.* 426; the doctrine was held by heathen philosophers, 3 *Tyn.* 191, as by Aristotle, 1 *Tyn.* 108, 155, 276; it is maintained by Jews, 1 *Brad.* 323, 329, 1 *Ful.* 126, 3 *Tyn.* 193, by Mahometans, 1 *Brad.* 323, 329, 3 *Tyn.* 193, by divers Greek fathers, 1 *Whitg.* 188, by Pelagians and semi-Pelagians, 1 *Ful.* 377, 3 *Whitg.* 613; the errors of Pelagius refuted by Augustine, 3 *Bul.* 11, 102; the views of the latter perverted by Papists, 1 *Ful.* 386—389 (see Augustine, viii); the doctrine of free-will opposed by Prosper, 1 *Tyn.* 487 n.; boastfully maintained by the church of Rome, 1 *Brad.* 323, 329, *Sand.* 23, *Tyn.* 191, 193; maintained by More, but denied by Tyndale, 3 *Tyn.* 210, 211; supported by Latimer, 2 *Lat.* 206; the errors of Hart and his fellows, 2 *Brad.* 170, 171; free-willers, or free-will men, 2 *Brad.* 128, 244, 1 *Whitg.* 94; reference to certain free-will men, schismatics and disturbers, *Phil.* 247; Bradford composes a letter concerning the free-willers, which is also signed by Ferrar, Taylor, and Philpot, 1 *Brad.* 305, 2 *Brad.* 169, *Phil.* xiv; other letters to free-willers, 2 *Brad.* 128, 164, 180, 181, 194; caution against the leaven of free-will, 1 *Tyn.* 466

Free-will offerings: 2 *Bul.* 205

Freher (Marquard): Theatrum Virorum, 2 *Lat.* 349 n

Freke (Edm.), bp of Rochester, afterwards of Norwich: *Park.* 318, 319; his opinion on prophesyings, *ib.* 459 n.; he meets the queen at Canterbury, *ib.* 475; his translation, *ib.* 477 n

Frembe: strange, foreign, 1 *Cov.* 139

Freming (......): a friend of Sir Phil. Sidney, 2 *Zur.* 292

Fremund (St), of Dunstable: *Bale* 192, 1 *Lat.* 55 n

French: *v.* France.

The French land in the Isle of Wight, and at Newhaven, 2 *Cran.* 495 n.; French refugees, 1 *Zur.* 288, 291, 327; as to their churches, see Canterbury, London, Norwich.

French language: the language of ancient Gaul, 1 *Jew.* 298; French much used in England, *ib.* 293; used in pleading at the bar, 2 *Cran.* 170

Frensham (Hen.): mentioned, 1 *Zur.* 22 bis, 25, 36, 42, 47, 58, 68, 70, 78; eulogized, 2 *Zur.* 21; extract from his will, *ib.* n.; letter to him, 1 *Zur.* 37; corrected copy of the same, 2 *Zur.* xi.

Frentike: frantic, mad, *Calf.* 81

Freres: friars, *Pil.* 205

Frey (Agnes): wife of Albert Durer, *Pra. Eliz.* xvii, xviii.

Freyamt, Zurich: 4 *Bul.* 546

Fria, a Saxon idol: *Pil.* 16

Friar Mantuan: *v.* Baptista Mantuanus (S.).

Friars: *v.* Monks.

Their origin, 2 *Ful.* 102; their various colours, 3 *Tyn.* 107; their exemption, *Pil.* 380; their pranks and knavery, *Rid.* 55; on burial in their coats and cowls, which they sold for that purpose, *Bale* 329, *Calf.* 287, 2 *Cran.* 147, 2 *Ful.* 13, 1 *Lat.* 50, 2 *Lat.* 200, 332, 1 *Tyn.* 48, 122 n., 2 *Tyn.* 92; their coats were supposed to preserve from diseases and ensure salvation, 2 *Cran.* 147; a friar's cowl said to take away part of purgatory, 2 *Lat.* 362; a feigned armour, 1 *Lat.* 29, 32; friars bound to say service, but not to preach, 1 *Tyn.* 329

Augustine: not instituted by St Augustine, 2 *Ful.* 102; their writers on the Apocalypse, *Bale* 257

Barefoot: *v.* Observants.

Begging: the Mendicant or begging friars, 4 *Bul.* 516, 1 *Hoop.* 526, 1 *Lat.* 292, *Rid.* 67; their beginning and procedure, 2 *Tyn.* 277, 278; the people duped by them, 3 *Tyn.* 76; four orders of them, *Bale* 171; the Carmelites, a branch of them, 4 *Bul.* 516 n.; limiters, or friars sent to gather alms within certain limits, 1 *Tyn.* 212, 2 *Tyn.* 277; they said "In principio erat Verbum," from house to house, 3 *Tyn.* 62; story of a friar limitour, 1 *Lat.* 524

Black: *v.* Dominicans.

Grey: *v.* Franciscans.

Jerome: some called by the name of St Jerome, but under the Augustinian rule, 2 *Ful.* 103 n

Minors: *v.* Franciscans.

Preaching: *v.* Dominicans.

White: *v.* Carmelites.

Friday: *v.* Fasting, Good-Friday.

The day named from Fria, *Pil.* 16; the four holy Fridays, or ordination fasts, 2 *Tyn.* 98; the golden Fridays, *Pil.* 80, 551

Frideswide (St): her bell at Oxford, 4 *Jew.* 824

Friend (Tho.): *v.* Frynd.

Friends: the friendship of men to be preserved, 1 *Bul.* 197; when most needed friends are asleep, 1 *Lat.* 228; the value of a faithful friend, *Phil.* 231; on the knowledge of friends in another life, 3 *Bec.* 152, &c.; no certainty in worldly friends, *ib.* 151; false friends are worse than enemies, 1 *Lat.* 222

Fries (Augustine), or Frisius: printer at Zurich, 1 *Hoop.* 96, 98, at Strasburgh, *Grin.* 221

Friesland: Scory and others had an English church there, *Rid.* 387; East Friesland receives the Interim, 3 *Zur.* 61; Enno, count thereof, *ib.* 512 n

Friesland, in the North sea: probably Cape Farewell, Greenland, 2 *Zur.* 290

Frisius (Augustine): *v.* Fries.

Frisius (Ger.): 3 *Zur.* 251

Frisius (James): saluted, 2 *Zur.* 225

Frisius (Jo.): saluted, 2 *Zur.* 107

Frisius (......): saluted, 1 *Zur.* 17, 30, 32, & sæpe; mentioned, *ib.* 305 n

Frisius (Otho): *v.* Otho.

Frith (Jo.): mentioned, 1 *Tyn.* xxxvii, 37 n.; king Henry's opinion of him, as recorded by Cromwell, *ib.* xlviii; said to have printed Tyndale's answer to More's Dialogue, *ib.* l; he leaves Tyndale to come into England, *ib.* liii; is seized and imprisoned, *ib.*; Tyndale's first letter to him as "brother Jacob," *ib.*; Tyndale's second letter to him in the Tower, *ib.* lvii; he is burned, for denying the corporal presence in the sacrament, *Bale* 394, 586, 3 *Bec.* 11, 1 *Brad.* 283, 288, 2 *Cran.* 246, 2 *Hoop.* 376, 1 *Tyn.* lx; defamed by Gardiner, 1 *Hoop.* 245; his books, *Bale* 164, 2 *Bec.* 421; his answer to More, 1 *Tyn.* lvi; his Disputation of Purgatory,

3 *Tyn.* 3 ; he expounds Tracy's testament, *ib.* 271; his name in connexion with the question of the authorship of a treatise on The Supper of the Lord, *ib.* 218—220

Frittenden, co. Kent: Frensham's bequest, 2 *Zur.* 21 n

Frobenius (Jerome), printer, son of John: *Grin.* 231, 2 *Zur.* 299 n

Frobenius (Jo.), printer: 2 *Zur.* 299 n

Frobisher (Sir Martin): notice of his voyages, 2 *Zur.* 290, 291

Froissart (Jo.): *Bale* 7

Fronsberg (The count): 2 *Zur.* 207

Frorne: frozen, 3 *Jew.* 597

Froschover (Chr.), printer at Zurich: notice of him, 3 *Zur.* 719 n.; mentioned, sometimes by his Christian name only, *Grin.* 221, 232 n., 4 *Jew.* 1199, 1200, 1 *Zur.* 30, 43, 70, 2 *Zur.* 24, 106, 180, 243, 294, 305, 3 *Zur.* 216, 307, 334, 502, 627, 719 n.; his shop, 2 *Cov.* 505; he was probably the printer of Coverdale's Bible, 1535, *ib.* x ; he prints the edition of 1550, *ib.* xiii, 2; he manufactures paper, 3 *Zur.* 222 ; visits Oxford, *ib.* 194, 504, 719 ; Hooper orders books from him, *ib.* 89; he receives twelve English exiles into his house, 1 *Zur.* 11 n., 42 n., 43, 2 *Zur.* 108 n., 3 *Zur.* 751 n. ; letters by him, 3 *Zur.* 719—727

Froschover (Chr.?), the younger : 2 *Brad.* 403, 1 *Zur.* 117

Frugality: a duty, *Sand.* 342

Fruier (......): martyred, *Poet.* 170

Fruit, Fruits: prayer for the preservation of the fruits of the earth, 3 *Bec.* 44, 45; "fruit of the vine," what, 3 *Jew.* 521, 522; "fruit of the belly," 2 *Hoop.* 7; fruits worthy of repentance, 3 *Bul.* 106

FRUITFUL LESSONS, by Coverdale, 1 *Cov.* 195, &c.

Frump: to mock, or insult, *Hutch.* 344 ; frumps, taunts, 2 *Whitg.* 147

Fryer (......): v. Fruier.

Fryer (Jo.), M.D.: 2 *Brad.* 209 n

Frynd (Tho.), of New coll. Oxon : proctor, 2 *Jew.* 952 n

Fryth (Jo.): v. Frith.

Fuchsius (Leon.): 1 *Hoop.* 278

Fugatius, or Fagan, apostle of the Britons: 3 *Jew.* 163, 2 *Whitg.* 128

Fulbertus Carnotensis : said to have sucked our lady's breast, and been made whole by it, 4 *Jew.* 938

Fulbrooke, co. Warwick: the free chapel there, 2 *Lat.* 383 n

Fulco, a French priest: *Pil.* 591

Fulgentius (St): his works, *Jew.* xxxvii; he was the author of a book De Fide ad Petrum, sometimes attributed to Augustine, 1 *Bec.* 207 n., 2 *Cov.* 200 n., 2 *Ful.* 86 n., *Rid.* 40 n.; he wrote against the Novatians, 1 *Bec.* 95; says that there is in the scriptures plenty for the strong to eat, and for the babe to suck, 2 *Cran.* 34, 2 *Jew.* 684, *Whita.* 400; writes, to hold the truth of God, is to worship the only God; to turn the truth of God into a lie, is to do homage to a creature, 3 *Jew.* 482; affirms that the flesh of Christ which he took unto him is of none other nature than man's flesh is, 3 *Bec.* 455 n. ; his doctrine concerning our Lord's ascension, 2 *Cov.* 153; he says that, as concerning substance of his manhood, Christ was not in heaven when he was on earth, and forsook the earth when he ascended into heaven, 2 *Bec.* 278, 279, 3 *Bec.* 453, 1 *Cran.* 98, (51), 3 *Jew.* 252, 254, 260, 263; writes, according to his humanity he was locally on earth, according to his divinity he filled heaven and earth, &c., 3 *Bul.* 270, 3 *Jew.* 263; declares that, according to the whole man which he took, he left the earth and sits on the right hand of God, 3 *Bec.* 454; teaches that his humanity is local, but his Godhead incomprehensible, 1 *Bul.* 151 ; asserts that God gives grace to the unworthy freely, 1 *Bec.* 73 ; utters a golden sentence concerning remission of sins, *ib.* 97 ; says Judas lost the fruit of repentance because he had not faith, *ib.* 98; recites a saying of Cyprian, that God is a hearer not of the voice but of the heart, *ib.* 133; contrasts the sacrifices of the law with that of the gospel, *Coop.* 94, 95, *Grin.* 68, *Rid.* 40 n.; declares it to be an error to say that the sacrament is but a substance, *Bale* 93; calls it a commemoration, *Rid.* 179 ; advises that the garment of a holy maid be such as to be a witness of her inward chastity, 2 *Bec.* 370; states that whoever in this life shall not please God, shall in the world to come have repentance for his sins, but no pardon, 3 *Jew.* 568; his opinion with regard to the future punishment of the ungodly, 2 *Cov.* 200; his conclusion from a sermon of Augustine's, 3 *Bec.* 443 n., 1 *Jew.* 132 n.; quoted by P. Lombard, 3 *Bec.* 443 n., 455 n

Fulgosus (B.): Fact. et Dict. Memorab. Libri, *Jew.* xxxvii; he says pope Anastasius II. was an Arian heretic, 3 *Jew.* 345

Fulham, co. Middlesex: the bishop's palace, 1 *Zur.* 211; Ridley's mode of living there, *Rid.* vii; Bradford made deacon there, 2 *Brad.* xxii.

FULKE (Will.), master of Pembroke hall,

Cambridge: his birth, 1 *Ful.* i; education, *ib.* ii; ejected from his college, *ib.* iii; he goes to Paris with the earl of Lincoln, *ib.*; master of Pembroke hall, *ib.*; his death, and epitaph, *ib.* iv; list of his works, *ib.* v; A DEFENCE OF THE SINCERE AND TRUE TRANSLATIONS OF THE HOLY SCRIPTURES INTO THE ENGLISH TONGUE, AGAINST THE CAVILS OF GREGORY MARTIN: edited by the Rev. Cha. Hen. Hartshorne, M.A., 1 *Ful.*; STAPLETON'S FORTRESS OVERTHROWN: A REJOINDER TO MARTIALL'S REPLY: A DISCOVERY OF THE DANGEROUS ROCK OF THE POPISH CHURCH COMMENDED BY SANDERS: edited by the Rev. Rich. Gibbings, M.A., 2 *Ful.*; references to works of his, *Calf.* 19, 235, 2 *Ful.* 70, 168, 308, 384, 385 nn., *Jew.* xx; he says that although in scripture a bishop and an elder is of one order and authority in preaching, &c., yet in government, by ancient use of speech, he is only called a bishop, to whom ordination was always principally committed, *Rog.* 332 n.; his catalogue of Popish books, dispersed in England during the time of queen Elizabeth, 2 *Ful.* 3, 4; reference to it, *Coop.* v.

Fuller (Tho.): Church History, 2 *Ful.* 6 n., 9 n., 37 n., *Grin.* xi, 360 n., 2 *Lat.* 368 n.; Worthies, 1 *Lat.* 113 n.; Abel Redivivus, 2 *Brad.* xii. n.; Fuller cited about Geoffrey of Monmouth, 2 *Ful.* 6 n.; his list of Primers, &c., corrected, *Pra. Eliz.* vii. n.; cited about the massacre of St Bartholomew, *Rog.* 8; on prophesyings, *Grin.* xi. n., xiii, on Grindal's death and character, *ib.* xv.

Fulthorp (J.): executed at York, 1 *Zur.* 225 n

Fulvius (Aulus): anecdote of him, *Wool.* 29; his impartiality, *Sand.* 227

Funckius (......): 1 *Zur.* 30, 2 *Zur.* 90, 95, 168; his exhibition, 2 *Zur.* 329

Funerals: v. Burial, Supper.

Furius (Frid.), Cæriolanus: Bononia, *Jew.* xxxvii; on the acts of the Spanish inquisition against the Jews, 2 *Jew.* 690

Furness, co. Lancaster: the abbey, *Sand.* i; Furness fells, *ib.* i, xxix; Furnes fools, 2 *Lat.* 417

Furours: 1 *Brad.* 40

Furstenburg (Will. de), grand master of the knights sword-bearers in Livonia: 3 *Zur.* 687 n

Fust (Jo.), printer at Mayence, *Sand.* 224 n

Fust (Tho.), or Fusse: martyred at Ware, *Poet.* 163

Fynes family: v. Fienes.

Fynk (Friar): *Bale* 154

Fysher (Jo.), canon of St Mary's, Warwick: 2 *Lat.* 396 n

Fyssher (Jo.): Cranmer writes to the abbot of Westminster for him, 2 *Cran.* 251, 270

G

G. (A.): v. Gilby (Ant.).

G. (E.): notice of him, *Poet.* li; da pacem, Domine; verses from the Old Version of the Psalms, *ib.* 505

G. (E.), a sectary: *Rog.* 203

G. (G.): v. Gifford (Geo.)

Gaberdines: 3 *Jew.* 612

Gabriel, the angel: prince of a kingdom, 3 *Bul.* 343; sent to Zacharias, and to Mary, *ib.* 341; what he said of John, 4 *Bul.* 95

Gabriel (The), one of Frobisher's ships, 2 *Zur.* 291 n

Gadara: the lake, 3 *Bul.* 353, 364

Gads: spears, *Rid.* 145

Gage (Sir Jo.): at court, 2 *Cran.* 490; a privy councillor, *ib.* 531; named, *ib.* 241

Gage (Tho.): Survey of the West Indies, 2 *Ful.* 22 n

Gaged: impawned, 2 *Bul.* 36

Gagneius (......): on the intercession of saints: 1 *Ful.* 537, 538

Gaguinus (Rob.): account of him, *Bale* 320 n.; De Orig. et Gest. Franc., *Jew.* xxxvii, 4 *Jew.* 112; Sarmatiæ Europ. Descriptio, *Grin.* 56 n

Gaid: withes, 1 *Bul.* 302

Gainas: 1 *Bul.* 391

Gainsford (Mrs), an attendant on queen Anne Boleyn: 1 *Tyn.* 130

Galatians (Epistle to the): v. Paul (St). How they were bewitched, 1 *Brad.* 386

Galatinus (Pet.): disputed learnedly on the first verse of Genesis, 1 *Bul.* 200 n.; referred to about Jonathan Ben Uziel, 3 *Whitg.* 343 n

Galeazzo Maria [Sforza], duke of Milan: slain, *Calf.* 339

Galen (Cl.): his rules to preserve health, 1 *Hoop.* 297; he describes the causes of pestilence, 1 *Hoop.* 318, 2 *Hoop.* 160; mentions preservatives against it, 1 *Hoop.* 333; advises to fly from the air that is infected, 2 *Hoop.* 167; says contraries are holpen by contraries, *ib.* 169; was wont to say, take nothing, and hold it fast, 4 *Jew.* 885; other references, 1 *Hoop.* 278, 286

Galeotus (Martius): his error respecting justification, *Rog.* 109, 160

Galerius, emperor: v. Maximian.

Galerius: judges Cyprian, 1 *Jew.* 362
Galesinius (Pet.), his blunder about St Synoris, 2 *Ful.* 44 n
Galfridus: *v.* Gaufridus.
Galfridus Britannicus: *v.* Geoffry of Monmouth.
Galgalath: one of the magi, *Whita.* 560 n
Galilee: several prophets rose out of it, 3 *Jew.* 242
Gallandius (And.): 2 *Bec.* 281 n., 3 *Bec.* 454 n.; 2 *Ful.* 70 n
Gallars (Nic. de), or Gallasius, minister of the French church in London: notice of him, 2 *Zur.* 49 n., 96 n.; letter from him to Calvin, 2 *Zur.* 49
Galley half-pence: 1 *Bec.* 235 n., 2 *Bec.* 435
Gallia Antarctica: *v.* Brazil.
Galloway (Alex. bp of): *v.* Gordon.
Gallus (Nic.): narrates words of card. Hosius about the scriptures, 4 *Jew.* 757; complains of sects amongst professors of the gospel, 2 *Jew.* 686; says the strifes amongst us are not of light matters, but of the high articles of Christian doctrine, 3 *Jew.* 621
Gallus (Rich.): *v.* Vauville (R.).
Gallus (Rob.): imagines Christ to say of the pope, "Who set this idol in my room?" 4 *Jew.* 1009
Galtropes: a military engine for maiming horses, *Rid.* 368
Gamaliel: 4 *Bul.* 482
Gaming: *v.* Cards, Sports.
  Prevalence of dicing, &c., *Hutch.* 7; dicing houses, 1 *Lat.* 196; certain games forbidden by law, *ib.* 372; cards, dice, &c., forbidden to be used by all but gentlemen, except in the time of Christmas, 3 *Zur.* 285 n.; gaming not to be permitted in the church, &c., 2 *Hoop.* 129; forbidden to the clergy, *Grin.* 130, 166, 2 *Hoop.* 145; forbidden on Sundays and holy days, *Grin.* 138; Haddon's opinion respecting it, 3 *Zur.* 282, &c.; it is worthily condemned of all good divines, 2 *Bul.* 40; often the occasion of sin, *Sand.* 118; gamesters, dicers, &c., who would overreach and win of their neighbours, are thieves, 2 *Bec.* 108, 162; how they swear, 1 *Bec.* 360; their duty, 2 *Bec.* 115
Gang days: procession days, *Pil.* 556; what ceremonies to be used on such days, *Grin.* 141, 168
Gang week: *v.* Rogation-week.
Gangra: *v.* Councils.
Ganlyne (Frere): 2 *Lat.* 388
Gaping Gulph: *v.* Discovery.
Garanza (Barth.): *v.* Carranza.
Garbrand (Jo.): notice of him, 3 *Zur.* 68; legatee of Jewel's papers, 4 *Jew.* xxv, 1276 n., some of which he published, *ib.* xxvii; dedicatory prefaces by him, 2 *Jew.* 815, 966, 4 *Jew.* 1129; a short dedication in Latin verse by him, 2 *Jew.* 1099 n
Garcia (Jo. à): *v.* Villa Garcia.
Garden of the Soul: *v.* Hortulus Animæ.
Gardens: meditations for them, 1 *Lat.* 225, 236
Gardiner (......): a friar of Stoke-Clare, 2 *Cov.* viii. n
Gardiner (Steph.), bp of Winchester: not of noble birth, 4 *Jew.* 1146; probably alluded to as "a bastard," *Calf.* 331; master of Trin. hall, Cambridge, *Rid.* 327 n.; ambassador to the pope, 2 *Cran.* 332 n.; he meets Cranmer at Waltham, 1 *Cran.* ix; assists him in the matter of the king's divorce, 2 *Cran.* 244; present at Anne Boleyn's coronation, *ib.* 245; Cranmer commends himself to him on his appeal against the pope, *ib.* 268; he objects to Cranmer visiting his diocese, and to his style of "primate of all England," *ib.* 304; apparently concerned in the betrayal of Tyndale, 1 *Tyn.* lxix. n.; his conference with Bucer at Ratisbon, on the king's supremacy, 1 *Ful.* 489; his book De Vera Obedientia, 1536, in support of the king's supremacy, 2 *Hoop.* 268, 557, 559, 567, *Jew.* xxxvii, 1 *Jew.* 38, 3 *Zur.* 298 n., 347 n.; commended by Bonner's preface, Tonstall's sermons, Cole's oath, 1 *Jew.* 34, 60; in this book he defends the breaking of oaths made to the pope, shewing that no man is bound to perform an unlawful oath, &c., 1 *Brad.* 469 n., 480, 484, 592, *Pil.* 621; says that he is compelled by the mighty power of the truth, &c., 4 *Jew.* 1074; the Bishops' Book (or Institution) ascribed to him, *Rid.* 135, but see 511; he conformed to Henry VIII's changes, *ib.* 101; his tergiversation and inconsistency, *Calf.* 24 [see 3 Fox 454, ed. 1684], 2 *Cran.* 17 n., *Pil.* 621, 622; his blunders, 1 *Jew.* 53, 4 *Jew.* 635; a translation of the Bible committed to the examination of him and other bishops, 1 *Ful.* 98; in France, *Bale* 442; ambassador at Paris, 2 *Cov.* 493; concerned in drawing up a book of ceremonies, 1 *Lat.* 132 n.; he attends the Spital sermons, 3 *Zur.* 210 n.; a sermon by him answered by Barnes the next Sunday, *ib.* 317, see 631; Barnes's controversy with him on justification, purgatory, &c., *ib.* 616; Barnes prays for him, 2 *Cov.* 435; he examines persons charged with heresy, *Bale* 433, 1 *Tyn.* 33, 3 *Zur.* 232; his concern in the King's Book, or

Necessary Doctrine, *Rid.* 511; he questions Anne Askewe, *Bale* 198, 201, 202; letter from him to Parker and Smith, *Park.* 20; letters to Parker, *ib.* 22, 27; as chancellor of Cambridge he determines the pronunciation of certain Greek letters, *ib.* 28; signature as privy councillor, 2 *Cran.* 496, *Park.* 30; he impedes the abolition of vigils, &c., on pretence of making a league with the emperor and the French king, 2 *Cran.* 415 n., 416 n.; envoy to the emperor, 3 *Zur.* 37; with the emperor in Utrecht, *Bale* 182, 221; his works on the sacrament, 1 *Cov.* 429, *Pil.* 547, *Rid.* 308, &c.; Cranmer's controversy with him, 1 *Cran.* xx, 2 *Cran.* x, *Grin.* 232, &c., 3 *Zur.* 388; A Detection of the Devil's Sophistrie, 1546, *Bale* 154, 2 *Brad.* 284, 1 *Cran.* 107, 108, 194, 241, 256, 307, 308, 2 *Cov.* 263, *Jew.* xxxvii, 1 *Jew.* 54, 78, 205, 211, &c.; its title-page, 1 *Hoop.* 99; the preface to it, *ib.* 100; in it he corrupts a text in the Psalms, 1 *Ful.* 11, 1 *Jew.* 54; AN ANSWER UNTO MY LORD OF WYNCHESTER'S BOOK, by bp Hooper (including many passages of the work replied to), 1 *Hoop.* 97—247; Hooper's dedication to Gardiner, *ib.* 101; Gardiner's EXPLICATION AND ASSERTION OF THE TRUE CATHOLIC FAITH TOUCHING THE MOST BLESSED SACRAMENT OF THE ALTAR, 1551, referred to, 2 *Brad.* 274 n. (the whole treatise is included in the Answer to it, next mentioned), Cranmer's ANSWER TO A CRAFTY AND SOPHISTICAL CAVILLATION DEVISED BY STEPHEN GARDINER, 1 *Cran.* 1—367; the latter writes against Cranmer, under the name of Marcus Antonius Constantius, 2 *Brad.* 173 n., 274, 2 *Cov.* 253, 254, 1 *Cran.* 419 n., 2 *Cran.* x, 455—458, 1 *Jew.* 54, 3 *Jew.* 186, *Rid.* 16; Ridley replies, *Rid.* xvi; Cranmer's wish that he might live to write an answer, 2 *Cran.* x, 455—457; controversy with Bucer on the celibacy of the clergy, 2 *Brad.* 19, 2 *Cov.* 513, 520, 3 *Zur.* 178, 254; Gardiner a persevering opponent of the reformation, 2 *Cran.* viii, ix; called Diotrephes, *Rid.* 110, 113, 117, &c., a wild boar, successor to Ananias, 3 *Bec.* 228, a wolf, *ib.* 237, God's enemy, 2 *Hoop.* 621; letter from him to Ridley, respecting a sermon preached at court by the latter, *Rid.* 495; he alleged that laws made during the king's minority were not binding, 1 *Lat.* 118 n.; Ridley sent to exhort him, *Rid.* 260, 264; he is sent to the Fleet, 3 *Zur.* 384; deprived of his see, 2 *Cran.* x, 429 n., 1 *Lat.* 321 n., 3 *Zur.* 80, 256, 722; committed to the Tower, 1 *Lat.* 321 n.; while there he challenges Hooper to a disputation, 3 *Zur.* 80; released from the Tower, *ib.* 367; he sings a mass of requiem for Edward VI., *ib.* 368; letter to him from queen Mary, *Park.* 54 n.; letter from him to the university of Cambridge, *ib.* 56 n; he obtains leave for P. Martyr to quit England, 3 *Zur.* 506 n.; consents to the liberation of Sandys, *Sand.* x, xii; tries to arrest him again, *ib.* xii; lord chancellor, *Rid.* 394; as such refuses to swear in judge Hales, 4 *Jew.* 1190 n.; deceived by an image on the great seal, *Calf.* 36, 354; he preaches before Philip and Mary at Paul's cross, 3 *Zur.* 298, 347; again sent to negociate a peace with the emperor and the French king, *Rid.* 394; his persecution, 3 *Zur.* 171; his threats, *Pil.* 197, 254; he examines Hooper, 2 *Hoop.* xxvii, &c., 2 *Lat.* 270; his enmity to him, 2 *Hoop.* 620, 621; a conference with him at some former period, *ib.* viii; he examines Bradford, 1 *Brad.* 465; process and sentence against that martyr (in Latin), *ib.* 585; his enmity to the exiles, *Jew.* xiii; his horrible death, *Phil.* 86, 269, *Pil.* 655, 3 *Zur.* 301 n

He says that Christ is not yet fully possessed of his glory, 1 *Jew.* 461; his opinion on justification, *Hutch.* 96; he called the gospel a doctrine of desperation, 2 *Hoop.* 376, 377, 592; certain matters in which he varied from other Papists touching the Lord's supper, 1 *Cran.* 380, *Rid.* 307; matters wherein he varied from himself, 1 *Cran.* 381, *Rid.* 311; certain things which he granted, 1 *Cran.* 383, *Rid.* 315; matters wherein he varied from the truth, and from the old authors of the church, 1 *Cran.* 385; his doctrine on the sacrament generally, *ib.* 438; in one place he refers the word "Hoc" to the bread, in another to individuum vagum, 2 *Jew.* 789; he says neither the natural wine nor Christ's very blood, but the accidents and forms, are the fruits of the vine, 3 *Jew.* 520; declares that Christ drank his own very blood at the supper, and ever now drinketh the same in the kingdom of heaven, *ib.*; describes Christ's presence in the sacrament as natural, 1 *Jew.* 446; his opinion on a mouse eating the host, *Bale* 154; his notion how it became a general consent to abstain from the cup, 1 *Jew.* 65, 78, 211, 3 *Jew.* 182; his attempt to explain the words of Gelasius on the sacrament, 1 *Jew.* 54; how he disposes of a passage from Origen, 3 *Jew.* 517; he thinks Basil's liturgy disordered, 2 *Jew.* 579

Gardiner (Will.), alias Sandwich: notice of him, 2 *Cran.* 365 n
Gards: borders, 1 *Tyn.* 352
Garganus: *v.* Mons.
Gargrave (......), or Hargrave: recommended for vicar of Rochdale, *Pil.* vii.
Gargrave (Sir Tho.): one of the royal visitors for the North, 1 *Zur.* 73 n.; president of the North, *ib.* 217 n.; mention of him and his son, *Grin.* 325
Garlands: the use of garlands of bay forbidden by certain fathers, 3 *Jew.* 883
Garments: *v.* Apparel, Vestments.
Garner (Jo.), minister of the French church at Strasburgh: 3 *Zur.* 112, 492
Garnet (Hen.): *Calf.* 5 n.; executed, *Rog.* 10
Garnish (Lady): Anne Askewe taken to her, *Bale* 200
Garret (Tho.), or Garrard, or Gerrard: recommended to Cromwell for the parsonage of St Peter by Calais, 2 *Cran.* 310; sent to preach at Calais, *ib.* 376 n.; burned in Smithfield, *Bale* 394 (Garare), 3 *Bec.* 11, 1 *Brad.* 283, 288, 2 *Cran.* 310 n., 381 n., 2 *Lat.* 418 n., 3 *Zur.* 207, 209, 632
Garret (Sir Will.), lord mayor of London: *Grin.* 262, *Phil.* 150
Garrett (Jo.), of Oxford: 2 *Cran.* 383 bis
Garter (Bernard): *v.* B. (G.).
Garter (Order of the): the knights wear the image of St George, *Rid.* 498, 502, and keep St George's feast, *ib.* 502; the prelate of the order, 2 *Whitg.* 79, 188, 3 *Whitg.* 405
Gascoigne (Geo.): notice of him, *Poet.* xv; de profundis, *ib.* 33; good morrow, *ib.* 36; good night, *ib.* 38; notice of one G. Gaske, perhaps Gascoigne, *ib.* xxvii; a description of the world, by G. Gaske, *ib.* 307
Gascoyne (......): *Park.* 65
Gaske (G.), perhaps Gascoigne, *q. v.*
Gaspar: *v.* Jaspar.
Gastius (J.): against the Catabaptists, 1 *Whitg.* 87, 97, 133
Gataker (Tho.): his account of Whitaker, *Whita.* x.
Gate: road, 1 *Brad.* 280, 2 *Brad.* 293, 2 *Cov.* 271
Gates: those of cities, how named, *Pil.* 345; ministers compared to them, *ib.* 348; the strait gate and narrow way, 2 *Tyn.* 120
Gates (Sir Hen.), brother of the next: one of the royal visitors for the North, 1 *Zur.* 73 n
Gates (Sir Jo.), or Gate, or Yates: vice-chamberlain: *Rid.* 333, 535 n.; sheriff of Essex, *ib.* 529; letter to him, *ib.* 336; at Cambridge, *Sand.* ii, iv; "made deacon" (i. e. executed), *ib.* ii, see 3 *Zur.* 367 n
Gates (Rob.): *v.* Yate (Mr).
Gaudes: ostentatious rites, *Calf.* 268
Gaufridus, abbot: 1 *Jew.* 225 n
Gaufridus Antisiodorensis: wrote on the Apocalypse, *Bale* 256
Gaufridus de Bello-Loco, *q. v.*
Gaul: *v.* France.
Gaulminus (Gilb.): *Calf.* 69 n
Gauston (Rich.): *Rid.* 536 n
Gavantus (Barth.): Thesaurus, 1 *Brad.* 513, 2 *Brad.* 298—311, 2 *Ful.* 22 nn
Gavell (Rob.), keeper of Nonsuch park: *Park.* 387
Geason: scarce, rare, 4 *Jew.* 723; geson, 3 *Jew.* 622
Geche (Alex.): martyred at Ipswich, *Poet.* 173
Geddes (Mich.): *Calf.* 193 n., 2 *Ful.* 70 n., 225 n
Gee (Edw.): Answer to Gother, *Calf.* 188 n., 377 n
Gelasius I., bp of Rome: the Roman council under him, *Calf.* 21 n., 171, 324 n., 2 *Tyn.* 279 n. (*v.* Councils, *Rome*, 496); his epistles extravagant, *Whita.* 435; they are spurious, *Rid.* 180, 182; he proves, against Eutyches and Nestorius, that Christ is both God and man, 1 *Cran.* 289—295; spurious decree respecting the canonical books, 2 *Ful.* 221; it allows but one book of Maccabees, 1 *Ful.* 24; speaks of writings not read in the church of Rome, because thought to be written by heretics, 1 *Jew.* 113; condemns the Acts of Paul and Thecla, 2 *Ful.* 339 n.; calls the Canons of the Apostles apocryphal, *Whita.* 41; condemns apocryphal works of Clement and others, 1 *Jew.* 111, 112; he cites the council of Nice on the water of baptism, 3 *Jew.* 492, 541; calls the sacrament a similitude and image, 2 *Jew.* 609; says, we must think of Christ the Lord himself, that which we profess in his image (the eucharist), *ib.* 700, 3 *Jew.* 469; asserts that the image and similitude of Christ's body and blood is celebrated in the action of the mysteries, 1 *Cran.* 296, *Grin.* 66, 2 *Hoop.* 425, 2 *Jew.* 1113, 1115, 3 *Jew.* 508, *Rid.* 44; says the sacraments of the body and blood of the Lord pass over into a divine substance by the working of the Holy Ghost, yet remain they still in the propriety of their own nature, 1 *Jew.* 11, 3 *Jew.* 506, 508; affirms that the nature of bread and wine in the sacrament does not go away, 2 *Bec.* 267, 3 *Bec.* 424, 425, 1 *Brad.* 543 n., 548, 1 *Cran.* 261, 289, 293,

296, (33), *Grin.* 66, 2 *Hoop.* 425, 1 *Jew.* 11, 33, 52, 53, 248, 259, 2 *Jew.* 564, 599, 776, 792, 1030, 1066, 1115, 3 *Jew.* 482, 501, 504, 508, *Rid.* 44, 160, 174; this decree expounded by R. Tapper, *Jew.* 37, 52; testimony against some who received the bread but not the cup, of whom he says, either let them receive the whole sacraments, or else let them be driven from the whole, 2 *Bec.* 243, 3 *Bec.* 275, 413, 415, *Hutch.* 282, 3 *Jew.* 481, 597, *Sand.* 455; he declares that the sacrament cannot be divided (i. e. by abstaining from the cup) without great sacrilege, 2 *Bec.* 243, 1 *Brad.* 546 n., *Coop.* 138, 2 *Cran.* 174, *Hutch.* 282, 1 *Jew.* 9, 55, 56, 76, 225, 235, 255, 2 *Jew.* 990, 1030, 3 *Jew.* 478, 594, 597, 4 *Jew.* 820, 891, *Pil.* 541, *Sand.* 455; the gloss on the above decree pronounces it not superfluous to receive the sacrament under both kinds, 2 *Bec.* 243; writing to certain bishops, he declared those accursed who receiving the body of Christ abstained from the communion of the cup, *ib.*; parts of the mass attributed to him, 2 *Brad.* 306—309 (see 513 n.), 1 *Jew.* 9, 96; other directions about divine service ascribed to him, 4 *Bul.* 196, 201; he speaks of certain churches built in the names of dead men who were not altogether faithful, 1 *Jew.* 158; gives directions about the distribution of offerings, &c., 2 *Tyn.* 173 n.; cited as declaring that none may dispute the judgment of the Roman church, 1 *Jew.* 68, as saying that the pope, being a bishop, is above any temporal prince concerning his priestly office, 4 *Jew.* 673, and exempted from all law of man, 2 *Jew.* 919, 4 *Jew.* 833; he says a wrongful sentence may hurt no man, 2 *Jew.* 805, 3 *Jew.* 203; shews that Acacius was justly condemned, 4 *Jew.* 650; directs an offending clerk to be admitted only to lay-communion, *Coop.* 159 n.; on the council of Chalcedon, 1 *Jew.* 423; on conflicting councils, *ib.* 233; he opposed the Manichees, *ib.* 257

Gelasius Cyzicenus: Hist. Conc. Nic., *Jew.* xxxvii; cited, 2 *Bec.* 295 n., 3 *Bec.* 267 n., 433 n., *Coop.* 31 n., 1 *Jew.* 464 n., 466 n., &c., 3 *Jew.* 540 n

Gereh, or Geeras: a Jewish coin, 1 *Tyn.* 419

Geffrie (Will.): whipped, *Rog.* 162 n

Gehazi: 4 *Bul.* 124, 130

Gehenna: *v.* Hell.

Gemblacensis (Sig.): *v.* Sigebertus.

Geminus, an ancient astronomer: 2 *Zur.* 336

Genebrardus (Gilb.): *Calf.* 323 n., *Rog.* 93 n., *Whita.* 182, 186, &c.; calls the first and second books of Esdras canonical, *ib.* 103; on the time of Judith, *ib.* 86; on Desiderius of Bourdeaux, *Rog.* 162; he writes that fifty popes successively were apostates, *ib.* 182

Generians: heretics, 2 *Cov.* 184 n

Genesis: Tyndale's prologue, 1 *Tyn.* 398; contents of the book, 2 *Cov.* 17; a table expounding certain words therein, 1 *Tyn.* 405; Egyptian words occur in it, *ib.* 409; remarks upon portions of its narrative, *ib.* 400—402

Genesius, Diocletian's jester: *Pil.* 401

Geneva: the reformation established there, *Lit. Eliz.* 451; war with Berne, *Phil.* 389; extracts from the council book, 3 *Zur.* 765 n., 768 n.; Geneva besieged by the duke of Savoy, *Grin.* 429 n., 1 *Zur.* 334, 2 *Zur.* 315 n.; application to England for help, and consequent proceedings, 2 *Zur.* 315 n., *Grin.* 429 n.; letter of the privy council to the archbishop on behalf of it, *Grin.* 432; another, to the bishops, *ib.* 434; letter of archbishop Grindal to the bishops for a collection in behalf of it, *ib.* 429; the sums contributed by Grindal and other dignitaries, *ib.* 432 n., queen Elizabeth's letter to the Swiss cantons in behalf of it, 2 *Zur.* 315; the state admitted to the Swiss confederation, *ib.* 201 n.; the arms of Geneva ("the halfe egle and key"), 1 *Brad.* 220; the church of Geneva catholic and apostolic, *Phil.* 153; like Sion, despised, 4 *Jew.* 666, 667; disliked by queen Elizabeth, 2 *Zur.* 131; it communicated with wafer cakes, *Grin.* 208; a lay elder ministered the cup in the communion, *Rog.* 235; four thousand communicants at one time, 3 *Jew.* 370; the English church there, 1 *Whitg.* 251, 3 *Zur.* 166, 167 n., 766 n.; the form of Common Prayer used by the English there, *Grin.* 203, 208, 213, 316 n., 3 *Whitg.* 371, 372, 378; it condemns the private ministration of sacraments, and baptism by women, 3 *Whitg.* 546; the Italian church, 1 *Zur.* 47

Genevians: 2 *Jew.* 770, 787, &c.

Gennadius, patriarch of Constantinople: his encyclical letter, *Jew.* xxxvii, 1 *Jew.* 403, 3 *Jew.* 334, 4 *Jew.* 828, 841, 2 *Whitg.* 432

Gennadius of Marseilles: *Calf.* 69, 149 n., 177 n.; probably the author of a book De Defin. Orthod. Fidei, otherwise De Eccl. Dogmat. improperly ascribed to Augustine, 2 *Bec.* 258 n., 2 *Cov.* 185 n.; his words on justification, 2 *Cran.* 207, 208; he declares that holy men do truly in pronouncing themselves sinners, 2 *Cov.* 385; neither praises nor blames the daily reception of the sacrament, 2 *Bec.* 258 n.; in opposition to Origen, he maintains the resurrection of the same body, 2 *Cov.* 185 n.; says that the perpetual virginity of our lady is proved sufficiently by the scriptures, 3 *Jew.* 440; well-nigh charges Augustine with heresy, *ib.* 607; makes no mention of the epistles decretal, 1 *Jew.* 173

Gennesaret (The lake of): 3 *Bul.* 364

Genseric, king of the Vandals: 2 *Bul.* 109

Gentianus Hervetus, *q. v.*

Gentile (Alberic): professor of civil law at Oxford, 2 *Zur.* 329 n

Gentiles, Heathen: *v.* Idolatry, Philosophers.

Who they are, 2 *Lat.* 46, *Now.* (101); the times of the Gentiles, 2 *Lat.* 46; how they knew God, 1 *Bul.* 196; traces of true religion amongst them, *ib.* 202; their idolatry, 2 *Cran.* 144; they had not always images, 1 *Bul.* 200; their oracles and miracles, 2 *Cran.* 41; some of them in their sacrifices said, "Hoc age," 1 *Jew.* 119; their earnest study in bringing up their children, 2 *Bec.* 5, 382, &c.; honouring of parents among them, 1 *Bul.* 202; how they prepare themselves to battle, 1 *Bec.* 251; there have been many examples of virtue amongst them, *Wool.* 48, 51; their virtues deserve no reward, but rather punishment, *ib.* 49; whether the virtuous works of the heathen are sins or no, 2 *Bul.* 418; they cannot worship God, 1 *Tyn.* 115; they perish because they know not Christ, 2 *Lat.* 74; their condemnation, *Bale* 557; against Gentilism, or the heathen opinion respecting destiny, 3 *Bul.* 181; many Gentiles were saved under the old testament, *Whita.* 530; the heathen called into the church, *Pil.* 61, *Sand.* 254; their calling shewn to Peter by a vision, *Sand.* 275; they are not to be baptized until they believe, *Phil.* 281; they as well as Jews are justified by faith, 1 *Bul.* 115; heathen customs Christianized, *Calf.* 66; heathen princes may lawfully be served, *Pil.* 311; heathen poets cited in holy scripture, *Hutch.* 178 (*v.* Aratus, Epimenides, Menander); some heathen authors ought not to be read, 2 *Bec.* 382; some read warily, godliness being interlaced, profit much, *ib.* 383

Gentility: heathenism, 1 *Bec.* 10, *Calf.* 19, 2 *Cran.* 25, 101, 2 *Ful.* 58, 1 *Jew.* 544, *Sand.* 373

Gentlemen: *v.* Landlords, Noblemen, Prayers.

The origin of gentle blood, and the folly of boasting thereof, *Pil.* 125; gentlemen commonly ascend to their estate through knowledge, 2 *Cran.* 399; their duty, especially as landlords, 1 *Bec.* 256, 2 *Bec.* 115, 1 *Tyn.* 201; they should be trained to serve the king and state, 1 *Lat.* 68; have the same law to live after as the poor, *Pil.* 41; they should be peace-makers, 1 *Lat.* 486; their tenants and servants, 2 *Cran.* 185; an admonition to them against suffering swearers in their houses, 1 *Bec.* 361; their little delight in reading the word of God, 2 *Bec.* 420; popular complaints against them, 2 *Cran.* 194—197; their exactions, 1 *Bec.* 253; those who unreasonably raise their rents are thieves, 2 *Bec.* 108; their greediness censured in becoming sheepmongers, and causing the decay of towns, *ib.* 434; their oppressions alleged as a cause for rebellion, *ib.* 598, 599; advice to country people as to their conduct towards gentlemen who are tyrants, 2 *Tyn.* 21, 59; the character of those who are true gentlemen described, 2 *Bec.* 598, &c.; the character of those who are not really gentlemen described, *ib.*; Philpot claims the rank of a gentleman, *Phil.* 12

Gentlemen Pensioners, *q. v.*

Gentleness: better than sharpness, *Pil.* 183

Gentlewomen: *v.* Prayers.

Dorcas an example to them, 2 *Bec.* 585

Geoffry of Monmouth: Britan. Orig., *Jew.* xxxvii; a copy in MS., *Park.* 265; he says that the British flamines were changed for bishops, 2 *Whitg.* 127; his account of bishopricks in England before Augustine came, 3 *Jew.* 165; his statement respecting Augustine and the slaughter attributed to him, 1 *Jew.* 300, 3 *Jew.* 164, 165, *Pil.* 515; he speaks of him as a proud and cruel man, 2 *Ful.* 6, 186; not to be implicitly credited, *Calf.* 307 n

Geography: *v.* America, Arabia, Climates.

Ancient geography, 2 *Zur.* 89, 95

George (St): *v.* Garter.

Account of him, 2 *Bec.* 536 n., 1 *Hoop.* 313 n.; drawn on horseback, *Calf.* 35 n., 36, 287, 1 *Hoop.* 320, with the dragon, 1 *Ful.* 72, 1 *Hoop.* 313 n., 320; invoked in battle, 2 *Bec.* 536, *Calf.* 20; patron of England, 1 *Hoop.* 313; his festival expressly retained in 1536, *Pra. Eliz.* 5 n

George, king of Albania: *v.* Scanderbeg.

George, duke of Clarence, brother of Edward IV.: the treason of his great-grandsons, the Poles, *Lit. Eliz.* 655 n

George, marq. of Brandenburg: signed the confession of Augsburgh, 2 *Zur.* 15 n

George, count of Wirtemberg: 4 *Bul.* xxi.

George, patriarch of Alexandria: wrote the life of Chrysostom, *Jew.* xxxvii; speaks of his education at Athens, 4 *Jew.* 652

George, the Arian patriarch of Alexandria: 1 *Hoop.* 313 n., 2 *Whitg.* 385
George, bp of Laodicea: an Arian, 3 *Whitg.* 241
George ......: going to Padua, 3 *Zur.* 725
George Major: *v.* Major.
George of Trebizond: 2 *Bec.* 288 n., *Calf.* 378 n
George (Christian): martyred at Colchester, *Poet.* 172
George (David): *v.* Davidians.
 Founder of the Davidians or Davi-Georgians, 2 *Bec.* 379 n., 1 *Lat.* 229, *Rog.* 202, *Whita.* 229; he debased the credit of the holy scriptures, *Rog.* 78; preferred his own imaginations to them, *ib.* 79; said that Christ's flesh was dissolved into ashes, and rose no more, *ib.* 64; affirmed himself to be greater than Christ, *ib.* 49, 162; rumoured that himself, and not Christ, should be the future judge, *ib.* 67; would have women to be all common, *ib.* 307; taken up and burned after his death, 3 *Jew.* 187, 188
George (Sir Will.): 1 *Ful.* xi.
Georgians: their faith, 1 *Bul.* 98
Gerald (Sir Gilb.): *v.* Gerard.
Geraldus (Greg.) Lilius, *q. v.*
Gerard, abp of York: his letter to Anselm, on clerical celibacy, 2 *Ful.* 23, 94; a lecherous man and a witch, *Pil.* 591
Gerard (Sir Gilb.), or Gerald: letters to him, *Park.* 308, 325; an ecclesiastical commissioner, *ib.* 370 n
Gerard the merchant: saluted, 2 *Zur.* 42
Gerardus Lorichius, *q. v.*
Gerbellius (Nic.), Phorcensis: his works not found, *Jew.* xxxvii; referred to, 4 *Jew.* 665
Gerhardus, a Franciscan: author of Evangelium Æternum, *Rog.* 203 n
Gerhardus (Jo.): Patrologia, *Calf.* 74 n
Germanus (probably the patriarch of Constantinople who died about 740): his vain allegations respecting images, *Calf.* 345; his alleged address to the girdle of the virgin, 1 *Jew.* 535
Germanus, patriarch of Constantinople (fl. 1250): *Jew.* xxxvii; he declares that our daily bread is Christ, 1 *Jew.* 128, 169, and that the manna was Christ, 3 *Jew.* 499; speaking of the communion he says, we are no more on earth, but stand by the King in the throne of God in heaven, 2 *Jew.* 741; referred to about altars, 1 *Ful.* 518
Germanus (St), bp of Auxerre: invoked for the ague, *Bale* 348, for the evil, *ib.* 498; how he stilled the sea, 2 *Ful.* 116
Germany: *v.* Empire, Interim.

The Canaanites mentioned in Obad. xx. thought to be the Germans, *Pil.* 268; Tyndale observes that there are nations within the inclosure of Dutchland (i. e. Germany), who speak tongues unknown to the Dutchmen, 2 *Tyn.* 268; conspiracy of the boors against their lords, called Liga Sotularia, 4 *Jew.* 664; clergy in Dutchland licensed to live in sin, 3 *Tyn.* 40; the "Centum gravamina nationis Germanicæ," a remonstrance addressed to the pope by the diet of Nuremberg, *ib.* 40 n.; not of Lutheran origin, *Calf.* 16 n.; the war of 1525, 2 *Cran.* 199, 200, 4 *Jew.* 665; the reformation in Germany a hotch potch, 1 *Lat.* 147; the princes dissolved the monasteries, and set up schools and colleges, 2 *Jew.* 1011; wretched condition of the country, 2 *Cran.* 233, 234; its troubles falsely ascribed to Luther, 4 *Jew.* 664, 2 *Tyn.* 244, 3 *Tyn.* 188; embassy therefrom, 2 *Cran.* viii, 371 n., 377 n., 379; troubles shortly after the death of Luther, *Phil.* 416; disputes respecting ecclesiastical rites and ceremonies, *Rog.* 317; the preaching of Christ's gospel driven out of the churches there, 3 *Bec.* 10; two portions of five remained still in obedience to the see of Rome, 3 *Jew.* 195, 197; but where the churches were Popish, the people were often Protestant, *ib.* 197; the immorality of German courts, 2 *Zur.* 53; Germanical natures, *Park.* 125
Gerningham (Mr): arrests Sandys, *Sand.* vi.
Gerontochomia: 1 *Bul.* 286, 4 *Bul.* 498
Gerrard (Mr), a justice: *Park.* 375
Gerrard (Sir Gilb.): *v.* Gerard.
Gerrard (Tho.): *v.* Garret.
Gershonites: their service, 2 *Bul.* 132, 142
Gerson (Jo. Charlier, commonly called): Opera, *Jew.* xxxvii; De Auferibilitate Papæ, 2 *Cran.* 77; Contra Floretum, 1 *Jew.* 246; he calls scripture the rule of faith, *Whita.* 485; his opinion on the exposition of scripture by itself, *ib.* 495; he complains that the substance of divinity was brought to ostentation of wits, and sophistry, 4 *Jew.* 736; declares that we ought rather to believe a man well learned in holy letters than a council or pope, 3 *Bec.* 392, 2 *Cran.* 36, 37, *Pil.* 532 n., 626; defines ecclesiastical power, 4 *Bul.* 38; he held general councils to be above the pope, 1 *Jew.* 67; he says, to demand whether the authority of the pope be greater than the authority of the church, is as much as if a man would demand whether the whole be greater than a part, 4 *Jew.* 921; allowed the privilege of giving sentence in councils even to

laymen, 3 *Jew.* 207, 4 *Jew.* 1026; shews that the consideration of the faith pertains to them, 2 *Jew.* 677; he was the great promoter of the council of Constance, 1 *Jew.* 231; thought worthy to be director in it, 4 *Jew.* 736; he therein exhibited seventy-five abuses in the church of Rome, and earnestly desired that they might be reformed, *ib.* 1106; addressed the French king as judge in a cause ecclesiastical, *ib.* 967; referred to on a council holden in Paris, *ib.* 952; he says, both popes and bishops may wander from the faith, *ib.* 927; he and the school of Paris reproved pope John XXII., 1 *Jew.* 400, 3 *Jew.* 345, 4 *Jew.* 931, 936; speaks of an error of that pope respecting the soul, 3 *Jew.* 144, 4 *Jew.* 930, 1117, *Rog.* 181 n.; he allows that "Hoc" points at the substance of bread, 2 *Jew.* 788; says a brute beast eating the host receives the body of Christ, 2 *Jew.* 783; calls communion under both kinds heresy, 1 *Jew.* 231; his foolish arguments for withholding the cup from the laity, 1 *Jew.* 15, 231, 3 *Jew.* 597; he says, if laymen communicated under both kinds, the priestly dignity would be degraded, 1 *Jew.* 206; on opus operatum, 2 *Jew.* 750; on the origin of stone altars, 1 *Jew.* 310; he says that as there is but one God, all the world should pray to him in one tongue, *ib.* 14; states that the priest may say "Dominus vobiscum," though but one be present, *ib.* 174; sought to reduce the number of ceremonies, *Lit. Eliz.* xxvi; he says that through their number, the virtue of the Holy Ghost is utterly quenched, 4 *Jew.* 738; writes that some have killed themselves because of the irksomeness of them, *Rog.* 180; says the Flagellants held that none could be saved without the baptism of voluntary blood by whipping, *ib.* 277 n.; his character as a casuist, 1 *Brad.* 564; praised by Trithemius, 3 *Jew.* 133, and by Curio, *Phil.* 393

Gertrude (St): account of her, 1 *Bec.* 139 n.; invoked against rats and mice, *Bale* 498, 1 *Bec.* 139, 2 *Bec.* 536; her nuns, *Bale* 192

Gervase of Tilbury: Parker sends a transcript of a treatise by him to lord Burghley, *Park.* 424

Gervase (Father): at Lentzburg, 3 *Zur.* 153

Gervasius (St): martyred, 2 *Jew.* 654

Gervayes abbey: *v.* Jervaulx.

Gerves (Mr): 2 *Cran.* 258

Geskinbuge (......): 3 *Zur.* 617

Gesner (Conrad), mentioned: 1 *Zur.* 12, 17, 25, 31 n.; 2 *Zur.* 95, 3 *Zur.* 56, 64, & sæpe; he studies Welsh, 3 *Zur.* 73; married, 2 *Zur.* 90; sends to England for MSS. of ancient ecclesiastical authors, 1 *Zur.* 137 n., his Bibliotheca and Epitome, *Jew.* xxxvii, 3 *Jew.* 130, 1 *Zur.* 305, 3 *Zur.* 89; his book on birds, 3 *Zur.* 89; letter to him, 1 *Zur.* 31

Geson: *v.* Geason.

Gesse: guests, *Calf.* 300

Gesta Romanorum, 1 *Tyn.* 80 n., 328

Gestas, or Gismas: the impenitent thief, *Whita.* 560 n

Geste (Edm.), bp: *v.* Gheast.

Gests: acts, exploits, 1 *Tyn.* 450

Gestures: *v.* Ceremonies, v, Prayer, Supper.

Gethsemane: our Saviour's agony there, 1 *Lat.* 217, &c.; the tears of our Saviour in the garden; verses, *Poet.* 422

Geufræus (Ant.): Aula Turc., *Rog.* 243 n

Geveren (Schelto à): his discourse Of the End of the World, translated by Rogers, *Rog.* v, vii.

Gheast (Edm.), or Geste, bp of Rochester, afterwards of Salisbury: notice of him, *Park.* 123 n.; mentioned, *Grin.* 269; he disputes at Cambridge, *Grin.* 194, *Rid.* 169, and at Westminster, 4 *Jew.* 1199, 1 *Zur.* 11; assists at the funeral solemnity of the emperor Ferdinand, at St Paul's, *Grin.* 32; to preach at Paul's cross, *Park.* 240; his share in the Bishops' Bible, *ib.* 250; present at Grindal's confirmation as primate, *Grin.* x; he replenishes the library at Sarum, *Jew.* xxv; letter by him, *Park.* 250

Ghent: 2 *Zur.* 105

Ghinucci (Jerome de), bishop of Worcester: deprived by act of parliament, 2 *Cran.* 330 n

Ghost (Holy): *v.* Holy Ghost.

Ghostly enemies: *v.* Enemies.

Ghosts: *v.* Demons, Samuel, Spirits.

Giants: *v.* Tyrants.

Giants before the flood, 1 *Lat.* 245; the sons of Ham, 1 *Tyn.* 311; those mentioned by Ezekiel, *Bale* 579ʹ

Gibbes (Mr): defames the dean of Exeter, *Park.* 261

Gibbes (Will.): *v.* Gybbes.

Gibbings (Rich.): editor of Calfhill's Answer to Martiall, *Calf.*; likewise of Fulke's Answers, 2 *Ful.*; his Roman Forgeries, *Whita.* 41 n., 43 n

Gibbon (Edw.): Decline and Fall, 2 *Ful.* 98 n., 101 n., 361 n.; he respected Parker, *Park.* xiv.

Gibbon (Maurice), alias Reagh, titular abp of Cashel: takes flight, 1 *Zur.* 309 n

Gibeah: case of the Levite's concubine, 1 *Bul.* 417

Gibeonites: deceived Joshua, *Pil.* 392; their burying of Saul, *ib.* 318

Gibson (Jo.): letter to him, 1 *Brad.* 591, 2 *Brad.* 194; in prison for debt, 2 *Brad.* 244

Gibson (Jo.?), prebendary of Botevant: enjoined to view the statutes of the church of York, *Grin.* 151; legacy to him, *ib.* 460

Gibson (Rich.): martyred in Smithfield, *Poet.* 171

Gibson (Tho. and Will.): *v.* Gybson.

Gibson (Will.): notice of him, *Poet.* liv; verses from A Description of Norton's Falsehood of Yorkshire, *ib.* 542

Gidding (Little), co. Hunts: the Ferrar family, 1 *Brad.* 258 n., *Pra. B.* vi.

Gideon: called to judge Israel, *Pil.* 47, 109; a type of Christ, *Sand.* 394; his fleece, 4 *Bul.* 222, 231; it was a type of the Jewish nation, 2 *Bul.* 287, *Calf.* 336; his victory, *Pil.* 29

Gieseler (J. C. I.): Text Book of Eccl. Hist., *Calf.* 6 n., 2 *Ful.* 33 n., 81 n., *Rog.* 203 n

Giffe-gaffe: 1 *Lat.* 140

Gifford (Geo.), or Gyfford: translator of Fulke's work on the Apocalypse, 1 *Ful.* vii; his Catechism, published under the initials G. G., *Rog.* xvi; his Plain Declaration, against the Brownists, *ib.* 326; his Reply to Barrow and Greenwood, *ib.* 141, 142, 273

Gifford (Hum.): notice of him, *Poet.* xxi; verses; the life of man compared to a ship in a tempest, *ib.* 211; in praise of the contented mind, *ib.* 212; of the vanity of the world, *ib.* 213; a lesson for all estates, *ib.* 215; a godly discourse, *ib.* 215; the complaint of a sinner, *ib.* 217; a dream, *ib.* 218

Gifts: *v.* Grace, Holy Ghost. The gifts of God are not to be gloried in, 1 *Bec.* 202, 203, 2 *Bec.* 442; they are bestowed that we may use them for our neighbour's benefit, 1 *Tyn.* 24

Gigas (Herm.): *v.* Hermannus.

Gigglot: a wanton, 1 *Bul.* 398

Gigli (Sylvestro de), bp of Worcester: 1 *Tyn.* xviii.

Gilberd (Rob.): *Bale* 16

Gilby (Ant.): wrote an answer to Gardiner, under the initials A. G., 1 *Hoop.* 100; in exile, 1 *Cran.* (9); a leader amongst the Puritans, *Grin.* 326 n., 1 *Zur.* 285 n.; A Pleasant Dialogue between a Souldier of Barwicke and an English Chaplain, 1581, [ascribed to him by Dr Maitland, Index of Engl. Books at Lambeth], *Rog.* 310, 331, 332 n

Gildas: De Excidio Brit., *Jew.* xxxvii, 2 *Whitg.* 127; he says Britain received the gospel in the time of Tiberius, *Pil.* 510; a passage contained in his epistle on this subject generally misunderstood, 2 *Ful.* 186 n.; he states that Joseph of Arimathea preached in this realm, 1 *Jew.* 305, 3 *Jew.* 163; the preaching of Gildas to the Britons, 3 *Bec.* 10, 11; he laments their miserable state, *Pil.* 517; his testimony against their clergy, 1 *Tyn.* 143 n., 458; the ordering of ministers in his time, *Pil.* 584; falsely cited respecting Augustine, *ib.* 618, 619

Gilderde (Jo.): *v.* Gylderde.

Giles (St): invoked for women that would have children, *Rog.* 226; his bowl, *Bale* 527

— St Giles's fields: *v.* London.

Giles (Jo. and others): *v.* Egidius.

Giles (Steph.): *v.* Gyles.

Gilgal: 4 *Bul.* 481

Gilgate (Phil.): 3 *Zur.* 341

Gill: a ludicrous name for a woman, 1 *Bul.* 398

Gillam (Sir): *v.* Whitehead.

Gillebert: shews that the church is taught by the sufferings of martyrs, *Bale* 187 n

Gillingham, co. Kent: the benefice let to farm, 2 *Cran.* 284, 285

Gilpin (......), of Cambridge: presented to Bebington, Cheshire, *Grin.* 346

Gilpin (Bern.): denounces unfaithful patrons, 2 *Lat.* 29 n.; declines the bishoprick of Carlisle, *Grin.* 268 n.; his Life by bishop Carleton, *Calf.* 237 n

Gilpin (Geo.): his warning to Sandys at Antwerp, *Sand.* xv.

Gilpin (Geo.), the elder: translated The Beehive of the Romish Church, from the Dutch, *Rog.* 225 n

Gilpin (Josua): witness to Grindal's will, *Grin.* 463

Gipps (Rich.): notice of him, *Poet.* xxx; Psalm vi. in metre, *ib.* 337

Giraldus Cambrensis: a copy of his work in MS., *Park.* 265

Giraldus, abp of York: *v.* Gerard.

Gird: to sneer, or reproach; girdeth, 2 *Ful.* 153; girding, 1 *Brad.* 387

Girding of the loins: what signified by the expression, *Grin.* 6

Girtias: story of her, 1 *Bec.* 234

Giselbert: referred to on original sin, *Rog.* 100; he maintains justification by faith only, *Wool.* 35

Gladness: *v.* Joy.

Glaiton (Rafe): *v.* Allerton (R.).

Glaive: a broad-sword or falchion, 2 *Brad.* 48 n., 71; gleyve, 2 *Bec.* 216

Glaris, Switzerland: 3 *Zur.* 628, 629
Glasgow: the plague there, 2 *Zur.* 335; James, abp of Glasgow: *v.* Beaton.
Glastonbury, co. Somerset: the abbey, its revenue, 3 *Zur.* 627 n.; abbot Whiting and two monks hanged on the Tor, *ib.* 614 n., 627; the abbey granted to the strangers who fled from Strasburgh, *ib.* 737 n., 738 n
Glauberg (Jo. à), senator of Frankfort: 3 *Zur.* 765 n., 766; the same (?) saluted, 2 *Zur.* 298
Glaucus: 2 *Jew.* 803
Glaverer: a flatterer, *Bale* 19
Gledal (Reg.): servant to Grindal, *Grin.* 462
Glede: a kite, 2 *Cov.* 487
Glemham (Cha.): translates P. Martyr's Preces ex Psalmis, *Pra. Eliz.* 419
Glencairn (Earls of): *v.* Conyngham.
Gleyve: *v.* Glaive.
Glikes, nips, scoffs, &c.: 1 *Jew.* 91, 99
Glin (Will.): *v.* Glyn.
Gloria in excelsis: made by Hilary, 2 *Brad.* 307; by whom appointed in the mass, 3 *Bec.* 263, 2 *Brad.* 307, *Pil.* 503; used at the communion, 3 *Whitg.* 99; in English verse, by Coverdale, 2 *Cov.* 564, and by Sir N. Breton, *Poet.* 187
Gloria Patri: its use enjoined by Damasus, 1 *Jew.* 264, 2 *Whitg.* 469; a protest against the Arians, *ib.* 481; why another form of doxology was anciently used after the Benedicite, *Pra. Eliz.* 26 n., 141
Glorify (To): glorificare, *Now.* (101)
Glorious: used for vain-glorious, 1 *Tyn.* 453
Glory: *v.* Heaven.
Glory (Vain): *v.* Boasting, Pride.
Gloss: *v.* Law (Canon), Lyra (N. de).
What, *Hutch.* 344; a fair gloss makes not good an evil thing, 1 *Hoop.* 30
Glossa ordinaria: a collection of notes upon the scriptures, made by Walafrid Strabo, or Strabus, in the ninth century, and printed with the exposition of N. de Lyra, *Jew.* xxxiv; it confesses that errors have crept into the text of scripture, 1 *Ful.* 43; on the justification of Abraham, 2 *Cran.* 209; on Luke viii. 10, Christ's speaking in parables, *Whita.* 240; its interpretation of Luke xv. 8, "evertit domum," *ib.* 202; it declares that Paul learned not of the other apostles as his betters, 3 *Jew.* 288; says the people must choose, and the bishop must ordain, 1 *Whitg.* 441; speaks of the agreement of the people with the priest in their responding "Amen," 3 *Bec.* 409; on superstition (cited by Aquinas), *Pil.* 562, 563

Glossa ordinaria (Nova): a commentary not identified, 3 *Whitg.* 228 n.; cited on the συνέδριον, *ib.* 228; on the origin of the word battologizare, *ib.* 516
Glossary: of obsolete words in the works of Hutchinson, *Hutch.* index; of words in the Elizabethan poets, *Poet.* 557
Gloucester: partially rebuilt, 2 *Lat.* 393 n.; the grammar school of St Mary de Crypt, *ib.* 393 n., 418; the New Inn, lines written there by Hooper with a coal, 2 *Hoop.* xxx, and see 2 *Brad.* 363; Hooper's martyrdom, 2 *Hoop.* xxv, &c.; part of the stake recently discovered, *ib.* xxx; other martyrs there, *Poet.* 167
Gloucester (Hum. duke of): *v.* Humphrey.
Gloucestershire: contained six mitred abbots, 2 *Tyn.* 288 n.; ignorance of the clergy of Gloucester diocese in Hooper's time, 2 *Hoop.* 151
Glove (......): Glove's wife, martyr at Lewes, *Poet.* 170
Glover (......): letter possibly addressed to one of the name, 2 *Brad.* 60
Glover (......): martyred at Norwich, *Poet.* 172
Glover (......), a Brownist: he seems to have impugned the deity of the Holy Ghost, *Rog.* 70 n.; held that love is come in place of the ten commandments, *ib.* 92, that concupiscence is but venial sin, *ib.* 102, 103, that the regenerate may fall from the grace of God, *ib.* 147, that God has predestinated all to eternal death who are not in the state of true repentance, *ib.* 157
Glover (Jo.), of Bexterly hall, brother to Robert, the martyr: 2 *Lat.* 84 n., 419 n
Glover (Rob.), martyr: letter of Philpot to him, *Phil.* 243; extract from his last letter to his wife and children, 3 *Zur.* 360 n.; burned at Coventry, 2 *Lat.* 84 n., *Poet.* 164 bis, *Rid.* 384 n., 1 *Zur.* 86 n
— Mrs Glover, wife of the martyr: Ridley's letter to her, *Rid.* 383
Glover (Rob.), Somerset herald: *Park.* xiii.
Gloves: worn by laymen in receiving the sacramental bread, 2 *Bec.* 301; Oxford gloves sent as presents, 1 *Zur.* 130; some sent by Lady Jane Grey as a present to Bullinger's wife, 3 *Zur.* 454, 456
Gluttony: *v.* Eating.
The vice censured, 2 *Lat.* 15, *Pil.* 52, *Sand.* 137, 393; against gluttony and drunkenness; with sentences and examples of scripture, 1 *Bec.* 449, &c.; gluttony prevalent in abbeys, *Pil.* 610; a proverb respecting it, 2 *Bec.* 548; it should be restrained by law, 2 *Tyn.* 92, 93; the great evils of

belly-care, 2 *Bec.* 602; gluttony and drunkenness the root of all evil, 2 *Jew.* 1039, 1040; prayer against them, 3 *Bec.* 60

Glycerium: a name used by Jewel in his letters to denote queen Elizabeth, 4 *Jew.* 1228, &c., 1 *Zur.* 82, 93, &c.

Glyn (Will.), bp of Bangor: notice of him, *Phil.* xxix; a doctor at Cambridge, *Park.* 18, 38; one of the Romish disputants there, 1549, *Grin.* 194, *Rid.* 169; he disputes with Ridley at Oxford, *Rid.* 191; an old friend of Ridley's, *ib.* 234, yet very contumelious to him, *ib.* 235

Gnatho: 1 *Lat.* 124, *Pil.* 400

Gnomograph: a maxim-writer, 2 *Bec.* 401

Gnostics: why called Docetæ, *Grin.* 59 n.; sometimes called Barbelitæ, 2 *Ful.* 375; their founder, *Grin.* 59 n.; their heresy, 1 *Bul.* 132, 1 *Cov.* 21 n., 1 *Ful.* 215, *Grin.* 59 n.; they held a plurality of Gods, *Rog.* 44; worshipped images, 1 *Ful.* 194; carried about an image of Christ, *Calf.* 42, 43, 371, 2 *Jew.* 646, *Park.* 86, *Rid.* 88; disallowed matrimony, *Rog.* 261, 306; rejected the Psalms, *Whita.* 31; comparison between them and the Papists, *Phil.* 417

Go forth: to go on, continue, 1 *Bec.* 175

Goad (Roger): made provost of King's college, Cambridge, in the room of Dr Philip Baker, deprived, *Grin.* 308 n.; recommended as visitor for St John's college, *ib.* 359; he disputes with Campion, in the Tower, 1 *Ful.* xi; vice-chancellor, 3 *Whitg.* 611, 616

Goar (Jac.): 2 *Bec.* 257 n., 3 *Bec.* 388 n., 482 n., 483 n., *Grin.* 26 n

Goat: *v.* Scape-goat.

Gobbetts: fragments, 1 *Brad.* 209, *Phil.* 408

GOD: *v.* Armour, Commandments, Creeds, Kingdom, Prayer, (especially the Lord's).

  i. *His Name.*
  ii. *Similitudes.*
  iii. *His nature, power, glory.*
  iv. *The Trinity in Unity.*
  v. *His goodness, love, mercy.*
  vi. *His truth, justice, holiness, vengeance.*
  vii. *His works, and providence.*
  viii. *His grace.*
  ix. *His revelation of his will.*
  x. *Our duty to him.*

i. *His Name* (see also x. *b*, below): the Name of God, what is to be understood thereby, 3 *Bec.* 608, 1 *Bul.* 238, 3 *Bul.* 126, 4 *Bul.* 210, (see the several expositions of the third commandment and the Lord's prayer), 2 *Cov.* 303, 1 *Lat.* 345; what is meant by the Name of the Lord, 3 *Bec.* 622; the names of God, 3 *Bul.* 130, &c., *Hutch.* 16,

Jehovah, 1 *Brad.* 43, 3 *Bul.* 130, 136, *Pil.* 27, 1 *Tyn.* 408; the use of the word vindicated, 1 *Ful.* 590; this name called $\tau\epsilon\tau\rho\alpha\gamma\acute{\alpha}\mu\mu\alpha\tau\sigma\nu$, 3 *Bul.* 130, *Calf.* 284, *Grin.* 41; the Divine name is in four letters in many languages, 3 *Bul.* 131, *Hutch.* 17; the names Jah, and Hu (i. e. He), 3 *Bul.* 132, 155; I am: ΩΝ: est, *Hutch.* 17, 131, 1 *Tyn.* 420; Adonai, Dominus, commonly used by the Jews instead of Jehovah, 3 *Bul.* 132, *Hutch.* 17; El, and Elohim, 3 *Bul.* 133, 134, 2 *Tyn.* 165; El Schaddai, God Almighty, 2 *Brad.* 318, 1 *Bul.* 215, 3 *Bul.* 134, 135, 136, 1 *Hoop.* 293, 2 *Hoop.* 442: the Greek, ΘΕΟΣ, 3 *Bul.* 131; whence derived, *ib.* 134; the Latin, Deus, *ib.* 131, 134; the German, Gott, *ib.* 131, 135; the English, God, *ib.* 135 n.; Egyptian and Persian words for God, *ib.* 131, 136; the Lord of Sabbaoth, or of Hosts, *ib.* 132, *Pil.* 27, &c., 132, 138; the name is rarely used in the New Testament, and why, *Pil.* 27; the Most High, 3 *Bul.* 133; why he designates himself the God of Abraham, Isaac, and Jacob, *ib.* 136; why in the preface to the decalogue he calls himself the Lord our God, 2 *Bec.* 56, 57; why he is called Father, and our Father, 2 *Bec.* 17, 145, 1 *Brad.* 118, 1 *Bul.* 125, 4 *Bul.* 206, 208, 1 *Lat.* 342, *Lit. Edw.* 501, (550), *Now.* (71, 72), 191; what it profits us that he is our Father, 2 *Bec.* 145, 146; what we learn by calling him our Father, *ib.* 146; why he is called a shepherd, see viii. below.

ii. *Similitudes* of God made in the scriptures, 3 *Bul.* 152, *Hutch.* 159, &c.; they often speak of God after the manner of men, 1 *Tyn.* 88; though he is a Spirit, the scriptures attribute to him the parts of a man's body, 3 *Bul.* 138, *Hutch.* 18; the spiritual meaning of those several parts explained, 3 *Bec.* 609, *Hutch.* 18—20; the face of God, 3 *Bec.* 609, 1 *Bul.* 179, *Hutch.* 19; his mouth, 3 *Bec.* 609, 1 *Bul.* 38, *Hutch.* 19; his arm, 3 *Bec.* 609, *Hutch.* 19; his right hand, 2 *Bec.* 37, 3 *Bec.* 452, 1 *Bul.* 146, 148, 2 *Cov.* 154, 155, 162, 1 *Hoop.* 66, 67, *Hutch.* 19; the finger of God, 3 *Bec.* 609, *Hutch.* 20; his feet, *Hutch.* 20; he is compared to man's soul, *ib.* 164; other figures explained, *ib.* 21, 22; he is of a pure nature, and immutable, *ib.* 25; yet said to be angry, to laugh, sleep, awake, *ib.* 26; what it is for him to sleep, 3 *Bec.* 610; he is said to forget, remember, sit, stand, go, walk, *Hutch.* 27; how he is said to have rested the seventh day, *ib.* 88; how he is said to repent, 3 *Bul.* 56, *Hutch.* 90; he is invisible, *Hutch.* 29; yet Moses, Micaiah and Stephen are said to have seen God, *ib.* 30; the Anthropomorphites, Epicureans, &c., supposed him to be corporeal, *ib.* 12; he is likened to the sun, *ib.* 160, to fire, and light, *Hutch.* 163, 184, *Poet.* 240, 2 *Tyn.* 149, to a flood, *Hutch.* 185; he is called a rock, 2 *Hoop.* 260; errors of those who worship the sun, moon, fire, saints, bread and wine, &c., for God, *Hutch.* 13; God's image in man, 2 *Bul.* 377, 3 *Bul.* 53, *Hutch.* 164; it is defaced, *Lit. Edw.* 502, (551); the blotting out of this image is our depravation, 2 *Bul.* 394; it is defaced by sin, but restored by Christ, *Lit. Edw.* 499, (549); it is renewed by the gospel, 3 *Bul.* 53; God did all things with those of old by the Son, *ib.* 143; how the patriarchs did see him, *ib.* 142; how he was shadowed in visions, *ib.* 137, 143; how he shewed himself to Moses, *ib.* 145; he doth most evidently open himself through Christ, *ib.* 147; the image of God in Christ and in us different, *Phil.* 118; it is not lawful to make a representation of God, 2 *Bec.* 66, &c., 3 *Bul.* 235, *Now.* (10), 123, (*v.* Images); he will not be likened to anything, 1 *Bul.* 224; he did not give the Israelites his image, 2 *Bec.* 62; he cannot be represented by any image, 2 *Cran.* 101

iii. *His nature, power, glory, &c.*: there is a God, 3 *Bul.* 125; what he is, 2 *Bec.* 16, 3 *Bec.* 602, 614, 3 *Bul.* 146, *Lit. Edw.* 496, (546), *Now.* (101); a measure to be kept in this inquiry, 3 *Bul.* 125; dangerous disputations arose even in the primitive church, *ib.* 157; sundry opinions, *ib.* 124; fantasies of the Epicureans and Stoics, 1 *Jew.* 501; these follies reproved by Plato, *ib.*; the thoughts of believers and unbelievers concerning him, 2 *Tyn.* 210; knowledge of him surpasses all other science, *Hutch.* 2; the form and manner of knowing him, 3 *Bul.* 129; his existence shewn by the works of creation, *Whita.* 316; how he is known by them, 3 *Bul.* 150; his glory, majesty, and power are seen in his creatures, 1 *Hoop.* 45; whence the true knowledge of him must be fetched, 3 *Bul.* 124; we must learn what he is, and judge of him, from his word, 2 *Hoop.* 71, *Hutch.* 11, &c.; all things to be believed of him are contained therein, 3 *Bul.* 160; he is learned by the sayings of the prophets and apostles, *ib.* 153; THE IMAGE OF GOD, OR LAYMAN'S BOOK, by R. Hutchinson, *Hutch.* 1, &c.; God defined out of the scriptures, *ib.* 118; he is revealed by Christ, (*q. v.*), 2 *Tyn.* 26, &c.; he dwells in Christ bodily, in us spiritually, 2 *Lat.* 134; our God is the true God, 1 *Bul.* 218; our Maker, Lord, and Saviour, *Now.* (8), 121; his perfection is absolute, *Sand.* 421; he is unsearchable, *Hutch.* 28, infinite and incomprehensible, 2 *Bec.* 146; his nature cannot be expressed by words, *Now.* (29), 144; he alone is self-existent, *Hutch.* 16; he is a spirit, 1 *Bul.* 238, *Hutch.* 18, 25; he is invisible, *Hutch.* 29; a comparison between him and man, 1 *Bec.* 358, 2 *Hoop.* 315; his superiority to the idols of the heathen, 1 *Bec.* 206; Papists have false conceptions of his character, 1 *Tyn.* 278, 291—296, 2 *Tyn.* 156; "God shall be all in all," i. e. the Holy Trinity, 1 *Brad.* 272; God eternal; verses by Jo. Davies, *Poet.* 243; he only is immortal, *Hutch.* 61; he is unchangeable, *ib.* 25, *Rid.* 75; his omnipresence, *Hutch.* 31, 1 *Lat.* 332, *Lit. Edw.* 520, (567,) 3 *Tyn.* 86; he alone can be in all places at once, 2 *Bec.* 271, 3 *Tyn.* 232; how present with the wicked, *Hutch.* 31; a meditation of the presence of God, 1 *Brad.* 193, *Pra. B.* 112; he is alone omniscient, 2 *Lat.* 173, 332; he sees all things, *Sand.* 233, 234; is the searcher of hearts, *Rid.* 68; his wisdom, 3 *Bul.* 148; he is full of understanding, *Hutch.* 45; his wisdom not according to the wisdom of the world, 2 *Lat.* 126; his judgment, and civil judgment, not alike, *Phil.* 48; his foreknowledge, 3 *Bul.* 185; his will, see ix. below; his power, 3 *Bul.* 149; he is almighty, 2 *Bec.* 16, 18, 280, 609, 3 *Bec.* 273, 1 *Bul.* 125, 4 *Bul.* 263, 3 *Jew.* 498, 499, *Hutch.* 110, 2 *Lat.* 173, and therefore he cannot sin, lie, be deceived, or die, *Hutch.* 111; answer to the objection that he cannot revoke what is past, *ib.* 117; some things are not possible to him, *e. g.* he cannot break his decrees or promises, 3 *Tyn.* 232, 233; his omnipotence acts not contrary to his nature, 4 *Bul.* 451; his omnipotence pleaded by heretics, 2 *Jew.* 583, *Phil.* 61, 62; the resort of those who maintain transubstantiation, 2 *Jew.* 581; in that controversy his will, not his power, is the subject of dispute, 1 *Cran.* 15; he is an almighty helper, *Pil.* 431; how his almighty power is attributed to the word, 4 *Bul.* 266; his kingdom, see vii. below; his majesty, *Pil.* 296, 297; his glory, *Now.* (81), 203; God's glory and goodness inexplicable; verses by Jo. Davies, *Poet.* 247; a meditation of his power, beauty, goodness, &c., 1 *Brad.* 194, *Pra. B.* 113; the kingdom and power and glory are his, 2 *Bec.* 196; all things of, by, and in him, 2 *Bul.* 383

iv. *The Trinity in Unity :* on the unity of God, 3 *Bul.* 154, *Hutch.* 178, &c., *Now.* (29), 145, *Rog.* 35—38; the term Trinity, *Now.* (103); the doctrine of the Trinity in Unity, or how the Father, the Son, and the Holy Ghost are one God, 2 *Bec.* 16, 17, 1 *Bul.* 43, 124, 3 *Bul.* 137, 156, 325, 2 *Hoop.* 22, 70, 71, 120, *Hutch.* 178, 3 *Jew.* 252, 1 *Lat.* 456, *Now.* (29), 145, *Phil.* 302; on the Unity of God, and the Trinity of persons (an article, 1538), 2 *Cran.* 472; the sum of things to be believed concerning the Holy Trinity, 3 *Bul.* 168; why this truth is obscure to us, *Whita.* 376; it is not to be joined with curious disputations, 3 *Bul.* 172; its certainty, *ib.* 167; the distinction of persons in the Godhead proved from scripture, *ib.* 156, &c., *Hutch.* 121, &c.; the doctrine of the Trinity in Unity proved by scripture, *Rog.* 42, *Whita.* 534, &c.; the truth is denoted by ELOHIM in conjunction with the singular, 1 *Bul.* 200, 3 *Bul.* 135, *Hutch.* 169, 182; taught in the name "the God of Abraham, of Isaac, and of Jacob," 3 *Bul.* 137; the unity of the persons proved by their having the same attributes, *Hutch.* 183, &c.; the saints of the Old Testament knew and worshipped the Holy Trinity, *ib.* 122; the mystery was known to the patriarchs and prophets, 3 *Bul.* 169; it is proved by testimonies of the gospel, *ib.* 160, and by the teaching of the apostles, *ib.* 163; the doctrine is held by all churches, *Rog.* 43; this is the only point on which Romanists are sound, *Phil.* 150; what a person in the Godhead is, *Hutch.* 11, 129, 130; words used by the church to signify the persons, 3 *Bul.* 158, *Hutch.* 131; the term ὑπόστασις used by Gregory of Neocæsarea, 2 *Jew.* 607; Jerome consulted Damasus on the propriety of speaking of three hypostases, *Whita.* 442; the terms Trinity, person, hypostasis, consubstantial, &c., may be received, *ib.* 588; the three persons ever work inseparably, *Hutch.* 164; their work in baptism, *ib.* 11, 156, 199, 200, in creation, *ib.* 11, 62, 165, in providence, *ib.* 11, in the incarnation of Christ, *ib.* 165, in his miracles, *ib.* 166, and resurrection, *ib.*; the mystery of the Trinity shadowed by similitudes, 3 *Bul.* 165, as in Abraham's vision (Gen. xviii), *Hutch.* 126, 160, in the sun, *ib.* 160, in fire and light, *ib.* 163, *Poet.* 240, in man's soul, *Hutch.* 164; the ternarius numerus of Pythagoras, *ib.* 123, 176; unto the Trinity, (a hymn), 2 *Cov.* 543; hymn to the glorious honour of the most blessed Trinity, by B. Barnes, *Poet.* 51; heresies respecting the Holy Trinity, *Rog.* 43—45, 202; the Trinity said by Peter of Antioch to have been crucified, *ib.* 57; popish images of the Holy Trinity, *ib.* 223; erroneous statement that some held a quarternity of persons, *ib.* 44

God the Father, as confessed in the creed, 1 *Brad.* 140, 2 *Hoop.* 22, *Now.* (29), 145

God the Son : v. Christ.

God the Holy Ghost: v. Holy Ghost.

v. *His goodness, love, mercy :* how he alone is good, *Hutch.* 170; good in himself, 2 *Bul.* 366; his goodness to men, 1 *Bec.* 199, 292, 3 *Bul.* 148; his liberality, 1 *Lat.* 397; all good things are his gifts, 2 *Bec.* 18, 19 ; he gives all good things for Christ's sake, *ib.* 45; he does good for his promise sake to the unworthy, *ib.* 608, 609; his goodness not to be mistrusted, *Pil.* 353; his kindness in feeding his servants, 3 *Bec.* 52; his benefits towards us, 1 *Bec.* 179; the rehearsal of them, *ib.* 184, 185; we should ever set them before our eyes, *ib.* 280; his benefits towards man, in creation, 2 *Bec.* 443 ; his love shewn therein, 1 *Brad.* 68; his benefits towards man, in the promise of redemption, 2 *Bec.* 444, in giving the law, and dealing friendly with him, *ib.* 445 ; his love in giving his Son, 1 *Bec.* 74, 2 *Bec.* 28, 3 *Bec.* 64, 1 *Brad.* 74, 1 *Hoop.* 17, in sending him in the fulness of time, 2 *Bec.* 445; thanksgiving to him for sending his Son, 3 *Bec.* 63, &c.; the love of God, verses, *Poet.* 346; his exceeding love towards us, 3 *Bul.* 8, 1 *Lat.* 333, 2 *Lat.* 86, 205, *Pil.* 189, 2 *Tyn.* 186, 198, 199; he loved us first, 2 *Tyn.* 199, 3 *Tyn.* 196, 198; he sets forth his love that we may have confidence in him, 1 *Tyn.* 294; the preaching of his kindness makes men earnestly to love him, 1 *Bec.* 81; his love greater than a parent's, 1 *Lat.* 535, &c.; he loves repenting sinners as well as the angels in heaven, 3 *Tyn.* 88 ; loves the good deeds of believers, because he first loved them, 1 *Tyn.* 295; his love unchangeable, 2 *Brad.* 88, &c., 113, 122, 154; his mercy and pity, 1 *Brad.* 319, 3 *Bul.* 149, 2 *Cov.* 129, 1 *Hoop.* 489; his free mercy to men, 1 *Bec.* 71, 72; he is full of mercy, *Hutch.* 56; full of compassion, *ib.* 60; he is of himself inclined to have mercy, 2 *Hoop.* 256; the greatness of his mercy, 1 *Brad.* 342, &c.; divine mercy as great as God's divinity, verses by Jo. Davies, *Poet.* 247, greater than his anger, 2 *Bec.*

76, and greater than our iniquity, 1 *Lat.* 267; his mercy and his justice, 1 *Brad.* 319; examples of his mercy, 3 *Bec.* 110, 111; his mercy to Adam, &c., 1 *Brad.* 69, 70; shewn in the fire descending on the sacrifices, 1 *Hoop.* 48; his mercy the sole cause of the deliverance of Israel, *ib.* 257; to whom he is merciful, 2 *Hoop.* 362; his mercy alone delivers us out of our misery, 1 *Bec.* 145; two manner of mercies, outward and inward, 2 *Hoop.* 343; his mercy on our repentance, 1 *Bec.* 249; caution against presumption therein, *Wool.* 143; he is a merciful and loving Father, 1 *Tyn.* 280, 3 *Tyn.* 111; not a tyrant, 2 *Hoop.* 369, 1 *Tyn.* 280, 3 *Tyn.* 111, though represented as such by Romanists, 3 *Tyn.* 120; he delights not in pain suffered by his creatures, 2 *Tyn.* 96; his long forbearing, 2 *Bul.* 429, 3 *Bul.* 149, 2 *Cran.* 200, *Pil.* 11, 119, 179; he is slow to anger, ready to forgive, *Now.* (12,) 126; turns to us when we turn to him, *Pil.* 182; he dries up the seas of mistrust and heaviness out of the soul, 2 *Hoop.* 368; in the midst of judgments he always preserves penitent sinners, *ib.* 369; he loves and helps the poor afflicted, *ib.* 316; despises not a troubled and broken heart, *ib.* 218; hears the cry of the oppressed, 1 *Lat.* 357; can help when man cannot, *ib.* 543; he is the Father of widows and orphans, *ib.* 145; careful of his afflicted faithful, 2 *Hoop.* 370; no less favourable to his people in adversity than in prosperity, *Rid.* 75

vi. *His truth, justice, holiness, vengeance:* his truth, 3 *Bul.* 148; he is truth, *Hutch.* 51; he can neither lie nor deceive, 1 *Bec.* 148; he is full of righteousness, *Hutch.* 57; his righteousness described, 3 *Bul.* 40; sin repugnant to his law, 2 *Bul.* 406; he is not the author of evil, 1 *Brad.* 213, 214, 321, 2 *Bul.* 365, 373, 2 *Cov.* 341, 1 *Ful.* 563, *Hutch.* 65; how he is said to do evil—not the sin, but the punishment, 2 *Bul.* 382; his justice, 1 *Brad.* 319, 2 *Brad.* 129, 3 *Bul.* 149, 2 *Cran.* 129; his righteousness is not satisfied by our penance, but by the death of Christ, 2 *Tyn.* 156; he is a righteous sovereign, *Hutch.* 59, 68; a righteous judge, 2 *Jew.* 1068, 1 *Lat.* 364; no respecter of persons, 1 *Lat.* 337, 391, 2 *Lat.* 93, 201, *Sand.* 278, 1 *Tyn.* 101; not partial, *Pil.* 132, 133; he regards no more a pope than a potter, a cardinal than a carter, a bishop than a butcher, &c., 2 *Cran.* 18; why he is called a jealous God, 2 *Bec.* 73, 74, 3 *Bec.* 612, *Now.* (11), 124; he suffereth not a mate, 1 *Bul.* 233; is jealous for his religion, *Pil.* 258; not to be tempted, 1 *Lat.* 205, 528; he visits sins of the fathers on the children, 1 *Bul.* 235; he declared his hatred of sin by the death of Christ, 1 *Hoop.* 49; faithful and just, though he delay his promises, 2 *Bul.* 91; faithful and just to his people, see viii. below; the presence of his favour towards his own, is the destruction of the wicked, 2 *Hoop.* 266; his justice twofold, corrective and retributive, 1 *Hoop.* 266; vengeance belongeth to him, *Pil.* 249, *Sand.* 289, 1 *Tyn.* 332, 404; his righteous retribution, *Pil.* 226, 257; he is slow in punishing, but sure, 1 *Hoop.* 24, *Pil.* 248, 258; though long-suffering, he will recompense, 1 *Lat.* 106; compared to a shooter, "He hath bent his bow," *Hutch.* 22; he sends prophets and preachers to exhort to repentance before inflicting judgments, 3 *Bec.* 6, &c.; he visits by preaching and vengeance, 1 *Lat.* 146; plagues following the contempt of his word, 3 *Bec.* 206, 207; his ire against the impenitent, 1 *Hoop.* 18; examples of his anger against such, 3 *Bec.* 206; remedies against his wrath, *ib.* 208, 209, 220; how we may be delivered from his great ire, 2 *Hoop.* 99; men's various ways of pacifying his wrath against sin, *Sand.* 219, 220; the way prescribed by himself, *ib.* 220, 221; righteousness of his judgments, *Pil.* 346; he punishes sinners justly, 2 *Bul.* 427; punishes most sharply, *ib.* 428, 1 *Hoop.* 18; examples of this, 2 *Bul.* 429; to whom he is severe, 2 *Hoop.* 362; how he punishes sin, 3 *Bec.* 605, 606, by his creatures, *Pil.* 177, 220, 221, by the offending parts, *ib.* 226; he hates not the troubled man for his trouble, but for his sin, 2 *Hoop.* 317; he delivers wicked men up to their own lusts, *ib.* 579, gives them over to a reprobate sense, 2 *Bul.* 380; how he makes men blind, *ib.* 380; how he hardened Pharaoh's heart, *ib.* 382; he leaves desperation to his enemies, 2 *Hoop.* 265; what his curse is, 3 *Bec.* 604; the remembrance of his justice for sin, a greater pain than the death of the body, 2 *Hoop.* 335

vii. *His works and providence* (v. Creation, Providence): he made the world, and all things, 2 *Bec.* 18, 19, 3 *Bec.* 614, 1 *Bul.* 126, *Hutch.* 62, *Rog.* 39; his works two ways considered, 3 *Bul.* 150; he created all things by his Word, *Now.* (31), 146; he created all things good, 2 *Bul.* 366; in what state he created man, 3 *Bec.* 614; he preserves all things, *Rog.* 39; his providence, 3 *Bul.* 178, *Now.* (31), 147, *Pil.* 93; it is over all, 1 *Lat.* 263, 2 *Lat.* 30; he rules the world thereby, *Hutch.* 69; God to be looked to in all things, good or evil, *Pil.* 227; a meditation on the providence of God towards mankind, 1 *Brad.* 191, *Pra. B.* 109; he is not subject to necessity, 1 *Brad.* 212, 213; his will, 2 *Bec.* 155, 156, 1 *Brad.* 310, 4 *Bul.* 212, 213, *Now.* (76), 196; it is the cause of all things, *Pil.* 674; it is in part unsearchable, in part revealed, 1 *Lat.* 369, in part known, in part unknown, 1 *Brad.* 129; nature is his ordinary will, miracles his extraordinary will, *ib.* 359; natural causes are only the instruments of God's will, 1 *Jew.* 501; his permissive will, *ib.* 441; his will is to be submitted to, 2 *Lat.* 185, to be preferred to ours, 3 *Bec.* 113; example hereof in Christ, *ib.* 114; what is meant by praying that his will may be fulfilled in earth as in heaven, 2 *Bec.* 154, 155 (v. Prayer, The Lord's); his will immutable, 2 *Brad.* 129, 130; he casts away that which is contrary thereto, 1 *Bec.* 152; he governeth all things, 3 *Bul.* 178; his kingdom (*q. v.*), in respect of his power, his grace, his glory, 1 *Brad.* 127; he works his will and uses his creatures as it seems to his wisdom most meet, 2 *Hoop.* 365; he uses the ministry of angels, 3 *Bul.* 338; that which his servants do, is his deed, *Pil.* 234; he overrules the purposes of men, 2 *Lat.* 96, 97; laughs to scorn the intent of the wicked, 2 *Hoop.* 269; overrules the acts of men and the devil, *Pil.* 178; he is against private authority and disorderly doings, 1 *Lat.* 115; the pains of the world are his servants, 2 *Hoop.* 585; nothing happens without his foresight, *Rid.* 79; his foreknowledge is no cause of things, *Hutch.* 85; his predestination (*q. v.*), 3 *Bul.* 185; he is the doer of wonders, 2 *Hoop.* 360; his doings to be marked, whether they be blessings or plagues, *Pil.* 173—175; various ways of considering his works, 2 *Hoop.* 353, 409; they comfort the faithful, but not the unfaithful, *ib.* 353; his tuition of us here and in the life to come compared, *ib.* 196, 263, 264; all troubles come by his providence, *ib.* 217; why he punishes the good with the evil, 2 *Bul.* 75; his punishments at first are gentle, *Pil.* 178; why he exercises the afflicted in their troubles, 1 *Hoop.* 490; two impediments that keep him from helping the troubled, 2 *Hoop.* 311; he hides his consolations for a time to try us, *ib.* 337; why he defers to give that which he means to give, 4 *Bul.* 171; how his temptations differ from Satan's, 2 *Bec.* 185, 186; he tempts in two manner of ways, *ib.* 186; he is not the author of temptation to evil and damnation, *ib.* 194; reasons why he tempts us, *ib.* 191, &c.; he chiefly helps in great extremities, 3 *Bec.* 213, &c.; he is mysterious in his deliverances, 1 *Hoop.* 489; examples of his deliverance, 2 *Bul.* 96; he gives wisdom to escape snares, 1 *Lat.* 293; his good-will learned by his providence, 3 *Bul.* 184; the good hand of God, *Pil.* 331; we have all things of his hand, 2 *Cran.* 87; his will is the first cause of all good, *Pil.* 195; he is the giver of all good things, *ib.* 85; his temporal and spiritual gifts, 1 *Bec.* 281, 282; he upholds and defends his people, 2 *Bec.* 633, 634, 1 *Lat.* 264, 2 *Lat.* 153; his watchfulness over them, *Pil.* 422; his fatherly care and good-will to them, 2 *Bec.* 165, 166; he saves them in all dangers, *Pil.* 191, 196; he sends for the best whatever comes upon them, 2 *Bec.* 158; the assurance of his defence and comfort must be learned out of his word, 2 *Hoop.* 193; by him we are preserved from evil, 1 *Bec.* 179; his providence to be depended on, 1 *Brad.* 439; he will supply his servants with necessary things, 2 *Bec.* 466, 467; he is wise in his distribution of riches, *Pil.* 153; his storehouse, 1 *Lat.* 399, 404; his liberality evidenced in the provision made for his creatures, 2 *Bec.* 603; the histories of scripture confirm this, *ib.* 603; hereby he encourages poor married men, *ib.* 605, 614; this should encourage men to stay at home and not wander, *ib.* 606, and should assure travellers that he will not forsake them, *ib.* 606, 607; godly preachers are encouraged to look for his liberality, *ib.* 611, 614; also their wives, *ib.* 612; and those that are imprisoned for his glory, *ib.* 613, and that love his word, *ib.*; none should despair of his liberality, *ib.* 610; his blessing prospers labour, *Pil.* 50, 133, makes food serviceable, *ib.* 53; he watches upon his ministers, 1 *Bec.* 218; they that do things at his commandment can take no harm, 2 *Hoop.* 371; for whom he fights, 1 *Bec.* 252; he the only stay of the country, *Rid.* 143; ways for England to obtain his favour, 1 *Bec.* 127, 128; he and the world judge not alike, *ib.* 137; the ways of God unsearchable, verses by Edm. Spenser, *Poet.* 30

viii. *His grace* (v. Covenants, Faith, Gospel, Grace, Justification, Predestination, Promises, &c.): what his grace is, 3 *Bec.* 616; he is the worker of all good things in man, 1 *Tyn.* 498, 3 *Tyn.* 34 ; he gives his gifts freely, 3 *Bul.* 144; our goodness springeth out of his, 3 *Tyn.* 196; he is the God of our salvation, 1 *Brad.* 286 ; able and willing to save, 2 *Hoop.* 255, 259; salvation is of him only, 1 *Bec.* 72, 2 *Hoop.* 71, 275, 348; his justice and his mercy therein, 1 *Brad.* 319, 2 *Cov.* 129; everlasting life is his free gift, 2 *Bec.* 50; probations out of scripture that he freely saves the faithful, 3 *Bec.* 297, &c.; his election, 1 *Bec.* 72 ; his sovereignty, *Phil.* 339; on his decrees and man's imbecility, *ib.* 402 ; he foreknew the fall of man, 2 *Bul.* 377 ; he gave his Son that we, being cleansed from sin, might serve him in holiness, 2 *Bec.* 636, 637; his grace exhibited in Christ, 3 *Bul.* 12; once angry with the world, now pleased with it in Christ, *ib.* 26; he has performed through him what he promised to our forefathers, *ib.* 19; he hath given in him all heavenly treasures, 1 *Bul.* 156; God is our Father, Christ our Brother, 1 *Lat.* 328 ; none can come to Christ unless the Father draw him, 3 *Tyn.* 224, 225 ; he alone can open the heart, 1 *Lat.* 285; his property in his elect to wound before he heals, 3 *Bec.* 160, 213; how we were reconciled to him, *ib.* 614; his grace and Spirit are not bound to any external ceremony, 2 *Bec.* 220; not tied to circumcision, 2 *Bul.* 175; conversion to God, 3 *Bul.* 56; he alone converts man from evil and keeps him in goodness and virtue, 2 *Hoop.* 208; he alone forgives sins, *Bale* 117, 2 *Bec.* 45, 172, 173, 557, 560, 1 *Bul.* 166, 2 *Hoop.* 60, 351, *Hutch.* 92 (v. Sin); probations of this out of scripture, 3 *Bec.* 299, 300; his mercy in forgiving sins, 2 *Bec.* 175, 176, 3 *Bec.* 50, 51; he remits sins of his free favour, 2 *Bec.* 45, 181, 182; he releases both à pœna and à culpa, *ib.* 174, 3 *Bec.* 144, 233, 1 *Lat.* 426, 1 *Tyn.* 271, 3 *Tyn.* 154; faith is his gift, 1 *Bul.* 263; nothing can quiet the comfortless spirit but God, 2 *Hoop.* 323; hope is his gift, 2 *Bul.* 90; he sanctifieth, 1 *Bul.* 266; he is the only teacher of true knowledge, *Sand.* 114; who are "taught of God," *Whita.* 454; he hides his truth from the wise and prudent of the world, 3 *Bec.* 39; why God leaves one blind and opens the eyes of another, is a question too deep for us, 3 *Tyn.* 191; to whom his benefits in Christ belong, 1 *Bec.* 292; his promises are made to the godly and not the ungodly, 2 *Bec.* 618, 619; his delight in his people, *Pil.* 71; his relations to them, *ib.* 259; he is especially their God, *ib.* 331, 351; his presence with them, *ib.* 108; his love to them, *ib.* 189; nothing but his grace and presence can defend them, 2 *Hoop.* 224; he is all to them, 2 *Bul.* 170; he is all-sufficient, 1 *Bul.* 215 ; why he is called the God of Abraham, Isaac, and Jacob, 3 *Bul.* 136; he is the Father of all the faithful, 1 *Lat.* 337 ; why he is called a shepherd, 2 *Cov.* 287, &c. 2 *Hoop.* 187, &c.; what it is to be his sheep, 2 *Hoop.* 195; his friendship and familiarity towards them, *ib.* 227; he exercises them in dangers and troubles, *ib.* 214, 265, 587 ; their troubles are known and appointed by him, *ib.* 215, 581; how his voice and teaching heal their minds, *ib.* 196; he will never permit his sheep to be deadly wounded, *ib.* 230; why he is called a husbandman, *Hutch.* 23 ; his favour in this world is joined with troubles, 2 *Hoop.* 265, 587 ; why he lays his cross upon the faithful, 2 *Bec.* 189, 190; he afflicts those whose sins he has forgiven, 3 *Bul.* 91; he punishes his elect, 2 *Hoop.* 225; but not without just cause, *ib.* 292, 369; his chastisements are sent in love, 3 *Bec.* 94, &c., 102, 104, &c., 2 *Hoop.* 292, 363, *Pil.* 181; his punishments are for our good, *Pil.* 179; he punishes a Christian in order to his repentance and salvation, 3 *Bec.* 105; examples of this, *ib.* 106, &c.; his faithfulness in times of extreme distress, 2 *Cran.* 457 ; the afflicted by his commandment take courage to approach his mercy, 2 *Hoop.* 257 ; what his blessing is, 3 *Bec.* 604; the liberty of the sons of God, 3 *Bul.* 102; how he is said to reward good works, 2 *Bul.* 346 ; he is just to reward according to his promise, 1 *Ful.* 340

ix. *His revelation of his will* (v. Covenants, Gospel, Law, Scripture, Word, &c.) : what his will is, 1 *Hoop.* 445; it must be known in order to be practised, *ib.* 443; it is sufficiently revealed, *Pra. B.* 26; what his word is, 3 *Bec.* 614, 1 *Bul.* 37; his law, what, 1 *Bul.* 209; to what end he gave law to Adam, 2 *Bul.* 375; of the use and effect of his laws, *ib.* 237; his covenant with man, 1 *Bul.* 44, 113, 2 *Bul.* 169; the different ways in which he spoke to the fathers, 2 *Jew.* 968; he sets forth to sinful men both the law and the gospel, 2 *Bec.* 628 ; his will and pleasure as set forth in scripture to be submitted to in all articles of Christian faith, 1 *Cran.* 34; none of his writings lost, *Whita.* 525; he would have his word understood, 1 *Bul.* 71, but hides the mysteries thereof from the wise and prudent, 2 *Lat.* 93; his general will expressed in the decalogue,

1 *Lat.* 537; his special will, *ib.*; his teaching to be praised, 1 *Bul.* 60; his people must hear Christ's voice, 1 *Hoop.* 19; what it is to shew his word, 3 *Bec.* 608; why his preachers are contemned of the world, 2 *Hoop.* 202; his messengers cruelly intreated, *Sand.* 187, 188; the despising of his word and preachers never escapes unplagued, 3 *Bec.* 7

x. *Our duty towards Him:* we are all debtors to him, 2 *Bec.* 178, both in body and soul, 2 *Hoop.* 574; our duty towards him, 1 *Bec.* 206, 3 *Bec.* 619, *Now.* (9), 122

(*a*) To believe in him (*v.* Faith):—what it is to do so, 2 *Bec.* 19, 3 *Bec.* 609, 620; faith in him, what it is, 1 *Bul.* 124; we see him now by faith, 1 *Lat.* 485; faith joins to him, 1 *Bul.* 103, and brings salvation, 2 *Hoop.* 262; by faith we obtain all good things from him, 2 *Bec.* 45, 46

(*b*) To fear him, *Sand.* 279, 280; what fear we ought to have towards him, 1 *Bec.* 208, 3 *Bec.* 604, 619; his fear is in all penitents, 3 *Bul.* 59; it is twofold, *ib.* 60; his name to be hallowed, 1 *Brad.* 125, 1 *Bul.* 238, *Now.* (73), 194; by whom it was and is hallowed, 1 *Lat.* 347; it cannot be made more glorious than it is, 2 *Bec.* 148; it is to be had in reverence, *Now.* (13), 126, 1 *Tyn.* 24; how esteemed by the Gentiles, 1 *Bul.* 202; it is not to be taken in vain, 1 *Brad.* 10, 154; what it is to take his name in vain, 1 *Bec.* 359, 2 *Cran.* 102; to go to mass is to take God's name in vain, 2 *Brad.* 321; how it is abused, 1 *Bul.* 240; the punishment of those who abuse it, *ib.* 241; he most chiefly detests idolatry and the abusing of his name, 2 *Bec.* 79; what is to be taken heed of in naming him, 1 *Hoop.* 322; what it is to swear by him, 2 *Tyn.* 55; he alone is to be sworn by, and only on necessary occasions, *Hutch.* 21; an oath is a special honour to him, 1 *Bul.* 248; a Christian may swear for his glory, 1 *Bec.* 378

(*c*) To love him (*v.* Love):—our love of God, 1 *Bec.* 226, 227, 1 *Bul.* 181; he alone is to be loved, 1 *Bul.* 183; how he is to be loved, 3 *Bec.* 619, 1 *Bul.* 182, 1 *Hoop.* 299, *Now.* (22), 137; he that hath his love and fear sealed in his heart liveth an angelical life, 2 *Hoop.* 219

(*d*) To worship him (*v.* Worship, Temple): the worship of God, 3 *Bec.* 609, 620, 1 *Bul.* 45, 2 *Bul.* 128, 3 *Bul.* 200; rewards for them that worship him, 3 *Bul.* 204; punishments for them that do not worship him, *ib.* 204; he alone is to be worshipped, *ib.* 201; probations out of scripture that he only is to be worshipped, in spirit and in truth, 3 *Bec.* 300, 301; when the soul of man doth wait upon or have silence towards him, 2 *Hoop.* 247; prayer to him should be directed to heaven, 1 *Tyn.* 383, 385; heaven is his dwelling-place, 2 *Bec.* 146, 147, 1 *Brad.* 123, *Now.* (73), 193, 1 *Tyn.* 382; his throne is there, *Bale* 298, &c.; how he was present in the temple, 3 *Tyn.* 86, and in the pillar of fire, *ib.*; he dwells not in temples made with hands, *Bale* 149, 169, 211, 611, *Calf.* 131, 1 *Tyn.* 382; his temple, what it is, 3 *Bec.* 608, 3 *Bul.* 225; who are the house of God, 4 *Bul.* 82; the building of his house, *Pil.* 3; it must be built before our own, *ib.* 39; his priest and sacrifices, 3 *Bul.* 226; he cannot away with any hypocrisy, 2 *Hoop.* 573; looks not at the gift, but the giver, 2 *Lat.* 202; delights not in outward pomp, *Sand.* 347; when he liketh, and when misliketh ceremonies, 2 *Bul.* 128; his commands and man's inventions, 2 *Lat.* 354; his wisdom shines in the institution of the sacraments, 4 *Bul.* 244; he is to be praised for instituting them, *ib.*

(*e*) To give him thanks (*v.* Thanksgiving):—what thanksgiving to him is, 3 *Bec.* 620; thanksgiving due to him alone, 4 *Bul.* 221; how the godly give thanks to him, *ib.* 222

(*f*) To trust in him (*v.* Faith):—what it is to do so, *Rid.* 68; it is the first commandment, and first article of our creed, 3 *Tyn.* 273, 274; we should trust him for all things, 2 *Bec.* 614, 615, both for soul and body, 1 *Lat.* 402, 2 *Lat.* 154; to distrust his promises is to make him a liar, 2 *Lat.* 36; to those that trust in him he is most beneficial, 2 *Bec.* 619

(*g*) To call upon him (*v.* Prayer):—to be called on, 3 *Bul.* 206, and he alone, 1 *Bec.* 139, 165, 2 *Bec.* 126, 127, 3 *Bec.* 228, 3 *Bul.* 208, 4 *Bul.* 172, 2 *Hoop.* 100; probations of this out of scripture, 3 *Bec.* 301, 302; the holy fathers of the old and new testament prayed to him only, 1 *Bec.* 141; before him all are beggars, 1 *Lat.* 397; invocation of God, or calling upon him, what it is, 3 *Bul.* 206, 1 *Cov.* 402; he commands us to call unto him for help, 2 *Hoop.* 256; help not to be asked or sought any where saving of him, *ib.* 224, 256, 349; he commands us to call upon him in sickness, 3 *Bec.* 112, 113; examples of the benefit of doing so, *ib.* 113; how to come to him in adversity, 1 *Lat.* 142; by whom he is called upon, 4 *Bul.* 172; what things provoke men to call upon him, *ib.* 174; how to draw near to him, *Sand.* 134; we cannot do this without his grace, *ib.* 133; comfort in drawing near unto him, *ib.* 143; on seeking God, *ib.* 144; he is to be sought and found by faith, *ib.* 152, by hearing, *ib.* 153, by prayer, *ib.* 155; the fruit of seeking him, *ib.* 159; with what abilities he must be furnished that comes to pray to him, 4 *Bul.* 174; what we must ask of him, *ib.* 187; why we must express our desires in words, *ib.* 203; he alone hears everywhere, all persons, and always, 3 *Bul.* 211; how he hears not sinners, 2 *Bec.* 626; the Intercessor with him, 3 *Bul.* 212

(*h*) To honour him :—his honour always foremost, 1 *Bul.* 269; how he is to be honoured, 1 *Tyn.* 106, 3 *Tyn.* 57; we should be grieved to see him dishonoured, 1 *Lat.* 518; what it is to glorify him, 1 *Bec.* 389, 2 *Bec.* 148, 149; his glory and the promotion of his word must be sought in prayer, 1 *Bec.* 165

(*i*) To serve him :—he is not only a Saviour, but also Lord, *ib.* 127; a master and teacher, 2 *Hoop.* 193; he is to be obeyed rather than man, *Pil.* 24, 41, yea, before all, 1 *Hoop.* 31; probations of this out of scripture, 3 *Bec.* 302, &c.; he is to be served, *Sand.* 181, and he alone, 3 *Bul.* 226, *Sand.* 182—184; God himself prescribes how men shall serve him, *Sand.* 189, 221; scripture our only rule in this matter, *ib.* 190—222; what his true service is, 3 *Bec.* 609, 620, *Lit. Edw.* 515, 516, (562, 563); it is twofold, 3 *Bul.* 223, inward, *ib.*, outward, *ib.* 227; what it is to be his servant, 1 *Bec.* 292; who is his handmaid, *ib.* 293; he may be served in every kind of living, 2 *Hoop.* 194; he judges not the person of the act, but the act of the person, 1 *Bec.* 137; he judges the work of the heart, and not the heart of the work, 2 *Bec.* 539; he is to be served with childlike, not slavish, fear, *Sand.* 184; how God is served in the church, *ib.* 252; how to please him, 1 *Tyn.* 332; what it is to walk before him, 1 *Bec.* 206, 208; what it is to walk with him, *Sand.* 231; what it is to follow him and fight under his standard, 3 *Bec.* 620; he is to be followed absolutely, *Sand.* 375; humility most acceptable to him, 2 *Hoop.* 213; he requireth pureness in man, 2 *Bul.* 123; what he is to us we must be to our neighbour, 2 *Bec.* 182; what is his, and what Cæsar's, *Hutch.* 325, 1 *Lat.* 295, 303, 511; he will be served of all nations, *Sand.* 253, &c.; what it is to serve him unlawfully, 3 *Bul.* 237

(*k*) Some opposite sins (*v.* Sin, &c.):— wrong done unto him, 2 *Hoop.* 280; nothing disobeyeth him but man, 1 *Lat.* 387, and the devil, 2 *Hoop.* 366; his promises are not believed, 1 *Lat.* 269; we must not tempt him, 1 *Lat.* 205, 528, nor murmur against him, 2 *Hoop.* 585; what murmuring against him is, 3 *Bec.* 604; who hinder his glory, 1 *Bec.* 321; Rome robs him of his honour, *Sand.* 27; what the despising of him is, *ib.*; in our deeds too many of us deny him, 1 *Lat.* 106; what it is to forsake him, 3 *Bul.* 233

Goddard: a cup or goblet, 3 *Bec.* 282

Goderanus, a priest: 2 *Jew.* 784

Godfathers: *v.* Baptism, Gossips, Sponsors.

Godfrey of Boulogne, king of Jerusalem: his victory at Antioch, *Lit. Eliz.* 449

Godfrey, (......): probably an officer of the Exchequer, *Grin.* 253

Godfrey (......): his book of benefices, *Park.* 348

Godfridus Viterbiensis: Chronicon, 4 *Jew.* xxxvii. 648

Godliness: *v.* Prayers.

True godliness and false: *Lit. Edw.* 524, (570); contrast between those who are godly before the world, and those who are so before God, 1 *Bec.* 137; what it is to live godly, *ib.* 326; the necessity of godliness, 3 *Bec.* 48; who is godly, *ib.* 602; the rule of true godliness, 1 *Cov.* 505; perfection to be sought therein, *Sand.* 425

Godly: *v.* Christians.

Gods: *v.* Idols.

Rulers and magistrates are called gods in scripture, 1 *Bec.* 212, 2 *Brad.* 255, *Sand.* 225, 1 *Tyn.* 175, 2 *Whitg.* 82; but they are mortal gods, *Pil.* 476; the name ascribed to Moses, 2 *Whitg.* 82; polytheism refuted, *Hutch.* 170, &c.; all other gods besides the true God forbidden, 1 *Brad.* 150, 1 *Bul.* 219; what strange gods are, 2 *Bec.* 618, 3 *Bec.* 602, 1 *Bul.* 220; there is no cause to choose them, 1 *Bul.* 232; what it is to serve them, 3 *Bul.* 233; God's properties not to be assigned to them, *ib.* 236; his gifts not to be attributed to them, *ib.*; Israel served strange gods with the true God, *ib.* 235; the gods of the Egyptians and Philistines, 1 *Bul.* 224; the many gods of the heathen, *Hutch.* 170; minores dii, *ib.* 174; the notion of the Manichees respecting two contrary principles, *ib.*; Papists covertly bring in many gods, *ib.* 171; to some the belly is a god, 1 *Tyn.* 299, 300, *Wool.* 44

Godsalve (......), of Norwich: a persecutor, *Bale* 395
Godstow, near Oxford: *Phil*. xxix.
Godwin (Fra.), bp of Llandaff, afterwards of Hereford: De Præsulibus, 1 *Lat*. 123, 272, 321, 369, 377, 379, 384 nn., *Wool*. iii.
Godwin (Tho.), bp of Bath and Wells: falsely charged, when dean of Canterbury, with the misappropriation of church-plate and ornaments, *Park*. 303; an ecclesiastical commissioner, *ib*. 370 n.; he suspects an interpolation in Bede, *Calf*. 306 n
Godwyn (Tho.): Rom. Antiq. *Calf*. 108 n
Goff (Jo.): *v*. Gough.
Gog and Magog: *Bale* 570, &c., 2 *Hoop*. 477; mentioned by poets, *Hutch*. 178
Goidge (T.), or Goyge: 2 *Cran*. 383 bis
Gold: *v*. Magi.
Supposed discovery of gold in a Northern island, 2 *Zur*. 290, 297; said to exist in Holy Island, 3 *Zur*. 435; Gardiner's opinion about the virtues of gold and certain precious stones, 1 *Cran*. 333
Goldastus (Melch. H.): Monarchia Rom. Imp., *Jew*. xxxvii, 4 *Jew*. 680, &c.; Polit. Imp. *Jew*. xxxvii: Imperialia Decreta de Cultu Imaginum, *Park*. 90 n.; mistaken as to the author of the feigned Donation of Constantine, 2 *Ful*. 360 n
Golde (Gervis): 2 *Cran*. 367 n
Golde (Hen.): chaplain to abp Warham, 1 *Tyn*. xxvii, 483; interpreter between the maid of Kent and the pope's orator, 2 *Cran*. 277
Golden-Fleece (Order of the): 1 *Zur*. 205 n
Golden Legend: *v*. Legend.
Golden Rule: *v*. Rule.
Goldsmith (Fra.): *Jew*. xi.
Goldsmiths' Company: *v*. London.
Goldwell (Tho.), prior of Canterbury: 2 *Cran*. 271
Goldwell (Tho.), bp of St Asaph: notice of him, *Phil*. xxvii.
Goletta: *v*. Guletta.
Golgotha: *v*. Jerusalem.
Goliath: slain, *Pil*. 30, 120, 246, 360, 415 *Sand*. 371, *Whita*. 406
Gomorrah: *v*. Sodom.
Gonell (......): *Park*. 38
Gonour (Mons. de): ambassador from France, *Park*. 212; received by Parker, *ib*. 214
Good: it is the nature of God and his people to return good for evil, *Pil*. 261; how men are good, 3 *Bec*. 603; every good thing in us is Christ's gift, purchase, doing, and working, 1 *Tyn*. 23, 27, 111; all power to do good is of God only, 3 *Tyn*. 34; to whom we should do good, 2 *Bul*. 63; how, *ib*. 64; how far, *ib*.; good and evil mixed in the church; *Pil*. 388

Good Friday: how it may be observed, 1 *Bul*. 260; every day should be Good Friday to a Christian, 1 *Lat*. 225; the day called Parasceve, 1 *Jew*. 107; the Popish ceremonies used thereon, 2 *Cran*. 158; the peculiar mass, *Pil*. 507, 508; no consecration or oblation on that day, 1 *Jew*. 128, 246; the sacrament received under one kind, having been consecrated the preceding day, *ib*. 245; creeping to the cross thereon, *Rid*. 497, 498; the pope curses us every Good Friday, *Pra. Eliz*. 467; a sermon for the day, 1 *Lat*. 216

Good intent: things invented thereby are useless to obtain remission of sins, 1 *Bec*. 49, 151, 152, 348
Good-man of the house: the term, 1 *Bul*. 258
Good men: *v*. Righteous.
Good works: *v*. Works.
Goodacre (Anne), wife of Jo. Baron, *q. v*.
Goodacre (Jo.), abp of Armagh: 2 *Cran*. 438 n
Goode (Hue): 2 *Cran*. 382, 383
Goode (Will.): editor of bp Cooper's Answer against Private Mass, *Coop*.; his Rule of Faith, 1 *Brad*. 520 n., 529 n.; a letter of P. Martyr, first published by him, 2 *Brad*. 403 n
Goodfellow (R.): *v*. Robin.
Goodman (Chr.): divinity reader at Oxford in king Edward's days, 4 *Jew*. 1192 n.; in exile, 3 *Zur*. 347; pastor at Geneva, 3 *Zur*. 769 n; admitted a citizen there, *ib*. 768 n.; letter of Jewel to Whittingham and Goodman at Geneva, 4 *Jew*. 1192, 1193; letter from Goodman thence to P. Martyr, 3 *Zur*. 768; his tract, How Superior Powers ought to be Obeyed, printed at the same place, *Grin*. 327, 4 *Jew*. 1193 n., *Park*. 61 n., 449, 1 *Zur*. 21 n., 2 *Zur*. 34 n., 131; Bullinger's answer to questions, probably by him, on civil government, 3 *Zur*. 745; returned to England, 4 *Jew*. 1207, 1208, 1 *Zur*. 21; preaches in the Scots' camp, 1 *Zur*. 60; appointed minister of St Andrew's, 2 *Zur*. 364 n.; a leader among the Puritans in England, *Grin*. 326 n., *Park*. 382
Goodman (Gabriel), dean of Westminster: has the charge of abbot Feckenham, *Grin*. 382; an ecclesiastical commissioner, *ib*. 201, *Park*. 370, 383, 390; his share in the Bishops' Bible, *ib*. 336 n.; not meet for the see of London, *ib*. 360; he signs a warrant for the apprehension of Cartwright, 1 *Zur*. 313 n.; recommended for the bishopric

of Norwich, *Park.* 473, 476, 477; mentioned, *Grin.* 365, 392 n., *Park.* 407, 409, 411, 438, 447, 469

Goodman (Will.), father of Christopher: 3 *Zur.* 768 n.; the same, apparently, is mentioned as an exile, 1 *Cran.* (9)

Goodrich (Tho.), bp of Ely: mentioned, 2 *Cran.* 270; sent to France, 1533, *ib.* 246; his election and consecration to the see of Ely, *ib.* 247 n., 264 n.; he signs a declaration respecting a general council, *ib.* 468; Sir Tho. Smith was his chancellor, *Park.* 30 n.; a royal visitor of Cambridge, 2 *Brad.* 370; a commissioner at the disputation there, *Grin.* 194, *Rid.* 169; he visits Joan Bocher, *Hutch.* iii, iv, n., v, n.; made privy councillor, 3 *Zur.* 675 n.; signature as such, 2 *Cran.* 524, *Rid.* 508; ambassador to France, 3 *Zur.* 497 n.; made lord chancellor, 2 *Cran.* 436 n., 3 *Zur.* 444, 447; upright in that office, *Park.* 315; his views on the eucharist, 3 *Zur.* 72, 76

Goodrick (Mr), a gentleman of Yorkshire: *Grin.* 325

Goodrick (Rich.), an eminent lawyer: 2 *Lat.* 428

Goodrik (Hen.?): a prebendary, *Park.* 202

Goodryche (Master): preaches against Latimer at Bristol, 2 *Lat.* 225 n

Goods: *v.* Church, I. xii.

Temporal goods, 4 *Bul.* 188; it is lawful to possess them, 2 *Bec.* 388, 389; they supply our necessity, 2 *Bul.* 55; serve to relieve the poor, *ib.* 61; are not kept by denying the truth, *ib.* 100; the division of them, *ib.* 228; every man is bound to preserve them from waste, because he is bound to maintain his family, and support his king, 2 *Tyn.* 66; all things were in common in the apostles' age, 2 *Bul.* 20 (*v.* Anabaptists); community of goods, 1 *Lat.* 406, 1 *Whitg.* 352, 521; it is not required amongst Christians, *Rog.* 352; enjoined by certain heretics, *ib.* 353, 354; there is a propriety of goods, so that they are not common, 2 *Bec.* 110, 111; the property of another man is not to be possessed, 2 *Bul.* 49; evil-gotten goods never thrive, *Pil.* 57, 58

Goodwin Sands: *v.* Kent, Tenterden.

Goodwin (Tho.): *v.* Godwin.

Googe (Barnaby): *v.* B. (G.).

Notices of him, *Park.* 198, *Poet.* xxxvi; the uncertainty of life, verses by him, *ib.* 391

Gordian, the younger, emperor: his burial, 1 *Jew.* 276

Gordian knot: the term explained, 1 *Jew.* 189, 192

Gordon (Geo.), 4th earl of Huntley: commands at Haldanrig, 3 *Zur.* 237 n.; taken prisoner at Pinkey, *ib.* 43; defeated at Corrichie, taken prisoner, and (accidentally?) killed, 1 *Zur.* 129; his daughter Jean, the divorced wife of James earl of Bothwell, 1 *Zur.* 193, 195

Gordon (Geo.), 5th earl of Huntley: mentioned, 1 *Zur.* 166 n.; he arms in defence of the queen of Scots, *ib.* 205 n

Gordon (Adam), son of the earl of Huntley: made prisoner at Corrichie, 1 *Zur.* 129 n

Gordon (Alex.), bp of Galloway: commissioner for the release of Mary queen of Scots, *Park.* 378

Gordon (Jo.), son of the earl of Huntley: made prisoner at Corrichie, and executed for treason, 1 *Zur.* 129 n

Gore (James): died in prison, *Poet.* 165

Goreway (......): martyred, *Poet.* 164

Gorgonia, sister of Gregory Nazianzen: skilful in the scriptures, 2 *Jew.* 676; her reception of the sacrament, and miraculous cure, *Grin.* 48 n., 1 *Jew.* 241, 249

Gorham (Nich. de): notice of him, 1 *Tyn.* 152 n.; his commentaries, 1 *Lat.* 199 n.; he wrote on the Apocalypse, *Bale* 257 [erroneously called Gallus]; mentioned as Nicolaus Gorranus, 2 *Bec.* 639

Gorionides: *v.* Hegesippus.

Gorranus (Nic.): *v.* Gorham.

Gorton (Rich.): recommended by Cranmer to Cromwell, 2 *Cran.* 310; also by Latimer, 2 *Lat.* 386, 387

Gosnold (Jo.), or Gosnal: a commissioner for the suppression of colleges, &c., *Park.* 33 n.; solicitor-general, 2 *Lat.* 428

Gospel: *v.* Law, Promises, Truth.

Of the gospel of the grace of God, 3 *Bul.* 1, &c.; what the word signifies, 1 *Bec.* 44; the term εὐαγγέλιον explained, 1 *Bec.* 113; 3 *Bul.* 1, 1 *Ful.* 549, *Lit. Edw.* 504 (553), *Now.* (101), 1 *Tyn.* 8, 9; what the gospel is, 3 *Bec.* 602, 616, 3 *Bul.* 3, 1 *Tyn.* 8, 9, 476; the vicar of Croydon on this, 2 *Cran.* 338, 340; the term is not to be limited to the writings of the evangelists, 1 *Tyn.* 213, 441, 477, 484, 2 *Tyn.* 144; the gospel is found in the Old Testament, 1 *Tyn.* 11, *Whita.* 618—620; Tyndale calls the epistle to Romans most pure evangelion, 1 *Tyn.* 484; the nature of the gospel, 3 *Bec.* 5; it is tidings from heaven, 3 *Bul.* 4; the word of God, though uttered by men, *ib.* 5; why it is called a witness, 4 *Bul.* 317, why a testament, 1 *Tyn.* 9; the cause of it, 3 *Bul.* 9; it was before the church, 3 *Tyn.* 24, 25

GOSPEL — GOSPELLERS 357

(see Church I. viii.); it has not its being of the church, but the church of it, *Phil.* 344; the sum of it, 3 *Bul.* 32; the use of it, *Pil.* 97, 107; the first announcement of it, 3 *Bul.* 13, 2 *Lat.* 3; it was promised in the Old Testament, 1 *Tyn.* 9; contained therein (see above); how it was made known to the old fathers by prophecy, types, and figures, 3 *Bul.* 15, &c., 2 *Lat.* 4, *Now.* (38), 155: there are not divers gospels, 3 *Bul.* 19; "another gospel," what, *Whita.* 626; the gospel distinguished from, and contrasted with, the law, *Now.* (5), 118, 1 *Tyn.* 389; it was prefigured by the law, 2 *Jew.* 615; a comparison between the law and the gospel, 1 *Brad.* 297; the gospel pertains to the new man, the law to the old, *ib.* 299; 2 *Brad.* 196; the gospel more effectual than the law, *Pil.* 354; what it does for him who is convinced by the law, 1 *Tyn.* 17, 22; the law bindeth, the gospel looseth, *ib.* 21, 119 (*v.* Absolution); the law condemneth, the gospel comforteth, *ib.* 83; the law and the gospel not to be separated, *ib.* 11; to affirm the liberty of the gospel is a good work, 2 *Brad.* 119; the gospel teaches repentance and faith, 3 *Bul.* 35; it preaches grace, *ib.* 6; it is not grounded on works, *ib.* 36; it alone opens unto us our salvation, 2 *Hoop.* 114; it gives life, *Pil.* 111; it is the ministration of life, 1 *Tyn.* 11, the ministration of righteousness, *ib.* 48; righteousness is set forth in it, and obtained by it, 2 *Bec.* 629; it is the word of peace, *Sand.* 285; a comfort to the penitent, 1 *Tyn.* 10; it purifies the heart, 2 *Tyn.* 35; what it is to preach the gospel, 2 *Bec.* 562; how Christ preached it, 3 *Bul.* 37, *Now.* (38), 155; how long, 2 *Hoop.* 30; how Paul preached it, 3 *Bul.* 39; it spread through the world, 1 *Jew.* 267, and that without the pope's or man's decrees, *Phil.* 331; it is the only light in the world, 2 *Tyn.* 34; it may not be hid, *ib.* 35; it cannot be too much opened unto the people, 2 *Hoop.* 80; it should be preached to all, 2 *Lat.* 205; the preaching of it makes a church pleasant to God, *Pil.* 156; purely taught in king Edward's days, *Phil.* 302; not to be suspected because it has entered into princes' courts, 3 *Jew.* 194; it must be spread abroad as in the apostles' time, *Bale* 457; it shall be preached throughout the world before the judgment, 2 *Lat.* 307; no other doctrine has been generally received, *Pil.* 145; Pilkington supposed that there was no people under heaven which had not once received it, *ib.*; the time of its preaching is the "acceptable time, and day of salvation," 2 *Jew.* 1087, *Sand.* 305; its invitations, *Sand.* 9; its freeness, *ib.* 11; how the salvation preached in the gospel belongs to all, 3 *Bul.* 32; how it is the savour of death, *Phil.* 57; why trouble follows its preaching, 1 *Tyn.* 164; will always meet with persecution, 2 *Lat.* 303, 307; hence called the word of the cross, *ib.* 303 (comp. 1 *Brad.* 264); it is increased by persecution, 3 *Jew.* 189, *Pil.* 264, *Sand.* 283; its enemies, *Pil.* 44; slandered by heretics, 1 *Jew.* 532; contempt of it the cause of tribulation, 2 *Cran.* 197; it is received by the simple and unlearned, 2 *Jew.* 1026; the insincere preaching of it, 3 *Bul.* 31; an admonition to lovers of the gospel, 1 *Brad.* 407; we must love and live it, 1 *Bec.* 121; it must be professed in heart and verity, 1 *Brad.* 436, and in holiness, *ib.* 437; why there are so few sincere and true professors of it, 2 *Hoop.* 217 (*v.* Gospellers); it is heard by some inwardly, by others only outwardly, 2 *Jew.* 822; received by some in vain, *Sand.* 299, &c.; its holiness less welcome to some than its freeness, 1 *Hoop.* 59; the little fruit which it produces is a token that the fear of God is wanting, *Sand.* 187; some follow the gospel for novelty, 2 *Lat.* 92, *Sand.* 338; some profess it for the sake of gain, 1 *Lat.* 502, 2 *Lat.* 203, *Sand.* 339, 3 *Whitg.* 581; it is not to be condemned for the froward lives of some of its professors, 2 *Lat.* 306

Gospellers: professors of the gospel, *Pra. B.* 25; the term used in disdain by Harding, 1 *Jew.* 148, &c.; remarks upon it, *ib.* 248; what gospellers should do, 1 *Bec.* 256, 257; they taught the grace of perfect redemption, 2 *Bec.* 637; were put to death for trifles, 3 *Bec.* 243; faint gospellers, their weakness, or rather infidelity, *Phil.* 266; many of evil life, 1 *Bec.* 256, 293, 1 *Hoop.* 58, *Rid.* 59; such are rather gospel-spillers, 2 *Brad.* 210; some were gospellers for the sake of novelty, 2 *Lat.* 92 (comp. *Sand.* 338)'; false gospellers, 2 *Cran.* 14, 1 *Lat.* 67, 360, 502, 2 *Lat.* 183, 203; some pretended gospellers among the rebels, 2 *Cran.* 195; talkers and not walkers are no true gospellers, 2 *Lat.* 92; lip-gospellers, 2 *Cran.* 9; mass-gospellers, 1 *Brad.* 381, 390, 391, 2 *Brad.* 53, 104, 230, 231; carnal-gospellers, 1 *Brad.* 9, 11, 12, 287, 1 *Lat.* 361, 2 *Lat.* 432; they looked for abbey-lands, and were worse than Papists, 1 *Lat.* 256 (comp. 3 *Whitg.* 581); gross-gospellers censured, 2 *Bec.* 206, 415, 416, 592, 617, 3 *Bec.* 5,

358 GOSPELLERS — GRACE

206; card-gospellers, dice-gospellers, pot-gospellers, 1 *Lat.* 286

Gospels: *v.* Epistles and Gospels, Matthew, Mark, Luke, John.

Why the people stand up at the reading of the gospel, 3 *Bec.* 264; what the reading it in the church-yard on Palm Sunday signified, 1 *Bec.* 113; superstitious use of gospels, 3 *Tyn.* 61, 62 (see especially John)

Gospels (Apocryphal): *v.* Apocrypha, ii.

Gossing: perhaps guzzling, perhaps gossiping, 1 *Bec.* 449

Gossip: a sponsor; derivation of the word, 2 *Zur.* 104 n.; (Lat. compater), *ib.* 104, 112; (Lat. commater), *ib.* 114; gossipry, i.e. sponsorship, *Bale* 537

Gosson (Steph.): notice of him, *Poet.* xxxi; speculum humanum, verses by him, *ib.* 345

Gostwyck (Mr, qu. Sir Jo.?): notice of him, 2 *Lat.* 368 n

Gother (Jo.): Nubes Testium, *Calf.* 199 n.; source of the authorities alleged in that work, *ib.* 63 n.; by whom answered, *ib.* 188 n., 377 n

Gothofredus (Jac.): *Calf.* 110 n.; his opinion respecting the Libra Occidua, 2 *Ful.* 364, 365 n

Goths: they and other barbarians assaulted Rome, 4 *Bul.* 200, and overran Christendom, 2 *Tyn.* 268; they were the scourge of God, *Lit. Eliz.* 493; why sent, *Grin.* 98; end of the Goths' kingdom in Spain, 1 *Bul.* 416

Gottofredus, duke of Athens: 4 *Jew.* 653

Gottofredus Pictaviensis: cited by Duns Scotus, 3 *Jew.* 273

Gough (Jo.): bookseller, 2 *Cov.* 319, 2 *Lat.* 465; printer, 1 *Bec.* 29 n., 4 *Bul.* xviii.

Gough (Jo.): eminent as a preacher among the Puritans, 2 *Zur.* 147; deprived, *ib.*; his controversy with abbot Fecknam, 1 *Ful.* 426, 2 *Ful.* 3, 2 *Zur.* 147 n.; cited before the commissioners, *Grin.* 326 n. (Goff), *Park.* 382 (Gouff).

Gould (David), professor at St Andrew's: 2 *Zur.* 364

Gounthorp (......), parson of Wetyng: 2 *Cran.* 336

Gourd: *v.* Jonah.

Gourders: probably whirlpools or violent rushings, 4 *Jew.* 715

GOVERNANCE OF VIRTUE, by T. Becon: 1 *Bec.* 393, &c.; reference to it, 2 *Bec.* 481

Governess of the Netherlands: *v.* Mary.

Government: *v.* Women.

Civil and ecclesiastical government, 3 *Whitg.* 189, 416, &c., 554; the three forms of civil government, 1 *Bul.* 309, &c., *Rog.* 335, 336, 2 *Whitg.* 356, 3 *Whitg.* 197; popular government the worst, 3 *Whitg.* 208; mischievous books on government, *Park.* 60, 61

Gower (Jo.), poet: *Rid.* 490, 494

Gown: *v.* Cap, Vestments.

Different sorts of gowns worn by the clergy, 3 *Jew.* 612; Parker is desired to bring a long one to court, *Park.* 2; the side gown and sarcenet tippet, 2 *Cran.* 38; the ordinary use of the gown required, *Grin.* 339, *Sand.* xx; Turkey gowns and hats worn by those who disliked the gown and square cap, 2 *Whitg.* 369

Goyge (T.): *v.* Goidge.

Grabe (Jo. Ern.): Prolegom. in edit. Alex. LXX. Interp., 2 *Ful.* 166 n.; Spicilegium, *Calf.* 21, 126, 2 *Ful.* 338, 339 nn

Grace: *v.* God, Christ; also Free-will, Good, Gospel, Justification, Merit, Perseverance, Prayers, Predestination, Sacraments, Salvation, Works; likewise Augustine, viii, and other fathers.

What grace is, 3 *Bec.* 608, 616, 3 *Bul.* 6, 7, 4 *Bul.* 301; the word is diversely taken in scripture, *Sand.* 297; it is the favour of God, 1 *Tyn.* 11, 286, 407, also the gifts of his Spirit, *ib.* 286; grace and gift distinguished, *ib.* 491; $\chi\acute{a}\rho\iota\varsigma$ and $\chi\acute{a}\rho\iota\sigma\mu a$, 1 *Ful.* 468, 469; what $\chi\acute{a}\rho\iota\varsigma$ means, 1 *Bec.* 311; Tyndale's reasons for using the word "favour" as a translation of $\chi\acute{a}\rho\iota\varsigma$, 3 *Tyn.* 22; the doctors speak of several kinds of grace; gratia gratum faciens, gratis data, operans, cooperans, præveniens, subsequens, 3 *Bul.* 11, 3 *Tyn.* 22; seven-fold grace, *Calf.* 226; the cause of grace, 3 *Bul.* 7; the sole cause of our deliverance is God's mercy, *Sand.* 180; grace is purchased by Christ, *ib.* 298; it comes by Christ, 1 *Bul.* 43; it is exhibited in Christ, 3 *Bul.* 12; the gospel preaches it, *ib.* 6; it is the work of God's Spirit, 1 *Ful.* 450; bestowed by the Holy Ghost, according to the secret pleasure of his will, *Sand.* 298; God is not unrighteous in giving it to some and withholding it from others, *Now.* (11), 125; the freeness of grace, *Pil.* 194, 445, *Sand.* 11, 21, 297; it is free every way, *ib.* 11; it excludes the merit of works, *Now.* (57), 176; salvation is by grace only, not by works or merits, *Lit. Edw.* 512, (560), *Sand.* 21, 2 *Tyn.* 156, 157; free-giving and deserving cannot stand together, 1 *Tyn.* 436; some would sell grace for money, *Sand.* 11; its working, 3 *Bul.* 9; it preventeth us, *ib.* 168;

till preventing grace be bestowed men cannot see God, 3 *Tyn.* 192, or consent to God's law, *ib.* 174; we have no free-will wherewith to anticipate the grace of God, *ib.* 174, 192; works are not a preparation to it, *Sand.* 267; we have no power except by grace, 3 *Tyn.* 174; we cannot draw near to God without it, *Sand.* 133; none can come to Christ except the Father draw him, 3 *Tyn.* 224, 225; the time of receiving grace, the "acceptable time and day of salvation," *Sand.* 305; it is offered and received by the word, *ib.* 299; the way of receiving it is repentance, *ib.* 309; the season of affliction an especial time of receiving it, *ib.* 307; of receiving grace in vain, 2 *Jew.* 1086, *Sand.* 297, &c.; what grace the wicked may have; the gift of understanding is one thing, that of regeneration another, 2 *Whitg.* 590, 591; we are justified by grace, 3 *Bul.* 12; grace is given to be exercised, 1 *Tyn.* 60; it cannot be increased by ceremonies, *ib.* 286; it is offered by the sacraments, *Sand.* 299, 302; how received by them, *ib.* 304; grace is not conferred by sacraments, 4 *Bul.* 301, &c., nor contained in them, *ib.* 305, but in the mind of the faithful receiver, *ib.* 308; they are the visible signs of invisible grace, 2 *Jew.* 1099, &c.; grace was not tied to circumcision, 2 *Bul.* 175; grace is freely given, and received by faith, 4 *Bul.* 303; they who are in a state of grace may know it, 2 *Tyn.* 172, 211, though this is denied by Popish doctors, *ib.* 172, 211, 213, 214; signs of grace, *ib.* 192; it frames the will of man to God's service, 1 *Ful.* 377; it is the only cause of faith, piety, and holiness, *Sand.* 257; it is necessary for worthily considering God's plagues, *Pil.* 174; the gifts of grace are for the benefit of our brethren as well as of ourselves, 1 *Tyn.* 466; graces and gifts grow in the hands of him that spendeth them, *Sand.* 345; Latimer teaches that justification, grace, and salvation, may be lost, 2 *Lat.* 7; doctrines of grace abused by carnal men, 2 *Brad.* 130; the apostles wrote against this abuse, 2 *Bul.* 338; Augustine and the Pelagian controversy, 3 *Bul.* 11 (and see Augustine, viii.); the kingdom of grace on earth, *ib.* 276

Grace: what the word means in the universities, 3 *Tyn.* 22

Graces: of prayer before meat, 1 *Bec.* 173; of grace or thanksgiving after dinner and supper, *ib.* 174, 175; graces ordered to be said in English, 2 *Cran.* 504; benedictio mensæ, *Pra. Eliz.* 132; precationes ante cibum; including one from Erasmus, and one (in verse) by Melancthon, *ib.* 399, 400; graces or prayers before meals, 1 *Bec.* 401, 402, 3 *Bec.* 18, 19, *Lit. Edw.* 372, &c., *Lit. Eliz.* 20, &c., 260, *Pra. B.* 54, 56, 57, 69, *Pra. Eliz.* 17, 18; forms in English verse, *Lit. Edw.* 374, 375; a prayer at meal-time, *Pra. B.* 70; post pastum gratiarum actio, *Pra. Eliz.* 132; gratiarum actiones à cibo; including forms from Chrysostom, Athanasius, and Erasmus (some in verse), *ib.* 400—402; graces or thanksgivings after meals, 1 *Bec.* 402, 403, 3 *Bec.* 19, *Lit. Edw.* 373, &c., *Lit. Eliz.* 20, &c., 260, &c., *Pra. B.* 55, 57, 58, 71, *Pra. Eliz.* 17, 18; forms in English verse, *Lit. Edw.* 374, 375

Graduale, or Graile: a part of the mass; its origin, 2 *Brad.* 306, 3 *Bec.* 264; the name was also applied to the book containing the graduales, &c., *Grin.* 135 n., *Sand.* iii; grayles ordered to be delivered up, 2 *Cran.* 523; grailes to be abolished, *Grin.* 135, 159

Graes (Ortwin): *v.* Gratius.

Grafton (Rich.): completes Matthews' Bible, 1 *Tyn.* lxxv; presents a copy to Cranmer, *ib.*; his letter to Cromwell, with six Bibles, 2 *Cran.* 346 n.; letter to Parker, *Park.* 295; mentioned, 3 *Whitg.* 600

Graham (Will.), earl of Montrose: arms in defence of queen Mary, 1 *Zur.* 205 n

Grahams (The): delivered the earl of Northumberland to the regent Murray, 1 *Zur.* 214 n

Graile: *v.* Graduale.

Grambsius (Jo.): *Calf.* 155 n

Gramercy: 1 *Lat.* 213

Grammars: none to be used but those set forth by authority, 2 *Cran.* 504; inquiry respecting them, *ib.* 158; that by Lily, *Grin.* 173

Grammatical Sense: *v.* Scripture.

Granada (city): not quite identical with the ancient Elvira, *Calf.* 154 n

Graney (Leonard visc.): *v.* Grey.

Grange (The laird of): *v.* Kirkaldy.

Granger (James): Biogr. Hist. of England, 4 *Jew.* 860 n., 1 *Tyn.* 395 n

Granvelle (Ant. cardinal of): *v.* Perrenot.

Grasdale (Rich.): *Bale* 16

Grate: grateful, 1 *Bec.* 197

Grathwick (Steph.): martyred in St George's Field, *Poet.* 169

Gratiæ expectativæ: *v.* Expectations.

Gratian, emperor: excellent in feats of war, 1 *Bul.* 384; he installed Gregory Nazianzen, 1 *Jew.* 408; allowed the cognizance of altercations to the bishops, *Whita.* 437; commended by Ambrose, *Grin.* 18; his errors, 3 *Jew.* 236, 237; the decree of Gratian, Valentinian, and Theodosius, for the establishment of St Peter's doctrine, 1 *Bul.* 34, 2 *Hoop.* 540; extracts from this decree and references to it, 2 *Bec.* 305, 1 *Bul.* 328, 331, 2 *Bul.* 281, 4 *Bul.* 63, 2 *Ful.* 362, 4 *Jew.* 1002, 1043; Valentinian, Valens, and Gratian forbade rebaptizing, 4 *Bul.* 394

Gratian (St): invoked for thrift losing, *Bale* 348, 498

Gratian, pope: i. e. Gregory VI., *q. v.*

Gratian, the canonist: *v.* Law (Canon).

    Who he was, 3 *Jew.* 186; called the foundation of canon law, *ib.* 132

Gratitude: *Now.* (101).

Gratius (Orth.): *v.* Fasciculus.

Gravamina (Centum): *v.* Germany.

Grave: *v.* Burial, Death, Hell (ᾅδης).

Grave-diggers: *v.* Fossarii.

Gravelines: Wolsey meets the emperor there, 2 *Tyn.* 314 n

Gray (Arth. and others): *v.* Grey.

Gray (Jo.), scribe of the general assembly of the church of Scotland: *Park.* 206, 207

Gray (Patrick, 5th lord): taken prisoner by the English, 3 *Zur.* 239 n

Gray (Tho.): MS. of his Scala Chronica, at Corpus Christi coll., Camb., *Jew.* xxxvii; extract respecting Augustine of Canterbury, 3 *Jew.* 164 n., 4 *Jew.* 779

Gray (Tho.), a child: slain by an earthquake, *Lit. Eliz.* 567

Grayle: *v.* Graduale.

Gray's Inn: *v.* London.

Graziers: landlords are become graziers, 1 *Lat.* 279; their greediness has caused the decay of towns, 2 *Bec.* 434; graziers, sheepmongers, and rich farmers, the cause of dearth, *ib.* 603

Greadly: greedy, 1 *Bec.* 449

Greece, Greeks: *v.* Church, II. i.

    The Grecian monarchy, *Bale* 423, *Hutch.* 147, 1 *Lat.* 356, *Pil.* 186, 187; the Greeks had famous schools, 4 *Bul.* 480; the faith brought to Rome from Greece, 4 *Jew.* 883; the Greeks are in subjection to the Turks, 3 *Bec.* 9, 10, 4 *Bul.* 20; poor Greeks in England; 4 *Jew.* 1276; hart of Greece, or rather grease, 2 *Bec.* 345

Greediness: *v.* Covetousness

Greek language: its importance as a means of understanding scripture, 4 *Bul.* 542, *Whita.* 468; as to the Septuagint, see Bible, *Greek;* reasons why the New Testament was written in that language, 4 *Bul.* 189, *Whita.* 127, 216, 217, 219; an index of Greek words explained in Fulke's Defence, 1 *Ful.* 603; Greek known in early Christian times in Egypt, Cyprus, Jerusalem, Gaul, Italy, and Africa, *Whita.* 217, and amongst the Parthians, *ib.* 218; the restoration of Greek learning opposed by the Scotists, 3 *Tyn.* 75; its revival at Cambridge, *Pil.* iv; Gardiner's determination (as chancellor of Cambridge) respecting the pronunciation of certain Greek letters not attended to, *Park.* 28; disputes respecting pronunciation at Oxford, *ib.* 138 n.; Greek books found, 3 *Zur.* 447; Sir T. More on the force of the article, 3 *Tyn.* 25 n.; Greek forms of Hebrew names, *Pil.* 11 n.; Greek dialects, *Whita.* 256

Green (Bartlet): noticed, 2 *Brad.* 251; Philpot writes to him, *Phil.* 109, 119; a letter concerning him, *ib.* 154; he was strong in scripture and the doctors, *ib.*; Fecknam's report of him, *ib.* 155; a letter possibly to him, 2 *Brad.* 60; his martyrdom, *ib.* 251 n., *Poet.* 165, 3 *Zur.* 175 n

Green (Roland): *v.* Grene.

Green (......), a sectary: *Rog.* 203

Greene (Tho.?): letter from Latimer to Dr Greene, 2 *Lat.* 295, (467); probably Dr Tho. Greene, master of Cath. hall, and vice-chancellor, *ib.* 295 n

Greenham (R.): a practical divine, 1 *Brad.* 564; notice of his Comfort for an Afflicted Conscience, *Poet.* xliv; lines by H. C. prefixed thereto, *ib.* 470

Greenland: discoveries there, 2 *Zur.* 290

Greenstead, near Ongar, co. Essex: the benefice, 2 *Lat.* 222 n (see also Grenstede).

Greenwall (Nich.), fellow of Ch. coll., Camb., *Park.* 25, 26

Greenwich, co. Kent: the monastery of Observants, 1 *Tyn.* xv, 38 n.; the royal palace, *ib.* 38 n.; here king Henry received the title of Defender of the Faith, 2 *Tyn.* 338; Latimer there, 2 *Lat.* 265 n., 268; king Edward's death announced to the lord mayor and citizens there, 3 *Zur.* 272; Whitgift's sermon before queen Elizabeth there, 3 *Whitg.* 566

Greenwood (Jo.): preached without authority, *Rog.* 231; thought the people might reform the church, *ib.* 344

Greenwood (Will.), opposes Latimer, 1 *Lat.* iv; Latimer's letter to him, 2 *Lat.* 356; notice of him, *ib.* n

Gregory (St), called the Great, bp of Rome:
    i. *His Life, Acts, and Writings.*
    ii. *On God.*

iii. *Scripture, Doctrine.*
iv. *The Church, and its Ministry.*
v. *Peter, Rome.*
vi. *Sacraments.*
vii. *Worship, Ceremonies, Images.*
viii. *Antichrist.*
ix. *Civil Power, &c.*

i. *His Life, Acts, and Writings*: he was a nobleman of the dignity or degree of a counsellor, 3 *Jew.* 410; he complains of worldly cares and businesses brought on him by his bishoprick, 2 *Jew.* 679, 680; his contest with John, patriarch of Constantinople, see v. below; he suffered great danger by the Lombards, 2 *Hoop.* 234; sent Augustine the monk to England, 1 *Jew.* 280, 299, 3 *Jew.* 163—166, 4 *Jew.* 777, &c., *Pil.* 482, 483, 515; advised him to gather the best constitution out of any churches, *Calf.* 197, 1 *Jew.* 301, 4 *Jew.* 1123; how he answered questions submitted to him by Augustine, 2 *Ful.* 10, 1 *Jew.* 301, 4 *Jew.* 1045, *Pil.* 517, 524; he gave him "codices plurimos," 2 *Ful.* 113; he speaks of the conversion of Britain, &c., 1 *Jew.* 302; exhorts Ethelbert to set forth the faith of Christ, 2 *Ful.* 24; story of 6000 children's heads found in his fishpond, and his act in consequence thereof, *Pil.* 570, 686

His works, *Calf.* 409, 2 *Ful.* 402, *Jew.* xxxvii; a MS. of his Pastoral, the Saxon version of Alfred, 4 *Jew.* 1273; character of his epistles, *Whita.* 436; his epistle to Martin Scholasticus, 1 *Jew.* 96; the Dialogues, their authenticity questioned, *Calf.* 89; perhaps by Gregory II., *Calf.* 89 n.; a passage of Origen's ascribed to him, 1 *Jew.* 338

ii. *On God*: he declares that God is omnipresent, yet far from the wicked, *Wool.* 96; shews that nothing can take place without the foreknowledge and determination of Almighty God, referring, as an example, to the lengthened life of Hezekiah, *Pil.* 675; teaches that whatever is outwardly future in deed, is even now inwardly completed in predestination, *ib.*; says God went in Paul's breast, as under a tent, 2 *Jew.* 769; states that Paul by preaching poured God into his hearers, *ib.*; says, that John spake of the Lamb by pointing, Isaiah by foreseeing, Abel by offering, 1 *Jew.* 488, 540, 3 *Jew.* 467, 546; speaks of Christ filling the manger, who gave himself as meat to the minds of men, 2 *Jew.* 767; says, our Lord were no* wall unto us,

if he had not been in the form of man, 3 *Jew.* 493; affirms that the Word goes away in his body, but tarries in his Godhead, 2 *Bec.* 275, 3 *Bec.* 429, 3 *Jew.* 263; declares that Christ though absent nowhere by the presence of his majesty, is not here by the presence of his flesh, 2 *Bec.* 274, 275, 278, 3 *Bec.* 429, 455, 1 *Cran.* 96, (50), 2 *Hoop.* 492; writes of his appearance to Thomas, and of that apostle's lack of faith, 1 *Cran.* 262; counsels to follow whither we believe Christ to have ascended in body, 3 *Bec.* 455; speaks of one as beholding Christ inwardly, and by meditation bearing him in the breast, 3 *Jew.* 546; mentions one who took money, and sold Jesus Christ our Lord to a heretic, *ib.* 553; explains the statement that the Son of Man knows not the hour of his return, *Rog.* 48 n.; approves the work of Paschasius De Spiritu Sancto, 1 *Bul.* 160

iii. *Scripture, Doctrine*: he calls the scriptures the epistles of God, *Whita.* 528; compares them to a river in which the elephant may swim, and yet the lamb may walk, 1 *Jew.* 331, 2 *Jew.* 684, *Whita.* 400 (and see 374); speaks of a holy man who lay bed-ridden for many years, and who, though illiterate, possessed a wonderful knowledge of the scriptures, 2 *Jew.* 684; writes on the use of the obscurities of the word of God, 4 *Jew.* 1184, *Whita.* 375; treats of the literal and mystic sense thereof, *Whita.* 404; says the letter hides the spirit as the chaff the corn, 2 *Jew.* 619; declares that true preachers must fetch the foundation of their matters out of the holy scriptures, 2 *Cran.* 34; mentions that the church used two Latin versions of the Bible, the old and the new, *Whita.* 128; reads Gen. iii. 15, "ipsa conteret," but does not apply it to the virgin Mary, 1 *Ful.* 533; says the Holy Spirit being the author of the book of Job, it is not needful to inquire who was the penman, *Whita.* 107; interprets a text in Job juxta spiritum, 1 *Jew.* 504; states why John Baptist is styled an angel by Malachi, 1 *Ful.* 483; his interpretation of Wisdom xii. 15, and of Sol. Song ii. 17, founded on mistaken readings, *Whita.* 155; he says the books of Maccabees are not canonical, *ib.* 60, 96; distinguishes between the sound and signification of words, 4 *Jew.* 765; says some things are small, and do small hurt; some are small, and do great hurt, 1 *Jew.* 96; cited as declaring that custom must yield to truth, 3 *Bec.* 390 n; he confesses

---

* Correct "now all" to "no wall."

original sin, 2 *Bul.* 390; shews how one sin follows another, 2 *Jew.* 1068; calls feigned holiness double iniquity, 1 *Bec.* 135, 3 *Bec.* 278, *Wool.* 47; says that humility is the beginning of virtues in us, 1 *Bec.* 201, 202; likens him that gathers virtues without humility, to one that brings dust into the wind, *ib.* 202; says our righteous Advocate will defend us in the judgment, because we acknowledge ourselves unrighteous, *ib.* 149; remarks that if God's working were comprehended by reason, it were not wonderful, 1 *Jew.* 504; says, they who know not the things of the Lord, are not known of the Lord, 2 *Jew.* 800, 4 *Jew.* 1178; affirms that faith is righteousness, 2 *Bec.* 638; says that the love of God is never idle, 1 *Bec.* 208, 227, 346, 1 *Lat.* 161; shews that in the common people it is not knowledge, but a good life that is necessary, *Whita.* 241; says it is better to offend than to forsake a truth, *Pil.* 45; exhorts not to be in love with signs which may be had in common with the reprobate, but to love the miracles of charity and piety, *Calf.* 332; says God spares some in this world to torment them afterward, 3 *Bec.* 104, 105; said to have thought that venial sins were purged in purgatory, *Rog.* 216 n.; cited by More to the effect that a man in purgatory procured help by praying to a saint, 3 *Tyn.* 121 n.; strange story of a ghost, adduced as proof of the efficacy of sacrifice for the dead, *Calf.* 89; story of his saying mass for the soul of Trajan, 2 *Brad.* 290, 2 *Cov.* 269; declares that God's chosen people shall know in heaven the righteous whom they never saw before, 3 *Bec.* 153

iv. *The Church, and its Ministry*: he speaks of the universal church as one flock under one Shepherd, namely Christ, 1 *Jew.* 378; allows, in effect, that the church of Rome is not the whole church, but only a part of it, 4 *Jew.* 922; says that the church after the days of her affliction, shall be strengthened with great power of preaching, *ib.* 1065; declares that at the end of the world, the church weakened with age, shall not be able to bear children, *ib.* 1063; feared that the devil would soon destroy the whole flock, *ib.* 732; as to the last persecution of the church, see viii. below; he honoured the first four general councils as the four gospels, 3 *Jew.* 225, 4 *Jew.* 772, 1109, *Rog.* 211; praises custom, *Calf.* 54 n., but replies to those who urge the authority thereof, 1 *Bec.* 376; remarks that Christ did not say, "I am custom," but "I am the truth," 2 *Cran.* 51; his caution to beware of the wicked novelties of words, and new things brought forth by heretics, 2 *Jew.* 795; he mentions a fourfold distribution of church-goods, 1 *Bec.* 24, 4 *Bul.* 488; warns pastors against being bold to receive wages and yet being no workmen, 1 *Bec.* 360, 361; declares it great condemnation, without labour to receive the reward of labour, *ib.* 4; says the priests must watch the Lord's sheep with great diligence, *ib.* 361; affirms that the shepherd who does not rebuke offenders slays them by silence, *ib.* 3, 4, 384; says he must be pure who takes on him to correct another's fault, *ib.* 16; asserts that the light of the flock is the flame of the shepherd, *ib.* 386; spoke to the citizens of Rome in their own tongue, 4 *Bul.* 190; some remarks on preaching, *Bale* 88, 89; he calls a priest who cannot preach, a dumb trumpeter, 1 *Bec.* 9; says there is no such pleasant sacrifice to God as earnest zeal to win souls, *Pil.* 344; asks when the wolf is become the shepherd, what may become of the flock, 4 *Jew.* 747; says that Christ entered into the temple (Matt. xxi.) to shew that the fault of the priests is the ruin of the people, *Sand.* 237; bitterly lamented that the order of priesthood having fallen inwardly, could not long stand outwardly, 4 *Jew.* 732; says, priests we are called, but priests we are not, 3 *Jew.* 309; speaks of the deposition of a bishop for niggardliness, 2 *Bec.* 325, 326; in a council held at Rome he decreed that nothing should be taken for ordination, &c., 4 *Bul.* 139; cited as saying that cardinals have their name à cardine, *ib.* 117, 118; he forbade presbyters and other clerks to be made abbots, *ib.* 113; declares that none can serve the ecclesiastical office and keep the rule of monkery, 4 *Jew.* 800; he allowed the marriage of the clergy, 2 *Ful.* 10; writes of Speciosus, a married deacon, *Calf.* 88; relates a notable story of Paulinus, *ib.* 117—119, *Pil.* 441; referred to for a statement concerning St Benet, 1 *Jew.* 7 n., 192; 2 *Jew.* 751

v. *Peter, Rome, the title of universal*: what primacy he grants to Peter, 2 *Ful.* 314; he says, it is evident that Christ committed the care of the whole church to Peter ...yet he was not called universal apostle, 1 *Jew.* 343, 344, 347, 354, 367, 3 *Jew.* 317, 319; writes, Peter the apostle was the first member (or rather, Peter the first of the apostles was a member) of the holy and universal church; Paul, Andrew, and John,

GREGORY I.

the heads of several nations...and none ever wished himself to be called universal, 1 *Jew.* 440, 3 *Jew.* 270, 4 *Jew.* 1120; says Paul forbade the members of the Lord's body to be subject to other heads, &c., 1 *Jew.* 439, 440; ascribes to Paul the headship of the nations, and the principality of the church, 1 *Jew.* 431, 438, 3 *Jew.* 269, 270, 288, 4 *Jew.* 824; says that he went to Rome bound with chains to conquer the world, 1 *Jew.* 431; he strenuously opposed the ambition of John, patriarch of Constantinople, who desired to be called universal bishop, *Bale* 503, 2 *Brad.* 145 n., 2 *Ful.* 49 n., 72, 258, 259, 2 *Hoop.* 234, 235, 546, 1 *Jew.* 46, 47, 76, 96, 344, &c., 3 *Jew.* 316, &c., 4 *Jew.* 730—733, *Pil.* 518, 2 *Whitg.* 171, 172; (most of the passages in the present section refer to this controversy; see also viii. below); he remarks that if one be called universal patriarch, the name of patriarch is taken from the rest, 1 *Jew.* 425; asserts that the said John would alone be called a bishop, *ib.* 427; speaks of him as following Lucifer, 1 *Jew.* 345, 3 *Jew.* 279; asks him what answer he will make to Christ, the head of the universal church, at the last judgment, 1 *Jew.* 346, 2 *Jew.* 992, 3 *Jew.* 284, 318, 4 *Jew.* 733; after reproving this patriarch for his ambition, he says to the emperor Mauritius, O my most gracious lord, do I herein quarrel for mine own right? 1 *Jew.* 346, 4 *Jew.* 734; says it is God's cause, it is not mine; not I only am troubled therewith, but also the whole church, 1 *Jew.* 346, 4 *Jew.* 734; affirms that none of the holy men in any dispensation would suffer himself to be called universal, 1 *Jew.* 32, 46; states that none of his predecessors would use that profane name, 1 *Jew.* 32, 37, 46, 47, 94, 346, 354, 366, 377, 426, 3 *Jew.* 311, 4 *Jew.* 734, 886, *Pil.* 519; declares that Leo refused the name of universal bishop, though it was offered to him by the synod of Chalcedon, 1 *Jew.* 47, 422, 424, *Pil.* 520; asks, who, contrary to the statutes of the gospel and the decrees of councils, presumes to take to himself this new name? 1 *Jew.* 76, *Pil.* 520; says, the godly laws, the reverend synods, yea, the commands of our Lord Jesus, are broken by the invention of this proud and pompous name, 1 *Jew.* 346, 2 *Jew.* 1001; he abhorred the name, *Calf.* 88, 1 *Jew.* 47, 434; calls it a proud name, *Sand.* 101, a name of blasphemy, *Pil.* 76, 520, and characterizes it by many other like epithets, 1 *Jew.* 345, 354; beseeches God to turn away that pride and confusion from the church, &c., 1 *Jew.* 423; intimates that if an universal bishop were to fall, the whole church would fall together, 1 *Jew.* 374, 2 *Jew.* 992, 1081, 3 *Jew.* 277, 4 *Jew.* 730, 731, 732, *Park.* 112; declares that to consent to that wicked word were to betray the faith, 2 *Brad.* 145 n., 2 *Hoop.* 546, 1 *Jew.* 47, 76, 345, 425, 4 *Jew.* 732; warned that to bear these things patiently would be to corrupt the faith of the universal church, 1 *Jew.* 345, 377; 4 *Jew.* 732; says that whoever calls himself universal priest is the forerunner of Antichrist, 1 *Brad.* 538, 4 *Bul.* 89, 2 *Cran.* 214, 452, 2 *Ful.* 72, 1 *Jew.* 47, 109, 339, 344, 2 *Jew.* 897, 914, 991, 4 *Jew.* 743, 1072, *Pil.* 76, 519; cited as saying, he that maketh himself a bishop over all the world is worse than Antichrist (no Latin given), *Rid.* 263; he styled himself servant of the servants of God, 1 *Jew.* 424; writes to Eulogius, patriarch of Alexandria, disclaiming authority over him, and rejecting the name of universal pope, 1 *Jew.* 346, 404, 3 *Jew.* 318, 1 *Tyn.* 216 n.; counsels him neither to write to him, nor to receive letters from him by the name of universal, 1 *Jew.* 407; speaks of certain bishops, not of all bishops, as pertaining to his charge, 4 *Jew.* 707, 708; complains of the consecration of a bishop of Salonæ without his knowledge, 1 *Jew.* 409, 4 *Jew.* 707; most of the bishops of Rome since Gregory have been wolves and devourers, 4 *Bul.* 29

vi. *Sacraments:* he deemed trine immersion in baptism unimportant, *Whita.* 592; speaking of this practice he says, the faith being one, the diversity of customs hurteth nothing, 2 *Jew.* 1106, 3 *Jew.* 616; mentions it as signifying the mystery of Christ's lying in the grave three days, 4 *Bul.* 364, 365; wrote to Leander against the practice, on account of the interpretation which the Arians put upon it. 2 *Bec.* 227 n.; he addresses Christ as the great and holy passover, 1 *Jew.* 535; does not think that the sacrament was ministered at Emmaus, *ib.* 232; shews how non-communicants must go out before the celebration of the eucharist, 2 *Bec.* 256, 3 *Bec.* 482, 1 *Jew.* 19, 33, 55, 202, 2 *Jew.* 640; says the apostles consecrated the host with the Lord's prayer only, 1 *Brad.* 513 n., 1 *Hoop.* 237, *Pil.* 498, 635; describes the celebration of the communion by Cassius, 1 *Jew.* 186; says Christ, living immortally in himself, dieth again in this mystery, &c., 2 *Jew.* 618, 726, 733, 743, 792, 3 *Jew.* 541;

affirms that this sacrifice, offered with tears and benignity of mind, singularly helps our pardon, 2 *Jew.* 743; referred to on the kind of bread used in the sacrament, *ib.* 588; he speaks of receiving unleavened and leavened bread, 3 *Bec.* 425; though his time was overcharged with superstition, yet communion of both kinds remained, 1 *Hoop.* 226, 227; addresses communicants as knowing what the blood of the Lamb is by drinking, 3 *Bec.* 414, *Hutch.* 282; speaks of the blood of Christ poured into the mouths of the faithful, 3 *Bec.* 414; says that Christ's body must be received by faith, *Grin.* 58; calls it the food of the mind, not of the belly, *ib.* 46; cited as affirming that the true flesh and blood of Christ are in them that receive unworthily, 4 *Jew.* 893; the passage declared to be spurious, *ib.* 892, 893; cited by Gratian as declaring that as to these words, "the truth of (Christ's) flesh and blood," some men not unaptly understand thereby the effect and force of Christ's flesh and blood, that is, the remission of our sins, 3 *Jew.* 487, 508, 541; he says part of the mass was made by Scholasticus (or a scholastic man), 1 *Brad.* 513, 2 *Brad.* 310, *Pil.* 503; his own additions to the mass, 1 *Brad.* 513, 2 *Brad.* 306—309, 1 *Jew.* 9, 96, 301, 302, *Pil.* 503; he celebrated mass three times on Christmas-day, 2 *Jew.* 632; referred to as naming private mass, 1 *Jew.* 106; said to have been the first founder thereof, *Hutch.* 227; as to mass for the dead, see iii. above; story of his seeing a child in the bread of the altar, 1 *Hoop.* 290; an alleged miracle respecting his mass-book, *Pil.* 508

vii. *Worship, Ceremonies, Images:* he says true prayer consists not in the voice of the mouth, but in the thoughts of the heart, 1 *Bec.* 133; calls it expedient to give thanks alway to God, *ib.* 180; seems not to have been very friendly to singing, 4 *Bul.* 196, 1 *Jew.* 266; writes on unknown tongues, 1 *Jew.* 315; he spoke to the people in their own tongue, 4 *Bul.* 190; says the faith being one, the diverse custom of holy church hurts nothing, 2 *Jew.* 1106, 3 *Jew.* 616; ordained the Kyrie eleeson, *Pil.* 503; appointed stations at Rome, 1 *Lat.* 49 n.; devised the greater litany, *Calf.* 297, 2 *Whitg.* 469, 480; why it is called sevenfold, *Calf.* 297; the Dirige ascribed to him, *Pra. Eliz.* 57 n.; he ordained fasting every day in Lent, *Pil.* 561; allows that confirmation may be administered by priests where there are no bishops, *Calf.* 220; compares penance to a court of justice, 3 *Jew.* 368; he sent to one a cowl and tunic of the blessing of St Peter, *ib.* 299, and to another a key taken from St Peter's body, *ib.*; he favoured images, 1 *Hoop.* 47; regarded them as laymen's books, 2 *Bec.* 60, 63, *Calf.* 21 n., 1 *Hoop.* 29, 41, 2 *Jew.* 657, 660; praised Secundinus for desiring an image of the Saviour, 2 *Jew.* 663; rebuked Serenus, &c. for breaking images, but would by no means have them to be worshipped, *Bale* 97, 2 *Bec.* 61, *Calf.* 9, 30, 379, *Park.* 89, *Rid.* 497, 3 *Tyn.* 183, *Whita.* 509; speaks against believing in colours, i. e. pictures, *Calf.* 144, 149; cited with reference to a faithless Jew, preserved from spirits by the sign of the cross, *ib.* 88, 89; quoted about the fall of the idol Dagon, and the setting of him up again, 4 *Jew.* 1075; the Western churches overflowed with image-worship from his time, *Rid.* 92

viii. *Antichrist:* as to the forerunners of Antichrist, see v. above; he deemed the pride of John, patriarch of Constantinople, a proof that the times of Antichrist were near, 1 *Jew.* 109, 345, 4 *Jew.* 743; he says, the king of pride is at hand, an army of priests is prepared, 2 *Ful.* 371, 1 *Jew.* 345, 2 *Jew.* 905, 914, 929, 991, 4 *Jew.* 674, 681, 688, 714, 743, 843; Jewel wrongly censured as corrupting this passage, 4 *Jew.* xxi; a false reading of it, 1 *Ful.* 371 n.; says Antichrist shall obtain the glory of the world, &c., 2 *Jew.* 917; asserts that he shall call himself God, &c., 2 *Jew.* 992, 4 *Jew.* 732; declares that though he is a cursed man and not a spirit, he falsely calls himself God, 2 *Jew.* 907; writes of the last affliction of the church, *ib.* 896

ix. *Civil power, &c.:* he called the emperor Mauritius his lord and master, &c., 2 *Ful.* 16, 4 *Jew.* 704, 705, 968; told that emperor that he had committed his priests into his hand, 4 *Jew.* 705; said that Christ had given power unto the emperor to bear rule, not only over soldiers, but also over priests, *ib.* 705; writing to Mauritius, against John, bishop of Constantinople, who claimed universal authority, he says, Your majesty must repress him that doth this wrong unto the holy universal church, *ib.* 675; complains to the empress Constantia of the bishop of Salonæ, 1 *Jew.* 411; speaks of the labarum, or imperial banner, 2 *Jew.* 650; describes the miseries of the empire, 1 *Jew.* 418; committed a spiritual matter to the French queen Brunichilda, *ib.* 396, 4 *Jew.* 961, &c.; says the council at Matiscon was convened by Gunthranus, *Rog.* 204 n.; intimates that lords should not interfere in the business of the priest, *Whita.* 444; says he that abuses his power deserves to lose it, 1 *Jew.* 443; would have men so to be honourable as that their honour should be no derogation to the honour of God, 1 *Jew.* 345, 4 *Jew.* 675

Gregory II., pope: not improbably the author of Dialogues ascribed to Gregory the great, *Calf.* 89 n.; patron of St Boniface, the apostle of Germany, 2 *Tyn.* 259 n.; his replies to inquiries sent to him by Boniface, 4 *Jew.* 1045

Gregory III., pope: added to the canon of the mass, 2 *Brad.* 309, 1 *Jew.* 9; made a law that images should be worshipped, 2 *Bec.* 60, 2 *Brad.* 309; granted a man license to marry his uncle's wife, *Pil.* 602; his league with the French king, 2 *Tyn.* 260

Gregory IV., pope: abused the emperor, 2 *Tyn.* 266

Gregory V., pope: regulated the election of the emperor, and constituted the seven electors, *Bale* 502, 2 *Tyn.* 269; the Gregorian singing ascribed to him, 4 *Bul.* 196

Gregory VI., pope: bought the popedom, *Sand.* 241; an enchanter, *Rog.* 180; his history written by cardinal Benno, 2 *Hoop.* 240; deposed by Henry the emperor, *Pil.* 640 [there called Gratian, his name being Giov. Graziano].

Gregory VII.*, pope: poisoned six popes his predecessors, 3 *Jew.* 250, 346, 4 *Jew.* 700; restricted the title "pope" to the bishop of Rome, *Calf.* 255 n.; declared disobedience to the pope to be idolatry and infidelity, 3 *Jew.* 201; condemned Berengarius, 1 *Hoop.* 526; appointed a three days' fast to get a sign from heaven respecting transubstantiation, 1 *Jew.* 534; wickedly burned the sacrament, 1 *Hoop.* 123, 2 *Jew.* 773, 3 *Jew.* 346, 4 *Jew.* 700; furthered prescript forms of prayer, 2 *Whitg.* 466; brought many wicked superstitions into the church, *Pil.* 521; replies to those who urge the authority of custom, 3 *Bec.* 390, 1 *Jew.* 49; forbade the marriage of priests, *Pil.* 564; the opposition offered to his decree, *ib.* 567; commanded that none should hear the mass of a married priest, 2 *Jew.* 989, *Pil.* 574, *Rog.* 272; says that if a priest be an adulterer his blessing is turned into a curse, 1 *Jew.* 550, 4 *Jew.* 801; took upon him authority to use two swords, 2 *Hoop.* 239; claimed the right to absolve subjects from their allegiance, 3 *Jew.* 172 n.; meddled with the empire, 2 *Hoop.* 236; kept the emperor Henry waiting three days at his gate, 4 *Jew.* 696; stirred up Rodolphus against him, 2 *Hoop.* 239; sent an imperial crown to Rodolphus, 3 *Jew.* 346, 4 *Jew.* 698; procured the deposition of Henry, *Grin.* 21, and sought to murder him, 3 *Whitg.* 592; his acts against that emperor confirmed by a council, 1 *Whitg.* 482; he was a sorcerer and raiser of devils, *Bale* 593, 1 *Jew.* 105, 3 *Jew.* 346, 4 *Jew.* 700, *Rog.* 180; the council of Brixia charged him with adultery, sacrilege, forging, murder, sorcery, and apostasy, 1 *Jew.* 400, 3 *Jew.* 129, 345, 346, and deposed him, 1 *Jew.* 406, 3 *Jew.* 129, 4 *Jew.* 700; a synod held at Rome against him, 4 *Jew.* 926; his life written by card. Benno, (*q. v.*) who relates horrible things of him, 2 *Hoop.* 240; his character the same by other writers, 3 *Jew.* 345—347; some write of his virtues, 4 *Jew.* 698; his extreme wickedness, 1 *Jew.* 400, 3 *Jew.* 346, 347, 4 *Jew.* 700; called hell-brand, *Pil.* 565, 574

Gregory IX., pope: his Decretals: v. Law (Canon).

Gregory X., pope: his election, 1 *Tyn.* 150 n

Gregory XI., pope: condemned a tenet respecting the consecration of the host, 2 *Ful.* 21 n

Gregory XII., pope: bought the popedom, *Sand.* 241; confirmed an order of friars, 2 *Ful.* 103; in his time there were three popes at once, 2 *Ful.* 103, 1 *Tyn.* 325 n.; his abdication or deposition, 1 *Tyn.* 325 n., *Whita.* 510

Gregory XIII., pope: excommunicated queen Elizabeth, *Rog.* 8; revised the canon law, *Calf.* 6 n

Gregory, bp of Nazianzum, father of the next, *q. v.*

Gregory Nazianzen (St):
  i. *His Life and Works.*
  ii. *On God.*
  iii. *Scripture, Doctrine.*
  iv. *The Church and its Ministry.*
  v. *Sacraments, &c.*
  vi. *Miscellanea.*

i. *His Life and Works*: his account of his father, 3 *Jew.* 391, who was bishop of Nazianzum before him, *Pil.* 565; he records that his father pacified a disturbance in the church at Cæsarea, 1 *Whitg.* 447; speaking of him, he says that a good and diligent bishop serves in the ministry none the

---

* Commonly called, Hildebrand. Canonized.

worse for being married, but rather better, 3 *Jew.* 411; he praises his mother, *ib.* 144, 413; speaking of the time of his father's infidelity, he says that his mother being a Christian woman, watched, fasted, sang psalms and prayed for her husband, and was careful for him, *ib.* 414; compares her to Sarah, *ib.*; commends her wisdom, *ib.*; says that she passed all others in godliness, *ib.*; remarks that as the sun-beams are fair and clear in the morning, and grow brighter and warmer towards noon, even so his mother, shewing first the pleasant firstfruits of godliness at the beginning, afterward shined out with greater light, *ib.*; tells that her husband gave her the charge of delivering his money to the poor, *ib.*; as to his sister Gorgonia, see iii. and v. below; Gregory was a student at Athens for thirteen years, 4 *Jew.* 652; his election to his bishopric, 1 *Jew.* 407; his installation, *ib.* 408; he held service in a small oratory at Constantinople, *ib.* 186, 187; funeral orations were used in his time, and he himself made such orations for Basil and others, *Grin.* 10, *Pil.* 543, 3 *Whitg.* 375; his Christian reply to a young man who attempted to assassinate him, 2 *Jew.* 1072; he was married, *ib.* 1128; his wife, 2 *Zur.* 280; his infirmities in age, *ib.* 97; Jerome praises him, 2 *Cran.* 124; he was called the glory of the world, 3 *Whitg.* 595; his works, *Jew.* xxxvii, 2 *Ful.* 402, 3 *Whitg.* xxviii; his Monodia corrupted by Volaterranus, 1 *Jew.* 193, 194

ii. *On God:* he says it is not the business of all to dispute concerning God, &c., *Whita.* 241; exhorts to honour that little Bethlehem, that hath led us into paradise, 4 *Jew.* 667; remarks that Christ is called the life, the way, the bread, the vine, the true light, &c., 1 *Jew.* 526, 2 *Jew.* 1042; writes of his fear, or reverence, 1 *Ful.* 324; speaks of his death as the great and unsacrificeable sacrifice offered as an eternal purgation for the whole world, 2 *Ful.* 84; refers to Christ as being in heaven till the times of restitution, 1 *Ful.* 131, 151; declares that according to his body, he is within the limitation of place, according to his Godhead, without the limits of any place, 1 *Jew.* 485; says, come boldly unto Christ and wash his feet, 2 *Jew.* 764; declares that although Christ shall come in the last day so as to be seen, yet there is in him no grossness, 1 *Cran.* 139, 141; proves the divinity of the Holy Ghost from scripture, 3 *Jew.* 265; speaks of certain heretics who called the Holy Ghost a strange God unknown to scripture, *Whita.* 534

iii. *Scripture, Doctrine:* his diligent study of the scriptures, *Whita.* 371; he exhorts to the reading of them, and to meditation, *ib.* 242; writes on the proper way of studying the scriptures, 2 *Cran.* 122—124; says his sister Gorgonia was skilful in them, 2 *Jew.* 676; compares their literal sense to the body, their mystic sense to the soul, *Whita.* 404; says inferences from scripture stand on the same footing with the natural words of scripture, *ib.* 515; his verses respecting the canon of the Old Testament, *ib.* 58; he numbers the second commandment among the ten, and holds it a moral law, 2 *Bec.* 60; says Matthew wrote his gospel for the Hebrews, *ib.* 126; cited in support of tradition, *ib.* 595; he asserts that the learning of a Christian ought to begin with the fear of God and end in matters of high speculation, 2 *Cran.* 124; declares that only believing is righteousness, 3 *Jew.* 244; says, if thou be a bond-slave, fear the whip; if thou be a hireling, look only for thy reward; but if thou be a child, reverence God as thy Father, *ib.* 583; speaks, allegorically, of defiling sacred vessels, 2 *Ful.* 114; says the time we have in this world is the time of working, the future the time of reward, 2 *Bec.* 395, 3 *Bec.* 460; says of the truth (?), by death it liveth, by wounding it springeth, by diminishing it increaseth, 3 *Jew.* 189

iv. *The Church, and its Ministry:* he appeals to the faith of four hundred years, and the doctrine of the church, 2 *Ful.* 63; says, we must make great account of all churches, even as of the body of Christ, 4 *Jew.* 1043; calls Cæsarea the mother of all churches, 1 *Jew.* 421, 4 *Jew.* 1043; notes that the grace of God goeth not by place, but by the Holy Ghost, 4 *Jew.* 1013; compares the church troubled with contentious persons to a sea-fight, 3 *Whitg.* 596; refers to Christians as fighting against each other, 2 *Jew.* 1073; speaks of defending the church against the church, and striving for Christ against Christ, 1 *Jew.* 98, 2 *Jew.* 1007, 4 *Jew.* 1121; laments the pitiful state of the church in his time, 3 *Jew.* 626; declares that he never saw any good end of a council, 2 *Cran.* 36, 464, 4 *Jew.* 772, 907, 908, *Pil.* 532, *Rog.* 210; condemns those who instruct others before they are taught themselves, 1 *Bec.* 5; complains of the number of clergy in his time, 1 *Jew.* 197, 2 *Jew.* 1019; referred to on the word χειροτονία, 1 *Ful.* 247, 248; said by Cartwright to prove that the election of the minister pertained to the church, 1 *Whitg.* 443, 444; speaks of a commotion at Cæsarea about the election of a bishop, *ib.* 447, 464; observes that the violence was mainly among the common people, *ib.* 447; says that his father pacified the sedition, elected, chose, &c., *ib.*; bids his fellow-citizens not to feed the pastor or judge the judge, *Whita.* 440; says to the prefect of the province, Thou art my sheep, &c., 3 *Jew.* 368; says, the spiritual power surpasses the temporal, as the soul excels the body and the heavens surmount the earth, 4 *Jew.* 837; speaking of the doctrine and the life of ministers he says, the print of a seal is all one, whether it be graven in iron or in gold, 4 *Bul.* 161, 1 *Jew.* 398; speaks of some as exercising priesthood together with Christ, 1 *Ful.* 268; he mentions the jurisdiction exercised by Cyprian, 3 *Jew.* 332, 2 *Whitg.* 164, 429; praises Athanasius, 3 *Jew.* 219 n.; calls him archpriest of priests, *ib.* 315, and, the eye of the world, 4 *Jew.* 1045; gives an account of Basil, 1 *Jew.* 189; styles him the pillar and buttress of the church, *ib.* 433, and, the eye of all the earth, 4 *Jew.* 1032; reckons up all his books, 1 *Jew.* 194; calls Eusebius Samosatensis the rule and standard of the faith, 4 *Jew.* 717

v. *Sacraments, &c.:* he affirms all sacraments to be seals, *Hutch.* 252; writes on the baptism to Moses, 2 *Brad.* 383 n.; says the mystery of baptism is greater than it appears to be, 1 *Jew.* 466; counsels that children should not be baptized till three years old, 2 *Cran.* 175; says the passover was the figure of a figure, 2 *Jew.* 613; calls the eucharist a divine table prepared against them that trouble us, 3 *Bec.* 388; speaks of the passover as partaken of by us in a figure, though more plain than the old passover, 2 *Bec.* 289, 3 *Bec.* 444; says it is not necessary to observe all things in it as Christ did, 1 *Hoop.* 240; terms it the unbloody sacrifice, 2 *Ful.* 84; speaks of offering to God the figure of great mysteries, the sacrifice of praise, 2 *Jew.* 716, 721, 737; exhorts to eat the Lord's body and drink his blood, *Coop.* 141; complains of some who turned the holy mysteries into a play or comedy, 3 *Jew.* 555; distinguishes between the eucharist and the agapæ, 2 *Lat.* 263; mentions that his sister Gor-

gonia reserved the tokens of Christ's body and blood, *Grin.* 48 n., 1 *Jew.* 241, 249; speaks of Christ drinking new wine with us in the kingdom of his Father, 2 *Bec.* 289, 2 *Jew.* 616; cited as saying to the people, I have offered you up for a sacrifice, 2 *Jew.* 709; speaks of a spiritual altar, and its acceptable sacrifices, *ib.* 617; describes the terrible sound of the people singing with one voice, 1 *Jew.* 266

vi. *Miscellanea:* he praises marriage, 2 *Jew.* 1128, 3 *Jew.* 416, 417, (and see i. above); says Basil's father, although married, yet so lived that he was hindered no whit from attaining perfect virtue and holy knowledge, 3 *Jew.* 412; declares that the privileges of a few make not a common law, 1 *Jew.* 334; his use of the word πρεσβυτικῶς (after the manner of old men), 4 *Jew.* 912; he censures some who were slow in judging themselves, quick in condemning others, 3 *Whitg.* 595; writes of the use of arguments, *Whita.* 30; says a kingdom grounded on good will stands fast, *Sand.* 53; declares peace to be the best thing, *ib.* 93; but says there is a peace that is unprofitable, and a discord that is profitable, 4 *Jew.* 1085; he saw the apostasy of Julian in his face, *Pil.* 312; forewarns that Antichrist will come in the desolation of the world, 4 *Jew.* 728

Gregory of Neocæsarea (St), called Thaumaturgus: his works, *Jew.* xxxviii; his canon on excommunication, 1 *Jew.* 143; his controversy with Ælian, an ethnick, 2 *Jew.* 607: he ascribes the origin of images to the heathen, *ib.* 646

Gregory Nyssen (St): he was married, 2 *Jew.* 1128; his account of his brother Basil, 1 *Jew.* 189; his works, *Jew.* xxxviii; the Testimonia adversus Judæos shewn to be genuine, 2 *Ful.* 295, 296 n.; his remarkable treatise De iis qui adeunt Hierosolyma, *ib.* 109 n.; he speaks of Christ as "the bread which came down from heaven," 1 *Jew.* 471, and of his human body as the bread brought forth without sowing, *ib.* 520; says he is made our bread, *ib.* 475; declares that he turns himself into whatsoever is convenient for the receiver, whether strong meat, herbs, or milk, *ib.* 475, 526; says that whoever has abundantly drunk of the apostles' springs, has received Christ, *ib.* 475; affirms that the body of Christ is the nature of every man (omnis humana natura), *ib.* 472; says he that worships a creature, notwithstanding he does it in the name of Christ, yet is he a worshipper of images, 4 *Jew.* 950; interprets the "rock" of Peter's confession, 1 *Jew.* 340, 2 *Ful.* 295, 296; expressions used by him with reference to St Stephen's vision, 1 *Jew.* 474; he calls baptism the divine bath, 2 *Jew.* 620; says Christ appointed water to signify the inward washing of our souls, *ib.* 566, 596; declares that it is not the water that benefits, but the commandment of God, and the Spirit, &c., *ib.* 566; states that the nature of water, the rod of faith going before, giveth life, *ib.*; speaks of the altar, bread and wine, and priests, after dedication to God, as peculiarly honourable, *ib.* 577, 579; refers to a kind of meat, bearing the likeness and resemblance of our bodily meat, but the pleasure and sweetness whereof passeth only into the soul, *ib.* 1117, 3 *Jew.* 529; says a priest, as to his outward form, is what he was before, 2 *Jew.* 579; praises the ornaments and pictures in a certain church, *ib.* 654; relates that he was much affected by beholding a picture of the offering up of Isaac, *Calf.* 173 n.; discommends pilgrimages, 2 *Ful.* 109 n.; shews how "est" is used for "operatur," 3 *Jew.* 467, 541

Gregory of Tours (St): quoted with reference to the true form of the cross, 2 *Zur.* 45 n.; he speaks of the tower wherein the Lord's body was reserved, 2 *Jew.* 560, 561; mentions Martial of Limoges, *Calf.* 69 n

Gregory, an intrusive bishop of Alexandria: 2 *Whitg.* 385 n

Gregory Presbyter: his life of Gregory Nazianzen, *Jew.* xxxviii, 1 *Jew* 190

Gregory of Haimburg: *Jew.* xxxvii; speaks of the pope assuming authority over the angels, 4 *Jew.* 846; says pope Paschalis raised up the son of Henry IV. and caused him to be crowned emperor against his father, *ib.* 698; mentions that Adrian refused to give the emperor Frederick his blessing, for holding his left stirrup instead of the right, *ib.* 691, 692

Gregory (Jo.): his Episcopus Puerorum, *Calf.* 237 n

Greis (i. e. steps): to be taken away, 2 *Hoop.* 135

Grendfield (......): at Calais, 2 *Cran.* 375 n

Grene (Roland): 2 *Cran.* 556

Grensted (Essex, or Sussex?): martyrs there, July 1556, *Poet.* 168

Grese: to graze, *Pil.* 595

Gresham (Sir Jo.), and

Gresham (Sir Rich.): 2 *Cran.* 258 n.; letter to one of them, *ib.* 258

Gresham (Sir Tho.): received cardinal Châtillon, *Grin.* 300 n.; named, 1 *Zur.* 93 n., 140 n.; Burgon's Life of him, *ib.* 93, 139, 140, &c. nn

Gresna, Poland: the archbishop, 3 *Zur.* 597

Gressans: *Pil.* 462

Gressop (Tho.): notice of him, *Poet.* xliv, 2 *Zur.* 147; verses prefixed to the Geneva Bible, *Poet.* 469

Gretserus (Jac.): maintains that latria should be rendered to the cross, *Calf.* 381 n.; defends a spurious epistle ascribed to pope Alexander I., *ib.* 16 n.; confesses that the second Nicene council relied on the fable of the image sent to Abgarus, *ib.* 171 n.; his hesitation with regard to Ben Gorion, 2 *Ful.* 339 n.; his intemperate notes, *ib.* 110 n

Greville (Fulke), lord Brooke: mentioned, 2 *Zur.* 294, 298; notice of him, *Poet.* xvii; nine sonnets by him, *ib.* 107

Grey (Tho.), 1st marq. of Dorset: 1 *Bec.* 125 n

Grey (Tho.), 2nd marq. of Dorset: 1 *Bec.* 125 n

Grey (Hen.), 3rd marq. of Dorset, afterwards duke of Suffolk: notice of him, 3 *Zur.* 3 n., 742; sprung from the royal line, 4 *Bul.* 545; mentioned as marquis, 3 *Zur.* 82; warden of the Marches, 2 *Tyn.* 278 n.; privy councillor, 3 *Zur.* 675; signature as such, 2 *Cran.* 523; Bullinger writes to him, *ib.* 430 n., and dedicates to him his 5th Decade, 3 *Zur.* 397, 399, 406, 409, 434; receives information respecting his style, *ib.* 399, 406, 409; the dedication, 4 *Bul.* 528; letter from him to Bullinger, 3 *Zur.* 3; he favours the gospel, *ib.* 76, 77; patronizes Jo. ab Ulmis, *ib.* 84, 392, 396, 404, 422 (see the letters of that individual, *passim*); goes into Scotland with cavalry to promote the reformation, *ib.* 428; created duke of Suffolk, *ib.* 3 n., 437, 454 n.; regulations of his household, *ib.* 282; Aylmer tutor in his family, 2 *Bec.* 424; report of his having joined Sir Tho. Wyat's rebellion, 3 *Zur.* 686; his execution, *ib.* 154, 290 n.; he confessed the Lord Christ with his latest breath, *ib.* 305; Calvin's commendation of him, *ib.* 716

— Frances (Brandon), his wife: godmother to queen Elizabeth, 2 *Cran.* 274

Grey (Hen.), de jure 4th earl of Kent: 1 *Bec.* 125 n

— Anne (Blennerhasset) his wife, *ib.*

Grey (Reg.), 5th earl of Kent: at the trial of Tho. duke of Norfolk, 1 *Zur.* 267 n

Grey (Will.), 14th lord Grey of Wilton: commands the cavalry at Pinkey, 3 *Zur.* 43; takes Haddington, *ib.* 264 n.; disperses the

rebels in Oxfordshire, *ib*. 391 n.; attacks Leith, 1 *Zur*. 86 n
Grey (Arthur), 15th lord Grey of Wilton; at the duke of Norfolk's trial, 1 *Zur*. 267 n.; patron of Spenser, *Poet*. xiv.
Grey (Leonard, lord), visc. Graney, deputy of Ireland: beheaded, 3 *Zur*. 220 n
Grey (Lord Jo.), brother of the duke of Suffolk: notice of him, 3 *Zur*. 715 n.; letter to him from Calvin, *ib*. 715
Grey (Lady Anne): married Sir Rich. Clement, 1 *Bec*. 125 n
Grey (Lady Anne), another: married Hen. Willoughby, 1 *Bec*. 125 n
Grey (Lady Cath.), ultimately countess of Hertford: *v*. Seymour.
Grey (Lady Jane): *v*. Jane.
Grey (Lady Mary), wife of Tho. Keyes, *q. v.*
Grey (Will.): a letter signed by him and others, 2 *Cov*. 493
Grey-friars: *v*. Franciscans.
Grey hairs: verses by W. Hunnis, *Poet*. 158
Grief: *v*. Sin, Trouble.
Griffith (Maurice), bp of Rochester: apparently referred to as "master Rochester," 1 *Brad*. 469; notice of him, *Phil*. xxvii.
Griffith (Will.), printer: 1 *Brad*. 556
Grigby (Justinian): Jane his wife, *Park*. 303
Grimbald (St): account of him, 3 *Bec*. 43; we are taught by God's word not to trust in him, *ib*.; idolatrous altars built to him, *ib*. 240, 265
Grimbold (Mr): chaplain to bishop Ridley, *Rid*. 361; Ridley's esteem and affection for him, *ib*. 337, 374; he advises him to undertake certain translations, 2 *Brad*. 160, *Rid*. 374; false reports concerning him, 2 *Brad*. 158, *Rid*. 373, 379; he recants, 1 *Brad*. 549, 2 *Brad*. 208, *Rid*. 372, 391, 541; is set at liberty, 2 *Brad*. 168, 174, *Rid*. 371, 379, 391; his treachery, *Rid*. 537, &c.
Grimsby (Great), co. Lincoln: Whitgift desires its prosperity, 3 *Whitg*. 620; it was his birthplace, *ib*. v.
Grimsthorp, co. Lincoln: the castle, the residence of Catherine, duchess of Suffolk, 1 *Lat*. 324; Latimer preached in the hall there, *ib*. 324, 326, 447, 2 *Lat*. 96, 111, 129
Grimston (Eliz.): *v*. Grymeston.
Grinæus (Barth.): *v*. Grynæus.
GRINDAL (Edm.), successively bp of London, and abp of York and Canterbury: biographical notice of him, *Grin*. i—xx; some account of him, *Rog*. 9; his birth, *Grin*. i; the house in which he was born, *ib*. 321; narrow escape of his life, *ib*. i; his career at Cambridge, *ib*., *Hutch*. i; his ordination, *Grin*. i; minor proctor at Cambridge, *Park*. 38; senior proctor, *Grin*. i; at the disputation there, 1549, *Grin*. ii, *Rid*. 169; appointed lady Margaret's preacher, *Grin*. ii; president (or vice-master) of Pembroke hall, *ib*.; chaplain to bishop Ridley, and prebendary and chanter of St Paul's, 2 *Brad*. xxv, *Grin*. ii, *Rid*. 331, 336; chaplain to king Edward, 2 *Brad*. xxvi, 2 *Cran*. xi, *Grin*. ii; a friend of Bucer, 2 *Zur*. 72 n., prebendary of Westminster, *Rid*. 332, *Grin*. iii; on king Edward's death he escaped into Germany, 2 *Brad*. 192, *Grin*. iii, *Rid*. 381; in exile, 1 *Brad*. 445, 1 *Cran*. (9), *Grin*. iii, *Rid*. 489, 493; at Frankfort, 3 *Zur*. 755; he writes thence to Ridley, *Rid*. 386; Ridley's answer, *ib*. 388, see also 533; the troubles at Frankfort, *Grin*. iii; Grindal at Strasburgh, *Jew*. xiii; he sends Bradford's examinations thence to Foxe, 1 *Brad*. 463; on the death of queen Mary he returned to England, *Grin*. iv, with Sandys, *Sand*. xvi; a commissioner for the revision of the Prayer Book, *Grin*. v, 2 *Zur*. 22 n.; at the disputation at Westminster, *Grin*. v, 1 *Zur*. 11, 2 *Zur*. 22 n.; a commissioner for the visitation of the North, *Grin*. v, 2 *Zur*. 22 n.; he preaches before the queen, 2 *Zur*. 16 n.; master of Pembroke college, *Grin*. vi; made bishop of London, *ib*., 1 *Zur*. 23, 40; his election, *Park*. 100 n.; his consecration, *Grin*. vi, *Sand*. xviii, 1 *Zur*. 63, 2 *Zur*. 27 n.; he takes part in a disputation concerning images, 1 *Zur*. 67; his intercourse with the French church in London, 2 *Zur*. 49, 50; a commissioner for the revision of the calendar, 1561, *Lit. Eliz*. xxxiii; he signs letters to the queen, *Park*. 100, 129, 294; advised her to marry, *Grin*. 19 n.; letter from him to Mr Mullins, archdeacon of London, about the plague, *ib*. 78; occasional forms of prayer set forth by him, *Lit. Eliz*. 460, &c.; he preaches at St Paul's, at the funeral solemnity of the emperor Ferdinand, *Grin*. viii, 32; an ecclesiastical commissioner, *ib*. 201, *Park*. 107, 298, 344 n., 345; he assists in the compilation of certain Advertisements, *ib*. 233; to be urged to execute the laws and injunctions, *ib*. 233, 234; supposed to favour the Puritans, *ib*. 237; he tolerated some irregularities, *Sand*. xx. n.; endeavoured to remove the vestments, 1 *Zur*. 169, 177; disapproved of organs and choral service, *ib*. 178; deemed by Parker too tolerant, *Park*. 284; his share in the Bishops' Bible, *Grin*. viii, *Park*. 335 n.; he shews favour to strangers, *Park*. 340; recommended for the see of York, *ib*. 350;

translated thereto, *Grin.* viii, ix, *Sand.* xix, 1 *Zur.* 224, 229, 233; his election, *Park.* 359 n.; confirmed archbishop, *ib.* 361 n.; he comes to York, *Grin.* 325; his illness, 1572, 1 *Zur.* 258; a supervisor of Pilkington's testament, *Pil.* xi; translated to Canterbury, *Grin.* x, 356, *Sand.* xxi, 2 *Zur.* 271; his disagreement with Sandys about dilapidations, *Sand.* xxii; his mandate respecting the publication of the articles agreed upon in convocation, 1575,6, *Grin.* 190; he falls under the queen's displeasure with respect to the exercises called prophesyings, *Grin.* xi, 3 *Whitg.* xii; his letter to the queen about these exercises, *Grin.* 376, &c.; a speech by him in council, being in her majesty's displeasure, *ib.* 471; confined to his house and sequestered, *ib.* xiii, *Rog.* 9 n., 1 *Zur.* 329 n., 332; documents relating to his sequestration, *Grin.* 372—403; the lord treasurer's message to him concerning his submission, *ib.* 469; his submission, *ib.* 394 n., 400; restored, to a certain extent, to the exercise of his jurisdiction, *ib.* xv; afflicted with blindness, *ib.* xv, 398; his proposed resignation, *ib.* 397—400; his last will, *ib.* 458; his decease, *ib.* xv, *Sand.* xxv, 3 *Whitg.* xii; his burial at Croydon, *Grin.* xv, xvi; inscriptions on his tomb, *ib.* xvi; bishop Tanner's account of him, *ib.* xvii. n.; references to him, 2 *Ful.* 41, 87, 1 *Zur.* 58, 69; referred to by the poet Spenser as Algrind, *Grin.* xiii, xiv. n.; a speaker in a feigned dialogue, 2 *Ful.* 164; his character, *Grin.* xiii, &c., *Rid.* 333

His REMAINS, edited by the Rev. Will. Nicholson, A.M., *Grin.*; list of his remains, *ib.* xviii, &c.; letters by him, 2 *Cov.* 529, *Grin.* 217, &c., *Park.* 165, 196, 201, 261, 267, 348, 394, *Rid.* 386, 1 *Zur.* 168, 175, 182, 191, 196, 201, 208, 215, 224, 258, 291, 293, 2 *Zur.* 17, 22, 51, 72, 96, 107, 170; letters to him, *Park.* 115, 120, 127, 134, 143, 152, 160, 227, 242, 272, 308, 323, 345, 474, *Rid.* 386, 533, 1 *Zur.* 356, 357, 2 *Zur.* 81, 98, 110, 166, 178, 244, 271, 273; Beza writes to him, 3 *Whitg.* 277, 278; dedications to him, 3 *Bec.* 400, *Now.* i*, 107

Grindal (Edm.), son of Robert: *Grin.* 321

Grindal (Rob.), of St Bee's: the archbishop's brother, *Grin.* 321; Elizabeth his wife, *ib.*; his daughters, Mabel, Anne, Barbara, Frances, *ib.* 461; Anne married Will. Dacres, *ib.* 321, 322

Grindal (Will.): servant to the archbishop, *Grin.* 462

Grinstead (E. and W.), co. Sussex, *v.* Grenstede.

Grisons: disturbances there, 1 *Zur.* 278

Groat: the price of a dirige, *Pil.* 543

Grofferus (Jo.): 1 *Ful.* 63 n

Groningen: the duke of Alva defeated near it, 1 *Zur.* 205

Gronnowe (Will.): his complaint against the governor of Calais, 2 *Cran.* 347, 356

Gropper (Jo.): De Præst. Altar. Sacram., *Jew.* xxxviii; Enchiridion, 1 *Bul.* 83; the Antididagma ascribed to him, 2 *Zur.* 18 n.; Lib. Propos. ad Comp. Relig., attributed to him, 1 *Jew.* 15 n.; his definition of faith, 1 *Bul.* 83; cited on opus operatum, 2 *Jew.* 750; Harding borrowed from him, *ib.* 714

Grosteste (Rob.), bp of Lincoln: appealed from the pope to Jesus Christ, *Pil.* 591; Lincoln (i. e. Grosteste?) on the sin of a priest who preaches not the word of God, *Bale* 89, 105

Groves: praying in groves forbidden, 2 *Jew.* 635

Gryese (Jo.), of Henley: 2 *Cov.* 501

Gryft: graft, 2 *Bec.* 214

Grymbald (St): *v.* Grimbald.

Grymeston (Eliz.), born Barney, or Bernye: notice of her, *Poet.* xxxix; Psalm li. in metre, *ib.* 412

Grymmus (Jo.): 2 *Cov.* 505

Grynæus (Barth.), or Grinæus: martyred, 1 *Zur.* 36, 42

Grynæus (Jac.): 1 *Whitg.* 409

Grynæus (Sim.): employed by Henry VIII. to collect the opinions of the Swiss divines respecting his divorce, 3 *Zur.* 552 n.; his letter to the king with those opinions, *ib.* 554; his letter of the same date to Bucer, *ib.* 552; a friend of Cranmer, 2 *Cran.* 342, 343, whom he reproves about the Six Articles, &c., 3 *Zur.* 526; named, *ib.* 609; his character as a divine, *ib.* 523

Guaguinus (Alex.): on the religion of the Russians, *Rog.* 169, 243, 285 nn

Gualther: i. e. G. Deloenus, *q. v.*

Gualter (Rodolph): visits England, 3 *Zur.* 124 n.; chosen minister of St Peter's at Zurich, 2 *Zur.* 231; Parkhurst lived four years in his house at Zurich, 1 *Zur.* 298 n.; he writes to Parkhurst on behalf of the Puritans, *ib.* 297 n., 2 *Zur.* 140; six years afterwards he writes to Cox on the same subject, but with altered views, *ib.* 362, see 3 *Whitg.* 496; writes again to Cox on the same question, 2 *Zur.* 225; recovers from a dangerous illness, *ib.* 196; he succeeds Bullinger as chief pastor of Zurich, 1 *Zur.* 318; saluted or mentioned, 2 *Brad.* 406, 1 *Zur.* 12, 17, 22, 154, & sæpe, 2 *Zur.* 90, 95, 170, 3 *Zur.* 42, 49, 504, 615

His commentaries on the minor prophets, 1 *Bul.* 8; dedicated to Parkhurst, *Rog.* 5; translated, 2 *Zur.* 148 n.; commentaries on St John's gospel, 1 *Zur.* 141, 2 *Zur.* 7; on the Acts, 3 *Whitg.* xxviii; on Romans, *ib.*; on 1 and 2 Corinthians, *ib.* xxix; 1 *Zur.* 279, 286, 288, 293, 365 n., 2 *Zur.* 226; on Galatians, 2 *Zur.* 275, 294; on all the epistles, 3 *Whitg.* xxviii; his treatise on Christ's presence, 1 *Zur.* 310; his book on Antichrist, 2 *Cran.* 63, 1 *Zur.* 282, 3 *Zur.* 174; this was translated by Sampson, 3 *Zur.* 176; letters by him, (a few jointly with Bullinger), 1 *Zur.* 357, 360, 362, 2 *Zur.* 3, 8, 11, 52, 60, 137, 140, 142, 154, 214, 225, 237, 249, 258, 273, 294, 312; letters to him, 4 *Jew.* 1219, 1 *Zur.* 48, 141, 205, 234, 279, 284, 286, 289, 293, 297, 306, 310, 312, 315, 316, 318, 320, 324, 326, 328, 331, 2 *Zur.* 36, 54, 55, 61, 75, 114, 146, 202, 222, 236, 256, 302, 304, 306, 307, 310, 3 *Zur.* 134, 163, 166, 184, 186, 191, 195, 358, 410, 418, 424, 434, 458, 484, 501, 637, 721, 723, 725; he thinks that none should bind all churches to one and the same form of discipline, 1 *Whitg.* 187; quotes and approves Augustine's rule, that a Christian should use the customs of the churches to which he may come, *ib.* 286, 287; condemns those who would set up one church as a model for all, 2 *Whitg.* 453; referred to about men disturbing the church under false pretences, 1 *Whitg.* 16, 17; thinks that Andronicus and Junia first planted religion at Rome, *ib.* 499; interprets χειροτονία, Acts xiv. 23, not merely of gathering of voices, but of laying on of hands, *ib.* 348; allows the title of archbishop, 2 *Whitg.* 333; admits that deacons might preach, 3 *Whitg.* 59; allows of their promotion to a higher grade, *ib.* 70; gives his opinion on ecclesiastical senates, *ib.* 177, 192; speaks at large on the inconvenience of an ecclesiastical magistracy or seigniory, *ib.* 210—213; deems the authority of the magistrate more weighty than that of elders, *ib.* 185; expounding 1 Cor. xii. 28, he supposes that Christian magistrates are included, *ib.* 160; asserts the ecclesiastical authority of magistrates, *ib.* 190; writes on excommunication, against the Anabaptists, 1 *Whitg.* 186, 187, 3 *Whitg.* 434; censures Ambrose's vehemence in singly excommunicating Theodosius, 3 *Whitg.* 244; sanctions a kind of civil excommunication, *ib.* 266; disapproves Paul's vow in the temple, and the use of Jewish rites, 3 *Whitg.* 550; admits the lawfulness of some things used by Papists, 2 *Whitg.* 40; recites ancient precedents for the use of vestments, *ib.* 22; entertains some scruples about portraits, 3 *Zur.* 190, 195; shews that some rich men are saved, 1 *Whitg.* 33; dedication to him and others, 4 *Bul.* 546

— Rachael his wife, 3 *Zur.* 188; daughter of Zuinglius, 1 *Zur.* 289

Gualter (Rodolph), the younger: comes to England, and visits bishop Parkhurst, 1 *Zur.* 264 n.; maintained at Cambridge, and afterwards at Oxford, by that bishop, *ib.* 271 n., 289, 299; his removal to Oxford, 2 *Zur.* 217, 225; made M.A. there, *ib.* 219; copy of his diploma, *ib.*; mentioned, 1 *Zur.* 321, 365, 2 *Zur.* 226, 253; letter from him to his father, 2 *Zur.* 202; his letter to Simler, *ib.* 208, 211, 217; letters to him, *ib.* 213, 279; he returns to Zurich, 1 *Zur.* 304, 307, 310, 312; his death, *ib.* 324, 2 *Zur.* 307; his character, 2 *Zur.* 256

Guardians: included in the term parents in the fifth commandment, 1 *Bul.* 268; the honour due to them, *ib.* 281

Guasto (The marq. dal): 2 *Cran.* 234 n

Guelder: the duke styled by Clement VII., the eldest son of the holy see of Rome, 2 *Tyn.* 264

Guerero (Alph. de): reckons the decretal epistles as a part of canonical scripture, *Whita.* 109

Guernsey: three women burned there, 2 *Zur.* 264 n.; state of the church there, with special reference to the case of E. Bonamy, *ib.* 264, &c.; presbyteries in the island, *ib.* 265; church affairs, *ib.* 269, 270; Sir Tho. Leighton, governor, 1 *Zur.* 323 n

Guerricus, abbot: 2 *Bec.* 259 n

Guest (Edm.), bp: *v.* Gheast.

Gueux: the name of a party, 2 *Zur.* 206 n

Guido de Bayso, or Baisius, archdeacon of Bologna: *Calf.* 174 n

Guido Cameracensis: wrote against the Albigenses, *Whita.* 31

Guido Columna, *q. v.*

Guido de Perpin: Summa de Hæres., *Jew.* xxxviii; mentions an error of the Greeks and Armenians about the state of the soul after death, 4 *Jew.* 931, 935; declares that the Greeks hold simple fornication to be no sin, *ib.* 636

Guienne: styled Gyan, 2 *Tyn.* 303; lost, *Calf.* 114

Guigo, a Carthusian: probably author of the Scala Paradisi ascribed to Augustine, 3 *Jew.* 379 n

Guildford, co. Surrey: the birth-place of

bishop Parkhurst, 1 *Zur.* 30; Arianism there, *ib.*
Guildford (Sir Hen.), K. G.: 1 *Tyn.* xxi; notice of him, *ib.* 395 n
Guillermus, or Guillelmus, abbot of St Theodoric: his remains are with Bernard's works, *Jew.* xxxviii; he desired to see and touch whole Christ, and not only so, but to come to the holy wound of his side, the door of the ark, that he might enter wholly, even to the heart of Jesus, 2 *Jew.* 608, 1042
Guilty: their punishment, 2 *Bul.* 231
Guimund, Guitmund, or Wimund, bp of Aversa: upheld transubstantiation, and wrote against Berengarius, 1 *Hoop.* 118, 3 *Jew.* 215; denies that the sacrament can be eaten by mice, *Bale* 154; says, our sacraments are in a manner the body of Christ, that is, the church, 2 *Jew.* 593 n; mentioned, 1 *Bec.* 376, 3 *Bec.* 390 n
Guise (Dukes of): *v.* Lorraine.
Guisnes: 3 *Zur.* 684, 685
Guitmund: *v.* Guimund.
Guiverra (Jo. de): 2 *Jew.* 667
Guldebeckius (......): saluted, 1 *Zur.* 110, 121, 2 *Zur.* 95
Guletta, or Goletta, in Africa: 1 *Zur.* 327 n
Gulielmus: *v.* Wilhelmus, William.
Gulielmus Affliginensis, or Haffliginensis: notice of him, 2 *Jew.* 797 n.; he says the Lord lies hidden under the species of bread, 2 *Jew.* 797
Gulielmus Altisiodorensis: cited by Duns Scotus, 3 *Jew.* 273
Gulph: *v.* Discovery.
Gundoforus, king: *Bale* 612
Gundulph, bp of Rochester: an epistle from Anselm to him and others, *Pil.* 573
Gunning (Pet.), bp of Ely: speaks of interpolations in the chronicle of Eusebius, 2 *Ful.* 236 n., 237 n
Gunthorp (......): *v.* Gounthorp.
Gunthranus: calls a council at Matiscon, *Rog.* 204
Gurney* (W.): signature as privy councillor, *Grin.* 423
Gusman (Don Diego): ambassador from Spain, 1 *Zur.* 139 n
Gusman (Don Martin de): *Grin.* 21 n
Guston (Will.): 2 *Cran.* 357
Guttenberg, Bohemia: silver mines there, 2 *Zur.* 292
Guy: *v.* Guido.
Guymund: *v.* Guimund.
Gweni, a river of Yorkshire: Paulinus baptizes there, *Pil.* 518

Gwent (Rich.): a letter signed by him, 2 *Cran.* 390; concerned in Cranmer's trial, *ib.* 560
Gwin (Jo.): martyred at Newbury, *Poet.* 168
Gwynne (Lewis): a prebendary, *Park.* 114, and parson of Llandewi-Brefi, *ib.* 266, 280
Gyan: *v.* Guienne.
Gybbes (W.), or Gibbes: dedication to him, 3 *Bec.* 353; account of his family, *ib.* n
Gybson (Tho.): printed the first concordance to the English New Testament, 2 *Lat.* 380 n
Gybson (Tho.): his balsam, *Grin.* 281
Gybson (Will.): his MS. translation of a book by Bullinger, 4 *Bul.* xviii.
Gyfford (Geo.): *v.* Gifford.
Gylderde (Jo.): presented to Sutton Magna, 2 *Cran.* 362
Gyles (Steph.), a monk of Canterbury: 2 *Cran.* 333
Gyllam (Sir): *v.* Whitehead (G.)
Gymnicus (Jo. and Gualter), of Duisburg: 2 *Zur.* 42
Gymnosophists: 1 *Bul.* 202, 2 *Bul.* 156, 1 *Jew.* 302, 2 *Jew.* 981
Gyves: fetters, 1 *Jew.* 149

H

H. (F.), esq.: translates a book by Viret, 2 *Brad.* 297 n
H. H. H.: horses, hawks, harlots, *Sand.* 401
H. (I.): probably Joyce Hales, *q. v.*
H. (M.): i. e. Mary Honywood, *q. v.*
H.: i. e. Rob. Harrison, *q. v.*
Haberdyne (M.); *v.* Hubberdine.
Haberman ab Unsleben (G. J. I. J. N. de): *Calf.* 97 n
Habet-Deum, bp of Tamallume: *Rid.* 147
Habitacles: dwelling-places, 1 *Brad.* 356
Habits: *v.* Vestments.
Hacket (Tho.), printer: 2 *Hoop.* 179
Hacket (Will.): a counterfeit Christ, *Nord.* 110, 113; he relied on visions, *Rog.* 196; his pretensions, *ib.* 68; his usual oath, *ib.* 357; his insurrection, *ib.* 344; his execution, *Nord.* v, 114, *Rog.* 162
Hackett (Sir Jo.): king Henry's agent in the Netherlands, 1 *Tyn.* xxxii, xxxiv; being enjoined by Wolsey, he endeavours to procure the suppression of Tyndale's writings at Antwerp, *ib.* xxxiii, and requests that Tyndale and Roye may be delivered into his hands, *ib.* xxxiv; suggests

---

* Doubtless an error for Burleigh.

a false charge of treason against an English merchant, *ib.*; travels in search of Tyndale, *ib.*; endeavours to seize copies of Tyndale's Testament on board Scottish ships, *ib.* xxxvi.

Hackney: a horse, 1 *Hoop.* 320

Haddington: besieged by the English, 3 *Zur.* 388; taken, *ib.* 264

Haddon (James): tutor to the lady Jane Grey, 3 *Zur.* 429, 431; prebendary of Westminster, dean of Exeter, *ib.* 289 n.; Hooper's commendation of him, *ib.* 103; a disputant in the convocation house, 1553, *Phil.* 170, 182, 200, 201, 3 *Zur.* 295 n., 373 n.; an exile, 1 *Brad.* 445, 1 *Cran.* (9); liberal to the poor, 3 *Zur.* 307; he extols Jewel, 4 *Jew.* 1194, 1195; letters from him to Bullinger, 3 *Zur.* 279—301

Haddon (Walter): some account of him, *Phil.* 170 [the disputant in the convocation house was James Haddon, *q.v.*]; references to him, 1 *Zur.* 111, 2 *Zur.* 51 n., 69 n., 70; he made an oration at Bucer's funeral, 3 *Zur.* 492 n.; executor to him, *ib.* 361; he denies that king Edward was poisoned, *ib.* 365 n.; an ecclesiastical commissioner under Elizabeth, *Grin.* vii, *Park.* 72, 133, 370 n., 439; concerned in the translation of the Latin Prayer Book of 1560, *Lit. Eliz.* xxiv, &c.; a commissioner for the revision of the calendar, 1561, *ib.* xxxiii; he answers the letter of Jerome Osorius to queen Elizabeth, *Park.* 216 n., 3 *Zur.* 365 n.; Osorius replied, *Park.* 217 n.; Haddon's rejoinder, completed, after his death, by Foxe, *Jew.* xxxviii, 4 *Jew.* 686, *Park.* 217 n.; in answering Osorius he speaks of indulgences found in the graves of the dead, *Grin.* 29 n.; commissioner at Bruges, 2 *Zur.* 115 n.; he turned some of Augustine's prayers into Latin verse, *Pra. Eliz.* 382 n.; a specimen, *ib.*; letters by him, *Park.* 218, 282; letters to him, *Park.* 284, 3 *Zur.* 364; saying of queen Elizabeth respecting him, 1 *Zur.* 240 n.; his death, 4 *Jew.* 1281, 1 *Zur.* 240

Hades: *v.* Hell.

Hadham, co. Herts: the bishop of London's house there, *Grin.* 266, 320, *Rid.* x. n

Hadleigh, co. Suffolk: Cranmer's letter to the inhabitants, rebuking them for their lack of charity towards Tho. Rose, their curate, 2 *Cran.* 280; Hugh Payne's preaching there, *ib.* 383; Dr Taylor rector there, 2 *Brad.* 103; his martyrdom, *Rid.* 489, 493

Hadrian: *v.* Adrian.

Hæcceitas: a term invented by the schoolmen, 1 *Tyn.* 158

Haerlem: besieged, 2 *Zur.* 222

Haffliginensis (Gul.): *v.* Gulielmus.

Hagar: relieved by an angel, 3 *Bul.* 342, 345; the allegory of Hagar and Sarah, *Pil.* 335, 1 *Tyn.* 307

Hagenbach (K. A.): referred to for an account of Jac. Hochstratus, *Rog.* 200 n

Haggai: he was a poor Levite, *Pil.* 19, 99; Pilkington's commentary on his prophecy; AGGEUS AND ABDIAS PROPHETS, &c., *ib.* 1, &c.; after the temple was repaired by Ezra, he caused the people to weep, 4 *Jew.* 1047, 1048

Hagiographa: the apocryphal books were so called, 1 *Ful.* 24

Hagustalden: *v.* Hexham.

Haile (Jo.), vicar of Thistleworth: condemned for treason, 2 *Cran.* 303 n

Hailes (Will.), or Hale: martyred at Barnet, *Poet.* 163

Haimburgensis (Greg.): *v.* Gregory.

Haimo: *v.* Haymo.

Haine (......): *v.* Hayne.

Haines (Simon): *v.* Haynes.

Hairs (Grey): verses by W. Hunnis, *Poet.* 158

Hake (Edw.): notice of him, *Poet.* xxxiii; stanzas from The Commemoration, *ib.* 368; a complaint, from Gold's Kingdom, *ib.* 369; stanzas from News out of Powles Churchyard, *ib.* 370

Hakluyt (Rich.): references to his Voyages, 2 *Zur.* 290 n., 291 n

Halcot (Rob.): *v.* Holkot.

Haldanrig: fight there, 3 *Zur.* 237 n

Halden (High), co. Kent: Frensham's bequest, 2 *Zur.* 21 n

Hale (Will.): *v.* Hailes.

Hale forth (To): a sea term, 1 *Brad.* 138

Hales, co. Gloucester: Cromwell sends for Coots, who preached at Hales, 2 *Lat.* 374; the imposture called the blood of Hales, 1 *Hoop.* 40, 41 n., 2 *Jew.* 652, 1 *Lat.* xi, 231, 232, 2 *Lat.* 407, 408, *Pil.* 551, 602, 1 *Tyn.* 383; flocks of people came to it from the West country, 2 *Lat.* 364; Burnet's account of it, 1 *Tyn.* 383 n.; a mistake of his corrected, 2 *Lat.* 408 n.; report of the commissioners appointed to examine it, 2 *Lat.* 407 n.; it was exhibited and denounced by bp Hilsey, at Paul's cross, *ib.* 408 n.; the abbey surrendered, *ib.* 380 n.; the chapel and shrine of St Kenelm, *ib.* 409

Hales (Alex. de): *v.* Alexander.

Hales (Chr.): 3 *Zur.* 83, 656, 660; he orders certain portraits, *ib.* 185, 186, 188, 668; Gualter's scruples on the subject, *ib.* 190,

195, and Burcher's, *ib.* 191—194; in danger from French pirates, *ib.* 184; expected at Oxford, *ib.* 724, 726; in exile at Frankfort, 2 *Cran.* 424 n.; his letters, 3 *Zur.* 184—195

Hales (Sir Chr.), a Kentish justice: 2 *Cran.* 349 n.; in a commission about the new foundation of the church of Canterbury, *ib.* 398; a persecutor, *Bale* 395; lessee of an hospital at Canterbury, *Park.* 167

Hales (Humf.), son of Sir James: letters to him, 2 *Brad.* 103, 106; his wife Joan, and children, *ib.* n

Hales (Sir James): notices of him, 1 *Brad.* 248, 2 *Brad.* 85 n., 2 *Cran.* 388 n.; mentioned as serjeant Hales, 2 *Lat.* 419 n., 428; a commissioner for the redress of enclosures, 1 *Lat.* 99 n., 101 n., 102 n.; one of Cranmer's counsel, 2 *Cran.* 388; made a judge, 2 *Lat.* 419 n.; deprived, 4 *Jew.* 1190; imprisoned for religion, 2 *Hoop.* 377, 379; intended to be burned, 3 *Zur.* 154; Bradford's letter to him, 2 *Brad.* 85; prevailed on to recant, *Rid.* 363; his terrors of conscience, 2 *Hoop.* 612; God's judgment on him, 2 *Brad.* 106, 108, 125; he tried to kill himself, 2 *Brad.* 85 n., 2 *Hoop.* 377, 378; Hooper's brief treatise, wherein is contained the truth that Mr Justice Hales never hurt himself until such time as he... waxed weary of the truth, 2 *Hoop.* 374—380; reference to this treatise, *ib.* 592; his lamentable end, 2 *Brad.* 85 n., 3 *Zur.* 177; letter by Bradford on his death, 2 *Brad.* 108

Hales (Jo.): mentioned, 2 *Zur.* 64, 65, 69, 93, 3 *Zur.* 19, 189; clerk of the hanaper, 2 *Cran.* 423, 424, 434, *Park.* 5 n., 1 *Zur.* 19 n.; the king's treasurer abroad, 3 *Zur.* 27; in exile at Frankfort, 2 *Cran.* 424 n., 3 *Zur.* 764; he writes a book on the succession to the crown, 1 *Zur.* 103 n

Hales (Joyce): a friend of Bradford, 1 *Brad.* 248, 591, 2 *Brad.* 216; treatises addressed to her, 1 *Brad.* 307, 351, 2 *Brad.* 195; letter to her on the death of Sir James, her father-in-law, 2 *Brad.* 108; other letters to her, *ib.* 147, 189, 203, 251

Hales (Will.): servant to Grindal, *Grin.* 462

Halford, co. Warwick: the benefice, *Park.* 138 n

Halforde (Jo.): *v.* Alforde.

Halifax, co. York: became loyal through good instruction, *Grin.* 380

Hall: an island in the North, 2 *Zur.* 291

Hall (......), a priest: tried for treason *Lit. Eliz.* 658 n

Hall (......), an officer in Frobisher's expedition: 2 *Zur.* 291 n

Hall (Edw.), the chronicler: 2 *Brad.* 248 n.; Mr Haw or Haule of Gray's Inn (apparently the same) visits Anne Askewe, *Bale* 165; his Chronicle, 2 *Lat.* 33, 301, 392, 402

Hall (Geo.): 2 *Brad.* 10

Hall (James): 2 *Brad.* 10

Hall (Jo.): letter to him, 2 *Hoop.* 597; letter to him and his wife, *ib.* 604; letter to them, being prisoners in Newgate, 2 *Brad.* 216; letter to Mrs Hall in Newgate, *ib.* 247; Mrs Hall greeted, *Phil.* 242; this Mrs Hall is conjectured by Strype to have been the mother of Edw. Hall, the chronicler, 2 *Brad.* 247 n.; her funeral, *ib.*

Hall (Jo.), M.D.: notice of him, *Poet.* xx; verses by him;—an example of prayer against idolatrous tyrants, out of the cxv. Psalm, *ib.* 197; Psalm cxv. in metre, *Poet.* 198; an wholesome warning for all men that bear the name of Christians to live Christianly, *ib.* 200; the faithful soldier of Christ desireth assistance of God against his ghostly enemies, *ib.* 202

Hall (Jos.), bp of Norwich: vindicates the genuineness of Udalric's epistle to Nicholas, and relates that between fifty and sixty children's skulls were found in the moat of an abbey, *Pil.* 687

Hall (Lau.), priest of Oldham: 2 *Brad.* 10, 77

Hall (Nich.): martyred, *Poet.* 162

Hall (Peter): edits the Harmony of Confessions, 1 *Zur.* 169 n., 2 *Zur.* 363 n

Hall (Rowland), printer: 1 *Brad.* 114, 220

Hall (Tho.): *v.* Baily.

Hall (Tho.), a priest: 2 *Brad.* 6, 15, 16, 18, 20, 77; letter to him, *ib.* 7

Hall (Tho.), rector of King's Norton: 1 *Brad.* 557

Hallelujah: in the latter Psalms, 1 *Ful.* 582; in the New Testament, Alleluia, *Bale*, 539, &c.; used in the service of the church, 1 *Jew.* 303; sung by the ancient church at funerals, but not by Papists, *Pil.* 320, 321, 543; used in the mass, 2 *Brad.* 306

Haller (Berthold): 4 *Bul.* xv, xvi.

Haller (Jo.): translates a book by Bullinger, 4 *Bul.* xxii; letter from him to Bullinger, 2 *Zur.* 2; saluted or mentioned, 4 *Jew.* 1214, 1215, 1233, 1235, 1 *Zur.* 17, 30, 40, & sæpe, 2 *Zur.* 90, 95, 3 *Zur.* 153, 743, 744

Halling (......): saluted, 4 *Jew.* 1190

Hallowing: *v.* Consecration, Holy.

Things hallowed by Popish bishops, *Pil.* 493; the vanity of Popish hallowing, *ib.* 163, 316, 496; hallowing of the fire and altar prohibited, 2 *Hoop.* 129, *Rid.* 320

Hallowmas: the feast of All Saints, *Park.* 473
Hallows: saints, 2 *Cran.* 281 n
Haloander (Greg.): *Calf.* 305 n., 2 *Ful.* 95 n., *Jew.* xxxix; 1 *Jew.* 284, 287
Haly: *v.* Albohazen Haly.
Ham: his name, 1 *Tyn.* 407; cursed, 1 *Bul.* 210, 287; the first idolater after the flood, 1 *Cov.* 34; compared to the pope, 1 *Tyn.* 311; his style, "servant of servants," assumed by the pope, 2 *Tyn.* 248
Haman: *Pil.* 242, 290
Hamant (Matth.): a heretic, burnt at Norwich, *Rog.* 49; he said that Christ was a sinful man and an idol, *ib.* 49, 133; denied his resurrection, *ib.* 64, and ascension, *ib.* 65; impugned the deity of the Holy Ghost, *ib.* 70; rejected the New Testament, *ib.* 83; held that justification is by God's mere mercy without respect to Christ's merits, *ib.* 109, 298; said that he was saved by his Helene, *ib.* 162; denied the necessity of sacraments, *ib.* 246, 275, 283
Hamber: hammer? *Park.* 425
Hambleton (Mr), probably James Hamilton, *q. v.*
Hamburgh: reformation there, 1 *Tyn.* xxv; Tyndale and Coverdale there, *ib.* xxxix, xl; the town holds out against Charles V., 3 *Zur.* 668 n.; English trade there, 1 *Zur.* 140, 210
Hamilton family: "the Ambletons," 1 *Zur.* 203 n.; several of them put to death the regent Lennox, *ib.* 262
Hamilton (James), 2nd earl of Arran: Chatelherault, his French dukedom, 1 *Zur.* 57 n.; he escapes from France, *ib.* 44 n., 56, 57 n.; suitor of queen Elizabeth, 4 *Jew.* 1228, 1 *Zur.* 34 n., 68 n.; referred to by Jewel under the name of Crito, 4 *Jew.*1224, &c., 1 *Zur.* 56, 57 n., 59, &c.; in a confederacy, 1 *Zur.* 149 n.; made a guardian of James VI., *ib.* 197 n.; his towns and castles wasted by the English, *ib.* 228
Hamilton (Claud): was leader of those who killed the regent Lennox, 1 *Zur.* 262 n
Hamilton (James), of Bothwellhaugh: shot the regent Murray, 1 *Zur.* 215, 218
Hamilton (James), brother of Patrick, 2 *Cran.* 325, 335
Hamilton (Jo.*), abp of St. Andrew's: a soldier, 1 *Zur.* 60; condemned to death for hearing mass, *ib.* 132; hanged for some other reason, *ib.* 257, 262; his death avenged by the Hamiltons, *ib.* 262
Hamilton (Patrick): martyred, *Bale*, 394, 2 *Cran.* 325 n

Hamilton (Rob.), minister of St Andrew's: 2 *Zur.* 364
Hamilton castle, Scotland: 1 *Zur.* 57 n., 219 n.; queen Mary flees thither, *ib.* 203
Hammond (Hen.): his opinion on the origin of presbyters, 2 *Tyn.* 256 n
Hammond (Jo.): martyred at Colchester, *Poet.* 167
Hammond (Dr Jo.): an ecclesiastical commissioner, *Park.* 447; mentioned, *Grin.* 3 70
Hamond, bp of Rochester: i. e. Haymo de Hythe, *q. v.*
Hamond (Mr): desired to make his child prebendary of York, *Park.* 361, 362
Hampshire: *v.* Winchester.
  Musters, 1588, *Coop.* xv.
Hampson (R. T.): Medii Ævi Kalend., 2 *Lat.* 100 n
Hampton ...., co. Warwick: the priest there, 2 *Lat.* 381
Hampton Court, co. Middlesex; 3 *Zur.* 729 n.; Fulke preaches there, 1 *Ful.* vii; the conference there, 3 *Whitg.* xix.
Hamsted (Hadrian): becomes the apologist of the Anabaptists, *Grin.* 243; cited before the bishop of London and openly censured, *ib.* 243 n.; a revocation offered to him, *ib.* 441, 443
Hanani: (rather Jehu his son), 1 *Bul.* 336
Hanau (The count of): 2 *Zur.* 298, 300
Hand: *v.* God, Hands.
  Significations of the word in Scripture, *Pil.* 21, *Sand.* 134, 135; our hands must be cleansed, *Sand.* 134
Hand-ball: *Rid.* 489, 493
Hands (Laying on of): *v.* Absolution, Blessing, Confirmation, Ordination.
  The phrase diversely used in scripture, 1 *Whitg.* 431; Moses laid his hands on those appointed to be judges, 2 *Bul.* 221; the gesture not used by the apostles only, *Calf.* 219, 220; it is used in ordination, 4 *Bul.* 138, 1 *Ful.* 468, 2 *Ful.* 117, but grace is not ordinarily given thereby, 1 *Ful.* 468; extraordinary gifts were bestowed thereby in the beginning of the church, *ib.* 469; hands anciently laid on converted heretics in token of their repentance, *Whita.* 497; the ceremony doth neither help nor hinder, 1 *Tyn.* 274, 275; χειροτονία, what, 1 *Ful.* 162, 466, 467, 1 *Whitg.* 345, &c.
Handson (......): licensed to preach, 3 *Whitg.* 600 (not the same as Hanson, named below).
Hanging: *v.* Execution.
Hangman: a decree of the university of

---

* Not James, as 1 *Zur.* 257 n.

Oxford (1683) burned by the hangman (1710), 2 *Zur.* 311 n
Hanibalis (Helias de): wrote on the Apocalypse, *Bale* 258
Hanmer (Meredith): his Great Bragge and Challenge of M. Champion confuted, *Calf.* 287 n.; Fulke defends him, 1 *Ful.* x.
Hannah: her prayer, 4 *Bul.* 180, 225, *Pil.* 322, 564; her song, versified by M. Drayton, *Poet.* 119
Hannibal: knew how to gain victory, and how to use it, 2 *Jew.* 1010; his answer on hearing the orator Phormio, 4 *Jew.* 885
Hanson (Jo.), of Trin. coll., Camb.: 3 *Whitg.* 600 (*v.* Handson).
Hanun, king of the Ammonites: *Grin.* 29
Happiness: who is happy, 3 *Bec.* 607; wherein felicity consisteth, 2 *Hoop.* 299, 300; a good part of happiness is to will that which God willeth, 4 *Bul.* 213; the felicity of this world is none otherwise good, than it standeth with God's favour, 2 *Hoop.* 618
Harbledown, co. Kent: the hospital, *Park.* 167
Harborough: harbour, refuge, 1 *Brad.* 105, 1 *Cov.* 318, *Pra. B.* xxvi.
Harborough for Faithful Subjects, [a book by bishop Aylmer, *q. v.*]: censured by M. Marprelate, *Rog.* 338
Harbourous: hospitable, 1 *Cov.* 35, *Sand.* 386, 1 *Tyn.* 479
Harden (To): what, 2 *Bul.* 381
Hardenberg (Alb.): notices of him, 2 *Cran.* 422 n., 3 *Zur.* 538 n.; invited by Cranmer to come and advise on the reformation of religion, 2 *Cran.* 421 n., 422, 425; banished from Bremen, 2 *Zur.* 73 n.; mention of him, 3 *Zur.* 22; letters to him, *ib.* 18, 538
Hardiman, (Jo.), vicar of Lydd: his evil behaviour, *Park.* 342
Harding (Tho.): some account of him, 4 *Jew.* xv, 3 *Zur.* 309 n.; ordained priest in the time of Edward VI., 3 *Jew.* 334; he signed Protestant articles, *Jew.* viii; how he once preached against Rome, 2 *Jew.* 809, 4 *Jew.* 694; in a sermon at Oxford he denounced purgatory, 1 *Jew.* 97; letter from him to Bullinger, 1551, 3 *Zur.* 309; his sudden change in religion, *Calf.* 2, 49, 1 *Jew.* 98, 1 *Zur.* 45 n., 3 *Zur.* 373; the lady Jane writes to him on his apostasy, 3 *Zur.* 304 n., 306 n.; he disputed with Ridley at Oxford, *Rid.* 191; chaplain to bishop White of Lincoln, 1 *Brad.* 501; made a doctor in queen Mary's time, 4 *Jew.* 694; supposed by Jewel to have voted for him in the chapter of Salisbury, *Jew.* xv, 3 *Jew.* 334; but he denied this, *ib.*; his retirement to Louvain, *Jew.* xviii; his controversy with Jewel, 2 *Ful.* 3, 113, 154, *Grin.* 169, *Jew.* xix, &c., xxvii, 4 *Jew.* 1262, 1263, 1273, *Now.* iv, 1 *Zur.* 139 n., 147; his ANSWER, with Jewel's reply, 1 *Jew.* 81, &c.; his conclusion, exhorting Jewel to stand to his promise, 2 *Jew.* 801; Jewel's answer to it, *ib.* 805; his doctrine, 3 *Jew.* 116; terms of reproach used by him, 1 *Jew.* 99; his flowers of speech, &c., collected, 3 *Jew.* 138, &c.; he sneers at Jewel's personal appearance, 4 *Jew.* 693; what he says against the public reading of scripture, 3 *Whitg.* 46; he maintains that no council should be kept without the consent of the bishop of Rome, *Rog.* 205 n.; declares that emperors and kings are the pope's summoners, but of themselves are no absolute callers of councils, *ib.* 205 n.; Dering's book against him quoted, 2 *Whit.* 470
Harding (Tho.): editor of the Decades of Bullinger, 1, 2, 3, 4 *Bul.*
Hardwick (Jo.), of Hardwick: his daughter Elizabeth, *Park.* 301 n
Hare (Hugh): Dr Parry attempts to murder him, *Lit. Eliz.* 583
Hare (Michael): a Popish guest, sent to bishop Grindal by the council, *Grin.* 319, 320
Hare (Raaf): accused of heresy, 2 *Cran.* 390, 392 n.; ordered to do penance at Calais, *ib.* 393
Hargrave (Geo.), Hargreves, or Gargrave: recommended to be vicar of Rochdale, *Park.* 221, *Pil.* vii.
Harington (Sir Jo.), of Exton: *v.* Harrington.
Harington (Sir Jo.), K. B.: notice of him, *Poet.* xvii; Psalms cxii. and cxxxvii. versified by him, *ib.* 115, 116
Harland (......): martyred, *Poet.* 167
Harleston (Rob.): Parker marries his daughter Margaret, *Park.* x, 46 n., 484
Harley (Jo.), bp of Hereford: chaplain to king Edward, 2 *Brad.* xxvi, 2 *Cran.* xi; mentioned, as it seems, 2 *Hoop.* xix; mentioned as "M. Harlow ep. Herfordiæ," *Park.* x, 483; deprived, 4 *Jew.* 1190; dead, *ib.* 1196
Harlot: what, 3 *Bec.* 612
Harlow (M.): *v.* Harley (Jo.).
Harman (Dirick), or Carver, *q. v.*
Harman (Jo.), alias Voysey, *q. v.*
Harman (Rich.), an English merchant at Antwerp: exports Tyndale's Testament, and is in peril thereby, 1 *Tyn.* xxxiv; Anne Boleyn writes a letter on his behalf, *ib.* lxiv.
Harmony of Confessions: *v.* Confession.
Harp: *v.* David.

Harp (Dorothy): 2 *Cran.* 250
Harpagus, and Astyages: their history, 1 *Lat.* 457
Harold, king of England: said to have banished Robert, abp of Canterbury, 2 *Tyn.* 294
Harpol (Jo.): *v.* Hartpoole.
Harpsfield (Jo.), archdeacon of London: notice of him, *Phil.* xxx; at Winchester college, *Phil.* i; he wrote the homily Of the Misery of Mankind, 2 *Cran.* 128 n.; abstract of his sermon before the convocation, *Phil.* xi; he argues with Philpot respecting the mass, *ib.* 94; disputes with Latimer at Oxford, 2 *Lat.* 250, and with Ridley, *Rid.* 191; comes with Bonner, whose chaplain he was, to the Compter, to degrade Dr Taylor, 1 *Brad.* 496; confers with Bradford, *ib.* 502, 508; engaged on the Popish side in the disputation at Westminster, 4 *Jew.* 1199, 1200, 1 *Zur.* 11
Harpsfield (Nich): opposes Jewel, *Jew.* xx, 4 *Jew.* 1263 n.; his Dialogi sex contra Summi Pont. Oppugnatores, published under the name of Alanus Copus, *Jew.* xxxv; he tells us that the apostles were monks, and Christ himself was the abbot, 4 *Jew.* 909; calls Christ the leader of monastic life, and Elias and Elizæus first captains of the Benedictine order, 3 *Jew.* 235, 4 *Jew.* 784; denies that the virgin is called upon to command her Son, 3 *Jew.* 577; says Peter denied not the faith of Christ, but he denied Christ, his faith nevertheless being safe, *ib.* 584; alleges notable stories with reference to the history of pope Joan, 4 *Jew.* 651, 656; speaks of pope John's error about departed souls, *ib.* 930; acknowledges that many good men mislike so many appeals to Rome, *ib.* 949; says that all the decrees of the councils of Carthage and Africa are abolished and trodden under foot as dreams and things superfluous, *ib.* 938; allows that Juvenalis and others were condemned at Chalcedon, *ib.* 1022; mentions that Bessarion and other Greeks at the council of Florence, spoke of the corruption of a Nicene canon, 3 *Jew.* 341, 937; states that there were fewer bishops in many famous councils than at Trent, *Whlta.* 40; makes contradictory statements about Epiphanius and his destruction of the picture, 4 *Jew.* 793; says he was a heretic and a Jew, *ib.*; denies that he wrote an epistle against image worship, *ib.*; reviles the Greeks for permitting the marriage of priests, 3 *Jew.* 420; speaks of the virtues of holy water, 3 *Jew.* 179, 197, 4 *Jew.* 1041; referred to about Theodore Balsamon, 3 *Jew.* 306; he says all the gospellers deny that Christ ever came in the flesh, 1 *Jew.* 134, 4 *Jew.* 760; charges Peter Martyr with denying that Christ is our intercessor, 1 *Jew.* 134, 4 *Jew.* 760

Harpies: what, 4 *Bul.* 122

Harpocrates: *Phil.* 421

Harrington (Sir Jo.), of Exton: treasurer of the camp at Boulogne, &c., 1 *Brad.* 32 n., 486 n., 2 *Brad.* xii, xiii, 1 n.; compelled to make restitution for a fraud, 2 *Brad.* xiv—xvi, 2 n., 6, 10, &c., 17, 25, 29

Harrington (Rob.), son of Sir Robert: an intimate friend of Bradford, 1 *Brad.* 258, 2 *Brad.* 187, 253, who called him Nathanael, 2 *Brad.* 55 n., 117, 216; letters to him and his wife, *ib.* 55, 63, 117; to him and another, *ib.* 60; letter of Philpot to him, *Phil.* 241

— Lucy his wife, 2 *Brad.* 55 n

Harris (......), a justice: *Grin.* 213

Harris (Rob.), pres. Trin. coll., Oxon: 1 *Brad.* 557; his preface to Bradford on Repentance, *ib.* 561

Harris (Seb.), curate of Kensington: 3 *Tyn.* 187 n

Harris (Will.): martyred at Colchester, *Poet.* 172

Harrison (Jo.): warden of the printers [i. e. of the Stationers' company], *Park.* 449

Harrison (Rob.): A Little Treatise on the first verse of the 122nd Psalm, published under his initials, *Rog.* 176 n.; this book says it is the calling of every Christian to join only where the Lord's worship is free, &c., *ib.* 185 n.; cited on lawful calling to the ministry, *ib.* 237 n.; an extract on the choice and deposition of ministers, and on discipline, *ib.* 273 n.; R. H. was of opinion that those who are able must preach, even without authority, *ib.* 231; his speculations censured, *ib.* 203

Harrow, co. Middlesex: 2 *Zur.* 329 n

Harrow: to plunder or destroy, *Pil.* 171; the harrowing of hell, *ib.* n

Harsnett (Sam.), abp of York: his library at Colchester, *Grin.* 478 n., *Lit. Eliz.* xxxv.

Hart (Hen.): a free-will-man, 1 *Brad.* 306, 318 n., 2 *Brad.* 128, 174, *Rid.* 379; an Anabaptist and Pelagian, 2 *Brad.* 173 n.; a treatise, ascribed to him, on THE ENORMITIES PROCEEDING OF THE OPINION THAT PREDESTINATION...IS ABSOLUTE, &c., with Bradford's reply, 1 *Brad.* 318, &c.; his errors, 2 *Brad.* 131; letter to him, 1 *Brad.* 591, 2 *Brad.* 194

Hart (Jo.), or Heart, a priest: deported into Normandy, *Lit. Eliz.* 658 n

Hart (Jo.): conference with Jo. Rainoldes, *q. v.*

Hart (Sir Perceval): entertained queen Elizabeth, 2 *Zur.* 220 n

Hart of grease: what, 2 *Bec.* 345

Harte (Hen.), of Pluckley, Kent: indicted, 2 *Cran.* 367 n

Hartgill (Jo. and Will.): murdered by Cha. lord Stourton, *Park.* 422 n

Hartipole (Ann): Philpot's letter to her, fallen from the sincerity of the gospel, *Phil.* 249

Hartlebury castle, co. Worcester: 2 *Lat.* 375, &c.

Hartpoole (Jo.), or Harpol: martyred, *Poet.* 166

Hartshorne (Cha. Hen.): editor of Fulke's Defence, 1 *Ful.*

Hartwell (Mr): answers Shacklock, 2 *Ful.* 4

Harvee (......), prebendary of Sarum: a layman, 4 *Jew.* 1262, *Park.* 176

Harvel (Rich.): 3 *Zur.* 158

Harvest: *v.* First-fruits, Fruits.
 The harvest great, the labourers few; a sermon, 2 *Jew.* 1016; the harvest of the world, *Bale* 464

Harvey (Hen.), LL.D.: *Grin.* 252, *Park.* 18, 196; a divine and preacher, *Rid.* 337, 340; a commissioner for a visitation in the North, 1 *Zur.* 73 n.; concerned in reforming the university statutes, 3 *Whitg.* 599 [qu. whether all these places refer to the same person?]

Harvey (Rob.): Cranmer's commissary at Calais, 2 *Cran.* 391 n.; hanged there, *ib.*

Harwich, co. Essex: 2 *Zur.* 290 n

Harwood (Steph.): martyred at Stratford-le-Bow, *Poet.* 163

Hasted (Edw.): Hist. of Kent, 2 *Cran.* 313, 330, 348, 411, 2 *Lat.* 221 nn

Hastings (Fra.), earl of Huntingdon: privy councillor, 2 *Cran.* 531

Hastings (Hen.), earl of Huntingdon: lord president of the North, *Grin.* 342, 345, 348, 351, 355; mourner at the funeral of the emperor Ferdinand, *Grin.* 32; he befriends Sampson, *Park.* 243, 245; present at the duke of Norfolk's trial, 1 *Zur*, 267 n.; letter to him, *Park.* 245; a book dedicated to him, 4 *Bul.* xxii.

Hastings (Edw. lord), of Loughborough: one of queen Mary's privy council, 1 *Zur.* 5 n

Hastings (Jo.), parson of Wittersham: imprisoned, 2 *Cran.* 306

Hastynges (Fra.): his pretended wife, 2 *Cran.* 277

Hatcher (......), M.D.: at Cambridge, *Park.* 18, 38

Hatcher (Dr): at Cambridge, (perhaps the same), *Grin.* 368, *Sand.* iv.

Hatfield, co. Herts: Parker preaches there, 1540, before the princess Elizabeth, *Park.* ix, 483; Hatfield park, 2 *Cov.* 529 n., *Grin.* 285

Hatfield (Tho.), bp of Durham: what he paid to the pope, *Pil.* 584

Hatfilde (Hen.): Cranmer's kinsman, 2 *Cran.* 287

Hatred: against it, with sentences and examples of scripture, 1 *Bec.* 458, 459; it is manslaughter, 2 *Bec.* 121

Hatto, bp of Mentz: eaten by rats, *Pil.* 30, 45 i, 612; referred to as "the merciless Moguntine," *Sand.* 159

Hatton (Sir Chr.), K. G.: mentioned, *Park.* 400, 442, 2 *Whitg.* addenda, 2 *Zur.* 303 n.; signature as privy councillor, *Grin.* 414, 417, 423, 429, 433, 435; he tries to get Ely house from bishop Cox, 1 *Zur.* 319 n.; Rogers dedicates to him, *Rog.* xi.

Haukes (Tho.): *v.* Hawkes.

Haule (Mr): *v.* Hall (Edw.).

Haut: haughty, 3 *Bec.* 621, 1 *Brad.* 183

Haverfordwest, co. Pembroke: a martyr there, *Poet.* 172

Haversham, co. Bucks: the benefice of abp Sandys, *Sand.* i.

Havre (Cha. Phil. marquis d'): *v.* Croy (C. P. de).

Havre-de-Grace: otherwise called Franciscopolis, but by the English Newhaven, 1 *Zur.* 115 n.; the protector Somerset neglects to defend it, 3 *Zur.* 728 n.; the French take it, *ib.* 658 n.; the French Protestants give up the town to Elizabeth, *Lit. Eliz.* 459, 1 *Zur.* 115 n.; it is held by the English under the earl of Warwick, *Park.* 179; besieged by the French, *ib.*; the plague rages there, *Grin.* 77, *Lit. Eliz.* 459, 1 *Zur.* 132; the town surrendered to the French, *Grin.* 260 n., *Park.* 183

Haw (Mr): *v.* Hall (Edw.).

Haward (Sir Geo.): *v.* Howard.

Hawarden (Will.), princ. of B. N. C., Oxon: at Cranmer's trial, 2 *Cran.* 547

Hawberk (Sir Nich.): 1 *Bec.* 264 n

Haweis (Tho.): Sketches of the Reformation, 2 *Brad.* xxx. n., xliv. n

Hawford (Edw.), master of Ch. coll., Cambridge: recommended as visitor for St John's college, *Grin.* 359; concerned in a revision of the university statutes, 3 *Whitg.* 599

Hawford (Phil.), or Ballard, abbot of Evesham: 2 *Lat.* 406

Hawkeherste (......), a monk of St Augustine's, Canterbury: 2 *Cran.* 274 n
Hawkes (Tho.): ready to die, 1 *Brad.* 410; martyred, *Poet.* 162
Hawkins (Hen.): letter by him and Tho. Savile to Wolfius, 2 *Zur.* 336
Hawkins (Sir Jo.): wounded by Birchet, 2 *Whitg.* addenda.
Hawkins (Nich.), archdeacon of Ely: designed to be made bishop of Ely, 2 *Cran.* 247 n.; letters to him, *ib.* 244, 272
Hawkins (Rob.), a Londoner: examined before the ecclesiastical commissioners, *Grin.* 201
Hawkshead, co. Lanc.: the school founded by abp Sandys, *Sand.* xxvi; prayers to be used there, *ib.* 443, 444
Hawthorn: superstitiously considered a defence against lightning, *Pil.* 177, 563
Hay (Andr.), earl of Errol: arms in defence of queen Mary, 1 *Zur.* 205 n
Hayburne (Jo.), parson of St Quintin de Spellache, Calais: 2 *Cran.* 349 n
Haydon (......): *v.* Heydon.
Haye (Mons. de la): *v.* La Haye.
Hayes: nets to catch rabbits, *Calf.* 274
Hayes, co. Kent(?): the benefice farmed, 2 *Cran.* 268
Hayle (Will.): *v.* Hailes.
Haymo: In Pauli Epist. Interp., *Jew.* xxxviii; he says Christ took the form of a servant, i. e. he in very truth took man, 3 *Jew.* 261; speaks of the greatness and sufficiency of his sacrifice, 3 *Bec.* 423; gives all the glory of justification to him, 2 *Bec.* 639; says the speech (used in the church) ought to be understood, 2 *Bec.* 255, 3 *Bec.* 409; declares that the cup is called the communication, because all partake of it, 1 *Jew.* 135, 261; referred to on 1 Cor. x, "the cup" and "the bread," 1 *Jew.* 236, on the text, "we have an altar," 1 *Ful.* 518, 519
Haymo Hirsueldensis: wrote on the Apocalypse, *Bale* 256
Hayne (......): martyred, *Poet.* 172
Haynes (Simon), or Heins: dean of Exeter: sometime president of Qu. coll., Camb., 2 *Lat.* 387 n.; a commissioner for reforming the liturgy, *Rid.* 316; commissioner at a disputation, 3 *Zur.* 391 n
Hayward (Chr.): expelled from Trin. coll., Camb., by Whitgift, 3 *Whitg.* 507 n
Hayward (Sir Rowland): *Park.* 465; lord mayor of London, *Poet.* liv.
Hayward (Tho.): *v.* Heyward.
Head: *v.* Christ, Church, Supremacy.
What it is to anoint the head, 2 *Bec.* 537, 538
Headlings: headlong persons, *Bale* 508

Health: *v.* Prayers.
Rules for preserving it, 1 *Hoop.* 297
Hearers, or Audientes: those in the ancient church who were allowed to hear the sermon, but not to be present at the eucharist, 1 *Jew.* 143, *Rid.* 160, 163
Hearing: Aristotle calls it the sense of understanding, 1 *Jew.* 178; the natural order of it, 3 *Jew.* 260; the benefit of it, *Pil.* 291
Hearne (Tho.): Ben. Abbat., 1 *Lat.* xi, 231 n., 2 *Lat.* 408 n
Heart: *v.* Man, Prayers, Purity, Sursum corda.
Jeremiah describes the heart of man, 1 *Lat.* 149, 159; it is inscrutable, *ib.*; deceitful, *Nord.* 162; it must be purged, *Sand.* 136, &c.; it is purified by faith, 1 *Lat.* 485; a broken heart is a pleasant sacrifice to God, *Phil.* 227; he looks on the heart rather than on the deed, 1 *Tyn.* 100, 118, 489; the heart must be kept clean, 2 *Bec.* 405; it is defiled by unclean thoughts, *ib.*
Hearts-ease: *Nord.* title.
Heart (Jo.): *v.* Hart.
Heath (......): persecuted, *Pil.* 242; Mrs Heath, *ib.*; Philpot's letter to her, *ib.* 245
Heath (Mr), dean of South Malling: 2 *Cran.* 399
Heath (Jo.): *v.* Heth.
Heath (Nich.), successively bishop of Rochester, and Worcester, and abp of York: notice of him, *Phil.* xxv; not of noble birth, 4 *Jew.* 1146; educated at St Anthony's school, London, 3 *Whitg.* v; ambassador to Smalcald (or elsewhere) in the king's great cause, 2 *Cran.* 276, 307, 332 n.; Melancthon's account of him, *ib.* 276 n.; he took part in the exposure of the maid of Kent, 2 *Cran.* 66; mentioned as bishop of Worcester, *Park.* 18, *Rid.* 111; his answer to certain questions, 2 *Cran.* 152 n.; commissioner for reforming the church service, *ib.* 414, 415; he forsakes Cranmer, and the adherents of the reformation, 1 *Cran.* xvii; disputes with him and others in London, 3 *Zur.* 323, 645 n.; imprisoned, *ib.* 80; in the custody of Ridley for a year, *Rid.* vi, 429; he attends the duke of Northumberland at his execution, 3 *Zur.* 367 n.; one of queen Mary's privy council, 1 *Zur.* 5 n.; he favours Geo. Shipside, *Rid.* ix; confers with Bradford, 1 *Brad.* 518; examines Philpot, *Phil.* 135; a commissioner to examine Cranmer, 1 *Cran.* xxi; made lordchancellor, 3 *Zur.* 175; as such he signed the warrant for Cranmer's death, 2 *Cran.* 66 n.; mentioned under Elizabeth, 1 *Zur.* 7, 10 n.; co-president with Sir Nich. Bacon

of the Westminster conference, *ib.* 16 n.; letter to him and other deprived bishops, *Park.* 109; prisoner in the Tower, *ib.* 122; afterwards he lived at Chobham, Surrey, 2 *Zur.* 182 n., [not Cobham, as in 2 *Cran.* 276 n., and *Phil.* xxvi]; his character, 3 *Zur.* 530 n

Heathen: *v.* Gentiles.

Heaven: *v.* Kingdom, Life everlasting, Paradise, Prayer (The Lord's).

Meanings of the word, 1 *Bul.* 145, 2 *Cov.* 152; 2 *Hoop.* 67, *Now.* (59, 99), 178; there are two heavens, the spiritual and the temporal, 1 *Lat.* 385; the former is where the angels are, *ib.*; the latter where the stars are, *ib.* 387; the heavens why made, 1 *Hoop.* 331; they shall be dissolved, *Sand.* 366; the third heaven, 1 *Ful.* 285; the new heaven, *Bale* 581, 1 *Brad.* 353, 356, 357; the testimony of scripture respecting heaven, 2 *Cov.* 211, &c.; it is a place, 4 *Bul.* 448, 1 *Hoop.* 66; a place of joy, 1 *Hoop.* 67; God's dwelling place, 1 *Brad.* 123, 4 *Bul.* 208, 1 *Lat.* 332, *Now.* (73), 193; his will done there, *Now.* (76), 197; where it is, 2 *Cov.* 212, 2 *Lat.* 86; in what sense it is to be understood with reference to the ascension of our Saviour, 2 *Cov.* 152, 153; he sits there in his natural body, 1 *Hoop.* 67, 2 *Hoop.* 444; how it was opened by him on his ascension, 1 *Ful.* 287; many of the fathers held that the saints of old did not enter it until after Christ's death, *ib.* 280; when it is to be entered on, 3 *Bec.* 623; whether the virgin Mary, Elias, &c., be there, 1 *Tyn.* 315; Tyndale declares that departed souls are not yet in glory, i. e. in heaven, 1 *Tyn.* lxiii, 3 *Tyn.* 118, 127, 180, and affirms that to say the souls of the departed are in heaven is a Popish doctrine, and subversive of the resurrection, 3 *Tyn.* 180; Hooper maintains that the spirits of departed saints are there, 2 *Hoop.* 63; how flesh and blood shall not be there, 1 *Bul.* 176; the eternal inheritance to be attained through the cross and trouble, 1 *Cov.* 340; we must enter it by many troubles, 2 *Hoop.* 337; glory is reserved for those who suffer with Christ, 2 *Tyn.* 28; the faithful shall know one another in heaven, 2 *Cov.* 221; the joys of heaven, 2 *Brad.* 149, 2 *Hoop.* 264, they pass all men's thoughts, 1 *Lat.* 531; its glories, 1 *Brad.* 341, 397; the glory of heaven; with sentences and examples of scripture, 1 *Bec.* 484, 485; on different degrees of glory, *Hutch.* 306; how the salvation shall be, 2 *Cov.* 213; heavenly mansions; verses by Jo. Davies, *Poet.* 246; a meditation concerning heaven, *Pra. B.* 101; another, *ib.* 106; another, with a prayer for heavenly-mindedness, *ib.* 17; a sweet contemplation of heaven and heavenly things, 1 *Brad.* 266; NEWS OUT OF HEAVEN, by T. Becon, 1 *Bec.* 35; Christians are citizens of heaven, 1 *Brad.* 416, 419, 2 *Cov.* 232, 235; the way to heaven, 1 *Lat.* 488; desires after it, *Pra. B.* 187; a prayer for the glory of heaven, 3 *Bec.* 84, 85, *Lit. Edw.* 475; a true Christian believes that heaven is his already, 1 *Tyn.* 21; "heavenly things" (Jo. iii), 4 *Bul.* 243, in sacraments, *ib.* 251

Hebb (Rich.): *Rid.* 536 n

Hebeonites: *v.* Ebionites.

Heberdynne (Mr): *v.* Hubberdine.

Hebilthwayte (Will.): servant to Tonstal, 1 *Tyn.* 395

Hebrew: *v.* Bible, Rabbins, Thau.

The holy tongue, 2 *Ful.* 224; the primitive language, *Whita.* 112, 113; known by the common people, 4 *Bul.* 189, 2 *Jew.* 678; the Hebrew scriptures understood by the people after the captivity, *Whita.* 213—215; Bellarmine affirms that the language ceased to be vernacular amongst the Jews in the time of Ezra, *ib.* 211; this statement is refuted, *ib.* 212; but it is admitted that the language became much corrupted, *ib.* 213, 214; on the dialect called Hebrew in the New Testament, *ib.* 214, 215; Hebrew used in divine service by Christian Jews, 1 *Jew.* 289; Matthew's gospel and the epistle to the Hebrews said to have been written in this tongue, *Whita.* 125—127; perhaps the Syriac is intended, *ib.* 126; Hebrew words in the service of the church, 1 *Jew.* 303; such words were used by Marcus and Heracleon in their prayers, *ib.* 316; the language not known in England in Henry VIIIth's time, 1 *Tyn.* xxv; studied by Philpot, *Phil.* ii; knowledge of it restored, *Bale* 335; its study at Cambridge, *Park.* 348, 467; it is most necessary to be known, 4 *Bul.* 542, 3 *Tyn.* 75, *Whita.* 468; remarks on some peculiarities of the Hebrew tongue, 1 *Tyn.* 148, 149; the present Hebrew letters not used till after the captivity, *Calf.* 107 n.; Ezra asserted to have invented them, *Whita.* 116, on the ancient form of the letter ה, *ib.*; on the origin of the vowel points, 2 *Jew.* 678; the points defended by Arias Montanus, 1 *Ful.* 55, and by Fulke, *ib.* 78, 578; Hebrew words, see the Indexes to 1 *Ful.* and *Tyn.*; Hebraisms in scripture, *Whita.* 378; they occur in the New Testament, 1 *Tyn.* 468

Hebrews: the epistle to the Hebrews; v. Paul (St.): the gospel of the Hebrews; v. Apocrypha, ii.
Hebron: 4 *Bul.* 524
Hecla: a mount in Ireland [Iceland?], *Rog.* 215
Hector and Troilus: a romance, 1 *Tyn.* 161
Hedge (Piers): 3 *Cran.* 390
Hedge priests: rustic clergy, 2 *Ful.* 235; 2 *Whitg.* 265, 382, 3 *Whitg.* 279
Hedio (Caspar): notice of him, 3 *Zur.* 50 n.; letter to him and the other ministers of Strasburgh, *ib.* 534; saluted, *ib.* 492; his death, *ib.* 682
Heedy : careful, 1 *Brad.* 77
Hegesippus, or Egesippus (fl. c. 170): Eusebius says he wrote five books of apostolical traditions, *Whita.* 574; his ecclesiastical history was the first ever written, but it is now almost entirely lost, *Rid.* 220 n.; his remains, 2 *Ful.* 338 n.; he testifies that the Lord, after his ascension, appeared to Peter, *Rid.* 220; gives an account of the continual praying of St James, 1 *Brad.* 24 n.; says he used neither wine nor strong drink, &c., 1 *Jew.* 237, 238; describes the corruption of the church, immediately after the death of the apostles, 2 *Whitg.* 183
Hegesippus, Egesippus, or Joseph Ben Gorion: often confounded with the last-mentioned, 2 *Ful.* 338, 339, *Whita.* 574; some account of him, 2 *Ful.* 338 n.; De Excidio Hierosolymitano, *Jew.* xxxvi.; he mentions Constantinople, therefore must have lived since the time of Constantine, 2 *Ful.* 339 n., *Whita.* 575; describes the subtle sleights of Simon Magus, *Bale* 445, 2 *Ful.* 338
Heidelberg: the palace of the electors Palatine, 2 *Zur.* 247 n.; tyranny in the church there, *ib.* 238, 251
Heiden (Seobald): a book by him, 2 *Cov.* 509
Heilbrunnen: 3 *Zur.* 638
Heins (Simon): v. Haynes.
Heirs, Inheritance: v. Primogeniture.
 The law of Moses on inheritance, 2 *Bul.* 226; all believers are heirs, 1 *Tyn.* 77; their assurance thereof, *ib.* 89, 113; the kingdom of God is not as the hire that is due to servants, but as the inheritance of the sons of God, 2 *Bul.* 346
Heiu, an Anglo-Saxon nun: 2 *Ful.* 12
Helchesaites: their heresy, *Bale* 210, *Phil.* 420; said to have held sundry Christs, at least two, 1 *Jew.* 481; they asserted the Holy Ghost to be the natural sister of Christ, *Rog.* 71; allowed perjury to escape persecution, *ib.* 119, 357

Heldelin (James): saluted, 2 *Zur.* 52
Helding (......): one of the framers of the Interim, 3 *Zur.* 383 n
Helena: stolen by Paris, 1 *Bul.* 417
Helena (St,) empress: said to have been an Englishwoman, *Bale* 156, 1 *Jew.* 306; Calfhill states that Ambrose calls her "stabulariam," *Calf.* 322, but his word "asserunt" refers to the enemies of Christianity, *ib.* 409; she was the wife, not the concubine of Constantius, *ib.* 322 n.; her invention of the cross, *ib.* 287, 321, &c., 1 *Ful.* 212, 2 *Ful.* 190, 193, 194, *Pra. Eliz.* 529 n.; different statements about this matter, *Calf.* 322—325; Ambrose says she worshipped not the cross, but the King, 2 *Bec.* 72, *Calf.* 192, 377, 1 *Ful.* 212, 2 *Ful.* 202, 2 *Jew.* 650, *Park.* 8; what she did with the cross, *Calf.* 326; what she did with the nails, *ib.* 327; she apparelled herself like a servant and ministered unto the holy virgins, 4 *Jew.* 1017
— Helen's day: the Invention of the Cross (May 3), *Pil.* 15
Helias de Hanibalis, *q. v.*
Heliodorus: v. Chromatius.
Heliogabalus, emperor: wished to unite all religions in one, 2 *Jew.* 646 n.; his gluttony, *Sand.* 393
Hell: v. Limbus.
 (*a*) The term generally:—it is diversely taken, 3 *Bec.* 604, *Hutch.* 57, 1 *Tyn.* 353; according to some Papists hell has four divisions, *Rog.* 154 n., 215, 249 n.; P. Dens on limbus, infernus, and purgatorium, 1 *Tyn.* 159 n.; the infernal regions of the poets, *Calf.* 14; the derivation of the English term "hell" appears in the word "unhele," to uncover, 2 *Tyn.* 322
 (*b*) Hades (ᾅδης) and its equivalents (v. Paradise):—the meaning of "sheol" (שאול), 1 *Ful.* 59, 128, 129, 158, 284, 286, 301, 305, 306, &c., *Hutch.* 57; the signification of ᾅδης, 2 *Cov.* 206, 1 *Ful.* 59, 128, 158, 280, 282, 284, 287, 305, 307, 311, 313, 314, 316; the meaning of "infernus," &c., 1 *Ful.* 81, 292, 305, 307, 320, *Now.* (101), 1 *Tyn.* 531; Jerome's distinction between "infernus" and "mors," 1 *Ful.* 306; Abraham's bosom, 1 *Bul.* 139, 2 *Cov.* 212, 1 *Ful.* 285, 295, 296, *Whita.* 537; on our Lord's descent into hell, 2 *Bec.* 33, 3 *Bec.* 139, 1 *Bul.* 137, 2 *Cran.* 89, 1 *Ful.* 81, 278, &c., 2 *Hoop.* 30, *Lit. Edw.* 504, (553), *Now.* (43), 160, *Rog.* 59, 60; translations respecting it examined, 1 *Ful.* 278—331; controversy on the subject, *Park.* 305, *Rog.* xiii; differences amongst Papists about it, *Whita.* 536; the

Institution of a Christian man explains the creed as referring to the place of torment, 2 *Cran.* 89; Latimer and others maintained the same opinion, 1 *Ful.* 284, 1 *Lat.* 233, 234, 1 *Whitg.* 29 n.; the article of 1552 affirms that he preached to the spirits in prison, *Lit. Edw.* 526, (572); some denied the fact of Christ's descent into hell, 1 *Lat.* 233; others considered it to mean no more than his burial, *Whita.* 537; thus thought Beza, 1 *Ful.* 280; the old metrical version of the creed upon it, *ib.* 283, 284; Fulke refers it to his sufferings in soul, *ib.* 279; various opinions as to the reasons of Christ's descent into hell, *Whita.* 537, 538; the profit we obtain thereby, 2 *Bec.* 33

(*c*) The place of eternal punishment (γέευνα):—what it is, 3 *Bec.* 604; what the word "gehenna" means, and whence it is derived, 1 *Tyn.* 531; the name Tartarus, 2 *Cov.* 206; why hell is not mentioned in the creed as the abode of the wicked, *Now.* (60), 179; on the death and damnation of the unrighteous, 2 *Cov.* 201; that there is an eternal death, and that the soul is passible, *ib.* 202; the bodies of unbelievers being raised are passible, *ib.* 204; hell stated to be under the earth, *ib.*; it cannot be represented by painters, 1 *Lat.* 220; the pains of hell, 2 *Cov.* 205, &c., 2 *Lat.* 191, 192; they are inexpressible, 1 *Lat.* 220, 235, 2 *Lat.* 191; they are eternal, *Hutch.* 56, 57; refutation of opinions to the contrary, 2 *Cov.* 208—210; on the nature of the fire there, *Bale* 576, 2 *Lat.* 235, 360; degrees of punishment, 1 *Lat.* 11, 12, 224; the fault of perishing is man's own, and not God's, 1 *Bec.* 94, 2 *Lat.* 192; sin is the cause of damnation, 1 *Hoop.* 264; affliction in this world is to keep us from the pains of hell, 2 *Bec.* 463, 464; they should be thought of, in order to produce humility, 1 *Bec.* 204; against hell, sin, and death; with sentences and examples of scripture, *ib.* 479, 480

Hellbusius (Tilman): *v.* Heshusius.

Hellopeus (......): condemned the use of the sign of the cross in baptism, *Rog.* 321 n

Helmoldus: Chronica Slavorum, *Jew.* xxxviii; cited about the emperor Henry IV., 4 *Jew.* 699, 700

Helvidius: denied the perpetual virginity of Mary, 4 *Bul.* 437, 2 *Cran.* 60, 1 *Hoop.* 161, 3 *Jew.* 441, 2 *Lat.* 105, *Phil.* 427, 2 *Tyn.* 339 n., *Whita.* 539; alleged Tertullian, 1 *Jew.* 22

Helvetia: *v.* Switzerland.

Hemerobaptists: a sect who baptized every day, 2 *Ful.* 390

Hemmingius (Nich.): works by him, 3 *Whitg.* xxix; his Exposition of the 84th Psalm, translated by Rogers, *Rog.* viii; he shews that the judicial law of Moses has expired, and only binds so far as it pertains to the law of nature, and as the civil magistrate may admit it for policy, 1 *Whitg.* 274, 275; speaks of degrees in the church, and the necessity of order, 2 *Whitg.* 326—331; admits difference of rank amongst ministers, *ib.* 266; states that the early bishops ordained patriarchs, &c., *Rog.* 329 n.; allows the promotion of deacons, 3 *Whitg.* 70; explains what the work of an evangelist is, 2 *Whitg.* 299; says, we acknowledge the pope neither as the head of the church nor the tail, *Rog.* 347 n

Heneage (Geo.), dean of Lincoln: 2 *Cran.* 265

Heneage (Mr): "master Hennage," perhaps Sir Tho., 2 *Cran.* 409

Heneage (Sir Tho.): 1 *Ful.* xi, *Park.* 320

Henley on Thames, co. Oxon: complaint of a picture of the death of Becket, in a window of the Lady chapel in the church there, and of other superstitions, 2 *Cov.* 501

Henley (Will.): servant to Grindal, *Grin.* 462

Henmarsh (Will.): legacy to him, *Grin.* 461

Henningius (Jo.): Archæologia Passionalis, *Calf.* 328 n

Henricians, otherwise Apostolics: a sect in Bernard's time, 3 *Jew.* 151; they said he was no bishop who was a wicked man, *Rog.* 270; condemned prelacy, *ib.* 330; denied baptism to infants, *ib.* 280; would have none to marry but virgins and single persons, *ib.* 307; allowed perjury in time of persecution, *ib.* 119

Henricus de Gandavo: 1 *Jew.* 457, 2 *Jew.* 667

Henricus de Hassia: wrote on the Apocalypse, *Bale* 256

Henricus Herfordiensis, or de Hervordia: his Chronicon Generalis, 1 *Jew.* 191 n

Henry III., emperor: caused four kings of Vindelicia to carry pans, &c., to his kitchen, 4 *Jew.* 702; deposed popes, *Pil.* 640

Henry IV., emperor: compelled by the bishop of Rome to make war sixty-two times, 2 *Hoop.* 239; his conflict with Rodolph, *Lit. Eliz.* 449; compelled to wait bareheaded at the gate of Hildebrand, 4 *Jew.* 696; shamefully used by his son, *ib.* 697; deposed by the pope, and sought to be murdered, 2 *Cran.* 12, *Grin.* 21, 3 *Whitg.* 592; his character, and the cause of his dispute with the pope, 4 *Jew.* 699; he vainly seeks a prebend in the church of Spires, *ib.* 700; his death, *ib., Lit. Eliz.* 451; burial refused to him, 4 *Jew.* 700

Henry V., emperor: raised against his father by the pope, 4 *Jew.* 697; constrained to surrender his authority to pope Paschal II., 2 *Hoop.* 238

Henry VI., emperor: Celestine III. crowned him with his feet, and then kicked the crown off again, 4 *Jew.* 697, 2 *Tyn.* 271

Henry VII.*, emperor: poisoned in the sacrament, *Grin.* 60, 1 *Hoop.* 123, 2 *Hoop.* 240, 1 *Jew.* 105, *Sand.* 66

Henry I., king of England: a learned prince, *Sand.* 81; he (or as Tyndale says, William II.) would have had a certain tax which was paid by the priests, but was obliged to yield to Ralph bp of Chichester, 2 *Tyn.* 295

Henry II., king of England: a forgiving prince, *Sand.* 81; vexed by prelates, 2 *Tyn.* 19; unworthily treated by the pope, 2 *Hoop.* 240, 4 *Jew.* 1076

Henry III., king of England: complained of the pope's exactions, 4 *Jew.* 1081; caused the chronicles to be searched concerning the superiority of the English crown over Scotland, *Park.* 327; his tomb, *Now.* 229

Henry IV., king of England: exiled in the time of Richard II., then being earl of Derby, 2 *Tyn.* 295; a traitor and usurper, 1 *Tyn.* 458, 2 *Tyn.* 296, 3 *Tyn.* 212; he renounced the jurisdiction of the bishop of Rome, *Rog.* 347

Henry V., king of England: an usurper, 1 *Tyn.* 458; he held the land by the sword, against all right, 3 *Tyn.* 212; cast off evil company, *Wool.* 127, 128; sent for lord Cobham, *Bale* 17; would not receive his confession of faith, *ib.* 22; the clergy complained to him of the spread of Wickliffe's doctrine, *ib.* 49; he called a parliament at Leicester, *ib.*; dispersed an assembly in St Giles' fields, *ib.* 50; was sent into France by his clergy, 1 *Tyn.* 338, 2 *Tyn.* 297, 302, 3 *Tyn.* 212; conquered more than they intended, 2 *Tyn.* 303; was counted a happy prince, *Sand.* 81; made a statute against swearing, 1 *Bec.* 390; built Sion and the Charter-house of Shene, 2 *Tyn.* 81; his funeral sermon preached by Walden, 1 *Bec.* 391 n

Henry VI., king of England: an usurper, 1 *Tyn.* 458; managed and deceived by prelates, 2 *Tyn.* 297, 303, &c.; reputed a holy prince, *Sand.* 81; said to have renounced the jurisdiction of the bishop of Rome, *Rog.* 347; his unhappy reign, *Bale* 12; miracles were ascribed to him after his death, yet he was not canonized, 3 *Tyn.* 122

Henry VII., king of England: a prudent prince, *Sand.* 81; the reason of his reputation for wisdom, *Park.* 461; he made use of cardinal Morton and other prelates to get at his subjects' secrets, and raise money, 2 *Tyn.* 305; anecdote of him and his cup-bearer, 2 *Lat.* 150

Henry VIII., king of England: *v.* Doctrine, Institution, Statutes.

He walks barefoot from Barsham to our lady of Walsingham, 1 *Hoop.* 40 n., 3 *Zur.* 609 n.; pope Julius sends him the golden rose, 1 *Tyn.* 186; he sends forces to assist king Ferdinand, 2 *Tyn.* 310 n.; his Assertio septem Sacramentorum, adv. M. Lutherum, 3 *Tyn.* 101, 2 *Tyn.* 339; translated and published by authority, 1687, *Calf.* 244 n.; an edition printed in Dublin, 1766, *ib.*; he receives the title of Defender (*q. v.*) of the the Faith; set on to war against the French king by the pope, 2 *Cran.* 12, who afterwards interdicted his whole realm, *ib.* 13; he claims the kingdom of France, 1 *Tyn.* 187; a loan forgiven him by the spiritualty and temporalty, 2 *Tyn.* 337; warned that Tyndale was printing a version of the scriptures, 1 *Tyn.* xxx; he cautions his subjects against the Bible (*q. v.*) in English, *ib.* xxxi, 131 n.; desires the princess regent of the Netherlands to procure the destruction of books intended to poison his subjects, *ib.* xxxii; compact between him and the princess, to prohibit the printing or selling of Lutheran books, *ib.* xxxvii; his proclamations against heresies, and forbidden books, 2 *Lat.* 304 n., 305 n., 1 *Tyn.* xl, 34, 131; he prohibits the translation and circulation of the scriptures in English, 2 *Lat.* 304 n., 1 *Tyn.* 35; letter to him from Latimer, for restoring liberty to read them, 2 *Lat.* 297; he reads and approves of Tyndale's Obedience, 1 *Tyn.* 130, in which the writer advises him to consider what his support of the pope has cost, *ib.* 335; his opinion of Tyndale's answer to More, *ib.* xlvi; he is ridiculed in a play at Paris, 2 *Tyn.* 341; Tyndale intreats him to cease from persecuting, *ib.*, and to take measures for the settlement of the crown, *ib.*; his supremacy admitted by archbishop Warham, 2 *Cran.* 214 n.; the question of the lawfulness of his marriage with Catherine (*q. v.*) of Arragon, considered at Cam-

---

* Not VI. as sometimes stated.

HENRY VIII.

bridge, 1 *Lat.* v; opinions of Bucer, Œcolampadius, Zuinglius, &c., on this marriage, 3 *Zur.* 551; letter of Simon Grynæus to the king, with opinions, *ib.* 554; he employs Sir Tho. Elyot to procure Tyndale's arrest, 1 *Tyn.* li; seizes the charters of Oxford, 2 *Cran.* 252; the question of his divorce agitated, *ib.* 216, 237, 2 *Lat.* 340, 1 *Tyn.* 38 n., 2 *Tyn.* 238, 319, &c.; bishop Stokesly favours it, 2 *Lat.* 333 n.; Tyndale's opinion was against it, 2 *Tyn.* 238; the question occasioned his Practice of Prelates, *ib.*; he therein declares that the king's vow of matrimony was more binding than Luther's vow of celibacy, *ib.* 340; the king seeks the opinion of Cranmer, 2 *Cran.* vii; his licence to Cranmer to proceed to the determination of the question, *ib.* 238 n.; Cranmer pronounces judgment, *ib.* viii, 242; the sentence, *ib.* 243; preaching against the king's marriage with Anne (*q. v.*) Boleyn prohibited, *ib.* 283, 296; preaching in favour of it enjoined, and the arguments to be used set forth, *ib.* 461; preamble to the act of succession, which confirms this marriage, *ib.* 285 n.; it was moreover confirmed by a papal bull, *Park.* 414, 420; the king's peremptory order to Bourchier, earl of Essex, to return Richard Stansby's copyholds, 2 *Cran.* 267 n.; his injunctions to all monasteries, 2 *Lat.* 240 n.; he writes to the bishops about settling his style of supreme head, 2 *Cran.* 306 n.; he is excommunicated by the pope, 4 *Jew.* 1076; accursed by a bull of Paul III., *ib.* 1131; message of that pope to him, 2 *Cran.* 126; his inhibition of ordinary visitation during his own visitation, 1535, *ib.* 463; he commands the publication of Coverdale's Bible, 1 *Ful.* 98; dedication to him of the Bible, 1535, 2 *Cov.* 3; his warrant for a doe for Parker, *Park.* 4; Cranmer's letter to him, excusing sir Tho. Baschurch, who had pronounced him a tyrant, 2 *Cran.* 319; another, on the misconduct of queen Anne Boleyn, *ib.* 323; he wills his true subjects to have no familiarity with cardinal Pole, 1 *Hoop.* 37; his marriage with Jane Seymour, *v.* Jane; Cranmer's letter to him on his preaching in Kent, and complaining of the prior of the Black Friars, who had answered him, 2 *Cran.* 325; the king's practice on receiving books presented for his perusal, *ib.* 341, 3 *Zur.* 15; he licenses the reading of the Bible in English, 2 *Lat.* 240, 1 *Tyn.* lxxv; his corrections of the Institution of a Christian Man, 2 *Cran.* 83, 358; he alters the Lord's prayer, " suffer not us to be led,"
&c., 2 *Cran.* 106, *Pra. Eliz.* 16 n.; minute of an answer of his to a letter from the commissioners, prefixed to the Institution, 2 *Cran.* 469; his answers to Latimer's arguments against purgatory, 2 *Lat.* 245; an argument of his against giving the cup to the laity, *Rid.* 106; Bullinger dedicates a book to him, 2 *Bul.* 15; dedication to him of the New Testament, 1538, 2 *Cov.* 24; he proposes to marry the duchess of Milan, 2 *Cran.* 375 n.; takes upon himself to answer the German religious embassy, *ib.* 379; the bishops decline answering them, for fear of contradicting him, *ib.*; he condemns Lambert in person, *ib.* 218 n., 3 *Zur.* 201; his Six Articles (*q. v.*), 2 *Cran.* 168; his marriage with Anne of Cleves, *v.* Anne; Cranmer's letter to him, bewailing the charge of treason against Cromwell, *ib.* 401; letter from Dantiscus, a Polish bishop, to Cranmer, condemning the king's conduct, *ib.* 402; his marriage with Cath. Howard, *v.* Catherine; questions attributed to him, *ib.* 115 n.; his judgment concerning Dr Crome, 3 *Zur.* 214; Cranmer's letter to him, in behalf of Edward Isaac, for an exchange of lands belonging to Christ church, Canterbury, 2 *Cran.* 458; he goes to the North, 3 *Zur.* 219; cause of his war with Scotland, *ib.* 634 n.; he marries Catharine (*q. v.*) Parr, *ib.* 242; issues a proclamation concerning white meat, 1 *Bec.* 107; sends a fleet to Scotland, *Pra. Eliz.* 567 n.; orders the English litany to be used at processions, *Pra. Eliz.* xxiv; copy of this litany, *ib.* 563, &c.; letter to the dean and prebendaries of Stoke, requiring them to send four able men to his army, about to invade France, *Park.* 15; the king's letter to the archbishop for the publication of his royal injunctions, 2 *Cran.* 494; he invades France, *Pra. Eliz.* 567 n.; takes Boulogne, *Park.* 15 n., 30 n.; the keys of that town given to him, *Hutch.* 99; his letter to the fellows of Corpus Christi college, Cambridge, recommending Parker as master, *Park.* 16; his preface to the Primer, 2 *Cran.* 496, another copy, *Pra. Eliz.* 10; his injunction for the use of the Primer, *ib.* 11; his privilege annexed to the same, *ib.* 113 n.; his commission to Parker, Redman, and May, to inquire into the possessions of the university of Cambridge, *Park.* 34 n.; minute of the king's letter to be sent to Cranmer, for the abolition of vigils, &c., 2 *Cran.* 414; he delays his reforms to propitiate the emperor and French king, *ib.* 415 n.; would not have

left a mass in all England if he had lived a little longer, *ib.* 416 n.; his death, 3 *Zur.* 257 n.; his executors, *ib.* 257; his praises, 1 *Bec.* 222, 240, 244, 2 *Cran.* 418, *Phil.* 322; the charges which he sustained, 1 *Bec.* 221; he fortressed England, *ib.* 245; renounced and banished the jurisdiction of the bishop of Rome, *Rog.* 347; his letter abolishing the pope's authority, 2 *Cran.* 369 n.; the reformation brought to pass by him, 1 *Bec.* 181, 193, 1 *Hoop.* 201, 438, 2 *Zur.* 158; he purged the church of many abuses, 3 *Bec.* 227; shook off monkish superstitions, 2 *Cran.* 418; in his time the pope was away, but not all Popery, 1 *Brad.* 527, 3 *Zur.* 36; his diligence in reclaiming the people from superstition, *Park.* 11; he allowed all licensed by the universities to preach without control of any, 2 *Lat.* 329; his conduct with respect to religion, abbey-lands, &c., 2 *Cran.* 16; his sacrilege, 3 *Whitg.* xv; letters to him, 2 *Cran.* 231, 232, 237, 238, 241, 242, 2 *Lat.* 297, 3 *Zur.* 554

Henry II., king of France: his proposed marriage (when Dauphin) with the princess Mary, 2 *Tyn.* 319; his marriage (before he became king) with Cath. de Medici, 2 *Cran.* 246 n.; Bullinger dedicates a book to him, 4 *Bul.* xxi; he protests against the council of Trent, 4 *Jew.* 905, 3 *Zur.* 497 n.; burns five persons for religion, 3 *Zur.* 655; at war with England, *ib.* 656, and with Charles V., 1 *Lat.* 390; he makes peace with England, 2 *Zur.* 19; mortally wounded in a tournament, on the day he intended to burn certain men for religion, *Pil.* 654, 2 *Zur.* 24

Henry III., king of France: when duke of Anjou he besieged Rochelle, *ib.* 223 n., and was elected king of Poland, *ib.* 223 n., 247 n., 250 n.; succeeding to the throne of France, he was deprived of that of Poland, *ib.* 273 n.; anecdote of him, *ib.* 247 n

Henry IV., king of France: queen Elizabeth assists him with men and money, *Lit. Eliz.* 470, 471; prayers for his success in war, *ib.* 647, 652

Henry, titular king of Scots (Hen. Stuart, lord Darnley, duke of Albany): mentioned as likely to succeed to the crown of England, 4 *Jew.* 1246, 1 *Zur.* 102; a mourner at the funeral of the emperor Ferdinand, at St Paul's, *Grin.* 32; he marries the queen of Scots, 1 *Zur.* 144; returns to the mass, *ib.* 149, 150; his part in the murder of Rizzio, *ib.* 166 n.; murdered by gunpowder, 3 *Jew.* 173, 1 *Zur.* 186, 192, 196, 197 n., 198, 2 *Zur.* 200

Henry, prince of Wales, son of James I.: 2 *Zur.* 331, 334

Henry, prince of Condé: 2 *Zur.* 281 n., 282

Hentenius (Jo.): Enarrationes vetust. Theologorum, 2 *Ful.* 88 n.; his edition of the Vulgate (Ant. 1567), 1 *Ful.* 74, 533

Hepburn (Adam), alias Bothwell, bp of Orkney: marries the queen to lord Bothwell, for which he is deposed, 1 *Zur.* 192; mentioned, *ib.* 195 n

Hepburn (James), earl of Bothwell, afterwards duke of Orkney, 3rd husband of Mary queen of Scots: mentioned, 1 *Zur.* 166 n.; suspected of the murder of lord Darnley, 3 *Jew.* 173, 1 *Zur.* 192, 197, 198; he divorces his wife (Jean Gordon), is made duke of Orkney, and marries the queen of Scots, *ib.* 192, 193; his flight from Scotland, *ib.* 195, 2 *Zur.* 168; prisoner in Denmark, 1 *Zur.* 197 n., where he dies miserably, *ib.* 195 n

Hepburn (Jo.), of Bantoun: 1 *Zur.* 195 n

Hepburn (Jo.), minister of Brechin: 2 *Zur.* 365

Heracleon, a heretic: used Hebrew words in his prayers, 1 *Jew.* 316

Heracleonites: denied baptism to infants, *Rog.* 280; used extreme unction, and other superstitious rites, *Phil.* 424

Heraclides, bp of Ephesus: 1 *Whitg.* 464

Herbert (Will.), 1st earl of Pembroke: privy councillor to Mary and Elizabeth, 1 *Zur.* 5 n.; signature as such, *Park.* 46, 103, 156; a commissioner, *Jew.* xv, 1 *Zur.* 39 n.; he recommends Dr Ellis for bishop of Bangor, *Park.* 258; claims an advowson, *ib.* 266

Herbert (Hen.), 2nd earl of Pembroke: mourner (as lord Herbert) at the funeral of the emperor Ferdinand, *Grin.* 32; present (as earl) at the duke of Norfolk's trial, 1 *Zur.* 267 n

— He married, when lord Herbert, the lady Cath. Grey, from whom he was divorced, 1 *Zur.* 103 n., 3 *Zur.* 304 n

— Mary, his 3rd wife, sister of Sir Ph. Sidney: notice of her, *Poet.* xvi; twenty-seven Psalms in metre by her and her brother, *ib.* 53, &c.; notice of The countesse of Pembroke's Yuychurch, and her Emanuel, both by Abr. Fraunce, *ib.* xxii.

Herbert (Phil.), 4th earl of Pembroke.

— Anne (Clifford) his wife: Sam. Daniel her tutor, *Poet.* xxxvii.

Herbert (Edw. lord), of Cherbury: his Life of Henry VIII., 1 *Lat.* 395 n., 402 n., 2 *Lat.* 367 n

Herbert (Will.): *v.* Ames (J.).

Herbst (Jo.): *v.* Oporinus.

Hercules: a romance so called, 1 *Tyn.* 161
Herd (Mr): preserves some writings of Cranmer, *Park.* 187; minute of a letter to him, from or by order of queen Elizabeth, respecting the said writings, 2 *Cran.* 459
Herebald, abbot of Wye: account of his baptism, 2 *Ful.* 14
Hereford: *v.* Missale.
  The bishop's first-fruits to the pope, 4 *Jew.* 1079; Cranmer's injunctions to the clergy of the diocese, sede vacante (1538), 2 *Cran.* 81; reference to them, 2 *Lat.* 242 n.; proposed visitation of the cathedral, *Park.* 165
Hereford (Nich.): *v.* Herford.
Hereford (Walter visc.): *v.* Devereux.
Heremites: *v.* Hermits.
Heresy: *v.* Doctrine, Error, Heretics, Sects; also Augustine, xxvii, and other fathers.
  Αἵρεσις deducitur ἀπὸ τοῦ αἱροῦμαι, 2 *Cov.* 411; the word used by Cicero for a sect of philosophers, 3 *Jew.* 214; the term applied to the first Christians, *ib.*; various definitions of it, *Bale* 217, 218, 3 *Jew.* 210, 211; translations respecting it examined, 1 *Ful.* 111; it is not mere error, 2 *Whitg.* 539; Tertullian's rule against it, 2 *Jew.* 1000; Hilary shews how we are to know it, *ib.* 998; Romanists affirm that certain doctrines are now matters of faith which were not always so; consequently, that some opinions are now heretical which were not so formerly, *Whita.* 281; heresy alleged to be a means of the preservation of tradition, *ib.* 657, 667; Christian truth and knowledge of God's word so called by Romish prelates, 2 *Cov.* 330, *Phil.* 124, 1 *Tyn.* 243; heresies and sects are many, 2 *Bec.* 525, 526, *Rid.* 367, *Rog.* passim; eighty reckoned up by Epiphanius, and (at least) eighty-eight by Augustine, 1 *Jew.* 334, 2 *Jew.* 687 n., 3 *Jew.* 603; various heresies described or referred to, 1 *Bec.* 278, 320, 412, 418, 2 *Ful.* 375; early ones, *Bale* 314, 316: some in the apostles' time, 2 *Whitg.* 183; John wrote against them, 1 *Tyn.* 530; divers agreeing with the Papists, 2 *Ful.* 390; the old heretics compared with the Papistry, *Phil.* 417, &c.; many sectaries crept in in king Edward's time, *Hutch.* 214, *Phil.* 304, &c., 3 *Zur.* 66; heresies in the days of queen Elizabeth, *Park.* 61, 474; the dangers of the time in regard of false doctrine, *Nord.* 107, even in the church of England, *ib.* 109; heresies are permitted that the elect may be tried, *Phil.* 305; they were foretold and denounced by the apostles, *ib.* 309; the real causes of heresy, 1 *Jew.* 334, 3 *Jew.* 603; it is spread abroad by Satan, 1 *Lat.* 151, 234; it comes of pride, 2 *Tyn.* 140; it is founded on the misinterpretation of scripture, 2 *Jew.* 1110, *Whita.* 229; there have never been any heresies so gross, but they were able to make some shew of God's word, 2 *Jew.* 563; heresy comes not of the scripture, but of the blindness of those who understand it not, 2 *Tyn.* 141, &c.; there is no other heresy save man's foolish wisdom, 1 *Tyn.* 160; some ascribe it to prayer in the vulgar tongue, 1 *Jew.* 334; it should be suppressed, *Now.* 226, and punished, 2 *Hoop.* 87; teachers of heresy are soul-murderers, *Sand.* 246; it separates from God, *Pil.* 642; entails everlasting destruction, *Whita.* 15; list of inquisitors of alleged heresy appointed in the time of Henry V., *Bale* 16; examinations of persons charged with heresy, *ib.* 43 n

Heretics: *v.* Burning, Magistrates.
  Who is a heretic, 3 *Bec.* 603, 4 *Bul.* 63, *Pil.* 619, 620; the character described in scripture, 2 *Cov.* 400—402; the term defined by Augustine, 1 *Brad.* 539, *Rid.* 155; Jerome's definition, 2 *Cov.* 334; Ruffinus says the man is not a Christian who would abide to be called a heretic, 2 *Jew.* 1029; heretics are the apes of catholics, *Whita.* 667; they have apparelled themselves with the name of the church, 3 *Jew.* 150, &c.; a speech touching them, *Poet.* 276; philosophers their patriarchs, 2 *Bul.* 407, 3 *Bul.* 124; they are not generally unlearned, *Pil.* 120; a learned heretic refuted by an unlearned man, *ib.* 267; their abuse of scripture (*q. v.*), 1 *Ful.* 7, &c.; they pretend to have God's word with them, 2 *Cran.* 217, 3 *Jew.* 240, 242; their errors ascribed by Stapleton to a most diligent collation of scripture, *Whita.* 480; they clout up (i. e. join) the scriptures without understanding, *Phil.* 308; they cannot defend their opinions thereby, *Whita.* 475; some have denied the scripture, *ib.* 298; they are grieved with the glory of the gospel, 1 *Jew.* 84; they do not reject traditions, *Whita.* 610; some falsely alleged the fathers for themselves, 1 *Jew.* 22, 83; their argument from the mysteries of religion, *Whita.* 614; they held conventicles, *Sand.* 191; were the first authors of half-communion, 1 *Jew.* 258; prepared the way for Mahomet, *Bale* 572; they slander the gospel on account of divisions, 1 *Jew.* 532; the devil builds his chapel in them, 3 *Bec.* 401; they are to be avoided, *Whita.* 16, 17; to be answered by the word

of God, *Phil.* 141; public disputations with them recommended, *Hutch.* 201, 202; the consent of the whole church a powerful argument against them, *Whita.* 313, 316, 317; how they were judged in the primitive church, *Phil.* 50, *Rid.* 61; whether it be lawful to kill them, 2 *Bec.* 312, &c., *Rog.* 350; the course which must first be taken, 2 *Bec.* 313; they are unworthy to live, *Sand.* 40; they cannot be martyrs, *ib.* 378; one heretic (says Bonner) may be witness against another, *Phil.* 84; the power to put heretics to death disclaimed by the church of Rome, *Phil.* 123, *Rid.* 267, (see 272); alleged heretics delivered over to the temporal power, 2 *Tyn.* 45; prayer used by Stokesley and Bonner at the condemnation of persons charged with heresy, *Phil.* 148; burial refused to such, *Bale* 394; we must not break faith with heretics, 1 *Tyn.* 206, 2 *Zur.* 173; "no promise to be kept with heretics" is the posy (or motto) of Papists, *Sand.* 98; sir T. More's opinion on this point, 1 *Tyn.* 3; heretics lose not their baptism, 3 *Whitg.* 141; those baptized by them are not to be baptized again, 4 *Bul.* 22, (*v.* Baptism, vi.)

Herford (Nich.), or Hereford: a follower of Wickliffe, *Bale* 43 n., 81, but an apostate, *b.* 123, 125

Herforde (Jo.), printer: 1 *Hoop.* 99

Hering (Jo.), proctor: 2 *Cran.* 491

Heriot (Adam), minister of Aberdeen: 2 *Zur.* 364 n., 365

Herkinalson: hermaphrodite, 4 *Jew.* 656

Herle (......): reveals a plot, 2 *Zur.* 198 n

Herle (Tho.): chaplain to the queen, and warden of Manchester; suggested for bishop of Bangor, *Park.* 259; he desires to surrender the college, *ib.* 365

Herlinus (......): 3 *Zur.* 509 n

Herman: i. e. H. Folkerzheimer, *q. v.*

Herman (St): his bones burned by Boniface VIII., *Bale* 394

Herman, abp of Cologne: *v.* Wied (H. de).

Herman (Rog.): 2 *Cran.* 261

Herman (Wolf.): says the scriptures, apart from the testimony of the church, are of no more avail than Æsop's fables, *Rog.* 197 n., *Whita.* 276

Hermannus: author of the sect called Fratricelli, *Pil.* 18

Hermannus Contractus: *Jew.* xxxviii, 1 *Jew.* 105, 4 *Jew.* 648

Hermannus Gigas: Flores Temporum, *Jew.* xxxviii; cited on the cross seen by Constantine, *Calf.* 110 n.; he says pope Liberius communicated with heretics, 4 *Jew.* 929

Hermas: his Pastor, 2 *Hoop.* 233 n., *Pil.* 601 n., *Whita.* 109; cited by Irenæus, *Whita.* 68; publicly read in the church of old, *Rog.* 325; accounted by Stapleton as deuterocanonical, *Whita.* 305; he says it might be made canonical, *ib.* 109, 330; Hermas places belief that there is one God before all things, 3 *Jew.* 256; prescribes that in fasting, an account of the food commonly eaten should be had, and so much given to the poor, 2 *Bec.* 545, 546; said to have deceived pope Pius I., and to have induced him to alter the keeping of Easter-day, 2 *Hoop.* 233

Hermes Trismegistus: believed in one God, *Hutch.* 176

Hermians: *v.* Seleucians.

Hermias: his error, 2 *Cov.* 160 n., 1 *Hoop.* 160

Hermits, or Eremites: their life censured, 1 *Bul.* 280; those of old unlike Popish ones, 2 *Ful.* 239; they were learned in the scriptures, 3 *Jew.* 435; Basil mentions their receiving the sacrament by themselves, 1 *Jew.* 152, 154; history of one, 3 *Bec.* 103, 104

Hermogeneans: no such sect, *Rog.* 45 n

Hermogenes: his fable of the ape, 2 *Hoop.* 86

Hermogenes: a heretic, 2 *Cov.* 160 n.; refuted by Tertullian, *Whita.* 689; he held the eternity of matter, *Rog.* 45 n.; ascribed original sin to God, *ib.* 99; sanctioned polygamy, *ib.* 307

Herne, co. Kent: Ridley's benefice, *Rid.* 407

Herod the Great: burned the sacred records of the Jews to conceal the baseness of his stock, 4 *Jew.* 761, *Sand.* 16; troubled at Christ's birth, 2 *Lat.* 130, 131, 152, *Pil.* 140, 335, 359, 423; his favourers, 1 *Lat.* 289; his death, 1 *Bul.* 318, 2 *Bul.* 79

Herod Antipas: troubled at the gospel preached by John, *Pil.* 141; his agreement with Pilate, *ib.* 410, 551; the similitude of Herod and Pilate used by Jerome, 2 *Ful.* 77 n.; he sought to place images in the Temple, *Park.* 82

Herod Agrippa: in killing James he despised justification by faith, *Rog.* 113; his miserable death, 1 *Bul.* 318, 2 *Bul.* 79, 3 *Bul.* 342, 4 *Bul.* 126, *Grin.* 8, 4 *Jew.* 1126

Herodian: pronounces civil sedition worse than war, 2 *Jew.* 1028

Herodotus: cited, 1 *Hoop.* 320, 417, 4 *Jew.* 845, *Pil.* 424

Heroldt (Jo.), called Discipulus: his sermons, 4 *Bul.* 557, *Calf.* 75 n.; his Promptuarium Exemplorum, 1 *Lat.* 497; he quotes a doctor who declares that the priest is higher than kings, happier than angels, the creator of his Creator, 2 *Jew.* 773; relates marvels concerning holy water, 1 *Lat* 497 n; referred to on the sign of the cross, *Calf.* 75 n

Heron (Sir Geo.): slain, *Grin.* 355 n

Hertford: letter therefrom by prince Edward, 2 *Cran.* 413

Hertford (Edw. earl of): *v.* Seymour.

Hertfordshire: Cranmer's letter to certain gentlemen of Hertfordshire, 2 *Cran.* 267

Heruli (The): 2 *Bul.* 109

Hervæus Natalis: *v.* John of Paris.
De Potestate Eccles. et Papal., *Jew.* xxxviii; probably the author of commentaries ascribed to Anselm, 2 *Cran.* 207 n.; he says that while Christ was on earth, Peter had not the pope's authority, 3 *Jew.* 287; maintains that all power is subject to that of the pope, *Rog.* 191, 192 n.; declares that he is virtually the whole church, 3 *Jew.* 234, 4 *Jew.* 729, 863, 921; maintains that he has authority so to expound the scriptures, that it may not be lawful for any man to hold or to think the contrary, 3 *Jew.* 599, *Rog.* 191; says Christ or the pope only is lord of the common state (i. e. the church), 4 *Jew.* 918

Hervetus (Gent.): notice of him, *Sand.* 249 n.; his description of the sacramental bread, 2 *Jew.* 588; he says that in a Greek church there is but one altar, *ib.* 636; his version of Clement Alex., *Calf.* 370 n

Heshusius (Tilemanus): styled by Parkhurst Hellhusius, 1 *Zur.* 109 n.; notice of him and his works, *ib.*; his Sexcenti Errores, *Calf.* 19 n.; said to have rejected the Apocalypse, *Rog.* 84; he maintains that infants believe, *ib.* 281 n.; his controversy with Zanchius, 2 *Zur.* 111

Hesiod: cited, 1 *Bec.* 369, 2 *Bul.* 28, 3 *Bul.* 356, 1 *Ful.* 142

Heskins (Tho.): notice of him, 1 *Ful.* 4 n.; a pillar of the Popish synagogue, 1 *Ful.* viii; he opposes Jewel [by a sermon called The Parliament of Christ], *Jew.* xx; his Parliament repealed by Fulke, 2 *Ful.* 3, 81, &c.

Hesperius: evil spirits ejected from his house, 2 *Ful.* 86

Hesse (Landgraves of): *v.* Christina, Philip, William.
The Hesse family at Marpurg, 3 *Zur.* 719

Hester (Andr.): publishes Coverdale's Bible, Lond., 1550, 2 *Cov.* xiii.

Hesterbergh (Pet.): 3 *Zur.* 617

Hesychius, or Isychius: In Leviticum libri vii, *Jew.* xxviii; he says that we should search no further than the gospel, 2 *Cran.* 24; calls the incarnation of Christ a sacrifice, 1 *Jew.* 521; asserts that he offered up himself in his last supper, 1 *Jew.* 521, 2 *Jew.* 717; says that he brought his blood into heaven, 2 *Jew.* 719; designates the mysteries of Christ the holiest of holy things, 1 *Jew.* 521; terms the sacrament of the Lord's supper the Lord's mystery, 3 *Bec.* 388; refers to it as eaten in memory of Christ's passion, 3 *Jew.* 493; explains the command (Lev. viii. 31) that bread is to be eaten with flesh, 3 *Bec.* 426, 3 *Jew.* 514, *Phil.* 183, *Rid.* 174; testifies that in his time the bread remaining of the sacrament was burned, 2 *Bec.* 252, 3 *Bec.* 373, *Coop.* 150, 1 *Cran.* 59, 60, 2 *Jew.* 554, 773, *Grin.* 60 n.; speaks of the grace of God as given only of mercy and compassion, and embraced only by faith, not by works, 2 *Cran.* 210, 3 *Jew.* 244, 559; says that not one sin only, but many, are forgiven us through the sacrifice of Christ, 1 *Bec.* 336, 337, 3 *Bec.* 421; teaches that where pride and hypocrisy reign, humility has no place, 3 *Jew.* 311; declares that in the world to come there is no working, 2 *Bec.* 395, 3 *Bec.* 460; sometimes strains the scriptures, 2 *Jew.* 718

Heth (Jo.): married a niece of Parker, *Park.* xiii.

Hethe (H. de): *v.* Hythe.

Heton (Tho.): *v.* Eaton.

Hewald the Black: and

Hewald the White: martyrs, *Bale* 191

Hewet (Andrew): burned for denying the corporal presence, 2 *Cran.* 246

Hewet (Tho.): proposed for the see of Bangor, *Park.* 257, 261

Hewicke (D.): *v.* Huick (Tho.).

Hewis (Dr): counsel in the matter of the king's divorce, 2 *Cran.* 244, [probably Jo. Hughes].

Hexham, co. Northumberland: 2 *Ful.* 11; the rebels there, 1569, 1 *Zur.* 214 n., 247 n

Hextall (Marg.): married Will. Whetenhall, 1 *Bec.* 191 n

Hey nony nony, &c.: 2 *Cov.* 537

Heyden (Jo.): says the Ossenes compelled people to marry against their will, *Rog.* 306 n

Heydon (Chr. ?): his son and heir, *Park.* 417

Heydon (Will.): made a great stir about the suppression of prophesyings, *Park.* 459

Heylin (Pet.): Hist. of the Reformation, *Calf.* 418

Heynes (Simon): *v.* Haynes.

Heywarde (Tho.): martyred, *Poet.* 164

Hezekiah, king of Judah: his reign and acts, 2 *Bul.* 9; he despised not faithful admonishers, *ib.* 15; his reformation, 1 *Bul.* 325, 4 *Bul.* 481, 1 *Lat.* 76; he broke the brazen serpent, *Park.* 89, 3 *Tyn.* 183; cleansed the Temple, 4 *Jew.* 988; kept the passover, 4 *Bul.* 407, 475; commanded priests and Levites, 1 *Bul.* 330; was careful for their stipends, *ib.* 335; not a church-robber, 2 *Bul.* 45; a valiant captain, 1 *Bul.* 384; prevalence of his prayer, 2 *Bul.* 95, 4 *Bul.* 168, 170, 225, 2 *Cov.* 380, 2 *Hoop.* 164; why he alleged his righteousness, 4 *Bul.* 175; his days were lengthened, but not contrary to God's foreknowledge and determination, *Pil.* 675; he was rebuked by Isaiah, *ib.* 113; commendation of him, *ib.* 360

Hickes (Geo.): Jorian, *Calf.* 87 n

Hickscorner: 3 *Bec.* 281, 361; his logic, 3 *Jew.* 529, 626; the word used in the plural for scoffers, *Pil.* 357

Hidden: the godly so called in scripture, 2 *Hoop.* 307

Hide (Annis or Margaret): martyred in Smithfield, *Poet.* 169

Hide (Tho.), schoolmaster of Winchester: *Calf.* 276

Hieracites: said none were saved who died before they came to years of discretion, *Rog.* 137, 154, and that none should be saved in the body, *ib.* 145; condemned marriage, *ib.* 261, 306

Hierarchas: founder of a sect, 3 *Bec.* 401

Hierarchics: heretics, 2 *Cov.* 184

Hierax: said Melchisedec was the Holy Ghost, *Rog.* 71; his Ascensorium Esaiæ, *ib.* 82

Hiero I., king of Syracuse: *Hutch.* 12

Hierocles: commends marriage, 1 *Bul.* 396, 399, 408; says it must be contracted with prudence, *ib.* 403, 404; enjoins the honouring of parents, *ib.* 203; calls our country a second God, our first and chiefest parent, *ib.* 278

Hieroglyphics: 2 *Jew.* 648

Hierome (Will.): v. Jerome.

Hieromonachus (M.): *v.* Matthæus.

Hieronymus: *v.* Jerome.

Hieronymus (......), preacher in the Italian church in London: his dispute with Corranus, *Grin.* 309 n., 312

Hieronymus Cathalanus: says that Constantine's Donation is utterly false, 4 *Jew.* 678

Higden (Ranulph): Polychronicon, *Jew.* xxxviii; stolen from Roger of Chester, *Calf.* 296 n., *Pil.* 597 n.; translated by Jo. de Trevisa, and continued by Will. Caxton, *Pil.* 598 n.; the work mentions the first institution of litanies, *Calf.* 296; ascribes the institution of extreme unction to pope Felix III, or IV, *Pil.* 527; narrates that England was once under flamines and heathen priests, *ib.* 597; speaks of an ordinance of Lucius on meats, *ib.* 514; mentions disputes in Britain respecting Easter, *ib.* 512; says Gregory I. ordained fasting every day in Lent, *ib.* 561; relates the conduct of Augustine in England, *ib.* 516; speaks of certain questions submitted by him to Gregory, *ib.* 517; mentions his baptizing ten thousand people in the Swale, 4 *Jew.* 780; declares that Northumberland was many years without a bishop or altar, *Pil.* 583; makes mention of several early English versions of the scriptures, 2 *Jew.* 694; relates stories of St Edmund, *Pil.* 588, and other English saints, *ib.* 590, &c.; speaks of the ejection of married clerks before the conquest, *ib.* 575; tells of the misdeeds of John the pope's legate, sent to enforce clerical celibacy, *ib.* 572; states the origin of Salisbury use, *ib.* 535; says pope Honorius sent the pall to Honorius * abp of Canterbury, *ib.* 585; notices that Celestine crowned the emperor Henry VI. with his foot, and kicked the crown off again, 4 *Jew.* 697; records great and destructive fires and whirlwinds in London and elsewhere, *Pil.* 607; describes the Cistercian order, *ib.* 509; charges abbeys with gluttony and outrage, *ib.* 610; describes a dearth in Henry VI's days, *ib.* 611

Higham (Sir Clement): one of queen Mary's privy council, 1 *Zur.* 5 n

Highgate, co. Middlesex: Sandys a benefactor to the free-school, *Sand.* xxvi.

High-places: what it is to sacrifice in them, 2 *Bul.* 264; the sin of doing so, *ib.* 151

Highways: the making of them commended, 1 *Lat.* 23; repaired out of church-revenues, 2 *Cran.* 160, 398

Higinus, bp of Rome: said to have brought in sponsors, 2 *Bec.* 210, *Calf.* 212, 3 *Whitg.* 109, 120, 473; he (or Pelagius) ordered that no metropolitan should condemn a bishop unheard, 2 *Whitg.* 369

Hilaria (St), virgin: 1 *Jew.* 162

Hilarion, a hermit: 3 *Jew.* 435

Hilary (St), bp of Poictiers.

i. *His Life and Works:* he was bishop of Poictiers, 3 *Jew.* 390, *Rog.* 329; he was married, 2 *Jew.* 1128, *Pil.* 570; he writes to his daughter Abra, 2 *Jew.* 728, 3 *Jew.* 390; his works, *Calf.* 410, 2 *Ful.* 403, *Jew.* xxxviii; he wrote to the bishops of Britain, 3 *Jew.* 165; made hymns, 1 *Jew.* 265; said to have composed the Gloria in

---

* The date 1127 is an error; archbishop Honorius ruled from 634 to 653.

excelsis, 2 *Brad.* 307; a commentary ascribed to him, 1 *Bec.* 337 n.; Cranmer accused of falsifying him, 1 *Cran.* 413, 1 *Jew.* 53

ii. *God, Scripture, Doctrine:* he declares that it is not less (sinful) to make God than to deny him, 3 *Jew.* 122; shews that God is nigh unto those who are of a contrite heart, but far from the proud, 1 *Hoop.* 235; concludes, against Arius, that Christ is one with the Father, not in purpose and will only, but also in very nature, 1 *Cran.* 161; says that unless God had taken man, he could never have been known to man, 1 *Jew.* 530, 3 *Jew.* 537; seems to speak erroneously respecting the nature of Christ's body, 1 *Jew.* 481, 497, 3 *Jew.* 623; writes on our union with God the Father and the Son, 1 *Jew.* 476; speaks of Christ dwelling naturally in us, and says we are naturally in Christ, *ib.* 470, 476; in matters touching God would have reference only to the word of God, 4 *Jew.* 1019; dwells on the authority of scripture, 2 *Jew.* 1058; refers the emperor Constantius to the books of God, 3 *Jew.* 234; intimates that we should not put a meaning upon scripture, but receive it from scripture, *Whita.* 461; says that scripture should be interpreted by scripture, *Phil.* 377; admonishes that in discovering the meaning of scripture we must regard the context, *Whita.* 492; calls it the order of the apostles' doctrine to preach God out of the law and the prophets, 3 *Jew.* 238; says the words of God are the things which they utter, 1 *Jew.* 547; declares that all God's words are true and wonderfully fiery, &c., *Rid.* 227; reckons the Old Testament as consisting of two and twenty books, *Whita.* 58; compares the book of Psalms to a promiscuous heap of keys, 1 *Jew.* 330; mistakes the meaning of the words "Bereschith" and "hosanna," 2 *Jew.* 678; speaking of Christ's saying that his Father would, if he asked, give him twelve legions of angels, he says, twelve thousand legions, 4 *Jew.* 195; admits the use of words not found in scripture, *Whita.* 603; says heresy comes from the understanding, not from the scripture, 2 *Jew.* 681, 3 *Jew.* 241; states that we must yield an account, not of God's words, but of our own expositions, 3 *Jew.* 242; intimates that if things written be denied, things not written must be allowed, 3 *Jew.* 480, 4 *Jew.* 775; declares that the tradition of men, for which they have broken the precepts of the law, shall be uprooted, 3 *Jew.* 180; speaking of some matter he says, the archangels know it not, the angels have not heard it, the prophet has not felt it, the Son himself has not uttered it, 2 *Jew.* 695; says, the truth admits no lie, neither can religion abide impiety, *Rog.* 362; confesses original sin, 2 *Bul.* 390; affirms that repentance is ceasing from sin, 1 *Ful.* 437; his rule of faith, 2 *Jew.* 998; he shews that forced faith is no faith, *ib.* 810; says there are many who feigning faith, are not subject to faith, &c., *Calf.* 249; speaks of faith alone justifying, 2 *Bec.* 639, 2 *Cran.* 130; says our eternal life is easy and ready,—to believe that Jesus Christ is raised from the dead, 3 *Jew.* 256; complains, if we fast once, we think we have satisfied; if out of the barns of our household, we give somewhat to the poor, we believe we have fulfilled the measure of righteousness, *ib.* 583; calls falling grievous and dangerous in many, 1 *Jew.* 523, 524; does not mention purgatory, 2 *Lat.* 247

iii. *The Church, &c.:* he declares that what is set up by man's workmanship will not endure, but that the church is otherwise built, 2 *Jew.* 1023, 4 *Jew.* 1058; says it is grounded upon the foundation of the prophets and apostles, 4 *Jew.* 1058; writing of Christ's sleep in the ship he says, churches in which God's word does not keep watch suffer wreck, 1 *Jew.* 318, 2 *Jew.* 994, 1081, 4 *Jew.* 747; remarks that many barbarous nations have attained the true knowledge of God, 2 *Jew.* 673; says the spoils of the heathen, taken from the devil, are divided to the furniture and the ornament of the church of God, 3 *Jew.* 616, 2 *Whitg.* 37; praises peace and unity, but warns against false peace, 4 *Jew.* 1085, 1 *Lat.* 487, *Rid.* 120, *Sand.* 94; speaks of Peter as the porter of heaven, whose earthly judgment is a fore-judged authority in heaven, &c., 3 *Jew.* 367; says Peter lieth under the building of the church, 2 *Ful.* 283; addresses that apostle as the foundation of the church, happy in having the new name pronounced, &c., *ib.*; says, Peter, by confession of his blessed faith, deserved an exceeding glory, *ib.* 289, 290, 291, 1 *Jew.* 367; holds that the rock is the faith confessed by Peter's mouth, 2 *Ful.* 284, 297, 1 *Jew.* 340, 4 *Jew.* 1118; writes, this faith is the foundation of the church, 4 *Jew.* 1119; says, on this rock of confession is the building of the church, 2 *Ful.* 284, 297, 1 *Jew.* 340, 368; speaks of the apostles as holy and blessed men who for the worthiness of their faith obtained the keys, &c., 2 *Ful.* 290; his testimony as to Peter and the rock of the church dreaded by Romanists, *ib.* 289 n.; in his legend it is said that pope Leo was an Arian heretic, 4 *Jew.* 926; he says the ears of the people are more holy than the hearts of the priests, 2 *Jew.* 777, 1044; censures monks, 4 *Jew.* 798, 799

iv. *Sacraments, Worship*: he speaks of the sacrament of prayer, of fasting, of thirst, of weeping, of the scriptures, 1 *Jew.* 225, 2 *Jew.* 1103, 1104, 3 *Jew.* 458; says of the fathers of old they were under the cloud, and were drenched with Christ, the rock giving them water, *ib.* 447; writes of union with Christ by baptism, 1 *Jew.* 478, 519, 2 *Jew.* 565; judges that Judas was not present at the supper, 3 *Bec.* 382, 4 *Bul.* 464, 3 *Jew.* 532; warns against separation from the medicine of the body and blood of the Lord, 3 *Bec.* 414, 473; explains how there is a figure and a truth in the sacrament, 2 *Bec.* 286, 3 *Bec.* 424, 437, 1 *Cran.* 247, 272, (31); calls it the Lord's meat, 3 *Bec.* 388; says, in our Lord's meat we receive the Word made flesh, 1 *Cran.* 160, 1 *Jew.* 520; asserts that we receive Christ verily under a mystery, 1 *Jew.* 475, 2 *Lat.* 267; writes on our union with Christ by the Lord's supper, 1 *Brad.* 97, 1 *Cran.* 160, (68), *Rid.* 201; speaks of the receiving of the body and blood of Christ as causing us to be in Christ, and Christ in us, 2 *Bec.* 293, 294, 3 *Bec.* 464, *Coop.* 141; says the bread that came down from heaven is received only of the members of Christ, 2 *Jew.* 786, 1121; speaks of drinking of the fruit of the vine, 3 *Jew.* 522; says that one standing without, might hear the voice of the people praying and singing in the church, *Calf.* 294

v. *Heretics, Antichrist*: he distinguishes between simple error and wilful opposition to the truth, 3 *Jew.* 211; declares that heresy is from the understanding, not from the scripture, 2 *Jew.* 681, 3 *Jew.* 241; notes that all heretics profess to follow scripture, *Whita.* 229; states that in his time there were as many faiths as wills, &c., 3 *Jew.* 253; speaks of some who often change their faith, 2 *Lat.* 277; says heretics live by dry bread, 3 *Jew.* 528; writes against the Arians, 1 *Cran.* 161, 1 *Jew.* 127, 3 *Jew.* 450; declares that they know not God, yet wishes that it were so, 3 *Jew.* 203; requires them to produce another gospel, 1 *Jew.* 27; tells that they called themselves the church of Christ, though indeed the synagogue of Antichrist, 3 *Jew.* 151; speaks of their religion as the faith of the times rather than that of the gospels, 1 *Jew.* 261, 262, 3 *Jew.* 248, 4 *Jew.* 706; he was opposed by the heretics Auxentius and Saturninus, *ib.* 1052; Auxentius alleges multitudes of bishops against him, *ib.* 1053; he challenges him to call what councils he likes against him, *ib.* 952; terms a synod held at Milan, the synagogue of the malignant, *Rog.* 210; says of some people deceived by the Arians, they believe what they believe not, &c., 3 *Jew.* 255; speaks against the errors of Tertullian, *Whita.* 599; says that he who repudiates the authority of scripture is an antichrist, *Sand.* 15; expounding Christ's words, "When ye shall see the abomination of desolation standing in the holy place," he refers them to the time of Antichrist, 4 *Jew.* 728; says Antichrist shall be contrary to Christ under the colour of preaching the gospel, &c., 2 *Jew.* 916; cautions against the veneration of walls and buildings, declaring that in them Antichrist shall sit, 1 *Brad.* 529, *Coop.* 183, 184, 2 *Jew.* 916, 1080, 4 *Jew.* 729, 730

Hilary (St), bp of Rome: on the body of Christ received from the altar, 2 *Jew.* 603

Hilary (St), bp of Arles: perhaps the composer of the Athanasian creed, 1 *Brad.* 371 n.; some ascribe to him the books De Vocatione Gentium, 2 *Ful.* 353 n

Hilary, bp of Chichester: *Pil.* 589

Hilary the Deacon: perhaps the author of commentaries on the epistles, attributed to Ambrose, *Calf.* 235 n., 2 *Ful.* 183 n

Hilary, a deacon: leader of a sect, 3 *Jew.* 321, 322

Hilasmos, (ἱλασμός): what it means, 1 *Bec.* 335; 2 *Tyn.* 153

Hilda (St): *Bale* 156, 2 *Ful.* 19, 26, *Pil.* 512 n

Hildebrand: *v.* Gregory VII.

Hildebrand (Joach.), Rituale, *Calf.* 66 n., 297 n

Hilderic: *v.* Childeric.

Hildeshen (Jo.): *Bale* 520

Hildesley (Jo.), bp: *v.* Hilsey.

Hilkiah, high priest: 2 *Bul.* 10

Hill (Adam): his controversy with Richard Humes on Christ's descent into hell, 1 *Lat.* 233 n

Hill (Albayn): letter to him, 2 *Brad.* 208

Hill (Rich.): notice of him, *Poet.* xxvi; a friendly admonition, *ib.* 305

Hill (Sir Rowland), lord mayor of London: *Rid.* 410

Hill (Mr): *Park.* 223
Hill (......): an astrologer, 1 *Ful.* v.
Hill (......), or Hills: his Quatron of Reasons of Catholic Religion (Antw. 1600), *Rog.* 106 n.; he states what he affirms to be the marks of the true church, *ib.* 176; says the catholic religion affirms that we have free-will, *ib.* 106 n., that it maintains worshipping of saints, relics, images, &c., *ib.* 224 n., that it teaches confession to a priest of all deadly sins which we can remember under pain of damnation, *ib.* 258 n.; he says that all Christian men in England were Papists till the age of Henry VIII., *ib.* 173; asserts that Protestants deny the baptism of children to be necessary, *ib.* 279
Hill (......): Olive-branch, of Peace, *Calf.* 243 n
Hilles (Barnabas), son of Richard: 1 *Zur.* 241, 270, 2 *Zur.* 180, 196
Hilles (Gershom), son of Richard: 1 *Zur.* 271, 2 *Zur.* 196, 3 *Zur.* 243
Hilles (Rich.): notice of him, 2*Cov.* 502 n.; little skilled in Latin, 3 *Zur.* 196, 197, 199; persecuted for religion, *ib.* 230—232; partner with Burcher, *ib.* 259 n.; commended by Cranmer, 2 *Cran.* 424; he frequented mass in queen Mary's time, 3 *Zur.* 345; noticed or mentioned, 2 *Cov.* 512, 1 *Zur.* 224, 308, 2 *Zur.* 17, 118, 3 *Zur.* 20, 38, 592, 594, 627, 628; his letters to Bullinger, 1 *Zur.* 171, 211, 241, 270, 2 *Zur.* 14, 82, 164, 180, 195, 3 *Zur.* 196—272; a letter to R. Gualter, 2 *Zur.* 304; his wife, 3 *Zur.* 38, 267, 269, &c., 658, 659, &c.; birth of a daughter, 3 *Zur.* 639
Hilley (Dr Rich.): 2 *Lat.* 322
Hilsey (Jo.), bp of Rochester: notices of him, 2 *Cran.* 295 n., 2 *Lat.* 369 n.; being prior of the Dominicans at Bristol, he preaches against Latimer, 2 *Lat.* 225 n.; as bishop he signs a declaration respecting a general council, 2 *Cran.* 468; exposes the rood of grace in a sermon at St Paul's, 3 *Zur.* 606, 609 n.; exhibits and denounces the blood of Hales at the same place, 2 *Lat.* 408 n.; his Primer, 2 *Lat.* 369 n., *Pra. Eliz.* 507 n., 511 n
Hiltinus, bp of Augsburgh: Udalric succeeds him, 3 *Jew.* 424
Hin: what, 2 *Bul.* 35
Hincmar, abp of Rheims: Opera, *Jew.* xxxviii; his view of a provincial council, 4 *Jew.* 1054, of the council of Frankfort, *ib.* 1055; he calls image-worship "puparum cultum," *Calf.* 175 n
Hinds: husbandmen, 2 *Bul.* 39

Hinham: a word used at the feast of asses, 1 *Tyn.* 92 n
Hinkesell (Jo.): v. Hynkesell.
Hippinus (Jo.): v. Æpinus.
Hippo: v. Councils.
    Once overrun with Donatism, but reduced to catholic unity, 1 *Bul.* 365; besieged and taken, *Pil.* 612
Hippocras: v. Ipocras.
Hippocrates: 1 *Hoop.* v, 286, 297, 2 *Hoop.* 164
Hippolytus (St): how he, when a layman, distributed the communion to his family, 1 *Jew.* 155; his caution against the heresy of Novatus, reported by Prudentius, 2 *Ful.* 346; his constancy in martyrdom, 2 *Bec.* 472; he is said to have written on the Apocalypse, *Bale* 255; the tract De consummatione Mundi attributed to him is spurious, though its authenticity is maintained by bp Bull, 2 *Ful.* 282 n.; remarks on this book, 1 *Jew.* 85, 116, 117; it speaks of bishops sacrificing Christ, *ib.* 109, 117; its statements about Antichrist, 2 *Ful.* 391, 1 *Jew.* 116, 2 *Jew.* 914, 4 *Jew.* 728
Hire: v. Wages.
Hirelings: hireling shepherds, 4 *Bul.* 162; they flee in time of pestilence, 1 *Lat.* 265
Hirter (......): 1 *Zur.* 62
His: formerly used for its, *Sand.* 285 n
Hish: to make an insulting objection, 1 *Tyn.* 432
Hiske: to open the mouth, 1 *Bec.* 294
Hispalen: Seville so called, 1 *Brad.* 508
Historia Longobardica: a work annexed to the Golden Legend, *Jew.* xxxix; it recounts five inventions of the cross, *Calf.* 321 n.; says pope Liberius so consented to the commandments of the Arian emperor, that he communicated with heretics, 4 *Jew.* 229
Historia Scholastica, q. v.
Historia Tripartita: v. Cassiodorus.
Historical sense: v. Scripture.
Histriones: v. Drama.
Hitchins (Will.), or Tyndale, q. v.
Hith (H. de): v. Hythe.
Hitton (Tho.): martyred at Maidstone, *Bale* 394, 2 *Tyn.* 340, 3 *Tyn.* 113
Ho! stop, or halt, 1 *Tyn.* 25; "no ho," no stop, bound, limit, 2 *Bul.* 126
Hoare (Sir Rich. Colt), bart.: Ancient Wilts, 2 *Lat.* 364
Hoarders of corn: cruel murderers, 1 *Bec.* 253
Hobberton (Mr): v. Hubberdine.
Hoby (Sir Phil.): mentioned, 2 *Cran.* 195 n., 521, 522; ambassador to Germany, 3 *Zur.* 57, 379 n., 645 n.; one of an embassy to

France, *ib.* 497 n.; sent to bring over king Philip, *ib.* 511

Hochin (Will.), or Tyndale, *q. v.*

Hochstraten (Jac.): says he is a heretic that cleaveth to the scriptures, *Rog.* 200

Hodgkin (Jo.), suffragan of Bedford: assists at the consecration of Scory and Coverdale, 2 *Cov.* xiii, n., at that of Parker, *ib.* xv, at that of Grindal, *Grin.* vi, n., at that of Jewel, *Jew.* xv.

Hody (Hum.): De Bibliorum Text., *Jew.* xxxviii; the work contains some letters of Rog. Bacon, 4 *Jew.* 736 n

Hoffman (Melch.): declares that the baptism of infants is of the devil, *Rog.* 280; affirms that sin after baptism is unpardonable, *ib.* 141; says that our salvation is of ourselves, *ib.* 298; wrote on the Apocalypse, *Bale* 258

Hogeson (Tho.): Cranmer's servant, 2 *Cran.* 299, Tho. H. *ib.* 300

Hohensaxe: *v.* Alt-sax.

Hokam (Gul.): *v.* Occam.

Holbech (Hen.), alias Rands, bp of Rochester, afterwards of Lincoln: notices of him, 2 *Cran.* 310 n., 3 *Zur.* 576; he succeeds More as prior of Worcester, 2 *Lat.* 371 n., 373 n.; a commissioner respecting the blood of Hales, *ib.* 407 n.; having been made suffragan of Bristol, he desires to preach before the king, *ib.* 412; commissioner in a disputation on the eucharist held at Oxford, *Phil.* 213 n., 3 *Zur.* 391 n.; his views on the eucharist, 3 *Zur.* 72, 76

Holbein (Hans): his dance of death, *Pra. Eliz.* xvii, xviii; his decease, *ib.* xix.

Holcot (Rob.): *v.* Holkot.

Holcot (Will.): present at Cranmer's disputation at Oxford, 1*Cran.* 428; he preached a funeral sermon for Jewel, *Jew.* xxv.

Holcroft (Sir Tho.), knight marshal: procured the liberation of Sandys, *Sand.* x, &c.

Holgate (Rob.), abp of York: the only rich prelate in Cranmer's time, 2 *Cran.* 437 n

Holidays: *v.* Holy days.

Holiman (Jo.), bp: *v.* Holyman.

Holiness, Sanctification: *v.* Prayers, Saints. The nature of sanctification, 1 *Hoop.* 71; the term sanctificare explained, *Now.* (103); holiness is the end of our election, *Sand.* 190; it must appear, *ib.*; it is required of those who profess the gospel, 1 *Brad.* 437, 2 *Brad.* 122: holiness of life enforced, 1 *Bec.* 342, &c.; whence perfect holiness proceeds, 4 *Bul.* 6; it is only in and from Christ, *Pil.* 164; it is through Christ's blood, 1 *Hoop.* 72; the Christian is holy, by reason of the Spirit dwelling in him, 1 *Tyn.* 340; holiness is a mark of the true church, *Poet.* 276 (see Church, I. vi. *a* and *c*); holiness and righteousness have respect to the two tables of the law, *Sand.* 190; ceremonial holiness in the law of Moses, *Pil.* 165; the vanity of Popish holiness, *ib.* 262; sanctification not by the bishop of Rome nor by holy water or the like, 1 *Hoop.* 73; in what sense the unfaithful are said to be made holy by the faithful, 2 *Bul.* 389, *Pil.* 164

Holinshed (Raphael): his Chronicle, 1 *Hoop.* 455, 1 *Lat.* xi, 81, 266, 2 *Lat.* 367, 392, 394, 408, 415, *Rog.* 49, 64, &c., 1 *Jew.* 247 nn

Holkot (Rob.): some account of him, 1 *Tyn.* 151 n.; he was a cardinal, 3 *Jew.* 132; reference to him, 2 *Lat.* 319; his works; Super Libros Sapientiæ, *Jew.* xxxviii; Super IV. Libros Sentent., *ib.*; he reproves a determination of Thomas Aquinas on worship, 2 *Jew.* 667; says, latria is due only to God, not to an image, 2 *Jew.* 667, 4 *Jew.* 950; comments on the words "This is my body," 2 *Jew.* 606, 787, 788; declares that if there had been a thousand hosts when Christ hung upon the cross, then had Christ been crucified in a thousand places, &c., 1 *Jew.* 496; doubts whether Christ in one host, can see himself in another, 2 *Jew.* 628; states that if a layman erroneously adore an unconsecrated wafer, that faith will suffice, 1 *Jew.* 13; speaks of the application of the mass, 2 *Jew.* 747; asserts that to make confession of venial sins is more of devotion than of necessity, 3 *Jew.* 372; strongly censures priests for their lechery, *ib.* 426; says, the priests of this time are like the priests of Baal, they are renegate angels, they are like the priests of Dagon, they are the priests of Priapus, they are the angels of hell, 4 *Jew.* 746; cites a remark of Bernard, about the wound of the church, *ib.* 724, 906; moves the question whether love be hatred, 3 *Jew.* 183; says the emperor is king of kings, 4 *Jew.* 1014

Holland: *v.* Netherlands.

Holland (Rog.): martyred in Smithfield, *Poet.* 172

Holland (Garland), a bookseller at Oxford: 1 *Zur.* 328

Holland (H.): Herωologia, 2 *Brad.* xii. n., xiii. n., 1 *Lat.* xiv.

Holland (Jo.): his cause in the Arches against Will. Porter, 2 *Cran.* 411

Holland (Rob.), minister of Prendergast: notice of him, *Poet.* xlvi; the Lord's prayer, in verse, *ib.* 477

Holland (Tho.), reg. prof. of divinity, Oxon: *Lit. Eliz.* 463

Hollingday (......): martyred in Smithfield Oct. 1557, *Poet.* 171

Hollowel (Will.): *v.* Holywell.

Hollyday (......): martyred in Smithfield, June 1558, *Poet.* 172

Holme, co. Lancaster: Whitaker's birthplace, *Whita.* ix.

Holmes (......): a rebel, 2 *Cran.* 187 n

Holocaust: what, 2 *Bul.* 189

Holofernes: *v.* Judith.

Holstein (Adolph duke of): *v.* Adolph.

Holstenius (Lucas): Codex Regularum, 1 *Lat.* 189 n.; he observes that the Pontifical has been wrongly ascribed to Luitprandus, 2 *Ful.* 99 n

Holt (Sir Jo.): letter to him, *Park.* 231

Holt (......), a traitorous priest: *Lit. Eliz.* 658

Holy: *v.* Holiness.

Holy ashes: *Pil.* 163, 493, 1 *Tyn.* 225; used in Lent, and what they signified, 1 *Bec.* 110; forbidden, 2 *Cran.* 417, 2 *Hoop.* 129, *Rid.* 320; demanded by the rebels of Devon, 2 *Cran.* 176

Holy bread: 1 *Lat.* 497, 2 *Lat.* 286, 294, 1 *Tyn.* 284; the conjuration of it, 1 *Hoop.* 283, 284, *Rid.* 107; what it signified, 3 *Zur.* 624; ministered every Sunday by the Papists, with holy water, instead of the sacrament, 2 *Bec.* 260; superstitiously borne about the body, 2 *Cran.* 158, 503; Latimer's verses on giving it, 2 *Lat.* xviii, 294; forbidden, 2 *Hoop.* 129, *Rid.* 320; demanded by the rebels of Devon, 2 *Cran.* 176; the holy loaf, a shadow of the ancient oblations at the eucharist, *Coop.* 89, *Lit. Edw.* 98

Holy cream: *v.* Unction.

Holy days: whether lawful, *Grin.* 215, 216; controversy respecting them, 2 *Whitg.* 565, &c.; the holy days of the Jews, 2 *Bul.* 159, &c., 2 *Whitg.* 578; the law being abrogated, the holy time is free, 2 *Bul.* 264, 265; though no holy days are now commanded, their observance is not inconsistent with Christian liberty, if they are not observed legally, 1 *Bul.* 260; with regard to them discipline with charity is constantly to be observed, 4 *Bul.* 504; Augustine on the origin of the great annual festivals, *Whita.* 606; they are commendable as free customs, but of no great moment, *ib.*; the apostles determined nothing concerning festivals, *ib.* 540, 607; their original institution and subsequent abuse, 1 *Lat.* 52, 53, 471, 1 *Tyn.* 231; solemn assemblies were ordained to the praise of God for special benefits, *Sand.* 55; their use, 1 *Tyn.* 24, 146, 226; the observance of feast-days is in itself indifferent, 1 *Hoop.* 32; feastful days appointed by magistrates are to be observed, 2 *Bec.* 83; how they should be kept, 2 *Cran.* 158; in what works they should be spent, 2 *Lat.* 39; Latimer's excuse for not attending church on holy days, *ib.* 157; of labour on them, 2 *Bec.* 83; they must not hinder work in harvest time, 2 *Cran.* 157, 468, 502; Henry VIII.'s order respecting certain feast-days, *ib.* 468; publication of it, *ib.* 348; Cranmer's mandate against observing those abrogated, *ib.* 470; abrogated holy days kept by the people and at court, *ib.* 347; the holy days of tailors, bakers, brewers, and the like, forbidden, 2 *Cran.* 158, 503, *Rid.* 532; abrogated feasts and fasts not to be observed, *Grin.* 128, 160, 2 *Lat.* 244; many saints' days restored to the calendar, temp. Eliz., *Pra. Eliz.* 4, &c., nn.; difference between Papists' holy days and ours, 2 *Whitg.* 595; holy days observed in some other reformed churches, *ib.* 583; disallowed by the church of Scotland, 2 *Zur.* 364; controversy especially concerning saints' days, 2 *Whitg.* 573; Bullinger disapproves festivals in honour of any creatures, 1 *Bul.* 260

HOLY GHOST: *v.* Prayers, Sin.

i. *His Nature and Attributes, and to what he is compared*: what he is, 3 *Bul.* 298, *Lit. Edw.* 514, (561); confession of him in the creed, 1 *Bul.* 155, 1 *Brad.* 145; what it is to believe in him, 2 *Bec.* 38; he is a distinct person or substance, not an accident or inspiration, 3 *Bul.* 305, 2 *Hoop.* 39, *Hutch.* 134, 155, &c.; very and eternal God, not a creature, 2 *Bec.* 39, 3 *Bec.* 141, 1 *Brad.* 90, 3 *Bul.* 300, &c., 1 *Cran.* 97, 102, 2 *Hoop.* 39, *Hutch.* 193, 3 *Jew.* 264, *Now.* (29), 145, *Rog.* 69; of one substance with the Father and the Son, *Hutch.* 158, *Rog.* 71; he proceeds from the Father and the Son, 3 *Bul.* 306, *Hutch.* 124, *Phil.* 378, *Rog.* 73; his proceeding, 3 *Bul.* 305; it is twofold, temporal and eternal, *ib.* 307, 308; the error of the later Greeks about the procession of the Holy Ghost, *Rog.* 74, *Whita.* 536; all the attributes of Deity are ascribed to him in scripture, *Hutch.* 193, *Rog.* 69; he is the Creator of all things, *Hutch.* 63, 137, 196; he is eternal, *ib.* 195; unsearchable, *ib.* 194; everywhere, 1 *Brad.* 90, 1 *Cran.* 97, 102, *Hutch.* 135, 194; infinite, not limited, 3 *Bul.* 309; the Spirit of life which quickeneth all other spirits, 2 *Hoop.* 40; he knows all things, *Hutch.* 198; governs all things,

HOLY GHOST

ib. 135, 197, 198; he is to be worshipped, *ib.* 205; to be prayed to, *ib.* 136, 199, 200, 204; hymns to the Holy Ghost; Veni Creator Spiritus, 1 *Cov.* 471 n.; the same in English, *Lit. Edw.* 172, 342, *Lit. Eliz.* 286; three hymns by Coverdale, 2 *Cov.* 541, 542, 543; one by F. Kinwelmersh, *Poet.* 292; the profit his Deity brings, 2 *Bec.* 40, 41; heresies respecting it, *Phil.* 302, *Rog.* 70, 71; he is called the Spirit of God, and of the Son, 3 *Bul.* 312, the Spirit of truth, *ib.* 314, the Spirit of promise, *ib.* 314, the finger of God, *ib.* 315, 2 *Hoop.* 39, *Hutch.* 20, 162, 206; he is compared to fire, 3 *Bul.* 316, 317, *Pil.* 266, 342, 2 *Whitg.* 521, to the wind, 3 *Bul.* 317; passages in which it is alleged that the word rendered "wind" signifies the Holy Spirit, 1 *Ful.* 571, &c.; he is compared to water, 3 *Bul.* 316, 2 *Whitg.* 521, to oil, 3 *Bul.* 318, 2 *Hoop.* 228; he is the only spiritual unction, *Rog.* 255, 264, the "unction from the Holy One," *Whita.* 452; why he appeared in the likeness of a dove, 3 *Bul.* 318, *Hutch.* 155, 156; not made a dove because of the words of St John, 1 *Cran.* 306; he is the "seed" spoken of in 1 Jo. iii. 9, 3 *Tyn.* 32; supposed by Theophylact to be "the porter" (Jo. x.), *Whita.* 465

ii. *The promise of the Holy Ghost, his coming, &c.*: the promise of the Holy Ghost, 1 *Cov.* 383, 388, *Pil.* 136; the sending of the Holy Ghost, 1 *Cov.* 387—420, *Lit. Edw.* 504, (553); why he came at Pentecost (*q. v.*), 1 *Cov.* 388; the manner of his coming, *ib.* 389; the hour, 4 *Bul.* 198; his mission a proof of our Saviour's ascension, 1 *Cov.* 407, and a commodity which we have thereby, 2 *Bec.* 459; the Spirit is given by God, 1 *Tyn.* 492; granted in answer to prayer, 1 *Cov.* 420; given through prayer, as well without laying on of hands as with, 1 *Tyn.* 274—275; not received by works or ceremonies, *ib.* 424; given to those who in fervent love and unity are gathered together, 1 *Cov.* 393; given not only to the learned, but to the simple and unlearned, *ib.* 398; why fleshly men receive not the Spirit, *ib.* 227

iii. *The Spirit in the church, collectively and individually*: he dwells in the church, *Nord.* 90; his power therein, 1 *Hoop.* 21; he is the guide of the church, *Rid.* 123, and ruler in the church, *Sand.* 241; spoken of as the vice-gerent of Christ, 4 *Bul.* 68, as Christ's vicar on earth, 2 *Hoop.* 39; so Philpot wrote in his Bible, *Phil.* 108, 125; by his virtue strength and operation the catholic church is preserved from all errors, 2 *Hoop.* 74; he sends true ministers, and prepares them for their work, *Sand.* 285; the Holy Ghost, speaking in the scriptures, is the judge of controversies, 2 *Ful.* 135, *Whita.* 445; he is the supreme interpreter of scripture, *Whita.* 415; said by Papists to direct all councils, *Rog.* 208; what it is to have the Holy Ghost, 3 *Bec.* 604; some have had the Holy Ghost from their birth, 3 *Tyn.* 207; when he accompanies baptism, 1 *Tyn.* 424; he dwells in all believers, *Bale* 151, 2 *Hoop.* 39, whose bodies are his temples, 3 *Bec.* 622, *Hutch.* 204, *Pil.* 48, 62 (v. Temple); proofs of his presence, *Phil.* 121, 1 *Tyn.* 76, 78, 117, 223, 262, 308, 499; the Spirit not to be quenched, 2 *Jew.* 880

iv. *His operations*: his office and work, 3 *Bec.* 141, 142, 1 *Brad.* 147, 3 *Bul.* 319, 1 *Cov.* 226, 229, 239, 240, 2 *Cran.* 90, 94, 3 *Jew.* 264, *Lit. Edw.* 504, 514, (553, 562), *Now.* (52), 170, 1 *Tyn.* 78, 79, 111, 112, 417, 487, 488, 498, 499, 2 *Tyn.* 183, 184, 201; his effect and power, 3 *Bul.* 311; he makes the word effectual to whom he will, 2 *Tyn.* 181; doth mortify and quicken, 3 *Bul.* 320; makes God's people willing, 2 *Tyn.* 250; regenerates, 2 *Hoop.* 39; works repentance, 1 *Cov.* 409; gives life, *ib.* 392; produces faith, 1 *Tyn.* 488, 493, 3 *Tyn.* 139; accompanies faith, 1 *Tyn.* 54, 111, 275; forgives sin, *Hutch.* 137, 199; restores the image of God, 1 *Cov.* 392, 393; makes a man spiritual, 1 *Tyn.* 487; sanctifies, 3 *Bul.* 312, 1 *Tyn.* 340; strives against the flesh (*q. v.*) and sin, *Phil.* 252, 1 *Tyn.* 492, 500, 503, 3 *Tyn.* 113; looses the bands of Satan, and gives power to love the law, and to do it, 3 *Tyn.* 276; writes the lively law of love upon the heart, 1 *Tyn.* 297; works obedience, 1 *Cov.* 493; causes all good works, 2 *Hoop.* 39; prepares the heart to prayer, *Pra. B.* xix; helps in prayer, *Nord.* 34; he is the teacher of the ignorant, 2 *Hoop.* 40; by his teaching men unskilled in tongues may understand the doctrine of scripture, *Whita.* 140; he is the teacher of all truth, *Pil.* 329; cannot teach things contradictory, *Phil.* 375; how he brought all things to the disciples' remembrance, *Whita.* 542; his illumination is essential to true religion, *ib.* 364; without him all reading and doctrine are in vain, 1 *Cov.* 228; we cannot judge what is truth without him, *Calf.* 60, 61, nor can we understand or do God's will, 1 *Tyn.* 78, or know the things of God, *ib.* 88; he is the supreme interpreter of scripture, *Whita.* 415; his teaching is the great evidence of scripture, *ib.* 295, the most certain argument, *ib.* 317, 318, 321, more excellent than all authority, *ib.* 345; it is the only testimony which will ever produce entire acquiescence in the great articles of our faith, *ib.* 308; his testimony is private, internal, secret, *ib.* 346; Augustine writes on the necessity of this inward teaching, *ib.* 453, 454; he teaches all the faithful, *ib.* 290, 433; but all have not the Holy Spirit in the same measure,—hence many religious differences, *ib.* 532; if men are in error, it does not follow that they are without the Spirit, *ib.* 296; he is the Paraclete, i. e. the comforter, advocate, or admonisher, 3 *Bul.* 313, *Phil.* 374 n., *Pil.* 137; he is the comforter of the poor, 2 *Hoop.* 40; a comforter in persecution, 2 *Lat.* 213; he supports against adversaries of the truth, 1 *Lat.* 268; bears witness in the hearts of the faithful, *Lit. Edw.* 511, (559); certifies the conscience of adoption, 2 *Tyn.* 211; produces joy, 2 *Jew.* 823; is the pledge and earnest of the heavenly inheritance, 3 *Bul.* 318, 1 *Cov.* 384, 388, 2 *Hoop.* 39, 1 *Tyn.* 101; how he seals, 4 *Bul.* 325; he is the Spirit of wisdom, understanding and counsel, 3 *Bul.* 319; the Spirit of strength, knowledge, and fear, *ib.* 320; he is love or charity, *ib.* 319, the fountain of unity, 1 *Cov.* 393; he reveals the mysteries of the kingdom, 3 *Bul.* 320; foreshews things to come, *ib.* 321; his divers gifts, *ib.* 321, *Lit. Edw.* 514, (562); his seven-fold gifts, *Calf.* 226; nine manifestations of the Spirit, *ib.* n.; on his extraordinary gifts in the primitive church, 1 *Jew.* 307, &c.; the gift of healing, 4 *Bul.* 231 (*v.* Miracles, Tongues); his gifts and graces given to every member of the church, 2 *Hoop.* 41 (*v.* Grace); they are to be exercised, 2 *Tyn.* 195; his increasings, 3 *Bul.* 311

Holy ground: *v.* Holy places.
Holy, holy, holy: *Hutch.* 123, *Pra. B.* 108
Holy island: *v.* Lindisfarne.
Holy land: *v.* Canaan, Jerusalem.
Holy loaf: *v.* Holy bread.
Holy oil: *v.* Unction.
Holy orders: *v.* Orders.
Holy places: *v.* Burial, Churches, Consecration, Temple.

On the holiness of places, 1 *Tyn.* 340; we acknowledge the holiness of places which God sanctified, 1 *Ful.* 371; the holy place, 2 *Bul.* 143, 4 *Bul.* 83; the holiest of all, 2 *Bul.* 144, 145, 4 *Bul.* 82; holy ground, *Pil.* 64, 316, 317, 530, 1 *Whitg.* 535

Holy salt: *Rid.* 107, 3 *Tyn.* 7; its alleged signification, 3 *Tyn.* 74

Holy strange gestures: an expression used by More for certain ceremonies, 3 *Tyn.* 85
Holy things: under the law, 2 *Bul.* 224; what are required in churches, 4 *Bul.* 501; holy things of the church of Rome, as holy cowls, girdles, beads, shoes, &c., 2 *Cran.* 147; holy beads, bells, boughs, candles, crosses, fire, moulds, palms, relics, wax, and various other things, many of which are here separately enumerated, 2 *Cran.* 63, 148, 1 *Lat.* 75, 478, *Pil.* 163, 493, *Rid.* 55, 1 *Tyn.* 225, 283, 462, 3 *Tyn.* 109 (*v.* Hallowing); such things forbidden, *Rid.* 320

Holy Thursday: *v.* Thursday.
Holy vessels: *v.* Chalices.
Holy water: *Calf.* 16, 17, *Pil.* 163, *Rid.* 55, 1 *Tyn.* 48; verses on it, *Calf.* 17; its invention ascribed (falsely) to pope Alexander I., 2 *Ful.* 117, 1 *Lat.* 75, *Rid.* 500; the exorcism or conjuration of it, 1 *Hoop.* 283, *Rid.* 107, 1 *Tyn.* 284; its alleged signification, 3 *Tyn.* 70, 3 *Zur.* 624; foolish arguments for it, 1 *Jew.* 15; the virtue ascribed to it, 3 *Jew.* 179; it is substituted by the pope for the blood of Christ, 2 *Cran.* 176, 177; the blasphemous doctrine of Durandus, *ib.* 177; said to forgive venial sin and drive away devils, *Pil.* 527; miracles alleged to have been wrought by it, 2 *Ful.* 116, *Rid.* 500; it is no defence against the devil, 1 *Lat.* 342, 497, *Rid.* 500; its superstitious use, 2 *Cran.* 158, 503; recognized by Henry VIII., 1 *Lat.* 132; Latimer's verses on giving it, 2 *Lat.* xviii, 294; Gardiner's opinion on it, *Rid.* 500, &c.; forbidden, 2 *Cran.* 158, 503; its restoration demanded by the rebels of Devon, *ib.* 176; holy-water-clerks, 4 *Bul.* 114; holy-water-stocks to be destroyed, *Grin.* 135, 159

Holy-workmen: such as trust in their imagined good works, 1 *Tyn.* 278, 305, 496, 3 *Tyn.* 140
Holybushe (Jo.): an edition of Coverdale's Testament published under this name, 1538, 2 *Cov.* xi, 23
Holyman (Jo.), bp of Bristol: a commissioner to examine Ridley, *Rid.* 255
Holyrood house: *v.* Edinburgh.
Holywel (Will.?): martyred, *Poet.* 168
Holywell, co. Flint: St Winifred's well, *Phil.* xxvii.
Homberg (...... von), a Frenchman: 3 *Zur.* 223
Home: *v.* Hume.
Homer: represents Jupiter as menacing the gods, *Sand.* 48; calls Pluto Hades, 1 *Ful.*

316; speaks of the gods appointing their shields to defend princes, 2 *Hoop.* 85; declares it not good to have many rulers, 1 *Jew.* 376; refers to Minos the lawgiver, *Calf.* 13 n.; adorns noble personages with the name demon, 3 *Bul.* 356; mentions an instance of punishment for want of duty to parents, 1 *Bul.* 288; speaks of the furies being invoked against one for the dishonour of his father's wife, 1 *Hoop.* 184; held souls to be immortal, 3 *Bul.* 385; he died of grief, or shame, 2 *Cov.* 132, 1 *Hoop.* 298; a temple built to him at Smyrna, 2 *Jew.* 981

Homilies: on reading them in the church, 1 *Bec.* 9, 3 *Jew.* 110, *Rog.* 323—325, 3 *Whitg.* 338, &c.; their use ancient and profitable, 1 *Bec.* 9, 10, 2 *Whitg.* 75; those of the fathers were publicly read in the church of old, *Rog.* 325; but reading homilies is not comparable to preaching, *Grin.* 382

The Anglo-Saxon Paschal homily shews that the English church did not hold transubstantiation, 2 *Ful.* 7, 20, 21, 247; it contains many passages taken from Ratramn, *ib.* 20 n.; the translator from the Latin was Ælfric, either the archbishop, or the abbot, *ib.*; the homily rendered into English and printed under the patronage of archbishop Parker, *ib.* 7, 247; editions of it, *ib.* 7 n., 20 n

The homilies of the church of England: Book I., &c.:—Cranmer engaged in composing homilies, 1539, 3 *Zur.* 626; the first book published 1547, 2 *Bec.* 643 n.; the three homilies (of salvation, faith, and good works) ascribed to Cranmer, 2 *Cran.* 128—149; the homily against whoredom, made by Tho. Becon, 2 *Bec.* 641—650; reference to it, 1 *Lat.* 244 n.; that on the misery of mankind was made by Jo. Harpsfield, 2 *Cran.* 128 n.; matrimony called a sacrament in the 1st part of the sermon against swearing, 2 *Ful.* 168 n.; Latimer assists in the composition of the first book of homilies, 1 *Lat.* xii; these homilies directed to be read in churches, 2 *Cran.* 504, 505, 512, 513, 2 *Hoop.* 128, *Rid.* 320; they contain a godly and wholesome doctrine, 3 *Bec.* 231, 1 *Brad.* 277, 400, 404, 1 *Bul.* 10, 2 *Cran.* 128 n., *Rid.* 400, *Rog.* 323; they were homely handled, 1 *Lat.* 121; notes for a homily on rebellion, 1549, 2 *Cran.* 188; a homily to be read in the time of pestilence, by bishop Hooper, 1553, 2 *Hoop.* 157—175; Homilies set forth by the right reverend ... Edmunde (Bonner), bishop of London, 1555, 2 *Cran.* 128 n.; a homily concerning the justice of God, in punishing of impenitent sinners, &c., written by dean Nowell, on occasion of the plague of 1563, *Grin.* 95—110, *Lit. Eliz.* 491—502; reference to it, *Now.* iii.

Book II., &c.:—publication of the second book, printed 1563, *Park.* 177 n.; names of the homilies therein, *Rog.* 323; they contain a godly and wholesome doctrine, *ib.*; the two tomes to be provided by churchwardens, *Grin.* 133, and to be placed in parish churches and chapels, *ib.* 157; articles respecting the reading of them, *ib.* 127, 161; their use, 3 *Jew.* 110; certain homilies (from both tomes) directed to be read in order on Wednesdays during the plague, 1563, *Grin.* 85; misstatement about the date of the council of Eliberis, in the homily against peril of idolatry, 2 *Ful.* 153 n.; in the second part of that homily the name Crinitus was printed Erinilus, 2 *Ful.* 159; the homily of sweeping of churches, as Cartwright styles it, 3 *Whitg.* 53, 491; the homily against wilful rebellion was occaisoned by the revolt of the earls of Northumberland and Westmoreland, 1569, *Lit. Eliz.* 462, 1 *Zur.* 227 n.; reference to it, *Grin.* 133; the fourth part issued by king Charles I., *Lit. Eliz.* 536 n

Homoüsion ('Ομοούσιον): the term is not in scripture, but the doctrine is, 1 *Jew.* 533, *Phil.* 117, 118, *Whita.* 564, 588, 603, 2 *Whitg.* 102; the term used before the council of Nice, 1 *Jew.* 533; approved by the council of Nice, but condemned by that of Rimini, *Whita.* 535; Ruffinus says none of the bishops at Rimini understood the word, *ib.* 139; meaning of the term, 3 *Bul.* 242, 3 *Jew.* 224, *Phil.* 299 n.; Luther on it, *Whita.* 611; the doctrine vindicated from scripture by the fathers, but ascribed by some Papists to tradition, 3 *Bul.* 246, *Coop.* 198, *Phil.* 117, 118, *Whita.* 534, &c., 563, 564; the Arians reproachfully styled the orthodox Homoüsians, 2 *Ful.* 375, 1 *Jew.* 465, 2 *Jew.* 807, *Rid.* 134

Hone (R. B.): Lives, 2 *Brad.* xii. n

Honesty: 1 *Bul.* 402

Honey: used by Romanists in baptism, 4 *Bul.* 359

Honorius, emperor: v. Law (Civil).

He submitted disputed questions to synods, 1 *Bul.* 331, 1 *Jew.* 390; recognized the bishop of Constantinople as equal to the bishop of Rome, 4 *Jew.* 1031; gave directions in the event of there being rival bishops of one city, 1 *Jew.* 350; made a law against rebaptizing, 4 *Bul.* 394; mentioned, 2 *Bul.* 109, 4 *Bul.* 539

Honorius I., pope: called the emperor Heraclius his sovereign lord, 2 *Ful.* 16; sent the pall, &c., to Honorius, archbishop of Canterbury, *Pil.** 585; took order that the archbishop might be consecrated in England, 2 *Ful.* 24; fell into schismatical error, 3 *Jew.* 342, viz. the heresy of the Monothelites, 1 *Jew.* 399, 3 *Jew.* 344, *Rog.* 181; styled an Eunomian, 1 *Jew.* 381; condemned by the sixth general council, 2 *Ful.* 312, 334, 1 *Jew.* 399, 400, 4 *Jew.* 926

Honorius II., pope: his legate in England, *Pil.* 572, *Sand.* 224

Honorius III., pope: promoted transubstantiation, *Bale* 168, 3 *Bec.* 274; first decreed that the sacrament should be lifted up and worshipped, 3 *Bec.* 359, 361, 2 *Brad.* 310, 1 *Cran.* 238, 1 *Hoop.* 526, *Hutch.* 258, 1 *Jew.* 10; ordained that the host should be kept in a clean place and sealed up, 2 *Cran.* 172; made a decree respecting the carrying of the sacrament in procession, 2 *Bec.* 253 n.; said to have commanded kneeling at the communion, 3 *Whitg.* 88, 89; approved the Carmelites, 4 *Bul.* 516

Honorius of Autun: on Stephen's vision of Christ (ascribed to Augustine), 1 *Jew.* 542

Honorius, abp of Canterbury: receives the pall, *Pil.** 585

Honorius (Ant.): president of a college at Ripen, 3 *Zur.* 621

Honour: v. Worship.

Honour is a gift of God, yet used as a snare by the devil, 1 *Lat.* 430; dignities not to be sought, yet not to be refused if we are called to them, 2 *Lat.* 214; to honour, what it is, 1 *Bul.* 269

Honywood (Mary): letters to her, 2 *Brad.* 98, 131, 151; her history, *ib.* 98 n

Hood: directed to be worn, *Grin.* 148, *Lit. Edw.* 157, 2 *Whitg.* 50 n.; 2 *Zur.* 362

Hood (......): v. Houde.

Hood (Robin): 1 *Lat.* 107, 1 *Tyn.* 80, 161, 220, 306, 328, 400, 450, 3 *Tyn.* 51; his gestes, 1 *Hoop.* 77; his day, 1 *Lat.* 208; Robinhood pastimes, *Rid.* 304; (scenicis vanitatibus, *ib.* 434); disorders about a Robin Hood in Edinburgh, *Rog.* 311 n

Hooke (Rich.): martyred at Chichester, *Poet.* 162

Hooker (Rich.): Jewel his early patron, *Jew.* xxiii; recommended by Sandys for the mastership of the Temple, *Sand.* xxvi; disputes there between him and Travers,
3 *Whitg.* xvi; his Ecclesiastical Polity, *ib.*; reference to him respecting the sign of the cross, *Calf.* 108 n., on a passage of Ignatius about fasting, 2 *Ful.* 237 n., as to stations, *ib.* 238 n.; his mistake respecting the council of Florence, *Calf.* 247 n.; he quotes and comments upon Jewel, 4 *Jew.* 887 n.; eulogizes Whitgift, 3 *Whitg.* xi; speaks of Puritans refusing to take oaths which might turn to the molestation of their brethren, *Rog.* 359 n

Hooper (Dan.), son of the martyr: 3 *Zur.* 105, 111, 114

Hooper (Geo.), bp of Bath and Wells: Disc. conc. Lent, *Calf.* 97 n

HOOPER (Jo.), bp of Gloucester and Worcester: v. Martyr (P.).

Brief biographical notices, 1 *Hoop.* iii, iv, v, 2 *Hoop.* 181; a more extended memoir, 2 *Hoop.* vii—xxx; his name spelled Hoper, Houper, and Howper, 1 *Hoop.* iii; his birth, 2 *Hoop.* vii; his father a Papist, 3 *Zur.* 75; his uncle was, at a later period, favourable to religion, *ib.* 86; he studies at Oxford, and becomes a monk at Gloucester, 2 *Hoop.* vii; his conversion, *ib.*, 3 *Zur.* 34; he returns to Oxford, *ib.*, but is compelled to retire, *ib.* viii; becomes steward to Sir Tho. Arundel, 2 *Hoop.* viii, 3 *Zur.* 33 n., 35 n.; his conference with Gardiner, 2 *Hoop.* viii, 3 *Zur.* 35 n.; he escapes to Paris, but returns, 2 *Hoop.* vii; goes to Germany, *ib.*; his doubts respecting attendance at mass, 3 *Zur.* 39; satisfied by Bullinger, *ib.* 40; his marriage, 2 *Hoop.* ix; his perilous journey to England, *ib.*; he settles at Zurich, *ib.*; quits that city, *ib.*; his prophetic words to Bullinger, *ib.* x; he returns to England, *ib.*; made chaplain to the duke of Somerset, *ib.*, 3 *Zur.* 739 n.; a witness against Bonner, 3 *Zur.* 660; he preaches in London, and at court, *ib.* 635, 659, 662, several times a day, *ib.* 108, 557; his preaching and manners, 1 *Hoop.* 549, 2 *Hoop.* x, xi, 3 *Zur.* 185; his public lectures, 3 *Zur.* 73, 75, 79, 80, 88, 560; he preaches at court on the book of Jonah, 2 *Hoop.* xii, 431—558, 3 *Zur.* 75, 559, and in his preaching attacks the ordination book and the vestments, 2 *Hoop.* xii, 479; his disagreement with Traheron, 3 *Zur.* 426; nominated bishop of Gloucester, 1 *Hoop.* 434, 3 *Zur.* 87, 271, 559; he refuses to accept the see, 2 *Hoop.* xii, 3 *Zur.* 665; his zeal against pontifical ceremonies, 3 *Zur.* 466, 468; his scruples and controversy about ecclesiastical apparel,

* See the note on p. 389.

and the oath, 2 *Cran.* x, 428, 431, 3 *Jew.* 612 n., 3 *Zur.* 87, 410, 426, 466, 566, 567, 571, 573, 585, 665, 674; his opinion on vestments opposed by the privy council, *Park.* 234, 280; he is supported by J. à Lasco, but opposed by Bucer, 3 *Zur.* 675, and by the bishops, *ib.* 676; he disputes with Ridley on the vestments, 2 *Cran.* 430, 431, 2 *Hoop.* xiii, 3 *Zur.* 91 n., 426, 486, 673; Ridley's REPLY to him respecting them, 2 *Brad.* 375, &c.; their subsequent reconciliation, 3 *Zur.* 91 n., 486; his letter to Bucer and Martyr on the vestments, 2 *Hoop.* xiv; he is cautioned by P. Martyr, *ib.*; forbidden to preach, *ib.* xv; imprisoned for disobedience, *ib.*, 3 *Zur.* 107 n.; he submits to the privy council and is consecrated in the usual way, 2 *Hoop.* xv, xvi, 3 *Zur.* 107 n., 271, 410, 415, 482, 587; conditions on which he accepted his bishoprick, 3 *Zur.* 187; his vestments,—a scarlet chimere, &c., *ib.* 271; busy in his bishoprick, *ib.* 563; he entertains some scruples, *ib.*; visits his diocese, 2 *Hoop.* xvi; ignorance of his clergy, *ib.* 151 n., 3 *Tyn.* 75 n.; he preaches diligently, 3 *Zur.* 494; rides in a merchant's cloak, 2 *Brad.* 390; attacked by the sweating sickness, 2 *Hoop.* xvii, 159 n.; a commissioner for the reform of the ecclesiastical law, 2 *Hoop.* xvii, 3 *Zur.* 503, 590; being made also bishop of Worcester, he visits that diocese, 2 *Hoop.* xvii, 3 *Zur.* 23; he held the last-named see during good behaviour, 1 *Hoop.* 481 n.; he resides awhile with Cranmer, 3 *Zur.* 24; his controversy with Joliffe and Johnson, 2 *Hoop.* xix; his fidelity and diligence as a bishop, *ib.* xxi, 3 *Zur.* 497, 500, 582, 586, 588, 591; he supports the title of queen Mary, 2 *Hoop.* xxii, 556, 557; refusing to flee, he is summoned before the council, insulted by Gardiner, and committed to the Fleet, *ib.* xxii. (see 2 *Lat.* 270); deprived, 2 *Brad.* 83, 2 *Hoop.* xxii; sent to the Compter in Southwark, 2 *Hoop.* xxiv; condemned, and sent to Newgate, 2 *Hoop.* xxiv, 3 *Zur.* 171; degraded by Bonner, 2 *Hoop.* xxiv; his imprisonment, 1 *Brad.* 403, 3 *Zur.* 100 n., 505; his sufferings in it, 3 *Zur.* 101, 102 n., 292 n.; his writings in prison, 2 *Hoop.* xxiii; he sends writings thence to Bullinger for correction, 3 *Zur.* 105; these have not been found, *ib.* 106 n.; he signs a declaration concerning religion, 1 *Brad.* 374; Ridley inquires about him, 2 *Brad.* 159; Ridley's letter to him in prison, *Rid.* 355; in peril of death, 1 *Brad.* 190, 290; false report of his execution, 2 *Brad.* 172, 174, *Rid.* 373, 379; his journey to Gloucester, 2 *Hoop.* xxiv; his interviews with Sir Anth. Kingston and others, *ib.* xxv; his speech to the mayor and sheriffs, *ib.* xxvi; the order for his execution, *ib.*; his last prayer, *ib.* xxviii; lines written with a coal on the wall of the New Inn at Gloucester the night before his death, *ib.* xxx, 2 *Brad.* 363; his martyrdom, 1 *Brad.* 410, 2 *Brad.* 192, 2 *Hoop.* xxix, *Rid.* 380, 391, 3 *Zur.* 772; part of the stake recently discovered, 2 *Hoop.* xxx; Hilles's character of him, 3 *Zur.* 251; many false and erroneous opinions concerning him, 2 *Hoop.* 67, 68, 74; Harding reviles him, 4 *Jew.* 822; his character by Foxe, 2 *Hoop.* xxi; his doctrine respecting the eucharist, 3 *Zur.* 47; his opinion on divorce, *ib.* 64, 416, 422; some of his books came into the possession of Tho. Sampson, 1 *Zur.* 155

His works:—bishop Tanner's list, 1 *Hoop.* v; his EARLY WRITINGS, edited by the Rev. Sam. Carr, M.A., 1 *Hoop.*; his LATER WRITINGS, TOGETHER WITH HIS LETTERS AND OTHER PIECES, edited by the Rev. Cha. Nevinson, M.A., 2 *Hoop.*; references to his writings, 2 *Brad.* 297, 394, 1 *Bul.* 49, 197, 198, 216, 221, 252, 272, 288, 307, 308, 347, 401, 412, 432 nn., *Hutch.* 325; his letters (besides those printed in 3 *Zur.* as mentioned below), 2 *Hoop.* 568—622; letter to Cranmer, *ib.* xv; letters to Cecil, 2 *Brad.* 395, 397, 2 *Hoop.* xviii, xix; letter to Jo. à Lasco, 2 *Hoop.* ix, n.; letters to foreign divines, mostly to Bullinger, 3 *Zur.* 33—104 (and see *ib.* 742, and 3 *Bul.* 115); letter to him, *Rid.* 355 (and see 365).

— Anne (de Tserclas) his wife, 2 *Hoop.* viii, xvii, 1 *Zur.* 36 n., 3 *Zur.* 63, 105, 558, 562, 563; to be exhorted not to entangle herself with the cares of this life, 3 *Zur.* 576; she escapes, with her children, to Frankfort, 2 *Hoop.* xxii, 3 *Zur.* 110; an exhortation to patience sent to her by her husband, 2 *Hoop.* 578; six letters from her to Bullinger, 3 *Zur.* 107—114; the original Latin of one of them, in which she speaks of her husband's martyrdom, *ib.* 774; a letter to a faithful woman, and late wife to one of the bishops [probably Hooper], which gave their lives in the Lord's quarrel, *Phil.* 251

— Hooper's children; see Daniel and Rachel Hooper: Joanna, mentioned 3 *Zur.* 51, 64, 74, 563, 564, and Martin, named *ib.* 64, 74, do not seem to have been children of bishop Hooper.

Hooper (Rachel), dau. of the martyr: born abroad, 3 *Zur.* 92; her sponsors, *ib.* 50 n.,

73, 88, 92; her education, *ib.* 74, 75, 79, 105, 107; mentioned, *ib.* 64, 90

Hooper (W.): *v.* Hopper.

Hoore (Rich.): *v.* Hore.

Hoornbeeck (Jo.): Examen Bullæ Innoc. X., *Jew.* xxxvi; cited about a bull of Clement VI., 3 *Jew.* 560 n.; Miscell. Sacra, *Calf.* 69 n

Hope: *v.* Assurance, Faith, Prayers.

Of hope: 2 *Bul.* 88, &c., 2 *Cov.* 86; what it is, 3 *Bec.* 602, 616, 2 *Bul* 88; it is of things absent, 2 *Bul.* 89; but of things most certain, *ib.* 89; it is the gift of God, *ib.* 90; the companion of faith, *Nord.* 18; its office, 2 *Tyn.* 14; needful in penitents, 4 *Bul.* 553; he that has it will purify himself, 2 *Brad.* 122

HOPE OF THE FAITHFUL: a treatise on the resurrection, written by Wermuller, translated by Coverdale, 2 *Cov.* 135—226

Hopkins (Jo.): notice of him, *Poet.* xlviii; Psalm xlvi. in metre, *Lit. Eliz.* 566; Psalm lxxxiv. in metre, *Poet.* 485

Hopkins (Rich.), sheriff of Coventry: letters to him, 1 *Brad.* 389, 2 *Brad.* 244; an exile at Basle, 1 *Brad.* 389 n

Hopkins (Will): translates the book of Ratramn, 2 *Ful.* 20 n

Hopper (W.), or Hooper: martyred at Canterbury, *Poet.* 163

Hopton (Jo.), bp of Norwich: called Norwich Nobody, *Poet.* 166; he died in debt, *Park.* 58

Hopton (Sir Owen): 1 *Ful.* xi.

Hopton (Rob.): *Park.* 307 n

Hopton (Will.): *Park.* 307

Horace: cited, 1 *Bec.* 10, 93, 173, 222, 233, 2 *Bec.* 56, 162, 3 *Bec.* 261, 389, 619, 1 *Bul.* 289, 302, *Calf.* 2, 49, 340, 354, 389, *Grin.* 7, 1 *Hoop.* 356, 403, 418, 428, 430, 2 *Hoop.* 84, 487, 2 *Jew.* 581, 660, 1 *Lat.* 92, 431, *Pil.* 39, 584

Horæ: *v.* Hours.

Horæ B. V. M. ad usum Sarum: notice of the edition of Paris, 1510, *Pra. Eliz.* xxi; prayers to saints from the Horæ B. V. M., *Rog.* 227; address to Thomas à Becket, *ib.* 38 n.; address to souls in Purgatory, *ib.* 214, 220, 221; a citation respecting indulgences, *ib.* 220

Horapollo: *v.* Orus Apollo.

Horarium: *v.* Manuale.

ORARIUM, SEU LIBELLUS PRECATIONUM, 1560, *Pra. Eliz.* 115—208; why set forth, *Pra. B.* iii; notice of various editions of it, *Pra. Eliz.* xii.

Hore (Rich.), or Hoore: chaplain to lord Lisle, 2 *Cran.* 298, 320

Horims (Deut. ii. 12): what, 1 *Tyn.* 446

Hormisdas, pope: the father of pope Silverius, 2 *Ful.* 98, 99 n.; his decree respecting the authority of councils, *Rog.* 211; his address to Epiphanius of Constantinople, 1 *Jew.* 420; he warns the church of Rome against forsaking God, 4 *Jew.* 726

Horn (Phil. count of): *v* Montmorenci.

Horne (Geo.), bp of Norwich: Comm. on Psalms, 2 *Bul.* 6 n

Horne (Rob.), bp of Winchester: some account of him, 3 *Bec.* 194 n.; at a disputation on the sacrament, 1551, *Grin.* ii; chaplain to king Edward, 2 *Cran.* xi; his account of the services of the church of England, temp. Edw. VI., addressed to Bullinger, 2 *Zur.* 354; Bullinger's remarks in reply, *ib.* 357; dean of Durham, 1 *Cran.* (9); in exile, 1 *Brad.* 445, 1 *Cran.* (9); at Zurich, 3 *Zur.* 752; letter from him and others to the magistrates there, *ib.* 751; at Frankfort, *ib.* 128, 755; he returns to England, 1 *Zur.* 6; disputes at Westminster, 4 *Jew.* 1199, 1200, 1 *Zur.* 11, 15, 27; appointed bishop of Winchester, 1 *Zur.* 93; an ecclesiastical commissioner, *Park.* 72, 383, 439; he assists in the compilation of certain Advertisements, *ib.* 233; signs a letter to the queen, *ib.* 294; his Answer to Feckenham, 1 *Ful.* 75 n., 2 *Ful.* 3, 378, *Jew.* xxxviii, 4 *Jew.* 635, 1 *Whitg.* 22 n.; appointed to preach, *Park.* 318; his share in the Bishops' Bible, *ib.* 335 n.; present at Grindal's confirmation to the see of Canterbury, *Grin.* x; his letter to certain troublers of the church, 1 *Zur.* 321; very infirm, 2 *Zur.* 307; his death, 1 *Zur.* 332 n.; references to him, 2 *Ful.* 356, 380, *Grin.* 261, 1 *Zur.* 188, 191, 2 *Zur.* 108, 118; dedication to him, 3 *Bec.* 194; his letters, 1 *Zur.* 134, 141, 175 (with Grindal), 245, 276, 320, 321, 2 *Zur.* 354, 3 *Zur.* 125—131; letters to him from Bullinger and others, 3 *Whitg.* 496, 1 *Zur.* 341, 356, 357, 2 *Zur.* 264

— Margery his wife: an exile at Zurich, 3 *Zur.* 752; her death, 1 *Zur.* 321

Horner (M.), of Zurich: 4 *Bul.* xxvii. 2 *Zur.* vii.

Horninger, or Horningsheath, co. Suffolk: T. Rogers rector there, *Rog.* v; he died and was buried there, *ib.* ix.

Horsemen: in the Apocalypse, *Bale* 361, &c.

Horses: on the commandment not to multiply them, 1 *Lat.* 92; their masters should see them fed, *ib.* 395; Eligius invoked for their cure, *ib.* 139, 2 *Bec.* 536, 1 *Hoop.* 310, *Rog.* 226; commonly bled on St Stephen's day, 2 *Lat.* 100; those of the Apocalypse; white, *Bale* 312, 546, 549; red, *ib.* 314; black, *ib.* 317; pale, *ib.* 320, 321, 325

Horsey (Dr): murdered Rich. Hunne, but was pardoned, 3 *Tyn.* 166.
Horton (Jo.): *v.* Houghton.
Horton (Tho.), fellow of Pembroke hall: 1 *Brad.* 31, 195 n., 2 *Brad.* xvii; a dispenser of the bounty of Chambers and others, 4 *Jew.* vii, 1302
Hortulus Animæ: *Pra. Eliz.* 202, 242, 243, 272, 484, 507, 512, 546 nn
Hoshea, king of Israel: 2 *Bul.* 12
Hosiander (Andr.): *v.* Osiander.
Hosius, bp of Corduba: his authority and estimation, 4 *Jew.* 999; he drew up a creed substantially the same as the Nicene, *Phil.* 310 n.; once gave his hand to the Arians, 4 *Jew.* 908; subscribed in a council before the bishop of Rome, *ib.* 999; cites words of Guimund respecting the sacrament as a figure of the church, 2 *Jew.* 593 n., 624
Hosius (Stanisl. card.): notice of him, 1 *Zur.* 113 n.; his works, 2 *Ful.* 4, *Jew.* xxxviii, 1 *Zur.* 113 n.; he tells why Peter calls scripture a lamp, *Whita.* 7; states that the gospels are not to be believed but on account of the voice of God speaking to us within, *ib.* 346, 358; complains of the profanation of the scripture by its being made accessible to artizans and women, *ib.* 249; allows that Jerome translated the Bible into Sclavonic, 1 *Jew.* 270, 2 *Jew.* 692; says Matthew's gospel was written in Hebrew, *Whita.* 125; charged with denying the scriptures, 1 *Ful.* 8, 4 *Jew.* 754, &c.; he debases their authority, *Rog.* 197 n.; calls them a creature, and a certain bare letter, 4 *Jew.* 753; styles them beggarly elements, &c., *Whita.* 36; when objection was made that David, being a temporal prince, composed the Psalms, he replied, Why should he not write them? and cited the words of Horace, " scribimus indocti doctique poemata passim," 4 *Jew.* 759; he places the church above scripture, *Whita.* 277; observes that the apostles, delivering the creed, never said, I believe the holy Bible, but, I believe the holy church, 3 *Jew.* 247; declares the interpretation of the church of Rome to be the very word of God, *ib.* 247, 441, 4 *Jew.* 753, 759, 760; calls the scripture as it is alleged by Protestants, the word of the devil, 4 *Jew.* 752, 753, 759, 760; makes Peter the foundation, *Rog.* 171 n.; teaches that without one pope the church could not be one, 3 *Jew.* 120, 221, 4 *Jew.* 751; declares that no pope ever professed any manner of heresy, 4 *Jew.* 928; says God never bade us be careful whether the pope were Judas, or Peter, or Paul, 3 *Jew.* 120, 4 *Jew.* 943; asserts that the council which condemned the Saviour had the Holy Ghost, and did not err, 4 *Jew.* 941, 942; teaches that from the time our first father tasted of the forbidden fruit, Christ the Son of God became guilty of death, *ib.* 942; states that though the wickedness of bishops be never so great it cannot hinder the promise that they shall shew the truth of judgment, *ib.*; asks, what if Paul teaches rightly to believe in saints? 3 *Jew.* 256; maintains that the chief duty of priests is to sacrifice, *Calf.* 229; calls it heresy to teach the receiving of both kinds in the eucharist, 1 *Jew.* 64; his confession relative to the inferior orders of the clergy, *Calf.* 228; he affirms that the apostles appointed orders of monks, 3 *Jew.* 235, 4 *Jew.* 784; says our works are sprinkled with the blood of Christ, 3 *Jew.* 492; speaks of the substitution of crosses for images of Mercury, *Calf.* 66 n.; reproves Vergerius, 1 *Whitg.* 392; slanders Luther, 1 *Jew.* 106; calls the flock of Christ a wild beast of many heads, &c., 2 *Jew.* 685; Harding borrowed greatly from him, 1 *Jew.* 214 n.; reference to him, 4 *Jew.* 641; some of his books translated into English, 2 *Ful.* 4; Fulke answers him, 1 *Ful.* viii.
Hospinian (Hadr.), or Wirt: 4 *Bul.* 546
Hospinian (Rod.): De Templis, *Calf.* 42 n.; De Orig. Monach., 2 *Ful.* 103 n., 1 *Lat.* 189 n., 2 *Lat.* 196 n.; Hist. Sacram., 2 *Lat.* 265 n
Hospitality: a noble virtue, necessary for all, 2 *Bec.* 326; scripture gives examples to encourage to it, *ib.* 584; that of the patriarchs, 2 *Bul.* 59; it is a fruit of love, *Sand.* 400; a way of feeding Christ's flock, 1 *Bec.* 19, &c.; if it be disregarded, weaklings will be discouraged, *ib.* 26; it is to be shewn to godly strangers, *Sand.* 266; especially enjoined on bishops and ministers, 1 *Bec.* 22, &c., 2 *Bec.* 326; its decay lamented, 1 *Bec.* 174; that of the abbeys, *Pil.* 610; that of the inhabitants of Sandwich commended, 3 *Bec.* 599, 600
Hospitals: *v.* Canterbury, London.
Hospitalia, 1 *Bul.* 286, 2 *Bul.* 44, 4 *Bul.* 498; the original institution of hospitals, &c., 1 *Tyn.* 231; many founded since the reformation, 2 *Ful.* 122, *Pil.* 610; inquiry respecting them, *Grin.* 172
Host: *v.* Mass, Transubstantiation.
Called a singing-loaf, and why, 2 *Tyn.* 301, 3 *Tyn.* 227, or a singing-cake, *Coop.* 152; why made round, 1 *Jew.* 15, 78, 2 *Jew.* 991; why broken into three parts at the

celebration of mass, 3 *Bec.* 267, 268, 278, *Coop.* 77, 2 *Jew.* 584, &c.; called God, 1 *Tyn.* 248 n.; it is a deaf and dumb god, *Rid.* 409; worshipped, 1 *Cran.* 229, 2 *Cran.* 172, 1 *Jew.* 10, &c.; pretended miracles of its bleeding, &c., 2 *Cran.* 66; miraculous respect said to have been rendered to the host by beasts, birds, and insects, *Calf.* 86 n

Hostelry: hospitality, *Phil.* 391

Hostia: *v.* Ostia.

Hostiensis (Hen. de Segusio, card.): Super Decretal. Comm., *Jew.* xxxviii; he affirms that the pope is all, and above all, 1 *Jew.* 69, 4 *Jew.* 939; says God and the pope make one judgment-seat, and, sin only excepted, the pope can, in a manner, do all things that God can do, 1 *Jew.* 380, 381, & corrig., 3 *Jew.* 135, 145, 599, 4 *Jew.* 830, 831, 882 n., 899, 939, 940, 1137; affirms that the pope may sell any ecclesiastical title or dignity, without danger of simony, 4 *Jew.* 869; allows that if the pope commands anything savouring of heresy he is not to be obeyed, *ib.* 927; but says that he cannot be brought into order by any man, though he be accounted a heretic, 4 *Bul.* 119; asserts that all men ought to obey the pope unless he command sin, 3 *Jew.* 201; states that appeals may be made from equal to equal, 1 *Jew.* 395; declares it unlawful to say mass at night, save on that of the Nativity, *ib.* 117; speaks of the ordination of a reader, 3 *Jew.* 380; says the emperor is a vassal of the church of Rome, 4 *Jew.* 836

Hostmasterus (......): 1 *Jew.* 52

Hostrie: an inn, *Calf.* 322

Hosts of the Lord: what, 3 *Bul.* 132, *Pil.* 27, &c., 132, 138

Hotchens (Will.), alias Tyndale, *q. v.*

Hottinger (Jo. Hen.): Helvet. Hist. Eccl., 4 *Bul.* xi, *Pil.* 142 n.; Schola Tig. Carolina, 4 *Bul.* ix. n.; Dissert. misc. Pent., 2 *Ful.* 296 n.; his account of pope Adrian's offers to Zuinglius, *Pil.* 684

Houde(......): martyred in Smithfield, *Poet.* 172

Houghton (Jo.), prior of the Charter-house: condemned for treason, 2 *Cran.* 303 n

Hours for prayer: used by holy men, and commendable, 1 *Bec.* 171, 172, 4 *Bul.* 183, 197, &c.; the canonical hours, 4 *Bul.* 197, 201; [1] matins and lauds, *Pra. Eliz.* 19, 26,133, 139 n.; midnight matins, *Pil.* 483, 528; the Papists' rule about matins, *ib.* 528; the name laudes erroneously applied to part of an evening service, *Pra. Eliz.* 266; [2] prime, *ib.* 33, 145; [3] the third hour, or tierce, *ib.* 35, 147; [4] the sixth hour, or sext, *ib.* 36, 148; [5] the ninth hour, or none, *ib.* 37, 149; [6] vespers, *ib.* 38, 151; [7] compline, *ib.* 43,154; the hours chanted in churches in king Edward's time, 3 *Zur.* 72; Horæ B. V. M., *v.* Horæ.

House of God: *v.* Temple.

Housed, unhoused: with or without housings, i. e. hosen, stockings or boots, 2 *Bec.* 65

Householders: *v.* Prayers.

Their office, 1 *Bul.* 261, (*v.* Parents); they should garnish their houses with scripture, 1 *Bec.* 66; what they may pray for for themselves, *ib.* 166; counsel to householders in captivity, 1 *Bul.* 290

Household rules: *v.* Grey (H.), duke of Suffolk.

Housel: the eucharist, *Coop.* 10, 11, 85, &c., 2 *Cran.* 281 n.; 1 *Jew.* 117; sometimes hushel, 3 *Bec.* 4 n.; More calls it howsyll, 3 *Tyn.* 96; housel-sippings, *Bale* 526; houseling, 2 *Ful.* 11, 105, houseling at Easter, 3 *Bec.* 269; to be houselled, 3 *Tyn.* 179

Houses: delight in gorgeous houses is vain, 2 *Bec.* 430; those of princes and nobles may be according to their degree, *Pil.* 42; what the word means in a text in Exodus, 1 *Tyn.* 419; the parable of the two houses, 2 *Tyn.* 129; whole houses, i. e. families, baptized by the apostles, 4 *Bul.* 391

Hoveden: *v.* Howden.

Hoveden (Rob.), warden of All Souls' college: *Park.* 398

Hoveden (Rog. de): referred to about the second council of Nice, 2 *Ful.* 23 n.; he speaks of the burning of heretics in France, *Bale* 3; his account of the coronation of the emperor Henry VI., 2 *Tyn.* 271 n.; he preserves Joachim Abbas' account of Antichrist, 2 *Jew.* 915 n., 4 *Jew.* 714

Howard (Catherine), queen: *v.* Catherine.

Howard (Tho.), 2nd duke of Norfolk:

— Agnes (Tilney), his widow: godmother to queen Elizabeth, 2 *Cran.* 274; letters to her, *ib.* 254, 294; sent to the Tower, 3 *Zur.* 226

Howard (Tho.), 3rd duke of Norfolk: ambassador to France, 2 *Cran.* 246; his letter to Cranmer for the documents relating to the king's cause with queen Catherine, *ib.* 255; Cranmer's answer, *ib.* 256; letter to him from his daughter Mary, duchess of Richmond, *ib.* 360 n.; he invades Scotland, 3 *Zur.* 237 n., 634 n.; besieges Montreuil in France, 1 *Brad.* 493 n., 2 *Brad.* xii; committed to the Tower, 3 *Zur.* 42 n., 256, 639; released, *ib.* 367

Howard (Hen.), earl of Surrey, son of the

3rd duke: 1 *Bec.* 232 n.; his trial, 2 *Bec.* 554 n.; his execution, 3 *Zur.* 42 n., 257

Howard (Tho.), 4th duke of Norfolk: desires P. Martyr to return to England, 1 *Zur.* 20 n.; P. Martyr writes to him, 2 *Zur.* 57; he makes Greg. Martin tutor to his children, 1 *Ful.* xii; part of a letter from him to Parker, *Park.* 255 n.; letter from Parker to him, *ib.* 255; his signature as privy councillor, *ib.* 328 n., 330; mentioned, *ib.* 310; the patron of bishop Hughes, 1 *Ful.* 283 n; he proposes marriage to the queen of Scots, *Lit. Eliz.* 655 n., 1 *Zur.* 216, 2 *Zur.* 172; committed to the Tower in consequence, 1 *Zur.* 216; an insurrection for his deliverance, *Lit. Eliz.* 656 n., 1 *Zur.* 229 n.; his trial, *Park.* 391, 1 *Zur.* 261, 267, 2 *Zur.* 193, 198; names of the peers who tried him, 1 *Zur.* 267 n.; condemned, 1 *Zur.* 267, 2 *Zur.* 201; beheaded, *Lit. Eliz.* 655 n., *Park.* 394 n., 1 *Zur.* 261 n., 269 n., 272, 2 *Zur.* 198, 207; his attainder terminates a dispute about the stewardship of the archbishop's liberties, *Park.* 452

— Margaret, his second wife, daughter of Tho. lord Audley of Walden, and widow to lord Hen. Dudley: her death and unceremonious funeral, 1 *Zur.* 137

Howard (Phil.), earl of Arundel, son of the last duke: Greg. Martin was his tutor, 1 *Ful.* xii.

Howard (Will.), 1st lord Howard of Effingham: imprisoned, 1542, 3 *Zur.* 226; privy councillor to Mary and Elizabeth, 1 *Zur.* 5 n.; signature as such, *Park.* 77, 103, 106, 117, 155, 328 n., 330, 357, 381; at the duke of Norfolk's trial, 1 *Zur.* 267 n.; ambassador in France, 1 *Zur.* 273 n

Howard (Cha.), 2nd lord Howard of Effingham, and afterwards earl of Nottingham: sent to Cadiz as lord admiral, *Lit. Eliz.* 472

Howard (Hen.), earl of Northampton: Parker begs for his liberty, when lord Hen. Howard, *Park.* 394

Howard (Lord Edmund): father of queen Catharine, 3 *Zur.* 201 n

Howard (Lord Tho.), probably the 3rd visc. Bindon: letter to him, *Park.* 136

Howard (Lady Mary), afterwards duchess of Richmond: *v.* Fitzroy.

Howard (Sir Geo.): mentioned, *Sand.* iii; letter to him, *Park.* 197; a mourner at the funeral of the emperor Ferdinand, *Grin.* 33

Howden, co. York: the manor, "Hoveden," *Grin.* 399 n

Howe (......): 2 *Zur.* 333

Howel (Cha.), of Rochdale: *Park.* 232

Howell (Tho.): notice of him, *Poet.* xxiii; the office of the mind, verses, *ib.* 256

Howland (Rich.), afterwards bp of Peterborough: at Cambridge, *Grin.* 366—369; recommended by Whitgift as his successor at Trinity, 3 *Whitg.* xi.

Howlet (Jo.), i. e. Rob. Parsons, *q. v.*

Howley (Will.), abp of Canterbury: record of his confirmation as bishop of London, *Grin.* vi. n

Howsyll: *v.* Housel.

Hrabanus: *v.* Rabanus.

Hubberdine (Mr), otherwise Haberdyne, Heberdynne, Hobberton, or Hyberden, prior of St James's at Bristol: some account of him, 2 *Lat.* 229 n.; he was a man of little learning and unstable wit, *ib.* 365; opposed Latimer at Bristol, 2 *Cran.* 308 n., 1 *Lat.* viii, 2 *Lat.* 225, 232, 234, 358, 365; Latimer's letter to him, 2 *Lat.* 317

Hubert (St): invoked for dogs, *Rog.* 226; his rents, 1 *Tyn.* 237

Hubert (Conrad): some account of him, 2 *Cov.* 503, 594 n.; reference to him, 3 *Zur.* 331; he was assistant to Bucer, *ib.* 473; one of Bucer's administrators, 2 *Cran.* 435, *Park.* 46 n., 3 *Zur.* 26 n., 364; he edits Bucer's Scripta Anglicana, 2 *Zur.* 17 n.; in the preface to that book he refers to Grindal's providential escape when a boy, *Grin.* i. n., and to his exile, *ib.* iii; letter from him to T. Blaurer, 2 *Zur.* 27; one from him and Chelius to Parker and Haddon, 3 *Zur.* 364; letters to him, 2 *Cov.* 503—525, 527, (593, &c.), 2 *Cran.* 435, *Park.* 46, 2 *Zur.* 17, 22, 51, 72, 107, 3 *Zur.* 28, 333, 361, 490

— Margaret his wife, 2 *Cov.* 515

Hubert (Jo.): 2 *Cov.* 508, 518

Hubert (Sam.): 2 *Cov.* 505

Hubner (Pet.): letter to him, 2 *Zur.* 309

Huche (Gervase): 2 *Cran.* 382

Hucker-mucker: *v.* Hugger-mugger.

Huddle: confusedly, *Rid.* 304

Huddlestone (......), or Hurlestone: the lady Mary has mass in his house, *Sand.* iii; he takes one of Sandys' horses, *ib.* vi.

Huet (Pierre Dan.): *Calf.* 78 n

Huet (Tho.): *v.* Hewet.

Hugger-mugger: secrecy, 2 *Brad.* 283, *Phil.* 231; hucker-mucker, 2 *Cov.* 262; hukermuker, 1 *Tyn.* xxvii.

Hugh (St), of Cluny: 2 *Jew.* 784

Hugh (St), of Lincoln: a youthful martyr, *Bale* 192

Hugh (Will.): translates the book of Bertram, *Rid.* 159

Hughes (Jo.): an ecclesiastical commissioner, *Grin.* 294 (D. Hughs. See also Hewis).
Hughes (Will.), bp of St Asaph: notices of him, 1 *Ful.* 283, 284, *Park.* 446 n
Hugo Barchinonensis: wrote on the Apocalypse, *Bale* 257
Hugo, 2nd abbot of St Augustine's, Canterbury: *Park.* 166
Hugo de Fleury: 1 *Jew.* 120 n. & corrig. [but the author intended to be cited is Richard de S. Victore; see Hugo de S. Victore, below.]
Hugo Lingonensis: wrote against Berengarius, 1 *Hoop.* 248
Hugo de Sancto Charo, cardinal: his works, *Jew.* xxxviii; he teaches that man is not vile, since God delighted in him, *Wool.* 82; writes on the justification of Abraham, 2 *Cran.* 209; explains why Moses was called a priest, though indeed he was not one, 4 *Jew.* 982; comments on the direction given in Deut. xvii. about the king's copy of the law, *ib.* 980; rejects the Apocrypha, *Whita.* 65; expounds Luke viii. 10, "unto you it is given," &c., 2 *Jew.* 677, *Whita.* 240; states why the Lord's supper is called the communion, 1 *Jew.* 135; declares that the sacrament is one, on account of the unity of the institution, *ib.* 256; says there must be one table for all, *ib.* 133; declares that anciently those who would not communicate departed after the offertory, 3 *Jew.* 477; refers to the practice of consecrating two hosts on Thursday in Holy week, and reserving one until next day, 1 *Jew.* 246; speaks of the sacrament of bishopdom, *Rog.* 259; states why Paul went to visit Peter, 1 *Jew.* 375; says, because Paul went to Jerusalem to see Peter, the bishops made a vow to visit the pope, *ib.* 376; inculcates the cruel usage of Jews and the burning of heretics, 3 *Tyn.* 215; cites Gregory about babbling, 1 *Jew.* 315
Hugo de Sancto Victore: *Jew.* xxxviii; notice of him, 1 *Tyn.* 152 n.; he reckons the canonical books of the Old Testament as twenty-two in number, *Whita.* 65; testifies to the sufficiency of scripture, *ib.* 703; does not allow the Apocrypha as of authority, *ib.* 64; says, original sin is ignorance in the mind, and concupiscence in the flesh, 2 *Bul.* 385; states that faith, as a cause, precedes hope and charity, 2 *Cran.* 204; wrote on the sacraments, 1 *Hoop.* 118, see 248; references to him on the eucharist, 1 *Cran.* 41, 42, 56; he defines how long the bodily presence of Christ remains in the sacrament, 2 *Jew.* 786; cited as saying that if any man come to the communion without confession, he eats and drinks damnation, 3 *Bul.* 80, 1 *Jew.* 120 (but the words are those of Richard de S. Victore, 3 *Bul.* 80 n.); he says the sentence of Peter remitting sins, goes before the sentence of heaven, 3 *Jew.* 368; cited by Bonaventure, with reference to opus operatum, *Rog.* 248 n.; he reproves luxurious bishops, 1 *Bec.* 22

Hugo de Vienna: says death is more cause of rejoicing than of weeping, 2 *Lat.* 245

Hugo (Jo.): 4 *Bul.* 546

Huguenots: *v.* Church, II. v., France, French, Paris.

Huick (Tho.): mentioned as D. Hewicke, 4 *Jew.* 1262, *Park.* 177; an ecclesiastical commissioner, *Grin.* 294, *Park.* 107; vicar-general of the diocese of London, *Grin.* 318 n

Huker-muker: *v.* Hugger-mugger.

Hulderic, king: *v.* Childeric.

Hulderic, bp: *v.* Udalric.

Huldrich (Jo.): 1 *Zur.* 324 n., 326

Hull: *v.* Kingston-upon-Hull.

Hulliarde (Jo.), or Hullier: martyred at Cambridge, *Poet.* 166

Humaniformarians: *v.* Anthropomorphites.

Humanatio: a term not in the scriptures, 1 *Jew.* 533

Humbertus, a cardinal: *Jew.* xxxviii; legate of Leo IX., *Whita.* 42 n.; he declares that, for a perfect remembrance of Christ, there must be distribution as well as blessing and breaking of the bread, 2 *Bec.* 252, 3 *Bec.* 456, 1 *Jew.* 166, 3 *Jew.* 553

Hume castle, Scotland: taken by the English, 3 *Zur.* 387, 651; retaken, *ib.* 387

Hume (Alex. lord), and afterwards earl of Hume: one of the confederate-lords, 1 *Zur.* 193 n

Hume (......), a Scots nobleman: seizes the English rebel earls, 1 *Zur.* 214

Hume (Dav.): Hist. of Engl., 1 *Zur.* 3 n., 5 n

Humes (Alex.): denies Christ's descent into hell, 1 *Lat.* 233 n., *Rog.* xvi.

Humfrey (Lau.): *v.* Humphrey.

Humfrey (Phil.): martyred at Bury, *Poet.* 173

Humility: *v.* Prayers, Pride.
What it is, 1 *Bec.* 198, 3 *Bec.* 621, *Sand.* 103; a godly sweet flower, 1 *Bec.* 198; practised by God himself, *ib.* 199; that of Christ, *ib.* 199; that of the Holy Ghost, *ib.* 199, 200; the virtue, strength, and profit of humility, *ib.* 200; its excellence, 1 *Brad.* 559; its blessedness, 2 *Jew.* 1093, 1094; the praise of humility, verses by Sir

N. Breton, *Poet.* 184; without it nothing comes well to pass, 1 *Bec.* 205; it is necessary to be humbled and cast down, 3 *Bul.* 59, 4 *Bul.* 549, *Sand.* 141; humility is the door whereby we enter into Christ, *Phil.* 135; it is needful in prayer, 1 *Bec.* 160, *Nord.* 21, 2 *Whitg.* 476; it goes before exaltation, 1 *Lat.* 544; humbling of oneself before God is an argument and token of salvation, 3 *Bec.* 100, 115; it is the mother of all virtue, 2 *Jew.* 1093; a mean to preserve unity, *Sand.* 103; it preserves the church of God, and upholds all good commonweals, 2 *Jew.* 1094; examples of it, and of the benefits derived from it, 1 *Bec.* 200, *Pil.* 47; how to obtain it, 1 *Bec.* 204; counterfeit humility, *Nord.* 22, *Sand.* 103, 104; superstitious humility, *Sand.* 104; the name falsely applied to unbelief, *Phil.* 140

Humpard (Conrad): letter to him, 3 *Zur.* 605

Humphrey, duke of Gloucester: quarrelled with card. Beaufort, 1 *Lat.* 118; the tale of his detecting a pretended miracle, 2 *Tyn.* 298 n.; he died suddenly, not without suspicion of murder, 1 *Lat.* 119, 2 *Tyn.* 297, 304, *Wool.* 113

Humphrey (Lau.): in exile at Zurich, *Jew.* xiii, 1 *Zur.* 11 n., 3 *Zur.* 752 n.; president of Magdalene college, Oxford, *Grin.* 269, *Pil.* 682, 2 *Zur.* 210, 218, 308; (some diplomas in his name as vice-chancellor will be found under the title Oxford;) his learning, 1 *Ful.* 507, 509; his scruples about the habits, *Jew.* xix, *Now.* ii; a conference to be held with him, *Park.* 233; he remains immovable, *ib.* 234; appointed to preach at Paul's cross, *ib.* 239; his nonconformity, *ib.* 240; Jewel hesitates about admitting him to a benefice, in consequence of his opinion respecting. apparel, 4 *Jew.* 1265; he remains in his place, 1 *Zur.* 176; is permitted to officiate without the vestments, *ib.* 202 n.; entirely opposed to the more violent Puritans, *ib.* 292; his life of Jewel quoted or referred to, 2 *Brad.* xxi, n., *Jew.* vii, &c., xix, 4 *Jew.* 1194 n., *Rid.* xi. n., *Rog.* 266 n., 1 *Zur.* 310 n.; his praise of a Latin sermon by Jewel, 2 *Jew.* 949; letters by him, 1 *Zur.* 133, 151, 157 (with Sampson), 289, 310, 324, 326, 2 *Zur.* 20, 121 (with Coverdale and Sampson), 298, 301; letters to him from Bullinger, 1 *Zur.* 345, 360

Hun (Rich.): *v.* Hunne.

Hundred: a perfect number, *Bale* 468

Huneric, tyrant of the Vandals: *Rid.* 147

Hungary: wars with the Turks there, 2 *Cran.* 232, *Grin.* 13, 14, *Lit. Eliz.* 451, 454, 461, 524, 527, 533 n., *Pra. Eliz.* 463; professors of the gospel dispersed there, 4 *Bul.* xxi; affairs of the country, 3 *Zur.* 633, 634, 699; Ferdinand elected king, *Grin.* 14 n

Hungate (Mr): *Grin.* 325

Hunger: the force of it, *Pil.* 456, 458; threatened as a punishment against the despisers of God's word, 1 *Bec.* 469, 470; what it is to break bread to the hungry, *ib.* 108; spiritual thirst, 1 *Bec.* 64; hunger and thirst of the soul, 1 *Cran.* 38; not easily perceived of the carnal man, his mind being in the kitchen and buttery, *ib.* 39

Hungerford (Walter lord), of Heytesbury: he (Sir Walter Hungerford, Jan. 1532) sends a citation to Latimer, 2 *Lat.* 350; his offence and execution, 3 *Zur.* 202

Hungerford (Ant.), of Downe Ampney: 2 *Zur.* 328 n

Hungerford (Sir Ant.), son of the last, *ib.*

Hungus, a Scottish prince, 1 *Hoop.* 314 n

Hunne (Rich.): charged with heresy, and murdered in prison, 2 *Lat.* 362, 3 *Tyn.* 146, 166, *Wool.* 113 (there John); condemned for heresy after his death, and his body burned, *Bale* 395, 3 *Tyn.* 167; Dr Horsey, the supposed murderer, obtained the king's pardon, 3 *Tyn.* 166

Hunnings (Mr): 2 *Cran.* 520

Hunnis (Will.): notice of him, *Poet.* xix; poems by him, viz. Psalm vi. paraphrased, *ib.* 143; Psalm li. paraphrased, *ib.* 147; certain short and pithy prayers unto Jesu Christ our Saviour, *ib.* 152; a lamentation touching the follies and vanities of our youth, *ib.* 153; a dialogue between Christ and a sinner, *ib.* 154; a meditation, *ib.* 155; an humble suit of a repentant sinner for mercy, and, a psalm of rejoicing for the wonderful love of Christ, *ib.* 157; gray hairs, *ib.* 158; God's covenant with Noah, *ib.* 159

Huns: their devastations, 2 *Bul.* 109, 4 *Bul.* 200, *Grin.* 98, 2 *Tyn.* 268

Hunsdon, co. Herts: Parker preaches there, 1535, before the princess Elizabeth, *Park.* ix, 483; Ridley visits the princess Mary there, *Rid.* x. n

Hunsdon (Hen. lord): *v.* Carey.

Hunt (......): saluted, *Phil.* 227 (probably the next).

Hunt (Martin): died in the King's Bench, *Poet.* 168

Hunt (Tho.), of Huntscourt: 1 *Tyn.* xiv.

Hunt (Walter): Contra Doctrices Mulieres, *Bale* 156

Hunter (Jo.): procured the Zurich letters, 1 *Zur.* ix, 2 *Zur.* v, xi.

Hunter (Jos.): Hist. of South Yorkshire, 2 *Lat.* 292 n

Hunting: by bishop Jewel's guests, 2 *Zur.* 86; his opinion on it, *ib.*

Huntingdon (Jo.), or Huntington: a priest who wrote a poem called the Genealogy of Heretics, *Bale* 429; he afterwards became a gospeller, *ib.* 157, 162

Huntingdon (Earls of): *v.* Hastings.

Huntley (Earls of): *v.* Gordon.

Hurlestone (......): *v.* Huddlestone.

Hurlestone (......), a skinner in Cornhill: an acquaintance of Sandys, *Sand.* xiii, xiv.

Hurly-burly: *Rid.* 305

Hurst (......), martyr: *Poet.* 168

HURT OF HEARING MASS, by Jo. Bradford, 2 *Brad.* 297, &c.

Hurting: forbidden, 1 *Bul.* 303

Hurtzel (Peter): 3 *Zur.* 225, 235

Husbandmen: those who sell their corn, &c., for unreasonable gain, are thieves, 2 *Bec.* 108; their duty, *ib.* 115

Husbandry: that of God, 1 *Brad.* 379, &c.

Husbands: *v.* Marriage, Obedience, Prayers.

The husband is the head of his wife, 1 *Tyn.* 334; the duty of husbands, 1 *Bec.* 287, 2 *Bec.* 334, &c., 1 *Lat.* 343, 352, 538, 2 *Lat.* 6, *Sand.* 202, 317, &c.; their duty, with probations of scripture, 2 *Bec.* 518; the office of a husband, and how he ought to rule, 1 *Tyn.* 200; husbands must not be tyrants or churlish to their wives, 2 *Bec.* 337; they must love them, and why, *ib.* 334; they must be faithful to them, *ib.* 335; they must make provision for them and for their families, *ib.* 336; they must provide for the souls' health of their wives, *ib.* 337; they must defend them from injuries, *ib.*; they must bear with them after the example of Christ, *ib.* 338; husbands and wives should pray for each other, 1 *Lat.* 393; what kind of husbands fathers must provide for their daughters, 2 *Bec.* 356

Husen, near Cappel: 4 *Bul.* x.

Husenbeth (F. C.): attempts to avail himself of the spurious seventh book against Parmenian attributed to Optatus, 2 *Ful.* 323 n

Hushel: *v.* Housel.

Huskyne (Friar), i. e. Jo. Œcolampadius, *q. v.*

Huss (Jo.): denied transubstantiation, *Rid.* 158; his exposition of an opinion held by Wickliffe, 3 *Jew.* 309; he wrote on the Apocalypse, *Bale* 256; his doctrine condemned at Constance, 3 *Jew.* 162; himself burned there, *Bale* 9, 10, *Lit. Eliz.* 450, *Phil.* 120; he was betrayed and murdered by the council, 2 *Bec.* 244, 4 *Jew.* 955, *Sand.* 64

Hussey (Jo. lord): in the Tower, 1 *Lat.* 163; his dau. Bridget, 2 *Bec.* 622 n

Hussey (Ant.): Cranmer's register, 2 *Cran.* 395; a proctor, *ib.* 491 (there called Hussaws); probably one of the examiners of Philpot, *Phil.* 104

Hussey (Tho.), of Lincolnshire: 1 *Brad.* 493

Hussites: followers of Huss, *Phil.* 424 (there called Ussites); persecuted on account of the cup, 2 *Jew.* 979

Hut (Kath.): martyred with two maids, Elizabeth and Jone, *Poet.* 167

Hutchins (Hugh), alias Tyndale, *q. v.*

Hutchinson (Anne), daughter of Roger: *Hutch.* viii, x.

Hutchinson (Eliz.), daughter of Roger: *Hutch.* viii, x.

Hutchenson (Jo.), at Roklyf: *Hutch.* i, x.

HUTCHINSON (Roger): the time and place of his birth unknown, *Hutch.* i; educated at St Jo. coll. Cambridge, *ib.*; one of those who sought to convert Joan Bocher, *ib.* ii, iii; made fellow of Eton, *ib.* vi; his dying charge to Jo. Day, *ib.* viii, 213; his death, *ib.* viii; his character by Ascham, *ib.* ix; his will, *ib.* x; his WORKS, edited by Jo. Bruce, esq., F.S.A., *Hutch.*

— Agnes his wife, and his children, *Hutch.* viii, x.

Hutchenson (Tho.), son of Roger: *Hutch.* viii, x.

Hutchinson (Will.), father of Roger: *Hutch.* i, 128

Hutten (Josua): *Rog.* vi. n

Hutten (Ulric de): published a treatise by Laurentius Valla against the Donation of Constantine, 2 *Ful.* 361 n

Hutton (......): Cranmer's friend, 2 *Cran.* 314 (probably David or John)

Hutton (Mr), a grocer of London: 2 *Cran.* 256

Hutton (David): 2 *Cran.* 275

Hutton (Hen.): farms the manor of Chipley, *Park.* 20

Hutton (Jo.): named, 2 *Cran.* 287; his embassy in the Netherlands, *ib.* 375 n.; Cranmer recommends him for an abbot, and his wife for an abbess, *ib.* 375, 376, 377; he recommends him to Wriothesley, *ib.* 378; his wife coming to England, *ib.* 381 bis

Hutton (Matt.), abp of York: mentioned as a professor at Cambridge, *Park.* 252; Margaret professor of divinity, 3 *Whitg.* vi; master of Pembroke hall, *ib.* vii; regius professor of divinity, *ib.*; not meet for the see of London, *Park.* 360; enjoined to examine the statutes of the church of York, *Grin.* 151; letters to him as dean, *ib.* 394—396; his disputes, when dean of York, with archbishop Sandys, *Sand.* xxiii, xxvi; his opinion on the Lambeth Articles, 3 *Whitg.* 612, 613

Huyck (Tho.): *v.* Huick.
Hyberden (Mr): *v.* Hubberdine.
Hychins (Will.), alias Tyndale, *q. v.*
Hyde (Nich.): 2 *Cov.* 501
Hyde (Tho.): *v.* Hide.
Hydroparastatites: administered water instead of wine in the Lord's supper, *Rog.* 296
Hyginus: *v.* Higinus.
Hyll (Adam): *v.* Hill.
Hymenæus: 4 *Bul.* 8
Hymn of the Three Children: *v.* Daniel.
Hymns: *v.* Poetry.
Hynkesell (Jo.): 2 *Cran.* 367 n
Hypanis: a river, 1 *Hoop.* viii.
Hyperbole: used in scripture, *Whita.* 546
Hyperdulia: *v.* Worship.
Hyperius (And. G.): Methodus Theologiæ, 3 *Whitg.* xxix; a book of his on the study of theology altered and published by L. à Villa-vincentio, *Whita.* 637; he regards the Jewish high-priest as an authority for an archbishop, 2 *Whitg.* 348, 420; mentioned, 1 *Zur.* 131
Hypocrisy, Hypocrites: *Now.* (101); on hypocritical profession of the gospel, 1 *Brad.* 436, 437; it is a double wickedness, *Rid.* 60; dissimulation prevalent, 1 *Bec.* 40; what hypocrites are, 3 *Bec.* 610, 4 *Bul.* 11, &c., *Now.* (101); different sorts of them, 4 *Bul.* 12; how they are in the church, *ib.* 11, 51; they are like chaff and rotten members, *ib.* 13; cannot always be well known in this world, 2 *Lat.* 62; their salutation and conduct, 1 *Lat.* 289; they hate the light of God's word, 2 *Bec.* 468; excuse themselves, 3 *Bul.* 106; extol their own works above the law of God, 2 *Tyn.* 127; are great observers of rites and ceremonies, *Wool.* 45; are puffed up, *ib.* 46; their alms, prayers, and fastings, 2 *Tyn.* 78; they seek to be praised of men, 1 *Tyn.* 73; hunt after vain glory in their prayers, 1 *Bec.* 130; outwardly abstain from sin, 1 *Tyn.* 80; are impure in heart, 2 *Tyn.* 26; think themselves pure in respect of open sinners, 1 *Tyn.* 496; they have works to sell, 1 *Lat.* 482, 2 *Lat.* 200; their faith, 2 *Tyn.* 11, 130; they have the world on their side, 1 *Tyn.* 133; their judgment of others, 2 *Tyn.* 112 —114; they must be rebuked, before open sinners are dealt with, *ib.* 44; their wisdom made foolishness, 1 *Tyn.* 134; in time of persecution they fall away, 3 *Bec.* 203

Hypostasis: *v.* God, iv.
Hyssop: 2 *Bul.* 184
Hysteron proteron: *Grin.* 197
Hythe, co. Kent: hospital of St Bartholomew, *Park.* 169; hospital of St John, *ib.*
Hythe (Haymo de), or Hethe, bp of Rochester: founded St Bartholomew's hospital near Hythe, *Park.* 169

I

I. (H.): translator of the Decades of Bullinger, 1, 2, 3, 4 *Bul.*
I. P. L. C. D.: these initials explained, *Pil.* 10
I AM: *v.* God.
Iceland: stockfish brought therefrom, 2 *Lat.* 339; (*v.* Hecla)
Ichthyophagi: 1 *Jew.* 222
Iconoclasts: *v.* Images.
Idiot: a private or unlearned person, 2 *Bec.* 568, 1 *Bul.* 71, 2 *Bul.* 3
Idleness: *v.* Prayers, Vagrants.
   The vice condemned, 2 *Bul.* 27, 2 *Jew.* 864, 2 *Lat.* 40, *Pil.* 44, *Sand.* 337; against it, with sentences and examples of scripture, 1 *Bec.* 444, &c.; it must be eschewed, 2 *Bec.* 101, 401, 406, 1 *Hoop.* 506; we must not be idle, 1 *Bec.* 346, 349; no man ought to live idly, 2 *Bec.* 162, 616, 617, especially in a Christian commonweal, 3 *Bec.* 505; the evil effects of idleness, 2 *Bec.* 368, 3 *Bec.* 60, 2 *Jew.* 941, *Pil.* 437, *Wool.* 130, &c.; its evil to commonwealths and individuals, *Sand.* 117; it leads to other sins, *ib.* 138; that of labouring men, *Pil.* 446; that of soldiers, *ib.* 447; that of servants, *ib.*; that of the Popish spiritualty, 3 *Bec.* 505; idleness exiled from Sandwich, *ib.* 599
Idleness: the word used for ailing, or illness, 3 *Tyn.* 282
Idle words: an account of them to be rendered, 1 *Bec.* 135
Idolatry: *v.* Commandments, Idols, Images, Mass, Worship.
   What it is, 3 *Bul.* 223, 234, 1 *Hoop.* 307, *Now.* (101), 2 *Tyn.* 214, &c., 3 *Tyn.* 125; God has forbidden it, 2 *Bul.* 224, 1 *Hoop.* 309, &c., *Now.* (9, 10), 121, 123; it is a grievous sin, 1 *Bec.* 359; whence it springs, 3 *Tyn.* 64; its origin according to the book of Wisdom, *Rid.* 85; it was devised by blind reason, 2 *Tyn.* 201; it springs from man's wisdom, 1 *Tyn.* 160; the steps to-

wards image-worship, 1 *Ful.* 541; the finding out of images was the beginning of it, 2 *Hoop.* 57; idolatry reigns in many parts of the world, 1 *Bec.* 254; different degrees or kinds of it, 1 *Ful.* 180, *Hutch.* 13; it is spiritual, or corporal, 2 *Brad.* 319; of the latter there are three sorts, *ib.* 319, 320; another statement as to three kinds or degrees of idolatry, 1 *Whitg.* 335; translations respecting idols and idolatry examined, 1 *Ful.* 100—107, 179—216; idolatry is older than the law of Moses, 2 *Cran.* 62; that of the Gentiles, *Bale* 215, 3 *Bul.* 233, *Calf.* 39, 185, 2 *Cran.* 144, 1 *Whitg.* 333, &c.; gods of the Egyptians and Philistines, 1 *Bul.* 224, 1 *Hoop.* 320; Tiberius wished Christ to be enrolled amongst the gods, 1 *Jew.* 217; the idolatry of the Jews, 3 *Bul.* 233, 2 *Cran.* 144, 1 *Whitg.* 333, &c.; they served other gods with the true God, 3 *Bul.* 235, 1 *Whitg.* 335; Christians should beware of idolatry, 1 *Hoop.* 457, 2 *Lat.* 233; we should flee from it, 1 *Brad.* 393; remedy against it, with sentences and examples of scripture, 1 *Bec.* 404, 405; various ancient heretics possessed idols, 1 *Ful.* 215; idolatry has infected all the Latin church, 1 *Hoop.* 310; Romish idolatry compared with the kinds before mentioned, 1 *Whitg.* 333, &c.; Turks and Saracens hate Christians for their idolatry, *Calf.* 44, *Wool.* 26; it is committed by the worship of images, *Bale* 25, *Calf.* passim, 2 *Cran.* 178, 2 *Ful.* 127, *Rid.* 81—96, 2 *Tyn.* 214, 3 *Tyn.* 62, by the worship of the host, *Bale* 215, 3 *Bec.* 274, 275, 278, 1 *Cran.* 229, 1 *Hoop.* 311, 1 *Jew.* 11, 12, 13, by the invocation and worshipping of saints, 1 *Hoop.* 312, &c., 457, 2 *Tyn.* 164; the distinctions made by Romanists are but shifts, *Sand.* 28; image worship re-established in England, *Rid.* 52; all occasions and tokens of it should be removed, 1 *Hoop.* 30, 37, 488; how many idolaters are in the world, 1 *Bec.* 321; idolaters warned, *ib.* 126; how they should behave, *ib.* 257; an example of prayer against idolatrous tyrants, out of the cxv. Psalm, by Jo. Hall, M.D., *Poet.* 197; inward idolatry forbidden, 1 *Hoop.* 318; idolatry may exist without images, 2 *Tyn.* 214; some make an idol of God himself, 1 *Tyn.* 106, 121; to worship God in a manner not commanded is idolatry, 2 *Hoop.* 56, *Hutch.* 254; to believe that a visible ceremony is a service to the invisible God is idolatry, 1 *Tyn.* 362; to serve God with mere bodily service is idolatry, *ib.* 373, 374

Idols: *v.* Gods (Strange), Idolatry, Images.

What they are, 1 *Ful.* 113, 2 *Ful.* 127, *Now.* (101); images abused, 1 *Ful.* 183; scripture calls them "signs," 4 *Bul.* 229; they teach not, 1 *Bul.* 232; on things offered to idols, 2 *Whitg.* 39

Ignatius (St): he was bishop of Antioch, *Rog.* 329; his alleged vision of angels singing antiphonally, 3 *Whitg.* 385; he expressed his desire of martyrdom (ep. ad Rom.), 2 *Bec.* 472; exhorted to adhere to apostolic tradition, meaning the apostles' writings, 1 *Ful.* 165, *Whita.* 570; at his martyrdom he said, Now I begin to be Christ's disciple, 3 *Jew.* 163; torn of wild beasts, 2 *Brad.* 191, 2 *Bul.* 105

His works, *Jew.* xxxviii; the epistles ascribed to him not accounted genuine by Fulke, 1 *Ful.* 254, 417; Whitaker doubts of them, *Whita.* 571; various texts of them, 2 *Brad.* 305 n., 2 *Ful.* 235 n., *Whita.* 571 n.; the epistle to the Ephesians, *Whita.* 572 n.; that to the Magnesians, *ib.* 572 n., 574; that to the Trallians, *ib.* 572 n., 573; that to the Romans, *ib.* 572 n.; that to the Philadelphians, *ib.* 572 n., 573; it is interpolated, 2 *Ful.* 235 n., 236 n.; how the Vatican Index and the Bibliothecæ Patrum deal with a remarkable sentence in it, *ib.* 236 n.; the Epistle to the Smyrneans, *Whita.* 572; it is interpolated, 2 *Ful.* 235 n.; cited, 1 *Ful.* 417; the epistle to Polycarp, *Whita.* 572; the spurious epistle to Mary, *ib.* 572, 573; that to the Tarsensians, spurious, *ib.* 572; that to Hero, spurious, *ib.*; but cited as genuine by Calfhill and Mr I. Taylor, *Calf.* 290 n.; the spurious epistle to the Antiochenes, 2 *Ful.* 236 n., *Whita.* 572, 573; that to the Philippians, spurious, *Whita.* 508, 572, 573; but adduced as authentic by Mr Taylor, 2 *Ful.* 236 n.; Papists, though they cite his writings, reject his authority, *Whita.* 573; errors in the writings ascribed to him, *ib.* 573, 574

He calls Jesus Christ his antiquity, &c., *Calf.* 280 n., 2 *Jew.* 926, 4 *Jew.* 778; speaks of the full persuasion or assurance of faith and love, 1 *Ful.* 417; writing to the Romans, shortly before his martyrdom he says, my Love is crucified, *Whita.* 578; says whosoever speaks more than is written, although he do miracles, &c., should be deemed a wolf (pseud.), *Calf.* 290; assumes not apostolic authority, *Whita.* 573; professes to understand heavenly things, yet declares himself inferior to Peter and Paul, *ib.* 574; calls the church most chaste, 2 *Jew.* 898; says that they who are Christ's are with the bishop, 1 *Jew.* 349; admonishes that no man do anything pertaining to the church without the consent of the bishop, 2 *Whitg.* 304; teaches that neither presbyter, deacon, nor layman, should do anything without the bishop, even as Christ does nothing without the Father (interpol.), *Whita.* 574; writes, do nothing without the bishops, for they are priests (pseud.), 1 *Ful.* 268; says, he that attempts to do anything without the bishop, breaks peace, and confounds good order (interpol.), 3 *Whitg.* 304, 305; writes, it is not lawful without the bishop either to baptize or to celebrate the supper (ἀγάπην ποιεῖν), 2 *Bec.* 231 n., 2 *Ful.* 235; instead of the last phrase, the interpolated copy reads, to sacrifice, &c., 2 *Ful.* 235, 3 *Zur.* 146 n.; he declares that a bishop has power over all (interpol.), 1 *Jew.* 350, 2 *Whitg.* 304, 306; says he is the form of God the Father of all (interpol.), 1 *Jew.* 349; calls him prince of priests (interpol.), 2 *Whitg.* 171, 304, 306, 310, 428; exhorts to honour God first, as the author and Lord of all things, then the bishop, as the prince of priests bearing the image of God, &c., then the king (interpol.), 1 *Ful.* 489, 2 *Whitg.* 304; would have the emperor obey the bishop (interpol.), 2 *Ful.* 235; says a bishop should be chosen by the church, *Whita.* 573; mentions Clement as bishop of Rome (pseud.), *ib.*; speaks of bishops, presbyters, and deacons, 1 *Ful.* 262, 2 *Tyn.* 256 n.; says there is no elect church without them, *Whita.* 573, 574; requires laymen to be subject to deacons; deacons to presbyters, presbyters to bishops, the bishop to Christ (interpol.), 2 *Whitg.* 304; describes the presbytery (interpol.), 1 *Jew.* 197; speaks (besides other orders) of chanters, labourers, and confessors (pseud.), 3 *Jew.* 272; cited as a witness for minor orders, *Rog.* 260 n.; he uses the word χειροτονία, 1 *Ful.* 247, 248; speaks of being made partakers of Christ's resurrection by baptism (interpol.), 3 *Jew.* 470, 593; calls the Lord's supper (or perhaps the feast of charity accompanying it) ἀγάπη, 2 *Bec.* 231 n. (see above); exhorts oftentimes to come to the eucharist, *ib.* 258, 3 *Bec.* 473, *Coop.* 67; calls the eucharist the flesh of our Saviour Jesus Christ, that hath suffered for our sins, 1 *Cran.* 149, 151, 1 *Jew.* 517, 518, *Whita.* 571; terms it a medicine of immortality, 3 *Bec.* 387; speaks of one bread being broken, and one cup divided to all, and of there being one altar for the whole church, 1 *Jew.* 116, 261, 2 *Jew.* 588, 636, 1114, *Rid.* 173; an interpolation noticed in this passage, 1 *Jew.* 261 n.; he mentions Lent (pseud.), 2 *Ful.* 237, *Whita.* 508; says he who fasts on the Lord's day or the sabbath, except the one sabbath of Easter, is a murderer of Christ (pseud.), *Whita.* 573, 1 *Whitg.* 223; Fulke, citing this passage, erroneously reads, who shall *not* fast, 2 *Ful.* 237; he condemns those who keep Easter with the Jews (pseud.), *Whita.* 573; speaks of virgins who had consecrated themselves to God (interpol.), 2 *Ful.* 235; censures revilers of lawful marriage (interpol.), 3 *Jew.* 404; wishes to be found meet for God, as were Peter and Paul, and the other apostles that were married (interpol.), 2 *Ful.* 236, 2 *Jew.* 727, 883, 989, 3 *Jew.* 392, 421, 3 *Zur.* 116, 146 n.; thinks St Paul by the phrase "true yoke-fellow" meant his wife (interpol.), 3 *Jew.* 414

Ignorance: a peculiar heritage of man by reason of his corruption, 3 *Bul.* 100; often a great sin, 2 *Bul.* 410, 1 *Jew.* 324, 2 *Lat.* 211; an impediment in the way of obedience to God's law, 1 *Hoop.* 426; wilful ignorance excuseth not, 1 *Lat.* 385, *Pil.* 146, 2 *Tyn.* 129; ignorance is the mother, not of devotion, but of superstition, unbelief, hypocrisy, and all errors, 3 *Bec.* 489, 1 *Jew.* 57, 78, 2 *Jew.* 799, 800, *Nord.* 16, 113, *Pil.* 499, *Sand.* 113; it is a cause of evil, 2 *Hoop.* 173; much trouble and danger arise from it, *ib.* 78; horrible blasphemy is sprung of it, *ib.* 311; the remedy against it, *ib.* 312; the comparative ignorance of Popish and Protestant times, *Pil.* 611; the ignorance of Hooper's clergy, 2 *Hoop.* 151

Ignoratio elenchi: a logical term, *Whita.* 287

Illeya (Tho. de): *v.* Ylleya.

Illiberis: *v.* Councils, *Elvira.*

Illness: evil conduct, 2 *Brad.* 345

Illumination: 3 *Bul.* 100

Illyricus (M. F.): *v.* Flacius.

IMAGE OF BOTH CHURCHES, by bp Bale, *Bale* 249—640

Image of God: *v.* God.

THE IMAGE OF GOD, OR LAYMAN'S BOOK, by R. Hutchinson, *Hutch.* 1—208

Images: *v.* Cross, Crucifix, Idolatry, Idols, Pictures.

(*a*) The question of their lawfulness; on their worship, &c.:—the subject of images is handled in *Calf.* passim, see the Table, p. 393; translations respecting images examined, 1 *Ful.* 100—107, 179—216; the word used figuratively, 2 *Jew.* 656; the

410 IMAGES

word "simulacrum," how used by Cicero, 1 *Ful.* 101; how by various Christian writers, *ib.* 102, &c.; Romish doctrine concerning images, *Rog.* 221, 223; card. Wiseman declares that the Pontificale "embodies in the most perfect manner the doctrine of the church concerning them," *Calf.* 415; this book ordains their hallowing, *ib.* 47, 48; lord Cobham on them, *Bale* 25; an article about them, 1538, 2 *Cran.* 484; a treatise on images, ascribed to Ridley, *Rid.* 81, &c.; perhaps not his, *ib.* 543; verses on images, by Dr W. Bill, *Hutch.* 10; letter from Parker and others to queen Elizabeth on images, *Park.* 79—95; images forbidden by God, 1 *Brad.* 152, 1 *Bul.* 223, 228, 4 *Bul.* 68, *Lit. Edw.* 497, (546), *Phil.* 406, *Rid.* 83, &c.; why forbidden, 3 *Zur.* 191, 192, it is neither lawful to make images for religion's sake, nor to worship them, 2 *Bec.* 69, 70; those of God plainly forbidden, *ib.* 66, &c.; it is a dishonour to the divine nature to make any similitude thereof, *Hutch.* 12; images of Christ more perilous than any, *Rid.* 91; images of the true God and of saints are as idolatrous as the images of the heathen, 2 *Tyn.* 214; what images are lawful, and where and how they are lawful, 2 *Bec.* 68, *Calf.* 44, 1 *Ful.* 191, 1 *Hoop.* 44, *Now.* (10), 123; how far not lawful, 1 *Bul.* 231; their lawfulness debated, *Bale* 94; their use allowed, at one time, by Latimer, not as objects of worship, but as laymen's books, 2 *Lat.* 233, 353, 359; Tyndale writes to the same effect, 3 *Tyn.* 60, 88; so the Institution of a Christian man, 2 *Cran.* 101; Gardiner says that those who press the commandment too far condemn printed books, *Rid.* 499; images allowable as memorials, 2 *Zur.* 44; images of the dead are signs, 4 *Bul.* 229; images defended by absurd arguments, 2 *Jew.* 657, 658, 664; called laymen's books, or the books of the unlearned, *Calf.* 21, 292, 346, 2 *Cran.* 101, 179, 1 *Hoop.* 39, 41, *Hutch.* 3, 2 *Lat.* 233, 359, *Now.* (10), 123, *Park.* 93, *Pil.* 146, 3 *Whitg.* 32; the phrase traced to Gregory the Great, *Calf.* 21 n., 2 *Jew.* 657, 660; a similar expression used by John Damascene, 1 *Hoop.* 39; they are not profitable as laymen's books, 2 *Bec.* 61, &c.; they are blind books and dumb schoolmasters, *Rid.* 95; Gardiner defends them, *ib.* 495, &c.; they are not tolerable in Christian churches, 2 *Bec.* 60, 65, 3 *Bec.* 233, 2 *Cran.* 178, 1 *Hoop.* 36, &c., 85, 2 *Hoop.* 57, 58; themselves to be avoided as well as the worship of them, 1 *Hoop.* 320; reasons against them, *Rid.* 83; they are not necessary for God's worship, or our instruction, 2 *Cran.* 10; are not needed to shew God unto us, 1 *Hoop.* 321; move not to devotion, 2 *Bec.* 63, 64, *Rid.* 87; cannot effectually teach, *Calf.* 345, &c., 1 *Hoop.* 30; are not things indifferent, *ib.* 85, *Rid.* 90; are needless to the learned, dangerous to the unlearned, *Rid.* 86; their danger is great, *ib.* 87; their ill effects, *Calf.* 358, &c., 1 *Hoop.* 30, 38, &c.; they are a stumblingblock to our brethren, 3 *Tyn.* 183, and to the Turks and Jews, *ib.* 184; images and pictures particularly objectionable over the Lord's table, *Rid.* 86, 91; their ill effect is not counteracted by sincere preaching, *ib.* 87; they are rightly termed "meretrices," *ib.*; against the worship of images, *Bale* 39, 2 *Bec.* 58, 59, 1 *Hoop.* 38, 317, 2 *Jew.* 644, &c. 4 *Jew.* 791, &c., 1 *Lat.* 76, *Phil.* 406, 3 *Tyn.* 59; their abuse, by pilgrimage, &c., 2 *Cran.* 499, 1 *Lat.* 53, by being vainly trusted in, 2 *Lat.* 233, 333; what great honours used to be paid to them, 2 *Bec.* 413; Antichrist maintains the lawfulness of bowing to them, 3 *Bec.* 521; what it is to bow before them, 2 *Bec.* 72; what it is to honour or worship them, *ib.* 72, 73, 1 *Hoop.* 317; image-worship condemned by L. Vives, *Calf.* 20 n.; More's argument to prove that men may worship an image without being idolaters, and Tyndale's reply, 3 *Tyn.* 125; their servants are God's enemies, 2 *Bec.* 74; the image-server is an idolater, 3 *Tyn.* 62, 125; the worshipping of images revenged with hideous plagues, *Phil.* 406; their destruction is not out of hatred to saints, 3 *Tyn.* 183, nor is it any dishonour to Christ, *Calf.* 338, &c.

(*b*) Their history: (for fuller statements of the decrees of the councils here mentioned, see Councils):—their invention the beginning of idolatry, 2 *Hoop.* 57; the heathen made images of aches and fevers, and sacrificed thereto, 3 *Tyn.* 163; heathen reasons for images, *Calf.* 39, 185; images, and all occasions of idolatry, forbidden to Israel, 1 *Tyn.* 413; none allowed in the tabernacle or temple, *Rid.* 84; the cherubim, &c., in the tabernacle and the temple, no warrant for them, 2 *Cran.* 178, 2 *Jew.* 645; attempt of Herod, Pilate, and Petronius, to place images in the temple, *Park.* 82, *Rid.* 84, 85; various old heretics had images, 1 *Ful.* 215; the Gnostics carried about an image of Christ, *Rid.* 88; none allowed in the primitive church, 2 *Jew.*

IMAGES 411

989, *Rid.* 88, 3 *Tyn.* 182; the absence of them remarked by the heathen, particularly by Celsus, *Park.* 86, *Rid.* 88; Christians had none in the days of Origen, *Calf.* 80; proofs against them from the fathers, councils, and histories, 1 *Ful.* 194, *Park.* 79, &c., *Rid.* 88, &c.; laws and decrees of princes, bishops and councils against them, 2 *Bec.* 61, 69, 71, 305, 312; pictures, &c., prohibited by the council of Eliberis, 2 *Bec.* 71, 2 *Brad.* 308, *Calf.* 154, 2 *Cran.* 179, 2 *Ful.* 153, 154, 1 *Jew.* 69, 70, 2 *Jew.* 659, 990, 4 *Jew.* 791, 1110, *Park.* 93, *Phil.* 407, *Rid.* 94; representations of the sign of Christ forbidden by Valens and Theodosius, 2 *Bec.* 71 n., *Calf.* 190, 2 *Ful.* 159, 2 *Jew.* 659, *Park.* 90, *Rid.* 92; when images were first placed in churches, 2 *Cran.* 178, 179; the placing of them in churches came from idolaters, 2 *Bec.* 61; Epiphanius destroyed a picture of Christ, or of some saint, hanging in a church at Anablatha, 2 *Bec.* 60, & al. (*v.* Epiphanius, vii.); Augustine disallows images, see p. 81 of this Index; they were not allowed by the church in the time of Jerome, 3 *Tyn.* 182; images broken by Serenus, bishop of Marseilles, 2 *Bec.* 61, 1 *Hoop.* 41, *Rid.* 92; sanctioned by Gregory the Great, *Rid.* 92, 3 *Tyn.* 183; he said that they should not be broken, but that they should by no means be worshipped, *Bale* 97, 1 *Hoop.* 41, *Whita.* 509; he called them laymen's books, 2 *Bec.* 60, 2 *Jew.* 657 (see p. 410, col. 1); image-worship condemned by the council of Constantinople, A.D. 680, *Phil.* 407, *Rid.* 497, also by the council held at Toledo the next year, 2 *Bec.* 71 n., *Phil.* 407; the Quini-Sext council allowed pictures of our Saviour to supersede typical representations by a Lamb, *Calf.* 137 n.; image-worship enjoined by a council at Rome under Gregory III., 2 *Bec.* 60, 2 *Brad.* 309, *Calf.* 48; images abolished by the emperor Leo III. and publicly burned at Constantinople, *Rid.* 93; condemned by the council held there, A.D. 754, *Calf.* 138, &c., 2 *Jew.* 659, 4 *Jew.* 1110, *Park.* 91, *Rid.* 93, 3 *Tyn.* 183 n., *Whita.* 509; they divided the church and the empire, *Park.* 93, *Rid.* 94; the popes persuaded the Eastern emperors to admit them, 2 *Cran.* 179; the Greek church never willingly consented to them, 1 *Hoop.* 40; their adoration decreed by the second Nicene council, *Calf.* 48, 1 *Jew.* 548, 4 *Jew.* 791, 792, 1055, 1109, 1110, *Park.* 91, 92, *Rid.* 94, *Rog.* 209, 3 *Tyn.* 183 n., *Whita.* 509; images forbidden by the council of Frankfort, 4 *Jew.* 1049, &c., which condemned the second council of Nice, *Calf.* 155, &c.; they were condemned by Charlemagne, *ib.* 311; controversy on this subject as recorded in his Capitular, *ib.* 156—175; a synod at Mayence allowed images, but forbade them to be worshipped, 2 *Jew.* 647, 657, 668; a council at Sens preferred images to books, *ib.* 660; how the churches came to be so full of them, 2 *Cran.* 178; not allowed in the Greek church in Russia, 3 *Zur.* 691; there were, in Popish churches, images of the Father, *Calf.* 40, 1 *Hoop.* 320, *Rog.* 223, of the Son, *Rog.* 223, & al., of the Holy Ghost, *ib.* 223, of the Trinity, *Bale* 95, 97, 99, 3 *Bec.* 521, 522, *Rog.* 223; the holy rood, with St Mary and St John, 1 *Ful.* 190, 204; the images of saints and their emblems, 2 *Bec.* 65; why images were covered in Lent, 1 *Bec.* 111; idols at Canterbury, Walsingham, &c., 1 *Hoop.* 41 (and see below); the gilding and painting of images of Christ and the saints, 1 *Lat.* 22—24; dead images gilded, clothed, and lighted with wax candles; Christ's lively images neglected, *ib.* 36, 37; the sin of this, 4 *Bul.* 503, 3 *Tyn.* 59, 62, 82; images of Job, 3 *Tyn.* 105; deceitful and juggling images, 1 *Lat.* 54; moving and speaking ones, 2 *Jew.* 665 (*v.* Miracles); the devotion of image-makers, *Bale* 96; king Henry's injunction against images, &c. 2 *Cran.* 372 n.; images of the Father disallowed by the Institution, *ib.* 101; other images approved, as books for the unlearned, *ib.*; images destroyed in England, 3 *Zur.* 604; the rood of grace and other images broken at Paul's cross, *ib.* 606, 609; our lady of Walsingham and certain other idols burned at Chelsea, 2 *Brad.* 2 n., 2 *Lat.* 393 n.; the images of our lady of Worcester, Walsingham, Ipswich, Doncaster, and Penrice, would have made a jolly muster in Smithfield, 2 *Lat.* 395 (see those names, and also Willesden); mandates for removing shrines and images, 2 *Cran.* 490, 503, 509; their abolition in king Edward's time, 2 *Zur.* 158, 159 n., 3 *Zur.* 377; injunctions against them by the king and Cranmer, 2 *Cran.* 161, 499, 503, by Hooper, 2 *Hoop.* 121, 129, 143; their restoration demanded by the rebels of Devon, 2 *Cran.* 176; fraud at Christ church, Dublin, *Park.* 95; numbers of idols set up in queen Mary's time, 2 *Hoop.* 316, 3 *Zur.* 177 n.; queen Elizabeth desired to retain the crucifix, with St Mary and St John, 1 *Zur.* 73, 74; (see also p. 294, col. 2, of this

Index); letter from Parker and others to her containing reasons from scripture, the fathers, and councils, against the use of images in churches, *Park.* 79—95; images removed from churches in the time of Elizabeth, 1 *Ful.* 182, 184, 1 *Zur.* 63; those upon the rood-loft commonly replaced by a text (1 Jo. v. 21), 1 *Ful.* 193; Grindal enjoins fat (i. e. solid) images to be destroyed, *Grin.* 135; inquiry about images, *ib.* 159; images are retained by some churches which worship them not, *Whita.* 509, as in the churches of Germany, 2 *Zur.* 48 n., the Lutherans retain the crucifix with St Mary and St John, 1 *Ful.* 204; there are none any where but where the pope is [or was] head of the church, 2 *Cran.* 179

Imbraiding: upbraiding, reproach, 1 *Bec.* 131
Immanity: savageness, *Calf.* 353
Immarcescible: unfading, 1 *Brad.* 265
Immortality: *v.* Soul.
Impanation: 1 *Cran.* 251, 253, 280, 305
Impatience: *v.* Patience.
Impenitence: final impenitency, 2 *Bul.* 425
Imperfection: *Now.* (101)
Impery: empire, dominion, absolute command, 1 *Brad.* 341, 2 *Jew.* 964
Importable: that cannot be borne, 1 *Bec.* 53, 1 *Bul.* 3
Imposition of Hands, *q. v.*
Impossible: sometimes used in scripture for what is very hard to be done, *Hutch.* 112, 114
Impravable: not to be corrupted, 1 *Bec.* 105
Impress: a device, 3 *Whitg.* xvi.
Improper (v. a.): to appropriate, 2 *Jew.* 671
Impropery: impropriety, upbraiding, 1 *Bec.* 131
Impropriations: *Park.* 99; what, 1 *Lat.* 100 n.; condemned, *Pil.* 105, 2 *Zur.* 32, 360; they are against the word of God, *Pil.* 62; their evil effects, 3 *Bec.* 536, 537, 1 *Lat.* 100, 203, *Sand.* 155; a return of them required, 2 *Cran.* 428
Improve: to reprove, disprove, or disallow, 1 *Bec.* 3, 1 *Brad.* 329, 498, 2 *Brad.* 143, 1 *Bul.* 3, 1 *Jew.* 227, *Park.* 130, *Pil.* 629, 1 *Tyn.* 41, 258, 329, 3 *Tyn.* 128, 2 *Whitg.* 516, 3 *Whitg.* 550
Imps: young offspring, *Bale* 292; godly and virtuous ones, 2 *Bec.* 205; the first imps of the faith, i. e. the first Christians, 2 *Ful.* 18; Edward VI. styled a virtuous imp, *Now.* 229
Imputed Righteousness: *v.* Justification.
Ina, king of the West Saxons: gave Peter-pence to Rome, and became a monk there, *Bale* 447

Inaquation: 1 *Cran.* 305, 306
Incantation: *v.* Witchcraft.
Incarnation: *v.* Christ.
  The term not in scripture, 1 *Jew.* 533; its meaning, 1 *Cran.* 288; Gardiner makes the sacramental bread incarnate, *ib.* 306
Incense: what it denotes, 2 *Bul.* 157; Eusebius interprets it of praise, *Coop.* 92; the altar of incense, 2 *Bul.* 157; incense mentioned in the Apocalypse, *Bale* 342; burned by Tertullian in his chamber, *Rid.* 90; when first used at mass, 2 *Brad.* 311, *Pil.* 503
Incent (Dr): probably the dean of St Paul's, 2 *Cran.* 305
Incent (Jo.), Parker's registrar: *Park.* 161, 214, 328 n.; a notary, *Grin.* 463
Incest: 1 *Bul.* 417; the names of incestuous persons to be presented to the ordinary, *Grin.* 143
Inclosure: *v.* Commons.
Inconstancy: *v.* Youth.
Inculk: to inculcate, 3 *Tyn.* 245
Incute: to strike in, 1 *Bec.* 63
Ind: India, *Pil.* 643
Indent: to make an agreement, *Sand.* 276; indented, i. e. bargained, agreed for, 2 *Brad.* 318, 2 *Tyn.* 166
Indexes (Prohibitory and Expurgatory): references to some early prohibitory lists, published in England, *Rid.* 494 n., 1 *Tyn.* 3 n., 31, 33 n., 39 n.; Cathalogus librorum hæreticorum de commiss. Tribunal. sanctiss. Inquisit. Venetiarum, 1554, republished by the Rev. Jos. Mendham, 1840; it censures the Recognitions, *Calf.* 21 n.; proscribes the Commentaries of Æneas Sylvius, and the Fasciculus of O. Gratius, 2 *Ful.* 302 n.; Index lib. prohib. Rom. 1559, condemns the Hist. Certaminis Apostolici, *Calf.* 126 n.; interdicts the Opus Imperfectum, *ib.* 95 n.; prohibits a book called Unio Dissidentium, *Rid.* 494 n.; decree in it (or in the next) concerning vernacular versions of the scriptures, *Whita.* 209; the Tridentine prohibitory Index, 1564, releases books from censure, *Calf.* 95 n., 126 n.; the same, Antv. 1570, forbids the perusal of the Caroline Capitular, *ib.* 155 n.; the Belgic Index Expurgatorius, Antv. 1571, *Calf.* 20 n.; it condemns a declaration that to adore the wood of the cross is manifest idolatry, *ib.* 376 n.; the Index Expurgatorius of card. Quiroga, Madriti, 1584, *Calf.* 20 n.; it expurgates P. Crinitus, *ib.* 190 n.; erases a declaration of Erasmus that ancient monks were not bound by vows, 2 *Ful.* 103 n.;

the Index Expurgatorius, Lugd. 1586, censures statements that priests are by God's law subject to princes, *Rog.* 339 n., that the care of religion pertains to kings, *ib.* 342 n., that the godly cannot be punished after death, *ib.* 214 n.; the Vatican Expurgatory Index, Romæ, 1607, *Calf.* 20 n.; this, and the ed. of Bergom. 1608, erase a passage in the interpolated epistle of Ignatius to the Philadelphians, 2 *Ful.* 236 n., and strike out the term "magus," applied to pope Silvester, *Calf.* 91 n.; the Index auctorum damnatæ memoriæ, issued by Mascaregnas, inquisitor general of Portugal, Ulyssip., 1624, *ib.* 20 n.; it admonishes that the works of Æneas Sylvius be read cautiously, 2 *Ful.* 302 n.; the Index lib. prohib. et expurg. of card. Zapata, Hispali, 1632, *Calf.* 20 n.; it condemns a statement that God alone is to be adored, *ib.* 375 n.; censures a passage of Polydore Vergil about ancient monks, 2 *Ful.* 103 n.; forbids the Colloquies of Erasmus, *ib.* 194 n.; the Index lib. prohib. et expurg., Matriti, 1640, *Calf.* 20 n.; the reprint, Matriti [Genevæ], 1667, 2 *Ful.* 290 n.; it censures a note of Erasmus stating the "rock" to be Peter's profession, *ib.*; the edition, Madriti, 1707, *Calf.* 20 n.; Indice ultimo, Madrid, 1790, *ib.*; various Indexes expurgate the Enchiridion of Erasmus, *ib.* 314 n.; D. Franci Disq. de Papistarum Indicibus, 1684, *ib.* 96 n

India: *v.* Church, II. ii., Thomas (St).

Its geography, 2 *Zur.* 95; Christianity there before the Jesuits, 3 *Jew.* 198

Indies (West): *v.* West Indies.

Indifferently: impartially, *Grin.* 21

Individuum vagum: a term applied to the object denoted by the word "Hoc" in the form of consecration, 1 *Cran.* 106, 108, 2 *Jew.* 787—790; some call it individuum in genere, 1 *Cran.* 106; other names, 2 *Jew.* 789

Indolentia: that of the Stoics, 2 *Bul.* 82

Indract (St): murdered at Shapwick, *Bale* 191

Induction to benefices: 2 *Zur.* 360

Indulgences: *v.* Pardons.

Ineptly: foolishly, *Calf.* 216

Infallibility: *v.* Church, I. ix.

Romish claims to it, 2 *Tyn.* 289

Infants: *v.* Children.

Infernus: *v.* Hell.

Infidelity: *v.* Unbelief.

Infidels: *v.* Unbelievers.

Infirm: to weaken, 1 *Brad.* 544

Infirmity: sins of infirmity, 2 *Bul.* 417

Informers: *v.* Promoters.

Infortiatum: *v.* Law (Civil).

Infundeth: poureth into, 2 *Bec.* 562

Infymacion: a confirmation, *Park.* 268

Ingeam (Vincent): a Kentish justice, 2 *Cran.* 367

Ingenitus: the word not found in the scriptures, 3 *Jew.* 440

Ingeny: disposition, 1 *Bec.* 277

Ingram (Rob.): Hooper kept in his house at Gloucester before his martyrdom, 2 *Hoop.* xxv.

Ingratitude: what it is, 1 *Bec.* 186; a foul crime, *Sand.* 156; nothing displeases God so much, 1 *Bec.* 185

Ingworth (Rich.), or Yngworth, suffragan of Dover: Cranmer's instrument proposing him and another to the king, 2 *Cran.* 471; Cranmer's commission to him as suffragan, *ib.*; a visitor of monasteries, 2 *Lat.* 378 n., 395 n., 400 n

Iniquity: *v.* Mystery, Sin.

Injunctions: *v.* Articles of Inquiry.

Injuries: two ways of doing them to the souls of men, 2 *Hoop.* 67

Inhiate: to gape, 1 *Bec.* 253

Inn: to be at inn, what, 1 *Brad.* 79

Innocency: what it is, 3 *Bec.* 606, 620; commendation of it, 1 *Bec.* 206; how to practise it, *ib.* 206, 207; it is the security of princes, *Sand.* 405; how alleged by David, *ib.* 404

Innocent I., pope: many of the epistles ascribed to him are clearly and confessedly spurious, *Whita.* 435; that to Decentius considered so, 2 *Ful.* 90 n.; that to Victricius, *ib.* 179; that to Exuperius, cited by Gratian, *ib.* 244; his Pontificale, *Calf.* 381 n.; he excommunicated the emperor Arcadius, 1 *Jew.* 405; erased the name of Arsacius, bishop of Constantinople, from the calendar, 4 *Jew.* 650; his judgment in the case of Chrysostom and Theophilus, 1 *Jew.* 387, 394; what he wrote to the bishops of Africa touching Pelagius, 2 *Ful.* 351, 1 *Jew.* 394, 405; he complains of his want of authority to force Pelagius to come before him, 4 *Jew.* 996; how addressed by one of the synods of Carthage, 2 *Ful.* 351 n.; he calls other bishops co-disciples and copresbyters, 1 *Jew.* 419; his decree for the authority of the church of Rome, 3 *Bec.* 513 n.; he received apocryphal books, *Whita.* 39, 46; condemned the Gospel of Peter, *ib.* 312; cited in support of tradition, *ib.* 609; he confessed original sin, 2 *Bul.* 390; forbade the sacrament to be celebrated on Good Friday or Holy Saturday, 1 *Jew.* 246;

thought the eucharist necessary for infants, 2 *Ful.* 41, 392; ordained the use of the pax, 2 *Brad.* 311, *Pil.* 503; calls extreme unction a sacrament, 3 *Jew.* 457; permits it to be ministered by any Christian, *Calf.* 246

Innocent II., pope: a dissension between him and Peter compounded by Bernard, 1 *Jew.* 382; an indulgence granted by him, *Rog.* 220, 221

Innocent III., pope: *v.* Councils, LATERAN IV.

Before his election to the popedom, he was called Lotharius Levita, 3 *Bul.* 82, 2 *Hoop.* 521; he licensed the emperor Otho to marry his niece, *Pil.* 603; compelled king John to pay him tribute, 2 *Hoop.* 48, 522; excommunicated and insulted him, 1 *Ful.* 36 n.; absolved his subjects from their allegiance, and declared him deposed, 1 *Tyn.* 339 n.; his works, *Jew.* xxxviii; his creed published in the Lateran council, 3 *Bul.* 82, 4 *Bul.* 557; he questions whether, and in what sort, a man, either in his madness or in his sleep, may be baptized, 3 *Jew.* 358; inquires whether many species be one sacrament, 2 *Jew.* 794; was the father, and a great promoter, of the doctrine of transubstantiation, 1 *Cran.* 240, (88), 4 *Bul.* 278, 1 *Hoop.* 118, *Rid.* 16, 17, 246, 509; his decree affirming that doctrine, 2 *Bec.* 260, 268, 290, 3 *Bec.* 232, 261, 274, 361, 373, 374, 426; he recounts various opinions as to the words of consecration, 2 *Bec.* 263, 1 *Hoop.* 518, 1 *Jew.* 123, 2 *Jew.* 789, *Park.* 251, *Rid.* 18, 26; declares that those words were commanded to be said in silence, lest they should be despised, 2 *Jew.* 703; reports a fable respecting certain shepherds using the words over their bread, *ib.* 705; says none can make the sacrament but a priest duly ordained, &c., 1 *Hoop.* 192 n.; refers to cases of non-consecration, 1 *Jew.* 550 n.; cited with reference to opus operatum, 2 *Jew.* 750; he would prove transubstantiation by a miracle, 1 *Hoop.* 225; mentions some as affirming that after consecration the very substance of the bread remains, 3 *Jew.* 490; asserts that Christ's body is made from bread, 1 *Cran.* 194; said to teach that the body of Christ remains no longer than the sacrament is in the eating, *ib.* 56, (24); he refers to Judas receiving the sacrament, 3 *Bec.* 466; writes about a mouse eating the sacramental bread, &c., 4 *Bul.* 306, 1 *Hoop.* 167 n., 168, 225; declares that the canon of the mass came from Christ and his apostles, 1 *Jew.* 9; elsewhere states that pope Gelasius made a part of it, and he did something therein himself, 2 *Brad.* 309, 310; testifies that the Greek church did not use the mixed cup, 1 *Jew.* 139; ordains that the sacrament, and also chrism, be kept under lock and key, 2 *Bec.* 253, 3 *Bec.* 373, 2 *Brad.* 310, 1 *Cran.* 238, 2 *Cran.* 172, 2 *Jew.* 556; mentions priests who scarce said mass four times a year, 1 *Jew.* 199; gives a reason why the priest may say " Dominus vobiscum," though there be but one at mass, *ib.* 174; admits that the vestments were taken from Judaism, 4 *Bul.* 421, 1 *Zur.* 158; commands that meet men be provided to minister according to the diversities of languages, 3 *Bec.* 409, 1 *Jew.* 291; referred to on ecclesiastical orders, 4 *Bul.* 114; in the council of Lateran he enforced auricular confession, 2 *Brad.* 310, 1 *Jew.* 120, 2 *Jew.* 1133; writes on the making of chrism, 3 *Jew.* 178; declares it is not Jewish as some assert, *ib.*; forbids priests to marry, *ib.* 386; declares marriage to be unholy, *Calf.* 238, 239, 240, 1 *Jew.* 77; says that they that be in the flesh, that is to say, in marriage, cannot please God, *Calf.* 239, 3 *Jew.* 420; by the "defiled and unbelieving," Tit. i. 15, he understands married people, *Calf.* 239, 3 *Jew.* 420; to the question whether priests having several concubines are to be accounted bigami, he replies in the negative, 4 *Jew.* 636; interprets the name Cephas as meaning caput, 2 *Ful.* 301 n.; says the pope is not a bare man, 2 *Jew.* 575; asserts that the pope may be judged by no man, 1 *Jew.* 68, 93, 442, 3 *Jew.* 205, 4 *Jew.* 968, 1116; declares that his will only must stand for law, 4 *Jew.* 1052; says that he may make a layman his delegate to hear and determine in priests' causes, *ib.* 961; declares that the emperor holds his empire of the pope, 2 *Jew.* 917, 4 *Jew.* 836, 837; his absurd estimate of the superiority of the papal power over the imperial, 1 *Ful.* 36 n., 1 *Jew.* 14, 143, 414, 4 *Jew.* 672, 673, 675, 676, 847; he ordered that no archbishop should have his pall without an oath of obedience to the pope, 2 *Brad.* 310; thinks that though a reason cannot be given for everything brought in by our forefathers, profound mysteries lie hidden in them, 3 *Jew.* 552; declares that our virtues are dyed in the blood of the cross of Christ, *ib.* 492

Innocent IV., pope: claimed the right to depose princes, 1 *Jew.* 443 n.; sent ambassador to Tartary, *Wool.* 28

Innocent VI., pope: gave benefices only to such as were throughly proved in life and learning, 1 *Bec.* 384, 385
Innocent VIII., pope: bought the popedom, *Sand.* 241; dispensed with the priests of Norway to consecrate without wine, 1 *Jew.* 137, 222; his incontinency, *Rog.* 304
Inns: *v.* Taverns.
Inns of Court: *v.* London.
Inquisition: established in Spain, 2 *Jew.* 690, *Rog.* 291; English merchants in peril from it, 1 *Zur.* 233; three of them burned, 3 *Zur.* 626; the Inquisition in the Low-Countries, *ib.* 417 n., 568, 670; attempt to establish it at Antwerp, *ib.* 417 n
Inspiration: *v.* Scripture.
Instant (v. a.): to importune, *Bale* 242
Institutes of Justinian: *v.* Law (Civil).
Institution of a Christen man, 1537: a godly book, 2 *Cran.* 16; often called the Bishops' Book, 2 *Cran.* 83 n., 337 n., *Hutch.* 231 n.; some account of it, 2 *Cran.* 337 n.; by whom written, 1 *Lat.* x, 2 *Lat.* 369 n., 376 n., 379 n., *Rid.* 511; ascribed by Ridley to bishop Gardiner, *Rid.* 135, but probably he meant the King's Book, or Necessary Doctrine, *ib.* 511; minute of an answer of Henry VIII. to a letter from the commissioners, 2 *Cran.* 469; how far the book was authorized by the king, *ib.* 337 n.; the clergy enjoined to procure it, 2 *Lat.* 243; opposition of magistrates to it, 2 *Cran.* 350, 352, 354; it affirms that holy scripture alone sheweth men the right path to come to God, 2 *Cov.* 335; asserts the equality of bishops and presbyters, 2 *Bec.* 319 n.; speaks against masses of scala cœli, &c., 3 *Zur.* 212; said to sharply reprove the Florentine council, *Rid.* 135, 511; corrections by Henry VIII., with Cranmer's annotations thereon, 2 *Cran.* 83, and see 358, 359; this book superseded in 1543 (not 1540) by the Necessary Doctrine, 2 *Cran.* 16 n
Institution to benefices: 2 *Zur.* 360
Insurrection: *v.* Rebellion.
Intention: the Romish doctrine of the priest's intention, 2 *Brad.* 283, 1 *Cov.* 453, 2 *Cov.* 262, 1 *Jew.* 13, 139, 2 *Jew.* 705
Intentions (First and second): terms in logic, 1 *Tyn.* 157 n
Intercession: *v.* Christ, iii. c. 2; also Angels, Saints.
 Intercession a part of prayer, *Sand.* 77
Interdict: lands interdicted by the pope, and given to other princes, 1 *Tyn.* 235, 338; interdict of the diocese of Chichester, by Ralph, bishop, temp. Will. II., 2 *Tyn.* 295; of all England, by archbishop Langton, *ib.*;
the realm interdicted in Henry VIII's time, 2 *Cran.* 13; towns interdicted, *ib.* 282 n.; churches interdicted on blood being spilled in them, *ib.* 281 n., till the raising of money to pay for the hallowing, 1 *Tyn.* 340; Rye church not interdicted after manslaughter committed in it, 2 *Cran.* 357
Interest: *v.* Usury.
Interim: an ordinance of Charles V. temporarily settling the differences between the Protestants and the Papists in a manner favourable to the latter, 3 *Bec.* 260, 2 *Cran.* 421 n., 1 *Lat.* 147 n., 305, *Park.* 141, *Rid.* 120, 3 *Zur.* 18 n., 335, 379, 470 n., 532, 540, 646, 649, 650; some account of it, 3 *Bec.* 260 n., 1 *Lat.* 147 n., 305 n., 2 *Zur.* 125 n., 3 *Zur.* 383 n.; its provision respecting married priests, *Pil.* 574, 657; its order about confession, 3 *Jew.* 363; persecutions consequent upon it, 2 *Cov.* 526, 3 *Zur.* 18, 32; Bucer and Fagius obliged to quit Germany, *ib.* 329 n.; it is received at Constance, *ib.* 641 n., in East Friesland, *ib.* 61, at Strasburgh, *ib.* 667; confuted by Calvin, *Rid.* 120
Interludes: played in the church, 3 *Whitg.* 384
Intermediate state: *v.* Hell.
Intervallum: the time between Christmas and Quinquagesima, *Pra. Eliz.* 232
Introits: ordained by pope Celestine, 3 *Bec.* 263, 2 *Brad.* 305, *Pil.* 503 n., 3 *Whitg.* 73; what they are, *Lit. Edw.* 41 n
INVECTIVE AGAINST SWEARING, by T. Becon, 1 *Bec.* 350
Invention of the Cross (*q. v.*), or Helen's day: *Pil.* 15
Invention of man: the evil of it contrasted with God's word, 3 *Bec.* 490—496
Inventory: one of Bucer's property, *Park.* 47, 3 *Zur.* 362; A short Inventory of certain Idle Inventions, by C. T., 1581; notice of it, *Poet.* xxxvii; an extract, *ib.* 395
Invination: 1 *Cran.* 305, 306
Invisible: *Now.* (101)
Invitations: *v.* Gospel.
Invitatories: what, *Lit. Edw.* 18 n., *Lit. Eliz.* 34 n
Invocation: *v.* Prayer, Saints.
 What it is, 3 *Bul.* 204, 206, 4 *Bul.* 163, *Now.* (101); it springs from faith, 3 *Bul.* 212
Ipocras, or Hippocras: a kind of piment, or spiced wine, 2 *Bec.* 534
Ipswich, co. Suffolk: the image of our lady of Ipswich, 1 *Hoop.* 40, 1 *Lat.* 53 n., 2 *Lat.* 395, 3 *Tyn.* 125; idolatry there, *Pil.* 63; the maid of Ipswich, *v.* Wentworth; two

women burned there, *Poet.* 166; other martyrs there, *ib.* 173

Ireland: *v.* Church, II. v. *f.*

The people anciently called Scots, 2 *Ful.* 16, 19; pilgrimage thither, *ib.* 12; Ireland instigated by the clergy to rebel against king John, 2 *Tyn.* 295, and against Richard II., *ib.* 296; copper coinage used there as early as the reign of Edward III., *ib.* 231 n.; a wild country, *Hutch.* 73; More says the wild Irish prayed when they went to steal, 3 *Tyn.* 126; Parker fears the people of the North of England will become too much Irish and savage, *Park.* 123; the title of king of Ireland acknowledged by the French king, 3 *Zur.* 563 n.; the prince of this realm (England) reported to be not lord, but king, of Ireland, by ancient right, *Park.* 328; an attempted invasion by the French, 1551, 3 *Zur.* 107; unsettled state of the country, 1 *Zur.* 140, 329, 332; rebellions of the O'Neales, *Lit. Edw.* 473, *Pil.* 74 n., 1 *Zur.* 186, 194, 195, 2 *Zur.* 335; rebellion in Ulster, 1573, 2 *Zur.* 222 n.; English colonies established, *ib.* 224; the rebellion of N. Saunders, J. Fitzmaurice, &c., *Lit. Eliz.* 657 n.; the pope would wrest Ireland from the queen of England, 1 *Ful.* 487, 510; war there, 1599, *Lit. Eliz.* 473; the Spanish army defeated by lord Mountjoy, 2 *Zur.* 335; Campion's History of Ireland, *Park.* 407

Ireland (Earl of), i. e. B. Fitzpatrick, *q. v.*

Ireland (James), a Londoner: examined before the ecclesiastical commissioners, *Grin.* 201

Irenæus (St):

i. *His Life and Works:*—he was a disciple of Polycarp, who was a disciple of St John, 1 *Cran.* 265; his account of Polycarp and his doctrine, *Calf.* 270, *Whita.* 581 (see also iv. below); he was bishop of Lyons, *Rog.* 329; held a provincial council in France, 4 *Jew.* 1125; his mission to the churches of Phrygia, 2 *Whitg.* 312, 314; his martyrdom, 2 *Bul.* 105; his body falsely stated to have been burned by the Huguenots in 1562, 4 *Jew.* 1042, 1047; his works, *Jew.* xxxviii, 2 *Whitg.* xxix; he forbids additions to them, *Bale* 638; he wrote on the Apocalypse, *ib.* 255; he cites the Shepherd of Hermas, *Whita.* 68

ii. *Scripture, Tradition, Doctrine:* he compares the Jews, or their economy, to the sowing of the seed, 2 *Jew.* 615; considers that the law was lost in the captivity, and that Ezra restored it, *Whita.* 115; asserts the miraculous unanimity of the LXX. interpreters, *ib.* 120; writes that all which the Lord did, taught, and suffered, may be found in the prophets, *ib.* 620; says the precepts of a perfect life are the same in both testaments, *ib.* 675; asserts that the apostles delivered to their successors a certain gift of truth, *ib.* 585, 674; states that they most plentifully conferred on the church all things pertaining to the truth, *Calf.* 287; says they preached the gospel, and afterward by God's will they delivered the same to us in writing, to be a foundation and pillar to our faith, 2 *Jew.* 988, 3 *Jew.* 437, *Whita.* 528, 670; teaches that the pillar and buttress of the church is the gospel, and the Spirit of life, 3 *Jew.* 153; declares that to lean to the scriptures is to build upon a rock, but that to leave them is to build upon the sand, 2 *Cran.* 22, *Phil.* 368; speaking of an erroneous doctrine he says, this thing neither did the prophets publish, nor our Lord teach, nor the apostles deliver, 4 *Jew.* 886; affirms that he is happy who follows the doctrine of both the testaments, and not the traditions of men, 2 *Cran.* 22; says the scriptures are perfect, *Whita.* 675; denies that Christ and the apostles taught some things openly and some secretly, *ib.* 668; declares that the whole scriptures, both of the prophets and the evangelists, are open and without ambiguity, 2 *Ful.* 220; says the scriptures are without doubtfulness, and may be heard indifferently of all, 2 *Jew.* 684, 4 *Jew.* 1185; characterizes the doctrine of the apostles as manifest and firm, keeping nothing back, *Whita.* 398; writes on the obscurities of scripture, *ib.* 370, 371; shews that scripture is to be interpreted by itself, *ib.* 461, 491; compares the church in this world to Paradise, and the scriptures to the trees of the garden, 2 *Jew.* 691, 695, *Whita.* 675; speaks of making void the law of God by addition, subtraction, and misinterpretation, *Rog.* 195 n.; shews how heretics act when reproved by the scriptures, 2 *Ful.* 219, 3 *Jew.* 248, 4 *Jew.* 759, 762; Erasmus says he fights with no other defence than scripture, against a host of heretics, *Whita.* 675; he censures the heretic Valentinus for his treatment of scripture, 1 *Jew.* 260; says Matthew wrote his gospel in Hebrew, *Whita.* 126; speaks of the date of it, *ib.* 520, 552; whether he ascribes the epistle to the Hebrews to Paul, *ib.* 107; he explains " things new and old," and the "new song," 2 *Jew.* 724; his testimony to tradition considered, *Whita.* 583

—585; he says the tradition which is from the apostles is kept in the churches by priests that succeed them, 4 *Jew.* 1042; by apostolic tradition he means, in substance, what we call the creed of the apostles, 1 *Bul.* 28, 4 *Bul.* 535; he speaks of certain barbarous nations who received the faith without writing, by the power of the Holy Ghost, 2 *Jew.* 672—674, *Whita.* 520, 585, and says that they would not abide the inventions of heretics, 2 *Jew.* 674; his declaration of faith, 1 *Bul.* 26, 2 *Hoop.* 537; approval of it, 1 *Brad.* 371; he confesses original sin, 2 *Bul.* 390; thinks that man was imperfect when first created, 3 *Jew.* 606; speaks of the promise of mercy, the grace of God, &c., as a spiritual substance, 3 *Jew.* 507; thinks Abraham saw the day of Christ's death, 1 *Hoop.* 212; understands "the Word" to denote the divine nature of Christ, *ib.* 17, 83; shews that he was crucified and dead, but not in his Divinity, *ib.* 17; considers that he was near fifty years old when he suffered, 4 *Bul.* 536, 4 *Jew.* 695, *Whita.* 585, 665; referred to on the true form of the cross, 2 *Zur.* 45; he shews how God blinds the hearts of the unfaithful, 2 *Jew.* 676, 677; says it is better for men to be ignorant, and by love to draw near to God, than to think themselves to know much, and yet to be found blasphemous against God, 4 *Jew.* 910; shews that when Paul said "knowledge puffeth up," he did not find fault with the true knowledge of God, 2 *Jew.* 680; declares that Paul meant not a spiritual body, when he said "we are members of (Christ's) body, of his flesh, and of his bones," 1 *Cran.* 285; he was a chiliast, or millenarian, *Whita.* 391, 585; speaks of the seven ages of the world, 1 *Lat.* 365 n.; maintains that the righteous will rise and reign 1000 years before the last judgment, *Coop.* 147; his argument against those who denied the resurrection of the body, 1 *Cran.* 149, 150, *Sand.* 453; said to assert that faith and hope will remain in the life to come, *Whita.* 585; he condemns those who pretend to describe the heavenly hierarchy, *ib.* 577; shews that the powers are ordained by God, and that Satan lied when he claimed authority to bestow them, 3 *Whitg.* 588

iii. *The Church:* he speaks of churches founded by the apostles in various countries, *Whita.* 216; to stay the errors of his time, he refers to the most ancient churches, 3 *Bec.* 393, 1 *Brad.* 520, 1 *Jew.* 79, 364, 4 *Jew.* 1042, 1043; alleges the doctrine of the church in opposition to heretics who denied the scriptures, 1 *Brad.* 520, *Whita.* 326, 438, 439, 583; speaks of the church as possessing the gifts of the Lord, viz. apostles, prophets, and teachers; and says that where these are placed, there we must learn the truth, &c., *Phil.* 367; says we ought to obey those presbyters who succeed the apostles, and with the succession of the bishopric have received the gift of truth, 1 *Jew.* 402, 3 *Jew.* 349, *Whita.* 585; speaks of the apostolic doctrine as conveyed by succession of bishops, and as contained in the scriptures, *Rog.* 329 n., *Whita.* 461 n.; shews the difference between true and false Christians, *Wool.* 24, 25; declares that, as in the old testament so in the new, many are called, few chosen, 4 *Jew.* 877; says the apostles appointed bishops in all churches, 2 *Whitg.* 136, 138; calls the church of Rome the greatest and most ancient, and ascribes its foundation to Peter and Paul, 2 *Ful.* 340, 341, 1 *Jew.* 365, 4 *Jew.* 1042, *Phil.* 24, 25, *Whita.* 438 n.; says, to this church every church must needs agree, 2 *Ful.* 340, 1 *Jew.* 364; the pre-eminence that he gives to the church of Rome stands in consent and unity, not in superiority or government over all the world, 4 *Jew.* 1043; he declares that in it the tradition which is from the apostles has been always kept, 2 *Ful.* 340; enumerates the early bishops of Rome *Calf.* 251, 3 *Jew.* 326; declares that Peter and Paul appointed Linus, 2 *Ful.* 335, 340; speaks of the writings of Clement, 2 *Whitg.* 119; (as to Anicetus, see iv, below); he wrote to pope Victor about the keeping of Easter, 1 *Jew.* 144, 1 *Whitg.* 216; rebuked him for his intolerance, 1 *Brad.* 525, 2 *Brad.* 389, *Calf.* 269, 2 *Ful.* 69, 238, 308, *Whita.* 539, 2 *Zur.* 340, 347; prevented him from excommunicating the Eastern churches, 2 *Hoop.* 233; sought advice from him about the excommunication of certain heretics, *Phil.* 39; he says that a difference as to fasting should not break the agreement of faith, 1 *Brad.* 525

iv. *Sacraments, Worship:* he speaks of only two sacraments, baptism and the eucharist, 3 *Jew.* 459; of the latter he writes figuratively, 2 *Hoop.* 48; calls the bread wherein thanks are given, the body of the Lord, 1 *Cran.* 104, (30), 2 *Jew.* 606; says Christ confessed bread to be his body, and the cup his blood, 1 *Brad.* 589, 1 *Cran.* 33, 104, (54), 1 *Hoop.* 226, 2 *Jew.* 1115; calls the bread of the sacrament a creature, and an earthly thing, 1 *Brad.* 589, 1 *Hoop.* 226, 1 *Jew.* 518, 2 *Jew.* 1118; declares that when the mingled cup and broken bread receive the word of God, they become the eucharist of the blood and body of Christ, 1 *Cran.* 104 n., 265, 266, (30, 54), 1 *Ful.* 503, 505, 523, *Grin.* 47, also *Coop.* 194 n.; says that of this eucharist the substance of our flesh is stayed and increased, 2 *Bec.* 267, 3 *Bec.* 424, *Coop.* 194 n., 1 *Cran.* 104, 149 n., (54), *Grin.* 47, 2 *Jew.* 596, 599, 795, 3 *Jew.* 516; another like sentence, 1 *Brad.* 589, 1 *Cran.* 149 n., 1 *Hoop.* 226, 2 *Jew.* 1115; he states that as the bread, receiving the invocation of God, consists of two things, earthly and heavenly; so our bodies, receiving the eucharist, are no more corruptible, having hope of an eternal resurrection, 2 *Bec.* 267, 3 *Bec.* 424, 1 *Brad.* 87, 543, 4 *Bul.* 249, 1 *Cran.* 104, 265, 337, 338, (30, 54), 1 *Ful.* 503, 505, *Grin.* 66, 1 *Hoop.* 224, 2 *Hoop.* 419, 420, *Hutch.* 39, 271, 273, 277, 2 *Jew.* 759, *Rid.* 173, *Sand.* 453; uses this doctrine against some heretics who denied the salvation of the body, 1 *Cran.* 149, 150, *Sand.* 453; mentions that the bishops of Rome were wont to send the eucharist to other bishops who came there, in token of concord, 4 *Bul.* 430, 1 *Jew.* 144, 145, 161; (Jewel does not think that the sacrament is here intended, 1 *Jew.* 145); he says Anicetus granted the eucharist (probably meaning the ministration of it) to Polycarp, 1 *Jew.* 146, *Whita.* 217; speaks of one Marcus enchanting the sacramental cup, 1 *Jew.* 6; calls the Lord's supper a sacrifice, *Coop.* 89; speaks of the eucharist as the new oblation of the new testament, 3 *Bec.* 388, *Coop.* 89, 1 *Cran.* 104 (54), and as a pure oblation, &c., *Coop.* 89, 1 *Ful.* 271; how he interprets Malachi's "pure offering," 4 *Bul.* 224, 1 *Jew.* 109, 2 *Jew.* 722, 723; he does not speak of a propitiatory sacrifice amongst Christians, 1 *Ful.* 271, 2 *Ful.* 245; teaches that God is not pleased with sacrifice (of man's invention), 2 *Hoop.* 523; speaks of sacrifices in both the old and the new testament, but says the former were offered by bondmen, the latter by freemen, 2 *Jew.* 724; says it behoves us to offer to God the first-fruits of his creatures, &c., *Coop.* 90; remarks that we offer not to God as to one that needeth, but as giving thanks for his benefits, *ib.* 91; says that we should offer sacrifice daily, 1 *Jew.* 128; declares that our altar and temple are in heaven, and that we must offer our prayers and oblations there, *Coop.* 92, 1 *Jew.* 128, 311, 2 *Jew.* 723, 740; affirms that sacrifices do not sanctify the man, but that the conscience of him who offers, being pure, sanctifies the sacrifice, 2 *Hoop.* 527, 2 *Jew.* 723, 755

v. *Heresies, Antichrist*: he says that heretics abused the text, "we speak wisdom amongst them that are perfect," *Whita.* 674; declares that they professed to be wiser than the apostles, 1 *Jew.* 320; censures those who lead the blind out of the way, 2 *Jew.* 674; describes the error of some who denied the Lord's true humanity, 2 *Cov.* 348 n.; speaks of various heretics who denied the resurrection, *ib.* 186 n., and of some who used images and other superstitions, 1 *Ful.* 194 n.; as to the treatment of scripture by heretics, see ii, above; referred to about the Basilidians, *Calf.* 285 n., *Rog.* 57, 118, 119 nn.; on Carpocrates, *ib.* 40, 52, 101 nn.; on Cerinthus, *ib.* 48 n.; on the Ebionites, *ib.* 83, 89 nn.; he says they received only the gospel of Matthew, and rejected Paul as an apostate from the law, *Whita.* 35; describes the Gnostics or Docetæ, 1 *Cov.* 21 n.; rebukes them for having an image of Christ, *Calf.* 43, 371, 1 *Ful.* 194, 2 *Ful.* 127, *Park.* 86, *Rid.* 88; says they condemned marriage, *Rog.* 306 n.; tells of the heresy of Marcion, *ib.* 84, 85, 133 nn., *Whita.* 31; reproves the opinion of his sect that man's body is not capable of happiness, but the soul only, *Rog.* 297 n.; cited on the heresy of Marcus, *ib.* 135 n.; he says the Marcosians at the ministration of baptism used certain Hebrew words, to terrify and astonish the minds of the ignorant, *ib.* 242 n.; speaks of the errors of Menander, *ib.* 40 n.; states that the Nicolaitans would have women to be common, *ib.* 307 n.; speaks of the heresy of Saturnius, *ib.* 40 n., 51 n., *Whita.* 30; writes of Simon Magus and his evil doctrine, *Rog.* 40, 71, 118, 162 nn., *Whita.* 30; describes the Valentinians, 1 *Jew.* 400, *Rog.* 52, 84, 121, 145 nn.; states that they allowed no gospel but that of John, *Whita.* 34; says they called ignorance of the truth, knowledge, 2 *Jew.* 800; tells them that their errors arose from not knowing the scriptures, *ib.* 682; mentions how their founder treated the scriptures, 1 *Jew.* 260; records their conduct when confuted by the word of God, 2 *Ful.* 219; mentions their superstitious veneration of the cross, *ib.* 139; speaks of their follies as void of substance, 3 *Jew.* 507; tells of a deceptive miracle wrought by a juggler, 2 *Cran.* 45; referred to about the great apostasy, 2 *Ful.* 374; said to take Antichrist to be probably the Roman kingdom, *ib.* 368; he says the name of the beast is Λατεινος, which is the name of the last kingdom, 2 *Jew.* 915, 4 *Jew.* 743; mentions an opinion that Antichrist shall be of the tribe of Dan, 2 *Ful.* 370; says though an apostate and a robber, he will be worshipped as God, and though a servant, will proclaim himself a king, 2 *Jew.* 905, 4 *Jew.* 714, 843

Irene, empress of the East: a heathen born, 2 *Jew.* 653; an upholder of image-worship, *ib., Rid.* 93; she convoked the second council of Nice, *Calf.* 175, 177, *Park.* 92; burned the bones of her father-in-law Constantine V., *Calf.* 31, 175, 176, *Park.* 92, *Rid.* 94; put out the eyes of her son Constantine VI., *Calf.* 176, 2 *Jew.* 653, *Park.* 92, *Rid.* 94, and at length murdered him, *Calf.* 31, 175, 176

Irish: *v.* Ireland.

Irish (Mr), mayor of Oxford: Ridley prisoner in his house, *Rid.* xi, 286, 292, 376, 391, 392; his wife, 2 *Brad.* 158, 172, *Rid.* 292, 373, 391, 392; her sorrow for Ridley's approaching death, *Rid.* 292

Ironside (Gilb.), bp of Hereford: when vice-chancellor of Oxford, he published an account of the disputation there, 1554, from a MS., *Rid.* xv; his preface to that book, 1 *Brad.* 583

Irony: used in scripture, 2 *Cov.* 333, 366

Isaac: interpretation of his name, *Phil.* 257; instructed by his father, 4 *Bul.* 388; his afflictions, 2 *Bul.* 103

Isaac ..., emperor of the East: 2 *Jew.* 1028 n

Isaac (Edw.): notice of him, 2 *Lat.* 221 n.; visits Bainham in Newgate, *ib.* 221; executor to Mrs Wyate his mother, 2 *Cran.* 389; Cranmer writes to the king about an exchange of his lands, *ib.* 458; a friend of Sandys, *Sand.* xv, xvi; an exile at Frankfort, *Jew.* xii, 2 *Lat.* 221; death of his son there, *Sand.* xv

Isaac (Jo.): confutes Lindanus, *q.v.*; his opinion on the text, "They pierced my hands," &c., 1 *Ful.* 45; on the purity of the Hebrew text, *Whita.* 162

Isaac (Tho.): brother to Edward, 2 *Cran.* 389

Isabella, queen of Castile: affianced to king Edward IV., 2 *Tyn.* 304; married to Ferdinand V., *q.v.*

Isabella of Arragon, duchess of Milan, 3 *Zur.* 689 n

Isabella (The lady): mentioned, 4 *Jew.* 1197, 1198, 1 *Zur.* 8, 9

Isacius: robs the church of St John Lateran, 2 *Tyn.* 255

Isaiah: 4 *Bul.* 70, 122, 480; not only a prophet, but an evangelist, 1 *Bul.* 51, 3 *Bul.* 17, 1 *Cov.* 66; he meddled with the coin of the mint, and with vintners, 1 *Lat.* 137; sawn asunder, 2 *Jew.* 839, *Pil.* 361; the Ascension of Isaiah, an apocryphal book, *Rog.* 82

Isauria: 3 *Bul.* 257

Isbrandus, Dutch minister at Norwich: *v.* Balkius (Jo.).

Iscan (B.), bp: *v.* Bartholomew.

Ischyras, a pretended priest: 3 *Jew.* 321, 334, 2 *Whitg.* 161

Isengrenius (......): 3 *Zur.* 218, 223

Ishmael: circumcised, 4 *Bul.* 378; his mocking, *Pil.* 358; how he and his mother were mercifully relieved, *Grin.* 106; he was an archer, *Pil.* 428

Isidore (St), called Pelusiota, or of Damietta: referred to, *Calf.* 285 n.; absurd arguments for images ascribed to him, 2 *Jew.* 658

Isidore (St), of Seville, or Hispalensis: Opera, *Jew.* xxxviii, 3 *Whitg.* xxix; he asserts that if one in authority command anything besides the will and meaning of God's word, he must be taken as a false witness against God, &c., 3 *Jew.* 600; declares that whoever understands holy scripture otherwise than the sense of the Holy Spirit requires, may be called a heretic, though he depart not from the church*, *Bale* 218; speaks of the scriptures as read in all Christian tongues, 2 *Jew.* 692; says Jerome's version is preferred to all others, *Whita.* 131, 136, 137; states that Ezra settled the Old Testament in two and twenty books, *ib.* 64; yet he is referred to as an authority for the Apocrypha, *ib.* 39; by the sun he understands the kingdom, by the moon the priesthood, 4 *Jew.* 677, 838; calls the appearance of Samuel's ghost a piece of Satan's jugglery, *Whita.* 92; explains Ezekiel's reference to Tubal, *Bale* 571; expounds the meaning of Θ and T, *Calf.* 107; mistakes the origin of the name Cephas, 2 *Ful.* 302 n.; calls Timothy bishop of Ephesus, 2 *Whitg.* 294, and says he was buried there, *ib.* 303; wrote on the Apocalypse, *Bale* 255; bears testimony against the Canons of the Apostles, *Whita.* 41 n.; mentions various ecclesiastical orders, 4 *Bul.* 114, 3 *Jew.* 273; dwells on the responsibility of priests, *Bale* 89; denies that he ought to rebuke the vices of

---

* Compare Jerome, p. 427 below.

others who is himself vicious, 1 *Bec.* 16; speaks of the vestments, 3 *Bec.* 262; argues for a priest's shaven crown, 1 *Jew.* 14; says acoluthes are wax-bearers, so called because they carry wax-candles at the reading of the gospel, &c., 4 *Bul.* 115; describes the office of door-keepers, *Rog.* 258 n.; speaks of the bread and wine as consecrate to the remembrance of the Lord's passion, 2 *Bec.* 287, 3 *Bec.* 437; ascribes the mass to Peter, *Pil.* 503; describes the order of the church in singing, praying, &c., 1 *Jew.* 289, 4 *Jew.* 857, *Whita.* 226, 273; says reading brings no small profit to the hearers, 3 *Whitg.* 46; would have the reader's voice loud and clear, 3 *Jew.* 274; describes exomologesis, i. e. public confession or penance, 3 *Bul.* 75, 76; inculcates either chastity or marriage, 3 *Jew.* 406; but, according to another citation in the Canon Law, he allows a Christian man to have either a wife or a concubine, 4 *Jew.* 631, 632; teaches that in evil promises faith may be broken, 1 *Bec.* 372, 1 *Bul.* 250; advises that, if a man intends to do what pleases not God, his determination should be called back again, 1 *Bec.* 372; says many men, giving judgment before they can understand, by entangling themselves fall into a maze of error, 3 *Jew.* 565; describes the Angelici, 2 *Ful.* 41 n., speaks of the Cathari, 1 *Hoop.* 547 n., *Rog.* 115 n.; creeds taken out of a book of his, 1 *Bul.* 19, 22, 24, 2 *Hoop.* 535, 536; shews the origin of idolatry, 1 *Ful.* 104; the Dirige ascribed to him, *Pra. Eliz.* 57 n

Isidore Mercator, or Peccator: *Jew.* xxxviii; he says it is manifest that matters happening in a province, may be ordered in a provincial council, 4 *Jew.* 1054; referred to on the canons of Nice, *Coop.* 30 n., 223, 2 *Ful.* 105 n., 107 n., 2 *Whitg.* 151; his forgeries, 2 *Ful.* 360 n

Isidore, metropolitan of Syria: at the council of Florence, 3 *Jew.* 126, 341

Isidore, abp of Kiow: deposed from his office for advocating submission to the pope, 2 *Jew.* 578, 4 *Jew.* 740

Isidore de Clario: *v.* Clarius.

Islebius (Jo.): said that Christ suffered in both natures, *Rog.* 57; objected to the preaching of God's law, *ib.* 92

Isle of Wight: the French land at St Helen's point, 2 *Cran.* 495 n.; the isle visited, *Park.* 478; great clerical irregularities there, 1 *Zur.* 323 n

Isleworth, co. Middx.: *v.* Sion.

Islington, co. Middx.: mentioned as a small village, 1 *Lat.* 241; martyrs there, *Poet.* 171

Islip (Jo.), abbot of Westminster: 1 *Tyn.* 32

Islip (Simon), abp of Canterbury: 1 *Lat.* 55 n

Ismas: *v.* Dismas.

Isocrates: 1 *Bec.* 379, 398, 1 *Bul.* 273; Tyndale translates an oration of his, 1 *Tyn.* xxi, 395

Israel, Jews: *v.* Hebrew, Jerusalem, Law, Synagogue, Tabernacle, Temple.

(a) Before Christ (*v.* Covenants, Fathers before Christ): the great privileges of the Jewish nation, 4 *Jew.* 1162, *Sand.* 346; their time was nevertheless (comparatively) a time of darkness, 2 *Jew.* 1036; their state compared by Paul to childhood, *ib.* 615; they had the promise of what we have the fulfilment of, *ib.*; the Jews (or some of them) were indeed Christians, though not in name, *Hutch.* 218, 248, 325, 326, 2 *Jew.* 614; why the Law was given to them only, *Lit. Edw.* 500, (549); why God suffered the rest of the world to be in blindness is a deep mystery, 2 *Jew.* 1087; some were saved beside Israel, but not without Christ, 2 *Bul.* 401; why ceremonies were imposed upon the Jews, *Calf.* 122; the signification of their ceremonies, 1 *Tyn.* 351, &c.; their mistaken views of the purport of them, 3 *Tyn.* 66; the sacrifices, circumcision, &c. were their sacraments, *Rog.* 251; they erroneously supposed these sacraments to justify, 4 *Bul.* 302, and put all their confidence in them, 1 *Hoop.* 211, yet they never perverted them as Christians have perverted theirs, *ib.*; their holy-days, 2 *Whitg.* 578; the yellow [rather blue] borders of their garments, 1 *Tyn.* 352; their laws more definite in some respects than the rule of the church, 1 *Whitg.* 266, &c.; their polity, whether a pattern for the church, 2 *Whitg.* 345, &c.; whether examples of Jews appertain to Christians, 1 *Bul.* 326; how the precepts given to them belong to us, *Now.* (8), 121; they preserved the scriptures, *Whita.* 52; Israel in the desert termed an excellent church of God, 4 *Bul.* 37; their wanderings typical, *Sand.* 171, *Whita.* 408; their perils and deliverances, *Grin.* 106, 1 *Tyn.* 134—136; their sins and correction, *ib.* 142; their frowardness, *Grin.* 106, 3 *Tyn.* 43; their frequent captivities, 2 *Cran.* 198; how the Israelites overcame the Benjamites, 1 *Bul.* 375, 376; they were successively governed by judges, kings, and princes of the house of Judah, *Pil.* 23; their offence in asking a king,

ISRAEL — ITALY 421

1 *Lat.* 187, 192; the kings of Israel and Judah, 2 *Bul.* 5—12; the good kings prosperous, *Pil.* 75; why the Jews went thrice a year to Jerusalem, 2 *Bul.* 163, 2 *Lat.* 155, *Pil.* 69, 159; their monuments, &c., 1 *Tyn.* 347, 376—378; their covenants, *ib.* 347, 348; their schools of the prophets, synagogues, &c., 2 *Jew.* 981; scripture used in their public worship, *Pil.* 533, 534; their mode of reckoning years and months, *ib.* 15; the apostasy of Judah and Israel, 3 *Tyn.* 122; the Israelites destroyed for forsaking Jerusalem and going to Bethel, *Phil.* 220; their idolatry and other sins, *Calf.* 23, 24, 32, 33, 2 *Cran.* 144; their usury, heathen marriages, &c. reproved, *Pil.* 162; why God cast away their fasts, 1 *Bec.* 109; Israel wasted and overthrown for sin, *Sand.* 258; their captivity at Babylon, 1 *Bul.* 279, 292, 4 *Bul.* 11, 73, 75, 481, *Pil.* 12, 291; their backwardness in building the Temple, *Pil.* 37; they were given up to spiritual idolatry, when they had relinquished idols, 1 *Tyn.* 473, 3 *Tyn.* 43; their division into sects, 2 *Cran.* 145; it is said that they forbade any to read certain parts of the Bible till they were 30 years old, 2 *Jew.* 693; they expected Messiah to be a temporal king, 2 *Lat.* 146

(*b*) Since Christ (*v.* Rabbins): they were very corrupt in the time of our Lord, *Rid.* 137; burdened with ceremonies, *ib.* 138; their carnal understanding of Christ's words in the sixth of John, 4 *Bul.* 289, 447, 462, 1 *Cran.* 24, &c., 116, 185, 231, 249, 307, 372, *Grin.* 44, 2 *Hoop.* 191, 450, 1 *Jew.* 451, *Rid.* 175, *Rog.* 289, 3 *Tyn.* 227, 238, &c.; their traditions rejected by Christ and the apostles, *Whita.* 637; they accused Christ of various sins, *Rog.* 133; were guilty of his death, 1 *Cov.* 404; Judas their type, 1 *Brad.* 211; in persecuting the apostles they despised justification by faith, *Rog.* 113; the early Jewish converts clave to ceremonies, and thereby injured the church, 3 *Tyn.* 68—71; many of those who seemed to be converted, had only attained to an historical faith, *ib.* 70; God's vengeance on the Jews for their rejection of Christ, 3 *Bec.* 9, 2 *Tyn.* 241; their Temple forsaken, desecrated and destroyed, *Bale* 611, 2 *Bul.* 259, 2 *Jew.* 994, *Sand.* 347; their fall a warning to us, 3 *Bec.* 9, *Sand.* 259, 349, &c.; Pliny, Tacitus, and others, on the religion of the Jews, 2 *Jew.* 1025; some accused them of worshipping a sow or an ass, 3 *Jew.* 154; Juvenal says, "Nil præter nubes et cœli Numen adorant," 2 *Ful.* 209;

their dispersion, 2 *Lat.* 47, 49, *Pil.* 74, *Sand.* 149; thirty sold for a penny, 2 *Lat.* 46; their attempted restoration of the Temple defeated by Constantine, 4 *Jew.* 1074; again frustrated, miraculously, in the time of Julian (*q. v.*), 2 *Bul.* 260, *Calf.* 115; they claim to be alone the people of God, *Rog.* 171; deny the Trinity, *ib.* 43; feign unto themselves a God, *Wool.* 54; call upon God without the Mediator, 4 *Bul.* 173; are enemies of the Christian religion and of Christ, *ib.* 11, 12; pervert all the prophecies about Messiah, 1 *Ful.* 311; deny that Christ is come, and that Jesus is the Christ, 3 *Bul.* 24; oppugn our Saviour's deity, *Rog.* 49; deny his resurrection, *ib.* 64; look for a Saviour who shall be a great ruler, 2 *Lat.* 124; they tear their garments when they hear God's name blasphemed, 1 *Bec.* 367; reverence the scriptures, 4 *Jew.* 763, and teach them to their children, 1 *Hoop.* 189; hold that the ceremonial law is yet in force, *Rog.* 89; adhere to the Talmud, 2 *Hoop.* 393; their traditions, the Mishnah, &c., *Whita.* 611; they use their books of religion in the vulgar tongue, 2 *Hoop.* 207; lend freely to their brethren, *Sand.* 231; believe as much as the carnal sort of them ever did, 3 *Tyn.* 53; their faith is vain, 2 *Lat.* 3; they cannot do good works, 4 *Bul.* 83; they deny original sin, *Rog.* 97; maintain free-will, 1 *Brad.* 323, 329, 1 *Ful.* 126, 3 *Tyn.* 193; some deceived at Candie by Satan in the form of Moses, 2 *Cran.* 50; expelled from England (1293 —1655), 1 *Tyn.* xxv, 3 *Tyn.* 68 n.; the popes gave harbour to a great number, who lived by usury, and paid him yearly pensions, 4 *Jew.* 1148, 1149; they were numerous in Hamburgh, 1 *Tyn.* xxv; story of a Jew and a Christian, 3 *Bec.* 281, 282; the Jews are said to imagine that before the judgment there shall be a golden world, *Rog.* 68; whether they will receive Antichrist, 2 *Ful.* 369; they are to be converted and restored, *Bale* 137, 335, 341, 1 *Brad.* 364, *Pil.* 267; their restoration to Jerusalem denied, 2 *Lat.* 46, 47

The twelve tribes sealed (Rev. vii), *Bale* 334

Isuard, a monk: said to have selected lessons, 4 *Bul.* 201

Isychius: *v.* Hesychius.

It: formerly used for its, *Sand.* 285

Itala Versio: *v.* Bible, *Latin*.

Italian band (The): 4 *Bul.* 80, 95

Italy: outline of events in the early part of the sixteenth century, 1 *Tyn.* 186;

Calabria, &c. pillaged by the French, 3 *Zur.* 741

Ithamar : 2 *Bul.* 132, 141

Ithel (Tho.), master of Jesus college, Cambridge : recommended as a visitor for St John's college, *Grin.* 359 (see 358 n.); mentioned, 3 *Whitg.* 599

Ittigius (Tho.) : *Calf.* 21 n., 96 n., 2 *Ful.* 70 n

Ivo, bp of Chartres : *Jew.* xxxviii, 4 *Jew.* 938; speaks of the bread being dipped into the cup, 1 *Jew.* 253; his Decretum, *Calf.* 135 n., 154 n.; he is the supposed author of a sermon ascribed to Augustine, 3 *Jew.* 457 n

Izaulus : married the duchess of Athens, and got the city, 4 *Jew.* 653

Jabesh Gilead : neutral, *Pil.* 344

Jack : Jack-an-apes, 3 *Tyn.* 85; Jack Napes, 2 *Tyn.* 158; Jack of Napes, 3 *Tyn.* 61; Jack and Gill, 4 *Jew.* 915; Jack in the box, 1 *Cov.* 426, *Rid.* 265

Jacks : a kind of armour, *Rid.* 145; jacks of iron mail, *Bale* 356

Jackson (Hen.), of Merton college : *Park.* 301, 302

Jackson (Jo.) : Cranmer's tenant, 2 *Cran.* 299

Jackson (Roger ?) : martyred, *Poet.* 168

Jackson (Tho.) : his Works, 2 *Ful.* 247 n

Jacob : his life, 1 *Bul.* 41; promise of the Seed made unto him, 2 *Hoop.* 6; he worshipped Christ before he was born, 1 *Cran.* 235; his obtaining Esau's blessing mystically expounded, *Hutch.* 53; his afflictions, 2 *Bul.* 103; banished by Esau, *Pil.* 256; his ladder, 4 *Bul.* 253; it was a type of Christ, *Hutch.* 35; he married two sisters, 1 *Bul.* 405; took away idols, *ib.* 210; built an altar, 4 *Bul.* 165; prayed most ardently, *ib.* 224; said to have drunk freely, 2 *Bul.* 57; his staff (or bed), translations concerning it examined, 1 *Ful.* 539, &c.; the text alleged in the second council of Nice, *Calf.* 158; said to have blessed his sons with the sign of the cross, 2 *Ful.* 171; his prophecy of Shiloh, 3 *Bul.* 15, 20, 2 *Lat.* 75, 1 *Tyn.* 408

— Jacob's-staff : an astronomical instrument, *Poet.* 250

Jacob (Brother) : a name given to Jo. Frith, 1 *Tyn.* liii.

Jacobites : their fantasies respecting the passion of Christ, *Rog.* 58; they use a strange language in the congregation, *ib.* 243; imprint upon themselves the sign of the cross as a distinction from pagans, *ib.* 246

Jacobson (Will.) : Patres Apostolici, 2 *Ful.* 189 n., 235 n

Jacobus Andreas, *q. v.*

Jacobus Payva, *q. v.*

Jacobus de Valentia, *q. v.*

Jacobus de Voragine, *q. v.*

Jaddus, high priest : his interview with Alexander the Great, *Calf.* 117, *Pil.* 69

Jairus : a sermon on Jairus and his daughter, 1 *Lat.* 533

James (St), the Great : slain by Herod, *Rog.* 113

James (St), the Less : his part in the council at Jerusalem, 2 *Bul.* 277, &c., 2 *Cran.* 76, 2 *Ful.* 249, 4 *Jew.* 917, *Whita.* 432, 2 *Whitg.* 276, 277; said to have been bishop of Jerusalem, 1 *Jew.* 238, *Rog.* 328, 1 *Whitg.* 359, 459, 2 *Whitg.* 136, 252, 277, 302, 428; styled by pseudo-Clement, bishop of bishops, 1 *Jew.* 427; it is not likely that he took authority of Peter (as some say), for he had taken sufficient authority of Christ, *ib.* 431; Athanasius says he translated Matthew's gospel into Greek, *Whita.* 126; his knees were hard with continual praying, 1 *Bec.* 143, 2 *Bec.* 140, 1 *Brad.* 24, *Sand.* 38; what Egesippus says of him, 1 *Jew.* 237, 238; he is asserted to have said mass at Jerusalem, *Pil.* 482, 495, 498; how, 1 *Jew.* 23, 24; alleged to have worn a πέταλον or plate of gold, 1 *Zur.* 160 n., 350 n.; his martyrdom, 3 *Bec.* 8, 2 *Cov.* 132; this was before Clement became bishop of Rome, *Rid.* 180, 182; his chair esteemed as a monument of antiquity, 2 *Ful.* 239

— His Epistle :—argument of it, and contents of each chapter, 3 *Bec.* 590, 591; Tyndale's prologue to it, 1 *Tyn.* 525; some at an early period rejected it, *ib.*; Jerome mentions that there were doubts in the primitive church respecting it, 3 *Jew.* 433, *Phil.* 413; what Eusebius says of it, 1 *Ful.* 16 n., 33, 222, 2 *Ful.* 384, 3 *Jew.* 433; it was publicly received by many churches when disallowed by others, *Whita.* 306; Cajetan rejects it, *ib.* 105; Luther at one period rejected it, or at least doubted its authenticity, 1 *Ful.* 14, 15, 2 *Ful.* 384, *Whita.* 105; Calvin's opinion on it, 1 *Ful.* 16, 33; see also Confession, Justification, Unction.

— The Gospel of St James : *v.* Apocrypha, ii. The Liturgy of St James : *v.* Liturgies. His shrine : *v.* Compostella.

James I., king of Great Britain, &c. : *v.* James VI., king of Scotland.

James II., king of Great Britain, &c. : caused an accession service to be composed, *Lit. Eliz.* 463

James IV., king of Scotland : made Defender of the Faith by pope Julius II., 1 *Tyn.* 187 slain, *Pil.* 251

James V., king of Scotland: his death, 3 *Zur.* 239 n

James VI., king of Scotland; afterwards king of Great Britain, &c.: his birth, 1 *Zur.* 167, 170, 2 *Zur.* 120 n.; his baptism, 1 *Zur.* 183; proclamation of his style on that occasion, *ib.* n.; crowned king of Scotland, *ib.* 197; his tutors, 2 *Zur.* 302 n.; Gualter dedicates a book to him, *ib.* 275, 294; his message in return, *ib.* 310; he orders thanksgivings for the defeat of the Spanish armada, *Lit. Eliz.* 470; renews the solemn covenant, 2 *Zur.* 331 n.; sends ambassadors to queen Elizabeth, *ib.* 332; his accession to the throne of England, *Rog.* 21; his declaration about lawful sports on the Lord's day, *Grin.* 142 n.; he was the first king of this realm who issued a copper coinage, 2 *Tyn.* 231 n.; he renounced and banished out of England the jurisdiction of the bishop of Rome, *Rog.* 347

James, 3rd husband of Mary queen of Scots: *v.* Hepburn.

James, a deacon of York: taught singing in the church after the Roman manner, 1 *Jew.* 303; when he lived, *ib.* 304

James (Tho.): *Calf.* 96, 188, 200, 2 *Ful.* 277, 283, 360, 371 nn

Jameson (Tho.), minister of Largo: 2 *Zur.* 365

Jane Grey (The lady): Bradgate, her birthplace, 3 *Zur.* 429 n.; mention of her, *ib.* 428, 429; her admirable character, studies, and accomplishments, *ib.* 304, 406, 422, 432, 433, 451; she would not wear a costly dress, *ib.* 278 n.; Bullinger recommended to dedicate a book to her, *ib.* 423; she translated into Greek part of Bullinger's book on matrimony, 4 *Bul.* xix, 3 *Zur.* 427; report of her intended marriage with king Edward, 3 *Zur.* 430, 432; that sovereign left the crown to her, *ib.* 273; she is proclaimed queen, 1 *Brad.* 40 n., 2 *Cran.* 441—443, 3 *Zur.* 274, 366, 684; proclaimed in Cambridge, *Sand.* ii; queen nine days, 3 *Zur.* 367 [thirteen, according to Sir N. H. Nicolas]; tried, 2 *Cran.* 442 n., 3 *Zur.* 507; condemned, 3 *Zur.* 374; her discourse with Feckenham, &c., *ib.* 294, 304, 306 n.; an exhortation written by her the night before she suffered, in a Greek Testament, which she sent to her sister, the lady Katharine, 2 *Cov.* 133; her execution, 1 *Brad.* 282, 283, 2 *Brad.* 63, *Now.* 229, 3 *Zur.* 154, 515, 686; letters from her to Bullinger, 3 *Zur.* 4, 7, 9; her letters to Harding and to her sister, &c., sent to Bullinger, *ib.* 306 n.; Calvin commends her, *ib.* 716

Jane Seymour, third queen of Henry VIII.: mentioned in a prayer, 1 *Lat.* 40

Jane (Mother): called by Postell the saviour of women, *Rog.* 58, 298

Jane ......: 1 *Zur.* 65

Jannes and Jambres: *Whita.* 560

Jannizers: 1 *Jew.* 99

Jansenius (Corn.), bp of Ghent: remarks on Jo. v. ult., *Whita.* 340; on Jo. xvi. 12, *ib.* 543; on Jo. xx. ult., *ib.* 629; he says all we are required to know of a future life may be learned from the scriptures, *ib.* 643

Janson (Mr): *Grin.* 213

Janson (D. M.): declares that the bishop of Canaglion (1593) very catholicly accursed the mute fishes, *Rog.* 311 n.; says the Sorbonists held that subjects might be discharged from their oath of allegiance, and gather forces against their sovereign, *ib.* 360 n

Janua (Jo. de): *v.* Joannes.

Janus Cornarius, *q. v.*

Jarchi (R. Sol.): *v.* Solomon.

Jarnac: the battle, 2 *Zur.* 250 n

Jarret (Mr): at Zurich with P. Martyr, *Sand.* xvi.

Jason: how he won the golden fleece, 2 *Hoop.* 603

Jason of Cyrene: the 2nd book of Maccabees an epitome of his history, *Whita.* 98

Jaspar, or Gaspar, one of the three kings or Magi, *q. v.*

Javell (Chr.): says in time of necessity any one may baptize, *Rog.* 235, 236

Jaye (Geo.): *v.* Joye.

Jealousy: *v.* Zeal.

Whence it springs, and why God is called a jealous God, 3 *Bec.* 612

Jebusites: account of them, *Pil.* 371; Jesuits so called, 1 *Ful.* 568

Jechonias: *v.* Jehoiachin.

Jedburgh, Scotland: the castle taken, 3 *Zur.* 387

Jeffrey (Will.): *v.* Geffrie.

Jehoahaz, king of Judah: 2 *Bul.* 11

Jehoiachin, king of Judah: taken prisoner by Nebuchadnezzar, 1 *Bul.* 242, 2 *Bul.* 11, 4 *Bul.* 20, 2 *Hoop.* 102

Jehoiada, high priest: 1 *Bul.* 330, 358, 2 *Bul.* 8

Jehoiakim, king of Judah: burned the word of God, 4 *Jew.* 1165; was rebuked by Jeremiah, *Grin.* 28

Jehoram, king of Judah: 1 *Bul.* 236, 2 *Bul.* 7

Jehoram, king of Israel: 1 *Bul.* 336, 3 *Bul.* 208

Jehoshaphat, king of Judah: 1 *Bul.* 313, 324, 349, 378, 384, 2 *Bul.* 7, 95, 4 *Bul.* 170, 481, 4 *Jew.* 989

JEHOVAH — JEROME

Jehovah: v. God.
Jehovah nissi: explained, 1 *Tyn.* 420
Jehu, king of Israel: 1 *Bul.* 336, 2 *Bul.* 12, 4 *Jew.* 989, *Pil.* 7
Jehu, son of Hanani, *q. v.*
Jelf (R. W.): his edition of Jewel, 2 *Ful.* 369 n
Jenins (Will.), or Jennings, dean of Gloucester: Hooper's epistle to him and others, 2 *Hoop.* 95
Jenkins (Rob.): Hist. Exam. of Gen. Councils, *Calf.* 137 n
Jennet: a kind of horse, 2 *Jew.* 558
Jeremiah: commends Josiah and rebukes Jehoiakim, *Grin.* 28; prays for Jehoiakim and Zedekiah, 1 *Bul.* 316; forbidden to pray for the Jews, 4 *Bul.* 177, 552; his prophecy of the captivity, *Pil.* 12; his signs, 4 *Bul.* 232; a prayer for sin, which he teacheth the Israelites to say (ch. iii), *Lit. Edw.* 479; a prayer of Jeremy (ch. xvii), *ib.* 477; another (ch. xxxi), *ib.*; he was cast into a dungeon, but delivered, 4 *Jew.* 1167; stoned to death, 2 *Jew.* 839; his name in Matt. xxvii, whether an erroneous reading, 2 *Ful.* 386, 4 *Jew.* 635, *Whita.* 37 n
— Lamentations: the apocryphal preface in the Greek, *Whita.* 103; his prayer (Lam. v.) versified by M. Drayton, *Poet.* 121; also by Tho. Drant, *ib.* 417
— Part of the (apocryphal) epistle of Jeremy (Baruch, ch. vi), versified by Jud Smith, *Poet.* 518
Jericho: sermon on the taking of it, 2 *Jew.* 968; description of its fall, *ib.* 969, *Pil.* 29; the city accursed, 2 *Whitg.* 53, 54; rebuilt by Hiel, in spite of the curse, 2 *Jew.* 970; allegorical signification of the history, *ib.* 970, &c.; the school of Jericho, 4 *Bul.* 481
Jerk: to lash, 1 *Cov.* 108
Jerningham (Sir Hen.), or Jernegam: one of queen Mary's privy council, 1 *Zur.* 5 n
Jerningham (Jo.): Katherine (Brooke) his wife, 1 *Bec.* 264 n
Jerningham (Mr), or Gerningham: arrests Sandys, *Sand.* vi.
Jeroboam I., king of Israel: pulled down schools, 4 *Bul.* 481; ordained a new religion and mode of worship, 1 *Bul.* 335, 2 *Bul.* 11, 12, 126, 3 *Bul.* 237, 4 *Bul.* 22, 70, 72, 73, 101, 517; threatened, 1 *Bul.* 335, 336; his sins visited upon his house, *ib.* 235
Jeroboam II., king of Israel: 2 *Bul.* 12
Jerom (Steph.): *Calf.* 78 n
Jerome (St):
   i. *His Life and Works.*
   ii. *On God, and Christ.*
   iii. *Scripture.*
   iv. *Tradition.*
   v. *Sin.*
   vi. *Grace, &c.*
   vii. *The Church.*
   viii. *Bishops, and other Clergy, &c.*
   ix. *Peter, Rome.*
   x. *Saints, Ecclesiastical Writers.*
   xi. *Sacraments, particularly Baptism.*
   xii. *The Eucharist.*
   xiii. *Worship, Ceremonies, Tongues.*
   xiv. *Festivals, Fasting.*
   xv. *Celibacy, Marriage.*
   xvi. *Confession, Absolution.*
   xvii. *Affliction, Persecution, Death, Judgment, &c.*
   xviii. *The Cross, Images.*
   xix. *Heresies, real and alleged.*
   xx. *Antichrist.*
   xxi. *Civil Power, &c.*
   xxii. *Miscellanea.*

i. *His life and works*: he was sent to Rome, as to the principal school-mistress in those days, both of religion and learning, 4 *Jew.* 654; Victorinus the rhetorician and Donatus the grammarian were his instructors, *ib.* 653; his learning, 1 *Jew.* 278; he was a great man, although not a bishop, 1 *Ful.* 264; some part of the appointment of scripture lessons, &c., ascribed to him, 2 *Brad.* 307, 4 *Bul.* 201, *Pil.* 503; Damasus, bishop of Rome, wrote to him in doubtful cases to learn his counsel, 4 *Jew.* 1044; he speaks of one Apodemius coming from the furthest coast of France for his advice, *ib.*; says he went to Alexandria to see Didymus, 1 *Jew.* 376, 382, *Whita.* 373; his disputes with Augustine, 1 *Jew.* 532, 2 *Bul.* 116, 1 *Ful.* 35, *Phil.* 401, and see ix, below; Augustine commends him, 2 *Bul.* 390; he instructed Blesilla and Eustochium, 3 *Zur.* 5; his time, *Calf.* 8; date of his death, 4 *Bul.* 541; editions of his works, *Jew.* xxxviii, 3 *Whitg.* xxix; as to his versions of scripture, see Bible, Latin (Vulg.), and *Sclavonic;* also iii, below; his prologue Galeatus, 4 *Bul.* 540; the commentary on Leviticus, not his, 3 *Bec.* 439 n.; the counterfeit exposition of the Psalms, *Calf.* 259, *Whita.* 693; the judgment of Erasmus and Amerbachius concerning it, 2 *Ful.* 207, 208; Flores Psalmorum, quos Psalterium Hieronymi appellant, *Pra. Eliz.* 311—317; the suppositititious commentary on Proverbs, 4 *Jew.* 878 n.; the fictitious commentaries on Mark, *Calf.* 178 n.; the commentaries on 1 Cor. generally allowed to be spurious,

3 *Jew*. 143 n.; the commentary on Colossians not his, *Whita*. 239 n.; he wrote on the Apocalypse, *Bale* 255; epistles to pope Damasus, two authentic and one counterfeit, 2 *Ful*. 120, 349; his genuine epistle, and the spurious one, to Demetrias, *ib*. 44 n.; his genuine epistle to Oceanus, and the spurious one, *ib*. 97 n., 339 n.; his epistle ad Evagrium (or rather ad Evangelum), *ib*. 33; his treatise against Helvidius, 2 *Lat*. 105 n.; his book against Ruffinus, 4 *Jew*. 1073; Catal. Script. Eccles., 2 *Hoop*. 109; interpolations in it, *Calf*. 128 n.; the Vitæ Patrum falsely (when all together, as was formerly the case) ascribed to him, *ib*. 74 n., 252 n.; what Erasmus thought of the Life of Paul the Hermit, *ib*. 252; the spurious Regula Monachorum, 4 *Jew*. 878; interpolations of his Latin version of the Chronicle of Eusebius, 2 *Ful*. 337 n.; he translated the epistle of Epiphanius to John, bp of Jerusalem, *Calf*. 42 n., 254, 255, 1 *Hoop*. 41, 42, *Park*. 88, *Rid*. 91, and approved it, 3 *Tyn*. 182; he requests his reader to consider only the justice of his cause, 1 *Jew*. 85; forbids additions to his works, *Bale* 638; his writings much corrupted by his editor M. Victorius, *Whita*. 222; he says, I am not ashamed, in that thing that I know not, to grant mine ignorance, 4 *Jew*. 697; Palladius foolishly charged him with falsehood for certain free translations, *ib*. 1062; how he replied, *ib*.; he says of some captious quarrellers, albeit I in haste of penning have let escape a word or two, yet that shall not hazard the state of the church of God, *ib*. 693, 694; his opinion received in opposition to the council of Chalcedon, 1 *Jew*. 227, 423, 3 *Jew*. 219, *Rog*. 207; his authority refused as a man writing rashly he knew not what, 4 *Jew*. 924; his errors, *Calf*. 259; severely censured by Capito, 3 *Zur*. 235; some words of his cited, 3 *Whitg*. 587; perhaps erroneously cited for Ambrose, 2 *Bec*. 540 n

ii. *On God and Christ:* he declares that the heathen knew God, either by nature, or by creation and reason, 3 *Jew*. 198; and that man may naturally know that God is, and that he is just, *ib*.; says the heathens point out their gods with their finger, but (David) has God hidden in his heart, 2 *Jew*. 774; speaks of the name Jehovah being called tetragrammaton, *Grin*. 41; disallows the adoration of any creatures, 1 *Ful*. 546; why he consulted Damasus, bishop of Rome, on the use of the expression "three hypostases," *Whita*. 442; how he translates and expounds Zech. xiii. 7, "the Man that is my fellow," 3 *Bul*. 243, 244; he calls the stone that lay under Jacob's head, Christ, 2 *Jew*. 765; asserts that Christ, who was once born of Mary, is born in us every day, *ib*. 730, 733; addresses Paula and Eustochium, on their abode at Bethlehem, 1 *Jew*. 540, 543; describes their visit to the stable, 2 *Jew*. 740; imagines Christ to say, "I went down unto them, that I might eat with them, having received the form of man," *ib*. 618, 797; speaks of Christ being wounded to heal our wounds, 3 *Bec*. 419, 420; says the gospel is dedicated in the passion and blood of the Lord, 2 *Jew*. 732; declares that to us Christ is daily crucified, *ib*. 726, 733, 3 *Jew*. 527; says Christ is ever sacrificed to believers, 2 *Jew*. 726; speaks of Christ receiving sacrifice upon the cross, and also when accepting our praises and thanksgivings, *ib*. 737, 3 *Jew*. 337; says to the Pharisees, yea, although he should come down from the cross, yet would ye not believe him, 4 *Jew*. 1041; denies that the darkness at the crucifixion was caused by an eclipse, *Whita*. 579; declares that, as often as we enter into the sepulchre of the Lord, we see the Saviour lying in his shroud, 1 *Jew*. 467; writes on Christ's victory over death and hell, 1 *Ful*. 303; avows that Christ is not bodily in the church, but ascended into heaven, 1 *Jew*. 506; expounds Matt. xxvi. 11,—"me ye have not always,"—of Christ's corporal presence, 2 *Bec*. 274, 3 *Bec*. 428; writes, my husband is not at home, i. e. Christ is not now corporally in the church, for he is ascended into heaven, 4 *Jew*. 855; declares that Christ ascended with the same nature of flesh in which he was born and suffered (pseud.), 3 *Jew*. 257; speaks of Christ sitting at the right hand of God, the same nature of his flesh remaining in which he suffered, 3 *Bec*. 454, 455; his words on the right hand of the Father, 1 *Bul*. 150; he proves, that the body of Christ must needs be contained in some place, *Grin*. 54; says, let him (a persecutor) touch us with his finger, and we will go out,...Christ is not confined to a place, 1 *Jew*. 499; speaks of Melania as worshipping at Christ's feet, *ib*. 486: asserts that according to the mystical understanding, Christ entereth daily into the temple of his Father, 4 *Jew*. 791; says, I will neither hear father, mother, nor brother, against my Christ, *ib*. 662; says to one, Christ is thy banquet, thought, joy, desire, reading, and rest, 3 *Jew*. 470; affirms that the second coming of our Saviour shall be declared in glory; seeing therefore he is the Light of the world, it is great folly to seek him in any small corner, 3 *Bec*. 439, *Grin*. 54, 3 *Jew*. 536

iii. *Scripture* (see also vii, viii.)

(*a*) He gives lists of the canonical books in his prologue Galeatus, and the epistle to Paulinus, 4 *Bul*. 540, *Whita*. 60, 62; uses the term "canonical" in the ordinary sense, *Whita*. 45, 48; declares that the church knows not the Apocrypha, and that we must have recourse to the Hebrew, from which the Lord spoke, and the disciples took their examples, *ib*. 62; states that what is not found amongst those books must be thrown away, *ib*.; rejects the book of Tobit, *ib*. 80, 81; will not receive the book of Judith, *ib*. 82, 83, 2 *Whitg*. 152; thinks the book of Wisdom was written by Philo, 1 *Ful*. 354; censures the apocryphal additions to Daniel, *ib*. 26, *Whita*. 77, 79; asserts that the books of Maccabees are not canonical, 3 *Bul*. 396; ascribes them to Josephus, *Whita*. 96; declares that as the church reads Judith, Tobit, and Maccabees, but receives them not amongst the canonical scriptures, so she may read (Wisdom and Ecclesiasticus) for the edification of the people, but not to confirm the authority of ecclesiastical doctrines, 4 *Bul*. 450, 2 *Cov*. 426, 427, 1 *Ful*. 24, 2 *Ful*. 221, *Grin*. 23, 3 *Jew*. 431, 432, 433, *Whita*. 87; says, the Wisdom vulgarly attributed to Solomon, and that of Jesus the son of Sirach, and Judith, and Tobit, and the Pastor, are not in the canon, *Whita*. 60; states that the Roman church once rejected the epistle to the Hebrews, *ib*. 505 (see p. 428, col. 1, below); mentions doubts in the early church as to the epistle of St James, 3 *Jew*. 433, *Phil*. 413; condemns a false epistle to the Laodiceans, *Whita*. 108, 303, 531; rejects the apocryphal pieces attributed to Peter, *ib*. 304; censures the fabulous Acts of Paul and Thecla, 2 *Ful*. 339 n.; says that John, the survivor of the apostles, condemned this apocryphal story, *Whita*. 311

(*b*) Its authority and sufficiency:—he states that in the scriptures God daily speaks to believers, *Whita*. 701; declares that what is set abroad in the canonical scriptures, is the doctrine of the Holy Ghost, 4 *Jew*. 773; says of the scripture, This is the way, walk ye in it; go neither to the right hand, nor to the left, then shalt thou break and scatter all errors and idols, &c., *ib*. 1064; desires to kill the children of heretics, and of all that be deceived, with spiritual arrows, that is to say, with the testimonies of the scriptures, *ib*. 770, 771; declares that the sword of God cuts off all things invented without the authority of the scriptures, 2 *Cran*. 27, 3 *Jew*. 440, *Whita*. 693; says, that things that have no testimony of the scriptures are beaten down with the hammer of God's word, 1 *Jew*. 79, 2 *Jew*. 991, 3 *Jew*. 231, &c.; affirms that whatever is beside the scriptures, may in no wise be received among holy things, 2 *Cran*. 27; teaches that a statement which has not authority of the scriptures is despised with the same easiness with which it is proved, 2 *Bec*. 263, 3 *Bec*. 391, 404, *Calf*. 134, *Coop*. 189, 2 *Cran*. 28, 528, 2 *Lat*. 249, *Rid*. 113, *Sand*. 222, *Whita*. 590, 693; states that the apostles confirmed by the oracles of the law and prophets whatsoever they preached, 2 *Cran*. 28; says, wheresoever I expound not the scriptures ...let any man that list reprove me, *Calf*. 60; reminds that what we affirm must be established with testimonies of scripture, 1 *Bec*. 87, 88, 3 *Bec*. 391, *Phil*. 370; asserts that everything we speak, we should prove from the holy scriptures, 2 *Cran*. 28; declares that without authority of the scriptures prattling is not to be credited, 2 *Bec*. 264, 3 *Bec*. 391, *Whita*. 692; says, that building which is not founded on a rock, but is built on the sand, is undermined, and overthrown with the word of God, 4 *Jew*. 1151; shews that the testimony of the scriptures is to be preferred to that of dreams and soothsayers, 2 *Cran*. 44; intimates that to build upon any doctor's saying, without scripture, is to follow Pythagoras rather than Christ, *ib*. 28; judges that what councils may establish against the doctrine contained in the canonical letters is a wicked error, 2 *Bec*. 261, 3 *Bec*. 392, 398; counsels to believe no man without God's word, 2 *Cov*. 448, 2 *Cran*. 27; tells one to seek for nothing but the scriptures, 2 *Cran*. 27

(*c*) The original text, and versions thereof:— he repeatedly asserts the superior authority of the Hebrew and Greek originals, *Whita*. 156, 157 n.; highly esteemed the LXX. version, 1 *Ful*. 51, 52; explains certain of its variations, *ib*. 54; in some things he complains of it, *ib*. 49, 53; says the LXX. sometimes erred in numbers, *Whita*. 122; denies their alleged miraculous unanimity, 1 *Ful*. 53, 80, *Whita*. 120, 121;

complains of the variety of texts of the old Latin versions of the Bible, *Whita.* 128; censures their barbarisms, *ib.* 150; translated the scriptures into Latin, 2 *Ful.* 390; Augustine would have dissuaded him from translating from the Hebrew, 1 *Ful.* 26, 47; he gives an account of his translation, *Whita.* 131; the present Vulgate is not entirely his, *ib.* 129, 130; he censures many of its readings, *ib.* 132, 133; the Vulgate version of the Psalms is not his, *ib.* 180; he is said to have turned the scriptures into Dalmatic or Sclavonian, 2 *Ful.* 390, 1 *Jew.* 270, 2 *Jew.* 690, 691, 692; this assertion is erroneous, *Whita.* 221; he says Psalms were chanted at Paula's funeral in Hebrew, Greek, Latin, and Syriac, 2 *Ful.* 224, 1 *Jew.* 268, 2 *Jew.* 692, *Pil.* 321, *Whita.* 222

(*d*) Interpretation :—he says, the scriptures stand not in the reading, but in the understanding, 3 *Jew.* 242; affirms that the gospel is not in the words of the scriptures, but in the sense; not on the surface, but in the marrow; not in the leaves of the words, but in the root of the reason, *Bale* 114, 1 *Jew.* 447 n., 2 *Jew.* 1112, 3 *Jew.* 222, 243, 4 *Jew.* 764, *Whita.* 402; speaks not only of Moses, but of the apostles and evangelists, as veiled to some, *Whita.* 390; says Jesus lay hid in the letter, *Bale* 115, 2 *Jew.* 594, 765; shews that the knowledge of scripture was opened by the death of Christ, *Whita.* 389; says, whatever we read in the Old Testament we find also in the gospel, *ib.* 621; observes that it is usual in scripture to subjoin plain words to obscure ones, 3 *Jew.* 227, *Whita.* 494; explains what a figurative speech is, 2 *Jew.* 594; insists on the plainness of scripture, 3 *Whitg.* 55, yet maintains that there are in it many things obscure, *Whita.* 373; shews the way to unlock its mysteries, *ib.* 494; says, let reading follow prayer, and prayer reading, *ib.* 468; explains the difference between a prophet and an interpreter, *ib.* 147; calls Rheticus an eloquent man, but a fond interpreter, 3 *Jew.* 305; complains of the audacity of ignorant persons in expounding scripture, *Whita.* 233, 234; declares that whoever understands scripture otherwise than the sense of the Holy Ghost requires ...may well be called a heretic*, 1 *Jew.* 261, 3 *Jew.* 211, 4 *Jew.* 927, *Whita.* 452; intimates that to follow the simple letter is to kill the Son of God, 1 *Jew.* 452, 4 *Jew.* 764; warns of the danger of making Christ's gospel the gospel of a man, or even of the devil, *ib.* 247; falsely accused of corrupting scripture, 2 *Lat.* 341

(*e*) Remarks on some particular books and passages:—his rendering and exposition of Gen. iv. 7, 1 *Ful.* 391, 392; he says Noah was not righteous absolutely, but according to the righteousness of his generation, *Whita.* 166; mentions that the rabbins say, that the same night that Israel departed out of Egypt, all the idolatrous temples were destroyed, either by earthquake or lightning, 4 *Jew.* 880; says, Moses held the rule of the law, Aaron the rule of priesthood, *ib.* 982; writes, God sent out before our faces Moses, the spiritual law, and Aaron, the great priest, *ib.*; describes Aaron's garments, 2 *Brad.* 380, 2 *Bul.* 133; gives his opinion on the descent of Job, *Whita.* 104; expounds Eccles. xii. 11, "the words of the wise," &c., *ib.* 422; calls Isaiah not only a prophet, but an evangelist, 1 *Bul.* 51, 1 *Cov.* 66; comments on Isa. xxxii. 20, "Blessed are ye that sow beside all waters," *Phil.* 368; interprets Jer. xi. 19, "Mittamus lignum in panem ejus," 1 *Ful.* 519, 520; in Ezek. xxx. he uses the name "Alexandria" instead of "No," employing the figure called prolepsis, 4 *Jew.* 694; referred to about Tubal, *Bale* 571; he says Porphyry attacked the book of Daniel, *Whita.* 33 n.; understands Hosea i. 10, 11, of Christ, 3 *Jew.* 280; expounds Hos. vi. 7, "sicut Adam," &c., 1 *Bec.* 68; speaks of the gourd of Jonah, which he renders "hedera," 1 *Jew.* 292, *Whita.* 129, 145; explains the word "mountains" (Micah vi. 2), *Sand.* 216; expounds the first chapter of Haggai, speaking of the sword of God, 3 *Jew.* 232; as to the "pure offering" of Malachi, see xii, below; remarks on the mode of citation used by the writers of the New Testament, 1 *Ful.* 30 n.; maintains a loose opinion on this subject, *Whita.* 38; says that Christ and his disciples cite from the scriptures of the Hebrews, *ib.* 52; states that Julian objected to the Christians the discordance of the evangelists, 1 *Jew.* 532; says Matthew's gospel was written in Hebrew, 1 *Ful.* 30 n., *Whita.* 125, 126, or Syriac, *Whita.* 126 n., that the Hebrew text was extant in his time in the library of Cæsarea, 1 *Jew.* 237, *Whita.* 126, and that he made a copy from a Hebrew MS. in the library of Nicomedia, *Whita.* 127; this

---

* See the note on p. 419 above.

Gospel was an interpolated one, as appears by Jerome's extracts from it, 1 *Jew.* 237; he writes concerning St Matthew's citations from the Old Testament, 1 *Ful.* 30 n., 50, *Whita.* 525; does not expound the doxology in the Lord's prayer, 4 *Bul.* 220; reference to his exposition of the parable of the householder, Matt. xx, 2 *Lat.* 198 n.; he thinks that in ch. xxvii. 9, Matthew erred as to the name of Jeremy, 4 *Jew.* 635, *Whita.* 37 n.; says Mark alleges Abiathar for Abimelech, 4 *Jew.* 635; remarks that Luke was learned in the art of medicine, and expert in Greek, 1 *Ful.* 30 n.; speaks of the object of John's gospel, 2 *Brad.* 263; refers to the supposed quotation in Jo. vii. 38, on "living water," 1 *Ful.* 30 n.; enumerates the canonical epistles, *ib.* 19 n.; considers that the epistle to the Romans is involved in great obscurity, *Whita.* 373; differs from Augustine as to "the works of the law" (Rom. iii. 8), *ib.* 455; allows that in Rom. vii. the apostle speaks in his own person, 2 *Bul.* 247; refers to an objection by Porphyry, about Paul rebuking Peter (Gal. ii. 11), 1 *Jew.* 532; excuses the dissimulation of Peter, there referred to, 2 *Bul.* 115, & al., see ix, below; explains "beggarly elements" (Gal. iv. 9), 1 *Jew.* 138; interprets the word $ἀρραβὼν$ (Eph. i. 14), &c., *Whita.* 133 n., 134; explains Phil. iii. 1, "to write the same things," &c., 3 *Jew.* 437; on 2 Thess. ii. 15, he says that Paul will have his own things to be kept, and no strange things added, *ib.*; differs from Augustine on 1 Tim. iii. 2, where it is said that a bishop must be "the husband of one wife," *Whita.* 455; says that some rejected the epistle to Philemon, *ib.* 35; ascribes the epistle to the Hebrews to Paul, but mentions doubts that once existed as to it, 1 *Ful.* 30, *Whita.* 106, 107; says Paul wrote the epistle to the Hebrews in Hebrew, *Whita.* 125, but allows that his quotations follow the LXX, 1 *Ful.* 30 n.; refers to the seven catholic epistles, *ib.* 222 n., 223 n.; mentions that there were doubts in the ancient church as to the epistle of James, 3 *Jew.* 433, *Phil.* 413; says that the Apocalypse has as many mysteries as words, *Bale* 380

(*f*) The reading of scripture, &c. (see also *d*):—he says that if David confessed his ignorance of God's law, much more should we, and acknowledge the necessity of Divine assistance, *Whita.* 367, 368; writes on the story of Philip and the Ethiopian eunuch, *ib.* 369; states that whomsoever the devil hath deceived and enticed to fall asleep, God's word doth awake up, &c., 4 *Jew.* 1059; says of one, he will inclose himself with the doctrine of the scriptures, as with a strong wall, that the enemy may not enter into his heart, *ib.* 1064; affirms that the knowledge of the scriptures is the food of everlasting life, *Rid.* 132; censures certain men of his time for thinking it sin to read the scriptures, 2 *Jew.* 680; says ignorance of the scriptures is ignorance of Christ, 1 *Bec.* 383, 384, 2 *Jew.* 800; declares that it is the mother of errors, *Rid.* 132; doubts of the salvation of him who is negligent in hearing the word of God, 2 *Jew.* 1090; declares that the Lord hath spoken by his gospel, not that a few should understand, but all (pseud.), *ib.* 684; says the apostles and prophets wrote not like Plato for a few, but for the whole people, and that the scripture is read by all people that all may understand (pseud.), 4 *Jew.* 896, *Phil.* 369, *Whita.* 245, 398; says, we must read the scriptures with all diligence, that, as good exchangers, we may know the lawful coin, 2 *Cran.* 28, 2 *Jew.* 682, 3 *Jew.* 238; writes, we are taught that the lay people ought to have the word of God, not only sufficiently, but with abundance, and to teach and counsel one another, 2 *Jew.* 685, 696, 4 *Jew.* 796, 1186; advises the learning of verses of holy scripture, 2 *Ful.* 240; says men, monks, and women strove who should learn the most, 4 *Jew.* 797, *Pil.* 609; describes the poor husbandman as singing Psalms at his plough, 1 *Jew.* 331; exhorts Paula, Eustochium, and divers other women, to the constant study of the scriptures, *Whita.* 248; says none of the sisters at Bethlehem with Paula might be ignorant of the Psalms, or pass over the day without learning some part of scripture, 2 *Jew.* 670, 676, *Whita.* 248; states that the Jews forbade any to read some parts of scripture till they were thirty years old, 2 *Jew.* 693; says, at the coming of Christ the people, who were laid asleep under their teachers, shall resort to the mountains of the scriptures, 1 *Jew.* 327, 2 *Jew.* 688, 1019, 4 *Jew.* 1059, &c., 1064, 2 *Lat.* 343; declares that when they shall be turned, and shall behold the clear light of Christ, they shall feed in the paths and ways of holy scripture, and shall say, "The Lord feedeth me, and I shall want nothing," 4 *Jew.* 1064; affirms that when we shall obtain to be with Christ, and shall be like the angels, the doctrine of

JEROME

books shall give place, 3 *Jew.* 371; explains that though the paper and letters of the scriptures shall be abolished, the things that are promised shall last for ever, *ib.* 435

iv. *Tradition:* his testimony for Lent and tradition considered, *Whita.* 605; he shews that anything spoken after the apostles' time has no authority, and may be cut off (pseud.), *Coop.* 190, 2 *Cran.* 28, *Whita.* 694; declares that the writings of those who came after the apostles and evangelists are of no authority (pseud.),*Phil.* 369; asks one why he brings forth that which Peter and Paul never taught, 2 *Ful.* 63, 3 *Jew.* 192; speaks of the creed delivered by the apostles as written not with ink, but in the heart, *ib.* 133; speaks of human devices set forth as of apostolic origin, 2 *Jew.* 991; judges that anything which councils may establish against the doctrine contained in the canonical letters is a wicked error, 2 *Bec.* 261, 3 *Bec.* 392, 398; says that ecclesiastical traditions are to be observed as delivered of the elders, the custom of one not being overthrown by the contrary custom of others, 1 *Whitg.* 218; speaks of certain customs observed by tradition, 2 *Cran.* 58; says that many vices please through old custom, *ib.* 51; (Paulinus, not Jerome,) speaks of the force of evil habit, *Wool.* 106

v. *Sin:* he confesses original sin, and describes concupiscence, 2 *Bul.* 392; distinguishes between "peccatum" and "delictum," *ib.* 358; declares, on the authority of the scriptures, that there is no man without sin, 3 *Jew.* 581; says the souls of the young are without (actual) sin, *Calf.* 259; allows that in Rom. vii. Paul is speaking of his own person, 2 *Bul.* 247; had a controversy with Augustine on the question whether any lying or dissimulation is allowed in holy scripture, *ib.* 116; states that one who does not take an expression in the sense intended, bears false witness, 2 *Jew.* 770, 2 *Lat.* 315, 325; declares that slanderers are filled with live flesh, 3 *Jew.* 619; denounces gluttony, and the sins to which it leads, *Sand.* 138; says that abundance often breeds luxury, *ib.*; would not believe a great wine-drinker to be chaste, 2 *Lat.* 63; mentions the execution of an adulteress, 1 *Bul.* 412; calls hypocrisy a double evil, *Rid.* 60; speaks of some who take to themselves a part of the high looks of the Pharisees, see p. 432, col. 2, below; says pride is changed into humility, *ib.* 505; affirms that many follow the shadow of humility, but few the truth, 1 *Bec.* 205;

cautions against those men who go in chains, that wear long hair, as women, 3 *Jew.* 615; counsels against idleness, *Sand.* 117

vi. *Grace, Faith, Works* (see also ii): he declares that, as it is more to do the will of our Lord than to know it, so the knowledge of the same goeth before the doing (pseud.), 4 *Jew.* 796; cited as stating that Cain had free-will, 1 *Ful.* 390; said to have thundered out a most horrible curse against those who taught that the law commands impossibilities, 2 *Bul.* 246; he teaches, in several places, that no man ever fulfilled the commandments, 3 *Jew.* 580, 581; says it is man's true wisdom to know himself imperfect, 1 *Bec.* 71; asserts that the righteous are not saved by their own merits, 3 *Bec.* 170; affirms that it is most certain that every man needs the mercy of God, 3 *Jew.* 581, 582; says, if we consider our own merits, we must despair, 2 *Jew.* 1041, 3 *Jew.* 587; teaches that our righteousness consists not of our merit, but of the mercy of God, 1 *Bec.* 71; calls the righteousness which men shall seek, none other than Christ himself, 2 *Bec.* 639; writes on the grace of God which was with Paul, 1 *Ful.* 376, 377; maintains that God justifies by faith only, *Wool.* 34; other places to the same effect, 2 *Cran.* 205, 208, 211; by "the works of the law" he understood ceremonies, *Whita.* 455; elsewhere he allows that "the law of God" means everything commanded, 2 *Cran.* 208; he shews that we have access to God, not through our righteousness, but through faith in Christ, 3 *Jew.* 588; says, every holy man hath in himself the altar of the Lord, which is faith, 2 *Jew.* 735; declares that if we believe we shew the truth by our works, 2 *Lat.* 343; says that just men are so called because they are furnished with the greater part of virtues, 3 *Jew.* 581; explains what it is to do judgment (Mic. vi. 8), *Sand.* 223; speaks of the reverence due to mothers, 1 *Bul.* 274, 275; inculcates charity to the poor, see vii, below.

vii. *The Church* (see also viii. and ix, below): he says we must remain in that church which was founded by the apostles, &c., *Pil.* 618, 619; speaks of the church as circumscribed by the bounds of scripture, *Whita.* 701; declares that the church of Christ, containing the churches through all the world, is joined together in the unity of the Spirit, &c., 2 *Jew.* 819; expounds the text "One Lord, one faith, one baptism," 1 *Jew.* 256; shews that he, in Bethlehem, could hold communion with the presbyters at Rome, *ib.* 133; his use of the word "communion," *ib.* 132; he remarks that every province has peculiar manners, and rites, and feelings, which you cannot alter without great trouble, 4 *Jew.* 1125; calls the faithful the true vine, 1 *Jew.* 468; says, we are verily one bread, *ib.*; thinks that Christian is the "name" foretold by Isaiah, *Wool.* 21; honoured the father of Furia more for the name of a Christian, than for his worldly dignities, *ib.*; says that we are of Christ's flesh and of his bones, for he is the head of his body the church, 3 *Jew.* 494; declares that whosoever is a member of Christ's body is a priest, *ib.* 336; says, Christ, naked and hungry, lying before our gate, dieth in the poor, *ib.* 541; advises, while others build churches, &c., to clothe Christ in the poor, 1 *Bec.* 23; declares it the glory of a bishop to provide for the poor, *ib.* 21; describes the charity of Exuperius, *ib.* 32; says whatever the clerks have, that is the poor's, 1*Bec.* 23, 2 *Bec.* 325; calls it sacrilege not to give to the poor things that appertain unto them, 1 *Bec.* 24; likens those who with the goods of the poor satisfy their own pleasure to the Pharisees, *ib.*; remarks they are not always the children of holy men that sit in the places of holy men, but they that do the works of holy men, 1 *Jew.* 401, 3 *Jew.* 201, 323, 4 *Jew.* 703, 1070, 1117, 1134, 2 *Lat.* 313 n.; says that whoso believeth that man to be holy that is not holy, and joineth him to the fellowship of God, doth violence to Christ, &c., 3 *Jew.* 324, 4 *Jew.* 703; affirms that the church, after she was come to Christian princes, was indeed greater in wealth and riches, but in virtue and holiness less than she was before, 4 *Jew.* 723; speaks of the darkness of his time, 1 *Hoop.* 27; complains of the condition of the Eastern churches, 4 *Jew.* 1074; declares that by the exchangers (in the temple) are signified the sellers of ecclesiastical benefices, who make the house of God a den of thieves, *ib.* 869; writes, we say "there shall no hurt come upon us:" let us hear the saying of the Lord: "Sion and Jerusalem ... shall be consumed, and brought to an end," *ib.* 1062; warns that the watch-tower of the Lord shall be turned up with the enemy's plough, and the temple of the Lord turned into briars and thorns, &c., *ib.* 870; says the Lord will take away the names of vain glory and false admiration which are in the church, &c., 3 *Jew.* 310, 4 *Jew.* 929, 1063; affirms that in the end of the world our Lord will search Jerusalem, i. e. his church, with a candle, and punish those who have despised his commandments, 3 *Jew.* 597; states that the pin, or bar, (meaning Christ) shall be taken away from the place of faith, i. e. the church, because of the wickedness that daily groweth; and those who before hung upon him by faith, shall afterwards by infidelity be broken down, and fall and perish, 4 *Jew.* 1062; so small, he says, shall be the number of holy men, *ib.* 877

viii. *Bishops and other Clergy, Monks, &c.*: he calls the apostles fathers, 1 *Jew.* 77; denies that any holy man has authority like them, 3 *Jew.* 231; speaks of James as bishop of Jerusalem, 1 *Ful.* 222 n., 1 *Jew.* 238; calls Timothy bishop of Ephesus (pseud.), 2 *Whitg.* 294; exhorts bishops to hear the charge given to Titus, 1 *Whitg.* 433; says bishops hold the place of the apostles, *Whita.* 417; affirms that presbyters succeed the apostles, and that bishops are in the place of Christ, 2 *Whitg.* 258; declares that among the ancients presbyters and bishops were the same, but that gradually, that the plants of dissensions might be plucked up, all the care was brought to one, 4 *Bul.* 87 n., 1 *Jew.* 373; admonishes that as presbyters know themselves to be subject to him who is set above them, by the custom of the church; so bishops should know that they are greater than presbyters rather by custom than by the truth of the Lord's ordinance, 4 *Bul.* 87 n., 112, 2 *Ful.* 315, 316, 388, 1 *Jew.* 340, 379, 3 *Jew.* 292, 294, 2 *Whitg.* 225; says that a presbyter is the same as a bishop, and that before factions were made in religion by the instinct of the devil ... the churches were governed by the common counsel of the presbyters; but that afterwards, when every one thought those whom he had baptized were his own, not Christ's, it was decreed in all the world that one chosen from among the presbyters should be set above the others, and that to him should belong the whole care of the church, and the seeds of schisms be taken away, 4 *Bul.* 111, 1 *Ful.* 265, 1 *Jew.* 348, 3 *Jew.* 272, 294, 301, 4 *Jew.* 912, *Pil.* 494, 2 *Whitg.* 221, 225, 255, 265, 266, 267; again, he says that one was chosen and set above the others as a remedy of schism, 2 *Whitg.* 91, 117, 222, 238, 256; adduces a testimony by which, he says, it is very manifestly proved that a bishop and a presbyter are the same, 4 *Bul.* 87 n.; mentions one who was so peevish that he set deacons before priests, i. e. before bishops; whereas the apostle plainly teaches us that presbyters and bishops are the same, 3 *Jew.* 272, 439; remarks that among those of old bishops and presbyters were the same, the one being a name of dignity, the other of age, 2 *Tyn.* 152 n.; uses other words to the same effect, 2 *Whitg.* 254; declares that bishops ought to govern the church in common (with the priests), imitating Moses, who chose seventy, &c., 4 *Bul.* 112, 1 *Jew.* 349, 383; shews how the clergy of Alexandria used to choose one of themselves, whom they placed in a higher degree and called bishop, 2 *Whitg.* 222, 249—251, 256, 428; states that a bishop does nothing which a presbyter does not, except ordination, 3 *Jew.* 293, 1 *Whitg.* 437 —440; says that superintendent is an ancient name for a bishop, 4 *Jew.* 906; speaks of the safety of the church hanging on the dignity of the high priest (i. e. the bishop), 1 *Jew.* 372, 3 *Jew.* 221, 315, 4 *Jew.* 731, 734, 822, 823, 2 *Whitg.* 222, 240, 256; declares that whereever there is a bishop, whether at Rome, or Eugubium, &c., he is of the same merit, and the same priesthood, 2 *Hoop.* 237 n., 1 *Jew.* 373, 2 *Jew.* 1001, 3 *Jew.* 290, 293, *Phil.* 45, *Pil.* 494, 1 *Tyn.* 216 n., 2 *Whitg.* 255, 257; says, the power of riches, or the lowliness of poverty, makes a bishop neither higher nor lower, but all bishops are the apostles' successors, 1 *Jew.* 379, 3 *Jew.* 293, 610, 4 *Jew.* 1066, 1069; admonishes that if a man would be a bishop he should follow Moses and Aaron, by reading the scriptures, praying and teaching the people, 1 *Bec.* 382; says all that God's bishop does ought to be sermons, *ib.* 12; speaking of certain bishops he says, they themselves are to themselves both laymen and bishops too, 4 *Jew.* 971; declares that, as if they were placed in some high castle, they scarcely vouchsafe to look upon poor mortal men, and to speak to their fellow-servants, *ib.* 688; often refers to the order of presbyters, 1 *Ful.* 262, 263; states that the presbyter is contained in the bishop, 2 *Whitg.* 254; says we have in the church our senate, a company of presbyters, 3 *Whitg.* 201; writes concerning presbyters "who labour in the word," *ib.* 152; considers "pastors and teachers," as the same, 1 *Whitg.* 474; condemns those who enter the ministry without qualification, 1 *Bec.* 5; says he that knows not the law of the Lord is no priest, *ib.* 6, 383; asserts that such should be chosen pastors, in comparison of whom the others may right well be named the flock, *ib.* 9; declares that the captains of the church have the keys of knowledge to open the scriptures; therefore commandment is given that the masters should open, and the scholars enter, 3 *Jew.* 364; says the works of a minister must not confound his words, 1 *Bec.* 16; asks how the president of a church can take away evil out of it, if he have offended in the like fault, *ib.*; considers that priests who take tithes deny that Christ is come in the flesh, *Bale* 108; asks, dost thou consider Peter? consider Judas also: dost thou allow Stephen? mark also what Nicolas was: ecclesiastical dignity makes not a Christian, 4 *Jew.* 1117; condemns the pride and gluttony of the clergy, 2 *Whitg.* 388, 389; says of certain pastors, that they worship the Lord and Melchom both together, thinking they may serve both the world and the Lord, and satisfy two masters at once, God and mammon, 4 *Jew.* 971; complains that the soldiers of Christ bind themselves to worldly affairs, and offer the same image to God and to Cæsar, *ib.* 820, 971; speaks of some who assume such authority, that whether they teach good things or evil, they will not have their disciples to seek a reason, but only to follow them, their leaders, 3 *Jew.* 122, 4 *Jew.* 1039; refers to certain men who are taken for elders of the church, and chiefs of the priests, following the plain letter, and killing the Son of God, 1 *Jew.* 452, 4 *Jew.* 764; states that the king of Assyria, i. e. the devil, knows that he can never deceive the sheep, unless he first cast the shepherds into a trance, 4 *Jew.* 1063; says, the prophets of Jerusalem have never a word of prophecy in their mouths, &c., *ib.* 870; declares that when the prophets fell to taking of money, their prophecy became a soothsaying, *ib.* 1083; says, touching the clergy, the priests themselves that ought to teach the law of our Lord, and to defend the people committed to their charge, being amazed, and bereft of their wits, shall be turned into madness, *ib.* 1063; foretells that God will take away the names of vain glory and false credit, that are in the church, and the names of priests, together with the priests themselves, that vainly boast of the names of bishops, and of the dignity of priesthood, but do nothing, *ib.* 1063; says that the priest is made from the deacon, not the deacon from the priest, 2 *Whitg.* 258; speaks of archpriests and archdeacons, 1 *Jew.* 372, 2 *Whitg.* 431; refers to the latter, 2 *Whitg.* 173, 175, 177; reproves a deacon for setting himself above the elder, *ib.* 253; reckons five orders in the church, bishops, presbyters, deacons, the faithful, and the catechumens, 3 *Jew.* 272; compares Aaron, his sons, and the Levites, to bishops, priests, and deacons, 1 *Ful.* 262, 263; speaks of the honour due to bishops, presbyters, and deacons, *ib.* 262; says that honouring and trusting in ministers are different, 2 *Lat.* 347; the spurious treatise De septem Ordinibus speaks of fossarii as the first order, 3 *Jew.* 272; he says every ecclesiastical order is subject to its governors, 1 *Jew.* 372, 2 *Whitg.* 257; explains χειροτονία, as meaning the ordination of clerks by prayer and laying-on of hands, 1 *Ful.* 247, 248, 1 *Whitg.* 349; speaks of choice either by the bishop or the people, 1 *Whitg.* 442; mentions choice by the bishop, *ib.* 443, 460; complains that much cost was bestowed in adorning churches, and that little regard was had to the choice of ministers, *ib.* 482; a passage by Musculus on clandestine ordinations erroneously referred to him, *ib.* 441, 442; he treats of the origin of monks, 4 *Bul.* 514; declares that the state of a monk is one thing, and the state of a priest is another, 4 *Jew.* 800; says, a monk's office is not to preach, but to mourn, *ib.*; some account of the life and apparel of the monks of his time, 3 *Jew.* 617, 4 *Jew.* 945; of some he says, they are loth to be abjects and in servile state; for idleness they will not labour, and to beg they are ashamed, *ib.* 799; speaks of the incontinence of some who were girded and went in black, and had long beards, 2 *Jew.* 830; describes the three kinds of monks in Egypt, 2 *Tyn.* 42 n.; says, it was a law among the monks there, that whoso would not labour should not eat, 4 *Jew.* 800; replies to the accusation of severity and sadness, 3 *Whitg.* 523; the spurious Regula Mon. in his name charges monks to pronounce every word distinctly and warily, lest by their foolish utterance they should make the angels to fall a laughing, 4 *Jew.* 878; repeatedly mentions that companies of solitary virgins sang the Psalter in order daily at certain hours, 4 *Bul.* 198, 199

ix. *Peter, Rome:* he declares that the church is built on all the apostles, and that all received the keys of the kingdom of heaven; but allows that one was chosen as chief, to avoid schism, 2 *Ful.* 285, 292, 1 *Jew.* 435, 437, 3 *Jew.* 288, 290, 297, 4 *Jew.* 1136, 2 *Whitg.* 230; says bishops and priests, not understanding the words "Upon this rock," &c., take to themselves some of the pride of the Pharisees, &c., 1 *Jew.* 340, 3 *Jew.* 213, 375, 380, 4 *Jew.* 1119, 1 *Tyn.* 217 n., 269 n.; Baronius considers him shamefully astray, and Spondanus represents him as heretical, with reference to Peter's primacy, 2 *Ful.* 292 n.; he speaks of the agreement between Peter and Paul as to preaching, 3 *Jew.* 327; considers that Peter's ordinary vocation was to the Jews, Paul's to the Gentiles, *ib.* 329; explains why Paul went to Jerusalem to see Peter, &c., 1 *Jew.* 375, 4 *Jew.* 917; differs from Augustine about Peter's dissimulation, 2 *Bul.* 115, 116, 1 *Jew.* 532, 1 *Ful.* 35, *Phil.* 401, *Whita.* 455; affirms Paul to be in nothing inferior to Peter, 3 *Jew.* 328; says Peter was bishop of Antioch, *Rog.* 328 n.; strangely interpolates the Chronicon of Eusebius, as to Peter's long continuance at Rome, 2 *Ful.* 337 n.; expresses his attachment to the chair of Peter, *ib.* 349; says it is not easy to stand in the place of Paul, and to hold the rank of Peter, who are now reigning with Christ, 3 *Jew.* 327, 4 *Jew.* 923, 1134; asks counsel of the chair of Peter, calling it the rock on which the church is built, &c., 2 *Ful.* 349; confesses that pope Liberius was an Arian, 2 *Ful.* 349, 3 *Jew.* 342, 343, 4 *Jew.* 926; calls pope Damasus teacher of the virgin church, 1 *Jew.* 433; preserves his creed, 1 *Bul.* 32, 2 *Hoop.* 538; says if we agree with the bishop of Rome we are catholics, 1 *Ful.* 222; makes no mention of the bishop of Rome as supreme, *Phil.* 45; falsely alleged to call the pope chief-priest, 4 *Jew.* 822 (see p. 431, col. 1, above); he speaks of a certain peerless and high power in the church, but not with reference to the pope, 2 *Ful.* 253; mentions the church of Rome as the house in which the Lamb must be eaten, the ark of Noah, &c., *ib.* 349, *Pil.* 617 n.; says we are not to think that the church of the city of Rome is one, and the church of the rest of the world another, 3 *Jew.* 293; asks, why do you bring me the custom of one city? *ib.* 285, 293, 294, 4 *Jew.* 828; says, if authority is sought, the world is greater than the city, 1 *Jew.* 413, 3 *Jew.* 293, 333, 4 *Jew.* 920, 1119, 1 *Tyn.* 216 n.; said on one occasion, not only the bishop of one city, but also the bishops of all the world, are deceived, 4 *Jew.* 828; addresses

Augustine as pope, 2 *Hoop.* 236, 2 *Whitg.* 86 n.; calls Origen master or teacher of the churches, 1 *Jew.* 433, 3 *Jew.* 269, 4 *Jew.* 1045; speaks of the pride of the Romans, 1 *Jew.* 355; declares that Peter in his first epistle meant Rome, under the name of Babylon, 4 *Jew.* 1063; considers that Rome is the Babylon of the Apocalypse, 2 *Ful.* 371, 4 *Jew.* 1064, 1 *Lat.* 173, 174, *Rog.* 182

x. *Saints, Ecclesiastical Writers:* he is alleged to have believed in the intercession of saints, 3 *Jew.* 572; said to have prayed to saints, 3 *Tyn.* 126; tells why John Baptist is styled an angel by Malachi, 1 *Ful.* 483; says, we believe not that Mary was married again after her child-bearing, because we read it not, 3 *Jew.* 441; condemns the doctrine of Helvidius respecting her, 2 *Cran.* 60, 1 *Hoop.* 161, 1 *Jew.* 22 n.; he (or Sophronius) declares the story of the virgin's assumption to be apocryphal, *Whita.* 667; records the death of James and Peter, 1 *Jew.* 342 n.; calls the bodies of Peter and Paul the altars of Christ, 1 *Ful.* 516 (as to both of them, see ix, above); says that Paul, though not eloquent, bore the cross of Christ, and subdued the world, 4 *Jew.* 911; mentions the decease of John, *Calf.* 130; speaks of the epistles ascribed to Clement, 1 *Jew.* 111, *Whita.* 566; cites Ignatius (or Barnabas), *Whita.* 572; gives an account of Hegesippus, 2 *Ful.* 338 n., *Whita.* 574; says that Origen, Tertullian, &c., may be read, choosing the good in them, and shunning the contrary, 3 *Jew.* 233; as to Origen, see also xvii. and xix, below; he thinks that when he wrote well, nobody wrote better, 2 *Cran.* 342, 344; calls Pamphilus a martyr, before his martyrdom, 4 *Jew.* 694; wishes that Lactantius had been as able to confirm (the truth) as to overthrow the contrary, *Calf.* 180; mentions the public reading of Ephrem's homilies, 1 *Jew.* 269; declares that the work of Optatus De Schism. Donat. was in *six* books, 2 *Ful.* 323; speaks of Gregory Nazianzen, 2 *Cran.* 124; what Erasmus thought of his Life of Paul the Hermit, *Calf.* 252; he scoffs at Ambrose and his writings, 1 *Jew.* 314, 3 *Jew.* 176; gives a character of Epiphanius, *Calf.* 255, 3 *Tyn.* 182; speaks scornfully of Ruffinus, 3 *Jew.* 391; charges him with heresy, 4 *Jew.* 1006; marvels much that he does not call himself "the prisoner of Jesus Christ," &c., *ib.* 1073; expresses himself loath to write against Augustine, he being a bishop of his communion, 1 *Jew.* 130, 132; writing to Augustine, says, I judged that there were certain heretical errors in your epistle, 3 *Jew.* 607; addresses him as the most notable bishop in the world, 4 *Jew.* 1044, and as pope, 2 *Hoop.* 236, 2 *Whitg.* 86 n.; rails at Vigilantius, 3 *Jew.* 167; see also xix.

xi. *Sacraments, particularly Baptism:* he warns that if the sacraments are violated, then is he violated whose sacraments they are, 1 *Cran.* 228, 1 *Jew.* 517; said to consider the worthiness of the priest essential to a sacrament, *Calf.* 259; he asserts that out of Christ's side the sacraments of baptism and martyrdom are poured forth together, 3 *Jew.* 457; says that to those who are to be baptized the Holy Trinity is openly delivered, 2 *Jew.* 769; affirms that in baptism our faces are marked with the blood of Christ, 1 *Jew.* 488; says man gives the water only, but God gives the Holy Ghost, whereby sins are washed away, 3 *Jew.* 463; writes, if any man have received only the bodily washing of water, he has not put on the Lord Jesus Christ, *ib.*; declares that they who receive not baptism with full faith, receive the water, but not the Spirit, 2 *Jew.* 1106, 3 *Jew.* 462; says, we all are the priestly and kingly kindred, who having been baptized in Christ, are called by the name of Christ, 4 *Jew.* 984; declares that by the water of baptism, or by the fire of the Holy Ghost, Christ is made the body of the everlasting bread, 3 *Jew.* 484; explains "first faith" to be the faith of baptism, *ib.* 386; states that we are baptized not only for remission of sins, but also for the resurrection of our flesh, *ib.* 470; how baptism was celebrated in his time, *Calf.* 213; he mentions and approves the baptizing of infants, 2 *Bec.* 210, 4 *Bul.* 392, *Pil.* 279; speaks of Cyprian's conclusion that infants might be baptized immediately after their birth, 4 *Bul.* 392; says laymen may baptize if need require, 2 *Whitg.* 526; explains the meaning of trine immersion, 1 *Jew.* 256 n.; speaks of wine mingled with milk being given to those newly baptized, 4 *Bul.* 359; cautions against trusting merely in baptism and the spiritual food, 2 *Jew.* 757; shews that in his time baptism and the eucharist were ministered together, 1 *Jew.* 250

xii. *The Eucharist:* he speaks of the sacrament as Christ's last remembrance, 2 *Jew.* 591; terms it a Christian mystery, 3 *Bec.* 389, 2 *Jew.* 730, 732; calls it wheat and wine, which is not eaten without praising the Lord, nor drunk save in his holy courts, 2 *Hoop.* 431; says it ought to be common to all, 2 *Bec.* 240, 3 *Bec.* 414, 1 *Jew.* 18, 105, 129, 134, 202, 230, 3 *Jew.* 143; speaks of Christ as representing, in the sacrament, the truth of his body and blood, 2 *Bec.* 285, 3 *Bec.* 271, 436, 1 *Brad.* 590, 4 *Bul.* 440, 1 *Cran.* 122, 123, (59), 2 *Hoop.* 405, 472, *Hutch.* 238, 2 *Jew.* 609, 1113, 3 *Jew.* 453, *Sand.* 454; writes of Melchisedec's offering, 1 *Ful.* 148 ; refers to his bread and wine as a type of Christ's, 1 *Brad.* 590, 4 *Bul.* 440, 2 *Jew.* 730, 732, 3 *Jew.* 453; compares the shew-bread with the body of Christ, 1 *Cran.* 192, 342, (75); marks that the bread which the Lord brake was his body, *ib.* 33, 104, (54), 1 *Hoop.* 233, 2 *Hoop.* 439; speaking of Christ's words, "This is my body," &c., he says, let that saying be expounded by a figure, &c., 3 *Jew.* 446; adds, when I say it is a figure, then I say it is not the truth, *ib.* 447; calls Christ's flesh true meat, &c., 1 *Cran.* 24; observes that our Lord, as a type of his blood, offered not water but wine, 2 *Ful.* 83, 2 *Jew.* 592, 3 *Jew.* 521; says that the blood of Christ and his flesh are understood two ways, the spiritual, and that which was crucified, 3 *Bec.* 446, 1 *Brad.* 98, 1 *Cran.* 232, 233, 1 *Ful.* 272 n., 273, 1 *Jew.* 460, 462, 2 *Jew.* 621, *Rid.* 202; declares that it is lawful to eat of the oblation made in commemoration of Christ, but not of that which Christ made on the altar of the cross (pseud.), 3 *Bec.* 439, 1 *Jew.* 463; admonishes that we abandon Jewish fables, and ascend up with our Lord into that great parlour adorned and made clean, and there receive of him the cup of the new testament, 1 *Jew.* 12, 454, 2 *Jew.* 1121, 3 *Jew.* 474, 546; speaks of eating Christ's flesh and drinking his blood, not only in mystery, but also in the reading of the scriptures, 3 *Bec.* 439, 440, 1 *Brad.* 100, 2 *Hoop.* 486, and even prefers the latter interpretation to the former (pseud.), 1 *Brad.* 100, 1 *Jew.* 519, 2 *Jew.* 771; says, when we hear the word of the Lord, the flesh and blood of Christ are poured into our ears, 2 *Jew.* 600, 724, 1087, 1119; describes the strong in Christ as eating this bread, and virgins (i. e. the holy) as drinking this wine, 2 *Bec.* 293, 3 *Bec.* 462, 463; declares that the unholy do not eat Christ's flesh, *Hutch.* 265; says, lovers of pleasure eat not the flesh of Jesus nor drink his blood, 2 *Bec.* 292, 293, 3 *Bec.* 462, 1 *Cran.* 210, 225, (80), 2 *Hoop.* 498; states that heretics eat not the Saviour's body, 2 *Bec.* 293, 3 *Bec.* 462, 1 *Cran.* 210, (80), 2 *Hoop.* 498; says that Christ's flesh is the meat of faithful men, 3 *Bec.* 462, 1 *Cran.* 210, (81); censures some priests who defile the holy things of the Lord, 3 *Jew.* 596; affirms that holy men eat the heavenly bread, and are filled with every word of God, having the same Lord that is their meat, 2 *Jew.* 767 ; says those who eat and drink the body and blood of the Lord, are turned into the princes of the church, 2 *Hoop.* 431, 432; speaks of the union of God's inheritance through the mystery of Christ's body and blood, 1 *Jew.* 142; writes on the wheat of which the heavenly bread is made, *ib.* 474; says, we feast in sincerity, without leaven, 2 *Jew.* 734; speaks of priests making the Lord's body, 1 *Ful.* 272, *Rid.* 180, 182: asserts that they do wickedly against the law of Christ who think that the eucharist is made by the priest's words, not by his life, 2 *Jew.* 755; says the priest, who must always offer sacrifice for the people, must always pray, 2 *Ful.* 83 ; calls the sacrament of bread and wine a pure and simple sacrifice, 2 *Jew.* 735; notes that St Paul (1 Cor. x), speaks first of the cup, 1 *Jew.* 236; speaks of the apostles celebrating the communion with the Lord's prayer, 1 *Hoop.* 237; commends Exuperius, bishop of Toulouse, who carried the Lord's body in a wicker basket, and his blood in a glass, 4 *Bul.* 420, 2 *Ful.* 115, 1 *Hoop.* 233, 1 *Jew.* 239, 245, 249, 2 *Jew.* 554; says the mixed cup in the eucharist was foreshewn by Solomon, 1 *Ful.* 522; declares that a bishop ought not to refuse the eucharist of a priest (pseud.), 2 *Jew.* 626; speaks of the priests dividing the blood of the Lord to the people, 3 *Bec.* 413, *Coop.* 142, *Hutch.* 282, *Sand.* 455; testifies that the people received daily, 2 *Bec.* 258, 1 *Jew.* 17, 125, 174; refers to the custom at Rome of the faithful always receiving the body of Christ, which he neither blames nor approves, 3 *Bec.* 474, *Coop.* 126 n., 1 *Jew.* 156; wishes that we could at all times receive the eucharist without a pricking conscience, 2 *Bec.* 259; testifies that what remained after the communion was eaten in the church, *ib.* 251, 3 *Bec.* 456, 2 *Jew.* 553, 554; mentions that in his time a portion of the sacrament was sent from the church to the newly married, 1 *Jew.* 6; speaks of the reception of the communion by the married, in which passage he reproves those who received the sacrament at home, *Coop*. 126, 1 *Jew*. 156, 157; a spurious passage on the mass, 2 *Jew*. 640 n

xiii. *Worship, Ceremonies, Tongues:* he considers the incense prophesied of by Malachi to be the prayers of saints, 1 *Jew*. 110, 2 *Jew*. 713, 723; says incense and a pure sacrifice are offered daily, &c., 2 *Jew*. 725; verses put forth in his name on prayer, 1 *Bec*. 164; he says, in prayer we are not declarers, but cravers, 4 *Bul*. 204; does not expound the doxology in the Lord's prayer, *ib*. 220; compares the response "Amen" to a thunder clap, 3 *Bec*. 410, 1 *Brad*. 529, 1 *Jew*. 281, 286, *Whita*. 260; declares that we ought to praise the Lord rather in mind than in voice, 1 *Bec*. 134; describes the singing at the funeral of Fabiola, *Pil*. 320, 543 (as to that of Paula, see below); perhaps he arranged the epistles and gospels used in the church, 2 *Brad*. 307, 308 n., *Pil*. 503; mentions the custom of the church in confirmation, 1 *Jew*. 372, 3 *Whitg*. 64, 72, 359, 360, 479, 480, 493; speaks of white garments as worn by bishops, priests, and deacons at the sacrifice, 3 *Jew*. 616, 2 *Whitg*. 48, 49, 2 *Zur*. 166; refers to one garment being worn in ministration, another in common life, 2 *Whitg*. 48, 49; says the priests of Egypt wore linen garments, not only in the church but without, 2 *Zur*. 166; condemns sumptuous cost, even in churches and temples, 1 *Bul*. 422; says, of the house of God they have made a stage-play of the people, 4 *Jew*. 813; allows not the burning of candles in the day time, *Calf*. 214, 2 *Ful*. 240, 2 *Jew*. 178; declares that Hebrew is the mother of all languages, *Whita*. 113, 114; says that Ezra changed the Hebrew letters, *Whita*. 116; reproves Hilary for mistaking the word "Osanna," 2 *Jew*. 678; his testimony as to the form of the Samaritan Thau, see xviii, below; on the Punic tongue, 1 *Jew*. 293, 294, *Whita*. 223; on the tongue of the Galatians, 1 *Jew*. 274, 275; on the language of Gaul, *ib*. 297; on the term "barbarian" as used by Paul, *Whita*. 273; he shews that various nations worshipped God in their own tongues, 1 *Jew*. 337; speaks of the Christian worship of the Bessians and other barbarous people, *ib*. 290; describes the singing of Psalms in various languages at Paula's funeral, 2 *Ful*. 224, 1 *Jew*. 268, 2 *Jew*. 692, *Pil*. 321, *Whita*. 222; says of the Valentinians, with a barbarous sound of words, they terrify the simple, that, whatsoever they understand not, they may the more wonder at, 4 *Jew*. 813

xiv. *Festivals, Fasting:* he writes on the institution of the Lord's day, fasting days, &c., 2 *Brad*. 391; shews why Sunday and other holidays were appointed, 2 *Cran*. 61; says that it is uncertain whether the feast of the Nativity is the day whereon Christ was born, or that of his baptism (dub.), *Whita*. 667; mentions but few saints' days, 1 *Hoop*. 347; defends the observance of such festivals, 2 *Whitg*. 576 n., 579; cautions against satiety, as nothing so much overwhelms the mind, 2 *Bec*. 545; denounces gluttony and satiety, see v, above; gives advice about fasting, reproving those who eat no oil, but seek dainty fruits, &c., 2 *Bec*. 535, 1 *Bul*. 429, 430, 3 *Jew*. 528; affirms that the abstinence of the body is commendable when the mind fasts from vices, 2 *Bec*. 540; says to one, thou art afraid to lay thy body, worn out with fasting, upon the bare ground; yet the Lord lieth there with thee, 3 *Jew*. 541; mentions the mode of the Jews' fasting, 2 *Bec*. 533; declares the fasting of the Manichees to be worse than fulness, 3 *Jew*. 170

xv. *Celibacy, Marriage:* he allows that marriage is in many cases necessary, 3 *Jew*. 399; often speaks of it with disapprobation, *Calf*. 259, 1 *Jew*. 156, 157, 3 *Jew*. 389, 390, 404, 420; remarks that our Lord says, "He that can receive it, let him receive it," that every man may consider his own strength, &c., 3 *Jew*. 398; advises to abstain from the ungodly act, rather than stiffly to perform perilous vows, 1 *Bec*. 372; asks, what avails the chastity of the body when the mind is defloured? 3 *Jew*. 428; says the report of some who behave not well slanders the holy purpose of virgins, and declares that such persons should marry, 1 *Ful*. 481, 2 *Ful*. 104, 3 *Jew*. 400; speaks of some who make brags of their chastity with whorish countenance, 4 *Jew*. 768; denies not but widows and married women may be holy, 3 *Jew*. 390; declares that Paul forbids married men to put away their wives, *ib*. 422; allows that by the apostles' doctrine priests may be married, 2 *Ful*. 97; shews that a bishop or priest may be the husband of one wife, *Park*. 159, 160; comments on the text "a sister, a wife" (1 Cor. ix. 5), arguing that the latter word should be rendered "woman," 1 *Ful*. 471 n.; speaks of some men as thinking that by the custom of the Jews it was lawful for a man to have two wives or more at once; and as supposing the apostle's commandment to be, that one chosen to be a bishop should not have two wives at once, 3 *Jew.* 406; seems to have stated that the rule directing a bishop to be "the husband of one wife," means that he must have had but one wife after baptism, *Whita.* 455 n.; considers the direction that a deacon shall be the husband of one wife as permissive, not compulsory, 3 *Jew.* 406; says, if I should name severally all the married bishops, they would be more in number than the multitude of the council of Ariminum, 4 *Jew.* 1142; shews that those twice married could not be priests in his time, 2 *Ful.* 240; rebukes those who refused orders to men twice married, 3 *Tyn.* 152; says, many priests live in matrimony, 2 *Jew.* 728, 3 *Jew.* 393, 410, 4 *Jew.* 1143; affirms that married men are chosen into the priesthood, because there are not enough unmarried, 2 *Ful.* 97, 4 *Jew.* 1143, *Park.* 160, *Pil.* 567 n.; gives reasons why married men were preferred to orders before others who carried the shew of celibacy, 4 *Jew.* 1143; as to the Vigilantian opinion on this subject, see xix; he reproves bishops and priests who make their children read comedies, &c., 2 *Ful.* 98, 3 *Jew.* 393, *Pil.* 567; speaks of rulers of the church providing for their children and possessions, and neglecting the building of God's temple, 2 *Ful.* 98; as to the reception of the communion by the married, see xii, above; what he says of concubines, 4 *Jew.* 633; his indelicate language censured by Tyndale, 1 *Tyn.* 438, and by Erasmus, *ib.* n.; he says that Antichrist shall feign chastity, and deceive many, 2 *Jew.* 911, 990, 3 *Jew.* 420, 4 *Jew.* 767

xvi. *Confession, Absolution:* there was no auricular confession in his days, 2 *Jew.* 1134; he speaks of the public confession of sin made by Fabiola, 3 *Tyn.* 213 n., 214 n.; does not call penance the second table after shipwreck, 2 *Ful.* 170; says the apostles loosed with the word of God and testimonies of the scriptures, 3 *Jew.* 354, 357; affirms that the priest...knows who is to be bound, who to be loosed, *ib.* 367; writing of the keys, he says, this place bishops and priests not understanding, take to themselves some of the pride of the Pharisees, 1 *Jew.* 340, 3 *Jew.* 213, 375, 380, 4 *Jew.* 1119, 1 *Tyn.* 217 n., 269 n.; shews, from the law concerning leprosy, that absolution is only declaratory, 1 *Ful.* 273, 1 *Tyn.* 217 n., 270 n.; says it is not the absolution of the priest, but the life of the sinner, that is regarded before God, 3 *Jew.* 375, 376, 605

xvii. *Affliction, Persecution, Death, Judgment, &c.:* he consoles himself under suffering for the truth, 2 *Lat.* 352; shews that tribulation is needful for the exercise and probation of the Christian soldier, 1 *Lat.* 480; says none may joy with this world and reign with Christ, *Bale* 103; declares that the spiritual man never persecutes the carnal, but forgives him, 2 *Cran.* 13; speaking of union amongst the church's enemies, he employs the similitude of Herod and Pilate, 2 *Ful.* 77 n.; speaks on the origin of the soul, 3 *Bul.* 374, 375; distinguishes between death and hell, 1 *Ful.* 305, 306; defines "infernus," *ib.* 298; writes on hell, and the abode of Abraham, &c. before Christ's death, *ib.* 289—294, 297, 298; refers to Jonah in the whale's belly, *ib.* 319; does not mention purgatory, 2 *Lat.* 246, 247; ever thought he heard the last trumpet and the call to judgment, 1 *Lat.* 530, 2 *Lat.* 60, *Sand.* 174, 368; shews that while in this present world we may help one another, but not before the judging-place, 2 *Bec.* 394, 3 *Bec.* 459; affirms that in Matt. xxiv. not only the calamities of the Jews but the destiny of all the world is prophesied of, 4 *Bul.* 449; mentions many ancient fathers who were chiliasts or millenarians, 3 *Jew.* 606; writes against Origen and various heretics who denied the resurrection, or erred respecting it, 2 *Cov.* 185, 186, 189; attacks the opinions of John bp of Jerusalem on this subject, 1 *Bul.* 169, 2 *Cov.* 169, 185, 190; says that the future rewards of the just will differ in degree, *Hutch.* 306; maintains the eternity of punishment, 2 *Cov.* 208, 3 *Jew.* 563

xviii. *The Cross, Images:* he says the "standard" mentioned by Isaiah (xlix. 22) is the banner of the cross, *Calf.* 94, 2 *Ful.* 137; so he speaks of the standard of Jeremiah (iv. 6), *Calf.* 95, 2 *Ful.* 137; says the letter ת was anciently like a cross, *Calf.* 106 n., 107 n., 2 *Ful.* 138, 147, 2 *Jew.* 647, *Whita.* 116; declares the mystic signification of the "thau" of Ezekiel, *Calf.* 108; writes concerning the title on the cross, 1 *Jew.* 277; says Paula worshipped, lying before the cross, as though she had seen Christ hanging thereon, 2 *Ful.* 181 n., 202; recommends the use of the sign of the cross,

Calf. 195, 259; compares together phylacteries and pieces of the cross, and equally condemns the use of both, *Calf.* 283, 2 *Ful.* 181; his alleged adoration of the manger of our Lord, 2 *Ful.* 181, 208; he speaks of the images stolen by Rachel, 1 *Ful.* 105 n.; writes concerning Jacob's staff (Heb. xi), *ib.* 545, 546; numbers the second commandment among the ten, and holds it a moral law, 2 *Bec.* 60; condemns idols, *Calf.* 181; speaks against image worship, *ib.* 378; narrates a Jewish story that the Ammonites and Moabites took the cherubim in the Temple for idols, 1 *Ful.* 185; mentions the curiosity of the heathen in adorning images, and says their error has come over to us, 2 *Jew.* 654; approves the conduct of Epiphanius in destroying a picture in a church, 3 *Tyn.* 182, & al., see i.

xix. *Heresies, real and alleged:* notes that Christianity was called by wicked men a heresy, as mentioned in the Acts, 3 *Jew.* 215; would have no man patient under the suspicion of heresy, *ib.* 209; says to a presbyter named Marcus, I am (as thou sayest) a heretic,—what is that to thee? hold thy peace, 4 *Jew.* 952; pronounces a woe on teachers of perverse doctrine, *ib.* 1061; thinks that all heresiarchs are antichrists, teaching under the name of Christ things that are contrary to Christ, 2 *Cov.* 334; declares that there is no heresy that is not framed on account of the throat and belly, *Bale* 218; remarks that falsehood evermore imitates the truth, 3 *Jew.* 159; speaks of some closing their eyes (to the truth), *ib.* 181; declares that he who understands the scriptures otherwise than the sense of the Holy Ghost requires is a heretic, even though he depart not from the church, see iii. *d*, above; says that followers of heretics find not the mid-day light, but the mid-day demon [Psa. xc. 6, Vulg.], *Bale* 34; rebukes a maintainer of new doctrine, such as Peter and Paul never taught, 2 *Ful.* 93, 3 *Jew.* 192; censures heretics for blending new things with the old, 2 *Jew.* 790; asserts that in heresy, both old and new, the people hear one thing, the priests preach another, *ib.* 777; says a sincere faith requires not the artifice of words, *Whita.* 19; compares heretics to spiders, *ib.* 20; likens them to idolaters, 1 *Ful.* 213, 214, 215; remarks that under Constantius...infidelity was written by the name of unity and faith, *Calf.* 261, 1 *Jew.* 83, 383; a singular various reading in this passage, *Calf.* 261 n.; cautions against reading heretical books, *Whita.* 18; quoted by the Rhemists with reference to the prayer and service of heretics, *Rog.* 272 n.; he would have heretics killed with spiritual arrows, 4 *Jew.* 770, 771; considers the charge of madness brought against opponents of error, 3 *Jew.* 250; mentions the Alogians, *Phil.* 420; says the whole world mourned, and wondered that it was Arian, 2 *Jew.* 909, 4 *Jew.* 908; declares that Arianism was confirmed by councils, as that of Ariminum, *Rog.* 209 n.; censures Basilides, 3 *Jew.* 403; refers to an error of Cerinthus and Ebion, *Rog.* 89 n.; writes against Helvidius and his doctrine, 2 *Cran.* 60, 1 *Hoop.* 161, 1 *Jew.* 22 n.; speaks of the schism of one Hilary, a deacon, 3 *Jew.* 321, 322; mentions the Jovinians, *Rog.* 137 n.; calls Jovinian the Epicure of Christian men, *Phil.* 426; imagines him to say, "That the bishops condemn me, there is no reason, but a conspiracy," &c., 4 *Jew.* 956; tells the Luciferians that he could dry up all their streams with the sun of the church, 2 *Ful.* 63; on an error of the Manichees, &c., *Rog.* 135 n.; censures their doctrine respecting Christ's resurrection, 1 *Jew.* 483; calls their fasting worse than fulness, 3 *Jew.* 170; condemns Marcion for refusing the faith of Christ, *ib.* 403; writes on the Montanists, *Rog.* 141 n.; mentions the errors of Tertullian, *Whita.* 600; says the Nazarene heretics were circumcised with the Jews, and baptized with Christians, and so were neither Jews nor Christians, *Rog.* 275 n.; he says they held that the Jewish ceremonies were to be observed by Christians, *ib.* 314 n.; as to Origen, see x. and xvii, above; he notes the errors of that father, *Rid.* 30; says that he, and those who followed him, permitted a wise and godly man to lie, if it were for the welfare of them for whom the lie was made, 2 *Bul.* 115; as to Pelagius, see that title; he mentions an error of Priscillian, *Rog.* 135 n.; writes against the superstitious works of the Tatians, 3 *Jew.* 236; as to the Valentinians, see xiii, above; he says the Vigilantian bishops would take no men into the clergy, except they would first be married, *Rog.* 261 n.; says they maintained that all the clergy should be married, *ib.* 303 n

xx. *Antichrist:* he considers that the name of blasphemy, written in the forehead of the purple harlot, is "Rome everlasting," 2 *Ful.* 372; says the abomination of desolation may be taken for any perverse doctrine; which, when we shall see standing in the holy place, i. e. the church of Christ, then we must flee from Jewry to the mountains (of the scriptures), 4 *Jew.* 728, 1062; declares that the abomination of desolation shall be in the temple until the consummation of time, *ib.* 728; asks concerning those whom God hath grafted into the church, if they forget themselves, and worship Antichrist, why may not God overthrow them? *ib.* 1062; says Antichrist will be not the devil or a demon, but one man in whom Satan will dwell bodily, 2 *Ful.* 367; considers "the idol shepherd," Zech. xi, to be Antichrist, 2 *Jew.* 918; applies the prophecy of Daniel (xi. 37) to Antichrist, who, he says, shall feign chastity and deceive many, 2 *Jew.* 911, 990, 3 *Jew.* 420, 4 *Jew.* 767; says he shall tread under his feet all true religion, 2 *Jew.* 916, 4 *Jew.* 743; declares that he shall sit in the temple of God, either in that at Jerusalem, or (which he thinks more probable) in the church, 2 *Jew.* 916, 4 *Jew.* 743; declares that Antichrist shall stand in the holy place, i. e. in the church, and shall shew himself as if he were God, 4 *Jew.* 729; teaches that Elias shall come in his time, 2 *Ful.* 370; says the truth of Christ shall devour and consume the falsehood of Antichrist, 4 *Jew.* 893, 1041; describes his destruction, 2 *Jew.* 928

xxi. *Civil Power, &c.:* he says the Roman empire holds all nations, 1 *Jew.* 432; relates that Constantine was baptized by Eusebius, bishop of Nicomedia, 4 *Jew.* 1004; mentions that, to stay certain ecclesiastical dissensions, the emperor's writs caused the bishops, as well of the East as of the West, to draw to Rome, *ib.* 1005; speaks of a council held at Rome as summoned by the emperor, 2 *Whitg.* 363; when Ruffinus alleged a certain synod, Jerome asked what emperor ordered it to be called, 4 *Jew.* 1098; mentions Codrus and Decius, who died for their countries, 3 *Jew.* 538; speaks of the outrages of the Vandals, 1 *Ful.* 263; commends Nebridius, a courtier, *Pil.* 294; understands the kings whom Isaiah names as "nursing fathers" to be the apostles, 4 *Jew.* 978; asserts that the evangelical truth receives no oath, 1 *Bec.* 379; says that an oath ought to have three companions, *ib.* 374, 375

xxii. *Miscellanea:* he thinks cherubims are so called from their exceeding knowledge, 3 *Bul.* 338; states that religion took her name à religando, of tying together, and binding into the Lord's bundle, *ib.* 231; declares that first-born children had the privilege of offering sacrifice, 4 *Jew.* 983; mentions that Bethel came to be called Bethaven, *ib.* 1046, 1047; tells of the origin of the scribes and Pharisees, 3 *Jew.* 323; says it is no praise to have been at Jerusalem, but to have lived well there, 2 *Ful.* 109; remarks that the court of heaven is equally open from Britain, *ib.*; states that blessed Hilarion, though born in Palestine, saw Jerusalem but one day, &c., *ib.*; says the devil never shews himself with his whole face, 2 *Jew.* 556; declares that a man's learning is known by his patience (pseud.), 4 *Jew.* 878; says with Socrates, I know, that I know nothing, 1 *Jew.* 100; expresses his desire to learn, *ib.* 101; a proverb occurring in his works, "Simile habent labra lactucam," *Whita.* 187 n

Jerome of Ferrara: *v.* Savonarola.
Jerome of Prague: burned at the council of Constance, *Bale* 9, 10, 2 *Bec.* 244, 4 *Jew.* 955, *Phil.* 120, 426
Jerome, a friar of Greenwich: *v.* Barlow (J.).
Jerome (Will.), vicar of Stepney: burned in Smithfield, *Bale* 394, 3 *Bec.* 11, 1 *Brad.* 283, 288, 2 *Cran.* 310 n., 381 n., 3 *Zur.* 207, 209, 632
Jersey: fortified, 3 *Zur.* 722 n
Jerusalem: *v.* Councils, Temple.

Of old called Salem, or Solyma, *Pil.* 370, and Jebus, *ib.* 371, and afterwards Jerusalem, *ib.* 372; the name expounded in its four senses, 1 *Tyn.* 303 n.; it means the vision of peace, 1 *Cov.* 199 n., *Hutch.* 49; another explanation, *Pil.* 372; Sion and Jerusalem figuratively interpreted, *ib.* 261; Adam supposed to have been buried there, *ib.* 373; Salem, the kingdom of Melchisedec, 3 *Bul.* 282; Isaac offered on Moriah, 2 *Bul.* 151, *Pil.* 374; Sion explained as meaning the church, 3 *Bul.* 275, *Pil.* 261—264, *Poet.* 418; the city won by David from the Jebusites, *Pil.* 371; why called the holy city, *ib.* 315, 316, 372; the Jews went there thrice a year, 2 *Bul.* 163, 2 *Lat.* 155, *Pil.* 69, 159; it had a famous school, 4 *Bul.* 480; contained many schools, 2 *Jew.* 679; the city destroyed by Nebuchadnezzar, *Pil.* 89, 346, as foretold by Jeremiah, *ib.* 12; its lamentable state when viewed by Nehemiah, *ib.* 345; the new building thereof in the time of Nehemiah, what it teaches, *ib.* 370, 452; there were many enemies to its building, *ib.* 335; its hills and walls, *ib.*

87, 372, 373; the compass of its walls, *ib.* 443; its gates, &c., *ib.* 345; the Sheep-gate, *ib.* 378; the Fish-gate, *ib.* 379; the Dung-gate, *ib.* 387; Bethesda, 2 *Bul.* 98; Tyndale assumes that Bethesda and Siloam were the same, 3 *Tyn.* 88; Calvary, or Golgotha, 2 *Bul.* 151, 152; the disciples question Christ about the destruction of Jerusalem, and the end of the world, *Sand.* 351; the church here ordained not only deacons, but Matthias the apostle, 4 *Bul.* 131; the city asserted to have been a bishoprick in the apostles' time, 2 *Whitg.* 252 (*v.* James); signs preceding its destruction, 2 *Lat.* 45, *Lit. Eliz.* 568, *Sand.* 352; contentions between Simon, John, and Eleazar, *Sand.* 101; the city destroyed by the Romans, 3*Bec.* 8, 9, 2 *Bul.* 259, 2 *Jew.* 1028, 2 *Lat.* 46, *Pil.* 88, 89, 346, 372, *Sand.* 347, 348; escape of the Christians, and their flight to Pella, 1 *Brad.* 39, 1 *Whitg.* 380; the city trodden under foot, *Bale* 385; the Jews attempted to rebuild it in the days of Adrian, but their work was miraculously hindered, 2 *Lat.* 47, *Pil.* 375, 376; Adrian builds Ælia or Capitolina, 2 *Lat.* 48, *Pil.* 372, 375; the Jews again attempting the restoration of their temple, are overthrown by Constantine, 4 *Jew.* 1074; Jerusalem made a patriarchate, *Phil.* 43, 2 *Whitg.* 220, 221 n.; Constantine builds a church there, *Calf.* 182; the hallowing of that church, *ib.* 207; Julian's attempt to rebuild the temple frustrated by a miracle, *Calf.* 115, 121, 123, 2 *Jew.* 648, 978, 2 *Lat.* 48; on pilgrimages to Jerusalem, 2 *Ful.* 108, 238; for our false faith in visiting the monuments of Christ, the land was given to the infidels, 3 *Tyn.* 86; a nominal patriarch still appointed by the pope, 4 *Jew.* 842

Jerusalem (New): description of it, *Bale* 583, 594, &c., 3 *Bec.* 184, 1 *Brad.* 266, 272, 341, 1 *Zur.* 277; the description of heavenly Ierusalem, verses, *Poet.* 427; its measurement, *Bale* 600; no temple therein, *ib.* 610; the gold and precious stones, *ib.* 605; analogy between the earthly and heavenly Jerusalem, *Pil.* 375

Jervaulx or Jorvalles abbey, Yorkshire: made a stable, 1 *Lat.* 93 n

Jervis (......): *v.* Gerves.

Jess: what, *Nord.* 47 n

Jesse: the virgin Mary a branch of the stock of Jesse, 2 *Hoop.* 8

Jest, or Gest: exploit, 1 *Tyn.* 80

Jesters: *v.* Fools.

Jesting: unseasonable, 4 *Jew.* 915, &c.; jests distinguished from lies, *Hutch.* 52

Jesuitæ: enumerated among Protestant sects, 2 *Jew.* 686

Jesuits: referred to, *Bale* 352, *Lit. Eliz.* 656, *Poet.* 273, 290; styled Jebusites, 1 *Ful.* 568; established by Paul III. in 1540, 4 *Jew.* 1106; their rise, character, and work, *Whita.* 3, &c.; they have changed the character of popery, *ib.* 18; their missions and alleged miracles, 3 *Jew.* 179, 195, 197, &c.; they flock into this kingdom, *Rog.* 9; exercise papal jurisdiction here, *ib.* 10; cannot brook episcopal pre-eminence, *ib.* 331; in their high court of reformation in England, are said to have made a statute for abrogation of all episcopal dignity, *ib.*; were for putting all Europe into the hands of the king of Spain to preserve the (pretended) catholic faith, *ib.* 203; their equivocations for the deception of Protestants, *ib.* 120, 359; their unclean life, *ib.* 305; they allow whoredom at Rome, *ib.* 119; their provincials, Parsons, Weston, and Garnet, *ib.* 10

Jesus: *v.* Christ.

Jesus, son of Sirach: *v.* Ecclesiasticus. Augustine's opinion as to his writings, *Whita.* 46

Jethro: 4 *Bul.* 133

Jetted abroad: stalked up and down, 2 *Jew.* 922

Jewel (Jo.), father of the bishop: *Jew.* v.

JEWEL (Jo.), bp of Salisbury: biographical memoir, *Jew.* v, &c.; a brief memoir in Latin by Tanner, *ib.* xxvi; notice of him by Dr Garbrand, 4 *Jew.* 1129, 1130; his birth and early education, 4 *Jew.* v; he goes to Oxford, *ib.* vi; curate of Sunningwell, *ib.* viii; he proceeds B.D. a year before Harding, 1 *Jew.* 98; his sermon on that occasion preserved, *Jew.* viii; his (?) signature, 2 *Brad.* 397 n.; he is chosen public orator, *ib.* ix, x; notary to Cranmer and Ridley at their examination, *Rid.* 194; he signs Romish articles, *Jew.* xi; escapes from Oxford, *ib.*; his life saved through Bernhere and Mrs Warcup, 2 *Brad.* 45 n., *Jew.* xi; probably the bearer of Cranmer's last letter to Peter Martyr, 2 *Cran.* 457 n., addenda xv, *Jew.* xii; at Frankfort, *Jew.* xi, 3 *Zur.* 181; here he makes public confession of his fault of subscribing, *Jew.* xii, 1 *Jew.* 61; at Strasburgh and Zurich, *Jew.* xiii; his device, designed by himself when at Zurich, a book and a cross, 1 *Zur.* 21; he returns from exile, *Jew.* xiv, 1 *Zur.* 9; one of the disputants at Westminster, *Jew.* xiv, 1 *Zur.* 11; made a royal visitor for the establishment of religion, *Jew.* xiv, xv,

1 *Zur.* 24, 39; his celebrated challenge, *Coop.* 45, 1 *Ful.* 165, 442, 2 *Ful.* 28, 58, *Jew.* xvi, 1 *Jew.* 20, 21, 1 *Zur.* 147 n.; correspondence with Dr Cole thereon, *Coop.* 4, 50, 1 *Jew.* 26, &c., *Pil.* 523; elected and consecrated bishop of Salisbury, *Jew.* xv, 1 *Zur.* 40, 50, 63; mentioned, 2 *Zur.* 37, 85, 94; his palace and garden at Salisbury, 2 *Zur.* 86; his hospitality, *ib.* 86, 87; his opinion on hunting, *ib.* 86; his closing scene, *ib.* xxi; his death, *Jew.* xxii, 1 *Zur.* 260, 2 *Zur.* 193, 209; his will, *Jew.* xxiv, xxv, 2 *Zur.* 262; an epitaph upon his death, by W. Elderton, *Poet.* lii, 512; notice of an epitaph on him by N. Boweman, *ib.* lvi; a portion of that epitaph, *ib.* 554; his character, *Jew.* xxiii, 2 *Zur.* 181; his wonderful memory, *Jew.* xxiv; his life written by Humphrey, 2 *Brad.* xxi. n., *Jew.* vii, &c., xix, 4 *Jew.* 1194 n., *Rid.* xi. n., *Rog.* 266 n., 1 *Zur.* 310 n.; by Le Bas, 2 *Ful.* 371 n

His WORKS, edited by the Rev. Jo. Ayre, M.A., 1, 2, 3, 4 *Jew.*; list of them, *Jew.* xxvi, &c.; some of them mentioned, 1 *Ful.* 75 n.; references to them, *Calf.* 410, 2 *Ful.* 404, *Rog.* 272 n., 1 *Whitg.* 8, 22, 157, 2 *Whitg.* 119, 152, 153, 257, 3 *Whitg.* 308, 313; his Apologia Ecclesiæ Anglicanæ, *Calf.* 260, *Jew.* xviii, *Park.* 148, 161, 1 *Zur.* 101 n., 121, 339; said to have been set forth without order and unlawfully, 3 *Jew.* 185; translated into English by lady Bacon, *Park.* 219; translated into many tongues, and read at Trent, 3 *Jew.* 186; he wishes the Latin Apology to be reprinted, 4 *Jew.* 1274, 1275; the Apology attacked by Harding and others, 2 *Ful.* 3, *Grin.* 169 n., *Jew.* xix, &c., xxvii; attacked by Dorman, defended by Nowell, *Jew.* xx, *Now.* iii, iv; slandered by Martiall, 2 *Ful.* 175; the Defence of the Apology published, *Park.* 319; placed in churches, *Jew.* xxviii, *Park.* 417; he publishes a letter to Scipio, containing reasons why the English refused to send representatives to Trent, *Jew.* xviii, 1 *Zur.* 101 n.; an anonymous book ascribed to him, 1 *Zur.* 263; bishop Jewel's letters, 4 *Jew.* 1189—1281, 1 *Zur.* 6, 9, 13, 17, 19, 23, 32, 38, 44, 48, 50, 52, 54, 59, 67, 70, 77, 80, 88, 91, 96, 99, 104, 106, 114, 117, 120, 123, 125, 126, 138, 146, 155, 184, 226, 238; a letter to Parker, *Park.* 176, 4 *Jew.* 1262; a letter to Robert, earl of Leicester, 3 *Whitg.* 624 (not in Jewel's Works); a letter to Jewel from P. Martyr, 1 *Zur.* 339; one to him, Grindal, and Cox, from Bullinger, 2 *Zur.* 178; a letter to Jewel from H. Zanchius, *ib.* 185; his opinion on the "rock,"

2 *Ful.* 274, 281; his exposition of a place of Cyprian, 2 *Whitg.* 216, 217; he speaks of the unity of the church of England in the earlier part of the reign of Elizabeth, *Rog.* 7; his judgment concerning archbishops, &c. defended against Cartwright, 2 *Whitg.* 336; his opinion about the union of civil and ecclesiastical jurisdiction in one person, 3 *Whitg.* 450, &c.; An Apology of Private Mass (against bp Jewel), *Coop.* 2—41; an answer thereto, by bp Cooper, but by some improperly ascribed to Jewel, *ib.* 43—223, see 2 *Ful.* vii, ix, 45 n.; the anonymous writer depreciates Jewel's learning and experience, *Coop.* 4, &c.; Cooper's reply to this, *ib.* 192

Jewel (Jo.), of Northcote, Devon: brother to the bishop, *Jew.* xxv.

JEWEL OF JOY, by T. Becon, 2 *Bec.* 411, &c.

Jewels: *v.* Stones.

Jezebel, queen: *Bale* 282, 1 *Bul.* 242, 307; comparison between her time and that of queen Mary, 3 *Bec.* 238, &c.; queen Mary called by her name, 3 *Zur.* 115

Jezler (......): says that from the beginning of the reformation all orders burned with the love of truth, *Rog.* 4; on transubstantiation and some kindred errors, *ib.* 289; his peculiar opinion about excommunication, *ib.* 309 n

Joab: 1 *Bul.* 276

Joachim (St): the alleged father of the virgin Mary, Anna being, as it is said, her mother, 2 *Cran.* 30, 2 *Lat.* 228; Augustine will not allow the assertion, because it is not found in scripture, 2 *Cran.* 30

Joachim Abbas: account of him, *Bale* 305 n.; he wrote on the Apocalypse, *ib.* 256; his account of Antichrist, 2 *Jew.* 915, 4 *Jew.* 714, 740, 742, 744, 1115

Joachim, elector of Brandenburg: 3 *Zur.* 640 n

Joachim, servant to Burcher: 3 *Zur.* 686

Joan, pope: her history, *Calf.* 6 n., 1 *Jew.* 114, 3 *Jew.* 648, &c.; Martin Polonus calls her "Joannes Anglicus, natione Maguntinus," and relates her history, 4 *Jew.* 648, 651, 654; said to be John VIII., *Pil.* 602; being reckoned by some as the successor of John VII. she is the source of confusion in the numbering of the popes named John, 2 *Ful.* 269 n.; referred to, 1 *Tyn.* 285 n.; "merry as pope Joan," *Park.* 222, *Pil.* vii.

Joan of Kent: *v.* Bocher (J.).

Joan good fellow: 2 *Brad.* 288 (in 2 *Cov.* 267 "Hail good fellow").

Joanna I., queen of Naples: her history, 3 *Jew.* 174 n

Joannes: v. John.
Joannes Andræ: v. Andreas.
Joannes Angelus, or Parisiensis: v. Angelus.
Joannes Anglicus, Maguntinus: v. Joan, pope.
Joannes Aventinus, q. v.
Joannes de Balbis, Januensis: his Catholicon, a Latin vocabulary, *Jew.* xxxv, 4 *Jew.* 861
Joannes de Burgo, q. v.
Joannes Carnotensis: v. John of Salisbury.
Joannes de Cremona: makes no mention of pope Joan, 4 *Jew.* 648
Joannes de Magistris: 4 *Jew.* 635
Joannes Major: Super Libb. Sententiarum, *Jew.* xl; In Quartum Sententiarum Quæstiones, *ib.*; Magnum Speculum Exemplorum, 1 *Lat.* 426 n.; he says pope Boniface VIII. has falsely concluded with great shew of reason, that in temporal causes the pope is above kings, 4 *Jew.* 706, 836; calls papal pardons for twenty thousand years foolish and superstitious, 2 *Jew.* 920, 3 *Jew.* corrig., 4 *Jew.* 851; calls it a human custom for three bishops to ordain another, 3 *Jew.* 334
Joannes Moschus: his Limonarium, or Pratum Spirituale, *Calf.* 174 n., 2 *Jew.* 658 n
Joannes ad oppositum: a factious opponent, 2 *Brad.* 387, *Grin.* 233, 235, 3 *Whitg.* 72
Joannes Parvus: *Whita.* 495
Joannes Roffensis: v. Fisher.
Joannes Sabaita: 2 *Ful.* 287 n
Joannes Stella, q. v.
Joannes de Temporibus: said to have lived 361 years, 1 *Jew.* 112
Joannes Teutonicus: a scholiast on Gratian, 1 *Jew.* 249, 250
Joannes de Turrecremata, a cardinal: calls the pope king of kings and lord of lords, 2 *Lat.* 349; some account of him, *ib.* n
Joannes Vitalis, q. v.
Joannes de Wassalia, q. v.
Joannes Zonaras, q. v.
Joash, king of Judah: his career, 2 *Bul.* 8; he commands the priests, 1 *Bul.* 330
Job: supposed by some to have dwelt in Teman and married Dinah, *Pil.* 244; his afflictions, 2 *Bul.* 67, 2 *Cran.* 107; the devil could not afflict him without God's permission, 3 *Bul.* 364; he waited upon the Lord, 2 *Hoop.* 247; looked for the resurrection, 2 *Cov.* 170—172; his oration (prayer) in his most grievous adversity, *Lit. Edw.* 482; verses from Job, ch. vii, by W. Samuel, *Poet.* 312; Job referred to in the book of Ezekiel, 4 *Bul.* 177; invocation of him, *Bale* 348, 498, 1 *Bec.* 138, 2 *Bec.* 536, *Hutch.* 171, *Rog.* 226; his name used in a charm, 1 *Hoop.* 328; his image regarded as a remedy against some diseases, 3 *Tyn.* 105
— The book of Job: its antiquity, 1 *Bul.* 39; what we learn from it, 2 *Cov.* 18; certain rabbins say it is a fiction, *Whita.* 33; the book rejected by the Anabaptists, *Rog.* 81, *Whita.* 33; vindicated, *Whita.* 33; the apocryphal appendix in the Greek, *ib.* 103, 104
Jobelæa: of the Scythians, *Rog.* 202
Jochebed: 2 *Bul.* 176
Jochim (Herr), miller: 3 *Zur.* 617
Jodocus, a monk mentioned by Erasmus: 2 *Cran.* 38
Joel: joins prayer and fasting, 4 *Bul.* 179; his prophecy of the outpouring of the Spirit, 1 *Cov.* 399, &c.
Johai (Rabbi): 1 *Jew.* 509
Johannes: v. Joannes, John.
Johannites: the orthodox so called by Arians, 2 *Jew.* 807
John (St), the Baptist: foretold, 1 *Cov.* 63; an eminent saint, 1 *Bul.* 53; not without sin, 3 *Tyn.* 206; his mission and preaching, 1 *Cov.* 74; why styled an angel by Malachi, 1 *Ful.* 483; he came in the spirit of Elias, *Rid.* 70; preached repentance, 1 *Tyn.* 121; how he turned the hearts of the fathers to the children, 3 *Tyn.* 45; he restored the scriptures to their true sense, *ib.* 46; his fasting and strait living, 1 *Tyn.* 103; called John the Christener, *Hutch.* 217, 234; his baptism was from heaven, 4 *Bul.* 241; it was the baptism of repentance, *ib.* 250; he baptized without any words, *ib.* 259 (see further, in Baptism, iii); his disciples esteemed him as greater than Christ, 2 *Lat.* 69; his question to Christ, *ib.* 70; he makes a difference between himself and Christ, 4 *Bul.* 97, 273; Herod troubled at his preaching, *Pil.* 141; his martyrdom and burial, 3 *Bul.* 400; his body cast out by Julian the Apostate, *Bale* 57; his relics worshipped, *Rog.* 225; represented with a lamb, *Bale* 523
— Order of St John: v. Knights.
John (St), the Evangelist: why he laid his head on Christ's bosom, 2 *Brad.* 263; origin of the opinion that he would remain alive till Christ's coming, *Whita.* 203; he was bishop of the Asian churches, *Rog.* 328; called by Chrysostom the pillar of all the churches, 3 *Jew.* 319; was cast into burning oil, but miraculously delivered, 4 *Bul.* 32; banished to Patmos, 2 *Bul.* 105; ruled the church after his return therefrom, *Rog.* 328, 2 *Whitg.* 140, 230, 427, 428; he placed Polycarp at Smyrna, 4 *Bul.* 31; alleged to have worn on his head a plate ($\pi\acute{\epsilon}\tau\alpha\lambda\text{o}\nu$), 2 *Brad.*

381, 2 *Ful.* 113, 2 *Whitg.* 16, 22, 23, 25, 27, 1 *Zur.* 160 n., 350; he opposed Cerinthus the heretic, 2 *Brad.* 263; would not stay where he was, *ib.* 329, 1 *Bul.* 363, 2 *Bul.* 329, 4 *Bul.* 535, 4 *Jew.* 1100 n.; opposed the heresy of Ebion, *Bale* 265, 1 *Bec.* 278; said by Jerome to have condemned the apocryphal story of Thecla, *Whita.* 311; how he sought out and recovered a young man who had departed from the right way, and become a robber, 1 *Hoop.* 170 n., *Hutch.* 114, 2 *Jew.* 945; in his last days he exhorted his disciples to love one another, *Sand.* 398; his decease, *Lit. Eliz.* 455; his tomb known in the time of Chrysostom, *Calf.* 130; Polycarp followed his custom as to the keeping of Easter, 4 *Bul.* 57; Irenæus professes to follow his tradition as to the age of our Lord, *ib.* 536; fables concerning him, in the work of the false Abdias, *Calf.* 126—131; a sermon on his day, 2 *Lat.* 111; St John's hold, a sanctuary, 1 *Tyn.* 180

He never speaks of any other law but love, 1 *Tyn.* 475; his writings rejected by certain heretics who are termed Alogians, 1 *Ful.* 7, 8, *Whita.* 34

— Gospel of St John: written after his return from exile, *Whita.* 43; rejected by the Ebionites, *ib.* 35; Tyndale's prologue to it, 1 *Tyn.* 482; argument of it, and contents of each chapter, 3 *Bec.* 575, 576; a fragment upon it, 2 *Brad.* 263; our Lord's discourse in ch. vi. is considered in all the treatises, &c. concerning the Lord's supper; the history of the adulteress, Jo. viii, rejected by Cajetan, *Whita.* 105; John does not record the institution of the Lord's supper, 3 *Tyn.* 236; his gospel hung about the neck, superstitiously carried, and used as a charm, *Bale* 525, *Calf.* 17, 111, 1 *Cov.* 511, 2 *Cran.* 503, *Pil.* 563, 3 *Tyn.* 61 bis, 62, 110

— Epistles: Tyndale's prologue to them, 1 *Tyn.* 529; argument of them, and contents of each chapter, 3 *Bec.* 592, 593; Tyndale's exposition of the first epistle, 2 *Tyn.* 136, &c., 145, &c.; Augustine supposed that John wrote his first epistle to the Parthians, *Whita.* 218; the ancients sometimes called his second epistle "ad virgines," or πρὸς παρθένους, whence the mistake of Augustine, *ib.* 218 n.; a certain exposition of the second and third epistles is not Tyndale's, 2 *Tyn.* 134, 135; the second and third epistles rejected by Cajetan, *Rog.* 84, *Whita.* 105, and by some Lutherans, *Whita.* 296

— Revelation: proof that this book was written by St John the Evangelist, 1 *Ful.* 34; it was written in exile, *Bale* 253, 254; thought to have been all seen in one day, *ib.*; its peculiar excellence, *ib.* 251, &c., 1 *Bul.* 170 n.; Cerdon and other heretics rejected it, 1 *Ful.* 8, *Whita.* 34; it was interpreted by Justin and Irenæus, *Whita.* 391; the first book on which a comment was written, *Bale* 254; a list of writers on it, *ib.* 255, &c.; it is not named by the council of Laodicea, *Whita.* 54; Bullinger calls it "Theologia Domini," 1 *Bul.* 170 n., 418 n.; argument of the Revelation, and contents of each chapter, 3 *Bec.* 593, 594; THE IMAGE OF BOTH CHURCHES, an exposition of the Revelation, *Bale* 249—640; contents of ch. i—x, *ib.* 379, 380, of ch. xi—xvii, *ib.* 511, 512, of ch. xviii—xxii, *ib.* 514, 515; a note on the Apocalypse, 3 *Whitg.* 623; it foretells the pope, *Poet.* 285 (v. Antichrist, Babylon, &c.); on the caution not to add to it, *Whita.* 621

John V. [Cantacuzenus], emperor of the East: 2 *Jew.* 1028 n

John VI. [Palæologus], emperor of the East: 2 *Jew.* 1828 n

John VII. [Palæologus], emperor of the East: attended the council at Ferrara, *Rid.* 135 n

John, king of England: his history, 1 *Tyn.* 338, 339; he forbade appeals to Rome, and endeavoured to suppress clerical immorality, 2 *Tyn.* 19; evil-treated by the pope, 4 *Jew.* 1076; excommunicated, 1 *Ful.* 36 n.; the pope gave his realm to the king of France, 2 *Tyn.* 295; his submission to the pope, *ib.*; compelled to pay tribute to him, 2 *Hoop.* 522; supposed to have been poisoned, 4 *Jew.* 687; reference to an interlude of king John, probably Bale's, 2 *Cran.* 388

John, king of Hungary: v. John Zapolia, infra.

John (Don) of Austria, nat. brother to Philip II.: 1 *Zur.* 325, 2 *Zur.* 288, 303 n., 304; he defeats the Turks at Lepanto, 1 *Zur.* 270 n.; his death, *ib.* 327 n., 2 *Zur.* 308 n

John, duke of Finland, brother of Eric XIV., king of Sweden: comes to England, 1 *Zur.* 90 n

John Casimir (Duke), son of Frederick III., count Palatine: his marriage, 2 *Zur.* 173 n.; mention of him, *ib.* 272, 286, 298, 300; he besieges Deventer, 1 *Zur.* 325; visits England, and is made K. G., *ib.* 330 n., 2 *Zur.* 308; favours Calvinism, 2 *Zur.* 156 n

John Frederick, duke of Saxony: 2 *Cran.* 236 n.; signed the confession of Augsburgh, 2 *Zur.* 15 n.; war against him, 3 *Zur.* 258;

JOHN (Princes, Popes, &c.) 443

taken prisoner at Muhlberg, *ib.* 260; prisoner at Brussels, *ib.* 57, 58 n

John Galeazzo [Sforza], duke of Milan: his wife Isabella, and daughter Bona, 3 *Zur.* 689 n

John Zapolia, vaivode of Transylvania: *Grin.* 14 n

John I., pope: was an Arian ambassador, *Pil.* 601; erroneously called John the fourth, *ib.* 527 n

John VIII., pope: said to have been the woman-pope, *Pil.* 602 (v. Joan).

John IX. or X., pope: revoked the acts of Stephen against Formosus, 1 *Hoop.* 217, 1 *Tyn.* 324 n

John X. or XI., pope: more bent on war than on religion, 1 *Hoop.* 218

John XII., pope: said to have given occasion to the proverb, "as merry as pope Joan," *Pil.* vii. n.; an indulgence granted by him, *Rog.* 220, 221

John XII. or XIII., pope: the emperor Otho's oath to him, 2 *Tyn.* 269; he was deposed by that emperor, for a time, *Pil.* 640; being condemned by a council, he fled, and was succeeded by Leo, 1 *Whitg.* 403; his horrible wickedness, 4 *Jew.* 651; he was more wicked than any pope before him, 1 *Hoop.* 218; he cut off one of his cardinals' right hand, and another's nose, 3 *Jew.* 250; slain in adultery, 4 *Jew.* 702

John XIII. or XIV., pope: first gave names to bells in baptism, *Calf.* 15 n.; baptized the bell of St John Lateran, *Rog.* 266

John XV., pope: 1 *Hoop.* 124; son of a priest, 2 *Ful.* 98 n

John XIX., pope: an enchanter, *Rog.* 180
John XX., pope: an enchanter, *Rog.* 180
John XXI., pope: an enchanter, *Rog.* 180

John XXI., XXII. or XXIII., pope [Jac. d'Euse or de Ossa, 1316]: dispute as to his number, 4 *Jew.* 934; his election, *ib.* 931; asserted to have denied the consciousness of the soul between death and the resurrection, 1 *Jew.* 400, 3 *Jew.* 144, 4 *Jew.* 923, 925, 930, &c., *Pil.* 603, *Rog.* 181 n.; reproved by Gerson and the school of Paris for a heretic, 1 *Jew.* 400, 3 *Jew.* 345; forced to recant to Philip the French king, 4 *Jew.* 967; he lived in France, *ib.* 933; his decretals called Extravagantes, 1 *Lat.* 212, see Law (Canon); an indulgence granted by him, *Rog.* 220, 221

John XXII., XXIII. or XXIV., pope, [Balth. Cossa, 1410]: variously numbered, 4 *Jew.* 934; his election, whether regular, *ib.* 931, 935, 937; said to have poisoned his predecessor, *Bale* 47, 593; condemned and deposed by the council of Constance, 2 *Ful.* 269, 334, 1 *Jew.* 35, 67, 4 *Jew.* 702, 927, 955, 1097, 1 *Tyn.* 325 n., *Whita.* 510

John V., patr. of Alexandria, called the Almoner: 1 *Jew.* 147, 182, &c., *Sand.* 193 n

John I., patr. of Antioch: 2 *Ful.* 295, *Whita.* 678

John I., patr. of Constantinople: v. Chrysostom (St Jo.).

John II., patr. of Constantinople: calls Hormisdas, bp of Rome, his brother, 1 *Jew.* 385

John IV., patr. of Constantinople, surnamed the Faster: assumed the style of universal bishop, *Bale* 317, 503, & al. sæpe; denounced by St Gregory as the forerunner of Antichrist, 1 *Brad.* 538, & al.; v. Gregory (St).

John II., patr. of Jerusalem: Epiphanius writes to him about the picture destroyed by him, *Calf.* 253, &c., 2 *Ful.* 173, 174, *Park.* 88, 3 *Tyn.* 182; his quarrel with Epiphanius and Jerome, 1 *Ful.* 263; Jerome attacks his heterodox opinions respecting the resurrection of the body, 2 *Cov.* 169, 185 n

John the Almoner: v. John V., patr. of Alexandria.

John of Beverley (St), abp of York: 2 *Ful.* 14, 25

John of the Burnt Tower: v. Joannes de Turrecremata.

John, a cardinal, and the pope's legate: sent to enforce divorces of the clergy, *Pil.* 572; his infamous conduct, *ib.*, *Sand.* 224

John Cassian (St): v. Cassian.

John, bp of Chalcedon: ordains Coverdale at Norwich, 2 *Cov.* vii.

John the Chanter: came from Rome to Britain, and introduced the Roman service, 2 *Ful.* 14, 1 *Jew.* 303, 304

John of Chartres: v. John of Salisbury.

John Chrysostom (St): v. Chrysostom.

John Climacus (St): Scala Paradisi, 2 *Ful.* 287 n

John Damascene (St): v. Damascene.

John the Deacon: his life of Gregory cited, 1 *Brad.* 513 n

John the Deacon, called Digitorum Mutilus: whether the author of the feigned Donation of Constantine, 2 *Ful.* 360 n

John Isaac, *q. v.*

John, locum-ten. episc. Orient.: says there are not two kinds of adoration, but one only, due as well to the image as to the pattern of the image, 4 *Jew.* 792

John (Mass): v. Mass-Johns.

John of Paris: De Potestate Reg. et Papal.,

Jew. xxxviii; he cites a statement of Isidore that by the sun is meant kingly dignity, and by the moon is meant priesthood, 4 *Jew.* 677, 838; says the first-born (under the law) were not priests in dignity and office as Aaron was; yet in case of necessity they did some part of the priests' office, as Moses consecrated Aaron, *ib.* 983; affirms that in the old law the priests' office was inferior to the prince's, and subject unto him, *ib.* 980, 983, 984; declares that the priests who anointed the kings were undoubtedly subject to the kings, *ib.* 992, 1004; says, Jeremiah deposed no king, but was placed over nations and kingdoms, as having authority over the same in opening and preaching the truth, *ib.* 676; explains that a passage relating to that prophet is not to be understood of the overthrowing of kingdoms, but of the destruction of vices, &c., *ib.* 1151; says it appears by the holy expositors that Christ had neither authority nor judgment in things temporal, *ib.* 984; asserts that Peter calls us a kingly priesthood, of the kingdom of heaven, not of the kingdom of this world, *ib.* 985; notes that in the council at Jerusalem James gave sentence, *ib.* 917; understands Hos. i. 11, of Christ, not of the pope, 3 *Jew.* 281; expounds the text "there shall be one flock, and one shepherd," not of Christ, but of some other minister (viz. the pope), *ib.* 221, 4 *Jew.* 751; allows that the apostles received of Christ equal power of the keys and jurisdiction, but says that the matter wherein to use it none had but Peter, and to whomsoever he would commit the same, 3 *Jew.* 385; declares that the virtue of Christ's passion is contained in the sacraments of the church, *ib.* 445; refers to a statement that all manner of temporal power is given immediately to the pope, 4 *Jew.* 706; says Bernard allows no power to the pope, but he allows the same to inferior bishops; yet he allows the chief power to the pope, *ib.* 832; declares that Bernard says the pope has the temporal sword at his commandment, *ib.* 825; allows that Peter never touched the sword of temporal power, *ib.*; says the pope has the civil sword by the commission of the prince, *ib.* 835; speaks of an opinion that the pope is lord of the world by force of Constantine's donation, 2 *Jew.* 917, 919, 4 *Jew.* 678, 839; mentions a voice of angels heard when that donation was made, 4 *Jew.* 840; explains that when it is said that pope Zacharias deposed the French king, it is only meant that he consented to his deposition, *ib.* 683; speaks of some who say that the pope only is the true lord of temporal possessions, other bishops and princes being not lords, but overseers, bailiffs, and stewards, *ib.* 837, 1078; holds that the popedom is the highest virtue or power that ever God made, *ib.* 1036; admits that those things which belong to the pope's jurisdiction are not above nature, *ib.* 1037; states that kingly government came not from God, for he only suffered it in anger; and that it were more acceptable to him that the world were governed by the pope, *ib.* 677, 838; says that ecclesiastics ought to judge by those who are contemptible, i. e. by the laity, *ib.* 838; mentions an opinion that to judge of the pope's deeds is to touch the holy mount, *ib.* 834; says we must expound every act of the most holy father for the best, though it be theft, &c., *ib.* 833; blames an assertion that a pope spake certain words out of humility, *ib.* 847; allows that the pope may sometimes be such a one as may be removed, as a woman, or a heretic; and states that such are not reckoned in the calendar of popes, *ib.* 927; says the emperor, being required by the cardinals, is bound to deprive the pope, *ib.* 682, 1034, 1035; affirms that Henry the emperor deposed pope Benedict IX. by imperial and canonical censures, *ib.* 1034; denies that the emperor receives his power of the pope, *ib.* 836; affirms that to say the prince cannot either make or use his laws before the pope have allowed them is plainly false, *ib.* 1032; allows that in temporal affairs the temporal power is greater than the spiritual, *ib.* 836; pronounces it false to imagine that the prince's power is only bodily and not ghostly, *ib.* 1037; says, we do not read in the New Testament that priests ought to anoint kings, and mentions that the kings of Spain are not anointed, *ib.*; says that pope Cyriacus gave up his office that he might suffer martyrdom with Ursula and other virgins, and gives a reason why he is not reckoned amongst the popes, *ib.* 650; speaks of Boniface obtaining of Phocas that the church of Rome should be the head of all churches, 3 *Jew.* 312; gives testimony respecting pope Joan, 4 *Jew.* 656; Hervæus wrongly cited for him, 3 *Jew.* 131, 4 *Jew.* 825, 847, &c.

John, bp of Portua: 2 *Jew.* 773 n
John (Prester): *v.* Prester John.
John (Saint) family: *v.* Saint-John.

John of Salisbury, bp of Chartres: his Polycraticus, *Jew.* xliii; dispute as to his name Carnotensis, often miscalled Camotensis or Camocensis, 3 *Jew.* 130, 4 *Jew.* 925, 938, 1268, 1269, 1 *Zur.* 156; he is sometimes called Rupertus Carnotensis, 4 *Jew.* 938, 1080; he complains of the wresting of the scriptures, 1 *Jew.* 54, 385, 4 *Jew.* 923, 1115; remarks that Rome now sheweth herself not so much a natural mother as a step-dame, 4 *Jew.* 1082; says, in the church of Rome sit the scribes and Pharisees, 3 *Jew.* 130, 347, 385, 4 *Jew.* 679; states that the popes enter not into the holy of holies without shedding of blood, 3 *Jew.* 250; says the pope commands the angels, and has power over the dead, 4 *Jew.* 846; complains of the intolerable conduct of the pope and his legates, comparing the latter to Satan, sent abroad to scourge the church, 3 *Jew.* 130, 4 *Jew.* 679, 746, 747, 1080, 1147; censures flattery, 3 *Whitg.* 571
John (Sir): *v.* Sir John.
John the Subdeacon, 2 *Ful.* 360 n
John Ten-Commandments (Friar): 1 *Lat.* 524
John Zapolia: *v. supra.*
Johnson (......): had four prebends, *Park.* 450
Johnson (Mr): Bonner's registrar, *Phil.* 14, 79, 104
Johnson (Jo.): possessed lands in the Isle of Thanet, 3 *Bec.* 487 n
Johnson (Jo.), the canonist: 2 *Ful.* 81 n
Johnson (Paul), son of Jo. Johnson of the Isle of Thanet: dedication to him, 3 *Bec.* 487; account of him and his family, *ib.* n.
Johnson (Pet.): Grindal's registrar, *Pil.* 481 n
Johnson (Rob.), proctor: 2 *Cran.* 492
Johnson (Rob.), canon of Worcester: refused to subscribe bp Hooper's articles, 2 *Hoop.* xix; his reasons subsequently published at Antwerp, *ib.* xx. n
Johnson (Rob.?): a leading man among the Puritans, yet allowed to hold church preferment, *Grin.* 348
Johnson (Tim.): sold the manor of Fordwich, 3 *Bec.* 487 n
Johnston (......), of Annandale: his lands ravaged by the English, 1 *Zur.* 225 n
Johnston (Jo.): account of him, 2 *Zur.* 330 n.; his letters to C. Waser, *ib.* 330, 334
Johnston (Edw.), son of John: 2 *Zur.* 334
Johnston (Nath.): The King's Visitatorial Power asserted, *Park.* 485
Join: to enjoin, 1 *Tyn.* 281
Joliffe (Hen.): being canon of Worcester, he refused to subscribe bishop Hooper's articles, and afterwards published his reasons at Antwerp, 2 *Hoop.* xix, xx; concerned in Cranmer's trial, 2 *Cran.* 543
Joliffe (......), keeper of the wardrobe at Whitehall, *Pra. Eliz.* xx.
Jolle: a name applied to fools or jesters, 4 *Jew.* 860
Jonah: AN OVERSIGHT AND DELIBERATION UPON THE HOLY PROPHET JONAS; sermons by bp Hooper, 1 *Hoop.* 431—458; Jonah sent to Nineveh, 2 *Cov.* 368, 1 *Hoop.* 446; flees to Tarshish, 1 *Hoop.* 450; God's dealing with him, and its purport, 1 *Tyn.* 454; he is cast into the sea, 1 *Hoop.* 480; in the whale's belly, 1 *Ful.* 319—321, 1 *Hoop.* 489, 4 *Jew.* 1167; his prayer, 4 *Bul.* 225, 1 *Hoop.* 490, &c.; his song in the whale's belly, versified by M. Drayton, *Poet.* 129; delivered out of the body of hell by prayer, *Grin.* 106, 1 *Hoop.* 501; he was a type of Christ, 3 *Bul.* 17, 1 *Hoop.* 490, 2 *Hoop.* 32, 1 *Tyn.* 457, an evidence of the resurrection, 1 *Bul.* 170; he threatens Nineveh, 1 *Hoop.* 509, &c., *Pil.* 89; his short and pithy sermon, 1 *Lat.* 239; Nineveh's repentance, 4 *Bul.* 167, 179, 554, 1 *Hoop.* 512; his gourd, what plant it was, 1 *Jew.* 292, *Whita.* 129, 145; God's remonstrance with him, 2 *Bul.* 427, 428; on the question whether Tyndale translated Jonah, 1 *Tyn.* 447; his prologue to that book, *ib.* 449; how to read profitably, *ib.* 453, 465; many Jonases to be found in the realm, 1 *Hoop.* 466; who they are, *ib.* 466, 469; they ought to be cast out, *ib.* 480
Jonas, bp of Orleans: wrote against Claudius of Turin, *Calf.* xi, 2 *Ful.* 208
Jonas (Justus): *v.* Catechisms, *Cranmer's.*
His doctrine on the sacrament, 1 *Cran.* 106, 2 *Cran.* 218
Jonas (Justus), the younger: kindly treated by Cranmer, 2 *Cran.* 425 n., 3 *Zur.* 22
Jonathan: a captain, 1 *Bul.* 384; an example to sons, *ib.* 270, 271; his feigning, 2 *Bul.* 115
Jonathan Ben Uziel: *Whita.* 117, 3 *Whitg.* 343, 344
Joner (Wolfg.), abbot of Cappel: 4 *Bul.* ix; a book dedicated to him, *ib.* xv; slain in the battle of Cappel, *ib.* x. n
Jones (Geoffry): in exile, 1 *Cran.* (9)
Jones (Hugh), bp of Llandaff: *Park.* 257
Jones (Nich.): at Cambridge, *Park.* 339 n
Jones (Tho.): was deputy clerk to the ecclesiastical commissioners, *Grin.* 318 n
Jonson (Ben.): ridicules Becon's tracts, 1 *Bec.* xv.

Jordan: 4 *Bul.* 241, 255, 263
Jordan (......): 2 *Zur.* 293
Jordanes Botergius, *q. v.*
Jordanes Saxo: wrote on the Apocalypse, *Bale* 257
Jordayn (Isabella), abbess of Wilton: 2 *Cran.* 258 n
Jortin (Jo.): Life of Erasmus, 2 *Ful.* 319 n., 1 *Lat.* 46 n
Jorvalles abbey: *v.* Jervaulx.
Joscelin (Jo.), or Josseline: wrote the volume De Antiquitate Britannicæ Ecclesiæ, *Park.* xiii; Mr Joscleyn mentioned, *ib.* 298; notice of his book, *ib.* 425, 426
Joscelin (Sir Tho.), or Josseline, brother of the last, *Park.* xiii.
Joseph: refused Potiphar's wife, 1 *Bul.* 210, 410; exalted because he reverenced his father, *ib.* 287; his conduct as governor of Egypt, *ib.* 466; on his Egyptian name Zaphnath-paaneah, *Whita.* 178; his conduct in taking the lands of the people justified, 1 *Tyn.* 410; how he drank wine with his brethren, 2 *Bul.* 57; his burial, 4 *Bul.* 524; the removal of his remains, *Calf.* 312
Joseph (St): his breeches worshipped as relics, *Rog.* 225
Joseph of Arimathea: a good man, though a noble senator and rich, 1 *Bul.* 386, 2 *Bul.* 22; he waited for the kingdom of God, 3 *Bul.* 278; said to have preached in Britain, 1 *Jew.* 162, 280, 305, 3 *Jew.* 163, *Pil.* 511
Joseph (R.), the Blind: his paraphrase, 1 *Ful.* 79, 314, *Whita.* 117; account of him, *Whita.* 117 n
Joseph Ben-Gorion: *v.* Hegesippus.
Joseph of Egypt: referred to about Helena, *Calf.* 322 n
Joseph, patriarch of Constantinople: at the council of Florence, 3 *Jew.* 126, 341, *Rid.* 135 n
Joseph (Jo.): one of the six preachers at Canterbury, 1 *Bec.* x. n.; an exile, 1 *Cran.* (9)
Josephus (Flav.): his works, *Jew.* xxxix, 3 *Whitg.* xxix; a Latin version ascribed to Rufinus, *Calf.* x; he speaks of two inscribed columns erected before the Flood, *Whita.* 516; cites the testimony of a sibyl concerning the tower of Babel, *ib.* 112; says Magog was the beginner of the Scythians, *Bale* 571; records the history of Abraham delivering Lot, 1 *Hoop.* ix; states that Melchisedec feasted Abraham's soldiers, and received Abraham to his table, 2 *Jew.* 731; says he ministered to his army the duties of hospitality, &c., 1 *Ful.* 149; tells who were the guests at the eating of the paschal lamb, 2 *Bul.* 181; how he divides the ten commandments, 1 *Bul.* 213, 1 *Hoop.* 349; he describes the priests' garments, 2 *Bul.* 134; speaks of the ephod, *ib.* 136; describes the high-priest's breast-plate of judgment, *ib.*; likewise the golden plate worn by him, *ib.* 137; he says (as Rabanus Maurus states) that Solomon found out the mode of exorcism, 4 *Bul.* 114; affirms that the LXX. only translated the Law, *Whita.* 118; his statement as to the Old Testament canon and the Apocrypha, *ib.* 60, 61; he says Theotectus was struck blind and Theopompus fell mad, because they had irreverently touched the word of God, 1 *Bul.* 48; Lyra thinks he wrote the Rest of Esther, *Whita.* 71; the books of Maccabees ascribed to him by Jerome, *ib.* 96; he gives an account of the interview of Jaddus the high-priest with Alexander the Great, *Calf.* 117, *Pil.* 69; describes the sufferings of the Jews under Ptolemy Lathyrus, 2 *Hoop.* 82; writes of the name Pharisee, 3 *Whitg.* 522; says the Pharisees were first brought to the government of the state by the policy of Alexandra, 3 *Jew.* 323; relates how Herod, Pilate, and Petronius sought to place images in the Temple, and how the Jews opposed them, *Calf.* 44 n., *Park.* 82; does not state that Caiaphas was a Sadducee, 2 *Ful.* 246 n., 326 n.; speaks of the public reading of scripture in his time, 3 *Whitg.* 50; states that at the siege of Jerusalem a woman ate her own child, 4 *Jew.* 1179; his enumeration of the Jews slain there, 2 *Jew.* 1028; he was an eye-witness of the destruction, 2 *Bul.* 261; his counsel against swearing, 1 *Bec.* 391; references to him, 2 *Lat.* 89, 146, *Pil.* 682
Joshua: 1 *Bul.* 324, 4 *Bul.* 37; he was commanded to go in and out, and to be directed by the voice of Eleazar the high-priest, 4 *Jew.* 986; set before Eleazar, 1 *Bul.* 328, 329; a captain, *ib.* 375, 384, 386; he placed stones in Jordan, 4 *Bul.* 229; circumcision renewed in his time, *ib.* 395; he took Jericho, 2 *Jew.* 969; built an altar on mount Ebal, 1 *Bul.* 325; destroyed the Amorites, *Pil.* 28; in the destruction of the heathen nations he acted by the command of God, 1 *Cov.* 51; overthrew the altar of the Reubenites, 1 *Bul.* 362, 377; his prayers, 4 *Bul.* 225; he was a type of Christ, 1 *Cov.* 50; the book of Joshua, 2 *Cov.* 17

Josiah, king of Judah: his history, 2 *Bul.* 10; defended by God in his tender age, 2 *Hoop.* 102; his example in reforming, 1 *Bul.* 325, 3 *Bul.* 121; he set forth the word of God, 2 *Hoop.* 388; put the priests, &c., in mind of their duties, 4 *Jew.* 989; how he kept the passover, 4 *Bul.* 407; destroyed the false priests, 1 *Bul.* 335, 358; was slain in war, *ib.* 375; removed from evil to come, 3 *Bul.* 212; commended by Jeremiah, *Grin.* 28

Jot: the letter ϟ or ι, 2 *Tyn.* 229

Jotham, king of Judah: 2 *Bul.* 8

Jouress: duress, *Bale* 83

Joverius (Fra.): his Sanctiones Ecclesiasticæ, 2 *Ful.* 96, 113, 269, 312, 322 nn., *Jew.* xxxix; he says pope Liberius communicated with heretics, 4 *Jew.* 929; his account of the variation in the numbering of the popes named John, 2 *Ful.* 269 n

Jovinian, emperor: *v.* Athanasius, x.

As soon as he was created emperor, he made his first law for the restoring of banished Christians, 4 *Jew.* 1125

Jovinian, monk of Milan: charged with heresy, 1 *Ful.* 214; called by Jerome the Epicure of Christian men, *Phil.* 426; erred respecting marriage, making it equal to virginity, 2 *Ful.* 43, 388; taught that all future rewards will be equal, *Hutch.* 306

Jovinians: the sect of Jovinian, *Phil.* 404; they thought all sins to be equal, 2 *Bul.* 407, *Rog.* 137; maintained that the baptized can no more be tempted, *Rog.* 277; said that the regenerate cannot sin, *ib.* 138; mistaken for the Manichees, *ib.* 303

Jovius (Paul.): set aside from the bishoprick of Como, 4 *Jew.* 659; his works, *Jew.* xxxix; on Galeotus Martius, *Rog.* 109; referred to about what kind of men were made cardinals, 4 *Jew.* 659; on archery in England, 1 *Lat.* 197

Joy: *v.* Consolation, Jewel.

Gladness of heart, what it is, 3 *Bec.* 611; joy in God and joy in this world compared, *Phil.* 263; all rejoicing ought to be in God, 1 *Bec.* 176; joy in the Holy Ghost, 2 *Cov.* 314, &c.; the joy of the righteous, 2 *Jew.* 878; Paul exhorts to joy, 2 *Bec.* 428; our joy should be in the Lord, *ib.* 427, 428, 443; it should be continual, *ib.* 461, 462, 473; on the command to rejoice in the Lord, *ib.* 417; such rejoicing is banished from the heart by embracing worldly vanities, *ib.* 416; cause for joy and sorrow to those who consider the state of the time, *ib.* 413

Joyce: juice, *Calf.* 88

Joye (Geo.), or Jaye: 1 *Tyn.* l, liv, 4; once a friar, but wedded, *ib.* 37 n.; he prints two leaves of Genesis in a large form, *ib.* lx; his surreptitious edition of Tyndale's New Testament, *ib.* lxi; his Apology for the same, *ib.* lxii; he translated Osiander on the End of the World, 1 *Lat.* 365 n.; said by some to be author of the treatise on the Supper of the Lord, commonly ascribed to Tyndale, 3 *Tyn.* 218

Jubilee: the year of jubilee, 2 *Bul.* 166; the Christian jubilee, *ib.* 265; the Romish jubilee, *ib.* 266, 1 *Lat.* 49 n

Jucundus (Jac.): 2 *Cov.* 505, &c.

Juda (Leo): mentioned or saluted, 4 *Bul.* x, and n., 3 *Zur.* 317, 621; notice of him, 3 *Zur.* 235 n., 623 n.; his death, 4 *Bul.* xii.

Judæa: the spiritual Jewry is the truth of the gospel, *Rid.* 63

Judah: *v.* Israel.

The tribe, 4 *Bul.* 108; it grew fainthearted, as mentioned by Nehemiah, *Pil.* 415, 416; a type of Judas the traitor, *ib.* 417; kings of Judah, 1 *Bul.* 324

Judas Maccabæus: *v.* Maccabees.

He fought for the people of God against Antiochus, 1 *Bul.* 377, 384; ordained the feast of dedication, 2 *Bul.* 162; procured sacrifice for the dead, 1 *Lat.* 515; not to be followed in this respect, *Grin.* 24; the passage wanting in some ancient copies, *ib.*; slain in war, 1 *Bul.* 384

Judas the Traitor: prefigured by the tribe of Judah, *Pil.* 417; he was in the church, 4 *Bul.* 8, 16; preached and baptized, though a thief, *ib.* 349, 394; carried the bag, *ib.* 489; whether present at the last supper, *Whita.* 568; said to have been admitted to the Lord's table, and to have partaken, 4 *Bul.* 60, 463, 464, 476, 1 *Jew.* 142; said not to have been present at the institution of the sacrament, 3 *Bec.* 381, &c.; whether he received the body and blood of the Lord, 1 *Cran.* 221, 222, 223, 224, 225; Hilary is of opinion that he did not partake of the eucharist; Augustine and most of the fathers think the contrary, 4 *Bul.* 464, *Whita.* 455; said to have received our price, 4 *Jew.* 892, 893; he did not eat bread which was the Lord, 4 *Bul.* 271; what he received, *ib.* 464, 3 *Jew.* 531, 532; he had no fruit of the sacrament, 4 *Bul.* 341, but took it to his condemnation, *Rid.* 247; how the devil entered into him, 4 *Bul.* 473; he was a wilful apostate, 2 *Bul.* 424; his kiss, 4 *Bul.* 230; his treason, *Poet.* 427; the betrayal of Christ, verses by Jo. Markham, *ib.* 361; Judas was a figure of the Jews, 1 *Brad.* 211; called Satan, 4 *Bul.* 465;

those who attend idolatrous worship, knowing it to be so, compared to Judas, *Phil.* 221; his repentance, 1 *Brad.* 51, 3 *Bul.* 61, 111, *Calf.* 243; contemning Christ's admonitions, he died in horrible despair, 2 *Hoop.* 324, 350; a tradition concerning his death mentioned by Œcumenius and others, *Whita.* 664; the fall and repentance of Judas and Peter contrasted, 1 *Lat.* 379, 3 *Tyn.* 208, 209; an apocryphal Gospel called his, *Whita.* 312; Judas' chapel, *Pil.* 541.

Judd (Sir And.): founds a school at Tonbridge, *Park.* 210

Jude (St): his epistle doubted of by Eusebius, 1 *Ful.* 16 n., 222; received by some churches when disallowed by others, *Whita.* 306; Luther's doubts respecting it, *ib.* 105; Cajetan rejected it, *ib.*; so did some Lutherans, *ib.* 296; Wigand does so, *Rog.* 84; Tyndale's prologue to this epistle, 1 *Tyn.* 531; argument of it, 3 *Bec.* 593; Jude speaks of the fallen angels, 3 *Bul.* 350; cites Enoch, 1 *Bul.* 39, *Whita.* 70, 114, 516

Judex (Matthias): a writer of the Magdeburg Centuries, 3 *Jew.* 128; letter to him and the others, *Park.* 286, 2 *Zur.* 77

Judge of controversies: *v.* Church, Faith, Scripture.

Judge over sin: 3 *Jew.* 373, &c.

Judges: *v.* Magistrates, Prayers, Terms.

Their office described, 1 *Bul.* 346; they are only ministers of the law, 2 *Ful.* 134, 135; their duty, 1 *Bec.* 223, 224, *Sand.* 99, 225, 1 *Tyn.* 203—205; how they should behave in a matter brought before them, 1 *Bec.* 371; they must hear and know, 1 *Bul.* 347; must judge justly, *ib.*; must have discretion and clemency, *ib.* 356; must be without partiality or foolish pity, and be neither too hasty nor too slow, *Sand.* 226; must avoid bribes and delays, 1 *Lat.* 171, *Sand.* 225; must minister justice speedily, 1 *Lat.* 155; should not make men accuse themselves, 1 *Tyn.* 335; ought to have God for their pattern, 1 *Bul.* 348; preachers may admonish them, 2 *Lat.* 325; an admonition for them, 1 *Bec.* 370; their laws, 2 *Bul.* 220; of old they could be easily approached, 1 *Lat.* 156; if just they are to be honoured, *ib.* 157; their faults, 1 *Bul.* 348; some follow gifts, 1 *Lat.* 140; some favour the rich, *ib.* 145; some would not hear poor men's causes unless bribed, *ib.* 127, 128; those who are corrupt in judgment are thieves, 2 *Bec.* 108; a corrupt judge flayed alive, 1 *Lat.* 146; the sign of the judge's skin, *ib.* 181, 260; the place of punishment of unjust judges, *ib.* 158

Judges on mount Esau (Obad. 21), *Pil.* 270; the parable of the unjust judge expounded, 1 *Lat.* 142, &c., 150, &c.

Judges (Book of): by whom written, *Whita.* 302; what it declares, 2 *Cov.* 17; what the judges were, *Pil.* 23; they made war, 1 *Bul.* 384

Judgment: what it is, 1 *Bul.* 345, 2 *Bul.* 219; to be exercised, 2 *Lat.* 347; power of judgment, 4 *Bul.* 40; rash judgment condemned, 1 *Lat.* 382; that of God and that of the world not alike, 1 *Bec.* 137, *Pil.* 97; how far we may judge others, *Bale* 33, &c., 1 *Brad.* 6; what judgment is forbidden, and what not, 2 *Tyn.* 112; Christ forbids not public judgments, but only uncharitable private ones, *Sand.* 228; judgment pertains to the magistrate, 1 *Bul.* 346, *Sand.* 224; is not abrogated among Christians, 1 *Bul.* 350; what it is to do judgment, *Sand.* 223, &c.

— Private judgment: how it differs from public, *Calf.* 61; it is not true that each individual should follow the interpretation dictated by his own private spirit (which would lead to fanaticism), but we should follow the Holy Spirit's teaching in scripture, *Whita.* 433; the judgment of individuals taught by the Holy Spirit, not to be censured as mere private judgment, *ib.* 460, 461

Judgment (The): *v.* Christ, vi, Works, World.

The day of doom to be considered, *Wool.* 140; much to be desired, 2 *Hoop.* 38; one parliament will reform and put in order all things, 1 *Lat.* 362; certainty of the judgment, *Sand.* 353, 355; the day is not far off, 2 *Hoop.* 114, 1 *Lat.* 102, *Pil.* 258, *Sand.* 213, 2 *Tyn.* 179, 180; its time not known, not even to the angels, 2 *Lat.* 45, *Sand.* 355, 356; warnings and preparations for it, *Sand.* 368, 369; signs of its approach, *Pra. Eliz.* 506—509, margin (see Bede, ii), *Sand.* 356, &c.; the last sign before it is the preaching of the gospel throughout the world, 2 *Lat.* 307; some will remain alive until that day, 2 *Hoop.* 38, *Now.* (50), 168; it will be joyful to those who are prepared, but terrible to the wicked, 1 *Lat.* 530; of boldness in the day of judgment, 2 *Tyn.* 202, 203; the day of the Lord, 3 *Bec.* 613; the last day, 3 *Bul.* 405; the judgment day, *Bale* 576, 1 *Bul.* 44, 152, 2 *Bul.* 219, 2 *Hoop.* 36, *Lit. Edw.* 511, (559), *Rog.* 66; the judgment of the quick and dead, 1 *Bul.* 154, *Now.* (50), 168; an article de judicio extremo, &c., 2 *Cran.* 480; on the statements respecting it in 1 and 2 Thess., 1 *Tyn.* 516, 517; the form of the judgment, 2 *Lat.* 191; the elect shall be judges, not judged, *ib.*; the books which shall be opened, *Sand.* 367; heresies respecting the judgment, *Rog.* 67, 68

Judica (Dominica): Passion Sunday, 1 *Jew.* 107

Judith: an example of devotion, *Rid.* 139; she reproved Osias the priest, 4 *Bul.* 181; her fall hindered by the Lord, 2 *Hoop.* 296; her faith, 1 *Lat.* 348, 378; she sanctified the name of the Lord, *ib.* 348; slew Holofernes, 2 *Bul.* 115, 4 *Bul.* 225, *Pil.* 29, 360

— The book of Judith: its claims to be canonical considered, *Whita.* 82; it is not canonical, 4 *Bul.* 540, 1 *Ful.* 20 n.; mentioned in one copy of the Apostolic Canons, *Whita.* 43 n.; disallowed by Jerome, 1 *Ful.* 24, 2 *Whitg.* 152; its chronology uncertain, *Whita.* 83, &c.

Jueren (Sch. à): his book on the End of the World, transl. by T. Rogers, 2 *Lat.* 51 n (rather Geueren, *q. v.*)

Jugge (......), a preacher: in exile, 1 *Cran.* (9)

Jugge (Rich.), printer: *Bale* 640, *Grin.* 258, 260, 261, 264, 1 *Hoop.* 430; one of the queen's printers, *Park.* 281; Bibles printed by him, 2 *Cov.* xiii, 2, 1 *Ful.* 422, *Park.* 337

Julian, emperor, called the Apostate: once a reader in the church, 2 *Jew.* 845; how he counterfeited religion, 2 *Ful.* 116; his apostasy, 4 *Bul.* 77, *Sand.* 362; it was seen in his countenance by Gregory Nazianzen, *Pil.* 312; his objections against Christianity, 1 *Bul.* 532, 2 *Jew.* 687; he found fault with the simplicity of God's word, 2 *Jew.* 1026; fought against the people of God, 2 *Hoop.* 231; illtreated the Christians, 1 *Brad.* 407, 2 *Jew.* 977; accused them of sedition and treason, 4 *Jew.* 666; condemned the reasons of certain Christian bishops, 3 *Jew.* 203; banished Athanasius, *Pil.* 440; persecuted Artemius, 2 *Whitg.* 303; reproved Christians for suffering women and children to read the scriptures, 2 *Jew.* 696; forbade them to bring up their children in learning, *ib.* 982; charged them with a superstitious regard of sepulchres, 2 *Ful.* 88; took away the goods of the church, *Pil.* 596; cast out the body of John the Baptist, *Bale* 57; licensed the Jews to rebuild the temple, but they were interrupted by miracle, 2 *Bul.* 261, *Calf.* 115, 121, 123, 2 *Jew.* 648, 978, 2 *Lat.* 48; caused the priests of the pagans to order their lives according to the example of the Christian priests, 2 *Hoop.* 119; thought in his frenzy that the great Alexander's soul was come to dwell in him, 1 *Jew.* 439; made an edict against sorcery, 1 *Hoop.* 329; put demons to flight by the sign of the cross, *Calf.* 85—88, *Whita.* 591; the miraculous shower of rain which overtook him, *Calf.* 114, 115, 120, 2 *Ful.* 148, 2 *Jew.* 647; his image struck by lightning, 2 *Jew.* 652, 653; his defiance of Christ, 2 *Jew.* 845; his saying when he received his death-wound, 2 *Hoop.* 292, 1 *Jew.* 190, 2 *Jew.* 978; a warning to persecutors, 4 *Jew.* 1126

Julian, a lieutenant in Spain: 1 *Bul.* 416

Julian, president of the East: miraculously smitten with disease, 2 *Jew.* 653

Julian, a cardinal: sent to Germany with card. Beaufort, to seek aid against the Hussites, 2 *Jew.* 979; his epistle to the pope, *ib.*

Julian, bp of Ostia: granted to the university of Cambridge power to license twelve preachers, *Park.* 238

Julian, bp of Toledo: on the new commandment (wrongly cited as Angelomus), 2 *Jew.* 724, *Jew.* xxxix. n

Julian, the Pelagian: 1 *Ful.* 264, 3 *Jew.* 230

Julianites: *Hutch.* 247

Julianus (Ant.): on our Lord breaking bread after his passion, 1 *Jew.* 233

Juliers: invaded, 3 *Zur.* 633

Juliers (Will. duke of): v. William.

Julitta: her confession and martyrdom, 1 *Brad.* 554

Julius Cæsar, emperor: his declaration, "Veni, vidi, vici," 2 *Jew.* 806; engaged in civil war, 3 *Bul.* 18; his contest with Pompey, 2 *Jew.* 1094; he called his army fellow-soldiers, *Pil.* 451; would not be called king, 3 *Jew.* 318; reached out his foot to be kissed that folks might see his golden slipper set with stones, 4 *Jew.* 689; robbed the treasury, 2 *Jew.* 628; declared that as touching any wrong done by him to any one, he was as a private man, 4 *Jew.* 670; commended, *Pil.* 286

Julius I., pope: summoned to Nice, 3 *Jew.* 225; referred to by Harding to shew that Zosimus did not corrupt the council of Nice, 4 *Jew.* 925; he reproved the Arian bishops assembled at Antioch, 1 *Jew.* 352; was not present there, 4 *Jew.* 826; declared that council void, 1 *Jew.* 412; his judgment in the case of Eusebius and Athanasius, *ib.* 386, 393, &c., 415, 416; he was excommunicated and deposed by the bishops of the Eastern church, *ib.* 407, 4 *Jew.* 834; two spurious epistles ascribed to him, 2 *Ful.*

160 n., *Whita.* 435; he extols Peter, 3 *Jew.* 300; says the holy church of Rome has power granted her to open and shut the gates of the kingdom of heaven to whom she listeth, *ib.* 379; commands that the people receive both the bread and cup severally, 2 *Bec.* 243; forbids intinction, or dipping of the sacramental bread, 3 *Bec.* 415, 1 *Jew.* 212, 252, 253, 4 *Jew.* 816, 817, &c.; speaks against the use of milk, &c., in the communion, *Coop.* 137

Julius II., pope: forbade appeals from the pope to a council, 1 *Jew.* 68; determined that he who appeals from the pope to a general council is a heretic, 3 *Jew.* 216; called a council at Rome to overthrow that of Pisa, 1 *Jew.* 70; his oppressions and persecutions, 1 *Lat.* 181, 2 *Lat.* 333; he caused 16,000 to be slain in one battle, 3 *Bec.* 510; his ignorance, 4 *Jew.* 910; he sent Henry VIII. the golden rose, 1 *Tyn.* 186; quarrelled with Louis XII. of France, 2 *Tyn.* 310; offered to transfer the title of Most Christian King from the French king to Henry VIII., 1 *Tyn.* 187 n.; gave the title of Defender of the Faith to James IV. of Scotland, *ib.* 187

Julius III., pope: *v.* Councils, TRENT.

His election, 4 *Bul.* 29, 3 *Zur.* 344 n.; he convened the council of Trent, 4 *Bul.* 529; commanded that no reformers should be heard at the council of Trent, unless to recant their errors, 1 *Jew.* 62, 4 *Jew.* 1114; saying of Julius III. (or II.) on oaths, 2 *Zur.* 173

Julius Capitolinus: *Jew.* xxxix, 1 *Jew.* 276

Julius Paccius, *q. v.*

Julius Sancterentianus, *q. v.*

Julius, an Italian monk: 3 *Zur.* 699

June: a misprint for inne? 2 *Bec.* 633

Junia, or Junias: *v.* Andronicus.

Juniper-berries: sold for pepper, 1 *Cran.* 262

Junius (Fra.): 2 *Zur.* 190 n

Jurer: a swearer, *Bale* 466

Juris Canonici Corpus: *v.* Law (Canon).

Juris Civilis Corpus: *v.* Law (Civil).

Jurisdiction: power thereof, 4 *Bul.* 39

Jurors: called questmongers, 1 *Bec.* 370, & al.; advice to them, 1 *Lat.* 379; an admonition for them, 1 *Bec.* 370; what men they ought to be, *ib.* 371; they should not fear displeasure, 1 *Lat.* 488; an honest jury, 1 *Brad.* 406; a jury bribed with twelve crowns, 1 *Lat.* 190, 380; another case, *ib.* 190

Just: *v.* Righteous.

Justellus (Chr.): 2 *Ful.* 42 n

Justice: *v.* Judges, Law, Righteousness.

Divine justice is either corrective or retributive, 1 *Hoop.* 267; there must be justice in the dealings of all men, *Sand.* 227; it must be done by all to all, 1 *Lat.* 503; should be neither too hasty nor too slow, *Sand.* 226; sometimes delayed or denied to the poor, 1 *Lat.* 127; not to be sacrificed to mercy, *Sand.* 148; to be administered, and how, *ib.* 224, &c.; better administered under Edward VI. than under Mary, *Pil.* 614; the sword and balances of Justice, *Sand.* 201

Justices: *v.* Judges, Magistrates.

Justiciaries: those who seek to justify themselves, 1 *Tyn.* 13; they are not fit guests for the holy table, 1 *Bec.* 118

Justification: *v.* Christ, Faith, Grace, Law, Righteousness, Salvation, Works.

i. *Generally:* the doctrine stated, and explained, 3 *Bec.* 291, 603, 616, 1 *Bul.* 104—121, 3 *Bul.* 41, 49, 2 *Cov.* 338, 339, 379, &c., 2 *Ful.* 391, 1 *Hoop,* 49, &c., *Now.* (101), *Sand.* 268, 290, 291, 3 *Tyn.* 195—197; translations respecting it examined, 1 *Ful.* 332—342; "justifications," the Romish rendering of "ordinances," *ib.* 118, 157; how Abraham was justified, see his name; what David thought of justification, 3 *Bul.* 47, 49; for the doctrine of Ambrose, Augustine, Bernard, and other fathers and divines, see their names; the papal and scriptural doctrines contrasted, 3 *Tyn.* 111; Romish divines call the first receipt of grace the first justification, the increase thereof the second justification, *ib.* 203 n.; More says, that the first faith, and the first justifying are given us without our deserving; not so the second, *ib.* 203, 210; THE PARABLE OF THE WICKED MAMMON, a treatise on justification, by W. Tyndale, 1 *Tyn.* 29—126; notes on justification, with authorities from scripture, and passages from the fathers and schoolmen, 2 *Cran.* 203; an article on justification, 1538, *ib.* 473; the doctrine as taught in the Institution of a Christen man, *ib.* 112—114; the doctrine stated by Calvin, *Grin.* 255 n.; illustrated by a parable, 4 *Bul.* 320; another similitude, 3 *Tyn.* 197; three things are requisite in justification, justice, mercy, faith, 2 *Cran.* 129; it brings peace, 1 *Tyn.* 294; errors respecting it, *Rog.* 109—111, 113—115, 116; by-paths to it, 2 *Cran.* 114; Latimer says it may be lost, 2 *Lat.* 7; carnally secure worldlings hope to be saved without either faith or works, *Rog.* 114

JUSTIFICATION

ii. We are justified, efficiently,

By Grace: justification is a free gift, 1 *Bul.* 117, 3 *Bul.* 41, 1 *Hoop.* 51; it is freely given, though a ransom was paid for it, 2 *Cran.* 129; to justify is the work of God alone, 1 *Brad.* 217, 2 *Cran.* 131; we are justified freely by his grace, 3 *Bec.* 170, &c., 3 *Bul.* 12, 2 *Cran.* 95, 2 *Jew.* 1026, 3 *Jew.* 243, 2 *Lat.* 194; probations out of scripture that so many as are justified, are justified and saved solely by the mercy of God through faith, 3 *Bec.* 329, &c.; justification is consequent upon election, 1 *Brad.* 314; justification considered with reference to baptism, 2 *Tyn.* 90; free-will is clean contrary to free justification, 3 *Whitg.* 552; the cause of justification and its effects distinguished, *Lit. Edw.* 512, (560)

iii. We are justified, meritoriously,

By the Righteousness of Christ: we are righteous neither of ourselves nor in ourselves, 1 *Ful.* 342, but only by the merit or righteousness of Christ imputed unto us, 3 *Bec.* 616, 3 *Bul.* 46, 2 *Cov.* 379, 2 *Cran.* 128, 1 *Hoop.* 51, 2 *Jew.* 1041, *Now.* (60), 179, *Rog.* 108; he takes our sins, and gives us his righteousness, 1 *Lat.* 330; the greatest sinner is righteous when in Christ, 1 *Tyn.* 198; Abraham and all the faithful saved by imputed righteousness, 1 *Hoop.* 21,

iv. We are justified, instrumentally,

By Faith: by faith alone, not by works, *Bale* 543, 2 *Bec.* 638, 639, 1 *Brad.* 371, 1 *Bul.* 112, 113, 2 *Cov.* 339, 1 *Cran.* 113, 128, 1 *Ful.* 121, 2 *Ful.* 242, 2 *Hoop.* 121, *Lit. Edw.* 500, (549), *Now.* (28, 60), 144, 179, *Phil.* 409, &c., *Pil.* 167, *Rog.* 111, 1 *Tyn.* 46, 49, 119, 125, 192, 278, 294, 342, 375, 431, 488, 508, 509, 2 *Tyn.* 14, 15, 76, 90, 137, 3 *Tyn.* 172, 195—206, 274, 276, 3 *Zur.* 212; this is the doctrine of the fathers and old writers, 2 *Bec.* 638, 639, 2 *Cov.* 339, 340, 389, 390, 2 *Cran.* 130, 133, 203, 3 *Jew.* 244, *Wool.* 34; it is misrepresented by adversaries, 2 *Jew.* 1026; Standish calls it damnable, 2 *Cov.* 338; More's arguments against it, and Tyndale's replies, 3 *Tyn.* 197—210; the doctrine upheld by Barnes and Latimer, 3 *Zur.* 617; the elect were justified by faith in the promised Saviour from the first, 1 *Tyn.* 417 (*v.* Fathers before Christ); faith is said to justify, because it receives the justifying, 2 *Tyn.* 89; it is not the cause, but the instrument of justification, *Now.* (61), 180; the doctrine of justification without works must be kept uncorrupted, 3 *Bul.*

49; evils arising from the denial of it, 1 *Hoop.* 56

v. On justification

By works:

(*a*) We are not justified before God by our works, merits, or deservings, 3 *Bec.* 291, 2 *Cov.* 382, 2 *Cran.* 128, 1 *Hoop.* 51, *Rog.* 115, *Sand.* 268, 1 *Tyn.* 52, 56, 192, 497, 3 *Tyn.* 204; no work of ours can deserve anything of God, 2 *Cov.* 379; justification comes not by the deeds of the law, 1 *Bul.* 113, *Lit. Edw.* 500, (549), 1 *Tyn.* 51, 114, 487, 496, 3 *Tyn.* 193; answer to the statement that by "the deeds of the law," Paul means ceremonial observances, 1 *Tyn.* 51; one who came to Christ trusting in his own righteousness was deservedly referred to the law, *Whita.* 471; the law would justify if it were perfectly kept, *Now.* (24), 139; but no man is justified in this way, because none can keep the law, 1 *Hoop.* 51, *Now.* (25), 140; the Jews thought that the work of their ceremonies justified them, 4 *Bul.* 302, 1 *Hoop.* 211, 1 *Tyn.* 276; Papists maintain a similar doctrine, 3 *Bec.* 291, *Sand.* 25, 1 *Tyn.* 276, 3 *Tyn.* 111; this is a detestable and dangerous doctrine, 2 *Lat.* 147; it is stirred up by Satan, *Nord.* 115; it is taught by Jews, Turks, and Papists, 3 *Tyn.* 193, 194; cavils of those who uphold it, 2 *Bul.* 329; justifiers of themselves described, 1 *Tyn.* 13, 114, 432; they are sorely deceived, *ib.* 12; monks trust in their merits, *ib.* 431; monkish rhymes on justification, *Rog.* 110, 111; on certain scriptures which are alleged in favour of justification by works, 2 *Bul.* 335, 2 *Cov.* 379, &c., 2 *Ful.* 227, 1 *Tyn.* 63, &c.; the case of Hezekiah, 2 *Cov.* 380; that of the Ninevites, *ib.* 381; that of Cornelius the centurion, *ib.* 379, 380, *Sand.* 256, &c.; the "commandments and justifications," mentioned in Luke i. 6; in our version, "commandments and ordinances," 1 *Ful.* 118

(*b*) Though justification is by faith alone, repentance, hope, love, &c., are not excluded, 2 *Cov.* 342, 2 *Cran.* 129, 131; those who are justified must live in good works, 2 *Cov.* 389, 390, 1 *Hoop.* 57, *Wool.* 30, &c., (see Faith, *e.*); justification does not render good works unnecessary, or discourage them, 1 *Bul.* 118, 2 *Cov.* 341, 2 *Jew.* 1026, *Now.* (63), 182; it gives no liberty to sin, 2 *Cran.* 131, 133, 136, 139, but is productive of holiness, 1 *Hoop.* 57; good works necessarily follow it, *Now.* (61), 180; it brings love, 3 *Tyn.* 195—199; they who will not do good works because they are justified

JUSTIFICATION — JUSTINIAN

by faith, are not the children of God, nor children of justification, 2 *Cov.* 341; good works are marks of a justified man, 1 *Tyn.* 56, 192, 497, 3 *Tyn.* 197; true faith works through godly love and charity, 2 *Cov.* 342

(c) We are, however, justified by works, in the sight of man, 1 *Tyn.* 61, 119, 223, 417, 526, 3 *Tyn.* 200—203; the doctrine of the apostle James on justification is not opposed to that of Paul, 2 *Bul.* 327, 2 *Cov.* 485, 2 *Cran.* 208, 1 *Ful.* 405, 407, 424, 2 *Ful.* 384, 385, 3 *Jew.* 244, 4 *Jew.* 765, *Phil.* 412, *Whita.* 471, 1 *Tyn.* 61, 119, 120, 125, 223, 470, 526, 3 *Tyn.* 200—203, *Wool.* 30; the objection of difference between Paul and James is made by those who understand neither, 4 *Jew.* 765

Justin Martyr:

i. *His Life and Works:* he was impressed by seeing Christians go fearlessly to death, 3 *Jew.* 190, 558, *Rid.* 101; was turned to Christ through the godly life of Christians, 2 *Jew.* 1033; he preached the gospel, being apparelled as a heathen philosopher, 3 *Jew.* 615, 2 *Whitg.* 37; his works, *Calf.* 411, *Jew.* xxxix, 3 *Whitg.* xxix; he wrote on the Apocalypse, *Bale* 255; the treatise called Ζητήματα Ἀναγκαῖα is spurious, *Whita.* 583

ii. *Scripture, Doctrine, Miscellanea:* on the perspicuity of scripture, *Whita.* 397, 398; his firm faith in One God, 2 *Jew.* 998; he speaks of Christ as reigning from the cross, 4 *Jew.* 981; supposed that angels fell through the love of women, *Coop.* 146, 3 *Jew.* 606; was a chiliast or millenarian, maintaining that the righteous will rise and reign 1000 years before the last judgment, *Coop.* 147, *Rog.* 154, *Whita.* 391, 583; alleged in support of tradition, *Whita.* 582; he speaks of the fury of the heathen against the Christian name, *Wool.* 20; says Christians were called godless people, or atheists, 3 *Jew.* 624; speaks of some who made themselves eunuchs for the kingdom of heaven, *ib.* 398; calls the bishop προεστώς, 2 *Bec.* 239, &c., 2 *Whitg.* 277, 307—309; speaks of wine being distributed in the feast of Bacchus, 2*Whitg.* 39; referred to respecting the statue erected to Simon Magus, *Calf.* 343 n

iii. *Sacraments, Worship, Ceremonies:* he speaks only of two sacraments, 3 *Jew.* 459; describes the mode of baptizing, 1 *Whitg.* 215; calls baptism the water of regeneration, 3 *Bec.* 376, &c., 1 *Cran.* 263; speaks of the prayers used after baptism,

2 *Whitg.* 467; refers to an oblation of the Mosaic law as a figure of the bread of thanksgiving, which we do in the remembrance of Christ's passion, 3 *Bec.* 457; describes the celebration of the Lord's supper in his time, 2 *Bec.* 239, 3 *Bec.* 376, 387, 416, 474, 475, *Coop.* 81, 82, 125, 127, 139, 156, 1 *Cran.* 263, 264, 265, (30), 1 *Ful.* 503—506, 1 *Jew.* 17, 115, 146, 147, 2 *Jew.* 1114, 1 *Whitg.* 215, 237, 3 *Whitg.* 64—66; calls it eucharist, 2 *Bec.* 232 n., 3 *Bec.* 387, & sæpe; speaks of oblations at the communion, *Coop.* 90; refers to the mingled cup, 2 *Bec.* 239, &c., *Coop.* 81, 1 *Ful.* 503, 523, 2 *Ful.* 237, 1 *Jew.* 139, 2 *Whitg.* 308; declares that the communion is not common bread and wine, but the body and blood of Christ, *Coop.* 194 n., 1 *Cran.* 263, 264, 2 *Jew.* 599, *Rid.* 231; this passage asserted to have been corrupted by Cranmer, 1 *Cran.* 263, 264, *Rid.* 231; he mentions that deacons distributed the bread and wine, 2 *Bec.* 239, &c., 1 *Cran.* 263, 2 *Jew.* 1114, 3 *Whitg.* 64—66; declares that the elements in the eucharist are converted into our flesh and blood, 1 *Cran.* 263, 2 *Hoop.* 420; says, by dry and moist food we are taught what things God the Son of God hath suffered for us, 2 *Jew.* 772, 1114; speaks of sending the sacrament in both kinds to those who were absent, 2 *Bec.* 239, &c., *Coop.* 82, 1 *Jew.* 239; says nothing of a reservation of the host for sick persons, as Gardiner reports, 1 *Cran.* 146; referred to by Harding as a witness for the mass, 1*Jew.* 109; speaks of the kiss of peace, *Coop.* 81, 1 *Jew.* 265, 1 *Whitg.* 215; describes the prayer of the early Christians, 2 *Whitg.* 493; speaks of the people responding "Amen" to the prayers of the minister, 3 *Bec.* 407, *Coop.* 82, 1 *Cran.* 263, 1 *Ful.* 504, 1 *Jew.* 18, *Whita.* 260; shews how singing was practised in the church, and that kneeling was dispensed with on Sundays (pseud.), 1 *Whitg.* 215, 237; says Isaiah promises not the restoring of bloody sacrifices, but the true and spiritual oblations of praise and thanksgiving, 2 *Jew.* 735; speaks of the public reading of scripture, *Coop.* 82, 4 *Jew.* 856, 3 *Whitg.* 47, 343, 344; referred to respecting the figure of the cross, *Calf.* 178 n., 2 *Ful.* 164

Justin, the historian: 1 *Bul.* 278, *Calf.* 317 n., 1 *Hoop.* 423

Justina, empress: favoured the Arians, *Calf.* 301; oppressed Ambrose, 4 *Bul.* 195

Justinian, emperor: v. Law (Civil).

He was utterly unlearned, *Calf.* 305

rebuked for heresy, 1 *Jew.* 405; Rome recovered by him, 2 *Bul.* 109; he called Rome the head of the world, 4 *Jew.* 1032; used to say that he had no less care for the Christian religion than for his own life, *ib.* 1125; willed the pope to take knowledge of his laws, *ib.* 1032; deposed two popes, Sylverius, and Vigilius, 1 *Jew.* 406, 4 *Jew.* 682, *Sand.* 40, 1 *Zur.* 18 n.; called the bishop of Constantinople universal patriarch, 4 *Jew.* 1032; esteemed Epiphanius, bp of Constantinople, the more, because his ancestors had been priests and bishops, 3 *Jew.* 392; applied great diligence in prescribing such laws as might best govern the people, 1 *Hoop.* 352; made many ecclesiastical laws, *ib.* 78, 3 *Whitg.* 307; published laws respecting monasteries and monks, 4 *Bul.* 515; restricted the number of priests and deacons, 1 *Jew.* 121, 197, 2 *Jew.* 1019; commanded that churches should not be built without episcopal licence, and the erection of a cross, *Calf.* 135, 136, 189; in order to suppress conventicles he required a procession when a church was to be consecrated, *Calf.* 304, 305; made a law to correct the behaviour of the clergy, 4 *Jew.* 1029; his conduct with respect to councils, 3 *Whitg.* 304; he gave licence to a bishop to release a priest from penance, 4 *Jew.* 1030; commanded blasphemers to be put to death, 1 *Hoop.* 334; his laws said to have been made under papal influence, *Bale* 447; the Lord's supper not privately celebrated in his time, 1 *Hoop.* 171

Justinian (St): was father of St David, *Bale* 192

Justiniana: a bishoprick, 1 *Jew.* 363

Justiniani (Bernard): notice of him, 3 *Zur.* 228 n

Justinianus (Pet.): his Chronicle, *Jew.* xxxix, 4 *Jew.* 692

Justus Orgelitanus: shews how Christ is not always to be seen in the body, 2 *Bec.* 275, 276, 3 *Bec.* 430

Justus, bp of Rochester: consecrated by Augustine, 4 *Jew.* 779, 780

Juthware (St), virgin and martyr: *Bale* 191

Juvenal (D. J.): cited, 1 *Bec.* 222, 382, 2 *Bec.* 383, 399, 421, 535, 599, 3 *Bec.* 509, 1 *Bul.* 205, 339, *Calf.* 14 n., *Grin.* 389, 1 *Hoop.* 423, 1 *Jew.* 457, 544; supposed the Jews to worship the clouds, 2 *Ful.* 209

Juvenalis, bp of Jerusalem: condemned by the council of Chalcedon, 3 *Jew.* 145, 4 *Jew.* 1022; by a civil magistrate, 4 *Jew.* 1021

K

K. (I.): dedication by him to archbishop Bancroft, 4 *Jew.* 1314

K. (J.): put faith and love in the place of the sacraments, *Rog.* 177

Kabuenachi: 1 *Ful.* 315

Kaddow: *v.* Caddow.

Kahad: *v.* Kohath.

Kaiser: emperor, 1 *Bec.* 31; keser, *Sand.* 168

Kale (......): a traitor, *Lit. Eliz.* 658

Kampswell (Tho.): *v.* Camsele.

Karlington: a place for pilgrimages, *Bale* 99

Karne (Sir Edw.): ambassador to the pope, 2 *Cran.* 233 n

Karow (......): *v.* Carew.

Katherine: *v.* Catherine.

Kaye (Jo.): *v.* Caius.

Keeling (Will.): Liturgiæ Britannicæ, *Calf.* 224 n., *Lit. Edw.* ix, 1 *Hoop.* 479 n., 1 *Zur.* 235 n

Keep: to take care, 1 *Tyn.* 24

Keith (Geo.), earl Marischal of Scotland: 2 *Zur.* 295 n

Keith (Will.), son of Will. Keith, and brother of the preceding: killed near Geneva, 2 *Zur.* 295

Kellison (Matth.): *Calf.* 290 n

Kelly (Walter): letter signed by him, 3 *Zur.* 170; ordained by Grindal, *ib.* n

Kelso castle: taken by the English, 3 *Zur.* 387

Keltridge (Jo.): on the Septuagint, 1 *Ful.* 78, 530, 531

Kemnitius (Mart.): *v.* Chemnitius.

Kemp (......), a servant of king Philip: 3 *Zur.* 175 n

Kemp (W.), prebendary of St Paul's: *Rid.* 331 n

Kemp (Will.): letter to him, 1 *Brad.* 591, 2 *Brad.* 194

Kempe (......), a friar: preaches the gospel in Hamburgh, 1 *Tyn.* xxv.

Kempe (A. J.): Hist. Not. of St Martin-le-grand, 1 *Lat.* 196 n

Kempe (Jo.), doctor of canon law: [probably afterwards archbishop, and cardinal], *Bale* 28, 37

Kempe (Jo.), dedication to him: 3 *Bec.* 542; account of his family, *ib.* n

Kempe (Sir Tho.): *Park.* 169

Kempe (Sir Will.): 3 *Bec.* 542 n

Kempe family, of Spain's hall, Finchingfield, Essex, 3 *Bec.* 542 n

Kempis (Tho. à): *v.* Thomas.

Kendal, co. Westmoreland: Pilkington vicar there, *Pil.* ii.

Kendall (Tim.): notice of him, *Poet.* xxxv; verses to Jesus Christ, *ib.* 384
Kenelm (St): *Bale* 192: his shrine, 2 *Lat.* 409 n
Kennedy (Gilb.), 3rd earl of Cassilis: taken prisoner at Solway Moss, 3 *Zur.* 239 n
Kennedy (Gilb.), 4th earl of Cassilis: declines to attend mass, 1 *Zur.* 104 n.; arms in defence of the queen of Scots, *ib.* 205 n.; sworn to the earl of Mar, regent, *ib.* 262 n
Kennell (Dr): *Grin.* 252
Kennet (White), bp of Peterborough: Case of Impropriations, 1 *Lat.* 100 n
Kennington, co. Surrey: Henry V. there, *Bale* 17
Kent: *v.* Canterbury, Cinque Ports, Lambard (W.), Wyat (Sir Tho.)

The affection to their country of the gentlemen and commons there, 1 *Bec.* 235; the justices opposed the reformation, 2 *Cran.* 349, &c., 367; disturbances (1538), *ib.* 367; a priest martyred there, 2 *Lat.* 321; Cranmer requests that the coast may be fortified, 2 *Cran.* 496 n.; Pelagian sectaries there, 2 *Brad.* 173 n.; Frensham's benefactions to several parishes, 2 *Zur.* 21 n.; plague there, 1563, *Grin.* vii; defenceless condition of the coast, *Park.* 202; state of the castles, *ib.* 203; salt works there, *ib.* 258; letters to lord Burghley and the queen against spoiling the woods of the see of Canterbury, *Grin.* 363, 364 (*v.* Correll's wood); the Goodwin Sands, 1 *Lat.* 251 (see also Tenterden); the apple-maker of Kent, 3 *Bec.* 267, 530

The holy maid of Kent, *v.* Barton (Eliz.); Joan of Kent, *v.* Bocher (Joan).
Kent (Earls of): *v.* Grey.
Kentish-town, Cantlers, or Cantrells, co. Middx.: a prebend in St Paul's, held by Bradford, 2 *Brad.* xxiv, *Rid.* 331, and by Grindal, *Grin.* ii.
Kercheor: a kerchief, 3 *Tyn.* 124 n
Kerdeston (Sir Tho.): his dau. Elizabeth, 2 *Bec.* 583 n
Kerned: formed into corns, 2 *Jew.* 1017
Kerr (Tho.), of Fernihurst: 1 *Zur.* 214 n., 223 n.; his castles destroyed, *ib.* 225 n
Keser: *v.* Kaiser.
Ket (Fra.): said that no sufficient sacrifice was yet offered for the sins of the world, *Rog.* 298; asserted that Christ should suffer again, *ib.* 58; denied his ascension, *ib.* 65; impugned the deity of the Holy Ghost, *ib.* 70; was burned at Norwich for heresy, *ib.* 49
Ket (Will.): his rebellion, 2 *Cran.* 189 n., 190 n., 4 *Jew.* 915; the story of it written by Alex. Nevile, *Park.* xiii; he refuses the king's pardon, 2 *Cran.* 196 n
Kethe (Will.): notice of him, *Poet.* xlix; Psa. cxxv. in metre, *ib.* 492
Ketley (Jos.): editor of the Liturgies of king Edward VI., *Lit. Edw.*
Keyes (......): Parker's messenger, *Park.* 441
Keyes (Mr): perhaps Dr Jo. Caius, *Park.* 295
Keyes (Tho.), serjeant porter to queen Elizabeth: letter to Parker respecting his marriage with lady Mary Grey, *Park.* 366 n
Keys: *v.* Absolution, Gospel, Law, Peter.

Meaning of the keys, Matt. xvi., 2 *Bec.* 565, 566, 4 *Bul.* 146, 1 *Cov.* 373, 374, 2 *Cov.* 466, *Hutch.* 98, 1 *Lat.* 30, 31, *Now.* (100); they are given to the whole church, 2 *Hoop.* 51, *Whita.* 425; they represent the law and the gospel, 1 *Tyn.* 21; they are a mark of the church, *Lit. Edw.* 513, (561); their use is rather to open than to shut, 1 *Jew.* 331; the key of knowledge is the scriptures, *Hutch.* 100, 1 *Jew.* 331, 8 *Jew.* 363, 364
Kidder (Jo.): *v.* Kydder.
Kidderminster, co. Worcester: the town-clerk of Kethermyster, 2 *Lat.* 398
Kiffin (Howell): *v.* Kyffin.
Kilburn (Sir Pet.): *Park.* 417 n
Kildare (Gerald earl of): *v.* Fitzgerald.
Kilian (St): martyred, *Bale* 192
Kilkenny, Ireland: Bale's plays acted there, *Bale* ix.
Killigrew (Sir Hen.), brother-in-law to lord Burghley: sent to assist the escape of the earl of Arran, 1 *Zur.* 57 n.; ambassador in Scotland, *ib.* 167, 290 n.; sent abroad, 2 *Zur.* 174
Killing: *v.* Murder.
Kimbolton, co. Huntingdon: the castle and manor, 2 *Lat.* 295
Kimchi (R. Dav.): *v.* David.
Kindness: *v.* Love.
Kindred (Spiritual): *v.* Sponsors.
King (Allayn): 1 *Zur.* 223 n
King (Geo.): *v.* Kyng.
King (Tho.): Elynour Saygrave his wife, 2 *Cran.* 318
King (Rob.): in exile, 1 *Cran.* (9)
King (Dr): 2 *Lat.* 380
Kingdom of God, or of Heaven: *v.* Keys, Prayer (The Lord's), Prayers.

The kingdom of God, 3 *Bul.* 275, 4 *Bul.* 211, *Hutch.* 270, 1 *Lat.* 357, *Nord.* 80, *Now.* (74), 195, *Pra. B.* 22; it may be two ways considered, 3 *Bul.* 276, 1 *Lat.* 361; the kingdom of grace on earth, 3 *Bul.* 276,

KINGDOM — KINGS

1 *Lat.* 361, *Pra. B.* 22; that of glory in heaven, 3 *Bul.* 280, 1 *Lat.* 361, *Pra. B.* 22; the spiritual kingdom of God, 3 *Bul.* 277; the kingdom of God on earth, 4 *Bul.* 211, 1 *Lat.* 358; we desire his kingdom to be set up and enlarged, 2 *Bec.* 152, 153; for the kingdom of God, verses by Jo. Norden, *Nord.* 85, *Poet.* 461; this kingdom to be first and principally sought, 1 *Lat.* 302, 359, *Nord.* 79; the kingdom of heaven, *Bale* 115, 3 *Bec.* 603, 622, 623, 1 *Lat.* 477, 2 *Tyn.* 40; "He that is least in the kingdom of heaven;"—Tyndale interprets this of Christ, 2 *Tyn.* 232, 3 *Tyn.* 116; the kingdom of Christ, see Christ, iii. *d.*

Kingdom of Satan, *q. v.*

Kingdoms: earthly kingdoms, 4 *Bul.* 211; whence their felicity and calamity, 2 *Bul.* 5; they are preserved by the means by which they were first gotten, 2 *Jew.* 1010; whence their destruction, 4 *Bul.* 528; they are ruined by internal dissension, 2 *Jew.* 1328, 1094; why power is translated from one to another, *Sand.* 258; the four great monarchies, *Bale* 423, *Hutch.* 147, 1 *Lat.* 356, *Pil.* 186

Kings, Princes: *v.* Magistrates, where the same matters are set forth at greater length, under the same divisions; also Monarchy, Prayers, War.

i. *Their institution, power, and authority:* what a king is, 3 *Bec.* 615; the name not unlawful, 1 *Lat.* 173, 174; the title given to a queen regnant, 2 *Tyn.* 304; de rebus civilibus, an article concerning princes, governors, &c., 2 *Cran.* 478; the origin of kingly power, 2 *Ful.* 260; kings and rulers are appointed by God, 2 *Cran.* 478, 2 *Ful.* 260, 1 *Tyn.* 173, &c., 194—197, 332—334, 2 *Tyn.* 64, 66, 3 *Tyn.* 180, 3 *Whitg.* 588; he setteth them up and pulleth them down, 1 *Lat.* 356; they are chosen by God, not by the people, 2 *Tyn.* 65; why they are ordained, 1 *Tyn.* 174, 185; kings, &c. are the ministers of God, 1 *Bec.* 218, 1 *Brad.* 401; his vicars, 1 *Lat.* 204, *Pil.* 513, 514; his deputies, 1 *Lat.* 444; his lieutenants, *Sand.* 147; his generals, *ib.* 164; they are in the stead or place of God, 2 *Lat.* 299, 1 *Tyn.* 177; they represent God, 1 *Tyn.* 202; their hearts are in God's hand, 1 *Lat.* 356; God alone may judge them, *ib.* 300, 371; they are accountable to him alone, 1 *Tyn.* 178; their power, *Sand.* 48, &c.; it is derived from God, 1 *Lat.* 355; their authority proved by scripture, 1 *Bec.* 212; the sword delivered to them, *Rid.* 266; their law is God's law, 1 *Tyn.* 240; they are lords of the bodies and goods of their subjects, 2 *Tyn.* 66; they have a right to the common treasures of their countries, 1 *Bul.* 392; may exact tribute, 1 *Bec.* 220, 1 *Lat.* 97, 299; their honour, wherein it standeth, 1 *Lat.* 99; they cannot give any part of their dignity to another, 2 *Hoop.* 546, 559; their position dangerous, 3 *Zur.* 714; they stand not by their own power, *Pil.* 188, but by the favour of God, 2 *Tyn.* 244; kings though children, are still kings, 1 *Lat.* 117, 3 *Zur.* 745; a realm may be well governed under a child, 1 *Lat.* 268; laws provided for a king in Israel, 2 *Bul.* 222, &c.; his election appointed by God, 1 *Lat.* 87, &c.; the law was given in thunder, and so God gave Israel a king, 1 *Tyn.* 194, 334; kings are a great benefit, even though tyrants, *ib.* 179; foreign kings are a judgment from God, 1 *Lat.* 91; one king entitled with another's dominions, 1 *Tyn.* 187

ii. *Their duty:* the office of kings, 1 *Bec.* 286, 299, 1 *Lat.* 119; their office great and chargeable, 1 *Lat.* 193; their duty, 1 *Hoop.* 360, 1 *Lat.* 85, &c., *Nord.* 169, *Sand.* 41, &c., 1 *Tyn.* 202, 239, 250, 334, 335, 3 *Tyn.* 58; a king's labour, 1 *Lat.* 215; an exhortation to kings, *Hutch.* 71; lessons for them, 1 *Lat.* 386; those who have submitted themselves and their kingdoms to Jesus Christ, the King of kings, have flourished; those who have not done so have met with calamity, 2 *Bul.* 5, &c.; this principle illustrated in the history of the kings of Judah, *ib.* 5—11; in that of the kings of Israel, *ib.* 11, 12; in that of other kings, *ib.* 13; they are bound to obey the scriptures, 1 *Lat.* 85, 86, 250; they stand in need of the merits of Christ's passion as much as their subjects do, 2 *Lat.* 298; their duty towards the commonwealth, *Sand.* 46, 47; they should remember that they are not ordained of God for themselves, but for their subjects' welfare, 1 *Tyn.* 239; their responsibility before God, 1 *Tyn.* 180, 202 —204, 334, &c., 2 *Tyn.* 86; they should remember that their subjects are their brethren, 1 *Tyn.* 239; they must execute the laws, *Sand.* 51, 52, and should observe the law, 2 *Hoop.* 101; their duty in the administration of justice, 1 *Lat.* 273, &c.; they must restrain and punish malefactors, *Rog.* 345, 346; must not look at faults through their fingers, 1 *Lat.* 152; must study to make their people live in peace, *Sand.* 83, in piety, *ib.* 84, in honesty, *ib.*; they must care for others, *ib.* 108, 109; should be examples, *ib.* 84, 85; the im-

KINGS

portance of their example, 4 *Jew.* 1206; they should be learned, 1 *Lat.* 184; should not be proud, *ib.* 124, 132; have need of patience, *Hutch.* 297; may require too much, 1 *Lat.* 98; should break unlawful oaths, 1 *Tyn.* 240; those who govern well are generally disliked by their subjects, *Sand.* 36; the wife a king should choose, 1 *Lat.* 94; the dishonour of a king, *ib.* 94; kings too often follow the devil, *ib.* 357

iii. *Their office in relation to religion and the church* (*v.* Supremacy): to win them to the truth is great gain, *Sand.* 276; David an example to kings, 2 *Lat.* 308, and see David; the office and power of princes in religion and matters ecclesiastical, 2 *Ful.* 119, 3 *Jew.* 167, 4 *Jew.* 986, &c. *Rog.* 204, 1 *Zur.* 343, 354; on the office and authority of Christian kings, 2 *Cran.* 116, 2 *Zur.* 9; examples of Christian kings, *Bale* 612; Augustine states the way in which a king should serve God, see p. 84, above; kings are God's servants, to execute his laws, 1 *Tyn.* 334; the prince is keeper of the law of God, and head both of laity and clergy, 2 *Jew.* 997, 4 *Jew.* 975; they should be foremost in the way of truth, *Sand.* 123, 124; are bound to set forth the truth, 2 *Tyn.* 35; should maintain true religion, *Pil.* 640, 642, 2 *Zur.* 341, and provide that their people be taught the gospel, *Sand.* 44, 45; in some sense they are shepherds, 2 *Ful.* 266; their rightful power denied by Papists, 3 *Jew.* 116, 117; on their position in the church, 3 *Whitg.* 191; a certain writer says that they should be the pastors and head rulers of the congregations committed to their care, and should place curates over them, 3 *Tyn.* 265; Cranmer says they may make bishops and priests, 2 *Cran.* 117; they are constituted by God (says the Institution) to overlook priests and bishops, *ib.* 98; how princes are above bishops and priests, 2 *Ful.* 354, &c., 378, &c.; the clergy owe them obedience, as well as the laity, 1 *Tyn.* 333, 2 *Tyn.* 67; they are bound to provide for Christian ministers, 1 *Lat.* 303; their duty in relation to the reformation of the church, *Sand.* 42, 43, 237, 238; they may not change religion at their pleasure, *Pil.* 434; nor may they execute ecclesiastical duties, 1 *Bul.* 329, *Rog.* 341; the king ought not to be made a pope, 1 *Lat.* 148; how the king may correct the preacher, and how the preacher the king, *ib.* 86; on the subjection of princes to the church, *Rog.* 340, 3 *Whitg.* 189, 554; they are subject to the spiritual authority of bishops, &c., 4 *Jew.* 991, 992, *Pil.* 491; kings receive titles, &c. from the pope, and are too often his slaves, *Bale* 444, 1 *Tyn.* 186; they are made drunk by the popes with vain names and baubles, 1 *Tyn.* 204; the pope would have them many and weak, *ib.* 235; where the pope rules they are but his hangmen, *ib.* 242, 243, and their power but a shadow, *ib.* 186, 239, 337; they have been released from their treaties by the pope's dispensations, 1 *Tyn.* 205, 206, 2 *Tyn.* 301, 311; on their deposition by the pope, 4 *Jew.* 681, &c.; kings corrupted by prelates, 1 *Tyn.* 136; they become servants to the prelates, 2 *Tyn.* 178; their authority used by prelates as a cloak for their designs, 2 *Lat.* 305; the authority of kings and bishops inverted, 1 *Tyn.* 282; the Canon Law declares that princes ought to obey the bishops and decrees of the church, 2 *Cran.* 73, and says princes ought not to set bishops beneath them, but to assign them an honourable seat by them, *ib.*; who are the queen's enemies, 2 *Lat.* 260

iv. *The obedience due to them* (*v.* Obedience, Subjects, Tribute): kings are the supreme powers to whom obedience is due, 1 *Brad.* 435; our duty towards the king, his laws and authority, 1 *Lat.* 148, 373, 2 *Lat.* 260; kings and princes must be honoured and obeyed, 1 *Bec.* 82, 211, &c., 2 *Bec.* 475, 1 *Brad.* 411, 435, 478, &c., 2 *Cran.* 164, 1 *Lat.* 265, *Nord.* 167, 170; obedience to them required by the fifth commandment, 2 *Cran.* 103; the king is to be obeyed as supreme head of the state, 1 *Bec.* 180; kings must be obeyed, by high and low, 2 *Lat.* 329; how kings are to be obeyed, *Bale* 87, 1 *Brad.* 478, 3 *Jew.* 173, 4 *Jew.* 703, &c.; they must be implicitly obeyed, even in unjust demands, 1 *Lat.* 300; they are to be obeyed in all things not against God, 1 *Lat.* 512, 2 *Lat.* 17; to be obeyed usque ad aras, *Sand.* 264; they are to be actively or passively obeyed in all things, 1 *Brad.* 373, 2 *Brad.* 45, even to death, 1 *Brad.* 378; not to be actively obeyed if they command wickedness, 2 *Bec.* 90, 91, 1 *Tyn.* 332, 3 *Zur.* 746; for we must obey God rather, 2 *Lat.* 260; the authority of his word is above the king, 2 *Tyn.* 36; the law of princes has no power to force the conscience, 2 *Jew.* 1130; but kings may not be resisted, 2 *Lat.* 260, 1 *Tyn.* 173, &c., 194—197, 332—334, 2 *Tyn.* 64—66, 3 *Tyn.* 180, even though they break their engagements, 2 *Tyn.* 65; whether a tyrant may be resisted, 2 *Zur.* 169; princes

must not be resisted though they rule unjustly, God is their only ruler, 1 *Lat.* 371; we may not fight against them for religion, *Pil.* 433, 434; heathen princes may not be resisted, 1 *Tyn.* 177; Bullinger is inclined to an opposite opinion with regard to kings who command idolatry, 3 *Zur.* 746; it is not lawful for any man to arise against his prince, be he never so much a tyrant, 1 *Bec.* 219; it is impossible for traitors to escape, *ib.* 218; the people's proper remedy against evil princes, 1 *Tyn.* 196, 197, 336; what it is to honour the king, 1 *Bec.* 219; kings are to be prayed for, 1 *Lat.* 391, *Pil.* 434; their dues must be paid, 1 *Lat.* 307; paying the king his dues makes no man poorer, *ib.* 301, 513; fighting against the king's enemies is God's service, *ib.* 416, 496; princes are not to be trusted in, *Pil.* 231; suits to princes should be commended by prayer to God, *ib.* 308; not only is the king to be obeyed, but all his inferior magistrates, 1 *Hoop.* 101, 1 *Lat.* 373
— The king of Denmark styled himself king of England, 1 *Tyn.* 187, 2 *Tyn.* 334; kings of England (*v.* Defender, England, Supremacy); their alleged power to cure by means of cramp-rings, *Rid.* 500—503; the kings of France, being anointed, received the sacrament in both kinds, 1 *Jew.* 206; they were styled Most Christian, 1 *Tyn.* 186, 187 n., 2 *Tyn.* 263, 3 *Zur.* 683, and Eldest Son of the Holy See, 2 *Tyn.* 187 n.; Julius II. offered to transfer the last mentioned title to Henry VIII., *ib.*; king of Ireland, *q. v.*; the kings of Israel and Judah, see p. 455 above; the kings of Spain, not anointed, 4 *Jew.* 1037
Kings (The Books of): their contents, 2 *Cov.* 17; the first, otherwise the third book of Kings, by whom written, *Whita.* 301
Kings (The three): *v.* Magi.
Kings in the Apocalypse: seven, *Bale* 501; ten, *ib.* 505
King's book: *v.* Book, Doctrine.
King's college: *v.* Cambridge.
King's hall: *v.* Cambridge.
Kingsley (Sir Edw.): *v.* Kyngisley.
Kingsmill (Andr.): Latin letter to him, *Pil.* 679
Kingsmill (Dame Constance): and
Kingsmill (George), her son: *Pil.* xi.
Kingsmill (Sir Jo.): Alice his daughter married to bp Pilkington, *Pil.* iv, xi.
Kingsmill (Rich.): *Pil.* xi; one of the royal visitors for the North, 1 *Zur.* 73 n
Kingsmill (Sir Will.): *Pil.* xii.
Kingston-upon-Hull, co. York: the castle, *Grin.* 351

Kingston (Sir Ant.): notice of him, 3 *Zur.* 442 n.; his treacherous execution of Bray (or Boyer), 2 *Cran.* 187 n.; his cruelty, *ib.* 250 n.; his conduct when cited before bp Hooper, 2 *Hoop.* xxi; his interview with Hooper before his martyrdom, *ib.* xxv; he receives the order for execution, *ib.* xxvi.
Kingston (Sir Will.): notice of him, 1 *Tyn.* xxiii; constable of the Tower, 2 *Lat.* 411; letter to one Kyngeston, probably the same, 2 *Cran.* 250
Kington (West), co. Wilts: Latimer's benefice, 1 *Lat.* vi, 2 *Lat.* xv; styled by him his little bishoprick, 2 *Lat.* 328
Kinlochy (Patrick), minister of Linlithgow: 2 *Zur.* 365
Kinloss (Edw. abbot of): *v.* Bruce.
Kinnaston, co. Hereford: an earthquake or landslip there, *Lit. Eliz.* 569 n
Kinsale, Ireland: the Spaniards land there, 2 *Zur.* 335 n
Kinsfolk: included in the meaning of the fifth commandment, 1 *Bul.* 269; honour due to them, *ib.* 284
Kinwelmersh (Ant.): brother of the next, *Poet.* xxv.
Kinwelmersh (Fra.): notices of him, *Poet.* xxv, xxviii; verses by him; for Christmas day, *ib.* 291; for Whitsunday, *ib.* 292; all things are vain, *ib.* 293
Kirby (Monks'), co. Warwick: burial place of the Fieldings, 3 *Bec.* 89 n
Kirjath-jearim: 2 *Bul.* 148
Kirk (Jo.): Faith of Catholics, by Berington and him, 2 *Ful.* 282 n
Kirkaldy (Sir Will.) of Grange: one of the confederate lords, 1 *Zur.* 193 n., 198; queen Mary confers with him, *ib.* 195 n., 198; governor of Edinburgh castle, *ib.* 262; hanged at Edinburgh, with his brother and eleven goldsmiths, *ib.* 292 n
Kirkham (Walter de), bp of Durham: *Grin.* 399 n.; his (?) acts, *Pil.* 591
Kirkmen: ecclesiastics, *Pil.* 380
Kirton (Will.): witness to Grindal's will, *Grin.* 463
Kiss: the kiss of charity after the communion, 1 *Jew.* 265, *Whita.* 609; practised in the time of Justin Martyr, *Coop.* 81, 1 *Jew.* 265, 1 *Whitg.* 215; mentioned by Augustine, 1 *Jew.* 154; the practice abused and discontinued, 1 *Tyn.* 219; turned into kissing the pax (*q. v.*), 3 *Tyn.* 126; interrogatory about kissing the vestments, book, chalice, &c., 2 *Hoop.* 145; kissing the pope's foot, *v.* Pope.
Kitchen (Anth.), alias Dunstan, bp of Llandaff: mentioned, 1 *Zur.* 10 n.; he kept his

place through all changes of religion, 2 *Ful.* 118; the only bishop who retained his see on Elizabeth's accession, 4 *Jew.* 903, 908, *Phil.* xxxvi; his death, *Park.* 208 n
Kneeling: *v.* Prayer, Supper.
Knel (Joan), alias Bocher, *q. v.*
Knells: *v.* Bells.
Knewstub (Jo.): answers a Popish book, 3 *Ful.* 4
Knight (Sam.): Life of Colet, 1 *Lat.* 58 n
Knight (Tho.): letter to Bullinger, 3 *Zur.* 357; mentioned, *ib.* 676
Knightley (Sir Rich.): Elizabeth (Seymour) his wife, 1 *Bec.* 396 n., 3 *Zur.* 341 n
Knight-service: the archbishop's tenants by knight-service, *Park.* 388 n., 452
Knights: on winning spurs, 3 *Tyn.* 17 n.; what knighthood should be, *Bale* 21; the religious orders, *Bale* 505; THE CHRISTIAN KNIGHT, by T. Becon, 2 *Bec.* 620
— Knights of the Bath: 18 made at the coronation of Anne Boleyn, 2 *Cran.* 245
— Knights of the Garter, *q. v.*
— Knights of the Golden Fleece, *q. v.*
— Knights of the Round Table: *Calf.* 271
— Knights of St John: had much land in England, 1 *Tyn.* 236; their defence of Malta, *Lit. Eliz.* 460
— Knights Sword-bearers, in Livonia: 3 *Zur.* 687 n
— Knights (Teutonic): Luther's advice to them, 1 *Jew.* 217

— Knights of the Post: perjurers so called, *Rog.* 359
Knokes (Jo.): *v.* Knox.
Knollys (Sir Fra.), or Knowles: notice of him, 2 *Zur.* 54 n.; privy councillor to queen Elizabeth, *Grin.* 405, 408, 412, 417, 423, 427, 429, *Park.* 73, 75, 76, 77, 103, 106, 298, 357, 457 n., 1 *Zur.* 5 n.; vice-chamberlain, and a pious man, 2 *Zur.* 61, 62, 63; mourner at the funeral of the emperor Ferdinand, *Grin.* 32; sent to Carlisle to receive the queen of Scots, 1 *Zur.* 203 n., 204 n.; letter from him to Parker, *Park.* 96
—Cath. (Carey) his wife: verses from an epitaph on lady Knowles, by Tho. Newton, 1568, *Poet.* 553
Knollys (Hen.), or Knowles: queen Elizabeth's envoy in Germany, 2 *Zur.* 91 n.; Zanchius dedicates a book to him, *ib.* 110; he was sponsor to Zanchius' daughter, *ib.* 104, 112; letter to him, 2 *Zur.* 112; mentioned, *Park.* 333, 2 *Zur.* 271
Knonau (Gerold Meyer de): *v.* Meyer.
Knots: Trinity knots and St Katharine's knots, *Pil.* 80; injunction against wearing or praying upon beads or knots, *Grin.* 140
Knowle, co. Kent: 2 *Cran.* 297 n.; the archbishop's house there taken in exchange by the king, *ib.* 348 n
Knowledge: *v.* Prayers, Scripture, Word of God.
It is necessary for all degrees, *Hutch.* 1, 2; the means whereby God leadeth to it, *Sand.* 113; men's contempt of those means, *ib.*; both meditation and prayer are needful in order to it, *ib.* 114; God the only teacher of it, *ib.*; certain knowledge and clear knowledge are different, 2 *Lat.* 337; perfection to be sought, *Sand.* 424; knowledge should be practical, 1 *Hoop.* 152; the old saying declares that it is no burden, but to put it in experience, is painful, 2 *Hoop.* 347; knowledge without zeal is blameable, 2 *Lat.* 337; knowledge of ourselves, how attained, 1 *Hoop.* 88, 89; it makes us fly to God, 1 *Bec.* 42; leads to Christ, *ib.* 50, 145; its necessity, *ib.* 69, 83; it is the beginning of wisdom, *ib.* 194; knowledge of ourselves, and of God, would lead us to ascribe all the glory of creation, &c. to God, *ib.* 338; worldly knowledge, without that of the gospel, hinders rather than profits, 2 *Bec.* 350; it puffeth up, or maketh proud, 2 *Jew.* 680, 1 *Lat.* 230; the devil exceeds all men in knowledge, *Whita.* 613; knowledge of one another after this life, proof that we shall have it, 3 *Bec.* 152, &c.; the heathen doubted not of this, *ib.* 154; the word "knowledge" used in Tyndale's New Testament instead of confession, 3 *Tyn.* 22; the word used for acknowledge, 1 *Tyn.* xxvii, 57
Knowles (Sir Fra.): *v.* Knollys.
Knox (Jo.): *v.* Book of Common Order.
Called Knokes, *Calf.* 50, 2 *Ful.* 121; chaplain to king Edward VI., 2 *Brad.* xxvi; his account of Bradford's preaching before that prince, 1 *Brad.* 111, 2 *Brad.* xxviii; possibly he was chaplain to the duke of Northumberland, 3 *Zur.* 591 n.; the Articles submitted to him, 2 *Cran.* xi; he disliked the Common Prayer, *Rid.* 533; was opposed to kneeling at the Lord's supper, 3 *Zur.* 591 n.; his preaching in England, *Rid.* 59, 3 *Zur.* 760 n.; an exile, 1 *Cran.* (9); at Frankfort, *Jew.* xii; sent away therefrom, *ib.* xiii, 3 *Zur.* 760; pastor at Geneva, 3 *Zur.* 769 n.; a galley slave three years, 2 *Ful.* 121; his return to Scotland, 1 *Zur.* 39; his banishment proclaimed by sound of horn, *ib.* 24, 4 *Jew.* 1209, 1210; he preaches in the Scots' camp,

1 *Zur.* 60; his turbulent reformation, *Park.* 105; he declaims against idolatry, 1 *Zur.* 150; letter from him and others to archbishops Parker and Young, *Park.* 205; he signs a letter to Beza approving of the Helvetic confession, 2 *Zur.* 362, 364; again banished from Edinburgh, 1 *Zur.* 167, 170; he returns to his church there, *ib.* 198; his Admonition of Christians, *Jew.* xiii; the substance of it preached in Bucks, 3 *Zur.* 760 n.; he published, in 1556, his First Blast against the monstrous Regiment and Empire of Women, 4 *Jew.* 664 n., *Park.* 61 n., 2 *Zur.* 34 n.; in it he says a woman's government is a monstriferous empire, most detestable and damnable, *Rog.* 338 n., and declares that to keep the oath of allegiance made to women governors is nothing but plain rebellion against God, *ib.* 361; the book answered by bishop Aylmer, 2 *Ful.* 37 n., *Rog.* 338, 2 *Zur.* 34 n.; Bullinger's answer to queries by him (or more probably Goodman) on civil government, 3 *Zur.* 745

Kocher (......): Bibl. Theol. Symbolicæ, 3 *Zur.* 513 n

Kohath: his life, 1 *Bul.* 41

Kohathites: their service, 2 *Bul.* 132, 142

König (Geo. Matthias): *Calf.* 285 n

Korah: consumed by fire, together with Dathan and Abiram, whilst offering incense, 2 *Bul.* 131, 4 *Bul.* 11, 2 *Hoop.* 321, *Pil* 28, 360, 482, 624, *Sand.* 138; mass-priests his followers, 2 *Brad.* 329

Koran: *v.* Mahomet.

Kortholt (Christian.): Disquisitiones anti-Baronianæ, 2 *Ful.* 44 n

Krantz (Albert): Rerum Germ. Hist. Saxon., *Jew.* xxxix; he mentions popes who poisoned one another, *Pil.* 247; relates that pope Gregory VII. stirred up Rodolphus against the emperor Henry IV., 2 *Hoop.* 239; reports that Boniface VIII. affirmed that the power of both swords was in him alone, 4 *Jew.* 1135

Krasinski (......): Reformation in Poland, 3 *Zur.* 513, 689, 690 nn.; correction of a statement in it, *ib.* 596

Kraus (Dr): despaired of salvation, *Rog.* 142

Kydder (Jo.): 2 *Cran.* 253

Kyffin (Howell), doctor of canon law: *Bale* 28

Kyme (......), husband to Anne Askewe: *Bale* 198, 199.

Kyng (Geo.): died in prison, *Poet.* 164

Kyngeston (......): *v.* Kingston (Sir Will.)

Kyngisley (Sir Edw.): 2 *Cran.* 316

Kyrie eleeson: 2 *Brad.* 307, *Pil.* 503, 1 *Tyn.* 305

L

LABARUM: the imperial standard of the Romans, 2 *Ful.* 140, 148, 2 *Jew.* 648, 650, 651

Labbe (Phil.): 1 *Bec.* 6, 109, 337, 384, 2 *Bec.* 60, 71, 244, 245, 253, 259, 260, 264, 266, 295, 3 *Bec.* 267, 275, 373, 414, 415, 416, 417, 433, 455, 2 *Ful.* 23 nn.; an error respecting the acts of the 2nd Nicene council, *Calf.* 138 n

Labeo: *Jew.* xxxix.

Labour: *v.* Work.

Labourers: *v.* Artificers, Prayers, Vineyard. Their duty, 2 *Bec.* 115; their hire, 2 *Bul.* 37; their idleness, *Pil.* 446; those who do their work negligently are thieves, 2 *Bec.* 106, 107

Lacedemonians: their valour, 4 *Jew.* 1121; their law for training up their children, 1 *Bec.* 398; no images allowed in their council-chamber, *Park.* 85; the affection of a woman of Lacedemon to her country, 1 *Bec.* 234

Lacells (Jo.): *v.* Lascells.

Lacius (......): translator into Latin of a work by Calvin, 1 *Cov.* 422

Lack-Latin: a name applied to unlearned priests, 2 *Jew.* 1000, 1 *Lat.* 304 (and see Sir John).

Lactantius (L. C. F.): Opera, *Calf.* 411, *Jew.* xxxix; his book de Ira Dei, *Pil.* 477, 2 *Zur.* 233; the treatise De Mortibus Persecutorum, perhaps by Lucius Cecilius, *Calf.* 105 n., 2 *Ful.* 336; it is the source of an extraordinary error, 2 *Ful.* 336 n.; the verses ascribed to him De Passione Domini, fictitious, *Calf.* 180, &c., 375, 2 *Ful.* 156, 206; the Carmen de Resurrectione Domini, 1 *Hoop.* 46; his works reckoned as apocryphal in some copies of the Gelasian decree, *Calf.* 181; he exhorts to worship the living God and live, *Calf.* 344; passages on the anger of God, 3 *Zur.* 233; he speaks of God's vengeance long delayed, 1 *Lat.* 106; says, we are born that we may do to God just and due service, that we should know him alone and follow him, 3 *Bul.* 231; declares that in the knowledge of God and his service consists all the hope and salvation of man, *ib.* 225; affirms that by the soul we live, and that with the mind we understand, *ib.* 367; denies that man can attain to the reason and nature of the soul, *ib.* 368; shews that men are to be loved because they are men, 1 *Bul.* 185; expatiates on the workmanship of God in the frame of man, 3 *Bul.* 151, 1 *Hoop.* 86; refers to his upright posture, *Calf.* 25, 26; says some tumble on the earth, and regret that they were not born four-footed beasts, *ib.* 341, 342; says the nature of man seems to wish to sin, not only with excuse, but even with reason, 2 *Jew.* 608; says sins ought to be abolished by perpetual almsgiving, 3 *Zur.* 233; enumerates various works of mercy, 1 *Bul.* 185, 191; explains what patience is, 2 *Bul.* 85; states that God is pacified by the mending of our manners, *Sand.* 157; teaches that good deeds will be weighed with evil ones, 3 *Zur.* 233; speaks of degrees of virtue amongst heathen men, *Wool.* 48; writes of the first day, 1 *Hoop.* 342; refers to the blood on the door posts, 2 *Ful.* 142; expounds the meaning of circumcision, 2 *Bul.* 177; teaches that figures are vain and serve to no purpose, when the things signified by them are present, 1 *Cran.* 288, 297; says, it is only the catholic church which retains true religion, and out of this there is no salvation, 4 *Bul.* 52; calls every bishoprick the chief priesthood, 1 *Jew.* 373, 3 *Jew.* 315; is a witness against Romish rites, *Phil.* 390; says silent rites were devised by crafty men, that the people might not know what they worshipped, 2 *Jew.* 704, 813; explains what superstition is, 3 *Bul.* 232, 233; condemns the heathen practice of lighting candles in the day time, *Calf.* 302—304; asks whether he is to be thought in his wits who offers candles and tapers to the author and giver of light, 4 *Bul.* 502, *Calf.* 303, 3 *Jew.* 178; says, if any man think that apparel, precious stones, or other like things that we have in estimation, are pleasant or delectable unto God, undoubtedly he knoweth not what God is, 3 *Jew.* 615; shews, by the example of Canaan, that ignorance of God is the primary cause of idolatry, 1 *Hoop.* 318; reproves the use of images, 2 *Bec.* 61; how he uses the word "simulacrum," *Calf.* 40, 1 *Ful.* 102, 104; asks, is any man so foolish as to think that there is anything of God in an image? *Calf.* 341; condemns images as earthly, and therefore void of religion, *ib.* 183; advises to condemn and despise the earth, i. e. not to worship images, *ib.* 342; says it is a perverse and absurd thing that the image of a man should be worshipped by the image of God, 3 *Bul.* 197, 198 ; declares that the Gentiles make images because they fear their religion would be void, if they did not see what they adore, *Calf.* 40, 2 *Jew.* 646; exclaims, what madness it is either to make those things which they afterwards fear, or to fear what they

have framed! and replies to the objection that images represent unseen beings, *Calf.* 374, 2 *Jew.* 664; declares, without doubt, that where an image is there is no religion, 2 *Bec.* 61, 65, 69, *Calf.* 25, 1 *Hoop.* 43, 46, 2 *Jew.* 659, *Park.* 86, *Rid.* 89 ; says that if idolaters deck images, much more should we deck the images of the living God, i. e. give alms to Christians, *Wool.* 138; maintains some strange opinions respecting angels, 3 *Zur.* 233; says they are not willing to be called gods, since their office is to attend upon God with their service, and do nothing but his commandments, 3 *Bul.* 344, 345; declares that they will have no honour given unto them, all their honour being in God; but that those who fell, challenge to themselves the name and worship of gods, *ib.* 346; speaks of a certain perverse power always opposed to the truth, and taking pleasure in man's error, *Calf.* 25; considers that evil spirits insinuate themselves into men's bodies, and vex their minds that they may run to them for help, &c., 2 *Cran.* 41; says that they work miracles through which men give to images the faith of the godhead, *ib.*; affirms that devils are chased by the name of Christ and the sign of his passion, *Calf.* 83, 2 *Ful.* 142, 144; says that if, at sacrifice to idols, any one stands by who has his forehead signed, the wizard cannot give answer, *Calf.* 91; reproves superstitious honour of the dead, *ib.* 310, 2 *Ful.* 187; says the rude sort suppose that men's spirits wander about their tombs, 2 *Cran.* 43; declares that evil spirits assume the names of dead men, *ib.* 41; maintains that the righteous will rise and reign 1000 years before the last judgment, *Coop.* 147, 3 *Zur.* 233, 234; deems it unlawful for a Christian to go to war, or to accuse any one of a capital crime, *Rog.* 351; disallows the use of flowers and perfumes, 3 *Zur.* 233; says Mercurius (or Thoth) slew Argus who had so many eyes, and then fled into Egypt, 2 *Bul.* 218; writes of the knavery of Minos, *Calf.* 13 n., mentions Carneades, 4 *Jew.* 1103; referred to for an account of the miserable end of Maximian, 2 *Bul.* 80; states the use of eloquence, 2 *Jew.* 983; says, our words once uttered dissolve into air; but let them be put once in writing, and for the most part they remain unto all succeeding ages, 4 *Jew.* 1314; refers to the speech of animals, 1 *Jew.* 263; his errors, *Calf.* 180, 3 *Zur.* 233

Lacy (Alex.): printer, *Grin.* 477, 478 n
Lacy (Edw.): servant to Edm. Cranmer, 2 *Cran.* 301
Ladies: *v.* Gentlewomen.
Ladislaus, king of Hungary: slain, *Lit. Eliz.* 454
Lady (Our): *v.* Mary (B. V.)
Lady-fast: what, 2 *Tyn.* 98
Lady psalter: *v.* Psalms.
Lælius (......): 1 *Zur.* 72
Lælius Tiphernas: 2 *Ful.* 110 n
Læta: 4 *Bul.* 199, 392
Lætus (Erasm.), a divine of Copenhagen: 2 *Zur.* 226
La Ferte (M. le baron de): hostage for the French king, *Park.* 172
La Fontaine (Nic. de): prosecutor of Servetus, 3 *Zur.* 622 n
La Haye (Mons. de): *Park.* 170
Laity, or Laymen: *v.* Image of God, Images, Ministers, Parishioners, Prebendaries.
 They are the church as well as the priests, 3 *Tyn.* 158; lay people are members of Christ's church, for whose salvation he shed his blood as well as for that of the clergy, 2 *Bec.* 241; they have as large a share in God's love and covenant as ecclesiastics, 1 *Tyn.* 258; their interference in religion justified by the example of David and others, *Pil.* 625, &c.; they should not minister the sacraments in the congregation, *Rog.* 234; a layman remits sin, 3 *Jew.* 356, 357; the covetousness of temporal men, 2 *Bec.* 432, 587; they swallow up spiritual benefices, 1 *Lat.* 317; the Canon Law says they may not be judges of the clergy, 2 *Cran.* 72, 73, 1 *Tyn.* 178, 240, 2 *Tyn.* 272; nor meddle with their election, 2 *Cran.* 72, 167; nor impose any taxes upon them, *ib.*; nor have benefices to farm, *ib.*; laymen were of old permitted to preach, 1 *Whitg.* 453, 2 *Whitg.* 531; they may preach in infidel lands, 2 *Cran.* 117; many are able and willing to fill the place of bishops, 1 *Lat.* 122; laymen preached at Bristol, c. 1534, 2 *Cran.* 308 n.; ordered not to minister sacraments, &c., *Grin.* 122, nor to perform divine service unless tolerated by the ordinary in writing, *ib.*, and see 161; they should not be ignorant of the gospel, 2 *Tyn.* 35; profit of the scriptures being read by them, 3 *Bec.* 542, &c.; a layman alleging scripture, to be believed against a whole council, *Pil.* 532; they are not necessarily inferior in knowledge to the clergy, 1 *Tyn.* 241; if they are too ignorant to judge, blame is due to the clergy, *ib.*; not all children of the devil, 1 *Lat.* 43; Whitaker, after several fathers, supposes that "the place of the unlearned" (1 Cor. xiv. 16) means the place assigned to the laity, *Whita.* 260; clerical offenders were of old reduced to lay communion, *Coop.* 159; laymen kept in superstitious fear by Antichrist, 1 *Tyn.* 224; entreated to have forged sacrifices, 2 *Lat.* 259; they are not to be discouraged from reading good books, *ib.* 241, 244; injunctions for the laity, *Grin.* 132; how they should behave themselves, 1 *Bec.* 257; they should reverence bishops and ministers, *ib.* 261

Lake (Dr): Grindal's commissary, *Grin.* 428, 430 n
Laken: *v.* Luke.
Laker (Roger): *Hutch.* x.
Lakin (Dr), prebendary of Wistow: enjoined to view the statutes of the church of York, *Grin.* 151
Lakin (Tho.): in exile at Strasburgh (perhaps the same), 2 *Zur.* 20 n
Lamb: *v.* Christ, iv., Passover.
 A type of Christ, 2 *Bul.* 183; anciently used as a typical representation of our Lord, *Calf.* 137 n
Lamb (Jo.): Hist. Acc. of the XXXIX. Articles, *Lit. Edw.* xi, xii, nn.; Collection of Letters, 1 *Lat.* v, 2 *Lat.* 356, 378
Lambard (Will.): Dict. Angl., 1 *Lat.* 476 n.; De priscis Anglorum Legibus, *Calf.* 53 n., 2 *Ful.* 22 n.; Parker sends his Perambulation of Kent, not then published, to lord Burghley, *Park.* 424, 441
Lambert (St), his legend referred to: 1 *Ful.* 572
Lambert of Schaffnaburg: De Rebus Germ., *Jew.* xxxix; referred to, 3 *Jew.* 129, 347, 4 *Jew.* 648, 698
Lambert (Franc.): account of him, *Bale* 283 n.; he wrote on the Apocalypse, *ib.* 258; his opinion on the seven angels with the plagues, *ib.* 470
Lambert (Jo.), alias Nicholson: praises the Unio Dissidentium, 3 *Tyn.* 187 n.; his examination, 1 *Lat.* x. (corrected 2 *Lat.* xxxii.); judged by the king in person, 2 *Cran.* 219 n., 3 *Zur.* 201; Cranmer concerned in his condemnation, 1 *Cran.* xxix; his martyrdom, *Bale* 394, 1 *Brad.* 283, 288, 2 *Cran.* ix, 219, 3 *Zur.* 201
Lambeth, co. Surrey: smoky atmosphere and sickness there, 2 *Cran.* 338; the archbishop's palace, 1 *Cran.* xii, xiv; Gardiner there, *ib.* 182; card. Pole sets up the figure Y [doubtless the archiepiscopal pall]

in some windows there, *Calf.* 105; queen Elizabeth dines there, *Park.* 120; conference in the chapel respecting the vestments, *ib.* 268—270; the burial and monument of abp Parker, *ib.* xi; the Lambeth articles, *Whita.* x; Grindal's gift to the poor of Lambeth, *Grin.* 460; bishop Thirlby buried there, 2 *Zur.* 181 n.; the Norfolk chapel in Lambeth church, *Park.* x, 369, 484; Lambeth bridge, i. e. landing-place, *ib.* 311; watermen there, 1 *Lat.* 205; martyrdoms in St George's fields, *Poet.* 169

Lambley, co. Northumberland: the nunnery, 1 *Tyn.* xv. n

Lamentations: *v.* Jeremiah, Youth.

A PITEOUS LAMENTATION OF THE MISERABLE ESTATE OF THE CHURCH IN ENGLAND, by bishop Ridley, *Rid.* 47, &c.; the lamentation of a sinner; from the Old Version of the Psalms, *Poet.* 473; note thereon, *Pra. Eliz.* 374 n.; stanzas from the Lamentation of the Lost Sheep, by G. Ellis, *Poet.* 408

Lamoral (......), count of Egmont: executed at Brussels, 1 *Zur.* 204; some account of him, *ib.* n

Lampatians: say that men shall be saved by following any religion they have a mind to, *Rog.* 160

Lampridius (Ælius): speaks of the emperor Adrian granting the Christians one church in Rome, 4 *Jew.* 892; speaks of certain Roman emperors having in their oratories images of Moses, Christ, &c., 2 *Jew.* 646, 4 *Jew.* 1108 n.; on the golden rule of Alexander Severus, 1 *Bul.* 197; he mentions a Druidess warning that emperor of his death, 1 *Jew.* 297; speaks of the election of Christian bishops, 4 *Bul.* 135, 136

Lamps: *v.* Lights.

Lampugnan (Andr.): struck the image of the duke of Milan, *Calf.* 338, 339

Lancashire: Bradford's labours there, 2 *Brad.* xxvi, xxvii; his farewell to Lancashire, especially to Manchester, 1 *Brad.* 448; condition of the clergy in the time of Elizabeth, *Park.* 221, *Pil.* vii.

Lancaster (Tho.), abp of Armagh: chancellor of Sarum, and Jewel's proxy for his enthronization, *Jew.* xv; allowed, for the poverty of his see, to hold his English preferments in commendam, *ib.* 1274 n; mentioned in Jewel's will, *ib.* xxv; being archbishop elect he ordains ministers at Salisbury, and Jewel writes to archbishop Parker begging him to stay him from so doing, *ib.* 1274

Lancea sacra: 2 *Jew.* 585

Lances: abp Parker's poor lances at York, *Park.* 388

Landaff: *v.* Llandaff.

Landbeach, co. Cambridge: *Park.* vii, viii, 481, 482

Landlords: *v.* Commons, Gentlemen, Prayers, Sheep, Tenants.

Their duty, 1 *Bec.* 256, 2 *Bec.* 115, 1 *Tyn.* 201; accumulation of lands condemned, 2 *Cran.* 196, 1 *Lat.* 278, 279; landlords should be peace-makers, 1 *Lat.* 486

Landulphus Sagax: confounded with Eutropius, *Calf.* 71, 138, 176 nn. *Park.* 92

Lane (Jo.): at Oxford, 2 *Cran.* 382

Lane (Mr), of Westchester: exorcises a maid, 2 *Ful.* 76

Lanfranc, abp of Canterbury: De Euch. Sacram., *Jew.* xxxix; he was one of the inventors of transubstantiation, 1 *Hoop.* 117, 124, *Pil.* 573, 588; writes on the sacrament against Berengarius, 1 *Hoop.* 117, 118, 1 *Jew.* 458, 3 *Jew.* 215, 505; procures the condemnation of Berengarius as a heretic, 1 *Hoop.* 124, 524; claims supremacy for Peter, 1 *Lat.* 209; speaks of St Elphege, *Bale* 191; writes on heresy, *ib.* 217; the clergy were married in his time, *Pil.* 571; his decree in the synod of Winchester respecting sacerdotal celibacy, 2 *Ful.* 23, 93; mention of him, 4 *Jew.* 783

Langdale (Alban): one of the Romish disputants at Cambridge, *Grin.* 194, *Rid.* 169; one of the disputants at Westminster, 1 *Zur.* 11 n

Langdon (Jo.), monk of Canterbury: *Bale* 16

Langhern (Rich.), letter signed by him: 3 *Zur.* 170; ordained by Grindal, *ib.* n

Langrige (Peter): in prison for nonconformity, *Park.* 103

Langside, near Glasgow: battle there, 1 *Zur.* 203 n., 205, 218 n.; queen Mary's thorn there, *ib.* 206 n

Langton (Steph.), abp of Canterbury: interdicts the realm, 2 *Tyn.* 295

Langton (Tho.): a supervisor of Pilkington's testament, *Pil.* xi.

Languages: *v.* Tongues.

Languet (Hubert): account of him, 2 *Zur.* 289 n.; letter from him to P. Hubner, *ib.* 309; letters to him, *ib.* 289, 296, 300

Lanquet (Tho.): his Chronicle, *Coop.* xi.

Lanscade (Chr.): 2 *Zur.* 239, 276, 281, 285

Lanspergius (Jo.), Carthusian: prayers from his Pharetra Divini Amoris, *Pra. Eliz.* 380, 381

Lantern: the prison of Lantern, *Bale* 122
Lantschadius (Chr.): *v.* Lanscade.
Laodicea: *v.* Councils.
The apocalyptic epistle to the church, *Bale* 292; the apocryphal epistle, *v.* Paul.
Lap: to secure, 2 *Bec.* 626
Lardner (Nath.): 2 *Cov.* 348 n
Large (Edw.): in exile, 1 *Cran.* (9)
Large (Sir): a poor priest (possibly the same), 2 *Lat.* 383, 384
Larroquanus (Matt.): Adversaria Sacra, 2 *Ful.* 371 n
Lascells (Jo.): Anne Askewe's answer to his letter, *Bale* 228; martyred in Smithfield, *Bale* 138, 142, 243, 1 *Brad*, 283, 288, 3 *Zur.* 41 n
Lascells (Jos.): martyred, 2 *Hoop.* 376 (the same?)
Lasco (Jo. à): a baron of Poland, 1 *Lat.* 141, 3 *Zur.* 578; notices of him, *Grin.* 254 n., 3 *Zur.* 187 n., 262, 483 n., 560 n.; Cranmer's letter inviting him over to give his advice in the reformation of religion, 2 *Cran.* 420, 421, 3 *Zur.* 17 n.; his arrival in England, 3 *Zur.* 483, 560; resident here, 2 *Cran.* 421 n., 425, 426, 3 *Zur.* 187 n.; his friendship with Cranmer, *ib.* 22, 187 n., 383, 483; first minister of the foreigners' church in Austin Friars, London, *Grin.* 254 n.; superintendent of the foreign church in London, 3 *Zur.* 483; chief pastor of the foreign congregations in England, *Rid.* 535; he was opposed to clerical vestments, 1 *Zur.* 161; the reason he assigns for sitting at the communion, 3 *Whitg.* 94; his intercourse with Hooper, 2 *Hoop.* ix; he encourages him in opposition to the vestments, *ib.* xiv, 3 *Zur.* 95; disputes with Bucer about the eucharist, 3 *Zur.* 572; a commissioner for the reform of the canon law, *ib.* 503, 590; he departs from England for a time, 1 *Lat.* 141, 3 *Zur.* 61, 187 n., 483 n.; on Mary's accession he again quits England, embarking at Gravesend, with many of his flock, 3 *Zur.* 512 n.; his reception in Denmark, *ib.*; at Frankfort, *ib.* 131; dangerously ill there, *ib.* 516; he visits Poland, *ib.* 592; his interview with king Sigismund, *ib.* 596; how honoured by that prince, *ib.* 599; he labours in Poland, *ib.* 687, 688, 690, 693, 694, 696, 697, 702; instructs the nobles there, *ib.* 688; preaches at Wilna, *ib.* 600; his Brevis et dilucida de Sacramentis eccl. Christi Tractatio, *ib.* 578; Forma ac Ratio tota ecclesiastici Ministerii, in Peregr., potissimum vero Germ., Ecclesia, instituta Londini, 3 *Whitg.* xxix; letters to him, 2 *Hoop.* ix n., 3 *Zur.* 16, 101; Bucer writes to him, 2 *Whitg.* 38, 55, 57
— His second marriage, 3 *Zur.* 581; his daughter, *ib.* 599
Lashford (Joan), alias Warne, *q. v.*
Lashing: lavishing, 2 *Bec.* 108
Lassels (Jo.): *v.* Lascells.
Last times: *v.* World.
Latched: caught, 2 *Whitg.* 53
Lateran: *v.* Councils.
Latham (R.), fellow of Merton college: *Park.* 308, 326
Latimer (Hugh), father of the bishop: 1 *Lat.* i, 101, 197, 2 *Lat.* ix.
LATIMER (Hugh), bp of Worcester: memoir of him, 1 *Lat.* i; his life and acts, from Foxe, 2 *Lat.* ix; Bernher's account of him, 1 *Lat.* 319; his birth and parentage, *ib.* i, 101, 2 *Lat.* ix; his father taught him to shoot, 1 *Lat.* 197; he goes to Cambridge, *ib.* i. n., ii, 2 *Lat.* ix; ordained at Lincoln, 1 *Lat.* 298; his superstition and ignorance, 2 *Lat.* 332, 333, 348; how scrupulous he was in saying mass, 1 *Lat.* 138; when sick he often wished to be a friar, 2 *Lat.* 332; believed that images could help, *ib.* 333; his conversion, 1 *Lat.* ii, 2 *Lat.* x, 137; Morice's account of it, 2 *Lat.* xxvii; Bilney's confession the cause of it, 1 *Lat.* 334, 2 *Lat.* x, *Rid.* 118; his friendship with Bilney, 1 *Lat.* i, ii, 222, 334, 2 *Lat.* xiii, 52; his commendation of Bilney, 2 *Lat.* 330; his preaching at Cambridge, &c., 1 *Bec.* vii, viii, ix; he is godfather to a child born in prison, 1 *Lat.* 335; the bishop of Ely forbids his preaching; he preaches in the church of the Austin Friars at Cambridge; his opponents complain to Wolsey, 1 *Lat.* iii, 2 *Lat.* xi, xiv, xxix; one of the Cambridge divines appointed to consider the question of the king's marriage, 1 *Lat.* v, 2 *Lat.* xv, 340 n.; he first preaches before the king at Windsor, 1 *Lat.* v, 2 *Lat.* xiii; Latimer justified from Wharton's charge of subscribing the declaration that it was not necessary that the people should have the scriptures in English, 1 *Tyn.* 35; he writes to the king pleading for the restoration of the liberty of reading the word of God, 1 *Lat.* vi; his letter, 2 *Lat.* 297; thankful for the king's sanction of its use (conceded some years afterwards), 2 *Cran.* 346, 1 *Tyn.* lxxvi; made a royal chaplain, 1 *Lat.* vi; presented to the church of West Kington, *ib.*; letter to him there, 2 *Cran.* 296; cited to appear before the bishop of London, 1 *Lat.* vii, 2 *Lat.* xvi, 219, 323, 334 n.; articles to which he was required to subscribe,

2 *Lat.* 218; another copy, *ib.* 219; the Latin copy, *ib.* 466; he appeals to his own ordinary, is excommunicated and imprisoned, 1 *Lat.* vii, 2 *Lat.* xvi; appeals to the king, is absolved, but nevertheless inhibited in the diocese of London, 2 *Cran.* 308 n., 1 *Lat.* viii; he visits Bainham in Newgate, 2 *Lat.* 222; his preaching at Bristol, and the disturbance made thereby, 2 *Cran.* 308 n., 1 *Lat.* viii, 2 *Lat.* 225 n., 358; articles imputed to him by Dr Powell of Salisbury, 2 *Lat.* 225; he answers them, *ib.* 225, 358; appointed to preach before king Henry, 2 *Cran.* 308, 309; called a seditious fellow, and accused to the king as such, 1 *Lat.* 134; his answer to the king, *ib.* 135; favoured by Cranmer; made bishop of Worcester, 1 *Lat.* ix, 2 *Lat.* xviii; he writes to Cranmer, to urge him on in the king's cause against the pope, 2 *Cran.* 314; his arguments against purgatory with king Henry's answers, 2 *Lat.* 245; he subscribes a declaration about a general council, 2 *Cran.* 468; gives injunctions to the prior and convent of Worcester, and to his diocese, 1 *Lat.* x, 2 *Lat.* 240, 242; takes cognizance of Crewkehorne and Lambert, 1 *Lat.* x; preaches at the execution of friar Forest, 2 *Cran.* 366 n., 1 *Lat.* xi, 2 *Lat.* 392; he exposes the imposture called the blood of Hales, 1 *Hoop.* 41, 1 *Lat.* xi, 2 *Lat.* 407; exposes images at St Paul's, 3 *Zur.* 607; gives an account of his income as bishop, 2 *Lat.* 412; opposes the Six Articles, resigns his bishoprick, and is placed in ward, *Bale* 510, 1 *Lat.* xi, 135 n., 319, 2 *Lat.* xx, 3 *Zur.* 204 n., 215; thanks God that he became a quondam honestly, 1 *Lat.* 154; examined before the council, *ib.* 276; his answer on transubstantiation, *ib.*; the subtle manner of his examination before the bishops, *ib.* 294; committed to the Tower, 1 *Lat.* xii, 162, 163, 2 *Lat.* 258; on king Edward's accession he declines to take his former bishoprick, 1 *Lat.* xii, 3 *Zur.* 330, and, as it seems, another, 3 *Zur.* 465; resides with Cranmer at Lambeth, 3 *Zur.* 330; much troubled with poor men's suits, 1 *Lat.* 127; his faithful preaching and character, 2 *Bec.* 424, 425, 426, *Pil.* 427, 461, 462, *Rid.* 59; his exhortation to restitution, and its effect on Bradford, 1 *Brad.* 32, 2 *Brad.* xiv—xvi, 1, 2 n., 5, 11, 12; mentioned by Bradford, 2 *Brad.* 34; called the apostle of England, *Rid.* 99; his manner of teaching, 1 *Lat.* 341; his diligence in preaching, *ib.* 320, and in prayer, *ib.* 322; a bishop angry with him for his preaching,

ib. 154; he has to give place to Robin Hood's men, *ib.* 208; was a true prophet, *ib.* 92; foretold the troubles that occurred in queen Mary's time, 1 *Lat.* 320, 2 *Lat.* xxi; his ultimum vale, or last sermon before king Edward, 1 *Lat.* 237, 243, 252, 257; on Mary's accession he is summoned before the council, 3 *Zur.* 371 n.; his conduct and behaviour there, 1 *Lat.* 321; sent to the Tower, 2 *Brad.* 74 n., 1 *Lat.* xiii, 2 *Lat.* xxii; here he studies the New Testament, with Cranmer, Ridley, and Bradford, 2 *Brad.* xxxiii, 2 *Lat.* 259; sent from the Tower, together with Cranmer and Ridley, to Oxford, 1 *Cran.* 391, 1 *Lat.* xiii, 2 *Lat.* xxiii, 3 *Zur.* 515, where he disputes with Smith and others, 1 *Brad.* 494, 2 *Cran.* 445, 2 *Hoop.* 593, 2 *Lat.* 250—278, (479—494); Dr Weston takes part in the disputation, 2 *Lat.* 262; the record of it, *Park.* 160; his ignominious treatment at the disputation, 2 *Hoop.* 401; his imprisonment, and his treatment in it, 1 *Brad.* 445, 2 *Lat.* 256, 265, 284, 3 *Zur.* 505; his conferences with Ridley, during their imprisonment, *Rid.* 97, &c.; in peril of death, 1 *Brad.* 290; his prayers for himself, for the church of England, for the lady Elizabeth, *Rog.* 5; his examination before the commissioners, 2 *Lat.* 278—293, *Rid.* 255; his dress on that occasion, 2 *Lat.* 279; his last appearance before the commissioners, *ib.* 289; infamous character of his judges, 1 *Zur.* 12; he is excommunicated, committed to Bocardo, and condemned, 1 *Lat.* xiii, 323; condemned, at first, illegally, 2 *Cran.* 446 n.; ready to die, 1 *Brad.* 410, 1 *Lat.* 164; his martyrdom with Ridley, 1 *Lat.* xiii, 323, 2 *Lat.* xxiv, *Poet.* 165, *Rid.* 293—299, 3 *Zur.* 143 n., 154, 301, 751; his poor attire at his burning, *Rid.* 293; his last prayers, *ib.* 297; lamentation of the people on his death, *ib.* 299; Ridley's exalted opinion of him, 2 *Brad.* 372; his alleged dependence on Cranmer, *Rid.* 283; his memory reviled by Bonner, *Phil.* 129

His WORKS, edited by the Rev. Geo. Elwes Corrie, B.D., Norrisian professor of divinity, [now D.D. and master of Jesus college], 1, 2 *Lat.*; list of his works, 1 *Lat.* xiv; references to his sermons, 3 *Bec.* 280 n., *Calf.* 9, 47, 52, 154; his letters, 2 *Lat.* 295 —444, (467—478); a letter to Parker, *Park.* v; part of a letter respecting the Institution of a Christen Man, 2 *Cran.* 337 n.; extract from a letter to Cromwell, *ib.* 338 n.; a letter by him, or perhaps by Bradford, 2 *Brad.* 45, 2 *Lat.* 435; reference to his letter to Mrs Wilkinson, 2 *Brad.* 39 n.; letters to him, 2 *Brad.* 169, 190, 406, 2 *Cran.* 296, 308 (?), *Rid.* 361; in 1532 he allowed the use of images, pilgrimages, praying to saints, and the remembrance of souls in purgatory, 2 *Lat.* 353; afterwards argued against purgatory, *ib.* 245; stood forward (1540) in defence of justification by faith alone, 3 *Zur.* 617; his views on the eucharist, *ib.* 320, 322; his arguments against the sacrifice of the mass, *Rid.* 110; he maintained that Christ descended into the place of torment, 1 *Ful.* 284, 1 *Lat.* 234, 1 *Whitg.* 29 n.; spoke of strawberry preachers, 2 *Brad.* 9 n., 3 *Whitg.* 5; his saying respecting watchmen, *Park.* 353

Latimer (Jo. lord): *v.* Neville.

Latimer (Will.): witness against Bonner, 3 *Zur.* 660 n

Latin tongue: *v.* Prayer.

Its alleged majesty, *Whita.* 251; Cicero's Latinity, 4 *Jew.* 861, *Now.* i*, ii*, 97, &c.; vocabulary of Christian forms of speech in the Latin tongue, *Now.* 99; it was well known in early Christian times in Africa, 1 *Jew.* 56, 297, *Whita.* 224, and in the West, *ib.* 225; now a dead language, *ib.* 227; the Latin of the middle ages, 4 *Jew.* 861; examples of barbarous Latin, 1 *Jew.* 316; true Latin opposed by the Scotists, 3 *Tyn.* 75; why Latin is used by Papists, 2 *Hoop.* 392; absurd legends in the church-service, 2 *Cran.* 180; the priests speaking Latin are thought of the people to be marvellous well learned, *Rid.* 109; the tongue not understood by teachers of grammar in Tyndale's youth, 3 *Tyn.* 55; nor by certain lay lords in queen Mary's time, *Phil.* 56; Latin English, 1 *Cran.* 309, 310

Latinus (Λατεῖνος): *v.* Antichrist.

Latomus (Barth.): Adv. M. Bucer. Defens., *Jew.* xxxix; he says Socrates, Plato, and other heathen philosophers had as good understanding and faith in Christ as had Abraham, 3 *Jew.* 583; complains of the obscurity of scripture, *Rog.* 199; declares that in the times of the apostles the church as yet was rude, and barbarous, and out of order, 4 *Jew.* 855; confesses a great abuse in the communion in one kind, 1 *Jew.* 62, 2 *Jew.* 642, 3 *Jew.* 182

Latomus (Jac.): Opera, *Jew.* xxxix; he was opposed to communion in one kind, 1 *Jew.* 62, 2 *Jew.* 993

Laton (......), a traitor: *Lit. Eliz.* 658

Latoun (The laird of): 2 *Zur.* 331 n

Latria: *v.* Worship.

Latten: a mixed metal resembling brass, *Bale* 437 [misprinted Latin], 527; not iron tinned over, as stated, *Calf.* 300 n

La Turre (Nic. de): 4 *Jew.* 1276

Laud (Will.), abp of Canterbury: Conf. with Fisher, *Calf.* 255 n., 2 *Ful.* 71 n

Lauds: *v.* Hours.

Launcelot du Lake: *Calf.* 271

Launder (Jo.): martyred at Steyning, *Poet.* 162

Launder (......): martyred in Smithfield, *Poet.* 172

Launoy (Jean de): Varia de duobus Dionysiis Opuscula, *Calf.* 211 n.; he rejects the supposititious acts of the council of Sinuessa, 2 *Ful.* 364 n.; his satirical language respecting the "exempt," *Calf.* 97 n

Launson (Eliz.): martyred at Ipswich, *Poet.* 173

Laurence*, bp of Rome: *Pil.* 640

Laurence (St), the deacon: his history, 2 *Tyn.* 254 n.; he was a deacon, 4 *Bul.* 497; yet he consecrated the sacrament, 1 *Jew.* 240; he called the poor the treasures of the church, *Pil.* 157; what he said to Sixtus the martyr, a few days before his own decease, *ib.* 144; his martyrdom, *Bale* 586, 2 *Bul.* 106, *Pil.* 144, 2 *Tyn.* 254 n.; he was feared by the people in Tyndale's time, 2 *Tyn.* 165; collect for his day, 1 *Tyn.* 231 n

Laurence, second abp of Canterbury: his acknowledgment of the British and Irish clergy, 2 *Ful.* 16, 26

Laurence (Rich.), abp of Cashel; Authentic Documents, 2 *Brad.* xlvii.

Laurence (Giles): aids Jewel's escape in queen Mary's time, *Jew.* xi; preaches his funeral sermon, *ib.* xxv.

Laurence (H.): martyred at Canterbury, *Poet.* 163

Lawrence (Rob.), prior of Beauvale: condemned for treason, 2 *Cran.* 303 n

Laurence (Tho.), or Lawrence: an abettor of the maid of Kent, 2 *Cran.* 272; his book about her miracles, *ib.* 272, 273

Lawrence (Will.): letter to him, 1 *Brad.* 591, 2 *Brad.* 194

Laurence (......): martyred June 1556, *Poet.* 168

Lawrence (......); a friend of Foxe, abroad, 1 *Zur.* 35, 41

Lawrence (Mr), a preacher near Ipswich: removed by the archbishop's visitors, *Park.* 307

---

* Laurence and Lawrence are arranged together. One of the name is mentioned in the Canon Law, 4 *Jew.* 969.

Laurentius Valla, *q. v.*
Laurentius à Villa-Vincentia, *q. v.*
Laus Tibi Domine: the period from Septuagesima to Lent, 2 *Tyn.* 92
Lavacre: *v.* Laver.
Lavarocke (......): martyred, *Poet.* 167
Lavater (......), mayor of Zurich: 3 *Zur.* 103 (perhaps the mayor referred to, *ib.* 62, 67, &c.).
Lavater (Felix): grandson to Bullinger, 4 *Bul.* xxvii.
Lavater (Louis): minister at Zurich, 1 *Zur.* 13, 17; noticed, 3 *Zur.* 250, &c.; saluted, 1 *Zur.* 12, 17, 34, 2 *Zur.* 90, 95, & sæpe; his book on Joshua, 1 *Zur.* 150; that on Proverbs, *Jew.* xxxix; he translates a tract by Bullinger, 4 *Bul.* xxiv; his statement respecting the use of the angelical salutation, *Pra. Eliz.* viii; letters to him and others, 1 *Zur.* 94, 109; he married the second daughter of Bullinger, 4 *Bul.* xiv, 1 *Zur.* 30 n., 171 n., 2 *Zur.* 165 n.; his wife, 3 *Zur.* 596
Lavers: text appropriate to one, 1 *Bec.* 65; the brasen laver, 2 *Bul.* 159; lavacre, 3 *Bec.* 612; lavacrum, lavatio, *Now.* (102)
Law (Divine):
    i. *The Law of Nature.*
    ii. *The Law of God* (or his revealed will, generally).
    iii. *The Law of Moses.*
    iv. *The Law of Christ.*

i. *The Law of Nature:* what it is, 1 *Bul.* 194, *Lit. Edw.* 499, (548), *Now.* (23), 138; two especial points of it, 1 *Bul.* 196; it is the law of God written in the hearts of the Gentiles, *ib.* 194, 1 *Tyn.* 114; it is answerable to the written law, 1 *Bul.* 197; blessings or curses follow the keeping or breaking of it, 1 *Tyn.* 418

ii. *The Law of God* (or his revealed will, generally*: *v.* Covenants, Promises, Works): what the law of God is, 2 *Bec.* 53, 3 *Bec.* 602, 614, 1 *Bul.* 193, 209, 1 *Hoop.* 271—280; what it is, with confirmations of scripture, 2 *Bec.* 496; the names given to it in scripture, *ib.* 54; it is called a light, *ib.* 54, a glass, or looking-glass, *ib.* 54, 55, 1 *Brad.* 54, 1 *Lat.* 370, 2 *Lat.* 6, 10; under the term "law" is often comprehended the whole scripture, *Whita.* 641; how the term is used by St Paul, 2 *Lat.* 348, 1 *Tyn.* 484; to what end God gave his law to Adam, 2 *Bul.* 375; what law was given before Moses' time, 1 *Bul.* 210, 1 *Cov.* 40; laws given to Noah, 1 *Cov.* 33; the law of God was written in the hearts of the Gentiles, see i, above; the nature and property of God's law, 2 *Hoop.* 205; wherein the law of God differs from man's law, 1 *Hoop.* 26, 274; the estimation of it, *ib.* 290; its meaning must be rightly understood, *ib.* 291; diligence and circumspection required in interpreting it, *ib.* 271; it is to be interpreted by consent of other places, and allegory of the letter, *ib.* 292; the right understanding of the law is the strait gate, 2 *Tyn.* 120; to live according to this knowledge is the narrow way, *ib.*; sin is repugnant to it, 2 *Bul.* 406; it teacheth perfect righteousness, *ib.* 241; its perfection, 1 *Hoop.* 105, 1 *Tyn.* 300; nothing is to be added to or taken from it, 1. *Hoop.* 292; they who would destroy any portion of it, are to be abhorred, 2 *Tyn.* 39; though perfect, yet it bringeth nothing to perfection, 3 *Bec.* 15, *Sand.* 421; it is spiritual, 1 *Bec.* 48, 2 *Bec.* 95, 120, &c.; therefore it requireth the heart, 1 *Tyn.* 81, 192, 451, 485—487, 503; it has respect to the affections of the heart, *Now.* (21), 135, 136; it requires more than outward observance, 1 *Brad.* 54; the observance of the letter is not sufficient, *Nord.* 70; it must be fulfilled spiritually, 1 *Tyn.* 74, 488; hypocrites are satisfied with the outward work, 1 *Tyn.* 449, 2 *Tyn.* 10, 11; the use of the law, 2 *Bul.* 237, 1 *Hoop.* 281, 2 *Hoop.* 26, 1 *Lat.* 521, *Lit. Edw.* 499, (549), *Pil.* 104, 354; it is a bridle to restrain the evil, 2 *Bec.* 56, 2 *Bul.* 244; the full and perfect rule of righteousness, *Now.* (7), 120, (24), 139; the mark at which we ought all to aim, 1 *Tyn.* 300; the office of God's law, 3 *Bec.* 602; it was not given that God might profit by its being kept, but for our profit, 1 *Tyn.* 474; life is promised to them that keep it, 2 *Bul.* 250; it would justify if it were perfectly kept, *Now.* (24), 139; but no man is so justified, *ib.* (25), 140; it does not and cannot justify, 2 *Bec.* 631, 2 *Bul.* 247, 3 *Bul.* 36, *Lit. Edw.* 500, (549), 1 *Tyn.* 51, 52, 114, 415, 416, 2 *Tyn.* 4, for no man can fulfil it, it requires what no sinner can perform, 1 *Brad.* 213—215, 2 *Bul.* 237, 245, 2 *Cov.* 388, &c., 1 *Hoop.* 281, 411, *Lit. Edw.* 500, (549), *Now.* (25), 140, 1 *Tyn.* 10, 47, 76, 81, 86, 485, 502, 503, *Whita.* 382; it

---

* This division comprises everything of the kind thus indicated, and not appearing to refer *specifically* to the Law of Moses.

requires absolute perfectness, 2 *Bul.* 237, 241; it was not given that man might get life by it, 1 *Brad.* 215, 216; it delivers not from sin, 1 *Hoop.* 92; it gives not the power to obey, 1 *Tyn.* 52, 115, 416; it detects the evil in our hearts, *ib.* 51; makes sin manifest, 2 *Bul.* 238, 239; it is given to shew men their sinfulness, 2 *Bec.* 55; it convinces and condemns, *ib.* 628, 629, 1 *Hoop.* 282, 1 *Tyn.* liii, 52, 2 *Tyn.* 147; it is to be kept in view that we may be self-condemned, 1 *Tyn.* 10—12, 81, 416; it condemns our works, as worthy of death, *ib.* 113, 464; it causes wrath, *ib.* 51, 498, 2 *Tyn.* 4; it leads to hell's mouth, 1 *Brad.* 6; it kills, 2 *Bul.* 239, *Pil.* 111; hence it is called the ministration of death, 1 *Tyn.* 47, and the letter that killeth, *ib.* 308, 309; it pertains to the old man, 1 *Brad.* 299, 2 *Brad.* 196; Satan lays it against the conscience, 3 *Bec.* 161, 162; against temptation for not satisfying it, with sentences and examples of scripture, 1 *Bec.* 477, 478; it prepares the way for Christ, 2 *Tyn.* 146, 147; drives us to Christ, *ib.* 26, 120, that we may seek Christ, 1 *Tyn.* 114, 416, 2 *Tyn.* 26; by proving us guilty and helpless, it disposes us to receive mercy with thankfulness, 3 *Tyn.* 195; remedies against the curse of it, 3 *Bec.* 162, &c.; believers are delivered from its curse by Christ, 1 *Hoop.* 94; Christ hath performed the law for us, *ib.* 411; proofs of this, 3 *Bec.* 162, &c.; Christ is the fulness, end, and accomplishment of the law, 2 *Hoop.* 26; he came not to destroy the law, 2 *Tyn.* 38; the law is not destroyed through faith, 3 *Bul.* 44; believers must observe the law of God, 1 *Hoop.* 95, 2 *Lat.* 326, though no law is needed to compel the believer, 1 *Tyn.* 297, 506; it is a rule of life, 2 *Bul.* 243, 1 *Hoop.* 273; a law of liberty, 1 *Tyn.* 119, 488; he that is renewed keepeth the law without any law written, by the leading of the Spirit only, *ib.* 185; God's law is written in the hearts of his people, 3 *Tyn.* 137; the saints delight in it and love it, 1 *Tyn.* 301, 2 *Tyn.* 11, 3 *Tyn.* 191; the faithful consent unto it, and desire to fulfil it, 1 *Tyn.* 16; those who abide in grace, purpose to keep it, 2 *Tyn.* 7; he that hath a right faith delighteth in the law, though he cannot fulfil it, 1 *Tyn.* 13; he who hath the law of faith and love graven on his heart, keepeth all God's laws, 2 *Tyn.* 325; the true fulfilling of it, 2 *Bec.* 631, 2 *Bul.* 251; it is accomplished through faith, and not through works, 2 *Hoop.* 27; it is fulfilled by love, 1 *Bul.* 190, 2 *Hoop.* 111, 112, 1 *Lat.* 452, 1 *Tyn.* 192, 442, 475, 506, 2 *Tyn.* 11, 12, 118, 119, 173, 202, 203, 325; the sum of all God's laws—to love God and our neighbour, 2 *Bec.* 505, 506, 1 *Lat.* 327, to believe in Christ, and to love our neighbour, 2 *Tyn.* 188; we should let love interpret the law, 1 *Tyn.* 403, 475; John never speaks of any other law but love, *ib.* 475; the reception of God's law by different kinds of men, *ib.* 181, 185; whence it is that some hate, and others love it, 3 *Tyn.* 191; what it is to the unbelieving, and what to the godly, *Now.* (25), 140; they who love it not, can have neither faith nor hope, 2 *Tyn.* 7; nor can they understand the scriptures, *ib.* 7, 8; they who hate it, thereby break it, 3 *Tyn.* 57; certain objections that keep men from obedience to God's laws, solved; [1] of time and place, 1 *Hoop.* 413; [2] exception of persons, *ib.* 414; [3] presumption, *ib.* 415; [4] curiosity, *ib.* 419; [5] desperation, *ib.* 422; [6] ignorance, *ib.* 426; man erreth from it many ways, *ib.* 275; by ignorance, *ib.*; by the power of the world, *ib.* 276; by mistaking of the time, *ib.*; to obtain strength to walk in it, we must ask for the Holy Spirit, 2 *Bec.* 123; the profit that it bringeth, 1 *Hoop.* 290; what temporal blessings still follow its observance, and what curses its neglect, 2 *Tyn.* 52; every one must learn it, 1 *Hoop.* 274; like obedience is required of all, *ib.* 415; all realms should be governed by it, *ib.* 280; laws general and special, 2 *Lat.* 6; the virtue of a general law is not taken away by a particular commandment, 2 *Bec.* 69; in matters of faith, the conscience of man is bound only to the law of God, 1 *Hoop.* 277

iii. *The Law of Moses**:

(*a*) Generally (*v.* Commandments, Covenants, Israel, Works): what it is, 2 *Bec.* 53, & al., see ii, above; see also Tyndale's prologues to the five books of Moses, 1 *Tyn.* 392, &c.; when and why it was given, 1 *Bec.* 48, 2 *Bec.* 53, &c., 496, 497, 3 *Bec.* 162, 1 *Cov.* 39, 43, 1 *Hoop.* 256; the law given on Sinai; a poem, by M. Drayton, *Poet.* 134; it was given in thunder, and so God gave Israel a king, 1 *Tyn.* 194, 334; for whom given, 1 *Hoop.* 256;

---

* Many of the sentences in the former division have reference, in a greater or less degree, to the Law of Moses.

LAW (DIVINE — HUMAN)

why given only to Israel, *Lit. Edw.* 500, (549); given to be a certain doctrine, 2 *Bec.* 53, 54; given to further the promise, 1 *Cov.* 43; its excellence, 1 *Tyn.* 414; what it teacheth, 1 *Hoop.* 272; its use, see ii, above; Moses' forcible persuasions to obey, 1 *Hoop.* 413; the keeper of it had temporal promises, 1 *Tyn.* 415; its precepts called "the rudiments of the world," 2 *Bul.* 242; the law of Moses leadeth unto Christ, 1 *Cov.* 37—48; it was a school-master to lead to Christ, 2 *Bec.* 55, 56, 1 *Brad.* 5, 2 *Hoop.* 26, *Hutch.* 219; the law expounded by Christ, 1 *Hoop.* 271; the bondage of the law, 2 *Bul.* 296; what is meant by not being under the law, 1 *Tyn.* 501; how far and in what manner the law pertains to us, *Rog.* 91, 1 *Whitg.* 265, &c.; of the abrogation of the law, 2 *Bul.* 252; it is buried with Christ as touching the faithful, 2 *Hoop.* 33; but wicked men are under the law, *Hutch.* 326; the curse attached to it, 1 *Brad.* 57, and see ii, above; why written in tables, *Now.* (24), 139; the two tables, 2 *Bec.* 497, 500, 1 *Bul.* 212, *Lit. Edw.* 497, (546, 547); it contains ten commandments, 2 *Bec.* 56; the sum of them, 2 *Bec.* 123, 1 *Hoop.* 271, *Lit. Edw.* 499, (548); the contents of the law, 1 *Bul.* 214; it may be divided into the law of ceremonies, the law of penalty, and the law natural, (or of faith and love); all now superseded except the last, which was before Moses, and continues ever, 2 *Tyn.* 324, 326; another division to the same effect—the moral, ceremonial, and judicial law, 1 *Bul.* 210

(*b*) The Moral Law, 1 *Bul.* 209; how common to all men, *Lit. Edw.* 500, (549); the law contained in the ten commandments (*q. v.*) was required (in substance) of the fathers before the law, 1 *Cov.* 40; the majesty and dignity of the moral law, 1 *Bul.* 212; the excellence of its precepts, 1 *Tyn.* 414; its use, see ii, above; Moses gave laws, but not the spirit to fulfil them, 1 *Lat.* 453; how the moral law pertains to Christians, 2 *Lat.* 348, *Rog.* 91; it endureth still, 1 *Bul.* 211, 2 *Bul.* 225, 255, being, in substance, the law referred to in the first division.

(*c*) The Ceremonial Law (*v.* Altars, Priests, Sacrifices, Temple): what it is, 1 *Bul.* 209, 2 *Bul.* 125, 1 *Cov.* 47; its mysteries not concealed by Moses, *Whita.* 611, 612; mention is made of a certain place appointed for God's service, *Calf.* 32; the sacrifices could not put away sin, 1 *Bec.* 49, 58; ceremonial holiness, *Pil.* 165; ceremonial defilement, *ib.* 166; clean and unclean creatures, 2 *Bul.* 210, &c.; why the eating of certain meats is forbidden, *ib.* 211; on the Mosaic precepts against sowing two kinds of seed in one field, &c., 2 *Brad.* 196; the ceremonial law is abrogated, 2 *Bul.* 257; it is not to be observed by Christians, *Rog.* 88; they are made free from it, 3 *Bec.* 339, &c.; Tyndale maintains that the ceremonies of the law may still be observed if we will, provided we regard them as things indifferent, 2 *Tyn.* 327; Levitical matters are put away from the Christian church, 4 *Bul.* 421; the law prefigured the gospel, 2 *Jew.* 615; terms of the old law are often used by the fathers in a figurative sense, *ib.* 709

(*d*) The Judicial Law, 1 *Bul.* 210, 2 *Bul.* 217, &c., 1 *Cov.* 47; it is profitable, 2 *Bul.* 217; the most ancient of judicial laws, *ib.* 218; how it pertains to the ten commandments, *ib.* 220; the law as to inheritance, *ib.* 226; directions about the division of goods, *ib.* 228; laws of war, 1 *Bul.* 380; the judicial law is abrogated, therefore it binds not in any respect by its own force, 1 *Bul.* 342, 2 *Bul.* 280, *Rog.* 90, 1 *Whitg.* 270, &c., 3 *Whitg.* 552, 576; some of the Puritans held the judicial law of Moses to be binding, 1 *Zur.* 296

(*e*) The Law and the Gospel (*q. v.*) distinguished and contrasted, *Hutch.* 15, *Lit. Edw.* 496, (546), *Now.* (5), 118, *Pil.* 96, 97, 108, 111, 1 *Tyn.* 21, 308, 389, 476; an allegory of the law and gospel, 1 *Tyn.* 306; another (that of Hagar), *Pil.* 335, 1 *Tyn.* 307; both the law and the gospel are needful to be known, 1 *Brad.* 5; they are not to be separated, 1 *Tyn.* 11; a comparison between them, 1 *Brad.* 297; the law pertains to the old man, the gospel to the new, *ib.* 299; the law bindeth, the gospel looseth, 1 *Tyn.* 21, 119 (*v.* Absolution); the law condemneth, the gospel absolveth, *ib.* 83

iv. *The Law of Christ*: his summary of the commandments, 2 *Bec.* 123, 505, *Lit. Edw.* 499, (548), *Now.* (22), 136, 1 *Tyn.* 85, 470, *Wool.* 70; there are many causes to provoke to the study of the law of Christ, 1 *Hoop.* 215; the gospel called the new law, *Coop.* 112, *Hutch.* 234, *Phil.* 107

Law (Human):
    i. *The Law of Man, generally.*
    ii. *The Law of Nations.*
    iii. *The Civil Law.*
    iv. *The Law of England.*
    v. *Ecclesiastical Law, generally.*
    vi. *The Canon Law.*

LAW (HUMAN — CIVIL)

i. *The Law of Man, generally*: what law is, 1 *Bul.* 193, 1 *Hoop.* 273; the division of laws, 1 *Bul.* 193; the law of nature, *ib.* 194 (and see p. 466, above); the law of God, *ib.* 197 (and see the same page); the difference of man's law and God's law, 1 *Hoop.* 26, 274; the laws of men, 1 *Bul.* 206; laws are necessary for kingdoms, *ib.* 337; written laws are needful, *ib.* 341; civil laws, *ib.* 343; laws of policy, *ib.* 206; ecclesiastical laws, *ib.* 207 (and see v, below); superstitious ones, *ib.* 207; laws of honesty, *ib.* 343, of justice and equity, *ib.*, of peace and unanimity, *ib.* 344; what manner of law the magistrate ought to use, *ib.* 341; laws made for the punishment of the evil and the defence of the good are the very work of God, 2 *Hoop.* 81; the civil law must not repugn the law of God, *ib.* 77; (it too often happens that) in making laws, major pars vincit meliorem, 1 *Brad.* 427, 2 *Cov.* 243; the form and manner of law are not alike in all places, 2 *Hoop.* 77; laws must be general, 1 *Jew.* 222; the mind of the law to be followed, not the rigour of the words, 2 *Lat.* 178; the reason of it is the soul of it, 1 *Lat.* 182; against laws prescribed for the conscience for a time, until the settlement of points by a council or otherwise, 1 *Hoop.* 276; the law must be kept and executed by the magistrates, *Sand.* 51, 52; it must be executed without respect of persons, *ib.* 85; it must be received obediently, 1 *Lat.* 148; the law of man to be observed, but not made equal with God's law, 2 *Cran.* 145; all laws not contrary to God's word must be obeyed, none may be resisted, 1 *Lat.* 371; the law of man, if contrary to God's law, cannot bind the conscience, 1 *Brad.* 391, 1 *Hoop.* 277, *Rid.* 142; the law maketh meum and tuum, 1 *Lat.* 404, 406; it may be appealed to, *ib.* 145, 151; it is lawful for a Christian to go to law in a just cause, *Hutch.* 323, &c.; to do so is no breach of charity, 2 *Jew.* 863; how a Christian may go to law, 1 *Lat.* 481, 2 *Tyn.* 64; how suitors should be affected towards each other, *Hutch.* 331; a merry and wise tale on going to law, 1 *Lat.* 89; laws against swearing, 1 *Bec.* 390, 391; the law employed to punish heretics, *Rid.* 141; Anacharsis' web, *Sand.* 52; law will I, i.e. arbitrary law, 2 *Bec.* 313

ii. *The Law of Nations*: to be respected, 1 *Hoop.* 289; its observance enjoined on the Israelites, *ib.*; the maxim "Silent leges inter arma" devilish, *ib.* 290; how wealth may be gotten by the law of nations, 2 *Bul.* 14

iii. *The Civil Law*:

(*a*) Generally:—the Corpus Juris Civilis contains, Institutiones, Digesta (Vetus, Infortiatum, Novum), Codex, Authenticæ, seu Novellæ Constitutiones, Edicta, &c., *Jew.* xxxix; the Institutions of Justinian, 1 *Hoop.* 78; the Pandects, or Digests, what, and when published by Justinian, 2 *Bul.* 281 n.; the Code, or Codex of Justinian, what, and when published, *ib.* 280 n.; reference to it, 2 *Ful.* 364; the Novellæ Constitutiones of Justinian, 2 *Bul.* 281 n., *Jew.* xxxix; the Code and Novellæ of Theodosius II., 2 *Bul.* 281 n., *Jew.* xlii; lex Cornelia de falsis, 1 *Hoop.* 407; lex Julia majestatis, *ib.* 368; lex Julia de adulteris coercendis, 1 *Bul.* 203, 412, 1 *Hoop.* 376 n., 387, 2 *Jew.* 635; lex Pompeia de paricidiis, 1 *Bul.* 288, 1 *Hoop.* 368 n.; lex talionis, 1 *Bul.* 304; lex Voconia, 4 *Jew.* 665; "jus" defined, 1 *Hoop.* 273; the precepts of law, to live honestly, to hurt no man, to give every man his due, 1 *Bul.* 197, 1 *Hoop.* 275; Justinian commands certain of his laws to be generally received, 1 *Jew.* 286, 2 *Jew.* 702; his order for reading the laws, 2 *Jew.* 675; against defrauding the law, by following only the bare words of it, 1 *Jew.* 447, 2 *Jew.* 792, 1112; on ambiguous words, 1 *Jew.* 229; disjunctives stand for copulatives, and vice versâ (Paulus), *ib.* 236; Pomponius shews that laws must be general, *ib.* 222; a thing spoken generally must be taken generally, *ib.* 286; custom declared to be the best interpreter of the law, *ib.* 210, 229; the study of the civil law at Cambridge necessary for the king's service, *Rid.* 506

(*b*) Temporal concerns:—on the authority of the emperor and his laws, 4 *Jew.* 1033; on treason against the emperor or the state, 1 *Hoop.* 368; Rome called the head of the world, 4 *Jew.* 1032; Justinian's esteem for Constantinople, 1 *Jew.* 362; marriage of children not to be without the consent of parents, 3 *Bec.* 532, *Sand.* 281; on the marriage of clerks, 2 *Ful.* 95; against adultery, &c., 1 *Bul.* 203; a woman condemned for adultery not to be a witness, 2 *Jew.* 635; adultery punished with death, 1 *Bul.* 412, 1 *Hoop.* 376, 387; polygamy forbidden, 1 *Hoop.* 386, 387; on divorce, *ib.* 383; he that keeps one concubine said to live chastely, 4 *Jew.* 638; a concubine distinguished from a wife, *ib.*

632; whoremongers banished from all towns, *ib.* 647; the punishment of parricides, 1 *Bul.* 288, 1 *Hoop.* 368; on monsters (Ulpian), 1 *Jew.* 191; on bondage, 2 *Bul.* 301, 302; no Jew to hold a Christian slave, *Phil.* 149; on plagium, or manstealing, 2 *Bul.* 47; the crime capital, *ib.* 48; against cattle-stealing, 2 *Bul.* 48, 230; on property in wild animals, 1 *Hoop.* 390; the accessory follows the principal, *Calf.* 245; one thing by force of greater weight draws another with it, 2 *Jew.* 576; Ulpian referred to on the change of wine into vinegar, 1 *Cran.* 251, 254, 330, 332; on the understanding of a bargain, 1 *Jew.* 178; rule on tacit consent, 1 *Whitg.* 349; the allowance of a thing done, as good as a commission for doing it, 4 *Jew.* 1036; how riches may be gotten lawfully, 2 *Bul.* 25; as to sewers and the like, *ib.* 231; servitutes luminum, 2 *Zur.* 94 n.; the lex Voconia forbade a man to convey his inheritance to a woman, even to his daughter, 4 *Jew.* 665; on the will of the dead, 1 *Jew.* 423; laws for the relief of the poor, orphans, &c., 2 *Bul.* 281; the rich and noble forbidden to engage in trade, 1 *Hoop.* 392; against monopolists, 2 *Brad.* 396, 1 *Hoop.* 391; usury forbidden, 1 *Hoop.* 393; gaming prohibited, 2 *Bul.* 40; against forgery, 1 *Hoop.* 407 n.; a party to be heard in his own province, 1 *Jew.* 391; no jurisdiction without coercion, *ib.* 395; the competent tribunal for ecclesiastics, *Phil.* 36 n.; exceptio fori, *ib.* 7, 35; no man to be his own judge, 3 *Jew.* 294, 4 *Jew.* 956; the use of Latin required in all causes, 1 *Jew.* 295; but fidei commissa might be left in any language, *ib.* 296; the penalty of a false suggestion by a plaintiff, *ib.* 101, 102; suitors obtaining the help of great men to lose their suits, 1 *Hoop.* 394; the rule, qui mutum exhibet, &c., 1 *Jew.* 185; distinction between "recte" and "rite," the former having respect to the justice of a cause, the latter to the order of it, *Calf.* 206; provisions on appeals, 1 *Jew.* 390, 404, *Phil.* 149; an appeal allowed in the case of bribed witnesses, 1 *Hoop.* 408

(c) Ecclesiastical affairs:—the Civil Law contains many ecclesiastical enactments, 3 *Whitg.* 307; the Christian emperors provided for the state of religion in the church, 2 *Bec.* 305, 312, 1 *Bul.* 331, 332, 2 *Bul.* 281; edict of Gratian, Valentinian, and Theodosius, commanding their subjects to be of the religion which Peter delivered to the Romans, 2 *Bec.* 305, 1 *Bul.* 34, 328, 331, 2 *Bul.* 281, 4 *Bul.* 63, 2 *Ful.* 362, 2 *Hoop.* 540, 1 *Jew.* 80, 365, 4 *Jew.* 1002, 1043, *Phil.* 75; priesthood and empire declared to be the greatest gifts of God, 4 *Jew.* 1036; idolatry a capital offence, 2 *Bec.* 305, 312, 1 *Bul.* 359, 360, 2 *Bul.* 281; pardon granted to the repentant, 1 *Bul.* 362; blasphemy capitally punished, *ib.* 243, 1 *Hoop.* 334; magical arts forbidden, 1 *Hoop.* 327, 329, &c.; Sunday to be observed, 1 *Bul.* 264, 265, 1 *Hoop.* 338; husbandmen permitted to labour on that day, 1 *Bul.* 265, 266; heretics disqualified from various employments, *ib.* 320; rebaptizing forbidden, 4 *Bul.* 394; against the celebration of sacred rites in private houses, 1 *Bul.* 332, 1 *Hoop.* 171, 172; constitution of Justinian how bishops and priests should celebrate the holy oblation, 1 *Jew.* 284, &c.; he speaks of deacons as ministering the same, *ib.* 240; his law commanding ministers to speak in a clear voice, 2 *Bec.* 255, 441, 3 *Bec.* 409, 4 *Bul.* 190, 2 *Cran.* 450, 451, 1 *Jew.* 8, 57, 284—287, 309, 312, 333, 2 *Jew.* 701, 990, 997, 4 *Jew.* 810, 811, 963, 979, 1031, *Pil.* 499, *Whita.* 270; a law against paying money for admission to the priesthood or episcopate, 4 *Bul.* 130; directions of Justinian concerning the choice of bishops, *ib.* 133, 1 *Whitg.* 396, 398; the ordination of a bishop to be stayed, in the event of any charge being brought against him, until examination, 4 *Bul.* 136; laws against bishops absenting themselves from their churches, 1 *Bul.* 332, 1 *Jew.* 406, 4 *Jew.* 1026, 1033; bishops not to sell the goods of their churches, 1 *Bul.* 331, 332, 2 *Bul.* 281; Justinian gives licence to a bishop to release a priest from part of his penance, and to restore him to the ministry, 4 *Jew.* 1030; metropolitans mentioned by Justinian, 2 *Whitg.* 166; what that emperor says touching the pre-eminence of the bishop of Rome, 1 *Jew.* 361–363, 432, 4 *Jew.* 839; he labours to advance the honour of the see (of Rome), and to unite to it all the priests of the East, 4 *Jew.* 1032; ecclesiastical matters to be laid before the pope as the head of all the holy churches, *ib.*; intimation that the pope may not intermeddle with temporal causes, *ib.* 1031; the church of the city of Constantinople declared by Justinian to enjoy the prerogative of Rome the elder, 3 *Jew.* 307, 4 *Jew.* 841, 1031; Constantinople designated the perpetual mother of faith and religion, 4 *Jew.* 883, and the mother of all Christians of the catholic faith, *ib.*; Justinian styles Epiphanius of Constantinople universal patriarch, 1 *Jew.* 363, 4 *Jew.* 1032, and assigns to him the disposition of all things, agreeable to holy scripture, touching the ordering of bishops and clerks, 1 *Bul.* 331; the churches of Illyricum to appeal to Constantinople, not to Rome, 4 *Jew.* 1031; edict of Justinian limiting the number of the clergy at Constantinople, 1 *Jew.* 121, 197, 2 *Jew.* 1019; his order respecting the jurisdiction of the bishop of Justiniana, 1 *Jew.* 363; on the decision of doubts amongst bishops, *ib.* 390; on councils of bishops, 1 *Bul.* 331; a synod to be held yearly in every province, 4 *Bul.* 506, 4 *Jew.* 1124, 1125; the lieutenants of provinces empowered to convene councils in case of the neglect of the bishops to do so, 1 *Bul.* 332, 4 *Bul.* 506; Justinian's order about setting up a cross before building a church, *Calf.* 135, 136, 189, 2 *Ful.* 150, 158, 159, 185; in order to suppress conventicles, he required a procession when a church was to be consecrated, *Calf.* 304, 305; Valens and Theodosius forbade representations of the sign of Christ, 2 *Bec.* 71 n., *Calf.* 190, 2 *Ful.* 159, 2 *Jew.* 659, 668, *Park.* 90, *Rid.* 92; on the tribunal proper for bishops, clerks and monks, *Phil.* 36 n.; no bishop to be brought against his will before a civil judge, unless by the commandment of the prince, 4 *Jew.* 960; a priest sued in law, might, with the consent of the plaintiff, be judged by the bishop, *ib.* 961; clergymen forbidden to engage in games and pageants, 1 *Bul.* 332; monks to be driven to study the scriptures, or forced to bodily labour, 4 *Jew.* 1031; as to marriage, and some other matters which may be regarded as partly ecclesiastical, see *b*, above; Justinian commands that the holy canons be holden for laws, 4 *Jew.* 1033; a gloss asks, wherefore does the emperor busy himself with spiritual matters, seeing he knows they are no part of his charge? and answers, that he does it by the pope's authority, *ib.* 1031

iv. *The Law of England:* v. Courts, Execution, Jurors, Lawyers, Statutes, Tenure, Terms, Writs.

The Ancient Laws and Institutes of England, 1 *Lat.* 54 n.; complaint of the corrupt administration of the law, *ib.* 128; some good penal laws repealed under Mary, *Pil.* 614; the laws of real property, 2 *Zur.* 197; the law as to felony, the thief and the receiver, 1 *Brad.* 388; on law-suits, *Now.* (79, 80), 201; those who fail in their causes should be burdened with heavy costs, *Sand.* 227; suggestions for legislators, *Now.* 226; as to the ecclesiastical law of England, see the next division; also Lyndwode (W.).

v. *Ecclesiastical Law:* v. Canons, Church, Courts; also iii. *c*, above.

The church not burdened by God with infinite laws, 4 *Bul.* 478; ecclesiastical laws, what, 1 *Bul.* 207; much of the Canon Law remains in force here, 3 *Whitg.* 278; the burdens of our spiritual lawyers, 1 *Tyn.* 245; an act passed for revising the Canon Law, 1544, 2 *Cran.* 68 n.; commission proposed for making new laws ecclesiastical, 1546, *ib.* 415; king Edward's commission for the reformation of ecclesiastical law in England, 3 *Zur.* 447, 503, 580, 590; a new code proposed, *Hutch.* 6 n.; the Reformatio Legum Ecclesiasticarum, 2 *Cran.* xi, *Hutch.* 6 n., 1 *Lat.* xii, 3 *Zur.* 503 n., 580 n.; the validity of the Canon Law in England denied by Puritans, *Rog.* 361; controversy on chancellors and other ecclesiastical officers, 3 *Whitg.* 543

vi. *The Canon Law:*

(a) Generally:—one king, one law, is God's ordinance in every realm, therefore the clergy should not have a separate law, 1 *Tyn.* 240; this law was made only in favour of the clergy, 2 *Cran.* 166, 167; how the pope made him a law, 2 *Tyn.* 278; its authors, 3 *Jew.* 132; the Corpus Juris Canonici contains, Decretum Gratiani, Decretales Gregorii IX., Sextus Decretalium, Clementinæ, Extravagantes Joannis XXII., Extravagantes Communes, *Jew.* xxxix; its parts referred to, *Bale* 48; Decretum Gratiani, its character, 3 *Bul.* 81; allowed by Eugenius III., and commonly called fundamentum juris canonici, 3 *Jew.* 132, 312; its "distinctions," and "canons" or "capitula," 1 *Tyn.* 46 n.; references to Gratian, *Calf.* 409, 2 *Ful.* 402; he allows that the so-called canons of the apostles are apocryphal, *Whita.* 41; his forgeries, *Bale* 571; he was a common falsifier of the doctors, 1 *Jew.* 545; for example, he corrupted a canon of the second council of Milevis, 2 *Ful.* 71 n., shamelessly depraved a canon of the council of Chalcedon, *ib.* 288, and falsified an epistle of pope Leo the Great, *ib.* 82 n.; he bears witness against the interpolations in a treatise by Cyprian, *ib.* 291 n.; mistakes of his, 2 *Jew.* 568, 3 *Jew.* 394, 476, 4 *Jew.* 635, *Whita.* 157 n.; some errors of his allowed by Papists, 3 *Jew.* 177; the decretal epistles ascribed to the early bishops of Rome are not genuine, 2 *Bec.* 238 n., 1 *Jew.* 173, 341, &c., 388, *Rid.* 180—182, *Whita.* 435, 609, 2 *Whitg.* 136, 137, 141 ; they are futile and absurd, *Whita.* 509 ; not reckoned as scripture by Augustine (as falsely alleged by Gratian), *ib.* 109 ; Gratian's low estimate of them, 1 *Jew.* 173, 341; on the credit due to them, 1 *Whitg.* 532 n.; Bellarmine's cautious statement regarding them, *Calf.* 222 n. ; Decretals, letters of popes, c. 1150—1300, 3 *Jew.* 132, 1 *Lat.* 212; they contain marvels and mysteries, 1 *Hoop.* 291 ; Alexandrines, probably the decretal epistles of Alexander III. (a portion of the above), 1 *Lat.* 212; Sextus Decretalium, collected in the time of Boniface VIII., 1 *Hoop.* 569, 3 *Jew.* 132 ; Clementines, the decretal epistles of Clement V., 3 *Jew.* 132, 1 *Lat.* 212 ; Extravagantes, or Extravagantines, 3 *Jew.* 132, 1 *Lat.* 212, *Rid.* 164; a collection of tenets extracted from the Canon Law, 2 *Cran.* 68—75 ; it is wicked and full of tyranny, *ib.* 165 ; nevertheless it contains many truths strangely misplaced, *ib.* 76; the decrees, decretals, &c. censured, *Bale* 48, 2 *Cran.* 148, 163, 2 *Ful.* 237, 1 *Hoop.* 284; valued by Romanists as highly as the Bible, *Calf.* 18, 206, 2 *Cran.* 48, *Whita.* 109; popes, fathers, councils, &c. cited in the Canon Law, see 1 *Bec.* 493, 2 *Bec.* 660, 3 *Bec.* 635, 4 *Jew.* 1332; for fuller statements, see the names of the several popes, fathers, and councils in this Index; the gloss, see 2 *Bec.* 659, 3 *Bec.* 634, 4 *Jew.* 1338; the absurd gloss, "statuimus, i. e. abrogamus," 2 *Ful.* 236 n., 1 *Jew.* 33, 37, 54, 55, *Rid.* 36; Censura in Glossas (Manriq), *Calf.* 6 n.; the Decretals burned by Luther, 1 *Tyn.* 221; much of the Canon law remains in England, 3 *Whitg.* 278 (see v, above); how studied at Louvaine, 4 *Jew.* 1089

(*b*) As to Scripture, &c. :—declaration that as the correctness of the Old Testament is to be tried by the Hebrew, so is that of the New by the Greek, 4 *Bul.* 542; on the four senses of scripture, 1 *Tyn.* 303; the church often placed above scripture, *Whita.* 276 ; the decretal epistles reckoned as a part of canonical scripture (falsely citing Augustine), *ib.* 109 ; apocryphal gospels mentioned, *ib.* 108

(*c*) The Church :—distinction between believing the church and believing *in* God, 1 *Bul.* 159; on being in the church nominally and really, *Rid.* 127; the church stated to be one, as having one supreme head, 3 *Jew.* 221, 4 *Jew.* 751; the church often affirmed to be above scripture, *Whita.* 276; declaration that the church of Rome was consecrated by the martyrdom of both Peter and Paul, 2 *Tyn.* 285 n.; the authority of the Roman church asserted by several popes, 3 *Bec.* 511, 513, 526; statement that she has authority to judge all things, and that no one may judge her judgment, 4 *Bul.* 67, *Rog.* 192 n.; whatever the Roman church ordains, to be observed by all, 4 *Bul.* 67; whosoever is not obedient to the laws of the church of Rome, to be deemed a heretic, 4 *Jew.* 768; assertion that he doubtless falls into heresy who goes about to take away the privilege of the church of Rome, *ib.* 1148; disallowance of whatever is done against the discipline of the church of Rome without discretion of justice, 3 *Jew.* 285, 4 *Jew.* 873; the writings of the fathers to be held to the last iota, *Calf.* 260 n.; there is a list of fathers deemed authorities, *Whita.* 413; distinction between "ecclesia parochialis" and " ecclesia baptismalis," 1 *Jew.* 181

(*d*) The Pope:—none of the patriarchs ever used the name of universal, 2 *Hoop.* 234; the title of high priest formerly given to all bishops, *ib.* 237; St Cyprian called pope, *ib.*; a gloss ascribes the origin of the word papa to "Papæ interjectio admirantis," 3 *Tyn.* 324 ; the bishop of the first see not to be called prince of priests, 2 *Ful.* 323 n., 2 *Hoop.* 235, 1 *Jew.* 442; the bishop of Rome himself not to be called universal bishop, 3 *Jew.* 310, 314; the pope calls himself a servant, 4 *Jew.* 847; exposition of the text "Thou art Peter," *Rid.* 164, 2 *Tyn.* 281 n.; an absurd derivation for Cephas, 2 *Ful.* 301 n., *Rid.* 164; declaration that the Lord had not been discreet if he had not left a vicar behind him, 1 *Jew.* 380, 3 *Jew.* 276; statement that Peter's see was first at Antioch, but that it was translated to Rome by the Lord's command, 2 *Tyn.* 285 n.; the authority of Peter and Paul claimed for the pope's anathemas, *ib.*; statement that it is plain the church is one, for that in the universal church there is one head, that is, the pope, 3 *Jew.* 221, 4 *Jew.* 751; foolish arguments for his supremacy, 1 *Jew.* 14, 77, 339; his claims and pretensions, 2 *Cran.* 68, &c., 165; scriptures alleged in support of them, *ib.* 75; assertion that the Roman pontiff is the bishop of the whole world, 4 *Jew.* 827 ; that our Lord the pope is the ordinary judge of all men, 4 *Bul.* 120, 1 *Jew.* 442, 3 *Jew.* 317, 319, 4 *Jew.* 827;

LAW (CANON)

on appeals to Rome, 1 *Jew.* 389; on obedience to the pope, 3 *Bec.* 514; declaration that to be subject to the pope is necessary to salvation, 4 *Bul.* 120, 2 *Cran.* 68, *Grin.* 22, 1 *Jew.* 339, 442, 3 *Jew.* 196, 4 *Jew.* 1137, 2 *Lat.* 348 n., *Rid.* 164; that whoever is saved is under the pope, 1 *Jew.* 339, 3 *Jew.* 196, 284; that whosoever will not submit to the pope acknowledges himself to be none of Christ's sheep, 2 *Tyn.* 280 n.; that whoever denies the pope to be the head of the church, is to be holden as a heretic, 4 *Jew.* 739; that whosoever obeys not his commandments, falls into the sin of idolatry and infidelity, *ib.* 685; all men affirmed to be subject to the pope's will, and to be in him as members of a member, *ib.* 829; the pious emperor Constantine said to have called the pope God, and declared him consequently irresponsible to man, *Calf.* 5 n., 2 *Ful.* 356 n., 369, 1 *Jew.* 96, 438, 2 *Jew.* 773, 906, 4 *Jew.* 843, 3 *Tyn.* 231 n.; in a notorious and uncensured gloss the pontiff is styled "our Lord God the pope," *Calf.* 5 n., 2 *Ful.* 247, 369, 1 *Jew.* 96, 374, 443, 2 *Jew.* 773, 906, 4 *Jew.* 831, 843, 899, *Rog.* 38, 348; editions containing these words, *Calf.* 6 n.; in the latter editions the word "God" is omitted, 1 *Jew.* 96 n.; other references as to the name of God being applied to the pope, 2 *Jew.* 773 n.; the inquiry, who dares to say...to God or to the pope? 4 *Jew.* 831; statement that the pope is not a man, *ib.* 844; that he is neither God nor man, 2 *Jew.* 907, 991, 4 *Jew.* 843, 844; that he is the wonderment of the world, 4 *Jew.* 682, 844; the pope said to have a heavenly power, and the fulness of power, 4 *Bul.* 121; assertion that as all power in heaven and earth is given to Christ, so it is to the pope, 1 *Jew.* 93 n., 380; that the pope and Christ have one tribunal, *ib.* 381; the pope claims power to make new laws, 3 *Bec.* 527; he is asserted to be free from all human law, 2 *Jew.* 907, 919; to be the fountain of all law, &c., 1 *Jew.* 68; he is held to have all laws in the coffer of his breast, 4 *Bul.* 120, 1 *Jew.* 68, 93, 381, 442, 4 *Jew.* 768, 2 *Whitg.* 510; assertion that he may dispense against the law of nature, 3 *Jew.* 218, 599, against the divine law, *ib.* 218, 599, 4 *Jew.* 1245, against the canons or rules of the apostles, 3 *Jew.* 599; statement that he judges all things by authority, because he has authority over all men, and he is judged by none, because no man has authority over him, 1 *Jew.* 94 n.; that he may even change the nature of things, of nothing make something, of injustice make justice, &c., 4 *Bul.* 121, 1 *Jew.* 68, 69, 442, 2 *Jew.* 919, 3 *Jew.* 222, 599; all the sanctions of the Roman see to be received as if confirmed by the voice of Peter, 3 *Bec.* 511, 513, 4 *Bul.* 119, 2 *Cran.* 68, *Rog.* 202 n.; the decretal epistles of the popes to stand upon like foundation with the scriptures, 2 *Tyn.* 289 n.; whatsoever the pope decrees, whatsoever he establishes, to be observed of all men for ever, inviolably, 4 *Bul.* 67; statement that whatsoever the pope either allows or disallows, we are bound to allow or disallow the same, 4 *Jew.* 768; in what he will his will is instead of reason, and no man may say, "Lord, why doest thou so?" 4 *Bul.* 121, 1 *Jew.* 381, 442, 2 *Jew.* 919, 3 *Jew.* 205, 4 *Jew.* 739, 769, 898, 933, 1137; assertion that there is a certain spiritual holiness according to the state most holy and spiritual, and in this state is only the pope, 4 *Jew.* 702; that though the pope be not always a good man, yet he is ever presumed to be good, *ib.* 1009, 1010, 1116; that if the pope lack goodness acquired by merit, that is sufficient which he has from his predecessor, 1 *Jew.* 400, 401, 4 *Jew.* 703, 1109, 1110; Peter said to have made the pope heir of his goodness, 3 *Jew.* 201, 324; it is affirmed that the pope receives holiness from his chair, 1 *Jew.* 401, 3 *Jew.* 324, 4 *Jew.* 1009, 1068; that it is like sacrilege to dispute about his deeds, 2 *Jew.* 907, 4 *Jew.* 702, 768, 899, 907, 1116; his deeds excused as Samson's murders, the Jews' robberies, and Jacob's adultery, 2 *Jew.* 919, 4 *Jew.* 702, 802; declaration that if a pope be so wicked as to lead innumerable people with him to hell, no man may rebuke him, 3 *Bec.* 527, 2 *Cran.* 70, 165, 1 *Hoop.* 284, 471 n., 1 *Jew.* 400, 2 *Jew.* 919, 991, *Rog.* 202, 1 *Tyn.* 328, 329, 2 *Tyn.* 299, 3 *Tyn.* 41; that no mortal may presume to accuse the pope, for he is to judge all men, and to be judged of none, 1 *Hoop.* 285, 471 n., *Rog.* 191 n., 202 n., unless he depart from the faith, 2 *Ful.* 365 n., 1 *Jew.* 400, *Phil.* 420, 3 *Tyn.* 329 n.; arguments to prove that no man may accuse the pope, 4 *Jew.* 834; admission that it is certain the pope may err, 1 *Jew.* 399, 4 *Jew.* 927; the pope claims to be above councils, 2 *Cran.* 70, 1 *Jew.* 442, 3 *Jew.* 205; statement that a council cannot judge the pope, 4 *Bul.* 119; canons affirming that any council not authorized by the pope, is to be deemed a conventicle, 2 *Tyn.* 272 n.; yet it is stated

LAW (CANON)

that when the case is moved in a matter of faith, then is the council greater than the pope, 4 *Jew.* 704; all councils said to be held by the authority of the Roman church, 1 *Jew.* 93 n., 442 n.; assertion that the pope may be judged neither by the emperor nor by the whole clergy, nor by kings, nor by the people, 4 *Bul.* 119, 2 *Cran.* 69, 1 *Jew.* 68, 93 n., 442, 2 *Jew.* 907, 4 *Jew.* 968, 1116, 3 *Tyn.* 232 n.; it is said, other men's causes God would have to be determined by men; but the bishop of this see without question, he reserved to his own judgment, 1 *Jew.* 68; declaration that if the whole world should pronounce sentence in any matter against the pope, we must stand to the pope's judgment, 4 *Bul.* 119, 1 *Jew.* 68, 400, 2 *Jew.* 919, 3 *Jew.* 205, 600, 4 *Jew.* 768, 921, 1116; admission that he ought not to be judge in his own cause, 3 *Jew.* 294; Constantine's Donation, 2 *Ful.* 360 n., 3 *Jew.* 394, 4 *Jew.* 840, 2 *Lat.* 349 n., 2 *Tyn.* 279; reference about Phocas making the bishop of Rome head of the church, 2 *Hoop.* 235; after the emperors had made the bishop of Rome head of the church, he made himself head of emperors and kings, *ib.* 239; the emperor had the right of choosing the pope, 2 *Tyn.* 263; Louis le Débonnaire's alleged release of such right, *ib.* 279; he decreed that the bishop of Rome should be chosen by the people, 1 *Whitg.* 397, 400; Otho's oath to the pope, see *m*, below; the pope claims the right of both swords, 4 *Bul.* 120, 2 *Cran.* 71, 2 *Hoop.* 239, 1 *Jew.* 14, 228, 442, 4 *Jew.* 820; though it is said, Christ by several duties, and distinct honours hath set a difference between the offices of both powers, 4 *Jew.* 826, 985; the gloss declares this to be an argument that the pope has not both swords, *ib.* 985; statement that the pope has the principality of all the world, 3 *Jew.* 319, 4 *Jew.* 706, 827, 1013; that unto Peter were committed the rights both of heavenly and earthly empire, 3 *Jew.* 270, 4 *Jew.* 677, 682, 825, 958; the pope compared to the sun, the emperor to the moon, 1 *Jew.* 14, 443, 4 *Jew.* 671, 672, 847, 983; the pope said to be as much superior to the emperor, as the soul to the body, 4 *Jew.* 673; the pope claims power to depose kings, 2 *Cran.* 69, 1 *Jew.* 443; Zachary deposed the French king, 4 *Jew.* 683, 2 *Tyn.* 261 n.; the pope claims to be heir of the empire, 1 *Jew.* 443; statement that he may give the emperor power to depose him, and may in all things submit himself to him, 4 *Jew.* 968; that the pope may make a bishop only by his word, 3 *Jew.* 329; that the court of Rome hath an universal study, and the privileges of the same, 4 *Jew.* 654; that false Latin vitiates the pope's rescripts, 1 *Jew.* 343; all things sold at Rome, 4 *Jew.* 867

(*e*) Bishops:—of the precedence of the patriarchs in synods, 4 *Jew.* 1002; patriarchs and primates different names of the same office, 3 *Jew.* 313; patriarchs and primates declared to have no privilege above other bishops, except what the sacred canons allow, or as the pope may grant, 3 *Bec.* 510 n.; on the authority of the patriarch of Constantinople, 1 *Jew.* 404; on the places which should be made bishops' sees, 2 *Whitg.* 118 n., 377; there should be but one bishop in a diocese, 2 *Ful.* 363, 1 *Jew.* 372; episcopal power extolled, 3 *Bec.* 508; bishops called high priests, 2 *Hoop.* 237; on their appointment, 1 *Whitg.* 460, 462; Charlemagne directed that they should be chosen by the clergy and people, *ib.* 396, 400; Louis his son decreed that the bishop of Rome should be chosen by the people, *ib.* 397; the laity not to interfere in the election of prelates, 2 *Tyn.* 263 n.; statement that if a man be made bishop without the consent of his metropolitan, the great council (of Nice) has decreed that such a one may not be bishop, 3 *Jew.* 333; the bishop's oath to the pope, 3 *Jew.* 205, 4 *Jew.* 1113; if a man will be a bishop let him follow Moses and Aaron, 1 *Bec.* 382; hospitality necessary for bishops, *ib.* 23, 24, 2 *Bec.* 325; bishops commanded to minister to the poor and sick, 2 *Bec.* 326; admonished to have a liberal hand, *ib.*; a bishop deprived for niggardliness, 1 *Bec.* 23; the lay sort not to be heard in the accusation of a bishop, 4 *Jew.* 639

(*f*) Clergy:—Gratian interprets presbyter by senior, 4 *Jew.* 912; in old time golden priests used wooden cups, but now contrariwise wooden priests use golden cups, 4 *Bul.* 420, 1 *Hoop.* 521; priests, &c., anointed, 2 *Cran.* 62 n.; priests must watch the Lord's sheep with great diligence, 1 *Bec.* 361; ignorance most of all to be eschewed in the priests of God, *ib.* 384; an evil priest compared to a raven, 2 *Jew.* 628; the priest above the prince as touching his priestly office, 4 *Jew.* 673; the pope inferior to his confessor, *ib.* 992; flattering clerks to be deposed, 3 *Whitg.* 579; a clerk who commits a capital crime, or forges a charter, or bears false-witness, to be confined in a monastery, and reduced to lay communion, *Calf.* 273, and see *Coop.* 159 n.; laymen not to be judges of the clergy, 2 *Cran.* 72, 73, 1 *Tyn.* 178, 240, 2 *Tyn.* 272; the laity not to investigate their lives, 1 *Tyn.* 178 n., 2 *Tyn.* 272 n.; the lay sort not to be heard in the accusation of a bishop, 4 *Jew.* 639; a layman not to accuse a priest of fornication, *ib.*; a layman not to be the assessor of a bishop, *ib.* 1015; canons in regard to imposts upon the clergy, 3 *Bec.* 514, 2 *Cran.* 72, 167; laymen not to meddle with their elections, 2 *Cran.* 72, 167; nor have benefices to farm, *ib.*; on titles for ordination, 1 *Whitg.* 480, and priests without benefices, 3 *Whitg.* 246; on the canon of the second council of Nice against pluralities, 1 *Whitg.* 531; pluralities allowed in certain cases, *ib.*; what things are Simoniacal of their own nature, and what by law positive, 4 *Jew.* 868; the heresy of Macedonius more tolerable than the heresy of Simonists, *ib.* 869, 870; church goods not to be alienated, 2 *Cran.* 73; the ancient mode of dividing tithes and offerings, 1 *Bec.* 24, 2 *Tyn.* 173; on monks, *Calf.* 220; canon forbidding them to taste any kind of flesh, 2 *Tyn.* 276 n.; statement that no man can serve the ecclesiastical office, and orderly keep the rule of monkery, 4 *Jew.* 800

(*g*) Sacraments, especially Baptism:— definition of a sacrament, 2 *Jew.* 591; declaration that the sacraments of the new law bring to pass that which they figure, *Calf.* 243; all sacraments to be perfected with the sign of the cross, *ib.* 206; baptism ordinarily celebrated at Easter and Whitsuntide, 4 *Bul.* 367, 542, 2 *Cran.* 175 n.; mention of one who baptized "In nomine Patria," &c., 4 *Jew.* 910; reference to various fathers with respect to trine immersion, 2 *Bec.* 227 n.; that practice deemed unimportant, *Whita.* 593; reference respecting the forgiveness of sins in baptism, 4 *Bul.* 399; in baptism Christ is sometimes put on sacramentally, sometimes unto sanctification of life, 2 *Bec.* 294, 3 *Bec.* 465; every one of the faithful becomes partaker of the body and blood of the Lord when he is made a member of Christ in baptism, 3 *Bec.* 443 n., *Coop.* 121 n.; on sponsors, 2 *Bec.* 210 n., *Calf.* 212; question whether a man may be baptized in his madness or sleep, 3 *Jew.* 358; those who have been baptized of heretics not to be priests, *Rog.* 241 n.; that minister who by unlawful usage shall iterate holy baptism, accounted unworthy of an ecclesiastical function, 4 *Bul.* 394

(*h*) The Eucharist:—Christ is mystically sacrificed for us every day, i. e. adds the gloss, the sacrifice of Christ is represented in the sacrament of his body and blood, 2 *Bec.* 250, 3 *Bec.* 458; Christ was once sacrificed in himself, and yet is daily sacrificed in the sacrament,—he is sacrificed, i. e. his sacrifice is represented, 2 *Bec.* 250, 3 *Bec.* 458, 2 *Jew.* 726; Christ dies and suffers, i. e. the death and passion of Christ is represented, 2 *Jew.* 618, 726; all to communicate who would not be excommunicated, 3 *Bec.* 416, 474, *Coop.* 219 n., 2 *Cran.* 171; the sacrificer referred to as a *catholic* priest, 1 *Hoop.* 517; as many hosts to be offered as will suffice for the people, *Coop.* 151 n.; the mixed cup, 3 *Bec.* 359 n., 1 *Hoop.* 519; on the word "Hoc" in the form of consecration, 1 *Hoop.* 529; consecration affirmed to be instantaneous, *ib.* 522; said to be effected when the last syllable of the words is uttered, 2 *Bec.* 264; referred to the last letter of the formula, 1 *Hoop.* 522; cases of non-consecration, 1 *Jew.* 550; the change of the bread into the body of Christ compared with regeneration, 2 *Hoop.* 430, *Hutch.* 241 n.; distinction between the sacrament and the thing signified, 2 *Bec.* 268 n., 2 *Hoop.* 427; the Lord as to his body must needs be in one place, 2 *Hoop.* 488; till the world be ended the Lord is above; yet the truth of the Lord is with us here, 1 *Hoop.* 515; how the bread is Christ's body, 3 *Bec.* 437; the heavenly bread...in its manner is called the body of Christ, when indeed it is the sacrament of the body of Christ, 2 *Bec.* 250 n., 2 *Hoop.* 428; the heavenly sacrament...is called the body of Christ, but improperly...it is called the body of Christ, i. e. it signifies, 2 *Bec.* 284, 3 *Bec.* 437, *Coop.* 204, 205, 1 *Jew.* 503, 504, 2 *Jew.* 611, 621, 790, 1113, 3 *Jew.* 500, 514, 602, 4 *Jew.* 765, 790; the sacrament upon the altar is improperly called the body of Christ, as baptism is improperly called faith, 3 *Bec.* 450; the body of Christ eaten from the altar is a figure, &c., 2 *Bec.* 286; after consecration Christ's body is signified, *Coop.* 207 n.; the offering called the figure of the body and blood of Christ, *ib.* 207, 208 n.; the sacrament received as a similitude, *ib.* 208 n.; the blood interpreted as the sacrament of the blood, 3 *Bec.* 437, 438; mention of the species of bread under which the body of Christ lieth, and the species of wine under which, &c., 2 *Jew.* 797; neither the bread signifies the blood, nor the wine the body, 3 *Bec.* 450; reference to the bread as transubstantiated into the body, and the wine into the blood, 2 *Hoop.* 522; the sacrament is divided by parts, not so the body itself, 1 *Hoop.* 526 n.; on the distinction of parts in the body of Christ in the sacrament, 2 *Jew.* 779; exhortation to look on the holy body and blood of our God by faith, 2 *Bec.* 295, 3 *Bec.* 432 n., 444; admission that the material bread is not the body of Christ which supports the substance of the soul, 3 *Jew.* 471; the soul is fed principally with the body and blood of Christ, 3 *Bec.* 434; Christ has become our bread, because he has taken our flesh, 1 *Jew.* 530; how Christ is eaten, 3 *Bec.* 434, 465; he cannot be devoured with teeth, 2 *Bec.* 296, 3 *Bec.* 434; statement that as soon as the forms are touched with the teeth, the body of Christ is caught up into heaven, 1 *Hoop.* 517, 529, 1 *Jew.* 479, 2 *Jew.* 786, 3 *Jew.* 471, 488; Christ is eaten two manner of ways, 2 *Bec.* 296, 3 *Bec.* 434; of evil persons he is eaten only sacramentally, 2 *Bec.* 294, 3 *Bec.* 434, 465; the reprobate do not eat the living bread, 3 *Bec.* 434, 465; they that eat and drink Christ eat and drink life, i. e. in the kind of bread and wine, *ib.* 414, 465; to believe in Jesus Christ is to eat the bread of life, *ib.* 465; to eat the living bread is to believe in Christ, that is, by love to be incorporate in him, *ib.* 434, 465; as to the elevation of the host, *ib.* 359 n., 361, 1 *Hoop.* 526; order for kneeling at the elevation, 3 *Whitg.* 88 n.; statement that it is a most wicked custom for the priest not to communicate, 2 *Jew.* 640; on the meaning of the three parts of the broken host, *Coop.* 77 n., 4 *Jew.* 818; the distribution of the bread referred to, 3 *Bec.* 416; it was the old order, that the people should receive together, 4 *Jew.* 784; mention of priests going to the graves of the dead, and there distributing the sacrament, which custom was used among the heathen, 3 *Jew.* 555; on the sacrament being received in the kind of bread and wine, 3 *Bec.* 414; it is not superfluously received under both kinds, 2 *Bec.* 243, 3 *Bec.* 413, 414; the division of the sacrament declared to be great sacrilege, 2 *Bec.* 243 n., 3 *Bec.* 275 n., 413, 415 n., 4 *Bul.* 416, *Coop.* 138 n., *Sand.* 455; against intinction or dipping of the sacramental bread, 2 *Bec.* 243 n., 3 *Bec.* 415 n.; against the use of milk, intinction, and other abuses in the communion, *Coop.* 137 n.; order in the event of spilling the Lord's blood, 3 *Bec.* 437; canons requiring communion at least thrice a year, 2 *Bec.* 259 n., 3 *Bec.* 380, *Coop.* 102 n., 2 *Cran.* 174, *Pil.* 543; Christ gave not his body to his disciples that they should reserve it, 3 *Bec.* 456; canon forbidding reservation and directing the remains of the sacrament to be eaten, 1 *Hoop.* 522; canon directing the bread to be carefully kept, 2 *Hoop.* 418; a Nicene canon quoted in connexion with this subject, 2 *Ful.* 107; why the wine is not reserved, 2 *Jew.* 555 n., 556; the mass ascribed to St James and Eusebius of Cæsarea, *Pil.* 501, 502; the expression "missas celebrare" cited from pseudo-Clement, 2 *Ful.* 81 n.; mass not to be celebrated except on an altar and in a holy place, 2 *Cran.* 62 n., *Pil.* 496; the attendance of two clerks required at public mass, 1 *Jew.* 174; mass to be ordinarily said only in the day-time, *ib.* 117 n.; on a plurality of masses in one day, 2 *Jew.* 626; canon on giving the communion to excommunicate persons before death, 2 *Ful.* 105 n.; reference to the decree for transubstantiation, 3 *Bec.* 359 n., 361 n.; gloss on certain words in the canon of the mass, affirming transubstantiation, 1 *Hoop.* 518; the recantation of Berengarius, and gloss thereon, 3 *Bec.* 361 n., 1 *Hoop.* 525, 526, 3 *Jew.* 538, 539, 618, *Wool.* 27; the accidents said to be in the air, as in their subject, 3 *Jew.* 509; these forms or accidents are not mingled with other meats, *ib.* 518; statement that corpus Christi potest evomi, 2 *Jew.* 784; on the body of Christ being eaten by mice, 2 *Hoop.* 418, 3 *Jew.* 454; institution of the feast of Corpus Christi, 4 *Bul.* 423; indulgences for keeping that day, 2 *Jew.* 774

(*i*) Ceremonies, Customs:—decree for the celebration of service in diverse languages, 3 *Bec.* 409; reference to the reading of scripture, 4 *Bul.* 201; passages on confirmation, *Calf.* 216, 219, 220, 222, 2 *Cran.* 74, *Rog.* 254 n., *Whita.* 609; decree for Lent, 3 *Bec.* 511, 513, 2 *Brad.* 307 n.; a canon on fasting therein, 1 *Bec.* 533; the alleged institution of holy water, *Calf.* 16 n.; on the linen corporal, 1 *Jew.* 15; on the vestments used at mass, 2 *Tyn.* 221; vestments not to be put to profane uses, 2 *Cran.* 62 n.; whether a sacred garment mended with an unhallowed thread needs to be reconsecrated, 3 *Jew.* 614, 615; secular priests have no certain apparel appointed them, since no mention is made either of the colour or form; by which two

LAW (CANON) 477

differences, or by one of them, apparel must be discerned, *ib.* 617; no church to be built till the bishop has fixed a cross, *Calf.* 135 n.; on holy places, &c., *2 Cran.* 62 n., 74, *Pil.* 496; the feast of the dedication of a church to be observed, *2 Cran.* 62 n.; standing enjoined at the gospel, *3 Bec.* 409; defence of images, *Calf.* 21 n.; on the invention of the cross, *ib.* 322, 323; the cross to be used in all sacraments, *ib.* 206; reply to those who urge the authority of custom, 1 *Bec.* 376, 3 *Bec.* 390; custom not to be preferred to reason and truth, *Calf.* 191; it must give place to the truth, *Calf.* 191, 1 *Bec.* 376; praise of custom which is not against the catholic faith, *Calf.* 54; custom without truth an old error, 1 *Bec.* 376, 3 *Bec.* 390

(*j*) Marriage, Concubinage, &c.:—declaration that only virginity is able to present the soul of a man unto God, 3 *Jew.* 404; a man allowed to forsake his betrothed for a monastery, 1 *Tyn.* 171 n.; in what the sacrament of matrimony consists, *Calf.* 240; declaration that in marriage there are two sacraments, *ib.* 238; yet it is said to be unholy, *ib.* 238—241; marriage spoken against, 3 *Bec.* 364 n., 3 *Jew.* 420; the apostles took no order touching the not using of matrimony already contracted, 3 *Jew.* 423; marriage forbidden without the consent of parents, *Sand.* 281; reference about marriage with two sisters, 4 *Jew.* 1244; the marriage of co-sponsors prohibited, 3 *Bec.* 533 n., 1 *Tyn.* 245; canons forbidding marriage at certain times, 3 *Bec.* 533 n.; canons against marriage after divorce, *ib.* 532 n.; statement he who hath not a wife, instead of her ought to have a concubine, 4 *Jew.* 630; the passage altered in editions subsequent to the reformation, 3 *Tyn.* 41 n.; he that hath not a wife, but instead of a wife hath a concubine, not to be put from the communion, 4 *Jew.* 631, 3 *Tyn.* 41 n.; a concubine defined, 4 *Jew.* 631, 632, 3 *Tyn.* 41 n.; unless the solemnities of the law appear, concubinage is ever presumed to be adultery, 4 *Jew.* 632; bigami, i.e. persons who have been twice married, not to be admitted to orders, *Calf.* 19, 3 *Tyn.* 165 n.; statements about second marriage with reference to St Paul's direction, 3 *Jew.* 407; admission that the marriage of priests is forbidden neither by the authority of the law, of the gospel, nor of the apostles, 2 *Jew.* 882, 3 *Jew.* 403, 422; in old times before pope Siricius, it was lawful for priests to marry, 3 *Jew.* 408, 411, 423, 4 *Jew.* 807, 809; confession that the celibacy of the clergy was not introduced at the time of the synod of Ancyra, &c., 2 *Ful.* 96; proof that sundry popes were priests' sons, 3 *Jew.* 130; constitution of a council at Constantinople that the lawful marriage of bishops and priests should stand in force, *ib.* 404, 422; passages declaring that Greek priests make no vow of single life, 3 *Jew.* 396, 407, 408, 423, 4 *Jew.* 805; those who say that a married priest should not minister, accursed, *Pil.* 566; likewise those who teach that a priest should despise his wife, *ib.*; mention of a priest who took a wife, and lived with her without any offence of law, 4 *Jew.* 809; reproof of bishops and priests that bring up their children in worldly learning, 3 *Jew.* 393; a foolish reason against the marriage of priests, *ib.* 222; decree of Urban II. on clerical celibacy, 1 *Whitg.* 482 n.; inquiry what wise man will judge them to be priests who abstain not from fornication, 4 *Jew.* 802; caution to a man not to hear the mass of the priest whom he undoubtedly knoweth to keep a concubine, *ib.*; the gloss says this decree in old times stood as a ruled case, but now it is not so, *ib.*; a layman may not accuse a priest of fornication, *ib.* 639; if a priest embrace a woman, a layman must judge that he doth it to the intent to bless her, 2 *Ful.* 211, 4 *Jew.* 634; declaration that although the fornication of the priest be notorious, we are not on that account to abstain from his services, 3 *Jew.* 158; no man ought now to be deposed for fornication unless he persist in it, 4 *Jew.* 636, 637; a reason given for this, *ib.* 637; a man not to be deprived for simple fornication, forasmuch as few (priests) are found without that fault, 3 *Jew.* 162, 427, 4 *Jew.* 636, 637, 638, 802; ten years' penance once appointed for fornication, 4 *Jew.* 636, 637; the penalty commuted for a fine, *ib.* 637; touching adultery and other small faults the bishop, after penance done, may dispense with a priest, *Calf.* 18 n., 4 *Jew.* 638; the bishop dispenses with him that offends (having sundry concubines) but with him that offends not (having married two wives) he dispenses not, *ib.* 639; admission that lechery has more privilege than chastity, *Calf.* 19, 4 *Jew.* 639; pope Pelagius gives a reason why the ancient penalties are not to be exacted, *ib.* 637; it is not coming to widows or maids, but the often haunting unto them, that is forbidden, *ib.* 639; women having company with priests, to be removed by the bishop, sold, and made slaves, *ib.*; the gloss restricts this to women marrying priests, *ib.*; a priest having several concubines not accounted guilty of bigamy, *ib.* 636; with priests having sundry concubines the bishop may dispense, that they may nevertheless do their office, *ib.* 638; he that keepeth sundry concubines is not thereby made irregular, *ib.*; bastards made legitimate by the subsequent marriage of their parents, *ib.* 904; what may be done with the reward of a harlot, *ib.* 644

(*k*) Confession, Excommunication, &c.: —it is not proved that secret sins are of necessity to be uttered in confession unto the priest, 3 *Jew.* 372, 4 *Jew.* 977; proof, from Ezek. xviii. 27, 28, that sorrow of heart brings pardon, *Calf.* 242, 243; it appears most evidently that only by contrition of heart, without confession of mouth, sin is remitted, *ib.* 243; that confession which is made to God alone, purgeth sins, *ib.*; others on the contrary bear witness, saying, that without confession of the mouth and satisfaction of deed, none can be cleansed, &c., 3 *Bec.* 509; whether of these two opinions (in favour of, or against private confession) it were better to follow, is left to the discretion of the reader; for either side is favoured by wise and godly men, 3 *Bul.* 82, 3 *Jew.* 352, 377; the better opinion considered to be that confession was instituted by the church, not commanded in the scriptures, 2 *Jew.* 1134, 3 *Jew.* 352, 377; on the time when confession was instituted, whether in Paradise or subsequently, 1 *Hoop.* 536; perhaps (in the time of Ambrose) the manner of confession that now is used, was not appointed, 3 *Jew.* 377; among the Christians in Greece confession of sins is not necessary, because this tradition never came among them, 3 *Jew.* 353, 4 *Jew.* 977; some say we ought to confess our sins only unto God, as do the Grecians, 3 *Jew.* 353, 377; before we open our mouth unto the priest, the leprosy of our sin is made clean, *ib.* 377; although we utter nothing with our mouth, yet we may obtain pardon of our sins, *ib.* 363, 372, 4 *Jew.* 977; confession is made to the priest in token of forgiveness already obtained, not as a cause whereby to procure forgiveness, 3 *Jew.* 360, 4 *Jew.* 977; confession is made, not to obtain forgiveness thereby, but to declare our repentance, 3 *Jew.* 360; the sinner is made clean, not by the judgment of the priest, but by the abundance of divine grace, *ib.* 376; the word of God forgiveth sins, the priest is judge, 2 *Bec.* 174 n., 3 *Jew.* 378, 379; the judgment of the president is true when it followeth the judgment of the everlasting Judge, 3 *Jew.* 376; the merit of the priest can neither further nor hinder, but the merit of him that desireth absolution, *ib.* 358; statement that venial sins may be taken away either by a Pater noster, or by holy water, *ib.* 372; in necessity a layman may hear confession and absolve, 3 *Jew.* 357, 4 *Jew.* 977; excommunication called the sword of a bishop, 3 *Jew.* 356; he that is excommunicated cannot excommunicate, 3 *Jew.* 203, 4 *Jew.* 890; to slay an excommunicate man not murder, 2 *Cran.* 74; claim of the power of binding and loosing those buried under the earth, *Rog.* 68 n.; mention of some crimes which may be judged after death, as heresy, *ib.*; if any excommunicated person have been buried in an ecclesiastical cemetery, his bones are to be dug up, and cast out, 3 *Tyn.* 270; mention of absolution after death, 3 *Jew.* 359; Unigenitus, on which is founded the alleged power of the pope to sell pardons and indulgences, 1 *Tyn.* 74 n., and see 2 *Cran.* 74

(*l*) Oaths:—as in an oath there must be no falsehood, so in words ought there to be no lie, 1 *Bec.* 379, 380; passages against swearing by creatures, 1 *Hoop.* 478; it is a point of wisdom for a man to call that again which he hath evil spoken, 1 *Bec.* 372; in evil promises faith may be broken, 1 *Bec.* 372, 1 *Bul.* 250, 3 *Jew.* 399; it is sometimes contrary to a man's duty to perform the oath he has promised, 1 *Bec.* 372, 1 *Bul.* 250; that oath must not be kept whereby any evil is unwarily promised, 1 *Bul.* 250, 251; it is better not to fulfil the vows of a foolish promise, than by the observance of them to commit wickedness, 1 *Bec.* 372; we ought rather to forswear ourselves, than for the eschewing of perjury fall into any other more grievous sin, *ib.* 374; David commended for breaking his rash oath, *ib.*, 1 *Bul.* 251; the wicked vow of Hubaldus, 3 *Jew.* 400

(*m*) Civil power:—assertion that Christ, by several duties and sundry dignities, has severed the offices of both powers, 4 *Jew.* 826, 985; the heathen emperors were called pontifices maximi, *ib.* 983, 984; the emperor has not his sword of the pope, but the empire is from God alone, *ib.* 835, 836; statement that the common laws say the emperor is the lord of the world, *ib.* 1008, 1014; the emperor is a true emperor by the election of the princes only, before he be confirmed by the pope, *ib.* 836; there is no kind of thing but it may be thoroughly examined by the authority of the emperor; for he receives from God a general government and principality over all men, *ib.* 1033; assertion that the emperor has the right of choosing the pope, 2 *Tyn.* 263 n.; a priest sometimes called to make answer before a temporal judge, 4 *Jew.* 961; the pope by the consent of the prince exempts priests from subjection to the emperor, *ib.* 969, 974; the case of a bishop committed to the judgment of the French queen Brunichildis, 1 *Jew.* 396, 4 *Jew.* 961 —963; even the emperor calls himself a servant, 4 *Jew.* 847; declaration that the control both of the spiritual and material sword belongs to the church, 2 *Hoop.* 239 n., 2 *Tyn.* 272 n.; the emperor claimed as the pope's subject, 3 *Bec.* 507, 2 *Cran.* 69; the pope says the emperor is as far inferior to him, as the moon is to the sun, see in *d*, above; the emperor said to be the proctor or defender of the Roman church, 1 *Jew.* 443, 3 *Jew.* 311, 4 *Jew.* 836, 847, 981, 1013; princes ought to obey the bishops and decrees of the church, 2 *Cran.* 73; assertion that princes ought not to set bishops beneath them, but to assign them an honourable seat by them, *ib.*; every king, prelate, and potentate, who may think himself allowed to violate any decision of a pope accursed, 2 *Cran.* 69, 2 *Tyn.* 282 n.; princes not to tax ecclesiastics, without the pope's permission, 1 *Tyn.* 179, 2 *Tyn.* 277; yet the law says, if the temporal governor demand tribute, we deny it not, 1 *Bec.* 221; the bringing of any accusation against an ecclesiastic before a secular judge prohibited, 2 *Tyn.* 307 n.; any lay judge who shall have distrained or condemned an ecclesiastic to be suspended, 1 *Tyn.* 178 n.; Constantine stated to have conceded royal dignity to pope Silvester, 2 *Tyn.* 279; the alleged Donation of Constantine, 2 *Ful.* 360 n., 3 *Jew.* 394, 4 *Jew.* 840, 2 *Lat.* 349 n., 2 *Tyn.* 279; declaration that Constantine the emperor was president of the council of Nice, 4 *Jew.* 1018; statement that emperors have been present at councils, faith pertaining to them as well as to priests, *ib.* 1026, see 2 *Cran.* 70; transfer of the empire to Charlemagne, 2 *Hoop.* 238; Louis le Débonnaire's feigned release of the right of electing the pope, 2 *Tyn.* 279; Otho's oath to pope John, 3 *Bec.* 512, 513, 2 *Tyn.* 269; the pope's law annuls all the laws of temporal princes, 2 *Cran.* 68, 165; it is contrary to the law of the land, *ib.* 213, 214, 221, 222, 448, 449

(*n*) Rules of Law, &c.:—that what touches all ought to be allowed by all, 1 *Jew.* 412, 4 *Jew.* 826, 1 *Whitg.* 370; on tacit consent, 1 *Whitg.* 362; the matter is not subject to the word, but the word to the matter, 1 *Hoop.* 528; when the propriety of words is forced, the meaning of the truth is lost, *ib.*; a thing once bad cannot be amended by time, 1 *Jew.* 79; as to possessors malæ fidei, *ib.* 49, 50; a man ought to make his purgation where he is defamed, 4 *Jew.* 963; exceptio judicis incompetentis, 1 *Jew.* 62; a wrongful sentence bindeth no man, 4 *Jew.* 1152; appeals allowed from equal to equal, 1 *Jew.* 395 n.; in the presence of the superior, the power of the inferior ceases, 2 *Tyn.* 285; vain remedies, that are more grievous than the true and manifest dangers, to be rejected, 4 *Jew.* 647

(*o*) Miscellanea:—truth is known by little and little, 3 *Jew.* 595; whoever conceals the truth through the fear of any power provokes the anger of God against himself, because he fears man more than God, 2 *Lat.* 298 n.; assertion that if the Jews had not crucified Christ, they had sinned deadly, 3 *Jew.* 183, 4 *Jew.* 942; the sin against the Holy Ghost declared to be final impenitence, 2 *Bul.* 425; the Angelici mentioned, 2 *Ful.* 42 n.; a man said to lose that he never had, 4 *Jew.* 885; public disputations forbidden, *Phil.* 27, 34; mention of several universities, 4 *Jew.* 654; Rome designated the head of covetousness, *ib.* 867; all things sold there, *ib.*; Joachim Abbas condemned, *ib.* 741; explanation of the word apocrisiarii, *ib.* 878; unseemly heaviness for the dead, attributed to despair of the resurrection, 2 *Cov.* 123; statement that some have chosen rather to endure the miseries of this world a hundred years, than the pains of purgatory for one day, *Rog.* 218 n

La Warr (Tho. lord de): *v.* West.

Lawes (Tho.): prebendary of Canterbury, *Park.* 442; Grindal's commissary, *Grin.* 415 n., 416, 424

Lawish sprinkling: that sprinkling which was prescribed and practised under the law, 2 *Bec.* 227

Lawney (Tho.): 2 *Cran.* 301, 367

Lawrence: *v.* Laurence.

Lawse (Tho.): *v.* Lawes.

Lawson (Geo.): 2 *Cov.* 491

Lawyers: v. Prayers.
Their pleading at the bar, 3 *Jew.* 124; they pleaded in French, 2 *Cran.* 170; they were made parsons, vicars, prebendaries, *Hutch.* 4; their practice condemned, 1 *Brad.* 406, 2 *Ful.* 129, 130, 1 *Lat.* 344, *Pil.* 464; the delay of justice charged upon attorneys, proctors, counsellors, and advocates, *Sand.* 226; lawyers called horse-leeches, *Pil.* 238; their covetousness, 1 *Bec.* 253, 1 *Lat.* 98, 110, 344; it hath almost devoured England, 1 *Lat.* 318; anecdote of a covetous serjeant, *Sand.* 383; lawyers keep their old trade, *Park.* 352; said to be like Switzers (hirelings), 1 *Lat.* 127; those who counsel wrongly for gain are thieves, 2 *Bec.* 108; what they should do, 1 *Bec.* 256, 2 *Bec.* 114, 115; counsellors at the law must be righteous, *Sand.* 193; lawyers shall be judged, 2 *Lat.* 56

Layfield (......): *Sand.* iii.

Laying-on of Hands, q. v.

Laymen: v. Laity.

Layton (Rich.): prebendary of St Paul's, *Rid.* 331 n

Layton (Will.): prebendary of St Paul's, 2 *Brad.* xxiv. n., *Rid.* 331 n

Lazarus: on the parable of the rich man and Lazarus, *Pil.* 52, *Whita.* 642; the rich man's burial, *Whita.* 202

Lazarus, the brother of Martha and Mary: 2 *Bul.* 69; said to have preached at Marseilles, 1 *Jew.* 162

Lazius (Wolfg.): asserts that Abdias was one of the seventy disciples, *Calf.* 126

Lazy lordanes: 2 *Jew.* 922

Lea (Sir Hen.): v. Lee.

Leach (......), a Scotchman: his case, *Grin.* 260; recommended to Sir Will. Cecil, *ib.* 275

Leaf (Jo.): an apprentice, burned with Bradford, 1 *Brad.* 556, 2 *Brad.* xli; called by Bryce Jo. Least, *Poet.* 162

League: v. France.

Leagues: v. Covenants.

Leake, co. Lincoln: 2 *Cran.* 368

Leander: 2 *Bec.* 227 n

Leare: learning, lore, skill, 2 *Jew.* 626

Learning, Learned: v. Abbeys, Children, Scholars.
Learning not to be despised, 2 *Jew.* 1026, 1027; comparison of learning, 4 *Jew.* 878; two sorts of learners, 4 *Bul.* 154; on the Christian education of the young, 2 *Cran.* 419; they ought to be trained in Christian learning, 1 *Bec.* 10, in the knowledge of God's will, 2 *Bec.* 480; education to be enjoined by the clergy, 2 *Cran.* 499; its force, 1 *Lat.* 116; on the education of nobles and gentlemen, *ib.* 69; Cranmer objects to the exclusion of poor men's children from grammar-schools, 2 *Cran.* 398; none are learned unless they know Christ, 2 *Lat.* 258, 260; heretics not generally unlearned, *Pil.* 120

Learning (New): the gospel so called, 1 *Lat.* 30; against those that so call the gospel, with sentences and examples of scripture, 1 *Bec.* 439; the new learning proved to be old, 2 *Lat.* 318—320; the term afterwards applied to classical learning, 1 *Lat.* 30 n

Lease, or Leash: a cord or thong by which dogs are held, 2 *Tyn.* 84

Leases: *Pil.* 289; under the seals of chapters, *Grin.* 179

Least (Jo.): v. Leaf.

Leaven: the old leaven, 3 *Whitg.* 230; the leaven of the Pharisees, what it is, 1 *Lat.* 257, 258; leaven interpreted in a good sense, 1 *Tyn.* 113, 2 *Tyn.* 87, 233

Leaver (Mr): v. Lever.

Le Bas (C. W.): Life of Jewel, 2 *Ful.* 371, 1 *Zur.* 100, 139 nn

Lechery: v. Adultery.
The king requested to punish it, 1 *Lat.* 276

Le Chevalier (Ant. Rod.): v. Cavallerius.

Le Clerc (Jean): v. Clericus.

Lectern: a desk for reading, *Grin.* 155

Lectors, or Readers: 4 *Bul.* 113, 114, 1 *Whitg.* 541, 542, 2 *Whitg.* 174, 342, 456, 458; mentioned in the so-called apostolic canons, *Whita.* 509; also by Eusebius, 2 *Whitg.* 174; children under fourteen anciently admitted as such, 4 *Jew.* 911; the Romish order, *Rog.* 258; how they are ordained, 3 *Jew.* 273, charged on their ordination to read the gospel for the quick and the dead, 2 *Jew.* 745

Ledbury, co. Hereford, 2 *Zur.* 329 n

Ledington: v. Lethington.

Lee (Edw.), abp of York: preaches at Paul's cross, 2 *Lat.* 378; opposes Bale, *Bale* viii; present at Anne Boleyn's coronation, 2 *Cran.* 245; letter to him, to suspend the quarterly reading of the general curse, *ib.* 281

Lee (Rowl.), bp of Coventry and Lichfield: referred to, *ib.* 259 n., 271 n.; elected bishop of Chester (meaning Coventry and Lichfield), *ib.* 274

Lee (Tho.), or Legh: visits religious houses, 2 *Cran.* 315 n., 319 n., 2 *Lat.* 372 n.; cites queen Catharine, 2 *Cran.* 244; sent to Canterbury to inquire about Becket's blood, *ib.* 378; complains of the prevalence of open adultery, 1 *Lat.* 244 n

Lee (Sir Hen.), K. G.: Ridley's dying gift to him, *Rid.* 296; Parker favours him, *Park.* 354, 359
Lee (......): a rebel, 2 *Cran.* 187 n
Leech: a healer; dog-leeches, *Bale* 236
Leeds castle, co. Kent: *Bale* 18 n
Leeds (Edw.): letters to him and others, *Park.* 63, 64
Leese: to lose, 1 *Brad.* 72, 1 *Bul.* 44
Le Faucher (Mich.): De la Cene du Seigneur, 2 *Ful.* 115 n
Lefèvre (Jac.), of Étaples: *v.* Faber.
Legates: remarks on them, 4 *Jew.* 679; sin of one in England, *Pil.* 572, *Sand.* 224; legates à latere, 2 *Zur.* 149; pole-axes borne before them, 1 *Tyn.* 251
Legatinæ Constitutiones: *v.* Lyndewode.
Legatio: *v.* Adrian VI.
Legenda Aurea: 1 *Bec.* 139 n., 3 *Bec.* 200, 234, 519, 535, 1 *Hoop.* 182, *Hutch.* 171 n., *Jew.* xxxix, 1 *Jew.* 162, 265, 3 *Jew.* 344, 1 *Lat.* 435 n., 2 *Tyn.* 98 n., 3 *Whitg.* 348; it is a legend of lies, *Pil.* 18; opinion of Lud. Vives on it, 4 *Jew.* 816, *Sand.* 18
Legenda Sanctorum: 2 *Lat.* 132 n
Legenda Nova Sanctorum: this seems to be the Nova Legenda Angliæ of Jo. Capgrave, *q. v.*: cited on Oswin's synod at Whitby, *Pil.* 625; on St Etheldreda, *ib.* 590; on St Anselm, *ib.* 589; on St William, *ib.* 587, 588; on the burning of Canterbury, *ib.* 607
Legendaries: to be abolished, *Grin.* 135, 159
Legends: foolish legends in the Latin service, 2 *Cran.* 180, 181; their authority shaken by the diffusion of the scriptures, *Sand.* 18
Legh (Tho.): *v.* Lee.
Legion (The Thundering): 1 *Bul.* 383
Leicester: Brocvale, king of Leicester, 4 *Jew.* 780; Augustine of Canterbury there, *ib.*; a parliament there in the time of Hen. V., *Bale* 4, 49; a martyr there, *Poet.* 168; the hospital of Will. de Wigston; Sampson master of it, 2 *Zur.* 118 n
Leicester (Rob. earl of): *v.* Dudley,
Leicestershire: how they called swine to their food there, 1 *Lat.* 147
Leichtenaw (Conr. à), commonly called Urspergensis: *Jew.* xliv; describes the mission of Augustine to Britain, 1 *Jew.* 307; speaks of the crimes of Phocas, *ib.* 363, 364; says that at the request of pope Boniface, Phocas appointed the see of the apostolic church of Rome to be the head of all churches, before which the church of Constantinople was chief, 4 *Jew.* 733; asserts that Rome conquered the world not by religion but malice, *ib.* 685; relates certain acts of pope Sergius, 3 *Jew.* 276; describes the cruelty of Irene, 2 *Jew.* 653; says the council held at Constantinople against the image-breakers was repealed by one held at Frankfort, 4 *Jew.* 1050; does not mention pope Joan, *ib.* 648; mentions that Udalric succeeded Hiltinus in the see of Augsburg, 3 *Jew.* 424; says the emperor Henry III. coming into Italy, deposed three popes unlawfully made, 4 *Jew.* 682; relates the history of pope Hildebrand, and records his treatment of the emperor Henry IV., 2 *Hoop.* 239, 3 *Jew.* 129, 143, 4 *Jew.* 696, 699, 700; describes the character of that emperor, 4 *Jew.* 699; refers to papal intrigues, *ib.* 698; says Boniface VIII. entered into the popedom as a fox, reigned as a wolf, died as a dog, *ib.* 684
— Rerum mem. Paraleip. annexed to his Chronicon, *Jew.* xli; this work records the declaration of Louis IV., that his power depended not on the pope, but on God only, 4 *Jew.* 836; tells how Boniface VIII. went in procession attired as an emperor, and had a naked sword borne before him, *ib.* 684, 820, 825, 972; states that the emperor Henry of Luxemberg was poisoned in the sacrament, *ib.* 686, 687; says that pope Clement V. was an open whoremaster, *ib.* 874, and that from that time discipline and religion decayed in the cardinals, and three roots of vices, pride, avarice, and lechery, bare the sway, *ib.* 642, 874, 880; mentions a pope's claim of power to depose kings, *ib.* 932; records a complaint of the bad character of chaplains and canons, 3 *Jew.* 426; contains a chapter about exactions for suffering concubines, 4 *Jew.* 644; says, in the history of the council of Constance, that the bishops oppressed the Spirit of God, defied the voices of the prophets, persecuted Christ in his members, *ib.* 874; records the assertion of pope Pius II. that we must withstand any man to the face, whether Peter, or Paul, if he walk not after the truth of the gospel, *ib.* 875, and his remark that if a bishop speak against the pope, yea, although he speak the truth, yet he sins against his oath to the pope, *ib.* 948; describes the Liga Sotularia, *ib.* 665; mentions a decree of Maximilian against swearing, 1 *Bec.* 391; speaks of Cajetan requiring Luther to recant an article on the sacrament, 2 *Jew.* 751, 3 *Jew.* 557
Leigh (Edw.): Annot., *Calf.* 95 n.; Crit. Sac., *ib.* 107 n

Leigh (Rich.): his pious fraud at Christ church, Dublin, *Park.* 95 n
Leigh (Tho.), sheriff of London: *Phil.* 150
Leigh (Tho.), of Adlington: *Poet.* 364
Leighton (Sir Tho.): governor of Guernsey, 1 *Zur.* 323
Leighton (Sir Will.): his Teares, *Rog.* ix, x.
Leighton (Edw.), archdeacon of Sarum: signs a declaration respecting a general council, 2 *Cran.* 468
Leighton (Rich.), or Layton: a visitor of monasteries, 2 *Cran.* 315 n., 326
Leipsic: beseiged, 3 *Zur.* 258 n
Leith: intended to be fortified, 1 *Zur.* 59; defended by queen Mary, *ib.* 60; beseiged and taken by the English, *ib.* 82, 86, 88, 89, 91 (see *Calf.* 114); levelled to the ground, *ib.* 89; fortified by the king's party, *ib.* 262
Leith (James): a letter to Bullinger, 1 *Zur.* 230
Leland (Jo.): Itinerary, 2 *Lat.* 295, 368, 395, 402 nn
Lelius (......): 3 *Zur.* 355
Le Long (Jac.): Bibliotheca Sacra, 2 *Ful.* 166 n
Leman: a sweetheart, 1 *Lat.* 42 n
Le Mangeur (Pierre): v. Petrus Comestor.
Lemann (......): 2 *Zur.* 225, 262
Le Moyne (Osias), vicar of Roydon: 2 *Cran.* 368 n
Le Moyne (Steph.): *Grin.* 72 n
Lemster: v. Leominster.
Lending: rules for lending, 2 *Tyn.* 68
Le Neve (J.): 2 *Lat.* 370, 377, 378, 387 nn.; 3 *Whitg.* vi. n
Lenglin (Jos.), one of the ministers of Strasburgh: 3 *Zur.* 334, 534
Lennox (Earls of): v. Stuart.
Le Nourri (Nich.): *Calf.* 21, 69, 110, 211 nn.; claims for Cecilius the treatise De mortibus Persecutorum, commonly ascribed to Lactantius, 2 *Ful.* 336 n
Lent: v. Fasting.
 Supposed by Ambrose to be binding by force of our Lord's example and various scripture types, *Whita.* 604; referred by some Papists to Christ, by some to apostolic tradition, by others to the church, *ib.* 501; not ordained by the apostles, 3 *Tyn.* 258; traced by Bellarmine through the fathers up to Clement, *Whita.* 508; Platina ascribes its institution to Telesphorus, *ib.*; not instituted by Telesphorus, 2 *Ful.* 236, 237; at first enjoined on the clergy only, 2 *Brad.* 307; its observance of old, 3 *Jew.* 170, 2 *Whitg.* 556; the manner of observing it formerly various and uncertain, *Whita.* 508; ancient diversities of fasting in it, *Pil.* 560; disregard of it deemed heresy in early times, 3 *Jew.* 430; how kept by Romanists,—their absurd distinction between meats, *Whita.* 604; ceremonies used in the churches in Lent, and their signification, 1 *Bec.* 110, &c.; the monastic services in Lent, 2 *Tyn.* 81; images covered during Lent, 1 *Bec.* 111, 2 *Cran.* 414; a proclamation for abstaining from flesh in Lent, 2 *Cran.* 507; religious examination enjoined in it, *ib.* 500; its strict observance in king Edward's time, 3 *Zur.* 723; letters of the archbishop and council on the observance of Lent and fish day, *Grin.* 406, 407; flesh eaten in it, *Pil.* 484, 551, 560; dispensations touching white meat, 2 *Lat.* 413; Lent licences sought for Sir Rog. North, *Park.* 108, for the baron de la Ferte, *ib.* 172, for the lord of Lethington, *ib.*, for Jo. Fox, *ib.* 230, for Philip Sidney, *ib.* 316; what it requires of Christian men, 1 *Bec.* 91; usually appointed to abstinence, 2 *Bec.* 526; on fasting therein, 2 *Cran.* 156; it is a time of mourning for sin, 1 *Bec.* 111; we keep it when we live well, *ib.* 106; ancient canons respecting baptism and the offering of bread in Lent, 2 *Cran.* 39; marriage not permitted in Lent, except by dispensation, 2 *Lat.* 162, 1 *Zur.* 164; A POTATION FOR LENT, by T. Becon, 1 *Bec.* 85
Lent: offered (but perhaps an error for bent), 2 *Bec.* 165
Lentulus: the spurious epistle in his name, *Calf.* 46 n
L'envoy: the lenvoy, by Nic. Boweman, *Poet.* 555
Leo I., emperor of the East: was against images, *Phil.* 407
Leo III., emperor of the East, called the Isaurian: *Calf.* xii, 138; he forbade images, 2 *Bec.* 71, 312, 1 *Hoop.* 47, *Park.* 90, *Rid.* 93; a treatise De Re Militari erroneously ascribed to him, *Park.* 90, *Rid.* 93
Leo VI., emperor of the East, called the Philosopher, the Wise, and the Pacific: his book De Apparatu Bellico, or Tartica, *Rid.* 93 n., see *Park.* 90; he (?) maintained philosophers, 2 *Jew.* 981
Leo I., pope, called the Great: was too much addicted to the dignity of his see, 2 *Ful.* 327; but in a case of doubt he conferred with other bishops, 1 *Jew.* 382; confessed himself unable to remove Eutyches from his abbey, *ib.* 414; sent clergy to certain councils, 4 *Jew.* 995; was summoned to the Council (*q. v.*) of Chalcedon, 3 *Jew.*

225, 4 *Jew.* 996; his credit therein, 3 *Jew.* 219, 220; humbled by the council, 2 *Ful.* 288, 289, 308, 326, 327, 332, 363, 364; he would not assent to a decree of it, 1 *Jew.* 413, 423, 3 *Jew.* 220; charged the synod with rashness, 1 *Jew.* 423, 4 *Jew.* 1109; was required by the emperor to declare his consent to it, 1 *Jew.* 412, 413; his works, 2 *Ful.* 405, *Jew.* xxxix; his epistles, *Whita.* 436; an emendation in one of them proposed by Quesnel, 2 *Ful.* 319 n.; he wrote an epistle against Eutyches, which it is said St Peter corrected, 3 *Jew.* 299; one of his epistles corrupted by Gratian, 2 *Ful.* 82 n.; supposed to have written a discourse ascribed to Jerome, *Whita.* 667; he quotes from Ambrose, 3 *Jew.* 261 n.; Quesnel claims for him the composition of the books De Vocatione Gentium, 2 *Ful.* 353 n.; he speaks of the Seed of the woman bruising the serpent's head, *Whita.* 165 n.; cites Ambrose against the heresy of Eutyches, who asserted the flesh of Christ and his divinity to be of one nature, 1 *Jew.* 482; asserts that although John says "The Word was made flesh," yet the Word was not turned into flesh, 2 *Jew.* 566; regards "the form of God" as meaning the nature of God, 3 *Jew.* 261; exclaims, ye foolish scribes and wicked priests, the power of our Saviour was not to be shewed at the discretion of your blindness, 4 *Jew.* 1040; says, Christ suffered not in the Godhead, but in the infirmity of human nature, 1 *Jew.* 527; speaks of the shedding of Christ's blood as sufficient to deliver all the prisoners in the world, 3 *Bec.* 422, 423; declares that although the death of many saints is precious in the sight of the Lord, yet the slaughter of no innocent is a propitiation for the sins of the world, 3 *Bul.* 95, 3 *Jew.* 574; says that in one Lord Jesus Christ all are crucified, dead, buried, and raised again, 3 *Bul.* 95; warns the true worshipper of our Lord's passion so to behold Christ crucified with the eyes of his heart, that he may understand that Christ's flesh is his flesh, 3 *Jew.* 538; states that the flesh of Christ is the same (that it was) for essence, not the same for glory, *ib.* 258; says, Christ by unspeakable means began to be the nearer to us by his divinity, the further he is made from us by his humanity, *ib.* 496; cites Augustine respecting Christ's coming again in his true human nature, 1 *Cran.* 94 n., (48); censures the folly of not going to the prophets, to the apostles, &c., 4 *Jew.* 851; asks what needs it to believe that thing that neither the law hath taught, nor the prophets have spoken, &c., *ib.* 886; shews that the scriptures were read in the church, *ib.* 857; condemns apocryphal writings, 1 *Jew.* 111; intimates that it is better not to express our belief in the holy church, 1 *Bul.* 160; observes that the whole church has one prayer, and one confession, 4 *Jew.* 812; censures those who under the name of the church fight against the church, 1 *Jew.* 98, 500, 2 *Jew.* 819, 3 *Jew.* 152; says the devil is sore grieved with the calling of the heathen, and with the daily decreasing of his power, therefore he causes dissensions, 3 *Jew.* 610; affirms that every observance (of the church) is from divine teaching, &c., 2 *Ful.* 182; his canon on the appointment of bishops, 1 *Whitg.* 460; he speaks of a bishop named Juvenal obtaining the princehood of the province of Palestine, 4 *Jew.* 824; says, that bishop works himself greater condemnation who promotes an unworthy person to the ministry, 1 *Bec.* 6; declares that ignorance is worthy neither of excuse nor forgiveness in them that bear rule, *ib.* 384; says, unto frantic masters the truth is a slander, and to blind doctors light is darkness, 3 *Jew.* 250; directs that after the solemn reading of the most holy lesson there follow the sermon or exhortation of the priest, 4 *Jew.* 857; says, he that knows himself to be set over some men, let him not disdain to have some man preferred before him, &c., 2 *Ful.* 259, 311; affirms that it was given to one apostle to be over the rest, &c., 3 *Jew.* 291, &c.; says Christ took Peter into the fellowship of the undivided unity, *ib.* 120, 296; (similar words are ascribed to Nicholas III., *q.v.*), and by various other expressions greatly exaggerates the power of Peter, *ib.* 296; declares that Christ called Peter the rock, that the building of the everlasting temple might stand in the soundness of Peter, *ib.* 297; his statement as to the rock of the church shamefully perverted, 2 *Ful.* 293, 294; he declares that Peter had a special care of feeding the sheep committed to him, *ib.* 319; says Peter properly governs all priests, and uses other expressions to the same effect, 3 *Jew.* 299; his epistle to Anastasius, bp of Thessalonica, quoted by Harding for the supremacy, 1 *Jew.* 402; he is falsely stated to have been called universal bishop, 1 *Jew.* 422, 424; he was however by some styled universal patriarch, *ib.* 425 n., 426; he declined the title of universal bishop, 1 *Jew.* 47, 2 *Jew.* 632,

3 *Jew.* 300; claims to have decreed certain things by the inspiration of God and of the most blessed apostle Peter, 3 *Jew.* 296, 298; his decree for the authority of the Roman church, 3 *Bec.* 511 n.; he says sacraments were altered according to the diversity of times, but the faith whereby we live, was never different, 2 *Jew.* 1119, 3 *Jew.* 447; calls the cross of Christ both a sacrament and an example, 2 *Jew.* 1103, 3 *Jew.* 457; terms a promise of virginity a sacrament, 3 *Jew.* 458; speaks of God granting us the marvellous sacrament of regeneration, 1 *Jew.* 487; says that as our Lord was made our flesh, by that he was born, so are we made his flesh, by that we are new-born, 3 *Jew.* 494; declares that a man received of Christ is not the same after baptism as before, but that the body of the regenerate is made the flesh of the crucified, 1 *Brad.* 89, 1 *Jew.* 474, 2 *Jew.* 566, 3 *Jew.* 468; affirms that Christ gave unto the water (of baptism) what he gave unto his mother, 1 *Jew.* 455, 2 *Jew.* 567, 1102, 3 *Jew.* 468, 498; says, thou art washed in the blood of Christ, when thou art baptized in his death, 3 *Jew.* 529; directs baptism to be administered at Easter and Whitsuntide, 4 *Bul.* 367; a decree of his referred to about sponsors, 2 *Bec.* 210 n.; referred to about the eating of Christ in the sacrament of the eucharist, 1 *Cran.* 195, (75); he admonishes so to communicate of the holy table as to doubt nothing concerning the verity of Christ's body and blood, &c., 3 *Jew.* 466; says the same thing is received by the mouth that is believed by our faith, 1 *Jew.* 286 n., 3 *Jew.* 466, 468; declares that we are changed into the same thing that we receive, 3 *Jew.* 469; he (or Ambrose) speaks of eagles flying about the body with spiritual wings, 1 *Jew.* 451, 3 *Jew.* 546; he asks what hope they leave themselves in the help of the sacrament who deny the verity of human substance in the body of our Saviour, 2 *Jew.* 700; speaks of the communicants responding "Amen," 1 *Jew.* 286 n., 2 *Jew.* 698, 699; said to have made part of the canon of the mass, 2 *Brad.* 309, 1 *Jew.* 9, 96; alleged to have commanded the sacrament to be censed, 2 *Brad.* 311; ordered that the names of Dioscorus, Juvenalis, and Thalassius, should not be rehearsed at the altar, 4 *Jew.* 1022; directed that in case the church could not hold all that came, there might be two or more communions in one day, *Coop.* 70, 1 *Jew.* 17, 120, 2 *Jew.* 626, 629, &c., 641, 4 *Jew.* 821; it is said he was wont to communicat seven or eight times in one day, 3 *Bec.* 381, 474; he testifies that the Manichees used not the cup, 1 *Jew.* 257, 260, 3 *Jew.* 158 n., 481, *Rog.* 295 n.; speaks of the confirmation of converts from heresy, 3 *Whitg.* 479; favours private confession, 3 *Jew.* 369; speaks of the absolution of men bereft of speech and reason, *ib.* 355, 359; calls the fast of forty days an apostolical institution, *Whita.* 610; asks, what shall become of them that have broken the covenant of the heavenly sacrament (the promise of virginity)? 3 *Jew.* 458; said to have cut off his hand because a woman kissed it, *Pil.* 601; he allowed the marriage of priests, 2 *Brad.* 309; expounds the direction that a bishop is to be the husband of one wife, 3 *Jew.* 422; says of one, as we are informed, he is at one time the husband of two wives, we think him meet to be deprived of his promotion, *ib.* 406; mentions that the Priscillianists condemned marriage, *Rog.* 306 n.; says that to render to God the things which are God's is not to rebel against Cæsar, but to help him, 3 *Jew.* 173; beseeches the emperor to call a general council, 1 *Jew.* 411, 416, 4 *Jew.* 996, 997, 1098, 2 *Whitg.* 363; says the great council of Chalcedon was summoned by the travail of the emperor, 4 *Jew.* 1005; speaks of an emperor using the authority of the apostolic see to achieve the effect of a holy purpose, *ib.* 995

Leo ... , pope: stated to have been an Arian, 3 *Jew.* 344

Leo II., pope: confirmed the condemnation of pope Honorius, 2 *Ful.* 312

Leo III., pope: being accused by Paschalis and Campulus, he pleaded his cause before Charlemagne at Rome, 4 *Jew.* 967; after this he released the Romans of their oath to the emperor of Greece, and made Charlemagne emperor, *ib.* 672, 680; crowned him, 2 *Hoop.* 238 n.; allowed the pretended blood of Christ at Mantua, *Pil.* 602; appointed the censing in the mass, *ib.* 503; the institution of the rogation days attributed to him, *Calf.* 295 n

Leo IV., pope: humbly submitted himself to the emperor Lewis, 4 *Jew.* 705, 967, 968; confirmed the third council of Carthage, *Whita.* 39; speaks of the pix, &c., 2 *Jew.* 560 n

Leo V., pope: his history, 1 *Hoop.* 217

Leo VIII., pope: chosen by the people, 1 *Whitg.* 401—403; his acts, 2 *Tyn.* 269

Leo IX., pope: a wicked man, 2 *Hoop.* 240;

he promoted the error of transubstantiation and censured Berengarius, 1 *Hoop.* 118, 124, 524, 2 *Hoop.* 48; condemned the marriage of priests, *Rog.* 181; referred to in connexion with the apostolic canons, *Whita.* 42; his epistle to Peter and John, bishops of Africa, 3 *Jew.* 313

Leo X., pope: bought the popedom, *Sand.* 241; expressed infidel opinions, 2 *Cov.* 139 n.; called Christianity "that fable of Christ," 1 *Ful.* 66, 3 *Jew.* 469, *Rog.* 78, 181; his bull against Luther, 3 *Bul.* 119 n.; in it he calls whole communion the heresy of the Greeks and Bohemians, 1 *Jew.* 231, 248, and denounces appeals from the pope to a council as heretical, 3 *Jew.* 216 n.; he bestowed on Henry VIII. the title of Defender of the Faith, 1 *Tyn.* 186, 2 *Tyn.* 264, 338; extract from the bull, 1 *Tyn.* 187 n.; reference to him, *Pil.* 142 n

Leo Byzantius: his affection to his country, 1 *Bec.* 233

Leo Ostiensis: Chronic. Monast. Casin., *Jew.* xxxix, 4 *Jew.* 648, 698

Leodium: *v.* Liege.

Leominster, co. Hereford: Elizabeth, the woman of Lymster or Lemster, her pretended miraculous sustenance, 2 *Cran.* 64, 1 *Tyn.* 325, 326

Leonard (St): his bowl, *Calf.* 287

Leonard (Jo.), and Leonard (Tho.): *Park.* 198

Leoni (Pet.): *v.* Anacletus, antipope.

Leonicus (Nic. Tho.), or Leonicenus: De Var. Hist., *Jew.* xxxix; says the priests of Isis in Egypt used to wear linen surplices, and had their heads shaved, 3 *Jew.* 555

Leonicus Chalcocondylas, *q. v.*

Leonidas: his martyrdom, 2 *Bul.* 105

Leontium, a courteghian: 4 *Jew.* 645

Leontius, bp of Antioch: a heretic, 2 *Ful.* 381; a concealed Arian, *Sand.* 183

Leontius, bishop of Neapolis: wrote the life of St John, patriarch of Alexandria, called the Almsgiver, 1 *Jew.* 182; referred to, *ib.* 85; he says, Christians, in a manner, know not what an altar or a sacrifice is, 2 *Jew.* 735

Leontius, Scholasticus: declares that there are only twenty-two books of the Old Testament, *Whita.* 64; says that the scriptures were lost in the captivity, and restored by Ezra, *ib.* 115

Leopold, duke of Austria: killed at Sempach, 4 *Jew.* 671, 2 *Zur.* 263 n

Leovicius (......): his Varia Historia, *Pil.* 281

Lepanto: the battle there, 1 *Zur.* 270 n

Lepidus (M.): 1 *Hoop.* 297

Lepreyans: their law against adultery, 2 *Bec.* 649, 650

Leprosy: a type of sin, 2 *Lat.* 171; the law respecting it, *ib.* 179; this is analogous to the power of absolution, 1 *Ful.* 274, 1 *Tyn.* 217 n., 269; lepers cleansed by Christ, 4 *Bul.* 255; why he sent them to the priest, 1 *Tyn.* 264

Lese: to lose, 2 *Bec.* 588 (*v.* Leese).

Leslie (And.), earl of Rothes: upholds the Protestant cause, 1 *Zur.* 149 n.; arms on behalf of the queen of Scots, *ib.* 205 n

Leslie (Jo.), bp of Ross: queen Mary's agent in England, account of him, *Grin.* 315, 320; De Reb. Gest. Scot., *Calf.* 290 n

Lesse (Jo.): *v.* Leyes (Tho.).

Lessons: *v.* Calendar, Reading.

Read from the pulpit, 2 *Cran.* 156; places not edifying to be omitted in public reading, *Park.* 336 n.; bp Cooper's Brief Exposition of the first lessons for Sundays, *ib.* 462

FRUITFUL LESSONS, by bp Coverdale, 1 *Cov.* 195, &c.; a lesson for all estates, a poem, by Hum. Gifford, *Poet.* 215

Leston (Simon), proctor: 2 *Cran.* 492

Lethingdon (The lord of): *v.* Maitland.

Letoius, bp of Melita: styled governor of the churches of Militia, 2 *Whitg.* 165; vanquished the Messalians or Euchites, 1 *Jew.* 188, 193; overthrew and burnt their monasteries, and said they were dens of thieves, 4 *Jew.* 800

Letter: *v.* Scripture.

Lettern: a reading desk, *Grin.* 132 (*v.* Lectern).

Letters: *v.* Zurich.

Letters on the Suppression of Monasteries (Camd. Soc.): 1 *Lat.* x, 93, 244, 474; 2 *Lat.* 225, 37 2, 378, 386, 394, 406, 417 nn

Letters dimissory: *Grin.* 449; an article respecting them, *ib.* 186

Letters, or hinderers of true religion: their names to be presented to the ordinary, *Grin.* 144

Lettuce: such lips, such lettuce, *Calf.* 251

Leunclavius (Jo.): *Calf.* 45 n

Lever (......), brother of Ralph and Thomas: an exile, 1 *Cran.* (9)

Lever (Chr.): notice of him, *Poet.* liii; a prayer, *ib.* 523

Lever (Ralph): an exile, 1 *Cran.* (9)

Lever (Tho.): notices of him, 1 *Brad.* 565 n., 2 *Zur.* 147 n., 3 *Zur.* 685 n.; Mr Leaver (probably Tho.) at Cambridge, *Sand.* ii, iii; his friendship with Hutchinson, *Hutch.* i—iii; they visit Joan Bocher, *ib.* 146; his faithful preaching, *Rid.* 59; made master of St John's college, Cambridge, 3 *Zur.* 151; in exile, 1 *Brad.* 445, 1 *Cran.* (9); at Frankfort, 3 *Zur.* 755; at Zurich, *Jew.* xiii, 3 *Zur.* 750, 752; chosen pastor at Wesel, but declines the office, 3 *Zur.* 160; minister of an English congregation at Aran, 1 *Zur.* 88 n., 2 *Zur.* 3, 3 *Zur.* 165; married of late, *Park.* 66; on his suggestion, queen Elizabeth declines the title of supreme head, *ib.*; invited to be minister at Coventry, 1 *Zur.* 86; he preaches at the funeral of Dr Turner, *ib.* 206; a leader among the Puritans, *Grin.* 326 n.; about to be examined, *Park.* 382; connived at in his non-conformity as to habits, *Grin.* 205, 1 *Zur.* 202 n.; supposed to have been concerned in the Admonition to the Parliament, 1 *Zur.* 285; he complains of the state of Sherborne hospital, *Park.* 348; Grindal's commendation of his suit for it, *Grin.* 351; commended by Bullinger, 3 *Zur.* 744; mentioned, *Rid.* 389, 394, 1 *Zur.* 224; letters by him, 3 *Zur.* 150—169; letter from him to Bradford, 2 *Brad.* 137; letters to Bullinger, 1 *Zur.* 84, 2 *Zur.* 28; he was writer of certain prayers, *Pra. B.* v; his preface to Bradford's Meditations, 1 *Brad.* 565; his meditation on the tenth commandment, *ib.* 569; his Right Way, 3 *Zur.* 158 n

Levers (......): farms Aldborough benefice, *Park.* 404

Levi: slew Shechem, 1 *Bul.* 416, 2 *Bul.* 131; cursed by his father, 4 *Bul.* 295

Levi (Rabbi): 1 *Ful.* 313, 315

Levites: their ministry, 2 *Bul.* 131, 132, 4 *Bul.* 108, 191, 480; they were appointed to bear the ark, 4 *Bul.* 296; they lived by their ministry, 2 *Bul.* 31; a blessing rested upon them till they became greedy of gain, *Sand.* 243; their offerings out of their tithes acceptable to God, 4 *Bul.* 489; their cities, 2 *Bul.* 142, 4 *Bul.* 480

Leviticus: Tyndale's prologue to it, 1 *Tyn.* 421; what it contains, 2 *Cov.* 17

Lewd: misled, ignorant, 1 *Tyn.* 380, 2 *Tyn.* 105

Lewes (Joyce), martyr at Lichfield: called by Bryce Joyce Bowes, *Poet.* 171

Lewes, co. Sussex: martyrs there, *Poet.* 168, 170

Lewin (Will. ?): letters to Sturmius, 2 *Zur.* 276, 281; named, *ib.* 285

Lewis: *v.* Louis.

Lewis (......): *v.* Losius.

Lewis (......), one of the ministers of Strasburgh: 3 *Zur.* 534

Lewis (Dav.): at Cranmer's examination, 2 *Cran.* 542; mentioned as Dr Lewes, *Park.* 257; an ecclesiastical commissioner, *Grin.* 294, *Park.* 277, 370 n

Lewis (Jo.): Hist. of Translations, *Calf.* 35 n., 2 *Cov.* x.

Lewisham, co. Kent: the advowson, *Park.* 239

Leyes (Tho.), called by Bryce Jo. Lesse: died in Newgate, *Poet.* 164

Liars: *v.* Lying.

Libanius: 3 *Jew.* 534

Libanius the Sophist: bestowed great praises on Julianus the Renegate, 4 *Jew.* 700

Libel: the term defined, 3 *Whitg.* 521

Liberatus, archdeacon of Carthage: Breviarium, *Jew.* xxxix; he wrote the story of the council of Ephesus, 1 *Jew.* 67; describes the mode of ordination of the bishops of Alexandria, *ib.* 409; says Flavianus the bishop (of Antioch) commanded Eutyches to come to his council, 4 *Jew.* 952; speaks of a decree of the council of Chalcedon standing in spite of pope Leo, 1 *Jew.* 413, 3 *Jew.* 220, 4 *Jew.* 918, 1031; records the answer of the Alexandrians to Timotheus, 1 *Jew.* 99, 144; records the reconciliation of Moggus to Acacius, *ib.* 419; describes the heresy of Nestorius, *Rog.* 48 n.; says the pope ordered Mennas bishop of Constantinople by the licence of the emperor, 3 *Jew.* 331

Liber Festivalis: 2 *Lat.* 132 n

Liberian (......): 1 *Zur.* 62

Liberius, bp of Rome: his contention with Felix for the see of Rome, 1 *Jew.* 377; an Arian heretic, 2 *Ful.* 334, 349, 1 *Jew.* 381, 399, 3 *Jew.* 127, 144, 341, 342, 344, 4 *Jew.* 908, 923, 924, 926, 929, *Pil.* 601, *Rid.* 127, *Rog.* 181, *Whita.* 431 n.; beseeches Athanasius to subscribe a confession, 4 *Jew.* 841; made his humble appearance before the emperor Constantius, *ib.* 967; condemned for heresy, 2 *Cran.* 77

Libertines: a sect, 3 *Jew.* 602; their synagogues, 4 *Bul.* 482; some of them in Germany, 1 *Ful.* 123; they assert that the Holy Ghost is but an inspiration, *Hutch.* 135; teach that whosoever hath God's Spirit in him cannot sin, *Rog.* 139; say that, seeing man is justified by faith, he may live as he listeth, *ib.* 118; despise the scriptures, *Whita.* 36; interpret them allegorically, *Rog.* 197; say the Old Testament is abrogated, *ib.* 87; consider written commentaries vain, *ib.* 196; deprave the office of preaching, *ib.* 233; imagine the church militant is not visible at all, *ib.* 167; explain away the resurrection, heaven, and hell, *Hutch.* 138; deny spirits to be substances, i. e. distinct persons, *ib.* 134; their heresy respecting destiny, *ib.* 79

Liberty: naturally desired by all, *Pil.* 455, 456; Christian liberty, 2 *Brad.* 377, 378, 1 *Bul.* 260, 265, 2 *Bul.* 300, &c., 305, 3 *Whitg.* 488; testimonies of scripture concerning it, 2 *Bul.* 306; who they are that Christ sets at liberty, *ib.* 301; a bondman may be the Lord's freeman, *ib.* 303; the liberty of the sons of God, 3 *Bul.* 102; the freedom wherewith Christ makes his people free, 1 *Tyn.* 501; how far Christ has made us free, 2 *Bul.* 305; probations out of scripture that Christians have liberty from the law of Moses, 3 *Bec.* 339, &c., i. e. from the ceremonies, *ib.* 339, 340, from the choice of meats, *ib.* 340, 341, from the choice or difference of days, *ib.* 341, from the curse of the law, *ib.* 341, 342, from the devil, *ib.* 342, from death, *ib.*, from sin, the wrath of God, &c., *ib.* 342, 343; so that they have everlasting righteousness, *ib.* 343, 344; our liberty is spiritual, 1 *Bec.* 220; we are free from laws and ordinances of men in matters of religion, 2 *Bul.* 310; the estate, property, or duty of them whom Christ has made free, *ib.* 313; our liberty must be used according to the rule of charity, 2 *Lat.* 80; it must not be made an occasion to any of falling, 1 *Bec.* 19; the abuses of Christian liberty, 2 *Bul.* 314, &c.; the law of liberty, 1 *Tyn.* 119; liberty of conscience, 2 *Whitg.* 570

Libra Occidua: 2 *Ful.* 364 n

Libraries: attached to heathen temples, 2 *Jew.* 981; inquiry as to the library at Canterbury, 2 *Cran.* 161

Libya: the sands there, 4 *Bul.* 116

Licences: *v.* Cambridge, Dispensations, Lent, Marriage, Preachers.

Licentiousness: 2 *Brad.* 130, 2 *Bul.* 314, &c., 338

Lichfield, co. Stafford: martyrs there, *Poet.* 171; the first-fruits paid by the bishop of Lichfield and Coventry to the pope, 4 *Jew.* 1079

Lichfield (Clem.), abbot of Evesham: pawns his mitre, cross, &c., 2 *Lat.* 400

Lichtenstein (Hen. baron of): 2 *Zur.* 294

Licinius, emperor: called learning the poison and overthrow of commonweals, 2 *Jew.* 982; a persecutor, 2 *Bul.* 106, *Sand.* 109, 1 *Whitg.* 407; plagued by God for his cruelty to the Christians, 2 *Jew.* 977

Lictors: what they were, 4 *Jew.* 805

Lidley (Jo.): his prayers, *Pra. B.* v, 167; letter to him, 1 *Brad.* 591, 2 *Brad.* 194

Liefer: rather, 3 *Bul.* 131

Liege: Epist. Leod. Cler. adv. Paschal. II. 4 *Jew.* 834

Liell (Rich.), or Lyel: dean of the peculiars, 2 *Cran.* 490

Lieutenants (Lords): introduced, 1 *Lat.* 175 n

Life:

i. *The present life* (*v.* Death, Man): of life, and similes on the same, by Jo. Bodenham, *Poet.* 457; ten similes of man's life, *Wool.* 108; the vanity thereof, 2 *Bec.* 397; its shortness and uncertainty, *ib.* 161, 3 *Bec.* 89, 90, 92, 93, 118, 1 *Brad.* 335, 337; the uncertainty of life, verses by Barn. Googe, *Poet.* 391; men presume upon life, 3 *Bec.* 90; stanzas on this vain fleeting life, by L. Stavely, *Poet.* 376; life compared to a flower, *Nord.* 152; to a vapour, a shadow, &c., *Grin.* 109; we are taught in the Lord's prayer that life is not maintained by our own forecast, 2 *Bec.* 165; the life of man is a warfare, *ib.* 542, 1 *Cov.* 495, *Sand.* 164, &c.; the life of man compared to a ship sailing in a tempest, verses by Hum. Gifford, *Poet.* 211; the pleasure and ease of this life, 3 *Bec.* 605; its pleasures are but vanity, 1 *Brad.* 334; the commodities of life are mixed with evils, lest we should love them too much, *ib.* 338; God's elect must not look to live in pleasure and felicity, *ib.* 387; this life is full of misery, 2 *Cov.* 59; the miseries of the body and the soul, 1 *Brad.* 335, &c., 2 *Brad.* 127; lack of faith makes us love life, 1 *Brad.* 341; how much of it is wasted, *Sand.* 392; the promise of long life annexed to the fifth commandment, *Now.* (17), 131; inconveniences attending the hope of a long life, *Grin.* 4; the hope of its being long makes many unmerciful, 2 *Bec.* 396; life is not to be thrown away for trifles, 2 *Lat.* 223; the miserable end of a wicked life, 3 *Bec.* 90, 91

ii. *Spiritual life* (*v.* Man, Regeneration, Resurrection): life is by Christ, 1 *Bul.* 43; he is alone our life, 3 *Bul.* 29, 2 *Tyn.* 146

iii. *New, or holy life* (*v.* Amendment, Holiness, Works): a new life, *Now.* 103; it is the will of God that we should lead such a life, 2 *Bec.* 156; the life of him that prayeth must be answerable to his faith, 4 *Bul.* 177; what it is to live soberly, 1 *Bec.* 324; an honest frame of life described, *Lit. Edw.* 523, (570)

iv. *Life everlasting*: of eternal life, 2 *Bec.* 49, &c., 1 *Bul.* 44, 178, 2 *Cov.* 210, &c.; there is such a life, 2 *Bec.* 50; what it is, 3 *Bec.* 603; its blessedness, 1 *Brad.*

339, 2 *Brad.* 127; where the place of the faithful shall be, 2 *Cov.* 212; how the salvation shall be, *ib.* 213; it is to be enjoyed in body as well as soul, 2 *Bec.* 51; promised to them that keep the law, 2 *Bul.* 250; given only to the faithful. 2 *Bec.* 50, 51; it is God's free gift, *ib.* 50, 2 *Lat.* 74; all things requisite to it are given in Christ, 3 *Bul.* 27; often to be thought upon, 1 *Brad.* 348; a meditation of the life everlasting, the place and the joys thereof, 1 *Brad.* 269, *Pra. B.* 101; a meditation of the blessed state and felicity of the life to come, 1 *Brad.* 273, *Pra. B.* 106; Christ's body said to be a figure of the life to come, 2 *Jew.* 597

Liffley (......): warns Ridley, 2 *Brad.* 158

Liffort (Cha.): 2 *Zur.* 200

Lift up your hearts: *v.* Sursum.

Liga Sotularia: a conspiracy so called among the boors of Germany, 4 *Jew.* 664, 665

Light: *v.* Lights.

Whether created or an accident, 2 *Jew.* 581, 582; it is an image of God, *Hutch.* 163; an emblem of the Trinity, *Poet.* 240; the word of God a light, *Whita.* 383, 386; how the word light is used in scripture, 2 *Tyn.* 149; the light of the world, what it is, *ib.* 34; the patriarchs, &c., were such, 1 *Bul.* 40; the apostles were such, *Whita.* 384; how ministers are to be such, 3 *Bec.* 293, &c.; what it is to abide in the light, 2 *Tyn.* 175; meditations on light, *Pra. B.* 61, 74; a simile (on light), by Anth. Fletcher, *Poet.* 475

Lightfoot (Jo.): Temple Service, 2 *Ful.* 113 n., 246 n

Lightly: easily, 1 *Cov.* 519

Lightning: *v.* Thunder.

Lights: *v.* Candles.

Great and strange ones seen, *Lit. Eliz.* 570

Lignitz (The duke of): 3 *Zur.* 513 n

Ligon (Will.): 2 *Hoop.* 557

Lilius (Greg. Gyraldus): on Greek accents, *Jew.* xxxix. n., 2 *Jew.* 679

Lilius (Pet.): on discord, 2 *Jew.* 1094

Lily (......): *v.* Lylye.

Lily (Will.): notice of him, 2 *Bec.* 383; article respecting his Grammar, *Grin.* 173; it was originally written for St Paul's school, *ib.* n

Limacius (Lau.): 2 *Zur.* 112

Limbo: a prison, *Phil.* 160

Limbus patrum, the alleged abode of the fathers who departed before Christ's death, 1 *Ful.* 83, 84, 129, 158, 286, 293, 2 *Hoop.* 31, *Rog.* 62, 215, 249 n., *Whita.* 643; Peter Dens thereon, 1 *Tyn.* 158 n.; translations concerning it examined, 1 *Ful.* 278—331

Limbus puerorum: a place supposed to be assigned to children dying without baptism, 2 *Hoop.* 31, *Pil.* 427 n., *Rog.* 137 n., 154, 215 n., 249 n., *Whita.* 643

Limiters: *v.* Friars.

Limoges: a book Martial of Bourdeaux found there, 1 *Jew.* 113

Linacre (Tho.): his lecture at Merton college, Oxford, *Park.* 326

Lincoln: *v.* Missale.

The bishoprick, *Rid.* 263; it is mother to the bishoprick of Oxford, *ib.* 264; the bishop's first-fruits to the pope, 4 *Jew.* 1079; Anne Askewe reads the Bible in Lincoln cathedral, *Bale* 173; notice of articles and injunctions for the diocese, set forth by bishop Cooper, *Coop.* xii; value of the deanery, *Park.* 51; misconduct of a certain lady of Lincoln, *ib.* 147

Lincoln, i. e. R. Grosteste, *q. v.*

Lincoln (Edw. earl of): *v.* Clinton.

Lincolnshire: 1 *Lat.* 298; rebellion there, *Bale* 326, 2 *Cov.* 329, 2 *Cran.* 351, 352, 354, *Park.* 8 n. (*v.* Pilgrimage of Grace); Latimer's sermons preached in Lincolnshire, 1 *Lat.* 455, &c., 2 *Lat.* 1, &c.; Lincolnshire bagpipes, *Bale* 102

Lindanus (Will.), bp of Ruremond: notice of him, 1 *Ful.* 11; he speaks against the sufficiency of scripture, *Rog.* 78 n.; compares it to a nose of wax, *ib.* 196 n.; expatiates on its obscurity, *ib.* 199; says the true sense of it is to be fetched from the (Roman) catholic church, *ib.* 192 n.; states that the gospel cannot be committed to writing, *ib.* 197; prefers the Vulgate to the Hebrew and Greek, *Whita.* 111; confesses that there are many errors and various readings in the Vulgate, 1 *Ful.* 74, 4 *Jew.* 907; would have corrected it, 1 *Ful.* 62; thought the common Greek Psalter to be the version not of the LXX., but of Symmachus, *Whita.* 192; his opinion of the Vulgar Latin Psalter, *ib.*; he charges some Lutherans with corrupting scripture, 1 *Ful.* 122 n.; enumerates various alleged apostolical traditions, *Whita.* 512; says that but for tradition scripture would be of no validity, *Rog.* 200; charges Protestants with dissension amongst themselves, *Rid.* 307; references to him, 1 *Ful.* 42, 45, 79, & sæpe.

Lindau: the church there, 2 *Cov.* 519

Lindisfarne, or Holy Island: 3 *Zur.* 433, 435 n

Lindsay (Jo.), earl of Crawford: arms in

defence of the queen of Scots, 1 *Zur.* 205 n.; takes the oath to the regent Mar, *ib.* 262 n
Lindsay (...... lord), present at the murder of Rizzio, 1 *Zur.* 166 n.; one of the confederate lords, *ib.* 193 n.; his behaviour to the queen of Scots, *ib.* 197 n
Lindsay (Sir Walter): a leader at Haldanrig, 3 *Zur.* 237 n
Lindsay (Dav.): *v.* Lyndesay.
Lindsay (Jo.): his ed. of Mason, 2 *Ful.* 118 n., 128 n., 265 n., *Jew.* xl.
Lindwood (Will.): *v.* Lyndwode.
Lingard (Jo.): animadverts on Latimer, 1 *Lat.* 161 n
Linley (......): *v.* Lynley.
Linlithgow: the regent Murray slain there, 1 *Zur.* 215, 218
Linn: to cease, 2 *Cran.* 119
Linney (Rog.), vicar of Blackburn, *Park.* 222
Linus, bp of Rome: *Pil.* 588, 2 *Whitg.* 253; cited for transubstantiation, 2 *Lat.* 273; his story of St Peter, *Rid.* 221; the writings ascribed to him are spurious, *ib.* 220 n
Linwood (Will.): *v.* Lyndwode.
Lion (......): martyred, *Poet.* 168
Lipomanus (Aloysius): his reception as legate at Cracow, 3 *Zur.* 700: Sanctorum Historia, 1 *Hoop.* 310 n., 313 n., 457 n., *Jew.* xxxi; his Mariolatry, 1 *Jew.* 535 n., 536; he exclaims, behold how mighty is the holy mother of God! 4 *Jew.* 949; speaks of Theodore Balsamon, 3 *Jew.* 306
Liriensis episcopus: a bishop of Portugal, 4 *Jew.* 787
Lisle: a piece of the cross in the collegiate church there, *Calf.* ix.
Lisle (Arthur visc.): *v.* Plantagenet.
Lisle (Jo. visc.), afterwards duke of Northumberland: *v.* Dudley.
Lisle (Will.): his edition of the Paschal Homily, 2 *Ful.* 7 n
Lismanini (Dr): notice of him, 3 *Zur.* 602 n
Lister (......): martyred, *Poet.* 167
Litanies: used long before processions, *Calf.* 294; their institution ascribed to Mamercus, bp of Vienne, *ib.* 295 n., 2 *Whitg.* 480; set forth by pope Leo I., 2 *Whitg.* 480; appointed by Gregory I., *ib.* 469; that of Augustine the monk contrasted with the popish litany, *Calf.* 308; a cross borne at the singing or saying of the latter, 2 *Ful.* 182, &c.; the greater litany and the less, *Calf.* 296, 297; notices of the litany of 1544, viz. that next mentioned, 2 *Cran.* ix, 412, 494 n., *Pra. Eliz.* xxiii; AN EXHORTATION UNTO PRAYER,...TO BE READ AFORE PROCESSIONS. ALSO A LITANY WITH SUFFRAGES, &c., *Pra. Eliz.* 563; inquiry about this litany, 2 *Cran.* 157; injunction to use it, *ib.* 502; the English litany is found in king Edward's first Prayer Book, and in all subsequent Prayer Books and Ordination services, *Lit. Edw.* and *Lit. Eliz.*; THE LITANY AND SUFFRAGES, 1558, probably unauthorized, *Lit. Eliz.* 1; notes concerning it, *ib.* ix; THE LITANY USED IN THE QUEEN'S CHAPEL, 1559, (with various occasional prayers, the Lord's prayer, the Creed, the Commandments, and several graces), *ib.* 9; notes respecting it, *ib.* xi, xii; the Litany and suffrages, in the Primer of 1559, *Pra. Eliz.* 51; and in the Book of Christian Prayers, 1578, *ib.* 548; the litany (temp. Eliz.) with prayers for the queen, for pastors and ministers of the church, for rain, for fair weather, in time of dearth and famine, and in time of war, and (after certain other prayers of private composition), a prayer of Chrysostom, *Pra. B.* 193; the litany used in English under the reformation, 3 *Bec.* 231; some objected to confess themselves "miserable sinners," *Grin.* 255; no certain place appointed for it in the church of England, 2 *Whitg.* 463; the litany in Latin, in the Orarium, 1560, *Pra. Eliz.* 166; also, in the Preces Privatæ, 1564, *ib.* 257
Literal sense: *v.* Scripture.
Lither: lazy, 2 *Bul.* 32, *Pil.* 447; litherly, 1 *Cov.* 130
Lithuania: various religions there, 3 *Zur.* 690
Little-ease: 1 *Brad.* 273 n., 1 *Lat.* 250
Litton (Tho.): *Bale* 63 (an error for Hitton, *q. v.*)
Liturgies: *v.* Litanies, Responses.
Liturgy (λειτουργία) denotes any ministry or public service, 4 *Jew.* 805; Liturgiæ Veteres SS. Patrum, ed. Cl. de Sainctes, *Jew.* xxxix; various ancient liturgies were in the vulgar tongue, *Pil.* 499; they prove that those who did not communicate were obliged to go out, 2 *Bec.* 256, 3 *Bec.* 482, 483, 1 *Jew.* 19; examples of forged ones, *ib.* 114

Ambrose: his liturgy miraculously discarded, *Pil.* 508, 509; still used at Milan, *ib.* 508, and by the Cistercians, *ib.* 509

Armenia: the deacons' warning to non-communicants to depart and pray before the church door, 2 *Bec.* 256, 3 *Bec.* 482, 4 *Jew.* 887

Bangor: v. Breviary.

Basil: his liturgy written in Greek, *Pil.*

499; referred to, 1 *Jew.* 109; it is a communion, and no mass, *ib.* 156, 194; it calls the sacrament ἀντίτυπον, 2 *Hoop.* 406, 2 *Jew.* 574, 579, 593, 596, 597; the shutting of the doors, 3 *Bec.* 483; the exclamation "Holy things for the holy," 1 *Jew.* 511; thanksgiving is for being made worthy to be ministers of the altar, 1 *Ful.* 363, &c.; it contains a prayer for meetness to offer the sacrifice of praise, 2 *Jew.* 721; prayer to Christ, invisibly present, for the impartation of his body and blood, 1 *Jew.* 485; the form of consecration, 1 *Ful.* 502; prayer for the departed, 3 *Jew.* 561; the breaking of the bread, 1 *Jew.* 116, 2 *Jew.* 588; the reception of it, 2 *Jew.* 588; the mixed cup, 1 *Ful.* 523; mention is made of all receiving of one bread and one cup, 1 *Jew.* 116, 4 *Jew.* 887; cited for the elevation, 1 *Jew.* 507, 512.

Chrysostom: his liturgy written in Greek, *Pil.* 499; referred to, 1 *Jew.* 109; it is of later date than Chrysostom's time, 1 *Ful.* 434, *Whita.* 260; prayer is made for pope Nicolas, who lived 500 years after Chrysostom was dead, and for the emperor Alexius, who lived 700 years after Chrysostom, 1 *Jew.* 114, 2 *Jew.* 653; but these passages are not in the Greek text, 1 *Jew.* 114 n.; warning to non-communicants to depart, 3 *Bec.* 482; the shutting of the doors, 2 *Bec.* 256; the holy vessels brought to the altar by the deacons, 1 *Jew.* 198; prayer made for the dead, for the departed, *Coop.* 97, *Grin.* 26, 3 *Jew.* 561, 4 *Jew.* 886; the offering called a reasonable service, *Coop.* 97; the form of benediction, 1 *Ful.* 502; prayer for the descent of the Holy Ghost upon the elements, 2 *Jew.* 772; prayer to Christ, invisibly present, 1 *Jew.* 485, 486, 538; adoration and prayer by the priest, deacon, and people, *ib.* 486, 538; cited for the elevation, *ib.* 507, 508, 512; the loaf, and its division, 2 *Jew.* 588; the lancea sacra, *ib.* 585; the communion of the clergy, 1 *Jew.* 116, 198; the holy mysteries brought to the place where the people must receive together, *ib.* 116, 4 *Jew.* 887; the invitation to the people to approach, 1 *Jew.* 116, 195, 511; a prayer on receiving the sacrament, *ib.* 538; the people respond, *ib.* 116, *Whita.* 260; the concluding prayer, 1 *Jew.* 185, 186; this liturgy alleged for image worship, 2 *Jew.* 653.

Cologne: v. Cologne.

England: (v. Book of Common Prayer, Horarium, Litanies, Order): the ancient liturgies of England, 2 *Brad.* 298; the word "papa," and the name of Tho. Becket ordered to be obliterated from church books, 2 *Cran.* 157; steps towards their reformation, 1538, &c., *ib.* 366 n.; the cost of church books to be divided between the parson or proprietor, and the parishioners, *ib.* 499; mandate for bringing in and defacing popish rituals, *ib.* 522; a committee for reforming the offices of the church, 1548, *Rid.* 316; superstitious church books at All Souls' college, *Park.* 297; THE TWO LITURGIES, A.D. 1549, AND A.D. 1552; WITH OTHER DOCUMENTS SET FORTH BY AUTHORITY IN THE REIGN OF KING EDWARD VI.; edited by the Rev. Jos. Ketley, M.A., *Lit. Edw.*; LITURGIES AND OCCASIONAL FORMS OF PRAYER SET FORTH IN THE REIGN OF QUEEN ELIZABETH; edited by the Rev. Will. Keatinge Clay, B.D., *Lit. Eliz.*

Ethiopia: the deacons' warning to non-communicants to depart, 2 *Bec.* 256, 3 *Bec.* 482.

Geneva: v. Geneva.

Hereford: v. Missale.

James (St): he never used the Popish mass, *Pil.* 495—498; the liturgy called his was written in Greek, *ib.* 499; referred to, 1 *Jew.* 108, *Pil.* 482; the order of it, 1 *Jew.* 23, 24, 114; it testifies against the mass, *ib.* 114; confession of the people, 2 *Jew.* 700; the deacons take up the dishes and the cups to minister the sacrament unto the people, 4 *Jew.* 887; the mixed cup, 1 *Ful.* 523; the mode of consecration, *ib.* 504; the liturgy ascribed to St James is of later date than his time, 1 *Jew.* 114; his liturgy has a prayer for those that live in monasteries, *ib.*

Knox (J.): v. Book of Common Order.

Rome (v. Breviary, Missale, Rituale): the Ordo Romanus, 2 *Bec.* 256, 3 *Bec.* 482; Romish service-books, 2 *Cran.* 523, *Grin.* 135, 159; fables, fooleries, and witchcrafts in them, *Pil.* 536; references to liturgical writers, 2 *Brad.* 298—311.

Sarum: v. Breviary, Horæ, Manuale, Missale.

Scotland: v. Book of Common Order.

Strasburgh: notices of the French liturgy prepared by Calvin for his congregation there, and of a Latin translation by Pollanus, *Pra. Eliz.* 458, 477, 488 nn.

York: v. Breviary, Missale.

Livelihood: v. Prayers.

Liveries: referred to, *Bale* 222, 1 *Lat.* 448; men desired to wear the livery of noblemen, *Pil.* 191, 193; the badge on the sleeve, and the tyrannical conduct of some who wore it, *ib.* 356; archbishop Parker receives permission to retain forty persons with his livery badge or cognizance, *Park.* 175

Liverpool, co. Lancaster: 1 *Brad.* 454
Livish: living, lively, 1 *Bec.* 37
Livonia: Popish war there, 3 *Zur.* 599 n., 687 n., 688; invasion thereof, by Russia, *ib.* 699
Livy (Titus): cited, 1 *Bul.* 252, 2 *Bul.* 125, *Calf.* 14, 295, 316, 317, 2 *Cov.* 124, 1 *Cran.* 257, 1 *Hoop.* 327, 417, 2 *Lat.* 146, 2 *Jew.* 1028, 4 *Jew.* 908, 1071
Llandaff, co. Glamorgan: vacancy of the see, *Park.* 208
Llanddewi-Brefi, co. Cardigan: the advowson, *Park.* 266, 271, 280
Llanthony abbey, near Gloucester: 2 *Lat.* 418
Llewhaden castle, Wales: 3 *Bec.* 501 n
Lloyd (David, or Rob. ap David): receiver to Booth, bp of Hereford, 2 *Cran.* 263
Lloyd (Tho.): notice of him, *Poet.* xxxix; The inconstancy of youth, *ib.* 415
Lloyd (Will.), bp of Worcester: *Calf.* 306 n
Loadsman: *v.* Lodesman.
Loaf (Holy): a shadow of the ancient oblations at the eucharist, *Coop.* 89, *Lit. Edw.* 98; provided by the parishioners by turn, *Rid.* 67
Loaf (Singing): *v.* Host.
Locarno, in Italy: 4 *Bul.* xiii.
Lochleven castle, Scotland: queen Mary imprisoned there, 1 *Zur.* 196; her escape, *ib.* 202; the earl of Northumberland's imprisonment, *ib.* 214 n
Locke (......): *Grin.* 266
Locke (Hen.): *v.* Lok.
Locke (Mr), of Antwerp: *Sand.* xv.
Locks: *v.* Doors.
Lockwood (Hen.): *Park.* 25, 26
Locris: Pliny saith pestilence was never there, 2 *Hoop.* 168; law of the Locrensians against adultery, 2 *Bec.* 649
Locusts: in the Apocalypse, *Bale* 352, &c.
Lodesman: leading man, or pilot, 1 *Brad.* 235, 383; lodisman, *Phil.* 331; Christ a most true loadsman and guide, *Pra. B.* 67; the ten commandments a lodesman, *Wool.* 71
Lodge (Edm.): Illustrations, 1 *Zur.* 257 n.; Shrewsbury Papers, *ib.* 239 n
Lodowicke (St): *v.* Louis.
Loene (Pet. de): *v.* Deloenus.
Loftus (Adam), abp of Armagh: *Park.* 117 n
Logic: *v.* Arguments.

Its usefulness, *Hutch.* 28; terms of the scholastic logic, 1 *Tyn.* 157; mnemonic verses containing the moods, "Barbara, Celarent," &c., *Grin.* 43 n., *Rid.* 197 n.; fallacia æquivocationis, 1 *Jew.* 134; ignoratio elenchi, *Whita.* 287; intentions, first and second, 1 *Tyn.* 157 n.; petitio principii, 1 *Cran.* 333, 371, 2 *Ful.* 168, 1 *Jew.* 121, 2 *Tyn.* 206, 1 *Whitg.* 39, 66, 70, &c.
Lok (Hen.): notice of him, *Poet.* xviii, xxxix; poems by him, viz. Psalm xxvii, *ib.* 136; Psalm cxxi, and a version of the Lord's prayer, *ib.* 137; avarice, *ib.* 138; the miserable state of the wicked, *ib.* 139; six sonnets, *ib.* 140
Lollards: *Bale* 75; loller, 1 *Brad.* 11; as to Lollard's tower, see London, *St Paul's.*
Lomas (Jo.), or Lowmas: martyred, *Poet.* 165, 3 *Zur.* 175 n
Lombard (Pet.): *v.* Peter.
Lombardy: *v.* Historia Longobardica.
The kingdom divided between the pope and Charlemagne, 2 *Tyn.* 263; the Lombards, 2 *Bul.* 109
Lomeward, co. Kent: a manor, 1 *Bec.* 307 n
Lonche (λόγχη): mistake respecting the word, 1 *Jew.* 150, *Whita.* 560
London: see also Southwark, Westminster.

i. GENERAL HISTORY.

Great fires in popish times, *Pil.* 606, 607, 648; one in king Stephen's reign, 3 *Jew.* 574; many houses and churches thrown down by a whirlwind, *Pil.* 607; one of the Albigenses burned in London, 1210, *Bale* 3; pestilence in 1548, 3 *Zur.* 646; the plague or sweating sickness of 1551, 1 *Brad.* 61 n., 445, 2 *Brad.* xxiv, 2 *Cran.* 531, 2 *Hoop.* 139, 159, *Lit. Eliz.* 450, 3 *Zur.* 94, 496, 575 n., 679, 727; Bradford's farewell to the city of London, 1 *Brad.* 434; a congregation of godly men in London throughout queen Mary's reign, *ib.* 434 n., 2 *Brad.* 187 n., *Grin.* 203, 1 *Zur.* 7 n., 2 *Zur.* 29, 160, 3 *Zur.* 360 n.; some of them taken in Bow church yard, see in iii, below; a great plague in 1563, *Grin.* vii, 77, 78, 79, *Lit. Eliz.* 459, 460, 493, 1 *Zur.* 132 n., 2 *Zur.* 109, 114 n., 132; letters respecting it, *Grin.* 257, &c., *Park.* 182—184; prisoners removed from the Tower, *Park.* 192—195; fires made in the streets, *Grin.* 270; occasional services for this plague, *ib.* 75, &c.; a form of meditation for householders, *Lit. Eliz.* 503; separatists in London, 1 *Zur.* 201; examination of certain Londoners before the ecclesiastical commissioners, 1567, *Grin.* 199; Puritan assemblies in Bartholomew fair-time, *Rog.*

206 n.; London preachers, 3 *Whitg.* 2, &c., (and see Ministers); exiles in London, 4 *Jew.* 1274; articles of inquiry respecting strangers, *Grin.* 296; the plague of 1574, *Park.* 466; pompous reception of the duke Casimir, 1579, 1 *Zur.* 330 n.; the plague of 1593, *Lit. Eliz.* 471; Bartholomew fair not kept that year, *ib.*; twelve thousand carried away by the plague (at that time?), *Poet.* 465; London a sinful city, *Sand.* 259; full of pride, cruelty, malice, and other sins, 1 *Lat.* 63—65; full of whoredom, *ib.* 196; the city and suburbs full of vagrants, *Nord.* 176; play-houses, bowling-alleys, bear-gardens, &c., *ib.* 177

ii. The Cathedral, and its precincts, the Diocese, &c.

St Paul's cathedral: the church alleged not to be in the diocese of London, *Phil.* 21; several times burned, 2 *Ful.* 155, *Pil.* 485, 606; the steeple, 3 *Bec.* 257, *Hutch.* 80; men sometimes descended from it on ropes, *Pil.* 540; it was thrice burned, notwithstanding its cross and relics, *Calf.* 180; burned with lightning in Henry VI.'s time, *Pil.* 607; the rood at the North door, *Bale* 98; the altar of the Holy Ghost, *Pil.* 483, 539; Jesus chapel underground (called Judas chapel), *ib.* 541; masses, prayers, and anthems at St Paul's, *ib.* 483, 522, 527 —530; postles' mass at four or five in the morning, 2 *Jew.* 630; anthems in the steeple, *Pil.* 540; a Romish writer speaks of great communions there, at several altars, *Coop.* 21, and see 119; Rich. Hunne murdered in a chamber belonging to the church, 3 *Tyn.* 166; letter to the dean and chapter on thanksgiving for a victory over the Scots, 2 *Cran.* 417; funeral service for Francis I., *Rid.* v. n.; Ridley breaks down the wall by the high altar, *ib.* 324; public lectures at St Paul's, 3 *Zur.* 65; disputation in the convocation there, 1553, *Phil.* 179; the three martyrs of St Paul's, Rogers, Bradford, Ridley, 2 *Brad.* 192, *Rid.* 381; The burning of Paul's church in... 1561, *Pil.* v, 479—616; account of the fire, *Grin.* 246 n., *Pil.* 481 n.; whether by lightning or by accident, *Pil.* 648; letter of bishop Grindal to the archdeacons of the diocese of London about contributions for repairing it, *Grin.* 246; queen Elizabeth was much affected at the misfortune, and resolved to have the damage speedily repaired, *ib.* 246 n.; her letter to archbishop Parker about its re-edification [repair] after the fire, *Park.* 142; letters by Parker on the same, *ib.* 143, 152; the works at a stand for want of money, *ib.* 178; proposal to bring lead from St Bartholomew the Great, *Grin.* 272; inconvenience of a thanksgiving communion at St Paul's, *ib.* 267, *Park.* 201; abuses there, as talking, buying, selling, &c., *Pil.* 483, 539, &c., 648; talk of Papists there, *Poet.* 526; funeral solemnity of the emperor Ferdinand, *Grin.* viii, 2, 3; that of king Charles IX. of France, *Sand.* 161; prebends in this church, *Rid.* 332, 336; bills set up there, 2 *Hoop.* xi, 3 *Whitg.* 246

Lollard's tower, *Phil.* 7, 8, &c., 87, *Pil.* 540, 1 *Tyn.* 33; called Loler's tower, 2 *Brad.* 363; Lowlar's tower, *Poet.* 164, 165; Philpot describes his prison in another tower there, *Phil.* 87; the bishop's prison worse than purgatory, 2 *Lat.* 237, 361

Paul's cross:—the cross in St Paul's churchyard overthrown by an earthquake, 1382, *Pil.* 606; rebuilt by means of indulgences, *ib.*; English Bibles and other books burned near the North porch, bishop Fisher preaching, 1 *Tyn.* xxxi; preaching there, 2 *Cran.* 293, 319, 418, *Hutch.* 5, 1 *Lat.* 49 n., *Park.* 239, 261, 275, 318, 2 *Whitg.* 463; Will. Thorpe preaches there, *Bale* 119; letter to a preacher, 2 *Cran.* 289; bishops preached there in 1534 on the king's supremacy, *ib.* 308 n.; Parker appointed to preach, *Park.* ix. n., 5, 39, 45, *Rid.* 335; penance done there, 2 *Cran.* 372; alleged heretics bore faggots there, 2 *Lat.* 326; exposure and destruction of the rood of grace and other images, 3 *Zur.* 604, 606, 609; of the blood of Hales, 2 *Lat.* 408 n.; Barnes preaches at Paul's cross, 2 *Cov.* 349, 433; Latimer preaches there, 1 *Lat.* x; in the Shrouds, *ib.* xiv; Ridley preaches at Paul's cross, *Rid.* 119, 162, 260, 265; Bradford does the same, 1 *Brad.* 31 (*v.* Bourne (G.), bp); the gospel preached there on the Sunday after Elizabeth's accession, 1 *Zur.* 4; singing there, *ib.* 71; Jewel's famous sermon, 1 *Jew.* 1; peace proclaimed, 1564, with a sermon and other solemnities, 1 *Zur.* 133 n.; Sandys's sermon there on coming to the bishoprick of London, *Sand.* 331; seditious preachers there, *ib.* xx; penance done there by two girls who pretended to be possessed, *Park.* 465 n.; Sandys's farewell sermon there, on removing to York, *Sand.* 418; banners taken from the Spanish Armada displayed there during sermon, *Lit. Eliz.* 469; the Shrouds, a place for preaching, 1 *Lat.* xiv, 59 n

St Paul's churchyard:—the ill effects of burial there, 2 *Lat.* 67; tombs destroyed by protector Somerset, *Grin.* 29 n.; News out of Powles churchyard; by Edw. Hake; noticed, *Poet.* xxxiii; stanzas therefrom, *ib.* 370; the Brasen Serpent, R. Wolfe's, 3 *Zur.* 523 n.; Day's little shop, *Park.* 411, 412

The bishop's palace:—the bishop's chapel, *Phil.* 88; the bishop's coal-house used as a prison, *Lit. Eliz.* 339 n., 352 n., *Phil.* 12, 13, 70, 227; Jo. Felton affixed Pius V.'s bull of excommunication to the gates of the palace, and was executed there, 4 *Jew.* 1129, *Lit. Eliz.* 655 n., *Park.* 445 n., 3 *Whitg.* 503 n., 1 *Zur.* 221, 254

St Paul's school:—two Latin prayers composed for the scholars by Erasmus, *Pra. Eliz.* 171, 372, and 394; Lily's Grammar composed for it, *Grin.* 173 n

Bishoprick and Diocese (*v.* Articles, Lincoln): foundation of the see, 2 *Whitg.* 127, 128; the bishop's first-fruits to the pope, 4 *Jew.* 1078; extracts from registers, 1 *Tyn.* xv; Ridley's farewell to the bishoprick, *Rid.* 408; it was the spectacle of all England, *ib.* 336; in league with the seat of Satan, *ib.* 410; many Puritans in the diocese, *Grin.* 347 (see in i, above); the archbishop's peculiars, *Grin.* 415 n

iii. PARISH CHURCHES, AND PARISHES.

Christ church: formerly the church of the Grey Friars, *Rid.* xiii. n.; bishop Christopherson's funeral there, 1 *Zur.* 4 n.; two children killed there by an earthquake, *Lit. Eliz.* 567; Jesus church, apparently meaning Christ church, *Coop.* 119

Holy Sepulchre parish: Holborne Conduit, 1 *Cov.* 529

Saint Alphage within Cripplegate: Fulke preaches there, 1 *Ful.* vii.

Saint Andrew Holborn: Rod. Zuinglius buried there, 2 *Zur.* 205

Saint Antholin: morning service there, in the time of Elizabeth, 1 *Zur.* 33 n

Saint Bartholomew by the Exchange: Coverdale buried there, 1 *Cov.* viii, 2 *Calf.* xvi; the church destroyed, 2 *Cov.* xvi.

Saint Bartholomew the Great: orders conferred there, 1503, 1 *Tyn.* xv. n.; partial destruction of the church, and subsequent erection of the tower, *Grin.* 272 n.; proposal to remove the lead from the church and send it to St Paul's (then lately burned), and to substitute the fratrie as the parish church, *ib.* 272, 273, 274; eminent persons who resided in the precinct, *ib.* 272

Saint Benet Sherehog: 2 *Brad.* 247 n

Saint Botolph Bishopsgate: Fulke preaches there, 1 *Ful.* vii.

Saint Clement Danes: *v.* Westminster.

Saint Dunstan in the East: letter relative to dues and oblations there, 2 *Cran.* 263

Saint Dunstan in the West: Tyndale preaches there, 1 *Tyn.* xxiv.

Saint Giles Cripplegate: disorder at a funeral there, *Park.* 275, 276; Bartlett, divinity lecturer there, suspended, yet continues to read, *Grin.* 288

Saint Giles in the Fields (Middx.), St Giles's fields, *Bale* 50; many persons hanged and burned there, *ib.* 51; so lord Cobham, *ib.* 52; Babington and others executed there, *Lit. Eliz.* 468

Saint Helen Bishopsgate: see in v.

Saint Magnus: mentioned, 2 *Hoop.* xi; bishop Griffyth buried there, *Phil.* xxvii; bishop Coverdale presented to the rectory, 1 *Cov.* viii, 2 *Cov.* xv; he seeks the remission of the first-fruits, 2 *Cov.* 529, *Grin.* 284 n.; Coverdale's final burial-place, 2 *Cov.* xvi.

Saint Mary Abchurch: Latimer preaches there, 2 *Lat.* 323; his trouble in consequence, *ib.* 324; Barton, the parson, suspended, *Grin.* 266

Saint Mary le Bow: the Arches court there, 1 *Lat.* 52 n.; the election of bishops confirmed there, *Grin.* vi. n.; Bradford preaches there, 1 *Brad.* 485, 2 *Brad.* xxxii; a company of worshippers taken at a house in Bow churchyard, 2 *Brad.* 216 n., 2 *Hoop.* 555; letter to Hooper about the taking of a godly company in Bow churchyard at prayer, 2 *Hoop.* 612; his reply, *ib.* 613; his letter to the prisoners, *ib.* 614

Saint Mildred Bread-street: letter to Mr Earl, minister there, *Grin.* 293

Saint Stephen Coleman street: apparently referred to by Gardiner, *Rid.* 499

iv. FOREIGN CHURCHES.

The foreign Protestants restricted as to ceremonies, 3 *Zur.* 569; the restriction removed, *ib.* 570; their church government, *ib.* 571, 587

Dutch, Flemish, Belgic, or German church (*v.* Confession, Jo. à Lasco): king Edward's letters patent, 3 *Zur.* 337 n.; grant to it of the church of the Austin Friars, *ib.* 565, 567; its privileges, *ib.* 568; the church repaired and decorated by the king, *ib.* 569, 570; its services and discipline, *ib.* 575, 581, 587; Hooper's friendly converse with it, 2 *Hoop.* ix. n.; letter from bishop

Grindal to the ministers, *Grin.* 242, 243; erroneous opinions defended by H. Hamsted, *ib.* 243 n.; disturbance caused by Velsius, *ib.* 254, 438 nn.; dissensions, 1 *Zur.* 208, 2 *Zur.* 170; certain articles agreed upon, 1 *Whitg.* 198; the superintendence of this church claimed by Sandys, *Sand.* xx; letter of the ministers to the Lord Treasurer, 2 *Zur.* 320

French church: privileges granted to it by king Edward, 3 *Zur.* 568; character of Rich. Vauville, minister there, 3 *Zur.* 339; at the desire of Grindal, Calvin recommends de Gallars as minister, 2 *Zur.* 49 n.; Pet. Alexander, prebendary of Canterbury, preaches there, 1 *Zur.* 79; the church located in Threadneedle-street, *ib.* 93 n.; references to it, *ib.* 93, 190; Cousins succeeds de Gallars as pastor, 2 *Zur.* 96; collection for it; contribution of the chapter of Canterbury, 1 *Zur.* 288 n.; Acta Consistorii Eccl. Londino-Gallicæ, &c., 1571, *Grin.* 313 n.; the French ministers interfere in disputes between Sandys and the Puritans, *Sand.* xx; a French church in Lombard-street, *Grin.* 311 n

Italian church: Michael Angelo minister, 2 *Cran.* 440 n.; Corranus a member of it, *Grin.* 309 n

Spanish church: 2 *Zur.* 175 n., 254; Corranus preacher in it, *Grin.* 309 n

v. RELIGIOUS HOUSES, COLLEGES, HOSPITALS, INNS OF COURT, &c.

Austin Friars: they murdered one of their fellows, 2 *Tyn.* 128

Bethlehem hospital, otherwise *Bedlam: Phil.* 112, 206, 212, *Rid.* 411, 1 *Tyn.* 7, 184

Black Friars: the Dominican friars without Ludgate, *Bale* 28

Bridewell hospital: founded, *Pil.* 611, *Rid.* xiii. n., 411 n.; formerly a house of the king's, *Rid.* 535; separatists confined there, *Grin.* 216 n

Charter house: 2 *Cran.* 292 n., 2 *Lat.* 392, (*v.* Carthusians).

Christ's hospital: founded, *Rid.* xiii. n., 411 n.; (see Christ church in iii).

College of Arms: arms granted to Whitgift, *Lit. Eliz.* 594 n

Crutched Friars' church: Dr Turner's monument there, 1 *Zur.* 206 n

Gray's Inn: v. Inns of Court.

Grey Friars: v. Christ's hospital.

Inns of Court: 1 *Whitg.* 312, 314; disordered about religion, *Park.* 384, 385, 2 *Zur.* 201; as to the Temple, see Corranus (A.), and Hooker (R.).

Minories: the nunnery there, 3 *Tyn.* 90 n

Saint Anthony's hospital, Threadneedle-street: the French church established there, 1 *Zur.* 93 n.; St Anthony's school, 2 *Ful.* 164; eminent scholars, 3 *Whitg.* v.

Saint Bartholomew's hospital: founded, *Rid.* xiii. n., 411 n.; (see in iii).

Saint Helen, Bishopsgate: leases of the priory lands held by Hutchinson, *Hutch.* viii, x.

Saint Martin le Grand: a sanctuary, 2 *Bec.* 438 n., 1 *Lat.* 196 n.; the college granted to the abbey of Westminster, 2 *Cran.* 240 n

Saint Mary's hospital, Bishopsgate: the mayor and aldermen attended sermons there at Easter, 2 *Lat.* 341 n.; sermons at the Spital, *Hutch.* 5, *Park.* 263, *Sand.* 256, 2 *Whitg.* 463, 3 *Zur.* 210 n.; Barnes preaches there, 2 *Cov.* 355, 357, 433

Saint Paul's school, see in ii.

Saint Thomas of Acres: an hospital in Cheapside on the site of the birthplace of Tho. à Becket, 2 *Brad.* 350 n., 1 *Lat.* 201; Packington shot there, *Bale* 441; the Mercers' chapel now occupies the site, 1 *Lat.* 201 n

Savoy: v. Westminster.

Spittle: v. Saint Mary's hospital, Bishopsgate.

Temple: v. Inns of Court.

Whittington college: Bale 429; Jo. Standish, a fellow, 2 *Cov.* 322; Dr Smyth, master, *Park.* 72 n.; Sampson lecturer there, 2 *Zur.* 119 n

vi. THE CORPORATION, GUILDHALL, &c.

The mayor, *Bale* 153, 2 *Tyn.* 66; he and the sheriffs had their lords of misrule, *Grin.* 141 n.; the magistrates exhorted to relieve the poor, *Sand.* 344; the sword-bearer, 2 *Cran.* 307, 332; the chamber of London, *ib.* 293

Guildhall: the epistle of Eleutherius alleged to be preserved there, 2 *Ful.* 128; Anne Askewe condemned there, *Bale* 179, 212; arraignment of Cranmer, the lords Ambrose and Guilford Dudley, and the lady Jane, 3 *Zur.* 374 n.; the lord mayor's perch, i. e. chandelier, *Calf.* 300

vii. COMPANIES, THEIR HALLS, &c.

Goldsmiths': required to view the pix of the mint at Canterbury, 2 *Cran.* 357

Mercers': their chapel on the site of the hospital of St Thomas of Acres, 1 *Lat.* 201 n.; the image of Becket set up there, 3 *Zur.* 177

Merchant-Taylors': queen's day observed

at Merchant-Taylors' school, *Lit. Eliz.* 558 n

Plumbers': meeting of separatists at Plumbers' hall, *Grin.* 201 n

Saddlers': Anne Askew examined at their hall, *Bale* 148

Skinners': letter to archbishop Parker respecting a grammar school at Tonbridge, *Park.* 210

Stationers': their contest with Regnault, 2 *Cov.* 495; they sell corrupt primers, *ib.* 501; Harrison their warden, *Park.* 449

viii. THE TOWER, AND PRISONS.

The Tower, (v. Mints): lord Cobham confined there, *Bale* 45; Latimer there with Sir Rob. Constable, lord Hussey, and lord Darcy, 1 *Lat.* xii, 162, 163; Barnes, Garrard, and Jerome confined there, 3 *Zur.* 632; Anne Askewe imprisoned there, and racked, *Bale* 220, 224; various martyrs and confessors imprisoned there, 1 *Brad.* 421; Bradford and Sandys, 2 *Brad.* xxxii, xxxiii; Cranmer, Latimer, Ridley, 2 *Brad.* xxxiii, 74 n., 2 *Cran.* xi, 1 *Lat.* xiii, 2 *Lat.* xxii, 258, *Rid.* xi, 390, 3 *Zur.* 371, 505, 506; queen Elizabeth's prayer there, before proceeding to her coronation, *Lit. Eliz.* 666 n.; prisoners in the Tower for ecclesiastical causes, in the time of Elizabeth, *Park.* 121, 122; story of a soul-priest there, *Calf.* 285; disputation there, 1581, 1 *Ful.* xi; a prison called Nun's-bower, 2 *Brad.* xxxii, *Sand.* vii; honourable personages beheaded on Tower-hill, 2 *Ful.* 202; execution of the earl of Essex, *Lit. Eliz.* 474

The prisons were gaming houses, *Hutch.* 7; for some prisons not mentioned here, *v.* Southwark.

Compters: in Bread-street, 2 *Hoop.* 613, 614; in the Poultry, 1 *Brad.* 83 n., 411, 496, 2 *Brad.* xxxiv; by the Stocks, 2 *Hoop.* 556; Anne Askewe sent to one of these prisons, *Bale* 156, 222

Fleet: a poor prisoner there, 1 *Lat.* 128; various martyrs confined there, 1 *Brad.* 289, 367, 421, 2 *Cov.* 238

Ludgate: a prison for debt, 1 *Lat.* 223

Newgate: divers executions there, 1 *Lat.* 164; Anne Askewe imprisoned there, *Bale* 206, &c., 231, 239; Bradford there, 2 *Brad.* xxxviii; various martyrs confined or put to death there, 1 *Brad.* 289, 367, 2 *Cov.* 238, *Poet.* 164; Philpot examined at Newgate session hall, *Phil.* 4, &c.

ix. HOUSES OF THE NOBILITY, &c.

Bacon house: v. *Shelley house.*

Bedford house, in the Strand: 2 *Bec.* 622 n

Bergavenny house: *Park.* 49, 52

Ely house: 2 *Zur.* 203—205; the vidame of Chartres there, *Grin.* 305; its alienation from the see, 1 *Zur.* 319 n

Shelley house: afterwards Bacon house, *Park.* 49 n

Somerset house: many churches, &c., pulled down for the building of it, *Grin.* 29 n., 3 *Zur.* 728; mentioned, 2 *Cran.* 510

Worcester house: a Protestant meeting there, 2 *Zur* 161 n

Sir Jo. Champneis, his high tower of brick, 2 *Cran.* 307 n

Inns: v. *Cheapside, Crown,* below.

x. VARIOUS LOCALITIES.

Aldersgate: Day's shop there, *Grin.* 2, 33

Aldgate: reference to it, 3 *Bec.* 282

Baynard's castle: 3 *Tyn.* 106

Billingsgate: named of Billinus, *Pil.* 345

Birchin lane: *Sand.* xiii.

Bloomsbury, (Middx.): dead men's bones carried away by cart-loads from churches desecrated by protector Somerset, and buried in Blomesbury, *Grin.* 29 n

Bow churchyard: v. *St Mary le Bow,* in iii.

Bread-street: v. *Compters,* in viii.

Bull head: v. *Cheapside.*

Cheap or *Cheapside*: one side being in Canterbury diocese, and the other in London, they differed as to fasting days, *Pil.* 557; the cross in Cheap, 2 *Whitg.* 180; it was worshipped, 2 *Brad.* 350; the standard in Cheap, 1 *Whitg.* 56; Hacket hanged in Cheap, *Nord.* 114; the Bull head in Cheape, *Rid.* 391; the Nag's head; story of the Nag's head consecration, 2 *Ful.* 117

Crown: an inn, *Bale* 218

Fleet: see amongst the prisons.

Holborn: the conduit, 1 *Cov.* 529

Lollard's tower: see in ii.

London bridge: heads of malefactors set up there, 3 *Zur.* 209

Lothbury: v. Pinder (R.).

Ludgate: named of Lud, *Pil.* 345; a prison, 1 *Lat.* 223

Mark-lane: *Sand.* xii.

Minories: 3 *Tyn.* 90 n

Mint: v. Mints.

Nag's head: v. *Cheapside.*

Newgate: see amongst the prisons.

Paternoster-row: *Phil.* 159

Paul's cross: see in ii.

Poultry: v. *Compters,* in viii.

Red Cross-street: *Calf.* 331; Dr Williams's library there, 2 *Hoop.* 117, *Lit. Eliz.* xxxiv.

Royal Exchange: 3 *Whitg.* 246

Saint Giles' fields: see in ii.
Saint Lawrence-lane: Jewel writes thence, 4 *Jew.* 1275
Saint Martin le Grand: see in v.
Saint Paul's churchyard: see in ii.
Shadwell, (Essex): an unhealthy spot, *Grin.* 294
Smithfield: a place of burning, 2 *Brad.* 324; martyrs there; Claydon, and Turmyne, *Bale* 51; Jerome (*q. v.*) and others, *Bale* 394, & al.; Anne Askewe, *Bale* 243, & al.; Bradford and Leaf, 1 *Brad.* 556, 2 *Brad.* xl, *Poet.* 162, 3 *Zur.* 772; Philpot's martyrdom, *Phil.* 161; other martyrs, *Poet.* 165, 169, 171, 172; Anabaptists burned there, 1 *Tyn.* lxx; Bartholomew fair, *Lit. Eliz.* 471, *Rog.* 206 n
Smithfield (East): Edm. Spenser's birthplace, *Poet.* xiv.
Soper-lane: now New Queen-street, 2 *Brad.* 39 n.
Steelyard: 2 *Brad.* xxxiv.
Stocks: v. Compters, in viii.
Temple-bar: Pil. 606
Thames-street: famous for oil, 2 *Tyn.* 194
Tower-hill: see in viii.
Tower-street: Sandys suppressed the mass at the Portuguese ambassador's, *Sand.* xx.
Vintry: the Three Krayned wharfe, 1 *Tyn.* 36
Williams's (Dr) library: v. Red Crossstreet.
London (Geo.): concerned in the process against Cranmer, 2 *Cran.* 546; his deposition, *ib.* 550
London (Jo.): a visitor of monasteries, 2 *Cran.* 315 n.; condemned for perjury, *Calf.* 332, [see Foxe, ii. 469, ed. 1684].
Long: to belong, 2 *Tyn.* 61
Longbeach: a wood in Kent, *Park.* 372
Longdale (Alban): *v.* Langdale.
Longinus: a name given to the soldier who pierced Christ's side, 1 *Jew.* 150, *Whita.* 560; derived from λόγχη, a spear, *ib.*
Longland (Jo.), bp of Lincoln: examines Jo. Tewkesbury, 1 *Tyn.* 32; was promoted by Wolsey, 2 *Tyn.* 309; used by him to injure queen Catharine, *ib.* 320; he flatters him, *ib.* 334; assists Cranmer in the matter of the divorce, 2 *Cran.* 244; present at Anne Boleyn's coronation, *ib.* 245; charged with negligence, 2 *Cov.* 501; his oppressive conduct towards the king's justices of peace, 2 *Cran.* 316; letter to him, *ib.* 248, 249
Longobardica Historia, *q. v.*
Longolius (Chr.): buried in a friar's cowl, *Calf.* 287

Longolius (Gybertus: mistake respecting his translation of the acts of the 2nd Nicene council, *Calf.* 138 n
Longsho (Eliz.): letter to Bradford, 2 *Brad.* 226
Longueville (Louis duke of): *v.* Orleans.
Longus à Coriolano (Fra.): adopts Carranza's false catalogue of canonical books ascribed to the council of Florence, 2 *Ful.* 222 n
Lonicerus (Phil.): on the Turks, *Rog.* 109, 110, 160, &c. nn
Looe, co. Cornwall: Nowell elected member, *Now.* i.
Lopen: leaped, 1 *Tyn.* 267
Lopez (Roderigo), physician to queen Elizabeth: hanged at Tyburn, *Lit. Eliz.* 658 n
Loque (Bertrand de): says the sacrament is not a sacrament if it be not joined to the word of God preached, *Rog.* 271 n
Lord: on the title, 1 *Whitg.* 152; the meaning of κύριος, &c., 2 *Whitg.* 386; who is a lord or master, 3 *Bec.* 610
LORD of Hosts: *v.* GOD.
Lordennes, or Lourdanes: a term of reproach, from lord Danes, 3 *Bec.* 207; lazy lordanes; slothful, clownish fellows, 2 *Jew.* 922
Lord's day: *v.* Sunday.
Lords Lieutenants, *q. v.*
Lords of Misrule, *q. v.*
Lord's Prayer, *q. v.*
Lords Presidents, *q. v.*
Lords (Summer): *v.* Summer.
Lord's Supper: *v.* Supper.
Loretto, Italy: running to Lauret, 1 *Cov.* 410
Lorichius (Gerard.): De Missa Publica proroganda, *Jew.* xxxix; he mentions that Clement forbade the offering of any liquor but wine, 3 *Bec.* 359 n.; censures the abuses of the mass, *ib.* 366; proves that every mass ought to be common, and none private, 2 *Jew.* 585; calls private masses rather an abomination than a sacrifice, 1 *Jew.* 513, 2 *Jew.* 634; declares it a thing worthy to be laughed at when the priest reading his mass alone speaks as to a congregation, 3 *Bec.* 379; says the very institution of the sacrament wills that we eat and drink all together, 3 *Jew.* 479; explains the word communion, 1 *Jew.* 135; speaks of the prayers called secreta, 2 *Jew.* 707; refers to the elevation of the host, 1 *Jew.* 509, 513; says, the breaking of the bread in the sacrament signifies that all we are one body, 2 *Jew.* 589; writes on both kinds, 1 *Jew.* 211, 229; states his opinion on the torments of purgatory, *Rog.* 216; affirms that the council of Constance decreed against Christ, 1 *Jew.*

214; says they are false catholics who hinder reformation, 3 *Jew.* 182
Lorraine (Fra. de), duke of Guise: takes Calais by treachery, *Calf.* 114, *Pil.* 70, 86, 1 *Zur.* 91 n., 3 *Zur.* 139 n.; he and his brother meditate the conquest of England for the queen of Scots, *Lit. Eliz.* 458; a conspiracy against the Guises in France, makes them desirous of recalling their army from Scotland, 1 *Zur.* 79 n.; their rage, *ib.* 83; the duke's manœuvres, especially in Scotland, 1 *Zur.* 114, 115, 116, 118, 2 *Zur.* 66; the faction opposed by Elizabeth, *Lit. Eliz.* 459, 2 *Zur.* 91; the butchery at Vassey, 2 *Ful.* 73, 74, *Rog.* 6; the duke takes Rouen, 2 *Zur.* 83 n.; his faction, and its obstinacy, *Grin.* 280, *Rog.* 212; the duke assassinated at the siege of Orleans, by Poltrot, 2 *Ful.* 121, 4 *Jew.* 1258 n., 1 *Zur.* 124 n., 2 *Zur.* 116 n
Lorraine (Hen. de), duke of Guise: attacked in Paris, 2 *Zur.* 115; mischief of his family, 1 *Zur.* 150; his persecutions, *ib.* 325
Lorraine (Cha. card. of): made cardinal at twelve years of age, 2 *Cran.* 39; recommended Rizzio to the queen of Scots, 1 *Zur.* 170; attacked in Paris, 2 *Zur.* 115; his opinion of the Prayer Book, *Park.* 398
Loseby (T.), called by Bryce Jo. Lothesby: martyr in Smithfield, *Poet.* 169
Losels: lost or worthless persons, knaves, cheats, *Bale* 76, *Brad.* 406, *Calf.* 133: madlosell, *Bale* 63
Losius (......) or Lewis: saluted, 1 *Zur.* 136
Lot: rescued by Abraham, 1 *Bul.* 308; his hospitality, 2 *Bul.* 59; his deliverance from Sodom, 2 *Bul.* 95, 4 *Bul.* 555; his times corrupt like the last times, 4 *Bul.* 162; his wife, 4 *Bul.* 275
Lotharius I., emperor, oppressed his brethren, and was afterwards deposed and made a monk, 4 *Jew.* 683
Lotharius II., emperor: two Latin verses written of him, 4 *Jew.* 692
Lotharius the Levite: *v.* Innocent III.
Lothesby (Jo.): *v.* Loseby (T.).
Lots: their use considered, 1 *Tyn.* 456
Louis I., emperor, called le Débonnaire: his history, 2 *Tyn.* 265; he conceded too much to the pope, *ib.* 266; his alleged release of the right of electing the pope, *ib.* 279, 1 *Whitg.* 397, 400; deposed and made a monk, 4 *Jew.* 683; he wrote a book against images, 4 *Jew.* 1054; private mass came in during his time, 1 *Hoop.* 228
Louis II., emperor, called the Young: commended the Romans for choosing their own bishop, 1 *Whitg.* 401; unfortunate in all his doings and shamefully conquered by his brother, 4 *Jew.* 683
Louis III., emperor: commonly called Ludovicus nihili, 4 *Jew.* 684
Louis IV., emperor: last of the house of Pepin, 4 *Jew.* 684
Louis, king of Bohemia: *Grin.* 3 n., 14 n
Louis IX. (St), king of France: his chastity, 1 *Lat.* 95; his complaint of Romish exactions, 4 *Jew.* 1081; his law against swearing, 1 *Bec.* 390; invoked for horses, *Rog.* 226
Louis XI., king of France: his saying on dissembling, 4 *Jew.* 1101, 1102; 1 *Zur.* 120
Louis XII., king of France, his quarrel with the pope, 2 *Tyn.* 310; he marries the princess Mary of England, *ib.* 313
Louis II., king of Hungary and Bohemia: slain, *Bale* 575, *Grin.* 14 n.; his widow: *v.* Mary.
Louis II., duke of Bavaria: 2 *Zur.* 274 n
Louis, duke of Bavaria: joins the league against the Protestants, 3 *Zur.* 526 n
Louis V., elector Palatine, called the Pacific: his esteem for dogs, 2 *Cran.* 296
Louis VI., elector Palatine: *Park.* 471 n., 2 *Zur.* 286; favours the Lutheran doctrine, 2 *Zur.* 156 n., 274 n
Louis of Nassau, brother of Will. prince of Orange: a commander, 2 *Zur.* 247; he occupies Valenciennes, 1 *Zur.* 274
Louis de Bourbon, first prince of Condé: *Grin.* 280, 2 *Zur.* 91 n.; queen Elizabeth's contract with him, 1 *Zur.* 115 n., 116 n
Lourdanes: *v.* Lordennes.
Lout: to bow, or do reverence to, 3 *Bec.* 529, 2 *Bul.* 28
Louth, co. Lincoln: the rebellion called the pilgrimage of grace broke out here, 2 *Cran.* 363 n
Louvain, the university: Ridley there, *Rid.* 488, 492; the divines there draw up a confession of faith, to which Luther replies, 3 *Zur.* 670 n., 671; they dispute with Tyndale, 1 *Tyn.* lxxiv; they correct the Latin Vulgate, *Whita.* 154; the study of canon law there, 4 *Jew.* 1089; the Popish seminary, *Calf.* 51, 2 *Jew.* 701, 1 *Zur.* 184, 239, 3 *Zur.* 416; fugitives there, *Grin.* 169, 1 *Zur.* 147, 148, 153; treasons fomented by them, *ib.* 223; they publish conclusions against the power of the civil magistrate in religion, *Pil.* x.
Louvre: *v.* Lover.
Love and Charity: *v.* Faith, Prayers.
More urges, and Tyndale objects to employing the word charity as equivalent to

LOVE

'Αγάπη, 2 *Tyn.* 135, 3 *Tyn.* 14, 20, 21; meaning of the word dilectio, *Now.* (101); description of charity or Christian love, 2 *Hoop.* 111, 112; see Tyndale's exposition of 1 John, passim, 2 *Tyn.* 133—225; the nature of love or charity, 2 *Bec.* 341, 348, 583, 584, 3 *Bec.* 602, 616, 2 *Jew.* 862; an order and measure in love, 1 *Bul.* 185; what love we ought to have among us, 1 *Bec.* 226; Christian charity, a flower of the Nosegay, *ib.*; its excellency, *ib.* 3 *Bec.* 42; love is more excellent than knowledge, 1 *Cov.* 510; it is a natural and continual debt, *Sand.* 204; a principal part of Christian religion, *Now.* (6), 118; the commandment of Christ, 1 *Cov.* 236: the beginning and end of his commandments, *ib.* 417; the badge of Christians, 1 *Bec.* 37, 3 *Bec.* 81, 1 *Lat.* 448, *Now.* 19; the livery of Christ, 1 *Lat.* 448, 2 *Lat.* 1, *Sand.* 98, 286; by it we are known to be God's disciple, 3 *Bec.* 46, 47; love is a bond of the church, 4 *Bul.* 25; true love is only among the godly, *Pil.* 240; Christians cannot but love, 1 *Tyn.* 298; Christian love not carnal, 1 *Lat.* 448; love is the most necessary of all qualifications for a preacher, *Hutch.* 103, 104; examples of love, 1 *Bec.* 228, 2 *Bec.* 177 ; whence it is, 1 *Bul.* 180; it springs from faith, 1 *Lat.* 449, 454, 1 *Tyn.* 192, 2 *Tyn.* 88, 130, 173, 174, 198, 204, 3 *Tyn.* 195—199; it is an evidence or sign of faith, 1 *Cov.* 234, 2 *Tyn.* 88, 130, 198; the instrument wherewith faith maketh us children of God, 2 *Tyn.* 200; it is the surest evidence of justification, 3 *Zur.* 44; without love, faith and hope are dead, *Now.* 19; what it does, 1 *Bec.* 166, 2 *Tyn.* 14, 192; it casts out fear, 2 *Tyn.* 203, 204; fulfils the law, 1 *Bul.* 190, 2 *Hoop.* 111, 112, 1 *Lat.* 452, 1 *Tyn.* 192, 442, 475, 506, 2 *Tyn.* 11, 12, 118, 119, 173, 202, 203, 325; we should let love interpret the law, 1 *Tyn.* 403, 475; John never speaks of any law but love, *ib.* 475; it is above all laws, 2 *Tyn.* 188, 232 ; it draws to earnestness in religion, *Pil.* 354; causes good works, 2 *Tyn.* 88; things done without charity please not God, 1 *Bec.* 154; love seeketh not her own profit, 1 *Tyn.* 98, but maketh all things common, *ib.* 95—99; is prone to hospitality, *Sand.* 400; communicates gifts and graces to others, *ib.* 401; hides a multitude of sins, *ib.* 106, 206 ; the text misinterpreted by the Rhemists, *Whita.* 470; it cannot hide our sins from God, but hides the faults of our neighbours, *Sand.* 399; it fashions to the will of God, 1 *Bul.* 182; makes all things easy to be borne, 3 *Tyn.* 95; overcomes all evils, 1 *Bul.* 182; exhortations to love and charity, 1 *Bul.* 191, *Sand.* 398; godly counsels to continue in it, 1 *Bec.* 156; sermon on "Love one another," 1 *Lat.* 447 ; we must seek perfection in brotherly kindness and love, *Sand.* 425; we are to owe nothing else, 2 *Hoop.* 111; the necessity of love in prayer, *Pra. B.* xvi; it must be shewn, as is signified in the Lord's supper, 2 *Bec.* 231, 235; it must spring from repentance and faith in preparation for the same, *ib.* 235, 236 ; the love of God to man, 1 *Bec.* 45, 1 *Bul.* 181, (v. God, v.); gave his Son, that we might see love, and love again, 3 *Tyn.* 196; love is a duty which all men owe to God, 2 *Bec.* 403; it is the believer's motive, 1 *Tyn.* 21, 182, 297, 298, 434, 2 *Tyn.* 203, 208 ; our love to God springs from his love to us, 1 *Tyn.* 84, 108, 109, 222, 441, 2 *Tyn.* 198, 199, 200, 3 *Tyn.* 195, 196, 198; it is the consequence, not the cause of pardon, 1 *Tyn.* 83, 87; it proceeds from God's goodness deeply pondered, 1 *Bec.* 43; love to God is a mark of grace, 2 *Tyn.* 173; how it is manifested, 1 *Tyn.* 107, 108, 112, 2 *Tyn.* 173, 193; viz. by outward working, 1 *Bec.* 37, 38, 43; he that loves God will love his neighbour, 1 *Lat.* 422, 1 *Tyn.* 84; of the love of God and our neighbour, 1 *Bul.* 180, &c., *Now.* (22), 137; charity, or love of our brethren, *Lit. Edw.* 524, (571), 2 *Tyn.* 170, 171, 191, &c.; its necessity, 1 *Tyn.* 375; it is a sign of grace, 2 *Tyn.* 192, 205; charity between brethren who differ, 2 *Brad.* 197, 215; charity to those in error, *ib.* 180; we must use our liberty according to the rule of charity, 2 *Lat.* 80; love to our neighbour, 1 *Bec.* 227, 228, 2 *Bec.* 111, 112, 1 *Bul.* 186, 1 *Lat.* 20, 1 *Tyn.* 25, 26, 404 ; it is a duty which all men owe, 2 *Bec.* 404 ; it springs from the love of God, 1 *Bec.* 39, 40, 2 *Tyn.* 46, 192, 198, 206, 207, 325, 3 *Tyn.* 6; it is a new command, and yet old, *ib.* 174; the commandment set aside by Pharisees, *ib.* 41; how love is due to our neighbours, *Sand.* 205 ; we must not be hasty with them when they fall, 2 *Lat.* 187 ; it will seek to amend them, 1 *Lat.* 451; love for those who do us evil is true godly love, 1 *Tyn.* 193; a caution or exception with regard to love to men, *Sand.* 206; paternal and filial love, 2 *Cran.* 85; double charity, 1 *Bul.* 181; the pith of charity, *ib.* 190; the great want of love in these times, *Sand.* 206, 207; the love of many is cold, 1 *Bec.* 39 ; key-cold charity, *Coop.* 11, 59, &c.; love must not be feigned, 1 *Bec.* 227; false charity, 2 *Brad.* 343;

the duty of love, not understood by the natural man, 3 *Tyn.* 8
— The love of God (a poem): notice thereof, *Poet.* xxxi; stanzas from it, *ib.* 346; an hymn of heavenly love, by E. Spenser, *ib.* 6; verses on charity by W. Warner, *ib.* 380; verses thereon by Tho. Churchyard, *ib.* 402; St Charity, 3 *Tyn.* 21; faithful love seeks no delays, *Pil.* 119; love me love my dog, 1 *Tyn.* 84
— Love of Self, *q. v.*
— Love of the World, *q. v.*
Love (W.) a priest at St Stephen's, Norwich: *Park.* vi, 481
Love-day: a day appointed for the amicable adjustment of disputes, 1 *Tyn.* 440, 2 *Tyn.* 215
Love-feasts: *v.* Agapæ.
Lovelace (Will.): in a commission for a royal visitation, *Jew.* xv, 1 *Zur.* 39 n.; recommended to be steward of abp Parker's liberties, *Park.* 405
Lovell (Sir Ralph): father of Sir Thomas, 2 *Lat.* 295 n
Lovell (Sir Tho.), K. G.: notice of him, 2 *Lat.* 295 n
Lover, Loover, Louvre: an opening to let out smoke, 2 *Whitg.* 181
Lovus (......): an astrologer, 1 *Ful.* v.
Low Countries: *v.* Netherlands.
Lowenberger (Urban): 2 *Zur.* 201
Lowlars: *v.* Lollards.
Lowliness: *v.* Humility.
Lowmas (......): *v.* Lomas.
Lowth: lowness, 1 *Bec.* 272
Lowth (......), or Lowther: exercises spiritual jurisdiction without ordination, *Park.* 474; archbishop Grindal's account of him, and hope that his pardon will be stayed, *Grin.* 353
Loy (St): *v.* Eligius.
Loys (St): *v.* Louis.
Lubeck: holds out against the emperor, 3 *Zur.* 668 n
Lubetius (......): 2 *Zur.* 293
Lucan (M. A.): mentions a miracle, 1 *Hoop.* 328; and a case of necromancy, *ib.* 329
Lucane: perhaps a dormer-window, 4 *Jew.* 905
Lucas of Bruges: *Whita.* 148
Lucentius: papal legate at Chalcedon, 3 *Jew.* 220, 4 *Jew.* 1022
Lucerne: the republic at war, *Phil.* 390
Lucia (St): martyred, 1 *Jew.* 162
Lucian: cited or referred to, 4 *Bul.* 77, *Park.* 445, *Pil.* 312, 3 *Whitg.* 134 n., *Wool.* 130, 3 *Zur.* 607; killed by dogs, *Grin.* 8, *Wool.* 112

Lucian, presbyter of Antioch, and martyr: revised the text of the LXX, *Whita.* 124
Lucianists: 3 *Bul.* 112
Lucifer: assumed to mean the devil, *Sand.* 362, 297; his pride, 2 *Jew.* 1092; Gregory compares John of Constantinople with him, 3 *Jew.* 279, 320; Lucifer and the fallen angels said to have their being in aëre caliginoso, 1 *Lat.* 27
Luciferians: 2 *Ful.* 389; Augustine does not call them heretics, *Phil.* 426
Lucilius (Caius): a saying of his, 2 *Hoop.* 544
Lucius, king of Britain: his alleged conversion, and embassy to Rome, *Bale* 614, *Calf.* 53 n., 1 *Jew.* 267, 305, 3 *Jew.* 163, *Pil.* 482, 510, 2 *Whitg.* 129; the alleged embassy and imaginary rescript to him from pope Eleutherius, *Calf.* 52, 53, 305, 2 *Ful.* 53, 128, 186, 366, *Jew.* xxxvi, 1 *Jew.* 163, 267, 306, 438, 4 *Jew.* 974, 1124, *Park.* 295, *Pil.* 482, 510—513, 2 *Whitg.* 128, 3 *Whitg.* 592; copy of the letter, *Pil.* 512, 513; Lucius is said to have changed flamines for bishops, *Pil.* 597
Lucius, bp of Rome: *Rid.* 180
Lucius, an Arian: 2 *Ful.* 388
Luck (Jo.): *Bale* 16
Lucke (Rich.); 2 *Cran.* 367 n
Lucretia: 1 *Bul.* 417, 1 *Hoop.* 284, 1 *Tyn.* 183
Lucullus: 1 *Jew.* 22, *Sand.* 394
Lucy (Mr): commended by Latimer, 2 *Lat.* 381, 383; mentioned, *ib.* 399, 410, 413, 414, [probably Sir Tho. of Charlecote].
Lud: built Ludgate, *Pil.* 345
Ludham, co. Norfolk: a residence of the bishop of Norwich, 1 *Zur.* 98 n., 265 n.; fall of a great barn, 2 *Zur.* 117
Ludlow, co. Salop: the very cross of Ludlow, *Calf.* 35, 274; the school there, 2 *Cran.* 380
Ludlowe (J.): *v.* Lidley.
Ludovicus: *v.* Louis.
Ludovicus, canon of the Lateran: *Jew.* xxxix; extract from his oration at Trent, 4 *Jew.* 758
Ludovicus, cardinal of Arles; on councils, 3 *Jew.* 206
Ludovicus Patritius: *Jew.* xxxix, 2 *Jew.* 578
Ludulphus Saxo: De Vita Christi, *Jew.* xxxix; he tells a story about the devil entering a church during mass, 2 *Lat.* 109 n.; says the body of Christ is present in the sacrament in as great a quantity as on the cross, 2 *Jew.* 797
Luft (Haus), a printer of Marburgh: employed by Tyndale, 1 *Tyn.* xxxvii, xxxix, xl; also by Frith, *ib.* xxxvii; he printed for Tyndale

an edition of The Parable of the Wicked Mammon, *ib.* 31; and the Obedience, *ib.* 129; also the sixth edition of his New Testament with prologue to Romans [Anderson's Annals of Eng. Bib. ii. app. vii.]; Genesis and Numbers, *ib.* xxxix—xli; likewise the Practice of Prelates, 2 *Tyn.* 238; perhaps also an exposition of 1 Cor. vii, 1 *Tyn.* xxxvii.

Lugdunum: *v.* Lyons.

Lugentes: *v.* Excommunication.

Luidhard, a bishop: queen Bertha's chaplain, *Calf.* 306 n

Luitprandus Ticinensis: Rerum gestarum per Europeas, *Jew.* xxxix; records certain acts of pope Sergius, 3 *Jew.* 276; testifies as to the immorality of the Lateran, 4 *Jew.* 647, 651; says we see by experience that the emperor understands God's causes, &c., *ib.* 1029; not the author of the Pontifical, 2 *Ful.* 99 n

Luke (St): wrote Greek well, 1 *Whitg.* 346; the epistle to the Hebrews ascribed by some to him, 1 *Ful.* 29, 31, 33, *Whita.* 106; others suppose him to have translated that epistle into Greek, *Whita.* 125; his burial and translation, 2 *Whitg.* 303; invoked for oxen, 1 *Bec.* 138, 2 *Bec.* 536, *Hutch.* 171

— Gospel: Tyndale's prologue to it, 1 *Tyn.* 481; argument of it, and contents of each chapter, 3 *Bec.* 571, &c.; the address to Theophilus, *Whita.* 641; this gospel rejected by the Valentinians, *Whita.* 34; by the Ebionites, *ib.* 35; many parts of it refused by Marcion, 1 *Ful.* 7

— Acts of the Apostles: summary of the book, and contents of each chapter, 3 *Bec.* 577, &c.; the address to Theophilus, *Whita.* 645; the book rejected by Cerdon, &c., *ib.* 34; also by the Severians, *ib.* 35; and the Manichees, 1 *Ful.* 7, *Whita.* 318; its excellency, *Phil.* 361, &c.

Luke: Lucca so called, 2 *Jew.* 917

Luke, a town; perhaps Laken: martyrs there, 1 *Tyn.* lix.

Lukewarmness: *v.* Zeal.

Lumey (Will. lord of): *v.* Vandermarke.

Lumley (Jo., last lord): mourner at the funeral of the emperor Ferdinand, *Grin.* 32

Lunatics: *v.* Madmen.

Luncher (......): 1 *Zur.* 131

Lunenburg (Ernest duke of): *v.* Ernest.

Lupoldus de Bebenburg: De Jure et Transl. Imperii, *Jew.* xl; mentions that cardinal Hostiensis says the emperor is a vassal of the church of Rome, 4 *Jew.* 836

Lupton (D.): Modern Protestant Divines, 1 *Bec.* vii, xi, 2 *Brad.* xii, xvii, *Whita.* x. nn

Lupus (Christian.): Synodorum Decreta, *Calf.* 137 n., 2 *Ful.* 70 n., 1 *Hoop.* 376 n

Lurde: lurid, *Calf.* 361

Lure: to betray or deceive, 1 *Brad.* 262

Luskish: inclined to laziness, 2 *Bul.* 70

Lusts: forbidden to be nourished in the heart, 2 *Bec.* 121, &c.; they are to be denied, 1 *Bec.* 323, *Sand.* 374; they will be punished, 2 *Bec.* 142; the word used for will, or desire, whether holy, or unholy, 1 *Tyn.* 16, & passim.

Luther (Martin): born, *Lit. Eliz.* 454; called of God to his work, 2 *Ful.* 377, 4 *Jew.* 666; ordinarily called to teach before the coming of the pope's pardoner, 2 *Ful.* 72; before he began to publish the gospel, there was a general quietness in the church, 3 *Jew.* 174; he was sometime in agony of spirit, 2 *Lat.* 52; the first beginning of his reformation, 3 *Jew.* 193; in what sense he was the first publisher of the gospel, *ib.* 213; a certain person would have dissuaded him from the reformation as impracticable, 2 *Jew.* 995; his propositions to the university of Wittenberg, *Lit. Eliz.* 453; his part in the conference of Augsburg, 2 *Zur.* 15 n.; he appealed to the next general council, 3 *Tyn.* 185; his appeal disallowed, 2 *Jew.* 996; Harding accuses him of passing the bounds of modesty in his disputation with Eckius, 4 *Jew.* 899; Jewel defends him, *ib.*; he burned the decretals, 1 *Tyn.* 221; his preaching, *Pil.* 265; he was called on to work miracles, 1 *Lat.* 212; cursed by the pope for preaching the Gospel, 4 *Jew.* 1097; the tale about his conference with Satan refuted, 1 *Jew.* 105, 106; his controversy with Henry VIII, (*q. v.*) 2 *Tyn.* 338—340; he wrote a letter of apology for his rough reply to that king, 1 *Tyn.* xxxi, 2 *Tyn.* 340; his controversy with Erasmus on free-will, 3 *Tyn.* 233; More rails at his marriage and reviles his wife, Kath. Boren, 3 *Tyn.* 3, 5, 170; Tyndale's alleged conference with him, 1 *Tyn.* xxv, xxvi; he is falsely charged by Papists with inciting rebellion, 2 *Tyn.* 244; his alleged opinions on magistracy, 4 *Jew.* 669, 670, 671; he wrote vehemently against the German rebels, *ib.* 665, 669, 671; said Munzer was set to work by the devil, *ib.* 671; no man more advanced the authority of the civil magistrate, *ib.* 670; review of the controversy between Luther, Zuingle, and Œcolampadius on the Lord's supper, 1 *Cov.* 463—465; his part in it, 3 *Zur.* 681 n.; the conference at Marpurg, *Grin.* 251 n.; he meets Zuinglius there, 1 *Tyn.* xxxviii; dissension between them on

LUTHER 501

the sacrament, 1 *Brad.* 525, *Coop.* 39, 1 *Jew.* 531, &c.; conference in his house at Wittenberg on the same subject, 1 *Jew.* 468; he dissuaded Melancthon from coming to England, 3 *Zur.* 616 n.; his want of firmness towards the landgrave Philip, *ib.* 666 n.; a false story concerning him 1 *Ful.* 38; he prophesied of the troubles of Germany, *Phil.* 416; his death and burial, *Lit. Eliz.* 445; lamented, *Phil.* 415; Hooper's character of him, 3 *Zur.* 46; slandered and reviled by Popish writers, *Coop.* 23, 1 *Ful.* 38, 1 *Jew.* 106, 216, 3 *Jew.* 265, 607, 4 *Jew.* 673, 1040 n, *Poet.* 278, 3 *Tyn.* 3, 5, 187 n.; alleged to have been the founder of the reformed churches, 3 *Jew.* 265, 607, *Phil.* 386; where the church, or reformed faith, was before Luther, *Phil.* 391, *Poet.* 286; his reformation not without faults, *Poet.* 288; a proclamation issued by Henry VIII. against his disciples, 2 *Lat.* 305; his doctrine not come to an end, 2 *Ful.* 377

His works, *Jew.* xl; his German Bible, the word "only" inserted in the text (Rom. iii.), 1 *Ful.* 425; but in his later translation corrected, *ib.* 154; his EXPOSITION OF PSALM XXII. (Heb. xxiii.) translated by Coverdale, 2 *Cov.* 279—319; his preface to the Romans followed by Tyndale, 1 *Tyn.* 483; Sandys' advertisement to his Commentary on Galatians, *Sand.* 435; he wrote on the Apocalypse, *Bale* 258; his Kirchen-postilla, and Hus-postilla, 2 *Ful.* 18 n.; his treatise De Missa Privata, 1 *Jew.* 105; Brevis Confessio de Cœna Domini, 3 *Zur.* 681 n.; his book Ad Nobiles Ord. Teutonici, 1 *Jew.* 217; republished Jerome's epistle to Evagrius or Evangelus, 2 *Ful.* 33; a work by Erasmus ascribed to him, *Calf.* 314 n.; at the diet of Worms, 3 *Tyn.* 185, 186; charged with omitting a passage in 1 Peter, 1 *Ful.* 551; expounding Zech. xiii. 3, says that Christians must retain pure doctrines, without respect of persons, whether of kinsman or friend, 1 *Whitg.* 331, and shews that he who prophesies falsely is to be destroyed, not with iron weapons, but with the word of God, *ib.* 332; on the term Homoüsion, *Whita.* 611; he distinguishes between the obscurity of passages and the obscurity of dogmas in scripture, *Whita.* 361; the statement unjustly blamed by Stapleton, *ib.* 362; he says that the perspicuity or obscurity of scripture is either internal or external, i. e. in the heart or in the words, *Whita.* 363; admits that there are many difficulties in scripture, and assigns a reason for them, *ib.*

364; calls the Bible the book of heretics, *ib.* 229, 231; maintains that all the epistles of St Paul pertain to the universal church, 1 *Tyn.* 213; accused of rejecting various books of the New Testament, 2 *Ful.* 130, 384; at one time he erred (in common with some ancient churches) in rejecting certain books, *Whita.* 105; his alleged denial of the epistle of St James, 1 *Ful.* 14—18, 2 *Ful.* 384, *Phil.* 412; his doctrine and conduct censured by More in various particulars, and Tyndale's replies, 3 *Tyn.* 185—190, 212; quoted by bp Fisher (*q. v.*), 1 *Tyn.* 213, who feared he would burn the pope if he could, *ib.* 221; his theological defects, 2 *Zur.* 73; he was preeminent in preaching justification, 1 *Hoop.* 29, 144, 246; his doctrine thereon, 1 *Ful.* 122; misrepresented by Papists, *Phil.* 411; defended by Curio, *ib.* 412; he condemns servile fear, 1 *Ful.* 573; referred to on the church, 2 *Lat.* 313, 314; says, we honour the church of Rome in all things, only we withstand those that instead of the church, have thrust in the confusion of Babylon, 3 *Jew.* 223; his defence (in an early work) of the pope's supremacy, 1 *Jew.* 440; his opinion of the fathers, 2 *Jew.* 682, 683, 3 *Tyn.* 187; his alleged saying, that if the world lasted long, it would be necessary to receive the decrees of councils, *Whita.* 140; what he thought of the Waldenses, 3 *Zur.* 694 n.; cited by Gardiner as condemning the reformed doctrines in Germany, 1 *Cran.* 13; said to have acknowledged that his followers were worse than they had been when Papists, 2 *Ful.* 18, 121; speaks of prayer, meditation, and temptation as requisite to make up a preacher, 1 *Brad.* 563; he maintains that there are strictly but two sacraments, 3 *Jew.* 460; his opinions on the eucharist, and the real presence, 1 *Brad.* 511, *Coop.* 37, 1 *Cran.* 19, 281, 285, 2 *Lat.* 265, 3 *Whitg.* 328, 1 *Zur.* 182, 186, 3 *Zur.* 46; he differed from other reformers as to the manner of Christ's presence in the sacrament, *Phil.* 401; he differed, but not heretically, 2 *Ful.* 376; on communion in both kinds, 1 *Jew.* 214, 215; in an early work he disapproves of pronouncing the canon of the mass aloud, 2 *Jew.* 705; his opinion of confession, as cited by More, 1 *Tyn.* 263 n.; an opinion on absolution ascribed to him, 3 *Jew.* 355; he allows ceremonies, so that they be not taken for the principal points themselves, 2 *Brad.* 393, 394; allows images, &c., 3 *Whitg.* 328; venerated the sign of the cross, *Calf.* 304; whether he believed in purgatory, *Whita.*

541; his views on that subject, *Rog.* 215 n., 216 n.; his sayings about Jo. Marbach, 2 *Zur.* 81 n.; on the despair of Dr Kraus, *Rog.* 142 n.; he calls Aristotle sceleratus nebulo, 2 *Ful.* 57 n

Lutherans: *v.* Consubstantiation.
Censured, 2 *Zur.* 125, 241, 3 *Zur.* 251; classed with Papists, 2 *Zur.* 143; their errors, 3 *Whitg.* 549, 550, 1 *Zur.* 169, 177, 342; some of them rejected the epistles of Jude, 2 Peter, and 2 and 3 John, *Whita.* 296; they hold that infants believe and are therefore to be baptized, *Rog.* 281; the Lutheran view of the Lord's supper explained, and compared with other views, 1 *Tyn.* 367, &c.; dispute between them and the Zuinglians, 3 *Jew.* 620, 621, 623, 2 *Zur.* 245; their struggles with the Calvinists, *ib.* 156 n.; their opinion refuted, 1 *Zur.* 321; they attribute to Christ's humanity properties which belong only to his divine nature, 3 *Zur.* 682; the Lutheran controversy on the real presence avoided by Tyndale, 1 *Tyn.* liii, 346; Tyndale and Roye said by Robert Ridley to be manifestly Lutherans, *ib.* 483; they retain images, 1 *Ful.* 204, 205; the term Lutherans reproachfully used by Romanists, 2 *Ful.* 375, *Phil.* 417; they give the name to the spiritual, 3 *Tyn.* 107; called Martinists at Antwerp, 1 *Zur.* 174

Lutterworth: co. Leicester, *Bale* 15
Luttrell (Sir Jo.): his death, 3 *Zur.* 496 n
Lux mundi: *v.* Wassalia (Jo. de).
Lyall (Lord), i. e. Arth. Plantagenet, (*q. v.*) visc. Lisle.
Lycaonia: "the speech of Lycaonia," opinions respecting it, *Whita.* 256 n.; the people there spoke and prayed in their own tongue, 1 *Jew.* 277
Lychfield (Clem.): *v.* Lichfield.
Lycosthenes (Conrad), or Wolfhart: De prodigiis, 2 *Ful.* 143; he abridged Gesner's Bibliotheca, 1 *Zur.* 305 n
Lycurgus, king of Lacedemon: a lawgiver, 2 *Bul.* 219, 1 *Hoop.* 351, 4 *Jew.* 1164; he set down no punishment for ingratitude, *Sand.* 156; his answer about the bringing up of his children, 2 *Bec.* 5
Lydd, co. Kent: letter from Parker to the bailiff and jurats on the evil behaviour of Dr Hardiman the vicar, *Park.* 342
Lydford, co. Devon: Lydford law, 2 *Jew.* 627
Lydia: sold purple, 1 *Bul.* 31; her heart opened, 2 *Hoop.* 201, 2 *Jew.* 822, 936; her baptism, 4 *Bul.* 366; she sold not her house, 2 *Bul.* 22; was wealthy, *ib.* 23
Lydley (Jo.): *v.* Lidley.

Lygon (Will.): *v.* Ligon.
Lying, Lies, Liars: *v.* Deceit.
Lying forbidden, 2 *Bec.* 117; is forbidden under all circumstances, *Hutch.* 51; censured, 1 *Bec.* 447, 448; it agrees not with love, and is therefore damnable, 2 *Tyn.* 56; condemned among the Gentiles, 1 *Bul.* 204; allowed by Turks and Jesuits, *Rog.* 120; Origen permitted lying in some cases, and Jerome seems to follow him, 2 *Bul.* 115; Tyndale thinks there are cases in which dissembling is allowable, 2 *Tyn.* 57; scriptural examples explained, 2 *Bul.* 115, *Hutch.* 52; the prevalence of falsehood, 1 *Lat.* 451, 500; how every man is a liar, 1 *Bec.* 277; what leasing or falsity is, 3 *Bec.* 604; a lie defined, 2 *Bul.* 114, *Hutch.* 52; kinds of lies, 2 *Bul.* 114; jesting lies, *ib.*; they should be avoided, 1 *Lat.* 503; officious lies, 2 *Bul.* 115; the authors of false sects are liars, 1 *Bec.* 280; lies openly preached, 1 *Lat.* 501; use of lies among the faithless, 2 *Hoop.* 271; lies do harm three manner of ways, *ib.* 270; what is gained by lying, 4 *Jew.* 640; falsehood fearfully punished, 1 *Lat.* 407; why liars are not punished now as they were in the days of Ananias, *ib.* 503; lying children should be punished with stripes, 1 *Ful.* 324, 1 *Lat.* 501; Cranmer's play upon lies and adverbs in "ly," 1 *Cran.* 157

Lyle (Lord): *v.* Lyall.
Lylye (......), an artist: skilful in supplying wanting portions of MSS., *Park.* 254
Lymster: *v.* Leominster.
Lynde (Sir Humph.): Case for the Spectacles, *Calf.* 290 n., 2 *Ful.* 236 n
Lyndesay (Dav.), minister of Forfar: 2 *Zur.* 365
Lyndesay (Dav.), minister of Leith: 2 *Zur.* 365
Lyndewode (Will.), bp of St David's: Provinciale, seu Constitutiones Angliæ, 1 *Cran.* 143, *Jew.* xl, 1 *Tyn.* 394; this book begins with these words, "Ignorantia sacerdotium," 4 *Jew.* 877; refers to the elevation, 1 *Jew.* 509; says the sacrament is exposed that it may be worshipped, 2 *Jew.* 556; finds fault with the canopy over it, 1 *Cran.* 143, 2 *Jew.* 557; writes of daily communion, 1 *Jew.* 199; says, that in small churches only the priests receive the blood, 1 *Jew.* 261; describes Gradales or Grails, *Grin.* 135 n.; mentions a constitution of Edmund, archbishop of Canterbury, on vows by married women, 1 *Lat.* 54, an injunction of abp Winchelsea respecting church-books, vestments, &c., *Grin.* 159 n.; a mandate of arch-

bishop Islip forbidding the sale of masses, 1 *Lat.* 56 n
Lyner (Jo.), of St Gall : 3 *Zur.* 693
Lynley (Mr), prebendary of Husthwaite: enjoined to examine the statutes of the church of York, *Grin.* 151
Lynn, co. Norfolk: a Scotch preacher there, 1 *Zur.* 131
Lynne (Gwalter), printer: 1 *Brad.* 2, 4 *Bul.* xx, 2 *Cran.* 218
Lyons: the poor men of Lyons, or pauperes de Lugduno, a sect, 2 *Ful.* 247, 2 *Jew.* 689, 3 *Jew.* 81 n.; spoken of by Pius II., 4 *Jew.* 737; they affirmed that the Romish church was the harlot of Babylon, &c., 4 *Jew.* 736, 737; the hollow pillar of our Lord's length there, *Bale* 518
Lyra (Nic. de): Biblia cum Gloss. Ord. et Expos. N. de Lyra, *Jew.* xl, 3 *Whitg.* xxx; said to have been an Englishman, 1 *Jew.* 213; styled a German, *Bale* 258; notice of him, in which he is more correctly stated to have been a Jew, and to have received his name from his native place in the diocese of Evreux, 1 *Tyn.* 151 n.; reference to him, 4 *Jew.* 982; in the prologue to Genesis he (or Doring?) describes the advantage of a diversity of expositors, 1 *Jew.* 533; remarks about hearkening to " many " in judgment, Exod. xxiii. 2, 2 *Jew.* 688; on Deut. xvii. he reports the common opinion of the Jews on the expositions of their rabbins, 3 *Jew.* 248, 4 *Jew.* 864; thinks marriage with a deceased wife's sister (Deut. xviii.) lawful, 4 *Jew.* 1243; shews on Jos. v., why circumcision was not practised in the wilderness, 1 *Jew.* 224; speaks of the alleged omission of the feast of tabernacles, Neh. viii., 1 *Whitg.* 31; on Esther iii. he mentions an opinion that we may bow one knee to any great man, but two only to God, 2 *Jew.* 666; on Prov. xxx. he says that the scripture contains all things needful to salvation, as a merchant's ship does the necessaries of life, 2 *Cran.* 35; on Dan. xiv. (apoc.) he affirms that many feigned miracles have been wrought in the church, 1 *Jew.* 105, 2 *Jew.* 666, 3 *Jew.* 143, 197; expounds Hosea i. 11, " one head," 3 *Jew.* 280; rejects the Apocrypha, *Whita.* 65; thinks Josephus wrote the rest of Esther, *ib.* 71; expounds the text " Upon this rock," Matt. xvi. 18, that is, says he, upon Christ, 2 *Jew.* 1000, 4 *Jew.* 1119; in his exposition of this text he describes the true church, 1 *Brad.* 529, 2 *Jew.* 819, 1000, 4 *Jew.* 928, 2 *Lat.* 313, *Rid.* 127; and says that many popes have been apostates, 1 *Jew.* 381, 400, 3 *Jew.* 345, 4 *Jew.* 923, 928, 1117, 1119, 2 *Lat.* 313, *Rid.* 127; explains Lu. xi. 29, the text " They have Moses and the prophets," *Whita.* 643; thinks one of the disciples who went to Emmaus (Lu. xxiv.) was Luke himself, 1 *Jew.* 234; his opinion on Christ breaking bread at that place, *Hutch.* 283; he interprets those words of Christ, "Except ye eat," &c. (Jo. vi.) spiritually, and declares that directly they pertain nothing to the sacramental or corporal eating, 1 *Jew.* 212, 453, 454, 3 *Jew.* 589, 590, 4 *Jew.* 766 (the words are really Doring's, 3 *Jew.* 589); on Jo. vi. he writes, so far as we are united unto God by the sacrament of thanksgiving we live spiritually; but the union that is between him and us is by faith and love, 3 *Jew.* 496; on the same chapter he censures the Greek custom of giving the communion to infants, 1 *Jew.* 249; on Jo. vii. he shews that several prophets rose out of Galilee, 3 *Jew.* 242; understands the "one shepherd," mentioned in Jo. x, to be Christ, *ib.* 280; observes that the title on the cross, described Jo. xix, was in three languages, that all might read it, 1 *Jew.* 277; his comment on Jo. xx. ult., *Whita.* 629; on Acts xxiv. he writes of the term " heresy" as applied to the first Christians, 3 *Jew.* 214; expounds 1 Cor. vi. 17, " he that is joined unto the Lord is one spirit," *ib.* 496; on 1 Cor. xiv. he remarks that if the people understand the prayer, they can with more devotion say " Amen," and allows that in the primitive church the service was in the vulgar tongue, 1 *Jew.* 57, 289, 309, 333, *Whita.* 264; explains blessing " with the spirit," 1 Cor. xiv. 16, 1 *Jew.* 329, 330; writes upon St Paul being " rude in speech," 2 Cor. xi. 6, *Whita.* 101; on 2 Thess. ii. he declares that it is long since the grace of God has departed from the church of Rome, 3 *Jew.* 348; on the same chapter he says that the wickedness of Antichrist is mystical, that is to say, cloked under the name of godliness, 4 *Jew.* 743, and affirms that he shall be possessed of the devil, *ib.* 728; expounds " having a form of godliness" (2 Tim. iii.) that is to say, a shew of the religion of Christ, *ib.* 743; calls Titus archbishop of the Cretians, 2 *Whitg.* 352; on Heb. x. he declares that in the altar there is no doing again of Christ's sacrifice, 2 *Bec.* 250, 3 *Bec.* 459; (and the ordinary gloss affirms that what we do is the commemorating of a sacrifice, 2 *Bec.* 250 n.); his statement respecting the justification of Abraham,

James ii, 2 *Cran.* 209; on 1 Pet. iii. 19, he expresses an opinion that many of those drowned in the flood were saved, 3 *Tyn.* 134 n.; he wrote on the Apocalypse, *Bale* 258; declares that the opinions of the fathers may be rejected in things not determined by scripture, 2 *Lat.* 248; says there were few honest preachers in his time, *ib.* 347; writes upon the proof of doctrine by scripture, *Whita.* 465

Lysander: his theft, 2 *Jew.* 628

Lysimachus of Jerusalem: son of Ptolemy and Cleopatra, *Whita.* 73

Lythe: small, humble, *Phil.* 392

M.

M. (J.), i. e. John Markham, *q. v.*

M. M.: apparently a lady, 2 *Zur.* 95, 107 n

M. (P.): perhaps P. Morice, 2 *Cran.* 259

M. (P.): his death, 1 *Zur.* 324

M. (T.): perhaps Matthew, Massye, or Moor, 1 *Brad.* 374

Mabillon (Jo.): Mus. Ital., 2 *Bec.* 256 n.; Vetera Analecta, *Calf.* 128 n.; Præf. in iv. sæc. Bened., *ib.* 155 n.; he refutes errors respecting the time when Hegesippus lived, 2 *Ful.* 338 n.; his opinion as to the genuineness of the Gelasian decree, *ib.* 221 n

Macaber: an imaginary German poet, the alleged author of the verses accompanying the Dance of Death, *Pra. Eliz.* xviii. n

Macarius (St), the Egyptian anchorite: 4 *Bul.* 514, *Pra. Eliz.* xviii. n

Macarius, a priest of Alexandria: said to have pulled Ischyras from the altar, 3 *Jew.* 321

Macbee (Jo.), or Machabæus: chaplain to the king of Denmark, 2 *Cov.* xiv.

Macbrey (......): in exile, 1 *Cran.* (9)

Maccabees: referred to, *Pil.* 23, 68, 181, 207; examples of valour for the Lord's sake, *Rid.* 139; martyrs, 2 *Bul.* 413

— The books of Maccabees: not canonical, 3 *Bul.* 396, 4 *Bul.* 538, 1 *Ful.* 20, 77, *Grin.* 23, 3 *Jew.* 431, &c.; their claims to be canonical examined, *Whita.* 93, &c.; they contain doctrinal errors, *ib.* 97; also fabulous and contradictory stories, *ib.* 98, &c.; three books set down in the Apostolic Canons, *ib.* 43, 94, 103, but perhaps the passage is interpolated, *ib.* 93 n.; Gelasius allowed only one book, 1 *Ful.* 24; Jerome denied the books of Maccabees to be canonical, see p. 426, col. 1; he ascribed them to Josephus, *Whita.* 96; Augustine's opinion on them, see p. 52, col. 2; the second book is an epitome of a larger work by Jason of Cyrene, *Whita.* 98; it is cited in support of prayer for the dead, 2 *Brad.* 290, 2 *Cov.* 271, *Grin.* 23; the passage wanting in some ancient copies, *Grin.* 24; the third book ascribed to Lysimachus of Jerusalem, *Whita.* 73 n.; the third and fourth books rejected by Romanists, *ib.* 103; the fourth mentioned by Athanasius, *ib.*

M'Crie (Tho.): Life of Knox, 3 *Zur.* 760 n., 764 n.; Hist. of Reform. in Italy, 4 *Bul.* xiii. n., xv.

Mace (......): martyred, *Poet.* 167

Macedonians: heretics, 1 *Jew.* 246; their errors respecting the Trinity, *Rog.* 45; they denied the Son to be of one substance with the Father, *ib.* 48; affirmed the Holy Ghost to be a mere creature, *ib.* 70, and a servant to the Father and the Son, *ib.* 72

Macedonius, bp of Constantinople: his heresy, 3 *Bec.* 401, 1 *Bul.* 13, 4 *Jew.* 731, *Phil.* 382 n., 423, 424; he persecuted the orthodox, *Pil.* 637; his heresy condemned, 3 *Jew.* 224, 4 *Jew.* 1095, *Whita.* 449

Macedonius, a monk or hermit: appeased the anger of Theodosius, 1 *Bul.* 305, *Calf.* 22

Macham (Jo.), sheriff of London: merciful to Philpot in Newgate, *Phil.* 160

Macheson (Eliz.), the wife of bp Coverdale, *q. v.*

Machiavelli (Nic.): Hist. Florent., *Jew.* xl; prefers statutes, &c., of man to the holy scriptures, *Rog.* 80; censures the bishops of Rome for stirring up wars among Christian princes, 3 *Jew.* 171, 4 *Jew.* 679; his policy, *Sand.* 153; politic Machevils, 3 *Whitg.* 508; Machiavel government, *Park.* 391, 414

Machivilian atheists: are doubtful whether there be a God, *Rog.* 37; they cast off all virtue, *ib.* 118

Mackie (Cha.): Castles of Mary queen of Scots, 1 *Zur.* 193, 203, 205, 206 nn

Mackquhirrie (Alex.), a priest: 2 *Zur.* 331 n

Maclaine (Peter): bookseller at Basle, 1 *Zur.* 35, 41

Mac Phelim (Brian): his rebellion in Ulster, 2 *Zur.* 223 n

Macrobius (Aur.): says the wines of Egypt are extremely cold, 1 *Jew.* 248; declares that the altar of Saturn was decked with candles, *Calf.* 302; speaks of images of madness suspended at doors, *ib.* 333; speaking of holy garments, says, crafty man, crafty coat, 4 *Jew.* 614; referred to, 2 *Bul.* 125 n

Madew (Jo.): a Protestant disputant at the disputation held at Cambridge, 1549, *Grin.* 194, *Rid.* 169; master of Clare hall, *Park.* 38 n., *Rid.* 327 n

Madmen: on their absolution, 3 *Jew.* 359;

the church assoiled them not, but only pronounced them to be assoiled before, *ib.* 355
Madness: alleged against Paul and other Christians, 3 *Jew.* 250
Mæstræus (Martialis): 2 *Ful.* 286 n
Maestricht: 1 *Tyn.* lxx.
Magalath: one of the magi, *Whita.* 560 n
Magdalen ......: 1 *Zur.* 302, 305
Magdalene (St Mary): *v.* Mary.
Magdeburg: *v.* Centuriators.
   The siege, 3 *Zur.* 668 n., 679
Magdeburg (The duke of): 2 *Zur.* 214
Magellan (Ferd.), the navigator: 2 *Zur.* 290
Magi: what they were, 2 *Tyn.* 227; whence they sprung, 4 *Bul.* 480; there were certain wise men so called in Persia, 2 *Jew.* 981; how many came to Christ, 4 *Jew.* 695; Chrysostom says there were twelve, *ib.*; their offering of gold, frankincense, and myrrh, its mystic import, *Hutch.* 81, 255, 2 *Lat.* 132, 154; falsely called kings, 2 *Lat.* 143, *Poet.* 49, *Whita.* 560; called by various names, *Whita.* 560; a prayer to the three kings, *Rog.* 228
Magic: *v.* Witchcraft.
Magister Sententiarum: *v.* Peter Lombard.
Magistrates, Rulers: *v.* Kings, where the same matters are set forth under the same divisions; also Judges, Temporalty.
   i. *Their institution, power, and authority:* of the civil magistrate, *Rog.* 334, &c.; what magistrates are, 1 *Bec.* 215, 2 *Bec.* 302, 3 *Bec.* 610, 611, 1 *Bul.* 308; three kinds of them, 1 *Bul.* 309; their causes and beginnings, *ib.* 312; they are needful, 1 *Lat.* 390; necessary for the right institution of the common weal, 1 *Bec.* 214, 215; needful because the people cannot rule themselves, 2 *Tyn.* 95; ordained of God, 2 *Bec.* 302, 2 *Hoop.* 53, 85, 86, 103, 104, *Sand.* 198; the office grounded on God's word, 1 *Lat.* 298, 299; temporal powers not disannulled by Christ, 2 *Tyn.* 58, but approved by the New Testament, 1 *Bec.* 213; they are God's ministers, 2 *Hoop.* 107; God's lieutenants, even though evil men, *Hutch.* 331; they are in God's stead, 1 *Tyn.* 25; represent the person of a great Lord, 2 *Hoop.* 54; are not only ordained but also preserved by God, *ib.* 83; the will of God sometimes made known through them, *ib.* 388; God is in them, *ib.* 85; the magistrate is law endued with life, 1 *Bul.* 339; temporal rulers have the chief power in all commonwealths, *Pil.* 23; scripture calls them gods, 1 *Bec.* 212, 2 *Brad.* 255, *Sand.* 225, 1 *Tyn.* 175, 2 *Whitg.* 82; but they are mortal gods, *Pil.* 476; they bear the sword, see ii. below; are like the walls of a city, *Pil.* 348; have authority to abridge external liberty, 2 *Whitg.* 570; their laws are of two sorts, 2 *Hoop.* 102; the commodities we receive by them, 1 *Bec.* 216, 2 *Bec.* 330; of their election, 1 *Bul.* 318, 1 *Whitg.* 372; what kind of men to be chosen, 1 *Bul.* 319; they should be chosen for worthiness, *Sand.* 47; the manner of consecrating them, 1 *Bul.* 322; Christians may be magistrates, *ib.* 385 (*v.* Anabaptists); good and bad magistrates, *ib.* 314; evil rulers and officers, *Sand.* 121; whether they are of God, 1 *Bul.* 314; they are given to punish the wickedness of the people, 2 *Bec.* 302, *Hutch.* 74, and are a sign that God is wroth with the people, 1 *Tyn.* 194, 196, 334, 2 *Tyn.* 111, 112

   ii. *Their duty:* their office and duty, (*q.v.*) 1 *Bec.* 256, 260, 286, 2 *Bec.* 114, 302, &c., 1 *Bul.* 323, 1 *Lat.* 67, 349, 537, 2 *Lat.* 6, *Pra. Eliz.* 235, 1 *Tyn.* 479, 2 *Tyn.* 61; their duty, with probations of scripture, 2 *Bec.* 511, &c.; what manner of men they ought to be, *ib.* 303; their duty in worldly matters, *ib.* 306, &c.; they are ordained for man's good, 1 *Bul.* 313, 2 *Hoop.* 106, 107; for the support of the weak, 2 *Tyn.* 8; they owe a debt to the people, *Sand.* 201; must care for them as fathers for their children, 2 *Bec.* 514; how they may become esteemed, 1 *Lat.* 381; must keep their oath, as if they neglect their duty they are forsworn, 1 *Bec.* 371; qualities required in them, *Sand.* 201; they ought to be righteous, *ib.* 192; must rule justly, 2 *Bec.* 307; what it is so to rule, *ib.*; they must judge equally, *ib.* 513; they are the keepers of discipline and peace, 2 *Hoop.* 81; the magistrate called by Aristotle φύλαξ νόμου, *ib.* 86; magistrates must use the law indifferently, *ib.*; must not oppress or plunder their subjects, 2 *Bec.* 308, 309, 513, 514; may not take away their subjects' goods at their pleasure, *ib.* 329; those who overcharge their subjects are thieves, *ib.* 107; some magistrates and judges follow gifts, 1 *Lat.* 140; they must not take bribes, 2 *Bec.* 512; some are painful and good, 1 *Lat.* 142; they must deliver the oppressed, *Pil.* 471, 472, 476; must do judgment, *Sand.* 224; judgment pertains to them, 1 *Bul.* 346, 4 *Bul.* 509; they bear the sword, 1 *Bul.* 351, 352, 2 *Hoop.* 108; are called to rule with the temporal sword, 2 *Bec.* 616; the sword of government should be wielded with discretion, *Sand.* 135; they must avenge evil and punish the

MAGISTRATES

wicked, 2 *Bec.* 310, 311, 514, 515, 1 *Bul.* 351, 1 *Hoop.* 369, 475, 1 *Lat.* 481, 495, 2 *Tyn.* 21; it is their office to punish, not the office of the church, 2 *Lat.* 195, 196; the punishment inflicted by them is the very hand and will of God, 2 *Hoop.* 108, who by them punishes transgressors, *Hutch.* 307; when they ought to punish offenders, 1 *Bul.* 355; they should punish sin with mercy and sorrow, 1 *Tyn.* 102; must not punish for malice, 2 *Tyn.* 62; must not shew mercy in judgment, 1 *Lat.* 484; may lawfully punish with death, 2 *Bec.* 95, 1 *Bul.* 307, 352, 354, 356, 1 *Jew.* 228, 1 *Lat.* 484, *Rog.* 348—350, *Sand.* 72; but the magistrate who kills any man that is not worthy by the law to die is a murderer, 2 *Hoop.* 108; they may make war, 1 *Bul.* 370; when they do so the people must obey them, *ib.* 373; they may lawfully require an oath, *Rog.* 357 (and see Oaths); must not abuse their power, 1 *Lat.* 373; nor wax arrogant and proud, 2 *Hoop.* 106, 107; God will revenge the abuse of his office in them, *ib.* 104; some censured for little regarding public affairs, 1 *Bec.* 253; they are blameable if the people offend through their negligence, *Pil.* 34; admonitions to them, 1 *Bec.* 272, 380, 2 *Tyn.* 243; they were told their faults in king Edward's days, *Rid.* 58; the importance of their godly example, *Hutch.* 7; their sacrifice, *Sand.* 412

iii. *Their office in relation to religion and the church* (v. Anabaptists, Church, I. xi, Heretics, Supremacy): whether the temporal magistrates may meddle with matters of religion, 2 *Bec.* 303, &c.; whether the care of religion belongs to them, 1 *Bul.* 323; rulers are appointed to look on divine matters as well as worldly, 1 *Bec.* 392; they ought diligently to read God's word, 2 *Bec.* 303; to be learned in the laws of God, *ib.* 511; should be sound in religion, 1 *Bul.* 319; it is their duty to defend religion, *Pil.* 360, 361; to maintain it, 2 *Bec.* 511, 512; to support God's word, 2 *Hoop.* 388; they should defend the two testaments as their own life, *ib.* 87; must maintain good and godly people, 2 *Bec.* 309, 310, 514, 515; godly magistrates would have all men to be saved, 1 *Hoop.* 472; on the authority of Christian magistrates, 3 *Whitg.* 160, 165, &c.; Papists make them no better than swineherds, 2 *Bec.* 304; what is to be done by them for the conservation of religion, *ib.* 305, &c., 511, &c.; what laws concerning religion they ought to appoint, 1 *Bul.* 333; their duty and authority with regard to the church and matters of religion, 2 *Brad.* 378, 2 *Hoop.* 54, 1, 2, 3 *Whitg.* passim, especially 1 *Whitg.* 389, 466, 3 *Whitg.* 295, &c., 485, 486; they owe a duty to the church, 4 *Bul.* 434; it is their duty to care for it, *Pil.* 429; they should see the people instructed in true religion, 1 *Lat.* 316; should provide preachers, 2 *Bec.* 305, and schools, *ib.* 306; no farther liberty granted to them in the church of England than is given by the word of God, 4 *Jew.* 973; their office not to be confounded with that of the minister, 1 *Bul.* 329; when they come within the temple, they are as private men, 4 *Jew.* 670; what ecclesiastical functions they may not take upon them, 1 *Whitg.* 22; their ordinances in the church not articles of faith, *Pil.* 25; magistrates said to bear the sword in the Christian church, 4 *Bul.* 509; examples of their interference in matters of religion, 2 *Bec.* 304, &c.; they condemned Dioscorus, Juvenalis, and Thalassius, and gave judgment to put them from the dignities in the church, 4 *Jew.* 1021, &c.; and subscribed in councils, *ib.* 1025; how temporal rulers are above spiritual, *Pil.* 22, 116, 124; a bishop convented before a civil judge, 4 *Jew.* 960, &c.; how far they may constrain their subjects in matters of religion, *Sand.* 192; whether they may punish for breach of religion, 1 *Bul.* 357; they must find a remedy that God's name be not blasphemed, 1 *Bec.* 380; how they should deal with such as are not of the church, 1 *Whitg.* 386, 388; whether they may lawfully punish idolaters and false teachers, 2 *Bec.* 311, &c., 512; how the old godly magistrates handled heretics, *ib.* 316; they were desirous of their conversion, *ib.* 316, 317; magistrates should be circumspect whom they punish as heretics, *ib.* 315; they may punish Anabaptists for civil considerations, *Hutch.* 201; have power to command their subjects to fast in urgent cause, 2 *Bec.* 530, 531

iv. *The obedience due to them* (v. Obedience, Subjects, Tribute): our duty towards them, 1 *Bec.* 211, 218; we must honour them, 2 *Bec.* 88, 89, 1 *Bul.* 279, 1 *Hoop.* 357, *Now.* (16, 17), 130, 131, 3 *Tyn.* 57, 3 *Whitg.* 591; they are included in the term parents, 1 *Bul.* 268; the fear and honour we should pay them, 1 *Bec.* 219; obedience must be shewn to them, *ib.* 216, 1 *Brad.* 162, 1 *Bul.* 311, *ib.* 390, 1 *Hoop.* 357, 2 *Hoop.* 101, 2 *Lat.* 96, 111, 135; every man should be obedient to the higher powers,

2 *Hoop.* 101, 127, 1 *Tyn.* 506; the spiritualty not exempt from obedience to them, 1 *Bec.* 216, 217, 2 *Bec.* 89; ecclesiastical laws cannot exempt any person from obedience, 2 *Hoop.* 101; there are many great and weighty causes why they should be obeyed, *ib.* 103; obedience is to be yielded to them because they are ordained of God, *Sand.* 198; they are to be obeyed for conscience' sake, 2 *Hoop.* 108, *Sand.* 199, 3 *Whitg.* 576; inferior magistrates must be obeyed, 2 *Hoop.* 101, 1 *Lat.* 373; examples of obedience to magistrates, 2 *Bec.* 89; scriptural examples of men who have well or ill discharged the debt due to them, *Sand.* 200: Christ himself was subject to rulers, 1 *Tyn.* 188, 2 *Tyn.* 245; he and his apostles never withstood their authority, 2 *Bec.* 302, but taught obedience to them, 2 *Tyn.* 241; a sermon on obedience to magistrates, 3 *Whitg.* 586; the commodities of obedience, *ib.* 588; how far magistrates are to be obeyed, 3 *Bec.* 285; in what obedience consists, 3 *Whitg.* 589, &c.; to be obeyed whether Christian or heathen, *Sand.* 197; obedience to be paid not only to the faithful, but also to infidel and wicked tyrants, 2 *Hoop.* 54, 80, 102, 104; they must be obeyed, though never so evil, 2 *Cran.* 188, 4 *Jew.* 668, 1 *Tyn.* 116; they are to be obeyed in all worldly things, 2 *Cran.* 188, i. e. in all things not contrary to God's word, 1 *Brad.* 438, *Phil.* 223, 1 *Tyn.* 25; not to be obeyed if they command things contrary to the law of God, 2 *Bec.* 328, 329, 2 *Hoop.* 102, 103, 109; to be obeyed when they command war, 1 *Bul.* 373; tribute a debt due to them, *Sand.* 199; the evils of disobedience to them, 2 *Hoop.* 109; against speaking evil of them, 3 *Whitg.* 594; the sin of seditious talking, *Sand.* 119; disobedience punished, 2 *Bec.* 89, 90, 3 *Whitg.* 588; the powers are not to be resisted, 1 *Brad.* 438, 2 *Hoop.* 103, 1 *Lat.* 371, 1 *Tyn.* 25; we must not strive nor fight with them, 2 *Hoop.* 102, 104; we must not resist them though they be evil, but submit to them as to God's chastening, 1 *Tyn.* 196, 197, 332, 334, 336; resistance to them damnable, 2 *Hoop.* 105; rebellion against them worse than against parents, *Now.* (18), 132; damnable iniquity for any man to depose them, 2 *Hoop.* 104; by whom they are to be feared, *ib.* 106, 108; they are not to be flattered, *ib.* 564; their deeds to be judged of charitably, 1 *Lat.* 148; authorities to be prayed for, *Sand.* 82, 3 *Whitg.* 590 (*v.* Prayers for magistrates, and for the whole church); petition for them, 3 *Bec.* 36

v. *Justices of the peace:* called justices because they must be righteous, *Sand.* 192; an unjust justice reproved, 2 *Lat.* 419, &c.; they should encourage archery, 1 *Lat.* 197; those of Kent opposed the reformation, 2 *Cran.* 349, &c., 367; whether clergymen should hold the office, 2 *Whitg.* 394

Magistris (Jo. de): 4 *Jew.* 629

Magistris (Mart. de): De Temperant. Lib., *Jew.* xl; 4 *Jew.* 629, 630, 635

Magna Charta: protects church-lands, 3 *Whitg.* xiv, xv.

Magnificat: *v.* Mary (B. V.).

Magog: *v.* Gog.

Magusæi: Persians who abhor the sight of idols, yet worship them, 4 *Jew.* 949

Mahomet: his rise, *Bale* 562, *Pil.* 76, 77; his imposture, *Bale* 572; the Mahometan apostasy, *Lit. Eliz.* 493, *Pil.* 337, *Pra. Eliz.* 463, *Sand.* 388; when he first spread his religion in Arabia, 1 *Jew.* 184, 363; his doctrine a pestilence, *Phil.* 423; it spread through the sins of the clergy, 2 *Tyn.* 254; it was established by the aid of false miracles, 3 *Tyn.* 129, 130; he was the deceiver of the world, *Grin.* 98; a wicked monster and damned soul, *Lit. Eliz.* 522, 533; God's plague in the East, *Pil.* 75; he overran and oppressed various Christian churches, 4 *Bul.* 21, 73; his Alcoran, *Bale* 263, 572, 1 *Brad.* 329, *Calf.* 44, *Phil.* 422; its pretensions false, *Whita.* 530; Mahomet compared with the pope, *Bale* 262; he and the pope arose together, 2 *Tyn.* 259; declared to be Magog, *Bale* 571; said by some to be Antichrist, 2 *Jew.* 903; the Turks rejoice and glory in him, 2 *Bec.* 447

Mahomet II., sultan: takes Athens, 4 *Jew.* 653

Mahometanism: its antiquity, consent, &c., 2 *Ful.* 79; why Mahometists choose rather to be called Saracens, 4 *Jew.* 713; Christianity not extinguished where they prevail, 4 *Bul.* 21, 73

Mahounds: mahomets, idols, *Bale* 438; Mahometans, *ib.* 416 (*v.* Mawmets).

Maid of Kent: *v.* Barton (E.).

Maid of Lothbury: *v.* Pinder (R.).

Maid of Lymster, or Leominster, *q. v.*

Maid of Saint Alban's, *q. v.*

Maids: *v.* Prayers, Women.

They must have the fear of God before their eyes, and seek to please him, 2 *Bec.* 367; must be obedient to their masters and mistresses, *ib.*; must never be idle, *ib.* 367, 368; must not run to vain spectacles, plays, &c., *ib.*; must not keep company with light persons, *ib.*; they must observe a discreet silence, *ib.* 369; they must avoid early marriages, *ib.*; they must not take in hand marriage without the counsel and consent of parents and guardians, *ib.* 371; their diet, *ib.* 369; they must content themselves with seemly apparel, *ib.* 370, 371

Maidstone, co. Kent: a martyr there, *Bale* 63, 2 *Tyn.* 340; certain commissioners meet there, 2 *Cran.* 301; lands there taken from the archbishop in exchange by the king, *ib.* 348; martyrs there in queen Mary's time, *Poet.* 162, 169, 170; the grammar-school, *Park.* 170; the rood of grace near Maidstone, *v.* Boxley.

Maienne (The marquis of), or Maine: a French hostage, 3 *Zur.* 559 n

Maimonides: *v.* Moses.

Mainard (Augustin): accused of heresy by Calistus, *Phil.* 387

Mainarde (Will.): martyred at Lewes, *Poet.* 170

Maine: an earldom in France, 2 *Tyn.* 304

Maine: *v.* Maienne.

Mainour: *v.* Maner.

Maintenance: *v.* Caps.

Mair, the Idomite: said to have made the Talmud, *Bale* 479

Maitland (Sir Will.), of Lethington: one of the confederate lords, 1 *Zur.* 193 n.; mentioned, *ib.* 203 n.; sent from the queen of Scots, *Park.* 172

Maitland (Sam. Roffey): Dark Ages, *Calf.* 237 n.; Puritan Thaumaturgy, 2 *Ful.* 76 n.; his note on the prologues to Cranmer's Bible, 2 *Cran.* 125 n

Maitland (Will.): Hist. of London, 2 *Bec.* 438 n., *Grin.* 272 n

Maizers: *v.* Bowls, Masers.

Major (Geo.), minister at Eisleben: notices of him, 2 *Cran.* 433, 3 *Zur.* 26 n.; he held that Christ ascended with a multitude, *Rog.* 66 n.; says Thomas Monetarius depended wholly upon visions and revelations, *ib.* 196 n.; cited, 1 *Whitg.* 413

Major (Jo.): *v.* Joannes.

Majoranus (Lud.): speaks of the Roman pontiff as in primacy Abel, in government Noah, &c.; *Rog.* 347 n. (comp. Bernard, 1 *Jew.* 438 n. & al.); mentions an opinion that the inferior orders are not grounded upon scripture, but some come by tradition, *Rog.* 260 n

Majoristæ: a sect, 2 *Jew.* 686

Make: a mate, match, or partner, 1 *Tyn.* 278

Makebates: quarrelsome persons, 2 *Cran.* 160

Malabar: Nestorian or Chaldean Christians there, *Phil.* 202 n

Malachi: the "pure offering," or "clean oblation" foretold by him, 2 *Ful.* 381, *Hutch.* 46, 47, 1 *Jew.* 110, 2 *Jew.* 712, 713, 722, &c., *Phil.* 408

Malachias, an Irish bishop: *v.* O'Molana.

Malcham, or Malcom: 1 *Bul.* 248

Malcolm (J. P.): Lond. Rediviv., *Grin.* 273 n

Malchus: his story allegorized, 1 *Tyn.* 306

Maledicere: *Now.* (102)

Maler (Joshua): 3 *Zur.* 459

Malet (Fra.): *v.* Mallet.

Malice: *v.* Envy.

Against it, with sentences and examples of scripture, 1 *Bec.* 458, 459; it blinds men, *Pil.* 407; not to be removed by a pennyworth of ale, 1 *Lat.* 20; malitia, *Now.* (102)

Malkin: *v.* Maukin.

Mallet (Fra.): notice of him, 2 *Cran.* 318 n.; master of Michael-house, Cambridge, *ib.* 318; employed upon the church-service, *ib.* 366; prosecuted for saying mass as chaplain to the princess Mary, *ib.* 318 n., 529; dean of Lincoln, *Park.* viii, 482

Mallet (James), precentor of Lincoln: 2 *Cran.* 265 n

Malliet (......): letter to H. Bullinger the younger, 2 *Zur.* 199

Malling (East and West), co. Kent: one of them possibly referred to, 2 *Cran.* 251

Malling (South), co. Sussex: the college, 2 *Cran.* 249; the deanery given by Cranmer to Heath, *ib.* 399; gathering for repairing the church of [South?] Malling, *ib.* 251

Mallocke (Jo.), fellow of All Souls': *Park.* 300

Mallot (......): branded, 2 *Ful.* 121

Malmesbury (Will. of): *v.* William.

Malpas (Edw.): 2 *Cran.* 390

Malta: besieged by the Turks, *Grin.* 287; the Turkish news of Malta, 1 *Jew.* 85; prayers for its deliverance ordered in several dioceses, *Lit. Eliz.* 460; the form of prayer used on that occasion in Sarum, *ib.* 519; the island delivered; thanksgivings ordered in the province of Canterbury, *ib.* 461; the form of thanksgiving, *ib.* 524; an invasion feared, 1573, 2 *Zur.* 246

Malt-horses: slow, dull drudges of horses, 2 *Bec.* 611

Maltravers (Mr): *v.* Matravers.

Malveren (......): parson of St Dunstan's, *Bale* 70; he disputes with Thorpe, *ib.* 112, 115, 121, 122, 123

Malvern (Great), co. Worcester: the priory, subject to the abbot of Westminster, 2 *Lat.* 410 n.; the prior (through Latimer) begs

MALVERN — MAN

that the house may continue, *ib.* 411; St Blesis's heart at Malverne, 1 *Lat.* 55

Mamelukes: 2 *Tyn.* 177

Mamercus, bp of Vienne: said to have instituted litanies, *Calf.* 295—297, 2 *Whitg.* 480

Mammæa, mother of Alex. Severus: 3 *Zur.* 6

Mammer: to hesitate, 1 *Brad.* 432 (in 2 *Cov.* 275, stagger); mammering, 1 *Brad.* 47, 2 *Brad.* 106, 113

Mammets: *v.* Mawmets.

Mammon: the word explained, 1 *Tyn.* 68, 2 *Tyn.* 104, *Wool.* 139; why it is called "unrighteous," 1 *Tyn.* 69, *Wool.* 139; it is not to be served, *Sand.* 182; the servants of the great god Mammon, 2 *Cov.* 305; God and mammon cannot be served together, 2 *Tyn.* 104—106; THE PARABLE OF THE WICKED MAMMON, by W. Tyndale, 1 *Tyn.* 29—126; Mammon; verses by Edm. Spenser, *Poet.* 29

Mammotrectum: *v.* Marchesinus (Jo.).

Man: *v.* Heart, Mind, Soul, Reason, Will; Life, Death; Gentlemen, Noblemen, Poor, Rich; Aged, Young; also Duty, Vocation.

(*a*) Of man generally:—of the knowledge of man, 1 *Hoop.* 86; de microcosmo; man is a little world, &c.; verses by T. Bastard, *Poet.* 306; speculum humanum; verses on man, by S. Gosson, *ib.* 344; man; verses by Jo. Norden, *ib.* 459; his different names in Hebrew, &c., *Pil.* 94, 245; two parts of man, 1 *Cov.* 503; three parts, body, soul, and spirit, *ib.* 504; the diversity of his affections, *ib.* 502; the power of man, 3 *Bul.* 98; what his work is, 3 *Bec.* 611; what work passes his power, *ib.*; why he is born a babe, *Hutch.* 149; his nativity, of itself altogether unclean and defiled with sin, is made holy by Christ's, 2 *Hoop.* 28; man is born for man, 1 *Lat.* 81; his life a warfare (Job vii. 1, "militia"), *Sand.* 164, &c.; what misery and misfortune mankind is continually subject unto; verses, *Poet.* 478; we must shew pity to all men, 1 *Tyn.* 99; all are beggars before God, 1 *Lat.* 397; every man belongs to the temporalty, and also to the spiritualty, 2 *Tyn.* 60, 67; the duties of all estates one towards another, 1 *Lat.* 503 (*v.* Duty); every man is born either of God or of the devil, 2 *Tyn.* 190; the most are ever the worst, 2 *Lat.* 4; men to be followed only as they follow Christ, 1 *Lat.* 514; not to be followed in things which do not pertain to our own vocation, *ib.* 516; man's nature being now consumed, effeminated, and worn out, is unable, says Hooper, to do what former ages have done, 2 *Hoop.* 83; the last day of man, 3 *Bul.*

405; wherefore all men are not saved, *ib.* 33; man is but vanity, 2 *Bec.* 442

(*b*) Of man as created (*v.* Creation): his creation, 1 *Bec.* 46, 1 *Brad.* 120, 141, 149, *Lit. Edw.* 501, (551), *Now.* (32, 100), 147; to what end he was created, 2 *Hoop.* 24, 2 *Jew.* 1004; for God's glory, *Now.* (32), 147; to serve and honour God, *Sand.* 293; made in the image of God, 2 *Bul.* 377, 3 *Bul.* 53, *Hutch.* 24, 164, *Lit. Edw.* 501, 502, (551); therefore he must be loved, 1 *Tyn.* 18; his soul is an image of God, *Hutch.* 164; he was made God's lieutenant, or deputy, *Lat.* 375; he is the head of creation, 1 *Brad.* 352; the chief of the works of God, 3 *Bul.* 151, 175; the head of woman, 2 *Bec.* 337; the dignity of man, verses by Sir Jo. Davies, *Poet.* 95; in what state God created him, 3 *Bec.* 614; why created frail, 2 *Bul.* 375; God foreknew his fall, *ib.* 377

(*c*) Of man as fallen (*v.* Fall, Sin, Wicked):—he fell from his excellency, 2 *Hoop.* 24, 71, 1 *Tyn.* 14, 17, 22; lost the image of God, 1 *Brad.* 215, 2 *Bul.* 394, *Lit. Edw.* 502, (551); he is ruined by the devil, 1 *Lat.* 375; his universal corruption and depravity, 2 *Hoop.* 24, 25, 2 *Lat.* 102; what man is of himself, 2 *Hoop.* 204; probations out of scripture that every man is by nature a sinner and a child of wrath, 3 *Bec.* 326, 327; he is condemned before he is born, 1 *Tyn.* 89; born in sin, 2 *Lat.* 101; his natural sinfulness, perverseness, and misery, 1 *Bec.* 97, 126, 277, 3 *Bec.* 15, 137, 2 *Bul.* 122, 1 *Hoop.* 89, 548; natural corruption and wilful malice are joined in him, 1 *Hoop.* 304; by nature the devil possesses his whole heart, 2 *Tyn.* 190; his captivity through sin, 1 *Bec.* 50, 70, 90; by nature he is spiritually dead, 1 *Ful.* 397, 2 *Tyn.* 199; of his own power he can do nothing according to God's will, 1 *Lat.* 354, 388, 433, 1 *Tyn.* 111; he can do nothing but sin, 1 *Lat.* 429, 2 *Lat.* 113; there is nothing in him that might allure or provoke him to the help of his salvation, 2 *Hoop.* 72; his nature is to go astray, *ib.* 191; to feed on unwholesome and infected pastures, *ib.* 192; his heart is inclined to evil, 1 *Jew.* 100, 2 *Jew.* 1084, 2 *Tyn.* 85; yet he is not without an inclination to religion, 3 *Jew.* 199; his misery is increased by the malice of the devil, 1 *Hoop.* 90; his deserving is everlasting damnation, 1 *Bec.* 49; the old man, 3 *Bec.* 607, 621, 622, 1 *Brad.* 297, 2 *Brad.* 196, 3 *Bul.* 98—100, *Now.* (99); the carnal man, 2 *Tyn.* 180; the natural man, *Now.* (99),

1 *Tyn.* 185, 2 *Tyn.* 132; he understandeth not the things of God, 1 *Tyn.* 88, 3 *Tyn.* 6; is unable to do good, 1 *Tyn.* 111

(*d*) Of man as restored (*v.* Christ, Grace, Predestination, Redemption, &c.; also Christians, Church, Righteous, Saints): redeemed by Christ, 2 *Lat.* 109; quickened by grace, 2 *Tyn.* 199; how the old man is mortified and man is renewed by the Spirit, 3 *Bul.* 104; how he is brought to feed in the pastures of God's word, 2 *Hoop.* 204; he cannot merit heaven, 1 *Lat.* 521, 2 *Tyn.* 76; he must be made good ere he can do good, 2 *Tyn.* 186, 190; he is as an axe in the carpenter's hand, yet he must be diligent, *Pil.* 445; his greatest promotion in this world is to suffer for the truth, 1 *Lat.* 294, 361; the new man, 3 *Bec.* 606, 622, 1 *Brad.* 297, 2 *Brad.* 196, 3 *Bul.* 98—100, *Now.* (99); an unregenerate man is called soul or carnal ($\psi\upsilon\chi\iota\kappa\acute{o}\varsigma$), a renewed man spirit or spiritual ($\pi\nu\epsilon\upsilon\mu\alpha\tau\iota\kappa\acute{o}\varsigma$), 2 *Tyn.* 132; the spiritual man, 1 *Tyn.* 185, 2 *Tyn.* 180, 3 *Tyn.* 6, 7; Christian faith consists in the consideration of two men, viz. Adam, and Christ, 2 *Bul.* 401; with man all things shall be restored, 1 *Brad.* 358, &c.

Man (Isle of): order for the removal of rood-lofts, &c., *Grin.* 154 n

Man (Jo.), warden of Merton college: translated the Common Places of Musculus, 2 *Zur.* 148 n

Man in the moon: 4 *Jew.* 1050, *Park.* 404, 2 *Whitg.* 7

Man of Sin: *v.* Antichrist.

Manardinus (Mars.): *v.* Marsilius.

Manasseh, king of Judah: his history, 2 *Bul.* 9; the apostasy of himself, and the kingdom, 4 *Bul.* 70; a godly remnant remained in the midst of it, *ib.* 73; the troubles that befel him for idolatry, 1 *Bul.* 236; mercy shewn on his repentance, 4 *Bul.* 169, *Grin.* 106; his deliverance, 2 *Bul,* 95

—The Prayer of Manasseh, *Lit. Eliz.* 271; rejected by Romanists, *Whita.* 103; its character, *ib.* 104

Manasseh Ben Israel: *Whita.* 33 n

Manchester: Bradford born, and intended to be burned there, 1 *Brad.* 434 n., 448, 492 n., 2 *Brad.* 187, 191, 193, 199, *Rid.* 369, 378; Blackley, in Manchester, probably his birth-place, 2 *Brad.* xi; his last prayer there, *ib.* xxviii; Herle desires to surrender the college, to be annexed to some college at Cambridge, *Park.* 365; a new charter procured for it by dean Nowel; Woolton named the first warden, *Wool.* iii.

Manchet, or Maunchet: a small loaf, a wafer, 2 *Tyn.* 210, 3 *Tyn.* 179; used in the mass, 2 *Tyn.* 222; used in the communion in prison, *Sand.* viii.

Mancipation: 2 *Bul.* 229

Mandere, mandi: *Now.* (102).

Manducator (Pet.): *v.* Petrus Comestor.

Maner, or Mainour: a law term, 2 *Tyn.* 142

Manes, or Manichæus: founder of the Manichees, 1 *Lat.* 201 n., *Phil.* 347, 382 n., 421; his heresy, 3 *Bec.* 401, 4 *Bul.* 77; he held that there were in the Godhead two opposing principles, 1 *Hoop.* 65 n.; denied the true humanity of Christ, 1 *Bec.* 320, *ib.* 412, *ib.* 418, 2 *Bec.* 446, 3 *Bul.* 257, 1 *Cran.* 277; said to have professed to be Christ, *Rog.* 162; he had twelve apostles and seventy disciples, *Phil.* 422; called himself the Holy Ghost, 4 *Jew.* 842, 843, *Phil.* 421, *Rog.* 71; claimed to be an apostle, *Phil.* 421, 3 *Tyn.* 49 n.; said the apostles saw but as in a glass, 1 *Jew.* 76; affirmed that none were saved before the 15th year of Tiberias, *Rog.* 137, 163, 297; denied free-will, 3 *Jew.* 166; in what sense, *ib.* 167; condemned marriage and meats, 1 *Bec.* 278; denied the resurrection, 2 *Cov.* 186; his mysteries, *Rog.* 82; he rejected parts of the New Testament, 1 *Ful.* 7, 8; his Epistola Fundamenti, 2 *Cov.* 420, 3 *Tyn.* 49 n

Mangering: perplexing, *Phil.* 315

Mangeur (Pierre le): *v.* Petrus Comestor.

Manichæus: *v.* Manes.

Manichees: *v.* Augustine, and some other fathers.

Their heresy, 1 *Cov.* 51, 1 *Hoop.* 263, 1 *Lat.* 201 n., *Phil.* 347 n.; they yielded more credit to their own devices than to God's word, 3 *Jew.* 158, *Rog.* 79; espoused the error of the Gnostics, *Grin.* 59 n.; were in many respects like the Papists, 3 *Jew.* 157, &c.; their heresy not a fulfilment of 1 Tim. iv, 2 *Ful.* 50; how they deceived, 3 *Jew.* 156, 157; they were rebuked by Augustine for seeking a cause for the will of God, *Pil.* 674; maintained that there were two Gods, or contrary principles in the Godhead, 1 *Brad.* 212, 2 *Hoop.* 74, *Hutch.* 170, 1 *Jew.* 484, 1 *Lat.* 201 n., *Phil.* 347 n., 382 n., *Rog.* 37, 41, 1 *Whitg.* 329; affirmed the world and man to have been made by the latter, *Rog.* 41; denied the true humanity of Christ, 2 *Cov.* 348, 1 *Cran.* 277, 289, 1 *Jew.* 256, 257, 481, 2 *Jew.* 562, *Rog.* 51; rejected the truth of his passion, *Rog.* 51; said that demons, and not Christ, suffered on the cross, *ib.* 57;

denied that he rose in his own proper body, 1 *Jew.* 483; maintained that he ascended only to the sun, 2 *Cov.* 160 n.; made no material idols, but ideal ones, *Poet.* 108; denied a providence, *Rog.* 41; their opinion of the soul of man, 3 *Bul.* 374, *Hutch.* 24, 3 *Jew.* 167; they denied man's free-will to sin, *Rog.* 105; affirmed that original sin proceeds not from our corrupted nature, *ib.* 99; thought themselves free from sin, *ib.* 135; although heretics, and false teachers, they lived well outwardly, 1 *Jew.* 399; denied the resurrection of the flesh, 2 *Cov.* 184, *Rog.* 64, 145, 154, and the general judgment, *Rog.* 67; rejected the Old Testament, *ib.* 80, 87, *Whita.* 30; publicly attacked it, *ib.* 319; declared the law of God to proceed from the prince of darkness, *Rog.* 92; stated the books of the apostles and evangelists to be full of falsehoods, *Whita.* 34; rejected the Acts, *Rog.* 84; preferred their imaginations to the scriptures, 3 *Jew.* 158, *Rog.* 79; set forth and read apocryphal forgeries, 1 *Jew.* 113, 2 *Jew.* 894, 3 *Jew.* 442, *Whita.* 315; they did not baptize, 4 *Bul.* 397, *Rog.* 275; ministered communion in one kind, 1 *Jew.* 257—259, 3 *Jew.* 158, 595; their profanation of the eucharist, *Rog.* 295; their mysteries, *ib.* 202; forbade marriage, and allowed fornication, 1 *Ful.* 479, 2 *Jew.* 1129, 3 *Jew.* 157, *Rog.* 261, *Sand.* 321; their elect or priests might not marry, but their hearers might, 3 *Jew.* 157, *Rog.* 303 n.; their fastings, 2 *Zur.* 122; they fasted on Sunday, 1 *Jew.* 257, 1 *Whitg.* 229; abstained from flesh and wine, but had all manner of delicate fruits, and liquors more dainty than wine, 3 *Jew.* 159; condemned magistracy, 2 *Hoop.* 76, 78, *Rog.* 337; said no man should be put to death for any offence, *Rog.* 349; they thought no man ought to be compelled in religion, 1 *Bul.* 357; deemed all war unlawful, *Rog.* 351; enjoined community of goods, *ib.* 353; refused alms to any not of their sect, *ib.* 355; how they were confuted, *Rid.* 283

Manilius (Marcus): wrote a poem on astronomy, 2 *Jew.* 872

Maniple, Fannel, or Fanon: a sort of small scarf worn by a priest on his arm while saying mass, 2 *Bec.* 300, 3 *Bec.* 259, 3 *Tyn.* 73

Manipulus Curatorum: *Jew.* xl; opus operatum defined, 2 *Jew.* 751; on the exhortation "Sursum corda," 3 *Jew.* 534; strange mistake respecting the word "eleemosyna," 4 *Jew.* 878

Manlius: the name taken away, 1 *Ful.* 198

Mann (Jo.), warden of Merton college: ambassador to Spain, *Park.* 326

Manna: bread from heaven, 4 *Bul.* 410; a type, *Sand.* 371; Christ eaten therein, 1 *Jew.* 545, 546, 2 *Jew.* 577, 617; manna was eaten by the good and bad, but none eat Christ but they have everlasting life, 1 *Cran.* 207, 220

Manners (Hen.), 2nd earl of Rutland: Bridgit (Hussey) his widow, 2 *Bec.* 622 n

Manners (Edw.), 3rd earl of Rutland; sent against the rebels in the North, 1 *Zur.* 214 n

Manners (Rog.), 5th earl of Rutland: married Eliz. daughter of Sir Philip Sidney, 2 *Zur.* 326 n

Manning (......): Manning's wife, martyred at Maidstone, *Poet.* 169

Manning (Jo.): v. Manyng.

Manning (Rob.): his admission relative to the cross borne by the monk Augustine, 2 *Ful.* 17 n

Manqueller: a murderer, 1 *Brad.* 56, *Phil.* 307

Manred: man-rent, *Park.* 99

Manriq (Tho.): Censura in Glossas Juris Canonici, *Calf.* 6 n

Manthorp (R.), clerk of St Stephen's, Norwich, *Park.* vi, 481

Mantua: some of Christ's blood was once pretended to be kept there, *Pil.* 602

Mantuanus: v. Baptista Mantuanus (S.)

Mantzinsky (Jo.), a Polish nobleman: 3 *Zur.* 689

Manuale, or Enchiridion, Manuals. Orarium, or Enchiridion præclaræ Ecclesiæ Sarum, Par. 1528; English verses from it, *Pra. Eliz.* 139 n., &c.; a prayer from it, *ib.* 317 n.; references to it, *ib.* 201, 387, 392, 538, 546 nn. Manuale ad usum Ecclesiæ Sarisb., Roth. 1555, *Jew.* xl; prayer at the hallowing of the font, 2 *Jew.* 567; words from the marriage service, 4 *Jew.* 840 n.; prayer for the deliverance of the dead from hell, 3 *Jew.* 561. Manuale Sarisbur., Duaci, 1610; referred to about the consecration of salt and water, *Calf.* 17 n.; manuals to be abolished, 2 *Cran.* 523, *Grin.* 135, 159

Manuaries: consecrated gloves, 1 *Lat.* 50

Manumission: 2 *Bul.* 229

Manuscripts: many dispersed and destroyed, 2 *Zur.* 79, 80; sold by covetous stationers and spoiled in poticaries' shops, *Park.* 264; rare MSS. should be brought together into well-known places, *ib.* 140; letter from the council respecting writings and records formerly kept in divers abbeys, but then in private hands, *ib.* 327; Bale's and other

MSS., *ib.* 140; Bale's were purchased by abp Parker, *ib.* 198, 287, 2 *Zur.* 78 n.; those of Tilius, *Park.* 141; MSS. at Rome, *ib.*; no old ones at St David's, *ib.* 265; a curious one of the Old Testament, or part thereof, in Latin and Anglo-Saxon, *ib.* 253; one sent by Jewel to Parker, 4 *Jew.* 1274; Cranmer's written books, 2 *Cran.* 459, *Park.* 186, 187, 191

Manwood (Sir Rog.), afterwards lord chief baron: willing to endow a school at Sandwich, *Park.* 187, 188, 192; he founds one accordingly, 3 *Bec.* 601 n.; letter to him when serjeant, *Park.* 338; made a justice of the Common Pleas, *ib.* 405 n

Manworth (Mr), of Barking: 2 *Lat.* 409

Manyng (Jo.): 2 *Cran.* 300

Maozim (מעוים): guardian deities, 1 *Brad.* 92; Mauzim, 3 *Bec.* 240

Mar (Jo. earl of): *v.* Erskine

Marah: its bitter waters made sweet, 4 *Bul.* 262

Maramaldus (Fabr.): his devastations in Germany, 3 *Cran.* 233

Marbach (Jo.), a Lutheran: 3 *Zur.* 251, 334, 663; Luther's saying about him, 2 *Zur.* 81 n.; he appears to have blasphemed the Marian martyrs, *Rog.* 163 (*v.* Marpach).

Marbeck (Jo.): notice of him, *Poet.* xliv; 2 Sam. xxii. 2—7 in metre by him, *ib.* 468

Marburg, in Hesse: sometimes spelled Marlborowe, Marlborough, and Marborch, &c., 1 *Tyn.* xxxvii, xl, xlii, 129; Tyndale goes thither, *ib.* xxxiv; and employs the press of Hans Luft, *ib.* xxxvii; conference there between Luther and Zuinglius respecting the eucharist, 2 *Ful.* 376, *Grin.* 251 n., 1 *Tyn.* xxxviii, 2 *Zur.* 72 n.; the Hesse family there, 3 *Zur.* 719

Marca (Pet. de), abp of Paris: 2 *Ful.* 71 n.; agrees with Scaliger in his opinion that the Babylon mentioned by St Peter was not Rome, *ib.* 336 n. his conjecture with regard to the Donation of Constantine, *ib.* 360 n; observes that the words of Paschasinus, the papal legate at the council of Chalcedon, have been vitiated, *ib.* 288 n

Marcellians: denied the Trinity, *Rog.* 43

Marcellina, the partner of Carpocrates: worshipped the image of Jesus, and those of Paul, Homer, and Pythagoras, *Calf.* 188, 2 *Jew.* 667, 4 *Jew.* 950

Marcellinus, bp of Rome: charged with having sacrificed to idols, 1 *Jew.* 400, 3 *Jew.* 339, 344, 4 *Jew.* 833, 834, 1117, *Pil.* 601, *Rog.* 181; upon what evidence accused of this, and by whom defended, 2 *Ful.* 364, 365; his martyrdom, 1 *Jew.* 342 n.; he ascribes Ecclesiasticus to Solomon (pseud.), *Whita.* 47; the decretal epistles in his name are spurious, 1 *Jew.* 342

Marcellinus (Amm.): *v.* Ammianus.

Marcellus I., bp of Rome: 2 *Ful.* 347; calls himself bishop of the holy and apostolic and catholic church of the city of Rome (pseud.), 1 *Jew.* 426; his decretal epistles spurious, *ib.* 342

Marcellus, bp of Apamea: how it is said that he drove away demons and effected the burning of Jupiter's temple, 2 *Ful.* 116 n., 239, *Rid.* 500, 504

Marcellus, the heretic: 1 *Cran.* 278, *Hutch.* 121 n

Marcellus, a Latin poet: 2 *Cov.* 214 n

Marcellus Sidetes, a Greek poet: his(?) verses on heaven, 2 *Cov.* 214; on the goodness of God, *ib.* 217

Marcellus (Chr.): addressed the pope as another God on earth, 2 *Jew.* 906, 3 *Jew.* 284 n; 4 *Jew.* 831, 843

Marchesinus (Jo.): his book called Mammotrectum, or Mammotrepton, *Jew.* xl, 4 *Jew.* 861

Marchetti (Gio.): Official Memoirs, on miracles at Rome, 1796—7, *Calf.* 274 n

Marcian, emperor: *v.* Valentinian.

He summoned the council of Chalcedon, 1 *Jew.* 411, 4 *Jew.* 992, 1098, *Rog.* 204; brought Theodoret into it, 1 *Jew.* 374; confirmed the council, *ib.* 412; forbade a cause once adjudicated to be subjected to fresh disputation, *Whita.* 437; declares that whosoever, after the truth is found, seeks further, seeks for a lie, 1 *Jew.* 229; his ordinance respecting the sueing of priests in law, 4 *Jew.* 960, 961

Marcion: his heresy, 3 *Bec.* 401, *Hutch.* 121 n., *Phil.* 418; his apostasy, 4 *Bul.* 77; he espoused the error of the Gnostics, *Grin.* 59 n.; maintained that there were in the Godhead two opposing principles, 1 *Hoop.* 65, 2 *Hoop.* 74; denied our Lord's true humanity, 1 *Bec.* 412, 418, 2 *Bec.* 446, 3 *Bul.* 256, *Coop.* 202, 1 *Cran.* 177, 215, 262, 277, 285, 297, 1 *Hoop.* 70, 520, 521, 2 *Hoop.* 73, *Hutch.* 259, 2 *Jew.* 578, 601, 609, *Rid.* 200, 3 *Tyn.* 254, 259; said that Simon of Cyrene was crucified instead of Christ, 1 *Cran.* 256; was called mus Ponticus for gnawing or corrupting the scriptures, 1 *Ful.* 11, 42, 138; thought the Old Testament and the New Testament contrary, 1 *Jew.* 532; devised a book of contrarieties between them, 2 *Jew.* 687; rejected the law and the prophets, *Whita.* 30, as well as a great part of the New Testament, 1 *Ful.* 7, 8, *Whita.* 34; is alleged to have corrupted the epistles to the Corinthians, 1 *Ful.* 138; charged Paul with opposing ceremonies, 1 *Jew.* 217; of Paul's epistles it is said he accepted only those to Timothy and Titus, *Rog.* 84; the epistle to which he gave the name of the Laodiceans is that to the Ephesians, *Whita.* 303; he based his teaching on tradition, *Sand.* 15; Papists agree with him in this, *Whita.* 614; he defended his errors by mistaking of the scripture, 1 *Hoop.* 162; erred as to repentance, 1 *Ful.* 437; permitted women to baptize, 2 *Whitg.* 535; condemned marriage and meats, 1 *Bec.* 278; taught that the creatures of God, as flesh, bread, &c., are nought and unclean, *Grin.* 69; his heresy respecting hell, 1 *Ful.* 296, 297, 299, 302; he denied the resurrection, 2 *Cov.* 186; said that none should be saved in body and soul together, *Rog.* 145 n.; Manifestations (wrongly quoted for the Manifestations of Apelles), *ib.* 82, 202; his fury against magistracy, &c., 2 *Hoop.* 76, 78; his heresy confuted by Polycarp, 1 *Hoop.* 28, and by Tertullian, *Coop.* 202, 1 *Hoop.* 168, 282, 521, 3 *Tyn.* 254, 259

Marcionites: held a plurality of gods, *Rog.* 44; said the world was too base a thing for God to create, *ib.* 40; taught that Christ was man in appearance only, 2 *Lat.* 98, *Rog.* 51; referred to (it seems wrongly) as distinguishing between Jesus and Christ, *Rog.* 162; said to have affirmed that there were two Christs, *ib.* 163; implied, by their teaching, the sinfulness of Christ, *ib.* 133; received no Gospel but St Luke's, *ib.* 84, and rejected passages in that, *ib.* 85; also rejected the epistles to Timothy, Titus, and the Hebrews, *Whita.* 35; allowed baptism by private persons, and even by women, 2 *Ful.* 391, *Rog.* 236; thought that one man might receive a sacrament for another, 1 *Jew.* 23; said to have baptized living men as the substitutes of the dead, *ib.* 23 n., 2 *Jew.* 744, *Rog.* 266, 275; remark as to this statement, *Rog.* 266 n.; they disallowed marriage, 2 *Ful.* 391, *Rog.* 261; denied baptism to married folks, *Rog.* 265, 275; their opinion as to the resurrection of the body, 2 *Cov.* 183; they affirmed that man's body is not capable of happiness, and that no souls should be saved but their own, *Rog.* 297; confounded with the followers of Marcus, *ib.* 135 n.; Papists are plain Marcionists, 3 *Bec.* 273, 450, 2 *Ful.* 391

Marcolphus: 3 *Jew.* 133

Marcosians: deemed themselves as pure as Paul, &c., *Rog.* 135 n.; used certain Hebrew words at the ministration of baptism, 1 *Ful.* 89, *Rog.* 242; their relics, 2 *Ful.* 390

Marcus, bp of Rome: his alleged additions to the mass, 2 *Brad.* 308

Marcus, a holy monk: 1 *Jew.* 191

Marcus the heretic: espoused the heresy of the Gnostics, *Grin.* 59 n.; used Hebrew words in his prayers, 1 *Jew.* 316; held that the wine of the Lord's Supper was converted into blood, *Rog.* 287; Marcus, a necromancer, mentioned by Irenæus (the same person?) enchanted the sacramental cup, 1 *Jew.* 6

Marcus Antonius Constantius: v. Gardiner (S.)

Marcus Aurelius Antoninus Verus, emperor: 4 *Bul.* 540

Marcus Ephesius, i. e. abp of Ephesus: *Jew.* xl; at the council of Florence, 3 *Jew.* 126; cited for transubstantiation, 2 *Jew.* 574; he denied the proceeding of the Holy Ghost from the Son, *ib.*; his reference to the decree falsified by Zosimus, 3 *Jew.* 341; he runneth altogether ad Ephesios, 2 *Jew.* 579

Mardley (Jo.): notice of him, *Poet.* 1; Psalm cxlv. in metre, *ib.* 497

Mardocheus: v. Mordecai.

Mare-lady: May-lady, queen of May, 2 *Bec.* 346, 370

Mares (Rich.): a defendant in Chancery, 2 *Cran.* 257

Margadud, duke of South Wales: *Pil.* 516

Margaret, St: invoked for women with child, 1 *Bec.* 139, *Rog.* 226; account of her, 1 *Bec.* 139 n

Margaret [of Anjou], queen of Henry VI.: 1 *Lat.* 119, 2 *Tyn.* 304

Margaret [of Valois], queen of Navarre: Tyndale says she knew too much of Christ to consent to supersede Catharine of Arragon, 2 *Tyn.* 321; she wrote (in French) A Godly Meditation of the Christian Soul, *Poet.* xiii; verses were written on her decease by the ladies Seymour, 1 *Bec.* 386 n

Margaret, queen of James IV. of Scotland: daughter of king Henry VII., 1 *Zur.* 144 n

Margaret of Austria, governess of the Netherlands: Henry VIII. urges her to concur in measures for the destruction of heretical books, 1 *Tyn.* xxxii, xxxvii; Wolsey directs his agent to request her to give up Tyndale and Roye, *ib.* xxxiv, at a diplomatic conference at Cambray, *ib.* xxxvii; another English envoy to her, S. Vaughan, *ib.* xlii.

Margaret, duchess of Parma, governess of

the Netherlands: 1 *Zur.* 139 n., 204 n., 2 *Zur.* 206 n

Margaret, countess of Richmond: *v.* Tudor.

Margaret, countess of Salisbury: *v.* Pole.

Margarita Decreti: *Jew.* xl, 4 *Jew.* 637 n

Margarite: a pearl, 1 *Bec.* 16

Maria Theresa, "king" of Hungary: 2 *Tyn.* 304

Mariale: *v.* Bernardinus de Busti.

Mariana (Jo.): De Rebus Hisp., *Calf.* 273 n

Marianus, a bishop: 4 *Bul.* 190

Marianus Scotus: Chronicon, *Jew.* xl; speaks of the invention of the cross, *Calf.* 323; gives an account of the coming of Augustine into this country, 1 *Jew.* 307, 4 *Jew.* 874; mentions the death of Benedict, 4 *Bul.* 515; testifies in proof of pope Joan, 4 *Jew.* 650, 656; mentioned, 3 *Jew.* 346

Marie (Honoré de S.): *Calf.* 211 n

Marinarius (Ant.): said, in the council of Trent, if the faith of the gospel were a rule unto our life, then should we be Christians indeed, as now by titles and ceremonies we are called Christians, 4 *Jew.* 874; in the same council he affirmed his assurance of salvation, 3 *Jew.* 245

Mariners: *v.* Sailors.

Marischal (Geo. earl): *v.* Keith.

Marius (Caius): his cruelty, 1 *Cov.* 194 n.; he offered up his daughter, 2 *Jew.* 734

Marius Victorinus, *q. v.*

Mark (St): report of his preaching by Eusebius, 1 *Jew.* 353; said to have been bishop of Alexandria, *Rog.* 328; his scholars there, 2 *Jew.* 981; popes have of late devised a fast on his day, *Pil.* 557; his day not to be fasted, 2 *Cran.* 156; Cranmer's mandate for the celebration of it, *ib.* 468

— His Gospel: Tyndale's prologue to it, 1 *Tyn.* 480; argument of it, and contents of each chapter, 3 *Bec.* 570, 571; it was rejected by Cerdon, Marcion, &c., *Whita.* 34, and by the Ebionites, *ib.* 35; the last chapter rejected by Cajetan, *ib.* 105

Markeshall, co. Essex: 2 *Brad.* 98 n

Markets and Fairs: wares not to be sold on Sundays in service-time, nor in churchyards, and other like regulations, *Grin.* 138, 171, 2 *Hoop.* 136, 137, 142; market-set, i. e. market-stead, or place, 2 *Lat.* 116

Markham (......): preferred to farm Newsted priory, 2 *Cran.* 384

Markham (Sir Jo.): recommended to Cromwell for support in a Chancery suit, 2 *Cran.* 315; commended to the king's favour, *ib.* 358

Markham (Jo.): notice of him, *Poet.* xxxii; the betrayal of Christ, *ib.* 361

Markham (Rob.): 2 *Cran.* 286

Marks: *v.* Beast.

Sheep marks used by persons who could not write, 2 *Cran.* 291

Marlborough, in the land of Hesse: *v.* Marburg.

Marler (Anth.): king Henry VIII. gives him a Bible, 2 *Cran.* 118 n

Marler (Walter): Mary his wife makes a shirt for Bradford's burning, 2 *Brad.* xl, 181 n.; letter to her, *ib.* 181; salutation of her, *ib.* 215

Marley (......): called Cecil's old master, *Park.* 260

Marloratus (Augustine): notice of him, 1 *Bul.* 8 n.; Novi Test. Cathol. Expos., 3 *Whitg.* xxx; his comment upon St John translated, 1 *Bul.* 8, 2 *Zur.* 148 n.; his Thesaurus, *Park.* 455; he cites Calvin's exposition of χειροτονεῖν, 1 *Whitg.* 348

Marnix (Phil. de), lord of Mont St Aldegond: 2 *Zur.* 289 n

Maromaus (Fabr.): *v.* Maramaldus.

Maronis (Fra. de), or de Mayro: notice of him, 2 *Cov.* 421; Super Libros Sentent., *Jew.* xxxvii; gathers from Augustine that the authority of the church is greater than that of scripture, 2 *Cov.* 421; denies that the sacraments of their own virtue cause grace, 2 *Bec.* 219, 3 *Bec.* 469; speaks of the pope's plenitude of power, 3 *Jew.* 600

Marpach (......), one of the ministers of Strasburgh: 3 *Zur.* 534; the same (probably) saluted or mentioned, 2 *Zur.* 19, 23, 52 (qu. if Jo. Marbach?)

Mar-people (Sir Martin): notice of Sir Martin Mar-people; his Collar of Esses; by Jo. Davies, *Poet.* xxxiii; stanzas therefrom, *ib.* 363

Mar-prelate (Martin): says the bishops bid battle to Christ and his church, *Rog.* 170; that bishops are not to be obeyed when they cite, excommunicate, &c., *ib.* 310; censures bp Aylmer's Harborough for Faithful Subjects, *ib.* 338, see 2 *Ful.* 37 n.; his speculations opposed to the sufficiency of scripture, *Rog.* 203; virulence of some writers in the mar-prelate controversy, 3 *Whitg.* xviii; notice of bp Cooper's Admonition, against Martin the Libeller, *Coop.* xiii.

Marpurg: *v.* Marburg.

Marriage: *v.* Celibacy, Husbands, Unmarried, Wives; also Law (Canon).

   i.   *On Marriage generally.*
   ii. *Prohibited degrees and times.*
   iii. *The contracting of marriage.*
   iv. *Its solemnization.*
   v. *Duties of the married.*

MARRIAGE

vi. *Second marriage, &c.*
vii. *Judicial cognizance of marriage, &c.*
viii. *The marriage of the clergy.*

i. *On marriage generally:* on virginity, matrimony, and widowhood, 1 *Tyn.* 313—315; of wedlock or matrimony, 1 *Bec.* 103, 1 *Bul.* 393, &c., 4 *Bul.* 509, 1 *Hoop.* 374, &c., 2 *Jew.* 1128, 1129; what it is, 3 *Bec.* 611, 618, 1 *Bul.* 394, 1 *Hoop.* 380; the teaching of scripture respecting it, 2 *Cran.* 116; some passages concerning it examined, 1 *Ful.* 115—117; alleged heretical translations against the sacrament of matrimony examined, *ib.* 492—496; provisions of the law of Moses, 2 *Bul.* 226; reference to The Christian State of Matrimony, a book translated from Bullinger, 1 *Bec.* 29 n.; Tyndale wrote a treatise on matrimony, and on 1 Cor. vii, now lost, 1 *Tyn.* x, xxxvii; questions about marriage, 3 *Zur.* 315; matrimony is not (except in a wide sense) a sacrament, *Calf.* 235—241, 2 *Ful.* 229, 243, *Rog.* 260, 1 *Tyn.* 254; not a sacrament, yet not a mere civil contract, 1 *Ful.* 492; not a sacrament, though a sign of the kingdom of heaven, 3 *Tyn.* 175; sometimes called a sacrament, as in the homilies, 2 *Ful.* 168; in what the alleged sacrament consists, *Calf.* 240; it is only a sacrament of will, says Durandus, 2 *Jew.* 1125; it is declared by the Canon Law to have two sacraments, *Calf.* 238; on the word "sacramentum" in Eph. v. 32, *Whita.* 197, 489; marriage represents the union of Christ and the church, 1 *Bul.* 397, *Phil.* 246, *Sand.* 317, 1 *Tyn.* 254, 3 *Tyn.* 153, 154; the excellence or dignity of marriage, 1 *Bul.* 394; it is not unholy, *Hutch.* 148, 2 *Lat.* 162, though it is declared to be so by the Canon Law, *Calf.* 238—241, but honourable in all, 1 *Bul.* 396, 1 *Hoop.* 375, 2 *Hoop.* 55, 1 *Jew.* 158, 2 *Jew.* 1128, 1 *Lat.* 366, 393, 2 *Lat.* 160, 162, *Sand.* 313, 314, &c.; chaste and pure, 4 *Jew.* 803; good in the sight of God, 2 *Tyn.* 125; sanctioned by Christ's first miracle, 1 *Bul.* 396, 2 *Lat.* 160; as pleasing to God as chastity, 3 *Tyn.* 157, 162; yet not equal to virginity in all respects, 1 *Ful.* 492, 2 *Ful.* 228, 383, 1 *Hutch.* 148, 1 *Lat.* 393, 394, 1 *Tyn.* 21, 3 *Whitg.* 293; various notions respecting its lawfulness, *Sand.* 322; it is lawful for all Christian men and women, *Rog.* 305—307; no man is forbidden to marry, 1 *Bul.* 402; the views of Clement of Alexandria respecting marriage, p. 214, col. 2; of Tertullian and Origen, 1 *Jew.* 157, & al.; of Cyprian, p. 263, col. 2; of Epiphanius, p. 300, col. 2; of Ambrose, p. 22, col. 1; of Augustine, p. 78, col. 2; of Jerome, p. 435, col. 2; of Cyril of Alexandria, p. 267, col. 2; of Gregory Nazianzen, p. 365, col. 2, p. 367, col. 2; of Basil, p. 101, col. 2; of Augustine, p. 196, col. 2; some of the fathers censured it, 1 *Jew.* 157, 3 *Jew.* 387, &c.; the councils of Melchidense and Aquisgranum erred about it, 2 *Cran.* 87; various errors respecting it, *Rog.* 261, 262; marriage disallowed or dishonoured by divers heretics, *Rog.* 261, 306, *Sand.* 321; forbidden by the Manichees, 2 *Jew.* 1129; likewise by the pope, 2 *Tyn.* 189; the forbidding of it is a doctrine of devils, 4 *Bul.* 509, 2 *Hoop.* 126, 2 *Lat.* 162; God is the author of marriage, 3 *Bec.* 27; why he has ordained it, 1 *Brad.* 167, 1 *Tyn.* 254; its causes or ends, 1 *Bul.* 397, 1 *Hoop.* 381; first, for commodity and happiness, 1 *Bul.* 397; secondly, for the begetting and bringing up of children, 1 *Bul.* 400, 408, 1 *Hoop.* 381; thirdly, as a remedy against sin, 2 *Bec.* 103, 1 *Bul.* 400, 1 *Hoop.* 381; marriage regarded as a civil contract, 3 *Zur.* 517; discreditable proceedings respecting marriage in the papal courts, 1 *Tyn.* 170; marriage much abused in England, 1 *Lat.* 243, 244

ii. *Prohibited degrees, and forbidden times:* on the prohibited degrees, 3 *Bec.* 199, 532, 533, 2 *Cran.* 94, 328, 329, 359 n.; kindred may not intermarry, *Rog.* 262, *Sand.* 323; a man is forbidden to marry any woman to whom he owes obedience, 2 *Tyn.* 329, 330; marriage of brother with sister, why forbidden, *ib.* 331; regarded by Tyndale as not absolutely unlawful in all cases, *ib.*; of a brother and sister-german, *Park.* 353; on marriage with a brother's widow, 2 *Lat.* 333, 340; Tyndale's argument that such marriage is not unlawful, 2 *Tyn.* 323, &c.; marriage between uncles and nieces, whether utterly forbidden, *ib.* 331; on marriage with a deceased wife's sister, 4 *Jew.* xvii, 1243, 1262, *Park.* 176, 2 *Tyn.* 328, 3 *Zur.* 166; marriage with a wife's niece unlawful, 2 *Cran.* 328; papal impediments to marriage, 1 *Tyn.* 245; spiritual kindred (i. e. persons ecclesiastically related to each other through co-sponsorship) forbidden to intermarry by the church of Rome, v. Sponsors; the table of affinity to be affixed in the parish church and sometimes read, *Grin.* 126, 143; injunctions and inquiries directed against unlawful marriages, 2 *Cran.* 158, *Grin.* 143, 175; marriage prohibited at certain times, except by licence or dispensation, 3 *Bec.* 198, 199, 533, 2 *Cran.*

364, 3 *Whitg.* 276, 1 *Zur.* 164, 358, 2 *Zur.* 149; ordered to be solemnized at all times in the year, *Grin.* 189

iii. *The contracting of marriage:* it ought not to be avoided for poverty, or any such cause, 1 *Hoop.* 381; exhortation for a right choice, 3 *Bec.* 133; advice to king Edward on this subject, 1 *Lat.* 243; beauty or wealth not to be too much respected, *Sand.* 324, 325; how marriage is to be contracted, 1 *Bul.* 403; contracts to be made soberly, 4 *Bul.* 510; marriage is not to be carelessly or improperly entered on, *Sand.* 323; it must be begun with religion, 1 *Bul.* 409; against wicked and unlawful marriages, 2 *Hoop.* 149, 1 *Lat.* 366; children should not contract marriage without the consent of parents, 2 *Bec.* 355, 358, 371, 372, 3 *Bec.* 199, 532, *Sand.* 50, 281, 325, 326, 455, 1 *Tyn.* 169, 170, 199, 3 *Zur.* 315; untimely marriages injurious, 2 *Bec.* 369; the marriage of old doting widows objectionable, 3 *Bec.* 131; ungodly marriages, and stealing of wards, 1 *Lat.* 169, an act passed concerning this, *ib.* 170; privy contracts, forbidden or censured, 2 *Cran.* 82, 159, 2 *Hoop.* 137, 149, 2 *Lat.* 243; betrothing and the use of the ring therein, 1 *Zur.* 164; breaking a ring as a pledge of marriage, 1 *Tyn.* 361; persons contracted to be compelled to marry with all convenient speed, 2 *Hoop.* 138; banns required, 2 *Cran.* 159, *Grin.* 126, 2 *Hoop.* 126, 138, 149, *Rid.* 531, *Sand.* 434; dispensed with in a certain case, 2 *Cran.* 260

iv. *The solemnizing of holy matrimony:* marriage valid if contracted in lawful age per verba de præsenti, 2 *Cran.* 359, 360; Silvester commands that the wife be blessed by the priest, *Pil.* 569, 686; the popish marriage service partly in English, *ib.* 500, 544; on the service of the English church, *ib.* 544; forms will be found in the several Prayer-Books, *Lit. Edw.* and *Lit. Eliz.*; the English service described by bp Horn, 2 *Zur.* 356; matters concerning the solemnization of matrimony, 3 *Whitg.* 353, &c.; not to be solemnized except in the parish where the parties, or the woman at least, reside, nor without banns, (synod, 1562), *Sand.* 434; partly solemnized in the body of the church, 2 *Whitg.* 461, 462; old marriage customs, 3 *Whitg.* 353, 357, 493; the ring, its signification, *ib.* 353, 354, and see 1 *Tyn.* 361, 1 *Zur.* 164; articles, &c. respecting the solemnization of marriage, 2 *Cran.* 159, *Grin.* 126, 132, 163, 2 *Hoop.* 126, 138, 149, *Rid.* 531; order for the ministration of holy wedlock in the church in Denmark, 1 *Cov.* 480; persons united by Protestants remarried by Popish priests, *Rog.* 236 n., 262

v. *The duties of the married,* (v. Husbands, Wives): the duty of married persons, 2 *Bec.* 104, 476; they must dwell together with knowledge, 1 *Bul.* 406, must not break their marriage vow, but be faithful to each other, 2 *Bec.* 97, 1 *Bul.* 406; if they be not true to each other, they are forsworn, 1 *Bec.* 371; wedlock must be undefiled, 1 *Bul.* 400; reverend behaviour required in the state of marriage, *ib.* 405; there must be affection and religion in it, *Sand.* 329; how every man should esteem his wife, 2 *Tyn.* 51; the duty of a Christian towards an unbelieving partner, 2 *Hoop.* 609; marriage places the woman in subjection, 1 *Tyn.* 171; married women should be so apparelled as to please their husbands, 2 *Bec.* 439; the adversities of marriage, 2 *Lat.* 161; poor married men should not despair of a living, or seek it by unlawful means, 2 *Bec.* 605, 614; offences in marriage, 1 *Hoop.* 381; remedies against offences in it, *ib.* 382; admonition to married persons, for faith, 1 *Bec.* 272

vi. *Second and third marriage:* second and third marriages, 1 *Bul.* 405; second marriage condemned by some of old, 3 *Jew.* 390, *Sand.* 322; persons twice married called in the Canon Law bigami, *Calf.* 19, 3 *Tyn.* 165; and excluded from holy orders, *Rog.* 241 n., 3 *Tyn.* 165 n.; as to Bigamy, and Polygamy, see those titles.

vii. *The judicial cognizance of marriage and divorce:* to whom the judicial decision of matrimony pertains, 3 *Whitg.* 543; on the cognizance thereof by the ecclesiastical courts, *ib.* 267; their jurisdiction in matrimonial causes, 2 *Cran.* 249, 252, 253; a suit respecting a woman married to two husbands, *ib.* 364; wedlock indissoluble, except for adultery, 1 *Bul.* 403, 1 *Hoop.* 382, or (it is said) for infidelity in religion, 1 *Hoop.* 385; what the law should do in the event of husbands and wives forsaking one another, 2 *Tyn.* 54; see also Divorce.

viii. *The marriage of the clergy:* the marriage of priests is lawful, 3 *Bec.* 235, &c., 2 *Cov.* 483—485, 2 *Hoop.* 126, 1 *Lat.* 293, 2 *Lat.* 77, 162, *Pil.* 564, *Rog.* 302—305, 3 *Tyn.* 29, 151, 156; in general they should be married, 1 *Tyn.* 230; the canon law allows that their marriage is not forbidden by the authority of the law, the gospel, or the apostles, 2 *Jew.* 882; it is sanctioned by St Paul, *Phil.* 404; his doctrine on the subject explained, 3 *Tyn.* 155; Chrysostom's judgment upon his words, "the husband of one wife," 3 *Jew.* 406, 407; opinions of Augustine and Jerome on the same passage, *Whita.* 455; the marriage of priests sanctioned even by the Rhemish version, 1 *Ful.* 71; translation concerning it examined, *ib.* 471, &c.; most of the apostles were married, 3 *Bec.* 235, 1 *Bul.* 396, 421, 2 *Jew.* 727, 989, 3 *Jew.* 392, 421, 4 *Jew.* 803; the office of a bishop is not contrary to matrimony, 3 *Jew.* 404; the bishops and ministers of the primitive church were married, 3 *Bec.* 236, 2 *Jew.* 989, 1128, 3 *Jew.* 157, 390, &c., 4 *Jew.* 804, &c.; so are those of the Greek church to this day, 3 *Bec.* 236, *Coop.* 171, *Pil.* 564; the marriage of the clergy defended from the fathers, 2 *Jew.* 728; Tertullian a married priest, 1 *Jew.* 149; the marriage of the clergy vindicated by Paphnutius in the council of Nice, 2 *Ful.* 240, *Pil.* 532 (& al. v. Councils); allowed by that and other councils, 2 *Cran.* 169; the ordinance ascribed to pope Siricius, 2 *Ful.* 243; pope Felix III. or IV. was married, *Pil.* 527; the marriage of priests forbidden by Boniface III., 2 *Tyn.* 258; permitted in the Anglo-Saxon church, 2 *Ful.* 10; it continued for 1000 years, 2 *Jew.* 989; the epistle of Udalric or Hulderic to pope Nicholas, *Pil.* 568—570; in Latin, *ib.* 685 —687; the marriage of priests forbidden by Gregory VII., *Pil.* 564, 567; opposition to his decree, *ib.* 567; also forbidden by the council of Winchester, (1076), 2 *Ful.* 23, 93; the burden of compulsory celibacy was brought in by violence, 3 *Tyn.* 158; the epistle of Anselm respecting it, *Pil.* 571; that of pope Paschal, *ib.* 572; marriage accounted a sacrament, yet denied to priests of the church of Rome, *Pil.* 553; Antichrist cannot abide it, 3 *Bec.* 198, 505, 523, 524, 533; a foolish reason against it, 3 *Jew.* 222; admission into the priesthood refused by the church of Rome to persons who had been married more than once, *Calf.* 19, *Sand.* 322, 3 *Tyn.* 152, 155, 165; Jerome rebukes the error, 3 *Tyn.* 152; answer to the assertion that the Romish church does not forbid to marry, because no man is bound to be a priest, *ib.* 161; priests excommunicated if married, and burnt if they do not forsake their lawful wives, 2 *Cran.* 39; to forbid marriage to any is a devilish doctrine, 2 *Hoop.* 55, 56; consequences of its disallowance, 3 *Jew.*

417, &c., 2 *Tyn.* 123, 3 *Tyn.* 52 (and see Celibacy); unmarried priests often scandalous, *Hutch.* 202; concubinage sanctioned by the papal law, 1 *Tyn.* 232, 3 *Tyn.* 40; Campegius and Pighius say that the priest who keeps a concubine lives more holily than he who has a wife, 4 *Jew.* 627; More says that marriage defileth a priest more than triple whoredom, 3 *Tyn.* 29 n.; a tax paid by priests to their bishops for permission to keep concubines, 2 *Tyn.* 295; provision of the Six Articles as to the marriage of the clergy, 2 *Cran.* 393 n.; Cranmer's efforts to abolish compulsory celibacy, *ib.* viii; the marriage of the clergy allowed by law in the reign of Edward VI. and their children made legitimate, *ib.* x, 1 *Lat.* 529 n., 2 *Zur.* 159; disliked by Elizabeth, *Park.* 148, 157, 2 *Zur.* 61 n.; scarcely allowed in her time, 1 *Zur.* 164, 179, 358, 2 *Zur.* 129; proposed to be winked at, not established by law, *Park.* 66; clergymen were permitted to marry with the consent of the bishop and two justices, 2 *Zur.* 359; bishops' wives not permitted to live in the palaces, nor the wives of deans, canons, &c., within the precincts of cathedral churches, *ib.*; the marriage of the clergy defended by bp Cox, *Park.* 151, and by abp Parker, *ib.* 157; pensionary concubinage continued in Wales, notwithstanding leave of marriage, *ib.* 257

Marriage-Feast: sermon on the parable, Matt. xxii, 1 *Lat.* 455

Marry, or Mary: an oath, 1 *Brad.* 9, *Calf.* 82

Marsch (Walter): governor of the English factory at Antwerp, 1 *Tyn.* lxviii.

Marseilles: none admitted citizens of Massilia but such as had learned an occupation, 1 *Bul.* 294: meeting of the pope and French king, 2 *Cran.* 462

Marsh (Geo.): called a Lancashire martyr, 2 *Brad.* 236 n.; burned at Chester, *Pra. Eliz.* 373 n

Marsh (Jo.): *v.* Mershe.

Marshal: used by Tyndale as a translation of שר הטבחים, 1 *Tyn.* 408

Marshall (Dr): with Wolsey at York place, 2 *Lat.* xxx.

Marshall (Mr): at Calais, (perhaps an officer so called), 2 *Cran.* 411

Marshall (Mr): he and his wife saluted, *Phil.* 227

Marshall (Cuthb.): his Primer noticed, *Pra. Eliz.* viii, 507 n

Marshall (Jo.): *v.* Martiall.

Marshal (Rich.), dean of Christ Church, Oxon: notices of him, 2 *Cran.* 382 n., 1 *Zur.* 12 n.;

mentioned, 2 *Cran.* 382—384; he succeeded Cox as dean, 3 *Zur.* 373; laid snares for Jewel, *Jew.* xi; was at Cranmer's examination, 2 *Cran.* 543, 546; his deposition against him, *ib.* 552, 567; at Ridley's degradation, *Rid.* 286; he refused to allow him to speak at his martyrdom, *ib.* 295; his brutal treatment of the remains of P. Martyr's wife, 2 *Cran.* 382 n., *Grin.* 169 (see corrig.) 1 *Zur.* 12 n

Marshall* (Rog.): keeper at Nonsuch, *Park.* 387

Marshal (T.), poet: notice of him, *Poet.* xxviii; verses written in trouble, *ib.* 313

Marshall (Will.): servant to abp Grindal, *Grin.* 357

Marshalsea: *v.* Southwark.

Marsilius of Batavy: a witness for the truth, condemned by the council of Constance, *Phil.* 393 (qu. if intended for the next?)

Marsilius Manardinus Patavinus: De Translat. Imp., *Jew.* xl; speaks of the policy of pope Stephen in the translation of the empire, 4 *Jew.* 680; what he says of the errors of pope John XXII., *ib.* 925; he speaks of the pope as Antichrist, *ib.* 740, 1115; called a heretic by Harding, but defended by Jewel, *ib.* 741, 742

Marsilius of Parma: poisoned Alexander V., *Bale* 593

Marsus (Gualt.): founded a religious order, 2 *Ful.* 103

Marten (Ant.): a witness, 2 *Cran.* 388

Marten (Ant.), sewer of the queen's chamber: wrote a prayer on the Spanish armada, *Lit. Eliz.* 470

Martha: 4 *Bul.* 107

Martial, the poet: 1 *Bec.* 144, *Calf.* 264, 1 *Hoop.* 393, 2 *Lat.* 330

Martial of Limoges: alleged to have been one of the seventy-two disciples, *Calf.* 69, 271, 2 *Ful.* 177, 180, 1 *Jew.* 108; his counterfeit epistles, 2 *Ful.* 141, 142, 177, 180; when first heard of, and published, *Calf.* 69; his book found at Limoges, 1 *Jew.* 113; referred to for the mass, *ib.* 108; on the offering spoken of by Malachi, 2 *Jew.* 723; on the cross, *Calf.* 69, 70, 271, 2 *Ful.* 141, 142, 177, 180

Martiall (Jo.): notices of him, *Calf.* ix, 88; sometime usher at Winchester, 2 *Ful.* 150, 152, 163; his treatise of the Cross referred to, *ib.* 3, 107, *Grin.* xx; Calfhill's ANSWER TO THE TREATISE OF THE CROSS, edited by the Rev. Rich. Gibbings, M.A.; his reply to M. Calfhill's Blasphemous Answer, 2 *Ful.* 4; Fulke's REJOINDER TO his REPLY AGAINST THE ANSWER OF MASTER CALFHILL TO THE BLASPHEMOUS TREATISE OF THE CROSS, edited by the same, *ib.* 125—212; Fulke's books against him, 1 *Ful.* ix. bis; his address prefixed to a revised edition of Harding's Answer, 2 *Jew.* 812

Martian, emperor: *v.* Marcian.

Martin: *v.* Martinus, Martyn.

Martin I. pope: established image-worship, 1 *Hoop.* 47; his council, see Councils, Rome (650).

Martin II., pope: an enchanter, *Rog.* 180

Martin V., pope: his election, 1 *Tyn.* 325 n., *Whita.* 510; stated to have dispensed with an unlawful marriage, 3 *Jew.* 599

Martin (St), bp of Braga: born in Pannonia, and sometime abbot and bishop of Dumium, 1 *Bul.* 427 n.; canons collected by him, 1 *Whitg.* 460 (see Councils, *Braga II.*); his doctrine of continency, 1 *Bul.* 424—427

Martin (St), bp of Dumium: see the preceding.

Martin (St), bp of Tours: his election as bishop, 1 *Jew.* 298, *Whita.* 226; he found a chapel dedicated to a common thief, who was esteemed a martyr, 1 *Jew.* 158; crossed himself, *Calf.* 252; was preserved from death by the sign of the cross, *ib.* 329; his answer to the devil, 1 *Jew.* 551; a foolish tale of him, 2 *Cran.* 180; he told the emperor Maximus that it was impious for the temporal judge to take cognizance of an ecclesiastical cause, *Whita.* 443; his prayer when he saw death to be nigh, 3 *Tyn.* 279

Martin (Ant.): *v.* Marten.

Martin (Greg.): notice of him, 1 *Ful.* xli; list of his works, *ib.* xiii; discovery, *Calf.* 235 n., 2 *Ful.* 385 n

Martin (Tho.), or Martyn: probably referred to, 1 *Brad.* 516; queen Mary's commissioner against Cranmer, 2 *Cran.* 212, 446 n., 447, 542; he charges Cranmer with making a bargain with the king for the archbishoprick, *ib.* 217; Cranmer's letter to him and Story, *ib.* 446; his controversy with Ponet, 3 *Zur.* 116; his book on priests' marriages answered by Ponet, *Pil.* 549; Parker also wrote a defence of the marriage of priests in reply to him, *Park.* ix, 483

Martin: Hooper's friend, 3 *Zur.* 67

Martin, a German: servant to bishop Grindal, and recommended by him to Utenhovius, *Grin.* 286

Martin (......): saluted, 3 *Zur.* 334

* Marshall and Marshal are arranged together.

Martin (......): young Martin, *Park.* 470
Martin Mar-prelate, *q. v.*
Martin chain: one of counterfeit or base metal, 2 *Bec.* 438
Martinengo (The abbot of): the pope's nuncio to queen Elizabeth, who would not permit him to enter the kingdom, 4 *Jew.* 1246 n., 1 *Zur.* 102 n., 105
Martinists: Lutherans so called, 1 *Zur.* 174
Martinus de Magistris, *q. v.*
Martinus Polonus: a Cistercian monk, 4 *Jew.* 648; made penitentiary by pope Nicholas III., *ib.* 637 n.; his Chronicon, *Jew.* xl; reference to it, *Calf.* 323 n.; the "true" copy of it in the Vatican, *ib.* 6 n.; his Margarita Decreti, 4 *Jew.* 637 n.; records the history of pope Joan, *Calf.* 6 n., 4 *Jew.* 648, 649, 656; gives a reason why she is not reckoned in the calendar of popes, 4 *Jew.* 650; mentions that pope Boniface VIII. told the French king that he (the pope) was lord both in spiritual and temporal matters throughout the world, and therefore that the king should hold the empire at his hand, *ib.* 685; says the church has blown away many canons, as too burdenous, *ib.* 637
Martinus Scholasticus: *v.* Scholasticus.
Martyn (Tho.): *v.* Martin.
Martyn (......), a goldsmith in Cheapside: *Grin.* 348
Martyr (Isaac), son of Peter: 1 *Zur.* 58
Martyr (Pet.), Mediol.: De Insulis nuper Inventis, *Jew.* xli; on West Indian heathenism, 3 *Jew.* 198
Martyr (Pet.), Vermilius:
  i. *His life*: once a Carthusian monk in Italy, 3 *Zur.* 495 n.; Cranmer defends him against Smith's charge of mercenary motives, 1 *Cran.* 374; he abandoned a great income in his own country, and went into strange countries to promote the truth and glory of God, *ib.*; expenses of his journey to England, 3 *Zur.* 541 n.; resident in England, 1 *Lat.* 141; he lodged with Cranmer before he went to Oxford, 1 *Cran.* 374; confers with Ridley, *Rid.* ix; his acts at Oxford, *Jew.* viii, 3 *Zur.* 412, 414, &c.; regius professor of divinity, *Phil.* 213 n., 3 *Zur.* 420; he describes his duties in the university, 3 *Zur.* 481; he lectures there, *ib.* 721; lectures on the Romans, *ib.* 401, 419; concerned in a disputation on the eucharist, *ib.* 344 n., 478; assisted in it by N. Cartwright, 2 *Lat.* 250 n.; defends Lutheran opinions, 3 *Zur.* 61; as canon of Christ Church he would not wear white vestments in the choir, 2 *Zur.* 33, & corrig.; his opinions on the vestments, 2 *Hoop.* xiv, 1 *Zur.* 158, 2 *Zur.* 120, 3 *Zur.* 487, 585; in danger of trouble for his opposition to them, 3 *Zur.* 426; extracts from his letter to Hooper on them, 2 *Whitg.* 27, 35, 63, 65; his opinion of the Book of Common Prayer, 1 *Zur.* 234 n., 235; a patron of Froschover, 3 *Zur.* 723, 726; in a commission for reforming the ecclesiastical law, *ib.* 447, 503, 590; his illness, and the death of his wife, *ib.* 99; on Mary's accession he is confined to his house, *ib.* 369; obtains leave to depart from England, *ib.* 372, 506; his labours at Oxford destroyed by Spanish monks, 1 *Zur.* 33; he lectures at Strasburgh, *Grin.* 239, *Jew.* xiii, *Rid.* 387; opposition to him there, 2 *Zur.* 111 n., 113 n., 3 *Zur.* 509 n.; he is invited to Zurich, 3 *Zur.* 137 n.; made Hebrew professor there, succeeding Pellican, *Jew.* xiii, 3 *Zur.* 509 n., 518; Sandys dwelt in his house at Zurich, *Sand.* xvi; Jewel writes thence, 4 *Jew.* 1193; on Elizabeth's accession he is invited to return to England, 1 *Zur.* 20 n., 45, 55, 71, 77 n., 81; queen Elizabeth desires his return, 2 *Zur.* 13; he sends a book to her, 1 *Zur.* 25; her reception of it, *ib.* 53; letter to a nobleman (Tho. duke of Norfolk?) who had invited him to return, 2 *Zur.* 57; he writes to the Dutch church in London against Hadr. Hamsted, *Grin.* 243 n.; Parker desires his attendance at a conference in France, *Park.* 147; he attends the conference at Poissy, *Grin.* 244 n., 1 *Jew.* 88, 94, 4 *Jew.* 1245 n., 1 *Zur.* 99 n.; salutations of him, 1 *Zur.* 37, 42, 62, 2 *Zur.* 90; his death, 4 *Jew.* 1257 n., 1 *Zur.* 123, 130, 136, 2 *Zur.* 94; his image in silver [probably a medal] sent by Simler to Jewel, 1 *Zur.* 126; Parkhurst returns for the image, a golden Elizabeth, *ib.* 136; commendations of him by bishop Hooper, 3 *Zur.* 97, by bishop Grindal, *Grin.* 245; his doctrine slandered by A. Cope, 4 *Jew.* 760; Martyr vindicated from Gardiner's charge of want of learning, 1 *Cran.* 195, 196
— Catherine (Dampmartin) his wife: her death, 3 *Zur.* 99, 582; her body brutally cast out of her grave in Christ Church, Oxford, by dean Marshal, 2 *Cran.* 382 n., 1 *Jew.* 60, 1 *Zur.* 12 n.; Catherine Merenda, his second wife, 4 *Jew.* 1217, 1218, 1 *Zur.* 47 n., 66, 74; his children by her, *ib.* 54 n.; a son of his called Eliperius, who died an infant, 4 *Jew.* 1232, 1 *Zur.* 78; his servant Julius, 1 *Zur.* 41, 61, 232 n. (& al. *v.* Sancterentianus). Anna, saluted, *ib.* 41, 69, seems to have been the wife of Julius. See Martyrillus.

ii. *His Works:* Comm. in Genesin, 1 *Zur.* 127, 3 *Zur.* 504; Comm. in Exodium, 1 *Zur.* 504; Comm. in Lib. Judicum, 1 *Bul.* 8, *Jew.* xli, 4 *Jew.* 646, 3 *Whitg.* xxx, 1 *Zur.* 46, 112; Comm. in duos Lib. Samuelis, 3 *Whitg.* xxx, 1 *Zur.* 46; Melachim, i. e. Regum Libri duo, &c., 3 *Whitg.* xxx, 1 *Zur.* 112; Comm. in Ep. ad Romanos, 3 *Whitg.* xxx, 3 *Zur.* 504; Comm. in I. ad Cor. Epist., 1 *Whitg.* xxx, 3 *Zur.* 504; writings on the sacrament, 2 *Cran.* 220 n., 3 *Zur.* 478 n., 678, 680; Disputatio de Eucharistiæ Sacramento, 2 *Cran.* 220 n.; translated into English, *ib.*; Tractatio de sacramento Eucharistiæ, 2 *Cran.* 220 n., 3 *Zur.* 561; translated by N. Udall, 2 *Cran.* 220 n.; his dialogue on the ubiquitarian question, 1 *Zur.* 100, 4 *Jew.* 1245; his adhortatio ad cœnam Domini mysticam (in his Loci Comm.) is the original of the exhortation in the English communion service directed to be used when the people are negligent to come, *Lit. Eliz.* 186; his book on vows, against R. Smith, 1 *Zur.* 46, 58; his Latin sermons on rebellion, 2 *Cran.* 190 n.; apparent reference to them, 4 *Jew.* 665; his reply to Smith, 3 *Zur.* 495; Loci Communes, 2 *Bec.* 252 n., 266 n., 649 n., 3 *Whitg.* xxx, 3 *Zur.* 404 n., 478 n.; he turned the psalms into prayers, *Pil.* 670; preces sacræ ex Psalmis i. ii. iii. et li., *Pra. Eliz.* 419; prayers taken out of Psalms i. and ii., *Pra. B.* 205; A Treatise of the Cohabitation of the Faithful with the Unfaithful, ascribed to him, 2 *Brad.* 297 n.; Simler prepares an edition of his works, 1 *Zur.* 137; character of them, *Pil.* 682; certain of his writings translated into English, 1 *Zur.* 162; Gardiner intimates that he did not wish his writings to appear in English, 1 *Cran.* 222, 224; his translation of Chrysostom, *ib.* 287; he first published Chrysostom's epistle to Cæsarius, *Rid.* 509; books written against him by Rich. Smith, &c., 3 *Zur.* 479 n., 495 n.; Diacosio-Martyrion, an attack on him by bp White, 2 *Jew.* 590, 1 *Zur.* 16, 3 *Zur.* 479 n.; his letters, 2 *Brad.* 400, 403, 3 *Jew.* 3, 1 *Zur.* 339, 2 *Zur.* 25, 32, 38, 47, 57, 3 *Zur.* 468—519; letters to him, 2 *Cran.* 457, 2 *Hoop.* xiv, *Jew.* xii. n., 4 *Jew.* 1196, 1198, 1201, 1204, 1206, 1209, 1213, 1216, 1221, 1224, 1226, 1228, 1230, 1232, 1235, 1238, 1240, 1245, 1254, 1 *Zur.* 1, 6, 9, 13, 17, 19, 23, 38, 44, 52, 54, 59, 62, 65, 67, 70, 72, 75, 77, 80, 88, 91, 99, 112, 117, 2 *Zur.* 13, 76, 3 *Zur.* 29, 30, 118, 139, 181, 182, 768

iii. *His opinions:* on the declaration that "no man can say that Jesus is the Lord, but by the Holy Ghost," and on regeneration, 2 *Whitg.* 591; he collected passages from various old writers on justification, *Wool.* 35; expounds the text, "Christ sent me not to baptize," &c., 2 *Whitg.* 457; his sentiments upon the eucharist, 3 *Zur.* 388, 517, 544 n.; on a passage of Theodoret concerning the consecrated elements, *Phil.* 184 n.; cited by Gardiner as shewing that the doctrine of the real presence was maintained by others as well as Papists, 1 *Cran.* 20; his part in the Ubiquitarian controversy, 1 *Zur.* 100 n., 307; he writes on the celebration of the Lord's supper at Corinth, 2 *Whitg.* 548, 3 *Whitg.* 546; approves communion of the sick, 2 *Whitg.* 545; writes of "much speaking" in prayer, 3 *Whitg.* 516; on Rom. x. 15, "except he be sent," he says that St Paul is speaking of extraordinary calling, 2 *Whitg.* 530; on Rom. xii. he asserts that the apostle describes the functions and gifts which are at all times necessary for the church, 1 *Whitg.* 494; supposes, on Rom. xii. 8, that there were many governments in the church, 3 *Whitg.* 162; expounding 1 Cor. xii. 28, he states that St Paul is rehearsing the parts which the body, i. e. the church, has, 2 *Whitg.* 101; thinks that Andronicus and Junia were called "notable among the apostles," because they had spread the gospel through many places, 1 *Whitg.* 499; writes of deacons with reference to Rom. xii. 8, 3 *Whitg.* 282 n.; compares the elders and deacons of the apostolic church with Romish taper-bearers, &c., *ib.* 539, 540; considers it expedient for a minister to take the accustomed stipend though able to live of himself, 1 *Whitg.* 484; affirms that the laws of the church are unchangeable, 3 *Whitg.* 533; numbers three kinds of traditions, and shews with what cautions the church must be obeyed with respect to those which he calls "neuters," 1 *Whitg.* 252, 253, 286; would not have the power of excommunication committed to the pope or to one bishop, 3 *Whitg.* 542; on the civil jurisdiction of bishops, *ib.* 544; on the union of ecclesiastical and civil jurisdiction in one man, *ib.* 545; he calls Saul rude and ignorant because he did not know Samuel, who was the chief magistrate of Israel, 2 *Whitg.* 12; compares Papists to the idolatrous Israelites, 3 *Whitg.* 148; blames the Lutherans for defending several of their errors, *ib.* 549; his lectures and opinions on divorce, 3 *Zur.* 404; he tells how courtesans live at Rome, 4 *Jew.* 646; disproves purgatory, 3 *Zur.* 378; says the brasen serpent was set up only for a time, 2 *Whitg.* 71; speaks of circumcision amongst the Egyptians, 3 *Whitg.* 147

Martyrillus: a name familiarly applied to a son of the above-named Julius Sancterentianus and Anna his wife, 4 *Jew.* 1214, 1 *Zur.* 13, 41, 47, & sæpe [see the Latin].

Martyrologies: Martyrologium Romanum, 2 *Ful.* 287 n.; Martyrologe after the use of the chirche of Salysbury, 2 *Lat.* 80 n

Martyrs: *v.* Burning, Persecution, Prayers, Saints.

The ecclesiastical use of the word is too restricted, 1 *Ful.* 218; some are martyrs though they die not, *Hutch.* 302; a heart willing to suffer martyrdom is the inestimable gift of God to his elect, *Rid.* 397; tokens of a martyr, *Bale* 193; verses on the martyrs by Gef. Whitney, with the motto "Sic probantur," *Poet.* 207; the martyrs, verses by Will. Byrd, *ib.* 224; no small number of God's children are gone that way, 2 *Brad.* 62; they are witnesses for the truth, *Sand.* 292; nevertheless some true martyrs have maintained erroneous opinions on certain points, 1 *Whitg.* 29 n.; they have ever been put to death by the temporal power at the request of false prophets, 1 *Tyn.* 242; cruelly tormented, 2 *Jew.* 839; their boldness and constancy, 4 *Jew.* 1172; examples of it, *Bale* 586; the stedfast and joyful hearts of them that have suffered for the Lord, 2 *Cov.* 316; the martyrs of old would not purchase freedom from the cross, 2 *Lat.* 434; their example to us, *ib.* 438; martyrs more than conquerors, 2 *Tyn.* 20; martyrdom a cause of rejoicing, 1 *Brad.* 436; the great power of it, 3 *Jew.* 558; its blessedness, 2 *Brad.* 62, *Rid.* 378; the happiness of those who die for God's sake, 2 *Lat.* 444; the crown of martyrdom, 2 *Brad.* 239; death for righteousness is not to be abhorred, but rather to be desired, *Phil.* 219; Satan tempts to vain glory in the hour of martyrdom, 2 *Lat.* 223; martyrs always much commended, *Bale* 5; death in Christ's cause is a high honour, *Rid.* 77; but not precious in the eyes of carnal men, *Bale* 52; martyrs' birthdays (natalitia),—the days on which they suffered, *Calf.* 257; many blessed martyrs have died without baptism, *Coop.* 73, 2 *Jew.* 1107, 2 *Zur.* 195; such were baptized with blood, 2 *Bec.* 225; the blood of martyrs is the seed of the church, 2 *Cov.* 313, 2 *Ful.* 234, *Pil.* 144, 1 *Whitg.* 381, the seed of gospel-fruits, 1 *Lat.* 361; martyrs nothing the worse for wanting burial, *Pil.* 320; their shrines or tombs, 1 *Jew.* 156—158; miracles have been worked by their bodies, 2 *Cran.* 48, 1 *Jew.* 158; yet their shrines and reliques became instruments of superstition, 1 *Jew.* 158; their bodies or reliques deposited beneath the altar, 1 *Ful.* 268, 269; martyrs of the early church, 2 *Bul.* 105; all the Roman bishops to Sylvester were martyrs, *Bale* 316; a list of early martyrs who were hanged, *ib.* 57; of others who were burned, *ib.* 58; early writers of their lives, *ib.* 187; martyrs of the ancient British church, *ib.* 188; English martyrs, real or alleged, *ib.* 190—192; true martyrs in England, *ib.* 189; from their ashes thousands were stirred up, 1 *Lat.* 105; Anne Askewe compared with Romish martyrs, *Bale* 190; the martyrs of the English Reformation, 1 *Brad.* 283, 288, &c., 2 *Jew.* 728, *Pil.* 70; asserted to have sealed the Prayer Book with their blood, 3 *Whitg.* 327 —330; 288 persons burned from 1555 to 1558, *Grin.* 227 n.; Tho. Bryce's Register of the Marian martyrs, *Poet.* 161; account of certain English martyrs, 3 *Zur.* 772; two godly martyrs mentioned, *Phil.* 264; the martyrs referred to in Rev. xx., *Bale* 565; false martyrs, *Bale* 5; such were the Donatists and Anabaptists, 1 *Lat.* 160; it is not the death, but the cause that makes a martyr, 3 *Jew.* 188, 2 *Lat.* 281, *Sand.* 378; certain apostates, who thought that their sufferings ought to be accepted as satisfaction for the offences of others, were called by Cyprian the devil's martyrs, 3 *Tyn.* 199; a common thief regarded as a martyr, 1 *Jew.* 158; Romish martyrs, *Bale* 562, 1 *Tyn.* 291; no martyrs ever died to confirm Romish doctrines, 3 *Tyn.* 113, 170; false martyrs in England, *Bale* 189; the pseudo-martyr Becket contrasted with lord Cobham, *ib.* 55, &c.

Maruphus (Raphael): seller of dispensations and indulgences in London, 2 *Lat.* 349

Marven (......), of Chichester diocese: *Park.* 371

Marwin (Edm.): *v.* Mervyn.

Mary, sister of Moses: *v.* Miriam.

Mary (The Blessed Virgin): translations respecting her considered, 1 *Ful.* 526—538; she is "the woman" of the promise made to Adam, 1 *Bec.* 71, 3 *Bul.* 14, *Hutch.* 146, *Lit. Edw.* 503, (552); on the text Gen. iii. 15, corrupted "*ipsa* conteret caput tuum," 1 *Ful.* 74, 531, &c., *Whita.* 163, &c.; she was a branch of the stock of Jesse, 2 *Hoop.*

MARY

8; her parents traditionally called Joachim and Anna, 2 *Cran.* 30, 2 *Lat.* 228; the controversy respecting her alleged immaculate conception; divisions in the Romish church thereon, 1 *Ful.* 36, 3 *Jew.* 611, 4 *Jew.* 1045, 1053, *Rog.* 99, 100, 1 *Tyn.* 91 n., 159, 313, 3 *Tyn.* 131, *Whita.* 504; the doctrine strenuously maintained by Romanists in the time of Whitaker, e. g. by the university of Paris, and in Spain, *Whita.* 505 on the angelical salutation, "Ave Maria," &c., 1 *Ful.* 148, 149; it is a greeting, not a prayer, 2 *Lat.* 229, 360; its use defended, *ib.*; passages relating to it from Marshall's Primer, and L. Lavater, *Pra. Eliz.* viii; the abuse of it, 2 *Lat.* 230; " Magnificat," its use defended, 2 *Whitg.* 477, 482, 485; a copy in English verse, by Coverdale, 2 *Cov.* 565; the song of Mary the mother of Christ, &c. (poems), notice thereof, *Poet.* xl; extracts therefrom, *ib.* 422; her blessedness, 2 *Cov.* 350, *Pra. Eliz.* 530; her singular gifts and graces, 2 *Lat.* 227; she was full of grace, 1 *Ful.* 528; a virgin immaculate, and a vessel elect, 2 *Cov.* 414; her lowliness, 2 *Lat.* 92, *Pil.* 47; her faith, 2 *Lat.* 93; she was not without sin, 1 *Lat.* 383, 2 *Lat.* 117, 157, 225, 228, 358, *Rog.* 134, 1 *Tyn.* 316, 3 *Tyn.* 207; she confesses this in calling God her Saviour, 1 *Bec.* 316, 2 *Bec.* 170; many doctors admit that she was not faultless, and some of them declare that she was somewhat vainglorious, 1 *Lat.* 383, 515, 2 *Lat.* 117, 163, 164, 226, 359, 3 *Tyn.* 207; she was rebuked by Christ, 3 *Tyn.* 207; she was justified by faith, 1 *Ful.* 529; saved through faith, 1 *Lat.* 384, 2 *Lat.* 93, 116, 227; saved by Christ, 2 *Lat.* 226; not by her maternity, *ib.* 227; her obedience to the magistrates, 2 *Lat.* 96, 111; her poverty, *ib.* 107, 300; Mary the mother of our Lord, 2 *Cov.* 347, 350, *Now.* (34, 38), 151, 154, 155; the title θεοτόκος or Deipara vindicated by the fathers from scripture, *Whita.* 538; Nestorius would not call her by this name, 3 *Jew.* 224; the term allowed by Whitaker, *Whita.* 603; she suffered as other mothers, 2 *Lat.* 115; it is not so great a grace to be the mother of God as to be the child of God, 3 *Jew.* 578; she was blessed because she carried Christ in her heart, 2 *Jew.* 757, 3 *Jew.* 578; likened to a saffron-bag, 2 *Cov.* 347, 350, 1 *Lat.* 60; her perpetual virginity asserted, *Bale* 568, 4 *Bul.* 437, 2 *Cran.* 60, 88, 1 *Lat.* 517, 2 *Lat.* 105, *Phil.* 380, 2 *Tyn.* 227, 3 *Tyn.* 33; denied by Helvidius, 4 *Bul.* 437, 2 *Cran.* 60, 1 *Hoop.* 161, 3 *Jew.* 440, 441, 2 *Lat.* 105, *Phil.* 427, 2 *Tyn.* 339 n., *Whita.* 539, and by the Antidico-Marianites, *Whita.* 539; defended from scripture by the fathers, 2 *Cran.* 60, 3 *Jew.* 440, 441, *Whita.* 502, 539; not an article of faith according to Basil, *Whita.* 502, 539; maintained by Henry VIII., 2 *Tyn.* 339; it is not certain, 2 *Ful.* 273; no necessary article of faith, 3 *Tyn.* 96; she went to Jerusalem to hear the word of God, 2 *Lat.* 156; her heart pierced at the Saviour's passion, *Phil.* 270; some say that at the time of Christ's passion, the whole faith remained only in her, 3 *Jew.* 268; the Festival says time was when holiness was in her only, *Rog.* 172; More says that her faith alone never failed, 3 *Tyn.* 39 n.; Salmeron says she offered her Son, as Abraham offered Isaac, *Whita.* 164 n.; the story of her assumption fabulous, *ib.* 579, 580; declared by Jerome or his contemporary Sophronius to be apocryphal, *ib.* 667; Romish arguments for it, 1 *Tyn.* 159 n., 315; scripture does not teach that her body is in heaven, 3 *Tyn.* 28; she is not the "woman clothed with the sun" mentioned in the Apocalypse, *Bale* 404; old English verses on the life of the virgin Mary, from the Enchiridion Eccl. Sarum, *Pra. Eliz.* 139 n., 151 n., 155 n.; she is to be honoured, 2 *Cov.* 351; her true honour, 2 *Lat.* 228; superstitious honours paid to her, *ib.* 227; she is not to be worshipped, 3 *Jew.* 576, 2 *Lat.* 153; if a living woman loved God as much as our lady, her prayers would avail as much, 3 *Tyn.* 184; cardinal Bembo calls her our lady and goddess, 3 *Jew.* 577, 4 *Jew.* 949; she was called by a speaker in the council of Trent, God's most faithful fellow, 3 *Jew.* 121; said to be the saviour of men and women through her virginity, *Rog.* 298; Lipomanus says, no man may be saved but by her, 4 *Jew.* 949; a form of salutation of the virgin from the Horæ B. V. M., secundum usum Sarum, *Rog.* 220, 221; blasphemous addresses to her, 2 *Jew.* 899, 900, 1044, 1083; prayer offered to her for women with child, *Hutch.* 172; besought to command her Son, 1 *Tyn.* 316 n.; prayer for heaven through her compassion, *Rog.* 111; her relics worshipped, *ib.* 225; address to her girdle, 1 *Jew.* 535; popish images of the virgin, *Rog.* 223 (see Images, p. 411, col. 2); Officium Beatæ Virginis, 1 *Lat.* 426 n.; Lady Psalters or Rosaries, 1 *Brad.* 45, 588, 1 *Lat.* 425; ascribed to Urban II., 1 *Whitg.* 482; injunction against them, *Grin.* 163; the blasphemous Psalter of Bonaventure, 1 *Brad.* 588, 1 *Ful.* 528, 2 *Jew.* 899, 900,

1083, 3 *Jew.* 571, 1 *Tyn.* 150 n.; that of Brigit, *Pil.* 535; a blasphemous book called Mariale, by Bernardinus de Busti, 1 *Ful.* 528, 2 *Jew.* 900, 3 *Jew.* corrig.; The Mirror of our Lady cited, *Pra. Eliz.* 26 n.; the two St Mary days, the Conception and Purification, 1 *Tyn.* 91, 2 *Tyn.* 98; the feast of the Visitation of our Lady, commonly called the new-found Lady-day, decreed by Urban VI., *Pil.* 535

Mary Magdalene (St): mentioned as an example of repentance, *Poet.* 408, *Sand.* 310; notice of Mary Magdalene's Lamentations, (a poem, perhaps by Sir Nic. Breton): *Poet.* xl; extracts, *ib.* 434; why persuaded to implore Christ's mercy, 2 *Hoop.* 259; forgiven by Christ, *Hutch.* 92; we all be Magdalenes in falling into, but not in forsaking sins, 1 *Lat.* 16; said to have anointed Christ's feet, *Hutch.* 336, 1 *Lat.* 15; mention of the same event, 1 *Tyn.* 56; question whether Mary Magdalene was indeed the woman referred to as a penitent and spoken of in Luke vii. as anointing the Saviour's feet, 1 *Cov.* 329 n.; on the Lord's appearance to Mary Magdalene after his resurrection and his words "Touch me not," 1 *Cov.* 330, 1 *Jew.* 499, *Pra. B.* 150; images of her, *Calf.* 346

Mary, sister of Martha: chose the good part, 1 *Tyn.* 87

Mary, mother of John Mark: 2 *Bul.* 21

Mary (St), of Egypt: 1 *Jew.* 162

Mary, queen of England, *v.* Philip II., Privy Council, Statutes.

Reference to the lady Mary, afterwards queen, 1 *Lat.* 91; a prayer translated by her in the eleventh year of her age, *Lit. Eliz.* 250, *Pra. Eliz.* 107, 201 n.; a prayer commonly used by her, *Pra. Eliz.* 202 n.; the same in English, *ib.* 109; Ridley's interview with her at Hunsden, *Rid.* x. n.; letter from the council of Edward VI. to her when princess, on her using the mass, and admonishing her to conformity, 2 *Cran.* 526; two of her chaplains prosecuted for saying mass, *ib.* 526, 529; baptism performed in her house contrary to law, *ib.* 528; her mass-priests tolerated by Somerset, but sent to prison by Northumberland, 3 *Zur.* 439; attempt to carry her out of the kingdom, 3 *Zur.* 564 n., 568; she had been declared illegitimate, 2 *Cran.* 286, 3 *Zur.* 273; her accession and proclamation, 1 *Brad.* 16 n., 40 n., 2 *Brad.* xxx, 34 n., 3 *Zur.* 366, 367; her proclamation in Norfolk, *Sand.* ii; proceedings on her accession, 3 *Zur.* 100; she was styled supreme head of the church of England, 1 *Jew.* 61; she consents to Sandys being set at liberty, *Sand.* x; submits herself to the pope's authority, 2 *Cran.* 16, 2 *Lat.* 280; recalls cardinal Pole, 3 *Zur.* 741; letter from her to bp Gardiner, about disorders in the university of Cambridge, *Park.* 54 n.; her coronation, 3 *Zur.* 373; contradictory oaths taken by her, 2 *Cran.* 454; her precept to bp Bonner for the dissolution of the convocation, *Phil.* 214; proposals and preparations for her marriage, 2 *Tyn.* 319, 3 *Zur.* 343, 509, 510; her marriage solemnized, 1 *Brad.* 399 n., 580; it was a plague to England, *Now.* 228; Philip and Mary, their style, 2 *Cran.* 543; called Ahab and Jezebel, 3 *Zur.* 115; they issue a proclamation against books opposed to the pope, *Rid.* 280 n.; state of religion in queen Mary's days, contrasted with that of king Edward's days, *ib.* 49, &c.; the persecution under her, 2 *Zur.* 160, 249 n., violent, but of short duration, *Rog.* 5; a congregation of the faithful in London in her time, 1 *Brad.* 434 n., 2 *Brad.* 187 n., *Grin.* 203, 1 *Lat.* 313, 1 *Zur.* 7 n., 2 *Zur.* 29, 160, 3 *Zur.* 360 n.; she issues a proclamation for the apprehension of heretics, 3 *Zur.* 773; a compendious register in metre of the martyrs in her reign, by Tho. Bryce, *Poet.* 161; 288 persons burned from 1555 to 1558, *Grin.* 227 n.; declaration of the prisoners, addressed to her, 1 *Brad.* 399; Bradford acknowledges her to be the Lord's anointed, *ib.* 370, and prays for her, *ib.* 164; his letter to her sent with a supplication, *ib.* 401; the supplication to the king, queen, and parliament, *ib.* 403; Ridley's letter to her in behalf of certain poor men, tenants under the see of London; and of his sister, *Rid.* 427; Cranmer's letter to her, excusing the part he took under the will of Edward VI., 2 *Cran.* 442; his letter to her council on the same, and on his condemnation at Oxford, *ib.* 445; his letter to her on his being cited before the pope, and protesting against foreign jurisdiction and popish doctrines, *ib.* 447; his letter to her concerning her contradictory oaths, *ib.* 454; question whether God would change her heart or take her away, 3 *Bec.* 214, 215; her message to Elizabeth, shortly before she died, 1 *Zur.* 3; her death, *ib.*; her funeral, *ib.* 7; her tomb, *Now.* 229

Mary, queen of Scots: concealed in the mountains, 3 *Zur.* 37; her proposed marriage with Edward VI., 2 *Cran.* 154 n., 155 n.; carried into France, 3 *Zur.* 387 n., 643 n.; the wife of Francis II., king of France,

1 *Zur.* 89, 102; she banishes Jo. Knox, *ib.* 24; disputes between the queen and her subjects about the fortifying of Leith, *ib.* 59; she defends Leith, *ib.* 60; she retains the mass, *ib.* 104, 116, 124, 140, 167, 169, 2 *Zur.* 116; her intended marriage with Edm. Pole, *Lit. Eliz.* 655 n.; she seeks an interview with Elizabeth, 1 *Zur.* 115; their intended meeting at York, *ib.* 109; she sends queen Elizabeth presents, *ib.* 115, 120; demands of her parliament permission to hear mass, to declare war against England, and to retain her German guards, all which is refused, *ib.* 132; the conduct of her nobles, 3 *Jew.* 170, justified, *ib.* 173, 174; she marries lord Darnley, 1 *Zur.* 144; the heir presumptive to the crown of England, *ib.* 102; her devotion to popery, *ib.* 149; the murder of David Rizzio, 4 *Jew.* 1147, 1 *Zur.* 166 n., 170; birth of her son, afterwards king James, 2 *Zur.* 120; she is suspected of the murder of her husband lord Darnley, 1 *Zur.* 193, 197, 229, 251; marries the earl of Bothwell, *ib.* 192; escapes from Borthwick castle to Dunbar, *ib.* 193 n.; confined in Lochleven castle, *ib.* 196; she resigns the crown to her son, *ib.* 197, 2 *Zur.* 168; escapes from Lochleven, 1 *Zur.* 202; flees to castle Hamilton, *ib.* 203; association of nobles for her defence, *ib.* 205 n.; her letter to the laird of Nether Polloc, *ib.* 203 n.; her arrival in England, after the battle of Langside, *Park.* 325; she escapes to Carlisle, and is detained there, 1 *Zur.* 203; a prisoner in England, *ib.* 229, 239, 2 *Zur.* 308; at Bolton castle, 1 *Zur.* 210 n.; at Tutbury castle, *ib.*; transferred to Coventry, *ib.* 217, 247 n.; at Sheffield castle, *ib.* 260 n., 2 *Zur.* 223 n., 262 n.; the earl of Shrewsbury's regulations respecting her imprisonment there, 1 *Zur.* 260 n.; her intended marriage with Tho. duke of Norfolk, *Lit. Eliz.* 655 n., 1 *Zur.* 216, 229, 2 *Zur.* 172; rising in Norfolk for the deliverance of the queen and the duke, *Lit. Eliz.* 656 n., 1 *Zur.* 229; report of her being sought in marriage by the brother of the French king, 1 *Zur.* 239; she is declared the enemy of the kingdom, *ib.* 269; proposal to charge her with treason, *ib.* 278 n.; a plot for her deliverance, *Lit. Eliz.* 656 n.; reference to her, *Park.* 398, 446 n.; her character by Jewel, 4 *Jew.* 1279; her wickedness, 3 *Jew.* 173

Mary [of England], wife of Louis XII. of France: married by proxy to the emperor Charles V, 2 *Tyn.* 312; the marriage broken off, and the princess wedded to Louis XII., *ib.* 313

Mary [of Guise], 2nd wife of James V. of Scotland: 1 *Zur.* 39

Mary [of Portugal], 1st wife of Philip II. of Spain: 3 *Zur.* 510 n

Mary, queen dowager of Hungary, and governess of the Netherlands: 2 *Cran.* 231; she remonstrates with her brother, the emperor Charles V., against the establishment of the Inquisition in the Low Countries, 3 *Zur.* 417 n.; expected at Calais, *ib.* 343, 509; about to visit England, *ib.* 133; notice of her, *ib.* 343 n

Mascall (Rob.), bp of Hereford: *Bale* 7, 44

Mascall (Rob.), servant to R. Hilles: 2 *Zur.* 196

Mascaregnas (Ferd. Mart.): *v.* Indexes.

Mascelzer: a godly general, 1 *Bul.* 381 n

Masers: *v.* Bowls.

Maskell (Will.): *Lit. Edw.* xiii, *Lit. Eliz.* xxiii, *Pra. Eliz.* xi, &c.; Ancient Liturgy of the Church of England, 1 *Brad.* 8, 160, 2 *Brad.* 299, 310, 311, 2 *Cov.* 525 nn., *Lit. Eliz.* xxix; Monumenta Ritualia, 1 *Brad.* 46, 58, 589, *Lit. Eliz.* 250 n., *Pra. Eliz.* 26, 27, 57, &c. nn

Mason (Fra.): Works, by Lindsay, 2 *Ful.* 118 n., 128 n.; Of the Consecration of Bishops, by Lindsay, *Jew.* xl; his error with regard to the deposition or banishment of Abiathar, 2 *Ful.* 265 n

Mason (Sir Jo.): chancellor of Oxford, 1 *Bec.* 232 n.; mentioned, 3 *Zur.* 370; privy councillor to Mary and Elizabeth, 1 *Zur.* 5 n.; signature as such, *Park.* 155; appointed to examine into a complaint against bishop Bonner, 1 *Zur.* 7 n.; extract from a letter by him, *ib.* 185 n.; prayers by him, *Lit. Eliz.* 508 n., 516 n

Mass: *v.* Altars, Host, Intention, Liturgies, Massmongers, Missale, Opus operatum, Priests, Sacrifices, Transubstantiation; also Supper of the Lord.

The name unknown in the time of the apostles, 2 *Cov.* 469, 3 *Tyn.* 96; not used in the early church, 2 *Ful.* 81, 82; the old doctors used not the name, 1 *Jew.* 109, 110, 114, 3 *Jew.* 338, 4 *Jew.* 887; the word alleged to be taken from the Hebrew, 2 *Brad.* 304, 1 *Hoop.* 243, *Phil.* 94, *Pil.* 505, 506, 3 *Tyn.* 177, not from the Syriac, 2 *Brad.* 305; not used in Greek, *ib.* 304, 305; it is Latin, denoting the dismissal of the non-communicants, 2 *Bec.* 256, 3 *Bec.* 482, 2 *Brad.* 304, 2 *Jew.* 640, *Phil.* 94, *Pil.* 507; when first employed, 1 *Hoop.* 226; not named till c. A.D. 400, and then it meant a communion, 2 *Ful.* 81, 1 *Jew.* 23, 2 *Jew.* 640; first used by Ambrose, 2 *Ful.* 81 n.,

MASS

Pil. 507; employed by Augustine for the dismissal of the catechumens, 2 *Ful.* 82 n.; anciently used for the holy communion, *ib.* 7; sometimes it means an assembly of the people, 1 *Jew.* 180; alleged to mean a sending of Christ to his Father, 2 *Bec.* 454; the term used in reformed liturgies, *Lit. Edw.* 4, 76; the Romish doctrine of the mass, 2 *Bec.* 454, 3 *Bec.* 228, 229, 1 *Brad.* 373, 1 *Tyn.* 373; its four pillars, 1 *Brad.* 431 n., 2 *Brad.* 271, 2 *Cov.* 248, 250; its marrowbones, 2 *Lat.* 257, *Rid.* 112, 122; it is no ceremony of God's appointment, 1 *Hoop.* 174; not a sacrament of Christ, 2 *Hoop.* 451; very far from his institution, *Bale* 628; it is not, neither can be, the holy supper of the Lord, 1 *Brad.* 450, 2 *Brad.* 157, 1 *Cov.* 530, 531, 2 *Hoop.* 50, 51, 394, 413, but it is a horrible profanation thereof, 1 *Brad.* 85, 160, 2 *Brad.* 315, 1 *Hoop.* 31, 181, *Phil.* 221, 409, *Rid.* 401, 2 *Tyn.* 217, &c.; a mere enemy against God's word and Christ's institution, 2 *Hoop.* 126; it is not the Lord's supper, being deficient in several essential points, *Phil.* 66, 96; it is not a communion, *Rid.* 104; not the sacrament of unity, but of singularity, *ib.* 123; it doth not shew forth the Lord's death, *ib.* 104; the mass and the Lord's supper cannot go together, 2 *Brad.* 316, 345; contrast between the Lord's supper and the mass, 2 *Bec.* 455—457, 3 *Bec.* 283, 284, 356, &c., 387, &c., 2 *Hoop.* 465; A COMPARISON BETWEEN THE LORD'S SUPPER AND THE POPE'S MASS, by T. Becon, 3 *Bec.* 351; Christ compared with massmongers, 2 *Bec.* 451, 3 *Bec.* 267; the mass is no sacrament, *Phil.* 92, 118; it overthrows the sacrament, 1 *Brad.* 456; Papists assert that the first mass was said by Christ, *Pil.* 504; they report that Peter said mass at Rome, and James at Jerusalem, 1 *Jew.* 23; but the mass is never mentioned in the New Testament, *Rid.* 112; it is a new kind of sacrifice, 3 *Bec.* 265, *Rid.* 52; a yesterday's bird, 1 *Hoop.* 112; never heard of in early times, 2 *Cov.* 469; there were no papistical masses in the primitive church, 1 *Cran.* 352; how they entered, *ib.* 353; authorities alleged for the mass, 1 *Jew.* 108, 109; it is not catholic, *ib.* 80, *Pil.* 548; not sanctioned by true councils of the universal church, *Rid.* 130; it is the invention and ordinance of man, 1 *Cov.* 531, 2 *Hoop.* 32; set up by Antichrist, 3 *Bec.* 523; the sacrifice of Antichrist, 2 *Hoop.* 32; the device and doctrine of the devil, 2 *Brad.* 312, 1 *Cran.* 422, 1 *Lat.* 411; a delusion, *Rid.* 409; the blindness of Papists in celebrating it, 2 *Hoop.* 392; its sinfulness, 3 *Bec.* 207; to be abhorred of all good men, *ib.* 257; a monster of lies, *ib.* 263; sacrilegious, 2 *Hoop.* 508; horrible and blasphemous, 2 *Bec.* 448, 2 *Brad.* 231, 1 *Cran.* 348, 1 *Ful.* 241, 1 *Lat.* 445, *Rid.* 52, *Sand.* 43; masses are blasphemous fables and dangerous deceits, *Rog.* 299—301; the mass is a foul abomination, 1 *Lat.* 237; abominable and idolatrous, *Bale* 171, 215, 235, 236, 3 *Bec.* 253, 264, 267, 270, 274, 275, 278, 1 *Brad.* 280, 392, 2 *Brad.* 44, 48, 141, 227, 317, 318, 1 *Cran.* 229, 349, 350, 2 *Cran.* 172, 1 *Hoop.* 152, 311, 312, 2 *Hoop.* 395, 451, 518, 589, 610, 1 *Jew.* 10—13, 2 *Lat.* 440, *Rid.* 401, 409, 1 *Tyn.* 248, 2 *Tyn.* 217, 220; it makes the creature into the Creator, *Rid.* 51; it is a fellowship with devils, 2 *Brad.* 334, 3 *Bec.* 352; the table of devils, 3 *Bec.* 352, *Phil.* 250; the sacrifice of the devil, *Calf.* 231, 2 *Ful.* 166; like the groves in the old law, 2 *Brad.* 337; forbidden in scripture, *Grin.* 211; it does not appease, but provoke God's wrath, *Sand.* 12; Christ is thereby crucified afresh, *Bale* 393; there is nothing in the mass after God's word, 2 *Brad.* 336, 337, 1 *Hoop.* 140; it is a destruction of the true worshipping of God, 2 *Brad.* 313; it has no preaching, 3 *Bec.* 256; true preaching and massing cannot go together, 2 *Brad.* 314, 324; of the mass as a sacrifice, 2 *Jew.* 708, &c.; against the sacrifice of the mass, 2 *Bec.* 246, 414, 3 *Bec.* 196, 232, 265, 366, 1 *Brad.* 6—8, 2 *Brad.* 270, 285, 290, &c., 2 *Cov.* 249, 264, 269, &c., 1 *Cran.* 81, &c., 345, 362, 2 *Hoop.* (500), *Rid.* 206, &c.; the mass is neither a sacrifice propitiatory, nor of laud and praise, 1 *Cran.* 352; it agrees not with God's word, 2 *Bec.* 449, 450; the prophet Malachi spoke nothing of any offering propitiatory to be made by the priests when he said that everywhere should be offered unto God a pure sacrifice and oblation, 1 *Cran.* 351; St Paul's saying that " every high priest is ordained to offer gifts and sacrifices for sins," refers not to priests of the new testament, but of the old, *ib.*; on the doctrine that the priest has authority to offer up Christ to his Father, 3 *Bec.* 372, 377, 2 *Jew.* 708; difference between the sacrifice of Christ on the cross and that of the priests in the mass, 2 *Hoop.* 509; the latter cannot be propitiatory, 1 *Cran.* 345, 2 *Hoop.* 517; it is styled an unbloody sacrifice, *Rid.* 276; probations out of the old fathers that the mass is no propitiatory

MASS

sacrifice for the sins of the quick or dead, 3 *Bec.* 456, &c.; it is an enemy to Christ, his priesthood and sacrifice, being opposed to the all-sufficiency thereof, 2 *Bec.* 247, 248, 2 *Brad.* 312, 2 *Cov.* 264, 1 *Cran.* 348 —350, 1 *Ful.* 241, 2 *Ful.* 381, 1 *Hoop.* 500, 2 *Hoop.* 513, 1 *Lat.* 275, 445, *Rid.* 23, 52, 107, 275; on application of the virtue of Christ's passion thereby, 2 *Jew.* 746, &c.; refutation of the doctrine that the sacrifice of the mass is the principal means to apply the benefit of Christ's death to the quick and dead, 2 *Cov.* 266; questions concerning some abuses of the mass, with answers, 2 *Cran.* 150; questions and answers on some points connected with it, *ib.* 152; causes which moved Ridley to abstain from it, *Rid.* 103—110, 119; his answers to certain queries touching the abuses of the mass, *ib.* 316; arguments against the mass by Latimer, *ib.* 110; Romanists have a plurality of masses in one church in one day, 2 *Jew.* 625; but mass may be said by a priest once a day only, fasting, *Rid.* 56 n.; not to be said at night except on that of the Nativity, 1 *Jew.* 117; not to be said by married priests, *Pil.* 574; THE DISPLAYING OF THE POPISH MASS, by T. Becon, 3 *Bec.* 251; its histrionic character, *Phil.* 408; it is an acting of the sacrifice of Christ, 3 *Tyn.* 149; is a foolery and of no avail, 2 *Lat.* 58, 192; its manifold abuses, corruptions, and abominations, *Bale* 236, 1 *Brad.* 513, 1 *Cran.* 353, 354, 362, 1 *Jew.* 7, 8, *Rid.* 401; admitted even by its defenders, 1 *Jew.* 7, 8; the people are mocked at it, 3 *Bec.* 257, 258; the absurdity of saying it in Latin, 2 *Cran.* 169, *Rid.* 103; trifling forms, ceremonies, and gestures used in it, 3 *Bec.* 260, 265, 275, 276, 282, 283, 361, 362, 1 *Jew.* 15, 16, 2 *Jew.* 991, 2 *Lat.* xxiii, *Pil.* 498, *Rid.* 107, 108, 109, 110, 1 *Tyn.* 226, 247, 248, 2 *Tyn.* 220, &c., 3 *Tyn.* 73, 74, 96; it is full of prayers to saints, *Pil.* 498, 502; the massmonger's trinkets, 3 *Bec.* 362; apparel worn at mass, *ib.* 259, 262, 361, 2 *Tyn.* 221 n., 3 *Tyn.* 73, 117; the mass ascribed by the canon law to St James and Eusebius of Cæsarea, *Pil.* 501, 502; its antiquity denied, *ib.* 502; it was not complete till 700 years after Christ, *ib.* 504; it took longer in patching than Solomon's temple in building, *Hutch.* 21; its parts, and their origin, 2 *Brad.* 305, &c., 3 *Bec.* 257, 263, &c., *Pil.* 503; the confiteor, 3 *Bec.* 263, 2 *Brad.* 306, 2 *Tyn.* 220; the introit, 3 *Bec.* 263, 2 *Brad.* 305, 1 *Jew.* 302; the Kyrie, 3 *Bec.* 263, 2 *Brad.* 306, 1 *Jew.* 302, *Pil.* 503; the gloria in excelsis, 3 *Bec.* 263, 2 *Brad.* 307, *Pil.* 503; the collects, 3 *Bec.* 263, 2 *Brad.* 307; the epistle, 3 *Bec.* 263, 2 *Brad.* 307; the grail, 3 *Bec.* 264, 2 *Brad.* 306; the alleluia, 3 *Bec.* 264, 2 *Brad.* 306; the tract or sequence, 3 *Bec.* 264; the gospel, 3 *Bec.* 264, 2 *Brad.* 307; the creed, 3 *Bec.* 264, 2 *Brad.* 308; censing of the altar, 3 *Bec.* 264; the offertory, 3 *Bec.* 264, 2 *Brad.* 308; the prayer, "suscipe Sancta Trinitas," 3 *Bec.* 264; the washing of hands, 3 *Bec.* 265; the address, "orate pro me fratres," 3 *Bec.* 265, *Rid.* 108; the secreta, 2 *Jew.* 707; the preface, 3 *Bec.* 266, 2 *Brad.* 308; the sanctus, 3 *Bec.* 266, *Pil.* 503; the canon, by whom made, 3 *Bec.* 266, 1 *Brad.* 513, 2 *Brad.* 308, 1 *Jew.* 9, 96, 97, 302; attributed by a bishop of Sidon to the apostles, 3 *Jew.* 235, 4 *Jew.* 783; it recognizes the sacrifice of the people, 2 *Jew.* 737; abuses and blasphemous petitions in it, 1 *Jew.* 9, 10, 2 *Jew.* 738, *Rid.* 109, 110; ringing to sacry, 3 *Bec.* 266; memorial of the living, *ib.*; the words of consecration, 3 *Bec.* 269, 1 *Hoop.* 518, 1 *Tyn.* 96, 97; of consecration under silence, 2 *Jew.* 697, &c.; (*v.* Transubstantiation); the elevation, 3 *Bec.* 267, 270, 2 *Brad.* 310, 1 *Jew.* 507, &c.; not ordained by Christ, *Hutch.* 230; the adoration of the sacrament, 3 *Bec.* 267, 270, 1 *Cran.* 228, 229, 234, 235, 1 *Jew.* 514, &c., *Rid.* 106; it is a new device, 1 *Jew.* 10; the memorial of the dead, 3 *Bec.* 276; prayer for them, 1 *Hoop.* 518, 535; the second sacring, 3 *Bec.* 277; the breaking of the host, *ib.* 267, 278, 1 *Jew.* 18; the Agnus Dei, 3 *Bec.* 278; the kissing of the pax, *ib.* 279; of the priest receiving for others, 2 *Jew.* 739, &c.; commencement of the custom, 2 *Cran.* 151; the language of the mass itself implies a communion, 3 *Bec.* 279, 2 *Cran.* 171, 172; the cup denied to the laity, *Rid.* 105, 2 *Tyn.* 222; the rinsing of the chalice, &c., 3 *Bec.* 282; the post communion, *ib.* 279; the address "Ite missa est," *ib.* 282, *Rid.* 108; St John's gospel, 3 *Bec.* 282; hanging the host over the altar, a modern practice, and not used in Italy, 2 *Cran.* 172, 173; of the canopy, 2 *Jew.* 553; of private mass, 2 *Bec.* 453, 3 *Bec.* 365, 367, 4 *Bul.* 417, 1 *Jew.* 504, &c.; the term denotes sole receiving by the priest, *Coop.* 8, 9; an article de missa privata, 2 *Cran.* 480; AN APOLOGY OF PRIVATE MASS, *Coop.* 1—41; AN ANSWER thereto, by bp Cooper, *ib.* 43—224; against private mass, 1 *Jew.* 16, &c., 80, 104—203; it is of the devil, not of God, 3 *Bec.* 280; can by no means stand with the institution of Christ, 1 *Cov.* 531; not catholic, 1 *Jew.* 80; there was none in the primitive church, as Harding acknowledges, *ib.* 118; it is contrary to ancient canons, 2 *Cran.* 38; all the ancient liturgies bear witness against it, 2 *Bec.* 256, 3 *Bec.* 482, 483, 1 *Jew.* 19; the mass-book itself testifies against it, 1 *Jew.* 18; the ancient church of Rome knew none, 2 *Bec.* 239; it is of late origin, 2 *Brad.* 312; no mention made of it before pope Gregory I., 3 *Bec.* 418, to whom its institution is ascribed, *Hutch.* 227; said to have proceeded first of the negligence of the people, 1 *Jew.* 117, 118; the negligence of the people not a sufficient argument for it, *ib.* 121; the practice chiefly sprang from lucre, 1 *Cran.* 353; it is not used by the Eastern churches, 1 *Jew.* 18; the Greeks have none, 2 *Bec.* 239; the Armenians and Indians know it not, *ib.* 240; question respecting the practice of the Eastern churches and the Greeks at Venice, 4 *Jew.* 887, 1269, 1270; against the opinion that the priest's receiving of the bread and wine is the application of Christ's merits to us, 1 *Cov.* 530; private masses do not help the dead, *Bale* 152, 171; different kinds of masses, 3 *Bec.* 372, 1 *Lat.* 50, *Pil.* 80, 496; forenoon masses at St Paul's, *Pil.* 483, 528; a morrow-mass chaplain, *Phil.* 93; Good Friday mass, 1 *Jew.* 128, 245, 246, *Pil.* 507, 508; mass of requiem, *Pil.* 80, 496; mass for the dead, 2 *Cran.* 151; introduced by a delusion of Satan in the time of pope Gregory, 3 *Zur.* 212; it cannot help the dead, *Bale* 152, 171, 1 *Tyn.* 424, 425; (see Annals, Minds, Trentals; also Prayer for the dead); mass of scala-cœli (*q. v.*), 1 *Bec.* 191 n., 1 *Lat.* 50, 97, *Pil.* 80, 496; missa sicca, 3 *Bec.* 372; mass of the Holy Ghost, *Rid.* 129; the term explained, *ib.* 511; the sale of masses, and their price, 3 *Jew.* 552, *Pil.* 506; masses forbidden to be sold, 1 *Lat.* 55; why masses serve, 3 *Bec.* 229; the supposed virtues of the mass, *ib.* 283, 284; it serves for all purposes, *ib.* 284; all fortunate events ascribed to the virtue of it, *ib.* 242; it is alleged that masses purchase the assistance and favour of God, 1 *Cov.* 530; that being present at the sacrifice will give us speed in all our affairs, *ib.*; on " hearing mass," 1 *Jew.* 177—179; against so doing, 2 *Hoop.* 577; no goodness is learned at it, 3 *Bec.* 256; no man is the better for hearing it, *ib.* 256, 257; letter on the mass, to Hopkins and others at Coventry, 1 *Brad.* 389; THE HURT OF HEARING MASS, by J. Bradford, 2 *Brad.* 297—351; reasons used to prove that a man may go to mass, *ib.* 301—303, 335—350; we must not partake of it, and why, *Pil.* 171, 633; it is not to be attended by those who profess the gospel, 2 *Whitg.* 34; the sin of attending it, 2 *Brad.* 49, 52, 53, 125, 230—232, 317, 2 *Lat.* 441; the like question as to matins and evensong, 2 *Brad.* 200; going to mass is a breach of all the commandments, *ib.* 317—327; other scriptural reasons against going to it, *ib.* 327—334; to partake of it is idolatry, 1 *Hoop.* 152, 312; exhortation to cease from it, 3 *Bec.* 284, &c.; it is better to read the Bible than to hear it, *Bale* 149; how many mass-hunters there are, 2 *Bec.* 448; if a man attend mass he is deemed a good catholic, though his life be evil, 2 *Brad.* 314; the mass admired by the people, 3 *Bec.* 354; defenders of it transgress the commandments of God for the traditions of men, 2 *Hoop.* 390; against trusting in the popish mass, 1 *Bec.* 420; why Papists are loth to forego it, 2 *Bec.* 448; the incommodities that follow of it, *ib.*; it is the nurse of all vices, 3 *Bec.* 256; the fruits of it, *ib.* 366, 389; poison has been administered therein, *Sand.* 66; the mass ought to be overthrown, and the true use of the Lord's supper restored, 3 *Bec.* 394, 395; the epistle and gospel directed to be read in English, 2 *Cran.* 501; the mass abolished in England, 3 *Zur.* 377; massmongers thereupon caused the insurrection in Devonshire, 2 *Bec.* 596; a priest imprisoned for celebrating mass at Oxford, and the hearers fined, 3 *Zur.* 467; verses, de missa apud Anglos per evangelium e medio sublata, 3 *Bec.* 352; epitaphium missæ, *ib.* 395; all the rites of it should be taken away, 1 *Hoop.* 440; it should not be counterfeited in the communion, 2 *Hoop.* 127; imitations of it in king Edward's time, 3 *Zur.* 72; the mass established again on the accession of queen Mary, 2 *Hoop.* 589, 3 *Zur.* 373; its abolition on the accession of Elizabeth, 1 *Zur.* 29, 2 *Zur.* 19; its rites still imitated by some in England, 2 *Zur.* 26; names of hearers or sayers of mass to be presented to the ordinary, *Grin.* 144; Mistress Missa, a book ascribed to Dr Turner, *Rid.* 108, 510; its proper title is, A new Dialogue wherein is contained the Examination of the Mass, &c., 2 *Brad.* 287 n., *Rid.* 510 (see also *Cov.* 266); A newe Dialogue called the Endightment agaynste Mother Messe, 1548, *Rid.* 511; The

Burying of the Mass, by W. Roye, 1 *Tyn.* 39, 40; epitaphium missæ, 3 *Bec.* 395

Mass-Johns: *Calf.* 52 n

Massmongers: the character of massmongers, 3 *Bec.* 389, 390; they mass not except well rewarded, *ib.* 365, 366; celebrate in a corner privately, *ib.* 379; stand at an altar, *ib.* 356; come to the altar with no previous examination of themselves, *ib.* 384; use gorgeous furniture, and divers trinkets, *ib.* 362; celebrate mass put together by divers popes, *ib.* 372; minister in an unknown tongue, *ib.* 362, 363; provoke God's anger by their many profanations of the mysteries, *ib.* 384, &c.; use cake and wine mingled with water, *ib.* 359; deprave Christ's words, *ib.* 357, 358; do nothing of that which Christ commanded, *ib.* 358; deny Christ, 1 *Lat.* 522; declare that they offer a propitiatory sacrifice, 3 *Bec.* 366; boast that they offer Christ for the sins of the quick and dead, *ib.* 372, 377; usurp Christ's office, 1 *Lat.* 275; invoke dead saints, 3 *Bec.* 356; consecrate the bread and wine to saints departed, *ib.* 373; deny that the substance of bread and wine remains after consecration, *ib.* 369, &c., 378, 379; lift up the sacrament to be gazed at and worshipped, *ib.* 359, &c.; insist that the eating of the priest alone profits others, *ib.* 375; make the Lord's supper a private breakfast, 2 *Bec.* 453; give nothing to those that stand by, 3 *Bec.* 365, 367; apply the sacrament to the dead, *ib.* 379; declare that Easter is the time to receive the Lord's supper, moving the people to partake but once a year, *ib.* 380, 381; put back no man, however wicked, *ib.* 383, 384; assert that the unfaithful, and even animals may eat the body of Christ, *ib.* 378, 379; at communion time they distribute to persons kneeling at an altar, *ib.* 364; deliver the sacrament privately, *ib.* 374; suffer not the people to take the bread into their hands, *ib.* 363, 364; take the cup away from the laity, *ib.* 364; declare that the sacrament gives grace ex opere operato, *ib.* 358, 380; so patch up their mass as to allure rather to Antichrist than to Christ, *ib.* 376; so that those who hear go away the more disposed to sin, *ib.* 376, 377; neither have weak consciences any consolation, *ib.* 377, 378; reserve the sacrament, *ib.* 373—375; heap mass on mass, *ib.* 368, 369; have innumerable kinds of masses, *ib.* 372; make the mass a salve for all diseases, *ib.* 372; handle their mass so as to be an occasion of enmity, *ib.* 374; inflame to earthly not heavenly things, *ib.*; go away (from the mass) prepared for any evil, *ib.* 366; the fearful state they are in, *ib.* 284; they are double dissemblers, *ib.* 257; never preach, *ib.* 356; mislead the people, 1 *Lat.* 314, 2 *Lat.* 441; declare that Christ's death puts away only original sin, 2 *Bec.* 368; caused the insurrection in Devonshire, 2 *Bec.* 596; frequent houses filled with evil company, 3 *Bec.* 358, 359; comparison between them and Christ, 2 *Bec.* 451, 3 *Bec.* 267

Massacre: *v.* Paris.

At Vassey, and other places in France, *Rog.* 6

Massæus (Christian.): Chronic. Libri, *Jew.* xl, *Whitg.* xxx; he mentions the patriarchate of Antioch, 2 *Whitg.* 201; speaks of pope Joan, 4 *Jew.* 656; refers to the error of pope John XXII., *ib.* 932, 933, 934, 936

Massarius (Hierome): letter to Bullinger, 3 *Zur.* 342

Masser: Sir John Masser; one who offers mass, 2 *Brad.* 324

Massers: *v.* Masers.

Massey (......): his illegal contract of marriage, 2 *Cran.* 328

Mass-Johns, and Massmongers: *v.* supra.

Massurius Sabinus: on the word religion, 3 *Bul.* 230

Massye (Tho.): a Protestant member of parliament, 1 *Brad.* 374 n

Master (Rich.), parson of Aldington: concerned in the imposture of Eliz. Barton, 2 *Cran.* 272 n., 1 *Tyn.* 327 n

Master (Will.): in exile at Frankfort, 3 *Zur.* 764

Master of the Sentences: *v.* Peter Lombard.

Masters: *v.* Householders, Obedience, Prayers, Servants, Schoolmasters.

Their duty, 1 *Bec.* 287, 2 *Bec.* 359, &c., 520, 1 *Bul.* 281, 1 *Lat.* 351, 394, 538, 2 *Lat.* 6, *Pra. Eliz.* 237; their duty to their servants, with probations of scripture, 2 *Bec.* 520; the office of a master, and how he ought to rule, 1 *Tyn.* 201; masters must not be over-rigorous, 2 *Bec.* 362; must perform their covenants, and not over-burden their servants, *ib.* 362, 363; must govern their servants godly, *ib.* 359; the order of prayers in their households, *ib.* 359, 360; must carry their households to church on Sundays, &c., *ib.* 360; must take care that no vice creep in their households, *ib.* 361; must take care that there be no filthy singing in their households, but that psalms be sung, *ib.* 361; must not suffer their servants to swear, 1 *Bec.* 388; must set a good example, 2 *Bec.* 361, 362, imitating the pattern of David, *ib.* 362; their commandments when contrary to God's word are not to be obeyed, *ib.* 364; petition for them, 3 *Bec.* 37

Masters of Arts: 1 *Jew.* 29

Masters (......), father of Richard: his death, 3 *Zur.* 359

Masters (Rich.): converted by means of Bullinger, 2 *Zur.* 63; his illness, 1550, 3 *Zur.* 359, 419; physician to queen Elizabeth, 2 *Zur.* 11; his letters, *ib.* 55, 61, 114, 3 *Zur.* 358; letter to him, 2 *Zur.* 11

Masters (......): Hist. of C. C. C. Cambridge, 2 *Lat.* 376 n., *Park.* 16 n., 19 n

Masting: feeding on mast, 2 *Bec.* 425; masty; full of mast, or eating mast, 3 *Bec.* 383

Matchett (......), parson of Thurgarton: Parker writes to him against prophesyings, *Park.* 456, 457 n

Maternus (Firmicus): his books on astronomy, 2 *Jew.* 872

Mathematicals: astrologers, 1 *Bul.* 221, 2 *Bul.* 232, 1 *Hoop.* 330

Mather (......): hired by the Spanish ambassador's secretary to murder lord Burghley and the queen, *Grin.* 332 n.; executed, 2 *Zur.* 198 n

Mathewe (......), vicar of Howe: sent to the Marshalsea, *Park.* 76

Mathilda, wife of Lewis II. of Bavaria: 2 *Zur.* 274 n

Matins: *v.* Hours.

Matravers (Mr): 3 *Zur.* 612, 618

Matrimony: *v.* Marriage.

Matthæus Blastar, or Hieromonachus: *Jew.* xl; he speaks of Constantine honouring the pope, 4 *Jew.* 690, 692; his account of Constantine's Donation, *ib.* 839, 841

Matthæus à Michovia: De duobus Sarmat., *Jew.* xl; he says the emperor Henry III. caused four kings of Vindelicia to carry pans to his kitchen, 4 *Jew.* 702; declares that Isidore, abp of Kiovia in Russia, was deposed and put to death for attempting to move his people to submit to the pope, *ib.* 740

Matthæus Palmerius, *q. v.*

Matthæus (Jo.): commanded men to burn all books except the Bible, *Rog.* 326 n

Matthew (St): Chrysostom says he had the care of all the world, 3 *Jew.* 319

— His Gospel written in Hebrew, 1 *Ful.* 30 n.; testimonies respecting the Hebrew original, *Whita.* 125, 126; Whitaker thinks them not conclusive, *ib.* 126; some think he wrote his gospel in Hebrew, and that St John translated it into Greek, 1 *Jew.* 237; the Hebrew gospel of St Matthew confounded by Harding with the apocryphal gospel of the Hebrews, *ib.* 238; Irenæus on the date of St Matthew's gospel, *Whita.* 552; Theophylact and others on its date, *ib.* 519; Tyndale's prologue to it, 1 *Tyn.* 468; his exposition of chapters v. vi. vii., with a prologue, 2 *Tyn.* 1; notice of the same, 1 *Tyn.* li, lii; his marginal notes on chapters i.—xxi., 2 *Tyn.* 226—236; argument of St Matthew's gospel, and contents of each chapter, 3 *Bec.* 567, &c.; Jerome's remarks on his citations from the Old Testament, 1 *Ful.* 30 n., 50; the imperfect commentary cited, *ib.* 589; (i. e. the Opus Imperfectum, wrongly ascribed to Chrysostom, *q. v.*); this gospel rejected by Cerdon, Marcion, &c., *Whita.* 34

Matthew, archdeacon of Antioch: aids Mahomet, *Bale* 572

Matthew, prefect of Barbelrode: 2 *Cov.* 510, 521, &c.

Matthew (......): *v.* Mathewe.

Matthew (Rich.): servant to Grindal, *Grin.* 462

Matthew (Tho.): the supposed name of a merchant who contributed towards the publication of the Bible called Matthew's, 1 *Tyn.* lxxiv; see Bible, *English*, 1537.

Matthew (Tho.): a Protestant member of parliament, 1 *Brad.* 374 n

Matthew (Tobias), abp of York: sometime dean of Christ Church, *Grin.* xiv, 473; he married Frances (Barlow), widow of Matthew, son of abp Parker, 3 *Bec.* 501 n., 2 *Zur.* 263 n

Matthew Paris: supposed to have been born in Bohemia, 4 *Jew.* 651; his Historia Major, *Jew.* xl; extracts from his chronicle sent to Parker, *Park.* 140; Parker borrows his chronicle of Cecil, *ib.* 353; it is printed, *ib.* 388 n.; what he says of pope Urban II., 1 *Whitg.* 482 n.; he speaks of the misconduct of a papal legate, in the time of Henry I., *Sand.* 224; gives an account of king John's attempts at reformation, 2 *Tyn.* 19 n.; shews that the pope called that prince his vassal, 4 *Jew.* 1078; and that he sentenced him to be deposed, *ib.* 687; writes of papal exactions, *ib.* 1079, 1080, 1081; records the resignation of N. de Farnham, bishop of Durham, *Grin.* 399 n.; says that Edward I. forbade bishops to go to Rome, &c., *Pil.* 583, 584

Matthew of Westminster: Flores Historiarum, 2 *Ful.* 23, *Jew.* xl; he records the death of Augustine of Canterbury, 4 *Jew.* 780, 782; repeats the falsehood of Malmesbury concerning Bede's journey to Rome, 2 *Ful.* 119 n.; says the pope had the tenths of all the spiritual livings in England during the space of ten whole years, 4 *Jew.* 1080

Matthias (St): *v.* Apocrypha, ii.
    His election, 4 *Bul.* 131, 132, 133, 1 *Ful.* 465, 466, 1 *Tyn.* 259, 328, 1 *Whitg.* 296, 339, 357, 469; Abdias says he desired two of the stones he was martyred with to be buried with him, 1 *Jew.* 245

Matthias, king of Hungary: 1 *Zur.* 47 n

Matthias Paris: *v.* Matthew.

Matthias (......): his widow, 3 *Zur.* 44

Mattishall, co. Norfolk: *Park.* x, 484; abp Parker's benefaction to the poor, *ib.* xiii.

Maudlin (Dr): 3 *Zur.* 202 n

Maugre: examples of the use of the word, *Hutch.* 346

Maukin, or Malkin: a slattern, *Calf.* 236; mother Maukin, *ib.* 236, 251, 284

Maunchet: *v.* Manchet.

Maund: a hand-basket, *Grin.* 51 n., *Hutch.* 346

Maunder (......), a rebel: 2 *Cran.* 187 n

Maundvyld (Tho.), rector of Petworth: letter to him, 2 *Cran.* 278

Maundy [mandatum]: *Grin.* 51, *Hutch.* 221, 259, 346, 1 *Tyn.* 259, 3 *Tyn.* 236

Maundy Thursday: altar-stones washed on that day, *Bale* 528, 1 *Bec.* 116; consecration of the sacrament thereon in the Latin church, *Coop.* 18, 2 *Cran.* 174, 1 *Jew.* 245; the pope's bull, In cœna Domini, 2 *Cran.* 74, 167; the day styled Shere, or Shire, Thursday [i. e. Shrive-Thursday, from confession on it], *Coop.* 18, 2 *Cran.* 174, 1 *Jew.* 246

Maurice (St): his martyrdom, 2 *Bec.* 91, 473

Maurice, elector of Saxony: 2 *Cran.* 439, 2 *Zur.* 125 n., 3 *Zur.* 258, 456 n., 650, 679

Mauritania: Leo writes to the bishop (or bishops) thereof, 3 *Jew.* 406

Mauritius, emperor: *Bale* 503, 4 *Bul.* 139, 515, 2 *Hoop.* 234, 235, 293, 555, 1 *Jew.* 363, 3 *Jew.* 310, *Pil.* 518, 521

Maurus (R.): *v.* Rabanus.

Mauzim: *v.* Maozim.

Mawmet, or Mammet [from Mahomet]: a puppet, *Bale* 438 n., 1 *Bec.* 285, *Calf.* 31; mawmetry; i. e. idolatry, *Calf.* 175 n., 176; mammetrous, *Bale* 165

Maxentia (St): *Bale* 192

Maxentius, emperor: a persecutor, 1 *Lat.* 129, 1 *Whitg.* 407; his death, 1 *Bul.* 318

Maxentius: says that heretics when they cannot give a reason for their perversity, fall to railing, 3 *Jew.* 131

Maxfield, near Winchelsea: the birthplace of Greg. Martin, 1 *Ful.* xii.

Maximian, emperor: 1 *Hoop.* 387; supposed inscription to him and Diocletian, 2 *Ful.* 217; his appointment of idolatrous priests, 2 *Whitg.* 391, 392

Maximilian I., emperor: became king Henry's soldier, 2 *Tyn.* 311; his law against swearing, 1 *Bec.* 391

Maximilian II., emperor: crowned king of the Romans, *Grin.* 19; he opposes the Turks in Hungary, *Lit. Eliz.* 533 n.; seeks the crown of Poland, 2 *Zur.* 278 n

Maximin, emperor: 1 *Bul.* 378, 2 *Bul.* 105, 1 *Hoop.* 169, *Hutch.* 113; burned the scriptures, 2 *Jew.* 690; burned a church where many were assembled to celebrate the nativity of Christ, *ib.* 976; a judgment upon him caused him to call in his proclamation against the Christians, *ib.* 977

Maximin, an Arian bishop: opposed by Augustine, 2 *Cran.* 36

Maximinian, emperor: 2 *Bul.* 73, 79, 106

Maximus, emperor: *Whita.* 443

Maximus: his martyrdom, 2 *Bul.* 105

Maximus, bp of Jerusalem: led out of the council of Palestine by Paphnutius, 4 *Jew.* 951

Maximus Taurinensis: Homiliæ, *Jew.* xl; sermons of his attributed to Ambrose and others, *Calf.* 177 n., 2 *Ful.* 154, 155, 340 n., 1 *Jew.* 499, 4 *Jew.* 1078 n., *Whita.* 667; he says, I read of Peter's tears, not of his satisfaction, 2 *Jew.* 1135; remarks that the tear washes away the offence which shame would not suffer to confess with speech, *ib.* 1134; is uncertain whether Peter or Paul should be preferred, 1 *Jew.* 430; says, Mary could not touch Christ, because she sought him upon the earth; but Stephen touched him, because he sought him in heaven, 1 *Jew.* 499, 542, 2 *Jew.* 741, 1043, 3 *Jew.* 548; declares that a church cannot stand without a cross, &c., *Calf.* 177, 179, 2 *Ful.* 155

Maximus the Scholiast: wrote scholia on the pseudo-Dionysius, *Jew.* xl, *Whita.* 252; says the elements are symbols, not the truth itself, 2 *Jew.* 611, 624; cited for the elevation, 1 *Jew.* 507, 511, 512; speaks of the bread and cup as set forth covered, *ib.* 510; and of their being shewn, *ib.* 511

Maximus, an Arian: the alleged author of the "Opus imperfectum" ascribed to Chrysostom, *Whita.* 684

Maxwell (...... lord): taken prisoner at Solway moss, 3 *Zur.* 239 n.; mentioned, *ib.* 429

Maxwell (......), brickmaker: 1 *Tyn.* 33

May: mare (i. e. May) lady, 2 *Bec.* 346, 370; May bishops, 4 *Jew.* 997

May games: *Grin.* 141, 175; thought sufficient cause for excommunication by the Scottish presbytery, *Rog.* 311

May (Jo.), bp of Carlisle: 2 *Cran.* 264 n

May (Will.): vicar-general of Ely, 2 *Cran.* 264 n.; his interview with Henry VIII., *Park.* 34; president of Queens' college, *ib.* 38 n., 67; a commissioner for the revision of the Prayer Book, *Grin.* v, *Rid.* 316; a royal visitor of Cambridge, 2 *Brad.* 370, *Grin.* 194, *Rid.* 169; dean of St Paul's, *Phil.* xxx, *Rid.* 328; an ecclesiastical commissioner, *Park.* 107, 439; queen Elizabeth's almoner, *Now.* 229; nominated abp of York, but died unconsecrated, *ib.* 229, *Park.* 123 n.; his death, 1 *Zur.* 93; letter to Parker, *Park.* 38

Maydewell (......), a Scotch friar: 2 *Cran.* 339

Mayence: *v.* Councils.

What the archbishop paid for his pall, *Pil.* 583; the Golden Swan, 3 *Zur.* 52

Mayer (Wolfg.): *v.* Meyer.

Mayfield, co. Sussex: Cranmer's manor, 2 *Cran.* 253; probably meant by Maxfield, *q. v.*

Maynard (......): *v.* Mainarde.

Maynard (Hen.): *Park.* 469

Mayro (Fra. de): *v.* Maronis.

Mazzoreth: the use thereof, 1 *Ful.* 78

Meadows (James): account of him, 2 *Zur.* 327 n

Meagher (Andr.): Popish Mass, *Calf.* 302 n

Meale: to melt, 2 *Bec.* 501

Means: must be used, 3 *Bul.* 181, 1 *Lat.* 528, 543, *Pil.* 328; to be used, not trusted in, *Pil.* 194; to be joined with prayer, *ib.* 412

Mearing (Marg.): *v.* Mering.

Meat: *v.* Graces.

Continency in it, 1 *Bul.* 423; the choice of it, *ib.* 431; why God forbad the eating of certain meats, 2 *Bul.* 211; the choice abrogated, *ib.* 271; Popish differences in meats, 2 *Hoop.* 56, *Pil.* 46; sumptuary agreement made by the bishops and church dignitaries, 2 *Cran.* 491

Meat-offering: 2 *Bul.* 191

Meath (H. bp of): *v.* Brady.

Medals: *v.* Coins.

Meddled: mingled, *Phil.* 330

Meddows (James): *v.* Meadows.

Mede, or Meed: reward, 3 *Bec.* 196

Mede (Jos.): *Calf.* 32 n., 1 *Cov.* 451 n., 2 *Ful.* 386 n

Medes: kingdom of the Medes and Persians, *Pil.* 186, 187; the Medes had famous schools, 4 *Bul.* 480

Media vita: verses, apparently a translation from the Latin, 2 *Cov.* 554

Media Villa (Rich. de), or Middleton: notice of him, 1 *Tyn.* 153 n.; on the four divisions of hell, *Rog.* 215 n

Mediators: *v.* Christ.

The term, *Now.* (102); the two mediators, of the law and of the gospel, 2 *Cran.* 177; vain distinction between mediators of intercession and of redemption or salvation, 1 *Hoop.* 35, 3 *Jew.* 573, &c., 2 *Lat.* 233; there is only one, viz. Jesus Christ (*q. v.*), 3 *Jew.* 571, 573; the pope sets himself up for one, 2 *Cran.* 177

Medici family: 2 *Cran.* 331 n

Medici (Giulio de), afterwards pope Clement VII., *q. v.*

Medici (Hipp. card. de): 2 *Cran.* 234, 2 *Tyn.* 275 n

Medicine: *v.* Physic.

Medina Cœli (The duke of): 1 *Zur.* 275, 2 *Zur.* 206 n

Meditation: the benefit of it, 1 *Brad.* 559, 566

Meditations: *v.* Affliction, Christ, Commandments, Creed, Death, God, Heaven, Life everlasting, Prayer, Prayer (The Lord's), Supper.

GODLY MEDITATIONS, by J. Bradford, 1 *Brad.* 113, &c.; CHRISTIAN PRAYERS AND MEDITATIONS, *Pra. B.* 1, &c.; meditations concerning the sober usage of the body, 1 *Brad.* 187; concerning the pleasures of this life, *ib.* 188; for the exercise of true mortification, *ib.* 190, *Pra. B.* 96; for the different times of the day, 1 *Brad.* 230, &c.; daily meditations (from Lud. Vives), on rising, *Pra. B.* 60; on the daylight, *ib.* 61; on rising, *ib.* 62; on dressing, *ib.* 63; on beginning the day, *ib.* 64; on going abroad, *ib.* 67; on a journey, *ib.* 68; before meat, *ib.* 69; at meal-time, *ib.* 70; after meat, *ib.* 71; at mid-day, *ib.* 72; on returning home, *ib.* 73; at sunset, *ib.*; on lighting candles, *ib.* 74; on undressing, *ib.* 75; on retiring to rest, *ib.* 76; meditations written by Bradford in a copy of Tyndale's Testament, 1 *Brad.* 248—257; A FORM OF MEDITATION for the plague, *Grin.* 264, 477; a meditation (penitential), by W. Hunnis, *Poet.* 155; de vitæ hujus fragilitate, et spe resurrectionis vitæque æternæ, from scripture and the burial service, *Pra. Eliz.* 358; mors, tua mors, Christe, &c., verses thereon by C. T., *Poet.* 395

Medman (Peter): 3 *Zur.* 538

Medowes (James): *v.* Meadows.

Medwel (Jo.): in exile, 1 *Cran.* (9)

Medwin (St): sent from Rome to Lucius, *Park.* 295

Medy: Milan, *Phil.* 373
Meed: to deserve, 1 *Jew.* 13
Meek: who they are, 1 *Lat.* 480; their reward, *ib.* 482; how they inherit the earth, 2 *Tyn.* 20
Meer-stone: a boundary-stone, 2 *Bul.* 230
Megander (Gasp.): 3 *Zur.* 236, 250, 615, 633; his widow, *ib.* 252
Meghem (The count): 1 *Zur.* 205 n
Megil: 2 *Bul.* 135
Meier (Wolfg.): *v.* Meyer.
Mekerchius (Adolph): 1 *Ful.* xiv.
Mekim (Rich.): burned, 3 *Zur.* 221 n
Melancthon (Phil.): his birth, *Lit. Eliz.* 445; one of the principal champions at the conference at Marpurg, *Grin.* 251 n.; he drew up the confession of Augsburg, 2 *Zur.* 15 n.; wrote an apology for it, *ib.* 103 n.; at Paris, 1 *Tyn.* liv; notice of the Simplex ac pia deliberatio, &c., 1535, drawn up by him and Bucer, *Lit. Eliz.* xxix. n., 2 *Zur.* 18 n.; he attends a conference at Wittenberg, 1 *Jew.* 469; his want of firmness in the case of the landgrave Philip, 3 *Zur.* 666 n.; present at his marriage, 2 *Cran.* 405 n.; invited to England, *ib.* 420 n., 421 n., 422, 423, 431, 3 *Zur.* 17, 18, 21, 725; expected to come, 1 *Lat.* 141; dissuaded from coming, 3 *Zur.* 616; he proposes a synod of Protestant divines, *ib.* 713 n.; letter inviting him to a conference to form a declaration of faith on the sacrament, 2 *Cran.* 433; he went to the council of Trent, *Whita.* 10; his opinion of the Interim, 2 *Zur.* 126 n.; his death, *ib.* 71 n.; references to him, 2 *Lat.* 314, *Rog.* v.n.; his Loci Communes, 1 *Brad.* 20, 2 *Brad.* 7, *Rid.* 280; reference to an epistle on the Eucharist by him, 3 *Tyn.* 258 n.; wrote a treatise De integri usu sacramenti, *Coop.* 167; notice of his Responsiones ad impios articulos Bavaricæ Inquisitionis, 1 *Zur.* 110 n.; reference to MS. notes by him, *Calf.* 305 n.; letter from him to Bucer, 3 *Zur.* 556; letters to him, 2 *Cran.* 433, 3 *Zur.* 21, 25; Bradford's preface to his Treatise of Prayer, 1 *Brad.* 19; the Introduction to Bull's Prayers, taken in great part from him, *Pra. B.* vii; precatio ante cibum, carmine reddita, *Pra. Eliz.* 400; his works burned in Oxford, *Rid.* 280; his doctrine, 2 *Ful.* 377; on Gen. i. 2, "the spirit of God moved," &c., *Hutch.* 65, 196; his opinion respecting Christ's humanity, 3 *Zur.* 688; he opposes the error of Stancarus, 1 *Zur.* 127 n.; his early views on predestination, 3 *Zur.* 325; his opinion on the number of sacraments, 3 *Jew.* 455, 456, 460; upon the eucharist, *Coop.* 37, 1 *Cran.* 20, *Rid.* 160, 3 *Zur.* 544 n.; on transubstantiation, *Rid.* 158; he says Ambrose would never have travailed to accumulate so many miracles as he did, had he not thought the nature of bread to be changed in the mystery of the Lord's supper, 1 *Cran.* 178, he means a sacramental change, *ib.* 179; on communion under one kind, 1 *Jew.* 217—219; upon figurative speeches, 1 *Cran.* 137; he expounds Heb. vi. of the sin against the Holy Ghost, *Hutch.* 117; on the church's rejection of apocryphal writings, 3 *Whitg.* 621; his opinion of the old doctors, 2 *Lat.* 268; he explains a statement by Augustine respecting the authority of the church, *Rid.* 128; describes disorders in Germany about things indifferent, *Rog.* 317 n.; declares that when the opinion of holiness, of merit, or necessity, is put unto things indifferent, then they darken the light of the gospel, and ought by all means to be taken away, *Grin.* 210; relates a vision he had read of, 3 *Bec.* 390; discusses questions respecting magistracy, &c., 1 *Bul.* 308, 323 n.; writes of community of goods, 2 *Bul.* 21

Melancthonici: an alleged sect, 2 *Jew.* 686
Melchiades, bp of Rome: *v.* Melciades.
Melchior: one of the three kings, *Rog.* 228, *Whita.* 560
Melchizedek, king of Salem: a type of Christ, 1 *Brad.* 590, 3 *Bul.* 282, 1 *Cov.* 55, 56, 2 *Ful.* 260, *Pil.* 370, *Whita.* 168, 169; how said to be without father and mother, &c., *Grin.* 41, 2 *Jew.* 1111; his priesthood, 2 *Jew.* 720; his bread and wine, whether a sacrifice, 4 *Bul.* 439, 1 *Ful.* 148, 149, 513—515, *Hutch.* 238 n., 1 *Jew.* 110, 2 *Jew.* 712, 730—732, *Sand.* 454, 1 *Tyn.* 256 n., *Whita.* 167, 168; erroneously thought by some to be the Holy Ghost, 3 *Jew.* 233, *Rog.* 71; compared by Durandus to the pope, 4 *Bul.* 118, 1 *Jew.* 373
Melciades, bp of Rome: refers to a supposed authority given by Christ to Peter, 1 *Jew.* 339 n.; his decree about the communion, *ib.* 159, 160, 239; he calls confirmation a sacrament, *Calf.* 222, 3 *Jew.* 456; an epistle bearing his name contradicts St Luke, 1 *Jew.* 342; the Donatists referred to him, *Whita.* 436; he sat, to determine a cause, with divers other bishops, 1 *Jew.* 394
Meletius, bp of Lycopolis: called archbishop of Egypt, 2 *Whitg.* 160, 161; erred on sin after baptism, 1 *Hoop.* 169, *Hutch.* 113; was deposed from his bishoprick, 1 *Whitg.* 408
Melito, bp of Sardis: on the canon of the

Old Testament, 4 *Bul.* 540, 2 *Ful.* 222 n., *Whita.* 56, 62; he wrote on the Apocalypse, *Bale* 255
Mell: meddle, *Rid.* 415
Mellitus, bp of London: sent to preach in England, 3 *Jew.* 163; consecrated by Augustine, 4 *Jew.* 779, 780
Melor (St), of Cornwall: *Bale* 192
Meltiades, bp of Rome: *v.* Melciades.
Melvil (Sir James): 1 *Zur.* 195, 2 *Zur.* 311 n
Melville (Andrew): 2 *Zur.* 331 n., 333
Melville (James), minister of Fernie: 2 *Zur.* 331 n., 365
Melvin (Mr): 2 *Zur.* 333; the Melvins, *ib.* 335
Membra Christi: *Now.* (102)
Memoriale Historiarum: a manuscript, 3 *Jew.* 276
Memorials: *v.* Dead.
Memories: months' minds, and the like, *Grin.* 136 n.; commemorations; so in the communion service, *Pil.* 535; memoriæ; monuments, shrines, or tombs, 2 *Tyn.* 161, 3 *Tyn.* 60, 272 n
Memory: natural, artificial, spiritual, 2 *Hoop.* 461; all the kinds employed upon the substance of things absent, *ib.*; two things to be noted in the word "memoria," 1 *Hoop.* 209; Jewel's memoria technica, *Jew.* xxiv.
Menahem, king of Israel: 2 *Bul.* 12
Menander: cited, 1 *Bec.* 15, 203, 222, 366, 3 *Bec.* 365; alleged by St Paul, 4 *Jew.* 737, *Whita.* 70, 2 *Whitg.* 36; verses on honouring parents, 1 *Bul.* 289; his Phasma, 1 *Zur.* 139
Menander, a heretic: 3 *Bec.* 401, 1 *Cran.* 262, 277, *Phil.* 417; he ascribed the creation of the world to angels, *Rog.* 40
Menandrians: ascribe the creation to angels, *Hutch.* 68
Mendham (Jos.): *v.* Indexes.
Memoirs of the Council of Trent, *Calf.* 16 n.; Spiritual Venality of Rome, *Rog.* 219 n
Mendicants: *v.* Friars.
Mendoza (Fernando de): *Calf.* 302 n
Mendoza (Hurtadus): 4 *Jew.* 948
Menecrates: called himself Jupiter, 4 *Jew.* 842
Menelaus: 1 *Bul.* 417
Menevia: *v.* Saint-David's.
Mengus (Hieron.): Flagellum Dæmonum, &c., *Calf.* 318 n
Mennas, abp of Constantinople: 1 *Hoop.* 171; his consecration, 1 *Jew.* 408, 3 *Jew.* 331; he excommunicated pope Vigilius, 4 *Jew.* 834

Mennes (Sir Matth.) or Mennys: account of his family, 3 *Bec.* 597 n
Menno Simonis: 1 *Hoop.* 246
Mennonians: a sect, 3 *Jew.* 602
Men-stealers: 2 *Bul.* 47
Mentz: *v.* Mayence.
Merarites: their service, 2 *Bul.* 132, 142
Merati (......): on the mass, 2 *Brad.* 306, &c. n
Mercator (Marius): some books among the works of Augustine ascribed to him, 1 *Bec.* 316 n
Mercerus (Jo.): well skilled in Hebrew, *Whita.* 172; he supposes the "one pastor" of Eccles. xii. 11 is Christ, *ib.* 423
Merchandize (Monstrous) of the Romish Bishops: referred to, 3 *Bec.* 198 n
Merchants: *v.* Prayers.
Too covetous, 1 *Lat.* 98; their craft, 1 *Bec.* 253; merchants and chapmen who deceive in trade are thieves, 2 *Bec.* 108; what they should do, 1 *Bec.* 256, 2 *Bec.* 115; they must deal truly, *Sand.* 204; merchants of the staple, and merchants-adventurers, 3 *Zur.* 272 n
Merchant-Taylors' school: *v.* London.
Merciable: merciful, 1 *Bec.* 421
Merciful: *v.* Mercy.
Mercurius Trismegistus: 2 *Bul.* 218, 3 *Bul.* 385, *Jew.* xl, 2 *Jew.* 577
Mercury: 4 *Bul.* 68; way-side crosses substituted for images of Mercury, *Calf.* 66
Mercury (St): 1 *Jew.* 190
Mercy: *v.* God, Magistrates, Prayers.
God's mercy the only source of Israel's blessings, 1 *Hoop.* 257; the sole cause of our deliverance, *Sand.* 180; ready to all that are repentant, *Pil.* 101; means to provoke it to him that shall pray, 1 *Bec.* 160, &c.; mercy and truth meeting together, *ib.* 148; former mercy a pledge of future mercy, *Pil.* 136; we must love mercy, *Sand.* 228; mercy better than oblations, 1 *Lat.* 23; where it is, there are all good things, 1 *Bec.* 158; its fruits, *Sand.* 228, 229; without justice it is folly, *ib.* 147; the blessedness of the merciful, 1 *Lat.* 484, 2 *Tyn.* 23; blessed be the merciful, &c.; verses by Jo. Davies, *Poet.* 249
Mercy-seat: 2 *Bul.* 154
Mercy-stock: propitiation, 2 *Bec.* 459
Mere: a boundary, 2 *Bul.* 38, 230
Mere (Jo.): letter to Parker, *Park.* 17; notice of him, *ib.* 19 n.; mentioned, *ib.* 38
Mere (Jean Poltrot de): *v.* Poltrot.
Merell (......): 2 *Zur.* 298
Merenda (Cath.): second wife of P. Martyr, *q. v.*

Mereworth, co. Kent: 1 *Bec.* 61 n
Merick (Rowl.), bp of Bangor: consecrated, *Sand.* xviii, 1 *Zur.* 63 n
Mering (Sir Will.), or Merynge: letter to Cranmer on bishop Longland's oppression of him, 2 *Cran.* 316 n.; recommended to Cromwell for support against the bishop, *ib.* 316
Mering (......): saluted, *Phil.* 227
Mering (Marg.): martyred in Smithfield, *Poet.* 171, 2 *Zur.* 160 n
Merit: *v.* Grace, Works; also Saints.
 Translations concerning merit examined, 1 *Ful.* 343—374; of merits, 2 *Bul.* 342; what they are, 3 *Bec.* 608; angels have none, 2 *Tyn.* 169; the merits or deserts of man, 1 *Bec.* 49, 70, 3 *Bec.* 170, &c., 2 *Bul.* 342; merit and mercy, 3 *Jew.* 583, &c.; the former not compatible with grace, 1 *Tyn.* 436; merit disclaimed, 2 *Bul.* 342, *Hutch.* 95, *Lit. Eliz.* 257, *Now.* (57), 176, (62), 182, *Poet.* 515, *Pra. B.* 156, 1 *Tyn.* 75, &c., 2 *Tyn.* 76; there can be none between us and God, *Whita.* 198, 199; the merits of man are the mercies of God, 1 *Bec.* 54; merits are of God, not of men, 1 *Ful.* 353; God crowns his gifts, not our merits, *Bale* 590, 1 *Ful.* 341; Abraham had no deserts when the promise was made him, 1 *Bec.* 311; the word often used by the Catholic doctors, but in a sound sense, 1 *Ful.* 352; thus Augustine, *Bale* 590; Bernard on the term, *Sand.* 214 n.; dispute of the Scotists and Thomists about meritum congrui and meritum condigni, 3 *Jew.* 611; the Romish doctrine, *Sand.* 25; merit-mongers, 1 *Lat.* 521; their arrogance, *ib.* 368; they are murmurers against God, 2 *Lat.* 200; monks and friars were such, *ib.*; to claim merit is treason against Christ, 1 *Lat.* 419; trust in men's merits leads to desperation, 3 *Jew.* 247; remedies against the want of merits, 3 *Bec.* 169, &c.; Christ has promised all his to them that repent and believe, 3 *Tyn.* 204
Merle d'Aubigné (J. H.): Hist. of the Reformation, 4 *Bul.* viii, &c.
Merley (Sir Rob.): takes lord Cobham to the Tower, *Bale* 45
Merlin: his prophecies, 2 *Jew.* 880, *Sand.* 67, 1 *Tyn.* 305, 2 *Tyn.* 141
Merlinus (Jac.): Concilia, 2 *Ful.* 90 n., 105 n. 107 n.; shamefully corrupts an old canon, *ib.* 42 n
Mermaids: 2 *Brad.* 288, 2 *Cov.* 267, *Hutch.* 178
Mersburg: conflict there, 1080, *Lit. Eliz.* 449

Mershe (Jo.): an ecclesiastical commissioner, *Park.* 383
Merston, co. Kent: *v.* Shorne.
Merton, co. Surrey: the provision of Merton, 4 *Jew.* 904
Merula (Gaud.): on the gods of Egypt, &c., *Rog.* 37 n
Mervyn (Edm.): 2 *Cran.* 382—384
Merynge (Sir Will.): *v.* Mering.
Meslin: mixture, 1 *Whitg.* 201
Messages of God: how sent, *Pil.* 222
Messalians, Euchites, Psallians: founded by Simeones, 1 *Jew.* 245; their heresy, 1 *Brad.* 23, 1 *Cran.* 172, 173, 1 *Jew.* 188, 193, 458, *Phil.* 425, *Sand.* 263, 2 *Whitg.* 561; they acknowledged a plurality of gods, *Rog.* 37; trusted to their own lying revelations, *ib.* 158; hence they were called Enthusiasts, 4 *Bul.* 94, 345; did nothing else but pray, *ib.* 182; said that prayer only should be used, not the sacraments, *Rog.* 251; thought that sacraments should be received only for obedience to magistrates, *ib.* 246, 251; their error on baptism, 2 *Ful.* 388, *Rog.* 277; they set it at nought, 4 *Bul.* 345, 397; affirmed that the regenerate cannot sin, *Rog.* 141; their error respecting the Lord's supper, *Rid.* 9, *Rog.* 284; the sect vanquished by Letoius and others, 1 *Jew.* 188, 193; confuted by Amphilochius, 2 *Whitg.* 165
Messiah: *v.* Christ.
Metaphors: *v.* Figures.
 Similitudes, not images, are used by Christ for instruction, 1 *Hoop.* 45; he often used them, but chiefly when he spoke of the sacraments, 1 *Cran.* 135; argument upon the use of them, *ib.* 124, 127; whether God's mysteries can be thoroughly expressed by them, *ib.* 89; they are not to be pressed in all points to purposes for which they are not used, *ib.* 283, 284; Christ's words in the sacraments are not to be taken without a trope, 1 *Hoop.* 115; papists deny a trope, but use one, *ib.* 121, 528
Metaphrastes (Sim.): *v.* Simeon.
Metcalfe (Nich.), master of St John's college, Cambridge: opposes Latimer, 2 *Lat.* xii.
Metcawffe (Jo.), skinner: *Park.* 211
Metellus, a Roman noble: choked by a hair, 2 *Jew.* 980
Meteors: fiery, airy, and watery ones, 3 *Bul.* 183; great and strange lights seen, *Lit. Eliz.* 570; Fulke writes on them, 1 *Ful.* vi.
Metherk (Adolph.): 2 *Zur.* 290 n
Methodius: on the martyrdom of Dionysius, *Whita.* 578

Methodius: *v.* Cyril the monk.
Methonensis: *v.* Nicholas.
Methusaleh: length of his life, 1 *Bul.* 40
Metonymy: the figure often used in scripture, *Coop.* 199, 2 *Hoop.* 48
Metropolis: a metropolis, 4 *Bul.* 118; the name anciently conferred on cities by the prince, 3 *Jew.* 315
Metropolitans: *v.* Archbishops.
Metusiasts: believed in transubstantiation, *Rog.* 289
Metz: besieged and taken, 2 *Zur.* 305 n., 3 *Zur.* 456 n., 590 n
Meuccius (Sylv.): wrote on the Apocalypse, *Bale* 257
Mey (Will.): *v.* May.
Meyer family: saluted, 1 *Zur.* 305
Meyer (Jac.), or Maiorus: 1 *Bec.* 391
Meyer (Seb.): wrote on the Apocalypse, *Bale* 258
Meyer (Wolfg.): account of him, 2 *Zur.* 322 n.; De Vulneribus Eccles. Rom., *Calf.* 6 n.; letter to him, 2 *Zur.* 322; salutation of him, 1 *Zur.* 30
Meyer de Knonau (Gerold): 1 *Zur.* ix, x.
Meyrick (Dr): *v.* Myrrick.
Micah: instituted a strange worship, 3 *Bul.* 237
Michael, the archangel: the nation of the Jews committed to him, 3 *Bul.* 348, 1 *Jew.* 430; he fights with the dragon, *Bale* 411; meaning of his name, *ib.* 412; images of him, *Rog.* 223; painted as weighing souls, 3 *Tyn.* 163; his balance, *Bale* 523; temple erected to him in mount Garganus, 3 *Bul.* 348
Michael, an emperor of the East: made a law that no monk should serve the ministry in any cure, 4 *Jew.* 1030
Michael III., emperor of the East: rebuked by pope Nicholas I., 1 *Jew.* 267
Michael VIII. [Palæologus], emperor of the East: it is said that his clergy would not suffer him to be buried, because he would have submitted to the pope, 1 *Jew.* 404, 4 *Jew.* xli n.; 740
Michael Angelo: *v.* Buonarrotti.
Michael Angelo, minister of the Italian church in London: 2 *Cran.* 440
Michael Anglus: *v.* Coverdale.
Michael Choniates, bishop of Athens: 4 *Jew.* 653
Michael (The): one of Frobisher's ships, 2 *Zur.* 291 n
Michael house: *v.* Cambridge.
Michaelis (......): 1 *Zur.* 305
Michal, David's wife: her lie, 2 *Bul.* 115
Micher: a pilferer, *Pil.* 290

Michovia (M. à): *v.* Matthæus.
Michtam: 2 *Bul.* 290
Microcosm: man is a little world, &c., verses by T. Bastard, *Poet.* 306
Micrologus: De Eccles. Observat., *Jew.* xl; he describes how communicants alone were wont to be present at the divine mysteries, 2 *Bec.* 255, 256, 3 *Bec.* 481; says, it cannot justly be called a communion, unless many receive together, 1 *Jew.* 135; declares it not a thing authentic that the bread should be dipped in the wine and so distributed for a perfect communion, 3 *Bec.* 415
Micronius (Mart.): his preaching at the German church in London, 3 *Zur.* 587; supports Hooper in his opposition to the vestments, 2 *Hoop.* xiv; complains of his severity, *ib.* xxi; letters to Bullinger, 3 *Zur.* 557—581, see 4 *Bul.* 142 n
Middleburg: invaded by the Walloons, 1 *Zur.* 273
Middlemore (......): *v.* Mydelmore.
Middleton, co. Lancaster: 1 *Brad.* 454; Nowell went to school at Middleton, *Now.* i.; and afterwards founded a free school there, *ib.* viii.
Middleton (Conyers): letter from Rome, *Calf.* 66 n., 67 n
Middleton (Erasmus): Biographia Evangelica, 2 *Brad.* xii. n
Middleton (Hen.), printer: 2 *Hoop.* 177
Middleton (Humph.): letter to him, 1 *Brad.* 591, 2 *Brad.* 194; he is martyred, *Poet.* 162
Middleton (Rich.): *v.* Media Villa (R. de)
Middleton (Tho.): notice of him, *Poet.* liv; a portion of his Wisdom of Solomon Paraphrased, *ib.* 534
Midsummer: the cressets on Midsummer night, *Calf.* 301
Midwives: were licensed by the archbishop or bishop, *Grin.* 174 n., 2 *Lat.* 114 n.; their superstition, 2 *Hoop.* 141, 2 *Lat.* 114; whether they may baptize, 4 *Bul.* 370; inquiries respecting them, *Grin.* 174, 2 *Hoop.* 141; those of the Egyptians, 2 *Bul.* 115
Mieczlaus, king of Poland: *Grin.* 56 n
Milan: the use of the church granted by Justina to the Arians, *Calf.* 301; Ambrose forbade Theodosius to enter the church there, 3 *Bec.* 478, &c., *Coop.* 140 n.; he took order for the service there, 1 *Jew.* 265; his liturgy still used there, *Pil.* 508; taken from the French by Ferdinand, the emperor's brother, 2 *Tyn.* 315; the duchy invaded by Charles V., 2 *Cov.* 512; the motto "Vel in ara," *Calf.* 339
Milciades: *v.* Melciades.

Milden, co. Suffolk: the rectorial library, 1 *Cov.* 198
Mildenham (Tho. de), prior of Worcester: 2 *Lat.* 371 n
Mildmay (Tho.): arrests Sandys, *Sand.* vi.
Mildmay (Sir Walter): a privy councillor, *Grin.* 417, *Park.* 357, 457 n.; mentioned, *Grin.* 392 n.; dwelt in the precinct of St Bartholomew the Great, *ib.* 272 n.; his monument in the church there, *ib.*
Milerus, an Irish priest: committed to the custody of bishop Grindal, *Grin.* 307, 315
Miles Monopodios: *Rog.* 331
Miletus: 4 *Bul.* 30, 44, 106
Milhoffen: the church there, 2 *Cov.* 522
Millenary petition: *Rog.* 21
Millennium: on the reign of 1000 years, *Bale* 566, 567; controversy respecting an earthly reign, *ib.* 587; ancient opinions concerning the millennium, 2 *Cov.* 184; most of the ancient bishops and fathers believed that the kingdom of Christ would be on earth for 1000 years after the resurrection, 2 *Whitg.* 434; this was held by Justin, Lactantius, Irenæus, and many other fathers, but generally denied by the reformers, 4 *Bul.* 537, *Coop.* 147, 3 *Jew.* 606, *Whita.* 391; the chiliastic doctrine keenly defended by Justin Martyr, *Whita.* 583; Irenæus was a Chiliast, *ib.* 585; the sentiments of Lactantius, 3 *Zur.* 233, 234; the ancient Chiliasts, 2 *Cov.* 186, 1 *Hoop.* 161, 3 *Jew.* 606; this doctrine asserted to have been invented by Papias, 4 *Bul.* 537, *Whita.* 664; article of 1552 against certain heretics designated millennarii, *Lit. Edw.* 537, (582); these are stated to have denied the eternity of happiness, *Rog.* 154; opinion that Satan was loosed 1000 years after Christ, *Bale* 94, 559, 1 *Brad.* 92, 2 *Brad.* 274, 312, 2 *Cov.* 253, 2 *Hoop.* 48
Miller (Simon), or Milner: martyred at Norwich, *Poet.* 170
Miller (Walter), a martyr in Scotland: 1 *Tyn.* 277 n
Miller (Will. Hen.): his library, *Poet.* vii.
Milles (Mr): 2 *Cran.* 260
Milles (Jo.), of Chevening: 2 *Cran.* 319
Milles (Tho.): martyred at Lewes, *Poet.* 168
Mills (Mr), of All Souls' college: *Park.* 297 n
Milner (Jo.), bp of Castabala: *Calf.* 21 n
Milner (Jos.): Ch. Hist., 1 *Bul.* 363
Milner (Simon): *v.* Miller.
Milton, co. Kent: the vicarage, 2 *Cran.* 265
Milwright (......): martyred, *Poet.* 167
Mimnermus: 2 *Cov.* 109
Mincha, Minhah, (מנחת): 2 *Brad.* 304, 1 *Hoop.* 241

Mind: *v.* Affections, Contentment.
The office of the mind: verses by Tho. Howell, *Poet.* 256; no joy comparable to a quiet mind, verses by one Candish, *ib.* 308; the mind must be lifted up to heavenly things in prayer, 4 *Bul.* 178
Mind: to desire, *Sand.* 40
Minds: days' minds, *Grin.* 136, *Pil.* 318; months' minds, 3 *Bec.* 126, 1 *Brad.* 49, *Grin.* 136, *Pil.* 318, 1 *Tyn.* 238; month ends, 2 *Hoop.* 146; years' minds, 3 *Bec.* 126, *Grin.* 136, *Pil.* 318, *Pra. Eliz.* 59 n., 1 *Tyn.* 238
Miner (......): his butchery of the Waldenses, *Pil.* 653
Minge (......): martyred at Maidstone, *Poet.* 162
Mingle-mangle: 4 *Bul.* 201, *Hutch.* 346, 1 *Lat.* 147, 290
Minhah: *v.* Mincha.
Mining: 2 *Zur.* 292
Minion: darling, delicate, 1 *Bec.* 285
Ministers: *v.* Apostles, Bishops, Clergy, Curates, Deacons, Evangelists, Preachers, Prelates, Priests, Prophets.
i. *The ministry in general:* ordinary and extraordinary ministers, 1 *Whitg.* 471; minister Dei, seu ecclesiæ, what, *Now.* (102); an article, de ministris ecclesiæ, 2 *Cran.* 477; of ministering in the congregation, *Rog.* 229; there is a lawful ministry in the church, *ib.* 236; the ministry of the word of God remains therein, 4 *Bul.* 103; wherefore God useth the ministry of men in the building of his church, *ib.* 93; the beginning and worthiness of the ministry, *ib.* 102; it is not appointed in vain, *ib.* 97; the end of it, *ib.* 101; it is the means whereby the elect are brought to the obedience of Christ, *Sand.* 342; zeal for maintaining it, and the contrary, *Pil.* 9; some exalt the ministry too much, 4 *Bul.* 96; some take from it, *ib.*; it must be duly limited, *ib.*; the scripture makes a difference between it and the operations of the Spirit, *ib.* 273; ministers are no better than records and testimonies and servants of God's word and sacraments, 2 *Hoop.* 91; they are tied to the word of God alone, 1 *Hoop.* 22; names given to ministers, 2 *Bec.* 91; they are called angels, ambassadors, overseers, 1 *Bec.* 13; pastors, see iv. below; watchmen, see iii. below; "stewards of the mysteries of God" (a sermon), 2 *Jew.* 1046; the names of ministers are interchanged, 4 *Bul.* 108; "minister" a more fit name than "priest," 2 *Lat.* 264; use of the word by English translators, 1 *Ful.* 460, &c.; Cranmer signs himself

MINISTERS

"minister of the church of Canterbury," for which he is rebuked by Dantiscus, a Polish bishop, 2 *Cran.* 400—403; ministers said by Cartwright to be the mouth of God to the people, and of the people to God, 2 *Whitg.* 490; their office a holy service, 2 *Jew.* 1129; the importance of it, 1 *Cov.* 250, 359; their charge the greatest of all charges and vocations, 2 *Hoop.* 118; they are appointed to rule with the sword of the Spirit, 2 *Bec.* 616; they have the keys of the kingdom of heaven, *ib.* 566, (*v.* Absolution); they alone should administer the sacraments in the congregation, *Rog.* 234; the ministration of sacraments properly belongs to those to whom public teaching is committed, *Now.* (94) 217; how curates should administer the Lord's supper, 3 *Tyn.* 265, &c.; ministers are not sacrificing priests, 2 *Jew.* 1131; they are not Christ's vicars, 1 *Hoop.* 22; preachers called so, 1 *Lat.* 349; their office not a lordly one, 2 *Brad.* 255; unprofitable, in a worldly view, *Pil.* 105, 593; on the equality of ministers, 2 *Whitg.* 401, &c.; whether Christ forbids rule and superiority, 1 *Whitg.* 148; he forbids ministers to exalt themselves above each other; the pope's doctrine is exactly contrary, 1 *Tyn.* 207; the ministry is of equal dignity in all, *Pil.* 493, 494; all have one authority, 2 *Bec.* 319; all are equal as to their ministry, but not as to order and polity, 3 *Whitg.* 535, 536; not all equal in every respect, 2 *Zur.* 233; there are divers degrees in the church, 3 *Jew.* 271; three orders are allowed by scripture, bishops, priests, and deacons, *Hutch.* 50; the litany of 1544, (like several subsequent litanies) has, "bishops, pastors, and ministers," *Pra. Eliz.* 572; another reckoning; ministers, seniors, and deacons, 3 *Whitg.* 295; the seven orders of the church of Rome, *Hutch.* 50; the sacrifice of ministers, *Sand.* 412; persecution comes upon them first, *ib.* 379; the discipline and correction of them; 4 *Bul.* 135, 504; of ministers having no pastoral charge, 1 *Whitg.* 469; character of the ministers of England, 2 *Zur.* 163; Harding calls them tinkers, tapsters, fiddlers, and pipers, 4 *Jew.* 873, 909; Jewel admits their want of learning, *ib.* 910; many of them made of "the basest sort of the people," 1 *Whitg.* 316; many had been idolatrous sacrificers and mass-mongers, *ib.* 317, &c.; artificers and unlearned men admitted to the ministry, *Park.* 120; many come out of the shop into the clergy, 2 *Ful.* 118; order to ordain no more artificers, *Grin.* 241 n.; some beneficed ministers neither priests nor deacons, *Park.* 128, 154, 308, (*v.* Lowth); laymen presented to benefices, *ib.* 311, and made prebendaries, *ib.* 312; an archdeacon not in orders, *ib.* 142 n.; the names of counterfeit ministers to be certified to the bishops, *Grin.* 186; there was however a learned ministry in England, *Sand.* 245; some ministers refuse conformity, *Park.* 268, 269, 270, 272, (*v.* Declaration, Puritans); certain London ministers summoned to Lambeth, *ib.* 233; dedication to the ministers of Norfolk and Suffolk, 3 *Bec.* 290

ii. *The calling of ministers:* their mission (Rom. x. 15), 2 *Whitg.* 530; their ordinary and extraordinary calling, 1 *Hoop.* 447; they must be lawfully called and sent, 2 *Bec.* 318, 319, 4 *Bul.* 128, &c., 2 *Hoop.* 123, 3 *Jew.* 320, *Rog.* 229, 1 *Whitg.* 84, &c.; must not run unsent, 2 *Lat.* 28, *Phil.* 315, nor usurp the office of preaching, 2 *Whitg.* 531; if they thrust themselves into office they are thieves, *Pil.* 102; against calling by favour and gifts, 4 *Bul.* 129, or of private affection, *ib.* 131; the lawful calling of God, *Calf.* 230; heavenly or secret calling, 4 *Bul.* 128; ministers must be lawfully sent, as Christ was, i. e. prepared by the Holy Ghost, *Sand.* 285; on the election of ministers, 4 *Bul.* 128, &c., 1 *Whitg.* 296, &c., 3 *Whitg.* 9, 501, 537; they must be chosen and called before ordination, *Rog.* 239—241; fit persons ought to be chosen, 1 *Bec.* 8; two ways for providing for their fitness, 2 *Hoop.* 118; what sort of persons should be appointed curates, and what their work should be, 3 *Tyn.* 265; their office, and requisites for it, 1 *Lat.* 35; who may choose them, 4 *Bul.* 131; of their election by the people, 4 *Bul.* 128, 1 *Whitg.* 339, 370, &c., 1 *Zur.* 280, 292, 2 *Zur.* 229, 233; the opinion of Calvin respecting it, 3 *Zur.* 758 n.; how they were appointed in the apostles' time, 2 *Cran.* 116; on their election in the early church, 1 *Bec.* 7, 1 *Ful.* 466, 1 *Jew.* 408; the people's consent required in many places, to Cyprian's time and later, 1 *Whitg.* 358; why their election was taken from the people, *ib.* 463; Whitgift says that ministers are chosen by the people, in England, for they are chosen in a way allowed by the parliament, *ib.* 372, and that the diversity between the apostles' times and ours requires a different government, &c., *ib.* 378; popular election not necessary, the contrary sometimes convenient, *ib.* 456; no certain form of election and calling commanded, *ib.* 363, 457; censure and examination of ministers, 4 *Bul.* 135, 504; their examination in the church of England, 1 *Whitg.* 299; articles of convocation touching their admission, *Grin.* 185; curates not to be made hastily, 1 *Lat.* 152; what manner of men should be ordained, 4 *Bul.* 134; the ordination (*q. v.*) of ministers, *ib.* 128, 138; they ought to be ordained by men lawfully appointed for that purpose, *Rog.* 238; there is no promise that grace is given with the office, 2 *Cran.* 116; ministers are not made by chance, *Sand.* 334; rulers should provide that there be learned curates, 1 *Bec.* 254; on their presentation and nomination, (*v.* Patronage), 2 *Cran.* 97, 98; ministers not allowed to preach without licence, *Grin.* 340, (*v.* Preachers); churchwardens, &c. not to suffer unlicensed persons to minister, *Park.* 383; as to laymen occupying the place of ministers, see i. above; the ministers of the reformed churches do not preach without commission, 2 *Ful.* 377

iii. *Their duty generally* (see also Bishops, Prelates): the duty of ministers, 2 *Bec.* 317, &c., 1 *Hoop.* 26, 1 *Lat.* 35, 350, 2 *Lat.* 38, 120, *Sand.* 99; their study, *ib.* 333; they are commanded diligently to study the scriptures, *Whita.* 523; they cannot be learned unless they know Christ, 2 *Lat.* 258; their duty is to pray incessantly, *Sand.* 38, and to teach, *ib.* 39; what they must pray for, 1 *Bec.* 166; the life required of a minister, 2 *Lat.* 26, *Sand.* 332; he must take as much heed to a virtuous life as to his doctrine, 1 *Bec.* 16; ministers must not only teach well, but live well, *Sand.* 246; the people are narrow-eyed in considering their lives, 1 *Bec.* 18; how ministers should behave, *ib.* 257; what sort of men they ought to be, *ib.* 101, 2 *Bec.* 319, 320; they must be righteous, *Sand.* 103; they are to be the salt of the earth, 3 *Bec.* 290, &c.; lights, 2 *Bul.* 157; the light of the world, 3 *Bec.* 293, &c., 2 *Tyn.* 34; they are trumpeters, *Sand.* 165; their duty as watchmen, *ib.* 383, 439, 1 *Whitg.* 511; they must be witnesses to the truth, *Sand.* 291; must not flatter for benefices, 2 *Lat.* 28; must accuse sins, 4 *Bul.* 546; may not use violence to turn the people to goodness, 2 *Lat.* 195; must be vigilant that Satan sow not his tares, 2 *Bec.* 526, 2 *Lat.* 189; must not forsake their flocks, *Pil.* 441, 1 *Whitg.* 506; should not be long absent from them, 2 *Lat.* 121; the evils of non-residence, *Hutch.* 338, 2 *Jew.* 984, 2 *Lat.* 384; spiritual men do not sufficiently shew hospitality, 2 *Bec.* 432; they should be more liberal to the poor, *ib.* 590, 591; their office especially in time of pestilence, 2 *Hoop.* 174; they must not flee from their flocks then, 1 *Lat.* 416; they should not be occupied with secular business, 3 *Whitg.* 430, &c.; nor be tenants-at-will, 2 *Whitg.* 460; on their exercise of civil offices, 1 *Whitg.* 153, 2 *Whitg.* 394, &c., 3 *Whitg.* 544; they ought not to wear delicate apparel, 2 *Lat.* 82, 83; ministers exhorted, 2 *Jew.* 1085, 1 *Lat.* 65, 286, they will have to give account, 1 *Lat.* 38, *Sand.* 245; who they are that occupy the ministry faithfully, 1 *Bec.* 2; true ministers are few, 1 *Lat.* 31

iv. *The pastoral work:* pastors, their office, 4 *Bul.* 88, 106, 1 *Ful.* 486, *Pil.* 489, 490, &c., 1 *Whitg.* 512, &c.; it is not a lordly dignity, 4 *Bul.* 89; the term applied by Romanists to bishops only, *Whita.* 415; "pastors and teachers" (Eph. iv.) regarded as the same order by several fathers, 1 *Whitg.* 474, 504, but not by Cartwright, *ib.* 503; the word "pastors" means feeders, 1 *Bec.* 22, 26, 3 *Jew.* 281; Christ's charge to them, 2 *Bec.* 325; the scope and drift whereunto they should aim, 4 *Bul.* 153; they should desire nothing but the weal of the flock, *Sand.* 242; the authority of pastors, 4 *Bul.* 160; they must feed the people faithfully, *Sand.* 342; the feeding of Christ's sheep, various kinds thereof, 1 *Bec.* 3, &c., 3 *Bec.* 33, 2 *Hoop.* 197; they must preach and teach out of the scriptures, 1 *Bec.* 3, &c., 2 *Bec.* 320, 2 *Hoop.* 277, (see v. below); their condemnation if they preach not, 2 *Bec.* 321; must administer the sacraments duly and faithfully, 1 *Bec.* 11, 2 *Bec.* 320, 322, (see i. above); must edify in work and life, 1 *Bec.* 12, &c.; the need of pastoral watchfulness, 1 *Bul.* 3; the rod as needful as the staff, *Sand.* 247; must be hospitable, 1 *Bec.* 19, (see iii. above); must pray for the people, 2 *Bec.* 322, 323; must have earnest consideration of the lambs of Christ, 1 *Bec.* 9; must drive away wolves, 2 *Bec.* 322, *Sand.* 397; must lead a virtuous life, 2 *Bec.* 323, 324, (see iii. above); their debt to the flock, and the flock's to them, *Sand.* 202; of the residence of the pastor (with his flock), 1 *Whitg.* 506, &c., (see also iii. above); a true shepherd described, 3 *Bec.* 21, 23

v. *The office of preaching:* the preaching of God's word, 2 *Bec.* 320; the ministry of the word is God's ordinance, *ib.* 318; a mark of the church, 4 *Bul.* 17, 18; termed the mystery of the kingdom, 4 *Bul.* 237; not a sacrament, 1 *Ful.* 459; the excellency

MINISTERS

and utility of it, *Rog.* 323; errors respecting it, *ib.* 230, 234; it is the ordinary means of salvation, 1 *Lat.* 200, 291, 306, 349, 418 (*v.* Faith, *c.*); a means of regeneration, *ib.* 202; by it we are called to God's kingdom, *ib.* 358; the power of it, 4 *Bul.* 40; it is compared to a fisher's net, 1 *Lat.* 285; preachers cannot tell who will receive the word, and who not, 2 *Tyn.* 181; they can only call sinners to repentance, 1 *Lat.* 285; God alone can make it fruitful, *ib.* 155; the preaching of Christ himself brought forth little fruit, *ib.*, 2 *Lat.* 209; it is the chief kind of feeding, 1 *Bec.* 3; the preaching of Christ's benefits is a provocation to live well, *ib.* 44; makes us new and bold men, *Pil.* 117; moves more than plagues, *ib.* 183; conquers more than fighting, *ib.* 265; what preaching should be, 1 *Ful.* 402; it must be in a language that the people understand, 2 *Cran.* 170; what kind is most effectual, 3 *Whitg.* 1, &c.; the gentle kind wins most to God, *Pil.* 354; what ministers should teach, *Sand.* 39; how they should teach, 1 *Bec.* 42, 43; they should employ similitudes suited to their hearers, 2 *Lat.* 210; on written sermons, 1 *Bul.* 9, 3 *Whitg.* 40, 42, 1 *Zur.* 281; preaching compared with reading, 3 *Whitg.* 28, &c.; reading homilies not comparable to preaching, *Grin.* 382; of ministers that cannot preach, 1 *Whitg.* 538, &c.; the word may be preached privately as well as in public, *ib.* 207, &c.; preaching should not be confined to sacred places, 1 *Lat.* 207; the utility of daily preaching, 2 *Hoop.* 80; of preaching before the administration of sacraments, 3 *Whitg.* 14, &c.; a sermon should be preached before the holy supper, 1 *Hoop.* 177, 178; of sermons at funerals, 1 *Zur.* 281 (and see Burial); secular princes should command or suffer true preachers of God's word to preach the gospel purely and plainly, and that once or twice in the week, 3 *Tyn.* 265; there should be some preachers among soldiers in time of war, 1 *Bec.* 252; sermons should be made in time of war, with admonitions for amendment of life, *ib.* 259; also after the victory, with praises to God, *ib.*; the high titles of preachers, *Pil.* 106, 107; said to be Christ's vicars, 1 *Lat.* 349; are but God's instruments, *ib.* 155, and servants, *Pil.* 21; the properties of true preachers, 3 *Bec.* 243, 244, 1 *Lat.* 290, &c.; a faithful preacher is a great jewel to a Christian commonwealth, 3 *Bec.* 598; better than ten thousand massmongers, *ib.* 160; the office, work, and duty of preachers, 1 *Bec.* 353, *Calf.* 229, 2 *Cov.* 308, 1 *Lat.* 61, *Lit. Edw.* 518, (565); how great, hard, and difficult it is, 1 *Hoop.* 450, 549, *Hutch.* 200; it requires the whole man, 1 *Tyn.* 207; their most necessary qualification for it is love, *Hutch.* 103; not every man should take the office, but only such as are called thereto, 1 *Tyn.* 283, 2 *Tyn.* 36; none may preach except he be called, 2 *Lat.* 38; none should preach without the allowance of the church of God, *Phil.* 315; preachers should be chosen after Paul's rule, 1 *Tyn.* 283; how to know who are sent of God, *ib.* 282; preaching is the bounden duty of all prelates, &c., *ib.* 101, 207; the old fathers were diligent preachers, *Hutch.* 6; preaching scandalously neglected by some bishops, 1 *Hoop.* 143; ministers are bound to preach, *Rog.* 232; it is the duty of priests, *Bale* 84—88, the curate's office, not that of monks and friars, 1 *Tyn.* 300; laymen permitted to preach in the ancient church, *v.* Laity; every man should be a preacher in his sphere, 2 *Tyn.* 36; preachers and teachers most necessary, *Now.* (3), 116, *Pil.* 112; they ought to be provided by magistrates, 2 *Bec.* 305, 2 *Tyn.* 265; preachers have two offices, to teach and to confute, 1 *Lat.* 129; what they must preach, *Pil.* 59, 218; how and what they should speak, 2 *Jew.* 952, &c.; their duty is to teach what God commands, *Sand.* 274; they should always be able to say, "my doctrine is not mine, but his that sent me," 1 *Hoop.* 508; must neither add to, nor take away from God's law, 2 *Cran.* 25, 27; Christ commands his precepts to be taught, not man's inventions, 2 *Lat.* 355; preachers ought to be sure of the truth of their preaching, *ib.* 336, and have deep knowledge thereof, *ib.* 338; their discourse should be salt, 2 *Tyn.* 31, 32; they require boldness, and should never fear, 1 *Lat.* 86, 507, 2 *Lat.* 26; must speak the truth though it give offence, 2 *Lat.* 77; must rebuke sin without respect of persons, *ib.* 420; must rebuke all estates, 1 *Lat.* 468, 506, 509; may admonish judges, 2 *Lat.* 325; must rebuke wicked magistrates, 1 *Lat.* 374, 381; must be bold, even to princes, *Rid.* 95; may correct the king, 1 *Lat.* 86; what they should rebuke, *Sand.* 274; hearing of vice they ought to reprove it, 2 *Lat.* 40; they must rebuke prevalent false doctrines and superstitions, 2 *Tyn.* 32; must call the nation to repentance, *ib.* 95; must not use violence against oppressors, *ib.* 68; have no other sword than that of the Spirit, *ib.* 196; when preachers rebuke sin, sinners are displeased, 2 *Bec.* 598; true preaching stirs up persecution, 2 *Tyn.* 32; Satan (*q. v.*) greatly opposes it, *Nord.* 115, 116; faithful preachers slandered in England, 1 *Lat.* 240; they will be persecuted, 2 *Lat.* 302, 303; to abolish preaching is against the fourth commandment, 1 *Hoop.* 345; in queen Mary's days preachers were miserably handled for speaking truth, 3 *Bec.* 240, 244; they were thrust out of their livings and compelled to flee, *ib.* 239; those only that flattered were allowed to preach, *ib.* 243; preachers slandered as though they caused rebellion and trouble to the state, 2 *Bec.* 596, 1 *Lat.* 249, 2 *Tyn.* 245; it was thus in the primitive church, 2 *Bec.* 597, 598, and in queen Mary's time, 3 *Bec.* 240; the cause of ignorance and rebellion is the lack of preaching, 2 *Bec.* 595, 1 *Lat.* 273; preaching God's word makes loyal subjects, *Grin.* 379; preachers must be of good life, 2 *Lat.* 26 (see iii. above); ought to be mouth-stoppers, 1 *Lat.* 131; how to stop their mouths, *ib.* 374; there were few preachers in the time of popery, *ib.* 130; preaching was superseded by the mass, *ib.* 203; the lack of preachers lamented, *Hutch.* 5, 1 *Lat.* 269, 291, 3 *Zur.* 485; when the people will not learn, God sends no preachers, *Pil.* 184; preaching begun to be renewed in England, *Hutch.* 6; preachers persecuted in queen Mary's time, see above; the true preachers of God's word banished, 3 *Bec.* 240; the scarcity of preachers lamented in the time of queen Elizabeth, 2 *Jew.* 999, 1000, *Sand.* 154; papists and false prophets were better provided for formerly than true preachers afterwards, 2 *Bec.* 585, 586; learned ones should be placed in parishes, or sent to itinerate, *ib.* 422; preachers directed to be appointed in vacant dioceses, *Park.* 119; certain godly preachers were preserved in persecution, 3 *Bec.* 563, &c.; God has special care over them, *ib.* 564; they are encouraged by the comfortable histories of God's liberality, 2 *Bec.* 611, 614; their wives encouraged that God will not let them lack, *ib.* 612; preachers must be reverenced, *ib.* 475, *Sand.* 270; but not unduly honoured, *Sand.* 271; they were reverenced under the reformation, 3 *Bec.* 238; their office worshipful, *Pil.* 106; not to be despised, 1 *Lat.* 470; they are not to be disdained for their simplicity, *Pil.* 99, 100; the world neglects and sets nought by them, 2 *Bec.* 611; preaching must be maintained, *Hutch.* 201, 1 *Lat.* 504; it is not to be despised, *Pil.* 12, 114; all men ought to hear it, *ib.* 114; scruples against hearing it reproved, *Sand.* 271; preachers are to be followed only as they follow Christ, 1 *Lat.* 514; not in false doctrine, *ib.* 523; what he is that neglects preaching, 1 *Bec.* 3; strawberry preachers, 2 *Brad.* 9, 1 *Lat.* 62; of ministers that cannot preach, 1 *Whitg.* 538; the scriptures admonish us to beware of false preachers, 3 *Bec.* 501; the craft and subtilty of such, *ib.* 501, 502; their intermixture of false doctrine with true, *ib.* 502; the popish preachers wolvish shepherds, *ib.* 236; masterly curates preach their own doctrine, and endeavour to make the people sleep, 2 *Lat.* 344; preachers of human imaginations break the third commandment, 1 *Hoop.* 325; covetous preachers are always false prophets, 2 *Tyn.* 17; negligent preachers bring in popery, 1 *Lat.* 153; they are worthy of double dishonour, *ib.* 154; worldly-minded preachers are enemies of the cross, *ib.* 529; those who have lost their salt are disallowed of God, 2 *Tyn.* 33; evil preachers to be refused, 1 *Lat.* 87; he that preaches truly the scriptures is to be heard, whatever be his life, 1 *Bec.* 386; if preachers live ill, but preach well, their word is not to be despised, 2 *Bec.* 324; the punishment of unfaithful preachers, 1 *Lat.* 524, 529; false preachers shall be confounded at Christ's coming, 2 *Tyn.* 184

vi. *Unworthy ministers* (see also in v.): of their unworthiness and evil life, 4 *Bul.* 161, 2 *Jew.* 755; there are many evil walkers among them, *Sand.* 120; careless and slothful pastors, 1 *Whitg.* 517; idle and negligent ministers reproved, *Hutch.* 224, *Pil.* 35; ad pastores otiosos et somnolentos, verses (in English) by And. Willet, *Poet.* 394; their slackness in their office censured, 1 *Bec.* 254; curates who neglect their duty are thieves, 2 *Bec.* 107; if they regard their vocation only as a way or trade to live by, they steal what they receive, *Sand.* 242, 243; the lack of good curates is the cause of all mischief, 2 *Lat.* 307; mischiefs of ignorant ministers, 1 *Bec.* 9; unable ones are unprofitable, *Pil.* 36; popish guides, and they who cannot or will not teach, are no pastors, *Sand.* 344; many curates come unto their benefices for the desire of filthy lucre, 1 *Bec.* 254; spiritual men are covetous of rich benefices, 2 *Bec.* 431, 587; some flatter for them, 2 *Lat.* 28; curates, vicars and parsons often leave their flocks in time of sickness, 1 *Lat.* 416; non-residence the cause of much evil, *Hutch.* 338, 2 *Lat.* 384; if ministers teach not the truth which saveth, they are murderers, *Sand.* 244; the blind curate and his blind parishioners fall together, 1 *Lat.* 523; negligent curates should be complained of, *ib.* 304; prayer a remedy against them, *ib.*; wicked ministers not to be allowed, *Sand.* 240; they must be deposed, 1 *Bec.* 6, *Rog.* 272, 273, *Sand.* 40; ministers should retain their office only so long as they behave well therein, 1 *Hoop.* 481; whence the ministry is contemned, 1 *Bec.* 2; the unworthiness of ministers derogates not from the service of God, 4 *Bul.* 22; their wickedness impairs not Christ's ministry or sacraments, 2 *Brad.* 345, 2 *Hoop.* 125, *Pil.* 170, 636, *Rog.* 269—272, 2 *Whitg.* 520; whether the minister be a good or an evil man, a heretic or a catholic, &c., the effect of baptism is all one, 2 *Jew.* 1106; good doctrine is not to be rejected for the scarce good life of them, 4 *Bul.* 161; whether the prayers of an evil priest are profitable, 3 *Tyn.* 148; the error of the Donatists and Anabaptists respecting evil ministers, *Hutch.* 97; opinion of the Anabaptists on the ministry, 1 *Whitg.* 412

vii. *Duty towards ministers:* the duty of the flock to their pastors, *Sand.* 202; ministers are to be had in honour, 2 *Bec.* 91, 565, 1 *Bul.* 283; they are included under the term parents, 1 *Bul.* 269; how to be esteemed, 1 *Hoop.* 20; they should not only be reverenced of the people, but also honoured by the magistrates, 2 *Hoop.* 91; pastors are to be honoured of parishioners, 2 *Bec.* 330; obedience to be paid to them, *ib.* 91, 2 *Jew.* 876; disobedience to them punished, 2 *Bec.* 92; how far they are to be obeyed, *ib.* 92, 93; though unworthy, must be obeyed and honoured in their office, 2 *Lat.* 346; teaching contrary to God's word, they are not to be obeyed, 2 *Bec.* 332; the order not to be despised for the faults of some, *Hutch.* 310; if good, they are entitled to double honour, 1 *Lat.* 153; how to be heard, 4 *Bul.* 102; how far they are to be followed, 1 *Hoop.* 21, 2 *Hoop.* 371; not blindly, 2 *Tyn.* 129; they are to be believed only so far as they preach God's word, 1 *Hoop.* 28; their words, when according to the word of God, are to be taken for an oracle, 2 *Bec.* 566; on contempt of ministers, 1 *Bul.* 284; their office highly esteemed by Christ, though contemned by men, *Sand.* 35, 350; ministers must be provided for, 1 *Lat.* 303, *Sand.* 45, 96, 412; they ought to be rewarded, 4 *Bul.* 488; those who fulfil their office have a right to maintenance, 1 *Tyn.* 230, 236, 437; Hezekiah careful for their stipends, 1 *Bul.* 335; the duty of the laity towards unlearned curates, 1 *Lat.* 503; ministers must be prayed for, 1 *Bec.* 165, 1 *Cov.* 250 (*v.* Prayers, including those for the whole church).

Ministry : *v.* Vocation.
Minories : *v.* London.
Minorites : *v.* Franciscans.
Minos : 2 *Bul.* 219, *Calf.* 13, 14, 4 *Jew.* 1164
Minshull (......): 2 *Bec.* 438 n
Minstrels : their use, 1 *Lat.* 546; such should be chosen by men of honour, as would sing David's songs, 1 *Bec.* 267; their chief point is to lie and flatter, *ib.* 276; minstrels and morris-dancers in church, 1 *Zur.* 259 n
Minstrelsy : *v.* Music.
Mints : that in the Tower, and the abp's mint at Canterbury, 2 *Cran.* 294; the latter, *ib.* 357; that at Bristol, 3 *Zur.* 649; bishops made comptrollers of the mint, 1 *Lat.* 67; minting priests, *ib.* 68
Minucius Felix : remarks that we put a difference between nations and people, but to God the whole world is one house, 3 *Jew.* 200; says, crosses we neither worship nor wish for, *Calf.* 178, 184, 380, 2 *Ful.* 206; on the worship of God, in reply to the objection that Christians had neither temples nor altars, *Calf.* 183; on heathen processions, &c., *ib.* 295
Minutes : small coin, mites, 1 *Bec.* 194
Miracle-plays : 2 *Bul.* 194
Miracles : *v.* Antichrist, Constantine, Demons, Host, Julian, Prophesyings, Signs, Witchcraft.

What, 2 *Hoop.* 411; they are the extraordinary will of God, 1 *Brad.* 359; not to be supposed without necessity, 1 *Cran.* 255; those of the Old Testament, their signification, *Calf.* 334—337; those of the New Testament, *ib.* 337; miracles joined to the word of God as seals, 4 *Bul.* 451; they were not always employed to confirm the teaching of the prophets, 3 *Tyn.* 131; those recorded in scripture were not done to sanctify the place, but for the sake of the people, *ib.* 87; they led not to idolatry, *ib.* 83; Christ's miracles were seals of his doctrines, 1 *Lat.* 211, 2 *Lat.* 160; yet Christ and his apostles, for all their miracles, required not to be believed without scripture, 3 *Tyn.* 111; Christ's miracles have a spiritual signification, 2 *Lat.* 170;

MIRACLES

miracles are in some respects like sacraments, *Calf.* 320; they are no proof of doctrine, *ib.* 316, &c., 333, 334, 2 *Cran.* 45, 47, 48, 64, 3 *Jew.* 197, *Sand.* 17, nor a sure probation of holiness, 2 *Cov.* 477, 478; they who consent to the word only because of miracles, will fall away, 3 *Tyn.* 132; the use of miracles, 1 *Tyn.* 184; true and false ones distinguished, *ib.* 286; distinguished by their purposes, *ib.* 287, 289, 3 *Tyn.* 89—92; some miracles are sent to confirm men in the truth, others to try how they will stick to it, 1 *Brad.* 428; true miracles are done to draw men to God's word, false ones to confirm doctrine that is not God's word, 3 *Tyn.* 91; true miracles to be known from false ones by the scriptures, 2 *Cran.* 66, 3 *Tyn.* 128; miracles are wrought by faith, 1 *Tyn.* 274; but the faith which works miracles is not necessarily saving faith, 3 *Tyn.* 197, 199; the working of them neither makes nor hinders holiness, 2 *Cran.* 50; there is none in the sacrament of the eucharist, 2 *Hoop.* 410; if transubstantiation were a miracle, it would be such a miracle as scripture never knew, 3 *Tyn.* 261, 262; miracles are always cognizable by the senses, *Coop.* 195; miracles were at the first wrought through ceremonies, as anointing, 1 *Tyn.* 226; miracle on the reception of the sacrament by an apostate, related by Cyprian, 2 *Jew.* 761, 785; the cure of Gorgonia, sister of Gregory Nazianzen, *Grin.* 48 n.; Chrysostom affirms that true miracles had utterly ceased in his time, 2 *Cran.* 46; yet mention is made of a hypocrite miraculously discovered at Constantinople in the time of Chrysostom, 1 *Jew.* 246; some in the time of Augustine, 2 *Cran.* 48 (see p. 77, col. 2; and see in like manner the names of other fathers); it is related that when Deuterius, an Arian, was about to baptize a man, the water dried up, 2 *Jew.* 761; Marcellus stated to have miraculously burned Jupiter's temple, 2 *Ful.* 116; Germanus said to have stilled the sea, *ib.*; miracles alleged to have been wrought by the cross, *Calf.* 316, &c., 2 *Ful.* 189, 3 *Tyn.* 84; miracles wrought by the bodies of saints, or at their tombs, 1 *Jew.* 158, 3 *Tyn.* 83; miraculous dreams or visions (*q. v.*), *Calf.* 117, 119; miracles declared to have ceased, *ib.* 217; true ones said to have ceased as soon as the faith was spread abroad, 1 *Tyn.* 287; opinion that they endured only till the scripture was authentically received, 3 *Tyn.* 128, 130, 136; the church, says Tyndale, knew true scripture from false by miracles, *ib.* 135; why there are none, or but few, now, *Calf.* 333, 2 *Hoop.* 45, 2 *Lat.* 160, *Rid.* 75; Tyndale says those whom the pope calls heretics shew no miracles, because they bring no new learning, 3 *Tyn.* 103, and that miracles are not needed to prove doctrine drawn from scripture, *ib.* 128, 129; those which are adduced to confirm false doctrine are either feigned, or done of the devil, 2 *Jew.* 922, 1 *Tyn.* 325—327; false ones wrought by demons to turn men from the truth, 3 *Tyn.* 92; miracles wrought by the working of Satan to confirm idolatry and error, 2 *Hoop.* 45, 3 *Tyn.* 128, 129; such have been permitted by God to try the faith of the elect, 3 *Tyn.* 89—91, or sent to call men to repentance, 1 *Hoop.* 417, or permitted as a punishment, 1 *Tyn.* 195; God sends false miracles to those who believe not, as in the case of the Mahometan apostasy, 3 *Tyn.* 129, 130; those of the heathen, wrought by evil spirits, *Calf.* 316, &c., 2 *Cran.* 41, 1 *Tyn.* 287; such were those of the Egyptian sorcerers, 2 *Tyn.* 85; those of the priests of Serapis, *Calf.* 274; of a priest of Saturn, *ib.* 275; some related by Pliny, 1 *Hoop.* 328, 329; the imposture of Agesilaus, 1 *Jew.* 101; diseases have been healed by charms, 2 *Ful.* 157; a deceptive transformation of wine mentioned by Irenæus, 2 *Cran.* 45; Augustine speaks of delusive miracles wrought at tombs, *ib.* 47; a false miracle wrought by illusion of the devil, and exposed by the prayer of Astyrius, 2 *Brad.* 341; Lyra says many feigned miracles have been wrought in the church, 1 *Jew.* 105, 3 *Jew.* 197; More claims a continued succession of miracles for the church of Rome, 3 *Tyn.* 100; his confidence that they prove its doctrine, *ib.* 127, 130; the alleged miracle concerning the Gregorian and Ambrosian missales, *Pil.* 508; false popish miracles, *Calf.* 274, 2 *Cran.* 64—66; they would make a horse laugh, *Pil.* 587; miracles alleged to have been wrought in proof of saint-worship, 3 *Tyn.* 127, 128; some wrought by the devil in the preaching of purgatory, 1 *Lat.* 212; false ones wrought with roods and images, *Bale* 98, *Calf.* 134, 171, 2 *Jew.* 665, 666; miraculous roods, 2 *Ful.* 210; the rood of grace, an image in Kent which used to weep, move its eyes, &c., 3 *Zur.* 604, 606, 609; a false miracle at Dublin, *Park.* 95 n.; false juggling ones in the West of England, 1 *Lat.* 55; miracles of the Jesuits, 3 *Jew.* 179, 195, 197, &c.; many of the miracles in the last times wrought by the devil, *Bale* 98; in these latter days they have oftener been wrought by the devil than by God, *Calf.* 316; false miracles performed at Rome in 1796, 97 (Marchetti), *ib.* 274 n.; the lying wonders of Antichrist, 2 *Hoop.* 45, 2 *Jew.* 922, 923

Miræus (Aubertus): *Calf.* 69 n., 2 *Ful.* 282 n
Mirammelinus: 1 *Bul.* 416
Mirandola (Jo. Picus): *v.* Picus.
Miriam: *Sand.* 148; called Mary, 1 *Bul.* 48, 2 *Bul.* 176, *Pil.* 361
Mirror: a mirror of mutability, by T. Proctor, *Poet.* 400
Miscreants: unbelievers, 1 *Bec.* 22
Miseries: against the temptation to complain of the miseries of the faithful; with sentences and example of scripture, 1 *Bec.* 463, &c.
Misers: miserable persons, 1 *Bec.* 172, 1 *Brad.* 73, 150, 2 *Brad.* 85
Mishnah: exceedingly foolish, *Whita.* 611
Misrule (Lords of): account of them, *Grin.* 175; injunction against them, *ib.* 141
Missa: *v.* Mass.

The word anciently used for a dismissing, 1 *Jew.* 202; sometimes employed for a meeting of the people, *ib.* 180; sometimes for any kind of prayers, *ib.* 180, 185

Mistress Missa: 2 *Brad.* 287, 2 *Cov.* 266, *Rid.* 108, 510
Missah (מסה): its meaning, 2 *Brad.* 304, 1 *Hoop.* 243, *Phil.* 94, *Pil.* 505, 3 *Tyn.* 177
Missale: *v.* Mass.

Missale Romanum: referred to, 1 *Hoop.* 283, 284; the cross in it, *Calf.* 202; an alteration in the instructions prefixed to it, 2 *Ful.* 21 n

Missale ad usum Sarum: cited or referred to, 2 *Bec.* 72 n., 1 *Brad.* 8, 2 *Brad.* 298, 299, *Jew.* xl, 2 *Jew.* 597, 4 *Jew.* 818, 859, *Phil.* 148, *Pil.* 81, *Pra. Eliz.* 232 n.; the prayer of oblation, 1 *Brad.* 8; prayer that God would look favourably upon the offering, 2 *Jew.* 773; rubric on mixing the wine with water, 1 *Lat.* 138; the missale shews that the papists have changed the words of consecration, 3 *Bec.* 357, 2 *Bec.* 456; it calls the eucharist bread after consecration, 2 *Bec.* 268; shews that anciently there was a communion, and not a private mass, *ib.* 240, 1 *Jew.* 18, 19; and that communion was in both kinds, 2 *Bec.* 245; quoted for the worship of the host, 3 *Bec.* 359

The other English uses, viz. Hereford, Bangor, York, and Lincoln, 2 *Brad.* 298, 299; the uses of York and Bangor, *Pil.* 81; the Lincoln missale not known to exist,

2 *Brad.* 299; mass-books to be abolished, *Grin.* 135, 159
Mis-sense: to misunderstand, or pervert, 1 *Jew.* 3
Missions: of Papists, Nestorians, &c., 2 *Ful.* 60; of the Jesuits, 3 *Jew.* 179, 195, 197, &c.; of Protestants, 2 *Ful.* 61
Mitch (Mr): tries to pull Sandys from the vice-chancellor's chair, *Sand.* v.
Mitchell (Mr): apprises Sandys that he may escape from the Tower, *Sand.* vii.
Mitford (Will.): Hist. of Greece, *Calf.* 13 n
Mithridates, king of Pontus: knew twenty-two languages, 1 *Jew.* 276; his stratagem, *ib.* 22
Mitres: *Bale* 526, 1 *Tyn.* 252; why cloven, 2 *Jew.* 1020, or horned, *Pil.* 584, 1 *Tyn.* 233; the two-horned order of bishops, *Bale* 615; mitres worn by some abbots, 2 *Tyn.* 288; Pilkington had neither cruche nor mitre, *Pil.* 586
Moabites: build with the Jews, *Pil.* 384; overthrown for sins, 1 *Bul.* 374, 4 *Bul.* 496
Moazim (......): altars built to them, 3 *Bec.* 240
Mocket (Rich.), warden of All Souls' college, Oxon: reference to his Doctrina et Politia Ecclesiæ Anglicanæ, 1617, *Lit. Eliz.* xxxii.
Mocking: *v.* Scoffing.
Modwina (St), account of her: 3 *Bec.* 240 n.; altars built to her, *ib.* 240
Mœvius, a foolish poet: 2 *Bec.* 419
Mohais: the battle there, *Grin.* 14 n
Moichers: perhaps mouchers, *Coop.* 221
Moile (Sir Tho.), a Kentish justice: 2 *Cran.* 349 n
Molanus (Jo.): affirms that the laity need not read the scriptures, *Whita.* 210; refers to the letter Thau, *Calf.* 107 n.; quotes the spurious epistle of Lentulus, *ib.* 46 n.; mentions the release of the pseudo-Abdias from censure, *ib.* 126 n.; speaks of the substitution of crosses for images of Mercury, *ib.* 66 n.; referred to, *ib.* 202 n
Molineux (......), chaplain to the duchess of Norfolk: 2 *Cran.* 255
Molyneux (......): cousin to Cranmer, 2 *Cran.* 295
Momus: 1 *Cran.* 294, 2 *Jew.* 554, *Pil.* 312
Momus, or Zoilus: opposes Bale, *Bale* 381, 515
Monarchies: *v.* Kingdoms.
Monarchy: 1 *Bul.* 309, 1 *Whitg.* 390, 2 *Whitg.* 244, 3 *Whitg.* 181, 196, 197; Christ and the gospel no enemies to it, 3 *Whitg.* 192
Monasteries: *v.* Abbeys.
Monday: named from the moon, *Pil.* 16
Monetarius (Tho.): depended upon visions,

Rog. 196; took upon himself the ordering and reformation of the church, *ib.* 343

Money: *v.* Coinage, Covetousness, Restitution, Riches.

Generally sought, 1 *Bec.* 222; Aristotle thereon, 3 *Zur.* 284; it will not buy mercy in the day of judgment, 1 *Lat.* 107, but may witness against us, *ib.* 108

Money (*v. a.*): to bribe, 2 *Tyn.* 302

Monger (Mr): in Bread-street counter, 2 *Hoop.* 613

Monhemius (......): attacked by the Censors of Cologne, *Whita.* 360

Monica, mother of Augustine, 2 *Bec.* 343, 344, 1 *Brad.* 540, 2 *Cov.* 218, *Pil.* 557

Moniepennie (David), dean of faculty at St Andrew's: 2 *Zur.* 333 n., 335

Monks: *v.* Abbeys, Benedictines, Carthusians, &c.; also Friars.

Of monasteries and monks, 4 *Bul.* 513; their origin, *ib.* 514, 2 *Lat.* 196; differences between ancient monks and modern ones, 2 *Ful.* 17, 18, 25, 102; anciently very few, if any, of them were priests, 4 *Bul.* 113, 514, 3 *Tyn.* 149 n.; laws about monks made by Justinian, 4 *Bul.* 515; those of the ancient British church, *Calf.* 306; religious orders and their founders, 4 *Bul.* 515, 516; the infinite number of monastical sects, *Bale* 352, 1 *Bec.* 180, 2 *Bec.* 413, 3 *Bec.* 40, 41, 3 *Jew.* 611, *Pil.* 550; their orders said to be from the prophets and apostles, 3 *Jew.* 235, 4 *Jew.* 784; monks styled the apostles' vicegerents, *Calf.* 220; their pretended service of God, 4 *Jew.* 798, &c.; their "rules" praised as though Christ's rule were lost, or were not sufficient, *ib.*; these rules were directed to be accessible in the vulgar tongue, for the benefit of monks who knew no Latin; but not so the scriptures, 1 *Tyn.* 162 n.; why monks run to the cloister, 2 *Tyn.* 32, or, as they call it, into religion, *ib.* 22; they praise their profession or solitary life, 1 *Bul.* 280; their lip labour, 2 *Tyn.* 81; their preaching, 1 *Tyn.* 300; their habits, *ib.* 160; monachism, not acceptable to God, *ib.* 279, 280, but repugnant to Christ's gospel, 4 *Bul.* 516; monks resemble the Pharisees of old, 2 *Tyn.* 42; their counterfeit holiness, 1 *Bul.* 406, 2 *Tyn.* 91; their professed zeal for righteousness, 2 *Tyn.* 24; they sell an interest in their merits, 1 *Tyn.* 212, 227, 2 *Tyn.* 24; their hypocrisy, 1 *Lat.* 392; their false professions of poverty, chastity, and obedience, 2 *Cran.* 147, 1 *Tyn.* 430 (*v.* Vows); their profession and their practice, 2 *Tyn.* 276; they do the devil's work, 2 *Cran.* 64; they are covetous, and stir up rebellion, 2. *Lat.* 301; they love their neighbours in proportion to their gifts, 1 *Tyn.* 299, 343; their love is extended only to their order and benefactors, 2 *Tyn.* 71; they fulfil not the law of love, therefore their prayers avail not, *ib.* 41, 42; their god is their belly, 1 *Tyn.* 299; they are forbidden by the canon law to taste any kind of flesh, 2 *Tyn.* 276; a story of one who was a great faster, 2 *Bec.* 534; the merry monk of Cambridge, 1 *Lat.* 153, 170; monks accounted dead in law, 2 *Tyn.* 182 [Co. Litt. 132 a.]; brought into the cathedral churches, *Pil.* 574; profession under twenty-four years of age prohibited by Henry VIII., 2 *Cran.* 317, and monks forbidden to quit their precincts, *ib.* 312; Russian monks of St Basil persecuted, 3 *Zur.* 600

Monmouth (Hum.), sheriff and alderman of London: anecdote of him, 1 *Lat.* 440; his good example, *ib.* 441; a friend of Latimer, 2 *Lat.* 387 n.; persecuted for befriending Tyndale, 1 *Tyn.* xxii—xxiv, xxvi.

Monophysites: heretics, *Phil.* 185 n

Monopolies: hurtful, 2 *Brad.* 396

Monothelites: their heresy, 1 *Bul.* 14, 3 *Bul.* 261, *Calf.* 137; they denied two wills, divine and human, in Christ, *Rog.* 54; pope Honorius maintained their heresy, *ib.* 181

Mons, or Bergen: 2 *Zur.* 305

Mons Garganus: the church of St Michael there, 3 *Bul.* 348

Monson (B.*): an ecclesiastical commissioner, *Park.* 390

Monson (Gilb.): *v.* Mounson.

Monson (......): *v.* Munson.

Monsters: monstrous births frequent, 4 *Jew.* 1253, 1 *Zur.* 116; both of children and cattle, *Lit. Eliz.* 569; horrible and monstrous shapes, *Pra. B.* 84; a maid with two heads, &c., *Hutch.* 81; a supposed monster set up by Papists to amuse the people, *Grin.* 306, bis.

Mont (Chr.): a diplomatic agent of Henry VIII., Edward VI., and Elizabeth, 2 *Cran.* 377 n., 1 *Zur.* 173 n., 212, 242, (142), 2 *Zur.* 91 n., 173 n., 174, 186, 3 *Zur.* 1, 51, 528, 671, 675, 682, 683, 717; letters by him, 2 *Zur.* 168, 171, 206; his death, *ib.* 210

Mont-St-Aldegonde (Phil. lord of): *v.* Marnix (P. de)

Montacute (Hen. lord): *v.* Pole.

---

* R. in Strype. Doubtless Robert Monson, judge of the Common Pleas.

Montague (Ant. visc.): *v.* Browne.
Montallinus (......): burned at Rome, 1 *Zur.* 182 n
Montanists, called also Cataphrygians, and Pepuzians: their heresy, 1 *Ful.* 84, 2 *Ful.* 389; their name Cataphrygians, 2 *Ful.* 375, *Phil.* 420, 421; their name Pepuzians, 4 *Bul.* 371, 410, 2 *Ful.* 375; they relied on their own dreams, &c., and left the word of God, *Rog.* 158; denied the Trinity, *ib.* 43; held that Christ ascended only in soul, *ib.* 65; taught that sin after baptism is unpardonable, *ib.* 141, 298, 312; baptized dead men (C.), *ib.* 266; added blood to the elements in the eucharist (C.), *ib.* 295; observed stated fasts, 2 *Ful.* 390; condemned matrimony, *Rog.* 261, 306; held that women might be bishops and elders (P.), *ib.* 236 n., 240; took bribes commonly under the name of oblations, 3 *Jew.* 347; originated the idea that the sign of the cross protects from evil spirits, *Whita.* 591; believed in a purgatory, 2 *Ful.* 390, *Rog.* 214
Montanus, a heretic: 1 *Bec.* 278, 3 *Bec.* 401, 2 *Ful.* 238, 3 *Jew.* 337, *Phil.* 419; pretended to have a better revelation than the apostles, 1 *Jew.* 76; said he was the Holy Ghost, *Phil.* 421, 3 *Jew.* 335, *Rog.* 71; added many things to scripture, *Whita.* 688; invented and maintained various traditions, *Calf.* 257, *Whita.* 599; appointed set days and rules of fasting, 1 *Bul.* 434, 2 *Ful.* 388, *Phil.* 405, *Whita.* 596, 665, 1 *Whitg.* 224; called second marriage fornication, 3 *Jew.* 335; prayed for the dead, 2 *Ful.* 388
Montanus (Jo. F.): *v.* Fabricius.
Montanus (Phil.): corrects Theophylact, 1 *Ful.* 234
Montauban: Protestants tolerated there, 2 *Zur.* 224 n
Montcontour: the battle there, 2 *Zur.* 250 n
Monte Regio (Jo. de): *v.* Regiomontanus.
Montfaucon (Bern. de): Diarium Italicum, 2 *Ful.* 110 n., 372 n.; Bibliotheca Biblioth. MSS., *ib.* 361 n.; his statement respecting the Samaritan thau, *Calf.* 107 n.; his opinion of the counterfeit Liber de passione Imaginis Christi, attributed to Athanasius, 2 *Ful.* 200 n.; on the Opus Imperfectum, *Calf.* 96 n
Montford (Tho.): *v.* Mowntforde.
Montgomerie (Gabr. count): a French Protestant exile, *Park.* 420
Montgomery (Hugh), earl of Eglinton: arms in defence of the queen, 1 *Zur.* 205 n.; mentioned, *ib.* 262 n
Months: *v.* Days, Minds.

How reckoned in scripture, *Pil.* 287, 307; their names and reckoning amongst the Jews and in England, *ib.* 15; on the names now used, *ib.* 16
Montjoy (Lords): *v.* Blount.
Montmorenci (Ann, 1st duke of): constable of France, 2 *Zur.* 115
Montmorenci (Fra. 2nd duke of): probably referred to, 3 *Zur.* 559, 683; governor of Paris, 2 *Zur.* 115; ambassador to queen Elizabeth, 1 *Zur.* 34, 273, 2 *Zur.* 201
Montmorenci (Philip de), count of Horn: executed at Brussels, 1 *Zur.* 204; some account of him, *ib.* n
Montpellier: miraculous sights seen about it in 1573, *Lit. Eliz.* 569
Montreuil: "Muttrel journey," the siege by the duke of Norfolk, 1 *Brad.* 493 n., 2 *Brad.* xiii.
Montrose (Will. earl of): *v.* Graham.
Moon: *v.* Signs.
  Darkened by the earth intercepting the sun's light, 1 *Tyn.* 58; the new moon, 2 *Bul.* 162; the moon a figure of the church, *Bale* 327, *Sand.* 360; turned into blood by persecution, *Sand.* 360; signs of the moon, 4 *Bul.* 231; if suppositions be allowable, the moon may be supposed to be made of green cheese, 3 *Whitg.* 390; the man in the moon, 4 *Jew.* 1050, *Park.* 404, 2 *Whitg.* 7
Moor (Tho.), a Protestant member of Parliament: 1 *Brad.* 374 n
Moore (The): a manor of Cranmer's, 2 *Cran.* 493
Moore family, of Ireland: originally of Kent, 3 *Bec.* 563 n
Moore (Jo.): professed to be Christ, *Rog.* 162
Moore (Tho.), parson of Wethringset: dedication to him, 3 *Bec.* 563; conjectures as to his family, *ib.* n.; his diligence, *ib.* 566
Moore (Will.), or More, prior of Worcester: account of him, 2 *Lat.* 371 n
Moore (Mr): a bedel at Cambridge, and a friend of Sandys, *Sand.* iii, vi.
Moore (......), the king's servant: 2 *Lat.* 415
Moors: in Spain.
Moors: in noblemen's houses, 3 *Whitg.* 134
Moot-hall, or Mote-hall: 1 *Brad.* 198
Mopsuestus (Theod.): *v.* Theodorus.
Moptyd (Lau.), master of C. C. C. C.: *Park.* viii, 482
Moquot (Etienne): *Calf.* 236 n
Morant (Will.): martyred in St George's Field, *Poet.* 169
Moravia: *v.* Church, II. ii. *g.*
Moray: *v.* Murray.
Mordaunt (Sir Jo.): one of queen Mary's

privy council, *Phil.* 88, 1 *Zur.* 5 n.; one of Philpot's examiners, *Phil.* 88

Mordaunt (Lewis, 3rd* lord): at the duke of Norfolk's trial, 1 *Zur.* 267 n

Mordecai, or Mardocheus: 2 *Bul.* 162, 2 *Hoop.* 297, *Pil.* 384, 423, 660

Morden (......), a monk of Feversham: *Bale* 118

Morden (James): 1 *Tyn.* 13 n

Morden (Marian): 1 *Tyn.* 13 n

More: greater, 2 *Tyn.* 228

More (De la): a family long seated at Ivychurch in Kent, 3 *Bec.* 563 n

More (Avys): *Hutch.* x.

More (Sir Tho.): at St Anthony's school, London, 3 *Whitg.* v; he inquires about the cause of Goodwin sands, 1 *Lat.* 251; is proposed as high steward of Cambridge, but gives place to Sir R. Wingfield, 2 *Lat.* 296; knew the truth, and forsook it, 2 *Tyn.* 100; Cromwell meets Coverdale in his house, 2 *Cov.* 490, and see 491; he persecutes H. Munmouth, 1 *Tyn.* xxiii; has a license from Tonstal to read heretical books, *ib.* xxxvi, 34, 3 *Tyn.* 2; engaged in collecting alleged heresies from the works of Tyndale and Frith, 1 *Tyn.* 34; his objections to Tyndale's version of the New Testament, 3 *Tyn.* 14 n.; is sent ambassador to Cambray, with Tonstal, 1 *Tyn.* xxxvii; persecutes Jo. Tewkesbury, *ib.* 32; examines G. Constantine, *ib.* xxxviii; made lord chancellor, 2 *Tyn.* 335, 3 *Tyn.* 2; his severity to Bainham, who was racked in his presence, 2 *Lat.* 221, 1 *Tyn.* 35; referred by Henry VIII. to bishop Stokesley as to the divorce, 2 *Lat.* 333 n.; for a time he credited the holy maid of Kent, 1 *Tyn.* 327 n.; his fool, 4 *Jew.* 860 n.; he refuses to swear to the preamble of the act of succession, 2 *Cran.* viii, 285; a false martyr, *Bale* 139; his works, *Jew.* xl; he writes against the gospel, 2 *Lat.* 307 n.; his Dialogue, 1 *Tyn.* xxvi, 41 n., 286 n., 325; Tyndale's ANSWER UNTO SIR T. MORE'S DIALOGUE, 3 *Tyn.* 1 —215; references to it, 1 *Tyn.* xlii, xlv, 1; More's Confutation of Tyndale's Answer, *ib.* xxvii, 1, lii, 4, & passim, 2 *Tyn.* 134, 3 *Tyn.* 2, 3, & passim; his writings against Tyndale referred to, 1 *Lat.* 251, 2 *Lat.* 374; his attack on Frith, and Frith's reply, 1 *Tyn.* lvi; his Supplication of Souls, 1 *Tyn.* 41 n., 2 *Tyn.* 297, 3 *Tyn.* 263, 268 n., for which Tyndale calls him "the proctor of purgatory," 2 *Tyn.* 297; his opinion on the torments of purgatory, 3 *Jew.* 567, *Rog.* 216; his History of Richard III. quoted, 1 *Tyn.* 326 n.; his Utopia referred to, 1 *Bul.* 385, 4 *Bul.* 52, 2 *Tyn.* 84, 100, 225, 302, 3 *Tyn.* 166, 193, 263, & sæpe; allusion to his Book of the fair Gentlewoman, Lady Fortune, *Park.* 60; imploratio divini auxilii contra tentationem, ex Psalmis Davidis, *Pra. Eliz.* 318 n.; precationes ex Novo Test., perhaps collected by him, *ib.* 353; he acknowledges that papal pardons may prove to be of no use to the purchaser, 3 *Tyn.* 28 n.; his abusive language when speaking of Luther, *ib.* 3, 5, 187 n.; he asserts that Bilney died a Roman catholic, 1 *Lat.* 222 n.; says Barnes ought to have been burnt, notwithstanding the king's safe-conduct, 1 *Tyn.* 3; affirms that no reformer would abide by his faith to the death, 2 *Tyn.* 340; declares that there should have been a great many more burned than there had been, 3 *Tyn.* 97 n.; complains of the confusion produced by scholastic metaphysics, 1 *Tyn.* 157 n.; speaks of the prevalence of open adultery, 1 *Lat.* 244 n.; his eloquence and wit, *Park.* 315; his juggling with words, 3 *Tyn.* 79, and with scripture, *ib.* 82; styled M. Mocke, *ib.* 267

More (Will.): *v.* Moore.

Morecroft (Rich.), a Londoner: examined before the ecclesiastical commissioners, *Grin.* 201

Morelius (......): interprets scripture mystically, *Rog.* 197

Morell (Claude): 2 *Ful.* 110 n

Moreman (Jo.), dean of Exeter, and coadjutor to the bp: some account of him, 2 *Cran.* 183 n., *Phil.* 167; perverted justice Hales, *Rid.* 363; required by the Devon rebels as a teacher, 2 *Cran.* 183; his answer in the convocation house, *Rid.* 36 n.; he affirms that Christ ate his own body, *Phil.* 190

Moren (Jo.): *v.* Morwen.

Moreri (Louis): 2 *Ful.* 74 n., 1 *Lat.* 426 n

Mores (M.): *v.* Griffith (M.), bishop of Rochester.

Moresinus (Tho.): Papatus, Edinb. 1594, *Rog.* 266 n

Moreton (Jo.): *v.* Morton.

Morgan (Hen.), bp of St David's: notice of him, *Phil.* xxix; one of the examiners of Philpot, *ib.* 88, 104; sharply rebuked by him, *ib.* 122

Morgan (Phil.): *Bale* 28

Morgan (......): disputes with P. Martyr, *Jew.* viii.

---

* Qu. John 2d lord?

Morgan (Sir Rich.), chief justice of the Common Pleas: went mad after the execution of lady Jane Grey, whom he condemned, *Rid.* 362

Moriah: *v.* Jerusalem.

Morian: a follower of More, *Pil.* 638

Morice (James), of the household of Margaret, countess of Richmond: father of Ralph and William, 2 *Lat.* 222 n

M[orice?] (P.): 2 *Cran.* 259

Morice (Ralph), secretary to abp Cranmer: 2 *Cran.* 259 n.; probably referred to, *ib.* 349 n.; his account of Latimer's conversion, 2 *Lat.* xxvii.

Morice (Will.): 2 *Cran.* 389, 2 *Lat.* 222 n.; letter from Latimer to him, 2 *Lat.* 357

Mories (Margery): she and her son, martyrs at Lewes, *Poet.* 170

Morinus (Jo.): on the writings ascribed to Dionysius the Areopagite, *Calf.* 211 n

Morinus (Steph.): on the Ethiopic thau, &c., *Calf.* 107 n

Morison (Sir Rich.): mentioned, 2 *Zur.* 69; a commissioner at a dispute at Oxford, 3 *Zur.* 391 n.; letter from him to Calvin, *ib.* 147; one to Bullinger, *ib.* 148; dead, *ib.* 173; Bridget his widow, 2 *Bec.* 622 n

Morison (Tho.): *v.* Moresinus.

Morley (Hen. lord): *v.* Parker.

Morley (Sir Rob.), lieutenant of the Tower: brings lord Cobham before abp Arundel, *Bale* 23, 29

Mornay (Phil. de), sieur du Plessis: his work on the eucharist, *Rid.* 509; Tract. de Eccles., *Rog.* 298 n.; his character of H. Languet, 2 *Zur.* 289 n

Morning: *v.* Meditations, Prayers.

How a man should behave when he rises in the morning, 1 *Bec.* 401

Morocco: the straits, 1 *Bul.* 416

Morrice (i. e. Moorish) dance: 1 *Cov.* 4 n., *Grin.* 142, 175, 1 *Zur.* 259 n

Morris (Mr): slandered, *Park.* 368

Morrison (Sir Rich.): *v.* Morison.

Morrow-priest: one who said morrow-mass, 3 *Bec.* 530

Mortification: *v.* Meditations, Prayers.

Mortifico, mortificatio, *Now.* (102); mortification of sinful affections, *Nord.* 66; verses thereon, *ib.* 77; that of Christians, represented in baptism, 4 *Bul.* 329; a meditation for the exercise of true mortification, *Pra. B.* 96

Mortlake, co. Surrey: letters thence, 2 *Cran.* 240, 241; exchange thereof between Cranmer and Cromwell, *ib.* 333

Mortmain: statutes of mortmain, 1 *Lat.* 522; repealed in queen Mary's time, 2 *Cran.* 17

Morton (James, earl of): *v.* Douglas.

Morton (Jo. card.), abp of Canterbury: mentioned, 2 *Tyn.* 302 n.; licensed by the pope to study necromancy, *ib.* 305; said to have betrayed the confessions of the nobility to Henry VII., *ib.* 305

Morton (Tho.), bp of Durham: Works, *Calf.* 6, 64, 96, 202, 255, 290, 2 *Ful.* 49, 70, 71, 82, 86 mn

Morton (James), or Mourton: a rebellious priest, 2 *Cran.* 187 n

Morton (Nic.): stirs up a rebellion in the North, *Lit. Eliz.* 657 n

Mortuaries: what, 1 *Tyn.* 235 n.; a satisfaction for forgotten tithes, 2 *Tyn.* 43; oppressively exacted, 1 *Tyn.* 237, 338; checked by statute, 2 *Lat.* 301 n., 1 *Tyn.* 235 n., 3 *Tyn.* 269

Morwen (Jo.), or Moren: notice of him, 2 *Cran.* 383; his estimation of Jewel, *Jew.* vi; his Addition, &c., a libel upon the burning of St Paul's, *Pil.* 481—486; Pilkington's Confutation of it, *ib.* 487, &c.

Morwent (Rob.), pres. C. C. C. Oxon.: *Jew.* vi, 2 *Jew.* 952; concerned in Cranmer's examination, 2 *Cran.* 547; sent to the Fleet, *Jew.* ix.

Morwin (Pet.): in exile, *Grin.* 221

Morynge (Sir Will.): *v.* Mering.

Moschus (Jo.): *v.* Joannes.

Moscow: persecution there, 3 *Zur.* 600

Moses: *v.* Genesis, Exodus, &c.; also Law.

His age, 1 *Bul.* 42; references to him, 4 *Bul.* 28, 37, 102, 122, 133, 165, 180, 434, 479, 487; the Finding of Moses, a poem by M. Drayton, *Poet.* 130; he forsook Pharaoh's court, *Pil.* 341, 425; his marriage, *Rid.* 84; his punishment for neglect of circumcision, 4 *Bul.* 345, 366, 372, *Calf.* 335; God appears to him in a bush, *Calf.* 334; his miracles, 4 *Bul.* 232; his rod turned into a serpent, *ib.* 262; the song of Moses (Exod. xv), versified by M. Drayton, *Poet.* 124; his office extraordinary, *Whita.* 416, 417; he was a type of Christ as supreme ruler, *ib.* 418; a captain, 1 *Bul.* 384, 386; a worthy magistrate, *Sand.* 147; the lifting up of his hands, and what it prefigured, *Calf.* 104—106; whether he was a priest, 2 *Ful.* 270, 4 *Jew.* 982, &c.; not a priest subsequently to the unction of Aaron, *Whita.* 417; he and Aaron were associated as rulers, *Pil.* 35; his reception of the law, 2 *Bul.* 169, 4 *Jew.* 1164; bp Fisher says, Moses in the mount and Aaron below were types of Christ and of Peter or the pope, 1 *Tyn.* 208, 209; the true meaning of the type, *ib.* 209; his desire to see God in his majesty, 3 *Bul.* 144; how God shewed himself to him in the cleft of the rock, *ib.* 145, 4 *Bul.* 253; Moses represented with horns [through the rendering of the Vulgate, Exod. xxxiv. 30], *Rog.* 223; his making of the tabernacle, *Pil.* 8, 78; how he did sanctify, 4 *Bul.* 273; his character, 1 *Tyn.* 412; his afflictions, 2 *Bul.* 103; his hope, *ib.* 89; his prayers, 4 *Bul.* 170, 224, 225; he was the earliest writer, *Whita.* 114; though some suppose that there were scriptures before his time, *ib.* 114, 516; he was the first of the holy writers, 1 *Bul.* 39; wrote by the Spirit, *ib.* 46; requires a high and perfect righteousness, 2 *Bec.* 630; inculcates the teaching of God's word, *Pil.* 26; is jealous for God's word, *ib.* 24; his authority very great, 1 *Bul.* 47; he not only slays, 2 *Bul.* 239; but also leads to Christ, *ib.* 240; his smiting of the rock, *Calf.* 336; he offended, so that he entered not into the land of promise, 1 *Hoop.* 23; why God hid his body, 3 *Tyn.* 125; his sepulchre concealed, *Calf.* 312; how the devil has attempted to subvert the credit of his mission, *ib.* 13, 14; to be baptized into Moses, what it means, 4 *Bul.* 299; what it is to sit in the chair or seat of Moses, 1 *Bec.* 386, 4 *Bul.* 161, 2 *Cran.* 54, *Whita.* 426

Moses Ben Maimon (R.), or Maimonides: *Bale* 479, 3 *Bul.* 135, 1 *Hoop.* 350, *Whita.* 33 n., 3 *Whitg.* 343

Moses (Miles), B.D.: *Rog.* vii.

Mosheim (Jo. Lau.): 2 *Bec.* 379, 3 *Bec.* 401, 2 *Brad.* 382 n., 2 *Ful.* 5, 101, 225, 319, *Grin.* 21, 251, 254, 256, 1 *Hoop.* 47, 246, 263, 375, 524, 2 *Hoop.* 76, 4 *Jew.* 656, 1106, 1 *Lat.* 160, 274, 425, 465, 2 *Lat.* 98, *Pil.* 19, 513, 684 nn

Mosse (Jo.): 2 *Brad.* 10, 22

Mote-hall: *v.* Moot-hall.

Moten: meted, *Bale* 386

Mothers: *v.* Parents.

Mottram, co. Chester: called Mottrine, 1 *Brad.* 454; the parson of Mottram, 2 *Brad.* 77

Mouchers: self-will moichers, or mouchers, *Coop.* 221

Moulin (P. du): *v.* Du Moulin.

Mounson (Gilb.): notary to Cranmer and Ridley at their examination at Oxford, *Rid.* 194; see *Jew.* xiv.

Mounson (Rob.): *v.* Monson.

Mount (Chr.): *v.* Mont.

Mount of Olives: *v.* Olivet.

Mountains: the word, in Micah vi. 2, said to mean the angels, *Sand.* 216; alleged to denote, in Matt. xxiv. the holy scriptures, 2 *Cran.* 24, 25, 1 *Jew.* 327, *Whita.* 684, & al.

Mounteyn (Tho.?): in exile, 1 *Cran.* (9)

Mountjoy: *v.* Montjoy.

Mourning: what sort maketh blessed, 1 *Lat.* 479, 2 *Tyn.* 18; mourning for the dead, to be bridled, *Pil.* 319 (and see Dead); on mourning apparel, 3 *Whitg.* 368, &c.; mourning gowns commonly used at funerals, 3 *Bec.* 120, 124; not meet to be worn for those who have entered the kingdom of God, *ib.* 120, &c.

Mourton (James): *v.* Morton.

Mouse (Dr): *v.* Mowse.

Mow: a heap of corn, 2 *Bul.* 231

Mower (James), of Milton shore: Sandys lodged at his house, *Sand.* xv.

Mowing: making grimaces, *Bale* 352, 1 *Brad.* 283, 1 *Tyn.* 226; mows, grimaces, 1 *Brad.* 395, 1 *Cran.* 226

Mowling: moulding, 2 *Brad.* 285, 2 *Cov.* 264

Mowll (Edw.): chaplain to Dr Benet, the king's ambassador in Italy, 2 *Cran.* 289, 290

Mownt (......): servant to Cecil, *Park.* 258

Mownteforde (Tho.): committed to the Fleet, 2 *Cran.* 291

Mowse (Will.), master of Trinity hall: one day a Protestant, the next a Papist, *Sand.* iv; mentioned, 2 *Cran.* 437

Moyne (O. and S. le): *v.* Le Moyne.

Mozzelini (Sylv.), otherwise Prierias, *q. v.*

Mucktar (מקטר): its meaning, 1 *Hoop.* 241

Mugnos (Giles de): *v.* Clement VIII., antipope.

Muhlberg: battle there, 3 *Zur.* 260 n

Mule: 1 *Lat.* 140

Muller (Jo.): called Regiomontanus, *q. v.*

Mullins (Jo.): in exile at Zurich, 3 *Zur.* 752 n.; dean of Bocking, archdeacon of London, &c., 2 *Zur.* 307; bp Grindal's letter to him about the plague, 1563, *Grin.* 78; mention of him, *Park.* 377

Multitude: not always to be followed, 1 *Hoop.* 84; no proof of truth, 1 *Brad.* 426, 2 *Cov.* 243

Mumble-matins: *v.* Sir John.

Mummoth (Hum.): *v.* Monmouth.

Mumpsimus: 2 *Lat.* 16, 211; origin of the expression, 2 *Lat.* 16 n., 2 *Tyn.* 320 n

Muncer (Tho.), or Munzer: a leader of ungodly Anabaptists, 1 *Hoop.* 246 n.; said the Anabaptists only were the elect of God, *Rog.* 169; taught that scripture is not the true word of God, *ib.* 78 n.; pretended to have revelations, 2 *Ful.* 73; condemned preachers, 1 *Whitg.* 83 n.; affirmed that the word is not taught by preaching but by revelation, *Rog.* 231; his rebellion, 4 *Jew.* 670, 671, *Park.* 426, 2 *Tyn.* 244 n.; he declared that the sword of Gideon was given to him for the overthrowing of all tyrants, and setting up the kingdom of Christ, *Rog.* 343

Mundani, mundus, seculum: *Now.* (102)

Munday (Ant.): notice of him, *Poet.* xxi; a ditty declaring the uncertainty of our earthly honour, the certain account that we must all make of death, &c., *ib.* 226; a ditty shewing that neither strength nor any transitory things can save from the stroke of death, *ib.* 228; a ditty wherein the brevity of man's life is described, &c., *ib.* 230; stanzas from his Complaint of Jonas, *ib.* 231

Mundt (Chr.); *v.* Mont.

Mungey (Mrs), sister to bp Bonner, *Rid.* viii.

Muñion (Giles de): *v.* Clement VIII., antipope.

Munmouth (Hum.): *v.* Monmouth.

Munson (......): *Jew.* xiv. (perhaps G. Mounson).

Munster: seized by the Anabaptists, *Grin.* 256 n.; the rebels there not gospellers, but enemies to the gospel, 4 *Jew.* 665

Munster (Seb.): writes to Henry VIII., 2 *Cran.* 340; his character as a translator of scripture, *Park.* 257

Munzer (Tho.): *v.* Muncer.

Muralt (......): 1 *Zur.* 9, 25

Murdach (Hen.) abp of York: *Pil.* 588

Murder: *v.* Commandments.

Forbidden, 1 *Brad.* 164, 1 *Lat.* 9, *Now.* (19), 133; how murder is committed, 1 *Bul.* 304, 1 *Hoop.* 474; it may be of the heart, 1 *Hoop.* 372, or of the tongue, *ib.* 373; hatred is murder, 2 *Tyn.* 192; all things in which it consists are forbidden, 1 *Bul.* 299, 1 *Lat.* 10; its causes, 1 *Bul.* 304; how great an offence it is, *ib.* 305 wilful murder unpardonable, 2 *Bec.* 94; there are several kinds of murder, 2 *Bul.* 233; on the killing of tyrants, 1 *Bul.* 318; murder distinguished from chance-medley, 1 *Lat.* 195; murder condemned among the Gentiles, *ib.* 203; the pope's doctrine commands it, 1 *Tyn.* 166; its proper punishment, *Now.* 226; it must be punished with death, 1 *Hoop.* 474, 1 *Lat.* 190

Murderer: a name of the devil, 3 *Bul.* 356

Murray (James earl of): *v.* Stuart.

Murray (Will.), of Tullibardin: one of the confederate lords, 1 *Zur.* 193 n

Murray (......): 2 *Zur.* 333, 335

Murus: a British river named by Bede, 1 *Jew.* 303

Musæus: 3 *Bul.* 385

Muscovy: *v.* Russia.

Musculus (Abr.): letters to him, 2 *Zur.* 298, 301

Musculus (Andr.): said that Christ suffered in both natures, *Rog.* 57

Musculus (Wolfg.): notices of him, 2 *Zur.* 3 n.; 3 *Zur.* 335 n.; mentioned, 4 *Jew.* 665; perhaps named, 1 *Zur.* 84, 2 *Zur.* 301; invited to England, 3 *Zur.* 336, 680, 725; Comm. in Matthæum, 3 *Whitg.* xxx; Comm. in Evang. Joannis, *Jew.* xl; Comm. in Ep. ad Philipp., 3 *Whitg.* xxx; Loci Communes, 1 *Bul.* 8, 3 *Whitg.* xxx; translated by Man, 2 *Zur.* 148 n.; his book called Proscerus, 3 *Zur.* 572; his Precationes, *Pra. Eliz.* 442, 507, 513 nn.; a work of his referred to, 3 *Bec.* 375; notice of his translations, 2 *Zur.* 299 n.; his version of Eusebius, &c. *Calf.* 28, 69, 111, 269, 299, 2 *Ful.* 112, 115, 347, 358, 366, 379 nn.; an argument of his in support of scripture, *Whita.* 351; his division of the judicial law of Moses, 1 *Whitg.* 268; he gives a reason for the Jews' ceremonies, *ib.* 271; he says that the law of Moses has given place to the law of Christ, *ib.* 274; explains the command "Tell it unto the church," 3 *Whitg.* 170; considers that Timothy was a bishop, 2 *Whitg.* 298; denies that Timothy and Titus ordained by their own authority, 1 *Whitg.* 428, 435; defines an evangelist, *ib.* 493, 2 *Whitg.* 299; considers pastors and doctors the same, 1 *Whitg.* 474, 504; defends the discontinuance of apostolic church government, *ib.* 418, 420, 3 *Whitg.* 215—217; shews how, though there must be inequality in the church, &c., Christ forbids that men should desire greatness, 1 *Whitg.* 148, 155, 158, 159; thinks the episcopal honour was the first step to the papacy, 3 *Whitg.* 536; interprets Acts xiv. 23, they ordained those chosen by the faithful, 1 *Whitg.* 345; allows that the election of ministers remained until Cyprian's time, *ib.* 360; states why they are not chosen by the people, as at first, *ib.* 414, 421; does not think it convenient for any to take upon him public office in the church, without the magistrate's authority; if it was otherwise in the primitive churches, it was, says he, because they had not a Christian magistrate, *ib.* 394, 414, 422; writes about apostolic times, 3 *Whitg.* 195; writes of the magistrate's duty with reference to the election of ministers, *ib.* 397, 398; censures those who being chosen of none, get ordained for a sum of money, 1 *Whitg.* 441, 442; describes the election of ministers in the church of Berne, *ib.* 309, 418, 421, 422; commenting on the text, "Christ sent me not to baptize, &c.," he declares that in some churches some were admitted to minister the sacraments who were not admitted to preach, 2 *Whitg.* 457; notes that communion of the sick is retained in many reformed churches, *ib.* 545, 546; writes of Christ and his disciples singing a hymn, *ib.* 491; speaks of fervour in prayer, 1 *Lat.* 344, 362, 370; commends the public reading of scripture, 3 *Whitg.* 49—51; says that the epistle of the Laodiceans was publicly read in the primitive church, *Rog.* 324 n.; expounds texts on binding and loosing, 3 *Whitg.* 236; censures schism and contention, 1 *Whitg.* 42, 138, 196; speaks of the authority of Christian magistrates, 3 *Whitg.* 298, 300; disapproves a distinction between the church and a Christian commonwealth, 1 *Whitg.* 388, 389; denies that things which concern religion may be done without the magistrate's consent, *ib.* 393, 394, 420; distinguishes three kinds of idolatry, *ib.* 335; denies that Lucifer is Satan, 3 *Bul.* 350 n.; censures Millenaries, *Rog.* 154; records two verses about pope Alexander, 4 *Jew.* 867; letter from him to Bullinger, 3 *Zur.* 336; letters to him, *ib.* 334, 336

Musgrave (Sir Will.): Eliz. his wife, 2 *Cran.* 368

Music, Psalmody, Singing: *v.* Minstrels, Psalms.

Music declared to be a vain and trifling science, 2 *Bec.* 429; the delight of it is soon gone, *ib.*; it may be used, if not abused, *ib.* 430; a lesson for musicians, 1 *Bec.* 134; ditties and descants, 1 *Brad.* 160; descant and plain song, 1 *Tyn.* 307; descant, prick song, counterpoint, faburden, *Bale* 536, *Rid.* 511; harps, lutes, fiddles, virginals, viols, chimes, recorders, flutes, drones, trumpets, waites, shawms, organs, bells, *Bale* 536; Lincolnshire bagpipes, *ib.* 102; bagpipes, harps, lutes, fiddles, 3 *Whitg.* 322, 353; singing and piping, *ib.* 106; piping, playing, and curious singing, 2 *Lat.* 348; the music and minstrelsy of David to be interpreted ghostly, *Bale* 102; Christ put out the minstrels, *ib.*; the right use of singing, 2 *Cov.* 536, &c.; on singing in the church, 4 *Bul.* 190; the ancient manner, *ib.* 193; always free in the church, but not universal, *ib.* 194; agreement in it, *ib.* 195; what things to be discommended in it, *ib.* 196; on the spiritual songs of the apostolic church, *Whita.* 260; remarks on the singing of the church of old, 1 *Jew.* 265, &c.; Gregory's singing, 4 *Bul.* 196; singing after the Roman manner taught in Britain, 1 *Jew.* 303; directions of the council of Aix respecting psalmody, *Whita.* 273; singers in the Romish church, 4 *Bul.* 114; the singing of children on Palm Sunday, 1 *Bec.* 113, 114, 116; song and instruments approved, *Hutch.* 285; Cranmer's opinion on the composition of church music, 2 *Cran.* 412; on organs in the church, and curious singing, *Bale* 102, 2 *Lat.* 348, *Rid.* 511, 3 *Whitg.* 392; allusions to organs, *Phil.* 235, 1 *Tyn.* 234; music not expelled from the church of England, *Park.* 215; congregational singing encouraged; its beneficial influence, 1 *Zur.* 71; part-singing and organs commonly used, *ib.* 164 (see corrig. 2 *Zur.* x.); organs and chanting disapproved of by Grindal and Horn, 1 *Zur.* 178, as well as by Bullinger and Gualter, *ib.* 358; and objected to by the Puritans, 2 *Zur.* 150; singing in the reformed churches, 3 *Whitg.* 107; music on pilgrimages, *Bale* 102, 103

Musonius: on marriage, 1 *Bul.* 396

Musselburgh: *v.* Pinkie.

Mutability: *v.* Mirror.

Muttrel: *v.* Montreuil.

Muzta, a Saracen captain: 1 *Bul.* 416

Myconius (Fred.): an envoy from Germany, 2 *Cran.* 377 n., 378 n., 3 *Zur.* 612 n

Myconius (Mr): perhaps the same, 3 *Zur.* 218, 223

Mydelmore (Mr): 1 *Zur.* 204 n

Myrrh: *v.* Magi.

Myrrick (......): an unlearned Welsh doctor of law beneficed in Cheshire, *Grin.* 346

Mysteries: *v.* Sacraments.

What mysteries are, 4 *Bul.* 236; mysteries in religion, *Whita.* 614; "the mysteries of God," 1 *Ful.* 495, 496, 2 *Whitg.* 519; Gardiner deprecates inquiry into them, 1 *Cran.* 334; the mystery of the kingdom, 4 *Bul.* 237; sacramental mysteries, *ib.* 233, &c.; Christ our chief interpreter of mysteries, *ib.* 237; mystical divinity, *ib.* 238

Mysteries, or Miracle Plays: 2 *Bul.* 194 n

Mystery of Iniquity: what, 2 *Jew.* 909; its pretence of chastity, *ib.* 911; the practice of single communion, *ib.*; the doctrine of the keys, *ib.*; its abuse of prayer, *ib.*; the doctrine of purgatory, *ib.* 912; its use of the name of the church, *ib.*; the supremacy of Rome, *ib.*

Mystic sense: *v.* Scripture.

N

N. (H.): v. Nicholas.
N. (T.): v. Norton.
N. (W.): author of a work not found, *Rog.* 73 n
Naaman: reply of the king of Israel to the king of Syria's message, 3 *Bul.* 208; he is healed, *Calf.* 337, 4 *Bul.* 255; Elisha refuses his gift, 4 *Bul.* 124, 489; he is sent away in peace, 2 *Brad.* 338, 3 *Zur.* 39
Nabal: his death, *Grin.* 8
Naboth: 1 *Bul.* 307
Naclantus (Jac.), bp of Chioca: Ennar. in Epist. ad Rom., *Jew.* xl; on the worship of images, 2 *Jew.* 667, 3 *Jew.* 121, 4 *Jew.* 950; compelled to crave the pope's pardon, 4 *Jew.* 955
Nadab, and Abihu: 2 *Bul.* 187, 4 *Bul.* 239, 408, *Pil.* 629
Nag's head: v. London.
Nahash, king of the Ammonites: 1 *Bul.* 379, *Grin.* 29, 4 *Jew.* 1066
Nails: v. Cross.
Naioth, in Ramah: 4 *Bul.* 481
Naiton, king of the Picts, 2 *Ful.* 8
Nalle: an awl, 1 *Bec.* 5
Name, Names: v. God.
A good name passes all worldly riches, 2 *Bec.* 116; prayer for a good name, 3 *Bec.* 83; names in scripture not given in vain, *Pil.* 216; names given in circumcision, 2 *Bul.* 176; also in baptism, 4 *Bul.* 329, 2 *Jew.* 1108; many surnames in England derived from the names of foreign countries, 4 *Jew.* 651; names of blasphemy, *Bale* 422, 496
Namely: especially, expressly, *Grin.* 8, *Pil.* 34, 40, 2 *Tyn.* 83
Nanchiantes (Jac.): v. Naclantus.
Nangis (Guillermus de): 1 *Bec.* 390 n
Nantwich, co. Chester: a great fire there in 1593, *Poet.* xxi.
Naomi: a good example, 1 *Bul.* 285
Naper (And.), a Papist in Edinburgh: 2 *Zur.* 331 n
Napes: v. Jack.
Naples: 40,000 killed there, *Pil.* 607; taken by Louis XII., 2 *Tyn.* 310; strange things which befel there in 1566, *Lit. Eliz.* 569: poverty of its bishopricks, 4 *Jew.* 971
Narbonne: an abp or archdeacon thereof, 4 *Jew.* 685
Nares (R.): *Bale* 294, 394, 2 *Bec.* 345, 438, 3 *Bec.* 260, 276, 282, 284, 535 nn., 1 *Whitg.* 516 n., 3 *Whitg.* xxxi.
Narses: 2 *Bec.* 441

Nash (Tho.): on English hexameter verses, *Poet.* xxii.
Nashe (Tho.): his Christ's Teares cited, *Rog.* 78 n., 148 n
Nash (T.): Hist. of Worc., 2 *Lat.* 372, 375, 376, 387, 389, 394, 398, 400, 401, 403, 409, 410, 414 nn
Nasica: *Hutch.* 51
Nassau: the family, 2 *Zur.* 207 n (v. William).
Natalibus (Pet. de): v. Petrus.
Natalis, or Natalius, a martyr: his penance, 3 *Bul.* 76
Natalis Alexander, *q.v.*
Natalis (Herv.): v. Hervæus.
Natalitia: the days on which martyrs suffered, *Calf.* 257
Nathan: reproves David, 2 *Hoop.* 358, *Pil.* 12, 112, 161; speaks of Christ, 2 *Bul.* 159; none of his writings lost, *Whita.* 525
Nathanael, i.e. Rob. Harrington, *q.v.*
Nathaniel: said to have preached at Treves and Bourges, 1 *Jew.* 162
Nations: v. Sin.
Nativity: v. Christmas.
Natolia: 4 *Bul.* 20
Natural Man: v. Man.
Nature: what it is, 1 *Bul.* 194, *Hutch.* 277, 278; it is nothing but the ordinary will of God, 1 *Brad.* 359; Plato's definition, 1 *Jew.* 500, 501; how far it can teach men, 2 *Jew.* 198, 199; its corruption, 1 *Bul.* 194; the law a light of nature corrupted by sin, *Lit. Edw.* 499, (548); the nature of man (*q.v.*) is not the cause of sin, 2 *Bul.* 362; how greatly it is corrupted, 1 *Bec.* 46, 47, 3 *Bec.* 605, 2 *Bul.* 393, 394; nature powerless without grace, 1 *Bul.* 205; arguments upon transubstantiation from the operation of nature, 1 *Cran.* 250, 251, 252, 253, 254; whether the natures of things are changed by consecration, 4 *Bul.* 261
Nauclerus (Jo.): Memorabilium Chronic. Comment., *Jew.* xl; referred to on Constantine's Donation, 2 *Ful.* 361 n.; on the invention of the cross, *Calf.* 323 n.; he mentions the disinterment of Formosus, *Pil.* 652; tells how the Roman missale was approved, and the Ambrosian missale rejected by a miracle, *ib.* 509; speaks of a decree of Gregory VII. against priests' marriages, and the opposition of the clergy to it, *ib.* 567; declares that the clergy said that the pope, for good causes, was excommunicate, &c., 3 *Jew.* 129, 347; refers to the poisoning of pope Victor III., 1 *Jew.* 105 n.: what he says of pope John XXI. or XXII., or both, 4 *Jew.* 931, 932, 933, 934, 936; he tells how the French king

treated the insolent demands of Boniface VIII., *ib.* 685; mentions the poisoning of the emperor Henry VII., 1 *Jew.* 105 n., 4 *Jew.* 686

Naumberg (Julius bp of): *v.* Pflug.

Navarre: taken by the king of Spain, 2 *Tyn.* 310

Naveta, or Navicula: 1 *Tyn.* 238 n

Navy: greatly increased by queen Elizabeth, *Sand.* 81, 2 *Zur.* 67; the Christian navy; by Anth. Nixon, *Poet.* 543

Naworth castle, co. Cumb.: the rebels there, 1 *Zur.* 214 n

Nay and No: More's remarks on the difference between them, 3 *Tyn.* 25 n

Nazarene: the quotation in Matt. ii. 23, referred to Judges xiii. 5, but as it seems erroneously, *Whita.* 302; the opinion of pseudo-Chrysostom, *ib.* 525

Nazarenes: were both circumcised and baptized; *Rog.* 275; observed Jewish ceremonies, *ib.* 314; the Gospel of the Nazarenes, *Whita.* 108

Nazarites: 2 *Bul.* 207, 271, 4 *Bul.* 113, 481, 3 *Jew.* 170; complained of by Amos, 4 *Bul.* 494; the Greek forms of the word, *Whita.* 302 n

Nazianzen (Greg.): *v.* Gregory.

Neal (Dan.): Hist. of the Puritans, 2 *Ful.* 37 n

Neale (Shan O'): *v.* O'Neale.

Neander (Aug.): 2 *Brad.* 379, 382, 2 *Ful.* 101, 1 *Lat.* 201 n

Neare: nearer, 3 *Jew.* 260

Nebridius: a courtier commended by Jerome, *Pil.* 294

Nebuchadnezzar, king of Babylon: carried the Jews captive, 2 *Bul.* 11, 4 *Bul.* 20, *Pil.* 8, 12, 75; offended God though he was his instrument, *Pil.* 221; his golden image, *v.* Shadrach; his decree for the worship of God, 1 *Bul.* 325, *Pil.* 361; his vision, 3 *Bul.* 344; he is exhorted by Daniel to repentance, *ib.* 92, 2 *Cov.* 367; his pride, punishment, and restoration, 2 *Bul.* 72, 343, *Grin.* 106, 2 *Hoop.* 303, *Pil.* 231, 233; his prosperity, 2 *Bul.* 13; his death, *Grin.* 8

Necessary Doctrine: *v.* Doctrine.

Necessity: *v.* Fortune.

It sets aside law, 3 *Tyn.* 18; every one may lawfully pray for his own necessities, 2 *Bec.* 160; God allows us to hope for the supply of corporal necessaries, *ib.* 614, 615

Neck verse: *v.* Clergy (Benefit of).

Necromancy: *v.* Witchcraft.

Nectarius, patr. of Constantinople: his election, 1 *Jew.* 407, 409, 1 *Whitg.* 410; he desired the blessing of his bishop on his departure, 2 *Ful.* 108; his jurisdiction, 2 *Whitg.* 315; he abolished private confession, and the office of penitentiary, 3 *Bul.* 77, 2 *Ful.* 91*, *Pil.* 553, 1 *Tyn.* 263 n.; advised how to bring men to unity of faith, 4 *Jew.* 1019

Need: *v.* Necessity.

Negatives: examples of negatives by comparison, 1 *Cran.* 313, 314, 315; when a negative argument is of force, 1 *Jew.* 175

Negelin (......), a consul: 2 *Zur.* 3

Negelin (Matth.): notice of him, 3 *Zur.* 333 n

Negligence: in building God's house, *Pil.* 11, 13, 90; deprecated in captains and preachers, *ib.* 438

Negroo (Sir Peryn): his death, 3 *Zur.* 496 n

Nehemiah: meaning of his name, *Pil.* 285; he asked nothing before he prayed, 4 *Bul.* 225; his prayer for the sins of the people, *Lit. Edw.* 479; his prayer paraphrased, *Pil.* 296—305; his promotion in the Persian court, *ib.* 310, 325; his reverence to his prince, *ib.* 314; his love to his country, *ib.* 315; his prayer for divine guidance, *ib.* 322; he requests permission to go to Jewry, *ib.* 327; his zeal in leaving the court, *ib.* 332; his conduct on arriving at Jerusalem, *ib.* 337, 338; his secresy, *ib.* 341, 349; his zeal inspired by God, *ib.* 342; he views Jerusalem, *ib.* 345; his boldness in withstanding its enemies, *ib.* 360, 362; he seeks comfort in prayer, *ib.* 403; his labour in building, *ib.* 425, 450; he was a wise captain, *ib.* 426; his address to the nobles, *ib.* 430, 443; his diligence, *ib.* 444; his example recommended, *ib.* 286, 443; especially to courtiers, *ib.* 440

— Book of Nehemiah: otherwise called the second book of Esdras, 2 *Cov.* 18; Pilkington's EXPOSITION OF CERTAIN CHAPTERS, *Pil.* 276—468 (see above).

Neighbour: *v.* Duty, Love.

Who is our neighbour, 3 *Bec.* 610, 616, 1 *Bul.* 184, *Now.* (23), 102, 137, 138, *Sand.* 205, 1 *Tyn.* 85; our duty towards him, 1 *Bec.* 223, 1 *Tyn.* 98, 2 *Tyn.* 119, 3 *Tyn.* 57, 58; this duty not to be deserted by voluntary seclusion, 1 *Tyn.* 279, 280; our neighbour to be loved, and how, 1 *Bec.* 227, 228, 2 *Bec.* 111, 112, 1 *Bul.* 186, 1 *Lat.* 20, 1 *Tyn.* 25, 26, 404, 2 *Tyn.* 46; to be loved for God's sake, 2 *Tyn.* 47; as ourselves, 1 *Bul.* 187; as Christ loved us, *ib.*;

---

* Nestorius in this place is an error for Nectarius.

NEIGHBOUR — NEVILLE 553

how we ought to stand our neighbour in stead, *ib.* 188; we should do good works to win him to Christ, 1 *Bec.* 347 ; God's gifts are bestowed upon us for our neighbour's benefit, 1 *Tyn.* 24
Neither nother: neither the one nor the other, 2 *Tyn.* 129, 342, 3 *Tyn.* 125
Nelson (Tho.): notice of him, *Poet.* lv; a godly prayer (in verse) given to her majesty, *ib.* 551
Nemesis: 1 *Bul.* 273, 1 *Whitg.* 166, 167
Neophytes, or Novices: 1 *Ful.* 463
Nepos, a bp in Egypt: a chiliast, *Rog.* 154 n
Nepotian, a presbyter: 1 *Ful.* 263
Nere nother: neither nor other; or more probably, never neither, *Calf.* 73
Nero, emperor: 4 *Bul.* 124, 4 *Jew.* 1117; caused his mother to be slain, 2 *Bec.* 441; saw gladiators in an emerald, *Calf.* 47; whether Simon Magus practised sorcery before him, 2 *Ful.* 338, 339; he called Rome Neronopolis, 4 *Jew.* 918; his cruelty and persecutions, 2 *Bul.* 105, 108, 2 *Jew.* 1008, 3 *Jew.* 155, 189, 1 *Lat.* 27, 129, *Pil.* 254; Paul submitted to him, 2 *Hoop.* 80, 102, 4 *Jew.* 973, *Pil.* 314; Peter and Paul were martyred under him, 1 *Bul.* 315, 2 *Bul.* 105; he was deposed by the Romans, 1 *Hoop.* 284; lamented his love of music, 2 *Bec.* 429; supposed inscription to him (apud Gruterum), 2 *Ful.* 217
Nerva, emperor: 2 *Bec.* 437
Nestorians: their heresy, 2 *Jew.* 759, 3 *Jew.* 450; their doctrine respecting Christ's two natures, *Rid.* 314, *Rog.* 55; they denied that he had a natural body, 2 *Lat.* 253; said that he became God by merit, *Rog.* 48; corrupted the 1st epistle of John, 1 *Ful.* 11; alleged the council of Nice, 1 *Jew.* 83; pope Anastasius favoured them, 3 *Jew.* 343; they converted great nations, 2 *Ful.* 60; the Nestorians or Chaldean Christians in Malabar, *Phil.* 202 n
Nestorius, sometime patr. of Constantinople: his heresy, 1 *Bul.* 14, 3 *Bul.* 261, 267, 4 *Bul.* 455, *Calf.* 46, 141, 1 *Cran.* 22, 25, 278, 280, 289, 293, &c., 1 *Hoop.* 64, 65, 1 *Jew.* 525, 527, 529, 3 *Jew.* 536, 4 *Jew.* 731, *Phil.* 202 n., 423; he divided Christ's flesh from the Deity, 1 *Cran.* 172, 338, 3 *Jew.* 538; held that there were two Christs, one very God, and the other very man, *Rog.* 163; said to have allowed Christ to be God in the sense in which he himself could be, 2 *Jew.* 593; his opinions on the eucharist, 1 *Cran.* 22, 25, &c., 1 *Jew.* 220—222; he alleged the council of Nice, 1 *Jew.* 22; his heresy condemned by councils, 1 *Bul.* 14, 2 *Hoop.* 74, 3 *Jew.* 224, *Phil.* 185 n.; confuted by many, 1 *Jew.* 221
Nether Court, in the Isle of Thanet: 3 *Bec.* 487 n
Netherlands: *v.* Alva (F. duke of), Margaret, Mary.
  The Inquisition set up there, 3 *Zur.* 417 n., 568, 670; disorders there, 1 *Zur.* 139 n.; religious wars, *Lit. Eliz.* 578 n., *Rog.* 236; various affairs, 1 *Zur.* 183, 273 —275, 2 *Zur.* 165, 303, 321; children rebaptized by Papists, *Rog.* 236; embassy to England from the churches of Flanders, *Park.* 332; the duke of Alva's cruelty, 1 *Zur.* 204, 205, 208, 209, 273 n., 274, 2 *Zur.* 165, 207; inundations, 1 *Zur.* 233; the earl of Essex sent there with an army, *Lit. Eliz.* 467
Nethinims: *Pil.* 391, 392
Nets: to be used by ministers, *Sand.* 70, &c., 437, 441
Netter (Tho.), à Walden: what he was, *Bale* 28, 51; disputes with lord Cobham, *ib.* 28, 33, &c.; opposes Wickliffe, 3 *Jew.* 215; speaks of his disinterment, *Bale* 394; the Fasciculus Zizaniorum Wiclevi is not his, *ib.* 43 n.; his falsehood exposed, *ib.* 54; his Doctrinale, *Calf.* 63 n., 2 *Ful.* 22 n., *Jew.* xliv; Sermones, *Calf.* 81 n.; writes on the cross, *ib.* 63 n., 81 n.; his strange argument respecting fragments thereof, *ib.* 95 n.; on the canon of scripture, *Whita.* 330; on transubstantiation, *Bale* 154; he says that he is the more faithful catholic, and more agreeable to the scriptures, who denies merit, 3 *Jew.* 587; on heresy, *Bale* 217; he condemns Epiphanius, *Calf.* 42 n
Nettesheym (Hen. Corn. de): *v.* Agrippa.
Neuberg: conference there, 2 *Zur.* 177
Neubrigensis (Gul.): *v.* William.
Neuserus (......): revolted unto Turcism, *Rog.* 162
Neuters, Uterques, Omnia: *Pil.* 344
Neve (Will.), of Norwich: *Park.* vi, 481
Nevinson (Cha.): editor of the later writings of bp Hooper, 2 *Hoop.*
Nevinson (Chr.), Nevyson, or Newinson : notice of him, 2 *Cran.* 394 n.; commissioner in a disputation at Oxford, 3 *Zur.* 391 n.; dead, *ib.* 150
Nevinson (Steph.): letter to him as commissary of Canterbury, *Park.* 165; he had certain MSS. of Cranmer, *ib.* 191, 195; prebendary of Canterbury, *ib.* 319
Neville (Geo.), abp of York: his great feast, *Grin.* 328

Neville (Rob.), bp of Salisbury: of noble birth, 3 *Jew.* 410

Neville (Rich.), earl of Warwick: sent ambassador to Spain, 2 *Tyn.* 304 n

Neville (Ralph), 1st earl of Westmoreland: 1 *Bec.* 61 n

Neville (Hen.), 5th earl of Westmoreland: a commissioner, *Park.* 105; case of his marriage, *Jew.* xvii.

Neville (Cha.), 6th earl of Westmoreland: his rebellion, 2 *Jew.* 874, *Lit. Eliz.* 462, 538, 657, 1 *Zur.* 213, 217, 222, 227, 247; he escapes into Scotland, 1 *Zur.* 214, 223, 227, dies in the Netherlands, *ib.* 214 n

Neville (Geo.), lord Abergavenny: his daughter Elizabeth, 1 *Bec.* 191 n

Neville (Geo.), next lord Abergavenny: notice of him, 1 *Bec.* 61 n.; he investigates the case of the maid of Lymster, 2 *Cran.* 64; commissioner for a subsidy, *ib.* 301; letters to him, *ib.* 253, 270

Neville (Hen.), lord Abergavenny: his supposed rights under the see of Canterbury, 2 *Cran.* 387—389; he claims the stewardship of the liberties of the archbishops of Canterbury, *Park.* 285 n.; an ecclesiastical commissioner, *ib.* 370 n.; letter to him, *Park.* 285

Neville (Edw.), lord Abergavenny: 2 *Cran.* 389

Neville (Jo.), lord Latimer: his daughter Dorothy, 2 *Bec.* 480 n

Neville (Sir Edw.): 2 *Cran.* 64; high steward of the franchises of the see of Canterbury, &c., *ib.* 386, 388, 389; executed, *ib.* 386 n., 3 *Zur.* 625 n.; Katherine his (?) daughter, 1 *Bec.* 307 n

Neville (Sir Jo.): heads a rebellion in the North, 3 *Zur.* 219 n

Nevelle* (Sir Tho.): dedications to him, 1 *Bec.* 61, 87; his descent and history, *ib.* 61 n., 307 n

Nevile (Alex.): Parker gave him £100 for writing the story of Kett's rebellion, *Park.* xiii.

Nevell (Ant.): 2 *Cran.* 348

Nevil (Edm.): an accomplice of Will. Parry, whom he betrayed, *Lit. Eliz.* 465

Nevell (Rich.): Cranmer's servant, 2 *Cran.* 332; the same apparently, *ib.* 297, 348, 374, 388, 400

Neville (Tho.), master of Trin. coll. Cambridge, 2 *Zur.* 323; letter to him, 3 *Whitg.* 615

Nevell (Mr), fellow of St John's college, Cambridge: 2 *Cran.* 338 n., 2 *Lat.* 377, 380,

383, 389, 391, 393, 409; his suit for friars' lands, &c., 2 *Lat.* 393 n., 395; he takes a pardoner, *ib.* 400

Newark, co. Notts.: 2 *Cran.* 316 n

Newberrie (Raph.): 4 *Bul.* xxviii.

Newburgh (Hen. de), earl of Warwick: intended to make, and

Newburgh (Rog. de) earl of Warwick: made St Mary's church, Warwick, collegiate, 2 *Lat.* 396 n

Newbury, co. Berks: Coverdale there, 2 *Cov.* xi; popish books there, *ib.* 499, 500; Coverdale asks whether they shall be burned at the market cross, *ib.* 502; martyrs there, *Poet.* 168

Newbury (Will. of) v. William.

Newcastle upon Tyne, co. Northumberland: proposed to be made a bishop's see, *Grin.* iii; rebels executed there, *Lit. Eliz.* 538 n

Newcourt (R.): Repertorium, 1 *Bec.* x, xiii, *Grin.* 272 n., 2 *Lat.* 323, 324, 365, 370 nn

Newdigate (Fra.): married the widow of the protector Somerset, 1 *Bec.* 396 n

Newell (Mr): v. Nevell (Rich.).

New-fangled men: 1 *Lat.* 90

Newgate: v. London.

Newhaven: v. Havre de Grâce.

Newhaven, co. Sussex: the French land there, 2 *Cran.* 495 n

Newington, co. Surrey: the advowson, *Grin.* 462; this or another Newington referred to, 2 *Whitg.* 147

New life: v. Life.

New man: v. Man.

Newman (......): a friend of Cranmer's, 2 *Cran.* 237, 239 n., 262, 269; received into Cromwell's service, *ib.* 309

Newman (Jo.): martyred at Walden, *Poet.* 163

Newman (Jo. Hen.): *Calf.* 110 n., 287 n.; he cites a spurious epistle of Pius I., 2 *Ful.* 81 n

Newman (Rog.): letter to him, 1 *Brad.* 591, 2 *Brad.* 194

Newmarket, co. Cambr.: the heath, 3 *Bec.* 277

NEWS OUT OF HEAVEN, by T. Becon, 1 *Bec.* 35; the occasion of making it, and its profit, *ib.* 43

Newsham, co. Lincoln: the monastery, 2 *Cran.* 290, 291

Newstead (probably Newstead in Axholme, co. Linc.): the priory farmed by Markham, 2 *Cran.* 384

Newton (Frances), wife of Will. Brooke, (*q. v.*) lord Cobham.

---

* The different forms of the name Neville are arranged together.

Newton (Francis), dean of Winchester: made prebendary of Canterbury, in the room of his brother, *Park.* 341
Newton (Theodore), prebendary of Canterbury: *Park.* 340
Newton (Tho.): notice of him, *Poet.* lvi; verses from his epitaph on Lady Knowles, *ib.* 553
Newton Longueville, co. Bucks: *Phil.* xxix.
New-year's day: 1 *Bul.* 260
New-year's gifts: 2 *Lat.* 412: a godly custom to give them, 1 *Bec.* 307; A NEW-YEAR'S GIFT, by T. Becon, *ib.* 304—349; reference to it, 2 *Bec.* 446
Nibley (North), co. Gloucester: Tyndale's birthplace, 1 *Tyn.* xiv.
Nicagoras: 4 *Jew.* 842
Nice: *v.* Councils.
Nicephorus I., emperor of the East: was against images, *Phil.* 407
Nicephorus Callistus: Eccl. Hist., *Jew.* xl, 3 *Whitg.* xxxi; calls the scriptures ἐνδιαθήκους, *Whita.* 28; on the Old Testament canon, *ib.* 64; on the date of Matthew's gospel, *ib.* 519; he says that Matthew departing, recompensed his absence by present writing, 3 *Jew.* 436; refers to the fable of Abgarus, king of Edessa, *Calf.* 41 n.; tells a story about Paul communicating with Denis, 3 *Whitg.* 110; says Paul, what things being present, he had plainly taught by mouth, the same things afterward being absent, he shortly called to remembrance by writing an epistle, 3 *Jew.* 436; referred to on Paul's expression, "true yoke-fellow," 1 *Ful.* 476; he witnesses that Andrew went into Scythia, *Calf.* 128; records the martyrdom of Bartholomew, *ib.* 133; speaks of the labours of Simon Zelotes, 1 *Jew.* 353; says he preached in Britain, *ib.* 305, 3 *Jew.* 129, 164; writes of the preaching of Mark, 1 *Jew.* 353; referred to about Abdias, *Calf.* 126 n.; calls Timothy bishop of Ephesus, 2 *Whitg.* 294; speaks of the translation of the bones of Andrew, Luke, and Timothy, *ib.* 303; relates the martyrdom of Polycarp, *Pil.* 365 n.; records the building of Ælia, *Pil.* 375, and its miraculous interruption, *ib.* 376; how he speaks of Victor bishop of Rome, 2 *Whitg.* 134, 135; he relates that Adauctus, lieutenant under Diocletian, overthrew idols in Phrygia, 2 *Bec.* 305 n.; describes the banner of Constantine, 2 *Jew.* 650; speaks of the conversion of Helena, *Calf.* 322; refers to messengers sent to the council of Nice by pope Julius, 4 *Jew.* 1000; says Athanasius, being one of the chief deacons of Alexandria, was not the least part of that council, *ib.* 912; relates how Gregory Nazianzen saw the apostasy of Julian in his countenance, *Pil.* 312; tells of a miraculous event in that emperor's history, *Calf.* 87 n.; gives the saying of Athanasius, when banished by the same prince, *Pil.* 440; tells of the request of Terentius to Valens, *ib.* 324; imagines Valentinian to say, "For me, being thus occupied with business, and public cares, it is not easy to inquire of (ecclesiastical) matters," 4 *Jew.* 1001; narrates the excommunication of Theodosius, *Pil.* 381; writing of Gregory bishop of Nyssa, he says, although he had a wife, yet in other things he was nothing inferior to (St Basil) his brother, 3 *Jew.* 391, 416; relates a miracle at Constantinople, in the time of Chrysostom, 1 *Jew.* 247; records that Chrysostom's name being erased from the calendar of bishops of Constantinople was restored by Theodotus at the request of the people, 4 *Jew.* 650; tells what Simeones said when he saw Arsacius placed in the room of Chrysostom, *ib.* 1070; gives the history of the council of Ephesus, 1 *Jew.* 66; shews that Cyril of Alexandria sat in that council in the stead of pope Celestine, 4 *Jew.* 995; declares that in the fifth council of Constantinople, Menna the bishop of the same city was president, and not the pope, *ib.* 1003; mentions the condemnation of Theodoret by a general council at Constantinople, 1 *Jew.* 374; addresses the emperor Emmanuel Paleologus as leader of the profession of our faith, &c., 4 *Jew.* 1016; tells a story of a Jew baptized by laymen, 2 *Whitg.* 528; says that what remained of the sacrament was given to children, 2 *Jew.* 554; speaks of prayers at Alexandria on Wednesdays and Fridays, 1 *Jew.* 185; referred to on the names of various bishops, 3 *Jew.* 410; he declares the dignity and honour of the bishops of Rome and Constantinople to be equal, 3 *Jew.* 307, 4 *Jew.* 841; reckons that the pope has no possessions or privileges, which he received not from princes, 4 *Jew.* 835; states the succession of Constantinopolitan bishops, *Whita.* 510; says the bishop of Alexandria was entitled the judge of the whole world, 1 *Jew.* 427; mentions the prerogative of Justiniana Prima, 4 *Jew.* 707; speaks of Philæas, a bishop expert in civil matters, 3 *Whitg.* 455; mentions married priests, 4 *Jew.* 805; referred to about the tonsure, 2 *Ful.* 115 n.; on the use of the cross among the Egyptians, *Calf.* 65 n.;

he intimates that the Acephalians would not yield obedience unto bishops, *Rog.* 330 n.; says the Contobaptites allowed of no bishops, *ib.*; speaks of the heresy of Eutyches, *ib.* 51, 54, 57 nn.; writes of the Jacobites, *ib.* 58 n.; on the Macedonians, *ib.* 72 n.; on the heresy of Nestorius, *ib.* 55 n.; his account of Novatus, or Novatian, 1 *Whitg.* 173; he records an epistle of Dionysius Alex., to Novatus, 4 *Jew.* 872 n.; says that Socrates the historian favoured the Novatians, 2 *Whitg.* 185; on the Severites, *Rog.* 53 n., 54 n.; on the Theopaschites, *ib.* 52 n

Nicephorus Gregoras: Hist. Rom., *Jew.* xl.; Byzant. Hist., 3 *Whitg.* xxxi; records a saying of Andronicus, *ib.* 572; mentions sundry dukes of Athens, 4 *Jew.* 653

Nicetas Choniates: Annales, *Jew.* xl, 4 *Jew.* 653

Nicholas: *v.* Nicolas, Nicolaus.

Nicholas (St): account of him, 2 *Bec.* 536 n.; invoked for little children, *Rog.* 226; also to save from drowning, 2 *Bec.* 536

Nicholas I., pope*: claims supremacy for Peter, 1 *Lat.* 209; calls himself the prince over all the earth, 1 *Jew.* 403; declares that the pope cannot be judged, *ib.* 69, 443, 4 *Jew.* 847, 919, *Pil.* 602; says neither emperor nor king may judge the pope, for the servant is not above his lord, 4 *Jew.* 834, 847; asks, shall the saw boast against him that draweth it? i. e. the pope, 1 *Jew.* 442, 3 *Jew.* 222, 4 *Jew.* 834; declares that the pope was called God by Constantine, 4 *Bul.* 125, 1 *Jew.* 96, 438, 2 *Jew.* 906, 4 *Jew.* 843; says the church of Rome does not derive its privileges from any council, 1 *Jew.* 356; reproves Sigedodus, archbishop of Narbonne, for the assumption of judicial power, 3 *Bec.* 510 n.; decreed that no secular prince should assist at church councils, 2 *Tyn.* 266; says Christ by several duties and sundry dignities hath severed the offices of either power, 4 *Jew.* 826; allows that faith is universal, and pertaineth not only unto priests, but also laymen, *ib.* 913, 1026, 1029; forbids the laity to judge ecclesiastics, 1 *Tyn.* 178 n., 2 *Tyn.* 272 n.; states that he that is excommunicated cannot communicate, 4 *Jew.* 890; says we must sprinkle the heavenly seed, to whom the distribution is enjoined, 1 *Bec.* 3, 384; remarks that evil custom is taken by the ungodly for law, 2 *Cran.* 51; denies that the Latin tongue is barbarous, 1 *Jew.* 267; he is the first who mentions the synod of Sinuessa, 2 *Ful.* 364 n.; certain Anabaptists say that he invented baptism, *Rog.* 280

Nicholas II., pope: 2 *Ful.* 372; forced Berengarius to recant, 3 *Bec.* 360, 1 *Cran.* 14, 46, 1 *Hoop.* 193, 524, *Wool.* 27; was the first to condemn the true doctrine of the sacrament, 1 *Cran.* 14; brought in transubstantiation, 3 *Bec.* 232, 261, 274; teaches that Christ's body is torn in the sacrament, 2 *Bec.* 264, 290, 3 *Bec.* 361, 1 *Cran.* 113, 203; would have made transubstantiation the thirteenth article of faith, *Grin.* 73, 1 *Jew.* 95; declares that Christ has given to blessed Peter the right as well of the worldly as of the heavenly empire, 4 *Jew.* 677, 682, 825, 958; says, not any worldly sentence, but the self-same word whereby heaven and earth were made, was it that founded the church of Rome, *ib.* 726, 1036; asserts that whosoever attempts to abridge the authority of the church of Rome falls into heresy, 1 *Jew.* 95, 2 *Jew.* 692, 3 *Jew.* 152, 211, 296, 4 *Jew.* 1148, 1 *Whitg.* 283; Udalric, bp of Augsburgh, writes to him against his decree forbidding the marriage of priests, 4 *Jew.* 926, *Pil.* 568—570, 685 —687; he forbids attendance on the mass of an adulterous priest, 1 *Jew.* 70 n., 401, 4 *Jew.* 801, 802

Nicholas III., pope: extols Peter, 3 *Jew.* 300; says our Lord took Peter into the fellowship of the undivided Unity, and would have him called the same that he was himself, 1 *Jew.* 439 n., 3 *Jew.* 287; the same words are in an epistle by Leo I., *q. v.*; his decree in regard to the decretals, 3 *Bec.* 513 n

Nicholas (Dr): 2 *Cov.* 513

Nicholas (Hen.), or Nicolai: founder of the Familists, or Family of Love, 1 *Ful.* 37, *Grin.* 360 n., *Rog.* 13 n., 82, 202, *Sand.* 130 n., *Whita.* 298 n.; his writings, *Rog.* nn. passim; his Evangelium Regni, *ib.* 13; Instr., a work not met with, *ib.* 58; maintains that Christ's sufferings must be fulfilled in us, *ib.* 59, 163; calls the Holy Ghost the being of Christ, &c., *ib.* 73; says the scripture-learned preach the letter, but not the word of the living God, *ib.* 194, 325; censures all interpretations and writ-

---

* It is rather uncertain to which of the popes named Nicholas some of the passages from the Canon Law should be ascribed. See Law (Canon).

ten commentaries upon the scriptures, *ib.* 196; says the word is not taught by the sermons of ministers, but only by the revelation of the Spirit, *ib.* 231; styles public preachers, scripture-learned, licentious-scripture-learned, good-thinking-wise, ceremonial and letter-doctors, teaching masters, *ib.* 78, 177, 194, 233; says it is great presumption, that any man, out of the learnedness of the letter takes upon him to be a preacher, *ib.* 233; would have none to be preachers who have not been trained up in the Family, *ib.* 241; declares that to the elders of the Family it is given to know the truth, &c., *ib.* 194; says no man can minister the upright service or ceremonies of Christ but the renewed, *ib.* 271; thinks that the Jewish priesthood and service are to be observed of Christians, *ib.* 89, 315; dislikes and labours to make contemptible the outward admission of ministers, *ib.* 333; calls our liturgies and manner of serving God, foolishness of taken-on services, *ib.* 186; terms churches common houses, *ib.* 186, 320; calls the Family of Love a free people, &c., *ib.* 185; considers them alone as the people of God, *ib.* 169; affirms that they have no several religions or ceremonies, *ib.*; maintains that the regenerate do not sin, *ib.* 101, 141; teaches that men may be saved in any religion, if their affections are with the Family, *ib.* 160; calls the water of baptism elementish water, *ib.* 177, 278; teaches that there is no true baptism except in his sect, *ib.* 275; speaks of the ceremonies of the church of Rome as the prefiguration of true Christianity, *ib.* 188; calls a king the scum of ignorance, *ib.* 337; condemns war, *ib.* 351; says no man among the Familists claims anything as his own for his own private use, *ib.* 354; speaks of the general judgment as a doctrine mystical, *ib.* 68; denies the resurrection, *ib.* 145; allegorizes the land of promise, *ib.* 88, 351

Nicholas (Jo.): *v.* Nycholas.

Nicholas bishop: a mock bishop, 2 *Bec.* 320, 1 *Ful.* 218

Nicholls (Jo.), a recanting Jesuit: letter of archbishop Grindal for him, *Grin.* 421; notice of him, *ib.* n.; letter from the council about him, *ib.* 422

Nicholls (Will.): Comm. on the Common Prayer, 2 *Cov.* 316 n

Nichols (Benedict), bp first of Bangor, then of St David's: *Bale* 28

Nichols (Jo.): Hist. of Leic., 2 *Lat.* 375 n., 410 n.; Royal Wills, *ib.* 296 n

Nicholson (......): in prison for the truth, c. 1531, 2 *Lat.* 321

Nicholson (James): *v.* Nycolson.

Nicholson (Jo.), alias Lambert, *q. v.*

Nicholson (Tho.): *v.* Nicolson.

Nicholson (Will.): editor of the Remains of archbishop Grindal, *Grin.*

Nicodemus: his dialogue with Christ by night, 3 *Bul.* 37, 98, 4 *Bul.* 157, 243, 378, 2 *Hoop.* 171; Nicodemes can speak of Christ in the night, but openly they will confess nothing, 2 *Hoop.* 357; he and the Capernaites understand not Christ, nor any spiritual act, 1 *Cran.* 185; story of an image of Christ made by him, 2 *Jew.* 651

— Gospel of Nicodemus: *v.* Apocrypha, ii.

Nicol (......): martyred at Colchester (?), *Poet.* 167 (see also Nicoll).

Nicolai (Hen.): *v.* Nicholas.

Nicolai (Jac.): *v.* Nycolson.

Nicolaitans: allowed open lechery, *Phil.* 418; would have women to be common, *Bale* 275, 280, 1 *Cran.* 145, *Rog.* 307; they ascribed the creation to angels, *Hutch.* 68; rejected the Psalms, *Whita.* 31; John wrote his gospel against them and Cerinthus, 2 *Brad.* 263 n

Nicolas, the deacon: spoken of as founder of the sect of the Nicolaitans, *Bale* 275, 1 *Tyn.* 42

Nicolas (Dr), i. e. N. de Burgo, *q. v.*

Nicolas (Sir N. H.): Privy-purse Expenses, 1 *Lat.* v; Synopsis of the Peerage, 2 *Lat.* 382 n., 386 n.; Testam. Vetust., *ib.* 388

Nicolaus: *v.* Nicholas.

Nicolaus de Alsacia: wrote on the Apocalypse, *Bale* 257

Nicolaus Cabasilas, *q. v.*

Nicolaus de Clamengiis, *q. v.*

Nicolaus de Cusa, *q. v.*

Nicolaus Gallus, *q. v.*

Nicolaus Gerbellius, *q. v.*

Nicolaus Leonicus, *q. v.*

Nicolaus de Lyra, *q. v.*

Nicolaus Methonensis: *Jew.* xl; cited for transubstantiation, 2 *Jew.* 574

Nicoll (Will.): martyred at Haverfordwest, *Poet.* 172 (see also Nicol).

Nicolson (Will.), abp of Cashel: Engl. Hist. Lib., *Calf.* 296 n.; Correspondence, 2 *Ful.* 20 n.; on Bale's conversion, *Bale* viii.

Nicolson (Tho.): usher of Grindal's hall, *Grin.* 462

Nicostratus: called himself Hercules, 4 *Jew.* 842

Niem (Theodoric. à): De Schism. inter Urban. VI. et Clement., *Jew.* xli; he says the pope cannot commit simony, 1 *Jew.* 78 n.,

3 *Jew.* 147, 4 *Jew.* 868; relates the history of pope Joan, 4 *Jew.* 654, 655
Nifels: things of nought, *Coop.* 22
Niger (Bernard): one of the Magdeburgh centuriators, 2 *Zur.* 77 n., 79 n
Night: *v.* Bed, Darkness, Prayers.
   In Rom. xiii. it may signify the time of false doctrine, 2 *Hoop.* 114; far spent, *ib.*
Nile: turned into blood, 4 *Bul.* 262; its source, *Whita.* 370
Nill: to be unwilling, 1 *Brad.* 417
Nilus, abp of Thessalonica: Libell. de Primat. Papæ, *Jew.* xli, 1 *Jew.* 133; refers to the Nicene decree respecting patriarchs, and denies that the other patriarchs are under Rome, 3 *Jew.* 307, 308, 4 *Jew.* 707, 841; says the bishop of Constantinople doth order the bishop of Cæsaria and other bishops under him, but the bishop of Rome orders neither the bishop of Constantinople nor any other metropolitan, 3 *Jew.* 330
Nimiety: over-abundance, 1 *Bec.* 67
Nineveh: on its dimensions, 1 *Tyn.* 460; Jonah's preaching there, 1 *Hoop.* 509, &c., 1 *Lat.* 239, *Pil.* 89, 1 *Tyn.* 460; the repentance of the Ninevites, 3 *Bul.* 109, 4 *Bul.* 167, 179, 554, 2 *Cov.* 368, 1 *Hoop.* 512; they were spared partly for the sake of the children, 4 *Bul.* 373; their subsequent punishment for cruelties, 1 *Bul.* 374
Nisan: a Jewish month, *Pil.* 307
Nismes: Protestants tolerated there, 2 *Zur.* 224 n
Nix: a nag, *Grin.* 460
Nix (Rich.), bp of Norwich: an expression used by him, 2 *Brad.* 160 n.; he opposes Tyndale's New Testament, 1 *Tyn.* xxxiii. n.; Latin letter to him from queen Anne Boleyn, *Park.* 4
Nixon (Ant.): notice of him, *Poet.* liv; the Christian navy, *ib.* 543; stanzas from his Elisæ's Memorial, *ib.* 556
Nixon (Tho.): *v.* Nyxon.
Nixson (Will.), a Londoner: examined before the ecclesiastical commissioners, *Grin.* 201
No: *v.* Nay.
No: Alexandria so called, 4 *Jew.* 694
Noah: a righteous man, 4 *Bul.* 177; his time wicked, *ib.* 162; his ministry, *ib.* 102; he warned the world, *Pil.* 89; was delivered when the world was drowned, 2 *Bul.* 95, 3 *Bul.* 193 (*v.* Ark, Flood); the covenant renewed with him, 2 *Bul.* 169, 4 *Bul.* 434; God's covenant with Noah, a poem by W. Hunnis, *Poet.* 159; the law in his time, 1 *Bul.* 210; he offered sacrifice, 2 *Bul.* 187; the rainbow a sacrament to him, 2 *Jew.* 1100; the conduct of Ham, 1 *Bul.* 210, 287, 1 *Tyn.* 311; length of his life, 1 *Bul.* 41
Noailles (......): French ambassador to queen Mary, 2 *Cran.* 568
Nob: 2 *Bul.* 149
Nobilitatula: 1 *Zur.* 305
Nobility, Noblemen: *v.* Gentlemen.
   Rejoicing in nobility is vain, 2 *Bec.* 435, 436; wherein nobility really consists, *ib.* 436, 437, 600, 1 *Cov.* 513, 4 *Jew.* 1147; noble birth not of absolute necessity in princes' counsellors, 4 *Jew.* 1146; the nobility of England diminished by the wars of the Roses, 2 *Tyn.* 53; Ridley's reverence for nobility, *Rid.* 257; the office and duty of noblemen, *Sand.* 99; the chief point of great men's calling, 2 *Lat.* 37; they should admit poor suitors, [1 *Lat.* 255; were not in general sufficiently educated to be lords president, *ib.* 69; their sons become unpreaching prelates, *ib.* 102; the favour of noblemen uncertain, and not to be rejoiced in, 2 *Bec.* 441, 442; men desired to wear their livery, *Pil.* 191, 193; not many of them called, 2 *Brad.* 79, 85, 135, 246; some, however, have set forth God's word, 1 *Lat.* 141
Nod: the land of Nod, *Whita.* 174
Noel (Alex.): *v.* Nowell.
Noëtians: their heresy concerning the Trinity, *Rog.* 45
Noetus: his heresy, 3 *Bul.* 156
Noifull: noisome, injurious, guilty, 2 *Jew.* 856 n
Nominalists: their disputes with the Realists, 3 *Jew.* 611, &c., 1 *Tyn.* 157, 1 *Zur.* 53
Nonce: occasion, purpose, 1 *Cov.* 128
Nonconformists: *v.* Puritans.
None: *v.* Hours.
Nonest: nonce, purpose, *Pil.* 644
Nonnus, a Christian Greek poet: 1 *Ful.* 316
Non-residence: *v.* Benefices.
   Censured or treated of, 2 *Jew.* 984, 1 *Whitg.* 506, &c.
Nonsuch park: the earl of Arundel's, *Park.* 387
Noosel: (v. n.) to find shelter, 1 *Tyn.* 505; (v. a.) to bring up, *ib.* 508
Norden (Jo.): notice of him, *Poet.* xliii; further notice of him, *Nord.* vi; probably the same as the topographer, *ib.* (and see 176); list of his works (not topographical), *ib.* vii; his PROGRESS OF PIETY, *ib.* passim; poems by him,—man, *Poet.* 459; a psalm, wherein is set forth the love of God towards us, &c., *Nord.* 32; a praise for her majesty's most gracious government, *ib.* 44; to the praise of God for the forgiveness of our

sins, *ib.* 63, *Poet.* 460; this tendeth to a true denial of ourselves, in mortifying our affections, &c., *Nord.* 77; for the kingdom of God, *ib.* 85, *Poet.* 461; a praise of God's favour in protecting his church, *Nord.* 104; against false prophets and deceitful teachers, *ib.* 123, *Poet.* 462; for God's direction in our callings, *Nord.* 133; a song of praise for God's present help in trouble, being an acrostic of his name, *ib.* 150; before we go to bed, (verses), *Nord.* 160, *Poet.* 463

Nores (Will.): 2 *Cran.* 301

Norfolk: the insurrection there at the beginning of king Edward's reign, *Bale* 245, 2 *Bec.* 593 n., 596, 2 *Cran.* 188 n., 189 n., *Hutch.* 7 n., 1 *Lat.* 247 n., 265, 371 (*v.* W. Ket); reference to this rebellion, Mount Surrey, and the oak of reformation, 4 *Jew.* 915; those who remained faithful suffered miserably, 1 *Lat.* 376; rebellion in 1570, for the rescue of the duke of Norfolk, &c., 1 *Zur.* 229, 248 n.; inundations in Norfolk, *ib.* 233; a late harvest and scarcity, *ib.* 301; dedication to the ministers there, 3 *Bec.* 290

Norfolk (Dukes of): *v.* Howard.

Norgate (Rob.), master of C. C. C. C.: extract from a letter to abp Parker, *Park.* 469; letter to him, *ib.*

Norham castle, co. Northumb.: rebuilt by means of a pardon from Rome, 2 *Tyn.* 278

Nori, Sardinia: taken by the French, 3 *Zur.* 741

Noriture: nurture, *Calf.* 72

Norlingen: surrendered, 3 *Zur.* 638 n

Norma Concilii: see Flacius, *Jew.* xxxvii.

Normandy: lost by England, 2 *Tyn.* 304; it belongs of right to England, 2 *Zur.* 293

Normandy (......): 3 *Zur.* 144

Normanton, near Southwell, co. Notts.: the benefice, 2 *Cran.* 254

Nornburg: *v.* Nuremburg.

Norrie (Jo.), minister of Lorn: 2 *Zur.* 365

Norris (Sir Hen.): writes to queen Elizabeth, 2 *Zur.* 165 n.; ambassador in France, 1 *Zur.* 231

Norris (Jo.): his gallantry in Flanders, 1 *Zur.* 325 n

Norris (Silvester): *Calf.* 190 n

North: *v.* England.

North (Edw. 1st lord): mentioned as Sir Edw. North, *Rid.* 505; a privy councillor, 2 *Cran.* 505, 511, *Hutch.* v. n

North (Rog. 2nd lord): requires a Lent licence, *Park.* 108; at the duke of Norfolk's trial, 1 *Zur.* 267 n.; he obtains letters ordering the bp of Ely to sell him the manor of Somersham, *ib.* 319 n

North. (Will.), i. e. Will. Parr (*q. v.*), marq. of Northampton.

Northam, (qu. Norton, co. Kent?); Frensham's bequest, 2 *Zur.* 21 n

Northampton (Hen. earl of): *v.* Howard.

Northampton (Will. marq. of): *v.* Parr.

Northfolk (Will.): deprived by bp Sandys, *Park.* 125

Northumberland: the kingdoms of Northumbria and Deira, 1 *Lat.* 271; Northumberland many years without bishop, pall, or altar, *Pil.* 583; the people instructed in singing by Eddi, 1 *Jew.* 303; the dialect, *Rid.* 488, 492; Tyndale, a border country, *Rid.* 145, 1 *Tyn.* xiii; fights frequent in the borders, *Rid.* 398

Northumberland (Jo. duke of): *v.* Dudley.

Northumberland (Tho. earl of): *v.* Percy.

Norton, co. Kent: *v.* Northam.

Norton, co. Durham: *Pil.* 574

Norton (Chr.): executed for rebellion, 1 *Zur.* 225 n

Norton (Jo.): printer, 4 *Jew.* 1128

Norton (Rich.): cross-bearer to the rebels in the North, 1 *Zur.* 214 n

Norton (Tho.): executed for rebellion, 1 *Zur.* 225 n.; notice of and extract from a broadside by W. Gibson, called A Description of Norton's Falsehood of Yorkshire [1569], and presumed to refer to him, *Poet.* liv, and 542

Norton (Tho.), a lawyer: notice of him and his works, *Now.* viii, *Poet.* xlviii; he translates Nowell's Catechism, *Now.* viii; his dedication thereof to the archbishops and bishops, *ib.* 107; Psalm cxlvii. in metre by him, *Poet.* 487; letter from him (as it is supposed) to Calvin, 3 *Zur.* 339

Norton (Tho.): called by Strype a minister, but probably identical with the last, *Now.* viii; his advice respecting the Admonition, *ib.* ix, 3 *Whitg.* x.

Norway: a dispensation given to consecrate the sacrament there without wine, 1 *Jew.* 137, 222

Norwich: the martyrdom of Will. Wyght, 1428, *Bale* 12; this city was Parker's birthplace; mention of some localities, *Park.* vi, 481; martyrs under Mary, *Poet.* 170, 171, 172, 173; heretics burned there under Elizabeth, *Rog.* 49; the Green Yard, a place for preaching, *Park.* 313

The cathedral, &c.: injured by lightning, 1 *Zur.* 132; funeral of the duchess of Norfolk, 1564, without candles or torches, *ib.* 137; a serving man made prebendary, *Park.* 312; miserable state of the church, only six prebendaries, only one at home, some of them Puritans, *ib.* 450; the diocese visited by Parker, *ib.* 473; dispute between the archbishop and the chapter about visitation, *ib.* 476

Foreign churches: foreigners at Norwich, *Park.* 247 n.; a church assigned to them, *ib.* 255; the Dutch church, disturbances in it, 1 *Zur.* 256, 266; peace restored, *ib.* 278; cases of possession there, *ib.* 303; the French church, peaceable, *ib.* 256

Nosegay: A PLEASANT NEW NOSEGAY, by T. Becon, 1 *Bec.* 188—229; written in a few days, *ib.* 195

Nose of wax; the scriptures so called (by A. Pighius, *q. v.*), 1 *Ful.* 8, 539, *Hutch.* 236, 2 *Tyn.* 103, and al.

Nosel, or nowsle: to nurse, 1 *Tyn.* 318, 384; noosel, 1 *Tyn.* 508; nosylled, 2 *Cran.* 119; nousled, nuzzled, 2 *Bec.* 350

Nosocomia: 1 *Bul.* 286, 4 *Bul.* 498

Nostradamus (Mich.): threatened the world with peculiar evils in 1559—60, *Park.* 59 n.; Fulke wrote against him, 1 *Ful.* v.

Notaries: their marks or devices, 2 *Cran.* 556, 557; application of one to be a notary, *Park.* 392

Notaris (Dr), master of Clare hall: opposes Latimer, 2 *Lat.* xii.

Nottingham: great storms there, *Pil.* 607; a royal visitation commenced at St Mary's church, 1 *Zur.* 73 n

Nottingham (Cha. earl of): *v.* Howard.

Nottingham (Hen. earl of), afterwards duke of Richmond: *v.* Fitzroy.

Nourises: nurses, 3 *Whitg.* 189

Nourry (Nich. le): *v.* Le Nourry.

Nourtring: nourishing, chastening, *Grin.* 101

Nousled: *v.* Nosel.

Nova Villa (A. de): *v.* Arnoldus.

Novatian: one of the founders of the Novatian sect, 1 *Lat.* 425 n.; styled Catharus, 1 *Bec.* 94, 95, 278; compared by Cyprian (*q. v.*) to an ape, 3 *Jew.* 150, *Whita.* 667; his heresy, *Coop.* 147; he professed to be a bishop, which Cyprian denied, 3 *Jew.* 322; his remains, in Tertullian's works, *Jew.* xli; extracts from his abridgment of Tertullian's book on the Trinity, 3 *Bul.* 129, 141, 142, 176, 177, 252, 310, 324, 325 nn

Novatians: called also Cathari, and why, 4 *Bul.* 59, 2 *Ful.* 375, 1 *Hoop.* 169, 547, *Rid.* 120, 1 *Whitg.* 114 n., 171, 172; they separated from the church, and why, 4 *Bul.* 59, *Rid.* 120; they said the regenerate cannot sin, *Rog.* 138; thought themselves perfect, *ib.* 257; imagined that they could not sin even in thought, *ib.* 135, 138, 257; taught that sin after baptism is unpardonable, 3 *Bul.* 66, *Hutch.* 113, 117, *Rog.* 141, 298, 312; denied repentance and remission to the fallen, 2 *Bul.* 424, 1 *Ful.* 437, 438, 1 *Hoop.* 169, 547, 3 *Jew.* 353, 1 *Lat.* 425, 2 *Whitg.* 202, 203; abused the passage in Heb. vi. on apostasy, 1 *Ful.* 31, *Hutch.* 113, 117; their views respecting absolution, 1 *Ful.* 272; they rebaptized infants afore baptized, *Rog.* 266, 277; their pretended purity, and straitness of living, *Phil.* 419, 420; they condemned marriage, *Rog.* 261 n., especially second marriages, *ib.* 262, 307; maintained that the righteous have Christ inherent within them, *ib.* 115; Cyprian (*q. v.*) opposed them, 2 *Whitg.* 202, 203; their opposition to him, *Whita.* 441

Novatus: one of the founders of the Novatian sect, 1 *Lat.* 425 n.; his errors, 1 *Bec.* 94, 95, 278, 3 *Bec.* 401, 412, 3 *Jew.* 353, 354, *Rid.* 120; he would not receive the chrism after baptism, 2 *Ful.* 389; how he ministered the communion, 1 *Jew.* 153; his first coming into Italy, *ib.* 173 n.; he made a schism at Rome, *ib.* 348; desired the bishoprick of Rome, 1 *Whitg.* 172; forsook his ministry, *ib.* 173

Novellæ: *v.* Law (Civil).

Novellius Tricongius: made proconsul, 4 *Jew.* 659

Novelty: to be avoided in doctrine, *Phil.* 316

Novices: *v.* Neophytes.

Noviomagus (......): chaplain to the king of Denmark, 3 *Zur.* 512 n

Novus homo: *Nord.* (99)

Novus Orbis: Basil 1537, *Jew.* xli, 4 *Jew.* 1055, 1056

NOWELL (Alex.), dean of St Paul's: memoir of him, *Now.* i—ix; his birth and early education, *ib.* i; sent to Oxford, *ib.*; master of Westminster school, and prebendary there, *ib.*; returned member for Looe, but displaced, *ib.*; goes into exile, 1 *Cran.* (9), *Now.* ii; at Strasburgh, *Jew.* xiii, *Now.* ii; the troubles at Frankfort, *Now.* ii; on queen Mary's death Nowell returns to England, and is appointed a royal visitor, archdeacon of Middlesex, &c., *ib.*; made dean of St Paul's, *ib.* iii; his preaching, *ib.*; he preaches at the consecration of Grindal, Sandys, and other bishops, *Grin.* vi, *Sand.* xviii; prolocutor of the convocation, *Now.* iii; he assists at the funeral solemnity of the emperor Ferdinand at St Paul's, *Grin.* 32; approves rules for Tonbridge school,

Park. 211 n.; the queen is offended with a sermon by him, *ib.* 235; offended with him on another occasion, *Pra. Eliz.* xvii. n.; he will not preach before her unless she will favour him, *Park.* 254; being occupied against Dorman, (see below), he begs to be discharged from Lent preaching, *ib.* 260; at Hadham with Grindal, *Grin.* 320; he attends the duke of Norfolk at his execution, 2 *Zur.* 198 n.; signs a warrant for the apprehension of Cartwright, 1 *Zur.* 313 n.; he and others confer with Campion, *Now.* vii; he will not answer the book De Disciplina, *Grin.* 353; he obtains a new charter for the collegiate church of Manchester, *Wool.* iii; his contribution in aid of Geneva, *Grin.* 432 n.; legacy to him, *ib.* 459; president of Brasenose, *Now.* i, and a benefactor to that college, *ib.* viii; his death, *ib.*; mention of him, *Park.* 145; he was nearly related to Whitaker, *Whita.* ix; bishop Woolton was his nephew, *Wool.* iii.

His writings:—a sermon preached before queen Elizabeth, at the opening of parliament, Jan. 1563, (appended to the P. S. ed. of his Catechisms), *Now.* 223; he composes a homily for the plague of 1563, *Grin.* vi, 79, 258; viz. an homily concerning the justice of God, in punishing of impenitent sinners, &c., which is printed in *Grin.* 96, *Lit. Eliz.* 491; his controversy with Dorman, *Calf.* 2, 1 *Ful.* 75 n., 2 *Ful.* 3, *Jew.* xx, *Now.* iii, 3 *Whitg.* xxxi; controversy with Sanders, 2 *Ful.* 3, 356, *Now.* iv; his CATECHISM in Latin, and the same CATECHISM translated by Tho. Norton, edited by G. E. Corrie, D.D., master of Jesus college, Cambridge, *Now.*; notice of this Catechism, *Now.* iv—vii; whether sanctioned by convocation, *ib.* v; letter from Nowell to Sir Will. Cecil on its being printed, *ib.* vi; editions and abridgments of it, *ib.* vii; Whitaker translated it and the abridgment of it into Greek, *Whita.* xii; articles, &c., respecting it, *Grin.* 142, 152, 174; ministers enjoined to learn it, 1 *Whitg.* 336, 3 *Whitg.* 471; references to it, 1 *Whitg.* 68, 69; Nowell supposed by some to have been the writer of king Edward's Catechism, *Phil.* 180 n.; letter by him, *Park.* 251; his opinion on a place of Cyprian, 2 *Whitg.* 217, 218; on the pope's supremacy, *ib.* 245; he regards the Jewish high priest as an authority for an archbishop, *ib.* 348; declares the history of Paul's cross, *Pil.* 607; his view of Jewel's challenge, 2 *Ful.* 58

Nowell (Jo.), the dean's father: *Now.* i.

Nowell (Lau.), brother of Alexander: an exile, 1 *Cran.* (9)

Nowls: heads, *Pil.* 292

Noy: to hurt, to annoy, *Bale* 559, 1 *Bec.* 117

Nuffield, co. Oxon: the manor of English, 2 *Brad.* 45 n., *Jew.* xi.

Nullatenses: bishops without sees, some at Trent, 4 *Jew.* 997

Nullifidians: 3 *Bul.* 112

Numa Pompilius, king of Rome: 1 *Bul.* 201, 2 *Bul.* 219, *Calf.* 13, 14, 362, 363, 1 *Hoop.* 284, 352, 4 *Jew.* 1047, 1164, 1 *Lat.* 104

Numantines: 1 *Bul.* 252

Number: *v.* Beast, Six, Seven, &c.

Numbers: what the book contains, 2 *Cov.* 17; Tyndale's prologue to it, 1 *Tyn.* 429

Numenius: styles Plato an Attic Moses, *Whita.* 118

Nunc dimittis: *v.* Simeon.

Nuns: their beginning, 2 *Bec.* 376; nuns in the time of Augustine, 2 *Ful.* 100; in the Anglo-Saxon church, *ib.* 12; popish ones, *ib.* 99; at least 10,000 in England in Henry VIII.'s time, 3 *Zur.* 36

Nuremberg: diets or assemblies there, 3 *Jew.* 182, 4 *Jew.* 737, 3 *Tyn.* 40 n.; the Centum Gravamina, *v.* Germany; Tyndale there, 1 *Tyn.* lvii; he mentions it as Nornburg, 3 *Tyn.* 218; the city consents to the confession of Augsburg, 2 *Zur.* 15 n.; the Nuremberg Chronicle, *v.* Schedel (H.)

Nussbaum (Valentine): 3 *Zur.* 644, 667, 669, 677, 681

Nycholas (Jo.): 2 *Cran.* 390

Nycols (......): sent to preach at Calais, 2 *Cran.* 320

Nycolson (James): printer in Southwark, 2 *Cov.* x, xi, 2, 23, 319, 2 *Lat.* 465 (Jac. Nicolai); he seeks a privilege, 2 *Cov.* 498

Nyssen (Greg.): *v.* Gregory.

Nyxon (Tho.): *Rid.* ii. n

O

O: a superstition of the fifteen oos, 2 *Cran.* 148 (*v.* Brigit).

O. (I.), i. e. Jo. Old, *q. v.*

Oaths, and Swearing: *v.* Perjury, Prayers.
Jurisprandum, juramentum, *Now.* (101); of an oath, 1 *Bul.* 244; what it is, *ib.* 246; how swearing first came up, 1 *Bec.* 377; it is the ordinance of the Lord, 2 *Hoop.* 54; a special honour to God, 1 *Bul.* 248; whether it is lawful, *ib.* 244; whether all oaths are taken away from Christians, 1 *Bec.* 378; how and for what causes we may swear, and how

OATHS

and for what causes we may not, 1 *Bec.* 378, 2 *Bec.* 76, 78, 1 *Bul.* 245, &c., 1 *Hoop.* 324, 476, 477, 2 *Hoop.* 55, 1 *Jew.* 228, 2 *Lat.* 64, *Now.* (13), 127, 2 *Tyn.* 56, 57, 229; conditions of a holy oath, 1 *Bul.* 249; the faithful may holily and justly use oaths in matters of controversy, 2 *Hoop.* 54, 124; a Christian may swear for the health of himself or his neighbour, 1 *Bec.* 379; religious oaths are to be kept, 1 *Bul.* 252; large reward to those who keep them, *ib.* 253; oaths may not be taken vainly and rashly, 2 *Hoop.* 124, *Rog.* 356; needless ones are sinful, 1 *Hoop.* 335; the name of the Lord abused by vain oaths and by perjury, 1 *Bul.* 241; magistrates may lawfully require oaths of their subjects, 1 *Bec.* 380, 2 *Bec.* 78, 2 *Hoop.* 54, *Rog.* 357; how we may swear, and with what ceremonies, 1 *Bul.* 247; an oath ought to have three companions, 1 *Bec.* 374; on swearing by God, 2 *Tyn.* 55; why God suffered the Jews to swear by him, 1 *Bec.* 377; what is meant by the scripture expression, "swear in God," *ib.* 376, 377; God only to be sworn by, *Hutch.* 21; why men swear uncovered, 2 *Ful.* 210; against swearing by the saints, or any creatures, 1 *Hoop.* 477, *Hutch.* 21, *Now.* (14), 128; saints sworn by at sessions and courts, *Hutch.* 21; swearing by the mass, *ib.*; swearing by or on a book, *Bale* 74, 110, 111, by the gospels, by bread, salt, &c., *ib.* 56; bishops (says Bonner) may swear by looking on the gospel book, without touching it, *Phil.* 89; to make men swear by compulsion is not agreeable to God's word, 1 *Bec.* 380; compulsory oaths as to the amount of a man's property condemned, 1 *Tyn.* 187; no man should be compelled to swear against himself, *ib.* 203, 2 *Tyn.* 56; Tyndale says no man ought to be compelled to swear against another, 3 *Tyn.* 147; violation of oaths allowed by Papists, *Rog.* 119, 359, 360; pope Julius said they were binding on merchants, but not on princes, 2 *Zur.* 173; oaths dispensed with by the pope, 2 *Hoop.* 240; swearing lightly thought of by various heretics, *Rog.* 357; what kind of oaths may be broken, 1 *Bec.* 372, 1 *Bul.* 250, 2 *Cran.* 215, 2 *Hoop.* 55; it is our duty to repent of and break all oaths and vows which are sinful, 1 *Tyn.* 206, 240, 246, 2 *Tyn.* 57; errors about swearing, *Rog.* 358—361

Oaths:—that of Roman soldiers was termed a sacrament, 4 *Bul.* 235; tyrannical oaths exacted by the see of Rome from the emperors, 2 *Cran.* 74; the oath to the pope taken by Otho, the first German emperor, 3 *Bec.* 512, 513 n., 2 *Tyn.* 269; the oath of obedience to the pope, taken by Romish bishops, 4 *Bul.* 141, 530, 2 *Jew.* 996, 3 *Jew.* 205, 4 *Jew.* 948, 1113, *Pil.* 555; Cranmer's oaths of fidelity to the pope, on his consecration, 2 *Cran.* 559, 561, 562; his protestation, *ib.* 560; his oath to the king for his temporalities, *ib.* 460; the English coronation oath, 2 *Cran.* 126, 454; oath of fealty to Henry VIII. and his heirs according to the act of succession, *ib.* 285 n.; dispute as to oaths against the pope's supremacy, 1 *Brad.* 468, 475, &c., 483, &c.; Gardiner calls them Herod's oaths, *ib.* 468; the oath of the king's supremacy, *Lit. Edw.* 168, 338; the form in king Edward's ordination book objected to by Hooper, and altered by the king with his own hand, 2 *Hoop.* xii, 6 *Zur.* 81, 87, 416, 559, 566; the oath of the queen's sovereignty, *Lit. Eliz.* 281; reference to the oath taken by the council to queen Elizabeth, 4 *Jew.* 1144; a bishop's oath of obedience to the metropolitan, *Lit. Eliz.* 182, 350, *Lit. Eliz.* 294; the oath of churchwardens, *Grin.* 177; oath to be taken by every governor of Rivington school, *Pil.* 664; that of the schoolmaster and usher, *ib.* 667; that of a midwife, *Grin.* 174 n.; the Book of Oaths, 4 *Jew.* 1144 n., 2 *Lat.* 114 n

Profane swearing censured as an evil practice, 1 *Hoop.* 476, 2 *Lat.* 79; forbidden, 1 *Bec.* 357, 358, 2 *Bec.* 77; opposed to the word of God, 1 *Bec.* 38; against it, with sentences and examples of scripture, *ib.* 446, 447; AN INVECTIVE AGAINST SWEARING, by T. Becon, *ib.* 350; it and idolatry are most grievous sins, *ib.* 359; the world and God's word judge diversely of swearers, *ib.* 362; among the faithful oaths need not, among the unfaithful profit not, *ib.* 378; excuses made for swearing, *ib.* 375, &c.; what evils chance of vain swearing, *ib.* 389; swearers are enemies to God's word, *ib.* 366; they shall not escape unpunished, *ib.* 363; they are like thieves condemned to be hanged, *ib.* 365; examples of their punishment, *ib.*; there is enough swearing in England to bring destruction on the realm, *ib.* 355; profane oaths, 1 *Brad.* 10, 1 *Lat.* 231; laws for the punishment of swearing, 1 *Bec.* 390, 391; remedies against it, *ib.* 392; an exhortation to swearers, *Hutch.* 20; swearers of custom, and for other reasons, must leave the practice, 1 *Bec.* 388, 389; swearers to be excluded (after admonition) from the communion (synod, 1562), *Sand.* 434; to be presented to the ordinary, *Grin.* 143

Obadiah the prophet: 1 *Bul.* 374, 4 *Bul.* 95; some think him the same as Ahab's steward, *Pil.* 217; meaning of his name, *ib.* 216; commentary on his book, *ib.* 201—273

Obedience: *v.* God, Kings, Law, Magistrates, Parents, Vows.

What it is, 3 *Bec.* 621; when and to whom it is due, 2 *Tyn.* 61—63; it is required of us by the law of God, 3 *Jew.* 579, 580; it is thereby required alike of all, 1 *Hoop.* 415; it is better than sacrifice, *Sand.* 144; a principal part of Christian religion, *Now.* (6, 7), 118, 120; instant obedience due to God's commands, *Sand.* 269; it is due to God rather than to man, *Rid.* 143, 144; God rewards it, 1 *Tyn.* 175; THE OBEDIENCE OF A CHRISTIAN MAN, by W. Tyndale, *ib.* 127—344; summary of its contents, *ib.* 331, &c.; references to it, *ib.* 32—36, 41 n.; obedience to powers; faithful obedience a pleasant flower, 1 *Bec.* 211; it is due to rulers, *ib.* 216, 1 *Bul.* 390, *Nord.* 167, 1 *Tyn.* 173, 332—336; the spiritualty must pay it, 1 *Bec.* 216, 217; none are exempt from it, *ib.* 216; the limit of our obedience to the civil power, *Sand.* 199, 2 *Tyn.* 245; the rule of obedience, 3 *Whitg.* 590; canonical obedience not to be kept if opposed to the obligations of baptism, *Pil.* 621, or to our allegiance to our prince, *ib.* 622; popish obedience, 2 *Cran.* 147, 2 *Tyn.* 123; obedience of servants to their masters, 1 *Tyn.* 172; that of wives to their husbands, *ib.* 171; that of children to their elders, *ib.* 168; its reward, *ib.*; inobedientia, *Now.* (101)

Object: an obstacle, 3 *Bec.* 380

Object (adj.): obvious, *Sand.* 252

Oblations: *v.* Offerings, Sacrifices, Supper of the Lord.

Obruted: overthrown, 1 *Bec.* 57

Obsecrations: entreaties, 1 *Bec.* 187

Observants: a division of the Franciscans, 2 *Cran.* 292, 330 n., 333, 384, 1 *Lat.* 287, 1 *Tyn.* 301 n., 2 *Tyn.* 42, 44; the mode of profession, 1 *Tyn.* 227; they set Christ but little above Francis, 2 *Tyn.* 5; were Romish spies, *Bale* 221, 1 *Lat.* 287; their vigilance and tyranny, 2 *Tyn.* 249; their treacherous practices, *ib.* 305; one of them sent by Wolsey in search of Tyndale, 1 *Tyn.* xxxiv; they were not permitted even to handle a penny, *ib.* 301; banished the kingdom, *ib.* 38 n.; their house at Greenwich, *ib.* xv, 38 n.; the Cistercians were called White Observant monks, *Pil.* 509

Observare leges: *Now.* (102)

Obsign: to seal or ratify, 1 *Brad.* 262, 395

Occam (Will. de): his opinion on Maccabees, *Whita.* 97; he refers "Hoc" to the body of Christ, 2 *Jew.* 788; wrote on the errors of John XXII., *Jew.* xli, *Rog.* 181; condemned as a heretic, 1 *Jew.* 52, 4 *Jew.* 925

Occamists: 1 *Zur.* 53

Occupations: sundry kinds, 2 *Bul.* 30; needless ones, *ib.* 28; what occupation a godly man ought chiefly to use, *ib.* 31; men of occupation do not fear to swear bargaining, 1 *Bec.* 359; they must abstain from swearing, *ib.* 388

Ochinus (Bernardine): notice of him, 3 *Zur.* 334 n.; being invited into England by abp Cranmer, he came with P. Martyr, 4 *Jew.* 1224 n., 1 *Zur.* 22, 25, 26, 40, 58, 64; expenses of his journey hither, 3 *Zur.* 541 n.; his pension, 1 *Lat.* 141; Bradford goes to his house, 2 *Brad.* xxi, 352, 353; mentioned, 1 *Zur.* 30, 47, 60, 72, 78, & sæpe, 2 *Zur.* 31, 48, 76, 3 *Zur.* 353; his dangerous opinions, 4 *Bul.* xiv; he impugned the deity of the Holy Ghost, *Rog.* 70, and said that he is God's favour and virtue, *ib.* 73; defended polygamy, *ib.* 307; his opinion on a book ascribed to Clement of Rome, *Calf.* 368 n.; his Dialogi xxx, 2 *Zur.* 261; a Dialogue of his translated by Ponet, *Calf.* 368 n.; two letters from him to Musculus, 3 *Zur.* 334, 336; his wife, *ib.* 55

Ocivity: indolence, 2 *Hoop.* 92

Ockam (Gul. de): *v.* Occam.

O'Cullen (Pat.): hanged at Tyburn for treason, *Lit. Eliz.* 658 n

Odible: hateful, *Bale* 518

Odo (St), or Odilo: notice of him, *Bale* 320 n

Odoacer: 2 *Bul.* 109, 4 *Jew.* 952, 1001

Œcolampadius (Jo.): referred to, 2 *Lat.* 314, 3 *Zur.* 414; called by More friar Huskyne, 3 *Tyn.* 5; his part in the conference at Marpurg, *Grin.* 251 n.; his doctrine, 2 *Ful.* 377; cited about the fall of Satan, 3 *Bul.* 350 n.; his views on the sacrifice of Christ set forth by Gardiner, 1 *Cran.* 355; he speaks of Christ's converse with the disciples after his resurrection, *Whita.* 548; his controversy with Luther on the Lord's supper, 1 *Cov.* 463—466, 3 *Zur.* 46; his opinions with regard to the presence of Christ therein, 1 *Cov.* 469, *Phil.* 401; he wrote an epistle or treatise on the words, "This is my body," 3 *Tyn.* 258 n.; denied transubstantiation, *Rid.* 158; quoted upon justification, 2 *Cran.* 211; he explains how St Paul was "rude in speech," *Whita.* 101; expounds his anathema against those who should preach another gospel, *ib.* 627; he censures factious opposition to the custom of the church, 1 *Whitg.* 137; speaks of indifferent ceremonies, 3 *Whitg.* 107, 108; says the Jewish priests when not ministering wore the same kind of garments as laymen, 2 *Bul.* 133; desires the revival of excommunication, 2 *Zur.* 252; his opinion respecting the divorce of Henry VIII., 3 *Zur.* 551 n.; his commentary on Daniel, &c. (the copy given by Bradford to Rob. Harrington), 2 *Brad.* 55 n.; Parkhurst advises Simler to translate his German works, 1 *Zur.* 110; he is defended against the charge of falsifying fathers, 1 *Cran.* 171, 172, 3 *Jew.* 491, 494, 495; letter from him to Zuinglius, 3 *Zur.* 551; reference to an epistle of Melancthon to him, 1 *Cran.* 20

Œcumenius: notice of him, 1 *Ful.* 340 n.; Opera, *Jew.* xli; he enforces the duty of searching the scriptures, *Whita.* 240; mentions a tradition concerning Judas, *ib.* 664; on Acts xiv. 23, he affirms that Paul and Barnabas created and ordained the elders, 1 *Whitg.* 349; speaks of the conduct of Peter in the council at Jerusalem, 2 *Whitg.* 273, 275; says James was bishop of Jerusalem, *ib.* 277; on Rom. iii. he calls the flesh of Christ the propitiation of our sins, 2 *Jew.* 752; does not understand Rom. xii. 8, of deacons, 3 *Whitg.* 283; writes of the benediction of the cup, 1 *Cov.* x, 1 *Ful.* 501, 502; writes of unknown tongues, *Whita.* 262, 264; understands "the place of the unlearned," 1 Cor. xiv. 16, to mean the place assigned to the laity, *ib.* 260; expounds 1 Cor. ii. 16, "the savour of life," &c., 1 *Cran.* 202, 206; explains the text, "If our gospel be hid," &c., 2 Cor. iv. 3, *Whita.* 388; explains how we are "made meet," or counted worthy, Col. i. 12, 1 *Ful.* 363, 364; states his opinion on "the epistle from Laodicea," Col. iv. 16, *Whita.* 303; on 2 Thess. i. he says that suffering for Christ procures the kingdom of heaven according to justice, not by grace, 1 *Ful.* 339; says Paul, in writing to Timothy, calls bishops presbyters, 1 *Whitg.* 433, 487; styles Timothy and Titus bishops, 2 *Whitg.* 296; states that Paul would not have the whole island of Crete governed by one, *ib.* 283, 315, 317; allows the promotion of deacons, 3 *Whitg.* 70; writing on Heb. v. he shews (from Psa. cx.) how Christ is offered in the holy supper, 2 *Jew.* 732, 733; expounds Heb. x. 1, "the very image of the things," *ib.* 614, 616; speaks of Jacob and his staff, Heb. xi. 21, 1 *Ful.* 541; comments on the text, "Marriage (is) honourable in all," *ib.* 478, 479; dotes on the place, "we have an altar," *ib.* 519; tells why some epistles are called catholic, *ib.* 223; expounds James i. 13, "God cannot be tempted," *ib.* 560; on 2 Pet. i. 15, he mentions the opinion that the saints in heaven remember us on earth, *ib.* 537, 2 *Ful.* 88; cites Photius, *Whita.* 662

Œdilred, king: *v.* Edilred.

Œpinus (Jo.): *v.* Æpinus.

Œtenbach: the convent, 4 *Bul.* xi.

Offence: of offences, 2 *Bul.* 315; they are to be avoided, 2 *Brad.* 327, 328; we must walk without offence, *Sand.* 310, &c.; distinction between offence given and offence taken, 2 *Brad.* 343, 2 *Bul.* 318, 2 *Lat.* 77, 78, 2 *Whitg.* 60; to give offence is a great sin, 2 *Bul.* 319; how and by what means offences are given, *ib.* 316; they arise not of the gospel but of its enemies, *ib.* 319

Offenders: *v.* Punishment.

How they are to be dealt with, 2 *Tyn.* 46

Offendicle: a stumbling-block, 3 *Bec.* 610, *Pil.* 484

Offendiculum Sacerdotum: *v.* Anselm.

Offerings, Oblations: *v.* Sacrifices.

What the word "oblations," includes, 1 *Lat.* 17; what oblations we ought to offer, *ib.* 74; forgiveness of enemies needful before offering them, *ib.* 18; they must be our own property and not another man's, *ib.* 22; offerings to the clergy, 1 *Tyn.* 237, 2 *Whitg.* 557; oblations anciently divided into four portions, 2 *Ful.* 93; offering-days, 2 *Hoop.* 145, 1 *Lat.* 23 n., *Lit. Eliz.* 185

Offertory: its first appointment, 3 *Bec.* 264, 2 *Brad.* 306, 308

Office: *v.* Duty.

The humblest office is received from God, 1 *Tyn.* 101; offices not to be sought, 2 *Lat.* 26, 27; the sale of them censured, 1 *Lat.* 185, 2 *Lat.* 26, *Sand.* 47; of civil offices in ecclesiastical persons, 3 *Whitg.* 404, &c.; Cartwright's reasons against them examined, *ib.* 421, &c.

Officers: *v.* Judges, Magistrates.

How they should be chosen, 2 *Lat.* 26; what they ought to be, *ib.* 27; their duty to those under them, 3 *Tyn.* 58; they dishonour God when they abuse their power, *ib.*; some give and take bribes, 1 *Lat.* 261

Officina: *v.* Textor.

Officium Beatæ Virginis: *v.* Mary.

Oftfor, bp of the Victians: consecrated at the command of king Edilred, 2 *Ful.* 17, 24, 119

Og, king of Bashan: 1 *Bul.* 378

Oglethorp (Owen), bp of Carlisle; sometime vice-chancellor of Oxford, 3 *Zur.* 448; letter from him to Bullinger, *ib.* 124; he is imprisoned for superstition, *ib.* 187; disputes with Ridley at Oxford, *Rid.* 191; also with Cranmer, 1 *Cran.* 391, 400, 1 *Jew.* 53; mentioned, 1 *Zur.* 10 n., 3 *Zur.* 425; his death, 1 *Zur.* 69

Oil: *v.* Unction.

What is meant by oil in the scriptures, 2 *Hoop.* 228, 229; how it is used in Eastern countries, *Pil.* 526; hallowed, *ib.* 525; two sorts thereof, *ib.* 526; prayer on blessing it, 2 *Jew.* 1127, 1136, 3 *Jew.* 177; lofty terms applied to it, 2 *Jew.* 575, 576; address to it,—"Ave sanctum oleum," 1 *Jew.* 534, 3 *Jew.* 243

Ointment: *v.* Unction.

Meaning of the similitude, 2 *Cov.* 314

Okenfold wood, co. Kent: 2 *Cran.* 312, 313

Old (Jo.): notices of him, 1 *Bec.* ix, 2 *Bec.* 422, 424; in exile, 1 *Cran.* (9); J. O. (i. e. Old): translates a book on Antichrist, 2 *Cran.* 63; J. O. (perhaps the same): signs a conclusion to Ridley's Conferences, *Rid.* 151

OLD FAITH: translated from Bullinger by bp Coverdale, 1 *Cov.* 1, &c.

Old man: *v.* Man.

Old men and women: *v.* Aged.

Old ways: *Pil.* 537

Oldcastle (Sir Jo.), lord Cobham: notice of him, 1 *Bec.* 264 n.; Polydore Virgil's account of him, *Bale* 9; his father (?), and his youth, *ib.* 7; verses from his first book in the parliament-house, *ib.* 53, 54; he circulates the works of Wickliffe, &c., *ib.* 11; accused by the synod of 1413, *ib.* 16; abp Arundel complains to the king of him, *ib.* 17; his conference with the king, *ib.*; being cited by archbishop Arundel he refuses to appear, *ib.* 18; is excommunicated, *ib.* 19; his confession of faith, *ib.* 20; he offers to purge himself by combat, *ib.* 23; appeals to the pope, *ib.*; sent to the Tower, *ib.*; brought before abp Arundel, *ib.*; his first examination, *ib.* 24; his words respecting the real presence, 3 *Tyn.* 243; again brought before the archbishop, *Bale* 28; his latter examination, *ib.* 29; sentence against him, *ib.* 41; he speaks to the people, *ib.* 44; his manifesto from the Tower, *ib.* 45; an abjuration counterfeited by the bishops, *ib.* 46; he escapes from the Tower, and continues four years in Wales, *ib.* 51; retaken, condemned, and executed, *ib.* 52, 351, 394; A BRIEF CHRONICLE CONCERNING his EXAMINATION AND DEATH, &c., by bp Bale, *ib.* 1—59; causes of his condemnation and death, *ib.* 4, 10; his death compared with that of Tho. à Becket, *ib.* 55, &c.; England punished for it, *ib.* 12

Olearius (Jo. Gottf.): Biblioth. Scriptt. Eccles., 2 *Ful.* 336 n

Oleastro (Hieron. ab): prescribes rules for the interpretation of scripture, *Whita.* 495; on Deut. xvii. 12,—the judgment of the priest, *ib.* 421; on Deut. xxx. 11—"For this commandment," &c., *ib.* 382

Olesnicki (Nic.), lord of Pinczov: notice of him, 3 *Zur.* 690 n

Olevianus (Gasper): minister at Heidelberg, 2 *Zur.* 238 n

Olfridde: *v.* Ethelfride.

Oligarchy: 1 *Bul.* 310

Oliphant (Lau. lord): taken prisoner by the English at Solway, 3 *Zur.* 239 n

Olisleger (Hen.): vice-chancellor to the duke of Cleves, 2 *Cran.* 409; his letter to Cranmer in the cause of Anne of Cleves, *ib.* 410

Olive leaves: what they signified on the cross in ceremonies on Palm-Sunday, 1 *Bec.* 113, 114

Olive tree: never without leaves and fruit, 1 *Bec.* 114, 343; the Christian compared to it, *ib.* 347

Oliver (Jo.): consulted by the king about Cranmer's scrupling to swear to the pope, 2 *Cran.* 224; counsellor for the king in the matter of the divorce, *ib.* 244; mentioned, *ib.* 261

Oliver (Friar): *v.* Olyver.

Olivet: 4 *Bul.* 191

Olivetan (Pet. Rob.): notice of him, 3 *Zur.* 622 n

Olympia: her sufferings, *Pil.* 637, 638

Olympiodorus: says that a man shall continue in the state in which he dies, 3 *Jew.* 568

Olympius: confesses original sin, 2 *Bul.* 390

Olysleger (Hen.): *v.* Olisleger.

Olyver (Friar), prior of the Black Friars in Cambridge: preaches against the king's cause, 2 *Cran.* 295

O'Molana (Malachias), bp of Ardagh: *Park.* 421

Omri, king of Israel: 1 *Bul.* 336, 2 *Bul.* 12

On: used for against, 2 *Tyn.* 119

Once: at some time, 2 *Hoop.* 292

O'Neale (Con), earl of Tyrone: 1 *Zur.* 186 n

O'Neale (Matt.), illeg. son of Con, earl of Tyrone: 1 *Zur.* 186 n

O'Neale (Shan), illeg. son of Con, earl of Tyrone: his rebellion in Ireland, *Pil.* 74 n.

1 *Zur.* 186 n.; his submission, 1 *Zur.* 186 n., 194 n.; his death in an affray, *ib.* 186 n., 195

O'Neale (......), earl of Tyrone: his rebellion suppressed, *Lit. Eliz.* 473, 2 *Zur.* 335

Onerate: to load, 1 *Bec.* 67

Ongar (Chipping), co. Essex: the benefice, 2 *Lat.* 222 n

Onkelos: his Targum, 1 *Hoop.* 351, *Whita.* 117, 3 *Whitg.* 343

On-live, on-lyve: alive, 1 *Cov.* 465

Onslow (Fulke), and Mary (Whetenhall) his wife: 1 *Bec.* 191 n

Onslow (Rich.), solicitor-general: "Mr Onssley," *Park.* 302, 303 n

Onuphrius Panvinius: Epitome Pont. Rom., *Jew.* xli; Annot. in Platin. de Vit. Pont., *ib.*; cited, 4 *Jew.* 648, 659, 686, 698, 700, 934, 936

Opere operato (Ex): *v.* Opus.

Opitius (Mart.): *Calf.* 135 n

Oporinus (Jo.), or Herbst: a printer at Basle, 2 *Zur.* 112 n., 3 *Zur.* 106, 595 n., 638

Oppression: two sermons of oppression, affliction, and patience, *Hutch.* 295, &c.; Dr Somes' godly treatise against oppression, *Pil.* 468, &c.; what it is, *ib.* 469; why God suffers it, *Hutch.* 304; it is unlawful, and a grievous sin, *Pil.* 649, *Sand.* 135; complained of in Nehemiah's time, *Pil.* 454—458; various kinds in England, *ib.* 461, 462; practised by many classes of men, *ib.* 464, 465, brethren and countrymen, *ib.* 459; oppressors have no religion in them, *ib.* 474; restitution required of them, *ib.* 470, 471; the voice of the oppressed cries for vengeance, *ib.* 463; oppressors shall be punished, *ib.* 473; magistrates should deliver the oppressed, *ib.* 471, 472, 476; it is better to suffer than to oppress, *Hutch.* 302; how the oppressed should behave themselves under tyrannical princes, 1 *Bul.* 316

Opsopæus (......): *Whita.* 112 n

Optatus, bp of Milevis: Opera, *Jew.* xli; in a question concerning rebaptizing, he asserts that scripture must be the sole judge, *Whita.* 464; calls the sacrament of the Lord's supper a pledge of everlasting salvation and hope of the resurrection, 3 *Bec.* 387, 388; speaks of the body and blood of Christ as wont to be laid upon the altar, 3 *Bec.* 601; enumerates the bishops of Rome from Peter, 2 *Ful.* 348, 349, 3 *Jew.* 326; cited about Peter's primacy, 2 *Ful.* 311, 331, 332; an unfounded allusion to the origin of the name Cephas, supposed to be an interpolation in his text, 2 *Ful.* 302 n., which has been otherwise corrupted, *ib.*

348 n.; he says there are four sorts of heads in the church, bishops, priests, deacons, and the faithful, 3 *Jew.* 270; affirms that in apparel there is a token of the will, not a help towards chastity, *ib.* 428; the seventh book De Schismate Donatistarum referred to, though Optatus wrote but six, 2 *Ful.* 323

Opus aureum: 2 *Bec.* 472 n

Opus operans: 2 *Jew.* 750, 754

Opus operantis: 2 *Jew.* 750, 754

Opus operatum: remarks on it, *Bale* 159, 2 *Brad.* 278, 2 *Cov.* 257, 2 *Hoop.* 125, 2 *Jew.* 749, &c., *Rog.* 248, (and see Sacraments); the mass held profitable ex opere operato, 2 *Bec.* 454, 3 *Bec.* 358, 380

Opus Imperfectum: *v.* Chrysostom.

Opusculum tripartitum: *v.* Councils, *Lateran III.*

Or: ere, *Grin.* 16, *Pil.* 86

Oracles: those of the heathen the work of Satan and evil spirits, 3 *Bul.* 362, 2 *Cran.* 41; that of Apollo, 4 *Jew.* 1068; that of the Pythian Apollo said to Philippize, *ib.* 1113; Sibyllarum Oracula, *Jew.* xliii; who the sibyls were, and whence their name, *Hutch.* 177; their oracles often alleged by the fathers, 3 *Jew.* 132, 4 *Jew.* 737; sibylline utterances respecting God, *Hutch.* 177; testimony of the sibyls respecting the tower of Babel, cited by Josephus, *Whita.* 112; their utterance respecting the cross, *Calf.* 95 n.; they say that Antichrist shall be πολιόκρανος, and that his name shall be like *pontus*, 2 *Jew.* 914; declare that his greatest wo shall be by the banks of Tiber, 2 *Jew.* 915, 4 *Jew.* 743

Orange (Princes of): *v.* René, William.

Orarium: *v.* Horarium.

Orarium: a vestment, 2 *Tyn.* 221 n

Oratio: *Now.* (102)

Orator: one who petitions or prays, 2 *Brad.* 241, 2 *Bul.* 16, *Phil.* 157, 1 *Tyn.* 331

Oratories: *v.* Chapels.

Oratory: a fair and well-ordered oration very persuasive, 1 *Hoop.* 102; custom and manner of orators, *ib.* 413

Orbellis (Nich. de), commonly called Dorbel: notices of him, 2 *Lat.* xxvii, 1 *Tyn.* 151 n.; passages on faith and justification, 2 *Cran.* 204

Orbis (Novus): *v.* Novus.

Order: what it is, 3 *Bec.* 618; what manner of it remains in the church, 4 *Bul.* 108

Order (Book of Common): *v.* Book.

Order of the Church in Denmark, *q. v.*

ORDER OF THE COMMUNION, 1548, *Lit. Edw.* 1—8; reference to it, and to Latin versions of it, 2 *Cov.* 525 n

Orders, Ordination: v. Ministers, Bishops, Priests, Deacons, &c.
What orders the Lord hath instituted in his church, 4 *Bul.* 104; translations concerning orders examined, 1 *Ful.* 460, &c.; ecclesiastical orders said to be an apostolical tradition, *Whita.* 508; discussion as to the number of holy orders, 3 *Jew.* 271, &c.; they are variously reckoned by ancient writers, *ib.* 272, 273; the offices of apostle, bishop, priest, deacon, and widow, are of God, 3 *Tyn.* 176; five orders are mentioned in the so-called Apostolic canons, and by Ambrose, *Whita.* 509; Romanists make seven, *Hutch.* 50, *Rog.* 258, four lesser, three greater, 3 *Jew.* 271, *Rog.* 258; clerks of the minor orders carry tapers, &c., and drive dogs out of church, 3 *Jew.* 273; on the ordination of ministers, 4 *Bul.* 128; of consecration of bishops and ministers, *Rog.* 327; it must be lawful, *ib.* 238—241; power of ordination, 4 *Bul.* 43; on the authority of bishops to ordain ministers, 1 *Whitg.* 425; it is the only peculiar work of a bishop, according to Jerome and Chrysostom, *ib.* 439, 440; bishops must be most careful in it, 1 *Bec.* 4; ordination by the bishop and presbyters, 1 *Ful.* 249, 250, *Sand.* 434; ordination by bishops without the concurrence of the church disapproved by Beza, 2 *Zur.* 129; the people should consent, 1 *Ful.* 247; the alleged sacrament of orders, 4 *Bul.* 247, *Calf.* 227—231; some call it the sacrament of priesthood, of bishopdom, or of archbishopdom, *Rog.* 259; the doctrine of the Institution on the sacrament of orders, 2 *Cran.* 96—98; orders not a sacrament, 2 *Hoop.* 127, *Rog.* 258, 1 *Tyn.* 254; but a holy service, 2 *Jew.* 1129; each order called a sacrament, *Rog.* 259; how ordination may be termed a sacrament, *Calf.* 229; the order of it, 4 *Bul.* 138; the scripture method, *Pil.* 580; divers modes of appointment and ordination in the apostles' time, 1 *Whitg.* 428; on the signification of χειροτονία, and some other words, 1 *Ful.* 246, &c., *Pil.* 580, 1 *Whitg.* 345, &c.; putting on of hands is a sign, but not essential, 1 *Tyn.* 259 (v. Hands); ordination as described by ancient writers, *Pil.* 584, 585; popish rites, *ib.* 581; Romanists cannot agree as to what makes the priest, 1 *Tyn.* 258; Tyndale knew priests who went through the form of ordination a second time, because the bishop had omitted some ceremony, *ib.* 277; shaving, oiling, and vestments, and minor orders, are men's traditions, 3 *Tyn.* 176; ordination said to confer character, which is affirmed to be indelible, *Calf.* 230, 1 *Tyn.* 255; who are excluded from orders by the church of Rome, *Rog.* 241; why orders are not to be received at the hands of popish bishops, 4 *Bul.* 140; on the calling of ministers in the church of England, 1 *Whitg.* 299, &c.; THE FORM OF MAKING AND CONSECRATING ARCHBISHOPS, BISHOPS, PRIESTS, AND DEACONS, 1549, *Lit. Edw.* 159; the preface to it, ascribed to Cranmer, 2 *Cran.* 519; some things in this form attacked by Hooper, 1 *Hoop.* 47, 2 *Hoop.* xii, 3 *Zur.* 81, 87, 559, 566, 673; THE FORM OF MAKING AND CONSECRATING BISHOPS, PRIESTS, AND DEACONS, 1552, *Lit. Edw.* 329; THE FORM AND MANNER OF MAKING AND CONSECRATING BISHOPS, PRIESTS, AND DEACONS, 1559, *Lit. Eliz.* 272; notes respecting it, *ib.* xxi; of the services and ceremonies used in ordaining ministers, *Grin.* 340, 1 *Whitg.* 485, 2 *Whitg.* 408, 409; on the words "Receive the Holy Ghost," 1 *Whitg.* 488—491, 3 *Whitg.* 280, 487; on giving authority to preach, 3 *Whitg.* 40, 41; the English service censured by Romanists, *Pil.* 484, 578; the orders of the English church denied by Harding, 3 *Jew.* 320; Bradford's orders, for example, were not acknowledged by his judges, 1 *Brad.* 492; defence of the orders of the English church, *Poet.* 288, 289; the Book of Consecration is lawful, *Rog.* 327, 332; no bishop to ordain any without consent of six learned ministers, who should all lay on their hands (synod, 1562), *Sand.* 434; directions about ordination, *Grin.* 186; inquisition to be made for forged letters of orders, *ib.*; irregular ordinations by Lancaster, archbishop elect of Armagh, 4 *Jew.* 1274

Ordinale, or Directorium Sacerdotum: *Lit. Eliz.* 304 n

Ordinances: v. Advertisements.

Ordinaries: ecclesiastical rulers, 3 *Tyn.* 169

Ordination: v. Orders.

Ordo Romanus: 2 *Bec.* 256 n., 3 *Bec.* 482

Orenburg (The count von): killed at Groningen, 1 *Zur.* 205

Orestes: 1 *Hoop.* 184

Organs: v. Music.

A pair of organs, (the stocks), *Phil.* 235

Orichovius (Stanisl.): Chimæra, *Jew.* xli; he says that as God is above the priest, so the priest is above the king, 3 *Jew.* 117, 4 *Jew.* 674, 675, 1036

Origen:
    i. *His life and works.*

ii. *On God.*
iii. *Scripture, Tradition.*
iv. *Sin, Grace.*
v. *The Church, and its Ministry.*
vi. *Baptism.*
vii. *The Eucharist.*
viii. *Ceremonies and Worship, both legal and ecclesiastical.*
ix. *Fasting, Marriage, Confession, Absolution.*
x. *The Soul, a Future State, &c.*
xi. *Images, the Cross.*
xii. *Celsus, Heretics, Antichrist, &c.*
xiii. *Miscellanea.*

i. *His life and works:* his father Leonidas a martyr, 2 *Bul.* 105; he was sometime a student in Athens, 4 *Jew.* 652; a disciple of Clement of Alexandria, *Whita.* 586; preached while yet a layman, 1 *Whitg.* 452—454, 2 *Whitg.* 531; was a catechist, 2 *Jew.* 673; called to Antioch by Mammæa, 3 *Zur.* 6 n.; his ordination, 1 *Whitg.* 460; his high reputation, *Rid.* 28; he was called the informer or master of the churches, 4 *Jew.* 1045; his error respecting a saying of our Lord, 1 *Jew.* 228; he held a provincial council against Beryllus in Arabia, 4 *Jew.* 1125; the year of his death, *Calf.* 81 n.; his works, *Jew.* xli, 3 *Whitg.* xxxi; his Tetrapla, Hexapla, and Octopla, *Whita.* 124, 125; the Hexapla, 2 *Jew.* 692; he is the first known commentator (at least the first whose works remain), *Whita.* 391; the Homilies on Leviticus sometimes ascribed to Cyril of Alexandria, 2 *Jew.* 553 n.; his commentary on John vi. mangled by Romanists, 4 *Jew.* 788, 789; some of his works condemned, 1 *Tyn.* 154; errors and perilous doctrines in them, *Calf.* 78, *Coop.* 147, 2 *Cov.* 185, &c.; *Rid.* 30, 163, 1 *Tyn.* 220, *Whita.* 587, and see several places below; they were translated by Ruffinus, who was therefore charged with heresy, 4 *Jew.* 1006; cited by the Arians, 3 *Jew.* 226; falsified by Harding, *ib.* 515

ii. *On God:* he says we must first believe that there is one God who created all things, 3 *Jew.* 256; asserts that the power of God is the soul of the world, &c., 1 *Jew.* 501; says God is with us by the preaching of the evangelists and apostles, by the sacrament of his holy body and blood, by the glorious sign of the cross, *ib.* 492, 499, 536; mentions a tradition that our Lord's countenance assumed diverse appearances according to the worthiness of the beholders, *Whita.* 587; declares that Christ is in one sense every where, in another absent from us, 1 *Jew.* 492, 506; proves that Christ as to his divinity is present every where, as to his humanity gone from us into heaven, 2 *Bec.* 272, 273, 3 *Bec.* 427, 1 *Cran.* 94, (47); says it is not (Christ as) man that is wherever two or three are gathered together...but the Divine power that was in Christ, 1 *Jew.* 506, 3 *Jew.* 258; declares that the power of Jesus is present with them that are gathered in his name, 1 *Jew.* 492, 500; shews how Christ speaks in every congregation, *ib.* 493, 499; declares that, if we desire to follow any man, Christ is set before us, that we should follow him, 4 *Jew.* 882; says they are not to be heard which shew Christ in houses, *Grin.* 54; yet shews how, in a mystical sense, Christ enters into our house (see vii, below); states why Christ is called the Light, the Word, the Bread of life, 1 *Jew.* 451, 452, 2 *Jew.* 1042; says he that betrays Christ's disciples betrays Christ, 2 *Jew.* 760; denies that the darkness at the crucifixion was caused by an eclipse, *Whita.* 578; says Christ is the truth, Antichrist the truth counterfeit, 3 *Jew.* 159: speaks of some who thought that Christ should be crucified in the world to come, see iv, below; says the Holy Ghost is not changed into a turtle, but is made a dove, *ib.* 566

iii. *Scripture, Tradition:* he counts twenty-two books of the Old Testament, 4 *Bul.* 540, *Whita.* 57; says the books of the Old Testament were delivered by the apostles to be read in the churches, 4 *Jew.* 856, 3 *Whitg.* 47; teaches that no man ought, for the setting up a doctrine, to use any books but the canonical scriptures, 2 *Cran.* 23; speaks of honouring the bodies of the prophets, laid in their books and letters, as in graves, 2 *Jew.* 618; says that Paul sets an example to the teachers of the church, to bring forward what they have to say fortified by divine testimony, *Whita.* 676; calls him circumcised and clean who brings forward sound doctrine fortified by the rules of the evangelists and apostles *ib.* 677, 678; declares that our judgments and expositions without the scriptures have no credit, 1 *Bec.* 87, 2 *Bec.* 261, 3 *Bec.* 390, 391, *Coop.* 189, 2 *Cran.* 23, 3 *Jew.* 228, 231, 239, 4 *Jew.* 1173, *Whita.* 676; affirms that the discussing of our judgments must be taken only of the scriptures, 3 *Jew.* 239; says that if the scriptures do not establish anything, we ought to leave it to God, 2 *Cran.* 23; his way of interpreting scripture, *Whita.* 403, &c.; he compares scripture to the temple of God, and its meaning to the gold in the temple, *ib.* 677; says that as whatever gold was outside the temple was not sanctified, so every sense which is without the divine scripture is not holy, 3 *Jew.* 248; he is noted for drawing his text to allegory, 1 *Cran.* 113, (56), 1 *Tyn.* 307; a mystical exposition of his followed by Cyril, *Whita.* 687; though too much given to mystic interpretations, he understood some texts literally, and that in a very absurd manner, *ib.* 405; cautions that certain things written in John vi. are figures, 2 *Jew.* 591, 592, 1112; says there is even in the gospels, a letter which killeth, e. g. "Except ye eat my flesh and drink my blood," &c., 2 *Bec.* 287, 3 *Bec.* 430, 1 *Cran.* 113, 158, (56), *Grin.* 63, 2 *Hoop.* 499, 1 *Jew.* 456, 525, 2 *Jew.* 776, 4 *Jew.* 790, *Rid.* 31; admits obscurities in scripture, *Whita.* 371; shews how simple folks are deceived in the understanding of scripture, 1 *Jew.* 452, 2 *Jew.* 572, 1121, 3 *Jew.* 526; recommends the collation of parallel places, *Whita.* 493; speaks of scripture being read in the church, 1 *Jew.* 271; blames the people for not attending to the scripture at church and meditating on it at home, *Whita.* 247; says it had not been necessary to have these things read in the church unless thereof might grow some profit to the hearers, 4 *Jew.* 857; exhorts the people to read the scriptures, 1 *Jew.* 270, 326, 328; frequently admonishes all to search them, 2 *Jew.* 670, 696, 4 *Jew.* 796, 1186, *Whita.* 247; says we should come daily to the well of scripture, *Whita.* 677; affirms that the word of God is not only called flesh, but bread, milk, and herbs, 1 *Jew.* 526, 2 *Jew.* 762, 1042; says we must seek to understand the scriptures not only by study, but by supplication, *Whita.* 467; speaks of scripture as shut from the negligent, but opened to those who seek, 2 *Jew.* 684; warns of the danger of neglecting to be exercised therein, *ib.* 689, 3 *Jew.* 228, *Whita.* 700; says souls unskilled in the word of justice cannot stand before the abomination of desolation, 2 *Jew.* 688; admonishes that there is no less danger in despising the word of God, than the body of God, *ib.* 771; held singular views respecting the reading of scripture, supposing that it might be profitable, after the manner of a spell, even to those who did not understand it, *Whita.* 266; says, the very reading and hearing of God's word, though without understanding it, profits much, rejoices the angels within us, preserves us from serpents, &c., 1 *Jew.* 325; states that even they are saved who follow the letter of scripture, *ib.* 326, 327; says it is to the demons a torment above all kinds of torment if they see any man reading the word of God, *ib.* 57, 327, 2 *Jew.* 800, 4 *Jew.* 1178; shews how all that are like Pharaoh cry out that men are seduced, if Moses and Aaron (whom he takes mystically) call them to the service of God, 4 *Jew.* 1153; speaks of the shadows of the law, and "the very image," 2 *Jew.* 613, 616; agrees with our division of the commandments, 1 *Bul.* 213; numbers the second commandment among the ten, and holds it a moral law, 2 *Bec.* 60; expounds it, *Calf.* 372; referred to about "the least" precepts, 2 *Lat.* 314; plays with the word "begun," in Matt. xxvi. 37, 1 *Lat.* 218; on St Paul's quotation from Psa. xiv, in Rom. iii, 1 *Jew.* 314; quotes the book of Wisdom, 2 *Jew.* 604; whether he defended the history of Susanna, *Whita.* 78; mentions the gospel of the Hebrews, 1 *Jew.* 238; testimonies from him against traditions, *Whita.* 675, &c; cited in favour of them, *ib.* 586, 587

iv. *Sin, Grace:* he declares that all men being in the loins of Adam deserved death in him, 1 *Bec.* 68; some particular sins are mentioned in other divisions; he says that forasmuch as all men are shut up under sin, the salvation of man stands not in man's merits, but in God's mercy, 3 *Jew.* 587, 588; says Christ only is the sacrifice for sins; he is the sacrifice, the holy of holies, *ib.* 574; speaks of Christ as the priest, the atonement, and the victim, and says that his atonement comes to us by the way of faith, 1 *Jew.* 23, 3 *Jew.* 556; exhibits the profit of faith, 3 *Jew.* 584; maintains justification by faith alone, 2 *Bec.* 639; expounds that doctrine, referring to the penitent thief, and other examples in the scriptures, 2 *Bul.* 339, *Wool.* 34; some other passages, 2 *Cran.* 205, 211; he is not at all times consistent on this doctrine, *Calf.* 78; says with the holy shekel, viz. faith, we must buy Christ, who puts away our sins, 2 *Jew.* 748, 3 *Jew.* 559; declares the doctrine of St Paul to be that a man only believing may be justified though he have done no good works at all, 3 *Jew.* 244; will not allow any good deed of ours to be called good, rightly or duly, but only by abuse of speech, *ib.* 587; does not believe that there can be any work that may of duty require reward, *ib.*; mentions an erroneous opinion of some men that in the world to come Christ must suffer in his body, or be crucified again, 2 *Jew.* 719, 3 *Jew.* 560, 623

v. *The Church, and its Ministry:* he says the apostles were the heavens, 1 *Jew.* 468; calls Peter that great foundation and most sound rock whereon Christ has built his church, 2 *Ful.* 282; shews that the gates of hell prevailed not against any of the apostles, and that what was said to Peter was common to all, 2 *Ful.* 282, 283, 299, 1 *Jew.* 340, 401, 3 *Jew.* 288, 4 *Jew.* 929; teaches that the promise to Peter of the keys of the kingdom of heaven is common to the other apostles, 1 *Jew.* 360, 3 *Jew.* 289, 297, 4 *Jew.* 711, 717, 977; says that to Peter were given the keys of many heavens, *Calf.* 78, 3 *Jew.* 384; he does not limit the keys to Peter, 3 *Jew.* 384; says, let no man think we set John before Peter, 1 *Jew.* 428; declares that if we speak what Peter spoke we are made Peter, 3 *Jew.* 384, 4 *Jew.* 977, 1 *Tyn.* 218 n.; states that the rock is whoever is a disciple of Christ, 2 *Ful.* 273, 298, 1 *Jew.* 340, 385, 3 *Jew.* 297, 384, 4 *Jew.* 1118, 1 *Tyn.* 218 n.; speaks of all priests as the foundation of God's church, 1 *Jew.* 434; says that that against which the gates of hell prevail is neither the rock nor the church, *ib.* 338 n.; says all who are anointed with the holy unction are made priests, as Peter saith, 2 *Jew.* 737, 3 *Jew.* 336; he explains "no people," as meaning those who believe in Christ, a few in this city, and a few in another; and asserts that there never was any nation that was taken whole at the first beginning of the faith, 3 *Jew.* 595; says that Britain was subject to Christ in his time, 1 *Jew.* 305; mentions it as having agreed in the religion of one God, 3 *Jew.* 165; observes that the wise men of this world seeing the walls of the gospel rise up without grammar and profound knowledge in philosophy, say scornfully amongst themselves, that all this, by subtlety of speech, crafty shifts, and logical arguments, may easily be shaken down, 4 *Jew.* 911; refers to the danger of a church without the gospel, 2 *Jew.* 994; mentions bishops, priests, and deacons, 2 *Whitg.* 205; speaks of their duties, and on those of laymen, 1 *Jew.* 350; declares that the presence of the people is required in the admission of a priest, 1 *Bec.* 7, 8; says, that if Paul thought his authority not sufficient for a doctrine, how much more should others take heed what they teach, 2 *Cran.* 23; desires the lay-people to examine and judge whether he speaks well or otherwise, 2 *Jew.* 696; says a bishop is called not to a principality but to the service of the whole church, 1 *Jew.* 350, 365, 426; rebukes bishops for pride and stateliness, 4 *Jew.* 912; complains of the corruption of the clergy, 3 *Jew.* 424, 425; censures their worldly ambition, 1 *Jew.* 442; his erroneous opinion respecting evil ministers, 3 *Jew.* 385, 2 *Lat.* 347, *Rog.* 270

vi. *Baptism:* he says the (Red) sea is baptism, the cloud is the Holy Ghost, the lamb the Saviour, 2 *Jew.* 765; speaks of John's baptism as seen, but of Christ's as not seen, *ib.* 596; affirms that the baptism of infants was the doctrine of the apostles, 2 *Bec.* 209, 4 *Bul.* 392, *Phil.* 278; shews that the grace of the Holy Ghost does not always accompany baptism, 3 *Bec.* 467, 468; considers that baptism will be needed after our resurrection, 3 *Jew.* 560, 562, *Rog.* 275

vii. *The Eucharist:* although he says that manna signified Christ to come, who is now come indeed, and is manifested to us in the sacrament of his word, in the sacrament of regeneration, and of bread and wine, yet he meant not that Christ is corporally either in his word, in the water of baptism, or in the bread and wine, &c., 1 *Cran.* 154, (68); he calls the Lord's supper the bread of life, and banquet of salvation, 3 *Bec.* 387; says the Lord gave bread to his disciples, 2 *Jew.* 606; speaks of the bread remaining as material substance, 2 *Bec.* 265, 3 *Bec.* 423; calls the sacrament very meat, 1 *Cran.* 24; declares that the words of eating Christ's flesh and drinking his blood must be understood spiritually, and that if we follow them after the letter, this letter killeth, 2 *Bec.* 287, & al., see iii, above; says, the bread that is sanctified by the word of God and prayer, enters into the belly, &c., and shews that it is not the bread that profits, but the word of God said over it, 1 *Brad.* 589, *Coop.* 508, 509, 1 *Cran.* 261, 266, (30), *Grin.* 69, 70, 2 *Hoop.* 421, *Hutch.* 40, 272, 2 *Jew.* 566, 771, 1115, 3 *Jew.* 146, 452, 483, 515, 516, *Phil.* 183, *Rid.* 29, &c., 160; affirms that the bread which God the Word confesses to be his body is the nourishing word of souls, 3 *Bec.* 439, *Grin.* 68; calls the words he speaks the flesh of Christ, 1 *Jew.* 547, 548; says that Christ is called the bread of life, that the taste of our soul may have what to taste, 3 *Jew.* 532; cautions against abiding in the blood of the flesh, 3 *Bec.* 439, *Grin.* 69; says, he was wounded whose blood we drink, that is to say, the words of whose doctrine we receive, 3 *Jew.* 539; says, the blood of the testament is poured into our hearts, *ib.* 486; terms the bread and cup the holy of holies, and adds, how much more may we say this of God's word, 1 *Jew.* 522; referred to about the real presence, 2 *Lat.* 276; he speaks of the sacrament as Christ coming under our roof, 2 *Jew.* 758—761, 4 *Jew.* 789, 790; remarks that the Lord enters under our roof, both when we receive holy men, and also when we receive the holy sacrament, 1 *Jew.* 536, 537, 2 *Jew.* 760, 4 *Jew.* 790; and he says repeatedly that Christ comes by his word, 2 *Jew.* 760; warns against entering to the holy supper with filthy garments, 3 *Bec.* 475; affirms that the Word was made flesh and very meat...which no evil man can eat, 1 *Cran.* 208, (80), 2 *Jew.* 1120, 3 *Jew.* 454, 455; says it cannot be that he that continues evil may eat the Word made flesh, 2 *Bec.* 292, 3 *Bec.* 462, 1 *Cran.* 208, (80); asserts that, if any man touch the flesh of Christ's sacrifice, he is made holy straightways, 2 *Bec.* 292, 3 *Bec.* 462; admonishes to take the body of the Lord with all reverence, and not to suffer any part of it to fall, 1 *Jew.* 148, 150, 248, 4 *Jew.* 790; referred to on the grace of the eucharist, *Rid.* 241; he calls it the commemoration which makes God propitious to men, 2 *Ful.* 85, 2 *Jew.* 754, 755; the passage explained by his remarks on the shew-bread, 2 *Ful.* 85; he denies that what is sanctified by the word of God and prayer can of its own nature sanctify him that useth it, 2 *Jew.* 756, 3 *Jew.* 510; says the often using of the communion, and such like, are not righteousness itself, 2 *Jew.* 757; remarks that the Lord did not command the bread he gave to be reserved until the morrow, 2 *Bec.* 251, 3 *Bec.* 455, 456, *Coop.* 149, 1 *Jew.* 175, 2 *Jew.* 553, 780; in his time the bread that remained was burned, 2 *Bec.* 252, 3 *Bec.* 373, 1 *Hoop.* 521, 2 *Hoop.* 417; calls the heart "our altar," 1 *Jew.* 311

viii. *Ceremonies and Worship, both legal and ecclesiastical*: he shews that the reasons of holy rites should be opened, 3 *Jew.* 444; speaks of observances that are to be kept, though the reason of them is unknown, 2 *Cran.* 57; tells why circumcision is called a sign, 2 *Jew.* 595; states that unless a reason be rendered for it, it is but a dumb labour, *ib.* 757; mystically expounds the legal sacrifices, *Sand.* 414; states why the priest had the part that covered the heart, 2 *Jew.* 1017; shews that the sin-offering denotes Christ himself, 1 *Jew.* 521; calls it a sacrificial work to preach the gospel, 2 *Jew.* 709; says, God in prayer does not weigh so much our words as the heart, 1 *Bec.* 134; remarks that he who prays has trust in God, not for the words of his prayer or psalm, but because he hath well made up the altar of his heart, 1 *Jew.* 328; shews that various nations worshipped God in their own tongues, *ib.* 290; says no man can offer the sacrifice of prayer unless he be devoted to perpetual chastity, *ib.* 157; by continual sacrifice, he means faithful prayer, 3 *Jew.* 397; he distinguishes worship from adoration, *Calf.* 372, 373

ix. *Fasting, Marriage, Confession, Absolution*: he declares what kind of fast pleases God, 1 *Bec.* 105, 2 *Bec.* 540, 4 *Jew.* 1141; recommends that fasting which leaves more to nourish the poor, 2 *Bec.* 546; defines sobriety, *Sand.* 391; speaks of vows of chastity, 3 *Jew.* 398 n.; says none may offer the continual sacrifice (i. e. prayer) but such as have vowed continual chastity, *ib.* 897; speaks of some who teach chastity, but keep it not, 2 *Jew.* 830; declares that not only virgins or others that live in single life (but also married folks) offer up their bodies a holy sacrifice, 4 *Jew.* 804; says, that St Paul and his wife were called to the faith, both at one time, 3 *Jew.* 392; censures those who forbid men to marry, *ib.* 398, 399; speaks of marriage as if it were unholy, *ib.* 404; condemns second marriages, *ib.* 390, *Rog.* 262; describes the order of open confession, 3 *Jew.* 360; often speaks of private confession, *ib.* 368; as to the keys, see v, above; maintains that a wicked minister binds and looses, but in vain, 3 *Jew.* 385, *Rog.* 270

x. *The Soul, a Future State, &c.*: he says that man consists of three parts, the flesh, the spirit, and the soul, 1 *Cov.* 504; his opinion of the soul, 3 *Bul.* 374; thinks that we all must needs come into the fire of purgatory, even Paul and Peter, 3 *Jew.* 562; his errors about the resurrection, 2 *Cov.* 185, &c.; he says although the heavens shall be changed, yet that which is changed is not utterly abolished, 2 *Jew.* 569; errs in imagining that the pains of devils and the lost will cease, 1 *Bec.* 278.

279, 315, *Calf.* 78; his opinions on angels, 1 *Jew.* 325, 326

xi. *Images, the Cross:* he assigns the reason why image-makers were not suffered to dwell among the Jews, *Calf.* 44, 80; mentions that Celsus objected to the Christians, that they had neither images, altars, nor temples, and admits the statement, *ib.* 79—81, 1 *Jew.* 310, 2 *Jew.* 658, *Park.* 86, *Rid.* 88; says, we make no image of God, 2 *Jew.* 658; declares that it is not possible to worship both God and an image, *ib.* 667; expounds the mind of the law against images, *Calf.* 372; thinks that the cross was prefigured by the rod of Aaron, *ib.* 103; speaks of the ancient form of the thau mentioned by Ezekiel, *Whita.* 116 n.; enlarges on the power of the cross, i. e. the death of Christ, *Calf.* 77—79, 2 *Ful.* 144

xii. *Celsus, Heretics, Antichrist, &c.*: he intimates that Celsus charged the Christians with insanity, 3 *Jew.* 250; notices that he despised their religion because it had its origin among the Jews, *ib.* 193, 194, 4 *Jew.* 667; states that he scoffed at the gospel as a novelty, 4 *Jew.* 776; says that he affirmed that the sacraments of the Christians were taken from the sacrifices of Mithra, 3 *Jew.* 552; speaks of Celsus, &c., assuming the name of truth, *ib.* 159; as to his objection of the lack of images, &c., see xi, above; he refers to the scorn of the enemies of the truth, 1 *Jew.* 469; he says the Helchisaites to avoid troubles and persecution will swear and forswear themselves, *Rog.* 357 n.; speaks of the Seleucians, 1 *Hoop.* 160; says that heretics of good life are especially dangerous, 1 *Whitg.* 139; as to his own errors, see above, particularly in i. and x; he laments the existence, amongst Christians, of men who were scrupulous about small faults, and careless about great ones, 3 *Jew.* 618; declares that apostates betray the Saviour, 4 *Jew.* 791; calls Antichrist the truth counterfeit, 3 *Jew.* 159; declares that he is the abomination of desolation, 4 *Jew.* 728

xiii. *Miscellanea:* he thanks God that he is not ignorant of his own ignorance, 1 *Jew.* 98; speaks of zeal without knowledge, 2 *Jew.* 1007; asserts that, if love pass the measure of charity, he that loves and he that is loved are in sin, 3 *Jew.* 578; states his opinion of a lie, 2 *Bul.* 115; intimates that no remnant of the Chaldeans should be suffered to remain, 3 *Jew.* 617; explains giving "with simplicity," 3 *Whitg.* 283; asserts that the government of the people ought to be committed to him whom God chooses, 1 *Bec.* 8; admonishes those who have either money or lands to give tribute to Cæsar, 4 *Jew.* 705

Origenists: interpreted scripture allegorically, *Rog.* 197; held that the devils and ungodly shall all finally be saved, *Hutch.* 56, *Rog.* 67, 147

Original Sin: v. Sin.

Orismada: the holy fire of the Persian kings, *Rog.* 291

Orkney isles: 1 *Zur.* 195 n., 196

Orkney (James, duke of): v. Hepburn.

Orleans: v. Councils.

Some of the wine of Cana said to be preserved there, 1 *Jew.* 249; story of the provost's wife and the friars, 2 *Cran.* 64; the siege, 1563, 1 *Zur.* 124 n., 2 *Zur.* 116 n

Orleans (Cha. duke of): v. Charles.

Orleans (Louis d'), duke of Longueville: raises an army in the dukedom of Cleve, 3 *Zur.* 633 n

Ormanet (Nich.): datary of pope Julius III., *Calf.* 331, 413

Ormerod (Oliver): Picture of a Papist, *Calf.* 221 n

Orosius (Paulus): his history contains many examples of God's judgment, 2 *Bul.* 429; he speaks of Scipio at Carthage, 2 *Hoop.* 79; says the famine in the time of Augustus was because Caius refused to honour God, *ib.* 166; declares that there was peace in all the world at Christ's nativity, *Sand.* 286; speaks of the punishments which were inflicted on the Roman emperors for their persecution of the Christians, 2 *Bul.* 67; bears witness, that so many of the Roman emperors as persecuted the preaching of the gospel and advanced idolatry, died a shameful death, *ib.* 13; asserts that Philip was the first Roman emperor who was a Christian, 2 *Ful.* 355 n.; relates the successes of Constantine, and other Christian emperors, 1 *Bul.* 385; speaks of Helena, *Calf.* 322 n

Orphanotrophia: 1 *Bul.* 286, 4 *Bul.* 498

Orphans: 1 *Bul.* 288, 3 *Bul.* 385

Orpington, co. Kent: 2 *Zur.* 220 n

Orthuinus Gratius: v. Fasciculus.

Orus Apollo, or Horapollo: says Serapis had the figure of a cross upon his breast, *Calf.* 107

Osborn (Pet.): an ecclesiastical commissioner, *Park.* 277, 302, 383; his office, *ib.* 280; mentioned, 2 *Cov.* 532

Osburne (Mr): saluted, 2 *Brad.* 59

Osculatorium: v. Pax.

Oseney, co. Oxon: the great bell, 2 *Jew.* 809
Osiander (And.): account of him and his system, *Grin.* 254 n.; his errors, 2 *Ful.* 377, 3 *Jew.* 265, 622; his dogma respecting justifying righteousness, 3 *Zur.* 712; his calumnies against the Lutherans, *Whita.* 379, 380; he opposes the error of Stancarus, 1 *Zur.* 127 n.; expounds Micah v. 2, *Whita.* 173; his Conjecture of the End of the World, 1 *Lat.* 365 n.; Cranmer married his niece, 2 *Cran.* viii, 356; Cranmer's Latin letter to him against polygamy and concubinage, *ib.* 404, the same in English, *ib.* 406
Osiandrians: a sect, 1 *Ful.* 59, 2 *Jew.* 686; they affirmed Christ and his righteousness to be inherent in the righteous, *Rog.* 115
Osias: v. Ozias.
Osius (Stanisl. card.): v. Hosius.
Oslynger (Hen.): v. Olisleger.
Osmande (......): martyred, *Poet.* 162
Osmund (St) [de Seez], bp of Salisbury and earl of Dorset: 3 *Jew.* 410; author of the Salisbury use, *Pil.* 535
Osorius (Hieron.), bp of Silvas: says king Edward was poisoned, 3 *Zur.* 365 n.; his letter to queen Elizabeth answered by Haddon, *Grin.* 29 n., *Park.* 216 n., 3 *Zur.* 365 n.; his reply, *Park.* 217 n.; Haddon's rejoinder, completed, after his death, by Foxe, *Jew.* xxxviii, 4 *Jew.* 686, *Park.* 217 n
Ossenes: prayed in a strange language, *Rog.* 242; required all to marry, *ib.* 306; their relics, 2 *Ful.* 390
Ostend: blockaded, 2 *Zur.* 335
Ostend (Jo. van): burned at Antwerp, 3 *Zur.* 578
Ostering (Fra.): his widow Katherine, 2 *Cov.* 524, 525
Ostfor: v. Oftfor.
Ostia: the bishop of Hostia consecrates the bishop of Rome, 3 *Jew.* 331
Ostia (Julian, bp of): v. Julian.
Ostiarii: v. Porters.
Ostiensis (Hen. card.): v. Hostiensis.
Ostiensis (Leo): v. Leo.
Ostrogoths: 2 *Bul.* 109
Oswald (St), king of Northumberland: 2 *Ful.* 10, 11, 12, *Pil.* 583 n.; called St Oswald of Gloucester, *Bale* 192
Oswald (St), bp of Worcester, afterwards abp of York: a great helper of monks, *Pil.* 574
Oswen (Jo.), printer at Worcester: 2 *Hoop.* 94, 175, *Lit. Edw.* iv, &c.
Oswin (St), king of Deira: called St Oswin of Tynemouth, *Bale* 192

Oswold (Jo.): martyred, *Poet.* 167
Oswy, or Oswine, king of Northumberland: called a synod at Whitby about Easter, 2 *Ful.* 16, *Pil.* 625; Wighard (otherwise Dimianus) nominated abp of Canterbury, by him and Egbert, king of Kent*, 2 *Ful.* 16, 119
Osyth (St), or Syth: slain by the Danes, *Bale* 192; some account of her, 1 *Bec.* 139 n.; she was invoked for things lost, *ib.* 139, 2 *Bec.* 536, *Hutch.* 171; why, *Hutch.* 172 n.; St Sithe's key, *Bale* 498
Otford, co. Kent: manor, 2 *Cran.* 250 & passim; taken from Cranmer by the king in exchange, *ib.* 348
Otho, emperor of Rome: 1 *Bec.* 234
Otho I., emperor of Germany: his oath to the pope, 3 *Bec.* 512, 513 n., 2 *Tyn.* 269; he said that it pertained to the people of Rome to choose their bishop, 1 *Whitg.* 401, 402; yet took the power from them, *ib.* 403; deposed pope John XII. or XIII., 4 *Jew.* 682, *Pil.* 640; his epistle to that pope, 4 *Jew.* 651
Otho IV., emperor: licensed by the pope to marry his niece, *Pil.* 603
Otho, or Otto, Frisingensis: Chronicon, *Jew.* xli; says Constantine's Donation is false, 4 *Jew.* 678; does not mention pope Joan, *ib.* 648; tells how the Romans wrote to the emperor Conrad, *ib.* 1014; commends Gregory VII., *ib.* 698; speaks of Prester John, 2 *Ful.* 226 n
Otho, a cardinal: on the three holy tongues, 1 *Jew.* 271
Otho, the canonist: in his work the vestments are declared to be of popish invention, 1 *Zur.* 158; incontinent priests are ordered to be suspended, 4 *Jew.* 638; the gloss declares that this does not apply to simple fornication, *ib.*; priests directed to put away their concubines within a month, *ib.* 637, *Rog.* 119 n.; curious gloss on this, 4 *Jew.* 638; direction that the priest who openly keeps concubines shall be deposed, *ib.* 639, *Rog.* 119 n.; gloss on this, 4 *Jew.* 639, 802, *Rog.* 119 n.; the gloss declares that clerks commonly hold and have concubines in honest behaviour, under the name of their sisters, 3 *Jew.* 426; inquires whether a priest may be forced to forswear his concubine, and replies negatively, 4 *Jew.* 642; states that the church ought to dissemble the crime of whoredom, and acknowledges that the pope's marshall receives tribute from it, *ib.* 633, 644; decides that

---

* So read at p. 292 of this Index.

574   OTHO — OXFORD

no man may avoid a priest's services, unless he be convicted of fornication otherwise than by eye-witness, *ib.* 802; recommends priests to act, if not chastely, yet cautiously, 3 *Jew.* 136, 420, 4 *Jew.* 633, 639

Otilia (St): invoked for the headache, *Rog.* 226

Otter: counted fish on fast-days, 2 *Tyn.* 97 n

Ottius (Jo. Hen.): Examen perpet. in Annales Baronii, 2 *Ful.* 44 n

Otto Henry, elector palatine: 4 *Bul.* xix.

Ottoman: founder of the Turkish empire, 2 *Bul.* 268

Oudin (Cas.): the date he assigns to the pseudo-Abdias, *Calf.* 126 n.; greatly astray as to the time when Ben Gorion existed, 2 *Ful.* 338 n.; mistaken concerning the Testimonia adversus Judæos, by Gregory Nyssen, *ib.* 296 n.; he gives an account of the Liber Pontificalis, *ib.* 98 n.; his charge against Claude Morell, *ib.* 109, 110 n.; referred to, *Calf.* 235 n

Ought: awed, 1 *Bec.* 154, 2 *Bul.* 371, 3 *Bul.* 46

Oughtred (Sir Ant.): Elizabeth (Seymour) his wife, 3 *Zur.* 340 n

Ousel: a blackbird, 1 *Jew.* 283, 330

Out of: without, 1 *Bec.* 154

Outasing: making a tumult, *Bale* 244

Overall (Jo.), bp of Coventry and Lichfield, and afterwards of Norwich: concerned in the dispute with Barret at Cambridge, and declared to be somewhat factious, 3 *Whitg.* 615; his dedication of the collected works of Jewel, 4 *Jew.* 1306—1312

Overhipped: passed by, skipped over, 1 *Jew.* 368

Overly: used for over (as an adverb), 1 *Brad.* 548; superficially, cursorily, 3 *Bec.* 374

Overset: to overcharge, 2 *Tyn.* 71

Overton (Will.), bp of Coventry and Lichfield: controversy between him and certain persons about the chancellorship of his diocese, *Grin.* 370

 Margaret (Barlow) his wife, 3 *Bec.* 501 n., 2 *Zur.* 263 n

Ovid: cited or referred to, 1 *Bec.* 144, 182, 203, 261, 2 *Bec.* 101, 383, 1 *Bul.* 257, 303, *Calf.* 14, 25, 316 nn., *Grin.* 13, 1 *Hoop.* 58, 120, 138, 278, 407, *Hutch.* 176, 1 *Lat.* 415, *Pil.* 51, 1 *Tyn.* 438, 455

Owe: to own, 3 *Bul.* 70, & add.

Owen (Howell ap): *v.* Abowan.

Owen (Tho.), notary: 2 *Cran.* 547

Owl: story of one, 4 *Jew.* 915, 916

Ox: an emblem of a good labourer, *Pil.* 380

Oxenbridge (......): preaching at Paul's cross, laments the state of Oxford, 1 *Lat.* 62 n

Oxford: the council of Oxford, A.D. 1222; a deacon degraded for apostasy, and afterwards burned, *Bale* 3; notice of a sermon at Oxford by a great clerk, 2 *Tyn.* 206; a strange story of an execution, 1 *Lat.* 149, 163; the disputation concerning the eucharist in king Edward's time, 3 *Zur.* 391, 478 n.; punishment of a priest and others for celebrating mass, *ib.* 467; a story about searchers for popish books at Oxford, 1 *Ful.* 132, 137; the disputation with the martyrs in queen Mary's reign, 1 *Cran.* 391, &c., 1 *Jew.* 45, 53, 2 *Lat.* 250, &c., *Park.* 160, *Pil.* 400, *Rid.* 189, &c.; Latimer, Ridley, and Cranmer burned at Oxford, *Poet.* 165, 166, (and see their names); Oxford gloves, 1 *Zur.* 130, 3 *Zur.* 630, &c.

University: v. Caius (T.), Universities. Ordered to surrender its liberties to Henry VIII., 2 *Cran.* 252 n.; its opposition to that king's injunctions, *ib.* 382—384; the university said to live quietly with fewer privileges than Cambridge, *Park.* 24; declared to be more perverse than Cambridge, 3 *Zur.* 680; hypocritical hymnals were sung round the Christmas fire, *Calf.* 298; mode and expense of study there, 3 *Zur.* 190, 194, 419, 420, 424, 459; exhortatio ad Oxonienses, 4 *Jew.* 1302; ill will of the university to the martyrs, *Rid.* 359; its depressed and lamentable state after the death of Mary, 1 *Zur.* 11, 33; Parkhurst describes it as a den of thieves, *ib.* 29; its piteous condition as to preachers, 1566, 1 *Lat.* 62 n.; queen Elizabeth visits it, *Coop.* xiv; diploma to the baron of Alt-Sax, 2 *Zur.* 216; one to R. Gualter the younger, *ib.* 219; the university commended by his father, *ib.* 280; in 1683 the university condemned, amongst other books, that of Buchanan De Jure Regni, 2 *Zur.* 311 n.; the decree burned, in 1710, by the hangman, *ib.*; list of the colleges and halls, 3 *Jew.* 110, the professorships, &c., *ib.* 111

    COLLEGES, &c.:

All Souls' college: the founder ordered that the fellows should all be priests, *Park.* 396, but in 1572 only two of the forty were priests, *ib.*; variance between the warden and another about a chantry in the diocese of Lincoln, 2 *Cran.* 249; letter from Cranmer to the warden, Roger Stokeley, desiring a lease of Les Wydon for a friend, *ib.* 279; letter from Parker to the warden, Rich. Barber, requiring an inventory of superstitious plate and vestments retained by the college, *Park.* 296; letter from

Parker and others requiring the warden to deliver up certain superstitious books, *ib.* 297; letter from Parker and other ecclesiastical commissioners to the warden citing several fellows before them, *ib.* 300; order of the commissioners respecting the plate, &c., *ib.* 301 n.; disposal of the plate and church books, *ib.* 304; letters from Parker to the warden to procure the renewal of a lease for the widow of an old tenant, *ib.* 320, 324

Brasenose college: Nowell a benefactor, *Now.* viii; for a short time principal, *ib.* i.

Broadgates hall: Jewel sheltered there on his expulsion from Corpus, *Jew.* ix, 1191 n.; merged in Pembroke college, 1 *Zur.* 327 n

Canterbury college: some account of it, 2 *Cran.* 365 n.; merged in Christ-church, *ib.*

Christ-church: commission respecting its statutes, *Park.* 118; certain injunctions directed to be observed there till the completion of their book of statutes, *Grin.* 282; as to the church, see the *Cathedral,* below; Latin prayers used there, *Lit. Eliz.* xxxii; the dean's house, 1 *Cran.* xxii.

Corpus Christi college: concio in fundatoris Foxi commemorationem, 4 *Jew.* 1304; the college popishly inclined, *Jew.* ix; the ejection of Jewel, *ib.*

Exeter college: 1 *Cran.* 393

Lincoln college: 1 *Cran.* 391, 392, 393

Magdalene college: 1 *Cran.* 393, 1 *Zur.* 289, 290; notice of orders by bp Cooper as visitor, *Coop.* xiv.

Merton college: an order made that only three priests should be within the college, *Park.* 325; one physician there for reading Linacre's lecture, *ib.* 326

Pembroke college: v. Broadgates hall.

Queen's college: Grindal a benefactor, *Grin.* 459

St John's college: a dispute there, *Park.* 436

University college: 1 *Cran.* 393, 423; lord Bedford's benefaction, 2 *Bec.* 622 n

Schools: Latimer examined in the Divinity school, 2 *Lat.* 291, *Rid.* 256; the Parvise, or Logic school, *Coop.* 55, 1 *Jew.* 48, 3 *Jew.* 612; disputations in parvis, or in parviso, *Phil.* 98

CHURCHES, &c.:

The Cathedral: the bishoprick once a part of the diocese of Lincoln, *Rid.* 264; Harding, while he professed the doctrines of the reformation, wished his voice had been equal to the great bell of Frideswise, 4 *Jew.* 824, or of Osney, *ib.* 1310; this bell was baptized by Dr Tresham, and named Mary, *Jew.* x, *Rog.* 266; the quiremen, 1 *Cran.* 391; the see long vacant, *Park.* 145 n.; letter from Grindal to the dean and chapter, about certain recusants, *Grin.* 362

St Mary's church: 1 *Cran.* 391, &c.; Latimer and Ridley examined there, 2 *Lat.* 288, *Rid.* 276, 277; examination of Cranmer there, 2 *Cran.* 212, &c., 542, &c., *Rid.* 255; Dr Cole's sermon before Cranmer's burning, 1 *Cran.* xxiii, &c.; Amy Robsart buried there, 2 *Bec.* 583 n

St Mary Magdalene church: the martyrs' aisle, 1 *Brad.* 273 n

Bocardo, or the North gate: notices of it, 1 *Brad.* 83, 273 n.; Cranmer, Latimer, and Ridley, prisoners there, 1 *Brad.* 83, 2 *Brad.* 82, 1 *Cran.* xxii, xxiii, 2 *Cran.* 563, 1 *Lat.* xiii, 323, 2 *Lat.* 435, 444, *Rid.* xi, 293, 359; Ridley describes it as a college of quondams, 2 *Brad.* 84, *Rid.* 560; the word Bocardo used for a prison generally, or figuratively for affliction, 1 *Brad.* 273, 1 *Lat.* 250, 293, *Pra. B.* 106

The Castle (?): abp Parker desires the sheriff, that as there is no convenient prison within the diocese for clerks convict, such may be lodged in the common jail at Oxford, *Park.* 145

The Bear: Park. 138 n.; bishop Cooper born in Cat street, *Coop.* x.

Oxford (Jo. earl of): *v.* Vere.
Oxfordshire: rebellion there, 3 *Zur.* 391
O yes: oyez, 1 *Whitg.* 281
Oysters, 1 *Zur.* 264 n
Oza: *v.* Uzzah.
Ozias: a priest mentioned in the book of Judith, 4 *Bul.* 181

P

P. (E.): edited the Confutation of Unwritten Verities, 2 *Cran.* 2, 5

P. (I.): perhaps Pilkington or Parkhurst, 1 *Brad.* 374

P. (R.), perhaps Rob. Pownall: 1 *Brad.* 242 n.; a prayer by him, *ib.* 578

P. (W.): notice of him, *Poet.* xlvii; a fragment of the xcv. Psalm in metre, *ib.* 484

P. (W.): letter to W. P., probably Punt, or Porrege, 2 *Brad.* 38; letter to W. P., perhaps the same, 2 *Hoop.* 592

Pace (Rich.): persecuted by Wolsey, 2 *Tyn.* 317; his book De Fructu qui ex Doctrina percipitur, 2 *Lat.* 16 n.; he translated a sermon by bishop Fisher, 1 *Tyn.* 189 n
Pachette (......), widow: 2 *Cran.* 293
Pachymeres, the scholiast on the pseudo-Dionysius: speaks of union with Christ by baptism, 1 *Jew.* 473; says the holy oil is Christ, 2 *Jew.* 576, 3 *Jew.* 499; says Dionysius calls presbyters sacrificers, 2 *Jew.* 709, and that by λειτουργούς he means deacons or subdeacons, 4 *Jew.* 805; expounds a passage on the figurative sacrifice, *ib.* 721; says Judas was not at the last supper, *Whita.* 568; explains the word κοινωνία, 1 *Jew.* 135; declares that this common diet brings us into remembrance of the Lord's supper, *ib.* 131; speaks of the holy gifts remaining covered till the time of distribution, &c., *ib.* 510; calls them symbols of Christ, *ib.* 511, 512; explains an address of Dionysius to the sacrament, *ib.* 535; his use of the word ἀγάλματα, 2 *Jew.* 656
Pacius (Jul.): describes various kinds of theft, 2 *Bul.* 34 n.; mentions a kind called peculatus, *ib.* 46, and another kind called plagium, *ib.* 47; speaks of abigei or robbers of cattle, *ib.* 48; describes the crime called ambitus, *ib.* 46; treats of usury, *ib.* 40; refers to laws made for the relief of the poor, *ib.* 281
Pack: a lewd person, 2 *Bul.* 69
Packingham (Patr.), or Pattenham: martyred at Uxbridge, *Poet.* 163
Packington (Augustine), merchant at Antwerp, where he is said to have bought up Tyndale's New Testament for Tonstal, 1 *Tyn.* xxxvii.
Packington (......): shot in London, *Bale* 441
Pad: to travel on foot, 2 *Brad.* 46
Padley (Jo.): a kinsman of Cranmer, and sanctuary-man in Westminster, 2 *Cran.* 257
Padley (Steph.): priest at Malling, 2 *Cran.* 249 n
Padua: the university erected by Charlemagne, 2 *Jew.* 981
Pagans: v. Heathen.
Paganus (M. Ant.): notice of him, *Sand.* 249 n
Paganus Bergonensis: wrote on the Apocalypse, *Bale* 258
Paget (Sir Will., afterwards lord): servant to king Henry VIII., 2 *Cran.* 232; secretary to that prince, *ib.* 412; a privy councillor, *ib.* 496, 505, 510, 522, *Park.* 30, 1 *Zur.* 5 n.,

2 *Zur.* 159 n.; he questions Anne Askewe, *Bale* 203, 205; made comptroller of the household, 3 *Zur.* 77 n.; president of Wales, *ib.* 661; one of king Edward's visitors at Cambridge, 1549, *Grin.* 194; at Windsor, 3 *Zur.* 729 n.; ambassador from queen Mary to France and Germany, *Rid.* 394; letter to him, 2 *Cran.* 414
Paget (Tho. 3rd lord): being concerned in a rebellion, flees into France, *Lit. Eliz.* 656 n
Paget (......): his Catechism, *Rog.* 61
Pagi (Ant.): Crit. in Annales Baronii, *Calf.* 9 n.; his conjecture as to the source of the fable that St Peter was for twenty-five years at Rome, 2 *Ful.* 336 n.; rejects the counterfeit acts of the synod of Sinuessa, *ib.* 364 n.; his words concerning the authorities adduced by the 2nd council of Nice, *Calf.* 345 n
Pagi (Fra.): Breviar. Gest. Pontiff. Rom., 2 *Ful.* 337 n
Pagitt (Eph.): Christianography, 2 *Ful.* 328 n
Pagninus (Sanctes): v. Bible, *Latin.*
Reference to him, 4 *Jew.* 982
Painime: pagan, 2 *Cran.* 15
Painswick, co. Gloucester: 2 *Lat.* 417 n
Painter (Geo.), and Jone his wife, martyrs: v. Catmer.
Painter (Greg.): v. Paynter.
Pair: to impair, 2 *Brad.* 29
Palat. (Bapt.): testifies that the Illyrians and Slavonians use their common tongue in divine service, 3 *Bec.* 410
Palatinate of the Rhine: religious changes there, 2 *Zur.* 156 n., 274
Palea: in Gratian, 3 *Jew.* 394
Paleologus (Jo.): v. John.
Palgrave (Sir Fra.): Parliamentary Writs, 4 *Jew.* 904 n
Pall: a vestment worn by [arch]bishops, *Calf.* 305; Damasus ordered metropolitans to fetch their palls from Rome, 2 *Whitg.* 173; Gregory I. ordained that the pall should be freely given, 4 *Bul.* 139; Innocent III. required an oath of fidelity from those who received it, 2 *Brad.* 310; the pope sells it, 4 *Bul.* 139; its cost has often beggared the whole diocese, *Pil.* 582; many sees have been a long time without it, *ib.* 583; what the English archbishops paid to the pope for it, 4 *Jew.* 1078 (see also Pallium).
Palladius, bp of Helenopolis: the alleged biographer of Chrysostom, 1 *Jew.* 387; his Historia Lausiaca, *Pil.* 26 n
Pallas: defended Achilles, 2 *Hoop.* 85
Pallgrave (Jo.), or Pawlesgrave, rector of

St Dunstan's in the East: letter to him, 2 *Cran.* 263
Pallium: whether common to all Christians or peculiar to the priests, 1 *Zur.* 160, 350; worn by certain ascetics, *ib.* 350 n.; as to the archiepiscopal pallium, see Pall.
Palm Sunday: explanation of the ceremonies used on that day, 1 *Bec.* 112; the procession with the veiled cross, *ib.*; the carrying of palms, 2 *Cran.* 509, 1 *Bec.* 112; inquiries about the hallowing of them, 2 *Cran.* 157, *Rid.* 532; the reading of the gospel in the churchyard, 1 *Bec.* 113; the singing of the children before the naked cross, *ib.*; the green olives and palms upon that cross, *ib.*; the singing of the people, &c., *ib.* 114; flowers used in the ceremonies, *ib.* 115; the casting down of cakes, &c., *ib.*; the spearing (i. e. barring) of the church door, *ib.*; the singing in the church, *ib.* 116; the uncovering of the crucifix, *ib.*; the practice of lifting the veil (which covered it) upon this day abolished, 2 *Cran.* 414; the making of wooden crosses on this day, *ib.* 503; the leading up and down of an ass, *Rog.* 180
Palm-tree, Palms: the nature of the palm-tree, 1 *Bec.* 112, 113; why victory is signified by it, *ib.* 112; palms forbidden, 2 *Cran.* 417, 2 *Hoop.* 129 (and see Holy things); their restoration demanded by the rebels of Devon, 2 *Cran.* 176; they were indeed boughs of a sallow tree, 1 *Bec.* 112
Palmas: held a provincial council in Pontus, 4 *Jew.* 1125
Palmer (Sir Tho.): imprisoned, 3 *Zur.* 577 n.; executed, *ib.* 367 n
Palmer (......): martyred at Newbury, *Poet.* 168
Palmer (Pet.): servant to Grindal, *Grin.* 462
Palmer (Tho.): warden of the minor canons of St Paul's, *Bale* 28; he questions lord Cobham, *ib.* 39
Palmer (Will.), chancellor of the church of York: enjoined to view the statutes of the said church, *Grin.* 151
Palmer (Will.): Orig. Lit., 1 *Cov.* 452 n., 456 n., *Grin.* 135 n.; a mistake in this book corrected, *Pra. Eliz.* x, xii; Treatise on the Church, 2 *Ful.* 324 n.; Jurisdiction of Brit. Episc. vindicated, *ib.* 118
Palmere (Rob.): parson of St Quintin de Spellache, Calais, 2 *Cran.* 349 n
Palmerius (Matth.) Florentinus: Chronicon, *Jew.* xl; he relates how Stephen disinterred Formosus, 3 *Jew.* 276; says it was ordained (in the time of Boniface III.) that the church of Rome should be head of all churches, though the church of Constantinople had before claimed it, 3 *Jew.* 278, 4 *Jew.* 733; supplies evidence in proof of pope Joan, *ib.* 656; tells of the imprisonment and death of the emperor Henry IV., *ib.* 700

Palmes (Dr), master of Nicholas hostel, Camb.: opposes Latimer, 2 *Lat.* xii.
Palmio (......): *Lit. Eliz.* 584 n
Palmistry: looking of men's hands condemned, 2 *Cran.* 100
Palms: *v.* Palm Sunday, &c.
Palude (Pet. de): *v.* Petrus.
Pambo, a monk of the 4th century: stories of him, *Pil.* 26, 688, 3 *Whitg.* 585
Pamelius (Jac.): *Calf.* 202 n., 203 n
Pammachius: a tragedy so called, played at Cambridge, *Park.* 21—29
Pamphilus: martyred, 2 *Bul.* 105, 4 *Jew.* 694
Pamphilus: the pseudonym of Tho. Randolph, 4 *Jew.* 1224 n., 1 *Zur.* 56, 57 n., 59, &c.
Pan (To savour of the): to be suspected of heresy, 2 *Brad.* 160 n
Pancras (St): *v.* Saint Pancras.
Pandects: *v.* Law (Civil).
Pandulph: 4 *Jew.* 648
Pandulph: the pope's legate to king John, 2 *Tyn.* 316
Panecuis (Bapt.): *Bale* 593
Paneitas: a word devised by the schoolmen, 1 *Tyn.* 158 n
Panormitanus (Abbas): i. e. Nic. Tudeschi, *q. v.*
Panormitanus (Ant.): De Dict. et Fact. Alphons., *Jew.* xli; he shews how Alphonsus V. esteemed books, 2 *Bec.* 5 n.; a story about his reservation of the host, 2 *Jew.* 556 n
Pantaleo (Heinr.): Chronographia Christianæ Eccl., *Jew.* xli; cited, 4 *Jew.* 740, 1051
Panter, or Pantner: keeper of the pantry, 1 *Tyn.* 466
Pantheon: *v.* Rome.
Pantin (T. P.): *Calf.* 306 n
Paolo (Fra): *v.* Paul.
Papa: *v.* Pope.
Papalins: supporters of the pope, *Lit. Eliz.* x.
Papebrochius (Dan.), rejects the fictitious Sinuessan council, 2 *Ful.* 364 n.; records the testimony of cardinal Bona relative to the font of Constantine, *ib.* 360 n.; states his opinion as to the date of the death of St Ambrose, *ib.* 81 n.; speaks of pope Silverius as son of a Roman bishop, *ib.* 99 n
Paper: made by Froschover, 3 *Zur.* 222

Paphnutius: though an unmarried man he vindicated the marriage of priests in the council of Nice, and prevailed over the whole synod, 1 *Bul.* 401, 2 *Cran.* 169, 1 *Ful.* 480, 2 *Ful.* 153, 240, 1 *Hoop.* 376, 1 *Jew.* 227, 425, 3 *Jew.* 405, 4 *Jew.* 1053, 1 *Lat.* 288, *Pil.* 532, 576, *Rog.* 207, 3 *Tyn.* 157 n., 165; the statement denied or doubted by some Romanists, 1 *Hoop.* 376 n.; he allowed it to be an old tradition of the church, that such as came to the order of priesthood single, should not marry, 3 *Jew.* 386; led Maximus, bishop of Jerusalem, out of the heretical council of Palestine, 4 *Jew.* 951

Papias: said to have greatly regarded traditions, 4 *Bul.* 537; styled the father of tradition, *Whita.* 664; his statement concerning Judas, *ib.* 664; asserted to have been the first who taught that Peter was at Rome, *ib.*; his belief respecting the millennium, 4 *Bul.* 537, *Rog.* 154, 2 *Whitg.* 434

Papists: v. Church (especially the church of Rome), Clergy, Mass-mongers, Pope, Popery, Priests, Recusants, and numerous other heads.

Papist is a foul name of heresy, according to Calfhill, but a sublime title of glory, in the opinion of Baronius, *Calf.* 290 n.; references to many books on this point, *ib.*; description of Papists, 2 *Bec.* 315; their false doctrine, *ib.* 380, 3 *Bec.* 207, 234, 263; their intermixture of false doctrine with true, 3 *Bec.* 502; some articles of their belief, 2 *Lat.* 332; comparison between them and various ancient heretics, 2 *Ful.* 390, *Phil.* 417, &c.; in many things they are like the Manichees, 3 *Jew.* 157, &c.; they are Marcionists, 3 *Bec.* 273; follow Pelagius, 1 *Ful.* 377; differ but little from Jews, *Pil.* 630; their doctrine commonly stands on false reports, *Grin.* 40; they cannot agree in what they assert, 3 *Bec.* 263; their stubborn opposition to God's word, *ib.* 5, 6; they cannot abide it, or the preachers of it, 2 *Bec.* 617; they fear the gospel, *Pil.* 142; their manner of alleging the scripture, 3 *Bec.* 175; their juggling with words, 3 *Tyn.* 22; they untruly usurp the name of the church, *Phil.* 54, 55; advance and rejoice in the pope, 2 *Bec.* 447; make him their god, *Pil.* 420; their disregard of councils, 1 *Jew.* 69, 70; they are wresters and misreporters of the doctors, *Phil.* 115; have tampered with history, 1 *Tyn.* 337, 338, 3 *Tyn.* 48; they abuse the name of the Lord, 1 *Lat.* 288; make Christ half a Saviour, 2 *Lat.* 124, 125, 146, not a Redeemer, but a judge of men's merits, *ib.* 125, 146; in effect they deny him to be God, *Pil.* 142; they cannot brook the doctrine that he has offered a sufficient sacrifice, 2 *Bec.* 448; maintain that men must doubt of their salvation, 3 *Bec.* 174, &c.; are corrupters of Christ's testament, *ib.* 269, 270; abuse the sacraments, 1 *Bec.* 11, *Phil.* 116; their baptism not so evil as their mass, *Pil.* 171; they have not the sacrament of the Lord's body, *Phil.* 54; have corrupted God's word and brought in heresy about the sacrament, 3 *Bec.* 402, 405; what they do at mass, *ib.* 262, &c.; they offer a strange sacrifice, *ib.* 240; their juggling in the mass, *Rid.* 401; they do not tarry for the people, 3 *Bec.* 280; their doctrine concerning the presence of Christ in the sacrament is new, 3 *Bec.* 274; they ascribe all things to the virtue of the mass, *ib.* 242; are loath to forego the same, 2 *Bec.* 454; their wafer god, or idol of bread, 3 *Bec.* 240, 241, 261, 262; their worship, *Pil.* 129; their long prayers, 3 *Bec.* 534; they call not on God in the name of Christ, but by the mediation of saints, 2 *Bec.* 135, 4 *Bul.* 173; their erroneous doctrine as to the power of forgiving sins, 2 *Bec.* 556, 558; their objections in behalf of priestly absolution, answered, *ib.* 563, &c.; their cruelty against the dead, *Pil.* 217, 652; their tyranny in divorcing priests and their wives, 3 *Bec.* 235; in what their godliness consists, 2 *Bec.* 536; what they delight in, *ib.* 428; their vain inventions, 1 *Lat.* 292; their fondness in their fasting, 2 *Bec.* 536; their manner of drinking at night, *ib.* 534, 535; their manner of dining, *ib.* 534; they are enemies of the cross of Christ, 1 *Lat.* 520; schismatics, *Pil.* 541, 544; thieves and robbers, *Rid.* 401; comparison between and the border thieves in the North, *ib.* 398, 402, &c.; they are church robbers, *ib.* 402, &c.; bloody men, *Pil.* 420; compared to Edomites, *Pil.* 211, 238, 255, 256; more cruel than they, *ib.* 218, 253; they come of Hagar the bond-woman, *ib.* 335; their arrogant pretensions, *ib.* 208; their ambition and security, 3 *Bec.* 239; their cruelty in defending their kingdom, *ib.* 230, 511, 512, 527, 528; their obedience in wicked matters, *ib.* 243; they would have faith to be compelled, *Phil.* 104; are grievous enemies to Christians, 3 *Bec.* 401; Romish hypocrites are the pestilences of the Christian commonwealth, *ib.* 226; they are double-minded, *Sand.* 130; cannot abide reformation, 3 *Bec.* 516; are ashamed of repentance, 1 *Lat.* 314; hard to be converted, *Pil.* 448; they are to be avoided, *Whita.* 16; warned, 1 *Bec.* 127; warned that the gospel of Christ would rise again, 3 *Bec.* 216; none were suffered to preach but they, 3 *Bec.* 243; they subscribed and conformed in the days of Henry and Edward, *Pil.* 550; they should be disarmed, *Park.* 399; stanzas from Jo. Phillip's Friendly Larum... discovering the acts and malicious minds of those obstinate and rebellious Papists, &c., *Poet.* 525; their pestiferous humours to be purged out, 3 *Bec.* 290, &c.

Pappus (......): an opponent of Sturmius, 2 *Zur.* 314 n

Para: the earth of it said to cure all wounds, 2 *Hoop.* 164

Parables: what, 2 *Lat.* 188; they are feigned, but not lies, *Hutch.* 55; the Jews taught commonly by them, 2 *Lat.* 210; why Christ spoke to the people in parables, 4 *Bul.* 242, 2 *Jew.* 676; every one hath a certain scope, 2 *Lat.* 199; whether they are to be expounded word by word, 1 *Tyn.* 85; (see Samaritan, Sower, Talents, Vineyard, &c.)

Parable of the Wicked Mammon, *q. v.*

Paraclete: *v.* Holy Ghost.

Paradinus (Claud): Symbola heroica, *Calf.* 339 n

Paradise: the sweet rest of God for those who depart hence in faith, *Bale* 387; the souls of the righteous go there straightway, 2 *Lat.* 247; it was opened by Christ's death, *Whita.* 389; considered as identical with the "third heaven," 1 *Ful.* 285, *Whita.* 538

The Paradise of Dayntie Deuises: anonymous contribution thereto, *Poet.* xxvii, 310; "a foolish paradise," *Rid.* 160, 3 *Whitg.* 316

Parage: parentage, kindred, *Bale* 334

Paraleipomena: *v.* Leichtenaw (C. à).

Paralogism: in logic, 1 *Jew.* 31, 43

Paramo (Lud. à): shews that the highest degree of worship is rendered to the material cross, *Calf.* 381 n

Paramour (Tho.): bought the manor of Fordwich, 3 *Bec.* 487 n

Parascene: Good Friday, 1 *Jew.* 107

Paratoras: one of the magi, *Whita.* 560 n

Parayte (Bertrand): wrote on the Apocalypse, *Bale* 257

Parclose: closet, parlour, 1 *Bec.* 63

Pardie: *v.* Perde.

Pardon: *v.* Absolution, Sin.

Pardon bowls: *v.* Bowls.

Pardoners: *Bale* 28, *Rid.* 55, 67; one taken and deprived of his seal, 2 *Lat.* 400

Pardons, Indulgences: the Romish doctrine concerning them, *Rog.* 219—221, 4 *Jew.* 848, &c., 1 *Tyn.* 86, 122, 244; it is against the commandments of God, 2 *Hoop.* 121; references to many authorities respecting them, 1 *Brad.* 588; it is not known from whom pardons first began, 4 *Jew.* 851; they are not known by the authority of scripture, &c., *ib.*; the devising of them said to be a godly guile, &c., *ib.* 852; they are sold by the popes, *ib.* 848, &c., 1 *Tyn.* 74; on the alleged power of the pope to sell indulgences, 1 *Tyn.* 74 n.; the sale of pardons has turned godliness into gain, 4 *Jew.* 852; their price, &c., *Rog.* 219; pardons or indulgences reprehended, 1 *Brad.* 49, 3 *Brad.* 93, 1 *Tyn.* 48; they are the cause of much sin, 2 *Lat.* 306; they are filthy and detestable, 3 *Bul.* 95; the pope's pardons help not, 2 *Tyn.* 84; some popish writers are ashamed of them, 2 *Jew.* 920, 4 *Jew.* 851, 852; More acknowledges that the purchaser cannot be sure that they will profit him, 3 *Tyn.* 28 n.; Latimer preached against them, 2 *Bec.* 425; the Romish Indulgentiary, 2 *Bul.* 153; examples of indulgences, 2 *Bec.* 72, 1 *Tyn.* 122 n., *Rog.* 220, 221; pardons or indulgences were buried with the dead, *Grin.* 29, 2 *Hoop.* 147

Parents: *v.* Children, Commandments, Duty, Obedience, Prayers.

Whom the name includes, 1 *Bul.* 268; the fifth commandment extends to all superiors, *Cran.* 104, *Nov.* (16), 130, 2 *Tyn.* 325; meaning of the word "parentes" among civilians, 3 *Jew.* 392; parents are in God's stead, 1 *Tyn.* 168; on being born of holy ones, 2 *Bul.* 389; good and evil children born of the same father, *Pil.* 219; the duty of parents, 1 *Bec.* 287, 2 *Bec.* 346, &c., 1 *Bul.* 291, 1 *Hoop.* 360, *Pra. Eliz.* 236; their duty to their children, with probations of scripture, 2 *Bec.* 519; they should be present at their baptism, *ib.* 347; must take care that no harm chance to them, *ib.* 348; ought not to be too careful of them, nor too careless, 2 *Lat.* 157, 158; how they must teach them to speak, 2 *Bec.* 348; they are commanded to bring their children up virtuously, *ib.* 8, 481; they must train them in the knowledge of God's word, *ib.* 348, 349, and in the fear of God, *Sand.* 263, 264, 270; must give earnest diligence that they reverence God's name, 1 *Bec.* 388; their general corrupt and negligent education of their children lamented, *Wool.* 103; they must devise convenient pastimes for them, 2 *Bec.* 349; must take heed with whom they keep company, *ib.*; must teach their children good manners, *ib.*; must send them to school to a good school-master, *ib.* 350, &c.; must train them in good letters and knowledge of God's will, 1 *Bec.* 396, 397; must prepare them godly books, 2 *Bec.* 351; must let them read the Bible at dinner and supper, *ib.* 351; should correct them if they do amiss, *ib.* 353, 354; must put them into some honest godly way of life, *ib.* 355; must provide proper marriages for them, *ib.* 355, 356; must give them a portion in marriage, *ib.* 356; some abuse their authority in marrying their children for gain, *ib.* 372; it is their duty to lay up for their children, *ib.* 164; prodigal parents are thieves, *ib.* 108; they must set their children a good example, *ib.* 356, 357; must commend them in prayer to God, *ib.* 357; examples of their godly bringing children up, *ib.* 352, 353; those who neglect the godly bringing up of their children are wicked, *ib.* 4; the love of parents to their children, *Pil.* 456; their affection for their children less than God's for us, 1 *Lat.* 535, &c.; some love the bodies of their children better than their souls, *Sand.* 339; parents are sometimes unnatural, 1 *Lat.* 536; Jairus an example to them, *ib.* 537; the duty of children to their parents, 1 *Bec.* 287, 1 *Bul.* 297, 2 *Bul.* 225; their duty, with probations of scripture, 2 *Bec.* 519; parents are to be honoured, 2 *Bec.* 357, &c., 1 *Brad.* 161, *Now.* (16), 130, 1 *Tyn.* 168; commands in scripture to honour them, 2 *Bec.* 86; what it is to honour them, *ib.* 85, 357, 358; the honour due to them, 1 *Bul.* 271; the honouring of parents among the Gentiles, *ib.* 202; promise to them that honour, and threatenings to them that despise them, *ib.* 286; examples of obedience to them, 2 *Bec.* 86; how far they are to be obeyed, *ib.* 87, 2 *Lat.* 158, 164, 203; not to be followed further than they follow the scriptures, *Phil.* 129; children who are disobedient to their parents ought to be punished, 2 *Bec.* 88

Fathers: their duty, 1 *Bec.* 287; their power and authority, 2 *Bul.* 226; the office of a father, and how he should rule, 1 *Tyn.* 199; the sick man's exhortation to his children, 3 *Bec.* 131—134

Mothers should nurse their own children, 2 *Bec.* 347; their turmoils, 1 *Bul.* 274

Parfew (Rob.), alias Warton, *q. v.*

Paris: the synod, A.D. 825, *Calf.* 42 n. (as to others, see Councils); persecution there, five doctors taken, 1 *Tyn.* lix; the reformed worship prohibited, 1 *Zur.* 250 n.; the massacre of St Bartholomew, *Lit. Eliz.* 462, 569 n., *Park.* 399, 401, *Rog.* 7, 8, 1 *Zur.* 276 n., 291, 2 *Zur.* 210 n.; the constable of France burned the pulpits of the Huguenots, 4 *Jew.* 988; blockaded by king Henry IV., *Lit. Eliz.* 471

University, &c.: the university erected by Charlemagne, 2 *Jew.* 981; its appeal from pope Leo X., 4 *Jew.* 916, 923; Ridley went there, *Rid.* iii; it strenuously maintained (in Whitaker's time) the immaculate conception of Mary, *Whita.* 505; the doctors of the Sorbonne reproved John XXII., 1 *Jew.* 400; they censure Luther, *ib.* 66; their declaration on Christ's body in the sacrament, *Rid.* 509; on oaths of allegiance, *Rog.* 360; on councils, 4 *Jew.* 1037; a dispute respecting the Hebrew language and professorship, 3 *Zur.* 416; clamours there, *Rid.* 303

Montmartre (Mons Martyrum), 1 *Hoop.* 314 n.; St Lewis's mantle in the Grey Friars, *Bale* 518; the Holy Chapel; part of the cross there, *Calf.* 326

Paris (Matth.): *v.* Matthew.

Paris (Rob. de): 1 *Brad.* 31

Paris (W.): speaks of the sacrament of archbishopdom, *Rog.* 259

Paris Garden: *v.* Southwark.

Parish-priests: 4 *Bul.* 9, 116

Parishens: parishioners, 1 *Tyn.* 257

Parishes: *v.* Rogation week.

What, 4 *Bul.* 9; on the meaning of the word παροικία, 1 *Jew.* 159, 160; the word used by Tyndale for "God's heritage" (1 Pet. v. 3), 1 *Tyn.* 235; elsewhere he says "parishens," *ib.* 257, 1 *Whitg.* 534; παροικία formerly meant a diocese, 1 *Jew.* 161; Alexandria and Egypt called parishes by Eusebius, 2 *Whitg.* 205; parishes said to have been divided by pope Dionysius, 1 *Whitg.* 534, 535; Sandys enjoins that no parishes receive strangers to the communion, *Sand.* xx; the perambulation of parishes, 1 *Zur.* 259 n. (see Gang days).

Parishioners: their duty, 2 *Bec.* 114; their duty to ministers, with probations of scripture, *ib.* 517, 518; they owe their pastors honour and reverence, *ib.* 330, 331, and all things necessary for their living, *ib.* 331, 332, and obedience, *ib.* 332; they must dissemble their pastors' faults, *ib.* 333; those who withhold their lawful payments from ministers are thieves, *ib.* 108; parishioners

PARISHIONERS — PARKER

to be exhorted to contribute to the relief of the poor, *Grin.* 128, and to obedience towards their prince, and all in authority, and to charity and mutual love among themselves, *ib.* 130; their custom of swearing censured, 1 *Bec.* 362; petition for them, 3 *Bec.* 37

Parisiensis: *v.* Peter.

Parisiensis (Jo.), or Angelus, *q. v.*

Parisiis (Jo. de): *v.* John.

Park (Will.): registrar of the Court of Faculties, *Grin.* 446

Parke (Rob.): translates from the Spanish a history of China, *Poet.* xxvii.

Parker family: the archbishop's parents, *Park.* vi, 481; his descendants, *ib.* x, xi, 484

PARKER (Matt.), abp of Canterbury: his autobiographical memoranda in English, *Park.* vi; the original Latin, *ib.* 481; notice of him, *Poet.* xiii; his birth, education, and ordination, *Park.* vi, vii, 481; he is summoned to court by queen Anne Boleyn, *ib.* vii, 1, 2, 482; being recommended by the king, he is elected master of Corpus Christi college, Cambridge, *ib.* viii, 16, 17, 482; chosen vice-chancellor, *ib.* viii, 17, 482; dean of Stoke-by-Clare, *ib.* vii, 4, 482; often appointed to preach at Paul's cross, 2 *Cran.* 418, *Park.* 5, 39, 45, *Rid.* 335; chaplain to Henry VIII., *Park.* vii, ix, 6, 482; article against him sent to lord chancellor Audley, *ib.* 7; his preferments, *ib.* vii, viii, 482; his letter to the council of queen Catharine Parr against the dissolution of Stoke college, *ib.* 31; minute of an interview with Henry VIII., *ib.* 34; his marriage, *ib.* x, 46 n., 484; again chosen vice-chancellor, *ib.* viii, 37, 38, 482; appointed to preach before king Edward, 2 *Cran.* 425, 429, *Park.* ix, x, 40, 41, 43, 483; he preaches at Bucer's funeral, 3 *Zur.* 492 n.; extract from his sermon on that occasion, 2 *Brad.* xxiv; he was one of Bucer's executors, *Park.* 46, 3 *Zur.* 361; made dean of Lincoln, *Park.* viii, 482; with the duke of Northumberland at Cambridge, *Sand.* ii; deprived of his deanery, 2 *Cran.* 318 n., *Park.* viii, 482; his retired life in queen Mary's time, *Park.* viii, 199, 483; his version of the Psalter, *ib.* ix, 483, *Poet.* xiii, xiv; Psalms xcii. and cx. versified by him, with arguments and collects, *Poet.* 2, 4; summoned to London on the accession of Elizabeth, on the queen's service, *Park.* 53; he preaches before the queen, *ib.* ix, x, 2 *Zur.* 16 n.; a commissioner for the revision of the Prayer Book, *Grin.* v; unwilling to accept the archbishoprick, *Park.* 57, &c.; resolution that he should be archbishop, *ib.* 68, 1 *Zur.* 23; he is summoned to court, *Park.* 68, 69; he writes to the queen begging to be discharged from the office, *ib.* 69; but refers himself to the queen's pleasure, *ib.* 71; a second resolution that he should be archbishop, *ib.*; the queen assents to his election, *ib.* 76; his consecration, 2 *Cov.* xv, *Park.* x, 484, 1 *Zur.* 63; Tonstal committed to his custody, *Park.* 77, 78; consecrates Sandys, *Sand.* xvii; an exchange effected between the queen and the archbishop, *Park.* 102 n.; he takes part in a disputation concerning images, 1 *Zur.* 67 (see *Park.* 79, &c.); in a commission for reformation, *Grin.* vii; he and others write to the university of Cambridge for the restoration of Bucer and Fagius deceased, 2 *Zur.* 51 n.; he is displeased with Sandys, *Sand.* xviii; he and other bishops advise Elizabeth to marry, *Grin.* 19 n., *Park.* 129; he is nominated a commissioner for the revision of the Calendar, 1561, *Lit. Eliz.* xxxiii; refuses a dispensation to allow a child to hold a benefice, *Park.* 136; gives directions to search out those who do not comply with the true religion, 1 *Zur.* 122; the queen thought him too easy, his brethren thought him too sharp, *Park.* 173; the queen grants him permission to retain forty persons with his livery badge, *ib.* 175; he appoints days for prayer on account of war, pestilence, and famine, *Lit. Eliz.* 458, &c., *Park.* 182; assists at the funeral solemnity of the emperor Ferdinand, at St Paul's, *Grin.* 32; his armoury, *Park.* 216; he publishes Jewel's Apology, translated by lady Bacon, *Jew.* xviii; his dedicatory letter to lady Bacon, with her translation, 3 *Jew.* 51, *Park.* 219; he was a principal contriver of uniformity in religion, *Rog.* 6; perplexed through want of support in his endeavours to enforce it, *Park.* 262; his measures for that purpose, *ib.* 270, 272—274, 278; he (it is supposed) published a book on the lawfulness of vestments, 2 *Zur.* 120; he desires the suppression of the Court of Faculties, 1 *Zur.* 180 n.; intercedes on behalf of Sampson, 2 *Zur.* 118 n.; sets forth the Saxon Paschal homily, together with parts of the two epistles of Ælfric, 2 *Ful.* 7, 20, 247; his two editions of the Flores Historiarum of Matth. of Westminster, *ib.* 119 n.; his part in the Bishops' Bible, *Park.* 335 n., 336 n.; he refuses a dispensation to make a child a prebendary, *ib.* 362; his lances at York, *ib.* 388; he sanctions the publication of the Reformatio Legum Ecclesiasticarum, *Hutch.* 6 n.; letters forged in his name, *Park.* 418; he sends the Antiquitates Britannicæ Ecclesiæ to lord Burghley, *ib.* 425; meaning and object of that book, *ib*; he intends to keep it private during his life, *ib.* 426; suspects a remarkable interpolation in Bede's Ecclesiastical History, *Calf.* 306 n.; Acad. Hist. Cant., ed. Drake, 2 *Lat.* 378 n.; he has various artists and workmen in his house, *Park.* 426; selects Whitgift to answer the Admonition, 3 *Whitg.* x; his seal, *Park.* 452 n.; statement of his yearly expenses, *ib.* 455; his son's statement of his revenue and expenditure, *ib.* xii; his illness, *ib.* 464, 477; he publishes Asser's Ælpedi Res Gestæ, *ib.* 468; disliked by the precisians, *ib.* 472; he spends his time in copying books, devising ordinances for scholars, in genealogies, &c., *ib.* 474; receives the queen at Folkestone and Canterbury, *ib.* 475; visits in the diocese of Winchester, *ib.* 478, 1 *Zur.* 323 n.; cared neither for cap, tippet, surplice, nor wafer bread, but for the laws established, *Park.* 478; how addressed by Sanders, 2 *Ful.* 215, 216; advised by him to revolt to the popish church, *ib.* 247; references to him, 1 *Zur.* 61, 2 *Zur.* 20, 282, &c.; his death and burial, *Grin.* 356 n., *Park.* xi, *Sand.* xxi, 1 *Zur.* 317; his character, 1 *Zur.* 317 n.; dates of sermons preached by him on remarkable occasions, *Park.* vii, ix, 481, 483; his CORRESPONDENCE, edited by Jo. Bruce, esq., and the Rev. Tho. Thomason Perowne, A.M., *Park.*; letters by him (and in the Correspondence), 2 *Zur.* 77, 3 *Zur.* 361; letters to him, 1 *Bec.* xiii, 2 *Cov.* 529, 2 *Cran.* 418, 425, 429, *Grin.* 252, 267, 290, 294, 299, 326, 347, 353, 4 *Jew.* 1262, 1265, 1273, 1274, *Park.* v. n., 1, & passim, *Pil.* vii, 3 *Whitg.* 600, 3 *Zur.* 364; dedications to him, *Now.* i*, 107

— Margaret, his wife, daughter of Rob. Harleston, *Park.* 46 n., 483, 484; Mere's legacy to her, *ib.* 19; her death and burial, *ib.* 369 n., 484; the archbishop's children and descendants, *ib.* 484

Parker (Hen.), lord Morley: a fugitive beyond sea, 1 *Zur.* 309 n

Parker (Sir Jo.), son of the abp: his birth, *Park.* x, 484; More's legacy to him, *ib.* 19 n.; his statement of his father's revenue and expenditure, *ib.* xii; a note by him, *ib.* 115 n.; he marries Joanna, daughter of bp Cox, *ib.* x, xi, 484; his children, *ib.* xi, 484

Parker (Sir Jo.), the abp's grandson: a note by him, *Park.* 103 n

Parker (......): one of the disputants at Cambridge, 1549, *Grin.* 194, *Rid.* 169

Parker (......): decoys Story into a ship, and brings him to England, 1 *Zur.* 253 n

Parker (Mr), dean of Tamnworth: brother to the abbot of Gloucester, 2 *Cran.* 380

Parker (Greg.), martyr at Canterbury: called by Bryce, Greg. Paynter, *Poet.* 165

Parker (Jos.), 4th son of the abp: died an infant, *Park.* 484

Parker (Matt.), 2nd son of the abp: died an infant, *Park.* 484

Parker (Matt.), 3rd son of the abp: his birth, *Park.* 484; Frances (Barlow), his wife, afterwards married to abp Matthew, 3 *Bec.* 501 n., *Park.* 484, 2 *Zur.* 263 n

Parker (Tho.), chancellor of Worcester: summons Tyndale, 1 *Tyn.* xvii; reviles and threatens him, *ib.* 395; burns Tracy's dead body, *ib.* xviii, 3 *Tyn.* 270, 271, 282; is heavily fined for it, 3 *Tyn.* 270

Parker (Tho.), mayor of Norwich, the archbishop's brother: *Park.* 19 n

Parker (Will.): he and Alice his wife were the archbishop's parents, *Park.* vi, 481

Parkhurst (Ant.): *Jew.* vii.

Parkhurst (Jo.), bp of Norwich: was Jewel's tutor at Oxford, *Jew.* vi; a document signed by him, 2 *Brad.* 397 n.; his escape from England, *Jew.* xi. n., in exile, 1 *Brad.* 374 n., 1 *Cran.* (9); a friend of P. Martyr, 3 *Zur.* 518; at Zurich, *Jew.* xi. n., xiii, 1 *Zur.* 11 n.; at Baden, with his wife, 4 *Jew.* 1196; he returns from exile, 2 *Zur.* 12, 55; references to him about this period, 1 *Zur.* 9, 2 *Zur.* 7, 10, 12, 37; he becomes rector of Cleve, 1 *Zur.* 48, 51 n., 61, 69; refuses a bishoprick, *ib.* 61; is made bishop of Norwich, *ib.* 61 n., 76, 79; preaches at the funeral of the duchess of Norfolk at Norwich cathedral, *ib.* 137; behaves with moderation towards the Puritans, 2 *Zur.* 141, 144; said by Cecil to wink at schismatics and anabaptists, *Park.* 149; to be pressed to execute the laws, *ib.* 234; his share in the Bishops' Bible, *ib.* 248, 335 n.; he interposes in the dissensions in the Dutch church at Norwich, 1 *Zur.* 256 n.; is embarrassed by the misconduct of his agent, *ib.* 265; patronizes R. Gualter, 2 *Zur.* 218, 222; his death, *Park.* 446 n., 1 *Zur.* 317; his character, 3 *Bec.* 294, 2 *Zur.* 7, 10; note respecting his Ludicra, sive Epigrammata Juvenilia, 1573, *Pra. Eliz.* 238 n., and see 1 *Zur.* 49; Latin poems by him, viz. decem plagæ Ægypti, *Pra. Eliz.* 415; decem precepta, decem versibus comprehensa, *ib.* 404; ad Deum Opt. Max.

precatio, *ib.* 238; ad Jesum Christum precatio, *ib.*; cursus vitæ D. N. Jesu Christi, *ib.* 413; distichs,—iræ Dei adversus pios brevis, *ib.* 238; ad Christianum, *ib.* 239; de morte, *ib.* 418; verses prefixed to Cranmer's Answer to Gardiner, 1 *Cran.* 8; verses addressed to Becon, 1 *Bec.* 33; his commendation of queen Elizabeth, *Rog.* 5, 6; his letters, *Park.* 247, 1 *Zur.* 29, 31, 49, 61, 90, 94, 97, 98, 107, 109, 110, 121, 128, 131, 136, 143, 165, 194, 205, 232, 255, 266, 277, 300, 302, 303, 304, 2 *Zur.* 117, 127, 177, 199; letters to him, 4 *Jew.* 1190, 1191, 1193, 1195, *Park.* 389, 401, 403, 415, 416, 417, 457, 459, 2 *Zur.* 140; letter to him, Grindal, and Sandys, from Bullinger and Gualter, 2 *Zur.* 166

Parks: *v.* Commons.

Parliament: *v.* Statutes.

On parliament, 4 *Jew.* 902, &c.; the term explained to a foreigner, 2 *Zur.* 181; the parliament represents the nation, 1 *Whitg.* 372; its use, *Sand.* 34; its authority, *Grin.* 339; it has been variable in its decisions, *Rid.* 130; may err, 1 *Lat.* 148, 182; how managed by the private councils of kings, 3 *Tyn.* 159; on liberty of speech in parliament, 1 *Lat.* 183, *Phil.* 33, 51; the consent of the bishops not needful to make a law, *Pil.* 627; convocation no part of the parliament, *Phil.* 52; plain parliament, pleno parliamento, 2 *Tyn.* 256; parliament religion, 4 *Jew.* 903, 904; the parliament at St Edmund's Bury, temp. Edw. I., *ib.* 904; from a parliament held in this reign the clergy were excluded, *ib.*; one at Cambridge, 12 Ric. II., *Park.* 300 n.; one at Leicester, 2 Hen. V., *Bale* 4, 49; its proceedings, *ib.* 50; meetings of parliament in king Edward's time, 3 *Zur.* 468 n., 508 n.; proceedings in the time of queen Mary, 4 *Jew.* 904; meetings and proceedings in the reign of queen Elizabeth, 1 *Zur.* 185 n., 2 *Zur.* 13, 17, 114, 132 n.; a sermon before the parliament, 1563, *Now.* 223; a sermon before a parliament at Westminster, *Sand.* 34; abp Parker and lord Cobham ordered by the council to confer with the sheriff and principal persons in boroughs that fit persons might be chosen, *Park.* 380; the judgment compared to a parliament, 2 *Lat.* 55

Parma (Dukes, &c. of): *v.* Alexander, Mary, Peter Aloisius.

Parmenian: opposed by Augustine, 4 *Bul.* 60; he made the bishop a mediator between God and the people, 3 *Jew.* 575, 576

Parmenides: believed in one God, *Hutch.* 176

Parnell (Tho.): Barnes at his house in London, 3 *Zur.* 617

Parochia: *v.* Parish.

Parr (Catherine), queen: *v.* Catherine.

Parr (Will.), earl of Essex, afterwards marq. of Northampton: brother to queen Catherine, 3 *Zur.* 93 n.; he questions Anne Askewe, *Bale* 201; a privy councillor (sometimes he signed "W. North,"), 2 *Cran.* 496, 523, 524, *Park.* 73, 75, 76, 106, 122, 155, 328 n., 330, 357, 381, *Rid.* 508, 1 *Zur.* 5 n.; ambassador to France, 3 *Zur.* 497 n.; lord chamberlain, *ib.* 93; active in the cause of Christ, *ib.* 88; his death, 1 *Zur.* 257; a book dedicated to him, as it appears, but not published till after his decease, *Poet.* xxviii.

— Elizabeth (Brooke), his 2nd wife, 1 *Bec.* 264 n.; Helen (Suavemberg), his 3rd wife, 1 *Zur.* 257

Parr (Will.), lord Parr of Horton (?): questions Anne Askewe, *Bale* 201

Parr (......): "young Mr Parre," 2 *Cran.* 367

Parr (......): an exile, 3 *Zur.* 144

Parret (Tho.): died in the King's Bench, *Poet.* 168

Parry (Sir Tho.): a privy councillor, *Park.* 74, 75, 76, 77, 103, 106, 117, 122, 1 *Zur.* 5 n.; letter from him and Cecil to Parker, *Park.* 104

Parry (Hen.): in exile at Frankfort, 3 *Zur.* 763; a commissioner for visitation, 4 *Jew.* xv, 1 *Zur.* 39 n

Parry (Will.): tried and convicted for attempting to murder Hugh Hare, but pardoned, *Lit. Eliz.* 583; engages to shoot the queen, *ib.* 465, 466, 658; thanksgiving on the discovery of his plot, with an extract from his confession, *ib.* 583; his execution, *ib.* 465, 466

Parrys (Thos.): imprisoned, 2 *Zur.* 160 n

Parse: to pierce, *Pil.* 273

Parsonages: *v.* Benefices.

No taverns, alehouses, or the like, to be kept in them, *Grin.* 130, 166; to be kept in good repair, *ib.* 131

Parson (St): S. Parson's breech, *Calf.* 287

Parsone (Anth.): *v.* Person.

Parsons: *v.* Clergy, Curates.

Rectors so called in distinction from vicars, 2 *Tyn.* 37 n., 260; persons, *Bale* 321; the practice of little master parson, 2 *Tyn.* 293

Parsons (Rob.), or Persons, alias Cowbuck: notice of him, *Lit. Eliz.* 658 n.; sometime provincial of the Jesuits in England, *Rog.* 10; his Warn-word, *Calf.* 5 n.; his Three

Conversions of England, *Calf.* 53 n.; *Phil.* iii; A brief Disc. containing certain Reasons, &c., publ. under the name of Jo. Howlet, *Rog.* 239; Fulke answers this, 1 *Ful.* x, 96 n., and see *ib.* 113, 189, 190; A Treatise tending to Mitigation, &c., by P. R., *Jew.* xli, 4 *Jew.* 1309; his account of Jo. Philpot, *Phil.* ii; he says all or most part of the ministers of England are merely laymen, *Rog.* 239

Parthians: Augustine supposed that John wrote his first epistle to them, *Whita.* 218; origin of the mistake, *ib.* n

Partiality: *v.* Judges, Persons.

Participation: 2 *Hoop.* 11

Partlet: *v.* Pertelet.

Partridge (Sir Miles): hanged, 2 *Brad.* xxvii, 3 *Zur.* 579 n

Partridge (Nich.), of Lenham, Kent: at Zurich, 4 *Bul.* xii; Gualter came to England with him, 2 *Zur.* 7 n., 3 *Zur.* 124, 608 n.; about to return to Switzerland, 3 *Zur.* 617; afterwards in the service of Barlow, bp of St David's, *ib.* 608 n., 626, and in that of a mayor of Dover, *ib.* 608 n.; his death, *ib.* 608 n., 637; three letters from him to Bullinger, *ib.* 608, 610, 614

Parvis: *v.* Oxford.

Paschal I., pope: his history, 2 *Tyn.* 266

Paschal II., pope: stirred up rebellion, *Grin.* 21 n., 3 *Whitg.* 592; constrained the emperor Henry V. to surrender his authority to him, 2 *Hoop.* 238; condemned the marriage of priests, *Rog.* 181; his letter to Anselm on the promotion of priests' children to holy offices, *Pil.* 572; his (?) decree for the authority of the see of Rome, 3 *Bec.* 526 n.; he places the pope's authority above all councils, 1 *Jew.* 93 n., 442, 4 *Jew.* 919, 1115

Paschal lamb: *v.* Passover.

Paschal taper: *v.* Candles.

Paschal time: *v.* Easter.

Paschasinus: 4 *Jew.* 1021

Paschasius Radbertus: Opera, *Jew.* xli; he says we believe the church as the mother of regeneration, not *in* the church as the author of salvation, 1 *Bul.* 159, 160, 3 *Jew.* 256; declares that baptism and the body and blood of the Lord are the sacraments in the catholic church, 3 *Jew.* 459; says, Christ is mystically offered for us daily, 2 *Bec.* 250, 3 *Bec.* 458; was one of the authors of the doctrine of transubstantiation, 1 *Hoop.* 118; tells of a priest who beheld the real presence, *ib.* 291 n.; considers that Christ's words "Drink ye all of this," apply as well to the rest of the faithful as to ministers, 3 *Jew.* 479, 480, 4 *Jew.* 766; affirms that Christ did not give his body to be reserved, 2 *Bec.* 252, 3 *Bec.* 456; Bertram and Jo. Scotus wrote against him, 1 *Hoop.* 118 n., 524 n

Pasetes, the juggler: his banquet, 3 *Jew.* 474

Pashur, the false prophet: advanced by the people, 2 *Hoop.* 269

Pasquils: whence the term is taken, 2 *Bul.* 117; pasquyls, 1 *Lat.* 110; pasquil poets, *Rog.* 180

Pass: to care, 1 *Brad.* 402, *Calf.* 248, *Phil.* 8, *Rid.* 367; past upon; cared for, 2 *Brad.* 42

Passalorynchitæ: a sect of heretics described by Augustine, *Phil.* 421 n

Passau: the pacification of Passau, 2 *Cran.* 437, 3 *Zur.* 456 n

Passe-lamb: paschal lamb, 3 *Tyn.* 245

Passion: suffering, 2 *Tyn.* 110; passio, passus, *Now.* (102)

Passion Sunday, otherwise Dominica Judica: the Sunday before Palm Sunday, 1 *Jew.* 107

Passions: The Passions of the Spirit (a poem); notice thereof, *Poet.* xxxv; stanzas therefrom, *ib.* 381

Passover: what it was, 2 *Bul.* 164, 178, &c.; meaning of the name, 1 *Tyn.* 353 n.; the author and beginning of the ordinance, 2 *Bul.* 179; its institution, 1 *Tyn.* 353; the time of it the same as that of Christ's death, 2 *Bul.* 180, *Now.* (41), 158; the place for eating it, 2 *Bul.* 181, 186; it was celebrated only at Jerusalem, 4 *Bul.* 431, 1 *Hoop.* 172; the guests at it, 2 *Bul.* 181; none were admitted to eat it who could not demand what it meant, 1 *Jew.* 230; the manner of eating it, 2 *Bul.* 181; why the Jews stood at the eating of it, 3 *Bec.* 260; the end whereto it tended, 2 *Bul.* 182; it was eaten in memory of the great benefit of God, when he destroyed the Egyptians, *Grin.* 42; it kept the Lord's benefit in memory, 2 *Bul.* 182; was a testimony of God's good-will to his people, *ib.*; a badge and confession of faith, *ib.* 185; it warned the communicants of their duty, *ib.* 186; its signification and fulfilment in the death of Christ, 1 *Tyn.* 353—356; the lamb was called the passover, yet it was only a remembrance of the passover, 4 *Bul.* 280, 441, *Grin.* 41; it was a type of Christ, 2 *Bul.* 183, 1 *Cov.* 39, 211; a token and figure of the shedding of Christ's blood then to come, 1 *Cran.* 135, 136; the passover compared with our eucharistic sacrament, 4 *Bul.* 246, 402, 427,

PASSOVER — PAUL

Coop. 112, 1 *Hoop.* 125, 190, *Hutch.* 217, 3 *Tyn.* 242, 246, 247, 250; the Christian passover, i. e. Easter, 2 *Bul.* 265

Pastance : pastime, or feasting, the state of one bene pastus, 2 *Bec.* 427

Pastimes: *v.* Sports.

Pastor Nuntius, i. e. Hermes, *q. v.*

Pastors: *v.* Ministers.

Pasture: used for the word of God, 2 *Hoop.* 198

Patch: an appellation commonly bestowed on fools, 4 *Jew.* 860 n

Pate (Rich.), or Pates, bp of Worcester: notice of him, *Phil.* xxvii; made bishop, 4 *Jew.* 905 n., *Phil.* ix; mentioned as such, 2 *Brad.* 83, *Rid.* 359, 1 *Zur.* 10 n.; at the council of Trent (twice), 4 *Jew.* 905, 1056, *Phil.* xxvii, 1 *Zur.* 79 n.; sent to the Tower (twice), 4 *Jew.* 1233, *Park.* 122, 1 *Zur.* 79 ; " patesing," a supposed allusion to his name, *Park.* 124

Pater-noster: *v.* Prayer (The Lord's).

Pater-nosters numbered up on beads, 4 *Bul.* 205; a still pater-noster as good as a loud, 2 *Cov.* 399; the devil's pater-noster, 1 *Lat.* 350, 377

Pathway: A PATHWAY INTO THE HOLY SCRIPTURE, by W. Tyndale, 1 *Tyn.* 1—28; THE PATHWAY UNTO PRAYER, by T. Becon, 1 *Bec.* 123—187; reference to it, 2 *Bec.* 492

Patience: *v.* Affliction, Cross, Prayers.

What it is, 3 *Bec.* 621; there are two kinds, *Hutch.* 299, 320; the image of it, 2 *Bul.* 86; the need of it, 4 *Bul.* 553; it is necessary for all, *Hutch.* 295; Christians must have patience, and be long sufferers, 3 *Tyn.* 36; its original, 2 *Cov.* 96; its fruit, *ib.*; its force and effects, 2 *Bul.* 87 ; its commodity, 2 *Cov.* 125; exhortations to it, 1 *Brad.* 375, 2 *Cov.* 94, 227, &c., 1 *Hoop.* 578; one in verse, by H. C., *Poet.* 479; ensamples of it, 2 *Cov.* 123; the patience of the godly, *Pil.* 248; patience in adversity, 1 *Cov.* 169; patience under scoffing, *Pil.* 402; patience under the cross, the will of God, 2 *Bec.* 156, 157; examples of it, *ib.* 157; our best service is sometimes to bear the cross patiently, 2 *Lat.* 185; "the word of thy patience," what, *Phil.* 253; impatience of the mind many ways known, 2 *Hoop.* 249

Patmore (Tho.): in prison for the truth, 2 *Lat.* 321

Patraca (Steph. abp of): *v.* Stephen.

Patriarchs : *v.* Fathers before Christ.

Patriarchs (in the church): their dignity, 4 *Bul.* 117, *Rog.* 329; Gratian says they and primates are the same in office, though not in name, 3 *Jew.* 313; their origin, 2 *Tyn.* 257; Cyprian said to refer to them, *Phil.* 74; what the council of Nice decreed respecting them, 1 *Jew.* 69, 386, 3 *Jew.* 304, &c., *Phil.* 43, 2 *Whitg.* 142, 148, 220, 380; the word does not occur till above a century afterwards, 2 *Zur.* 228 n.; in the time of Augustine there were four,—Alexandria, Constantinople, Antioch, and Rome, *Rid.* 263; these were stairs to the popedom, 2 *Whitg.* 379, 1 *Tyn.* 257; the council of Chalcedon (451) mentions the patriarchs of every diocese, 2 *Zur.* 228 n.; examples of the title universal patriarch, 1 *Jew.* 427; four titular ones still appointed by the pope, Alexandria, Constantinople, Antioch, Jerusalem, 4 *Jew.* 842; other mock patriarchs in the church of Rome, *ib.* 1056

Patrick (St): his fast, 2 *Tyn.* 98; his purgatory, 2 *Bec.* 600, 1 *Hoop.* 290, *Rog.* 215 n., 1 *Tyn.* 290; a modern Romish prayer through "his merits and intercession," 3 *Tyn.* 117

Patrick (Jo.): Devotions of the Romish Ch., *Calf.* 287 n

Patripassians : the name, 2 *Ful.* 375; their heresy, *Rog.* 45, 57, 3 *Bul.* 156, *Hutch.* 121, 128, 207; Cyril called men back from their council, 4 *Jew.* 951, and appealed therefrom, *ib.* 1101

Patritius (Lud.): *v.* Ludovicus.

Patronage, Patrons: *v.* Benefices.

How patronage came to bishops, abbots, &c., 2 *Zur.* 230; how controlled in Zurich, *ib.* 230, 231; the duty of patrons, 1 *Lat.* 290, 2 *Lat.* 28, *Pil.* 36; their sin in presenting unfit persons, 2 *Bec.* 423; their corrupt practices, 1 *Bul.* 7, 2 *Jew.* 999, 1000, 1011; they sell or shamefully abuse their benefices, 1 *Lat.* 290; story of one, *ib.* 186; many of them believe not in hell or heaven, *ib.* 187; covetous ones a plague, 3 *Whitg.* 456; Christ an example to patrons, 1 *Lat.* 292

Patrons (Heavenly): *v.* Angels, Saints.

Pattalornichites: *v.* Passalorynchitæ.

Pattenham (Patr.): *v.* Packingham.

Patteson (Tho.): fool to Sir T. More, 4 *Jew.* 860

Paul: *v.* Paulus.

Paul (St): *v.* James, Justification, Peter.

He was brought up at Gamaliel's feet, 4 *Bul.* 482; his conversion ascribed to the prayer of Stephen, 1 *Lat.* 338; thrown down a persecutor, raised up a preacher, 2 *Jew.* 1134; joined to the twelve apostles, 1 *Bul.* 53; his vision of Christ, *Rid.* 219; he went to Jerusalem, to see Peter, 1 *Jew.*

375; not merely to confer with Peter, *Whita.* 432; he was nothing inferior to the chief apostles, 1 *Jew.* 384; called head, prince of the apostles, &c., *ib.* 438, 3 *Jew.* 270, 288, 4 *Jew.* 824; not inferior to Peter, 4 *Bul.* 123; in labours his superior, 1 *Tyn.* 210, 217; the whole world said to be committed to him (see p. 190, col. 2, of this Index); he was the apostle of the Gentiles, 3 *Jew.* 327, &c.; struck Elymas blind, 1 *Bul.* 359, 363, 377; withstood Peter to the face, 1 *Jew.* 384, 4 *Jew.* 834; his preaching at Philippi by the water-side, *Pil.* 263 (*v.* Lydia); his imprisonment there, *ib.* 145; handkerchiefs brought from him to the sick, who were healed thereby, *Calf.* 337, 1 *Tyn.* 226; he restores Eutychus to life, More says by his merits, 3 *Tyn.* 145; his vow in the Temple, 3 *Whitg.* 550; he availed himself of the protection of the magistrate, 1 *Bul.* 377, 4 *Bul.* 35, 3 *Zur.* 747; delivered from the Jews, *Pil.* 423; his preaching and doctrine, 3 *Bul.* 39, 1 *Tyn.* 96, 210, 211, 219, 288, 292, 312, 2 *Tyn.* 148, 170; his preaching misreported, 2 *Lat.* 326, 327; he might have borne a fagot at Paul's cross, *ib.* 326; his doctrine commended to the churches, 2 *Bul.* 274; he cites profane authors, 2 *Jew.* 680, 3 *Jew.* 132, 4 *Jew.* 737, *Whita.* 70, 2 *Whitg.* 36; his life and conversation an example, 1 *Bec.* 14; his zeal, *Pil.* 24, 343; his weeping, 1 *Lat.* 518; his prayers, 4 *Bul.* 226; his example in afflictions, 2 *Bul.* 104; how he was delivered out of tribulations, *ib.* 96; his holiness or prayers are not to be our confidence, 1 *Tyn.* 288; how he used means, *Pil.* 328; he exercised discipline, *Pil.* 7; his doctrine of the sacrament of the Lord's Supper, 4 *Bul.* 60, 3 *Tyn.* 251, 255, &c.; he rebuked not them that sung in churches, 4 *Bul.* 192; received wages, *ib.* 493; used the benefit of judgment, appealing unto Cæsar, 1 *Bul.* 351; early writers say he was married, 1 *Ful.* 117, 2 *Jew.* 727; whether he preached in Britain, 1 *Jew.* 280, 305, 3 *Jew.* 164, *Poet.* 289; his martyrdom, 1 *Bul.* 315, 2 *Bul.* 105, 4 *Bul.* 32, 2 *Cov.* 132, *Rid.* 76; his tomb, *Calf.* 130; his sword and handkerchief worshipped, *Rog.* 225

His epistles: some things in them are hard to be understood, 1 *Ful.* 558, *Whita.* 369; Ebion rejected them, 1 *Ful.* 7, *Whita.* 35; most of them were disallowed by Marcion, *Rog.* 84; as to spurious writings in his name, *v.* Apocrypha, ii.

— Romans: its excellency, *Phil.* 362, 1 *Tyn.* 484, 507; it is an epitome of the gospel, *ib.* 508; the manner of his teaching in it, *ib.* 495; its alleged obscurity, *Whita.* 373; Tyndale's prologue to it (taken in a great measure from Luther's), 1 *Tyn.* 483 —510; argument of this epistle, and contents of each chapter, 3 *Bec.* 580, 581; St Paul's conflict (Rom. vii), 1 *Tyn.* 503, 2 *Tyn.* 159; on his expression "I am carnal, sold under sin," *Whita.* 455; how he wished himself "accursed from Christ," *Pil.* 424

— 1 Corinthians: Tyndale's prologue, 1 *Tyn.* 511; argument of the epistle, and contents of each chapter, 3 *Bec.* 581; Paul's doctrine of the Lord's supper, 4 *Bul.* 60, 3 *Tyn.* 251, 255, &c.

— 2 Corinthians: Tyndale's prologue, 1 *Tyn.* 512; argument of the epistle, and contents of each chapter, 3 *Bec.* 582; Paul's farewell to the Corinthians, *Sand.* 418

— Galatians: Tyndale's prologue, 1 *Tyn.* 513; argument of the epistle, and contents of each chapter, 3 *Bec.* 583, 584

— Ephesians: Tyndale's prologue, 1 *Tyn.* 514; argument, and contents of each chapter, 3 *Bec.* 584, 585; this is the epistle which Marcion called the epistle to the Laodiceans, *Whita.* 303 n., and which Tertullian supposed to be "the epistle from Laodicea," *ib.* 304

— Philippians: Tyndale's prologue, 1 *Tyn.* 514; argument, and contents of each chapter, 3 *Bec.* 585

— Colossians: Tyndale's prologue, 1 *Tyn.* 515; argument, and contents of each chapter, 3 *Bec.* 586

— 1 Thessalonians: on the date of this epistle, *Whita.* 552; Tyndale's prologue to it, 1 *Tyn.* 516; argument, and contents of each chapter, 3 *Bec.* 586; Jewel's EXPOSITION UPON THE TWO EPISTLES TO THE THESSALONIANS, 2 *Jew.* 813, &c.

— 2 Thessalonians: on the date of this epistle, *Whita.* 552; Tyndale's prologue to it, 1 *Tyn.* 517; argument, and contents of each chapter, 3 *Bec.* 587; what Paul taught in this epistle, *Phil.* 363; Jewel's exposition of it, 2 *Jew.* 887—946

— 1 Timothy: Tyndale's prologue, 1 *Tyn.* 517; argument, and contents of each chapter, 3 *Bec.* 587; this epistle is supposed by Theophylact to be "the epistle from Laodicea," *Whita.* 304; rejected by the Marcionites, *ib.* 35

— 2 Timothy: Tyndale's prologue, 1 *Tyn.* 519; argument, and contents of each chapter, 3 *Bec.* 588; this epistle was rejected

PAUL —PAULET

by the Marcionites, *Whita.* 35; on the subscription to it, 2 *Whitg.* 294
— Titus : Tyndale's prologue, 1 *Tyn.* 519; argument, and contents of each chapter, 3 *Bec.* 589; this epistle was rejected by the Marcionites, *Whita.* 35
— Philemon : Tyndale's prologue, 1 *Tyn.* 520; argument, and sum of the epistle, 3 *Bec.* 589; it has been rejected by some, *Whita.* 35; vindicated by Chrysostom, *ib.* 35, 36
— Hebrews: whether written by Paul, 1 *Ful.* 8, 1 *Tyn.* 521, *Whita.* 106, 107; various opinions as to its authorship, 1 *Ful.* 28–30, 3 *Jew.* 186; some affirm it to have been written in Hebrew, *Whita.* 125; it is thought to have been written or translated by Clement, 2 *Whitg.* 120; Tyndale's prologue to it, 1 *Tyn.* 521; argument of the epistle, and contents of each chapter, 3 *Bec.* 589, 590; it was once disallowed, or at least doubted of, by the church of Rome or some therein, 1 *Ful.* 30, *Whita.* 505; it was rejected by Marcion and the Arians, 1 *Ful.* 8, *Whita.* 35, 323; and by Cajetan, *Whita.* 105; its canonicity and authority defended, 1 *Ful.* 29 n., 30, 1 *Tyn.* 522, &c.

Paul I., pope: 2 *Ful.* 360 n
Paul II., pope: reduced the interval between the jubilees, 2 *Bul.* 268, 1 *Lat.* 49 n.; his arrogance, *Pil.* 99, 602 n.; his incontinency, *Rog.* 304
Paul III., pope: *v.* Clement VII.
He accursed king Henry VIII., 4 *Jew.* 1131; his message to that king, 2 *Cran.* 126; he consulted with Reg. Pole about a general council, *ib.* 331; appointed some cardinals (including Pole) to consider of the state of the church, 1 *Jew.* 469, 2 *Jew.* 728, 807, 1019, 4 *Jew.* 800, 1107; set forth a new portus, *Pil.* 535; his epistle to Charles V., *Jew.* xli; in it he asserts exclusive authority over wicked priests, 4 *Jew.* 959, 1030; the council of Trent held under him, *ib.* 1051; in his bull for the summoning of it he left out the name of Christ, *ib.* 1052; decrees of his confirmed by the council, 4 *Bul.* 29, 529; he would not punish the wickedness of his son Peter Aloisius, 4 *Jew.* 658; derived a revenue from prostitutes, *Rog.* 181; his death, 3 *Zur.* 344 n
Paul IV., pope [Giampietro Caraffa, nuncio in England for three years]: he would not admit the validity of the renunciation of the emperor Charles, nor the election of his brother, *Grin.* 20 n.; cast Moronus into prison, 4 *Jew.* 1146; imprisoned certain Augustine friars, &c., for religion's sake, *ib.* 661; maintained stews at Rome, 3 *Jew.* 337; reproached king Sigismund Augustus of Poland, 3 *Zur.* 599 n.; his bull "Rescissio alienationum," *ib.* 149 n.; his Index Romanus, *Calf.* 95 n., 126 n

Paul, bp of Apamea: 4 *Jew.* 974
Paul of Burgos: his comments are with Lyra's, *Jew.* xxxiv; referred to, *Whita.* 148; what he says of light, 2 *Jew.* 581, 582; he wrote on the Apocalypse, *Bale* 256
Paul, bp of Constantinople : 2 *Ful.* 112
Paul the Deacon: De Gestis Longobard., *Jew.* xli; he says the bishop of Ravenna prepared the way to Antichrist, 2 *Hoop.* 235; tells how Phocas gave the supremacy to Rome, *ib.*, 1 *Jew.* 361; relates how when an Arian bishop would have baptized a man, after his blasphemous sort, the water dried up, 2 *Jew.* 761; tells of princes who banished idols, 2 *Bec.* 71 n.; his additions to Eutropius, *Calf.* 71 n
Paul the Deacon, monk of Cassina: said to have chosen lessons, 4 *Bul.* 201
Paul the Hermit : 4 *Bul.* 514, *Calf.* 252, 3 *Jew.* 435
Paul of Samosata : *v.* Samosatensians.
His heresy, 1 *Bec.* 278, 3 *Bec.* 401, 3 *Bul.* 267, 1 *Cran.* 278, 1 *Hoop.* 83, 2 *Hoop.* 74, *Whita.* 27; he denied the Holy Trinity, *Hutch.* 132; impugned the deity of the Holy Ghost, *Rog.* 70; his train of attendants, 2 *Whitg.* 384; he was condemned in the council of Nice, 1 *Hoop.* 64; the pope likened to him, *Phil.* 423
Paul (Father): his history of the council of Trent cited, 2 *Tyn.* 272 n.; adduced to shew that Romanists depressed the power of bishops, 2 *Bec.* 319 n
Paul (......): saluted, 1 *Zur.* 75; and Paullus (probably the same), 4 *Jew.* 1235, 1 *Zur.* 80
Paul (Sir Geo.), or Paule : 3 *Whitg.* v, xi.
Paula (St): her daughters instructed by Jerome, 3 *Zur.* 5; her abode in Bethlehem, 1 *Jew.* 540, 543; her visit to the stable, 2 *Jew.* 740; her conduct alleged for the use and worship of the cross, *Calf.* 252, 253, 255, 256, 2 *Ful.* 174: a fool for Christ's sake, 3 *Jew.* 251; Psalms sung in various languages at her funeral, 2 *Ful.* 224, 1 *Jew.* 268, 2 *Jew.* 692, *Pil.* 321, *Whita.* 222
Paulet (Will.), lord St John of Basing, then earl of Wiltshire, and at length marq. of Winchester: in an embassy to France (master Paulet), 2 *Cran.* 246, 505, 511, 523, 524, 530; privy councillor, *Park.* 46, 155,

Rid. 508, 1 *Zur.* 5 n.; lord treasurer, *Grin.* 32, 1 *Zur.* 5 n., 7; chief mourner at the funeral of the emperor Ferdinand, *Grin.* 32; letter from him to Parker, *Park.* 119; his religious character, 3 *Zur.* 341

Paulet (Jo.), 2nd marq. of Winchester: while lord St John he was one of the examiners of Philpot, *Phil.* 50; present as lord St John at the duke of Norfolk's trial, 1 *Zur.* 267 n

Paulet (Sir Amias): ambassador to France, 2 *Zur.* 277, 281 n., 282, 283, 285

Paulet (Sir Hugh): being governor of Calais he had the Common Prayer translated into French, 2 *Cran.* 439

Paulet (Mr): see the 1st marquis, above.

Paulians, or Samosatenes: disciples of Paul of Samosata, 2 *Hoop.* 74; the former name used, *Hutch.* 134, 161; they thought that Christ was not the Son of God before his incarnation, *Rog.* 48; declared the Holy Ghost to be nothing but the motion of God in his creatures, *ib.* 72

Paulianus: Jerome's brother, 1 *Ful.* 263

Paulicians: held that the wicked are not to be excommunicated, *Rog.* 309; corruptly called publicans, *Bale* 322

Paulinus, bp of Antioch: *Grin.* 53 n

Paulinus (St), bp of Nola: was rich for the poor, 1 *Hoop.* 397; by his voluntary captivity he obtained liberty for his flock, *Calf.* 117—119, *Pil.* 441; he brought images into the church, *Calf.* 26, 29; praised painted images, 2 *Jew.* 654; set up the cross in certain churches, 2 *Ful.* 158; speaks of a church, &c., saved from fire by a piece of the cross, *Calf.* 329; writes to Alypius, 1 *Jew.* 365; Jerome writes to him, 4 *Bul.* 540; he sent loaves to Augustine, 1 *Jew.* 145, 2 *Jew.* 588; the year of his death, *Calf.* 188; Opera, *Jew.* xli; his life of St Ambrose, 1 *Jew.* 242; remarks of Erasmus thereon, *ib.* 243; his language on the water of baptism, *ib.* 537, 2 *Jew.* 576, 763; he refers to the union of Christians through the eucharist, 1 *Jew.* 140; speaks of the Trinity as contained in bread, 2 *Jew.* 604; says we are incorporate in Christ by faith, 1 *Jew.* 140; shews how Paul was present by his letters, 2 *Jew.* 604; speaks of the force of evil habit, *Wool.* 106; questions Augustine concerning burial, 3 *Tyn.* 272 n.; held some erroneous opinions, *Calf.* 189

Paulinus, bp of Trier: refused to attend the council of Milan, 4 *Jew.* 951

Paulinus (St), abp of York: baptized in the rivers Gweni and Swale, *Pil.* 518

Paullus: *v.* Paul......

Paul's cross: *v.* London.

Paulsen (H. C.), and J. L. Mosheim: Hist. Tartar. Eccl., 2 *Ful.* 225 n

Paulus: *v.* Paul.

Paulus Æmylius, *q. v.*

Paulus Æmilius, the Roman: 2 *Cov.* 124

Paulus Burgensis; *v.* Paul of Burgos.

Paulus Jovius, *q. v.*

Paulus the Jurist: *v.* Law (Civil).

Paulus de Palatio: *Rog.* 99

Paulus Sergius: 1 *Bul.* 363

Paulus Thebius: 4 *Bul.* 514

Paulus (Andr.): 2 *Zur.* 293

Paulus (Marcus), Venetus: says the body of St Thomas is preserved in India, 4 *Jew.* 950

Paulus (Sim.): on Antinomians, *Rog.* 92, 152; on an error of Valla, *ib.* 104

Pauperes à Lugduno: *v.* Lyons.

Pausanias: 4 *Jew.* 865

Pavia: the battle there, and Wolsey's treacherous dealing respecting it, 2 *Tyn.* 317, 318; the university erected by Charlemagne, 2 *Jew.* 981

Pawlesgrave (Jo.): *v.* Pallgrave.

Pawns: pledges, *Sand.* 94; the Mosaic law respecting them, 2 *Bul.* 36, 228

Pax: what the pax or osculatorium was, *Grin.* 135 n., 1 *Jew.* 265, *Pil.* 495 n., 3 *Tyn.* 126; the primitive custom, which it superseded, 1 *Jew.* 265; its introduction, 2 *Brad.* 311, *Pil.* 503; the kissing of it, *Bale* 320, 2 *Brad.* 311, 1 *Tyn.* 279, 2 *Tyn.* 194, 3 *Tyn.* 71, 126; [its use enjoined, 1548, Burnet. Ref. rec. I. xxi.]; its meaning, 3 *Zur.* 624; paxes to be destroyed, *Grin.* 135, 159; oscularies, 1 *Lat.* 50

Payne (Hugh), curate of Hadleigh: his popish preaching, and excommunication by Cranmer, 2 *Cran.* 333; he is presented to Sutton Magna, and dies, *ib.* 362

Payne (Jo.), or Pain: a rebel, 2 *Cran.* 187 n

Paynil ('Tho.): sent to the German princes, 2 *Cran.* 377 n

Paynter (Greg.), or Parker, *q. v.*

Payva (Jac.), Andradius: Orthod. Explic. libri x., *Jew.* xli, *Rog.* 223 n.; answered, *Whita.* passim; on the authority of scripture and of the church in relation to it, *ib.* 278; he admits scripture to be a rule, *ib.* 662; speaks of its difficulty, *ib.* 360; admits that the chief heads of faith are plain, *ib.* 400; calls the Holy Spirit the sole and faithful interpreter of scripture, *ib.* 466; on the purity of the Hebrew text, *ib.* 162; on the authority of the Vulgate, *ib.* 111; on the priesthood of Melchizedek, *ib.* 168; on Augustine's citation from the book of

Wisdom, *ib.* 89; he condemns a passage in Gratian, *ib.* 109; maintains the merit of good works, *Rog.* 122, 127 ; says that the heathen philosophers had the righteousness of faith and everlasting life, 3 *Jew.* 584; declares that the cross of Christ is to be worshipped with latria, 2 *Jew.* 667, 3 *Jew.* 121, 4 *Jew.* 950

Peace : *v.* Mind, Unity, War.
It is double, outward and inward, *Sand.* 86; our God is the God of peace, 2 *Jew.* 884; peace was promised in Christ, *Pil.* 157; it comes by Christ, *Sand.* 282; it is found in Christ, *ib.* 340; his diligence in preaching it, *ib.* 287; he died and rose again to procure it, *ib.* 288; we are made partakers of it by faith, *ib.* 290; it is the fruit of forgiveness, 1 *Tyn.* 294; man's conscience cannot be at peace until settled in a full persuasion of the remission of sins, *Sand.* 287; peace with God is an incomparable blessing, *Phil.* 256; peace is the badge of God's people, *Sand.* 286; it is the fruit of the gospel, *ib.* 60, 61; how we should behave to enjoy it, 1 *Bec.* 260 ; what it is to live peaceably, *Sand.* 86; an exhortation to peace and unity, *ib.* 428 ; worldly peace is grievous to the church, *Pil.* 158; Christ's peace cannot be kept with the world's peace, 1 *Brad.* 389; the cry "Peace, peace," a token of danger, *Sand.* 211

Peace with France, 2 *Tyn.* 318, 1 *Zur.* 24, 75 n., 133, 139, 273, 3 *Zur.* 480, 559 ; the peace of Câteau Cambresis, 2 *Zur.* 19

Peaced: appeased, 2 *Tyn.* 110
Peace-makers: their blessedness, 1 *Lat.* 485, 2 *Tyn.* 26
Peacock (Reynold), bp: *v.* Pecocke.
Peacock (......), president of Queens' college, Cambridge: resigns, *Park.* 67
Pead (Eleanor): extract from the oath taken by her before being licensed as a midwife, *Grin.* 174 n
Peak: *v.* Derbyshire.
Peakishness : *Pil.* 436
Pearl: A SPIRITUAL AND MOST PRECIOUS PEARL, translated from O. Wermuller, by bp Coverdale, 1 *Cov.* 84, &c.
Pears (Steuart A.): commenced the editing of Bullinger's decades, 1 *Bul.* viii; his report to the Parker Society respecting the archives of Zurich, &c., 2 *Zur.* v.
Pearson (Jo.), bp of Chester: On the Creed, 2 *Bec.* 49 n., 1 *Bul.* 137 n., 1 *Cov.* 21, 50 nn., 2 *Cov.* 150, 160, Vindiciæ Ignat., *Calf.* 211, 1 *Cov.* 21 n., Opera Posth., *Calf.* 251 n.; when he believed that Hegesippus flourished, 2 *Ful.* 338 n.; his opinion as to the author of the Pontifical, *ib.* 98 n
Pearson (Geo.): editor of the Writings and Translations of bp Coverdale, and of his Remains, 1 & 2 *Cov.*
Peasants: *v.* Ploughmen.
Pease: to appease, 1 *Bec.* 49
Peason: peas, 4 *Jew.* 944
Peccator, peccatum originis : *Now.* (102)
Peckes (Will.): martyred at Bramford, *Poet.* 173
Peckham (Jo.), abp of Canterbury : *Jew.* xli ; he requires every priest to consecrate at least once a week, 1 *Jew.* 199; enjoins priests to change the bread in the pix every seventh day, 2 *Jew.* 561
Peckham (Sir Edm.): one of queen Mary's privy council, 1 *Zur.* 5 n
Peckham (Sir Rob.): one of queen Mary's privy council, 1 *Zur.* 5 n
Pecocke (Reg.), bp of Chichester: persecuted, *Bale* 351, 394, *Pil.* 591
Peculiar People, *q. v.*
Peculiars : certain churches so called, 2 *Cran.* 490, 2 *Lat.* 323; a return of them required, *Park.* 181
Pedaries : consecrated sandals, 1 *Lat.* 50
Pedder (Jo.), dean of Worcester : once in exile, 1 *Cran.* (9)
Pedlers : not to sell their wares in the churchyard, nor anywhere during divine service, *Grin.* 138
Peerson (And.): *v.* Pierson.
Pegge (Sam.): Life of Grosseteste, 1 *Lat.* 56, 122, 203, 2 *Lat.* 408 nn
Pegnafort (R. de): *v.* Raymond.
Pegson (Tho.): mention of him and his wife, *Park.* 303
Peiresius (Mart.) : *v.* Peresius.
Peise: to poise or weigh, *Sand.* 306 (*v.*Pese).
Pekah, king of Israel : 2 *Bul.* 12
Pekahiah, king of Israel : 2 *Bul.* 12
Pekins (Jo.): in exile, 1 *Cran.* (9)
Pelagians: their error on grace and free-will, 1 *Hoop.* 263, 3 *Jew.* 580, &c., *Rog.* 105, 3 *Whitg.* 613; their equivocal confession of the grace of God, 2 *Jew.* 593; they declared the doctrine of election to be dangerous, *Rog.* 155; held that the number of the predestinate may increase or be diminished, *ib.* 147 ; greatly erred respecting original sin, 2 *Bul.* 386, 4 *Bul.* 376, 2 *Cran.* 108, 1 *Hoop.* 263, *Lit. Edw.* 527, (573), *Rog.* 94, 99, 277 ; hence they, or some of them, denied the baptism of infants, 4 *Bul.* 376, *Rog.* 280; some allowed infant baptism, but denied it to be for the remission of sins, 2 *Bec.* 210 n., see *Rog.* 277;

their opinion about infants dying unbaptized, 3 *Jew.* 564; they said that being once baptized we can no more be tempted, *Rog.* 277; affirmed the righteous to have no sin in this life, 2 *Cov.* 387, *Rog.* 135, 257; deemed concupiscence no sin, *Rog.* 102; considered all sins to be equal, *ib.* 137; erred with regard to justification, 1 *Ful.* 403; maintained the possibility of fulfilling the law of God, 2 *Cov.* 388, 389, 3 *Jew.* 580, 581; taught that men might merit heaven, *Bale* 316; said heretics were not to be excommunicated for their private and singular opinions, *Rog.* 309; enjoined community of goods, *ib.* 353; falsely alleged Augustine, 1 *Jew.* 22; also Ambrose and Jerome, *ib.* 83; false translations by them, 1 *Ful.* 12; their doctrine condemned at Ephesus, 1 *Bul.* 14; how censured by Prosper, *Whita.* 443; followed by Papists, 1 *Ful.* 377, 2 *Ful.* 391, 2 *Tyn.* 122, 181; followers of their error in England, in queen Mary's time, 2 *Brad.* 171, 213, *Rid.* 367; the Pelagian worthily called the enemy of grace, 2 *Hoop.* 73

Pelagians (Semi-): maintain free-will, 3 *Whitg.* 613

Pelagius I., bp of Rome: *v.* Damasus, Higinus. The commemoration of the dead in the mass ascribed to him, 2 *Brad.* 311

Pelagius II., bp of Rome: censures the title of "universal patriarch," 2 *Hoop.* 234, 546, 1 *Jew.* 427, 3 *Jew.* 316, 2 *Whitg.* 172; says that councils ought not to be held without the sentence of the bishop of Rome, 2 *Tyn.* 272 n.; his decree concerning second marriage, *Calf.* 18; his additions to the mass, 2 *Brad.* 307

Pelagius, the heretic: 1 *Bec.* 278; his doctrine is darkness, 2 *Tyn.* 104; his errors on grace and free-will stated and refuted, 3 *Bul.* 11, *Phil.* 427, *Sand.* 24; he declared that men are born without virtue, and without vice, 2 *Bul.* 386; hence he denied the baptism of infants, 4 *Bul.* 376, *Phil.* 274; Augustine's controversy with him, 3 *Bul.* 11, 4 *Bul.* 201, *Coop.* 148, 2 *Cov.* 388; he was vanquished by a council, 4 *Jew.* 1095; writings ascribed to him, but found in Jerome's works, 1 *Brad.* 589, 2 *Ful.* 44 n., *Sand.* 138

Pelbart (......): his Sermons, 4 *Bul.* 557; his Golden Rosary, *Whita.* 465

Pelemke (Jo.): zum Rynberch, 3 *Zur.* 260

Peleus: 1 *Hoop.* 184

Pella: the Christians escape thither from Jerusalem, 1 *Brad.* 39 (Peltis), 1 *Whitg.* 380

Pellican (Conr.): on the tabernacle, 2 *Whitg.* 93; on the alleged omission of the feast of tabernacles, 1 *Whitg.* 30; on 2 Chr. xxix, xxx, *ib.* 35; on white garments (Eccles. ix), 2 *Whitg.* 26; on the office of Timothy, *ib.* 296; he calls Titus an archbishop, *ib.* 132; he revises and edits the Bible of Leo Judæ, 3 *Zur.* 235 n., 623 n.; translates the Talmud into Latin, *ib.* 432; references to him, 4 *Jew.* 1243, 2 *Lat.* 246; letters to him, 3 *Zur.* 451, 624; the same Pellican (?) saluted, 2 *Brad.* 406, 3 *Zur.* 38, 42, 44, 49, 621; his death, *Jew.* xiii, 3 *Zur.* 138 n., 509 n

Pellican (Sam.): son of Conrad, 3 *Zur.* 452; the same Pellican (?) saluted, 1 *Zur.* 30, 62, 110, 2 *Zur.* 90, 95

Pellicia (......): *Calf.* 181 n

Pelting: paltry, *Calf.* 10

Peltis, i. e. Pella, *q. v.*

Pembroke (Earls of): *v.* Herbert.

Penance: what commonly so called, 1 *Brad.* 45; the word is not a right translation of μετάνοια, 1 *Ful.* 257; but penance was called μετάνοια by metonymy, *ib.* 162, 258; the word was often used for repentance (*q. v.*), e. g., 1 *Bec.* 92, 2 *Cov.* 19, 29, 343 *Now.* (102); it is a deceitful term, 1 *Tyn.* 260, 3 *Tyn.* 172; translations concerning penance examined, 1 *Ful.* 428—449; false and true penance, 3 *Tyn.* 22, 23; without faith it is vain, 2 *Tyn.* 162; its right use is to tame the flesh, *ib.* 163; penance called a sacrament, 3 *Jew.* 456; it is not so properly, *Rog.* 255—257, 3 *Tyn.* 171; on the alleged sacrament, *Calf.* 241—244, 2 *Jew.* 1131; such as fall said to be relieved by it, 1 *Cran.* 360; Martiall (not Jerome) calls it the second table, i. e. plank, after shipwreck, *Calf.* 241, 2 *Ful.* 170; the fathers sometimes called baptism the sacrament of penance, *Calf.* 242; penance is said to be divided into contrition, confession, and satisfaction (see those words), 1 *Bec.* 97, 1 *Brad.* 46, 2 *Cran.* 116, *Rog.* 257, 1 *Tyn.* 261, 265, 267, 2 *Tyn.* 162, 3 *Tyn.* 171; so the council of Trent, 1 *Brad.* 46 n.; all these parts were in the repentance of Judas, *ib.* 51; a modern Romish definition, 1 *Tyn.* 342 n.; the Romish doctrine thereon is blasphemous, 1 *Ful.* 429; lord Cobham on penance, *Bale* 25; references to English divines thereon, 1 *Brad.* 46 n.; on the public use of penance, *Now.* (96), 219; it is a wholesome rite, 4 *Bul.* 249; its origin and abuse, 2 *Tyn.* 161; its use in the primitive church, *ib.* 219; the place for penitents in the ancient Latin church [comp. Art. xvi, Ch. of Eng., "penitentiæ locum,"], and the manner of their absolution, 1 *Ful.*

431 ; open penitential discipline should be restored, 3 *Zur.* 547; penance done at Paul's cross, 2 *Cran.* 289, 372, *Park.* 465 n.; faggot-bearing there, 2 *Lat.* 326 (and see Faggots); penance performed in the church or market-place, 1 *Brad.* 50; archbishop Grindal's direction for penance, *Grin.* 455; a form of public penance was drawn up by him, *ib.* xiv; penance to be done by the incontinent, *ib.* 143; penance for adultery, &c., 1 *Brad.* 50, 2 *Zur.* 360; Dr Turner, dean of Wells, enjoins an adulterer to do penance in a priest's square cap, *Park.* 241, 2 *Zur.* 125 n.; unmarried women not to be churched without penance, *Grin.* 127, 164; article of convocation against the commutation of penance, *ib.* 189

Pendleton (Hen.): notice of him, *Phil.* xxx; references to him, 1 *Brad.* 86, 487; his inconstancy, *ib.* 449; he confers with Bradford, *ib.* 541; one of the commissioners to examine Philpot, *Phil.* 31

Peneman (Rob.): executed at York, 1 *Zur.* 225 n

Penitence: *v.* Penance, Repentance.

Penitents: what things necessary in them, 3 *Bul.* 108; the fear of God is in them, *ib.* 59; faith is needful in them, *ib.* 62; their external signs, 1 *Hoop.* 542; true penitents are in a happy case, 3 *Bul.* 111; there is pardon for them, 1 *Hoop.* 486, 493; God always preserves them, 2 *Hoop.* 369; he will save them, 1 *Hoop.* 533; instances of penitents, 4 *Bul.* 554

Of old, penitents (pœnitentes, persons under penance) might not be present at the eucharist, 2 *Bec.* 256, 2 *Jew.* 705, *Rid.* 160, 163; there are now none to be sent away, *Rid.* 207

Penn (Tho.): his errors, 2 *Brad.* 397

Pennaforti (R. de): *v.* Raymond.

Penner: a pen-case, *Phil.* 87

Penny: no penny, no pater-noster, 2 *Brad.* 280, 2 *Cov.* 259

Penny (Dr): suffered to enjoy a prebend in St Paul's, though he had become a physician, *Grin.* 348, 2 *Zur.* 147 n., 203 n.; suspected of nonconformity, *Park.* 264

Penrice, co. Glamorgan: pilgrimage to an image there, 2 *Lat.* 395

Penruddock (Sir Geo.): *Grin.* 332

Penry (Jo.), a Puritan: *Rog.* 203, 231; cited, *ib.* 345

Pensioners (Gentlemen), or Spears: 2 *Cran.* 399 n

Pensiveness: *v.* Care.

Pentateuch: *v.* Bible.

Pentecost, Whitsuntide: the Jewish feast, 2 *Bul.* 164; the great day of Pentecost described, 1 *Cov.* 388, 389; Peter's discourse thereon, *ib.* 397, &c.; verses for Whitsuntide, by F. Kinwelmersh, *Poet.* 292; how the festival may be kept, 1 *Bul.* 260, 2 *Bul.* 265; of old it was a time for baptism, 4 *Bul.* 367

Pentecostal: what it was, 1 *Lat.* 135

People: *v.* Prayers.

They are for the most part prone to sedition, 1 *Whitg.* 467; tumultuous and variable, *ib.* 468; inconstant in all ages, 3 *Whitg.* 568—571; given to complaining, *Pil.* 455; their complaints are often groundless, *Sand.* 226; for the most part they are unapt to govern, 3 *Whitg.* 274; the duty of the common people, *Bale* 21; their duty towards God, towards the higher powers, and towards the commonwealth, *Sand.* 52; their duty under princes, *ib.* 85, 86 (*v.* Kings, Magistrates, Subjects); the increase of the commons, the honour of the king, and vice versâ, 2 *Bec.* 601; the people (or Laity, *q. v.*) should be constrained to hear the word, *Sand.* 46; the common people followed Christ, *ib.* 340

— People of God: who are such, 4 *Bul.* 382; they are called a peculiar people, 1 *Bec.* 49, 340; they are gathered together by baptism, 4 *Bul.* 399

Pepin, king of France: his usurpation, 2 *Tyn.* 260; his gift to the pope, 4 *Jew.* 680, 692, 2 *Tyn.* 261

Pepuzians: *v.* Montanists.

Perambulation: *v.* Rogation week.

Perbreak: to break forth, eject, vomit, 3 *Bec.* 384, 4 *Jew.* 945

Percase: perchance, *Phil.* 198

Perch: a chandelier, *Calf.* 300

Perchers: large wax candles, 1 *Bul.* 199, 238, *Calf.* 300

Percy (Tho.), 7th earl of Northumberland: one of the royal visitors for the North, 1 *Zur.* 73 n.; he heads the rebellion in the North, 2 *Jew.* 874, *Lit. Eliz.* 462, 538, 657, 1 *Zur.* 213, 217, 222, 227, 247; is supplied with money by the duke of Norfolk, 2 *Zur.* 198; his flight and confinement in Lochleven, 1 *Zur.* 214 n., 223; his execution, *ib.* 217 n.; his wife, 2 *Zur.* 198 n.; his daughter Joan, 1 *Bec.* 396 n

Percy (Hen.), 8th earl of Northumberland: he was (when Sir Hen. Percy) one of the royal visitors for the North, 1 *Zur.* 73 n.; extract from a letter to him, *ib.* 223 n

Percy (Hen.), 9th earl of Northumberland: Sion house granted to him, 3 *Zur.* 3 n

Perde, or Perdie: an oath, par Dieu, *Phil.*

352, 373; perdy, 1 *Jew.* 63; pardie, *Calf.* 192, *Coop.* 23

Perdue (......): martyred at Canterbury, *Poet.* 169

Peresius (Mart.): De Div. Apost. atque Eccles. Tradit., *Jew.* xli; he gives his opinion on the apostolic canons, *Whita.* 42; how he divides traditions, *ib.* 500; he says that many godly men would have the laws of single life abolished, 3 *Jew.* 428

Perfection, Perfect: the law requires absolute perfectness, 2 *Bul.* 237; perfection is not attainable in this life, 2 *Bul.* 237, 1 *Tyn.* 301, 2 *Tyn.* 150; what is meant by the charge to be perfect, 1 *Bec.* 209, 2 *Tyn.* 71; in what sense men are said to be so, 3 *Jew.* 581; Christian perfection explained, 1 *Cov.* 203, 205; there are various degrees, or rather kinds, of perfection, 1 *Bec.* 209, 210, 3 *Jew.* 580, &c.; perfection considered as of two kinds, divine and human, *Sand.* 421; there is perfection in God, *ib.* 421, in his word, *ib.*, in all his works, *ib.* 422; it is in us by imputation, *ib.*; we must aim at it, 1 *Bec.* 209; it must be sought for by industry, *Sand.* 423; inward perfection, *ib.*, &c.; we should seek perfection in knowledge, *ib.* 424, in faith, *ib.*, in godliness, *ib.* 425, in brotherly kindness and love, *ib.*, outward perfection in doing, *ib.*, in speaking, *ib.* 426, in suffering, *ib.* 427; an exhortation to perfection, *ib.* 420; τέλειος τελειόω, τελείωσις, used by the fathers to express the condition of the more advanced Christian, 1 *Cov.* 203 n.; τέλειον used with reference to the eucharist, *ib.*

Perfumes: *Bale* 528, *Lit. Eliz.* 503

Pergamos: the epistle to the church there, *Bale* 278

Pericles: an example of patience, 2 *Cov.* 123

Perin (W.): *v.* Peryn.

Perionius (Joach.): cites Chrysostom corruptly, *Calf.* 368

Peritsol (R. Abr.): 1 *Ful.* 315

Perjury: *v.* Oaths.

It is forbidden, *Now.* (13), 126; permitted by certain heretics in time of persecution, *Rog.* 119; it is a dreadful sin, 1 *Bec.* 368; it thirsteth for innocent blood, *ib.* 370; what incommodities rise out of it, *ib.* 375; its prevalence lamented, 1 *Lat.* 380; caused by Wolsey making men swear what they were worth, *ib.* 301; how punished in England, *Pil.* 550; that of priests in the time of Henry, Edward, and Mary, 1 *Lat.* 315; national perjury in queen Mary's time, *Rid.* 50

Perkins (Will.): an eminent divine, 1 *Brad.* 564; Præpar. ad Demonst. Problem., *Calf.* 211 n

Perlous: perilous, 1 *Cov.* 277

Perne (And.): some account of him, *Phil.* 169; one of the disputants at Cambridge, 1549, *Grin.* 194, *Rid.* 169; chaplain to king Edward, 2 *Brad.* 2 *Cran.* xi; master of Peter-house, and dean of Ely, *Park.* 261, 3 *Whitg.* vi, x, 599, 600, 2 *Zur.* 51 n.; as vice-chancellor of Cambridge he pronounced sentence against Bucer and Fagius, *Pil.* 657; Bradford exhorts him to repent, 1 *Brad.* 446; he is nominated to preach at Paul's cross, *Park.* 261; his share in the Bishops' Bible, *ib.* 335 n

Perne (And.), minister of Wilby, Northamptonshire, *Phil.* 169

Perne (And.), LL.D.: *Phil.* 169

Perne (Peter): 1 *Zur.* 41, 3 *Zur.* 182, 183

Pernel: the plant pimpernel, *Pil.* 56

Perowne (J. J. S.): editor of Rogers on the Articles, *Rog.*

Perowne (Tho. Thomason): one of the editors of the Correspondence of abp Parker, *Park.*

Perpin (Guido de): *v.* Guido.

Perpoynt (Geo.): *v.* Pierpoint.

Perrenot (Ant.), bp of Arras, and cardinal of Granvelle: minister of Charles V., 2 *Cran.* 231, &c., 235; his rule in Flanders, 4 *Jew.* 1147, 1 *Zur.* 139

Perrin (Jo.), bookseller: 1 *Hoop.* iii. (title).

Perry (Tho.): his suit with Jane Benbowe, 2 *Cran.* 249, 252, 253

Pers (Jo.): 2 *Cran.* 260

Perse (James): in exile, 1 *Cran.* (9)

Persecution: *v.* Affliction, Cross, Exhortation, Martyrs, Prayers, Prisoners, Thanksgivings.

It is not to be thought strange, 1 *Brad.* 416, &c., 2 *Cov.* 233, &c.; it was foretold by Christ, *Rid.* 420; he promised not promotion but persecution, 2 *Lat.* 302; the highest promotion in this life is to suffer for the truth, 1 *Lat.* 294; persecution always accompanies God's word, 1 *Tyn.* 131; it follows confession thereof, 1 *Bec.* 273; it is a sure mark of true preaching, 2 *Lat.* 303; true preaching stirs it up, 2 *Tyn.* 32; false doctrine was never persecuted, 3 *Tyn.* 129; persecution is ever the lot of the righteous, 1 *Brad.* 377, 2 *Brad.* 234, 359, 2 *Jew.* 890, *Nord.* 91, 117, *Pil.* 142, 204, *Rid.* 423, *Sand.* 361, 377; shews who are God's people, 2 *Brad.* 210; the children of light seldom lack it, 1 *Lat.* 42; the carnal ever persecute the spiritual, 3 *Tyn.*

107, 110; the persecution of the prophets, 2 *Bec.* 469, 470; that of Christ and his apostles, *Bale* 315, 2 *Bec.* 470, 471; that of martyrs and confessors in the early church, 2 *Bec.* 472, 473, 2 *Jew.* 976, 977; the ten persecutions, 2 *Bul.* 105; to persecute is a sign of Antichrist's church, 3 *Bec.* 202; papal persecutions, *Bale* 574, *Pil.* 142, 205; heathen rulers were more merciful than some Christian ones, 2 *Lat.* 65, 66; these pretend to persecute for love, 3 *Jew.* 183; opinions of the Papists for which they persecute, 2 *Cov.* 248; persecution in England for God's word;—under king Henry V., *Bale* 49, &c.; under king Henry VIII., *ib.* 138, &c., 394, 3 *Bec.* 11, 1 *Brad.* 283, 288, 2 *Cov.* 327, &c.; 2 *Cran.* 310 n., 1 *Tyn.* xxii, &c., 2 *Tyn.* 341; persecution looked for, 2 *Brad.* 35, &c.; that in queen Mary's time, 3 *Bec.* 203, 204, 2 *Brad.* 399, *Grin.* 227 n., *Poet.* 161, *Rog.* 5, 2 *Zur.* 160, 249 n., 3 *Zur.* 773; (see many letters of Bradford, Cranmer, Hooper, Latimer, Philpot, and Ridley); the prelates persecuted Christ in his members, 1 *Brad.* 436, 441, 449, 456, 2 *Brad.* 188, 190, 250; Ridley's counsel to the godly in time of persecution, *Rid.* 62, &c.; his letter to the brethren dispersed in sundry prisons, *ib.* 342; another to the brethren which constantly cleave unto Christ in suffering affliction with him, *ib.* 349; his farewell to the prisoners and exiles, *ib.* 419; Philpot's letter to certain godly women forsaking their own country in time of persecution, *Phil.* 236; A COMFORTABLE EPISTLE TO THE AFFLICTED PEOPLE OF GOD, by T. Becon, 3 *Bec.* 192; persecution in France, 2 *Bul.* 105, *Rog.* 6, & al.; in Germany, 2 *Cov.* 526, 3 *Zur.* 18, 32; in the Netherlands, see p. 553; in Russia, 3 *Zur.* 600; in Asia, 2 *Bul.* 105; that of Christians by the world, 3 *Bec.* 194, 195; the true church must suffer persecution, 1 *Brad.* 526, *Nord.* 89, (see p. 200, col. 1, of this Index); it follows the true church, *Bale* 67; it is a mark thereof, 1 *Brad.* 526, 2 *Lat.* 290, *Sand.* 361; the true church cannot be long without it, 2 *Cran.* 62; all Christians must bear it, 2 *Lat.* 429, &c.; persecution will befall the righteous, but they merit not heaven thereby, 2 *Tyn.* 28, 29; neither is it a satisfaction for their sins, *ib.* 29; different forms of persecution, *Hutch.* 301; sometimes it comes in the form of scoffing, *Pil.* 402; persecution shews who are faithful, 2 *Lat.* 82, 168, 213; it proves who have received God's word in truth, *ib.* 435; the devil tempts us to avoid it, *ib.* 439; hot gospellers cannot bear it, *ib.* 213; it diminishes the number of professors, 1 *Whitg.* 380; many of them in time of persecution fall away, *Sand.* 300; exhortations to constancy under persecution, 1 *Brad.* 385, 2 *Cov.* 227, &c., 1 *Tyn.* lviii; against the storms of persecution, with sentences and examples of scripture, 1 *Bec.* 459, &c.; encouragements under it, 2 *Lat.* 431, 433, 436, &c.; it cannot destroy God's people, *Pil.* 207; God alway provides a place for worship in it, *ib.* 263; Christ's cross must be embraced, 2 *Lat.* 434; we should rejoice in persecution, 1 *Bec.* 274, 275; the faithful exhorted so to do, 2 *Bec.* 468, &c.; it is a token of God's love, 1 *Bec.* 275; a happy state, 2 *Brad.* 245; the blessedness of those who suffer it, 1 *Lat.* 487, 2 *Tyn.* 27, 29; the happiness of suffering, not for evil, but for Christ's sake, 2 *Brad.* 75; Christians have peace in it, *Pil.* 158, 197; persecutors, when they imprison men's bodies, set their souls at liberty, *Phil.* 261; persecution is the highway to heaven, 1 *Brad.* 383; we may lawfully flee from persecutors, 2 *Cran.* 444, 445, *Rid.* 62, 65, 383, *Sand.* 335; flight counselled by Christ, *Rid.* 63; examples of flight,—Christ, Paul, Elijah, *ib.* 62;—Athanasius, *ib.* 63; carnal objections to flight answered, *ib.* 71, 72; examples of God's ready hold in extreme perils, *ib.* 73, &c.; against dissembling in time of persecution, *ib.* 66; how to answer magistrates, 2 *Brad.* 156; persecution makes God's word and the church to flourish, 1 *Bec.* 274; it spreads the gospel, *Pil.* 143, 264; persecutors;—Cain and his successors in all ages, *Pil.* 204; ancient ones, *Bale* 315; whose children persecutors are, 1 *Bec.* 29, 30; their threats brought to nought, *Pil.* 197, 254; they are recompensed for their tyranny, 2 *Bul.* 107; opposers of God's truth are always overthrown, *Pil.* 206; persecutors warned, *ib.* 197; dreadful deaths of several, *ib.* 655; remonstrance against persecution, *ib.* 212; false complaints of persecution, 3 *Whitg.* 320, 462

Perseverance: *v.* Prayers, Predestination.

Perseverance, or endurance to the end, is needful to salvation, 1 *Bec.* 121, 2 *Bec.* 461, 462, 571, 2 *Brad.* 176, *Sand.* 196; it distinguishes God's children from hypocrites, 2 *Brad.* 165; it is consequent upon election, 1 *Brad.* 315; on the perseverance of the elect, *Phil.* 307, 3 *Tyn.* 36—39; the doctrine strongly asserted by Tyndale,

1 *Tyn.* 78, 79; by Bradford, 1 *Brad.* 76, 298, 317, 379, 380, 2 *Brad.* 109, 113, 122, 123, 134, 139; by Foxe, 1 *Tyn.* 79 n.; also in the Lambeth articles, 3 *Whitg.* 613; Latimer seems to deny it, 1 *Lat.* 229, 2 *Lat.* 7, 8, 362; the elect though they fall, shall be restored, 1 *Brad.* 298, 2 *Cran.* 91, 92, 2 *Hoop.* 274, 3 *Tyn.* 36; they cannot perish, *Rog.* 146; the doctrine gives no place to carnal liberty, *Phil.* 307; though it be true, we must use the means appointed, 1 *Whitg.* 524; when Christians pray that God will give them again his Spirit, they pray according to their sense, 1 *Brad.* 298; to doubt of final perseverance is to dishonour God, *Pra. B.* 38; for perseverance is solely attributable to God's faithfulness, 2 *Brad.* 113, 2 *Jew.* 885; as Satan prevailed not against Christ, no more shall he against any of his members, 1 *Brad.* 317; an objection answered, *ib.* 251

Persia: origin of the Persian name, *Pil.* 428; the Persian monarchy, 1 *Lat.* 356, *Pil.* 186, 187; its destruction, *Pil.* 185; Persia had famous schools, 4 *Bul.* 480; the royal cities, &c., *Pil.* 281; institutions and customs, *ib.* 282, 283; the country was famous for its archers, *ib.* 428; Constantine wrote letters on behalf of Christians persecuted there, *Sand.* 109; contest of Persia with the Turks, 2 *Cran.* 440; the church not extinct there, 4 *Bul.* 20; the Persians called God Σύρη, 3 *Bul.* 131; allegation that they worship a dragon, *Rog.* 37, and trust in their soldan, *ib.* 38; the orismada, a holy fire, carried before the king, *ib.* 291

Persius (A. F.): cited, 1 *Bec.* 23, *Calf.* 4, 108, 341, *Pil.* 156

Person (Ant.), or Parsone, or Persons: burned, 3 *Bec.* 11, 3 *Zur.* 242 n

Person (......): 2 *Brad.* 161

Persons: *v.* God.

Persons: parsons, *Bale* 321; see 1 *Bec.* 9 n

Persons: not to be respected, *Sand.* 278, 440

Persons (Rob.): *v.* Parsons.

Persuasions: of two kinds, *Pil.* 349, 350; more effectual than threatenings, *ib.* 354

Pertelet, or Partlet: what, 1 *Tyn.* 226

Perusinus (Pet.), or of Perugia: *v.* Bizarro.

Perusio (Bald. de): *v.* Baldus.

Peryn (Will.): was master of the Blackfriars in Smithfield, 1 *Cran.* 68 n.; he maintains (in his Three godly and notable Sermons, 1546) that a beast may eat Christ's body, *Bale* 146, 154, 159, 1 *Cran.* 68, *Rid.* 309; these sermons referred to, *Bale* 181, 182; Bale's intention to write against him, *ib.* 171, 236

Pesah (פסח): the passover, 2 *Bul.* 178, 1 *Hoop.* 125, 172, 190, 1 *Tyn.* 353

Pese: weight, *Sand.* 287, (*v.* Peise).

Pesth, Hungary: besieged, 3 *Zur.* 634

Pestilence: *v.* Plague, Prayers.

Petalum (πέταλον): alleged to have been worn by St John, 2 *Brad.* 381, 2 *Ful.* 113, 3 *Jew.* 615, 2 *Whitg.* 16, 22, 23, 25, 27; also by St James, 1 *Zur.* 160 n., 350 n

Petavius (Dion.): referred to concerning the stations of the ancient church, 2 *Ful.* 183; his description of the counterfeit tract De Vitis Prophetarum, ascribed to Epiphanius, *ib.* 207 n.; referred to, *Calf.* 9 n

Peter: *v.* Petrus.

Peter (St): *v.* Paul, Pope.

First mentioned in the lists of apostles, 1 *Ful.* 41, 553, 2 *Lat.* 91; why named Cephas, 4 *Bul.* 491, *Hutch.* 102; alleged derivation of that name from κεφαλὴ, 2 *Ful.* 301, 302; Christ preferred Peter's boat, *ib.* 304, 1 *Lat.* 198, 205; the Rhemish explanation thereof, 1 *Lat.* 205 n.; Peter walked on the sea, 2 *Ful.* 305; on our Lord's address to him, "Thou art Peter, and upon this rock I will build my church," 3 *Bul.* 50, 51, 4 *Bul.* 81, 122, 491, 2 *Cov.* 465—468, 2 *Ful.* 228, 249, 250, 272, 303, *Hutch.* 100, 101, 1 *Jew.* 340, &c., 367, 368, 2 *Jew.* 895, 1000, 3 *Jew.* 297, 2 *Lat.* 309 n., 312, *Lit. Edw.* 513, (561), *Phil.* 37, *Rid.* 261, 1 *Tyn.* 216—218, 318, 2 *Tyn.* 234, 281, 284; on the promise to him of the keys of the kingdom of heaven, 2 *Bec.* 565, 566, 4 *Bul.* 146, 1 *Cov.* 373, 374, 2 *Cov.* 466, 2 *Hoop.* 51, *Hutch.* 98, 99, 1 *Lat.* 30, 31, *Now.* (100), *Phil.* 75, *Rid.* 266, 1 *Tyn.* 205, 216—218, 2 *Tyn.* 282; the delivery of the keys to Peter did not make him an authoritative judicial interpreter of scripture, *Whita.* 425; Peter addressed by Christ as "Satan," *Pil.* 604; not only Peter, but Christ himself was subject to the temporal power, 1 *Tyn.* 188; bp Fisher, however, says that he paid tribute as the head of the apostolic family, *ib.* 190; why the tribute was paid, 2 *Ful.* 303; sometimes he was arrogant, 4 *Bul.* 476; on Christ's prayer for him, 2 *Ful.* 304, *Hutch.* 106, 4 *Jew.* 710, 711, *Whita.* 430, 431; his faith failed not, 3 *Tyn.* 38; More says it failed in himself, but was preserved in our lady, *ib.* n.; he cuts off Malchus' ear, *Pil.* 433; the story of Peter and Malchus allegorized, 1 *Tyn.* 306; his denial of Christ, 1 *Brad.* 72, 1 *Cov.* 272—274, 2 *Hoop.* 348; how Christ looked upon him, *Hutch.* 107; his repentance, 1 *Brad.*

PETER

72, 2 *Bul.* 424, 4 *Bul.* 549, 2 *Cov.* 366, 367, 376; Peter's tears at the cock's crowing, verses by S. Rowlands, *Poet.* 347; Saint Peter's Ten Tears (a poem, 1597), notice of it, *ib.* xli, extracts from it, *ib.* 447; his fall and repentance contrasted with those of Judas, 1 *Lat.* 379, 3 *Tyn.* 208, 209; his restoration to the apostleship, 2 *Brad.* 143; Christ's commission to him to feed his sheep and his lambs, *ib.* 142, 143, 4 *Bul.* 122, 2 *Cov.* 467, 2 *Ful.* 305, *Hutch.* 102, 3 *Jew.* 175, 201, 281, &c., *Phil.* 76, 131, 2 *Tyn.* 280, *Whita.* 428, 429; his discourse at Pentecost, 4 *Bul.* 250, 1 *Cov.* 397, &c.; he, with John, healed the lame man by Christ's power, 4 *Bul.* 255, 2 *Ful.* 306; he gave sentence against Ananias and Sapphira, 1 *Bul.* 359, 2 *Ful.* 306; his shadow healed the sick, *Calf.* 337, 2 *Ful.* 306; he denounced Simon Magus, 2 *Ful.* 306; raised Dorcas or Tabitha, 2 *Bul.* 23, 2 *Ful.* 306; his vision at Joppa, 2 *Ful.* 306, *Sand.* 275; his sermon to Cornelius, *Sand.* 276, &c.; the baptism of the latter, 4 *Bul.* 312; Peter's deliverance out of prison by an angel, 2 *Bul.* 96, 4 *Bul.* 226; why Paul went to Jerusalem to visit him, 2 *Ful.* 307, 1 *Jew.* 375; whether Peter was president in the council at Jerusalem, 2 *Cran.* 76, 2 *Ful.* 249, 307, 4 *Jew.* 917, 2 *Tyn.* 250, *Whita.* 432, 2 *Whitg.* 276, 277; styled a pillar, 4 *Bul.* 123, 2 *Cov.* 468; reproved by Paul for dissimulation, 2 *Brad.* 144, 1 *Jew.* 384, 4 *Jew.* 834, *Phil.* 401, 2 *Tyn.* 251, *Whita.* 455; said to have sat at Antioch as bishop, 2 *Brad.* 144, *Rog.* 328, 2 *Tyn.* 285; it is doubted whether he ever was at Rome, though he is alleged to have been the first bishop there, 2 *Brad.* 144, 145, 4 *Bul.* 63, 2 *Cov.* 469, 2 *Cran.* 76, 2 *Ful.* 307, 335, &c., 2 *Hoop.* 545, 560, *Phil.* 26, 78, 2 *Tyn.* 285, *Whita.* 512; whether he wrote his first epistle from Rome, and continued there for five and twenty years, 2 *Ful.* 336, &c.; Whitaker asserts that Papias was the first who taught that he was at Rome, *Whita.* 665 (but see the note); he was not the first pope, *Poet.* 274; not bishop of Rome even, but an apostle, 2 *Jew.* 908; as such he had universal power jointly with the rest, 1 *Jew.* 431; he had no more authority over all churches than any other apostle, 2 *Brad.* 143, *Phil.* 74; his see apostolic was specially over the Jews, 3 *Jew.* 326; on his primacy and alleged supremacy, 4 *Bul.* 122, 2 *Cov.* 465—468, 2 *Cran.* 76, 1 *Ful.* 41, 86, 87, 553, 2 *Ful.* 249, 250, 303—308, 310, &c., *Hutch.* 98, &c., 1 *Jew.* 366, &c., 383, 384, 428, &c., 435, &c., 1 *Lat.* 205, 210, 2 *Lat.* 91, *Park.* 110, 2 *Tyn.* 249, 250, 280, &c., *Whita.* 418, 2 *Whitg.* 123, 273, 279; the former admitted by Calvin, 2 *Whitg.* 279; he did not arrogantly assume it to himself, 1 *Jew.* 372; Bellarmine considers him to have been an ordinary pastor, while the other apostles were extraordinary, *Whita.* 417; his alleged order that women should come to church veiled, 1 *Jew.* 75; said to have met Christ long after his ascension, *Rid.* 221; his martyrdom under Nero, 1 *Bul.* 315, 2 *Bul.* 105, 4 *Bul.* 32, 2 *Cov.* 132, 2 *Ful.* 305, *Rid.* 76; his body buried by pope Cornelius, 1 *Jew.* 173; his wife continued with him to his dying day, 1 *Ful.* 475; she became a martyr, 2 *Jew.* 727; his daughter, *v.* Petronilla; collect for the octave of St Peter and Paul, from the Roman Breviary, 3 *Tyn.* 117 n.; Peter supposed to open heaven-gates, 2 *Bec.* 536; his chains canonized [Aug. 1], *Rog.* 225; the feast of Cathedra S. Petri [Jan. 18], 2 *Cov.* 500; St Peter's patrimony, 4 *Bul.* 110, 1 *Tyn.* 207, 271; legend of his consecrating Westminster abbey in person, 1 *Tyn.* 326; why recourse was had, in days of old, to Peter's chair, 3 *Jew.* 608, &c.; who are his successors, 2 *Hoop.* 546; Peter said, by Sixtus II., to dwell in the bishop of Rome, 1 *Jew.* 401; the joint authority of Peter and Paul claimed by the pope, 2 *Tyn.* 285; the pope's claims to be Peter's successor examined, 4 *Bul.* 29, &c., 2 *Tyn.* 281, &c.; the popes have been most unlike him, 4 *Jew.* 1009, &c., *Pil.* 271, except in his faults, *Pil.* 604; his seat and his keys are his doctrine, 2 *Tyn.* 286

— His 1st Epistle: Tyndale's prologue to it, 1 *Tyn.* 527; argument of it, and contents of each chapter, 3 *Bec.* 591; whether written from Rome, 2 *Ful.* 336

— His 2nd Epistle: Tyndale's prologue to it, 1 *Tyn.* 528; argument and contents, 3 *Bec.* 592; this epistle rejected by Cajetan, *Whita.* 105, and by some Lutherans, *ib.* 296

— Apocryphal pieces in his name: *v.* Apocrypha, ii.

Peter, duke of Savoy: built the Savoy hospital, London, *Grin.* 302 n

Peter Aloisius, duke of Parma, son of pope Paul III.: his wickedness, 3 *Jew.* 657, 658

Peter (St), bp of Alexandria: believed as Athanasius and Damasus did, and approved the creed of the latter, 1 *Bul.* 34, 4 *Bul.* 63, 2 *Hoop.* 539; styled archbishop,

2 *Whitg.* 160; put to death by Maximin, 1 *Hoop.* 169, *Hutch.* 113

Peter Aloisius, see above.

Peter, chanter of Paris, see below.

Peter of Cluni: opposes Peter Bruse, 3 *Jew.* 215

Peter the Eater: *v.* Petrus Comestor.

Peter the Fuller, bp of Antioch: said that the Holy Trinity was crucified, *Rog.* 57

Peter Leoni: *v.* Anacletus, antipope.

Peter Lombard, bp of Paris, commonly called the Master of the Sentences: his Libri Sententiarum, 3 *Bul.* 81, 4 *Bul.* 484, *Jew.* xxxix, 1 *Tyn.* 151 n., 3 *Whitg.* xxx; he was author of a new divinity, *Bale* 571; much quoted by the school-authors, 1 *Cran.* 351, (94); his authority, 1 *Jew.* 381; allowed to be not infallible, 3 *Jew.* 177; he says (quoting Fulgentius) that the flesh of Christ is of the same nature whereof all men's flesh is, 3 *Bec.* 455; affirms that the Holy Ghost is the affection of love within us, *Rog.* 73; says that there is a temporal and an eternal proceeding of the Holy Ghost, *ib.* 74; speaks of seven deadly sins, 2 *Bul.* 410; distinguishes between pœna and culpa, 3 *Bul.* 90; says that concupiscence after baptism is no sin, but a punishment, *Rog.* 102; referred to about faith, *Calf.* 86; passages on justification, 2 *Cran.* 204, 206, 207, 210; he defines a sacrament as the sign of a holy thing, 1 *Jew.* 219, 515; gives three reasons for the institution of sacraments, 4 *Bul.* 241, 242; says sacraments are instituted not only to signify, but also to sanctify, *Calf.* 237; declares that they have received power to confer grace by the merit of the passion of Christ, 4 *Bul.* 304; says, that which is consecrated of the priest is called a sacrifice because it is a remembrance and representation of the true sacrifice, 2 *Bec.* 250, 264 n., 278 n., 3 *Bec.* 459, 1 *Cran.* 351, 357, &c., (94), 2 *Hoop.* 530; his doctrine on this passage and its context, 1 *Cran.* 358, 359; he affirms that excommunicate persons, heretics, schismatics, &c., though priests, cannot consecrate the sacrament, and states why, 1 *Hoop.* 517, 518; he promoted transubstantiation, *ib.* 118; his doctrine in relation to this and some kindred points, 1 *Cran.* 279, 280, 328, 1 *Hoop.* 167, 168, 192, 193, 224, 3 *Jew.* 490; terms used by him with reference to the manner of Christ's presence, 4 *Bul.* 443; he asks, what becometh of the substance of the bread and wine? and replies, they say either that it is resolved into the matter that was before, or else it is consumed into nothing, 3 *Jew.* 504; thinks that the accidents have their being without a subject, 3 *Jew.* 510; explains the meaning of the breaking of the host into three parts, 1 *Hoop.* 228; recites various opinions on the breaking of the bread, 2 *Jew.* 584; teaches that our eyes are deceived, and that nothing is broken, 4 *Jew.* 818; thinks that the body of Christ may possibly be eaten by a beast; an opinion which has been condemned, 1 *Cran.* 67, 2 *Ful.* 21 n., 2 *Jew.* 783, 3 *Jew.* 488, *Rid.* 309, 509; explains why Christ is received under two kinds, 3 *Bec.* 414, 443, 1 *Hoop.* 229; is supposed to have first spoken of the seven sacraments, *Calf.* 237 n.; his enumeration, 4 *Bul.* 246; he teaches that many things are improperly called sacraments, *Calf.* 215; declares that confirmation is said to be a greater sacrament than baptism, *ib.* 221, 222 n.; states that in it the Spirit is given for strength, 3 *Whitg.* 359; writes on penance, *Calf.* 242—244; cites a Sermo de Pœnitentia, falsely attributed to Chrysostom, *ib.* 64 n.; also the fictitious treatise De vera et falsa Pœnitentia bearing the name of Augustine, 2 *Ful.* 240 n.; declares that without confession, there is no way to heaven, 3 *Bul.* 81, 1 *Jew.* 120; says it is not sufficient to confess to God without a priest, neither is he truly humble and penitent that does not desire the judgment of a priest, 3 *Bul.* 81; mentions Bede as saying, let us open our small and daily sins unto our fellows, and the greater unto the priest, 3 *Jew.* 457; states that, without confession of the mouth and absolution of the outward pain, sins are forgiven by the contrition and humility of the heart, *ib.* 377; cites Ambrose respecting absolution, 2 *Bec.* 174 n.; notes that it appears plainly that God himself looses the penitent when, by giving him inward light, he inspires into him the true contrition of the heart, 3 *Jew.* 358; affirms that Christ has given power to priests to bind and loose, that is, to declare unto men who are bound and who are loosed, *ib.* 380; says, although a man be assoiled before God, yet is he not accounted assoiled in the sight of the church, but by the judgment of the priest, *ib.* 360, 374; writes, if thou want a priest thou must make thy confession unto thy neighbour or unto thy fellow, *ib.* 357; states that all priests have not knowledge to discern between sin and sin, *ib.* 356, 363, 373; teaches that spiritual kindred may not intermarry, *Rog.* 262; allows that many priests are ignorant, and have not the key of knowledge, 3 *Jew.* 356, 363, 382 ; confesses that the five inferior orders were not primitive, *Rog.* 260; gives a reason for doorkeepers and acolythes, 3 *Jew.* 273; enumerates seven orders, which he says are called sacraments, consequently he makes thirteen sacraments out of seven, *Calf.* 228, *Rog.* 259; speaks of two sorts of holy oil, *Pil.* 526 n.; on the fallen angels, 1 *Lat.* 27 n.; his division of the ten commandments, 1 *Bul.* 213, 1 *Hoop.* 350; on the religious standing of women under the law, *Whita.* 529; his opinion as to whether Mary was sinless or not, 2 *Lat.* 226 n

Peter, bp of Nicomedia : adored images, 2 *Jew.* 664

Peter, chanter of Paris : 1 *Brad.* 564 n., 3 *Jew.* 347 n

Peter of Perugia : *v.* Bizarro.

Peter Thomas, patriarch of Constantinople : *Bale* 520

Peter the Venerable : *v.* Peter of Cluni.

Peter ... (Sir) : *Grin.* 395

Peter-pence : first given by king Ina, *Bale* 447; paid in consequence of king John's submission, 1 *Tyn.* 339; a mark of slavery, *Bale* 529; referred to, 4 *Jew.* 1077, &c.

Peterborough : the Saxon History, or Chronicle of Peterborough, 2 *Ful.* 23 n., 4 *Jew.* 780

Peterbrusians : *v.* Bruse (Pet.).

Peterson (Will.) : letter to C. Pulbert, 3 *Zur.* 604; mentioned, *ib.* 217, 381, 627, 628, 629

Petilia : the citizens there, 1 *Bul.* 252

Petilian, the Donatist : opposed by Augustine, 3 *Jew.* 229, 2 *Lat.* 261; he charged Augustine with burning the holy gospel, 1 *Jew.* 463, 4 *Jew.* 764, *Sand.* 16 n

Petilians : taught that the sacraments are holy only when administered by holy men, *Rog.* 270

Petit (Jac.) : *Calf.* 212 n

Petitio principii : *v.* Logic.

Petition : a part of prayer, 4 *Bul.* 163; a petition by certain Puritans to king James, *Rog.* 21, 26

Peto (Will. card.) : confessor to queen Mary, 1 *Tyn.* 38 n

Petrarcha (Fra.) : Opera, *Jew.* xli ; he reproves the church of Rome as adulterous, *Phil.* 423 ; terms Rome (rather Avignon) the whore of Babylon, 4 *Jew.* 628, 744 ; speaks of it as the fountain of sorrow, the temple of heresy, false Babylon, &c., 3 *Jew.* 345, 4 *Jew.* 740, 874, 928, 1115, *Phil.* 430 ; describes its immorality, *Phil.* 418 ; calls glorying in the nobility of others, a boasting to be laughed at, 2 *Bec.* 436

Petre (Sir Will.) : notice of him, 2 *Cran.* 315 n.; allusions to him, *ib.* 338, 4 *Jew.* 1229, 1230, 3 *Zur.* 77 n.; proposed to Cranmer for master of his faculties, 2 *Cran.* 394; a privy councillor, and secretary of state, *ib.* 505, 511, 520, *Park.* 75, 117, 155, 1 *Zur.* 5 n., 71, 80; letter from him to Parker, *Park.* 118

Petrikow, Poland : 3 *Zur.* 700

Petronilla (St) : daughter of St Peter, 3 *Bec.* 257, 265, 1 *Ful.* 475 ; invoked for the ague, 2 *Jew.* 923, *Rog.* 226

Petronius : wished to set up an image in God's temple, 1 *Bec.* 17, *Park.* 82, *Rid.* 85

Petrus : *v.* Peter.

Petrus de Alliaco, *q. v.*

Petrus de Aquila, *q. v.*

Petrus Aureolus, *q. v.*

Petrus Camaracensis : *v.* Alliaco (P. de).

Petrus Chrysologus, *q. v.*

Petrus Comestor, or Manducator, (Pierre le Mangeur) : mentioned (no doubt erroneously) as the brother of P. Lombard and Gratian, *Bale* 573 ; he held transubstantiation, 1 *Hoop.* 118, 518; mentions different opinions as to the words of Christ in consecration of the eucharist, 2 *Bec.* 263 ; his Historia Evangelica, 2 *Lat.* 116 n

Petrus Crinitus, *q. v.*

Petrus Ferrariensis : complains that kings are slaves to the pope, 4 *Jew.* 1039

Petrus Joannis, Catalanus : wrote on the Apocalypse, *Bale* 258

Petrus Manducator : *v.* Petrus Comestor.

Petrus Martyr, *q. v.*

Petrus de Natalibus : Catalogus Sanctorum, *Jew.* xl ; says the body of Christ contained corporally in heaven, is contained sacramentally in the host, 2 *Bec.* 286, 472 n., 473 n., 3 *Bec.* 449 ; states a reason for believing the assumption of the Virgin, 1 *Tyn.* 159 n.; tells how St Ambrose quitted a house, the master whereof had never been in trouble, 3 *Bec.* 103 n., 1 *Lat.* 435 n. ; tells how St Bartholomew confounded a demon which inhabited an idol, 3 *Tyn.* 92 n.; says St Bernard denounced sentence of excommunication against flies, *Rog.* 311 n. ; gives a legend of St Brandon, 2 *Tyn.* 98 n.; records St Martin's dying prayer, 3 *Tyn.* 279 n.; gives an account of St Patrick's purgatory, 1 *Tyn.* 290 n.; what he says of St Thecla, 4 *Jew.* 651; he speaks of miracles wrought by St Thomas Aquinas, 3 *Tyn.* 131 n

Petrus de Palude : a poor friar observant called patriarch of Jerusalem, 4 *Jew.* 1056 his book De Caus. Immed. Eccles. Potest., *Jew.* xli; he exalts Peter above the rest of the apostles, 3 *Jew.* 287; calls him the superintendent of the whole world, 4 *Jew.* 906; teaches that, next after Christ, spiritual grace and power is derived from Peter, *ib.* 829; expounds the words " Whatsoever thou shalt bind," &c., 3 *Jew.* 383, 384; states that the church has no power of jurisdiction but only from Peter, 4 *Jew.* 829; says the pope's power exceeds that of all the rest of the church, 3 *Jew.* 234, 4 *Jew.* 921; declares that none may judge the pope, 2 *Jew.* 907, 919, 4 *Jew.* 833, 898, 1033; maintains that the pope is chosen by the law of God, but that other bishops are chosen by the law of man, 4 *Jew.* 1036; asserts that no man may believe that the church of Rome may err from the faith, *ib.* 1057, 1058; says the church of Peter cannot wholly fail from the faith, but all other churches may, *ib.* 726; affirms this from Christ's prayer for Peter, *ib.* 710; says that in the church one bishop is sufficient to consecrate another, but for solemnity three are devised, 3 *Jew.* 334; writes on a mouse eating the sacrament, 2 *Jew.* 784

Petrus Parisiensis: *v.* Peter, chanter.

Petrus Perusinus: *v.* Bizarro.

Petrus Ravennas: Compend. Jur. Canon., *Jew.* xlii; cited, 4 *Jew.* 634

Petrus Urbevetanus: speaks of one mass only being said, after the manner of the Greeks, 2 *Jew.* 635, 4 *Jew.* 888

Pett (Peter): notice of him, *Poet.* xxxv; all creatures praise God; verses by him, *ib.* 386

Petworth, co. Sussex: the benefice farmed, 2 *Cran.* 278

Peucer (Caspar): son-in-law to Melancthon, and head of the university of Wittemberg, 1 *Zur.* 302 n.; with Melancthon he edits Carion's Chronicle, *Jew.* xxxiv, 4 *Jew.* 1051

Pews: seats, *Bale* 527, 2 *Brad.* 49, 340, *Grin.* 175 n., 2 *Lat.* 441; pews for prayer, *Sand.* 237; pew-fellows, 1 *Ful.* 65, 3 *Jew.* 341; pue-fellows, 1 *Ful.* 204

Peyto (Will. card.): *v.* Peto.

Pewter ware: 3 *Zur.* 195

Peyton (Sir Hen.): Mary (Seymour) his wife, 1 *Bec.* 396 n

Pez (Bern.): Thesaurus Anecdot. Novis., *Jew.* xlii, 4 *Jew.* 678

Pezelius (Chr.): 1 *Zur.* 302 n

Pfaffus [Germ. Pfaffe]: a contemptuous term for priest, 2 *Hoop.* 413

Pflug (Jul.), bp of Naumberg: named, 1 *Ful.* 63 n.; one of the compilers of the Interim, 2 *Zur.* 125 n., 3 *Zur.* 383 n

Phagius (Paul): *v.* Fagius.

Phanons: to be destroyed, *Grin.* 135, 159; what, *ib.* 135 n. (*v.* Maniple).

Pharaoh [Amun-m-ha II.?]: punished for taking Sarai, 1 *Bul.* 410

Pharaoh [Thothmes III.?]: gave an Egyptian name to Joseph, 1 *Tyn.* 409, *Whita.* 178

Pharaoh [Rameses III.?]: his daughter Termuth, *Poet.* 130

Pharaoh [Osirei-men-phthah?]: afflicted, 2 *Bul.* 79; his impenitence, *ib.* 261, 1 *Cov.* 118; God hardens his heart, 2 *Bul.* 381, 382; he is drowned in the Red sea, 4 *Bul.* 329; he represents the devil, 1 *Brad.* 149, *Now.* (8), 121; and the pope, *Sand.* 146

Pharaohs: alleged meaning of the name, 1 *Bul.* 352; destroyed for rebellion, 2 *Bul.* 13

Pharisees (generally associated with the scribes): the origin of both, according to Josephus and Jerome, 3 *Jew.* 323; why the Pharisees were so called, 2 *Jew.* 1017, 3 *Whitg.* 522; their name marks their character, 3 *Tyn.* 108; their austerity, 2 *Jew.* 1017; their lip-service, 4 *Bul.* 180, 184; their hypocrisy, *ib.* 12; although hypocrites, yet they instructed the congregation, 1 *Jew.* 399; Cyprian remarks that Christ never blamed the priests except under the name of scribes and Pharisees, *Whita.* 427; how they esteemed men's traditions, 2 *Hoop.* 271; how they set aside God's commandments by their glosses, 1 *Tyn.* 460, 461, 2 *Tyn.* 41, 42, 3 *Tyn.* 47; they saw the day of Messiah's birth, and were sad, 2 *Hoop.* 477; felt not the consolation of Christ, *ib.* 325; were troubled at his preaching, *Pil.* 140; drove sinners from him, 1 *Tyn.* 293; though they had the clearness of Christ's coming, yet they put him to death, 2 *Hoop.* 331; their false righteousness, 1 *Tyn.* 74, 2 *Tyn.* 40; Pharisees and scribes compared with monks, 2 *Tyn.* 42, 43; their practice followed by prelates, *ib.* 240, 241; the Pharisee and publican, *Hutch.* 335; Pharisees think scripture may be expounded as men list, *Rog.* 195; hold free-will, *ib.* 105; think that we are justified by external righteousness, *ib.* 109, 116; suppose that God is pleased with lip-service, *ib.* 120; desire their works to be seen of men, *ib.* 124

Phavorinus: 2 *Jew.* 803

Phebe: was a servant of the church, 2 *Bul.* 219

Phelps (Will.), of Cirencester: articles subscribed by him, 2 *Hoop.* 152

Pheneux (......): servant to Cromwell, 2 *Cran.* 400

Phenomena: arguments from divers examples of natural phenomena, 1 *Cran.* 259
Pherecydes : 3 *Bul.* 385
Phicinus (M.) : *v.* Ficino.
Phidias : his statue of Jupiter Pisanus, 2 *Jew.* 1010
Philadelphia : the epistle to the church there, *Bale* 288
Philastrius, or Philaster : speaks of the Aerians, 2 *Brad.* 382 n. ; condemns Aerius as an Arian, 3 *Bul.* 399 ; says the Arians condemned marriage, *Rog.* 306 ; describes the Semi-Arians, *ib.* 70; speaks of the Basilidians, *ib.* 119; on Cerinthus, *ib.* 64, 160; on the Eunomians, *ib.* 44; on the Manichees, *ib.* 67, 154; on the Marcionites, *ib.* 51 ; he says the Cataphrygians (the same sect) baptized the dead, *ib.* 266, and added blood to the Lord's supper, *ib.* 295; on the Montanists, *ib.* 65; on Simon Magus, &c., *ib.* 41; he mentions heretics who rejected Ecclesiastes and the Song of Solomon, *Whita.* 31 ; speaks of certain heretics who went barefoot, *Phil.* 426; contends that there were many languages from the beginning, *Whita.* 113
Philautia : used satirically for philosophy, 1 *Tyn.* 154, 157
Phileas, a bishop and martyr : he was married, *Pil.* 565; determined civil matters, 3 *Whitg.* 455
Philemon : had property, 2 *Bul.* 22; as to the epistle to him, *v.* Paul.
Philemon, the poet: blames unseemly sorrow for the dead, 2 *Cov.* 126
Phileni: 1 *Bul.* 278
Philip (St), the apostle: fable concerning him, *Calf.* 134; Acts of Philip, *Rog.* 82
Philip, the deacon : baptized, 3 *Whitg.* 58 ; in what manner, 4 *Bul.* 310, 311, 395, 396 ; baptized Simon Magus, *ib.* 383; was an evangelist, 3 *Bul.* 278, 4 *Bul.* 105; had a house and daughters, 2 *Bul.* 22
Philip, king of Macedon : 3 *Bec.* 5, 386, 429, 2 *Bul.* 219, 2 *Cov.* 59, *Sand.* 154
Philip, Roman emperor : by some considered to have been a Christian; fiction as to his baptism, 2 *Ful.* 355
Philip, emperor of the East: *v.* Philippicus.
Philip (......), king of France : his law against swearing, 1 *Bec.* 390
Philip VI., king of France : when crowned, 4 *Jew.* 933
Philip II., king of Spain : at Brussels with the emperor, 3 *Zur.* 52, 57 ; wounded at a tournament, *ib.* 61; his excesses at Antwerp, *ib.* 175; he arrives in London, *ib.* 177; names queen Mary (*q. v.*), 1 *Brad.* 399 n., 580 ; conditions of the match, 3 *Zur.* 510; Philip and Mary, their style, 2 *Cran.* 543 ; a supplication to them, 1 *Brad.* 403 ; he demands to be crowned, &c., but is denied, 3 *Zur.* 174, 179, 180; beheads two noblemen, *ib.* 750; is made protector to the prince that should be born, 2 *Brad* 167, *Rid.* 371; proposes marriage to queen Elizabeth, 1 *Zur.* 5 n., 2 *Zur.* 1; makes peace with France and England, *ib.* 19 ; asks Elizabeth's permission to bring three regiments of infantry through the English channel, *ib.* 172 ; sends an Italian abbot to Scotland to oppose the Reformation, 1 *Zur.* 149, but the ship is wrecked, *ib.* 150; is expected in Brabant, *ib.* 173 ; blockades Geneva, *ib.* 334; the invincible armada, 1588, *v.* Spanish armada; he prepares to invade England and Ireland, 1596, *Lit. Eliz.* 472, 473

— Mary of Portugal his 1st wife, 3 *Zur.* 510 n.; Mary, queen of England, his 2nd wife: *v.* Mary.
Philip, archduke of Austria : consort of Joanna of Spain, 2 *Bec.* 622 n
Philip, earl of Flanders : his law against swearing, 1 *Bec.* 391
Philip, landgrave of Hesse : invited Luther, Zuingle, and others, to a conference concerning the eucharist at Marpurg, *Grin.* 251 n.; signed the confession of Augsburg, 2 *Zur.* 15 n.; Bullinger dedicated a book to him, 4 *Bul.* xvi; he married Margaret de Sala, his first wife living, 2 *Cran.* 405 n., 3 *Zur.* 666 n.; imprisoned, 3 *Zur.* 58; his character, *ib.*
Philip of Mantua : wrote on the Apocalypse, *Bale* 257
Philip (Tho.) : persecuted, 3 *Tyn.* 269
Philip Flatterer, *q. v.*
Philippi : the jailor there, 4 *Bul.* 366
Philippians (Epistle to the) : *v.* Paul.
Philippicus, emperor of the East : was against images, 2 *Bec.* 71, *Phil.* 407
Philipps (Morgan) : concerned in Cranmer's trial, 2 *Cran.* 553
Philips (Hen.) : sought Tyndale's friendship in order to betray him, 1 *Tyn.* lxv; borrowed money from him, *ib.* lxvii; brought the emperor's officers to arrest him, *ib.*; had Gabriel Donne for his coadjutor, *ib.* lxix n.; procured the arrest of Poyntz, as a succourer of Tyndale, *ib.* lxxi; was a scholar of Louvaine, 3 *Tyn.* 271
Philips (Walter), last prior and first dean of Rochester : *Phil.* 64, 170, 3 *Zur.* 373 n
Philips (......) : in prison for the truth, 2 *Lat.* 321

Phillip (Anne): witness to Hutchinson's will, *Hutch.* x.
Phillip (Jo.): notice of him, *Poet.* iii; Stanzas from his Friendly Larum, *ib.* 525
Phillips (Anne), of Picton: a book dedicated to her, *Poet.* xlvi.
Phillips (Roland), vicar of Croydon: his examination before Cranmer, 2 *Cran.* 338
Phillips (......): Sir E. Carew's gaoler, 3 *Zur.* 625 n
Philistines: their God, 1 *Bul.* 224; their priests, 4 *Bul.* 480; they take the ark of God, *ib.* 295
Philo, a Gentile philosopher: mentioned by Josephus, *Whita.* 88
Philo, the Jew: what he says on Job's country and wife, *Pil.* 245; he mentions the Therapeutæ, 2 *Ful.* 101; referred to, *Bale* 534; thought to have written the Book of Wisdom, 1 *Ful.* 354, *Whita.* 88
Philo (Dr), master of Michael house, Cambridge: 2 *Lat.* xii.
Philoromus, martyr: *Pil.* 565 n
Philosophers: they were ignorant of true wisdom, *Wool.* 4; preferred their inventions to revelation, *Rog.* 79; some held that God thinks not of our affairs, 1 *Lat.* 34; some made themselves laughing-stocks, 1 *Cran.* 254; their opinions concerning death and a future state, 2 *Cov.* 40; concerning these things they write foolishly and childishly, *ib.*; their opinions on a future state investigated by bp Warburton, *ib.* n.; they were the patriarchs of heretics, 2 *Bul.* 407, 3 *Bul.* 124, 1 *Jew.* 334
Philosophy: distinguished from theology, *Whita.* 364; the difference between divine and philosophical precepts, *Wool.* 121; philosophy teaches that every corporal thing has two substances, the matter and the form, 1 *Cran.* 337; that of Aristotle, Plato, and Pliny, referred to by Cranmer, *ib.* 331; conclusions from it, *ib.* 333; Gardiner argues that philosophy should not move the faith of a Christian, *ib.* 252; how philosophy is spoken against by Paul, *Hutch.* 29, 1 *Tyn.* 155; false philosophy, 1 *Tyn.* 154, &c.
Philotus (Laur.): *Park.* 60 n
Philpot (Sir Peter), K. B.: father of Jo. Philpot, *Phil.* i.
PHILPOT (Jo.), archdeacon of Winchester: biographical notice of him, *Phil.* i—xxii, (and 3, 4); he was a knight's son, *ib.* i; and of kin to the lord Riche, *ib.* 58, 102; studies at Winchester, *ib.* i, ii; is admitted "true fellow" of New coll., Oxford, *ib.* iii; takes the degree of B.C.L., *ib.*; forfeits his fellowship for absence, *ib.* iv; goes into Italy, *ib.* iv, v, 3; encounters a Franciscan friar, v, 41; change in his religious views, *ib.* vi; he lectures on the epistle to the Romans at Winchester cathedral, *ib.* vii; is made archdeacon of Winchester, *ib.* ix, 5; being archdeacon he excommunicates bp White, of Lincoln, for preaching false doctrine, *ib.* 82; is wounded by Cook the register, *ib.* x; his disputation in the Convocation, Oct. 1553, against transubstantiation, *ib.* 179, &c.; see 3 *Zur.* 373 n.; his freedom of speech there the cause of his persecution, *Phil.* xiii, xiv, 52, 156; he is illegally deprived of his archdeaconry, *ib.* xiv, 11; excommunicated by Gardiner, *ib.* 101; committed to the King's Bench, *ib.* xiv, 156; removed to the sessions-house by Newgate, *ib.* xvi; committed to the custody of Bonner, *ib.*, and laid in his coal house, *ib.* 13, 70, 227, 267, &c.; in prison, 1 *Brad.* 403, 2 *Brad.* 74 n., 96; his examination at several times during his imprisonment, *Phil.* 3, &c.; his examiners, *ib.* xxv, &c.; he sings in prison for joy, *Bale* 102, *Phil.* 17, 268, 270; his prayer for wisdom to answer his accusers, *Phil.* 19; his prophecy of the increase of the gospel, *ib.* 30; he is put in the stocks, *Bale* 102, *Phil.* 81, 85, 230, &c.; Bonner illegally declares himself to be his ordinary, and proceeds accordingly, *Phil.* 83; articles feigned against him, *ib.*; he is conveyed into a close tower joining Paul's, *ib.* 87; searched for writings, *ib.*; sentences written in his Bible and another book, *ib.* 108, 125; false charges against him, *ib.* 109; he sharply rebukes Morgan, *ib.* 122; is denied candle-light, *ib.* 125, 267; again rebuked for singing, *ib.* 127; he rebukes and warns his persecutors, *ib.* 143; his vision, *ib.* 272; his further examination in the consistory at St Paul's, *ib.* 146, &c.; three articles objected against him, *ib.* 146; his last examination, *ib.* 148; Bonner's exhortation to him, and his reply, *ib.* 151; his bill of complaint to the parliament, *ib.* 156; mentioned as in peril of death, 1 *Brad.* 290; he is condemned, *Phil.* 158; sent to Newgate, and cruelly used there, *ib.* 159; warned by the sheriffs to prepare against the next day, *ib.* 161; his words when going to the stake, *ib.*; his martyrdom, *ib.* xvii, 161, *Poet.* 165; on his prayer at the stake, 1 *Brad.* 258; his EXAMINATIONS AND WRITINGS, edited by the Rev. Rob. Eden, M.A., *Phil.*; Grindal's opinion on his examinations, *Grin.* 223; his writings

characterized, *Phil.* xviii, &c.; his letters from prison, *ib.* 217—292; a letter which seems to be his is also assigned to Bradford, 2 *Brad.* xlvii; a letter to a sister of his exhorting her to stick to the truth, and to abide trial, *Phil.* 238; a declaration concerning religion signed by him, 1 *Brad.* 374; his views on election, *ib.* 305, 2 *Brad.* 169; his opinion respecting the sacrament of the body and blood of Christ, *Phil.* 53, 61, &c.; cited about a place of Cyprian, 2 *Whitg.* 220; he defends Calvin, *Phil.* 46; letters to him, 2 *Brad.* 179, 243, 2 *Hoop.* 592; reference to him, 2 *Brad.* 129; play upon his name, *Phil.* 234

Philpot (Jo. ?): suspended for nonconformity, *Grin.* 289, 2 *Zur.* 147 n

Philpot (Tho.): brother of the martyr, *Phil.* 240

Phillpotts (Hen.), bp of Exeter: source of an extract from the Canon Law adduced by him with reference to purgatory, 2 *Ful.* 240 n

Phinehas: zealous for God, *Pil.* 7, 343, 477

Phines (Eliz. lady): *v.* Fineux.

Phocas, emperor: murdered his lawful sovereign Mauritius, together with his wife and family, *Bale* 503, 2 *Hoop.* 235, 293, 555, 1 *Jew.* 363, 3 *Jew.* 310, *Pil.* 76, 521; is said to have conceded supremacy to the church of Rome, Boniface III. being bishop, *Bale* 503, 562, 2 *Brad.* 146, 2 *Ful.* 72, 354, 365, 1 *Hoop.* 226, 2 *Hoop.* 235, 555, 1 *Jew.* 184, 361, 363, 3 *Jew.* 311, *Pil.* 76, 521, *Poet.* 284, 2 *Tyn.* 258, 1 *Whitg.* 232; the authority for this statement, 2 *Ful.* 365, and see 371; he was slain by the people, and thrown into the fire, 1 *Jew.* 364

Phocylides: 1 *Bec.* 375

Phoroneus: gave laws, 2 *Bul.* 219

Photinians: their heresy, 1 *Bec.* 418, 2 *Jew.* 759

Photinus: his heresy, 3 *Bec.* 401, 3 *Bul.* 267, 1 *Cran.* 278, *Hutch.* 121, *Phil.* 423; he impugned the deity of the Holy Ghost, *Rog.* 70; added to the gospel, *Bale* 638

Photius, patr. of Constantinople: Bibliotheca, *Calf.* 89 n., 2 *Ful.* 101 n.; Nomocanon, *Jew.* xlii; Epistolæ, *ib.*; he speaks of the declaration of the council of Constantinople respecting the divinity of the Holy Ghost, 3 *Jew.* 224; alludes to the confidence of our works, our faith, &c., 1 *Ful.* 369, 370; compares faith to a rule, *Whita.* 662; writes on being "guilty of the body and blood of the Lord," 1 *Cran.* 408, 409; he converted the Bulgarians, 2 *Ful.* 60; writes to the prince of Bulgaria about the council of Constantinople, 4 *Jew.* 994; mentions that Cyril presided at the synod of Ephesus, in the stead of pope Celestine, *ib.* 995; praises Theodosius as a defender of godliness, 4 *Jew.* 994; his constitution how priests, &c., were to be sued, *ib.* 960, 967; his remark respecting the Angelics, 2 *Ful.* 42 n

Phœnician: *v.* Punic.

Phœnix: 1 *Hoop.* 184

Phrygians: probably Cataphrygians, or Montanists, *Rog.* 158

Phrygio (Paul Const.): notice of him, 3 *Zur.* 554 n.; his testimony in proof of pope Joan, 4 *Jew.* 656

Phrygium: a mitre; one made of a peacock's tail delivered to Sylvester, 4 *Jew.* 841

Phylacteries, *Calf.* 283, 1 *Jew.* 327 n

Physic: chargeable and painful, 1 *Lat.* 539; its use lawful, *ib.* 541; the practice of medicine, 2 *Zur.* 205

Physicians: to be honoured, 1 *Lat.* 540, *Wool.* 93, but not trusted in, 1 *Lat.* 541, 3 *Tyn.* 119; they may not pray that many may fall sick, 1 *Bec.* 167; too many of them seek their own profit, 1 *Lat.* 98, 541; physicians, surgeons, and alchemists, use strange languages to hide their sciences from others, 1 *Cran.* 311

Physiognomy: a forbidden art, 2 *Cran.* 100, 1 *Hoop.* 329

Picards: *v.* Adamites, Beguardi.
 Referred to, 2 *Brad.* 161 n., 1 *Jew.* 227, 228, 2 *Jew.* 689; exterminated by Zisca, *Whita.* 229 n

Piccolomini (Æn. Sylv.): *v.* Pius II.

Pickback: *Calf.* 103

Pickering (Sir Will.): one of queen Elizabeth's suitors, 1 *Zur.* 24, 34 n

Pickeringe (Rich.): mention of him and his wife, *Jew.* xxv.

Pickmote: Doctor Pickmote and his fellows, 1 *Lat.* 133

Pictures: *v.* Images.
 They move men's hearts, 2 *Jew.* 661; portraits ordered by Chr. Hales, 3 *Zur.* 185, 186, 188, 668; Gualter's scruples on the subject, *ib.* 190, 195, and Burcher's, *ib.* 191—194; graving and painting not forbidden by the second commandment, 1 *Hoop.* 44, *Now.* (10), 123, 124
 — In churches (see the names of the fathers, &c., here mentioned): testimonies of fathers and councils against them, *Calf.* 145, 149, 154; the council of Eliberis forbids them, 2 *Bec.* 71 (&c. *v.* Councils); Gregory Nyssen mentions them, *Calf.* 173 n., 2 *Jew.* 654; Epiphanius destroys a picture of

Christ, or of some saint, in a church at Anablatha, 2 *Bec.* 60, & al.; many rejected them till Jerome's time, *Calf.* 8; Augustine censures them, *ib.* 188; Paulinus introduces them, *ib.* 29; Charlemagne condemned them, *ib.* 311; Greek church allows them, 3 *Zur.* 691; images in glass windows, 2 *Ful.* 208; pictures of saints not to be painted in church windows, 2 *Hoop.* 138; pictures on the walls to be defaced, *ib.*

Picus (Jo.), prince of Mirandula: Opera, *Jew.* xlii; he besought the pope to reform the church, and to restrain the luxury of priests, 4 *Jew.* 949, 1106; says, we ought to believe a simple plain husbandman, or a child, or an old woman, rather than the pope and a thousand bishops of the pope, if his bishops speak against the gospel, and the others speak with the gospel, *ib.* 921; quotes Jerome on heresy, 3 *Jew.* 210 n.; translated a spurious work of Hippolytus, 2 *Ful.* 282

Picus (J. F.): Opera, *Jew.* xlii.

Pie, or Pica: the term explained, 3 *Bec.* 535, *Lit. Edw.* 18 n., *Lit. Eliz.* 33 n., 304 n.; pies to be delivered up, 2 *Cran.* 523

Pie (Will.): v. Pye.

Piece: a castle, 1 *Jew.* 485

Picernus de Monte Arduo (Barth.): published the feigned Donation of Constantine, 2 *Ful.* 361 n

Pierpoint (Mrs): 2 *Brad.* 253

Pierpount (Sir Geo.): dedication to him, 1 *Bec.* 37; notice of him and his family, *ib.* n

Perpoynt (Geo.): presented to a prebend of Lincoln, *Park.* viii, 482

Pierrepont, in Picardy: 1 *Bec.* 37 n

Pierrepont family: some account of it, 1 *Bec.* 37 n

Pierroceli (......): 2 *Ful.* 121

Piers (Jo.), bp of Rochester, then of Salisbury, and ultimately abp of York: recommended for the see of Norwich, *Park.* 476, 477; mentioned, *Grin.* 397; he aids Geneva, *Grin.* 430 n., 432 n., 433

Piers Plowman: mention of The Ploughman's Complaint, turned into modern English, *Rid.* 490, 494

Pierson (And.): prebendary of Canterbury, *Park.* 197 n., 442, 444; his supposed share in the Bishops' Bible, *ib.* 335 n (bis).

Piety: v. Godliness, Religion.

Pighius (Alb.): Hierarch. Eccles. Assertio, *Jew.* xlii, 3 *Whitg.* xxxi; Explic. Cathol. Controv., *Jew.* xlii; De Lib. Hom. Arbitrio, et Div. Grat. *ib.*; De Actis VI. et VII. Synodorum, *Calf.* 137 n.; his exposition of "Lo, here is Christ," *Hutch.* 34; he places the church above the scriptures, *Whita.* 276; teaches that their authority depends on that of the church, 4 *Jew.* 754, 861, 862, 863; affirms that the church has power to give canonical authority unto certain writings, which otherwise they have not, *ib.* 758, &c.; says that without the authority of the church we ought not to believe the clearest scripture, *ib.* 863, 1114; declares the sense of the church to be the inflexible rule, 3 *Jew.* 247; calls the scriptures a nose of wax, 1 *Ful.* 8, 539, *Hutch.* 34, 236, 347 bis, 3 *Jew.* 431, 4 *Jew.* 748, 758, 759, 863, *Rog.* 195, 2 *Tyn.* 103, 2 *Whitg.* 172 n., 3 *Whitg.* 33, 34, 157; terms them a shipman's hose, a dead letter, &c., 3 *Jew.* 431, 4 *Jew.* 748, *Rog.* 195 n.; says they are dumb judges, &c., 4 *Jew.* 748, 758, 773, 863; declares that the writings of the apostles should not be above, but subject to, our faith, 3 *Jew.* 218, 4 *Jew.* 759, 863, *Park.* 110; speaks of the obscurity of scripture, *Rog.* 199; affirms that the word of God is so dark that it cannot be read with any profit, 1 *Bul.* 70; says the apostles knew all things, but only taught them by word of mouth, *ib.* 63; his opinions on predestination answered by Calvin, 3 *Zur.* 325; he denies original sin, 4 *Jew.* 787; declares that Augustine's judgment thereon is false, *ib.* 786, 787; his statement of Augustine's doctrine respecting concupiscence before and after baptism, 3 *Jew.* 464; he asserts that sacraments benefit ex opere operato, 2 *Jew.* 750; alleges the "clean offering" of Malachi in favour of the mass, *Hutch.* 46; confesses that there are errors and abuses in the mass, 1 *Jew.* 7, 8, 62, 106, 108, 2 *Jew.* 642, 683, 993, 3 *Jew.* 182, 4 *Jew.* 738, 739, 948, 1107; on Peter's keys, *Hutch.* 99; on Christ's prayer that Peter's faith might not fail, *ib.* 106; he treats of the authority of the Roman church, 4 *Jew.* 863; maintains that the authority of the pope is greater than that of a general council, &c., *ib.* 921; says, that certain general councils determined wickedly, &c., 1 *Jew.* 35, 65, 67, 69, 233, 254, 4 *Jew.* 1053, 1109; on the 6th and 7th councils, *Calf.* 137; he rejects the acts of the council of Constantinople (691) as spurious, *Whita.* 41; declares that those who have vowed chastity may not marry, 4 *Jew.* 640; writes on the text "it is better to marry than to burn," *Pil.* 570; prefers adultery before wedlock, 1 *Hoop.* 32; his sentiments respecting heavenly patrons, 3 *Bul.* 211; he juggles with Augustine, 1 *Cran.* 127,

1 *Jew.* 53, 54; slanders Luther, 1 *Jew.* 106; charges us with dissension, *Rid.* 307
Pight : pitched, 4 *Bul.* 96
Pigot (Rob.): martyred at Ely, *Poet.* 164
Pigot (Tho.): *v.* Pygott.
Pike (Mother): 2 *Brad.* 76
Pilate (Pontius): desired to place images in the Temple, *Calf.* 44 n., *Park.* 82 ; judged Christ, 3 *Bul.* 14, 23 ; he and Herod agreed in doing so, *Pil.* 410, 551 ; the simile of Herod and Pilate used by Jerome, 2 *Ful.* 77 n. ; he was troubled about Christ, *Pil.* 141; bore witness of his innocency, yet condemned him, *Now.* (40), 157; despised justification by faith, *Rog.* 113; named in the creed, 1 *Bul.* 134, 135; why, *Now.* (40), 157; the Acts of Pilate, otherwise called the Gospel of the Nazarenes, *Calf.* 321 n., 3 *Jew.* 441, *Pil.* 683, *Rog.* 82, *Whita.* 108, 560 n.; Mistress Pilate, 2 *Lat.* 123
Pilches : skins, *Rid.* 423
Piled : what, 1 *Tyn.* 117 n
Pilgrimage : *v.* Shoe.
    Made to holy places, 2 *Cov.* 479, 2 *Ful.* 108, 210, 238 ; anciently to Ireland, 2 *Ful.* 12 ; termed pilgrimage gate-going, 1 *Brad.* 280; it was considered meritorious, *Bale* 27; made in the jubilee for remission of sins, 2 *Cran.* 74 ; commended or allowed, 1 *Lat.* 23, 24, 2 *Lat.* 353, 359 ; not to be required unless vowed, 2 *Lat.* 233 ; when and how to be made, *ib.* 360; how it was practised, 2 *Bec.* 413 ; pilgrims were accompanied by bagpipes, Canterbury bells, &c., *Bale* 101, 102; how abused, 1 *Lat.* 54 ; juggling to get money from pilgrims, 2 *Lat.* 364; lord Cobham questioned on the subject of pilgrimage, *Bale* 39; Will. Thorpe examined thereon, *ib.* 99 ; pilgrimage forbidden, 2 *Zur.* 158; all men are pilgrims, *Bale* 25; who are true pilgrims, *ib.* 99, 3 *Tyn.* 63 ; the Christian man's pilgrimage, 1 *Lat.* 474 ; my pilgrimage, verses by Sir W. Raleigh, *Poet.* 235
Pilgrimage of Grace : an insurrection in Lincolnshire and Yorkshire, *Bale* 326, 2 *Cran.* 332 n., 1 *Lat.* 25 n., 29, 2 *Lat.* 390, 392 n., *Park.* 8 n.; it broke out at Louth, 2 *Cran.* 362 n
PILKINGTON (James), bp of Durham : biographical notice of him, *Pil.* i; his birth, *ib.*; sent to Cambridge, *Hutch.* i, *Pil.* i; mention of him there, *Park.* 38; master Pylkington senior (apparently the same) at Cambridge, 2 *Brad.* xviii; one of the disputants there, 1549, *Grin.* 194, *Rid.* 169 ; vicar of Kendal, *Pil.* ii ; in exile, 1 *Brad.* 374 n., 445, 1 *Cran.* (9), *Grin.* 224, &c., *Jew.* xiii, *Pil.* ii, 3 *Zur.* 752 n.; his expositions at Basil, *Pil.* ii; he returns to England, and is made a commissioner for revising the Prayer Book, *Grin.* v, *Pil.* iii; master of St John's college, Cambridge, and regius professor of divinity, *Pil.* iii ; he preaches at the restitution of Bucer and Fagius, *ib.* iv, 651, 2 *Zur.* 51 n. ; privately marries Alice Kingsmill, *Pil.* iv; made bishop of Durham, *Park.* 123 n., *Pil.* v, 1 *Zur.* 63 n.; his sermon at Paul's cross, on the church being [as it was supposed] struck by lightning, *Pil.* v, 647 ; he sends money to the house where he had dwelt at Zurich, 2 *Zur.* 109; his conduct in the controversy about habits, *Pil.* viii; his moderation towards the Puritans, 2 *Zur.* 141, 144 ; supposed to favour them, *Park.* 237, *Pil.* viii; he signs a letter to the queen, *Park.* 294 ; the popish insurrection at Durham, and destruction of his property, *Pil.* ix, 1 *Zur.* 218 ; his illness and recovery, 1 *Zur.* 260; the foundation of Rivington school, *Pil.* xi; his death, *ib.*, 1 *Zur.* 321, 325, 2 *Zur.* 270; his will, *Pil.* xi; his epitaphs at Durham, *ib.* xi, xiii; his character, *ib.* xiii; references to him, *Grin.* 234, *Park.* 264, 2 *Zur.* 247; commemoration of him at Rivington school, *Pil.* 671
    His WORKS, edited by the [late] Rev. James Scholefield, A.M., regius prof. of Greek, Cambridge, *Pil.* ; list of his works, *ib.* xiv—xvi ; his answer to the man of Chester, 2 *Ful.* 3, *Pil.* 481, 487; letters* by him, *Park.* 221, 1 *Zur.* 222, 286, 3 *Zur.* 134, 136; other letters by him, *Pil.* ix, x, 658, 679; he wrote certain prayers*, *Pra. B.* v.
— Alice (Kingsmill) his wife, *Pil.* iv ; his children, Deborah, Ruth, Isaac, Joshua, *ib.* xi.
Pilkington (Jo.) : brother of the bishop, and an archdeacon, *Pil.* v.
Pilkington (Lau.) : brother of the bishop, and vicar of Norham, *Pil.* v.
Pilkington (Leon.) : succeeds his brother, the bishop, as master of St John's, *Park.* 147 n., *Pil.* v; legacy to him, *Pil.* xi.
Pilkington (Rich.), of Rivington park: the bishop's father, *Pil.* i; built Rivington church, *ib.* xi.
Pilkinton (Barth.), alias Traheron, *q. v.*

---

* Not in his Works, save that a part of the letter in *Park.* 221, is in *Pil.* vii. A defect in the former copy (*Park.* 222 n) is supplied by the latter.

Pill: to peel, strip, plunder, rob; pilleth, 2 *Brad.* 346; pilled, i. e. stripped, bald, *Bale* 36, 1 *Brad.* 44, 2 *Brad.* 218, 1 *Tyn.* 117 n., 227
Pillars: the badge of some order of prelates, 1 *Tyn.* 246, 3 *Tyn.* 81; pillars and pole-axes carried before cardinals, 2 *Jew.* 1020; Peter, James, and John called pillars, 4 *Bul.* 123
Pill-pates: pilled or polled heads, shavelings, 2 *Bec.* 315
Pin (L. E. du): *v.* Du Pin.
Pinamonti (J. P.): Exorcista rite edoctus, *Calf.* 318 n
Pinczov, Poland: 3 *Zur.* 687; a synod there, *ib.* 602 n.; reformation there, *ib.* 690
Pindar: calls God ἀριστότεχνον, 1 *Jew.* 501; terms life σκίας ὄναρ, *Wool.* 108; believed the soul to be immortal, 3 *Bul.* 385; his house at Thebes spared by Alexander, 2 *Brad.* 372 n
Pinder (Rachel): does penance at Paul's cross for pretending to be possessed, *Park.* 465 n
Pindfools: pixes so called, 1 *Hoop.* 527
Pining (v. a.): wearing out, 1 *Brad.* 387
Pinkie: a great victory over the Scots there, 2 *Cran.* 417, 1 *Hoop.* xi, 3 *Zur.* 43
Pinsons: pincers, 2 *Bec.* 65
Pipes: rolls, "the rolls and pipes of memory," 3 *Jew.* 330
Pirithous (......): *Grin.* 234 n
Pisanus (Barth.): *v.* Bartholomew.
Piscator (Jo.): on Christ's descent into hell, *Rog.* 61 n
Pistorius (Jo.): Vet. Script. Germ., *Jew.* xlii.
Pistorius (......): concerned in abp Hermann's book of reformation, 2 *Zur.* 18 n
Pit (The bottomless): opened, *Bale* 351
Pitcairn (Rob.): 2 *Zur.* 365 n
Pitho, Suada, or Suadela: 4 *Bul.* 265
Pithœus (Fra.): Codex Canonum vetus, *Calf.* 246 n
Pits (Jo.): notice of him, *Poet.* xxxv; Psalm c. in metre, *ib.* 387
Pits (Jo.): his library, 1 *Ful.* xiv.
Pity: foolish pity not to be shewn by magistrates, 2 *Bec.* 310, 311, 1 *Bul.* 353, *Sand.* 226
Pius I., pope: praises custom, *Calf.* 54 n.; prescribes what must be done if in the eucharist any of the blood drop upon the ground, 3 *Bec.* 437; says, it profits a man nothing to fast and pray, except the mind be refrained from ungodliness, 1 *Bec.* 109, 2 *Bec.* 534; supposititious order about the keeping of Easter-day, 2 *Ful.* 237, 2 *Hoop.* 233, *Pil.* 601; the chronicle of Eusebius corrupted to maintain the falsehood, 2 *Ful.* 237 n.; the third spurious epistle adduced by J. H. Newman, *ib.* 81 n

Pius II., pope (previously called Æneas Sylvius, and surnamed Piccolomini): forbade appeals to a council from the pope, and determined that any one so appealing is a heretic, 1 *Jew.* 68, 3 *Jew.* 216; said that evil physicians kill bodies, unwise priests souls, 1 *Bec.* 9; monopolized the alum trade, 1 *Lat.* 181 n

— Æneæ Sylvii Opera, *Jew.* xxxii; De Origine Bohemorum, *Bale* 11; De Gestis Basil. Concil., 2 *Brad.* 160 n., *Rid.* 374; he declares that before the council of Nice small regard was had to the church of Rome, 1 *Jew.* 386, 441, 3 *Jew.* 306, 4 *Jew.* 996; calls it ruin to the church to say that no council may be kept without consent of the pope, 4 *Jew.* 827, 998 (when pope, he spoke differently; see above); says others besides bishops had a voice in councils, 3 *Jew.* 206, 4 *Jew.* 1026; rejects the papistical etymology of the name Cephas, 2 *Ful.* 302 n.; declares that the decree containing Constantine's donation is utterly false, 4 *Jew.* 678; says, we are bound to withstand any man to the face, whether he be Peter or Paul, if he walk not after the truth of the gospel, 3 *Jew.* 285, 4 *Jew.* 875; asks what should be done if a wicked pope teach things contrary to the faith, 4 *Jew.* 928; states that if the bishop of Rome will not hear the church, he will not hear Christ, and must be taken as a heathen and a publican, 3 *Jew.* 223; asserts that many popes have been found heretics, or defiled with other devices, *ib.* 345; says that if a bishop speak against the pope, although he speak the truth, he sinneth against his oath, 2 *Jew.* 996, 4 *Jew.* 948; shews how the Hussites were persecuted on account of the cup in the sacrament, 2 *Jew.* 979; testifies that consent was given to the Bohemians to have communion in both kinds, 2 *Bec.* 245 n.; speaks of permission being conceded to the Sclavonians, &c., of having service in their own tongue, 3 *Bec.* 410, 1 *Jew.* 291, 335, *Pil.* 500; mentions an opinion that at Christ's passion the faith remained only in Mary, 3 *Jew.* 268; says charity is waxen cold, and faith is dead, 4 *Jew.* 874; acknowledges abuse in restraining priests' marriage, and would have it restored, 1 *Jew.* 62, 2 *Jew.* 830, 993, 3 *Jew.* 182, 417, 424, 427, *Pil.* 566, 656; mentions the epistle of Udalric on this subject, *ib.* 687; says, a married man, having his wife alive, may be chosen pope, 3 *Jew.* 395; describes the Adamites, *Rog.* 101 n.; speaks of the poor men of Lyons, 4 *Jew.* 737; his retractations, 2 *Ful.* 302 n.; his writings censured, *ib.*

Pius IV., pope: murdered cardinal Caraffa in prison, 4 *Jew.* 1146; set up the cross in the church, 2 *Ful.* 159; confirmed the empire to Ferdinand, *Grin.* 21 n.; his alleged offer to confirm the English Prayer Book, *Lit. Eliz.* xxii; he reassembled the council of Trent, but prejudged all Protestants for heretics, 4 *Jew.* 1114, 2 *Zur.* 60 n.; copy of his creed, 4 *Jew.* 1310, 1311; his Index, *Calf.* 95 n.; his cardinals sought to depose him, 3 *Jew.* 202

Pius V., pope: declared Rome " magis Gentilizare quam Christianizare," *Rog.* 182; baptized the duke of Alva's standard, *ib.* 266; subsidized the duke of Savoy, 2 *Zur.* 171; copy of his bull against queen Elizabeth, 4 *Jew.* 1131; notices of it, and remarks upon it, *Grin.* 328, 2 *Jew.* 906, *Lit. Eliz.* 655 n., 657 n., *Pil.* 623 n., 1 *Zur.* 221, 229, 238, 2 *Zur.* 179; A VIEW OF A SEDITIOUS BULL, &c., by bp Jewel, 4 *Jew.* 1127—1160; the bull answered by Bullinger, 4 *Bul.* xxv, *Grin.* 328, 4 *Jew.* 1129 n., 1 *Zur.* 221, 242—244, 258, 266, 268, 269, 2 *Zur.* 178 n., 179, 183, 192; the Missale published by his command, 2 *Ful.* 21 n.; his Censures of the Gloss, *Calf.* 6 n

Pix, or Pyx: the box in which the host is reserved, *Bale* 168, 1 *Brad.* 88, 392, *Hutch.* 253, 347, 3 *Tyn.* 268; distinguished from the tabernacle or ciborium, 4 *Bul.* 449 n., 2 *Jew.* 560; the pix, and canopy, 2 *Jew.* 553, &c.; the pix suspended over the altar, *Hutch.* 347, *Pil.* 129; sometimes made in the form of a dove, 1 *Jew.* 188, 192, 2 *Jew.* 559, &c.; called a monster [monstrance], 2 *Jew.* 561; pixes to be destroyed, *Grin.* 135, 159; the pix of the mint at Canterbury, 2 *Cran.* 357

Placard: edict, proclamation, 1 *Brad.* 60, 73

Placcius (Vinc.): Theatrum Anon. et Pseudon., *Calf.* 69 n., 2 *Ful.* 103 n

Placebo: the office for the dead, *Bale* 330 (*v.* Dirige).

Placidia (Galla), empress: her epistle to Theodosius her father, 2 *Ful.* 363

Placilla, wife of Theodosius: her piety, *Pil.* 386

Plague: *v.* Prayers, Psalms, Thanksgivings.

Pestilence threatened to despisers of God's word, 1 *Bec.* 469, 470; it is an extraordinary magistrate to reform and punish sin, 2 *Hoop.* 166; the causes of it, *ib.* 161, 165; its nature and condition, *ib.* 163; sundry occasions of it, *ib.* 166, 167; precepts in plague-time, *Grin.* 258; the only remedy for it, 2 *Hoop.* 165, 168; who may not flee from it, *ib.* 168; the best preservative from pestilence, *ib.* 169; Christ's medicine for it, *ib.* 170, 173; the plague in 1537, 2 *Lat.* 380; in London, 1548, 3 *Zur.* 646; the plague or sweating-sickness in London and throughout England, 1551, 1 *Brad.* 61, 445, 2 *Brad.* xxiv, 66, 2 *Hoop.* 139, 159, *Lit. Eliz.* 450, 3 *Zur.* 94, 496, 575 n., 679, 727; letter from the king to the bishops respecting it, 2 *Cran.* 531; direction for service on Mondays, Wednesdays, and Fridays, during the sweating sickness, 2 *Hoop.* 139; Hooper's homily for the occasion, *ib.* 161; plague in London and elsewhere, 1563, *Grin.* vii, 77, 78, 79, *Lit. Eliz.* 459, 460, 493, *Park.* 182—184, 1 *Zur.* 132, 2 *Zur.* 109, 114 n.; it first appeared among the English army, at Newhaven, near Boulogne, *Grin.* 77, 1 *Zur.* 132; Thirlby and Boxall removed from the Tower, *Park.* 192—195; letters about the fast, *Grin.* 257, &c.; services for the occasion, *ib.* 75, &c., *Lit. Eliz.* 478, &c.; notification to be given to the curates of London, *Grin.* 78; dean Nowel's homily for the occasion, *ib.* 79, 96, *Lit. Eliz.* 491; a form of meditation...to be daily used of householders, *Lit. Eliz.* 503; remedy against infection suggested by bishop Grindal, *Grin.* 268; fires in the streets, *ib.* 270; perfumes, &c., recommended as a precaution against contagion, *Lit. Eliz.* 503; the plague in Chiavenna, 1563, 2 *Zur.* 110 n., 113; feared at Canterbury, 1564, *Park.* 208; in London and Lambeth, 1574, *ib.* 466; the plague of 1593, Bartholomew fair not kept, *Lit. Eliz.* 471; great mortality (at that time?), *Poet.* 465; plague in Scotland, 1602, 2 *Zur.* 335

Plagues: *v.* Prayers.

Plagues must constrain those whom benefits will not win, *Sand.* 151; they cannot be resisted, *Pil.* 72; if despised, they bring greater, *ib.* 176; they are to be considered, *ib.* 173—175, 180; the cause of them to be searched out, *ib.* 50, 180; they come from God,—yet man sins in plaguing, *ib.* 220; the wicked plague one another, *ib.* 246; they are commonly brought by false religion, *ib.* 73; by evil teaching, 2 *Cran.* 14; their difference under popery and the gospel, *Pil.* 85; were greater then than since, *ib.* 606; the plague of one a warning to others, *ib.* 175

Plain as a pack-staff: 2 *Brad.* 319
Plancher: cornice, *Park.* 231
Plantagenet (Geo.), duke of Clarence: *v.* George; and so with other princes of the family.
Plantagenet (Arthur), visc. Lisle: notice of him, 2 *Cran.* 298 n.; his government at Calais, *ib.* 376 n.; extracts from his letters to the king, *ib.* 495 n.; he opposes the gospel at Calais, 3 *Zur.* 220; is sent to the Tower, *ib.*; letters to him, 2 *Cran.* 298, 316, 318, 320, 322, 324, 390, 391, 393
Plantagenet (Marg.), countess of Salisbury: *v.* Pole.
Plat: plot, *Calf.* 48; its derivation, *ib.* n
Plate: Cranmer refers to Cromwell a proposition concerning the weight of plate, 2 *Cran.* 335
Platform: The Piteous Platforme of an Oppressed Mynde, by G. C.; notice thereof, *Poet.* xxiv; an extract, *ib.* 266
Platina (B.): De Vitis et Gestis Summ. Pontif., *Jew.* xlii, 3 *Whitg.* xxxi; he tells what Anacletus decreed about the sacrament, 2 *Bec.* 258, 3 *Bec.* 474; says that Alexander I. brought in wafer-cakes, 3 *Whitg.* 82; and ordained holy water, *Pil.* 601; in Sixtus I. he tells how the mass was pieced together, 3 *Jew.* 434, *Pil.* 503, 3 *Whitg.* 73 n.; he ascribes the institution of Lent to Telesphorus, *Whita.* 508, and says that he ordained the Gloria in excelsis, 3 *Whitg.* 99; his account of the supposed ordinance of Hyginus respecting sponsors, *Calf.* 212 n.; he tells of an order of Pius I. respecting Easter, 2 *Hoop.* 233, *Pil.* 601; in Eleutherius, he speaks of the British flamines, 2 *Whitg.* 127; he mentions an ordinance of pope Lucius on meats, *Pil.* 514; declares that Marcellinus sacrificed to idols, *ib.* 601; reference to the life of Silvester, 1 *Hoop.* 276; he states that Liberius was an Arian heretic, 3 *Jew.* 342, 343, 4 *Jew.* 929, *Pil.* 601; says that the emperor Constantius deposed Liberius, and afterwards, restoring Liberius, deposed pope Felix, 4 *Jew.* 682; affirms that Felix was an Arian, *Pil.* 601; mentions riots at the election of Damasus I., 1 *Whitg.* 463; says that Damasus ordained the antiphonal singing of the Psalms, 3 *Whitg.* 385 n.; mentions that Anastasius I. ordered standing at the gospel, 3 *Whitg.* 384 n.; says pope Boniface I. was the son of Jucundus a priest, 3 *Jew.* 394; states that he first divided priest from people in the time of the ministration of the sacrament, 1 *Jew.* 311; in Celestine I. he relates how Satan destroyed certain Jews in Crete, 2 *Cran.* 50; says that this pope brought in the introit, 3 *Whitg.* 73 n.; in Leo I. he refers to Mamercus of Vienne, *Calf.* 295 n., 2 *Whitg.* 480; he notices that Gelasius condemned the Manichees to exile, 1 *Jew.* 257; declares that Anastasius II. was an Arian, *Pil.* 601; says that John I. went on an embassy in favour of the Arians, *ib.* 602; speaks of sedition at the election of Boniface II., 1 *Whitg.* 463; on Agapetus, *Calf.* 259 n.; on Silverius, 2 *Ful.* 99 n.; he says that this pope was the son of bishop Hormisda, 3 *Jew.* 394; relates the opposition of Gregory I. to the name of universal bishop, 2 *Hoop.* 234; mentions that Sabinian the pope commanded all Gregory's writings to be burned, 4 *Jew.* 1110; in Boniface III. he says it was the custom to ask how much the bishoprick was worth, not how many sheep were in it, 2 *Tyn.* 255 n.; speaks of this pontiff obtaining of the emperor Phocas that Rome should be called the head of all churches, 1 *Hoop.* 226, 2 *Hoop.* 235, 3 *Jew.* 311, 316, 2 *Tyn.* 258 n., 1 *Whitg.* 232; testifies, in Boniface V., to the covetousness of the papal clergy, 2 *Tyn.* 255 n.; in Severinus I. he says, without the emperor's letters patent the pope was no pope, 3 *Jew.* 334, 4 *Jew.* 699, 2 *Tyn.* 255 n.; and tells how Isacius seized the treasures of the Lateran, 2 *Tyn.* 255 n.; in Agatho he refers to the first Latin mass at Constantinople, 2 *Brad.* 311; mentions riots at the election of Conon, 1 *Whitg.* 463, and at that of Sergius I., *ib.*; mentions that this pope introduced the Agnus Dei in the mass, 2 *Jew.* 586 n.; says that pope Constantine approved images, and had certain saints painted in St Peter's, 2 *Bec.* 71 n.; states that Zachary absolved the French from their allegiance, and made Pepin king, *Pil.* 602; on Stephen II., *ib.*; in Stephen III. he mentions riots at the election of Constantine, 1 *Whitg.* 463; he speaks also of disorders when Paul I. was chosen, *ib.*; in Adrian I. he mentions how Corsica came to the see of Rome, 2 *Tyn.* 261 n.; he says that the feet of this pope were kissed by Charlemagne, 4 *Jew.* 688; states that Leo III. made Charlemagne emperor, *ib.* 672, 680; that he instituted rogation days, *Calf.* 295 n.; and allowed the (so-called) blood of Christ at Mantua, *Pil.* 602; says that Adrian II. was son of a priest, 3 *Jew.* 394; in his life he relates how the emperor praised the Roman people for their choice of the high priest,

1 *Whitg.* 402; he relates the story of pope Joan, *Pil.* 602; allows that almost all affirm that history, 4 *Jew.* 655, 656; tells of Adrian III.'s encroachments on the power of the emperor, 2 *Tyn.* 267 n.; says, in Formosus I., that the emperors had lost their power, and the popes their virtue, 1 *Jew.* 415, 2 *Jew.* 1081, 3 *Jew.* 172; says that Stephen disinterred Formosus, 3 *Jew.* 249, 276, 1 *Tyn.* 234 n.; tells how he persecuted the name of Formosus, and speaks of petty popes who did nothing but deface the names of their predecessors, 1 *Hoop.* 217, 3 *Jew.* 219, 276; says that after Stephen it became customary for popes to abolish the acts of those who went before them, 4 *Jew.* 750, 751, 773, 1 *Tyn.* 324 n.; affirms that Romanus abrogated the decrees of Stephen, 1 *Hoop.* 217, 1 *Tyn.* 324 n.; in his life, he calls some popes monsters, 3 *Jew.* 347; says that Theodore II. restored the acts of Formosus, 1 *Hoop.* 217; tells that John IX. did the like, 1 *Tyn.* 324 n.; in Benedict IV. he calls some popes monsters, &c., 4 *Jew.* 702, 1013; he tells that Leo V. was cast into prison by Christopher, who assumed his place, but soon fled, 1 *Hoop.* 217; declares that John X. was son of a priest, 3 *Jew.* 394; says that he restored the acts of Formosus, 1 *Hoop.* 217; in Agapetus II. he tells how Otho became emperor, 2 *Tyn.* 269 n.; in John XII. he speaks of the translation of the empire to Germany, *ib.*; he says the emperor Otho I. deposed pope John XIII., 4 *Jew.* 682, 1034; censures him, 4 *Jew.* 702; tells that after him the emperor chose Leo to be pope, 1 *Whitg.* 403; relates the history of Leo VIII., his election, deposition, and restoration, 1 *Whitg.* 401; says John XV. was son of a priest, 3 *Jew.* 394; in his life he praises Odilus and Berengarius, 1 *Hoop.* 124; tells of Gregory V.'s institution of the seven electors in Germany, 2 *Tyn.* 270 n.; says that Silvester II. was a sorcerer, and sold himself to the devil, *Calf.* 91, 92, 1 *Jew.* 381, *Pil.* 602; censures Benedict IX. and says he sold the popedom to John the archdeacon, 4 *Jew.* 702; declares that he sold himself to the devil, *Pil.* 602, 603; in Sylvester III. he says that popes were then elected, not for learning or holiness, but through friendship and money, 4 *Jew.* 702; says Victor III. died not without suspicion of being poisoned, 1 *Hoop.* 451; states that Alexander III. moved men to sedition, 2 *Hoop.* 240; censures Boniface VIII.,

1 *Hoop.* 569 n.; says that he brought in the Romish jubilee, 2 *Bul.* 266; speaks of the multitudes who crowded the city of Rome in the year of jubilee, *ib.* 267, 268; how Innocent VI. gave benefices, 1 *Bec.* 384; says that he forbade non-residence, *ib.* 385; relates the history of pope John XXIV., 4 *Jew.* 934, 937; records Pius II.'s approval of the marriage of priests, 1 *Jew.* 62 n., 3 *Jew.* 419, *Pil.* 566; mentions a saying of his, 1 *Bec.* 9; describes the pride of Paul II., *Pil.* 99, 602 n.; referred to as censuring Adrian VI., 4 *Jew.* 737; he mentions many interruptions and schemes in the popedom, *Whita.* 510; speaks of St Bridget, 1 *Hoop.* 291 n.; his evidence concerning litanies and the rogation-days, *Calf.* 295 n

Plato: cited, 1 *Bec.* 4, 2 *Bec.* 5, 137, 382, 420, 421, 1 *Brad.* 360 n., 376 n., 1 *Bul.* 273, 274, 338, 2 *Bul.* 219, 393, 3 *Bul.* 134, 356, 385, 4 *Bul.* 480, *Calf.* 25 n., 1 *Cov.* 503, 1 *Cran.* 331, 1 *Ful.* 232 n., &c., 1 *Hoop.* 351, 2 *Hoop.* 84, 85, *Hutch.* 176, 1 *Jew.* 96, 500, 501, 2 *Jew.* 1018, 3 *Jew.* 179, 560, 4 *Jew.* 651, 700, 2 *Lat.* 317, *Sand.* 137, *Whita.* 118, 3 *Whitg.* 428, *Wool.* 13, 99 n., 3 *Zur.* 310

Platonists: their opinion of the soul, 3 *Bul.* 374; the later ones, 1 *Lat.* 202 n

Plausible: giving applause, rejoicing, 1 *Bec.* 141

Plautus cited, 1 *Cran.* 262, 4 *Jew.* 854, *Pil.* 215

Play wily beguile (To): 1 *Brad.* 375, 2 *Brad.* 49, 340

Players: *v.* Drama.

Playhouses: tolerated, *Nord.* 177

Playter (Tho.): letter signed by him, *Park.* 307

Pleasure: *v.* Meditations.

To abound in pleasures in this life is dangerous, 2 *Bec.* 633; granted pleasures, 1 *Bul.* 420, 2 *Bul.* 55; our pleasures are vanities; verses by D. Sand, *Poet.* 300; true pleasure, 1 *Cov.* 513

Pleat: to plead, *Bale* 325

Plebani: secular parish priests, 4 *Bul.* 116

Pledges: 2 *Bul.* 36, 228

Plessis (Phil. du): *v.* Mornay.

Pliny the elder: Nat. Hist., 1 *Bec.* 114, 343, 2 *Bul.* 144, 4 *Bul.* 261, *Calf.* 47, 1 *Cran.* 24, 331, 2 *Ful.* 339, *Grin.* 7, 1 *Hoop.* 297, 328, 359, 365, 2 *Hoop.* 164, 168, *Jew.* xlii, 1 *Jew.* 57, 272, 274, 276, 283, 528, 4 *Jew.* 861, 892, *Sand.* 396, *Whita.* 516, *Wool.* 111

Pliny the younger: 1 *Cov.* 101, 1 *Hoop.* 392, *Pil.* 231, 428; he (?) calls the religion of the Jews the despising of all gods, 2 *Jew.* 1025; writes to Trajan about the Christians,

1 *Bec.* 17, 4 *Bul.* 166, 193, 2 *Hoop.* 615, *Hutch.* 228 n., 2 *Jew.* 1002, 1089, *Phil.* 19, *Pil.* 333, 2 *Whitg.* 492

Plot: *v.* Plat.

Plough, Ploughmen: Latimer's sermons on the plough, 1 *Lat.* 59, &c.; ploughing on the sabbath (die solis), 1 *Bul.* 265; ploughmen and princes equal before God, 1 *Lat.* 249, 343; what food, &c. is requisite for the former, *ib.* 249; they are instructed in the resurrection by corn sown, better than by a crucifix, 1 *Hoop.* 45; Tyndale's New Testament for the use of ploughmen, 1 *Tyn.* lxxiii; specimen of it, 3 *Tyn.* 287; The Ploughman's Prayer, mentioned by More, 1 *Tyn.* 3

Plowland, or Carucate: 1 *Tyn.* 236

Plowman: *v.* Piers.

Pluckley, co. Kent: 2 *Cran.* 367 n

Plumbe (Will.): 1 *Bec.* 61 n

Plumtree (......), a priest: executed at Durham, 1 *Zur.* 225 n

Pluralities: *v.* Benefices, Church II. iv, Councils, *Nice II.*

On pluralities of benefices, 4 *Bul.* 144, *Hutch.* 5, 1 *Lat.* 122, 1 *Whitg.* 506, &c.; they are hurtful to the church, 2 *Brad.* 395, 2 *Jew.* 984; papists hunt for them, *Pil.* 255; popes have sanctioned them, 2 *Tyn.* 275, 288, 3 *Tyn.* 42; Antichrist dispenses with them, 3 *Bec.* 534, 535; an act of Henry VIII. for restraining them, 2 *Lat.* 301 n., 2 *Tyn.* 336; it contains a clause making employment at court an excuse for non-residence and pluralities, 2 *Tyn.* 256, 336; Clement VII. authorizes his nephew to take possession of all vacant benefices throughout Christendom, and to hold them for six months, *ib.* 275 n.; Whitgift defends them, 1 *Whitg.* 528, &c.; dispensations for them, *Grin.* 449

Plutarch: cited, 1 *Bul.* 201, 309, 338, 347, 3 *Bul.* 124, *Calf.* 14 n., 317 n., 1 *Hoop.* 297, 484, 1 *Jew.* 22, 50, 2 *Jew.* 991, 4 *Jew.* 805, 865, 912, *Pil.* 377, *Sand.* 38, *Whita.* 218

Pluto: called 'Αἴδης, 1 *Ful.* 316

Pneumatomachi: a term applied to the Arian and Macedonian heretics, *Phil.* 382 n., *Rog.* 45, 70

Pocularies: what, 1 *Lat.* 49 n

Pœna et culpa: 2 *Bec.* 174, 3 *Bec.* 144, 233, 605, *Rid.* 55, 418, 1 *Tyn.* 271, 342, 3 *Tyn.* 103, 141, 154

Poetry: *v.* Psalms.

SELECT POETRY, CHIEFLY DEVOTIONAL, OF THE REIGN OF QUEEN ELIZABETH; collected and edited by Edw. Farr, esq., *Poet.*;

extracts from Spenser respecting Grindal, *Grin.* xiii. n.; the word poetry used for fiction or falsehood, 2 *Tyn.* 268, 3 *Tyn.* 121, 122, 131

INDEX

of the first lines of the English poetry.

A blast of wind, a momentary breath, *Poet.* 49
A husbandman within thy church by, *ib.* 141
A joyful thing to man it is, *ib.* 2
A lofty heart, a lifted eye, *ib.* 77
A mighty spire, whose top doth pierce, *ib.* 203
A new-year's gift more precious, 1 *Bec.* 306
A righteous man still feareth all his, *Poet.* 242
Adieu, deceitful world, thy pleasures, *ib.* 209
Adieu, my former pleasure, *ib.* 228
Alack, when I look back, *ib.* 153
Alas! poor fame, in what a narrow room, *ib.* 398
Alexander our holy father, the pope, *Rid.* 54
All creatures of the eternal God but, *Poet.* 386
All English hearts rejoice and sing, *ib.* 420
All flesh is grass, and withereth like, *ib.* 207
All glory unto God, *ib.* 546
All people to Jehovah bring, *ib.* 60
All that is and shall be set upon, *Lit. Edw.* 374
Although the purple morning brags, *Poet.* 398
And is there care in heaven? And is, *ib.* 30
An hundred tongues, 2 *Cov.* 205
As candles light do give, *Poet.* 475
As falls the tree, so prostrate still it lies, *ib.* 458
As for thy gifts we render praise, *Lit. Eliz.* 560
As I lay musing in my bed, *Poet.* 213
As rain makes every ground bring, *ib.* 456
As Sion standeth, very firmly stedfast, *ib.* 75
As those three kings, touch'd with a, *ib.* 49
At last he came unto a gloomy glade, *ib.* 29
At the rivers of Babylon, 2 *Cov.* 571
Awake, each English wight, *Poet.* 399
Awake from sleep, and watch awhile, *ib.* 154
Aye, now I see that mourning follows, *ib.* 358
Be glad now, all ye Christian men, 2 *Cov.* 550
Be light and glad, in God rejoice, *Lit. Eliz.* 558
Be thankful, O my soul, unto the, 3 *Bec.* 221
Because ye have committed sin, *Poet.* 518
Before the world I here recant my life, *ib.* 339
Before thy face, and in thy sight, *ib.* 155
Behold and see, forget not this, 2 *Cov.* 583
Behold now give heed, such as be, *Poet.* 502
Behold the blast which blows, *ib.* 300
Blessed are all that fear the Lord, 2 *Cov.* 573
Blessed are all that fear the Lord, *ib.*
Blessed Creator! let thine only Son, *Poet.* 41
Both gods and men abhor, 2 *Bul.* 28
Break thou the jaws of old Levyathan, *Poet.* 47
But human pureness none is such, *ib.* 377
But stay, my muse, I fear my Master's, *ib.* 434
But wilt thou know what is the sin of, *ib.* 372
But yet the good which we by sin receive, *ib.* 248
By Adam's fall, 2 *Cov.* 556

By Babel's brooks we sit and weep, *Poet.* 116
By Euphrates' flow'ry side, *ib.* 328
By thee the path of heavenly health, *ib.* 554
Call unto mind, O mighty Lord, *ib.* 121
Calm thy tempestuous thoughts, my, *ib.* 321
Care for thy soul as thing of greatest, *ib.* 223
Charity is the only staff and stay, *ib.* 402
Christ died and suffer'd great pain, 2 *Cov.* 563
Christ is now risen again, *ib.*
Christ is the only Son of God, *ib.* 553
Cloth'd with state, and girt with might, *ib.* 71
Come all the world, *ib.* 381
Come, Holy Ghost, eternal God, *Lit. Edw.* 172, 342, *Lit. Eliz.* 286
Come, Holy Ghost, eternal God, *Poet.* 292
Come, Holy Ghost, our souls, *Calf.* 226 n
Come, Holy Spirit, most blessed, 2 *Cov.* 542
Come, let us lift up our voice, *Poet.* 484
Come sharpest griefs, employ repentant, *ib.* 347
Come wend unto my garden gay, *ib.* 516
Content thyself with patience, 2 *Hoop.* xxx.
Corrupt and filthy are we all, *Nord.* 77
Could He begin, beginnings that, *Poet.* 243
David in this psalm doth exhort, *ib.* 387
Dear dames, your senses to revive, *ib.* 178
Dear David's Son! whom thy forefathers, *ib.* 43
Death made her free from worldly carke, *ib.* 553
Do not correct me in thy wrath, O God, *ib.* 337
Do tyrants teach their people's hearts, *ib.* 547
Doubt not of this; forget it not, 1 *Bul.* 289
Down in the depth of mine iniquity, *Poet.* 116
Drooping and dying in depth of despair, *ib.* 369
England is blest and loved of God, *ib.* 346
Eternal Time that wastest without, *ib.* 453
Eternal Truth, almighty, infinite, *ib.* 108
Even as a flower, or like unto the grass, *ib.* 209
Even such is Time, which takes on trust, *ib.* 236
Except the Lord had been with us, 2 *Cov.* 571
Except the Lord himself will deign, *Poet.* 334
Except the Lord the house do build, *ib.* 449
Faith's best is trial, then it shineth most, *ib.* 455
Fellow of thy Father's light, *Pra. Eliz.* 33
Fools, that true faith yet never had, *Poet.* 1
For Thy name's sake be my refuge, *Bale* 184
Fortress of hope, anchor of faithful, *Poet.* 45
From deep gulphs of misfortune, *ib.* 326
From depth of dole wherein my soul doth, *ib.* 33
From out the depth of misery I cry, *ib.* 335
From pasture unto pasture he did the, *ib.* 540
From thence almost comes every, 1 *Bul.* 204
From virgin's womb this day did, 2 *Poet.* 291
Full of celestial syrups, full of sweet, *ib.* 48
Give ear, O Lord, to hear, *ib.* 157
Give laud unto the Lord, *Lit. Eliz.* 561
Give me my scallop-shell of quiet, *Poet.* 235
Give peace in these our days, O Lord, *ib.* 505
Go, little book, &c., 2 *Cov.* 534
Go on our days, we do on earth, *Poet.* 312

Go, soul, the body's guest, *ib.* 233
God be merciful unto us, 2 *Cov.* 580
God is my strength; in him I will, *Poet.* 468
God sits above and sees the sons, 1 *Bul.* 288
God, th' eternal God, no doubt is, *Poet.* 237
God the Father, dwell us by, 2 *Cov.* 543
God unto goodness so greatly is, 2 *Bec.* 174
God, who the universe doth hold, *Poet.* 319
Grace groweth after governance, 1 *Bec.* 395
Hast thou desire thy golden days to, *ib.* 215
Haste homewards, man, draw nearer, *Poet.* 211
Hatred eternal, furious revenging, *ib.* 452
Have mercy, O good God, on me, *ib.* 412
He did not nourish as he should, 1 *Bul.* 288
He that is King of glory, and, *Lit. Edw.* 374
Hear me, O hear me, when I call, *Poet.* 53
Heavenly Messias! sweet anointed King! *ib.* 43
Help now, O Lord, and look on us, 2 *Cov.* 567
Her only end is never-ending bliss, *Poet.* 86
Her sceptre was the rule of righteousness, *ib.* 556
Here is the spring where waters flow, *ib.* 469
Here man, who first should heavenly, *ib.* 208
Here man with axe doth cut the bough, *ib.* 208
Here they that did their brethren, 1 *Bul.* 289
Hereof hath God, 2 *Cov.* 217
Hereout, O Lord, the right request, *Poet.* 202
How do I use my paper, ink, and pen, *ib.* 224
How far that mercy reacheth, erst we, *ib.* 247
How good, and how beseeming well, *ib.* 77
How is the faithful city chang'd, *ib.* 520
How long, O Lord, shall I forgotten be? *ib.* 55
How Mary, &c., *Pra. Eliz.* 139 n., 151 n., 155 n
How need the soul to stand upon her, *Poet.* 245
How pleasant is thy dwelling-place, *ib.* 485
I am confest unto the priest, *Rog.* 110
I appeal, O God! to thee, *Poet.* 320
I call on thee, Lord Jesu Christ, 2 *Cov.* 560
I lift my soul, Lord, up to thee, *ib.* 578
I musing in my careful mind, *Poet.* 376
I praise my God who lends his ear, *Nord.* 150
I pray thee, Protestant, bear with me, *Poet.* 267
I saw an image, all of massy gold, *ib.* 24
I wailing, *ib.* 450
I will sing praise unto the Lord for aye, *ib.* 124
If all the joys that worldly wights, *ib.* 212
If deepest learning, with a zealous, 1 *Ful.* iv.
If ever Thou me love, *Poet.* 384
If God command the winds to cease, *ib.* 542
If greedy gaping after gain, 1 *Bul.* 204
If in a three-square glass, as thick as, *Poet.* 240
If unto us poor mortal men, *ib.* 197
Ill-favour'd envy, ugly hag, 1 *Bul.* 302
Images are made to put us in mind, *Hutch.* 10
Imaginary Muses, get you gone, *Poet.* 447
In God I trust, for so I must, 2 *Cov.* 547
In grief and anguish of my heart, *Poet.* 129
In heart where envy's seed takes, 1 *Bul.* 301
In loathsome race, pursued by, *Poet.* 308

In terror's trap with thraldom, *Poet.* 313
In th' act of sin the guilt of, *ib.* 242
In the midst of my misery, 2 *Brad.* 368
In the midst of our living, 2 *Cov.* 554
Inhabitants of heav'nly land, *Poet.* 84
It is a sweet and seemly thing, 1 *Bul.* 289
Jacob did see a ladder high, *Poet.* 394
Judas, that treason harbour'd in his, *ib.* 361
Judge not before, 2 *Cran.* 20
Laid in my quiet bed to rest, *Poet.* 218
Lamentably do I now proceed, 1 *Bec.* 352
Let go the whore of Babylon, 2 *Cov.* 586
Let us be glad, and clap our hands, *Poet.* 157
Life is a frost of cold felicity, *ib.* 457
Life is a wand'ring course to doubtful, *ib.* 457
Like as the armed knight, *Bale* 238
Like as the thief in prison cast, *Poet.* 217
Like as the wight, far banish'd from, *ib.* 215
Lion of Judah! which dost judge, *ib.* 42
Lo! how I grovelling under burden lie, *ib.* 142
Lo! how that thou art fair, *ib.* 341
Lord, at thy voice my heart for fear, *ib.* 127
Lord, how long, how long wilt thou, *ib.* 318
Lord, in thy house who shall for ever, *ib.* 332
Lord Jesus, let thy holy eyes reflect, *ib.* 523
Lord, let not me a worm by thee be, *ib.* 54
Lord, when I think how I offend thy, *ib.* 195
Love, lift me up upon thy golden wings, *ib.* 6
Make the great God thy fort, and, *ib.* 338
Man, dream no more of curious, *ib.* 107
Man is a little world, and bears the, *ib.* 306
Man, wilt thou live virtuously, 2 *Cov.* 545
Man's pleasures pass, respect them not, *ib* 266
Men talk of love that know not, *Poet.* 190
Mighty Lord, from this thy land, *ib.* 68
Mighty ruler, God most true, *Pra. Eliz.* 35
Most glorious Lord of life! that on, *Poet.* 32
My body in Christ, 2 *Cov.* 195
My heart doth in the Lord rejoice, *Poet.* 119
My heavenly Love, from that high, *ib.* 196
My soul doth magnify the Lord, 2 *Cov.* 565
My soul, give laud unto the Lord, *Poet.* 481
My sweet little baby, what meanest, *ib.* 506
My thirsty soul desires her drought, *ib.* 427
My wicked flesh, O Lord, with sin full, *ib.* 140
Nigh seated where the river flows, *ib.* 80
No kind of pain, 2 *Bec.* 447
No vainer thing there can be found, *Poet.* 391
Not unto us, Lord, not to us, *ib.* 198
Now blessed be these days of thine, *ib.* 368
Now blessed be thou, Christ Jesu, 2 *Cov.* 562
Now hath the great Creator, for, *Poet.* 253
Now is our health come from above, 2 *Cov.* 552
Now Pharaoh's daughter Termuth, *Poet.* 130
Now the cheerful day doth, *Pra. Eliz.* 20
Now when to Sina they approached, *Poet.* 134
O art, not much unlike the fowler's, *ib.* 315
O be ye joyful in the Lord, *ib.* 387

O benign Father! let my suits ascend, *ib.* 44
O blessed is the man at each, 3 *Bec.* 222
O Christ, that art the light and day, 2 *Cov.* 584
O Creator most benign, *Pra. Eliz.* 36
O endless power! O well-spring, *Poet.* 370
O false and treacherous probability, *ib.* 113
O Father, full of might and love, *Nord.* 160
O Father ours celestial, 2 *Cov.* 548
O Frenchmen, which were once, *Poet.* 467
O glorious conquest, and thrice, *ib.* 47
O glorious Patron of eternal bliss! *ib.* 45
O God be merciful to me, 2 *Cov.* 576
O God, from them that grudge me, *Poet.* 333
O God, my strength and fortitude, *ib.* 480
O God of gods, O Father great, *Nord.* 133
O God, that guid'st thy, *Nord.* 123, *Poet.* 462
O gracious God, and heavenly, *Poet.* 508
O gracious God, bow down thine ear, *ib.* 551
O great Creator of the starry pole, *ib.* 393
O hark awhile unto my style, *ib.* 200
O heaven, O earth! to thee I call, 3 *Brad.* 364
O heaven that art, 2 *Cov.* 214
O heavenly God! O Father dear! *Poet.* 316
O heavenly God that governs every, *ib.* 433
O heavenly Lord, thy godly word, 2 *Cov.* 584
O holy essence of all holiness, *Poet.* 187
O Holy Spirit our Comforter, 2 *Cov.* 541
O ignorant poor man! what dost, *Poet.* 96
O Jesu, if thou do withdraw, *ib.* 152
O Jesu, oft it grieveth me, *ib.* 152
O Jesu sweet, grant that thy grace, *ib.* 152
O Lamb of God, Christ, which, *Lit. Edw.* 375
O Lord, consider my distress, *Poet.* 489
O Lord God, have mercy on me, 2 *Cov.* 574
O Lord, how long wilt thou forget, *Poet.* 223
O Lord, in thee is all my trust (O. V.)
——— note thereon, *Pra. Eliz.* 374 n
O Lord, the Maker of all things, *ib.* 44
O Lord, the world's Saviour, *ib.* 41
O Lord, turn not away thy face, *Poet.* 473
O Lord, turn not thy face away (O. V.)
——— note thereon, *Pra. Eliz.* 374 n
O Lord, when I myself behold, *Poet.* 143
O Lord, who in thy sacred tent, *ib.* 222
O Nature, careful mother of us all, *ib.* 250
O our Father celestial, 2 *Cov.* 549
O praise the Lord where goodness, *Poet.* 79
O sinful soul, the cause of Jesus', *ib.* 349
O the glory eternal, *Pra. Eliz.* 37
O thou, that mad'st the world of, *Poet.* 147
O! what is man, great Maker of, *ib.* 95
O what is man? or whereof might, *ib.* 344
O you that serve the Lord, *ib.* 74
Of all the plagues that rain on mortal, *ib.* 451
Of Christ's body this is a token, 2 *Lat.* 294
Of Sabbath day the solemn feast, *Poet.* 2
Of things unseen how canst thou deem, *ib.* 30
Oft, and ever from my youth, *ib.* 76

POETRY   611

O Father, full of might and love, *Poet.* 463
O heavenly Lord! who plain dost, *ib.* 181
O heavenly Spirit of especial power, *ib.* 264
O! how profound are all thy judgments, *ib.* 443
O living Lord, I still will laud thy, *ib.* 126
O loving Lord, thou only didst defer, *ib.* 438
O! the sweet sense of love's humility, *ib.* 184
O! what a joyful thing it is, *Nord.* 32
O! why should man, that bears the, *Poet.* 408
On sweet and savoury bread of, *ib.* 142
Our Father which in heaven art, *ib.* 137
Our Father, which in heaven art, *ib.* 503
Our God is a defence and tower, 2 *Cov.* 569
Our God is good; why should we, *Nord.* 104
Out of the deep cry I to thee, 2 *Cov.* 577
Perhaps you think me bold, *Poet.* 297
Peruse with patience, I thee pray, *ib.* 161
Pity, O Lord, thy servant's heavy, *ib.* 184
Plant, Lord, in me the tree of godly life, *ib.*
Prais'd be the Lord of might, *ib.* 82
Praise him that aye, *ib.* 74
Praise the Lord, O ye Gentiles all, *ib.* 501
Praise thou the Lord, Hierusalem, 2 *Cov.* 582
Praise ye the Lord, for it is good, *Poet.* 487
Pray thus, when ye do pray, therefore, *ib.* 477
Pray we to God, the almighty, *Lit. Edw.* 375
Prepare a place above the skies, *Poet.* 365
Preserve us, Lord, by thy dear word, *Poet.* 494,
    Pra. Eliz. 412
Put not your trust in fading earth, *Poet.* 359
Rapt with the rage of mine own, *ib.* 15
Read me, and be not wroth, 1 *Tyn.* 39 n
Rejoice, O England blest! *Nord.* 44
Rejoice, rejoice, with heart and voice, *Poet.* 291
Relieve my soul with thy dear mercies', *ib.* 50
Remember, Lord, what hath betide, *ib.* 417
Remember your promise in baptism, 2 *Lat.* 294
Repair to Pilate's hall, *Poet.* 352
Ride on in glory, on the morning's wings, *ib.* 50
Rise, sinful man, look on the heavenly, *ib.* 390
Sacred, dear Father of all things created, *ib.* 51
Save, Lord, and bless with good, *Lit. Eliz.* 560
Save me, Lord; for why? thou art, *Poet.* 56
Shall clammy clay shroud such a gallant, *ib.* 400
Since God hath fix'd our days and years, *ib.* 511
Since thou hast not, O Lord, left me, *ib.* 406
Sing, and let the song be new, *ib.* 71
Sing unto the Lord with hearty accord, *ib.* 495
Sion lies waste, and thy Jerusalem, *ib.* 113
Sith God is ever changeless as He's good, *ib.* 246
So blind, O Lord, have my affections, *ib.* 141
Soiled in sins, O Lord! a wretched, *ib.* 514
Sole hope and blessing of old Israel's, *ib.* 44
Such as in God the Lord do trust, *ib.* 492
Such providence hath nature secret, *ib.* 205
Sweet Saviour! from whose fivefold, *ib.* 41
Teach the king's son, who king himself, *ib.* 62
That Christ did, that thou must die, *ib.* 395

The apostles have for help evangelists, *ib.* 466
The bird of day messenger, *Pra. Eliz.* 28
The bruiser of the serpent's head, *Poet.* 377
The foolish wicked men can say, 2 *Cov.* 581
The God of bliss, *Nord.* 85, *Poet.* 461
The God that fram'd the fixed pole, *Poet.* 396
The heav'nly frame set forth the fame, *ib.* 57
The highest tree is seldom times most, *ib.* 555
The house Jehovah builds not, *ib.* 75
The jewel of our joy is gone; the happy, *ib.* 512
The life is long which loathsomely doth, *ib.* 299
The lights of heaven (which are the, *ib.* 97
The Lord! He is my saving light, *ib.* 136
The Lord is our defence and aid, *Lit. Eliz.* 566
The Lord, most high, the Father, thus, *Poet.* 4
The Lord, the Lord my shepherd is, *ib.* 59
The Manicheans did no idol make, *ib.* 108
The meek and gentle pledge of mortal, *ib.* 422
The office of the mind is to have power, *ib.* 256
The ofter sin, the more grief shews, *ib.* 242
The pastor which the souls do feed, *ib.* 394
The pastors good, that do glad tidings, *ib.* 204
The pitiful compassion of God's best, *Rog.* 11
The poor man belov'd, for virtue, *Poet.* 471
The raging sea, that roars with fearful, *ib.* 206
The retchless race of youth's, *ib.* 415
The roaring sea doth fret and fume, *ib.* 465
The serpent sin, by shewing human, *ib.* 110
The sharpest edge will soonest pierce, *ib.* 359
The shepherd good doth watch his, *ib.* 394
The Sicil tyrants never found, 1 *Bul.* 302
The sin of pride made Lucifer, *Poet.* 379
The stately pine, whose branches, *ib.* 230
The sturdy rock, for all his strength, *ib.* 310
The thirsty soul that fainteth in the, *ib.* 470
The travelling man uncertain where, *ib.* 205
The wife that gads not, gigglot wise, 1 *Bul.* 398
The wishes of the wise, *Poet.* 175
The wretch is worse than mad, 1 *Bul.* 289
The wretched seas of worldly, *Poet.* 543
Thee will I laud, my God and King, *ib.* 497
Then let us leave this wretched world, *ib.* 363
These are the holy commandments, 2 *Cov.* 544
These hairs of age are messengers, *Poet.* 158
They that their faith's foundation lay, *ib.* 325
This is my steadfast creed, *ib.* 258
This wondrous Trinity in unity, *ib.* 247
This work is finished, thanks, 3 *Whitg.* 498 n
Those that do put their confidence, *Poet.* 493
Those which at home scorn'd Pharaoh, *ib.* 132
Thou Holy Spirit, we pray to thee, 2 *Cov.* 543
Thou knowest God; now, 3 *Bul.* 225, 226
Though David's reign be somewhat, *Poet.* 4
Though I be small in quantity, 2 *Bec.* 3
Though late, my heart, yet turn, *Poet.* 454
Though Sathan strive with all his main, *ib.* 207
Three furies fell, which turn the world, *ib.* 203
Thrice puissant General of true, *ib.* 46

612   POETRY

Through torments strange and, *Poet.* 207
Thy mercy, Lord, my faith persuades, *ib.* 364
'Tis only faith doth justify, *ib.* 380
To all the old and Catholic, *ib.* 549
To bed I go from you, *ib.* 403
To die, dame Nature man did frame, *ib.* 311
To him that while he lives doth love, 1 *Bul.* 289
To him the Highest keeps, *Poet.* 69
To mine humble supplication, *ib.* 322
To Noah and his sons with him, *ib.* 159
To pray to God continually, *ib.* 257
To say the soul is God, or part, 3 *Bul.* 373
To the intent the mighty power, *Poet.* 312
To thee my crying call, *ib.* 65
To thee, O God, we yield all, *Lit. Eliz.* 559
True love is charity begun to be, *Poet.* 241
Unto my spirit lend an angel's wing, *ib.* 48
Unto the hills I lift my eyes, *ib.* 137
Vouchsafe, O Lord! to be our guide, *ib.* 180
Wake up, wake up, in God's name, 2 *Cov.* 558
We believe all upon one God, *ib.* 546
We give thee thanks, O Father, *Lit. Edw.* 374
Weep not, but weep; stint tears, *Poet.* 357
Well were it with mankind, if what, *ib.* 397
Were man's thoughts to be measured, *ib.* 240
What if nations rage and fret? *ib.* 73
What is so sweet, so amiable, *ib.* 327
What is the world? A net to snare, *ib.* 307
What kind of state can any choose, *ib.* 478
What meanest thou, my friend, 1 *Bec.* 190
What means the raging minds, *Poet.* 525
What shall we do to thee, *Nord.* 63, *Poet.* 460
What state so sure, but time subverts, *Poet.* 226
What though the world, through, *ib.* 138
What wit hath man to leave that wealth, *ib.* 249
When Adam dalve and Eve span, *Pil.* 125
When after Christ's birth there, *Rog.* v, vi, n
When as contrariwise the wicked, *Poet.* 139
When as man's life, the light of human, *ib.* 107
When griping griefs do grieve the mind, *ib.* 479
When I behold the bier, *ib.* 303
When I look back, and in myself, *ib.* 302
When man is sick, then doth he seek, *ib.* 309
When shall this time of travail cease, *ib.* 175
When the angels all are singing, *ib.* 194
When thou hast spent the ling'ring day, *ib.* 38
When worthy Watts with constant cry, *ib.* 162
Where is thy mercy which exceeds, *ib.* 447
Where righteousness doth say, *ib.* 499
Where shall I, vex'd, my sinful head, *ib.* 51
Wherefore do the heathen now rage, 2 *Cov.* 568
Whiles in my soul I feel the soft, *Poet.* 241
Whilst in the garden of this earthly, *ib.* 140
White spotless Lamb! whose precious, *ib.* 42
Whitegift, whom gracious honour, *ib.* 306
Who dost desire to life to come, *Calf.* 391
Who doth not see the state of fickle, *Poet.* 459
Who fear the Lord are truly blest, *ib.* 115
Who fears not God shall not escape, *ib.* 139
Who loveth gold shall lack, and he, *ib.* 138
Who may, but will not help, doth hurt, *ib.* 380
Who seeks to tread that happy path, *ib.* 388
Who shall profoundly weigh or scan, *ib.* 314
Who would not travail all his life, *ib.* 389
Whoso will be accounted wise, *ib.* 295
Why did my parents send me to, *ib.* 100
Wisdom, elixir of the purest life, *ib.* 534
With misery enclos'd, *ib.* 324
With sobbing voice, with drowned eyes, *ib.* 330
Within did devilish envy sit, 1 *Bul.* 302
Within my garden plot, *Poet.* 117
Wrapt up, O Lord, in man's, *ib.* 109
Ye stately wights, that live in quiet rest, *ib.* 305
Yet shall my soul in silence still, *ib.* 61
You, readers, mark this well, and print, *ib.* 541
You that have spent the silent night, *ib.* 36
You that Jehova's servánts are, *ib.* 78
You therefore that remain on earth, *ib.* 231

INDEX

of the first lines of the Latin poetry.

Absque viro facta est fœcunda, *Pra. Eliz.* 413
Accipe præclarum, 1 *Cran.* 8
Æterni cœli gloria, *Pra. Eliz.* 149
———— O the glory eternal, *ib.* 37
Ales diei nuncius, *ib.* 141
———— The bird of day messenger, *ib.* 28
An ego campana nunquam, *Calf.* 15 n
Benedictus Deus in donis suis, *Pra. Eliz.* 400
Certius incerta nihil est mortalibus, *ib.* 418
Christe, qui lux es et dies, *ib.* 269
———— note on it, *ib.* 156 n
———— O Christ, that art the light, 2 *Cov.* 584
Christus ad æthereas cum vellet, *Pra. Eliz.* 404
Clamitat in cœlum, vox sanguinis, *Pil.* 463
Cognostis ipsum? nunc colendi, 3 *Bul.* 226
Confiteor, tundo, conspergor, *Rog.* 110
Consors paterni luminis, *Pra. Eliz.* 145, 254
———— Fellow of Thy Father's light, *ib.* 33
Corpora qui solito satiasti nostra, *ib.* 402
Credo in Deum Patrem, creavit omnia, *ib.* 403
Crucem tuam adoramus, 2 *Bec.* 72
Cum possit dubiis ecclesia pressa, 1 *Bec.* 33
Da, Deus, lætæ bona sancta, *Pra. Eliz.* 411
De cruce deponitur hora vespertina, *ib.* 151 n
Dolos maligne qui struunt, *ib.* 238
Dona tui serva nobis, Deus optime, *ib.* 412
Dulcis Iësu, *ib.* 238
Gratia magna tibi, Pater, et Rex, *ib.* 402
Hinc quæ ferre quæas, scitaris, 1 *Bec.* 33
His epulis donisq. tuis, *Pra. Eliz.* 400
Hoc est nescire, &c., *Rid.* 124
Hora completorii datur, *Pra. Eliz.* 155 n
Hostis non lædit, &c., *Pil.* 436
In primis, pueri, Christum, *Pra. Eliz.* 413

POETRY — POLE 613

Jam lucis orto sidera, *Pra. Eliz.* 134, 247
——— Now the cheerful day doth spring, *ib.* 20
Jam noctis umbras lucifer, *ib.* 406
Jam quinta lunæ cornua, *ib.* 417
Jam sol citato sidere, *ib.* 408
Jam vesper ortus incipit, *ib.* 409
Jam video peragenda mihi, &c., 4 *Jew.* 1305
Jesu beate, numinis, *Pra. Eliz.* 407
Jesu benigne, fervidas, *ib.* 406
Missa, malum, pejus quo secula, 3 *Bec.* 352
Mors, tua mors, Christe, *Poet.* 395
Nocte qua Christus rabidis, *Pra. Eliz.* 405
Nosco meum in, 2 *Cov.* 197 n., *Pra. Eliz.* 418
Numinis ira brevis, &c., *Pra. Eliz.* 238
O crux ave, spes unica, 1 *Jew.* 534
O Deus, appositis apponendisq., *Pra. Eliz.* 400
Omnes gentes laudent Dominum, *ib.* 401
Omnis in humanis vana est sapientia, *ib.* 408
Omnipotens, clemensque Deus, *ib.* 382
Omnium in hoc uno versatur summa, *ib.* 413
Patris sapientia, veritas divina, *ib.* 133 n
Perlege Bæconum, patria tibi voce, 1 *Bec.* 33
Præteriens hospes vacuum mirere, 3 *Bec.* 395
Primum sanguinei latices, *Pra. Eliz.* 415
Quæ nunc sumemus membris alimenta, *ib.* 400
Qui bibit inde, furit: procul hinc, 4 *Jew.* 1209
Qui cupis ad vitam renovari morte, *Calf.* 390
Quod sumus utilibus dapibus, *Pra. Eliz.* 402
Rector beate cœlitum, *ib.* 418
Rector potens, verax Deus, *ib.* 147
——— Mighty Ruler, God most true, *ib.* 35
Rerum Creator omnium, *ib.* 156, 264
——— note on it, *ib.* 131 n
——— O Lord, the maker of all things, *ib.* 44
Rerum Creator optime, *ib.* 148
——— O Creator most benign, *ib.* 36
Rex venit ad fores, jurans per urbis, 4 *Jew.* 692
Salva festa dies, 2 *Cran.* 412, 1 *Lat.* 207
Salvator mundi Domine, *Pra. Eliz.* 153
——— with a doxology, *ib.* 272
——— O Lord, the world's Saviour, *ib.* 41
——— a Latin prayer founded on it, *ib.* 131
Se nascens, dedit [in] socium, *ib.* 416
Summa Dei pietas veniam non, 2 *Bec.* 174
Summam quæ doceant salutis, *Pra. Eliz.* 416
Summe Parens, qui tecta tenes sublimia, *ib.* 403
Te lucis ante terminum, *ib.* 156 n
Te, sancte Jesu, mens mea, *ib.* 410
Tutela præsens omnium, *ib.*
Unum agnosce Deum, colas et unum, *ib.* 404
Unum crede Deum, nec jures vana per, *ib.*
Ut modo ponuntur languentia corpora, *ib.* 410
Veni Creator Spiritus, 1 *Cov.* 471 n
——— Come, *Lit. Edw.* 172, 342, *Lit. Eliz.* 286
——— Come, Holy Ghost, our souls, *Calf.* 226 n
——— Come Holy Spirit, most, 2 *Cov.* 542
Vidi et perlegi doctos, Bæcone, 1 *Bec.* 33
Vitam quæ faciunt beatiorem, *Pra. Eliz.* 416

See also the verses attached to the Calendars, *Lit. Eliz.* 326, *Pra. Eliz.* 213—234; likewise epitaphs in 3 *Bec.* 501 n., *Grin.* xvii, *Pil.* xiii, and some verses in 2 *Bec.* 174, 393, 3 *Bec.* 128, 2 *Bul.* 28, *Grin.* xiii. n., *Rog.* 110, 111, 3 *Whitg.* 498 n
Poets: *v.* Heathen.
 Their lying, 2 *Jew.* 660; hence the word poet is used for a feigner of things not true, 3 *Jew.* 249; their fantasies concerning musicians, 1 *Bec.* 264, &c.; notices of anonymous English poets, *Poet.* xxvii, xxxi, xxxv, xl bis, xli, xlii, xlv, li bis, lv.
Poh! horson knave, or, Poz! hosenknopf: a vulgar exclamation, 4 *Jew.* 1202, 1 *Zur.* 14, *ib.* (8)
Poinet (Jo.), bp: *v.* Ponet.
Poinings (Sir Tho.): *v.* Poynings.
Pointell: a pen, *Phil.* 376
Points: tags, or pins, *Park.* 472
Poison: administered in the sacrament, 1 *Cran.* 250, 255, 1 *Hoop.* 123, 451, 4 *Jew.* 685, &c.; the word used as an adjective, 1 *Tyn.* 17
Poissy: conference there, 2 *Ful.* 73, *Grin.* 244, 1 *Jew.* 89, 94, *Park.* 147, 1 *Zur.* 99 n
Poitiers: part of the cross there, *Calf.* 326
Poke: a bag or sack [whence pocket], 1 *Brad.* 71, 2 *Brad.* 319
Poland: its affairs, 3 *Zur.* 687—702; when the gospel was read, it was a custom for the king and others to stand up with naked swords, *Grin.* 56; reformation there, 3 *Zur.* 596, &c., 688, 690; Henry, duke of Anjou, elected king, 2 *Zur.* 223, 247, 250 nn.; the crown given to Stephen Batori, 2 *Zur.* 273 n.; a king there moved to take the style of head of the church, 1 *Whitg.* 392; various religions, 3 *Zur.* 690; the Polish diet, *ib.* 700
Polanus (Amandus): Sylloge Thes. Theol., 2 *Ful.* 291 n
Pole (Sir Rich.), K. G.: father of lord Montague and the cardinal, 3 *Zur.* 220, 625 n
——— Margaret (Plantagenet) his wife, daughter of Geo. duke of Clarence, created countess of Salisbury, *ib.* 220, 625 n
Pole (Hen. de la), lord Montacute or Montagu: 2 *Cran.* 386 n.; executed, 3 *Zur.* 625
Pole (Reg. card.): 1 *Bec.* 233, 4 *Jew.* 801, 1 *Lat.* 58, 173, 2 *Lat.* 411, 3 *Zur.* 207; a man of regal blood, and many excellent qualities, 2 *Cran.* 184, *Rid.* 257, 258, 277; his family, 3 *Zur.* 220; his quarrel with Henry VIII., 1 *Hoop.* 37; his treason, *Calf.* 49; in favour with pope Paul III., 2 *Cran.* 331, 4 *Jew.* 800; sent from prince to prince by the pope to stir up war against Henry

VIII., 2 *Cran.* 13; he counsels the emperor to make war against England, 3 *Jew.* 171; nobles beheaded for joining in his conspiracy, 3 *Zur.* 625; he was cardinal-deacon of St Mary in Cosmedin, *Rid.* 270; his pardon and promotion required by the Devonshire rebels, 2 *Cran.* 184; his recall by queen Mary, 3 *Zur.* 347, 741; privy councillor to her, 1 *Zur.* 5 n.; ambassador to France and Germany, *Rid.* 394; legate à latere, 2 *Lat.* 279, *Rid.* 255; he sent commissioners to Cambridge to purge the churches, *Pil.* 65; a priest accused before his commissioners, *Calf.* 331; on his letters to Cranmer, 2 *Cran.* 454 n.; his letter to Cranmer in answer to Cranmer's to the queen, *ib.* 534; made archbishop of Canterbury in the place of Cranmer, 3 *Zur.* 743; he placed the figure Y [the archiepiscopal pall] in the windows at Lambeth, *Calf.* 105; his income as archbishop, *Park.* xii; his death, 1 *Zur.* 3; carnal fool, a play upon his name, *Pil.* 77; his book Pro ecclesiast. Unitatis Defensione, against Henry VIII., 2 *Cran.* 184, *Jew.* xlii, 1 *Lat.* 173 n., 174, 198, *Pil.* 497; his arguments against the king's divorce stated, 2 *Cran.* 229—231; his reasons for the pope's supremacy, 1 *Jew.* 339; he says the name of king is odious, 1 *Lat.* 174; he wrote also De Baptismo Constantini, &c., *Jew.* xlii, 2 *Ful.* 360 n.; on the cross seen by Constantine, *Calf.* 110 n

Pole (Sir Geof.), brother of the cardinal: indicted for treason, 2 *Cran* 386 n

Pole (......), son of Hen. lord Montagu: attainted, 3 *Zur.* 207; not mentioned by historians, *ib.* x.

Pole (Arth.): convicted of treason, but pardoned, *Lit. Eliz.* 655 n., 1 *Zur.* 129 n.; his conspiracy instigated by the bishop of Aquila, the Spanish ambassador, 1 *Zur.* 102 n

Pole (Edm.): designed to marry Mary queen of Scots; was convicted of treason, but pardoned, *Lit. Eliz.* 655 n., 1 *Zur.* 129 n

Pole (Joan de la): her marriages and issue, 1 *Bec.* 264 n

Pole-axes: borne before legates à latere, 1 *Tyn.* 247, 251, 3 *Tyn.* 81 (*v.* Pillars).

Policy: joined with prayer, *Pil.* 413, 415; THE POLICY OF WAR, by T. Becon, 1 *Bec.* 230; also called The True Defence of Peace, *ib.* 238 n

Politian (Angelus): his death, *Lit. Eliz.* 452

Politian (Bern.): said to have poisoned the emperor Henry VII., in the eucharist, *Grin.* 60 n

Poll : to plunder, 2 *Bul.* 47

Pollanus (Valerandus): notices of him, *Pra. Eliz.* 458 n., 3 *Zur.* 82 n., 737 n.; pastor at Frankfort, 3 *Zur.* 111; he baptizes his son in the Rhine, *ib.*; in England, 2 *Cran.* 421 n.; *Pra. Eliz.* 458 n., he translates into Latin the Disputation in the Convocation-house, *Phil.* 173; English version of his preface thereto, *ib.* 174; letter from him to Calvin, 3 *Zur.* 737

Pollard (......): one of the disputants at Cambridge, 1549, *Grin.* 194, *Rid.* 169

Pollard (Jo.): 2 *Cran.* 547

Polley (Jone, or rather Margery): martyred at Dartford, *Poet.* 162

Polling: plundering, taxing, 1 *Brad.* 33, 2 *Tyn.* 59, 60, 258

Polloc (Nether-): 1 *Zur.* 203 n

Polsted (Mr): a commissioner to visit religious houses, 2 *Lat.* 368; the two Polsteds, 3 *Zur.* 612, 618

Poltrot de Mere (Jean): murders the duke of Guise, 2 *Ful.* 121, 4 *Jew.* 1208 n., 2 *Zur.* 116 n

Polwhele (......): *v.* Poule Wheele.

Polycarp (St): 1 *Hoop.* 39, *Whita.* 572; he was bishop of Smyrna, 4 *Bul.* 31, 2 *Ful.* 335, 2 *Whitg.* 119 n., 428; he maintained the true doctrine, and confuted Marcion, 1 *Hoop.* vi, 83; testimony of Irenæus as to his doctrine, *Calf.* 270, *Whita.* 581; he trusted that the people were well instructed in the holy scriptures, 2 *Jew.* 696; how he disagreed, but yet maintained communion with Anicetus, 4 *Bul.* 57, 58, *Calf.* 269, 270; permitted by Anicetus to administer the sacrament at Rome, 1 *Jew.* 146, *Whita.* 217; his controversy with Victor about Easter, 1 *Jew.* 144; his answer when commanded to blaspheme Christ, 2 *Jew.* 884, *Rid.* 144, *Sand.* 217, 218; he refused to swear by Cæsar's fortune, 1 *Bul.* 248, 1 *Hoop.* 478; his martyrdom, 2 *Bul.* 105, 1 *Hoop.* vi, 28, *Pil.* 364; his remains refused to those who wished for them, *Calf.* 314, 2 *Ful.* 188, 1 *Hoop.* 347

Polychronicon: *v.* Higden (R.).

Polycletus: his two images, 3 *Whitg.* 570

Polycrates, bp of Ephesus: seven of his ancestors or cousins bishops before him, *Pil.* 565; he rebuked Victor, 2 *Ful.* 69, 238, *Park.* 111; mentions St John's πέταλον, 2 *Brad.* 381 n., 2 *Ful.* 113; calls Timothy bp of Ephesus, 2 *Whitg.* 295; and says he was stoned at Ephesus, *ib.* 303

Polycraticus: *v.* John of Salisbury.

Polycreta: 1 *Hoop.* 297

Polydore Vergil, *q. v.*

Polygamy: censured, 1 *Bul.* 404; true matrimony forbids plurality of wives, 1 *Hoop.* 386; it is forbidden to Christians, 1 *Lat.* 94; Tyndale thought it was tolerated by the apostles, 1 *Tyn.* 229; Cranmer's letter to Osiander against it, (Lat. and Engl.), 2 *Cran.* 404, 406

Polymius: a fictitious king, *Calf.* 133

Polytheism: *v.* Gods.

Pomander: a ball of perfumes, 3 *Bec.* 75, 2 *Brad.* 288, 2 *Cov.* 267; THE POMANDER OF PRAYER, by T. Becon, 3 *Bec.* 72; notice of another book so called, *Pra. Eliz.* xxi.

Pomeroy (Sir Tho.): a rebel, 2 *Cran.* 187 n

Pomfret: *v.* Pontefract.

Pompey: 3 *Bul.* 18, 1 *Hoop.* 329, 1 *Jew.* 50, 2 *Jew.* 1010, 1031, 1094, 4 *Jew.* 689

Pompon de Believre (......): French minister to the Netherlands, 2 *Zur.* 303 n

Pomponius: shews that laws must be general, 1 *Jew.* 222; on bondage, 2 *Bul.* 301, 302

Pomponius Lætus: Rom. Hist. Compend., *Jew.* xlii, 4 *Jew.* 689, 701, 842

Ponder (......): legacy to him, *Grin.* 462

Ponet (Jo.), bp of Winchester: previously bp of Rochester, 3 *Zur.* 87 n.; being bp of Winchester he made Philpot his archdeacon, *Phil.* ix; he translates Ochine's Dialogue, *Calf.* 369 n.; his Catechism, 1 *Cran.* 422, *Lit. Edw.* xii, *Phil.* 180 n., 3 *Zur.* 142 n.; followed to some extent by Nowell, *Now.* vii; in exile, 1 *Brad.* 445, 1 *Cran.* (9); at Strasburgh, *Jew.* xiii; his controversy with Dr Martin, *Phil.* 549, 3 *Zur.* 116 n.; two letters from him to Bullinger, 3 *Zur.* 115, 117

— Maria, his wife: sells her husband's books, 3 *Zur.* 118; letter from her to P. Martyr, *ib.*

Ponnes (Mr): 2 *Lat.* 383

Ponsonby (Will.): 4 *Bul.* xxi.

Pont (Rob.), minister of Elgin: 2 *Zur.* 365

Pontefract, co. York: the castle, 2 *Cran.* 363; the Dominican priory; grant of the site, *ib.*

Pontianus, bp of Rome: his decretals spurious, *Rid.* 180, 182; his alleged expression "conficere corpus Domini," *ib.*

Pontificale Romanum : *Jew.* xlii; ceremonies touching kings and emperors, 4 *Jew.* 691; the oath taken by Romish bishops, 4 *Bul.* 141, 142; question and answer about persons to be ordained, *ib.* 145; charge to the reader to pronounce the holy lessons distinctly and plainly, to the understanding and profit of the faithful, 4 *Jew.* 858; ceremonies prescribed for the consecration of churches, *Calf.* 208—210; order for the hallowing of images, *ib.* 47, 48, (and see 415); assignment of supreme worship to the cross, *ib.* 381 n.; direction for the baptism of bells, *ib.* 15 n.; form used in hallowing priests' vestments, 3 *Jew.* 614

Pontificalis Liber: some account of this important record, 2 *Ful.* 98 n.; it bears witness that some bps of Rome were the children of priests, and one pope the son of another, *ib.*; declares that St Marcellinus was an idolater, *ib.* 365 n.; reference to it concerning the baptism of Constantine, *ib.* 360

Pontius, the deacon: on the martyrdom of Cyprian, 2 *Whitg.* 22, 25, 26, 1 *Zur.* 160 n., 350 n

Pontius, the martyr: his worthless Acts, 2 *Ful.* 355 n

Pontius Pilate: *q. v.*

Poole (Geo. A.): 2 *Ful.* 331 n

Poole (Reg.): *v.* Pole.

Poor, Poverty: *v.* Alms, Prayers.

Who are poor, 3 *Bec.* 607, 2 *Bul.* 225; their miserable state through death, 2 *Bec.* 583, 591; wants of their children, *Pil.* 455, 456; poverty is God's gift, 3 *Bec.* 26; we should not murmur against it, but rather rejoice, 2 *Bec.* 464, &c.; why God sends it, or takes away goods, *ib.* 465; when the faithful feel it, it is sent to prove their faith, *ib.* 467; it does not of itself secure God's blessing, 2 *Tyn.* 16; it is used by Satan as a snare, 1 *Lat.* 430; the poor are equal to the rich in things pertaining to salvation, *Pil.* 124; both have equal privileges in Christ, 2 *Lat.* 201; the poor as well as the rich are builders in God's house, *Pil.* 33, 46; they are most diligent in hearing the gospel, 1 *Lat.* 477, 2 *Lat.* 72; Christ must be sought amongst the poor, 2 *Lat.* 127, (*v.* Christ, vii); what sort of poor are blessed, 2 *Bec.* 111; 1 *Lat.* 476, 478, 2 *Lat.* 127; the poor in spirit, 2 *Bec.* 111, 2 *Lat.* 300, 2 *Tyn.* 16, 17; the duty of the poor, how they should live, *Hutch.* 318; they serve God by living uprightly in their vocation, 2 *Lat.* 215; they must not bear it heavily that they are forced to labour, 2 *Bec.* 398, 399; they must labour faithfully without craft, *ib.* 399; they must not spend what they get wastefully, but warily, *ib.* 399, 400; they must eschew superfluous expenses, *ib.* 400; they must have their apparel decent and seemly, *ib.*; they may sometimes make merry, 2 *Lat.* 162; they must beware of idleness, 2 *Bec.* 401; they must seek to live honestly and quietly among their neighbours, *ib.* 401, 402; seeking, if any offences chance, reconciliation, and checking false reports, *ib.* 402; they may not rob the rich, 1 *Lat.* 398; what they may pray for for themselves, 1 *Bec.* 167; duty towards the poor, 1 *Lat.* 406, 1 *Tyn.* 103; what we are to them, the same will God be to us, 2 *Bec.* 391; mercy to them enforced, *Sand.* 159, 160; they should find gentleness at the hands of the rich, 1 *Bec.* 64; care of them, 4 *Bul.* 157, 497; they are not to be defrauded of their portion, *ib.* 495; they are to be comforted and relieved, 2 *Bec.* 619; godly men seek to relieve them, *ib.* 584, 585; they should be provided for, *Now.* 228; how they should be maintained, *Sand.* 230; they were provided for by Christ and his apostles, 1 *Bec.* 20; ancient bishops were careful for them, *ib.* 21; their support out of church-revenues, 2 *Cran.* 160; one fortieth of the revenues of benefices over £20 enjoined to be given to them, *ib.* 500; parishioners to be exhorted to contribute to their relief, *Grin.* 129; on laws for their relief, *Sand.* 51, 2 *Whitg.* 389, 3 *Whitg.* 290; the act 5 Eliz. cap. 2, *Lit. Eliz.* 593 n.; collections to be made for them according to this statute, *Grin.* 140; provision made for them at Sandwich, 3 *Bec.* 599; justice too often denied to them, 1 *Lat.* 127; unmercifulness towards them prevalent, 1 *Bec.* 40; the coldness of love to them is a sign of the approach of the day of judgment, 2 *Bec.* 587; God can easily enrich them, *ib.* 467; on religious profession of poverty, *ib.* 388, 2 *Cran.* 147, 1 *Lat.* 478, 2 *Lat.* 127, 1 *Tyn.* 430, 435, 2 *Tyn.* 123 (*v.* Vows).

Poor men of Lyons: *q. v.*

Poor men's box: to be fixed near the high altar, 2 *Cran.* 157, 503; gifts to it, enjoined in lieu of pilgrimages, &c., *ib.* 157, 158, 503 (*v.* Chests).

Poore (Rich.), bp of Sarum: his constitutions, 2 *Bec.* 253 n

Pope: *v.* Antichrist, Dispensations, Indulgences, Peter (St), Purgatory, Supremacy; and especially Law (Canon), p. 472

Harding's reasons for a pope, 3 *Jew.* 274; on unity by one pope, *ib.* 277; order of the early bishops of Rome, *Calf.* 251, 3 *Jew.* 326; list of popes in the Palatine library, 4 *Jew.* 648; great deference paid by the early church to the bishop of Rome, and why, *Whita.* 435; the advice of bishops of Rome sought by godly men of old, 2 *Ful.* 119; thirty of the first were faithful martyrs, *Pil.* 605; there was no heretical bishop of Rome to Augustine's time, *Whita.* 427; the decretal epistles of the early popes, mostly spurious, *Calf.* 222 n., 2 *Ful.* 59, 281, *Jew.* xxxvi. n.; several early popes were the sons of priests, 2 *Ful.* 98; bishops of Rome addressed by other bishops as brethren, 1 *Jew.* 385, 386; popes have been excommunicated and deposed by other bishops, *ib.* 406; their jurisdiction anciently limited to a part of Christendom, 4 *Jew.* 707; how the pope's usurped authority arose, *Rid.* 262, &c.; steps by which he ascended, 2 *Whitg.* 379; how he became greatest, 2 *Tyn.* 257; his beginning and proceedings were of the devil, 2 *Hoop.* 238; he began to flourish about Mahomet's time, *Pil.* 75; progress of the papal power, 2 *Tyn.* 257, &c.; compared to the growth of ivy, *ib.* 270, 274; Phocas grants him the supremacy, *Bale* 503, 2 *Ful.* 72, 365, 2 *Hoop.* 235, 555, 1 *Jew.* 184, 363, *Pil.* 76, 521, *Poet.* 284, 2 *Tyn.* 258; appeals from the pope; case of the Donatists in France, 4 *Jew.* 965; appeals from him to the emperor, 1 *Jew.* 397; popes have been corrected or deposed by emperors, *Pil.* 640; the bishops were once subject to, and made by the emperors, 2 *Hoop.* 236, 238; the right of electing the pope given to Charlemagne and his successors, 2 *Tyn.* 263, but virtually relinquished by Louis-le-Débonnaire, *ib.* 266; advances towards rendering the election of the pope independent of the emperor, *ib.* 266, 267; disputes between the popes and the German emperors, *ib.* 298, 301; the pope's power established, *Bale* 561; he has climbed above kings and emperors, extolled himself above God, and dispensed with his laws, 2 *Cran.* 15, 39, 222; the crimes by which he effected his designs, *ib.* 178; his pretended authority and tyranny in England, 1 *Bec.* 181, 2 *Bec.* 413, *Rid.* 266; England cursed by him, 2 *Hoop.* 567; his jurisdiction renounced by many of our kings and parliaments, *Bale* 11, *Rog.* 347; Henry VIII.'s letter abolishing his authority in England, 2 *Cran.* 369 n.; substance of Cranmer's sermons in Kent against his authority, and of the defence of it by the prior of the Black Friars at Canterbury, *ib.* 326; opposition at Oxford to the name of pope being obliterated from books, *ib.* 382—384; two priests punished by Cranmer for retaining the name in books, *ib.* 387; a league against the pope proposed by Henry VIII., 3 *Zur.* 612 n.; Cranmer's letter to queen Mary, protesting against his jurisdiction in this country, 2 *Cran.* 447; card. Pole's reply to the assertion that the pope's authority is a foreign power, *ib.* 540; there was good cause to repeal the law of his pre-eminence, *ib.* 77; princes, although

POPE

sworn to him, under a common mistake, as head of the church, may pull their necks out of his yoke, *ib.* 78; he hath no jurisdiction in this realm of England, 2 *Hoop.* 127, 547, *Rog.* 346; the oath against his authority, 2 *Hoop.* 232, 397, 566; he discharged all Papists from their obedience to queen Elizabeth, *Rog.* 348; his power is declining, *Pil.* 77, 206; his seat shaken, and his fall begun, *ib.* 30, 421; he shall be destroyed, 2 *Bec.* 415; the pope's titles and designations, *Rog.* 347, 348; on the word "papa," 4 *Bul.* 118, 1 *Jew.* 362; its origin, according to a gloss in the Canon Law, 3 *Tyn.* 324; the earliest known instance of the name being applied to a Christian minister, 2 *Tyn.* 259 n.; all bishops once so called, 2 *Hoop.* 236, 4 *Jew.* 1299, 2 *Tyn.* 259, 2 *Whitg.* 86; or at least many bishops, 2 *Whitg.* 196; the name restricted to the bishop of Rome by Gregory VII., *Calf.* 255 n.; the titles of prince of the priests, &c., forbidden by councils, 2 *Whitg.* 168; some early popes were styled bishops of the universal church, 1 *Jew.* 422, 427; as to the name of universal bishop, see p. 122, col. 2, and p. 362, col. 2; the pope called Lord and God, 4 *Bul.* 72, 2 *Jew.* 1020, 4 *Jew.* 842, and see above, p. 473, col. 1; instances in which the name of God has been usurped by kings and others, 4 *Jew.* 842; the pope styled king of kings and lord of lords, 4 *Bul.* 120, 4 *Jew.* 847, 2 *Lat.* 349; said to be neither God nor man, 2 *Jew.* 907, 991, 4 *Jew.* 843, 844; said to have one consistory with God, 4 *Bul.* 119, 1 *Jew.* 381; Tho. Aquinas asserts that the pope's dominion is above all human authorities, and that he may properly be called Christ, king, and priest, 2 *Tyn.* 291; called "the light" which is "come into the world," 1 *Jew.* 385; it is affirmed that he hath no fellow, 4 *Bul.* 120; he is said to have no superior in spiritual causes, 4 *Jew.* 704; he assumes the title of cursed Ham, servus servorum, 2 *Tyn.* 248; he calls himself servant of servants, but would be accounted lord of lords, *Phil.* 396; by whom elected, 2 *Ful.* 269; riots at the election of popes, 1 *Whitg.* 463; his investment, 3 *Jew.* 319; his coronation, 2 *Tyn.* 258 n.; his excessive pomp, 4 *Jew.* 1069, *Sand.* 26; the kissing of his feet, 4 *Jew.* 687, 688, *Sand.* 272, 1 *Tyn.* 285, 3 *Tyn.* 56 n.; the sacrament carried before him on a horse, *Rog.* 291; he succeeds the heathen emperors as pontifex maximus, 2 *Ful.* 218; is no preaching prelate, 3 *Bec.* 508; what power he claims, 1 *Tyn.* 268—269, 328; his power said to be supernatural, 4 *Jew.* 1035; his alleged "plenitude of power," and the like, 2 *Brad.* 144, 4 *Bul.* 121, 1 *Jew.* 93 n., 380, 385, 4 *Jew.* 829; many preposterous statements respecting the pope's authority, 3 *Bul.* 118, &c., 2 *Cran.* 68, 1 *Jew.* 68, 93, 442, 443, 2 *Jew.* 907, 919, 991, and see Law (Canon), p. 472—474 above; he pretends to be lord over Christ's merits, 1 *Tyn.* 271; claims power over the angels of God, 4 *Jew.* 846, likewise over kings and emperors, 4 *Bul.* 120, 2 *Cran.* 69, 70, 222, 226, 2 *Hoop.* 239, 2 *Jew.* 917, *Rog.* 209, 1 *Tyn.* 186, 328, 339, 2 *Tyn.* 269, 3 *Tyn.* 104; he claims both swords, 4 *Bul.* 120, 1 *Jew.* 228; like the devil, he assumes to give away the kingdoms of the world, 2 *Cran.* 452; tempts Christendom as the devil tempted Christ, 2 *Tyn.* 274, 275; he transferred the empire into France, 2 *Hoop.* 238; the emperor receives his power from him, 4 *Jew.* 836—838; it is said that he can depose the emperor, 4 *Bul.* 120; an emperor received his crown from the feet of a pope, who kicked it off again, 2 *Tyn.* 271; he commands kings to wait on him, 4 *Jew.* 688, &c.; his bridle and stirrup held by an emperor, *ib.* 690, 691; he confers titles and presents on kings, *Bale* 444, 1 *Tyn.* 186—187; he is a king, 4 *Jew.* 982, &c.; a temporal ruler, 2 *Ful.* 268, 269; his kingdom is of this world, 2 *Tyn.* 249; he received it from the devil, *ib.* 274; the policy of his kingdom, *Bale* 181; what his triple crown signifies, 3 *Bec.* 507, 1 *Jew.* 403, *Poet.* 463; territories possessed or claimed by him, 2 *Jew.* 917; is really inferior to princes, 4 *Jew.* 705, 706; obedience to the pope inconsistent with loyalty to kings, 2 *Lat.* 285; he teaches disobedience to the civil ruler, 1 *Tyn.* 166; procures rebellion against princes, 3 *Whitg.* 592; claims power to absolve subjects from their oath of fidelity, &c., 2 *Cran.* 70; stirs up war and bloodshed, *Phil.* 388, 1 *Tyn.* 186 —188, 2 *Tyn.* 294, 295; four millions of men supposed to have been slain for the popes' quarrels, 2 *Tyn.* 267; his authority the trouble of all Christian souls, 2 *Hoop.* 232; claims the right to judge in temporal things, and to give authority to arrest and manacle men, 2 *Cran.* 71; he has a realm in every realm, *ib.* 213; receives intelligence secretly and rapidly from all parts of Christendom, 2 *Tyn.* 296; claims power to compel princes to receive his legates, 2 *Cran.* 71; his exactions and rapacity, 4 *Jew.* 1077,

&c., *Pil.* 584; his usurped power, 3 *Bec.* 488, *Rid.* 136; his authority according to abp Arundel, *Bale* 27; lord Cobham questioned about it, *ib.* 38; the pope's false power condemned, 1 *Tyn.* 188; his pretensions opposed by Fra. Zabarella, 2 *Jew.* 992; his claim of supremacy, resting chiefly on his alleged succession of St Peter, 2 *Brad.* 142, &c., 4 *Bul.* 119, &c., 2 *Cov.* 464, 465, 2 *Ful.* 231, 248, &c., 335, *Hutch.* 100, 1 *Jew.* 338, &c., 2 *Jew.* 991, 1001, 2 *Lat.* 280, 332, 348, *Phil.* 74; he is most unlike St Peter, *Pil.* 271, *Sand.* 277; the pope's claim to supremacy is incompatible with scripture, 2 *Tyn.* 247, 261, 280, &c.; it is contradicted by the language of Cyprian, Augustine, Ambrose, Jerome, Origen, and Gregory I., 1 *Tyn.* 214, &c.; seven general councils in which the bishop of Rome was not taken for supreme head, *Phil.* 39; the question of his succession, 3 *Jew.* 348—350; it is disproved by certain councils, *Poet.* 274; ridiculous arguments for his supremacy, 1 *Zur.* 14, 77, 339; the pope compared to Abel, Noah, Abraham, Melchisedec, &c., and to Christ himself, 4 *Bul.* 118, *Rog.* 347; Christ and the pope compared, 2 *Tyn.* 273; he is not the foundation of the church, 4 *Bul.* 81; he claims to be head of the church, 4 *Bul.* 86, 2 *Cov.* 464, 1 *Jew.* 428, *Rid.* 164; he is termed by some the basilisk of the church, neither the head nor the tail, *Rog.* 347; he is not the "one shepherd" mentioned Eccles. xii. 11, *Whita.* 423; he calls himself Christ's vicar, 2 *Cov.* 464, 1 *Hoop.* 22, 1 *Jew.* 378, 379; he is declared to be the under bridegroom of the church, 3 *Jew.* 267, 270; the church alleged to be dependent on him, *ib.* 220; his supremacy not sanctioned by the high priesthood of the Jews, *Phil.* 395; distinction between the pope's supremacy and the office of an archbishop, 2 *Whitg.* 99, 245, &c.; he exercises his supremacy with great lordliness, 1 *Lat.* 206; he governs not according to God's will, but his own, 2 *Lat.* 282; he sets himself above God's word, 3 *Jew.* 218; he and his prelates think themselves wiser than God, 2 *Cran.* 10; he claims to be the only true interpreter of scripture, *Rog.* 197; Bellarmine's opinion on this, *Whita.* 414; pretends authority to dispense with the word of God, 1 *Cran.* x, 2 *Cran.* 222; instances of the perversion of scripture by the pope, 2 *Cran.* 75; he is a forger, 1 *Jew.* 356, &c.; he corrupts Christianity, *Bale* 347; his doctrine as contrasted with that of Christ, 3 *Bec.* 520, &c.,

2 *Tyn.* 273; it is worldly, 2 *Tyn.* 198; it cannot be true, because it is not persecuted, 1 *Tyn.* 131; what truths he denies, 2 *Ful.* 392; he forbids the reading of the word of God, 2 *Hoop.* 44; founds all his falsehoods and superstitions upon unwritten verities, 2 *Cran.* 10; breaks the third commandment, 1 *Hoop.* 325; agrees with Pelagius, 2 *Tyn.* 181; belies God's mercy, *ib.* 157; substitutes his holy water for the blood of Christ, 2 *Cran.* 176, 177; he has set up the sacrifice of the mass, 3 *Bec.* 523; his abuses of the eucharist, *ib.* 524, &c., 1 *Lat.* 209; his doctrine of the eucharist is opposed to Christ's, 1 *Hoop.* 120; the popes by whom the parts and ceremonies of the mass were introduced, 3 *Bec.* 262, &c., 2 *Brad.* 305, &c.; the pope has added five more sacraments, 3 *Bec.* 524; has devised purgatory, *ib.* 523; remarks on his pardons, 4 *Jew.* 851, &c., *Rog.* 219; popes have often granted remission of sins to those engaging in wars for their ends, 2 *Tyn.* 294, 295, 301; he curses us on Good Friday, *Pra. Eliz.* 467; his pardons help not, 2 *Tyn.* 84; his curses hurt not, *ib.* 87; he claims authority to open and shut heaven, 2 *Cran.* 70; he hath not Peter's key, but a picklock, *Hutch.* 100; sets forth saints as mediators, 3 *Bec.* 522, 523; would have prayers made at the shrines of saints, *ib.* 533; teaches to honour images and reliques, *ib.* 521, 522; his pedlery, *ib.* 4; the pope is subject to a general council, 2 *Cran.* 77, but he claims to be above all councils, 1 *Jew.* 67, &c., 410, 4 *Jew.* 921, &c.; asserts authority to summon and confirm them, *Rog.* 205, 206; greater authority is ascribed to him by papists generally, than to a council, *Whita.* 414, 415; it is said that there can be no council of bishops without his authority, 2 *Cran.* 70; and that where he is there is a general council, 4 *Bul.* 120; assumes power to make laws, claims exemption from all laws, says he can dispense even with the law of God, &c., see p. 473, col. 1 above; thinks his laws better than Christ's, *Pil.* 80; his laws are at variance with the law of the land, 2 *Cran.* 213, 214, 221, 222, 448, 449; he calls himself the ordinary of all men, bishop of all the world, &c., see p. 472, col. 1; all bishops said to derive from the pope, and receive of his fulness, 4 *Jew.* 829; he confirms the election of bishops, 1 *Jew.* 406; papists always make him the judge in the last resort, *Whita.* 445; he claims to judge all men, and to be judged or rebuked of none, &c., 4 *Bul.* 119, 2 *Cran.* 69, 70,

2 *Jew.* 907, *Rog.* 191, 202, 348, 3 *Tyn.* 232 n., and see p. 473 above; he has been called judge of the quick and dead, *Rog.* 68; he judges God and his word, 2 *Hoop.* 442; judges what oaths ought to be kept, and what may be broken, 2 *Cran.* 70, 2 *Hoop.* 240, 2 *Tyn.* 301, 311; he is exempt from all order and obedience, 2 *Hoop.* 238; without check, 4 *Jew.* 833; he suffers no man to dispute his power, 3 *Tyn.* 231; it is held to be heresy not to acknowledge him, 2 *Cran.* 67, 165; and stated that every man must be subject to him of necessity of salvation, 4 *Bul.* 120 (& al. see p. 473, col. 1); he is not the judge of controversies, *Whita.* 447; he is the subject of controversy, therefore not the judge, *ib.* 449; he is an incompetent judge of controversies because a party to them, *ib.* 464; on appeals to him, 3 *Bul.* 120, 2 *Ful.* 70, 71, 308, 1 *Jew.* 386, &c., 3 *Jew.* 216; his alleged infallibility a falsehood, 2 *Cran.* 69, 1 *Jew.* 398, &c., 4 *Jew.* 925, &c., *Pil.* 115, *Rog.* 202; not taught by the catholic fathers, 2 *Jew.* 901; many popes have erred even when teaching ex cathedrâ, *Whita.* 430; as certain papists admit, *ib.* 431; the decisions of one pope have frequently reversed those of another, 1 *Tyn.* 324, 3 *Tyn.* 99; the wickedness of popes, 2 *Cran.* 178, 4 *Jew.* 702, *Pil.* 247, 601—603; Genebrard's testimony against them, *Rog.* 182; their tragical acts, 3 *Jew.* 249, 250; they have poisoned each other, 2 *Bul.* 110, *Pil.* 247; near 50 popes in 160 years, and only 13 emperors, 2 *Brad.* 274, 2 *Cov.* 253; eight popes in twelve years, *Pil.* 247; two and three popes at once, each denying the authority of the other, *Pil.* 545, 618, 1 *Tyn.* 324; a woman-pope, *Pil.* 602 (v. Joan); the pope protects wickedness, 2 *Tyn.* 275, yet it is said that he is ever holy, 4 *Jew.* 702; the bishops of Rome have been the devil's great guns, 1 *Lat.* 27; many have been worldly and profane, *Rog.* 181; divers have been heretics, 1 *Ful.* 11, 1 *Jew.* 381, 399, 400, 3 *Jew.* 339, &c., *Pil.* 601—603, *Rog.* 181; some have been conjurors and sorcerers, *Rog.* 180; many have been incontinent, *ib.* 304, 305; the pope receives evil-doers into the ministry, 2 *Tyn.* 275; his swarm of hypocrites, 3 *Bec.* 506; his creatures all superstitious, *Pil.* 563; popes, bishops, and others, who enter not by the door, are thieves and robbers, 2 *Lat.* 309—312; the pope's haughtiness, pride, tyranny, and cruelty, 1 *Bec.* 180, 3 *Bec.* 507, 508, 515, 518, 519, 527, 528, 538, 1 *Jew.* 109, *Pil.* 99; petition for deliverance " from the tyranny of the bishop of Rome, and all his detestable enormities," *Calf.* 315 n., *Lit. Edw.* 101, 163, 233, 234, *Lit. Eliz.* ix. and 4, *Pra. Eliz.* 572, *Rid.* 50; it occurs in a litany of Mary's time, *Pra. Eliz.* 52 n.; the popedom has been frequently obtained by simony, *Sand.* 241; money can do all things with the pope, 3 *Bec.* 488, 507, 509, 531, 535; he would deliver men from their sins for a little money, 2 *Bec.* 174; he offers to sell the grace of God, *Sand.* 11; yet it is affirmed that he cannot commit simony, 4 *Jew.* 867, &c.; he sanctions and encourages the holding of enormous pluralities, 3 *Bec.* 505, 534, 2 *Tyn.* 275, 288, 3 *Tyn.* 42; he commits the cure of souls to boys, 3 *Bec.* 535; is the author of impropriations of benefices, *ib.* 536, 537; dispenses with the clergy's performance of their duties, 1 *Tyn.* 148; requires not the consent of parents to marriage, 3 *Bec.* 532; forbids the marriage of Christian gossips (i. e. co-sponsors), *ib.* 532, 533; he cannot abide the marriage of priests, *ib.* 505, 523, 533; will not suffer such divorces as that marriage may follow, *ib.* 532; the pope compared to Pharaoh, *Sand.* 146, to Balaam, *ib.* 150, to Tobiah the Ammonite, *Pil.* 410, to Simon Magus, *Phil.* 417, to Mahomet, *Bale* 262; the pope, equally with the Turk, persecutes Christ's followers, 2 *Cran.* 62; the pope and his sect are not the church, 3 *Tyn.* 9, 39—42; he is an excommunicate person, 2 *Hoop.* 560; he cannot abide reformation, 3 *Bec.* 516; there is no truth where he is chief head, 2 *Hoop.* 559; wheresoever he hath supremacy Christ is dishonoured, *ib.*; he is an old grey fox, *Sand.* 63; a false apostle and deceitful worker, 3 *Bec.* 487, 488; the devil's chaplain, 1 *Lat.* 74; a high priest after the order of Satan, *Bale* 562; the pope said to be the firstborn of Antichrist, 2 *Hoop.* 396, 465; alleged to be Antichrist himself, *Bale* 325, 4 *Bul.* 122, 2 *Cran.* 178, 213, 222, 452, 2 *Ful.* 393, *Pil.* 279, *Rog.* 347, *Whita.* 414 (and see Antichrist); how he sits in the temple of God, &c., *Hutch.* 108; is painted in the scriptures as the enemy of God, 2 *Cran.* 223; his religion is against Christ's religion, *ib.* 449; the pope said to be the beast of the Apocalypse, 1 *Hoop.* 24; his power derived from the bottomless pit, 2 *Hoop.* 546; declared to be Gog, *Bale* 571; the pope to be killed with the staff of God's word, 2 *Hoop.* 238, 240; the person of the pope not so much to be detested as the papacy,

2 *Cran.* 322; though a pope may mean well, he can never bring a good design to issue, *ib.* 78; a paper which came from the pope, *Sand.* 130
Pope (Mr): confers with Barnes, 2 *Cov.* 417; present at his death, *ib.* 440; he disputes with Ridley, *Rid.* 161 (perhaps Sir Tho. Pope).
Pope (Rich.), a priest at Norwich: *Park.* vi, 481
Pope (R. T. P.): 2 *Ful.* 86 n
Popery: *v.* Prayers, Questions, Reformation. It began in the apostles' time, 2 *Ful.* 69, *Poet.* 284; is grounded on tradition, *Sand.* 16, &c.; its doctrines, *Rog.* passim; they are based on tradition, but opposed to scripture, *Sand.* 19; it is Antichristianism, and includes all heresies, *Whita.* 20; difference between it and true Christianity; in the foundation, *Sand.* 12, in the end, *ib.* 20, in the means, *ib.* 28; confutation of four Romish doctrines, 2 *Brad.* 267, 2 *Cov.* 248; its two chief pillars; the mass, and the papacy, 2 *Brad.* 161, 162, *Rid.* 366; it is opposed to the grace of the gospel, *Pil.* 20; teaches distrust in God, *Sand.* 185; foments rebellion and commotion, 1 *Zur.* 246; its abominations, *Rid.* 150; its absurdities asserted to be catholic, *Sand.* 359; some of the pope's pomp borrowed from the Jews, and some from Gentiles, 1 *Tyn.* 336, 3 *Tyn.* 20; miserable state of men under it, 2 *Jew.* 1066, 1083; many of those educated in popery preserved from perishing, 1 *Lat.* 305, 525; God's mercy the cause of our deliverance therefrom, *Sand.* 180; injunction of Edward VI. for its abolition, 2 *Cran.* 498; men still fond of its dregs, *Pil.* 121, *Sand.* 208, 1 *Zur.* 343; all remains of papistry should be taken away, 1 *Hoop.* 438, 2 *Zur.* 342, &c.; semi-popery deprecated, 2 *Zur.* 5, 11
Popetry: puppetry, 3 *Tyn.* 27
Popham (Sir Jo.), lord chief justice: *Rog.* 20
Popinjay (from the Spanish papagayo): a parrot, 3 *Tyn.* 72; one that could say the creed, 3 *Jew.* 255
Population: the king's honour standeth in the multitude of people, 2 *Bec.* 601, 1 *Lat.* 100
Porey (Jo.): *v.* Pory.
Porkets: pigs, 2 *Brad.* 64, 212
Porphyry: excused the errors and follies of the heathen, 4 *Jew.* 1108; denied the authenticity of the book of Daniel, *Whita.* 33; what he said of St. Paul, 1 *Jew.* 73; he objected the disagreement between him and Peter, *ib.* 532; accused all Christians of sedition and treason, 4 *Jew.* 666

Porrege (Rich.): letter to him, 1 *Brad.* 591, 2 *Brad.* 194
Porrege (Will.): named, 2 *Brad.* 108, 117; letters to him, 1 *Brad.* 591, 2 *Brad.* 38 (?), 194, see P. (W.)
Porreta (Gilb.): wrote on the Apocalypse, *Bale* 256
Port (Fra.): Greek professor at Geneva, 1 *Zur.* 231
Port-de-Grace: *v.* Havre-de-Grace.
Port-sale: a public sale or auction, as of fish when fishermen return to port, 2 *Jew.* 912, 922
Portasse, Portesse, Portuis, &c.: the Breviary, *Bale* 262, 2 *Bec.* 135, *Calf.* 16 n., 159, 298, 2 *Cran.* 523, *Grin.* 9 n., 135—159, 213, 2 *Hoop.* 86, 1 *Jew.* 106, 107, *Pil.* 17, 630, 1 *Tyn.* 230 n., 2 *Whitg.* 589, 3 *Whitg.* 52, 490
Porter (Will.): in the Arches court, 2 *Cran.* 411
Porters: ministers and rulers the porters of the church, *Pil.* 382, 383
Porters, Ostiaries, or Doorkeepers: an ecclesiastical order, 4 *Bul.* 113, 3 *Jew.* 273, *Rog.* 258, *Whita.* 509, 2 *Whitg.* 174
Portesius (Jo.): corrupted a passage in Eusebius, *Calf.* 278 n
Portiforium: the Breviary (*q.v.*), *Calf.* 16 n.; portifolium, *Bale* 175; portifoliome, *ib.* 369
Portman (Sir Will.), chief justice: 2 *Hoop.* 378
Portraits: *v.* Pictures.
Ports (Cinque): *v.* Cinque Ports.
Portsmouth, co. Hants: 2 *Cran.* 495 n
Portugal: an ambassador therefrom has mass in his house, many English being present, *Grin.* 300; Sandys suppresses the mass there, *Sand.* xx.
Portuis: *v.* Portasse.
Portured: portrayed, 3 *Bec.* 518
Pory (Jo.), master of C. C. C. and vice-chancellor: letters to him and others, *Park.* 63, 64; mentioned, *ib.* 298; he desires to resign his prebend at Westminster to Mr Aldrich, *ib.* 358
Possession: *v.* Demons, Energumeni.
Possevinus (Ant.): his remarkable confession as to the expurgation of MSS., *Calf.* 6 n.; references to him, *ib.* 64, 104, 181 nn
Possidonius: says Valerius, bishop of Hippo, had small skill in Latin, 1 *Jew.* 295; mentions that Augustine heard causes, 3 *Whitg.* 450; describes his apparel, 3 *Jew.* 618, 619
Possinus (Pet.): a shameful interpolation noted in his Catena Græcorum Patrum, 2 *Ful.* 286 n

Post: rates of postage from abroad, 3 *Zur.* 270, 677, 678; postmasters' endorsements, *Park.* 289
Post: perhaps a game at cards, 1 *Jew.* 429
Postellus (Will.): maintained that one mother Jane was the saviour of women, *Rog.* 58, 298
Postillæ Majores: *Jew.* xlii, 1 *Jew.* 233
Postils: comments, *Bale* 352
Posts: text appropriate to them, 1 *Bec.* 66
Posy: motto, *Sand.* 98, 3 *Whitg.* xii.
Pot (To go to): i. e. to ruin, 3 *Tyn.* 110
POTATION FOR LENT, by T. Becon, 1 *Bec.* 85, &c.
Potten (Agnes or Ann): she was one of the two women burnt at Ipswich, *Poet.* 166
Potter (Tho.): translated sermons by Bullinger, 4 *Bul.* xxiii.
Pottkyns (......), Cranmer's registrar: 2 *Cran.* 254; letters to him, *ib.* 249, 264, 265, 348
Pouldering: powdering, 3 *Tyn.* 222
Poule Wheele (......): a traitor, *Lit. Eliz.* 658
Pouling: polling, 2 *Tyn.* 258
Poultney (Sir Tho.): Elizabeth his daughter, 3 *Bec.* 89 n
Poverty: *v.* Poor.
Powell (Edm.): 2 *Cran.* 543, 547
Powell (Edw.): opposes Latimer at Bristol, 2 *Cran.* 308 n., 2 *Lat.* 225, 358; upholds pilgrimages, 2 *Lat.* 366; imputes various articles to Latimer, *ib.* 225; burned for denying the king's supremacy, 2 *Cran.* 310 n., 2 *Lat.* 225 n., 3 *Zur.* 209
Powell (Tho.), printer: *Coop.* 223
Powell (Will.), printer: *Rid.* 80
Power: *v.* Kings, Magistrates.
What it is, 4 *Bul.* 41; two kinds of power, absolute, and limited, *ib.* 42; ecclesiastical power, *ib.* 38, &c.; power of consecration, *ib.* 39; of the keys, *ib.* 39, 44; of jurisdiction, of preaching, of judicial correction, to receive, *ib.* 40; of ordination, *ib.* 43; to teach, *ib.* 44; to administer the sacraments, to judge of doctrines, to call a council, *ib.* 45; to dispose of the affairs of the church, *ib.* 46
Powers: a name of angels, 3 *Bul.* 338
Powis (Edw. lord of): *v.* Cherleton.
Powis (Edw. Grey, lord): his death, 3 *Zur.* 496 n
Pownall (Rob.): 1 *Brad.* 578; an exile, 3 *Zur.* 167; letter signed by him, *ib.* 170; ordained by Grindal, *ib.* n
Poynes (Sir Nic.): 1 *Ful.* xi.
Poynet (Jo.), bp: *v.* Ponet.
Poynings (Sir Adrian): sent with an army to Newhaven, 2 *Zur.* 92 n

Poynings (Sir Tho.): his death, 3 *Zur.* 36 n
Poynt (......), a doctor of law at Cambridge: *Park.* 18
Poyntz (Jo.): *v.* Poyntz (Tho.)
Poyntz (Tho.), an English merchant at Antwerp: receives Tyndale into his house, 1 *Tyn.* lxv; writes to his brother John to procure Tyndale's deliverance, *ib.* lxvii, &c.; his efforts for that purpose, *ib.* lxx; he is imprisoned for his kindness to Tyndale, *ib.* lxxi; but makes his escape, *ib.* lxxii.
PPP. SSS. RRR. FFF.: 1 *Jew.* 421 n
Practice: *v.* Prelates.
Præmunire: incurred by those who hinder the execution of our laws by any authority from Rome, 2 *Cran.* 449; taken away in Mary's time, *ib.* 17
Prague: a terrible and miraculous sight there, *Lit. Eliz.* 569; the university erected by Charlemagne, 2 *Jew.* 981
Praise: *v.* Exhortation.
True praise, 1 *Cov.* 513; what it is to offer the sacrifice of praise, 1 *Bec.* 298, 299
Praised: appraised, *Bale* 286
Prateolus (Gab.): says it is the common article of all sectaries to affirm that scripture is clear and needs no interpretation, *Whita.* 361; declares that the Anabaptists condemn magistracy, *Rog.* 337 n
Praxeas, a heretic: alleged God's omnipotence, 1 *Jew.* 490, 2 *Jew.* 798; opposed by Tertullian, 2 *Whitg.* 226
Praxeneans: their heretical views on the Trinity, *Rog.* 45
Prayer: *v.* Confession of sins, Faith, Thanksgiving; also Ambrose, Augustine, and other fathers and doctors.
(*a*) *On Prayer generally*: of prayer, 3 *Bul.* 32, 2 *Cov.* 87, *Now.* (64), 183, 1 *Tyn.* 296—303, *Wool.* 134; what prayer is, 1 *Bec.* 128, 130, 2 *Bec.* 125, 3 *Bec.* 607, 608, 621, 4 *Bul.* 163, 1 *Lat.* 326, 507, *Nord.* 11, *Sand.* 76, 1 *Tyn.* 93, 2 *Tyn.* 78; what it is, with probations out of scripture, 2 *Bec.* 490; its parts, 1 *Bec.* 128, 1 *Lat.* 311, 312, *Sand.* 76, 77; kinds of prayer, *Nord.* 12, *Pil.* 564; deprecation, 1 *Lat.* 311, *Nord.* 12; *precor* and *deprecor* distinguished, 1 *Lat.* 415; supplication, 1 *Lat.* 312, *Nord.* 12, *Pil.* 564, *Sand.* 77; petition, 1 *Bec.* 128, *Sand.* 76; intercession, *Nord.* 12, *Sand.* 77; thanksgiving, 1 *Bec.* 128, 1 *Lat.* 312, *Nord.* 13, *Now.* (82), 203, *Pil.* 564, *Sand.* 77; common or public prayer, 4 *Bul.* 164, 183, 1 *Jew.* 333, *Sand.* 261, 2 *Tyn.* 79 (*v.* Book of Common Prayer, Liturgies); its advantage and

PRAYER

excellency, 1 *Jew.* 333, 1 *Lat.* 337, 338; how it should be conducted, 2 *Tyn.* 79; the manner of some reformed churches, 2 *Whitg.* 489; the question of set forms, *ib.* 466; Gualter's opinion respecting it, 2 *Zur.* 231; on responses, 1 *Jew.* 281, 282, 2 *Whitg.* 489, &c.; the Puritans held that extempore prayer should be permitted, 1 *Zur.* 281, 291; in the Romish church there is no public prayer, *Whita.* 268; prayer ought to be common, 1 *Bec.* 166; articles and injunctions respecting it, 2 *Hoop.* 128, 130, 131, 136, *Rid.* 320; attendance on customary prayers not sufficient without private prayer, 1 *Brad.* 34; of private prayer, 4 *Bul.* 164, 1 *Jew.* 333, *Sand.* 261, 2 *Tyn.* 79; its peculiar advantage, *Sand.* 262; household prayer should likewise be maintained, 1 *Lat.* 229; we must pray, 4 *Bul.* 167; prayer is a duty, 1 *Hoop.* 458, *Rog.* 225; God has expressly commanded it, 2 *Bec.* 129, 1 *Lat.* 166; this is a great comfort, 1 *Bec.* 146; though commandment without a promise to hear, would avail but little, *ib.*; our unworthiness not to be objected against God's commandment, 2 *Bec.* 130; those who do not pray deny God, 1 *Lat.* 311; prayer is necessary, 3 *Bec.* 12, 4 *Bul.* 169; no will-work, but absolutely necessary, 1 *Lat.* 508; especially needful for understanding the scriptures, *Whita.* 467; objections against prayer answered, 4 *Bul.* 168, 169; as, for example, that God knows whereof we have need, 1 *Bec.* 169, 170; it is true that prayer cannot alter God's decrees, yet we must pray, *Pra. B.* 6, 7, 8; God is to be sought in prayer, *Sand.* 155; it must be made to God only, 1 *Bec.* 139, 140, 4 *Bul.* 171, *Nord.* 13 (see *d.* below); to the Father, 2 *Cov.* 275, &c.; to the Son, *Hutch.* 192; to the Holy Ghost, *ib.* 136, 199, 200, 204; prayer must be offered through Christ alone, and all things must be asked in his name, 1 *Bec.* 149, 2 *Bec.* 134, 4 *Bul.* 173, *Now.* (66), 186; prayer is acceptable only through Christ, 1 *Lat.* 167, 330; Jews, Mahometans, and Papists, do not make their prayers in the name of Christ; consequently they are not acceptable, 2 *Bec.* 135, 4 *Bul.* 173; how God hears the prayers of the heathen, 3 *Tyn.* 181; what it is to pray in Christ's name, 1 *Bec.* 149, 2 *Bec.* 134; the Holy Ghost is the author of prayer, 1 *Bec.* 143, 2 *Bec.* 125; instructions concerning prayer, 1 *Brad.* 116; Becon's prayer that God would direct his pen to speak of it, 1 *Bec.* 141; an exhortation to prayer, *ib.* 187; an exhortation unto prayer, to be read afore processions, 1544, *Pra. Eliz.* 565; Bradford's preface to Chrysostom's orations on prayer, 1 *Brad.* 13; his preface to Melancthon's treatise, *ib.* 19; an introduction to prayer (in part from Melancthon), *Pra. B.* xiii; an address on prayer by Richard Daye, *Pra. Eliz.* 431; a treatise on prayer, its nature, efficacy, &c., by Jo. Norden, *Nord.* 9; meditations concerning prayer, *Pra. B.* 1, 1 *Brad.* 173; considerations to stir us up to pray, 1 *Brad.* 21; things which move us to pray, 4 *Bul.* 174, 2 *Lat.* 177; the cause which moves us to it must be diligently considered, 2 *Bec.* 128; how we should prepare ourselves to it, *ib.* 128, &c.; what things are to be considered in preparation for it, 1 *Bec.* 145; heads for consideration before prayer, by Thos. Cottesforde, *Lit. Edw.* 375; he that intends to pray must consider in what case he stands, 1 *Bec.* 145; to pray aright is a thing of great difficulty, *ib.* 128, 1 *Hoop.* 144; yet, though false prayer is painful, true prayer is a comfort, 2 *Tyn.* 80; how we ought to pray, 4 *Bul.* 201, 1 *Cov.* 247; the rule and form of prayer, *Now.* (70), 190; faith in prayer, 2 *Bec.* 132, 133; it springs from faith, 1 *Tyn.* 118, 2 *Tyn.* 115; it must be offered in faith, *Now.* (67), 187, 2 *Tyn.* 118; faith makes it acceptable, 1 *Lat.* 172; without faith it profits not, *ib.* 419; how to pray with a faithful mind, 1 *Bec.* 137; prayer must be grounded on God's promises, 2 *Whitg.* 473; he promises to hear and answer it, 1 *Bec.* 147, 2 *Bec.* 130, 131, 1 *Tyn.* 293; the promises must be embraced, 2 *Bec.* 132; if the promises be not obtained, it is owing to our unfaithfulness, 1 *Bec.* 148; in prayer we must submit to the will of God, *ib.* 167, 168, 2 *Whitg.* 474; how to pray according to the will of God, 2 *Bec.* 138, &c.; all things are to be asked according to his will, 1 *Bec.* 151, 2 *Bec.* 136, 137; some things must be asked conditionally, others not so, 2 *Lat.* 173, 174—185; temporal things must be left to the will of God, 2 *Bec.* 139, 140, 3 *Bec.* 114, 2 *Whitg.* 474; spiritual things may be asked without condition, 2 *Bec.* 139; we may appoint God no time in prayer, 1 *Bec.* 152, 153; why prayer is not always immediately answered, 2 *Brad.* 73, 1 *Lat.* 547; we must be in quiet for it, 1 *Bec.* 130; we must abide the Lord's leisure in it, 2 *Bec.* 143; no time of granting must be appointed in it to God, *ib.* 142, 143; why they that pray do not always receive that they ask, 4 *Bul.*

PRAYER 623

170; prayer is fruitless where repentance is not, *Sand.* 157; it must be offered with a pure mind, 1 *Bec.* 136; sin must be put away, or prayer will not be heard, 1 *Brad.* 22; we must put out of our mind infidelity, wrath, contention, 1 *Bec.* 138; he that prays aright cannot sin, *ib.* 143; God will not hear the wicked, 1 *Lat.* 344, 507; he punishes our sin by not hearing our prayers, *ib.* 230; if not offered in love and charity, prayer is not acceptable to God, 2 *Bec.* 180, 181; if we hope to be forgiven we must forgive, 1 *Bec.* 153, &c., 2 *Bec.* 140, &c. (see the Lord's prayer, below); with how great reverence we should pray, 1 *Bec.* 171; prayer must be with humility, *ib.* 260, 2 *Whitg.* 476; a feeling of helplessness is necessary, *Pil.* 411; we must pray with understanding, 1 *Lat.* 344, 507, with fervent affection, *Now.* (69), 189, *Pil.* 292; the earnestness of the heathen in their prayers, *Sand.* 262; the slothfulness and coldness of the prayers lamented, 2 *Lat.* 173; prayer must proceed from love, 4 *Bul.* 179; on lifting up of the mind to heavenly things, 1 *Bec.* 130, 4 *Bul.* 178; outward forms and inward dispositions, *Pil.* 295; prayer is the work of the mind, 1 *Bec.* 132, 136, 1 *Lat.* 507; examples of it in the mind, 1 *Bec.* 132; when we may pray with the voice, *ib.* 164; prayer must not be with the mouth only, but also with the heart, 4 *Bul.* 180, *Now.* (68), 188; mouth-prayer proceeding from the heart is commendable, 2 *Bec.* 125; prayer not proceeding from the heart is vain and unfruitful, 1 *Bec.* 133, 134, 135, 163, 2 *Tyn.* 80; external gestures in prayer, 1 *Bec.* 131, 132, 164, 4 *Bul.* 185, 1 *Jew.* 319, *Whita.* 587, 3 *Whitg.* 92; the ancient custom of standing on Sundays, and at Paschal time, *Calf.* 257, 271, 413, 2 *Cran.* 38, 39, 56 n., *Whita.* 587, 593, 666, 1 *Whitg.* 215; kneeling on Sundays, &c., accounted wicked by Tertullian, *Calf.* 257, 270; prayer sometimes made with the head covered, 2 *Cran.* 55; toward what part of the world we must pray, 4 *Bul.* 500; the place of prayer, 1 *Bec.* 156, &c., 4 *Bul.* 183; we may pray everywhere, *Nord.* 25, *Pil.* 323, 1 *Tyn.* 118; examples of prayer in solitary places, 1 *Bec.* 130, 131; the temple was, and the church is, the house of prayer, *Sand.* 251, &c.; against the notion that prayer offered in certain places is especially availing, 3 *Tyn.* 84—89; God hath not respect to the place, but to the heart and faith, 1 *Hoop.* 491; yet places dedicated to prayer are not to be despised, 1 *Bec.* 159; when we ought to pray, *ib.* 172, 4 *Bul.* 183; our prayer must be continual, or without ceasing, 1 *Bec.* 168, 170, 3 *Bec.* 212, 213, 1 *Brad.* 23, 4 *Bul.* 181, 2 *Cov.* 275, 2 *Hoop.* 317, 2 *Jew.* 878, 1 *Lat.* 509, *Nord.* 26, *Sand.* 38, 263, 2 *Tyn.* 117; importunity is needful, 1 *Lat.* 144, 229, 346, 547, 2 *Lat.* 164; the opportunity of prayer not to be let pass, 4 *Bul.* 186; prayer is hourly needed, 2 *Tyn.* 77; set hours for prayer used by holy men and to be commended, 1 *Bec.* 170, 171, 172, 4 *Bul.* 183, 197, &c.; we should pray in the morning, 1 *Bec.* 173; before labour, *ib.*; before going to bed, *ib.* 175; before sleep, *ib.* 176; prayer is to be resorted to in adversity and trouble, 1 *Cov.* 125, 1 *Lat.* 165, 2 *Lat.* 177; we must call upon God in all afflictions, 1 *Cov.* 247, 2 *Lat.* 185, 213; the order of prayer in adversity, 1 *Lat.* 143; in affliction we must pray conditionally, 2 *Lat.* 185; prayer among soldiers, 1 *Bec.* 252; it is necessary in preparing for war, *ib.* 257, 258; prayer is necessary to support us in the hour of death, 2 *Cov.* 121; we must pray for princes, *Sand.* 38, 78, &c., 83, &c.; for the ministers of the word, 1 *Cov.* 250; for ourselves, *ib.* 247; for all that are given and committed to us of God, *ib.*; for our brethren and neighbours, 1 *Bec.* 166, 1 *Tyn.* 93; for the people, *Sand.* 38, 83, &c.; for all men, *ib.* 78; when referred to no certain end, prayer is unprofitable, 1 *Bec.* 140; a man must ask for somewhat in it, *ib.*, 2 *Bec.* 126; what we must seek in it, 1 *Bec.* 165; what men may pray for for themselves, *ib.* 166, 167; we ought to pray that God would make us one by his Holy Spirit in the faith, 1 *Cov.* 253; that he may sanctify our bodies, our souls, and our whole lives to his service, *ib.*; that he may defend us from evil, *ib.*; we should pray that faithful pastors may be sent, 4 *Bul.* 158; especially we ought to pray, that our heavenly Father may be glorified, 1 *Cov.* 247; on prayer for vengeance upon the wicked, 1 *Brad.* 177; on prayer that all men may be saved, 3 *Whitg.* 383; what we must not pray for, 1 *Bec.* 167; we must require no unworthy thing for God to grant, and contrary to his laws, 4 *Bul.* 181; the commendation of prayer, 1 *Bec.* 128; it is a Christian exercise, *Sand.* 275; one of the most excellent works required of Christian men, 2 *Hoop.* 615; it passeth all good works, 1 *Lat.* 338; it is the widow's weapon, *ib.* 157; a sovereign salve for all sores, *Pil.*

405, 411; may be compared to a perfume, 1 *Bec.* 131; it adorns the state of a commonwealth, 3 *Bec.* 12; what it does, 1 *Bec.* 144; it is the means whereby we obtain all things necessary, 1 *Brad.* 14; the benefit we receive of God in it, 2 *Bec.* 490, 491, 492; through prayer we receive the Holy Ghost, 1 *Lat.* 444; it certifies the conscience of being in the number of the elect, 3 *Bec.* 174; by it all things are easy, 1 *Bec.* 143, 144; it is the Christian's special weapon, 1 *Lat.* 506; a means to resist the devil, 3 *Bec.* 157; the only remedy against his fiery darts, *Phil.* 264; there is a victory to be gained by it, 2 *Tyn.* 116, 120; it is a remedy against sin, 1 *Brad.* 135, *e. g.* against adultery, 2 *Bec.* 101; it is a remedy against God's wrath, 3 *Bec.* 211, 212; prayer is heard, 2 *Cov.* 91; why God hears it, 2 *Bec.* 131, 132; it is acceptable to God, *Lit. Edw.* 518 (565); he is moved with it, 4 *Bul.* 170; of what virtue and strength it is, 1 *Bec.* 141, 2 *Bec.* 127, 4 *Bul.* 244, 1 *Hoop.* 184; examples of prayer and its efficacy, 1 *Bec.* 140, 141, 257, 258, 1 *Lat.* 508; examples of deliverance thereby, 3 *Bec.* 212; what great things the old fathers brought to pass through it, 1 *Bec.* 141, 142, 143; the prayers of Jacob, 4 *Bul.* 224, of Moses, *ib.* 170, 224, 225, 1 *Lat.* 143, of Joshua, 4 *Bul.* 225, 1 *Lat.* 144, of Samuel, 4 *Bul.* 225, of David, 1 *Bec.* 171; the tenor of his prayer in Psa. li., 1 *Hoop.* 57, 2 *Hoop.* 358; his desire to be heard for his righteousness, explained, 1 *Bec.* 150, 4 *Bul.* 175, *Sand.* 404; the prayers of Josaphat, 1 *Lat.* 144; of Hezekiah, 2 *Bul.* 95, 4 *Bul.* 168, 170, 225, 2 *Cov.* 380, 2 *Hoop.* 164; of Manasseh (see his name); of Daniel, 1 *Bul.* 292; 4 *Bul.* 175, 225, of Nehemiah, 4 *Bul.* 225, *Lit. Edw.* 479, *Pil.* 296—305, 322, 403; Christ an example of prayer, 1 *Cov.* 247; he prayed, and taught others to pray, 1 *Bec.* 143; Stephen's prayer the cause of Paul's conversion, 1 *Lat.* 338; the prayers of Paul and Silas, 4 *Bul.* 226; examples of confession of unrighteousness in it, 1 *Bec.* 149, 150; prayer must be joined with means, *Pil.* 412; with study, 1 *Lat.* 125; with labour, *ib.* 402; with fasting and alms, 1 *Bec.* 161, 2 *Tyn.* 93, 94; prayer, fasting, and alms, are our spiritual sacrifices, 1 *Bec.* 138; it must be joined with watchfulness, *Sand.* 397, 398; the command to use not many words in prayer expounded, 1 *Bec.* 169; faithful men make short prayers, 1 *Lat.* 352; against vain babbling, 2 *Tyn.* 80, 81; lip-labour forbidden in prayer, 4 *Bul.* 204; on "vain repetitions," and "much speaking," 3 *Whitg.* 513—517; the most part of the Popish clergy neither pray, nor know what true prayer is, 1 *Lat.* 314; none may be hired to pray, 1 *Tyn.* 280; intercessory prayer cannot be bought with money, *ib.* 96; though hypocrites will pray for hire after their manner, 2 *Tyn.* 81; the Christian desires the prayers of others, but does not trust in them, 3 *Tyn.* 277—278; prayer has been termed a sacrament, 4 *Bul.* 247

(*b*) *On the language in which public prayer should be offered:* the question concerning public prayer and sacred rites in the vulgar tongue, *Whita.* 250; prayer in the congregation should not be in an unknown language, but in a tongue understood by the people, 3 *Bec.* 230, 231, 1 *Brad.* 372, 2 *Brad.* 201, 202, 4 *Bul.* 188, 2 *Ful.* 223, 2 *Hoop.* 391, 555, 564, 1 *Jew.* 33, 56, 76, 263, &c., 4 *Jew.* 811, &c., 2 *Lat.* 261, *Now.* (69), 188, *Rid.* 103, 104, 401, *Rog.* 241—243, *Whita.* 258, &c.; we should not use prayers which we do not understand, *Whita.* 266; Romish explanations of St Paul's teaching in unknown tongues, *ib.* 6; prayer in an unknown tongue is not primitive, 2 *Jew.* 989; it is not common prayer, *ib.* 990; it is unreasonable, 4 *Bul.* 188, 189, 2 *Cran.* 169, &c.; it is unprofitable, 2 *Tyn.* 221; testimony of the fathers against it, 1 *Jew.* 33, *Whita.* 270, &c.; probations out of the old fathers that common prayer ought to be in a tongue understood by the people, 3 *Bec.* 407, &c.; the Armenians, Egyptians, Ethiopians, Indians, Moravians, Muscovites, &c. had their service in the vulgar tongue, 1 *Jew.* 289, 334, 335, *Pil.* 499, 500, *Rog.* 243, *Whita.* 269; arguments for service in a foreign tongue confuted, *Whita.* 251, &c.; foolish reasons for it, 1 *Jew.* 271, 1 *Zur.* 14; the unknown tongue of the mass, an abuse, 1 *Jew.* 8, 9; opinion that the vulgar tongue should be used in the mass, except perhaps in certain secret mysteries, 2 *Cran.* 151; against the Latin service, *ib.* 450; its barbarisms, 1 *Jew.* 316; it is a mark of Antichrist's synagogue, 2 *Brad.* 202; buzzing in Latin helps not the people, 3 *Tyn.* 126; its restoration under queen Mary, 3 *Bec.* 207; request that it may be taken away, *ib.* 247; debate upon it at the Westminster conference, 1 *Zur.* 14; prayer in a foreign tongue disallowed in the church of England, *ib.* 178 (see 358); Justinian's edict against prayer in a low tone of voice, see p. 470, col. 2

PRAYER

(c) *On Prayer for the Dead:* departed saints may be remembered in prayer, 1 *Lat.* 40, 217, 284; the true doctrine on this point, 2 *Brad.* 279, 2 *Cov.* 258; the ancient practice of memorials of the dead, 2 *Cov.* 249, 270; it is opposed to the Romish doctrine of praying for the dead, *ib.*; offering for the dead in the ancient church was an offering of thanksgiving for their salvation, *Coop.* 96; what the fathers meant by prayer for the dead, 2 *Brad.* 291, 2 *Cov.* 270, *Grin.* 24, 25; Ambrose prayed for the repose of Theodosius, 2 *Ful.* 87; what Augustine says of the practice, 3 *Bul.* 397; it is supported by Chrysostom, *Whita.* 596; the Romish doctrine, 2 *Brad.* 270, 3 *Bul.* 395, 2 *Cov.* 249; confutation of the papists' sacrificing and praying for the dead, 2 *Brad.* 290, 2 *Cov.* 269; it is superstitious and without warrant of God's word, 3 *Bul.* 395, 396, *Grin.* 23, 24, 2 *Jew.* 743, *Phil.* 405; but, on the contrary, opposed to his commandments, 2 *Hoop.* 121; Judas Maccabæus not to be followed in this respect, 2 *Cov.* 473, *Grin.* 24, 1 *Lat.* 515 (the passage is wanting in some ancient copies, *Grin.* 24); prayer for the dead is useless, 3 *Bec.* 459, &c., 3 *Bul.* 399; the vanity of making provision for it, 3 *Bec.* 124, 1 *Tyn.* 331; some are prayed for and prayed to also, 1 *Tyn.* 244; masses for the dead, see p. 527, col. 1; strange story of a ghost, adduced in proof of the efficacy of sacrifice for the dead, *Calf.* 89; prayer for the departed enjoined to be used before all sermons, 2 *Cran.* 460; it is found in the form of bidding prayer, 1547, *ib.* 504; commendatory prayer for the faithful departed retained in king Edward's first Prayer Book, *Lit. Edw.* 88; so in the order of burial, *ib.* 145—148; in the Dirige, 1559, *Pra. Eliz.* 59 n., 67; asserted to be in the English burial service, 3 *Whitg.* 362, reply to this, *ib.* 364; memorial of the departed in our communion service, 2 *Brad.* 291, 311, 2 *Cov.* 269

(d) *On the Invocation of Saints and Angels:* prayer must be offered to God alone, and not to saints or angels, 2 *Bec.* 144, *Now.* (64), 184; against prayer to angels, *Bale* 544, 626, 2 *Bec.* 58, 59, 3 *Bul.* 219, 347, *Calf.* 375, 2 *Lat.* 86, 2 *Tyn.* 169; against the invocation of saints, 1 *Bec.* 138, 2 *Bec.* 380, 536, 3 *Bec.* 43, 263, 268, 356, 1 *Brad.* 372, 2 *Brad.* 270, 281, 294, 4 *Bul.* 539, 2 *Cov.* 249, 260, 272, 422, 423, 475, 1 *Hoop.* 35, 36, 85, 458, *Hutch.* 93, 200, 1 *Lat.* 235, 2 *Lat.* 88, 99, 153, 172, 186, 234, *Now.* (65), 184, *Rog.* 225, &c.; it began by rhetorical exornation, 2 *Ful.* 87; it is said to receive some sanction from Augustine, 3 *Tyn.* 126 n.; Latimer speaks dubiously on prayer to saints, sometimes allowing it, 2 *Lat.* 234, 235, 353; it is allowed by the Institution, so that we make no invocation of them, 2 *Cran.* 102; it is commanded by Antichrist, 3 *Bec.* 522, 523; it is to bring in many gods, *Hutch.* 171, for if we pray to them we make them gods, 2 *Lat.* 172, 186; it is idolatrous, 2 *Ful.* 187, 1 *Hoop.* 85; injurious to the honour of Christ, 2 *Hoop.* 121; damnable, 3 *Tyn.* 278; some are prayed to and prayed for also, 1 *Tyn.* 244; those who pray to saints made by the pope may be praying to the damned, 3 *Tyn.* 122; the Romish doctrine of praying and sacrificing to the dead refuted, 2 *Cov.* 269, &c.; if they who pray to saints received what they pray for, yet would not such prayers be thereby proved lawful, 3 *Tyn.* 181; invocation of the virgin, angels, saints, &c. omitted from the litany, *Pra Eliz.* vii; the clauses of invocation required by an act of parliament to be blotted out, *ib.*

(e) *Manuals of prayer:* Horæ B. V. M. ad usum Sarum, see p. 400, col. 1; Orarium, Enchiridion, Manuale eccl. Sarum, see p. 511, col. 2; Erasmi Precationes aliquot, *Pra. Eliz.* 98 n., &c.; his Modus Orandi Deum, *Calf.* 66 n., 389 n.; Precationes Christianæ ad imitationem Psalmorum, *Pra. Eliz.* 154 n.; the Exercitationes of Jo. Lud. Vives, 1 *Brad.* 223, 572, &c., *Pra. B.* vii, 60, 76, *Pra. Eliz.* 440, &c.; ORARIUM SEU LIBELLUS PRECATIONUM, 1560, *Pra. Eliz.* 115, &c.; notices of different editions, *Pra. B.* iii, *Pra. Eliz.* xii; PRECES PRIVATÆ, 1564, *Pra. Eliz.* 209, &c.; notice thereof, and of subsequent editions, *Pra. B.* iv, *Pra Eliz.* xv; Musculi Precationes, *Pra. Eliz.* 442 n., 507 n., 513; Precationum Piarum Enchiridion, Antw., 1573, *ib.* 272 n., 545 n.; Variæ Meditationes et Preces Piæ (Lat. Ital. Gall. et Angl.), Lond. 1582, *ib.* 475 n., 518 n.; Lanspergii Pharetra Divini Amoris, *ib.* 380 n., 381 n.; Saliceti Antidotarium Animæ, *ib.* 545 n.; Hortulus Animæ, *ib.* 202, &c.; Viridarium Spirituale, *ib.* 272 n

Bishop Hilsey's Primer, 2 *Lat.* 369 n., *Pra. Eliz.* 507 n., 511 n.; Marshall's Primer, *Pra. Eliz.* viii, 507 n.; Godly Prayers, notice of two series of prayers so called, *Lit. Eliz.* xix; one of the sets so designated, *ib.* 246, &c.; A PATHWAY UNTO PRAYER, by T. Becon, 1 *Bec.* 123; &c;

THE FLOWER OF GODLY PRAYERS, by T. Becon, 3 *Bec.* 1, &c.; THE POMANDER OF PRAYER, by T. Becon, *ib.* 72, &c.; another book so called, *Pra. Eliz.* xxi; Certain Godly Exercises, Meditations and Prayers, *Pra. B.* iv, *Pra. Eliz.* 520; Godlie Meditations upon the Lord's Prayer, the Beliefe, and Ten Commandmentes, &c., *Pra. B.* iv; Ludlowe's or Lidley's Prayers, *ib.* v, 167; Book of Christian Prayers, 1569, and subsequent editions, 1 *Brad.* 223, *Pra. Eliz.* xvi; history of Elizabeth's own copy, now at Lambeth, *ib.* xx; A BOOK OF CHRISTIAN PRAYERS (the second edition), 1578, *Pra. Eliz.* 429, &c.; Bull's CHRISTIAN PRAYERS AND HOLY MEDITATIONS, 1570, *Pra. B.*; Norden's PROGRESS OF PIETY, *Nord.*; Cosin's Collection of Private Devotions, *Pra. B.* iii, *Calf.* 226 n., *Pra. Eliz.* x. n., xii, &c.

Notices of early reformed manuals of private prayer, *Pra. B.* iii, iv; PRIVATE PRAYERS, PUT FORTH BY AUTHORITY DURING THE REIGN OF QUEEN ELIZABETH, edited by the Rev. Will. Keatinge Clay, B.D., *Pra. Eliz.*

(*f*) *Occasional Services:* occasional forms come into use, 2 *Cran.* 493, 494 n.; prayers were set forth 2 Edw. VI., for peace with Scotland, 2 *Cran.* 154; a thanksgiving ordered for a victory over the Scots, *ib.* 417; notes respecting occasional services, *Lit. Eliz.* xxxiii, &c.; a list of occasional forms of prayer and services used during the reign of Elizabeth, *ib.* 457—474; copies or abstracts of many of these forms, *ib.* 475—695; occasional services for the plague, 1563, *Grin.* 75—120; letters respecting them, *Grin.* 258, &c., *Park.* 182—185, 201; a form prepared for the preservation of Christian countries invaded by the Turks, 1566, *Park.* 289; notice of a form set forth in 1572, *ib.* 402; notes on accession services, *Lit. Eliz.* 463

Prayer (The Lord's): why so called, 2 *Bec.* 144; it was offered by Christ, 4 *Bul.* 207; the excellency of it, 2 *Bec.* 144; it is the sum of all prayers, 1 *Lat.* 327, 341, 443, 2 *Whitg.* 469; a compendium of all the Psalms and prayers in scripture, 1 *Hoop.* 428; Tertullian calls it a lawful prayer, *Pra. B.* xxxii; the Lord's prayer expounded, 4 *Bul.* 206—220, 2 *Cran.* 106—112, *Lit. Edw.* 518, &c., (565), *Now.* (70), 190, 2 *Tyn.* 82—86; paraphrased, 1 *Brad.* 180, 246, *Pra. B.* 133; a prayer to God the Father, founded on the Lord's prayer, *Pra. Eliz.* 450; the Lord's prayer in Latin verse, by G. Æmylius, *ib.* 403; the common people of the North have ever used it in English metre, *Pil.* 501; in metre, by Coverdale, 2 *Cov.* 548; another of the same, *ib.* 549; by Henry Lok, *Poet.* 137; by Rob. Holland, *ib.* 477; paraphrased by D. Cox, *ib.* 503; meditations on it, 1 *Brad.* 118, *Pra. B.* 9, 41; a short speech before the Lord's prayer, *Pra. Eliz.* 449; why it is in the plural, 4 *Bul.* 208, *Coop.* 19; on its order, 1 *Lat.* 302; how it is divided, 4 *Bul.* 206; the preface, "Our Father which art in heaven," 2 *Bec.* 143, 492, 4 *Bul.* 206; sermon on those words, 1 *Lat.* 326; why we call God "Father" in it, 2 *Bec.* 145, 146, 4 *Bul.* 206; few can truly say "Our Father," 1 *Lat.* 339; why it is said that he is "in heaven," 2 *Bec.* 146, 147, 4 *Bul.* 208; the first petition, "hallowed be thy name," 2 *Bec.* 147, 492, 493, 4 *Bul.* 209; sermon on this petition, 1 *Lat.* 341; the second petition, "thy kingdom come," 2 *Bec.* 149, 493, 4 *Bul.* 211; sermon on this petition, 1 *Lat.* 354; the third petition, "thy will be done in earth, even as it is in heaven," 2 *Bec.* 154, 493, 4 *Bul.* 212; sermon on this petition, 1 *Lat.* 368; the fourth petition, "give us this day our daily bread," 2 *Bec.* 158, 493, 494, 4 *Bul.* 214; sermon on this petition, 1 *Lat.* 389; why we say "give," 2 *Bec.* 159, 4 *Bul.* 215; why we say "us," 2 *Bec.* 159, 160, 4 *Bul.* 215; why we say "this day," 2 *Bec.* 160, 161, 4 *Bul.* 215; why we say "our," 2 *Bec.* 161, &c., 4 *Bul.* 214; what is meant by "daily," 2 *Bec.* 163, &c., 4 *Bul.* 214; what is understood by "bread," 2 *Bec.* 166, &c., 4 *Bul.* 214; "daily bread," 1 *Brad.* 100, 131, 181, 2 *Cran.* 109, 1 *Lat.* 389, *Now.* (77), 197, & al.; the fifth petition, "and forgive us our trespasses, as we forgive them that trespass against us," 2 *Bec.* 168, 494, 495, 4 *Bul.* 215; sermon on this petition, 1 *Lat.* 413; why we say "forgive us," 2 *Bec.* 176, 177; the sixth petition, "and lead us not into temptation," *ib.* 183, 194, 495, 4 *Bul.* 217; sermon on this petition, and the next, 1 *Lat.* 428; why we are taught to pray against being led into temptation, 2 *Bec.* 183, &c.; this petition altered by king Henry VIII. ("and suffer not us," &c.), 2 *Cran.* 106, *Pra. Eliz.* 16 n.; the seventh (or sixth) petition, "but deliver us from evil," 2 *Bec.* 195, 196, 495, 4 *Bul.* 218; sermon on it, see the preceding petition; what "evil" we pray to be delivered from, 2 *Bec.* 195, 2 *Whitg.* 484; two petitions omitted in some copies of Luke, 2 *Cov.* 36; portions omitted in the Vulgate,

1 *Ful.* 58; the conclusion or doxology, 2 *Bec.* 196, 495, 496, 1 *Brad.* 138, 4 *Bul.* 219, 1 *Lat.* 444, *Now.* (81), 202; "Amen," its meaning, 2 *Bec.* 197, 198, 4 *Bul.* 218, *Now.* (81), 202; the Lord's prayer used by the apostles in the communion, 3 *Whitg.* 99; said by the Greeks all together, in the Latin church by the priest alone, 1 *Jew.* 185; mode of saying it, directed by the Sarum breviary, *Lit. Eliz.* 72; Latimer used to examine the people in it after sermon, 1 *Lat.* 307; the Lord's prayer with the creed and ten commandments styled the sum of scripture, *Whitg.* 388; whether we be tied to it, 4 *Bul.* 203; it is lightly esteemed by many, 1 *Lat.* 389

Prayers: *v.* Meditations, Thanksgivings.

Brevis, sed efficax, oratio, *Pra. Eliz.* 381; a prayer by R. P. (perhaps Pownall), 1 *Brad.* 578; a prayer (in verse), by Sir N. Breton, *Poet.* 184

Adversity (*v. Prosperity*): in rebus adversis, *Pra. Eliz.* 199, 388; in angustiis et extremis periculis, *ib.* 387; in adversity, *Lit. Edw.* 480, *Pra. Eliz.* 106, (199); for our brethren that are in adversity (from Vives), *Pra. Eliz.* 485

Affliction (*v. Adversity, Care, Patience, Persecution, Sermon, Sickness*): in afflictione, *Pra. Eliz.* 190, 369; oratio afflicti in tribulatione; ex Augustino, *ib.* 382; de vitæ hujus miseriis querela; ex Augustino, *ib.* 395; in tristitia, morbis, et adversitatibus, *ib.* 190; in affliction or adversity, *ib.* 536 (190); for a faithful man being in trouble, 3 *Bec.* 34, 35; in time of trouble, crosses, and afflictions, *Nord.* 144, 179; to be said of such as be under the cross, *Pra. Eliz.* 545; under any trouble or cross, either private or common, *Pra. B.* 136; for deliverance from trouble, 1 *Brad.* 276; when we are punished of God for our sins or trial, *Lit. Edw.* 477; in great trouble of conscience; from Ps. cxliii, *Pra. Eliz.* 93

Agreement: v. Church.
All Christians: v. Christians.
All men: v. Intercession.
All times: v. Times.
Angels: for the help of God's holy angels, 3 *Bec.* 84, *Lit. Edw.* 474
Anger: contra iram, *Pra. Eliz.* 199— 385; against anger, *ib.* 105, (199)
Assurance (*v. Faith*): for assurance of election, *Pra. B.* 160; for sure hope of the life everlasting, *Lit. Eliz.* 253, *Pra. B.* 202, 204
Autumn: v. Times.
Avarice: v. Covetousness.

Beatitudes: v. Graces.
Biblical: v. Scripture.
Bidding: v. Bidding.
Bishops: v. Ministers.

Calling (*v. Labourers, &c.*): that all may walk in their vocation and calling, 3 *Bec.* 36, &c.; that every man may live uprightly in his calling, *Nord.* 129; another, *ib.* 180

Captives: of any captive, according to the form of David, Ps. cxlii, *Pra. Eliz.* 92; for a faithful man being in endurance, 3 *Bec.* 34

Care: adversus curam mundanam, *Pra. Eliz.* 198, 384; against worldly carefulness, *Lit. Eliz.* 250, *Pra. Eliz.* 104 (198)

Charity: v. Graces, Love.
Cheerfulness: v. Graces.

Children (*v. Husbands, Intercession, Parents*): of children, 3 *Bec.* 77; of children for their parents, *Lit. Edw.* 462, *Pra. Eliz.* 483; for children, 3 *Bec.* 29, 30, 37, *Pra. B.* 176

Christ (*v. God, Love, Mercy, Perseverance*): ad Deum Filium, *Pra. Eliz.* 375; to God the Son, 3 *Bec.* 76, *Pra. Eliz.* 453; devota oratio ad Jesum Christum, by St Bernardine, (O bone Jesu), *Pra. Eliz.* 202; the same in English, *ib.* 108; ad Jesum Christum, in verse, by bp Parkhurst, *ib.* 238; a prayer to Christ, in verse, by Chr. Lever, *Poet.* 523; certain short and pithy prayers (in verse) unto Jesu Christ our Saviour, by W. Hunnis, *ib.* 152; a confession of sins to Jesus Christ, 3 *Bec.* 16; de passione Christi, *Pra. Eliz.* 144, 180, &c., 283; upon the passion of our Saviour Christ, 1 *Brad.* 206, *Pra. Eliz.* 33, 85—88, 504— 512; to Christ crucified, *Pra. B.* 149; on Christ's resurrection and ascension, *Pra. Eliz.* 513, 514; to Christ ascended, *Pra. B.* 150

Christians: of all Christians, 3 *Bec.* 79, *Lit. Edw.* 466; meet for all men, at all times, *Lit. Edw.* 466; containing the duty of every true Christian, *Lit. Eliz.* 269 (comp. *Pra. B.* 191); necessary for all persons, partly translated by queen Mary from Tho. Aquinas (see under *Wisdom*), *Lit. Eliz.* 250

Church (*v. Adversity, Enemies, Gospel, Persecution, Sin*): pro statu ecclesiastico, *Pra. Eliz.* 370; for the universal church, &c., *Lit. Eliz.* 266, 576, 616, 643, *Nord.* 98, 105, *Pra. B.* 126, 129, *Pra. Eliz.* 98, 462, 468, 469; for the whole realm, and the body of the church, *Pra. Eliz.* 458; pro concordia et unitate ecclesiæ Christi, *ib.* 377; pro concordia et consensu...in rebus divinis, *ib.* 188; pro consensu dogmatum, et contra adversarios veræ fidei, *ib.* 377; for the concord of Christ's church, *Lit. Eliz.* 254, *Pra. Eliz.* 90, (184); for the peace of the church, *Pra. Eliz.* 98, 469; for unity and brotherly love in the church, 1 *Cov.* 385; for agreement in matters of Christian religion, 3 *Bec.* 40, &c.; against false prophets, errors, and schisms, *Nord.* 119, 178; for the continuance of our religious blessing, and the building of the spiritual Jerusalem, *Pil.* 393; for the restoration of the mystical Jerusalem, 2 *Jew.* 1004; for love to Jerusalem, *Pil.* 368; for love of God's house, 2 *Jew.* 1015; templum ingrediens, *Pra. Eliz.* 394

Cleanness : v. Purity.
Commandments : on the ten commandments, 2 *Brad.* 256
Commons : v. People.
Communion: v. Supper of the Lord.
Concord : v. Church.
Confession : succincta confessio peccatorum; confessions of sins, *Pra. Eliz.* 373, 1 *Brad.* 200, 202, *Lit. Eliz.* 265, 483, 486, 487, *Nord.* 51, 53, *Pra. B.* 46, *Pra. Eliz.* 110, (204), 488; for the morning, 1 *Bec.* 401, *Lit. Eliz.* 246, *Pra. B.* 45; to God the Father, 3 *Bec.* 15; to Jesus Christ, *ib.* 16, &c.; to the Holy Ghost, *ib.* 18
Conscience: v. Affliction, Peace.
Continuance: v. Perseverance.
Council : for the council, 3 *Bec.* 20, *Lit. Edw.* 455
Courtiers : for our courtiers, &c., *Pil.* 305
Covetousness (v. Sin) : adversus avaritiam, *Pra. Eliz.* 397; against covetousness, 3 *Bec.* 59, 60
Cross : v. Affliction.
Day : v. Morning.
Death (v. Martyrdom): upon the minding of death, *Pra. Eliz.* 537; in mortis periculo, *ib.* 368; in peril of death, 2 *Bec.* 578, *Pra. Eliz.* 537; the last prayer of king Edward VI., *Phil.* 178; in hora mortis, *Pra. Eliz.* 202, 397; in the hour of death, *Lit. Eliz.* 256, *Pra. B.* 155, *Pra. Eliz.* 109, (202); prayer and thanksgiving in the hour of death, 2 *Cov.* 88, 91; to be said by a sick person when joyful and glad to die, *Lit. Edw.* 481; for such as lie at the point of death, 3 *Bec.* 68, 186, *Lit. Edw.* 481; a prayer on behalf of queen Elizabeth, composed by Whitgift, the day before his death, *Lit. Eliz.* 695
Deliverance : v. Enemies.

Despair : v. Hope.
Devil : v. Enemies (Ghostly).
Dinner : v. Meat.
Direction: v. Prosperity.
Docility : pro docilitate, *Pra. Eliz.* 171, 172; pro docilitate pietatis, *ib.* 368; for knowledge and understanding, being a translation of Erasmus's prayer, pro docilitate, *ib.* 516
Drunkenness : v. Gluttony.
Election : v. Assurance.
Enemies (v. Intercession, War): for adversaries of God's truth, 3 *Bec.* 38, &c.; contra inimicos veritatis Christi, *Pra. Eliz.* 185; adversus consilia inimicorum Dei et divinæ illius veritatis, *ib.* 186; against the enemies of the truth, *Lit. Eliz.* 255, 628, 636, 647, *Pra. B.* 158, *Pra. Eliz.* 91, (185); against the enemies of the church, *Pil.* 452; against the enemies of the gospel, *Lit. Eliz.* 628, 630; in hostium periculo, *Pra. Eliz.* 395; contra malorum insectationem, *ib.* 369; for deliverance from our enemies, *Lit. Eliz.* 613, 640, 642; for deliverance from our enemies, taken from various parts of the Psalter, *ib.* 543, 545, 610, 611, 627, 634, 635; for enemies, 3 *Bec.* 38; for our evil-willers, *Pra. Eliz.* 487; for God's justice on enemies, *Pil.* 404, 405
Enemies (Ghostly): against the world, the flesh, and the devil, and their temptations, 3 *Bec.* 48, &c., 84, *Lit. Eliz.* 252, *Pra. B.* 124; against the world, *Pra. Eliz.* 541; against the pomps and pleasures of the world, *Pra. B.* 175; a heavenly prayer in contempt of the world and the vanities thereof, in verse, *Poet.* 433; against the flesh, *Pra. Eliz.* 542; contra diabolum, *ib.* 206, 397; against the devil, *ib.* 112, (206), 543; see also *Temptation,* below.
England (v. Sovereigns): ad Deum Opt. Max.; verses, *Pra. Eliz.* 238; a Latin prayer for the defence of the nation against the malice of Satan, *Lit. Eliz.* 466, 596 n
Envy (v. Sin) : contra invidiam, *Pra. Eliz.* 385, see 199; against envy, *ib.* 105, (199)
Error : v. Church.
Eucharist : v. Supper of the Lord.
Evening and Night (v. Morning, Private, School): preces vespertinæ; partly the Common Prayer, and in part from some ancient form, *Pra. Eliz.* 263; other evening prayers in Latin, *ib.* 154, 157, 271; a motion to an evening prayer, *Nord.* 156; prayers for the evening, 3 *Bec.* 14, 75, *Lit. Eliz.* 262, *Nord.* 157, *Pra. B.* 50—54, *Pra. Eliz.* 445; in occasu solis, 1 *Brad.* 576; at the

setting of the sun, *ib.* 239, (576), *Pra. B.* 73, *Pra. Eliz.* 444; quum accenduntur lucernæ, 1 *Brad.* 577; at the lighting up of candles, *ib.* 240, (577). *Pra. B.* 74, *Pra. Eliz.* 445; cum exueris, 1 *Brad.* 577; on unclothing, *ib.* 240, (577), *Pra. B.* 75, *Pra. Eliz.* 447; preces dicendæ, cum itur cubitum, &c., *Pra. Eliz.* 272, &c.; precatio cubitum euntis, in verse, *ib.* 409; cum intras lectum, 1 *Brad.* 577; on going to bed, 1 *Bec.* 403, 1 *Brad.* 241, (577), *Lit. Edw.* 379, 380, 381, 540, *Lit. Eliz.* 256, *Pra. B.* 76, *Pra. Eliz.* 89, (183), 448; sub noctem, *Pra. Eliz.* 131, 372; for the night, 3 *Bec.* 14, 75, *Pil.* 339, *Pra. Eliz.* 446, (372); quum obdormiscis, 1 *Brad.* 578; quum itur dormitum, *Pra. Eliz.* 131; when ready to sleep, 1 *Brad.* 242, (578), *Pra. B.* 77, *Pra. Eliz.* 448

Faith (v. Assurance, Graces): pro vera fide, *Pra. Eliz.* 378; for faith, 3 *Bec.* 45, 46, 81, 1 *Brad.* 65, 209, *Lit. Edw.* 469, *Pra. B.* 138, 203, *Pra. Eliz.* 522; pro veræ fidei augmento, *Pra. Eliz.* 379, comp. 187; pro augmento et constantia in vera fide, *Pra. Eliz.* 187, *ib.* 379; for increase of faith, *Lit. Eliz.* 253; for strength and increase of faith, *Pra. B.* 88; for faith and assurance, 2 *Brad.* 153; pro fiducia in Deum, *Pra. Eliz.* 183, 378; for trust in God, *Lit. Eliz.* 254, *Pra. Eliz.* 89, (523), (183)

Fame: v. *Name*.

Family, Household (v. Intercession, Pestilence): of householders, 3 *Bec.* 79, *Lit. Edw.* 465; certain prayers (for every day in the week, &c.) from the service daily used in the house of queen Catherine Parr, *Lit. Eliz.* 252; daily prayers for household use, from Sternhold and Hopkins's Psalms, 1566, *ib.* 258

Fathers: v. *Parents*.

Fear of God: pro timore pio, *Pra. Eliz.* 367; for the fear of God, 3 *Bec.* 45, *Pra. Eliz.* 523

Flesh: v. *Enemies (Ghostly)*.

Forgiveness: v. *Pardon*.

Fruits: for the preservation of the fruits of the earth, 3 *Bec.* 44, 45

Gentlemen: for gentlemen, 3 *Bec.* 24, *Lit. Edw.* 457, see also *Landlords*, below.

Gentlewomen: of gentlewomen; in verse, *Poet.* 180, 184

Glory: v. *Heaven*.

Gluttony: against gluttony and drunkenness, 3 *Bec.* 60

God: v. *Fear, Presence*.

God: a prayer to God the Father, the Son, and the Holy Ghost, *Pra. B.* 120; a form of prayer to God the Father, (including confession, desire of grace, and patience, prayer for enemies, and for every man,) to the Son, and to the Holy Ghost, 2 *Cov.* 89, 90; a form of prayer and thanksgiving, to the Father, the Son, and the Holy Ghost, *ib.* 91; ad Deum Patrem, *Pra. Eliz.* 375; to God the Father, 3 *Bec.* 75, *Pra. Eliz.* 450; another, in Jesus our Redeemer, (Augustine) *Pra. Eliz.* 452

Godliness (see also *Fear of God, Life*): pro vera pietate, *Pra. Eliz.* 376; pro docilitate pietatis, *ib.* 368; for true godliness, 3 *Bec.* 82, *Lit. Edw.* 471; for a godly life, 3 *Bec.* 47, *Pra. B.* 172, 203

Good name: v *Name*.

Goodness: for God's goodness, and continuance of the same, *Pra. Eliz.* 545

Gospel (v. Enemies, Ministers): for the increase of the gospel, 2 *Jew.* 1034

Grace (v. Prosperity): pro gratia et misericordia, *Pra. Eliz.* 187; oratio, qua nos Deo commendamus, et gratiam ab eo poscimus; ex Augustino, *Pra. Eliz.* 383; for grace, 3 *Bec.* 80, *Lit. Edw.* 467, *Pra. B.* 147, *Pra. Eliz.* 521; for grace and remission of sins, *Pra. B.* 191; the same enlarged, *Lit. Eliz.* 269

Graces (v. Holy Ghost): pro fide, spe, et caritate; from Jo. Lanspergius, *Pra. Eliz.* 380; for patience, cheerfulness, charity, illumination, and other graces, *Pra. B.* 169, &c.; referring to the eight beatitudes, *Pra. Eliz.* 35, &c., (148, &c.); pro Christiana perfectione, *ib.* 380

Health (v. Pestilence): for the health of the body, 3 *Bec.* 83, *Lit. Edw.* 472; for health both of body and mind, *Pra. Eliz.* 535

Heart: v. *Purity*.

Heaven: pro alterius vitæ cupiditatem, *Pra. Eliz.* 206, 397; for the desire of the life to come, *ib.* 113, (206); in desire of the life to come, from L. Vives, *ib.* 556; for the kingdom of God, *Nord.* 82, 87; for the glory of heaven, 3 *Bec.* 84, 85, *Lit. Edw.* 475

Holiness: v. *Godliness, Life*.

Holy Ghost (v. God): for the gift of the Holy Ghost, 3 *Bec.* 80, *Lit. Edw.* 468, *Pra. B.* 202; for God's Spirit, and grace to pray effectually, *Pra. Eliz.* 457; for the assistance of the Holy Spirit, 1 *Bec.* 67, *Nord.* 35; for the witness of the Holy Ghost, and that by his operation we may overcome carnal lusts, *Lit. Eliz.* 254; for his gifts, 3 *Bec.* 80; ad Spiritum Sanctum, *Pra. Eliz.*

186, 376; ad Spiritum, ut corda nostra sibi in templum dedicatum inhabitet, *ib.* 187; to the Holy Ghost, 3 *Bec.* 76, *Pra. Eliz.* 456; confession of sins to the Holy Ghost, 3 *Bec.* 18

Home: v. Journey.

Hope (v. *Assurance, Graces*): contra desperationem, *Pra. Eliz.* 368; against despair, *ib.* 504

Household: v. Family.

Humility: viri fidelis oratio de se humiliter sentientis; ex Augustino, *Pra. Eliz.* 381; for humility, 3 *Bec.* 82, *Lit. Edw.* 470

Husbands and Wives (v. *Intercession, Parents*): pro felici conjugio, *Pra. Eliz.* 393; of the married, 2 *Lat.* 161; of husbands, 3 *Bec.* 79, *Lit. Edw.* 463, 464; of wives, 3 *Bec.* 79, *Lit. Edw.* 464; for the married, 3 *Bec.* 27, 28; petition for husbands, *ib.* 37; for wives, *ib.*; prayer for a wife and children, *Pra. B.* 176; quum legitur evangelium de nuptiis in Cana Galileæ, *Pra. Eliz.* 371

Idleness: against it, 3 *Bec.* 60, 61

Idolatry: against it, 3 *Bec.* 56

Illumination: v. Graces.

Intercession (v. *Calling*): for all men, for enemies, for the persecuted, for wife, children, and family, *Pra. B.* 171, &c.

Jericho: v. Popery.

Jerusalem: v. Church.

Journey: iter ingressurus, *Pra. Eliz.* 394; ingrediens iter, 1 *Brad.* 574; on going any journey, *ib.* 235, (574), *Pra. B.* 67, 68; dum es in via aut itinere, *Pra. Eliz.* 394; for travellers by land, 3 *Bec.* 34; reversus domum, 1 *Brad.* 576, *Pra. Eliz.* 395; on coming home, 1 *Brad.* 238, (576), *Pra. B.* 72, *Pra. Eliz.* 443; after a journey; by queen Elizabeth, *Lit. Eliz.* 667 n

Joy: pro gaudio spirituali; from Erasmus, *Pra. Eliz.* 377; for spiritual joy; the same, *ib.* 531

Judges: v. Magistrates.

Judgment: in contemplation of the judgment, 2 *Lat.* 61; the fear of the judgment and judgment day; from Augustine, *Pra. Eliz.* 557

Justice: v. Enemies.

King: v. Sovereigns.

Kingdom of God: prayers for it, *Nord.* 82, 87

Knowledge (v. *Docility, Life, Redemption, Scripture*): for knowledge of God and his word, *Pra. B.* 203; for the knowledge of ourselves, 3 *Bec.* 80, *Lit. Edw.* 468

Labourers: for labourers and men of occupation, 3 *Bec.* 25, *Lit. Edw.* 459; to be said before a man begins his work, *Lit. Eliz.* 265

Landlords (v. *Gentlemen*): for landlords, 3 *Bec.* 24, *Lit. Edw.* 458

Lawyers: for lawyers, 3 *Bec.* 25, *Lit. Edw.* 459

Laymen: v. Parishioners.

Life (v. *Godliness*): for newness of life, *Pra. Eliz.* 525; for a life agreeable to our knowledge, 3 *Bec.* 83, *Lit. Edw.* 472

Life to come: v. Heaven.

Living: for competent and necessary living, 3 *Bec.* 51, 52, 83, *Lit. Edw.* 473; a prayer of Solomon for sufficiency of livelihood, *Lit. Edw.* 478

Love, Charity (v. *Church, Graces*): pro vere Christiano amore, *Pra. Eliz.* 189, 379; for love towards Christ, *ib.* 523; for charity, 3 *Bec.* 46, 81, *Lit. Edw.* 470; for charity, or love, towards our neighbours, *Pra. Eliz.* 483, 484

Magistrates (v. *Sovereigns*): pro Christianis magistratibus, *Pra. Eliz.* 388; for magistrates, 3 *Bec.* 20, 21, 36, *Pra. Eliz.* 482; of magistrates, 3 *Bec.* 76; for the judges, 3 *Bec.* 20, *Lit. Edw.* 456

Maids: of maids, 3 *Bec.* 78, *Lit. Edw.* 463

Mariners: v. Sea.

Marriage, and Married: v. Husbands.

Martyrdom: of one standing at the stake, 1 *Brad.* 292, *Phil.* 162; Cranmer's prayer a little before his death, 1 *Cran.* xxvi, 2 *Cran.* 565; Hooper's prayer at the stake, 2 *Hoop.* xxviii.

Masters: for masters, 3 *Bec.* 30, 37, *Lit. Edw.* 463; of masters, 3 *Bec.* 77, 78, *Lit. Edw.* 462

Meat: sumpturus cibum, 1 *Brad.* 575; before meat, 1 *Bec.* 173, 1 *Brad.* 236, &c., *Pra. B.* 69; in convivio, 1 *Brad.* 575; in the meal time, 1 *Brad.* 237, *Pra. B.* 70; sumpto cibo, 1 *Brad.* 576; after meat, 1 *Brad.* 237, *Pra. B.* 71; see also Graces.

Meditation: v. Private prayers, Meditations.

Merchants: for merchants, 3 *Bec.* 25, *Lit. Edw.* 458

Mercifulness: for mercifulness, 3 *Bec.* 82, *Lit. Edw.* 471

Mercy (v. *Goodness, Grace, Pardon, Rebellion, Repentance*): penitentis et divinam misericordiam implorantis; ex Augustino, *Pra. Eliz.* 373; pro divina misericordia, *ib.* 370; a petition for mercy, *Pil.* 347; for the mercy of God (in remission of sins), 1 *Brad.* 203; to Christ for mercy,

Lit. Edw. 481; for the avoiding of God's wrath for our sins, *Pra. B.* 154; a comfort after craving of mercy, (Psa.), *Pra. Eliz.* 500; in commendation of God's mercy received (Augustine), *ib.* 501, (373)

Mid-day (v. *School*): cogitations for about the mid-day, 1 *Brad.* 238

Mind (*Sound*): v. *Wisdom*.

Ministers (v. *Sermon*): pro fidelibus ministris, et fructu evangelii, *Pra. Eliz.* 188; pro ministris verbi, et fructu evangelii, *ib.* 388; quum legitur evangelium de seminante semen suum, *ib.* 371; for bishops, pastors, and ministers, 3 *Bec.* 21, &c., 36, *Lit. Edw.* 456, *Pil.* 121, *Pra. Eliz.* 481, *Pra. B.* 127, 130; for more labourers, 2 *Jew.* 1024; for the restoration of preachers, 3 *Bec.* 247; for faithful preachers, *Pil.* 452; of ministers, 3 *Bec.* 77; pro annunciando verbum Domini confidenter, *Pra. Eliz.* 197; to speak the word of God boldly; from Acts iv, *ib.* 98, (197)

Misery: v. *Affliction*.

Morning, Day (v. *Confession, Labourers, Private, School*): quum expergiscimur, 1 *Brad.* 572; on waking, *ib.* 230, (572), *Pra. B.* 60, *Pra. Eliz.* 440; ad primum intuitum lucis, 1 *Brad.* 573; on first beholding the daylight, 1 *Brad.* 231, (573), *Pra. B.* 61; quum surgis, 1 *Brad.* 573; on rising, *ib.* 231, (573), *Lit. Edw.* 379, *Pra. B.* 61, 62, *Pra. Eliz.* 88, (183), 441; quum induimur, 1 *Brad.* 573; oratio inter vestiendum, *Pra. Eliz.* 244; at the putting on of clothes, 1 *Brad.* 232, (573), *Pra. B.* 63, *Pra. Eliz.* 442; inter lavandum manus, *Pra. Eliz.* 244; indutus pro auspicio diei, 1 *Brad.* 574; when made ready to begin the day, *ib.* 232, (574), *Pra. B.* 63; cogitations meet to begin the day with, 1 *Brad.* 233, *Pra. B.* 64; pia meditatio ante preces, *Pra. Eliz.* 245; precationes matutinæ, *ib.* 130, 242, 243, 244; preces matutinæ; taken in part from the Common Prayer-book, partly from some ancient manuals, *ib.* 245; precatio in aurora, petens protectionem Domini, *ib.* 182; for the morning, 1 *Bec.* 401, 3 *Bec.* 14, 75, 1 *Lat.* 433, *Lit. Edw.* 380, 538, *Lit. Eliz.* 258, 268, *Pra. B.* 45—48, *Pra. Eliz.* 88, (182), 441, 442; a prayer to be used in private houses every morning, *Lit. Eliz.* 258; a confession and other prayers to be said in the morning, *ib.* 246, &c.; a prayer to be said both morning and evening, *Pra. Eliz.* 437; egrediens domo, 1 *Brad.* 574; on going abroad, *ib.* 234, (574), *Pra. B.* 66, *Pra. Eliz.* 443

Mortification: for mortification, 1 *Brad.* 190, *Nord.* 72, 88, *Pra. B.* 92, *Pra. Eliz.* 526

Mothers: v. *Parents*.

Name: pro bona fama conservanda, *Pra. Eliz.* 197; pro tuenda bona fama, *ib.* 393; for a good name, 3 *Bec.* 83; for the keeping of a good name, *Pra. Eliz.* 103, (197)

Nation: v. *England, Realm*.

Night: v. *Evening*.

Oppression: v. *Sermons*.

Pardon (v. *Grace, Mercy, Repentance*): a prayer and lamentation of a sinner, *Pra. B.* 142; pro venia delictorum, *Pra. Eliz.* 368; devota oratio, *ib.* 202; for the remission or forgiveness of sins, 3 *Bec.* 50, 51, 75, *Lit. Eliz.* 252, *Nord.* 59, 64, *Pra. B.* 139, 172, *Pra. Eliz.* 489, 490, 492, 493, (202), 494, 495, 496, 498, 499, 500; prayers for pardon, selected from various parts of the scriptures, canonical and apocryphal, *Lit. Eliz.* 541, 609, 633; for deliverance from sin, and to be restored to God's favour, *Pra. B.* 188

Parents (v. *Husbands*): of fathers and mothers, 3 *Bec.* 77, *Lit. Edw.* 462; pro parentibus nostris; composed by Erasmus for St Paul's School, *Pra. Eliz.* 394; prayer for fathers and mothers, 3 *Bec.* 29; petition for fathers, *ib.* 37

Parishioners: petition for them, 3 *Bec.* 37

Parliament: a prayer and thanksgiving for the queen used in parliament, *Lit. Eliz.* 581; a prayer used in parliament only, *ib.* 582; bidding prayer in a sermon before parliament, *Sand.* 34

Passion: v. *Christ*.

Patience (v. *Graces, Sermons, Sickness*): for patience, 3 *Bec.* 81, 82, *Lit. Edw.* 470; for patience in trouble and affliction, 2 *Bec.* 464, *Lit. Edw.* 256, *Pra. B.* 182, *Lit. Edw.* 474, *Pra. Eliz.* 89 (184)

Peace (v. *Church*): for a quiet conscience, 3 *Bec.* 81, *Lit. Edw.* 469; for peace and quietness of realms, 3 *Bec.* 42, 43

Penitence: v. *Psalms, Repentance*.

People (v. *Sovereigns*): for the commons, 3 *Bec.* 26; for subjects, 3 *Bec.* 36; to be used by the commons, *ib.* 77; the prayer of a good subject, *Lit. Edw.* 461

Perfection: v. *Graces*.

Persecution (v. *Intercession, Martyrdom*): in the time of persecution, 1 *Brad.* 278, 578; of the afflicted for the profession of God's word, *Pra. B.* 159; of Anne Askewe, *Bale* 210, 237, 238; of Ridley, for support under persecution, *Rid.* 142; of Philpot, for wisdom to answer his accusers,

Phil. 19; for persecuted Christians, *Lit. Eliz.* 546; for the scattered and persecuted flock of Christ, *Pil.* 273; for the faithful afflicted in France, 1 *Brad.* 571, *Pra. B.* 161, *Pra. Eliz.* 484

Perseverance: for continuance in seeking after Christ; by Augustine, *Pra. Eliz.* 528; for true perseverance, *Pra. B.* 204

Pestilence (v. Psalms): tempore pestilentiæ, *Pra. Eliz.* 391; for deliverance from pestilence, *Lit. Eliz.* 507, *Pra. B.* 84, *Pra. Eliz.* 534 (391); for preservation from plague and other diseases, 3 *Bec.* 43, 44; family prayers in time of pestilence, *Lit. Eliz.* 503; a form of meditation, *Grin.* 477

Piety: v. Godliness.
Plague: v. Pestilence.
Poor: for the poor, 3 *Bec.* 26, *Lit. Edw.* 461, *Pra. Eliz.* 486

Popery: for the removal of popery, 3 *Bec.* 247, &c.; for the confusion of all popery and false doctrine, *Pil.* 615; for the fall of the mystical Jericho, 2 *Jew.* 986

Preachers: v. Ministers, Sermons.
Presence: for the presence of God, 1 *Brad.* 264

Pride (v. Sin): contra superbiam, *Pra.* 198, 384; against pride, 3 *Bec.* 57, 58, *Pra. B.* 168; against pride and unchasteness, *Pra. Eliz.* 104 (198)

Princes: v. Sovereigns.
Prisoners: v. Captives.

Private: an order of private prayer for morning and evening every day in the week, (in K. Edward's Primer,) *Lit. Edw.* 382, &c.; private prayers and meditations for various times of the day, 1 *Brad.* 230, &c., *Pra. B.* 60, &c., (1 *Brad.* 572, &c.)

Prosperity: for good success, and the direction of Christ in all our doings, *Pra. Eliz.* 538; in rebus prosperis, *ib.* 200, 389; in prosperity, *Lit. Edw.* 479, *Pra. Eliz.* 106, (200); for grace in prosperity and adversity, *Lit. Eliz.* 253

Protection: for divine protection, 1 *Brad.* 242

Psalms (v. Psalms): Latin prayers from Psalms i. ii. iii. and li. by P. Martyr, *Pra. Eliz.* 419; his prayers from Psalms i. and ii. in English, *Pra. B* 205; the seven penitential Psalms in Latin, with a short prayer upon each, *Pra. Eliz.* 297; a prayer on Psalm cxv., 1 *Bec.* 301, &c.

Public: a preparation, or preface to public prayer, *Pra. Eliz.* 449

Purity: pro munditia cordis, *Pra. Eliz.* 369; for purity of heart, 3 *Bec.* 81, *Lit. Edw.* 469, *Pra. Eliz.* 524; pro custodia pudicitiæ, *Pra. Eliz.* 392

Queen: v. Sovereigns.
Realm (v. Church, England).

Rebellion: in a time of rebellion, *Lit. Eliz.* 536; prayer for mercy annexed to a homily on rebellion, 2 *Cran.* 202

Redemption: for the true knowledge of the mystery of our redemption, *Pra. B.* 87

Remission: v. Pardon.

Repentance (v. Confession): resipiscentis, *Pra. Eliz.* 370; alia pro eodem, ex Hieremia, *ib.*; penitentis, et divinam misericordiam implorantis; ex Augustino, *ib.* 373; alia ex eodem, *ib.* 374; for repentance, 1 *Brad.* 210, *Lit. Eliz.* 542, 543, *Pra. B* 139; for true repentance and mercy, *Lit. Eliz.* 612, 613, 640; for contrition, *ib.* 252; a prayer meet for our time and state (c. 1555, in exile?) to move us to true repentance, &c., *Pra. B.* 78; a solemn and repentant prayer for former life misspent, by Sir N. Breton, *Poet.* 181; a prayer of a repentant sinner, by W. A., in verse, *Poet.* 508; a complaint of a sinner in that he sinneth again after repentance (Augustine), *Pra Eliz.* 503

Reputation: v. Name.
Rich: for rich men, 3 *Bec.* 25, 26, *Lit. Edw.* 460
Rulers: v. Magistrates.
Schism: v. Church.

School: two prayers composed for St Paul's school, London, by Erasmus—pro docilitate, *Pra. Eliz.* 171, 372—pro parentibus nostris, *ib.* 394; prayers to be used at Hawkshead school (one for the morning and two for the evening), *Sand.* 443, 444; for the scholars at Rivington; morning, *Pil.* 664, midday, *ib.* 665, evening, *ib.* 666; other morning and evening prayers to be used in the same school, *ib.* 668; quum adeunda est schola, *Pra. Eliz.* 207; a prayer to be said of children before they study their lesson at school, *Lit. Edw.* 539

Scripture (v. Psalms, Jeremiah, Manasseh): precationes biblicæ; sc. Neemiæ, Moseh, Danielis, Manassis, Asæ, Tobiæ, et aliorum, *Pra. Eliz.* 362, 367; prayers from scripture, viz., those of Asa, Manasses, Job, Hieremy, and Solomon, *ib.* 94—96 (193 – 195); those of Nehemiah paraphrased, *Pil.* 296—305, 403; precationes ex Novo Testamento; perhaps collected by Sir Tho. More, *ib.* 353; before reading the scriptures, 2 *Hoop.* 3; for understanding of God's word, 3 *Bec.* 82, 83, *Lit. Edw.* 472, *Lit. Eliz.* 253, *Pra. B.* 203

Sea (v. *War*): for mariners, 3 *Bec.* 33
Seasons: v. *Times*
Sermons: ante concionem (auditam), *Pra. Eliz.* 386; before hearing a sermon, 3 *Bec.* 52, 53, *Pra. B.* 125, 135, *Pra. Eliz.* 515; bidding prayer, in a sermon before the parliament, *Sand.* 34; prayers offered by the preacher after sermons on the sacrament, 1 *Brad.* 110, *Hutch.* 233, 234, 287; after sermons on oppression, *Hutch.* 312, 339; prayer for queen Elizabeth in a sermon, *Sand.* 416; prayers occur in other sermons, as in 2 *Jew.* 986, 1004, &c.; post auditam concionem, *Pra. Eliz.* 387; after sermon, for the whole state of Christ's church, *Pra. B.* 126; thanksgiving after sermon, 3 *Bec.* 53

Servants: of servants, 3 *Bec.* 78, *Lit. Edw.* 463; for servants, 3 *Bec.* 30, 31, 37

Sickness (v. *Affliction*): in morbo, *Pra. Eliz.* 370; in gravi morbo, *ib.* 192, and see 202 n.; of the sick, 3 *Bec.* 100, 114, 115, 116, 130, 155, 158, 159, 164, 178, 179, 185, 187, 188, 2 *Lat.* 174, *Pra. Eliz.* 531, 533, (192); for a patient and thankful heart in sickness, 3 *Bec.* 83, 84, *Lit. Edw.* 474; for the sick, 3 *Bec.* 31, 146, 155, 158, 179, *Lit. Edw.* 399, *Pra. B.* 155; apud ægrotum, dum invisitur, *Pra. Eliz.* 190; at the visitation of the sick, *ib.* 554, (190)

Sin (v. *Affliction, Confession, Pardon, Repentance*): on the wrath of God against sin, 1 *Brad.* 224; pro tollenda morum pravitate, et vita melius instituenda; ex Augustino, *Pra. Eliz.* 380; the same in English at greater length, *ib.* 438; quum recitatur locus Pauli, "expurgate vetus fermentum," &c., *ib.* 371; of the church against sins, from Wisd. xv, *ib.* 94, (193); to keep the tongue, and to eschew the infection of the world, *ib.* 92; against pride, unbelief, envy, covetousness, and various other sins, *Pra. B.* 168, &c.; generally for avoiding of all sin, 3 *Bec.* 62, 63, *Pra. B.* 177

Single (v. *Maids*): of single men, 3 *Bec.* 78, 79, *Lit. Edw.* 463; for the unmarried, 3 *Bec.* 27; pro felici conjugio, *Pra. Eliz.* 393

Slander: against slandering and backbiting, 3 *Bec.* 61, 62

Soldiers: v. *War.*

Sound mind: v. *Wisdom.*

Sovereigns (v. *Council, People*): for all kings and rulers, *Lit. Eliz.* 267; for all kings, princes, countries, and people, which do profess the gospel, *ib.* 580; for the king (Edward VI.), 3 *Bec.* 19, *Lit. Edw.* 406, 454; precatio ad exemplar orationis Salomonis pro regina (Elizabeth), *Pra. Eliz.* 310; for the queen, *Lit. Eliz.* 580, *Nord.* 41, 45, *Pra. B.* 128, 130, *Pra. Eliz.* 32, 475, 477, 479; in a sermon, *Sand.* 416; for the queen's birthday, *Lit. Eliz.* 556; for the preservation of the queen's majesty, *ib.* 659, 660, 662, 683—695; for the preservation of the queen's majesty, and for her armies both by sea and land, *ib.* 624; for the queen, and all in authority, *ib.* 269, *Pra. B.* 191; a prayer and thanksgiving for the queen used in parliament, *Lit. Eliz.* 581; a godly prayer for queen Elizabeth, by Tho. Middleton, in verse, *Poet.* 551; for the queen on her sickness and recovery, *Lit. Eliz.* 516, 517; on the discovery of Dr Parry's plot, *ib.* 585, 587; for queen Elizabeth and England, *Pil.* 198, *Pra. Eliz.* 559; thanksgiving and prayer for the preservation of the queen and the realm, *Lit. Eliz.* 544, 644; pro principe adolescente, ex oratione Salomonis, *Pra. Eliz.* 370

Spring: v. *Times.*
Study: v. *School.*
Subjects: v. *People.*
Success: v. *Prosperity.*
Summer: v. *Times.*
Supper: v. *Meat.*

Supper of the Lord: on the holy communion, in sermons, 1 *Brad.* 110, *Hutch.* 233, 234, 287; ante sacram communionem, *Pra. Eliz.* 385; before receiving the communion, 1 *Bec.* 119, 3 *Bec.* 53, &c., *Pra. B.* 90, *Pra. Eliz.* 517, 518, 519, (385); one from Eusebius, *Pra. Eliz.* 519; on receiving, by Chrysostom, 1 *Jew.* 538; at receiving the mystery of Christ's body, 3 *Bec.* 56; at receiving the mystery of Christ's blood, *ib.*; for prayers after receiving, see Thanksgivings.

Swearing: against it, 3 *Bec.* 57
Teachableness: v. *Docility, School.*
Temptation (v. *Enemies* (*Ghostly*), *Sin*): against temptation, *Lit. Eliz.* 248, *Pra. Eliz.* 540; for present help in temptation, *Pra. B.* 151

Thanksgivings: v. *Thanksgivings.*

Times and Seasons: fructuosa precatio quovis tempore dicenda, *Pra. Eliz.* 201, see 107; precatio efficacissima, quovis tempore, et a quibusvis, sæpe dicenda, *ib.* 396; at all times, 1 *Brad.* 245, *Lit. Edw.* 476, *Lit. Eliz.* 251, 264, *Pra B.* 147, 189, *Pra. Eliz.* 107; tempore veris, *Pra. Eliz.* 389; in æstate, *ib.* 390; in autumno, *ib.* 391; in hyeme, *ib.*; for fair weather, *Pra. B.* 200; (for prayers adapted to different parts of the day, see *Morning* and *Evening*); quoties horam sonare audis, *Pra. Eliz.* 394

Tongue: v. *Sin, Slander, Swearing.*
Travellers: v. *Journey.*
Trouble: v. *Affliction, Patience.*
Trust: v. *Faith.*
Truth: for understanding of the truth, *Rid.* 5
Tumult: v. *Rebellion, War.*
Unbelief: v. *Sin.*
Unchasteness: v. *Whoredom.*
Understanding: v. *Knowledge, Scripture, Truth, Wisdom.*
Unity: v. *Church.*
Unmarried: v. *Single.*
Vanity of the world: v. *Enemies.*
Vices: v. *Sin.*
Vocation: v. *Calling.*
War (v. *Enemies, Peace, Sovereigns*): in time of war, *Lit. Eliz.* 615, 628, &c., 636, &c., 644; in war, tumult, &c., *Lit. Eliz.* 476, 536, 645, 650; for soldiers, 3 *Bec.* 33; of Constantine's soldiers, *Pil.* 413; of Theodosius, *ib.*; in behalf of Henry IV. of France, *Lit. Eliz.* 647, 652; for the success of the Protestants in France, *ib.* 649; for the prosperous success of her majesty's forces and navy, *ib.* 665, 671—678; two by the queen herself, *ib.* 666, 671, *Nord.* 188
Weather: v. *Times.*
Whoredom: against it, 3 *Bec.* 58; against pride and unchasteness, *Pra. Eliz.* 104, (198)
Winter: v. *Times.*
Wisdom (v. *Knowledge, Persecution*): for wisdom, &c., *Hutch.* 208, *Lit. Eliz.* 249; for obtaining of wisdom, from Wisd. ix, *Pra. Eliz.* 96, (195); of Jesus the son of Sirach, in necessity and for wisdom, Ecclus. ult., *ib.*; for the obtaining of a sound mind, *ib.* 524; a fruitful prayer to be said at all times (being in part a translation of the precatio aurea B. Tho. ab Aquino pro gratia divinæ sapientiæ, made by queen Mary, when 11 years old), *ib.* 107, see *Lit. Eliz.* 250; the original Latin, or an adaptation of it, *Pra. Eliz.* 201
Wives: v. *Husbands, Women.*
Women (v. *Gentlewomen, Husbands and Wives, Maids, Parents*): for women with child, 3 *Bec.* 28, *Pra. B.* 157; of a woman with child, *Pra. Eliz.* 544
Word of God: v. *Scripture.*
Workmen: v. *Labourers.*
Works (*Good*): v. *Godliness, Life.*
World: v. *Enemies* (*Ghostly*).
World to come: v. *Heaven, Judgment.*
Preachers, Preaching: v. *Ministers*; also London (Paul's cross, and Spittle), *Sermons.*
Preaching without licence forbidden in the time of Henry V., *Bale* 85; twelve preachers licensed by Cambridge university, 2 *Lat.* 324, 329, *Park.* 238; Cranmer's advice on preaching before king Henry, 2 *Cran.* 308; preaching forbidden for a time, in consequence of sermons on the king's divorce, *ib.* 283; preaching for or against purgatory, and other disputed subjects, forbidden for a year, *ib.* 460; what to be preached, *ib.* 461, 462; preaching in favour of the king's marriage enjoined, *ib.* 461; order for preaching, and bidding of the beads in all sermons, *ib.* 460; the preaching of friar Brenchley, *ib.* 302; sermons to be made against popery, at least four times a year, *ib.* 498; parsons enjoined to preach once a quarter at the least, *ib.* 154, 155; inhibition against all preaching for a time, 1548, 2 *Cran.* 513, *Lit. Edw.* xi. n., 3 *Zur.* 645 n.; letter from king Edward's council to all licensed preachers, 2 *Cran.* 512; king Edward's itinerant chaplains, 2 *Brad.* xxv; Ridley's letter to the preachers in his diocese, on the sins of the times, *Rid.* 334; articles of inquiry concerning preaching, *ib.* 530; article respecting preaching and prayers every Sunday and festival-day, 2 *Hoop.* 129; preaching prohibited by queen Elizabeth at the beginning of her reign, *Lit. Eliz.* xi, 1 *Zur.* 7, 2 *Zur.* 16 n., 29; preaching restored, 2 *Zur.* 30, but discouraged by her, *Grin.* xii; few preachers in Suffolk, *Park.* 307; seditious ones at Paul's cross, *Sand.* xx; preachers bred at Cambridge in the time of Elizabeth, 1 *Whitg.* 313; the number of preachers restrained, *Grin.* 376, &c.; what sort allowed by Grindal, *ib.* 380; to be deacons at the least, *ib.* 188; preachers of corrupt or popish doctrines to be presented to the ordinary, *ib.* 144; injunctions about sermons, *ib.* 128, 160; some preachers refused to administer sacraments, *ib.* 413; eminent ones in England, 1 *Brad.* 562; licenses to preach, *Bale* 85, *Park.* 242, 383, 389, 1 *Whitg.* 544, 3 *Whitg.* 40, 41, 2 *Zur.* 148, 162; those dated before 8 Feb. 1575—6, to be void, *Grin.* 187

Prebendaries: their duty, 2 *Cran.* 162; they are bound to keep hospitality, *ib.* 160; Cranmer condemns their idleness and fondness for belly-cheer, *ib.* 396, 397; question whether the king and parliament may not reform them, if they use not their prebends as they ought, *ib.* 466; article to be inquired respecting them, *Grin.* 179; those of Christchurch, Canterbury, allowed to change their houses for life, 2 *Cran.* 417; serving-men made prebendaries, *Park.* 176,

312; a dispensation sought for a child to be made one, *ib.* 362
Precautes: *v.* Excommunication.
Precepts: golden precepts, by A. Bourcher, *Poet.* 297
PRECES PRIVATÆ, 1564: *Pra. Eliz.* 209—317
Precisians: *v.* Puritans.
Predestinates: heretics so called, *Rog.* 156
Predestination and Election: *v.* Free-will, Perseverance.

A treatise of election and free-will, 1 *Brad.* 211; a brief sum of the doctrine of election and predestination, *ib.* 219; the DEFENCE OF ELECTION, *ib.* 307; notes thereon, *ib.* 305, 591; Ridley composed a treatise De Electione et Prædestinatione, but it is not extant, 2 *Brad.* 171 n., 214, 220, *Rid.* xv, 368; Latin tract on the words "Deus cujus vult misereatur, quem vult indurat," *Pil.* 673; the Lambeth articles, 3 *Whitg.* 612; the question of predestination stated, *Whita.* 24; the doctrine stated, asserted, explained, defended, 3 *Bec.* 608, 616, 2 *Brad.* 133, 195, &c., 3 *Bul.* 185, *Calf.* 350, 2 *Hoop.* 40, *Now.* (53, 54, 56, 101, 102), 171, 172, 174, *Rog.* 142—157; on the word "predestination," *Now.* (102), *Phil.* 403; election is the doctrine of God's word, 1 *Brad.* 311; scriptural examples of it, *Rog.* 144; the case of the penitent thief, 3 *Tyn.* 210; it is a deep mystery, 2 *Bec.* 481, 1 *Tyn.* 89; curious inquiries respecting predestination condemned, 2 *Lat.* 175, 204; the doctrine is perilous when made the subject of rash inquiry, 1 *Tyn.* 505; we should not go beyond the scripture, 2 *Brad.* 214; the deep secrets of predestination are not to be known further than God has revealed them in his word, 2 *Ful.* 229; repentance is the grammar school, predestination the university, 2 *Brad.* 134; the elect angels, 1 *Brad.* 322; the manner and order of our election, 3 *Tyn.* 35—39; election is of two kinds, to office, as that of Saul and Judas, and to eternal life, 1 *Brad.* 315; God's eternal book of predestination, 1 *Ful.* 329, 330; the Lamb's book of life, *Bale* 434, 578, 615; the cause of election and predestination to eternal life is only the good-will and mercy of God, 1 *Brad.* 180, 312, 1 *Hoop.* 264, *Rog.* 148; his glory is the sole end thereof, 1 *Brad.* 314, 3 *Tyn.* 191; probations out of scripture that God's election is free and undeserved, 3 *Bec.* 316, &c.; he did not choose men for any goodness either past or to come, 1 *Bec.* 72, *Pil.* 194, 195, 674, 2 *Tyn.* 190, 3 *Tyn.* 208—210; but election is sovereign and free, 1 *Bec.* 79, *Sand.* 257; God chooseth whom he will, 1 *Tyn.* 113, 2 *Tyn.* 181; his choice was before the world began, even from everlasting, 1 *Brad.* 312, 2 *Brad.* 92, *Pil.* 674, 1 *Tyn.* 65, 110; his will is determined and immutable, 2 *Brad.* 129; his predestination to life is not of all men, 1 *Brad.* 313; nor of all that are outwardly called, or in the visible church, *Now.* (57), 175, 3 *Tyn.* 107, 109, 114; but of a certain number, 3 *Bec.* 84, 2 *Hoop.* 25, *Lit. Edw.* 475, of individuals, *Pra. B.* 11, who were chosen in Christ, 1 *Brad.* 220, 312, 1 *Tyn.* 65; and who constitute the church properly so called, 4 *Bul.* 7, *Phil.* 136, 332 (and see Church, i, ii; also Christ, vii); for their sake the world was made, *Phil.* 335; the commodities proceeding from election, 1 *Brad.* 308; it is the beginning of salvation, 1 *Bec.* 72; by it the work of our salvation is taken out of our hands, and made the work of God only, 1 *Tyn.* 505; without it none would be saved, *ib.*; God's love for his elect, and what he does for them, 1 *Tyn.* 14, 77, 3 *Tyn.* 191, 192; the method of their salvation, 2 *Tyn.* 183; Christ's work for the elect, *ib.* 168, 169; God seeketh them, not they God, 3 *Tyn.* 112; Mary being first chosen of God, chose the good part, 1 *Tyn.* 87; his work in his chosen, *ib.* 54, 89; the drawing of the predestinate, 3 *Bul.* 189; God teaches them to know and to follow him, 3 *Tyn.* 49; in God's time they are called and justified, 1 *Brad.* 314, 1 *Hoop.* 264, *Now.* (62), 181; their hearts melt at the preaching of God's mercy, 1 *Tyn.* 19; the cause why some believe and others do not in God's predestination, 3 *Tyn.* 139, 140; by election God is our Father, 1 *Brad.* 119; it leads to holiness, 2 *Brad.* 166, *Phil.* 224, *Sand.* 190, *Wool.* 29; those whom God has chosen he makes holy, *Now.* (54), 172; he gives his Spirit to them, 1 *Tyn.* 449; how we are to make our calling and election sure, 2 *Ful.* 92, *Phil.* 224, 1 *Tyn.* 60, 2 *Tyn.* 87, 193; it cannot be known by those who only honour God with their lips, 1 *Tyn.* 78; it is made sure to ourselves by diligence, 1 *Ful.* 72, 85; evidences or tokens of election, 1 *Brad.* 302, 3 *Bul.* 187, 2 *Jew.* 821, 934, 2 *Lat.* 205, 206, *Phil.* 230, 1 *Tyn.* 107; no man can consent to God's law except he be chosen, *ib.* 80; holiness is an evidence, *Phil.* 286; it is proved by good works, *Sand.* 214 n., 1 *Tyn.* 71, &c., 77, 80, 85; restitution is a token of it, 1 *Lat.* 263; the Spirit is the seal and sign of it, 1 *Brad.* 79, and a witness of it, 1 *Ful.* 415, 420; faith is the demonstration of it, 1 *Brad.* 313; God's people feel in themselves the earnest of salvation; they judge not of others, except by their works, *ib.* 328; the elect cannot be distinguished by us in this world, 2 *Lat.* 56; we must judge of election by the event, and not otherwise, 1 *Hoop.* 264; as many as are stedfast in the faith were forechosen to everlasting life, *Lit. Edw.* 511, (559); they that are in heaven know the elect, and for them only pray, 3 *Tyn.* 279; petition to be (manifestly) of the number of the predestinate, 3 *Bec.* 84; their character and privileges, 1 *Tyn.* 77, 78, 263, 264, 3 *Tyn.* 30, 109, 111—114, *Whita.* 613; the scripture is their light and life, 2 *Tyn.* 143; they only understand it, *Whita.* 613, 614; how God trieth his elect; Jonah an example, 1 *Tyn.* 455; their temptation, 3 *Tyn.* 36, 37; temptations respecting predestination, 2 *Brad.* 101, 102, 3 *Bul.* 187; fear expressed in regard to being in the number, 3 *Bec.* 172; the struggles of the elect against sin, 3 *Tyn.* 113; how God punishes them, 2 *Hoop.* 225; they are punished here, that they may not be condemned with the world, *Phil.* 270; probations out of scripture that God's election is certain and unchangeable, 3 *Bec.* 316; it is unto eternal life, 1 *Brad.* 313; it is certain for ever, *ib.* 314, 2 *Jew.* 933, ensuring perseverance to the end, 2 *Brad.* 113—115; they are preserved by the hand of God, 3 *Tyn.* 103; the fear of God is their keeper, *Phil.* 334; nothing chances to them without the singular providence of God, 3 *Bec.* 565; he will keep his chosen from delusion, 2 *Jew.* 933; how they may err, *Phil.* 334; God sometimes permits them to fall, 1 *Tyn.* 144; they may fall, but they arise again, 2 *Cran.* 92, 2 *Hoop.* 274, 2 *Tyn.* 171, 3 *Tyn.* 36, 37; they shall never perish, 1 *Ful.* 420; probations out of scripture that they cannot perish, 3 *Bec.* 318, 319; they are saved by Christ, 1 *Cov.* 70; they shall be judges, not judged, at the last day, 2 *Lat.* 191; a thanksgiving for election and other benefits consequent thereon, *Pra. B.* 147; God had his chosen people in the times of darkness, 1 *Lat.* 306, 527; he chose some out of Sodom, Egypt, Babylon, &c., *Sand.* 257; election is required in infants who are baptized, 2 *Brad.* 290, 2 *Cov.* 268; it is not made frustrate by the want of outward baptism, 2 *Bec.* 221, 222; the doctrine of predestination misrepresented by heretics, *Phil.* 307; how some abuse it, 2 *Lat.* 175, *Phil.* 223; a carnal opinion deduced from it, 2 *Lat.* 175, 204; answer to certain enormities alleged to proceed from it, 1 *Brad.* 318; it occasions neither licentiousness nor despair, *ib.* 303; but promotes holiness and joy, *ib.* 303, 304; it does not set aside means, 1 *Whitg.* 524; it is not opposed to the invitations of the gospel, 1 *Brad.* 67; in what sense the salvation preached in the gospel belongs to all, 3 *Bul.* 33; the reprobate will be without excuse, 1 *Brad.* 219, 220; prayer cannot alter God's decrees, *Pra. B.* 6, 7, 8; the pope says that God chooseth us for our good qualities, 2 *Tyn.* 190; More says God remitteth not the sin of his chosen, because they are his chosen; but chose them because he foresaw their repentance, 3 *Tyn.* 208; Tyndale's reply, *ib.* 209, 210; disputes concerning predestination, 1550, 1 *Brad.* 306 n.; disagreement of Hooper and Traheron, 3 *Zur.* 406; argument against predestination, *Hutch.* 85, 86; Latimer asserts that we may be in the book of life at one time, and afterward out of it, 2 *Lat.* 175; on the errors of Hart and others, 2 *Brad.* 170; views of Calvin and others, 3 *Zur.* 325, 326; Calvin's doctrine agreeable to that of all the doctors of the church, *Phil.* 46; P. Martyr's views, 3 *Zur.* 506; Beza's sentiments, 3 *Whitg.* 142, 143; dispute on predestination at Strasburgh, 1563, 2 *Zur.* 99, 102; controversy at Cambridge, 1595, occasioned by a sermon by W. Barret, *Whita.* x, 1 *Whitg.* xvii, 3 *Whitg.* 611, &c.

Predicaments, or categories: 1 *Tyn.* 157

Prefract: obstinate, 1 *Brad.* 474

Prelates: *v.* Bishops.

What prelates are, viz. all that have any spiritual charge, 1 *Lat.* 61; who are right prelates, *ib.* 51; what they should be, 2 *Lat.* 24; prelates likened to ploughmen, 1 *Lat.* 61; admonition to them, *ib.* 65; evil ones a proof of God's anger, 1 *Tyn.* 195

Unpreaching prelates have been long suffered, 1 *Lat.* 193; they are made by the devil, *ib.* 202; they have not the zeal of Paul, *ib.* 520; how they are occupied, *ib.* 66, 67, 2 *Lat.* 24; they are the cause of commotions and rebellions, 1 *Lat.* 275; one of them angry with Latimer, *ib.* 154; one finds fault with a bell without a clapper, *ib.* 207; Christ an example to unpreaching prelates, *ib.* 199, 475; a terrible saying to them, *ib.* 63; their place of punishment, *ib.* 158

— The Practice of Prelates, by W.

Tyndale, 2 *Tyn.* 237—344; notices of it, 1 *Tyn.* xxxix, xli, 2 *Tyn.* 238; they obtain office by the service of kings and great men, in secular employments, 2 *Tyn.* 256; become clerks of kitchens, 2 *Lat* 120; their pompous badges and names, 1 *Tyn.* 246; the signification of their mitres, crosses, and ornaments, *ib.* 233, 234, 251, 252; if they were true apostles they would sell their mitres, crosses, &c., and give to the poor, 3 *Tyn.* 93; their pride and covetousness, 2 *Tyn.* 178, 254; they follow the Pharisees, *ib.* 240, &c.; call themselves the church, and claim infallibility, *ib.* 289; have left preaching, but reserve to themselves certain ceremonies, 1 *Tyn.* 274; stop the gospel on pretence of insurrections and heresies, 2 *Lat.* 304; declare it heresy to know God's word, 1 *Tyn.* 243; their crafty pretences to stop the reading of the scriptures, 2 *Lat.* 303; their secret organization, and communications with each other, and with the pope, 2 *Tyn.* 296; they are a bicorporeum, or corpus neutrum, *ib.* 342; are occupied with secular offices, 2 *Lat.* 24; hold great places in the state, 1 *Tyn.* 274; become lords presidents and the like, 1 *Lat.* 68, 176; when employed as ambassadors, they consider nothing but the advantage of their church, 2 *Tyn.* 303, 342; care for the prosperity of no realm, and bear no true allegiance but to the pope, *ib.* 303; they flatter and seduce kings, 1 *Tyn.* 136, but trouble their realms, 2 *Tyn.* 245, 294, &c., 333, and destroy their authority, 1 *Tyn.* 239, 247, 249, 2 *Tyn.* 178; or usurp it, to put down their opponents, 1 *Tyn.* 185, 242, 337, 3 *Tyn.* 73; they exhort rulers to slay such as they have chosen to condemn, 1 *Tyn.* 242; issue their own proclamations under the king's name and authority, 2 *Lat.* 305; their plotting against the emperor Charles V., 2 *Tyn.* 312; mischiefs resulting from their influence in this country, *ib.* 225, 294, &c., 302, 3 *Tyn.* 138, 166; their use of the mass, 2 *Tyn.* 224; their use of penance and purgatory, *ib.* 161—163; they often use astrology and necromancy, *ib.* 308; their sinful courses, *ib.* 161, &c., 254, 293, 342; summary of their evil ways, 1 *Tyn.* 336; admonition to them, 2 *Tyn.* 242

Premonstratensians: Newesham, the first house of the order in England, 2 *Cran.* 290 n

Prendergast, co. Pembroke (?): Rob. Holland, minister there, *Poet.* xlvi.

Presbyterians: *v.* Puritans.

Presbyterium: part of a church, 1 *Jew.* 311

Presbyters: *v.* Priests, viii, ix.

Presbytery: why the original word not rendered priesthood, 1 *Ful.* 240, &c.; Beza on the word, 1 *Whitg.* 488; "presbyterium" used by Cyprian for a consistory of elders, 1 *Ful.* 153; of seigniory or government by elders, 3 *Whitg.* 150, &c.; on presbyteries or consistories, *ib.* 538, &c.; there were consistories of elders in the primitive church, and there are such in some churches now, but not in the church of England, 1 *Ful.* 255; whether government by seniors ought to be perpetual, 3 *Whitg.* 164; a presbytery or consistory in every parish desired by the Puritans, *Grin.* 341, *Rog.* 340, 1 *Zur.* 245, 292, 295, 296; not permitted by queen Elizabeth, 1 *Ful.* 276; the inconvenience of the seigniory in the time of Christian princes, especially in the state of this church, 3 *Whitg.* 209; such consistories would not be able to correct the great, *Pil.* 380, 381; presbytery existed in Guernsey, 2 *Zur.* 265; private presbyteries first erected in England, *Rog.* 8; Bullinger's opinion of presbytery, 2 *Zur.* 241; Gualter's opinion, 2 *Zur.* 238, 251, 258

Prescription: makes a title in law, but not in religion, *Phil.* 48; it cannot make falsehood to be truth, *Jew.* 50

Presence (Real): *v.* Supper of the Lord, Transubstantiation.

Presidents (Lords): those of Wales and the North, 1 *Lat.* 175

Press-money: taken by soldiers, *Phil.* 226

Prest: ready, prepared, 2 *Bec.* 389, 1 *Whitg.* 504

Prestall (Jo.): condemned for treason, 1 *Zur.* 129 n

Prestall (......): a magician, 1 *Zur.* 253 n (perhaps the same).

Prester John: *Bale* 320, 2 *Ful.* 225; called Peter (or Preter) Gian, 4 *Jew.* 1055; styled Precious John, 2 *Bec.* 258; the vulgar tongue used in prayer in his dominions, 1 *Jew.* 334, *Pil.* 499, 500; spoken of as a heathen prince, *ib.* 205

Prestibulous: deceitful, *Bale* 427

Prestwich, co. Lancaster: 1 *Brad.* 454; called Prestige, 2 *Brad.* 228

Presuls: a name of bishops, 4 *Bul.* 118

Presumption: forbidden, *Rid.* 65; blamed, 1 *Lat.* 551, 2 *Lat.* 182, 254; its original cause, 1 *Hoop.* 416; how it is nourished, *ib.*; the occasion of it is continuance in sin, *ib.*; against presumption in God's mercy, *Wool.* 142

Pretend: to allege, 2 *Tyn.* 90

Pretie (Jo.): letter signed by him, 3 *Zur.* 170
Prevenient Grace, *q. v.*
Prevent: to go before, 1 *Tyn.* 498
Price (......): *v.* Aprice.
Prices: complaint of the high prices of commodities, 2 *Brad.* 395, 396, 2 *Cran.* 195, 436, 437, 1 *Lat.* 99
Pricklingham: the prior, 3 *Bec.* 281
Pride: *v.* Apparel, Boasting, Prayers.

    Pride censured, 1 *Cov.* 526; it is a great sin, *Sand.* 137; an ugly sin, *Nord.* 172; the cause of Satan's fall, 2 *Lat.* 169, *Sand.* 137, 138; how Sathan by the sin of pride hath ever prevailed, verses by W. Warner, *Poet.* 379; against pride, or vain-glory, with sentences and examples of scripture, 1 *Bec.* 448, 449; it is the beginning of sin, *Pil.* 227; the headspring of all evil, 1 *Bec.* 198; the source of heresies, 2 *Tyn.* 140; its evil effects, 2 *Jew.* 1092; it has been the cause of many kings doing evil, 1 *Bec.* 201; that of the Pharisee contrasted with the humility of the publican, *ib.*; why it so much reigns now, *ib.* 198; preservatives against it, *Sand.* 104, 105; a remedy against it, 2 *Tyn.* 74; some reasons against it, *Pil.* 293; the folly of it, 3 *Bec.* 57, 58;

    arises of good things, *Pil.* 228, of beauty, strength, &c., *ib.* 229, 230; it must not be nourished by riches, wisdom, or any other advantage or gift of God, 1 *Bec.* 202, 203; there is nothing in us of which we may be proud, *Sand.* 141; we must glory in nothing, because nothing is ours, *Pil.* 245; the pride of England in attire, *Nord.* 172, 173; the desire of vain-glory poisons all good works, 1 *Bec.* 110, 2 *Bec.* 541; God throws down the proud, *Pil.* 233

Prierias (Sylv. Mozzelini, called): his works, *Jew.* xliii; he calls the Romish church the square and rule of faith, and says that scripture hath received thence authority and credit, 1 *Jew.* 216, 2 *Jew.* 987, 3 *Jew.* 218, 4 *Jew.* 719, 861; says, whosoever leans not to the doctrine of the Roman church and of the bishop of Rome is a heretic, 4 *Jew.* 862; allows that pardons have no ground of God's word, but of the Roman church, which he says is greater, 1 *Jew.* 76, 3 *Jew.* 218, 4 *Jew.* 851; gives a reason for making the corporal of fine linen, 1 *Jew.* 15

Priests: *v.* Sacrifices.

    i. *Generally, and before the Law*: ἱερεύς is equivalent with the Hebrew כהן and the Latin " sacerdos," 1 *Tyn.* 255; כהן is considered to denote prince as well as priest, *ib.* 255 n., *Whita.* 417; πρεσβύτερος denotes "elder" or "senior," 1 *Tyn.* 256; they should have different names in English, 1 *Tyn.* 255; translations concerning priests and priesthood examined, 1 *Ful.* 240—277, (see below); without priests in the former sense there can be no sacrifice, *Sand.* 411; kinds of priesthood allowed by God, *ib.*; it originally pertained to the first begotten, 2 *Bul.* 130; as to the priesthood of Melchizedek, see his name; there is but one priest after the order of Melchizedek, namely, Christ, 2 *Brad.* 313, *Rid.* 208, *Sand.* 411, 2 *Tyn.* 283; the priesthood forfeited by Reuben, 2 *Bul.* 131, 1 *Tyn.* 310; faith poetically spoken of as God's priest, 3 *Bul.* 226

    ii. *The Priesthood of the Law:* the Levitical priesthood, 2 *Bul.* 130; who were rejected from being priests in the old law, 1 *Bec.* 100; why they were to have no blemish, 2 *Bec.* 323; their office, 2 *Bul.* 139; to sacrifice, &c., *ib.* 141; to answer inquiries concerning the law, *Whita.* 423; to teach and bless, 2 *Bul.* 139; to judge causes, *ib.* 142; to carry the tabernacle and its vessels, *ib.* 141; to serve in war, *ib.* 142, *Pil.* 414; their ministrations typical of the work of Christ, *Whita.* 254; their raiment, 2 *Bul.* 133—135, 137; they were married, 3 *Bec.* 235; their stipends and dwellings, 2 *Bul.* 143; their houses, *Pil.* 391; certain degrees among them, 2 *Bul.* 132; the high priest was a figure of Christ, *Whita.* 254, 2 *Whitg.* 346, (see p. 172, col. 1, above); his robes, 2 *Jew.* 1017; his megil, 2 *Bul.* 135; his ephod, *ib.*; his breast-lap of judgment, *ib.* 136; the urim and thummim, *ib.*; his golden plate, *ib.* 137; the priests admonished by Nehemiah, *Pil.* 378; the Jewish priesthood abrogated, 2 *Bul.* 262, 2 *Hoop.* 30, *Pil.* 505, *Rid.* 208, 2 *Tyn.* 283; it is no figure of the gospel ministry, 1 *Whitg.* 368; all (sacrificing) priesthood save that which belongs to all Christians, is abolished by Christ, *Hutch.* 46

    iii. *Heathen Priests:* the Chemarim or priests of Baal, 4 *Bul.* 73, 75, 481, 1 *Ful.* 565; Romish priests their successors, 1 *Brad.* 281, 2 *Brad.* 313; comparison between those and these, 3 *Bec.* 261; the priests of the Romans as described by Cicero, 2 *Whitg.* 128

    iv. *The priestly office of Christ:* see Christ, iii.

    v. *The term* ἱερεύς *and its equivalents as pertaining to all believers:* all Christians are spiritually priests, 2 *Brad.* 313, 2 *Cov.* 471, 1 *Ful.* 114, 241, 243, 2 *Ful.* 357, *Hutch.* 46, 50, 1 *Jew.* 117, 2 *Jew.* 737, 3 *Jew.* 335, 336, 2 *Lat.* 255 n., 309 n., 313

PRIESTS 639

Phil. 406, *Sand.* 411, 1 *Tyn.* 255, 256, 506, 527, 3 *Whitg.* 476; the priesthood of all Christians stated by Bede, 1 *Tyn.* 265 n.; this priesthood is not to offer up Christ, but spiritual sacrifices acceptable by Christ, 2 *Ful.* 242, 243; Peter's use of the term does not bear on the question of vestments, 2 *Brad.* 386

vi. *The term* ιερεὺς, &c. *as applied to Christian ministers:* never so applied in the New Testament, *Calf.* 225, 1 *Ful.* 109, 242, 269, *Hutch.* 50, 3 *Tyn.* 20; "sacerdos" is never so used in the Vulgate, 3 *Tyn.* 20; the apostles alleged to have been made priests at the last supper, 1 *Ful.* 241; on "the offering up of the Gentiles" (Rom. xv. 16), *Calf.* 230; on the meaning of λειτουργοί, 4 *Jew.* 805; the Jewish priesthood no figure of the gospel ministry, 1 *Whitg.* 368; there are no sacrificing priests in the church (except as the term is applied to all Christians), 2 *Lat.* 264, *Rid.* 107, 3 *Whitg.* 350, 351; sacrificing priests should cease for ever, 2 *Lat.* 255; there is no outward priesthood in the church, *Bale* 569; the Christian ministry is not a priesthood, *Phil.* 406, *Pil.* 581; it was not ordained to offer sacrifice, 2 *Jew.* 1131, *Rid.* 111, 112; no special class of priests, in this sense of the word, is any longer needed, 1 *Tyn.* 255; the fathers often termed ministers ιερεῖς, 1 *Ful.* 243, 251; Levitical language was often used by them figuratively or loosely, *ib.* 262, 270, 2 *Jew.* 709; this has led to much mischief, which they never dreamed of, 1 *Ful.* 269, 270; the evil consequences of the doctrine of a sacrificing and mediatorial priesthood, *Coop.* 87, 88; ιερεὺς used in the Greek liturgies, 1 *Ful.* 268; the word, in its ecclesiastical acceptation, includes bishops, *ib.*, 3 *Jew.* 272; ἀρχιερεὺς was often used for a bishop, 2 *Whitg.* 310

vii. *Romish priests* (v. Clergy, Mass, Mass-mongers, Sacrifices): Romish sacrifices, 4 *Bul.* 116; external priesthood is a Romish error, 2 *Ful.* 244; Peter and Paul were no priests of the popish order, *Rid.* 19; the office of such, *Rog.* 259; Romanists make the priest a mediator between God and Christ, 1 *Jew.* 97; More says the name "priest" has always signified an anointed person, 3 *Tyn.* 19, and that few durst be priests in old time, *ib.* 150; how men are led to become priests in the Romish church, *ib.* 161; Romanists cannot agree as to what makes the priest, 1 *Tyn.* 258; the manner of consecrating them is borrowed partly from the Jews, partly from the heathen, 3 *Tyn.* 20; they are greased with oil, *Pil.* 163; words with which the popish order is conferred, *Rid.* 19; the blasphemy of mass-priests, 2 *Bec.* 246, 1 *Brad.* 392; they claim a power exceeding that of angels, and say that they can create the Creator, 1 *Tyn.* 380; they take upon themselves to make both God and man, 1 *Cran.* 303; the wickedness of their masses, &c., *Pil.* 126, 161; they are said to offer Christ's body, 3 *Tyn.* 149, and to apply the benefit of Christ's passion to the people, 1 *Cran.* 353; they pretend to receive the sacrament for others, *Hutch.* 228; how they spend the day after saying mass, 3 *Bec.* 282; they sell heaven, &c., *Pil.* 20; the makers are the successors of the priests of Baal, 2 *Brad.* 313, priests after the order of Baal and Antichrist, 1 *Brad.* 281, and are followers of Korah, 2 *Brad.* 329; the popish priesthood is of Antichrist, *Sand.* 411; comparison of the old idolatrous ones, and those amongst us, 3 *Bec.* 261; the influence of priests in popish times, *Pil.* 6; their perjuries in Henry, Edward and Mary's reigns, 1 *Lat.* 315; in queen Mary's days they were the chief in the country, 3 *Bec.* 238; their want of learning, 4 *Jew.* 910; their ignorance and superstition, 2 *Bec.* 421, &c.; their neglect of their duty, *Bale* 130; they sought the pleasure of the world, *ib.* 129; spent their time in hawking, hunting, and frequenting ale-houses, 1 *Lat.* 383; their wickedness, *Rid.* 150; their swearing, 1 *Bec.* 360; their incontinence, 2 *Cran.* 37, 38, *Rog.* 305; a complaint of the unchastity of two priests, 2 *Lat.* 391; complaints against their shameful practices in Wales, 2 *Cran.* 37; a priest turns midwife, 1 *Lat.* 334; the signs of proud priests, *Bale* 109; priests were usually styled Sir (*q. v.*), and scornfully Sir John, 1 *Tyn.* 277 n.; regular priests, 4 *Bul.* 116; secular priests, *ib.*; soul priests cannot sing men out of hell, 2 *Lat.* 238; legacies to them are of no avail, 2 *Bec.* 394; chantry priests enjoined to teach youth, 2 *Cran.* 504, 2 *Lat.* 244; made beneficed clergymen to save their pensions, 1 *Lat.* 123 n.; hedge priests, 2 *Ful.* 235, 2 *Whitg.* 265, 382, 3 *Whitg.* 279; the title "Summus sacerdos," applied to the pope, 4 *Jew.* 822, &c.

viii. *The term Priest as applied to Christian ministers*, for the most part ambiguously (v. Clergy, Ministers): on the Christian priesthood, *Phil.* 405; an article, de ordine et ministerio sacerdotum et episcoporum, 1538, 2 *Cran.* 484; of the name "priest" given to ministers of the gospel, 2 *Whitg*. 310, 311, 3 *Whitg*. 350, &c.; what priests should be, *Bale* 21; they ought to have no blemish in them, 1 *Bec*. 101; they are called the salt of the earth and light of the world, 1 *Bec*. 385; their duty, 2 *Bec*. 432; office of the priest or minister, 1 *Hoop*. 183; to preach, *Bale* 88; it is not necessary that a priest have a shaven crown and long gown, 1 *Hoop*. 245; he should be known by his tongue preaching God's word, and not by cap or vesture, *ib*. 511; whether there were any priests in the primitive church who exercised themselves in prayer, without preaching, 2 *Cran*. 153; they too generally preached according to the faith of the emperors, kings or rulers, *ib*. 15; priests must preach sincerely and live godly, 1 *Bec*. 385; what great purity ought to be in their life, 1 *Bec*. 386; they forgive not sin, but are the ministers of God appointed to utter and declare forgiveness, 2 *Bec*. 561, &c.; they ought to be learned in the law of God, 1 *Bec*. 383, *Pil*. 160; the unprofitableness of unable ones, *Pil*. 36; priests ought not to meddle with worldly things, 2 *Cran*. 38, 56 n.; why they are now so little regarded, 1 *Bec*. 255; why they are despised, 2 *Bec*. 432; they are become blind and careless, 1 *Bec*. 354; the prayers of many are cold, *ib*. 382, 383; a priest, with Cranmer's approbation, renounces his priesthood, 2 *Cran*. 380; priests required to be twenty-four years old, *Grin*. 186

ix. *Priests, Presbyters, Seniors, or Elders* (πρεσβύτεροι): meaning of the name, 4 *Bul*. 106, 3 *Tyn*. 16; on the elders of the Jews and those of the church, 1 *Tyn*. 478; "presbyter" distinguished from ἱερεύς or "sacerdos," 1 *Ful*. 109, 110, 219, 242, &c., 1 *Tyn*. 255; the two words often confounded by the fathers, 1 *Ful*. 243, 251; Christ has disannulled all such priesthood as is called sacerdotium, but presbyterium remaineth, *Hutch*. 49; why πρεσβύτερος is not rendered "priest," 1 *Ful*. 240, &c., 3 *Tyn*. 16, 17, 20; the word "senior" is sometimes used for it in the Latin Vulgate, 3 *Tyn*. 16; the name "priest" is sometimes used as equivalent to presbyter or elder, 1 *Tyn*. 229, 256; in this sense it is a lawful name for ministers, 3 *Whitg*. 350, 351; alleged danger of applying the name to Christian ministers, 2 *Whitg*. 310; its use defended, *ib*. 311; the office of priests, presbyters, or elders, 1 *Tyn*. 229, 256, 436, 3 *Tyn*. 19, 1 *Whitg*. 473; the office thought by Tyndale to be less ancient than the episcopal office, 2 *Tyn*. 256; and so Hammond thought, *ib*. n.; the names of bishop and presbyter are used for the same in scripture and primitive antiquity, 1 *Tyn*. 229, 253; see also p. 120, col. 1, above; the word "priest" includes bishops by the Romish reckoning, *Rog*. 259; and the word "bishop" includes priests, *ib*. 304 n.; elders were in apostolic days both of the ministry and the laity, *Calf*. 247; they need no outward anointing, 1 *Tyn*. 256; their office in ecclesiastical government, *Now*. (96), 218, (*v*. Presbytery); the word "priests" as used in the Prayer Book does not mean sacrifice, 1 *Ful*. 467; nevertheless in the Puritan editions of the Prayer Book the word is changed to "minister," *Lit. Eliz*. xvi — xviii; "minister" and "sacerdos" interchangeable in the Latin Prayer Book, *ib*. 329, 337, &c.; in some cases the word "priest," found in king Edward's early Books, has since been changed to "minister," e. g. the exhortation to the communion, *Lit. Edw*. 4, 82; no other term than "presbyter" is used in letters of orders, 1 *Ful*. 245

— Priests (Arch): *v*. Archpriests.
— Priests (Chantry): see in vii, above.
— Priests (Hedge): *ib*.
— Priests (Regular): *ib*.
— Priests (Secular): *ib*.
— Priests (Soul): *ib*.

Primasius, bp of Uticina: wrote on the Apocalypse, *Bale* 255; he speaks of Christ's reverence (Heb. v. 7), 1 *Ful*. 325; says that the bread of idols is the partaking of demons, 1 *Jew*. 474; declares that no man sins more than he that stands in defence of sin, 4 *Jew*. 647; says Babylon shall fall when last of all she shall take power to persecute the saints, 2 *Jew*. 896, 4 *Jew*. 1063

Primates: *v*. Archbishops, Canterbury, Patriarchs.

Meaning of the word "primatus," 1 *Jew*. 366, &c.

Primer: references to the Sarum Primer, *Lit. Eliz*. 268 n., *Pra. Eliz*. 311 n.; a Prymer mentioned by More, 1 *Tyn*. 3; primers in English, 1535, 1537, 2 *Cran*. 392 n.; (Hilsey's and Marshall's Primers are mentioned p. 625, col. 2, above); The Primer in English moste necessary for the Educacyon of Chyldren, (1539?), 1 *Brad*. 264 n., 2 *Cran*. 393 n.; the Primer of 1545, *Pra. Eliz*. vii; Henry VIII.'s preface to his Primer Book, 2 *Cran*. 496; copies were set forth both in English and in Latin, *ib.* 497, 504; prayers from it, *Lit. Eliz.* 248, 249, 250, 254, 256; king Edward's first Primer, 1547, *Pra. Eliz.* vii; inquiry, 1548, respecting the English and Latin Primers, 2 *Cran.* 158; the sentences of prayer to saints in the preceding primers directed by an act of parliament to be blotted out, *Pra. Eliz.* vii, viii; the Primer of 1549, *ib.* vii; that of 1551, *ib.* viii; that of 1552, *ib.*; A PRIMER, OR BOOK OF PRIVATE PRAYER, 1553, *Lit. Edw.* 357, &c.; notices of it, *ib.* ix, *Pra. Eliz.* ix; reference to it, 3 *Bec.* 20 n.; THE PRIMER, 1559, *Pra. Eliz.* 1, &c; notice of it, *ib.* x, &c.; the Primers of 1566, 1575, and others, *ib.* xi; rubric primers forbidden, *Rid.* 320; popish primers not to be maintained or used, *Grin.* 140, 169, 2 *Hoop.* 129, 135

Primogeniture: the law thereof, 1 *Lat.* 271; the elder brother's privileges, *Pil.* 223; the priesthood originally descended to the firstborn, 2 *Bul.* 130; yet the elder brother was often refused by God, *Pil.* 224

Princeps: how used in the Latin tongue, 1 *Jew.* 371

Princes: *v.* Kings, Magistrates, Supremacy.

Principalities: a name of angels, 3 *Bul.* 338

PRINCIPLES OF CHRISTIAN RELIGION, by T. Becon, 2 *Bec.* 477, &c.

Princocks: pert, forward youths, *Pil.* 523

Printers: their carelessness and want of skill censured, 1 *Hoop.* iv, viii, 101 n., 429, 4 *Jew.* 1275

Priorius (Phil.): 2 *Ful.* 302 n

Priour (Will.), of St Benedict's church, Norwich: *Park.* vi, 481

Priscian: affirms that sound is a body, 3 *Jew.* 260

Priscilla: a mad heretic, *Phil.* 421 n

Priscillian: his opinion of the soul, 3 *Bul* 374

Priscillianists: their heresy, 4 *Bul.* 410, *Phil.* 426; they brought in other names of Deity beside the Trinity, *Rog.* 45; considered man to be made of the substance of God, *Hutch.* 24; yet it is said that they affirmed him to be the workmanship of the devil, *Rog.* 41; they supposed man's body to be under the influence of the zodiacal signs, 2 *Bul.* 363; condemned marriage, *Rog.* 306; thought it lawful to lie in some circumstances, *Hutch.* 51; allowed perjury to escape persecution, *Rog.* 119, 357

Prised: overturned, destroyed, 2 *Bec.* 312

Prises: prizes, trials of strength, *Calf.* 47

Prisoners: *v.* Captives.

They should be instructed and exhorted, 1 *Lat.* 164; prisoners for God's glory encouraged by comfortable histories of God's liberality, 2 *Bec.* 613; intercession for such, 3 *Bec.* 248; Cranmer and others were prisoners for confessing God's truth, *ib.* 244; Bradford and others relieved by certain godly men, 1 *Brad.* 379; their declaration concerning king Edward's reformation, *ib.* 399

Prisons: *v.* Cambridge, London, Oxford, Southwark.

Incarceration a proper mode of punishment, *Sand.* 74; Bocardo, the Gate-house, and other prisons alluded to, *Pra. B.* 106; bishops' prisons, 3 *Whitg.* 405, 447, 449; curates should be appointed for prisons, 1 *Lat.* 180; visiting prisons a good work, *ib.*; the body a prison, *Pra. B.* 106

Private Judgment: *v.* Judgment.

Privatus, a heretic: his condemnation, 2 *Whitg.* 198, 200

Privy Council: *v.* Prayers.

Letters from the lords of the council in the reign of Edward VI., 2 *Cran.* 505, 510, 511, 512, 520, 522, 524, 526, 530, 531, *Rid.* 507; letters to the lords of the council, 2 *Cran.* 440, 445; functions of the council during the king's minority, 3 *Zur.* 88; proceedings relative to Joan Bocher, *Hutch.* v; a list of queen Mary's council, and the changes which were made therein on the accession of Elizabeth, 1 *Zur.* 5 n.; letters from the lords of the council during the reign of queen Elizabeth, *Grin.* 405, 407, 414, 416, 419, 422, 425, 428, 432, 434, *Park.* 103, 105, 117, 121, 179, 180, 182, 192, 195, 217, 327 n., 328, 355, 379, 384, 457 n.; letters to the council, *Grin.* 316—320, 392, 396, *Park.* 330

Proba: 4 *Bul.* 203

Probate: *v.* Wills.

Probe: printer's proof, *Grin.* 268

Probianus: refused to adore the cross, *Calf.* 198, 199, 2 *Ful.* 161

Procere: large, 1 *Bec.* 204

Processionals: Processionale Romanum, *Grin.* 140 n.; to be given up and destroyed, 2 *Cran.* 523, *Grin.* 135, 159

Processions: *v.* Rogation week.

Procession, a Romish ceremony, 1 *Ful.* 564, 2 *Ful.* 182—189; to whom the institution is ascribed, 2 *Bec.* 253, *Calf.* 295, 305, 2 *Ful.* 182, &c.; borrowed from heathenism, *Calf.* 295, 2 *Ful.* 182; used by the heretics, *Calf.* 296, 2 *Ful.* 182; said to have been used by Chrysostom at Constantinople, in the night, *Calf.* 298, &c., 2 *Ful.* 184; why Justinian required that a procession should take place when a church was to be consecrated, *Calf.* 304, 305, 2 *Ful.* 185; litanies used long before them, *Calf.* 294, 1 *Ful.* 183; the procession of the monk Augustine, *Calf.* 308, 2 *Ful.* 17 n., 120, 186; processions with banners, torches, &c., *Bale* 524; popish ones disorderly, *Calf.* 298; women sung songs of ribaldry in processions in cathedral churches, 3 *Tyn.* 125; mandate for keeping processions in English, 2 *Cran.* 495; processions with the litany, temp. Hen. VIII., *Pra. Eliz.* xxiv, 51 n., 561; the term only means supplications, *ib.* 570 n.; processions forbidden, 2 *Cran.* 502

Proclamations: see the names of the sovereigns.

Proclus: comment on Plato, 3 *Bul.* 134

Proclus Cyzicenus: *Whita.* 539

Procopius: on the evils of wicked company, *Wool.* 127 n

Procrastination: its evil, *Sand.* 172, &c.

Proctor (Mr), of the Black Friars, Cambridge: 1 *Lat.* iv.

Proctor (T.): notice of him, *Poet.* xxxviii; a mirror of mutability, *ib.* 400

Proctors: Cranmer's statute regulating the number of proctors in his courts, 2 *Cran.* 491

Prodicus, a heretic: 4 *Jew.* 630, *Whita.* 229 n

Prodigal son: the parable, 2 *Hoop.* 253, 257; what caused him to resort unto his father, *ib.* 259

Prodigality: to be avoided, 2 *Bul.* 32; forbidden, *ib.* 53

Prodigies: v. Comets, Eclipses, England, Miracles, Monsters, Signs.

Wonders have been seen before great events, 4 *Bul.* 231, *Hutch.* 81; strange wonders in the skies, *Pra. Eliz.* 471; signs beheld in Germany during war with the Turks, 2 *Cran.* 235; signs and tokens seen in England in queen Mary's time, *Lit. Eliz.* 569; signs in the sun, moon, seasons, &c., in the time of queen Elizabeth, 4 *Jew.* 1253, 1 *Zur.* 116; a cow brings forth a fawn, 1 *Zur.* 305; crosses, horsemen, trees, &c., have been seen in the heavens, 2 *Ful.* 148, 149

Profano, profanatio: *Now.* (102)

Profession, Professors: v. Persecution.

Wherein profession consists, 2 *Hoop.* 357; why there are so few sincere and true professors of the gospel, *ib.* 217

Profligate: to drive off, 1 *Bec.* 66

Prognostications: v. Astrology.

Proine: to prune, 1 *Jew.* 502

Prometheus: custom at the feast of Prometheus at Athens, 1 *Zur.* 123 n

Promises: all are not to be kept, 1 *Lat.* 116

Promises of God: they are of two kinds, —the conditional promises of the law, and the free promises of the gospel, 1 *Brad.* 66, 218, 219; how God's promises imply a covenant, 1 *Tyn.* 470, 471, 2 *Tyn.* 6; promises under condition, 1 *Cran.* 206; examples of God's free promises, 1 *Brad.* 66, 67; open and hidden ones, 3 *Bul.* 16; the promises touching Christ, *ib.* 13; that made to Adam and Eve, 1 *Bec.* 71, 3 *Bul.* 13, 1 *Hoop.* 258; the promise is co-extensive with the curse 1 *Hoop.* 258; howbeit within certain limits, *ib.* 259; how any are excluded from the promise that is made to all, *ib.* 263; it is made in and for Christ, *ib.* 258; it is made to faith, *ib.* 261; it is not without effect, 1 *Bul.* 117; whom God's promises help, 1 *Tyn.* 121, 423, 464; they are made to the godly, and not to the ungodly, 2 *Bec.* 618, 619; to the penitent, 1 *Hoop.* 263; to godly worshippers, 1 *Bul.* 236; to the afflicted, 2 *Bul.* 263; promises to hear prayer, 2 *Bec.* 130, 131; Christ's promise to be with his church, *Pil.* 110; promise in the sacraments, 4 *Bul.* 251; in the Lord's supper, *ib.* 405, 434; the promises are to be remembered and believed, 1 *Bec.* 119; to be laid hold on, *ib.* 98; to be embraced and pleaded when we pray, 2 *Bec.* 132, *Pil.* 301, 2 *Tyn.* 167; when believed, they justify, 1 *Tyn.* 52; faith given to them establishes the mind, 1 *Bec.* 147; they bring quietness to the conscience, *ib.* 146; satisfy the conscience in all doubts, *Pil.* 186; comfort, 1 *Bec.* 147; stir up to enterprise great things, *Pil.* 109; promises given to rulers pertain to their successors, *ib.* 185; those made to fathers belong to their children, *ib.* 190; the certainty of God's promises, *ib.* 445; they cannot be stolen from us, 2 *Lat.* 155

Promoters (i. e. informers): much wanted, 1 *Lat.* 279

Properties: communication of them, 3 *Bul.* 270

Property: v. Goods.

The law makes it, 1 *Lat.* 406; we may not do what we list with it, *ib.* 398, 407, 414

Prophecy: what, *Now.* (102); not to be despised, 2 *Jew.* 880; whether to be taken literally, *Rid.* 70; the prophecies concerning Christ accomplished, *Sand.* 7; that of Daniel, chap. ix, considered, 1 *Cov.* 67, 68; the spirit of truth in Annas and Caiaphas, 4 *Jew.* 941, &c.; the prophecy of St Paul (1 Tim. iv.) fulfilled, 3 *Bec.* 236; Augustine refers to the sacrament of prophecy, 4 *Bul.* 247; Luther prophesied of the troubles of

Germany, *Phil.* 416; Bradford foretells certain plagues, 1 *Brad.* 453, 2 *Brad.* xxviii; Latimer's prediction of the troubles of queen Mary's time, and his own death, 2 *Lat.* xxi; he was a true prophet, 1 *Lat.* 321; Hooper's prophecy of his death, 2 *Hoop.* x; prediction by Mrs Moore at Cambridge, *Sand.* iii; a remarkable one by Sandys, *ib.* xv; an old verse which ran in Parker's head, *Park.* 479; feigned prophecies, as those of Merlin, were used to deceive the people, *Sand.* 67; such prophecies censured, 2 *Jew.* 880; pretended prophecies forbidden by law, 2 *Lat.* 375 n.; those of astrologers condemned, 2 *Jew.* 872 (*v.* Nostradamus).

Prophesyings: the name used in scripture, *Grin.* 385; account of the exercises so called, *ib.* 383; the orders and ground of them, *ib.* 384; their benefit, and abuses, *ib.* 386; they were encouraged by Grindal, 1 *Zur.* 329; his orders for reformation of abuses about them, *Grin.* 373; they were favoured by Parkhurst, *Park.* 457, 459; approved, within certain limits, by Sandys, *Park.* 457 n., *Sand.* xxiv, xxvi; sanctioned by many of the bishops, *Grin.* 385; favoured by several of the privy council, *Park.* 457 n.; the queen's displeasure with archbishop Grindal respecting them, *Grin.* xi, 372; his letter to the queen about them, *ib.* 376; he refuses to suppress them, and solemnly remonstrates with the queen, *ib.* 386, &c.; she would have them suppressed, *Park.* 456, 457; her letter sent to the bishops for suppressing them, *Grin.* 467; speech to Grindal in council on the subject, *ib.* 471; stir made by Will. Heydon on their suppression, *Park.* 459; lord Bacon's opinion on them, *Grin.* xi.

Prophet (The false): thrown into the lake of fire, *Bale* 554

Prophets: why called seers, and prophecies visions, *Pil.* 214; they speak of the future as past, *ib.* 226, 241; they preached the old faith, 1 *Cov.* 62; all holy prophets point to Christ, *ib.* 59, &c.; they speak of his godhead and manhood, *ib.* 63; likewise of his office, *ib.* 64; of his sacrifice, death, burial, resurrection, and ascension, *ib.* 65, 66, and of his kingdom, *ib.* 64; they speak, moreover, of the calling of the heathen, *ib.* 66; they allow the righteousness of God by faith, *ib.* 62; they sought salvation in Christ, *ib.* 67; they ate and drank Christ's flesh and blood, 1 *Cran.* 75, 76; it is thought they were all married except Jeremiah, *Rog.* 302; they were ungently entreated of the Jews, 1 *Bec.* 184; many of them left no writings, *Whita.* 302; they wrote the Old Testament, but not the Apocrypha, *ib.* 50; their books, 2 *Cov.* 18; many prophets were engaged in writing the books of Judges, Ruth, Samuel, and Kings, *ib.* 302; the twelve minor prophets formerly reckoned as one book, *ib.* 292; their authority is very great, 1 *Bul.* 50; several rose out of Galilee, 3 *Jew.* 242; none appeared between Malachi and John the Baptist, *Whita.* 51; their schools, 2 *Jew.* 981; their apparel, 2 *Whitg.* 12, 13; prophets in the Christian church, 4 *Bul.* 105, 1 *Whitg.* 473, 493, 494; Stapleton says the prophets mentioned in Eph. ii. 20, are those of the New Testament; this Whitaker denies, *Whita.* 348; and so Chrysostom, Ambrose, and others, *ib.* 349; the word sometimes means interpreters, *Grin.* 385, *Now.* (102), 1 *Tyn.* 80, 2 *Tyn.* 121; some of the Christian prophets foretold; others were endued with a singular gift of interpreting the scripture, 4 *Bul.* 105; Whitaker supposes the word to mean preachers, *Whita.* 259; the miraculous gift of interpretation having now ceased, study is requisite, *Grin.* 385

Prophets (False): there are many false ones, 2 *Tyn.* 195; not Turks, nor Jews, but popish doctors, *ib.* 121; against false prophets and deceitful teachers; verses by Jo. Norden, *Poet.* 462; they are agents of Satan, *Sand.* 396; suffered for the trial of the elect, *Pil.* 615; are sent to them who will not hear the truth, 1 *Tyn.* 272; where no love of truth is, there are they, 2 *Tyn.* 129; their impudency, *Nord.* 110; it is dangerous to dispute with them, *ib.* 111; they shall come, as is foretold, *Hutch.* 33, 1 *Tyn.* 318; the remedy against them is prayer, 2 *Tyn.* 116

Propitiation: ἱλασμός, or propitiation, what, 1 *Bec.* 335, 2 *Tyn.* 153; the Christian feast of propitiation, 2 *Bul.* 265

Proponed: propounded, 1 *Cov.* 216

Proportion: in sacraments, 4 *Bul.* 244

Proprium in communi: a monkish fiction, 2 *Cran.* 147

Proselytes: those of the Jews, *Whita.* 530

Prosopography of God: 3 *Bul.* 137, 138

Prosopopœia: 3 *Bul.* 138, 153

Prosper of Aquitaine: some account of him, 1 *Tyn.* 487 n.; it is stated, on the evidence of a poem of doubtful genuineness, that he was married, 3 *Jew.* 391; called bishop of Rhegium, 2 *Ful.* 353, 3 *Ful.* 891; probably a layman, 2 *Ful.* 353 n.; Opera, *Jew.* xlii; his Chronicon, *Calf.* 9 n.; whether the author of the treatise De Vocatione

Gentium, ascribed to Ambrose, 1 *Bec.* 81 n.; an epistle ascribed to him and also to Ambrose, 3 *Jew.* 464 n.; his Sententiæ ex Augustino, 2 *Bec.* 250, 268, 284, 292, 3 *Bec.* 413, 433, 434 n., 437, 458, 463 n., 464, *Grin.* 59, *Park.* 381; Pro Aug. Doct. Resp., 3 *Bec.* 419 n., 422 n.; he says we neither come to nor depart from God by distance of places, 2 *Jew.* 761; writes upon the bondage of man's will, 1 *Tyn.* 488 n.; says that if the grace of the Saviour overpass some persons, and the prayer of the church be not received for them, this must be referred to the secret judgments of divine justice (dub.), 3 *Jew.* 557; censures the Pelagians, *Rog.* 155, 309; his arguments against them, *Whita.* 443; passages on justification, 2 *Cran.* 206, 207, 209, 210; he refers to the reception of the blood of Christ as a proof that he died (pseud.), 2 *Jew.* 700; says that the wicked do not eat Christ's body (from Aug.), *Hutch.* 265; says Peter was a rock, 2 *Ful.* 288; declares that Rome, the see of Peter, first cut off the plague of Pelagius, *ib.* 353; mentions the council of Constantinople, 1 *Bul.* 13, and certain synods in Africa, 2 *Ful.* 354 n.; says they, unto whom the world is crucified, &c., wait for the day of judgment without fear (pseud.), 3 *Jew.* 245

Prosper of Orleans: whether the author of the books De Vocatione Gentium, 2 *Ful.* 353 n

Prosperity: *v.* Prayers, Wicked.

It is a perilous thing, 1 *Tyn.* 138; entire worldly prosperity a bad sign, 1 *Lat.* 435, 483; the temptation of it, 2 *Bec.* 186, 187; such temptation more dangerous than that of adversity, *ib.* 187; how to behave in it, 1 *Hoop.* 301; Moses' rule therein, *ib.* 301, 302

Prostibulous: *Bale* 517

Protagoras: doubts whether there be a God, *Rog.* 37

Protasius, martyr: 2 *Jew.* 654

Proterius, bp of Alexandria: 1 *Whitg.* 465

Protestants: the term employed, *Calf.* 134, *Poet.* 267; specially applied to the Germans, 2 *Zur.* 48; its origin, 2 *Jew.* 686; it is a party name, *Rid.* 9; Ridley cared not for it, *ib.* 14; Protestants declared by Sanders to be members of Antichrist, 2 *Ful.* 373; those so called are not to be charged with all the opinions of Luther, 1 *Ful.* 16, 18, 122; our religion older than that of Rome by 1000 years, *Phil.* 120; variances amongst Protestants, 2 *Ful.* 77 (*v.* Sects); popish Protestants, 2 *Brad.* 334; fainthearted ones, *Pil.* 416

Protestatio Concionatorum: see Flacius, *Jew.* xxxvii.

Protoflamines: *v.* Flamines.

Protogenes: gave David's Psalms to children instead of poets' fables, 1 *Jew.* 332

Proude (Rich.), or Prowde: 2 *Brad.* 108; letter to him, *ib.* 194

Provence: olim Gallia Narbonensis, *Calf.* 30

Proverbs: *v.* Erasmus, vii, Solomon.

What a proverb (משל) is, 2 *Hoop.* 453; ἐπὶ θύρας τὴν ὑδρίαν, *Whita.* 365; τὰ πέρυσι βελτίω, 3 *Jew.* 218; dimidium plus toto, 1 *Lat.* 277; honores mutant mores, *ib.* 437; similis simili gaudet, *ib.* 357; plain as Dunstable way, *ib.* 113; some common English proverbs cited, 2 *Bec.* 583, 601, 602, 1 *Lat.* 280, 363, 410, 431, 482, 502, 506, 2 *Lat.* 150, 1 *Tyn.* 304, 305, 2 *Zur.* 293; a monkish one, 2 *Whitg.* 478, 483; unexplained proverbial allusions, 3 *Bec.* 267 n

Providence: *v.* God, vii.

What it is, *Phil.* 403; divina providentia, verses (in English) by And. Willet, *Poet.* 394; a meditation thereon, *Pra. B.* 109; God rules the world thereby, *Hutch.* 69, &c., *Now.* (31), 147; he only can preserve us, 2 *Tyn.* 117; he will provide for his people, *ib.* 106, &c.; he will provide for the widow and the fatherless, 2 *Lat.* 224; mistrust of God's providence is a root of all evil, *Sand.* 343

Provinciale: *v.* Lyndewode.

Provincials: chiefs of religious orders within a province, 1 *Lat.* 296

Provision: not to be carefully made for a long time to come, 2 *Bec.* 161; necessary provision may be made, *ib.* 164

Prowde (Rich.): *v.* Proude.

Prowest: wisest, or most prudent, *Phil.* 360

Prowet (Steven): *Bale* 429

Prudentius (Aur.): his works, *Calf.* 415, *Jew.* xlii; he censures the notion that the soul is God, or a part of God, 3 *Bul.* 373; describes God's temple in the mind of man, *Calf.* 131, 132; the verses at length, with a metrical translation, 3 *Bul.* 225—227; speaks of Christ as written in the law by figures, 2 *Jew.* 604; says it was the woman who subdued the serpent, *Calf.* 259, and that the virgin deserved to bring forth God, *ib.*; calls Bethlehem the head of the world, 1 *Jew.* 439, 3 *Jew.* 270; refers to the use of the sign of the cross, *Calf.* 195, 259; verses exhorting to flee the errors of Novatus, with a metrical translation, 2 *Ful.* 346; verses, de resurrectione carnis humanæ, 2 *Cov.* 197 n., *Pra. Eliz.* 418; the same in

English metre, 2 *Cov.* 195; part of his hymn, ad galli cantum (Ales diei), *Pra. Eliz.* 141; an English version of it, *ib.* 28; verses on the banner, &c. of Constantine, 2 *Jew.* 648, 649, 651; he mentions pictures in a church, *Calf.* 29, 30; speaks of the cortyna, *ib.* 51 n.; referred to, *ib.* 26 n.; Parkhurst seems to imitate his Utriusque Testamenti Dipticon, *Pra. Eliz.* 413 n

Prynne (Will.): writes against Cosin's Hours of prayer, *Calf.* 226 n., *Pra. Eliz.* x. n., xiii, xiv.

Przibram (Jo.): Lib. de Prof. Fidei Cath., *Jew.* xlii; on communion in one kind, 1 *Jew.* 218

Psallians: *v.* Messalians.

Psalmists: singers, 4 *Bul.* 114

Psalmody: *v.* Music.

Psalmograph: psalm writer, 1 *Bec.* 12

Psalms:

i. *Generally:* what we learn from them, 2 *Cov.* 18; on the Greek and Latin mode of numbering them, 1 *Tyn.* 160 n.; many of them directed "To the chanter," or "chief singer," *Pil.* 533; torculares Psalmi, or those "upon Gittith," 2 *Bul.* 166; alleged obscurity of the Psalms, 1 *Jew.* 330; on the prayers for vengeance on the wicked, 1 *Brad.* 177; the seven (penitential) Psalms, *Pra. Eliz.* 45—50; these Psalms in Latin, with a short prayer upon each, *ib.* 297—304; notes respecting them, 1 *Brad.* 45 n., *Pra. Eliz.* 45 n.; Psalmi, &c., de nativitate, passione, resurrectione, et ascensione Christi, *Pra. Eliz.* 274, &c.; the Psalms of the passion, *ib.* 75, &c., (172, &c.), see also (277, &c.); Psalms of consolation named, 2 *Hoop.* 583, 584; the Psalms sung of old by husbandmen, artificers, and children, 1 *Jew.* 331, 332; how Damasus ordered them to be sung in the church, *ib.* 264, 2 *Whitg.* 469; on the alternate singing of them, 3 *Whitg.* 384—388; remarks on the reading of them, 1 *Jew.* 331; sitting at them, 2 *Hoop.* 146; reference to a curious MS. (apparently a Psalter), Latin and Anglo-Saxon, *Park.* 253

ii. *Expositions, &c.:*

CERTAIN COMFORTABLE EXPOSITIONS, &c., 2 *Hoop.* 176, &c.; written in the time of Hooper's trouble, *ib.* 182; the Psalms in the Primers generally have brief expository notes prefixed to them, *Pra. Eliz.* 19, &c.;

Psa. i.: prayers out of it, *Pra. B.* 205, 206, 207; a Latin prayer, *Pra. Eliz.* 419

Psa. ii.: prayers out of it, *Pra. B.* 207, 209 a Latin prayer, *Pra. Eliz.* 420

iii.: a Latin prayer out of it, *Pra. Eliz.* 421

xxiii.: EXPOSITION OF PSA. XXII. (xxiii.) by Luther, translated by Coverdale, 2 *Cov.* 279, &c.; another exposition, 2 *Hoop.* 184, &c.

li.: Latin prayers out of it, *Pra. Eliz.* 421, 422

lxii.: an exposition, 2 *Hoop.* 243, &c.

lxxiii.: an exposition, 2 *Hoop.* 283, &c.

lxxvii.: an exposition, 2 *Hoop.* 309, &c.

lxxix.: **a paraphrase of it,** 1 *Brad.* 282, &c.

cx.: expounded, 1 *Cov.* 53—58

cxv.: a prayer on it, 1 *Bec.* 301

cxvi.: DAVID'S HARP, an exposition of this Psalm, 1 *Bec.* 262; why this Psalm is called David's harp, *ib.* 267

cxix.: alphabetical, 2 *Bul.* 6

cli.: apocryphal, *Whita.* 103; yet included in the Metaphrase of Apollinarius, *ib.* 104

iii. *Metrical Versions:* whether the word of God, *Grin.* 216; the metrical Greek version of Apollinaris, 1 *Jew.* 332 n.; Psalms set forth in English metre, 2 *Bec.* 361; notices of some early English metrical versions, 2 *Cov.* 535, *Poet.* xiii, &c.; GHOSTLY PSALMS AND SPIRITUAL SONGS, by bp Coverdale, 2 *Cov.* 533, &c.; notice of Psalms (thirty-seven in number) drawn into metre by T. Sternhold, *ib.* 535; notices of the writers of the old metrical version of the Psalms, *Poet.* xlv—li; Norton's share in it, *Now.* viii, *Poet.* xlviii; the Psalms were turned into metre by Parker, *Park.* ix, 483, *Poet.* xiii; the Scottish version, Will. Kethe a contributor thereto, *Poet.* xlix; notice of the Psalms of David, translated into divers and sundry kinds of verse, by Sir Ph. Sidney, and his sister, Mary, countess of Pembroke, *ib.* xvi.

INDEX

of Psalms in metre.

Psa. ii. by bp Coverdale, 2 *Cov.* 568

iv. by Sidney, &c.*, *Poet.* 53

vi. by the same, *ib.* 54

— by Will. Hunnis, *ib.* 143

— by Richard Gipps, *ib.* 337

— by Richard Robinson, *ib.* 364

xii. by bp Coverdale, 2 *Cov.* 567

xiii. by Sidney, &c., *Poet.* 55

— by Will. Byrd, *ib.* 223

— by Fra. Davison, *ib.* 318

---

* That is, Sir Philip Sidney, and his sister the countess of Pembroke.

Psa. xiv. by bp Coverdale, 2 *Cov.* 581
— by queen Elizabeth, *Poet.* 1
xv. by Will. Byrd, *ib.* 222
— by Chr. Davison, *ib.* 332
xvi. by Sidney, &c., *ib.* 56
xviii. by Tho. Sternhold, *ib.* 480
— by Jo. Marbeck*, *ib.* 468
xix. by Sidney, &c., *ib.* 57
— by Will. Samuel, *ib.* 312
xxiii. by Sidney, &c., *ib.* 59
— by Fra. Davison, *ib.* 319
xxv.† by bp Coverdale, 2 *Cov.* 578
xxvii. by Hen. Lok, *Poet.* 136
xxx. by Mich. Cosowarth, *ib.* 406
xliii. by Fra. Davison, *ib.* 320
xlvi. by bp Coverdale, 2 *Cov.* 569
— [by Jo. Hopkins], *Lit. Eliz.* 566
xlvii. by Sidney, &c., *Poet.* 60
li. by bp Coverdale, 2 *Cov.* 574
— another, by the same, *ib.* 576
— by Will. Hunnis, *Poet.* 147
— by Eliz. Grymeston, *ib.* 412
— by Will. Whittingham, *ib.* 489
liv. by Anne Askewe, *Bale* 184
— by Jos. Bryan, *Poet.* 333
lxii. by Sidney, &c., *ib.* 61
lxvii. by bp Coverdale, 2 *Cov.* 580
lxxii. by Sidney, &c., *Poet.* 62
lxxiii. by Abr. Fraunce‡, *ib.* 237
— by Fra. Davison, *ib.* 321
lxxvii. by Sidney, &c., *ib.* 65
lxxxiv. by Jo. Hopkins, *ib.* 485
lxxxv. by Sidney, &c., *ib.* 68
lxxxvi. by Fra. Davison, *ib.* 322
xci. by Sidney, &c., *ib.* 69
— by T. Carey, *ib.* 338
xcii. by abp Parker, *ib.* 2
xciii. by Sidney, &c., *ib.* 71
xcv. by W. P. (a fragment), *ib.* 484
xcvi. by Sidney, &c., *ib.* 71
xcix. by the same, *ib.* 73
c. by Jo. Pits, *ib.* 387
ciii. by Tho. Becon, 3 *Bec.* 221
— by Tho. Sternhold, *Poet.* 481
cx. by abp Parker, *ib.* 4
cxii. by Tho. Becon, 3 *Bec.* 222
— by Sir Jo. Harington, *Poet.* 115
cxiii. by Sidney, &c., *ib.* 74
cxv. by Jo. Hall, M.D., *ib.* 198
cxvii. by Sidney, &c., *ib.* 74
cxxi. by Hen. Lok, *ib.* 137
cxxiii. by Fra. Davison, *ib.* 324
cxxiv. by bp Coverdale, 2 *Cov.* 571
cxxv. by Sidney, &c , *Poet.* 75
— by Fra. Davison, *ib.* 325

Psa. cxxv. by Will. Kethe, *ib.* 492
— by Rob. Wisdom, *ib.* 493
cxxvii. by Sidney, &c., *ib.* 75
— by Jos. Bryan, *ib.* 334
— by Hen. Dod, *ib.* 449
cxxviii. by bp Coverdale, 2 *Cov.* 573
— another, by the same, *ib.*
cxxix. by Sidney, &c., *ib.* 76
cxxx. by bp Coverdale, 2 *Cov.* 577
— by Fra. Davison, *Poet.* 326
cxxxi. by Sidney, &c., *ib.* 77
cxxxiii. by bp Coverdale, 2 *Cov.* 583
— by Sidney, &c., *Poet.* 77
— by Fra. Davison §, *ib.* 327
cxxxiv. by Sidney, &c., *ib.* 78
cxxxvi. by the same, *ib.* 79
cxxxvii. by bp Coverdale, 2 *Cov.* 571
— by Sidney, &c., *Poet.* 80
— by Sir Jo. Harington, *ib.* 116
— by Fra. Davison, *ib.* 328
cxlii. by the same, *ib.* 330
— by Jos. Bryan, *ib.* 335
cxliv. by Sidney, &c., *ib.* 82
cxlv. by Jo. Mardley, *ib.* 496
cxlvii. by bp Coverdale, 2 *Cov.* 582
— by Tho. Norton, *Poet.* 487
cxlviii. by Sidney, &c., *ib.* 84
cxlix. by Jo. Pullain, *ib.* 495
A Psalm, wherein is set forth the love of God towards us, &c., *Nord.* 32; a psalm of rejoicing for the wonderful love of Christ, by W. Hunnis, *Poet.* 157
iv. *Composed Psalms:* flores Psalmorum, quos Psalterium Hieronymi appellant, *Pra. Eliz.* 311; fifteen composed Psalms in Latin, by Jo. Fisher, bp of Rochester, *ib.* 318; penitential, *Lit. Eliz.* 541, 609, 633; in plague time, *Grin.* 85, *Lit. Eliz.* 482, *Pra. B.* 162; on the withdrawal of the plague, *Grin.* 111, 116, *Lit. Eliz.* 508, 510, 513, *Pra. B.* 164; for deliverance from enemies, *Lit. Eliz.* 543, 545, 610, 611, 627, 634, 635; used daily in the English army in France, *ib.* 627, see also 635; on the invasion of Malta by the Turks, *ib.* 520; for Hungary, invaded by the Turks, *ib.* 529, 530, 531; on victories over the Turks, *ib.* 524; for the anniversary of the queen's accession, *ib.* 555; on a thanksgiving for the preservation of the queen and realm from the bloody practices of the pope, *ib.* 599, 600, 601, 602; thanksgiving, 1588, *ib.* 619
Psalters (Lady): *v.* Mary (B. V.).
Psellus: cited by Theodoret, 2 *Ful.* 287
Pseudo-Christs: *v.* Christs (False).

---

* 2 Sam. xxii. 2—7, corresponding with a part of Psa. xviii.
† Psa. xxv. was turned into metre by the princess Elizabeth, and published 1542, 2 *Cov.* 535.
‡ Called lxxii.   § Called cxxxii.

Ptochotrophia: 1 *Bul.* 286, 4 *Bul.* 498
Ptolemeans: the sect so called, *Phil.* 418; they rejected the books of Moses, *Whita.* 31
Ptolemy II., called Philadelphus, king of Egypt: *v.* Bible, Greek (LXX).
Ptolemy VIII., called Lathurus, king of Egypt: his cruel treatment of the Jews, 2 *Hoop.* 82
Ptolemy (Claudius): his Cosmography, *Calf.* x; his canon, 2 *Zur.* 336
Ptolemy (or Bartholomew) Lucensis: *Calf.* x, 128
Publicans: what they were, 2 *Tyn.* 71
Publicans: the Paulicians corruptly so called, *Bale* 3, 322
Publius Syrus: *q. v.*
Pudsey (Hugh de), bp of Durham: founder of Sherborne hospital, *Grin.* 352 n
Pues: *v.* Pews.
Puine: *v.* Punie.
Pulbert (Conrad): letter to him, 3 *Zur.* 604
Pullain (Jo.): notice of him, *Poet.* 1; archdeacon of Colchester, *Calf.* vii; Psalm cxlix. in metre by him, *Poet.* 495
Pulleon (Jo. Ant.): ambassador from the pope, 2 *Cran.* 272 n., 277 n
Pulpit: that of Ezra, 1 *Whitg.* 205, 206; necessary in a church, 4 *Bul.* 501; advisable, but not necessary, 1 *Lat.* 207; a low pulpit to be made for the minister to read prayers; in small churches his stall in the choir will do; the form to be referred to the archdeacon or his official, *Grin.* 132, 155; the pulpit to be provided by the churchwardens, *Grin.* 133; lessons, epistles, gospels, &c., read from the pulpit, 2 *Cran.* 156, 501, *Grin.* 132; a pulpit without a preacher compared to a bell without a clapper, 1 *Lat.* 207
Pulton (......): Hist. of Engl. Franciscans, 1 *Lat.* 287, 2 *Lat.* 319, 391 nn
Punic tongue: 1 *Jew.* 292, &c., *Whita.* 223
Punie: inferior, junior, 3 *Jew.* 284; puine, *Calf.* 200
Punishment: *v.* Death (Punishment of), Hell. Temporal punishment, why sent by God, 3 *Bec.* 34; how laid on us, 1 *Bul.* 110; that of sinners just and certain, 2 *Bul.* 426; that of those who do not worship God, 3 *Bul.* 204; of those who abuse God's name, 1 *Bul.* 241; of blasphemers, *ib.* 242; of little foxes that spoil the church, *Sand.* 72, &c.; of those that eat and drink the Lord's supper unworthily, 4 *Bul.* 472; eternal punishment, *Pil.* 250; punishment belongs to the magistrate, 1 *Bul.* 346, 2 *Hoop.* 127; admonition before it, *ib.* 361; kinds of it, *ib.* 355; certain kinds appointed to certain sins, 2 *Bul.* 72; what is to be punished in offenders, 1 *Bul.* 357; what order must be had in punishment, *ib.* 360

Punned: pounded, 3 *Whitg.* 34
Punt (Will.): named, 2 *Brad.* 58, 94, (*Rid.* 364), 129 n., 179, 213; Ridley's messenger, *Rid.* 364 n.; letters to him, 2 *Brad.* 38 (?), 2 *Hoop.* 592 (?), *Rid.* 376
Pupilla oculi: *v.* Burgo (Jo. de).
Purdue (......): *v.* Perdue.
Purfles: embroidered borders (from "pour filles"), *Calf.* 161
Purfoot (Tho.), printer: 2 *Zur.* 254
Purfoy (Rob.) alias Warton, *q. v.*
Purgations: *v.* Holy ashes, salt, water, &c.
Purgatory: the Romish doctrine, 1 *Lat.* 37, 2 *Lat.* 332, *Rog.* 214, &c.; scriptures adduced to prove it, 2 *Cov.* 473—475, 3 *Jew.* 565; translations concerning it examined, 1 *Ful.* 278—331; falsely alleged to be the "last farthing" of the parable, 2 *Tyn.* 49; proved to be contrary to scripture, *Rog.* 212, 1 *Tyn.* 269 n., 3 *Tyn.* 281; the doctrine is against God's commandments, 2 *Hoop.* 121; it is taken out of the books of the heathen, not found in those of the Old and New Testaments, 2 *Cov.* 473; errors of Montanists, &c., respecting it, *Rog.* 214—218; the doctrine is maintained by feigned apparitions, &c., contrary to the scriptures, *Grin.* 24, 1 *Lat.* 212; when and how far it was believed by Luther, *Whita.* 541; once allowed by Latimer, 2 *Lat.* 239, 353; he describes the state of the souls therein, *ib.* 236; he deems it preferable to the bp of London's prison, *ib.* 237, 361; P. Dens on purgatory, 1 *Tyn.* 159 n.; its supposed locality, *Rog.* 215, 2 *Tyn.* 287; what sin is supposed to be punished there, *Rog.* 216, 218; its duration indefinite, 1 *Tyn.* 244; it was said that seven years were appointed in purgatory for every deadly sin, *ib.* 271, 3 *Tyn.* 47; its pains, 2 *Cran.* 63; the pope claims power over it, 2 *Jew.* 920, 1 *Tyn.* 235, 269, 271, 2 *Tyn.* 287; it is said to be his peculiar possession, 4 *Jew.* 845; popes have bidden the angels to fetch men out, 1 *Tyn.* 269; they have promised deliverance from it for killing Frenchmen, *ib.* 301, 311; it was believed that men could be delivered from it by masses, 2 *Bec.* 414, 1 *Cran.* 349; deliverance for money, *Pil.* 21, 77; it is a fire that may be quenched at a low price, 3 *Tyn.* 28, 141; shew the pope a little money, and God is so merciful that there is no purgatory, *ib.* 143; More (citing Gregory) says that a man procured help by

praying to a saint in purgatory, *ib.* 121 n.; address to souls there (Horæ B. V. M. ad us. Sar.), *Rog.* 214; a tale concerning it, 1 *Lat.* 36; it is a falsehood, *ib.* 426, 550; a folly found out by man, 2 *Hoop.* 31; a place of the Papist's devising, 3 *Bec.* 129, 523, 1 *Cran.* 353; rise of the doctrine, 2 *Tyn.* 162, 163; the doctrine condemned, 2 *Bec.* 175, 1 *Brad.* 49, 372, 588, 3 *Bul.* 389, 390, 2 *Cran.* 182, 2 *Lat.* 191; the pope's purgatory is needless, 3 *Tyn.* 142, 143; the opinion of it is vain and dangerous, *Sand.* 162, 163; it is a most pestilent ill, 1 *Hoop.* 566; its use in the mystery of iniquity, 2 *Jew.* 912; evils arising from the doctrine, 1 *Hoop.* 567; purgatory devoureth all things, 1 *Tyn.* 244; it is a source of wealth to the clergy, *ib.* 244, 303, 318, 2 *Tyn.* 162; purgatory pick-purse, 2 *Brad.* 292, 2 *Cov.* 270, 1 *Lat.* 36, 50, 71, 1 *Tyn.* 342; purgatory-rakers censured, 3 *Bec.* 119; the doctrine prevents men from confiding in God, 2 *Tyn.* 159; it is contumelious to Christ, 1 *Cran.* 349, 2 *Cran.* 181; it causes men to fear death, *Pil.* 321; they who fear purgatory cannot but utterly abhor death, 3 *Tyn.* 281; in providing for purgatory some forget hell, 2 *Lat.* 339; provision for it has brought thousands to hell, and caused much evil upon earth, *ib.* 363; charity to the living better than provision against purgatory, *ib.* 238; it is a cause of doubt to survivors, 1 *Hoop.* 561; how such doubts are removed, *ib.* 562; purgatory is a new doctrine, 3 *Jew.* 559, &c.; not mentioned by the apostles, *Phil.* 414; fathers quoted against it, 2 *Lat.* 246 —248; it was not held by Augustine, 1 *Ful.* 278, *Phil.* 415; his doubts about it, 3 *Jew.* 565, 566, 1 *Tyn.* 269 n.; he denies it, 3 *Jew.* 568; lord Cobham's opinion on it, *Bale* 21; it is not held by the Greek church, *Rog.* 213, 1 *Tyn.* 269 n.; it is denied by the reformed churches, *Rog.* 213; Latimer's arguments against it, with Henry VIII.'s answers, 2 *Lat.* 239; P. Martyr disproves it, 3 *Zur.* 378; God's purgatory and the pope's, 3 *Tyn.* 121; what the true purgatory is, 2 *Bec.* 577; the true purgatory is in this life, 3 *Tyn.* 214; the scripture knows none after this life, 2 *Bec.* 394; the right purgatory is to purge our appetites, &c., 1 *Tyn.* 321; how bodily pain purgeth the body, 3 *Tyn.* 141; there is (properly) no purgatory but the blood of Christ, 2 *Bec.* 381, 3 *Bec.* 126, 2 *Hoop.* 32, 3 *Tyn.* 180; St Patrick's purgatory, 1 *Hoop.* 290, 1 *Tyn.* 290

Purification: v. Churching, Purity.
Purim: 2 *Bul.* 162
Puritans: v. Admonition, Uniformity, Vestments.

On the name, 1 *Whitg.* 171; the name employed, *Poet.* 268; they were termed Precisians, *Park.* 377, 472, &c.; and sometimes Disciplinarians, *Rog.* 280, &c.; statements respecting them, *ib.* 8, &c., 1 *Zur.* 175, 202, 237, 249, 280, 283, 284, 287, 291, 295, 298, 320, &c.; persecutions of the Nonconformists in the reign of Elizabeth, *Lit. Eliz.* xxxiv, xxxv; ministers deprived at different times, *Rog.* 8, 2 *Whitg.* 458, 2 *Zur.* 119, 121, 125, 130, 147, 148, 162, 167; the Puritans send messengers to Switzerland, 1 *Zur.* 297 n.; Beza proposes a deputation from the foreign churches to queen Elizabeth and the bishops on their behalf, 2 *Zur.* 131, &c.; his further opinions on this, *ib.* 143; Bullinger and Gualter intercede for them, *ib.* 167; some of them separate from the established church, on account of the vestments, 1 *Zur.* 202;-the leaders imprisoned, *ib.*; many Puritans in London, *Grin.* 347, 348, 2 *Zur.* 162; examination of certain Londoners before the ecclesiastical commissioners, 1567, *ib.* 199; Grindal's opinion respecting the Puritans, *ib.* 339, &c.; he tolerated private preaching, and celebration of the sacraments without the liturgy, *Sand.* xx. n.; testimony of this party to the purity of doctrine in Elizabeth's days, *Rog.* 21, 1 *Zur.* 287; some went to Scotland, but soon returned dissatisfied, *Grin.* 295; they disliked fonts and brasen eagles, *Park.* 450; certain ministers refuse to subscribe, and why, *Rog.* 8, 3 *Whitg.* 319; the Puritans commonly regarded as persecuted, *Park.* 410; their influence exercised upon the Prayer-Book, *Lit. Eliz.* xv, &c.; in 1583 they allowed subscription to the articles, *Rog.* 10; their controversy with the prelates, 1, 2, 3 *Whitg.* passim; Whitgift opposes them, 3 *Whitg.* 581; and justifies his proceedings, *ib.* 602, &c.; they are opposed by learned men, *Rog.* 17; number of nonconforming ministers in each of the counties of England, in 1604, *ib.* 317; they refuse to subscribe in 1605, *ib.* 25, 26; they petition king James, *ib.* 21, 26; their device to shun subscription, *ib.* 28; virulent pamphlets published by them, 1 *Zur.* 291; queen Elizabeth offended with their dissolute writing, *Park.* 426; their books denounced as schismatical and seditious by her, *Rog.* 16; their private press, *Park.* 410; their works found in the Low Countries, *Park.* 283; some of their writers, *Rog.* 203; opinions ascribed to them; their uncouth doctrine, *ib.* 13; they said themselves were the church in England, *ib.* 170; their objections against the established government and rites, 1 *Zur.* 280, 292, 295; they abhorred archbishops, &c., *Rog.* 331; some detested parsons and vicars also, *ib.* 331, 332; they affirmed the bishops not to be sent by God, *ib.* 334; urged inferior ministers to seek at their classis a new approbation, which they termed the Lord's ordinance, *ib.* 334; pretended that they affected not parity in the church of God, *ib.* 332; their conceits of their discipline, *ib.* 15; they thought the advancement of their presbyterial kingdom a testimony that they should have part in future glory, *ib.* 152; their views on church assemblies or councils, *ib.* 206; they denied the validity of the canon law, *ib.* 361; considered that civil magistrates have no power to make ecclesiastical constitutions, &c., *ib.* 343, 344; said that princes must be servants unto the church, *ib.* 340; some preached without authority, *ib.* 231; they preached on fast-days and made very long sermons, *Lit. Eliz.* 480 n., 490 n.; objected to homilies, *Rog.* 326, 327; said ministers should not read anything in the congregation, but the scriptures, *ib.* 326; declared reading without preaching to be as evil as playing upon a stage, and worse too, *ib.* 326; considered that none might minister the sacraments who did not preach, *ib.* 235, 271, 281; taught that sacraments are no sacraments unless joined to the word of God preached, *ib.*; their doctors did not minister the sacraments, *ib.* 235; their sabbatarian opinions, *ib.* 18, 19; this doctrine censured and forbidden, *ib.* 20; they said that without preaching, the sabbath could not be hallowed in the least measure, *ib.* 326; their views of excommunication, *ib.* 310; they found fault that excommunication was not exercised against kings and princes, *ib.* 311; the Scotch presbytery excommunicated for May-games, &c., *ib.* 311, 312; the Puritans denied baptism to the children of those who obeyed not their decrees, *ib.* 280; their scruples on funeral rites, *Pil.* 321; some would have had all ceremonies left at liberty, *Rog.* 185, 317; some said that a promise was not to be kept when God's honour and preaching of his word were hindered, *ib.* 360; they would not take a lawful oath if it might injure their brethren, *ib.* 359; some used horrible imprecations, *ib.* 357; some said the people might reform the church, and that they must not tarry for the magistrate, *ib.* 344; others affirmed parliament to have power to reform the abuses of the church without the prince, *ib.*; hence their manifold petitions to the parliament, *Rog.* 344, *Sand.* xxvi, 3 *Whitg.* 620; a question among them on obedience to the prince, *Park.* 377; their faction democratic, *ib.* 437; danger to the state apprehended from them, *ib.* 418, 419, 426; disturbances and divisions caused by them, *Rog.* 317; under colour of reformation they sought the ruin of learning and religion, and sought a popular state, *Park.* 434

Purity: *v.* Prayers.

What pureness God requireth, 2 *Bul.* 123; the pure in heart are blessed, 1 *Lat.* 485, 2 *Tyn.* 25; the manner and order of our purification, 3 *Bul.* 41, 49; purity of life follows the true knowledge of God, 1 *Bec.* 26; cleanness of life to be observed by soldiers, *ib.* 252

Purre, or Pur: a word of invitation to hogs, 3 *Bec.* 280

Purvey (Jo.): a follower of Wickliffe, *Bale* 11; persecuted, *ib.* 44 n.; neither hot nor cold, *ib.* 80; he recanted, *ib.* 123; called Tom Purvey, *ib.* 125

Put case: to suppose, 2 *Bul.* 52

Puteo (Jac. card. de): deputed by the pope to judge Cranmer, 2 *Cran.* 212 n., 541, 1 *Zur.* 12 n.; called "cardinal of the pit," 2 *Cran.* 225

Putta, bp of Rochester: 1 *Jew.* 303

Puttock: 2 *Cran.* 193

Pye (Jo.): seeks and obtains the land of Droitwich priory, 2 *Lat.* 395 n., 397, 398

Pye (Will.), dean of Chichester: account of him, *Phil.* 169; in the convocation, 1553, *ib.* xiii; he took part in the disputation with the martyrs at Oxford, 1 *Cran.* 391, 2 *Lat.* 271, *Rid.* 191

Pygot (Rob.): *v.* Pigot.

Pygott (Tho.): 2 *Cran.* 543, 547

Pylkington (Mr): *v.* Pilkington (James), bp.

Pyriphlegeton: an infernal river, *Calf.* 14 n

Pyrrhus: *Calf.* 317

Pyrrhus, king of Epirus: 2 *Jew.* 1031

Pythagoras: his definition of God, *Hutch.* 176; his teaching respecting him, 1 *Hoop.* 285; he said we should not speak of God without light, 1 *Jew.* 119; his ternarius numerus, *Hutch.* 123, 176; his opinion of the soul, 3 *Bul.* 374, 385; his symbols, 4 *Bul.* 232, 238; he was a lawgiver, 2 *Bul.* 219; his injunction to his scholars, *Wool.* 101; made a king, *Hutch.* 308; αὐτὸς ἔφη, 3 *Bul.* 168, 1 *Jew.* 101

Pytho: 1 *Dec.* 259
Python: the witch of Endor called Pythonissa, 1 *Bul.* 242; pope Hildebrand mentioned by the council of Brixia, as Pythonico spiritu laborantem, 3 *Jew.* 129
Pyx: *v.* Pix.

Q

Quadring, co. Lincoln: the benefice, 2 *Cran.* 278
Qualmire: *v.* Quavemire.
Quarles (Fra.): his lines concerning Ridley, *Rid.* xii.
Quarry (......), the pardoner: *Bale* 429
Quartadecimans: *v.* Easter.
Quarter-service: proscribed by Latimer, 2 *Lat.* 243
Quasi: force of the word, 2 *Ful.* 173
Quasy: queasy, sick, 2 *Ful.* 173; queysie, *Calf.* 209
Quavemire: quagmire, 2 *Cran.* 67, 3 *Whitg.* 276; qualmire, 2.*Cran.* 67
Queenborough, co. Kent: state of the castle, *Park.* 203
Queens: *v.* Kings, Women.
Queen's day: the anniversary of Elizabeth's accession, *Lit. Eliz.* 558 n
Quell: to kill, *Phil.* 307 n.; queel, 1 *Hoop.* 552
Quene (Mr): at Paris, 2 *Cov.* 496
Quentel (Pet.): printer for Tyndale at Cologne, 1 *Tyn.* xxviii, 4, 5
Querele: complaint, *Grin.* 289
Quesnel (Pasch.): 2 *Ful.* 71, 319, 353 nn
Questionists: scholastic writers, *Hutch.* 16
Questions: some questions with answers by certain bishops, 2 *Cran.* 152; questions in order to the correcting of several abuses, *ib.* 465; questions and answers concerning the sacrament, *ib.* 115; concerning some abuses of the mass, *ib.* 150; queries concerning confirmation, with Cranmer's answers, *ib.* 80; some Popish questions cast abroad at Chester, (viz. those which follow), *Park.* 163 n.; Popish questions answered; which is the catholic church? *Pil.* 617; who is a heretic? *ib.* 619, 620; who is a schismatic? *ib.* 620; whether the priests who have subscribed be in schism? *ib.* 621; whether their ministering the communion &c. according to the Common Prayer be schism? *ib.* 623; whether reading chapters and psalms, &c., instead of "divine service" be schism? *ib.* 628, 629; whether priests that say the communion may also celebrate mass? *ib.* 630, 633; whether priests who say no communion but only read psalms and chapters, may celebrate mass? *ib.* 631; whether it be a wicked time, in which such heresy and schism reign? *ib.* 632, 633; whether the laity may receive the communion as now used? *ib.* 634; whether the people, compelled with fear of punishment, may receive the communion as mere bread and wine? *ib.* 636, 638; what should they do, who cannot have the mass? *ib.* 637, 638; whether all, as well priests as laity, are bound to obey the queen and her laws? *ib.* 639, 640; dark and doubtful questions not to be too curiously debated, 2 *Cran.* 14; unprofitable ones to be avoided, 3 *Whitg.* 573—577
Questmongers: *v.* Jurors.
Quew: cue, humour, *Calf.* 209
Qui pridie, &c.: 2 *Brad.* 309
Quick and dead: *v.* Judgment.
Quickness: *v.* life, *Bale* 616
Quidditas: a term invented by the schoolmen, 1 *Tyn.* 158
Quintilian (M. F.): names certain Punic words, 1 *Jew.* 294, and Gallic words, *ib.* 298; referred to, 1 *Hoop.* 221
Quintilians: heretics, 4 *Bul.* 371, *Phil.* 420
Quintin (......): Cecil's man, *Grin.* 260
Quintin (St): invoked for the cough, *Rog.* 226
Quintinus (Jo.): 2 *Ful.* 95 n
Quintus: a presumptuous man mentioned by Eusebius, *Rid.* 66
Quintus Curtius: 3 *Jew.* 453
Quiresters: choristers, *Bale* 437
Quiroga (Gasp. card.): *v.* Indexes.
Quod: the past tense of quoth, 3 *Bec.* 121
Quodlibetical Questions: 1 *Brad.* 589, *Rog.* 331 n
Quondams: Bocardo, a college of quondams, 2 *Brad.* 84, *Rid.* 360
Quoth he: the absurd frequency of these words in More's Dialogue, 1 *Tyn.* 286, 2 *Tyn.* 297, 3 *Tyn.* 20

R

R. (E.), i. e. E. Rawlins, *q. v.*
R. (J.), i. e. J. Rogers, *q. v.*
R. (P.): *v.* Parsons (R.)
Rabanus Maurus, bp of Mentz: Opera, *Jew.* xlii; a work of his in the library at Salisbury, 4 *Jew.* 1273; cited on the Old Testament canon, *Whita.* 64; he wrote on the Apocalypse, *Bale* 256; explains why baptism and the unction, and the eucharist, are called sacraments, 4 *Bul.* 248; mentions many ceremonies used at baptism, 4 *Bul.* 361,

362, *Calf.* 213; says that, though God gives the sacrament of grace by evil men, the very grace he gives not, but by himself alone, 3 *Bec.* 469; shews why bread is called the body of Christ, and the wine referred to his blood, 2 *Bec.* 286, 287, 3 *Bec.* 425, 437, *Grin.* 65, 66, 2 *Jew.* 793, 3 *Jew.* 446; referred to on spiritual eating, 1 *Cran.* 41 n (21); he declares that the thing itself of the sacrament is to every man life, the sacrament being one thing, and the virtue of it another, 2 *Bec.* 464, 465, 3 *Jew.* 471; says, the sacrament is received with the mouth, the virtue thereof filling the inner man; the sacrament is turned into the nourishment of the body; by the virtue of the sacrament we obtain eternal life, 1 *Jew.* 453, 516, 529, 2 *Jew.* 571, 562, 596, 1116, 3 *Jew.* 487, 516, *Rid.* 175 n.; proves that, though all men receive, one eats spiritually Christ's flesh, another does not, 3 *Bec.* 465, 466; says that the things which are consecrate unto the Lord are the food only of them which are in the Lord, *ib.* 466; declares that by the sacrament of his body and blood Christ is proved to dwell in us, *ib.*; describes the orders of the clergy, 4 *Bul.* 114, 115, *Rog.* 258; speaks of the vestments worn by priests, 3 *Bec.* 259 n.; affirms that it is for fleshly-minded men's sake, and not for such as are guided by the Spirit, that the custom of singing is instituted in the church, 4 *Bul.* 196; describes the singing of the primitive church, *ib.* 193, 194; holds that the bodies of saints are to be honoured as the members of Christ, *Rog.* 224 n.; states on the authority of Gregory and Bede, that the souls of dead men have often appeared, and taught that oblations and prayers profit them very much, 3 *Bul.* 400; explains the word "statio," 2 *Ful.* 183 n.; is said to have maintained that magistrates were a human institution for the hurt of men, *Rog.* 346; referred to, 1 *Whitg.* 413

Rabasses: *Bale* 479
Rabbi: on the title, 2 *Whitg.* 386
Rabbins: *Bale* 479, 1 *Ful.* 311—315; opinions of R. Abraham and Lyra upon the reception of their expositions, 3 *Jew.* 248; their superstitious discretion in limiting the people what they might read, and what not, 2 *Jew.* 695; they were patrons of freewill, 1 *Ful.* 393
Rabboni: 2 *Whitg.* 387
Rabina: *Bale* 479
Race of Britaine: 1 *Hoop.* 497
Racha (ריקה): its meaning, 2 *Tyn.* 45, 229

Rache, or Rachett: a dog that pursues by the scent, 3 *Bec.* 509
Rachel: 2 *Bul.* 176
Rack: *Bale* 224
Radbertus, (Paschasius), *q. v.*
Radcliffe, co. Lancaster: 1 *Brad.* 454
Radcliffe (Tho.), earl of Sussex: *v.* Ratcliffe.
Radclyff (Randall): recommended by queen Catharine Parr as bailiff of Stoke College, *Park.* 16
Raderus (Matth.): 2 *Ful.* 287 n
Radulph: *v.* Ralph, Rodolph.
Radzivil (Nich.), palatine of Wilna, grand marshal and chancellor of Lithuania: defends the gospel, 3 *Zur.* 597, 599, 601, 687, 690, 691, 701
Ragazzoni (......): *Lit. Eliz.* 584 n
Rahab, the harlot: 2 *Bul.* 115, 4 *Bul.* 229, 1 *Tyn.* 119
Railing: taunts and threats, to be borne, *Hutch.* 334
Railton (Greg.): exile at Frankfort, 3 *Zur.* 764
Raiment: *v.* Apparel.
Raimond (......): *v.* Raymond.
Raimund (Jo.): so Foxe styles Chr. van Ruremund, *q. v.*
Rain: order for public prayers for its ceasing, 2 *Cran.* 493
Rainbow: it is a sign of God's covenant, 4 *Bul.* 230, 231; a sacrament of God's promise to Noah, 1 *Hoop.* 134, 2 *Jew.* 1100; what it teacheth, 1 *Lat.* 269, 270
Raines: fine linen made at Rennes or Rheims, *Bale* 526, 542; raynes, 2 *Bec.* 415; reins, 2 *Jew.* 931
Rainford (Sir Jo.): 2 *Cran.* 280 n
Rainolds (Jo.), pres. C. C. C., Oxon: notices of him, 2 *Zur.* 279 n., 330; defended against G. Martin, 1 *Ful.* 38; his mistake about the Pontifical, 2 *Ful.* 99 n.; his conference with Hart, *Calf.* 126 n., 361 n., 2 *Ful.* 283, 319, 361, 364 nn.; letter from him to R. Gualter, junior, 2 *Zur.* 279
Rainolds (Tho.): *v.* Raynolds.
Rainolds (Will.): Whitaker writes against him, *Whita.* xii.
Raleigh (Sir Walter): notice of him, *Poet.* xxii; the farewell, *ib.* 233; his pilgrimage, *ib.* 235; an epitaph on himself, *ib.* 236; notice of some poems ascribed to him, *ib.* xlii.
Ralph, bp of Chichester: interdicted his diocese, 2 *Tyn.* 295
Rama: 4 *Bul.* 480
Rampinton (Phil. of): *v.* Repingdon.
Ramsay (Will.), professor at St Andrew's: 2 *Zur.* 364

Ramsden (......): chaplain to abp Grindal, *Grin.* 351
Ramsey (Lady Mary): notice of an epitaph on her, *Poet.* lvi.
Ramsey (H.), martyr in Smithfield: *Poet.* 169
Ramsey (Lau.): notice of him, *Poet.* lii; a short discourse of man's fatal end, *ib.* 511
Randall (Jo.): an eminent divine, 1 *Brad.* 564
Randall (Phil.), princ. of Hart hall, Oxon: 2 *Cran.* 547
Randall (Tho.): *v.* Randolph.
Randau (...... count): plenipotentiary from Francis II. of France, 1 *Zur.* 89 n
Randolph (Edw.): marshal of Newhaven, *Park.* 180 n
Randolph (Tho.), or Randal: princ. of Broadgates hall, Oxon, *Jew.* ix, 4 *Jew.* 1191; queen Elizabeth's agent in Scotland, &c., 1 *Zur.* 44, 57 n., 70, 104 n., 144 n., 165 n.; referred to by Jewel under the name of Pamphilus, 4 *Jew.* 1224 n., 1 *Zur.* 56, 57 n., 59, 68 n., &c.; dedication to him, 2 *Jew.* 1099 n
Randolph (Tho.): Enchiridion Theologicum, *Lit. Edw.* xi.
Rands (Hen.), alias Holbech: *q. v.*
Rangone (Guido): 2 *Cran.* 331
Ranulph, monk of Chester: *v.* Higden (R).
Rape: forbidden, 1 *Bul.* 415
Raphael, the archangel: *Hutch.* 90, 1 *Jew.* 23
Rappenstein (Andrew): 3 *Zur.* 225
Rascal: one of the common people or mixed multitude, or the whole of them collectively, 2 *Brad.* 145, *Calf.* 52, 2 *Tyn.* 306, 3 *Tyn.* 12, 114; rascals, 1 *Jew.* 96, 2 *Jew.* 1018; rascalitie, *Rog.* 230 n
Rascal (Justice): [doubtless Will. Rastal], *Pil.* 628
Rascall: a Romish writer so called [Jo. Rastal], *Calf.* 51
Rasheth: plucketh, 2 *Jew.* 839
Rastal (Jo.), or Rastell: a Romish writer, *Calf.* 2; a pillar of the popish synagogue, 1 *Ful.* viii; his books, 2 *Ful.* 3, 4, 45 n.; he opposes Jewel, *Jew.* xx; Jewel answers him, 1 *Ful.* 75 n.; called Rascall, *Calf.* 51
Rastal (Will.), or Rastell, justice of the Common Pleas: named, *Park.* 114, 3 *Tyn.* 263; called justice Rascal, *Pil.* 628; his edition of More's works, 3 *Tyn.* 2, 3
Rastell (Jo.), alderman of Gloucester: 2 *Brad.* 397 n., 398
Ratcliffe (Rob.), 1st earl of Sussex: mentioned, 2 *Cran.* 324; signature as privy councillor, *ib.* 490
Ratcliffe (Hen.), 2nd earl of Sussex: sent against the gospellers of Norfolk and Suffolk, 3 *Zur.* 179 n
Elizabeth (Howard) his wife: her life sought, 1546, *Bale* 220, 242
Ratcliffe (Tho.), 3rd earl of Sussex: in Dublin, *Park.* 95 n.; mourner at the funeral of the emperor Ferdinand, *Grin.* 32; he seeks the preferment of Mr Rush, *Park.* 283; commands an army against the rebels in the North, *ib.* 388 n., 1 *Zur.* 213 n., 214 n., 247 n.; invades Scotland, 1 *Zur.* 225, 228; signature as privy councillor, *Grin.* 414, 417, 427, 429, *Park.* 381; at the duke of Norfolk's trial, 1 *Zur.* 267 n.; lord chamberlain, *Park.* 442, 443; letters to him, *ib.* 416, 458, 466, 467
Ratcliff (Rich.): servant to Grindal, *Grin.* 303; his comptroller, *ib.* 462
Rathe: soon, early, 1 *Jew.* 114; rather, i. e. earlier, 2 *Jew.* 632, 2 *Tyn.* 332
Ratisbon, or Regensburg: conference there, *Bale* 449, 525, 3 *Zur.* 37
Ratlif (Cha.), of Rochdale: *Park.* 232
Ratramn: *v.* Bertram.
Rats' tower: in the Rhine, *Pil.* 30, 456, 612
Raught: reached, 1 *Cov.* 17 n., 3 *Tyn.* 241
Ravenna: the bishop began amongst the Latins to prepare the way to Antichrist, 2 *Hoop.* 235
Ravennas (Pet.): *v.* Petrus.
Ravisius, Textor, *q. v.*
Rawlins (Erkynnold): letter to Bradford, 2 *Brad.* 97; letter to him and his wife, *ib.* 221
Rayleigh, co. Essex: J. Ardeley or Ardite was burned there, *Poet.* 162
Rayment (B.): *Calf.* 274 n
Raymond (Mr): 1 *Zur.* 190
Raymond (St) de Pennaforti, otherwise de Rochefort: notice of him, 1 *Tyn.* 150 n
Raynaudus (Theoph.): Erotemata, 3 *Bec.* 415 n., *Calf.* 74, 200, 2 *Ful.* 86, 200, 287 nn.; Heptas Præsulum, 2 *Ful.* 86, 340 n
Rayner, i. e. R. Wolfe, *q. v.*
Raynes: *v.* Raines.
Raynesburg: *v.* Ratisbon.
Raynold (Richard), a monk of Sion: condemned for treason, 2 *Cran.* 303
Raynolds (Tho.), warden of Merton college: dean of Exeter, *Phil.* 168; nominated bp of Hereford, but set aside, 2 *Jew.* 952
Read: used for advise, 1 *Tyn.* 324; rede, 2 *Tyn.* 342
Read (Dr): *v.* Rede.
Read (Tho.): *v.* Reede.
Reade (Mr): recommended to bp Parkhurst, *Park.* 460
Readers: *v.* Lectors.

Reading: v. Lessons, Scripture.
  On reading in the church, 3 *Whitg.* 48, 317, 475, 505, 4 *Jew.* 856
Reading, co. Berks: a martyr there, *Poet.* 163; the abbey, 2 *Cran.* 275; its revenue, 3 *Zur.* 627 n.; the abbot (Faringdon) executed, 3 *Zur.* 317 n., 614 n., 627
Reading desk: v. Lettern, Pulpit.
Reagh (Maurice), or Gibbon, q. v.
Real Presence: v. Supper of the Lord.
Realists: their disagreement with the Nominalists, 3 *Jew.* 611, &c., 1 *Tyn.* 157, 1 *Zur.* 53
Reason: at the beginning men obeyed and were ruled by it, 2 *Hoop.* 82; how they descended from the regiment of it, *ib.* 83; man's reason is opposed to the will of God *Rid.* 133; until amended and removed from natural blindness it can do none other than condemn God and his people, 2 *Hoop.* 307; man's sensual reason cannot perceive the virtue of Christ's blood, 1 *Tyn.* 16; it cannot understand the victory of the faithful, 2 *Cov.* 311; the faith of religion cannot be proved by discourse of reason, 1 *Jew.* 505; some matters of faith are repugnant to reason, 3 *Tyn.* 234; conclusions from reason and natural operation, 1 *Cran.* 251, 252, 253, 254; Christ appealed to them to prove his resurrection, *ib.* 252; although they do not prevail against God's word, yet when they join with it they are of great moment to confirm the truth, *ib.* 250, 252; reason is the handmaid of faith, *ib.* 371
Rebated: beaten back, 1 *Brad.* 199
Rebecca: 2 *Bul.* 176
Rebellion: v. Democracy, Prayer (*f*), Prayers.
  Against rebellion and disobedience, with sentences and examples of scripture, 1 *Bec.* 456, &c.; against seditious rebels, 1 *Bul.* 280; provisions of the law of Moses against them, 2 *Bul.* 233; the causes of rebellion and insurrections, 2 *Cran.* 191, &c., 2 *Lat.* 306, 2 *Tyn.* 244; they come from the devil, 2 *Bec.* 593; rebellion caused by covetousness, 1 *Lat.* 247; by ignorance, *ib.* 371; by the enclosure of lands formerly belonging to monasteries, 3 *Zur.* 391; not the effect of reformed religion, 3 *Jew.* 170, but rather of popery, *ib.* 171; the treason of popish priests, 1 *Ful.* 491; sedition has been often charged against those who preached the truth, *Rid.* 143; the preaching of God's word is the chief remedy against it, 2 *Hoop.* 79; rebels warned, 1 *Bec.* 126; they generally pretend nothing against the king's person, 1 *Lat.* 163; seditious talkers, *Sand.* 119; insurrections are not to be excused, 2 *Bec.* 601, 602; rebellion discovered, 1 *Brad.* 373, 2 *Hoop.* 549, &c.; the evils of it, 1 *Lat.* 391; it is sinful, 1 *Brad.* 411; a grievous sin, *Now.* (18), 132; an offence most detestable, 2 *Cran.* 444; it displeases God, 2 *Bec.* 594; it is striving against God, 1 *Lat.* 538; it is the devil's service, *ib.* 496; it is damnable, 2 *Hoop.* 105; conspiracies not generally contrived by the meanest men, *Sand.* 405, 406; seditions and insurrections never have good success, 2 *Bec.* 328; but are always visited with judgments, 2 *Cran.* 199; examples of this, 2 *Bec.* 594, 595; traitors and seditious persons punished, 1 *Bec.* 218, 2 *Brad.* 69, 1 *Lat.* 149, *Pil.* 188; Absalom's rebellion against David, *Sand* 407 & al.; Cornish rebels defeated at Blackheath, 1497, 1 *Lat.* 101; rebellion in Lincolnshire, &c., 1536, see Lincolnshire, Yorkshire; rebellion in the North, 1541, and execution of the rebels, 3 *Zur.* 219, 220; rebellion in Devon and Cornwall, 1549, see Devonshire; in Norfolk, &c., about the same time, see Norfolk, Yorkshire; notes for a homily against rebellion, 2 *Cran.* 188; a sermon concerning the time of rebellion, *ib.* 190; mandate for the publication of an act of parliament against rebellion, 3 Edw. VI., *ib.* 530; Sir Tho. Wyat's rebellion, 3 *Zur.* 514, 686 (and see his name); a list of traitors against queen Elizabeth, *Lit. Eliz.* 657; another list, *ib.* 680; a supposed conspiracy against nigh friends of the queen, *Park.* 461; the rebellion in the North, 1569, led by the earls of Northumberland and Westmoreland, 2 *Jew.* 874, 4 *Jew.* 1146, 1277, 1279, *Lit. Eliz.* 462, 538, 657, *Park.* 388, *Poet.* liv, 542, *Sand.* 65, 1 *Zur.* 213, 217, 222, 225, 227, 247; the banner of the rebels had the cross and five wounds, 2 *Jew.* 883; Edm. Eluiden's New Year's Gift, *Poet.* 547; notice of An Answer to the proclamation of the Rebels in the North, 1569, *ib.* lv; stanzas therefrom, *ib.* 549; the rebellion utterly defeated, 1 *Zur.* 239; rebels executed, *ib.* 225 n.; rebellion in Norfolk, 1570, for the rescue of the duke, *ib.* 229, 248 n.; the plot of Babington and Ballard, 1585, *Lit. Eliz.* 468, 595, 658; sermon on it, *Sand.* 403; the great rebellion, *Lit. Eliz.* 536 n
Recantation: open recantation of superstitions enjoined on the clergy, 2 *Cran.* 500
Recognitiones: v. Clement of Rome.
Reconciliation: true import of the word, 1 *Jew.* 419; reconciliation to God, *Nord.* 55; to the pope, 1 *Jew.* 416, &c.

Record: to remember, to meditate, 2 *Bec.* 303, 1 *Tyn.* 508, 2 *Tyn.* 108
Records: v. Manuscripts.
Rectors: called parsons, 2 *Tyn.* 37 n., 260
Recusants (Popish): employed themselves in writing very dangerous and seditious books against queen Elizabeth, and her government, *Grin.* 169; articles of inquiry for them, *ib.* 418, 424; letters of archbishop Grindal to his officers respecting them, *ib.* 417, 423, 427; letter of Grindal respecting certain recusants in the diocese of Oxford, *ib.* 362
Redact: reduced, 1 *Bec.* 46
Rede: v. Read.
Rede (Dr), of Beccles: *Bale* 528
Rede (Eliz.), abbess of Malling: 2 *Lat.* 409
Rede me and be not wrothe: or, The Burying of the Mass: a satire on Wolsey, 1 *Tyn.* 39 n.; extracts from it, *ib.*
Redemption: v. Christ (p. 172, col. 2, &c.), Prayers, Thanksgivings.
What it is, 1 *Bec.* 329, 330; it is by Christ, 1 *Bul.* 43; the deliverance out of Egypt a type of this redemption, 1 *Cov.* 39; God's mercy its sole cause, *Sand.* 180; Christ the mediator of redemption, 3 *Bul.* 213; the ransom paid, 2 *Cran.* 129; redemption is by the blood of Christ, not by that of martyrs, 2 *Lat.* 234; whether shed for all;—for many, not for all, *Nord.* 57; Christ gave himself for the redemption of all men, i.e. (says Tyndale) some of all nations, 2 *Tyn.* 154; the schoolmen's distinction of "sufficient" and "effectual," 1 *Brad.* 320; "world" used in divers senses, *ib.*; we were redeemed that we might serve God, *Sand.* 181; redemption is through faith, which cometh by hearing, 1 *Lat.* 418; redemption nearer than it was, 2 *Lat.* 55
Redesdale, co. Northumb.: *Rid.* 489, 494
Redman (Edm.): probably for John, 3 *Zur.* 264
Redman (Jo.), master of Trinity college, Cambridge: notice of him, 3 *Zur.* 150, 264; a commissioner for reforming the liturgy, *Rid.* 316; he preaches at Bucer's funeral, 3 *Zur.* 492; mentioned, 3 *Jew.* 127, *Park.* 34, 38; letter to him from Latimer, 2 *Lat.* 297, (468); his death, *Now.* i; his dying declaration, 3 *Zur.* 151
Redman (Rob.): printer, 2 *Cov.* 323
Redman (Tho.): a notary, *Grin.* 463
Redman (Will.): archdeacon of Canterbury, *Grin.* 360; letter to him as such, *ib.* 415, 423, 427; legacy, &c., to him, *ib.* 462
Red Sea: 4 *Bul.* 180; the passage of the Red Sea; a poem, by M. Drayton, *Poet.* 132; it is a figure of the blood of Christ, 2 *Jew.* 732; a type of baptism, 4 *Bul.* 364, 390
Redstone Ferry, co. Worc.: v. Ashley.
Reduced: brought back, 1 *Bec.* 113
Redus, comes Montis Granelli: founds a religious order, 2 *Ful.* 103
Reede (Tho.), martyr: *Poet.* 167
Refectory: v. Fratry.
Refelled: confuted, 2 *Bec.* 314
Reflections on the Devotions of the Rom. Ch.: 2 *Lat.* 132 n., 200 n
Reformatio Legum Ecclesiasticarum: v. Law (p. 471)
Reformation: v. Church, I. ix, and II. iv, v; also Denmark, France, Germany, Poland, Scotland, Switzerland; as to the English reformation, v. Henry VIII., Edward VI., Elizabeth.
Reformation of churches to be made, 4 *Bul.* 498; Papists cannot abide it, 3 *Bec.* 516; it must be according to God's word, 1 *Hoop.* 29, 1 *Jew.* 79, *Sand.* 250; the best is to restore as things were in the beginning, 1 *Jew.* 4; the changes made by it, not new things, but old usages restored, 2 *Cran.* 351; countries in which it prevailed, 2 *Jew.* 808, *Phil.* 316; its slow progress complained of, *Pil.* 37, 38; Philpot's prophecy of the increase of the gospel, *Phil.* 30; the second temple not comparable with the first, 3 *Zur.* 485; the reformation was not received in England without consent of the clergy, *Pil.* 627; considerations offered to Henry VIII. to induce him to proceed to further reformation, 2 *Cran.* 466; further reformation proposed by Cartwright, 3 *Whitg.* 8; desired by the puritans, *ib.* 314, &c., 2 *Zur.* 163, 167
Reformed: informed, 2 *Bec.* 39
Reformers: v. Gospellers, Witnesses.
They were raised up by God, *Calf.* 50; what they did, 2 *Ful.* 245; their weapons, *Pil.* 265; Dr Weston's railing account of them, 2 *Lat.* 277; terms applied to them by Harding, 3 *Jew.* 268; early reformers quoted in support of the papists on some points, although accounted heretics by them, 1 *Cran.* 21; More says he never heard of any who would not forswear themselves to save their lives, 3 *Tyn.* 113, 115; why some of them fell away, *ib.* 115
Reformers: a class in the ancient church, 1 *Cov.* 205
Refuge: v. Sanctuaries.
The refuge of a sinner; by Rob. Burdet, *Poet.* 514
Regeneration: use of the term, *Now.* 99;

general references, 1 *Brad.* 175, 256, 301, 302, 327, 569, 2 *Lat.* 7, 8, *Pra. B.* 4, 11; regeneration or second birth described, 3 *Bul.* 37, 98, 101, 102, 4 *Bul.* 378, 1 *Tyn.* 111, 2 *Tyn.* 199, 200; new creation by the Spirit, 3 *Tyn.* 6; a meditation on the second birth, 1 *Brad.* 250; regeneration is a heavenly thing, 4 *Bul.* 243; in some sense it is an earthly thing, 1 *Ful.* 17; it consists rather in the spirit than in the flesh, 2 *Bec.* 224; regeneration distinguished from mere understanding, 2 *Whitg.* 590, 591; the term "spiritual" in scripture, denotes those who are regenerate, *Whita.* 452; the regenerate child of God described, *Sand.* 184; the regenerate have in them a double life, *Rog.* 288; a comparison between the old man and the new, 1 *Brad.* 297; the wicked have not regeneration, *ib.* 303; the nature of man cannot be contented until regenerated, 2 *Hoop.* 581; the knowledge of God is not attainable by labour or study before regeneration, 1 *Brad.* 119; regeneration in connexion with free-will, *ib.* 216, &c.; justification goes before it, *ib.* 217; it is wrought by the Holy Ghost, 2 *Hoop.* 39, 2 *Jew.* 895, *Now.* (61), 181; God regenerates his elect with his Spirit, 1 *Tyn.* 27, *Wool.* 64; David was thus regenerated, *Whita.* 472; it is ascribed to the word of God, *Hutch.* 15, 1 *Lat.* 202, *Rid.* 56, *Sand.* 272, 1 *Tyn.* 27; it comes through the doctrine of the gospel, *Pra. B.* xvi, by hearing and believing, 1 *Lat.* 471; how it is by water and the Holy Ghost, *Lit. Edw.* 514, (562); its connexion with baptism, *Pra. Eliz.* 546 n.; whether children are regenerated before baptism, 2 *Brad.* 405; as to regeneration in baptism, see Baptism, xii; it is not merely to be christened in water, 1 *Lat.* 202; on doubting of regeneration, 1 *Brad.* 147; the Lord's supper, if we receive it worthily, should assure us thereof, *ib.* 107; no man can be fed by the Lord's supper except he be regenerate, *Rid.* 9; regeneration is needful in order to do good works, *Rog.* 105, 106, 126; the works of men not regenerate are evil, *Whita.* 166; till born again man cannot work God's will, 1 *Tyn.* 277, 2 *Tyn.* 190; he cannot even think that God is righteous, 1 *Tyn.* 18; in regeneration we are made brethren, and fellow-heirs with Christ, *Sand.* 204; on the weakness of those who are lately born anew in the Spirit, 1 *Tyn.* 454; the regenerate are not without sin, *Rog.* 133, 134; they may fall into sin, *ib.* 137; how they cannot sin, 1 *Brad.* 250; they cannot finally fall, *ib.* 298, *Rog.* 147; prayer for the daily increase of regeneration, 1 *Brad.* 145, 304, *Pra. B.* 24, 25, 170; the new birth is not perfect in this life, 1 *Brad.* 251; nor till the resurrection, *ib.* 297; errors of Velsius on it, *Grin.* 437, 440, 475

Sometimes the term denotes the restitution of all things, *Bale* 584, 604, 1 *Ful.* 373

Regensburg: *v.* Ratisbon.

Regensperg, in Zurich: 4 *Bul.* 546

Regestion: a retort, *Calf.* 60

Regiments: governments, 1 *Brad.* 163

Reginald (Will.): *Calf.* 256 n., 415

Regino: Libri II. de Ecclesiast. Discipl., *Jew.* xlii; Chronicum, *ib.*; he states that pope Liberius bare good will to heretics, 3 *Jew.* 342, 343; does not mention pope Joan, 4 *Jew.* 648; reports the words of the council of Nantes, that it is a peevish thing to whisper those things to the walls that pertain to the people, *ib.* 812; says the false council of the Greeks was repealed in the council of Frankfort, *ib.* 1055

Regiomontanus (Jo.), or Müller: notice of him, 1 *Tyn.* 152 n

Register: that of the builders (Nehemiah), *Pil.* 393; A Parte of a Register, Edinb. 1593, *Grin.* 201 n., *Pil.* 658 n

Registers (Church): to be kept for christenings, marriages, and burials, 2 *Cran.* 156, 158, 500; injunctions, &c. respecting them, *Grin.* 128, 134, 166, 2 *Hoop.* 149

Regius (Urban): his Declaration of the twelve Articles of the Christian Faith, 1548, 2 *Brad.* 19; his book De Locis Communibus, 1 *Jew.* 220, 221

Regnault (Fra.), printer at Paris: 2 *Cov.* x, xi, 2 *Cran.* 125 n.; he prints many English books, 2 *Cov.* 495; amongst others, Coverdale's Testament, *ib.* 23, 32

Regnier, duke of Anjou, and titular king of Sicily, Naples, and Jerusalem: 2 *Tyn.* 304 n

Regno: *v.* Tiara.

Regrating: what, *Pil.* 464

Regrators: 2 *Hoop.* xviii, 1 *Lat.* 279

Regula Clericorum: an extract, on priests' marriage, *Pil.* 569, 686

Regula (St): 4 *Bul.* xvii; her martyrdom, 2 *Bul.* 106

Regulars: 4 *Bul.* 116

Regulus (Marcus): 1 *Hoop.* 336, *Hutch.* 321

Rehoboam, king of Israel: 1 *Bul.* 236, 2 *Bul.* 7

Reins: *v.* Raines.

Reiserus (Ant.): Launoii anti-Bellarminus, *Calf.* 211, 2 *Ful.* 44, 71 nn
Reiskius (Jo.): *Calf.* 46 n
Reisner (......): on the Ossenes, *Rog.* 306 n.; on the Essenes, *ib.* 353 n
Reister: a trooper, 2 *Zur.* 293
Rejoicing: *v.* Joy.
Reland (Adr.): Palestina, 1 *Bul.* 85 n
Related: referred, enrolled, 1 *Bec.* 137
Relic Sunday: the third Sunday after Midsummer day, *Park.* 7
Relics: on them, *Calf.* 311—314, 2 *Ful.* 188, 389, 1 *Lat.* 50; how far to be reverenced, 2 *Ful.*112; there was no worshipping of relics among the ancient fathers, 4 *Bul.* 523; relics placed in churches at consecration, *Calf.* 210; superstitiously abused, 2 *Tyn.* 216, 3 *Tyn.* 60; popish errors respecting them, *Rog.* 223—225; Antichrist digs them out and honours them, 3 *Bec.* 521; More affirms that miracles have been wrought to encourage their worship, 3 *Tyn.* 123, 124; kinds of relics enumerated, *Bale* 524; some of the wine of Cana kept at Orleans, 1 *Jew.* 249; Christ's coat in many places, 1 *Tyn.* 278; Christ's garments avail not, 1 *Lat.* 544; citation [from the Opus Imperfectum in Matthæum, wrongly ascribed to Chrysostom] against those who esteem the garments of Christ more than his body, *Park.* 8; the blood of Hales, *q. v.*; pieces of the cross enclosed in gold, 2 *Ful.* 180; relics of saints, nails, and fragments of the cross discovered by queen Elizabeth's commissioners, 1 *Zur.* 44; More's account of some small kerchiefs discovered at Barking, and affirmed to have belonged to the Virgin, 3 *Tyn.* 124 n.; relics set forth at Canterbury, in spite of the king's injunctions, 2 *Cran.* 334; those of Becket, *ib.* 378; St Algar's bones, St Blesis's heart, 1 *Lat.* 55; some saints had two or three heads, and so forth, *Pil.* 147; by God's law dead bones polluted those who touched them, 3 *Tyn.* 83; worshippers of relics may reverence pigs' bones, 1 *Lat.* 53, 3 *Tyn.* 122 n.; relics not to be maintained, 2 *Hoop.* 129, 143, *Rid.* 320; the true relics, 1 *Bul.* 212
Reliques of Rome: referred to, 2 *Bec.* 413 n., 3 *Bec.* 41 n., 257 n
Religion: 1 *Brad.* 566, 1 *Bul.* 233, 4 *Bul.* 517; what it is, 3 *Bul.* 232; no man has authority to make a religion, *Pil.* 627; in the antiquity of their religion pagans have the advantage over Christians, 2 *Cran.* 62; of true religion, 3 *Bul.* 230, 1 *Lat.* 392, 2 *Lat.* 354; the formation and origin of it, 1 *Hoop.* 306; its foundation, *ib.* 294; principal points of religion, by Tho. Tusser, *Poet.* 257; the first point of it is fear of God, 1 *Hoop.* 298; the second point is faith and confidence in God's word, *ib.* 298; the third point is love, *ib.* 299; we are commanded to confess and set forth true religion, 2 *Bec.* 79; to exercise diligence bringeth credit to religion, 2 *Hoop.* 80; princes have dealt in it, 1 *Bul.* 330; they may not change it at their pleasure, *Pil.* 434; whether it is lawful to compel men's faith, 1 *Bul.* 364, *Sand.* 192; Papists would have faith to be compelled, *Phil.* 104, 105; forced faith is not true faith, 2 *Jew.* 1023; whether we should fight for religion, *Pil.* 433; what the Christian religion is, *Lit. Edw.* 495, 496, (545, 546), *Now.* (1,2), 113, 114 (*v.* Gospel); it standeth in faith and ardent charity, *Phil.* 326; its principal parts, *Now.* (6, 7), 118, 119; PRINCIPLES OF CHRISTIAN RELIGION, by T. Becon, 2 *Bec.* 477; CERTAIN ARTICLES OF CHRISTIAN RELIGION PROVED AND CONFIRMED, by T. Becon, 3 *Bec.* 396; a declaration concerning religion signed by Ferrar, Hooper, Bradford, Saunders and others, 1 *Brad.* 367; complaints of the heathens of the disquiet introduced by Christianity, 2 *Cran.* 198; the corruption and decay of the Christian faith were predicted, and occurred, 3 *Bec.* 487; causes why the Christian religion decays, 1 *Bec.* 42; the cause of taking away the true religion in England, 3 *Bec.* 208; how it may be recovered, *ib.*; its restoration, *Pil.* 3; against strange religion, with sentences and examples of scripture, 1 *Bec.* 432, &c.; in matters of religion manifest lies do take place, 2 *Hoop.* 271; worldlings judge their religion by their belly, *Pil.* 612; false religion how maintained, *ib.* 78; it withholds blessings, *ib.* 85; it brings plagues, *ib.* 73; Turks, Jews, Anabaptists, &c., expect to attain eternal felicity by their religion, 1 *Brad.*502; sundry religions, 1 *Bul.* 98; where religion differs, there is no true love, *Pil.* 224; such difference makes nearest friends extreme foes, *ib.* 223; diversity of religion should not hinder charity, *Grin.* 28; foreign religions forbidden by the Romans, *Sand.* 263
Religion: the name applied to the monkish profession, or to any monastic order, 2 *Cran.* 147, 1 *Tyn.* 119, 2 *Tyn.* 128, 3 *Tyn.* 5
Religious: monks and friars, 1 *Tyn.* 163
Religious houses: *v.* Abbeys.

What true ones are, 1 *Lat.* 391, 393
Remigius (St): his holy oil, 1 *Jew.* 191
Remission: *v.* Absolution, Sin.

Rempington (Phil.): *v.* Repingdon.
Renatus: 4 *Bul.* 375
Renaudot (Euseb.): 2 *Bec.* 256 n., 257 n., 3 *Bec.* 482 n
René of Nassau, prince of Orange: invades Juliers, 3 *Zur.* 633 n
Reniger (Mich.): notices of him, 3 *Zur.* 374 n., 425; expelled from Magd. coll., Oxon., by bp Gardiner, 2 *Zur.* 308 n.; exile at Zurich, 3 *Zur.* 752; archdeacon of Winchester, 2 *Zur.* 308; letter from him to Bullinger, 3 *Zur.* 374
Renner (......): 1 *Zur.* 62
Rennes: *v.* Raines.
Renold (Hen.): *v.* Reynolds.
Renoldes (......), D.D.: an exile, 1 *Cran* (9)
Rents: against raising them, 2 *Bec.* 108, 1 *Lat.* 98, 107, 203, 317, *Pil.* 461, 462, 1 *Tyn.* 201

Rents: tenements, 2 *Tyn.* 275
Repentance: *v.* Meditations, Penance, Prayers, Sin.

What it is, 1 *Bec.* 75, 76, 92, 2 *Bec.* 10, 3 *Bec.* 613, 618, 1 *Brad.* 45, 3 *Bul.* 55, 56, 4 *Bul.* 552, 2 *Cov.* 365, 2 *Cran.* 201, 475, 1 *Ful.* 257, 2 *Jew.* 1131, 1132, *Now.* (58), 177, *Rog.* 139, *Sand.* 140, 157; what it is, with probations of scripture, 2 *Bec.* 506; it is a principal part of Christian religion, *Now.* (6), 119; diverse use of the word, 3 *Bul.* 56; its meaning in Latin, Greek, and Hebrew, 1 *Brad.* 45; various Latin renderings of μετανοέω, 1 *Tyn.* 477; various English renderings of μετάνοια, ib. 478, 3 *Tyn.* 23; it signifies change of mind, 1 *Ful.* 155; so says Tertullian, ib. 437; the word was figuratively used by the ancient church for penance, ib. 431; Tyndale's translation of the word, 1 *Tyn.* 268; Wycliffe's, ib. n.; Tyndale's defence of his rendering,—"repentance," and not "penance," 3 *Tyn.* 22, 23; pœnitentia, *Now.* (102); resipiscentia, ib.; false repentance and true, 3 *Bul.* 110, 552; that of Judas, 1 *Brad.* 51; that of Peter, 2 *Cov.* 366, 367; when it is true and unfeigned, 1 *Bec.* 92; true repentance is to turn from sin, *Sand.* 157; it is the return of the sinner from sin into a new life in Christ, 2 *Hoop.* 174; that of the reprobate is not true repentance, 2 *Bec.* 12; sum of the doctrine of it, 3 *Bul.* 68; it is necessary in order to salvation, *Nord.* 57, 58, *Sand.* 139, 140, 207; it is taught by the gospel, 2 *Bec.* 10, 3 *Bul.* 35; it was preached by our Lord, 1 *Bec.* 75; how scripture speaks of penance, 2 *Cran.* 116; the order of repentance as set down in scripture, *Sand.* 134; it followeth from the preaching of the word, 1 *Cov.* 409; the preaching of the truth is needful to it, 3 *Bul.* 57; it is not of man's free-will, 1 *Brad.* 53; it is the gift of God, 1 *Bec.* 93, 2 *Bec.* 11, 12, 1 *Brad.* 325, 2 *Brad.* 13, 1 *Ful.* 156, 433; God works it in us, 1 *Bec.* 178, 179; it is a fruit of the Holy Spirit, 1 *Cov.* 409; the first effect of grace, *Sand.* 309; it goes before faith, 1 *Tyn.* 261; hence it is spoken of as the gentleman-usher of lady Faith, 1 *Brad.* 41; it must be joined with faith, 1 *Bec.* 78, 3 *Bec.* 209; true repentance has faith for its companion, 2 *Bec.* 12; with faith it is the only means to obtain remission of sins, 1 *Bec.* 79, 83; where it and faith are, there is God's mercy, 3 *Bec.* 108, &c.; without faith, it is unprofitable, 1 *Bec.* 98; it begins of the love of virtue, ib. 93; the practice of it, *Sand.* 309, 310; how penance ought to be done, 1 *Bec.* 93; it must be voluntary, 3 *Bul.* 110; it is a work of all our life, ib. 107; its parts, what it comprises, 1 *Bec.* 97, 3 *Bul.* 106, 2 *Hoop.* 60, 174, 2 *Lat.* 9, &c., 1 *Tyn.* 477, 478; the outward exercises of it, 3 *Bul.* 108; public and private repentance, ib. 109; the signs of repentance, 1 *Bec.* 77, 78, 3 *Bec.* 613; it is conjoined with fasting and almsgiving, *Calf.* x; what and how it works, 1 *Bec.* 76, 77, 1 *Tyn.* 261, 3 *Tyn.* 23; it is a remedy to put away sin, 3 *Bec.* 209; a salve for all sin, 2 *Lat.* 9; the remedy of all plagues, 2 *Cran.* 200; its fruits, 1 *Bec.* 92, 2 *Bec.* 506, 507, 1 *Brad.* 76, 3 *Bul.* 105, 2 *Cov.* 360, &c.; there can be no true repentance without restitution, 1 *Brad.* 50 (& al., *v.* Restitution); without amendment of life, it profits not, 1 *Bec.* 90, 2 *Cov.* 93; the end of it, 1 *Bec.* 78; the repentance of Christians, *Wool.* 12; Bradford's daily exercise, 1 *Brad.* 33; the repentance of believers is not vain, 4 *Bul.* 555; it is a testimony of salvation, 3 *Bec.* 172; whosoever repenteth is heir of Christ's merits, 1 *Tyn.* 271; the praise of repentance, 1 *Bec.* 77; the fruit of the doctrine of it, 2 *Bec.* 11; examples of it, 1 *Bec.* 76, 3 *Bec.* 209, 3 *Bul.* 111; it is necessary in prayer, *Pra. B.* xix; it is a part of preparation to the Lord's supper, 2 *Bec.* 232; it is necessary in the prospect of death, 2 *Cov.* 81; it is not to be deferred, 3 *Bul.* 113, *Wool.* 109; of sickbed repentance, 1 *Lat.* 443, 2 *Lat.* 58; it may be wrought in the very hour of death, 1 *Lat.* 526; some consent to the truth at their latter end, 3 *Tyn.* 36; repentance (if it be true) never cometh too late, 3 *Bul.* 113; but late repentance not to be trusted to,

2 *Lat.* 193; remedies against late repentance, 3 *Bec.* 167, &c.; there is no repentance after this life, 1 *Lat.* 162, 246, 549; God, when he threatens, gives time for repentance, *ib.* 242, 541; exhortations to it, 1 *Bec.* 127, 1 *Brad.* 445, &c.; it is the will of God, 2 *Bec.* 156; recommended as acceptable to God, 3 *Bec.* 164; a sermon of repentance, 1 *Brad.* 43; questions on it, 2 *Cran.* 465; an article de pœnitentia, *ib.* 475; recantation; penitential verses by Geo. Whetstone, *Poet.* 339; a repentant poem (by an unknown contributor to Davison's Poetical Rhapsody), *ib.* xlii, 454; it is made unnecessary by the Romish doctrine of pardons, *Rog.* 220; it is changed into penance, 2 *Jew.* 1131; repentance is set by papists on three feet, confession, contrition, satisfaction, *Sand.* 157; papists substitute for it a purpose to do good works, 3 *Tyn.* 204; how and what repentance is in God, 3 *Bul.* 56, *Hutch.* 90

Repingdon (Phil. de), bp of Lincoln, a cardinal: while at Leicester a follower of Wycliffe, but when bishop a persecutor, *Bale* 79, 81, 123, 592

Reppes (Will.), alias Rugge, *q. v.*

Reprobation: asserted, *Bale* 576, 1 *Brad.* 324, 325, *Pil.* 673, *Rog.* 148, 3 *Whitg.* 612, 613; the reason of it pertains not to us, 1 *Brad.* 324, 325; it, as well as election, shews forth the glory of God, *ib.* 315, 316; God does wrong to no man, and cannot condemn the just, nor the penitent and believing, *ib.* 316; sin is the sole cause thereof, *ib.* 219, 220; the reproved cannot choose but err, *Phil.* 335; we may not judge who are reprobate, *Rog.* 148

Reps (Will.), alias Rugge, *q. v.*

Republicanism: *v.* Democracy.

Requiem: *Bale* 330

Rescissio Alienationum: *v.* Paul IV.

Reserve: More asserts that the apostles spoke with reserve before pagans, 3 *Tyn.* 28 n.; it is practised by heretics, not by sound catholics, *Whita.* 668

Respect of persons: 1 *Bul.* 348, *Sand.* 278, 440

Responses: 1 *Jew.* 281, 282

Rest: ease or rest, 1 *Bul.* 257

Restitution: to God, 1 *Hoop.* 554; to man, *ib.* 555; required by the law of Moses, 2 *Bul.* 230; its necessity, 1 *Brad.* 50, 2 *Bul.* 49, 1 *Lat.* 404, 405, 414, 452, 2 *Lat.* 13, 41, 63, 211, 238, 427, *Pil.* 468, 470; when, to whom, how much is to be made, 2 *Bul.* 50, 51; it must be made secretly or openly, 1 *Lat.* 262; an example of secret restitution, *ib.*; one of open restitution, *ib.* 263; the case of Bradford, 1 *Brad.* 32, 2 *Brad.* 2, &c., xiv—xvi, 1 *Lat.* 262 n

Restoration: means prepared by God for the restoration of man, 1 *Hoop.* 15; THE RESTORATION OF ALL THINGS; Bradford's cygnea cautio, mostly translated from Bucer, 1 *Brad.* 350, &c.

Resurrection: what it is, 1 *Bul.* 141; resurgo, resurrectio, *Now* (103); two sorts mentioned in scripture,—from sin and from death, *Hutch.* 138; the resurrection of Christ, see p. 178, col. 2; errors respecting our Saviour's resurrection, *Rog.* 64; the resurrection of the body, 2 *Bec.* 46, &c., 3 *Bec.* 144, 145, 1 *Bul.* 168, &c., 2 *Cov.* 168, &c., 2 *Hoop.* 61, 1 *Jew.* 460, 2 *Jew.* 866, &c., 2 *Lat.* 53, 444, *Lit. Edw.* 511, (559), 3 *Tyn.* 576; the article of the creed respecting it differently worded in the Aquilian and Carthaginian churches, 2 *Bec.* 49; verses of Prudentius on it, 2 *Cov.* 195—197, *Pra. Eliz.* 418; THE HOPE OF THE FAITHFUL, a treatise on the resurrection, by Wermuller, translated by bp Coverdale, 2 *Cov.* 135, &c.; an article de corporum resurrectione, &c., 2 *Cran.* 480; but little known concerning it, 1 *Brad.* 363, 364; the certainty and proofs of it, 3 *Bec.* 180, 181; how proved by Christ's argument from the declaration, "I am the God of Abraham," &c., 3 *Tyn.* 118; it will be of the flesh, not of the spirit, 2 *Hoop.* 61; it will be of these very bodies, 1 *Bul.* 76, 169, 2 *Cov.* 181, 2 *Hoop.* 62; in what sort they shall rise again, 1 *Bul.* 172, 2 *Cov.* 176, 1 *Cran.* 141, 150, 177; our bodies and souls are not to be merely spiritual, 1 *Cran.* 177; our bodies will be changed, 1 *Lat.* 531; what a glorified body is, 2 *Cov.* 177, &c.; our resurrection often to be thought upon, 1 *Brad.* 348; meditations on it, on awaking out of sleep, *Pra. B.* 60; what profit we have by it, 2 *Bec.* 49; it is a joyful hope, 2 *Brad.* 51, 198; not yet brought to pass (article of 1552), *Lit. Edw.* 537, (581); to be looked for, says Tyndale, every hour, 3 *Tyn.* 180; the dead in Christ shall rise first, 2 *Jew.* 870; the first resurrection, *Bale* 564, 568 (*v.* Millennium); resurrection is necessary in order to perfect joy and immortality, *Now.* (59), 178; heaven not the abode of the saints until after the resurrection, see Heaven; the resurrection in connexion with the restoration of all things, 1 *Brad.* 354, 357; all shall rise, 1 *Lat.* 548, 2 *Lat.* 59; the bodies of the wicked shall rise again, 1 *Bul.* 177, 2 *Cov.* 197, &c., 2 *Jew.* 868,

2 *Lat.* 59; the bodies of unbelievers being raised will be passible, 2 *Cov.* 204; the second resurrection, 2 *Hoop.* 61; the doctrine of the resurrection mocked by the heathen, 3 *Tyn.* 28; denied by some heretics, *Rog.* 64, 154; against them that deny the resurrection of the body, with sentences and examples of scripture, 1 *Bec.* 480, &c.; divers errors about it, 2 *Cov.* 183, &c.; the truth of it is subverted by Romish teaching, 1 *Tyn.* lxiii, 3 *Tyn.* 118, 127, 180

Retchless: careless, 1 *Brad.* 409, *Sand.* 287, 300

Reticius: confessed original sin, 2 *Bul.* 390

Reuben: his incest, 1 *Bul.* 210; he forfeited the priesthood, 2 *Bul.* 131; his saying respecting his brother Joseph, *Grin.* 41; his history not unprofitable, 1 *Tyn.* 310

Reubenites: 2 *Bul.* 158

Reuchlin (Jo.), or Capnio: the earliest German Hebraist, 1 *Tyn.* xxx. n

Reutlingen: the city consents to the confession of Augsburg, 2 *Zur.* 15 n

Revel: besieged by the Russians, 3 *Zur.* 699

Revelation: *v.* John (St).

Revelations: it is dangerous to look for instruction by revelations as various heretics do, *Rog.* 158, *Sand.* 115

Revenge, Vengeance: *v.* Prayers (The Lord's).
Against desire of vengeance, 1 *Cov.* 527; it is forbidden by God, 1 *Tyn.* 174, &c.; those who seek it have not their sins forgiven, 2 *Bec.* 183; lawful redress may be sought, but not in a spirit of revenge, 2 *Tyn.* 27, 62, 63; public vengeance allowed, private forbidden, 1 *Lat.* 145, 151, 481, 495, 2 *Tyn.* 21, 27, 58, 61, 62; those who revenge themselves are servants of the devil, 1 *Lat.* 375; vengeance belongs to God, *Pil.* 249, *Sand.* 289, 1 *Tyn.* 332, 404; it must be left to God, 1 *Lat.* 465; some sins cry for it especially, *Pil.* 463; it will be taken of blood, 2 *Bul.* 108; the day of vengeance not far off, *Pil.* 258

Reverence: in the time of popery there was some reverence, now none at all, 1 *Lat.* 230

Reverend: reverendus, *Now.* (103); Athanasius called "most reverend," 2 *Whitg.* 387

Revestry: vestry, *Calf.* 136, 317

Revet (Dr), parson of Hadleigh: 2 *Cran.* 333

Rew: row, 1 *Jew.* 398

Reward: *v.* Works.
Reward and punishment most certain, 1 *Bul.* 154; places which confirm it not to be abused, 2 *Bul.* 345; how God is said to give it, *ib.* 346; he gives it of mere grace, 1 *Ful.* 369—371, *Now.* (63), 183; in scripture the word means what is given freely, rather than what is deserved, 1 *Tyn.* 116, 434; to whom rewards are promised, 2 *Bul.* 344; to them that worship God, 3 *Bul.* 204

Reyley (Hugh), or Riley: house-steward and executor to Jewel, *Jew.* xxii, xxv.

Reyna (Cassiod. de): a preacher of the Spanish church in England, and author of a Spanish version of the Bible, 2 *Zur.* 175

Reyner, i. e. R. Wolfe, *q. v.*

Reynolds (......), D.D.: *v.* Renoldes.

Reynolds (Hen.), or Renold: in exile,1 *Cran.* (9)

Reynolds (Tho.): *v.* Raynolds.

Rhadamanthus: 2 *Bul.* 218

Rhegino: *v.* Regino.

Rheims: *v.* Raines.
The traitorous seminary there: 1 *Ful.* ix, 2, *Lit. Eliz.* 656 n., 688; G. Martin professor there, 1 *Ful.* xii; the rabble of Rheims, *ib.* 28; the Rhemish Testament, *v.* Bible, *English;* also Rhemists.

Rhelican (......): 3 *Zur.* 317

Rhemists (i. e. the annotators on the Rhemish Testament): their doctrine on original sin, *Rog.* 100; on faith, *ib.* 113; they call justification by faith the doctrine of Simon Magus, *ib.* 114; maintain free-will, *ib.* 106; teach that good works are meritorious, and that they justify, *ib.* 114, 124; say that Christ's pains have not so satisfied for all, that Christians are discharged of their particular satisfying, *ib.* 58; affirm that the works of one may satisfy for another, *ib.* 257; say that sins venial are taken away by sacred ceremonies, *ib.* 110, 180; teach that they are taken away by a bishop's blessing, *ib.* 299; commend works of supererogation, *ib.* 130; maintain that we should always be uncertain about salvation, *ib.* 113, 151; on the church, *ib.* 166; they affirm the infallibility of the church of Rome, *ib.* 183; say that the church never errs, never hath erred, and never can err, *ib.* 178, 179; their views as to the authority of the church, and her pastors, *ib.* 78, 79; speak of the title of universal bishop as refused, but of universal jurisdiction as always acknowledged, *ib.* 348; allow that certain popes were heretics, *ib.* 181; affirm that popes have authority to make ecclesiastical laws, and call councils, *ib.* 206; say councils cannot err, *ib.* 208; state that all must be subject to some bishop, priest, or prelate, *ib.* 339 n.; call those who preach without lawful sending thieves and murderers, *ib.* 333; declare that the king's power is in respect of the laity, and not of popes, bishops, or priests, *ib.* 339; say that the emperor of the whole world, if he take upon him to give laws to the clergy, shall be damned except he repent, *ib.* 343; affirm that the clergy should be free from tribute, *ib.* 339; they state that Christ instituted the seven orders, &c., *ib.* 259; observe that the water bearing up the ark was a figure of baptism, which saves the worthy receivers from perishing, *ib.* 268; say baptism gives grace and faith, *ib.* 250; declare that the mass is a sacrifice, *ib.* 299; affirm that it is the only sovereign worship due to God in his church, *ib.* 301; teach that whole Christ is contained in the eucharist, *ib.* 287; affirm that all communicants, bad or good, receive the body and blood of Christ, *ib.* 293; call the supper of the Lord, "the cup of devils," &c., *ib.* 283; maintain that prayers not understood are acceptable, *ib.* 243; assert that the saints hear our prayers, and have care of us, *ib.* 226; say the sermons of heretics must not be heard, *ib.* 272, and that their prayers are no better than the howling of wolves, *ib.*; call marriage a sacrament, *ib.* 260; forbid the clergy to marry, *ib.* 262, 306; say that after orders, it was never lawful in God's church to marry, *ib.* 304; assert that deacons, subdeacons, and priests, are bound to chastity, *ib.*; state that for those to marry which are professed, is to turn back after Satan, *ib.*; speak of bigami, *ib.* 241; say such as willingly die without the sacrament of penance shall never be forgiven, *ib.* 258; write on the sign of the mass, *ib.* 152; teach that no man ought to take an oath to accuse a catholic, *ib.* 358, 359; make contradictory statements respecting purgatory, *ib.* 217; on limbus patrum, *ib.* 62, 66; what they say of Antichrist, *ib.* 169; Fulke against the Rhemists cited, *ib.* 324; an answer to their ten arguments for the authority of the Latin Vulgate, *Whita.* 141

Rhenanus (Beatus), or Bilde: wrote annotations on Tertullian, *Jew.* xliii, 3 *Whitg.* xxxii, 253; he speaks of stone altars as a novelty, 3 *Jew.* 602; refers to the canon of the mass, 2 *Brad.* 310; says that pope Leo was wont to communicate seven or eight times in one day, 3 *Bec.* 381, 474; declares it evident that the eucharist was in times past touched with the hands of the lay-people, *ib.* 412; refers to canons respecting the reservation of the sacrament, *ib.* 373; says that laymen in times past used with a reed to draw the Lord's blood from the chalice, *ib.* 415; refers to the ancient custom as to confession, 3 *Jew.* 354, 374; observes that Tertullian says nothing of secret confession, 2 *Jew.* 1134, 3 *Jew.* 376; thinks the use of lights and tapers on candlemas-day came from the heathen, 3 *Jew.* 178; speaks of the bishop of Rome favouring Montanus, 4 *Jew.* 926; approves of the early church refraining from things indifferent, 3 *Jew.* 616

Rheticus: 3 *Jew.* 305

Rhetorians: say that no sect ever erred, *Rog.* 161

Rhetoric: Oratio contra rhetoricam, 4 *Jew.* 1283—1291

Rhine: *v.* Palatinate, Rats' tower.

Rhodes: taken by the Turks, 3 *Bec.* 10, 1 *Lat.* 13, 2 *Lat.* 33, 3 *Tyn.* 136; legend respecting an island near it, 2 *Ful.* 155

Rhodes (J.): notice of him, *Poet.* xxiv; his Answer to a Romish Rime, *ib.* 267

Rhodiginus (Lud. Cælius): *v.* Cælius.

Rhyme and reason: *Calf.* 199, 3 *Tyn.* 92, 2 *Whitg.* 483

Rial: *v.* Royal.

Ricarbie (......): martyred in Smithfield, *Poet.* 172

Riccall, co. Yorkshire: a prebend in the cathedral church, *Park.* 361

Rice (Will.), or Rise: sent to the Tower, *Park.* 155

Rich: *v.* Poor, Prayers, Riches.

Who are so, 3 *Bec.* 607; their duty, 1 *Bec.* 225, 2 *Bec.* 112, 113; they must be thankful to God, *ib.* 387, 388; what they may pray for, 1 *Bec.* 166; they must pray for daily bread, 2 *Tyn.* 117; how they ought to behave themselves, 1 *Bec.* 256; they should be righteous, *Sand.* 193; how they should live, *Hutch.* 317; they must consider of whom they have received their riches, 2 *Bec.* 387; also why God has given them their goods, *ib.* 389; they are God's almoners, stewards, or treasurers, *ib.* 538, *Hutch.* 297, 1 *Lat.* 399, 411, 477; their riches are not given to them to distribute to monks, &c., 2 *Bec.* 390; but to bestow them on the poor, *ib.* 390, 391; the reward to those who bestow their goods on the poor, *ib.* 391, 392; how they should bestow their goods, *ib.* 390; they should distribute in this life, *ib.* 393, 394; not after death, *ib.* 394; they must take heed and beware of covetousness, *ib.* 397, 398; they need patience, *Hutch.* 296; popular complaints against them, 2 *Cran.* 194; most rich men obtain their riches wrongfully, 1 *Lat.* 98; many misuse their goods, *Pil.* 41; their oppression censured, 2 *Bec.* 432, 433; their unmercifulness, 1 *Bec.* 127; unmerciful ones are thieves before God, 2 *Bec.* 106; the reward to those who are unmerciful, *ib.* 392; threats against rich men, *ib.* 433; ungodly rich men in the Lord's prayer mock God, *ib.* 163; they contemn the gospel, 2 *Lat.* 72, 91; false doctrine concerning the rich censured, 2 *Bul.* 24; scripture condemns not the riches, but those who abuse riches, 1 *Lat.* 545, 2 *Lat.* 202; sentences of scripture for those who are godly to remember, 2 *Bec.* 588, 589; sentences of scripture for the ungodly, *ib.* 589, 590; if these sentences were minded it would go much better with the poor, *ib.* 590; a rich murderer escapes by bribery, 1 *Lat.* 189; a terrible example of a rich man, *ib.* 277; the rich in spirit are accursed, 2 *Tyn.* 17

Rich (Rich. 1st lord): referred to, 2 *Cov.* 417; chancellor of the court of augmentation, 2 *Cran.* 398; lord chancellor, 2 *Cran.* 523, 530, 3 *Zur.* 258 n., 263 n.; his cruelty to Anne Askewe, *Bale* 142, 218; he sends her to the Tower, *ib.* 220; he racks her, *ib.* 224; compared to Pilate, *ib.* 241; privy councillor to king Edward, 2 *Cran.* 505, 511, and to queen Mary, 1 *Zur.* 5 n.; one of the examiners of Philpot, *Phil.* 50; he owns Philpot as his kinsman, *ib.* 58; he dwelt in the precinct of St Bartholomew the Great, *Grin.* 272

Rich (Rob. 2nd lord): ambassador to France, 2 *Zur.* 201 n.; at the duke of Norfolk's trial, 1 *Zur.* 267 n.; he goes on an expedition into Ireland, 2 *Zur.* 223 n

Richard I. king of England: taken prisoner, *Pil.* 372; his three daughters (pride, covetousness, lechery), *ib.* 591; Joachim's conversation with him respecting Antichrist, 2 *Jew.* 915 n

Richard II. king of England: his history, 2 *Tyn.* 295, 296; he renounced the jurisdiction of the bishop of Rome, *Rog.* 347; his epistle to pope Boniface, *Pil.* 640; he was subverted by evil counsellors, *Wool.* 129; wickedly deposed by the clergy, 1 *Tyn.* 458, 2 *Tyn.* 224; slain by them, 3 *Tyn.* 166; the land punished by God for his murder, 2 *Tyn.* 53

Richard III. king of England: murdered his nephews, 3 *Zur.* 220

Richard duke of York: murdered by king Richard, 3 *Zur.* 220

Richard of Armagh: *Whita.* 130, 148

Richardson (Jo.): Prælectiones Eccl., 2 *Ful.* 360 n

Richardus de S. Victore: Opera, *Jew.* xlii; on the Old Testament canon, and the Apocrypha, *Whita.* 65; on Maccabees, *ib.* 97 wrote on the Apocalypse, *Bale* 256; he says, if any man come to the communion before the priest's absolution, he eats and drinks his own damnation, 3 *Bul.* 80 n., comp. 1 *Jew.* 120; his distinction between "dimittere" and "remittere peccata," 3 *Jew.* 380; he says that Paul foresaw there should be many that would think lightly of fornication, 4 *Jew.* 630

Richelius (......): 2 *Cov.* 505

Richelius (Windelicius): 3 *Zur.* 364

Richerius (Edm.): Apologia pro Jo. Gersonio, 2 *Ful.* 371 n.; Hist. Conciliorum Gen., *ib.* 70 n

Riches: v. Goods, Money, Property, Vanity. The desire of riches dangerous, 1 *Lat.* 442; they are not to be greedily sought, 2 *Lat.* 214, 300; yet not to be refused if sent, *ib.* 214, 300; not to be wrongfully gotten nor wastefully used, *Pil.* 150, 151; ill-gotten riches are a curse, 1 *Lat.* 410; the lawful getting of them, 2 *Bul.* 24; wealth by inheritance, *ib.* 29; all belong to the Lord, *Pil.* 150; they come from God, 2 *Bec.* 387, 3 *Bec.* 25, 2 *Bul.* 53, 1 *Lat.* 398, 2 *Tyn.* 16; yet they are used as a snare by Satan, 1 *Lat.* 430; they are commonly esteemed a blessing, *ib.* 476, 477; it is a dangerous thing to have them, *ib.* 477, *Sand.* 302; they draw men backward from heaven, 2 *Lat.* 214; why God gives them, 1 *Bec.* 108, 2 *Hoop.* 281; outward appearances shew not who are in God's favour, 1 *Lat.* 403; riches do not shut out God's blessing, 2 *Tyn.* 16, 101, 106; the miseries that follow riches, *ib.* 101; they make no man's life happy, but rather troublous, 1 *Lat.* 277, 280, 303; they are neither to be condemned nor esteemed too highly, 1 *Lat.* 430, 2 *Lat.* 19; the mind not to be set upon them, 2 *Bul.* 52; delight in them is in vain, 2 *Bec.* 431, &c.; the true use of them, 3 *Bec.* 116, 117; they must serve to do honour, and shew courteous behaviour between man and man, 2 *Bul.* 58; they must not be abused, 2 *Bec.* 435; they are vainly bestowed on images, &c., 1 *Lat.* 292; an account must be given of them, 1 *Bec.* 108; they are fleeting and uncertain, 2 *Bec.* 435, 2 *Lat.* 214; worldly and godly riches, 1 *Lat.* 280; true riches, 1 *Cov.* 513

Richmond, co. Surrey: the Charterhouse of Shene founded by Henry V., 2 *Tyn.* 81;

services there, *ib.*; idolatry there, *Pil.* 63
Richmond (Henry, duke of), and Mary his wife: *v.* Fitzroy.
Richmond (Marg. countess of): *v.* Margaret.
Richmond (Legh): Fathers of the English Church, 2 *Brad.* xlvii, *Lit. Edw.* xi.
Rickmansworth, co. Herts: *Hutch.* 86; the advowson, *ib.* i, viii, ix, x.
Rid (Anselm): *v.* Ryd.
Riddle Family: *v.* Ryedale.
Riddleston (Tho.): 2 *Brad.* 236
Riding-fools: the allusion explained, 3 *Bec.* 264 n
Ridle (Hugh and Nich.): *Rid.* ii. n
Ridle (Will.), of Morale: slain by Nic. Featherston, &c., *Rid.* ii. n
RIDLEY (Nich.), bp of Rochester, afterwards of London: biographical notice of him, *Rid.* i; dates of the chief events in his life, *ib.* ii; his descent, and early education, *ib.*; his sisters, *ib.* 396; he goes to Cambridge, *ib.* ii; fellow of Pembroke college, *ib.* iii; he goes to Paris and studies at the Sorbonne, *ib.*; also to Louvain, *ib.* 488, 492; turned from Romish error by reading Bertram, *ib.* 206; was the means of a change in the views of Cranmer, 2 *Cran.* 218, 3 *Zur.* 383 n.; one of the six preachers at Canterbury, 1 *Bec.* x. n.; vicar of Herne, *Rid.* iv; master of Pembroke college, *Rid.* v, see 1 *Brad.* 31 n., 2 *Brad.* xvii, 27; candidate for the vice-chancellorship of Cambridge, *Park.* 17; chaplain to the king, *Rid.* v, x. n.; bishop of Rochester, *ib.* v, see 1 *Brad.* 31 n.; 2 *Brad.* xvii, 27; he disputes on the eucharist, 3 *Zur.* 323; a commissioner and visitor at Cambridge, 2 *Brad.* 370, *Grin.* 194, *Pil.* 522, *Rid.* 169; bishop of London, *Rid.* v, 3 *Zur.* 79 n., 185 n.; he visits his diocese, 3 *Zur.* 187; extract from his register as to Bradford's ordination, 2 *Brad.* xxii; as to that martyr's promotion to a prebend, *ib.* xxiv. n.; his friendship with Bradford, 1 *Brad.* 31; his statement about his preaching, 2 *Brad.* xxix; he makes Grindal one of his chaplains, and gives him a prebend, *Grin.* ii, *Rid.* 331; his opposition to the foreign churches in London, 3 *Zur.* 568, 569, 586; he grants leases to Hutchinson and others, *Hutch.* viii, ix; visits Joan Bocher, *ib.* iii, iv. n.; blamed by the Famulists for burning her, *Rog.* 350; sent by the council to exhort Gardiner, *Rid.* 260, 264; his letter to the preachers in his diocese, *ib.* 334; his controversy with Hooper about the vestments, 2 *Hoop.* xii, xiii, 3 *Zur.* 91 n., 486, 567, 673, (and see below); his conduct towards him before the council, 3 *Zur.* 573; their subsequent reconciliation in time of persecution, 2 *Hoop.* xvi, 3 *Zur.* 91 n., 486; he acknowledged his fault to him, *Grin.* 211; his courtesy to bp Heath, *Rid.* vi; his domestic arrangements at Fulham, *ib.* vii; his kindness to bp Bonner's mother, *ib.* viii; his influence with king Edward, *ib.* xiii. n.; he visits the princess Mary, *ib.* x. n.; is in displeasure for shewing his conscience in the duke of Somerset's case, *ib.* 59; nominated to the see of Durham, *ib.* iii; his foreboding of his death, *ib.* xi. n.; on the death of king Edward he is arrested, 3 *Zur.* 684; committed to the Tower, 2 *Lat.* 258, 390, *Rid.* xi; imprisoned there with Bradford, &c., 2 *Brad.* xxxiii; conference between him and secretary Bourn, &c., there, *Rid.* 153; he is sent with Cranmer and Latimer to dispute at Oxford, 1 *Cran.* 391, *Rid.* xi, 3 *Zur.* 515; in prison, 1 *Brad.* 445, 2 *Brad.* 74 n.; his conferences with Latimer, during their imprisonment, *Rid.* 97, &c.; the disputation there, 2 *Cran.* 445, 2 *Hoop.* 401, 593, *Rid.* 185, &c., 303, &c., (433, &c.); reference to the record of it, *Park.* 160; his confession of faith as to the true presence of Christ in the eucharist, *Rid.* 201; he asserts that he compelled no man to subscribe to king Edward's catechism, *ib.* 226; stated to have been much perplexed with the Romish argument about succession of bishops, *Phil.* 140; in peril of death, 1 *Brad.* 290; his letter from Bocardo to West, sometime his chaplain, but who had recanted, *Rid.* 337; his letter to the brethren remaining in captivity, *ib.* 342, (346); to the brethren which constantly cleave unto Christ in suffering affliction with him, *ib.* 349, (357); his last farewell to his kindred, *ib.* 395; his farewell to Cambridge, and to Pembroke hall, *ib.* 406; to Herne, *ib.* 407; to Canterbury, *ib.*; to Rochester, *ib.* 408; to Westminster, *ib.*; to London, *ib.*; to the temporal lords, *ib.* 412; another farewell to the prisoners and those exiled, *ib.* 419; farewell to Soham vicarage, *ib.* 536; his letter to the queen in behalf of certain poor men tenants under the see of London, and of his sister, *ib.* 427; his last examination at Oxford, *ib.* 253, &c.; references to it, 1 *Brad.* 369, 494, 2 *Brad.* 136; the scandalous character of his judges, 1 *Zur.* 12; he refuses to uncover his head to the pope's legate, *Rid.* 256—259, 277, 278; the articles against him and Latimer, *ib.* 270, 271; he is condemned as a heretic, 2 *Cran.* 446 n.; his sentence against

him, *Rid.* 286; ready to die, 1 *Brad.* 410; his degradation from the priesthood, *Rid.* 288; he intercedes on behalf of his sister and her husband and others, *ib.* 290; his behaviour the night before his suffering, *ib.* 292; his attire, *ib.* 293; his martyrdom, together with Hugh Latimer, 1 *Lat.* xiii, *Poet.* 165, *Rid.* iii, 293—299, 3 *Zur.* 143, 154, 301, 751; his parting gift, *Rid.* 295, 296; his dying prayer, *ib.* 296, &c.; his dying request to lord Williams on behalf of his sister and others, *ib.* 297; his painful death, *ib.* 298; the lamentation of the people, *ib.* 299; his learning, appearance, &c., *ib.* vi; his singular wit, *ib.* xii, 283; his character, *ib.* xii; his memory abused by Dr Story, *Phil.* 48; Quarles's lines concerning him, *Rid.* xii; his executors' complaint against bishop Bonner, 1 *Zur.* 7

His WORKS, edited by the Rev. Hen. Christmas, M.A., F.S.A., *Rid.*; some remains, appended to the works of Bradford, edited by the Rev. Aubrey Townsend, B.D., 2 *Brad.* 369, &c.; his reply to Hooper on the vestment controversy, *ib.* 375, &c.; discovery of this treatise, 2 *Cran.* 428 n.; his lost treatise on Election, 2 *Brad.* 171 n., 214, 220, *Rid.* xv, 368, 542; he wrote De abominationibus sedis Romanæ, *Rid.* 371, 373; his annotations on Tonstall, and other writings in prison, *ib.* 373; list of his works from Tanner, *ib.* xiii; works ascribed to him, but perhaps erroneously, *ib.* 543; he revised a sermon by Bradford, 1 *Brad.* 28 n., 82 n.; he mentions as absurd the papistical derivation of Cephas from κεφαλή, 2 *Ful.* 301 n.; was careless as to being called a Protestant, *Rid.* 15; his judgment of popish apparel, *Grin.* 211 n.; his testimony concerning the Prayer-Book, 3 *Whitg.* 329, 330; his opinion of the homilies, 1 *Bul.* 10, 3 *Whitg.* 347; his views on the eucharist, *Pil.* 547, 3 *Zur.* 72, 76; on the position of communicants, 1 *Whitg.* ii, 64; his letters, 1 *Brad.* 464, 2 *Brad.* xxvii, 82, 93, 161, 167, 172, 173, 192, 193, 198, 206, 213, 220, 398, *Park.* 45, *Rid.* 325—429, 532—542, (some of them particularly mentioned above); letters to him, 2 *Brad.* 24 (?), 169, 190, *Grin.* 238

Ridley (Alice), sister of the bp, married Geo. Shipside, *q. v.*

Ridley (Gloucester): *Rid.* ii, 159, &c.

Ridley (Hugh), brother to the bishop: *Rid.* 396

Ridley (Jo.), uncle to the bishop: *Rid.* ii.

Ridley (Jo.), of the Waltowne, brother to the bishop: farewell to him, *Rid.* 396

Ridley (Lancelot), nephew to the bishop: mentioned, *Rid.* ii, 490, 494; a preacher, *ib.* 337; one of the six preachers at Canterbury, 1 *Bec.* x. n

Ridley (Nich.), of Unthanke: kills Alex. Featherston, *Rid.* ii. n

Ridley (Nich.), of Willimountswick: cousin to the bishop, and head of the family, *Rid.* 396; mentioned, *ib.* 385 n.; he married Mabel, granddaughter of lord Dacre, *ib.*

Ridley (Rich.), of Aardriding: *Rid.* i. n

Ridley (Rob.), uncle to the bishop: *Rid.* ii, 1 *Tyn.* xxvii, 483; celebrated by Polydore Vergil, *Rid.* 488, 492

Ridley (Tho.), of the Bull head in Cheape: *Rid.* 391

Ridley family: *Rid.* i. n

Ridley hall: *v.* Willymotswick.

Rifely: 3 *Bul.* 181

Riga: an archbishop thereof, 3 *Zur.* 599 n.; imprisoned, *ib.* 687

Rigaltius (Nic.): 2 *Ful.* 113 n., 339 n

Righteous: who are so, 3 *Bec.* 603, 1 *Tyn.* 95, 3 *Tyn.* 205; they are just who believe in Christ, 2 *Lat.* 154

Righteousness: *v.* Justification.

Righteousness distinguished from holiness, *Sand.* 190; that of God, 3 *Bul.* 40; that of Christ, and its virtue, 3 *Bec.* 15; original justice, 3 *Bec.* 605; the righteousness of the ancient world, 2 *Bul.* 242; inherent justice denied, 1 *Ful.* 400; the righteousness of works described, 1 *Tyn.* 15, 112; the apostles speak against it, 2 *Bul.* 337; righteousness proceeds not from man's own strength, but from God, 1 *Tyn.* 494; ours consists in our unrighteousness being forgiven, 2 *Lat.* 140, 193, 194; we must forsake our own righteousness, and embrace God's, 2 *Tyn.* 228; the righteousness of the Pharisees and true righteousness, 1 *Tyn.* 74; righteousness before God by faith in Christ, 2 *Bec.* 631, 632; what it is to believe unto righteousness, 2 *Hoop.* 218; the righteousness which avails before God is belief in his promises, 1 *Tyn.* 16, 2 *Tyn.* 108; imputed righteousness, 1 *Brad.* 372, 3 *Bul.* 46, 4 *Bul.* 319; it is of mere grace, *Phil.* 281; the righteousness of Christ cometh upon us through faith, 1 *Tyn.* 496; translations respecting imputative justice and inherent justice examined, 1 *Ful.* 401—414; the righteousness of believers is both perfect and imperfect, 2 *Tyn.* 90; it is outward and inward; these two are mingled by the spiritualty, *ib.* 109; the pope's doctrine of righteousness and Christ's doctrine are clean contrary, *ib.* 186; there is an inherent righteousness, shewn forth by faith, 1 *Brad.* 372; this is to be distinguished, though inseparable, from the righteousness with which Christ endueth us in justification, *ib.*; what it is to hunger and thirst for righteousness, 1 *Lat.* 482, 2 *Tyn.* 22; he that thirsteth after it, trusting to Christ's blood, is accepted for full righteous, 1 *Tyn.* 94; what it is to live righteously, 1 *Bec.* 325, 326; righteousness comprises all our duty to our neighbour, *Sand.* 280; it pertains to magistrates, *ib.* 192; to ministers, *ib.* 193; to the rich, *ib.*; to lawyers, *ib.*; and to all, *ib.* 194

Right hand: *v.* God.

The right hand of fellowship, 4 *Bul.* 230; how the right hand is to be cut off, 2 *Tyn.* 50

Rightwisely: righteously, *Phil.* 409; rightwise-making, i. e. righteous making, 1 *Bec.* 421

Rikel (Dion.): wrote on the Apocalypse, *Bale* 256

Riley (Hugh): *v.* Reyley.

Rimini: *v.* Councils.

Rimmon: the house of, 2 *Brad.* 337, 338

Rincke (Herman): a personage of importance at Cologne, whence he drives Tyndale, 1 *Tyn.* xxix; he warns the king, Wolsey, and Fisher, of Tyndale's labours, *ib.* xxx; enjoined by Wolsey to search for him, *ib.* xxxiv; his letter to Wolsey in reply, *ib.*; he bribes the magistrates of Frankfort to get possession of Tyndale's books, *ib.* xxxv.

Ring: a token of marriage, *Pil.* 192 (*v.* Marriage, iv); mentioned by Bernard as a symbol of the seisin of an inheritance, 2 *Jew.* 1102; given to doctors when created, *Pil.* 192; the ring of Macham the sheriff, *Phil.* 160; cramp-rings, *Rid.* 501; a ring of a rush, used as a token, 2 *Tyn.* 215

Ringing: *v.* Bells.

Ringsley (Sir Edw.), or Ringeley, or Ryngsley: 2 *Cran.* 345, 361, 372, 387

Rinian (St): *v.* Ronan.

Ripen, Denmark: 3 *Zur.* 621 n

Ripon, co. York: the rebellious earls there, 1 *Zur.* 247 n

Rise (Will.): *v.* Rice.

Riselles, in Flanders: four martyrs there, 1 *Tyn.* lix.

Rishton (Edw.), or Riston: his Challenge, answered by Fulke and Carter, 2 *Ful.* 3; reference to it, 1 *Ful.* viii.

Rites: *v.* Ceremonies.

Rither: rudder, 3 *Jew.* 136

Rituale Romanum: 4 *Bul.* 523, *Calf.* 17 n., 1 *Hoop.* 345, 533

Rivelled: wrinkled or shrivelled, 2 *Jew.* 1075

Rivet (Andr.): *Calf.* 69, 89, 195, 202, 258, 2 *Ful.* 296 nn

Rivington, co. Lancaster: the birthplace of Pilkington, *Pil.* i; he founds a grammar-school there, *ib.* xi; extracts from the statutes of it, *ib.* 663; commemoration of the founder, *ib.* 671

Rivius (Jo.): *Rog.* viii.

Rix (Mr): desired as chaplain by the earl of Wiltshire, 2 *Cran.* 302; Cranmer's letter to him, *ib.*

Rizzio (David): his murder, 4 *Jew.* 1147, 1 *Zur.* 166 n., 170

Roads: *v.* Ways.

Roan: *v.* Rouen.

Roast: *v.* Rule.

Roath (Jo.): *v.* Roth.

Roating: coarse, *Pil.* 490

Robbery: *v.* Stealing.

Robert (St), of Bury: *Bale* 192

Robert, king of Sicily: said to have wrought the poisoning of the emperor Henry of Lucenburg, 4 *Jew.* 687

Robert, abp of Canterbury: exiled, 2 *Tyn.* 294

Robert, or Radbert, *q. v.*

Roberts (Nich.): a friend of Cranmer's, 2 *Cran.* 278; made vicar of Quadring, *ib.* 284; Cranmer's admonitory letter to him, *ib.*

Robertson (Tho.), or Robinson, archdeacon of Leicester: *Bale* 206 (?), *Rid.* 316, 3 *Zur.* 264 n

Robertson (Will.): Hist. of Scotland, 1 *Zur.* 219 n.; Charles V., *Grin.* 15 n., 1 *Lat.* 305 n

Robertus Carnotensis: 4 *Bul.* 196

Robertus de Collo-Torto, *q. v.*

Robertus Gallus, *q. v.*

Robertus Tuicensis: wrote on the Apocalypse, *Bale* 256

Robertus (Magister): *Calf.* 42 n

Robin (......): saluted, 4 *Jew.* 1190

Robin Goodfellow: named, 1 *Brad.* 427, *Calf.* 70, 2 *Cov.* 243, 1 *Tyn.* 321, 2 *Tyn.* 139; the reference explained, 1 *Brad.* 427 n., 1 *Tyn.* 321 n

Robin Hood, *q. v.*

Robin (Round): 1 *Cov.* 426, *Rid.* 265

Robinson (Hen.), bp of Carlisle: sometime provost of Queen's coll., Oxon., provision for him, *Grin.* 461

Robinson (Nich.), bp of Bangor: was chaplain to abp Parker, letter to him, 2 *Cov.* 532; mentioned, *Park.* 261; he signs a letter to the queen, *ib.* 294; likewise a letter to lord Burghley, *ib.* 394

Robinson (Ant.): servant to Jewel, *Jew.* xxv.

Robinson (Hastings): translator and editor of the Zurich Letters, 1, 2, 3 *Zur.*
Robinson (Jo.): *v.* Robynson.
Robinson (Rich.): notice of him, *Poet.* xxxiii; Psalm vi. in metre, *ib.* 364; time fleeting, *ib.* 365
Robinson (Tho.): *v.* Robertson.
Robinson (Dr): *Bale* 206 [perhaps Thomas].
Robsart (Sir Jo.): dedication to him, 2 *Bec.* 583; notice of him, his ancestors, &c., *ib.* n
Robsart (Amy or Anne), wife of Rob. Dudley (*q. v.*), earl of Leicester.
Robynson (Jo.): servant to lord Wiltshire, 2 *Cran.* 369
Roccha (Angelus) à Camerino: *Calf.* 178 n
Rocester abbey, co. Stafford: its suppression, 2 *Cran.* 379
Roch (St): invoked against pestilence, *Bale* 348, 1 *Bec.* 139, *Calf.* 20, 1 *Hoop.* 457, *Hutch.* 171, 2 *Jew.* 922, *Pra. Eliz.* 392 n., 535; prayer for his intercession, *Rog.* 228; some account of him, 1 *Bec.* 139 n.; we are forbidden by God's word to trust in him, 3 *Bec.* 43
Rochdale, co. Lanc.: the living, *Park.* 221, 231 n., *Pil.* vii; the school, *Park.* 231, 232
Roche (Tho.): presented to Sutton Magna, 2 *Cran.* 362 n
Rochefort (R. de): *v.* Raymond (St).
Rochelle: named, 2 *Zur.* 84; synod of the reformed church of France there, 1 *Zur.* 250 n.; besieged, 2 *Zur.* 223 n., 250 n
Rochester, Kent: martyrs there, *Poet.* 170; a citation to lord Cobham affixed to the gates of the cathedral, *Bale* 18; several of the bishops were archdeacons of Canterbury, *Grin.* 360 n.; a benefice annexed to the bishoprick, *Park.* 100; Ridley's last farewell to it, *Rid.* 408
Rochester (Master): perhaps Maurice Griffith, bp of Rochester, 1 *Brad.* 469
Rochet, or Rochette: a vestment worn by bishops, 1 *Jew.* 91, 1 *Lat.* 208, 264, 2 *Lat.* 348, *Lit. Edw.* 157, 217, *Park.* 475, 1 *Tyn.* 252, 1 *Zur.* 164, 3 *Zur.* 585 n.; stated to have been introduced by Sisinius, a Novatian bishop, *Pil.* 661
Rochford, co. Essex: J. Simpson was burnt there, *Poet.* 162
Rochford (Tho. visc.), afterwards earl of Wiltshire: *v.* Boleyn.
Rock: *v.* Christ, iv, Peter (St).
  That smitten by Moses, *Calf.* 336; that on which Christ built his church said to be faith, 3 *Tyn.* 31; he who cometh to this rock is safe, *ib.*
Rock: an instrument used in spinning, 2 *Cov.* 537

Rocke (St): *v.* Roch.
Rod: what is understood by it in scripture, 2 *Hoop.* 225
Rodbert, or Robert: founded the order of Fontevraud, 3 *Bul.* 295 n
Rodborne (Tho.), afterwards bp of St David's: *Bale* 16
Roderic, king of the Goths: 1 *Bul.* 416
Rodolph II., emperor: *Rog.* 49
Rodolph, duke of Suabia: stirred up by the pope against his brother-in-law the emperor, 2 *Hoop.* 239, 3 *Jew.* 346, 4 *Jew.* 698, *Lit. Eliz.* 449
Rodolph (Ant.): rejects the Apocrypha, *Whita.* 64
Rodolph (Jo.): 3 *Zur.* 97
Roestius (Diethelm), consul of Zurich: 4 *Bul.* x. n
Roffensis: *v.* Fisher (Jo.), bp of Rochester.
Rogation week: its institution, *Calf.* 295, 296; commonly called Gang-week, 3 *Whitg.* 276, &c.; sometimes Cross-week, *Calf.* 66; Gang-week at Rome, 2 *Jew.* 915 (see *Calf.* 295 n.); heathen custom, *Calf.* 66, 2 *Zur.* 40; processions or perambulations, 3 *Whitg.* 276, 277, 278, 495, 2 *Zur.* 40, 361; superstitious ceremonies sometimes used, surplices, banners, bells, &c., *Grin.* 168, 241, 3 *Whitg.* 276, 277, 495; formerly gospels were said to the corn in the fields, 3 *Tyn.* 62, 234; letter to the archdeacon of Essex on perambulations in Rogation week, *Grin.* 240; the right use of such perambulations, 2 *Zur.* 40; what psalms to be said, *Grin.* 141, 168
Roger of Bishopsbridge, abp of York: *Pil.* 589
Roger, bp of Worcester: *Pil.* 589
Roger of Chester, or Chichester: notice of him, 4 *Jew.* 697 n.; his works copied by R. Higden, *Calf.* 296 n
Rogers (Sir Edw.): privy councillor to queen Elizabeth, *Park.* 75, 76, 77, 103, 106, 117, 1 *Zur.* 5 n.; comptroller of the household, *Grin.* 32; mourner at the funeral of the emperor Ferdinand, *ib.*
Rogers (Sir Rich.): 1 *Bec.* 396 n
Rogers (And.): Mary (Seymour) his wife, 1 *Bec.* 396 n
Rogers (Dan.), son of the martyr: notice of him, 2 *Zur.* 296 n.; mentioned, *ib.* 293 n., 300 (?)
Rogers (Jo.), the martyr: chaplain at Antwerp, 1 *Tyn.* lxxiv; editor of the Bible called Mathewe's, 2 *Cov.* x, 1 *Tyn.* lxxiv; prebendary of St Paul's, 2 *Brad.* xxv, *Rid.* 331 n., 336; in prison, 1 *Brad.* 403, *Hutch.* viii; he signs a declaration concerning

religion, 1 *Brad.* 374; intention to take him to Cambridge to dispute, *Rid.* 363; he is examined at St Mary Overy's, 1 *Brad.* 473; degraded by Bonner, 2 *Hoop.* xxiv; in peril of death, 1 *Brad.* 289, 2 *Brad.* 83; condemned, 3 *Zur.* 171; his martyrdom, 1 *Brad.* 282 n., 410, 445, 2 *Brad.* 190, 192, 194, *Rid.* 378, 380, 391, 3 *Zur.* 772

Rogers (Jo.): Displaying of the Family of Love, by J. R., *Rog.* 41, 271, 350 nn

Rogers (Matth.): exhorts his children, 2 *Brad.* 363

Rogers (Rich.), suffragan of Dover: an ecclesiastical commissioner, *Park.* 370 n.; he attends queen Elizabeth at Canterbury, *ib.* 475

ROGERS (Tho.): notice of his life and works, *Rog.* v; THE CATHOLIC DOCTRINE OF THE CHURCH OF ENGLAND; AN EXPOSITION OF THE XXXIX. ARTICLES; edited by the Rev. J. J. S. Perowne, M.A., *Rog.*; he translated a work by Scheltco à Jueren on the end of the world, 2 *Lat.* 51 n., *Rog.* v; his opinion on the cross in baptism, *Rog.* 321 n

Rogers (Tho.), student of Ch. ch., Oxon.: *Rog.* ix.

Rogers (Tho.), another: *Rog.* ix.

Roging: insidious, knavish, 3 *Whitg.* 139

Rohan (M. de): queen Elizabeth's contract with him, 1 *Zur.* 115 n

Rokeby (Jo.), or Rookbye, precentor of the church of York: enjoined to view the statutes of the said church, *Grin.* 151

Rolfe (Mr): a gentleman of Kent, *Park.* 258

Roll up: to chaunt, 1 *Tyn.* 243

Roma (Aug. de), abp of Nazareth: at the council of Basil, 4 *Jew.* 1056

Romances: some mentioned, 1 *Tyn.* 161

Romanists: v. Church, II. iii, Papists. The term used, *Sand.* 64; differences among them, 3 *Jew.* 610, &c.

Romans: their monarchy the last of the four, 1 *Lat.* 356; what countries the empire comprised, 2 *Jew.* 915; its civil wars and contentions, 2 *Hoop.* 78; the disquiet raised by the introduction of Christianity, 2 *Cran.* 198; according to divers fathers it was this which hindered the revelation of Antichrist, 2 *Jew.* 913; the monarchy usurped by the pope, *Pil.* 186; why the Romans never received the God of the Jews, 3 *Bul.* 203; they had famous schools, 4 *Bul.* 480; they trained their children in good letters, 1 *Bec.* 398; they said their ancilia were sent from heaven, 1 *Jew.* 510; their law against perjury, 1 *Bec.* 391; against whoredom, 2 *Bec.* 649; Gesta Romanorum, 1 *Tyn.* 80 n., 328

Romans (Epistle to the): v. Paul (St).

Romanus, pope: 1 *Hoop.* 217, 3 *Jew.* 276, 1 *Tyn.* 324 n

Romanus, martyr: his address to his judge, as stated by Prudentius, 3 *Bul.* 225

Romanus (St): Romane [one of several saints so named] invoked for madness, 2 *Jew.* 923

Romanus Patritius: v. Patritius, Vartomannus.

Rome: v. Church, II. iii, Councils, Empire, Pope, Romans.

The head of the world, 4 *Jew.* 1032; an epitome of the world, 1 *Jew.* 420; names given to it by Cicero, ad Frontinum, *ib.* 432; it is the seven-hilled city, 4 *Jew.* 879, *Lit. Eliz.* 655, *Phil.* 429; it was built on seven hills, but Sander says the site is removed, the present city being on the other side of the river, 2 *Ful.* 372; the hills particularly mentioned, *ib.* 372, 373, 2 *Jew.* 915; Rome declared to be the Babylon of St John, *Poet.* 275, *Rid.* 53, 54 (v. Babylon); called Babylon by Augustine, *Rog.* 181, and by Jerome, *ib.* 182; it is said to be the beast of St John, *Bale* 426, the great whore, *ib.* 493, 2 *Hoop.* 554, *Rid.* 53, the seat of Satan, *Rid.* 415, and of Antichrist, 2 *Cran.* 63; its anagram,—Amor, *Rog.* 179, 180; Bede's exposition of S. P. Q. R., 1 *Jew.* 421; the city beautified by Augustus, 1 *Bec.* 245, *Grin.* 17, 2 *Jew.* 1015; many times assaulted and sacked by barbarians, 2 *Bul.* 109, 4 *Bul.* 200, 1 *Jew.* 416, 418; whether Peter was there, 2 *Brad.* 144 (&c. v. Peter); number of clergy in the church at Rome in the time of Cornelius, 1 *Jew.* 197, 2 *Whitg.* 215; language of the clergy in an epistle to Cyprian, 2 *Ful.* 159; simple order of the church in the time of Damasus and Jerome, 1 *Jew.* 174, 265; Rome a patriarchate, 4 *Bul.* 112, *Rid.* 263, 2 *Whitg.* 220, 221 n.; recognized by the Nicene council as equal with Alexandria and Antioch, 3 *Jew.* 304, &c.; its primacy, 1 *Jew.* 368, &c., 412; the faith of the West came not first from Rome, *ib.* 161; Rome declared the chief church by the emperor Phocas (q. v.), 2 *Tyn.* 258; the see of Rome is a tyranny of body and soul, 1 *Hoop.* 23; jubilees instituted, 2 *Bul.* 266, 1 *Lat.* 49 n.; corrupt state of the church, 4 *Jew.* 745, &c.; Rome said by Pius V. " magis Gentilizare, quam Christianizare," *Rog.* 182; the awful corruption of manners there, *Phil.* 389, 418; harlots harboured there, and brothel-houses openly maintained, and made a source of revenue, &c., *Bale* 518, 2 *Jew.* 707, 728, 4 *Jew.* 627, 644, *Rog.* 119 n., 3 *Tyn.* 52, 171; priests and prelates wait on courtezans, 2 *Jew.* 728, 807; it is the nest of abomination, 1 *Hoop.* 447; all things are venal there, *Rid.* 54; Rome gives trifles, but receives gold, *Pil.* 272; a letter by Knox, professedly printed there, 1 *Brad.* 111; false miracles performed there in 1796, 97, *Calf.* 274 n.; manuscripts there, *Park.* 141

CHURCHES.

Churches and monasteries on the seven hills, 2 *Ful.* 372, 373; Serramus De septem Urbis Romæ Ecclesiis, *Rid.* 510; the stations, appointed by Gregory I., 1 *Lat.* 49 n

St Peter's: limina Petri et Pauli, 1 *Jew.* 173 n.; the pix made by Gregory, 2 *Jew.* 560

All Saints': formerly the Pantheon, *Calf.* 66

St Andrew: pix there, 2 *Jew.* 560

St John Lateran: robbed by Isacius, 2 *Tyn.* 255; indulgence for visiting it, 1 *Brad.* 372 n.; the great bell baptized by John XIV., *Rog.* 266

St Mary in Cosmedin: Pole cardinal deacon thereof, *Rid.* 270

St Mary Rotunda: *Calf.* 67 n

St Mary Scala Cœli: 1 *Brad.* 372 n., 1 *Lat.* 97 n

St Paul: St Brigit's prayers there, *Pra. Eliz.* 507 n

St Sylvester: pix there, 2 *Jew.* 560

OTHER LOCALITIES.

The Tarpeian rock, 1 *Bul.* 204; the theatre of Pompeius, 2 *Jew.* 1010; there was a library in the Capitol, *ib.* 981; the Pantheon, now St Mary Rotunda, *Calf.* 67 n.; the Lateran (*v.* Councils, and *St John,* among the churches, below), 2 *Ful.* 372; the alleged baptistery of Constantine there, *ib.* 360; Ara Cœli, *ib.* 373; the castle of St Angelo, 2 *Lat.* 180; the English college, *Lit. Eliz.* 656 n., 1 *Zur.* 254 n.; the image called Pasquil, 2 *Bul.* 117; that of pope Joan, 4 *Jew.* 649, 655

Rome (New): *v.* Constantinople.

Romney (New), co. Kent: unlawful exaction of 3*d.* per acre for tithes in Rumney Marsh, 2 *Cran.* 289

Romney (Old), Kent: the living, *Park.* 339 n

Romulus: 2 *Bul.* 219

Ronan (St): "St Tronian's fast," *Pil.* 80; "St Rinian's," *ib.* 551

Roo (Geo.), rector of Winchcomb: 3 *Tyn.* 75 n

Roo (Geo.), or Row: chaplain to abp Grindal, *Grin.* 331

Rood: a crucifix, 2 *Jew.* 922; from roʊ, cross, *Calf.* 35 n.; the holy rood with St Mary and St John, *Bale* 612, 1 *Ful.* 190, 204, 1 *Zur.* 73, 74; various roods are mentioned at p. 255, col. 2 of this Index; the book of the rood, 2 *Cran.* 101

Rood-lofts: what they were, *Calf.* 35 n., *Grin.* 154 n.; lights set therein, *Rid.* 67; order of the ecclesiastical commissioners for their removal, *Grin.* 154 n.; directed to be taken down and altered, *ib.* 134, 158, *Sand.* 250; commonly removed and texts set up, 1 *Ful.* 193

Roodd (Mr): subscribes the book of the king's succession, and promises to preach nothing doubtful without consulting Cranmer, 2 *Cran.* 287

Roode (Mr), of Gray's Inn: 2 *Cran.* 306

Rook (St): *v.* Rochus.

Rookbye (Jo.): *v.* Rokeby.

Roost: *v.* Rule.

Rooth (Rich.): *v.* Roth.

Rooty, or Rowty: coarse, *Pil.* 490

Roper (Geo.): martyred at Canterbury, *Poet.* 165

Roper (Jo.): sometime attorney-general, *Phil.* xxxi.

Roper (Jo.?): a Puritan, *Grin.* 204

Roper (Will.): notice of him, *Phil.* xxxi; he was one of the commissioners for the examination of Philpot, *ib.* 4; he married Margaret, dau. of Sir Tho. More, and wrote his life, *ib.* xxxi; his Life of Sir T. More, 2 *Lat.* 333 n

Rosa Solis: *Poet.* 193

Rosaries: what, 4 *Bul.* 204 n

Rosaries, or Lady Psalters: *v.* Mary (B. V.)

Roscoe (Will.): his Leo X., *Calf.* 6 n

Rosdell (Chr.): 1 *Hoop.* iv, v.

Rose (Tho.), or Ros, or Rosse, curate of Hadleigh: persecuted by his parishioners, 2 *Cran.* 280; proposed as abp of Armagh, *ib.* 438; persecuted by Gardiner in queen Mary's time, 3 *Zur.* 773

Rose of gold: presented by the pope to kings, 1 *Tyn.* 186

Rosell (Harold): apparently clerk of Cranmer's kitchen, 2 *Cran.* 321; he married Dorothy Cranmer, sister of the archbishop, *ib.* 256 n.; Cranmer recommends him to send his son Thomas to a free school, *ib.* 262

Rosell (Tho.): 2 *Cran.* 262

Rosellis (Ant. de): Monarchia, *Jew.* xlii; he extravagantly exalts the pope, 4 *Bul.* 120; declares that he is prince of the kings of the earth, 4 *Jew.* 671; asserts, by implication, that he is king of kings and lord of lords, *ib.* 682

Rosogan (James): and

Rosogan (Jo.): rebels, 2 *Cran.* 187 n
Rosse (Tho.): *v.* Rose.
Rossem (Martin van): raises an army in the dukedom of Cleve, 3 *Zur.* 633 n
Rosso (Pietro Maria): 2 *Cran.* 234 n
Rosweydus (Heribertus): his valuable edition of the Vitæ Patrum, *Calf.* 252 n
Rotaker (Chr.): 1 *Zur.* 62, 3 *Zur.* 698
Rotenberg: surrendered, 3 *Zur.* 638 n
Roth (Jo.): martyred, *Poet.* 168
Roth (Rich.), or Rooth: martyred at Islington, *Poet.* 171
Rothbury, co. Northumb.: birthplace of the martyr Taylor, *Rid.* 489, 494
Rothes (And. earl of): *v.* Leslie.
Rothman (Bernard): an ecclesiastic of Münster, who introduced the reformation into that city, but was afterwards infected with the enthusiasm of the Anabaptists, *Grin.*256
Rotomage: *v.* Rouen.
Roudbery (Rob.): *Bale* 16
Rouen: *v.* Councils.
  Persecution there, 1 *Tyn.* lix; a letter of Hooper's printed there, 2 *Hoop.* 570; the city taken and sacked by the duke of Guise, *Grin.* 253 n., 2 *Zur.* 83 n.; mentioned, 1 *Zur.* 115 n., 118 n
Rough (Jo.): in exile, 1 *Cran.* (9); martyred in Smithfield, *Poet.* 171, 2 *Zur.* 160 n., 3 *Zur.* 360 n.
Round: to whisper, 2 *Bul.* 69, *Lit. Eliz.* 495 n.; roun, 2 *Bul.* 69 n.; rown, *Lit. Eliz.* 495 n.; rounded, 1 *Jew.* 45, *Phil.* 198; rowned, i. e. consulted, *Bale* 125
Roustius (......): 3 *Zur.* 421
Rout: crowd, 2 *Jew.* 869; rout, to make a stir, *Pil.* 356
Routh (Mart. Jos.), pres. Magd. coll. Oxon.: Reliquæ Sacræ, 1 *Bul.* 132 n., *Calf.* 154 n., 2 *Cov.* 132 n., 184 n., 2 *Ful.* 338 n
Row (Geo.): *v.* Roo.
Row (Jo.), minister of Perth: 2 *Zur.* 364
Rowland: proverb on Rowland and Oliver, *Calf.* 374
Rowlands (Sam.): notice of him, *Poet.* xxxii; Peter's tears, *ib.* 347; the death of death, sin's pardon, and soul's ransom, *ib.* 349; the high way to mount Calvarie, *ib.* 352; Christ to the women of Hierusalem, *ib.* 357
Rowned: *v.* Round.
Rowty: *v.* Rooty.
Roxburgh castle: taken by the English, 3 *Zur.* 387
Royal, or Rial: a gold coin, *Rid.* 382
Royard: qu. Ruardus Tapper? 1 *Jew.* 38, 52, 55
Royden (......): a friend of Bradford, 1 *Brad.* 36 n.; letter to him, 2 *Brad.* 67; to him and his wife, *ib.* 124

Roydon (Tho.): dedication to him, 1 *Bec.* 307; notice of him and his family, *ib.* n
Roydon, co. Essex: the vicarage, 2 *Cran.* 368
Roydon, co. Suffolk: 1 *Bec.* 307 n
Roye (Will.): once a monk of Greenwich, and afterwards Tyndale's associate in his translations, 1 *Tyn.* xv, xxii, xxiii, 37—41, 3 *Tyn.* 187 n.; he offends Wolsey by his satire, 1 *Tyn.* xxxvi, 39 n.; with Tyndale at Cologne, *ib.* xxviii; sought for abroad by Wolsey's orders, *ib.* xxxiv, xxxv; burned in Portugal, *ib.* 42 n.; Tyndale's character of him, *ib.* 37—39
Royston (Dr): chaplain to Tonstal, 1 *Tyn.* xxiv.
Ruardus Tapper, *q. v.*
Rubbidge: rubbish, *Sand.* 59
Rubric primers: *v.* Primers.
Ruchat (Abr.): Hist. de la Ref. de la Suisse, 3 *Zur.* 622 n
Rudder (S.): Hist. of Gloucestershire, 2 *Lat.* 393, 415, 417, 418 nn
Ruddock: a robin red-breast, metaphorically a gold coin, 2 *Bul.* 59
Ruding (Rogers): Annals of the Coinage, 3 *Zur.* 615 n
Ruff (In his): in his best attire, at his highest exaltation, 2 *Jew.* 846 n
Ruffin (St): invoked for lunacy, *Rog.* 226
Ruffinus, or Rufinus: his dispute with Jerome, 4 *Jew.* 1098; called a heretic, *ib.* 1006, 1007; he was tinctured with the heresy of Origen, *ib.* 1007; Hystoria Ecclesiastica, *Jew.* xlii; mistaken for Eusebius, 3 *Jew.* 411, 951 n.; his Exposition of the Creed, formerly ascribed to Cyprian, 2 *Bec.* 49 n., 2 *Cran.* 23; his Latin version of Josephus, *Calf.* x; his Latin version of the Recognitiones, *ib.* 21 n.; he enumerates the canonical books of the Old Testament, 4 *Bul.* 541; divides the scriptures into canonical, ecclesiastical, and apocryphal books, 2 *Cran.* 23; allows the books termed ecclesiastical to be read in the church, but not to be alleged for doctrine, *ib.*, 3 *Jew.* 433, *Whita.* 59, 62; bears witness against the Apocrypha, 2 *Cran.* 23, 1 *Ful.* 20 n., 3 *Jew.* 452, *Whita.* 59; says that apostolic tradition required to be written for the benefit of posterity, *Whita.* 570; maintains the scriptures to be a sufficient rule of faith, *Sand.* 222 n., *Whita.* 28; ascribes the creed to the apostles, 1 *Bul.* 123; shews why we profess our belief *in* God, the Father, the Son, and the Holy Ghost, but not *in* the church, &c., *ib.* 159; describes a controversy about the difference of substances

and subsistences (οὐσίας et ὑποστάσεις), 3 *Bul.* 158; says that the clause, "he descended into hell," is not in the creed of the church of Rome, nor is it used in the churches of the East, 1 *Bul.* 137, *Whita.* 536, 537; on the ascension of Christ, 2 *Cov.* 150, 2 *Hoop.* 482; on his sitting on the right hand of the Father, 1 *Bul.* 148, 2 *Cov.* 156; he says in some Eastern churches they professed to believe "the resurrection of *this* flesh," 2 *Bec.* 49 n., 1 *Bul.* 168, 169, 2 *Cov.* 168; calls it a cavil to say, that the body of man is "any other thing but flesh," 3 *Jew.* 535; said to have held that God committed the government of the world to certain celestial powers, *Rog.* 42 n.; referred to on ecclesiastical ranks, 2 *Whitg.* 432; he speaks of deacons dividing the sacrament in the absence of the presbyters, 1 *Jew.* 239, 241; referred to about hermits, 2 *Ful.* 239; he relates that Constantine at the time of sermons stood upright, 4 *Jew.* 1017; a passage in his history misapplied in the Canon Law to prove that the pope is God and above human judgment, 2 *Ful.* 356 n.; he speaks of the invention of the cross, *Calf.* 322, 323, 326; says that the emperor called the council of Nice together according to the determination of the priests, &c., 4 *Jew.* 993, 1000, *Rog.* 204 n.; on the Nicene decree respecting patriarchs, 3 *Jew.* 307, 4 *Jew.* 828; words added in his abridgment of a Nicene canon, 2 *Ful.* 107; he calls Athanasius the greatest or highest bishop, 3 *Jew.* 315, 4 *Jew.* 824; on the administration of baptism by him in pastime, when a child, *Hutch.* 116; on George of Alexandria, 2 *Whitg.* 385; he mentions two bishops of Alexandria at one time, 4 *Jew.* 994; says when Maximus sat in the council of Palestine, Paphnutius put him out, saying that it is not lawful to confer matters with wicked men, *ib.* 951; speaks of the vain endeavour of the Jews to rebuild the temple in the reign of Julian, 2 *Bul.* 260, 261; states that none of the bishops at Rimini understood the word ὁμοούσιος, *Whita.* 139; states that the father of Gregory of Nazianzum was bishop there before him, *Pil.* 565; describes the scriptural studies of Basil and Gregory, *Whita.* 371; quoted for Jerome's censure on Ambrose, 1 *Jew.* 314 n.; he gives a prayer of Theodosius, *Pil.* 414; mentions a law made by him, *ib.* 409; on the patience of Theodorus, *ib.* 333; tells how the cross recommended Christianity to the Egyptians, *Calf.* 65, 276, 277; says the man is not a Christian who would bear to be called a heretic, 2 *Jew.* 1029, 3 *Jew.* 184, 210; speaks of a learned heretic who was confuted by a simple man, *Pil.* 267; speaks of the heresy of Apollinaris, *Rog.* 52 n.; of that of the Macedonians, *ib.* 72 n.; relates some heathen miracles, *Calf.* 274, 275

Rugge (Rob.): vice-chancellor of Cambridge, *Rid.* 327 n

Rugge (Will.), or Reppes, bp of Norwich: notice of him, 2 *Cran.* 336 n.; he was once abbot of St Benedict at Hulme, 1 *Lat.* 123 n.; when abbot he signed a declaration about a general council, 2 *Cran.* 468 [a footnote ascribes the signature to Will. Boston, alias Benson, abbot of Westminster, but as it seems erroneously]; his conduct as bishop denounced by Cranmer, *ib.* 336

Ruinart (Theod.): Acta martyrum, 2 *Ful.* 189 n

Ruins: *v.* Time.

Ruinus (Car.): says the pope has power to decree against the epistles of St Paul, *Rog.* 191 n

Rule and charge: 4 *Jew.* 959

Rule (Golden): 2 *Tyn.* 118

Rule of Clerks' Lives: *v.* Regula.

Rule of Faith: *v.* Faith.

Rule (To) the roast: 4 *Jew.* 744, *Rid.* 115; or the roost, *Phil.* 46, 291

Rulers: *v.* Kings, Magistrates.

Runcorn (Mr): 1 *Brad.* 494

Rupe Scissa (Jo. de): wrote on the Apocalypse, *Bale* 258

Rupertus: 4 *Jew.* 873

Rupertus Carnotensis, i. e. John of Salisbury: *v.* John.

Rupertus Tuitensis: De Divinis Officiis, *Jew.* xlii, 1 *Jew.* 179

Ruremond (Chr. van): printer at Antwerp, 1 *Tyn.* xxxiii.

Rush (Mr): recommended to be teacher in the grammar-school at Canterbury, *Park.* 144; notice of him, *ib.* n.; recommended for preferment, *ib.* 283

Rush-bearing: the wake, or feast of dedication, *Grin.* 142

Rushbrough (Eliz.): *v.* Brown (E.)

Russell (Jo.), 1st earl of Bedford: sheriff of Worcester, 2 *Lat.* 393 n., 395 n., and see 405; he makes suit for abbey-lands, *ib.* 395 n.; his advancement, 2 *Bec.* 622 n.; a privy councillor, 1 *Cran.* xix, 2 *Cran.* 490, 510, 511, 523, 524, 530, 531, *Park.* 30, 46, *Rid.* 508, 2 *Zur.* 159 n.; he defeats the rebels at Exeter, 2 *Cran.* 163 n.; sent to the Tower on the accession of queen Mary, *ib.* 441 n., 442

Russell (Fra.), 2nd earl of Bedford: notices of him, 2 *Bec.* 622 n., 2 *Brad.* 77 n., 2 *Zur.* 215 n.; mentioned, *Park.* 464, 1 *Zur.* 29, 78, 326; he was some time at Zurich, 2 *Zur.* 8 n.; concerned in the correction of the liturgy, *ib.* 9 n.; privy councillor to queen Elizabeth, *Grin.* 405, 417, 423, 427, *Park.* 73, 357, 381, 1 *Zur.* 5 n.; he invites P. Martyr to return to England, 1 *Zur.* 81 n.; governor of Berwick, 2 *Zur.* 116, 145; extracts from his correspondence, 1 *Zur.* 165 n., 167 n.; ambassador in Scotland at the baptism of James VI., *ib.* 183 n.; a supervisor of Pilkington's testament, *Pil.* xi; at the duke of Norfolk's trial, 1 *Zur.* 267 n.; patron of Gualter's son, *ib.* 289; letters by him, 2 *Zur.* 36, 54, 63, 74, 75, 306, 3 *Zur.* 138; letters to him, 2 *Brad.* 77, 138, 2 *Zur.* 8, 52, 57 (?), 60, 137, 214; dedication to him, 2 *Bec.* 622

Russell (Fra.? lord): apparently Francis, heir app. of the 2nd earl of Bedford, 1 *Zur.* 20, 34; taken prisoner by the Scots, *Grin.* 355 n

Russia: v. Church, II. ii.
   Invaded by the Tartars, 3 *Zur.* 692; the Russe Commonwealth, cited, *Rog.* 38 n., 79 n., 81 n., &c.; the Ruthenians, or Little Russians, and their tongue, 2 *Bec.* 245, 3 *Zur.* 600, 691

Rustandus: papal legate in England, 4 *Jew.* 1080

Rusticus (St): martyred at Paris, 1 *Hoop.* 314 n

Rusticus: set up in the place of a deprived bishop, 1 *Bec.* 23, 2 *Bec.* 325, 326

Rutenes: 2 *Bec.* 245

Ruth: marries Boaz, *Rid.* 84; an example to daughters in law, 1 *Bul.* 285; the book of Ruth; by whom written, *Whita.* 302

Ruthall (Tho,), bp of Durham: 2 *Tyn.* 315

Ruthenians: v. Russia.

Rutherford (Jo.), principal of St Salvator's college, St Andrew's: 2 *Zur.* 364

Rutherius, bp of Verona: 1 *Hoop.* 160 n

Ruthven (Patrick, lord): took part in the murder of Rizzio, 2 *Zur.* 166 n

Rutilius (P.): his death, 1 *Hoop.* 297

Rutland (Earls of): v. Manners.

Rutter: a rider, a knight, 2 *Tyn.* 292; ruffling rutters, *Bale* 388

Rycall: v. Riccall.

Rych (Rich. lord): v. Rich.

Ryd (Herman.): De Vit. et Honest. Cleric. *Jew.* xlii; declares that for the multitude of lechery (in priests) other faults are taken for no sin, 4 *Jew.* 642; says the clergy understand not the words of their canon, *ib.* 878; mentions that Brigitta says, in her revelations, Christ shall take his blessing from the clergy of Rome, and shall give the same unto a people that shall do his will, *ib.* 874; referred to about Rupertus Carnotensis, *ib.* 938

Ryd (Val. Anselm.), or Rid: Catalogus Annorum, *Jew.* xlii; he says pope Liberius was the first that forsook the pure doctrine of the bishops of Rome, 3 *Jew.* 342; relates how the council of Frankfort cursed that of Constantinople, which censured images, 4 *Jew.* 1051; affords testimony in proof of pope Joan, *ib.* 656; says pope Hildebrand had made the leaden sword of the pope's authority so mighty, that it had utterly dulled the iron sword of the empire, 3 *Jew.* 346; speaks of the wealth of John XXII., 4 *Jew.* 932

Rye, co. Sussex: manslaughter in the church there, 2 *Cran.* 357

Ryedale, or Riddle family: *Rid.* i. n

Rymer (Tho.): Fœdera, 2 *Lat.* 368, 370, 386, 394 nn

Ryngsley (Sir Edw.): v. Ringsley.

Rynthelen (Corn. à): *Calf.* 135 n

S

S: Philpot wrote to him concerning infant baptism, *Pil.* 274

S. (D.): v. Sand.

S. (J.): "J. T. [and] J. S." 3 *Whitg.* 498 n

S. (Rich.): 2 *Cran.* 288

Sabbaoth: what it means, 3 *Bul.* 132; though a Hebrew word, it is used in English service, 1 *Jew.* 303

Sabbatarians: their doctrines, *Rog.* 18, 19, 97, 233, 234, 271, 315, 327; they maintain that the sabbath was none of the ceremonies which were abrogated, *ib.* 89; say that the church hath no authority to sanctify any other day, *ib.* 187, 322; hinder people from attending churches upon holy days, *ib.* 322; hold all must keep the sabbath as they prescribe on pain of damnation, *ib.* 319; Rogers styles them demi-Jews, *ib.* 315; their books called in and forbidden, *ib.* 20

Sabbath: on the sabbath, 2 *Bul.* 161, 162; called by Tyndale saboth, and by More sabbaoth, 3 *Tyn.* 97 n.; what the word signifies, 2 *Bec.* 80; the sabbath was made for man, 1 *Bul.* 265, 2 *Bul.* 264; it was made for rest, *Pil.* 338; the Lord rested on it and blessed it, 1 *Bul.* 258, 259; the fourth commandment, 2 *Whitg.* 569, &c., 593; the precept expounded, 2 *Bec.* 80, &c., 500,

1 *Bul.* 253, &c., 1 *Hoop.* 337, &c., *Lit. Edw.* 497, (546), *Now.* (14), 128; a meditation on it, 1 *Brad.* 157; prayer on it, 2 *Brad.* 259; the day commanded to be sanctified, and how, 1 *Bec.* 38, 2 *Bec.* 81, 500, 2 *Cran.* 103, *Pil.* 18; sabbath-breaking rebuked by Nehemiah, *Sand.* 251; promises and threatenings added to the sabbath, 1 *Bul.* 263; it was a sign to the Israelites that they were God's people, 1 *Tyn.* 351; but they supposed that they were justified by keeping it, 3 *Tyn.* 67; the Maccabees fought on that day, 1 *Jew.* 224; Dion mentions certain Jews who would not do so, *ib.*; it was superstitiously kept by the scribes and Pharisees, 2 *Cran.* 146; the sabbath of the Jews referred to by Seneca, 1 *Hoop.* 346; it was not violated by Christ, *Rog.* 133; whether Christians be bound to observe it as the Jews were, 2 *Bec.* 82; controversy on the subject, *Rog.* ix, 18, 19; the opinions of Whitgift and Cartwright, 1 *Whitg.* 200—202, 228, 229, 2 *Whitg.* 446, 579, 580; what of the precept was temporary, and what continues, 1 *Hoop.* 341, 2 *Brad.* 323, *Now.* (14, 15), 128, 129; it is partly ceremonial, 2 *Bec.* 82, *Park.* 81; the sabbath has two parts, the outward rest from bodily labour, which was ceremonial; and the inward rest from our own wills, which remains, 2 *Cran.* 60, 61; the ceremonial sabbath is abrogated by Christ's coming, *Rog.* 89; the commandment is now to be observed spiritually, 2 *Tyn.* 325; Augustine says its literal observance pertained only to the Jews, 2 *Cran.* 102; the spiritual import of the precept, 2 *Bec.* 82, 1 *Bul.* 254, *Lit. Edw.* 515, (563), *Now.* (16), 129, 130; what it is, in the Christian sense, to keep it, 3 *Bec.* 608; the sabbath of the Jews was not observed by the first Christians, 2 *Zur.* 122; Eusebius declares that Christians have no care of corporal circumcision, nor of keeping the sabbath, nor of abstaining from meats, 3 *Bul.* 292, 293; our sabbath is not the Jews' sabbath, 2 *Whita.* 446; the sabbath of Christians is not corporal but spiritual, not outward but inward, 2 *Bec.* 82; Tertullian affirms that the Christian sabbath is to be kept every day, 1 *Jew.* 128; every day is the sabbath to the godly, 2 *Bec.* 83; Augustine censures as carnal those who, when they hear of the sabbath, understand nothing thereby but one day in seven, 4 *Bul.* 287; all days are proper for good deeds, 2 *Tyn.* 113; the sabbath (i. e. Saturday) and the Lord's day confounded by Cartwright, 1 *Whitg.* 223, 228; distinguished by Augustine, *Coop.* 101 n., 1 *Whitg.* 228, 2 *Whitg.* 581 n.; in early Christian writings the word sabbath means Saturday, *Whita.* 569, 573; the sabbath turned into Sunday, *q. v.*; the commandment expounded with reference to holydays, 1 *Tyn.* 24; the holy-day subservient to God's word, *ib.* 25, 26; the holy time said to be free, 2 *Bul.* 264; assertion that we may change the sabbath to Monday or any other day, as we see need; or, if necessary, make only every tenth day holy, or have two every week, 3 *Tyn.* 97; statement that Christian magistrates may appoint what day they will, 2 *Bec.* 82; assertion that it pertaineth nothing to salvation; and the magistrate or the church (says Curio) may appoint any other day for prayers to God, and to receive his doctrine and sacraments, *Phil.* 379; the term sabbath applied to the Lord's day, 2 *Bec.* 82, &c., 1 *Bul.* 259, &c., *Calf.* 269, 271, 1 *Hoop.* 342, 2 *Hoop.* 136, 137, 1 *Lat.* 473, *Lit. Eliz.* 573, *Park.* 189, *Poet.* 2, 276, 2 *Whitg.* 579, 580, &c., 3 *Whitg.* 610; "the first day of the week" (Acts xx. 7), is so called in a treatise dubiously ascribed to Tyndale, 3 *Tyn.* 264; Sunday so designated by Harpsfield, chaplain to Bonner, *Phil.* 93; profanation of the sabbath in this sense, 1 *Brad.* 55, 60, 1 *Bul.* 262, 1 *Lat.* 472, *Lit. Eliz.* 573, *Nord.* 177, *Poet.* 375, by games, &c., *Grin.* 176 n., 215; by bear-baiting, and the like, *Lit. Eliz.* 574, *Nord.* 177; alehouse more frequented on this day than churches, *Pil.* 6; judgment for bear-baiting on it, 1 *Brad.* 31; the sabbath (or Lord's day) is God's ploughing day, 1 *Lat.* 473; the sabbath is a type of rest to come, 1 *Hoop.* 339; the sabbath at the end of the world, *Bale* 449, 450; the eternal sabbath, *ib.* 581, 587, 622

Sabellians: deny the Trinity, *Rog.* 202; their heresy on the persons in the Godhead, *Hutch.* 121, 143; refuted by the text, "I and My Father ARE one," *Whita.* 482

Sabellicus (Marc. Ant.): Opera, *Jew.* xlii; Rapsod. Hist., *ib.*; says Andrew suffered in Scythia, *Calf.* 128; referred to about early persecutions, 1 *Lat.* 129; he says Liberius was an Arian, 3 *Jew.* 127, 342, 343; writes of Boniface III., 1 *Jew.* 363; tells of the grant of the emperor Phocas to the church of Rome in his time, 4 *Jew.* 733; says, the Greeks claimed the dignity (now claimed by the pope), 3 *Jew.* 278; writes of pope Joan, 4 *Jew.* 650, 655, 656, 688; mentions the disinterment of pope Formosus,

3 *Jew.* 276, 277; records tragic acts of John XII., *ib.* 250; notices the conduct of pope Hildebrand to the emperor Henry IV., *ib.* 346, 4 *Jew.* 965; relates that of Boniface VIII. towards Philip, king of France, 4 *Jew.* 685; mentions the temporary removal of the papal court to Avignon, *ib.* 933, 936; states how Clement V. treated F. Dandalus, *ib.* 692, 696, 931; says Urban IV. took five of his cardinals, tied them up in sacks, and threw them into the sea, *ib.* 931; speaks of evil deeds of Urban VI., 3 *Jew,* 250; referred to, 2 *Cran.* 50, 1 *Hoop.* v, 4 *Jew.* 835, 934; mistake of Jewel in regard to his works, 3 *Jew.* 147, 4 *Jew.* 693 n

Sabellius: his heresy, 1 *Bec.* 278, 3 *Bec.* 401, 3 *Bul.* 156, 1 *Cran.* 63, 67, 278, 1 *Hoop.* 161, *Hutch.* 121 n., 132 n., *Phil.* 382 n., 423; said he was Moses, and that his brother was Aaron, *Phil.* 422

Sabie (Fra.): notice of him, *Poet.* xxxvi; stanzas from David's Ode, *ib.* 393

Sabinian, pope: would have burned all Gregory his predecessor's books, 1 *Jew.* 532, 3 *Jew.* 276

Sabinus, king of the Bulgarians: condemned and abolished image-worship, 2 *Bec.* 71

Sabinus, a bp in Spain: mentioned by Cyprian, 1 *Ful.* 40 n., 3 *Jew.* 331

Saccas (Ammonius): v. Ammonius.

Sacellani: 4 *Bul.* 116

Sacerdotale: a false epistle adduced therein, *Calf* 16 n.; benediction against birds, worms, &c., *ib.* 17 n

Sacerdotale Novum: what is said therein of Mary, *Whita.* 579

Sackcloth: 1 *Hoop.* 538

Sackville (Tho.), lord Buckhurst, afterwards earl of Dorset: the queen dines with him, *Park.* 219; at the duke of Norfolk's trial, 1 *Zur.* 267 n.; his writings, *Now.* viii.

Sackville (Sir Rich.): privy councillor to Mary and Elizabeth, *Park.* 171 n., 1 *Zur.* 5 n.; mourner at the funeral of the emperor Ferdinand, *Grin.* 33; he obtains a lease of Charing, *Park.* 372; his physic, *Grin.* 281

Sackville (Edw.*): signature as privy councillor, *Park.* 103, 117, 122

Sacrament of the Altar: v. Mass, Supper of the Lord.

Sacramentaries: a term of reproach used by Romanists, 1 *Jew.* 85, 465; applied to those who affirm transubstantiation, *Rid.* 175; a sect, 2 *Jew.* 686; divided into eight sects, *ib.*

Sacraments: see their names; also Ceremonies, Signs.

i. *What sacraments are, properly and otherwise;* meaning and diverse uses of the word, 4 *Bul.* 248, 1 *Cran.* 3, 1 *Ful.* 493 —496, 2 *Hoop.* 45, *Now.* (103); translations concerning the sacraments examined, 1 *Ful.* 450, &c.; μυστήριον never used in scripture for what we call a sacrament, *Whita.* 197; Paul applies the word μυστήριον, or "sacramentum," to marriage, to the preaching of the gospel to the Gentiles, and to the incarnation of Christ, 2 *Cran.* 115, 2 *Ful.* 229; "sacramentum" is sometimes taken for an oath, 4 *Bul.* 235; it is used in several places in the Vulgate for "mystery," *Calf.* 236; on the limited ecclesiastical meaning of the word, *Phil.* 407; what sacraments are, 2 *Bec.* 109, 3 *Bec.* 612, 616, 4 *Bul.* 233, 234, 240, 2 *Cran.* 115, 2 *Hoop.* 88, *Hutch.* 236, 2 *Jew.* 1099, 3 *Jew.* 442, &c., *Lit. Edw.* 516, (563), *Now.* (83, 84), 205, *Rid.* 239; definitions of the term by the fathers, 1 *Brad.* 87; the outward form was never called a sacrament by them, 2 *Jew.* 758, 796; definitions by Augustine, see p. 66, col. 2; a sacrament defined in the Canon Law as a holy sign, 2 *Jew.* 591; the schoolmen's definition, *Rog.* 250; A BRIEF DECLARATION OF THE SACRAMENTS, by W. Tyndale, 1 *Tyn.* 345, &c.; a treatise of the sacraments, gathered out of sermons preached by Jewel at Salisbury, 2 *Jew.* 1099, &c.; questions and answers concerning them, 2 *Cran.* 115; an article de sacramentorum usu, *ib.* 477; they are holy, and not profane things, 4 *Bul.* 314; badges or tokens of our Christian profession, *Rog.* 245, 246; not sacrifices, *Hutch.* 49; not confirmations of our obedience to God hereafter, but of his grace to us, 2 *Hoop.* 89; sacraments called by various names by the fathers, *ib.* 405; they are called mysteries, 4 *Bul.* 237, antitypes, 2 *Hoop.* 406, symbols, 4 *Bul.* 238, signs (see below), visible words, *ib.* 317, *Wool.* 22; all signs are not sacraments, 2 *Whitg.* 66; mere similitudes are not properly speaking sacraments, *Hutch.* 236, 1 *Tyn.* 254; many things improperly so called, 4 *Bul.* 247, *Calf.* 215, 2 *Cran.* 115, 2 *Jew.* 1103; as the washing of feet, by Ambrose and Bernard, 2 *Cran.* 79, 1 *Jew.* 223, 225, 2 *Jew.* 1103; the cross of Christ, by Leo, 2 *Jew.* 1103; the scriptures, by Hilary, *ib.*; Christian religion, by Tertul-

* Query?

SACRAMENTS

lian, *ib.*; prayer, by Hilary, 4 *Bul.* 247 n., 1 *Jew.* 225, 2 *Jew.* 1103; fasting, &c., by Hilary, 1 *Jew.* 225, 2 *Jew.* 1103; unction, orders, &c., by Augustine, 4 *Bul.* 247, *Calf.* 215; Calfhill allows that the term may be, in a sense, applied to the ordering of ministers, *Calf.* 229; wedlock, &c., so called, 2 *Tyn.* 91; one of the homilies of the church of England speaks of the sacrament of matrimony, 2 *Ful.* 168 n.; the name of Christian is as it were a sacrament, *Wool.* 20, 22; the forgiveness of such as offend against us is, as it were, a sacrament to assure us of the pardon of our sins, 1 *Brad.* 133, *Pra. B.* 31; good works are, as it were, sacraments, being signs of God's work in us, 2 *Tyn.* 90; man's head is a sacrament of Christ, *Hutch.* 281; Jerome considers that the water and blood denoted the sacraments of baptism and martyrdom, 3 *Jew.* 457; repentance not a sacrament, 1 *Tyn.* 261; preaching not one, 1 *Ful.* 459; sacraments and sacramentals, 2 *Cran.* 499

ii. *How many there are:* they are few in number, *Pil.* 130; how many, 3 *Bec.* 616, 4 *Bul.* 246, 3 *Jew.* 455, &c., *Now.* (85), 207; difference of opinions as to their number stands rather in terms than in the matter, 2 *Jew.* 1102; there are properly but two, 2 *Bec.* 199, 1 *Brad.* 82, 4 *Bul.* 246, 2 *Hoop.* 45, 88, 127, *Sand.* 87; two only were ordained by Christ, 1 *Cov.* 79, 2 *Jew.* 1103, *Rog.* 250; only two are mentioned by Tertullian, Ambrose, and Augustine, 2 *Bul.* 246, *Calf.* 223, 2 *Jew.* 1103 (the latter, however, sometimes uses the term in a wider sense; see above); no man ought to invent more, 2 *Hoop.* 127; ancient writers never speak of "seven sacraments," though, using the term in a wide sense, they speak of many more than seven, 2 *Cran.* 115; seven sacraments asserted by Romanists, 2 *Bec.* 199, *Pil.* 484, 522, 524, 553, *Rog.* 252; they attempt to prove them by tradition, *Whita.* 500; they were first mentioned (it is said) by Peter Lombard, *Calf.* 237 n.; first authoritatively asserted by the council of Florence, *Whita.* 512; remarks on the seven reputed sacraments, 2 *Jew.* 1124, &c., 3 *Jew.* 458, 1 *Tyn.* 252—286; they are five more than the word of God allows, 3 *Bec.* 524, 618, 2 *Ful.* 233; they are all celebrated with the sign of the cross, *Calf.* 210—248; some Papists reckon seven sacraments of orders, therefore thirteen in all, *Rog.* 259; P. Lombard calls the seven orders sacraments, *Calf.* 228; the Institution reckons seven sacraments, but asserts that baptism, penance, and that of the altar, are of superior dignity, 2 *Cran.* 99; some (say Romanists) are standing, as orders, others transitory, as baptism, (i. e. the water), 1 *Brad.* 533, 534; they who affirm matrimony and orders to be sacraments, teach that one sacrament defileth another, 3 *Tyn.* 29

iii. *Their parts; the sign, and the thing signified:* in what sacraments consist, 2 *Bec.* 199, 3 *Bec.* 616, 4 *Bul.* 249, 278, 3 *Whitg.* 129, 130; their essential parts are found in scripture, *Whita.* 538; each of them consists of the word and of the element, 2 *Bec.* 270; or the word and the rite, 4 *Bul.* 251; or the promise and the ceremony, *ib.* 252; or the sign and the thing signified, *ib.* 250; the sign and the thing signified, retain their several natures, *ib.* 270; how they are joined together, *ib.* 281; they are joined in signification, but not inseparably linked in any other manner, *ib.* 278; sacraments must have outward elements, 1 *Ful.* 459; they are signs, representing things, 4 *Bul.* 233, 250, &c., 327, 1 *Tyn.* 357, 2 *Tyn.* 216; analogous to the signs of covenants amongst the Jews, 1 *Tyn.* 347, &c.; signs of God's promises, *ib.* 252, 409; not bare signs, see viii, below; the nature of signs illustrated by the banners of an army, 1 *Hoop.* 195; by the keys of a city, *ib.*; by the ringing of bells, *ib.* 197; by the crowing of a cock, *ib.*; sacraments are as visible words offered to the senses, *ib.* 513; we are not to look at the things which are seen, but at those not seen, 2 *Jew.* 569; analogy of the sign and thing signified, 4 *Bul.* 244, 280; the former must bear a resemblance to the latter, 2 *Jew.* 780; where there is no signification, there is no sacrament, 3 *Tyn.* 30, 175, 176; sacraments are spoken of sacramentally, 1 *Hoop.* 62, 528; the signs are commonly called by the names of the things signified, 2 *Bec.* 283, 290, 297, 1 *Brad.* 87, *Coop.* 203, 1 *Cran.* 335, 2 *Hoop.* 495, 531, 3 *Tyn.* 247; sacramental speeches, and how they are to be expounded, 4 *Bul.* 283, &c.; the sacraments of the old testament were not the things which they were called, 1 *Hoop.* 403

iv. *The Sacraments of the old testament:* the sacraments of the old testament and those of the new; in what respects alike, and in what different, 2 *Bec.* 201, 202, 217, 4 *Bul.* 298, 1 *Cran.* 75, 1 *Hoop.* 126, 190, 200, 2 *Hoop.* 50, 88, 520, *Hutch.* 41, 218, 250, 2 *Jew.* 610, 613, 3 *Jew.* 447, 1 *Tyn.* 350, 3 *Tyn.* 245, &c., *Whita.* 408; all the ceremonies, ornaments, and sacrifices of the old testament were sacraments, 3 *Tyn.* 64, 82; the tree of life (e. g.) was a sacrament to Adam, *Rog.* 251; Noah's ark, &c., termed sacraments, 2 *Whitg.* 497; the rainbow was a sacrament to Noah, *Rog.* 251, 3 *Tyn.* 27; Christ to come was eaten in sacraments by the ancient fathers, 1 *Hoop.* 127; of the sacraments of the Jews, especially circumcision and the passover, 2 *Bul.* 167, &c., *Rog.* 251; there were two kinds of sacraments,—standing ordinances, as circumcision and the passover; and signs extraordinary, as the bow in the clouds, 1 *Hoop.* 198; in the latter sense the brasen serpent was a sacrament, 1 *Jew.* 5; those of the old testament are abrogated, 2 *Bul.* 269, *Hutch.* 218; Christian sacraments succeed them, 1 *Tyn.* 350; of arguments from the sacraments of the old testament to ours of the new, 4 *Bul.* 289

v. *The institution and purpose of sacraments:* by whom ordained, 1 *Cov.* 79, 2 *Jew.* 1100; God the only author of them, 4 *Bul.* 239; why ordained, 2 *Bec.* 199, 200, 201, 4 *Bul.* 239, &c., 352, 1 *Cov.* 79, &c., 1 *Cran.* 41, 2 *Jew.* 1100, *Now.* (83, 84), 205; they are given because of our weakness, 2 *Tyn.* 90; because we are in the body, 2 *Jew.* 1101; the need we have of them, 2 *Bec.* 201; to what end they serve, 3 *Bul.* 32, 4 *Bul.* 316, 1 *Hoop.* 133; what it availeth to have them, *ib.* 530; they visibly gather together into one religion, and distinguish from others, 4 *Bul.* 332, 1 *Jew.* 131, 2 *Jew.* 1100; it was the will of Christ through the word and sacraments to gather his church together, 1 *Cov.* 80; he ordained them, that his people might be associated together in the unity of faith, 1 *Cov.* 345

vi. *Administration of them:* the form and manner of celebrating them, 1 *Hoop.* 533; the manner of observance to be decided by the word of God, *ib.* 213; they should be administered only as God commandeth, *ib.* 236; the right administration and use of them is a mark of the church, 4 *Bul.* 17—19, 2 *Hoop.* 43, 88, *Rog.* 174; their ministration according to the Common Prayer not schismatical, *Pil.* 623, &c.; of power to administer them, 4 *Bul.* 45; to whom their ministration properly belongeth, *Now.* (94), 217; they are not to be administered by women, 1 *Hoop.* 133; they should not be administered in the congregation but by a lawful minister, *Rid.* 321, *Rog.* 234; yet the being of the sacraments depends not on this point, *ib.*; on their administration by other than regular ministers, 2 *Whitg.* 519; on their ministration in private, *ib.* 508, 3 *Whitg.* 546; of preaching before their administration, 3 *Whitg.* 14, &c.; the administration of the word and sacraments should go together, 2 *Whitg.* 497; how they are consecrated, 4 *Bul.* 269; they should not be ministered in a tongue not understood by the people, *Rog.* 241—243; their meaning and nature should not be hidden from the people, but explained, *Whita.* 252; objection against divulging them from the pseudo-Dionysius answered, *ib.* 253; sacraments which preach not, profit not, 1 *Tyn.* 423; the effect of sacraments is not hindered by the badness of ministers, *Rog.* 269—272, 2 *Whitg.* 525

vii. *The right use of them and their abuse:* those who are moved by the Holy Spirit do not despise the outward sacraments, 1 *Cov.* 411; how they are to be contemplated, 1 *Cran.* 366; they are necessary to believers, *Bale* 22, 4 *Bul.* 345; they are to be received as at the hands of Christ, *ib.* 240; they are easy to be kept and most august and excellent, 2 *Hoop.* 124; who should be admitted to them, *Now.* (95), 217; without their use there are no sacraments, *Phil.* 67, 68, 95; they are sacraments only so long as rightly used, 1 *Brad.* 372; how they are to be used, 4 *Bul.* 21, 2 *Hoop.* 124, *Rog.* 264; they must be used with faith, 1 *Cov.* 80, (see viii, below); by whom they are used devoutly and reverently, *ib.* 411; the opinion that their true use is not to be understood by the unlearned, is false, 1 *Hoop.* 214; every man is bound to know it, *ib.* 216; this true use is to be known by scripture, *ib.* 218; how they are sanctified, 2 *Hoop.* 406; reverence is to be used in disputing of them, 4 *Bul.* 294; they are not to be abused but rightly used of us all, *Rog.* 264; though we condemn the abuse of sacraments, we must not contemn them, 1 *Bul.* 175; when not rightly used they are abhorred by God, 1 *Hoop.* 146; to abuse them is a breach of the fourth commandment, *ib.* 345; they ought not to be reserved, nor to be worshipped, 2 *Hoop.* 125, nor to be gazed upon, *ib.* 124; by abuses they are made idolatry, 2 *Tyn.* 217, 3 *Tyn.* 175; they are abused by the Papists, 1 *Bec.* 11, 2 *Tyn.* 143, who have defiled them with a multitude of superstitious ceremonies, 1 *Jew.* 138; Fulke says they have but one sacrament at the most, and that horribly profaned, 2 *Ful.* 242; the mass is no sacrament, *Phil.* 92; God's sacrament and the pope's, 1 *Tyn.* 273; Christ's and Antichrist's, *ib.*

283; those who are partakers of unlawful sacraments are members of the devil, 4 *Bul.* 338

viii. *The grace of sacraments :* too much not to be attributed to them, nor too little, 4 *Bul.* 294, 2 *Hoop.* 441; to add too much to them or to take from them, is sacrilege, 1 *Hoop.* 399; too much is added to them when as much is attributed to them as to the grace and promise that they confirm, *ib.*; they are not to have Christ's office given to them, *ib.* 76; nor are they to be honoured for the things they represent, *ib.* 208; not to attribute to them what scripture attributes to them, is a sin, 4 *Bul.* 295; they are not merely naked signs, 1 *Brad.* 92, 1 *Hoop.* 399, 2 *Hoop.* 45, 88, 127, 1 *Jew.* 448; but also seals, &c., 1 *Bec.* 12, 4 *Bul.* 240, 318, 1 *Ful.* 450—452, 1 *Hoop.* 194, 2 *Hoop.* 88, *Hutch.* 251, 252, *Pil.* 192, *Sand.* 303; they may be compared to the titledeeds of an estate, *Coop.* 213; they have a more effectual force than any sealed charter, 4 *Bul.* 321; but they seal nothing to unbelievers, *ib.* 327; Christ is present in them, 1 *Cran.* 11; they are witnesses and signs of grace and God's good will towards us, 2 *Bul.* 240, 317, 1 *Hoop.* 211, 2 *Hoop.* 125, *Rog.* 247, 248; witnesses to God's promise, 1 *Hoop.* 136; visible evidences of his promise and grace, 1 *Cov.* 411; witnesses of the truth, 4 *Bul.* 316; grace is more abundant in our sacraments than in those of the law, 1 *Ful.* 450; grace is offered by them, *Sand.* 302; they depend not on our worthiness or unworthiness, 4 *Bul.* 342; they strengthen and confirm faith, *ib.* 327, 331, 1 *Cran.* 41, 1 *Ful.* 450—452, 2 *Ful.* 169, *Now.* (94), 217, *Rog.* 248—250; they are aids to the spiritual memory, 2 *Hoop.* 462; they put the faithful in mind of their duty, 4 *Bul.* 339; certify them of immortality, and life everlasting, 1 *Cran.* 161; how grace is received by them, *Sand.* 304; of themselves they give not grace, 2 *Bec.* 218, &c., 2 *Brad.* 403, &c., 4 *Bul.* 202, 296, *Calf.* 73, 1 *Hoop.* 127, 208, 2 *Hoop.* 125, 406, 3 *Tyn.* 172, 3 *Whitg.* 382; probations out of the old fathers that the sacraments of the new law do not confer grace, but set forth the things which God gives to the faithful, 3 *Bec.* 466, &c.; they confer not grace ex opere operato, *Bale* 159, 2 *Brad.* 278, 2 *Cov.* 257, 1 *Ful.* 450, 2 *Hoop.* 125, 2 *Jew.* 749, &c., *Rog.* 247, 248, 250, 268; the work of the sacraments saveth not, but faith in the promises signified by the sacraments, 1 *Tyn.* 342, 423, 2 *Tyn.* 90, 103; they are not made effectual by the words spoken, 4 *Bul.* 259; the grace not to be ascribed to the outward elements, 1 *Cov.* 345; there is no promise made to the mere symbol, *Rid.* 240; the grace of God is not contained in them, 4 *Bul.* 305, 310; they signify God's grace, but do not contain it, as a vessel contains water, 2 *Jew.* 781; grace is given by a sacrament, only as by an instrument, *Rid.* 239—241; they profit nothing without faith, 4 *Bul.* 327, 340, 1 *Cov.* 411, 1 *Hoop.* 134, 135, 146, 200, 2 *Jew.* 1101; without faith they are hurtful, 3 *Jew.* 445; they do but increase the damnation of the unbelieving, 1 *Tyn.* 358; their recipients receive not always the thing signified, 4 *Bul.* 271, *Rog.* 267; affinity of sacraments with the word of God; as the latter may be heard without profit, so the former may be received without profit, 4 *Bul.* 272; to some they are as a book to one who cannot read, 2 *Jew.* 1101; they cannot join those to Christ who were not joined to him before, 1 *Jew.* 133; the godly are justified and accepted before they be made partakers of them, 4 *Bul.* 311; in what way they are necessary, and in what way not necessary, 2 *Hoop.* 122; faith and salvation not tied to sacraments, *Rog.* 249, *Whita.* 530; God is not bound to them, *Hutch.* 108; they are only "generally necessary to salvation," 1 *Tyn.* 359, 369; some receive them not, and yet are partakers of the things signified, *Rog.* 267; many are sanctified without visible sacraments, 4 *Bul.* 347; they are not to be thought indifferent or unnecessary, *ib.* 346, *Now.* (85), 206; they are not made void by the reformed, 4 *Bul.* 313

Sacre: to consecrate, *Pil.* 572 n (*v.* Sacring).

Sacrifice, Sacrifices :

i. *In general* (v. Altars, Priests) : sacrifices have been usual in all ages, *Sand.* 410; what offered by Aaron, what by Christ, and what by us, *ib.* 411, &c.; sacrifices are of two sorts—of expiation, and of confession, 4 *Bul.* 432, 433, or propitiatory, and eucharistic, 2 *Hoop.* 521; four kinds noted; propitiatory, penitential, eucharistic, and the consecration of ourselves, *ib.* 523, &c.; the distinction of bloody and unbloody sacrifices, 2 *Jew.* 733, 734, &c., *Rid.* 210; propitiatory sacrifice, what, 2 *Hoop.* 516; there is none without shedding of blood, *ib.* 506, 508, 509, 516, 1 *Lat.* 73, 74; unbloody sacrifices are eucharistic, 2 *Hoop.* 517; propitiatory sacrifice must not only be pure, but also be offered by one free from sin, *ib.* 503, 504, 506; God is not propitiated by man's sacrifice, *ib.* 526, &c.; no sacrifice is acceptable where there is not the love of our neighbour, 2 *Tyn.* 48; there can be no sacrifice without a priest, *Sand.* 411; it is to be offered to God only, 3 *Bec.* 265

ii. *Those of the Patriarchs:* the beginning of sacrifices, 2 *Bul.* 186, 1 *Cov.* 27, 3 *Tyn.* 27; those of the old fathers were figures of the sacrifice of Christ, figures of things to come, 1 *Cov.* 28; were signs of the testament, 3 *Tyn.* 27; they were used by the patriarchs in faith, 1 *Lat.* 236; that of Abel considered, 1 *Cov.* 27, 28, 2 *Hoop.* 325 n.; the offering of Melchisedec, *q. v.*; Abraham's sacrifice of Isaac mystically expounded, *Phil.* 257

iii. *Those of the Law* (v. Passover): commanded to the Jewish priests, 2 *Bul.* 141; not lawful without the temple, 4 *Bul.* 75; offered on altars, *Pil.* 547; they have some things common, and some things peculiar, 2 *Bul.* 187; why they were called "sin," 4 *Bul.* 281, 441; they were not really propitiatory, but only ceremonially so, 1 *Cran.* 347, 2 *Hoop.* 511, 3 *Tyn.* 65, or capable of obtaining remission of sins, 1 *Bec.* 49; but they were sacraments, and preached unto the people, 3 *Tyn.* 82; their meaning, 2 *Tyn.* 215; they could not take away sins, but signified the sacrifice of Christ to come, 1 *Cran.* 347; they were figures, or shadows, of the true and everlasting sacrifice of Jesus Christ, 2 *Jew.* 708, *Lit. Ed.* 500, (549), *Pil.* 546; the burnt-offering, or holocaust, 2 *Bul.* 189; the altar thereof, *ib.* 158; the daily sacrifices, *ib.* 190; the sin offerings, *ib.* 193; the yearly atonement, *ib.* 194; the sacrifice of the red cow, 2 *Bul.* 201, 4 *Bul.* 281; other cleansing sacrifices, 2 *Bul.* 203; that of jealousy, *ib.*; sacrifices of thanksgiving, *ib.*; free-will offerings, *ib.* 205; the meat offering, *ib.* 191; the drink offering, *ib.* 192; Jewish and all carnal sacrifices were accomplished and taken away by Christ's sacrifice, *ib.* 269, 1 *Ful.* 241, 277, *Hutch.* 46

iv. *That of Christ* (v. Christ, iii): the death of Christ is the alone sacrifice for sin, 3 *Bec.* 265, 1 *Cran.* 345, 346; there is but one propitiatory sacrifice, viz. that of Christ once offered, and never to be repeated, 1 *Cran.* 344, 2 *Hoop.* 32, 123, 500, 501, 523, 1 *Lat.* 73, 74, *Rid.* 207—211, 275, 1 *Tyn.* 370; his priesthood is ἀπαράβατον (Heb. vii); his sacrifice, therefore, cannot be offered by another, 2 *Bul.* 195, 2 *Ful.* 245, 2 *Hoop.* 501, 502, 508; its effect is both to give and to continue life, 1 *Cran.* 364; its virtue never ceases, 1 *Bec.* 53; our salvation is the fruit thereof, 2 *Hoop.* 502

v. *Spiritual and Christian sacrifices* (v. Priests, Supper): what kind God requires, 1 *Bec.* 97; the sacrifices of God, as described by Prudentius, 3 *Bul.* 226; what kind we have to offer, 1 *Cran.* 346, 349, 1 *Lat.* 74, *Rid.* 211, *Sand.* 412; what offerings are acceptable, 1 *Tyn.* 433; spiritual sacrifices, 1 *Cran.* 349, 2 *Ful.* 243; such are prayer, fasting, and alms, 1 *Bec.* 138; that of a broken spirit, sighs, tears, &c., 3 *Bec.* 246, 2 *Hoop.* 524; the sacrifices of righteousness, *Sand.* 403, &c.; prayer that we may offer them, *ib.* 416; the sacrifice of praise and thanksgiving, 1 *Bec.* 298, 299, *Coop.* 87, 2 *Ful.* 245, 2 *Hoop.* 525, 1 *Lat.* 445, *Now.* 224; "the calves of our lips," 1 *Brad.* 23; the sacrifice of praise is acknowledged even in the canon of the mass, 2 *Jew.* 737; it is acceptable to God, 1 *Bec.* 298; the sacrifice of ourselves and all we have, 2 *Hoop.* 526, *Sand.* 413, &c.; all the works that Christian people do to the glory of God, are sacrifices of the church, 1 *Cran.* 88, 346; the sacrifice of the minister, *Sand.* 412, of the magistrate, *ib.*; what kind the death of martyrs is, 2 *Hoop.* 517; distinction between sacrifices propitiatory and gratificatory, 1 *Cran.* 361; the sacrifice of the church is gratulatory; that for the church, propitiatory, 1 *Brad.* 513; we have no propitiatory sacrifice to offer, 2 *Lat.* 275, 292; Latimer shews that Christ made no sacrifice in his last supper, *Rid.* 111, 112; the papistical doctrine of a daily expiatory sacrifice confuted, 1 *Cran.* 344, &c., 1 *Lat.* 73, 2 *Lat.* 251; of the sacrifice, i. e. of the priests' supposed authority to offer up Christ to his Father, 2 *Jew.* 708, &c.; against the sacrifice of the mass, 2 *Hoop.* (500, &c.); Gardiner asserts that the mass, as well as all good works, is propitiatory, 1 *Cran.* 360; but denies that the daily sacrifice of Christ's body and blood is an iteration of the sacrifice on the cross, *ib.*; the mass styled an unbloody sacrifice, 1 *Cran.* 364, *Rid.* 211, 276; papists have made a new sacrifice, 3 *Bec.* 265; in what sense the eucharist has been and may be called a sacrifice, 2 *Ful.* 245, 2 *Hoop.* 528, 529, 1 *Tyn.* 371; it is indeed no sacrifice, but the memorial of a sacrifice, 3 *Tyn.* 177; in what sense the term "sacrifice" is used by the old fathers, 1 *Ful.* 270, 1 *Jew.* 171, 2 *Jew.* 709, 1 *Lat.* 167, 1 *Tyn.* 371; by the phrase "daily sacrifice" they meant Christ's sacrifice, which lasts for ever, 1 *Jew.* 128, 129,

167; what they meant by "unbloody sacrifice," 2 *Jew.* 733, 734, &c.; none of them ever taught that "Hoc facite" was "Hoc sacrificate," *ib.* 990; they applied the name of sacrifice to prayer, thanksgiving, and every good work, *Coop.* 91; the Christian sacrifice is one in all places, *Rid.* 216; the "clean-offering" foretold by Malachi, 2 *Ful.* 381, *Hutch.* 46, 47, 1 *Jew.* 110, 2 *Jew.* 712, 713, 722, &c., *Phil.* 408

vi. *Those of the Gentiles:* derived from the patriarchs by tradition, 2 *Bul.* 187; unbloody sacrifices to Fides and Terminus, 2 *Jew.* 734; bread and wine offered to devils, 2 *Whitg.* 39; human sacrifices, 2 *Jew.* 734

Sacrilege: the spoils of heathen temples not to be devoted to private use, 2 *Whitg.* 31, &c.; sacrilege caused by the covetousness of the clergy, *Sand.* 243; robbery of church-livings, *ib.* 155; the spoil of colleges, churches, &c., 3 *Whitg.* 581; the sacrilege of Henry VIII., *ib.* xv; sacrilege charged on Protestants, 2 *Ful.* 122, 123; lamented, *Hutch.* 4; deprecated, *Sand.* 97; condemned, 2 *Bul.* 44, 230, 1 *Hoop.* 395; rebuked by Jewel, *Jew.* xvii; robbery of the church thought a pastime, *Pil.* 466; church goods not to be taken away, *ib.* 61; church robbers under the name of church visitors, *Sand.* 122; Whitgift's remonstrance to queen Elizabeth, 3 *Whitg.* xiii—xv; sacrilege punished by God, 2 *Ful.* 114

Sacring: the elevation of the host, 1 *Brad.* 160 n., 2 *Brad.* 314, 1 *Cran.* 229, 2 *Jew.* 846 n.; the worst part of the mass, 3 *Bec.* 270; the second sacring, *ib.* 277; ringing to sacry, *ib.* 266; sacring bells, *Bale* 91, 1 *Brad.* 160 n.; forbidden, *Grin.* 135, 159, 2 *Hoop.* 128, *Rid.* 319

Sad: grave, 3 *Bec.* 375, 1 *Jew.* 528, 3 *Tyn.* 19; firm, solid, *Pil.* 418

Sadducees: Tyndale's derivation of their name, 3 *Tyn.* 107; they held free-will, *Rog.* 105; denied angels and devils, 3 *Bul.* 348; looked only for temporal blessings, *Rog.* 88; denied the resurrection, *Hutch.* 138, *Rog.* 64; it is said that they received only the five books of Moses, *Rog.* 80, *Whita.* 30; certain English Sadducees taught that the Holy Ghost is merely an inspiration, *Hutch.* 135, *Rog.* 72; denied spirits to be substances, i.e. distinct persons, *Hutch.* 134; explained away the resurrection, heaven, and hell, *Hutch.* 138

Sadeel (A. C.): De Legit. Vocat. Past. Eccl. Ref., *Rog.* 329 n

Sadler (Sir Ralph): his correspondence, 2 *Cran.* 360 n., 1 *Lat.* 164 n., 1 *Zur.* 57 n., 2 *Zur.* 34 n.; a privy councillor, *Hutch.* v. n., *Park.* 357; a commander in the army against the rebels in the North, 1 *Zur.* 247 n.; supposed to be a supporter of the Puritans, *Park.* 428

Sadly: gravely, 3 *Jew.* 344

Sadness: gravity, 2 *Bec.* 334, 2 *Bul.* 51

Sadoc: founder of the Sadducees, 3 *Tyn.* 107 n

Sadoletus (James card.) bp of Carpentras: 2 *Cran.* 331

Saenz (Jos.): *v.* Aguirre.

Safe-conduct: of the pope, not to be relied on, 4 *Jew.* 953, &c.

Saffron-bag: 2 *Cov.* 347, 350, 1 *Lat.* 60

Saffron-Walden: *v.* Walden.

Sage (Jo.), bp: *Calf.* 52 n

Saguntum: besieged, *Pil.* 456; the Saguntines died rather than forswear themselves, 1 *Bul.* 252, 1 *Hoop.* 336

Sailors: *v.* Prayers.

In peril of death they confessed to the mast, 1 *Tyn.* 245

Sainctes (Claud. de): Liturgiæ SS. Patrum, *Jew.* xxxix, 1 *Jew.* 114, 3 *Jew.* 555

Sainsed: censed, incensed, *Calf.* 124

Saint-Alban's, co. Hertford: duke Humphrey's detection of a pretended miracle at St Alban's shrine, 2 *Tyn.* 298; story of the maid of St Albans, an impostor, 2 *Cran.* 65; the abbey held by Wolsey in commendam, 2 *Tyn.* 337 n.; Geo. Tankerfield, martyr there, *Poet.* 163; Tho. duke of Norfolk taken there; 2 *Zur.* 172 n.; Michaelmas term held there 1593, on account of the plague in London, *Lit. Eliz.* 471

Saint-Aldegonde (P. lord of Mont-): *v.* Marnix (P. de).

Saint-Amand: the barons, 2 *Lat.* 322 n

Saint-Andre, (M. le mareschal): ambassador from France, 3 *Zur.* 497 n

Saint-Andrew (Master): his labours at Frankfort, 3 *Zur.* 766

Saint-Andrew's, Scotland: why so named, 1 *Hoop.* 314 n.; assembly there, 2 *Zur.* 363

Saint-Andrew's (J. abp of): *v.* Hamilton.

Saint-Asaph, co. Flint.

Saint-Bee's, co. Cumberland: situated in Cowpland, *Grin.* 256; rights of the abbey, *ib.* 323; the birthplace of Grindal, *Grin.* i, *Sand.* xxix; he founds a free-school there, *Grin.* xv; leaves a chalice and Bible to the church, and money to the poor, *ib.* 460

Saint-Cher (H. de): *v.* Hugh.

Saint-Colme (...... lord): *v.* Stewart.

Saint-David's, co. Pembroke: the archiepiscopal pall taken away by Sampson, *Pil.* 583; bishop Bernard submits to the see of Canterbury, 3 *Tyn.* 158 n.; bp Barlow strips the cathedral of its leaden roof, 3 *Bec.* 501 n.; no old MSS. in the library there, *Park.* 265

Saint-George's-Fields: *v.* Lambeth.

Saint-Giles's-Fields: *v.* London.

Saint-John (Lords), of Basing: *v.* Paulet.

Saint-John (Oliver), 1st lord St John of Bletshoe: at the duke of Norfolk's trial, 1 *Zur.* 267 n.; his sister Margaret, 2 *Bec.* 622 n

Saint-Leger (Sir Ant.), K.G. : 2 *Cran.* 398; Agnes (Warham) his wife, *Park.* 113 n

Saint-Leger (Sir Warham): letter to him, *Park.* 113; notice of him, *ib.* n

Saint-Leger (Mr), prebendary of Canterbury, *Park.* 319

Saint-Loe (Sir Will.): Elizabeth (Hardwick) his wife, *Park.* 301 n

Saint-Pancras, Middx.: the prebend, *Rid.* 331 n.; Kentish-town (*q. v.*) is in this parish.

Saint Valeri, in Picardy: 3 *Tyn.* 124

Saint-Victor (H. de): *v.* Sancto Victore.

Saints: *v.* Christians; likewise All Saints, Canonization, Martyrs, Relics.

Christian men so called by Paul, 2 *Jew.* 1002; all faithful Christians are saints, 1 *Lat.* 507; why the faithful are so called, 2 *Bec.* 43; they do not neglect good means, 3 *Bul.* 181; must abstain from some things, 2 *Bul.* 278; their sins, *ib.* 74, 2 *Lat.* 163; the sins of saints extenuated by popish writers to the diminishing of the glory of God's mercy, 1 *Tyn.* 450; their good works, whether they be sins, 2 *Bul.* 419; why they are afflicted, *ib.* 69; they are persecuted by the wicked, *Pil.* 204; their cruel treatment, and their constancy under it, 4 *Jew.* 1172; in suffering the cross they feel no new miseries, 2 *Bul.* 102; their suffering is not for the redemption of others, 3 *Bul.* 95; their discommodities recompensed with commodities, 2 *Bul.* 99; saints of More's church, were not saints till they were dead, 3 *Tyn.* 131; that church makes some to be saints who were none at all, 1 *Tyn.* 291; some are shrined for holy saints whose deeds were abominable blasphemies, 2 *Tyn.* 174; departed saints see not down from heaven, 1 *Lat.* 332; they are not in heaven until the resurrection, 1 *Tyn.* lxiii, 3 *Tyn.* 118, 127, 180; opinion to the contrary, 2 *Hoop.* 63; we shall know them in heaven, 2 *Cov.* 223; the Romish church makes hirelings of the saints, 1 *Tyn.* 289; represents them as vindictive, *ib.* 453, 2 *Tyn.* 165; sells their merits, 1 *Tyn.* 74 n.; they could not stand on their own merits, 2 *Lat.* 193; those merits did not save themselves, much less can they save others, 1 *Tyn.* 271, 2 *Tyn.* 166, 167; prayers asking favours through their merits, and the like, *Rog.* 111, 227, 1 *Tyn.* 231, 290, 3 *Tyn.* 117 n.; of the worshipping of saints, 1 *Tyn.* 288—296, 2 *Tyn.* 163, &c.; translations concerning the honour of saints examined, 1 *Ful.* 526—538; an article de veneratione sanctorum, 2 *Cran.* 482; they are to be honoured, 2 *Hoop.* 35, 2 *Lat.* 232, 234; the right worship of them, 3 *Bul.* 230, 2 *Lat.* 88, 99, 359, 2 *Tyn.* 164, 166, 3 *Tyn.* 80; their monuments and volumes are to be reverenced, 2 *Hoop.* 180; saints unduly regarded, 1 *Tyn.* 184, 450; they were at the first commemorated without superstition, but afterwards made gods, *ib.* 231; made to succeed heathen deities, *Calf.* 19, 20; superstitious worship of them censured, 1 *Bec.* 134, 2 *Bec.* 144; such worship is contrary to their will and teaching, 3 *Bul.* 344, 1 *Tyn.* 289, and can only be a great offence to them, 3 *Tyn.* 279; it shews distrust of Christ, 2 *Tyn.* 211, 212; it is idolatry, *ib.* 164, 165, 216, 217, 3 *Tyn.* 81; superstitious observances in their honour, 2 *Tyn.* 216; offerings to them, *ib.* 163; honour is not to be given to them as to God, 2 *Bec.* 58, 59; arguments in behalf of saint-worship examined, 1 *Tyn.* 290—293, 3 *Tyn.* 79, 80, 116—131, 181; More's defence thereof, 3 *Tyn.* 79, 116—127, 181; saints chosen as protectors, 1 *Brad.* 284, 1 *Lat.* 225, 2 *Tyn.* 166, &c.; they are not to be looked to for protection, *Pil.* 92; against the doctrine of heavenly patrons, 3 *Bul.* 211; patrons of particular countries and places, 1 *Hoop.* 313, 3 *Jew.* 572; they are not our advocates or mediators, 2 *Tyn.* 166; on the doctrine that they are intercessors, 4 *Bul.* 172, 2 *Cran.* 93, 2 *Tyn.* 5; their intercession used frequently to be sought, 2 *Bec.* 414; their intercession, in some sort, allowed, 2 *Lat.* 234, 359; against trusting in their intercession, with sentences and examples of scripture, 1 *Bec.* 420, &c.; that they pray for us in heaven, is not to be proved by scripture, 3 *Bul.* 221; they cannot help us, 1 *Tyn.* 66, 3 *Tyn.* 117; their intercession is a dream of the Romanists, 3 *Bec.* 291, 292; vows to saints, 4 *Bul.* 517; as to prayer to them, see p. 625, col. 1, above; the Romish church divides saints departed into canonized and uncanonized; and More says that we may pray to the former, but not for them; and that we

SAINTS — SALVATION

may pray both to and for the latter, 3 *Tyn.* 121; he also says, that if we should thereby happen to worship a wicked man, that would not hurt us, *ib.* 122; lists of saints once invoked against various diseases and misfortunes, and for other purposes, *Bale* 348, 498, 1 *Bec.* 138, 139, 2 *Bec.* 536, *Calf.* 20, 1 *Hoop.* 457, *Hutch.* 171, 172, *Rog.* 226; the example of patriarchs, prophets, apostles, martyrs, &c., 2 *Lat.* 438; the example of the saints is to be followed, *Hutch.* 93, 2 *Lat.* 88; but only as they followed Christ, 1 *Lat.* 514; they are not to be followed in things which do not belong to our own vocation, *ib.* 516; Christ is to be followed in his saints, 1 *Cov.* 512; they are better remembered by writings than by days, *Pil.* 18 (*v.* Holy days); on their commemoration at the eucharist and otherwise, 2 *Ful.* 88; their images or pictures not to be painted in church windows, 2 *Hoop.* 138 (*v.* Images, Pictures); their emblems or symbols, *Bale* 523, 2 *Bec.* 65, 1 *Hoop.* 320; the Papists are themselves ashamed of their lying legends, 3 *Tyn.* 129; young saints, *Bale* 192; an imaginary saint called Synoris, 2 *Ful.* 44 n

Sala (Margaret de): married the landgrave of Hesse, his first wife living, 2 *Cran.* 405 n., 3 *Zur.* 666 n

Salamis: 4 *Bul.* 370

Salcot (Jo.), alias Capon, bp of Bangor, afterwards of Salisbury: notices of him, 2 *Cran.* 274, *Jew.* xvi, 3 *Jew.* 339, 1 *Lat.* 123 n.; referred to as "another learned man," 2 *Cran.* 66 (see the addenda); he signed a declaration respecting a general council, 2 *Cran.* 468

Salem: *v.* Jerusalem.

Salerno: an archbishop thereof, 2 *Cran.* 331

Salford, co. Oxon(?): an estate belonging to All Souls' college, *Park.* 320 n

Salicetus (Nic.), abbas: a prayer from his Antidotarium Animæ, *Pra. Eliz.* 545

Salied: danced, 1 *Bec.* 373

Salisbury: martyrs there, *Poet.* 166; Holkersheimer's account of his visit to Salisbury, 2 *Zur.* 85, &c.; queen Elizabeth there, *ib.* 258 n

The Cathedral: the spire injured by lightning, 4 *Jew.* xvi, 1233, 1 *Zur.* 78; the bishop's throne, 2 *Jew.* 557; the bishop's first-fruits to the pope, 4 *Jew.* 1079; Jewel elected bishop by the chapter, *Jew.* xv, 3 *Jew.* 334; a serving man prebendary there, *Park.* 176; Salisbury use, 2 *Cran.* 518, 523; invented by Osmund, the second bishop, *Pil.* 535 (*v.* Breviary, Horæ, Manuale, Missale, Primer); the Salisbury Martyrology, 2 *Lat.* 80 n.; the cathedral library, built by Jewel, replenished by Gheast, *Jew.* xxv; books there, 4 *Jew.* 1273

The Bishop's palace: described, 2 *Zur.* 86

Salisbury (Marg. countess of): *v.* Pole.

Salisbury (Rob. earl of): *v.* Cecil.

Salisbury (Jo. of): *v.* John.

Salisbury (Jo.): suffragan of Thetford, *Phil.* xxx; afterwards bishop of Sodor and Man, *Park.* 265 n

Salisbury (Tho. of): *v.* Thomas.

Salisbury (Will.): an antiquary, *Park.* 265 n., 271

Salkyns (Will.): servant of R. Hilles, 2 *Zur.* 17, 19, 22, 24, 74; two letters from him to Bullinger, 3 *Zur.* 345, 346

Sallet: a kind of helmet, 1 *Brad.* 348, *Calf.* 327, *Lit. Eliz.* 255

Sallust (C. C.): cited, 3 *Bec.* 598, 1 *Bul.* 278, 1 *Hoop.* 353, 1 *Jew.* 109, 2 *Jew.* 662, 4 *Jew.* 1068, *Wool.* 29

Sallust, a Roman prefect, *Pil.* 333

Salmeron (Alph.): says that Mary offered her Son to God, as Abraham offered Isaac, *Whita.* 164 n

Salmonicus: *v.* Serenus.

Salonius: says the "one pastor" of Eccles. xii. 11, is God, *Whita.* 422

Salt: *v.* Holy salt.

Made in Kent and Norfolk, *Park.* 258; the nature of it, 3 *Bec.* 290, 292; why it was ordered to accompany offerings, 1 *Tyn.* 433, 436, 439; used by Romanists in baptism, 4 *Bul.* 361; how our communication should be savoured with salt, 1 *Bec.* 366; the salt of the earth, what, 3 *Bec.* 290, 292, 2 *Tyn.* 31—33; not the Popish clergy, but all believers, 3 *Tyn.* 95; ministers are to be so, 3 *Bec.* 290, &c.; the corrupt cannot endure it, 2 *Tyn.* 31, &c.; what salt is to be trodden under foot, *ib.* 33

Saltmarsh (......): legacy to him, *Grin.* 462

Saltwood, co. Kent: the castle, *Bale* 69; the constable thereof, *ib.* 126

Salvart (......): 2 *Zur.* 298

Salvation: *v.* Grace, Justification, &c.

What it is, 3 *Bec.* 616; salvare, salvator, salvatio, meaning of the words, *Now.* (103); Cranmer's homily of salvation, 2 *Cran.* 128; salvation is the work of God, 1 *Tyn.* 498; the free gift of God, 2 *Lat.* 74, 140; it is entirely by grace, 1 *Bec.* 177, 2 *Brad.* 130, 1 *Cov.* 42, 1 *Ful.* 340, 1 *Tyn.* 466; yet a debt due, because of God's promise, 1 *Ful.* 341; the bye way and the right path to it, 2 *Lat.* 147; the way appointed by God himself, *Sand.* 221; it must be sought in

Christ alone, 3 *Tyn.* 109; Christ first promised to Adam is the beginning of it, 1 *Bec.* 50, 1 *Hoop.* 15; all things requisite to it are given in him, 3 *Bul.* 27; he alone is our salvation, *ib.* 29; he fully works the same, *ib.*; there is none but through Christ's death, 3 *Tyn.* 31; it is his free gift, 1 *Lat.* 420; it was not only promised to the fathers, but performed, 2 *Bul.* 288; it is by faith, 3 *Bul.* 34; by faith only, 1 *Tyn.* 15, 3 *Tyn.* 197; not by works or merit, 2 *Lat.* 73, *Wool.* 30; there is none without a special faith, 2 *Lat.* 10; many of our ancestors in times of darkness were saved by God's grace, 1 *Lat.* 305, 525; salvation is not tied to sacraments, *Rog.* 249, *Whita.* 530; things pertaining to salvation are given to all sorts of men alike, *Pil.* 124; how salvation is offered to all, 1 *Brad.* 67, 3 *Bul.* 32; wherefore all men are not saved, 3 *Bul.* 33; how salvation is nigh unto us, 1 *Tyn.* 281; how it is to be wrought out with fear and trembling, 3 *Jew.* 246; assurance of salvation, see p. 44, col. 1; the helmet of salvation, 1 *Lat.* 505; how salvation is nearer than it was, 2 *Hoop.* 114, 2 *Lat.* 3, *Sand.* 212; eternal salvation, what it is, 3 *Bul.* 28 (*v.* Heaven, Life everlasting); heresies respecting salvation, *Rog.* 160, 162, 163; some confound its effects with its cause, 2 *Brad.* 170; it is not by the profession of every religion, *Rog.* 159; but only by the name of Jesus Christ, *ib.* 161; there is no salvation out of the church, 2 *Bec.* 44, 3 *Bec.* 144, 4 *Bul.* 51, 2 *Cov.* 393, 2 *Lat.* 182, 279, 281, 282, *Now.* (57), 176, *Phil.* 16, 40; there are only two ways, that of salvation, and that of perdition, 1 *Cov.* 507; all men shall not be saved at the length (article of 1552), *Lit. Edw.* 537, (582)

Salve festa dies: reference to its music, 2 *Cran.* 412

Salve Regina: a blasphemous address, 3 *Tyn.* 184

Salvian: *Jew.* xlii; he says all human things need arguments and witnesses, but the word of God is its own witness, *Whita.* 357; says, under colour of religion men are made slaves to worldly vices, 3 *Jew.* 425

Samaria: the people of Samaria knew not God, *Hutch.* 13; they embraced only the law, *Rog.* 81; the disciples would have called down fire upon them, 4 *Bul.* 44; Samaria the type of heresies, 1 *Ful.* 215; the Samaritan alphabet, the ancient Hebrew, *Whita.* 116 (*v.* Thau).

Samaria, city: the siege and famine, *Pil.* 28

Samaritan (The Good): the parable explained, 1 *Bec.* 70, 1 *Ful.* 397, *Hutch.* 49, 1 *Tyn.* 85, 3 *Tyn.* 93; his gift, the "two pence," interpreted by some to mean the Old and New Testament, 1 *Tyn.* 86; so More explains it, and he considers the further sum to be tradition, 3 *Tyn.* 93 n

Samaritans: *v.* Samaria.

Samatius: feigned himself a fool for 30 years, *Hutch.* 87

Samford (Jo.), alderman of Gloucester: 2 *Brad.* 396, 397 n

Sammonicus: *v.* Serenus.

Samona: *Jew.* xlii; cited for transubstantiation, 2 *Jew.* 574

Samosaten: *v.* Paul of Samosata.

Sampson, last abp of St David's: took away the pall, and became bp of Dol in Britanny, *Pil.* 583

Sampson (Rich.), bp of Chichester: dean of the chapel to Henry VIII., 1 *Tyn.* 130; mentioned, 2 *Lat.* 295 n.; at Lambert's condemnation, 2 *Cran.* 218 n.; Latimer committed to his custody, 1 *Lat.* xi; he is sent to the Tower, *ib.* xi, 164; maintains the pope's supremacy, 3 *Zur.* 208; a letter signed by him, 2 *Cran.* 390

Sampson (Tho.): account of him, 1 *Brad.* 29 n.; a student of law, *ib.* 30 n.; surety for Bradford at the Temple, 2 *Brad.* xiii. n., and the means of his conversion, 1 *Brad.* 30, 2 *Brad.* xiii; a distributor of Chambers's bounty, 4 *Jew.* vii, 1302; a preacher, *Rid.* 337; dean of Chichester, 1 *Cran.* (9); an exile, *Rid.* 389, 394, 3 *Zur.* 753; at Frankfort, *Jew.* xii, 3 *Zur.* 755; he studies Hebrew, *Sand.* xvi; returned to England, 1 *Zur.* 69; P. Martyr writes to him on the vestments, &c., 2 *Zur.* 25, &c.; the bishoprick of Norwich is offered to him, but he declines it, 1 *Zur.* 75 n.; as dean of Christ church, Oxon, he sends to bishop Grindal a copy of certain injunctions delivered him by the lord keeper, *Grin.* 282; appointed to preach at the funeral of the duchess of Norfolk, but bp Parkhurst preached instead, 1 *Zur.* 137 n.; appointed to preach at Paul's cross, *Park.* 239; he refuses the habits, *Now.* ii, *Park.* 240; a conference to be held with him, *Park.* 233; he remains immovable, *ib.* 234; the earl of Huntingdon applies to Cecil that he may be set at liberty, *ib.* 243, 245; he writes to abp Parker, *ib.* 243; that prelate's clemency to him, *ib.* 244; his reply to his letter, *ib.*; he is deprived of his deanery, 1 *Zur.* 176, 2 *Zur.* 118 n., 162; afterwards made lecturer at Whittington college, 2 *Zur.* 118 n.;

connived at in his nonconformity as to habits, *Grin.* 205, 1 *Zur.* 202 n.; prebendary of St Paul's, 2 *Zur.* 118 n.; cited before the ecclesiastical commissioners, *Grin.* 326 n., *Park.* 382; was opposed to the more violent Puritans, 1 *Zur.* 292; master of Wigston's hospital at Leicester, 2 *Zur.* 118 n.; Bullinger's character of him, *ib.* 152; letters by him, *Park.* 243, 1 *Zur.* 1, 62, 75, 130, 153, 3 *Zur.* 170—182; and with Humphrey, 1 *Zur.* 157; letter, jointly with Coverdale and Humphrey, to Farell, &c., 2 *Zur.* 121; letters to him, *Park.* 244, 1 *Zur.* 345, 2 *Zur.* 25, 32, 38, 47; saluted, *Pil.* 682, *Rid.* 394; his preface to two sermons by Bradford, containing some account of their author, 1 *Brad.* 29; extracts from the same, 2 *Brad.* xiii, &c.; reference to it, *Rid.* 363 n.; he answered Fowler's Psalter, 2 *Ful.* 3; translated Gualter's book on Antichrist, 3 *Zur.* 176; is supposed to have had a hand in the Admonition to the Parliament, 1 *Zur.* 285 n

Samson: a Nazarite, 2 *Bul.* 209; a type of Christ, *Sand.* 370; his jaw-bone, *Calf.* 336

Samuel: *v.* Saul.

He was a captain, 1 *Bul.* 384, 386; a minister, magistrate, prophet, and prince, *Sand.* 35—37; governor of Naioth, the college of prophets, 4 *Bul.* 480; vanquished the Philistines by prayer, *ib.* 225; rebuked Saul, 3 *Bul.* 237; sacrificed, 2 *Bul.* 152; Samuel and Eli compared, 1 *Lat.* 188; the ghost raised by the witch of Endor was not Samuel, but the devil or an evil spirit in his likeness, 3 *Bul.* 403, 2 *Cran.* 45, 1 *Ful.* 299, 300, 312, 313, 1 *Hoop.* 326, 329, *Whita.* 91, 92

— Books of Samuel, what they contain, 2 *Cov.* 17; written by others besides Samuel, *Whita.* 301; none of Samuel's writings lost, *ib.* 525

Samuel (Will.): notice of him, *Poet.* xxviii; Psalm xix. and Job vii. versified by him, *ib.* 312

Samuell (Rob.): martyred, *Poet.* 163

Sanballat: his name and country, *Pil.* 334; his violent rage, *ib.* 397

Sancroft (Will.), abp of Canterbury: reburied the bones of abp Parker, and restored his monument, *Park.* xi.

Sancterentianus (Jul.): *v.* Santerentianus.

Sanctification*: the manner and order of it, 2 *Bul.* 337, 3 *Bul.* 41, 49; wherein it consists, *Lit. Edw.* 514, (562); what it is to sanctify, 4 *Bul.* 210, *Now.* (103); we must sanctify ourselves if we would have victory over our enemies, 1 *Bec.* 250; it must be throughout, 2 *Jew.* 885; it is begun, but not completed, in this life, 1 *Ful.* 411; sanctification in the sacraments, 4 *Bul.* 267

Sancto Charo (H. de): *v.* Hugo.

Sancto Victore (H. de): *v.* Hugo.

Sancto Victore (R. de): *v.* Richardus.

Sanctuaries: cities, or other places, of refuge, 1 *Bul.* 305, 2 *Bul.* 234; places which afforded protection to criminals, 1 *Tyn.* 180, 2 *Tyn.* 275; called franchises, 1 *Tyn.* 333; right of sanctuary, *Phil.* 72 (*v.* Westminster).

Sanctus: appointed (in the mass) by Sixtus I., 3 *Bec.* 266, *Pil.* 503; the black sanctus, a burlesque hymn, *Pra. Eliz.* 472

Sanctus-bell: *v.* Bells.

Sanctus Secundus (... count): 2 *Cran.* 233

Sand (D.): notice of him, *Poet.* xxvi; verses by him; think to die, *ib.* 299; our pleasures are vanities, *ib.* 300

Sander (Nich.), or Sanders, or Saunders: some account of him, of his works, and of his rebellion in Ireland, *Lit. Eliz.* 657 n.; a pillar of the popish synagogue, 1 *Ful.* viii, ix; he opposes Jewel, *Grin.* 169, *Jew.* xx; several books by him, 2 *Ful.* 3, 4; De visibili Monarchia Ecclesiæ, *Park.* 409, 410, 3 *Whitg.* xxxi, 1 *Zur.* 281, 2 *Zur.* 227 n., 235; he therein says that it is heretical to affirm that the scriptures ought necessarily to be translated into the vulgar tongues, *Whita.* 210; the work cited about the authority of Christian magistrates, 3 *Whitg.* 297, 299, 302, 311, 312; answered by Dering, *Park.* 410; by Dr B. Clerk, *ib.* 411—414, 430; by Acworth, *ib.* 440 n.; his Rock of the Church, 2 *Ful.* 4; A DISCOVERY OF THE DANGEROUS ROCK OF THE POPISH CHURCH, COMMENDED BY N. SANDERS, by W. Fulke, *ib.* 213, &c.; Whitaker writes against him, *Whita.* xii; Fulke replies to him, 1 *Ful.* viii. bis, ix, 15, 16, 134, 2 *Ful.* 4; Nowell answers him, 2 *Ful.* 3, *Now.* iv.

Sandes (Rich.): 2 *Cran.* 390

Sandwich, co. Kent: decay of the haven through its being stopped up with sand, 1 *Lat.* 251, 3 *Tyn.* 77; irruption of the sea, 1 *Brad.* 61 n.; the town visited by Parker, *Park.* 188, 189; dedication to the mayor, &c., 3 *Bec.* 597; commendation of the people, *ib.*; Christian doctrine honoured there, *ib.*; provision made for the poor, *ib.*

---

* See Holiness, where these entries should have been placed.

599; idleness exiled, *ib.*; the bells rung in a great thunderstorm, 1464, 1 *Lat.* 498 n.; service at the church on Parker's visitation, *Park.* 189; state of the refugees and their church, *ib.* 189; some members thereof excommunicated, *ib.* 247; dissensions among the Dutch, 1 *Zur.* 256; hospital of St Bartholomew, *Park.* 168; Ellys's hospital, *ib.*; St John's house, *ib.* 169; Sir Rog. Manwood's free school, 3 *Bec.* 601, *Park.* 187, 188

Sandwich (Sir Jo.): founder of an hospital, *Park.* 168

Sandwich (Rob.), of Stillington: legacy to him, *Grin.* 461

SANDYS (Edwin), bp of Worcester, then of London, and at last abp of York: his birth, family, and education, *Sand.* i, xxix, xxx, n.; at Cambridge, *Hutch.* i, *Park.* 38; master of Cath. hall, 2 *Brad.* 27; vice-chancellor of Cambridge, where he preached at the proclamation of queen Jane, *Sand.* ii, xxix; he prepares his sermon for the press, *ib.* iii; his answer to the duke of Northumberland on his preparing to proclaim queen Mary, *ib.* iv; he expostulates with the university, *ib.* v; resigns his office of vice-chancellor, *ib.*; sent to the Tower, *ib.* vi; with Bradford, 2 *Brad.* xxxii, xxxiii; he refuses to escape, *Sand.* vii; celebrates the communion in the Tower, *ib.* viii; is removed to the Marshalsea, 2 *Brad.* xiii, *Sand.* viii; finds favour with the keeper, and celebrates the communion there also, *ib.*; in peril, 2 *Brad.* 83; particulars of his release, *Sand.* x—xii; he goes into Essex, *ib.* xiv; sails to Antwerp, *ib.* xv; in exile, 1 *Cran.* (9), 4 *Jew.* 1196, 2 *Zur.* 1; he goes to Augsburgh, and thence to Strasburgh, *Sand.* xvi; loses his wife and child, *ib.*; at Frankfort, *Jew.* xii, 3 *Zur.* 755; at Strasburgh, *Jew.* xiii; at Zurich, *Sand.* xvi; on queen Mary's death he returns to England, *ib.* xvi, 1 *Zur.* 6; preaches before the queen, 2 *Zur.* 16 n.; disputes at Westminster, 4 *Jew.* 1199, 1200, 1 *Zur.* 11; in the commission for revising the Common Prayer, *Grin.* v, *Sand.* xvii; one of the royal visitors for the North, 1 *Zur.* 24, 73 n.; he has scruples about rites and ceremonies, *Sand.* xvii; nominated bishop of Carlisle, and afterwards of Worcester, 1 *Zur.* 73; consecrated bishop of Worcester, *Sand.* xvii, 1 *Zur.* 63; mentioned as such, 1 *Zur.* 58—69, 2 *Zur.* 94, 105; has a dispute with Sir Jo. Bourne, concerning a stone altar, *Sand.* xviii; quarrels with abp Parker about visitation, *ib.*; marries again, *ib.*; signs a letter to the queen, *Park.* 294; his share in the Bishops' Bible, *ib.* 256, *Sand.* xix; he is translated to the see of London, *Grin.* ix, *Park.* 369 n., *Sand.* xix, 1 *Zur.* 229, 233, 2 *Zur.* 181; issues strict injunctions, *Sand.* xix; an ecclesiastical commissioner, *Park.* 383, 390, 434, *Sand.* xx; thought by Parker not sufficiently severe against the Puritans, *Park.* 382; his dispute with Dering, *Sand.* xxi; he recommends a national synod, *ib.*; is embarrassed in circumstances, 1 *Zur.* 265; signs a warrant for the apprehension of Cartwright, *ib.* 313 n.; receives a legacy from abp Parker, *Sand.* xxi; present at Grindal's confirmation to the see of Canterbury, *Grin.* x; translated to York, *Sand.* xxi; his farewell sermon at Paul's cross on removing thither, *ib.* 418, &c.; mentioned as archbishop, 2 *Zur.* 313; his disagreement with Grindal and Aylmer, *Sand.* xxii; his visitation refused by dean Whittingham of Durham, *ib.* xxiii; he gives an account of his visitation to lord treasurer Burghley, *ib.* xxiii; a foul plot devised against him by Sir Rob. Stapleton, *ib.* xxiv, xxv; he answers in parliament the petition of sixteen articles, *ib.* xxvi; favours prophesyings, *Park.* 457 n. 459 n., *Sand.* xxvi; has a controversy with dean Hutton, *Sand.* xxvi; his hope of his successor, *ib.* 420; preamble to his will, *ib.* 446; his decease, and burial at Southwell, *ib.* xxvii; his epitaph, *ib.*; notice of him (in Latin) from a MS. catalogue of bishops who have belonged to St John's coll. Camb., *ib.* xxix, xxx.

His works, *Sand.* xxx, xxxi; his SERMONS, and MISCELLANEOUS PIECES, edited by the Rev. John Ayre, M.A., *ib.*; on the excellence of his sermons, *ib.* 3; letters by him, *Park.* 65, 124, 256, 1 *Zur.* 3, 72, 145, 264, 294, 311, 312, 331; letters signed by him and others, *Park.* 294, 390, 394, 434, 3 *Zur.* 755; letters to him, 2 *Brad.* 24 (?), *Park.* 384, 402, 451, 2 *Zur.* 189, 191, 237, 240; letter to him, Grindal, and Parkhurst, from Bullinger and Gualter, 2 *Zur.* 166; dedication to him as bishop of London, *Now.* 107

— His first wife, *Sand.* ix, xiii; she died in exile, *ib.* xvi; his second wife, Cecilia, daughter of Sir Tho. Wilford, *ib.* xviii, 1 *Zur.* 74 n

Sandys (Will. 3rd lord): at the duke of Norfolk's trial, 1 *Zur.* 267 n.; ambassador to France, 2 *Zur.* 201 n

Sandys (......), of Essex: his daughter married Edwin Sandys, afterwards archbishop, *Sand.* ix, xiii.

Sandys (Edwin), son of the abp: instructed by Hooker, *Sand.* xxvi.
Sandys (Will.): he and Margaret his wife, parents of the abp, *Sand.* i.
Sandys (Will.), F.S.A.: *Park.* xi. n
Sanhedrim, or συνέδριον: 3 *Whitg.* 226, 227; appointed after the return from Babylon, 2 *Whitg.* 91
Santerentianus (Jul.), or Terentianus: the friend and attendant of Peter Martyr, 4 *Jew.* 1220, 1232, &c., 1 *Zur.* 8, 9, 13, 14, 17, 24, 51, 58, 77 n., 147, 150, 224, 232, 271, 2 *Zur.* 27, 33, 41, 55 n., 90, 95, 180, &c.; with P. Martyr at Lambeth, 3 *Zur.* 535; a corrector of the press, 2 *Zur.* 305; letter from him to Jo. ab Ulmis, 3 *Zur.* 365; his death reported, 1 *Zur.* 187; Anna, his wife, *ib.* 69, 805, 2 *Zur.* 41, &c.
Santrinus (......): 2 *Zur.* 278, 284
Sapcoates (Sir Guy): his daughter Anne, 2 *Bec.* 622 n
Sapidus (......): 3 *Zur.* 51, 509 n., 605, 609
Sapor, king of Persia: persecuted Simeon, and slew Ustazardes, 2 *Brad.* 347, 348, 2 *Whitg.* 168; his treatment of the emperor Valerian, 2 *Jew.* 978, 4 *Jew.* 701; he called himself the brother of the sun and the moon, 4 *Jew.* 842
Sapphics: Saphickes upon the passion of Christ, by A.W., *Poet.* 452
Sapphira: *v.* Ananias.
Saracens: *v.* Turks.
They pretend to be the children of Sarah though indeed the seed of Hagar, 4 *Jew.* 713; persecutors, 2 *Bul.* 106; why sent against the Christians, *Grin.* 98; they cannot do good works, 4 *Bul.* 83
Saracin: one of the magi, *Whita.* 560 n
Sarah: the allegory of Sarah and Hagar, *Pil.* 335, 1 *Tyn.* 307; how she was preserved by God, 1 *Bul.* 410, 2 *Hoop.* 296
Saravia (Hadrian): mentions some who said the sacraments appertained only to the first planting of the church, *Rog.* 246
Sarcerius (E.): 3 *Bec.* 381, 418, 474
Sarctorius (Nich.): *v.* Schneider.
Sardanapalus: 1 *Hoop.* 422, 423
Sardis: the epistle to the church, *Bale* 285
Sarisburiensis (Jo.): *v.* John.
Sarisburiensis (Tho.): *v.* Thomas.
Sarum (New): *v.* Salisbury.
Sarum (Old): its remains, 2 *Zur.* 88
Satan: *v.* Prayers.
What he is, 3 *Bul.* 349, 1 *Lat.* 42; not a mere affection of the flesh, *Hutch.* 140, but a person, *ib.* 141; his nature, 1 *Lat.* 493; he is a creature, 3 *Bul.* 349; an evil and unclean spirit, *ib.* 357; not created evil, *ib.* 349; created an angel, *Hutch.* 67; his fall, *Sand.* 186; he fell through pride, 2 *Hoop.* 70, 2 *Lat.* 123, 169, *Sand.* 137, 138; the devil is said by the Manichees and Priscillianists to have made man, *Rog.* 41; the name Devil or Diabolus; whence it comes and what it means, 2 *Bul.* 118, 3 *Bul.* 355, *Now.* (101); the name Beelzebub, 3 *Bul.* 357, 4 *Bul.* 159, 2 *Jew.* 1025, &c.; he is called Demon for his cunning, 1 *Brad.* 376, 3 *Bul.* 356; he is "the evil one" mentioned in the Lord's prayer, 2 *Bec.* 195; 1 *Lat.* 443, 2 *Whitg.* 483; he is a serpent, 3 *Bul.* 356, *Pil.* 419; why he appeared in that form, *Pil.* 407; the serpent's head, and the bruising of it, 1 *Bec.* 296, 313, 1 *Cov.* 22, 2 *Hoop.* 5, *Lit. Edw.* 503 (552), *Now.* (35), 151, *Sand.* 8, 1 *Tyn.* 10; he is called the Dragon (*q. v.*), 3 *Bul.* 356; a roaring lion, 2 *Brad.* 256, 3 *Bul.* 356; a wolf, 1 *Bul.* 5; the adversary, 3 *Bul.* 355; a crafty and experienced enemy, 1 *Lat.* 429, 438, 493; a murderer, 3 *Bul.* 356; his malice and rage, 3 *Bec.* 48, 49, 401; illustrated by Christ in a parable, 2 *Bec.* 525; overruled, *Pil.* 178; his power, 3 *Bec.* 48, 49; he is quick, crafty, and mighty, 3 *Bul.* 354; but his power is limited, *ib.* 363; has no power except by God's permission, 2 *Cran.* 107, 1 *Lat.* 438, 442, *Pra. B.* 34, 41; his cunning, 1 *Brad.* 376, 3 *Bul.* 356; he exceeds all men in knowledge, *Whita.* 613; his subtleties, 3 *Bul.* 192, 1 *Hoop.* 294; his craft cannot prevail against God, 1 *Lat.* 360; he is a liar from the beginning, so that speaking truth he lies, 2 *Bec.* 627, 628; a deceiver, 3 *Bul.* 356; the father of lies, 1 *Lat.* 500; he never seems to be what he is, *Calf.* 87; changes himself into an angel of light, 3 *Bec.* 405, 1 *Jew.* 549, *Nord.* 107; is a great prince, 2 *Bec.* 149, 150; figured by Pharaoh, 1 *Brad.* 149, *Now.* (8), 121; he is the prince, lord or ruler of this world, 3 *Bul.* 359, 1 *Lat.* 357, 374, *Phil.* 175; the god of this world, 3 *Bul.* 358; his kingdom, 4 *Bul.* 211; the kingdom of the world is his, 3 *Bul.* 281; he taketh upon him to be lord over all things in earth, 2 *Lat.* 42; he is an usurper and a liar, 1 *Lat.* 375; his vigilance, 2 *Jew.* 953; he is a vigilant watchman, *Park.* 353; his activity, 2 *Bec.* 593, 623; his operations, 3 *Bul.* 360; he works by blinding the mind, 3 *Tyn.* 191; he is the author of all evils and mischances, 2 *Bec.* 633; he beguiled Eve, *Now.* (33), 148; we were brought into captivity to him, by the fall of Adam, 1 *Bec.* 296; he is the author

of man's sinful state, 2 *Bec.* 629; not the author of original sin in the sense maintained by the Valentinians, *Rog.* 99; insurrections come from him, 2 *Bec.* 593; his temptations, 2 *Brad.* 81, 3 *Bul.* 357, 2 *Jew.* 845, 846, *Sand.* 166 (*v.* Temptation); the devil alone is not the cause of sin in us, 2 *Bul.* 362; the devil, the flesh, and the law, are man's great enemies, 1 *Tyn.* 359, 360; he is old Adam's great counsellor, *Coop.* 47; how Sathan by the sin of pride hath ever prevailed; verses by W. Warner, *Poet.* 379; he is our tormentor, 2 *Whitg.* 485; an enemy to the Christian, 1 *Bec.* 125, 2 *Bec.* 184; he will disquiet him if he cannot hinder his salvation, *ib.* 633; a dialogue between Satan and our conscience, 1 *Brad.* 210; he argues that God does not hear sinners, 2 *Bec.* 626; suggests that he who has not kept the commandments must perish, 2 *Bec.* 626, 627, 628; urges that sinners are damned, *ib.* 630; asserts that the promise is to those only that walk not after the flesh, *ib.* 632; his objections against Christian doctrine and hope, *ib.* 634, 635; he labours to make us doubt of salvation, 1 *Brad.* 316; alarms with the fear of backsliding, 2 *Bec.* 632; tempts us to despair, *Sand.* 381; maketh weapons of everything, 1 *Lat.* 430—432; hath overthrown many saints for a time, 1 *Brad.* 137; his arts to hinder prayer, 1 *Lat.* 329, 342; he calumniates and depraves the scriptures, 2 *Bec.* 628; seeks to cast us into persecution and affliction, 1 *Lat.* 467; would have us avoid persecution, 2 *Brad.* 48, 2 *Lat.* 439; ready to tempt at the hour of death, 1 *Lat.* 284; his assaults when death approaches, 2 *Lat.* 148; how to resist them, *ib.* 149; how he appeared to a dying man in Germany, and was defeated through faith, 2 *Lat.* 149; when he has the upper hand he rules quietly, 1 *Lat.* 130, 151, 234; chiefly desires to rule religion, 1 *Brad.* 427, 2 *Cov.* 243; how he hinders, 2 *Jew.* 842; he labours to banish peace and introduce discord, 3 *Bec.* 33; his practices to hinder the building of God's house, *Pil.* 356, 418, 454, 455; his malice exhibited in Nehemiah's enemies, *ib.* 419, and in the papists, *ib.* 420; his rage against God's kingdom, *ib.* 467; his opposition to every good work, *Nord.* 115, especially to the preaching of the word, *ib.* 116; he is an enemy to preaching, 1 *Lat.* 202, 2 *Lat.* 210; attempts to evacuate Christ's death, 1 *Lat.* 72, 73; sows tares amongst the wheat, 2 *Lat.* 189; is no unpreaching prelate, 1 *Lat.* 77; but the most diligent prelate and preacher in England, *ib.* 70; goes to the university to teach, not to learn, *ib.* 203; never shews himself so right a devil as when ministers are absent or negligent, 2 *Bec.* 526; invented fee-farming of benefices, &c., 1 *Lat.* 203; imitates the ordinances of God, *Calf.* 12, &c.; has corrupted the true use of fasting, 2 *Bec.* 526; may be served by saying the paternoster, 1 *Lat.* 377; is the author of all superstition, *ib.* 70—72; invented holy water, holy bells, &c., *ib.* 498; pretends to fear the sign of the cross, 2 *Ful.* 143—145, 172, *Whita.* 591; counterfeits a flight from the holy water-bucket, and nestles in the bosom of the priest, *Calf.* 87; is driven away by faith, not by bells or holy water, 1 *Tyn.* 226; how Christ confounds him, 2 *Lat.* 185; his power was annihilated by the coming of Christ, 1 *Bec.* 296; he was overthrown by Christ in the wilderness, 1 *Lat.* 505; Christ by his death destroyed the power of the devil, see p. 178, col. 1; how victory over him is to be gotten by us, 2 *Bec.* 624; he must be avoided by conformity to God's word, 1 *Hoop.* 109; remedies against his temptations, 3 *Bec.* 156; he must be resisted, 1 *Lat.* 439, 2 *Lat.* 11, 12, 149, *Pil.* 436; we must fight manfully against him, but not fear, 3 *Bul.* 363; how to resist him with faith, prayer, and the word of God, 3 *Bec.* 156, 167; the scriptures are our arms against him, 1 *Lat.* 505, *Whita.* 237; he cannot withstand them, 2 *Lat.* 149; he dwells in the air, 1 *Lat.* 497; there is a saying that every man sees him before he dies, 2 *Bec.* 624; some ascribe their gains to the devil, 1 *Lat.* 213; miracles have been wrought by his power, see Miracles; deceived the monk Valens, 2 *Cran.* 42; he deceived certain Jews in Crete by appearing to them in the form of Moses, *ib.* 50; his appearance to St Martin, 1 *Jew.* 551; he once confessed that he could do nothing in the presence of a Christian, 2 *Jew.* 978; he would have himself worshipped, 3 *Bul.* 210; on his being bound for a thousand years, *Bale* 559, and loosed in the last days, 1 *Lat.* 517; opinion that he was loosed 1000 years after Christ, *Bale* 94, 559, 1 *Brad.* 92, 2 *Brad.* 274, 312, 2 *Cov.* 253, 2 *Hoop.* 48; he stirs up Gog and Magog, *Bale* 570; we desire in the Lord's prayer that his kingdom may be subdued, 2 *Bec.* 151; he shall be cast into the fire, *Bale* 575; he is everlastingly condemned, 3 *Bul.* 352; his time not long, 1 *Brad.* 415, 2 *Cov.* 231; his army are wicked spirits, the world and the flesh, 2 *Bec.* 543; (*v.* Demons, Enemies); who are the people of the devil, 2 *Hoop.* 71 ; the wicked are born of the devil, 2 *Tyn.* 190— 192; they are members of the devil, 4 *Bul.* 338; what it is to have the devil, [3 *Bec.* 604; an incarnate devil worse than Satan in his own nature, *Pil.* 363; he has many servants, 1 *Lat.* 375, 376 ; monks and friars do his work, 2 *Cran.* 64 ; false teachers are his agents, *Sand.* 396; the livery of his servants, 1 *Lat.* 448; danger of being his servant, 1 *Hoop.* 107 ; the devil's chaplains, 1 *Cov.* 484; his wages, 1 *Tyn.* 140; his great guns and serpentines, 1 *Lat.* 27 ; he and his synagogue have custom, multitude, riches, &c. on their side, 1 *Brad.* 376

Satisfaction : *v.* Propitiation, Restitution.

Translations concerning it examined, 1 *Ful.* 428—449; the scripture doctrine respecting it, 2 *Cov.* 363, &c. ; satisfaction for sin cannot be made by works or sufferings, 3 *Bul.* 90, 1 *Hoop.* 348, 2 *Tyn.* 29 ; none can be made for punishment, 1 *Bul.* 167 ; what they are to do who cannot make it, 1 *Bec.* 103 ; Christ is the only satisfaction, *ib.* 102, 1 *Tyn.* 228, 267 ; satisfaction may be made to men, but not to God, 2 *Jew.* 1134; he who would make satisfaction to God for his sins, is faithless, 1 *Tyn.* 228 ; whoever has injured his neighbour ought to make satisfaction to him, 1*Bec.* 103, 2 *Bec.*105, 1 *Tyn.* 228, 267, 478; on satisfaction to the congregation, 1*Brad.* 50; use of the word satisfaction in the ancient church, 1 *Ful.* 431; the word is employed by Augustine, but he does not teach the Romish doctrine, *Calf.* 75; satisfaction is a part of the Romish sacrament of penance, 1 *Brad.* 46, 588, 1 *Tyn.* 267, 2 *Tyn.* 162 ; a modern popish definition of it, 1 *Tyn.* 342 n

Sator : one of the Magi, *Whita.* 560 n

Sattled : settled, *Bale* 496

Saturday : *v.* Fasting.

Named from Saturn, *Pil.* 16

Saturn : derivation of the name, 3 *Bul.* 135

Saturnians : ascribed the creation to angels, *Hutch.* 68 ; condemned marriage, *Rog.* 306

Saturninus: a heretic, 3 *Bec.* 401; called Saturnil, *Phil.* 417 ; he espoused the heresy of the Gnostics, *Grin.* 59 n.; rejected the Old Testament, *Whita.* 30; ascribed the creation of the world to angels, *Rog.* 40; said that Christ was man in appearance only, *ib.* 51; taught that he was opposed to the god of the angels, *ib.* 133; wrongly stated to have called himself the Christ, *ib.* 162

Satyrus, brother of St Ambrose : being shipwrecked, he hanged the sacrament about his neck in a stole, *Coop.* 27, 134, 141, 2 *Ful.* 105, 556, 2 *Jew.* 554, 3 *Jew.* 552, 554

Saul, king of Israel : *v.* Samuel.

Head over Israel, 4 *Bul.* 86 ; he spares Agag, 1 *Bul.* 307, 2 *Bul.* 351, 2 *Jew.* 855; runs to witches, 1 *Bul.* 242, *Pil.* 25; kills himself, 1 *Bul.* 242, 2 *Bul.* 79; his burial, *Pil.* 319

Saul (Mons.) : ambassador from France, *Grin.* 244

Saunce-bell : a corruption of "sanctus," 1 *Jew.* 292

Saunders (Sir Edw.), lord chief-baron: *Park.* 164

Saunders (......), a parson : *Park.* 18

Saunders (Lau.) : 1 *Brad.* 555; in prison, *ib.* 403, 2 *Hoop.* 594, *Sand.* ix, xii; he signs a declaration concerning religion, 1 *Brad.* 374; in peril of death, *ib.* 290, 2 *Brad.* 83 ; examined at St Mary Overy, 1 *Brad.* 482; excommunicated, *ib.* 496; condemned, 3 *Zur.* 171; martyred, 1 *Brad.* 410, 445, 2 *Brad.* 192, *Rid.* 380, 391, 3 *Zur.* 772; mentioned as "sincere Saunders," 2 *Brad.* 190; letter from him to Ferrar and others, *ib.* 179 ; letters to him, *ib.* 175, 177

Saunders (Nich.) : *v.* Sander.

Sauromanus (Jo.) : Latin verses, de sacro baptismo, *Pra. Eliz.* 404

Sautre (Will.) : persecuted, *Bale* 44 n.; burned, *ib.* 3, 76, 394

Savage (Sir Jo.) : slain at Boulogne, 2 *Tyn.* 306 n

Saverne, near Strasburgh ; 3 *Zur.* 49 n.; a convocation there, *ib.* 651

Saverson (......): a doctor of Bologna, *Phil.* 41; one of the commissioners to examine Philpot, *ib.* iv, 31

Savile (Sir Hen.) : his edition of Chrysostom, *Calf.* 64 n.; he publishes Will. of Malmesbury, 2 *Ful.* 22 n

Savile (Tho.): letter from him and Hawkins to Wolfius, 2 *Zur.* 336 ; notice of him, *ib.* n

Savile (......) : *Grin.* 325

Saviours: promised in Obadiah, *Pil.* 269— 271

Savonarola (Jerome) : a trumpet of the gospel, *Phil.* 393 ; a casuist, 1 *Brad.* 564 ; he complains of the tyranny of the bishops of Rome, 4 *Jew.* 740; wrote on the Apocalypse, *Bale* 258; burned, *ib.* 398

Savoy hospital : *v.* Westminster.

Sawtre (Will.) : *v.* Sautre.

Sax (Alt): *v.* Alt-Sax.

Saxo (Ludolphus): De Vita Christi, 2 *Lat.* 109; a prayer therefrom, *Pra. Eliz.* 545

Saxon Chronicle, *q. v.*

Saxons (Anglo): *v.* Anglo-Saxons.

Saxony, electors: *v.* Augustus, John Frederick, Maurice: the prince of Saxony (son of duke John Frederick), a suitor to queen Elizabeth, 1 *Zur.* 24 n., 34
   The churches of Saxony, 2 *Zur.* 39; religious persecution there, 1 *Zur.* 315, 317, 319

Say: an assay, 3 *Tyn.* 78

Say (Will.): register of Oxford, 1 *Cran.* 391, 393; (the same?) registrar of convocation, *Grin.* 274

Sayer (Greg.): Clavis Regia, 2 *Lat.* 63 n

Sayer (......), a deputy of London: *Park.* 276

Saygrave (Elynour): wife of Tho. King, *q. v.*

Saynsure: censer, *Calf.* 124

Scævola (Q.): 3 *Whitg.* 323

Scaffold, or stage erected for the performance of religious dramas, *Hutch.* 349, 1 *Tyn.* 422

Scala cœli: *Rid.* 55, 1 *Tyn.* 244; that at Rome, 1 *Bec.* 191 n., 1 *Brad.* 372 n., 1 *Lat.* 97 n., *Rid.* 510, 1 *Tyn.* 244 n.; a similar privilege granted to the church of Boston, 1 *Tyn.* 244 n.; masses of scala cœli, 1 *Bec.* 191, 1 *Brad.* 372, 2 *Brad.* 293, 2 *Cov.* 271, 1 *Lat.* 50, 97, 2 *Lat.* 238, 239, 362, *Pil.* 80, 496, 3 *Zur.* 212; scalary loosings, 1 *Lat.* 51; the true scala cœli, 1 *Lat.* 97, 123, 178, 200, 470

Scala Cronica: *v.* Gray (Tho.).

Scala inferni: 1 *Lat.* 178, 179

Scaliger (Jos.): *Calf.* 9 n., 107 n.; his conjecture as to the Babylon mentioned by St Peter in his first epistle, 2 *Ful.* 336 n.; he maintained the identity of the Essenes and Therapeutæ, *ib.* 101 n.; his opinion concerning Ben. Gorion, *ib.* 338 n.; he points out interpolations in the chronicle of Eusebius, *ib.* 236 n., 237 n., 337 n

Scalled: the meaning uncertain, 1 *Bec.* 374

Scambler (Edm.), bp of Peterborough, afterwards of Norwich: was a preacher in London in queen Mary's time, 1 *Zur.* 7 n., 2 *Zur.* 160 n.; to preach at Paul's cross, *Park.* 261; his share in the Bishops' Bible, *ib.* 335 n.; Rogers dedicates to him, *Rog.* xi.

Scamlings: meals obtained by shift, *Pil.* 558

Scandal: *v.* Offence.

Scanderbeg [Geo. Castriot], king of Epirus or Albania: his death, *Lit. Eliz.* 444

Scape-goat: 2 *Bul.* 194

Scapular: indulgence to those who wear it, 1 *Tyn.* 123 n

Scarcity: *v.* Famine, Prices.

Scarecrows: 1 *Brad.* 380, 381

Scarlet (Tho.), printer: 1 *Cov.* 196

Scepper (......), or Shipperius: an admiral sent by the emperor to carry off the Lady Mary, 3 *Zur.* 568

Sceva: 4 *Bul.* 115, 256

Schaffnaburg (Lambert of): *v.* Lambert.

Schard (S.): De Jurisd. Imper. ac Potest. Eccl. Scripta, *Jew.* xliii, 2 *Jew.* 992, 4 *Jew.* 969, &c.

Schedel (Hartmann): his Chronicon, commonly called the Nuremberg chronicle, 2 *Ful.* 103; mentions the Acephali, *Rog.* 54 n.; speaks of pope Joan, 4 *Jew.* 656

Schelhornius (Jo. Geo.): *Calf.* 49 n., 290 n

Scheltco à Jueren, otherwise Schelto à Geveren: *v.* Jueren.

Schentzius (......): 3 *Zur.* 628, 630, 631

Schism, Schismatics: *v.* Prayers.
   Passages on schism, *Phil.* 283, 1 *Whitg.* 4, 2 *Whitg.* 240, 3 *Whitg.* 595; translations concerning it, 1 *Ful.* 221; it is a great sin, *Now.* (57), 176, *Rid.* 120, *Sand.* 246; dissensions amongst Christians cause the gospel to be spoken against, 1 *Jew.* 532; it must be avoided, 4 *Bul.* 61; not to be made for diversity of doctrine in matters not essential to the faith, *ib.* 53; nor for vices of ministers, or for diversity of ceremonies, *ib.* 56; nor for impurity of life of men in the church, *ib.* 58; nor for unworthy partakers of the Lord's supper, *ib.* 60; there have been many schisms between rival popes, *Pil.* 545, 618, 1 *Tyn.* 324; some apply the term to the reformation of abuses, 2 *Jew.* 998; divisions in the church of England lamented, *Sand.* 381; schismatics, 4 *Bul.* 11, 12; who are such, *ib.* 63, *Pil.* 620; differing in substance makes one, not merely differing in ceremonies, *Pil.* 620; Papists are such, *ib.* 541, 544; a speech touching schismatics, *Poet.* 276; they should be reproved, 3 *Whitg.* 464

Schisure: schism, *Park.* 14

Schmidius (Jo. Andr.): 2 *Ful.* 339 n

Schmidt (Eras.): *v.* Fabricius.

Schmutz (Alex.): 3 *Zur.* 289, 361 n., 396 n., 402, 406, 409, 443, 445; why he came to England, *ib.* 402; patronized by bp Coxe, *ib.* 427; fellow of St John's college, Oxford, *ib.* 449 n

Schmutz (Jo.): 3 *Zur.* 290

Schneeberger (......): 2 *Zur.* 201

Schneider (Jo.): 1 *Zur.* 105

Schneider (Nich.): 4 *Bul.* 546

Schœnemann (Car. T. G.): *Calf.* 235 n

Schoham (שוהם): onyx stone, 2 *Bul.* 136

Scholars: *v.* Schools.

They must be maintained, 1 *Lat.* 307, 358, 418, 504; a supplication for their maintenance, *ib.* 179; required to be maintained by beneficed clergymen, 2 *Cran.* 156, 161, 501, 2 *Hoop.* 148, *Rid.* 530; students to be maintained by the wages of the church, 4 *Bul.* 494; the duties of scholars, 1 *Bul.* 281; they must pray at their uprising, commending themselves to God, 2 *Bec.* 385; must attend sermons, 2 *Bec.* 306; must love and reverence their school-masters, 2 *Bec.* 385, 386; must be diligent in applying their books, *ib.* 386; must make orations or themes, 2 *Bec.* 306; must have their lives garnished with good manners and godly virtues, 2 *Bec.* 387

Scholastic Divinity: *v.* Schoolmen.

Scholastica Historia: on Melchisedec's offering, 1 *Ful.* 148

Scholasticus: said to have made part of the canon of the mass, 1 *Brad.* 513, 2 *Brad.* 310, 1 *Jew.* 9, 96, *Pil.* 503; not a proper name, 1 *Brad.* 513 n.; called Martinus Scholasticus, 1 *Jew.* 96 n

Scholefield (James), regius prof. of Greek, Cambridge: editor of bp Pilkington's works, *Pil.*

Scholiast (The Greek): *v.* Œcumenius.

Scholies: mention of some ancient Greek ones, 2 *Ful.* 87, 88; supposed to refer to the Enarrationes of Hentenius, *ib.* 88 n

Schomberg (... count): 2 *Zur.* 207

Schoolmasters: there ought to be wise and godly ones provided, 1 *Bec.* 260; provision must be made for them, 2 *Bec.* 306; the duty of masters or teachers, *Nov.* (1), 113; what kind they are to be, 2 *Bec.* 306, 378; how wise ones will act, *Pil.* 355; they must instil into their scholars' minds true persuasions of God, 2 *Bec.* 378; must enarm them against heresies, *ib.* 379; especially against the Romish heresy, *ib.* 379, 380, 381; they must read the scriptures, history, &c., to their scholars, *ib.* 378, 379; must read some godly catechism to them, *ib.* 378; must teach good letters, *ib.* 382; must teach those authors that are profitable, *ib.* 382; must teach good manners, *ib.* 383; must shew a good example of conduct, *ib.* 384; how they must chastise their scholars, *ib.* 384, 385; they are worthy of honour, *ib.* 386; king Edward's injunction to all schoolmasters to use his Catechism, *Lit. Edw.* 493, (544); injunctions, &c., respecting them, *Grin.* 142, 173; recusant ones, *ib.* 419, 420, 425

Schoolmen: *v.* Doctors, Merit, &c.

Many of them mentioned, *Bale* 328, 2 *Jew.* 667; they had no devotion but to the pope, the god that made them, 1 *Cran.* 327; they differed in their teaching from the Jesuits, *Whita.* 19; the study of them discountenanced by Cranmer, 1 *Cran.* viii; they are disowned as authorities by Stapleton, *Whita.* 413; specimens of their inquiries, and terms of their art, *Bale* 350, 1 *Tyn.* 157—158, 3 *Whitg.* 575; their blunders, 4 *Jew.* 877, 878; their absurd conclusions from errors of the Latin Vulgate, *Whita.* 140; their distinction of "via" and "domus," or this life and the life to come, *ib.* 198; their distinctions with regard to faith, *Phil.* 412 (and see p. 316, col. 1, above); a lesson concerning the sacraments from one of them (not named), 4 *Bul.* 239; what made them take up the doctrine of transubstantiation, 1 *Cran.* 302; scholastic terms used with relation to that doctrine, *Grin.* 44, 3 *Tyn.* 254

Schools: *v.* Prayers, Universities.

Of schools, 4 *Bul.* 113, 479, 2 *Jew.* 981, 1011; in Israel, 1 *Bul.* 334, 2 *Bul.* 143, 4 *Bul.* 480; those of the prophets, 4 *Bul.* 480, 2 *Jew.* 981; a hundred schools in Jerusalem, 2 *Jew.* 679; what schools were instituted by Christ and his apostles, 4 *Bul.* 482; schools appertain to the preservation of the ministry, *ib.* 483; the true end of them, *ib.* 485; discipline in them, *ib.* 485; their corruption, *ib.* 484; schools ought to be established by the temporal magistrates, 2 *Bec.* 306; they are not sufficiently maintained, 1 *Lat.* 291, 349; the books of holy scripture must be read in them, 2 *Bec.* 306; sixteen grammar-schools founded by Edward VI., who intended also to found twelve colleges, *Rid.* xiii. n.; inquiry respecting grammar-schools in cathedral churches, *Grin.* 180; that of Bangor, *ib.* 184; some should be set up for women-children, 2 *Bec.* 376, 377

Schorne (Mr Jo.): *v.* Shorn.

Schottus (P. Gaspar): his Physica Curiosa, a record of prodigies, *Lit. Eliz.* 569 n

Schröck (......), Jesuit: *Whita.* 331

Schuendi (Lazarus): 3 *Zur.* 58 n

Schwartzenberg (The count): imperial minister to the Netherlands, 2 *Zur.* 303 n

Schweitzer (Christophel): 2 *Zur.* 328, 330

Schwenckfeldians: referred to, 2 *Jew.* 686; 3 *Jew.* 67, 187, 189, 265, 602; they thought that our Saviour retained not both natures after his resurrection, but that he is only God, *Rog.* 64; despised the scripture, 2 *Jew.* 671, *Whita.* 36, 298; trusted to immediate revelations, *Rog.* 152; objected to written

commentaries, *ib.* 196; contemned the sacraments as superfluous, *ib.* 251, 265
Schwenckfeldt (Caspar): notice of him, *Whita.* 36 n.; his errors, 2 *Cov.* 519, 4 *Jew.* 755, *Rog.* 196 n., 3 *Zur.* 513 n.; himself and his sect referred to, 3 *Jew.* 265
Science: liberal science not to be despised, 1 *Cov.* 498
Scilurus, the Scythian: *Sand.* 49
Scipio Africanus: not idle in his leisure, *Hutch.* 1, *Wool.* 94; sayings of his, 1 *Hoop.* 365, 2 *Hoop.* 79, *Sand.* 372
Scipio (D.): probably Scipione Biondi, *Jew.* xviii; Jewel's letter to him in the council of Trent, *ib.* 1094
Sclavonians: their conversion by Cyril and Methodius, 1 *Jew.* 291, 334, 335; their tongue, *ib.* 334; permitted by the pope to minister the Lord's supper in their own tongue, *Pil.* 500
Scoffing: v. Mocking.
The sin of mocking, *Pil.* 357, 401; that of Ishmael, *ib.* 358; mockers not to be feared, *ib.* 365; mockers in the last days, 2 *Jew.* 869
Scoggin (Jo.): his jest-book, 4 *Jew.* 860
Scoloker (Will): printer, *Bale* 2
Scorce, or Scorse: exchange, 1 *Jew.* 518
Scorners: of God's word warned, 1 *Bec.* 126, see also Hickscorner.
Scory (Jo.), bp of Hereford: consecrated bp of Rochester, 2 *Cov.* xiii, 2 *Cran.* 429 n.; deprived of the see of Chichester, *Phil.* xxvii; he disseminates Cranmer's declaration against the mass, 1 *Cran.* xx, 3 *Zur.* 371 n.; an exile, 1 *Brad.* 445, 1 *Cran.* (9); in Friesland, *Grin.* 239, *Rid.* 387; one of the disputants at Westminster, 1 *Zur.* 11, 4 *Jew.* 1199, 1200; appointed and confirmed bishop of Hereford, *Grin.* vi. n., 1 *Zur.* 23, 40; consecrated, *ib.* 63 n.; he signs letters to the queen, *Park.* 101, 294; forbidden to visit his diocese, *ib.* 117 n.; he often conferred with Sandys, *ib.* 126; Parker and Grindal seek the queen's permission for him to visit the cathedral of Hereford, *ib.* 165; not fit for the see of London, *ib.* 359; mentioned, 1 *Zur.* 69
Scot family: v. Scott.
Scotists: disciples of Duns Scotus, opponents of the Thomists, 1 *Jew.* 70, 3 *Jew.* 611, 4 *Jew.* 1046, 3 *Tyn.* 75, 131, 1 *Zur.* 53; the Franciscans took this side, 1 *Tyn.* 159 n
Scotland: v. James IV., V., VI., Mary; also Edinburgh, Leith, &c.
Andrew, why its guardian saint, 1 *Hoop.* 314 n.; the ancient supremacy of the crown of England, *Park.* 328; the Scots invade England, 1513, *Pil.* 251; Tyndale's Testament sent to Scotland, 1 *Tyn.* xxxvi; the Scots, notwithstanding their dialect, read and understood the English Bible, *Whita.* 215; occasion of Henry VIII.'s war with Scotland, 1 *Hoop.* xii. n.; the country invaded, 3 *Zur.* 236—240, 634; fight at Haldanrig, *ib.* 237 n.; war with Scotland, 1544, *Pra. Eliz.* 567 n.; the land again invaded by the English, 3 *Zur.* 643, 645, 647; castles taken by them, *ib.* 387; prayer ordered for peace with Scotland, 2 *Cran.* 154; the title of king of Scotland assumed by Francis II., king of France, 1 *Zur.* 40; war with Scotland, and its termination, *Lit. Eliz.* 458; public affairs, 1 *Zur.* 60, 68, 89, 193, 195, 225, 228, 251, 2 *Zur.* 120; religious disturbances and progress of the reformation, see p. 209, col. 1 above; state of religion, *Grin.* 280; the protestants assisted by queen Elizabeth, *Now.* 226, 227; monasteries abolished, 2 *Zur.* 116; the confederate Scots lords, 1 *Zur.* 193 n., 197 n.; their standard, *ib.* 195; summary of statutes regarding the reformation of religion, *ib.* 198, &c.; the English, under the earl of Sussex, blow up 50 castles, and burn 300 villages, *ib.* 225; on the succession to the crown, 2 *Zur.* 200; war, 1575, *Grin.* 355; the Scots defeated, *Pil.* 86, 251; not good archers, *ib.* 427
Scots: the ancient Irish so called, 2 *Ful.* 16, 19
Scott* of Scott's hall and elsewhere, in Kent, (anciently Balliol): notice of many of the family, 1 *Bec.* 353 n
Scot (Cuthb.), bp of Chester: a commissioner for the condemnation of Bucer and Fagius, 2 *Zur.* 20 n.; he opposes the reformation, 1 *Zur.* 10 n.; disputes, on the Romish side, at Westminster, 1 *Jew.* 60, 1 *Zur.* 11 n.; apparently referred to as Mr Scot, *Park.* 25, 26, 28, 29; he absconds without regard to his sureties, *ib.* 218
Scot (Sir Reg.): his daughter Elizabeth, 3 *Bec.* 487 n
Scot (Sir Walter), of Buccleugh: 1 *Zur.* 214 n., 225 n
Scot (Geo.), minister of Kirkaldy: 2 *Zur.* 365
Scott (Greg.): notice of him, *Poet.* liii; stanzas from his Brief Treatise against certain Errors of the Romish Church, *ib.* 520; Mr Scot (believed to be the same) recommended by Grindal to be a prebendary of Carlisle, *Grin.* 285

---

* Scott and Scot are arranged together.

Scott (Jo.): steward of Grindal's house, *Grin.* 461, and his executor, *ib.* 463

Scott (Rich.), or Skotte: dedication to him, 1 *Bec.* 353; notice of him and his family, *ib.* n.; mention of him, 3 *Bec.* 487 n.; Mary (Whetenhall) his wife, 1 *Bec.* 191 n

Scott (Tho.): notice of him, *Poet.* xxviii; to art; verses, *ib.* 315

Scot (Mr): supposed to be Cuthbert, afterwards bp of Chester, *Park.* 25, 26, 28, 29

Scot (Mr): v. Scott (Greg.).

Scotus: v. Duns (Jo.).

Scotus (Jo.), Erigena: called Jo. Scotus the elder, in distinction from Duns Scotus, *Bale* 398; he wrote on the eucharist against Paschasius, 1 *Hoop.* 118 n.; his opinion on the sacrament, *ib.* 524, 1 *Jew.* 458; he was condemned for a heretic, 200 years after his death, *Grin.* 74

Scriba (......): 3 *Zur.* 331

Scribes: v. Pharisees.

Scriptores post Bedam: *Jew.* xxxii, 4 *Jew.* 697 & al.

Scripture: v. Bible, Word of God; also Church, viii, Prayers, Prophecy, Tradition; likewise Augustine, Jerome, and all the fathers and doctors.

i. *Generally, the canon, &c:*

(*a*) What the scripture is, *Now.* (2, 103), 114, 1 *Tyn.* 88; various names by which the word of God is called, 3 *Bec.* 603, *Calf.* 356, 3 *Jew.* 364; names by which it is designated in Psa. cxix, *Whita.* 383; why termed a Testament, *Now.* (2), 14; why the books of scripture are called testamentary, *Whita.* 28; scripture styled God's indenture, *Pil.* 192; its original, 1 *Cov.* 48; why it is given to us, *ib.* 394, *Now.* (2), 14; its office, *Rid.* 56; The Sum of Scripture, a book forbidden by Henry VIII., 1 *Tyn.* 3 n., 4; A PATHWAY INTO THE HOLY SCRIPTURE, by W. Tyndale, *ib.* 1, &c.; A TREATISE OF THE HOLY SCRIPTURE, by bp Jewel, 4 *Jew.* 1161, &c.; A DISPUTATION ON HOLY SCRIPTURE, AGAINST THE PAPISTS, ESPECIALLY BELLARMINE AND STAPLETON, by W. Whitaker, D. D., translated by the Rev. W. Fitzgerald, A. M., *Whita.*; THE COMMON PLACES OF THE HOLY SCRIPTURE, by T. Becon, 3 *Bec.* 587, &c.; THE DEMANDS OF HOLY SCRIPTURE, WITH ANSWERS TO THE SAME, by T. Becon, *ib.* 595, &c.; the antiquity of scripture, *Pil.* 428, *Whita.* 293; it can by no means decay, *Phil.* 345; it cannot be corrupted, *ib.* 346; God has preserved his word at all times, *Poet.* 279, 288; it did not perish in the Babylonian captivity, *Whita.* 103, 114, 115; it has been preserved by miracle, 1 *Hoop.* 138, 1 *Lat.* 120, *Whita.* 653; by the mercy of God, not by the heads of the church, 3 *Tyn.* 48, 138; it is sound and uncorrupted, 1 *Bul.* 55; not mentioned in the creed, because the creed is itself an epitome of it, *Whita.* 299; summed up in the creed, Lord's prayer, and ten commandments, *ib.* 388; a brief description of the contents of the Old and New Testaments, 1 *Tyn.* 8; what the several books contain, 2 *Cov.* 17, &c.; scripture divided into two parts, the law, and the promises, or gospel, 1 *Bec.* 97, *Now.* (5), 118; it contains three things; the law, the gospel, and histories, 1 *Tyn.* 449; use of the histories, *ib.* 451, &c.

(*b*) The Old Testament:—as to the evidence of scripture, see in ii, below; not contrary to the New, *Rog.* 86; the likeness and difference between them, 2 *Bul.* 282, 293, &c., 4 *Bul.* 249; they mutually support and confirm each other, *Whita.* 291, 292; the Old Testament is given to Christians, 1 *Bul.* 59; it is not to be refused, 1 *Cov.* 71; whether we are bound by proofs out of it, 2 *Bul.* 19; Christ is set forth in it, 1 *Tyn.* 144; the whole of Christian doctrine can be found in it, *Whita.* 619, 620; and the Christian sacraments too, *ib.* 620; it is perfect, *ib.* 641

(*c*) The New Testament:—its origin, 2 *Cran.* 514; its writers added nothing to the law of God, *Whita.* 618; THE SUMMARY OF THE NEW TESTAMENT, by T. Becon, 3 *Bec.* 560, &c.; list of the books of it, with their contents, *ib.* 562, &c.; Jerome's remarks on the quotations in the New Testament, 1 *Ful.* 30 n., *Whita.* 38, 52; it is "the word of the cross," 1 *Brad.* 264

(*d*) The canon (see the names of the several books, and the title Apocrypha):—list of the canonical books, 1 *Bul.* 54, *Rog.* 75; in what sense the word "canonical" is used by fathers and councils, *Whita.* 27, 44, 658, 662; Augustine's rule for distinguishing canonical scripture, 1 *Ful.* 19, *Whita.* 45, 308; the Romish distinction of canonical (or proto-canonical) and deutero-canonical, *ib.* 49, 305; history of the canon, 4 *Bul.* 538, &c.; on certain books supposed to be referred to in the Old Testament, and yet never received as canonical, *Whita.* 301; some canonical pieces may have been lost, *ib.* 302, 525; the Old Testament possibly corrected and arranged by Ezra, *ib.* 116; Tertullian says the autographs of the apostles were preserved in his time, *ib.* 311; Papists cannot assign the period when the canon was defined, *ib.* 69; it was, according to Augustine, fixed in the apostles' times, *ib.* 310, 311; the power of fixing the canon belonged to the apostles, not as ministers of the church, but as the organs of the Holy Ghost, *ib.* 311; many flourishing churches had doubts for a time concerning certain books, *ib.* 105, 285, 293; as in later times the Lutherans had, *ib.* 296; none of the fathers cited by Stapleton really say that the canon depends only on the authority of the church, *ib.* 323, &c.; Stapleton says the present church has the power of constituting the canon of scripture; Durandus and Driedo ascribe that power only to the ancient church, *ib.* 330; some Romanists assert that the church can even add a book to the canon, *ib.* 505; yet Canus and Bellarmine say that the church is not governed by new revelations, *ib.* 504; the arguments of Papists for the church's authority over scripture stated and refuted, *ib.* 285, &c.; the true office of the church in relation to scripture, see in ii, below; all reformed churches are agreed about the canon, *Rog.* 80; they allow as many books as the catholic church ever did, 2 *Ful.* 219; only the canonical scriptures should be read in churches, 1 *Bul.* 9, 2 *Cran.* 39; heresies respecting the canon, *Rog.* 80, &c.; those who reject any part of scripture are refuted by that part which they allow, *Phil.* 353, 354

ii. *The authority of scripture:* on its authority, 2 *Cov.* 335, 2 *Hoop.* 43, 1 *Lat.* 85, *Rid.* 171, *Whita.* 275, &c.; theses on its authority, 3 *Whitg.* 621; it claims to be of divine authority, *Whita.* 289; in Christ's church its authority is conclusive, 2 *Tyn.* 251, 333; it is in the church, what law is in the state, *Whita.* 27; it must be our direction, *Rog.* 157; one clear text is as weighty as a thousand, *Rid.* 172; inferences from scripture are of equal authority with express statements, *Whita.* 514, 515; on the inspiration of scripture, *ib.* 101, 102; all scripture is given by inspiration of God, 1 *Tyn.* 88, *Whita.* 526, 632, &c.; the writers were by nature quite unfitted for their work, but qualified for it by the Holy Ghost, *Whita.* 294; the writers free from all error, *ib.* 37; there are no other writings free from error, 1 *Whitg.* 173; on the style of various inspired writers, *Whita.* 478; Ascham thought the inspired writers superior in style, &c. to the classical, 2 *Zur.* 71; scripture may be recognized as divine by all who are taught of God, *Whita.* 290; it is God's letter to us, *Pil.* 286; the word or voice of God, 2 *Cran.* 52, 4 *Jew.* 1631, *Whita.* 296; he speaks in it, *Whita.* 445, 450; it is not only to be heard, but to be embraced as the truth of God, *Now.* (4), 117; the authentic scripture was attested by miracles, 3 *Tyn.* 135; scripture (like Christ) requires not the testimony of man for its probation, *Phil.* 356, *Whita.* 336; scripture is its own evidence, *Whita.* 335, 357, 3 *Tyn.* 136, 137; its unity, *Whita.* 661; it is the voice of God, and therefore never inconsistent with itself, *Phil.* 353; Calvin's enumeration of the evidences of scripture, *Whita.* 293; no evidences are sufficient without the teaching of the Holy Ghost, *ib.* 294, 295; Augustine, Chrysostom, Jerome, and other fathers on the sole authority of scripture, *Coop.* 187, &c.; when he tempted Christ, the devil was not so vain as to attempt to teach anything without its authority, 2 *Cran.* 52; its authority is internal, *Whita.* 279; and sealed not by the church, but by the Holy Ghost, *ib.* 280; it is not dependent on or subject or inferior to the church, but above it, 1 *Brad.* 519, 2 *Hoop.* 43, 3 *Jew.* 218, *Whita.* 275, 276, 459, 460; one Hermann affirms that the scriptures, apart from the testimony of the church, are of no more avail than Æsop's fables, *Whita.* 276; Cochlæus mentions many things therein which he says would not be credible, but for the authority of the church, *ib.* 282; its authority is not dependent on that of the church, 2 *Tyn.* 289, 3 *Tyn.* 49, 50, *Whita.* 332, &c.; the offices of the church in relation to the scriptures, *Phil.* 375, *Rog.* 193, *Whita.* 270, 283, 284; how much authority with respect to scripture is attributed to the church by the Papists and ourselves, *Whita.* 280, &c.; it is more ancient than the church, *ib.* 351, 352; the word is the foundation of the church, *Phil.* 135; the church is the witness and keeper thereof, *Rog.* 198; the church does not judge it, but according to it, *Whita.* 353; man cannot give authority to scripture, *Phil.* 357; it has authority in the reformation of the church, and is the rule to be followed therein, 3 *Bul.* 121, 122, 1 *Hoop.* 29, 1 *Jew.* 79, *Sand.* 250; scripture is a judge, 2 *Ful.* 134, &c.; the judge of faith and practices, 1 *Brad.* 393; the judge in all controversies, *ib.* 370, 2 *Brad.* 9, 1 *Hoop.* 278, 2 *Hoop.* 82, 282, *Rid.* 131, &c.; the judge of the doctors' writings, 1 *Hoop.* 30; the judgment of the doctors is not to be received without the authority of

SCRIPTURE

scripture, 1 *Bec.* 87; scripture is to be followed in preference to them, 1 *Lat.* 121; difference to be made between scripture and the writings of the bishops or fathers of the church, 2 *Cran.* 32; councils and doctors are nothing in comparison with the majesty and authority of scripture, *Phil.* 396; the fathers' doctrine must be tried by it, 1 *Tyn.* 154; and the doctrine of all preachers, 2 *Tyn.* 195; the pope will not have his doctrine tried thereby, *Sand.* 15, 16; it is to be preferred above all other writings, 2 *Cran.* 30, 31; More would have it tried by the catholic faith, not the faith by scripture, 3 *Tyn.* 111 n.; scripture is the divine balance, 2 *Cran* 30; it is the rule of faith, see iii, below; the only standard, 2 *Jew.* 988; the touchstone to try all doctrines, 1 *Bec.* 87, 2 *Cran.* 14, 47, 48, 51, *Hutch.* 14, 15, 1 *Tyn.* 398; doctrines to be believed no farther than they accord with it, 2 *Cran.* 18; all religious councils have ascribed the supreme decision to scripture, *Whita.* 434, 435; it was always appealed to by the fathers, 2 *Cran.* 77; its authority, as the final decider of Christian doctrine, depreciated by More, but maintained by Tyndale, 3 *Tyn.* 96—100, 110, 133—145; reference to an anonymous book on the Authority of Scripture and of the Church, 1 *Zur.* 267

iii. *The sufficiency of scripture:* the word of God is perfect, 3 *Bul.* 28, *Sand.* 421; probations out of scripture that there is therein a doctrine sound and in all parts perfect, 3 *Bec.* 319, &c.; its perfection proved by various texts, *Whita.* 615, &c.; from the uncertainty of tradition, *ib.* 651—669; from the rejection by Christ and the apostles of Jewish traditions, *ib.* 637, &c.; shewn by the testimony of the fathers, *ib.* 669—704; testimonies alleged from the fathers to the contrary considered, *ib.* 565, &c.; its sufficiency, 1 *Brad.* 435, 2 *Cran.* 528, 3 *Jew.* 222, &c., *Phil.* 358, &c., 1 *Whitg.* 180; asserted by Jerome and Augustine, *Rid.* 113; by Anne Askewe, *Bale* 234; how asserted by the reformed, *Whita.* 514; it is alone sufficient for doctrine and practice, 1 *Hoop.* 105, 111; sufficient for our instruction without images, 2 *Cran.* 10; sufficient for salvation without man's doctrine, 1 *Bec.* 134; it is a rule, the perfect and the only rule of faith and duty, 1 *Bul.* 13, 4 *Bul.* 248, 2 *Hoop.* 43, *Hutch.* 253, 2 *Jew.* 996, 998, *Rid.* 113, *Sand.* 12, 190, 222, *Whita.* 19, 474, 484, &c., 657, 658, 662; said by Bellarmine to be a commonitory, not a rule, *Whita.* 657, &c.; holy scripture contains all things necessary to salvation, 2 *Bec.* 15, 2 *Cran.* 21, 2 *Hoop.* 120, 130, 186, 543, *Now.* (2), 115, *Rid.* 53, *Rog.* 76, 3 *Tyn.* 26, 96—99, 226, 231, *Whita.* 629; all things which are to be believed of God, 3 *Bul.* 160; all things that concern faith, good living, and charity, 2 *Cran.* 17; of scripture only is Christ and his truth learned, 1 *Bec.* 87; it is the sole foundation of our faith, *Phil.* 194; the foundation and rule of religion, *Sand.* 12, 222; the only necessary treasure, *Park.* 338; Christian religion only to be learned from it, *Now.* (2), 114; it teaches all points of true godliness, 1 *Bul.* 61; it is not to be added to, *Phil.* 372; without the word we must do nothing, to it add nothing, 1 *Tyn.* 330; words not found in it, how far to be received, *Whita.* 588; there are many things not settled in scripture, 1 *Whitg.* 216; the perfection of scripture denied by ancient heretics, *Whita.* 544, &c.; its sufficiency denied by Papists, 2 *Ful.* 162; Romish evasions with regard to it, *Whita.* 157; true Christians rest their faith on it, not on unwritten traditions, *Sand.* 12—14; Romanists say that scripture is insufficient without tradition; their arguments considered, *Whita.* 524, &c.; some make tradition equal to scripture, *Rog.* 78, 79; the word of God forsaken for the writings of doctors in the ninth century, 1 *Hoop.* 524; DIVERSITY BETWEEN GOD'S WORD AND MAN'S INVENTION, by T. Becon, 3 *Bec.* 484, &c.; men first act without scripture, afterwards against scripture, 1 *Jew.* 24, 25

iv. *The original text, and versions thereof* (v. Bible): the authentic scripture is contained in the Hebrew and Greek originals, not in the Latin Vulgate, *Whita.* 135; no version can be authentic in the fullest sense, *ib.* 138, 140; the original scriptures much decried by Papists, *ib.* 157; it is admitted that errors have crept into their text, 1 *Ful.* 43; scripture should not be read to the people in an unknown tongue, *Now.* (4), 116; but it should be translated into every language, 1 *Tyn.* 7, 144; all men should know it, *ib.* 241 (see below); the state of the question concerning vernacular versions, *ib.* 208; reasons for them, *ib.* 235; arguments against them refuted, 1 *Tyn.* 146, *Whita.* 211; the advantage of various translations, 2 *Cov.* 13; testimonies of the fathers respecting many, *Whita.* 245; divers versions of the Greeks and Latins, 2 *Cov.* 13, 1 *Ful.* 73, 439, 2 *Jew.* 692,

Whita. 123, 128; translations were used by the Armenians, Russians, Ethiopians, Dalmatians, and Goths, 1 *Jew.* 270, 2 *Jew.* 690, &c., *Whita.* 221, 245; they were common in Africa in early times, *Whita.* 217, 218; they are not injurious to the people, *ib.* 229, &c.; they should be corrected when obsolete, *ib.* 232; they are permitted by the church of Rome under certain conditions, *ib.* 140; suffered in some Romish countries, *Bale* 336; crafty pretences of the prelates to stop the reading of scripture, 2 *Lat.* 303; the subtle shifts of the popish clergy in opposition to its circulation, 1 *Tyn.* 392, 393; the earliest papal law against the laity possessing the word of God in their native tongue, *ib.* 132 n.; the prohibition came not from love to their souls, *ib.* 161; Erasmus would have it removed, *ib.* 161 n., 162, *Whita.* 249; a decree concerning vernacular translations in Pius IV.'s Index, *Whita.* 209; Sanders says it has always been a trick of Jews and heretics to be still in hand with translations, 2 *Ful.* 370; the opinion of the reformed concerning versions of scripture, *Whita.* 211; the Bible should be in the English tongue, 1 *Tyn.* 144; More says that the church does not forbid the scripture in English, but orders that no man shall translate or read it without authority, 3 *Tyn.* 166; yet he acknowledges that none dare print even an unproscribed translation, *ib.* 168; to possess the Bible in English was deemed a sign of heresy, 2 *Jew.* 993; attempts to suppress it, *Bale* 440, 441; the privilege of having it, 1 *Lat.* 369; no translation perfect, 2 *Jew.* 831; alleged mistranslations by Beza, 1 *Ful.* 594; alleged mistranslations in the English Bible, *ib.* 592, 2 *Jew.* 831

v. *The reading, study, and exposition of scripture:* the knowledge of scripture belongs to all men, *Phil.* 326, 327; it is necessary for all, 2 *Cran.* 119, *Pil.* 120, 608, 1 *Tyn.* 241, *Whita.* 516, 517, 521, &c.; needful as a remedy against ignorance, 2 *Hoop.* 312; the fathers confess that it is necessary for all Christians, *Whita.* 289, &c.; they exhort the people to read the scripture, 4 *Jew* 795, *Whita.* 244, &c.; remarkable knowledge of scripture gained by the hermit Anthony, 2 *Jew.* 684, 3 *Jew.* 430, 435; also by a bedridden slave*, 2 *Jew.* 684; it must be diligently read and studied by the clergy, 2 *Hoop.* 129; laymen to be encouraged to study the Bible, 2 *Cran.* 81; the profit of the scripture being read by them, 3 *Bec.* 542, &c.; it ought to be read by all in the vulgar tongue, 2 *Bec.* 424, 2 *Cran* 122, 2 *Hoop.* 44, 391, 2 *Jew.* 669, &c., 4 *Jew.* 895, 896, *Whita.* 212, 243; what it is to have all scripture locked up, and what to have it unlocked, 1 *Tyn.* 27, 464, 469, 2 *Tyn.* 7; it is now lawful to read it, 1 *Bec.* 82; how it is to be read, 2 *Bec.* 608; Origen supposed that the reading of scripture might be profitable, after the manner of a spell, even to those who understood it not, *Whita.* 266 n.; on the alleged danger of reading, 2 *Jew.* 682; the true use of reading, 3 *Bec.* 107; directions for reading profitably, 1 *Tyn.* 8—11, 389, 398, &c., 403—405, 463, 469; it must be read believingly, 1 *Hoop.* 287; obediently, *ib.* 289; it must be diligently searched, *Whita.* 25, 235, 236, 644; it needs application, 4 *Bul.* 155; whether necessary for the government of the people, 1 *Lat.* 121; it should be read by those who go to the wars, 1 *Bec.* 252; children (*q. v.*) should be taught the Bible, 1 *Hoop.* 32; it must not be forgotten in pastime, 1 *Lat.* 121; of the public reading of scripture in the church, 3 *Whitg.* 28, &e., 2 *Zur.* 234; only the canonical books to be read, 1 *Bul.* 9, 2 *Cran.* 39; the profit of public reading, 3 *Whitg.* 46; it should be heard with reverence and fear, *Jew.* 1182; the Ethiopian eunuch and the scripture, 2 *Cran.* 121; the Bible written out by command of Constantine, and sent to all parts, 2 *Jew.* 690; knowledge of scripture encouraged by Cranmer in opposition to the study of school-authors, 1 *Cran.* viii; the curates knew not what a whole Bible was, 1 *Tyn.* 146; on the obscurity and perspicuity of scripture, 1 *Bul.* 70; scripture said to be hard, 2 *Jew.* 683; it contains innumerable mysteries, *Phil.* 407, many difficulties, 1 *Bul* 71, and some apparent contradictions, *Whita.* 377; whether too dark to be profitable, 1 *Bul.* 70; controversy on its perspicuity, *Whita.* 359, &c., reasons why God would have many obscurities in it, *Whita.* 365, 366; notwithstanding these obscurities scripture is, in general, plain and easy to be understood, 1 *Bul.* 72, 1 *Ful.* 77; there are some places in which an elephant may swim, and others through which a lamb may wade, *Whita.* 374 (this similitude is Gregory's, 1 *Jew.* 331, 2 *Jew.* 684, *Whita.* 400); Luther distinguishes between the obscurity of passages, and the obscurity of

---

* Gregor. Magni Papæ I. Op. Par. 1705. In Evang. Lib. I. Hom. xv. 5. Tom. I. col. 1491.

SCRIPTURE

doctrine, allowing that many texts are difficult, but affirming that all dogmas are plain, *Whita.* 361; he also says that the perspicuity or obscurity is either internal or external, *i. e.* in the heart or in the words, *ib.* 363; he admits that there are many difficulties in scripture, and assigns a reason for them, *ib.* 364; the perspicuity of scripture is not disproved by experience, *ib.* 379, 380; it is proved from several passages of the scripture itself, *ib.* 381—388; from the clearness of its principal points, *ib.* 388; from the difference between the two Testaments, one sealed, the other opened, *ib.* 389; from its having been understood in the first ages without any commentaries, *ib.* 391; by the object of all writing, *ib.* 392; by a consideration of the two classes of readers, the faithful and unfaithful, *ib.*; from its argumentative use by the fathers, *ib.* 390; from the testimonies of the fathers, *ib.* 393—400; and even from the admissions of Romanists, *ib.* 400, 401; supposed testimonies of the fathers against the perspicuity of scripture considered, *ib.* 370—376; nothing defined on this subject by the council of Trent, *ib.* 359; general sentiments of the Papists concerning it, *ib.* 360; in their estimation scripture is dark, 1 *Jew.* 381; Romish evasions with regard to it, *Whita.* 5, &c.; our sentiments concerning it generally misrepresented, *ib.* 361; our real sentiments, *ib.* 364; the senses of scripture; Augustine enumerates the historical (or grammatical, or literal), the ætiological, the analogical, and the allegorical, *ib.* 403; other mystical senses are mentioned as the tropological, and the anagogic, *ib.*; some speak of the analogical, allegorical, historical and moral exposition, *Rog.* 197; the schoolmen assign to scripture four senses; the literal, tropological, allegorical, and analogical, 1 *Tyn.* 303, &c., 343; eminence in each of these four senses assigned to Gregory, Ambrose, Augustine, and Jerome, respectively, *ib.* 343 n.; Tyndale says that it has but one sense, viz. the literal, though it uses figures, *ib.* 304; Whitaker, not wholly rejecting the above distinctions, yet maintains that there is properly but one sense of scripture, viz. the literal, *Whita.* 404—410; the literal sense to be taken, 1 *Tyn.* 399; what is truly the literal sense, *Whita.* 404, 405; the literal sense is all spiritual, 1 *Tyn.* 309; scripture consists not in bare words, but in the sense, 1 *Hoop.* 401, *Whita.* 402; the histories (especially Christ's miracles) have a spiritual signification, 2 *Lat.* 170; the letter and the spirit, 1 *Brad.* 567, *Rid.* 31, 32; the letter and the spirit compared to the humanity and divinity of the begotten Word, *Whita.* 404; knowledge of scripture is twofold, in the letter and in the spirit, *ib.* 613; in the spirit it is understood by the elect only, *ib.* 613, 614; only by such as have their baptismal profession at heart, 2 *Tyn.* 138, &c.; the schoolmen and their followers slight the literal sense, 1 *Tyn.* 303, 308, 393; scripture is not to be taken always as the letter soundeth, *Grin.* 40; the literal meaning not always the true one, 3 *Tyn.* 229, 243, 249; scripture often speaks as men speak, but must be understood spiritually, 1 *Tyn.* 88; many things in it have first a carnal fulfilling, then a spiritual one, *ib.* 355; when we are to depart from the letter, 4 *Bul.* 437; how the letter killeth, *ib.* 287, *Hutch.* 15, 2 *Jew.* 1111, 1112, *Phil.* 57, 1 *Tyn.* 308, 2 *Tyn.* 141; the tropological sense, 1 *Tyn.* 303, &c., *Whita.* 403, 406; the figures or metaphors of scripture, *Bale* 261, *Grin.* 42; they are not obscure, *Whita.* 379; the allegorical sense, 1 *Tyn.* 303, &c.; examples of scripture allegories (or types), *Whita.* 405; Sandys's allegorical or moral application of the "signs in the sun," &c., *Sand.* 358; the analogical sense, *Rid.* 233; divers expositions are allowable, so that they agree with the catholic faith, 2 *Lat.* 198; concerning the exposition or interpretation of scripture, 1 *Bul.* 72, 4 *Bul.* 154, *Whita.* 402, &c.; it ought to be expounded, 1 *Bul.* 70, &c., *Now.* (3), 116; how to be interpreted, 1 *Hoop.* 28, 84; rule of the council of Trent, *Whita.* 402, 403; Stapleton's cautions respecting its interpretation, *ib.* 411—414; Bellarmine's rules, *ib.* 414; we should search for the meaning of scripture, 2 *Lat.* 189; it is not to be expounded after private conceit, 1 *Ful.* 9; or according to men's fantasies, 1 *Bul.* 75 (*v.* Judgment); it should be expounded as Christ and his disciples expounded it, *Phil.* 376; its proper sense restored under the reformation, 1 *Cran.* 6; its manner of speaking to us, 1 *Tyn.* 107; how its terms are to be understood, 2 *Cov.* 19; an exposition of certain words and phrases in the New Testament, 1 *Tyn.* 531; scripture contains nothing superstitious or unprofitable, *Pil.* 370; there is nothing in it which is not precious, 1 *Tyn.* 310; two things to be marked in doubtful texts, 1 *Hoop.* 292; how we must understand if one sentence seems to repugn a multitude, 2 *Bec.* 290; in what manner we ought to understand the examples contained in it, 2 *Cov.* 15; we are not to approve or imitate whatever is there recorded, *Calf.* 281, 282; scripture is of no private interpretation, *Rid.* 114, 1 *Tyn.* 317; it cannot be understood except by the special help of God's Spirit, 2 *Jew.* 685, 1 *Tyn.* 88; the scripture being inspired, only the Spirit can infallibly interpret it, *Whita.* 451; faith in scripture is produced by the Holy Spirit, as the fathers confess, and even the Papists themselves, *ib.* 355—358; scripture makes a difference between the ministry of men and the operation of the Spirit, 4 *Bul.* 273; all have not the gift of public interpretation, but all the faithful understand, *Whita.* 433; men cannot try doctrine by the scripture unless they have the Spirit, *Calf.* 60; it availeth nothing without faith, 1 *Lat.* 544; scripture is the outward instrument, but faith is the work of the Spirit, 3 *Tyn.* 139; scripture cannot be understood by those who deny justification through faith in Christ's blood, 3 *Tyn.* 169; application of scripture necessary, 4 *Bul.* 155; on the means of finding the sense of scripture, *Whita.* 466; prayer is a means, 1 *Bul.* 78, *Now.* (5), 117, *Whita.* 467; another means is knowledge of the original tongues, &c., *Whita.* 362, 468; another means is consideration whether the words are proper or figurative, *ib.* 470; another means is to mark the scope, and context, and circumstances, 1 *Bul.* 77, *Whita.* 470; another means is the collation of different places, 1 *Bul.* 78, *Whita.* 471, both of like places and of dissimilar ones, *Whita.* 472; scripture is to be interpreted by itself, 1 *Ful.* 9, 1 *Hoop.* 271, *Hutch.* 353, *Tyn.* 249, *Whita.* 415, 445, 488, &c.; dark places in it are to be expounded by others more plain, 2 *Cran.* 17; the Old Testament is declared by the New, 1 *Cov.* 71; collation of scripture not the cause of heresies, *Whita.* 480; another means is attention to the analogy of faith, 1 *Ful.* 37, *Rog.* 195, *Whita.* 472; scripture must not be expounded contrary to the articles of belief, 1 *Bul.* 75; no exposition must be repugnant to the love of God and of our neighbour, 1 *Bul.* 76; another means is recourse to the learned, *Whita.* 473; Romish arguments against these means, *ib.* 474, 476, &c.; the Jews (says Whitaker) had no commentaries on the prophets, in the time of Christ, *ib.* 391; no Christian commentary known before Origen, *ib.*; expositions are not forbidden, *Bale* 637, 1 *Bul.* 74; exposition is necessary, 1 *Bul.* 70—72; what expositors are to be preferred, 1 *Cov.* 409; some said that they could not be understood without Aristotle, 1 *Tyn.* 154; on the authority of the church in relation to the interpretation of scripture, *Phil.* 375, *Rog.* 193; it rests not with the church authoritatively, *Whita.* 416, &c.; Romish arguments from the Old Testament refuted, *ib.*; the Romish means of interpretation resolve themselves into the authority of the pope, *ib.* 484; he is no sufficient interpreter, *ib.* 460; no man or set of men may challenge an exclusive right to interpret it, *Phil.* 377; scripture is not to be interpreted by the alleged unanimous consent of the fathers, (*q. v.*), *Whita.* 448; Cajetan denies that the exposition of scripture is so tied by God, *ib.* 466; there is no such thing as the unanimous consent of the fathers, *ib.* 455, 456; to admit all the interpretations of the doctors is to refuse any certain sense, 1 *Ful.* 545; to interpret scripture by the doctors, is to measure the meteyard by the cloth, 1 *Tyn.* 153; there was a time when the fathers were not extant, *Whita.* 456; the interpretation of scripture rests with the Holy Spirit and scripture itself, *ib.* 415, 447, &c.; proofs that the supreme decision belongs not to the church, but to scripture and the Holy Spirit, *ib.* 447, &c.; it is proved from various texts, *ib.* 457, &c.; from the absurdity of resolving faith into human judgment, *ib.* 459; from the principle that the lawgiver has supreme authority to expound the law, *ib.*; from the absurdity of making the church superior to scripture, *ib.* 459, 460; from the testimony of the fathers, *ib.* 461, &c.; scripture is the law, the interpreter, in a sense, the judge, *ib.* 446; some errors respecting the interpretation of scripture, *Rog.* 193—197; scripture not to be corrupted with foreign expositions, 1 *Bul.* 74; why it is not understood by the prelates, 3 *Tyn.* 98; false interpretations are to be avoided, 1 *Hoop.* 110; it must be cleared from perverse interpretations, 2 *Tyn.* 144; errors from the misinterpretation of scripture, 2 *Jew.* 1110

vi. *The use and benefits of scripture:* scripture was written for our learning, 4 *Jew.* 1166, 1 *Lat.* 59, 85, 112, 129, 171, 194, 216, *Sand.* 113, *Whita.* 392; its excellence, 3 *Bec.* 490, &c., 2 *Cov.* 311, 2 *Jew.* 1034, 1 *Lat.* 85; its importance, 2 *Brad.* 8; its profit, 4 *Jew.* 1166; instruction to be derived from it, 2 *Cov.* 21, 2 *Hoop.* 312, 4 *Jew.* 1175, &c.; it was given that man might be led to salvation, 1 *Cov.* 394; it is intended to bring men to God, 2 *Tyn.* 147; God is to be sought in it, *Sand.* 153; in it the ignorant may learn what they should know, 2 *Cran.* 121, 2 *Hoop.* 312; it teaches about God, 2 *Hoop.* 71; it teaches what Christ is, also what man, heaven, and hell are, 1 *Hoop.* 26; it engenders faith, *Whita.* 448; the knowledge of it is practical, 1 *Hoop.* 95; it leads to virtue, *ib.* 109; it is for holiness as well as for wisdom, *ib.* 77; it is edifying to all, 2 *Cran.* 120; a lamp, and a light, *Whita.* 383—387; the light and life of God's elect, 2 *Tyn.* 143; the true manna, the bread which came down from heaven, the key of the kingdom of heaven, &c., 4 *Jew.* 1164; a precious jewel, *Sand.* 113; the instrument of salvation, and a better jewel than gold or silver, 2 *Cran.* 120; the only medicine for all diseases, *ib.*, 4 *Jew.*1174; it is our spiritual sword, 1 *Lat.* 505; the sword of the Spirit, 1 *Tyn.* 398; our weapon against Satan (*q. v.*), 3 *Bec.* 158, *Whita.* 237; its power against error, 4 *Jew.* 1166; it is a remedy against adultery, 2 *Bec.* 101; heretics must be confuted by it, *Phil.* 141; all heresies and false doctrines may be so confuted, 1 *Hoop.* 111; the Arians refuted out of it, *Whita.* 481, 534, &c., 562, &c.; the pope to be resisted by it, 2 *Hoop.* 240; heretics who deny scripture, must be met with other arguments, *Whita.* 441; the mere words have no power against demons, 1 *Jew.* 327

vii. *Some abuses of scripture* (others in the preceding divisions): abusing of the scriptures, 4 *Jew.* 752; the truth of God's word is darkened by man's wisdom, 1 *Hoop.* 27; scripture darkened by Pharisees and hypocrites, 2 *Tyn.* 5; altered by their glosses, *ib.* 41; its true sense corrupted by the scribes, and by the church of Rome, 3 *Tyn.*43—48; darkened by Romish doctors, 2 *Tyn.* 102, 103, 140, &c.; its meaning concealed by Latin and false glosses, 3 *Tyn.* 136; wrested by Papists, 1 *Lat.* 60, 2 *Lat.* 283, 320; made to serve a wicked purpose, 1 *Hoop.*140; their manner of perverting it, *ib.*, 1 *Tyn.* 449, 450, 2 *Tyn.* 280; absurd popish interpretations, 1 *Ful.* 36; six heretical opinions concerning scripture held by them, *Whita.* 705; Romish blasphemies against scripture, 1 *Ful.* 8, 4 *Jew.* 753, &c.; the popish clergy say it teaches disobedience, 1 *Tyn.* 163, 392; and that it makes heretics, *ib.* 28, 392; it makes no heretics, 2 *Tyn.* 141, &c.; the pope cannot dispense with it, 1 *Cran.* x; it has been burnt by Papists, 3 *Bec.* 65, 4 *Jew.* 761, 1 *Tyn.* xxxi; as it was by king Joachim and Antiochus, 3 *Bec.* 66, 4 *Jew.* 1165; it were as well burned as rendered useless, 1 *Hoop.* 139; condemned as new learning, 2 *Lat.* 318—320; called a nose of wax, *Rog.* 195 (*v.* Pighius); scriptures wiped out of the temples by the Papists, 3 *Bec.* 233; scripture alleged by heretics, and how, 3 *Jew.* 240, 242, *Phil.* 306; subverted by their proud free-will knowledge, *Phil.* 308; corrupted by them, 1 *Ful.* 11; abused and discredited by various heretics, *Rog.* 77—79; statement that all heretics profess to follow it, *Whita.* 229; but many heretics have rejected parts of it, and some the whole, *Rog.* 77, 80, 83, 84, 87, *Whita.* 298; sitting down upon the Bible, 3 *Tyn.* 169; contempt of God's word is the sin of sins, *Poet.* 372

Scrooby, co. Notts: a manor of the see of York, 2 *Cran.* 437 n

Scrope (Rich.), abp of York: a false martyr, *Bale* 189

Scrope (Hen. lord): invades Scotland, 1 *Zur.* 225 n

Scrope (Eliz. lady): 1 *Tyn.* 148 n

Scultetus (Abr.): *Calf.* 78 n., 2 *Ful.* 295 n., 2 *Zur.* 328 n

Scurfield (Jo.), of Bristol: examined by Latimer, 2 *Lat.* 404

Scute: a light boat, *Bale* 533

Scythians: their law against swearing and perjury, 1 *Bec.* 391; their Jobelæa, *Rog.* 202

Scythianus: the first originator of the Manichæan heresy, *Rog.* 79 n

Sea: *v.* Dead Sea, Red Sea.

Its creation and uses, 3 *Bul.* 175, 2 *Hoop.* 365; it is a figure of the troublous world, *Sand.* 370, 380; the Syrian sea, what, 1 *Bul.* 170; a prayer for mariners, 3 *Bec.* 33

Seage: a seat, 2 *Hoop.* 135

Seal, Seals: those of princes, *Pil.* 191; the great seal of England, *Calf.* 36; the Holy Ghost and the sacraments are God's seals, *Pil.* 193; seals in sacraments, 4 *Bul.* 318, 1 *Hoop.* 133 (& al. *v.* Sacraments); miracles as seals, 4 *Bul.* 451; opening of the seven seals, Rev. vi, *Bale* 312, &c.; the sealed, Rev. vii, *ib.* 334, *Calf.* 98, 2 *Ful.* 138, *Rid.* 69

Searchfield (Jo.): a wanderer for conscience' sake, 2 *Brad.* 58 n

Searle (Geo.), or Searles: martyred, *Poet.* 168

Seaton (Jo.): *v.* Seton.

Seats: necessary in a church, 4 *Bul.* 501, 2 *Hoop.* 135 (*v.* Pews).

Seats, i.e. Thrones: a name of angels, 3 *Bul.* 337

Sebald (Dr): 2 *Zur.* 19, 52, 74

Sebastian (St): invoked for the plague, *Rog.* 226; prayer to him, *ib.* 227
Sebastian, servant to lord Cromwell: 2 *Cov.* 494, 497
Sebastian, i. e. S. Westcote, *q. v.*
Sebastian (......): saluted, 1 *Zur.* 30
Secelles (......): *v.* Cechelles.
Seckendorff (Vit. Lud.): Comm. Hist. de Lutheranismo, *Jew.* xliii; on the character of Leo X., 2 *Cov.* 139 n
Seckford (Tho.): an ecclesiastical commissioner, *Park.* 370 n.; letter from him to Parker, *Park.* 142
Secreta: a term in the mass-book, 2 *Jew.* 707
Secrets: *Pil.* 341, 342; holy ones, 4 *Bul.* 236
Sectaries: *v.* Heretics.
Their prevalence, 3 *Bec.* 401; their licentiousness censured, *ib.* 6; ministers must warn against them, *ib.* 293; names of some writers, *Rog.* 203; the names of maintainers of sectaries to be presented to the ordinary, *Grin.* 143
Sects: *v.* Heresy.
αἱρέσεις, why translated sects, 1 *Ful.* 221, 224; Christians called a sect by Tertullian, 3 *Jew.* 212; in what sense, *ib.* 214; sects among the Jews, 2 *Bec.* 525, 2 *Cran.* 145; St Paul rebukes sect-makers, 1 *Tyn.* 511; many in the apostolic age and since, 2 *Bec.* 525, 526, 2 *Ful.* 375, 2 *Jew.* 687, 3 *Jew.* 603; many in the church of Rome, 2 *Bec.* 415, 2 *Ful.* 375, *Sand.* 17, 1 *Tyn.* 124, 128, 3 *Tyn.* 103, 128; many monstrous ones, 1 *Bec.* 254; that of Antichrist most pernicious, 3 *Bec.* 503; a great number of them in the age of the reformation, 2 *Bec.* 526, 2 *Jew.* 686, *Nord.* 114; more numerous in modern times than with the Jews, 2 *Cran.* 147; many amongst Protestants, 1 *Ful.* 34, 35, 3 *Jew.* 429, 602
Seculum: *v.* World.
Security: against carnal security, with sentences and examples of scripture, 1 *Bec.* 471; the danger of sleeping in security, *Sand.* 210
Sedgrave (Chr.), mayor of Dublin: *Park.* 95 n
Sedgwick (Tho.): one of the Romish disputants at Cambridge, 1549, *Grin.* 194, *Rid.*169; he disputes with Cranmer, 1*Cran.* 391; refuses the oath of supremacy, *Park.* 105
Sedition: *v.* Rebellion.
Sedon (Alice): 2 *Brad.* 228
Sedulius (Cælius): Collectan. in Pauli Epistolas, *Jew.* xliii; says God by nature is the God of all; but by will the God of few, 4 *Jew.* 662; on the Transfiguration, *Wool.* 133; referred to on the eucharist, 1 *Cran.* 195; likewise on justification, 2 *Bec.* 639; some of his verses introduced into a work untruly ascribed to Jerome, *Calf.* 178 n
Seed of the woman: *v.* Christ, iv.
Seely: simple, inoffensive, weak, 1 *Brad.* 283, *Phil.* 264, *Pil.* 595, *Rid.* 6 n., 3*Whitg.* 52; sely, *Grin.* 60, *Lit. Eliz.* 545, *Pil.*209; silly, 1 *Bul.* 286, 351, 2 *Bul.* 45, 98, 169, 3 *Bul.* 83; meaning of the word traced, *Rid.* 6 n
Seez (Osmund de): *v.* Osmund (St).
Segar (Will.): a rebel, 2 *Cran.* 187 n
Segrave (Elynour): *v.* Saygrave.
Segusio (Hen. de): *v.* Hostiensis.
Seigniory, and Seniors: *v.* Priests.
Seiler (Jo.): 4 *Bul.* 546
Seiti: Turkish priests, *Rog.* 120, 359
Seius (Caius): a Christian called by Jewel Marcus Sejanus, 2 *Jew.* 1089
Selah: 2 *Hoop.* 327
Seld: seldom, *Calf.* 54
Selden (Jo.): Titles of Honor, *Calf.* 6 n., 35 n
Seleucians, or Hermians: their opinions, 2 *Cov.* 160, 184, 1 *Hoop.* 160; they set baptism at nought, 4 *Bul.* 397
Self: *v.* Denial, Examination, Knowledge.
Love of self the root of all mischief, 1 *Lat.* 434
Selim II., sultan of Turkey: 2 *Zur.* 246
Sellerar: *v.* Cellarer.
Selling: *v.* Buying.
Sellum: *v.* Shallum.
Selneccerus (Ric.): thought bishops might summon councils, *Rog.* 206; answered by Beza, 1 *Ful.* 159
Sely: *v.* Seely.
Semblably: similarly, 1 *Bec.* 39
Semer (Lady Jane): *v.* Seymour.
Semi-Arians: *v.* Arians (Semi).
Semo Sancus: a Sabine god, *Calf.* 343 n
Semsted: separated, removed, 1 *Bec.* 136
Sempach: battle there, 1386, 2 *Zur.* 263 n
Sempil (Rob. lord): one of the confederate lords, 1 *Zur.* 193 n
Sempill (Helen): a Papist in Edinburgh, 2 *Zur.* 331 n
Senators: 4 *Bul.* 106
Seneca (L. A.): teaches that there is one God the Creator, 1 *Hoop.* 285; says that God is our observer, and ever with us, *Wool.* 95; shews how the gods are to be worshipped, 1 *Bul.* 199, 200; says the anger of God maketh those miserable upon whom it lighteth; not so the wrath of

man, 4 *Jew.* 1153; speaks of the torments of a guilty conscience, *Wool.* 99; declares that man was created to behold and gaze upon the stars, 3 *Bul.* 194; says that nature has mingled pleasure and necessity, *Wool.* 92; advises to mark not who speaks, but what is spoken, 2 *Bec.* 324; writes on the evils of bad company,*Wool.* 129; exhorts Lucilius to avoid the vulgar, *ib.* 84; instructs how to use riches, *ib.* 89; says, I lend myself to the things of the world, but do not give myself to them, &c., 2 *Cov.* 127; advises respecting gifts, *Hutch.* 3; describes how life is wasted, *Sand.* 392; says that death is always imminent, *Wool.* 141; counsels men in misery to dispatch themselves, 2 *Bul.*415; affirms and proves the immortality of the soul, 3 *Bul.* 385; other sayings of his, 3 *Jew.* 227, 614; he speaks of the sabbath of the Jews (quoted by Augustine), 1 *Hoop.* 346; commends Epicurus,*Wool.* 94; gives an account of Sextius, *Wool.*101; relates that Julius Cæsar reached out his foot for Pompeius Pœnus to kiss, that folks might see his golden slipper set with stones, 4 *Jew.* 689

Seniors: *v.* Priests, ix.

Sennacherib, king of Assyria: fights against Israel, and is overthrown, 2 *Bul.* 9, 3 *Bul.* 133, 2 *Hoop.* 231, 266, *Pil.* 28; slain, 1 *Bul.* 242

Sens: *v.* Councils.

Senses: *v.* Scripture, v.

The word "sensibilis" explained, *Now.* (104); articles of faith may be above, but not contrary to our senses, 1*Cran.* 245, 246, 262, 263; Romish doctrine is contrary to our senses, *ib.* 245, 246, 262, 263; if we may not trust them, the sensible sacrament is but a piece of jugglery, *ib.* 256; sensitive powers of the soul, 3 *Bul.* 376; a reprobate sense, 2 *Bul.* 380

Sensing: incensing, *Calf.* 343

Sentence (The general): *v.* Curse.

Sentences (The Master of the): *v.* Peter Lombard.

Sentleger (......): *v.* Saint-Leger.

Sentlow (Mr): harbours Hooper, 2 *Hoop.* viii.

Senwalch, king: *v.* Coinualch.

Separation: *v.* Water.

Separatists: *v.* Puritans.

Against them, 4 *Bul.* 52; the first in England, 2 *Brad.* 173 n.; some in the time of Elizabeth, *Grin.* 293, 316, 1 *Zur.* 202

Sepharad (Obad. 20): said to be Spain, *Pil.* 268

Septuagint: *v.* Bible, *Greek.*

Sepulchre: *v.* Easter.

Seraphics: an order of monks, *Phil.* 420

Seraphim: 3 *Bul.* 338

Serapion, bp of Antioch: rejects certain books falsely inscribed with the names of the apostles, *Whita.* 326

Serapion, or Syrapion, the sacrament sent to him, *Coop.* 28, 153, &c., 2 *Ful.* 105, *Grin.* 48, 1 *Hoop.* 172 n., 521, 1 *Jew.* 149, 151, 243, 244, 245, 2 *Jew.* 554, 556, *Phil.* 117, 2 *Whitg.* 542, 3 *Whitg.* 66

Serapis, the Egyptian idol: had a cross upon his breast, *Calf.* 65, 91, 107, 2 *Ful.* 148; how the cross recommended Christianity to the Egyptians, *Calf.* 276, 277; impostures connected with his worship, *ib.* 274; his temple at Alexandria destroyed, 2 *Jew.* 648

Serarius (Nich.): his idea as to the meaning of the word Cephas, 2 *Ful.* 301 n

Sere: dry, or late, *Calf.* 228, 279, 295

Serenus, bp of Marseilles: broke images, *Bale* 97, 2 *Bec.* 61, 71, *Calf.* 9, 30, 379, 1 *Hoop.* 41, 2 *Jew.* 655, *Park.* 89, *Rid.* 92, 497, 3 *Tyn.*183, *Whita.* 509

Serenus Salmonicus, or Sammonicus: *Calf.* 285

Seres (Will.), printer: *Bale* 2, 1 *Cov.* 529, *Pil.* 274

Sergeant (Jo.), [i. e. Smith]: Anti-Mortonus, 2 *Ful.* 70 n

Sergius I., pope: his additions to the mass, 2 *Brad.* 311, 1 *Jew.* 97, 2 *Jew.* 586, *Pil.* 503; orders the host to be broken into three parts, and explains the meaning thereof, *Coop.* 77, 2 *Jew.* 585, 586, 4 *Jew.* 818; he set forth a piece of the cross to be worshipped, *Pil.* 602; the fable respecting his interview with Beza, 2 *Ful.* 119 n

Sergius II., pope: called Os Porci, 2 *Jew.* 586; private masses were not known prior to his time, 1 *Hoop.* 228

Sergius III., pope: his treatment of the body of Formosus, *Bale* 394, 1 *Hoop.* 218, 2 *Jew.* 586, 3 *Jew.* 276 n., 277 n., *Pil.* 652

Sergius IV., pope: an enchanter, *Rog.* 180

Sergius, the monk: aided Mahomet, *Bale* 572, 2 *Ful.* 79

Serjeants: *v.* Lawyers.

Serle (......): uncle of Hutchinson, *Hutch.* viii, ix.

Serles (Rob.): vicar of St Peter's in Oxford, *Jew.* vi; his part in the process against Cranmer, 2 *Cran.* 546, 548

Sermons: *v.* Advent, Assize, Parliament, Prayers, Preaching.

Sandys' farewell sermon at Paul's cross on his removal to York, *Sand.* 418; as to

50

SERMONS — SEVERITY

funeral sermons, see Burial; Sermones Discipuli, see Heroldt (Jo.); Dormi secure, 3 *Bec.* 200, 234

Serpent: v. Satan.
    The wisdom of the serpent, *Pil.* 425; the curse upon it, 1 *Cov.* 19; the Egyptians worshipped serpents, 1 *Bul.* 224; those of the Egyptian enchanters, 4 *Bul.* 276

Serpent (Brasen): cause of its erection, its effect and use, 1 *Hoop.* 54; no argument for images, *Calf.* 9, 335, 336, 1 *Ful.* 183; it was a token, *Grin.* 42; a type of Christ, 1 *Cov.* 44, 2 *Ful.* 202, 1 *Lat.* 73, 1 *Tyn.* 426, 3 *Whitg.* 33; it came to be worshipped, 1 *Lat.* 75; destroyed by Hezekiah, 2 *Bec.* 69, 70, 2 *Ful.* 202, *Park.* 89, 3 *Tyn.* 183

Serpentines: what, 1 *Lat.* 27 n

Serranus (......): *Rid.* 510

Sertorius (Q.): his speech, 1 *Bec.* 233

Servant of God: a glorious name, *Pil.* 364

Servants: v. Masters, Offices, Prayers.
    What, 3 *Bec.* 610; theirs is an honest estate, 1 *Lat.* 350; in serving with a good mind they serve Christ, *ib.* 351; what kind Christian men ought to have, 1 *Bec.* 388; limitation of their number demanded by the Devon rebels, 2 *Cran.* 185; exhortation of the sick man to his servants, 3 *Bec.* 134, 136; good examples for them, 1 *Lat.* 396, 2 *Lat.* 119, *Sand.* 270; a true and faithful one described, 3 *Bec.* 610; their duty, 1 *Bec.* 287, 2 *Bec.* 115, 363, &c., 520, 3 *Bec.* 134, 1 *Lat.* 350, 538, 2 *Lat.* 6, 85, 87, 90, *Pra. Eliz.* 237; not to rule their masters, 2 *Cran.* 185, but to honour them, 2 *Bec.* 363; they must obey them, *ib.* 363, 364; they are commanded to obey them, though they be evil, 2 *Hoop.* 81; what obedience they owe to them, 1 *Tyn.* 172; they must obey them unless they command contrary to God's word, 2 *Bec.* 364; how they may become good, *ib.*; where many are in a house together, they must strive to excel each other in virtue and well-doing, *ib.*; the chief point of a serving-man's office is not shooting, 2 *Lat.* 37; servants must be overseen, 1 *Lat.* 394, 395; they follow the evil examples of masters, 2 *Lat.* 79; faithful and slothful servants contrasted, 1 *Lat.* 19, 20; slothful and idle ones, 3 *Bec.* 610, *Pil.* 447; those who do their work negligently are thieves, 2 *Bec.* 106, 107, and cursed, 1 *Lat.* 395; eye-servants shall be condemned, *ib.* 394; the oaths of servants, 1 *Bec.* 361; servants paid tithe of their wages, 1 *Tyn.* 237; serving-men after long service are often cast away, 2 *Bec.* 442; articles respecting servants, *Grin.* 124, 137, 161

Servetians: 1 *Bul.* 9, 2 *Jew.* 686, *Rog.* 265, 280, 2 *Zur.* 185

Servetus (Mich.): his heretical doctrine, *Hutch.* 121, *Rog.* 45; he taught falsely respecting the Word, 2 *Brad.* 265; said that Christ was but a figure of the Son of God, *Rog.* 55; impugned the deity of the Holy Ghost, *ib.* 70; considered the Holy Ghost to be God's favour and virtue, *ib.* 73; denied baptism to infants, *ib.* 265, 280; disliked commentaries, *ib.* 196; proceedings against him, 3 *Zur.* 622 n., 742; his burning at Geneva, 3 *Jew.* 187, 188; his errors refuted by Calvin, 1 *Ful.* 59, 3 *Zur.* 743

Service (Divine): v. Worship.

Servitutes luminum: a term in the Roman law, 2 *Zur.* 94 n

Servus servorum: the style of cursed Ham, assumed by the pope, 2 *Tyn.* 248; yet he would be accounted lord of lords, *Phil.* 396; Gregory the Great styled himself servus servorum Dei, 1 *Jew.* 424

Sesostris, king of Egypt: yoked kings and princes together, and forced them to draw his waggon, 4 *Jew.* 702

Seth: 1 *Bul.* 40, 41, 4 *Bul.* 102; the pillars of Seth, mentioned by Josephus, 3 *Tyn.* 27 n

Setlings: saplings, young trees, 1 *Bec.* 18

Seton (Alex.), or Seyton: examined by Gardiner, *Bale* 433; compelled to recant, *ib.* 441, 1 *Bec.* viii.

Seton (Jo.), or Seyton: confers with Bradford, 1 *Brad.* 494; disputes with the martyrs at Oxford, 1 *Cran.* 391, 2 *Lat.* 269, *Rid.* 191

Seton (Jo.): a writer on logic, 1 *Whitg.* 84 (perhaps the same).

Seven: v. Orders, Sacraments.
    Meaning of this number in scripture, *Now.* (16), 130, 1 *Tyn.* 431, 432; seven-fold grace, *Calf.* 226; seven climates of the world, *Bale* 269, 426, 501; seven deadly sins, v. Sin; seven hills, v. Rome.

Severians: heretics, *Calf.* 211 n.; they rejected the Old Testament, *Rog.* 80, *Whita.* 31; also the Acts, *Rog.* 84, *Whita.* 35; perverted the scripture, 2 *Ful.* 390; thought it might be interpreted as men listed, *Rog.* 195; confounded the divine and human nature in Christ, *ib.* 54; thought the human nature of Christ before his passion was devoid of human affections, *ib.* 53; used no wine in the Lord's supper, *ib.* 295; denied the resurrection, *Whita.* 31

Severity: not cruelty, 1 *Bul.* 354

Severus (M. A. Alexander), emperor: had images of Christ, &c., 2 *Jew.* 646, 4 *Jew.* 1108; a piece of land being claimed by the Christians for a church and also by the taverners, the emperor decided in favour of the former, 3 *Jew.* 199; he saved the life of Ulpian, 2 *Jew.* 981, 982; his golden rule, 1 *Bul.* 197; his watchword, "Laboremus," 2 *Jew.* 650; ascribed also to Pertinax, 4 *Jew.* 1304

Severus (L. Septimius), emperor: a persecutor, 2 *Bul.* 105

Severus (Sulpitius): *v.* Sulpitius.

Severus, a heretic: 3 *Bec.* 401; he removed certain gold and silver doves, 2 *Jew.* 559

Severus (......): saluted, 2 *Cov.* 512

Seville: *v.* Councils.
 Called Hispalen, 1 *Brad.* 508

Sewell (......): prebendary of Carlisle, *Grin.* 285

Sext: *v.* Hours.

Sextius: his nightly self-examination, *Wool.* 101, 108, 111

Sextons: 4 *Bul.* 114, *Rid.* 498

Sextus: *v.* Law (Canon).

Seymour family: descended from the protector, 1 *Bec.* 396 n

Seymour (Jane), queen: *v.* Jane.

Seymour (Edw.), earl of Hertford, afterwards duke of Somerset: notice of him, 1 *Bec.* 396 n.; he pillages Edinburgh, 3 *Zur.* 37; a governor of the realm in the absence of king Henry, 2 *Cran.* 315 n.; named, *ib.* 338; lord protector, *ib.* 498, 504, 507, 508, 510, 512, 524, 530, 531, *Park.* 40, 3 *Zur.* 258; made duke, 3 *Zur.* 256 n.; a request to the lord protector, 1 *Lat.* 127; his men guard the king's person, 2 *Cran.* 522; Hooper his chaplain, 2 *Hoop.* x; Becon his chaplain, 1 *Bec.* x; he pulls down many churches and religious fabrics for the building of Somerset house, *Grin.* 29 n.; his conduct towards his brother, 3 *Zur.* 735, and towards the duke of Northumberland, *ib.*; charges of maladministration against him, 1549, *ib.* 728; conspiracy against him, *ib.* 76; his imprisonment in 1549, 1 *Bec.* x, 2 *Cran.* 522, 3 *Zur.* 69 n., 71; prayer for him, 3 *Bec.* 34 n.; his deliverance, 1 *Bec.* x, 3 *Zur.* 77, 78, 338, 464 n., 480, 636, 704 n.; thanksgiving for the same, 3 *Bec.* 34 n.; his preface to Coverdale's Spiritual and most Precious Pearl written about this time, 1 *Cov.* 91; made a privy councillor again, 3 *Zur.* 559; signature as such, *Rid.* 508; the privy council move the king for the restitution of his lands, *Hutch.* v. n.; he settles a foreign congregation at Glastonbury, 3 *Zur.* 738; mentioned, 2 *Brad.* 390; commended by Calvin, 3 *Zur.* 711; praised for godly bringing up of his children, 1 *Bec.* 399; too pliable in religious matters, 3 *Zur.* 439; his case, *Rid.* 59; sent to prison, 1551, 3 *Zur.* 577, 579, 729; tried, *ib.* 440, 579; his execution delayed, *ib.* 444; his execution, 3 *Bec.* 205, *Lit. Eliz.* 444, 3 *Zur.* 441 n., 449, 579, 731; his dying speech, and behaviour, 3 *Zur.* 731, 732; punished for his contempt of God's word, 1 *Brad.* 111, 2 *Brad.* xxix; his character, 3 *Zur.* 733, &c.; Calvin's sorrow at his death, *ib.* 737; letter by him, *Rid.* 505; extract from a letter to Sir Ph. Hobby, 2 *Cran.* 195 n.; letters to him, 2 *Brad.* 369, 370, *Rid.* 327, 3 *Zur.* 704; dedications to him, 1 *Hoop.* xi, *Phil.* 321

— Catherine (Fillol) his 1st wife: 3 *Zur.* 340; her (?) life sought, *Bale* 220, 242; she (?) sends Anne Askewe money, *ib.* 223

— Anne (Stanhope) his 2nd wife: account of her, 1 *Bec.* 396 n., 3 *Bec.* 3 n., 3 *Zur.* 340; imprisoned, 3 *Zur.* 342 n., 577; released, *ib.* 367; dedication to her, 3 *Bec.* 3

— His children, 1 *Bec.* 396 n., 3 *Bec.* 3 n., 3 *Zur.* 339, &c.

Seymour (Edw.), earl of Hertford (eldest son of the protector by his 2nd wife): 3 *Zur.* 341; his clandestine marriage with the lady Catherine Grey, the divorced wife of Hen. Herbert, and sister of the lady Jane, for which marriage he and his wife were committed to the Tower, 1 *Bec.* 396 n.*, *Park.* 149, 1 *Zur.* 103 n., 3 *Zur.* 304 n.; he was at the duke of Norfolk's trial, 1 *Zur.* 267 n.; dedication to him, 1 *Hoop.* v.

— Cath. (Grey) his wife, see above; an exhortation sent to her by the lady Jane, her sister, 2 *Cov.* 133

Seymour (Tho.), lord Seymour of Sudley: sent (when Sir Tho.) on an expedition to France, 2 *Cran.* 411 n.; lord admiral, *ib.* 496 n.; his proposed marriage with the duchess of Richmond, 2 *Bec.* 554 n., 2 *Cran.* 360 n.; a privy councillor, 2 *Cran.* 505, 510, 2 *Zur.* 159 n.; said to have attempted the life of king Edward, 3 *Zur.* 648; condemned, *ib.* 651; he was covetous, and a contemner of prayer, 1 *Lat.* 227; not content with his portion, *ib.* 271 n.; his character, *ib.* 160— 162; his pen, *ib.* 162; his wickedness, *ib.* 163, &c.; his downfall, 3 *Bec.* 3 n.; sent to

---

* For Frances read Catherine.

the Tower, 3 *Zur.* 477; beheaded, *ib.* 55 n., 648 n.; his horrible death, 1 *Lat.* 160—162; his death procured by his brother, the protector, 3 *Zur.* 735; his attainder defended, 1 *Lat.* 181

Seymour (Lord Edw.): eldest son of the protector, 3 *Zur.* 341; he takes flight, 1 *Zur.* 309

Seymour (Lord Hen.): son of the protector, 3 *Zur.* 341

Seymour (Lady Anne): married Ambrose, lord Lisle, afterwards earl of Warwick, 3 *Zur.* 340, 565 n.; afterwards became the wife of Sir Edw. Unton, or Umpton, K.B., 1 *Bec.* 396 n., 3 *Zur.* 340 n.; a book dedicated to her, *Poet.* xliii; letter to her, 3 *Zur.* 702

Seymour (Lady Elizabeth): 1 *Bec.* 396 n., 3 *Zur.* 341

Seymour (Lady Jane): some account of her, 1 *Bec.* 396 n., 3 *Zur.* 2 n., 340; her letter to Bucer and Fagius, 3 *Zur.* 2; dedication to her, 1 *Bec.* 396

Seymour (Lady Margaret): 3 *Zur.* 340

Seymour (Lady Mary): 1 *Bec.* 396 n., 3 *Zur.* 340

Seymour (Sir Jo.): his daughter, 3 *Zur.* 340 n., 341 n

Seymour (Dorothy), wife of Sir Clem. Smith, *q. v.*

Seymour (Eliz.), sister of queen Jane, and wife of Greg. lord Cromwell, *q. v.*

Seyst me and seyst me not: *Bale* 526

Seyton (A. and J.): *v.* Seton.

Sforza family: *v.* Galeazzo Maria, John Galeazzo.

Sgyropulus (Sylv.): 2 *Bec.* 266 n

Sh... (Mr): M. Sh. in Bread Street counter, 2 *Hoop.* 613

Shacklock (Rich.): books by him, 2 *Ful.* 4 and n

Shaddai: *v.* God.

Shadrach, &c.: *Pil.* 384

Shaftmond: a measure of about half a foot, 2 *Cran.* 66

Shake-bucklers: blusterers and bullies, 2 *Bec.* 355, 3 *Bec.* 509; otherwise swash-bucklers, 2 *Bec.* 355 n., *Pil.* 151, 2 *Whitg.* 28

Shalcross (R.): saluted, with his wife, 2 *Brad.* 76; letter to them, *ib.* 232

Shales: shells, 2 *Tyn.* 123

Shallum, king of Judah: 2 *Bul.* 12

Shalm, or Shawm: a sort of musical pipe, or hautboy, 1 *Cran.* 259

Shalmaneser, king of Assyria: places strangers in Judea, *Pil.* 12

Shapwick, co. Somerset: St Indract and others killed there, *Bale* 191

Sharington (Sir Will.): makes open restitution to the king, 1 *Lat.* 263; is pardoned and restored in blood, 3 *Zur.* 649 n

Sharp (......): 2 *Brad.* 161

Sharpe (Jo.): servant to Grindal, *Grin.* 462

Shaving: *v.* Tonsure.

Shaw (Dr): preaches on the bastardy of the sons of Edward IV., 1 *Lat.* 183

Shawm: *v.* Shalm.

Shaxton (Nich.), bp of Salisbury: notices of him, 2 *Cran.* 292 n., 293 n., 3 *Jew.* 339, 2 *Lat.* 369 n.; assigned to preach before the king, 2 *Cran.* 309; he signed a declaration respecting a general council, *ib.* 468; forbidden to preach, 3 *Zur.* 215; on the passing of the Six Articles he resigned his bishoprick, *Bale* 510, 2 *Lat.* xx, but afterwards acquiesced, *Bale* 142, 218, 219, *Rid.* 115 n

Sheba, son of Bichri: 1 *Bul.* 376

Shebna: 4 *Bul.* 555

Shechem: 1 *Bul.* 416

Shechemites: destroyed, 4 *Bul.* 295

Sheen, co. Surrey: *v.* Richmond.

Sheep: their simplicity, 2 *Jew.* 1016; sheep without a shepherd, *ib.*; sheep numerous, but dear, 1 *Lat.* 99 n., *Now.* 227; sheepmongers, their oppression of the people, 2 *Bec.* 432, 434, *Pil.* 86, *Now.* 227, 228

Sheep-marks: used in subscriptions, 2 *Cran.* 291

Sheep of Christ: *v.* Christ, Feeding, Peter. God's people so called, 1 *Bul.* 4, 2 *Cov.* 282, &c.

Sheep's clothing: what it is, 2 *Tyn.* 122, &c.

Sheffield (......): an officer of London, 2 *Cran* 339

Sheffield, co. York: the queen of Scots imprisoned in the castle, 1 *Zur.* 210 n., 260 n., 2 *Zur.* 223 n

Shelford, co. Notts: the priory suppressed, 2 *Cran.* 321

Shelley (Will.): condemned for treason, *Lit. Eliz.* 656 n

Shellmore (Tho.): curate of Wingham, 2 *Cran.* 301

Shem: 1 *Bul.* 41, 4 *Bul.* 102

Shene, co. Surrey: *v.* Richmond.

Shent: blamed, *Pil.* 146, *Rid.* 269

Shepherd: *v.* Christ.
  In what sense God may be so called, 2 *Cov.* 287; various opinions on Eccles. xii. 11, "one shepherd," *Whita.* 422, 423

Shepherd (Nich.), master of St John's coll., Camb.: 2 *Zur.* 189 n., 191, 213 n

Shepherds: *v.* Ministers.
  Tale of some who repeated the words of consecration over their bread, 2 *Jew.* 705

Sheppy, co. Kent: Cranmer's letters to the prioress, 2 *Cran.* 284, 285
Shepreve (......), Heb. professor, Oxon: 2 *Cran.* 383
Sherbourn, co. Durham: the hospital, Lever master, *Grin.* 351, 2 *Zur.* 147 n.; he complains of its state, *Park.* 348; Grindal's services to it, *Grin.* x, 352
Shere Thursday: *v.* Maundy Thursday.
Sheriffs: their office, 2 *Brad.* 246; often covetous, 1 *Lat.* 181; Grindal's remark respecting them, *Grin.* 345
Sherington (Sir Will.): *v.* Sharington.
Sherwood (Dr), or Sherwode: opposes Latimer, 2 *Lat.* xv; a letter to him from Latimer, *ib.* 309, (468)
Sherwood (......), a traitorous priest: *Lit. Eliz.* 658, 681
Sheterden (Nich.), or Chittenden: martyred, *Poet.* 162; letters to him, 1 *Brad.* 591, 2 *Brad.* 133, 194
Sheve: shiver, sherd, fragment, 1 *Bec.* 469
Shew-bread: *v.* Bread.
Shibboleth: 4 *Bul.* 230
Shilling: *v.* Coinage.
Shiloh: Jacob's prophecy of Messiah by this title, 3 *Bul.* 15, 20, 2 *Lat.* 75; meaning of the word, 1 *Tyn.* 408
Shiloh: the tabernacle there, 2 *Bul.* 148, 4 *Bul.* 480
Shimei: his malediction of David, 1 *Bul.* 290, 2 *Cran.* 107
Ship, Ships: a ship a figure of the church, *Sand.* 370, &c.; The Ship of Safeguard, by G. B., 1569, notice of it, *Poet.* xxxv; stanzas therefrom, *ib.* 388; ships baptized by Papists, *Pil.* 493, *Sand.* 19
Ship: a vessel or small dish for holding incense, so called from its resemblance to a boat or little ship, 3 *Bec.* 362, 1 *Tyn.* 238
Ship: a name for the coin usually styled an angel, 2 *Tyn.* 318
Shipperius (......): *v.* Scepper.
Shipside (Geo.), or Shiphead: 2 *Brad.* 193, *Rid.* 292, 427 n.; he married Alice, Ridley's sister, *ib.* viii, 292, 428; he is imprisoned at Oxford, 2 *Brad.* 168, 174, 208, *Rid.* 361, 372, 376, 379, 382, 541; released, but plundered, *ib.* 391; Ridley supplicates the queen on behalf of him and his wife, *ib.* 290; Ridley's farewell to him, *ib.* 395, and to his wife, *ib.* 396; he was present at Ridley's burning, *ib.* 295, &c.
Shire Thursday: *v.* Maundy Thursday.
Shitterdun (Nich.): *v.* Sheterden.
Shittim-wood: figured Christ's humanity, 2 *Bul.* 153, 154
Shoame: *v.* Soham.

Shoe: a cut shoe; a mark of having vowed a pilgrimage, 1 *Tyn.* 103
Shoham: *v.* Schoham.
Shooter's Hill, Kent: noted for robberies, 1 *Lat.* 139
Shooting: *v.* Archery.
Shore: a support, 2 *Ful.* 288
Shore up: to lift, 2 *Ful.* 144
Shorling: a sheep that has been shorn, hence a shaveling, a popish priest, 2 *Bec.* 260, 2 *Brad.* 276, 287; shorelings, *Bale* 494, 2 *Cov.* 255, 266
Shorn (Mr John): a popish saint who had an image at Shorne-and-Merston, Kent, 1 *Lat.* 474; his boot, *Bale* 498
Shorne-and-Merston, co. Kent: 1 *Lat.* 474
Shorton (Rob.), dean of Stoke by Clare: his death, *Park.* 4
Shotover, near Oxford: *Jew.* vi.
Shrewsbury: a plague begins there, 1 *Brad.* 61 n.; Thorpe's preaching at St Chad's, *Bale* 82, 90
Shrewsbury (Earls of): *v.* Talbot.
Shrift: confession, *Grin.* 140, & sæpe.
Shrines: mandates for removing shrines and images, 2 *Cran.* 490, 503
Shrive: to confess to a priest, *Phil.* 300 n.; shriven: heard at confession, 2 *Ful.* 90
Shrouds (The) at St Paul's: *v.* London.
Shrove Tuesday, *q. v.*
Shushan, or Susa: *Pil.* 281
Shut (Jo.): translates a book by Viret, 2 *Brad.* 297 n.; legacy to him, *Grin.* 462
Shuttle: light, volatile, giddy, 2 *Bul.* 128
Shyphead (Geo.): *v.* Shipside.
Si non caste, tamen caute: an infamous gloss, 3 *Jew.* 136, 420, 4 *Jew.* 633, 639
Siberus (Adam): the apostles' creed in Latin verse, *Pra. Eliz.* 403
Siberus (Urban. Godofr.): De Aquæ Benedictæ potu Brutis non denegando, *Calf.* 17 n
Sibill of Cleves: 3 *Zur.* 529 n
Sibylle (Bart.): places Purgatory in the centre of the earth, *Rog.* 215 n.; considers venial sins as the cause of the torments thereof, *ib.* 216 n.; says the punishment there is but temporary, *ib.* 217 n.; holds that infants dying unbaptized are not saved, *ib.* 249, 250 n.; speaks of limbus puerorum, 137
Sibyls: *v.* Oracles.
Who they were, and whence their name, *Hutch.* 177
Sichardus (Jo.): *Calf.* 20 n
Sicilian vespers: 1 *Zur.* 291
Sicily: the kingdom subject to the pope, 2 *Jew.* 917

Sicinius: v. Sycinius.

Sick, Sickness: v. Affliction, Death, Prayers.
Why sickness is sent, 3 *Bec.* 31, 32; the purpose of God in afflicting with it, 2 *Bec.* 463; against the troublous tempests of it, with sentences and examples of scripture, 1 *Bec.* 475, 476; we must not murmur in it, but receive it with thanksgiving, 2 *Bec.* 462, 463; the conflict of Christians with their enemies is most perilous in it, *ib.* 571; the book called the Solace of the Soul was especially intended to be placed in the hands of the faithful in it, *ib.* 571; letter of lord Burghley on occasion of severe illness, *Park.* 453; the sick healed in the name of Christ, 4 *Bul.* 255 (v. Miracles); they may use physic, 1 *Lat.* 541; how the church deals with them, 4 *Bul.* 521; they are to be visited, 2 *Jew.* 1103, 1 *Lat.* 479; forms of visitation, in the Prayer Books, *Lit. Edw.* and *Lit. Eliz.*; popish rites in visiting the sick, 2 *Hoop.* 147; how they are to be spoken to, 2 *Cov.* 103, 2 *Jew.* 1137; THE SICK MAN'S SALVE, by T. Becon, 3 *Bec.* 87, &c.; its popularity, *ib.* 92 n.; the sick man's complaint, *ib.* 94; his determination to make his will, *ib.* 116, &c.; exhortation to him, *ib.* 130, &c.; his confession of his faith, *ib.* 135, &c.; a dying Christian's exhortation to his son, 2 *Jew.* 1138; his farewell to wife, children, and servants, 3 *Bec.* 145, 146; exhortation to him to die willingly, *ib.* 147, &c.; his confession of his sins, *ib.* 165; his good-will to die, *ib.* 178, 185; exhortation to him when at the point of death, *ib.* 188, 189; his death, *ib.* 190; commendation of him when departed, *ib.*

Sicle: shekel. 2 *Bec.* 109, 2 *Jew.* 748
Siculus (Geo.): answered by Calvin, 3 *Zur.* 325
Sidall (Hen.): notices of him, 1 *Jew.* 1235, 1237, 1 *Zur.* 18 n., 81 n.; in Edward VI.'s reign he acted with the reformers, 4 *Jew.* 1205; at Oxford, 3 *Zur.* 460, 461, 468; letter from him to Bullinger, 3 *Zur.* 311; on Mary's accession he has charge of Peter Martyr, *ib.* 369; was one of the witnesses to Cranmer's recantation, 1 *Cran.* xxii, 2 *Cran.* 563, 567, 4 *Jew.* 1205; he changed with the times, 1 *Zur.* 45 n.; subscribed to the queen's supremacy, *ib.* 81 n

Sidney (Sir Hen.): notice of him, *Hutch.* 293 n.; sent to the queen of Scots, 1 *Zur.* 115 n.; he lent Parker a MS., *Park.* 388 n.; his signature as privy councillor, *Grin.* 412; lord president of the marches of Wales, and lord deputy of Ireland, 3 *Whitg.* xii; letter by him, *Park.* 316; dedication to him, *Hutch.* vii, 293

Sidney (Sir Phil.): notices of him, *Park.* 316 n., *Poet.* xvi, xlii; his parentage, *Hutch.* 293 n.; his father seeks a Lent licence for him, *Park.* 316; his education, 2 *Zur.* 309; his tutor at Ch. Ch. Oxon, *ib.* 329 n.; abroad, *ib.* 217; his "magnum negotium," *ib.* 292 n.; letters to H. Languet, *ib.* 289, 296, 300; wrote English hexameters, *Poet.* xxii; twenty-seven psalms in metre, by him and his sister Mary, countess of Pembroke, *Poet.* 53, &c.

Sidney (Sir Will.): father of Sir Henry, *Hutch.* 293 n.; the lady Mary his wife, daughter of Jo. Dudley, duke of Northumberland, *ib.*

Sidney (Mary), countess of Pembroke: v. Herbert.

Sidon: denounced by Christ, 2 *Hoop.* 209
Sidonius (Mich.): concerned in drawing up the Interim, 2 *Zur.* 125 n
Sigebertus Gemblacensis: Chronicon, *Jew.* xliii; he affirms that Innocent permitted all Christians to anoint the sick, *Calf.* 246; affords testimony in proof of pope Joan, 4 *Jew.* 656; speaks of the wickedness of pope Hildebrand (Gregory VII.), 3 *Jew.* 129; says he troubled the states of Christendom, *ib.* 129, 346; records that at his death he confessed to one of his cardinals that he had foully abused his pastoral office, *ib.* 129, 346; censures the covetousness of the clergy, *ib.* 347; states that the Acephalians maintained that women might be deacons, elders and bishops, *Rog.* 240 n.; referred to, *Calf.* 67, 138, 246, 296, 297, 323 nn.; apparently confounded with Jac. Ph. Forestus Bergomensis, *ib.* 67 n., 323 n

Sigedode, abp of Narbonne: 3 *Bec.* 510 n
Sighara, king of the East Saxons: previously a monk, 2 *Ful.* 18, 24
Sigismund, emperor, and king of Hungary: called a council at Constance, 4 *Jew.* 908; could not sleep while a chest of gold was in his chamber, *Sand.* 102; his death, *Lit. Eliz.* 455
Sigismund I., king of Poland: 2 *Cran.* 402; his queen Bona (Sforza), 3 *Zur.* 689
Sigismund II., surnamed Augustus, king of Poland: wishes Jo. à Lasco to return, 3 *Zur.* 592; his interview with him, *ib.* 596, &c.; his war with Russia, *ib.* 599 n., 687 n.; his intended reformation, *ib.* 601
Sigismund III., king of Poland: queen Elizabeth's letter to him in favour of Flemish exiles, 2 *Zur.* 321

Sigismund (......): speaks of the Muscovites using their common tongue in divine service, 3 *Bec.* 411; says they debar men twice married from the ecclesiastical function, *Rog.* 240 n
Significatists: think only bare signs are received in the Lord's supper, *Rog.* 289
Signs: *v.* Sacraments.
What signs are, 4 *Bul.* 227, 1 *Hoop.* 195; division of them, act of Augustine, and others, 4 *Bul.* 227, 228; some are ordained of God, some given of men, *ib.* 229; diversity of the signs of each class, *ib.* 230; signs are not the things signified, *ib.* 250, 251, 1 *Hoop.* 196, 2 *Tyn.* 184, though commonly called by the names of these things, 2 *Bec.* 282, 2 *Bul.* 172, 280, 1 *Cran.* 125, 335, 336, 1 *Tyn.* 365, 368, 371, 375, 379, 3 *Tyn.* 247—249, 251; sacramental signs are severed from other signs, 4 *Bul.* 233; in the sacraments they retain their own nature, *ib.* 270; difference between sacramental signs and vain outward shews, 1 *Cran.* 322; the visible signs of the sacraments are not to be worshipped, *ib* 134; paradigmatical signs, 4 *Bul.* 232; signs and wonders, *ib.* 231 (*v.* Prodigies), signs of the times, *Poet.* 465, 466; signs before the end of the world, see p. 179, col. 2, above; also the titles Sun and World; signs in the sun, moon, and stars, 4 *Bul.* 231, *Sand.* 356, &c., 388; how the sun and moon will be darkened, 2 *Lat.* 54, 98; the sign of the Son of Man; whether the cross, *Calf.* 95, 96, 2 *Ful.* 137
Sihon, king of the Amorites, 1 *Bul.* 378
Sikerness: *v.* Sykerness.
Silence: serveth best where nothing can be said, 3 *Jew.* 333; commendable in a maid, 2 *Bec.* 369; silence-gloom, what, *ib.* 455
Silesia (The duke of): 3 *Zur.* 650
Silius Italicus: verses against unkindness to one's country, 1 *Bul.* 290; on envy, *ib.* 302
Silly: *v.* Seely.
Siloam: *v.* Jerusalem.
Silvanus: revolted from Christianity to Turcism, *Rog.* 162
Silverius, pope: *v.* Sylverius.
Silverton, co. Devon.: bp Bourne buried there, *Phil.* xxix.
Silvester: *v.* Sylvester.
Simeon, the patriarch: 1 *Bul.* 416; cursed, 4 *Bul.* 295
Simeon, a just man who waited for Messiah, 3 *Bul.* 278; his song, Nunc dimittis; its use defended, 2 *Whitg.* 477, 482; a version in English metre by Coverdale, 2 *Cov.* 566

Simeon, son of Cleophas: James's successor as bp of Jerusalem, 2 *Whitg.* 252
Simeon of Durham: De Regibus Anglorum, 2 *Ful.* 23
Simeon Metaphrastes: a poor schoolmaster, and writer of lying legends, 2 *Jew.* 654; he speaks of Eugenia coming into the school in man's apparel to hear Plato, 4 *Jew.* 651; relates that Luke made images of Christ and Mary, 2 *Jew.* 653, 654; refers to the burial place of Timothy, 2 *Whitg.* 303; reference to his life of Dionysius, *Whita.* 578; he charges Epiphanius with Judaism, 4 *Jew.* 793; tells of the sufferings of St Barbara, 1 *Hoop.* 457 n.; gives an account of St George, 1 *Hoop.* 313 n
Simeon, abp of Seleucia: 2 *Brad.* 347, 348, 2 *Whitg.* 166, 168, 431
Simeones: his story, 1 *Jew.* 244, 245; founder of the Messalians, *ib.* 245
Similis, a late converted soldier: his epitaph, *Sand.* 173
Similitudes: *v.* Figures, Metaphors.
Simkin (......): 3 *Tyn.* 146
Simler (Jo. Jacob): his collection of letters at Zurich, 2 *Zur.* v.
Simler (Josiah): 1 *Zur.* 6, 12, 17, 120, 125, 302, 2 *Zur.* 212 n.; godson of Bullinger, 3 *Zur.* 261; his Astronomical Institutes, and some other writings, 1 *Zur.* 62; he translates some of Bullinger's works, 4 *Bul.* xxiv, xxvi, 1 *Zur.* 95, 96, 110; refutes Stancarus, 1 *Zur.* 127; prepares an edition of P. Martyr's works, 1 *Zur.* 137; publishes his Preces ex Psalmis, *Pra. Eliz.* 419; his oration concerning Peter Martyr's life and death, dedicated to Jewel, 4 *Jew.* 1260 n.; he opposes the Ubiquitarians, 1 *Zur.* 307; writes against Brentius, 2 *Zur.* 247, 256; his Bibliotheca referred to, *Rog.* 181 n.; extracts, 1 *Cov.* 88 n., 2 *Cov.* 505 n., 594 n., 607 n.; saluted, 1 *Zur.* 12, 17, 22, & sæpe; his wife, or wives, 4 *Bul.* xiv, 1 *Zur.* 30 n., 62, 171 n., 2 *Zur.* 90, 165 n., 3 *Zur.* 596; his death, 1 *Zur.* 125 n.; letters to him, 4 *Jew.* 1220, 1242, 1250, 1256, 1259, 1260, 1 *Zur.* 50, 61, 94, 96, 106, 109, 120, 125, 126, 136, 302, 304, 2 *Zur.* 84, 93, 105, 208, 211, 217, 224, 259, 268, 272
Simler (Peter): 4 *Bul.* xv, 546
Simnel (Lambert): overthrown, 3 *Bec.* 3 n
Simon (St), called Zelotes: said to have preached the gospel in Britain, 1 *Jew.* 305, 3 *Jew.* 129, 164, *Poet.* 289; to have preached in Africa, 1 *Jew.* 353; sermon on the festival of St Simon and St Jude, 1 *Lat.* 447
Simon of Cyrene: *v.* Basilides, Valentinians.
Simon Magus: was baptized, although a

hypocrite, 4 *Bul.* 383; was in the church, *ib.* 8; did not truly believe, 1 *Tyn.* 124; baptism did not profit him, 4 *Bul.* 271, 341, 347, *Rog.* 267; he offered money for the power of giving the Holy Ghost, 3 *Bul.* 96, 4 *Bul.* 130; was admonished by Peter, *Phil.* 380; was founder of the Gnostics or Docetæ, *Grin.* 59 n.; said the world was created by angels, *Rog.* 40; taught that Christ was not very man, although he appeared so, 1 *Cran.* 277; is stated to have assumed the title of the Holy Ghost, *Rog.* 71; said to have termed his Helene the Holy Ghost, *ib.*; he rejected the prophets, *Whita.* 30; boasted to be saved by himself, *Rog.* 162; is said by the Rhemists to have first taught justification by faith only, *ib.* 114; denied the resurrection of any flesh, *ib.* 64; fables concerning his sorcery, 2 *Ful.* 338, 339; it is stated that a statue was erected to him as a god, *Calf.* 343; mentioned by Eusebius, 2 *Whitg.* 183; compared to the pope, *Phil.* 417

Simon the Tanner: 2 *Bul.* 22

Simon (......) : *v.* Symon.

Simonians, or Simonists: erred about the resurrection, 2 *Cov.* 183; had idols, 1 *Ful.* 215; thought the practice of virtue an intolerable yoke, *Rog.* 118

Simonides: says God alone is supernatural, 1 *Jew.* 501; could not attain to the knowledge of God, *Hutch.* 12

Simons (Ant.), of South Molton : *Jew.* v.

Simony: *v.* Benefices, Patrons.

The sin so called, 4 *Bul.* 130; Simoniacs, 2 *Bul.* 45, 4 *Bul.* 82; thieves break into the ministry by simony, *Sand.* 240, 241; to buy the ministry of the church is a common practice in papistry, 1 *Hoop.* 447; they who enter by it, deal evilly after they have entered, *Sand.* 242; argument that a pope cannot commit simony, 1 *Jew.* 78, 4 *Jew.* 867, &c., (see p. 619, col. 2, above); simony lamented, *Hutch.* 5; condemned in all kinds of ministers, 2 *Hoop.* 123, 148; evasions which are practised, 1 *Tyn.* 171; the sin prevalent in Norfolk, *Park.* 311; inquiries respecting it, *Grin.* 166, 181; benefices to be forfeited for it, 2 *Cran.* 503; the church should be purged from it, *Sand.* 43, 44, 136; prayer for the confusion of all Simonites, &c., *Lit. Eliz.*

Simplex ac Pia Deliberatio : *v.* Cologne.

Simplicity : 4 *Bul.* 368

Simpson (Andr.) : *v.* Sympson.

Simpson (Jo.), or Simson : martyred at Rochford, *Poet.* 162

Simson (Cuth.) : *v.* Symson.

Simson (Dav.) : in exile, 1 *Cran.* (9)

Simson (Jo.) : *v.* Symson.

Sin : *v.* Christ, Confession, Evil, Penance, Prayers, Repentance, Temptation, Wickedness.

i. *In general :* whence the name "peccatum" comes, 2 *Bul.* 358; the word "sin" is used in scripture for a sin-offering, 2 *Bec.* 575, 1 *Tyn.* 377; what sin is, 3 *Bec.* 602, 605, 614, 2 *Bul.* 360, 2 *Lat.* 5; the nature of it, 1 *Bec.* 146; it is ἀνομία, or lawlessness, 2 *Tyn.* 188; it is repugnant to the law of God, 2 *Bul.* 406; false views of it inculcated by Pharisees and Papists, 1 *Tyn.* 461; the cause or beginning of sin, 2 *Bul.* 361, 368, 408; how sin and death came into the world, 1 *Bul.* 43; destiny not the cause of it, 2 *Bul.* 363; God is not the author of it, 1 *Brad.* 213, 214, 321, 2 *Bul.* 365, 373, 2 *Cov.* 341, 1 *Ful.* 563, *Hutch.* 65, 3 *Tyn.* 175; More charges Luther with teaching that God compels men to sin, 3 *Tyn.* 190; Tyndale's reply to this charge, *ib.* 190—193; the devil and Adam's will wrought it, 2 *Hoop.* 72; the nature of man was not the cause of it, 2 *Bul.* 362; the devil not alone the cause of it, *ib.*; it springeth of the devil's suggestion and our corrupt will, *ib.* 370; it came by free-will, 3 *Bec.* 614; its wilfulness, 1 *Brad.* 320, 321, 1 *Lat.* 195; excuses to cloak it, *Rid.* 67; it is not the outward work only, 1 *Tyn.* 489; its root is unbelief, *ib.*; outward abstinence from sin is but hypocrisy, *ib.* 80; the estimation of it, 3 *Bul.* 54; it is a horrible thing, 1 *Lat.* 232, 461; heinous in God's sight, 2 *Lat.* 103; is measured by the greatness of the person against whom it is committed, 1 *Ful.* 350; its greatness shewn by Christ's sufferings, 1 *Brad.* 143; it is hateful to the truly penitent, *ib.* 77; the sleep and death of the soul, *Pil.* 111; most men sleep in sin, *Sand.* 209; we cannot arouse ourselves, *Pil.* 12; insensibility to sin is dangerous, 1 *Hoop.* 87; the servitude of sin, *ib.* 261; nothing is worse than to be servant to sin, 1 *Cov.* 508; sin is a heavy and intolerable burden, 3 *Bec.* 166, 2 *Hoop.* 313, 1 *Lat.* 298; it is like a thorn, 1 *Bec.* 69; different kinds of sinners, *Sand.* 127, &c.; the kinds and sorts of sins, 2 *Bul.* 407; original sin, see ii, below; actual sin, 2 *Bul.* 404, &c.; scelera and delicta, *ib.* 409; crying sins, *ib.*; mortal and venial sins, 2 *Bul.* 416, 2 *Lat.* 7, 8, 2 *Tyn.* 10, 191; the seven deadly sins, 2 *Bul.* 409, 410; peccatum alienum, *ib.* 410; sin of ignorance, *ib.*; of infirmity, *ib.* 417; sin through frailty distinguished from wilful sin, 3 *Tyn.* 33; a caution against presumptuous sins, 2 *Lat.* 163; voluntary and involuntary sin, 2 *Bul.* 412; hidden and manifest sins, 2 *Bul.* 416, 1 *Tyn.* 203, 240; sins of the mind, *Pil.* 231; whether the virtuous works of the heathen are sins, 2 *Bul.* 418; sin after baptism, see iii. below; works done before the Spirit of God comes, are sin, 1 *Tyn.* 183; works before justification have the nature of sin, *Rog.* 127; whether the good works of the saints are sins, 2 *Bul.* 410; there are many sins which are accounted no sins, 1 *Tyn.* 122; the differences of sin, 2 *Bul.* 384; all sins are not equal, *ib.* 407; they are increased by degrees and circumstances, *ib.* 408; nations punished by God for sins, 2 *Tyn.* 53, 54; a prayer of Nehemias for the sins of the people (from 2 Esdr.), *Lit. Edw.* 479; the sinfulness of man, 2 *Bec.* 27, 28, 44, 3 *Bec.* 15, 61, 62, 100, 101, 2 *Cov.* 384, 385; it is shewn by the law, 2 *Bec.* 54, 55; it is necessary to know this end of the law, *ib.* 55; acknowledgment of it by holy men of old, 3 *Bec.* 101; all men are sinners (Christ alone excepted), 1 *Bec.* 315, 316, 2 *Bec.* 168, 169, 1 *Brad.* 342, 1 *Bul.* 114, 1 *Lat.* 417, *Rog.* 133—142, *Sand.* 133, 3 *Tyn.* 32, 150, 207, 208; man convinced of sin, 2 *Bul.* 122; God hath wrapped (or concluded) all under sin, 2 *Hoop.* 58; sin remains in the righteous and regenerate, 2 *Bul.* 60, 2 *Cov.* 384, &c., 2 *Hoop.* 122, *Pra. B.* 32; whatsoever is ours is sin, 1 *Tyn.* 23; our best deeds are defiled with sin, *Sand.* 136; no man is free from it in this life, 1 *Bec.* 136, 1 *Lat.* 537, *Phil.* 311, 2 *Tyn.* 150—152; it remains in us until utterly slain by the death of the body, 1 *Tyn.* 500; certain heretics profess to be without sin, *Phil.* 310; and therefore object to the penitential prayers of the church, the Psalms, and even to the Lord's prayer, *ib.* 312; the sins of the saints, 2 *Bul.* 74; why they are recorded in scripture, 1 *Tyn.* 311, 400; Papists extenuate them, and thereby diminish the glory of God's mercy, *ib.* 450; the faithful and unfaithful sin diversely, 2 *Hoop.* 60, 2 *Tyn.* 191; how "he that is born of God cannot sin," 1 *Brad.* 251, *Rid.* 56, 2 *Tyn.* 152; how a true member of Christ's church sinneth not, and how he is yet a sinner, 3 *Tyn.* 32, 113, 114; all are sinners, but the believer does not consent to sin, 1 *Tyn.* 311; some never consented to sin to follow it, having the Holy Ghost from their birth, 3 *Tyn.* 207; Christians cannot live in wilful sin, 2 *Tyn.* 189, 191, 212, 213; all Christians should beware of sin, 1 *Hoop.* 73; we may not sin because Christ has borne our sins, *Hutch.* 333; he did not die for our sins that we should still live in them, 1 *Tyn.* 510; he that sins willingly never tasted of Christ truly, 1 *Brad.* 78; relapse into sin is dangerous, *Hutch.* 285, 1 *Lat.* 429; the sins of the faithful are not imputed unto them, for Christ's sake, 2 *Hoop.* 274; believers fight against sin, unbelievers yield themselves to sin, 2 *Tyn.* 10; therefore the sins of the former are venial, but those of the latter deadly, *ib.*; the frailty of the flesh against which a believing soul fighteth, is forgiven, 3 *Tyn.* 142; mortification of sinful affections, *Nord.* 66; sin shall not be laid to the charge of the saints, 2 *Hoop.* 60; he is not a sinner in the sight of God that would be no sinner, 1 *Tyn.* 94; what sin does, 1 *Bec.* 46, 146, 199; it condemned man, 3 *Bec.* 614; produces all kinds of trouble, 1 *Hoop.* 459, 2 *Hoop.* 323; causes all calamities and plagues, 2 *Lat.* 145, *Sand.* 306, as the pains of child-birth, 3 *Bec.* 28, pestilence and all other diseases, 2 *Hoop.* 160, 165, 167, 172, 173, the corruption of the creatures, 1 *Brad.* 362, 363; through it the creatures will not serve man, *Pil.* 91; it is the cause of death, 1 *Brad.* 333, 362, 363, 1 *Bul.* 43, 2 *Cov.* 49, 1 *Ful.* 397, 1 *Lat.* 220, *Sand.* 168; it put Christ to death, 1 *Bec.* 177, 1 *Brad.* 143, *Pil.* 347; causes the persecution of the church, 2 *Bul.* 73; hinders everything from doing good, *Pil.* 54; defiles everything in the sinner, *ib.* 165, 166; even what God commands, *ib.* 162; it produces insensibility, *ib.* 49; one sin waits on another, 1 *Lat.* 245; sin is not easily perceived, unless we behold ourselves in the glass of God's law, 1 *Bec.* 98; knowledge of sin goes before faith, 1 *Lat.* 168; to feel and bewail it is the work of God's Spirit, 2 *Hoop.* 217; how it should be felt, *ib.* 218; sorrow for sin is a part of contrition, 1 *Bec.* 97; David's repentance and full forgiveness, 3 *Tyn.* 203, 204; grief for sin is a joyful sorrow; verses by Jo. Davies, *Poet.* 248; sorrow exhorted to draw nigh to God, *Sand.* 127; Satan's temptation that God does not hear them, 2 *Bec.* 131, 626; the greater sinners, the more welcome if penitent, 2 *Tyn.* 343; no sin is too great to be forgiven on repentance, 1 *Lat.* 267; sin must be acknowledged and confessed, 4 *Bul.* 549, 2 *Hoop.* 349; confession of sin, 1 *Brad.* 436, 438, 441, 448, 457, 2 *Brad.* 13, 30, 1 *Bul.* 164,

3 *Bul.* 59, 69 (see p. 223, col. 2, above); confession to God recommended, 3 *Bec.* 164; a motion to a confession of our filthiness and corrupt affections, *Nord.* 47; the confession, *ib.* 51; another, *ib.* 53; confession to God the Father, 3 *Bec.* 15, 16, to Jesus Christ, *ib.* 16, &c., to the Holy Ghost, *ib.* 18, 19; confession of various sins, and petitions for deliverance therefrom, *Pra. B.* 167; confession is necessary for those who come to the Lord's supper, 2 *Bec.* 234; confession made by the sick man, 3 *Bec.* 165; confession without faith is nothing worth, 2 *Hoop.* 350; men's various ways of pacifying God's wrath against sin, *Sand.* 219, 220; man cannot satisfy for his sin, *ib.* 220, 221; on recovery from sin, 1 *Tyn.* 465; those who repent after it are not excluded from grace, 2 *Bec.* 11; penitential remembrance of sin is good, *Pil.* 181; but some glory in their sins past, 1 *Brad.* 34; remedies against sin, 3 *Bec.* 164, &c., 1 *Cov.* 523—528; the principal remedy is to believe Christ's gospel, 1 *Hoop.* 109; his blood is the only effectual remedy, 1 *Lat.* 232, 343; we must flee the occasions of sin, 1 *Cov.* 504; sin must be rebuked, 4 *Bul.* 546, &c., 1 *Lat.* 241, *Pil.* 98; it flourishes where there is no correction for it, 1 *Hoop.* 90; outward sin should be punished by the king, 1 *Tyn.* 203, 240; profane writers declare that iniquity increases with the age of the world, 2 *Hoop.* 83; the sins of fathers hurt not penitents, 4 *Bul.* 555; against sin, death, and hell, with sentences and examples of scripture, 1 *Bec.* 479, 480

ii. *Original Sin* (v. Adam, Baptism, Corruption, Man): on it, 1 *Bec.* 330, 3 *Bec.* 605, 1 *Brad.* 57, 342, 2 *Bul.* 384, &c., 2 *Lat.* 101, *Now.* (33, 34), 102, 149, 150, *Pra. B.* 11, *Rog.* 94—103, 1 *Tyn.* 14, 64, 489; the catholic doctrine respecting it, 2 *Bul.* 389; all the holy fathers confess it, *ib.* 390; an article de peccato originali, 2 *Cran.* 472; doctrine of the Institution, *ib.* 107, 108; the doctrine may be from scripture, *Whita.* 536; the sin of our nature is the work of Satan, 2 *Bec.* 629; every man is partaker of it through Adam's fall, 2 *Bul.* 385, 386, 396, 2 *Cran.* 112, 2 *Hoop.* 24, 2 *Jew.* 1104, *Lit. Edw.* 503, (552), 1 *Tyn.* 113, 3 *Tyn.* 209; all men by nature are inheritors of hell, 1 *Lat.* 4; man is humbled by the true doctrine, *Sand.* 21; heresies respecting it, *Rog.* 97, 100, 102; Rome diminishes it, *Sand.* 23; how it is voluntary, 2 *Bul.* 388; it is the fountain and root of all other sins, 2 *Hoop.* 25; bringeth forth the fruits of the flesh, 2 *Bul.* 399; condemneth, *ib.* 394; its after-pains, or remains after baptism, 2 *Cran.* 182; its infection remains to the end, even in the faithful, 1 *Brad.* 423, 2 *Brad.* 57, 60, 2 *Cov.* 240, *Rog.* 99, 1 *Tyn.* 301; Christ redeemed us not from that only, but from all sin, 1 *Bec.* 330, &c., 3 *Bul.* 43; Flacius Illyricus sends a disputation on original corruption and free-will to Parker, *Park.* 140

iii. *Sin after Baptism:* on it, 2 *Bul.* 417, 3 *Jew.* 463, 464, *Pil.* 448, *Rog.* 136—142, 1 *Tyn.* 466; it is soon committed after baptism, 1 *Bec.* 204; it is not unpardonable, 2 *Bec.* 170, &c., *Hutch.* 113; a remedy for it, 1 *Bec.* 178; God forgives it, *ib.* 335; Christ is a Saviour not only before baptism, but after it, *ib.*; the case of Peter, *ib.* 96; the heresy of those who deny remission of sins after baptism confuted, *ib.* 95, 96, 2 *Bec.* 170, 171, &c.; the Arians so held, *Phil.* 313; whereof this heresy is gathered, 1 *Bec.* 96; texts alleged for it expounded, 1 *Bec.* 96, *Hutch.* 113, 1 *Tyn.* 521

iv. *The forgiveness of sins* (v. Absolution, Justification, Pardons, Prayer (The Lord's), Prayers): of the forgiveness of sins, 2 *Bec.* 43, 44, 168, 1 *Bul.* 164, &c., 3 *Bul.* 30, 36, 48, 4 *Bul.* 216, 550, 1 *Cov.* 375, 2 *Hoop.* 58, *Now.* (57, 100), 176, *Pra. B.* xxii, xxv, 31, 43; whence cometh the knowledge of sin, and whence the forgiveness, 2 *Hoop.* 58; there is no forgiveness but in the church, 2 *Bec.* 44, 2 *Hoop.* 60; how sins are forgiven, 1 *Bul.* 167; God alone forgives, *Bale* 117, 2 *Bec.* 45, 172, &c., 557, &c., 3 *Bec.* 144, 2 *Hoop.* 60; priests have not power to forgive sins, 2 *Bec.* 174; the apostles did not assume the power of remitting them, *ib.* 559, 560; the priest forgives them not, but utters the free remission purchased of God by Christ, *ib.* 561, &c.; God forgives of free favour, *ib.* 181, 182; he forgives for the sake and merits of Christ, 1 *Bec.* 97, 1 *Bul.* 164, 2 *Hoop.* 58, 1 *Lat.* 330, 342, *Sand.* 412, 2 *Tyn.* 76; who suffered for and redeemed us from *all* sin, 1 *Bec.* 332, 3 *Bul.* 43, 2 *Hoop.* 123, 2 *Tyn.* 188, 189; his blood is the only remedy, 1 *Lat.* 232, 343; he is alone the sacrifice for sin, 2 *Bec.* 574, 575; the only propitiation for it, 1 *Brad.* 49; it is put to flight through him, 1 *Bec.* 297; God forgives freely and fully, 2 *Bec.* 174, 3 *Bul.* 63, 1 *Lat.* 330, 342, *Now.* (79), 199, *Sand.* 290, 412, 2 *Tyn.* 155, 156, 158, 166, 168, 3 *Tyn.* 203, 204;

he forgives all sins, 1 *Bul.* 165; both original and actual, 2 *Tyn.* 155, 156; both the fault and the pain, 2 *Bec.* 174, 175, 3 *Bec.* 144, 1 *Bul.* 108, 1 *Lat.* 426, 1 *Tyn.* 271, 2 *Tyn.* 136—138, 155, 158—160; God forgives without merit on the sinner's part, 2 *Hoop.* 72; love to God is not the cause but the consequence of pardon, 1 *Tyn.* 83; Christ procured remission for many, viz. for those who believe, *ib.* 363; forgiveness is proclaimed for all believers, 1 *Lat.* 461; the sins of all believers are pardoned through Christ's death, *Lit. Edw.* 500, (549); sin is hidden through repentance, 1 *Lat.* 263, 417 (see in i. above); Christ suffered not for such as be impenitent, *ib.* 331; penitents must believe the forgiveness of sins for Christ's sake, 4 *Bul.* 550; we should believe that our sins are pardoned, 1 *Brad.* 347; the truly penitent should be assured thereof, 1 *Ful.* 421; nothing but a persuasion thereof can give peace, *Sand.* 287; how to be assured of forgiveness, 1 *Brad.* 342, &c., 1 *Tyn.* 263; to believe the remission of sins is by many accounted presumption, 1 *Brad.* 47; in what sense we are saved from sin, 2 *Lat.* 145; verses by Jo. Norden to the praise of God for the forgiveness of our sins, *Nord.* 63, *Poet.* 460; the forgiveness of sins to be prayed for, 1 *Lat.* 415; heretics who would not pray for it, *Rog.* 135; a man may ask forgiveness privately, 2 *Bec.* 177; sin may be forgiven without confession to man, 3 *Jew.* 361; the forgiveness of sins sought in the Lord's prayer, 1 *Brad.* 133, *Now.* (78), 199; we cannot be forgiven unless we forgive others, *Now.* (79), 200; the Canon Law says no forgiveness can be had but by supplication of a priest, 2 *Cran.* 75; the remission of our daily sins denoted by the washing of the disciples' feet, 2 *Jew.* 1103; what profit we have by believing the remission of sins, 2 *Bec.* 46; the remission of sins is to be preached to the people, *ib.* 565; what it is to preach it, *ib.* 13; why God is merciful to forgive sins, *ib.* 175, 176; Christ's readiness to forgive, 3 *Bec.* 166, &c.; there is hope of forgiveness as long as God speaks to us, *Pil.* 25; sins are not forgiven for the grievousness of disease, 2 *Bec.* 574; no sufferings of ours can make satisfaction for them, 2 *Tyn.* 29; they cannot be forgiven after this life, 3 *Bec.* 126, &c.; the papists' pestilent doctrine in respect to the forgiveness of them, 2 *Bec.* 558; sin is made by the Romish clergy a most profitable merchandise, 1 *Tyn.* 272; the pope's forgiveness contrasted with God's, 1 *Tyn.* 271, 2 *Tyn.* 156; the bishop of Rome takes upon him unjustly to forgive sins by bulls, 2 *Bec.* 172, 173; whether the mass be a satisfaction for sin, 1 *Cran.* 81, &c.; venial sin supposed to be put away by extreme unction, *Rog.* 264; sins are not put away by ceremonies, 1 *Tyn.* 284

v. *Sin against the Holy Ghost*: sin against the Father and the Son, 3 *Bec.* 611; sin against the Holy Ghost, 3 *Bec.* 611, 2 *Brad.* 321, 2 *Bul.* 417, 420, &c., 2 *Jew.* 1074, 1 *Lat.* 266, 2 *Lat.* 318, 320, 441, *Rog.* 136, 1 *Tyn.* 522, 2 *Tyn.* 152, 177, 199, 212, 232, 344, 3 *Tyn.* 24; on sin against the Holy Ghost, with sentences and examples of scripture, 1 *Bec.* 466, 467; various opinions on that sin stated by Augustine, 1 *Lat.* 463 n.; the beginning of it, 2 *Bul.* 421; it was committed by Judas and others, 1 *Lat.* 425, 462; it is not remissible, 2 *Bul.* 423; Melancthon supposes Heb. vi. to refer to it, *Hutch.* 116; of the sin which is said to be unto death, 2 *Hoop.* 560, 1 *Tyn.* 521—523, 2 *Tyn.* 212; that sin is not to be prayed for, 2 *Hoop.* 560; but we must not expressly judge that sin to be in any man, without a special testimony of the Holy Ghost, *ib.*; how sinners must be prayed for, *Pra. B.* 6; God's children cannot sin unto death, 2 *Brad.* 166; there is only one irremissible sin, viz. unbelief, 2 *Hoop.* 61

vi. *The punishment of sin* (v. Hell): what sin brings a man unto, 2 *Hoop.* 230 (see in i. above); it drives to desperation, 1 *Bec.* 146; sin will be known at length, 1 *Hoop.* 459; secret sin shall be revealed, 1 *Lat.* 259; the plague of sins, 2 *Bul.* 426; sin will not go unpunished, 2 *Lat.* 171; its punishment is just and certain, 2 *Bul.* 426, &c.; how God punishes it, 3 *Bec.* 605, 606; he punishes it in this world, not in purgatory, *ib.* 606; why sins are plagued with temporal punishments, although they have been forgiven by the grace of God, 2 *Bul.* 430; to live in sin unpunished is a sign of damnation, 2 *Brad.* 36; the punishment of secret sins pertains to God, 1 *Tyn.* 203; God's decree against sinners, 4 *Bul.* 554; God's judgment against sin is not to be extenuated, 1 *Hoop.* 92; sin is the cause of damnation, 2 *Lat.* 145, *Pil.* 169; it condemns, but good works do not save, *Pil.* 169

Sin-offering: 2 *Bul.* 193, 1 *Tyn.* 377
Sinai: v. Law (Divine), iii.
    The assembly there, 1 *Bul.* 46, 4 *Bul.* 94
Sindal: sindon, fine linen, *Pil.* 283.

Sindon: a wrapper, 3 *Tyn.* 74
Singer (Sam. W.): Hist. of Playing Cards, 1 *Lat.* 8 n
Singers: in the church of Rome, 4 *Bul.* 114
Singing: v. Music, Psalms.
Singing-loaf: v. Host.
Single: v. Bachelors, Maids, Prayers.
Singleton (Hugh), printer: 2 *Cov.* 39, 137
Sinistral: sinister, unsound, evil, 1 *Bec.* 95
Sinners: v. Complaint, Dialogue, Lamentations, Man, Prayers, Sin, Wicked.
    An humble suit of a repentant sinner for mercy, by W. Hunnis, *Poet.* 157; the complaint of a sinner, by Hum. Gifford, *ib.* 217
Sinope: a red stone found in Sinopis in Pontus, 1 *Bul.* 422
Sion, or Zion: called Tsion, *Poet.* 418; explained as meaning the church, 3 *Bul.* 275, *Pil.* 262; holiness in it, *ib.* 261—264
Sion, co. Middx.: a monastery of the order of St Bridget, 1 *Hoop.* 291 n.; founded by Henry V., 2 *Tyn.* 81; services there, *ib.*; shrift there, 1 *Tyn.* 337; contumacy of the friars, 2 *Cran.* 292 n., 303; obedience of the nuns, *ib.* 292 n.; Sion house, built on the site, 3 *Zur.* 2 n
Siphanus (Laur.): 2 *Ful.* 296 n
Sir: the three sirs,—king, knight, priest, 1 *Brad.* 589; priests so called, 2 *Brad.* 7 n.; the designation comes from "Dominus," the academical title of a B.A., *Bale* 394, 447; e. g. Sir John Flemyng, 2 *Cran.* 257; spiritual sir, *Bale* 496; sir John, sir Thomas, &c. *Bale* 447, 2 *Brad.* 279, 290, 2 *Cov.* 258, 269
Sir John: a familiar name for a priest, 1 *Brad.* 71, 589, 2 *Brad.* 120, 313, 2 *Cran.* 306, 1 *Lat.* 317, *Rid.* 104, *Sand.* 155, 1 *Tyn.* 146, 277, 2 *Tyn.* 249, 2 *Whitg.* 265; references to old writers, *Calf.* 52 n.; singing sir Johns, 1 *Brad.* 391; blind buzzard sir John, 2 *Brad.* 43; sir John Lack-Latin, 2 *Lat.* 28, *Pil.* 20, 160, 271; sir John Masser, 2 *Brad.* 324; sir John Mumble-matins, *Pil.* 26; sir John Smell-smoke, *ib.* 255
Siricius, pope: addressed by Cyprian as a brother, 1 *Tyn.* 216 n.; he censures marriage, *Calf.* 240, 3 *Jew.* 386, 404, 420, *Pil.* 570, *Rog.* 181; before his time it was lawful for priests to marry, 3 *Jew.* 411, 423; he says that after a time, a law was made that the infants of the faithful should not be baptized except at Easter and Whitsuntide, except in cases of necessity, 4 *Bul.* 367; his canon forbidding offenders to come to the Lord's table, 1 *Jew.* 182; the fourth epistle attributed to him, whence probably derived, 2 *Ful.*

179, 243; the text of Optatus which contains his name corrupted, *ib.* 348 n
Sirmondus (Jac.): Concilia Generalia, *Calf.* 41, 138, 2 *Ful.* 90, 288, 289, 359 nn
Sisinnius, a Novatian: 4 *Jew.* 1019; told by Chrysostom that there could be but one bishop in a city, 2 *Whitg.* 215; his advice in a council, *Calf.* 10, 3 *Jew.* 224; wore white apparel, *Pil.* 661, 2 *Whitg.* 23, 25, 1 *Zur.* 160, 350 n
Sistern: sisters, 1 *Brad.* 370
Sit: to be at rest, 1 *Bul.* 147
Sith, sithen: since, 1 *Brad.* 38
Sith (St): v. Osyth.
Sitselt (Rob.): 2 *Bec.* 480 n
Six: its mystic import, *Bale* 449
Sixtus I., or Xistus, bishop of Rome: made part of the canon, 2 *Brad.* 309, and ordered commemoration of the dead, *ib.* 311 n.; appointed the Sanctus to be sung, *Pil.* 503
Sixtus II., pope: introduced altars, 2 *Bec.* 297; or first consecrated them, 1 *Jew.* 310 n.; ascribes Ecclesiasticus to Solomon, *Whita.* 47; says Peter dwelleth in the bishop of Rome, 1 *Jew.* 401; calls Laurence an archdeacon, 2 *Whitg.* 173; martyred, 2 *Tyn.* 254; Laurence's saying at his martyrdom, *Phil.* 144
Sixtus III., pope: was accused and purged before Valentinian, 4 *Jew.* 967
Sixtus IV., pope: built stews at Rome, *Rog.* 181; how he settled the disputes of the Scotists and Thomists, 4 *Jew.* 1046; what he did with regard to the jubilee, 2 *Bul.* 268
Sixtus Senensis (Fra.): speaks of the difficulty of scripture, *Whita.* 361; admits that it is, to a great extent, plain, *ib.* 401; misled by Carranza with respect to a catalogue of canonical books, untruly assigned to the council of Florence, 2 *Ful.* 222 n.; he calls certain books deutero-canonical, *Whita.* 49; maintains the purity of the Hebrew text, *ib.* 161; on the Latin Vulgate, *ib.* 130; on the Rest of Esther, *ib.* 72, 75, and how he evaded the Tridentine decree, *ib.* 76; on the book of Judith, *ib.* 83; he confesses that Chrysostom sometimes speaks hyperbolically, *Calf.* 77 n.; is mistaken in ascribing five homilies on Job to that father, 2 *Ful.* 110 n.; his description of the commentaries on Mark falsely attributed to Jerome, *Calf.* 178 n.; references to him, *ib.* 74, 140, 107 nn
Skeffington (Sir Will.): 2 *Bec.* 554 n
Skelthrop (......): 2 *Brad.* 243
Skelton (......): a gentleman of Cumberland, *Grin.* 256
Skelton (Jo.): cited, 1 *Bul.* 312 n

Skill: to know, *Bale* 366; to matter, 1 *Jew.* 63, *Phil.* 343, *Pil.* 262, 1 *Tyn.* 67
Skinner (Ralph), dean of Durham: *Park.* 124; letter to Bullinger, 3 *Zur.* 313
Skinner (Rob.): 4 *Bul.* 544, 3 *Zur.* 393, 395, 401, 407, 409, 422, 431, &c.
Skinner (Tho.) : his daughter Anne, 1 *Bec.* 232 n
Skinners' company: *v.* London.
Skippe (Jo.), bp: *v.* Skypp.
Skrimsham (R.), of All souls' college: *Park.* 301 n
Sky: 3 *Bul.* 174
Skypp (Jo.), bp of Hereford: sometime chaplain to Anne Boleyn, *Park.* 3; his election, 2 *Cran.* 81 n., *Park.* 6 n.; mentioned, 1 *Cran.* xvii; his answers to certain questions, 2 *Cran.* 152; letters from him to Parker, *Park.* 1, 2, 6, 9; his death, *ib.* 81 n., 6 n
Slade (Jo.): martyred at Bramford, *Poet.* 173
Slander: *v.* Prayers.
 What it is, 3 *Bec.* 610, 1 *Lat.* 518; who is a slanderer, *Hutch.* 224; slander is a kind of persecution, *Pil.* 210; worse than the fire, *ib.* 361; it is forbidden, 2 *Bec.* 118, 2 *Bul.* 117, 233; against slandering and lying, with sentences and examples of scripture, 1 *Bec.* 447, 448; a sonnet of a slanderer's tongue; by James Yates, *Poet.* 451; the names of slanderers to be presented to the ordinary, *Grin.* 143
Slater (......) : his acts at Oxford, 2 *Cran.* 382—384
Slave: account of one who gained great knowledge of the scriptures, 2 *Jew.* 684
Slavery: *v.* Bondage.
 Abhorred by all, *Pil.* 456
Sleeke (Will.) : died in prison, *Poet.* 167
Sleep: *v.* Prayers, *Evening.*
 It is the image of death, 1 *Lat.* 548, *Nord.* 153, *Poet.* 404, *Pra. B.* 76; also a figure of sin, *Pil.* 111; it must not be indulged in, 2 *Lat.* 2, 5; the dangers of sleep, natural and spiritual, *Sand.* 382; sleepiness to be shaken off by magistrates, *ib.* 382; likewise by ministers, *ib.* 383; spiritual sleep, 2 *Lat.* 2; the sleep of the soul, *ib.* 13; what it is to be asleep, 3 *Bec.* 610; some sleep in error, but most in sin, *Sand.* 209, yet in security, *ib.* 210; against sleep in sin, *ib.* 395; it is time to awake, 2 *Hoop.* 113
Sleidan (Jo.): Cranmer procures him a pension, 3 *Zur.* 54 n.; he was a friend of P. Martyr, *ib.* 509 n.; Comment. de Stat. Relig. et Reip. Car. V., *Jew.* xliii; Hist. of the Ref. transl. by Bohun, 1 *Lat.* 147, 305, 425 nn.; states that cardinal Campeius said that for a priest to play the whoremaster was a less offence than to take a wife, *Rog.* 304 n.; refers to the blasphemies of Tetzel, 3 *Jew.* 194; speaks of a conference at Nuremburg, 4 *Jew.* 948; and of one at Augsburgh, 3 *Jew.* 208; mentions a remarkable confession of pope Adrian VI., 3 *Jew.* 182, 4 *Jew.* 737, 1107; gives an account of civil wars in Germany, 4 *Jew.* 665; speaks of Luther enjoining submission to the civil power, *ib.* 670; and of his rebuking Munzer, *ib.* 671; passages on the Anabaptists, *Rog.* 158, &c., 169, 231, 265, 326, 330, 354, 1 *Whitg.* 413; he writes of the conference of Marpurg, 2 *Ful.* 376; relates the history of Peter Aloisius, duke of Parma, 4 *Jew.* 658; narrates the murder of Jo. Diazius by his brother, *ib.* 659, 660; says pope Pius IV. cast cardinal Caraffa into prison, and there put him to death, *ib.* 1099; mentions princes who protested against the council of Trent, *ib.* 905, 1052; tells of some who spoke contemptuously of God's word, 3 *Jew.* 431, 4 *Jew.* 758; referred to, 4 *Jew.* 1146 n., 3 *Zur.* 529 n., 531 n., &c.; Sleidan attacked by Surius, 1 *Ful.* 63; report of a continuation of his work by Sturmius, 2 *Zur.* 92
Slibbersauce : 1 *Tyn.* 54
Slifter: a cleft, or crevice, 2 *Brad.* 333
Slime: used for mortar (Gen. xi.), 1 *Tyn.* 408
Slindon, co. Sussex: the manor and park, 2 *Cran.* 250, 255
Slingsby (Mr) : *Grin.* 325
Slops: trowsers, 2 *Bul.* 133, 1 *Whitg.* 62
Slorried: bedaubed, *Phil.* 233
Sloth: *v.* Idleness, Sleep.
Sluys: sea fight near it, 1 *Zur.* 274
Slyndon: *v.* Slindon.
Smacald: congress there, 1535, 2 *Cran.* 332 n., 3 *Jew.* 193, 3 *Zur.* 520 n., 521; bp Fox of Hereford sent thither, 2 *Lat.* 379 n.; the league of Smacald, and an embassy therefrom, 1 *Zur.* 21, 54; L. Humphrey going to a conference there, 1578, 2 *Zur.* 301
Smaragde: emerald, *Bale* 297
Smarden, co. Kent: 2 *Cran.* 367 n
Smedley (Edw.): Hist. of the Reformed Relig. in France, 1 *Zur.* 250 n.; an error noted, *Calf.* 314 n
Smell-smock: sir Saunder Smell-smock, *Bale* 395; sir John Smell-smoke, *Pil.* 255
Smerwick, co. Kerry: N. Saunders and other rebels land there, *Lit. Eliz.* 657 n
Smeton (Tho.): says Leo X. made a fable

SMETON — SNARLE

of the gospel of Christ, *Rog.* 181 n.; states that Calvin's catechism is read and expounded in several reformed churches, *ib.* 325 n

Smith (Sir Clem.): married Dorothy, sister of queen Jane Seymour, 3 *Zur.* 341 n

Smith (Sir Tho.): fellow of Queens' college, Cambridge, when 19 years old, *Park.* 64 n.; he lectures on Greek at Cambridge, 2 *Cran.* 322 n.; gives up the office of vice-chancellor, *Park.* 17, 18; chancellor to Goodrich, bp of Ely, *ib.* 30; secretary to king Edward, *Rid.* 328, 3 *Zur.* 77 n., 729 n.; an enormous pluralist, 1 *Lat.* 122; a visitor at Cambridge, 1549, *Grin.* 194; repeatedly ambassador in France, *Grin.* 285, 1 *Zur.* 91 n., 3 *Zur.* 497 n.; the commissioners for revising the liturgy met at his house in Westminster, *Grin.* v, *Sand.* xvii; dean of Carlisle, *Grin.* 285; secretary of state to queen Elizabeth, 1 *Zur.* 262 n., 2 *Zur.* 258; an ecclesiastical commissioner, *Park.* 370 n.; a privy councillor, *ib.* 457 n.; he induces the queen to send forces against Edinburgh castle, 1 *Zur.* 290 n.; mentioned, *Park.* 36 n.; letter from him to Porie, Parker, and Leeds, *ib.* 64; letter to him and Parker from Gardiner, *ib.* 20

Smith (Sir Tho.), master of requests to James I.: 2 *Bec.* 480 n

Smythe*(Chr.): a notary at Cranmer's examination, 2 *Cran.* 542

Smith (Jo.), father of Sir Thomas: 2 *Cran.* 322 n

Smith (Jo.), of Oriel college: disputes with Latimer at Oxford, 2 *Lat.* 250, 264, &c.; provost, *Park.* 138 n

Smith (Jo.), a Londoner: examined before the ecclesiastical commissioners, *Grin.* 201

Smith (Jo.?): Anti-Mortonus; publ. under the name of Jo. Sergeant, 2 *Ful.* 70 n

Smythe (Jo.), of the college of St Martin le Grand: his preferment solicited, 2 *Cran.* 240

Smith (Jo. Hen.): v. Fabricius.

Smith (Jud): notice of him, *Poet.* lii; paraphrase of the 5th chapter of the Song of Solomon, *ib.* 516

Smith (Rich.), reg. prof. of divinity, Oxon: some account of him, 4 *Jew.* 1191, *Park.* 72 n., 1 *Zur.* 12 n.; his letter, in 1550, to Cranmer, stating his intention to write a book in favour of the marriage of priests, *Rid.* 190; he disputed against P. Martyr, 3 *Zur.* 478 n.; assailed the works of Becon, 1 *Bec.* xv; persecuted Hooper, 2 *Hoop.* viii; his testimony to him, *ib.* x; was concerned in the disputation with the martyrs at Oxford, 1 *Cran.* 414, 424, 1 *Jew.* 33, 53; Ridley's principal opponent, *Rid.* 189; preached at the stake, before Ridley and Latimer, *ib.* 294; concerned in the process against Cranmer, 2 *Cran.* 546; his deposition, *ib.* 551; his conduct on the accession of Elizabeth, 4 *Jew.* 1218, *Park.* 72—74, 1 *Zur.* 45; he is deprived of his professorship, 1 *Zur.* 12, 4 *Jew.* 1201; reported to have married and kept a tavern in Wales, 4 *Jew.* 1237, 1 *Zur.* 81; his opinions on the sacrament, 1 *Cran.* 32, 33, 47, 53, 56 n., 71, 73, 78, 101, 108, 109, 150, 153, 173, 307, 329, 331, 362, 368, 375, *Rid.* 308, &c.; he furnished Gardiner with his authorities, 1 *Cran.* 163; De Cœlibatu Sacerd. et Votis Mon. contra P. Martyrem, 3 *Zur.* 478 n., 494 n.; Diatribe de Hominis Justif. adv. P. Martyrem, *ib.* 478 n.; Confutation of the True and Cath. Doctrine, against Cranmer, 1 *Cov.* 429, 1 *Cran.* 368, 3 *Zur.* 494 n.; Martyr writes against him, 2 *Brad.* 405, 1 *Zur.* 46 n.; his Confutation answered by Cranmer, 1 *Cran.* 9, 45; answer to his preface, *ib.* 368—379

Smith (Rich.): died in Lowlars' tower, *Poet.* 164

Smith (Rob.): martyred at Uxbridge, *Poet.* 163

Smith (Tho.): a persecutor, *Bale* 429

Smith (Will.), M.A., Camb.: recommended as a fellow of Eton, *Park.* 162

Smith (Will.), a tailor: persecuted, 3 *Tyn.* 270

Smythe (Will.): 2 *Cran.* 253

Smith (......): 4 *Jew.* 1194

Smyth (......): in prison for the truth, about 1531, 2 *Lat.* 321

Smyth (Mr), of the exchequer: perhaps Jo., father of Sir Tho., 2 *Cran.* 322

Smythe (Mr): at Oxford, 1538, 2 *Cran.* 383

Smythe (......): a layman, but prebendary of Norwich, *Park.* 312, 313

Smithfield: v. London.

Smoke-farthings: 4 *Jew.* 1079

Smyrna: the people built a temple and library in honour of Homer, 2 *Jew.* 981; the Apocalyptic epistle to the church there, *Bale* 275; Polycarp placed there by St John, 4 *Bul.* 31; the church writes to other churches on Polycarp's martyrdom, 2 *Ful.* 188 n., *Pil.* 365 n

Snape (Mr): *Rog.* 206 n

Snarle: to entangle, 1 *Bec.* 52, 1 *Brad.* 432

---

* Smith, Smyth, and Smythe, are arranged together.

(in 2 *Cov.* 275, "snare"), *Grin.* 483, *Lit. Eliz.* 507 n
Snecanus (Gall.): *Rog.* 341 n
Snede (......), vicar of Rye: letter to him, 2 *Cran.* 357
Snedysham (Rich.): *Bale* 16
Snoth (Agnes): martyred, *Poet.* 165, 3 *Zur.* 175 n
Snow: excessive, *Lit. Eliz.* 570
Soale (Joan): *v.* Sole.
Soames (Hen.): *Calf.* 53, 2 *Ful.* 20, 23, 225, 319, 1 *Zur.* 13, 15, 16, 158, &c., 3 *Zur.* 507, 508, &c., nn
Sobriety: *v.* Drunkenness, Gluttony, Temperance.
What it is to live soberly, 1 *Bec.* 324
Socheners: *v.* Switzerland.
Socinians: their heresy and that of the Arians distinguished, *Phil.* 298
Socinus (Lælius): mentioned, 3 *Zur.* 700
Socrates, the philosopher: was declared by an oracle to be the wisest of men, 3 *Bul.* 203; confessed that he knew nothing, 1 *Jew.* 100, 4 *Jew.* 1089, *Sand.* 112; taught by questions, *Lit. Edw.* 495, (545); his use of the word demon, 3 *Bul.* 356; he held souls to be immortal, *ib.* 385; says that every god is to be worshipped as he himself commands, *Calf.* 34, 263, *Hutch.* 254, *Sand.* 87; would have men only ask the gods for good things, without saying what, 2 *Bec.* 137; called a rich dolt a golden slave, *ib.* 600; his curst and shrewd wife, 1 *Cov.* 139; his words touching the eloquence of his accusers, 1 *Jew.* 83; he warned against believing every argument, *ib.* 84; his anticipations of a future state, 3 *Bec.* 154; poisoned, 2 *Cov.* 132, 222; his burial, *Pil.* 317
Socrates Scholasticus: *v.* Cassiodorus.
He speaks of the Jews attempting to rebuild the temple, *Sand.* 347; mentions a vision of angels seen by Ignatius, 3 *Whitg.* 385; speaks of the heresy of Paul of Samosata and Photinus, 3 *Bul.* 267; tells how Constantine summoned the council of Nice, 4 *Jew.* 1018; and how the bishops submitted their differences to his decision, *ib.*; recites the Nicene creed, 1 *Bul.* 15; approves the Nicene doctrine and terms used to express it, 3 *Bul.* 160, 243, 1 *Jew.* 533; says the council of Nice allowed the marriage of the clergy, 2 *Ful.* 153, 240, 1 *Hoop.* 376; writes of the synod of Gangra, *Coop.* 127; states that Constantine recalled the bishops from the council of Tyre, 4 *Jew.* 963, 1003; calls Athanasius the great star of Egypt, 3 *Jew.* 125; states that he appealed from the synod of Tyre to Constantine, 2 *Ful.* 358, 379; mentions his deposition, *ib.* 379; speaks of Antony the hermit, *Pil.* 146; says Libanius the sophist bestowed great praises upon Julian the renegate, 4 *Jew.* 700; states that he called the scriptures and all books of the Christian fathers but toys in comparison of the books of Julian, 3 *Jew.* 534; says Paulinus of Trier and many others refused to come to the council of Milan, 4 *Jew.* 951; shews how the emperor Theodosius sat amongst the bishops in a synod, *ib.* 1019; notices an assembly of the orthodox and heretical being summoned by Theodosius, who decided in favour of the former, 3 *Whitg.* 309; speaks of his conduct at the council of Aquileia, 4 *Jew.* 1020; says Jerome taught barbarians the scriptures, 2 *Jew.* 690; describes the acts of the council of Constantinople, 2 *Whitg.* 163, 315, 431; mentions the end of Arius, *Pil.* 29 n.; says Chrysostom succeeded Nectareus as bishop, 3 *Bul.* 78; mentions certain crosses and tapers used by him, 2 *Ful.* 121, 184; notes that he came not to the Arian council, though the emperor Constantius called him, 4 *Jew.* 1101; speaks of his banishment, *Coop.* 121 n.; mentions that Acacius melted the vessels of the church to redeem prisoners from the Persians, 2 *Ful.* 115; relates how certain Jews seeing the ready help of the Christians in preserving them from drowning, became Christians, 1 *Bec.* 18; he says, we believe in God according to the evangelical and apostolic tradition, 2 *Jew.* 673; declares that the simple unlearned people in cases of truth, judge oftentimes more uprightly than the deepest philosophers, 4 *Jew.* 897; asserts that Christians, because of their dissensions, were scorned at by the infidels, 1 *Jew.* 533, 2 *Jew.* 687; narrates how Chrysostom said that one city must have but one bishop, 2 *Whitg.* 215; says, that rules which bind the church are not made without the consent of the bishop of Rome, 1 *Jew.* 410, 4 *Jew.* 1001; mentions a rule of ecclesiastical rule that without the advice and will of the pope of Rome, no councils should be kept, 4 *Jew.* 826; says that long before his time the bishops' see of Rome, as well as of Alexandria, was grown beyond the bounds of priesthood into a foreign lordship, 2 *Ful.* 347; censures the conduct of the bishops of Rome and Alexandria towards the Novatians, 2 *Whitg.* 184; speaks of a decree that no man should be chosen

bishop without the consent of the bishop of Constantinople, 3 *Jew.* 333, 4 *Jew.* 827; calls all metropolitans patriarchs, 2 *Whitg.* 150; speaks of disorders at the election of bishops, 1 *Whitg.* 464, 465; mentions an archdeacon, 2 *Whitg.* 173; allows diversity of rites in the same religion, 4 *Bul.* 57, 1 *Whitg.* 219; says many things have been received by custom, now in one country, and now in another, 3 *Jew.* 570; declares it impossible to describe all the ceremonies of all the churches in each city and region, 4 *Bul.* 57; says, in all countries you shall not find two churches which in all points agree together in prayer, *ib.* 194; states that the gospel has laid on us no yoke of bondage, but that men for release of labour kept Easter and other festivals as they would, 2 *Brad.* 389 n., 4 *Bul.* 537, 538, 3 *Jew.* 438, *Whita.* 540, 1 *Whitg.* 219, 2 *Whitg.* 582; mentions some who deemed fornication a thing indifferent, but fought for the keeping of their holy days as for their souls, 4 *Jew.* 630; affirms that the ancient churches met together at the selfsame hour, 4 *Bul.* 183; mentions that at Antioch the church was set so that the altar looked towards the West, *ib.* 500; refers to vestments, 2 *Whitg.* 22, 23, 25, 28, 1 *Zur.* 350; says it was the custom in Thessaly to baptize only at Easter, 4 *Bul.* 367; speaks of the eucharist in holy week, 1 *Jew.* 246; gives an account of the origin of auricular confession, *Pil.* 553; speaks of its abolition at Constantinople, 4 *Jew.* 1053; mentions divers customs of fasting in Lent, 3 *Jew.* 170, *Pil.* 560; speaks of monks, 2 *Whitg.* 174; alludes to some idle ones, 4 *Jew.* 798; speaks of councils and other affairs of the church as dependent on Christian emperors, 2 *Ful.* 366, 1 *Jew.* 411, 2 *Jew.* 1022, 4 *Jew.* 991; gives an account of Pambo, 3 *Whitg.* 585; mentions the Gothic version of Ulphilas, *Whita.* 221; says the Arian heretics alleged the authority of Origen, 4 *Jew.* 783; speaks of their being overthrown by the holy scriptures, 3 *Jew.* 228, *Whita.* 679; describes the Manichees, *Rog.* 41 n.; refers to Montanus, *ib.* 43 n.; favoured the Novatians, 2 *Whitg.* 184, 185; speaks of the errors of Sabellius, *Rog.* 43 n.; referred to, 2 *Ful.* 160, 360, 1 *Hoop.* 169; wrongly alleged by Harding, 4 *Jew.* 1008, 1014

Sodbury (Little), co. Gloucester: 1 *Tyn.* xvi.
Sodom: its sin, 1 *Bul.* 418, 419; destroyed with Gomorrha, &c., 2 *Bul.* 429, 4 *Bul.* 496, *Pil.* 28; Lot rescued, 4 *Bul.* 555; the wicked church called Sodom and Gomorrha, *ib.* 11; the destruction of those cities a type of Christ's second coming, 2 *Jew.* 868
Soham, co. Cambridge: Ridley's farewell to it, *Rid.* 536; disputes about the advowson, *ib.* n
Soile: to solve, 4 *Jew.* 629; soyl, 1 *Tyn.* 71
Soiter (Melch.): *Rog.* 324 n
Soking: sucking, absorbing, 1 *Tyn.* 54
SOLACE OF THE SOUL, by T. Becon: 2 *Bec.* 569, &c.
Soldan: the sultan, *Bale* 590, *Pil.* 205
Soldiers: *v.* Archery, Billmen, Captains, Prayers.

Commendation of warriors, 1 *Bul.* 379; the oath of Roman soldiers, 4 *Bul.* 235; what manner of soldiers the ancient Christians were, 1 *Bul.* 382; mercenary soldiers, *ib.* 277; the wickedness of many in the wars, 1 *Bec.* 251; the idleness of some, *Pil.* 446, 447; soldiers of one kindred should be joined together, *ib.* 426, 427; soldiers admonished, *ib.* 414; description of a Christian soldier, 1 *Bul.* 381; there should be preachers among soldiers, 1 *Bec.* 252; they should read the scriptures, and give themselves to prayer, *ib.*; how they should prepare themselves for battle, *ib.* 251; how they should return after having gotten the victory, *ib.* 259; disbanded soldiers left to poverty and thieving, 2 *Tyn.* 302, 312; provision for them, *Now.* 227; all men are soldiers, *Sand.* 164, &c.
— Soldier of Barwicke: *v.* Gilby (A.).
— Soldiers of Christ: 4 *Bul.* 236; they must not put away the shield of prayer as long as the battle endures, 1 *Bec.* 168; the faithful soldier of Christ desireth assistance of God against his ghostly enemies; verses by Jo. Hall, M.D., *Poet.* 202
Sole (Joan): martyred, *Poet.* 165, 3 *Zur.* 175 n
Soleman (Jo.): a rebel, 2 *Cran.* 187 n
Solinus (C. J.): 1 *Bec.* 8, 1 *Hoop.* vi.
Solitude: dangerous, *Wool.* 85
Solœcophanes: a figure of speech, 1 *Ful.* 135, 146, 2 *Ful.* 385, 387; examples from Greek poets, 1 *Ful.* 141; from the New Testament, *ib.* 142
Solomon, king of Israel: *v.* Temple.

Interpretation of his name, *Grin.* 17; he was also called Jedidiah, 4 *Bul.* 372; made king, 1 *Lat.* 114; he prayed for wisdom, *ib.* 133; his prayer a precedent for kings, *ib.* 125; he was wisest of kings, 2 *Bul.* 6; wisest of all men, 3 *Bul.* 206, 4 *Bul.* 480; reverenced as such, 1 *Bul.* 50; his judgment, 1 *Cran.* 18, 92, 1 *Lat.* 126; he heard the complaints and causes of his people, 1 *Lat.* 133; judged in spiritual cases, 4 *Jew.* 988; banished Abiathar, the high priest, 1 *Bul.* 330, 2 *Ful.* 265; (Abiathar was not the legitimate high priest, 2 *Ful.* 265 n.); prayed in the tabernacle, 2 *Bul.* 149; built the temple, *ib.* 152; prayed at its dedication, 4 *Bul.* 166; became idolatrous, *Calf.* 347; punished, 1 *Bul.* 235

His writings : five books ascribed to him by a council at Carthage, 1 *Ful.* 19, *Whita.* 46; some of his writings are lost, *Whita.* 302, 525

— Proverbs: 4 *Bul.* 540, 2 *Cov.* 18; his prayer for sufficing of livelihood (Prov. xxx), *Lit. Edw.* 478

— Ecclesiastes, or the Preacher: 2 *Cov.* 18; vindicated against certain heretics, *Whita.* 31, 32

— Solomon's Song, 3 *Bul.* 153; called his Ballad, or Balettes, &c., 3 *Bul.* 153, 1 *Ful.* 571, 572, 2 *Ful.* 43, *Phil.* 317; vindicated against certain heretics, *Whita.* 31, 32; despised by Seb. Castellio, *Rog.* 81; ch. iv. in metre by D. Fenner, *Poet.* 341; ch. v. versified by M. Drayton, *ib.* 117; a paraphrase of the same chapter by Jud Smith, *ib.* 516

Apocryphal books : Ecclesiasticus has been ascribed to him, *Whita.* 46, 47

— Wisdom: its claims to be canonical considered, *Whita.* 86, &c.; it is not canonical, 4 *Bul.* 540, 541, 1 *Ful.* 20 n.; the most respected of all the apocryphal books, *Whita.* 56; ascribed by some to Philo, 1 *Ful.* 354, 3 *Jew.* 186, *Whita.* 88; whether received by Melito, *Whita.* 56 n.; mentioned by Epiphanius as doubtful, *ib.* 59; disallowed by Jerome, 1 *Ful.* 24; Augustine's opinion, *Whita.* 46; often cited as canonical by *Hutch.* (*e.g.*), 194, 206; extracts from The Wisdom of Solomon paraphrased, by Tho. Midleton, *Poet.* 534

Solomon Jarchi (R.): 1 *Ful.* 311, 313, 314, 315, 526

Solon: 2 *Bul.* 219, 1 *Hoop.* 351, 484, *Pil.* 462, *Sand.* 52

Solway moss: the raid there, 3 *Zur.* 239 n., 634

Solyman I., great Turk: *Grin.* 15

Solyman II., called the Magnificent: *Lit. Eliz.* 524 n., 2 *Cran.* 232, &c.

Some (Rob.): his treatise against the foul and gross sin of oppression, *Pil.* 468; Whitgift speaks of his foolery, 3 *Whitg.* 616

Some (Tho.): collects sermons by Latimer, 1 *Lat.* xiv; dedicates them to the duchess of Suffolk, *ib.* 81

Somer (Nic.): chauntry priest at Croydon, charged with lewdness, 2 *Cran.* 393, 394

Somer (Will.): *v.* Sommers.

Somerdine (Rich.): yeoman of Grindal's horse, *Grin.* 462

Somerfield (......): *v.* Somervile.

Somerset (Edw. duke of): *v.* Seymour.

Somerset house: *v.* London.

Somerset (Will.), 3rd earl of Worcester: said to have been at the duke of Norfolk's trial, 1 *Zur.* 267 n

Somersetshire: rebellion there, 3 *Zur.* 66

Somersham, co. Hunts: Somersham house, *Park.* 474; alienation of the manor from the see of Ely, 1 *Zur.* 319

Somervile (......): a traitor, *Lit. Eliz.* 588; strangled himself in prison, *ib.* 598 n., 658 n.

Somerville (...... lord): taken prisoner by the English, 1542, 3 *Zur.* 239 n

Sommers (Will.), or Somer: jester to Henry VIII., 4 *Jew.* 860, 871

Somner (......): *Park.* 400

Sonds (......): his vain prophecies, *Park.* 60

Songs: *v.* Ballads, Psalms.

Song of the three children, see Daniel; a spiritual song, containing a glorying of God, by Abr. Fleming, *Poet.* 546

Sons: *v.* Children.

The sick man's exhortation to his son, 3 *Bec.* 132, 133; sons are not always to walk in their fathers' ways, 1 *Lat.* 176

Sons of God: *v.* Children.

Those spoken of in Gen. vi. 2, 1 *Tyn.* 409; how the faithful are sons of God, 1 *Hoop.* 16

Sons of the prophets: 4 *Bul.* 481

Sonwalch: *v.* Coinualch.

Sooth: truth, *Bale* 81; sothfast, true, *ib.* 70; soothfastly, *Phil.* 423; sothfastness, *Bale* 66; sothly, *Phil.* 338

Soothsayers: *v.* Witchcraft.

Soper lane: *v.* London.

Soph, or Sophister: 2 *Lat.* xxvii.

Sophi: the title of the king of Persia, 2 *Ful.* 328 [not Cophti], *Pil.* 500; sophy, 2 *Cran.* 440, *Pil.* 205

Sophocles: cited or referred to, 2 *Bul.* 28, 2 *Cov.* 126, 1 *Hoop.* 285, 1 *Lat.* 491; his recitation of his Œdipus Colonæus before the judges, 3 *Jew.* 249; choked, 2 *Cov.* 132

Sophronius: turned Jerome's Latin Psalter and prophets into Greek, *Whita.* 137; perhaps the interpolator of Jerome's Catalogue of Eccles. Writers, *Calf.* 128 n.; he (or Jerome?) declares the story of the

assumption of the virgin to be apocryphal, *Whita.* 667
Sophronius, patr. of Jerusalem: asserts that Paul preached in Britain, 3 *Jew.* 128, 164; fables concerning images in the Limonarium or Pratum Spirituale, ascribed to him, 2 *Jew.* 658; whether he was the writer of that book, *Calf.* 174 n., 2 *Jew.* 658 n
Sopbronius, a heretic: *Hutch.* 121 n
Sopwell, co. Hertford: the nunnery, 2 *Cran.* 65
Sorbonne: *v.* Paris.
Sorcery: *v.* Witchcraft.
Sorocold (Tho.): 2 *Brad.* 41; himself and his wife, *ib.* 76
Sorocold (Tho.), rector of St Mildred's in the Poultry: his Supplications of Saints, 1610, *Lit. Eliz.* 622 n., 665 n
Sorrow: *v.* Affliction, Sin.
Two kinds, 1 *Lat.* 479; sorrow Godward, 3 *Bul.* 60; worldly sorrow, *ib.* 61; consolation to one in sorrow, *Phil.* 228; need of true sorrow, 4 *Bul.* 549
Sort: number, multitude, 1 *Bec.* 5, 4 *Bul.* 159, *Sand.* 45
Soter, bp of Rome: epistle of Dionysius to him, 3 *Whitg.* 345; his orders about the eucharist, ascribed also in part to Anacletus, 1 *Jew.* 172—176, 184
Sothfast: *v.* Sooth.
Soto (Dom. à); De Natura et Gratia, *Jew.* xlii; In Ep. ad Rom. Comm. et Apol. adv. Catharin., *ib.*; his controversy with Catharinus, 3 *Jew.* 620, 4 *Jew.* 956; he says Pighius is ill reported of as a man denying original sin, *ib.* 787
Soto (Petrus à); notice of him, 3 *Zur.* 58 n.; sent to Cranmer in Bocardo, *Rid.* 293, 3 *Zur.* 751 n; he destroyed P. Martyr's work in Oxford, 1 *Zur.* 33, 4 *Jew* 1212, 1213; he teaches that sin is purged by good works, *Rog.* 116; speaks on works of supererogation, *ib.* 130; says that of the ministers and members of the church is required neither grace nor other inward virtue, *ib.* 192; limits the church to bishops and prelates, *ib.* 172; his judgment on scripture, 3 *Jew.* 757, 758, *Whita.* 496; he talks of the obscurity thereof, *Rog.* 199; affirms that the sense of scripture is to be sought of the church, *ib.* 192; prefers tradition to scripture, *ib.* 200; enumerates apostolical traditions, *Whita.* 511; affirms that the council which condemned our Lord had the spirit of prophecy, 4 *Jew.* 941; allows swearing by things created, *Rog.* 357 n
Souchenars: *v.* Switzerland.
Soude (Will.): *v.* Sowode.

Soul: *v.* Solace, Spirits, Dead, Heaven, Man.
The word diversely taken, 3 *Bul.* 366; for breath and life, *ib.*; for a desire, *ib.* 367; for the spirit of man, *ib.*; for the mind, *ib.*; sometimes for the whole man, 1 *Ful.* 281; the soul is bodiless, 3 *Bul.* 372; a substance, *ib.* 369; what manner of substance, *ib.* 372; neither God, nor a part of God, *ib.* 373; its original, *ib.*, *Whita.* 394; its fall through Adam, 1 *Bec.* 204; the opinions of philosophers and others on the soul, 3 *Bul.* 374; operations and powers of the soul, *ib.* 376; two faculties of it, *ib.* 98; it must be fed as well as body, 1 *Lat.* 412; it is not nourished with corporal food, *Hutch.* 242; its health to be sought in prayer, 1 *Bec.* 165; it is passible, 2 *Cov.* 202; its immortality, 3 *Bec.* 181, &c., 3 *Bul.* 378; testimonies to this, *ib.* 381; all wise men have thought the soul immortal, *ib.* 385; the immortality of the soul, with sentences and examples of scripture, 1 *Bec.* 482, &c.; how mortal, and how immortal, 2 *Cov.* 201; the death of the soul, 3 *Bul.* 380, 2 *Cov.* 201; the soul separated from the body, 3 *Bul.* 379; where it lives when separated, *ib.* 386; whither went the soul of Jairus's daughter, 1 *Lat.* 550; how the soul is translated to its appointed place, 3 *Bul.* 388; the souls of the righteous are blessed immediately after death, *ib.* 404; souls do not sleep, *ib.* 389, 2 *Hoop.* 63; an article to this effect, *Lit. Edw.* 537, (581); at what time the righteous are carried up into heaven, 3 *Bul.* 389; they not carried into purgatory, *ib.* 390; the praying for souls departed at the mass, 3 *Bec.* 276; a practice not taught by the scriptures, *ib.*; why the Papists cherish it, *ib.* 277; souls do not wander in the earth, *ib.* 401, 2 *Cran.* 44, 45; the souls of the blessed know not our affairs on earth, 3 *Bul.* 212; the soul returns to the body at the day of judgment, *ib.* 388; the souls of the righteous are purged by the blood of Christ, *ib.* 391, 393; their works, *ib.* 378; the immortality of the soul; the worth of the soul; the soul; poems by Sir Jo. Davies, *Poet.* 86, 96, 97; care for the soul, verses by Will. Byrd, *ib.* 223
Sound: declared by Priscian to be a body; Aristotle says otherwise, 3 *Jew.* 260
Sound: to signify, *Phil.* 224
Southam: 1 *Lat.* 325
Southam (Rob.), martyr in Smithfield, *Poet.* 172
Southampton: *v.* Bevis, Hampshire.
Southampton (Tho. earl of): *v.* Wriothesley.

Southcoots (Mr), a justice, *Park.* 375
Southwark, co. Surrey: three martyrs there, 3 *Zur.* 200; the church of St Mary Overy (now St Saviour's); Bradford examined there, 1 *Brad.* 473, 482, 585; Hooper examined there, 2 *Hoop.* xxiii; Bonner buried in St George's churchyard, privily by night, *Grin.* 307; the King's Bench prison, 1 *Brad.* 83 n., 289, 367, 2 *Brad.* xxxiv, xxxv, *Poet.* 168; the Marshalsea, 1 *Brad.* 289, 367, 421, 2 *Brad.* xxxv, 2 *Cov.* 238, 1 *Lat.* 164; the Clink, a prison, 1 *Brad.* 492, 2 *Hoop.* xxiv, 181; the Compter, *ib.* xxiv, Winchester house, pillaged by the rebels under Sir Thomas Wyat, 3 *Zur.* 514; Winchester's rents, a place of ill fame, *Bale* 518, 531, 2 *Tyn.* 275; the stews at the Bank, or Bankside, 1 *Lat.* 133, 134, 196; stews suppressed, *Hutch.* 328; Paris Garden, a place for bear-baiting, 1 *Brad.* 31
Southwell, co. Notts: a manor of the see of York, *Sand.* xxv, xxvii; the epitaph of abp Sandys there, *ib.* xxvii, xxviii.
Southwell (Sir Rich.): one of queen Mary's privy council, 1 *Zur.* 5 n.; he (or Sir Rob.) was at the examination of Bradford, 1 *Brad.* 470
Southwell (Sir Rob.), master of the rolls: 1 *Bec.* 61 n
Southworth (Sir Jo.): some account of him, *Grin.* 305, 306; committed to prison, *Park.* 329; he refuses to submit, *ib.* 330
Sovereigns: *v.* Kings, Magistrates, Prayers.
Sower: the parable expounded, 2 *Lat.* 209, *Sand.* 299
Sowerby (Tho.): in exile at Frankfort, 3 *Zur.* 764
Sowode (Will.): master of C. C. C. C.: *Park.* 16
Soyl: *v.* Soile.
Sozomen (Hermias): *v.* Cassiodorus.
He states that the descendants of Hagar choose the name of Saracens, as though they came of Sara the free-woman, 4 *Jew.* 713; mentions an attempt of the Jews to rebuild their temple, *Sand.* 347; says the Eastern churches immediately after the time of the apostles, used to sing psalms and hymns to Christ our Lord, 4 *Bul.* 193; shews that their practice as to singing, prayer, and reading, varied, *ib.* 194; says that Polycarp and Victor thought it folly to be separated for ceremonies, 1 *Whitg.* 219; describes the constancy of the early Christians in their sufferings, 3 *Jew.* 190, 604; tells how barbarous nations were brought to the truth through the behaviour of Christian captives, *Sand.* 246; speaks of Helena, 4 *Jew.* 993; refers to the invention of the cross, *Calf.* 326, 327; gives some account of what became of the nails, *ib.* 327; referred to on the worship of the cross, *ib.* 198; he speaks of the labarum, which he calls λάβωρον, 2 *Jew.* 650; states how Constantine rebuked quarrelling bishops, 4 *Jew.* 968; affirms that he said to the bishops, you cannot be judged of men (i. e. laymen), *ib.*; says that he gave the clergy the power of appealing from the magistrate to their bishops, 3 *Whitg.* 454; states that Constantine summoned the council of Nice, and tells how, 4 *Jew.* 996, 999, 1004; says pope Julius excused himself from attending it, on account of age, *ib.* 996, 999; states that Vitus and Vincentius were the pope's legates there, *ib.* 999, 1000; relates how the emperor Constantine sat in the council, *ib.* 1015, 1017; mentions how Paphnutius vindicated the marriage of the clergy in this synod, 1 *Bul.* 401, 1 *Hoop.* 376, 3 *Jew.* 386, 389, 405, 424, 4 *Jew.* 1053, *Pil.* 532, *Rog.* 207 n.; speaks of twenty bishops being summoned to court by the emperor, that he might consider and decide upon the decrees of a council, 4 *Jew.* 1026, 3 *Whitg.* 309; states that Constantine called upon those who had kept the council at Tyrus to repair to him, 4 *Jew.* 1008; says he wrote letters to the Persian king in favour of Christians, *Sand.* 109; speaks of his building a church at Jerusalem, *Calf.* 182; refers to bishops assembled at Alexandria confirming the decrees of Nice, 3 *Bul.* 159; mentions that Athanasius appealed to pope Julius, 2 *Ful.* 346; says that Hosius, bishop of Corduba, was president in the council of Sardica, 4 *Jew.* 1003; refers to St Anthony, 3 *Bec.* 280 n.; tells how the body of Paul, bp of Constantinople, was mistaken by the people for that of the apostle, 2 *Ful.* 112; states that the bishops of the East deposed pope Julius, 4 *Jew.* 834; mentions the council of Ariminum, and states why it was disallowed, 3 *Jew.* 217; speaks of the heresy of pope Liberius, 4 *Jew.* 908, 924; says Constantius bewailed that many waxed worse when fallen to the religion of Christ, 3 *Jew.* 625; mentions a saying of his that men unfaithful to God could not be faithful to their prince, *Sand.* 97, 261, 441; tells how Julian condemned the reasons of some Christian bishops, and records their answer to him, 3 *Jew.* 203; affirms that Julian said, when princes and magistrates come within the temple, they are but as private men, 4 *Jew.* 670; mentions

a miraculous shower which fell on Julian, *Calf.* 114, 115, 120; narrates the conduct and answer of Valentinian when requested to examine certain matters of religion, 4 *Jew.* 670, 994, 1001, 2 *Whitg.* 363; mentions that Damasus, &c. writing to the bishops of Illyricum, said it is meet that all the teachers within the Roman jurisdiction should agree together, 3 *Jew.* 333, 4 *Jew.* 707, 828; speaks of the election of Nectarius, 1 *Jew.* 408; tells why confession was abolished at Constantinople, 3 *Bul.* 77, 78, 2 *Ful.* 91; speaks of Theodosius in a council, 4 *Jew.* 1020, 1021; says Chrysostom deposed certain bishops for simony, 2 *Whitg.* 315; records his banishment, *Coop.* 121 n.; cited a saying that there was no private confession in the church of Constantinople while Chrysostom was bishop (Socrates!), 3 *Jew.* 352; relates a miracle at Constantinople, 1 *Jew.* 246; describes the sufferings of Olympias, *Pil.* 637; speaks of Epiphanius bp of Salamine as expert in civil matters, 3 *Whitg.* 455; says that the cities of Scythia had but one bishop, 2 *Whitg.* 165, 430; speaks of an archbishop, and a metropolitan, *ib.* 166; speaks of disorders at the election of bishops, 1 *Whitg.* 463, 464; speaks of archdeacons, deacons, and other ministers reading the scriptures in the church, 2 *Whitg.* 173, 175, 3 *Whitg.* 64; writes of Spiridion, a married bishop, 2 *Jew.* 727, 3 *Jew.* 390, 411, 412, 413, *Pil.* 561, 562; speaks of the disciples of Eustathius despising married priests, *ib.* 565; mentions applications to emperors for leave to hold councils, 4 *Jew.* 994, 1001, 1005, 2 *Whitg.* 363; says a council at Milan was held by order of the emperor, 1 *Jew.* 382; alludes to a law of bishops that things done (in any council) without the advice and will of the bishop of Rome should be void, 4 *Jew.* 826; speaks of a council confirmed neither by the bishop of Rome nor any other bishop, 4 *Jew.* 998; mentions the origin of public penance, 3 *Bul.* 77; describes the manner of open confession, 3 *Jew.* 360; speaks of auricular confession, *Pil.* 553; alludes to the place for penitents in the Roman church, 1 *Ful.* 431; tells how one Eutropius fled to a church for shelter, and lay before the holy table, *Pil.* 546; mentions a golden vestment sold by Cyril, 2 *Whitg.* 24; alludes to processions of the Arians at Constantinople, 2 *Ful.* 184; says that Christians, because of their dissensions, were scorned at by the infidels, 1 *Jew.*

588; affirms that the Arians and Donatists did rebaptize, 4 *Bul.* 393; describes the heresy of Macedonius, *Rog.* 70 n.; intimates that kings are saved only by godliness, and that without it armies are nothing, 3 *Jew.* 194; referred to, *Calf.* 65, 193, 252, 388, 2 *Ful.* 347, 360

Spain: *v.* Cadiz, Inquisition, Sepharad.
    Ancient jurisdiction of the bishop of Rome there, &c., 3 *Jew.* 332, 334; the kings not anointed, 4 *Jew.* 1037; victories of the Moors, 1 *Zur.* 219, 239; the Spanish ambassador ordered to quit England, *ib.* 266; Drake's victories at Cadiz, &c., *Lit. Eliz.* 469; no need to fear Spain, *Poet.* 375

Spaniards: brought into England to maintain Popery, *Pil.* 242; hence Papists were called Spaniels, *ib.* 233; their pernicious influence in this country, 1 *Zur.* 32, and especially at Oxford, *ib.* 33; a Spanish Protestant church, *v.* London.

Spanish Armada, 1588: the invasion excited by cardinal Allen, *Lit. Eliz.* 657; the armada delayed a year, *ib.* 469; seen near the Lizard, *ib.*; defeated, and banners displayed at Paul's cross, *ib.*; queen Elizabeth's prayer of thanksgiving for its overthrow, *ib.* 622 n.; rejoicings in England and Scotland, *ib.* 470; reference to it, *Poet.* 134

Spalatinus (......): his account of Tyndale's New Testament, 1 *Tyn.* xxx.

Spalatro (Ant. abp of): *v.* Dominis (A. de).

Spanhemius (Ezech.): 2 *Ful.* 89 n., 199 n

Spanhemius (Frid.): *Calf.* 31 n., 361 n., 2 *Ful.* 98 n

Spar: to bar, to shut, 1 *Bec.* 54, 1 *Brad.* 417, 2 *Brad.* 46, 2 *Cov.* 233; spear, *Bale* 289, 385, 403, 561

Sparke (Tho.): Ans. to Albine, *Rog.* 181 n

Sparrow (Will.): burned, *Poet.* 171

Spaxton, co. Somerset: Woolton minister there, *Wool.* iv.

Spear: *v.* Spar.

Spears: gentlemen pensioners, 2 *Cran.* 399 n

Speciosus, a deacon: *Calf.* 88

Spectacles: More's referred to, 3 *Tyn.* 234, 236, 243

Speculator: *v.* Durandus (Gul.).

Speculum (Aureum) Papæ: *Jew.* xlii, 3 *Jew.* 273, 4 *Jew.* 868, 910

Speech: *v.* Tongue.

Speke (Sir Tho.): his death, 3 *Zur.* 496 n

Spellache, in the marches of Calais: parsonage of St Quintin, 2 *Cran.* 345, 349

Spelman (Sir Hen.): Concilia, *Calf.* 53 n., 2 *Ful.* 23 n.; Glossarium, *Calf.* 35 n., 305 n.; De non temerandis Ecclesiis, 2 *Ful.* 114 n

Spence: a battery, or store room, 1 *Hoop.* 388, 1 *Jew.* 87

Spencer (Hen.), bp of Norwich: besieged Ypres, *Bale* 171

Spencer (Tho.): in exile at Zurich, 3 *Zur.* 752 n.; perhaps mentioned, *ib.* 136, 157; archdeacon of Chichester, 1 *Zur.* 255; his death, *ib.*

Spencer (Dr), parson of Hadley: commended by Grindal to Cecil, *Grin.* 292

Spencer (Dr), prebendary of Riccall in the church of York: *Park.* 362

Spencer (......): martyred at Salisbury, *Poet.* 166

Spencer (......): martyred at Colchester, *Poet.* 167

Spens (Dav.), minister of Monimail: 2 *Zur.* 365

Spens (Will.), minister of Kilconquhar: 2 *Zur.* 365

Spensa (Ant.): 4 *Jew.* 656

Spenser (Edm.): biographical notice, *Poet.* xiv; an hymn of heavenly love, *ib.* 6; an hymn of heavenly beauty, *ib.* 15; the ruins of time, *ib.* 24; Mammon, *ib.* 29; the ministry of angels, *ib.* 30; the ways of God unsearchable, *ib.*; a sonnet, *ib.* 32; he repeatedly alludes to Grindal, calling him Algrind, *Grin.* xiii. n., xiv. n.; referred to, *Calf.* 47 n., 52 n

Spenser (Miles): *Rid.* 536 n

Spenser (Rich): burned, *Bale* 394

Spenser (......): abroad, 3 *Zur.* 136, 157

Sponsor (......), fellow of Gonville hall: *Park.* 252

Spials: spies, *Sand.* 166, 211

Spilman (Fra.?): *v.* Spylman.

Spilman (Tho.): grantee of the site of the Grey Friars, Canterbury, 2 *Cran.* 330 n

Spina (Alph. de): his Fortalitium Fidei, 2 *Ful.* 5 n (*v.* Fortalitium).

Spindle: to shoot with a long stalk, 2 *Bul.* 163

Spira (Fra.): notices of him, his desperation and dreadful end, 1 *Brad.* 433 n., 2 *Brad.* 80 n., 2 *Cov.* 276 n., 1 *Lat.* 425, *Rog.* 59, 142, *Sand.* 362

Spiridion: a married bishop, 2 *Jew.* 727, 1128, 3 *Jew.* 390, 412, 413, *Pil.* 561, 576

Spirit: *v.* Flesh, Man.

What it is, 3 *Bec.* 606, *Now.* (103), 3 *Bul.* 298, 299; exposition of the word in 1 Cor. xiv, 1 *Jew.* 313, 315; the spirit of faith, the same to Jews and Christians, 1 *Bul.* 327

Spirit (Holy): *v.* Holy Ghost.

Spirits: *v.* Angels, Demons.

To seek intercourse with evil spirits is a breach of the third commandment, 1 *Hoop.*
326; caution against lying spirits, *Sand.* 115; lying spirits of divination, *ib.* 373; seducing spirits, scripture is the sole remedy against them, *Whita.* 347; not every spirit to be believed, *ib.* 433; Whitaker asserts that by the word "spirit" John means "doctrine," *ib.*; the appearing of spirits, 3 *Bul.* 400; apparitions of the dead are insufficient to prove truth, 2 *Cran.* 43; they cannot establish new articles of faith, *ib.* 64; the appearing of spirits adduced in support of purgatory, 3 *Bul.* 400; the souls of the dead do not wander in these regions, *ib.* 401; the case of Samuel (*q. v.*), *ib.* 403; story of a ghost by Gregory I. (or II.?), *Calf.* 89; the apparition of Benedict IX. (*q. v.*), *Pil.* 603 n.; an alleged one at Blackburn, *Park.* 222; Sandys speaking of the reformation in England, says the gospel hath chased away walking spirits, *Sand.* 60

Spiritual: *v.* Pearl.

Meaning of the word, *Now.* (103); who may fitly be so called, 1 *Tyn.* 495, 2 *Tyn.* 128; the word denotes the regenerate, *Whita.* 452; spiritual things represented by outward and visible tokens, 1 *Cov.* 390; not to be grossly compared with corporal things, *Phil.* 68; they are not subject to the temporal power, *ib.* 72

Spiritual sense: *v.* Scripture.

Spiritualty: *v.* Clergy.

Spittle: *v.* London.

Spon (Huldric): 3 *Zur.* 425

Spondanus (Hen.): *Calf.* 42 n., 2 *Ful.* 292 n

Sponsors: *v.* Baptism.

Of godfathers and their promise, 3 *Whitg.* 118; the custom old and commendable, 2 *Bec.* 228; their invention ascribed to Hygenus, *Calf.* xi, 212, 3 *Whitg.* 109, 120, 473, 504; mentioned by the pseudo-Dionysius, *Calf.* 211; the decree of Theodore, abp of Canterbury, *ib.* 212 n.; injunctions respecting them, *Grin.* 126; co-sponsors termed by Papists spiritual kindred, and forbidden to intermarry, *Bale* 537, *Rog.* 262, 306, 1 *Tyn.* 245; Gualter's opinion of sponsors, 2 *Zur.* 233; some objected to them, *Grin.* 208; some were punished for refusing to choose them for their children, 2 *Zur.* 149; sponsors were called gossips, *Bale* 537, 2 *Zur.* 104 n.; of parents presenting and answering for their children, 3 *Whitg.* 134, 138

Sporis: spurs, *Park* 13

Sports: *v.* Cards, Gaming, Hunting.

Honest pastimes may be used temperately, *Phil.* 307; handball, *Rid.* 493 n.; games on Sunday afternoon, 3 *Whitg.* 384

Spottiswood (Jo.), superintendent of Lothian: 2 *Zur.* 364; letter from him and others to abps Parker and Young, *Park.* 205

S. P. Q. R.: 1 *Jew.* 421

Springal: a youth, 1 *Brad.* 556

Springham (Rich.): a contributor to the afflicted gospellers, *Jew.* xiii, 1 *Zur.* 9, 112 n.; mentioned, 1 *Zur.* 65

Sprites: the spiritualty or clergy, 1 *Tyn.* 330, 333, 341

Spurge (Rich. and Tho.): martyrs, *Poet.* 166

Spurs: the winning of them, *Park.* 13, 3 *Tyn.* 17 n., 151, 2 *Whitg.* 191; golden spurs a mark of knighthood, 3 *Tyn.* 17 n

Spylman (Mr): of Gray's Inn, *Bale* 164; surety of Anne Askewe, *ib.* 178

Squire: square, rule, or measure, 2 *Jew.* 1058, 1 *Whitg.* 191

Squire (Edw.): his horrible treason, and execution at Tyburn, *Lit. Eliz.* 473, 681, 682

Squire (Jo.): Lect. on 2 Thess., *Calf.* 6 n

Stacey (Tho.), proctor: 2 *Cran.* 491

Stackered: staggered, 1 *Bul.* 87

Stacy (Jo.), brickmaker: 1 *Tyn.* 33

Staff: what it means in scripture, 2 *Hoop.* 226

Stafford (Hen. lord): translates Fox De vera Differentia, 2 *Brad.* 16 n., *Rid.* 512

Stafford (Edw.), lord Stafford: letter to Wolfg. Meier, 2 *Zur.* 322

— Mary (Stanley) his wife, *Park.* 358

Stafford (Edw. lord), who succeeded, 1603: at C. C. C., Cambridge, *Park.* 358

Stafford (Geo.), or Stavert: lady Margaret's reader at Cambridge, and the first who read lectures on the scriptures there, 1 *Bec.* vii, 2 *Bec.* 425, 426, 1 *Lat.* 440, 2 *Lat.* xxvii.

Stafford (Mr): in exile, 3 *Zur.* 144

Staffordshire: superstition of the priests there, 2 *Bec.* 423

Stage-plays: on Sundays and holy days, *Lit. Eliz.* 574

Stainer (Pet.): 3 *Zur.* 126

Stainfield, co. Linc.: letters to the prioress, 2 *Cran.* 278, 284

Stairs: the emblem explained, *Pil.* 389

Stalbrydge (Hen.): a name assumed by Bale, 1 *Bec.* viii.

Stale: a bait, or decoy, *Grin.* 368

Stale: used for stole, *Calf.* 249

Stallard (......), of Benet college: *Park.* 344

Stalled: installed, *Calf.* 316

Stamford, co. Linc.: Latimer preaches there, 1 *Lat.* 282, 296, 511, 2 *Lat.* xvii; the mayor, 1 *Lat.* 449; the Dutch church, 1 *Zur.* 266 n

Stancariani: 2 *Jew.* 686

Stancarus (.....:.): his dangerous opinions, 4 *Bul.* xiii, 3 *Jew.* 265, 4 *Jew.* 1260, 1261; refuted by Simler, Osiander, Calvin, Bullinger, and Melancthon, 1 *Zur.* 127

Standgate hole [near Lambeth?]: noted for robberies, 1 *Lat.* 139

Standish (Hen.), bp of St Asaph: examines persons charged with heresy, 1 *Tyn.* 32; at Anne Boleyn's coronation, 2 *Cran.* 245

Standish (Jo.): notices of him, *Bale* 172, 1 *Ful.* 4 n.; his character, 2 *Cov.* 322; he charges Erasmus with heresy, 1 *Lat.* 46; his attack on the protestation of Dr R. Barnes, *Bale* 429, 2 *Cov.* 322; A CONFUTATION of that treatise, by bp Coverdale, 2 *Cov.* 320, &c.

Standysh (......): candidate for the vice-chancellorship at Cambridge, *Park.* 17

Stanfeld: *v.* Stainfield.

Stanghurst (Rich.): wrote English hexameters, *Poet.* xxii.

Stanhope (Sir Edw.): notices of him, 1 *Bec.* 396 n., 3 *Bec.* 3 n.; his dau. Anne marries the duke of Somerset, 1 *Bec.* 396 n., 3 *Zur.* 340 n

Stanhope (Sir Mich.): confined, 3 *Zur.* 77 n.; beheaded, *ib.* 579 n

Stanhope (Tho.): 1 *Zur.* 213 n

Stanislaus Hosius, *q. v.*

Stanislaus Orichovius, *q. v.*

Stanley (Edw.), 3rd earl of Derby: speaks against Bradford in parliament, 1 *Brad.* 469, 474, 2 *Brad.* 43, 44; sues for his life, 1 *Brad.* 517; was to have conveyed him into Lancashire, *ib.* 492 n., *Rid.* 382; favourably disposed towards him, 1 *Brad.* 499, 515, 530, 538, 2 *Brad.* xxxviii; privy councillor to Mary and Elizabeth, 1 *Zur.* 5 n.; one of the commissioners for the north, *ib.* 73 n.; his dau. Anne married Cha. lord Stourton, *Park.* 424 n.; his dau. Mary married Edw. lord Stafford, *ib.* 358

Stanley (Hen.), 4th earl of Derby: when lord Strange he sought the lady Margaret Seymour for his wife, 3 *Zur.* 340 n.; and was a mourner at the funeral of the emperor Ferdinand, *Grin.* 32; he succeeds to the earldom, *Park.* 424 n

Stanley (Tho.), bp of Sodor and Man: *Park.* 222, *Pil.* vii.

Stanley (Sir Rowl.): desires to be sheriff of Cheshire, *Grin.* 345

Stanley (Sir Will.): betrays Deventer to the Spaniards, *Lit. Eliz.* 656 n

Stanley (Agnes): martyred in Smithfield, *Poet.* 169

Stanly (......): concerned in Squire's treason, *Lit. Eliz.* 682

Stannaries: 2 *Jew.* 627

Stansby (Rich.): bailiff to the earl of Essex, 3 *Cran.* 266, 267

Stanstrete (Jo.): 2 *Cran*, 367 n

Stanton: *v.* Staunton.

Staphylus (Fred.): notices of him, 1 *Zur.* 339 n., 2 *Zur.* 70 n.; his apostasy, 2 *Ful.* 58, 1 *Jew.* 106, 2 *Jew.* 686, 687, 803, 808, *Sand.* 362; named, 4 *Jew.* 756 n.; translations of his Apology, 2 *Ful.* 76; he professes to have found out 34 sects sprung from Luther, 2 *Jew.* 686; reviles Luther's translation, 1 *Ful.* 60; the validity of his reference to a work by Luther questioned, 2 *Ful.* 18 n

Stapleton (Tho.): allusion to his name Thomas, 2 *Ful.* 51, 53, 59; Opera, *Jew.* xliii; books by him, *Calf.* 3, 51, 64 n., 2 *Ful.* 3, 3 n., 4, 3 *Jew.* 166; he attacks Jewel's Apology, *Grin.* 169, *Jew.* xx; departs from the expositions of the fathers, 4 *Jew.* 1306; writes on the authority of scripture, *Whita.* 277; confesses that scripture has its chief testimony from God, *ib.* 358; gives cautions respecting the interpretation of scripture, *ib.* 411—414; treats of the authority of the church with respect to scripture, *ib.* 280, 281; says, that is the only true sense of scripture, which is given by the church of Rome, *Rog.* 197 n.; maintains that the church is to be believed whether it teach truth or error, *ib.* 78; describes the marks of the church, *ib.* 176; says that the clergy only may judge of doctrine, *ib.* 192; teaches that Mary was sinless, *ib.* 134; states his opinion on The Shepherd of Hermas, and the Clementine Constitutions, *Whita.* 109; rebukes sacrilege, 2 *Ful.* 114; affirms that our bishops and ministers come not in by the door, but have stolen in like thieves, *Rog.* 333 n.; is indebted to Staphylus for a charge against Luther's followers, 2 *Ful.* 18 n.; contradicts himself, *Whita.* 352; he translates Bede's history, 2 *Ful.* 5; also the Apology of Staphylus, *ib.* 76 n.; Bridges replies to him, 1 *Ful.* 75 n.; Whitaker writes against him, *Whita.* title, and xii; Fulke answers him, 1 *Ful.* viii, ix, x; STAPLETON'S FORTRESS OVERTHROWN, 2 *Ful.* 1, 28, &c.

Stapleton (Sir Rob.): his foul plot against abp Sandys, xxiv, xxv

Stapleton (......), parson of Bingham: letter to him, 2 *Cran.* 262; his character, *ib.*

Stapulensis, i. e. J. Faber, *q. v.*

Starky (Tho.), skinner: *Park.* 211

Star Chamber: *v.* Courts.

Stars: *v.* Astrology, Signs.

The stars created, 3 *Bul.* 174; signs by them, 4 *Bul.* 231; the star which appeared at Christ's birth, *Hutch.* 81; opinions respecting it, *ib.* 82; a new star, which lasted 16 months, *Lit. Eliz.* 569; star said to denote the ministers of God's word, *Bale* 328; one falls from heaven, *ib.* 346; another, *ib.* 350; stars falling from heaven said to denote pastors falling away, *Sand.* 361, 362; another application, *ib.* 363; the woman crowned with twelve stars, *Bale* 405

State: *v.* Temporalty.

Evil walkers in the state, *Sand.* 121

State Papers: 2 *Lat.* 523

Statham (Mr): mentioned, with his wife, who is styled Latimer's nurse, 2 *Cran.* 375, 2 *Lat.* 386, 387, 391, 393, 397

Stationers' company: *v.* London.

Stations: what they were in ancient times, 2 *Ful.* 183, 238, 1 *Lat.* 49 n

Stationaries: 1 *Lat.* 49

Statutes: subjects should read the acts, 1 *Lat.* 372

20 Hen. III.: stat. of Merton, 4 *Jew.* 904 n., 1 *Lat.* 248

Edw. I.: 4 *Jew.* 904

7 Edw. I.: mortmain, 1 *Lat.* 522 n

13 Edw. I.: stat. Westm. II., 1 *Lat.* 248 n

9 Edw. II.: excommunication, *Grin.* 452

15 Rich. II.: mortmain, 1 *Lat.* 522 n

Hen. V.: against heresy, *Bale* 50

4 Hen. VII.: commons, 1 *Lat.* 101 n

7 Hen. VIII.: commons, 1 *Lat.* 101 n

21 Hen. VIII.: pluralities, 2 *Cran.* 365, *Park.* 136, 2 *Tyn.* 256 n., 336

23 Hen. VIII.: mortmain, 1 *Lat.* 522 n

25 Hen. VIII.: on succession to the crown, 2 *Cran.* 285 n

— commons, 1 *Lat.* 101 n

— marriage, prohibited degrees, 2 *Cran.* 329 n

26 Hen. VIII.: suffragans, 2 *Cran.* 471, 1 *Lat.* 175 n

27 Hen. VIII.: commons, 1 *Lat.* 101 n

28 Hen. VIII.: on succession to the crown, 2 *Cran.* 328 n

31 Hen. VIII.: the six articles, *q. v.*

33 Hen. VIII.: forbidding the use of cards, &c. to all but gentlemen, except at Christmas, 3 *Zur.* 285 n.; promoting archery, 1 *Lat.* 197 n

37 Hen. VIII.: usury, *Grin.* 172

1 Edw. VI.: sacrament, both kinds, *Lit. Edw.* iii.

3 and 4 Edw. VI.: commons, 1 *Lat.* 248 n

— against rebellion; mandate for its publication, 2 *Cran.* 530

5 and 6 Edw. VI.: uniformity, *Lit. Edw.* 213

— against regrators, forestallers, and ingrossers, 2 *Hoop.* xviii.

1 Mary: restoring the supremacy to the pope, 2 *Hoop.* 617 n

1 Eliz.: supremacy, 2 *Zur.* 13 n

— uniformity, *Lit. Eliz.* xxi, *Rog.* 7, 27, 2 *Zur.* 17 n.; copy of the act, *Lit. Eliz.* 27

— first-fruits, 2 *Zur.* 13 n

— poor, *Grin.* 129

— exchange of church lands, *Park.* 98 n

— against witchcraft, 1 *Zur.* 44 n

5 Eliz.: supremacy, *Park.* 174, 1 *Zur.* 124 n

— poor, *Grin.* 140, *Lit. Eliz.* 593 n., 1 *Zur.* 124 n

— fish days, 4 *Jew.* 1142

— for the translation of the Bible and Prayer Book into Welsh, 1 *Zur.* 124 n

— some other acts, 1 *Zur.* 124 n

8 Eliz.: declaring the ordination forms to be lawful, *Lit. Eliz.* xxi.

13 Eliz.: subscription, *Park.* 293 n

— usury, *Grin.* 172

Staunton, co. Gloucester: 2 *Hoop.* 154

Staunton (......): Ridley's receiver, *Rid.* 428

Stavely (Tho.): his Romish Horse-leech, 1 *Lat.* 50 n

Stavely (Leonard): notice of him, *Poet.* xxxiv; stanzas on this vain fleeting life, *ib.* 376

Stavert (Geo.): *v.* Stafford.

Stawn (Will.): *Bale* 429

Steady: an anvil, 1 *Jew.* 523

Stealing: *v.* Theft.

Steare: to stir, or arouse, *Phil.* 393

Stedfastness: *v.* Faith.

Steeples: *v.* Towers.

Steiger (......): 3 *Zur.* 163

Stein, Zurich: 4 *Bul.* 546

Steiner (Werner): 4 *Bul.* xvii.

Stella (Diego): teaches that predestination springs from works, *Rog.* 149; ranks the refusal of ecclesiastical tradition with refusal of the gospel, *ib.* 79; says the church of Rome never erred, *ib.* 182; teaches that the pope is infallible, *ib.* 197

Stella (Jo.): Vitæ Summ. Pontif. *Jew.* xliii, 2 *Bec.* 297 n., 3 *Bec.* 361 n., 365 n

Stella Clericorum: *Jew.* xliii; speaks of the priest as creating the Creator, 2 *Jew.* 773, 3 *Jew.* 453, *Rog.* 41

Stellartius (Prosp.): De Coronis et Tonsuris, 2 *Ful.* 115 n

Stephanus Bisuntinus: wrote on the Apocalypse, *Bale* 257

Stephen (St): his oration in Acts vii, 3 *Bul.* 24, 4 *Bul.* 208, 308; his vision of Christ, 1 *Jew.* 542, *Phil.* 189, *Rid.* 219; his martyrdom, 3 *Bul.* 400; his burial, 4 *Bul.* 523; his prayer resulted in Paul's conversion, 1 *Lat.* 338

Revelation of Stephen, an apocryphal book, *Rog.* 82; collect for his day, from the Breviary, 1 *Tyn.* 231 n.; sermon on his day, 2 *Lat.* 96; horses bled on St Stephen's day, *ib.* 100

Stephen I., pope: deceived by Basilides, 1 *Ful.* 40, 2 *Ful.* 342, 343; his controversy with Cyprian, 2 *Ful.* 376, 3 *Jew.* 331, 332, *Whita.* 691; Cyprian charges him with error, 1 *Tyn.* 216 n., see also p. 262, col. 1, above; and uses remarkable words in allusion to his conduct, 2 *Ful.* 322 n.; his martyrdom, 3 *Jew.* 551

Stephen II. or III.*, pope: increased the popedom, 2 *Tyn.* 251; was carried on men's shoulders, 2 *Brad.* 311

Stephen III. or IV., pope: his history, 2 *Tyn.* 262, 263; he anointed Pepin's sons, *Pil.* 602

Stephen IV. or V., pope: his election, 2 *Tyn.* 266

Stephen V. or VI., pope: decrees the removal of things turned to error and superstition, *Calf.* 67, 253, 2 *Ful.* 141, 3 *Jew.* 570

Stephen VI. or VII., pope: disinterred the body of Formosus, cast it into the Tiber, and abrogated his acts, *Bale* 394; 1 *Hoop.* 217; 3 *Jew.* 249, 276, 277, 4 *Jew.* 1110, *Pil.* 652, 1 *Tyn.* 324 n.; some ascribe the outrage to Sergius, 3 *Jew.* 276 n., 277 n.; it is said that he was himself disinterred by Sergius, *Pil.* 652

Stephen ......, pope: decree for the authority of the Roman church, 3 *Bec.* 511; he speaks of our holy lady the church of Rome, 1 *Jew.* 343; acknowledges that Greek priests, &c. are married, 3 *Jew.* 396, 408

Stephen [Batori], king of Poland: 2 *Zur.* 273 n

Stephen, abp of Patraca: ascribed "all

---

* Properly III., but generally called II., the second Stephen having sat only a few days.

power" to the pope, 1 *Jew.* 93, 94 n., 339, 385, 443, 3 *Jew.* 217, 284 n., 4 *Jew.* 832, 1137
Stephen (Edda): *v.* Edda.
Stephens (Dr): meaning Gardiner, 1 *Cran.* ix.
Stepney, co. Middx.: 2 *Cran.* 375 n.; a daily prayer used there, *Lit. Eliz.* 469; lord Cromwell's house there, 2 *Cran.* 385
Stepport: probably Stockport, 1 *Brad.* 454
Stercoranists: 1 *Cran.* 55
Stere (Will.): martyred at Canterbury, *Poet.* 163
Sternhold (Tho.): notice of him, *Poet.* xlvi; Psalms xviii. and ciii. in metre, *ib.* 481
Steuchus (Augustin.): Opera, *Jew.* xliii, 2 *Jew.* 774 n.; speaks of the exposition of scripture by itself, *Whita.* 495; shews that heathen writers confess the existence of angels, whom they call gods, 3 *Bul.* 328; writes on the pretended donation of Constantine, 4 *Bul.* 125, 126; mentions Charlemagne's book, 4 *Jew.* 1054; calls the pope king of kings, &c., 3 *Jew.* 153, 4 *Jew.* 671; speaks of hallowing water, with salt and prayers, for the forgiveness of sins, 3 *Jew.* 178, 179, 4 *Jew.* 859
Stevens (Jo.), notary: *Bale* 28
Stevens (Jo.): Hist. of Anc. Abbeys, 2 *Lat.* 380, 386, 389, 415, 418 nn
Stevens (......): martyred at Lewes, *Poet.* 170
Stevens (......), of Calais: 2 *Cran.* 372 n
Stevens (Will.): Life of Bradford, xii. n., xlvii.
Stevenson (Jos.): edits Bede, *Calf.* 306 n.; first discovers the source of the fiction of his journey to Rome, 2 *Ful.* 119, 120 n
Stew: a bathing house, 2 *Brad.* 54
Steward (Mr): perhaps a name of office, *Park.* 460
Steward (Dr): *Park.* 476
Stewards: the parable of the unrighteous steward, 1 *Cran.* 283, 1 *Tyn.* 70; ministers are stewards, 2 *Jew.* 1046, 1 *Lat.* 35; stewards must give account, *Sand.* 401
Stewart (Hen.), lord St Colme: a Scots nobleman, 1 *Zur.* 262 n
Stews: suppressed, 1 *Lat.* 133, (*v.* Rome, Southwark).
Steyning, co. Sussex: J. Launder was burned there, *Poet.* 162
Stifflers: sticklers, *Park.* 252
Stigelius (Jo.): pro pace; verses, *Pra. Eliz.* 411; de vita beata; verses, *ib.* 416
Stile (Chr.): collects four psalms of invocation for the preservation of the queen, *Lit. Eliz.* 609 n., 619 n
Still (Jo.), afterwards bp of Bath and Wells:

mentioned, *Grin.* 353; recommended for a prebend at Westminster, *Park.* 439; and for the deanery of Norwich, *ib.* 449; sometime master of St John's, and afterwards of Trin. coll., Cambridge, 3 *Whitg.* xi.
Stillingfleet (Edw.), bp of Worcester: *Calf.* 42, 53, 211, 237 nn.; he corrected a common error as to a passage in Gildas, 2 *Ful.* 186 n.; his opinion of Geoffrey of Monmouth, *Calf.* 307 n.; in error with regard to the council of Florence, *ib.* 247 n
Stilpo: *Wool.* 106
Stinchcombe, co. Gloucester: 1 *Tyn.* xiv.
Stiped: steeped, 4 *Jew.* 817
Stirling: king James VI. baptized there, 1 *Zur.* 183 n.; execution of the abp of St Andrews, *ib.* 257 n.; the regent Lennox put to death there, *ib.* 262
Stockewith (Humf.): 2 *Cran.* 247
Stockport, co. Chester: *v.* Stepport.
Stockton on Tees, co. Durham: the manor (Stoctuna), *Grin.* 399 n
Stockwood (Jo.) minister of Battel: 4 *Bul.* xxii; probably author of A short Catechism for Householders, p. 158, col. 1
Stoffler (Jo.): his Germanical rhythmes, *Rog.* v. n
Stoics: hold that God is nothing else but nature, 1 *Jew.* 501; deny his providence, *Hutch.* 69; say he has written fatal laws, 1 *Hoop.* 263; maintain destiny, fate, and fortune, *Rog.* 41; their opinion concerning necessity condemned, 1 *Brad.* 212; they deem all sins equal, 2 *Bul.* 407, *Rog.* 137, 2 *Whitg.* 45; condemn all pleasure, 2 *Bul.* 57; their opinion of the soul, 3 *Bul.* 374; against their indolentia, 2 *Bul.* 82
Stoke Charity, co. Hants: *Rid.* 536 n
Stoke by Clare, co. Suffolk: 2 *Cov.* viii; the college,—Parker made dean, *Park.* vii, 4, 482; letter from Henry VIII. to the dean and prebendaries requiring them to send four able men to his army, about to invade France, *ib.* 15; R. Radclyff recommended by queen Catherine Parr as bailiff, *ib.* 16; letter from queen Catherine Parr to the dean and fellows, desiring a lease of the manor of Chipley for Edw. Waldgrave, *ib.* 19; Parker opposes the dissolution of the college, but without success, *ib.* 31—33, 482; pensions granted to the dean, &c., *ib.* 40; the schoolmaster's stipend restored by Elizabeth, *ib.* 188
Stoke by Nayland, co. Suffolk: Payne's popish preaching there, 2 *Cran.* 333
Stokeley (Rog.), warden of All Souls' coll. Oxon.: letter to him, 2 *Cran.* 279
Stokes (Dr), Austin friar: letter from Parker

53

to him, *Park.* 10; he preaches against Parker, and is imprisoned, *ib.* 14 n
Stokes (Geo.): British Reformers, 2 *Brad.* xii. n
Stokesley (Jo.), bp of London: appointed to that see, 1 *Tyn.* xxxviii. n.; mentioned, *ib.* lvi, 32, 33; sent from court by Wolsey, 2 *Tyn.* 309; a persecutor, 2 *Lat.* 326; no preacher, *ib.* 328; he condemns Rich. Bayfield, 1 *Tyn.* 1; his prayer when he gave sentence against heretics, *Phil.* 148; he troubles Latimer, 2 *Lat.* 322, &c.; cites him to appear before him, 2 *Lat.* 218, 350; examines him, 2 *Lat.* xvi; inhibits him from preaching in his diocese, 2 *Cran.* 308 n., 1 *Lat.* viii; opposes Bale, *Bale* viii; denounces certain books, 1 *Tyn.* 447; signs a declaration respecting a general council, 2 *Cran.* 468; favours the king's divorce, 2 *Lat.* 333 n.; is sent to Rome about it, 1 *Cran.* x; present at Anne Boleyn's coronation, 2 *Cran.* 245; his death, 3 *Zur.* 231
Stolberg (The count): ambassador from the emperor, 1 *Zur.* 192
Stole: part of a priest's dress, 3 *Bec.* 259; worn by the priest at mass, baptism, and confession, 3 *Tyn.* 8; its alleged signification, *ib.* 73; stoles to be abolished, *Grin.* 135, 159
Stomached: inclined, encouraged, *Bale* 313
Stonden (......): *Park.* 464
Stone (Jo.), monk of Canterbury: 2 *Cran.* 333
Stonehenge, in Wiltshire: called Stonage, 4 *Jew.* 655; described, 2 *Zur.* 88
Stones: used as signs, 4 *Bul.* 314; precious stones, their mystical import, *Bale* 606—608; writers on them, *ib.* 609; lively stones, 2 *Brad.* 204
Stoning (......): 1 *Brad.* 493
Stonor (Sir Walter): justice at Henley, 2 *Cov.* 500
Stookes (Mr), junior: 2 *Cov.* 492
Stools: text appropriate to them, 1 *Bec.* 65
Storck (Nich.): a leader of the Anabaptists, 1 *Hoop.* 246; depended on visions, *Rog.* 196
Stork: the ensign of natural love, 1 *Bul.* 273
Storms: *v.* Sea, Thunder.
Story (Jo.): notice of him, *Phil.* xxxi; mentioned, 2 *Brad.* 251; a commissioner against Philpot, *Calf.* 246, *Phil.* 4, 46; likewise against Cranmer, 2 *Cran.* 212, 446 n., 447, 542; he confessed himself to have been the chief despatcher of all God's saints that suffered in queen Mary's time, *Phil.* 48; his treasonable speeches against Edward VI. and Elizabeth, 4 *Jew.* 665, 666; sent to the Fleet, 1 *Zur.* 79 n.; he escaped

to Flanders, *ib.* 253; but was afterwards arrested and executed, *ib.* 111, 254; canonized, *ib.* 254 n.; letter to him, 2 *Cran.* 446; his character, 1 *Zur.* 252 n
Stotes (Tho.), of Braunton: *Jew.* v.
Stoughton (Rob.): 4 *Bul.* xxvii.
Stour: assault, onset, 2 *Brad.* 192.
Stourton (Cha. lord): executed for murder, *Park.* 422 n
— Anne (Stanley) his wife, *Park.* 424 n
Stourton (Jo. lord): notice of him, *Park.* 422 n.; committed to the custody of Parker, *ib.* 422—424, 441; came to chapel and behaved orderly, *ib.* 448
Stow (Guy): 2 *Brad.* 397 n
Stowe (Jo.): Survey of London, *Grin.* 141, 272, 4 *Jew.* 1165, 1 *Lat.* 59, 223, 2 *Lat.* 341 nn
Stowell (Jo.): accused of bigamy, *Park.* 405, 406, 407, 408; imprisoned, *ib.* 447 n
Stowmarket, co. Suffolk: *Park.* 417 n
Stoxeth (Hen.): Cranmer's friend, 2 *Cran.* 337
Str. (D.): his preaching at York, *Pil.* 587
Strabo: Geographia, *Jew.* xliii; he speaks of colleges among the Egyptians, 4 *Bul.* 479; cited respecting Persia, *Pil.* 281—283, 288, 325; he tells that the Smyrnians built a temple to Homer, 2 *Jew.* 981; mentions nations without bread, 1 *Jew.* 222; what people he calls barbarians, *ib.* 267, 272—274
Strabo (Wal.), or Strabus Fuldensis: *v.* Walafridus.
Strachan (Will.), professor at St Andrews: 2 *Zur.* 364
Strada (Famianus): *Calf.* 287 n
Strafford (Sir Edw.): sent to France, 1 *Zur.* 331 n
Stralen (Jac.): wrote on the Apocalypse, *Bale* 256
Strange (Hen. lord): *v.* Stanley.
Strange fire: *v.* Fire.
Strange gods: *v.* Gods, Idols.
Strange tongues: *v.* Tongues.
Strange woman: *v.* Women.
Strangers: *v.* Exiles.
Strangers should be received with hospitality, *Sand.* 400; godly strangers are to be cheerfully received, but heretical and wicked ones should be cast out of the country, *ib.* 266; foreign divines invited to England, 2 *Cran.* 420, &c.; queen Elizabeth's proclamation against strangers, *Grin.* 297; articles of inquiry for them, *ib.* 296; bishop Grindal's remembrance concerning them, *ib.* 297; letter from the queen to abp Parker, enjoining him to

make inquiry respecting the numerous strangers in England, *Park.* 321, 323
Strangled things: *v.* Blood.
Strasburgh: called Argentine, 4 *Jew.* 801, 1 *Tyn.* 38; the bishop received money from priests who kept concubines, 4 *Jew.* 801; rejection of the mass there, 1 *Tyn.* 40 n., 3 *Zur.* 49; Tyndale's Obedience printed there, 1 *Tyn.* lxxiii; Calvin's congregation, and its liturgy, *Pra. Eliz.* 458 n., 477 n., 488 n.; the city visited with sickness, 3 *Zur.* 659; disputes respecting the Interim, *ib.* 470 n., 471 n.; the bishop takes orders, and says mass, *ib.* 651, 661 n.; degeneracy of the church there, *ib.* 475; letter from Bucer and Fagius to the ministers, *ib.* 534; another, from Bucer, *ib.* 549; the Interim received, *ib.* 667; many flee hence to England, and settle at Glastonbury, *ib.* 737 n.; English exiles there, 2 *Hoop.* viii, *Jew.* xiii, 4 *Jew.* 1194 n., *Rid.* 387; sermons preached there, *Sand.* 293, 313; enforcement of the confession of Augsburgh, 2 *Zur.* 81 n., 111; the college of St Thomas, 3 *Zur.* 471 n., 663, 667 n
Stratford-le-Bow, co. Essex: a martyr there, *Poet.* 163
Stratford-on-Avon, co. Warwick: the collegiate church, 2 *Lat.* 383 n.; recantation of the parish priest, *ib.* 414
Strawberry preachers: 2 *Brad.* 9, 1 *Lat.* 62
Streater (R.): *v.* Streter.
Stremer (Greg.): 2 *Cran.* 382, 383.
Strenaeshalch: *v.* Whitby.
Strength: little affiance to be placed in human strength, 1 *Bec.* 244; true strength, 1 *Cov.* 513; prayer for strength against the devil, the world, and the flesh, 3 *Bec.* 84
Streter (R.): martyr at Canterbury, *Poet.* 164
Strickland (Will.): legacy to him, *Grin.* 46 n
Strife: *v.* Discord.
Stringer (Anth.): *Grin.* 329
Strownd, i. e. Stroudend, in Painswick, co. Glouc.: 2 *Lat.* 417
Struvius (B. G.): Dissertatio de doctis Impostoribus, 2 *Ful.* 338 n
Strype (Jo.): very frequently cited or referred to, as, 2 *Bec.* 320, 539, 3 *Bec.* 199, 205, *Calf.* 7, 2 *Cov.* vii, x, &c., 2 *Ful.* 37, 45, *Grin.* 169, 293, &c., *Jew.* viii, 1 *Jew.* 34, 85, 4 *Jew.* 665, 666, 1129, 1190, 1205, 1243, 1299, 1 and 2 *Lat.* (see index), *Now.* ii, iii, v, *Pil.* ii—vi, viii, xiv, xvi, 254, 481, 495, 541, 623, 626, 627, 648, 658, 1 *Whitg.* vii, &c., 64, 198, 507, 2 *Whitg.* 41, 333, 545, 3 *Whitg.* 326 nn.; account of Grindal's Dialogue between Custom and Verity, *Grin.* 37, of the plague of 1563, *ib.* 77; of the queen's displeasure respecting exercises or prophesyings, *ib.* 372—375; his Annals corrected, *Pra. Eliz.* xiv, xv.
Stuart (James), earl of Athol: mentioned, 1 *Zur.* 166 n.; one of the confederate lords, 193 n., 197 n
Stuart (Hen.), lord Darnley, duke of Albany, 2nd husband of Mary queen of Scots: see p. 385, col. 1
Stuart (Cha.), earl of Lennox: married Eliz. Cavendish, by whom he had the lady Arabella Stuart, 2 *Zur.* 200 n
Stuart (Matth.), earl of Lennox: committed to the Tower, 1 *Zur.* 102; mentioned, *ib.* 197; chosen regent of Scotland, *ib.* 226, 262; takes Dumbarton castle, *ib.* 262; put to death by the Hamiltons, *ib.*
— Margaret (Douglas) his wife, niece of Henry VIII., 1 *Zur.* 144 n., 2 *Zur.* 200 n.; hostile to religion, 1 *Zur.* 102
Stuart (Lodowick), duke of Lennox: sent ambassador to France, 2 *Zur.* 332
Stuart (James), earl of Murray: his victory at Corrichie, 1 *Zur.* 129; he imprisons the abp of St Andrews, *ib.* 132 n.; upholds the protestant cause, *ib.* 149 n.; mentioned, *ib.* 167 n.; his religious character, *ib.* 170; declared regent during the king's minority, *ib.* 197, 199, 210; suspected of the murder of lord Darnley, *ib.* 197 n.; he defeats the queen's party at Langside, *ib.* 203; seizes the English rebel earls, *ib.* 214; moved the duke of Norfolk to marriage with the queen of Scots, *ib.* 216 n.; his cruelty, *ib.* 218 n.; he is slain, *ib.* 215, 218, 223
Stuart (Hen.), lord St Colme: *v.* Stewart.
Stuart (Lord James): quells a riot at Edinburgh, 1 *Zur.* 104 n
Stuart (Lady Arabella): 2 *Zur.* 200 n
Stubborn persons: 2 *Bul.* 317
Stubbs (Jo.): writes a violent book called The Discovery of a Gaping Gulph, &c., *Grin.* 408—412
Stubbs (Phil.): Anatomy of Abuses, *Grin.* 176 n., *Rog.* 91 n.; he holds that Christians are bound by some of the judicial laws of Moses, *ib.* 170
Stubner (......): a leader of the Anabaptists, 1 *Hoop.* 246
Stuckius (Jo. Will.): 2 *Zur.* 225, 333
Students: *v.* Scholars.
Studley (J.): reference to his Pageant of Popes, *Poet.* 270 n
Study: to desire, 2 *Tyn.* 25
Stumbling-blocks: not to be put in our brother's way, 1 *Bec.* 19
Stumphius (Jo.): father of Jo. R. Stumphius, 3 *Zur.* 98 n., 724; letters to him, *ib.*

67, 98.; dedication to him and others, 4 *Bul.* 546

Stumphius (Jo. Rod.): notice of him, 3 *Zur.* 98 n.; he accompanied Hooper to England, *ib.* 57; studied at Oxford, *ib.* 64, 84, 402, 412, 483, 719; a worthy youth, *ib.* 561; he often wrote to Bullinger, *ib.* 719; letters by him, *ib.* 460—467; recalled from Oxford by his father, *ib.* 724; his return to Switzerland, *ib.* 98, 125, 311, 437, 438, 496, 500

Stumphius (......): saluted, 1 *Zur.* 62

Stupre : rape, 3 *Bec.* 611

Sturbridge, co. Cambridge : the fair, *Rog.* 206 n

Sturmius (James) : 3 *Zur.* 372, 531 n.; letter to him, *ib.* 537

Sturmius (Jo.): mentioned, 2 *Zur.* 52, 3 *Zur.* 51, 509 n.; some account of him, 2 *Zur.* 281 n., 314 n.; agent to queen Elizabeth, *ib.* 211; his treatises, *ib.* 92; Quart. Antipapp., *Rog.* 163, 293; he comments on Aristotle, 2 *Zur.* 69; letters from him to queen Elizabeth, *ib.* 175, 231; one to Cecil, *ib.* 176; letters to him, *ib.* 64, 90, 174, 210, 216, 220, 257, 276, 281, 285, 286, 287, 303; Ascham names a son after him, *ib.* 90

Sturmius (Peter): his conduct at Strasburgh, 2 *Zur.* 82, 99

Sturmius (......) : 2 *Cov.* 512

Sturtle (......) : *v.* Thirtell.

Sturvey (Jo.), alias Essex, abbot of St Augustine's, Canterbury : 2 *Cran.* 265; letter to him, *ib.* 240

Suada, or Suadela : 4 *Bul.* 265

Suainton (Quinting): Sandys' servant, *Sand.* vii, xiii.

Suavemberg (Helen), 3rd wife of Will. Parr (*q.v.*), marq. of Northampton.

Subdeacons : 4 *Bul.* 112, 114, *Rog.* 259; mentioned by Eusebius, 2 *Whitg.* 174; allowed by Beza, 2 *Whitg.* 332, 433; one of the new bishops acts as subdeacon in the queen's chapel, 1 *Zur.* 63

Subduce : to withdraw, 1 *Bec.* 130

Subinco Lepus, abp of Prague : *Bale* 11

Subjects: *v.* Kings, Magistrates, Obedience, Prayers.

Their duty, 1 *Bec.* 260, 286, 2 *Bec.* 114, 327, &c., 1 *Bul.* 389, 1 *Lat.* 538, *Pra. Eliz.* 235; their duty, with probations of scripture, 2 *Bec.* 515, 516; they are called on to obey, *ib.* 616; they may not resist, 1 *Lat.* 163; they must love and reverence the civil magistrates, 2 *Bec.* 327; they must humbly obey them, *ib.* 328, 329; they must pray for them, *ib.* 327, 328; they must dissemble their faults, *ib.* 329, 330; they must pay tribute, *ib.* 329; those who grudge to pay taxes are thieves, *ib.* 107; if they disobey their rulers, they are forsworn, 1 *Bec.* 371, 372; admonition to them for faith, *ib.* 272

Subscription : *v.* Articles (XXXIX).

Of subscribing to the Communion Book, 3 *Whitg.* 326, &c.; subscription not required of the laity, but only of ministers, *Rog.* 24; refused in part by the Puritans, *ib.* 25, 26; devices for avoiding it, *ib.* 26—28; the views of Zanchius on subscription, 2 *Zur.* 102—104; the practice as to it in foreign churches, *Rog.* 24

Subsidies : are due to the prince, *Sand.* 53; granted to Henry VIII., 2 *Cran.* 265 n., 301, 336, 348, 3 *Zur.* 206; to queen Mary, *Pil.* 495; arrears of one granted in Mary's time, *Grin.* 252, *Park.* 196

Substance: *v.* Form, God, Homoüsion.

On substance, &c., 2 *Bul.* 18, 1 *Cran.* 256, 257, 259, 260, 298, 319, 322, 324; it cannot be without accidents, 1 *Cran.* 326; is not changed without change of accidents, 2 *Hoop.* 409

Succession : *v.* Bishops, Church, Popes; also England, Scotland.

Successus : Cyril's epistle to him, 3 *Bul.* 257

Sudary : a napkin, 2 *Hoop.* 128, *Rid.* 319

Suetonius Tranquillus : 1 *Bec.* 245 n., 2 *Bec.* 329 n., *Grin.* 17, 4 *Jew.* 659, 842, 918, 1 *Whitg.* 74

Suffenus : a foolish poet, 2 *Bec.* 419

Sufferate : to steal away, withdraw, 1 *Bec.* 195

Suffering : for the truth's sake is our greatest promotion in this world, 1 *Lat.* 294, 361; that of saints, not our redemption, 3 *Bul.* 95

Suffolk : three young men martyred, *Bale* 586; rebellion there in favour of the lady Elizabeth, 3 *Zur.* 133; inundations, 1 *Zur.* 233; only one preacher in an extensive district, *Park.* 307; dedication to the ministers there, 3 *Bec.* 290; desire of seventy-one "brethren" addressed to king James, *Rog.* 21

Suffolk (Dukes and duchesses of): *v.* Brandon, Grey.

Suffragans : their office, 4 *Bul.* 112, 2 *Cran.* 471, 1 *Lat.* 175, *Rid.* 55; confirmation committed to them, 1 *Tyn.* 274; suffragans authorized by an act of Henry VIII., 1 *Lat.* 175 n.; the abbot of Newesham, Cranmer's suffragan, 2 *Cran.* 290, 291; one appointed to Dover, under the act above mentioned, *ib.* 471; Parker had one [Rich. Rogers, bp of Dover], *Park.* 370, 475

Suffrages: *v.* Litany.

Sugill: to defame or slander, *Park.* 11, 157
Suicerus (Jo. Casp.): *Calf.* 285 n., 2 *Ful.* 235 n
Suicide: its unlawfulness, 2 *Bul.* 413, 414, *Hutch.* 85, 1 *Lat.* 435, *Whita.* 95; allowed by some heretics, 1 *Ful.* 23, 3 *Whitg.* 57; frequent, 1 *Brad.* 61; the death of madmen unwilful, 2 *Bul.* 414
Suidas: says Serapis had the figure of a cross upon his breast, *Calf.* 107; tells of Pasetes the juggler, 3 *Jew.* 474; relates an anecdote of the emperor Leo, 2 *Jew.* 981; referred to on Justinian, *Calf.* 305
Sulcer (Simon): *v.* Sultzer.
Sulphur: *v.* Brimstone.
Sulpicius Severus: his works, *Jew.* xliii; on the reading of scripture in the church of Tours, 1 *Jew.* 298, 2 *Jew.* 692; on the devil's appearance to St Martin, 1 *Jew.* 551; on some who set out their holiness to sale, 4 *Jew.* 945; on Jerome's remark as to the familiarity of certain virgins with monks and priests, 3 *Jew.* 425; on the derivation of the word ceremony, 2 *Bul.* 125; referred to, *Calf.* 322 n
Sultzer (Simon): 2 *Zur.* 98 n., 100, 3 *Zur.* 297; Sulcer, *Phil.* 390
Sum of the Scriptures: *v.* Fish (S.).
Summa Angelica: *v.* Angelus de Clavasio.
Summer lords and ladies: *Grin.* 141, 175
Sumners: summoners, *Grin.* 176, 3 *Whitg.* 246
Sumptuary agreement: *v.* Meats.
Sun: *v.* Signs.
 Meditations thereon, at mid-day and sunset, *Pra. B.* 72, 73; it is an image of the Holy Trinity, *Hutch.* 160; a figure of Christ, *Bale* 327, 482, 552, *Lit. Edw.* 507, (556), *Now.* (45), 162, *Rid.* 13, *Sand.* 358, 359; signs in the sun, *v.* Signs; rings seen about the sun, and divers suns seen at once, 2 *Lat.* 51; three at the same time, *Hutch.* 81; a strange appearance in the sun, seen by Bullinger, 2 *Zur.* 196; remarkable appearance observed in Poland, 3 *Zur.* 692; the sun used as a similitude in speaking of the sacrament, 1 *Cran.* 89, 90, 91
Sunday: *v.* Easter, Palm Sunday, Passion Sunday, Relic Sunday, Whitsunday.
 The name is derived from the sun, *Pil.* 16; the Lord's day was appointed by the apostles, or the church, instead of the ceremonial sabbath, 2 *Bec.* 82, 2 *Brad.* 391, 1 *Bul.* 259, 260, 2 *Cran.* 60, 61, 2 *Jew.* 641, 1 *Whitg.* 200; it is observed by custom, 3 *Whitg.* 368; it is not, however, an unwritten tradition, *Whita.* 570; there is scriptural authority for it, 1 *Hoop.* 342; it is called in the New Testament, the first of the sabbath, 1 *Bul.* 260, 1 *Hoop.* 342, *Pil.* 17; and the Lord's day, (Rev. i), *Bale* 268, 1 *Bul.* 260, *Pil.* 17; gatherings for the poor on this day were appointed by St Paul, 2 *Whitg.* 450; some call it the sabbath, *q. v.*; how the Lord's day should be sanctified and spent, 1 *Brad.* 158, 1 *Bul.* 259, &c., 2 *Lat.* 39; it was appointed for the public worship of God, and the hearing of his word, 2 *Bec.* 82, 1 *Bul.* 260, 1 *Lat.* 471, 1 *Tyn.* 226; Justin Martyr's account of the worship of the church on Sunday, *Coop.* 82, & al.; the ancient Christians stood in prayer on this day, see p. 623, col. 1; its observance commanded by Constantine, 1 *Bul.* 265, 2 *Jew.* 702; law of the emperors Leo and Anthemius for it, 1 *Bul.* 264; fasting is lawful on this day, but not expedient, see p. 321, col. 1; the holy day is servant to man, 3 *Tyn.* 7, 8; work on Sunday, *Grin.* 261; no common work should be done unnecessarily, or without urgent cause, 2 *Bec.* 83, 1 *Hoop.* 349; tillage allowed by an old imperial law, 1 *Bul.* 265; pedlars and others not to sell their wares during divine service, *Grin.* 138; fairs and markets not to be held in church-time, *ib.* 138, 171, 2 *Hoop.* 136; games on Sunday afternoon, 3 *Whitg.* 384; none to use pastimes, &c. in church-time, *Grin.* 170, 171; taverns, &c. not to be open except for travellers, 2 *Hoop.* 137; the Lord's day is much abused, 1 *Lat.* 471, *Now.* 226
Sundridge, co. Kent: 2 *Cran.* 260
Sunningwell, co. Berks: Jewel's cure, *Jew.* viii.
Superaltars: *v.* Altars.
Supererogation: *v.* Works (Good).
Superilluminate: an heretical sect in England, *Whita.* 298
Superintendents: the name is equivalent to bishops, 4 *Jew.* 906; some appointed by bp Hooper, 2 *Hoop.* xvii, xix; some in the church of Scotland, 2 *Zur.* 364 n
Superiors: of honour and obedience to them, 2 *Bec.* 88, 93; how far they are to be obeyed, *ib.* 93, 94; their duty, 1 *Hoop.* 360
Superstition: false religion, 3 *Bul.* 223, 232; it is to believe more than the Bible teaches, *Pil.* 562; on ἐθελοθρησκεία and δεισιδαιμονία, *ib.*; who are superstitious, according to Lactantius, 3 *Bul.* 232, *Calf.* 310; superstition has repressed many crimes, *Whita.* 255; it is hateful to God, 2 *Tyn.* 169; persons brought up in superstition

are more slow to believe God's word than infidels, 1 *Hoop.* 512; how much there was before the reformation, 1 *Bec.* 315; superstitions and superstitious usages enumerated, *Bale* 262, 320, 518, 519, 524— 529, 562, 1 *Bec.* 315, 3 *Bec.* 4, 66, 231, 1 *Brad.* 8, 393, 2 *Cran.* 63, 64, 147, 148, 155, &c., 498, 503, 2 *Hoop.* 129, 1 *Lat.* 57, 498, *Sand.* 220, 223, 359, 1 *Tyn.* 48, 90— 92, 122, 160, 184, 237, 238, 245, 274, 277, 279, 283, 313, 433, 462, 2 *Tyn.* 197, 3 *Tyn.* 7—9, 20, 40, 61, 62, 73, 74, 79, 80, 258, (*v.* Holy things); the mass-monger's trinkets, 3 *Bec.* 362; charms and the like, 4 *Bul.* 260, *Calf.* 284; superstition must be avoided, 1 *Hoop.* 85; it must be rooted out, *Sand.* 440; all monuments and tokens of it should be removed, 1 *Hoop.* 486; relics of superstition in the North of England, 1 *Zur.* 259 n.; superstitious practices at burials, 3 *Bec.* 124; superstitious bequests, *Grin,* 173

Supper: prayers before it, 1 *Bec.* 402, 3 *Bec.* 19; behaviour at table, 1 *Bec.* 403; thanksgivings afterwards, *ib.*, 3 *Bec.* 19; what is to be done after it, 1 *Bec.* 403

Supper of the Lord: *v.* Mass, Sacraments, Transubstantiation; also Councils, Law (Canon), Prayers, Thanksgivings, and the names of the fathers, especially Augustine.

i. *Name, institution, doctrine, abuse.*

(*a*) Called by various names, 4 *Bul.* 402, 2 *Hoop.* 463, 1 *Jew.* 287; Paul terms it "the Lord's supper," and "the Lord's table," and "the communion," 4 *Bul.* 402; the term "Lord's supper," cavilled at, 1 *Lat.* 122, 2 *Lat.* 262; "cœna Judaica" and "cœna Dominica" distinguished, 2 *Lat.* 263; the Lord's supper is spoken of in scripture as the "breaking of bread," 4 *Bul.* 276, 402, 429, 1 *Jew.* 18, 3 *Tyn.* 264; anciently called "eucharistia," 2 *Bec.* 232, 4 *Bul.* 224, 2 *Hoop.* 463, *Hutch.* 227, 285; meaning of that word as employed by Irenæus, 1 *Jew.* 145; termed "eulogia," *Hutch.* 227; styled the sacrament of thanksgiving, 1 *Bec.* 120; anciently called ἀγάπη, 2 *Bec.* 231, 251, 2 *Hoop.* 463; styled ἀντίτυπα by Basil and Theodoret, 2 *Hoop.* 406; so called in Basil's liturgy after consecration, 2 *Jew.* 574, 579; designated τὸ τέλειον, 1 *Cov.* 203 n.; called σύναξις, 2 *Bec.* 240, 3 *Bec.* 418, 4 *Bul.* 330, 402, *Calf.* xii, *Hutch.* 228; styled "collecta," *Calf.* xii; spoken of as a league or confederacy, 4 *Bul.* 467; termed a communion, and why, *ib.* 330, 402, 1 *Jew.* 130, *Phil.* 69, *Rid.* 104; styled a sacrament, or mystery, 2 *Hoop.* 463; why termed "missa," *ib.* (*v.* Mass); spoken of as a sacrifice, see vii, below; why called "viaticum," 2 *Hoop.* 463, 2 *Whitg.* 543; sometimes called the sacrament of the altar, of the holy table, of bread and wine, but most properly the sacrament of the body and blood of Christ, 2 *Jew.* 1109; lofty names given to it by the ancient fathers, 3 *Bec.* 387, &c.; irreverent names applied to it by Anabaptists, *Rid.* 255

(*b*) The supper instituted by Jesus Christ our Lord, and how, 2 *Bec.* 229, 231, 232, 3 *Bec.* 232, 1 *Brad.* 83, 4 *Bul.* 404, &c., 1 *Cov.* 79, 2 *Hoop.* 47, 2 *Tyn.* 218; why instituted, see in v, below; when instituted, 4 *Bul.* 405; on what day, 2 *Zur.* 237; why ordained after eating the Passover, *Hutch.* 217; ordained instead of the passover, 2 *Bul.* 269, 1 *Tyn.* 356, 3 *Tyn.* 242, 245, 2 *Whitg.* 514; compared with the paschal supper, 4 *Bul.* 246, 402, 427, *Coop.* 112, 1 *Hoop.* 125, 190, *Hutch.* 217, 3 *Tyn.* 246— 251; what Christ did when he ordained it, 3 *Bec.* 254, &c., 4 *Bul.* 406; how he blessed it, *Calf.* 231—233; how he administered it, 1 *Hoop.* 180; how he used and taught others to use it, 2 *Hoop.* 464; on the words of institution, 1 *Brad.* 489, 1 *Cov.* 429— 431, *Grin.* 35, &c., 2 *Jew.* 623, &c., *Rid.* 7, 8, 15, &c., 1 *Tyn.* 356, 363, &c., 3 *Tyn.* 241, 243, see also ii. and v.iii. *g*, below; Christ gave heavenly and earthly things to his disciples, 3 *Bec.* 365; he gave freely, *ib.*; to what uses he instituted it, 2 *Bec.* 509, 510; its institution described by the evangelists and St Paul, 1 *Cran.* 28, *Rid.* 6, &c., 3 *Tyn.* 241, 243; Harding asserts that the apostles departed in many respects from the letter of Christ's institution, 1 *Jew.* 223; Cyprian enforces the necessity of adhering to the Lord's tradition, see p. 262, 263, above; the things spoken and done by Christ, and written by the evangelists and St Paul, ought to suffice the faith of Christian people, 1 *Cran.* 30

(*c*) Of the sacrament of Christ's body and blood, or Lord's supper, 1 *Bec.* 117, &c., 1 *Cov.* 422, &c., 2 *Hoop.* 90, 2 *Jew.* 1109, &c., 1 *Tyn.* 345, &c., 3 *Tyn.* 218, &c.; what it is, 2 *Bec.* 228, 3 *Bec.* 612, 613, 617, 1 *Brad.* 84, 4 *Bul.* 403, &c., 1 *Hoop.* 175, *Lit. Edw.* 516, (564), *Now.* (90), 212; what it is, with probations of scripture, 2 *Bec.* 508, 509; de vera doctrina et usu cœnæ Domini, 2 *Hoop.* 400, &c.; the true doctrine concerning the holy sacrament, 2 *Cov.* 417; an assertion and defence of the true knowledge and use thereof, 1 *Hoop.* 154; the doctrine of scripture on it, 1 *Brad.* 394, 2 *Brad.* 271, 2 *Cov.* 250; an article de eucharistia, 2 *Cran.* 475; sermons on it, 1 *Brad.* 82, 4 *Bul.* 401, *Hutch.* 209, 235, 262, 1 *Jew.* 3; a meditation on it, 1 *Brad.* 260; de cœna Domini; verses by A. Ellinger, *Pra. Eliz.* 405; the Lord's supper coupled with baptism in scripture, 1 *Brad* 88, 534; the two sacraments compared, 1 *Cran.* 221, *Rid.* 275; denoted by "the water and the blood," 1 Jo. v. 6, 2 *Tyn.* 209; reference to a book entitled, Quid de Eucharistia Veteres senserunt...Dialogus, 3 *Tyn.* 258 n.; doctrine of the Anglo-Saxon church, 2 *Ful.* 7, &c.; abp Arundel's determination, *Bale* 27; lord Cobham examined on the sacrament, *ib.* 30, 37; his belief, *ib.* 22, 24; Will. Thorpe examined about it, *ib.* 91; Anne Askewe questioned on the subject, *ib.* 148—151, 199, 202, 203, 212; her letter on it, *ib.* 196; her faith as to it, *ib.* 207, 212, 214, 217, 232, &c.; THE SUPPER OF THE LORD, a treatise ascribed to W. Tyndale, 3 *Tyn.* 218, &c.; the subject is treated of in Tyndale's Brief Declaration of the Sacraments, 1 *Tyn.* 345, &c.; contrary doctrines held at different times by Cranmer, 2 *Cran.* 217, 218; change in his views, *ib.* 342 n., 3 *Zur.* 13; he desires an united declaration of the protestants, 2 *Cran.* 433; submits to the judgment of the old church, *ib.* 453; his ANSWER to Gardiner, 1 *Cran.* 1, &c.; his DEFENSIO VERÆ ET CATH. DOCTRINÆ DE SACRAMENTO, *ib.* (1, &c.); the doctrine of the reformed the same as that of the catholic fathers, 2 *Jew.* 1030; proclamation of Edward VI. against irreverent talking of the sacrament, 2 *Cran.* 505; a disputation (at London, 1548) respecting it, 3 *Zur.* 322 n.; disputation at Cambridge, 1549, *Grin.* ii, 193, &c.; Ridley's determination there, *Rid.* 167; his BRIEF DECLARATION OF THE LORD'S SUPPER, *ib.* 1, &c.; A FAITHFUL DECLARATION OF CHRIST'S HOLY SUPPER, IN THREE SERMONS, by R. Hutchinson, *Hutch.* 209, &c.; A TREATISE ON THE SACRAMENT OF THE BODY AND BLOOD OF CHRIST, translated from Calvin by bp Coverdale, 1 *Cov.* 422; title to another edition, *ib.* 529; errors which have crept into the church, 2 *Bec.* 260; the true doctrine never condemned by any council before the time of pope Nicholas II., 1 *Cran.* 14; the Romish doctrine confuted, 2 *Brad.* 269, 282, 2 *Cov.* 248, 261, *Pil.* 634 (v. Mass, &c.); the controverted points enumerated, *Rid.*

11; alleged heretical translations concerning it examined, 1 *Ful.* 497—525; a dialogue between Custom and Verity, on the words, " This is my body," *Grin.* 35, &c.; dissensions among Romanists touching the sacrament, *Rid.* 307; Gardiner denies that the Lord's supper is commanded, 1 *Brad.* 490; the strange notions of Rob. Cooch, 2 *Zur.* 236

(*d*) Some abuses of the Lord's supper (see also the title passim):—though a holy thing it may be abused, 1 *Jew.* 5; abuses and corruptions of the ordinance by men in various ages, and especially by Papists, 1 *Bec.* 11, 2 *Bec.* 237, &c., 3 *Bec.* 231, 232, 384, 385, 1 *Brad.* 373, 1 *Cran.* 23, 1 *Jew.* 6, 7, 2 *Jew.* 989, 1 *Lat.* 236, 2 *Lat.* 261, *Phil.* 116, 117, *Rog.* 267, 2 *Tyn.* 218, 3 *Tyn.* 73; the abuse of it is the conculcation of Christ's blood, 1 *Hoop.* 61; plagues sent on account of its abuse, *Lit. Eliz.* 505; it is horribly perverted by the mass, 2 *Brad.* 315, 3 *Bec.* 385, 386 (v. Mass, Massmongers); Romanists have not the supper of the Lord, *Phil.* 54; the mass is not the Lord's supper, being defective in several essential points, and contrary to Christ's ordinance, 2 *Hoop.* 51, 394, 414, 467, 500, *Phil.* 66, 96, 100; the Lord's supper contrasted with the mass, 2 *Bec.* 451, 455, &c., 3 *Bec.* 267, 283, 284, 356, &c., 387, &c., *Coop.* 98, 2 *Hoop.* 464, &c., *Rid.* 103, &c.; A COMPARISON BETWEEN THE LORD'S SUPPER AND THE POPE'S MASS, by T. Becon, 3 *Bec.* 351, &c.; the Lord's table contrasted with the table of devils, 3 *Tyn.* 255; the sacrament received as a purgation from slander, 1 *Jew.* 6; profanely used by princes, for the confirmation of treaties which are speedily broken, 2 *Tyn.* 301; made a market, 2 *Hoop.* 128; offered for the dead, 4 *Bul.* 431; administered to the dead, 1 *Jew.* 7, *Rog.* 266; buried with the dead, 1 *Jew.* 244, 245; it belongs to the dead no more than baptism, 3 *Bec.* 379; Papists carry it about in public processions, see viii. *l*, below; holy bread and holy water given instead of the Lord's supper, 2 *Bec.* 260; the abuses and errors introduced into it should be removed, 3 *Bec.* 386; various heresies about the sacrament, *Rid.* 9, *Rog.* 283, &c.

ii. *Of the sign and the thing signified, and how the elements are Christ's body and blood:* the supper is a sacrament; *v.* Sacraments; a visible word, 2 *Hoop.* 90; whether the forms be the sacrament, 2 *Jew.* 791, &c.; whereof it consists, 4 *Bul.* 405; it contains

SUPPER OF THE LORD

two things, the one earthly the other heavenly, 2 *Hoop.* 49, 433; the sign and thing signified, 4 *Bul.* 250, 329, 2 *Lat.* 267; the outward sign, and the inward grace, *Sand.* 88; the signs and the promises, 2 *Bec.* 199; meaning and importance of the outward signs, 1 *Cov.* 330, 331, 340; the hidden mysteries, 2 *Jew.* 1122; the threefold resemblance of the sign to that which it signifies, 1 *Brad.* 88; whether the blessing changes the natures of things, 4 *Bul.* 261; the fathers speak of the elements as changed or turned into the body and blood of Christ, i. e. sacramentally or mystically, 1 *Brad.* 94, 95; the schoolmen understood this literally, *ib.* 95; in what sense the elements are changed, *Hutch.* 276, &c.; nature of the sacramental mutation, *Rid.* 274; the bread and wine are changed in use, not in substance, 2 *Hoop.* 152, 394, 408, 460, 469, 531, *Now.* (91), 214, *Rog.* 285—287, *Sand.* 89, 90; they are changed sacramentally, *Rid.* 12; a great and marvellous change is made by the power of God's word, *Coop.* 194; passages of the fathers in which they speak of the eucharist as a figure, sign, or mystery of the body of Christ, *Sand.* 453, 454; it is a sacrament, sign, memorial, commemoration, representation, or figure effectual, of the body of Christ, *ib.* 88; a figure, pledge, token, or remembrance of Christ's body, 2 *Jew.* 590, &c.; the difference between the body of Christ and the sacrament of the body, 2 *Jew.* 1121; the sacrament of the Lord ought not to be separated from his substance and verity, 1 *Cov.* 439, 440; the elements are called bread and wine after consecration, 1 *Brad.* 85, *Hutch.* 266, 267, *Rid.* 16, 3 *Tyn.* 251, 255; the substance of bread and wine remains, *Bale* 168, 2 *Bec.* 264, 3 *Bec.* 232, 617, 618, 1 *Brad.* 86, 4 *Bul.* 276, *Grin.* 196, 2 *Hoop.* 152, 155, 402, 1 *Jew.* 11, 545, 547, 2 *Jew.* 1114; this the fathers testify with one consent, 1 *Jew.* 150; whether the bread and wine are so called after consecration for their *former* substance, 4 *Bul.* 276; they are not transubstantiated, 2 *Hoop.* 48, 122, 402; there is no miracle in the sacrament, *Grin.* 49, 1 *Hoop.* 164, 225, 2 *Hoop.* 410, 412, 3 *Tyn.* 261, 262; of the real presence, 1 *Jew.* 445, &c.; disputation on it, *Phil.* 34, 53, 60—69; three opinions on the presence of Christ's body,—the Romish, the Lutheran, and the third opinion, 1 *Tyn.* 366; these opinions examined, *ib.* 367, &c.; Philpot acknowledges the true catholic doctrine thereof, *Phil.* 130, 132, 133, 141, 192; the term "really" is ambiguous, *Rid.* 196; why the bread and wine are called Christ's body and blood, and in what sense they are so, 2 *Bec.* 282, 283, 3 *Bec.* 54, 67, 274, 1 *Brad.* 95, 96, 4 *Bul.* 282, 1 *Cov.* 440, *Grin.* 65, 2 *Hoop.* 441, 1 *Jew.* 167, 518, 2 *Jew.* 565, &c.; real presence, *Phil.* 399, *Rid.* 15; the bread is made Christ's mystical body, *Rid.* 157; Papists assert that the natural body of Christ though in heaven is yet invisibly in the eucharist, 2 *Bec.* 276, 279; they say his body spiritual is in the sacrament, *Grin.* 50; Dr Moreman affirms that Christ ate his own body, *Phil.* 190; the corporal presence in the sacrament of the altar, as taught in the Institution, 2 *Cran.* 96; there is no manner of local or corporal presence of Christ's body and blood in the sacrament, 2 *Bec.* 270, &c., 3 *Bec.* 271, &c., 1 *Brad.* 95, 96, 4 *Bul.* 253, 435, 452, *Grin.* 55, 67, 1 *Hoop.* 62, 68, 115, 119, 155, 157, 158, 400, 414, 514, 2 *Hoop.* 122, 153, 155, 443, &c., 1 *Jew.* 445, &c., *Now.* (93), 216, *Phil.* 192; against the notion of Christ's natural body being carnally eaten in it, with sentences and examples of scripture, 1 *Bec.* 418, &c.; the doctrine of the Lord's bodily presence is incompatible with what he said about going hence, and being no more in the world, 3 *Tyn.* 251—253; it is disproved by the words "till he come," 1 *Brad.* 394; it is not supported by John vi, 1 *Hoop.* 155 (see in iii, below); that passage makes much for the interpretation of Christ's words in the supper, 4 *Bul.* 289; the corporal presence establishes the Marcionite heresy, 2 *Bec.* 270; probations from the old fathers that the substance of the bread is not changed into the natural body of Christ, 3 *Bec.* 423, &c.; the article, temp. Edw. VI., against Christ's bodily presence, 1 *Zur.* 165 n.; protestation against the same in the liturgy of Elizabeth, *ib.* 180 n; the Papists' own doctors believe not that the very body of Christ is received in the sacrament, 1 *Hoop.* 530; the declaration, "This is my body," not a mere metaphor, *Hutch.* 36; how those words are to be expounded, and what they mean, 2 *Bec.* 282, 4 *Bul.* 253, 435, 438, 441, *Coop.* 199, *Grin.* 35, &c., 40, 197, 1 *Jew.* 446, 456, 2 *Jew.* 567, 1110; a vain quiddity of Duns respecting them, *Rid.* 24; Christ hesitated not to say, "This is my body," when he gave a sign of his body, *Grin.* 65; "This cup," &c., explained by a trope, 4 *Bul.* 445; the cup is the sign of Christ's blood,

1 *Tyn.* 365, 366, 379, 383; the cup is the new testament by metonymy, *Rid.* 20; Christ calls the cup the fruit of the vine, *ib.* 17; Christ's body and blood are not only represented, but presented, *Sand.* 302, 303; Christ is present spiritually, or by grace, to the faith of the receiver, 1 *Brad.* 95, 96, 435, 450, 456, 480, 488, 511, &c., 522, 531, 532, 585, 586, 4 *Bul.* 452, *Coop.* 130, 131, 1 *Hoop.* 121, 530, 2 *Hoop.* 394, 441, 453, *Hutch.* 33, 3 *Jew.* 558, 2 *Lat.* 251, &c., 285, *Lit. Edw.* 507, (556), *Now.* (91), 213, *Poet.* 375, *Rid.* 13, 201, 213, 236, 265, 273, 274, 1 *Tyn.* liii; probations out of the old fathers that Christ is truly present in the supper in grace, and not in body, 3 *Bec.* 427, &c.; he is present as a house is in a lease, *Hutch.* 251; another illustration, 1 *Tyn.* 372; Christ is not less present at baptism than at the supper, 3 *Bec.* 261, 1 *Cran.* 76, &c.; a difference to be made of the Lord's body, 4 *Bul.* 470; the elements are not simply Christ's body and blood, but his body broken and his blood shed, 1 *Brad.* 102; hence it teaches repentance, *ib.*, and faith, *ib.* 103, and shews Christ's love, *ib.* 104; the supper is not the only way of receiving Christ's body and blood, *ib.* 100; nevertheless necessary, *ib.* 101; difference amongst Protestants as to the manner of Christ's presence, *Phil.* 400; opinion of Zanchius, 2 *Zur.* 99, &c.; it was calumniously said of the reformed,—that they asserted the holy sacrament to be no better than a piece of common baken bread, and that they made it a mere figure, *Rid.* 10; denial of this, *ib.*; Christ said to be laid on the table, 1 *Jew.* 464, &c.; Christ to be worshipped in the sacrament, *Rid.* 235, 236; of calling it Lord and God, 2 *Jew.* 758, &c.

iii. *Of eating Christ's body, &c.* (see iii. above): Christ appointed the sacramental bread to be eaten of the faithful, 3 *Bec.* 374; why, *ib.* 375; the sacrament is a spiritual meat, 1 *Bec.* 117, &c.; heavenly bread, 2 *Jew.* 620, 621; in memory of Christ's passion in the flesh, not a distribution of flesh, 1 *Hoop.* 402; how the flesh of Christ is given for bread, 4 *Bul.* 456; what it is to eat his flesh and drink his blood, 2 *Bec.* 294; 3 *Bec.* 612, 4 *Bul.* 457, 1 *Cran.* 24, 40, &c., 1 *Hoop.* 62, 2 *Hoop.* 153, *Hutch.* 35, *Pil.* 552, 1 *Tyn.* 369; that Christ's natural body and blood are not carnally eaten and drunken in the Lord's supper, with sentences and examples of scripture, 1 *Bec.* 418, &c.; the body of Christ is eaten, not carnally, but spiritually by faith, 2 *Bec.* 295, 4 *Bul.* 456, 1 *Cov.* 207, 465, 466, 1 *Cran.* 35, &c., *Grin.* 46, 47, 198, 1 *Hoop.* 55, 69, 2 *Hoop.* 49, 451, 486, *Hutch.* 241, 1 *Lat.* 458, 2 *Lat.* 127, 252, 266, 292, 1 *Jew.* 449, 541, 543, 2 *Jew.* 572, 1110, 1117, 3 *Jew.* 531, &c., *Rog.* 288, 289, *Sand.* 89, 3 *Tyn.* 162, 163, 178, 179, 224, 226, 227, 236—238, 244; the old fathers confirm this, 2 *Bec.* 295, &c.; passages which appear to controvert this explained, *ib.* 296, 297; when we eat Christ's flesh and drink his blood, 1 *Cov.* 212, 331; there are two kinds of eating, spiritual and sacramental, 4 *Bul.* 463; a third kind of eating, maintained by Romanists, 4 *Bul.* 464; to receive worthily, is to receive with faith, 1 *Lat.* 237; the body of Christ may be eaten without the sacrament, 1 *Hoop.* 530; whether the sacrament is referred to in John vi., 1 *Jew.* 449, 516, 1 *Tyn.* 369; how the Capernaites took Christ's words, 4 *Bul.* 447, 1 *Cran.* 116, 185, 231, 249, *Grin.* 44, 2 *Hoop.* 191, 450, 1 *Jew.* 451, *Rid.* 175, *Rog.* 289

iv. *That Christ's body is eaten by the righteous, but not by the wicked:* whether Judas Iscariot was present at the supper, and if so, what he received there, see p. 447 above; coming to the supper without faith profits nothing, 3 *Bec.* 55, 1 *Tyn.* 252, 3 *Tyn.* 256; none are fed thereby, save the regenerate, *Rid.* 9; the body and blood of Christ are not eaten and drunken by the wicked, but by the faithful only, 2 *Bec.* 291, 292, 295, 3 *Bec.* 378, 379, 1 *Brad.* 91, 489, 511, &c., 537, 542, *Grin.* 55, *Hutch.* 41, 42, 43, 263, &c., 242, 243, 2 *Jew.* 1120, *Now.* (93), 215, *Phil.* 133, *Rid.* 12, 246, *Rog.* 292, 293; the old fathers confirm this, 2 *Bec.* 292, &c.; probations out of the old fathers that the ungodly do not eat his body or drink his blood, 3 *Bec.* 462, &c.; evil men eat the sacrament, but not the body of Christ, 1 *Cran.* 29; they receive the outward sign, but not the inward grace, *Sand.* 88; Christ's body is received of every man unto life, and of no man unto destruction, 1 *Jew.* 453; what it is to eat and drink unworthily, 4 *Bul.* 469, *Hutch.* 42, 1 *Tyn.* 358, 366, 3 *Tyn.* 256; in what sense persons are said to receive to their own damnation, 1 *Cov.* 432; who are guilty of the body and blood of the Lord, 3 *Tyn.* 267; unworthy recipients are guilty of the Lord's body, though they eat it not, *Hutch.* 280

v. *The benefits, &c. of the Lord's sup-*

per: why it was ordained; the ends of it, 2 *Bec.* 229, 231, 232, 284, &c., 509, 510, 3 *Bec.* 269, 1 *Brad.* 105, 4 *Bul.* 433, 467, 1 *Cov.* 436, 1 *Hoop.* 90, 1 *Lat.* 459, 2 *Lat.* 255, *Lit. Edw.* 516, (564), *Now.* (90) 212; Christ ordained his supper for a remembrance of himself and his benefits, 3 *Bec.* 370, 372, 4 *Bul.* 445, 468; as a memorial of his sufferings and death, 3 *Bec.* 230, 1 *Brad.* 393, 1 *Cov.* 418, 1 *Hoop.* 156, 190, 1 *Tyn.* 356, 371, 3 *Tyn.* 177, 264; as a token of mercy, 1 *Tyn.* 360; as a token of God's good-will, and to assure and stir up our minds to faith, 3 *Bec.* 377, 379, 380; Christ appointed the sacramental bread that each might enjoy by and for himself, *ib.* 375; he instituted the holy signs that we should look upwards to heaven, *ib.* 374, and that they might be exercises of faith to the living, *ib.* 379; the supper is instituted to represent God's gifts to the church, 4 *Bul.* 467; likewise to gather together the church and to unite it in one communion, *ib.* 467, 1 *Cov.* 418; and that all his people should openly testify that they belong to him, 3 *Bec.* 375, 376; and that they might lead a life worthy of his gospel, *ib.* 376; also to admonish Christians of their duty, 4 *Bul.* 468; and to help our weakness, 1 *Cov.* 532; it is necessary to be received, *ib.* 531, *Hutch.* 44; it is not rendered unnecessary by baptism, 1 *Tyn.* 359; it is not essential to salvation in an absolute sense, *ib.* 369; what things are to be remembered at it, 1 *Bec.* 119; the faithful Christian must lift up his soul from the outward elements to Christ, 1 *Cov.* 351; the right use of it is very profitable, 1 *Hoop.* 186, 2 *Hoop.* 433; how rightly to use it, 1 *Hoop.* 61, 127, 147, 182; its true use is to be learned from the doctrine of justification, 1 *Hoop.* 60; its benefits or fruits, 1 *Bec.* 119, 1 *Brad.* 99, 106, 1 *Cov.* 79, 437—439, 2 *Cov.* 267, 470, 471, 2 *Cran.* 116, 2 *Hoop.* 90, 218, *Hutch.* 41, 1 *Lat.* 460, 461, 2 *Lat.* 127; it preaches penitence and faith, 1 *Hoop.* 178; the promise belonging to it, 2 *Bec.* 199, 1 *Cov.* 461, 1 *Tyn.* 252; it has a promise of remission of sins, *Phil.* 190; to the faithful receiver it is a pledge or token of forgiveness, 1 *Tyn.* 357, 367, 2 *Tyn.* 223; breaking of bread in the supper, is the token of the new covenant confirmed by Christ on the cross, 1 *Cov.* 418; a sign of our redemption, 3 *Tyn.* 242, 250; a sacrament of our redemption, *Rog.* 283—285; not a mere sign, 1 *Brad.* 92, &c. 449; 1 *Cov.* 419, 1 *Hoop.* 190, 199, 3 *Zur.* 47; but a seal, 4 *Bul.* 393, 1 *Hoop.* 191; and the means of grace to the soul, and of resurrection to the body, *Coop.* 212; it is food for body and soul, 3 *Bec.* 378; grace is given thereby to those who receive worthily, 1 *Cov.* 352, *Rid.* 239, 240; faith is confirmed by it, 1 *Cov.* 532, 2 *Ful.* 169, 1 *Tyn.* 369; by it we are made partakers of the body and blood of Jesus Christ, 2 *Hoop.* 47, 49, 50, *Rog.* 283, 285; it is a spiritual nourishment, 2 *Bec.* 167, 168; Christians are strengthened by it to eternal life, 1 *Cov.* 211; the fruit of Christ's death is communicated to us in the Lord's supper, not on account of the merit of the work, but for the promises that are made to us therein, 1 *Cov.* 461; we are stirred up by it to consider the benefits we receive of Christ, *ib.* 442; we are more vehemently stirred up to holiness of life, *ib.*; by it we are fed unto life everlasting, *Sand.* 87; whoso receiveth it, receiveth life or death, *Rid.* 8, 9, 161; what goodness followed the ministration of it in king Edward's days, 3 *Bec.* 256; what we profess in receiving it, 1 *Bec.* 120; to the first Christians it was a token of perseverance in the Christian religion, 3 *Tyn.* 264; it is not profitable to the absent, *ib.* 179; it helps not the unbeliever, 3 *Bec.* 55, 2 *Hoop.* 49, 1 *Tyn.* 252, 3 *Tyn.* 256; it is only the faith of the receiver that makes him partaker of Christ's death, 3 *Jew.* 558; to attribute salvation to the sacrament is an ungodly opinion, 1 *Hoop.* 131; it maketh not, but ratifieth our peace, *ib.* 127; it hath no power to work salvation, or to cause a man to die well, 2 *Jew.* 243; it increases the guilt of those who come not to it with a right purpose, 1 *Tyn.* 358, 3 *Tyn.* 256; to the wicked it is damnable, *Now.* (93), 216; the wicked cautioned not to approach it, *Hutch.* 43, 2 *Jew.* 1124, *Sand.* 304

vi. *The sacrament as a type of unity:* it is a sacrament of love and concord, 3 *Bec.* 281; a sign of the love that Christians ought to have among themselves, *Rog.* 282, 283; a symbol of the church's unity, 2 *Whitg.* 546; in it there are three similitudes; nourishing, unity, conversion, *Hutch.* 37, 238, 245, *Rid.* 171, 175, 205; the "one bread" signifies that we are all one body, *Coop.* 120, *Hutch.* 37, 239; 3 *Tyn.* 255, 2 *Whitg.* 546; "the body and blood of the Lord" (1 Cor. xi. 27) interpreted to mean the congregation, 3 *Tyn.* 255; in what sense sacramental recipients become Christ's body, *Hutch.* 241, 244; some are very members of Christ's body who never received the sacrament thereof, 1 *Jew.* 142; the sacrament was ordained to move all men to friendship, love, and concord; but, through the enemies of Christ, nothing raises so much contention, 1 *Cran.* 30, 42, 43, 44

vii. *The eucharist as a sacrifice* (v. Mass, Sacrifice): of the sacrifice, 2 *Jew.* 708; in what sense the old fathers, &c. call the Lord's supper an oblation or sacrifice, 2 *Bec.* 249, *Coop.* 88, 93, 94, 104, 1 *Cov.* 451, 1 *Cran.* 353, 1 *Ful.* 262, 2 *Ful.* 381, 382, 2 *Hoop.* 394, 463, 528, 532, 2 *Jew.* 716, *Rid.* 207; it was termed an unbloody sacrifice by the council of Nice, *ib.* 250; it has been called a tremendous sacrifice, 2 *Jew.* 716; it is no new sacrifice, *Bale* 569; but is instead of all sacrifices, 2 *Bul.* 270; it is not truly and properly a sacrifice, 2 *Hoop.* 32, 47, 90, 394, 448, 460, 514, 515, 521, 528, 1 *Tyn.* 371, 424, 3 *Tyn.* 177; but a sacrament, 2 *Brad.* 289, 2 *Cov.* 267; the Romish opinion of the Lord's supper as an actual sacrifice for sin is opposed to the sufficiency of the sacrifice of Christ, 1 *Cov.* 453, 2 *Cov.* 470; Christ is not offered up therein, as Papists say, *Rid.* 12; it is not a sacrifice for sins, but a memorial of the sacrifice of Christ, *Coop.* 93, 94, 2 *Cov.* 471, *Hutch.* 48, *Now.* (92), 215; it may be called a sacrifice, because it is the sign of a sacrifice, 2 *Bec.* 249, 4 *Bul.* 432, 1 *Lat.* 167; it is a sacrifice mystically, *Rid.* 317; not a propitiatory, but a spiritual sacrifice, 2 *Bec.* 245, &c., 4 *Bul.* 432, 1 *Cov.* 426, 432, 451, 1 *Ful.* 241, 2 *Hoop.* 423, 2 *Lat.* 276, 287; a sacrifice of praise and thanksgiving, 4 *Bul.* 432, 433, 1 *Jew.* 491, *Rid.* 275; in it we offer up praises for the sacrifice of the cross, 2 *Jew.* 716; the lay people make a sacrifice as well as the priest, by thanksgiving and humble submission to the will of God, 1 *Cran.* 352; in the Lord's supper we offer up ourselves, our souls, our bodies, our alms, praises, and prayers, 1 *Jew.* 124; the sacrifice is specially named in the Prayer Book, *ib.* 122; "hoc facite," expounded, 3 *Bec.* 241, 2 *Hoop.* 460; "Do this" does not mean "Sacrifice this," 1 *Brad.* 514, 2 *Brad.* 286, 2 *Cov.* 265; the expression "is given" does not refer to a sacrifice, 2 *Jew.* 713

viii. *Celebration, rites, circumstances* (v. Altars, Liturgies, Tables):

(a) Order, &c., generally:—Christ's body must be received sacramentally as well as spiritually, *Hutch.* 243; the right use of the Lord's supper, 1 *Cov.* 443, 1 *Hoop.* 61, 127, 147, 182, *Rid.* 399; the sacrament consists in the use thereof, 2 *Hoop.* 48; except it be received it is no sacrament, *Phil.* 95, 96; description of the manner in which it should be administered, 1 *Hoop.* 533, &c., 3 *Tyn.* 265—267; its essential parts and accidental circumstances, *Coop.* 111, 113, 123, 1 *Jew.* 122, 124, 126, 127; after what manner it was celebrated by our Lord, see i. *b.* above; he delivered one manner of celebrating his supper, 3 *Bec.* 372; whether it be lawful to add anything to the rite of it, 4 *Bul.* 407; nothing is to be followed in celebrating it but that which we have received of Christ, *ib.* 412; some circumstances are not settled in scripture, 1 *Whitg.* 200; it was simply used by the apostles, 1 *Hoop.* 237, 3 *Tyn.* 97; it is said that they celebrated it with the Lord's prayer, p. 734, col. 2, below; its disorderly celebration at Corinth, and St Paul's commandment respecting it, 1 *Hoop.* 171, 1 *Jew.* 3, 2 *Whitg.* 506, 546, 551, 3 *Whitg.* 546, 547; how celebrated in old time, 4 *Bul.* 408, *Coop.* 81, 82, 83, 2 *Cov.* 469—472, 2 *Tyn.* 220 (v. Dionysius, Justin, and others); heathen misrepresentations of the Christians' practice, 2 *Jew.* 1026; the performing of it changed in latter times, 4 *Bul.* 409; how administered in king Edward's days, 2 *Cov.* 525, *Rid.* 281, 3 *Zur.* 31, 266; it was then often celebrated without the surplice, 1 *Zur.* 158; in some places vestments, lights, &c., were used, 3 *Zur.* 72; the godly order of king Edward's days abolished and the mass brought back, *Rid.* 51; petition that the true ministration of the Lord's supper might be restored, 3 *Bec.* 247; its administration in England described by bp Horn, 2 *Zur.* 354; of the orders and ceremonies used in the celebration thereof, 3 *Whitg.* 73, &c.; the English communion service agreeable to scripture, *Pil.* 541, 542; on the use of the ante-communion service alone, 3 *Whitg.* 381; order for the administration of the Lord's supper in the church of Denmark, 1 *Cov.* 470-478; the Lord's supper must be common, 1 *Jew.* 105; it ought to be administered publicly, 2 *Bec.* 200, 3 *Bec.* 374, 379; probations out of the old fathers that it is a public banquet, *ib.* 415, &c.; the faithful ought to receive together, as they did of old, and not the priest alone, *ib.* 229, 230, 275, 279, 280, 1 *Cov.* 432, 2 *Cran.* 171, 172, *Hutch.* 227, 228, 1 *Jew.* 107, 2 *Jew.* 989; communion of the priest alone, defended, *Coop.* 8, &c.; Christ ordained a

SUPPER OF THE LORD

communion, not a private mass, *Coop.* 8, &c., *Hutch.* 227, 1 *Jew.* 16, &c. (and see p. 526, col. 2, above); Christ did not eat up all himself, but Papists require us to believe, that the priest receives it for all, 1 *Cov.* 433; by mass-mongers it is made a private breakfast, 2 *Bec.* 453; the sacrament cannot be received by one man for another, 2 *Cran.* 150, 2 *Hoop.* 125, 133, *Hutch.* 228, *Rid.* 316; does not profit those who are absent, 3 *Tyn.* 179; single communion is a part of the mystery of iniquity, 2 *Jew.* 911; what tongue is to be used, 4 *Bul.* 421; Papists minister it in a strange tongue, 2 *Bec.* 253, &c.; injunctions respecting its administration, *Grin.* 124, 125, 137; injunction to the dean and chapter of York respecting it, *ib.* 148; the office of the minister in the communion, 1 *Hoop.* 534; the office of the people, *ib.* 535

(*b*) Who should be admitted to the Lord's supper, and who not:—for whom it was instituted, 4 *Bul.* 426; only the faithful ought to be admitted, 2 *Hoop.* 50; women are to be admitted, 2 *Lat.* 263, 1 *Whitg.* 254; the negligence of the people in regard to the communion, *Hutch.* 320, 1 *Lat.* 459; Rome increases it, 1 *Jew.* 119; the more wicked the people became, the more they withdrew from the communion, 2 *Cran.* 174; men come to it from custom, 1 *Lat.* 460; Cartwright would have men compelled by law to receive it, 2 *Whitg.* 552; Whitgift's opinion, *ib.* 553; attendance on the communion was formerly required by law, *Lit. Eliz.* 505; of shutting men from the communion, and compelling to communicate, 3 *Whitg.* 101; Cartwright says that those who are fit to hear, are fit to communicate, 2 *Whitg.* 554; this Whitgift denies, *ib.* 555; popish communicants in England, 3 *Whitg.* 102; what is required in those who receive,* 1 *Hoop.* 536; on the examination of communicants, 3 *Whitg.* 78, &c.: communicants required to know the creed, &c., 2 *Cran.* 82, 156, 500, 2 *Hoop.* 132, 2 *Lat.* 243: on the worthy receiving of the Lord's supper, 1 *Brad.* 108, 1 *Cov.* 433, 2 *Cov.* 87, 1 *Lat.* 237, *Sand.* 90; on receiving unworthily, 1 *Cov.* 432, *Grin.* 56; the plea of unworthiness considered, 1 *Cov.* 448, 449; who should fear to come, *Hutch.* 223; a comfort for afflicted consciences who fear to approach, 4 *Bul.* 475; no man receiveth damnation through it, who is not dead before, *Rid.* 9; on the necessary number of communicants, 2 *Whitg.* 546, &c.; mention is made of 4000 participating at once at Geneva, 3 *Jew.* 370, &c.; who are not to be admitted to the communion, *Grin.* 162; it is not to be administered to open sinners, *Grin.* 125, *Now.* (95), 217; probations out of the old fathers that wicked and notorious offenders ought to be put away from the Lord's table, 3 *Bec.* 474, &c.; swearers to be excluded, after admonition (synod 1562), *Sand.* 434; offenders were kept from the Lord's table in the ancient church, 1 *Jew.* 182; audientes, pœnitentes, catechumeni, and energumeni, not allowed of old to be present, 2 *Jew.* 705, *Rid.* 160, 163; none should be present but communicants, *Phil.* 97; probations of this out of the old fathers, 3 *Bec.* 481, &c.; proofs from the ancient liturgies, 2 *Bec.* 256, 3 *Bec.* 482, *Coop.* 107, 1 *Jew.* 19, 33, 4 *Jew.* 887; Papists admit gazers at the communion against the primitive practice, 2 *Bec.* 255, &c.; the presence of gazers and lookers-on formerly tolerated in England, *Grin.* 267, *Lit. Eliz.* 505 n.; the communion is not intended for infants, 4 *Bul.* 426; why they are not admitted to it, 1 *Jew.* 230; it was formerly administered to them, 2 *Bec.* 223, 3 *Bul.* 398, *Calf.* 213, 270, *Coop.* 10, *Whita.* 666, 2 *Whitg.* 521; the wine only, 1 *Jew.* 249

(*c*) Preparation (*v.* Prayers):—how we ought to approach the Lord's table, 1 *Cov.* 446, 447, *Now.* (93), 216; qualifications for approaching it, 1 *Cov.* 202—206; how we must prepare ourselves, 2 *Bec.* 232, &c., 4 *Bul.* 473, 1 *Jew.* 119, *Sand.* 90; how we ought to prepare our hearts, and with what faith and reverence we should resort to these holy mysteries, 2 *Jew.* 1122—1124; self-examination is needful before the communion, 3 *Bec.* 384, 1 *Brad.* 108, *Rid.* 9, *Sand.* 304; we must come with pure minds, 1 *Bec.* 118; having our minds garnished with godly virtues, *ib.*; not trusting in any good works, *ib.*; with thirsty souls, *ib.*; with faith, *Bale* 196, 1 *Bec.* 118; the coming with faith is an argument of God's choice of us to be his, 3 *Bec.* 173; how the minister should prepare himself, 1 *Hoop.* 534; it is convenient to receive the sacrament fasting, *Hutch.* 221, *Phil.* 379; but it is not forbidden to come after meat, *Hutch.* 222, *Phil.* 379

(*d*) Times and occasions of celebrating the communion: when to be celebrated, and how often, 4 *Bul.* 423, 424, *Coop.* 100, &c.; it should be often celebrated and received, 3 *Bec.* 381, 2 *Hoop.* 129, 1 *Whitg.* 512; probations out of the old fathers that we ought oftentimes to come to it, 3 *Bec.*

470, &c.; no certain time appointed, *ib.* 380, 1 *Whitg.* 200; when the church was most pure it was often received, 2 *Bec.* 259; it was received every day, in the apostles' time, at Jerusalem, 2 *Cran.* 174; and so by some in later times, 1 *Jew.* 17, 136, 157, 169, 2 *Jew.* 631, 1 *Whitg.* 217; communion four days a week mentioned by Basil, 1 *Jew.* 155; in Lent it was consecrated in the Greek church only on Saturdays and Sundays, *ib.* 246, 2 *Jew.* 555; at Alexandria it was celebrated on Sundays only, 1 *Jew.* 168; weekly celebration approved, 2 *Whitg.* 556; reception every Sunday advised by Augustine, *Pil.* 542; daily communion mentioned in king Edward's first Prayer Book, *Lit. Edw.* 80; old decrees direct it to be received at least three times a year, 2 *Cran.* 174, 1 *Hoop.* 228, 1 *Jew.* 176; to be received thrice a year at least, *Grin.* 124, 137, 172; communion once a year deemed sufficient in the church of Rome, 2 *Bec.* 257, &c., 1 *Hoop.* 228, *Hutch.* 220; commonly received at Easter, *Bale* 159, 2 *Cran.* 173, *Hutch.* 215; some of the Greeks received it but once a year in the time of Ambrose and Augustine, 1 *Jew.* 168; in the ancient church it was sometimes celebrated in the evening after supper, 2 *Cov.* 470, 1 *Jew.* 136; Tertullian on the time of ministration, 1 *Whitg.* 216; whether to be celebrated more than once in a day, 2 *Jew.* 625, &c.; it should be celebrated, as in the primitive church, but once on the same day, *Coop.* 70, 2 *Hoop.* 126; article respecting the times of administering it, *Grin.* 158; whether to be celebrated against imminent dangers, 4 *Bul.* 427; on its celebration at marriages, 3 *Whitg.* 356; communion at the burial of the dead in the ancient church, 1 *Lat.* 236; Celebratio cœnæ Domini in funebribus, *Lit. Eliz.* 433; not more than one communion to be celebrated at a funeral, 2 *Hoop.* 146

(*e*) Preaching before the sacrament:—Christ preached before it, 3 *Bec.* 254; it should be preceded by a sermon, 1 *Hoop.* 177, 178, 2 *Zur.* 232; what things ought to be preached at the ministration, 3 *Bec.* 256; (see the sermons mentioned in i. above); ministered without preaching it profits little, 3 *Bec.* 255

(*f*) Some other circumstances:—where the supper should be celebrated, 4 *Bul.* 418, 1 *Whitg.* 200; Christ ministered it at a table, and why, 3 *Bec.* 258; it ought to be ministered at a table, *ib.* 259; a table is more meet for the ministering of the Lord's supper than an altar, 2 *Bec.* 297, 298 (*v.* Altars, Tables); what vestures should be used, 2 *Bec.* 299, &c. (*v.* Vestments); Christ ministered his supper without cope or vestment, 3 *Bec.* 259; altar and mass vestments condemned by Bullinger, 1 *Zur.* 345; vessels belonging to the sacrament, 4 *Bul.* 419; what vessels may be used without superstition, 2 *Ful.* 114; extravagance in them reproved by the fathers, *ib.* (*v.* Chalices); ministers enjoined not to practise popish rites nor counterfeit the popish mass, *Grin.* 124, 159, 2 *Hoop.* 128, 145, 1 *Tyn.* 248 n.; superstitious practices in divers places in England, 3 *Whitg.* 85; on simple and pompous celebration, *ib.* 106; on the commemoration of saints and martyrs, 1 *Ful.* 269, 2 *Ful.* 88; the kiss of peace, see Kiss, Pax; the poor should be remembered at the time of communion, *Rid.* 320

(*g*) The elements:—why the sacrament was instituted in the form of bread and wine, 4 *Bul.* 410; Christ delivered bread and wine to his disciples, 3 *Bec.* 359, 369, *Rid.* 228; on the proper kind of bread, 3 *Whitg.* 82, &c.; whether it ought to be leavened or unleavened, 3 *Bec.* 262, 4 *Bul.* 410; Christ used unleavened bread, 3 *Whitg.* 86; manchets or wafers used by Romanists, 3 *Tyn.* 179; a question arose at Oxford whether they were bread, *ib.*; starch bread spoken of, 3 *Whitg.* 459; unleavened bread used in England and elsewhere, 1 *Zur.* 164, 2 *Zur.* 40; required by the Communion Book and also by the first Prayer Book of king Edward, *Lit. Edw.* 8, 97; either leavened or unleavened bread allowed by the council of Trent, according to custom, 1 *Jew.* 534 n.; wafer bread enjoined by Elizabeth, *Park.* 240, 277, 278, 2 *Zur.* 121, 161, 361; i. e. bread like singing cakes, but somewhat larger, *Park.* 375; form of sacramental bread appointed by Parker and Grindal, *ib.* 378; directions respecting it, *ib.* 458; loaf bread not to be permitted, *ib.* 460; the rubrick which speaks of "usual" bread regarded by Parker as permissive, not as forbidding wafer bread, *ib.* 376; wafer cakes used at Geneva, *Grin.* 208; on the mixture of water in the cup, 4 *Bul.* 410, *Coop.* 81, 82, 137, 1 *Ful.* 503, 522, 523, 1 *Jew.* 137, 139, *Rog.* 296, 3 *Tyn.* 96 n., 97, *Whita.* 602, 603, 2 *Whitg.* 435, 541 n.; the practice is not mentioned in scripture, 1 *Ful.* 523; Cyprian speaks of it as Christ's institution, *Coop.* 136 n.; the liturgies of

St James and St Basil do the same, 1 *Ful.* 523; Justin mentions it, *Coop.* 81, 82, 1 *Ful.* 503, 523, 2 *Ful.* 237, *Whita.* 582; so does Irenæus, 1 *Ful.* 503, 523; testimonies of Cyprian and others to the practice, *Whita.* 602; Cyprian advocated not so much the mixing with water as the use of wine, *ib.*; he presses on the Aquarii the necessity of observing the Lord's tradition, viz. the use of *wine* together with the water, *ib.* 498; yet he estimates the practice very highly, *ib.* 603; the mixed cup enjoined, as the apostolic practice, by the 3rd council of Carthage, and the 6th gen. council of Constantinople, 1 *Ful.* 261, 523; the origin of the practice ascribed to pope Alexander, 3 *Bec.* 262; rubric of the Salisbury missal respecting the mixed cup, 1 *Lat.* 138; water directed to be mixed with the wine by the Communion Book of K. Edward, *Lit. Edw.* 4; also by his first Prayer Book, *ib.* 85; some, instead of the elements ordained by Christ, have used water, others milk, others bread and cheese, 4 *Bul.* 410, *Coop.* 74, 110 n., 135, &c., 1 *Jew.* 252, 2 *Jew.* 588, *Phil.* 117, 420, *Rog.* 295; Innocent VIII. gave a dispensation to consecrate the sacrament without wine, 1 *Jew.* 137, 222; the consecration of metheglin forbidden, 2 *Jew.* 635; bread and wine anciently offered in the Lord's supper, 1 *Cov.* 451; the practice not agreeable to the institution of Christ, *ib.*; the holy loaf, a shadow of the ancient oblations, *Coop.* 89, *Lit. Edw.* 98; holy loaves were formerly provided by the parishioners by turns, 1 *Lat.* 460; order of the king in council (1550) respecting the finding of the bread and wine, 2 *Cran.* 523; communion bread and wine to be provided by the churchwardens, *Grin.* 134

(*h*) Consecration, elevation, the minister (*v.* Intention):—on the consecration of the elements, 4 *Bul.* 267, 416; wherein it standeth, 1 *Hoop.* 518, 2 *Ful.* 167, 1 *Jew.* 123; the Romish doctrine, 3 *Bec.* 269, *Phil.* 65, 66; this differs from that of the ancient churches, 1 *Ful.* 505, 506; some consider that it is in the word "benedixit," 1 *Hoop.* 518; to bless, is to give thanks, 3 *Bec.* 269, 1 *Ful.* 497, &c., 2 *Hoop.* (469), *Hutch.* 226, *Rid.* 111; what it is to bless the cup, 2 *Hoop.* (408); the words of consecration considered, 2 *Bec.* 281, &c., 4 *Bul.* 405, 1 *Hoop.* 529, *Phil.* 95, *Rid.* 18; the words regarded as those of consecration were spoken by our Lord after the delivery of the elements, 3 *Tyn.* 241, 243; Aquinas mentions some who affirmed that the Lord consecrated the bread with other words before he said, "This is my body," 3 *Tyn.* 241 (see in i. *b.* above); Ambrose says Christ the Priest doth daily consecrate the bread with his own words, 2 *Jew.* 772; the words of consecration not to be grossly interpreted, 2 *Bec.* 284, 1 *Hoop.* 115; how the ancient fathers took them, 2 *Bec.* 285, &c.; what the word "Hoc" denotes, 1 *Hoop.* 116, 148, 529, *Phil.* 99; some call the object individuum vagum, or individuum in genere, see p. 413, col. 1; Papists have added "enim" to the words of consecration, 2 *Hoop.* 470; and the words "mysterium fidei" to the blessing of the cup, *Rid.* 23; none of the words of consecration are wanting in the English service, *Pil.* 635; "Hoc est corpus" is true only to those who begin at "Accipite, comedite," 2 *Brad.* 336; consecration is in order to communion, 1 *Jew.* 126; the apostles are said to have consecrated with the Lord's prayer only, 2 *Cov.* 470, *Pil.* 498, 508, 635, 3 *Whitg.* 99; power of consecration, 4 *Bul.* 39; evidence that the sacrament was of old sometimes consecrated by deacons, 1 *Jew.* 240; of consecration under silence, 2 *Jew.* 697, 698, 702; Ridley thought the practice not inconvenient, *Rid.* 318; doubts touching consecration, 1 *Jew.* 550; some say that altar, superaltar, lights, &c., are requisite to it, and that the five words must be said with one breath, 2 *Jew.* 705; crossing and breathing over the bread and wine forbidden, *Grin.* 159; the sacrament not to be lifted up or worshipped, *Hutch.* 230, 253, *Rog.* 290, 291; of the elevation, 1 *Jew.* 507, &c.; Basil cited for it, but he does not refer to it, 1 *Brad.* 514; on the adoration, 1 *Jew.* 514, &c.; the practice condemned, 2 *Bec.* 301, 4 *Bul.* 422, 1 *Cov.* 433, 3 *Jew.* 550, 3 *Tyn.* 179, 180; it was unknown in the old church, 3 *Bec.* 360; Erasmus says the worship of the sacrament was prior to Augustine and Cyprian, *Rid.* 236; how Christ's body was worshipped by the old catholic fathers, 1 *Jew.* 12; worshipping the sacrament was brought in by Honorius, *Grin.* 48, & al.; whether there must be one chief dealer in the action of the supper, 4 *Bul.* 416, 1 *Whitg.* 216; how the minister ought to prepare himself, 1 *Hoop.* 534; the office of the minister, *ib.*; on receiving from an evil priest, *Bale* 167

(*i*) Communion in both kinds or in one: —of communion under both kinds, &c.,

1 *Jew.* 204, &c., *Phil.* 116; the communion ought to be ministered to all under both kinds; the cup is not to be denied to the laity, 2 *Bec.* 240, 241, 3 *Bec.* 230, 275, 1 *Brad.* 373, 528, 4 *Bul.* 68, 414, 1 *Cov.* 459, 460, 471, 2 *Cran.* 173, 451, 2 *Hoop.* 47, 1 *Jew.* 9, 204, &c., 3 *Jew.* 479, &c., 4 *Jew.* 766, *Rid.* 105, *Rog.* 294—296; it was instituted in both kinds, 2 *Cov.* 471, 1 *Jew.* 210, &c., 3 *Jew.* 479, &c.; the objection that Christ spoke to consecrate priests answered, 2 *Bec.* 241, 242; his blood was shed for laymen as well as for priests, *Rid.* 23; the laity received in both kinds in the ancient church, 2 *Bec.* 242, &c., 259, 1 *Jew.* 62 n.; probations out of the old fathers that it should be ministered under both kinds, 3 *Bec.* 412, &c.; other testimonies of the fathers, *Coop.* 138, &c., 141, &c., *Hutch.* 282, 2 *Jew.* 989, *Pil.* 541, 542, *Sand.* 455; the division of the bread and the cup forbidden by Gelasius, who calls it sacrilege, 2 *Bec.* 243, & al.; alleged scriptural examples for one kind, *Rid.* 269; alleged patristic authorities for the practice, *Coop.* 23, 24, 133, &c.; in scripture and the fathers both kinds are often meant, though but one is mentioned, *ib.* 159, &c.; the cup not denied to the laity for 1000 years, *Hutch.* 281; it was not forbidden in the twelfth century, 1 *Hoop.* 229; the denial is not to be traced farther back than Frederick Barbarossa, *Hutch.* 283; Romanists take away one half of the sacrament, 2 *Tyn.* 222; the Oriental church never consented to it, *Hutch.* 283; communion in both kinds is used in the Greek and various other churches, 2 *Bec.* 245, 3 *Bec.* 275; both kinds were received, by the pope's dispensation, in Austria, 2 *Ful.* 243; White, bp of Lincoln, says, that communion in both kinds was never forbidden in the church of Rome, *Rid.* 269; the question evaded by the council of Trent, *Grin.* 22, 3 *Jew.* 203; the cup taken from the laity by Mary, *Rid.* 51, 52; an act of parliament, 1547, for receiving in both kinds, *Lit. Edw.* iii; proclamation of king Edward VI. for it, *ib.* 1; letter missive from his council to the bishops, concerning, it, 2 *Cran.* 511; communion in one kind is an abuse, 1 *Jew.* 9; heretics the first authors of it, *ib.* 258; some arguments for one kind, *Coop.* 23, &c., 29, &c., *Hutch.* 283; foolish reasons for refusing the cup to the laity, 1 *Jew.* 231

(*j*) Administration, reception, gestures: the breaking of the bread, and why it is broken, *Hutch.* 267, 2 *Jew.* 584, &c., 623, 3 *Tyn.* 264; interrogatory respecting it, 2 *Hoop.* 145; what gestures to be used at the supper, 2 *Bec.* 298, 4 *Bul.* 421; of kneeling, 2 *Bec.* 298, *Hutch.* 232, 3 *Whitg.* 88, &c., 491; this posture forbidden in old councils, *Grin.* 47; enjoined in England, 1 *Zur.* 164, 2 *Zur.* 121; no worship of the bread is intended, 2 *Ful.* 205; notice about this, 2 *Bec.* 298, n., 1 *Zur.* 180; objected to by a preacher (perhaps Knox), 3 *Zur.* 591; conceded as indifferent by the episcopal party at Frankfort, *ib.* 754; bishops Grindal and Horn speak of the practice as tolerated until better times, 1 *Zur.* 179; used in Denmark, 1 *Cov.* 476; standing preferred to kneeling, 2 *Bec.* 298; sitting deemed the best posture, *ib.* 299; Christ sat, and why, 3 *Bec.* 260; sitting not practised in the ancient church, 2 *Bec.* 299 n.; a reason assigned for it, 3 *Whitg.* 93, 94; St Paul's rule for eating the Lord's supper, *Pil.* 529; prayer at receiving, *v.* Prayers; of receiving with the hand, 2 *Bec.* 300, 301, 4 *Bul.* 422, 1 *Jew.* 152, &c.; it is best and most in accordance with primitive usage for the people to receive it thus, *Hutch.* 230, 1 *Zur.* 178 n., (and see 358); probations out of the old fathers that it ought to be delivered to the laity, into their hands, 3 *Bec.* 411, 412; to handle the bread is forbidden by the Papists, *ib.* 268; the bread was not put into the people's mouths in the primitive church, *ib.* 268, 269; Ambrose mentions that the priest, in ministering it, said "The body of Christ," the communicant responding "Amen," 2 *Jew.* 698; Leo refers to the same custom, *ib.*; on the words of delivery to each communicant in the English church, 3 *Whitg.* 97, 98; the cup ministered by a lay elder in the church at Geneva, *Rog.* 235; on the ministration of the sacrament by deacons, 3 *Whitg.* 64—67; dipping of the bread in the wine, condemned by pope Julius, 1 *Jew.* 212, 252, 253; how the Anabaptists ministered their communion, *Rog.* 234, 235

(*k*) How to behave after we have received the sacrament, 1 *Bec.* 120; what is to be considered after we have received it, *ib.* 121; it should be followed by thanksgiving, *Hutch.* 43, 284, (*v.* Prayers, Thanksgivings).

(*l*) Of reservation, &c.:—Christ did not command the fragments of his supper to be kept, 3 *Bec.* 372, 373; how the remnants are to be used, 4 *Bul.* 422, 2 *Jew.* 554; anciently they were in some places burned, *Grin.* 60 n., 2 *Jew.* 773; Papists reserve the sacrament contrary to primitive practice, 2 *Bec.* 251, &c.; against reservation of the sacramental bread, hanging it up, and the like, *ib.* 251, 4 *Bul.* 422, 2 *Cran.* 152, 153 n., 172, 1 *Jew.* 148, &c., 2 *Jew.* 553, &c.; probations out of the old fathers that the sacrament was not reserved among the ancient Christians, 3 *Bec.* 455, 456; on the subject, *Coop.* 23, &c., 29, &c., 149, &c.; it is alleged to have been reserved of old in some places, 2 *Jew.* 241, 554; when the reservation was enjoined, 2 *Brad.* 310, *Calf.* 136; reservation defended, *Coop.* 23, &c.; diversely used in divers countries, 2 *Jew.* 555; carrying about the bread condemned, 2 *Bec.* 253, 3 *Jew.* 550, 555, *Rog.* 290, 291; what the Papists do if the bread corrupts or the wine is spilled, 2 *Bec.* 262

(*m*) Administration in private houses, communion of the sick:—on celebration in private houses, *Coop.* 124, &c., 2 *Whitg.* 514, 540, &c; the practice censured, 2 *Bec.* 238, &c., 4 *Bul.* 428, 1 *Cov.* 432, *Hutch.* 227; it is very ancient, 2 *Whitg.* 541; in what case it is lawful, 1 *Hoop.* 173; no man may receive alone, *ib.* 170; on communion of the sick, and houseling before death, 2 *Ful.* 11, 105, 2 *Hoop.* 147, 463, 1 *Jew.* 135—137, 2 *Whitg.* 543, &c., 3 *Zur.* 123; Hooper disapproves of it, 1 *Hoop.* 170—173; so does Coverdale, 2 *Cov.* 86; in the primitive church the sacrament was sent to the sick and others who were absent, 4 *Bul.* 430, *Coop.* 81, 125, *Grin.* 48, 1 *Jew.* 136; how it was carried home, *Grin.* 47, 48

Supplementum Chronicorum: *v.* Forestus (J. P.)

Supplication: *v.* Prayer.

AN HUMBLE SUPPLICATION UNTO GOD FOR THE RESTORING OF HIS HOLY WORD, by T. Becon, 3 *Bec.* 223, &c.

Supplication of Beggars: *v.* Fish (S.)
Supplication of Souls: *v.* More (Sir T.)
Supremacy:

i. *Of the pope* (*v.* Law (Canon), Peter, Phocas, Pope): contentions of the Greek and Roman churches about supremacy, 2 *Hoop.* 234; the pope cannot establish his, *ib.* 545, 546; it is abhorred by the Eastern church, 4 *Jew.* 740; the Greek church compelled for a time to acknowledge it, 2 *Hoop.* 238; where the pope hath supremacy kings suffer wrong, *ib.* 546, 559; the pope's supremacy abrogated by Henry VIII., 2 *Cran.* 369 n.; denied in the Institution, *ib.* 98; restored by act of parliament, under Mary, 2 *Hoop.* 617 n.; rejected by Elizabeth, *Rog.* 347

ii. *Of princes* (*v.* Kings, Magistrates, Oaths): on the supremacy of kings, 2 *Ful.* 354, &c.; men are called heads in scripture in respect of outward government, 3 *Jew.* 266; Cranmer says Nero was, in a temporal sense, head of the Roman church, and the Turk is head of the church of Turkey, 2 *Cran.* 219; the supremacy of Christian kings affirmed in the Institution, *ib.* 98; supremacy transferred to the kings of England, *ib.* 303 n., 2 *Zur.* 128, 149, 158 (*v.* Statutes): Parker's account of the first admission of the king's supremacy, 2 *Cran.* 214 n.; it is preached by Cranmer in Kent, *ib.* 326; affirmed by Gardiner, *Park.* 23; the title of "supreme head" acknowledged by the kings of France, 3 *Zur.* 563 n.; the king acknowledged by the Articles of 1552 as supreme head in earth of the church of England and Ireland, *Lit. Edw.* 536, (580); the title disliked by Calvin and at Magdeburg, 1 *Ful.* 488; in what sense it was allowed in England, 1 *Brad.* 478, 1 *Ful.* 489; nothing to be taught against the king's supremacy, 2 *Hoop.* 144; the title of "supreme head" used by queen Mary, 1 *Jew.* 61, 4 *Jew.* 974; question as to its lawfulness, 1 *Zur.* 1; Elizabeth (on Lever's suggestion) declines it, 4 *Jew.* 1144, *Park.* 66, 1 *Zur.* 24, 33; the title changed to "supreme governor," 2 *Cran.* 224, margin, 1 *Zur.* 29; the queen's supremacy required to be acknowledged by all ministers, 2 *Zur.* 358; secretly denied by the Puritans, 3 *Whitg.* 510; our sovereign hath the chief power in this realm of England, &c., *Rog.* 335, 336, and the chief government of all estates ecclesiastical and civil, *ib.* 338—341; of the prince's supremacy in ecclesiastical causes, 1 *Whitg.* 27, 391, 2 *Whitg.* 263, 3 *Whitg.* 295, &c., 592; on the title of "supreme head" or "governor," 4 *Jew.* 973, &c.; we grant no further liberty to our magistrates than is given them by the word of God, and confirmed by the examples of the best governed commonwealths, *ib.* 973; we need not search for scripture to excuse the title of "supreme head of the church," for we devised it not, we use it not, and our princes claim it not, *ib.* 974; the sovereign is supreme head of all the people of England, as well ecclesiastical as temporal, but Christ only is the head of the church, 2 *Cran.* 224; that title belongs to Christ alone, 2 *Whitg.* 84, 85; no king is head of the church, but in every particular church the king, being a Christian, is chief magistrate, 2 *Ful.* 261, 262, &c.; Hooper speaks to this effect of king

Edward, 2 *Hoop.* 127; monarchs alleged to be the heads of particular churches, 3 *Whitg.* 198; the supremacy is a chargeable dignity, 1 *Lat.* 152; the archbishop's style of "primate of all England," not derogatory to it, 2 *Cran.* 304; the prince has power by law to ordain ceremonies in certain cases, *Park.* 375

Suresby: to be depended on, 1 *Brad.* 63

Surfeiting: *v.* Gluttony.
 Admonitions against surfeiting and drunkenness, 1 *Bec.* 324, 325

Surius (Laur.): *Calf.* 324 n.; De Prob. Sanctor. Hist., *Jew.* xliii; Vita Sanctorum, 2 *Ful.* 355 n.; Comm. Brev. Rerum Gest. *Rog.* 93, 206, 207, 224, 296 nn.; he attacks Sleidan, 1 *Ful.* 63, 4 *Jew.* 1087; his version of the Apology of Staphylus, 2 *Ful.* 77 n

Surnames: *v.* Names.

Surplice: *v.* Vestments.
 Compared to the ephod, 2 *Bul.* 135; when introduced, 2 *Bec.* 99, 300, 2 *Zur.* 166, 2 *Whitg.* 47, 3 *Whitg.* 109; on its use, disputes about it, &c., 2 *Bec.* 99, 300, *Grin.* 271, 339, 2 *Whitg.* 1, &c., 1 *Zur.* 142, 146, 148, 158, 164, 345, &c., 2 *Zur.* ix. 121, 361; the Lord's supper often celebrated without it in king Edward's time, 1 *Zur.* 158; P. Martyr would not wear it in the choir at Oxford, 2 *Zur.* 33, and corrig.; articles &c. respecting it, *Grin.* 124, 155, 158; not required to be worn in preaching, but only at the sacraments, 2 *Zur.* 118; to be worn at the Lord's supper, *Lit. Edw.* 97, 157, 217; ordered by Sandys to be worn in all divine service, *Sand.* xx; to be worn in the choir at York, *Grin.* 148; not to be worn in perambulations, *ib.* 241; disapproved by Bullinger, 2 *Zur.* 357; Jewel desired its abolition, 1 *Zur.* 100; Cox defended it, *ib.* 236; it was opposed by some at Cambridge, *Park.* 226 n.; not borne in the diocese of Norwich, *ib.* 149; disorders at St Giles, Cripplegate, *ib.* 275, 276; Parker's chaplain, for lack of a surplice and wafer-bread, at certain places, did but preach, *ib.* 277

Surplice Fees, 2 *Whitg.* 557, 559

Surrey (Hen. earl of): *v.* Howard.

Sursum corda: 3 *Bec.* 266, 360, 407, 4 *Bul.* 309, 408, 1 *Jew.* 12, 119, 285, 292, 467, 3 *Jew.* 533—535, *Rid.* 318, *Whitg.* 260; mentioned by Cyprian and Augustine, and found in the ancient liturgies, 1 *Cov.* 456 n

Surtees (Rob.): History of Durham, corrected, *Ful.* 481 n

Susa: *v.* Shushan.

Susanna: falsely accused, 2 *Bul.* 114; her faith, 1 *Lat.* 378 (*v.* Daniel).

Suspicions: 2 *Bul.* 227

Suspire: its meaning illustrated from the Ritual Rom., 1 *Hoop.* 345, n

Sussex: *v.* Cinque Ports.

Sussex (earls of): *v.* Ratcliffe.

Sustentacles: supports, *Bale* 369

Sutcliffe (Matth.): *Calf.* 190 n., 381 n., *Rog.* 359 n

Sutherland (Jo.), earl of Sutherland: arms in defence of the queen of Scots, 1 *Zur.* 205 n

Sutor: ne sutor ultra crepidam, *Calf.* 263 n

Sutton (Edm.): exile at Frankfort, 3 *Zur.* 764

Sutton-Coldfield, co. Warwick: 1 *Lat.* 272

Sutton Magna, co. Essex: the benefice, 2 *Cran.* 361

Suychynars, or Suyzars: *v.* Switzerland.

Swaffham, co. Norfolk, *Bale* ix.

Swale, a river of Yorkshire: Augustine baptizes there, 4 *Jew.* 780, *Pil.* 518, and Paulinus, *ib.* 518 n

Swan: its singing, 1 *Brad.* 350, 1 *Ful.* 455

Swash-bucklers: *v.* Shake-bucklers.

Sweard: sword, *Calf.* 93

Swearing: *v.* Oaths.

Sweating sickness: *v.* Plague.

Sweden: *v.* Eric XIV., Finland (Jo. d. of).
 War with Denmark, 1 *Zur.* 150, 2 *Zur.* 106

Sweep-stake, 2 *Brad.* 292, 2 *Cov.* 271

Sweetlad: a mock saint, 2 *Bec.* 536

Swendius (...... baron): a military writer, 2 *Zur.* 300 n

Swerder (Will.): 2 *Cran.* 374; master of Eastbridge hospital, Canterbury, 3 *Zur.* 247

Swermerians: heretics, 3 *Zur.* 50; they condemned the outward ministry of the word and sacrament, *Rog.* 237; said the baptism of infants was of the devil, *ib.* 280

Swift (Rich.): *v.* Swyfte.

Swift (Rob.): Pilkington's chancellor, *Pil.* xii.

Swillings: food for swine, 1 *Brad.* 160

Swinbourne (Rowl.): *v.* Swynbourne.

Swine: the fleshly, 2 *Tyn.* 10, 114, 230; their faith, *ib.* 11; pearls not to be cast before them, *ib.* 115

Swink: labour, toil, 1 *Cran.* 293: swinked, laboured, 2 *Bec.* 7

Switzerland: *v.* Church, II. v., Confessions, Elizabeth; also Berne, Zurich, &c.
 Banishment of the nobles, 2 *Ful.* 121; wars and troubles, *Phil.* 388—391, 3 *Zur.*

552 n., 556; the decay of churches and monasteries, the destruction of masses, altars, vestments, &c., *Phil.* 388, 389; five cantons allied with France, 3 *Zur.* 68, 653, 656, 740; queen Elizabeth's letter to the thirteen cantons, 1 *Zur.* 333; the Swiss commended for their love of liberty, 2 *Zur.* 169; they freed their country, 4 *Jew.* 671; the people called Socheners, Souchenars, Suychynars, Suyzars, or Zwitzers, 1 *Tyn.* 186, 2 *Tyn.* 300, 311; Zwicers, 4 *Bul.* 229

Sword: *v.* War.

In the scripture generally taken for vengeance and punishment, 1 *Bul.* 352; delivered to kings and governors, *Rid.* 266; the temporal sword and the spiritual, 2 *Hoop.* 53, 1 *Lat.* 85; both usurped by Gregory VII., 2 *Hoop.* 239; the "two swords" (Luke xxii.), 1 *Tyn.* 323; the sword of the Spirit, 1 *Lat.* 439

Swyfte (Rich.): 2 *Cran.* 390

Swynbourne (Rowl.), master of Clare hall: account of him, 2 *Lat.* 378 n

Sybils: *v.* Sibyls.

Sycinius: *v.* Sisinnius.

Sydall (Hen.): *v.* Sidall.

Sydney family: *v.* Sidney.

Sykerness: entireness, *Phil.* 345

Sylvanus: *v.* Silvanus.

Sylverius, pope: son of pope Hormisdas, 2 *Ful.* 98, 99 n.; chosen by corruption and simony, contrary to the will of the clergy, 4 *Jew.* 1034; deposed by Justinian, *ib.* 1030, *Sand.* 40, 1 *Zur.* 18 n.; he says, he that usurpeth what he has not received, let him lose that he hath, 1 *Jew.* 443

Silvester I., pope: his Acts fictitious, *Calf.* 174 n.; the council of Nice alleged to have been kept in his time, 4 *Jew.* 695; statement that he sent Hosius there to represent him, *ib.* 993, 998, &c.; false statements about Constantine's Donation to him, acknowledgment of his supremacy, &c., see Constantine; feigned story of his having baptized Constantine, 2 *Ful.* 359, 4 *Jew.* 995, 1003, 1004; Gerson says he first caused stone altars to be made, 1 *Jew.* 310; his additions to the mass, 2 *Brad.* 306; his command that the wife be blessed by the priest, *Pil.* 569, 686; alleged to have said that the highest prelate may be judged of no man, 3 *Jew.* 339, 4 *Jew.* 1000; follies in the decrees ascribed to him, *Calf.* 193, 1 *Jew.* 15; reference to him, 1 *Hoop.* 278

Sylvester II., pope: was a sorcerer, and sold himself to the devil, *Bale* 560, 561, 593, *Calf.* 91, 1 *Jew.* 381, 400, 3 *Jew.* 340, 4 *Jew.* 926, *Pil.* 602, *Rog.* 180, *Sand.* 66; slain at mass, *Calf.* 92; he was probably the writer of a treatise De Dignitate Sacerdotum, falsely ascribed to Ambrose, 2 *Whitg.* 153 n.; it condemns Simoniacal ordination, *ib.* 153; other citations, *ib.* 156, 157

Sylvester III., pope: bought the popedom, *Sand.* 241, see 4 *Jew.* 702; was an enchanter, *Rog.* 180; his history written by card. Benno, 2 *Hoop.* 240

Sylvester Prierias, *q. v.*

Silvester (......): 3 *Zur.* 771

Sylvius (Æneas): *v.* Pius II.

Sylvius (Geo.), or Wood, a Scottish minister: 2 *Zur.* 365

Symbolical divinity: 4 *Bul.* 238

Symbolists: think nothing is received in the Lord's supper but bare signs, *Rog.* 289

Symbols: *v.* Creeds.

What symbols are, 4 *Bul.* 237; examples of them, *ib.* 238; those of Pythagoras, *ib.*

Symmachus, pope: his contest with Laurence for the popedom, *Pil* 640; he declares that God has reserved the pope to His own judgment, 1 *Jew.* 68; says that though the pope lack goodness acquired by merit, what he has from his predecessor is sufficient, *ib.* 400, 401, 3 *Jew.* 201, 324; asserts that the popes, together with the privileges of their see, have received liberty to do ill, 3 *Jew.* 339; is said to have ordered the Gloria in excelsis to be used, 2 *Brad.* 307, and to have made ciboria, 2 *Jew.* 559

Symmachus, the consul: his opposition to Christianity, 1 *Jew.* 84, 4 *Jew.* 666, 1108

Symmachus, the heretic: translated scripture, 2 *Ful.* 390, 2 *Jew.* 692; some account of him and of his version, *Whita.* 123

Symon (......): martyred at Norwich, *Poet.* 172

Sympson (Andr.), minister of Dunbar: 2 *Zur.* 365

Symson (Cuth.): deacon of the Christian congregation in London in queen Mary's days, and martyr, 1 *Brad.* 434 n., 2 *Brad.* 128, 2 *Zur.* 160 n.; called Symion, *Poet.* 172

Symson (Jo.), minister of Scoonie: 2 *Zur.* 365

Synagogue: a name applied to the congregation of the Jews, 4 *Bul.* 4; its officers, 2 *Whitg.* 345, 348; it erred, 2 *Ful.* 45—47; sometimes called "ecclesia," 1 *Ful.* 227, 228; it was a figure of the church, 4 *Jew.* 1299, 2 *Whitg.* 345; what synagogues were, 2 *Whitg.* 143, 482, 1 *Lat.* 533; those of the Libertines, and others, 4 *Bul.* 482; that of Antichrist, 1 *Cran.* 332; that of the devil, *ib.* 302

Synaxis: a name of the Lord's supper, 3 *Bec.* 418, 4 *Bul.* 402
Syncretism: 2 *Zur.* 362
Synecdoche: *Phil.* 117
Synesius: 2 *Jew.* 803, 4 *Jew.* 700
Synge (......): Rejoynder to the Jesuite's Reply, 1632, 2 *Ful.* 364 n
Synods: *v.* Councils.
Synoris (St): an imaginary saint, originating in a blunder of P. Galesinius, 2 *Ful.* 44
Synusiasts: called also Ubiquitaries, *q. v.*
Syrapion: *v.* Serapion.
Syriac tongue: when used, 1 *Jew.* 276; employed by Christ, 2 *Ful.* 225; Syriac words in the New Testament,—Talitha cumi, Abba, Aceldama, Golgotha, Pascha, *Whita.* 213
Syrian Sea: 1 *Bul.* 170
Syrians: worshipped a fish and pigeons, *Rog.* 37
Syricius: *v.* Siricius.
Syrophœnisse: 4 *Bul.* 182
Syrus (Publius): denounces ingratitude, *Sand.* 156
Syth (St): *v.* Osyth.

T.

T.: *v.* Thau.
T. (C.): author of A Short Inventory of certain Idle Inventions, 1581, *Poet.* xxxvii; an extract from this work, *ib.* 395
T. (J.) translates a book of Bullinger, 4 *Bul.* xxi.
T. (J.): " J. T. [and] J. S." 3 *Whitg.* 498 n
Tabarites: the canonists of the Jews, 2 *Jew.* 678
Taberer, and Tabering: *Calf.* 257
Tabernacle: 2 *Bul.* 143, &c., 4 *Bul.* 83; why commanded to be made according to the pattern shewed in the mount, *Sand.* 222; its ordinances, 1 *Tyn.* 414; things laid up in it, 2 *Bul.* 145; the veil, *ib.* 145; the mystery of the most holy place, 1 *Ful.* 288; the tabernacle a type of the church, 2 *Bul.* 147, 4 *Bul.* 82, *Sand.* 222, 2 *Whitg.* 93
Tabernacles (Feast of): 2 *Bul.* 165, 166; its alleged discontinuance, 1 *Whitg.* 29, &c.
Tabitha: *v.* Dorcas.
Table, Tables: texts appropriate to tables, 1 *Bec.* 64; how we ought to behave at table, *ib.* 174, 402, 403; the word diversely taken in scripture, 2 *Hoop.* 228; the golden table in the tabernacle, 2 *Bul.* 154; the table provided by the Lord our Shepherd, 2 *Cov.* 310, 2 *Hoop.* 227

Table of the Lord, or Communion table: *v.* Altar.
Of the Lord's table, 4 *Bul.* 418; Christ, the apostles, and the primitive church used a table at the communion, 3 *Bec.* 229; St Paul speaks of the Lord's table, 4 *Bul.* 402; it was called ἱερὰ τράπεζα, and mensa Dominica, 1 *Jew.* 98; termed God's board, *Hutch.* 225, *Lit. Edw.* 91, 278; the name table, as well as altar, commonly used by the fathers, 1 *Ful.* 517, 518, 1 *Jew.* 310, &c.; it was anciently of wood, and men stood around it, 1 *Ful.* 517, 1 *Jew.* 311, 3 *Jew.* 601, 602; a table is necessary in a church, 4 *Bul.* 501; tables set up instead of altars, 2 *Cran.* x, 524, 1 *Jew.* 90, *Rid.* 280, 281, 529, 2 *Zur.* 159 n., 3 *Zur.* 72, 79, 384, 466; the Lord's board should not be made in the form of an altar, 2 *Hoop.* 128, *Rid.* 320; reasons for this, 2 *Cran.* 524, 2 *Hoop.* 128, *Pil.* 545, *Rid.* 321, 322; the table for the communion not to be decked as the altars were, 2 *Hoop.* 142; its position indifferent, *Rid.* 281; the Lord's table irreverently spoken of by bp White, *ib.*, and by Weston, 2 *Lat.* 275; cast out by the Papists, 3 *Bec.* 240; restored temp. Eliz., 1 *Zur.* 63; complaint of unseemly tables with foul cloths, *Park.* 133; tables overthrown by the rebels in the North, 1 *Zur.* 214; enjoined to be placed within the quire, *Park.* 375, 376; articles respecting communion-tables, *Grin.* 133, 157, 2 *Hoop.* 142; what parts of the service to be read there, *Grin.* 132
Tables: a game, backgammon, *Grin.* 138, 166; tables, *ib.* 130
Tables (Twelve): forbade magical arts, 1 *Hoop.* 327
Tacitus (C. C.): on the worship of the Jews, 2 *Jew.* 1025, 3 *Jew.* 154; on the idolatry of the Germans, 1 *Bul.* 223, 224
Tack: spot, stain, 2 *Whitg.* 84
Tadcaster, co. York: the rebellious earls there, 1 *Zur.* 247 n
Tag and rag: 1 *Whitg.* 315
Tagasta in Numidia, now Tajelt: the birthplace of St Augustine, *Hutch.* 54
Tailarandus Petragoriensis, a French cardinal: *Bale* 520
Tailor (Will.): a priest condemned by Chichele, *Bale* 394
Tajelt: *v.* Tagasta.
Talarus: father of pope Adrian II., 2 *Ful.* 98 n
Talbot (Geo.), 4th earl of Shrewsbury: complaint against him, 2 *Cran.* 366
Talbot (Fra.), 5th earl of Shrewsbury: notice

of him, 1 *Zur.* 15 n.; privy councillor to Mary and Elizabeth, *ib.* 5 n.; president of the council in the North, and a royal visitor, *ib.* 73 n

Talbot (Geo.), 6th earl of Shrewsbury: the queen of Scots committed to his keeping, 1 *Zur.* 210 n., 2 *Zur.* 223 n.; his orders concerning her, 1 *Zur.* 260 n.; lord steward at the trial of Tho. duke of Norfolk, *ib.* 261 n., 267 n.; he married the lady St Loe, *Park.* 301 n

Talbot (Gilb.), 7th earl of Shrewsbury: ambassador to France (when lord Talbot), 2 *Zur.* 201 n.; letter to him, 3 *Whitg.* 620

Talbot (Sir Gilb.): sheriff of Worcestershire, 2 *Lat.* 414 n

Talbot (Sir Jo.): 2 *Hoop.* 557

Talboys (Gilbert lord): Elizabeth (Blount) his widow, 2 *Bec.* 554 n

Talcorne (Jo.), proctor: 2 *Cran.* 491

Talents: how to be employed, 2 *Bec.* 418; the purport of the parable, 1 *Tyn.* 472

Tales: carrying of them, 2 *Bul.* 117; taletellers shall be punished, 1 *Lat.* 334; tales of tubs, i. e. fabulous stories, 1 *Brad.* 418, 2 *Cov.* 234

Talkers: *v.* Tongue.

Tallow (The laird of): 1 *Zur.* 195 n

Tally-up: to score, reckon up, 1 *Bec.* 134

Talmud: 2 *Hoop.* 393; made by Mair the Idomite, *Bale* 479; it destroys the sense of scripture, *ib.* 319, 3 *Tyn.* 48; translated by Conrad Pellican, 3 *Zur.* 432

Tamars (...... de): 2 *Zur.* 289

Tamerlane, king of Scythia: 4 *Jew.* 701

Tamworth, co. Stafford: the college, 2 *Cran.* 380

Tamworth (Jo.), Cranmer's kinsman: 2 *Cran.* 368, 369

Tamworth (Tho.), of Lincolnshire: 2 *Cran.* 368

Tamworth (Mr): *Park.* 202

Tankard-bearers: in London, 3 *Jew.* 173

Tankerfield (Geo.): martyred at St Albans, *Poet.* 163

Tanner (Tho.), bp of St Asaph: Bibl. Brit. Hib., 2 *Brad.* xii. n., 2 *Lat.* 319 n., 379 n.; his account of Becon and his works, 1 *Bec.* xv; of Coverdale, 2 *Cov.* 19; of Cranmer, 1 *Cran.* xxx; of Fulke, 1 *Ful.* xiii; of Grindal, *Grin.* xvii, xviii; of Hooper, 1 *Hoop.* v; of Jewel, 4 *Jew.* xxvi; of Latimer, 1 *Lat.* xiv; of Pilkington, *Pil.* xiv; of Ridley, *Rid.* xiii; of Sandys, *Sand.* xxx, xxxi; Not. Mon., 2 *Lat.* 394 n., 397 n., 403 n

Tanner (Mr): *Park.* 18

Tantalus: 2 *Hoop.* 97

Tapers: *v.* Candles.

Tapper (Ruardus), dean of Louvaine: 1 *Jew.* 72; Opera, *Jew.* xlii; he teaches falsely respecting original sin, *Rog.* 97; likewise on good works, *ib.* 122—139; allows that communion under both kinds is more agreeable to the institution, 3 *Jew.* 479; on a decree of Gelasius, 1 *Jew.* 37, 52, 53; he wrote against Pighius, 4 *Jew.* 787; Harding borrowed from him, 2 *Jew.* 714; (*v.* Royard).

Tarasius: *v.* Tharasius.

Tares: *v.* Wheat.

Targums: 2 *Cran.* 183, 1 *Hoop.* 351, *Whita.* 117, 3 *Whitg.* 343; translated by Fagius, 2 *Jew.* 679 n

Tarpeian rock: *v.* Rome.

Tarquinius Priscus: *Calf.* 316

Tarquinius Sextus: 1 *Hoop.* 284

Tarquinius Superbus: 1 *Bul.* 417

Tarrieth you: awaiteth you, 1 *Bec.* 48

Tartaret (Pet.): extracts from his Lucidissima Commentaria, 1 *Tyn.* 158 n

Tartarus: *v.* Hell.

Tartary, Tartars: communications between Batus prince of Tartary and Innocent IV., *Wool.* 28; the Tartars invade Russia, 3 *Zur.* 692; their religion, *ib.* 690; that of the Turks borrowed by them, 3 *Jew.* 199; that of the Mord-wite Tartars, *Rog.* 38; the great cham after dinner causes a trumpet to be sounded, and gives all other kings and emperors leave to dine, 4 *Jew.* 842; laws of the Tartarians against adultery, 2 *Bec.* 649

Tassin (René Prosper): Hist. de la Congr. de S. Maur, 2 *Ful.* 101 n., 238 n

Tatian: his heresy, 3 *Bec.* 401, 1 *Hoop.* 375 n., 3 *Jew.* 232

Tatians: *v.* Encratites.

Tau: *v.* Thau.

Taunton, co. Somerset: Cranmer made archdeacon of Taunton, 2 *Cran.* vii.

Taunts: *v* Railing.

Taurus: 2 *Bul.* 281

Taverner (Jo.): exile at Frankfort, 3 *Zur.* 764

Taverns: *v.* Bush.
  Inns and hostlers: 1 *Lat.* 395; the clergy not to frequent taverns or alehouses, 2 *Cran.* 500, 2 *Hoop.* 144, *Grin.* 130; they were wont so to do, 1 *Cran.* xiii, 1 *Tyn.* 394; alehouses, tippling houses or taverns, not to be kept in parsonage-houses, *Grin.* 130, 166; taverns, &c. not to be open on Sundays during service, *ib.* 138, 2 *Hoop.* 137

Taxes: *v.* Tribute.

Taxis (Jo. Bapt. de): 2 *Zur.* 292 n

Taylor (Jo.), bp of Lincoln: *Park.* viii, 482; previously a commissioner for the reform of the liturgy, *Rid.* 316

Taylor (Jer.), bp of Down and Connor: Lib. of Pro., 2 *Ful.* 44 n

Taylor (Isaac): cites as genuine certain spurious epistles ascribed to Ignatius, *Calf.* 290 n., 2 *Ful.* 236 n.; likewise a counterfeit epistle bearing the name of pope Eusebius, *Calf.* 324 n

Taylor (Jo.), archd. of Buckingham: master of the rolls, 2 *Cran.* 306 n

Taylor (Rog.), alias Cooke, of Oxford: 2 *Cran.* 556

Taylor (Rowl.): born at Rothbury, Northumberland, 2 *Brad.* 93 n.; in prison, 1 *Brad.* 403, 493, 2 *Brad.* 74 n., 96; he signs a declaration concerning religion, 1 *Brad.* 374; a letter signed by him, 1 *Brad.* 305, 2 *Brad.* 169; letters to him, 2 *Brad.* 179, 2 *Hoop.* 592; in peril of death, 1 *Brad.* 290; degraded, 1 *Brad.* 496, 3 *Zur.* 171; his godly confession, 2 *Brad.* 82, *Rid.* 358, 364; his martyrdom, 1 *Brad.* 410, 445, 2 *Brad.* 192, *Rid.* 380, 391, 489, 493, 3 *Zur.* 772; mentioned as "trusty Taylor," 2 *Brad.* 190; his widow married a minister named Wright, *Park.* 221

Taylor (Will.): *v.* Tailor.

Teachers: *v.* Doctors, Ministers, Schoolmasters.

God provides them for such as desire to learn, *Sand.* 268; their necessity, *ib.* 244; things requisite in them, *Phil.* 366; doctors or teachers in the church, 4 *Bul.* 106, 116; "pastors and teachers," see p. 538, col. 2; false teachers are wolves, *Sand.* 397

Teaching: the word μαθητεύσατε expounded, *Phil.* 281, *Whita.* 527; power to teach, 4 *Bul.* 44; the manner of teaching in the church, 4 *Bul.* 154, 1 *Tyn.* 156; ministers should teach the good and right way, *Sand.* 39, 40; private teaching, 4 *Bul.* 157; how all may teach, *ib.* 104; what things to be joined to teaching, *ib.* 158

Tebold (Tho.), an agent of lord Cromwell's: 1 *Tyn.* lxix. n

Tedeschi (N.): *v.* Tudeschi.

Te Deum: 3 *Jew.* 255

Tekoah: the widow there, *Pil.* 161, 309

Tekoites: *Pil.* 379, &c.

Tela: *v.* Councils.

Telamon: denied providence, *Hutch.* 73

Telesphorus, bp of Rome: said to have instituted Lent, 3 *Bec.* 511 n., 2 *Ful.* 236, 237, *Whita.* 508; the chronicle of Eusebius corrupted to maintain the statement, 2 *Ful.* 236, 237; parts of the mass ascribed to him, 2 *Brad.* 307, 308, *Pil.* 503, 3 *Whitg.* 99, 100; he forbids mass at night, 1 *Jew.* 117 n

Tellez (Emman. Gond.): *Calf.* 302 n

Teman: means the South, *Pil.* 244

Temper: to govern, 1 *Tyn.* 328

Temperance: *v.* Continency, Drunkenness, Eating, Gluttony.

On temperancy, 1 *Hoop.* 349; Origen defines sobriety or temperance, *Sand.* 391; temperance in diet recommended, 2 *Bec.* 102, 103, 1 *Hoop.* 349, *Pil.* 52, *Sand.* 392; sobriety in attire, *Sand.* 394; in speech and gesture, *ib.* 395; inward sobriety, *ib.* 391

Tempest: *v.* Thunder.

Temple: why the temple was builded, 1 *Bec.* 156, 2 *Bul.* 143; the place of its erection, 2 *Bul.* 150; how long it stood, *ib.* 152; how God was present in it, 3 *Tyn.* 86; he did not dwell therein, but his name was there, 1 *Tyn.* 382; how the temple was honoured, *Pil.* 69, 70; why the people were specially called there, 3 *Tyn.* 84; the earnest longing of godly Jews for the Lord's house, 2 *Jew.* 1005, &c., *Sand.* 294; the superstitious Jews thought God heard nowhere else, 3 *Tyn.* 67, 68; no idolatrous images were allowed there, *Park.* 81, 82, *Rid.* 84; there were certain figures or images therein, by divine appointment, 1 *Ful.* 182, 184; the door-keepers of the temple, 2 *Bul.* 142; the temple several times desecrated, 2 *Jew.* 994; its rebuilding, *Pil.* 3, &c.; the first temple and the second, *ib.* 126—128; their comparative glory, *ib.* 155; what the second lacked, *ib.*; under what kings it was built, *ib.* 14; the forty-six years in building, how calculated, *ib.* 13, 14; the temple defiled by Antiochus, *ib.* 88; Christ approved of the temple, 1 *Bec.* 159; how it was purged by him, 2 *Jew.* 1009, *Pil.* 5, *Sand.* 236, &c.; the use to which he required it to be restored, *Sand.* 251; the veil rent at Christ's crucifixion, 2 *Bul.* 259, 1 *Cov.* 75; the temple destroyed, as he foretold, *Bale* 611, 2 *Bul.* 259, 2 *Jew.* 994, *Sand.* 347, 348; attempt of the Jews to restore it in the days of Constantine, 4 *Jew.* 1074; Julian's attempt to rebuild it miraculously frustrated, 2 *Bul.* 260, *Calf.* 115, 121, 123, 2 *Jew.* 648, 978, 2 *Lat.* 48

The spiritual temple or house of God, 3 *Bec.* 608, 3 *Bul.* 225, 4 *Bul.* 82, *Pil.* 65, 66, 2 *Tyn.* 210, 211; God's house,—general and particular; i. e. the whole company of Christians, and each particular man, *Pil.* 65; Christians, or the people of God, are his temple, 1 *Lat.* 24, 1 *Tyn.* 438; the temple was a figure of the church, 4 *Bul.* 82, *Sand.* 240, 371, 2 *Whitg.* 94; its desolation and restoration an emblem of the corruption and reformation of the church, 2 *Jew.* 986, &c., *Pil.*

277, 278; building the house of God,—what it consists in, *Pil.* 3, 7, 62, 73; it must be built as God commands, *ib.* 78, 79; God's delight in the building of it, *ib.* 68; all are required to build it, *ib.* 66, 94, 378; its building promoted by David, Cyrus, Constantine, &c., *ib.* 8; troubles are to be expected in building it, *ib.* 396, &c.; but the builders of it need not fear want, *ib.* 150, 154, 155; they are blessed of God, *ib.* 184; negligence in building it, *ib.* 11, 13, 90; vain excuses for such negligence, *ib.* 32, 42; men build their own houses rather than God's, *ib.* 83; its building hindered by sin, *ib.* 40; all that build it not sleep in sin, *ib.* 116

The soul of a Christian man is the temple of God, 1 *Bec.* 159; the bodies of the elect are the temple of the Holy Ghost, *Hutch.* 204—(*v.* Holy Ghost); whether a man can be both the temple of God and the temple of the devil, 1 *Cran.* 216, 217, 218

God dwells not in temples made with hands, *Bale* 149, 169, 211, 611, *Calf.* 131, 1 *Tyn.* 382, 438, 3 *Tyn.* 63 (*v.* Churches)

The temple in the Apocalypse; John measures it, *Bale* 384; the temple opened in heaven, *ib.* 402, 474; none in the New Jerusalem, *ib.* 610

In what temple Antichrist shall sit, 2 *Jew.* 916; and see Antichrist.

Temporalty: *v.* Church, I. xi., Laymen, Magistrates.

Tempsis: the Thames, *Park.* 250

Temptation: *v.* Adversity, Prayers, Satan.

What it is, 3 *Bec.* 608, *Now.* (103); why God sends or permits it, 2 *Bec.* 191, &c.; how God's temptations differ from those of Satan, 2 *Bec.* 185, 186, 4 *Bul.* 217; temptation to evil cannot proceed from God, 1 *Ful.* 561, &c.; those with which he proves us are tokens of his good-will, 2 *Bec.* 193, 1 *Cov.* 516, 1 *Lat.* 434; what temptations are to the godly, and what to the wicked, 1 *Brad.* 135; temptation is a good and necessary thing, 1 *Lat.* 433; appointed by God, *ib.* 466; sent for our profit, *ib.* 435; it never ceases, *ib.* 226; the danger of being continually assaulted with it, 2 *Hoop.* 305; it is of two kinds, 1 *Lat.* 437; the temptations of prosperity, 2 *Bec.* 186; those of adversity, *ib.* 188, &c.; the former more dangerous than the latter, *ib.* 187; temptations of the devil respecting the sacraments, 1 *Hoop.* 530; remedies against temptations of all kinds, 1 *Bec.* 404, &c., 1 *Cov.* 517, *Phil.* 258, *Pra. B.* 153; God can make the temptations of the devil, the world, and the flesh, light if we ask his help, 2 *Bec.* 193; why we pray against temptation, 1 *Brad.* 135, 183, *Now.* (80), 201, and see p. 626, col. 2; he will not suffer us to be tempted above what we can bear, 1 *Lat.* 436, 2 *Lat.* 141; those blessed who endure temptation; verses by Jo. Davies, *Poet.* 245; it should be an occasion of virtue, 1 *Cov.* 518; what is to be done if we be overcome, 2 *Bec.* 194, 195; accustomed sinners are not much tempted, 1 *Lat.* 441

Tenants: *v.* Landlords.

Hardly dealt with, 1 *Lat.* 317; advice to them as to behaviour to their landlords, 2 *Tyn.* 21, 59

Tenbury, co. Worc.: Sutton in this parish, 2 *Lat.* 416 n

Tender (To): to treat with tenderness, 1 *Brad.* 103, 404, 2 *Brad.* 99

Tenebræ: ceremonies on Tenebræ Wednesday, i.e. Wednesday in Holy Week, *Calf.* 300; why the Virgin's candle was not extinguished, 3 *Tyn.* 39 n

Tenison (Tho.), abp of Canterbury: Disc. of Idolatry, *Calf.* 66 n., 366 n

Tentation: an essaying, 1 *Cov.* 29

Tenterden, co. Kent: steeple said to be the cause of Goodwin sands, 1 *Lat.* 251, 3 *Tyn.* 77, 78; the grammar-school, *Park.* 170

Tenths: *v.* First-fruits.

Tenure: *v.* Knight-service.

Teraphim: what, 2 *Bul.* 135, *Calf.* 32

Terasius: *v.* Tharasius.

Terence: cited, 1 *Bec.* 276, 2 *Bec.* 102, 3 *Bec.* 243, 374, 598, 599, 1 *Hoop.* 370, 2 *Hoop.* 554, *Hutch.* 140, 141, 149, 3 *Jew.* 136, 543, 4 *Jew.* 627, 1 *Lat.* 124, 287, *Park.* 123, *Pil.* 349, 400, 495, *Sand.* 108, 168, 3 *Whitg.* 500, 1 *Zur.* 139

Terentianus (Jul.): *v.* Santerentianus.

Terentius, a Roman captain: his request to Valens, *Pil.* 324, 660

Termin: used for Thermopylæ, 1 *Hoop.* 356

Terminus a quo, and terminus ad quem: 1 *Cran.* 331

Terms (Law): when they began and ended, and on what days the judges did not sit, *Lit. Edw.* 364, *Lit. Eliz.* 45, 443, *Pra. Eliz.* 234

Termuth: Pharaoh's daughter, *Poet.* 130

Terouane, or Therouenne: taken by stratagem, 3 *Zur.* 683 n

Tertullian:
  i. *His Life and Works.*
  ii. *Of God and Christ.*
  iii. *Scripture, Truth, Doctrine.*
  iv. *Tradition.*

TERTULLIAN

v. *The Church.*
vi. *Sacraments, Baptism.*
vii. *The Eucharist.*
viii. *Worship, Ceremonies.*
ix. *Fasting, Marriage.*
x. *Confession, &c., Persecution.*
xi. *The Soul, or Future State.*
xii. *Images, the Cross.*
xiii. *Heresies.*
xiv. *Civil Power, Heathenism, &c.*

i. *His Life and Works:* he was a married priest, 2 *Jew.* 727, 1128; burned incense in private, but not as idolaters did, *Park.* 88, *Rid.* 90; fell into heresy on some points, *Rid.* 163, 3 *Jew.* 133; but in many respects was catholic, 3 *Jew.* 335, 337; his works, *Calf.* 417, 2 *Ful.* 410, *Jew.* xlii, 3 *Whitg.* xxxii; his writings and sentiments, 3 *Zur.* 229; his rule of faith, or creed, 1 *Brad.* 371, 1 *Bul.* 28, 29, 2 *Hoop.* 538, *Whita.* 484, 1 *Whitg.* 217; a valuable note on his Apology referred to, *Calf.* 188 n.; De Corona Militis, *ib.* 195 n., *Whita.* 600, 1 *Zur.* 85; De Jejunio, *Whita.* 665; De Monogamia, 2 *Ful.* 113; De Pallio, 2 *Whitg.* 23, 24, 1 *Zur.* 160 n., 351; Liber de Trinitate, an abridgement of a book of his by Novatian, 3 *Bul.* 129 n.; Cyprian's high opinion of him, *Rid.* 37; he is accused by Papists of writing carelessly, *ib.* 38; the scripture to be followed, not his authority, 1 *Hoop.* 29

ii. *Of God, and Christ:* he declares that concerning God, and those things that are of him and in him, the mind of man is not able to conceive, &c., 3 *Bul.* 127, 128; other passages from Novatian's abridgement of his book on the Trinity, *ib.* 126, 129, 141, 142, 176, 177, 252, 310, 324, 325; he teaches that for God to be able to do anything is for him to will so to do, and that for him to be unable, is for him to be unwilling, 1 *Bul.* 436, 1 *Hoop.* 168; observes that we are not to believe that God hath done all things because he can do them, 2 *Jew.* 583; uses various similitudes in illustration of the sonship of Christ, and the procession of the Holy Spirit, 3 *Bul.* 166, 167; thinks that all things in the Old Testament were done of God through the Son, *ib.* 143; refers Psa. cx. 3 to our Lord's immaculate conception, 1 *Cov.* 55; states that Christ is not a name, but an appellation, meaning Anointed, 3 *Bul.* 289; affirms that our Lord was 30 years old at his death, 4 *Jew.* 695, *Whita.* 665; his reflections on the ascension of Christ, 2 *Cov.* 166; he says that he sent the power of the Holy Ghost as his vicar, 1 *Jew.* 379; relates that Tiberius desired Christ to be worshipped as a god, *Pil.* 141, 683; sometimes uses dangerous language concerning God and Christ, *Coop.* 147; tells how the heathen painted the God of the Christians, 2 *Jew.* 1026

iii. *Scripture, Truth, Doctrine* (see iv.): he calls the scripture a rule of faith, *Whita.* 27; says, we are not permitted to indulge our own will in anything...we have the apostles of the Lord for our authors, 3 *Bec.* 391, 403, 4 *Bul.* 151, *Calf.* 27, 2 *Cran.* 22, *Whita.* 690; refers to the several epistles of St Paul as authorities, 4 *Jew.* 1043; denies that the apostles practised reserve, 3 *Jew.* 439, *Whita.* 668, 673; warns that there is nothing else to be believed after Christ's gospel once published, 2 *Cran.* 22, 56; remarks that we need search no farther than Christ, *ib.* 22; states that there is no certainty (that the angels have a bodily substance) because the scripture declares it not, *ib.* 23; remarks that scripture is in no such peril as to need help from reasoning lest it should contradict itself, *Whita.* 492; exclaims, Arise, O truth, expound thine own scriptures, *ib.*; asserts that the fewer places of scripture should be interpreted by the more, 1 *Bul.* 79, 1 *Jew.* 237, 3 *Jew.* 227; speaks of meeting to hear the scriptures, and of its advantages, 1 *Jew.* 336, 2 *Jew.* 898, 1059, 4 *Jew.* 857; intimates that faith is fed by the public reading of the scriptures, 2 *Jew.* 1081, 4 *Jew.* 857, 3 *Whitg.* 46 & corrig.; says, by the word of God we feed our faith, stir our hope, and strengthen our confidence, 4 *Jew.* 769; observes that scripture discloses the frauds of heretics, 1 *Jew.* 85 (see corrig.), 2 *Jew.* 696, 4 *Jew.* 767; describes heretics as shunners of the light of scripture, and everywhere (while a catholic) asserts the perfection and authority of scripture, *Whita.* 690; praises the fulness of scripture, *ib.* 689; his opinion on the epistle from Laodicea, *ib.* 304; he ascribes the epistle to the Hebrews to Barnabas, 1 *Ful.* 31, *Whita.* 106; says the autograph books of the apostles were preserved in his time, *Whita.* 311; mentions a priest of Asia who feigned a writing in the name of Paul, 2 *Ful.* 339; speaks of truth as a stranger in the world, 3 *Jew.* 154; says that she fears nothing but to be hid, *ib.* 204; declares truth requires but this, that no man condemn her before he know her, *ib.* 160; says of the wicked, they love to be igno-

TERTULLIAN

rant, they do not wish to know that which they hate, *ib.* 123; affirms that μετανοία means change of mind, 1 *Ful.* 155, 437, 443; says faith saves, not knowledge or expertness in scripture, *Whita.* 241; asks, What thing owe I, except the blood which the Son of God shed for me? 2 *Jew.* 163; says that we are washed in the passion of the Lord, see in vi. below; declares that, in order that we might be certified that we are the children of God, he hath sent the Holy Ghost into our hearts, crying, Abba, Father, 3 *Jew.* 245; often insists on the superior purity of a Christian's life, 2 *Jew.* 1033; says a Christian man ought not (only) to speak honourably, but to live honourably, 4 *Jew.* 661; describes patience, 2 *Bul.* 86, 87; censures vain curiosity, and unprofitable questions, 3 *Whitg.* 574

iv. *Tradition* (see iii.): he distinguishes between scripture and tradition, *Whita.* 499; passages on tradition and custom, *Calf.* 265, 266; he refers to some who believe without the scriptures, that they may believe against the scriptures, 1 *Jew.* 24, 25, 3 *Jew.* 597; shews how custom prevails over truth, and remarks that Christ said not "I am custom," but, "I am the truth," *Calf.* 280, 1 *Jew.* 205; declares that whatever savoureth against the truth is heresy, though it be an old custom, 3 *Bec.* 391, 398, 2 *Cran.* 50, 3 *Jew.* 211, 4 *Jew.* 778, *Whita.* 612, 2 *Whitg.* 227; says, whatever was first, is true, whatever afterwards, is spurious, 1 *Brad.* 544, *Coop.* 62, 2 *Cran.* 23, 1 *Jew.* 2, 25, 79, 320, 3 *Jew.* 350; declares that we are washed in the passion of the Lord, 1 *Jew.* 488, 521, 2 *Jew.* 1000, 3 *Jew.* 445, 4 *Jew.* 1042, *Park.* 93, *Rid.* 94, 105, 158, 2 *Whitg.* 225, 226, *Whita.* 601; refers to heretics as not to be disputed with out of scripture, *Whita.* 440, 441, 3 *Zur.* 229; said (while yet a catholic) that we should dispute against heretics out of tradition, not out of scripture, *Whita.* 601; calls the articles of faith an old tradition, 2 *Jew.* 673; speaks of various usages not commanded in scripture, *Calf.* 263, 264, 1 *Whitg.* 216; affirms that custom is the author of various traditional observances, 2 *Cran.* 56; when he became a Montanist he advocated various traditions, *Whita.* 599; enumerates various traditions asserted to be apostolical, but which are not so regarded by Papists, *ib.* 600, 666; explains the "deposit" committed to Timothy, *ib.* 556

v. *The Church* (see x.): he likens the ship (Matt. viii. 23) to the church, *Sand.* 371; terms the church a pure virgin, 4 *Jew.* 1040; calls Jerusalem the mother and the spring of religion, 1 *Jew.* 280, 353; speaks of doctrine which was most holy in the apostles' churches, 2 *Ful.* 131; says that what the apostles preached should not otherwise be proved than through those churches which they founded, *Whita.* 324, 3 *Zur.* 230; teaches that all true churches derive their succession from the apostles and apostolic men, as Smyrna from Polycarp placed there by John, and Rome from Clement appointed by Peter, 4 *Bul.* 31, 32, 2 *Ful.* 75, 238, 3 *Jew.* 321, 325; advises to behold the apostolic churches where the apostles' chairs are still continued, and their authentic writings openly pronounced, 4 *Jew.* 1043, 1044; refers to many great churches derived from that which was planted by the apostles, 1 *Jew.* 367, 4 *Jew.* 1044; by the rock he understood Peter himself, 4 *Bul.* 81, 2 *Ful.* 281, 282; on the charge to Peter, whether personal, 2 *Ful.* 136; considers that the power given to Peter belongs to spiritual men, either to an apostle, or to a prophet, *ib.* 282, 291; repeatedly praises the church of Rome as that to which apostles gave their doctrine, and that where they suffered, 4 *Bul.* 32, *Calf.* 267, 2 *Jew.* 898, 4 *Jew.* 1043; speaks of authority being received from the church of Rome, 4 *Jew.* 1044; charges the bishop of Rome with favouring certain heresies, *ib.* 926; mentions the spread of the gospel through many nations, including the places of the Britons inaccessible to the Romans, 1 *Jew.* 305, 3 *Jew.* 165, 200, *Pil.* 511; mentions bishops, priests, and deacons, 2 *Whitg.* 205; refers to Polycarp and Clement as having been made bishops by the apostles, *ib.* 119, 138, 428 (see above); calls the bishop the highest priest, 3 *Jew.* 380, 4 *Jew.* 823, 2 *Whitg.* 310, 311, 3 *Whitg.* 64, 72; says that any bishop who walks not in his fathers' steps is to be counted a bastard, *Pil.* 485, 597; remarks on this passage, *ib.* 604; speaks of approved elders presiding, having obtained that honour, not by money, &c., 4 *Jew.* 912; he is the first writer who is known to have applied the term "papa" to a Christian minister, 2 *Tyn.* 259 n., 2 *Whitg.* 86 n.; says that though there be but three together, and though they be laymen, yet there is a church, 3 *Jew.* 335, 336; says, in touching the brethren's knees, we touch Christ, 2 *Jew.* 760; refers to the love of Christians towards each other as noticed by the heathen, *ib.* 1072, 1089; calls Christians a sect, 3 *Jew.* 212, 595; in what sense, *ib.* 214; speaks of one Caius Seius, a Christian, 2 *Jew.* 1089; affirms that all Christians are priests, 3 *Jew.* 335, 336, 4 *Jew.* 984

vi. *Sacraments, Baptism:* he acknowledges but two sacraments, properly so called, 4 *Bul.* 246, *Calf.* 223, 3 *Jew.* 459; calls the helve wherewith Elijah recovered the axe out of the water, the "sacrament of wood," *ib.* 457; says it behoved the sacrament of (Christ's) death to be figured in preaching (under the law), *Calf.* 116; calls Christian religion a sacrament, 2 *Jew.* 1103; shews that Satan counterfeits the divine sacraments in his idol service, *Calf.* 13; calls baptism a divine substance, 3 *Jew.* 508; declares that they who understand the weight of baptism will fear the getting of it more than the delaying, 4 *Jew.* 894; says the chief priest, that is, the bishop, has authority to give baptism, 3 *Jew.* 380, 4 *Jew.* 823; declares that priests and deacons may baptize by the authority of the bishop, 3 *Whitg.* 64, 72; allows that laymen may baptize, 2 *Whitg.* 526; affirms that women may not teach or baptize, 4 *Bul.* 370, 2 *Whitg.* 535; speaks of Easter and Pentecost as the special times for baptism, 1 *Whitg.* 513; mentions the exorcism of infants, 1 *Zur.* 178 n; says that before persons were baptized they renounced the devil, his pomp and his angels, answering more than the Lord prescribed, 1 *Whitg.* 216; refers to trine immersion, 2 *Bec.* 227, 3 *Bul.* 161, 4 *Bul.* 357, 364, 1 *Whitg.* 216; refers to crossing in baptism, 3 *Whitg.* 125; says the flesh is signed, that the soul may be defended, the flesh is overshadowed by the imposition of hands, *Calf.* 224, *Whita.* 591; speaks of the use of milk and honey, and various other superstitious practices, 4 *Bul.* 359, *Calf.* 213, 270, 2 *Cran.* 56, 2 *Ful.* 161, 3 *Whitg.* 125; calls baptism the seal of faith, 3 *Whitg.* 113; affirms that the holy angel of God is present at it, 2 *Jew.* 741, 742; says the Holy Ghost comes down and hallows the water, 1 *Jew.* 466, 2 *Jew.* 763

vii. *The Eucharist:* he says that bread and wine were figures in the Old Testament, and so taken in the prophets, and now be figures again in the New Testament, and so used of Christ himself in his last supper, 1 *Cran.* 119, 120; on Melchisedec, and his bread and wine, 2 *Jew.* 731; he styles the sacrament the Lord's banquet, 3 *Bec.* 388; terms it the sacrament of the eucharist, or thanksgiving, 1 *Jew.* 150; calls it hospitalitatis contesseratio, *ib.* 145; how he understood the words of institution, 2 *Hoop.* 48, 472, 500; he calls bread a figure of Christ's body, 1 *Cran.* 119, 120, 121, (58), *Rid.* 173; declares that Christ refused not bread, but by it represented his body, 2 *Bec.* 285, 3 *Bec.* 435, 1 *Cran.* 119, 154, (58), *Grin.* 69, 1 *Hoop.* 227, 2 *Hoop.* 439, *Hutch.* 272, 1 *Jew.* 150, 2 *Jew.* 611, 3 *Jew.* 453, *Rid.* 38; says, in many places, that Christ called bread his body, 1 *Cran.* 33, 104, (54); affirms that Christ made bread his body by saying, "This is my body," i. e. a figure of my body, and argues that if Christ had not a true body, the bread would not be a figure, 2 *Bec.* 285, 3 *Bec.* 271, 369, 435, 1 *Brad.* 589, 4 *Bul.* 439, *Coop.* 202, 1 *Cran.* 106, 119, 154, 194, (58), *Grin.* 64, 65, 195, 198, 1 *Hoop.* 231, 2 *Hoop.* 439, 528, *Hutch.* 259, 1 *Jew.* 258, 447, 456, 517, 2 *Jew.* 567, 592, 600—611, 624, 759, 790, 1112, 3 *Jew.* 169, 243, 453, 468, 497, 502, 512, 4 *Jew.* 765, *Rid.* 37, 160, 162, 232, *Sand.* 453, 3 *Tyn.* 259; writes, he made the bread his body, i. e. he consecrated it to be a representation of his body, 1 *Hoop.* 232; is alleged to affirm that in the sacrament we eat the body and drink the blood of our Saviour Jesus Christ, 1 *Cran.* 153, 154, (67); says the flesh is fed with the body and blood, &c., *Coop.* 139; on Jo. vi. he affirms that Christ must be devoured by hearing, chewed by understanding, and digested by faith, 1 *Jew.* 452, 2 *Jew.* 572, 1119, 3 *Jew.* 486, 533, 3 *Tyn.* 228 n.; declares that Jesus hath another body than bread, for bread was not given for us, but the very true body of Christ was given upon the cross; which body was exhibited in the supper under the figure of bread, *Grin.* 71; calls the Lord's supper a sacrifice, *Coop.* 89; testifies that in his time the eucharist was administered in the morning, and only by those who were chief, 1 *Whitg.* 216, 237; says it was not usual to receive the bread of the Lord except from the hands of the presidents, *Rid.* 181, 183; mentions the common supper after the communion, 2 *Bec.* 251, 4 *Bul.* 423, 424; his exhortation to his wife, in which he mentions the case of a Christian woman, who, being married to a heathen, received the sacrament every morning secretly before meat, *Coop.* 23, 124, *Grin.* 47, 48, 1 *Jew.* 6, 148, 149, 150, 241, 2 *Jew.* 554, 610, 611

viii. *Worship, Ceremonies:* he expounds

the sacrifice prophesied of by Malachi, 1 *Jew.* 110, 124, 2 *Jew.* 712, 723; says we keep the sabbath not every seventh day, but every day, 1 *Jew.* 128; describes the manner of prayer amongst Christians in his time, 4 *Bul.* 136, *Calf.* 309; as to praying for the emperor, see in xiv. below; he calls the Lord's prayer a lawful prayer, *Pra. B.* xxxii; refers to certain songs used in the church in his day, *Whita.* 261; speaks of praises and thanksgivings proceeding from a pure heart, 4 *Bul.* 224; refers to certain orders of which there is no law out of the scripture, 1 *Whitg.* 216, 237 (see iv. above); allows that matters of discipline may be altered, 1 *Whitg.* 217, 2 *Whitg.* 226; reproves some for sitting after prayer, 2 *Whitg.* 449; mentions praying toward the East, 4 *Jew.* 708; says, let them that have no (spiritual) light, burn their tapers daily, 3 *Jew.* 178; thought it wicked to fast or kneel on Sundays, &c., *Calf.* 257, 1 *Whitg.* 223; refers to stations, 2 *Ful.* 238; speaks of "stationum semijejunia," *ib.* 183 n.; mistakenly cited about processions, *Calf.* 296; speaks against the notion of the holiness of places, *Pil.* 63; cited to shew that the dead were buried by ministers with prayer, 3 *Whitg.* 363

ix. *Fasting, Marriage:* he declares that God is not honoured with the belly nor with meats, 3 *Jew.* 528; admonishes to fast without compulsion, according as every man shall see time and cause, as the apostles did, *ib.* 438; being a Montanist, he blames the catholics for saying that men should fast of their own choice, not by command, *Whita.* 665, 666; considers it wicked to fast on Sundays, *Calf.* 257, 1 *Whitg.* 223; on the text " a sister, a wife " (1 Cor. ix. 5), he argues that the latter word should be rendered "woman," 1 *Ful.* 474 n.; he says that sons should not marry without consent of parents, *Sand.* 455; asks, what heathen can without mistrust suffer his Christian wife to be put away from him at the Easter prayers, 3 *Jew.* 405; condemns second marriages, 1 *Bec.* 279, *Rog.* 262; censures marriage altogether, 1 *Jew.* 157, 3 *Jew.* 388; refers to bishops among the catholics who had married two wives successively, 3 *Jew.* 407 (as to marriage, see also xiv. below); condemns fornication, 4 *Jew.* 647

x. *Confession, &c., Persecution:* he describes exomologesis or confession, 3 *Bul.* 76, 1 *Ful.* 457 n.; speaks of kneeling before the presbyters and the altar of God in penance, 1 *Ful.* 433; speaks of a key endued by Christ, 3 *Jew.* 373; declares the key to be the interpretation of the law, 1 *Jew.* 331, 3 *Jew.* 364, 4 *Jew.* 1134; alleged on excommunication, 3 *Whitg.* 252; he speaks of false charges against the ancient Jews, 3 *Jew.* 154; mentions similar charges against the early Christians, and refers to infamous names applied to them, and the rage of the people against them, 2 *Hoop.* 375 n., 376, 2 *Jew.* 1027, 3 *Jew.* 154, 214, 4 *Jew.* 664, 708; calls the heathens' cruelty the Christians' glory, 3 *Jew.* 189, 4 *Jew.* 770, 859; says, the more we are cut down, the more we become, and refers to the blood of Christians as a seed, 1 *Bec.* 274, 2 *Ful.* 234 n., 2 *Jew.* 1031, 3 *Jew.* 189, 595, 596, 4 *Jew.* 770, 859, *Pil.* 144 n., *Sand.* 283, 284, 1 *Whitg.* 381; on fleeing from city to city, 2 *Jew.* 808

xi. *The Soul, a Future State:* his opinion of the soul, 3 *Bul.* 374; he affirms that souls separated do not return again to this world, *ib.* 401; denies that the soul of any saint, much less the soul of a prophet, can be fetched up by the devil, *ib.* 403; speaks of Abraham's bosom, 1 *Ful.* 293, 295, 296; mentions prayers and oblations for the dead, 2 *Ful.* 238 (see Montanists, in xiii. below); writes on the resurrection, 2 *Cov.* 186 n.; says that resurrection is not properly spoken of anything, save of that which fell, 1 *Bul.* 141, 2 *Cov.* 167; shews that the body shall be partaker with the soul in judgment, of that whereof in this life it had been partaker with the soul, 2 *Brad.* 333; refers to the Elysian fields and the infernal regions, *Calf.* 14 n

xii. *Images, the Cross:* he expounds the second commandment, *Calf.* 371; says God forbade the substance of idolatry, 3 *Jew.* 507; affirms that he has forbidden an idol, as well to be made as to be worshipped, &c., 4 *Jew.* 794; expounds St John's caution against idols, 1 *Ful.* 194, *Park.* 83, *Rid.* 86; shews that in his time Christians abhorred images, 1 *Hoop.* 43, *Park.* 86, *Rid.* 88; his use of the word "simulacrum," 1 *Ful.* 102; he speaks of the brazen serpent, 2 *Jew.* 646, 647; refers to the letter tau or T, as like the cross, *Calf.* 106, 2 *Ful.* 147; speaks of the continual use of the sign of the cross in his day, *Calf.* 257, 2 *Jew.* 648, 3 *Whitg.* 126

xiii. *Heresies* (see iii, iv): he calls philosophers the patriarchs of heretics, 2 *Bul.* 407, 3 *Bul.* 124, 1 *Jew.* 334; warns that heresy should be avoided as a deadly fever, *Whita.* 17; says a heretic assaults the faith by the same words of God that breed the faith, 4 *Jew.* 752; declares that the doctrine of heretics, compared with the apostles' doctrine, will pronounce sentence against itself, 4 *Bul.* 32, 33, 3 *Jew.* 236, 4 *Jew.* 892; says heretics, conscious of their own weakness, never proceed in due order, 2 *Jew.* 629; observes that they persuade first, and teach afterwards, 1 *Jew.* 101; says they would provoke us to play the rhetorician, 3 *Jew.* 133; disallows disputation with them on the scriptures, see in iv. above; declares that by their conjectures they draw bare words whither they list, 2 *Jew.* 593; speaks of certain antitrinitarian heretics, *Rog.* 45; referred to on Apelles, *ib.* 81, 82; on Basilides, *ib.* 57; on the heresy of Cerdon, *Whita.* 34; he says the Cerdonites thought that the Jewish ceremonies were to be observed by Christians, *Rog.* 314; speaks of the Docetæ, 1 *Cov.* 21 n.; on Hermogenes, *Rog.* 99; he says the Hermogenians allowed a man to have many wives at the same time, *ib.* 307; referred to on Marcion and his sect, *ib.* 40, 163, *Whita.* 34; he says they condemned marriage, *Rog.* 261, and denied the sacraments to married persons, *ib.* 265, 266; says that the Montanists thought that the Holy Ghost uttered greater things in Montanus than Christ uttered in the gospel, 4 *Jew.* 760; shews that they held a purging of souls after this life, *Rog.* 214 n.; his reply to Praxeas, who alleged God's omnipotence, 1 *Jew.* 490, 2 *Jew.* 798; refers to the Valentinian heresy, 4 *Jew.* 926, *Rog.* 52

xiv. *Civil power, Heathenism, &c.*: he calls Rome Babylon, 2 *Ful.* 371; considers the Roman state to be the hinderer of the revelation of Antichrist, 2 *Jew.* 913; speaks of the honour due to the emperor, *ib.* 997, 4 *Jew.* 705, 975; declares him to be next to God, *Grin.* 12, 3 *Whitg.* 591; testifies that Christians prayed for the emperor, 1 *Bul.* 390, *Calf.* 308, 309, *Sand.* 80, 3 *Whitg.* 590; says, we sacrifice for the emperor with a pure prayer, 2 *Jew.* 725; says that when Marcus Aurelius was at war with the Germans, the prayers of the Christian soldiers obtained showers of rain, 1 *Bul.* 382; addresses the heathen Romans on their professed veneration of their forefathers, 3 *Jew.* 179; reproves them for making the divinity of their gods dependent on their own pleasure, 1 *Jew.* 217, 3 *Jew.* 264, 4 *Jew.* 901, *Whita.* 706; notices offerings made to heathen deities, 2 *Whitg.* 36, as the consecration of bread, *ib.* 39; says the devil imitates the sacraments in the mysteries of idols, *Calf.* 13; censures Christians for taking part in heathen festivals, 2 *Whitg.* 444; calls the upper garments of the heathen priests infulas, 2 *Ful.* 113; shews that Christians changed their apparel on changing their religion, 2 *Whitg.* 23, 24; inquires whether it be lawful for the servant of God to communicate with whole nations, in apparel, &c., 3 *Jew.* 616, 617; declares that a Christian man ought not to go with a laurel garland upon his head, like the heathens, *ib.* 616; says to the heathen, we have been of your company; men be made, and not born Christians, 4 *Jew.* 871; refers to a fault of conversation, not of preaching, 4 *Jew.* 701; observes that thieves always leave something behind them to be known by, 1 *Jew.* 190

Testament (New): *v.* Bible.

Testaments: *v.* Covenants, Wills.

Tester: a sixpence, 1 *Lat.* 137 n.; why so called, *ib.*

Teston, Testoon, or Testourn: a coin, 1 *Lat.* 137, 3 *Zur.* 727 n

Testwood (Rob.): martyred, 3 *Zur.* 242 n

Tetragrammaton: 3 *Bul.* 130, *Calf.* 284, *Grin.* 41

Tetzel (Jo.): dealer in indulgences, 3 *Jew.* 193, 194

Teutonic Knights: *v.* Knights.

Teutonicus (Jo.): *v.* Joannes.

Teversham, co. Cambr.: Whitgift rector, 3 *Whitg.* vii, xi.

Teviotdale, Scotland: the English ravage it, 1 *Zur.* 225 n

Tewkesbury, co. Glouc.: 2 *Lat.* 405

Tewkesbury (Jo.): mentioned, 2 *Lat.* 306 n.; charged with possessing and reading Tyndale's works, and finally burnt, 1 *Tyn.* 32, his examination, *ib.* 42—124, nn

Textor (J.), Ravisius: Officina, *Jew.* xliii; he writes of women who came in men's apparel to hear Plato, 4 *Jew.* 651; speaks of pope Joan, *ib.* 655, 656; says John XII. was slain in adultery, *ib.* 702; mentions the poisoning of Victor III. in the chalice, *ib.* 687

Teynham, co. Kent: called Tenam, 3 *Cran.* 312, and Denham, 313

Θ: *v.* Thau.

Th. (Jo.): signature attached to a prayer, 1585, *Lit. Eliz.* 582

Thacker: a thatcher, *Pil.* 381

Thacker (R.): notice of him, *Poet.* xl; a godly ditty, to be sung for the preservation of the queen's reign, *ib.* 420

Thaddeus: Jude so called, 4 *Bul.* 66; the Gospel of Thaddeus, *Bale* 314, *Rog.* 82

Thalassius, bp of Cæsarea: condemned for heresy, 3 *Jew.* 145, 4 *Jew.* 1022

Thales: believed in one God, *Hutch.* 176; gazing upon the skies fell into a pit, *Sand.* 392

Thames, river: *Park.* 250, 2 *Whitg.* 241

Thameseidos: a poem by E. W., 1600; notice thereof, *Poet.* xxxii; lines therefrom, *ib.* 358

Thanksgiving: *v.* Sacrifice.

Of thanksgiving, 4 *Bul.* 220; what it is, 3 *Bec.* 604, 620, 4 *Bul.* 163, 164, *Now.* (82, 83), 203, 204, *Sand.* 77; it is due only to God, 4 *Bul.* 221; should be perpetually given to him, 1 *Bec.* 115; it is to be rendered in all things, 2 *Jew.* 879; God requires it of us for his benefits, 1 *Bec.* 185; to be given through Christ, 4 *Bul.* 221; how we may be moved to it, 1 *Bec.* 176, &c.; God's benefits should move us to thankfulness, *ib.* 178; the sacrifice of thanksgiving, *ib.* 185, 186, 4 *Bul* 223; God desires this, and not bloody sacrifices, 1 *Bec.* 372; the creatures of God are sanctified by thanksgiving, 4 *Bul.* 268; exhortation to it, 1 *Bec.* 187; the grievous sin of unthankfulness, *Sand.* 156

Thanksgivings: *v.* Prayers, Psalms, iv.

Communis gratiarum actio pro cognitione donorum Dei accepta, *Pra. Eliz.* 208; the same, with the title, pro divinis in nos donis et beneficiis, *ib.* 398; for all God's benefits, 3 *Bec.* 68, 85, 1 *Brad.* 245, *Lit. Edw.* 475, *Pra. B.* 147; a general thanksgiving, *Pra. Eliz.* 546; a thanksgiving to God the Father, the Son, and the Holy Ghost, *Pra. B.* 123; the blessing and thanksgiving of Toby the elder, *Lit. Edw.* 478; thanksgiving appended to the Christmas Banquet, 1 *Bec.* 84

Childbirth: for the deliverance of a woman with child, 3 *Bec.* 28, 29

Christ: to Christ, for his incarnation, passion, and victory, *Lit. Edw.* 481

Deliverance: for bringing us out of the darkness of men's traditions, 3 *Bec.* 65, &c.; of a faithful man from trouble, *ib.* 35

Departure: for the departure of the faithful out of this world, 3 *Bec.* 69, 70, 190, 191

Meat: *v.* Graces.

Morning: a motion to a thanksgiving in the morning, *Nord.* 152; the thanksgiving, *ib.* 154

Persecution: in time of persecution, 1 *Brad.* 205

Pestilence: for withdrawing the plague, 1563, *Lit. Eliz.* 508; another, 1564, *ib.* 513

Queen: *v.* Sovereign.

Realm: *v.* Sovereign.

Rebellion: *v.* Victory.

Recovery: revalescentis, *Pra. Eliz.* 370

Redemption: for our redemption, *Pra. B.* 88

Sermon: after sermon, 3 *Bec.* 53

Sovereign (*v.* Victory): a thanksgiving and prayer for the preservation of the queen and the realm, 1572, 1588, *Lit. Eliz.* 618

Supper of the Lord: post communionem, *Pra. Eliz.* 386; after the communion, 1 *Bec.* 120, 3 *Bec.* 55, *Pra. B.* 92, *Pra. Eliz.* 520

Tradition: *v.* Deliverance.

Victory: a prayer of thanksgiving, and for continuance of good success to her majesty's forces, 1596, *Lit. Eliz.* 668; a collect of thanksgiving, 1588, *ib.* 622; another, by the queen herself, *ib.* n

— *over rebels:* for the suppression of rebellion, 1570, *Lit. Eliz.* 538

— *over spiritual enemies:* pro devicta tentatione, *Pra. Eliz.* 369

War: *v.* Victory.

Tharasius, patr. of Constantinople: 4 *Jew.* 916, *Park.* 92, *Rid.* 93

Tharsitius: tale of his bearing our Lord's body when he attended the martyr St Stephen, 3 *Jew.* 551, 554

Thau (תו): the sign or mark mentioned by Ezekiel, 2 *Brad.* 5, *Calf.* 97, 98, 106—109, 2 *Ful.* 138, 147, 2 *Jew.* 647, *Rid.* 70, 2 *Tyn.* 13 n., 20, *Whita.* 116; the letter ת was anciently cruciform, *ib.*; Jerome's explanation of the reasons why this sign was to be made, *Calf.* 108; remarks by bp Andrewes and Corn. Curtius on the meaning of the letter, *ib.* 108, 109 n.; Calfhill says, in a mystery it betokened the death of Christ, but has no relation to the sign of the cross, *ib.* 109; mystic signification of the Hebrew ת and the Greek T and Θ, *ib.* 107

Theatines: a religious order, *Phil.* xxvii, xxviii; when and by whom founded, 4 *Jew.* 1106 n

Theatrum Crudel. Hæret.: 1 *Lat.* 250

Theban legion: 2 *Bec.* 91 n., 4 *Jew.* 1172

Thebes: destroyed by Alexander, 2 *Brad.* 372 n

Thecla: *v.* Paul.

Theft, Thieves: *v.* Commandments, Restitution.

What theft is, 2 *Bul.* 34, 1 *Hoop.* 391, 2 *Lat.* 427; who is a thief, 1 *Tyn.* 99; divers kinds of theft and thieves, 2 *Bec.* 104, 105, 2 *Bul.* 34, &c., 1 *Lat.* 139; deceitful practices are theft, 1 *Lat.* 401; it is theft to defraud the king in taxes, *ib.* 299, 300,

512; it is theft to withhold the tithes lawfully due, *ib.* 304; sacrilege is the greatest thiefdom of all, 1 *Hoop.* 395; it is theft to misuse riches, 1 *Lat.* 478; if the rich help not the poor it is theft, 1 *Tyn.* 81; the realm is full of thieving, 1 *Lat.* 512; theft forbidden by God, 1 *Brad.* 168, 2 *Bul.* 230, *Now.* (19), 133; condemned among the Gentiles, 1 *Bul.* 203; we may not steal to eat, 2 *Lat.* 15; thieves change the name of things they have stolen, 2 *Jew.* 627; thieves detected, *ib.* 628; they ought to expose their confederates, 1 *Lat* 519; thieves warned, 1 *Bec.* 126; some reproved by Latimer, 2 *Lat.* 40; theft of thirteen pence halfpenny, 1 *Lat.* 410; theft punished, 2 *Bec.* 109, 110; honest men sometimes slain for thieves in the border country, *Rid.* 398

Themistocles: 2 *Bec.* 356, 1 *Jew.* 438, 4 *Jew.* 1104, *Sand.* 36, 53, 325

Theobald, abp of Canterbury: 2 *Tyn.* 292

Theobald (......): one of the ministers of Strasburgh, 3 *Zur.* 492, 534

Theocritus : cited, 1 *Ful.* 141

Theodora, empress : 1 *Zur.* 18 n

Theodore : *v.* Theodorus.

Theodore I., pope : son of a bishop, 2 *Ful.* 98 n.; he defended images, 1 *Hoop.* 47 n

Theodore II., pope : 1 *Hoop.* 217

Theodore, abp of Canterbury : the real author of an ordinance respecting sponsors ascribed to Hyginus, *Calf.* 212 n.; his Pœnitentiale, 1 *Lat.* 54 n.; he says the Greeks and other orientals confess only to God, 1 *Jew.* 120; speaks of the pix, 2 *Jew.* 560

Theodoret: *v.* Cassiodorus.

 i. *His Life and Works.*
 ii. *On God and Christ.*
 iii. *Scripture, Doctrine.*
 iv. *Bishops.*
 v. *The Eucharist.*
 vi. *Ecclesiastical History.*
 vii. *Heresies.*
 viii. *Miscellanea.*

 i. *His Life and Works:* his persecutions, 1 *Jew.* 387, 395; opposed by the bishops of Egypt, 2 *Whitg.* 318, 319; charged with Nestorianism, but acquitted in the council of Chalcedon, 1 *Cran.* 130, 1 *Jew.* 374, 2 *Jew.* 802, *Rid.* 36; he appealed to the pope, 1 *Jew.* 386; said he governed 800 churches, and had freed them from heresy, 2 *Whitg.* 318—320, 432; speaks of his poverty, *ib.* 321; the emperors write to Dioscorus concerning him, *ib.* 318—320; his works, *Calf.* 417, 2 *Ful.* 410, *Jew.* xliii, 3 *Whitg.* xxxii; Comment. in Cantica Canticorum, of uncertain authenticity, 2 *Ful.* 287 n.; the epistles to Dioscorus and pope Leo, said by Crakanthorp to be forged, *ib.* 307 n.; he wrote (as Papists say) before the determination of the church, *Rid.* 36; his authority refused in the disputation with Cranmer at Oxford, 2 *Jew.* 571; certain leaves of his torn and cast into the fire by John Clement, 1 *Jew.* 52, 4 *Jew.* 785; words of his falsified by Harding, 3 *Jew.* 513; his credit defended, 2 *Whitg* 318

 ii. *On God, and Christ:* on the order of persons in the Holy Trinity, 3 *Bul.* 301; he shews that God will do only such things as are agreeable to his nature, 4 *Bul.* 452; declares it most absurd to say, that God hath created all things, but that he hath no care of the things which he hath made, 3 *Bul.* 178; says the fathers (before Christ) did not see the divine nature or substance, but a certain glory and certain visions which were answerable to their capacity, *ib.* 142; referred to about the Word being made flesh, 4 *Bul.* 436; on Christ's fear, or reverence (Heb.v. 7), 1 *Ful.* 325; he shews that Christ suffered in his humanity, 3 *Bul.* 269; says the body of the Lord, after the ascension, was called a body, *ib.* 259; declares that, though free from suffering when it rose, it has the same circumscription it had before, 3 *Bec.* 454; proves that it must occupy space, *ib.*; 1 *Cran.* 129, 130; extract from a dialogue of his upon Christ's coming again in the same form as that in which his disciples saw him go to heaven, 1 *Cran.* 129

 iii. *Scripture, Doctrine:* he says, in our disputations of godly matters, we have laid before us the doctrine of the holy gospel, 4 *Jew.* 1019; admonishes that we take the resolution of our questions out of the words of the Holy Ghost, *ib.*; dares not to say anything upon which scripture is silent,*Whita.* 703; says the Greek version of the scriptures was published 301 years before Christ, *ib.*118; states that the Jews sent Ptolemy the whole scripture, written in golden characters, *ib.* 119; refers to the Greek version of Aquila, *ib.* 123; testifies to the existence of many vernacular versions of scripture, 4 *Jew.* 896, *Whita.* 245; says (as is alleged) that scripture explains itself, *Whita.* 495; declares that the doctrines of the gospel were understood not only by the teachers, but by artizans, rustics, and women, 2 *Jew.* 696, 4 *Jew.* 796, 797, 1186, *Whita.* 248; speaks of the term "barbarian" as used by Paul, *Whita.*

267; argues in support of the epistle to the Hebrews, *ib.* 323; says we do not reckon the angels in the number of gods, nor divide natures without bodies into male and female, 3 *Bul.* 333; declares that the ministry of angels is the praising of God, and singing of hymns or songs, *ib.* 341; proves that the devils are justly punished, *ib.* 351; maintains justification by faith only, 2 *Cran.* 205, 3 *Jew.* 244, *Wool.* 34; applies 2 Cor. viii. 14 to the communion of saints, 2 *Ful.* 92

iv. *Bishops. &c.:* he thinks that the name of apostle in the primitive church signified bishop, 2 *Ful.* 309; calls the episcopal office ἀρχιερωσύγη, *Whitg.* 310; mentions bishops addressed as "most honourable lords," 2 *Whitg.* 386; cited in support of the pope's supremacy, 1 *Jew.* 374; he speaks of a peculiar habit of the priesthood, 1 *Zur.* 350

v. *The Eucharist:* he shews how the names of things are changed in scripture, 1 *Cran.* 127, 128, 225, (61), is a witness against transubstantiation, *Rid.* 174; what things are principally to be noted in his writings on the sacrament, *ib.* 130; long extracts from dialogues of his on this subject, *ib.* 128—130; dispute about the translation of his words, *ib.* 132, 133, 134; he says that when Christ gave the holy mysteries, he called the bread his body, and the mingled cup his blood, 3 *Bec.* 439, 1 *Cran.* 33, 105, 128, (54); declares that the Saviour hath made exchange of the names; and unto his body hath given the name of the symbol, and unto the symbol the name of his body, 3 *Jew.* 509; uses the word ἀντίτυπα for the sacrament, 2 *Hoop.* 406 n.; calls the sacrament the image or figure, and Christ's body the pattern or truth, 1 *Jew.* 548; speaks of the divine mysteries representing that which is a body indeed, 3 *Bec.* 439; states that the tokens of Christ's body and blood do, after invocation, change their names, but continue the same substance, *Phil.* 203: says that the signs are understood to be the things that they are made, and are believed and adored, &c., 1 *Jew.* 546, 2 *Jew.* 570, 3 *Jew.* 506, 508; writes, he that called himself the vine, honoured the signs and symbols which are seen, with the name of his body and blood, not changing their nature, but adding grace to nature, 2 *Bec.* 266, 288, 3 *Bec.* 424, 439, 444, 1 *Brad.* 590, 1 *Cran.* 128, 261, 299, (34), *Grin.* 71, *Hutch.* 274, 1 *Jew.* 11, 2 *Jew.* 564, 571, 3 *Jew.* 501; says the church offers the symbols of the body and blood, 1 *Jew.* 522; declares that the mystical signs do not after sanctification depart from their own nature, but remain in their former substance, 2 *Bec.* 266, 288, 3 *Bec.* 424, 1 *Cran.* 130, 132, 133, 261, 299, (34), *Grin.* 71, 2 *Hoop.* 425, *Hutch.* 274, 1 *Jew.* 517, 547, 548, 2 *Jew.* 482, 571, 776, 1066, 1116, 3 *Jew.* 482, 509, *Phil.* 183, 201, *Rid.* 35, 36, *Sand.* 89; says with Chrysostom, that the bread remains after consecration, although we call it by a more excellent name of dignity, that is to say, by the name of Christ's body, 1 *Cran.* 249, (74); shews that when Christ called the bread his body, it was to cause the receivers to lift their minds from earth to heaven, *ib.* 336; holds that the bread and wine are sacraments of Christ's body and blood, not of his divinity, *ib.* 72; calls the Lord's supper a healthful sacrament, 3 *Bec.* 388; speaks of having communion with the Lord in the sacrament, *ib.* 395 n.; speaks of gifts offered at the holy table, and of Theodosius' offering, *Pil.* 546; says that we offer not another sacrifice, but celebrate a memory of the one healthful sacrifice, 3 *Bec.* 457, 458; explains on 1 Cor. xi. 26, the words "till he come," *ib.* 370

vi. *Ecclesiastical History:* he says Christians everywhere published the victory of the cross, 2 *Jew.* 649; refers to the nails of the cross, *Calf.* 327; alleges Psellus about Peter, 2 *Ful.* 287; calls Epaphroditus an apostle, 1 *Whitg.* 497; speaks of the office of Timothy, 2 *Whitg.* 296; likewise of that of Titus, *Rog.* 329, 2 *Whitg.* 284; seems to assert that Paul preached in Britain, 1 *Jew.* 280, 305, 3 *Jew.* 128, 164; speaks of the churches of Britain, 3 *Jew.* 165; cites Ignatius, *Whita.* 571; speaks of Ephrem Syrus, 1 *Jew.* 269, 270; praises the emperor Constantine, 4 *Jew.* 1016; relates his threat to repress errors, *ib.* 675, 964, 1018, 1031; records his declaration that he would hide the faults of the clergy, 2 *Bec.* 333 n.; relates some particulars respecting the council of Nice, 1 *Bec.* 358, 412, 4 *Jew.* 999, 1000, 1004, 1014—1016; records Constantine's address and instructions to the council, 3 *Jew.* 227, *Whita.* 678, 679; tells how he rebuked the bishops for their quarrels, 1 *Bul.* 327, 328; mentions the hypocrisy of Leontius, bishop of Antioch, *Sand.* 183; states that Vitus and Vincentius were sent to the council of Nice by the pope, 4 *Jew.* 1000, 1003; numbers but 20 canons of this council, 2 *Whitg.* 151; reports an epistle of the council to the church of Egypt, 1 *Whitg.* 408; says the Arians besought the emperor Constantius to summon another council at Milan, 4 *Jew.* 1005; states that Athanasius refused to come to the council of Cæsarea, though summoned by the emperor, *ib.* 951, 1100; relates how he was charged and cleared, 1 *Bec.* 18 n., *Sand.* 129; tells of the baptism of Constantine, 2 *Jew.* 1107; mentions proceedings of emperors in establishing true religion, 2 *Bec.* 305 n.; speaks of councils at Constantinople and Rome, 4 *Jew.* 1000, 1001; says that Hosius, bishop of Corduba in Spain, not by right of his place, but for the worthiness of his person, was appointed president in the council of Sardica, *ib.* 1003; gives an account of the judgment of pope Julius in the case of Eusebius and Athanasius, 1 *Jew.* 386; speaks of a golden cope sold by Cyril of Jerusalem, 2 *Whitg.* 23, 24; tells that Constans wrote a menacing letter to his brother Constantius on behalf of the Christians, *Sand.* 109; speaks of the council of Ariminum, 3 *Jew.* 217; says Liberius, bishop of Rome, said to the Arian emperor Constantius, "Although I be alone, yet the account of faith is therefore no whit the less," *ib.* 595; mentions the vain attempt of the Jews to rebuild the temple in the reign of Julian, 2 *Bul.* 260, 261; tells of Terentius's request to Valens, *Pil.* 324; narrates an anecdote of Basil and the cook Demosthenes, *Whita.* 232; words of Athanasius erroneously ascribed to him, 2 *Jew.* 681; states how Ambrose was elected bishop, 1 *Whitg.* 461; relates how Theodosius banished the Arians, *Sand.* 73; declares how Macedonius the hermit appeased the anger of Theodosius, 1 *Bul.* 305, 306; speaks of the ministers choosing Nectarius bishop of Constantinople, 1 *Whitg.* 410; says the council of Constantinople was called by Theodosius, *Rog.* 204 n.; recites an epistle of this council, 2 *Whitg.* 410; says that pope Damasus commanded the bishops of the East to come to Rome, not in his own name, but by the emperor's special letters, 4 *Jew.* 996; gives the confession of this pope, *Grin.* 53 n.; shews how Ambrose brought Theodosius to repentance, 3 *Bec.* 478, &c., *Coop.* 140 n., *Sand.* 72, 224, 455, 3 *Whitg.* 245; tells how Theodosius was admonished of his mortality, *Grin.* 389; speaks of the empress Placilla, wife of Theodosius, *Pil.* 386; praises Amphilochius, 1 *Jew.* 189; testifies that he governed all Lycaonia, 2 *Whitg.* 165; relates how Valentinian was angry with some who moved him to idolatry, *Pil.* 165 n.; mentions his counsel concerning the election of a bishop of Milan, 4 *Jew.* 674, *Rid.* 144; records what Chrysostom said to Gainas, 1 *Bul.* 391; describes the large jurisdiction of Chrysostom, 2 *Whitg.* 311, &c.; calls him the doctor of the world, 1 *Jew.* 433, 3 *Jew.* 269, 282; says, Nestorius, though a heretic, covered himself with a certain cloke or colour of the true faith, 4 *Jew.* 713; calls Leo president of the world, 1 *Jew.* 429; tells the story of Bassus and Simeones, *ib.* 244

vii. *Heresies:* on the Anthropomorphites, *Rog.* 38; on the heresy of Arius, *ib.* 52, 70; he states that the Arian heretics said that the catholic Christians, whom they called Homoüsians, were the cause of all division, 4 *Jew.* 952; on the controversy with his sect, and the use of the scriptures therein, *Whita.* 562 n.; on some Arians called Douleians, *Rog.* 47; on the heresy of Basilides, *ib.* 57; speaks of a sect of Donatists as Arians, and accustomed to commit suicide, 1 *Whitg.* 112, 114; Enthusiasts, see Messalians, below; Euchites, the same; on the Helcesæi, 1 *Jew.* 481; on the heresy of Macedonius, *Rog.* 48; on that of Marcellus, *ib.* 43; on the Messalians or Euchites, 1 *Jew.* 193, *Rog.* 246, 251, 277, 284, 2 *Whitg.* 561, otherwise called Enthusiasts, 4 *Bul.* 397, *Rog.* 196; he states that Letoius overthrew and burnt the Messalians' monasteries, and said they were dens of thieves, and chased the wolves away from the fold, 4 *Jew.* 800; on the Maximillians, *Rog.* 158; on the Montanists, *ib.*; on the Priscillians, *ib.*; on the Saturnians, *ib.* 133; on Simon Magus, *ib.* 118; he says the Tatians use no wine in the sacrament, *ib.* 295 n.; on the Valentinians, *ib.* 119; he calls Antichrist the abomination of desolation, 4 *Jew.* 728

viii. *Miscellanea:* he shews that the restriction of place in performing sacred rites is now done away, 1 *Hoop.* 242; speaks of the origin of antiphonal singing, 3 *Whitg.* 386; condemns words that are not understood, 3 *Bec.* 363; comments on the text "marriage (is) honourable in all," 1 *Ful.* 479; what he says of Paul's yoke-fellow, *ib.* 475; he shews that the soul of man is not buried, 3 *Bul.* 272; says the wicked shall not be able to prevail against God, but if they once get the over hand, yet shall they come down again, 4 *Jew.* 1075

Theodoric, king of the Goths, 2 *Bul.* 109, 3 *Jew.* 339, 4 *Jew.* 652, *Pil.* 640 (there called Theodosius), *Whita.* 438

Theodoricus Andree: wrote on the Apocalypse, *Bale* 258

Theodoricus à Niem, *q. v.*

Theodorus: *v.* Theodore.

Theodorus Anagnostes, or Lector: *Jew.* xliii; on a picture by St Luke, 2 *Jew.* 654; stated to have said that Barnabas translated the epistle to the Hebrews into Greek, *Whita.* 125

Theodorus Ancyranus: *v.* Theodotus.

Theodorus Cyreniacus: denied there was a God, *Rog.* 37

Theodorus Gazæus: *Whita.* 576

Theodorus, martyr: 2 *Jew.* 654; the same (?), *Pil.* 333

Theodorus Mesethenus, or Mesechius: denied Christ to be the same as the Word, *Rog.* 55; held him to be very man, and not God, 1 *Cran.* 278

Theodorus Mopsuestus: his error respecting the ancient prophets, 1 *Ful.* 9; his doctrine condemned, 1 *Bul.* 14

Theodosia: queen Elizabeth so called, *Calf.* 11

Theodosians: *v.* Theodotians.

Theodosius, emperor: *v.* Valens.

A valiant general, 1 *Bul.* 381, 384; Rome sacked in his time, 2 *Bul.* 109; he took the name of honour from the city of Antioch, 3 *Jew.* 315; was rebuked by Amphilochius, at whose instance he banished the Arians, *Sand.* 41, 73, 232; pacified by Macedonius, 1 *Bul.* 305, *Calf.* 22; in his anger he caused many to be slain at Thessalonica, *Pil.* 408, *Sand.* 224; Ambrose rebuked him, excluded him from the church, and brought him to repentance, 3 *Bec.* 478, &c., *Coop.* 140, *Grin.* 389, 1 *Jew.* 311, *Pil.* 381, 491, 546, 555, *Rid.* 95, *Sand.* 72, 3 *Whitg.* 242, &c.; he did penance in the presence of all the people, 3 *Jew.* 361; on his repentance he gave his consent to a law to do nothing without deliberation, *Park.* 157, *Pil.* 408, *Sand.* 224; he professed obedience to the law, 2 *Zur.* 169; his opinion of Ambrose, 1 *Jew.* 362; his prayer, *Pil.* 413; summoned the council of Constantinople, 1 *Jew.* 411, *Rog.* 204; his letter to council of Ephesus II., 1 *Jew.* 66; sat amongst bishops in council, 4 *Jew.* 1019; wished Florentius to be present at the council of Chalcedon, *ib.* 1029; confirmed councils, 1 *Jew.* 412; defended Flavianus, bp of Constantinople, *ib.* 407; decided a controversy between the orthodox and Arians and Eunomians, 3 *Whitg.* 310; he permitted litigants to refer their disputes to the church, *ib.* 455; his laws against idolatry, 2 *Bec.* 71, 305, 312, 4 *Jew.* 1125; law for the establishment of St Peter's doctrine, see p. 360, col. 1, above; a law against rebaptizing, 4 *Bul.* 394; law concerning figures of the cross, see p. 411, col. 1, above; on the epistles of Theodosius and Valentinian to Dioscorus, 1 *Jew.* 366, 2 *Whitg.* 318—320; he is commended by Ambrose, *Grin.* 11; Ambrose's funeral oration for him, *ib.* 25

Theodosius II., emperor: 1 *Bul.* 433; summoned the council of Ephesus, 1 *Jew.* 411, *Rog.* 204; wrote to it, *Whita.* 437; his Codex, *Jew.* xliii. See Law (Civil).

Theodosius, bp of Mira: allowed image worship, 2 *Jew.* 664

Theodotian: a translator of scripture, *Calf.* 107 n., 2 *Ful.* 390, 2 *Jew.* 692, *Whita.* 147; some account of him, and of his version of the Old Testament, *Whita.* 123; the apocryphal additions to Daniel ascribed to him, 1 *Ful.* 25

Theodotians: heretics, 1 *Bec.* 418, *Phil.* 420

Theodotus, or Theodorus, bp of Ancyra: against pictures, *Calf.* 145, 149

Theodotus, bp of Antioch: 4 *Jew.* 650

Theodotus, bp of Laodicea: excommunicated two persons named Apollinaris, 3 *Whitg.* 240

Theodotus: a heretic, 1 *Bec.* 418 n

Theodulphus: 2 *Bec.* 533 n

Theognis: cited, 1 *Ful.* 141, 1 *Zur.* 23

Theologia Domini: the Revelation, 1 *Bul.* 170, 418

Theology: *v.* Compendium, Doctors, Schoolmen.

Theology distinguished from philosophy by the internal light of the Holy Spirit, *Whita.* 364; mystical and symbolical divinity, 4 *Bul.* 238; metaphorical and symbolic theology is not argumentative, *Whita.* 409; English divinity, 1 *Lat.* 179

Theopaschites: heretics, 2 *Ful.* 359 n.; they denied the human soul of Christ, *Rog.* 52; said that another suffered in his place, *ib.* 57

Theophilus: St Luke's addresses to him, *Whita.* 641, 645

Theophilus, bp of Alexandria: his contention with the monks of Egypt, *Hutch.* 12; his opposition to Chrysostom, *Whita.* 596; he declares it the result of a diabolic spirit to think that anything is divine without the authority of the holy scriptures, *ib.* 688; speaks of the Lord's bread as that wherein the body of our Saviour is represented, 2 *Bec.* 288, 289, 3 *Bec.* 444; says that if Christ had been crucified for devils, his cup would not have been denied them, 2 *Cran.* 451, 1 *Jew.* 33, 56; speaks of the laws of fasting, *Whita.* 596; a saying of Theophylact falsely attributed to him, 1 *Cran.* 187, 190

Theophilus of Antioch: *Jew.* xliii; on the honour due to the emperor, 1 *Jew.* 551

Theophilus the Exile: a Familist, *Rog.* 202

Theophilus (......): a minister in the strangers' church at Norwich, 1 *Zur.* 256 n., 266 n

Theophrastus: 2 *Hoop.* 299, *Jew.* xliii, 1 *Jew.* 438, 4 *Jew.* 912

Theophylact: Opera, *Jew.* xliii, 3 *Whitg.* xxxii; he is but an abridger of Chrysostom, 3 *Jew.* 491; on his authority, *Phil.* 76, *Rid.* 229 n.; his works translated into Latin by Œcolampadius, 1 *Cran.* 188; he explains why Christ is called the Lamb of God which taketh away the sins of the world, 3 *Bec.* 421; erred respecting the procession of the Holy Spirit, *Hutch.* 279; speaks on the naming of our Lord by Joseph, 1 *Ful.* 536; describes a rule (κανών), *Whita.* 662; says nothing can deceive them who search the scriptures, 2 *Jew.* 682; explains why the gospel was delivered in writing, *Whita.* 655; declares that heresies are brought in by those who bring in anything beside the doctrine of the apostles, 1 *Bec.* 88, 3 *Bec.* 391, 2 *Cran.* 34; ascribes the opening of scripture to the Holy Spirit, and supposes him to be "the porter" (Jo. x), *Whita.* 465; shews that he who enters not by the door, i. e. by the scriptures, is a thief, 4 *Jew.* 1169, 1170; expounds the command to have our "lights burning," with reference to God's word, *ib.* 1170; calls God's word the candle whereby the thief is espied, 3 *Jew.* 431, 4 *Jew.* 767; says the light of the gospel dazzles the eyes of the impious, *Whita.* 388; writes on the date of St Matthew's gospel, *ib.* 519; says, St John translated St Matthew's gospel into Greek, 1 *Jew.* 237; shews that St Luke delivered written, what before he had spoken, 3 *Jew.* 437; his reading of Luke i. 42, "blessed... *for* blessed is the fruit of thy womb," 1 *Ful.* 515; he admits that Mary was not faultless, 2 *Lat.* 226, 359; following Chrysostom, he expounds the doxology in the Lord's prayer, 4 *Bul.* 219; on John v, the last verse, *Whita.* 340; he mentions a tradition concerning the death of Judas, *ib.* 665; on St Paul speaking in the Hebrew tongue, *ib.* 215; Gal. i. 8 expounded by him, *ib.* 627; on the epistle from Laodicea, *ib.* 304; said to teach that it is in man's power to be elected, *Rog.* 150; quoted upon justification, 2 *Cran.* 211; he speaks of faith alone justifying, 2 *Bec.* 639; says that the virtue of our neighbour cannot be sufficient for us, for each must be justified by his own works, 2 *Bec.* 395, 396, 3 *Bec.* 128, 460; asserts that God will render the crown of life as a just debt, 1 *Ful.* 339; speaks of calling sinners to repentance, *Whita.* 194; condemns doubtfulness, 1 *Ful.* 418; referred to about Peter, 2 *Ful.* 278; he says St Paul shews himself to be equal to Peter, 3 *Jew.* 328; is an enemy to the pope's primacy, 1 *Ful.* 86; speaks of baptism by trine immersion, 2 *Bec.* 227; calls the sacrament of the Lord's supper the blessed bread, 3 *Bec.* 388; observes that Christ said not "This is a figure," but, "This is my body," 1 *Cran.* 188, 2 *Jew.* 605, *Rid.* 228; teaches that the consecrated bread is changed into the flesh of the Lord, 1 *Brad.* 498 n., 1 *Cran.* 188, &c., 3 *Jew.* 496, *Rid.* 228—230; speaks of the bread as transformed, *Hutch.* 277; his words explained by other passages of his writings, *ib.* 279; he says the bread is transelemented into the body of the Lord, &c., 2 *Jew.* 574; uses similar language respecting ourselves, 2 *Jew.* 577, 3 *Jew.* 482, 495; says, the body of Christ is eaten, but the Godhead not eaten, and shews why, 3 *Jew.* 492; although he speaks of the eating of the very body of Christ, and the drinking of his very blood, he means a celestial and spiritual eating, and a sacramental conversion of the bread and wine, 1 *Cran.* (75), 187; he shews that Christ's words must be understood spiritually, for we are no devourers of flesh, 2 *Bec.* 289, 3 *Bec.* 444; says that the flesh of our Lord is life-making, 3 *Jew.* 491; speaks of the cup of blessing, 1 *Ful.* 504; says the reverend cup is in equal manner delivered to all, 3 *Jew.* 479; asserts that Christ was offered but once, and that we make a memory of his oblation, 3 *Bec.* 458; declares that we have one offering, not many, *ib.* 423; says that some thought Judas was not present at the sacrament, *ib.* 382; asserts that he tasted the Lord's flesh, *Rid.* 247; disallows a private reception of the Lord's supper, *Hutch.* 229; admonishes to frequent communion, 2 *Bec.* 259, 3 *Bec.* 474; explains what were the things which Paul declared that he would "set in order" at Corinth, 1 *Hoop.* 237; affirms that the foundation and ground of all prayer is faith, 1 *Bec.* 148; says Jesus, by casting out the oxen and doves, foreshewed that there should no longer be need of the sacrifice of beasts, but of prayer, 2 *Jew*. 708; expounds the text "marriage (is) honourable in all," 1 *Ful*. 477, 479; says the wife must regard the things within the house, *Sand*. 320; what he says of Paul's yoke-fellow, 1 *Ful*. 475 n., 477; he says it belongs to God alone to forgive sins, and that priests have no power to remit them, 2 *Bec*. 173, 174; allows that laymen may bind and loose, 3 *Jew*. 356, 357; declares that then (in another world) it will be no time to work, nor be honest to beg, 2 *Bec*. 396, 3 *Bec*. 460; shews that St Paul teacheth every man, priest, or monk, or apostle, to be obedient to princes, 1 *Bec*. 216; says that when we corporally obey the ruler, and pay tribute, which is debt, it hindereth nothing that we should spiritually well please God, *ib*. 221; on Christ's command to preach upon the house-tops, *Whita*. 669; on the sign of the Son of Man, 2 *Ful*. 138

Theopompus: 1 *Bul*. 48
Theotectus: 1 *Bul*. 48
Therapeutæ: a sect of Jews mentioned by Philo; mistakes concerning them, 2 *Ful*. 101
Therfe: unleavened, *Pil*. 54
Thermopylæ: the Lacedemonians' epitaph, 1 *Hoop*. 356
Therouenne: *v*. Terouane.
Thessalonians (Epistles to the): *v*. Paul (St).
Thessalonica: its bishop said to have been a vicar of the pope, 1 *Jew*. 402
Thetford, co. Norfolk: a martyr there, *Poet*. 164; the abbey, 2 *Bec*. 554 n
Theudas, the Egyptian: 2 *Ful*. 369
Thickpenny (David), curate of Brighthelmstone: a Familist, *Grin*. 359
Thieves (The two): names assigned to them, *Whita*. 560; the penitent, 4 *Bul*. 551, 1 *Cov*. 301, 302; he was sanctified without outward baptism, 4 *Bul*. 348
Thieving: *v*. Stealing.
Thilo (Jo. Car.): Cod. Apoc. N. T., *Calf*. 96, 126, 201 nn
Thirasius: *v*. Tharasius.
Thirkesson: *v*. Thurcaston.
Thirlby (Tho.), bp of Westminster, then of Norwich, lastly of Ely: *Park*. 18; chaplain to the king, 2 *Cran*. 244; sent to France, *ib*. 246; letter severely reprehending him for negligence as archdeacon of Ely, *ib*. 292; his election to the see of Westminster, of which he was the first and only bishop, *ib*. 115 n.; envoy to Charles V., 3 *Zur*. 37; he disputes with Cranmer and Ferrar, *ib*. 645; smells of the Interim, *ib*. 646; is made bishop of Norwich, *ib*. 185 n., 430; a commissioner against Cranmer, 2 *Cran*. 224; one of queen Mary's council, 1 *Zur*. 5 n.; a commissioner about the restoration of Calais, *ib*. 8 n.; sent to king Philip to negotiate a peace, 4 *Jew*. 1197; he opposes the reformation in the house of lords, *ib*. n., 1 *Zur*. 20; prisoner in the Tower, *Park*. 122; removed thence on account of the plague, *ib*. 192—195; lives with Parker, *ib*. 194 n., 203, 215, 217; his death, *ib*. 369 n., 2 *Zur*. 181; buried at Lambeth, *Park*. 194 n.; his letters to Parker, *ib*. 41, 193; letter to him, *ib*. 193

Thirst: *v*. Hunger.
Thirtell (T.): martyred in Smithfield, called by Bryce, Sturtle, *Poet*. 169
Tholouse: *v*. Toulouse.
Thoman (Caspar): account of him, 2 *Zur*. 324 n.; his interview with Sir Rob. Cecil, *ib*. 327; letter from him to C. Waser, *ib*. 326
Thoman (Hen.): 2 *Zur*. 329
Thomas (St): *v*. Apocrypha, ii.
His doubting and confession, 1 *Brad*. 72, 1 *Cov*. 345, 1 *Cran*. 255, 258, 261, 262; he was in India, *Calf*. 127, *Hutch*. 98, 349; his tomb known in the time of Chrysostom, *Calf*. 130
Thomas Aquinas (St): some account of him, 1 *Tyn*. 149 n.; called the angelic doctor, 4 *Bul*. 485 n., 2 *Jew*. 783; or doctor sanctus, 2 *Tyn*. 291; alleged appearance of Christ to him in a vision, 2 *Jew*. 783; he died on his way to the council of Lyons, *Whita*. 536; held in high estimation, 3 *Jew*. 610; miracles attributed to him, 3 *Tyn*. 131

Opera, *Jew*. xliii; he allows that the subject of theology is God, 1 *Tyn*. 107 n.; admits but one kind of worship for God and for images, 2 *Jew*. 666; gives reasons why Christ descended into hell, *Whita*. 537; says his soul was there as long as his body was in the grave, *ib*. 538; proves the procession of the Holy Spirit from the Son, *ib*. 536; terms scripture the rule of our faith, *ib*. 660; speaks of its being "written for our learning," *ib*. 524; gives reasons why the teaching of the apostles was written, *ib*. 655; says the doctrine of the apostles and prophets is our rule, *ib*. 28; explains "the foundation of the apostles and prophets," *ib*. 349, 649; affirms that we should have much (knowledge) of the word of God, *ib*. 240; says that in scripture not words only, but things, have a signification, *ib*. 404; writes about the literal sense of scripture, *ib*. 408; also on scripture metaphors, *ib*. 379; says that to try out the truth

THOMAS AQUINAS

by the scriptures, requires long study and exercise, 2 *Cran.* 35; states that the reason why many understand not the gospel is not in it, but in the malice and unbelief of men, *Whita.* 388; figuratively interprets "the crumbs which fall from the master's table," *ib.* 701; says "lex" is sometimes used for morals, 2 *Lat.* 348; draws absurd conclusions from errors of the Latin Vulgate, *Whita.* 141; on St Paul being "rude in speech," *ib.* 101; he expounds Eph. vi. 13, "having done all," *ib.* 198; on 1 Jo. v. 9, " the testimony of men," *ib.* 339; he speaks against adding to the scriptures, *ib.* 622; considers the citation of apocryphal books allowable, *ib.* 69; on the book of Ecclesiasticus, and Samuel's ghost, *ib.* 93; he says Christ has satisfied only for original sin, *Rog.* 298, (see 3 *Jew.* 557); states that original sin does not incur sensible punishment, *Rog.* 97 n.; teaches that baptism puts away original sin, penance actual sin, *ib.* 278 n.; speaks of some who say, with good reason, that a man may obtain remission of his venial sins by entering into a church that is consecrated, 3 *Jew.* 372; declares that the wearing of a monk's cowl can remove sin, *ib.* 614; passages on justification, 2 *Cran.* 204, bis, 208—211; he used in speaking of justification the old manner of speech, that faith alone justifies, 2 *Bec.* 639; his language about faith, *Calf.* 85; on the "one faith," *Whita.* 671; his explanation of St James on faith and works, 3 *Jew.* 245, *Wool.* 30; on attrition and contrition, 1 *Brad.* 46 n.; on works of supererogation, *ib.* 48 n.; he explains the profession of belief "*in* the holy catholic church," as referring to the Spirit who sanctifies the church, but says it is better to omit the word "in," 1 *Bul.* 160; considers the doctrine of the church an infallible rule, 2 *Jew.* 987 n.; says we are not bound on necessity of salvation to believe the doctors, as Jerome or Augustine, or even the church itself, except in things pertaining to the substance of the faith, 3 *Jew.* 176; affirms that the church may dispense with a vow of chastity solemnized by the receiving of holy orders, 4 *Jew.* 788; says that in case a vow be unprofitable, or a hindrance, it ought not to be kept, 3 *Jew.* 400; exalts the pope above all human dignities, and says he may be styled Christ, king, and priest, 2 *Tyn.* 291; declares that to say that the pope has not the primacy of the universal church is an error like the error of them who say the Holy Ghost proceedeth not from the Son of God, 4 *Jew.* 739; a passage respecting the Roman supremacy ascribed by him to Cyril, *Whita.*

440; he explains why bishops are so called, 4 *Jew.* 906; expounds the title presbyter, *ib.* 912; compares the vow and profession of a monk with baptism, *Rog.* 276; declares that God alone can institute a sacrament, 4 *Bul.* 239; calls the sacrifice of the mass a memorial of the Lord's passion, 2 *Bec.* 250; says that as the body of our Lord was once offered on the cross for the debt of original sin, so it is daily offered on the altar for the debt of daily sins, 3 *Jew.* 557; speaks of the sacrament of the altar as a sacrifice and gift to pacify God, 3 *Bec.* 377; mentions various opinions as to the words used by Christ in the consecration of the eucharist, 2 *Bec.* 263, 3 *Tyn.* 241; what he understands by "this," in the words of consecration, 2 *Jew.* 788; he recites opinions on the consecration of the sacrament in silence, *ib.* 697; says the words of consecration are spoken in silence, because they pertain only to the priest, *ib.* 703; greatly promoted the doctrine of transubstantiation, 3 *Bec.* 232, 3 *Tyn.* 227 n., 241; terms used by him descriptive of the manner of Christ's presence in the sacrament, 4 *Bul.* 443, 1 *Hoop.* 193; he says that whole Christ is under every part of the species of bread and wine, 1 *Cran.* 64; illustrates the doctrine of transubstantiation by comparing the presence of Christ's body to the reflection of a man's face in many glasses, or in all the broken pieces of a glass, at the same time, 3 *Tyn.* 235 n.; says the body of Christ is ex pane, not de pane, *Rid.* 307; states that in the body of Christ (in the sacrament) there is not distance of parts from each other, as in the *true* body of Christ, 2 *Jew.* 778; treats of the miraculous appearance of the real presence, 1 *Hoop.* 291; opines that if the substance of bread remained, the worship of the sacrament would be idolatrous, 1 *Jew.* 11 n.; says there must be a readiness to make the condition of consecration at the adoring of the eucharist, *ib.* 13; refers to the case of a priest neglecting to put wine into the chalice, *ib.* 550; speaks of the body of Christ going no farther than the stomach, 1 *Cran.* 56; allows that Judas was present at the last supper, 4 *Bul.* 464; asserts that beasts may eat the body of Christ, 1 *Cran.* 68, 2 *Jew.* 783, *Rid.* 309, *Rog.* 293 n.; says, if a man take too much of the consecrated wine he may be made drunk by a miracle, 2 *Jew.* 785; refers to the corruption of the sacramental elements, *Rid.* 310; says that, though whole Christ be under both kinds, yet is he not given in vain under both kinds, 2 *Bec.* 244, 3 *Bec.* 413; states that the reception of the communion in both kinds continued in divers churches until his time without controulment, 1 *Jew.* 212; asserts that in certain churches the blood was not given to the people, *ib.* 261; a hymn of his cited with reference to the communion of the laity, 1 *Hoop.* 229; he mentions an old decree that the faithful should communicate every day, 3 *Jew.* 475, 477; shews that the mass is neither better nor worse on account of the goodness or badness of the priest, 2 *Jew.* 755; says that the sacrifice of the priest is satisfactory in proportion to his devotion, 1 *Cran.* 84; thinks a priest, not charged with cure, need say mass only on great feasts, 1 *Jew.* 199; states why the sacrament should not be consecrated on Good Friday or Easter eve, *ib.* 246; speaks of private mass, *ib.* 106; declares it sufficient if one be present at such mass, *ib.* 107; says that service was once in the vulgar tongue, *ib.* 289; writes on giving thanks " with the Spirit," *ib.* 313; speaks of the private prayer offered by the priest in the presence of the people, *ib.* 107, 264; his precatio aurea pro gratia divinæ sapientiæ, or an adaptation of it, *Pra. Eliz.* 201, compare *ib.* 396; the same, or a similar prayer in English, *Lit. Eliz.* 250, *Pra. Eliz.* 107; he says that the observance of the Lord's day succeeds that of the sabbath, not by force of the commandment, but by the constitution of the church, and the custom of Christian people, 2 *Brad.* 391; sought to reduce the number of ceremonies, *Lit. Eliz.* xxvi; on superstition, *Pil.* 562; he says the pains of purgatory and hell-fire differ only in duration, *Rog.* 217; treats of limbus patrum, 1 *Tyn.* 159 n.; mentions certain heretics who looked for the redemption of demons, *Rog.* 58; speaks of the renewal of the earth, 1 *Brad.* 358, 360—362; denied that the virgin was conceived without sin, 1 *Tyn.* 91, 3 *Tyn.* 131; moves the question whether Mary were faultless or not, 2 *Lat.* 226; calls her arrogant, 1 *Lat.* 384 n.; cited about tot quots, *Rid.* 510; referred to, 4 *Jew.* 873, 2 *Lat.* 235 n., 317, *Pil.* 80, 550

Thomas of Canterbury: *v.* Becket.

Thomas à Kempis: De Imitat. Christi, *Pra. Eliz.* 453 n.; transl. by Rogers, *Rog.* viii, ix.

Thomas, earl of Lancaster: a false martyr, *Bale* 189

Thomas of Salisbury: notice of him, 1 *Jew.* 551 n.; a work by him in MS. in C. C. C. C., *Jew.* xliii; he says that the host should be believed to be the body of the Lord only conditionally, 1 *Jew.* 551

Thomas Theodonensis: *Bale* 398

Thomas Waldensis: *v.* Netter (T.).

Thomas, a preacher of England: withstood the pope, 4 *Jew.* 934

Thomas (Pet.): *v.* Peter.

Thomas (Tho.): printer to the university of Cambridge, *Pil.* 276

Thomas (Will.): clerk of the council, *Rid.* 332; his (?) Hist. of Italy, *Rog.* 179 n., 337 n

Thomists: disciples of Thomas Aquinas, opponents of the Scotists, 1 *Jew.* 70, 254, 3 *Jew.* 611, 4 *Jew.* 1045, 1046, *Pil.* 80, 550, *Rog.* 197, 1 *Tyn.* 91 n., 1 *Zur.* 53; the Dominicans took this side, 1 *Tyn.* 159 n

Thompson (Edm.): ordained by Ridley, 1 *Brad.* 446 n.; perhaps the Thomson whom Bradford exhorts to repent, *ib.*

Thompson (Jo.), or Tompson: a rebellious priest, 2 *Cran.* 187 n

Thomson (......): *v.* Thompson (Edm.).

Thorah (תּוֹרָה): the Law, 1 *Bul.* 49, *Calf.* 108, 2 *Ful.* 138, 1 *Hoop.* 88

Thorgau: 3 *Zur.* 405; convocation there, 1 *Zur.* 302 n., 315 n

Thorn (M.): notice of him, *Poet.* xxviii; the world vanity, *ib.* 314

Thorndike (Herbert): 2 *Ful.* 70 n

Thornidon (Dr): cellarer of Ch. Ch., Canterbury, 2 *Cran.* 312 (perhaps identical with the next).

Thornton (Rich.), suffragan of Dover: was a monk of Canterbury, 1 *Cran.* xx, 429

Thornton (Tho.), vice-chancellor of Oxon: account of him, 2 *Zur.* 329 n

Thorough: a passage, 1 *Brad.* 303

Thorp (Mr): 2 *Lat.* 295, 296

Thorpe (Jo.), Carmelite: wrote on the Apocalypse, *Bale* 257

Thorpe (Jo.): Cranmer's kinsman, 2 *Cran.* 261

Thorpe (Will.): the manner of his bringing up, *Bale* 77; his preaching at Shrewsbury, *ib.* 82; he preaches at Paul's cross, *ib.* 119; examined before abp Arundel, *ib.* 44 n., *Rid.* 490, 494, 1 *Tyn.* ix, xxvi; his EXAMINATION, by Bale, *Bale* 60, &c.; his preface, *ib.* 65; he confesses his faith, *ib.* 70; refuses to recant, *ib.* 123; is taken to prison, *ib.* 126; his testament, *ib.* 127; his end uncertain, *ib.* 133, 394

Thoth: an Egyptian deity, 2 *Bul.* 218, 3 *Bul.* 136

Thoughts: we should beware more of evil thoughts than of evil words and deeds, 2 *Brad.* 189

Thraall man: slave, *Phil.* 374

Thrace: the mode of choosing kings there, 1 *Bec.* 8; custom at birth and death, 3 *Bec.* 123

Thraso: *Pil.* 400, 431

Threape: to urge, 4 *Jew.* 1091

Threatenings: move the evil, *Pil.* 71; God's are conditional, *ib.* 89; their benefit. *ib.* 96

Throgmorton (Sir Clement): 1 *Zur.* 7 n

Throckmorton* (Sir Nich.): remarks on a memorable trial, probably his trial, 1 *Brad.* 405; his character, *ib.*; he aids Jewel, *Jew.* xi; ambassador in France, 1 *Zur.* 132 n.; put under restraint there, *Grin.* 260 n.; extracts from his state correspondence, 1 *Zur.* 56, 68, 91, 197 nn.; mourner at the funeral of the emperor Ferdinand, *Grin.* 33

Throgmorton (Sir Rob.): 2 *Lat.* 388 n

Throgmorton (Anth.): servant to cardinal Pole, 2 *Lat.* 388

Throckmorton (Fra.): hanged at Tyburn for rebellion, *Lit. Eliz.* 656 n

Throckmorton (Jo.): hanged for rebellion, *Lit. Eliz.* 656 n

Throgmorton (Mich.): servant to card. Pole, 2 *Lat.* 388

Thrones: a name of angels, 3 *Bul.* 337; the great white throne, *Bale* 576

Thuanus (Jac. Aug.): 1 *Bec.* 396 n., *Grin.* 14, 16, 19, 21, 22, 2 *Zur.* 289 nn

Thucydides: calls certain heathen oblations pure sacrifices, 2 *Jew.* 734

Thummim: *v.* Urim.

Thunder, Lightning: meaning of thunder in scripture, *Bale* 243—245; the law was given in thunder, and so God gave Israel a king, 1 *Tyn.* 194, 334; on prayer against thunder and lightning, 2 *Whitg.* 477—479, 482, 483; charms against lightning, *Pil.* 177, 536, 563

Thunsern (Will.): 3 *Zur.* 261

Thurcaston, co. Leic.: the birthplace of Latimer, 1 *Lat.* i; called Thirkesson, 2 *Lat.* ix.

Thurgau: *v.* Thorgau.

Thurland (Tho.): master of the Savoy hospital, *Grin.* x; he abuses his trust, *ib.* 302—304; Grindal's letter to lord Burghley respecting him, *ib.* 349

Thurlesby (Tho.): *v.* Thirlby.

Thurlow (Tho.), bp of Lincoln, afterwards of Durham: confirmation of his election to Lincoln, *Grin.* vi. n

Thursday (Holy): on the observance of Ascension day, 1 *Bul.* 260

Thursday (Maundy or Shere): *v.* Maundy-Thursday.

Thurstan, abp of York: consecrated by the pope, in defiance of the king's commands, *Pil.* 584

Thurston (......): Thurston's wife, martyr at Chichester, *Poet.* 170

Thurstone (Marg.), widow: martyr at Colchester, *Poet.* 172

Thwaites (Will.): his daughter Winifride, 1 *Bec.* 37 n

Thyatira: the epistle to the church, *Bale* 281

Thymelthorp (Geo.): his frauds on bp Parkhurst, 1 *Zur.* 265 n., 301

Thynne (Sir Jo.): imprisoned, 3 *Zur.* 77 n

Tiara: the pope's triple crown, what it signifies, 3 *Bec.* 507, 1 *Jew.* 403, *Poet.* 463; words used when the tiara or regno is placed on the pope's head, 2 *Tyn.* 258 n (see also Phrygium).

Tiberius Cæsar, emperor: our Lord began to preach in his reign, 4 *Bul.* 536; he is said to have been troubled at the preaching of Christ, and to have wished him to be worshipped as a god, 1 *Jew.* 217, *Pil.* 141, 683, 684; he said it was the property of a good shepherd to shear, not to devour the sheep, 2 *Bec.* 329

Tibullus: 1 *Bec.* 375

Tiburcius (St), or Tyburtius: his martyrdom, *Bale* 586, 2 *Bec.* 473

Tichonius: *v.* Tychonius.

Tierce: *v.* Hours.

Tigury: *v.* Zurich.

Tilius (Jo.), bp of Angoulême: possessed many ancient councils, *Park.* 141; published the Caroline Books, *Calf.* 155 n

Tillage: its decay, *Now.* 227, 228

Tillemont (L. Seb. Le Nain de): 2 *Ful.* 70, 183, 338, 353 nn

Tillet (Jean du): *v.* Du Tillet.

Tilney (Mr): seeks a dispensation, *Park.* 351

Tilney (Jo.), rector of Buckland, Herts: 1 *Bec.* xii.

Tilneye (Jo.), Carmelite: wrote on the Apocalypse, *Bale* 257

Tiltey, co. Essex: suit between the abbot and the bp of London's chaplain, 2 *Cran.* 261

Time: the ruins of time; verses by Edm. Spenser, *Poet.* 24; time fleeting; verses by Rich. Robinson, *ib.* 365; address to time, by A. W., *ib.* 453; we have no to-morrow, *Sand.* 171; the "acceptable time," *ib.* 305; the "time of amendment," or "reformation," Heb. ix, 1 *Bul.* 59

Timelings: time-servers, 3 *Bec.* 235

Times: *v.* Days, Prayers, Signs, World. The wickedness of the times: *Lit. Eliz.* 573, *Wool.* 141, 142

Timmes (Will.): martyred, *Poet.* 166

Timon of Athens: 3 *Zur.* 731

Timotheans: their heresy, 2 *Jew.* 566

Timothy: his office and jurisdiction, 4 *Bul.* 105, *Rog.* 328, 1 *Whitg.* 427, 430, 432, 501,

---

* Or Throgmorton. The forms are arranged together.

502, 508, 2 *Whitg.* 132, &c., 284, 286, &c., 293, &c., 427, 373; statements of the histories, *ib.* 294; of the fathers, *ib.* 295; of later writers, *ib.* 296; his decease, *ib.* 303; his bones translated, *ib.*; as to the epistles to him, see Paul.

Timothy, a bp of the Arians: 1 *Jew.* 99, 144

Tindale (Will.): *v.* Tyndale.

Tindale (Will.), of Carlisle diocese: 1 *Tyn.* xv.

Tingle (......): died in Newgate, *Poet.* 164

Tip: a fall, 2 *Brad.* 104; tip for tap, 1 *Bul.* 283

Tiphernas (Lælius): 2 *Ful.* 110 n

Tipler: an innkeeper, *Grin.* 138

Tippets: worn by the clergy, *Bale* 119, 1 *Brad.* 428*, 2 *Brad.* 225, 2 *Cran.* 321, *Grin.* 207, 339, 1 *Lat.* 300, *Phil.* 213, 2 *Whitg.* 1; made of sarcenet, 2 *Cran.* 38, *Park.* 268; worn by act of parliament, *Park.* 268; some preached before the queen without the tippet, *ib.* 264

Tir Oen: *v.* Tyrone.

Tiro Prosper: *v.* Prosper.

Tirrell (......), fellow of King's hall, Camb., opposes Latimer, 2 *Lat.* xxix.

Tischell (Jo.): 3 *Zur.* 669

Tisdale (Jo.), printer: 1 *Hoop.* 432, 2 *Hoop.* 179

Tisen (Jo.): servant to bp Stokesley, 1 *Tyn.* lvi.

Titans: mentioned by the prophets, *Hutch.* 178; a fable about Titan, 2 *Hoop.* 603

Titelmannus (Fra.): wrote on the Apocalypse, *Bale* 258

Titeshale (Jo.): *v.* Tyteshale.

Tithes: they were due to God by the law of Moses, 1 *Lat.* 303; they were appointed to be given to priests, *Bale* 104, 107, 108, 1 *Bec.* 20; whether they are to be paid under the gospel, *Bale* 103, &c.; St Jerome's opinion respecting them, *ib.* 108; inquiry by what law they are due now, 2 *Cran.* 465; they are not due by God's law, but by the law of the land, 1 *Lat.* 304, 1 *Tyn.* 230; none paid in the first ages of the church, 2 *Tyn.* 256; their original use in the church and subsequent misappropriation, *Bale* 105, 2 *Tyn.* 336; how the abuse should have been corrected, 2 *Tyn.* 336; the offering of the faithful, how anciently divided, 2 *Ful.* 93, 2 *Tyn.* 173 n.; tithes enjoined to be paid, 2 *Cran.* 501; of what to be paid, *Bale* 103, 2 *Cran.* 282 n.; for what purpose they are to be paid, 2 *Bec.* 432; priests should relieve the poor with them, *Bale* 106; tithes possessed by religious houses, &c., 2 *Zur.* 230; unlawful exaction of 3*d.* per acre for tithes in Romney marsh, 2 *Cran.* 289

Titian, the painter: *Phil.* 381

Titles: not unlawful, 1 *Whitg.* 105; conferred by popes on princes, *Bale* 444, 1 *Tyn.* 186, 187 (see Defender); ecclesiastical titles, 1 *Whitg.* 152 (and see Bishops, v); Κύριος, rabbi, monsieur, 2 *Whitg.* 386

Titus: his office and jurisdiction, 4 *Bul.* 133, *Rog.* 329, 1 *Whitg.* 427, 2 *Whitg.* 132, &c., 282, 352, 373, 427; as to the epistle to him, see Paul.

Titus Vespasian, emperor: destroyed the temple, 2 *Jew.* 994

Tobiah, the Ammonite: *Pil.* 409

Tobit: referred to, 2 *Bul.* 63, 64, *Pil.* 57, 58
— the Book of Tobit: its claims to be canonical considered, *Whita.* 80, &c.; it is not canonical, 4 *Bul.* 538, 1 *Ful.* 20, 24, 77; Jerome had seen a Chaldee copy, *Whita.* 81

Todd (J. H.): speaks of a fictitious tract ascribed to Hippolytus, 2 *Ful.* 282 n

Todington, co. Glouc.: the seat of the Tracys, 3 *Tyn.* 269

Tokens: their nature in scripture, 1 *Cran.* 16

Toledo: *v.* Councils.

Toleration: Sandys says that the liberty of openly professing diversity of religions is dangerous to the state, *Sand.* 49; clerks' tolerations, what, *ib.* xx. n

Toll: *v.* Tribute.

Tolwyn (Will.): compelled to recant, *Bale* 441, 1 *Bec.* viii.

Toman (Caspar): *v.* Thoman.

Tomkins (Tho.): martyred, 1 *Jew.* 59 n., *Rid.* 391, 3 *Zur.* 113 n [not Jenkins, as there printed].

Tompson (Jo.): *v.* Thompson.

Tomson (Lawr.): his reply to Feckenham, 1 *Ful.* 426, 2 *Ful.* 3

Tonbridge: *v.* Tunbridge.

Tone and tother: an antithetical form used by Tyndale and More, 2 *Tyn.* 296

Tongue: *v.* Lying, Oaths, Slander.

Of the tongue, 2 *Bul.* 111; why it was made, 1 *Bec.* 164, 366; the right use of it, 2 *Bec.* 118, 119; continency in its use, 1 *Bul.* 420; sobriety in speech, *Sand.* 395; perfection to be sought in speaking, *ib.* 426; abuse of the gift of speech, 3 *Bec.* 61; the tongue a slippery member, 1 *Brad.* 154; sins of the tongue, especially speaking against those set in authority, *Sand.* 119; against filthy talk; with sentences and examples of scripture, 1 *Bec.* 447, 448;

---

* The corresponding place, in 2 *Cov.* 144, has "appetites.'

TONGUE — TOULOUSE

evil talk censured, *ib.* 253; an account must be rendered of idle words, *ib.* 135; double-tongued men censured, *Sand.* 132

Tongues: *v.* Languages.

Only one before the building of Babel, *Whita.* 112, 113; seventy-two reckoned by some fathers, 1 *Jew.* 288; five in England, *ib.* 275; languages are continually changing, *Whita.* 656; on dialects, *ib.* 215, 256; the three holy tongues, Hebrew, Greek, and Latin, which were upon the cross, 3 *Bec.* 410, 2 *Ful.* 223, 224, 1 *Jew.* 15, 271, *Whita.* 257; Cajetan says these were on the cross as the representatives of all languages, *Whita.* 257; they are otherwise called the three learned or ecclesiastical languages, *ib.* 220, 267; all others denominated barbarous, 1 *Jew.* 266, 267, 2 *Jew.* 669, *Whita.* 356; on the gift of tongues, 4 *Bul.* 231, 2 *Cran.* 183, 514, 1 *Jew.* 307, &c., 313, *Whita.* 258, &c.; unknown tongues profit not, *Whita.* 238; it was not the ancient custom to minister in them, 2 *Bec.* 254; to speak in the church in an unknown tongue is contrary to Paul's command, 1 *Tyn.* 219, 234; the mass-monger ministers in a strange tongue, 3 *Bec.* 362, 363; Papists pray, christen, and bless in Latin, but curse in English, 1 *Tyn.* 272; the vulgar tongue is to be used in public prayer (see p. 624, col. 2), and at the Lord's supper, 4 *Bul.* 421

Tongues of fire: 1 *Cov.* 389

Tonstal (Cuthb.), bp of London, afterwards of Durham: notice of him, *Phil.* xxvi; references to him, 2 *Cran.* 490, 2 *Lat.* 295 n., 329, 2 *Tyn.* 278 n.; how he was flattered by Erasmus, 1 *Tyn.* xxi, 395; he was in Germany with Luther, *Phil.* 104; called Saturn, 4 *Jew.* 1228, 2 *Tyn.* 321, 337; he refuses to patronise Tyndale, 1 *Tyn.* xxi, xxiv, 396; prohibits certain books, *Rid.* 494 n.; preaches at Paul's cross against Tyndale's Testament, 1 *Ful.* 61, 1 *Tyn.* xxiv, 393 n.; orders all copies of it within his diocese to be delivered up, 1 *Tyn.* xxxii, 132 n.; is said to have bought them up at Antwerp, *ib.* xxxvii; goes with Sir T. More to Cambray as ambassador, *ib.*; licenses Sir T. More to read heretical books, *ib.* xxxvi, 34, 3 *Tyn.* 2; joins with Warham, Gardiner, and More in collecting alleged heresies from the writings of Tyndale, 1 *Tyn.* 34; examines Jo. Tewkesbury, on the charge of reading books by Tyndale, *ib.* 32; his London register referred to, 2 *Cov.* viii. n., 2 *Lat.* xvi; he burns copies of Tyndale's Testament in St Paul's church-yard, calling the contents "doctrinam peregrinam," 1 *Tyn.* xxxviii, 2 *Tyn.* 337; translated to Durham, 1 *Tyn.* xxxviii. n.; he signs a declaration respecting a general council, 2 *Cran.* 468; forswears the pope, 1 *Ful.* 61; preaches against the pope, 2 *Cran.* 13, 2 *Hoop.* 268, 557, 567, *Jew.* xliii, 1 *Jew.* 34, 60; he is sent to Picardy, 3 *Zur.* 37; examines Bradford, 1 *Brad.* 468; is committed to Parker's custody, *Park.* 77, 78, 106 n.; his death, 4 *Jew.* 1228, 1 *Zur.* 69; his executors and funeral, *Park.* 106; his Sermon made vpon Palme Sondaye, *Jew.* xliii (& al. see above); De Veritate Corp. et Sang. Christi in Euch., *ib.*; Ridley's lost Annotationes on this work, 2 *Brad.* 159, *Rid.* xv, 373; Tonstal allows that transubstantiation was not settled till the council of Lateran (1215), 1 *Brad.* 511, 524, 1 *Jew.* 549, 2 *Jew.* 562, 3 *Jew.* 489, 4 *Jew.* 784; says, if the sacrament be a figure of Christ's body, then was a figure crucified for us, and not Christ, 2 *Jew.* 590; speaks of the use of the Latin church in receiving the sacrament on Good Friday, 1 *Jew.* 245; mentions the forgery of Zosimus, 3 *Jew.* 127

Tonsure: its antiquity, 2 *Ful.* 115; its origin, &c., *ib.* 116; it was borrowed from the heathen, 1 *Tyn.* 232, 3 *Tyn.* 20; what it may be supposed to signify, 1 *Tyn.* 235; absurd reason of Isidore Hispalensis for it, 1 *Jew.* 14; the tonsure referred to, 3 *Bec.* 259; declared to be the mark of the beast, 2 *Brad.* 43, 1 *Tyn.* 173, 236; the Greeks shorn square, 2 *Ful.* 116

Tonvillanus (Pet.): 3 *Zur.* 157

Tooley (Jo.), a criminal: his body exhumed and burned for heresy, *Pil.* 217

Toot: to look, search, or pry, 2 *Bec.* 63, 1 *Brad.* 54, *Calf.* 47, 380

Tootle (Hugh): *v.* Dodd (C.).

Tooth and nail: *Bale* 130

Topley (......), a friar of Stoke-Clare: 2 *Cov.* viii. n

Torculares Psalmi: 2 *Bul.* 166

Tornierus (Count Phil.): 2 *Cran.* 233

Torquato (Ant.): prognosticates the ruin of Europe, 4 *Jew.* 1217, 1218, 1 *Zur.* 47 n

Torquemada (Jo. de): defends the revelations of St Bridget in the council of Basil, 1 *Hoop.* 291 n

Toshes: tusks, 3 *Bec.* 237

Totehill (Hen.): brought before Cranmer for supporting the pope and Becket, 2 *Cran.* 387, 388

Tot quots: *Bale* 519, *Hutch.* 350, 1 *Lat.* 49, 97 n., *Pil.* 255, *Rid.* 55, 510, 1 *Tyn.* 236, 3 *Tyn.* 102, 173

Totylas, a prince of the Goths: 2 *Bul.* 109

Toul: taken by the French, 3 *Zur.* 590 n

Toulouse: a place of pilgrimage, *Bale* 634;

the university erected by Charlemagne, 2 *Jew.* 981

Tournament: one at Brussels, 3 *Zur.* 61

Tournay: conquered, and the see given to Wolsey, 2 *Tyn.* 273; the city given up to the French, *ib.* 315

Tourner (......): *v.* Turner.

Tourney (Hen.), of Calais: 2 *Cran.* 311, 313, 334

Tours: *v.* Councils.

Tower of London, *q. v.*

Towers of churches: the steeple the poor man's sign, 1 *Bec.* 21; steeples to be well repaired, *Grin.* 134; round towers in Norfolk and Suffolk, 2 *Cov.* viii. n

Towker (......): physician to Cranmer, and to Ch. Ch. Canterbury, 2 *Cran.* 357

Towns: the old English meaning of the word, *Hutch.* 350; many in England have become desolate, 2 *Bec.* 434

Townsend (Aubrey): editor of the Writings of Bradford, 1, 2 *Brad.*

Townsend (Dr), a civilian: 2 *Cran.* 253

Toxites (Mich.): mentioned, 2 *Zur.* 64, 69, 71, 72

Toy (Humf.), printer: 3 *Whitg.* 498 n., 551, 600

Toy (Rob.), printer: 1 *Hoop.* 99

Tractatio: *Now.* (103)

Tracy (Hen.), of Todington: 2 *Lat.* 415

Tracy (Rich.): son of Will. the testator, 3 *Tyn.* 273; his suit against Dr Parker for burning the body of his father, *ib.* 270; he was a commissioner respecting the blood of Hales, 2 *Lat.* 407 n.; he is called the father of Traheron, 3 *Zur.* 613

Tracy (Will.): one of the murderers of Becket, 3 *Tyn.* 269

Tracy (Will.), a Gloucestershire gentleman: some account of him, 3 *Tyn.* 269—271; copy of his testament, *ib.* 272; his corpse disinterred, and burnt for heresy by Dr Parker, chancellor of Worcester, *Bale* 395, 1 *Lat.* 46, *Pil.* 653, 1 *Tyn.* xviii, 3 *Tyn.* 270, 271, 282; Parker is heavily fined for this, 3 *Tyn.* 270; Tyndale's exposition of his testament, 1 *Tyn.* lxxiii, 3 *Tyn.* 269, 273, 283

— Margaret his wife, 3 *Tyn.* 273

Tradition: *v.* Augustine, and other Fathers; also Ceremonies.

Meaning of the term, *Now.* (103), *Whita.* 497; use of the word in scripture, 4 *Bul.* 534, 2 *Ful.* 228, 2 *Jew.* 674, 3 *Jew.* 436, 1 *Tyn.* 219, *Whita.* 498; translations on the subject examined, 1 *Ful.* 107, 108, 164—178; meaning of the term as used by the fathers, 2 *Jew.* 673, 3 *Jew.* 436, &c., *Whita.* 497, 699; its signification as used by Romanists, *Whita.* 497; different kinds of tradition;

divine, apostolical, and ecclesiastical, *ib.* 500, 501; scriptural or apostolical, popish, ecclesiastical, *Calf.* 267; scriptural, antiscriptural, neuter, 1 *Whitg.* 252, 286; other divisions, *Whita.* 502; tradition before the time of Moses, *ib.* 517; the chief contents of the lively tradition of the holy fathers, 1 *Bul.* 42—45; Moses put this into writing, *ib.* 45; the traditions of the Jews, 4 *Bul.* 533; tradition was not used more than scripture by the ancient Jews, as is alleged, *Whita.* 518; no necessary things were left to oral tradition under the law, *ib.* 529, &c.; the traditions of the scribes and Pharisees, deemed by them equal to God's laws, 2 *Cran.* 146; traditions followed by the Jews to their ruin, 2 *Lat.* 51; their traditions rejected by Christ and the apostles, *Whita.* 637; the Mishnah, &c., *ib.* 611; the tradition of the Gentiles, *ib.* 612; whether Christ gave power to the church to teach anything besides that which he taught, *Phil.* 358; the church was not dependent on tradition for many years after Christ, *Whita.* 519; apostolic traditions, written and unwritten, 2 *Cran.* 57—60; the unwritten traditions of the apostles cannot be contrary to their written doctrine, 3 *Bul.* 396; they taught nothing that they were ashamed to write, 3 *Tyn.* 29; against the feigned traditions of the apostles, 1 *Bul.* 64, 3 *Bul.* 396, 4 *Bul.* 535, 3 *Jew.* 436, &c.; men's traditions, 3 *Bec.* 603, 1 *Bul.* 208; why they are commended, 2 *Bul.* 311; Paul teaches believers to beware of them, 1 *Tyn.* 508; of unwritten verities, 3 *Bec.* 520, *Hutch.* 124, 2 *Tyn.* 100; Cranmer's CONFUTATION OF UNWRITTEN VERITIES, 2 *Cran.* 1, &c.; another treatise Of Unwritten Verities, ascribed by some to Cranmer, *ib.* 514, &c.; the term is a new invention of the Papists, *ib.* 52; pretended unwritten verities broached by them, *ib.* 10, 515; the origin of unwritten verities, *ib.* 515; the danger of admitting them, *Sand.* 14, 15; they are not to be credited, 2 *Tyn.* 142; the traditions in the decretal epistles are empty trifles, *Whita.* 609; tradition considered by Papists to be of equal authority with holy scripture, *Rog.* 78; the Muscovites have the like opinion, *ib.* 79; our faith should be based on scripture, not on unwritten tradition, *Sand.* 12—14; the latter not so sure as the former, *Rid.* 221; Papists teach that some things, not written, must be believed for salvation, 3 *Tyn.* 26; More's attempt to prove this, answered, *ib.* 96, 97, 100; all that is necessary to salvation is contained in scripture, 1 *Ful.* 89, *Rog.*

76; to admit that tradition is necessary is to make scripture insufficient, 2 *Cran.* 10, 1 *Ful.* 172; concerning the perfection of scripture, against human traditions, *Whita.* 496, &c.; tradition to be received if consonant with scripture, but not otherwise, *Rog.* 316—321, *Whita.* 625; it must be tried by scripture, 3 *Tyn.* 133; it is not necessary that traditions be like in all places, *Rog.* 313, &c.; dogmas and practices alleged to rest upon tradition, *Whita.* 511, 2 *Zur.* 194; it is not needful to prove the authority or genuineness of the books of scripture, *Whita.* 530, &c.; it is not necessary to prove the Trinity, &c., *ib.* 534, &c.; it was not the ground of Arius' condemnation at Nice, *ib.* 562, 563; the descent of Christ into hell is not dependent on it, *ib.* 536, 537; the procession of the Holy Ghost from the Son is not derived from it, *ib.* 536; nor the doctrine of original sin, *ib.*; nor the virginity of Mary, *ib.* 538, 539; the sacraments are not dependent on it, *ib.* 538; the baptism of infants does not rest upon it, *ib.* 540; against the allegation that it is necessary in the interpretation of scripture, 3 *Jew.* 240, &c.; Romish arguments for tradition considered and refuted, *Whita.* 515; reasons against unwritten verities, 2 *Cran.* 52; against man's traditions and unwritten verities, with sentences and examples of scripture, 1 *Bec.* 434, &c.; scriptures alleged by the Papists for unwritten verities answered, 2 *Cran.* 53; the arguments from scripture whereby Bellarmine proves the existence of some true traditions refuted, *Whita.* 542, &c.; examination of certain texts alleged in favour of tradition, *Phil.* 363, &c.; More explains the "two pence" in the parable of the Samaritan to be the two testaments, and says the further sum to be expended denotes tradition, 3 *Tyn.* 93 n.; doctors alleged for unwritten verities, 2 *Cran.* 56; men's traditions censured by Chrysostom and Ambrose, 1 *Ful.* 171; arguments from councils examined, *Whita.* 562; answer to the objection that some barbarous nations have received the faith without writing, *ib.* 520; tradition is very hard to be preserved, *ib.* 651, &c.; means for preserving it specified by Bellarmine, viz. ecclesiastical writings, usage, ancient monuments, heresy, *ib.* 656, 657; it has always been various and uncertain, *Calf.* 212, *Whita.* 664—667; its uncertainty is the reason why the scriptures were written, *Whita.* 655; it was alleged by both parties, in the ancient disputes about Easter, *Sand.* 20, *Whita.* 539, 540; ancient traditions disregarded by the Romanists, *Calf.* 270, 3 *Jew.* 436; no popish tradition observed by all churches, *Whita.* 504, 506; tradition is a fallible token of a true church, 1 *Hoop.* 82; tradition not universally rejected by heretics, as some allege, *Whita.* 610; the old heretics based their doctrine on it, *Sand.* 15, *Whita.* 667, 668; the Valentinians relied on it, 2 *Ful.* 219; it is a ground of popery, *Sand.* 16, 19; tradition as to purgatory, *Whita.* 541; the mass falsely supported by it, 1 *Hoop.* 236; traditions relating to baptism, prayer, crossing the forehead, offices of bishops, &c., 2 *Cran.* 56—58; the council of Trent orders traditions to be received, but explains not what those traditions are, *Whita.* 511; statements by that council, *Rog.* 79, 200, 209; rules of the Papists for distinguishing true from false traditions, *Whita.* 503; probations out of scripture that those which fight with the word of God ought to be banished out of the congregation of true Christians, 3 *Bec.* 324, &c.; how much man's traditions were observed, 2 *Bec.* 414; they were esteemed as God's laws, 2 *Cran.* 146; the grievous burden of them, 3 *Tyn.* 94; thanksgiving to God for bringing us out of the darkness of them, 3 *Bec.* 65, &c.

Traditors: those who gave up the scriptures and sacred vessels to the persecutors, 1 *Tyn.* 144 n

Traheron (Barth.) v. Tracy (R).
Notice of him, 3 *Zur.* 316 n.; at Zurich, 4 *Bul.* xii; at Strasburgh, 3 *Zur.* 609; in the service of lord Cromwell, *ib.* 626; intends to marry and keep a school, *ib.* 226; mentioned, *ib.* 378, 382, 384, 387, &c.; in parliament, *ib.* 266; tutor to the young duke of Suffolk, *ib.* 465; occupied with Greek literature, *ib.* 431; his controversy with Hooper on predestination, 2 *Hoop.* xi, 3 *Zur.* 406, 416, 426; an exile (alias Pilkinton), 1 *Cran.* (9); at Frankfort, 3 *Zur.* 763; letters by him; *ib.* 316—328

Traitors: v. Rebellion.

Trajan, emperor: would be called pontifex maximus, 4 *Jew.* 983; persecution under him, 2 *Bul.* 105; Pliny wrote to him about the Christians, 1 *Bec.* 17, 4 *Bul.* 166, 193, *Hutch.* 228 n., 2 *Jew.* 1002, 1089, *Phil.* 19, 2 *Whitg.* 492; he became, through Pliny's report, more gentle towards them, 2 *Hoop.* 615, *Pil.* 333; his library called Ulpia, 2 *Jew.* 981; fable of the release of his soul by Gregory's massing, 2 *Brad.* 290, 2 *Cov.* 269

Translation: remarks thereon by Sir Jo. Cheke, 3 *Zur.* 146; it ought to be literal where the sense is ambiguous, 1 *Cran.* 190

Transubstantiation: v. Mass, Supper of the Lord.

The term a new one, 1 *Hoop.* 210, 1 *Jew.* 11, 44, 2 *Jew.* 990; what it means, 2 *Bec.* 262, 1 *Jew.* 534; the doctrine defined, 1 *Cran.* 45, 3 *Jew.* 497, &c.; defenders of the doctrine are not agreed among themselves, 1 *Hoop.* 116, 167, 3 *Jew.* 490, *Phil.* 99; different opinions as to the words which effect it, 2 *Bec.* 263, *Rid.* 11, 18, 26, 27; various scholastic phrases devised to cloak the difficulty of the bodily presence, *Grin.* 44, 3 *Tyn.* 254; it is said that the accidents of the bread and wine remain in the sacrament, but not their substance, 1 *Cran.* 45, 254, 256, 260, 261, 267, 273, 274, 284, 301, 323, 324, 326, 328, *Grin.* 44, 2 *Jew.* 562, &c.; accidents cannot be broken, eaten, &c., 1 *Cran.* 324; on the Romish doctrine that the body of Christ remains as long as the accidents of the bread remain without corruption, 2 *Jew.* 775, &c.; Romanists teach that the sacrament is God indeed, but only for a season, *ib.* 777, &c.; the doctrine of transubstantiation considered, condemned, and refuted, 2 *Bec.* 260, &c., 3 *Bec.* 369, 370, 524, 1 *Brad.* 456, 532, &c., 542, &c., 2 *Brad.* 157, 269, &c., 4 *Bul.* 274, 1 *Cov.* 453, 454, 2 *Cov.* 248, &c., *Grin.* 193, 2 *Hoop.* 394, 402, &c., *Hutch.* 245, 1 *Jew.* 445, &c., 480, &c., 2 *Jew.* 796, 1 *Lat.* 275, 2 *Lat.* 251, 286, *Phil.* 179, &c., 183, 398, *Rid.* 156, &c., 171, &c., 192, &c., *Rog.* 285, 287, 1 *Tyn.* 278, 366, 367, 380, 381, 2 *Tyn.* 221, 3 *Tyn.* 178, 222, &c.; unless it can be proved to have been received universally before the bishops of Rome defined it, it must be deemed a popish faith, 1 *Cran.* 22; it is plainly a papistical doctrine, *ib.* 305; a papistical, wicked, and devilish error, 2 *Bec.* 260, &c.; a carnal doctrine, *Sand.* 89, 3 *Tyn.* 239, &c., 244; it is antichristian, 1 *Brad.* 373; horrible and idolatrous, *ib.* 435, 442; the darling of the devil, *ib.* 450; simple and plain people cannot understand, nor the Papists defend it, 1 *Cran.* 328; arguments in favour of it, with replies thereto, *Hutch.* 269, &c.; it is not contained in scripture, but is contrary thereto, 2 *Bec.* 262, &c., 1 *Cran.* 12, 13, 95, 241, 304, 329, 1 *Hoop.* 112, *Hutch.* 267, *Phil.* 61, *Rid.* 171, 172, 198, 3 *Tyn.* 231, 234, 235; examination of scriptures alleged for it, 1 *Tyn.* 367, 368, 3 *Tyn.* 223—230, 236—244; it is not taught by Christ in the sixth chapter of John, 4 *Bul.* 447, *Grin.* 44, 2 *Hoop.* 191, 450, 1 *Jew.* 451, *Rid.* 175, *Rog.* 289, 3 *Tyn.* 227—230; the words of consecration do not prove it, for they are to be expounded mystically, 4 *Bul.* 253, 435, 438, 441, 445, *Coop.* 199, *Grin.* 39, 40, 1 *Hoop.* 114, &c., 119, 120, 147, 162, 528, 529, *Hutch.* 258, 2 *Jew.* 606, 787, 788, *Phil.* 95, 99, *Rid.* 157; what the word "This" refers to, 1 *Hoop.* 116, 148, 529, 2 *Jew.* 606, 607, 623, 788, 789, *Phil.* 99, *Rid.* 315 (see Individuum vagum); "est" is frequently equivalent to "significat," 3 *Tyn.* 249, 258, 261; it cannot be interpreted, in any language by "transubstantiare," *Coop.* 197; Papists play with syllables in a high mystery, teaching that the conversion does not take place till the last syllable of "Hoc est corpus meum," is pronounced, 1 *Cran.* 246, *Rid.* 27; the doctrine is not agreeable with a strictly literal interpretation of the words of institution, 3 *Tyn.* 243; if the bread be transubstantiated, so is the chalice, 1 *Hoop.* 122, *Rid.* 204; it is disproved by the circumstances of the institution, *Phil.* 398; Paul knew not of transubstantiation, 2 *Bec.* 264; his words prove that the bread remains bread after sanctification, 1 *Cran.* 250; transubstantiation is opposed to the analogy of faith, *Whita.* 472; it is not to be believed merely on account of God's omnipotency, *Coop.* 194, 196, 1 *Cran.* 34, 1 *Hoop.* 168, 2 *Jew.* 581; in this controversy, his will, not his power, is the subject of dispute, 1 *Cran.* 15; had the doctrine been only beyond our reason, faith would have received it, if expressly taught in scripture, 3 *Tyn.* 231; but it is to be rejected, because it is contrary to scripture, *ib.* &c.; it is not to be stablished from the nature of faith, 1 *Hoop.* 220; it is not proved by the real presence, 1 *Cran.* 241; antiquity is against it, 2 *Cran.* 453, 1 *Hoop.* 235, *Phil.* 40, 61; it is not affirmed by any ancient writer, but is contrary to the doctrine of all the fathers, 2 *Bec.* 262, &c., 3 *Bec.* 423, &c., 426, 427, 1 *Brad.* 99, 4 *Bul.* 438, 1 *Cran.* 13, 263, & passim, 2 *Hoop.* 440, *Hutch.* 271—275, 4 *Jew.* 765, *Rid.* 28, &c., 173, &c., 200, 3 *Tyn.* 228 n.; fathers untruly alleged in support of it, *Hutch.* 38, 39; such a speech was used by the old doctors, but not with a gross meaning, *Coop.* 38, 211, &c., 1 *Tyn.* 372; they spoke mystically, 1 *Tyn.* 370; the doctrine was not charged upon the church by any of the ancient heretics, *ib.* 372; not received by the Greek church, 2 *Bec.* 266, 3 *Bec.* 232, 426, 618, 1 *Jew.* 139, *Rid.* 237, 249; arguments against it, 1 *Brad.* 85—91, 544, 1 *Hoop.* 147, 514, 528, 2 *Hoop.* 402, 412, 443, *Rid.* 16—20, 171, &c.; from the nature of Christ's humanity, 1 *Hoop.* 113, 1 *Jew.* 480, &c., *Rid.* 175; from his ascension into heaven, and session

TRANSUBSTANTIATION — TREASON

at God's right hand, *Rid.* 176, 212; from the nature of a sacrament, 2 *Bec.* 270, 1 *Brad.* 395, 2 *Brad.* 273, 2 *Cov.* 252, 1 *Hoop.* 127, *Rid.* 175, *Rog.* 286; from reason and the evidence of our senses, 2 *Bec.* 262, 1 *Cran.* 255, 304, *Grin.* 59, 1 *Hoop.* 112; from nature's abhorrence of a vacuum, 1 *Cran.* 250, 251, 252, 330; from the operation of natural causes upon the sacramental meats, 2 *Bec.* 262, 1 *Cran.* 250, 251, 252, *Grin.* 61, 1 *Hoop.* 123, 224; the body of Christ is imprisoned by Papists in a box, and afterward burned when it is mouldy, *Grin.* 50; the burying of the sacrament, 1 *Jew.* 188, 192; whether a mouse or other beast can eat the body of Christ, *Bale* 154, 158, 2 *Jew.* 782, &c.; directions of the Romish church in case of the host being eaten by a mouse or other animal, with references to books on this point, 2 *Ful.* 21 n.; transubstantiation is a new doctrine, 2 *Bec.* 260, 262, 2 *Brad.* 282, 2 *Cov.* 261, *Grin.* 72, 1 *Hoop.* 526; brought in about 1000 years after Christ, 2 *Brad.* 274, 2 *Cov.* 253; when the corporal presence began to be discussed, 1 *Hoop.* 524; the church much troubled by controversies respecting it, *Rid.* 5; by whom transubstantiation was introduced into the church, 1 *Hoop.* 118; the mass book itself is a witness against the doctrine, *Bale* 92, 93; Rome its mother, 1 *Hoop.* 117; what moved the school-authors to take up the doctrine against all reason, 1 *Cran.* 302; Gregory VII. appointed a three days' fast to get a sign from heaven respecting the real presence, 1 *Jew.* 534; Erasmus says it was long and very late ere the church determined the article of transubstantiation, 4 *Jew.* 785; it was first authoritatively asserted in the council of Lateran, 1215, under pope Innocent III., 2 *Bec.* 260, 262, 268, 3 *Bec.* 274, 361, 426, 1 *Brad.* 511 n., 524, 545, 3 *Bul.* 82, 1 *Cran.* 239, 240, 1 *Hoop.* 526, 2 *Hoop.* 48, 522, 1 *Jew.* 11, 44, 549, 2 *Jew.* 549, 562, 564, 1067, 1116, 3 *Jew.* 488, 489, 4 *Jew.* 784, *Rid.* 16 n., 246, 315; promoted by Honorius III. and Urban IV., *Bale* 168; the doctrine as now maintained was laid down by Thomas Aquinas, 1 *Tyn.* 149 n.; statements of the Canon Law, see p. 475, col. 2, above; statements of Rob. Holket, see p. 393, col. 2, above; the doctrine was supported by the Six Articles, 1 *Cran.* 240; the defence of it not to be allowed, 2 *Hoop.* 134; doctrine of the council of Trent respecting it, 2 *Brad.* 227 n., 1 *Cov.* 453, 454; the papistical doctrine passes the fondness of all the philosophers, 1 *Cran.* 254; Papists called to be ashamed of it, 3 *Bec.* 426; it involves monstrous and unnecessary miracles, 2 *Hoop.* 410, *Rid.* 200, 3 *Tyn.* 261, 262; it is contrary to the nature of miracles, *Coop.* 195; it involves many absurdities and inconveniences, 2 *Brad.* 283, 284, 2 *Cov.* 262, 263, 1 *Cran.* 324—332, 1 *Hoop.* 122, *Rid.* 198, &c.; priests are said to create the Creator, *Rog.* 41; Christ is every day made anew by it, 1 *Cran.* 303; evils proceeding from it, 2 *Brad.* 276, 2 *Cov.* 255; it subverts our faith in Christ, 1 *Cran.* 43; encourages various heresies, *ib.* 339, 340, *Rid.* 175, 200; if the nature and substance of bread and wine remain in the sacrament after consecration, the doctrine must be given up, or else the error of the Nestorians must be followed, 1 *Cran.* 299, 301; transubstantiation involves idolatry, *Bale* 215, 3 *Bec.* 274, 275, 1 *Cran.* 329, 1 *Hoop.* 311, 1 *Jew.* 11—13 (v. Host, Mass); More says it would not hurt us, if we should in ignorance worship an unconsecrated host, 3 *Tyn.* 122 n., 123; the doctrine causes Turks and other unbelievers to reject Christianity, *Wool.* 26, &c.; it hangs on reason, 2 *Brad.* 272, 2 *Cov.* 251; Tho. Aquinas, and after him More, illustrate the doctrine by comparing the presence of Christ's body to the reflection of a man's face in many glasses at once, 3 *Tyn.* 235; the fallacy of this comparison, *ib.*; transubstantiation is the root of the corruption of Christianity, 1 *Cran.* 6; the foundation of all popery, 1 *Brad.* 84; it and constrained celibacy go together, *Pil.* 573; our conversion into Christ is the very transubstantiation that God delights in, 2 *Hoop.* 152

Trapezuntius (Geo.): v. George of Trebizond.

Trappes (Mr.), of London: *Park.* 167

Travail: to labour in argument, *Phil.* 135

Travellers: v. Prayers, Journey.

Encouraged by the promises of God that they shall have necessary things, 2 *Bec.* 606, 607

Travers (Walter): disputes at the Temple between him and Hooker, 3 *Whitg.* xvi; Eccl. Discipl.... Explicatio, *Grin.* 353 n., *Park.* 477 n., 2 *Whitg.* 106 n., 3 *Whitg.* xxxii.

Traves (Jo.), or Travers: 2 *Brad.* 1 n., 7 41, 44, 76, 77; his letters to Bradford, 2 *Brad.* 1, 16; letters to him, *ib.* 4, 10, 17, 20, 22, 25, 26, 28, 31, 33

Travise: traverse, 1 *Hoop.* 89

Treachery: the sin of treachery, *Sand.* 120

Treacle: a medicine, remedy, antidote, 2 *Bul.* 27; its use, 2 *Cran.* 86; more frequently spelled triacle, *ib.* 122, 1 *Jew.* 391, 2 *Jew.* 992, 3 *Whitg.* 147

Treason: v. Rebellion.

Treasure: common treasures, 1 *Bul.* 923; treasure in heaven, 2 *Tyn.* 101
Treate: a point treated of, *Phil.* 340
Treaties: *v.* Kings, iii.
Treatise: *v.* Fasting, Scriptures.
Tree (Mother): martyred at Grinstead, *Poet.* 168
Tree of life: *Bale* 617, *Calf.* 101, 102
Treen: wooden, 1 *Jew.* 121, 2 *Jew.* 993, 1 *Whitg.* 36
Trees: we are like trees, *Pil.* 67, 68
Tregonwell (Sir Jo.), or Dr Trygonell: 2 *Cran.* 244, 261, 560; prebendary of Westminster, and a member of parliament, *Now.* i; letter to him, 2 *Cran.* 256
Tremellius (Imm.): notice of him, *Park.* 333 n.; with Cranmer at Lambeth, 3 *Zur.* 535; Hebrew professor at Cambridge, 2 *Zur.* 97 n., 190 n., 3 *Zur.* 716; probably referred to as Emmanuel, *Sand.* xvi; letter from him to Parker, *Park.* 332
Trenchard (Sir Tho.): receives the archduke Philip, 2 *Bec.* 622 n
Trent: *v.* Councils.
Trental: a service of thirty masses, 1 *Brad.* 49 n., 71, 372, 2 *Cran.* 63, 147, 157, 273; *Grin.* 30, 1 *Lat.* 56 n., 2 *Lat.* 243, *Pil.* 20, *Rid.* 319, 510, 1 *Tyn.* 148 n.; the communion not to be used thus, 2 *Hoop.* 146
Trentham (Rich.): grantee of Roucester abbey, 2 *Cran.* 379 n
Tresham (Will.): vice-chancellor of Oxford, 2 *Jew.* 952 n; he disputes with P. Martyr, *Jew.* viii; baptizes the great bell at Christ church, Oxford, *ib.* x., *Rog.* 266; disputes with Ridley, *Rid.* 191; prays for his conversion, *ib.* 245; disputes also with Latimer, 2 *Lat.* 266, &c.; and with Cranmer, 1 *Cran.* 391; concerned in the process against the latter, 2 *Cran.* 546; his deposition against him, *ib.* 549
Trespasses: *v.* Debts, Forgiveness, Prayer (The Lord's), Sin.
Trethwiffe (Tho.): 1 *Tyn.* 148 n
Treveth (Nich.): *v.* Triveth.
Trevisa (Jo. de): translates Higden's Polychronicon, *Pil.* 598 n.; says Bede translated the gospel of John, *Whita.* 222
Trevison (Jo.), proctor: 2 *Cran.* 492
Trew (......): a free-will-man, 1 *Brad.* 318 n., 2 *Brad.* 243, 244, 358; letters to him, 2 *Brad.* 180, 181
Tria (Engelram de): 2 *Tyn.* 292 n
Triacle: *v.* Treacle.
Trial: *v.* Throckmorton (Sir N.).
Tribbechovius (......): De Doct. Scholast. Cor., 1 *Hoop.* 47 n
Tribulation, Trouble: *v.* Affliction.

The godly and the wicked are troubled, but in different ways, *Nord.* 135; man shall always have trouble in this world, 1 *Lat.* 436; it is to be expected in building God's house, *Pil.* 396, &c.; it is always the portion of the faithful, 2 *Lat.* 183; it is not expedient that Christian men should be delivered from the troubles of the world, 2 *Hoop.* 230; trouble cannot hurt God's children, 1 *Brad.* 419, 2 *Cov.* 235; it is profitable to them, 1 *Hoop.* 509; a blessing, and the gift of God, 1 *Tyn.* 138; the time of tribulation is better for them than the time of joy, *Phil.* 226; how they should behave in it, 2 *Hoop.* 313; their comfort in it, 1 *Tyn.* 141; by tribulation we are certified to be the children of God, *Phil.* 290; patient expectation in troubles declareth that we are bound unto God, 2 *Hoop.* 317; a song of praise for God's present help in trouble, *Nord.* 150
Tribute: *v.* Oaths.

What is meant by tribute, 1 *Bec.* 220; it is to be paid, *ib.* 219, 220, 1 *Lat.* 282, 301, 307, 513; it is due to princes, *Sand.* 53, 199; kings may impose taxes, 1 *Lat.* 299; we are bound to pay them though unjust, *ib.* 300; not to pay them is theft, *ib.* 299. 300, 512; compulsory oaths as to the amount of a man's property condemned, 1 *Tyn.* 187; the Jews paid taxes to the king of Persia, *Pil.* 457; tribute was paid by our Saviour, and by Peter, 1 *Tyn.* 189; Paul's command respecting it, *ib.* 191; if taxes ought to be paid to a heathen, much more to a Christian king, 1 *Lat.* 306; why we ought to pay tribute, 1 *Bec.* 220, 2 *Hoop.* 110; it is a note of our obedience, 2 *Hoop.* 109, 110; it is to be paid for conscience' sake, *ib.*; it is to be paid cheerfully, *Park.* 8; objection against paying it answered, 1 *Bec.* 220, 221; taxes generally avoided by the clergy, 1 *Tyn.* 189; Antichrist exempts his from toll and tribute, 3 *Bec.* 514
Tricennals: trentals, 1 *Lat.* 56
Triers: a place of pilgrimage, *Bale* 633
Trigonel (Sir Jo.): *v.* Tregonwell.
Trilia (Bern. de): *v.* Bernard.
Trindals: rolls of wax, 2 *Cran.* 155, 503; trindles, *Rid.* 532
Trinity (The Holy): *v.* God.
Trinity knots: *Pil.* 80
Tripartita Historia: *v.* Cassiodorus.
Tripartitum Opusculum: *v.* Councils, *Lat. III.*
Tritheites: not only distinguish, but divide the persons of the Trinity, *Rog.* 44; affirm the Holy Ghost to be inferior to the Father, *ib.* 72
Trithemius (Jo.), or à Trittenheim: notices of him, 4 *Bul.* 515 n., 1 *Hoop.* 327 n., *Rid.* 159 n.; his works, *Calf.* 69, 115, 258 nn., *Jew.* xliii; he makes the authority of the

church equal to that of scripture, *Rog.* 79; gives testimony as to the abandonment of Arian tendencies by Eusebius, 2 *Ful.* 359 n.; commends Bertram, 3 *Bec.* 449, *Rid.* 159; says Anselm wrote many books which never came to his knowledge, 4 *Jew.* 808; praises Gerson, 3 *Jew.* 133; his cabalistical writings censured, 1 *Hoop.* 327

Triumphed: made to triumph, 2 *Jew.* 933

Triveth (Nich.): on superstition, 1 *Hoop.* 314; his notes on Augustine De Civ. Dei, *Jew.* xxxiii, 1 *Jew.* 150 n

Trombeta (Ant.): notice of him, 1 *Tyn.* 152 n

Tronian (St): v. Ronan.

Tropes: v. Figures, Metaphors.

Trophimus: 4 *Bul.* 44

Trophonius: his case, 1 *Hoop.* 290

Tropicks: affirmed the Holy Ghost to be a mere creature, *Rog.* 70

Tropological sense: v. Scripture.

Trothes: truths, *Calf.* 48

Trouble: v. Tribulation.

Troy: 1 *Bul.* 417

Trullan synod: v. Councils, *Const.* (691).

Trumbett (Ant.): v. Trombeta.

Trumpets: their use and importance, *Pil.* 442; the blowing of trumpets amongst the Jews, 2 *Bul.* 142, 1 *Tyn.* 352; the feast of trumpets, 2 *Bul.* 165; the seven trumpets in the Apocalypse, *Bale* 343, &c.

Trunchfield (Joan): she was one of the two women burnt at Ipswich, *Poet.* 166

Trushman: substitute, 3 *Jew.* 357

Trust: v. Faith.

Not to be placed in physic, horses, &c., *Pil.* 230

Truth: v. Prayers.

What it is, 3 *Bec.* 604, 620: God is truth, *Hutch.* 51; assured knowledge of the truth is attainable by the teaching of God, 2 *Lat.* 336; the truth is ever certain and simple, 2 *Jew.* 593; it throws down men and advances Christ, *Sand.* 22; the doctrine of it is needful to repentance, 3 *Bul.* 57; its enemies, p. 297, col. 2, above; it is always assaulted by Satan, 1 *Hoop.* 26; how it must be judged, *Calf.* 60, 61; it is not afraid of the light, 1 *Cran.* 368; it is darkened by man's wisdom, 1 *Hoop.* 27; often hid in corners, *Phil.* 121; suppressed by the multitude in queen Mary's days, 3 *Bec.* 243; some were prisoners for confessing it, *ib.* 244; it cannot be burned or imprisoned, 1 *Brad.* 457; the complaint of Verity, verses, 2 *Brad.* 364; a dialogue between Custom and Verity, *Grin.* 35; custom must yield to it, 1 *Jew.* 49, 154, *Whita.* 613; it cannot be maintained with lies, *Rid.* 10; it is to be preferred to peace, 1 *Lat.* 487, 2 *Lat.* 347; we must walk in truth, *Sand.* 118, 122, &c.; the truth is to be testified by preaching, *ib.* 291; by writing, *ib.*; by suffering, *ib.* 292; it must be spoken always, 2 *Lat.* 90; must be truly uttered, *Pil.* 487; must be spoken though it give offence, 2 *Lat.* 77; the danger of withstanding it, 1 *Cov.* 501; to withhold the truth which we know, is treason to Christ, 2 *Lat.* 298; to deny it is not the way to keep our goods, 2 *Bul.* 100; it and falsehood are nigh neighbours, 4 *Jew.* 1167

Trygonell (Sir Jo.): v. Tregonwell.

Tserclas (Anne de): the wife of bp Hooper, q. v.

Tsion: for Zion, *Poet.* 418

Tubeta (Ant.): v. Trombeta.

Tubingen: 2 *Cov.* viii, xii.

Tubman (Will.): servant to Grindal, *Grin.* 462

Tuchyner (......), master at Winchester college, *Phil.* i.

Tudeschi (Nich. de), abbot of Palermo, commonly called Panormitanus: *Jew.* xli; he admits that the apostles gave the Holy Ghost without chrism, 3 *Jew.* 178; says Augustine had a wrong opinion of original sin, 4 *Jew.* 786, 787; observes that the true faith of Christ may remain in one alone; and *so* it is true to say that faith faileth not in the church, 4 *Jew.* 724; says, custom prevails not against the law of God, 3 *Jew.* 423; states that notwithstanding the priest say mass, with the intention that God would destroy some man, yet doth he consecrate, *ib.* 454; ascribes to the pope the fulness of power, 4 *Jew.* 832; calls him the bishop of all the world, *ib.* 827; says that he holds the place of God in the earth, &c., *Rog.* 38 n.; declares that Christ and the pope make one consistory, and says, that sin only excepted, the pope in a manner can do all things that God can do, 3 *Jew.* 270, 272, 284, 559, 560, 4 *Jew.* 831, 831, 939, 940; says he may dispense against the New Testament, 3 *Jew.* 218, 599, *Rog.* 191; moves a doubt whether he may deprive all the bishops in the world at one time, 3 *Jew.* 329, 330; declares that the pope, notwithstanding he take money for bestowing a bishoprick, &c., commits no simony, 4 *Jew.* 869; prefers the assertion of a private person, supported by scripture, to a pope or council, 2 *Bec.* 261, 3 *Bec.* 392, 2 *Cran.* 37, 2 *Jew.* 677, 3 *Jew.* 177, 4 *Jew.* 712, 775, 1054, *Phil.* 357, *Pil.* 532 n., 626; allows that the laws and determinations of popes and councils cannot, in strait manner of speech, be called the laws of God, 4 *Jew.* 1052; affirms that the pope may be a here-

TUDESCHI — TURKS

tic, and of heretics may be judged, 4 *Jew*. 928; says the pope is bound to confess himself, and that in so doing the priest is above him, *ib.* 674, 704, 1037; affirms that the cardinalship stands by the law of God, *ib.* 784; considers that a cardinal, for receiving a palfrey of a nobleman, is not thought to commit simony, *ib.* 869 (but see the note); allows that single life is not of the substance of holy orders, 2 *Jew*. 993, 3 *Jew*. 404, 417, 507; remarks that the priests of Greece, being within orders, do marry wives without sin or breach of law, either of God or of man, 3 *Jew*. 423, 4 *Jew*. 809; considers that the pope might have a wife, 4 *Jew*. 809; asserts that a priest is not to be deposed for simple fornication, 3 *Jew*. 145; says, a priest that keeps a concubine, unless notoriously, may not be refused in his service, 4 *Jew*. 637, 641; declares a bishop not bound to deprive a priest that keeps a concubine, *ib.* 639; would have those that cannot live chaste contract matrimony, 3 *Jew*. 427; concludes that a harlot may dispose of her goods, 4 *Jew*. 647; says that the prince's law, if it be prejudicial or hurtful to the church, is not extended unto the church, unless it be expressly allowed by the pope; but if it be profitable for the church, we must think it is allowed, unless it be expressly disallowed, *ib.* 1032; lays it down as a rule in law, that error in name marreth not the matter, so that the body or party be known, *ib.* 635

Tudor (Edm.), earl of Richmond: Margaret (Beaufort) his wife, 2 *Cran.* 358

Tudson (Jo.), or Tutson: martyred, *Poet.* 165, 3 *Zur.* 175 n

Tuesday (Shrove): why so called, *Grin.* 140

Tufton (Mr): *Park.* 198

Tuke (Sir Brian): 1 *Tyn.* xxxvi.

Tullibardin: *v.* Murray (W.), of Tullibardin.

Tully (M.): *v.* Cicero.

Tunbridge, co. Kent: the grammar-school founded by Sir And. Judd, *Park.* 210

Tunic: an ancient vestment, not peculiar to the clergy, 1 *Zur.* 350 n.; two different kinds, *ib.*

Tunicle: worn with the albe, *Lit. Edw.* 76, 170; to be abolished, *Grin.* 135, 159; the word used by Tyndale in Exodus, 1 *Tyn.* 420

Tunis: the kingdom desired by Don John of Austria, 1 *Zur.* 327 n

Tunstall (Cuthb.): *v.* Tonstal.

Turbervile (James), bishop of Exeter: 1 *Zur.* 10 n.; prisoner in the Tower, *Park.* 122

Turcas: turquoise, *Bale* 607

Turelupini: a medieval sect, 2 *Jew.* 689

Turkened, or Turkised: furbished, *Rog.* 24

Turkey: affairs of it, 2 *Zur.* 246; history of an emperor, 3 *Bec.* 278; the church not extinct there, 4 *Bul.* 73

Turkish stone: turquoise, 3 *Bul.* 336

Turks: *v.* Mahomet, Mahometanism.

Alleged to be Magog, *Bale* 571; their cruelty, 1 *Bec.* 239, 240, 2 *Bul.* 106; their boasting, 1 *Bec.* 289; they reckon their first emperor from the date of the first Romish jubilee, 2 *Bul.* 268; their enmity to the Christian name, *Grin.* 13; they have been the scourge of God, *Lit. Eliz.* 493; the dread of Christendom, *Pil.* 77; they overran the churches of the East, *Pra. Eliz.* 462; their ravages in Hungary (*q. v.*), and various other parts of Christendom, *Bale* 574, 2 *Bul.* 381, 2 *Cran.* 232, *Grin.* 13, 14, 98, *Lit, Eliz.* 451, 454, 461, 524, 527, 533 n., *Pra. Eliz.* 463, 2 *Tyn.* 254, 1 *Zur.* 269, 283; they take Rhodes, 3 *Bec.* 10, 1 *Lat.* 13, 2 *Lat.* 33, 3 *Tyn.* 136; war with them in Germany, 2 *Cran.* 233—236; their contest with Persia, *ib.* 440, *Grin.* 287, 1 *Jew.* 85; they attack Malta, *Lit. Eliz.* 460, 519; but are defeated, *ib.* 461, 524; invade Cyprus, &c. 1 *Zur.* 239 n., 269; defeated at Lepanto, *ib.* 270; they are not to be hated, 3 *Tyn.* 8; they may be resisted, 3 *Tyn.* 212; war against them is commendable, *Grin.* 13, 2 *Zur.* 169; their false religion, *Bale* 572; they are a great multitude, yet in error, 4 *Bul.* 155, 3 *Tyn.* 53; said to be five times as numerous as the Papists, 3 *Tyn.* 53, 70; a part of the devil's church, 4 *Bul.* 11; they do not worship the true God, *ib.* 173, *Wool.* 54; deny the Trinity, *Rog.* 43; say that Christ was a good man like Moses and Mahomet, *ib.* 49; are in error respecting his passion, *ib.* 58; imagine the Holy Ghost to be a bare power and efficacy of God, *Rog.* 72; prefer their own imaginations to the scriptures, *ib.* 79; deface the New Testament, *ib.* 85; think that justification is to be obtained by pilgrimages to Mecca, &c., *ib.* 109; and by works without faith, *ib.* 114; they cannot do good works, 4 *Bul.* 83; they say that all who live uprightly shall be saved, of whatsoever religion they be, *ib.* 160; also that the devils and ungodly in hell, who call upon God for mercy, shall be saved, *ib.* 67; they abhor images, *Calf.* 44, *Wool.* 26; will not suffer an image even in profane or civil things, 2 *Bec.* 68; use the Arabian language in their rites, *Rog.* 242; their priests count it meritorious to injure Christians by lies and forswearing, *ib.* 120; their law against adultery, 2 *Bec.* 649; a hymn, by Rob. Wisdom, for deliverance from

Turk and pope, *Poet.* 494; another petition to the same effect, *ib.* 531; prayer against the Turks, *Pra. Eliz.* 462 n.; woes and miseries coming upon them, 2 *Bul.* 106; Policy of the Turkish Empire, *Rog.* 44, 120, 160, &c. nn.; Aulæ Turcicæ Descriptio, *ib.* 85 n

Turmyne (Rich.): hanged and burnt, *Bale* 51

Turn, return, and half turn: gestures at mass, 2 *Bec.* 451

Turnbull (......), reader of logic at Oxford: 2 *Cran.* 383, 384

Turner (Rich.): a preacher, 2 *Cran.* 349 n.; one of the six preachers at Canterbury, 1 *Bec.* x. n.; he preached in the rebels' camp near Canterbury, 2 *Cran.* 439; proposed as abp of Armagh, *ib.* 438, 439; an exile, 1 *Cran.* (9)

Turner (Rob.): in exile, 1 *Cran.* (9)

Turner (Sharon): his History of Henry VIII., 1 *Hoop.* 38; he refutes imputations on Anne Boleyn, 3 *Zur.* 553 n

Turner (Will.), M.D., dean of Wells: notice of him, 1 *Zur.* 206 n: his birth and education, *Rid.* 488, 492; an exile, 1 *Cran.* (9), *Rid.* 389, 394; he makes one do penance in a priest's square cap, *Park.* 241; his book called Mistress Missa (A New Dialogue, &c.), 2 *Brad.* 287 n., *Rid.* 108, 510; his Preservative or Triacle against the Poison of Pelagius, 1 *Lat.* iii. n.; his Hunting of the Wolf, *Park.* 455; his book against Cooch, 2 *Zur.* 236 n.; letter to Foxe, chiefly concerning Ridley, *Rid.* (487), 491; letter to Bullinger, 2 *Zur.* 124; his death, 1 *Zur.* 206; bp Cox married his widow, 2 *Zur.* 181

Turner (Dr), a physician, son of the dean: 2 *Zur.* 203 n., 209

Turney (Hen.): *v.* Tourney.

Turntippets: 2 *Cran.* 15, *Pil.* 211

Turonense concilium: *v.* Councils, *Tours.*

Turpin (Tho.); letter signed by him, 3 *Zur.* 170; ordained by Grindal, *ib.* n

Turre (Nich. de la): *v.* La Turre.

Turrecremata (Jo. de): *v.* Joannes.

Turrhenus, king of Etruria: 1 *Jew.* 294

Turrianus (Fra.): 1 *Jew.* 351, 352; Advers. Magdeburg. Cent., 2 *Ful.* 301 n

Tusser (Tho.): notice of him, *Poet.* xxiv; principal points of religion, *ib.* 257; his belief, *ib.* 258

Tutbury, co. Stafford: suppression of the priory, 2 *Cran.* 379; the queen of Scots imprisoned in the castle, 1 *Zur.* 210 n., 217 n., 247 n

Tutor: guardian, 3 *Bul.* 5, 2 *Tyn.* 277

Tutson (Jo.): *v.* Tudson.

Tuttie (J.): martyr at Canterbury, *Poet.* 164

Twibytte, or Twibill: a two-edged bill or mattock, 2 *Bec.* 449

Twins: their fortune often unlike, *Hutch.* 87

Twonson (Nich,), printer at Nuremberg: 1 *Tyn.* lvii, 3 *Tyn.* 218

Twynn (Tho.): translates a book by Bullinger, 4 *Bul.* xxvi.

Twysden (Rog.): Hist. Angl. Scriptores Decem, 2 *Ful.* 23 n

Tybald (Tho.), or Tybbold: 2 *Cran.* 340, 341, 3 *Zur.* 16 n., 520 n

Tyburn tippet: 1 *Lat.* 119, 180

Tyburtius (St): *v.* Tiburcius.

Tychonius: his rules, in Augustine, *Whita.* 378, 494, *Rid.* 126; he wrote on the Apocalypse, *Bale* 255

Tyconius: a Donatist, 1 *Ful.* 147

Tyler (Rog.): 2 *Brad.* 397 n

Tyler (Tho.): died in prison, *Poet.* 172

Tyleshardes: tile-sherds, *Calf.* 208

Tyndale family: 1 *Tyn.* xiii, &c.

Tyndale (Hugh), alias Hutchins: 1 *Tyn.* xiii, xiv.

Tyndale (Jo.): arrested and fined for befriending his brother William, 1 *Tyn.* xlii

Tyndale (Tho.), of Kington St Michael: 1 *Tyn.* xiii.

TYNDALE (Will.): mentioned, 1 *Hoop.* 245; called Hitchins, 1 *Tyn.* 37, Hochin, *ib.* xxii, Hotchens, *ib.* xxiii, Hutchyns, *ib.* xxxiv, Hychens, *ib.* xxvi, Hychins, *ib.* xv; his descent, *ib.* xiii; his birth, *ib.* xiv; he studied in both universities, *ib.*; tutor in the family of Sir John Walsh, *ib.* &c.; not a monk, *ib.* xv; summoned to appear before Dr Parker, *ib.* xvii, &c., 395; he preaches at Bristol, *ib.* xviii; quits Gloucestershire for London, *ib.* xxi, 394; seeks the patronage of bp Tonstal, but in vain, *ib.* xxi, 395; befriended by H. Munmouth, *ib.* xxii; he quits England to return no more, *ib.* xxv; his life abroad, including his biblical labours, *ib.* &c.; his knowledge of Hebrew, *ib.* 68; he is shipwrecked, *ib.* xxxix; his epistles to Frith, *ib.* liii, lvii; his manner of life at Antwerp, *ib.* lx; his protestation touching the resurrection of the body, and the state of departed souls, *ib.* lxii; carried off prisoner to Vilvorden, *ib.* lxvii; his martyrdom, *Bale* 394, 3 *Bec.* 11, 1 *Brad.* 288, 1 *Tyn.* lxxv; his last prayer, 1 *Tyn.* lxxv; testimonies to his character and attainments, from Cochlæus, *ib.* xxix; from Herman Busche, as recorded by Spalatinus, *ib.* xxx; from Vaughan, *ib.* xliii, xlv; from Frith's letter to More, *ib.* lvi, 3 *Tyn.* 219; from Joye, 1 *Tyn.* lxii; from Mr Poyntz, *ib.* lxvii; from his jailor and prosecutor, *ib.* lxxii, lxxiv; *ib.* from Foxe, lxxvii; Sir Tho.

More's testimony to his labours, *ib.* lii; his humble estimate of himself, *ib.* lv; he was a Yorkist in principle, *ib.* 458; he had the spirit of Elias, *Bale* 138

His WORKS, edited by the Rev. Hen. Walter, B.D., F.R.S., 1, 2, 3, *Tyn.*; the known and reputed labours of his pen, 3 *Tyn.* 337; some books of his mentioned, 2 *Bec.* 421; works edited by him, 1 *Tyn.* ix; he published lord Cobham's examination, *Bale* 6; likewise that of Will. Thorpe, *ib.* 64; *Rid.* 494 n.; his (?) advertisement prefixed thereto, *Bale* 62; his biblical labours, 2 *Cov.* viii, 2 *Cran.* ix, 1 *Tyn.* xxv. &c., and p. 115, above; not assisted in them by Coverdale, 2 *Cov.* viii; More's objections to Tyndale's version, 3 *Tyn.* 14 n.; articles extracted from his Wicked Mammon by the bishops, with Foxe's remarks on them, and extracts from the examination of W. Tewkesbury, 1 *Tyn.* 46, &c. nn.; the Obedience of a Christian Man, written three years before the Practice of Prelates, 2 *Tyn.* 344; articles which the prelates affirmed to be contained in it, and pronounced heretical, 1 *Tyn.* 170, 173, &c. nn.; Tewkesbury and others condemned for possessing his books, *ib.* 32—36, 46, &c.; works erroneously ascribed to him, *ib.* x.

Tyndale (Will.), monk of Greenwich: 1 *Tyn.* xv, and perhaps another of the name, *ib.*

Tyndall (Humph.), master of Qu. coll. Camb., 3 *Whitg.* 611

Tynedale, a district in Northumberland: *Rid.* 145; the ancient barons of it, 1 *Tyn.* xiii.

Types: *v.* Allegories.

Types of Christ, p. 175, col. 2 above; see also Sacrifices; types of the church, p. 202, col. 2 above; the type of Abraham and his two wives (Gal. iv.), 1 *Tyn.* 307, *Whita.* 405; Israel in the wilderness, the water, the rock, the cloud, &c., *Whita.* 407, 408, David and Goliath, *ib.* 400; reasons grounded on types are uncertain, 2 *Whitg.* 92

Tyrants: an honourable name at first, 2 *Whitg.* 86, 1 *Bul.* 310; who are such, 3 *Bec.* 610; Tyndale uses the word in Gen. vi. 4, now rendered "giants," 1 *Tyn.* 409; a tyrant better than no king at all, *ib.* 180; tyrants are entirely in God's hands, *ib.* 140; why they are suffered to prosper, 2 *Tyn.* 111; God will be revenged on them, *ib.* 245; they cannot kill whom they please, 3 *Bec.* 564; whether they may be resisted, 2 *Zur.* 169; they must not be, 1 *Tyn.* 332, 336, 3 *Tyn.* 180, 188; of the killing of them, 1 *Bul.* 318

Tyre: denounced by Christ, 2 *Hoop.* 209

Tyrology: instruction for mere beginners, 2 *Bec.* 563

Tyrone (Earls of): *v.* O'Neale.

Tyronense concilium: *v.* Councils, *Tours.*

Tyrrell (......): *v.* Tirrell.

Tyteshale (Jo.): wrote on the Apocalypse, *Bale* 257

Tytler (A. F.): England under Edw. and Mary, 1 *Lat.* 161 n

U

Ubiquitaries: otherwise called Synusiasts, *Rog.* 289; Lutheran and Popish ones, *ib.* 293; they say, that Christ, as man, is wherever the Deity is, *ib.* 65; believe Christ's body to be eaten corporally, *ib.* 289, and that by the wicked as well as by the godly, *ib.* 293; they were opposed by Bullinger, *q. v.*; also by P. Martyr, and J. Simler, 1 *Zur.* 307 attacked by Sturmius, 2 *Zur.* 314; the Ubiquitarian controversy, 4 *Jew.* 1245 n., 1264, 1 *Zur.* 92 n., 98, 100, 123, 127, 135, 139, 302, 307, 2 *Zur.* 205, 245 n., 253, 3 *Zur.* 145

Ubiquity: the ubiquity of Christ's body a false doctrine, 4 *Bul.* 447; introduced by Antichrist, 3 *Bec.* 524; heretical, and consenting to Marcion, *ib.* 450

Udal (Jo.): a divine, 1 *Brad.* 562

Udalric, or Hulderic, bp of Augsburgh: writes to pope Nicholas against forbidding priests' marriage, 3 *Jew.* 211, 426, 427, 4 *Jew.* 641, 926; copy of the epistle in English, *Pil.* 568—570; the Latin original, *ib.* 685—687; the epistle is likewise ascribed, but as Cave judges erroneously, to Volusian, bp of Carthage, 3 *Jew.* 427 n., 4 *Jew.* 641, *Sand.* 316 n

Udalric (......): saluted, 3 *Zur.* 334

Udalricus Zazius, *q. v.*

Ufford (Will.), regent of the Carmelites: *Bale* 16

Ugsome: frightful, 3 *Bec.* 179

Ukraine: 3 *Zur.* 600 n

Uladislaus: *v.* Wladislaus.

Ullenson (Jo.): 3 *Zur.* 564

Ulmer (Jo. Rod.), or Ulmius, son of Jo. ab Ulmis: 1 *Zur.* 324, 326, 2 *Zur.* 306, 307

Ulmis (Hen. ab): comes to England, 3 *Zur.* 447 n

Ulmis (Jo. ab): 2 *Brad.* 403 n., 1 *Zur.* 87, 324 n., 2 *Zur.* 306 n., 3 *Zur.* 4 n., 123, 282, 311; patronized by the marquis of Dorset, 3 *Zur.* 84; he studies at Oxford, *ib.* 70, 719; admitted into the king's college (Ch. ch.), *ib.* 389; he often writes to Bullinger, *ib.* 719; takes degrees in arts, *ib.* 360, 389 n., 450; resigns his fellowship at St John's, *ib.* 396 n., 449; letters, mostly to Bullinger, *ib.* 377—457; a postscript by him, *ib.* 323; letter to him, *ib.* 365

Ulmis (Jo. Conrad ab), or Ulmer: comes to England, 3 *Zur.* 447 n.; preacher at Schaffhausen, 4 *Bul.* xxvi; two letters by him, 3 *Zur.* 458, 459

Ulmis (Jo. Gualter ab): 3 *Zur.* 702

Ulmis (Mistress ab): 3 *Zur.* 697

Ulphilas, an Arian bishop: 2 *Jew.* 691, 692; his Gothic version of the scriptures, *ib.* 690, *Whita.* 221

Ulpian, the lawyer: *v.* Law (Civil).
His life saved by Alexander Severus, 2 *Jew.* 981, 982

Ulric, duke of Wurtemberg: succours Brentius, 3 *Zur.* 543 n

Ulstat (Dan.): he and his firm at Antwerp contract for reforming the debased currency, 1 *Zur.* 93 n

Ulster: *v.* Ireland.

Ulstetter (Jo.): married Sarah, daughter to Fagius, 3 *Zur.* 331 n.; letters to him, *ib.* 331, 332

Ulysses: 2 *Bul.* 213

Umpton (Sir Edw.), or Unton: Anne (Seymour) his wife, dau. of the protector Somerset, and widow of Amb. Dudley, earl of Warwick, 1 *Bec.* 396 n., 3 *Zur.* 340 n*., 565 n.; letter to her, 3 *Zur.* 702; a book dedicated to her, *Poet.* xliii.

Unbelief, Infidelity: *v.* Faith.
Sometimes published among the simple under the name of faith, 1 *Jew.* 83; it is the result of ignorance or misunderstanding of God's word, 2 *Hoop.* 173; there is no true faith where there is doubtfulness, 3 *Bec.* 176, 177; two kinds of doubting, 1 *Bul.* 88; unbelief is the root of all evil, both of wickedness and of misery, 2 *Bec.* 396, 1 *Cov.* 240, 2 *Hoop.* 59, 173, *Phil.* 287, *Sand.* 343, 1 *Tyn.* 489—491, 494; mistrust offends God, *Pil.* 135; the greatest dishonour to God is to doubt him, 1 *Brad.* 119, 344; unbelief is emphatically declared in scripture to be sin, 1 *Tyn.* 490; the damning sin, 3 *Tyn.* 173; remedy against it, with sentences and examples of scripture, 1 *Bec.* 405, 406

Unbelievers, Infidels: meaning of the word infidelis, *Nov.* (101); unbelievers' thoughts of God, 2 *Tyn.* 210; their sins are not pardoned because of their infidelity, 2 *Hoop.* 60; how they are guilty of the body and blood of Christ, 4 *Bul.* 466; the Christian's duty towards infidels, 1 *Tyn.* 99; they may not be wronged, *ib.* 204; promises made to them must be kept, *ib.* 206

Unclean: creatures that were so, 2 *Bul.* 210; unclean things, 4 *Bul.* 268; the touching of them, 2 *Bul.* 216

Uncomber (St): his (or her) oats, *Bale* 498 [qu. if St Hunegunda? and see Concumbre].

Unction: *v.* Holy Ghost.
Holy oil, *Pil.* 163, 1 *Tyn.* 224, 225; declared by some of old to be Jewish, 3 *Jew.* 178; the institution of chrism ascribed by tradition to Christ, after the maundy, 2 *Cran.* 515, 516; chrism or holy oil, how made and used, 2 *Jew.* 1136, 3 *Jew.* 178; blasphemously termed the chrism of salvation, *Calf.* 218; Papists say that chrism is necessary to salvation, and yet have none, for Innocent III. says chrism is made of oil and balsam, but the balsam has been omitted for many ages, 3 *Jew.* 178; oil was used by the apostles and fathers, but not as the Romanists use it, *ib.* 235, 243; outward oil avails not, 2 *Tyn.* 184; anointing anciently joined with baptism, 4 *Bul.* 361, *Calf.* 224, 225; such anointing needful, according to Cyprian, *Whita.* 601, 602; introduced by the fathers, says Erasmus, *ib.* 602; not positively unlawful, 2 *Brad.* 385; not received by Novatus, 2 *Ful.* 389; anointing at baptism practised in king Edward's time, *Lit. Edw.* 112; article against its use in baptism, *Grin.* 160; anointing used by Papists in their confirmation, 3 *Bec.* 234, *Rog.* 253, 254, 3 *Tyn.* 20; such chrism not in scripture, 2 *Cran.* 80, 116; anointing of Romish priests, *Pil.* 163, 581, 3 *Tyn.* 19, 176; the ceremony borrowed from the Jews, 3 *Tyn.* 20; no outward anointing is necessary for Christian priests, 1 *Tyn.* 256; the apostles were anointed, not with oil, but with the Spirit, 1 *Tyn.* 229; the anointing of kings,—the chief bishop is the proper person to anoint the king, but any other may, 2 *Cran.* 126; the king a perfect monarch without anointing, *ib.*; the kings of France, being anointed, received the sacrament in both kinds, 1 *Jew.* 206; the kings of Spain not anointed, 4 *Jew.* 1037; anointing of the sick,—on the precept of St James, 3 *Bec.* 374, 619, 4 *Bul.* 521, 522, 2 *Cran.* 99, 2 *Ful.* 170, 2 *Jew.* 1135, &c., 3 *Jew.* 243, *Whita.* 199, 1 *Whitg.* 543; this anointing was a symbol of the gift of healing, *Calf.* 245; its effect has ceased, *ib.*; extreme unction was used by the old heretics called Heracleonites, *Phil.* 424; on the Romish sacrament of extreme unction, *Calf.* 244—248, 2 *Jew.* 1135; it is no sacrament, *Pil.* 524, &c., *Rog.* 263; whether sanctioned by St James, see above; anointing of the sick was a temporary sign, not a perpetual sacrament, 2 *Ful.* 170, 3 *Jew.* 243; Rogers affirms that extreme unction is allowed to be administered by any Christian, *Rog.* 263; this does not

---

* Misprinted Ampton, as at p. 24 of this Index.

appear to be the fact, *ib.* n.; but Innocent I. is said to have permitted it to be so ministered, *Calf.* 246; anoiling has no promise, and is altogether superstitious, 1 *Tyn.* 275; More maintains the contrary, *ib.* 276 n.; oil for anointing the sick, sold by the bishops to the inferior clergy, 3 *Tyn.* 20; the form of anointing, *Rog.* 263; the unction said to take away venial sin, 2 *Cran.* 117, *Pil.* 527; unction of the sick enjoined by the Institution, and styled a sacrament, 2 *Cran.* 99; unction in sickness not unlawful, 2 *Brad.* 385; permitted by king Edward's first Prayer Book, if desired, *Lit. Edw.* 139, 143, *Lit. Eliz.* xxvi; direction about it, 2 *Hoop.* 147; unction said to be abolished in the church of England, 1 *Zur.* 178 (see 358); we visit the sick and anoint them with the precious oil of the mercy of God, 2 *Jew.* 1103; on the ointment in Psa. xxiii, 2 *Cov.* 314, 2 *Hoop.* 228; Christ's anointing of his people, 2 *Tyn.* 180, 182, 184; meaning of the precept, "Anoint thy head" (Matt. vi.), *ib.* 92

Underhill (Tho.): a rebel, 2 *Cran.* 187 n
Underhill (Edw.): Hooper's champion, 2 *Hoop.* xi.
Underset: supported, 2 *Tyn.* 208
Understanding: *v.* Scripture, v.
  A faculty of the soul, 3 *Bul.* 98, 376
Undertree (......): scheme to take him, *Park.* 460, 462, 463; examined, *ib.* 464; should be hanged, *ib.*
Ungodly: *v.* Wicked.
Unhappy: who is so, 3 *Bec.* 607
Unhele: to uncover, 2 *Tyn.* 322
Uniformity: *v.* Statutes.
  Uniformity of doctrine in all the reformed churches earnestly desired by Cranmer and Calvin, *Rog.* 3; established in this kingdom under Edward VI., *ib.* 4; interrupted by Mary's reign, *ib.* 5; restored under Elizabeth, *ib.* 6; letter by her requiring uniformity in rites and ceremonies, *Park.* 223; letter of Parker on the same, *ib.* 227; proceedings, *ib.* 233, 234, 236, 237; Parker perplexed through want of support in his endeavours, *ib.* 262; course to be adopted, *ib.* 267; uniformity enforced by Parker, *ib.* 270, 272—274, 278; another letter of the queen, *ib.* 386; her care for uniformity, and proceedings to enforce it, *ib.* 451; uniformity of doctrine disturbed by disputes about subscription, *Rog.* 8, and by the Jesuits, *ib.* 10; Whitgift endeavours to promote it by enforcing subscription, *ib.* 11; it was maintained through Elizabeth's reign, *ib.* 20; furthered by James' approval of the canons, *ib.* 22
Unigenitus: *v.* Clement VI.

Unio Dissidentium, otherwise called The Union of Doctors: a book compiled by Herman Bodius, 3 *Tyn.* 187, 213; the same book, or another with a similar title, *Rid.* 490; Unio Dissidentium Tripartita, *ib.* 494 n
Union: *v.* Unity.
  The word used for oneness wherein there is but a single person, 3 *Bec.* 279
Unions: *v.* Chantries, Pluralities.
United Brethren: *v.* Moravians.
Unity: *v.* Church, vi, Love, Prayers, Schism.
  Of unity, 3 *Jew.* 620, &c., *Now.* (104); conjunction with Christ and the church, 4 *Bul.* 333, 1 *Hoop.* 153; true and false unity, *Calf.* 261, &c., 1 *Lat.* 487, *Rid.* 120, *Sand.* 94, 2 *Tyn.* 259; unity is in itself no evidence of truth, 1 *Lat.* 130; they cannot be truly one, who are not one in truth, *Sand.* 429; unity is nothing without verity, 1 *Brad.* 394, *Poet.* 269; to what unity St Paul exhorts, 3 *Tyn.* 123; unity a mark of the church, *Poet.* 275; Christians are all united by two bonds, *Pil.* 367; unity is required in religion and in affection, *Sand.* 93; it depends not on uniformity of rites, *Pil.* 538, 620; unity must be kept, 4 *Bul.* 61; it is to be maintained if possible, *Rid.* 121; to be embraced if it be with verity, *ib.* 157; hindrances to it, *Sand.* 100, &c.; preservatives of it, *ib.* 103, &c.; exhortations to it, 2 *Jew.* 1095, &c., *Sand.* 92, 428, 3 *Zur.* 45; union is almost banished, 3 *Bec.* 40, 41; unity by one pope, 3 *Jew.* 277; unity in the church of England, *Sand.* 95; unity among the reformed, 2 *Ful.* 123; much desired by Cranmer, 2 *Cran.* 420, *Rog.* 3; discord urged as an objection to Christianity, 1 *Lat.* 385; unity of religion, the strength of a state, *Sand.* 49; concord preserves a commonwealth, 3 *Bec.* 598
Universal: *v.* Catholic.
Universal Bishop: *v.* Bishops, Gregory I.
Universal History: 1 *Lat.* 13, 274
Universalism: condemned, *Rog.* 67, 147, 158, &c.; the faith of swine, 2 *Tyn.* 11; article of 1552 against those since called Universalists, *Lit. Edw.* 537, (582)
Universality: *v.* Church.
  Double meaning of the term, *Rid.* 158
Universals: a term in logic, 1 *Tyn.* 157
Universities: *v.* Cambridge, Oxford; also Benefactors, Colleges, Degrees.
  Schools and universities allowed by scripture, 2 *Whitg.* 343; no Christian ones in the apostles' time, *ib.* 354; several mentioned in the Canon Law, 4 *Jew.* 654; the English universities described, 3 *Jew.* 110, 111; they are the eyes of the realm, 1 *Brad.* 443; the seed-plots of future pastors, 3 *Zur.* 710; in Romish times they virtually

excluded the scriptures, 2 *Tyn.* 291; their oaths, *ib.*; their decay and sad condition, 1 *Lat.* 102, 203, 269; Cromwell advised to examine the statutes of the colleges, 2 *Lat.* 393; Bucer's account of the condition of the universities, 3 *Zur.* 543, 546; their state in the time of Elizabeth lamented, 1 *Bul.* 6, 2 *Jew.* 999, *Pil.* 593, 1 *Zur.* 40, 77; racket stirred up by Withers for the reformation of the university windows, *Park.* 234; the Wednesday fish day dispensed with in the universities, *ib.* 235; some improvement in them, 1 *Zur.* 207; controversy about their state, 3 *Whitg.* 395, 396; their possessions, 2 *Whitg.* 389; the devil goeth to the university to teach, not to learn, 1 *Lat.* 203

Unjust: sometimes overcome those who have the juster quarrel, 1 *Bul.* 375

Unkemmed: uncombed, 1 *Bul.* 55

Unless: lest, 1 *Bec.* 366

Unmarried persons: *v.* Prayers.
Their duty, 2 *Bec.* 98, 99, 104

Unneaths: scarcely, 2 *Brad.* 174 ("scantly," *Rid.* 379); unneth, *Phil.* 429; unnethes, *Lit. Eliz.* 256

Unrepentants: are unhappy, 3 *Bul.* 112; they perish, 4 *Bul.* 555

Unrighteous: *v.* Wicked.

Unthankfulness: a grievous sin, *Pil.* 30, 31, 460; the table of the Lord cannot abide it, 1 *Bec.* 120

Unto: until, *Pil.* 205

Unton (Sir Edw.): *v.* Umpton.

Unwellfulness: unhappiness, *Phil.* 387

Unwritten verities: *v.* Tradition.

Upaventure: in case, *Bale* 66

Upeher (T.): an exile, 3 *Zur.* 167 n

Uplandish people: those of higher Germany, 3 *Tyn.* 188

Upper Court, in the Isle of Thanet: 3 *Bec.* 487 n

Urban I., pope: gave the name of high priest to all bishops, 2 *Hoop.* 237; decreed that the Roman pontiff has power to make new laws, 3 *Bec.* 527; ordered the sacramental vessels to be of gold or silver, 1 *Jew.* 15; says the goods of the church ought not to be turned to other than ecclesiastical uses and the commodity of the poor, 1 *Bec.* 24

Urban II., pope: his acts, 1 *Whitg.* 482; he set on foot the crusades, *Pil.* 372; anathematized all clerks who should consent to do homage to any prince for an ecclesiastical preferment, 1 *Tyn.* 380 n., 1 *Whitg.* 482

Urban IV., pope: ordained the feast of Corpus Christi, *Bale* 168, 3 *Bec.* 232, 274, 361, 4 *Bul.* 423, *Grin.* 73, 1 *Hoop.* 527, 1 *Jew.* 10, 516, 549, 2 *Jew.* 774, 3 *Jew.* 553, *Pil.* 535; the ministration of the Lord's supper, under both kinds, to the lay people continued till his time, 2 *Bec.* 243, 244

Urban VI.*, pope: thrust five of his cardinals alive into sacks, and threw them into the sea, 3 *Jew.* 250, 4 *Jew.* 931, 1146; decreed the feast of the Visitation of our Lady, *Pil.* 535

Urban VIII., pope: his Missale, 2 *Ful.* 21 n.; his Pontificale, *Calf.* 15 n., 381 n

Urbanus Regius, *q. v.*

Urbevetanus (Pet.): *v.* Petrus.

Urceus (Ant. Codrus): Sermones, *Jew.* xliv, 1 *Jew.* 150; says, the pope is the greatest bishop, if not in virtue, at least in money, 4 *Jew.* 1082

Ure: use, *Calf.* 304, 1 *Cov.* 173

Uriah: 3 *Bul.* 91, 4 *Bul.* 30, 372

Urian (......): 4 *Jew.* 1190

Urijah, high priest: 4 *Bul.* 70

Urim and Thummim: what, 2 *Bul.* 136, *Pil.* 679; worn in the breastplate, 2 *Jew.* 1017; not in the second Temple, *Pil.* 155

Ursinus: his contention with Damasus, 1 *Jew.* 355

Ursinus (Zech.): compiled the Heidelberg Catechism, 2 *Zur.* 157 n

Urspergensis: *v.* Liechtenaw (Conr. à).

Ursula (St): an Englishwoman, *Bale* 156; martyred at Cologne, *ib.* 192, 4 *Jew.* 650

Uses: those of Salisbury, Hereford, Bangor, York, Lincoln, 2 *Cran.* 518, 523 (see Breviary, Horæ, Missale, &c.).

Usher (James), abp of Armagh: *Calf.* 53, 64, 96, 183, 211, 255, 269, 290, 322 nn., 2 *Ful.* 70, 87, 116, 236, 241, 319, 364 nn.; he published first the interpolated, and afterwards the genuine Ignatian epistles, 2 *Ful.* 235 n.; misapplies words in the epistle of Gildas, *ib.* 186 n.; remarks the identity of passages which occur in the Anglo-Saxon Paschal homily, and in the book of Ratramn, *ib.* 20 n.; his error respecting the Liber Canonum of Ælfric, *ib.* 22 n

Ussites: *v.* Hussites.

Ustadt (Hector von): 3 *Zur.* 698

Ustazardes, a Persian martyr: 2 *Brad.* 347, 348, *Pil.* 637, 638, 3 *Zur.* 198

Usury: of usury, 2 *Bul.* 40; a letter on it, 4 *Jew.* 1276; a paper on it found in Jewel's study, *ib.* 1293, &c.; it is forbidden and abhorred by God, 2 *Jew.* 854, 1 *Lat.* 303, *Sand.* 203; not sanctioned by Christ, 2 *Jew.* 859; condemned by the fathers, *ib.* 853, 856, 860; its wickedness, *ib.* 851, &c., 1043, 1 *Lat.* 410, *Pil.* 39, 162, 464, *Sand.* 136; it is allowed by law in some places,

---

* Not IV. as in 4 *Jew.* 931.

but not by God's law, 2 *Jew.* 858; it should be repressed by law, *Sand.* 50; laws respecting it in England, *Grin.* 172, 1 *Lat.* 279 n., 410; by our old law usurers were deemed excommunicate, 2 *Jew.* 853; Sandys remonstrates against usury, *Sand.* xxvi; it is not to be taken on wares, 2 *Jew.* 857; false pleas for it, *ib.* 855; what lawful interest is, 2 *Bul.* 41, 2 *Jew.* 857, 858; against usurers, 2 *Bul.* 43; they are merciless, *Sand.* 230; ten, twenty, thirty in the hundred taken by them, *ib.* 182, compare *Pil.* 40; some in England take 40 per cent. 1 *Lat.* 279; usurers are thieves before God, 2 *Bec.* 106, 162; they have their gains by the devil, 2 *Lat.* 42; their names to be presented to the ordinary, *Grin.* 143; godly usury, 1 *Lat.* 410

Utenhovius (Jo.): mentioned, 2 *Brad.* 352, 352, *Grin.* 266, 2 *Zur.* 17 n., 3 *Zur.* 56, 57, 85, 404, 565, 653; some account of him, 2 *Brad.* xx. n., 2 *Cran.* 421 n., he was a nobleman, 3 *Zur.* 36 n., 739; an elder in the strangers' church in London, *ib.* 572; resident with Hooper, *ib.* 562; present at the execution of the duke of Somerset, *ib.* 731; in Poland, *ib.* 693, 694, 696, 697, 702; his letters to Bullinger, *ib.* 583—596; letter of bishop Grindal to him, *Grin.* 243

Uterques: neuters, *Pil.* 344

Utopia: *v.* More (Sir T.).

Utter: to make manifest, 1 *Brad.* 321, 1 *Tyn.* 12, 3 *Tyn.* 128, 240, 258

Uxbridge, co. Middlesex: a martyr there, *Poet.* 163

Uzzah (Vulg. Oza): smitten with sudden death, 3 *Bul.* 237, 4 *Bul.* 296, 408; not a king, but a poor Levite, 3 *Jew.* 409, 4 *Jew.* 695

Uzziah, or Azariah, king of Judah; smitten with leprosy, 1 *Bul.* 328, 2 *Bul.* 8, *Grin.* 271

V

V. (R.): probably Vaux, *q. v.*

Vacuum: abhorred by nature, 1 *Cran.* 250, 251, 252, 330

Vadeth: departeth, fadeth, 3 *Bec.* 609, 1 *Jew.* 95

Vadian (Joachim): notice of him, 3 *Zur.* 11 n.; references to him, 4 *Bul.* xviii, 1 *Cran.* 195, 3 *Zur.* 698; letter to him, disapproving of his treatise on the eucharist, 2 *Cran.* 342, 343, 3 *Zur.* 11

Vadiani: *v.* Anthropomorphites.

Væhe (Mich.): *v.* Vehe.

Vagabonds: should be punished, *Now.* 228

Vaghamus (......): an astrologer, 1 *Ful.* v.

Vaghan (Hugh): 2 *Cran.* 280

Vaghan (Mr), of Chepe side: 2 *Cran.* 364

Vagrants: their great increase, *Nord.* 175

Vahan (......): 2 *Zur.* 69

Vain-glory: *v.* Boasting, Pride.

Vairus (Leon.): erroneously quoted as affirming that Christ was "venificus," *Rog.* 133

Vaivode (The): *Grin.* 14 n

Valdenses: *v.* Waldenses.

Valdensis (Tho.): *v.* Netter.

Valdesius (Jo.?): disliked commentaries, *Rog.* 196

Valdo (Pet.), of Lyons: no heretic, 2 *Jew.* 689

Valence: *v.* Councils.

Valence (A bishop of): plenipotentiary from Francis II. of France, 1 *Zur.* 89 n

Valenciennes: revolts from the duke of Alva, 1 *Zur.* 274

Valens, emperor of the East: favoured the Arians, 2 *Brad.* 325, 326; became an Arian, 4 *Jew.* 908; would not grant the orthodox a church for themselves, *Pil.* 324, 660; published an edict against making images, 2 *Bec.* 71; forbade the iteration of baptism, 4 *Bul.* 394; how he was turned from his intended cruelty, 2 *Brad.* 325, 326

Valens, the monk: deceived by the devil, 2 *Cran.* 42

Valentia (Jac. Parez de): Comm. in Psalm., *Jew.* xliv; he remarks that Jews, Saracens, and ill Christians, to excuse their wicked life, say simple fornication is no sin, 4 *Jew.* 635; wrongly cited for the next, 3 *Jew.* 557

Valentia (Vincentius de): Sermones Hyemales, *Jew.* xliv; he declares that the virgin Mary opened heaven once, the priest every day, 2 *Jew.* 747; says, the priest is the mouth of the body; therefore when the priest receiveth the sacrament, all the members are refreshed, *ib.* 744, 3 *Jew.* 557

Valentine (St): invoked for the falling sickness, 2 *Jew.* 923, *Rog.* 226

Valentine, the heresiarch: *v.* Valentinus.

Valentinian I., emperor: refused to be sprinkled with idolatrous holy water, *Pil.* 165; his counsel touching the election of a bishop of Milan, 4 *Jew.* 674, *Rid.* 144; his saying respecting Ambrose, 1 *Jew.* 407; he allowed that the prince must submit to the priest, 2 *Ful.* 380; yet intimated that ecclesiastics must be subject to the emperor, *ib.* 381; he disclaimed the right of interfering with synods, *Whita.* 437, 2 *Whitg.* 363 n.; confessed himself to be as one of the people, 4 *Jew.* 670; forbade the iteration of baptism, 4 *Bul.* 394; his division of the empire, and law as to the Libra, 2 *Ful.* 364 n

Valentinian II., emperor: admonished by Ambrose, *Rid.* 96; Ambrose's refusal to be judged by him, 4 *Jew.* 1027, *Whita.* 441, 3 *Whitg.* 308; he confessed himself subject to Christ, 1 *Jew.* 369; his decree for the establishment of St Peter's doctrine, see p. 360, col. 1, above; he made penal statutes against idolaters, 2 *Bec.* 312; professed obedience to the law, 2 *Zur.* 169; Ambrose commended him, *Grin.* 11, and doubted not of his salvation, though he died without baptism, 2 *Bec.* 224, 2 *Jew.* 1107, 3 *Jew.* 359; he offered for him when dead, though assured of his salvation, *Coop.* 96, 2 *Jew.* 742

Valentinian III., emperor: not the son, but the grandson of Theodosius the Great, 2 *Ful.* 363 n.; his edict in the council of Chalcedon, 1 *Jew.* 82; his decree respecting figures of the cross made upon the ground, see p. 411, col. 1, above; what he says about seeking truth, 1 *Jew.* 229

Valentinians: heretics, 1 *Ful.* 215, 2 *Hoop.* 74, *Phil.* 418; described by Irenæus, see p. 418, col. 2, above; they acknowledged many gods (æons), 1 *Hoop.* 65, *Rog.* 37, 44; held Christ to be very God, but not very man, 2 *Cran.* 277, 285, 339; said that he took not flesh of the virgin Mary, *Rog.* 52; affirmed that his flesh was spiritual, &c., *ib.*; taught that he was not crucified, but that Simon of Cyrene was in his place, 1 *Cran.* 256; worshipped images, 1 *Ful.* 194, 215; charged the scripture with obscurity, *ib.* 89, 164; received no gospel but John's, *Rog.* 84, *Whita.* 34; relied on tradition, 2 *Ful.* 219, *Sand.* 15; feigned three degrees of men, *Rog.* 122; said that men are elected by nature, *Rog.* 149; ascribed original sin to the devil, *ib.* 99; held that all who lead a moral life shall be saved, *ib.* 160; erred respecting good works, *ib.* 121, 162; allowed whoredom, *ib.* 119; superstitiously venerated the cross, 2 *Ful.* 139, 390; erred about the resurrection, 2 *Cov.* 183, &c., 1 *Cran.* 150, 157, 177, 215, 258, 262; said that none shall be saved in soul and body together, *Rog.* 145; affirmed themselves to be spiritual, and condemned all other men as gross and earthly, 1 *Jew.* 400, 2 *Jew.* 807

Valentinus: his heresy, 1 *Bec.* 320, 412, 418, 2 *Bec.* 446, 3 *Bec.* 401, 3 *Bul.* 256, 4 *Bul.* 77, 2 *Cov.* 186, *Grin.* 59 n., 1 *Jew.* 260, 2 *Jew.* 791, *Sand.* 15, *Whita.* 614

Valera (Cypr.): says John XIV. baptized the great bell of St John Lateran, *Rog.* 266 n.; describes the pope's mode of travelling with the sacrament before him, *ib.* 291 n

Valera (Cypr. de): republished, in 1702, the Spanish Bible of C. de Reyna, 2 *Zur.* 175

Valeri (St): his chapel in Picardy, 3 *Tyn.* 124

Valerian, emperor: a persecutor, 2 *Bul.* 106, 4 *Bul.* 514; his court compared to a church of God, 2 *Jew.* 1033, 3 *Jew.* 194; conquered and put to death by Sapor, king of Persia, 2 *Jew.* 978, 4 *Jew.* 701

Valerius, bp of Hippo: Augustine's predecessor, 1 *Jew.* 295; he associated Augustine with himself, 1 *Hoop.* 507

Valerius Maximus: cited or referred to, 2 *Bec.* 5, 137, 308. 356, 382 nn., 1 *Bul.* 252, 278, 294, *Calf.* 14 n., 316 n., *Grin.* 7, 1 *Hoop.* 24, 297, 298, 327, 328, 336, 357, 417, 483, 1 *Lat.* 146, *Sand.* 36, 52, 53, *Wool.* 111

Valesius (Hen.): 2 *Brad.* 381, 2 *Ful.* 101, 1 *Hoop.* 376 nn

Valla (Lau.): a witness for the truth, condemned by the council of Constance, *Phil.* 393; notice of him, 2 *Brad.* 160 n.; *Opera*, 4 *Jew.* xliv; his opinion as to the authorship of the books ascribed to Dionysius the Areopagite, *Whita.* 576; his famous Declamatio against the Donation of Constantine, 2 *Brad.* 160, 4 *Bul.* 125, 2 *Ful.* 361, 4 *Jew.* 678, *Rid.* 374; he speaks of the insatiable ambition and greediness of the church of Rome, 4 *Jew.* 972, 1081; mentions popes who were heretics, 3 *Jew.* 127, 344; complains of the vices of the bishops of Rome, and calls the pope Antichrist, 4 *Jew.* 740, 1115; says that he makes merchandize of church-goods, *ib.* 916; satirizes the apparel, pride, and riot of priests, *ib.* 972; allows that there are many errors in the old Latin translation of the Bible, *ib.* 907; referred to on the doxology in the Lord's prayer, 4 *Bul.* 219; said to have denied man's free-will to move, &c. *Rog.* 104; referred to about faith, 1 *Hoop.* 221; cited about marriage, 4 *Jew.* 630

Vallenses: v. Waldenses.

Valley of the shadow of death: 2 *Cov.* 304, 2 *Hoop.* 214

Valois: cruelty of the French king there, 2 *Jew.* 840

Valois (Tho.): commented on Aug. de Civ. Dei, *Jew.* xxxiii; his mistake about the word "apex," 1 *Jew.* 150; his remarks on superstition, 1 *Hoop.* 314

Valor: value, 1 *Bec.* 291

Valor Ecclesiasticus: 2 *Lat.* 383 n., 394 n., 409 n

Valteline: 3 *Zur.* 517

Valys (M. de): 3 *Zur.* 42

Vandals: why sent, *Grin.* 98; their ravages,

2 *Bul.* 109, *Calf.* 30, 118, 1 *Ful.* 263, 2 *Tyn.* 268; their persecuting spirit, *Rid.* 147

Vandermarke (Will.), lord of Lumey: takes the Brill, 1 *Zur.* 273

Vanderstad (Corn.): excommunicated from the strangers' church at Sandwich, *Park.* 247

Vandevelde (Jo. Fra.): 2 *Ful.* 61 n

Van Emmerson (Marg.): v. Emmerson.

Van Rossem (M.): v. Rossem.

Vane (Sir Ralph): sent to prison, 3 *Zur.* 577 n.; executed, 2 *Brad.* 91 n., 3 *Zur.* 579 n

Vane (Eliz. lady): probably the widow of Sir Ralph, 2 *Brad.* 91 n.; notice of her, *ib.*; her bright example in dangerous times, *Phil.* 262, 265; she was a liberal benefactor to God's saints, *ib.* 265 (see 2 *Brad.* 161, *Rid.* 374); letter from her to Philpot (signed F. E.), *Phil.* 155; letters to her, 2 *Brad.* 91, 96, 140, 142, 184, *Phil.* 259, 262, 264, 267, 269, and probably 289

Vanity: v. Pleasure, World.

All things are vain; verses by F. Kinwelmersh, *Poet.* 293; the vanity of riches; by Sam. Daniel, *ib.* 397; the vanity of fame; by the same, *ib.* 398

Vannius (......): declares that the sacrament received by the massmonger cannot profit him that is present, but does not receive, 3 *Bec.* 375

Varenius (Bern.): cited, 1 *Hoop.* viii. n

Varillas (Ant.): 3 *Zur.* 666 n., *Whita.* 32 n

Varinus: his definition of a rule, *Whita.* 662

Varna: battle there, *Lit. Eliz.* 454

Varro (M. Ter.): Opera, *Jew.* xliv; against images, 1 *Bul.* 201, *Calf.* 188, 2 *Jew.* 659, *Park.* 86, *Rid.* 89; other citations, 4 *Bul.* 235, 1 *Hoop.* 27, 4 *Jew.* 783

Vartomannus (Lud.), Bononiensis: cited as Romanus Patritius, 2 *Jew.* 578 n

Vassey: slaughter there, 2 *Ful.* 74, 3 *Jew.* 172, *Rog.* 6

Vatablus (Fra.): the Latin Bible edited by him and Pagninus, 1 *Brad.* 535, *Jew.* xxxiv, 4 *Jew.* 989; he supposes the "one shepherd" of Eccles. xii. 11, to be the Holy Spirit, *Whita.* 423; expounds the "pure offering," or spiritual worship, of the Gentiles, 1 *Hoop.* 242

Vaudois: v. Waldenses.

Vaughan (Sir Hugh): 2 *Cran.* 330 n

Vaughan (Ant.): Susan (Cranmer) his wife, 2 *Cran.* 330 n

Vaughan (David): canon of St Mary's, Warwick, 2 *Lat.* 396 n

Vaughan (Hugh): v. Vaghan.

Vaughan (Mr.), of Portsmouth: bp Gardiner's letters to him, [see Heylin, Ref. Edw. VI., p. 56], *Calf.* 36

Vaughan (Steph.): king Henry's envoy in the Netherlands, charged to search for Tyndale, 1 *Tyn.* xlii; his interview with Tyndale, *ib.* xliii; extracts from his letters to the king, respecting Tyndale, also from Cromwell's answers, 1 *Tyn.* xlii—l; More endeavours to prove him a disciple of Tyndale, *ib.* li.

Vaumure: outwork, 2 *Ful.* 30

Vaut: vault, *Bale* 494

Vautroullier (Tho.), printer: 2 *Ful.* 214

Vauville (Rich.), alias R. Gallus, or François: minister of the French church in London, 3 *Zur.* 337 n., 339 n., 737, 739; present at the execution of the duke of Somerset, *ib.* 731; he married Joanna the attendant on Hooper's wife, *ib.* 365 n (see p. 399, col. 2 above)

Vaux (Tho.), 2nd lord of Vaux of Harrowden: notice of him, *Poet.* xxvi; verses; on the instability of youth, *ib.* 302; bethinking himself of his end, *ib.* 303

Vaux (Will.), 3rd lord Vaux of Harrowden: notice of him, *Poet.* xxvi.

Vaux (Lau.): his Catechism, 2 *Ful.* 4; he errs respecting Christ's descent into hell, *Rog.* 62; what he says of faith, *ib.* 113; he states that to expect justification by faith is a breach of the first commandment, *ib.* 114; declares that sins are remitted by a priest's absolution, *ib.* 299; says none who have committed mortal sin can be saved without the sacrament of penance, *ib.* 258; affirms that sins venial are purged by prayer, almsdeeds, &c. *ib.* 110; teaches that to doubt the existence of purgatory is a breach of the first commandment, *ib.* 214; on the church, *ib.* 166; on seven sacraments, *ib.* 252, 259; on transubstantiation, *ib.* 287, 289; he calls marriage a sacrament, *ib.* 260

Vaux (Rich.): translation of a Latin sermon of Jewel, by R. V., probably Vaux, 2 *Jew.* 950

Vaux (......): 2 *Cran.* 241

Vavasor (......): one of the disputants at Cambridge, 1549, *Grin.* 194, *Rid.* 169; account of him, and of his committal to prison at Hull, *Grin.* 351

Vaward: the fore-part, 1 *Brad.* 408, 2 *Brad.* 70, 90

Vawte: vault, *Calf.* 274

Vedelius (Nic.): De Cathedra Petri, 2 *Ful.* 336 n

Vegetius: 4 *Bul.* 235

Vehe (Mich.), or Væhe: Assert. Sacr. Axiom., *Jew.* xliv; on sacramental eating, 1 *Jew.* 213 (see corrig.), 3 *Jew.* 592

Veil: v. Tabernacle, Temple.

Veils: worn at churching, 2 *Whitg.* 562—564

Velated: veiled, 1 *Bec.* 112
Velenus (Ulric.): his treatise (published 1520) intended to prove that St Peter was never at Rome, 2 *Ful.* 336 n
Velleius Paterculus: 1 *Bul.* 278
Velsius (Justus): notice of him, *Grin.* 254; Strype's account of him, *ib.* 438 n.; his errors, 3 *Zur.* 132; his Christiani Hominis Norma, *Grin.* 474; bishop Grindal's Animadversiones on it, *ib.* (436), 438
Venerandus, honorandus, reverendus: *Now.* (103)
Venew, or Venue: a bout in fencing, 1 *Jew.* 410
Vengeance: *v.* Revenge.
Veni Creator: see p. 613 above.
Venice: alliance of the Venetians with the pope, 2 *Tyn.* 299; notwithstanding it, they cared not for his blessing or cursing, 2 *Tyn.* 300; Greek rites at Venice, 4 *Jew.* 884, 887; no private masses, *Hutch.* 228; the gospel preached there, 3 *Zur.* 357; war with Turkey, 1 *Zur.* 239, 3 *Zur.* 246
Venison: spoken of, 2 *Cran.* 250, 255, 270, *Grin.* 266, 289, *Park.* 177; Hen. VIII.'s warrant for a buck for Cranmer, 2 *Cran.* 250; his warrant for a doe for Parker, *Park.* 4; queen Elizabeth sends him a deer killed with her own hand, *ib.* 190; order of Hen. earl of Arundel for the supply of deer to him, *Park.* 387
Venlo, in Guelderland: revolts from the duke of Alva, 1 *Zur.* 274
Vennard (Rich.): notice of him, *Poet.* xxiv; verses entitled, Laudetur Dominus in æternum, *ib.* 264
Venning (Ralph): The Heathen Improved, 2 *Brad.* xliii. n
Verbum: 1 *Bul.* 37
Verbum Dei, *Now.* (103)
Verdun: taken by the French, 3 *Zur.* 590 n
Vere (Jo. de), 15th earl of Oxford, 2 *Cran.* 324
Vere (Edw. de), 17th earl of Oxford: 2 *Zur.* 282, 283
Vere (Sir Fra.): holds Ostend, 2 *Zur.* 335 n
Vergerio (Gio. Batt.), bp of Pola: renounces popery, 3 *Zur.* 499 n
Vergerio (Pietro Paolo), bp of Capo d'Istria: renounces popery, 3 *Zur.* 499 n.; moves the king of Poland to take upon him to be the head of the church, 4 *Jew.* 1207 n., 1235, 1 *Whitg.* 392; mentioned, 1 *Zur.* 19, 3 *Zur.* 339, 376, 599 n., 603 n., 693, 695, 696; a work probably by him, *Jew.* xliv; he declares that the bishop of Vegla was threatened with deprivation in the council of Trent, for a little inkling of the truth, 3 *Jew.* 208

Vergers: injunction to those of the church of York, *Grin.* 152
Vergil (Polydore): account of him, *Bale* 8; Anglica Historia, *Jew.* xliv; his chronicle censured, *Bale* 8—10; De Rerum Inventoribus, *Jew.* xliv, 3 *Whitg.* xxxii; this work expurgated, 2 *Ful.* 103 n.; he burned the books which he had used in compiling his history, 2 *Zur.* 80 n.; on the baptism to Moses, 2 *Brad.* 383; he says the priesthood was appointed at Jerusalem long before Peter came to Rome, 1 *Jew.* 433; refers to the title on the cross found by Helena, *Calf.* 325 n.; speaks of queen Bertha, *Calf.* 306 n.; says Augustine arrived in England, A.D. 596, and continued abp of Canterbury fifteen years, 4 *Jew.* 783; tells when he died, *ib.* 780; mentions ordinances of Gregory VII. against the marriage of the clergy, *Pil.* 565; says the restraint of priests' marriage was first attempted in England about 1100, and never before, 3 *Jew.* 395; censures the enforcement of single life on priests, *ib.* 427; his account of king Henry Vth's rejection of evil company, *Wool.* 127; his false account of lord Cobham, *Bale* 9; he celebrates Robert Ridley, *Rid.* 488, 492; cites Fisher (Roffensis), 1 *Jew.* 101, 3 *Jew.* 568, 4 *Jew.* 886; writes of the origin of archbishops, 2 *Whitg.* 118; explains the meaning of the title cardinal, 4 *Jew.* 855; mentions three kinds of baptism, 2 *Bec.* 225 n.; referred to on the origin of sponsors, *ib.* 210 n.; he speaks of changes in the mass, 1 *Hoop.* 239, 3 *Jew.* 434, 3 *Whitg.* 73; gives an account of the origin of vestments used therein, 3 *Bec.* 262; declares that priestly rites, garments, &c., rehearse rather Hebrew than apostolic institutions, &c., 2 *Brad.* 381; says the use of linen vestments came to us from the Egyptians by the Hebrews, 2 *Brad.* 383; referred to about processions, &c., *Calf.* 295, 1 *Lat.* 49; censures the worshipping of images, 2 *Jew.* 668, 3 *Jew.* 121, 553, 4 *Jew.* 950; says that saints' lives are read although not written truly, 4 *Jew.* 816; mentions the denial of purgatory by the Greeks, *Rog.* 213
Verily: 4 *Bul.* 218
Verities (Unwritten): *v.* Tradition.
Verity: *v.* Dialogues, Truth.
Vernacle: the holy vernacle or sudary, 3 *Tyn.* 79 n
Vernerius (R.): *v.* Werner.
Verney (......), or Berny, or Berners: hired to murder lord Burghley and the queen, and executed, *Grin.* 332 n., 2 *Zur.* 198 n
Verney (Sir Rich.): 2 *Bec.* 583 n

Vernone (Jo. de), a French Carmelite: wrote on the Apocalypse, *Bale* 257

Veron (Jo.): noticed, 1 *Bec.* xi, 2 *Brad.* 83; portion of an epitaph upon him, by Jo. Awdelie, *Poet.* 540

Verona: the library of St Nazarius, 1 *Jew.* 189; a bishop of Verona: 2 *Cran.* 331

Veronica (St): reference to the legend, 2 *Ful.* 204; More alludes to the holy vernacle, or sudary, 3 *Tyn.* 79 n

Verractus (Jo. Mar.), or Verratus: Disp. adv. Lutheran., *Jew.* xliv; he says that the authority of the church is above the authority of the gospel, 4 *Jew.* 863; asserts that the determination of the church is called the gospel, 4 *Jew.* 759; admits the church of Rome to be a particular church, 1 *Ful.* 39

Verres: his policy, 4 *Jew.* 947, 1113

Verses: *v.* Poetry.

Verus, emperor: 2 *Bul.* 105

Veselus (Jo.): *v.* Wesselus.

Vesey (Jo.), bp: *v.* Voysey.

Vespasian, emperor: would be called pontifex maximus, 4 *Jew.* 983; his taxation, *Sand.* 343: his idea of the death befitting an emperor, *Jew.* xxi; a saying of his, *Wool.* iv.

Vespers: *v.* Hours.

The Sicilian vespers: 1 *Zur.* 291

Vesputius (Amer.): 3 *Jew.* 198, 4 *Jew.* 740

Vessels (Holy): *v.* Chalices.

Vestment: the word commonly means a chesible, as, 3 *Bec.* 259

Vestments, Habits: *v.* Albe, Amice, Birrus, Breast-plate, Cap, Cassock, Chesible, Chimere, Cope, Dalmatic, Ephod, Fanon, Gown, Hood, Maniple, Mitre, Pall, Petalum, Rochet, Stole, Surplice, Tippet, Tunic, Tunicle; also Bullinger (H.), Coverdale (M.), Grindal (E.), Hooper (J.), Humphrey (L.), Lever (T.), Martyr (P.), Ridley (H.), Sampson (T.); likewise Cambridge.

Those of the priests in the old law, and what they signified, 3 *Bec.* 259, 260; of the apparel of ministers, 2 *Whitg.* 1, &c.; whether it is Aaronical, 2 *Brad.* 380; bishops and priests should be known by their tongue, not by their cap or vesture, 1 *Hoop.* 511; ministers were known by distinct apparel in times past, 2 *Whitg.* 9; ancient testimonies as to this, 1 *Zur.* 350; the ancient writers examined, *ib.* 160; vestments said to be men's traditions, 3 *Tyn.* 176; called a doctrine of Antichrist, 2 *Hoop.* 56; the massing apparel described, 3 *Bec.* 259; its origin, *ib.* 262, 263; its professed meaning, 3 *Tyn.* 73, 117; great importance attached by Romanists to vestments, albs, tunicles, and stoles, *Coop.* 163; injunction of abp Winchelsea, respecting vestments, *Grin.* 159 n.; gorgeous Romish ones, *Bale* 526, 527; they were embroidered with flowers, birds, beasts, fishes, &c., 2 *Bec.* 300; superstitions about them, 3 *Jew.* 614; the vestments of a Romish bishop, 2 *Jew.* 1020, 1 *Lat.* 168, 2 *Lat.* 348, 1 *Tyn.* 252; Ridley inveighs against the foolish apparel of Rome, *Rid.* 289; a long gown and tippet worn in convocation, *Phil.* 213; the side gown and sarcenet tippet, 2 *Cran.* 38; the habits of monks, 1 *Tyn.* 160, (and see Friars); Romish vestments to be destroyed, *Grin.* 135, 159; the vestments and pastoral staff of bishops of the reformed church, *Lit. Edw.* 157; the episcopal vestments as worn by Hooper,—a scarlet chimere, &c., 3 *Zur.* 271 n.; controversy about the habits, 2 *Cov.* xv, 2 *Cran.* x, 428, 431, *Grin.* 205, 210, 211, 339, 340, 1 *Hoop.* 479, 554, 2 *Hoop.* xii, &c., *Jew.* xv, xix, 4 *Jew.* 1265, 1267, 1271, *Now.* ii, *Park.* 226 n., 240, 245, *Pil.* viii, 1 *Whitg.* 72, 2 *Whitg.* 1, &c., 3 *Whitg.* vii, viii, 1 *Zur.* 74, 100, 134, 142, 146, 148, 149, 151, 153, 157, &c., 160, 164, 168, 175, 176, &c., 185, 201, 221, 236, 248, 342, 345, 347, 350, 358, 360, 2 *Zur.* 25, 32, 38, 39, 118—121, 130, 133, 136, &c., 140, &c., 142, &c., 148, 153, 166, 186, &c., 221, 357, 361, 362, 3 *Zur.* 87, 91, 95, 426, 487, 488, 495, 571, 585, 665; Ridley's reply to Hooper, 2 *Brad.* 375, &c.; the habits conceded as indifferent by the episcopal party at Frankfort, 3 *Zur.* 754; judgment of the foreign reformers, 3 *Whitg.* 549—551; Becon's opinion, 2 *Bec.* 299; he thinks that popish apparel should be utterly put away, but that the surplice may be worn as a thing indifferent, if commanded by the magistrate, *ib.* 300; habits prescribed to the clergy by Elizabeth, 1 *Zur.* 84; objected to by many of the bishops, *ib.* n.; defended as the ordinance of the magistrate, *Grin.* 210, 1 *Whitg.* 69, 2 *Whitg.* 16; Grindal would rather minister without them, but for obedience to the prince, *Grin.* 211; Romish vestments retained at court, 1 *Zur.* 63; styled relics of the Amorites, *ib.* 52; the use of the cope enjoined, 2 *Zur.* 121; letter of Zanchius to queen Elizabeth against the popish vestments, *ib.* 339, &c.; his views about them, *ib.* 186, &c.; the use of the habits dispensed with in some instances, 1 *Zur.* 202 n.; Parker's proceedings in order to uniformity, *Park.* 267: notice of A brief Discourse against the outward Apparel, &c., 2 *Zur.* 119 n.; a work in defence of the vestments published by order of the queen's commissioners, *ib.* 120; Dr W. Turner, dean of Wells, enjoins an adulterer to do penance in a priest's cap, *ib.* 125 n.; Pilkington's letter to the earl of Leicester in behalf of the refusers of the habits, *Pil.* 658; Sandys's injunctions concerning them, *Sand.* xx; the apparel now used not popish or antichristian, 2 *Whitg.* 30; vestments were before the pope's tyranny, *ib.* 22; there should be no strife about vestments without superstition, lawfully appointed, 2 *Ful.* 113; neither alb, surplice, vestment, nor pastoral staff required by the ordination service, 1 *Whitg.* 488; turkey gowns and hats worn by those who disliked the gown and square cap, 3 *Whitg.* 369; what garment ought to be worn at the Lord's supper, 4 *Bul.* 420

Vestry: one to be called to hear a letter from the commissioners, *Grin.* 294

Vetus homo: *Now.* (103)

Vevay: 3 *Zur.* 167, 168

Veysy (Jo.), bp: *v.* Voysey.

Vials (The Seven): *Bale* 475, 478, &c.

Viaticum: *Coop.* 11, 29, 2 *Hoop.* 463

Vicar (M.): 2 *Brad.* 76

Vicars: 4 *Bul.* 112

Vicars general: 4 *Bul.* 112

Vice: a buffoon, or fool, fantastically dressed, *Calf.* 210, *Grin.* 211 n

Vicelius (Geo.): *v.* Wicelius.

Victor I., bp of Rome: 2 *Whitg.* 134; on the celebration of baptism, *ib.* 507; in his time it was ordinarily celebrated at Easter only, 1 *Whitg.* 513; he is said to have allowed baptism by women, 2 *Whitg.* 507, 523; a provincial synod held by him at Rome, 4 *Jew.* 1124; Irenæus seeks his advice, *Phil.* 39; his part in the controversy respecting Easter, for his intolerance in which he was rebuked by Irenæus, 1 *Brad.* 525, 2 *Brad.* 389, 4 *Bul.* 57, 537, *Calf.* 262, 269, 2 *Cran.* 77, 2 *Ful.* 69, 238, 308, 2 *Hoop.* 233, 1 *Jew.* 144, *Whita.* 539, 1 *Whitg.* 216, 2 *Zur.* 340, 347

Victor III., pope: poisoned in the sacrament, *Grin.* 60, 1 *Hoop.* 123, 451, 1 *Jew.* 105, 4 *Jew.* 686, 687, *Sand.* 66

Victor (Aur.): *v.* Aurelius.

Victor Uticensis: De Persec. Vand., *Jew.* xliv, *Rid.* 147, 305; he speaks of the church of Rome as head of all churches, 1 *Jew.* 436, 439, 4 *Jew.* 822

Victore (H. de S.): *v.* Hugo.

Victore (R. de S.): *v.* Richardus.

Victorinus (Marius): says many thousand bishops consented to the Nicene faith, 1 *Jew.* 358, 412, 4 *Jew.* 1025

Victorinus Pictaviensis: wrote on the Apocalypse, *Bale* 255

Victorinus, the rhetorician: Jerome's schoolmaster, 4 *Jew.* 653, 654

Victorius (Marianus): corrupted Jerome's works, *Whita.* 222

Victory: *v.* Thanksgivings.

How to obtain it, 1 *Bec.* 244; examples of its being given by God, *ib.* 245, &c.; by what means he may give it to us, *ib.* 248; to get it we must amend our manners, *ib.* 249, and seek to have God on our side, *ib.* 250; it is always God's, 1 *Lat.* 285; Victoria, a goddess of the Romans, 4 *Jew.* 865

Vidame of Chartres: *v.* Ferriers (J. de).

Vienna: defended by Ferdinand against the Turks, *Grin.* 15

Vienna (H. de): *v.* Hugo.

Vierdmuller (Otho): *v.* Werdmuller.

Vigilance: *v.* Watching.

Vigilantians: would admit no unmarried men to holy orders, *Rog.* 261, 303

Vigilantius: denied prayer to saints, the worship of relics, &c., 2 *Cran.* 175, 2 *Ful.* 44, 67, 188, 388, 3 *Jew.* 166, *Phil.* 427, *Rog.* 224; railed at by Jerome, 2 *Ful.* 44, 188, 3 *Jew.* 167; deemed a heretic by Papists, 1 *Ful.* 214

Vigilius, pope: 1 *Zur.* 18 n.; his character, 4 *Jew.* 1034; he accused pope Sylverius of treason, *ib.* 1034; was excommunicated by Mennas, *ib.* 834; deposed by Justinian, *ib.* 1030, *Sand.* 40; the decretals in his name are spurious, *Rid.* 180, 182; he commands the celebrant of the communion to look Eastward, 2 *Brad.* 311

Vigilius, bp of Thapsus: 2 *Zur.* 80 n.; probably the writer of the Athanasian creed, 1 *Bul.* 29 n.; author of a treatise wrongly ascribed to Augustine, 2 *Jew.* 769; his works published, *Park.* 288 n

Vigilius (St), bp of Trent, and martyr: 4 *Bul.* xviii; proves that Christ is God and man, *Phil.* 208; shews, in several passages, that Christ is absent as to his humanity, but present as to his divinity, 2 *Bec.* 275, 279, 3 *Bec.* 273, 429, 430, 453, 1 *Bul.* 152, 3 *Bul.* 266, 2 *Cov.* 154, 1 *Cran.* 73, 98, 99, 100, (51), 2 *Jew.* 497, 776, 1118, 3 *Jew.* 252, 254, 262, 485, 486, *Rid.* 177, 178; speaks of the faith and catholic profession which the apostles delivered, the martyrs confirmed, and the faithful keep to this day, 2 *Jew.* 811, 1118; shews that the council of Chalcedon is not contrary to the doctrine of Cyril, 1 *Bul.* 20; Gardiner quotes his account of the heresies of Eutyches and Nestorius, 1 *Cran.* 289

Vigils: 1 *Tyn.* 219; the ancient vigils discontinued for their abuse, 2 *Cran.* 175, 3 *Tyn.* 126; inquiry respecting vigils, 2 *Hoop.* 147; vigils abolished, 2 *Cran.* 414, 415 (see also Wake)

Vigor (......) : notes errors in French translations of the scriptures, 1 *Ful.* 61
Viguerius (......) : says the church was before, and is above the word, *Rog.* 173; denies the salvation of infants dying unbaptized, *ib.* 249 n
Vilfrid (St): *v.* Wilfrid.
Vilierius (Fr.): De Statu Primitivæ Eccl., 3 *Whitg.* xxxii; on patriarchs, 2 *Whitg.* 150
Vility: vileness, *Bale* 67
Villagagno (Nic.): an apostate, 2 *Jew.* 803 n
Villa Garcina (Jo. de), or Villa Garcia: a Spanish monk, sometime regius professor of divinity at Oxford, 1 *Cran.* xxii, xxviii, xxix, 2 *Cran.* 563, 567, 4 *Jew.* 1212 n., 1213, 1 *Zur.* 33 n
Villain: a bondman or servant, 2 *Bec.* 436; to walk a villain; the phrase explained, 2 *Tyn.* 309
Villanovanus (Mich.): *v.* Servetus.
Villany: servitude, 2 *Bec.* 185, 1 *Cov.* 300
Villars (......): preacher of the French church in London, 2 *Zur.* 261 n
Villavincentio (Laur. à): his book on the study of theology, *Whita.* 637 n.; he calls justification by faith the doctrine of devils, *Rog.* 114; says the common people are only to know that which pertaineth unto manners, *ib.* 192
Villegagnon (Mons. de): carries the queen of Scots into France, 3 *Zur.* 643 n
Villegaignon (Nich. Durand de): 2 *Ful.* 61
Villers (Ph. de): *v.* Vyllers.
Vilvorden: Tyndale imprisoned there, 1 *Tyn.* lxvii, lxxii, and burnt at the stake, *ib.* lxxv.
Vincent (St): his martyrdom, *Bale* 586
Vincentius: legate at Nice, 4 *Jew.* 999
Vincentius Bellovacensis: Speculum Quadruplex, seu Bibliotheca Mundi, *Jew.* xliv, 3 *Whitg.* xxxii; Speculum Naturale, *Phil.* 361; he tells the story of Thecla, wishing to attach herself to St Paul, 4 *Jew.* 651; mentions Phileas of Thmuis, a nobleman and rich, who being consecrated bishop, had a wife and children, 3 *Jew.* 410; says Jerome charged Ruffinus with the Pelagian heresy, 4 *Jew.* 1006, 1007; speaks of the gift of Phocas to Boniface, 1 *Jew.* 184; says Victor III. died of a dysentery, 4 *Jew.* 686; referred to, 1 *Bec.* 390, 1 *Jew.* 190
Vincentius Lirinensis: speaks of the rule of ecclesiastical and catholic sense, *Whita.* 443; mentions scripture as a rule, *ib.* 662; asserts the canon of scripture to be self-sufficient for all, and more than sufficient for all things, *ib.* 703; teaches that it is sufficient for the truth of the catholic faith, and that the church cannot make one article thereof, 1 *Cran.* 379; his rule respecting what is catholic, 3 *Jew.* 266; how it must be limited, *ib.* 267; on the duty of a catholic Christian in case a portion of the church, or the whole church, should fall from the faith, or be corrupted with heresy, 4 *Jew.* 723, *Rid.* 268; on judging false prophets, *Whita.* 459; on the deliberations of the council of Ephesus, 3 *Jew.* 224; on the heresy of Nestorius, *Rog.* 163; on the sect of Photinus, *ib.* 70 n.; on the errors of Tertullian, *Whita.* 600; he recommends recourse to the most ancient writers, 2 *Ful.* 175, 4 *Jew.* 723; states that Philip the Roman emperor was a Christian, 2 *Ful.* 355 n
Vincentius de Valentia, *q. v.*
Vincentius Victor: his opinion of unbaptized infants, 4 *Bul.* 375
Vindelinus (......): 2 *Cov.* 505, &c.
Vine: a name of the church, 4 *Bul.* 83; Christ's parable of the true vine expounded, *Hutch.* 35
Vineyard: the church so called, *Sand.* 57; the parable of the labourers in the vineyard, 2 *Lat.* 198; that of the vineyard let out, 1 *Tyn.* 473; the Lord's vineyard broken down and wasted, 2 *Cran.* 9; destroyed by foxes, *Sand.* 65
Vini: *v.* Wini.
Vinton: *v.* Gardiner (S).
Vio (Tho. de), card. Cajetan, *q. v.*
Violence: in what cases lawful, 2 *Tyn.* 63
Viret (Pet.): *Phil.* 390, 3 *Zur.* 548; against hearing mass, 2 *Brad.* 297 n.; letter to him and others, 2 *Zur.* 121
Virgil: cited, 1 *Bec.* 182, 2 *Bec.* 419 n., 1 *Bul.* 289, 301, *Calf.* 14 n., 86, 2 *Cov.* 205, 1 *Hoop.* ix, 353, 365, 393, *Hutch.* 175, 4 *Jew.* 743, 959, 3 *Zur.* 733
Virginals: text appropriate to them, 1 *Bec.* 65
Virginity: *v.* Celibacy.
Virgins: *v.* Maids.
What, 3 *Bec.* 612; virgins in the church, 4 *Bul.* 512; vestal virgins, 2 *Bul.* 288
Viron (Jo.): *v.* Veron.
Virtue, Virtues: what virtue is, 3 *Bec.* 612; knowledge and talk of it not sufficient, 2 *Hoop.* 219; it must be sealed in the conscience and loved, *ib.* 217; the putting of it in practice and use very hard, *ib.* 346; THE GOVERNANCE OF VIRTUE, by T. Becon, 1 *Bec.* 393; virtue immovable; verses, *Poet.* 310; virtues are all obtained from God, 1 *Bec.* 204, 205; they are to be exercised, *ib.* 115; without faith they are but sins, 2 *Bec.* 14; a pastor must take as much heed to a virtuous life as to his doctrine, 1 *Bec.* 16; such a life is the best way to re-edify the house of the Lord, *ib.*

194; four general virtues mentioned by Origen, *Sand.* 391 n
Virvesius (Alph.): Philippicæ Disputationes, *Jew.* xliv; on vows of chastity, 3 *Jew.* 400
Visellus (Jo.): *v.* Wesselus.
Visenomy: physiognomy, 2 *Tyn.* 127
Visibility: a mark of the church (*q. v.*), *Poet.* 273
Visions: prove no doctrine, 2 *Cran.* 47, 64; miraculous ones, *Calf.* 117, 119; how to know true ones from false, 2 *Cran.* 66; a vision revealed to Philpot, *Phil.* 272
Visitation, Visitations: *v.* Articles of inquiry, Canterbury, Commissions, Sacrilege, Sick. What it is to visit, 3 *Bec.* 609; God's two visitations, 1 *Lat.* 146; ecclesiastical visitations needful and profitable, *Sand.* 247; ordinary visitation forbidden during the royal visitation, 1535, 2 *Cran.* 463; Parker forbids the bishops of his province to visit their dioceses, *Park.* 115, 116; he is offended with the visitation of Worcester by bp Sandys, *ib.* 125, 126; sermon at a visitation, *Sand.* 235; visitation of the sick, 2 *Zur.* 356, 358
Vitas Patrum: 3 *Bec.* 234, 474, 1 *Hoop.* 144, 291 n., 1 *Jew.* 199, 2 *Jew.* 1094, 2 *Lat.* 73, *Pil.* 184, 642
Vitalianus: 4 *Bul.* 196
Vitalis (Jo.), a cardinal: Specul. Moral. totius S. Scripturæ, *Jew.* xliv; he complains of the priests of his time, 1 *Jew.* 121, 4 *Jew.* 746
Vitel (Chr.): a Familist, *Rog.* 202; he says that there are men as holy as Christ, *ib.* 135; affirms that the Marian martyrs were stark fools, *ib.* 163
Vitellius, emperor: his gluttony, *Sand.* 393
Vitruvius: on the river Hypanis, 1 *Hoop.* viii.
Vitus: legate at Nice, 4 *Jew.* 999
Vives (Jo. Lud.): notice of him, 4 *Bul.* 498 n.; Opera, *Jew.* xliv; his Commentary upon St Augustine's City of God corrupted, *Calf.* 20 n.; Bradford translates his prayers, *Pra. Eliz.* xxii; his Exercitationes, 1 *Brad.* 195, 223; his Preces et Meditationes Diurnæ, 1 *Brad.* 572—578; prayers taken from his works, *ib.* 230, &c., *Pra. Eliz.* 182, 183, 198, 199, 206, 378, 384, 385, 397, 440—448, 468, 482, 483, 485, 486, 487, 489, 490, 504, 506, 514, 515, 521, 522, 523, 524, 535, 537, 538, 540, 541, 542, 543, 544, 556; meditations from his works, 1 *Brad.* 195—*Pra. B.* vii, 60—76; he maintains the authority of the originals of scripture, *Whita.* 157; declares the account of the LXX. ascribed to Aristæus to be a modern fiction, *ib.* 117; thinks that if Paul were alive again, he would be thought a bad rhetorician, 4 *Jew.* 739, 740; considers image worship, though among Christians, to be idolatry, *Calf.* 20, 3 *Jew.* 553, 4 *Jew.* 950; writes on the Babylon of the Apocalypse, *ib.* 1064; doubts whether a Christian may bear arms, *Rog.* 351; says the name of heresy is laid upon very light matters, 3 *Jew.* 211; his opinion of the Legenda Aurea, 4 *Jew.* 816, *Sand.* 18; he says that for the space of some hundred years past, the less any book came into students' hands, the purer it came to us, 4 *Jew.* 877, 878; speaks of Augustine's opinion on the Roman law, *ib.* 645; says, at Rome, notwithstanding all things be bought and sold, yet may ye do nothing there without form and order, and that of most holy religion, *ib.* 867; states his opinion about government by women, *Rog.* 337 n.; calls beauty a little thin skin well coloured, 1 *Bec.* 203, 2 *Bec.* 437; terms gay raiment a very instrument of pride, 1 *Bec.* 203

Vively: vividly, 1 *Bec.* 234

Vix: sometimes means "non," 3 *Whitg.* 499, 500

Vladislav, king: *v.* Wladislaus.

Vocation: *v.* Duty. What calling or vocation is, 3 *Bec.* 608, 616; it is either general or special, 2 *Lat.* 37; we must not run uncalled, *ib.* 29; every man should fulfil the duties of his calling, 1 *Lat.* 359, 503, 537, 538, 2 *Lat.* 6, 94, 154, 159, 214, 215, 430, 1 *Tyn.* 100, 102; God will aid and defend therein, 2 *Lat.* 34, &c.; every man has *one* vocation, *Hutch.* 6; the danger of transgressing our vocation, 1 *Hoop.* 456; we must not leave our vocation, 1 *Lat.* 516; how calling follows election, 1 *Brad.* 314

Volaterranus (Ra.): Commentarii Urbani, *Jew.* xliv, 3 *Whitg.* xxxii; he calls Timothy presul Ephesinus, 2 *Whitg.* 295; says that pope Sixtus was the first that caused altars to be erected, 1 *Jew.* 310; declares that the decree containing Constantine's Donation is false, 4 *Jew.* 678; says that Celestine introduced the introit, 3 *Whitg.* 73; speaks of the institution of extreme unction, *Pil.* 527; bears testimony in proof of pope Joan, 4 *Jew.* 656; says that Urban II. confirmed, in a council, the acts of Gregory VII., 1 *Whitg.* 482; describes the Monothelites, *Rog.* 54 n.; corrupted the Monodia of Gregory Naz., 1*Jew.* 194; refers to Genesius, jester to Diocletian, *Pil.* 401; speaks of the fall of the kingdom of the Goths in Spain, 1 *Bul.* 416; says Petrarcha was made poet in the Capitol, 4 *Jew.* 742; references to him, 1 *Jew.* 137, 222 n

Volo: a response in the baptismal service, 1 *Tyn.* 253; hence a priest was sometimes called a volower, and baptism volowing, 1 *Tyn.* 276, 3 *Tyn.* 72

Volsius (Paul.), or Wolzius: 1 *Cov.* 491

Volusian, bp of Carthage: on Dionysius the Areopagite, 2 *Whitg.* 130, 428; Udalric's epistle ascribed to him, 3 *Jew.* 427, *Sand.* 316 n

Voragine (Jac. de): 1 *Jew.* 190; Legenda Aurea, p. 481, col. 1, above; Sermones Aurei de Sanctorum Festis, 2 *Lat.* 132 n

Vortiger, king of Britain: *Pil.* 253

Vossius (Ger. Jo.): his works, *Calf.* 69 n., 126 n., 2 *Ful.* 411; his perplexity concerning Ben Gorion, *ib.* 338 n.; manuscripts of his corrupted as to the name of the pseudo-Hegesippus, *ib.*; he claims the authorship of the books De Vocatione Gentium, for Prosper of Orleans, *ib.* 353 n.; is mistaken about the Pontifical, *ib.* 99; referred to about Theotectus and Theopompus, 1 *Bul.* 48

Vossius (Isaac): published the genuine epistle of Ignatius, 2 *Ful.* 235 n

Votaries: *v.* Vows.

Vouchers: seemingly for butchers, 3 *Tyn.* 262

Vows: *v.* Oaths,
On vows: 2 *Bul.* 206, 271, 1 *Tyn.* 433—440, 3 *Tyn.* 185, 186; they are often taken in scripture for praises and thanksgivings, 1 *Bec.* 186, 373; what vows must be paid to the Lord, *ib.* 284, 285; simple and solemn vows, 4 *Jew.* 786, &c.; monastical vows, and the evil of them, 1 *Bul.* 232, 4 *Bul.* 518, 2 *Cran.* 147, 1 *Lat.* 60, 1 *Tyn.* 430, 435, 438, 2 *Tyn.* 163, 3 *Tyn.* 185, 189; Latimer preached against them, 2 *Bec.* 425; how they were observed, *ib.* 414; on vows of virginity, 2 *Ful.* 102—104; Foxe on vows of celibacy, &c., 1 *Tyn.* 173 n.; vows rashly made are not binding, 3 *Tyn.* 160; rash vows of chastity may be broken, *ib.*, *Whita.* 593; all vows contrary to our engagements in baptism are void, *Pil.* 621; the pope gives license to break lawful vows, 3 *Tyn.* 189; translations concerning votaries examined, 1 *Ful.* 471, &c.

Voysey (Jo.), or Vesey, alias Harman, bp of Exeter: 1 *Lat.* 272 n.; rewards G. Donne, who was concerned in the betrayal of Tyndale, 1 *Tyn.* lxix. n.; Coverdale his coadjutor, 1 *Cov.* viii, 2 *Cov.* xiii; his death, *Phil.* 168; letter to him, 2 *Cran.* 428

Vulford (Rich.): 1 *Tyn.* 13 n

Vulgarius: what is to be understood by this name, 2 *Cov.* 13, & addenda.

Vulgate: *v.* Bible, *Latin*.

Vyllers (Philippe de): chos n grand-master of Rhodes, 2 *Lat.* 33

W

W. (A.): i. e. A. Warcup, *q. v.*

W. (A.), a contributor to Davison's Poetical Rhapsody: perhaps Arthur Warren, possibly Andrew Willet: notice of him, *Poet.* xlii; Saphickes upon the passion of Christ, *ib.* 452

W. (E.), author of Thameseidos, 1600: notice of him, *Poet.* xxxii; lines from the poem, *ib.* 358

W. (H.): i. e. Hen. Wilkinson, *q. v.*

Wacker (......): 2 *Zur.* 294

Wadding (Luc.): Annales Minorum, 1 *Lat.* 50 n

Wade (Chr.): martyred at Dartford, *Poet.* 162

Wæchtler (Christfrid): 2 *Ful.* 33 n

Wafer: *v.* Host, Supper of the Lord.

Wagelings: hirelings, *Bale* 439

Wages: hire is due, 2 *Bul.* 346; against the withholding of it, 2 *Bec.* 105, 2 *Bul.* 37, 230

Wagner (Mark): 2 *Zur.* 77 n

Waid (Chr.): *v.* Wade.

Wailing: of wailing, and not prevailing; verses by James Yates, *Poet.* 450

Wake: the feast of dedication, observed in honour of the patron saint, and called rush-bearing, *Grin.* 142; wakes, *Calf.* 257

Wake (Will.), abp of Canterbury: his Commentary on the Church Catechism cited, *Lit. Edw.* xi.

Wakefield (Jo.): controller of Cranmer's household, refuses to join in lord Darcy's rebellion, 2 *Cran.* 362, 363

Wakeman (Jo.), first bishop of Gloucester: 1 *Lat.* 123 n

Walafridus Strabo: *v.* Glossa ordinaria.
He states that the old fathers said mass in their common apparel, 3 *Jew.* 617; his testimony to the frequency of communion among the Greeks, 2 *Bec.* 258 n.; he speaks of Gregory's litania major, *Calf.* 297 n.; wrote on the Apocalypse, *Bale* 256

Walary (St): *v.* Valeri.

Waldegrave (Sir Edw.): notice of him, *Park.* 19 n.; privy councillor to queen Mary, 1 *Zur.* 5 n

Waldegrave (Rob.), printer: 1 *Hoop.* 252

Walden (Saffron), co. Essex: Bradford labours there, 2 *Brad.* xxvi; his farewell to it, 1 *Brad.* 455; a martyr there, *Poet.* 163

Waldenses, or Vaudois: *v.* Lyons.
Called Waldeans, *Bale* 322; otherwise pauperes de Lugduno, named, it is said, from Valdo, a merchant of Lyons, 2 *Jew.* 689; on their confession, 2 *Brad.* 161, *Rid.* 375; their doctrine on the sacrament,

1 *Jew.* 235; their opinion on oaths, &c., *ib.* 227; persecuted, *Bale* 563; butchered by French kings, *Pil.* 264, 653; Luther's opinion of them, 3 *Zur.* 694 n., and see 697

Waldensis (Tho.): *v.* Netter (T.) à Walden.

Waldensius (......): secretary to Charles V., 2 *Cran.* 235

Wales: *v.* England.
The pope's power of no ancient standing there, 3 *Tyn.* 158; wickedness of the priests, 2 *Cran.* 37; crowns paid by them for keeping concubines, 3 *Tyn.* 40; pensionary concubinage continued there notwithstanding liberty of marriage granted, *Park.*257; an instance, *Grin.* 346; the marriage of priests never altogether rooted out there, *Pil.* 570; custom of cursing thieves in the marches of Wales, 1 *Tyn.* 273; More says the Welsh of his time prayed when they went to steal, 3 *Tyn.* 126; a pilgrimage there, *Calf.* 24; the Bible and Prayer Book rendered into Welsh, 1 *Zur.* 124 n.; the prince of Wales's cognizance and motto, *Pra. Eliz.* 19 n

Waleran, bp of Medenburg: a witness against transubstantiation, *Bale* 563

Waleran, bp of Numburg, or Nicenburg: Anselm's epistle to him, *Pil.* 538

Waley (J.): *Park.* 265

Walk: use of the term in scripture, 1 *Bec.* 209, 2 *Tyn.* 149; what it is to walk with God, 1 *Tyn.* 409; walking in truth, *Sand.* 118, 122, &c.; walkers in bye-paths; as in heresy, *ib.* 118; after the flesh, *ib.*; after covetousness, *ib.*; in obstinacy, *ib.* 119; in the counsel of the wicked, *ib.*; walking with the tongue, *ib.*, walking in treachery, *ib.* 120; evil walkers among the clergy, *Sand.* 120, and the temporality, *ib.* 121; we must walk without offence, *ib.* 310, &c.; to walk a villain, what, 2 *Tyn.* 309

Walkeham (Jo.), a monk of Canterbury: 2 *Cran.* 333

Walker (Jo.), archdeacon of Essex: *Grin.* 463

Walker (Tho.), parson of Shadwell, Essex: his suit for non-residence recommended to archbishop Parker by bishop Grindal, *Grin.* 294

Walker (......), a preacher at Norwich, *Park.* 312, 313; a Puritan (probably the same), *Grin.* 326 n., *Park.* 382

Walker (......), M.D.: and another

Walker (......), M.D.: *Park.* 18

Wall (Cha. Will.): *Calf.* 276 n

Wallachia: 3 *Zur.* 650

Wallenus of Crowland: a false martyr, *Bale* 189

Walloons: 1 *Zur.* 273; at Sandwich, *Park.* 189

Wallop (Sir Jo.): sent on an expedition to France, 2 *Cran.* 411 n.; his death, 3 *Zur.* 496 n

Walltown, Northumberland, *Rid.* i. n

Wallys (Jo.), Franciscan: wrote on the Apocalypse, *Bale* 258

Walmer castle, Kent: *Park.* 203

Walpole (Edw.): Lucy (Robsart) his wife, 2 *Bec.* 583 n

Walpoole (......), a Jesuit: his treason, *Lit. Eliz.* 681, 682

Walsh (Sir Jo.): patronizes Tyndale, 1 *Tyn.* xiv, xvi—xxi.

Walsh (Maurice): son of the last, 1 *Tyn.* xxv. n

Walsh (......): 2 *Brad.* 187

Walsingham, co. Norfolk: the shrine and image of our lady of Walsingham, *Bale* 98, *Calf.* 35, *Hoop.* 40, 1 *Lat.* 53 n., 474 n., 2 *Lat.* 395, 1 *Tyn.* 436, 3 *Tyn.* 125, 3 *Zur.* 609 n.; pilgrimage thereto, *Bale* 25; idolatry there, *Pil.* 63; the image burned at Chelsea, 2 *Brad.* 2 n., 2 *Lat.* 395 n.; a martyr at Walsingham, *Poet.* 164; salt-works near thereto, *Park.* 258

Walsingham (Sir Edm.): lieut. of the Tower, 1 *Tyn.* xxiii.

Walsingham (Sir Fra.): 2 *Zur.* 276, 277, 300; privy councillor, *Grin.* 405, 408, 412, 414, 417, 423, 427, 429, 433, 435; secretary, *ib.* 360; ambassador in France, 1 *Zur.* 230; minister to the Netherlands, 2 *Zur.* 303 n.; letters from him to Sturmius, *ib.* 285, 286, 287, 303; a letter to him, *ib.* 313; dedication to him, 2 *Jew.* 815; legacy to him, *Grin.* 459

Walstone (St): invoked for good harvest, *Bale* 498

Walter: to roll, tumble, lie grovelling, 1 *Brad.* 77, 278, 422; welter, 2 *Cov.* 238

Walter, bp of Durham: apparently de Kirkham, *Pil.* 591

Walter, bp of Hertford [Hereford]: killed by a woman, *Pil.* 590

Walter (Hen.): editor of Tyndale's works, 1, 2, 3 *Tyn.*; his edition of King Edward's Primer, *Lit. Edw.* ix. n

Waltham abbey, co. Essex: 1 *Cran.* viii, ix, 2 *Cran.* vii; a pardon bowl there, 1 *Lat.* 75

Walton (Brian), bp of Chester: *Calf.* 107 n., 2 *Ful.* 166 n

Walton (West), co. Norfolk: *Park.* 18

Wan (i. e. faint) hope: *Bale* 582

Want: peculiar use of the verb, 3 *Jew.* 337, *Sand.* 34, 392

Wantonness: *v.* Chambering.

War: *v.* Arms, France, Peace, Prayers, Soldiers, Thanksgivings, Victory.
Full of peril, 1 *Bul.* 373; the mother of

all evils, 1 *Bec.* 238; kingdoms are wasted by it, *ib.* 239; war deprecated, 1 *Lat.* 390; it is the scourge of God, 1 *Bul.* 374; threatened to the despisers of God's word, 1 *Bec.* 469, 470; causes of it, *ib.* 240—242, 1 *Bul.* 376; war for profit, 1 *Bul.* 375; fighting in defence of our country, *ib.* 276; in defence of religion, *ib.* 376, *Pil.* 433; princes should give no cause of war, 2 *Tyn.* 26; commendation of war, 1 *Bul.* 379; examples of it, out of the scripture, *ib.* 384; provisions of the law of Moses respecting it, *ib.* 380, 2 *Bul.* 235; in what case it is lawful, 1 *Hoop.* 475; sometimes it is a duty, 2 *Tyn.* 27; it is lawful for Christian men, at the command of the magistrate, to serve in wars, *Rog.* 350—352; war against the king's enemies is God's service, 1 *Lat.* 416; we must go to war at the prince's command, 2 *Tyn.* 63; the use of weapons lawful, 2 *Hoop.* 127; Augustine not always consistent with himself on the question whether Christians should engage in war, *Whita.* 456; war against infidels commended, *Grin.* 13; what war is unjust, 1 *Bul.* 379; THE POLICY OF WAR, by T. Becon, 1 *Bec.* 230; the armours of war are to be neither neglected nor trusted in, *ib.* 244, 245; how soldiers should prepare for battle, *ib.* 251; how the heathens prepare themselves thereto, *ib.*; how the Christians, *ib.*; cleanness of life required in war, *ib.* 252; and reading of the scriptures, *ib.*; what those who tarry at home in time of, should do, *ib.* 252, 256, &c.; Christian warfare, 2 *Brad.* 161, *Rid.* 366; the two weapons necessary in this war are prayer and knowledge, 1 *Cov.* 497; the use of prayer, *ib.* 498; the use of knowledge, *ib.*; our weapons must be fetched out of the storehouse of God's word, 1 *Cov.* 499

Wars of the Lord: what so called in the scriptures, *Grin.* 13, *Whita.* 516

Warblington, co. Hants: 3 *Zur.* 220 n

Warburton (Will.), bp of Gloucester: Divine Legation, 2 *Cov.* 41 n

Warcup (......), and Anne his wife: letter to them and others, 2 *Brad.* 45; Mrs Warcup, *ib.* 41, 45 n., 72; she was instrumental in saving the life of Jewel, *Jew.* xi; she relieved the prisoners in Bocardo, 2 *Brad.* 84 (and see 95), *Rid.* 360 (and see 365), 382; letters to her, 2 *Brad.* 121, 151 (see n.), 163, 185, 2 *Hoop.* 602

Ward (Rob.), or Warde: disputes with the martyrs at Oxford, 1 *Cran.* 424, *Rid.* 191, 226; concerned in the process against Cranmer, 2 *Cran.* 546; his deposition, *ib.* 547

Ward (Sam.), master of Sidney college: 3 *Whitg.* xvii.

Ward (Tho.): Errata of the Prot. Bible, *Calf.* 236 n

Ward (......), the painter: *Pil.* 656

Wards: v. Courts.

An act against stealing of wards, 1 *Lat.* 170; wardship of the crown, 2 *Cran.* 389

Ware, co. Herts: a martyr there, *Poet.* 163

Ware (Sir James): his Hunting of the Romish Fox, &c., *Park.* 95 n.; he publishes Campion's History of Ireland, *ib.* 407 n

Ware (Hen.), official of Canterbury: *Bale* 28

Ware (Rob.): *Park.* 95 n., 109

Warefeld (Mr): legacy to him, *Grin.* 462

Warehorn, co. Kent: the benefice, *Park.* 214

Warham (Will.), abp of Canterbury: named, 2 *Cran.* 492; he condemns Tho. Hitton, 2 *Tyn.* 340; searches the works of Tyndale and Frith for heresies, 1 *Tyn.* 34; proscribes Tyndale's version of the New Testament, 1 *Tyn.* xxxii; endeavours to buy it up, *ib.* xxxiii; his reply to a priest who wished the people to have the New Testament in English, *ib.* 234; Latimer cited before him and examined by him, 2 *Lat.* xvi, xvii, 218; his admission of the right of the universities to license preachers, *ib.* 329; his conduct with reference to the maid of Kent, 2 *Cran.* 65; he is said to have admitted the king's supremacy, *ib.* 214; succeeded by Cranmer, 1 *Cran.* vii, xi; letter to him from Latimer, 2 *Lat.* 351 (474); his portrait bequeathed by Grindal to his successors, *Grin.* 459

Warham (Will.), archdeacon of Canterbury: letter to him, 2 *Cran.* 268

Warham (Agnes), wife of Sir A. Saint-Leger, *q. v.*

Warham (Eliz.): 3 *Bec.* 597 n

Warley (Great?), co. Essex: Fulke rector there, 1 *Ful.* iii.

Warne (Eliz), martyr at Stratford-le-Bow: called by Bryce widow Warren, *Poet.* 163

Warne (Jone), alias Lasheforde: martyr in Smithfield, *Poet.* 165, 3 *Zur.* 175 n

Warner (Sir Edw.): lieutenant of the Tower, *Park.* 121; letter to him, *ib.* 122

Warner (Fra.): 3 *Zur.* 243; letter to Bullinger, *ib.* 355

Warner (Jo.), warden of All Souls' college, Oxon: *Rid.* 292 n

Warner (Will.): notice of him, *Poet.* xxxiv; verses; of Christ, *ib.* 377; the flesh and the spirit, *ib.*; how Sathan by the sin of pride hath ever prevailed, *ib.* 379; charity, *ib.* 380; faith, *ib.*

Warner (Mr): *Park.* 114

Warrants: v. Venison.

Warren (Eliz.): v. Warne.

Warthon (......), of Bungay: a persecutor, *Bale* 395

Warton (Rob.), alias Parfew or Purfoy, bp of Hereford: notice of him, *Phil.* xxvii.

Warton (Tho.): Hist. of Engl. Poetry, *Now.* viii.

Warwick (Earls of): *v.* Dudley.

Warwick: St Mary's collegiate church; its history, 2 *Lat.* 396 n.; the Dominican priory, 1 *Tyn.* 212 n

Waser (Caspar): account of him, 2 *Zur.* 326 n.; letters to him, *ib.* 326, 330, 334

Washing of Feet: what it means, 3 *Bec.* 610, 1 *Jew.* 223, 225, 226; it denotes the remission of our daily sins, 2 *Jew.* 1103

Wassalia (Jo. de): *v.* Wesselus.

Wasselheim: 2 *Zur.* 52

Waste: *v.* Goods, Prodigality.

Waste must be avoided, *Sand.* 342

Watching, Watchfulness: *v.* Vigils.

True watching, 1 *Tyn.* 92; watchfulness enforced, 3 *Bec.* 89; the danger of neglecting it, *Sand.* 382; needful against error, superstition, and sin, *ib.* 395; against false teachers, *ib.* 396; that others be not deceived, *ib.* 397; over our lives, *ib.*; watching for Christ's coming, *Grin.* 5, *Sand.* 368

Watchmen: *v.* Ministers.

Water: *v.* Holy water.

Water is a figure of God, *Hutch.* 185; the water of separation, 2 *Bul.* 201; the water and blood from Christ's side, what signified thereby, 1 *Cov.* 75; why the Lord commanded to baptize with water, 4 *Bul.* 363; the water of life, *Bale* 616; men are invited thereto, *Sand.* 10; how they must come, *ib.* 30; commodities received by coming, *ib.* 31

Waterland (Dan.): Works, 2 *Cov.* 139 n., 2 *Ful.* 86 n

Waterman (W.): says the Esseis deem all swearing as bad as forswearing, *Rog.* 358 n

Watkins (Rich.): 2 *Cran.* 243, 491, 545

Watson (Tho.), bp of Lincoln: account of him, *Phil.* 168; at a disputation in king Edward's time, *Grin.* ii; he disputes with the martyrs at Oxford, 1 *Cran.* 391, *Rid.* 191; Ridley's Annotationes (not extant) on his two Lent sermons, *ib.* xv; he preaches before queen Mary in support of the mass, 2 *Brad.* 207, *Rid.* 538, 540; bishop elect of Lincoln, 2 *Zur.* 20 n.; notice of his work on the Seven Sacraments, *Coop.* xiii; he tries to procure the arrest of Sandys, *Sand.* xii; opposes the reformation, 1 *Zur.* 7; disputes, on the popish side, at Westminster, *ib.* 11 n.; prisoner in the Tower, 4 *Jew.* 1202, *Park.* 122, 1 *Zur.* 16, 79; transferred by order of council from Grindal's house to the care of bp Cox, *Grin.* 281; enlarged, *ib.* 351; imprisoned in Wisbeach castle, *Phil.* xxviii; his death, 4 *Jew.* 1196, 1197

Watson (Rob.): in exile, 1 *Cran.* (9)

Watson (Tho.): translated Sophocles' Antigone, *Phil.* 168

Watson (Dr), master of Christ's coll., Camb.: opposes Latimer, 2 *Lat.* xii.

Watson (Will.): Decacordon of Quodlib. Quest., 1 *Brad.* 589, *Rog.* 331 n

Watterton (Mr): *Grin.* 325

Wattis (......): in Canterbury Bridewell, 3 *Zur.* 627 (see the next).

Watts (Friar): forswears the pope, but changes again, *Bale* 510 (perhaps the same as Wattis, named above).

Watts (Tho.): martyred, *Poet.* 162

Watts (Tho.), or Wattes: an ecclesiastical commissioner, *Grin.* 201, *Park.* 344 n., 369; chaplain to bp Grindal, *Grin.* 269, 288; archdeacon of Middlesex, *ib.* 353; recommended as visitor for St John's college, Cambridge, *ib.* 359; named, *ib.* 459; rector of Bocking, *Calf.* viii.

Wattwood (......), or Wetwood, canon of Warwick: cared neither for statutes nor injunctions, 2 *Lat.* 397, 401, 406; reprimanded by Latimer, *ib.* 396; he reforms, *ib.* 416

Wauchop (Rob.): appointed archbishop of Armagh by Paul III., but he never had the see, 4 *Jew.* 905 n.; at the council of Trent, *ib.* 905, 1056; called blind Sir Robert of Scotland, *ib.* 1056

Wawling: squeaking, *Bale* 439

Wax: simile from its use in sealing, 4 *Bul.* 270, 314 (see Nose of wax).

Way: how the word is to be taken in scripture, *Sand.* 116; the narrow way found by few, 2 *Tyn.* 120, 121

Way (Tho.), keeper of the Marshalsea: his kindness to Sandys and others, *Sand.* viii.

Waydner (Wolfg.): *v.* Weidner.

Ways: repairing dangerous ways, a charitable work, 3 *Bec.* 119, 2 *Lat.* 238

Weak: how to be borne with, *Pil.* 45; weaklings distinguished from stubborn persons, 2 *Bul.* 317; they are discouraged if they see pastors wanting in hospitality, 1 *Bec.* 26

Weal (......): 1 *Brad.* 552

Wealth: *v.* Riches.

Weapons: *v.* Arms, War.

Wearish: sour, 2 *Tyn.* 33

Web (Jo.): martyr at Canterbury, *Poet.* 165

Webbe (Will.): Discourse of English Poetrie, cited, *Poet.* xxvi.

Webster (Aug.), prior of Axholme: 2 *Cran.* 299; condemned for treason, *ib.* 303

Webster (Mr): contest between him, Mr

Woodroff, and archbishop Grindal, respecting a prebend at York, *Grin.* 329 n.; the archbishop's opinion of his case, *ib.* 329
Weda (Herm. de), abp of Cologne: *v.* Wied.
Wedering: weather, 2 *Tyn.* 79
Wedlock: *v.* Marriage.
Wednesday: named from Woden, *Pil.* 16
Wednesday (Ash): ashes hallowed and used on it, 2 *Cran.* 157, 509, *Rid.* 532; ceremonies of the day, 1 *Lat.* 71
Weedon (Lois), co. Northampton: the benefice farmed, 2 *Cran.* 279
Weesel: to ooze, 1 *Brad.* 304
Weesing: oozing, 1 *Brad.* 303
Weet: "it doth us to weet,"—makes us know, *Pil.* 107
Weford (Tho.), prior of Coventry: his death, 2 *Lat.* 386
Weidner (Wolfgang): pastor at Worms, 4 *Bul.* xxii, 1 *Zur.* 26; letter to him, 1 *Zur.* 26
Weigh-house: custom-house, 3 *Tyn.* 76
Weight and measure: 2 *Bul.* 231
Weissenheim: 2 *Cov.* 523
Welaway: woe on woe, or alas! alas! 1 *Brad.* 39, 62
Welles (Mr): *Park.* 333
Wellesborne (Jo.): his dau. Agatha, wife of bp Barlow, 3 *Bec.* 501 n
Welsh: *v.* Wales.
Welsh (Sir Jo.): *v.* Walsh.
Welsh (......) of C. C. C., Oxon: *Jew.* ix.
Welsh (......): a rebel, 2 *Cran.* 187 n
Welsh language: 3 *Zur.* 73
Welsinger (Chr.): 3 *Zur.* 669 n
Welter: *v.* Walter.
Wendelin (......), printer at Strasburgh: Grindal's opinion of him, *Grin.* 221
Wendesley (Rich.): an ecclesiastical commissioner, *Park.* 383, 390, 447
Wendon (Nich.), archdeacon of Suffolk: *Park.* 142; not in orders, *ib.* n
Wendy (Tho.): mentioned, *Park.* 25, 26; commissioner at Cambridge, 1549, 2 *Brad.* 370, *Grin.* 194, *Rid.* 169
Wenefrida (St): *v.* Winifred.
Went (Jo.): martyred in Smithfield, 3 *Zur.* 175 n.; called Winter by Bryce, *Poet.* 165
Wentworth (Tho. 1st lord): instructs Bale, *Bale* vii.
Wentworth (Tho. 2nd lord): one of queen Mary's privy council, 1 *Zur.* 5 n.; he surrenders Calais, 3 *Zur.* 139 n.; lord lieut. of Suffolk, 1 *Zur.* 99 n.; at the duke of Norfolk's trial, *ib.* 267 n
Wentworth (Hen. 3rd lord?): a privy councillor, 2 *Cran.* 524, *Rid.* 508
Wentworth (Sir Roger), father of the maid of Ipswich, 1 *Tyn.* 327 n

Wentworth (Mr): at Calais, 2 *Cran.* 411
Wentworth (Ann), called the maid of Ipswich: tormented of the devil, and, as it was supposed, miraculously healed, *Bale* 440, 2 *Cran.* 65, 1 *Tyn.* 327, 3 *Tyn.* 90—92
Werdmuller (Otho), or Wermuller: mentioned, 2 *Zur.* 328; minister at Zurich 3 *Zur.* 85; a book of his translated into English, *ib.* 415 n.; A SPIRITUAL AND MOST PRECIOUS PEARL, translated by bp Coverdale, 1 *Cov.* 84; his TREATISE ON DEATH, translated by Coverdale, 2 *Cov.* 37; THE HOPE OF THE FAITHFUL, translated by bp Coverdale, *ib.* 135; the last-mentioned treatise is not his, but Bullinger's, 4 *Bul.* xix.
Werdmuller (Valentine), or Wormulus: in prison in England for theft, 3 *Zur.* 85, 561 n., 563, 569; an impostor, *ib.* 572
Werikon, Zurich: 4 *Bul.* 546
Werner (Rolewinck): attributes the erection of altars to Sixtus, bishop of Rome [Fasc. Temp. fol. 32. 2], 1 *Jew.* 310 (*v.* Fasciculus).
Werter (Phil. and Ant.): 2 *Zur.* 69 n
Wesalius (Andr.): 3 *Bul.* 151
Wesant: windpipe, 1 *Lat.* 262
Wesel: the church there, 3 *Zur.* 160, 163, 168; the duke and duchess of Suffolk exiles there, 2 *Cov.* 528
Wesselus (Jo.): called Lux Mundi, *Bale* 563, 1 *Brad.* 360 n.; works of his, *Jew.* xliv; he says no man can interpret scripture, *Rog.* 195; states that certain of the bishops of Rome have been in pestilent heresies, 4 *Jew.* 927; declares that the devising of pardons is a godly guile and a hurtless deceit, to the intent that by a devout kind of error the people may be drawn to godliness, 4 *Jew.* 852; says the prelates' keys do not open but shut heaven, 3 *Jew.* 363; on nature, 1 *Brad.* 359 n.; on the Nominalists and Realists, 3 *Jew.* 613
West: *v.* Empire.
West-Chester: *v.* Chester.
West Indies: heathenism there, 3 *Jew.* 198, 199
West-Kington: *v.* Kington.
West (Tho.), lord de la Warr: patron of Shepton Mallet, 2 *Cran.* 385
West (Will.), lord de la Warr: at the duke of Norfolk's trial, 1 *Zur.* 267 n
West (Nich.), bp of Ely: hears Latimer preach at Cambridge, 2 *Lat.* xxviii—xxx; forbids him to preach, 1 *Lat.* iii; preaches against him, 2 *Lat.* xii; examines alleged heretics, 1 *Tyn.* 32; his death, 2 *Cran.* 247 n., 264 n
West (Jo.), an Observant of Greenwich: sent to hunt out Roye, 1 *Tyn.* xxxiv, xxxv.
West (......), sometime chaplain to Ridley: turns Papist, *Rid.* 337; Ridley's letter to

him from Bocardo, *ib.*; he died for sorrow, *ib.* 391

Westcote (Sebastian), minor canon of St Paul's: letter of bishop Grindal to lord Robert Dudley, respecting him, *Grin.* 262 (and see 261); excommunicated, *ib.* 262, &c.

Westminster:

i. CHURCHES.

The abbey (now collegiate church) of St Peter (*v.* Coronation): built on the site of a temple of Apollo, 4 *Jew.* 1165; legend of its consecration by St Peter, in person, 1 *Tyn.* 326; his cope affirmed to be kept there, *ib.* n.; the abbey was a sanctuary, *ib.* 326 n.; tombs of the kings, *Now.* 229; agreement between Henry VII. and the convent for sermons on Sundays, &c., 2 *Lat.* 370 n.; Westminster bowl, *Bale* 527; letter from Cranmer to abbot Boston, 2 *Cran.* 240; Ridley's farewell to this church, *Rid.* 408; the disputation, 1559, *Grin.* v, 1 *Jew.* 39, 74, 75, 4 *Jew.* 1201, &c., *Pil.* 626, 1 *Zur.* 10, 11, 13, &c., 27, 2 *Zur.* 22 n.; in it Cole praised ignorance, 1 *Jew.* 57; a proposed disputation declined by the Romanists, *ib.* 34, 35, 59; Cole's explanation of the Romanist party giving up, *ib.* 38; peace concluded here, 1572, 1 *Zur.* 273

Westminster school: its claims on Trin. coll. Camb., 3 *Whitg.* vii; queen's day observed here, *Lit. Eliz.* 558 n

St Clement Danes: *Pil.* 606

ii. ROYAL PALACES.

Westminster palace: the chapel called the Old Chapel, 1 *Tyn.* 35; the preaching-place, 1 *Lat.* 79, 2 *Lat.* xx; walkers and talkers in it, 1 *Lat.* 204; Westminster hall, 2 *Whitg.* 213; see also Terms.

Whitehall palace: Holbein's Dance of Death there, *Pra. Eliz.* xviii.

iii. OTHER LOCALITIES.

Bridge [i. e. landing-place]: 1 *Lat.* 211

Cannon-row: the house of the abp of York, *Park.* 291 n.; Cranmer's residence when archbishop elect, 2 *Cran.* 237

Gate-house: a prison, *Park.* 465, 470, 1 *Whitg.* 14 n

Savoy hospital: account of it, *Grin.* 302 —304; saved from ruin by bishop Grindal, *ib.* x.; letter by him respecting it, *ib.* 349

York-place: the house of Wolsey, 2 *Lat.* xxix.

Westmonasteriensis: *v.* Matthew.

Westmoreland (Earls of): *v.* Neville.

Weston (Hugh): some account of him, *Phil.* 167; mention of him, *Bale* 178; once a curate near Bishopsgate, 2 *Lat.* 260; he attends the duke of Suffolk at his execution, 3 *Zur.* 305 n.; dean of Westminster, *Phil.* xiii, 3 *Zur.* 373; prolocutor in the disputation in the Convocation house, Oct. 1553, *Phil.* 179; he confers with Bradford, 1 *Brad.* 538, 550; is one of the examiners of Philpot, *Phil.* 104; obtains a commission against Cranmer, Ridley, and Latimer, 2 *Hoop.* 593, 594; prolocutor in the disputation with them at Oxford, 1 *Cran.* 391, 2 *Cran.* 445 n., 1 *Jew.* 115 n., *Rid.* 191; his preface to the disputation with Latimer, 2 *Lat.* 250; Latimer addresses him, *ib.* 257; he rails against the reformers, *ib.* 277; is concerned in the process against Cranmer, 2 *Cran.* 553; refuses to deliver his supplicatory letter to the council, *ib.* 445 n.; Ridley's letter to him, requiring performance of certain promises, *Rid.* 375; his promises to Ridley were not kept, *ib.* 305, 375; deprived of the deanery of Windsor for adultery, 1 *Zur.* 12 n

Weston (Rob.): this (?) Weston presides in civil law at Oxford, 3 *Zur.* 420; dean of the arches, *Park.* 129 n., 428, 430

Weston (......): provincial of the Jesuits in England, *Rog.* 10

Westphaling (Herb.), bp of Hereford: sometime canon of Christchurch, 2 *Zur.* 305; suggested as bp of Oxford, *Park.* 360; made bishop of Hereford, 1 *Zur.* 328 n
— Anne (Barlow) his wife, 3 *Bec.* 501 n., 2 *Zur.* 263 n

Westphalus (Joachim): a Lutheran, 4 *Bul.* xiii, xxiii, *Rog.* 163, 3 *Zur.* 513 n

Westwell, co. Kent: the manor, *Park.* 373

Wete: to know, 1 *Tyn.* 234; weet, *Pil.* 107

Wetherby, co. York: the rebellious earls there, 1 *Zur.* 214 n., 247 n.; rebels executed there, *Lit. Eliz.* 538 n

Wetheringset, co. Suffolk: 3 *Bec.* 563

Wettenhall family: *v.* Whetenhall.

Wetwood (......): *v.* Wattwood.

Weybridge, co. Surrey: the forest, *Park.* 4

Whalley, co. Lanc.: *Park.* 222, *Pil.* vii; the birthplace of Nowell, *Now.* i; the abbey-lands, 2 *Cran.* 253 n

Whalley (Steph.), last abbot of Hales: 2 *Lat.* 380; a commissioner respecting the blood of Hales, *ib.* 407 n

Whalley (Will.), canon of Lincoln: *Park.* viii, 482

Wharton (Sir Tho.): an officer to the lady Mary, *Rid.* x. n., xi. n.; one of queen Mary's privy council, 1 *Zur.* 5 n

Wharton (Hen.): works, *Calf.* 96 n., 2 *Ful.* 20, 22, 23 nn., *Rid.* xiv; mistaken as to the author of the supposed Donation of Constantine, 2 *Ful.* 360 n

Wharton (Mr): priests of his retinue, *Bale* 443

Wheat and Tares: sermon on the parable,

2 *Lat.* 188; by what fault the tares grow in the Lord's field, *Sand.* 439

Whelock (Abr.): *Calf.* 53 n., 306 n., 2 *Ful.* 22 n

Whet (sharpen): "whet them on thy children" (Deut. vi. 7), 1 *Tyn.* 446

Whetenhall family : 1 *Bec.* 191 n

Whetenhall (Geo.): dedication to him, 1 *Bec.* 191; account of his family, *ib.* 191 n., 307 n., 353 n

Whetenhall (Will.): his daughters, 1 *Bec.* 307 n

Whetstone: sharpens and yet has no sharpness in it, 1 *Cran.* 179; lying for the whetstone, 3 *Whitg.* 384

Whetstone (Geo.): notice of him, *Poet.* xxx; recantation, verses by him, *ib.* 339; his life of Fra. earl of Bedford, 2 *Brad.* 77 n

Wheych, i. e. Droitwich, *q. v.*

Whiborne (Perceval): *v.* Wiburn.

Whighthead (Dr Jo.): *v.* Whyghthead.

Whilom: in old time, *Phil.* 343

Whitacre (......), chaplain to bp Poynet: proposed as abp of Armagh (perhaps a mistake for Goodacre), 2 *Cran.* 438

Whitaker (T. D.): History of Richmondshire, 2 *Cov.* vii.

WHITAKER (Will.), master of St Jo. coll., Cambridge: notices of him, 1 *Ful.* 14 n., *Whita.* ix, &c.; his birth and education, *Whita.* ix; master of St John's, *ib.*; he opposes Arminianism in the church of England, *ib.* x; mentioned, 3 *Whitg.* 611, 614; his death, *Whita.* x, 3 *Whitg.* 615; his character, *Whita.* x; Gataker's description of him, *ib.*; Bellarmine kept his portrait in his study, *ib.*

His works, *Jew.* xliv, 4 *Jew.* 1309, *Whita.* xi, xii; his DISPUTATION ON HOLY SCRIPTURE, AGAINST THE PAPISTS, ESPECIALLY BELLARMINE AND STAPLETON, translated and edited by the Rev. Will. Fitzgerald, A.M., *Whita.*; this work cited, *Rog.* 197, 324; his answer to Campion, 1 *Ful.* 14, 440, et sæpe; his Greek and Latin version of the Prayer Book noticed, *Lit. Eliz.* xxii; cited on false doctrines in the Apocrypha, 1 *Ful.* 21, 22; how he is misrepresented by G. Martin, *ib.* 132, 133

Whitborne (Rich.), or Bedyll, last prior of Great Malvern: 2 *Lat.* 410

Whitby, co. York (formerly Streneshalch): a synod held there by Oswy, 2 *Ful.* 16, *Pil.* 625

Whitby (Dan.): Idol. of the Ch. of Rome, 2 *Ful.* 41 n

Whitchurch (Edw.), printer: 2 *Cran.* 395, 1 *Hoop.* 572, 2 *Hoop.* 18, *Lit. Edw.* 10, 11, 12, 188, 189, 354

White, or Witta (St): cheese offered to St White, 2 *Tyn.* 216, 217; who was painted with round cheeses, 1 *Hoop.* 320

White (Jo.), bp of Lincoln, afterwards of Winchester: once master at Winchester college, *Phil.* i; excommunicated by archdeacon Philpot for preaching false doctrine, *Phil.* 82; commissioned to examine Latimer and Ridley, 2 *Lat.* 279, *Rid.* 255; he called "only faith" a new doctrine, *Rid.* 260; pronounced sentence on Latimer, 2 *Lat.* 292; translated to Winchester, 3 *Zur.* 175; preached a turbulent sermon at queen Mary's funeral, 4 *Jew.* 1196, 1 *Zur.* 7; opposed the reformation, 1 *Zur.* 10 n.; disputed, on the popish side, at Westminster, *ib.* 11 n.; committed to the Tower, *ib.* 16; his death, 4 *Jew.* 1230, 1 *Zur.* 69, 71; his book entitled Diacosio-Martyrion, de Veritate Corp. et Sang. Christi in Euch., adv. P. Martyr, *Jew.* xliv, 3 *Jew.* 590, 4 *Jew.* 1196, 1 *Zur.* 16 n., 71 n., 3 *Zur.* 479 n

White (Sir Tho.): founder of St John's college, Oxford, 1 *Ful.* xii.

White (Tho.), archd. of Berks: subscribes, *Grin.* 257

White (Will.): *v.* Whyte.

White (Will.), a Londoner: examined before the ecclesiastical commissioners, *Grin.* 201

White (......): *v.* Whyte.

White (......): 3 *Zur.* 181

White (......): a notary at Cranmer's disputation, 1 *Cran.* 391, 393

White (......): martyred at Canterbury, *Poet.* 169

White-Friars: *v.* Carmelites.

White Observant monks: *v.* Cistercians.

Whitehall: *v.* Westminster.

Whitehead (David): notice of him, *Hutch.* i. n., 1 *Zur.* 11, 255 n.; at a disputation on the eucharist, 1551, *Grin.* ii; he visits Joan Bocher, *Hutch.* 146 n.; proposed as abp of Armagh, 2 *Cran.* 438; an exile, 1 *Cran.* (9); preacher to the exiles at Frankfort, 3 *Zur.* 128 n., 755, 763, 764; he disputes at Westminster, 4 *Jew.* 1199, 1200; preaches before the queen, 2 *Zur.* 16 n.; a commissioner for the revision of the Prayer Book, *Grin.* v; mentioned, *Bale* 64, *Rid.* 494 n., 1 *Tyn.* xxvi, 3 *Whitg.* 2; his death, 1 *Zur.* 242

Whitehead (Gyllam): a gospeller, *Bale* 157, 162

Whitehead (Jo.): *v.* Whyghthead.

Whitelocke (Bulstrode): Memorials, 1 *Zur.* 124 n

Whitfield (Ralph): cousin to Ridley, *Rid.* 397

WHITGIFT (Jo.), successively bp of Worcester, and abp of Canterbury: memoir of him, 3 *Whitg.* v, &c.; his birth, and early education, *ib.* v; sent to Cambridge, *ib.* vi; Bradford his tutor and patron, 2 *Brad.* xx; fellow of Peter-house, 3 *Whitg.* vi; his degrees, *ib.*; ordained soon after the accession of Elizabeth, *ib.*; Margaret professor of divinity, *ib.*; master of Pembroke-hall, *ib.* vii; of Trinity college, *ib.*, 1 *Zur.* 294; regius professor of divinity, 3 *Whitg.* vii; other preferments, *ib.* (and 1 *Whitg.* 507 n.); he deprives Cartwright of his fellowship, *ib.* viii, 507; dean of Lincoln, *ib.* ix; the Admonition controversy, *ib.* ix—xi; recommended for the see of Norwich, *Park.* 476, 477; proposed as visitor for St John's college, Cambridge, *Grin.* 359; appointed bishop of Worcester, 3 *Whitg.* xi; consecrated, *ib.*; arms granted to him by Sir G. Dethick (Strype's statement corrected), *Lit. Eliz.* 594 n.; vice-president of the marches of Wales, 3 *Whitg.* xii; abp of Canterbury, *ib.*; his archiepiscopate, *Rog.* 10, &c.; his remonstrance with the queen against sacrilege, 3 *Whitg.* xiii; he approves Whitaker's Disputation, *Whita.* 12; patronizes Hooker, *ib.* xv; his part in the Lambeth articles, *ib.* xvii; his alleged intolerance, *ib.* xviii; his opposition to the Puritans, 1 *Zur.* 297 n.; he requires subscription of all ministers in his province, *Rog.* 11; puts down sabbatarianism, *ib.* 20; crowns king James, *ib.* xix; present at the Hampton-court conference, *ib.*; his death and burial, *ib.* xx; his works, *ib.* xxi; a letter to him, *Grin.* 370; a dedication to him, *Poet.* liv; verses addressed to him, by T. Bastard, *Poet.* 306; a legacy to him, *Grin.* 459

His WORKS, edited by the Rev. Jo. Ayre, M.A., 1, 2, 3 *Whitg.*; references to his Reply to Cartwright, *Park.* 439, *Rog.* 234 n., 1 *Zur.* 291 n., 306, 309, 2 *Zur.* 227 n.; he writes against the popular election of ministers, 1 *Ful.* 465, 466; cites Ridley's reply to Hooper, 2 *Brad.* 390 n.; a prayer on behalf of queen Elizabeth, composed by him the day before her death, *Lit. Eliz.* 695

Whitgift (Hen.), father of the abp, and Anne (Dynewell) his wife: 3 *Whitg.* v.

Whitgift (Isabel), 3 *Whitg.* v.

Whitgift (Jo.), grandfather of the abp: 3 *Whitg.* v.

Whitgift (Rob.), abbot of Wellow or Welhove: 3 *Whitg.* v.

Whiting (Rich.), abbot of Glastonbury: hanged, 3 *Zur.* 317 n., 614 n., 627

Whitney (Geffrey): notice of him, *Poet.* xx; verses from his Emblems, *ib.* 203

Whitstable, co. Kent: brimstone made from stuff gathered on the shore there, *Park.* 341

Whitsuntide: *v.* Pentecost.

Whittaker (J. W.): his opinion on Coverdale's translation of the scriptures, 2 *Cov.* xvii.

Whittingham (Will.), dean of Durham: notices of him, *Poet.* xlviii, 3 *Zur.* 764 n.; references to him, *Grin.* 326 n., 3 *Zur.* 370, 764 n., 765 n.; his life exists in MS. in the Ashmolean Museum, 4 *Jew.* 1192; an exile, 1 *Cran.* (9); ordained by the English at Geneva, *Sand.* xxiii; at Frankfort, *Jew.* xii, 3 *Zur.* 762; he opposed the Communion Book, and wrote a preface to the book of Goodman against the lawfulness of women's government, *Grin.* 327 n.; refusing abp Sandys's visitation, he was excommunicated, *Sand.* xxiii; the abp called his ordination in question, *ib.* xxiv; Psalm li. in metre by him, *Poet.* 489; he translated Ridley on the Lord's supper into Latin, *Rid.* xiv; two letters from him to Calvin, 3 *Zur.* 764, 766; letter to him, 4 *Jew.* 1192

Whittington college: *v.* London.

Whittle (Tho.): *v.* Whitwell.

Whittled: sharpened, drunken, 1 *Bec.* 362

Whitwell (Jo.): almoner to Cranmer, 2 *Cran.* 248

Whitwell (Tho.), or Whittle: brutally treated by Bonner, *Phil.* 13; martyred in Smithfield, *Poet.* 165, 3 *Zur.* 175 n

Whod (......), martyr at Lewes: *Poet.* 168

Whoredom: *v.* Adultery, Homilies.

Whorle-pit: whirl-pool, 1 *Bec.* 442

Whote: hot, *Phil.* 414

Whyghthead (Jo.): *Bale* 28, 31

Whymple: *v.* Wimpole.

Whyte (......), an Irishman: *Grin.* 306

Whyte (Will.): persecuted, *Bale* 44 n

Wibrandis, wife of Bucer: *q. v.*

Wiburn (Perceval): some account of him, 1 *Zur.* 378, 2 *Zur.* 147 n.; a leading man among the Puritans, yet allowed to hold church preferment, *Grin.* 348; his account of the church of England, 2 *Zur.* 358; he goes to Geneva with a complaint against the English bishops, 1 *Zur.* 363; references to him, *Grin.* 326 n., *Park.* 382, 1 *Zur.* 178 n., 2 *Zur.* 128 n., 142, 147 n., 153 n.; letter from him to Bullinger, 1 *Zur.* 187

Wiccius (......): saluted, 2 *Zur.* 225

Wicelius (Geo.): 1 *Jew.* 15 n.; an apostate, 2 *Jew.* 803, 808; his Hagiologium, *Calf.* 126 n.; Via Regia, 1 *Lat.* 58 n.; quoted by Foxe, 2 *Ful.* 98

Wicliffe (Jo.): *v.* Wycliffe.

Wick: a Northern word, *Rid.* 488, 492

Wicked: *v.* Man, Unbelievers.

Who is ungodly, 3 *Bec.* 602; who is

unrighteous, *ib.* 603; who is evil, *ib.*; the wicked love darkness, *Hutch.* 32; God withholdeth his grace from them, 1 *Cov.* 255; their life is wholly defiled, *Pil.* 166; they plague one another, *ib.* 246; their cruelty, *ib.* 248; their infelicity, 2 *Bul.* 80; though cursed by God, yet they enjoy blessings in this world, 1 *Lat.* 363, 466; why they are suffered to prosper, *Hutch.* 58; they shall not prosper always, *Pil.* 224; the evils which follow when they bear rule in church and state, *Sand.* 120, 121; we may not desert the place where they dwell, 2 *Lat.* 196; they are subject to the power of God, *Now.* (30), 146; they are soon dismayed, *Pil.* 435, 436; how they are punished, 2 *Bul.* 432; the miserable state of the wicked; verses by Hen. Lok, *Poet.* 139; their miserable end, with sentences and examples of scripture, 1 *Bec.* 463, &c.; they are punished for ever, *Pil.* 250; what they should do, 1 *Bec.* 256; what a vicious man should pray for, *ib.* 167

Wickedness: *v.* Evil, Sin.

What unrighteousness signifies, 1 *Bec.* 330; prevailing ungodliness censured, *ib.* 354; the great increase of vices, *ib.* 357; corporal and spiritual vices censured, *ib.* 254; vice must be put away, *ib.* 348; what it is to deny ungodliness, *ib.* 321

Wickham (Will.), afterwards bp of Lincoln: recommended by archbishop Grindal to be master of the Savoy, *Grin.* 349; his wife, 2 *Zur.* 263 n

Wickius (Jo. James): 3 *Zur.* 176

Wickius (......): 1 *Zur.* 30, 58, 83, 94, 305

Wickliffe (Jo.): *v.* Wycliffe.

Wida, king of Hungary: his widow, 3 *Zur.* 699

Wideford (Wilh.), or Wodford: says it cannot be gathered that the bread which Christ brake after his resurrection was sacramental bread, 1 *Jew.* 233, 239

Widerkehr (Anna): mother of Hen. Bullinger, 4 *Bul.* vii.

Widowhead: widowhood, 3 *Tyn.* 157

Widowhood: *v.* Marriage.

Widows: their duty, with probations of scripture, 2 *Bec.* 520, 521; the duty of elder widows is to be occupied about matters of God and the congregation, 2 *Bec.* 365; that of the younger is to marry and guide the house, *ib.* 365; of the office of widows in the church, 4 *Bul.* 511, 2 *Tyn.* 253, 276, 3 *Tyn.* 155, 156, 1 *Whitg.* 319, 321, 3 *Whitg.* 281, &c., 292, &c.; of those who left their first faith (1 Tim.v.), *Whita.* 482, 483; letter to a certain godly woman, instructing her how to behave in her widowhood, 2 *Hoop.* 608; widows should not soon marry, 1 *Lat.* 548; old ones sometimes contract monstrous marriages, 2 *Bec.* 366; widows formerly went into religious houses, 1 *Lat.* 392; a rich widow condemned and converted, *ib.* 180; prayer the widow's weapon, *ib.* 157

Wied (Hermann de), abp of Cologne: notices of him, *Bale* 509, 2 *Cran.* 423 n., 437, 3 *Zur.* 19, 540; he invites Hardenberg to his city, 3 *Zur.* 538 n.; his Simplex ac Pia Deliberatio, a service-book drawn up by Bucer and others, *Lit. Eliz.* xxix, *Pra. Eliz.* xxv. n., 2 *Zur.* 18 n.; Antididagma, a work set forth by the canons of Cologne in opposition to the archbishop's reformation, 2 *Cran.* xv, 210, *Jew.* xxxiii, 3 *Jew.* 186, 451; ascribed to Jo. Gropper, 2 *Zur.* 18 n.; the archbishop's deprivation and death, 3 *Zur.* 540 n

Wiet (Sir Tho.): *v.* Wyat.

Wife: *v.* Wives.

Wigan, co. Lanc.: 1 *Brad.* 454; the birthplace of bp Woolton, *Wool.* iii.

Wigan (Edw.): *Park.* 25, 26

Wigandus (Jo.): one of the writers of the Magdeburg Centuries, 3 *Jew.* 128, 164, 2 *Zur.* 77 n.; letter to him, *Park.* 286; he rejected the 1st and 2nd epistles of John and that of Jude, *Rog.* 84

Wiggington (Giles): thought the people might reform the church, *ib.* 344

Wiggynton (Tho.), of Tring: 2 *Cran.* 267

Wighard, or Dimianus, abp of Canterbury: 2 *Ful.* 16, 119

Wight: *v.* Isle of Wight.

Wight (Jo.), or Wyght, printer: 1 *Brad.* 16, 18, 27

Wight (Will.): *v.* Wyght.

Wigston (Will. de): *v.* Leicester.

Wilbraham (Tho.): proposed as a commissioner, *Park.* 370

Wilcox (Tho.), or Wilcocks: a Puritan, *Sand.* xx; one of the writers of the Admonition, 3 *Whitg.* x, 1 *Zur.* 284 n

Wild (J.): 2 *Brad.* 76

Wildbaden: 3 *Zur.* 654

Wildbore (Mich.): grantee of part of Pontefract priory, 2 *Cran.* 363 n

Wilford (Sir Tho.): his daughter Cecilia, the second wife of abp Sandys, *Sand.* xviii, 1 *Zur.* 74 n (see also 1 *Bec.* 307 n).

Wilford (Fra.?): an exile, 3 *Zur.* 167 n

Wilford (Jo.): in exile, 3 *Zur.* 764, and perhaps 167 n

Wilfred (St), abp of York: *Pil.* 484; at a synod at Whitby, *ib.* 625 n.; he caused Etheldreda to leave her husband, and gave her the habit of a nun, 2 *Ful.* 12, *Pil.* 590; consecrated Oftfor at the command of king Edilred, 2 *Ful.* 17, 24; deposed by king

Ecgfrid, *ib.*; and again by king Aldfrid, *ib.* 24
Wilhelm Wideford, *q. v.*
Wilhelmus Haffliginensis: *v.* Gulielmus.
Wilhelmus Lugdunensis: his sermons cited, 1 *Lat.* 27 n
Wilkie (James): *v.* Wylkie.
Wilkins (Dav.): Concilia, 2 *Ful.* 22 n., *Grin.* vi, 189 n., 190, 1 *Lat.* v, vii, viii, 33, 45, 54, 56, 60, 132, 2 *Lat.* 240, 304, 356; Leges Anglo-Sax., 1 *Bec.* 390 n., 3 *Whitg.* xxxii.
Wilkinson (Hen.), canon of Ch. ch.: 1 *Brad.* 557; his preface to Bradford on Repentance (1652), *ib.* 558
Wilkinson (Hen.,) princ. of Magd. hall, Oxon: 1 *Brad.* 557
Wilkinson (Will.): his Confutation cited, *Rog.* 139, 153, 233, 271, 325
Wilkinson (Mrs), of Soper-lane, London: notices of her, 2 *Brad.* 39 n., 2 *Cran.* 444 n., *Rid.* 382, 385; she relieves the prisoners in Bocardo, 2 *Brad.* 84 (and see 95), 2 *Lat.* xxv, *Rid.* 360 (and see 365); letters to her, 2 *Brad.* 45, 72(?), 121, 182, 2 *Cran.* 444, 2 *Hoop.* 601, 2 *Lat.* 444
Will: the will of man, 3 *Bul.* 98, 100, 376; it cannot go before the wit, or judgment, 3 *Tyn.* 192, 210, 211; it is evil to follow our own will, 1 *Bec.* 151, 152
Will, or Testament: *v.* Wills.
Will (Free): *v.* Free-Will.
Will we nill we: *Grin.* 108
Will-works: *v.* Works.
Willerton (......), chaplain to Bonner: confers with Bradford, 1 *Brad.* 86, 497
Willesden: *v.* Wilsdon
Willet (Andr.): *v.* W. (A.).
Notice of him, *Poet.* xxxvii; Synopsis Papismi, *Calf.* 24, 85, 2 *Ful.* 122 nn., *Poet.* 269, 283; English verses entitled, divina providentia, and, ad pastores otiosos et somnolentos, *Poet.* 394
Willett (Tho.): *Hutch.* x.
William: *v.* Gulielmus, Wilhelmus.
William I., king of England: received a banner from the pope, to encourage him to invade England, 2 *Tyn.* 294; his army received the communion in both kinds, 1 *Jew.* 261; in a parliament holden by him it is written that the king is the vicar of the highest King, 4 *Jew.* 905
William II., king of England: *v.* Henry I.
Obliged by Anselm to surrender the investiture of bishops to the pope's vicar, 2 *Tyn.* 294
William, duke of Aquitaine: became a hermit, 1 *Hoop.* 313 n
William, duke of Bavaria: 2 *Cran.* 236; he joins the league against the Protestants, 3 *Zur.* 526 n

William, duke of Cleves and Juliers: at war with the emperor, 2 *Cov.* 512, 3 *Zur.* 235, 240 n
William, landgrave of Hesse: 4 *Bul.* xxiii.
William IX., prince of Orange: 1 *Zur.* 273, 276, 293, 2 *Zur.* 173, 207, 289, 300
William (St), abp of York: *Pil.* 484; story of him and his horse, *ib.* 587; his character, *ib.*
William (St), of Norwich: *Bale* 192
William (St), of Rochester: *Bale* 192
William, archdeacon of Canterbury: an epistle from Anselm to him and others, *Pil.* 573
William of Malmesbury: *Jew.* xl; his shameful depravation of a letter ascribed to pope Sergius I., 2 *Ful.* 119 n.; he says a child appeared to Gregory in the bread of the altar, 1 *Hoop.* 291; testifies that the creed, &c., were taught in the vulgar tongue amongst the Anglo-Saxons, 2 *Ful.* 22; says that king Canute being at Rome made his complaint to the pope that his archbishops should be vexed with such unreasonable sums of money required of them, 4 *Jew.* 1081; states that Victor III. was poisoned in the cup at the sacrament, 1 *Hoop.* 451 n.; cited about king Henry's dispute with Ralph, bp of Chichester, 2 *Tyn.* 295 n
William of Newbury: Rerum Anglic. Libri Quinque, *Jew.* xxxviii; his account of Becket, 3 *Jew.* 574, 575, 4 *Jew.* 960
W[illiam?] Paris, *q. v.*
Williams (Jo.), lord Williams of Thame: keeps order at the martyrdom of Latimer and Ridley, *Rid.* 293, 295; Ridley's last request to him, *Hutch.* ix; present at Cranmer's burning, 1 *Cran.* xxii, xxiii, xxix; one of the examiners of Philpot, *Phil.* 49; in his sickness he sent for Jewel, *Jew.* xiv.
Williams (Dan.): his library, Red-Cross-street, London, *Lit. Eliz.* xxxiv.
Willyams (Griffin): takes part in Cranmer's trial, 2 *Cran.* 547
Williams (Jo.), chancellor of Gloucester: Hooper's epistle to him and others, 2 *Hoop.* 95; his signature, 2 *Brad.* 397 n
Williams (Mr): in the Marshalsea, *Park.* 423
Williamson (Sir Jos.), secretary of state to Charles II.: 4 *Bul.* xxxi.
Willington (Will.): his dau. Godith, 3 *Bec.* 89 n
Willington, co. Beds.: 2 *Lat.* 368 n
Willis (Browne): Hist. of Abbeys, 2 *Lat.* 371, 383, 410, 413
Willis (Hen.): 2 *Brad.* 397 n
Willo: an instrument for catching fish, *Phil.* 385
Willobie (Hen.): notice of him, *Poet.* xxxvii; the praise of a contented mind, *ib.* 396

Willock (Jo.), superintendent of Glasgow and the West: 2 *Zur.* 364 n.; letter from him to Bullinger, 3 *Zur.* 311

Willoughby de Eresby (Pereg. lord): *v.* Bertie.

Willoughby de Eresby (Kath. lady), afterwards duchess of Suffolk: *v.* Brandon.

Willoughby of Parham (Will. 1st lord): sent against the rebels in the North, 1 *Zur.* 214 n

Willoughby (Hen.), of Woollaton: 1 *Bec.* 125 n

Willoughby (Dr), of Aldborough: *Park.* 404; spent £4 for painting a pulpit, *ib.* n

Wills, or Testaments: should be made, to prevent contention, 1 *Lat.* 540; ministers to exhort their parishioners to make them, 2 *Hoop.* 138; the clergy enjoined to exhort men to give alms to the poor, when they make their wills, 2 *Cran.* 503; the determination of the sick man to make his will, 3 *Bec.* 116; his provisions as to his body, *ib.* 117; as to his soul, *ib.*; for his wife, *ib.*; for his son, *ib.* 118; for his daughters, *ib.*; for his servants, *ib.*; for his debtors, *ib.*; for scholars of Cambridge and Oxford, *ib.* 118, 119; for the poor, *ib.* 119; for the highways, *ib.*; for sermons, *ib.* 119, 120; for mourning gowns, *ib.* 124; he appoints his wife executrix, *ib.*; desires to be buried simply in the churchyard, *ib.* 124, 125; rejects months' minds and years' minds, *ib.* 126; injunction against the use of a superstitious form, 2 *Hoop.* 148; on superstitious bequests, *Grin.* 173; wills not to be altered, 2 *Hoop.* 148; wills of founders set aside by the pope and monks, 2 *Tyn.* 287, 288; Romish ecclesiastics formerly denied Christian burial to those who left nothing to the church, 3 *Tyn.* 269; this rule checked by the lay courts in France, *ib.*; on the probate of wills in the province of York, *Grin.* 150; probate fees regulated, 2 *Lat.* 301 n

Willymotswick, Northumberland, (now Ridley hall): the seat of the Ridley family, *Rid.* i. n.; meaning of the name, *ib.* 488, 492

Wilna, Poland: 3 *Zur.* 596, 687; the palatine of Wilna, 4 *Bul.* xxiii; see Radzivil (N.).

Wilsdon, or Willesdon, co. Middx.: our lady of Wilsdon, an image, *Calf.* 35, 3 *Tyn.* 125

Wilsford (Tho.), or Wyllford (probably Sir Tho. Wilford, *q. v.*): his daughters, 1 *Bec.* 307 n

Wilson (Isabel): niece of abp Grindal, *Grin.* 461

Wilson (Lea): his collection of Bibles, 2 *Cran.* 125 n

Wilson (Nich.): master of Michael house, Cambridge, 2 *Cran.* 318 n

Wilson (Nich.), parson of St Thomas Apostle: maintains the pope's supremacy, 3 *Zur.* 208; attainted, 2 *Lat.* 365 n.; pardoned, 3 *Zur.* 211; he forswears the pope, but changes again, *Bale* 510; a letter of his prefixed to a sermon by Fisher, 1 *Tyn.* 189 n.; his (?) charge against Barnes, 2 *Cov.* 433

Wilson (R.), minister of Dalkeith: 2 *Zur.* 365

Wilson (Tho.): *Jew.* vii, *Park.* 420 (?); an ecclesiastical commissioner, *Park.* 383; a privy councillor, *Grin.* 412, 414, 417; letter to him, 4 *Jew.* 1276

Wilson (Will.), D.D., donor of Bull's Prayers, *Pra. B.* vi.

Wilson (......): chaplain to Grindal, who left him books, &c., *Grin.* 460, 461

Wilson (......): Wilson's wife martyred at Canterbury, *Poet.* 170

Wilton, co. Wilts: dispute about the appointment of an abbess, 2 *Cran.* 258, 297

Wiltshire (Tho. earl of): *v.* Boleyn.

Wiltshire (Will. earl of): *v.* Paulet.

Wimboldsley, co. Chester: *v.* Winsley.

Wimpled: wrapped, *Phil.* 383

Wimpole, co. Cambr.: *Wool.* 14

Wimsley (Jo.), or Wymbesly, archd. of London, *Phil.* xiii.

Wimundus Aversanus: *v.* Guimund.

Winchard (Mr.): *v.* Wynchard.

Winchcomb, co. Glouc.: ignorance of G. Roo, rector, 3 *Tyn.* 75 n.; lands of the abbey, 2 *Lat.* 415

Winchcombe (Mr): *v.* Wynchcombe.

Winchelsey (Rob. de), abp of Canterbury: 2 *Cran.* 492; his injunction respecting church books, vestments, &c., *Grin.* 159 n

Winchester: meeting of Henry VIII. and the bishops there, 2 *Cran.* 314, 326; arrival of some friars minor in the time of Mary, 3 *Zur.* 177; a martyr there, *Poet.* 173; Winchester goose, a swelling produced by a disease, 3 *Bec.* 284

The Cathedral and diocese: monks brought in, *Pil.* 574; the rood that decided a controversy between monks and married priests, *Calf.* 134; reference to the rood of Winchester, *ib.* 274; the bishop's first-fruits to the pope, 4 *Jew.* 1078; payment of the prior (1247) towards the pope's table, *ib.* 1079; epitaph on bp Horne, 3 *Bec.* 194 n.; the warden of the manors of St Swithin, 2 *Cran.* 312; the diocese visited by abp Cranmer, *ib.* 304, 305; also by abp Parker, *Park.* 478, 1 *Zur.* 323 n

Winchester college or school: *Calf.* 201, 274, 3 *Jew.* 111, *Phil.* i; Martiall usher there, 2 *Ful.* 150, 152, 163; the Wednesday fish-day dispensed with, *Park.* 235

Winchester (Marquises of): *v.* Paulet.

Winchingham (Hen.): wrote on the Apocalypse, *Bale* 257

Windless: out of breath, *Calf.* 213

Window: a blank space in writing, 2 *Cran.* 249

Windows: text appropriate to a window, 1 *Bec.* 63; nothing to be painted in church-windows but branches, flowers, and sentences of scripture, 2 *Hoop.* 138

Winds: red winds, i. e. blights, *Sand.* 103

Windsor, co. Berks: three martyrs there, 3 *Zur.* 242 n.; the castle, *ib.* 729 n.; king Edward's first Prayer Book drawn up there, 2 *Cran.* 450 n.; Wolsey's tomb referred to, 2 *Tyn.* 292

Windsor (Andr. lord): obtains the demesne of Bordsley, 2 *Lat.* 394 n

Windsor (Will. lord): one of the examiners of Philpot, *Phil.* 50

Wine: v. Bush.
  Wines of Egypt, 1 *Jew.* 248; of Naples, *ib.* 249; some of the wine of Cana said to be preserved at Orleans, *ib.* 249; wine purchased at Calais for Cranmer, 2 *Cran.* 316, 318, 411

Winfrid, or Boniface, q. v.

Wing (Godfrey): Grindal's commendation of him, *Grin.* 250

Wingfield (Sir Ant.): 2 *Cran.* 490, 2 *Zur.* 159 n.; captain of the king's guard, 2 *Lat.* 415 n.; a privy councillor, 2 *Cran.* 505, 510, 511

Wingfield (Sir Jo.): father of Sir Richard, 2 *Lat.* 295 n

Wingfield (Sir Rich.), K.G.: high steward of the university of Cambridge, &c., 2 *Lat.* 295 n

Wingfield (Sir Rob.): letter by him and others, *Park.* 306

Wingham, co. Kent: the case of Dr Benger, 2 *Cran.* 300, 301

Wini, bp of the West Saxons: deposed by king Coinualch, and afterwards, through simony, made bp of London, 2 *Ful.* 16, 24, 27, 118, 119

Winifred (St): martyred, *Bale* 192; invoked for virginity, *Rog.* 226; as to her well, see Holywell.

Winram (Jo.): v. Wynram.

Winslade (......): a rebel, 2 *Cran.* 187 n

Winsley: perhaps Wimboldsley, 1 *Brad.* 454

Winsloo (Mr): *Park.* 461

Winstan (St), of Evesham: *Bale* 192

Winter (Jo.): v. Wynter.

Winter (Jo.): v. Went.

Winterthur, Zurich: 4 *Bul.* 546

Winton: v. Winchester.

Winwick, co. ...... : the parson of Winwick, 2 *Cran.* 116

Wirt (Hadr.): v. Hospinian.

Wis (J.): I know, *Calf.* 47

Wisbeach, in the isle of Ely: the benefice, 2 *Cran.* 264; disputations at the castle, 1 *Ful.* iii, ix, 41; bp Watson and abbot Feckenham imprisoned there, *Phil.* 168

Wisdom: v. Prayers.
  Who are wise, 3 *Bec.* 607; the two principal parts of wisdom are to know one's self, and to know God, *Wool.* 3; wisdom is better than arms, *Pil.* 439; true wisdom, 1 *Cov.* 513; this is only found in God's church, *Wool.* 4; of perfect wisdom, verses by R. Edwardes, *Poet.* 295; the wisdom of God is the source of all good things, 1 *Cov.* 501; it is not revealed to the carnally wise, but to babes, 2 *Lat.* 338; it is to be obtained by prayer, 1 *Cov.* 501; the wisdom of the world, 1 *Brad.* 420, 426, 2 *Cov.* 236, 242; it is foolishness with God, 1 *Brad.* 448, 1 *Cov.* 500, 2 *Lat.* 308, *Pil.* 242, 243, 245, *Wool.* 4; how it is made foolish, 1 *Brad.* 428, 2 *Cov.* 244; it cannot comprehend the things of God, *Pil.* 243, 1 *Tyn.* 107; the wisdom of man is the source of all division, heresy, and idolatry, 1 *Tyn.* 160

Wisdom (Rob.): notices of him, 1 *Bec.* viii. n., ix, 2 *Bec.* 422, *Poet.* xlix; proposed as abp of Armagh, 2 *Cran.* 438; an exile, 1 *Cran.* (9); his books, 2 *Bec.* 423; Psalm cxxv. in metre by him, *Poet.* 493; his hymn, "Preserve us, Lord," &c., *ib.* 494, *Pra. Eliz.* 412 n.; the Latin of Cellarius, from which the above is taken, *Pra. Eliz.* 412

Wisdom of Jesus son of Sirach: v. Ecclesiasticus.

Wisdom of Solomon: v. Solomon.

Wise men: v. Magi.

Wiseman (Nich. card.): his declaration respecting the Pontificale so far as it relates to images, *Calf.* 415 n

Wiseman (Will.): died in the Lowlars' tower, *Poet.* 165

Wishes: the wishes of the wise, by Tho. Bryce, *Poet.* 175

Wisigoths: 2 *Bul.* 109

Wissemburg (Wolfg.): Antilogia Papæ, *Jew.* xliv, 3 *Jew.* 427

Wit: the reasoning faculty, 1 *Tyn.* 182, &c.

Witch of Endor: v. Samuel.

Witchcraft: v. Charms, Demons, Miracles.
  Against conjurors and witches, 1 *Bul.* 221; witchcraft, sorcery, and other magical arts condemned, 1 *Hoop.* 308, 327, 2 *Hoop.* 294, *Now.* (13), 127; such arts forbidden by God, 2 *Bul.* 232, 1 *Tyn.* 413; contrary to the third commandment, 1 *Hoop.* 326, &c.; forbidden by human laws,

ib. 327, &c.; encouraged by Satan, 3 *Bul.* 362; conjurors, witches, figure-flingers, &c., raised up by the devil, *Calf.* 14; witchcraft served by the mass, *Bale* 236, and by the Romish ceremonies, which are but sorcery and legerdemain, 3 *Bec.* 234; sorcerers and conjurors pretend to derive their art from Athanasius, Moses, Enoch, Abel, Adam, Raphael, 1 *Jew.* 23, 2 *Jew.* 991; witches and sorcerers consulted, 1 *Lat.* 345, 534; how they dishonour the name of God, *ib.* 349; witches abuse the Pater noster, *Calf.* 17; the existence of devils evidenced by conjurors, sorcerers, &c., *Hutch.* 142; circles, characters, and superstitious words of conjuration, 2 *Tyn.* 80; popish and other charms, 4 *Bul.* 261, *Pil.* 177, 536, 563 (*v.* Agatha, Holy things, John (St), Evang.—his Gospel); an example, 1 *Hoop.* 328; charms have healed diseases, 2 *Ful.* 157; the sin of necromancy, 1 *Hoop.* 326; sorcerers do not hold converse with the dead, but with the devil, 2 *Cran.* 44, 45; conjuring among the Jews, *Pil.* 385; the sin of Saul, 1 *Bul.* 242, *Pil.* 25, *Sand.* 129 (and see Samuel); Nero saw the fights of gladiators in an emerald, *Calf.* 47; witchcraft in the days of Charlemagne, 2 *Tyn.* 265; various popes have practised it, *Bale* 592, *Calf.* 91, *Rog.* 180; licence granted by the pope to card. Morton and thirteen others to study necromancy, 2 *Tyn.* 305; Wolsey's skill in witchcraft, *ib.* 308; necromancy avowed by Anne Wentworth, 2 *Cran.* 65; witchcraft should be removed, 1 *Lat.* 349; an act against it, 1 *Zur.* 44 n.; witches and sorcerers greatly increased; Jewel had seen many most evident marks of their wickedness, 2 *Jew.* 1028; many witches discovered by queen Elizabeth's commissioners, 1 *Zur.* 44; case of an old woman at Stowmarket, *Park.* 417 n.; inquiries about witchcraft, palmistry, and other forbidden arts, 2 *Cran.* 158, *Grin.* 175, 2 *Hoop.* 145; sorcerers shut out of the new Jerusalem, *Bale* 633

Wite: to blame, 1 *Tyn.* 164, 2 *Tyn.* 193
Witenbachius (Tho.): *Pil.* 684
With (Rich.): put to death, *Bale* 394
Withebroke, co. Warwick: 2 *Cran.* 259
Withers (Geo.), afterwards rector of Danbury: 2 *Zur.* 153 n.; he stirs up a racket for the reformation of the university windows, *Park.* 234, 236; his licence to preach informal, *ib.* 238; he goes to Geneva with a complaint against the English bishops, 1 *Zur.* 363; confutes the Rhemish glosses, 1 *Ful.* xiii; letter from him to the elector Palatine, 2 *Zur.* 156; a letter by him and Barthelot, *ib.* 146

Withers (Geo.), probably another: his interest in Croydon, *Grin.* 403
Withers (Matt.): died in prison, *Poet.* 172
Withsaveth: vouchsafeth, *Bale* 473
Witnam (Jo.), of New college: *Bale* 16, 28
Witness: of bearing witness, 2 *Bul.* 112, 225
Witness (False): *v.* Commandments, Lying. Forbidden, 2 *Bec.* 116, 117, 1 *Brad.* 170, *Now.* (19), 134; false-witness-bearers censured, 1 *Bec.* 254; warned, *ib.* 126; false-witness-bearing condemned among the Gentiles, 1 *Bul.* 204
Witnesses: the three heavenly and the three earthly witnesses, 2 *Tyn.* 209; the two witnesses mentioned in the Apocalypse, *Bale* 387, 2 *Ful.* 370; supposed by Hippolytus and others to be Elias and Enoch, *Bale* 387, 1 *Jew.* 117; witnesses for the truth, *Bale* 347, 349, 520, 563
Witney, co. Oxford: 2 *Cran.* 382; Jack Knacker of Witney, *Calf.* 274
Witta (St): *v.* White.
Wittemberg: the university, 3 *Jew.* 193, 2 *Zur.* 260; the concord of Wittemberg, 2 *Zur.* 102 n
Witterence (......): steward of Newgate, *Phil.* 160
Wittersham, co. Kent: the priest imprisoned, 2 *Cran.* 306
Wives: *v.* Husbands, Marriage, Obedience, Prayers.

Caution required in choosing them, 2 *Bec.* 346, 347; what kind fathers should provide for their sons, *ib.* 356; their duty, 1 *Bec.* 287, 2 *Bec.* 340, &c., 518, 519, 1 *Lat.* 352, 538, 2 *Lat.* 6, *Sand.* 202; their duty to their husbands, with probations of scripture, 2 *Bec.* 518, 519; they must love their husbands, *ib.* 341; must be subject to them, and reverence them, *ib.* 340, *Sand.* 319, &c.; owe no obedience to their husbands commanding wicked things, 2 *Bec.* 341; must forbear their husbands, *ib.* 343; must look well to their houses, *ib.*; must array themselves in modest and comely apparel, *ib.* 345, 346; why the Holy Ghost prescribes this, *ib.*; a wife the arm of her husband, 1 *Bul.* 398; the sick man's exhortation to his wife, 3 *Bec.* 130, 131; his farewell to her, *ib.* 145, 146; instructions for a woman whose husband was offended about her religion, 2 *Hoop.* 609
Wladislas, king of Bohemia and Hungary: 2 *Brad.* 161 n., 1 *Jew.* 235
Wladislaw, Poland: 3 *Zur.* 596
Woburn, co. Beds: the school, 2 *Bec.* 622 n
Woden: *Pil.* 16
Wodeness: madness, *Bale* 402
Wodford (Wilh.): *v.* Wideford.

Wodman (......): *v.* Woodman.
Woe: the first, *Bale* 350; the second, *ib.* 358; the third, *ib.* 400
Woe worth: the phrase explained, *Hutch.* 350
Wolcocke (Jo.): a rebellious priest, 2 *Cran.* 187 n
Wolf, Wolves: Satan is one, 1 *Bul.* 5; description of a head wolf (Gardiner), 3 *Bec.* 237; false teachers are wolves, *Sand.* 397
Wolfe (Rayner or Reginald), printer: 2 *Cran.* 429, 430, 440, 4 *Jew.* 1274, *Now.* xi, 3 *Zur.* 523 n., 609 n
Wolfgang, prince of Anhalt: signs the conf. of Augsburg, 2 *Zur.* 15 n
Wolfgang (Master), of Worms: 3 *Zur.* 682
Wolfhart (Conrad): *v.* Lycosthenes (C.).
Wolfius (Gaspar): 2 *Zur.* 178 n., 199
Wolfius (H.): letter to him, 2 *Zur.* 336
Wolfius (Jo.): *Pra. Eliz.* 404 n., 1 *Zur.* 17, 25, 30, 58, & sæpe, 2 *Zur.* 90, 329, 3 *Zur.* 386, 394; Lectiones Memorab., 1 *Lat.* 50 n., 2 *Lat.* 51 n., 149 n.; his commentaries, 2 *Tyn.* 127, 2 *Zur.* 177, 199; letters to him, 1 *Zur.* 49, 94, 2 *Zur.* 117, 127, 177, 199, 3 *Zur.* 125, 459, 519
Woll: for will, 2 *Tyn.* 196
Wollay (Edw.): notice of him, *Poet.* liv; verses from his Plain Pathway to Perfect Rest, *ib.* 541
Wolley (Sir Jo.): account of him, 2 *Zur.* 220 n.; letter from him to Sturmius, *ib.* 220
Wolley (Tho.), of Henley: 2 *Cov.* 501
Wolloc (Jo.): *v.* Wullock.
Wolsey (Tho. card.), abp of York: his ignoble birth, 4 *Jew.* 1146, 2 *Tyn.* 322; styled Thomas Curteis, though a churl, 2 *Tyn.* 182; Tyndale calls him Wolfsee, *ib.* 258, 307; he was an imitator of Becket, *ib.* 292; the arts by which he rose at court, *ib.* 307—310; said to have been skilled in astrology and necromancy, *ib.* 308; his pomp at the Field of the Cloth of Gold, *ib.* 314; his entry into Bruges, *ib.*; he came from bloodshedding to a bishoprick, viz. that of Tournay, *ib.* 273; pleased with flattery, 3 *Tyn.* 111; a seeming reference to his splendour, 2 *Tyn.* 123; he had two fools called Patch, 4 *Jew.* 860 n.; his episcopal pluralities, 2 *Tyn.* 273, 337; the honour which he required to be paid to his scarlet hat, *ib.* 339, 3 *Tyn.* 57, 93; his acts as minister, 1 *Tyn.* xviii, xxiii; he causes great perjury by making men swear what they are worth, 1 *Lat.* 301; suppresses monasteries, 2 *Ful.* 122, 4 *Jew.* 800, 801; solicits Cranmer to be fellow of his college at Oxford, 1 *Cran.* viii; is largely pensioned by the emperor, 2 *Tyn.* 316 n., but plays false with him, as well as with the king of France, *ib.* 316—318; Charles V. writes a book against him, *ib.* 322; he wrote to the emperor desiring the popedom, but finding that the emperor was not favourable to his claims, he menaced him, *ib.*; he procures for Henry VIII. the title of Defender of the Faith, *ib.* 338; seeks to raise money for war with France, 1 *Tyn.* 187 n.; is warned that Tyndale is about to give the people of England the scriptures in their native tongue, *ib.* xxx; burns copies of Tyndale's New Testament and other forbidden books, *ib.* xxxi; seeks the destruction of Tyndale's New Testament abroad, *ib.* xxxii, xxxiii; Roye's satires upon him, *ib.* 39 n., 41 n.; he endeavours to procure the arrest of Tyndale and Roye, *ib.* xxxiv; persuades the king to order that Tyndale's translations should be burnt, *ib.* 131 n.; his favour to Latimer, 1 *Lat.* iv; their interview, 2 *Lat.* xxix; he takes steps towards procuring the divorce of queen Catharine, 2 *Tyn.* 319, &c.; his proceedings with regard to the maid of Kent, 2 *Cran.* 65; Tyndale warns those sworn to him that it is their duty to repent, 2 *Tyn.* 341, 342; he gets possession of Anne Boleyn's copy of Tyndale's Obedience, 1 *Tyn.* 130; a petition presented to the king against him, 1 *Bec.* 125 n.; his treason, 2 *Tyn.* 334; Tyndale accuses him of secretly encouraging a marauding invasion of Scots, *ib.* 306; he is arrested at Cawood, 1 *Zur.* 259 n.; his death, 2 *Tyn.* 174 n., 177 n.; reference to his tomb, *ib.* 292; pretended revelations concerning his soul, 2 *Cran.* 272 n.; Tyndale feared he would be canonized, 1 *Tyn.* 291, 3 *Tyn.* 123, 131
Wolsey (Will.): martyred at Ely, *Poet.* 164
Wolstoncros (Nic.): *v.* Worsyncroft.
Wolton (Jo.): *v.* Woolton.
Wolves: *v.* Wolf.
Wolzius (Paul): *v.* Volsius.
Womberwell (Rob.): vicar of St Laurence in the Jewry, *Bale* 28
Women: *v.* Aged, Gentlewomen, Maids, Wives, Widows; also Apparel, Churching, Prayers, Thanksgivings.
They are often included in scripture under the term men, 2 *Lat.* 7, 82, 263, 264; woman and man were equal till the fall, 1 *Lat.* 252, 2 *Lat.* 161; as sin came by a woman, so did righteousness, *Hutch.* 143; as to the Seed of the woman, see p. 175, col. 1, above; the religious standing of women under the law, *Whita.* 529; Paul's advice to them, 2 *Lat.* 108; why their heads should be covered, 1 *Lat.* 253; silence

in a woman is a great virtue, 2 *Lat.* 92; many women have been learned in the scriptures, *Bale* 156; Theodoret rejoiced that many were well instructed in divine things, *Whitg.* 248; and so Eusebius, *ib.* 249; Hosius on the contrary accounts this a profanation of scripture, *ib.*; women may not teach publicly in the congregation, *Bale* 155, 2 *Bec.* 376; some heretics allowed the contrary, *Rog.* 236, 240; women have been employed about divine things by God's own appointment, 3 *Tyn.* 18; they offered for the tabernacle, *Pil.* 386; aided the building of Jerusalem, *ib.* 385; how they prophesied at Corinth, 2 *Whitg.* 504; Tertullian and Epiphanius speak against their teaching or baptizing, *ib.* 535 (see Baptism, v.); how and when they may teach, *ib.* 499, &c.; they may be employed, in case of necessity, to teach, and even to administer the sacraments, 3 *Tyn.* 18, 29, 30, 98, 176; Calvin, Knox, and Aylmer on government by women, 2 *Zur.* 34, 131; government by them regarded as a token of God's anger towards a nation, 3 *Bec.* 227; books on government by them, *Park.* 60; Bullinger's answer to questions of a certain Scotsman (Knox, or more probably Goodman) on this and other subjects, 3 *Zur.* 745; opponents to government by them, *Rog.* 337, 338; they are sometimes instruments of God's power, *Sand.* 149; but they ought not to rule in a man's office, 3 *Tyn.* 151; those who will rule their husbands, break God's injunction, 1 *Lat.* 252; women not to live in the houses of unmarried clergymen, except in certain cases, *Grin.* 130; not to reside within colleges, &c., *Park.* 146; a woman may soon bring a man into evil, 1 *Lat.* 94; some are fond of brawling, 2 *Bec.* 345; statement that the will of a woman must be followed, or else all the fat is in the fire, 2 *Cran.* 15 (side note); a woman offended at a passage in Ecclus. xxv, *Whita.* 229, 231; fond women addicted to superstition, 2 *Cran.* 179; some are unnatural, 1 *Lat.* 334; difference between an honest woman and a harlot, 2 *Bec.* 342, 343; a strange woman, what, 1 *Bul.* 221

A woman clothed with the sun, *Bale* 404; her man-child, *ib.* 409; she fleeth, *ib.* 410; is persecuted by the dragon, *ib.* 416, &c.; the church compared to a woman, p. 202, col. 2, above.

The woman sitting on the beast, *Bale* 496

Wonlichius (......): saluted, 1 *Zur.* 62, 196, 206, 305, 2 *Zur.* 178; his wife Susanna, 1 *Zur.* 62

Wonston, co. Hants: the advowson, *Grin.* 460, 461

Wood: wild, mad, furious, 1 *Bec.* 288, 1 *Brad.* 415, 2 *Cov.* 231, 2 *Jew.* 977, 3 *Jew.* 276, *Phil.* 315, *Pil.* 160; wodeness, *Bale* 402

Wood (Ant. à): *Coop.* ix, *Grin.* 421, 4 *Jew.* 1192, 2 *Lat.* 225, 229, 250, 297, 369, 371, 372, 376, 378, 386, 387, 392, 400, 406, 418 nn

Wood (Geo.): v. Sylvius.

Wood (Hugh): chaplain to lord Hungerford, 3 *Zur.* 202 n

Wood (Rob. à): killed at Rye, 2 *Cran.* 357

Wood (Mr): seeks to be placed in physic in All Souls' college, *Park.* 396

Wood (......): a Scotchman, and a factious fellow, *Grin.* 291

Woodchurch, co. Kent: Frensham's bequest, 2 *Zur.* 21 n

Woodcocke (Tho.): 1 *Hoop.* 252

Woodhal (Edm.): Grindal's godson, *Grin.* 461

Woodhal (Eliz.), Grindal's sister: her daughters, Dorothy, Katharine, Elizabeth, Isabel, *Grin.* 461

Woodhal (Will.), the elder: *Grin.* 461

Woodhal (Will.), the younger: executor to Grindal, who was his uncle, *Grin.* 463; legacies to him, *ib.* 460

Woodhouslie: 1 *Zur.* 218 n

Woodman (......), or Wodman: martyred at Lewes, *Poet.* 170; he, or another of his name, mentioned, *Phil.* 9

Woodrofe (Dav.): sheriff of London, 2 *Brad.* xli.

Woodroff (Mr): archbishop Grindal's opinion of his presentation to a prebend of York cathedral, *Grin.* 330

Woodroofe (Will.): at Zurich, 4 *Bul.* xii; the same, probably, 3 *Zur.* 610

Woods: v. Kent.

The policy of preserving them, *Pil.* 330

Woodstock, co. Oxon.: 1 *Brad.* 486

Wool: high price of it, 2 *Bec.* 432

WOOLTON (Jo.), bp of Exeter: biographical notice of him, *Wool.* iii; a dispensation for him (when a preacher) requested by bishop Grindal, *Grin.* 299; his works, *Wool.* v; his CHRISTIAN MANUAL; OR, THE LIFE AND MANNERS OF TRUE CHRISTIANS, *Wool.*; he ascribes certain homilies to Cranmer, 2 *Cran.* 128 n

Woolward-going: wearing wool by way of merit, 2 *Bec.* 321, 1 *Tyn.* 227, 433, 461, 2 *Tyn.* 158, 161, 3 *Tyn.* 80

Wootton family: v. Wotton.

Worcester: recommended to the care of lord Cromwell, 2 *Lat.* 403; an act passed to rebuild it (32 Hen. VIII.), 2 *Lat.* 403 n.; the school, the bridge, the wall, *ib.* 403;

WORCESTER — WORDE

the two friaries, Black and Grey, granted to the city, *ib.*; guild of the Holy Trinity, *ib.*; Jo. Oswen, printer at Worcester, 2 *Hoop.* 94, 175, *Lit. Edw.* iv, &c.

The Cathedral : monks brought in, *Pil.* 574; Italian bishops, 1 *Tyn.* xviii ; bp Latimer's injunctions to the prior and convent of St Mary, 1 *Lat.* x, xv, 2 *Lat.* 240 ; the image of our Lady at Worcester turned out to be that of some bishop, 2 *Lat.* 395, 402 n

The Diocese : Latimer's injunctions to all parsons, &c. 1 *Lat.* x, xv, 2 *Lat.* 242
Worcester (Will. earl of): *v.* Somerset.
Worcester house: *v.* London.
WORD : *v.* Christ, iv.
Word of God: *v.* Gospel, Preaching, Scripture; also Prayers.

What it is, 3 *Bec.* 603, 614, 1 *Bul.* 37, 2 *Hoop.* 43, 3 *Jew.* 364; written and spoken, the same, 1 *Bul.* 48; its causes and beginnings, *ib.* 38; how revealed, *ib.* 39; revealed by men, *ib.*; revealed by the Son of God, *ib.* 51; its proceeding, *ib.* 49; to whom revealed, *ib.* 57 ; to what end revealed, *ib.* 60; the will of God is revealed in it, 2 *Bec.* 137, &c.; its excellence as contrasted with man's invention, 3 *Bec.* 490, &c.; its power and efficacy, *ib.* 296, 1 *Bul.* 60, 4 *Bul.* 331, 2 *Cov.* 310; how the almighty power of God is attributed to it, 4 *Bul.* 266 ; it is a seed, *ib.* 91; faith is planted by it, 1 *Bul.* 84; it is the doctrine of faith, 3 *Bec.* 603; the fruits of it, *ib.* 489; salvation wrought by it, 4 *Bul.* 94; it is the nourishment of the soul, 1 *Bec.* 63, 2 *Bec.* 167; the heavenly manna, 2 *Hoop.* 46 ; the life of man consists in the food of it, *ib.* 198, 200, 201, 203; mercies in it, *ib.* 343 ; consolation in it, *ib.* 325; without God's word no man's conscience can be at rest, 2 *Cov.* 301; it does nothing comfort the unfaithful, 2 *Hoop.* 353; how the virtue and nature of it are sealed in the conscience, *ib.* 213; it is an excellent treasure, 1 *Bec.* 192, 2 *Cov.* 298; the eyes of Christians, 2 *Hoop.* 396; the star of light, *ib.* 603; green pastures, and fresh waters, 2 *Cov.* 296, &c., 2 *Hoop.* 197, &c.; knowledge of it needful to season our deeds and prayers, 2 *Tyn.* 77 ; every faithful man must be jealous for it, 3 *Bec.* 496, 497; every one is bound to defend it, 2 *Tyn.* 37 ; it must be practised and used, 2 *Cov.* 92; the office of such as teach it, 2 *Hoop.* 3; what it is to shew it, 3 *Bec.* 608; the preaching of it causes the Christian religion to flourish, 1 *Bec.* 381; the true preaching of it needs to be restored, 1 *Hoop.* 205 ; it alone is to be taught, *Pil.* 19, 24; it must be set forth to all the people, 2 *Hoop.* 131; grace is offered by it, but to most in vain, *Sand.* 299; what is offered in it, 2 *Hoop.* 203; the preaching of it is the chief remedy against sedition, *ib.* 79; how it must be used to profit us, *ib.* 355, 357 ; how to be heard, 1 *Bul.* 64, *Sand.* 273, 274 ; it is to be reverently heard and come to, 2 *Bec.* 549, 550, 1 *Cov.* 499; the profit of hearing it, *Pil.* 103 ; a mind to hear it is a token of predestination to salvation, 3 *Bec.* 174 ; those that love to hear it may be encouraged by comfortable histories of God's liberality, 2 *Bec.* 613; God sends it before judgments, 1 *Bec.* 183, 184; it either corrects or hardens, 1 *Tyn.* 471, &c.; it works either life or death, *Pil.* 266; kings, &c. bound to have it taught to those under their governance, 2 *Hoop.* 278 ; it was restored by king Henry, 1 *Bec.* 191; the preaching of it with the due administration of the sacraments was restored under queen Elizabeth, 3 *Bec.* 565 ; it is a great blessing to a nation, *ib.* 598; to have it is the greatest good upon earth, 2 *Cov.* 297 ; it is a mark of the church, 4 *Bul.* 21, 2 *Hoop.* 43; the taking of it away a just cause for lamentation, 2 *Hoop.* 252, 262; where it lacks, superstition reigns, 2 *Bec.* 54; what evils result if it be extinguished, 1 *Bec.* 191; he that would take the soul of man from it is the worst of all enemies, 2 *Hoop.* 231, 543; the ignorance of it brings a murrain and rot of the soul, *ib.* 200 ; the abuse of it provokes God's vengeance, *ib.* 252, 262; it is not enough for a man to hear it, but he must be ruled by it, *ib.* 209; they who profess to honour it, but mortify not their lusts, must expect heavy chastisements, 1 *Tyn.* 474 ; diseases and plagues of some hearers of it, 1 *Bul.* 66; plagues follow the contempt of it, 3 *Bec.* 206, 207 ; the wicked will be always at discord and variance with it, 2 *Hoop.* 214 ; it is ever hated by the world, 1 *Tyn.* 131; enemies, and abusers of it censured, 1 *Bec.* 82, 2 *Bec.* 550; despisers of it, 1 *Lat.* 385; despisers of it, and sliders back from the truth of it censured, 1 *Bec.* 255, 266 ; scorners of it warned, *ib.* 126 ; against such as go about to dissuade from the studying, reading or hearing of it, with sentences and examples of scripture, *ib.* 426, &c.; against the despising of it, with sentences and examples of scripture, *ib.* 468, &c.; the end of those that hate it, *ib.* 183, 184; not only the man that abuses it, but he that will not learn shall be damned, 2 *Hoop.* 210; those who refuse or repugn it are unworthy of all mercy and forgiveness, *ib.* 201; the word in sacraments, 4 *Bul.* 251, 254, 259
Worde (Wynken de): Dives and Pauper a book printed by him, *Rog.* 298 n

Words: for what purpose instituted, and of what force, 4 *Bul.* 264; how men are justified or condemned by their words, 1 *Tyn.* 80

Wordsworth (Chr.): Eccl. Biog., *Calf.* 175 n., 1 *Lat.* ii, viii, 317, 440, 2 *Lat.* 272, 277, 283, 304, 306, 322, 333, 351, 406, 417 nn

Work, or Labour: *v.* Prayers.

Labour is commanded, 2 *Bul.* 27; it is the duty of all, 2 *Lat.* 39; man is born to it, 3 *Bec.* 25; the yoke of it is laid on man's neck, 2 *Bec.* 83, 84; all men must labour in their vocation, *ib.* 615, 616, 1 *Lat.* 408; there is time enough allowed for it, 1 *Bul.* 256; examples of labour, 2 *Bec.* 84, 85, 616; all labour is not godly, 1 *Lat.* 376; work rests with us, the profit of it with God, *Pil.* 133; he giveth the increase, 1 *Lat.* 213, 404, 2 *Lat.* 39; labour is vain without his blessing, *Pil.* 50

Workington, co. Cumberland: Mary, queen of Scots, lands there, *Park.* 325 n., 1 *Zur.* 203 n

Workmen: *v.* Artificers.

Works: what they signify in scripture, 2 *Bul.* 321

Works (Good): *v.* Example, Good, Holiness, Law, Merit, Prayers, Salvation.

i. *What are good works, and what not*: of good works, 1 *Bul.* 119, &c., 2 *Bul.* 320, 353; what they are, 2 *Bul.* 321, 2 *Hoop.* 59, 1 *Tyn.* 90, 100, 434; the ten commandments a platform of them, 2 *Bul.* 353; what, according to the ancient prophets, *ib.* 354; Bernard's description of them, *Sand.* 214 n.; they are not the fantasies of man, but the commandments of God, 1 *Bec.* 81, 82; those that lead to heaven are God's commandments, 2 *Cran.* 144; works of mercy, 1 *Bul.* 190; works of humanity, 2 *Bul.* 321; works of light, *ib.*; good works are commended in scripture, 2 *Cov.* 402; to do the work of God, is to believe in Christ, 3 *Tyn.* 222; false notions of what are good and bad, inculcated by Pharisees and Papists, 1 *Tyn.* 461; God judges the work of the heart, and not the heart of the work, 1 *Bec.* 109; it is the purpose and intent of our deeds that makes them good or bad, 2 *Tyn.* 73; what we may do of ourselves and what not, 1 *Tyn.* 503; holy works of men's imagination, and those which are accepted by God, *ib.* 407; works considered with reference to three sorts of men working; pagans, false Christians, true Christians, *Wool.* 43; the dark doctrine of Pharisees, Pelagians, &c., 2 *Tyn.* 103—104; such have taught men to trust in works of imaginary holiness, 1 *Tyn.* 278—281; the Papists preach only such works as are profitable to themselves, 3 *Tyn.* 203; Christ rebuked the Pharisees not for gross sins, but for their holy deeds, 1 *Tyn.* 431; works of man's own devising are not accepted, 2 *Cran.* 144; Latimer's preaching against will-works, 2 *Bec.* 425; will-works preferred by some to Christian-works, 1 *Lat.* 37, 38; works of mercy, &c., distinguished from voluntary works, and the former preferred, *ib.* 23, 24, 37, 2 *Lat.* 243, 353; God's commands, and man's inventions, 2 *Lat.* 354; popish works, 2 *Tyn.* 157; holy-work men, 1 *Tyn.* 278, 305; they torment themselves to please God, *ib.* 278; holy works of men's imagination are injurious to the performers, *ib.* 429—431; some men reputed to be very holy, are found to have no hope when they see death at hand, 3 *Tyn.* 140; works of supererogation, 3 *Bec.* 200, 527, 1 *Brad.* 48, 1 *Lat.* 482, 521, 2 *Lat.* 200, *Rog.* 128—131, *Sand.* 25, 1 *Tyn.* 86, 87; references to English divines respecting them, 1 *Brad.* 48 n.; they subvert godliness, *Rog.* 131; no man has sufficient for himself, much less for others, 3 *Bec.* 126, &c.; undue works (opera indebita), 1 *Brad.* 46, 47

ii. *Works are not meritorious* (*v.* Grace, Justification, Law, Merit): our righteousness stands not in them, 2 *Lat.* 139; works deserve not grace or any good thing, 2 *Cov.* 365, 2 *Ful.* 91, 1 *Lat.* 488, 2 *Lat.* 74, 148, 193, 200, *Now.* (57), 176, 1 *Tyn.* 27, 112; to teach the merit of works is derogatory to God's glory, 2 *Cov.* 397; it is opposed to our Saviour's doctrine, *ib.*; also to that of the apostles, 2 *Bul.* 337, 2 *Cov.* 398; against the popish doctrine of works satisfactory, 3 *Bul.* 90, 1 *Lat.* 520; we may not set any works in the place of Christ, nor make them the satisfaction for our sins, 2 *Cov.* 365; good works cannot justify men before God, 2 *Bul.* 325, 3 *Bul.* 49, 2 *Lat.* 137, 138, 1 *Tyn.* 497, 2 *Tyn.* 74, 75, 103, 3 *Tyn.* 204; probations of this out of scripture, 3 *Bec.* 335, 336; they are not a preparation to grace, *Sand.* 267; they deserve not the remission of sin, 1 *Hoop.* 56; they cannot satisfy for sins committed after baptism, 1 *Bec.* 338; they cannot deserve eternal life, 1 *Tyn.* 82; what our works deserve, 2 *Tyn.* 157; good works do not save, though evil works condemn, *Pil.* 169; trusting to obtain righteousness by them is the error of the Pelagians, 2 *Bec.* 637; against trusting in the merits of them, with sentences and examples of scripture, 1 *Bec.* 420, &c.; we have no righteousness to boast, *Sand.* 404; our best deeds are imperfect, evil, and defiled with sin, 1 *Hoop.* 51, *Sand.* 22, 136; they all are unclean before God, 1 *Bec.* 192; they need washing in Christ's blood, 1 *Tyn.* 463; in their greatest perfection they need grace to pardon their imperfection, 2 *Hoop.* 73; trust in them can bring no peace, 1 *Tyn.* 330, 509; he who would worship God by them is an idolater, 2 *Tyn.* 157—158, 214, &c.; whether the good works of the saints be sins, 2 *Bul.* 419; they would be so if judged by the law, 1 *Tyn.* 113, 3 *Tyn.* 173

iii. *Whence good works spring, and what they shew:* their original cause, 2 *Bul.* 322, &c.; they are the gift of God, and the work of his Spirit, 1 *Tyn.* 56; every good thing in us is Christ's gift, purchase, doing, and working, *ib.* 23, 27, 111; good works spring from grace, 1 *Ful.* 367, 2 *Hoop.* 73; they do not precede the grace of God, 1 *Tyn.* 112; the grace of Christ and renewal by the Holy Ghost are necessary for their performance, *Rog.* 106; they are the fruits of the Spirit, 1 *Tyn.* 73, 83, 108, 497, 3 *Tyn.* 197; the fruits or necessary consequence of faith, 3 *Bec.* 291, 1 *Brad.* 76, 2 *Cov.* 365, 2 *Cran.* 141, 2 *Hoop.* 121, *Lit. Edw.* 513, (560), 1 *Tyn.* 62, 64, 417, 489, 497, 2 *Tyn.* 87, 125, 3 *Tyn.* 173; the fruits of the light of knowledge, *Sand.* 214; faith is the mother of them, 1 *Bec.* 80, 82, 270, 271; those who believe cannot but do them, 1 *Tyn.* 493; from faith springs love, and from love works, 2 *Tyn.* 194; hence they are the evidence of true faith, 2 *Lat.* 71, 1 *Tyn.* 497, 2 *Tyn.* 59—61, 71, 72, 77, 87, 89, 108, 125, 193, 195, 207; the outward signs of inward belief, *Rog.* 123; they do necessarily follow justification, 2 *Hoop.* 121, *Now.* (61), 180, *Pil.* 468, 1 *Tyn.* 295 (see more in v. below); homily of good works annexed unto faith, 2 *Cran.* 141; good and bad works come of good and bad doctrine, 2 *Tyn.* 38

On works before justification, 2 *Cov.* 431, *Rog.* 125—128; works done by a heathen, Jew, or heretic, are altogether fruitless, 2 *Cran.* 142; the virtues of the heathen, whether they be sins, 2 *Bul.* 418; works done before grace comes are sin, 1 *Tyn.* 183, 435, 487, 2 *Tyn.* 72; works without faith are sinful and offensive, 2 *Cran.* 141, 1 *Tyn.* 494, 495, 2 *Tyn.* 126; all deeds under the law are sin, 1 *Tyn.* liii; without love works are not acceptable, 2 *Lat.* 1; we cannot do good works until we are justified, *ib.* 142; there can be none before we are born again and renewed, *Now.* (61), 181; in an unregenerate state they are impossible, *Rog.* 105; we must be good, before we can do good,

Pil. 167, 1 *Tyn.* 23, 50, 62, 73, 497, 2 *Tyn.* 186, 3 *Tyn.* 173, 174, 204, 205; a good work maketh not a good man, but a good man maketh a good work [Augustine? cited by W. Tracy]. 3 *Tyn.* 273; heathen, Turks, and Papists, maintain the contrary, 1 *Tyn.* 108, 3 *Tyn.* 11; works declare what a man is within, but make him neither good nor bad, 1 *Tyn.* 23, 59, 62, 112, 113, 116; they must be done out of the mercy that we have received, and not that we may receive mercy, 3 *Tyn.* 204

iv. *Good works are necessary, and pleasing unto God:* the doctrine of justification by faith only is not opposed to good works, 2 *Bul.* 327, *Now.* (63), 182, *Wool.* 32, &c., 56, 78; Becon not to be slandered as teaching faith without them, 1 *Bec.* 91; their right place, 2 *Lat.* 74; the reformed doctrine places them where scripture places them, 2 *Bec.* 637; they may be taught when faith is laid as a foundation, *ib.* 638; they must be brought forth, *ib.* 210; they are no derogation from faith, 1 *Lat.* 235; they are not superfluous, but necessary to salvation, 2 *Cov.* 341, 2 *Cran.* 95, 129, 2 *Hoop.* 59, *Phil.* 412, *Sand.* 426; they are necessary to shew forth our profession, not to deserve immortality, 2 *Cov.* 403; none are saved without them, 1 *Bec.* 341, &c.; there is no true faith without them, 1 *Ful.* 419; those who do them not are not the children of God, nor the children of justification, 2 *Cov.* 341; we must do them, but not trust in them, 1 *Bec.* 118, 2 *Bec.* 635, 1 *Lat.* 521, 2 *Lat.* 141, 148, 194, 200; why, how, and to what end they must be done, 1 *Bec.* 110, 345—347, 2 *Bul.* 356, 2 *Hoop.* 59, 2 *Lat.* 141, 151, 200; we were redeemed that we might serve God, *Sand.* 181, 182; God hath called us unto good works to walk in them, 2 *Cov.* 365; Christians should excel in them, 1 *Ful.* 449; God's mercy to us deserves that we should work, to testify our thankfulness, 3 *Tyn.* 277; we must express faith, fear, and love by them, 1 *Bec.* 208, 209; Christ is dishonoured by a life not in accordance with our profession, *Sand.* 359; to stop the mouths of adversaries is an urgent cause why we should do good works, 3 *Bec.* 211; we must be earnest followers of good works, 1 *Bec.* 341, &c.; we must lose no opportunity to do them, 1 *Lat.* 545; the time has need of them, 1 *Bec.* 82, 205; there is great slackness among the people with regard to them, *Rid.* 60; probations out of scripture that they ought diligently to be done of all true Christians, 3 *Bec.* 336, &c.; against slackness in doing them, with sentences and examples of scripture, 1 *Bec.* 473, &c.; the study of them is to be excused, 2 *Bec.* 640; they are pleasing and acceptable to God, 2 *Hoop.* 121, *Now.* (61, 62), 181, 182, *Rog.* 117; but only when proceeding from a true faith in Jesus Christ, *Rog.* 120; how God accepts them, *Sand.* 268; all works done in faith are acceptable, but none without faith, 1 *Tyn.* 100, 102; the meanest works with faith are good and acceptable, *ib.* 495; they are accepted by God through Jesus Christ, 1 *Lat.* 420, 453, 2 *Lat.* 57, 140, 151; an exhortation to the doing of them, 1 *Bec.* 58, 80, 210

v. *The use of good works to ourselves and others* (see also iii. above): how they profit, 2 *Cov.* 341; they are an evidence of faith (see in iii. above); they assure us of our election, *Wool.* 73 (and see Predestination); in what sense justification is attributed to works, 2 *Bul.* 327; they justify us outwardly before the world, 1 *Tyn.* 61, 119, 223, 417, 526, 2 *Tyn.* 74, 75, 89, 3 *Tyn.* 200—203; they are our outward righteousness, 2 *Tyn.* 88; they may be done in the sight of men, if vain-glory be absent, 2 *Bec.* 540; they extend only to our neighbours, 1 *Tyn.* 476; we must beware of seeking glory of men by them, 2 *Tyn.* 73; the desire of vain glory poisons them, 1 *Bec.* 110; diligence in good works keeps from sin and promotes holiness, 2 *Tyn.* 76; they do us three kinds of service; certify us of everlasting life, kill sin in us, and relieve the necessity of our neighbour, 1 *Tyn.* 23; testify what we are, *ib.* 109, 116, 497, 2 *Tyn.* 149, 189, 193, 195; declare us to be created anew, 1 *Bec.* 81; prove that we are God's children and heirs, 1 *Tyn.* 83; declare us to be of charity, 1 *Bec.* 83; this is their reward, 1 *Tyn.* 100; thus they are as it were sacraments, 2 *Tyn.* 90, 91

vi. *Of their reward:* of the reward of good works, 2 *Bul.* 342, &c., *Wool.* 75, 76; on the judgment and reward according to works, 1 *Tyn.* 108, 110, 113, &c.; places which confirm the reward of works not to be abused, 2 *Bul.* 345; their reward stands in mercy and mere favour, 2 *Cov.* 432, 1 *Ful.* 369—371, 3 *Jew.* 586, *Now.* (63), 183, 1 *Tyn.* 116, 2 *Tyn.* 74, 75; Augustine and Chrysostom on this, 2 *Cov.* 432, 1 *Ful.* 353; what the reward is, 1 *Tyn.* 100; they will be rewarded in heaven, but cannot purchase it, 1 *Lat.* 420, 2 *Lat.* 140; they must be done of pure love, not for reward, 1 *Tyn.* 20, 21, 62, 63, 65, 110, 278—281, 3 *Tyn.* 173, 200

Works of darkness: 2 *Hoop.* 115, 2 *Jew.* 1035, *Sand.* 213

Works of supererogation: see p. 796, col. 2.

World: v. Creation, Geography; also Life, Redemption, Wisdom.

Created and preserved by God, 3 *Bul.* 173, &c., *Lit. Edw.* 501, (550), *Rog.* 39; heresies respecting its creation and preservation, *Rog.* 40—42; the three parts of the world, *Rid.* 279; its seven climates, *Bale* 269, 426, 501; or four, *ib.* 468; comparison of the old world and ours, 1 *Bec.* 242, 243; the miserable state of the world, *ib.* 238; its corruption, 1 *Cov.* 492; Bernard speaks of the whole world as within the net of Christ, *Whita.* 400; it is at the best that it ever will be till the harvest, *Bale* 464; we are strangers in it, 3 *Whitg.* 585; it is not our home, 1 *Brad.* 375, 2 *Brad.* 235, 415, 423, 459, 2 *Cov.* 231, 239; it is the place of trial of God's people and the devil's servants, 2 *Brad.* 210; what it is to live in it, 1 *Bec.* 309; its seven ages, 1 *Lat.* 365; opinion that it was made to endure 6000 years, which time shall be shortened, 2 *Lat.* 20, 52; it waxes old, *Sand.* 169; passeth away, *Rid.* 338; without doubt draweth towards an end, *ib.* 75; the end of it, 3 *Bec.* 613, *Now.* (51), 169; works on the subject, *Rog.* v, vi, vii; the disciples question Christ both concerning the destruction of Jerusalem, and his coming and the end of the world, *Sand.* 351; how far the end is off, 3 *Bec.* 624; the time is unknown, 2 *Jew.* 871, *Sand.* 388; the end of all things is at hand, *Sand.* 387; this consideration makes the heavy joyful, and the godly watchful, *ib.*; signs that the end approaches, 1 *Lat.* 172, 356, 364, 365, 2 *Lat.* 20, 53, *Sand.* 388; what is signified in scripture by the latter times, 3 *Bec.* 613, 623, 624; the reformers considered that the last times were come, 3 *Bec.* 613, 623, 624, 1 *Lat.* 517, *Lit. Eliz.* 259, 501 n., *Sand.* 439; the last days like those of Noah, 1 *Lat.* 366; views of Chrysostom and Sandys respecting the signs preceding the end of the world, *Sand.* 352; the effect of these signs in the hearts of men, *ib.* 364; the end of the world, the fulfilling of the kingdom of Christ, *Lit. Edw.* 510, (558); as to the latter times, the end of the world, and the coming of the Lord, see also p. 179, col. 2, above; on the burning and renewal of the world, 1 *Brad.* 357; opinion of Augustine, *ib.*; of Tho. Aquinas, *ib.* 358; it is not to be destroyed, but purged, at Christ's coming, *Sand.* 366; to be renewed, *Lit. Edw.* 511, (557); the new earth, *Bale* 581

Mundani, mundus, seculum, *Now.* (102), a description of the world, verses by G.

Gaske, *Poet.* 306; what it is, 3 *Bec.* 603; the term includes the so-called spiritualty, 2 *Tyn.* 177; Egypt a figure of it, 1 *Brad.* 149; it is a wilderness, 2 *Brad.* 206; it is a mighty prince, 2 *Bec.* 150; we desire in the Lord's prayer that its kingdom may be dispersed, *ib.* 151; it lieth in wickedness, 2 *Tyn.* 213; the manner of it described by Isaiah, 1 *Bec.* 248; it is crafty and deceitful, 1 *Lat.* 176; it is at enmity with God, 1 *Tyn.* 132; it is an enemy to the Christian, 2 *Bec.* 184; Christians cannot agree with it, 2 *Lat.* 184; of the vanity of the world; verses by Hum. Gifford, *Poet.* 213; the world vanity; verses by M. Thorn, *ib.* 314; all things in it are subject to vanity, 2 *Bec.* 474; the vanity of its possessions and pleasures, *Phil.* 286; a heavenly prayer in contempt of the world and the vanities thereof (in verse), *Poet.* 433; its blindness, notwithstanding the light, *Sand.* 208; whence the blindness of it comes, 3 *Bec.* 488; "all that is in the world," 2 *Tyn.* 177; its delights are nothing compared with the rewards of the righteous, *Phil.* 254; love of the world reproved, *Rid.* 340; it quencheth the love of God, 2 *Tyn.* 177; what it is to despise earthly things, 3 *Bec.* 620; how worldly things are to be used, 2 *Bec.* 188; inordinate attachment to them is improper, 2 *Cov.* 127; they are transitory, 3 *Whitg.* 584; worldly joys and delights soon pass away, 2 *Bec.* 428, 429; the world overcome by Christ, 2 *Brad.* 234; the world and the church, *ib.* 124

World, Flesh, and Devil: *v.* Enemies, Prayers.
Worldliness: decays the ministry, *Pil.* 105
Worldlings: hate the light of God's word, 2 *Bec.* 468
Worldly Goods: *v.* Goods.
Wormius (C.): Hist. Sabell., 1 *Hoop.* 161 n
Worms: Luther at the diet there, 1521, 3 *Tyn.* 185; what the bishop of Sidon said about the sale of masses, 3 *Jew.* 552; why Brentius and the Adiaphorists would not condemn Zuinglius and Osiander, *ib.* 621; an intended congress there, Nov. 1565, 1 *Zur.* 344
Wormulus (Val.): *v.* Werdmuller.
Wormwood: the star so called, *Bale* 346
Worship, and Divine Service: *v.* God, Prayer, Thanksgiving; also Ceremonies.
Of the worship of God, 2 *Bul.* 128; what worship is, 3 *Bul.* 195, &c., *Calf.* 366, 2 *Hoop.* 56, *Now.* (9), 122; what it is to serve, 1 *Bul.* 231, 3 *Bul.* 223, 2 *Hoop.* 56; what it is to bow down to, 1 *Bul.* 231; what it is to adore, 3 *Bul.* 195, *Calf.* 366; what the true honour to God is, 2 *Bec.* 58; worship is to be paid to God alone, *Calf.* 367; God only is to be served, *Sand.* 181, 182; not mammon, *ib.* 182; nor the belly, *ib.* 183; nor men, *ib.*; nor the world, *ib.* 184; what honour is due to God, what to rulers, and what to neighbours, 3 *Tyn.* 57; the distinction of latria and dulia, *Calf.* 381, 2 *Ful.* 126, 208, 2 *Jew.* 662, 666, 3 *Tyn.* 125; examination of translations concerning those expressions, 1 *Ful.* 258, 259, 539—546; examples of the words in scripture, 3 *Tyn.* 57 n.; latria, dulia, hyperdulia, *Bale* 546, 628, 3 *Tyn.* 56; scholastic distinctions between doulia and latria untenable, 3 *Tyn.* 57; all such distinctions disallowed by the 2nd council of Nice, and by Aquinas, 2 *Jew.* 666; latria due only to God, *ib.* 662; it is offered by Romanists to the material cross, *Calf.* 381 n.; how the worship of God is described in scripture, 3 *Tyn.* 57; what kind is acceptable, 1 *Tyn.* 106, 2 *Tyn.* 157, 158, 3 *Tyn.* 57; worship must be such only as God appoints, 1 *Brad.* 152, 372, 2 *Brad.* 233, 318, 319, *Hutch.* 253, 1 *Jew.* 24, *Sand.* 189, 221; this was affirmed by Socrates, *q. v.*; to worship otherwise is idolatry, 2 *Hoop.* 56, *Hutch.* 254; what sort of worship is forbidden, *Now.* (10), 123; true worship and false, 3 *Bul.* 223, 1 *Tyn.* 362, 3 *Tyn.* 66; that of believers, 2 *Tyn.* 210; that of unbelievers, *ib.* 211; we must serve God with childlike fear, not slavish, *Sand.* 184; popery teaches distrust, *ib.* 185; will-worship and outward shew, 1 *Tyn.* 103, 104, 119; will-worship is condemned in scripture, *Whita.* 97; devisers of new-fangled worship are accursed, 1 *Bul.* 335; idolatrous and carnal worship, 2 *Tyn.* 214, &c.; worshipping by works and ceremonies is idolatry, *ib.* 157, 158, 214, &c.; God is not honoured with copes, tapers, &c., 1 *Lat.* 305; scenic apparatus of divine worship agitated, 1 *Zur.* 23; God delights not in outward pomp, *Sand.* 347; popish worship, *Phil.* 389; that of papists gorgeous, that of the reformed church simple, *Pil.* 129; inward and outward worshipping, 3 *Bul.* 199; worship must be both in body and spirit, 2 *Brad.* 328, 335; on bowing of the body, 1 *Tyn.* 420; spiritual worship, 3 *Bul.* 198, 1 *Tyn.* 373—374, 3 *Tyn.* 125; worship in spirit and in truth, 2 *Brad.* 335; God must be worshipped in spirit, not by images, *Phil.* 406; places for worship are left free by God, 2 *Bul.* 263; God is worshipped in our hearts, not in any other place, 3 *Tyn.* 88; large promises to godly worshippers, 1 *Bul.* 236; worship of Christ's body, how paid by old fathers, 1 *Jew.* 12; honour not to be given to angels as to God, 2 *Bec.* 58,

59; worship of saints, 2 *Bul.* 222; of the worshipping of sacraments, ceremonies, images, relics, &c., 3 *Tyn.* 59—63; religious honour not to be given to creatures, *Sand.* 272; much less to images, *ib.* 273; the worshipping of idols and relics, *Bale* 546
Descriptions of divine service by ancient writers, *Calf.* 294, &c. (*v.* Justin, Pliny, &c.); as to the service of the English church, see Book of Common Prayer, Epistles and Gospels, Lessons, &c.; articles respecting divine service, 2 *Hoop.* 129, 141, 142, 145; enactments respecting attendance on it, &c., *Grin.* 170; churchwardens to mark who are absent, *ib.* 139; all persons not attending divine service every Sunday, to be presented to the ordinary, &c., *ib.* 129; inquiry whether it was said as the Latin service was, 2 *Hoop.* 145; reference to the practices of sitting at the Psalms, kneeling at Kyrie-eleyson, standing at Magnificat, &c., *ib.*; inquiry respecting divine service in cathedrals, *Grin.* 180; the names of disturbers of divine service to be presented to the ordinary, *ib.* 144
Worsyncroft (Nic.), or Wolstoncros, a priest: 2 *Brad.* 15, 16
Worter (Phil. and Ant.): *v.* Werter.
Worthiness and unworthiness: *Pil.* 47
Wotton (Sir Edw.), or Wootton: 3 *Zur.* 612; a privy councillor, 2 *Cran.* 511
Wotton (Sir Hen.): his dau. Margaret, 1 *Bec.* 125 n
Wotton (Nich.), dean of Canterbury: he was Cranmer's master of the faculties, 2 *Cran.* 394; privy councillor to Mary and Elizabeth, *Park.* 74, 75, 1 *Zur.* 5 n.; commissioner about the return of Calais, 1 *Zur.* 8 n.; plenipotentiary for a peace with France, *ib.* 89 n.; commissioner at Bruges, 2 *Zur.* 115 n.; he had his dividend of church plate, *Park.* 304; letter to him, *ib.* 144
Wotton (Tho.), or Wootton: *Park.* 304; an ecclesiastical commissioner, *ib.* 370 n.; visited by the queen in Kent, *ib.* 441
Wounds: the five wounds, 1 *Lat.* 29 n., *Sand.* 130, 1 *Zur.* 214 n., 218
Wrack: ruin, 3 *Bul.* 86
Wreight (......): martyred at Bramford, *Poet.* 173
Wren (Matt.), bp of Ely: his MS. account of the masters of Pembroke hall, 1 *Ful.* i. n., *Grin.* 37 n
Wright (Ann): *v.* Albright (Ann).
Wright (R.): martyred at Canterbury, *Poet.* 163
Wright (Rob.), rector of Dennington: 1 *Ful.* iv.
Wright (Tho.): Life and Times of Q. Eliz., 1 *Zur.* 185, 195, 219, &c. nn

Wright (Walter), archdeacon of Oxford: 2 *Cran.* 549, *Jew.* ix, *Park.* 138 n.; vice-chancellor, 2 *Jew.* 952 n.; he exhorts Philpot, *Phil.* 132
Wright (......): *v.* Wreight.
Wright (......): married Rowland Taylor's widow, *Park.* 221
Wriothesley (Tho. lord), earl of Southampton, lord chancellor: account of him, 2 *Cran.* 401 n.; reference to him, *Park.* 30; he was an apostate, *Bale* 226; compared to Pilate, *ib.* 241; his cruelty to Anne Askewe, *ib.* 142; he refuses to release her, *ib.* 161; questions her, *ib.* 199, 202; her letter to him, *ib.* 216; he racks her, *ib.* 224; reasons with her, *ib.* 225; he was a governor of the realm in the king's absence, 2 *Cran.* 315 n.; other letters to him, *ib.* 378, 401
Wrisley (Sir Tho.): the same.
Write: used apparently for wr.ting, 2 *Jew.* 804
Writhed with: turned away, 2 *Bec.* 75
Writing: taught by God to Moses, *Whita.* 114; Pliny says it existed always, *ib.* 516; believed by Tyndale to be older than the flood, 3 *Tyn.* 27; Josephus speaks of two inscribed columns erected before the flood, *Whita.* 516
Writs: de hæretico comburendo, *Hutch.* v, 3 *Tyn.* 270; ne injuste vexes, *Pil.* 470
Wroth (Sir Tho.): 2 *Cran.* 389, *Grin.* 280, *Jew.* xiii, 4 *Jew.* 1222 n., 1225 n., *Rid.* 333, 1 *Zur.* 5, 53 n., 59, 2 *Zur.* 76, 104, 114
Wrought: raught? 1 *Cov.* 17
Wulfher, king of Mercia: 2 *Ful.* 119
Wullock (Andr.): 4 *Bul.* 544, 3 *Zur.* 401, 407, 409
Wullock (Jo.): 3 *Zur.* 393, 395; in exile, 1 *Cran.* (9)
Wullock (......): preaches on the borders of Scotland, 3 *Zur.* 431
Wulstan, abp of York, 1 *Zur.* 259 n
Wurtemberg (Ulric duke of): *v.* Ulric.
Wurtzburgh: the bishoprick invaded, 3 *Zur.* 682 n
Wyat (Sir Hen.), of Allington: Anne (Skinner) his wife, 1 *Bec.* 232 n
Wyat (Sir Tho.), the elder: dedication to him, 1 *Bec.* 232; notice of him and his family, *ib.* n.; his death, 3 *Zur.* 36 n
Wyat (Sir Tho.), the younger: his rebellion against queen Mary, 1 *Bec.* 232 n., 264 n., 2 *Brad.* 67 n., 3 *Jew.* 171, *Rid.* 390, *Sand.* viii, ix, 3 *Zur.* 513, 514, 686; his overthrow, 1 *Brad.* 425, 428
Wyatt (Tho.): Margaret his widow, 2 *Cran.* 362, 389; wardship of his son, *ib.* 389
Wyatt (...... lady): assisted Ridley in prison, *Rid.* 385
Wych [Droitwich] (A prior of): 2 *Lat.* 378 n

Wycliffe (Jo. de): *v.* Bible, *English*, Netter (Tho.) à Walden.
Commended or otherwise mentioned, *Bale* 80, *Calf.* 50, *Phil.* 120; he preached repentance to our fathers in vain, 1 *Tyn.* 458; the effects of his preaching, 2 *Tyn.* 296; it somewhat checked the outward wickedness of the English clergy, 3 *Tyn.* 41; he set forth the truth of the gospel, 1 *Cran.* 14; opposed the friars, *Bale* 171; his doctrine holy, *ib.* 34; his opinion on the sacrament, 3 *Zur.* 221; he resisted the popish doctrine of the mass, 1 *Hoop.* 527; denied transubstantiation, *Rid.* 158; condemned university degrees, 1 *Ful.* 568; his death, *Bale* 15; errors ascribed to him after it, 3 *Jew.* 162; he is alleged to have maintained that no man is a temporal lord, or a prelate or bishop, while he is in mortal sin, *ib.* 308, 309; charged by More with having occasioned rebellion in Bohemia, 3 *Tyn.* 165; his doctrine was carried thither, *Pil.* 264, 654; his opinions condemned by the council of Constance, *Bale* 9, 2 *Bec.* 244, 1 *Cran.* 195, 196, 3 *Jew.* 162; his dead body excommunicated, *Rog.* 311; his bones dug up and burned, *Bale* 394, *Pil.* 653; his Apology for the Lollards, 2 *Bul.* 127 n., *Calf.* 36, 132, 330 nn.; De Solutione Sathanæ, *Bale* 560; Wickliffe's Wicket, 2 *Cov.* ix. n.; when first printed, 1 *Tyn.* lxxiii; Wycliffe cited by Gardiner, 1 *Cran.* 13; alleged by Harding, 2 *Jew.* 581, 582; his works circulated by lord Cobham, *Bale* 11; inquisitors appointed to search them, *ib.* 16; copies of his books burned, 3 *Bec.* 11; not one of his numerous books destroyed, *Bale* 140; followers of him, *ib.* 81; complaint of the spread of his doctrine, *ib.* 49; the persecution that followed soon after his death, *Pil.* 264; account of the Fasciculus Zizaniorum Wiclevi, *Bale* 43 n

Wydon (Les): *v.* Weedon.

Wye, co. Kent: martyrs there, *Poet.* 169; the almshouse, *Park.* 169; the grammar-school, *ib.* 170

Wye (Herewald, abbot of): 2 *Ful.* 14

Wye (Hen.): martyred, *Poet.* 168

Wye (Jo.): 2 *Cran.* 382

Wye (Rich.): 2 *Cran.* 382, 383

Wyght (Jo.): *v.* Wight.

Wyght (Will.): burned for being a married priest, *Bale* 12

Wykeham (Will. of), bp of Winchester: enlarges Cowling castle, *Bale* 19 n

Wykeham college: *v.* Winchester.

Wykes (Hen.), printer: *Park.* 319 n

Wylkie (James) of St Andrew's: 2 *Zur.* 364

Wymbesly (Jo.): *v.* Wimsley.

Wymondham, co. Norfolk: Ket's rebellion, 2 *Cran.* 189 n

Wyn: mirth, joy, 1 *Brad.* 70

Wynchard (Master): 3 *Bec.* 260

Wynchcombe (Mr): 2 *Cov.* 500, 502

Wynram (Jo.), prior of Portmoak: superintendant of Fife and St Andrew, 2 *Zur.* 364

Wynter (Jo.), parson of Staunton: assertion and defence of the true use of the sacrament made by him, 2 *Hoop.* 154

Wytesham: *v.* Wittersham.

Wytnam (Jo.): *v.* Witnam.

X

Xenarchus: his Pentathlus, *Whita.* 378 n

Xenodochia: 2 *Bul.* 44, 4 *Bul.* 498

Xenophon: 1 *Bul.* 268, 396, 2 *Cov.* 123, 1 *Ful.* 232 n., &c., 1 *Hoop.* 361

Xerxes: wept over his great army, 2 *Jew.* 1014, 4 *Jew.* 845; overcome by Themistocles, 1 *Hoop.* 417

Xistus: *v.* Sixtus.

Y

Yale (Tho.): letter to him as Parker's chancellor, *Park.* 128; an ecclesiastical commissioner, *Grin.* 294, *Park.* 300, 301 n., 344 n., 345, 370, 383, 447; dean of the arches, *Park.* 428

Yarn: a net made of yarn, 1 *Bec.* 464

Yate (Mr): placed in the custody of the earl of Sussex for nonconformity, *Park.* 458 (qu. if Rob. Gates?)

Yates (Sir Jo.): *v.* Gates.

Yates (James): notice of him, *Poet.* xli; of wailing, and not prevailing, *ib.* 450; a sonnet of a slanderous tongue, *ib.* 451

Yea and Yes: More's remarks on the difference between them, 3 *Tyn.* 25 n., 229

Year (Edw.): *Jew.* ix.

Years: *v.* New Year.

Diversely reckoned, *Pil.* 15, 308; on the time of the commencement of the year in official and other documents, 1 *Tyn.* xli. n.; the three years and a half, or 42 months, or 1260 days, p. 272, col. 1

Years-minds: *v.* Minds.

Yeax: hiccough, 1 *Jew.* 249

Yeman (Rich.): martyr at Norwich, *Poet.* 173

Yeomen: *v.* Ploughmen.

An example of the old English yeomanry, 1 *Lat.* 101; their sons have chiefly maintained the faith of Christ, *ib.* 102

Yer: ere, before, 2 *Bec.* 38, 2 *Bul.* 16, 1 *Tyn.* 51, 455, 2 *Tyn.* 235, 285

Yes: *v.* Yea.

Ylleya (Tho. de): wrote on the Apocalypse, *Bale* 257

Yngworth (Rich.): *v.* Ingworth.

Yong (......): *v.* Young.

York: Elizabeth and Mary queen of Scots were to go there, 1 *Zur.* 109, 115; the queen's army against the rebels there, *ib.* 247 n.; rebels executed there, *ib.* 225 n

The cathedral (*v.* Missale): a survey to be made of lands and revenues of the church, *Grin.* 149; four prebendaries to be annually appointed to survey the fabric, *ib.* 150; injunction respecting the statutes, *ib.*; dignitaries to be present at service, *ib.* 148; the vicars-choral and other inferior ministers to be daily present, &c. *ib.* 147, &c.; communion days, *ib.* 148; injunction to the precentor respecting the choristers, *ib.* 152; a table of sermons to be set up, *ib.* 147; the vergers to suffer no man to walk in the church in sermon time, *ib.* 152; the vicars-choral to abstain from unlawful games, *ib.* 149; muniments not to be taken out of the treasury, &c., unless under certain conditions, *ib.* 152; injunction respecting the accounts, *ib.*; houses of dignitaries not to be let to laymen, *ib.* 146; letter to the dean and chapter on their provision of armour, *Park.* 347

The archbishoprick, &c.: foundation of the see, 2 *Whitg.* 127, 128; it is mother to the Northern bishopricks, *Rid.* 264; what the archbishop paid to the pope for his first-fruits, and what for his pall, 4 *Jew.* 1078; instructions set forth to the curates of the diocese in the time of Mary, *Rid.* 417; relics of superstition in the diocese, 1 *Zur.* 259 n.; visitation of the province by abp Grindal, 1571, *Grin.* 123, &c.; injunction respecting testaments and administrations, *ib.* 150

Beddern: a house belonging to the dean and chapter, *Grin.* 148, 149

Ouse bridge: story of St William and his horse, *Pil.* 587

York (James, a deacon of): *v.* James.

York (Rich. duke of): *v.* Richard.

Yorke (Rowland): betrays a fort near Zutphen, *Lit. Eliz.* 656 n

Yorkshire: *v.* England (the North).

Aske's rebellion, or the pilgrimage of grace, 2 *Cov.* 329, 2 *Cran.* 332 n., 1 *Lat.* 25 n.; the rebels' badge, 1 *Lat.* 29 n.; rebellion in king Edward's time, 2 *Cran.* 188 n.; notice of, and extract from, A Description of Norton's Falsehood of Yorkshire [1569], *Poet.* liv, 542 (as to these outbreaks, see also Pilgrimage, Rebellion); superstition of the people, *Grin.* 326; Coverdale, a district in Richmondshire, 2 *Cov.* vii.

Young, Youth: *v.* Children, Education, Schools, Unmarried.

The inconstancy of youth; verses by Tho. Lloyd, *Poet.* 415; lines on its instability, by lord Vaux, *ib.* 302; the duty of young unmarried folk, with probations of scripture, 2 *Bec.* 521; young unmarried men must reverence their elders, *ib.* 366; must be ruled by them, *ib.*; must be, not proud, but meek, *ib.*; must not be idle or tavern-hunters, *ib.* 367; must abstain from fornication, *ib.*; petition for younger men, 3 *Bec.* 38; a lamentation touching the follies and vanities of our youth, by W. Hunnis, *Poet.* 153; young martyrs, *Bale* 192

Young (Tho.): successively bp of St David's, and abp of York, *Phil.* 171; sometime precentor of St David's, 3 *Zur.* 373 n.; in exile, 1 *Cran.* (9); his translation to York, *Park.* 115 n., 123 n., 134 n.; he took order for a survey of the revenues of the church of York, *Grin.* 149; signed a letter to the queen, *Park.* 294; on a grant by him, *Grin.* 329, 330; his letters to Parker, *Park.* 114, 291 n.; letters to him, *ib.* 205; his death, *ib.* 115 n., 328 n

Young (Jo.), afterwards bp of Rochester; chaplain to bp Grindal: *Park.* 275; to preach at court, *ib.* 378

Young (Jo.), master of Pembroke hall: one of the Romish disputants at Cambridge, 1549, *Grin.* 194, *Rid.* 169, 2 *Zur.* 18 n.; at the disputation of 1551, *Grin.* ii; his report of Dr Redman's dying declaration, 3 *Zur.* 151, 152; he disputes with Cranmer, 1 *Cran.* 391; deprived of the mastership of Pembroke college, *Grin.* vi.

Young (Jo.), rector of St Magnus, London: 2 *Cov.* xv. n

Young (Jo.): describes the repulse of the English exiles from Basle, 3 *Zur.* 164 n., and their reception at Arau, *ib.* 167 n

Young (Peter): preceptor of James VI., 2 *Zur.* 302 n.; his almoner, *ib.* 311 n

Young (Frances), widow: Grindal's niece, *Grin.* 461

Youngman (Dr), of Cambridge, *Grin.* 304

Youth: *v.* Young.

Yoxford, co. Suffolk: R. Cove was martyred there, *Poet.* 164

Ypres: besieged, 1381, by the bp of Norwich, *Bale* 171

Yren (......), martyred at Colchester: *Poet.* 167

Yvry: victory of Henry IV. of France there, *Lit. Eliz.* 471

Z

Zabarella (Fra. card.): says that the pope hath gotten all the rights of inferior churches, so that the inferior prelates stand for nothing, &c., 3 *Jew.* 320, 4 *Jew.* 828; declares that the pope doth whatsoever he listeth, although it be unlawful, 2 *Jew.* 919, 992, 3 *Jew.* 219, 4 *Jew.* 674, 734, 832, 1137; affirms that the pope may be accused before the emperor, and required to yield an account of his faith, 4 *Jew.* 969, 979, 1035

Zacagnius (Lau. Alex.): Collectanea, *Calf.* 92 n., 2 *Ful.* 296 n

Zaccaria (Fra. Ant.): Bibliotheca Ritualis, *Calf.* 202 n

Zacchæus, a pretended priest: 3 *Jew.* 321, 334

Zaccheus: his conversion, 2 *Jew.* 1062; he made restitution, 2 *Bul.* 50; an example of repentance, 3 *Bul.* 111, 551, 1 *Lat.* 405, 414

Zacharias: *v.* Benedictus.

Zacharias, son of Barachias: opinions as to his identity, 2 *Jew.* 839, *Sand.* 222 n., *Whita.* 589, 590

Zacharias, pope: said to have deposed Childeric, king of France, and set up Pepin, 4 *Jew.* 672, 681, 683, *Pil.* 602, 2 *Tyn.* 260, 3 *Whitg.* 592; stated to have translated the empire from Greece into Germany, 4 *Jew.* 677; he speaks of decrees against appointing bishops to villages and little cities, 2 *Whitg.* 376; denies them to be priests who abstained not from fornication, 3 *Jew.* 162, 4 *Jew.* 802; mentions a priest who baptized "In nomine Patria," &c., 1 *Jew.* 316, 4 *Jew.* 910; answers questions of Boniface, 4 *Jew.* 1045

Zadok: 1 *Bul.* 330

Zaleucus: 2 *Bec.* 649 n., 1 *Bul.* 198

Zamzumims (Deut. ii. 20): 1 *Tyn.* 446

Zana (......): 1 *Jew.* 443 n

Zanchius (Hieron.): account of him, *Grin.* 277 n., 1 *Zur.* 8 n., 2 *Zur.* 81 n., 111 n., 185 n.; references to him, 1 *Zur.* 182 n., 2 *Zur.* 52, 113; a friend of P. Martyr, 3 *Zur.* 509 n.; he succeeds Hedio at Strasburgh, *ib.* 553 n., 682 n.; enters on his charge at Chiavenna, where a great plague soon breaks out, 2 *Zur.* 110 n., 113; censures tritheism, *Rog.* 44 n., 72 n.; refutes the new Arians, *ib.* 93; speaks of the heretic Ochinus, *ib.* 70 n., 73 n.; also of Servetus, *ib.* 73 n.; allows the title of archbishop, 2 *Whitg.* 333; speaks of the restoration of religion by Elizabeth, *Rog.* 7; states his opinion on the vestments, 2 *Zur.* 186, &c.; disputation at Strasburgh concerning his doctrines, *ib.* 98, &c.; letters by him, *ib.* 81, 98, 110, 112, 185, 271, 313, 339; letters to him, *Grin.* 276—280, 333—342; his daughter Lælia Constantia, 2 *Zur.* 112

Zapata (...... card.): *v.* Indexes.
Zapolia (Jo.): *v.* John.
Zarephath (Obad. 20): said to be France, *Pil.* 268
Zazius (Udalr.): Opera, *Jew.* xliv; on Nominals and Reals, 3 *Jew.* 614
Zazius (Wolphg.), or Lazius: on Abdias, *Calf.* 126, 1 *Jew.* 112
Zeal: what it is, 3 *Bec.* 612, 2 *Jew.* 1006, *Now.* (104); zeal for God's glory commended, *Pil.* 5, 8, 351; lukewarmness reproved, *ib.* 342; examples of true zeal, *Sand.* 195; the nature of it, *Nord.* 24; it must be according to knowledge, 1 *Jew.* 25, *Sand.* 196; zeal of the godly to serve the Lord, *ib.* 294; the zeal of God's house, 2 *Jew.* 1004, &c.; it moved Christ to reform the Temple, *Sand.* 249; of faith and zeal; verses by J. Bodenham, *Poet.* 455; true zeal is wanting in the church of Rome, *Sand.* 249; knowledge without zeal is blameable, 2 *Lat.* 337; zeal without knowledge is not good, 2 *Jew.* 1007, 1 *Tyn.* 105; blind zeal, *Sand.* 194; works invented by blind zeal are not accepted before God, 1 *Bec.* 348; force of the word $\zeta\eta\lambda\omega\tau\dot{\eta}\nu$ in Tit. ii. 14, 1 *Hoop.* 94

Zedekiah, king of Judah: 4 *Bul.* 20; his history, 2 *Bul.* 11; punished for idolatry, 1 *Bul.* 236, 242; led captive, 4 *Bul.* 555

Zeni (Nic. and Ant.): old Venetian navigators, 2 *Zur.* 290

Zeno: thought the soul died shortly after the body, 3 *Bul.* 385; his servant, *Hutch.* 78

Zenocarus à Scauwenburgo (Gul.): *Calf.* 287 n

Zenzelinus (......): *Calf.* 6 n

Zephyrinus, bp of Rome: 3 *Bul.* 76; says, Christ commanded his apostles to appoint the seventy-two disciples, 1 *Jew.* 342

Zephyrus (Fr.): Paraphrasis Tertul. Apolog., *Jew.* xliv, 3 *Whitg.* xxxii, 253 n.; shews that the early Christians had no images, *Park.* 86, *Rid.* 88; says, we live as heathens under the name of Christ, 4 *Jew.* 874

Zerubbabel: 4 *Bul.* 319, *Pil.* 110, &c.; the first prince of Judah after the captivity, *ib.* 190

Ziegler (......): saluted, 3 *Zur.* 428

Zigabenus (E.): *v.* Euthymius.

Ziggius (Fra.): *Pil.* 684

Zilam (צלם): 1 *Hoop.* 104

Zimri: 1 *Bul.* 336

Zinchius (......), or Zinkius: he and his wife were the host and hostess of Hooper at Zurich, 3 *Zur.* 55, 70, 562

Zion: *v.* Sion.

Zipporah: circumcises her son, 2 *Bul.* 173, 4 *Bul.* 371

Zisca (Jo.): exterminated the Picards, *Whita.*

229 n.; ordered his body to be flain [not slain] to make parchment to cover a drum, *Pil.* 655

Zodiack: the supposed influence of the several signs upon the parts of man's body, *Hutch.* 77, *Pra. Eliz.* 227, &c.; the notion existed among the Priscillianists, 2 *Bul.* 363

Zoilus, the railer: *Bale* 381, 515, 3 *Jew.* 140

Zolle (Matt.): 3 *Zur.* 250, 251

Zonaras (Jo.): Annales, 2 *Ful.* 361 n.; Comment. in Canones, *ib.* 95 n.; he says the synod of Gangra condemned those who taught that faithful rich men could not be saved, unless they renounced their goods, 2 *Bul.* 24

Zornius (Pet.): *Calf.* 181 n

Zoroaster: 1 *Lat.* 201 n

Zosimus, pope: 2 *Hoop.* 237 n.; he decreed that deacons should not minister the eucharist in the presence of the bishop or priest, 1 *Jew.* 240; assumed the right of hearing appeals, *ib.* 356; claimed a sovereignty in judgment and jurisdiction over all Africa, 3 *Jew.* 340; his conduct in the case of Apiarius, 2 *Ful.* 70, 71, 308; he falsified the council of Nice, 1 *Jew.* 339, 356, 417, 3 *Jew.* 126, 296, 340, 341, 4 *Jew.* 923, 937; declares that the authority of the Roman see cannot order or change anything contrary to the orders of our fathers, 3 *Jew.* 600

Zouch (Edw. lord): student at Trin. coll., Cambridge, 3 *Whitg.* 599

Zouch (Geo.): 1 *Tyn.* 130

Zozomen: *v.* Sozomen.

Zuenckfeldians: *v.* Schwenckfeldians.

Zuicherland: Switzerland, 2 *Ful.* 121

Zuingerus (Theod.): his Theatrum Vitæ Humanæ, expurgated, *Calf.* 91 n

Zuinglians: the term used, *Poet.* 268; their doctrine on the sacrament as opposed to Luther's, 1 *Jew.* 531, &c., 3 *Jew.* 620, 621, 623; Luther writes against them, *Coop.* 39; Harding's statement of Zuinglian doctrine, 3 *Jew.* 241; Zuinglianism, 2 *Zur.* 128

Zuinglius (Huldric): *v.* Luther (M.).

His preaching, *Pil.* 265; Adrian VI. offered to make him a cardinal if he would be quiet, *ib.* 142, 684; he meets Luther at Marburg, 1 *Tyn.* xxxviii; opposed there by Melancthon, *Grin.* 251 n.; he opposes Luther's error, *Phil.* 401, 3 *Zur.* 46; lectures at Zurich, 4 *Bul.* x; his opinion on Henry VIII.'s divorce, 3 *Zur.* 551 n.; mention of him, 3 *Jew.* 607, 666, 671, 1 *Zur.* 36, 42; letter to him, 3 *Zur.* 551; his death in battle, 4 *Bul.* x. n., xvi, *Lit. Eliz.* 453, 3 *Zur.* 33 n., 221, 552 n., 556 n

His works, 3 *Whitg.* xxxii, 3 *Zur.* 33 n.;

Hooper seriously impressed by some of them, 2 *Hoop.* vii; he wrote on the Apocalypse, *Bale* 258; treats of original sin, 2 *Bul.* 398; distinguishes between original and actual sin, *ib.* 397—399; declares that through the blood of Christ original sin is made harmless to infants, *ib.* 398; says that sacraments are instead of an oath, 4 *Bul.* 338; declares that they bear witness of a thing that hath been done, *ib.* 324; speaks of the sacraments as upholding faith, but affirms that the visible things are nothing, unless the sanctification of the Spirit go before, *ib.* 332; is not offended, though all those things which the Holy Ghost worketh be referred to the external sacrament, so long as we understand them to be spoken figuratively, as the fathers spake, *ib.* 326; does not suppose that Christ instituted baptism in Matt. xxviii, or prescribed time, place, or circumstances, 2 *Whitg.* 498, 516—518; thinks that there are three errors about circumstances as regards baptism, and infers that laymen and women may minister it, *ib.* 503, 511, 526, 534; citing Augustine, he ascribes the institution of infant baptism to the apostles, 1 *Whitg.* 232; commenting on 1 Cor. i. 17, he thinks that some taught, and some baptized, 2 *Whitg.* 457, 3 *Whitg.* 24; says that preaching is necessary before baptism, when those to be baptized have discretion, but not otherwise, 2 *Whitg.* 518, 3 *Whitg.* 20, 26; exposes the weakness of the Anabaptists' reasons against baptizing infants, 1 *Whitg.* 279, 280, 3 *Whitg.* 76—78; shews how wrongly they argue who, from Matt. xxviii.19, maintain that teaching must precede baptism, 3 *Whitg.* 24—26; answers those who require evident testimony from scripture that children may be baptized, *ib.* 331, 332, 364; reproves Baltazar for having introduced re-baptization without the authority of the church, and contrasts his conduct with that of the Zurich ministers, 1 *Whitg.* 130, 131, 2 *Whitg.* 70, 71; approves of sponsors, 3 *Whitg.* 120, 121; says that the Anabaptists protest against witnesses in baptism, 1 *Whitg.* 130; censures them because they would have nothing added to the bare words of baptism, 3 *Whitg.* 99, 100; writes on the baptism of children in the faith of their parents, *ib.* 135—138; his opinions on the Lord's supper, 1 *Cov.* 463, 1 *Cran.* 195, 225, 273, 2 *Ful.* 376, *Phil.* 401; cited by Gardiner as supporting transubstantiation, 1 *Cran.* 239, 241, 244, 245, 279, 335; he says that the apostles placed bishops in the churches, 2 *Whitg.* 253; and that themselves became bishops in the end, *ib.* 302, 355; mentions the appointment of

James as bishop of Jerusalem, 1 *Whitg.* 359, 459; affirms that Timothy was a bishop, 2 *Whitg.* 296, 300; says there were three ways of electing ministers in the apostles' time, 1 *Whitg.* 343, 417, 429, 457; considers the work of an evangelist the same as that of a bishop, 2 *Whitg.* 299; exposes the subtlety of the enemy, who sows darnel when the Lord has revealed the light of his word, 1 *Whitg.* 11; declares who are heretics, *ib.* 137; defines schismatics as those who without the authority of the church conspire in some new opinion, *ib.*; describes a kind of men who are puffed with pride, contentious, and slanderers of others, professing to be endued with the Spirit of God, *ib.* 131, &c.; charges magistrates to let none trouble the gospel, *ib.* 9; thought that if every man might freely publish his own devices, there would soon be many errors, *ib.* 8, 9, 124, and many sects and factions, *ib.* 9; more sects than among infidels, *ib.* 124; compares the plague of contention to a mountain torrent, *ib.* 9, 10; censures troublers of the church as falsely pretending the purity of religion, *ib.* 54; calls those troublers of the church who strive about external matters, *ib.* 40, 80; describes the sword that Christ said he came to send Matt. x. 34, as having no place among the faithful, *ib.* 82, 128; defines "scandalum" as an offence joined with contempt, 2 *Bul.* 315; blames contention about ceremonies, 3 *Whitg.* 124; says that in controversies about external ceremonies, if nothing to the point be found in the New Testament, we should refer to the Old, *ib.* 440; shews that there are many external and indifferent things neither commanded nor forbidden by express word of God, which yet may be used without impiety, and answers some objections, 1 *Whitg.* 254, 255, 285, 2 *Whitg.* 228; declares that we may not suppose with the Papists that there are things necessary to salvation not contained in scripture, but that there are external things or ceremonies omitted, which yet may be used according to St Paul's rule, 1 *Whitg.* 256, 257, 285, 2 *Whitg.* 228; censures the Anabaptists for innovating unnecessarily about external things, 1 *Whitg.* 40; for going about innovations of their own private authority, *ib.* 251; says they inveigh more bitterly against the ministers of the word than against the Papists, *ib.* 46, 47, 125; says that if they had been sent of God they would have construed rightly the things not yet reformed, and would have become all things to all men, &c., *ib.* 81, 128, 251; shews what protestation the Anabaptists made of obedience to magistrates, and how disobedient they were like to be, *ib.* 83, 105, 128, 129, 249; says it is melancholy and wrath, not true zeal, of which they glory, *ib.* 86, 87, 126, 3 *Whitg.* 524; describes how they think magistrates and ministers their enemies, because they tell them of their faults, 1 *Whitg.* 87, 125, 126; and how they slander the ministers to win credit to themselves, being like Ate, seeking confusion of all things, *ib.* 87, 126, 129, 130; also how they say that such as have benefices cannot teach the gospel sincerely, their hope being themselves to succeed in their places, *ib.* 91, 127, 376; says that they boast of being moved with the Spirit, *ib.* 97, 128; and that they are fond of going to places where the gospel is diligently preached, and causing troubles there about external things, *ib.* 108, 125, 126, 127, 130; asserts that, if any man, however modestly, reproves them, they omit no reproach against him, *ib.* 125; says that they call us half-Papists, and condemn going to churches, *ib.* 126; that they are armed with hypocrisy and false reporting of others, *ib.*; that they glory that the multitude follow them, *ib.*; that they take upon them to teach others, but cannot abide to be taught, and as authors of contentions have not the God of peace, *ib.* 127, 2 *Whitg.* 243, 244; that they deserve the same discipline as the bishop of Rome, as their contention comes of envy, &c., 1 *Whitg.* 128; shews that as they, unlike Christ, make contention for external things among the faithful, they are not sent of God, *ib.* 128, 129, 251, 2 *Whitg.* 243, 244; that they have their secret conventicles in corners, without the consent of the church, 1 *Whitg.* 129; censures them for that in their secret meetings they pour out opprobrious speeches against magistrates and ministers, *ib.* 129, 130; observes that those who before were gentle, if they embrace their doctrine become contentious, *ib.* 129; that whoever withstands them, him they account an atheist, *ib.* 130; that they wander up and down like minstrels, loving to live at other men's provisions, *ib.*; that they are burdensome to the poor, and though seeming to contemn riches, live at other men's tables, *ib.* 127, 128; accuses them of reasoning foolishly, à factis et exemplis, yea à non factis et non exemplis, *ib.* 179, 316 2 *Whitg.* 15; denies that it is lawful to reason à facto ad jus, 1 *Whitg.* 316, 353 2 *Whitg.* 511, 3*Whitg.* 75, &c.; would have examples give place when against a general law, 1 *Whitg.* 354; censures the hypocritical humility of the Anabaptists, *ib.* 8, 129, in whom he found only a melancholy contumacy, *ib.* 8; says that they divide the church and trouble the state, *ib.* 131; would not have men moved by their reproaches, *ib.* 10, 11; knew that he exposed himself to reproaches, *ib.* 7; though marvellously slandered, would not leave off the defence of the truth, *ib.*; mentions several errors of the Catabaptists, *Rog*. 49, 80, 106, 153; is opposed to the revival of excommunication, 2 *Zur.* 252

Zuinglius (Huldric), the younger: 1 *Zur.* 34, 49, 62, 103, & sæpe, 2 *Zur.* 90, 95, 3 *Zur.* 108, 412; he married the eldest daughter of Bullinger, 4 *Bul.* xiv, 1 *Zur.* 30 n., 171 n., 2 *Zur.* 165 n

Zuinglius (Rod.): grandson of the great Zuinglius, 2 *Zur.* 188, and of Bullinger, *ib.* 189 n.; he studied at Cambridge, 1 *Zur.* 264 n., 267; letter from him to Sandys, 2 *Zur.* 189; his illness and death, 1 *Zur.* 269 n., 271, 2 *Zur.* 202, &c., 208; his funeral, 2 *Zur.* 205, 208

Zurich: the Tigurines at war, *Phil.* 390; freedom of the canton, 3 *Zur.* 246; its citizens were forbidden to receive money from foreign states, *ib.* 463, 484; Hooper's arrival at Zurich and sojourn there, 2 *Hoop.* ix; an unskilful printer at Zurich, 1 *Hoop.* viii; the Tigurines write a book against Luther, 2 *Lat.* 265; the Consensus Tigurinus, 1549, between Calvin, Bullinger, &c., 3 *Zur.* 121 n., 267, 479 n.; letter from Edward VI. to the senate, *ib.* 1; exiles at Zurich, *Jew.* xiii, *Rid.* 387, 3 *Zur.* 752; the hospitality of the magistrates to the English exiles, 1 *Zur.* vii. n.; letter from several exiles to the magistrates, 3 *Zur.* 751; letter of the ministers of the church there, on behalf of the English exiles, to certain Englishmen, 1554, *ib.* 747; Jewel's grateful remembrance of Zurich, 1 *Zur.* 23; he sends money for a public supper there, *ib.* 119; Parkhurst's love to Zurich, *ib.* 30, 108; Pilkington's affection for it, *ib.* 222; Lever's grateful remembrance of it, *ib.* 87; letter of the state to queen Elizabeth, in behalf of C. Thoman, 2 *Zur.* 323; THE ZURICH LETTERS RELATIVE TO THE ENGLISH REFORMATION...CHIEFLY FROM THE ARCHIVES OF ZURICH; translated and edited by the Rev. Hastings Robinson, D.D., 2 series, 1 and 2 *Zur.*; ORIGINAL LETTERS RELATIVE TO THE ENGLISH REFORMATION, &c.; translated and edited by the same, 3 *Zur.*; EPISTOLÆ TIGURINÆ, 1531—1558 (the Latin originals of the last-mentioned series), 1 *vol.*

The church of Zurich: its purity, 3 *Zur.* 84 (*v.* Confession); Lud. Lavater De Ritibus Ecclesiæ Tigurinæ, *Pra. Eliz.* viii; patronage of the churches, 2 *Zur.* 231; the election of ministers, 1 *Whitg.* 309; the tithes of Zurich possessed by the bishop of Constance, 2 *Zur.* 230; dedication to the ministers of the Zurich-see, and other places in the territory of Zurich, 4 *Bul.* 546

The Gross-munster or cathedral at Zurich — statue of Charlemagne there, 3 *Zur.* 192; St Peter's church — R. Gualter's, 2 *Zur.* 231; the Fish-market, &c., 3 *Zur.* 192

Zutphen: *v.* Yorke (R.).

Zwicers, &c.: *v.* Switzerland.

Zwickius (James): 3 *Zur.* 693, 694, 697

INDEX

OF THE PRINCIPAL TEXTS EXPLAINED OR ILLUSTRATED.

*** Many other texts are referred to in the General Index, under their subjects or leading words. See also the Indexes of Texts in 1 *Fulke*, 592, &c., *Grindal*, 502, &c., *Philpot*, 444, and 3 *Tyndal*, 289.

GENESIS, *q. v.*
  i. 2, *Hutch.* 63—65, 137, 196, *Whita.* 132
    30, *Whita.* 174
  ii. 8, *ib.* 174, &c.
    23, *ib.* 174
  iii. 6, 8, 17, *ib.*
    15, 1 *Ful.* 74, 531, &c., *Whita.* 163
  iv. 4, 5, 8, *Whita.* 132
    13, 15, 16, 26, *ib.* 174
  v. 22, *ib.* 175
  vi. 2, 1 *Lat.* 242
    2, 4, 1 *Tyn.* 409
    3, 6, *Whita.* 175
    5, *ib.* 165
  viii. 4, 7, *ib.* 175
  ix. 6, *ib.* 166
  xi. 12, *ib.* 175
  xiii. 2, 11, *ib.*
  xiv. 3, *ib.*
    18, *ib.* 167
  xviii. *Hutch.* 126, 160
  xxi. 9, *Whita.* 175
  xxiv. 22, 32, *ib.* 176
  xxvii. *Wool.* 36
    5, 33, *Whita.* 176
  xxviii. 34, *ib.*
  xxx. 32, *ib.* 133
  xxxi. 32, *ib.* 176
  xxxiv. 29, *ib.*
  xxxvi. 24, *ib.*
  xxxvii. 2, *ib.* 177
    36, 1 *Ful.* 286
  xxxviii. 5, 12, 23, *Whita.* 177
  xxxix. 6, 10, *ib.*
  xl. 5, 16, *ib.*
  xli. 45, *ib.* 178

EXODUS, *q. v.*
  xii. 46, *Whita.* 409
  xv. 1—17, *Poet.* 124
  xx. 1—17: *v.* Commandments.

LEVITICUS, *q. v.*
  xvii. 4, 1 *Brad.* 23
  xviii. 16, 2 *Tyn.* 323, 328
    16, 26, 3 *Zur.* 551, 555

NUMBERS, *q. v.*
  xxxvi. 7, 8, *Whita.* 169

DEUTERONOMY, *q.v.*
  iv. 2, *Whita.* 615
  vi. 7, 1 *Tyn.* 145 n
  xii. 32, *Whita.* 615
  xv. 4, *Sand.* 265
  xvi. 10, *Pil.* 505, 506
  xvii. 8—13, *Whita.* 418, &c.
    14, &c., 1 *Lat.* 87
  xxx. 11, *Whita.* 381

JOSHUA, *q. v.*
  vi. 1—3, 2 *Jew.* 968

JUDGES, *q. v.*
  ix. 53, *Calf.* 91
  xiii. 5, *Whita.* 302 n

RUTH, *q. v.*

1 SAMUEL, *q. v.*
  ii. 1—10, *Poet.* 119
  viii. 1, 1 *Lat.* 174, &c.
  xii. 23, 24, *Sand.* 34
  xxi. 13, 1 *Jew.* 502, *Whita.* 469

2 SAMUEL, *q. v.*
  xxii. 2—7, *Poet.* 468

1 KINGS, *q. v.*
  i. 5, &c., 1 *Lat.* 113

2 KINGS, *q. v.*

1 CHRONICLES, *q. v.*

2 CHRONICLES, *q. v.*
  xix. 10, 11, *Whita.* 424

EZRA, *q. v.*
  ix. 8, *Whita.* 170

NEHEMIAH, *q. v.*
  i. 1 to v. 5, *Pil.* 285, &c.
    5, &c., *Lit. Edw.* 479

ESTHER, *q. v.*

JOB, *q. v.*
  v. 1, *Whita.* 170
  vii. *Poet.* 312
  xiv. 14, *Sand.* 161
  xix. 23—27, 2 *Cov.* 170—172
  xxi. 13, *Whita.* 471

PSALMS, *q. v.*, especially as to metrical versions.
  i. *Pra. B.* 205—207, *Pra. Eliz.* 419
  ii. *Pra. B.* 207, 209, *Pra. Eliz.* 420
    12, *Whita.* 162, 181
  iii. *Pra. Eliz.* 421
  iv. 3, *Whita.* 181
    5, *Sand.* 403
  vii. 11—13, 2 *Jew.* 1068
  xvi. 8—11, 1 *Cov.* 406, 407
    10, 1 *Ful.* 81, 280, &c.
  xix. 4, *Poet.* 271, *Whita.* 159, 469
    8, *Whita.* 640
    9, *ib.* 383
  xxii. 1, 2 *Ful.* 225, *Whita.* 477
    16, 1 *Ful.* 45, 78—80, 521, *Whita.* 159
  xxiii. 2 *Cov.* 279, 2 *Hoop.* 187
  xxiv. 7, *Calf.* 150
  xxxii. 4, *Whita.* 182
    9, *ib.* 183
  xxxviii. 7, *ib.* 184
  xlv. 2, *Pil.* 287
  li. *Pra. Eliz.* 421, 422
    3 *Tyn.* 203, 204
  lxii. 2 *Hoop.* 243
  lxvii. 3, 4, 2 *Jew.* 1054
  lxviii. 6, *Whita.* 184, 185
    12, &c., *ib.* 186
    16, 18, *ib.* 188
    22, 27, *ib.* 189
  lxix. 9, 2 *Jew.* 1004
  lxxii. 16, 2 *Hoop.* 474
  lxxiii. *ib.* 283
    20, *Calf.* 164
  lxxvi. 4, *Whita.* 684 n
  lxxvii. 2 *Hoop.* 309

Psalms,
lxxix. 1 *Brad.* 282
lxxxvi. 11, *Sand.* 112
lxxxvii. 3 *Zur.* 714
    6, *Whita.* 604 n
lxxxix. 29, *ib.* 378
xc. *ib.* 191
xci. 13, *ib.* 404
xcix. 5, 1 *Jew.* 540, &c.
cx. 1 *Cov.* 53
cxv. 1 *Bec.* 262
cxix. 2 *Bul.* 6, *Whita.* 383, 109, *Whita.* 378
cxxxii. 15, *ib.* 190

PROVERBS: *v.* Solomon.
vi. 22, *Whita.* 383
xvi. 11, *ib.* 170
xxv. 27, 1 *Bul.* 65
xxx. 1, &c., *Lit. Edw.* 478

ECCLESIASTES: *v.* Solomon.
ix. 2, *Whita.* 171
xi. 3, 2 *Brad.* 279, 2 *Cov.* 258
xii. 11, *Whita.* 422
    12, 13, *Sand.* 1

SONG OF SOLOMON, *q. v.*
ii. 15, *Sand.* 55
iv. *Poet.* 341
v. *ib.* 117, 516

ISAIAH, *q. v.*
i. 12, &c., *Whita.* 133
viii. 7, *ib.* 379
ix. 6, *ib.* 158
xi. 6—8, *ib.* 405
xii. 1—6, *Poet.* 126
xlix. 21, 22, *Calf.* 92
liv. 13, *Whita.* 454
lv. 1, *Sand.* 7
    6, 7, *ib.* 144
lxii. 2, *Wool.* 17
lxiii. 1, *Hutch.* 21
lxv. 15, *Wool.* 21
    25, *Whita.* 405
lxvi. 1, *Calf.* 165
    8, *Wool.* 17

JEREMIAH, *q. v.*
iii. 22, &c., *Lit. Edw.* 479
iv. 4—6, *Calf.* 94
xi. 19, 1 *Ful.* 519
xvii. *Lit. Edw.* 477
xxiii. 6, *Whita.* 158
xxxi. 18, 19, *Lit. Edw.* 477
    32, 33, *Whita.* 561

LAMENTATIONS: *v.* Jeremiah.
v. *Poet.* 121, 417

EZEKIEL:
ix. 4, see Thau.
xiii. 3, *Whita.* 424
xviii. 20, *ib.* 377
xxxiv. 4, 2 *Whitg.* 414

DANIEL, *q. v.*
vii. 7, 8, 2 *Jew.* 918
xi. 37, *ib.* 911
    38, 1 *Brad.* 92 n

HOSEA:
i. 10, 11, 3 *Jew.* 280
xi. 1, *Whita.* 409

JOEL, *q. v.*
ii. 13, *Whita.* 173

AMOS, *q. v.*

OBADIAH, *q. v.*
    Passim, *Pil.* 201, &c.

JONAH, *q. v.*
ii. 1—10, *Poet.* 129

MICAH:
v. 2, *Whita.* 173
vi. 2, 8, *Sand.* 216

NAHUM, *q. v.*

HABAKKUK:
iii. 1—19, *Poet.* 127

ZEPHANIAH, *q. v.*

HAGGAI, *q. v.*
    Passim, *Pil.* 1, &c.
i. 11, 3 *Jew.* 232
    2—4, 2 *Jew.* 986
ii. 11, *Whita.* 423

ZECHARIAH:
xi. 17, 2 *Jew.* 918
xii. 2, 3, 2 *Bul.* 108 n
xiii. 3, 1 *Whitg.* 329, 331

MALACHI:
i. 11, 2 *Ful.* 381, *Hutch.* 46, 47, 1 *Jew.* 110, 2 *Jew.* 712, 713, 722, &c., *Phil.* 408, *Poet.* 270
ii. 7, *Whita.* 423
iv. 2, *Rid.* 13

---

1 or 3 ESDRAS: *v.* Ezra.

2 or 4 ESDRAS: *v.* Ezra.

TOBIT, *q. v.*
xiii. 3, *Lit. Edw.* 478

JUDITH, *q. v.*

REST OF ESTHER, *q. v.*

WISDOM: *v.* Solomon.
i. *Poet.* 534
ix. *ib.* 536
xix. *ib.* 538

ECCLESIASTICUS, *q. v.*
v. 5, *Whita.* 172
xvi. 15, *ib.* 172
xxiv. 30, *ib.* 151

BARUCH, *q. v.*
vi. *Poet.* 518

SONG OF THE THREE CHILDREN:
    v. Daniel.

SUSANNA: *v.* Daniel.

BEL AND THE DRAGON: *v.* Daniel.

PRAYER OF MANASSES, *q. v.*

1 MACCABEES, *q. v.*

2 MACCABEES, *q. v.*
xii. 44, 45, 2 *Brad.* 292, 2 *Cov.* 271, 473, *Grin.* 24, 1 *Lat.* 515

MATTHEW, *q. v.*
    Whita. 200, 201
i.—xxi. 2 *Tyn.* 227, &c.
ii. 1, 2, 2 *Lat.* 129
    15, *Whita.* 525, 23, *ib.* 302 n., 525
iii. 2, 1 *Brad.* 43
    11, 2 *Whitg.* 521
v. 1—3, 1 *Lat.* 474
    6, 1 *Tyn.* 79, 94
    7, *Poet.* 249
    11, 1 *Tyn.* 71
v, vi, vii. 2 *Tyn.* 16, &c.
v. 14, *Whita.* 384
    20, 1 *Tyn.* 74
    23, 24, 1 *Lat.* 17, 3 *Whitg.* 171
    29, 30, *Whita.* 405
    44, 45, 1 *Tyn.* 72
vi. 1, *ib.*
    5, *ib.* 73
    7, 3 *Whitg.* 513, &c.
    9—13, *v.* Prayer (The Lord's).
    12, 1 *Tyn.* 86
    14, *ib.* 76

INDEX OF THE TEXTS.

Matt. vi. 18, 1 *Tyn.* 73
    19, *ib.* 77
  vii. 15, *Whita.* 458
    21, 1 *Tyn.* 77
  viii. 1—3, 2 *Lat.* 167
    23—26, *ib.* 181
    23, 24, *Sand.* 370
  ix. 13, *Whita.* 193
    37, 38, 2 *Jew.* 1016
  x. 41, 42, 1 *Tyn.* 80, 101
  xi. 2, &c., 2 *Lat.* 65
  xii. 37, 1 *Tyn.* 80
  xiii. 24—30, 2 *Lat.* 188
    33, 1 *Tyn.* 113
  xv. 3, *ib.* 104
    6, *Whita.* 637
  xvi. 18, 19, see Peter.
    19, *Whita.* 425
    23, 1 *Tyn.* 105
    24, *Pra. Eliz.* 401 n
  xvii. 21, 1 *Tyn.* 82
  xviii. 17, *Whita.* 426, 3 *Whitg.* 225
    20, 2 *Cran.* 53
  xix. 17, 1 *Tyn.* 81, *Whita.* 471
    21, 1 *Tyn.* 81
    24, *ib.* 82
  xx. 14, &c., 2 *Lat.* 198
  xxi. 12, 13, *Sand.* 235
  xxii. 2, 3, 1 *Lat.* 455
    21, *ib.* 282, 296
  xxiii. 2, 2 *Cran.* 54, *Whita.* 426
    5, 1 *Tyn.* 104
    13, *ib.*
    14, *ib.* 105
  xxiv. 2 *Hoop.* 588, *Rid.* 63
    24, 3 *Tyn.* 103
    28, 1 *Jew.* 12
  xxv. 34, 1 *Tyn.* 82
  xxvi. 29, *Hutch.* 269, 270
  xxvii. 9, 2 *Ful.* 386
    46, *Whita.* 478
  xxviii. 16, 2 *Whitg.* 516
    18, 2 *Tyn.* 282
    19, *Whita.* 527, 3 *Whitg.* 24
    20, 2 *Cran.* 54

MARK, *q. v.*
    Whita. 201
  i. 15, 2 *Hoop.* 163
  x. 29, 30, 1 *Tyn.* 109

LUKE, *q. v.*
    Whita. 201, 202
  i. 3, 4, *ib.* 522, 641
    6, 1 *Ful.* 118
    74, 75, *Sand.* 177
  ii. 6, 7, 2 *Lat.* 84, 96
    8—12, *ib.* 111

Luke ii. 14, *Whita.* 468
    42, 2 *Lat.* 143
  iii. 36, 1 *Ful.* 43, 50, &c., 57
  v. 1—11, 1 *Lat.* 198
  vii. 19, &c., 2 *Lat.* 65
    47, 1 *Tyn.* 83
  viii. 5, 1 *Lat.* 59
    10, *Whita.* 240
  ix. 54, 55, 1 *Tyn.* 105
    60, 3 *Whitg.* 407
    62, 1 *Lat.* 59
  x. 21, 22, *Whita.* 454
    23, 24, 2 *Jew.* 1075
    28, 35, 37, 1 *Tyn.* 85
    42, *ib.* 86
  xi. 2—4: v. Prayer (The Lord's)
    15, 2 *Jew.* 1025
    53, *Whita.* 202
  xii. 14, 3 *Whitg.* 408, 409
    15, 1 *Lat.* 239
    32, 33, 1 *Tyn.* 87
  xiv. 14, *ib.* 106
  xvi. 1—12, 1 *Lat.* 34
    1—9, 1 *Tyn.* 45
    8, 1 *Lat.* 33, 41
    9, *Wool.* 139
    29, *Whita.* 642
  xvii. 21, 1 *Tyn.* 103
    37, 1 *Jew.* 12
  xviii. 1—8, 1 *Lat.* 142, &c., 150, &c.
    29, 30, 1 *Tyn.* 109
  xxi. 25—28, 2 *Lat.* 44
    25, *Sand.* 346
  xxii. 19, *Coop.* 38
    20, 1 *Ful.* 132, 599, 2 *Ful.* 385—387
    25—28, 2 *Lat.* 44
    32, *Whita.* 430, 449
  xxiv. 25, 27, *ib.* 368, 643
    30, 1 *Jew.* 232

JOHN, *q. v.*
    Whita. 203
  i. 9, 1 *Brad.* 319
    12, 1 *Tyn.* 111
    16, *ib.* 110
  ii. 1, 2 *Lat.* 160
  iii. 5, 1 *Ful.* 455, &c., 2 *Whitg.* 521, 522
    18, 2 *Whitg.* 521
  iv. 24, 1 *Tyn.* 106
  v. 29, *ib.* 110
    34, *Whita.* 336
    36, 1 *Tyn.* 112
    38, *Whita.* 337
    39, *ib.* 644
    47, *ib.* 339
  vi. 1, 2, *Sand.* 331
    25—27, 3 *Whitg.* 567

John vi. 35, 53, and other verses, 1 *Brad.* 91, 100, 4 *Bul.* 447, 1 *Cran.* 24, 25, 26, 27, 307, 372, *Grin.* 44, 2 *Hoop.* 191, 450, 1 *Jew.* 449, 451, 2 *Lat.* 266, *Lit. Edw.* 521, (568), *Phil.* 64, *Rid.* 175, *Rog.* 289, 1 *Tyn.* 368, 3 *Tyn.* 222, &c., *Whita.* 489
    45, *Whita.* 454
    63, *Coop.* 211
  vii. 17, 1 *Tyn.* 111
    38, 1 *Ful.* 52 n
  viii. 1, &c., *Whita.* 305
    25, *ib.* 377
    47, 1 *Tyn.* 88
  x. 3, *Whita.* 465
  xiii. 17, 1 *Tyn.* 112
    35, *ib.*
  xiv. 21, *ib.*
    26, *Whita.* 194
  xv. 10, 1 *Tyn.* 112
    12, 1 *Lat.* 447
    13, 1 *Tyn.* 86
    16, *ib.* 112
  xvi. 12, 2 *Cran.* 54, *Whita.* 542
  xx. 16, *ib.* 428
    17, *Pra. B.* 150
    30, *Whita.* 545
    31, *ib.* 628
  xxi. 15, &c., see Peter.
    22, *Whita.* 203
    25, 2 *Cran.* 55

ACTS: *v.* Luke.
    Whita. 203
  i. 1, *ib.* 645
  ii. 46, 3 *Whitg.* 83
  vii. 26, 1 *Tyn.* 9 n
    49, *Calf.* 165
  viii. 13, 1 *Tyn.* 124
  x. 31, *ib.* 118
    34, *Sand.* 256
  xiv. 23, 1 *Ful.* 246, 1 *Whitg.* 345
  xv. *Whita.* 431, 2 *Whitg.* 232
  xvii. 2, 3, *Whita.* 645
    11, *ib.* 457
  xviii. 24, 28, *ib.* 646
  xix. 3, &c., 1 *Ful.* 453, &c. *Hutch.* 116, 3 *Whitg.* 17
  xx. 35, *Whita.* 560
  xxvi. 22, *ib.* 647
  xxvii. 35, 1 *Jew.* 235

ROMANS: *v.* Paul.

Rom. i. 2, *Whita.* 647
    4, *ib.* 194
    32, *ib.* 195
  ii. 3, *ib.* 204
    6, 1 *Tyn.* 113
    13, *ib.* 114
  iii. 11, 1 *Jew.* 314
  iv. 2, *Whita.* 196
  v. 6, 13, *ib.* 204
    18, 1 *Ful.* 120, 159
  vi. 19, 2 *Jew.* 1061
  vii. 14, *Whita.* 455
    25, *ib.* 204
  viii. 18, 1 *Tyn.* 113, *Whita.* 204
    19—23, 1 *Brad.* 351, &c.
  ix. 18, *ib.* 324
  x. 2, 1 *Tyn.* 105
    9, *ib.* 123
    11, *ib.* 95
    15, 2 *Whitg.* 530
    17, *Whita.* 648
    18, *Poet.* 272, *Whita.* 160
  xi. 6, *Whita.* 196
  xii. 6, *ib.* 472
    7, 3 *Whitg.* 411
    8, *ib.* 282, 283
    16—18, 2 *Jew.* 1090
    19, *Whita.* 204
    20, 1 *Lat.* 439
  xiii. 2 *Hoop.* 93, &c.
    1, *Whita.* 204
    8, 9, 2 *Lat.* 1, *Sand.* 197
    12, 2 *Jew.* 1035
    12, 14, 2 *Hoop.* 114, 116
  xiv. 5, &c., *Whita.* 204, 2 *Whitg.* 594
  xv. 4, 1 *Lat.* 59, 85, *Whita.* 648
    16, *Calf.* 230, 2 *Jew.* 709
  xvi. 23, *Whita.* 204

1 CORINTHIANS: *v.* Paul.
  Whita. 204, 205
  i. 17, 2 *Whitg.* 456
  ii. 6, *Whita.* 614
    11, 1 *Tyn.* 78, 111
  iii. 10—12, *Calf.* 56, 57
    14, 1 *Tyn.* 115
  iv. 1, 2, 2 *Jew.* 1046, 2 *Whitg.* 519
  v. 7, *Pra. Eliz.* 371
  vii. 1, 1 *Ful.* 115
  viii. 8, *Rid.* 11
  ix. 5, 1 *Ful.* 115, 472, 474
    16, 17, 1 *Tyn.* 100
  x. 11, *Whita.* 407
    13, 1 *Tyn.* 92
    16, *Rid.* 8
    17, *Coop.* 77, 120
  xi. 3, 3 *Whitg.* 419
    16, *Whita.* 558
    20—34, *Coop.* 78

1 Cor. xi. 22, 1 *Jew.* 158
    23—25, *Rid.* 8
    23, 1 *Jew.* 3
    24, *Rid.* 15
    29, 1 *Cran.* 373
  xii. 3, 2 *Whitg.* 590, 591
    8, 9 &c., *Whita.* 433
    13, 1 *Brad.* 88, 534
    28, 2 *Whitg.* 98
  xiii. 1 *Lat.* 449
  xiv. *Whita.* 258, &c.
    16, 1 *Jew.* 313
    29, 2 *Whitg.* 234, 235
    40, 1 *Whitg.* 212
  xv. 3, *Whita.* 561
    28, 1 *Brad.* 272
    51, *Whita.* 205

2 CORINTHIANS: *v.* Paul.
  Whita. 205
  i. 24, 2 *Whitg.* 414
  iv. 3, *Whita.* 387
  v. 10, 1 *Tyn.* 116
  vi. 1, 2, 2 *Jew.* 1084, *Sand.* 293
  xiii. 11, *Sand.* 418

GALATIANS: *v.* Paul.
  Whita. 205
  i. 8, *ib.* 622
    9, *ib.* 559
    16, *ib.* 133
  ii. 2, *ib.* 432, 2 *Whitg.* 411
    6, 2 *Whitg.* 409, &c.
    14, 1 *Ful.* 35
  iii. 1, *Whita.* 133
    13, 1 *Ful.* 44
  iv. 10, 2 *Whitg.* 579, 586, 594
    24, *Whita.* 405
  vi. 14, 2 *Hoop.* 279

EPHESIANS: *v.* Paul.
  Whita. 205
  i. 3—14, 1 *Brad.* 311—318
    6, 1 *Ful.* 410
    14, *Whita.* 133
    22, 23, 3 *Whitg.* 483
    23, 1 *Ful.* 231, &c.
  ii. 8, *Wool.* 37
    10, *Whita.* 468
    19, 20, *ib.* 649
    20, *ib.* 347, &c.
  iii. 18, *Calf.* 205
  iv. 8, 1 *Cov.* 407
    11, 1 *Whitg.* 492, &c., 2 *Whitg.* 98, 235, 300, 338
    19, *Whita.* 133, 134
  v. 32, *ib.* 197
  vi. 8, 1 *Tyn.* 116
    10, &c., 1 *Lat.* 25, 490

Eph. vi. 13, *Whita.* 197

PHILIPPIANS: *v.* Paul.
  i. 18, 1 *Whitg.* 292, 294
  ii. 2—5, *Sand.* 92
  iii. 3, *Hutch.* 205
    17, 18, 1 *Lat.* 510

COLOSSIANS: *v.* Paul.
  i. 24, 2 *Bul.* 333, 2 *Ful.* 92
  ii. 8, 1 *Jew.* 137, 138
    14, *Whita.* 206
    16, 17, 2 *Cran.* 61
    21, *Whita.* 455
  iii. 24, 1 *Tyn.* 116
  iv. 16, *Whita.* 468

1 THESSALONIANS: *v.* Paul.
  Passim, 2 *Jew.* 817, &c.
  ii. 13, *Whita.* 337
  v. 12, 3 *Whitg.* 484
    21, *Whita.* 457

2 THESSALONIANS: *v.* Paul.
  Passim, 2 *Jew.* 887, &c.
  ii. 3, &c., *Coop.* 184
    9—11, 3 *Tyn.* 104
    13, *Whita.* 206
    15, 2 *Cran.* 55, *Whita.* 551

1 TIMOTHY: *v.* Paul.
  ii. 1, 2, *Sand.* 75
    4, 1 *Brad.* 324, 325, *Sand.* 284
    13, *Whita.* 206
  iii. 2, *ib.* 455, 1 *Zur.* 157, 347
    13, 3 *Whitg.* 69—71
  iv. 1, &c., 1 *Tyn.* 214
  v. 12, *Whita.* 482, 483
    22, 1 *Whitg.* 425
  vi. 3, *Whita.* 559
    11, 3 *Whitg.* 412
    20, *Whita.* 555

2 TIMOTHY: *v.* Paul.
  i. 13, *Whita.* 557
  ii. 2, *ib.*
    3, 4, 3 *Whitg.* 413
    4, *Whita.* 206
  iii. 1—5, 3 *Tyn.* 105
    8, *Whita.* 560
    16, 17, *ib.* 632
  iv. 10, 1 *Jew.* 162

TITUS: *v.* Paul.
  iii. 1, 3 *Whitg.* 586
    5, 1 *Ful.* 455, &c.

PHILEMON: *v.* Paul.
  9, *Whita.* 206

HEBREWS: v. Paul.
       Whita. 206
  i. 3, *Phil.* 118
  v. 4, 2 *Whitg.* 412
     7, 1 *Ful.* 323, &c.
  vi. 4, *Hutch.* 112, 117, 1 *Tyn.*
     521, 522
  vii. 12, 2 *Tyn.* 282
  ix. 28, *Whita.* 198
  x. 26, 1 *Tyn.* 521, 523
     30, 3 *Whitg.* 420
  xi. 21, *Calf.* 158, 1 *Ful.* 539
  xii. 20, 1 *Tyn.* 521, 523
  xiii. 4, *Sand.* 313
     10, *Phil.* 119
     16, *Whita.* 198

JAMES, *q. v.*
  i. 12, 1 *Lat.* 434
     18, 1 *Tyn.* 120
     19, *Whita.* 206
     25, 1 *Tyn.* 119
  ii. 14, *ib.* 120
     21, *ib* 119
     22, *Wool.* 29, 30
     24, see Justification.
     25, 1 *Tyn.* 119
     26, *ib.* 120
  iv. 8—10, *Sand.* 126
  v. 14, see Unction.
     15, *Whita.* 199

1 PETER, *q. v.*
      Whita. 206
  i. 9, 1 *Tyn.* 109
  ii. 19—25, *Hutch.* 295, 313
  iii. 15, 3 *Whitg.* 133
     19, *Lit. Edw.* 504, 526, (553, 572)
  iv. 7—10, *Sand.* 386
     8, *Whita.* 470
     11, 2 *Jew.* 950

2 PETER, *q. v.*
      Whita. 206
  i. 10, 1 *Ful.* 72, 85, *Wool.* 73
     15, 2 *Ful.* 87
     19, 1 *Brad.* 519, *Whita.* 337, 386, 650
     20, 1 *Tyn.* 317, 528
  ii. 1, *ib.* 124
     1—3, 3 *Tyn.* 102
  iii. 10, 1 *Brad.* 357
     16, *Whita.* 369

1 JOHN, *q. v.*
     Passim, 2 *Tyn.* 145, &c.
  i. 4, *Whita.* 650
    8, 9, 1 *Tyn.* 86

1 Joh. ii. 20, *Whita.* 452
  iii. 9, 1 *Brad.* 251, *Rid.* 56
     16, 1 *Tyn.* 86
  iv. 1, *Whita.* 433, 457
     20, 1 *Tyn.* 84
  v. 6, 9, *Whita.* 339
     7, *Hutch.* 167
     13, *Whita.* 199
     17, *ib.* 207

2 JOHN, *q. v.*
  12, *Whita.* 558

3 JOHN, *q. v.*
  4, *Whita.* 207

JUDE, *q. v.*
  5, *Whita.* 207
  9, *ib.* 561

REVELATION: *v.* John.
  Passim, *Bale* 250, &c.
  ii. 14, *Whita.* 207
  vii. 3, *Calf.* 98
  xiii. 8, 1 *Ful.* 329
  xiv. 13, 1 *Hoop.* 561
  xviii. 4 *Rid.* 64
  xx. 7, 1 *Lat.* 517
     18, *Whita.* 621

www.ingramcontent.com/pod-product-compliance
Lightning Source LLC
Chambersburg PA
CBHW052106010526
44111CB00036B/1485